ISBN 978-1-5281-6011-7
PIBN 10932083

AMERICAN STATE PAPERS.

CLASS I.

FOREIGN RELATIONS.

VOLUME V.

AMERICAN STATE PAPERS.

DOCUMENTS,

LEGISLATIVE AND EXECUTIVE,

OF THE

CONGRESS OF THE UNITED STATES,

FROM THE

FIRST SESSION OF THE FIRST CONGRESS TO THE SECOND SESSION OF THE THIRTY-FIFTH CONGRESS, INCLUSIVE:

COMMENCING MARCH 4, 1789, AND ENDING MARCH 3, 1859.

SELECTED AND EDITED, UNDER THE AUTHORITY OF CONGRESS,

BY

ASBURY DICKINS, Secretary of the Senate,

AND

JAMES C. ALLEN, Clerk of the House of Representatives.

SECOND SERIES.
VOLUME V.

WASHINGTON:
PUBLISHED BY GALES & SEATON.
1858.

188

CORNELIUS WENDELL, PRINTER.

TABLE OF CONTENTS.

FOREIGN RELATIONS—VOLUME V

FOR INDEX SEE THE CLOSE OF THE VOLUME

TABLE OF CONTENTS.

AMERICAN STATE PAPERS.

FOREIGN RELATIONS.

BRITISH WEST INDIA AND NORTH AMERICAN COLONIAL TRADE.

COMMUNICATED TO THE HOUSE OF REPRESENTATIVES FEBRUARY 9, 1818.

Mr. FORSYTH, from the Committee to whom was referred that part of the President's message which relates to the commercial intercourse of the United States with the British West India islands and North American colonies, and also the petition of the inhabitants of different parts of the District of Maine on the same subject, reported:

That by the statement marked A, annexed to this report, it appears that the average amount of duties upon merchandise annually imported into the United States from the British West India islands and North American colonial possessions from 1802 to 1816, excluding the period from the commencement of the restrictive system to the termination of the late war, exceeds two millions of dollars. The value of the merchandise upon which these duties accrued is supposed to be equal to seven millions of dollars per annum. The statement B shows that the average annual amount of exports to the same places, principally of domestic production, up to 1817, excluding the time of the operation of the restrictive system and the continuance of the war, has exceeded six millions five hundred thousand dollars. The statement C shows that in the year 1815 the amount of duties on merchandise imported in American vessels from the British West India islands and North American colonial possessions was to the amount of duties imported in British vessels as one to four; in 1816, as one to five and a half, or two to eleven. Taking the ratio of 1816 as the basis of calculation, and it is believed to afford the safest and most solid, as past experience shows, a constant diminution of the amount of duties on goods imported in vessels of the United States, it is estimated, supposing the same proportion exists in the exports, that American vessels are used in the transportation annually of $2,177,924 worth of merchandise, and British vessels $11,322,076 worth of the most bulky articles of commerce, one half of which are of the growth, production, or manufacture of the United States. This inequality in the advantages of this commerce, to the injury of the navigating interest of this country, arises from the rigorous enforcement of the colonial system of Great Britain as to the United States, while it is relaxed to all other nations who are friendly to the British empire and have colonial possessions. The portion of the commerce which is carried on in American vessels arises from accidental and temporary suspensions of the system which the governors of the islands, &c., are permitted, under the pressure of dire necessity, to direct—an employment for our seamen and vessels precarious and momentary, rather irritating and tantalizing than profitable. This intercourse appears to the committee in the worst possible state as it regards the navigation of the United States, while it is in the best for that of Great Britain. Justice and policy require on the part of every wise government its best exertions to secure to its own citizens a perfect equality in the transportation of merchandise with the people of every nation, respectively, with whom it has commercial intercourse. Some governments are governed by a policy more contracted, desiring to give to their navigation the exclusive transportation of their native products, while they desire their participation in carrying the productions of other countries. The committee are satisfied that the United States will never be governed by the selfish views of the latter class, but trust that it has not been, nor will it ever be, regardless of the just motives of the former: so far it is a duty to protect the navigating interest. This duty can be performed in relation to the subject of this report by conventional stipulation with Great Britain, formed upon the basis of reciprocity, or by legislative acts operating exclusively against the British navigator engaged in this trade. With the first mode this House has no further concern than to know that the other branch of the Government has performed its duty. Repeated and hitherto unavailing applications have been made to the British Government. It is not, however, surprising that they have been unsuccessful, since no adequate motive at present exists to induce Great Britain to arrange this intercourse by convention. The offer contained in the articles annexed to this report, the most rational and reciprocally advantageous of any ever made, may be considered as dictated by a spirit of accommodation which, under the pressure of adequate motives, might be fostered into a determination to grant all that we could reasonably ask or they be expected to yield. The three first articles, with some practicable modifications, would, by the adaptation of the commercial laws to the stipulation contained in them, confining the commerce strictly to those articles which Americans were permitted to carry, would place the trade upon as favorable grounds as could be expected. It would, no doubt, in a short time be followed by a complete abandonment of the residue of the present jealous system of exclusion. The committee cannot, however, but approve the prompt rejection of this proposition, since these articles are connected with another altogether inadmissible, without a departure from what they deem the settled policy of this country in relation to the trade with the Indians within its jurisdiction. The British ministry having assured this Government that these articles were all that could be granted consistent with their opinions of the best interest of the British empire, there is no longer any hope of effecting this desirable object by negotiation. It remains for Congress to determine what course is to be pursued. If it were possible to separate the interest of one class of the community from that of another, it must be obvious that, however fatal to the navigator, the present state of things is not injurious to the cultivator of the soil. The productions of his labor are carried with facility to a ready market, and he receives in return all those articles which taste and habit have rendered necessary to his comfort. But this separation is impossible, and the necessary connexion between the two interests is apparent, when it is remembered that the competition of American with foreign navigation is essential to keep down the expense of transportation always paid by the cultivator and consumer. If this injury is not now apparent, it will ultimately be felt when the total ruin of the navigation interest will deprive us of the power to remedy the evil. The committee forbear to press those important considerations of preparation for national defence so inseparably connected with the inquiry. They feel that there is on this point but one sentiment among the representatives of the people and in the nation. Experience, prudence, gratitude for the glory shed upon our country, and the confident and delightful anticipation of future renown, all conspire to insure the necessary sacrifices for the preservation and interest of the seamen of the United States. This object, so far as it may be promoted by a participation in the commercial intercourse with the British American colonies, may be effected by a trifling and temporary sacrifice of the interests of agriculture. A slight knowledge of the situation of the British West India colonies authorizes the position that a commerce with the United States is essential to their prosperity if not to their existence. The best market for the sale of their surplus products is found here, while the grain, provisions, and lumber, articles of the first necessity, received in return, are procured on terms infinitely more advantageous than they are to be had for their use in any other part of the world. But for occasional supplies of those articles from the United States some of the islands would be deserted by their inhabitants, or a change produced in their agriculture ruinous to their commercial interest. The people of the United States are in a very different situation. The British West India market is convenient, but not necessary to their accommodation. All the articles imported from them can be procured abundantly, upon terms equally advantageous, from other quarters. The annexed tables, marked D and E, show the amount of imports of the chief articles of their product from the British West Indies, &c., and the proportion it bears to the whole amount of imports of similar articles from other West India islands, &c. Many of these can be and are procured from other quarters of the world with which commerce in American vessels is not restrained. The demand for all can be supplied without a recourse to the British West India islands, and a supply from other quarters will be obtained by the employment of American vessels and American seamen in common with the vessels and seamen of the country from which it may be brought. The only danger to be apprehended is that the cultivator, losing the British West India market for the use of his exports, would lose with it the ability to procure the commodities he formerly received in return. The extent of this danger depends upon the correctness of the position laid down—that this commerce is essential to the British West India islands, and only convenient to the United States. If the necessaries of life can only be or are procured on terms infinitely more advantageons here than anywhere else, it follows they will still be carried to the British West Indies, if not directly under a convention between two governments, circuitously through some mutually friendly port. It is perfectly true that the West India islands are capable of producing all that is necessary for their own subsistence, but this must be at the expense of their commercial importance; the abandonment of the most profitable for, to them, an unprofitable cultivation. The general use and consequent high price of West India produce will insure a continuance of the usual course of agriculture, and will, as heretofore, operate as a bounty upon the growth of breadstuffs in the United States. In favorable seasons and in peaceful times Europe affords a surplus of human aliment, and supplies are to be found on the African coast of the Mediterranean; but these come loaded with the increased expenses and the dangers of the lengthened transportation of heavy articles. In the event of one of those desolating tempests of but too frequent occurrence in these otherwise favored regions, destroying in an instant the labors of a life, and scattering the hoards collected by prudence for the subsistence of the colony, the distance from these places of relief renders timely assistance to the unfortunate impossible. The North American colonies cannot furnish these necessary supplies. The navigation of the principal river which carries the greatest portion of her stores to the ocean is closed the better part of the year, and is not practicable at that season which is usually marked by these calamities. It is believed, too, that by far the largest portion of the apparent exports of Canada of breadstuffs, and even of lumber, &c., are carried from the United States. There must be at all times a dependence to a certain extent upon this country. And if a conventional relaxation is not produced by a prohibition of this direct intercourse, or the imposition of such charges as shall amount almost to prohibition, it follows that the trade will be circuitous. In this event the export trade, instead of being carried on exclusively in British bottoms, will be prosecuted in American vessels and the vessels of that foreign nation in whose ports the parties may, by tacit arrangement, meet for the exchange of their commodities. The return cargoes, if of British growth, will, under the navigation act of the United States, be brought wholly in American vessels.

The only question remaining to be examined is as to the mode of effecting this desirable result—by total prohibition of all intercourse, or by burdensome charges on the trade if confined to British vessels? The committee believe that the latter is to be preferred, and have accordingly reported a bill. There is no essential difference between them, except as the one or the other is more or less inconvenient in its execution. The effect of onerous duties is more slow but equally certain; the pressure will soon be felt, and the beneficial consequences gradually follow. The stream of commerce will easily and naturally flow into the desired channel without the risk of those dangers which a sudden and violent effort to divert it might produce. A short time will prove the efficacy of this arrangement, and justify its continuance, modification, or abandonment. It is recommended, too, by its facility of execution; it requires no further alteration in the existing laws; it is not necessary to arm for its enforcement the petty officers of the customs with powers dangerous and odious to a free people.

For further and more detailed information on the subject of this report, the committee refer the House to a document marked F, furnished from the Department of State.

FEBRUARY 19, 1818.—Accompanied with a bill supplementary to the "*Act regulating duties on imports and tonnage*," passed April 27, 1816.

A.

Statement of the amount of duties arising on merchandise imported into the United States from the British West Indies and their American colonies, from October 1, 1801, to September 30, 1816.

	1802.	1803.	1804.	1805.	1806.	1807.	1808.	1809.
British West Indies	$1,844,442	$1,770,651	$1,939,859	$1,864,119	$2,360,665	$1,948,672	$1,092,091	$611,612
British North American colonies	62,154	58,225	111,578	144,868	188,253	244,125	112,177	148,224
Total	1,906,596	1,828,876	2,051,437	1,008,987	2,548,918	2,192,797	1,204,268	758,836

A—Continued.

	1810.	1811.	1812.	1813.	1814.	1815.	1816.
British West Indies	$535,222	$453,188	$16,861	$33,736	$2,521	$1,304,308	$2,127,486
British North American colonies	79,602	44,915	55,780	26,552	184,794	1,386,020	317,298
Total	614,824	498,103	72,641	60,288	187,315	2,690,228	2,444,784

B.

Statement of the value of merchandise, the produce and manufacture of the United States, exported to the British West Indies and their American colonies, from October 1, 1801, to September 30, 1817.

	1802.	1803.	1804.	1805.	1806.	1807.	1808.	1809.
British West Indies	$6,228,464	$5,624,647	$6,315,667	$5,473,218	$5,092,288	$5,322,276	$1,427,510	$1,511,570
British North American colonies	512,561	1,005,846	983,306	970,610	1,124,835	1,338,199	308,635	672,743
Total	6,741,025	6,630,493	7,298,973	6,443,828	6,217,123	6,660,475	1,736,145	2,184,313

B—Continued.

	1810.	1811.	1812.	1813.	1814.	1815.	1816.	1817.
British West Indies	$2,322,720	$1,626,115	$1,775,037			$1,684,480	$3,050,729	$3,802,462
British North American colonies	1,310,586	1,670,515	643,350	$2,422	$10,050	1,396,815	3,019,171	3,691,292
Total	3,633,300	3,296,630	2,418,387	2,422	10,050	3,081,295	6,069,900	7,493,754

Value of foreign merchandise exported as above.

	1802.	1803.	1804.	1805.	1806.	1807.	1808.	1809.
British West Indies	$461,026	$90,973	$731,991	$518,189	$515,640	$630,361	$133,553	$154,429
British North American colonies	172,313	154,447	143,929	173,391	298,454	224,825	70,818	88,689
Total	633,339	245,420	875,920	691,580	814,094	855,186	204,371	243,118
Total American and foreign merchandise	7,374,364	6,875,913	8,174,893	7,135,408	7,031,217	7,515,661	1,940,516	2,427,431

B—*Value of foreign merchandise*—Continued.

	1810.	1811.	1812.	1813.	1814.	1815.	1816.	1817.
British West Indies	$71,443	$123,684	$22,203			$18,493	$89,355	$69,105
British North American colonies	132,250	177,929	17,382			865	40,279	27,527
Total	203,693	301,613	39,585			19,358	129,634	96,632
Total American and foreign merchandise	3,836,999	6,598,243	2,457,972	2,422	10,050	3,100,650	6,199,534	7,590,386

C.

Statement showing the amount of duties arising on merchandise imported into the United States from the British West Indies and British American colonies in American and foreign vessels during the years ending 30th September, 1815 and 1816.

On merchandise imported from—	In American vessels.		In foreign vessels.	
	1815.	1816.	1815.	1816.
British West Indies	$250,320	$313,218	$1,053,988	$1,814,268
British American colonies	431,849	135,430	954,771	181,868
	682,169	448,648	2,008,759	1,996,136

TREASURY DEPARTMENT, *Register's Office, January 7, 1818.*   JOSEPH NOURSE.

D.

Importations in American vessels from the West Indies, &c., during the year ending September 30, 1815.

	25 per cent.	30 pr. cent.	40 pr. cent.	Spirits.	Molasses.	Coffee.	Cocoa.	Sugar.			Salt.	
								Brown.	White.	Loaf.	Bushels.	Pounds.
British West Indies	$99,398	$30,850	$17	227,813	38,505	42,666	....	125,233	....	....	317,150	2,753,292
British American colonies	1,188,959	158,948	3,852	72,503	8,916	430	....	85,715	....	....	55,068	572,981
Other West Indies, &c.	2,999,702	572,547	40,459	1,814,650	3,516,851	17,687,856	89,042	33,750,094	2,471,840	....	519,799	4,596,961

Importations in foreign vessels from the West Indies, &c., during the year ending September 30, 1815.

	28-575 per cent.	34-650 per cent.	46-90 pr. cent.	Spirits.	Molasses.	Coffee.	Cocoa.	Sugar.			Salt.	
								Brown.	White.	Loaf.	Bushels.	Pounds.
British West Indies	$568,384	$138,159	$25,612	867,314	146,160	390,132	119,002	1,465,490	2,749	2,228	172,834	9,442,865
British American colonies	1,905,236	319,963	28,063	215,511	94,971	2,160	....	919,949	....	....	2,473	....
All other West Indies, &c.	2,746,059	568,500	62,472	1,353,419	1,934,949	1,754,589	163,421	7,580,632	1,010,394	....	202,376	3,676,364

E.

Importations in vessels of the United States from the West Indies and American colonies during the year ending September 30, 1816.

From—	Value of merchandise paying duties ad valorem.					Spirits.	Molasses.
	7½ per cent.	15 per cent.	20 per cent.	25 per cent.	30 per cent.		
British American colonies	$544	$12,382	$25,471	$300,213	$52,916	21,461	448
British West Indies	219	825	86	12,917	2,774	11,350	76,385
All other West Indies, &c.	1,822	130,331	8,942	306,771	114,331	2,214,050	6,255,342
	2,585	143,538	34,449	619,901	167,321	2,246,861	6,332,175

E.—*Importations in vessels of the United States—Continued.*

From—	Coffee.	Cocoa.	Sugar.		Pimento.	Salt.	
			Brown.	White clayed.		Pounds.	Bushels.
British American colonies	1,519	....	10,853	2,183	507	208,000	70,494
British West Indies	68,650	2,328	937,632	42,244	344	16,874,133	863,625
All other West Indies, &c.	21,089,410	1,257,496	29,036,044	5,097,257	19,584	1,092,945	69,079
	21,159,579	1,259,824	29,984,559	5,142,684	20,435	18,175,078	1,003,198

TREASURY DEPARTMENT, *Register's Office, February 10, 1818.*   JOSEPH NOURSE, *Register.*

E.—*Importations in foreign vessels from the West Indies and American coloni   dur ng the year ending September 30, 1816.*

| From— | Value of merchandise paying duties ad valorem. | | | | | Spirits. | Molasses. |
	8¼ per cent.	16¼ per cent.	22 per cent.	27½ per cent.	33 per cent.		
British American colonies	$9,384	$34,451	$9,987	$66,509	$17,377	74,539	4,171
British West Indies	....	19,447	4,153	316,180	75,266	1,651,291	500,594
All other West Indies	2,232	24,327	1,337	, 75,291	23,840	371,761	1,340,468
	11,616	78,225	15,457	477,980	116,503	2,097,591	1,845,233

E.—*Importations in foreign vessels—Continued.*

| From— | Coffee. | Cocoa. | Sugar. | | Pimento. | Salt. | |
			Brown.	White clayed.		Pounds.	Bushels.
British American colonies	39,309	6,395	57,048	....	29,331	209,123	1,816
British West Indies	1,872,532	139,460	5,318,977	224,409	1,411,818	2,508,818	425,683
All other West Indies	1,716,363	83,408	7,963,151	747,082	2,326	44,660	21,372
	3,621,204	229,263	13,339,176	971,491	1,443,475	2,763,601	448,871

TREASURY DEPARTMENT, *Register's Office, February 10, 1818.*

JOSEPH NOURSE, *Register.*

F.

Notes on the practical effect of the treaty lately made between Great Britain and the United States.

1. The duties and tonnage on British and American ships and goods are equalized, except as it respects the colonies of Great Britain in North America and the West Indies, to which the treaty does not apply.

2. Since the peace the colonial system of Great Britain has been enforced with unusual rigor, neither American vessels nor property being admitted into her colonies.

3. American vessels are admitted into the French, Spanish, Dutch, Danish, and Swedish colonies in the West Indies, under certain restrictions as to imports and exports; and the vessels of those nations are admitted under similar restrictions into the ports of the British colonies in the West Indies.

4. Very heavy duties have been recently imposed in the British West Indies on American produce, even when carried in British ships, and also on the exportation of plaster of Paris from the colony of Nova Scotia to the adjoining State of the Union.

Observations on the preceding facts.

1. In the agreement to equalize the duties on the carrying trade of the two countries it will be seen at the first glance that the positive advantages are on the side of Great Britain. Our exports are wholly composed of bulky articles, such as lumber, provisions, cotton, tobacco, tar, &c., &c., the whole of which are of primary necessity to the manufactures and colonies of Great Britain, and require for their transportation a quantity of tonnage ten-fold larger than that which would be requisite to bring back their value in British manufactures. Thus a single ship from London or Liverpool frequently brings to the United States twenty times the value of the cargo which the same carried from the United States; and of the one hundred sail of vessels which sailed for Ireland during the last season, not more than one would be requisite to bring back the returns in Irish linens, the only article of merchandise imported from that country. Now, the only advantage which the United States derives from the treaty is the removal of the duty imposed on their produce when carried to British ports in their own bottoms. It was found proper to remove this duty by giving up the immense advantages that would accrue from the exclusive carriage of our own productions. It may, however, be observed, with truth, that the British market has for many years been as necessary to our productions as those productions were to that market. But the period of monopoly has passed away, and our raw materials will find as ready a sale in the other parts of Europe as they have lately found in Great Britain. These observations apply more particularly to the intercourse between the United States and the European ports of Great Britain.

2. The seizure and condemnation of American vessels under the charge of violating the laws which regulate the West India trade leave no doubt as to the determination of the British Government to enforce its colonial system in the most rigid manner. This severity on the part of Great Britain will warrant a counteraction on ours.

3. We have at present an unrestricted entry into all the ports of the island of Cuba, and, although Spain may at a future day fix certain limits to our imports and exports, yet there can be no doubt of our having a partial entry for any lumber and other bulky commodities necessary to her colonists, as well as a free export of such as are not wanted for the commerce of the mother country. There is a mutual advantage in this exchange which will insure its continuance for many years.

We have also admission into the Dutch, French, Swedish, and Danish settlements in the West Indies, under such regulations, however, as the respective governments think proper to impose. These are of a nature to leave us many advantages and to employ a very large tonnage. We have also free admission into the Portuguese settlements in Brazil, where we might more reasonably expect a total seclusion. In a word, the other European nations have so far yielded to the course which Nature points out for the supply of their colonies with necessaries that they have no restrictions whatever as to the mode in which they are carried. Great Britain alone says that we shall not be the carriers of the articles which we ourselves furnish, although they are indispensable not only to the well being but frequently to the very existence of her colonies in the West Indies.

We should have less reason to complain if the rigor which is shown towards us were dealt out in equal measure to other nations. But this is so far from being the case, that vessels under the flag of any European nation having colonies in the West Indies are admitted under certain limitations as to the size and the nature of their cargoes, the latter of which, however, may be composed of the very articles generally carried from the United States, as well as of indigo, dye woods, specie, &c., and, what must appear very singular in the conduct of a nation affecting extraordinary morality in its public as well as private character, by far the greatest part of the commerce carried on under this admission of foreign vessels into her West India islands is in direct contravention of the laws of the respective governments to which they belong.

4. Does it accord with the spirit of liberality which we are to presume dictated the late treaty to impose most extraordinary duties on our productions, even when carried to her settlements in her own vessels? She may say, with apparent reasons, that she must encourage the consumption of the commodities which are of her own growth or of that of her North American colonies, and that ultimately the consumer must pay the duty. But I trust that before these observations are closed it will appear that this proceeding is grounded in jealousy and a reliance (I hope a mistaken one) in our apathy.

In considering the treaty without reference to the West Indies, it would at first appear that the carrying trade is left open to both the parties, and that there is a fair and equal chance for its emoluments. But on a nearer view, and in connexion with the excepted ports, it will be seen that Great Britain has such decided advantages over us that, unless some vigorous measures are adopted on our part, the shipping interest of this country must necessarily sustain incalculable loss. Instead of a gradual increase that might rationally be looked for in a country where every other branch of trade is progressive, we must be prepared to see our tonnage reduced at the end of four years to one-half its actual quantity. Great Britain leads annually six hundred sail of ships in her West India settlements, which make but one voyage a year. They sail from the West Indies generally between the months of May and August, and consequently arrive in England between June and October. Of those which arrive first, as many as are requisite are freighted to bring dry goods, &c., to the United States, and if freights do not offer they are loaded by the owners with salt, crates of earthen ware, coal, copperas, and a variety of bulky articles of small value, the profits on which generally afford a moderate freight. When these cargoes are landed in the United States, and others consisting of provisions, lumber of all sorts, stock, and such other articles as are admitted into the British colonies, are taken in, they proceed to their West India settlements with all the prospects of advantage afforded by an exclusive trade, and they arrive in season to take another freight to England. Now, if the trade between the United States and the West Indies in British ships were prohibited by our Government, all the British ships employed in making the indirect voyages of which we have just spoken would remain idle until the months of November and December, at which time they generally sail from Europe to the West Indies, or they must perform the intermediate voyage by proceeding to the British settlements on this continent to procure their lumber and provisions. But in this operation the advantage of the outward freight is lost, for those settlements cannot consume the great quantity of coarse goods which are readily disposed of in the United States, and, indeed, a sufficiency is supplied by vessels regularly employed between these settlements and the mother country. Thus every article of lumber and provisions carried from the North American colonies to the West Indies by vessels trading in this circuitous manner must be subject to the charge of double freight. But there is still a greater inconvenience which cannot be surmounted. Quebec is the only one of the colonies which can furnish breadstuffs for the West Indies. Now, it must be evident that the West India ships arrive in Europe too late to proceed to Quebec, as they would certainly be caught by the ice. In this event, therefore, of the seclusion of these ships from our ports, they would be unable to procure the profitable employment which they now enjoy by their circuitous voyages already described.

Again, a considerable tonnage is employed in carrying timber from the Bay of Fundy to Europe. The vessels employed in this trade, like those employed in that of the West Indies, bring freights or coarse goods to the United States, and then proceed to execute the main object of their voyage, after having secured one freight to the United States.

It must be seen on a moment's reflection that these operations produce an injury to our carrying trade commensurate to the benefit which they yield to that of Great Britain. For it is evident that in the instances here noticed the voyages to the United States are merely incidental to others of greater importance, and yet the cargoes brought to this country are precisely those which, under proper restrictions on our part, would be brought by our own vessels and by the other British ships employed in a regular trade between the two countries. In fact, it is an evil growing out of the British colonial system highly prejudicial to the maritime interests of this country. It is not even confined to the cases already noticed. British ships have brought freights or cargoes to the United States, where they have taken in lumber and provisions, with which they have proceeded to Jamaica, and, after landing their cargoes and finding freights scarce, they have gone in a few days to New Orleans for a load of cotton or tobacco for a European port; thus carrying three freights, two of which, at least, ought to have been carried by the ships of our own country. Now, the American tonnage proceeding from the northern and in fact from all the Atlantic States is compelled to proceed to New Orleans in ballast, because it cannot land cargoes of lumber and provisions in the West Indies as the British do. The case is equally strong when applied to the shipping belonging to the British colonies in North America. Vessels come from New Brunswick with cargoes of plaster, fish, &c., which yield a good freight and afford returns in provisions and lumber, which are carried to the West Indies and their value brought to us again in rum, &c. In these operations the American shipping cannot participate, and the singularity of this case is aggravated by the consideration that it is in the United States only that a market can be found for the plaster. There is something so unnatural in this restriction as to plaster that we should have supposed that even the jealous policy of Great Britain would have revolted at it, and surely great reliance must have been had on our forbearance when the experiment was hazarded. But one solid advantage is derived from the minuteness with which the British colonial system is enforced. It develops the views and intentions of Great Britain in a manner too clear to be misunderstood, and shows most forcibly the necessity of an early and vigorous reaction on our part.

In the formation of the treaty it is to be presumed that the parties, by relinquishing tonnage duties on the one side and bounties on the other, intended to leave the commerce of the two countries open to fair and open competition, and if one of the parties thought proper to make exceptions as to the trade of particular ports or places, it would not have been expected that those exceptions should in any way operate to the positive disadvantage of the other party. Thus, if Great Britain had reserved to herself and to her colonies in North America the privilege of directly supplying her West India settlements with provisions and lumber, however irrational and unnatural the scheme may have been, we had no right to complain. But when she avails herself of the exception of her colonies from the operation of the treaty, in order to destroy or diminish the apparent equivalent which we have or should have received in return for our concessions, it would be extreme folly to suppose that our Government would not take the necessary steps to remedy so serious an evil. The treaty would otherwise prove nothing more or less than an act of self-immolation.

.   .   But there is another feature in the treaty which, although it has excited but little observation, because its practical effects have not yet been felt, yet requires the immediate interference of the Legislature. British ships may import into the United States, on equal terms with our own ships, the productions, and manufactures of the whole globe; whereas we can carry to Great Britain, in our vessels, only *certain* articles of our own produce, and those, too, in an unmanufactured state. The staples of the eastern and middle States are virtually excluded from British ports by bounties granted in favor of her own and of her colonial productions. British ships may bring from the Baltic to the United States the bulky articles of hemp, iron, cordage, and coarse linens; from Holland and Germany a great variety of coarse goods, the wines and brandy and even plaster of France; and also the wines and fruits of Spain and Portugal, as well as the salt of the latter countries, the last and only resource of a great number of our vessels returning from Europe, together with all the productions of the countries bordering on the Mediterranean, and, in a word, as before observed, of the whole universe. Thus it appears that the operation of the treaty in its present form, and without interruption by restrictive measures on our part, will soon place us in nearly the same relation in which her colonies stand to Great Britain, with the additional and very convenient circumstance of our requiring no aid from her to support our establishment. We receive the produce and manufactures of Great Britain, of her colonies, and of the whole universe, in her own bottoms; we furnish the most precious raw materials to her manufactures, and to her colonies lumber and provisions of a quality suited to the habits of her colonists, such as can be procured with convenience in this country only, and such as are always necessary to their convenience and frequently to their very existence. We receive from their colonies in North America all their productions, and more especially one that has no value except in our country, and yet, being of a very bulky nature, requires and employs for its transport a very extensive tonnage. Thus we furnish a very extensive nursery for British seamen and an ample field for the employment of British capital, and what is the return for all these advantages and for all this complaisance on our part? Why, it is the privilege of carrying in our own bottoms a part of our own productions to Great Britain on the same terms that similar goods are carried from our country in her ships. And this is the same nation which but a short time ago threatened to drive our flag from the ocean, and from the ocean she will drive it, without firing a gun, if we sleep at our posts.

We are to presume from the character of the individuals who acted as our Commissioners in the formation of the treaty that they were fully aware of the consequences that might flow from the exclusion of the British colonies from its operation, and they must have been sensible that some moderate concessions would have been made by the British Government in regard to their colonial trade, or that the severity of its regulations would be met by a corresponding counteraction on our part. It appears, therefore, singular that no mention has been made relative to the subject in any of the official communications of the Government to Congress, nor, in fact, any notice taken of it, until a motion was made by Mr. King calling for some rigorous measures on our part to meet those already adopted by the British Government. From the sentiments expressed by some of the House it may be inferred that it is considered as a very delicate subject. It is certain that it is much to be regretted that the conduct of Great Britain should render it a subject of necessary legislation in our national councils. But it must be observed that the date of the British tariff of duties on our produce carried to the West Indies is subsequent to that of the treaty. We may therefore be considered at issue on the point of restriction, and we may as well commence our operations now as at some future period, when the minds of our people may be more irritated by the operations of the present system. There may be some difference of opinion as to the manner in which we ought to proceed in regard to the West India trade; but this, I think, will soon disappear when we look narrowly into the nature of the West India settlements and of the many local circumstances by which they are affected. Soon after the American Revolution Great Britain excluded the vessels of the United States from her West India ports. She had determined to try the experiment of supplying them from her colonies on this continent. She, however, permitted her own vessels to carry supplies from the United States; and yet so inadequate were these supplies to meet the extraordinary demand occasioned by hurricanes, that, according to the statements of Bryan Edwards, the historian, in the short period of six years no less than fifteen thousand human beings perished in her West India colonies from hunger and bad provisions. But there is now no longer a deficiency of tonnage or capital for the ample supply of those colonies, provided our ports are open as they then were. There is, on the contrary, a redundancy both of shipping and capital, and nothing is wanted but a continuance of our complaisance to insure the profitable employment of one and the other. The views of Great Britain have been developed by acts of an unequivocal character, and it now rests with us to show whether she has judged us correctly in calculating on our forbearance now, as she did on the former occasion. Then, if we are not arrested by any considerations in regard to her, we have only to settle the question as it respects the interest of our own country. This subject may be brought before us in a very simple form: *Can Great Britain support her West India colonies in comfort, or even in safety, without supplies from the United States?* I answer, with confidence, that she cannot; and that, consequently, we are entitled to and can obtain from her a reasonable participation in the carriage of the articles which we alone can furnish. If she monopolizes the carriage of her plaster, may we not as reasonably monopolize the carriage of our supplies, which are as useful to them as her plaster is to us.

.   We have already shown in what manner she now supplies her islands from the United States, and how much that mode of supply operates to our prejudice, and, from the single fact of her taking supplies from us in any form or manner, it might fairly be inferred that she is unable to furnish them from her own resources. For can any one, knowing the uniform course of her policy towards us, doubt for a moment as to the motives of her conduct on this occasion? Would she permit the importation of a barrel of meal or one stave from this country if she could furnish that barrel or that stave from her own possessions? But we shall endeavor to supply proofs of a more positive character. Let us then suppose all communication to be interdicted between the United States and the British West India islands, and that the latter are compelled to rely on their own resources or those of the mother country and her colonies on this continent for supplies of lumber and provisions.

It is well known that the West India islands are unable to support themselves, otherwise the question as to supplying them would never have been agitated. The single circumstance of their being liable to be occasionally visited by hurricanes is of itself sufficient evidence of their dependence on foreign aid. They must then depend on supplies from the mother country and her colonies in North America. Let us now see to what extent they may safely rely on the one and the other. England and Ireland can furnish salt provisions in abundance, and wheaten and rye flour. The latter are the only articles of dry provisions that can be furnished from Europe. Peas and beans have been tried frequently, but have been found a most unwholesome food for the slaves. Rye flour is also a bad food, as it proves uniformly sour before its arrival, and makes at best but a weak and unwholesome food in the manner in which it must be used by the negroes, as they cannot submit it to the process of fermentation before it is used. The mode of preparing food adopted by the negroes is, and necessarily must be, extremely simple, and must require but little time or fuel; a small earthen or iron pot composes the whole of a negro's culinary apparatus, and into this pot everything must go. During the late war the experiment was fully made with rye flour, and it was universally condemned and abandoned as soon as Indian meal could be procured. Wheaten flour, although wholesome and nourishing, yet, requiring more preparation than Indian meal or rice, is found less agreeable than the latter articles, even when perfectly sweet; but it will be seen that of necessity it must generally be delivered to the negro in an unsound state, and of course must prove an unwholesome diet. Thus we see that Great Britain can furnish but one article of dry provisions to her islands, and even that one of a doubtful character as to its effects on the health of the negroes. Of her means for supplying lumber I presume it is needless to say anything, as she relies on foreign supplies for her own consumption. The islands must then depend on Nova Scotia and Canada for all their lumber, and for such dry provisions as the mother country cannot supply. Nova Scotia can export no dry provisions; on the contrary, she imports for her own consumption. Fish she can supply in great variety and abundance. White pine lumber abounds in the Bay of Fundy, but good lumber of other kinds is very scarce there. The only and last resource, therefore, is Canada. Here flour and lumber of some kinds may be procured; but there are so many untoward circumstances attending the mode of supply from Canada that the object can only be attained in a very imperfect manner. Thus we see that the West Indies can be supplied with flour, fish, and a certain portion of lumber, from Canada and Nova Scotia; and we will, for argument's sake, suppose that these supplies may be fully equal to the demands of the islands; we will further suppose that the planters, as well as the slaves, are compelled to eat Canadian flour and to use none but Canadian and Nova Scotia lumber and fish; we will even go further, and suppose that a regular intercourse is established, and that the demands of the colonies in the West Indies are ascertained and the shipments duly proportioned to those demands. Are there then no contingencies which may occasionally diminish, if not wholly defeat, the object of this arrangement? It is well known that vessels of burden can make but one voyage annually to Quebec, and that, consequently, the whole supply of dry provisions, consisting only of bread and flour, for one year's consumption, must be deposited in the warm climate of the West Indies between the months of June and September, and that during the remaining eight months of the year the consumer must eat the flour of the preceding year's growth, under all its progressive and, I may add, rapid stages of deterioration, until the supplies of the ensuing year arrive. But this is not the only inconvenience attending this mode of supply; a much larger capital must be employed in the business, because the merchant in the West Indies who supplies the estates must make his investments for the remainder of the year during the four months in which the supplies are brought to market, and he will demand a price proportioned to the inconvenience sustained by his heavy advances and to the danger of totally losing whatever stock he may have on hand when new provisions arrive; thus the provisions which, under the most favorable circumstances, would be dear, become much more so. But we will even suppose that this inconvenience is obviated by a submission on the part of the planter; we will then have placed the matter in the most favorable point of view that our opponents could require.

It is well known that the island of Jamaica has more internal resources than any of the other British islands in the West Indies. She raises such large quantities of ground provisions and has such extensive plantation walks, as they are called, that she does not import one-tenth part of the provisions consumed by her black population. The clearances from our custom-houses will show that she receives from us proportionably less negro and more fine provisions than any other of the British islands. I make this assertion on the additional authority of the best-informed merchants of this city; but the weight of my observations on this particular point are but little affected by a supposition of the quantity of negro provisions being greater or less than that here stated.

According to the official returns of the number of negroes in that island in the year 1787, the latest official record that I can find, there were—

    250,000 negroes.
    40,000 white and colored persons in the island.
    —————
    290,000 being the whole population.
    ═════

We have already supposed that the whole of the white population shall receive its dry provisions from abroad, but that the negroes and colored people receive only one-tenth of their provisions in the same manner. Let us then suppose that under this order of things the island should be visited by one of those dreadful hurricanes by which it is so frequently ravaged and which destroy all the fruits of the earth that are exposed to the violence of their action. The consequences of this awful visitation cannot be contemplated without horror and without deprecating the blind and inveterate policy that could subject such an extensive population to all the miseries of famine and consequent insurrections and massacres that would ensue. If it is imagined that I speak in terms of exaggeration, let me refer to the authentic history of Bryan Edwards. But enough can be proved without any such reference; for it must be remembered that these scourges would only occur at those precise periods when the islands can receive no immediate supplies from Canada, and that they are too remote from England to receive aid from that quarter. Hurricanes prevail almost exclusively in the months of September and October, during which latter month the navigation of the St. Lawrence generally closes.

I have selected the island of Jamaica for the particular object of my observations because it is equal in value to all the other islands, and because it has proportionally greater resources. The same observations will apply with still greater force to the other insular possessions of Great Britain in the West Indies.

When we take into consideration the amount of British capital vested in the West Indies, estimated many years ago by Bryan Edwards at the enormous sum of 70,000,000 sterling; of the value and extent of the British shipping employed in the West India trade, which, in 1787, was no less than 1,069 vessels, or 155,009 tons; and also the amount of the mercantile capital actively and usefully employed in this trade, can we for one moment suppose that Great Britain will put in jeopardy the whole or any considerable part of these important possessions merely to preserve to herself the comparatively small consideration of monopolizing the carriage of our lumber and provisions, in which we have a rational claim to participate? Such a supposition but ill accords with the wary and calculating spirit that governs her commercial policy.

But let us admit that, deaf to all the suggestions of reason and common prudence, she should persist in this course of interdiction, are there no other considerations opposed to its operation? Will she lay aside all regard to the comfort, to the established habits and to the interests of her colonists, which are identified with her own? The charges incident to the cultivation of the favored island of Jamaica are already so high that, on an average, the estates of that island scarcely pay the legal interest of the capitals vested in them; and it is well known that her possessions in the Antilles have for many years been considered rather as splendid than useful appendages to the crown. Many of the sugar estates have lately been converted into pasture from the inability of the proprietors to support the heavy charges incident to the manufacture of sugar and rum, and from the decrease of population. Our embargo and the late war have contributed considerably to produce this effect. The preceding observations are made under a presumption that Great Britain is at peace with all the world. But if we represent her as engaged in a war with any of the maritime nations of Europe, her West India colonies must be absolutely dependent on the United States for their supplies. For even if Great Britain and her North American colonies could furnish the materials, the charges of carriage and insurance would render them insupportably dear. Whilst writing these notes I received from a friend the return of the naval officer of Jamaica of the imports and exports of that island for one year, viz: from the 30th September, 1803, to September 30, 1804; of some of the items of this document I may speak hereafter. At present I shall only observe that it was made at a time when Great Britain was at war with France, and when she found it necessary, *as she always must do on similar occasions*, to suspend the operations of her colonial system. From the part which we then performed in furnishing and carrying supplies to her islands, it may easily be imagined what must be the situation of these islands when the mother country is at war with us. The writer can state, on the authority of several respectable residents in the island of St. Croix, that, from the commencement of our embargo in —— to the conclusion of the late war, no less than 7,000 slaves perished from hunger and bad provisions; the island during that time was in possession of the British. Its proximity to Porto Rico gave it many advantages over the other British islands.

It may, however, be justly observed that the object is well worth the attention and even solicitude of Great Britain. By the return of which I have just spoken, and which will be found annexed to these notes, it appears that the amount of tonnage which entered Jamaica from America in one year was 69,525 tons, and we can form some estimate of the proportion of that tonnage which belonged to the United States by the proportion of goods stated to have been carried by American vessels. I should be disposed to consider the proportion at least as eight tons of American to one of British shipping. But if the tonnage employed in carrying to Jamaica 69,525 tons be doubled it will give a tolerably accurate view of the whole tonnage sent from America to the West Indies in one year, viz: 139,050 tons. This tonnage, divided, gives 1,390 vessels, of 100 tons, performing one voyage in a year, or 695, of the same burden, performing two voyages in a year; or 347, of 200 tons, performing two voyages in a year. Now, can it be reasonably expected that, as a maritime nation, we will permit Great Britain to load by far the largest part of this tonnage in our ports with articles which she cannot supply, and which are absolutely necessary to her colonies, without some equivalent? Are we to count for nothing the market which we afford for the consumption of her West India produce, and without which one most important item, viz: rum, must lose one-half its value?

The writer closes his observations on this very important subject with a personal one relative to himself. He has lived many years in the West Indies, and has been intimately connected with their commerce for the last thirty-five years.

St. Jago de la Vaga, Jamaica, *December* 1.

By the return of the naval officer laid before the House of Assembly, on Tuesday the 13th November, the following is a summary of the exports and imports of this island from the 30th September, 1803, to 30th September, 1804:

Imports from the United States of America in American vessels.

64,362 barrels of corn meal and flour.	267 quintals of fish.
16,119 bags ⎫	11,741 barrels of beef.
6,223 barrels ⎬ of bread.	17,038 barrels of pork.
3,895 kegs ⎭	5,247 firkins of butter.
3,063 tierces of rice.	65,435 bushels of corn.
2,275 hhds. ⎫	6,768,271 feet of lumber.
15,743 barrels ⎬ of fish.	7,997,957 staves and heading.
444 kegs ⎪	12,733,207 shingles.
2,743 boxes ⎭	

In British vessels.

12,937 barrels of corn meal and flour.
648 barrels ⎤
513 kegs ⎬ of bread.
561 tierces of rice.
261 hhds. ⎤
845 barrels ⎬ of fish.
100 kegs.
565 boxes.
667 barrels of beef.

1,596 barrels of pork.
49 firkins of butter.
162 casks.
3,892 bushels of corn.
400,845 feet of lumber.
411,902 staves and heading.
242,000 shingles.
93 casks of tobacco.
1,467 barrels of naval stores.

From British America.

816 barrels of flour.
100 bags ⎤
88 barrels ⎬ of bread.
109 kegs ⎟
10 quintals ⎦
1,904 hhds. ⎤
13,798 barrels ⎬ of fish.
324 kegs ⎟
368 boxes ⎦
362 barrels of bread.

191 barrels of pork.
80 firkins of butter.
4,300 bushels of corn.
719,971 feet of lumber.
302,750 staves and heading.
139,750 shingles.
153 logs.
60,000 feet of mahogany.
154 casks of oil.
92 hhds. of beer.

Exports—Total from Kingston.

41,562 hhds. ⎤
3,940 tierces ⎬ of sugar.
144 barrels ⎦
12,003 puncheons ⎤ of rum.
541 hhds ⎦
64 casks of molasses.

873 bags ⎤ of ginger.
1,024 casks ⎦
5,645 bags ⎤ of pimento.
632 casks ⎦
16,313,386 pounds of coffee.

Total from the out ports.

61,970 hhds. ⎤
8,862 tierces ⎬ of sugar.
717 barrels ⎦
30,204 puncheons ⎤ of rum.
372 hhds. ⎦
365 casks of molasses.

981 bags ⎤ of ginger.
70 casks ⎦
13,927 bags ⎤ of pimento.
785 casks ⎦
5,750,594 pounds of coffee.

GRAND TOTAL.

103,352 hhds. ⎤
12,802 tierces ⎬ of sugar.
2,207 barrels ⎦
42,207 puncheons ⎤ of rum.
913 hhds. ⎦
429 casks of molasses.

1,854 bags ⎤ of ginger.
1,094 casks ⎦
19,572 bags ⎤ of pimento.
1,417 casks ⎦
22,063,980 pounds of coffee.

Increase since last year, in coffee only, 4,240,977 pounds.
Decrease about—

6,000 hogsheads of sugar.
16,148 puncheons ⎤ of rum.
560 hhds. ⎦
93 casks of molasses.

2,644 bags of ginger.
1,537 bags ⎤ of pimento.
68 casks ⎦

The tonnage of vessels trading to this island between September 30, 1803, and September 30, 1804, was—

From Great Britain and Ireland.. 93,433 tons.
From America .... 69,525 "
From the Spanish Main... 4,101 "
Traders under free port act.. 14,826 "
Droggers .... 3,382 "

During the above period 1,813 horses, 2,182 mules, 218 asses, and 2,107 horned cattle have been imported, and from Great Britain and Ireland 54,507 barrels of herrings.

ARTICLE 1. His Britannic Majesty consents to extend to the United States the provisions of the free port act, as established by the 45 Geo. III, chap. 57, (except as far as relates to negro slaves, which, under the abolition acts, can no longer be lawfully exported from any British possession to any foreign country ;) that is to say, that any sloop, schooner, or other vessel whatever, not having more than one deck, and being owned and navigated by subjects of the United States, may import into any of the free ports in his Majesty's possessions in the West Indies, from the United States, any of the articles enumerated in the above act, being of the growth or production of the United States, and any coin, bullion, diamonds, and precious stones; and the said articles, being of the growth or production of the United

States, and also all other articles imported into the said free ports by virtue of this convention from the United States, shall be subject in all respects to the same rules, regulations, and restrictions, and shall enjoy the same advantages as to re-exportation as are now applied to similar articles when imported by authority of said act from any other foreign country, and re-exported from the said possessions of his Majesty. His Britannic Majesty further consents that any vessel of the United States, as above described, may export from any of the said ports to the United States rum of the produce of any British colony or possession; and also all manner of goods, wares, or merchandise which shall have been legally imported into those possessions of his Majesty in which the said free ports are established, except masts, yards, or bowsprits, pitch, tar, and turpentine, and also except such iron as shall have been brought from the British colonies or plantations in America.

And whereas, by an act passed in the 48th year of his Majesty's reign, chapter 125, rice, grain, and flour are added to the articles previously allowed to be imported into the said free ports, it is agreed that those articles may be imported from the United States into the said free ports in vessels of the United States, as above described; and it is agreed on the part of the United States that any facilities granted in consequence of this convention to American vessels in his Majesty's said colonies and possessions shall be reciprocally granted in the ports of the United States to British vessels of a similar description engaged in the intercourse so allowed to be carried on; and that if at any future period during the continuance of this convention his Britannic Majesty should think fit to grant any further facilities to vessels of the United States in the said colonies and possessions, British vessels trading between the said colonies and possessions and the United States shall enjoy in the ports of the latter equal and reciprocal advantages. It is further agreed that articles imported into the said free ports of the United States by virtue of this convention shall pay the same duties as are or may be payable upon similar articles when imported into the said free ports from any other foreign country; and the same rule shall be observed on the part of the United States in regard to all duties chargeable upon all such articles as may, by virtue of this convention, be exported from the said free ports to the United States.

But his Britannic Majesty reserves to himself the right to impose higher duties upon all articles so allowed to be imported into the said free ports from the United States, or from any other foreign country, than are or may be chargeable upon all similar articles when imported from any of his Majesty's possessions.

Art. 2. His Britannic Majesty engages to allow the vessels of the United States to import into the Island of Bermuda the following articles, viz: tobacco, pitch, tar, turpentine, hemp, flax, masts, yards, bowsprits, staves, heading, boards and plank, timber, shingles, and lumber of any sort; bread, biscuit, flour, peas, beans, potatoes, wheat, rice, oats, barley, and grain of any sort, such commodities being the growth or production of the Territories belonging to the United States of America; and to export from the said island to the United States, in vessels of the said States, any goods or commodities whatever which are now by law allowed to be exported from his Majesty's colonies and possessions in the West Indies to any foreign country or place in Europe; and also sugar, molasses, coffee, cocoa, nuts, ginger, and pimento; and also all goods the growth, produce, or manufacture of the United Kingdom of Great Britain and Ireland, upon the same terms and subject to the same duties only as would affect similar articles when imported from the United States into Bermuda, or exported from Bermuda to the United States in British ships. And it is agreed on the part of the United States that a similar equality shall prevail in the ports of the said States with regard to all British vessels trading in similar articles between the United States and the Island of Bermuda.

Art. 3. It is agreed that vessels of the United States may resort to Turk's Island for the purpose of taking in cargoes of salt for the United States; and that the vessels so resorting to the said island shall be allowed to import tobacco, cotton and wool, the produce of the said United States, upon the same terms and subject to the same duties as British ships when engaged in a similar intercourse. It is agreed on the part of the United States that a similar equality shall prevail in the ports of the said States with regard to all British vessels trading in the same articles between the United States and the said Turk's Island.

Art. 4. It is agreed that the navigation of all lakes, rivers, and water communications, the middle of which is or may be the boundary between his Britannic Majesty's territories on the continent of North America and the United States, shall, with the exception hereinafter mentioned, at all times be free to his Majesty's vessels and those of the citizens of the United States. The inhabitants of his Britannic Majesty's territories in North America and the citizens and subjects of the United States may freely carry on trade and commerce by land or inland navigation, as aforesaid, in goods and merchandise the growth, produce, or manufacture of the British territories in Europe or elsewhere, or of the United States, respectively, within the territories of the two parties, respectively, on the said continent, (the countries within the limits of the Hudson's Bay Company only excepted;) and no other or higher duties or tolls, or rates of carriage or portage, than which are or shall be payable by natives, respectively, shall be taken or demanded on either side. All goods or merchandise, whose importation into the United States shall not be wholly prohibited, may freely, for the purposes of commerce, above mentioned, be carried into the said United States in the manner aforesaid by his Britannic Majesty's subjects; and such goods or merchandise shall be subject to no other or higher duties than would be payable by citizens of the United States on the importation of the same in American vessels into the Atlantic ports of the United States; and in like manner all goods and merchandise the growth, produce, or manufacture of the United States, whose importation into his Majesty's said territories in America shall not be entirely prohibited, may freely, for the purposes of the commerce above mentioned, be carried into the same by land, or by means of such lakes, rivers, and water communications, as above mentioned, by the citizens of the United States; and such goods and merchandise shall be subject to no other or higher duties than would be payable by his Majesty's subjects on the importation of the same from Europe into the said territories.

No duties shall be levied by either party on peltries or furs which may be brought in the manner aforesaid by land or inland navigation from the said territories of one party into the said territories of another; but tolls or rates of ferriage may be demanded and taken in manner above mentioned on such peltries or furs. It is further agreed that nothing in this article contained as to the navigation of rivers, lakes, or water communication, shall extend to give a right of navigation upon or within the same in those parts where the middle is not the boundary between his Britannic Majesty's territories and the United States of America.

OCCUPATION OF AMELIA ISLAND.

COMMUNICATED BY THE CHAIRMAN OF THE COMMITTEE ON FOREIGN RELATIONS OF THE HOUSE OF REPRESENTATIVES
JANUARY 20, 1819.

*Communicated to the Hon. John Holmes, Chairman of the Committee on Foreign Relations of the House of
Representatives.*

DEPARTMENT OF STATE, *January* 20, 1819.

SIR: In answer to the questions in your letter of the 16th instant I have the honor to state that
Amelia Island is held under the authority of the act of Congress of January 15, 1811, and is intended to
be held as long as the reasons upon which it was taken shall continue, subject, of course, to any other
provision which Congress may deem necessary or expedient.[1] It is under a military government. No
customs are collected, no vessels being permitted to enter the port. Of its population the only evidence
possessed is contained in the extract of a letter from Colonel Bankhead, a copy of which is herewith
inclosed.

I am, very respectfully, sir, your most humble and obedient servant,

J. Q. ADAMS.

[Extract.]

FERNANDINA, AMELIA ISLAND, *December* 24, 1817.

SIR: Most of the inhabitants at this place at this time are followers of Aury and those persons who
have been drawn here from motives of speculation, who are, I suspect, of that profligate character
generally engaged in the violation or evasion of our revenue laws.

I have the honor to be, very respectfully, your most obedient servant,

JAMES BANKHEAD,
Major 1st Bat. Art. S. D., Com'g detachment United States troops.
GEORGE GRAHAM, Esq., *Acting Secretary of War.*

BRITISH WEST INDIA AND NORTH AMERICAN COLONIAL TRADE.

COMMUNICATED TO THE SENATE FEBRUARY 19, 1819.

Mr. MACON, from the Committee on Foreign Relations, to whom was referred so much of the documents
accompanying the Commercial Convention with Great Britain as relates to the colonial trade, made
the following report; which was read:

That the object of the negotiation with Great Britain respecting the colonial trade is the establishment
of a regulation whereby a trade in articles of the produce and manufacture of the United States and of
the British colonies may be carried on between them; and secondly, a regulation whereby the shipping
of the two countries may be placed on an equal footing in the carrying on of this trade.

In respect to the articles of the trade, the United States would agree that all articles of the produce
and manufacture of the United States and of the respective colonies should be included, and all other articles
excluded. But as Great Britain probably would not consent to this arrangement, the United States would
not object to the catalogue of articles of the produce and manufacture of the United States and of the
said colonies enumerated in the British acts of Parliament, and according to which the trade has heretofore
been carried on in British bottoms.

As respects duties and charges, they should be placed on a footing of reciprocal equality. If Great
Britain would consent to impose no higher or other duties on articles of the produce and manufacture of
the United States imported into the colonies than upon the like articles imported from her continental
colonies, (whence only they can be obtained,) the United States might agree to impose no greater or
other duties and charges on articles the produce and manufacture of her colonies than on the like articles
from other countries. To this adjustment Great Britain will probably disagree. In lieu thereof, and as a
compensation for the stipulation not to impose greater or other duties on the colonial articles of Great
Britain than on the like articles of other countries, it might be stipulated, on the part of Great Britain,
that the duties and charges on articles of the produce and manufacture of the United States should not
exceed by more than ——— per cent. those which should be imposed on the like articles imported from
the British continental colonies.

In no event should articles of the produce and manufacture of the United States pay higher duties
and charges in the direct voyage from the United States than in the indirect or circuitous voyage through
New Brunswick, Nova Scotia, Bermudas, or other intermediate ports; and as the direct trade should not
be more restrained in respect to the articles thereof than the indirect or circuitous trade, no article
should be allowed to go or come indirectly or circuitously which might not go or come directly.

.   There is nothing in principle or policy that forbids the confining of this trade, to articles of the produce or manufacture of the respective countries—that is, of the United States and of the British colonies. Articles of the produce and manufacture of other portions of the British territories coming through these colonies being excluded from the United States as articles not of the produce and manufacture of the United States are excluded from Great Britain, and would be excluded from the British colonies.

As respects the shipping employed in this trade, it must be placed on a footing of practical and reciprocal equality, both as respects duties and charges and the equal participation of the trade. On this adjustment, even there will exist an advantage in favor of the English navigation, as it will be exclusively employed in the transportation of articles of the produce and manufacture of the United States between the intermediate colonies aforesaid and the West India colonies, and likewise, in a disproportioned degree, in the distribution of these articles among the British West India colonies.

Furthermore, as the voyage from the United States to New Brunswick, Nova Scotia, and Bermuda is a short one, and would yield but little profit, the duties and charges must be as great on the British ships and the articles of the produce and manufacture of the United States composing their cargoes arriving in the British West India colonies through these intermediate colonies, as on the same ships and articles arriving directly from the United States; otherwise the direct trade will be deserted in favor of the circuitous trade, and thereby the object of the arrangement, an equality in the employment of the shipping of the two countries, will be defeated. So far as the operation of the late navigation law is understood it seems to have been advantageous, and especially in the increase of the American shipping engaged in the direct trade between the United States and Great Britain and the corresponding decrease of that of Great Britain; but sufficient time has not yet been afforded satisfactorily to ascertain this point, nor to determine other questions that are in a course of solution.

Perhaps it would be prudent to allow time for this important experiment; and, to suffer the negotiation on this subject to remain where it is for the present, it ought not to be forgotten that, without cutting off the trade with New Brunswick, Nova Scotia, and Bermuda, this experiment cannot be fairly made. Whether it would be expedient at the present session to adopt this measure is perhaps doubtful.

If the effect of our navigation law, reinforced according to the above suggestion, should prove to be such as it not improbably will be, it might and probably would be our true footing to adhere to the law and decline any convention with Great Britain touching the colony trade.

16TH CONGRESS.]   No. 335.   [1ST SESSION.

IMPRISONMENT OF WILLIAM WHITE, AN AMERICAN CITIZEN, AT
BUENOS AYRES.

COMMUNICATED TO THE HOUSE OF REPRESENTATIVES DECEMBER 15, 1819.

To the House of Representatives of the United States:

In conformity with the resolution of the House of Representatives of the 24th of February last, I now transmit a report of the Secretary of State, with extracts and copies of several letters touching the causes of the imprisonment of William White, an American citizen, at Buenos Ayres.

JAMES MONROE.

WASHINGTON, *December* 14, 1819.

DEPARTMENT OF STATE, *Washington, December* 14, 1819.

The Secretary of State, to whom has been referred a resolution of the House of Representatives of the 24th of February last, requesting the President to cause to be laid before that House, at the next session of Congress, any information which might be in his power touching the causes of the imprison-ment of William White, an American citizen, at Buenos Ayres, has the honor herewith to submit to the President extracts from a communication of Mr. John Graham, together with copies of several letters to and from Mr. W. G. D. Worthington, which contain all the information in possession of this Department upon that subject.

Respectfully submitted.

JOHN QUINCY ADAMS.

Extract from a communication of Mr. Graham, one of the Commissioners to South America, to the Department of State.

"3d. That of Mr. William White. This requires some detail. This gentleman made himself known to Judge Bland, at Montevideo, as an American citizen, and was by him introduced to me. He took an early occasion to state how much he had been injured by the government of Buenos Ayres; that to his exertion they were indebted for the fleet which gave them Montevideo; that they had refused to pay him the money due him; had thrown him into prison, and ultimately banished him. We, Judge Bland and I, explained to him that this was not a case on which we could act. He came on board the frigate, remained there all night in consequence of the wind, and before he went off gave me a large parcel of papers in relation to his case. I did not wish to take them, as I did not think it probable that I could make any use of them, for the reasons above stated, and because I saw on opening them that Mr. Worthington had made an unsuccessful attempt to obtain permission for him to visit Buenos Ayres to settle his affairs there, the object he seemed then to have in view. He requested me, however, to take them and read them; that they would be interesting as matter of history, and if I found I could do anything for him he would be obliged to me. Upon this consideration I took them. . I looked over them, and, so far as I understood them, did not find that they presented a case for us to act on." "Under these circumstances, Mr. White obtained permission from Captain Sinclair to come up to Buenos Ayres in the ship's tender, and very unexpectedly presented himself at our lodgings to ask our aid. We told him that he had embarrassed us exceedingly by coming up in the tender, a vessel which, from respect to us, had been exempted from search, and that an implied pledge, at least, had been given that no violation of the law should be permitted, and that he had now, without consulting us, presented himself at our house; that under such circumstances we could not interfere in his behalf or offer him any advice how he should proceed—the alleged object for which he called on us. . The only doubt was whether it was not our duty to state to the Government what had taken place. To this he said he would have no objection, particularly as his arrival was no longer a secret, and as any consequence would be less injurious to him than going back to Montevideo without obtaining for his family some relief. . We, accordingly, the next day informed the director what had taken place. He was evidently very seriously affected when he heard that Mr. White had come up—before he knew what was the object of our communication, remarked that he could not be permitted to land. After a little while he recovered himself and said, that, so far as he was individually concerned, he would have no objection, as White owed him money. He then put it upon the ground of popular indignation, observed that White was exceedingly obnoxious. On my remarking that, as a citizen of the United States, I hoped that justice would be done him as a fellow-citizen, he said that he did not know what he was; he sometimes claimed to be an English subject, and had certainly aided and assisted the British in getting into Buenos Ayres; that he was a notorious smuggler and violator of the laws, &c. White was afterwards arrested, and we left him in prison. There was some reason to think that he preferred being there, at least for the present, to going back to his family without accomplishing his object. He is understood to be a restless intriguer, and had, probably, political objects in view, as connected with his money affairs."

Copy of a letter from the Commissioners to William White, Esq.

BUENOS AYRES, *May* —, 1818.

SIR: Soon after we received the letter which you addressed to us, we sent you a message that we had been told by the director that you would not be permitted to land, but that you might appoint an attorney to manage any business you had there. We have now to add that a subsequent communication with the Secretary of State leads us to believe that this determination will not be departed from.

Under these circumstances, we deem it proper to return to you the papers which you sent us for perusal.

WM. WHITE, Esq.

Copy of a letter from Mr. Worthington to Mr. Adams, dated Baltimore, December 4, 1819.

SIR: On the receipt of your letter of the 30th June last, inclosing a copy of the resolution of the House of Representatives of the United States of the 24th February, calling for information on the imprisonment, at Buenos Ayres, of Mr. White, an American citizen, as I answered you on the 3d July, I immediately wrote to the Rio de la Plata for full and precise information on the case. I have yet received no answer, and as my letter may have miscarried, or an answer may arrive too late for the ensuing session of Congress, I feel it my duty to afford you all the knowledge I have on the subject, loose and unsatisfactory as it may be. In my letter of the 9th July, 1818, from Santiago de Chili, amongst nineteen packages of different papers forwarded to your Department, I sent a duplicate of Wm. P. White's case, marked "No. 4," which package, I presume, was composed of, 1st. A copy of White's letter from Montevideo, of the 29th November, 1817, to me. 2d. My answer to him of the 10th December, 1817. 3d. My memorial for him to his excellency Mr. Pueyrredon, the supreme director of the United Provinces of the Rio de la Plata, of the 13th January, 1818; and 4th. The answer to me from Mr. Secretary Tagle, of the 23d January, 1818.

From the press of business then before me I omitted to make a note on the case, as was customary with me. Now, all that I know, in addition to what those papers furnish, is simply this:

Mr. Tagle's answer was not handed till the very day, nay a few hours before I stepped into the coach to cross the Pampas for Chili, as will be seen by comparing dates with the second part of my diary, &c. So, if it had even been expedient and necessary, I had no chance to contest it. I never heard anything more of M. White (having sent him a copy of Tagle's letter) till my return, in March last, to Buenos Ayres, when his son brought me a letter from his father wishing me to meet him in a boat out in the roads of Buenos Ayres. I requested his son to tell him I would do no such thing; I had taken leave of the Government and was just about embarking for the United States; that I had appointed Mr. Strong consul, and should refer his letter to him, who would, no doubt, attend to anything right and proper in his case. I did so, and have sent Mr. Strong a copy of the resolution under consideration, but have not yet heard from him.

White has been in prison at least two or three times at Buenos Ayres, also at Montevideo; and I was told was put in prison while our Commissioners in the Congress were at Buenos Ayres. So that I know not on what particular imprisonment the resolution wants information.

I was told that he and a certain man named Larea were once hunted down in Buenos Ayres by the popular indignation for being the contrivers or authors of various odious proceedings, speculations, taxations, &c. There is some account given of him in the first volume of Brackenridge's Voyage to South America, page 239.

He is a native of Pittsfield, Massachusetts, said to possess splendid abilities; but in South America, for these ten or twelve years past, has always been in difficulties, with some short intervals of precarious affluence and show. My own opinion of him was that he had so commingled and identified himself with the fiscal and speculative concerns of Buenos Ayres and Montevideo, and certain men there, both natives and foreigners, both in power and out of power, that it was hard to unravel whether he "was a man more sinned against than sinning."

In speaking on his case to the supreme director, Mr. Pueyrredon, he said White was a man without principles. I replied: It is said he is a man of great talents. Pueyrredon answered that he was a man of showy but not of solid abilities; that he had been much overrated. I have heard it said he had claims against some men of weight and influence in Buenos Ayres, and, to get rid of being called to account or being compelled to pay him, they procured his imprisonment and banishment.

Others say that his having procured a high duty to be laid on *yerba*, and then monopolized it, having previously purchased up large quantities, was the cause, under the popular fury, of his being disgraced, imprisoned, banished, &c. A proceeding of this kind on yerba would have the same effect on the people of South America as a similar proceeding on whiskey in some parts of our country. So you may judge of his imprudence.

When he addressed his complaint to me, I nevertheless determined, noxious as he appeared to be to almost everybody, if, on investigating it, I found him entitled to redress as an American citizen, to enforce his claim. But I discovered, from the best information that I could procure, by his agencies in the affairs of Buenos Ayres, Montevideo, and countries with which the United States had always been neutral, that he had, in a manner, stepped beyond the line of neutrality in his negotiations and speculations in the struggles of those powers; and, if he had not absolutely forfeited, he had at most only a very equivocal claim on the protection and interference of the Government of the United States in his patriot and anti-patriot dilemmas.

Wishing to preserve the influence which I had with the Government of Buenos Ayres for the benefit of our citizens *bona fide* and unquestionably entitled to my services, I thought it best not rashly to jeopardize my fair standing by attempting to force Mr. White out of embarrassments of which he assumed to be chief author himself, and into similar or worse difficulties his own imprudence would again shortly plunge him. He never was imprisoned when I was in Buenos Ayres. The Commissioners can tell, I suppose, why he was when they were there. I did all for him that I could and ought to have done, both in the manner and the matter. I am sorry that it is not in my power to be as precise in this respect as I could wish. I inclose Mr. White's original letter to me; also Mr. Secretary Tagle's original letter, a translation of which I forwarded, is herein, as first mentioned.

Any further information on this or any other South American subject will be cheerfully furnished by me.

With the most distinguished consideration, &c.,

W. G. D. WORTHINGTON.

Mr. White to Mr. Worthington.

MONTEVIDEO, *November* 29, 1817.

SIR: The accompanying copies of proceedings against me by a political faction which preceded the Government of the Ex-Director Alvear, in April, 1815, I beg leave to lay before you; and I do this in the hope that you will not find the investigation of the subjects to which they refer foreign to the commission with which you are charged by the Government of our country.

It is unnecessary I should detail reflections on the subject of this process in order to demonstrate that in it are stamped the features of a despotism rendered more odious as it strikes at the root of individual rights, while it is pretended to be an effort towards the establishment of rational liberty; but I flatter myself with the hope that the present administration will adopt a more liberal policy, and that I shall, under your protection, be restored to the enjoyment of that, and also of the laws of a country to promote whose independence I have made efforts that were crowned with the most extraordinary success.

This agency, and in which I made so considerable disbursements, was always considered as that of a private character and myself as a subject of an independent Government, having uniformly resisted the idea of seeking the advancement of my fortune and happiness by attaching myself to the interest of any other Government in however small a degree opposed to those of our common country. In a word, I have never solicited nor received the honors of Argentine citizenship. There are many foreigners and some countrymen now in Buenos Ayres who were witnesses to the degree of eclat with which I acquitted myself in this agency; and everything which envy and malice can suggest, with regard to my accounts, must be considered as calumny until these accounts be dispassionately examined. From them must result a large balance in my favor; independent of which I was deprived of property of great value under authority of the Government of Buenos Ayres, and without a shadow of process, as far as regards two vessels and stores, which may be estimated at more than $40,000. I hope for a restitution not less summary; and, in whatever case, that you will not consider as incompatible with your public duty the requiring the recognizance of my rights to the protection of my person and property, conformably to law, during such periods as shall be necessary for me to regulate my accounts with the Government and private persons in Buenos Ayres, and that you will honor me with a communication on this subject of my address.

With considerations of profound respect, I have the honor to be, sir, your obedient servant,

WILLIAM P. WHITE.

W. G. D. WORTHINGTON, Esq.,
          Agent, &c., from the Government of the United States of America at Buenos Ayres.

Mr. Worthington to the Supreme Director, Pueyrredon.

BUENOS AYRES, *January 13*, 1818.

SIR: Permit me to lay before your excellency the request of William P. White, who claims to be a citizen of the United States. He alleges that his presence and personal attendance are actually necessary to enable him to settle certain commercial transactions which he heretofore had in this city; and that, in consequence of a decree under the Government of the Ex-Director Don Ignatio Alvares, he was sent out of the country and not permitted to return since. He requests that the decree against [him] may be repealed, and that he may be permitted (as are all other citizens of the United States) to come and reside in the city of Buenos Ayres in safety sufficiently long to close those old commercial concerns, &c. He confidently expects this from the justice of your administration, as may be seen by a copy of his letter to me of the 29th of November last; and viewing Mr. White simply as any other citizen of the United States, I bring before you this application, under the full persuasion that the most proper order will be taken in the premises.

I have the honor to be, with the most distinguished consideration, &c.,

W. G. D. WORTHINGTON.

His Excellency JUAN MARTIN DE PUEYRREDON,
 Supreme Director of the United Provinces of the Rio de la Plata.

[Translation.]

Mr. Tagle to Mr. Worthington.

To Señor Don W. G. D. WORTHINGTON, *Special Agent of the United States,*
 from the Secretary of State in the Department of Government:

MY DISTINGUISHED FRIEND AND SIR: I have submitted to the consideration of his excellency the Supreme Director your recommendation for the return of William P. White to this capital from Montevideo; and, on his view of the subject, his excellency has charged me to manifest to you that he is extremely sorry that he cannot accede to it, because the political circumstances of this country oppose the return of the said White to it. He was proscribed from these provinces for reasons of the greatest weight, and which, if he should return, would expose him to inconveniences which it might not be in the power of the Government to obviate. These considerations deprive his excellency of the satisfaction which he would have in complying with your wish on this occasion. I avail myself [of it] to protest to you the consideration with which I am de V. S. S. 2 S. M. B.

GREGORIO TAGLE.

BUENOS AYRES, *January 23*, 1818.

CLAIM OF JOSEPH KRITTMAN AGAINST THE CITY OF HAMBURG.

COMMUNICATED TO THE SENATE FEBRUARY 18, 1820.

The SECRETARY OF STATE, to whom, by a resolution of the Senate, was referred, on the 16th of February, last, the memorial of Joseph Krittman, to consider and report thereon, has the honor of submitting the following report:

From the statement of the memorialist it appears that in the month of October, 1811, while attempting to depart without a passport from Hohenfelde, a dependency of the city of Hamburg, where he had been some time residing, he was arrested and his effects were seized by a warrant from the mayor of Hohenfelde, which was then subject to the dominion of France. That after various proceedings in sundry subordinate tribunals, he obtained, first, a special order for the delivery to him of a part of his effects, and afterwards, on the 18th of November, 1811, an order from the prefect for the restoration of them all. He complains that these orders were ineffectual, and that, besides enduring much personal ill treatment from the mayor and other police officers, a part of his effects, to a very large amount in value, were never restored to him. It appears also that an attachment was laid upon them by the wagoner whom he had employed for their conveyance, upon which a judgment was obtained in the wagoner's favor against him.

The memorialist in 1812 applied to Mr. Barlow, then minister of the United States in France, for his official interposition in his favor; and at his instance Mr. Krittman's memorial and papers were referred to the consideration of the highest judicial officer of that country, and in March, 1813, the memorialist obtained from the tribunal of the first instance at Hamburg a new decree for the examination, appraisement, and restoration of his effects, which decree remained, however, without execution until the ancient authority of the senate of Hamburg was restored, in consequence of the occupation of that place by the Russian army under General Tettenborn.

From this restored government a third order for the restoration of his effects was issued on the 2d of April, 1813; but at the execution of the order, at which he states his opponents refused to be present, it appeared that the most valuable part of the effects had been stolen or ruined; and the memorialist alleges that his loss, in consequence thereof, with interest and expenses to the 10th of August, 1814, amounted to more than $15,000.

In September, 1814, the memorialist alleges that he petitioned the senate of Hamburg for a further decision upon his complaint, and at various times since he has urged his claims upon that body, without success. He states that a part of his effects remain there still under seizure, and that he has not been able to learn whether the senate of Hamburg have deemed it worth their while to reconsider his claims, but that his friends at Hamburg concur with him in the opinion that, if the Government of the United States would interfere in his behalf, a letter from the proper authority to the senate of Hamburg would enable him to obtain justice and to recover his losses.

It may be doubted whether the facts, as stated by the memorialist himself, are of a character to justify the abandonment of his cause, which has left him in the uncertainty with regard to the ultimate proceedings of the senate of Hamburg of which he complains. The only interference in his behalf by the Government of the United States which could be expedient or proper is believed to be by instructing the consul of the United States at Hamburg to represent to the senate the substance of his memorial to Congress, and the confidence with which the Government of the United States rely that the senate will do justice to his case, of the merits of which, from its nature, they must exclusively be the judges. This instruction will accordingly be given.

All which is respectfully submitted.

JOHN QUINCY ADAMS.

DEPARTMENT OF STATE, *February* 16, 1820.

16TH CONGRESS.]   No. 337.   [1ST SESSION.

CLAIM OF JAMES SMITH AND OTHERS AGAINST FRANCE.

COMMUNICATED TO THE SENATE MARCH 22, 1820.

To the honorable the Senate and House of Representatives of the United States in Congress assembled:

The memorial of the subscribers respectfully showeth:

That they are native citizens of the United States and were resident merchants within the same in the year 1806, and both before and since. In the month of November of that year the ship Bordeaux Packet, Spafford master, sailed from the port of Philadelphia, bound for Antwerp, with a cargo consisting of the produce of the United States and of colonial goods, consigned to the house of J. Ridgway, Mertens & Co., merchants at that place, where she arrived on the 27th of February, 1807. In the month of December, 1806, the brig Diamond, Manson master, sailed from the said port of Philadelphia with a similar cargo and destination, and arrived at Antwerp the 18th April, 1807. In the month of January, 1807, the ship Helena, Smith master, sailed from the port of Charleston with a like cargo and destination, and arrived at Antwerp the 10th April, 1807; and in the same month of January the ship North America, Dean master, sailed from the port of Savannah with a like cargo and destination, and arrived the said 10th April, 1807. In these cargoes your memorialists were, respectively, interested as proprietors, and both vessels and cargoes were, without exception, American property, duly documented as such, and were proceeding to the said port of Antwerp under the faith of treaties and the relations of amity subsisting between the United States and the several powers of Europe, and particularly with France. Your memorialists further state that, on their passage out, these vessels were detained by British cruisers and sent into different ports of England, when, after a short time, they were liberated, and from whence, without landing any of their cargoes, they proceeded to the port of destination and arrived at the respective dates before mentioned. At the port of Antwerp they were instantly seized, the cargoes were deposited in the custom-house stores under the exclusive control of the officers of Government, and, although repeated and faithful efforts were made by the consignees to obtain their release generally, and also to obtain permission for their reshipment and exportation from France, those efforts, as is notorious to all the world, proved abortive.

The ground upon which these seizures were made, though informally stated by a subordinate officer to have been the decree of Berlin of the 21st November, 1806, has never been made known from the Government of France. That the decree of Berlin by any of its provisions authorizes the seizure and detention it is impossible to contend; for the penalty of exclusion from the ports of France pronounced upon vessels and their cargoes in the predicament of those before mentioned was asked by the agents of your memorialists as a favor, and refused. It follows, of course, that the interdict of the Berlin decree could not be applied by the French Government to this property; and if it could have been, from any forced construction of that order, the invincible ignorance of it by your memorialists when their property left the United States would have constituted, with every just government, a ground of exemption from its penalties. Your memorialists, however, submit that the seizure was, and was known to be by those who made it, an act of lawless violence, without pretence of justification, and intended, through the restraint of American property, to produce an influence upon the American Government and upon her relations to the two great belligerents.

Your memorialists further submit that, after three years of nearly unremitted exertions by the consignees to save this property, the director general of the customs at Paris, on the 23d June, 1810, ordered the sale of all these cargoes, and that their proceeds should be lodged provisionally, according to the language of his mandate, in the *caisse d'amortissement;* and on the 9th July following the sale commenced, and was continued until the 15th of the same month, when the result in net proceeds was as follows, viz:

The cargo of the Bordeaux Packet produced, net		920,382 62	francs.
"	the Diamond	1,005,090 62	"
"	the Helena	631,065 28	"
"	the North America	1,003,300 40	"
	Making a total in francs of	3,559,836 92	
	and in dollars	667,469 43	

This sale was not, your memorialists beg leave to state, the consequence of any judicial proceeding whatever; for at no time after the arrival of the said vessels down to the present moment has there been a recourse by the officers of France to any tribunal of any kind, for the purpose of establishing against the property or its owners any charge of offence against the laws or ordinances of France or the decrees of the then Emperor. The cargoes were never libelled; the consignees were never cited to answer; the sale never purported to be the result of any judicial sentence or order; the property was taken from the possession of your memorialists by mere force, and the proceeds withheld from them by the continuance of the same force.

Your memorialists were induced to hope that, upon the establishment of a new order of things in France, the justice of that Government would have restored to them the proceeds of their property, which had been *provisionally* lodged in the *caisse d'amortissement,* and the interest from the time of its first detention; but they are compelled to make known that the most sedulous exertions to this effect have proved abortive, and that, unless the Government of the United States shall support by the weight of its name and authority the claims of your memorialists, there is no reason to expect that they can be made effectual. What France has granted to the citizens of other states in redress of wrongs proceeding from the same source, though far less flagrant in their character, your memorialists cannot believe will be withheld from citizens of the United States, if their Government shall think it proper to grant them its aid and protection; and a more reasonable case for such aid and protection your memorialists believe cannot be presented.

They therefore respectfully pray your honorable body to adopt such measures as shall have the effect of restoring to them the property of which they were wrongfully dispossessed by the authority of France, and of obtaining compensation for the detention of it from the year 1807:

PHILADELPHIA, *February* 10, 1819.

WILLIAM MONTGOMERY,	DAVID LEWIS,
JOSEPH INSKEEP,	ANTHONY STORKLE,
ROBERT McALESTER,	ISRAEL PLEASANTS,
ANDREW PELLET,	JAMES SMITH,
JAMES READ,	EDWARD SMITH,
WILLIAM NEWBOLD,	CHARLES PLEASANTS,
SAMUEL G. HAYS,	WILLIAM D. HODGE.
SAMUEL W. JONES,	

The SECRETARY OF STATE, to whom, on the 16th of February, 1819, by a resolution of the Senate, the memorial of James Smith and others was referred to consider and report thereon, has the honor of submitting the following report:

The claims of the memorialists belong to a class which, among many others, has been repeatedly and very earnestly pressed upon the attention of the Government of France. Copies are herewith submitted to the Senate of the correspondence between the minister of the United States at Paris and the minister of foreign relations upon this subject, before and since the reference of the memorial to this Department. From the grounds of resistance to the claims most recently assumed on the part of the French Government, it would appear that any relief which the memorialists may be entitled to expect can result only from measures within the exclusive competency of the legislative authority.

JOHN QUINCY ADAMS.

DEPARTMENT OF STATE, *Washington, March* 20, 1820.

Extracts of a letter from Mr. Gallatin, dated Paris, January 20, 1817, to Mr. Monroe, Secretary of State.

"Having received no answer from the Duke de Richelieu to my letter of the 9th November last, I addressed to him, on the 26th December, a short note, of which and of his answer, dated the 16th instant, copies are inclosed."

"In the interview which accordingly took place to-day the Duke for the first time declared that he did not consider us as being of right entitled to an indemnity from the present French Government on account of spoliations committed by that of Bonaparte on our commerce. In support of his position that the existing Government was not responsible for the acts of injustice done by the former, he alleged, 1st. The example of Naples in rejecting our application to the same effect. 2d. The conduct of the allied powers who, although dictating within the walls of Paris terms of peace to France, had not carried the demand of indemnities for their subjects to the extent claimed by us. 3d. The constant refusal of Bonaparte to indemnify us for these acts of injustice which he had committed himself. In the course of the conversation the Duke hinted, without positively expressing it, that any indemnity which might be allowed by the present Government would be a favor."

"After having repeated what had already been stated on former occasions, that the United States could not be bound by the acts of other powers to which they were not parties, and that the denial of justice by others could not justify a similar conduct on the part of France, I told the Duke that I thought it unnecessary, unless he thought proper to do it in an official shape, to enter into a discussion of the question of right, since he knew as well as myself that under all the circumstances of the case the present Government of France was, according to the acknowledged principles of public law, responsible for the acts of those who had been in the possession of the Government during the expulsion of the Bourbons, and who had been recognized by all the powers of Europe. I requested, therefore, that he would proceed to state what he had concluded to offer in answer to the basis proposed in my note of the 9th of November. He said that his offer would fall very short of our demands; that he would not go beyond an indemnity for vessels burnt at sea, and for those the proceeds of which had only been sequestered and deposited in the *caisse d'amortissement;* and that it would even be difficult to obtain from the Chambers the authority to pay to that extent. He added that he would make his proposal in writing, and that this could not be attended with much delay. I then said that I could not give any opinion on his proposal until I had received his note, but that I wished him to understand that if the Government of the United States thought it proper (which I could not at present promise) to accept an indemnity for certain classes only of our claims, this never would be purchased by a relinquishment of the other just demands of our citizens."

Extract of a letter from Mr. Gallatin to the Duke de Richelieu, dated Paris, November 9, 1816.

"Exclusively of other special orders of the same nature which may not be known to me, the cargoes of seven vessels arrived at Antwerp in the beginning of the year 1807, and which were permitted to be landed there, were also sequestered and finally sold by virtue of an order of Government, dated the 4th May, 1810. In all these cases there has been no condemnation, no final decision. The vessels and cargoes were only seized and sold by order of Government, and the proceeds of sales *deposited* in the *caisse d'amortissement* or in some other public chest."

"The right to demand and obtain a decision on all those suspended cases is undeniable. Either the proceeds of sales must be restored to the lawful owners by virtue of that decision, or the present Government of France must go beyond what has been done by the former Government and decree the final confiscation of property which even that Government had been unwilling to condemn. I will not permit myself for a moment to suppose that there can be any hesitation on that question."

Mr. Gallatin to Mr. Adams.

[Extract.]

PARIS, *February 19, 1819.*

"I had the honor to receive your despatches Nos. 10, 11, and 12. An indisposition which has confined me in my chamber for more than three weeks, and of which I am just recovering, has as yet prevented my using the arguments contained in the first in those quarters where it may be useful to remove unfavorable impressions, but I will not fail to attend to that subject whenever a convenient opportunity shall offer.

"The agitation which took place here after the termination of the Congress of Aix-la-Chapelle, the subsequent change of ministry, and afterwards my indisposition, had prevented my renewing my application on the subject of American claims. Immediately after the receipt of your despatch No. 12, although it would have been desirable to have had a previous conversation with Marquis Dessolle, I thought it advisable, upon the whole, to call his attention to the subject before the budget of this year was presented to the Chambers, and addressed him a letter, of which a copy is inclosed."

Mr. Gallatin to the Marquis Dessolle, Minister of Foreign Affairs.

[Translation.]

PARIS, *February 11, 1819.*

MONSIEUR LE MARQUIS: I have the honor to transmit to your excellency a memorial addressed by Mr. Parish, a citizen of the United States, to his excellency the minister of finance on the subject of a claim which it appears has been laid before that department.

Having been confined for the last three weeks by indisposition, I have been prevented from asking an interview of your excellency, with which I was desirous of being favored before I presented to you this memorial and renewed my application for the settlement of the American claims in general. But having recently received very special orders from my Government, accompanied by a particular recommendation of Mr. Parish's claim, I am no longer at liberty to defer the discussion of this interesting concern.

I have, therefore, to request your excellency to have the goodness to examine the official notes which I had the honor to address to the Duke of Richelieu upon the subject of these claims, and to which I have yet received no answer. I shall not now enlarge upon the view presented in my note of the 9th

November, 1816. By that of the 22d April, 1817, it will be seen that the negotiations on that subject were suspended solely in consideration of the trying situation in which France was then placed, and especially of the embarrassments of the administration by the enormous and unexpected mass of claims brought forward by the subjects of the allied powers. These obstacles are now happily removed; every demand of all the European powers and their subjects has been amicably adjusted and settled; the rights, so legitimate, of the citizens of the United States alone remain unsatisfied. My Government, preserving an unshaken confidence in his Majesty, cannot doubt that the time has at length arrived when ample justice will be rendered to its claims.

With respect to that of Mr. Parish, it may be remarked that it is very simple and is susceptible of being adjusted without waiting the result of or in the least interfering with a general settlement. In fact, the cargoes in question were never condemned, but were only sold for the joint benefit of all, and the proceeds deposited, provisionally, in the Sinking Fund. It is further important to remark that, by an order of the French Government, permission was granted to the consignees of cargoes sequestered at that period at Antwerp to take possession and dispose of them, on their giving an obligation to become responsible for the amount to the public treasury in the event of a decision pronouncing their confiscation. The house of Mr. Ridgway, consul of the United States, together with that of Mr. Parish, refused their assent to a condition which implied an admission of the legality of the seizure. The European consignees, with whom this consideration had no weight, received and sold their goods, and their obligations were subsequently returned to them. Thus, by refunding to the houses of Ridgway and Parish the proceeds of the cargoes consigned to them, the decision which was virtually carried into effect in the case of all others similarly situated will only receive its due application as it regards them.

I have to observe that, although the claims of both these houses are perfectly similar to each other, that of Mr. Parish is the only one which appears to have been taken into consideration by the department of finance.

In the hope that my health may soon permit me to confer personally with your excellency, I have the honor to be, &c.,

                                                            ALBERT GALLATIN.

                              ────────────

                    Mr. Gallatin to the Secretary of State.

                                                            PARIS, *July* 8, 1819.

SIR; I transmitted, in my despatch No. 100, the copy of the letter which I had addressed to Marquis Dessolle on the 11th of February last, on the subject of American claims in general, and more particularly of that of Messrs. Gracie and Parish.

On the 23d of March, in transmitting to the same minister a letter from Mr. Hyde de Neuville in behalf of Mr. Gracie, I reminded him of my preceding note, and requested that a report which the director general of the douanes was shortly to make on the claim might be communicated to me before the minister of finances should decide upon it. This was the more important as the director was known to be decidedly hostile to the claim and to the restitution of any sum which had, in any shape, found its way to the public treasury.

My request was not complied with, but Mr. Parish still thought that the affair had taken a favorable turn, and not expecting an immediate decision, left this city for Antwerp, and went thence on some business to England. From this last country he wrote me a few days ago and transmitted the inclosed copy of a letter addressed to him by the minister of finances, and by which he is informed that his claim is inadmissible.

The minister's letter is incorrect as to facts. The order to sell and to pay into the treasury the proceeds of the sales of sequestered property is not and was not by the then existing Government considered as a condemnation. When the vessels in question arrived at Antwerp, the only penalty to which they were liable for having touched in England was to be refused admission, and the only question was whether this exclusion should be enforced, or whether the consignées should be permitted to sell the cargoes. It was not at all by giving a retrospective effect to the Milan decree that the cargoes were sold. The sale took place about the same time that the property seized at St. Sebastian was sold; it was done by virtue of an order from Government, distinct from the Rambouillet decree, and for which no motive was assigned. I have requested Mr. Parish's lawyer to procure copies of the order of sale, and of that by which the money was paid into the public treasury instead of the *caisse d'amortissement;* for although the substance of the orders is known, the text has not been communicated.

But however easy it might be to answer the minister's letter, there would be some inconvenience in pursuing that course or in prosecuting further Mr. Parish's claim, distinct from others of the same nature.

I was, indeed, always averse to that discrimination, and did not share that gentleman's hopes of success; but as he was very sanguine, and we had heretofore failed in obtaining relief, I could not resist his solicitations, especially after the receipt of your despatch No. 12.

The decision of the minister of finances, founded on the assumed principle that no redress remains when the money has been paid into the treasury and been expended, would apply with equal force to all the American claims. If it becomes necessary to combat seriously that doctrine, it will be better to do it generally, and in a direct correspondence with the minister of foreign affairs, than by answering a letter which is not addressed to me, and applying my arguments to a single case.

I am still in hopes of receiving the instructions which I was led to expect from your despatch No. 12. If circumstances induce me to renew my application before these are received, it is my intention either not to take notice of the letter of the minister of finances, or to consider it merely as the proof that he could not, according to existing laws, on his sole responsibility, and without a diplomatic arrangement, order the claim to be liquidated.

His letter places, nevertheless, our claims on a still more unfavorable footing than that on which they heretofore stood. We had applied to this Government for indemnity; we had stated the arguments by which our claims were supported, and receiving no written answer, we had it, however, placed on record that we had been verbally answered that the pressure of the demands of the allies was the reason why ours were not yet taken into consideration. This was not much; but still this Government was not in the least committed by the decision of any of its ministers against us.

In the present state of things I will try, until I am positively instructed, to keep the negotiation alive, but without urging a decision, unless I can ascertain that a favorable result will be thus obtained.

I have the honor to be, with great respect, sir, your obedient servant,

ALBERT GALLATIN.

The Minister of Finance to Mr. Parish.

[Translation.]

PARIS, *May* 22, 1819.

SIR: You have applied, in behalf of Mr. Archibald Gracie, of New York, for the restitution of the value of the cargoes of three American ships, the Perseverance, the Hiram, and the Mary, sequestered by the Imperial Government in 1807, and the proceeds of which were afterwards confiscated by it.

Having had a detailed statement laid before me of the circumstances connected with this transaction, the documents exhibited establish the following facts:

On the 21st November, 1806, a decree was issued at Berlin by which the British islands were placed in a state of blockade. By articles seven and eight of this decree every vessel coming directly from England or from the English colonies, or having been there since the publication of the said decree, was refused admission into any port; and every vessel attempting to contravene that clause by means of a false declaration was, together with the cargo, subject to seizure and confiscation as if they were English property. It was while these legislative measures were in force that the three ships in question arrived to your address. They had put into England; a circumstance which was, however, not considered by the custom-house as an irremissible cause of confiscation, there being reason to presume that it was through stress of weather.

In the interval of time previous to the decision which was to be made by the chief of the State, a proposal was made to you to dispose, conditionally, of the cargoes of these vessels on your engaging to refund the proceeds in the event of their final confiscation. You refused your assent to this offer, and at a subsequent period claimed its execution. But things had then changed, the legislative measures having become more rigorous.

By a decree of November 23, 1807, it was declared (article 1) "That all vessels which, after touching in England from any cause whatsoever, shall enter the ports of France, shall be seized and confiscated, together with their cargoes, without exception or distinction of goods and merchandise."

By a retrospective effect, which I am certainly very far from wishing to justify, but to which it is proper to advert, because it forms one of the prominent features of the case, this decree of November 23 was enforced as to these three vessels. It was ineffectually that the director general of the customs represented to the head of the Government that the English had no interest whatever in these three vessels, and that they were solely and *bona fide* American property, an immediate sale of their cargoes having been ordered by the supreme authority on the 4th of May, 1810. This order was carried into execution on the 15th of June following; and the proceeds, at first deposited in the Sinking Fund, were subsequently withdrawn, in conformity also with the same superior orders, and placed in the public treasury as having definitively become the property of the State.

I admit, with you, sir, the iniquity of these measures, and, with you, I deplore their effects; but to repair them is not within the compass of my power. If the cargoes in question still existed in the custom-house stores, they should be immediately restored to you; but having been sold, their proceeds no longer exist. The whole transaction was terminated, irrevocably terminated, four years prior to the restoration; and it is not within the power of his Majesty's Government to revive an obsolete claim, to renew a discussion on rights which are extinct, or to repair individual losses by an augmentation of the public burdens.

With the expression of my regrets, be pleased, sir, to accept the assurance of my perfect consideration.

The Minister of Finance and Secretary of State,

THE BARON LOUIS.

16TH CONGRESS.]   No. 338.   [1ST SESSION.

DELAY OF SPAIN TO RATIFY THE TREATY OF 1819.

COMMUNICATED TO THE SENATE MARCH 27, 1820.

To the Senate of the United States:

I transmit to Congress an extract of a letter from the minister plenipotentiary of the United States at St. Petersburg, of the 1st of November last, on the subject of our relations with Spain, indicating the sentiments of the Emperor of Russia respecting the non-ratification by his Catholic Majesty of the treaty lately concluded between the United States and Spain and the strong interest which his Imperial Majesty takes in promoting the ratification of that treaty. Of this friendly disposition the most satisfactory assurance has been since given directly to this Government by the minister of Russia residing here.

I transmit also to Congress an extract of a letter from the minister plenipotentiary of the United States at Madrid of a later date than those heretofore communicated, by which it appears that at the instance of the chargé des affaires of the Emperor of Russia a new pledge had been given by the Spanish Government that the minister who had been lately appointed to the United States should set out on his mission without delay with full power to settle all differences in a manner satisfactory to the parties.

I have further to state that the Governments of France and Great Britain continue to manifest the sentiments heretofore communicated respecting the non-ratification of the treaty by Spain, and to interpose their good offices to promote its ratification.

It is proper to add that the Governments of France and Russia have expressed an earnest desire that the United States would take no step for the present on the principle of reprisal which might possibly tend to disturb the peace between the United States and Spain. There is good cause to presume, from the delicate manner in which this sentiment has been conveyed, that it is founded in a belief as well as a desire that our just objects may be accomplished without the hazard of such an extremity.

On full consideration of all these circumstances, I have thought it my duty to submit to Congress whether it will not be advisable to postpone a decision on the questions now depending with Spain until the next session. The distress of that nation at this juncture affords a motive for this forbearance which cannot fail to be duly appreciated. Under such circumstances the attention of the Spanish Government may be diverted from its foreign concerns and the arrival of a minister here be longer delayed. I am the more induced to suggest this course of proceeding from a knowledge that while we shall thereby make a just return to the powers whose good offices have been acknowledged, and increase, by a new and signal proof of moderation, our claims on Spain, our attitude in regard to her will not be less favorable at the next session than it is at the present.

JAMES MONROE.

WASHINGTON, *March* 27, 1820.

Extracts of a letter from Mr. Campbell to the Secretary of State, dated St. Petersburg, October 20, (November 1,) 1819, containing details of a conversation with Count Nesselrode.

"Your despatch, No. 3, of June 3, I had the honor to receive a few days ago.

"After some general conversation he* inquired (as I presumed he would do, and waited for him to introduce the subject) if I had any certain account of what Spain was doing or had done respecting the treaty lately concluded by her minister at Washington with our Government. I had shortly before received from Mr. Gallatin a letter confirming the account which had already reached me through the newspapers, that the King had refused to ratify the treaty until he should obtain some previous explanations relating, as stated by Mr Gallatin, to two points: First. The declaration Mr. Forsyth was instructed, on exchanging the ratifications, to put in, that the grant to the Duke d'Alagon for lands in the ceded territory which, though intended to be, was not, by the terms of the treaty, made null, should be considered as null; and second, an engagement required by Spain, on the part of our Government, not to recognize the independence of any of the Spanish colonies; and that to demand these explanations a minister extraordinary was to be sent to Washington, though Mr. Forsyth had offered, as instructed, to give full explanations on any point connected with the treaty. I therefore informed the Count I had received authentic information, though not from my Government, that the King had refused his assent to the treaty until he should obtain explanations on certain points, for which purpose he proposed sending a minister extraordinary to Washington. I took this occasion to remark further that by official information from my Government I felt myself authorized to state that Mr. Onis, the Spanish minister, was fully empowered to conclude the treaty, and might have yielded more than he did without exceeding his authority; and that the points on which it was now proposed to ask explanations had been fully discussed before the treaty was signed and their intent and meaning explicitly understood by both parties, of which the Spanish court was fully informed, and our minister there was instructed to give ample explanations, which he offered to do, on any points relating to the treaty that might be supposed to require them. I added that the treaty was undoubtedly, under all circumstances, highly favorable to Spain, and that I was satisfied a strong desire on the part of my Government to preserve peace alone induced them to agree to its provisions; that I presumed he had been informed respecting the terms of the treaty by Mr. Poletica, with whom I understood you had freely communicated on the subject. He said Mr. Poletica had advised him that, from the explanations received from you respecting it, the treaty was by him considered favorable to Spain. I then referred to the grant to the Duke d'Alagon, briefly stated the nature of it as made known to me, and observed that should the views of the King, as now avowed in relation to it, supposed the principal point on which the explanation was required be acquiesced in, the chief object of entering into the treaty would be thereby frustrated; that by one of its provisions the United States Government agreed to pay, on account of Spain, to their own citizens, for spoliations committed by her subjects or in her ports contrary to treaty, five millions of dollars out of the proceeds of the sales of lands in the ceded territory; but should this grant, said to include a very large portion of

* Count Nesselrode.

those lands, be confirmed, the sum assigned for that purpose would fail, and of course this provision of the treaty could not be complied with.

" He appeared to feel the full force of the remark, giving his consent to the conclusion drawn and proceeded to observe it was to be regretted that Spain did not understand her own interest better than she seemed to do; that it was difficult to conceive, in her present situation, what could induce her to take the course she had done and refuse to ratify a treaty favorable to herself and concluded by her minister vested with full power for the purpose. He then remarked on the great importance of preserving peace, as far as practicable, among the civilized nations of the world, inquired what Spain could now do in regard to the business by sending a minister to Washington, and what course our Government would be likely to adopt on the occasion.

"I replied that, as to Spain, I could form no opinion of the motives by which she was governed. I did not perceive what she could do, unless she receded from her objections to the treaty; and as to my own Government, though I was satisfied of its strong desire to preserve peace, I could not pretend to say what course it might conceive itself called on to take on the present occasion, though I presumed no decisive measures would be adopted to change essentially the relations between the two countries until Congress should convene, early in December, and the course then pursued would probably depend upon what Spain should in the meantime do.

"He then inquired how soon I expected to hear from my Government after it had been advised of the refusal on the part of Spain to ratify the treaty; and, being told that I could not state the precise time with any degree of certainty, but that it would undoubtedly be as soon as despatches could reach this from Washington, he expressed, with some earnestness, his wish that I should make known to him, at as early a day as might be convenient, such information as I might receive from my Government on this subject."

Extract of a letter from Mr. Forsyth to the Secretary of State, dated Madrid, January 3, 1820.

For this extract, see vol. 4, Foreign Relations, page 674.

The Duke of San Fernando and Quiroga to Mr. Forsyth.

PALACE, *December* 16, 1819.

[Translation.]

For this letter, see vol. 4, Foreign Relations, page 675.

Extract of a despatch from Count Nesselrode to Mr. Poletica, minister of H. I. M. the Emperor of Russia, in the United States, dated November 27, (December 9,) 1819.

[Translation.]

For this extract, see vol. 4, Foreign Relations, page 676.

16TH CONGRESS.]   No. 339.   [1ST SESSION.

COMMERCE WITH FRANCE AND WITH THE BRITISH AMERICAN COLONIES.

COMMUNICATED TO THE HOUSE OF REPRESENTATIVES APRIL 22, 1820.

DEPARTMENT OF STATE, *Washington, March* 28, 1820.

SIR: In answer to your letter of the 6th instant, I have the honor of stating that there appears to be no objection to the publication of the documents to which you allude; copies of which are accordingly herewith transmitted to you, together with some others not less essential to give the House a full view of the proceedings of the Executive, hitherto, in negotiation with Great Britain in relation to the commercial intercourse between the United States and the British American colonies, and with France in relation to the general commerce between that country and the United States.

I am, with great respect, sir, your very obedient servant,

JOHN QUINCY ADAMS.

THOMAS NEWTON, Esq., *Chairman of the Committee on Commerce of the House of Representatives.*

List of papers transmitted to the Hon. T. Newton, Chairman of the Committee on Commerce, with the letter of the Secretary of State of March 28, 1820.

The Secretary of State to Mr. Rush, dated May 21, 1818. Extract.
The same to Mr. Gallatin, dated May 22, 1818. Extract.
The same to Mr. Rush, dated May 30, 1818. Extract.
The same to Messrs. Gallatin and Rush, dated July 28, 1818. Extract.
The same to Mr. Rush, dated May 7, 1819.

DOCUMENT A.

Draught of two articles proposed by the American plenipotentiaries at the 3d conference, 17th September, 1818, for regulating the commercial intercourse between the United States, and first, the British islands in the west.

DOCUMENT B.

Counter projet, offered by the British plenipotentiaries at the 5th conference, 6th October, 1818, of an article for the intercourse between the United States and Nova Scotia, and New Brunswick.

DOCUMENT C.

Counter projet, offered by the British plenipotentiaries at the 8th conference, 19th October, 1818, of an article for the intercourse between the United States and the British West Indies.

DOCUMENT D.

Draught of an article proposed by the British Government 19th March, 1817, for the intercourse between the United States and the Island of Bermuda.
Mr. Rush to the Secretary of State, June 14, 1819.
The same to the same, September 17, 1819. Extracts.
Mr. Gallatin to the Secretary of State, May 21, 1819.
Mr. Gallatin to the Marquis Dessolle, dated May 5, 1819. Translation.
The same to the same, May 12, 1819. Translation.
The same to the same, May 14, 1819. Translation.
The Duke of Richelieu to Mr. Gallatin, September 12, 1819. Translation.
Mr. Gallatin to the Duke of Richelieu, July 28, 1818.
The same to the same, August 3, 1818.
The same to the same, August 10, 1818.
Mr. Sheldon to Count d'Hauterive, September 30, 1818.
Count d'Hauterive to Mr. Sheldon, October 17, 1818. Translation.
Mr. Gallatin to the Secretary of State, May 22–24, 1819.
The same to the Marquis Dessolle, May 17, 1819.
The same to the same, May 24, 1819.
The same to the Secretary of State, October 25, 1819. Extracts.
The same to the Marquis Dessolle, October 25, 1819.
The same to the Secretary of State, November 8, 1819. Extracts.
The Marquis Dessolle to Mr. Gallatin, November 6, 1819. Translation.
Mr. Gallatin to the Secretary of State, December 9, 1819.
The same to the same, January 15, 1820.
The same to the Baron Pasquier, January 6, 1820.
The same to the Secretary of State, January 20, 1820.
The Baron Pasquier to Mr. Gallatin, January 14, 1820. Translation.

DEPARTMENT OF STATE, *March* 28, 1820.

N. B. The correspondence and papers referred to in the above list relating to affairs with Great Britain are included in vol. 4, Foreign Relations, from page 370 to page 405.

The following relates to affairs with France:

Extract of a letter from Mr. Gallatin to the Secretary of State, dated.

PARIS, *May* 21, 1819.

"A set of officers is established by law in every port of France, known by the name of "Courtiers interpretes conducteurs de navires," who have the exclusive right of acting as ship-brokers, and\ as interpreters in all transactions and declarations, written or verbal, relative to vessels, whether with the custom-houses or elsewhere. A tariff, approved from time to time by the minister of the interior, determines their fees, which vary in the several ports, but are always much greater for foreign than for French vessels. Several complaints having been made both as to the principle and as to abuses flowing from that monopoly, Mr. Laine, then minister of the interior, decided, in October, 1817, as being a correct interpretation of the law, or a necessary exception to it, that every man might always act for himself without the interposition of the brokers, and that a foreigner acting with the assistance of the consul of his nation must be deemed to act by himself.

Gross abuses had prevailed at Havre, where the brokers had constantly extorted from the American captains fees more than double of those fixed by the tariff, a circumstance which had not been communicated to me. Mr. Beasley, in the summer of 1818, was induced to avail himself of the authority given by Mr. Laine's decision, and soon acted in behalf of all the American captains, who ceased to employ the brokers. Their usual declarations were received in that way at the custom-house, but rejected by the administration of the "octroi." The case having been stated to me, and the former abuses being at the same time brought to view, I made, in July and August last, the proper representations to the Duke of Richelieu. The administration of the "octroi" was instructed to receive the declarations of the captains through the consul or his chancellor; a new instruction confirming the former one was transmitted from the Department of the Interior; and the Duke of Richelieu, in a letter of the 12th of September, 1818, gave me the assurance that the brokers should be kept within the bounds of the tariff, and that all abuses in that respect would be suppressed. Considering the point as settled, and having about that time departed for England, I did not trouble you with a communication of these details.

The brokers, denying the power of the minister of the interior to give that construction to the law, had, in the meanwhile, instituted a suit against one of the captains and against the chancellor and secretary of Mr. Beasley for having infringed the provisions of the said law. Mr. Beasley having intervened as consul, and declared that they had acted by his direction, it was expected that the court would declare itself incompetent. This, however, has not taken place. The tribunal of Havre rejected the interposition of the consul, forbade the chancellor and secretary to interfere in future with the functions of the brokers, and condemned them to pay the expenses of the suit. On appeal to the royal court of Rouen, this tribunal reversed the decision of that of Havre, by admitting the consul's intervention, but not considering the letters of the minister of the interior as sufficient evidence, gave only an interlocutory decree, by which Mr. Beasley was directed to produce, within three months, a decision from the competent authority, showing that he was authorized to act and to delegate his authority in the manner he had done it. The brokers having appealed to the court of cassation, this last court has confirmed the decision of that of Rouen, on the special ground that the contended for exception to the law might result from a diplomatic arrangement, but not from a simple decision of the minister of the interior.

Previous to this decree of the court of cassation, Mr. Decazes, now minister of the interior, had, on the 17th February last, rescinded Mr. Laine's decision of October, 1817, on the ground that the law was peremptory; in consequence of which Mr. Beasley has ceased to act as interpreter, and the brokers again act exclusively as such. Mr. Decazes, by another decision of the 24th February, approved a new tariff, by which the fees of the brokers are more than doubled and made about equal to those which they had formerly illegally extracted from the American captains. Both decisions were made without any previous notice to me or to any other foreign minister, without any concert with the Department of Foreign Affairs, and without being brought before the council of ministers.

Several of the foreign ministers have made representations against those decisions of Mr. Decazes. I was obliged to wait for the decree of the court of cassation and for a copy of it, in order to bring before the Department of Foreign Affairs both the questions which arose from the lawsuit, and in which we were alone concerned, and those more immediately belonging to the brokers' fees and exclusive privilege. I have now the honor to inclose copies of the letters which I have addressed to Marquis Dessolle on those subjects, and also of the correspondence which had taken place last year.

You will perceive that with respect to the suit I have asked, first, a special decision from the King's Government which shall satisfy the court of Rouen that Mr. Beasley had been duly authorized to act as he did, and thus put an end to the suit now pending; second, a general decision which may shelter our consuls from any direct or indirect prosecutions before "correctional" or criminal tribunals for their official acts. It must, on this last point, be observed that no French public functionary can be either sued or prosecuted here for any of his official acts without the previous permission of the council of State.

As to the other questions I have asked, first, that our consuls might act as interpreters for their countrymen in their transactions with the custom-houses and other administrations; second, that the tariff should be reduced and fixed at the same rate for American as for French vessels. In those several demands I have chiefly dwelt on the principle of reciprocity.

The questions relative to the suit have, at my request, been referred to the minister of justice. I infer, from a long conference with Mr. Dessolle, that the ministry will support Mr. Decazes in his construction of the law, which they say cannot be modified even by a subsequent treaty without the assistance of the legislative body. Mr. Dessolle seemed to receive more favorably the application for a modification of the tariff.

That minister having no knowledge of the English language, I had hoped, by addressing him in French, to accelerate decisions in the business to be transacted with him.

Mr. Gallatin to the Marquis Dessolle, Minister of Foreign Affairs.

[Translation.]

PARIS, May 5, 1819.

SIR: I have the honor to transmit to your excellency a memorial, accompanied by eleven documents, addressed to you by Mr. Beasley, consul for the United States at Havre, in relation to the differences between him and the brokers-interpreters of that place, on the subject of which I had the honor to make communications to the Duke of Richelieu in my several letters of the 28th of July, 3d and 10th of August, 1818.

It is proper that I should recall to your excellency that, in consequence of the decision promulgated on the 25th October, 1817, declaring the right of every individual to act for themselves, and without the intervention of a broker, in their own affairs, every master of a vessel, being a foreigner, was considered as acting for himself when accompanied by the consular agents of his nation; it was, I say, solely in consequence of that decision that the consul of the United States at Havre officiated as an intermediate agent, either personally or by his chancellor, in making the customary declarations required of American captains by the administrations of the customs and of the direct contributions. This decision was further confirmed by one of the ministers of the interior, made upon a full investigation of the statements of the brokers and of my representations, and of the explanations furnished to him by his excellency the minister of foreign affairs.

The brokers had, notwithstanding, instituted a suit in the tribunal of correctional police at Havre against Captain Cowell, an American, and Messrs. Taylor and Touret, the former the chancellor and the latter the secretary of the consul of the United States, on the plea of their having made the customary declarations to the administration of the customs without resorting to them, and in conformity with the decision of October 25, 1817. It was to no purpose that the consul interposed by taking up their defence, the tribunal at Havre having, by sentence of August 26, 1818, set aside the interposition of the consul, condemned Taylor and Touret to pay the costs of the suit, and forbade them to interfere with the duties of the brokers in future.

On an appeal to the royal court at Rouen the correctional sentence of the court at Havre was reversed by a decree of December 8, 1818; but it went no further than to pronounce an interlocutory judgment, referring Messrs. Taylor and Touret to the competent authority to decide whether Mr. Beasley, as consul of the United States, has a right to exercise the functions of a ship-broker and interpreter in behalf of his countrymen in competition with the persons appointed by the French Government; and, in that case, whether he has the right of delegating such functions to his chancellor or to his secretary. This decree was confirmed on the 26th of March, 1819, by the court of cassation, to which the brokers had appealed. For the text of these two decrees I beg leave to refer your excellency to the documents annexed to the consul's memorial.

I am aware that the minister of the interior, by a circular bearing date February 17, 1819, appears to have annulled the decision of his predecessor; but this measure is applicable only to the grounds of the question, and can have no retroactive effect on the incidental difficulty growing out of the suit. It is not my intention to discuss the merits of the main question at present. I will have the honor to present to your excellency my remarks on that subject in a distinct shape and in a separate note. My sole object at present is to support the request of the consul, so far as it goes, to obtain either from your excellency, the council of State, or from any other competent authority, an official and formal decision which may serve to satisfy the royal court of Rouen, and terminate a vexatious suit which should never have been instituted.

It is not my intention now to request a decision to that precise effect which may authorize the consul to act in future in behalf of his countrymen concurrently with the brokers, but one declaring his right to do so as well at the period when he did so act as on the 8th of December, the date of the sentence of the court at Rouen. Such a decision is merely the declaration of the fact as it then stood; and the consul having acted, as I have before remarked, strictly in conformity with the decisions pronounced by his Majesty's Government, has an unquestionable right to its protection from all suits founded on this pretence either against him or his chancellor.

By the sentence of the royal court at Rouen Messrs. Beasley, Taylor, and Touret were bound to abide by or appeal from the decision to be given within the term of three months, commencing from the 8th of December, 1818, the date of the sentence. This term began effectually only on the 26th of March, 1819, the day of the date of the sentence of the court of cassation. I beg your excellency will be pleased to recollect that it will expire on the 26th of June, and that it is requisite that the decision should be submitted to the court at Rouen before that day.

To the request of the consul permit me, sir, to add a few remarks, which are, however, intended to apply only to the suit and not to the grounds of the main question.

The consuls of France in the United States could never have been exposed to what has been experienced by the American consul at Havre. With a view to protect the agents of foreign powers from local vexations, and to prevent their being dragged from court to court, it is provided, not by a temporary law but by the Constitution of the United States, that the Supreme Court, which in cases of personal concern is to be considered in the light of a court of cassation, should serve for all such agents and even for consuls as the first court to bring suit in, and the only one in which, even in criminal cases, they could be sued. In the cases in which other courts have attempted to take cognizance of offences charged on a consul, the Government has undertaken the defence by committing it to the Attorney General, whose duty it was made to oppose and prove the incompetency of the court. This was the course taken in the case of Mr. Kosloff, the Russian consul, when under a criminal accusation. It has been further determined that consuls were not liable to prosecution for acts done in the performance of their duties—a point on which, I think, Mr. Lescallier, late consul of France in the United States, is enabled to give some information.

Thus we find that in the United States, where all the national public officers may be prosecuted for their official acts by any individual thinking himself aggrieved by them, foreign consuls enjoy a special exemption; whereas, here, the consul of the United States has, in consequence of the suit brought against his chancellor when acting by his orders, been actually prosecuted, and his case has now for nine months been pending in the tribunals, for an official act performed with the express sanction of the Government, and without the smallest interposition having yet been manifested in his favor.

The suit has, however, been brought by persons bearing a public character, whose conduct had necessitated the interference of the consul of whom they complained. With my note of the 10th of August, 1818, I transmitted to the Duke of Richelieu several original documents establishing the fact that the brokers-interpreters at Havre had obliged the masters of six vessels only to pay a sum of 1,427 francs beyond what was authorized by the tariff; and I proved that, in the course of two years and a half, they must have illegally exacted and received from the American commerce nearly seventy thousand francs more than their lawful dues. The Duke of Richelieu, in his letter of the 12th September following, gave me an assurance that these abuses should in future be repressed. But the owners and captains, remotely situated as they are, were unable to commence two hundred suits against the brokers for the recovery of the sums thus unjustly exacted; and they, availing themselves of impunity, have become the complaining party; while, on the other hand, we see the consul of the United States arraigned before the tribunals.

Upon all these considerations, I conceive myself authorized to demand of his Majesty's Government not only the special decision required by the American consul at Havre to dismiss the present suit, but, in addition, that the consuls of the United States who have his Majesty's exequatur be protected in the free and unmolested exercise of their duties, and no longer exposed to be sued *for their official acts* in correctional or criminal courts.

I can offer the assurance that, leaving to their Government the care of making such representations as may be necessary, the American consuls will, in the discharge of their duties, confine themselves strictly within the limits prescribed by the established rules of his Majesty's Government.

I beg your excellency to receive the assurance of my perfect consideration,

ALBERT GALLATIN.

Mr. Gallatin to the Marquis Dessolle.

[Translation.]

PARIS, *May* 12, 1819.

SIR: By a letter of the 25th of October, 1817, from the ministry of the interior, it was declared, in reference to the duties of ship-brokers acting as interpreters, that every individual had the right of acting for himself, and without the intervention of a broker, in his own business, and that every foreign master of a vessel was considered as acting for himself if attended by the consular agents of his nation.

His excellency the minister of the interior, relying upon the authority of the law for the appointment of brokers, revoked, by his letter of February 17, 1819, the declaration above referred to. The question relating to the duties attributed by the common law of nations to consuls, or the exercise of which may, for reasons of convenience, be granted to them, remains untouched. Whether it be necessary, therefore, to annul a law unless it may have been modified by a diplomatic agreement is a question which I shall not take upon me to discuss.

It is sufficient that, by the decision of the 17th February, 1819, it is admitted that the law may be so modified by diplomatic agreement—a principle which has been further admitted by the tribunals, namely: by the royal court of Rouen, in a decree of the 8th December, 1818; by the court of cassation, in one of the 26th of March, 1819, and in the preambles thereto. I had the honor to inclose to your excellency copies of these decrees in my note of the 5th instant.

No difficulty, therefore, can exist to the forming such diplomatic arrangements as the case may require. I thought, indeed, that this was the light in which what had been done in 1818 was viewed. The decision of the minister of the interior, of the 31st of August of that year, explanatory of and confirming that of the 25th of October, 1817, was produced by the difficulties created by the brokers and by the representations addressed by me to his excellency the minister of foreign affairs, and was not given until the explanations communicated by him to the minister of the interior were fully considered. It might therefore be viewed as the result of a diplomatic arrangement; and from the total silence of the letter of the 17th of February, 1819, on that point, it is presumable that on this occasion neither the letter of August 31, 1818, nor the circumstances which produced it were communicated to his excellency the minister of the interior. However that may be, the exclusion which now affects the consuls appears to be at variance with the principles generally received as forming the common law of nations, and is at once highly injurious to the American commerce, and contrary to the principle of reciprocity.

Without enlarging on the first point, I shall only remark that the establishment of consuls having originated in the aid and protection to be afforded by them to the commerce and interests of their countrymen with the local authorities, the right of assisting them as interpreters in the custom-houses, excise offices, and other administrations, seems to be a necessary part of their duties.

The serious inconveniences resulting to the American commerce from the establishment of the brokers-interpreters have been already stated in my former note, a proof of which is afforded by the simple fact of the interposition of the American consuls. Receiving no salaries from their Government, they must necessarily receive a suitable compensation for their services when required by their countrymen; nor would they have been resorted to but for the extravagant demands of the brokers, which are to be traced to their possession of an exclusive right, and to the tariff.

Although the fees payable to the brokers have been regulated, yet there are unforeseen cases constantly occurring which serve as a pretext for demanding an additional compensation for some service not specified in the tariff. Enjoying a monopoly of the duty, their demands were unavoidably complied with. They even carried the practice so far for several years as to exact from the American captains more than double the fees allowed by the tariff. Of this fact I have exhibited proof in my note to the Duke of Richelieu of the 10th of August last. This proceeding having been remonstrated against, they presented a demand to the government to alter the tariff and raise their fees—a measure that would necessarily add to the burdens under which the trade already labored, and give the sanction of law to the abuses so justly complained of.

But the tariff itself, although requiring the approbation of the Government, is prepared and proposed by the local authorities, by the chambers and tribunals of commerce, which, being composed of French merchants, throw the whole burden upon the commerce of foreigners. This tariff, varying in different ports of the kingdom, is, however, uniformly higher for foreigners than for Frenchmen.

As long as the establishment of the brokers continues in force upon its present footing, there is no other remedy, either for the rates laid down by the tariff or for the abuses practiced under favor of the monopoly, than by resorting to the consuls. Let the brokers moderate their demands; let their compensation be proportioned to their services, and they alone will be employed. The right of the consuls to act as interpreters in behalf of their countrymen will only be exercised in cases where the fees demanded, either in virtue of the tariff or otherwise, shall be found to be exorbitant. That right alone can effectually check abuses, and will be specially exercised for that purpose.

I pass on to the principle of reciprocity.

In the United States, as in France, extraordinary duties are laid by the customs on foreign commerce for the benefit of the public treasury. I must remark, however, that they are more moderate than in France, and that the United States, as I have on former occasions given the assurance, are ready to form a convention with France stipulating the repeal of these extraordinary duties by both parties.

But, in the United States, when these duties are once paid, the subjects of France and the citizens of the United States are placed upon a perfect equality. All fees, for any service whatever, payable to public officers of every description, are precisely the same for both, and the Frenchman enjoys the right, in common with the American, of employing the services as an agent or interpreter of his consignee or one of his clerks, or of any other individual. In a word, the French consul may act in all these different ways in behalf of his countrymen. Hence we see that, in consequence of the facility enjoyed by Frenchmen to employ such interpreters as they find most convenient, and of their total exemption from the vexations produced by monopoly and extortion, they seldom apply to their consuls, whose interference is only required in cases of difference or dispute; their right, however, remains unimpaired, and has never been questioned.

I have therefore to request of your excellency that the Americans shall be placed by the tariff upon the same footing as Frenchmen in regard to the fees payable to the brokers-interpreters, and that the consuls of the United States shall enjoy the right of acting for their countrymen in the manner pointed out by the declarations of the 25th October, 1817, and 31st August, 1818, and especially that they may assist them as interpreters in the different administrations concurrently with the brokers-interpreters. I here offer the assurance that the most perfect reciprocity will, in every respect, be observed in the United States.

The Government of the United States has seen with satisfaction the great increase of the trade between the two countries in the latter years—a point on which the French custom-houses can furnish precise data. From America I have none more recent than those published in 1816, in which year the United States imported, exclusive of wines, brandies, dried fruits, and other articles of that nature, to an amount of about sixty millions in merchandise, the produce of French industry. More than two-thirds of these consist of articles of modes and luxury, manufactured at Paris, and of Lyons silks, exported from Havre. They imported into France at least an equal value in cotton and other raw materials. Your excellency will, doubtless concur with me in the opinion, that a trade so extensive and beneficial to both nations should not be shackled by local vexations or by those petty interests which have given rise to the representations forming the object of the present note and of that which I had the honor of addressing to you on the 5th of the present month.

I eagerly seize on this occasion to renew to your excellency the assurance of my distinguished consideration.   ALBERT GALLATIN.

Mr. Gallatin to the Marquis Dessolle.

[Translation.]

PARIS, *May* 14, 1819.

SIR: When I had the honor to address to your excellency my note of the 12th instant I was not informed that the brokers-interpreters at Havre had obtained an alteration of the tariff in their favor.

I am no less surprised than concerned to learn that, as far back as the 24th of February last, his excellency the minister of the interior approved this new tariff, which allows to the brokers-interpreters, for French ships when loaded, fifty centimes on every ton of goods entered and twenty-five centimes at clearing; for foreign ships, one franc (100 centimes) per *ton of measurement* at entry, and, if they clear out with cargo, fifty centimes per *ton of goods.*

By the former tariff, American ships, arriving from the United States, paid, altogether, from fifty to ninety centimes per ton.

An American ship of three hundred tons, which is about the medium tonnage of our vessels employed in the trade to Havre, paid, according to the former tariff, one hundred and fifty francs, and according to the present, four hundred and fifty francs on clearing out with cargo, and three hundred on clearing out in ballast.

By which it appears that the brokers are now authorized by law to demand the exorbitant fees which, for two years and a half, they had been receiving contrary to law, and, instead of being punished for their violations of the tariff, their extortions have received the sanction of the law.

I had the honor, in my note of the 10th of August, 1818, denouncing these abuses, to inform the Duke of Richelieu of the exertions then making by the brokers to obtain this alteration of the tariff, and I expressed the hope that they would be unavailing, and that no new burden would be imposed on the American commerce.

The Duke of Richelieu, in his answer of the 12th September following, says: "The administration will take measures that they" (the brokers at Havre) "shall strictly conform to the existing tariff, and the abuses they may have committed shall be repressed."

Relying on this assurance, I was far from expecting that the tariff would have been augmented without any previous notice.

I am persuaded that the greater part of these circumstances have been unknown, and that no hesitation will be felt in reducing and equalizing the tariff, and giving the requisite attention to the representations contained in my note of the 12th of the present month.

I request your excellency to accept the assurances, &c.,

               ALBERT GALLATIN.

The Duke of Richelieu to Mr. Gallatin.

[Translation.]

PARIS, *September* 12, 1818.

SIR: I have the honor to return to you the seven original acquittances inclosed in your letter of the 10th of August last, relative to the charges exacted by the brokers at Havre from American vessels.

The administration will take measures to enforce their strict observance of the existing tariff, and to put a stop to the abuses that may have been practiced by them.

Be pleased, sir, to accept the assurances, &c.,

               RICHELIEU.

Mr. Gallatin to the Duke de Richelieu.

PARIS, *July* 28, 1818.

MONSIEUR LE DUC: I am informed that his excellency the minister of the interior addressed a circular letter to the several Chambers of Commerce, bearing date the 25th of October, 1817, and intended to define the rights and duties of the brokers-interpreters, conductors of vessels. In that letter are the following paragraphs, which I beg leave to transcribe from the copy with which I have been furnished:

[Translation.]

"An exception to these privileges occurs at once upon considering the right attributed to every individual of acting for himself, and without the intervention of a broker in his own concerns.

"So that no French captain, no foreign captain or trader who speaks French, is bound to employ a broker, either in settling his freight or in making his declarations at the custom-house, or, in fine, for any other formality whatever if he acts in person.

"But if he employs another, he is to resort to the person designated by law; he can only be assisted by a broker, nor can the custom-house admit any other.

"Nevertheless, foreign consuls, acting personally or by their accredited vice consuls or chancellors, have claimed the right of assisting the shipmasters as well as other persons of their nation, and of acting for them as interpreters; and it has been admitted that this was precisely one of the principal objects of their establishment. By virtue of this reciprocal privilege, every foreign shipmaster is considered as acting in person when he is accompanied by the consular agents of his nation duly accredited, and that whether he speaks the French language or not.

' In regard to translations, it is exclusively the duty of the broker to translate all documents produced in disputes on commercial matters; but the exclusive right of interpreters is not to be understood as extending to any other act or to any other case, &c."

The consul of the United States at Havre has accordingly assisted lately several American captains in making the necessary declarations at the custom-house for the purpose only of entering and clearing the vessels; but he has been interrupted in the exercise of those functions, which he thought, indeed, inherent to his office, and which were so explicitly recognized by the instructions above quoted.

The officers of the custom-house, after some hesitation, and on the consul's formal demand and making himself responsible for the consequences, have received the declarations made by the captains with his assistance; but the brokers have not only entered a protest, of which I have the honor to inclose a copy, they have also, as therein intimated, actually brought suits before the tribunal of first instance against the American captain and consul's chancellor.

The controller of the indirect contributions (at one of whose bureaus it is necessary to make declarations of the wines and spirits which may be on board for the use of the captain and crew) has positively refused to admit such declarations through the consul; and in a letter, of which I have also the honor to inclose a copy, he has intimated his determination to seize all American vessels whose captains shall not have made the declarations with the assistance of the brokers.

This refusal and this determination on his part, rendering the instructions of his excellency the minister of the interior altogether nugatory, I beg leave to request your excellency that such orders may be given to the several administrations and authorities as will carry those instructions into effect, and as may protect the American consul and captains against the proceedings with which they are threatened.

It is proper to add, that the captains and owners of French vessels are at perfect liberty in the United States to use, in their transactions with the custom-house or with any other public office, the assistance of the consuls of their nation, and to employ such agents as they may think proper.

I request your excellency to accept, &c.,

ALBERT GALLATIN.

The same to the same.

PARIS, *August* 3, 1818.

MONSIEUR LE DUC: I had the honor to write to your excellency, on the 28th of last month, in relation to the opposition made to the consul of the United States at Havre by the controller of the indirect contributions and by the brokers of that place; I have now that of transmitting a copy of one of the seizures made by the controller aforesaid of part of the stores of the American vessels entered by the assistance of the consul, and also a printed copy of a letter said to have been addressed by the brokers to his excellency the minister of the interior, and which has been published and circulated at Havre.

It does not belong to my functions to discuss the questions which the brokers have raised respecting the construction of the laws of France and the validity of the orders which have emanated from his Majesty's Government. To those orders, leaving it to the minister of the United States to make such representations as the case might require, the American consul and captains must and will always submit. But whilst they act in conformity with such orders they are entitled to the protection of his Majesty's Government, and I beg leave to claim it for them in this instance.

Not only have they been summoned before the tribunals for having made declarations at the custom-house which had been actually received as legal by its officers, but the controller of the indirect contributions has, by his refusal to receive declarations made in the same manner, altogether defeated the object of the circular of the minister of the interior, and he subjects the American captains, by his seizure of stores and vessels, to indefinite expense and delays.

It is to this last circumstance that I wish more particularly to call your excellency's attention at this moment, as a letter from the director general of the indirect contributions would, it is presumed, be sufficient to compel the officers of that administration at Havre to comply with the orders of Government and to act in the same manner as the custom-house officers.

Permit me, therefore, to request that orders may be given to the controller aforesaid to receive the declarations made at any of the bureaus of his administration by the American captains with the assistance of their consul, and to release the stores, vessels, or other property which may have been seized by his orders under color of such declarations having been thus made without the assistance of the brokers.

The urgency of that measure induces me to confine this letter to that sole object, but I may hereafter add to it some representations concerning the rate of emoluments charged to American vessels by the brokers at Havre, and which has been the primary cause of the consul's interference.

I request your excellency to accept, &c.,

ALBERT GALLATIN.

The same to the same.

PARIS, *August* 10, 1818.

MONSIEUR LE DUC: In the letter which I had the honor to address to your excellency on the third of this month I alluded to the illegal fees charged by the brokers of Havre to the captains of American vessels.

I have now the honor to inclose a copy of the tariff and some of the brokers' accounts, showing that their charges have considerably exceeded the rates fixed by it. These legal rates vary from 40 to 87½ centimes per ton, according to the size of the vessels, and taking the average of the first six months of this year would have amounted to 56½ centimes per ton. The brokers have for several years demanded one franc and fifty centimes per ton.

Prior to this year this demand was always enforced without any reservation, in proof of which their books may be examined; and the inclosed accounts, No. 1 to 6, show that in some instances they have received even more. The difference between the legal charges, according to the tariff, and those made and received by the brokers, in these six vessels alone, amounts to 1,427 francs, as appears from the following statement:

	Tons.	Due by the tariff. *Francs.*	Charged by brokers. *Francs.*
Pocahontas	280	150	570
Ceylon	210	135	350
Chatsworth	266	150	380
Emmeline	212	135	315
Mary Augusta	234	135	370
Catharine	178	120	267
In six vessels	1,380	825	2,252

Although the statement of the vessels entered at Havre from 1st July, 1815, to the 31st December, 1817, is not in my possession, I believe that there could not have been, during that period, less than 300, measuring, together, about 75,000 tons, on which the legal charges of the brokers, as fixed by the tariff, could not have exceeded 45,000 francs, and on which they must have charged and received more than 110,000 francs.

In December last the American captains determined, with the advice of the consul, to resist these exorbitant and illegal demands, and the brokers so far yielded as to receive one franc per ton; they refused, however, to give final receipts, and made a reserve of the other fifty centimes in case they should be adjudged to them. But they have lately again required the payment of one franc fifty centimes per ton, and have given receipts of the form exhibited in the account No. 7, and by which they oblige themselves to refund the fifty centimes if they are not entitled to them by competent decision.

The statement of the American vessels entered at Havre from the 1st January to the 30th of June, 1818, is in my possession. They were in number 74, measuring 19,040 tons, on which the legal charge of the brokers, according to the tariff, was 10,720 francs, as appears by the following abstract:

	Francs.
From 90 to 120 tons, none	
From 120 to 150 tons, 6 vessels, at 105 francs per vessel	630
From 150 to 200 tons, 11 vessels, at 120 francs per vessel	1,320
From 200 to 250 tons, 19 vessels, at 135 francs per vessel	2,565
From 250 to 300 tons, 15 vessels, at 150 francs per vessel	2,225
From 300 to 350 tons, 16 vessels, at 165 francs per vessel	2,640
From 350 to 400 tons, 3 vessels, at 180 francs per vessel	540
From 400 and above 4 vessels, at 200 francs per vessel	800
74 vessels, by tariff	10,720

At the rate of one franc per ton, the brokers have received on these vessels 19,040 francs, or 8,320 francs beyond what they were entitled to; and their reserve of fifty centimes amounts to a further sum of 9,520 francs, which the captains have also been obliged to leave in the hands of their consignees. Lately, as has already been stated, the brokers again demand the immediate payment of the whole at the rate of one franc fifty centimes per ton.

These abuses were, till lately, but very partially known to me, and the tariff was communicated only a few days ago. I am sure that, being now brought to the knowledge of your excellency, they will be suppressed and their authors discountenanced. It is understood that they are endeavoring at this time to obtain an alteration in the tariff. It is hoped that this attempt will be defeated, and that no new charges will be authorized on the American commerce, whose growing importance is equally beneficial to both countries, and which should not be impeded by such petty vexations.

Permit me to request that the accounts No. 1 to 7, being original papers belonging to the parties, may be returned to me.

I request your excellency to accept, &c.,

ALBERT GALLATIN.

Mr. Sheldon to Count d'Hauterive, acting as Minister of Foreign Affairs in the absence of the Duc de Richelieu.

PARIS, *September* 30, 1818.

SIR: The consul of the United States at Havre informs me that the local authorities there refuse to recognize the chancellor of that consulate or to receive declarations or other official papers presented by him, alleging that no exequatur has been granted to him for the exercise of his functions.

The consul himself having duly received the exequatur of his Majesty, and in the regular exercise of his official duty appointed his chancellor, by an act or commission under his hand and seal, this appointment belonging, under our laws and usages, to the consul alone, the appointment was made known to the prefect of the department, and the recognition of the chancellor by that officer was signified to the consul, who supposed that no further formalities were requisite. But, either from some misapprehension on the part of the local authorities or from a formality, the necessity of which is now for the first time made known to this legation, they require an exequatur, or a superior order of some kind, to induce them to acknowledge the chancellor of the consulate officially. The mayor of Havre is particularly mentioned as having demanded the chancellor's exequatur to be represented to him.

I have the honor to inclose the commission furnished by the consul of the United States at Havre to his chancellor, and to request that an exequatur, if the usages of France render it necessary for that affair, may be granted upon it, or that such orders may be given that he may be duly recognized by all the subordinate authorities with whom he may have occasion, in the discharge of his official duties, to have any intercourse.

I have the honor to be, &c. [in the absence of the minister of the United States.]

D. SHELDON.

Count D'Hauterive to Mr. Sheldon.

[Translation.]

PARIS, *October* 17, 1818.

SIR: With the letter you did me the honor to write to me on the 30th September last, I received the document showing the appointment of Mr. Thomas Taylor as chancellor of the consulate of the United States at Havre.

In transmitting it to me for the purpose of obtaining the exequatur of the King, it may have escaped your recollection that, chancellors not being entitled to that credential, it would be impossible for me to comply with your request.

That request appears, further, to be connected with particular circumstances which have already been taken into consideration; and in consequence of the explanations given, both to the minister of the interior and to the director general of the administration of the customs, I infer that the chancellors of foreign consuls residing in France will, in future, experience no difficulty in the exercise of the duties specially assigned to them in that capacity.

I have the honor to return, inclosed, the commission of Mr. Taylor.

Be pleased, sir, to accept the assurance, &c.,

D'HAUTERIVE.

Mr. Gallatin to the Secretary of State.

PARIS, *May* 22, 1819.

SIR : A new quarantine of ten days has again been laid on our vessels, and I have again renewed my annual representation on that subject. I have the honor to inclose a copy of my letter to Marquis Dessolle, who, in a conference, has promised to pay immediate attention to the subject. They are at this moment much alive to anything connected with the importation of contagious diseases, a Swedish vessel having lately arrived from Tunis to Marseilles with persons on board having actually the plague; they and the vessel are under strict confinement at the lazaretto of Marseilles, and the circumstance has not been permitted to transpire publicly.

I have the honor to be, with great respect, sir, your obedient servant,

ALBERT GALLATIN.

P. S. *May* 24.—Mr. Dessolle informed me verbally last evening that it had been agreed to take off the quarantine on our vessels. An occurrence in relation to it at Havre induced me to write to him again on the subject to-day, and I annex a copy of this letter.

A. G.

Mr. Gallatin to the Marquis Dessolle.

PARIS, *May* 17, 1819.

MONSIEUR LE MARQUIS: A quarantine of ten days has again been imposed on all vessels arriving in France from any port of the United States, even though such vessels may have clean bills of health. The Nimrod, arrived lately at Havre from New York, with 27 passengers on board, is now in that situation. Those passengers are compelled to remain crowded on board the vessel, without any possible result but that of perhaps creating instead of preventing sickness.

No contagious disease is known to prevail in any part of the United States. No other reason is assigned for this measure than the existence of a malignant fever at St. Domingo, Martinico, or Guadaloupe. This is the fourth time within less than four years that a similar general measure has been adopted without sufficient motives. Every time Government has listened to my representations and removed the quarantine, but not till after considerable loss and inconvenience had been suffered by individuals.

I can only refer to my former letters and briefly repeat their substance.

The yellow fever is essentially a tropical disease. A year hardly elapses without its appearing in some of the West India islands. This in itself, considering the distance and difference of climate, affords no reason whatever for laying under an interdict vessels from the United States. It is only when that disease does actually extend to some of their ports that cautionary measures become useful and necessary so far as relates to such ports. The most southern ports of the United States, are, of course, on account of the great and long summer heats, most exposed. The yellow fever has never been known to exist north of the 43d degree of latitude; it has never, in any part of the United States, made its appearance before the latter part of the month of June; it always disappears with the first frost; it has not, during the last fourteen years, appeared once anywhere north of Charleston, in South Carolina.

Any quarantine laid on vessels coming with clean bills of health from ports of the United States where no contagious disease is known to exist is a measure wholly useless as it relates to the prevention of such diseases, and extremely prejudicial to the commercial intercourse between the two countries. Whenever it is generally known, the passengers will be landed in England, and arrive forty-eight hours afterwards in France, without any other result than causing them some additional expense and inconvenience. As the delay of ten days' quarantine is an extra charge, equal to about twenty per cent. on the freight, the vessels will also be induced to land their cargoes in England, whence the cotton will be brought in French vessels to France. The expense will fall on the consumer, and in some instances the return cargoes of the American vessels will be purchased in England instead of France.

Such is nearly the substance of the arguments which have already, on former occasions, been successfully used with your excellency's predecessor. Last year, during my absence, Mr. Sheldon having made a similar application, he was, in answer, informed, by a letter of 28th September, 1818, from Mr. D'Hauterive, that the quarantine was taken off, in pursuance of a decision taken by the council of ministers, and on the ground that no contagious disease then prevailed in the United States.

The circumstances being now the same, I hope that the determination will be similar, and that the quarantine will be taken off, and not hereafter be renewed, except with respect to such ports as may at the time be afflicted with a contagious disease and such vessels as may not have clean bills of health.

I request your excellency to accept, &c.,

ALBERT GALLATIN.

The same to the same.

PARIS, *May* 24, 1819.

MONSIEUR LE MARQUIS: Your excellency having informed me verbally that the quarantine on American vessels had been removed, I had not intended to trouble you again on the subject; but I receive daily representations in relation to it, and every day's delay is attended with some new inconvenience. I am informed by my letters of the 22d that one of the passengers on board the Nimrod, named Bourguency, was released and permitted to proceed to Paris by virtue of an order from the Department of the Interior. This fact, provoking with respect to all the American passengers and mortifying to myself, whilst it proves that no importance is attached by this Government to the quarantine, makes me still more anxious to receive the official information that it has been in fact removed.

I pray your excellency to accept, &c.,

ALBERT GALLATIN.

Mr. Gallatin to Mr. Adams.

[Extracts.]

PARIS, *October* 25, 1819.

"I had the honor, in conformity with your request, to transmit, in my despatches Nos. 40 and 51, copies of the French tariff and of the communications of our several consuls on the subject of the extra duties and charges laid in the ports of France on the commerce of the United States." "American vessels are daily withdrawing from the trade, and if the evil is not corrected the whole of the commerce between the two countries will be carried on almost exclusively in French vessels. Our counter-vailing system of extra duties is wholly inefficient to protect our navigation; and if they are still more increased on the same plan, the French duties continuing the same, the ultimate effect would be that all our importations from France would be made in American and all our exportations to France in French vessels. This, considering the respective bulk of both, would give to the French four-fifths of the navigation between the two countries.

"Although the general conversations I have had on the subject gave no hopes of obtaining relief through the medium of negotiations, and although I felt a reluctance to make an application that would not probably be favorably received, the circumstances appeared so urgent that I have thought it my duty to address to the minister of foreign affairs the letter of which a copy is inclosed. I hope to be able to communicate to you their determination in time for Congress to act during the ensuing session, if that course shall be deemed eligible.

"The difficulty in that case will be to find an efficient remedy. I have already alluded to it in my despatch No. 88, in which I suggested the utility of obtaining an amendment to the Constitution of the United States which would authorize Congress to lay a duty on produce of the United States when exported in foreign vessels; but that process is uncertain and dilatory. On reflecting on the subject it has appeared to me that another mode might be adopted, which I beg leave to submit to your consideration.

"It consists in repealing our existing discriminating duty (of ten per cent. on the ordinary duty) on merchandise imported in foreign vessels, and in substituting to it an additional duty on those vessels, equal, on an average, to the extra duty which foreign countries lay on our produce, when imported there in American vessels.

"To apply this to France, and taking the French extra duty on cotton, which is our principal export there, as the criterion, the difference between the duty laid here on cotton when imported in our vessels, and that laid on it when imported in French vessels, is about one cent and a quarter per pound. Supposing, then, that a vessel carries at the rate of about 1,000 pounds of cotton to the ton, the difference amounts to about twelve dollars and a half per ton; and this is the additional tonnage which, being laid in our ports on all French vessels, without regard to their inward or outward cargoes, would countervail in a direct manner the French extra duty. This statement shows the greatness of the evil to be corrected, since, even admitting some error in the estimated quantity of cotton which vessels carry on an average, the difference against the vessels of the United States is more than the whole price of the freight. Calculated on tobacco, that difference is still greater, and amounts to nearly seventeen dollars per ton; for although the duty, when imported in American vessels, is but two-thirds per pound of that laid on cotton, a vessel will carry at least twice as much tobacco per ton as cotton. There can be no doubt that, taking into consideration the whole trade, the additional tonnage duty of twelve dollars and a half per ton on French vessels generally substituted to our existing discriminating duties, will no more than countervail the extra duties laid by the French government on our vessels.

"But in order to render this plan altogether efficient, I think it would be necessary to authorize also the President, in case the Government of France should attempt to defeat it by laying additional duties on our vessels, to increase in the same proportion the proposed tonnage duty on French vessels; and a provision might be added that all those extra duties should cease on our part whenever France consented to repeal theirs.

"I have alluded only to the general extra duties paid into the public treasury; but there are various other local charges laid on our vessels, such as pilotage, brokerage, &c., which are sometimes heavy and always vexatious, but which it is more difficult to countervail, because they are not uniform. Their nature and amount are stated in the consular communications formerly transmitted. That which relates to the ship-brokers of Havre is fully explained in my despatch No. 103, and I must add, that to the letters which I addressed to the minister of foreign affairs on that subject I have received no further answer. The average amount of those various charges might be estimated and added to the suggested additional tonnage duty. But the most efficient mode to obtain redress in those cases would be to lay another specific duty on French vessels, equal to the charges which, in the ports to which those vessels respectively belong, are laid on American vessels. That specific duty would, of course, vary according to the French ports from which the vessels came; and although there might be some difficulty in the execution, it seems to me that it may be surmounted by making the certificate of our consuls legal evidence of the amount of the extra charges imposed in their respective consular districts on American vessels.

"The importance of this subject will be my apology for having offered these suggestions. Of the greatness of the injury sustained by our commerce, and of the necessity of applying without delay a remedy, there can be no doubt. I hope that I may be mistaken on one point, and no endeavors shall be omitted on my part to induce this Government to alter their policy, but I firmly believe that nothing will produce that effect but the adoption of countervailing measures on the part of the United States."

Mr. Gallatin to the Marquis of Dessolle.

PARIS, *October* 25, 1819.

MONSIEUR LE MARQUIS : I had the honor on my arrival here to communicate, verbally, to his excellency the Duke de Richelieu that I was authorized by my Government to conclude with that of France commercial arrangements founded on a footing of perfect equality, and such as might promote an intercourse equally advantageous to both countries. With that view I had requested him to examine the convention concluded in July, 1815, between Great Britain and the United States, the bases of which they were ready to adopt in their commercial relations with France. The peculiar circumstances which prevented at that time the further prosecution of that subject have fortunately ceased to exist, and I have now the honor to bring it again to the consideration of your excellency.

Both France and the United States have, in order to encourage their own navigation, passed laws laying extra duties on foreign vessels and on the merchandise imported in such vessels; but the inequality is at present so much greater in France than in the United States, and the mode heretofore adopted in America to counteract that inequality is so defective, that if this system was permitted to continue on both sides the commercial intercourse between the two countries would in a short time be carried on almost exclusively in French vessels. In order to obtain their due share in the navigation between the two countries, (and they claim nothing more than their share,) the United States will be compelled to alter their laws and to lay such additional extra duties on the tonnage of French vessels or on merchandise imported therein as will, in that respect, restore a perfect equality in the commercial intercourse of the two nations.

This plan, however, of each Government laying extra duties in order to countervail those laid by the other is attended with serious inconveniences on both sides. The ship owners of each country are always apt to think that the extra duties paid by them are greater and more oppressive than those laid on the vessels of the other. They claim the protection of their Government, and ask that these should be enhanced; a species of commercial hostility takes place, which may have an unfavorable effect on the friendly relations of the two countries, and the ultimate and unavoidable tendency of the system is to lessen their commerce and to throw it in other channels.

Any attempt on the part of either country to engross for its vessels the carrying trade between the two will certainly be defeated by the other; and if, as it is believed, they have no other aim than that of a fair reciprocal equality, this will be attained with much greater facility and certainty by both mutually agreeing to abolish altogether all extra duties, than by each trying to countervail those of the other.

The bases of an arrangement founded on that principle would be :

1. That in the United States no higher tonnage duties or other charges should be laid on French

than on American vessels, nor any higher duties on articles of the produce or manufacture of France, when imported from France into the United States in French vessels, than when imported in the same manner in American vessels.

And, reciprocally, that in France no higher tonnage duties or other charges should be laid on American than on French vessels, nor any higher duties on articles of the produce or manufacture of the United States, when imported from the said States into France in American vessels, than when imported in the same manner in French vessels.

2. That no higher duties should be laid in France on articles of the produce or manufacture of the United States than on similar articles of the same value of the produce or manufacture of any other foreign country.

And, reciprocally, that no higher duties should be laid in the United States on articles of the produce or manufacture of France than on similar articles of the same value of the produce or manufacture of any other foreign country. These being, in substance, the same principles on which the commercial convention between the United States and Great Britain is founded, have the advantage of being recommended by the experience of two great maritime nations, equally jealous of their commercial prosperity. I may add that they have, either by positive treaties or by mutual municipal laws, been adopted in the commercial intercourse between the United States and Sweden, the Netherlands, Germany, and Prussia.

The great inequality, to the disadvantage of America, which now exists in her intercourse with France renders it important that the determination of his Majesty's Government on this subject should be communicated as soon as possible. It would be with great reluctance that the United States would find themselves obliged, in self-defence, to lay additional extra duties on French vessels; and they have given satisfactory evidence of their earnest disposition to cultivate and promote their commercial relations with France by the reduction of duties on French wines, which, without any previous stipulation in favor of the American commerce, was decreed during the last session of Congress.

I request your excellency to accept the assurances of the distinguished consideration with which I have the honor to be,

Your excellency's most obedient and humble servant,

ALBERT GALLATIN.

His Excellency the Marquis Dessolle, *Minister of Foreign Affairs, &c.*

Extracts of a letter from Mr. Gallatin to the Secretary of State, dated

Paris, *November* 8, 1819.

"Marquis Dessolle invited me to a conference on the 6th instant on the subject of the commercial arrangement proposed in my note to him of the 25th of October. He appeared to admit generally the correctness of the principles therein assumed as the basis of a negotiation, but he added that other causes of inequality might exist besides those arising from discriminating duties, and alluded to the frequent desertion of French seamen in America, to our refusal to deliver them, and to the great inconvenience to which this circumstance subjected French vessels. This subject is not immediately connected with that of the equalization of duties, and I believe that the evil complained of is not of great magnitude. If in their tariff they had only gone far enough to balance in some degree our natural superiority, there would not perhaps have been much reason to complain; but the existing system is intolerable. The minister has promised to write, and I hope to be able to communicate the final result before the end of the year."

"I have received the inclosed answer to my letter of the 14th of May last on the subject of the fees of the ship-brokers of Havre. The new tariff is thereby confirmed, and the extortions of which they had been guilty are made, on the plea of usage, a justification of Mr. Decaze's decision. That we had submitted without remonstrance to that imposition, and that the fees bear a just proportion to the services rendered, are assertions contrary to fact. It would, however, be an error to suppose that either this measure or the disinclination to enter into commercial arrangements arise from a hostile spirit against the United States. The ministry's dispositions towards them are, on the contrary, rather friendly than otherwise. In the case of the brokers, the decision is consistent with the general principles by which France is administered." "It is only an additional tonnage duty, to be taken into consideration with other extra charges whenever they become the subject either of negotiation or of legislative measures."

The Marquis Dessolle to Mr. Gallatin.

[Translation.]

Paris, *November* 6, 1819.

Sir: In your note of the 14th of May last you did me the honor to address to me some observations relating to the new tariff given to the ship-brokers at Havre on the 24th of February.

The advance of the dues, as exhibited by it in their favor, is not so real as may seem at first view. In fact, it has long since been generally admitted that the rates of the old tariff were insufficient; and, in consequence, custom had sanctioned the demand of higher rates since the peace as being more adequate to the pains and trouble of the brokers. To these new charges, adopted with the consent of the parties, and even of the American consuls at Havre, no objection whatever had been made since 1814 until the present. These are the same rates which were formerly spontaneously agreed to by the parties concerned, and are now established by the new tariff, which only confirms and sanctions by law the practice hitherto observed in this particular.

If the rates fixed by it are higher for foreign than for French vessels, it is because the brokers require more time and trouble in managing the business of the former than of the latter. The difference, then, in the charge in either case is to be referred to an unquestionable principle of equity; this difference has always existed in France, and is founded in justice and proportioned to the trouble of the brokers, who, being subjected in the former case to double labor, are therefore entitled to a double compensation. With respect to the difference in the tonnage by measurement or by goods, it has been ascertained that it was always intended that the brokerage should be uniform, both in the case of Frenchmen and foreigners, and paid upon the tonnage by measurement only. Orders have, therefore, been given forthwith to rectify the error that has taken place on this point, so that the tonnage by measurement may serve as the only rule for the rate of brokerage to be charged on French and foreign ships indiscriminately.

Be pleased, sir, to accept the assurances of the high consideration with which I have the honor to be, &c.,

THE MARQUIS DESSOLLE.

Mr. Gallatin to Mr. Adams.

PARIS, *December* 9, 1819.

SIR: The change of ministry has thrown new delays in the discussion of the commercial propositions which I had made to this Government. Mr. Pasquier has promised to take them immediately into consideration, and seems to understand both the reasonableness of what we ask and the difficulty of acceding to it without giving great displeasure to the shipping interest of France. The council of commerce, (consisting of eminent merchants,) to whom the proposals had, in the first instance, been referred, have reported that a nominal equality would give a decided superiority to our navigation; that the French discriminating duties were, however, too high, and that they should be reduced to two-thirds of their present amount. I have explicitly declared that if, instead of abolishing all those duties on both sides, an equalization was attempted, the reduction proposed by the council of commerce was altogether insufficient, and I could not accede to it.

I have the honor to be, with great respect, sir, your obedient servant,

ALBERT GALLATIN.

Hon. JOHN QUINCY ADAMS, *Secretary of State, Washington.*

Mr. Gallatin to the Secretary of State.

PARIS, *January* 15, 1820.

SIR: I have spoken several times to Mr. Pasquier since my letter of the 9th ultimo on the subject of the discriminating duties. He always professed sentiments friendly to whatever might increase the commercial relations between the two countries, and appeared disposed to meet in some manner the overture made on our part; but he always added that the French merchants were extremely averse to a total abolition. I addressed to him, on the 6th instant, the letter of which a copy is inclosed, and he had positively promised to send me, yesterday, an answer, which is not yet received. The departure of the Stephania compels me to write to you without waiting for it. I understood that at all events that answer would not be decisive, and a project of a law making sundry alterations in the custom-house duties was yesterday presented to the Chamber of Deputies, which contains no alteration in the discriminating duties of which we complain. The effect of these becomes every day more manifest. At Nantes, where not a single American vessel has arrived within the last twelve months, eight French vessels have arrived with cargoes of American produce within the last six months of 1819. I am confident that this Government will make no sufficient alteration until they are compelled to do it by our own acts. A clause in your act leaving a contingent power to suspend its operation in case an arrangement should take place is all that appears necessary to obviate every objection.

I have the honor to be, with great respect, sir, your most obedient servant,

ALBERT GALLATIN.

Mr. Gallatin to the Baron Pasquier, Minister of Foreign Affairs.

PARIS, *January* 6, 1820.

SIR: I beg leave to recal to your excellency's attention the letter respecting the commercial relations between France and the United States, which I had the honor to address to your predecessor on the 27th of October last.

Marquis Dessolle, in a conference on the subject, informed me that it had been referred to the council of commerce, whose opinion has for a considerable time been transmitted to the Department of Foreign Affairs. Congress being now in session, it becomes urgent that I should, without delay, communicate to my Government the decision of that of his Majesty on the overture I had the honor to make. It is the earnest desire of the United States that an arrangement deemed equally beneficial to the commerce of both countries may be concluded; but I have already stated that if their endeavors in that respect should fail, they will be under an indispensable necessity of restoring, by a new modification of their discriminating duties, the equality to which their navigation is entitled.

I request your excellency, &c.,

ALBERT GALLATIN.

His Excellency BARON PASQUIER, *Minister of Foreign Affairs, &c.*

Extract of a letter from Mr. Gallatin to the Secretary of State, dated

PARIS, *January* 20, 1820.

"I have now the honor to inclose the copy of Mr. Pasquier's long-promised answer on the subject of our commercial relations, which was not received till after I had closed my last despatch to you. I am confirmed in the opinion that nothing will be done here until we shall have done justice to ourselves by our own measures. The ministry is, I think, well disposed; but they will not act in opposition to the remonstrances of the shipping interest and of the Chambers of Commerce, which have been consulted. That of Paris is averse to our proposals. Indeed, Mr. Pasquier informed me that that of Bordeaux alone had given an opinion favorable to them."

The Baron Pasquier to Mr. Gallatin.

[Translation.]

PARIS, *January* 14, 1820.

SIR: I have laid before his Majesty the proposal made by you in the name of your Government in the note which you addressed to my predecessor on the 25th October last, the object of which is the conclusion of a commercial convention founded on the principle of perfect equality and calculated to establish relations as comprehensive as may be found practicable, mutually advantageous to both nations.

His Majesty is disposed, sir, to adopt any arrangement which has for its basis a due reciprocity of advantages, and which, by reconciling the commercial interests of both people, may promote their mutual prosperity.

As soon, therefore, as the various points of information indispensably necessary to guide the decision of his Majesty's Government, as well in relation to the two stipulations proposed in your note as to the other clauses which it may be found expedient to insert in the intended convention, shall have been collected, I will lose no time in entering with you into more particular discussions, and I have every reason to believe that I may be enabled to do so speedily.

I beg you, sir, to accept the assurances, &c.,

PASQUIER.

16TH CONGRESS.] **No. 340.** [1ST SESSION.

CLAIMS OF CITIZENS OF THE UNITED STATES ON ACCOUNT OF SPANISH SPOLIATIONS.

COMMUNICATED TO THE HOUSE OF REPRESENTATIVES MAY 12, 1820.

To the Speaker of the House of Representatives:

I transmit to the House of Representatives a report from the Secretary of State, with the document prepared in pursuance of a resolution of the House of Representatives of the 14th ultimo, on the subject of claims of citizens of the United States for Spanish spoliations upon their property and commerce.

JAMES MONROE.

WASHINGTON, *May* 12, 1820.

DEPARTMENT OF STATE, *May* 12, 1820.

The Secretary of State, to whom has been referred the resolution of the House of Representatives of the 14th ultimo, respecting the communication of any information received by the Department of State, or other Executive Department, of the amount of claims of the citizens of the United States for Spanish spoliations upon their property and commerce, or those for which the Spanish Government are held responsible, has the honor of reporting to the President a list of the claims concerning which documents have been transmitted to this Department, together with the statement of their amounts, so far as they can be collected from them.

JOHN QUINCY ADAMS.

The PRESIDENT *of the United States.*

LIST OF CLAIMS, &c.

Name of vessel.	Description.	Name of master.	Of what port.	Voyage.	Where detained.	When detained.	Value, exclusive of interest.
Abeona	Brig	Joel Beeman	Portland	Dublin to Cadiz	Vigo	1807	
Abigail	Schooner	Woodbridge	Marblehead		St. Sebastian		
Abigail	Schooner	James Atwood	Boston		Carthagena	May 18, 1797	$14,620 00
Abigail	Ship	John Hildreth	New York		Santander	July 4, 1799	
Abo	Brig	B. Mezick		Jamaica to Baltimore	Havana	Aug. —, 1797	
Active	Schooner	John Holbrook	Penobscot		Gixon		
Adeline	Schooner	James Mathews	Baltimore	Jamaica to Portobello	Carthagena		
Agnes	Brig	James Neill	New York		St. Sebastian		
Albany	Barque	Emanuel Perady	Hudson		Coruna	April 24, 1798	110,000 00
Alert	Schooner	Jacob Oliver	Beverly	Jamaica to Santander	Bayonne	Jan. 17, 1799	
Alfred	Ship	Lister Askwith			Cadiz		
Albemarle	Ship	Laign			Algeziras	Mar. 1, 1797	
Alert	Brig	Benj. Rich	Boston		Algeziras	Feb. 21, 1798	
Alert	Ship	Wm. Mahon		Teneriffe to Malaga	Algeziras	Dec. 28, 1806	
Alert	Brig	Saml. Hericks	Newburyport	Marseilles home			
Alert	Brig	Samuel Smith	Baltimore	Jeremie to Baltimore	St. Jago de Cuba	April 2, 1805	
Alexander	Ship	Moses Griffin, jr.	Philadelphia		Rio de la Plata	Dec. 24, 1801	
Alexander	Brig	Wm. Laughion	Norfolk		Algeziras	1806	
Algol, or Argol		Nathl. Barker	Boston		Algeziras	Mar. 7, 1806	
Almy	Brig	Cusler		Jamaica to New York	St. Jago de Cuba	1797	
Amazon	Ship	Israel Trask	Boston		Coruna	July —, 1800	
Amelia	Brig	Thomas Logan	New York		Muros	Sept. 4, 1798	24,706 00
Amelia	Brig	Jas. R. Calendar	Philadelphia		Algeziras	Oct. 10, 1800	
Amelia	Brig	Saml. Williams	Seabrook	Mole to New York	St. Jago de Cuba	Feb. —, 1797	
American Packet			New York		Algeziras	Oct. 6, 1801	15,000 00
America	Ship	Silas Swain	Philadelphia		Rio de la Plata	April 20, 1802	
America	Brig	Ehrenstrom	New York		Cuba	Oct.,1804, or 5	
America	Ship	John Stenson			Malaga	1797	
Amity	Sloop	Josh. Ellery	Portsmouth,N.H		Cuba	Oct. —, 1804	
Ann and Mary	Ship	Thomas Hunt	Philadelphia		Santonia	Mar. 28, 1799	
Ann and Mary	Brig	John Mallory	Baltimore		La Guayra	1805	
Ann	Ship	Wm. Robinson	Baltimore		Cadiz	June 25, 1799	
Ann	Brig	D. Bythwood			Algeziras	July 6, 1797	
Ann Isabel	Brig	J. Williams	Virginia		Algeziras	June 22, 1805	
Ann	Brig	Wm. Carry		Charleston to ——	Algeziras	Mar. 7, 1806	
Andrew	Brig	Coggins	Philadelphia		St. Sebastian		
Ann	Schooner	Pliny Hamilton	Baltimore	Jeremie to Baltimore	Cuba	Nov. 6, 1803	
Ann		Chapman		Philadelphia to Leghorn	Algeziras		
Ann	Schooner	Robert Dobbin	Baltimore	Jeremie home	St. Jago de Cuba	April 27, 1805	
Ann	Ship	Caleb Johnson	New York	Savannah to Jamaica	St. Jago de Cuba	May 6, 1805	
Ann	Schooner	Prince	Falmouth	Portland to Canary	Teneriffe	Sept. 12, 1798	
Ann	Brig	Parker	Philadelphia	St. Ubes to Philadelphia	Teneriffe	Sept. 12, 1798	
Ann	Schooner		Charleston		Cuba		
Ann Ballard	Schooner	Benj. Gordon		Portsmouth, N.H.,to Jamaica	St. Jago de Cuba	1806	
Ann Maria	Schooner	Hugh Wilson		Baltimore to Jamaica	St. Jago de Cuba	1796	
Antelope		Obed Rich	Boston		Rio de la Plata	Dec. 13, 1801	
Antelope	Schooner	Morse		Gonaives to Philadelphia	St. Jago de Cuba	1805	
Apollo	Ship	John Walker			Rivedeo	Sept. 21, 1798	102,100 00
Apollo	Brig	Henry Waddell	New York		Malaga	May —, 1799	
Apollo	Schooner	Richards		New York to Jeremie	St. Jago de Cuba	1797	
Angel		Smith			Coruna		
Angel		Robert Young			Coruna		
Ardent	Ship	Alexander Smith	Baltimore		Algeziras	May 17, 1799	
Ariadne	Ship	John Le Bosquet	Boston		Santander	Mar. 13, 1800	
Argus	Schooner	Thomas Gordon	Baltimore	Jeremie to Philadelphia	Cuba	Nov. 14, 1803	
Arab	Ship	Donohue	Philadelphia	Philadelphia to Jamaica	Porto Rico		
Arrow	Ship	Fletcher	Newburyport		Villa Franca		
Asia (a)	Ship	Jacob Peterson	Philadelphia		Callao de Lima	Sept. 9, 1801	142,000 00
Atalanta	Brig	Epes Ellery			Algeziras	Sept. 5, 1797	
Atalanta	Schooner	W. Montgomery			Algeziras	Sept. 23, 1797	
Atalanta	Brig	Elnathan Minor	Yorktown, Va.		Carthagena, O. S.	Jan. 13, 1797	43,000 00
Atalanta	Brig	Samuel Taylor	Boston	Boston to Leghorn	Carthagena	Aug. 18, 1800	
Atalanta (b)	Ship	Durfee Turner	New York		Algeziras	Aug. 16, 1801	12,000 00
Atlantic	Ship		Charleston		Passages		
Atlantic	Ship	Michael Jose	Boston	Bermuda to Honduras	St. Jago de Cuba	June 9, 1797	
Atlantic	Ship	W. Montgomery	Norfolk	Norfolk to Leghorn	Teneriffe	1797	
Atlas	Schooner	Thomas Kimball			Algeziras	Mar. 22, 1798	
Aurora	Ship	Benj. Fernal	Boston		Vigo	Oct. 1, 1796	
Aurora	Brig	Wm. Todd	Boston		Coruna	Dec. 27, 1798	7,077 00
Aurora		Eve	Charleston		Algeziras	Feb. 20, 1801	12,000 00
Aurora	Ship	Geo. Thompson	Philadelphia		Rio de la Plata	Jan. 18, 1802	
Aurora	Brig	Frankfort		Philadelphia to Jamaica	St. Jago de Cuba	1797	8,330 00
Aurora	Brig	Vincent		Jamaica to Honduras	Havana	1797	
Buba Sidi	Brig	Thomas Clifton	Philadelphia		Malaga	Nov. 11, 1799	
Baltimore	Brig	Benj. Houston		Baltimore to Leghorn	Algeziras	July 5, 1806	
Baltimore	Schooner	Edward Veasey		Baltimore to Bordeaux	Santander	1812	

(a) Cargo.   (b) Vessel.

LIST OF CLAIMS—Continued.

Name of vessel.	Description.	Name of master.	Of what port.	Voyage.	Where detained.	When detained.	Value, exclusive of interest.
Baba Sidi	Brig				Alicante		
Barbara	Schooner	James Sharp	New York		Algeziras	April 23, 1798	
Barbara (a)	Ship	Henry Clark	Boston		Cadiz	July 2, 1799	$20,000 00
Betsy	Brig	Gideon Snow	Boston		Malaga	April 18, 1797	
Betsy	Brig	Fran. Blackwell	Baltimore		Algeziras	June 8, 1800	73,500 00
Betsy	Brig	Simkins		Antigua to Philadelphia	Porto Rico	1798	
Betsy	Brig	Cushing		Jeremie to Philadelphia	Baracoa	1799	
Betsy	Brig	Sproul		Jamaica to New York	Baracoa	1806	
Betsy	Brig	Clark	Boston		St. Domingo	Jan. —, 1797	
Betsy	Schooner		Philadelphia	Jeremie to Philadelphia	St. Jago de Cuba	Feb. —, 1797	
Betsy	Schooner				Campeachy	1799	
Betsy		Philips					
Betsy	Schooner	Hooper			Bilboa	1807-'8	
Betsy	Schooner	Holmes	Salem		St. Sebastian		
Betsy	Sloop	Burnham					
Betsy	Brig	Denabre					
Betsy Holland	Schooner	Hugh Nickol	Newbern		Cuba	1804	
Beaver	Ship	Robt. Moore		Jamaica to Spanish Main	Cuba	Aug. 24, 1799	
Beaver	Schooner	Oliver Hecks		New York to Jamaica	Cuba	1802	
Beaver	Ship	Cleveland	New York		Lima		
Bell	Brig	Jas. Woodend	Norfolk	Port au Prince to Jamaica	St. Jago de Cuba	April 26, 1797	
Benjamin	Ship	James Newell	New York		Cuba	April —, 1805	
Bethia	Ship	W. Jones			Malaga	1797	
Berbice Packet		J. Stewart	Charleston		Algeziras	July 24, 1805	
Birmingham	Ship	Ezra Pearce			Algeziras	Nov. 19, 1797	
Blossom	Brig	Fernald	Portsmouth	Madeira to St. Thomas	Teneriffe	Sept. 15, 1798	
Boston	Brig	L. Russel			Algeziras	Mar. 9, 1806	
Boston	Sloop	Seth W. Terry	Boston		Rio de la Plata	July 11, 1801	
Brothers (b)	Brig	Jas. Summer, Jr.	Charlest'n,Mass		Carthagena	June 6, 1797	£6,000 00
Brothers	Schooner	Wm. Fairfield	Annapolis	Annapolis to Havana	Matanzas	Dec. 28, 1799	
Brothers	Ship	Steinhall	Philadelphia		St. Sebastian		
Buckskin	Schooner	William Henry	Baltimore	Baltimore to Jeremie	St. Jago de Cuba	1806	
Bulia	Brig	Robert Perry	New York	New York to Cuba	St. Jago de Cuba	Mar. 21, 1805	
Byfield	Snow	Simon Kindsman			Algeziras	July 15, 1797	
Catharine	Schooner	James Cox	Marblehead		Santander	Feb. 20, 1799	
Catharine	Ship	James Mills	Baltimore		Barcelona	Sept. 4, 1800	40,000 00
Catharine	Ship	George Dowdall			Algeziras	July 6, 1806	
Calpe	Ship	Richard Jones	Norfolk		Algeziras	July 26, 1805	16,000 00
Carpenter	Ship	James Meyer	Salisbury,Mass		Algeziras	April 23, 1806	
Caroline	Brig	Elihu Cotton	Middletown	The Mole to Jamaica	St. Jago de Cuba	April 26, 1797	
Carnatic	Schooner	Joseph Watts		Baltimore to Aux Cayes	St. Domingo	1797	
Carolina	Ship	Cook	Charleston	London to Charleston	Teneriffe	Jan. 16, 1799	
Cato (c)	Schooner						
Canton	Brig		Salem	Salem to China	Talcahuano	1810	
Camilla					Passages	1810	
Camilla	Brig	Shaler	New York		St. Sebastian		
Calisto (d)	Brig	Edward Tyler		Philadelphia to Cadiz	Algezir	May 9, 1807	
Cargo of the Ann, English (e)	Ship	Andrew Müller			Ferrol	1799	
Cargo of the Patrona, Swedish (f)	Galiot	Elije Jac. Besser			Santander	1795	
Cargo of Louisa Joanna, Swedish (g)	Snow				Ceuta	Mar. 3, 1797	
Cargo of Spanish Sacra Familia (h)					St. Sebastian	1797	
Cargo of Count Bernstorf, (i)	Brig				Algeziras		72,000 00
Cargo of Swed. Nora (j)	Ship				Ceuta	June 26, 1797	
Cargo of Danish Concordia (k)	Brig				Algeziras		
Cargo of flour (l)	Ship			Philadelphia to Havana	Campeachy	July 22, 1802	
Cargo of Ufersaght (m)	Ship				Guarda	April 1, 1806	100,000 00
Cargo of Portland	Ship	Robert Peel	Boston		Alicante	Feb. —, 1799	
Cargo of ship Hawk	Ship				St. Sebastian	Oct. —, 1810	
Cargo of Julia	Schooner	John Alderson	Washing'n,N.C	Charleston to Jamaica	Baracoa		8,000 00
Cargo of Gilpin	Schooner	Baldwin			Puerto Cabello	June —, 1815	5,358 00
Cargo of New York (n)	Schooner				Ayamonte	1807 or 1808	6,000 00
Cargo of Paddy	Brig	Peter Caruth	Charleston		Cadiz	Oct. —, 1806	
Cargo of Hannah	Schooner				Coruna	Jan. —, 1799	
Cargo of Carlota Edwiga	Brig						
Cargo of Swedish Aurora	Galiot						
Ceres	Brig	Thomas Norton	New York	Port au Prince home	Cuba	Feb. 25, 1804	
Celia	Brig	Aaron Dean	Dighton, Mass	Dighton to Havana	Matanzas	Dec. 28, 1799	

(a) Cargo.
(b) Vessel.
(c) Condemned and sold, vessel and cargo.
(d) Liberated.
(e) Owners of cargo, O. Bowen, &c., New York.
(f) Owners, William Sontag & Co., Philadelphia.
(g) J. H. Rogers, of Boston, supercargo.

(h) Owned in Charleston.
(i) Day: Fairchild, of Boston, supercargo.
(j) Israel Trask, of Boston, supercargo.
(k) Alberganti, supercargo.
(l) Owned by Joseph Dunlap and others.
(m) Owned by John Mallebay, of New York.
(n) Pillaged by the Spaniards.

LIST OF CLAIMS—Continued.

Name of vessel.	Description.	Name of master.	Of what port.	Voyage.	Where detained.	When detained.	Value, exclusive of interest.
Cerberus	Brig	David Luskin	Newburyport	Dighton to Marseilles	Algeziras	Jan. —, 1808	
Chatham	Ship	James Peters	New York		Barcelona	July 25, 1797	$55,000 00
Charlotte	Brig	Dan'l McKenney	Philadelphia		Algeziras	Dec. 23, 1798	
Charlotte	Schooner	Adam Masterton	New York	Cape Francois home	Cuba	Oct. 25, 1803	
Charlotte		Daniel Maker	Boston	Liverpool to Leghorn	Cadiz	1799	
Chorus							
Chance	Schooner	Graves					
Chimera	Schooner			Norfolk to ——	Algeziras	May 26, 1805	
Chile	Ship	James Bunker	Nantucket	Norfolk to S. Pacific Ocean	Callao de Lima	1805	
Charles	Ship	Benjamin Worth	Nantucket	Norfolk to Lima	Valparaiso	Oct. —, 1815	
Charles Stewart	Schooner	Alfred Eastin	New Orleans		Santa Martha	1815	
Charles Carter (a)	Ship	John Tomkins	Norfolk		Lat. 35° 7′, long. 70° W	1805	
Clothier	Ship	Rose Campbell	Baltimore		Callao de Lima	May 6, 1800	
Commerce	Brig	Robert Caleff	Norfolk		Santander	Oct. 11, 1798	
Commerce (b)	Ship	Gideon Gardner	Baltimore	Lisbon to Calcutta	Cadiz	July 4, 1799	50,000 00
Commerce	Ship	W. McNeil Watts	Booth's bay		Santander		
Commerce	Snow	Henry Danglois	Boston		Algeziras	Nov. 15, 1796	
Commerce	Brig	George Golfink			Algeziras	April 23, 1797	
Commerce	Brig	Robert Mattacks	Charleston		Algeziras	June 15, 1805	
Commerce	Sloop		New London	Jamaica home	Campeachy	Aug. 2, 1798	
Commerce	Schooner	Hubbel		Havana to New York	Augustin	1808	
Commerce	Ship	Alex. Brennan	New York	Belfast to Leghorn	Algeziras	Jan. 16, 1807	
Commerce (c)	Brig	Daniel Green	Charleston	Aux Cayes home	St. Jago de Cuba	1805	
Commerce	Ship	Chas. Rockwell	New York		Batabano, Cuba	1805	
Columbia (d)	Ship	Thaddeus Pickens	New York		Algeziras		
Columbia	Brig	Samuel Weucock	Philadelphia		Algeziras	July 17, 1800	13,500 00
Columbia	Ship	John Bryan	Norfolk		Hyguerita or Cartaya	Aug. —, 1801	19,000 00
Columbia	Brig	William Torrey	Charleston	Aux Cayes to Carthagena	Cuba (St. Jago)	Feb. 7, 1804	
Columbia	Ship	Samuel Smith	Glastenbury, Ct.	Barcelona to Cadiz	Cadiz	Aug. 21, 1802	
Columbus	Ship	James Woods	New York	Cadiz to Havana	Nevitas	June 24, 1800	
Columbus	Ship	Sterry Cook	Dartmouth		Algeziras	Mar. 1, 1797	
Columbus	Ship	Lothrop					
Comet	Schooner	Jon. Shillaber	Baltimore		Carthagena de Indias	1815	
Comet	Brig		Charleston	Jeremie to Norfolk	San Sebastian	June 16, 1805	
Commodore Rogers	Brig	N. Shalor	New York		St. Sebastian		
Connecticut	Ship				Rio de la Plata		
Cornelia	Brig	S. Hathaway	Providence, R.I.	St. Petersburg home	St. Jago de Cuba	Mar. 8, 1804	
Clarissa	Brig	G. B. Dawson	Philadelphia	Charleston to Barcelona	St. Jago de Cuba	May 29, 1805	
Cumberland (e)	Brig	Eras. J. Pierce			Algeziras	Aug. 26, 1805	
Cyrus (f)	Ship	Eames			Alicante		
Davies	Polacre	Thomas Lovell	Boston		Ceuta	Mar. —, 1801	
Delaware	Brig	James Dumphy	Philadelphia		Santander	Jan. 13, 1799	
Delight	Brig	John Purkett			Ceuta	May 13, 1797	
Delight	Sloop	William Flag	Charleston		Cuba	1804 or 1805	
Debonnaire	Schooner	Charles Parsons	Boston		Algeziras		
Delaware	Ship	Smith					
Diana	Brig	Silvester Simons	New Haven		Algeziras	May 22, 1805	
Diana	Brig	James Freeman	Boston		Malaga	Jan. 24, 1799	
Diana	Ship		Boston			1801	
Despatch	Brig	Philip Brown	Philadelphia		Malaga	April 2, 1797	
Despatch	Brig	Philip Brown	Philadelphia		Algeziras	Mar. 3, 1797	
Despatch	Brig	William Harding	New Orleans		Cuba	July,1804 or '5	
Despatch	Schooner	William Wallace	Norfolk	Cadiz to Hamburg	Alicante		
Despatch	Ship				St. Lucar	1808	
Dido	Brig	Shail	Marblehead		Algeziras	Aug. 24, 1805	
Dig	Brig	William Guyson	Norfolk		Algeziras	May 22, 1805	
Dove	Brig	Samuel Eams	Boston	Jeremie to Boston	Cuba	Jan. 6, 1804	
Don Quixote	Schooner	William Alley	Charleston	Port au Prince home	Cuba	Feb. 9, 1804	
Dolphin	Brig	John Eave			Havana	1799	
Dorchester (g)	Schooner	Constant Booth	Baltimore		St. Jago de Cuba	April 4, 1797	
Dorchester	Schooner	Joseph White	Vienna		Cuba	Jan. —, 1804	
Drick	Brig	Hill	New York		Algeziras	May 28, 1805	
Dublin Packet	Ship	Henry Green	New York		Cadiz	May 18, 1800	
Eagle	Brig	C. Churchill	Nantucket		Coruna	Jan. 1, 1799	20,892 00
Eagle	Schooner	Josiah Ingersoll	New York		Algeziras	July 29, 1799	17,000 00
Eagle	Ship	N. Schaaler			Algeziras	April 2, 1805	222,222 22
Eagle	Schooner	Thomas Barber	New York	Port au Prince to Jamaica	Baracoa, Cuba	June 17, 1804	
Eagle	Ship	Alsten	Philadelphia		St. Sebastian		
Echo	Brig	T. T. Clark	Boston		Algeziras	Oct. 15, 1805	
Edward Graham	Schooner	Benj. Bissell		Norfolk to Martinique	Margarita	Dec. 14, 1815	
Emeline	Brig	Kim	New York		St. Sebastian		
Eliza	Schooner	William Flag	Charleston		Ceuta		

(a) Ordered to Porto Rico.
(b) Cargo.
(c) Cleared.
(d) Liberated.
(e) Liberated the following day.
(f) Acquitted by the council of prizes at Paris.
(g) Cleared.

LIST OF CLAIMS—Continued.

Name of vessel.	Description.	Name of master.	Of what port.	Voyage.	Where detained.	When detained.	Value, exclusive of interest.
Eliza	Ship	Neil McNeil	Charleston		Los Passages	July 5, 1796	
Eliza	Brig	Mugford	Salem		Carthagena	May 18, 1797	$25,360 00
Eliza	Brig	Michael	Philadelphia		Cadiz	June —, 1799	
Eliza	Brig		Norfolk		Santander	May 3, 1799	
Eliza	Snow	H. Perry Benson			Algeziras	April 23, 1797	
Eliza	Ship	Elisha Turner	Boston		Algeziras	June 13, 1797	46,030 00
Eliza	Ship	Caleb Loring	Boston		Montevideo	April —, 1801	
Eliza	Sloop	John Arden		Jacqmel to Aux Cayes	Cuba	Feb. 25, 1804	
Eliza	Schooner	Thomas Grandy	Charleston		Cuba	June 3, 1804	
Eliza	Schooner	Ab. Sasportas	Charleston		Cuba	Nov. —, 1804	
Eliza	Brig	Elias Britton	Charleston		Palma, Majorca	Aug. 15, 1801	
Eliza	Brig	Harrington		Amsterdam to Philadelphia	Porto Rico	1798	
Eliza	Brig	Solomon Norton		Pool to Leghorn	Algeziras	Feb. 9, 1807	
Eliza	Schooner	W. Manchester		Africa to New Orleans	Cuba	1806	
Eliza	Brig	John Powell	Baltimore	Baltimore to Bay Honduras	St. Jago de Cuba	Dec. 12, 1804	
Eliza	Brig	John Champlin	Warren, R. I.		Havana	Mar. —, 1798	
Eliza	Schooner	Mitchell		St. Jago to Charleston			
Eliza	Schooner	Edward Palmer	Norfolk	Gonaives to Charleston	St. Jago de Cuba	Mar. 29, 1804	
Eliza	Sloop	Samuel Slocum	Newport, R. I.	Gonaives to Charleston	Porto Rico	April 1, 1804	
Eliza	Schooner	Brown	New York		Rio de la Hacha		
Eliza	Brig	Macy	Boston		St. Sebastian		
Eliza	Ship	John Evans	Norfolk	Jamaica to Norfolk	Batabano	Mar. 29, 1805	
Eliza Myers	Schooner	Thomas Long			Off Malaga	Oct. 6, 1799	
Eliza and Sarah	Brig	A. R. Clarke	New York	Maracaybo to New York	Cuba	1805	
Ellice	Ship	Wm. Howey	New York		Porto Rico	1797	
Eleazer	Ship		New York		Passages		
Eleanor	Brig	Davidson					
Eleanor	Brig	Treat		Baltimore to Jeremie	St. Jago de Cuba	1799	
Eleanor	Schooner	Thomas Ring	Baltimore	The Cape home	St. Jago de Cuba	Dec. 20, 1804	
Eleanor	Schooner	Thomas Williams			St. Lucar		
Eleanor	Schooner	Gawen	Baltimore		St. Sebastian		
Eleanor	Schooner	John Yeaton	Alexandria	Portsmouth, N. H., to Cuba			16,789 00
Elizabeth	Snow	George Loring			Algeziras	July 2, 1798	
Elizabeth	Brig	John Gardner	Philadelphia		Cadiz	1796	
Elizabeth	Brig	Silvester Wilson	New York		Bayona	Sept. 24, 1797	
Elizabeth	Schooner	Thos. Howland	New York		Cuba	April 2, 1804	
Elk	Ship	John Jones	Baltimore	Baltimore to Cape Francois	Cuba	Oct. 21, 1803	
Enterprise	Brig	Nathaniel Wilcox	Killingworth		Rio de la Plata	Dec. 26, 1801	
Enterprise	Schooner	Reub. Newcomb	Hampden, Mass	New Orleans to Liverpool	Campo Santos	Mar. 15, 1807	
Enterprise	Brig	Brown	Boston		St. Sebastian		
Enterprise	Schooner	Wm. Lewis	Alexandria	Cape Francois, home	Baracoa	July 18, 1805	12,220 00
Endeavor	Brig	Sol. Pennock	New Haven		Cuba	Aug. 3, 1804	
Eraul Chil	Ship				Algeziras	Nov. 4, 1800	
Esther	Schooner	Zach. Morgan	Beverly		Camarinas	Mar. —, 1799	9,259 00
Experiment (a)	Brig	James Living	New York		Cadiz	Mar. —, 1800	30,000 00
Experiment	Brig	Abram Dolby	Philadelphia	— to St. Domingo	Porto Rico	Aug. 17, 1799	
Exchange	Schooner	Day	Baltimore		St. Sebastian		
Factor	Schooner	Wm. Chase	New York	New York to Aux Cayes	Cuba	Jan. 13, 1804	
Factor	Brig	Seth Wadsworth	New York		Cuba	Mar. 12, 1804	
Fair	Brig	Joseph Tod	Providence		Rio de la Plata	Sept. —, 1800	
Fair American	Brig	Richards	Philadelphia	Philadelphia to Jamaica	St. Jago de Cuba	1798	
Fair Manhattan		Wm. Woffendale		New York to Gibraltar	Algeziras	Mar. 7, 1807	
Fair Columbian	Brig	Charles Taylor	Alexandria, D.C	— to Havana	Havana	Sept. 5, 1798	
Fame	Ship	Wm. Story	New York		St. Sebastian	Mar. 17, 1799	
Fame	Brig	James P. Hunt	Lamerton	New Jersey to Madeira	Algeziras	Sept. 13, 1798	11,759 00
Fame	Brig	Thomas Newell	Savannah		Algeziras	Dec. 2, 1800	15,500 00
Fame	Brig	Joseph Bounds	Baltimore		St. Lucar	Dec. 2, 1799	
Fame	Brig	Thompson		Cape Francois to Philadelp'a	St. Jago de Cuba	1806	
Fame	Brig	John Powell	New York	St. Jago de Cuba home		April 25, 1805	
Fame	Brig	Andrew Spring	Biddeford	Boston to Baracoa		April 6, 1805	
Fame	Brig	James Misroon	Charleston	Cape — home	St. Jago de Cuba	Feb. 3, 1805	
Farmer	Ship	J. Whitemore	New York		Coruna	April 30, 1798	10,500 00
Fanny	Brig	Samuel Silvester	Alexandria, D.C		Rio Caminho	Sept. 17, 1801	5,000 00
Fermen Actel	Brig	Wm. Guyfelden	United States	Cape — to Gibraltar	Algeziras	Mar. 3, 1807	
Felicity	Brig	Wm. Boyd			Cadiz	June 9, —	
Pell's Point	Brig	John Brown	Baltimore		Vigo	Sept. 6, 1798	27,496 00
Felicity	Schooner	Hugh Wilson	Baltimore		Huelva	Sept. —, 1798	
Federal	Ship		Wilmington		Passages		
Federalist	Ship	John Pratt	Charleston		Los Passages	Dec. 9, 1797	
Five Brothers	Brig	Joseph Breck	Boston		Rio de la Plata	Dec. 20, 1801	
Five Sisters	Schooner	Ph. N. Brown	Norfolk	Trinidad to Norfolk	St. Jago de Cuba	1806	
Flora	Ship	Nic. Lepelley	Alexandria or Petersburg		Malaga	May 25, 1800	32,775 33
Flora	Brig	Creswell		Philadelphia to Cape Fran.	Porto Rico	1801	
Fox	Ship	Rich'd Penniston	Philadelphia	Charleston to Bilboa	Port Passage	April 8, 1799	
Fox	Brig	David Norie	New York		Vigo	May 4, 1797	
Fortitude	Ship	Thomas Smith	New York	New York to Madeira	Palma	Aug. 20, 1799	

(a) Compromised.

LIST OF CLAIMS—Continued.

Name of vessel.	Description.	Name of master.	Of what port.	Voyage.	Where detained.	When detained.	Value, exclusive of interest.
Fox	Brig	Cullen	Philadelphia		St. Sebastian		
Franklin	Brig	Gilbert	Wilming'n, N.C		Coruna	Mar. 10, —	$13,016 00
Franklin	Brig	Andrew Morris	Wilming'n, Del		Campeachy	July 3, 1799	
Frederick	Schooner	Daniel Bender	New York		Algeziras	Feb. 1, 1799	
Frederick	Schooner	J. Gilbert Clark	New York		Coruna	May 16, 1799	85,138 00
Friendship	Brig	John Proud	Providence, R.I.		Alicante	June 19, 1797	29,080 00
Friendship		Wm. Beacon			Rivadeo	Aug. 4, 1797	
Friendship	Brig	Gideon Guy Ren	Norfolk		Cadiz	May 18, 1800	
Friendship	Brig	Richard Keating	Boston		Malaga	Sept. 27, 1805	6,300 00
Friendship	Brig	John Bolter	New York		Vigo	May —, 1797	
Friendship	Schooner	Wm. Job Cook			Palma, Majorca	Oct. 16, 1801	
Friendship	Brig	Jacob Clemens		Leghorn to Madeira	Algeziras	Sept. 15, 1806	
Friendship	Brig	Smith	Charleston	Leghorn to Port au Prince	St. Jago de Cuba	Nov. 19, 1803	
Friend	Schooner	Guimeret	Virginia		Algeziras	May 11, 1805	
Francis Lewis	Schooner	David Evans	Philadelphia	Pt. Rep. to Philadelphia	Cuba	April —, 1804	
Francis and Mary		Wm. Peterkin	Baltimore		Cadiz	June 16, 1799	
Fredericksburg Packet	Ship	John Briard	Philadelphia		Cadiz or Algeziras		
Freedom	Schooner	Murray	New York		St. Sebastian		
Galen	Ship	McKay	Boston		Passages	April 25, 1798	
Gallant	Schooner				Rio de la Plata		
Gardner	Ship	Stephen Briggs	Nantucket	Pt. Rep. to Pacific ocean	Guayaquil	1806	
George	Ship	Francis Waite	Portland	North Carolina to Cadiz	Algeziras	Oct. 7, 1797	
George (a)	Brig	Isaac Howland	Philadelphia		Vigo	Mar. 23, 1799	13,187 00
George	Schooner	George Bowers	Somerset	North Carolina to Aux Cayes	Cuba	Jan. 18, 1804	
George	Barque	Stephen Hopkins		Cadiz to Alicante		June 26, 1807	
George	Schooner	N. M. Pedge	Washing'n,N.C	Jamaica to South Carolina	Cuba	April 1, 1805	
George	Brig	James Taylor		Norfolk to Lisbon	Alicante	Oct. 11, —	
George	Sloop	Thomas Read	Norfolk	Honduras home	Cuba	April 19, 1805	
George	Sloop	John Grant	Kennebunk		Porto Rico	Feb. 19, 1797	
George		Bray	Newburyport		Passages	Jan. 13, 1808	
George	Brig	Damien Abile		Trieste to ——	Algeziras	June 12, 1807	
George Washington	Ship	George W. Morse		Philadelphia to Bordeaux	St. Sebastian	1807	
General Butler	Ship	Lake		Greenock to New Orleans	La Vera Cruz	1809	
General Wilkinson	Schooner				Passages		
General Knox (b)	Ship	Augustus Liberal	New Orleans	Bordeaux to ——	Robbed at sea		
Governor Mifflin	Ship	John Dove	Philadelphia		Cathargena	April 27, 1797	85,000 00
Governor Carver		Nat. Spooner	Boston		Majorca	April 29, 1799	
Governor Sumner		Nathan Leech	Boston		Algeziras	June 30, 1800	
Governor White	Schooner	Mark Lynch	New York	Cape Francois home	Cuba	Feb. 23, 1804	
Governor Strong	Ship	James Miller	Boston		Salou	Jan. —, 1804	
Governor Brook		Whelan		New Providence to Havana	Havana	1799	
Governor Strong	Ship	Thomas Clerk	Alexandria	Liverpool to New Orleans	St. Jago de Cuba	April 1, 1805	
Governor Mifflin	Ship	John Dove	Philadelphia		Malaga		
Greyhound	Brig	Wm. Plummer	Boston		Majorca	April 29, 1799	
Government		Leach					
Good Intent	Schooner	Simon Baker	New York		Cuba	Mar.,1804,or 5	
Golden Age	Ship	Earl		Jamaica to Philadelphia	Havana	1797	
Good Hope	Schooner	Thomas Duplex	Boston	New Orleans to Havana	Campeachy	July 22, 1801	
Greenwich	Brig	Edward Landers	Newport	Newport to Havana	Mantanzas	Dec. 18, 1799	
Grand Turk	Brig	Samuel Staples		Alexandria to ——	Algeziras	Feb. 22, 1807	
Gun Boat No. 3					Algeziras	June 15, 1805	
Greenway	Ship						
Halcyon (c)	Ship	Wm. Fettyplace	Boston		Algeziras		
Hampton	Snow	Moses Andres			Algeziras	July 13, 1797	
Hancock	Ship	Wm. Johnston	New York		Algeziras	Sept. 14, 1797	
Hannah	Schooner	John Griste	Marblehead		Malaga	Dec. 10, 1798	
Hannah	Brig	John Norris	Savannah		Algeziras	April 6, 1799	
Hannah		White	Salem		Algeziras	Aug. 20, 1800	
Hannah	Brig	Harding		Demarara to Boston	Porto Rico	1798	
Hannah	Brig	Coxe	Philadelphia	Demarara to Port Republican	Porto Rico	1799	
Hannibal	Ship	Jos. D. Jenkins	Providence	Rio de la Plata	Rio de la Plata	Oct. 22, 1801	
Hannah	Schooner	George Barker			Coruna	Jan. —, 1799	
Harmony	Brig	Seth Clark			Algeziras	Nov. 6, 1797	
Harmony	Brig	Marshall	Charleston	Cadiz to Charleston	Teneriffe	April 10, 1799	
Harriet	Schooner	Tim. Crocker	Boston		Santander	June 26, 1798	
Harriet	Brig	Edward Slocum			Algeziras	Aug. 24, 1797	
Harriet	Schooner	Robert Williams		N. York to St. Jago de Cuba	St. Jago de Cuba	June 4, 1805	
Harriet		Flagg		Charleston to Tabasco		1805	
Harry	Brig	Linster Calender			Algeziras	Oct. 11, 1800	
Hawk	Brig	Jonathan Hall			Algeziras	April 1, 1797	
Hawk (d)	Ship	Brown	Philadelphia		St. Sebastian	1810	10,000 00
Hawk	Schooner	Goff	Baltimore		St. Sebastian		
Hawk	Brig	Bond	Baltimore		St. Sebastian		
Hazard	Ship	Richard Gardner			Alicante	April —, 1799	
Hazard	Brig	Rogers					
Hetty	Ship	Neill		New York to ——	Santander	May —, 1800	
Hetty	Schooner	Woodbury	Salem		St. Sebastian		

(a) Or ship.   (b) Royal Spanish squadron.   (c) Liberated.   (d) Cargo.

LIST OF CLAIMS—Continued.

Name of vessel.	Description.	Name of master.	Of what port.	Voyage.	Where detained.	When detained.	Value, exclusive of interest.
Henry	Sloop	James Rinker	New York		St. Jago de Cuba.	Aug. —, 1799	$14,600 00
Henrietta	Schooner	Sandys		Newbern to Antigua	Porto Rico	1799	
Hermon (a)	Schooner	Charles Hayt	Boston	Liverpool to Palmero	Cadiz		
Hector	Brig	Thomas Harding.	New York		Baracoa, Cuba	July 25, 1804	
Hercules Courtney (b).	Ship	Henry Hudson		Newport, R. I., to Leghorn	Algeziras	Jan. 22, 1801	100,000 00
Hibernia (c)			Boston		Algeziras	July 26, 1801	15,000 00
Hibernia	Ship	Macdonald		Waldoboro' to Jamaica	Porto Rico	Dec. —, 1800	
Hiland	Schooner	Joshua Yeaton		Alex. to St. Jago de Cuba	Baracoa	Mar. —, 1807	22,378 00
Hiram	Schooner	George Kinns	Newbern				
Hiram	Brig	Jas. Graisbury	Philadelphia	Cape — to Gonaives	St. Jago de Cuba	Jan. 28, 1805	
Hope	Ship	George Hastie	Philadelphia		Tariffa	April 21, 1799	
Hope	Ship	John Greenfield	New York		Algeziras	Nov. 3, 1800	12,000 00
Hope	Schooner	Charles Hazard	New London		Algeziras	June 25, 1801	37,500 00
Hope	Brig	Stephen Webber			Algeziras	Oct. 2, 1805	
Hope	Brig	W. Lyons			Algeziras	Mar. 11, —	
Hope	Brig	Prince		Surinam to Boston	City St. Domingo	1799	
Hope	Ship	Jno. Burnham	New York	Rotterdam to ——	Alicante		
Holker	Schooner	Jer. Tatem	Philadelphia		Omoa	Mar. —, 1799	60,000 00
Holly	Schooner	Thomas		Philadelphia to Hispaniola	St. Jago de Cuba	1804	
Hoppet	Brig	Ezra Lewis	Hingham, Mass	Tobago to Turk's Island	Porto Rico	April 16, 1804	8,624 00
Huntress	Ship	Cunningham			Cadiz	Oct. 22, 1805	
Hunter (c)	Ship	Wm. Whitlock	New York		Algeziras	Mar. 12, 1798	110,000 00
Hunter	Sloop	Joseph Starks	New London		River Oronoco	April —, 1799	
Hudson	Brig	Sam. G. Bailey	New York		Cadiz	May 12, 1805	
Intrepid	Ship	John Sutter	Baltimore		Passages		
Intrepid	Brig	Bowen	Salem		St. Sebastian		
Industry	Schooner	Robert Farquar			Algeziras		
Industry	Schooner	Butts		Alexandria to Montserat	Porto Rico	1798	
Industry	Schooner	Misroon	Charleston	Charleston to Jamaica	St. Jago de Cuba	April 6, 1797	
Independent	Pol. brig	John Robertson		Philadelphia to Algiers	Cadiz	1797	
Independent	Pol. brig	John Robertson		Alicante to Boston	Almeria Bay	April 26, 1798	
Independent	Schooner	Diskeley	Baltimore		St. Sebastian		
Iris	Barque	Conway	Salem		Algeziras	1807	
Iris	Brig	Cassayne					
Isabella	Schooner	Mercer		Surinam to Philadelphia	City of St. Domin.	1798	
Jane	Brig	Sam. Patterson	Wiscasset		Santander	Oct. 27, 1798	
Jane	Ship	John Whitby	Norfolk		Rivadeo	Sept. 19, 1798	110,494 00
Jane	Brig	Nathiel Knight	Boston		Vigo	April 6, 1799	11,960 00
Jane	Schooner	Lyman Berry	Norwich, Conn		Valencia	Dec. —, 1805	
Jane	Schooner	Saml. Ramsay	Baltimore	Cape Frans. to Gonaives	Cuba	Jan. 15, 1804	
Jane	Ship	Josiah Bragdon		New York to Smyrna	Algeziras	Jan. 28, 1807	42,602 71
Jane	Brig	Mois	Haverhill	Cadiz to Ostend	Alicante	Oct. 11, —	
Jane	Ship	Gardner		Massachusetts to Canary	Teneriffe	May —, 1798	
James	Schooner	Robert Gray	Boston		Rio de la Plata	April 18, 1801	
Jay	Schooner	Samuel Calder		Malaga to the United States	Alicante	Oct. 8, —	
Jefferson (d)	Brig	Simon Richmond			Algeziras	May 3, 1805	
Jenny	Schooner	Johnson		Philadelphia to Jamaica	Porto Rico	1797	
Jefferson	Schooner	Jos. R. Connel	Philadelphia	Jaquemel home	St. Jago de Cuba	Dec. 23, 1804	
Joseph (e)	Ship	Henry W. Bool	New York		Algeziras	July 5, 1798	30,000 00
Joseph	Ship	John Grant	Kennebunk		Rio de la Plata	July —, 1801	
Joseph	Brig	Alex. Beard	Baltimore		Bilboa	Sept. 28, 1805	
Joseph	Schooner	John Lurvey	Newburyport	Jaquemel home	St. Jago de Cuba	Mar. 26, 1804	
Joseph	Schooner	Samuel Stacey	Salem		Bilboa		
Joseph Harvey (c)	Brig	Benj. Monteith	Philadelphia		Algeziras	Aug. 22, 1801	50,000 00
Josephus	Ship	Wm. Lovelace	Charleston		Cadiz	July 18, 1800	48,000 00
John and Martha	Ship	Feltknap	Newburyport		Malaga	May 28, 1798	
John Adams	Ship	James Johnson			Coruna	Dec. 29, 1796	39,000 00
John	Schooner	Nehem. Roundsy			Algeziras	Aug. 26, 1797	
John	Brig	Mat. Dote	Newburyport	Jamaica to ——	Cuba	Mar. 9, 1804	
John	Brig	Smith		Philad. to St. Jago de Cuba	Havana	1799	
John	Brig	John Tucker	New York	Jeremie to New York	St. Jago de Cuba	Jan. —, 1797	
John and Evice	Ship	I. L. Baker			Algeziras	Nov. 4, 1805	
John and Ruth	Schooner	John S. Darrell	Charleston	Cape Francois to S. Marc	Cuba	Feb. 10, 1804	
John and James	Ship	C. Langford	Baltimore	Baltimore to Cuba	St. Jago de Cuba	April 11, 1805	
John and James	Ship	James Johnson	Petersburg	London to Madeira	Coruna	Jan. 9, 1799	
John Vining	Schooner		New York				
John and Charles	Brig	Rt. M'Williams			Ferrol	1808	
John and Charles	Brig	Ebenezer Dyer	Portland	Virginia to Cork	Barquero, Galicia	Dec. 14, 1807	52,309 00
Josiah Collins	Ship	George Blair			Near Ferrol	Sept. —, 1798	
Joanna Lance		John Rober		Tarragona to ——	Algeziras	June 18, 1807	
Juliet	Schooner	Nat. Horton	New York		Algeziras	Aug. 11, 1797	
Juliet	Schooner	John Alderson	Wash'n, N. C.		Cuba	June 6, 1804	
Julia and Ann	Brig				Santander		
Jupiter	Brig	Nicholls	Norfolk		Cuba	Nov., 1804-5	
Juno	Brig	Nicholls		New York to Jamaica	Cuba	1797	
Juno	Ship	Seth Toby		Amsterdam to Leghorn	Algeziras	1807	
John	Schooner	Reuben Wicks					

(a) Cargo, say £50,000 sterling.   (b) Compounded for $18,000.   (c) Compounded.   (d) Say £50,000 sterling.   (e) Cargo.

LIST OF CLAIMS—Continued.

Name of vessel.	Description.	Name of master.	Of what port.	Voyage.	Where detained.	When detained.	Value, exclusive of interest.
Kitty	Brig	Thos. Horton	Philadelphia		Almeria	Feb. —, 1797	
Kitty	Brig	T. or Jas. Carter.	Newburyport		Algeziras		
Kitty	Schooner	Harper		Jeremie to Philadelphia	St. Jago de Cuba.	1797	
Kitty	Schooner	Singleton		Philadelphia to Jamaica	St. Jago de Cuba.	1797	
Kitty	Ship	Thos. Carter	Boston	Philadelphia to Malaga	Algeziras	May 6, 1798	
Kitty	Ship	M'Pherson		C. of Good Hope to Philad.	Porto Rico	1798	
Lambert	Schooner	Ar. Stotesbury	Philadelphia	Philadelphia to Cadiz	Algeziras	Sept. 4, 1800	$19,000 00
Lark	Brig	Will. Church	Bristol, R. I	Africa to Charleston	Cuba	1806	
Lenox	Ship	Green	Philadelphia	Philadelphia to Cadiz	St. Lucar or Cadiz	Aug. —, 1799	
Levant	Ship	Dav. Fairchild	Boston		Ceuta	April 26, 1797	
Leffen	Schooner	William March	Virginia		Algeziras	May 16, 1805	
Leander	Schooner	Smith		New York to Havana	Monte Christo	1799	
Liberty	Ship	Philip Bonet	Philadelphia		Vigo	May 10, 1798	
Liberty	Brig	Duer		Trinidad to Philadelphia	Cumana	1800	
Little John Butler	Brig	James Smith	Philadelphia	Philadelphia to Havana	Porto Rico	Aug. 17, 1799	
Little Fanny		Fosdick		Philadelphia to Surinam	Porto Rico	1799	,
Little Jack	Sloop	John Jones	New York	Jeremie home	St. Jago de Cuba.	April 1, 1805	
Little John				New York to ———	Minorca		
Louisa		Moffet	Philadelphia		Ensenada	Oct. 12, 1801	
Lucy	Schooner	Charles Robbins	Plymouth, Mass		Puerto Marin	Mar. 26, 1801	
Lucy	Brig	Gore		Jamaica to New York	St. Jago de Cuba.	1798	
Lydia (a)	Schooner	Jesse Pearson	Baltimore		Trinidad, Cuba	Sept. 24, 1797	5,000 00
Lydia	Brig	Dav. Patterson	Charleston	Cape Francois to Charleston	Baracoa	May 23, 1804	
Lively	Schooner		Portland		St. Jago de Cuba.	Jan. —, 1797	
Marianne	Ship	Jos. Paul Smith	Philadelphia		Cadiz		
Marianne	Ship	Patterson	Salem		Passages		
Marianne	Brig	John Adams			Cadiz		
Marianne	Ship	Knowles Adams	New York		Cadiz	June 29, ———	
Marianne	Ship	Knowles Adams	New York		Algeziras	May 11, 1799	
Marianne	Brig	Benjamin Peak			Algeziras	June 11, 1797	
Marianne	Brig	Peter York			Algeziras		
Marianne	Ship	Daniel Olney	Providence		Ensenada	May 27, 1801	
Marianne	Schooner	John Anthony	Boston	Boston to Guadaloupe	Porto Rico	July 18, 1805	
Maria	Ship	Uriah Starbuck	New York		Carthagena		
Maria (b)	Schooner	Jacob Stone	Newburyport	Jeremie home	Algeziras	Feb. 13, 1799	94,000 00
Maria	Brig	Thomas Rindge	New York		Vigo	April 23, 1797	
Maria (c)	Brig	David Hardy	Philadelphia	Philadelphia to Cadiz	Algeziras	July 23, 1801	55,500 00
Maria	Schooner	Chace	Baltimore	Port au Prince home	Cuba		
Maria	Brig	Sterling	Philadelphia		Cuba	Aug. 1, 1804	
Maria	Brig	William Russell	Alexandria		Algeziras		
Maria	Schooner	B. Ripon	Charleston	Bayamo to Charleston	St. Jago de Cuba.	Mar. 14, 1805	
Maria	Brig	John Morgan	Savannah		Havana	July 9, 1797	
Martin	Schooner	N. Williams	Gloucester		St. Lucar	April 26, 1799	
Martin	Schooner	N. Williams			Ceuta		
Martin		Parcel	Norfolk		St. Sebastian		
Mary	Brig	Phineas Stoder			Algeziras		
Mary	Ship	John Hunter	Charleston		Passages	April 1, 1799	
Mary (d)		Smith		New York to St. Sebastian	Santander	Jan. —, 1800	
Mary	Snow	Thomas Barnum	Boston		Algeziras	Mar. 4, 1797	
Mary	Brig	Tim. Gardner			Algeziras	Dec. 2, 1797	
Mary (e)	Ship	Thomas Webb	Philadelphia		Omoa or Guatem.	Mar. —, 1799	60,000 00
Mary	Brig	Florence Douzat.	Newburyport		Algeziras	Oct. 26, 1801	
Mary	Brig	William Butler	Philadelphia		Algeziras	Feb. 18, 1806	
Mary	Ship	James N. Brown	New York		Bilboa	June 28, 1805	170,000 00
Mary	Brig	Willington		Philadelphia to C. Nicola mole	Porto Rico	1797	
Mary	Brig	Norton			Montevideo		
Mary	Brig	Scott	New York	C. Francis to Port au Prince	Cuba	Mar. 3, 1804	
Mary	Ship	Stephenson			Algeziras		
Mary	Ship	Robert Stevenson			Bilboa	Feb. 6, 1806	
Mary	Barque	Geo. W. Balch			Algeziras		
Mary	Sloop	John Miles	New Haven, Ct.	To Trinidad and R. Orono	Angostura		
Mary	Ship	Hunt			Cadiz	1806	
Mary	Ship	Bradford			Algeziras		
Mary Brownrig	Schooner	Samuel M'Grath		New York to Cuba	St. Jago de Cuba.	April 23, 1805	
Mary Anne	Brig	Lawson	New York		St. Sebastian		
Mary Torrens		Brown	Philadelphia		St. Sebastian		
Mary and Eliza	Ship	Smith	Baltimore		St. Sebastian		
Marcus	Schooner	Samuel Moody		Jamaica to Bath	Campeachy	May 17, 1799	
Margaret	Ship	Seth W. Terry	Boston		Rivadeo	April 21, 1796	
Mars	Ship	Charles Henry		Savannah to London	Los Passages	1808	
Marie Therese					Los Passages		
Mercury	Brig	Samuel Brooks	Boston		Malaga	July 26, 1796	
Mercury	Ship	Henry Hubbard	Philadelphia		Algeziras	May 8, 1801	
Mercury	Ship	Moses Pierson	Boston		Rio de la Plata	May 8, 1801	65,000 00
Mercury	Schooner		Charleston		St. Jago de Cuba.	Feb. —, 1797	
Mercury	Ship	Ben. Davidson	Boston		Montevideo	1801	
Mentor	Brig	Wm. Thompson			Algeziras	Sept. 5, 1797	

(a) Vessel.　　　(b) Cargo.　　　(c) Compounded.　　　(d) Ransomed.　　　(e) Say.

LIST OF CLAIMS—Continued.

Name of vessel.	Description.	Name of master.	Of what port.	Voyage.	Where detained.	When detained.	Value, exclusive of interest.
Merrimack	Ship	John Williams	Boston		Ensenada	Nov. 15, 1801	
Mehitabel	Snow	John Denny		Newburyport to Jamaica	Cuba	1806	
Mermaid	Schooner	Trouant	Boston		Teneriffe	Aug. 3, 1799	
Minerva (a)	Sloop	Geo. Keyler	New York		Algeziras	Aug. 9, 1798	$16,388 00
Minerva	Brig	David Bray	Philadelphia		Ceuta	April 22, 1797	
Minerva	Brig	William Riddell	Boston		Rivadeselle	Sept. 1, 1798	33,500 00
Minerva	Brig	Moody		Philadelphia to Jeremie	Cuba	1797	
Minerva	Ship	Hall	Boston		Ensenada	Oct. 23, 1801	
Minerva	Brig	Killbourn	Newburyport		Cuba	1805	
Minerva	Brig	Ingram	New York	Leghorn to New York	Alicante		
Minerva	Ship	John M'Shane	Philadelphia	—— to Barcelona	Alicante	Oct. 18	
Minerva	Brig	William Yaner	Montevideo	Montevideo	Algeziras	Aug. 19, 1807	
Minerva	Ship	Pearson	Boston	Montevideo to ——			
Milford		Sampson	Baltimore		Algeziras	July 24, 1801	10,000 00
Miantinomo	Ship	Valentine Swaine	Norwich, Ct.		Conception, Chili	1801	
Molly	Brig	Peter Kelly	Philadelphia		St. Jean de Luz	Mar. 11, 1799	
Molly	Ship	John Borrowdale	New York		Rivadeo	Feb. 20, 1800	
Molly	Ship	Richard Flyn	Philadelphia		Algeziras	July 25, 1801	280,000 00
Molly	Brig	Harding	New York	Rio Janeiro to Buenos Ayres	Buenos Ayres	1803	
Molly	Brig	D. Adams		Alicante to Torringen	Cadiz or Algeziras		
Molly		B. Shattuck			Cadiz		
Molly				Philadelphia to ——	Villa Franca		
Monongahela Farmer		John Waterman	New York		Algeziras	May 13, 1805	
Molly Farley	Schooner	Williams		Norfolk to Martinique	St. Domingo city	1797	
Montezuma	Ship	Isaacs	Boston		Montevideo	Sept. 16, 1801	
Mount Vernon	Schooner	Maley	Philadelphia		Cuba	Oct. 9, 1804	
Nancy	Brig	Samuel Brown	Boston		Algeziras	April 3, 1797	
Nancy	Ship	Jesse James	Salem		Passages		
Nancy	Schooner	Henry Atkins			Algeziras	July 1, 1798	
Nancy	Brig	Phil. Aremberg	Baltimore	La Vera Cruz home	Campeachy	June 18, 1799	
Nancy		Williams	Salem		Algeziras	Mar. 27, 1801	10,000 00
Nancy	Schooner	Job Palmer			Algeziras	Aug. 20, 1797	
Nancy	Brig	John Le Bosquet	Boston		Rivadeo	May 28, 1797	
Nancy			Marblehead		Algeziras	Aug. —, 1801	5,500 00
Nancy	Brig	George Dexter	Charleston		Guarda	Sept. 16, 1801	
Nancy	Ship	Gardner	New York				
Nancy	Schooner	B. Booth Foss	Charleston	Charleston to Havana	Matanzas, Cuba	June 28, 1800	
Nancy	Snow	Richard Pitt	Baltimore	Baltimore to St. Jago de Cuba	Cuba	Jan. 19, 1804	
Nancy	Brig	Jer. Tatem	Charleston	Charleston to Honduras	Cuba	Feb. 1, 1804	
Nancy	Sloop	Henry Bours	Nantucket	Norfolk to Jamaica	Cuba	April 17, 1804	
Nancy	Brig	Henry Burner	Philadelphia	Norfolk to Gibraltar	Algeziras	Jan. 10, 1806	
Nancy	Schooner		Norwich, Conn.		Conception, Chili		
Nancy	Schooner	Rd. B. Brandt		Port au Prince to Alexandria	Baracoa	Feb. —, 1805	35,899 69
Nancy	Brig	Parker Muren	Norfolk		Algeziras	1807	
Nancy	Brig	Fraser					
Nancy	Sloop	Geo. Sydleman	Norwich, Conn.	New London to Surinam	Angostura	1797	12,269 00
Nanina	Brig	Rich'd Garwood	Philadelphia	Jamaica to Philadelphia	St. Jago de Cuba	Feb. 6, 1804	
Nabby	Brig	John Lawrence	Hartford	Antigua to Demarara	Porto Rico	April —, 1797	
Nelly and Kitty	Ship	Samuel Church	Baltimore		Passages	Mar. 7, 1798	
New York Packet	Brig	Jos. Innes	Charleston		Huelva	Sept. —, 1798	
Newport	Ship	Henry Tew			Algeziras	Oct. 20, 1797	
Negotiator	Ship	Lindegreen	Boston		Muros	Oct. 8, 1798	
Neptune	Brig	Wm. Manson	Baltimore	Jacquemel to Baltimore	St. Jago de Cuba	Dec. 9, 1803	
Neptune	Brig	Asah. Denning	Hartford		Cuba	June 10, 1804	
Neptune	Brig	Stephen Clapp	Baltimore		Cuba	May 16, 1804	
Neptune	Schooner	Busker		Philadelphia to St. Thomas	Porto Rico	1800	
Neptune	Ship	James Jefferis	Philadelphia		Cadiz	1797	
Neptune	Ship	Tho. Mendenhall	Philadelphia		Montevideo	Mar. 1, 1814	
Neptune	Brig	Ray	Philadelphia	Santa Cruz home	Porto Rico	1805	
New Orleans Packet	Brig	Wm. Hancock	New Orleans		Cuba	1804 or 5	
New Jersey	Ship	Clay		Canton to Philadelphia	Porto Rico	1799	
Nelson	Schooner	Thomson		Jamaica to Charleston	Mariel in Cuba	1806	
Needham	Schooner	Wm. Grant	Charleston	Jamaica home	St. Jago de Cuba	April 1, 1797	
Neutrality	Brig	Clark	Bath, Kenneb'k	Savannah to Jamaica	St. Jago de Cuba	April 9, 1797	
Neutrality	Schooner	David Norie			Algeziras		
Nymph (b)	Brig	Charles Hardy	Philadelphia		Algeziras	Sept. 16, 1800	58,500 00
Nymph	Schooner	Nap. Raymond	New York	L'Anceveau to New York	Nevitas in Cuba	April 24, 1797	57,000 00
Nymph	Brig	Webb	Philadelphia	Philadelphia to Bordeaux	Fort Dauphin	1799	
Ocean	Ship	Vredenburg		Calcutta to Philadelphia	Porto Rico	1797	
Ohio	Brig	Wm. Rust		New York to Jamaica	St. Jago de Cuba	May 6, 1805	
Olive Branch	Ship	Alex. McConnell	Norfolk		Gizon	Aug. 1, 1799	
Olive Branch	Schooner	Joseph Owens	Norfolk	Cape Francois home	Cuba	Mar. 9, 1804	
Olive Branch	Schooner	I. C. Muirhead	New York	New York to Port au Prince	St. Jago de Cuba	Dec. 25, 1804	
Olive Branch	Brig	Wm. Furnan	New Hampshire	Norfolk to Lisbon	Alicante	Oct. 11	
Olive	Ship	James Laughton			Algeziras		
Olive	Ship	Enoch Conklin	New York		Rio de la Plata	Feb. 19, 1809	
Olive	Schooner	Smith		Boston to Martinique	Monte Christo	1797	

(a) Cargo.   (b) Ransomed for $6,000.

LIST OF CLAIMS—Continued.

Name of vessel.	Description.	Name of master.	Of what port.	Voyage.	Where detained.	When detained.	Value, exclusive of interest.
Oliver Ellsworth		Wm. Henry	New York		Rio de la Plata	April 20, 1802	
Olinda	Sloop	Wm. Darnell			Porto Rico	June 17, 1797	
Onico	Schooner	George Howe	Norwich, Conn.		Conception, Chili.	Sept. 27, 1801	$60,000 00
Orington	Schooner	Ambrose Atkins	Penobscot		Malaga	May 2, 1797	
Orion (a)	Ship	John Farmer	New York		Vigo	Oct. 18, 1799	20,000 00
Orange	Ship	Orange	New York		Teneriffe	April 12, 1799	
Otter	Ship	Daniel Bennet	Boston		Carthagena	Jan. 17, 1798	69,000 00
Otter	Ship	Clifton					
Outram (a)	Ship	Samuel C. Hill	Boston		Carthagena	June 23, 1797	10,000 00
Pacific	Ship	Sam'l Kennedy	Charleston		Ferrol	Dec. 9, 1798	85,000 00
Pacific	Brig	Shubal Dunham	Boston		Vigo		
Pacific Trader		Jos'a Woodbury.	Boston				
Parkman	Ship	Lewis McMillan.	Alexandria		Rivadeo	May 15, 1798	54,885 00
Patty	Brig	Arch. Campbell	New York		Malaga	June 1, 1799	
Patty	Ship	Martin Laughlin.	New York		Porto Rico	May 28, 1805	
Patty	Brig	Jon'n Hardin		Penzance to Leghorn	Algeziras	Nov. 18, 1806	
Patty	Ship		Providence, R.I.		River Oronoco	1801	10,000 00
Patsey (b)	Schooner	Kane	Charleston		Cuba	Feb. —, 1805	
Pattern	Ship	Joshua Nash	Boston		Porto Rico	July 21, 1798	
Pastly			New England		Algeziras	Oct. 31, 1800	10,000 00
Paddy	Brig	Peter Caruth	Charleston		Cadiz	Oct. —, 1798	
Palishore	Ship	Stephen Mumain.			Algeziras	April 15, 1797	
Paramaribo	Brig	George Creed	Baltimore		Algeziras	July 28, 1797	
Pamelia	Brig	Merihew		Philadelphia to Cape Francois	Porto Rico	1801	
Patience	Sloop	Ward Post		Washington, N.C., to Jamaica		1805	
Peggy	Sloop	Henry Leader	Richmond		Malaga	May 2, 1797	
Peggy	Barque	William Baird	Philadelphia	Philadelphia to Bilboa	Santander	May 31, 1798	133,500 00
Peggy	Barque	Wm. Davidson	Baltimore		Gixon	April 1, 1799	
Peggy	Schooner	Thomas Tucker	New York		Malaga	June 26, 1798	
Peggy	Schooner	Jacob Curtis	Baltimore	Charleston to St. Jago	Cuba	Feb. 20, 1804	
Peggy	Schooner	John Denny	Newburyport	St. Mark's home	Cuba	Feb. 17, 1804	
Pearl	Ship	Latimer	New York		St. Jean de Luz	Jan. 19, 1799	
Pearl	Brig	Horton		Philadelphia to St. Thomas.	Porto Rico	1800	
Perseverance (c)	Ship	B. Knox	Boston		Algeziras	Sept. 18, 1801	13,500 00
Pegasus (d)	Ship	Otis Liscombe	New York		Coquimbo, Chili.	Jan. 2, 1801	150,000 00
Penelope	Schooner	Reed	Charleston		Campeachy		
Phenix (e)	Ship	Josiah Roberts	Boston		Rio de la Plata	Dec. 17, 1801	80,000 00
Phenix	Brig	William Cottle	Boston		Rio de la Plata	Mar. 15, 1802	
Pigou	Ship	Collet	Philadelphia		Montevideo	April 27, 1802	
Pilgrim	Brig	John Thissell	Beverly	Santander to Bilboa			
Plato	Ship	And. Lawrence	Baltimore	Leghorn to Surinam	Almeria or Malaga	July 14, 1797	43,000 00
Port Packet	Sloop	Davis	Georget'n, S. C.	Leghorn to St. Barts	Porto Rico	1798	
Portland	Ship				Alicante	Feb. —, 1799	
Polly	Ship	Wm. Bradshaw	Salem	Salem to Vigo	Malaga	April 29, 1797	26,000 00
Polly		Dugget	Boston		Algeziras	Oct. 28, 1800	15,500 00
Polly	Snow	Benj. Labbree	Philadelphia	Philadelphia to Cadiz	Algeziras	July 21, 1801	47,000 00
Polly	Brig	J. Robinson	Virginia		Algeziras	May 11, 1805	
Polly	Schooner		Boston		Cuba		
Polly	Brig	Michael Smith	Newburyport	Baltimore to Cadiz	Alicante	Oct. 25, ——	
Polly	Sloop			New York to Jamaica	St. Jago de Cuba.	Jan. —, 1797	
Polly	Sloop	Wm. D. Wilson	Baltimore	Baltimore to Jamaica	St. Jago de Cuba.	April 26, 1797	
Polly (f)	Snow	Benj. Labbree	Philadelphia		Cadiz		32,000 00
Polly	Brig	Graves					
Polly and Nancy	Ship	J. M. Knight			Algeziras		
Polly and Nancy	Brig	John Croan	Baltimore		Algeziras	May 6, 1805	
Polly and Nancy	Schooner	Wm. Brinster	Charleston	Gonaives to Charleston	Cuba	Jan. 30, 1804	
Polly and Maria			Philadelphia		St. Jago de Cuba.	Feb. —, 1797	
Pomona (g)	Ship	John Cruft	Boston		Carthagena	May 18, 1797	47,000 00
Pomona	Ship	Robert Hooper	Baltimore	Baltimore to Cadiz	St. Lucar	Oct. 13, 1799	41,000 00
Pomona (h)		Craig	Charleston		Algeziras	Sept. 11, 1801	62,000 00
Portsmouth	Ship	John Milward			Campeachy	1799	
Post Boy	Schooner	Adams	Baltimore		St. Sebastian	May 1, 1810	
Post Boy	Schooner	Spencer	Philadelphia		St. Sebastian		
Prudent	Ship	B. Crowninshield.	Salem		Algeziras	Nov. 3, 1800	48,500 00
Prudence	Ship	Wm. Rogers		Boston to Kingston	Cabanos	May 6, 1801	
Prudence	Sloop	Paddock	Nantucket		Buenos Ayres	Oct. 20, 1801	
President	Ship	And. Pinkham	New Bedford	New York to Gibraltar	Algeziras	Mar. 30, 1801	55,000 00
President	Schooner	Jos. Gate	North Carolina.	—— to Jamaica	Cuba	Mar. 4, 1804	
President	Ship	William Penrose.	Philadelphia	—— to Cadiz	Alicante	Oct. 23, ——	
President	Ship	John A. Smith	Baltimore		Porto Rico	Oct. 29, 1797	
Prince	Schooner	Stephen Sears		Labrador to Mediterranean	Algeziras	1806	
Prosper	Schooner	Selby	New York	New York to St. Sebastian.	St. Sebastian	Jan. —, 1810	
Pulaski	Brig		New York		Ensenada		
Rachel	Ship	Joseph Ropes			Algeziras	June 27, 1797	
Raven	Schooner	Amb. B. Martin.			Algeziras	Oct. 4, 1797	
Rainbow	Sloop		Charleston	Charleston to New Orleans.	Havana	Aug. 22, 1801	

(a) Vessel. (b) Brig. (c) Vessel—compounded. (d) Say. (e) Cargo.
(f) Compounded for $10,000—second capture. (g) Barque ship. (h) Compounded.

LIST OF CLAIMS—Continued.

Name of vessel.	Description.	Name of master.	Of what port.	Voyage.	Where detained.	When detained.	Value, exclusive of interest.
Ranger		Henry Pease		Newport to Santa Cruz	Baracoa	April 8, 1797	
Ranger	Sloop	John Allen			Straits of Gibraltr	1805	
Retrieve	Schooner	Reuben Jones	Newburyport		Gixon	April —, 1798	
Republican	Ship	James Simpson	Baltimore		Coruna	Dec. 24, 1798	$100,240 00
Republic	Schooner	Robert B. Ward	Charleston		Havana	Aug. · 3, 1801	16,019 00
Recovery	Ship	Nat. F. Adams	Norfolk		Algeziras	June 25, 1805	
Resolution	Schooner	Isaac Judson		Jacquemel to Connecticut	Cuba	Jan. 18, 1804	
Resolution	Ship	Henry Only	Boston		Ensenada	Nov. 15, 1801	
Resolution	Schooner	Nichols		St. Thomas to Hispaniola	St. Jago de Cuba	1806	
Rebecca (a)	Ship	Henry Nimmo	Norfolk		Algeziras	Aug. 30, 1806	60,000 00
Rebecca	Schooner	Stone					
Rebecca	Sloop	Wm. Clark	Philadelphia	Jamaica to Philadelphia	St. Jago de Cuba	May 29, 1797	
Rebecca	Brig	Zeb. Tucker	Portland, Mass.	Portland to Honduras	Honduras	Dec. 24, 1805	
Regulator	Schooner	A. Donaldson	Philadelphia		Porto Rico	May 22, 1804	
Reward	Brig	Jon. Stout		Portland to Kingston	St. Jago de Cuba	1806	
Rising Sun	Brig	Josiah Gould	Boston		Buenos Ayres	April —, 1801	
Rio	Brig	Thos. B. Stevens	Portsm'th, N.H.		Rio de la Plata	Nov. 12, 1801	
Risk	Schooner	Warner		Cape Francois to Philadelphia	Balacoa, Cuba	1806	
Risk		Jones					
Richard	Barque	John Ordion					
Rover	Brig	Arthur Smith	Baltimore	Malaga home	Malaga	Oct. 9. 1796-'8	
Rover	Brig	John Wait			Algeziras	Nov. 13, 1805	
Robertson (b)	Brig	Geo. Wakefield	Norfolk		Cadiz	June 18, 1799	12,000 00
Robert	Sloop	Town		Philadelphia to Jamaica	St. Jago de Cuba	1798	
Robert and Mary	Brig	Israel		Philadelphia to Hispaniola	St. Jago de Cuba	1806	
Roboreus	Ship	Hall	Baltimore	Baltimore to —	Cuba		
Roe Buck	Brig	Sloan	Philadelphia		St. Sebastian		
Rosby	Ship						
Roanoke	Ship	Ebenezer Paine			Algeziras	July 15, 1797	
Rose Bud	Schooner	Priam Pease	Philadelphia		Rio de la Plata	Feb. 10, 1802	
Rolla	Ship	Israel Arnold	Providence		Rio de la Plata	Jan. 1, 1802	
Rose	Brig	Jacob Wing	Philadelphia	Jeremie to Philadelphia	St. Jago de Cuba	Nov. 13, 1803	
Rose	Brig	Andrew Miller	Philadelphia		Ensenada	July 15, 1801	
Romulus (c)	Ship	William Pryor	Duxbury		Algeziras	Oct. 11, 1806	
Ruby	Brig	James Art	Philadelphia	Baltimore to Cadiz	Gixon	May 24, 1796	
Rufus	Ship	John Holland	New York		Cadiz	July 10, 1799	
Sally	Schooner	Stacey	Marblehead				
Sally	Ship	J. Farrell	New London		St. Lucar	July 30, 1799	
Sally	Schooner	L. Stephenson	Boston		Algeziras	July 21, 1799	12,000 00
Sally	Brig	John Harrison	Newport, R. I.		Alicante	May 22, 1797	31,000 00
Sally	Schooner	John Patterson	Charleston		Cadiz	Oct. 27, 1799	
Sally	Brig	S. Turner		Boston to —	Algeziras	Sept. 10, 1805	
Sally	Brig	John Thott		Savannah to —	Algeziras	Mar. 7, 1806	
Sally	Ship	Dan'l McPherson	Philadelphia		Rio de la Plata	Jan. 7, 1802	
Sally	Brig	Venn		Wilmington, Del., to Jamaica	Porto Rico	1798	
Sally	Brig	George Taylor	Boston		Buenos Ayres	Feb. 14, 1802	
Sally	Brig	John Chase	Somerset	Jamaica home	St. Jago de Cuba	April 25, 1805	
Sally	Schooner	Robert Churn		Norfolk to Jamaica	St. Jago de Cuba	May 13, 1797	
Sally	Schooner	Stephen Betts	Baltimore		C. of St. Domingo		
Sally	Schooner	Page					
Sally	Ship	Scott	New York		St. Sebastian		
Samuel	Schooner	James Blake			Algeziras	Mar. 11, 1797	
Samuel	Schooner	Chubal Coan			Algeziras	July 13, 1797	
Samuel		Ware		Marseilles to —			
Sarah	Ship	Ph. Cowper	New York		Coruna	Dec. 31, 1798	152,620 00
Sarah	Brig	George Douglass	Boston		Algeziras	Dec. 15, 1796	
Sarah	Ship	Thomas Hopkins			Algeziras	Mar. 29, 1797	
Sarah	Schooner	Rose	Norfolk	Port au Prince home	Cuba	Feb. 23, 1804	
Sarah	Ship	Jona. Smyth			Algeziras	1806	2,000 00
Saint George	Ship	Joseph Pick			Coruna	Mar. 9, 1797	
Saint Tamany	Brig	Hussey	New York		St. Sebastian		
Saratoga	Schooner	C.W.Wooster			La Guayra	Dec. —, 1812	
Salem	Schooner	Cleaner	Salem		St. Sebastian		
Saucy Jack	Schooner	Blunt		Alexandria to Hayti		Jan. —, 1804	
Shrub	Sloop	John Russell	Middletown, Ct.		Havana	Apr. 30, 1797	
Sewell	Schooner	C. C. Ronewell	Charleston	Charleston to Honduras	La Vera Cruz	July 25, 1800	
Sea Flower		Clark	Newport		Cuba	Dec. —, 1804	
Seaman	Brig	J. B. Lasher		Philadelphia to Genoa	Algeziras	May 20, 1807	
Serpent	Schooner	Howlin		Philadelphia to Cape Francois	St. Jago de Cuba	May —, 1806	
Sea Nymph		George Hastie	Philadelphia	The Mole home	St. Jago	Apr. 14, 1797	
Semiramis (d)	Ship		Charleston		St. Jago de Cuba		196,000 00
Shepherdess	Ship	John S. Doan	New York		Bilbos	Aug. —, 1807	
Signet	Schooner	Wickham	Baltimore	Baltimore to Port au Prince	Cuba	Feb. 7, 1804	
South Carolina	Ship	Paul Post	Charleston	Charleston to Leghorn	Palma, Majorca	July 25, 1800	
Sophia	Brig	Matthew Kenney	Philadelphia		Algeziras	July 24, 1801	55,000 00
Sophia	Brig	Shirley		Norfolk to Jamaica	St. Jago de Cuba	1798	
Spackman	Brig	William Wren	Norfolk		Ceuta	Mar. —, 1797	

(a) Cargo.   (b) Vessel.   (c) Compromised for $5,500.   (d) Ship and cargo of slaves.

LIST OF CLAIMS—Continued.

Name of vessel.	Description.	Name of master.	Of what port.	Voyage.	Where detained.	When detained.	Value, exclusive of interest.
Speedwell	Schooner..	John R. Story...			Ceuta	Apr. 15, 1798	
Splash	Schooner..	John Ferguson...	New York	Porto Bello to New York...	St. Jago de Cuba.	1806	
Spencer	Schooner.	Moffit	Philadelphia		St. Sebastian		
Spring Bird	Schooner.	Tucker	Marblehead		St. Sebastian		
Sterling	Brig	Tim. Trafton	Portsmouth		Muros	Sept. 19, 1798	$10,083 00
Stag (a)	Ship	Thomas Dulton..	Norfolk	Kingston to Savannah	Puerto Cabello...	Apr. 13, 1798	190,000 00
Stapleman (b)	Ship	F. Blackwell		Baltimore to Lisbon...	Algeziras	June 30, 1807	
Stork	Sloop						
Superb	Ship	Jos. Barnet	Boston		Passages	Mar. 6, 1798	
Success	Schooner.	Samuel Shaw	Boston		Algeziras	April 17, 1798	
Success	Brig	Titus Conklin.	New York		Rio de la Plata.	June 1, 1801	
Success	Ship	Gorton		Jamaica to Philadelphia...	St. Jago de Cuba.	1797	
Success	Brig	Clark		Philadelphia to Cumana...	Cumana	1798	
Success	Brig	Nicholas Blum .	New York	Jamaica to New York	Campeachy	July 12, 1805	
Sultan	Ship	Wm. Cole	Boston		Rio de la Plata..	Dec. 26, 1801	
Sussex	Ship	Philip Atkins..	Philadelphia		Pontevedra	July 19, 1797	
Susanna	Brig	Samuel Criswell	Philadelphia	Jamaica to St. Jago de Cuba		May 22, 1805	
Susanna	Brig	Hunt					
Susanna	Brig	Samuel Franklin			Algeziras	April 12, 1807	
Sukey	Ship	Whipple		Hayti to ——		April 14, 1804	
Sukey Smith	Brig	Harris	Charleston	Charleston to Teneriffe...	Teneriffe	Aug. 20, 1799	
Swansboro'	Ship	Is. Vredenberg.	Philadelphia	Baltimore to Cadiz	Tariffa or Cadiz.	July 13, 1800	38,099 00
Swift Packet	Brig	Jer. Goodhue..	Newburyport	Jacqmel to New Orleans	St. Jago de Cuba.	Dec. 21, 1804	
Swallow	Schooner.	Benj. Waters...	Salem	Jacqmel to Boston	St. Jago de Cuba.	Mar. 26, 1804	
Swallow	Schooner.	Berry	Philadelphia		St. Sebastian		
Tapster	Brig	Thomas Tucker.			Malaga	Sept. 17, 1799	
Tartar	Schooner.	Nic. W. Easton..	Baltimore		Cuba	Nov. 9, 1803	
Tartar	Brig	Seth Wadsworth.	New York	Cape Francois to St. Thom.	St. Jago de Cuba.	Mar. 12, 1804	
Tantivy	Brig	Pearly	New York		St. Sebastian		
Telemachus	Brig	Wm. Plummer..	Boston		Carthagena	May 18, 1797	33,330 00
Telemachus	Schooner.	Wm. B. Lugs...	Norfolk		Cuba	Apr.,1804 or 5	
Telegraph	Brig	Jer. Freeman...	Baltimore		Santander	Oct. 16, 1798	94,200 00
Three Brothers	Ship	Lindal Smith ...	Portland		Malaga	April 1, 1797	
Three Sisters		Tim. Wood	Wiscasset			Feb. 27, 1798	
Three Sisters	Ship	David Driver.	Norfolk	Trieste to Liverpool	Algeziras	May 20, 1806	
Three Sisters	Ship	John Anesley..	Philadelphia		Rio de la Plata.	Jan. 25, 1809	50,127 00
Three Friends	Brig	John Endicott			Santander	1798	
Thomas Pinckney (c)	Brig	George Pelor.	New York		Algeziras	Sept. 17, 1798	15,512 00
Thetis	Schooner.	D. Dougherty...	Philadelphia		Cuba or Sp. St. Domingo		
Thetis	Brig	Peterkin		Baltimore to Jeremie	Baracoa	1797	
Thomas	Ship	Tim. Newman ..	Boston	Cadiz to Amsterdam	Alicante	Oct. 11, ——	
Thorn	Ship	Dan. Edes, jr ..	Boston	Boston to Truxillo	Truxillo	1798	
Tickler	Schooner.	Thomas Frost...	Baltimore	Gonaives to Port au Prince.	St. Jago de Cuba.	April 4, 1805	
Topaz	Ship		Boston		Lima		
Torrans				Philadelphia to ——	St. Sebastian		
Trent	Ship	N. Kingsman ...	Salem to ——		Algeziras	Sept. 2, 1805	
Tryal	Ship	Thos. Coffin, jr.	Nantucket		Pisco	Aug. 18, 1801	
Tryal	Schooner.	Jos. Harding....		Philadelphia to Gibraltar..	Algeziras	April 13, 1807	
Trio	Brig	White		Jamaica to New York	Havana	1797	
Trio	Brig	George Flume ...	New York	Liverpool to New Orleans...	St. Jago de Cuba.		
Trimmer	Schooner.	Bunbury	Baltimore		St. Sebastian		
True John	Schooner.	Warner	Marblehead		St. Sebastian		
Tuley	Brig	Alex. Robinson..	New York	Cork to Leghorn	Algeziras	Dec. 28, 1806	
Tuley	Brig	Wm. L. Lavender	Washington	Cork to Jamaica	St. Jago de Cuba.	April 10, 1804	
Two Friends	Snow	Gilbert Howland.	Boston		Malaga	April 13, 1797	
Two Sisters	Brig	Wm. Worth		Boston to Jamaica	St. Jago de Cuba.	Jan. —, 1797	
Two Sisters	Schooner.	Giles	Beverly		Havana	1805	
Two Brothers	Schooner.	Dixey	Boston		Sacos		
Two Brothers	Brig	Macey	Boston		St. Sebastian		
Twins	Brig	Samuel Crow ...			Baracoa, Cuba..	April 5, 1805	
Two Sons	Schooner.	John Warner...			Bilboa		
Tyre	Ship		Providence		Callao	1801	400,000 00
Uncle Toby	Ship			New York to Lisbon	Ceuta	1808	
Union	Schooner.	John Haynes....	Alexandria		Cuba	May 8, 1804	
Union	Brig	Lake		Jamaica to the United States	Baracos	1797	
Union	Brig	Winge	Marblehead	Jamaica to Malaga	Algeziras	Nov. 17, 1807	
Union	Brig	Ricardo			Cuba	Jan. —, 1805	
United States					Cuba	Jan. —, 1805	
Valeria (d)	Brig	Stover	Newburyport	Jamaica to West Indies	St. Jago de Cuba.	1797	
Veneris	Ship	Henry Dowriel.			Algeziras	Mar. 11, 1797	
Venus	Schooner.	Shields	Baltimore		Alicante		
Venus	Brig	John Percy...	Bath, Me			1800 or 1801	
Vererius		Pesa			Algeziras	July 1, 1805	
Vickelhadge	Polacre	Thomas Dasson..	Boston		Malaga	Jan. 1, 1799	
Victory	Brig	Robert Hatton...	Norfolk		Bilboa	Nov. 5, 1799	
Victory	Schooner.	Robt. Campbell..	Newburyport	Curacoa to Virginia	St. Jago de Cuba.	1806	

(a) Including damages.   (b) Discharged.   (c) Cargo.   (d) Schooner.

LIST OF CLAIMS—Continued.

Name of vessel.	Description.	Name of master.	Of what port.	Voyage.	Where detained.	When detained.	Value, exclusive of interest.
Vigilant	Brig.......	Robt. Clonkman .	New York	....	St. Jago de Cuba.	Mar. —, 1805	....
Vigilant	Ship	Stephen Essel ..	....	New York to Cadiz	Algeziras	Aug. 2, 1807	....
Virginia Packet	....	Robert Wells ...	....	Norfolk to Cadiz	Teneriffe	1797	....
Volunteer	Ship	Edmund Fanning.	....	New York to China........	Coquimbo	Feb. —, 1816	....
Vulture	....	James Rich.......	....	....	Muros	Mar. 12, 1797	....
Washington	Brig	John Bonnell	....	....	Algeziras	Aug. 3, 1798	....
Washington	Ship	Francis Roberts..	Boston	....	Algeziras	Feb. 1, 1799	....
Washington (a)..........	Brig	Atkins Adams ...	Marblehead ...	....	Malaga	June 29, 1805	$3,000 00
Washington	Brig	John Benfield....	....	....	Algeziras	Nov. 16, 1805	....
Washington	Ship	Jas. Williamson .	Philadelphia....	....	Rio de la Plata...	Dec. 9, 1801	....
Washington	Sloop	....	Norfolk.........	....	Cuba	....	....
Washington	Ship	....	Baltimore	New York to Santander..	Off the port of Santander	....	....
Washington	Brig	....	....	....	Baracoa	Sept. 13, 1806	...... ,...
Welcome Return	....	Vanneman	....	Philadelphia to Jeremie..	Porto Rico......	1798	....
Wells	Ship	Lamsen	Boston	....	St. Sebastian ...	....	....
White Oak	Brig	Joseph Montfort.	Boston	....	La Guayra	1805	....
Willard	Schooner .	Andrew Harrison.	Boston	....	Carthagena	Jan. 18, 1798	69,600 00
William	Snow	Benjamin Lord ..	Philadelphia...	....	Huelva.	Aug. —, 1798	....
William	Schooner.	Henry King	Charleston	Cape Fran's to Gonaives .	Cuba	Jan. 16, 1804	....
William (b)...............	Ship	Solomon Towne..	Salem	....	Alicante.........	Nov. —, 1799	24,000 00
William	Sloop	Hayward	....	Bermuda to Hispaniola..	St. Jago de Cuba.	1806	....
William	Brig	William Loveth..	Portland.......	Jamaica to Liverpool....	....	....	....
William	Schooner.	George Benton ..	Hartford, Ct...	Barbadoes to Turk's Island.	....	1805	....
William	Brig	Gid. Holbrook ..	Plymouth, Mass	Martinique home	Porto Rico	Sept. —, 1797	....
William	Schooner.	John Hanwert....	....	Benecario to Copenhagen .	Algeziras	....	....
William Pew	Brig	William Blair....	Philadelphia...	Port au Prince home	Cuba	....	....
Warren	Ship	And. Sterrett ...	Baltimore	Baltimore to Canton	Conception	Jan. 20, 1807	....
Walter	Schooner.	Berry	Philadelphia...	....	St. Sebastian ...	....	....
Wilmington	Schooner.	....	....	....	Rio de la Plata ..	....	....
Wilmington	Schooner.	....	....	....	St. Jago de Cuba.	Jan. —, 1797	....
Widow's Son	Schooner.	William Bell	Newbern, N. C.	....	Cuba	Aug. 17, 1804	....
Winthrop	Schooner.	William Doliver.	....	....	Algeziras	Oct. 4, 1797	....
Woolwich	Brig	Jas. MacCutchin.	Philadelphia...	....	St. Jago de Cuba.	Jan. —, 1797	....
Yankee	Ship	J. Killburn	Connecticut ..	....	Rio de la Plata ..	Sept. 3, 1801	....
Yorick	Ship	C. C. Rabotteau.	....	....	Malaga	1804	....
Young Connecticut	Ship	Rollins	New York	....	St. Sebastian ...	....	....
Young Lion	Schooner.	....	....	....	Baracoa	May 31, 1805	....
Zephyr	Brig	Henry Elkins....	Boston	....	Malaga or Algeziras	April —, 1798	....

(a) Cargo.   (b) Cargo ransomed.

LIST OF CLAIMS—Continued.

Claims of—	Amount, exclusive of interest.	Remarks.	Claims of—	Amount, exclusive of interest.	Remarks.
David Beveridge........	$20,944 00	Of Philadelphia..............	John F. Merisult........	....	Of New Orleans ....
James Barry............	214,702 00	Of Washington City........	Nicklin & Griffith.......	....	Of Philadelphia.............
Peter Bretagne	....	....	James Bruce Nichol	$6,100 00	Of Alexandria, D. C.... .....
John Craig and others....	....	Of Philadelphia.............	Robert Oliver	....	Of Baltimore ....
William Cook	63,500 00	Of Charleston	John Perry..............	....	Two cargoes flour at Natchez.
Joseph Forrest..........	3,000 00	Of Washington City........	Jos. Dunlap and others...	....	A cargo of flour at Campeachy.
William Gallagher	....	For 100 hogsheads flax seed....	Francis Pearson	....	....
David Green, &c........	1,590 00	Of Philadelphia.............	Abram Piesch...........	....	Of Philadelphia.............
Gregory & Scobie,.....	8,487 00	Of Massachusetts	Jas. Perkins and others..	....	Of Boston ....
Lewis Groning.........	11,217 34	Or Michael Kelly, of Charleston	William D. Robinson....	564,327 00	....
George Hunter..........	25,000 00	Of Philadelphia.............	Ross & Simpson's assign's	39,558 29	Of Philadelphia.............
Richard Hughes	45,000 00	Of Boston	John Henry Rogers......	....	Of Boston ....
Hollins & McBlair	....	Of Baltimore	John and Samuel Wells..	90,900 00	Of Boston.................
John Hollins............	....	Of Baltimore	Joseph B. Windsor......	....	Of New York.............
Hale	....	Cash seized or detained......	James Yard.............	....	Of Philadelphia.............
John Jubel & Co........	....	Of New York	Robert Young	....	Of Alexandria..............
John Lowry	....	Of Alexandria	Moses Young	1,222 31	Of Washington City ....
Jedediah Leads.........	....	Of Charleston	Stephen Kingston	19,060 00	Of Philadelphia, additional for the insurance office of North America.................
Linchecomb	....	Of Dorchester county, Md. ..			
Peter Lokra............	....	Of Philadelphia.............			
Richard W. Meade	400,000 00	Of Philadelphia.............	Stephen Kingston	3,150 00	Of Philadelphia, additional on his own account...........
Thomas Mendenhall	463 00	Of Wilmington, Del.........			

RECAPITULATION.

A.	B.	C.	D.	E.	F.	G.	H.	I.
$14,620 00	$20,000 00	$40,000 00	....	$20,822 00	$11,752 00	$13,187 00	$10,000 00	$110,424 00
110,000 00	73,500 00	16,000 00	....	17,000 00	15,500 00	85,000 00	14,650 00	11,980 00
74,706 00	6,000 00	72,000 00	....	222,222 23	10,500 00	....	100,000 00	42,692 71
15,000 00	....	100,000 00	....	25,360 00	5,000 00	....	15,000 00	30,900 00
109,100 00	....	8,000 00	....	46,030 00	27,496 00	....	22,378 00	50,000 00
142,000 00	....	5,358 00	....	16,789 00	32,775 33	....	12,000 00	48,000 00
43,000 00	....	6,000 00	....	12,220 00	13,016 00	....	37,500 00	39,000 00
12,000 00	....	55,000 00	....	9,282 00	85,128 00	....	60,000 00	52,209 00
7,077 00	....	50,000 00	....	30,000 00	22,080 00	....	8,624 00	....
12,000 00	....	13,500 00	....	....	6,300 00	....	110,000 00	....
8,330 00	....	12,000 00						
490,833 00	99,500 00	377,858 00	....	399,725 23	229,477 33	98,187 00	390,102 00	384,195 71

K.	L.	M.	N.	O.	P.	Q.	R.	S.
....	$19,000 00	$24,000 00	$10,000 00	$60,000 00	$65,000 00	....	$100,240 00	$12,000 00
....	5,000 00	55,500 00	5,500 00	20,000 00	54,885 00	....	16,019 00	31,000 00
....	....	60,000 00	33,899 69	69,000 00	10,000 00	....	60,000 00	152,690 00
....	....	170,000 00	12,969 00	10,000 00	10,000 00	....	12,000 00	2,000 00
....	....	65,000 00	52,500 00	....	133,500 00	....	....	126,000 00
....	....	16,388 00	57,000 00	....	13,500 00	....	....	55,000 00
....	....	33,500 00	....	....	150,000 00	....	....	10,083 00
....	....	10,000 00	....	....	80,000 00	....	....	190,000 00
....	....	280,000 00	....	....	43,000 00	....	....	38,099 00
....	....	....	....	....	26,000 00	....	....	....
....	....	....	....	....	15,500 00	....	....	....
....	....	....	....	....	47,000 00	....	....	....
....	....	....	....	....	32,000 00	....	....	....
....	....	....	....	....	47,000 00	....	....	....
....	....	....	....	....	41,000 00	....	....	....
....	....	....	....	....	62,000 00	....	....	....
....	....	....	....	....	48,500 00	....	....	....
....	....	....	....	....	55,000 00	....	....	....
....	24,000 00	714,388 69	173,168 69	159,000 00	953,885 00	....	188,259 00	616,802 00

T.	U.	V.	W.	X.	Y.	Z.	Claims.
$33,330 00	....	....	$3,000 00	....	....	....	$20,244 00
24,200 00	....	....	69,600 00	....	....	....	214,702 00
50,127 00	....	....	24,000 00	....	....	....	63,509 00
15,512 00	....	....	....	....	....	....	3,000 00
400,000 00	....	....	....	....	....	....	1,500 00
....	....	....	....	....	....	....	8,487 00
....	....	....	....	....	....	....	11,217 34
....	....	....	....	....	....	....	25,000 00
....	....	....	....	....	....	....	45,000 00
....	....	....	....	....	....	....	400,000 00
....	....	....	....	....	....	....	463 00
....	....	....	....	....	....	....	6,100 00
....	....	....	....	....	....	....	564,227 00
....	....	....	....	....	....	....	32,558 29
....	....	....	....	....	....	....	90,900 00
....	....	....	....	....	....	....	1,222 31
....	....	....	....	....	....	....	19,060 00
....	....	....	....	....	....	....	3,150 00
593,169 00	....	....	96,600 00	....	....	....	1,510,430 94

A............	$490,833 00	O............	$159,000 00
B............	99,500 00	P............	953,885 00
C............	377,858 00	R............	188,259 00
E............	399,725 23	S............	616,802 00
F............	229,477 33	T............	593,169 00
G............	98,187 00	W............	96,600 00
H............	390,102 00	Claims............	1,510,430 94
I............	384,195 71		
L............	24,000 00	142 claims............	7,499,580 90
M............	714,388 00		
N............	173,168 69		

Averaging nearly $52,321, including the eighteen claims other than those for vessels or cargoes.

No. 341.

EXPENSES UNDER TREATY OF GHENT.

COMMUNICATED TO THE HOUSE OF REPRESENTATIVES DECEMBER 19, 1820.

To the House of Representatives:

In compliance with a resolution of the House of Representatives of the 21st of November last, "requesting the President to lay before the House information relating to the progress and expenditures of the Commissioners under the fifth, sixth, and seventh articles of the treaty of Ghent," I now transmit a report from the Secretary of State, with documents containing all the information in the possession of that Department requested by that resolution.

                                                            JAMES MONROE.

Washington, *December* 14, 1820.

DÉPARTMENT OF STATE, *December* 11, 1820.

The Secretary of State, to whom has been referred a resolution of the House of Representatives of the 21st of November last, requesting the President to lay before the House information relating to the progress and expenditures of the Commissioners under the fifth, sixth, and seventh articles of the treaty of Ghent, has the honor of submitting to the President the papers containing the information in possession of this Department requested by that resolution.

                                                            JOHN QUINCY ADAMS.

List of the papers submitted.

Statement of moneys drawn from the Treasury of the United States by the Commissioners and agents under the treaty of Ghent:

No. 1. Account of P. B. Porter, Commissioner under the sixth and seventh articles of the treaty of Ghent, for 1817.
    Boundary Commissioner's account for same period.
    Statement of wages and salaries for same period.
    Account of expenditures and abstract of vouchers of S. Hawkins for 1817.
    Account of expenditures and abstract of vouchers of S. Hawkins for 1818.
    Account of expenditures and abstract of vouchers of S. Hawkins for 1819.
No. 2. General account of expenses for 1817, 1818, and 1819.
    Account of expenses for 1818.
    Account of salaries and wages for 1819.
    W. C. Bradley for 1817, 1818, and 1819.
Letter from J. Delafield to the Secretary of State, May 17, 1820.
Letter from Secretary of State to Mr. Delafield, May 19, 1820.
Letter from Mr. Delafield to Secretary of State, May 19, 1820.
Letter from same to same, October 13, 1820.
Letter from same to same, November 1, 1820.
Letter from C. P. Van Ness to Secretary of State, with inclosure, November 25, 1820.
Letter from Mr. Delafield to Secretary of State, with inclosure, November 27, 1820.
Letter from P. B. Porter to Secretary of State, December 2, 1820.

TREASURY DEPARTMENT, *Fifth Auditor's Office, December* 8, 1820.

SIR: I have the honor to transmit, in pursuance of a resolution of the House of Representatives of the United States, of which you have furnished a copy, a general statement of moneys drawn from the Treasury in the years 1816, 1817, 1818, 1819, and 1820, by the Commissioners and agents appointed in virtue of the fifth, sixth, and seventh articles of the treaty of Ghent; as also copies of the accounts of those Commissioners and agents as far as they have been received, containing all the information on the subject of the resolution which can be supplied by this office.

I have the honor to be, very respectfully, sir, your obedient servant,

                                        S. PLEASANTON, *Fifth Auditor of the Treasury.*

Hon. SECRETARY OF STATE.

Amount of money drawn from the Treasury of the United States by the Commissioners and agents under the fifth, sixth, and seventh articles of the treaty of Ghent in the years 1816, 1817, 1818, 1819, and 1820.

Cornelius P. Van Ness, Commissioner under the fifth article, viz:

October 15, 1816, paid him	$15,000 00
From May 7 to September 6, 1817, paid him	10,944 00
From April 28 to November 27, 1818, paid him	31,500 00
From March 30 to September 17, 1819, paid him	18,500 00
From January 1 to November 30, 1820, paid him	20,000 00
Carried forward	$82,444 00

Brought forward...........	....	$82,444 00

William C. Bradley, agent under the fifth article, viz:

From April 19 to September 3, 1817, paid him...........................	$2,000 00	
From April 20 to September 29, 1818, paid him........................	5,000 00	
From January 23 to December 2, 1819, paid him.......................	5,210 88	
From January 1 to November 30, 1820, paid him.......................	4,444 22	
		16,655 10
		99,099 10

Samuel Hawkins, agent under the sixth and seventh articles, viz:

From April 26 to December 26, 1816, paid him.........................	· 3,000 00	
From January 14 to November 21, 1817, paid him......................	8,481 00	
From April 13 to October 27, 1818, paid him..........................	9,000 00	
From January 19 to October 22, 1819, paid him.......................	8,410 80	
		28,891 80

Peter B. Porter, Commissioner under the sixth and seventh articles, viz:

From February 11 to November 27, 1817, paid him.....................	16,315 95	
From April 16 to August 26, 1818, paid him...........................	18,200 00	
From February 16 to July 31, 1819, paid him..........................	15,400 00	
From January 1 to November 30, 1820, paid him.......................	15,400 00	
		65,315 95

Isaac Roberdeau, Topographical Engineer, for extra services performed under Samuel Hawkins, agent under the sixth and seventh articles, viz: March 24, 1817, paid him...... 428 00

Joseph Delafield, secretary to the Commissioners executing the seventh article, viz:
1820. Paid him.. 402 78

	194,137 63

RECAPITULATION.

Amount paid under the fifth article..	$99,099 10
Amount paid under the sixth and seventh articles.................................	95,038 53
As above..	194,137 63

JOSEPH NOURSE, *Register.*

Treasury Department, *Register's Office, December 2, 1820.*

The United States in account with P. B. Porter, Commissioner under the 6th and 7th articles of the treaty of Ghent.

Dr.

October 29, 1817.—To the following expenditures on the part of the United States in execution of the commission, viz:

Cash expended in the purchase of camp equipage, including tents, bedding, blankets, table and kitchen furniture.............................	$743 24	
Cash paid for the purchase of boats, sails, and oars.....................	317 56	
Cash expended in purchasing books, maps, and stationery.....	236 50	
Paid the travelling expenses of the Commissioner, assistant secretary, surveyor and men, and transportation of camp equipage, surveyor's instruments, &c..	985 75	
Paid for the subsistence of the American Commissioner, assistant secretary, and surveyor and men, while engaged in surveying the line, from May to November, 1817..	1,493 42¼	
Paid the salaries and wages of the assistant secretary, surveyors, and other persons employed	6,580 92	
		$10,357 39½

Per abstracts and accounts at large, as settled by the Board of Commission, under date of October 29, 1817: ...   ·   ·   ·   · · · · ·

Paid Richard Gatteu's bill, under date of April 30, 1817, for mathematical instruments (instruments not being included in the joint expenses of the Government)...	153 50	
Paid Isaac Greenwood's bill of April 29 for repairing instruments........	10 00	
		163 50

To my salary from January 16, 1816, to January 16, 1818, two years, at $4,444 44 per year.......................................	8,888 88
	19,409 77½
To paid Colonel Hawkins, the United States agent, per his acknowledgment dated August 13, 1817	1,815 95
	21,225 72½

CR.

1818.—By the amount of my drafts on the Secretary of State and charged to me at the Treasury under the following dates, viz:

February 11, 1817...	$5,000 00
May 2	2,000 00
May 31	3,000 00
November 21...	1,000 00
November 21...	1,000 00
November 27...	2,500 00

	$14, 500 00
September 4.—By check on United States Branch Bank in New York, being the amount of advances made by me to Colonel S. Hawkins, per his receipt, &c..............	1,815 95
	16,315 95
Balance...	4,909 77½
	21,225 72½

Abstract of expenses paid and incurred by the Government of the United States in execution of the sixth article of the treaty of Ghent, in salaries and wages of persons employed by the Board of Commission, in the year 1847.

Names of assistants employed.	In what capacity.	Rate of pay.	Commencem't of service.	Termination of service.	Time employed.	Amount.
Donald Fraser	Assistant secretary.............	$2,200 per annum.	Mar. 13, 1817	Mar. 1, 1818	1 year.....................	$2,200 00
David P. Adams	Astronomical surveyor	2,000 ...do.....			1 year.....................	2,000 00
William A. Bird	Assistant surveyor	1,100 ...do.....			1 year.....................	1,100 00
Thomas Clinton........	Steward, &d................	365 ...do.....			1 year.....................	365 00
Elijah Wilder........	Chain-bearer	30 per month	May 1, 1817	Nov. 15, 1817	6½ months	195 00
C. Beleisle...........	Boatman, &c	12 ...do.....	May 12, 1817	June 12, 1817	1 month	12 00
Do..............	.......do.........	16 ...do.....	June 12, 1817	Nov. 9, 1817	4 months 27 days...........	78 50
Alexander Caicy......	.......do.........	12 ...do.....	May 12, 1817	June 12, 1817	1 month	12 00
John Ogden..........	.......do.........	12 ...do.....	May 13, 1817	June 13, 1817	1 month	12 00
Alexander Caicy......	.......do.........	16 ...do.....	June 13, 1817	Aug. 25, 1817	2 months 11 days...........	36 00
Francis Charaderimo..	.......do.........	12 ...do.....	May 13, 1817	June 13, 1817	1 month	12 00
Alexander Law........	Pilot (from La Chien to St. Regis.)	5 per trip....	May 16, 1817	May 20, 1817	5 days.....................	5 00
Guestia Plomedo......	Boatman	16 per month	June 9, 1817	Nov. 9, 1817	5 months	80 00
Joseph Plomedo.......	.......do.........	16 ...do.....	June 9, 1817	Nov. 9, 1817	5 months	80 00
Joseph Austin........	.......do.........	16 ...do.....	July 20, 1817	Aug. 31, 1817	1 month and 11 days (extra and work on Sunday)	22 19
Sylvester Plumley.....	.......do.........	16 ...do.....	July 21, 1817	Aug. 9, 1817	19 days...................	12 00
Charles Davenport....	.......do.........	16 ...do.....	July 20, 1817	Nov. 9, 1817	3 months 20 days...........	58 00
William Thurston.....	.......do.........	16 ...do.....	July 26, 1817	Aug. 9, 1817	15 days...................	9 93
John Polley, jr.......	(Pilot in Long Saut)	1 per day....	July 28, 1817	Aug. 3, 1817	6 days....................	6 00
Edward Bryan........	Boatman	16 per month	Aug. 24, 1817	Nov. 9, 1817	2½ months	40 00
John Barrett (boy).....	.......do.........	12 ...do.....	Aug. 31, 1817	Nov. 9, 1817	2½ months	28 00
Peter Joseph	.......do.........	16 ...do.....	Aug. 31, 1817	Sept. 7, 1817	8 days....................	4 00
Henry Jackson........	Servant.....................	12 ...do.....	April 7, 1817	July 7, 1817	3 months	36 00
Leonard Baker........	Cook	20 ...do.....	May 1, 1817	Nov. 15, 1817	6½ months	130 00
Jacob Miller	Servant.....................	12 ...do.....	July 7, 1817	Nov. 7, 1817	4 months	48 00
						6,580 92

Boundary Commission account under the sixth and seventh articles of the treaty of Ghent, 1817.

April 25, 1817.—To Mr. Adams for his expenses in travelling from Washington to New York, with instruments, as per bill and vouchers No 1...........................	$115 08½
April 27.—A. J. Goodrich's bill, mathematical books, &c., for the surveyor, Mr. Adams, as per bill and receipt No. 2	51 50
May 1.—Prior & Dunning's bill, stationery, &c., for Mr. Adams, No. 3.................	17 00
May 1.—E. M'Laughlin's bill for one marquee and six tents, No 4....................	335 54
May 1.—Cartage of the same to steamboat, as per bill and receipt...................	1 00
May 1.—Peter Burtsell's bill, stationery, as per bill and receipt No. 5...............	159 00
May 2.—John L. Everett's bill, chest with apartments for stationery, &c., as per bill and receipt No. 6	9 00
May 2.—William Deforest's bill, fishing tackle, &c., as per bill and receipt No. 7.........	10 87
May 2.—Needles, thread, &c., for repairing tents	2 50
May 17.—Shot, cord, &c., bought by Major Fraser at Montreal	1 87
May 17.—Travelling expenses and transportation of instruments, baggage, &c., of commissary, secretary, surveyors, and men from New York to St. Regis, as per bill and vouchers No. 8	629 16½
Carried forward............................	1,332 53

Brought forward.............................	$1,332 53

May 17, 1817.—Contingent expenses of Leonard Baker, (servant,) for himself and boatmen, from Montreal to St. Regis .... | 6 75
May 21.—J. & D. P. Ross' bill of sundries, as per bill and receipt No. 9 .... | 653 59
May 24.—Peter Bishop's bill for furniture, &c., 18s. 3d., per bill and receipt No. 10........ | 3 65
June 5.—Mr. Volevenoch, (carpenter,) making stands for astronomical instruments, tables, &c., as per bill and receipt .... | 10 87
June 5.—Cash to Indian Louis for damage to axes.................................... | 1 00
June 5.—Fish, 25 cents; fish, 50 cents; paid for paddle, 50 cents...................... | 1 25
June 5.—Paid for use of a room for Commissioners at St. Regis .... | 1 00
June 5.—Indian express for carrying letters to French Mills for Commissioners at Boston.. | 2 00
June 22.—To J. Gust for four chairs, as per bill and receipt No. 12..................... | 8 00
June 26.—Paid Indian express for carrying letters to French Mills and bringing two chests from thence to St. Regis .... | 4 00
July 7.—Paid four Indian boatmen and boat in assisting to remove from St. Regis to Point Ellicott... | 4 00
July 10.—Paid John Hoople's bill for furniture, transportation for lead, &c., from Montreal, 1l. 18s. 6d., No. 13....... | 7 70
July 10.—Paid a man with a canoe for transporting same from Mille Rouche to camp..... | 1 00
July 15.—Mr. Robertson, for plank for drawing table, measuring rods, and signal poles for surveyor.. | 2 50
July 15.—Jacob Colt for sundries, as per bill and receipt, 53l. 16s. 0¼d., No. 14.......... | 215 21
July 18.—T. Clinton's, sundry provisions, &c., purchased by him for the use of the camp, per bill and vouchers No. 15... | 186 46
July 19.—Eri Lusher for a boat, rigging, &c., per bill and account No. 16 .... | 287 35
July 22.—Belisle (boatman) going to Canada for men, including ferriages for himself and them .... | 2 50
August 3.—William A. Bird's account for moneys expended by him, &c., Mr. Adams while absent from camp, per bill and receipt No. 17................................ | 10 21
September 5.—Sill & Thompson for grindstone crank and transportation, as per bill and receipt No. 18 .... | 8 00
September 5.—Postage for letter addressed to Commissioners :........................ | 25½
October 1.—Barrel of flour, as per bill and receipt No. 19............................ | 8 50
October 2.—T. Clinton, sundry provisions, &c., purchased by him for the use of the camp, per bill and vouchers No. 20, under date of September 22, 1817 .... | 519 85½
October 2.—Mr. Commissioner Porter's expenses from Niagara to and at Albany to meet the British Commissioner, in November, 1816, and returning................... | 140 00
October 2.—To his expenses from Niagara to New York, in April, 1817, to meet the surveyors, &c., and make preparations for the commencement of the survey .... | 90 00
October 2.—Cash paid for a canoe purchased at St. Regis, No. 20 .... | 10 00
October 18.—Moneys expended by Mr. Adams while out surveying, as per bill and receipt No. 21.. | 19 50
October 18.—T. Clinton's account of sundry provisions, &c., purchased by him for the use of the camp, as per bill and vouchers No. 22.................................... | 237 99½
October 18.—To paid the salaries and wages of assistant secretary, surveyors, and other persons employed .... | 6,580 92

	10,357 39½

RECAPITULATION.

In stating the preceding account it was found impossible to arrange the different items under distinct heads of expenditure, owing to there being, in many instances, a great variety of articles in the same vouchers applicable to different branches of expenses.

The following recapitulation, however, which has been made on a careful examination of the vouchers, will show the amount of expenses incurred under the respective heads there mentioned.

The Boundary Commission under the 6th and 7th articles of the treaty of Ghent,
　　　　　　　　　　　　　　　　To the UNITED STATES,　　　　　Dr.

The following expenditures on the part of the United States in execution of said commission, as per accounts and vouchers at large, herewith exhibited, viz:

To cash expended in the purchase of camp equipage, including tents, bedding, blankets, table, and kitchen furniture, &c.. | $743 24
To cash paid for the purchase of boat, sails, oars, &c................................ | 817 56
To cash paid for books and stationery .... | 236 50
To cash paid for travelling expenses of Commissioner, assistant secretary, surveyor, and men for the years 1816 and 1817, and transportation of camp equipage, surveyor's instruments, &c... | 985 75
To cash paid for the subsistence of the Commissioner, assistant secretary, surveyor, and men while engaged surveying the line, from May to November, six months, including contingencies, under the above heads.. | 1,493 42½
To cash paid the salaries and wages of assistant surveyors, &c., and other persons employed, as per account herewith exhibited .... | 6,580 92

	10,357 39½

OCTOBER 29, 1817.

Dr.　*The United States to S. Hawkins, on account of his expenditures as agent, under the 6th and 7th articles of the treaty of Ghent, commencing May, 1817.*

Date.		No. voucher.	To whom paid and for what object.	Amount.
1817.				
May	9	1	Travelling expenses from New York to Montreal, as per account	$54 61
	11	2	John Baird, for transportation of astronomical apparatus of Professor Ellicott, and self and baggage	65 00
	12	3	S. Palmer, tavern expenses on the road	5 00
	14	4	H. Wiswall, steamboat passage	11 00
	14	5	J. P. Smith, travelling expenses	11 40
	22	6	M. Martin, steward, his expenses in Albany	8 75
July	1	7	A. Shoemaker, for a boat, sails, &c.	70 00
	2	8	S. Daniels, for lodging and board at Ogdensburg	8 25
	6	9	Joseph Ellicott, for travelling expenses of my steward	19 00
	7	10	Guy Wood, crackers for table	3 65
	9	11	R. Colquhoun, provisions for table	3 25
	13	12	H. Clark, board of boatmen	2 32
	15	13	R. Colquhoun, provisions	1 42
	22	14	Joseph Lee, his services with batteaux and crew	10 93
	22	15	D. Hutchins, board for marquee floor	4 49
	24	16	G. Hoople, for camp furniture	6 57
	24	17	J. Archibald, for camp furniture	2 28
	27	18	J. L. Everett, for a chest for records and stationery	9 00
	29	19	J. Archibald, for a lamb	4 00
August	4	20	J. Stoneburner, for wagon hire at Long Saut	3 00
	5	21	S. C. Wood, for transportation	2 00
	8	22	M. Martin, steward, his wages	98 90
	13	23	P. B. Porter, for camp equipage and groceries paid by him	638 45
	14	24	S. Wood, for bunting for signals	3 60
	23	25	J. C. Perkins, for butter	10 28
	27	26	Clarke & Diggins, provisions for boatmen	2 00
	28	27	D. Chesley, provisions and calash hire	5 40
Sept.	2	28	R. Colquhoun, ferriage, one bag and one earthen jug	2 89
	2	29	D. McCauley, for groceries	5 00
	3	30	J. Bradford, for veal	1 87½
	4	31	H. Showin, for vegetables	3 87½
	5	32	La Trace, groceries	2 60
	2	33	A. Baker, meat and vegetables	14 60
	10	34	H. Wilson, vegetables and his services	9 50
	10	35	J. Eaton, barrel of bread	7 16
	12	36	P. Cleveland, for half barrel pork	12 75
	12	37	A. Barrett, for boating	1 75
	12	38	Peter Wilson, for boating	1 75
	13	39	B. Franklin, his wages	9 85
	22	40	W. L. Gray, his expenses bringing boat from Montreal	22 41
	22	41	J. and D. P. Ross, groceries and repairs to boat	41 60
	22	42	John Hanes, tent poles, &c.	7 00
	30	43	William Loucks, board and lodging at his house	14 90
Oct.	1	44	Nichols & Sanford, for six hams	9 98
	4	45	R. Atwater, Son & Co., groceries, provisions, camp furniture	323 90
	5	46	J. Baker, his services and entertainment	2 70
	8	47	Thomas Clinton, wages as steward	81 51
	8	48	Thomas Brannan, his expenses travelling, with baggage	4 15
	8	49	L. Stowell, provisions	4 65
	8	50	S. Town, for stage fare	3 00
	11	51	P. Stonell, for washing	2 50
	12	52	L. Wilson, tavern expenses at Prescott	15 35
	20	53	G. Wood, sundry articles, as per bill	122 58
	22	54	Zerah Poor, his expenses as messenger to Ogdensburg	6 12½
	23	55	Thomas Clinton, to pay extra for bread	21 37
	24	56	W. L. Gray, his wages as boatman	38 40
	27	57	W. Price, his wages as boatman	63 76
	27	58	T. Brannan, his account petty expenses (steward)	23 23
	28	59	S. B. Anderson, board and lodging at St. Regis	113 30
	29	60	C. Clark, entertainment for self and boatman	3 77
	30	61	Lem. Warren, sundries, as per bill	2 17
Nov.	4	62	Zerah Poor, his wages as boatman	66 00
	5	63	S. B. Anderson, board and lodging at St. Regis	81 00
	15	64	Joseph Delafield, his travelling expenses to New York from line	98 61
	19	65	John Boyd, hire of wagon and horses ten days, returning to New York	40 00
	21	66	N. Kinniston, expenses at his house	31 70
	22	67	J. Putnam, transportation and provisions	9 00
	20	68	Theodore Bailey, postage on public account	13 87½
	24	69	E. Bailey, transportation and horse feed	6 62
	25	70	Joseph Delafield, his expenses going to St. Regis, and for stationery	9 35
		71	Amount petty expenses for supplying table, &c., during summer	115 43
	25	72	John Decatur, for a large marquee	125 00
	25	73	Amount travelling expenses from St. Regis to New York	94 52
Dec.	23	74	T. Brannan, his wages as steward, and for sundry expenses charged by him, as per his bill	104 28
			Agent's salary for the year ending April 11, 1818	4,444 44
			Salary for secretary to agency for same time	1,000 00
				8,335 58

The United States to S. Hawkins, agent under the 6th and 7th articles of the treaty of Ghent, for the following expenditures, during the year 1818, as per vouchers accompanying.

Date.	No. voucher.	To whom paid and for what object.	Amount.
1818.			
May 5	1	F. Bulius, for provisions, as per voucher..	$30 42
6	2	E. W. Wilkins, for hams..	20 12
6	3	P. Burtsell, for stationery...	32 00
18	4	Captain Bartholomew, steamboat passages..	28 50
19	5	N. Skinner, for entertainment...	8 50
21	6	R. Aimes, for stage fare...	50 00
21	7	J. Sherwood, steamboat fare...	27 00
21	8	N. Hotchkiss, stage fare..	8 00
22	9	Dyde & Martinans, Montreal...	14 50
22	10	P. S. Jossy, calash hire..	20 00
25	11	S. Smallman, wagon hire..	11 00
June 8	12	P. B. Anderson, entertainment...	32 30
8	13	S. Chesly...	10 20
15	14	J. Shivers, for provisions..	7 09
19	15	C. Lusher, transportation...	15 65
23	16	J. Fulton, storage...	4 00
24	17	J. F. Strong, wages...	16 00
28	18	S. W. Tucker, provisions..	15 00
30	19	C. Dillabogh, board, &c...	17 80
July 1	20	E. Adams, transportation...	8 00
4	21	J. Eaton, for bread..	7 75
8	22	L. Gray, wages...	24 00
14	23	H. L. Hazen, repairs to boat..	6 80
August 4	24	S. B. Anderson, entertainment...	11 00
4	25	N. Cleaves, provisions...	2 40
6	26	D. Truesdail...	5 57
6	27	N. Taylor & Co., provisions...	36 53
7	28	J. Colts, for stores, &c..	144 70
13	29	J. Kincaid, wagon hire...	8 00
21	30	L. Poor, for provisions...	13 82
30	31	J. Woodbury, board, &c...	35 50
Sept. 21	32	J. Delafield, travelling expenses..	50 00
Oct. 8	33	J. Landon, board and lodging..	75 00
13	34	J. Woodbury, provisions..	25 88
21	35	T. Colham, boat hire...	3 00
22	36	G. Brownson, entertainment...	11 14
24	37	L. Wilson, transportation...	7 75
Nov. 3	38	N. Hayes, entertainment..	4 07
Dec. 24	39	J. Brennan, steward, his board...	24 00
Oct. 19	40	C. Kelsey, provisions..	5 00
Nov. 25	41	J. Baird, for steward's board, omitted in 1817...	32 25
July 12	42	Joseph Delafield, his amount of disbursements for provisions and other uses of camp, in May, June, and July, including travelling expenses of party to the line...	108 49
August 13	43	A. Pawling, for freight, camp equipage, &c..	4 00
15	44	W. F. Pease, storage and cooperage...	2 25
26	45	D. White, sundries...	13 25
26	46	J. Mosier..	5 50
July 17	47	J. Kincaid, wagon hire...	3 50
Sept. 6	48	William Forsyth, sundries, board, &c..	29 50
July 15	49	J. Brennan, his account of provisions furnished...	38 85
August 25		*Michael Daws, wages as boatman..	24 00
25		*Walter Atkins...	23 50
25		*Z. Paer, as cook and boatman..	40 50
Oct. —	50	Thomas Brannan, his wages, and disbursements by him at sundry times as steward.................	263 44
—	51	S. Hawkins, his account of travelling expenses...	105 50
—	52	Joseph Delafield, his salary for the year ending April 10, 1819................................	1,000 00
			2,578 52
		Agent's salary, for the year ending April 10, 1819...	4,444 44
			7,022 96

* I certify that these three vouchers, for boatmen's wages, were taken by me at the time of payment, and that the sums set opposite their names were paid to the said boatmen; that these, with others, (belonging to the agents' accounts,) it is believed, were left on the line in a chest of papers, &c., of the agents, the amount of which cannot be ascertained.

JOSEPH DELAFIELD.

NEW YORK, *November* 12, 1819.

Account of expenditures made by S. Hawkins, United States agent, under the 6th and 7th articles of the treaty of Ghent, commencing May 21, and ending November 1, 1819.

Date.	No. voucher.	To whom paid and for what object.	Amount.
1819.			
May 21	1	P. B. Bentsell, for stationery..	$44 41
August 27	2	M. Noe, for postage..	5 39½
Sept. 23	3	Thomas Brannan, his salary...	200 00
Oct. 11	4	J. Delafield, his salary for half year..	500 00
Nov. 1	5	Joseph Delafield, his amount of travelling expenes and other expenditures on the lines this season...........	218 40
			968 20½
Oct. 11	....	S. Hawkins, for salary due for the half year ending October 11, 1819...............................	2,222 22
			3,190 42½

Peter B. Porter's general account of expenses under the 6th and 7th articles of the treaty of Ghent, beginning on November 1, 1817, and ending on March 13, 1819.

November 5, 1818.—To cash paid for the subsistence, transportation, travelling, and other contingent expenses of the American party employed in running the boundary line, under the 6th and 7th articles of the treaty of Ghent, from November 1, 1817, to November 5, 1818, as per account herewith... $3,019 58

To cash paid for salaries and wages of assistant secretary, surveyors, and men, from March 13, 1818, to March 13, 1819, as per account herewith 8,331 00½

                        11,350 58½

FEBRUARY 20, 1819.

                                  PETER B. PORTER.

An account of the expenses of the American Commissioner and his party, engaged in running the boundary line under the sixth and seventh articles of the treaty of Ghent, from November 1, 1817, to November 5, 1818.

November 1, 1817.—To cash paid for expenses of assistant secretary and self, from Hamilton to St. Regis, and back, to hold a meeting of the board; absent four days; voucher No. 1... $64 00
November 4.—To cash paid Thomas Clinton for sundry provisions; voucher No. 2........ 92 42
November 8.—To cash paid Elijah Wilder, chain-bearer, for his expenses to Albany; voucher No. 3,.. 30 00
November 14.—To cash paid for stage fare and expenses of assistant secretary and L. Baker, cook, from Sackett's Harbor to Albany; voucher No. 4..................... 47 50
November 14.—To cash paid D. P. Adams, for travelling expenses of himself, Mr. Bird, and Mr. Rich, from Hamilton to Albany; voucher No. 5.............................. 112 68
May 1, 1818.—To cash paid for stores, provisions, &c., including the whole travelling expenses of assistant secretary, self, and six men, from Hamilton to Sackett's Harbor, and of myself with four men to Black Rock; voucher No. 6........................ 157 86½
May 1.—To cash paid Prior & Dunning for stationery; voucher No. 7................... 21 56
May 2.—To cash paid Peter Burtsell for stationery; voucher No. 8..................... 59 00
May 4.—To cash paid D. P. Adams for having barometer and thermometer repaired, retouching compass magnets, &c.; voucher No. 9.............................. 28 00
May 4.—To cash paid William A. Bird for travelling expenses from Albany to Hamilton; voucher No. 10.. 33 32
May 4.—To cash paid D. P. Adams for travelling expenses of himself, Messrs. Darby, Delafield and Gedney, and L. Baker, cook, from Albany to Hamilton, and of A. Dickey, from Utica to Hamilton; voucher No. 11.. 194 17
May 6.—To cash paid D. P. Adams for his expenses while engaged in completing his map, including drawing paper, &c., from November 13, 1817, to May 6, 1818; voucher No. 12, 234 25
May 9.—To cash paid for expenses of assistant secretary at Montreal while collecting stores, shipping, and axemen; voucher No. 13....................................... 13 94
May 10.—To cash advanced to assistant secretary for passage of batteau through locks, up tow-paths, and other necessary expenses from Montreal to Hamilton; voucher No. 14, 19 85
May 11.—To cash paid Grant & Duff for repairing batteau, new oars, cable, poles, storage, &c., at La Chien; voucher No. 15.. 20 21
May 15.—To cash paid Thomas Clinton for expenses of camp, from December 23, 1817, to June 24, 1818; voucher No. 16.. 253 06
May 15.—To cash paid Guernsey & Clark for pork, beef, cheese, &c.; voucher No. 17..... 463 00
June 5.—To cash paid Noah Dickinson, at Cornwall, for pork; voucher No. 18........... 6 80

                     Carried forward............................. 1,851 62½

Brought forward............................ $1,851 62½
June 5, 1818.—To cash paid P. Taylor & Co., St. Regis, for bread, &c.; voucher No. 19....   6 12½
June 5.—To cash paid Guy C. Wood for transportation of stores, &c.; voucher No. 20....   4 00
June 8.—To cash paid for wagon hire to and from St. Regis, when the Board met on fifth
 instant; voucher No. 21..   10 62½
June 8.—To cash paid for expenses of boatmen while going to and at St. Regis; voucher
 No. 22...   5 10
June 22.—To cash paid P. Taylor & Co. for provisions, board, &c.; voucher No. 23........   34 29
June 24.—To cash paid P. Taylor & Co. for provisions, board, &c.; voucher No. 24.......   4 35
July 6.—To cash paid R. Gregory for a skiff; voucher No. 25..........................   10 00
July 8.—To cash paid Captain Lusher for transportation of stores from Genesee river to
 camp; voucher No. 26..   1 62½
July 8.—To cash paid L. &. S. Dennison for paint, &c.; voucher No. 27................   10 68½
July 10.—To cash paid for expenses of assistant secretary going to Ogdensburg to receive
 stores and direct the forwarding in future; voucher No. 28......................   5 50
July 19.—To cash paid C. Hutchinson for injury done his grass, encamping thereon; voucher
 No. 29..   2 50
July 27.—To cash paid Thomas Clinton for expenses of camp; voucher No. 30...........   158 68½
August 3.—To cash paid James Starkweather for medicine; voucher No. 31..........   6 71
August 4.—To cash paid L. & S. Dennison for cordage, lead, &c.; voucher No. 32........   10 08
September 10.—To cash paid Thomas Clinton for expenses of camp; voucher No. 33......   229 42
September 19.—To cash paid Alexander Jaffroi for three gallons of tar; voucher No. 34...   3 00
September 21.—To cash paid Jabez Colt for stores, at Montreal; voucher No. 35..........   367 15
October 2.—To cash paid J. & D. P. Ross, being a balance on former account; voucher No. 36,   22 17
November 5.—To cash paid Thomas Clinton for expenses of camp; voucher No. 37......   276 28½

    3,019 58½

*Account of salaries and wages of assistant secretary, surveyors and men, employed in running the boundary
line under the 6th and 7th articles of the treaty of Ghent, from March 1, 1818, to March 1, 1819.*

August 1, 1819.—To salary of Major Donald Frazer, assistant secretary to the Board, from
 March 1, 1818, to March 1, 1819, as per voucher No. 1........................... $2,200 00
August 1.—To salary of David P. Adams, astronomical surveyor to the Board, from March
 1, 1818, to March 1, 1819; voucher No. 2...................................   2,000 00
August 1.—To salary of William C. Bird, trigonometrical surveyor to the Board, from March
 1, 1818, to March 1, 1819; voucher No. 3..................................   1,200 00
August 1.—To salary of William Darby, trigonometrical surveyor to the Board, from May
 1, 1818, to July 31, 1818; voucher No. 4..................................   300 00
August 1.—To salary of Richard Delafield, draughtsman to the Board, from May 1, 1818, to
 November 15, 1818; voucher No. 5....................................   600 00
August 31.—To cash paid C. Swarz, draughtsman, for draughting map of St. Lawrence;
 voucher No. 6...   210 00
August 31.—To salary of Thomas Clinton, steward to the party; voucher No. 7.........   365 00
August 31.—To wages of Thomas Gedney, chain-bearer, at $30 per month, from May 1 to
 November 15; voucher No. 8.......................................   195 00
August 31.—To wages of Antonio Camara, chain-bearer, at $30 per month, from May 15 to
 June 12, 1818; voucher No. 9.....................................   30 00
August 31.—To wages of Charles Davenport, prime hand, at $22 per month, from May 20
 to November 15, 1818; voucher No. 10..............................   128 66
August 31.—To wages of Leonard Baker, cook, at $20 per month, from May 1 to November
 15, 1818; voucher No. 11...   130 00
August 31.—To wages of Adam W. H. Dickey, boatman and axeman, at $16 per month, from
 May 13 to November 15, 1818; voucher No. 12.......................   104 00
August 31.—To wages of Guesta Plomedou, boatman and axeman, at $16 per month, from
 May 5 to November 15, 1818; voucher No. 13.......................   101 33⅓
August 31.—To wages of Joseph Plomedou, boatman and axeman, at $16 per month, from
 May 5 to November 15, 1818; voucher No. 14.......................   101 33⅓
August 31.—To wages of Simon Plomedou, boatman and axeman, at $16 per month, from
 May 5 to November 15, 1818; voucher No. 15.......................   101 33⅓
August 31.—To wages of Joseph La Bonta, boatman and axeman, at $16 per month, from
 May 5 to November 15, 1818; voucher No. 16.......................   101 33⅓
August 31.—To wages of Michael La Riverre, boatman and axeman, at $16 per month, from
 May 5 to November 15, 1818; voucher No. 17.......................   101 33⅓
August 31—To wages of Basil Lombare, boatman and axeman, at $16 per month, from May 5
 to November 15, 1818; voucher No. 18.............................   101 33⅓
August 31.—To wages of John B. Le Tondre, boatman and axeman, at $16 per month, from
 May 5 to November 15, 1818; voucher No. 19.......................   101 33⅓
August 31 —To wages of Augustus Berion, boatman and axeman, at $16 per month, from
 May 5 to August 31, 1818; voucher No. 20.........................   61 41
August 31.—To wages of Edward Bryan, boatman and axeman, at $16 per month, from May
 12 to November 15, 1818; voucher No. 21..........................   97 60

    8,331 00⅓

[Inclosure in P. B. Porter's letter to Secretary of State, of December 2, 1820.]

The Boundary Commission, for moneys expended in execution of the sixth article of the treaty of Ghent, to Peter B. Porter. DR.

Date.		No. voucher.	To whom paid and for what object.	Amount.
1817.				
Nov.	1	1	To case paid for expenses of assistant secretary and self, from Hamilton to St. Regis, and back, to hold a meeting of the Board, (absent 9 days)	$64 00
	4	2	To cash paid Thomas Clinton, for sundry provisions, &c	92 42
	8	3	To cash paid Elijah Wilder, chain-bearer, for his expenses to Albany	30 00
	14	4	To cash paid for stage fare and expenses of assistant secretary, and L. Baker, cook, from Sackett's Harbor to Albany	47 50
	14	5	To cash paid D. P. Adams, for travelling expenses of himself, Mr. Bird, and Mr. Rich, from Hamilton to Albany.	112 68
	27	6	To cash paid for stores, provisions, &c., including the whole travelling expenses of assistant secretary, self, and *six* men, from Hamilton to Sackett's Harbor, and of myself with *four* men to Black Rock	157 86½
1818.				
May.	1	7	To cash paid Prior and Dunning, for stationery	21 56
	2	8	To cash paid Peter Burtsell, for stationery	59 00
	4	9	To cash paid D. P. Adams, for having barometer and thermometer repaired, retouching compasses, &c	28 00
	4	10	To cash paid William A. Bird, for travelling expenses from Albany to Hamilton	33 32
	4	11	To cash paid D. P. Adams, for travelling expenses of himself, Messrs. Darby, Delafield, and Gedney, and L. Baker, cook, from Albany to Hamilton, and of A. Dickey, from Utica to Hamilton	194 17
	6	12	To cash paid D. P. Adams, for his expenses while engaged in completing his map, including drawing paper, &c., from November 13, 1817, to May 6, 1818	234 25
	9	13	To cash paid for expenses of assistant secretary at Montreal, while collecting stores, shipping men, &c	13 94
	10	14	To cash paid assistant secretary for passage of batteau through locks, up tow paths, and other necessary expenses from Montreal to Hamilton	19 50
	11	15	To cash paid Grant and Duff, for repairs of batteau, new oars, poles, cables, &c	20 21
	15	16	To cash paid Thomas Clinton, for expenses of the camp, from December 23, 1817, to June 24, 1818	253 06½
	15	17	To cash paid Guernsey & Clark, for pork, beef, &c	422 05
June	5	18	To cash paid Noah Dickinson, for pork	6 80
	5	19	To cash paid P. Taylor & Co., for bread, &c	6 12½
	5	20	To cash paid Guy C. Wood, for transporting stores	4 00
	8	21	To cash paid for wagon hire to and from St. Regis, when Board met on the 5th instant	10 62½
	8	22	To cash paid for expenses of a waiter while going to and at St. Regis	5 10
	22	23	To cash paid P. Taylor, for provisions, boards, &c	34 29
	24	24	......do..............do..............do	4 35
July	6	25	To cash paid R. Gregory, for a skiff	10 00
	8	26	To cash paid Captain Lusher, for transportation of stores from Genesee river to camp	1 62½
	8	27	To cash paid L. and S. Dennison, for paint, &c	10 68½
	10	28	To cash paid expenses of assistant secretary going to Ogdensburg to receive stores, and direct the forwarding in future	5 50
	19	29	To cash paid C. Hutchinson, for injury done his grass, encamping thereon	2 50
	27	30	To cash paid Thomas Clinton, for expenses of camp	158 68½
August	3	31	To cash paid James Starkwether, for medicines	6 71
	4	32	To cash paid L. and S. Dennison, for cordage, lead, &c	10 08
Sept.	10	33	To cash paid Thomas Clinton, for expenses of camp	229 42
	19	34	To cash paid Alexander Jaffroi, for three gallons of tar	3 00
	21	35	To cash paid Jabez Colt, for stores at Montreal	367 15
Oct.	2	36	To cash paid J. and D. P. Ross, being a balance on former account	22 17
Nov.	5	37	To cash paid Thomas Clinton, for expenses of camp	276 28½
	5	38	To cash paid O. M. Hedden's bill, for transportation	38 00
	6	39	To cash paid for a theodolite, bought of Wm. Darby, per account and receipt	120 00
	5	40	To cash paid R. Delafield, for expenses and transportation from camp to Albany	20 00
	6	41	To cash paid T. R. Gedney..................do..................do	20 00
	6	42	To cash paid L. Baker ....do..................do	20 00
	13	43	Cash paid Capt. W. Merrit's bill, for passages and transportation of men and baggage of Mr. Bird's party from Sackett's Harbor to Niagara	40 00
	14	44	To cash paid I. & D. P. Ross, bill of sundries from Montreal	35 10
	25	45	To cash paid A. Dickey, for expenses and transportation fromNiagara to Albany	18 00
	26	46	To cash paid C. Clikeman's bill, for wood for office	5 50
	26	47	To cash paid for sawing wood	50
	26	....	To cash paid Spencer, Stafford & Co's. bill, for axe, candlesticks, &c	2 93½
1819.				
Jan.	15	48	To cash paid Mr. Bird's bill of stationery purchased by him	2 00
	22	49	Garrett Houghtailing's bill, for wood for office	2 75
	28	50	D. Hagler..........do............do	2 75
	29	51	Robinson & Vanderbilt, for drawing boards, &c	5 67½
Feb.	8	52	D. Steele's bill of stationery	1 37
	9	53	M. Smith's ....do	2 25
	25	54	D. Longworth's...do	44
	25	55	T. Dobson's bill, for drawing paper and other stationery	50 77
March	1	56	Wm. A. Bird's bill of expenses fromAlbany to Philadelphia, and back, to hire a draughtsman, procure drawing paper, &c	58 00
				3,424 67
			SALARIES AND WAGES.	
March	1	59	Major D. Frazer's salary as assistant secretary for one year from March 1, 1818, to this time.	2,200 00
	1	60	D. P. Adams, astronomical surveyor, for same time	2,000 00

ACCOUNT—Continued.

Date.	No. voucher.	To whom paid and for what object.	Amount.
1819.			
March 1	61	W. A. Bird, trigonometrical surveyor, for same time	$1,200 00
1	62	William Darby, trigonometrical surveyor, three months, from May to August...................	300 00
1	63	R. Delafield, draughtsman, from May 1 to November 15	600 00
1	64	C. Swarz, for draughting, in the spring of 1818	210 00
	65	Thomas Clinton, as steward, one year's salary..	365 00
	66	Thomas Gedney, as chain-bearer, from May 1 to November 15, at $30 per month	195 00
	67	A. Camara, as chain-bearer, from May 15 to June 15, at $30 per month........................	30 00
	68	C. Davenport, prime hand, May 20 to November 10, at $22 per month..........................	128 66
	69	L. Baker, cook, from May 1 to November 10, at $20 per month	130 00
	70	A. Dickey, boatman and axeman, May 1 to November 10, at $16 per month......................	104 00
	71	G. Plomedou, boatman and axeman, May 5 to November 15, at $16 per month....................	101 33½
	72	J. Plomedou.........do.................do.................do.....	101 33½
	73	S. Plomedou.........do.................do.................do.....	101 33½
	74	J. La Bonta ....do.................do.................do.....	101 33½
	75	M. La Riverre ....do.................do.................do.....	101 33½
	76	Basil Lombare ......do.................do.................do.....	101 33½
	77	J. B. Le Tondre .....do.................do.................do.....	101 33½
	78	A. Berion, boatman and axeman, August 31 to November 15, at $16 per month	61 41
	79	E. Brian, boatman and axeman, May 12 to November 15, at $16 per month......................	97 60
	80	L. Baker, for attending the office from November 11, 1818, to May 1, 1819, viz: five months and 20 days, at $10 per month.........	56 56
			8,387 66½
		CONTINGENCIES.	
April 29	81	J. Hank's bill, for repairing theodolite	2 50
10	82	Benj. Pike's bill, for a telescope bought of him..	30 00
24	83	Robinson and Vanderbilt, for draught boards, &c..	2 19
15	84	D. P. Adams' bill, travelling expenses, stationery, &c.	73 54
16	85	Minerva Library's bill, for quills...	2 00
17	86	Peter Burtsell's bill, for stationery...	101 25
20	87	W. Deforest's bill, for lines..	4 12½
22	88	Anthony & Arcularius' bill, for groceries	191 32
29	89	J. & A. F. Baird's bill, for boarding Mr. Adams from November to April.......................	155 50
30	90	J. & A. F. Baird's bill, for wood and sundries for office.....................................	36 67
30	91	C. A. Leseur, draughtsman, for his board and travelling expenses............................	92 50
30	92	J. Loomis's bill, for office rent, &c..	106 00
May 1	93	W. A. Bird, trigonometrical surveyor, bill for boarding......................................	65 00
1	94	L. Baker's (man attending office) bill, for boarding..	60 00
1	95	W. A. Bird's bill, for travelling expenses from Sackett's Harbor to Niagara, and thence to Albany, in November, 1818...........	35 00
4	96	James Ferguson, assistant surveyor, bill of boarding.......................................	60 00
4	97	To cash paid Mr. Bagg's bill, boarding a man with baggage	3 75
6	98	To cash paid bill of travelling expenses of Messrs. Bird, Ferguson, and party, from Albany to Sackett's Harbor	71 00
12	99	To cash paid sundry bills for board and other expenses of same party at Sackett's Harbor.....	81 93
	100	To cash paid L. & S. Dennison's bill, for freight and transportation of sundry articles from New York and Albany to Sackett's Harbor......	46 28
20	101	Seven small bills for sundries at Sackett's Harbor..	28 72
22	102	Small bills for sundries at Kingston..	7 36½
June 2	103	J. Charles, for transportation...	2 00
7		J. Shepherd, for board of Captain Douglass..	1 33½
17	104	J. Shepherd's bill, for transportation, &c..	3 00
24	105	Porter & Barton's bill, for transporting provisions, boats, &c...............................	54 97
		For a tin horn..	25
24	106	J. Delafield's bill, advertising for a theodolite	4 50
July 1	107	S. Hooker's bill, for repairing boats..	8 75
21	108	O. Newberry's bill, for shot, hooks, &c..	1 81
22	109	S. H. Salisbury's bill, for stationery...	8 70
23	110	S. Bosworth's bill, for repairing theodolite	50
23	111	J. Guiteau's bill, for paint for boats..	1 38
24	112	J. A. Coe's bill, for 12 tin caps or globes for station poles.................................	18 19
24	113	J. A. Coe's bill, for copper for row locks..	1 19
27	114	S. Tucker's bill, for making sails for new boat	6 00
	115	R. King's bill, for paints and painting ditto...	14 93
28	116	R. Ree's bill, for an axe and spear...	1 00
28	117	A. Stannard's bill, for the new boat "Lady of the Lake "....................................	156 99½
	118	H. & W. Delafield's bill, for a theodolite imported from England............................	212 96
	119	Guernsey & Clark's bill, for provisions for Commissioner....................................	495 00
29	120	For cheese, by Major Fraser..	1 05
August 6	121	W. A. Bird's bill of expenses, &c., with party from Black Rock to Cunningham's Island in a boat,............	5 94
8	122	Steamboat bill, for freight...	3 00
8	123	Austin, a hand, for clothes lost..	8 03
11	124	J. Guiteau's bill, for medicine...	68½
12	125	Steamboat bill, for freight...	1 50
14	126	...........do...	14 00
14	127	J. Sill's bill, for biscuit...	10 00
25	128	N. Brown, for transportation of theodolite from New York...................................	2 87
28	129	Steward of steamboat, for articles for the sick	2 75

ACCOUNT—Continued.

Date.	No. voucher.	To whom paid and for what object.	Amount.
1819.			
August 29	130	J. Adams, for twine	$0 50
Sept. 4	131	C. Johnson's bill, for fresh meat, &c..	17 25
4	·132	S. Johnson's bill, for meat, vegetables, &c..	10 86
10	133	D. Hill's bill, for butter and vegetables, milk, &c...	14 61
18	134	W. Delbitt's bill, for sundries for the camp...	11 93
18	135	Major Fraser, for provisions, &c., purchased...	1 00
20	136	Secretary Fraser's expenses to Detroit to get hands, &c..	10 00
29	137	D..Pastorus' bill, for powder, shot, &c...	4 00
Oct. 18	138	W. De Witt's bill, for provisions and articles for sick, &c...	65 60½
Nov. 1	139	Sill, Thompson & Co.'s bill, for transportation of the party from Detroit to Black Rock, schooner American Eagle, freight, &c..	169 04
3	140	W. De Witt's bill of boarding, while employed as copying clerk in the office, and expenses from Black Rock to Albany, while employed as a chain-bearer..	76 00
5	141	Steamboat for passages of three sick men from Detroit to Black Rock, and freight	25 00
5	142	R. Smyth's bill at Detroit...	11 00
5	143	D. B. Douglass, assistant surveyor, bill of travelling expenses..	94 00
5	144	Thomas Clinton, steward, bill of sundries...	683 66½
			3,517 29½
1820.		SALARIES AND WAGES.	
March 1	145	Donald Fraser, his salary as secretary for one year, from March 1, 1819, to this time.....................	2,200 00
1	146	D. P. Adams, assistant surveyor, his salary from March 1 to April 15, 1819, one and a half months, at $2,000 per annum	250,00
1	147	D. B. Douglass, assistant surveyor, his salary for six months, from April 15 to October 15, 1819, at $2,000 per annum	1,000 00
1	148	W. A. Bird, as trigonometrical surveyor, from March 1 to October 15, 1819, seven and a half months, at $1,200 per annum..................................... $750 00 W. A. Bird, as assistant surveyor, from October 16 to March 1, four and a half months, at $2,000 per annum 750 00	1,500 00
1	149	James Ferguson, assistant surveyor, from February 10 to November, 1819, eight and two-thirds months, at $1,000 per annum .... $722 23 James Ferguson, as trigonometrical surveyor, from November 1, 1819, to March 1, 1820, four months, at $1,200 per annum 400,00	1,122 23
1	150	C. A. Leseur, as draughtsman, fifty-eight days, at $3 per day, in March and April, 1819...................	174 00
1	151	Lewis G. De Russey, as draughtsman, from May 15, 1819, to this time, at $1,000 per annum...............	791 67
1	152	Thomas Clinton, steward, for one year...	365 00
1	153	W. H. De Witt, as copying clerk and chain-bearer, from January 4 to November 3, at $30 per month.........	300 00
1	154	Leonard Baker, cook, from May 1 to October 15, at $20 per month	130 00
1	155	David Gay, boatman and axeman, for three months and one day's services, from June 19 to September 20, at $14 per month...	42 47
1	156	L. Hurlbut, boatman and axeman, from May 11 to September 15, at $14 per month........................	70 20
1	157	J. Howk, boatman and axeman, from June 24 to October 11, at $14 per month............................	49 00
1	158	M. Banks, boatman and axeman, from May 10 to October 11, at $14 per month, and expenses home	75 00
1	159	J. Van Nonnan, axeman, from June 19 to October 11, at $14 per month	52 26
1	160	T. Case, boatman and axeman, from June 22 to October 11, at $14 per month	51 33
1	161	Thomas Horton, axeman, from June 25 to September 20, at $14 per month................................	39 96
1	162	Daniel·Austin, boatman and axeman, from May 10 to October 11, and expenses home......................	79 00
1	163	Henry Johnson, axeman, three and a half months...	49 00
1	164	A. Davis, boatman and axeman, from May 12 to October 12, and expenses.................................	75 00
1	165	G. W. Fisher, boatman and axeman, four days in May...	2 12½
1	166	A. Perry, boatman and axeman, May 10 to June 2..	10 72
1	167	S. P. Hill, boatman and axeman, June 2 to June 17..	7 46½
1	168	H. Hyde, boatman and axeman, two days...	1 00
1	169	E. Barrett, boatman and axeman, August 21 to September 4	7 00
1	170	S. Johnson, boatman and axeman, two days...	1 00
1	171	Vermilye, Hever, McPherson, and Devinne, four United States soldiers, for one month's work each, per receipts.	24 00
			8,469 13
		CONTINGENCIES.	
14	172	Peter Burtsell's bill of stationery	41 00
	173	Mulder and Montgomery's bill of groceries...	37 70
April 20	174	S. Clark's bill, 4 barrels 1 hog pork, at $14..	56 00
20	175	A. S. Clark's bill, 4 barrels mess pork, at $17...	68 00
22	176	J. Archer's bill for transportation of groceries, &c., from Albany to Black Rock...........................	11 58
May 1	177	D. Sackett's bill for a sextant bought of him...	80 00
1	178	J. Sill's bill for hard bread..	25 34
	179	P. D. Shouck's bill for attending surveyor's office during winter	15 00
5	180	Captain D. B. Douglass' bill for a chronometer..	210 00
8	181	J. Fairbank's bill in July, 1819..	7 50
11	182	J. Chamberlin's bill for fresh beef, &c...	20 95
	183	Sill, Thompson & Co.'s bill for transportation of the party, (15 persons,) with two boats, provisions, and baggage, from Black Rock to Detroit river, in schooner Michigan...................................	130 00
29	184	J. Scott's bill for coffee and tea	11 56

ACCOUNT—Continued.

Date.	No. voucher.	To whom paid and for what object.	Amount.
1820.			
May 29	185	A. Bryant's bill for tumblers...	$3 69¼
30	186	L. Brace's bill for butter and beans...	10 84
	187	H. Daw's bill for blacksmith work on boats, &c..	16 23
	188	James Mason's bill for carpenter's work..	24 87
	189	D. McGill's bill for painting boats..	5 00
July 3	190	Steamboat, for passage of Surveyor Best and freight..	15 00
17	191	D. G. Jones' bill for sundries..	4 93
18	192	Stannard and Bidwell's bill for building new boat, &c...	79 13
9	193	C. T. Payne's bill for mending telescope...	1 25
	194	T. J. Wendall's bill for sundries...	2 25
15	195	E. Brook's bill for hard bread...	1 50
27	196	J. Sill's bill for boarding Bird and Ferguson last spring.....................................	12 50
Sept. 12	197	J. Sill's bill for hard bread..	64 08
Oct. 16	198	B. Delavan, for medicine..	5 00
	198	E. Brooks, for hire of a large boat to move camp...	10 00
Nov. 8	199	W. A. Baird's account, with vouchers, for sundry articles of stationery purchased, and expenses while out surveying...	43 25
10	200	Secretary Fraser's five bills of expenses at sundry times.....................................	9 68¼
	201	Thomas Clinton's (steward) account, with 23 vouchers, for purchase of provisions, camp equipage, &c., for the use of the commission...	771 96
	202	Sill, Thompson & Co.'s bill for the charter of the schooner Red Jacket, while engaged in surveying the islands in Lake Huron and St. Mary's straits, from July 1 to October 20, 3⅔ months, at $300 per month..............	1,100 00
	203	Thomas Clinton's bill for the rent of an office and store-room for the past year................	60 00
			2,955 76
		SALARIES AND WAGES.	
		D. Fraser, secretary, one year's salary...	2,200 00
		W. A. Bird, assistant surveyor, one year's salary..	2,000 00
		J. Ferguson, trigonometrical surveyor, one year's salary.......................................	1,200 00
		L. G. De Russy, draughtsman, one year's salary...	1,000 00
	208	W. Best, assistant surveyor, from May 1 to October 22, at $3 per day..........................	525 00
	209	T. Clinton, steward, one year, to March 1, 1821...	365 00
	210	F. Cooper, cook, wages five months, at $15 per month	75 00
	211	J. Lille, boatman and axeman, five months and twenty-one days, at $13 per month...............	73 66
	212	J. Hale ....do....................do....................do....................................	73 66
	213	N. Wakefield..do....................do....................do....................................	73 66
	214	A. Russell......do....................do....................do....................................	73 66
	215	J. Fanshaw, boatman and axeman, five months and seventeen days, at $13 per month...............	72 12
	216	John Grant, boatman and axeman, four months, at $13 per month..............................	52 00
	217	Nich. Swan, boatman and axeman, four months, at $13 per month..............................	52 00
	218	A Davis, boatman and axeman, three months, at $13 per month	39 00
	219	M. Banks, boatman and axeman, two months and four days, at $13 per month....................	27 67½
	220	W. L. Bellinger, boatman and axeman, two months and nineteen days, at $15 per month	33 96
	221	C. Hilee, seaman, axeman and boatman, 3⅔ months, at $16 per month...........................	58 67
	222	E. Welsh, seaman, axeman and boatman, five months and twenty-one days, at $15 per month........	85 00
	223	C. Stannard, seaman, axeman and boatman, three months and twenty days, at $13................	47 67
	224	W. Miller, seaman, axeman and boatman, three months and twenty days, at $12................	44 00
			8,171 73¼
		Total expense from November, 1817, to March, 1821...	34,996 25

REMARKS.

These accounts embrace every species of disbursement by the American Government on account of the commission for the period to which they relate, excepting the salary of the Commissioner and the salaries and subsistence of the agency.

They do not exhibit the *equalized* expenses of the two Governments, but the actual expenditures of the American Government. It is known, however, that the expenditures by the two parties have not differed essentially in amount, and at the close of the commission they will be brought together and equalized.

A few barrels of pork and some other provisions charged in this account have been delivered over to the British party when in need of them, and charged. They will be hereafter accounted for by them.

For the first year I made some charges for my travelling expenses, in conformity with the practice which I was informed by one of the Commissioners under the treaty of 1794 had been pursued by him and his colleague. But since the year 1817 I have made no charges of this nature.

P. B. PORTER.

BLACK ROCK, *December 2, 1820.*

At a meeting of the Board of Commissioners under the fifth article of the treaty of Ghent, held at Burlington, in the State of Vermont, on the 21st day of May, 1818, the following account, exhibited by the British agent, together with the vouchers accompanying the same, from A to N inclusive, was examined, passed, and allowed, and ordered to be paid in moieties by the agents of the respective Governments, to wit:

The Commission under the fifth article of the treaty of Ghent
To WARD CHIPMAN, *H. B. M. Agent.*   DR.

		N. B. Currency.		
		£	s.	d.
A	1817. June. To amount paid Coolidge & Deblois for provisions, utensils, and equipments, furnished in Boston for the surveying parties, per their account	100	0	10
B	November. To do. paid Crookshank and Johnston for provisions, utensils, and equipments furnished, and expenses of transportation, board, and lodging of the men, &c., paid at St. John's, N. B., for the same, per their account	1,119	16	5½
C	To amount paid Peter Fraser, do. do., at Fredericktown, N. B., per his account	688	7	7¼
D	Amount of Colin Campbell, assistant surveyor's account of expenditures, made by him on the survey	42	6	4
E	Amount of Richard Smith's account for passages and freight on the river St. John	56	5	0
F	Amount of pay due the British party on the exploring survey in 1817, per abstract	580	15	0
H	Amount of Colin Campbell's pay as assistant surveyor in 1817, 150 days, at 25 s. per diem	187	10	0
G	Amount of pay due the British on the actual survey in 1817, per abstract	540	0	0
I	Amount of William Whitney's bill for copying accounts	3	5	0
K	Amount of W. Reynold's bill for stationery	5	16	4
L	Amount of J. C. F. Bremnel's bill for postage	2	15	6
M	Amount of W. Pagan's bill for do	1	5	0
N	Amount of Colonel Bouchitte's account for expense	51	10	9
		3,379	13	9
	Sterling	3,041	14	5
		$13,518	75	

BURLINGTON, *May* 21, 1818.   Signed,   W. CHIPMAN, *Agent for H. B. M.*

The following account exhibited by the American agent, together with the vouchers accompanying the same, from A to O inclusive, was examined, passed, and allowed, and in like manner ordered to be paid in moiety by the agents of the respective Governments, to wit:

The Commissioners under the fifth article of the treaty of Ghent
To WILLIAM C. BRADLEY, *Agent of the United States under said article.*   DR.

A	Paid Mr. Orne, secretary, his salary for nine months, ending June 27, 1817	$1,666 66
B	I. Dove & Co.'s bill for provisions, utensils, equipments, and transportation of parties from Boston to St. John's	2,047 22
C	R. Powers, for expenses and transportation of party from the portage to Burlington	554 16
D	Paid J. Johnson for expenditures by him on public account	253 57
E	Charles Turner, jr., for do. do. and for transportation of himself and men from St. John's to Boston	236 23
F	L. Murryman, for expenses and transportation of G. Willard, a chain-bearer	8 00
G	J. Jones & Co., for advances made at Quebec	12 50
H	Horatio Gates and nephew, on account do., at Montreal	51 62
I	To chain-bearers and laborers on the exploring survey, as per abstract furnished	2,728 21
K	Do. on the actual survey, as per do	2,827 50
L	The assistant surveyor, at rate fixed by the Commissioners, for 150 days	750 00
M	To carriage of packets to the British agent	1 00
N	Lyman Cummings, for copying papers, &c	15 00
O	Paid Horace Fletcher for copying papers, &c	10 00
		11,161 67

MAY 21, 1818.   WILLIAM C. BRADLEY, *Agent United States.*

At a meeting of the Board of Commissioners under the fifth article of the treaty of Ghent, held at the city of New York on the 20th of May, A. D. 1819, the following account, exhibited by the agent on the part of his Britannic Majesty, together with the vouchers accompanying the same, from I. to VII. inclusive, was examined, passed, and allowed, and ordered to be paid in moieties by the agents of the respective Governments, to wit:

The Commission under the fifth article of the treaty of Ghent
To WARD CHIPMAN, *H. B. M. Agent.*   DR.

	1819.	N. B. Currency.		
		£	s.	d.
I.	To amount of expenditure made by the British agent for the pay and supply of the British on the exploring survey in the year 1818, per the schedule and the abstract and vouchers accompanying the same	1,681	7	2
II.	To cash paid for the British party and the astronomers on the parallel of 45 degrees, per schedule and the vouchers accompanying it	477	19	5½
III.	To amount paid A. Rositer for copying in Montreal	2	0	0
	Carried forward	2,161	6	7½

	£	s.	d.
Brought forward............	2,161	6	7½

IV. To cash paid Peter Fraser, amount of two orders drawn upon him by the British and American surveyors for services in the year 1817, and not included in the accounts of last year... **3 0 0**

V. To cash paid Colonel Buchette, his expenses in attending the commission at Burlington, in May, 1818, by order of the Board................................. **15 0 0**

VI. To cash paid Mr. Odell, his expenses in going from New Brunswick to Burlington, by order of the Board.. **37 10 0**

VII. To cash paid do. expenses at Burlington and returning to New Brunswick......... **28 18 11**

To sum allowed British agent for passages, &c., from New Brunswick to Burlington, per order of the Board, May 22, 1818...................................... **37 10 0**

To the amount allowed Colonel Buchette by the Board for extra assistance and stationery in the winter of 1817 and 1818, in preparing plans, and not included in last year's accounts:... **15 0 0**

To amount, Mr. Campbell, assistant surveyor, by the Board, for extra services in settling accounts of the surveys, preparing his plan, &c., report, &c., in the winter of 1817 and 1818, not included in last year's accounts.................. **47 0 0**

To amount paid for postage... **2 7 3**

	£	s.	d.
	2,347	12	9
Sterling........	2,112	17	6
	$9,390	55	

WARD CHIPMAN, *H. B. M. Agent.*

The following account exhibited by the agent on the part of the United States, together with the vouchers accompanying the same, from I to IX inclusive, was examined, passed, and ordered to be paid in moieties by the agents of the respective Governments:

The Commission under the fifth article of the treaty of Ghent
To WILLIAM C. BRADLEY, *Agent of the United States.* DR.

I. To cash paid N. Hayes for session room in 1818............................... **$34 00**

II. To cash paid H. H. Orne, secretary, salary from June 23, 1817, to June 1, 1818.... **2,085 00**

III. To cash paid for pork, bread, utensils, and sundry outfits for the astronomical and surveying parties, as per abstract A, with vouchers numbered from 1 to 43.... **2,174 27**

IV. To cash paid wages of assistants and men employed with the astronomers, as per vouchers numbered from 1 to 14, accompanying abstract B................ **2,172 08**

V. To cash paid assistants and laborers employed in the exploring survey, as per abstract C and vouchers numbered from 1 to 17.......................... **2,752 50**

VI. To sum paid R. Powers for his expenditure for transportation, provisions, and occasional labor on the exploring survey, as per abstract B, with vouchers from 1 to 58... **1,533 00**

VII. To cash paid E. Chamberlain for board of men in 1817, not received in season for last account.. **42 85**

VIII. To sum paid H. Chittenden, commissary on the part of the British and American Governments, for his expenditures made on account of the astronomers of both Governments, with their respective parties, while engaged in their operation during the season of 1818, with abstract VIII and vouchers marked from 1 to 171 **3,062 11¾**

IX. To sum paid H. Burnham and W. Lewis for assistance and writing for the surveyors during the winter of 1818 and 1819.................................. **248 00**

	14,103 81¾

WILLIAM C. BRADLEY, *Agent for the United States.*

At a meeting of the Board of Commissioners under the fifth article of the treaty of Ghent, held at Boston, in the State of Massachusetts, the 25th day of May, 1820, the agent of his Britannic Majesty presented to the Board his account of expenditures in the words and figures following, to wit:

The Commissioners under the fifth article of the treaty of Ghent
To WARD CHIPMAN, *H. B. M. Agent.* DR.

To amount allowed the British agent for the hire of a vessel to convey himself and the British surveyor from St. John's to Boston, on their way to attend the session of the Board in New York in May, 1819, per order of the Board......................$240 **60 0 0**

To amount paid Mrs. Satterwhite for the rent of a room, fuel, &c., for the session of the Board, May, 1819, per order of the Board.................................... **25 0 0**

To amount paid Mr. Odell, his expenses in attending the session of the Board at New York, May, 1819.. **26 15 5**

To amount of expenditure made by the British agent for the pay and supplies of the British party on the exploring survey in the year 1819 and the spring of 1820, per the schedule and vouchers accompanying it.. **1,921 11 9½**

To amount paid for the parties under the astronomers under the parallel of 45 degrees, per the schedule and vouchers accompanying it...........................$2,232 47 **558 2 5**

	£	s.	d.
	2,591	9	7½
	$10,365	92½	

BOSTON, *May* 25, 1820.   WARD CHIPMAN, *H. B. M. Agent.*

Which account, being read and examined, was passed and allowed, and the Board order that the amount, to wit, two thousand five hundred and ninety-one pounds nine shillings and seven pence half-penny, New Brunswick currency, equal to ten thousand three hundred and sixty-five dollars and ninety-two and a half cents, be paid in moieties by the respective agents.

The agent for the United States presented to the Board his account of expenditures in the words and figures following, to wit:

The Commissioners under the fifth article of the treaty of Ghent
To WILLIAM C. BRADLEY, *United States Agent.*   DR.

1. To this sum paid secretary for his salary from the 1st day of June, 1818, to June 1, 1819, including sum paid secretary *pro tem*	$2,222 22
2. To amount paid R. Tillotson for stationery, copying, &c., by order of the Board	77 44
3. To amount paid for provisions, utensils, and sundry outfits for surveying parties, as per abstract A, with vouchers from 1 to 14 inclusive.	1,620 98
4. To pay of assistants, commissary, and laborers for the year 1819, as per abstract B, with vouchers from 1 to 20 inclusive....	3,533 00
5. To this sum paid R. Powers, commissary, for expenditures made by him for transportation, provision, maintenance of assistants and men and sundry articles furnished for exploring survey, as per his account marked C, with vouchers from 1 to 66 inclusive	2,824 51
6. To this sum paid Captain Partridge for his expenses going to New York, attending the Board, and returning therefrom	97 00
To amount paid for transportation of the Commissioners from Burlington to the Missisqui bay, by order of the Board	25 50
	10,400 65

Which account, being read and examined, was passed and allowed, and the Board order that the amount, viz., the sum of ten thousand four hundred dollars and sixty-five cents, be paid in moieties by the respective agents.

I certify that the foregoing are true copies from the records of the Board of Commissioners appointed pursuant to the fifth article of the treaty of Ghent.

S. HALE, *Secretary.*

Mr. Delafield to the Secretary of State.

WASHINGTON, *May* 17, 1820.

SIR: The following considerations have induced me to solicit that I might remain attached to the commission under the sixth and seventh articles of the treaty of Ghent:

As the office of the agent under these articles has been vacated, some embarrassments may arise that give me the more confidence in submitting the annexed suggestions.

That I be permitted to repair to the above described boundary commission—

To represent the United States, (during the absence of an agent more fully authorized,) under the direction of the Government or of the American Commissioner, so far as it may be necessary.

To meet any proceedings on the part of the British agent.

To continue the minutes and journal of the agency; keep a record of the proceedings and notes of the evidence upon which decisions are had.

To report to the Government the proceedings of the Board and other occurrences of moment.

To transact all such things as the American Commissioner should deem to require the interference of an agent on the part of his Government.

To avoid the allegation on the part of the British Government that the United States had not met the agent of his Britannic Majesty by a corresponding officer or person acting in such capacity.

To supply the American Commissioner with another officer, so that he might be enabled to retire from the personal superintendence of the survey and party of surveyors whenever it might seem to him proper and requisite for the furtherance of the proceedings of the Board.

To enable the Board to proceed to the consideration of cases that in their opinion require the appearance of the respective Governments by officers representing them. It may be proper here to add that such material is now matured for consideration by the Board, not perhaps involving questions of doubt or difficulty, and that whenever the Board shall conclude to act upon such cases, an embarrassment might arise from the non-appearance of an officer corresponding to the British agent.

To take charge of the public property left on the line by the American agent, and dispose of so much thereof as is liable to waste and not needed by the commission.

To submit the accounts of the late agent of the United States to the Board for their sanction, or to the American Commissioner.

It is not believed nor desired that this appointment should increase in any material manner the expenses of the commission. No additional establishment would be requisite. The travelling expenses to and from the line and such compensation as might be allowed would only accrue, and the appropriation for the present year, from my knowledge of the disbursements of the commission, it is believed would cover this expense.

It is not intended to convey the impression that all the above enumerated duties are considered indispensable; but it is believed that, should this appointment be made, considerable embarrassments will be avoided, and I feel it right to state my convictions that it would be agreeable to the views and wishes of the American Commissioner.

Permit me to conclude that I have continued with the commission from the commencement of its labors to the present time, and that a strong desire to make myself useful to the advancement of the interests of my country (so far as in my power lies) urges me to seek for instructions upon the subject proposed.

I have the honor to be, &c.,

JOSEPH DELAFIELD.

Hon. JOHN QUINCY ADAMS, *Secretary of State.*

The Secretary of State to Mr. Delafield.

DEPARTMENT OF STATE, *Washington, May* 19, 1820.

SIR: Having laid before the President of the United States your letter of the 17th instant, I am directed by him to authorize your attendance upon the commission under the sixth and seventh articles of the treaty of Ghent for the purposes mentioned in your letter, and subject to the consent of the Commissioner, General Porter, whose directions in relation to the objects of your attention in this employment you will be pleased to take and observe. Your compensation will continue as heretofore, with such further allowance for necessary expenses as the Commissioner shall approve and may be allowed within the existing appropriation.

I am, &c.,

JOHN QUINCY ADAMS.

JOSEPH DELAFIELD, Esq.

Mr. Delafield to the Secretary of State.

WASHINGTON, *May* 19, 1820.

SIR: I have had the honor to receive your communication, bearing date this day, authorizing my attendance upon the boundary line commission under the sixth and seventh articles of the treaty of Ghent for the purposes therein described. In pursuance of such authority I shall repair forthwith to the boundary commission and confer with General Porter, whose directions upon all subjects where my services may be required shall be observed.

I beg leave to assure you that it will be my greatest pride to deserve the trust confided to me, and to render myself useful to the commission.

I have the honor to be, &c.,

JOSEPH DELAFIELD.

Hon. JOHN QUINCY ADAMS, *Secretary of State.*

Mr. Delafield to the Secretary of State.

RIVER ST. CLAIR, *October* 13, 1820.

SIR: I had the honor of addressing you on the 24th day of June last from the Detroit river, giving information of the intended departure of the surveyors employed by the Board under the sixth and seventh articles of the treaty of Ghent from that river to the upper end of Lake Huron.

The survey having been conducted to the head of the river Detroit, I sailed with the surveyors in a light schooner that had been employed for our service on the 21st day of July, and on the 3d day of August we commenced a section of survey at the north end of Lake Huron.

The British party had already begun their work at the head of the lake. We consequently took a section some distance below them, embracing the island known as Drummond's island, where the British forces now have a garrison, several channels hitherto unexplored, the commencement of the great Manatoulin islands, and a great number of lesser islands.

I regret that it is not in my power, without the aid of maps, to give a satisfactory description of that country, nor do I know of any that have been published that give a true knowledge of that end of Lake Huron.

That end of the lake from the river St. Marie to the Great Manatoulin is included in the surveys of the two parties and is completed. I conceive that the survey effected this season upon Lake Huron will embrace by far the most essential parts of that lake to be surveyed, so far as it relates to the duties of this commission. Drummond's island and Isle St. Joseph are of the most considerable interest, as well on account of their position as of territory, and more particularly Drummond's island. To this island, now in possession of the British, the United States have reasons to maintain a claim.

The season having advanced so far as to become boisterous and inclement, which rendered the conduct of the survey uncertain, and also having concluded the survey commenced, we left Lake Huron and arrived on the river St. Clair on the 6th instant. The party is at present employed upon this river, but will soon be under the necessity of returning to Black Rock on account of the inclemency of the weather. The British party left Lake Huron a few days before us and proceeded direct to Black Rock.

I have, &c.,

JOSEPH DELAFIELD.

Hon. JOHN QUINCY ADAMS, *Secretary of State.*

Mr. Delafield to the Secretary of State.

NEW YORK, *November* 1, 1820.

SIR: Upon the return of the boundary line party of surveyors from the north end of Lake Huron to the river St. Clair I had the honor to forward a letter, under date of October 13, 1820, describing the progress we had made during the past season. That letter having been ordered to the charge of the postmaster at Detroit, and supposing its receipt may be prolonged, I have thought it right to inclose a duplicate of the same.

For the reasons stated in my letter of the 13th ultimo we were then engaged in bringing the active labors of the survey for the season to a close; accordingly, when that duty was performed, we sailed from the St. Clair river and arrived at Black Rock on the 20th of the same month. At the latter place the surveyors and draughtsmen will be employed for some time in the preparation of their notes of observation, and in the composition of their maps for exchange and records, agreeably to the regulations of the Board.

I take great satisfaction in stating that our operations during the summer have been, in all respects, prosecuted with industry and success, and that they have been sanctioned by the concurrence and assent of the Commissioner, General Porter.

Our surveys have extended from the mouth of the Detroit river to the north end of Lake Huron, and have embraced that district, excepting the small Lake St. Clair and river St. Clair, and those parts of Lake Huron that are not essential to the duties of this commission.

Upon a full exposition to General Porter of the surveys effected and that which remains to be effected within the limits just mentioned, I have also the satisfaction to state that he concurs with me in opinion that but little remains to be done to bring to a close the performance of the sixth article of the treaty under which we act; and from the arrangements that are anticipated I do not doubt but what all the surveys that are necessary from the parallel of forty-five degrees north latitude, on the St. Lawrence river, through the lakes, to the north extremity of Lake Huron, will, in the coming season, be completed; nor do I at present foresee any obstacles that may present a protraction of the boundary lines for that extent by the decisions of the Board immediately thereafter. In furtherance of this view of the progress of our duties, General Porter has been pleased to confide to me the preliminaries he would establish to regulate such decisions; and their application to the various questions that suggest themselves, regardful of the best interests of the United States, is now a subject of study and investigation.

The difficulty that occurred to prevent a settlement of the accounts of the late agent of the United States, Colonel Hawkins, to wit, that they had not been acted upon by the Board, was submitted by me to the Commissioner of the United States in conformity to my instructions. In order to present a just understanding of what has transpired relative to these accounts, I have reduced the same to a correspondence with General Porter. His promised reply in a few days will enable me to lay the result before the Department of State.

I have the honor to be, with the greatest respect, &c.,

JOSEPH DELAFIELD.

Hon. JOHN QUINCY ADAMS, *Secretary of State.*

Mr. Van Ness to Mr. Adams.

NEW YORK, *November* 25, 1820.

SIR: Perceiving by the newspapers that the House of Representatives of the United States has requested of the President certain information relative to the proceedings and accounts of the Commissioners and agents under the treaty of Ghent, I am induced to write you briefly on the subject.

It having appeared to me that no settlement of accounts was contemplated by the treaty or expected by the Government until the final settlement at the close of the commission, it has been considered at least unnecessary to render any accounts; but being at all times not only willing but anxious to satisfy any branch of the Government as to my public conduct or accounts, I herewith forward you an abstract of my accounts, except as to the expenses of the commission for the present year. This is made out from papers which I have with me, but the vouchers are not here. I will, on my return home, arrange and forward them to your office. The amount of expenditures during the present year cannot be ascertained until all the accounts on both sides are settled and brought together, which it has not yet been possible to do.

The agent left this city a few days ago on his return home. He has proper vouchers to show that the money which has been received by him has been expended for the purposes of the commission.

I have, in the accompanying statement, put my salary at $4,444 44, as that is generally supposed to be the amount. But the Commissioners of his Britannic Majesty under the treaty of Ghent receive 1,200*l.* sterling, equal to $5,333 28; and it is believed to be not only just but in accordance with the treaty that the Commissioners appointed on the part of the United States should receive the same salary. This principle has been most conclusively recognized by the United States in the case of the agents, whose salaries were raised from $3,000 to $4,444 44 per annum, to make them equal to the pay of the agents on the part of Great Britain. The propriety of an equality of compensation to the Commissioners is certainly, to say the least, equally strong, as they are the *joint* officers of the two Governments.

I have never claimed on my personal account anything over my salary, whatever that may be, and such I know is the fact as to the agent.

The Commissioners under the fifth article of the treaty have held two sessions the present year. With respect to the progress which has been made by the commission, I understand the agent has already given to the Government all the information which it would be in my power to communicate.

If any statement of the moneys drawn by me from the Treasury shall have been laid before the House of Representatives previous to the receipt of this communication, I beg leave respectfully to request that copies of my letter and statement may be also transmitted to that body.

I have the honor to be, with great respect, your obedient servant,

C. P. VAN NESS.

Hon. JOHN QUINCY ADAMS, *Secretary of State.*

Abstract of moneys received and paid out by C. P. Van Ness, Commissioner under the fifth article of the treaty of Ghent.

Received from the United States in the years 1816, 1817, 1818, 1819, and 1820...........		$82,444 00
Paid out for the United States:		
To Mr. Bradley, agent of the United States, to be disbursed by him for the purposes of the commission, and for which disbursements he has the vouchers, I having taken his receipts for my vouchers	$40,437 83	
For instruments	791 92	
To John Johnson towards salary and expenses, who was surveyor under the commission about two years......................................	2,297 35	
To F. L. Hasler for salary and expenses, including transportation of instruments, who acted as astronomer under the commission about a year	8,183 27	
For expresses	105 00	
To Andrew Ellicott, who acted as astronomer in the summer of 1819, after Mr. Hasler left the service	670 00	
To physician for attending to Mr. Ellicott, who was taken ill on the lines....	11 00	
To five years' salary, at $4,444 44 per annum...........................	22,222 20	
		69,718 57
Balance to be applied to the expenditures of 1820		12,725 43

Mr. Delafield to the Secretary of State.

NEW YORK, *November* 27, 1820.

SIR: In addition to my previous communications respecting the progress of the boundary line commission under the sixth and seventh articles of the treaty of Ghent, I have the honor to submit some facts that it did not heretofore occur to me were material at this time to communicate, and which will hereafter be presented more in detail when the accounts of the past season are in readiness to exhibit. I allude more particularly to the names of persons now employed by the Commissioner or agent, the purposes for which employed, their terms of service and compensation.

In order that the Department of State may be entirely possessed of such information as I have upon these points, I have the honor to inclose a list containing the names, the services and salaries, and compensation of all persons employed during this season by the Commissioner of the United States under the above articles of the treaty of Ghent.

This list is collected, so far as it respects the principal persons employed, from the proceedings of the Board, and is otherwise expressed with as much certainty as can be ascertained until the accounts of the last season are rendered by the Commissioner. To those accounts I must beg leave to refer for the most exact and detailed information that may be desired.

My own duties have not required the employ of either additional boatmen or extra establishment of any kind, as I constantly remained present with the party of surveyors.

And I take pleasure in stating that the agency with which I have the honor to be charged has not essentially increased the expenses of this commission. Upon this subject I beg leave to add that if it should seem fit to place the compensation of the agent upon a footing with other officers of the Board the extra expenses incurred would be amply covered by such compensation—a course that would be the more gratifying because it would enable me to dispense with an account for contingent or extra expenditures, and thus conform to a system that I believe to be the wish of this Board to adopt, which is to confine its extra expenditures exclusively to disbursements necessarily accruing whilst the party is actually employed upon the boundary line in the prosecution of the surveys.

I have been unwillingly led to make any observations upon the subject of my own compensation, but the state of the appropriation for the agent, and the tenor of my appointment recognizing extra expenses to be allowed, have induced me to this explanation.

When I parted with the Commissioner at Black Rock it was his intention to forward the accounts of the past season to me that I might present them at the proper Auditor's office, and they were in preparation for that purpose. I am in daily hope of the receipt of these accounts, and shall hasten to lay them before the Department.

I have, &c.,

JOSEPH DELAFIELD.

Hon. JOHN QUINCY ADAMS, *Secretary of State.*

Names of persons forming the Board of Commission under the sixth and seventh articles of the treaty of Ghent, on the part of the United States, and of persons employed by them, their services and salaries, for the year 1820.

Peter B. Porter, Commissioner, salary	$4,444
Joseph Delafield, acting agent..	
Persons employed by the Commissioners:	
Donald Frazer, secretary...	2,200
William Bird, principal surveyor..	2,000
James Ferguson, trigonometrical surveyor	1,000
L. G. De Russy, trigonometrical surveyor and draughtsman	1,000
J. Best, assistant surveyor, three dollars per diem whilst employed, say six months.	

Thomas Clinton, steward, charged with purchase and issue of supplies and care of public property. His compensation appears in Commissioner's accounts.

Captain Gillett, master of a light vessel, with a crew of three men, employed for the transportation of the party and stores upon the upper lakes. The crew acting as boatmen when not employed navigating the vessel. Employed about three months.

Nine boatmen, employed in the service of the surveyors and constantly on duty with them. One of the number being the cook for the vessel and the party. These men were engaged by the month, mostly at the rate of thirteen dollars per month, and were employed from the 1st of May to the 20th of October, 1820.

For the wages of the master of the vessel, reference is made to the accounts of the Commissioner.

Persons employed by the acting agent under sixth and seventh articles of the treaty of Ghent, 1820, none.

Peter B. Porter, Esq., to the Secretary of State.

BLACK ROCK, *December* 2, 1820.

SIR: The surveying parties under the sixth and seventh articles of the treaty of Ghent returned from Lake Huron to this place the latter part of October, and are now engaged, as has been customary during the winter, in calculating, platting, and arranging the work of the summer. We availed ourselves of the best part of this season to survey the islands (which are numerous and many of them large) in Lake Huron and in the straits of St. Mary's, which unite that lake with Superior. The only surveys that now remain to be executed under the sixth article are on the river and small lake St. Clair, which we calculate to complete in time to make a final decision and report upon the sixth article in the course of the next season.

The execution of the sixth article will have consumed considerable time and expense; but I flatter myself that the maps and surveys which will accompany our report will show that we have not been idle, and that, besides exhibiting a clear and distinct demarcation of the boundary, they will furnish the Government with a mass of the most useful information in respect to a very considerable line of navigation, which is daily and rapidly growing into importance, and for the direction of which there are not at present any charts the accuracy of which can be in the least relied on.

The seventh article relates to a country which is, comparatively, of little importance; and a system of operations is proposed to be adopted for designating the boundary which will greatly reduce both the time and expense of its execution.

I have been gratified in having, during the last season, the assistance of Major Delafield, whose intelligence, habits of business, and correct deportment have rendered him very useful. I hope that he may accompany us again the next season to assist in arranging and preparing the various points for adjudication, and in making out the necessary reports and documents for the respective Governments. The knowledge which, by his former situation, he has acquired of the various subjects connected with the sixth article would probably enable him to be more useful than any other person. It would be my wish, also, should he continue with us, that he should take a general management and superintendence of the operations and expenses of the surveying parties, &c. This was not done by the late agent for reasons which are already known to you.

Major Delafield has expressed a wish, suggested, no doubt, by my presumed knowledge of the duties which he has to perform, that I would give an opinion as to what would be a reasonable compensation for his services. This, however, is a subject on which I do not feel authorized to express an opinion further than to say that I believe the Board of which I am a member has heretofore considered that neither considerations of justice nor of national *etiquette* required that the compensation of the two agents should be the *same*. On the contrary, they have been inclined to consider the agents rather as officers of the respective Governments than of the Board, and that their labors, as well as their compensations, might be essentially different, depending upon the instructions they might severally receive, and the arrangements they might make with their respective Governments. I may, perhaps, be permitted to add, that while I presume that Major Delafield has no expectation of receiving the amount of salary allowed to the former agent, yet that the sum of a thousand dollars a year, which he has heretofore received, seems quite too small, when compared with the nature and extent of his services, and when it is considered, too, that six or eight months in the year must be spent in camp in an uninhabited and inhospitable country.

On the subject of the accounts of the late agent (Colonel Hawkins,) Major Delafield, as his agent, has requested that they should be audited and adjusted by the Board, and has intimated that such was the wish of the Government. I informed him, in reply, that the reason for not having originally included the expenses of the agents amongst the common expenses of the Board arose from the circumstance that no British agent was appointed until after the close of the first year of our operations; that doubts were then entertained by the British Commissioner whether one would be appointed, and a consequent unwillingness on his part to share in the payment for services which were rendered exclusively to the American Government. The British Government has, however, since employed an agent, and I have assured Major Delafield that on the final settlement of the accounts next season I will use my endeavors, should it still be the wish of the Government, to have the agents' accounts included, and entertain no doubt but that they may be adjusted in a manner that will be satisfactory and at the same time do justice to the two Governments.

I inclose herewith for Mr. Pleasanton, the Auditor of your Department, transcripts of the accounts of our expenditures for the last three years. The vouchers to which they refer are on file with the secretary of the Board, and will be transmitted to Washington on the closing of the sixth article.

I have, &c.,

PETER B. PORTER.

Hon. JOHN Q. ADAMS, *Secretary of State.*

No. 342.

CORRESPONDENCE RESPECTING SUPPRESSION OF THE SLAVE TRADE.

COMMUNICATED TO THE HOUSE OF REPRESENTATIVES JANUARY 5, 1821.

I communicate to the House of Representatives a report from the Secretary of State which, with the papers accompanying it, contains all the information in possession of the Executive, requested by a resolution of the House of the 4th of December, on the subject of the African slave trade.

JAMES M NROE.

WASHINGTON, *January 4,* 1821.

DEPARTMENT OF STATE, *January 4,* 1821.

The Secretary of State, to whom has been referred the resolution of the House of Representatives of the 4th ultimo requesting the communication to that House of any correspondence that the President does not deem it inexpedient to disclose, which may have existed between the Executive of the United States and the Government of any of the maritime powers of Europe in relation to the African slave trade, has the honor of submitting copies of the papers requested by the resolution. With the exception of a note from the late Spanish minister, Onis, communicating a copy of the treaty between Spain and Great Britain on this subject, the only Government of Europe with whom there has been such correspondence is that of Great Britain, and these papers contain all that has passed between them on the subject in writing. Since the arrival of Mr. Canning various informal conferences between him and the Secretary of State have been held, in which the proposals on the part of Great Britain have been fully discussed, without effecting a removal of the objections upon which the President had in the first instance found himself under the necessity of declining them. They have not yet terminated, nor have any written communications passed on the subject, with the exception of the note from Mr. Canning and the answer to it herewith submitted, both of a date subsequent to that of the resolution of the House.

JOHN QUINCY ADAMS.

List of papers.

Mr. Onis to the Secretary of State, May 14, 1818. Translation.
Mr. Rush to the same, February 18, 1818. Extract.
Same to the same, April 15, 1818. Extract.
Same to the same, June 24, 1818. Extract.
Lord Castlereagh to Mr. Rush, June 20, 1818. Copy.
Mr. Rush to Lord Castlereagh, June 23, 1818. Copy.
Secretary of State to Messrs. Gallatin and Rush, November 2, 1818. Extract.
Mr. Rush to Lord Castlereagh, December 21, 1818. Copy.
Same to the Secretary of State, March 5, 1819. Extract.
Same to same, November 10, 1819. Extract.
Mr. Canning to the Secretary of State, December 20, 1820. Copy.
The Secretary of State to Mr. Canning, December 30, 1820. Copy.

Don Luis de Onis to the Secretary of State.

[Translation.]

SIR: The introduction of negro slaves into America was one of the earliest measures adopted by the august ancestors of the King, my master, for the improvement and prosperity of those vast dominions, very shortly after their discovery. The total inaptitude of the Indians to various useful but painful labors, the result of their ignorance of all the conveniences of life, and the imperfect progress in civil society, made it necessary to have recourse to strong and active laborers for breaking up and cultivating the earth. With the double view of stimulating them to active exertion and of promoting the population of those countries a measure was resorted to by Spain which, although repugnant to her feelings, is not to be considered as having originated the system of slavery, but as having materially alleviated the evils of that which already existed in consequence of the barbarous practice of the Africans upon saving the lives of a considerable portion of the captives in war, whom they formerly put to death. By the introduction of this system the negroes, far from suffering additional evils or being subjected while in a state of slavery to a more painful life than when possessed of freedom in their own country, obtained the inestimable advantage of a knowledge of the true God and of all the benefits attendant on civilization.

The benevolent feelings of the sovereigns of Spain did not, however, at any time permit their subjects to carry on this trade but by special license; and in the years 1789, 1798, and on the 22d of April, 1804, certain limited periods were fixed for the importation of slaves. Although the last term had not expired when his Majesty our lord Don Ferdinand the Seventh was restored to the throne of which a perfidious usurper had attempted to deprive him, his Majesty, on resuming the reins of government, soon perceived that those remote countries had become a prey to civil feuds; and in reflecting on the most effectual means of restoring order and affording them all the encouragement of which they were susceptible, his Majesty discovered that the numbers of the native and free negroes had prodigiously increased under the mild regimen of the Government and the humane treatment of the Spanish slave owners; that the white population had also greatly increased; that the climate is not so noxious to them as it was before the lands were cleared; and, finally, that the advantages resulting to the inhabitants of Africa in being transported to cultivated countries are no longer so decided and exclusive since England and the United States have engaged in the noble undertaking of civilizing them in their native country.

All these considerations combining with the desire entertained by his Majesty of co-operating with the powers of Europe in putting an end to this traffic, which, if indefinitely continued, might involve them all in the most serious evils, have determined his Majesty to conclude a treaty with the King of the United Kingdom of Great Britain and Ireland by which the abolition of the slave trade is stipulated and agreed on, under certain regulations, and I have received his commands to deliver to the President a copy of the same, his Majesty feeling confident that a measure so completely in harmony with the sentiments of this Government and of all the inhabitants of this republic cannot fail to be agreeable to him.

In the discharge of this satisfactory duty I now transmit to you the aforesaid copy of the treaty, which I request you will be pleased to lay before the President, and I have the honor to renew the assurances of my distinguished respect.

God preserve you many years!

LUIS DE ONIS.

WASHINGTON, *May* 14, 1818.

Extract of a letter from Mr. Rush to the Secretary of State, dated

FEBRUARY 18, 1818.

"You will probably have perceived, by the proceedings in the House of Commons, that treaties have been formed between this Government and both Spain and Portugal securing, as far as may be done by treaty, the final abolition, after a specified time, not very remote, of the slave trade. Thus is a last hand to be put to the work of America, whose legislators led the way, with Europe against them, in this transcendent moral reform. But it is a triumph which as little the courts as the public of Europe seem willing, in any shape, to acknowledge. The palm is claimed by others. America is even placed in fault. In his speech on the Spanish treaty, delivered in the House of Commons on the 8th instant, Lord Castlereagh observed that it was in vain for Britain alone to shut the door of her colonies against the slave trade; for that, unless there was a concert of exclusion, the other islands of the West Indies 'and the southern *provinces* of the United States would become the asylum and depot of it.' I gladly caught the opportunity of this accidental meeting* to say what could not have been otherwise than acceptable to the zeal for abolition. I stated the nature of our laws. I said I felt sure that he would hear from me with pleasure that it was upwards of nine years since the traffic had been abolished throughout the Union, and that so far had our acts of Congress carried the prohibition that to import even a single slave into any of the States had, during the same period, been denounced as an offence and subjected to unusually rigorous penalties of fine and imprisonment. His lordship admitted the prohibitions, but intimated fears lest we could not enforce them, alluding to the recent state of things at Amelia. In the end he invited me to look into all their conventions with other powers upon this subject, with a view to future conversation, adding that he was well disposed himself to a proper concert of action between our two Governments for the more effectual extirpation of the traffic.

"I shall look into the conventions accordingly, and wait the renewal of the topic. Whether policy would dictate any concert is a point upon which, not being instructed, I will not presume to give any opinion. But I hope I do not misjudge in thinking that, for the present, I am merely bound to listen to, without seeking, any further conversation. I will take care punctually to communicate for the President's information whatever may be said to me, in like manner as my duty devolves it upon me to transmit this first sentiment so cursorily thrown out by Lord Castlereagh. It will be understood that in adverting to our municipal prohibitions I intended no advance to the point of national co-operation. It was barely for the sake of an incidental and gratuitous vindication after a public remark, which, to say no more, was susceptible of unjust interpretations. On his allusion to Amelia island I reminded him that it was the very anxiety to prevent the illicit introduction of slaves that had formed a ruling motive with the President for breaking up, with the public force itself, the establishment at that place."

Extract of a letter from Mr. Rush to the Secretary of State.

APRIL 15, 1818

"He (Lord Castlereagh) next spoke of the slave trade. The Government of Great Britain felt, he said, an increasing desire that the Government of the United States should lend itself to the measures of regulation going forward in Europe for its complete extirpation. These measures mean, in effect, a reciprocal submission to the right of search. He explained, by saying that only to a limited number of the armed vessels of each of the maritime States would a power to search be deputed, while the exercise of it would be strictly forbidden to all others. It was contemplated, he continued, to form out of an association of these armed vessels a species of naval police, to be stationed chiefly in the African seas, and from whose harmonious co-operating efforts the best results were anticipated. He added that no peculiar structure or previous appearances in the vessel searched, no presence of irons or other presumptions of criminal intention, nothing but the actual finding of slaves on board was ever to authorize a seizure or detention. He said that they had lately pressed France upon the subject, and that there was no doubt of her eventual agreement. The recent vote in both her Chambers on the broad principle of abolition he regarded as a full pledge of her ulterior steps.

"I replied that I was sure that the President would listen with an ear the most liberal to whatever distinct proposals were made, more especially as the United States had been long awake as well to the

* With Lord Castlereagh.

moral guilt as to the political and social evils of the traffic, and had, as was known, aimed against it the denunciations of their own laws. The distinct propositions, his lordship gave me reason to think, would be made known before long through Mr. Bagot."

Extract of a letter from Mr. Rush to Mr. Adams, dated

LONDON, *June* 24, 1818.

"In two former despatches I have mentioned what Lord Castlereagh has said to me relative to the slave trade. In my interview with him on the eleventh of this month he spoke of it in a manner more formal and definitive.

"He first alluded to the late treaties concluded between Great Britain and several of the powers of Europe upon this subject. Entering into conversation upon their particular nature and provisions, he said that the period had arrived when it was the wish of the British Government to invite the Government of the United States to join in the measures which Europe was so generally adopting for the more perfect abolition of this traffic, and that it was now his design to submit through me proposals to this effect. It will be perceived by my despatch, No. 14,* that at that period it had been contemplated to make them through the channel of the English mission at Washington. What may have led to a change in this respect his lordship did not state, nor did I deem it material to inquire.

"It had occurred to him, he said, to make the proposals by sending me, accompanied by an official note, entire copies of all the treaties in question. They would best unfold the grounds and principles upon which a concert of action had already been settled by the States that were parties to them, and it was his intention to ask the accession of the United States upon grounds and principles that were similar. He added, that he would willingly receive my suggestions as to any other course that might strike me as better adapted to the object. I replied that none appeared to me more eligible, and that whenever he would inclose me the treaties I would lose no time in transmitting them for the consideration of the President.

"It naturally occurred to me during our conversation that the detached and distant situation of the United States, if not other causes, might call for a modification in some parts of these instruments, admitting that the broad principle of concert met approbation. His lordship upon this point was full in assurances that the British Government would be happy to listen to whatever modifications the Government of the United States might think fit to propose. Its anxious and only desire, he said, was to see a convention formed that would prove free from all objection, and be conducive to the single and grand object to which both sides looked. He ended by expressing the belief which was felt that the maritime co-operation of the United States would usefully contribute to the advancement of this great work of humanity.

"Nothing further passed necessary to the full understanding of the overture beyond what the documents themselves and his lordship's note are calculated to afford. To these I have therefore the honor to refer, as disclosing in the most authentic and detailed manner the whole views of the British Government upon this interesting subject."

Lord Castlereagh to Mr. Rush.

FOREIGN OFFICE, *June* 20, 1818.

SIR: The distinguished share which the Government of the United States has from the earliest period borne in advancing the cause of abolition, makes the British Government desirous of submitting to their favorable consideration whatever may appear to them calculated to bring about the final accomplishment of this great work of humanity.

The laudable anxiety with which you personally interest yourself in whatever is passing upon this important subject will have led you to perceive that, with the exception of the crown of Portugal, all European States have now either actually prohibited the traffic in slaves to their subjects, or fixed an early period for its cessation, whilst Portugal has also renounced it to the north of the equator. From May, 1820, there will not be a flag which *can legally* cover this detested traffic to the north of the line, and there is reason to hope that the Portuguese may also ere long be prepared to abandon it to the south of the equator; but so long as some effectual concert is not established amongst the principal maritime powers for preventing their respective flags from being made a cover for an illicit trade, there is too much reason to fear (whatever be the state of the law upon this subject) that the evil will continue to exist, and, in proportion as it assumes a contraband form, that it will be carried on under the most aggravating circumstances of cruelty and desolation.

It is from a deep conviction of this truth, founded upon experience, that the British Government in all its negotiations upon this subject has endeavored to combine a system of alliance for the suppression of this most abusive practice with the engagements which it has succeeded in lately contracting with the Governments of Spain and Portugal for the total or partial abolition of the slave trade. I have now the honor to inclose to you copies of the treaties which have been happily concluded with those powers, together with the acts which have recently passed the Legislature for carrying the same into execution.

I have also the satisfaction to transmit to you a copy of a treaty which has been recently concluded with the King of the Netherlands for the like purpose, though at too late a period in the session to admit of its provisions receiving the sanction of Parliament. I am induced the more particularly to call your attention to this convention, as it contains certain provisions which are calculated to limit in some respects the powers mutually conceded by the former treaties in a manner which, without essentially weakening their force, may render them more acceptable to the contracting parties.

The intimate knowledge which you possess of this whole subject renders it unnecessary for me, in

* April 15, 1818.

requesting you to bring these documents to the observation of your Government, to accompany them with any more detailed explanation. What I have *earnestly* to beg of you is to bring them under the serious consideration of the President; intimating to him the strong wish of the British Government that the exertions of the two States may be combined upon a somewhat similar principle, in order to put down this great moral disobedience, wherever it may be committed, to the laws of both countries. I am confident this cannot effectually be done except by mutually conceding to each other's ships-of-war a qualified right of search, with a power of detaining the vessels of either State with slaves *actually on board.*

You will perceive in these conventions a studious and, I trust, a successful attempt to narrow and limit this power within due bounds and to guard it against perversion. If the American Government is disposed to enter into a similar concert, and can suggest any further regulations the better to obviate abuse, this Government will be most ready to listen to any suggestion of this nature, their only object being to contribute by every effort in their power to put an end to this disgraceful traffic.

I have the honor to be, with great truth, sir, your most obedient humble servant,

CASTLEREAGH.

Mr. Rush to Lord Castlereagh.

LONDON, *June* 23, 1818.

MY LORD: I have been honored with your lordship's note of the twentieth of this month, inclosing copies of treaties recently concluded between this Government and the Governments of Portugal, Spain, and the Netherlands, respectively, in relation to the slave trade, and designed to draw the attention of the Government of the United States to this subject, with a view to its co-operation upon principles similar to those held out in these treaties, in measures that may tend to the more complete and universal abolition of the traffic.

The United States, from an early day of their history, have regarded with deep and uniform abhorrence the existence of a traffic attended by such complications of misery and guilt. Its transcendent evils roused throughout all ranks a corresponding zeal for their extirpation. One step followed another until humanity triumphed; and against its continuance under any shape, by its own citizens, the most absolute prohibitions of their code have, for a period of more than ten years, been rigorously and, it is hoped, beneficially levelled. Your lordship will pardon me this allusion to the earnest efforts of the United States to put down the traffic within their own limits, falling in, as it merely does, with the tribute which you have been pleased to pay to their early exertions in helping to dry up this prolific source of human woe.

Whether any causes may throw obstacles in the way of their uniting in that concert of external measures in which Europe generally and this nation in particular are now so happily engaged the more effectually to banish from the world this great enormity, I dare not, in the total absence of all instructions, presume to intimate, much less have I any opinion of my own to offer upon a subject so full of delicacy and interest. But it is still left to me to say that I shall perform a duty peculiarly gratifying in transmitting, by the earliest opportunities, copies of your lordship's note, with the documents which accompanied it, to my Government, and I sufficiently know the permanent sensibility which pervades all its councils upon this subject to promise that the overture which the former embraces will receive from the President the full and anxious consideration due to its importance, and, above all, to the enlarged philanthropy on the part of this Government by which it has been dictated.

I have the honor to be, with the highest consideration, your lordship's obedient faithful servant,

RICHARD RUSH.

Extract of a letter from the Secretary of State to Messrs. Gallatin and Rush, dated

DEPARTMENT OF STATE, *November* 2, 1818.

"SLAVE TRADE.

"The President desires that you would make known to the British Government his sensibility to the friendly spirit of confidence with which the treaties lately contracted by Great Britain with Spain, Portugal, and the Netherlands, and the legislative measures of Parliament founded upon them, have been communicated to this Government, and the invitation to the United States to join in the same or similar arrangements, has been given. He wishes you also to give the strongest assurances that the solicitude of the United States for the accomplishment of the common object, the total and final abolition of that odious traffic, continues with all the earnestness which has so long and so steadily distinguished the course of their policy in relation to it. As an evidence of this earnestness, he requests you to communicate to them a copy of the act of Congress of the last session, in addition to the act of 1807, to prohibit the importation of slaves into the United States, (acts of the last session, chapter 86, page 81,) and to declare the readiness of this Government, within their constitutional powers, to adopt any further measures which experience may prove to be necessary for the purpose of obtaining so desirable an end.

"But you will observe that, in examining the provisions of the treaties communicated by Lord Castlereagh, all their essential articles appear to be of a character not adaptable to the institutions or to the circumstances of the United States.

"The power agreed to be reciprocally given to the officers of the ships-of-war of either party to enter, search, capture, and carry into port for adjudication, the merchant vessels of the other, however qualified and restricted, is most essentially connected with the institution by each treaty of two mixed courts, one of which to reside in the external or colonial possessions of each of the two parties, respectively. This part of the system is indispensable to give it that character of reciprocity without which the right granted to the armed ships of one nation to search the merchant vessels of another would be rather a mark of vassalage than of independence. But to this part of the system the United States, having no colonies either on the coast of Africa or in the West Indies, cannot give effect.

"You will add, that by the Constitution of the United States it is provided the judicial power of the United States shall be vested in a Supreme Court and in such inferior courts as the Congress may, from time to time, ordain and establish. It provides that the judges of these courts shall hold their offices during good behavior, and that they shall be removable by impeachment and conviction of crimes or misdemeanors. There may be some doubt whether the power of the Government of the United States is competent to institute a court for carrying into execution their penal statutes beyond the territories of the United States—a court consisting partly of foreign judges not amenable to impeachment for corruption, and deciding upon the statutes of the United States without appeal.

"That the disposal of the negroes found on board the slave-trading vessels which might be condemned by the sentence of these mixed courts cannot be carried into effect by the United States; for if the slaves of a vessel condemned by the mixed court should be delivered over to the Government of the United States as freemen, they could not but by their own consent be employed as servants or free laborers. The condition of the blacks being in this Union regulated by the municipal laws of the separate States, the Government of the United States can neither guaranty their liberty in the States where they could only be received as slaves, nor control them in the States where they would be recognized as free.

"That the admission of a right in the officers of foreign ships-of-war to enter and search the vessels of the United States in time of peace, under any circumstances whatever, would meet with universal repugnance in the public opinion of this country; that there would be no prospect of a ratification, by advice and consent of the Senate, to any stipulation of that nature; that the search by foreign officers, even in time of war, is so obnoxious to the feelings and recollections of this country, that nothing could reconcile them to the extension of it, however qualified or restricted, to a time of peace; and that it would be viewed in a still more aggravated light if, as in the treaty with the Netherlands, connected with a formal admission that even vessels under convoy of ships-of-war of their own nation should be liable to search by the ships-of-war of another.

"You will therefore express the regret of the President that the stipulations in the treaties communicated by Lord Castlereagh are of a character to which the peculiar situation and institutions of the United States do not permit them to accede. The constitutional objection may be the more readily understood by the British cabinet if they are reminded that it was an obstacle proceeding from the same principle which prevented Great Britain from becoming, formally, a party to the Holy Alliance. Neither can they be at a loss to perceive the embarrassment under which we should be placed by receiving cargoes of African negroes and be bound at once to guaranty their liberty and to employ them as servants. Whether they will be as ready to enter into our feelings with regard to the search by foreign navy lieutenants of vessels under convoy of our own navy commanders is, perhaps, of no material importance. The other reasons are presumed to be amply sufficient to convince them that the motives for declining this overture are compatible with an earnest wish that the measures concerted by these treaties may prove successful in extirpating that root of numberless evils, the traffic in human blood, and with the determination to co-operate to the utmost extent of our powers in this great vindication of the sacred rights of humanity."

Copy of a letter from Mr. Rush to Lord Castlereagh, dated

LONDON, *December* 21, 1818.

The undersigned, envoy extraordinary and minister plenipotentiary from the United States, has the honor to present his compliments to Lord Castlereagh.

In the note of the 23d of June, which the undersigned had the honor to address to his lordship in answer to his lordship's communication of the twentieth of the same month relative to the slave trade, the undersigned had great pleasure in giving the assurance that he would transmit a copy of that communication to his Government, together with the documents which accompanied it, being copies of treaties entered into on the part of Great Britain with Spain, Portugal, and the Netherlands, for the more complete abolition of the odious traffic in slaves. He accordingly lost no time in fulfilling that duty, and has now the honor to inform his lordship of the instructions with which he has been furnished by his Government in reply.

He has been distinctly commanded, in the first place, to make known the sensibility of the President to the friendly spirit of confidence in which these treaties and the legislative measures of Parliament founded upon them have been communicated to the United States, and to the invitation which has been given that they would join in the same or similar arrangements the more effectually to accomplish the beneficent object to which they look. He is further commanded to give the strongest assurances that the solicitude of the United States for the universal extirpation of this traffic continues with all the earnestness which has so long and steadily distinguished the course of their policy in relation to it. Of their general prohibitory law of 1807 it is unnecessary that the undersigned should speak, his lordship being already apprized of its provisions, amongst which the authority to employ the national force as auxiliary to its execution will not have escaped attention. But he has it in charge to make known, as a new pledge of their unremitting and active desire in the cause of abolition, that so lately as the month of April last another act of Congress was passed, by which not only are the citizens and vessels of the United States interdicted from carrying on or being in any way engaged in the trade, but in which also the best precautions that legislative enactments can devise or their penalties enforce are raised up against the introduction into their territories of slaves from abroad, under whatever pretext attempted, and especially from dominions which lie more immediately in their neighborhood. A copy of this act is herewith inclosed for the more particular information of his lordship. That peculiarity in the eighth section which throws upon a defendant the labor of proof as the condition of acquittal, the undersigned persuades himself will be regarded as signally manifesting an anxiety to suppress the hateful offence, departing, as it does, from the analogy of criminal jurisprudence, which so generally requires the independent and positive establishment of guilt as the first step in every public prosecution. To measures of such a character, thus early adopted and sedulously pursued, the undersigned is further commanded to say that the Government of the United States, acting within the pale of its constitutional powers, will always be ready to superadd any others that experience may prove to be necessary for attaining the desirable end in view.

· But on examining the provisions of the treaties which your lordship honored the undersigned by communicating, it has appeared to the President that their essential articles are of a character not adapted to the circumstances or to the institutions of the United States.

The powers agreed to be given to the ships-of-war of either party to search, capture, and carry into port for adjudication the merchant vessels of the other, however qualified, is connected with the establishment, by each treaty, of two mixed courts, one of which is to have its seat in the colonial possessions of the parties, respectively. The institution of such tribunals is necessarily regarded as fundamental to the whole arrangement, whilst their peculiar structure is doubtless intended, and would seem to be indispensable towards imparting to it a just reciprocity. But to this part of the system the United States, having no colonies upon the coast of Africa, in the West Indies, or elsewhere, cannot give effect.

Moreover, the powers of government in the United States, whilst they can only be exercised within the grants, are also subject to the restriction of the Federal Constitution. By the latter instrument all judicial power is to be vested in a supreme court and in such other inferior courts as Congress may, from time to time, ordain and establish. It further provides that the judges of these courts shall hold their offices during good behavior, and be removable on impeachment and conviction of crimes and misdemeanors. There are serious doubts whether, obeying the spirit of these injunctions, the Government of the United States would be competent to appear as party to the institution of a court for carrying into execution their penal statutes in places out of their own territory—a court consisting partly of foreign judges, not liable to impeachment under the authority of the United States, and deciding upon their statutes without appeal.

Again. Obstacles would exist towards giving validity to the disposal of the negroes found on board the slave-trading vessels condemned by the sentence of the mixed courts. If they should be delivered over to the government of the United States as freemen, they could not but by their own consent be employed as servants or free laborers. The condition of negroes and other people of color in the United States being regulated by the municipal laws of the separate States, the Government of the former could neither guaranty their liberty in the States where they could only be received as slaves, nor control them in the States where they would be recognized as free. The provisions of the fifth section of the act of Congress, which the undersigned has the honor to inclose, will be seen to point to this obstacle, and may be taken as still further explanatory of its nature. ·

These are some of the principal reasons which arrest the assent of the President to the very frank and friendly overture contained in your lordship's communication. Having their foundation in constitutional impediments, the Government of his Britannic Majesty will know how to appreciate their force. It will be seen how compatible they are with the most earnest wishes on the part of the United States that the measures concerted by these treaties may bring about the total downfall of the traffic in human blood, and with their determination to co-operate, to the utmost extent of their constitutional power, towards this great consummation, so imperiously due at the hands of all nations to the past wrongs and sufferings of Africa.

The undersigned prays Lord Castlereagh to accept the assurances of his distinguished consideration.
RICHARD RUSH.

_____

Mr. Rush to the Secretary of State.

[Extract.]

LONDON, *March* 5, 1819.

"Lord Castlereagh sent me, a few days ago, the inclosed printed parliamentary document. It will be found to comprise a variety of interesting papers relating to the slave trade, exhibiting all that has lately been done by the powers of Europe upon the subject, and the actual and precise footing upon which it now stands. Its receipt was the first notice that I had in any shape of the fact of the publication or of there being any intention to publish my notes to this Government of the twenty-third of June and twenty-first of December. It will be seen from one of the papers how unequivocal and animated has been the refusal of France to allow her vessels to be boarded and searched at sea for slaves. Now, there is nothing more evident, as may be collected from my despatch of the fifteenth of last April, than that this is a result which, at that period, Lord Castlereagh did not anticipate. Nevertheless, it would seem, from a passage in his lordship's letter to Lord Bathurst, from Paris, dated the 10th of December, the last paper in the collection, and written subsequently to all the conferences and declarations at Aix la Chapelle, that he still indulges a sanguine expectation that 'the French Government may be brought, at no distant period, to unite their *naval* exertions with those of the other allied powers for the suppression of the trade.' Some of the evidence furnished by the African Society in London and from Sierra Leone as to the extent in which the trade continues to be unlawfully carried on may probably command attention in the United States.

"What communications may, at any former periods, have been made to the Government of the United States by the Governments of France, Russia, or Prussia, through any channel, either in Europe or at Washington, of their intentions in regard to this naval combination for putting down the traffic, I am not informed. It is impossible to refrain from remarking that to me they remained utterly unknown until I saw them recorded in these pages of a document given to the world by England."

_____

Extract of a letter from Mr. Rush to the Secretary of State, dated

LONDON, *November* 10, 1819.

"On the seventh of this month I received a note from Lord Castlereagh, requesting that I would call upon him at his house on the ninth. I waited upon him at the hour appointed.

"His object, he stated, was to say to me that the Government of Great Britain had lost none of its anxiety to see produced among nations a more universal and effective co-operation than had yet been witnessed for the total abolition of the slave trade. It was still carried on, he observed, to an extent that was afflicting.' In some respects, as' the evidence collected by the African Institution and from other sources would show, the voyages were marked by more than all their original outrages upon humanity. It was the intention of the Prince Regent again to invite the United States to negotiate upon the subject, in the hope, notwithstanding what had heretofore passed, that some practicable mode might still be adopted by which they could consent to become, party to the association for finally extirpating the traffic. That I was aware of the addresses which had been presented to his royal highness by both Houses of Parliament at the close of the last session, for the renewal of negotiations with the Governments both of the United States and France to effectuate this most desirable end; that it was his lordship's design to inclose to me, at an early day, copies of these addresses as a foundation upon which to build in the new endeavor which this Government was now prepared to make. In doing so, his object, however, merely would be that of bespeaking my interposition towards making known to the President the measure contemplated, since it was intended that all further negotiation should be carried on at Washington. This he thought indispensable, after the past failure, as it could not be supposed that I was prepared with any new authority or instructions to resume it upon this side of the water; that the new minister, Mr. Canning, who, his Lordship now informed me, was to sail as early in the spring as practicable, would accordingly have the whole subject in charge, and be prepared to enter upon it on his arrival, under ardent hopes for an auspicious termination to his labors.

"I replied that I would, in the same spirit as before, make known the communication to my Government. I adverted again to the obstacles which the Constitution of the United States interposed to the project, and also to the peculiar and extreme caution with which the momentous question of search mingled with it would be looked at throughout every part of the country. I said that these reasons superadded themselves to that derived from the failure of the attempt already made here to give great propriety, as it struck me, to a change of the scene of negotiation; that if anything could be done, it could be done only, or at all events be done best at Washington. That the President, I was sure, continued to possess all his original sensibility to the importance of the subject, and would entertain any proposals, differently modified, that were submitted, with the same anxious dispositions as ever for a favorable result to their objects.

"The conversation went off by a reference on my part to the Holy League. I remarked that, as the Government of Great Britain had declared that the principles of that league had its entire approbation, although it had not formally become a party to it, so the United States, acting within their constitutional limits, had long and earnestly striven, and would, it might be confidently affirmed, though restrained from going hand in hand with Europe, always continue their efforts in the same beneficent spirit for putting down totally the slave trade. It is well known that the Earl of Liverpool, not longer ago than last February, described in the House of Peers the character of this league, as well as the insurmountable impediment which held back this country from signing it. He distinctly declared that, as the signatures were all in the autograph of the respective sovereigns, England, in point of form, could never accede to it, for it was not consistent with her constitution that the Prince Regent should himself sign such an instrument without the intervention of a responsible minister. Upon my reminding Lord Castlereagh of this declaration, which I was the more ready to do since it was your wish that the illustration should be brought into view, he candidly admitted that we, too, doubtless had our constitutional embarrassments, but he nevertheless hoped that such and all others might, by proper modifications of the plan, be overcome."

Mr. Canning to the Secretary of State.

The undersigned, his Britannic Majesty's envoy extraordinary and minister plenipotentiary, took an early opportunity, after his arrival in the city of Washington, to inform Mr. Adams that, in pursuance of Lord Castlereagh's note, dated the 11th November, 1819, communicating to Mr. Rush an address of both Houses of Parliament relating to the African slave trade, he was instructed to bring that important question again under the consideration of the American government, in the hope of its being found practicable so to combine the preventive measures of the two countries as materially to accelerate the total extinction of an evil which both have long united in condemning and opposing.

Mr. Adams will find no difficulty in recollecting the several conversations which have passed between him and the undersigned on this subject; he will remember that the last of those conversations, which took place towards the close of October, was terminated with an assurance on his part that the proposals of the English Government would be taken into full deliberation as soon after the meeting of Congress as the state of public business would allow, with a sincere disposition to remove any impediments which appeared at first sight to stand in the way of their acceptance.

An interval of considerable length having elapsed since that period, the undersigned is persuaded that Mr. Adams will shortly be at liberty to communicate the definitive sentiments of his Government on a subject which is of too deep and too general an importance not to engage the attention and benevolent feelings of the United States.

In this persuasion the undersigned conceived it unnecessary on the present occasion to go over the various grounds which formed the matter of his late conversations with Mr. Adams.

Notwithstanding all that has been done on both sides of the Atlantic for the suppression of the African slave trade, it is notorious that an illicit commerce, attended with aggravated sufferings to its unhappy victims, is still carried on, and it is generally acknowledged that a combined system of maritime police can alone afford the means of putting it down with effect.

That concurrence of principle in the condemnation and prohibition of the slave trade which has so honorably distinguished the Parliament of Great Britain and the Congress of the United States seems naturally and unavoidably to lead to a concert of measures between the two Governments the moment that such co-operation is recognized as necessary for the accomplishment of their mutual purpose. It cannot be anticipated that either of the parties, discouraged by such difficulties as are inseparable from all human transactions of any magnitude, will be contented to acquiesce in the continuance of a practice so flagrantly immoral, especially at the present favorable period, when the slave trade is completely abolished to the north of the equator, and countenanced by Portugal alone to the south of that line.

Mr. Adams is fully acquainted with the particular measures recommended by his Majesty's ministers as best calculated, in their opinion, to attain the object which both parties have in view; but he need not be reminded that the English Government is too sincere in the pursuit of that common object to press the adoption of its own proposals, however satisfactory in themselves, to the exclusion of any suggestions equally conducive to the same end, and more agreeable to the institutions or prevailing opinion of other nations.

The undersigned embraces this opportunity to offer Mr. Adams the assurance of his high consideration.

STRATFORD CANNING.

WASHINGTON, *December 20, 1820.*

The Secretary of State to Mr. Canning.

DEPARTMENT OF STATE, *Washington, December 30, 1820.*

SIR: I have had the honor of receiving your note of the 20th instant, in reply to which I am directed by the President of the United States to inform you that, conformably to the assurances given you in the conversation to which you refer, the proposals made by your Government to the United States inviting their accession to the arrangements contained in certain treaties with Spain, Portugal, and the Netherlands, to which Great Britain is the reciprocal contracting party, have again been taken into the most serious deliberation of the President, with an anxious desire of contributing to the utmost extent of the powers within the competency of this Government, and, by means compatible with its duties to the rights of its own citizens and with the principles of its national independence, to the effectual and final suppression of the African slave trade.

At an earlier period of the communications between the two Governments upon this subject, the President, in manifesting his sensibility to the amicable spirit of confidence with which the measures concerted between Great Britain and some of her European allies had been made known to the United States, and to the free and candid offer of admitting the United States to a participation in these measures, had instructed the minister of the United States residing near your Government to represent the difficulties, resulting as well from certain principles of international law of the deepest and most painful interest to these United States as from limitations of authority prescribed by the people of the United States to the legislative and executive depositaries of the national power, which placed him under the necessity of declining the proposal. It had been stated that a compact giving the power to the naval officers of one nation to search the merchant vessels of another for offenders and offences against the laws of the latter, backed by a further power to seize and carry into a foreign port and there subject to the decision of a tribunal composed of at least one-half foreigners, irresponsible to the supreme corrective tribunal of this Union and not amenable to the control of impeachment for official misdemeanor, was an investment of power over the persons, property, and reputation of the citizens of this country not only unwarranted by any delegation of sovereign power to the national Government, but so adverse to the elementary principles and indispensable securities of individual rights interwoven in all the political institutions of this country, that not even the most unqualified approbation of the ends to which this organization of authority was adapted, nor the most sincere and earnest wish to concur in every suitable expedient for their accomplishment, could reconcile it to the sentiments or the principles of which, in the estimation of the people and Government of the United States, no consideration whatever could justify the transgression.

In the several conferences which, since your arrival here, I have had the honor of holding with you, and in which this subject has been fully and freely discussed between us, the incompetency of the power of this Government to become a party to the institution of tribunals organized like those stipulated in the conventions above noticed, and the incompatibility of such tribunals with the essential character of the constitutional rights guarantied to every citizen of the Union, has been shown by direct references to the fundamental principles of our Government, in which the supreme unlimited sovereign power is considered as inherent in the whole body of its people, while its delegations are limited and restricted by the terms of the instruments sanctioned by them, under which the powers of legislation, judgment, and execution are administered, and by special indications of the articles in the Constitution of the United States, which expressly prohibit their constituted authorities from erecting any judicial courts by the forms of process belonging to which American citizens should be called to answer for any penal offence without the intervention of a grand jury to accuse and of a jury of trial to decide upon the charge.

But while regretting that the character of the organized means of co-operation for the suppression of the African slave trade proposed by Great Britain did not admit of our concurrence in the adoption of them, the President has been far from the disposition to reject or discountenance the general proposition of concerted co-operation with Great Britain to the accomplishment of the common end, the suppression of the trade. For this purpose armed cruisers of the United States have been for some time kept stationed on the coast which is the scene of this odious traffic, a measure which it is in the contemplation of this Government to continue without intermission. As there are armed British vessels charged with the same duty constantly kept cruising on the same coast, I am directed by the President to propose that instructions, to be concerted between the two Governments with a view to mutual assistance, should be given to the commanders of the vessels respectively assigned to that service; that they may be ordered, whenever the occasion may render it convenient, to cruise in company together, to communicate mutually to each other all information obtained by the one and which may be useful to the execution of the duties of the other, and to give each other every assistance which may be compatible with the performance of their own service and adapted to the end which is the common aim of both parties.

These measures, congenial to the spirit which has so long and so steadily marked the policy of the United States in the vindication of the rights of humanity, will, it is hoped, prove effectual to the purposes for which this co-operation is desired by your Government, and to which this Union will continue to direct its most strenuous and persevering exertions.

I pray you, sir, to accept the assurance of my distinguished consideration.

JOHN QUINCY ADAMS.

The Right Honorable STRATFORD CANNING,
Envoy Extraordinary and Minister Plenipotentiary from Great Britain.

FOREIGN VESSELS ENGAGED IN SMUGGLING THROUGH FLORIDA.

COMMUNICATED TO THE HOUSE OF REPRESENTATIVES JANUARY 13, 1821.

TREASURY DEPARTMENT, *January* 11, 1821.

SIR: In obedience to a resolution of the House of Representatives of the 20th ultimo, instructing the Secretary of the Treasury "to state to the House, so far as he has information, the number and tonnage of the French ships which have arrived and are expected to arrive in the course of the present year in the river St. Mary's since the 1st of July last; whether their cargoes are intended for the consumption of the United States and to be introduced within the territories of the same in evasion of the laws; and what further provision he deems necessary to be made by law for the more effectual collection of the revenue on the southern frontier," I have the honor to state that two vessels under the French flag have arrived in the river St. Mary's since the 1st day of July, 1820, and that several others were daily expected at the date of the last communications from that port. The tonnage of those vessels has not been ascertained. Their cargoes consist principally of wine and fruit; and no doubt is entertained that they were intended for the consumption of the United States, and to be introduced into their Territories in evasion of the revenue laws.

Information has been recently received, entitled to the highest credit, that it is contemplated by mercantile adventurers of other nations to establish depositories of West India articles and of slaves, especially of those who for the commission of crimes may be sentenced in those islands to transportation, on the rivers St. John's and Apalachicola and other positions upon the coast of East and West Florida, for the purpose of illicitly introducing them into the United States, and of drawing from thence all articles necessary to the support and convenience of the West India colonists.

The uncertainty of the final result of the negotiations which have been carried on for the acquisition of the Floridas is understood to be the sole cause why those establishments have not already been made. Should the convention for the cession of those provinces to the United States be ratified by the King of Spain the intended scene of operation will be changed, without changing or in any degree weakening the motives which originally suggested the idea of such establishments.

The supply of the West India islands from the United States with articles of indispensable necessity without the intervention of American navigation will continue to be the object of unceasing exertion. In the event of the occupation of the Floridas by the United States, the depositories necessary to effect that object will probably be transferred to the uninhabited shores of the Gulf of Mexico west of the boundary of the United States. In that position the object of an establishment of that nature will be more manifest, whilst the facilities it will afford of evading the laws will be less than those now contemplated. It is for the wisdom of Congress to determine how far a permission on the part of a foreign government to make such establishments within its territories for the manifest purpose of evading the laws of the Union and of corrupting its inhabitants, will justify the adoption of measures necessary to repress the evil, but which at the same time may be considered an invasion of the rights of jurisdiction and territory of such nation. It is probable that the establishment of a depot of foreign articles on the uninhabited shores of the Gulf of Mexico, within the territories of Spain, would become the habitual resort of smugglers and pirates, from whence a contraband trade of the worst description would be attempted to be carried on with the United States. The establishment of two or more military posts on the Sabine and on the Red River, and the active and vigilant exertions of the revenue cutters employed in the Gulf of Mexico might, in a great degree, repress the efforts which would be made to introduce from such depot every species of merchandise into the United States, in evasion of the revenue laws. Should such an establishment be attempted, and no extraordinary measure of repression be authorized, it will be indispensably necessary to establish a new collection district, comprehending the rivers, bays, and shores of the western part of Louisiana, and secure by a liberal salary the services of a man of integrity and enterprise to superintend and enforce the execution of the revenue laws within the district.

I remain, with respect, your most obedient servant,

WM. H. CRAWFORD.

Hon. JOHN W. TAYLOR, *Speaker of the House of Representatives.*

CORRESPONDENCE RESPECTING THE SUPPRESSION OF THE SLAVE TRADE.

COMMUNICATED TO THE HOUSE OF REPRESENTATIVES JANUARY 15, 1821.

To the House of Representatives:

I transmit to the House of Representatives a report from the Secretary of State with the inclosed documents relating to the negotiation for the suppression of the slave trade, which should have accompanied a message on that subject communicated to the House some time since, but which were accidentally omitted.

JAMES MONROE.

WASHINGTON, *January* 12, 1821.

DEPARTMENT OF STATE, *January* 11, 1821.

The Secretary of State has the honor of submitting to the President a copy of a despatch from the minister of the United States at London, inclosing documents relating to the negotiation for the suppression of the slave trade, which should have been transmitted with those accompanying the message of the President to the House of Representatives of the 4th instant, but which were accidentally omitted.

JOHN QUINCY ADAMS.

List of papers.

Extracts of a letter from Mr. Rush to the Secretary of State, dated November 19, 1819.
Lord Castlereagh to Mr. Rush, November 11, 1819.   Copy.
Address from House of Commons, July 7, 1819, to the Prince Regent.   Copy
Address from House of Lords, July 9, 1819, to the Prince Regent.   Copy,
Mr. Rush to Lord Castlereagh, November 16, 1819.   Copy.

Extracts of a letter from Mr. Rush to the Secretary of State, dated

LONDON, *November* 19, 1819.

"I received on the 14th instant a note from Lord Castlereagh, dated the 11th, on the subject of the slave trade.   The addresses from the House of Commons and House of Lords to the Prince Regent came with it.   As the whole purport of this communication has been detailed, beforehand, in my last despatch, I am not aware that any further explanations from me are now requisite.

"The distinct testimony which is borne in both these addresses to the United States, having been first in point of time among the nations of the world to abolish the trade, will be perceived with satisfaction.   It is, so far as I know, the first occasion upon which the acknowledgment has been made in any official or authentic manner by any State in Europe.

"It appeared to me prudent to frame an answer of entire conciliation to Lord Castlereagh's note; and I hope that the spirit which it breathes may meet the President's approbation.   It bears date on the 16th, and is among the inclosures transmitted herewith."

Lord Castlereagh to Mr. Rush.

FOREIGN OFFICE, *November* 11, 1819.

The undersigned, his Majesty's principal Secretary of State for Foreign Affairs, has the honor to transmit to Mr. Rush, by command of the Prince Regent, copy of addresses which were presented by both Houses of Parliament at the close of the last session to his royal highness, which his royal highness has to request Mr. Rush will lay before the President with an intimation that it is the Prince Regent's earnest desire to enter without delay into discussion with the Government of the United States upon the important subject to which those addresses refer, and in the successful accomplishment of which the common feelings and reputation of both States are equally and deeply involved.

It has occurred to the Prince Regent's Government that the difficulties which have hitherto operated to prevent a common system of concert and prevention as directed against the illicit slave trade between the two Governments could be most satisfactorily examined by selecting Washington for the seat of deliberation.   Under this impression the undersigned has delayed to transmit to Mr. Rush the addresses in question till he could accompany them with some proposition to be conveyed to the Government of the United States for giving practical effect to the views of Parliament.

The undersigned having lately had the honor of acquainting Mr. Rush that Mr. Stratford Canning had been selected by the Prince Regent to replace Mr. Bagot as his envoy and minister plenipotentiary in America, and as that gentleman will proceed to his mission early in the spring and will carry with him full instructions on this subject, the undersigned has to request Mr. Rush will invite his Government, on the part of the Prince Regent, to enter, as soon as may be after Mr. Canning's arrival, upon the proposed discussions.

Upon a subject so deeply interesting to humanity the Government of the United States can never require any other impulse than that of its moral principles to awaken it to exertion; but whatever of aid good offices can contribute to smooth the way for an amicable and advantageous proceeding on such a matter the undersigned is convinced will be supplied by Mr. Rush's zeal and enlightened attachment to the success of the great cause which this inquiry involves; and in this view the communication is specially recommended to his personal support and protection.

The undersigned avails himself of this opportunity to renew to Mr. Rush the assurances of his distinguished consideration.

CASTLEREAGH.

MERCURII, 7 *die Julie*, 1819.

Resolved, "That an humble address be presented to his royal highness the Prince Regent to assure his royal highness that we acknowledge with becoming thankfulness the zealous and persevering efforts which, in conformity with former addresses of this House, his royal highness has made for accomplishing the total annihilation of the African slave trade by all the foreign powers whose subjects have hitherto been engaged in it.

"That we also congratulate his royal highness on the success with which his efforts have been already attended; that guilty traffic having been declared by the concurrent voice of all the great powers of Europe, assembled in congress, to be repugnant to the principles of humanity and of universal morality.

"That consequently, on this declaration, all the States whose subjects were formerly concerned in this criminal traffic have since prohibited it, the greater part absolutely and entirely; some for a time, particularly on that part of the coast of Africa only which is to the north of the line; of the two States which still tolerate the traffic, one will soon cease to be thus distinguished, the period which Spain has solemnly fixed for the total abolition of the trade being near at hand; one power alone has hitherto forborne to specify any period when the traffic shall be absolutely abandoned.

"That the United States of America were honorably distinguished as the first which pronounced the condemnation of this guilty traffic, and that they have since successively passed various laws for carrying their prohibition into effect; that, nevertheless, we cannot but hear with feelings of deep regret that, notwithstanding the strong condemnation of the crime by all the great powers of Europe and by the United States of America, there is reason to fear that the measures which have been hitherto adopted for actually suppressing these crimes are not yet adequate to their purpose.

"That we never, however, can admit the persuasion that so great and generous a people as that of France, which has condemned this guilty commerce in the strongest terms, will be less earnest than ourselves to wipe away so foul a blot on the character of a Christian people.

"That we are, if possible, still less willing to admit such a supposition in the instance of the United States, a people derived originally from the same common stock with ourselves, and favored, like ourselves, in a degree hitherto perhaps unequalled in the history of the world, with the enjoyment of religious and civil liberty and all their attendant blessings.

"That the consciousness that the Government of this country was originally instrumental in leading the Americans into this criminal course must naturally prompt us to call on them the more importunately to join us in endeavoring to put an end to the evils of which it is productive.

"That we also conceive that the establishment of some concert and co-operation in the measures to be taken by the different powers for the execution of their common purpose may, in various respects, be of great practical utility, and that, under the impression of this persuasion, several of the European States have already entered into conventional arrangements for seizing vessels engaged in the criminal traffic, and for bringing to punishment those who shall still be guilty of these nefarious practices.

"That we therefore supplicate his royal highness to renew his beneficent endeavors, more especially with the Governments of France and of the United States of America, for the effectual attainment of an object which we all profess equally to have in view; and we cannot but indulge the confident hope that these efforts may yet ere long produce their desired effect; may insure the practical enforcement of principles universally acknowledged to be undeniably just and true, and may obtain for the long afflicted people of Africa the actual termination of their wrongs and miseries, and may destroy forever that fatal barrier which, by obstructing the ordinary course of civilization and social improvement, has so long kept a large portion of the globe in darkness and barbarism, and rendered its connexion with the civilized and Christian nations of the earth a fruitful source only of wretchedness and desolation."

Ordered, "That the said address be presented to his royal highness the Prince Regent by such members of the House as are of his Majesty's most honorable privy council."

'G. DYSON.

" U. D. Dom. Com."

An address precisely similar was voted about the same time and presented, in due course, by the House of Lords.

DIE VENERIS, *Julie* 9, 1819.

Ordered, Nemine Dissentiente, by the lords spiritual and temporal in Parliament assembled, That an humble address, &c.

Resolved, That an humble address be presented to his royal highness the Prince Regent to assure his royal highness that we acknowledge, with becoming thankfulness, the zealous and persevering efforts which, in conformity with former addresses of this House, his royal highness has made for accomplishing the total annihilation of the African slave trade by all the foreign powers whose subjects had hitherto been engaged in it.

That we also congratulate his royal highness on the success with which his efforts have been already attended; that guilty traffic having been declared by the concurrent voice of all the great powers of Europe, assembled in congress, to be repugnant to the principles of humanity and of universal morality.

That consequently, in this declaration, all the States whose subjects were formerly concerned in this criminal traffic have since prohibited it, the greater part absolutely and entirely; some for a time, partially, on that part of the coast of Africa only which is to the north of the line. Of the two States which still tolerate the traffic, one will soon cease to be thus distinguished, the period which Spain has solemnly fixed for the total abolition of the trade being near at hand. One power alone has hitherto forborne to specify any period when the traffic shall be absolutely abandoned.

That the United States of America were honorably distinguished as the first which pronounced the condemnation of this guilty traffic, and that they have since successively passed various laws for carrying their prohibition into effect. That, nevertheless, we cannot but hear with feelings of deep regret that, notwithstanding the strong condemnation of the crime by all the great powers of Europe and by the United States of America, there is reason to fear that the measures which have been hitherto adopted for actually suppressing these crimes are not adequate to their purpose.

That we never, however, can admit the persuasion that so great and generous a people as that of France, which has condemned this guilty commerce in the strongest terms, will be less earnest than ourselves to wipe away so foul a blot in the character of a Christian people.

That we are, if possible, still less willing to admit such a supposition in the instance of the United States, a people derived originally from the same common stock with ourselves, and favored, like ourselves, in a degree hitherto perhaps unequalled in the history of the world, with the enjoyment of civil and religious liberty and all their attendant blessings.

That the consciousness that the Government of this country was originally instrumental in leading the Americans into this criminal course must naturally prompt us to call on them the more importunately to join us in endeavoring to put an entire end to the evils of which it is productive.

That we also conceive that the establishment of some concert and co-operation in the measures to be taken by the different powers for the execution of their common purpose may, in various respects, be of great practical utility, and that, under the impression of this persuasion, several of the European States have already entered into conventional arrangements for seizing vessels engaged in the criminal traffic, and for bringing to punishment those who shall still be guilty of these nefarious practices.

That we therefore supplicate his royal highness to renew his beneficent endeavors, more especially with the Governments of France and of the United States of America, for the effectual attainment of an object which we all profess equally to have in view; and we cannot but indulge the confident hope that these efforts may yet ere long produce their desired effect; may insure the practical enforcement of principles universally acknowledged to be undeniably just and true, and may destroy forever that fatal barrier which, by obstructing the ordinary course of civilization and social improvement, has so long kept a large portion of the globe in darkness and barbarism, and rendered its connexion with the civilized and Christian nations of the earth a fruitful source only of wretchedness and desolation.

Ordered, That the said address be presented to his royal highness the Prince Regent by the lords with white staves.

Mr. Rush to Lord Castlereagh.

London, *November* 16, 1819.

The undersigned, envoy extraordinary and minister plenipotentiary from the United States, has the honor to present his compliments to Lord Castlereagh and to acknowledge the receipt of his note of the 11th of this month.

The copies of the addresses to his royal highness the Prince Regent from both Houses of Parliament, at the close of the last session, respecting the slave trade, which, by command of his royal highness, came inclosed in his lordship's note, with a request that they might be laid before the President, the undersigned will lose no time in transmitting to the Secretary of State with that view. The intimation of its being the earnest desire of the Prince Regent to enter without delay into discussions with the United States upon the important subject to which these addresses refer, and in the successful accomplishment of which the two nations have a common interest, will, the undersigned is persuaded, be met by his Government in the same spirit of elevated benevolence which has given birth to the desire in the mind of his royal highness.

The undersigned cannot avoid expressing his acquiescence in the opinion that the difficulties which have hitherto operated to prevent a system of concert against the illicit slave trade between the two Governments are most likely to be satisfactorily examined by selecting Washington as the seat of deliberation. If, happily, they are of a nature to be removed, it is by such a transfer of the scene of a new endeavor that the best hopes may be formed; and it is hence with a peculiar satisfaction that the undersigned learns that Mr. Canning, when proceeding on his mission to the United States, will carry with him such full instructions upon the whole subject as may prepare him for entering upon the interesting duty of giving effect to the views of Parliament. The undersigned will not fail to make known this intention to his Government by the earliest opportunity that he can command.

Upon a subject so universally interesting to humanity Lord Castlereagh has justly inferred that the Government of the United States can never require any other incentive than that of its own moral impulse to awaken it to exertion. But if upon the present occasion it needed any other, the undersigned must be permitted to say that it would be abundantly found in the friendly and enlarged spirit of this renewed overture from the Government of the Prince Regent, and in the liberal justice rendered to the early and steadfast efforts of the United States in the cause of abolition by the addresses in question from both Houses of the Parliament of this realm. Following up their uniform policy in this great cause, never tired of adopting new expedients of prohibition where new evasions have pointed to their necessity, the undersigned feels happy in being able to state, feeling sure that the information cannot be otherwise than acceptable to the unwearied and useful zeal of his lordship in the same cause, that, besides the law of April, 1818, of which the undersigned had the honor to speak in his note of the twenty-first of December of that year, a subsequent act of Congress, of date so recent as last March, has raised up additional means for the extirpation of the baleful traffic. By this act the President is specially authorized to employ armed vessels of the United States to cruise upon the coasts of Africa, and other new provisions are introduced for intercepting and punishing such delinquent citizens as may be found forgetful of the denunciations of their Government, no less than of their own moral duties, abandoning themselves to the enormity of this transgression. It is well known that the sentiments of the President are in full and active harmony with those of Congress in the beneficent desire of putting a stop to this deep-rooted and afflicting evil. With such pledges before the world, the undersigned cannot err in confidently anticipating that the fresh proposals of the Government of his royal highness will be promptly taken up at Washington under the deepest convictions of their importance, and with every anxious desire for a favorable result that can be made compatible with the Constitution and other interests of the republic.

The undersigned is happy to embrace this occasion of renewing to Lord Castlereagh the assurances of his distinguished consideration.

RICHARD RUSH.

　　　No. 345.　　　[2D SESSION.

BRITISH WEST INDIA AND NORTH AMERICAN COLONIAL TRADE.

COMMUNICATED TO THE SENATE FEBRUARY 7, 1821.

[Confidential.]

To the Senate of the United States:

　　I herewith transmit, in confidence, to the Senate reports from the Secretaries of State and of the Treasury, with the papers containing the correspondence and the information in possession of the Government, the communication of which was requested by the resolution of the Senate of the twenty-third of last month. It is desired that the original letters may, when the Senate shall have no further use for them, be returned.

　　　　　　　　　　　　　　　　　　　　　　　　　　JAMES MONROE.

WASHINGTON, *February* 5, 1821.

———

　　　　　　　　　　　　　　　　　　　DEPARTMENT OF STATE, *February* 3, 1821.

　　The Secretary of State, to whom has been referred the resolution of the Senate of the 23d of January last, requesting a *confidential* communication of correspondence with the British Government relating to the commercial intercourse between the United States and the British American colonies, and other information in the possession of the Government relative to any infraction of the laws imposing restrictions on those relations, &c., has the honor of submitting to the President sundry papers received at this Department and at the Treasury embraced within the objects of the resolution. The correspondence with the British Government preceding the last session of Congress having been then printed by order of the House of Representatives, a copy of that document is among the papers herewith submitted. Among the manuscript papers are several original letters which it is desirable should be returned when the Senate shall have no further occasion for them.

　　　　　　　　　　　　　　　　　　　　　　　　　　JOHN QUINCY ADAMS.

———

　　　　　　　　　　　　　　　　　　List of papers.

1. Printed copy of a letter of the Secretary of State to the Chairman of the Committee on Commerce of the House of Representatives, March 28, 1820, with documents.
2. Report of the Secretary of the Treasury, January 30, 1821, furnishing:
　　(a.) Anonymous, June 15, 1819.
　　(b.) Jehu Hollingsworth to Secretary of the Treasury, St. Eustatius, October 11, 1820.
　　(c.) Jehu Hollingsworth to Secretary of the Treasury, St. Eustatius, November 4, 1820.
　　(d.) Jehu Hollingsworth to Secretary of the Treasury, St. Eustatius, May 24, 1820.
3. Secretary of State to Mr. Rush, May 27, 1820. Extract.
4. Mr. Rush to Secretary of State, July 14, 1820. Extract.
5. Mr. Rush to Secretary of State, August 12, 1820. Original.
6. Letter dated St. Bart's, September 30, 1820.
7. Letter dated St. Bart's, October 14, 1820. Extract.
8. Letter to a gentleman in New York, dated St. Mary's, September 15, 1820.
9. Letter to a gentleman in New York, dated St. Mary's, September 17, 1820.

———

　　　　　　　　　　Report of the Secretary of the Treasury.

　　　　　　　　　　　　　　　　　　TREASURY DEPARTMENT, *January* 30, 1821.

　　The Secretary of the Treasury, to whom has been referred the resolution of the Senate of the 23d instant, requesting from the President of the United States information relative to the commercial relations between the United States and the British colonies in the West Indies and on the continent of North America, has the honor to submit three letters from Jehu Hollingsworth, now and at the date of those letters a resident of the Island of St. Eustatius.

———

　　　　　　　　　　　　　　Anonymous. (a.)

　　　　　　　　　　　　　　　　　　　　　JUNE 15, 1819.

　　The schooner Eliza, Captain Lincoln, entered two hundred and fifty chests of tea at the custom-house, from Boston, and cleared out in two or three days for Lubeck with the same cargo on board without landing, save a few chests. She entered at Boston about the 26th or 27th July from St. Eustatius, *via* St. Andrews; the names of the shippers are unknown to the writer, as well as the port she belongs, but may be discovered at the port she loaded, where her landing certificate must be deposited.

　　It is impossible smuggling can be done to any extent without the knowledge of the captain or mate, or both. The master of every vessel has to take an oath or affirmation to his citizenship, his chief mate does not; if they were both obliged to do this, and also to swear they would not suffer any smuggling on board or from on board, directly or indirectly, during their command, under the pain of never commanding an American vessel afterwards, besides the penalty of perjury, it would certainly have a tendency to check it. They seldom sail more than two or three voyages together before they quarrel; and if an accomplice in smuggling be pardoned and to receive a share as informer, there would be few masters and mates willing to put themselves in the power of each other.

Something in this way may be worth trying in revising the collection law you speak of. Smuggling will always be done with facility whilst the trade to Bermuda and those places so contiguous to our borders are open to our vessels—Lubeck, Halifax, and Campabello on one side, Bermuda and the southward on the other, where arrangements are made for that purpose and put in practice in a few hours at one place, and in six or eight days from the other.

The writer of this is certainly placed in a very delicate situation in the character of a merchant to give any particular information relative to the mode and noted places for smuggling, and regrets he is so, because he is well aware of the great disadvantage it is both to the fair trader and the Treasury.

Having had a good deal of conversation with several captains and supercargoes on the subject of smuggling rum, they all say the price in the States is so low if they had to pay the present duty they would be ruined, and that Congress promised to reduce the double duties laid on in the war at the old rates after peace, which they have not done on rum.

You are particularly requested to destroy this paper after you have taken such notes from it as may answer your purpose.

Jehu Hollingsworth to Secretary of the Treasury. (b.)

St. Eustatius, *October* 11, 1819.

Sir: Your favor of the 31st July has been duly received and contents noted. I beg you will excuse the liberty I take in offering a few remarks relative to the trade between the United States, the British and French islands, and the four free ports of St. Bart's, St. Eustatius, St. Thomas and Curaçoa, trusting they may be acceptable to you.

I have been thirty-seven years in the West India trade, five of that time I resided in this island, to which place I returned in December last, after an absence of twenty-nine years. I have had a fair opportunity in the course of all this time to observe the various unsuccessful attempts on the part of the United States and the British and French Governments to regulate the trade to their islands in American vessels. Since my arrival here I have three times visited St. Kitt's, Nevis, and Antigua, for the double purpose of information and business; the result is, I am satisfied that it is quite in the power of Congress to put the struggle at rest in a summary way, perfectly satisfactory to our merchants and more profitable to the Treasury, by placing the British and French islands exactly on a footing; they are both in the habit of opening their ports to our vessels to suit their own supplies as they may be in want of, and pay for the same in such articles as they see fit. It is impossible they can be made to feel the want of our trade whilst our vessels are only allowed to go there under such circumstances. I am confident that something like the following will fix a settled trade for American vessels to the four free ports above mentioned, which would be to stop the intercourse of American vessels and all vessels belonging to such islands and ports to which the Americans are not allowed to trade exactly on the same terms with their own, at the time of passing this act, unless special permission be given by the President in case any ports should be opened or other unforeseen occurrences in his judgment to make it necessary.

Should Bermuda, Halifax, &c., &c., be closed, the British Government would be obliged to open New Providence for the supply of Jamaica; the American vessels will then have the carrying trade of all her produce to their very doors and theirs back in return.

Whilst I was in Antigua, in February last, a circular came out, dated December 3, 1818, to the collectors of the British islands, ordering them to stop the exportation of all their produce to any foreign free port, save rum; this was done to foster their own carrying trade to Bermuda, Halifax, &c. The consequence is, that the American traders to those free ports can get nothing in return but rum, which has had a tendency to introduce so much of that article into the States that heavy losses are sustained.

As it respects the French islands, they prohibit, in American vessels, the importation of everything except lumber and codfish, and allow them to take away nothing but molasses, whilst their European and island vessels are permitted to bring out to them every other supply from the United States. I am told that an act was passed in Martinique, on the 9th of November, 1818, that in six months after date all foreigners should cease business, and not even be allowed to wind up their own concerns.

I have just received the inclosed proclamation, opening St. Kitt's and Nevis for six months, and am informed that they are apprehensive that Congress will stop our vessels from going there; I should not regret to see that one of the first acts; they cannot suffer for the want of supplies, as they are to be had in abundance at the free ports, this island being only nine miles from St. Kitt's and thirty from Nevis.

With a tender of my services when I can be useful, I am, respectfully, your humble servant,

JEHU HOLLINGSWORTH.

Hon. William H. Crawford, *Secretary of the Treasury of the United States.*

Same to same. (c.)

St. Eustatius, *November* 4, 1819.

I did myself this pleasure on the 11th ultimo, to which I beg leave to refer.

Since then there has been another hurricane at Barbadoes, with a slight touch at St. Vincent's, Grenada, and Tobago, where I am informed it has destroyed much of their ground provisions. Within a few days the British man-of-war brig Fly came down to St. Kitt's, where she met an American schooner laying off and on, flour laden, with a few barrels of herrings. The captain of the Fly gave the American captain liberty to go to Barbadoes with the flour, to which place he proceeded after throwing overboard his herrings.

You may rely upon it those islanders never can be made to feel the want of our trade whilst our vessels are allowed to supply them under any circumstances whatever [save] on equal terms with their own, throughout the whole West India islands. The French European and island vessels bring out more of those articles from America that our vessels are not allowed to take there than they can consume, and have been here and at several other islands with their surplus flour. The Spanish islands lay on a duty of near $10 per barrel on flour, whilst their own vessels pay but $2.

I am certain if Bermuda, Halifax, &c., were closed against our own vessels it would revive our commerce beyond anything our Government can conceive. Some of the British West India ships proceed from Europe to Halifax, St. John's, Quebec, &c., with as many passengers as they can stow, from whence the passengers have to pay a second passage to the States, the expense of which they are kept ignorant of, and by that means land on our shores penniless; the said ships return from these places to the West Indies laden with flour, corn, corn meal, peas, &c., (which our coasters are allowed to take there for them,) and fill up with lumber, codfish, and all sorts of pickled fish, and from the West Indies home, which gives them three freights.

Our vessels are limited to only one passenger to five tons. I presume nothing can in the reach of our Government so effectually foil them in all this as that of making a sweeping law; stop them from coming and our vessels from going to and from all ports and places that are not open to our trade exactly on the same terms with their own. None of them can in justice complain; they will be then all on the same footing, and perhaps there never was a more favorable time for this measure than the present. I am well aware this measure would make a great noise to the eastward, particularly in the coasting interest, because it will spoil some of their sport in that quarter; but if the President sees fit to recommend the measure it will go down in Congress, and will be one of the best commercial arrangements for our country that has been adopted for some time. You will perceive the stopping of our trade along shore will completely break up their treble freighting from Europe and the carrying trade for their West India islands; it will give our European vessels a better chance and our small vessels the carrying trade to the present four ports. This measure may and probably will have a tendency to open New Providence for the supply of Jamaica, or resort to Curaçoa.

Should you think well of this measure, Mr. Horsey, Mr. McLean, and Mr. Seargent, members of Congress, I believe, have some knowledge of the character of the writer, to whom you are respectfully referred.

I am, with much esteem, yours very truly,

JEHU HOLLINGSWORTH.

Hon. WILLIAM H. CRAWFORD, *Secretary of the Treasury.*

Same to same (d.)

ST. EUSTATIUS, *May* 24, 1820.

SIR: I did myself this pleasure on the 11th of October and the 4th of November last. Since then I have not heard from you; but seeing a bill reported to Congress by the Committee on Commerce relative to the trade between the United States and the West Indies, I am encouraged to address you again on the subject. I observed to you in my letter of the 11th of October, 1819, that I was satisfied it was quite in the power of Congress to put the struggle at rest perfectly satisfactorily to our merchants and more profitably to the Treasury. Should that bill pass, and it be agreeable to you, I will give you my ideas of the measures necessary to be adopted by our Government in the West Indies, which I think will effectually put a stop to smuggling along our coast and outports without any extra expense to them, though this certainly could be better done by a personal interview, and I would willingly make a sacrifice of six or seven weeks of my time could I meet with a comfortable vessel going to your neighborhood that would return here again about that time. If I thought such a visit would promote the views of Government and our trade I should not regret the expense and trouble. The bill is well as far as it goes; but from the experience I have had since my residence here (not being an idle spectator) I am certain it is time the United States should take her stand in relation to her trade in this quarter; no half-way measures will answer this purpose.

I know you are aware of much smuggling and abuse in trade from the West Indies, and I know of but one way to stop it, and the sooner this is done the better, because it is the fair traders that support Government, and Government is bound to support them. Let any unprincipled men taste the sweets of smuggling forty or fifty hogsheads of rum at a saving of from forty-five to fifty dollars the passage, and you will find it difficult to stop them *in the States;* it can only be done *here.* It was to this measure I alluded in my letter of the 11th of October, 1819.

ST. EUSTATIUS, *May* 30, 1820.

SIR: The foregoing is a copy of my respects of the 24th instant, per brig Two Brothers, Captain Laws, *via* Philadelphia, all of which I now confirm.

In that letter I stated my willingness to go to Washington for the purpose of having a personal interview with you relative to the trade with those islands. If you deem such a measure necessary, I foresee a visit to St. Bartholomew, St. Thomas, and Curaçoa will be indispensable, as I wish to bring with me all the information I can get to enable me to lay before you the ideas I have in view with more certainty, because, if the bill reported to Congress should become a law, our trade in this quarter will be limited and require immediate attention. It will be the interest as well as sound policy on the part of the United States to be on the best possible terms with the Governors of the four free ports, and I am certain measures may be introduced to answer the purpose of our Government and the Treasury, congenial to both parties, with facility, if well managed here.

I trust you will excuse this liberty; the anxiety I feel in this business will, I hope, be my apology. I cannot help taking deep interest in its fate, as I anticipate great advantage will result to the commerce of our country. Should it be deemed necessary to call me home for a few days, I must beg leave to suggest the propriety of your dropping my sons, Samuel & Thomas G. Hollingsworth, a few lines to that effect, (in confidence, if you choose, as they never require help to keep their secrets.) They have themselves a heavy stake in my hands, as well as others. I am altogether in the commission line. It will be requisite they should send out a suitable person to take charge of my concerns in my absence; there are but few here equal to the trust. I could in that case be off in four or five days—sooner if necessary—with an easy mind.

I am, with much respect, your obedient servant,

JEHU HOLLINGSWORTH.

Hon. WILLIAM H. CRAWFORD, *Secretary of the Treasury of the United States.*

Extract of a letter from Mr. Adams to Mr. Rush, dated

DEPARTMENT OF STATE, *Washington, May 27, 1820.*

"I have the honor of transmitting herewith a copy of the laws passed at the session of Congress which closed on the 15th instant, among which you will find one (page 116) entitled 'An act supplementary to an act concerning navigation,' which has an important bearing upon our commercial relations with Great Britain.

"The subject to which that act relates has so recently and so fully been discussed between the two Governments that it may be superfluous, though it cannot be unreasonable, to assure the British cabinet, as you are authorized to do, that it was adopted with a spirit in nowise unfriendly to Great Britain; and that if, at any time, the disposition should be felt there to meet this country by arrangements founded on principles of reciprocity, it will be met on the part of the United States with an earnest wish to substitute a system of the most liberal intercourse instead of that of counter-prohibitions, which this act has only rendered complete."

Extract of a letter from Richard Rush, envoy extraordinary and minister plenipotentiary of the United States at London, to the Secretary of State.

LONDON, *July 14, 1820.*

"SIR: On the day after receiving your number twenty-four, acknowledged in my last, I addressed a note to Lord Castlereagh requesting an interview, in order that I might proceed to express forthwith the sentiments which the President still continued to cherish in regard to the commercial intercourse between the United States and the British West India islands and North American colonies. He appointed yesterday for me to call upon him.

"I said to him that, after the ample but unfortunately abortive discussions that had taken place between the two Governments upon this subject, it might seem superfluous to recur to it again; but that, nevertheless, I had the instructions of my Government to do so.

"It was merely to reiterate assurances that the supplementary act of Congress, passed on the 15th of May last, for the purpose of rendering more complete the prohibitions which the United States had found it necessary to impose on this intercourse, had been adopted in no unfriendly spirit, but solely with a view to secure to themselves that equal share in the navigation called for by this trade which a just reciprocity was thought to dictate; and that whenever a disposition was manifested here to allow this object to be secured to us by a commercial arrangement between the two countries, it would be met by the President with a sincere and earnest wish to substitute a system of the most liberal intercourse in place of the positive interdictions by statute to which we now finally and with reluctance had resorted.

"His lordship replied that no unfriendly temper was inferred by this Government from the measure in question; far from it. It was considered simply as a commercial regulation of our own, adopted to meet theirs, and not incompatible with the relations of harmony existing between the two nations, and which he hoped to see long continue."

Mr. Rush to the Secretary of State.

LONDON, *August 12, 1820.*

SIR: To what is stated in my number one hundred and thirty, of the Military Academy at Woolwich, I have it now in my power to add, from information acquired since, that the cadets leave that institution at the age of eighteen; that one hundred and fifty is the greatest number that can be educated at it at one time; that it is the only seminary of military instruction in the kingdom for the artillery and engineers, and that it is found adequate for the supply of officers of this branch of the service in the British army, not only for peace, but when the army is upon its full war establishment.

I mentioned in a former despatch (that of the 15th of June) the peculiar situation of the Queen. All attempts at a compromise have as yet utterly failed, and her case has been transferred from the House of Commons to the House of Lords. Before the latter body it is expected to be definitively brought on the 17th of this month. There has been no abatement in the heats which it has produced. The proceedings have taken the shape of a bill of pains and penalties which a committee of the Lords reported against her, and it is under the allegations of this bill that she is to be put upon her trial. Its provisions go to deprive her of all her titles, rights, and prerogatives as Queen Consort of the realm, and to dissolve the marriage between herself and the King. The specific charge laid against her, as worthy to draw down this doom, is the having carried on, while out of the kingdom, an adulterous intercourse with one Bartholomew Bergami, an Italian whom she took into her service and advanced to a high station in her household.

Whatever may have been the degree of criminality in the Queen, the nature of the proceedings against her has been strongly objected to. A fundamental rule of British jurisprudence dictates in theory, and for the most part it is so in fact, a complete separation of the legislative and judicial powers. They are wholly confounded in bills of pains and penalties in like manner as in acts of attainder and confiscation, and the recollections of past history in this country make known that they have usually been the concomitants of fierce and arbitrary times. Thus there are those who, while professing to believe that the conduct of the Queen will prove, on investigation, to have been marked by serious aberrations, protest zealously against the course adopted by her accusers. They say that it is unjust in itself, that it oversteps all the ordinary barriers of the law, and is wounding to the constitution. No subject can obtain a divorce for the cause mentioned in this bill without allowing to the wife the privilege of recrimination, if she choose to avail herself of such a defence. The Queen is cut off from it. She has been refused a list of the witnesses to be produced against her, as well as any specification of the place or places where or of the time when the imputed offence was committed. All parts of continental Europe which she has visited, and that during a space of six years, are left open to her prosecutors on both these material heads of accusation. These things are thought to wear an aspect of harshness. On the other hand, after the trial has actually commenced it is understood that it is not to be unduly hurried to her disadvantage; and that when the testimony against her is closed, she is to be allowed such interval of time as may be deemed reasonable to take her measures for repelling it.

When the bill was reported in the House of Peers Earl Grey declared that their lordships, in consenting to act upon it, had placed themselves, for all that concerned the Queen's hopes of justice and their own responsibilities, in the three-fold and awful situation of legislators, prosecutors, and judges. The debates which were had upon it in the House of Commons were marked by peculiar point and animation. Not to be prolix in recapitulating them, the quotation of a single passage may serve as a sample of their character and also of the boldness of speech which prevails in this body. One of the members, Mr. Bennet, alluding to what had been called, in the course of the debate, the "vindictive feelings" of his Majesty towards the Queen, and to the former having lent himself to an accommodation respecting her alleged adulteries, said, in explicit words, *that no sovereign had ever been so publicly degraded.* The same member cautioned ministers against going on with a proceeding at the consequences of which the boldest mind might shudder.

Upon the whole, whilst I think that it belongs to the genius of this people to exaggerate the incidents of political evil as they do those of political good, yet this question relative to the Queen is, without doubt, one of great difficulty, and, according to present appearances, perhaps also of some peril. Should she be degraded and the King embrace the option that will then be open to him of another marriage, and issue spring from that marriage, there are not wanting those who carry their apprehensions so far as to imagine that the very succession to the monarchy may become ultimately endangered; for succeeding Parliaments have often been known to undo the acts of prior Parliaments passed in violation of the received and popular notions of constitutional right, and because not only the immediate brothers of the King but those who are to descend from them will have the great stake of a throne in the inculcation of this doctrine.

The session of Parliament may be considered as at an end. It has stood adjourned since the middle of last month, and although to meet again on the seventeenth of this, it is not supposed that any further business will be done beyond that which relates to the Queen. Her case, up to the present period, has occupied so much of the time of both Houses that all other proceedings have been diminished in amount and abridged in their general interest. The coronation itself has been postponed, not avowedly but obviously, upon this ground. Nevertheless, there is parliamentary matter, whether in the shape of official acts or authentic discussions, still left for notice. Upon some portion of this, sheltering myself under a practice heretofore not disapproved of in me, I shall again presume to touch, selecting such heads as may serve to denote the current condition of this country in a few of the more prominent features of its industry, power, or wealth, or be at all capable of bearing upon any interests or institutions of our own.

Commerce and shipping seem first to attract attention. There is nothing that can divert Great Britain from these momentous branches of her policy. It was one of the maxims of Sir Walter Raleigh, to which Hume has added his sanction by quoting it, that "whosoever commands the sea, commands the trade of the world; whosoever commands the trade of the world, commands the riches of the world, and, consequently, the world itself." England never for one single instant loses sight of this maxim. Notwithstanding all the causes that have been operating since the peace of Europe to depress foreign and domestic commerce, it appears that the tonnage of the United Kingdom keeps up at above two millions six hundred thousand. This enormous amount is distributed throughout twenty-five thousand vessels, the navigation of which calls for one hundred and seventy thousand seamen.

A committee of the House of Lords, charged with an examination into the business of foreign trade, stated, among other things, in their report, that it had been ascertained from sufficient sources that British vessels were able to enter successfully at the present time into competition as carriers with those of any other nation; that is, in other words, that they are now navigated upon terms more cheap and advantageous than those of any other nation. Upon this position the only comment I will offer is, that, as regards the United States, I imagine that it is not warranted by the fact. I know, from recent correspondence with our consuls, that so far as the direct trade between the United States and Britain is concerned, our vessels continue to have the decided preference inwards and outwards. If I were to say in the proportion of ten to one, I do not think that it would go beyond the truth. It being known that the duties upon the vessels of the two countries are equal, this would seem sufficiently to demonstrate the continuance of our superiority as carriers.

It may be worth while to pause a moment upon the very large proportion of British shipping which it appeared was last year engaged in the trade to her North American colonies. It amounted to fifteen hundred and twenty-five ships, making more than three hundred and forty thousand tons, and giving employ to nearly eighteen thousand seamen. This trade, now become so important to the maritime interests of Britain, and which is confined almost exclusively to the carrying of timber, has doubled itself within the last three years. The tonnage employed between Britain and her West India islands is computed at full two hundred and twenty-six thousand. Thus the extraordinary and awakening fact is set before us that nearly one-fourth part of the whole tonnage of this empire, and much more than a fourth of its foreign tonnage, is employed in sailing over the American seas.

Besides the importance which these colonies of Britain have assumed as auxiliary to her maritime power, it is known that they are also mainly looked to for the support of her West Indies; and it is the latter, in turn, which keep alive in its most beneficial branches her trade with South America. The rapid increase of the trade with the North American colonies is solely owing to the heavy duty with which timber coming from all other places is burdened. It may be proper to mention that Lord Liverpool declared, in debate, that the merchants engaged in this trade would have no claim to the exclusive indulgences which they enjoyed (those arising out of a comparative exemption from duty) longer than 1821, there having been a former understanding with the Board of Trade to that effect. But he did not go so far as to assert positively that they would not be renewed. An act was passed, in July, for authorizing the importation of timber from these colonies for naval purposes entirely free of all duty whatever.

The trade of China and the East Indies did not escape attention in the inquiries into commercial subjects. The footing of our flag in those seas has long attracted the zealous notice of the merchants of this nation. There are constantly new proofs occurring that a trade fettered by monopolies can hold no way with a trade that is free. Great Britain has received a lesson upon this point, in reference to her trade with the East Indies, which adds new force to those which we have taught her. It is a fact that the importations into this country from those regions during the last year by her free traders *transcended in amount the transportations by her East India Company.* It was only in 1815 that the former commenced their competition, and already it has reached this result. They are styled free traders, moreover, only as descriptive of their partial exemption from restraints; for, as yet, successful as have been their endeavors, they have maintained them under the disadvantage of being limited to ships of a particular size as well as to certain defined ports. From the trade to China it is known that the English free traders are still altogether excluded. An American ship can sail without impediment from the river Thames as well as from the Delaware or Hudson for Canton, and return again, not indeed to London, but to Amsterdam, for instance, and there sell her cargo. No private English ship is yet permitted to embark in such a voyage.

I have in former communications dwelt upon the evident anxiety of this country to check our progress in this growing trade, and especially as it has of late been carried on by us among the Asiatic islands and along the path of the Pacific ocean. I have, during my residence in this capital, witnessed the progress of opinion upon this subject, and now we are upon the eve of seeing opinion followed up by counteracting measures. Lord Liverpool declared in the House of Lords that it was in contemplation by ministers to open a direct trade for the benefit of British merchants between India and any part of Europe, Asia, Africa, or America, without the intervention of the company. Malta, he said, had formerly been a sort of depot for this purpose; but under the altered circumstances of this commerce (meaning the success of the Americans, as the English have no other rivals in it) he had now no scruple in saying that any articles that could be imported from India in British ships ought not to be conveyed either through Malta or Great Britain, but be carried directly to any other place. Thus is likely to fall to pieces at last the monopoly to India, which began so far back that I cannot recollect when; I believe in the time of Elizabeth. The monopoly to China, it may be confidently affirmed, will be the next in order to fall.

His lordship declared on this same occasion, whilst discussing the transit trade generally, that he saw no objections to goods coming through this country duty free, or at an impost so low as to be only nominal, with a view of making England henceforth a still greater emporium than she has been of the trade of the world.

I cannot here forbear the remark that the doctrine is rapidly gaining ground among this people that commerce and trade of every description will ultimately flourish best when unshackled. At the moment when a portion of the most enlightened and patriotic citizens of our own country are holding up for our imitation the example of restrictions in this, it seems fit to bring into view that the advocates of restriction here are swerving from their tenets; are beginning to say that England has, in the long run, prospered, not in consequence but in spite of such a system; and that a career of much greater opulence and power is likely to open to her, under its abandonment, provided she can struggle through the dangers with which, as many now begin to say, her very restrictive system itself has at last yoked her. The high duties upon foreign articles imported for use or consumption in the kingdom are, it is true, still kept up; but perhaps less, as is now frequently avowed, with the motive of fostering those made at home than to answer the imperious calls of a revenue made necessary by an overwhelming debt and an extravagant expenditure. That her system of positive prohibition will, at a period not very remote, be abolished, seems to the last degree probable. It will be understood that I rather aim at the duty of transmitting facts and opinions as I find them prevailing, not universally, but more and more in this meridian, than at obtruding any theories of my own on a disputed point of national policy. Perhaps I may add, in further allusion to this subject, that a law has passed removing all restraints upon the exportation from England of gold and silver coin. It will not escape attention that this is at a time when the Government stands pledged to the nation for the early renewal of specie payments.

The imports into the United Kingdom for the last year, calculated at the official rates of valuation, amounted to a fraction more than thirty millions of pounds sterling. The exports for the same period, according to the real and declared value, which stands always at a lower rate than the official value, to a fraction above thirty-five millions. Of this amount the produce and manufactures of the country was in the proportion of four-fifths of the whole. The cotton goods exported amounted to more than sixteen millions, being of about the same value as those manufactured for home use. The cotton manufactures, in 1818, rose as high as forty millions, of which twenty millions were exported: It appeared that the falling off in the exports to the United States for the last three years has been, upon the average, more than three millions sterling each year. Nevertheless, the great and existing importance of our market to the industry of this country may be inferred from the following fact: that of her woolen manufactures for 1819, which were under seven millions sterling, the United States took nearly two millions. The East Indies and China, standing next upon the list, took less than one million; and Germany, which holds the third place, took but half a million.

The finances.—As far as I have been able to follow and can condense, in a word, the statements, to most minds so dark as well as complicated, upon this subject, they exhibit the following result: The whole productive revenue of the three kingdoms amounted during the last year to fifty-four millions of pounds sterling. Great as this sum is, it appears to have been insufficient to meet all the expenses of the Government and keep down the interest upon the debt. Accordingly, a sum of from five to seven millions has been borrowed from contractors; and, as I further understand, the fixed debt has received an addition of seven millions by the recent funding of exchequer bills to that amount. Mr. Wilberforce, talking of the finances, expressed to me once the consolation which he felt from recollecting that the property tax always remained as a resource for Great Britain in a day of extremity. "We have borne it," said he, "heretofore, and can again; and we know that we have in it a clear addition of fifteen millions to our income whenever the chancellor of the exchequer chooses to call it up."

The navy.—This is a subject to which England is ever awake. To other nations, however thoughtless they may now be under it, it is surely also a fearful subject. Let the following declaration of a whig member of Parliament, and a constant advocate of economy and retrenchment, be taken in support of this remark: Mr. Hume, while urging upon the floor of the House of Commons the necessity of a reduction of the naval force, observed that he did not wish any hasty reduction. He only wished a reduction to that point which would leave England in possession of *twice* as many ships-of-war as could be sent forth by the combined efforts of the whole world!

This is an opinion in unison with that of every individual in the country, of whatever party he may be. It is also in unison with the present fact. It appeared from the statements that the navy of Britain consists of six hundred ships, of which number more than ninety are at sea or otherwise employed. The appropriations for building and repairing for the year 1820 amounted to one million five hundred and ninety-four thousand four hundred and eighty pounds. I mention this sum the rather because it exceeds the appropriation of any former year, either of peace or war, in the whole annals of the country, so far as I can hunt up the information. In 1798, when the nation was in the midst of her belligerent exertions upon the ocean, and fighting, as she used to say, for her existence, though it is plain that she was even then fighting for the annihilation of all the other navies of the world, it was but about one-fifth of this sum. Twenty-three thousand seamen were voted for 1820, inclusive of eight thousand marines. Upwards of six millions sterling was the appropriation to cover the entire naval expenditure of the year. Notwithstanding the number of ships, it was stated by the Earl of Darnley, in the House of Peers, that there are none answering to the description of the frigates of the United States of the first class, all being too large or too light to cope with them. The best sort of ship, he said, was that which bore the largest force in the smallest compass. Lord Melville, in reply, did not controvert the statement. He said that a motive of wise economy had restrained them from building ships of the class to which there had been allusion, it having been found cheaper, as well as in all respects more expedient, to repair in an efficient and durable manner ships already built than to build new ones. Yet, in point of fact, they have built new frigates, *and are now building* some, not of the exact size, but *larger* than ours. Should the day of conflict between us again come about, and these ships (being single deckers like our own) be matched against ours, England, who has a thousand tongues to our one, would insist upon it, if successful, that we had been vanquished in equal combat. I may be excused the single digression of remarking that the English historians themselves, in describing the great sea fights with the Dutch in the time of Cromwell and Charles the Second, admit the superiority in size and strength of their own ships over those of the Dutch. The coolness of history may make these admissions, but the gratified enthusiasm of the day will not. We here see that a part of the lasting renown in arms of this nation, where the ocean was the field, hinged, after all, (when we recollect the obstinacy and bloody character of those battles,) upon the size and construction of her ships as compared with those of her enemies; a fact of history that may bear being adverted to by a nation looking to great maritime destinies, and now engaged in the important work of fixing the foundations of her marine.

I understand that at present every vessel of the British navy is built or repaired under cover. I also understand it to be agreed that exposure to atmospheric air is the true remedy for dry rot. Hence their vessels, when laid up in ordinary, are now aired by means of removing the planks. I have myself observed them lying in the Thames, off Deptford, with a couple of the planks stripped off from stem to stern, immediately above the water line, in order to expose them as much as possible to the action of this remedy. The opinion here is, that ships laid up in ordinary under this kind of exposure grow better instead of worse; the excellence and durability of the hulls increasing, as far as the experiments have yet gone, in proportion to the time they remain. I will leave this head, upon which I fear that I may have been tedious, by stating as a fact, to show the anxiety with which this Government prosecutes improvements in its marine, that, besides the emoluments of a profitable office conferred upon him, Sir Robert Seppings has received a grant of five thousand pounds sterling from the House of Commons for the supposed improvements of which he has, within the last few years, been the author.

The army.—The appropriations for the support of the army were between six and seven millions, or about the same as for the navy. "How does it happen," said the chancellor of the exchequer to me one day, "that your army in the United States, which does not exceed ten thousand men, should cost annually the same sum in dollars that ours, which consists of very nearly an hundred thousand men, does in pounds sterling?" whilst the British, as he added, was by far the most expensive army in all Europe; fully six times more so than the Russian, which was the cheapest, and twice as much so as the Dutch, which, next to the British, was the dearest. Two answers were given. The one he supplied himself, viz: the greater proportion of artillery which our army contained, being about three thousand, whilst that for the whole British army in time of peace did not exceed seven thousand. The other was the more familiar one of the comparative dearness of all labor in the United States, and consequently of military labor. He thought that these causes would go some length towards the explanation, but that they would not account for the whole disparity. I was not well enough acquainted with the organization of our army, and all the disbursements that grow out of it, to assign, at the moment, any other causes. When he spoke of our navy being more expensive than theirs, though in a far less degree, I mentioned, as one of the reasons, the more complete equipment of our ships. This he did not gainsay, but admitted that heretofore it had certainly been the case.

There was nothing done by Parliament towards the further extirpation of the slave trade. But an incident occurred in connexion with this subject which may deserve a transient notice. It goes to manifest the sensibility of the British public at any proposal for the liberation of their slaves under circumstances that might interfere with the private rights of individuals to this unhappy species of property. On the 5th of July Sir James Macintosh gave notice in the House of Commons that he would, in the course of the next session, move an address to the throne relative to the manumission of slaves in all parts of the British dominions where slavery still existed. The bare notice of such a motion excited the greatest alarm out of doors. To such an extent did it go that Sir James felt himself obliged to rise on the following day for the purpose of entering into a distinct explanation. He said that it was no general manumission he had contemplated. This would be "a great and dangerous mistake" as to his object. He had only contemplated some alteration in those laws prevailing in the colonies by which the owners of slaves were restricted in the right of voluntary manumission. The public inquietude generally, and especially that in the neighborhood of the West India docks, was, by this explanation, pacified.

The Catholic question, the consideration of the poor laws, the establishment of an extensive system of national education, taken in hand by Mr. Brougham, the state of the criminal jurisprudence, with many other subjects of like general importance, went off until another session, on the express ground of the paramount interest of the discussions respecting the Queen. Contenting myself, therefore, with the summary notices taken of the proceedings, and which I have done in redemption of the promise in my number 123, I find it time to draw to a conclusion.

Regarding the internal condition of the country, I may report that, up to the moment of my writing, it remains rélatively tranquil. The taxed and starving manufacturers have for a while lost sight of their own sufferings in their sympathies for the Queen. Her case seems to have given a new direction to the popular uneasiness; stifling for the time being, though not curing, much of other complaints. What more formidable exasperations it may be feeding time must determine.

Abroad the political elements seem to be all gathering. The revolution of Naples has alarmed Austria. We have the most authentic, may I add the most appalling, evidence that that of Spain has drawn down the decided exprobation of Alexander. Whether the European alliance, with Russia leading the way, meditate a crusade against the freedom of nations is becoming an anxious problem. I have no lights to shed upon it. The part that England may intend to act it will be my duty to watch. If the counsels of her cabinet do not become known to me, it will not be for the want of sedulously improving all the opportunities I can command for ascertaining them. I need not add that my earliest information will always be communicated to the Government.

With the greatest respect, I have the honor to remain your obedient servant,

RICHARD RUSH.

Hon. John Quincy Adams, *Secretary of State.*

Copy of a letter dated St. Bartholomew's, September 30, 1820.

Your esteemed favor of the 20th ultimo has been received, and I have endeavored to meet your wishes, but in the attempt to execute this task am satisfied that I shall completely disappoint the favorable opinion you have been pleased to entertain of my capacity. It is an axiom in politics that all Governments possess the right of making such municipal regulations as may appear most conducive to their interests, without taking into account the inconvenience or even injury they might produce to others; but in exercising this power great circumspection and political sagacity will be found necessary, for as the same weapon may be wielded on the part of others, they may, by countervailing measures, more than counterbalance the benefits that were expected to result from the operation of our own. The late act, however, of the United States Government as applied to the British colonial possessions, particularly their insulated ones, is so plain in its character that there can be but one opinion as to its probable efficacy, for the fact has been substantially verified, not by abstract reasoning or vague supposition, but by fair experiment, founded almost in mathematical demonstration, that they cannot exist without having their wants supplied from the United States either by direct or indirect means. If, therefore, this law shall be vigilantly enforced, and this only for a short period, the British Government must be driven into the necessity of abandoning them, or compelled to *invite* a commercial treaty with the Government of America on grounds of reciprocity, and have no doubt on my mind that this object was in view when the measure now in force was contemplated. There are some, from want of local information, but more from national prejudice, who think the British islands are partially dependent on the United States; that many articles of present consumption may be dispensed with, or can be readily obtained from Europe or their possessions in Canada and Nova Scotia; and, on the whole, that the United States Government may be laughed at in any attempt to render them subservient to her views. The effects of the embargo acts and that of the non-intercourse law have, however, plainly evidenced that these suppositions are founded in error and have nothing of truth to support them; for *notwithstanding* the scandalous violation on the part of American individuals of these salutary and justifiable measures, and the shameful cupidity used by them to afford supplies to our enemy, the most severe distress and want were experienced in all their islands, the greater number in this neighborhood being at times but one remove from starvation; flour, breadstuff generally, rice, corn, lumber, tobacco, and other objects of West India consumption, were only to be had in the smallest quantities and at most extravagant prices. The standing prices were, in all the British Windward islands, for a length of time rarely under the following quotations, (which I know from operations at the time,) but not unfrequently, as greater scarcity prevailed, these prices were considerably augmented : Flour, $30; corn, $3 per bushel; rice, $12; tobacco,* $50; white pine lumber, $100; red oak staves, $80 to $100; white oak staves,* $120; shingles, the common cypress, $16; and every other item at the same high rates, bearing so dreadfully against their estates that no returns from them could meet their contingencies, and complete destruction must have been the consequence of these acts had they not been abused and violated by our own countrymen. Salted fish from Newfoundland, with beef, pork, and butter from Ireland, were the only articles that were or could be furnished by themselves, and they in no abundant quantity and at very exorbitant rates. These facts prove that the *very existence* of these islands, French as well as English, is in the hands of the United States, and that whenever our Government pleases it can dictate its own terms in regard to its trade with them, either by insisting on a free, unrestrained intercourse, or punishing the refusal of this favor by measures of retaliation like the one before us. In the operation of this act some imagine *that the United States will lose* more than what is likely they can gain. Not so in my opinion. On the contrary, it is in every way fraught with public and individual benefit; and this I am satisfied will be substantially proved if it continues any time in force, for the rum and molasses made by the English as well as the French planter *must* find its way to the United States and be eventually lodged there to the benefit of its revenue. These articles cannot be locked up or sent elsewhere, for the United States is the only mart for them, and either through this or other islands not shackled by restraints they will force a passage to their ultimate end and consumption. These articles also form the only resource by which the planter can find the means of immediate subsistence for himself and slaves and provide for the contingent wants of his estate, for the sugar is under such restraints that it must all be shipped to Europe, and none can be had but what is clandestinely obtained.

I have said that Great Britain, under the present restrictive measure, will either have to abandon her islands or have to surrender to the United States a portion of that political pride of which she is so tenacious. Here, however, I find myself, on reflection, at fault, for as long as these *islands* (I allude to those belonging to *Sweden, Holland,* and *Denmark*) can be used as a medium of intercourse with her

---

* Sales of these articles were effected at Trinidad, the former at $100 per cwt. and the other at $180 per M.

own, she will quietly look on, seeing that through them her wants can be supplied, although shackled with additional expenses, particularly as by their means her rum and molasses can be realized in their exchange for objects of supply brought in this indirect way from the United States. In this she will find a most essential accommodation, and without it the consequences I have already pointed out would follow. But in this interchange of commercial matter the United States will enjoy a most decided advantage, for American vessels will be the sole carriers of, in bringing to us and placing in depot here, the produce of its soil, say rice, flour, corn, peas, lumber generally, and a number of other items of West India consumption, to be exchanged for colonial returns, say rum, molasses, sugars,* coffee,* &c., of which again they will be the carriers back, thereby finding double employment and furnishing very handsome means of revenue to their country.

This, according to the sailor phrase, is plain sailing, and must be readily seen by all. I have heard it observed by several that the qualified manner in which this act applies to Bermuda will counteract all that was intended by our Government as bearing on things this way. I think otherwise, for although American vessels are permitted to proceed there with cargoes, they can only bring in return specie or articles the growth and produce of its soil. Now we know that Bermuda produces nothing to be named as objects of exportation, and therefore the spirit of the act extends with as much force against them as against any of their possessions in this neighborhood.

Reasoning from analogy, that is, from the effects of the embargo and non-intercourse acts, and these materially weakened by the cupidity I have mentioned, we can readily calculate on the probable results of this new experiment. I do not for myself believe that any countervailing measures will be adopted by the British Government, but that the islands, already most dreadfully oppressed by their own restraints will be left to work their own salvation. The consequences on this ground will be innocent to both parties, neither having the right to be offended; but, for the plain reasons I have stated, the United States will be the more substantial gainers.

For this poor island†—God put His blessings on it—we may here reap some benefit out of this political collision, for here must be the great storehouse of depot, provided our Governor plays his cards with judgment. Of this we can have no doubt, for he is known to be warmly interested in the success of our commercial operations and will be ready to adopt such measures as will bear against our rivals and be the means of turning matters into this channel. As a motive of policy to effect this end, the custom-house fees‡ should be reduced as low as possible and every encouragement held out to invite the visits of strangers, particularly those engaged in trade. This island enjoys many local advantages which neither Statia nor St. Thomas possess, and with the fostering kindness of its chief, whose virtues are known to all, these advantages may be improved and turned to general benefit. I am satisfied, by a little dexterous management on the part of the Government here, we may secure all the business from windward, that is, in receiving their produce, for it must come here or go to St. Thomas and Statia, and furnishing them with American supplies. This would be giving employment to many now idling time for the want of something to occupy their industry. But I forbear further observations, for you must be sufficiently fatigued with what has been already intruded on you. My only motive for using this freedom was to show you that I was not under the influence of affected modesty, though in fixing this point I have run the hazard of being questioned for my arrogance. I know you will judge me fairly on either of these points. Like yourself, I take a warm interest in the rising honor of our common country, and that its star-spangled banner may wave for ages over it and extend its benign blessings to the remotest parts of the world is the fervent prayer of, dear sir, your most obedient and humble servant.

Extracts of a letter dated St. Bartholomew's, October 14, 1820.

"The probability of this island becoming the depot for the supplies of the adjacent British colonies, and the prospect of commercial advantages which will be derived therefrom, have induced me to establish myself here, and I embraced the first opportunity and leisure moment to communicate to the Hon. Secretary of State all the information I have acquired and, in my opinion, may deserve his notice."

"The Swedes and Danes will, in some measure, become the carriers of provisions, &c., for the supply of the aforesaid colonies; for since my arrival here more than thirty British vessels have assumed the Swedish flag, and, no doubt, in St. Thomas to a greater extent.

"Most of the British merchants and planters with whom I have conversed assure me that there are immense supplies of provisions accumulated in Bermuda, sufficient to serve them for some time. They also calculate on being supplied by the *circuitous* route of the *mother country*, and have attempted to prove to me that the expenses that way will not exceed a direct freight from the United States. That they will receive considerable in that manner cannot be doubted, but by no means to the extent they calculate on. Their necessities now must be great, as the article of flour in Antigua is selling at $12, and corn meal at $40. You may therefore form some idea what will be the situation of the planters three or four months hence."

St. Mary's, September 15, 1820.

Dear Sir: It may interest you to know that we have a port of entry established on the immediate frontier of East Florida, and at a very eligible situation. The French ship Apollon, Captain Eow, from Havre de Grace, is now moored there, and regularly entered. Not having had a designating name we call it Port St. Joseph, and we expect this name to be approved of by our Governor.

It lies on the west side of Bell's river, (an arm of St. Mary's river,) at Low's plantation on the main, situated about midway between the town of Fernandina and St. Mary's, and a more safe and commodious harbor than either of them; entrance by St. Mary's bar; a good depth of water up Bell's river by the way of the harbor of Fernandina, and up Jolly's river by the way of St. Mary's river as far as Point Peter;

* Often taken off clandestinely and brought here.
† As I intend to make it my fixed residence.
‡ As they now are, they are less than at St. Thomas.

very convenient for supplies of fresh provisions from the back country; wood and water, and the latter excellent.

Duties on imports and exports not the growth of the province low, and those laid on very low rates of valuation, and the cargoes admitted by the captain's manifest; products of the province are free of duties; port charges reasonable.

As I promised you in my last letter by mail, I have delivered Captain Hollbrook, of brig Harmony, a large letter for you on the topography of East Florida. It is, I suppose, a fortnight since he has it, and that he has been kept and is still awaiting a termination of the very threatening state of the weather.

I will inform you from time to time how we progress with Port St. Joseph, (it is under my charge,) for if we shall realize our commercial anticipations it may be worth your while to take a stand among us. We have reason for considerable expectations in the French trade, but much more in that of the West Indies. Merchants of Jamaica who are here say that the British restriction on their trade with the Spanish North American colonies can be easily removed or got over once there is an opening this way. They can get hard wood from other places, but yellow pine only from Florida. Nor have we any reason to apprehend the acts of Uncle Sam, for the treaty is the rock we build on, and which supported us during the strong measures of Mr. Jefferson's embargo and non-intercourse and the war with Great Britain. This is but a continuation of the arrangement under which we acted to a vast extent from 1808 to 1815, a long practice and strong precedent.

You must excuse my hurried mode of writing, or I will write you less and take more pains.

Yours, sincerely.

At the moment of closing this letter I was informed that the brig Harmony was in a bad way; as her departure from hence, or her reaching New York, if she sailed, was very questionable, from leakage, I immediately went and got your letter from on board, and have this moment returned from delivering it into the care of Captain E. Ellingswood, of ship Dryade, waiting for a wind. I shall, notwithstanding the new arrangement, hold a residence here as Spanish vice consul.

Sr. Mary's, September 17, 1820.

Dear Sir: Since putting my other letter to you into this mail it has occurred to me to mention that you might render us much good service by getting into some of your public prints—suppose the "Evening Post"—an extract of some part of my letter, without mentioning names, or such observations on the subject as your better judgment may suggest. Our Government is averse to our meddling openly in the public prints of the United States, but the sooner it is known that we have a port of entry hereabouts the better. I have officially communicated to the collector of this place information of our establishment, in order to prevent embarrassment in the beginning that might grow out of instructions that may have been founded on our not having a port of entry, a copy of which he informs me will go to headquarters by this mail. The sooner this information circulates in the United States the sooner it will get to France, where it may have a great tendency to delay the negotiations on an adjustment of this tonnage quarrel, for I believe that French vessels can now get their cargoes in Florida under these new regulations on better terms than they did in the United States before the one hundred franc act was levied on them. This I say to you, who I consider as more than half a Floridian, and who, I hope, will be ere long participating fully in the privileges of a Spanish citizen. If a cession of Florida should be arranged in the next meeting of Congress, which, by the by, is very questionable, very well; and if not, let us have something else to go on. While we hope for the best let us prepare for the worst.

Yours, sincerely.

16th Congress.]   **No. 346.**   [2d Session.

SUPPRESSION OF THE SLAVE TRADE—CONFERENCE OF FOREIGN GOVERNMENTS ON THE SUBJECT.

COMMUNICATED TO THE HOUSE OF REPRESENTATIVES FEBRUARY 9, 1821.

Mr. Hemphill, from the Committee to which is referred so much of the President's message as relates to the slave trade, and to which are referred the two messages of the President transmitting, in pursuance of the resolution of the House of Representatives of the 4th of December, a report of the Secretary of State, and inclosed documents, relating to the negotiation for the suppression of the slave trade, reported:

That the committee have deemed it advisable, previous to entering into a consideration of the proposed co-operation to exterminate the slave trade, to take a summary review of the Constitution and laws of the United States relating to this subject. It will disclose the earnestness and zeal with which this nation has been actuated, and the laudable ambition that has animated her councils to take a lead in the reformation of a disgraceful practice, and one which is productive of so much human misery; it will, by displaying the constant anxiety of this nation to suppress the African slave trade, afford ample testimony that she will be the last to persevere in measures wisely digested to effectuate this great and most desirable object, whenever such measures can be adopted in consistency with the leading principles of her local institutions.

In consequence of the existence of slavery in many of the States when British colonies, the habits and means of carrying on industry could not be suddenly changed; and the Constitution of the United

States yielded to the provision that the migration or importation of such persons as any of the States now existing shall think proper to admit shall not be prohibited by the Congress prior to the year 1808.

But long antecedent to this period Congress legislated on the subject wherever its power extended, and endeavored, by a system of rigorous penalties, to suppress this unnatural trade.

The act of Congress of the 22d of March, 1794, contains provisions that no citizen or citizens of the United States, or foreigner, or any other person coming into or residing within the same, shall, for himself or any other person whatsoever, either as master, factor, or owner, build, fit, equip, load, or otherwise prepare any ship or vessel within any port or place of the United States, nor shall cause any ship or vessel to sail from any port or place within the same for the purpose of carrying on any trade or traffic in slaves to any foreign country; or for the purpose of procuring from any foreign kingdom, place, or country the inhabitants of such kingdom, place, or country, to be transported to any foreign country, port, or place whatever, to be sold or disposed of as slaves, under the penalty of the forfeiture of any such vessel, and of the payment of large sums of money by the persons offending against the directions of the act.

By an act of the third of April, 1798, in relation to the Mississippi Territory, to which the constitutional provision did not extend, the introduction of slaves, under severe penalties, was forbidden, and every slave imported contrary to the act was to be entitled to freedom.

By an act of the 10th of May, 1800, the citizens or residents of this country were prohibited from holding any right or property in vessels employed in transporting slaves from one foreign country to another on pain of forfeiting their right of property, and also double the value of that right in money, and double the value of their interest in the slaves; nor were they allowed to serve on board of vessels of the United States employed in the transportation of slaves from one country to another under the punishment of fines and imprisonment, nor were they permitted to serve on board of foreign ships employed in the slave trade. By this act, also, the commissioned vessels of the United States were authorized to seize vessels and crews employed contrary to the act.

By an act of the 28th of February, 1803, masters of vessels were not allowed to bring into any port (where the laws of the State prohibited the importation) any negro, mulatto, or other person of color, not being a native, a citizen, or registered seaman of the United States, under the pain of penalties; and no vessel having on board persons of the above description was to be admitted to an entry, and if any such person should be landed from on board of any vessel the same was to be forfeited.

By an act of the 2d of March, 1807, the importation of slaves into any port of the United States was to be prohibited after the first of January, 1808, the time prescribed by the constitutional provision. This act contains many severe provisions against any interference or participation in the slave trade, such as heavy fines, long imprisonments, and the forfeitures of vessels; the President was also authorized to employ armed vessels to cruise on any part of the coast where he might judge attempts would be made to violate the act, and to instruct the commanders of armed vessels to seize and bring in vessels found on the high seas contravening the provisions of the law.

By an act of the 20th of April, 1818, the laws in prohibition of the slave trade were further improved. This act is characterized with a peculiarity of legislative precaution, especially in the eighth section, which throws the labor of proof upon the defendant that the colored persons brought into the United States by him had not been brought in contrary to the laws.

By an act of the 3d of March, 1819, the power is continued in the President to employ the armed ships of the United States to seize and bring into port any vessel engaged in the slave trade by citizens or residents of the United States, and such vessels, together with the goods and effects on board, are to be forfeited and sold and the proceeds to be distributed in like manner as is provided by law for the distribution of prizes taken from an enemy, and the officers and crew are to undergo the punishments inflicted by previous acts. The President, by this act, is authorized to make such regulations and arrangements as he may deem expedient for the safe keeping, support, and removal beyond the limits of the United States of all such negroes, mulattoes, or persons of color as may have been brought within its jurisdiction, and to appoint a proper person or persons residing on the coast of Africa as agent or agents for receiving the negroes, mulattoes, or persons of color delivered from on board of vessels seized in the prosecution of the slave trade.

And, in addition to all the aforesaid laws, the present Congress, on the 15th of May, 1820, believing that the then existing provisions would not be sufficiently available, declared that if any citizen of the United States, being of the crew or ship's company of any foreign ship or vessel engaged in the slave trade, or any person whatever, being of the crew or ship's company of any ship or vessel owned in the whole or in part, or navigated for or in behalf of any citizen or citizens of the United States, shall land from any such ship or vessel, and on foreign shore seize any negro or mulatto not held to service or labor by the laws of either of the States or Territories of the United States with intent to make such negro or mulatto a slave, or shall decoy or forcibly bring or carry, or shall receive such negro or mulatto on board any such ship or vessel with intent as aforesaid, such citizen or person shall be adjudged a pirate, and on conviction *shall suffer death.*

The immoral and pernicious practice of the slave trade has attracted much public attention in Europe within the last few years, and in a congress at Vienna, on the 8th of February, 1815, five of the principal powers made a solemn engagement, in the face of mankind, that this traffic should be made to cease, in pursuance of which these powers have enacted municipal laws to suppress the trade. Spain, although not a party to the original engagement, did soon after, in her treaty with England, stipulate for the immediate abolition of the Spanish slave trade to the north of the equator, and for its final and universal abolition on the 30th of May, 1820.

Portugal likewise, in her treaty in 1817, stipulated that the Portuguese slave trade on the coast of Africa should entirely cease to the northward of the equator, and engaged that it should be unlawful for her subjects to purchase or trade in slaves, except to the southward of the line. The precise period at which the entire abolition is to take place in Portugal does not appear to be finally fixed; but the Portuguese ambassador, in the presence of the congress at Vienna, declared that Portugal, faithful to her principles, would not refuse to adopt the term of eight years, which term will expire in the year 1823.

At this time, among the European States, there is not a flag which can legally cover this inhuman traffic north of the line; nevertheless, experience has proved the inefficacy of the various and rigorous laws which have been made in Europe and in this country, it being a lamentable fact that the disgraceful practice is even now carried on to a surprising extent. During the last year Captain Trenchard, the commander of the United States sloop-of-war Cyane, found that part of the coast of Africa which he visited lined with vessels engaged, as it is presumed, in this forbidden traffic; of these he examined many, and five, which appeared to be fitted out on American account, he sent into the jurisdiction of the United States for adjudication; each of them, it is believed, has been condemned, and the commanders of two of them have been sentenced to the punishment prescribed by the laws of the United States.

The testimony recently published, with the opinion of the presiding judge of the United States court of the southern district in the State of New York, in the case of the schooner Plattsburg, lays open a scene of the grossest fraud that could be practiced to deceive the officers of Government and conceal the unlawful transaction.

The extension of the trade for the last twenty-five or thirty years must, in a degree, be conjectural; but the best information that can be obtained on the subject furnishes good foundation to believe that during that period the number of slaves withdrawn from western Africa amounts to upwards of a million and a half; the annual average would be a mean somewhere between fifty and eighty thousand.

The trade appears to be lucrative in proportion to its heinousness; and, as it is generally inhibited, the unfeeling slave dealers, in order to elude the laws, increase its horrors; the innocent Africans, who are mercilessly forced from their native homes in irons, are crowded in vessels and situations which are not adapted for the transportation of human beings, and this cruelty is frequently succeeded, during the voyage of their destination, with dreadful mortality. Further information on this subject will appear in a letter from the Secretary of the Navy, inclosing two other letters, marked 1 and 2, and also by the extract of a letter from an officer of the Cyane, dated April 10, 1820, which are annexed to this report. While the slave trade exists there can be no prospect of civilization in Africa.

However well disposed the European powers may be to effect a practical abolition of the trade, it seems generally acknowledged that, for the attainment of this object, it is necessary to agree upon some concerted plan of co-operation; but, unhappily, no arrangement has as yet obtained universal consent.

England has recently engaged in treaties with Spain, Portugal, and the Netherlands, in which the mutual right of visitation and search is exchanged; this right is of a special and limited character, as well in relation to the number and description of vessels as to space, and to avoid possible inconveniences no suspicious circumstances are to warrant the detention of a vessel; this right is restricted to the simple fact of slaves being on board.

These treaties contemplate the establishment of mixed courts formed of an equal number of individuals of the two contracting nations, the one to reside in a possession belonging to his Britannic Majesty, the other within the territory of the other respective power. When a vessel is visited and detained it is to be taken to the nearest court, and, if condemned, the vessel is to be declared a lawful prize, as well as the cargo, and are to be sold for the profit of the two nations; the slaves are to receive a certificate of emancipation and to be delivered over to the Government on whose territory the court is which passes sentence, to be employed as servants or free laborers. Each of the Governments binds itself to guaranty the liberty of such portion of these individuals as may be respectively assigned to it. Particular provisions are made for remuneration in case vessels are not condemned after trial, and special instructions are stipulated to be furnished to commanders of vessels possessing the qualified right of visitation and search.

These powers entertain the opinion that nothing short of the concession of a qualified right of visitation and search can practically suppress the slave trade. An association of armed ships is contemplated, to form a species of naval police to be stationed principally in the African seas, where the commanders of the ships will be enabled to co-operate in harmony and concert.

The United States has been earnestly invited by the principal Secretary for Foreign Affairs of the British Government to join in the same or similar arrangements, and this invitation has been sanctioned and enforced by a unanimous vote of the Houses of Lords and Commons in a manner that precludes all doubts as to the sincerity and benevolence of their designs.

In answer to this invitation the President of the United States has expressed his regret that the stipulations in the treaties communicated are of a character to which the peculiar situation and institutions of the United States do not permit them to accede.

The objections made are contained in an extract of a letter from the Secretary of State under date of November 2, 1818, in which it is observed that, "in examining the provisions of the treaties communicated by Lord Castlereagh, all the essential articles appear to be of a character not adaptable to the institutions or to the circumstances of the United States. The powers agreed to be reciprocally given to the officers of the ships-of-war of either party to enter, search, capture, and carry into port for adjudication the merchant vessels of the other, however qualified and restricted, is most essentially connected with the institution by each treaty of two mixed courts, one of which to reside in the external or colonial possession of each of the two parties, respectively. This part of the system is indispensable to give it that character of reciprocity, without which the right granted to the armed ships of one nation to search the merchant vessels of another would be rather a mark of vassalage than of independence. But to this part of the system the United States, having no colonies either on the coast of Africa or in the West Indies, cannot give effect. That by the Constitution of the United States it is provided that the judicial power of the United States shall be vested in a Supreme Court and in such inferior courts as the Congress may, from time to time, ordain and establish. It provides that the judges of these courts shall hold their offices during good behavior, and that they shall be removable by impeachment, on conviction of crimes and misdemeanors. There may be doubts whether the power of the Government of the United States is competent to institute a court for carrying into execution their penal statutes beyond the territories of the United States, a court consisting partly of foreign judges not amenable to impeachment for corruption, and deciding upon statutes of the United States without appeal.

"That the disposal of the negroes found on board of the slave trading vessels which might be condemned by the sentence of these mixed courts cannot be carried into effect by the United States; for if the slaves of vessels condemned by the mixed courts should be delivered over to the Government of the United States as freemen, they could not, but by their own consent, be employed as servants or free laborers. The condition of the blacks being in this Union regulated by the municipal laws of the separate States, the Government of the United States can neither guaranty their liberty in the States where they could only be received as slaves, nor control them in the States where they would be recognized as free. That the admission of a right in the officers of foreign ships-of-war to enter and search the vessels of the United States in time of peace, under any circumstances whatever, would meet with universal repugnance in the public opinion of this country; that there would be no prospect of a ratification by advice and consent of the Senate to any stipulation of that nature; that the search by foreign officers even in time of war is so obnoxious to the feelings and recollections of this country that nothing could reconcile them to the extension of it, however qualified or restricted, to a time of peace; and that it would be viewed in a still more aggravated light if, as in the treaty with the Netherlands, connected with a formal admission that even vessels under convoy of ships-of-war of their own nation should be liable to search by the ships-of-war of another."

The committee will observe, in the first instance, that a mutual right of search appears to be indispensable to the great object of abolition; for while flags remain as a cover for this traffic against the right of search by any vessel except of the same nation the chance of detection will be much less than it would be if the right of search was extended to vessels of other powers; and as soon as any one nation should cease to be vigilant in the discovery of infractions practiced on its own code, the slave dealers would avail themselves of a system of obtaining fraudulent papers and concealing the real ownership under the cover of such flags, which would be carried on with such address as to render it easy for the citizens or subjects of one State to evade their own municipal laws; but if a concerted system existed, and a qualified right of mutual search was granted, the apprehension of these piratical offenders would be reduced to a much greater certainty, and the very knowledge of the existence of an active and vigorous system of co-operation would divert many from this traffic, as the unlawful trade would become too hazardous for profitable speculation.

In relation to any inconveniences that might result from such an arrangement, the commerce of the United States is so limited on the African coast that it could not be much affected by it; and as it regards economy, the expense of stationing a few vessels on that coast would not be much greater than to maintain them at any other place.

The committee have briefly noticed the practical results of a reciprocal right of search as it bears on the slave trade, but the objection as to the propriety of ceding this right remains. It is with deference that the committee undertake to make any remarks upon it. They bear in recollection the opinions entertained in this country on the practice of searching neutral vessels in time of war, but they cannot perceive that the right under discussion is, in principle, allied in any degree to the general question of search; it can involve no commitment, nor is it susceptible of any unfavorable inference on that subject; and even if there were any affinity between the cases, the necessity of a special agreement would be inconsistent with the idea of existing rights; the proposal itself, in the manner made, is a total abandonment on the part of England of any claim to visit and search vessels in a time of peace, and this question has been unequivocally decided in the negative by her admiralty courts.

Although it is not among the objections that the desired arrangement would give any color to a claim or right of search in time of peace, yet, lest the case in this respect may be prejudiced in the minds of any, the committee will observe that the right of search in time of peace is one that is not claimed by any power as a part of the law of nations; no nation pretends that it can exercise the right of visitation and search upon the common and unappropriated parts of the sea except upon the belligerent claim. A recent decision in the British admiralty court in the case of the French slave ship Le Louis is clear and decisive on this point. The case is annexed to this report.

In regard, then, to the reciprocal right wished to be ceded, it is reduced to the simple inquiry whether, in practice, it will be beneficial to the two contracting nations. Its exercise, so far as it relates to the detention of vessels, as it is confined to the fact of slaves being actually on board, precludes almost the possibility of accident or much inconvenience.

In relation also to the disposal of the vessels and slaves detained, an arrangement perhaps could be effected so as to deliver them up to the vessels of the nation to which the detained vessel should belong. Under such an understanding the vessels and slaves delivered to the jurisdiction of the United States might be disposed of in conformity with the provisions of our own act of the 3d of March, 1819, and an arrangement of this kind would be free from any of the other objections.

An exchange of the right of search, limited in duration or to continue at pleasure for the sake of experiment, might, it is anxiously hoped, be so restricted to vessels and seas and with such civil and harmonious stipulations as not to be unacceptable.

The feelings of this country on the general question of search have often been roused to a degree of excitement that evinces their unchangeable character; but the American people will readily see the distinction between the cases. The one in its exercise to the extent claimed will ever produce irritation and excite a patriotic spirit of resistance; the other is amicable and charitable; the justness and nobleness of the undertaking are worthy of the combined concern of Christian nations.

The detestable crime of kidnapping the unoffending inhabitants of one country and chaining them to slavery in another is marked with all the atrociousness of piracy, and as such it is stigmatized and punishable by our own laws.

To efface this reproachful stain from the character of civilized mankind would be the proudest triumph that could be achieved in the cause of humanity. On this subject the United States, having led the way, owe it to themselves to give their influence and cordial co-operation to any measure that will accomplish the great and good purpose; but this happy result, experience has demonstrated, cannot be realized by any system except a concession by the maritime powers to each other's ships-of-war of a qualified right of search. If this object was generally attained, it is confidently believed that the active exertions of even a few nations would be sufficient entirely to suppress the slave trade.

The slave dealers could be successfully assailed on the coast upon which the trade originates, as they must necessarily consume more time in the collection and embarcation of their cargoes than in the subsequent distribution in the markets for which they are destined. This renders that coast the most advantageous position for their apprehension; and, besides, the African coast frequented by the slave ships is indented with so few commodious or accessible harbors, that, notwithstanding its great extent, it could be guarded by the vigilance of a small number of cruisers; but if the slave ships are permitted to escape from the African coast and to be dispersed to different parts of the world their capture would be rendered uncertain and hopeless.

The committee, after much reflection, offer the following resolution:

Resolved by the Senate and House of Representatives of the United States of America in Congress assembled, That the President of the United States be requested to enter into such arrangements as he may deem suitable and proper, with one or more of the maritime powers of Europe, for the effectual abolition of the African slave trade.

NAVY DEPARTMENT, *February* 7, 1821.

SIR: I have the honor to transmit to you such information as this Department affords upon the subject of the slave trade, in answer to your letter of the 30th of January last.

The inclosed copy, No. 1, of a circular to the United States district attorneys and marshals has been answered, generally, that no slaves have been brought into their respective districts, with the exception of Maryland, South Carolina, and Georgia; answers have not been received from Louisiana.

There appears to have been partial captures made upon the coast and in the neighborhood of Georgia by the public vessels of the United States; the slaves in some cases have been bonded out to individuals until adjudication.

The slave trade has been checked by our cruisers upon the southern coasts of the United States, and no great attempts appear to have been made to introduce slaves through illicit channels.

There are now in charge of the marshal of Georgia two hundred and forty-eight Africans, taken out of a South American privateer, the General Ramirez, whose crew mutinied and brought the vessel into St. Mary's, Georgia; sixty more are in the custody of the marshal, detained and maintained in the vicinity of Savannah; forty or fifty more have been sent out of that State; under what orders it is not known.

The ships cruising on the coast of Africa during the last year captured the following vessels engaged in the slave trade, but having no slaves on board at the time, viz: Schooners Endymion, Platts-burgh, Science, Esperanza, and brig Alexander.

These vessels have been condemned in the district courts of New York and Massachusetts, and their commanders sentenced to fine and imprisonment under the acts of Congress.[*]

The most detailed information that has been communicated to this Department in relation to the slave trade will be found in the inclosed copy, No. 2, from the late United States agent, then resident in Africa, but since deceased.

I have the honor to be, with great respect, sir, your most obedient servant,

SMITH THOMPSON.

Hon. JOSEPH HEMPHILL,
   Chairman of the Committee on the Slave Trade, House of Representatives.

No. 1.

NAVY DEPARTMENT, *January* 13, 1821.

SIR: I duly received your letter of 25th November last, an answer to which has been delayed by the urgency of public business.

I request you will be pleased to inform me what disposition has been made of the two hundred and fifty-eight Africans mentioned in your letter, and what expense, if any, has been incurred for their safe keeping. It is very desirable to save further expenses by an early decision of their case.

I wish also to be informed upon the cases of all others within your jurisdiction and coming within the execution of the laws for prohibiting and suppressing the slave trade.

I am, very respectfully, your obedient servant,

SMITH THOMPSON.

JOHN H. MOREL, Esq., *Marshal of the district of Georgia, Savannah.*

No. 2.

Extract of a letter from the Rev. Samuel Bacon to the Secretary of the Navy.

CAMPELAR, (SHERBRO ISLAND,) *March* 21, 1820.

"The slave trade is carried on briskly in this neighborhood; had I authority so to do, I could take a vessel lying within the floating of one tide, say 25 miles from us, in the Shebar, under American colors, taking in a cargo of slaves. Their policy is to come with a cargo of goods suited to the market, deliver it to a slave factor on shore, and contract for slaves. They then lay at anchor in the river or stand out to sea for a specified number of days, till the slaves are all procured and brought to the beach and placed under a hovel or shed prepared for the purpose, all chained two and two. At the appointed time, or on a concerted signal, the vessel comes in and takes her slaves on board, and is off in an hour. This is rendered necessary, as they cannot be seized unless they have slaves on board, and they are watched by the cruisers so as to be taken when they have slaves with them. The Augusta (the schooner I purchased) is a vessel of 104 tons, a swift sailer, and was intended to take a cargo of 100; she has a camboose fitted to boil rice in large quantities. Slaves receive one pint each per day."

UNITED STATES SHIP CYANE, *off Sierra Leone, April* 10, 1820.

During our stay at Sierra Leone, the European gentlemen who were residents at the place treated us with the utmost respect, striving who should be most forward in attention and hospitality. A party was formed by those gentlemen to show our officers the interior settlements, and from their report on their return I learned the extent of the colony and the benevolent philanthropy of the British nation in

[*] The information contained in this paragraph is not derived from any official source; it is nevertheless believed to be correct.

alleviating the miseries of the oppressed and ignorant Africans. Not less than six thousand captured Africans have been landed at this settlement by the British ships-of-war. On their arrival, those of a proper age are named and sent to the adjacent villages. A house and lot is appointed to each family, and they are supported one year by government, at the expiration of which they are obliged to look out for themselves. The captured children are also sent to the villages, where they are kept at school till married, which is always at an early age. At the head of each village is a missionary, who receives his annual support from the Government, and who acts in the double capacity of minister and schoolmaster.

Lieutenant Cooper and myself walked through the villages situated to the westward of Sierra Leone. We landed at King Town, the former residence of King Tom. The house in which the king resided is in ruins, and almost hidden from view by shrubbery. From thence we proceeded to Krow Town, a small village inhabited by about five hundred Krowmen. The British ships-of-war on this station have each from twenty-five to seventy of these men on their books.

The trade of this place is considerable. Several vessels entered and sailed during our short stay; many of them were loaded with ship timber, which is somewhat like our white oak. The other articles of trade are ivory, camwood, wax, and palm oil. We sent a boat from Sierra Leone for Mr. Bacon, who came up and remained with us two days. He has already settled himself with his followers (until after the rains) on Sherbro island. I fear this island will not answer his wishes; it is low, unhealthy, difficult of access for ships, and is not very fertile. There are many places to leeward possessing greater advantages, one of which I hope he will select for a permanent settlement.

After remaining nine days at Sierra Leone we sailed for the Gallinas, a place of resort for slave vessels, since which we have made ten captures, some by fair sailing, others by boats and stratagem. Although they are evidently owned by Americans, they are so completely covered by Spanish papers that it is impossible to condemn them. Two schooners, the Endymion and Esperanza, we sent home. We shall leave the coast in the course of three or four days for Port Praya, from whence we shall proceed to Teneriffe for provisions.

The slave trade is carried on to a very great extent. There are probably not less than three hundred vessels on the coast engaged in that traffic, each having two or three sets of papers. I sincerely hope Government has revised the law giving us more authority. You have no idea how cruelly these poor creatures are treated by the monsters engaged in taking them from the coast.

Case of the French slave ship Le Louis, extracted from the 12th annual report of the African Institution, printed in 1818.

This vessel sailed from Martinique on the 30th of January, 1816, on a slave trading voyage to the coast of Africa, and was captured near Cape Mesurado by the Sierra Leone colonial vessel-of-war Queen Charlotte, after a severe engagement, which followed an attempt to escape, in which eight men were killed and twelve wounded of the British; and, proceedings having been instituted against Le Louis in the vice admiralty court of Sierra Leone, as belonging to French subjects and as fitted out, manned, and navigated for the purpose of carrying on the slave trade after the trade had been abolished both by the internal laws of France and by the treaty between that country and Great Britain, the ship and cargo were condemned as forfeited to his Majesty.

From this sentence an appeal having been made to the high court of admiralty, the cause came on for hearing, when the court reversed the judgment of the inferior court and ordered the restitution of the property to the claimants.

The judgment of Sir William Scott was given at great length. The directors will advert to such points of it as are immediately connected with their present subject. "No doubt," he said, "could exist that this was a French ship intentionally engaged in the slave trade." But as these were facts which were ascertained in consequence of its seizure before the seizer could avail himself of this discovery, it was necessary to inquire whether he possessed any right of visitation and search; because, if the discovery was unlawfully produced, he could not be allowed to take advantage of the consequences of his own wrong.

The learned judge then discussed at considerable length the question whether the right of search exists in time of peace? And he decided it without hesitation in the negative. "I can find," he says, "no authority that gives the right of interruption to the navigation of States in amity upon the high seas, excepting that which the rights of war give to both belligerents against neutrals. No nation can exercise a right of visitation and search upon the common and unappropriated parts of the sea, save only on the belligerent claim." He admits, indeed, and with just concern, that if this right be not conceded in time of peace, it will be extremely difficult to suppress the traffic in slaves.

"The great object, therefore, ought to be to obtain the concurrence of other nations by application, by remonstrance, by example, by every peaceable instrument which men can employ to attract the consent of men. But a nation is not justified in assuming rights that do not belong to her merely because she means to apply them to a laudable purpose."

"If this right," he adds, "is imported into a state of peace, it must be done by convention; and it will then be for the prudence of States to regulate by such convention the exercise of the right with all the softenings of which it is susceptible."

The judgment of Sir William Scott would have been equally conclusive against the legality of this seizure, even if it could have been established in evidence that France had previously prohibited the slave trade by her municipal laws. For the sake of argument, however, he assumes that the view he has taken of the subject might in such a case be controverted. He proceeds, therefore, to inquire how far the French law had actually abolished the slave trade at the time of this adventure. The actual state of the matter, as collected from the documents before the court, he observes, is this :

"On the 27th of July, 1815, the British minister at Paris writes a note to Prince Talleyrand, then minister to the King of France, expressing a desire on the part of his court to be informed whether, under the law of France as it then stood, it was prohibited to French subjects to carry on the slave trade. The French minister informs him in answer, on the 30th July, that the law of the Usurper on that subject was null and void, (as were all his decrees,) but that his Most Christian Majesty had issued directions that, on the part of France, ' the traffic should cease from the present time everywhere and forever.' "

"In what form these directions were issued or to whom addressed does not appear, but upon such authority it must be presumed that they were actually issued. It is, however, no violation of the respect due to that authority to inquire what was the result or effect of those directions so given; what followed in obedience to them in any public and binding form? And I fear, I am compelled to say, that nothing of the kind followed, and that the directions must have slept in the portfolio of the office to which they were addressed; for it is, I think, impossible that if any public and authoritative ordinance had followed, it could have escaped the sleepless attention of many persons in our own country to all public foreign proceedings upon this interesting subject. Still less would it have escaped the notice of the British resident minister, who, at the distance of a year and a half, is compelled, on the part of his own court, to express a curiosity to know what laws, ordinances, instructions, and other public and ostensible acts, had passed for the abolition of the slave trade.

"On the 30th of November, in the same year, (1815,) the additional article of the definitive treaty, a very solemn instrument, most undoubtedly, is formally and publicly executed, and it is in these terms: 'The high contracting parties, sincerely desiring to give effect to the measures on which they deliberated at the Congress of Vienna for the complete and universal abolition of the slave trade, and having each, in their respective dominions, prohibited, without restriction, their colonies and subjects from taking any part whatever in this traffic, engage to renew conjointly their efforts with a view to insure final success to the principle which they proclaimed in the declaration of the 8th of February, 1815, and to concert without loss of time, by their ministers at the court of London, the most effectual measures for the entire and definitive abolition of the traffic, so odious and so highly reproved by the laws of religion and nature.'

"Now, what are the effects of this treaty? According to the view I take of it, they are two, and two only: one declaratory of a fact, the other promissory of future measures. It is to be observed that the treaty itself does not abolish the slave trade; it does not inform the subjects that that trade is *hereby* abolished, and that by virtue of the prohibitions therein contained its subjects shall not in future carry on the trade; but the contracting parties mutually inform each other of the fact that they have in their respective dominions abolished the slave trade, without stating at all the mode in which that abolition had taken place."

"It next engages to take future measures for the universal abolition.

"That with respect to both the declaratory and promissory parts, Great Britain has acted with the *optima fides* is known to the whole world, which has witnessed its domestic laws as well as its foreign negotiations.

"I am very far from intimating that the Government of this country did not act with perfect propriety in accepting the assurance that the French Government had actually abolished the slave trade as a sufficient proof of the fact; but the fact is now denied by a person who has a right to deny it, for, though a French subject, he is not bound to acknowledge the existence of any law which has not publicly appeared; and, the other party having taken upon himself the burden of proving it in the course of a legal inquiry, the court is compelled to demand and expect the ordinary evidence of such a disputed fact. It was not till the 15th of January, in the present year, (1817,) that the British resident minister applies for the communication I have described of all laws, instructions, ordinances, and so on; he receives in return what is delivered by the French minister as *the* ordinance, bearing date only one week before the requested communication, namely, the 8th of January. It has been asserted in argument that no such ordinance has yet up to this very hour even appeared in any printed or public form, however much it might import both French subjects and the subjects of foreign States so to receive it.

' How the fact may be I cannot say; but I observe it appears before me in a manuscript form; and by inquiry at the Secretary of State's office I find it exists there in no other plight or condition.

"In transmitting this to the British Government, the French minister observes it is not the document he had reason to expect, and certainly with much propriety; for how does the document answer his requisition?' His requisition is for all laws, ordinances, instructions, and so forth. How does this, a simple ordinance professing to have passed only a week before, realize the assurance given on the 30th of July, 1815, that the traffic ' should cease from the present time everywhere and forever;' or how does this realize the promise made in November that measures should be taken without loss of time to prohibit not only French colonists, but French subjects likewise, from taking any part whatever in this traffic? What is this regulation in substance?' Why, it is a mere prospective colonial regulation prohibiting the importation of slaves into the French colonies from the 8th of January, 1817.

"Consistently with this declaration, even if it does exist in the form and with the force of a law, French subjects may be yet the common carriers of slaves to any foreign settlement that will admit them, and may devote their capital and their industry unmolested by law to the supply of any such markets.

"Supposing, however, the regulations to contain the fullest and most entire fulfilment of the engagement of France, both in time and in substance, what possible application can a prospective regulation of January, 1817, have to a transaction of March, 1816?

"Nobody is now to be told that a modern edict which does not appear cannot be presumed, and that no penal law of any State can bind the conduct of its subjects unless it is conveyed to their attention in a way which excludes the possibility of honest ignorance. The very production of a law professing to be enacted in the beginning of 1817 is a satisfactory proof that no such law existed in 1816, the year of this transaction. In short, the seizer has entirely failed in the task he has undertaken, in proving the existence of a prohibitory law enacted by the legal government of France which can be applied to the present transaction."

No. 1.

Papers relating to the Slave Trade, presented to both Houses of Parliament, by command of the Prince Regent,
February, 1819.

Extract of the protocol of the conference between the plenipotentiaries of Austria, France, Great Britain, Prussia, and Russia, held at London on the 14th December, 1817.

Present: Lord Castlereagh, plenipotentiary of Great Britain; Count Lieven, plenipotentiary of Russia; Baron Humboldt, plenipotentiary of Prussia; Prince Esterházy, plenipotentiary of Austria; Count Caraman, chargé des affaires of France.

The plenipotentiaries of Great Britain, Russia, Prussia, and Austria, and the chargé des affaires of France, having agreed to meet together for the purpose of resuming the conferences relative to the abolition of the slave trade, Lord Castlereagh presents two conventions which his government has concluded during the present year: the one with Portugal, and the other with Spain, on the subject of the abolition of the slave trade; his excellency requests to defer to another day the consideration of these two transactions, with reference to the further measures which may, under the present circumstances, be to be taken respecting this question. The two said documents are annexed to this protocol, *sub litt.* A and B.

A note, dated the 19th February, 1817, addressed by the Portuguese minister to the plenipotentiaries, on the question of the abolition of the slave trade, is read; their excellencies agree to take into consideration the contents thereof, as soon as the subject shall again be proceeded in by them, and they order that it may in the meantime be inserted in the protocol, to which it is annexed, *sub litt.* C.

After which the sitting was adjourned.

HUMBOLDT.
LIEVEN.
CASTLEREAGH.
ESTERHAZY.
G. DE CARAMAN.

NOTE.—The annexes A and B to the protocol of the conference of the 4th December, 1817, (viz: the additional conventions between Great Britain, Portugal, and Spain, signed at London on the 28th July, 1817, and at Madrid on the 23d September, 1817, respectively,) have been already printed and laid before Parliament.

Annex C to the protocol of the conference of the 4th December, 1817. *(Inclosed in No.* 1.)

Note of the Count de Palmella to the plenipotentiaries of the five powers.

LONDON, *February* 19, 1817.

The undersigned, envoy extraordinary and minister plenipotentiary of his most faithful Majesty, having received from his court the instructions requested by his predecessor, M. de Freire, upon the subject of the invitation addressed to him by the plenipotentiaries of the powers who signed the additional article of the treaty of Paris of the 20th November, 1815, considers it his duty to make their excellencies acquainted with the tenor thereof, being persuaded that they will find therein satisfactory proof of the plain and candid line of conduct which the King his master has adopted from the beginning of this negotiation.

His Majesty the King of Portugal, not having signed the additional article of the treaty of Paris of the 20th November, 1815, does not consider himself bound to take a part in the conferences established in London by virtue of that article, and the less so as, at the time when the said conferences were proposed at the Congress at Vienna, the Portuguese plenipotentiaries positively refused to concur therein.

His Majesty being, nevertheless, desirous of giving this further proof of his wish to co-operate with the high powers who signed the additional article, in the accomplishment of the object proclaimed in the declaration of the Congress of Vienna of the 8th February, 1815, has authorized the undersigned, notwithstanding the efforts and the sacrifices which it has already and must still cost the Brazils to accomplish it, to accept the invitation of the plenipotentiaries of those powers who signed the above mentioned additional article, and to take part in their conferences whenever their excellencies shall have given him the assurance that the negotiation in question will be grounded upon the following principles:

1. That, in conformity to the solemn declaration of the Congress of Vienna, due regard shall be had in proceeding to the abolition of the slave trade to the interests, the customs, and even the prejudices of the subjects of those powers which still permit this traffic.

2. That each of the said powers having the right to enact the final abolition at the period which it may judge most expedient, that period shall be fixed upon between the powers by means of negotiation.

3. That the general negotiation which may ensue shall in no way prejudice the stipulation of the 4th article of the treaty of the 22d January, 1815, between his most faithful Majesty and his Britannic Majesty, wherein it is stated that the period when the said traffic is universally to cease and be prohibited in the Portuguese dominions shall be fixed by a separate treaty between the two high contracting parties.

The principles thus laid down appear to the undersigned to be so clear and so conformable to everything which the plenipotentiaries to whom he has the honor of addressing himself have themselves communicated to him, that he doubts not they will explicitly acknowledge them in the answer which he has been desired by the King his master to request they will favor him with, and in consequence of which he will consider himself duly authorized to accept the invitation addressed by their excellencies to his predecessor, and to take part in the negotiation proposed at the sitting of the Congress at Vienna, held on the 20th January, 1815.

The undersigned most readily avails himself of this opportunity to request their excellencies to accept the assurance of his highest consideration.

LE COMTE DE PALMELLA.

To their Excellencies the PLENIPOTENTIARIES *of the Powers*
who signed the additional article of the treaty of Paris of the 20th November, 1815.

No. 2.

Protocol of the conference between the plenipotentiaries of the five powers of the 4th of February, 1818.

Present: Prince Esterhazy, Marquis D'Osmond, Baron de Humboldt, Count Lieven, Lord Castlereagh.

Lord Castlereagh reads a note verbale, containing a proposition on the part of his Government, the object of which is to make a convention between the powers represented by the plenipotentiaries assembled for the purpose of abolishing illicit slave trade; and he accordingly invites his colleagues to request forthwith instructions on this subject from their respective courts, in the event of their not being provided with sufficient authority to negotiate such a convention.

Lord Castlereagh then reads several reports derived from different societies occupied in the abolition of the slave trade, relative to the extent and nature of this traffic on the coasts of Africa, and requests the insertion in the protocol of the proposition above stated, together with the said reports as annexes thereunto. All these documents are inserted, *sub litt.* A, B, C, D.

The plenipotentiaries agree to invite, verbally, Count Palmella, minister of Portugal, to assist at the ensuing conference on the abolition of the slave trade, and adjourn for the present the further consideration of the subject.

CASTLEREAGH.
LIEVEN.
ESTERHAZY.
OSMOND.
HUMBOLDT.

[First inclosure in No. 2.]

Annex A to the protocol of the conference of the 4th of February, 1818.

Memorandum of Viscount Castlereagh.

In laying before the conference the reports received from the African societies in London, in answer to the queries addressed to them by his Majesty's Government upon the present state of the slave trade, as connected with the improvement and civilization of Africa, Lord Castlereagh (the reports being read) called the attention of his colleagues to the following prominent facts:

That a considerable revival of the slave trade had taken place, especially on the coast of Africa north of the line, since the restoration of peace, and that the principal part of this traffic being now of an illicit description, the parties engaged in it had adopted the practice of carrying it on in armed and fast-sailing vessels.

That the ships engaged in this armed traffic not only threatened resistance to all legal attempts to repress the same, but by their piratical practices menaced the legitimate commerce of all nations on the coast with destruction.

That the traffic thus carried on was marked with increased horrors, from the inhuman manner in which these desperate adventurers were in the habit of crowding the slaves on board vessels better adapted to escape from the interruption of cruisers than to serve for the transport of human beings.

That as the improvement of Africa, especially in a commercial point of view, has advanced in proportion as the slave trade had been suppressed, so, with its revival, every prospect of industry and of amendment appears to decline.

That the British Government has made considerable exertions to check the growing evil; that during the war, and whilst in possession of the French and Dutch settlements on that coast, their endeavors had been attended with very considerable success, but that since the restoration of those possessions, and more especially since the return of peace had rendered it illegal for British cruisers to visit vessels sailing under foreign flags, the trade in slaves had greatly increased.

That the British Government in the performance of this act of moral duty had invariably wished, as far as possible, to avoid giving umbrage to the rights of any friendly power; that with this view, as early as July, 1816, the accompanying circular order had been issued to all British cruisers, requiring them to advert to the fact that the right of search (being a belligerent right) had ceased with the war, and directing them to abstain from exercising the same.

That the difficulty of distinguishing in all cases the fraudulent from the licit slave traders, of the former of whom a large proportion were notoriously British subjects, feloniously carrying on this traffic in defiance of the laws of their own country, had given occasion to the detention of a number of vessels upon grounds which the Prince Regent's Government could not sanction; and in reparation for which seizures, due compensation had been assigned in the late convention with Spain and Portugal.

That it was, however, proved beyond the possibility of a doubt, that, unless the right to visit vessels engaged in this illicit traffic should be established, by the same being mutually conceded between the maritime States, the illicit slave trade must, in time of peace, not only continue to subsist, but to increase.

That the system of obtaining fraudulent papers and concealing the real ownership was now carried on with such address as to render it easy for the subjects of all States to carry on the traffic, whilst the trade in slaves remained legal for the subjects of any one State.

That even were the traffic abolished by all States, whilst the flag of one State shall preclude the visit of all other States, the illicit slave trader will always have the means of concealing himself under the disguise of the nation whose cruiser there is the least chance of his meeting on the coast. Thus, the Portuguese slave trader, since the abolition north of the line took effect, has been found to conceal himself under the Spanish flag; the American and even the British dealer has in like manner assumed a foreign disguise. Many instances have occurred of British subjects evading the laws of their country either by establishing houses at the Havana or obtaining false papers. If such has been the case in time of war, when neutral flags were legally subjected to the visit of the belligerent cruiser, the evil must tenfold increase when peace has extinguished this right, and when even British ships, by fraudulently assuming a foreign flag, may, with every prospect of impunity, carry on the traffic.

The obvious necessity of combining the repression of the illicit slave trade with the measure of abolition, in order to render the latter in any degree effectual, has been admitted both by the Spanish and Portuguese Governments, and in furtherance of this principle the late conventions have been negotiated; but whilst the system therein established is confined to the three powers, and whilst the flags of other maritime States, and more especially those of France, Holland, and the United States, are not included therein, the effect must be to vary the ostensible character of the fraud, rather than in any material degree to suppress the mischief.

The great powers of Europe, assembled in Congress at Vienna, having taken a solemn engagement in the face of mankind that this traffic should be made to cease, and it clearly appearing that the law of abolition is nothing in itself unless the contraband slave trade shall be suppressed by a combined system, it is submitted that they owe it to themselves to unite their endeavors without delay for that purpose, and as the best means it is proposed that the five powers now assembled in conference under the third additional article of the treaty of Paris should conclude a treaty with each other upon such enlarged and at the same time simple principles as might become a conventional regulation, to which all other maritime States should be invited to give their accession. This convention might embrace the following general provisions:

1st. An engagement by effectual enactments to render not only the import of slaves into their respective dominions illegal, but to constitute the trafficking in slaves on the part of any of their subjects a criminal act, to be punished in such suitable manner as their respective codes of law may ordain.

2d. That the right of visit be mutually conceded to their respective ships-of-war, furnished with the proper instructions, *ad hoc;* that the visit be made under the inspection of a commissioned officer, and no vessel be detained unless slaves shall be found actually on board.

3d. The minor regulations to be such as are established in the conventions with Spain and Portugal, under such further modifications as may appear calculated to obviate abuse and to render the system, if possible, more unobjectionable as a general law amongst the high contracting parties applicable to this particular evil.

After the abolition shall have become general, in a course of years, the laws of each particular State may, perhaps, be made in a great measure effectual to exclude import. The measure to be taken on the coast of Africa will then become comparatively unimportant; but so long as the partial nature of the abolition and the facility to contraband import throughout the extensive possessions to which slaves are carried from the coast of Africa shall afford to the illicit slave trader irresistible temptation to pursue this abominable but lucrative traffic, so long nothing but the vigilant superintendence of an armed and international police on the coast of Africa can be expected successfully to cope with such practices.

To render such a police either legal or effectual to its object, it must be established under the sanction and by the authority of all civilized States concurring in the humane policy of abolition; the force necessary to repress the same may be supplied as circumstances of convenience may suggest by the powers having possessions on the coast of Africa, or local interests which may induce them to station ships-of-war in that quarter of the globe; but the endeavors of these powers must be ineffectual unless backed by a general alliance framed for this especial purpose. The rights of all nations must be brought to co-operate to the end in view by at least ceasing to be the cover under which the object which all aim at accomplishing is to be defeated.

At the outset some difficulty may occur in the execution of a common system, and especially whilst the trade remains legal within certain limits to the subjects both of the crowns of Spain and Portugal; but if the principal powers frequenting the coast of Africa evince a determination to combine their means against the illicit slave trader as a common enemy, and if they are supported in doing so by other States denying to such illicit slave traders the cover of their flag, the traffic will soon be rendered too hazardous for profitable speculation. The evil must thus cease, and the efforts of Africa be directed to those habits of peaceful commerce and industry in which all nations will find their best reward for the exertions they shall have devoted to the suppression of this great moral evil.

Lord Castlereagh, upon these grounds, invited his colleagues, in the name of the Prince Regent, should the powers under which they at present act not enable them to proceed to negotiate a convention upon the grounds above stated, to solicit, without delay, from their respective sovereigns the authority necessary to this effect; his royal highness confidently trusting that the enlarged and enlightened principles which guided the councils of these illustrious persons at Vienna, and which have now happily advanced the cause of abolition so nearly to its completion, will determine them perseveringly to conduct the measure to that successful close which nothing but their combined wisdom and continued exertions can effectuate.

Lord Castlereagh concluded by calling the attention of his colleagues to the indisputable proofs afforded both by the present state of the colony of Sierra Leone and by the increase of African commerce in latter years, of the faculties of that continent, both in its soil and population, for becoming civilized and industrious, the only impediment to which undoubtedly was the pernicious practice of slave trading, which, wherever it prevailed, at once turned aside the attention of the natives from the more slow and laborious means of barter which industry presented to that of seizing upon and selling each other.

It was therefore through the total extinction of this traffic that Africa could alone be expected to make its natural advances in civilization, a result which it was the declared object of these conferences by all possible means to accelerate and to promote.

NOTE.—The proposition made by Viscount Castlereagh in the preceding memorandum was immediately transmitted by the several plenipotentiaries for the consideration of their courts, but no answer was received from the respective governments previous to the meeting of the conferences at Aix-la-Chapelle, in September, 1818.

[Second inclosure in No. 2.]

Annex B to the protocol of the conference of the 4th of February, 1818.

Queries proposed by Viscount Castlereagh to and answers of the African Society in London, December, 1816:

Query 1. What number of slaves are supposed at present to be annually carried from the western coast of Africa across the Atlantic?

Answer 1. It would be impossible to give any other than a conjectural answer to this question. It has been calculated, but certainly on loose and uncertain data, that the number of slaves at present carried from the western coast of Africa across the Atlantic amounts to upwards of 60,000.

Query 2. State as far as you can the comparative numbers annually withdrawn for the last twenty-five years, either by giving the probable number withdrawn in each year or upon an average of years?

Answer 2. The number of slaves withdrawn from western Africa during the last twenty-five years is also necessarily involved in considerable uncertainty. It has probably amounted to upwards of a million and a half. During many of the early years of that period the number annually withdrawn is stated, on credible authority, to have amounted to near 80,000.

This agrees with the result of the evidence taken before the privy council in 1787 and 1788. Even this enormous amount, however, is more likely to fall below the real export than to exceed it; for, in the specification contained in the privy council report, the Portuguese are supposed to have carried off only 15,000 annually, whereas there is reason to believe that their export was much more considerable. The number carried off by ships of the United States is also, it is apprehended, rated too low.

The abolition of the British slave trade in 1808 must, of course, have materially lessened the extent of the slave trade.

The diminution in the price of slaves on the coast, however, which followed that measure, appears in no long time to have had the effect of tempting other nations to enlarge their purchases and to crowd their ships, and British capital also gradually found its way into this branch of trade through the medium of foreign houses. On the whole, it is supposed that the average export of the last eight years may have somewhat exceeded the rate of 50,000 annually.

Query 3. From what parts of the coast have these supplies been drawn? State, as far as may be, the approximated distribution of these numbers with respect to different parts of the coast of Africa.

Answer 3. Previously to the year 1810 these supplies were drawn from all parts of the African coast, without distinction.

About a fourth part of the whole, it is supposed, was drawn from that part of the coast extending from the river Senegal to the eastern extremity of the Gold Coast. Of the remaining three-fourths, one half is supposed to have been drawn from Whydaw, the Bight of Benin, the rivers Bonny, Calabar, Gaboon, and the intermediate districts north of the equator; and the other half from Congo, Angola, Benguela, and other parts of the south of the equator.

Subsequently to the year 1793 the slave trade between the Senegal and the eastern extremity of the Gold Coast was divided almost exclusively between the English and the Americans, probably more than three-fourths of it being engrossed by the former. The contemporaneous abolition of the slave trade, therefore, by these two nations, tended greatly to diminish the export of slaves from that line of coast. The Portuguese had previously confined their slave trade almost entirely to the Bight of Benin and the coast to the southward of it; but, in consequence of the reduction in the price of slaves on the windward and Gold Coasts which followed the abolition of the British and American slave trade, they were gradually drawn thither. Before, however, their expeditions to this part of the coast had become very frequent they were checked by the promulgation of the treaty of amity between Great Britain and Portugal of February, 1810, confining the Portuguese slave trade to places under the dominion of the crown of Portugal. The windward, and also the Gold Coast, were thus preserved for some years from suffering so severely by the ravages of the slave trade, as would otherwise probably be the case. Considerable cargoes, it is true, were occasionally carried away from these districts during the years in question, especially when it could be ascertained that there were no British cruisers in the way to obstruct their progress.

But still, from the year 1808 to the year 1815, the slaves carried from western Africa were principally taken from Whydaw, the Bight of Benin, and the coast southward of it, and the coast north of that line was comparatively exempt from the ravages of this traffic.

Query 4. By what nations and in what proportions is it understood that the gross annual supply has been purchased and carried away?

Answer 4. Previous to the Revolutionary war the number carried away in British ships was estimated at 38,000 annually. About 40,000 or 42,000 more were supposed to be carried away by the Portuguese, French, Dutch, Danes, and Americans.

This estimate, however, probably falls below the truth, as there is reason to believe that the annual export of the Portuguese alone usually amounted to 25,000, and the number of slaves introduced into St. Domingo by the French, for some time before the revolution in that island, is known to have been very large.

For about two years after the breaking out of the maritime war of 1793 the slave trade on the west coast of Africa suffered a considerable interruption.

The French and Dutch were entirely driven from it, and the captures made from the English greatly discouraged their trade on that open and unprotected coast. Our maritime successes, and the capture of Dutch Guiana, combined to revive it, and the English share of the slave trade rose to the enormous amount of 55,000 slaves in a single year. The only other nations that during this period, and down to the year 1810, were engaged in the slave trade of western Africa were the Portuguese and Americans.

The number carried off by the Portuguese has been estimated at from 20,000 to 25,000 annually, and by the Americans about 15,000. Notwithstanding the prohibitory act of America, which was passed in 1807, ships bearing the American flag continued to trade for slaves until 1809, when, in consequence of a decision in the English prize appeal courts which rendered American slave ships liable to capture and condemnation, that flag suddenly disappeared from the coast. Its place was almost instantaneously supplied by the Spanish flag, which, with one or two exceptions, was now seen for the first time on the African coast engaged in covering the slave trade.

This sudden substitution of the Spanish for the American flag seemed to confirm what was established in a variety of instances by more direct testimony, that the slave trade, which now for the first time assumed a Spanish dress, was in reality only the trade of other nations in disguise.

Query 5. To what parts of the continent of North or South America, or the islands in the West Indies, have these slaves been carried?

Answer 5. The slaves formerly taken from the coast by the French, Dutch, and Danes, were almost exclusively for the supply of their own colonies.

Until the abolition of the British and American slave trade, the Portuguese carried the slaves taken by them from the coast, with scarcely any exceptions, to the Brazils.

Subsequently to that event the Portuguese flag was for some years employed in carrying cargoes of slaves to the Spanish colonies.

This practice, however, was greatly checked at least, if not wholly suppressed, in consequence of instructions issued to British cruisers, authorizing them to bring in for adjudication such Portuguese ships as might be found carrying slaves to places not subject to the crown of Portugal.

For the last two or three years, therefore, the Portuguese flag has been almost exclusively used in carrying slaves to the Brazils.

Before the abolition of the American slave trade, a considerable number of slaves were constantly introduced into South Carolina and Louisiana. The chief part, however, of the American slave trade before that event, and nearly the whole of it afterwards, was carried on for the supply of the Spanish colonies.

From the year 1810, as has been already noticed, whatever slave trade may have been carried on by an American capital has been under the disguise of either the Portuguese or Spanish flag, but chiefly of the latter.

The English for many years were in the habit of supplying the colonies of Spain with a considerable number of slaves. The remainder of the slaves they carried from the coast was distributed throughout their own colonies. Between the years 1795 and 1805, the largest share of their slave trade was carried on for the supply of Dutch Guiana, then in the possession of Great Britain, Trinidad, and the conquered colonies. Cuba also continued to receive a considerable supply of slaves from the English.

In 1805 Great Britain prohibited the slave trade for the supply of the colonies she had captured during the war, and in the following year prohibited that for the supply of the colonies of any foreign power whatever. The whole of the slaves, therefore, taken from Africa by the English, in the year 1806 and 1807, excepting what may have been smuggled, must have been distributed among her old colonies, and in the prospect of the approaching abolition of the British slave trade, that number was very considerable.

Query 6. What is the present extent and nature of the contraband trade in slaves?

Query 7. By what description of persons, under what flag, upon what part of the coast, and for the supply of what market, is this illicit trade carried on?

Answer 6, 7. It would be impossible by any probable estimate to distinguish at the present moment the contraband slave trade from that which may be considered as legal. The whole of the slave trade, whether legal or contraband, which is now carried on from western Africa, passes, with a very few exceptions, under the Spanish and Portuguese flags; the former being seen chiefly to the north of the equator, and the latter to the south of it. The flag, however, affords but a very slight presumption of the real national character of the adventure. In the case of a very great majority of the vessels detained by our cruisers, it has proved a disguise assumed by the contraband trader in order to escape detention. Of the slaves exported from the western coast of Africa, at the present time, estimated, as has been already said, at upwards of 50,000, probably a half is carried off under the Spanish and the other half under the Portuguese flag. During the last months of 1814 and the first months of 1815 several ships bearing the French flag appeared on the African coast and carried off cargoes of slaves. Within the last twelve months, also, several vessels bearing the American flag have come upon the coast, professedly for the purpose of carrying on its innocent and legitimate commerce; meeting, however, as they conceived, with a convenient opportunity of carrying off a cargo of slaves for the Havana market, they have not scrupled to take them on board. Two vessels, under these circumstances, sailed from the Rio Nunez full of slaves, in January, 1816, and it is supposed reached the place of their destination in safety. Another vessel of the same description was captured in the Rio Pongas, in April, 1816, while employed in taking the slaves on board.

With these exceptions, the whole slave trade of western Africa, for the last six or seven years, has been carried on, it is believed, under the flags of Spain and Portugal.

The Spanish flag, however, is probably, in almost every case, a mere disguise, and covers not *bona fide* Spanish property, but the property of unlawful traders, whether English, American, or others.

It is a well known fact that until the year 1809 or 1810 the Spanish flag had not for a long time been engaged in the African slave trade, except in one or two instances. Its sudden and extensive appearance subsequently to that period furnishes, as has already been remarked, a very strong presumption of the fraudulent character of the adventurers which it is employed to protect.

The ordinary course of proceeding is this: the ship belonging to the unlawful trader calls at the Havana or Teneriffe, for the most part at the former port. A nominal sale of ship and cargo is there effected to some Spanish house, and regular Spanish papers and a nominal Spanish captain having been obtained, and her real captain having taken the character either of supercargo or passenger, she sails on her slave trading expedition as a Spanish ship.

Since the Portuguese have been restricted by treaty from trading for slaves on certain parts of the African coast, they have resorted to similar expedients for protecting their slave trading expeditions to places within the prohibited district. And at the present moment there is little doubt that a considerable part of the apparently Spanish slave trade which is carrying on to the north of the equator, where the Portuguese are forbidden to buy slaves, is really a Portuguese trade.

A further use is now found for the Spanish flag in protecting the French slave traders; and it is affirmed that the French ships fitted out in France for the slave trade call at Corunna for the purpose of effecting a nominal transfer of the property engaged in the illegal voyage to some Spanish house, and thus obtaining the requisite evidence of Spanish ownership.

In consequence of these uses to which the Spanish flag has been applied, a great increase of the apparently Spanish slave trade has taken place of late. And as the flag of that nation is permitted to range over the whole extent of the African coast, it seems to keep alive the slave trade in places from which it would otherwise have been shut out; and it has of late revived that trade in situations where it had been previously almost wholly extinguished.

The Portuguese flag is now chiefly seen to the south of the equator, although sometimes the Portuguese traders do not hesitate still to resort to the rivers between Whydaw and the equator, even without a Spanish disguise. The only two cruisers which have recently visited that part of the coast found several ships under the Portuguese flag openly trading for slaves in Lago and the Bight of Benin.

In a great variety of cases the Portuguese flag has been found to cover the property of British or American slave traders. It will doubtless be now employed to protect also the slave traders of other nations by which the trade is prohibited. The limitation of that flag to parts south of the line renders it less desirable for a general voyage to the unlawful trader than the Spanish flag, which is under no local restriction.

The extraordinary facility with which a change may be effected in the national character of a ship and cargo intended to be employed in the slave trade has been judicially established in a great variety of instances. The Brazils and the island of Cuba form the great marts of the sale of the slaves carried from the western coast of Africa, exclusive of those smuggled into the British and restored French and Dutch colonies.

Query 8. Has this trade been lately carried on to a considerable extent on the coasts north of the equator?

Answer 8. The slave trade, under the circumstances stated in the answer to the last question, has certainly been carried on during the last two years to a great extent on the African coast north of the equator.

Query 9. By what description of persons and under what flag?

Answer 9. This question has been already answered.

Query 10. Have those fraudulent slave traders come in armed vessels, and have they employed force in order to effectuate their purposes?

Answer 10. During the last two years many slave ships have come to the coast armed, and have employed force to effectuate their purposes.

Query 11. When interrupted, have they threatened to return with armed ships of a larger class?

Answer 11. They have, and in some instances have executed their threats.

Query 12. From whence are these armed contrabandists chiefly fitted out?

Answer 12. A few of these armed ships have come from the Brazils, and one or two from Martinique; but for the most part they have come from the United States, having first obtained a Spanish disguise at the Havana. They have consisted chiefly of vessels which had been employed as American privateers during the war, and which sail uncommonly fast. In more than one instance they have come in small squadrons of two or three vessels, for the purpose of attacking and carrying any armed vessel which might obstruct their proceedings.

Query 13. What has been the effect produced by their depredations on the coast north of the line?

Answer 13. The effects of these proceedings have been highly detrimental. Exclusive of all the evils which are inseparable from a slave trade, under any circumstances, they have discouraged and in some cases crushed the first efforts to extend agriculture and legitimate commerce which had been produced in this quarter by the cessation for a time of the slave trade. Even the innocent commerce of Sierra Leone with the surrounding districts, which had tended more than anything else to give a steady impulse to the industry of the neighboring natives, has been subject to outrage and spoliation, attended in some cases with the loss of life. They operate most fatally in another point of view. The native chiefs and traders who began at length to be convinced, by the evidence of facts, that the abolition was likely to be permanently maintained, and that it was therefore absolutely necessary to engage heartily in schemes of cultivation, if they would preserve their influence, have learnt from recent events to distrust all such assurances. Notwithstanding all that had been said and done, they now see the slave traders again sweeping the whole range of coast without molestation; nay, with the air of triumph and defiance. It will be long, therefore, before they are likely to yield to the same conviction respecting the purposes of the European powers to abolish the slave trade which they had been led to admit. Even if effectual means should now be adopted for totally and finally abolishing this traffic, years will probably elapse before they will be induced to forego the expectation of its revival. It would be difficult fully to appreciate the deep and lasting injury inflicted on northern Africa by the transactions of the last two or three years. And this injury will be the greater on this account, that in the interior of that country, at least, they do not discriminate with any accuracy between the different nations of Europe. They only know in general that the white men who had ceased to trade in slaves, and who they understood were to trade no more in that commodity except as smugglers, liable to be seized and punished, have now resumed the open, avowed, and uncontrolled practice of that traffic.

Query 14. What system do you conceive best calculated to repress this evil?

Answer 14. I do not apprehend that the evil can be repressed, or even very materially alleviated, unless the abolition be made total and universal; and even then unless the slave trade be pronounced to be felonious and punished as such. At present no check whatever exists, not even that very inadequate one which in time of war arises from the right of search exercised by belligerents. It may be expected, therefore, that the slave trade, instead of being diminished, will increase from day to day. More prohibitory acts, even should they be adopted by all the powers of Europe, would be eluded unless regulations adapted to the very peculiar circumstances of the case were devised for confirming them.

Query 15. What progress had there been made during the war to exclude the trade in slaves from the coast of Africa north of the line?

Answer 15. The progress had been very considerable, as has been shown above, and was shown more largely by authentic documents communicated to Lord Castlereagh and the Duke of Wellington in 1814. The restoration of peace in Europe has been attended with very disastrous effects to this part of Africa.

Query 16. What effects can be traced to have arisen from such exclusion upon the interior civilization of industry, or upon the external commerce of this part of the coast, compared with what existed twenty years before.

Answer 16. In some remarks drawn up in August, 1814, on the subject of the legitimate commerce of Africa, it was very clearly shown that at that period a very considerable effect had been produced by the exclusion of the slave trade from northern Africa, imperfect as that exclusion was, on the external commerce, and consequently on the industry of that part of the coast, as compared with what existed twenty years before. Since 1814 the slave trade in northern Africa has unhappily experienced a very considerable revival, and it is to be apprehended that a corresponding check may have been given to the progress of industry and legitimate commerce.

It is obviously only when the slave trade has been eradicated that any marked progress in civilization can be expected. The existence of that trade is necessarily a bar to improvement. Supposing, however, that it should be effectually abolished, we are already in possession of very satisfactory evidence to show that there is nothing in the local circumstances of Africa, and as little in the character of her inhabitants, which would prevent, in their case at least, as rapid an advance in the arts of civilized life, and in the acquisition of moral and religious habits, as the world has witnessed in any other similar instance. A part of this evidence is derived from the colony of Sierra Leone. The population of that colony in 1809 did not exceed 1,500 souls, chiefly Africans. Since that time it has swelled to upwards of 10,000. This large increase consists almost entirely of persons who, having been rescued at different periods during the last seven years from the holds of slave ships, may be supposed, at the time of their introduction, to have stood at the lowest point of mental and moral depression.

The population of Sierra Leone, therefore, at this time exhibits all the varying shades of civilization, (varying partly according to the time that has elapsed since their introduction into the colony, and partly according to the character and opportunities of each individual,) from the enterprising trader, skilful mechanic, or industrious farmer, supporting himself and his family in comfort, and performing respectably his social and even religious duties, to the almost brutish state of the recently liberated captive.

Of these 10,000 Africans, all, excepting those who may yet be too young to labor, or who may have been too recently introduced into the colony to be able as yet to reap the fruits of their labors, maintain themselves by their own industry, chiefly in the cultivation of farms of their own. Making due allowance for previous habits and the difficulties arising from difference of language, they are found to be as susceptible of moral and intellectual culture as any people whatever.

In the month of October last the schools in the colony contained 1,237 scholars, whose advancement in knowledge was satisfactory to their instructors and to the Government; and it is said that a great eagerness existed among them to avail themselves of the means of instruction within their reach. The general conduct of the liberated captives has been such as to merit the approbation and confidence of their governors, and not a few have already so far improved their advantages as to be capable of discharging such subordinate judicial functions as jurors, constables, &c.

From the foundation of the colony, indeed, these functions have been almost exclusively discharged by Africans; and Sierra Leone exhibits the important example of a community of black men, living as freemen, enjoying the benefits of the British constitution, maintaining themselves by the ordinary pursuits of commerce, agriculture, or some mechanical art, fulfilling their various social and civil relations by the means only of such sanctions as the administration of British law and the precepts of charity impose upon them, and gradually improving, by means of schools and other institutions, in knowledge and civilization.

"A population of 10,000 freemen," observes Dr. Hogan, the chief judge of the colony, in a letter dated in October, 1816, "collected upon one spot, *so favorably situated*, and governed with a view to such noble and ennobling objects, forms too grand a stride in the moral march of human affairs not to fix the attention of an enlightened observer. I take this colony, then, as it is, and, looking steadily to the great objects which it was from its first settlement intended to promote, am well content." He afterwards adds that, with so much to deplore as there necessarily must be in a population such as has been described, he distinctly perceives "all the principal elements of social order and effectual civilization in existence and vigor, requiring only the care of a skilful hand to mould them into form, and to collect from them the early fruits of a successful and rapid cultivation."

The case of Sierra Leone has been adduced chiefly for the purpose of showing that the African character is susceptible of improvement and civilization in a degree perhaps not inferior to any other. It was in that part of the coast adjoining to Sierra Leone that the slave trade was for a time most effectually extinguished; and the consequence of that suspension of the slave trade was a very considerable increase of innocent commerce, and particularly of the export of rice; of that article considerable quantities were carried, during the peninsular war, to Portugal and Spain, and many cargoes have also been carried to Madeira, Teneriffe, and the West Indies. The trade in rice was one which might have been indefinitely extended, provided the slave trade had not revived. There is reason to fear that its revival may destroy in the bud this promising branch of commerce.

Query 17. State what measures are now in progress for the improvement of Africa, and how they are likely to be affected by the continuance or discontinuance of this trade, partially or generally?

Answer 17. This question has received a partial answer above.

Sierra Leone and its immediate neighborhood may be considered as the only part of the African coast where plans of improvement can be pursued without immediately encountering the malignant influence of the slave trade. It is almost necessary, therefore, to confine within that sphere, at least for the present, the direct efforts made for the civilization and improvement of Africa. Even the establishment formed in the Rio Pongas for the instruction of the natives, it is feared, must be withdrawn in consequence of the revival of the slave trade.

At Sierra Leone between 1,200 and 1,300 African youths of both sexes, most of them rescued from the holds of slave ships, are now under instruction. These have been brought to Sierra Leone from all parts of Africa, from Senegal to Benzuela, so that there is scarcely a language spoken in that extensive range of coast which is not spoken by some of the Sierra Leone colonists.

In instructing these liberated captives, the views of their benefactors are by no means confined to the benefits which they themselves may derive from the instruction afforded them, but extend to the possibility that individuals may hereafter arise from among them who may convey to their own native regions that light which they have acquired at Sierra Leone.

Query 18. Is there any reason to apprehend that the contraband trade may become extensive in time of peace, even on the coast north of the line, where so considerable a progress had been made to suppress the slave trade generally, if some decisive measures are not adopted by the powers conjointly to repress the same?

Answer 18. There is the strongest reason to apprehend this consequence. Indeed, the event here only supposed possible is actually at this moment matter of history.

Query 19, 20. Has it not been found that the trade is conducted with peculiar inhumanity and waste of life by these illicit traders? State the instances that have latterly occurred to illustrate the fact.

Answer 19, 20. Undoubtedly. The slave ships are now crowded to excess, and the mortality is dreadful. The following are some of the instances which have come to our knowledge:

 1. The Venus Havannera, under Spanish colors, of the burden of about 180 tons, carried off from the river Bonny 530 slaves. When captured on her passage to the Havana and carried into Tortola, the mortality was found to have amounted to 120.

 2. La Manella, a ship of the burden of 272 tons, sailed under the Spanish flag and took on board in the river Bonny 642 slaves. The deaths on the passage to the West Indies, previous to her capture, amounted to 140.

 3. The Gertrudes, a ship sailing under the Spanish flag, took on board upwards of 600 slaves. This ship was taken while yet on the African coast and brought to Sierra Leone for adjudication. But notwithstanding the short time that had elapsed since the slaves were taken on board, such was the dreadful state of crowding, that about 200 died before the ship was brought in, or within a short time after her arrival; many even of those who survived were so much debilitated by their sufferings as never to be likely to enjoy sound health.

 4. Nneva Constitucion, a vessel under the Spanish flag, of only 30 tons burden, had on board 81 slaves; but having been brought in within a few days after the slaves had been taken on board, the bad effects which must have followed such a state of crowding on a very long passage were prevented.

 5. The Maria Primeira, a ship under Portuguese colors, took on board upwards of 500 slaves. This number was reduced to 403, in consequence of extreme crowding, before she was brought into Sierra Leone; and nearly 100 more died soon after in consequence of the diseases contracted on board.

 6. Portuguese brig San Antonio, of 120 tons, took on board 600 slaves; when captured, although she had only sailed 80 leagues, 30 slaves had already died and many more were found to be in a dying state, and died soon after. The capturing officer took 150 of the slaves on board his own ship to prevent the almost universal mortality he apprehended. When he first went on board the slave ship he found a dead body in a state of absolute putridity lying among the sick.

 7. The Spanish ship Carlos, under 200 tons burden, took on board 512 negroes, in addition to a crew consisting of 84. About 80 slaves had died, previous to her capture, and the rest were in a most deplorable state. Many more instances might be added, but these may be considered as exhibiting the ordinary rate of mortality on board the ships engaged in the illicit slave trade.

Query 21. What has been the general influence observable on the interior of Africa by the successive acts of abolition on the part of different States?

Answer 21. Very little is known of the interior of Africa, or of the moral or political changes which take place there. Our knowledge is almost entirely confined to the banks of navigable rivers and to the line of the seacoast. There, indeed, the influence has been very observable of all the variations in the policy of European nations in respect to the slave trade, and perhaps some corresponding effect may be assumed to be produced in the interior regions which are removed from observation. Many proofs might be given of the evil effects produced on the coast of Africa by the vacillation and uncertainty which has attended the measure of abolition. And if any truth be more than another fully demonstrated by experience with respect to Africa, it is this: that without an effective abolition of the slave trade by all the powers of Europe it will be in vain to expect the development of the immense agricultural and commercial facilities of that continent; or that, except in very partial instances, the many millions of men by whom it is peopled should rise a single step in the scale of civilization above their present degraded level.

Query 22. What do you conceive would be the particular effect of an abolition of the slave trade on the part of Spain?

Answer 22. An abolition on the part of Spain would at once deliver the whole of northern Africa from the slave trade, provided effectual measures were taken to seize and punish illicit traders. The Spanish flag being now the only flag that can show itself in northern Africa engaged in the slave trade, the beneficial effects of such an arrangement may be inferred from what has been already said.

Another effect would be this: no slave trade would be lawful but what was found moving in the line between southern Africa and the Brazils, and no slave trader, therefore, could navigate any part of the Atlantic north of the equator; so that the risk of smuggling into the West India islands would be greatly lessened.

By the prolongation of the Spanish slave trade, on the contrary, not only is the whole of northern Africa, which would otherwise be exempt, given up to the ravages of that traffic, and the progress already made in improvement sacrificed, but facilities are afforded of smuggling into every island of the West Indies, which could not otherwise exist, and which, while slave ships may lawfully pass from Africa to Cuba and Porto Rico, it would perhaps be impossible to prevent.

Query 23. What amount of slaves do the Portuguese import annually into the kingdom of Brazil?

Answer 23. The number has been estimated at from 20,000 to 30,000 annually.

DECEMBER, 1816.

[Third inclosure in No. 2.]

Annex C to the protocol of the conference of the 4th of February, 1818.

Answers from Sierra Leone to the queries of Viscount Castlereagh, dated April, 1817.

Query 6. What is the present extent and nature of the contraband trade in slaves?

Answer 6. For some time past, especially after the settlement was formed in the Gambia, and previous to the recent transfer of Senegal and Goree to France, the contraband slave trade was confined to the part of the coast southward of the river Sherbró in latitude seven degrees north, with the exception of a few vessels which now and then took off slaves from Bissao and the trade carried on in the Rio Pongas.

The expedition of 1814 crushed the trade in the Rio Pongas for two years, but as many of the Rio Pongas traders have settled in the Havana, they have, since their recovery from that shock, returned to it with more eagerness and rapacity than ever.

From Sherbró and the Gallinas to Cape Appolonia a most extensive and by far the most abominable slave trade is carried on; in this district the practice of kidnapping the natives who go off in canoes is chiefly pursued; the vessels employed for this part of the coast are generally under the Spanish flag, but connected with former and present slave factors on that part of the coast.

It is supposed that very little, if any, slave trade is carried on between Cape Appolonia and Popo, where the Portuguese factories commence, and from which place to their most southern settlements a very extensive trade is carried on.

It is generally carried on in large schooners and brigs, well armed and manned, and from the circumstance of slaves being cheaper on the coast than whilst the slave trade was permitted by Great Britain and America, and from the risks run in each voyage, they crowd their vessels to an inhuman and destructive degree.

The vessels are chosen for their force and swiftness, without the least regard to the accommodation or the comforts of the slaves; and the persons chosen to man and command these vessels are certainly far more celebrated for their ferocity and daring spirit than for their humanity.

There can be no doubt but that a very great proportion of the slaves carried from the coast are fairly purchased from the factories by the slave captains, however unjustly they may have come into the possession of the factors, still it is equally notorious that the Havana traders do, whenever there is an opportunity, kidnap and carry off the free natives.

Query 7. By what description of persons, under what flags, upon what part of the coast, and for the supply of what market, is this illicit trade carried on?

Answer 7. The greatest part of, indeed nearly the entire slave trade on the windward coast is carried on by vessel fitted out from the Havana and other ports in the island of Cuba, though many vessels come for slaves from Old Spain and Teneriffe, but their ulterior destination is ostensibly for the Havana.

Several vessels have been fitted out from France, as the "Rodeur," from Nantes, and from the French West India islands, as the "Louis."

Though the settlements of Senegal and Goree have been delivered up so very lately to France, yet there is a very active and extensive slave trade already carrying on from those places and the adjacent countries; some of the vessels are from France, some from Teneriffe; and there can be no doubt but that this last mentioned place, from its vicinity to these settlements, will, in a very short time, become the depot for vessels intended to be employed in this trade on the windward coast.

From experience in the trade, it has now become the practice to have their vessels manned, &c., as much as possible with Spanish subjects, and the voyage under the control of a Spaniard. But this is far from being universally the case. It has been clearly proved in many instances that the property was not Spanish: for instance, the Dolores proved to be English; the Paz, English and American; the Theresa, English and French; the Triomphante, Portuguese, &c., with many others, besides the vessels sent out by several English subjects resident in the Havana.

The Alexander and Triumverata were both under the command of American subjects, and came directly from North America to the coast, though documented with Spanish papers from the Spanish consuls residing in ports from whence they sailed.

The exertions of Captain Irby and Captain Scobell induced the Portuguese traders to confine themselves to their own factories in the Bight of Benin, or rather to those parts of the Bight which are considered as Portuguese.

With the exception of those places, where I fancy little but Portuguese slave trading is carried on, the greatest part of that trade from Sherbró to Cape Appolonia and among the rivers on the coast, as well as at Cape Formosa and Gaboon, is under the Spanish flag; and there is every reason to believe that three-fourths of the slaves carried from the coast north of the line (except by the Portuguese in the Bight of the Benin) are procured in the extensive rivers of Calabar, Cameroons, Bonny, Gaboon, &c.

A very extensive Portuguese slave trade is carried on in the Bight of Benin and Biafra, especially about Popo, Whydaw, and the Cameroons, and those vessels wishing to trade in slaves from the Gaboons and the places adjoining lie at Cape Lopez, in about one south, and send their large launches to those places to trade, and small craft are, also, constantly employed in carrying slaves from those places to St. Thomas, from whence they are shipped across the Atlantic; these facts have been repeatedly proved in the court of vice admiralty here, for instance, in the case of the Ceres, Joanna, Caroline, Dos Amigos, &c.

The islands of Cuba and Porto Rico are held out by the vessels under the Spanish flag as their ports of destination though there can be very little doubt but that many are intended for, and actually do unload at, the French West India islands. What becomes of the slaves after their arrival at the island of Cuba is no part of this question.

The Portuguese carry the greatest part of their slaves to Brazil, though many vessels, as the General Silveria and the Temerario, were intended for the Havana. It clearly appears, from the cases of the Intrepida and others, that a very considerable trade in slaves is carried on between the Brazils and that place. It may also be proper to remark that, from the open confessions of all the masters and super-cargoes of slave vessels brought in here, a most extensive slave trade is carried on at every part of the coast distant from a British settlement. So eager are the slave traders to carry on this trade, that after the cession of Goree and Senegal to France, but before the British troops had all left the former place, 200 slaves were actually exported from it. The Moorish princes are already ravaging the negro towns within their reach.

Query 8. Has this trade been lately carried on to a considerable extent on the coast north of the equator?

Answer 8. The preceding observations apply chiefly to the trade carried on north of the line; few of our cruisers go to the south of it, consequently very few vessels from that part of the coast are detained or sent in here. On this account it is difficult to form any opinion at this place on the trade carried on there, although no doubt can be entertained that it is still more extensive than that carried on to the north. Nearly all these observations are therefore intended for the trade north of the line; the extent and misery of which, though dreadful, are not one-half of what is entailed on the western coast of this continent.

Query 9. By what description of persons and under what flag?

Answer 9. It is impossible, from the art with which experience has taught them to cover their vessels, to say how much of the slave trade carried on is *bona fide* the property of the nation whose flag it bears; but from the proportion of vessels amongst those sent to this port for adjudication, which have been clearly proved to be fraudulently disguised, there is no doubt but that much English but more American property is engaged in it. The captain and supercargo are generally also Spanish subjects, though many instances have occurred to the contrary, and during the war the sailors were often of that nation. Since the war, however, this practice is altered. The large American privateers have been completely fitted out in America, with the exception, perhaps, of the gratings, and have come to the Havana fully manned, where a sale, or pretended sale having taken place, a Spanish subject or two are put on board, whilst the American mate and sailors remain, engage for a new voyage, and come upon the coasts; and there is too much reason to believe at present that many English sailors are also engaged in these vessels. With the exception of the Portuguese flag in the Bight of Benin and Biafra, and the rivers near the line, the trade carried on to the north is chiefly under the Spanish flag; though a few vessels, like the Louis, (French,) Rebecca, (American,) and two schooners (French) now said to be trading in slaves in the Gaboon, do now and then appear under their own flag. Some vessels, as the Catalina, have been also fitted out from Jamaica.

Query 10. Have these fraudulent slave traders come in armed vessels, and have they employed force to effectuate their purpose?

Answer 10. The fact is so notorious that the best answer to this query may be an enumeration of some cases concerning which we have certain information.

1. The schooner, name unknown, which destroyed the brig Kitty, of Liverpool, murdered the master, (Roach,) and carried the black people, two of whom were captured negroes of Sierra Leone, as slaves to the Havana.

2. The Campardown, a brig of sixteen guns, and a large complement of men, commanded by the same person as the preceding. She destroyed the sloops Rambler and Trial, belonging to this port, and carried the blacks off as slaves. It is supposed that she carried off at least two hundred free blacks in her different voyages, as she made slaves of all the people going off in canoes. She had several skirmishes with the Princess Charlotte, and was once chased by the Creole and Astrea.

3. The Laura Anna, taken in the Rio Nunez, where they were obliged to promise the sailors their wages to prevent an action.

4. The Venganza, which fought the party sent to the Gambia after her, and at last blew up whilst engaging.

5. The Moulatto, a large black-schooner from the Havana, which made two or three voyages to the coast, carried off a great number of free negroes, and beat the Princess Charlotte off.

6. A large black schooner, her companion, which also beat the Princess Charlotte off.

7. The Paz, which, under the American flag, beat off the Princess Charlotte and killed several of her men.

8. The Leal, Portuguese, a large brig under Portuguese colors, with twelve or fourteen guns, fought the Princess Charlotte off Lagos for a long time, but was taken.

9. The Rosa, formerly the American privateer Commodore Perry, fitted out in America and manned with Americans, but supposed to be the property of an Englishman, who was an old slave trader and partner of Boostock at Mesurado, fought the boats of his Majesty's ship Bann and the commissioned sloop Mary for some time, but was at length captured.

10. The schooner Guadaloupe, taken by the Young Princess Charlotte. Besides their regular charge of two round shot, ten guns were each of them loaded with bags of five hundred musket balls. She was taken by boarding.

11. Brig Temerario, from Brazil. She was built on purpose for this forced trade, has eighteen guns, which were cast on purpose with her name on them. She made one voyage to the coast, when she was chased by the Princess Charlotte, but escaped. On her second voyage she was taken, after an action of two hours, by his Majesty's ship Bann. She had a complement of eighty men.

12. Schooner Dolores, formerly American schooner Commodore M'Donough, said to belong to an English house in the Havana, taken after a severe action by his Majesty's ship Forrest.

13. Brig Nneva Paz, formerly the American privateer Argus, fitted from America, though supposed in part to be British property, and manned with Americans and English. She took and plundered the schooner Apollo, of this port, and made an attack on the Prince Regent, but was captured by boarding after a short but severe action.

14. Schooner Carmen, from Brazils, taken for slave trading to the north of the line.

15. Schooner Triumphante, from Havana, late the American privateer Criterion, of sixteen guns, commanded by a Portuguese subject, taken by the boats of the Prince Regent, after a severe action, in the river Cameroons.

16. American schooner Dorset, from Baltimore direct, called the Spanish schooner Triumvirate, with an American supercargo, a Spanish captain, and American, French, English, and Spanish crew, taken after a smart action in the Rio Pongas, last January, by a vessel from this place.

17. A large schooner, name unknown, supposed from the Havana, took and plundered the brig Industry, of this port, last November, and carried the greatest part of the crew off as slaves.

18. Saucy Jack, an American privateer, which carried off a cargo of slaves in 1814, and, I believe, convoyed several vessels to and from the coast. He boarded, but did not molest, a sloop from this place to Goree, with rice.

These are specific instances, which have all been proved before some court of justice, and it is notorious that these are not one-eighth part of the vessels of this description which come on the coast for the purpose of carrying on this trade.

It has also lately become the practice of these vessels to sail in company. Captain Lawson, of the ship Diana, wished last year to seize one in the river Bonny, (or Calabar,) but durst not, and Captain Hogan, during his last cruise in the Prince Regent, looked into their rivers, but durst not go in, though he had a crew of one hundred and twenty men.

Query 11. When interrupted, have they threatened to return with armed ships of a larger class?

Answer 11. Yes, almost uniformly; although, from the universality of the trade, it is difficult to remember every particular instance.

The Nueva Paz was one where the threat was put in execution; and one of the most violent of the slave traders has very lately returned to the Gallinas and sent up a message by an American that he was waiting for the Prince Regent. Unfortunately, she was unrigged and repairing at Bance Island, which gave an opportunity to the trader of carrying off a cargo of slaves. The Dolores and Temerario were avowedly fitted out for the destruction of the colonial brig, and there can be no doubt but that very violent and powerful attempts will be made for that purpose, as, from the great annoyance she has been to the slave traders, the constant terror which has existed of her being found between Cape Verd and Cape Palmas—a circumstance which has prevented many vessels from carrying on the slave trade in these limits—and from the number of vessels she has captured, she is the greatest object of hatred and detestation to the slave merchants.

Query 12: From whence are these armed contrabandists chiefly fitted out?

Answer 12. The Havana is the port from which the majority of these vessels are fitted out, though many of them, as the old American privateers, are fitted out in America, and only go to the Havana for papers; and whilst some, like the Triumvirata, also Dorset, have the papers carried from the Havana to America, a few, like the Louis, are fitted out from the French islands; and the Portuguese come from the Brazil.

Query 13. What has been the effect produced by their depredations on the north coast of the line?

Answer 13. The worst consequence of this contraband trade, as far as respects the civilization of the coast and the turning of the natives from this inhuman and destructive trade to the arts of social life and the pursuits of an innocent commerce, is, that the natives will never believe that the abolition is really to take place; and as long as one slave ship is allowed to visit the coast the natives will always be looking forward to more, and will never believe it to be for their interest to change their present pursuits.

There can be no doubt but that the natives, immediately after the English abolition act took place, were more inclined to believe in the probability of an universal abolition of the trade than they are now. A stop was put to the trade for some time, and it was nearly two years before the slave traders took to other flags, and in this interim the natives began to look forward to some other means of procuring the luxuries and necessaries of life; a few vessels, with American and English men and papers and a foreign flag, began at last to appear, and the hopes of the slave factors for a renewal of this trade to revive; and it has now increased to such an extent that the slave traders who frequent the part of the coast near Sierra Leone destroy every vessel they meet, unless of very considerable force, and these they drive away. This at first had merely the effect of injuring the owners of these vessels, but the practice being continued, and the slave traders having declared their determination to persist in it, whatever might be the consequence, no English vessel, especially if connected with this place, dare show itself on the neighboring coasts; the result of which is clear: the innocent coasting trade is completely destroyed, nothing but a large English vessel dare go, these go but seldom, and the natives, thus deprived of every other means of acquiring what to them have by habit become necessaries of life, must engage in the slave trade.

Query 14. What system do you conceive best calculated to repair this evil?

Answer 14. This certainly is a question which requires the greatest consideration and which will be very difficult to solve; as, however, we have the advantage of some experience to guide us, we may be more able to decide it now with the prospect of success than any person could have done in 1807.

The following points must be firmly established before any adequate success can be expected to follow the greatest efforts:

1. That the prohibition be positive and universal, and that all persons agree in the same regulations for its extinction.

2. That the penalties inflicted on persons and property engaged in it be severe and certain.

3. That power be given to all the contracting parties to enforce these regulations; that the force employed for this purpose be adequate to the object for which it is intended, and that the remuneration offered to the persons employed in this service be certain and easily obtained.

It must be clear and evident that whilst any one power is allowed to carry on the trade the subjects of the other powers (wishing to be engaged in it) will cover themselves under the flag of the permitting power, and, from the experience these men have had in the art of fraudulent disguise, will cover themselves beyond the possibility of detection. We need look no further for a proof of this than to the difference between the Spanish slave trade before the war, in the years 1808, 1809, and now.

It is also clear, that to make this a common cause, and not the cause of each State entering into the agreement, the regulations, provisions, and penalties attached to it should be the same in all; and that it should not only be agreed upon between the States, but that every individual State should make a positive internal law upon the subject, embracing all the regulations, &c. And this is the more necessary to prevent any future collisions or jealousies in enforcing the penalties, for if the parties are honest in the cause, and the penalties to be inflicted by all the parties are equal, no difficulties can arise; but if they are unequal, a very great ground is laid for complaints, reproaches, and disputes, which would at once destroy everything which had previously been done.

As this may be a matter of much dispute, the following plan is proposed as less liable to objection:

That all property found engaged in the trade, either in the inception, the prosecution, or the conclusion, be confiscated to the seizer's use, either by the courts of his own country or by a tribunal to be specially appointed for that purpose.

That the sentence of inferior courts be final and conclusive whenever slaves are found on board.

That an appeal be allowed if no slaves are on board. That some further punishment should be inflicted on the parties engaged, which, in case of resistance, should be much severer than when none was made; and that this punishment should be inflicted as agreed on between the contracting parties.

That death should be inflicted by the courts of the party's own country on the officers of any ship where free natives had been kidnapped or any persons killed by their piratical resistance.

Neither agreements, regulations, nor penalties will be of any use, unless the contracting parties are determined, one and all, to enforce them upon every person found engaged in the trade, and also to use every means of detecting them. This is an object which cannot be obtained with a small force.

A large one must at first be employed; but there is every reason to believe that this force, if actively and properly employed, would soon render it safe to reduce it.

The whole coast of Africa will be frequented by the smugglers, and smugglers there will be, unless some very energetic measures are adopted to prevent the importation of slaves into the trans-Atlantic world; and it is not to be supposed for a moment that the coast of Africa can be guarded by one ship.

Query 15. What progress had there been made during the war to exclude the trade in slaves from the coast of Africa north of the line?

Answer 15. Whatever exclusion has taken place during the last war must be attributed chiefly to the war itself and the activity of the officers employed. Generally one, sometimes two, and now and then three ships-of-war were on the coast. After the settlement was formed in the Gambia the slave trade was completely excluded to the northward of Bissao; the trade between that place and Popo was reduced from a most extensive and open trade to a comparatively small and smuggling one. It was entirely suppressed for a considerable distance round the British settlements.

Query 16. What effect can be traced to have arisen from such exclusion upon the interior civilization and industry, or upon the external commerce of this part of the coast, compared with what existed twenty years before?

Answer 16. The civilization, to a certain degree, of the natives, for some distance around the British settlements, and in those places where the trade was entirely excluded, is the effect of the partial abolition; the natives have also become more peaceable and quiet, and have turned their attention to the arts of a civilized life, and have left off those practices whose only object was to procure slaves. In places where the exclusion of the trade has only been partial these advantages have not arisen. Wars, kidnappings, and false trials have not been so frequent, because the demand for slaves was small; still they existed, and the natives, with minds unchanged, continued to have recourse to them when slaves were wanted. No doubt can exist but that these circumstances have affected the very interior of the continent, and that though not more civilized, yet they have been more peaceable and quiet since the abolition than before, for the slaves procured are not more in number than answer the present comparatively small demand. The effects upon the external commerce of the coast has been astonishing; compare the imports into England at present with what they were twenty years ago. Let it also be considered that not one third, perhaps not one quarter, of the trade goes to England, and then some ideas may be formed of the capabilities of the coast of Africa to carry on an immense traffic in innocent articles. A complete exclusion would do more to promote this object in five years than a partial one in fifty.

Query 17. State what measures are now in progress for the improvement of Africa, and how they are likely to be affected by the continuance of the trade, partially or generally?

Answer 17. Little can be here said upon the measures in progress for the civilization of Africa which is not known already. Since Senegal and Goree have been transferred, those measures are nearly confined to Sierra Leone. Here the greatest improvements have been and are still making, and hence must the civilization of Africa proceed. With common attention a large number of persons may be educated, anxious and capable of spreading the blessings they have received throughout their native continent. But where the slave trade is allowed no improvements can come; its pestiferous breath blasts at once the hopes of the philanthropist and the missionary, and a train of desolation, barbarity, and misery follows close on the steps of the slave trader.

Query 18. Is there any reason to apprehend that the contraband trade may become extensive in time of peace, even on the coast north of the line, where so considerable a progress had been made to suppress the slave trade generally, if some decisive measures are not adopted by the powers conjointly to suppress the same?

Answer 18. Of this not a doubt can exist. It will be carried on more extensively and more ferociously than ever. It is since the conclusion of the war that the large armed vessels have increased so very considerably. Whilst the war existed, and condemnation followed resistance, those persons who thought their property secure if taken before courts of justice sent out unarmed and heavy sailing vessels; now that there is no penalty attached to it, every person engaging in the trade will send to the coast vessels well armed and manned, with orders to fight their way through every obstacle. The wages they give are enormous, from seven to ten pounds per month; and, in consequence, their vessels will be soon manned with entire crews of American and English sailors. The greatest enormities will be perpetrated, and, unless not only the right of search, with condemnation for resistance, be allowed, but also very vigorous measures be adopted to enforce it, these crimes must all pass unpunished.

Sierra Leone, *April*, 1817.

[Fourth inclosure in No. 2.]

Annex D to the protocol of the conference of the 4th of February, 1818.

Letter of Z. Macauley, Esq., to Viscount Castlereagh, dated

London, *December* 20, 1817.

My Lord: I have been honored with your lordship's note of the 18th instant, acknowledging the receipt of the answers made on the 26th December, 1816, to the queries which your lordship had proposed relative to the then state of the African slave trade, and requesting the communication of such further intelligence as I might have since obtained. The answers to the same queries which I delivered last week to Mr. Planta were written on the coast of Africa in the month of April last, and therefore apply to a period six months later than that to which my answers refer. Since that time I have not received from Africa any detailed communications on this subject. Such as I have received I will now lay before your lordship.

Colonel Mac Carthy, the Governor of Sierra Leone, in a letter dated April 20, 1817, observes, "I am grieved to say that there is nothing favorable to state with respect to the slave trade, which has not only been renewed in those places from which it had been driven, but actually extended three times as far as at any period during the late war." This representation has been fully confirmed to me, and it is added, "that the slave trade is now openly and undisguisedly carried on both at Senegal and Goree."

·. Governor Mac Carthy, in a subsequent letter, dated June 10, 1817, says: "The slave trade is carried on most vigorously by the Spaniards, Portuguese, Americans, and French. I have had it affirmed from several quarters, and do believe it to be a fact, that there is a greater number of vessels employed in that traffic than at any former period." To the same effect are the letters I have received from Sierra Leone, which, under date of 28th June, 1817, state as follows: "The coast is crowded with slave ships, and no trade can be done where they are. We could get rice to leeward, but dare not go there, as we are certain of being plundered by them. I saw it mentioned in a London newspaper, that a Carthagenian pirate had been plundering our vessels. It was a Havana slave ship, and all the Spaniards who come on the coast swear to do the same whenever they have it in their power. If this should be suffered, we must give up all the trade, and leave the African coast to the slave dealers."

On the 20th of July, 1817, it is further stated as follows: "The slave trade is raging dreadfully on the coast. Goree has become quite an emporium of this traffic. Our merchants are losing the whole trade of the coast. The whole benefit of it accrues to the slave dealers. No other trade can be carried on where the slave trade prevails."

This view of the subject is confirmed in a report recently published by the Church Missionary Society in Africa and the east. The committee of that society, in communicating to its subscribers the substance of the information recently received from their missionaries on the windward coast of Africa, observes as follows: "The natives saw the missionaries sit down in the midst of them while the slave trade was yet a traffic, sanctioned by the laws of this country and of the civilized world. They utterly disbelieved at first the professions of the missionaries; and, when at length brought by their patient and consistent conduct to believe them, yet so debased were their minds by that traffic which our nation in particular had so long maintained among them, that they had no other value for the education offered to their children than as they conceived it would make them more cunning than their neighbors. But the missionaries gladly became the teachers of their children, in the hope that they should outlive the difficulties which then opposed their mission. The act of abolition seemed to open a bright prospect to the friends of Africa. The numerous slave factories which crowded the Rio Pongas vanished, and Christian churches began to spring up in their room. The country was gradually opening itself to the instruction of the missionaries, when the revival of the slave trade by some of the European powers proved a temptation too great to be resisted. At the moment when the natives began to assemble to hear the missionaries preach, and even to erect houses for the worship of God, at this moment their ancient enemy comes in like a flood, and, it is to be feared, will drive away our missionaries for a time. So great is the demoralizing effect of the slave trade, and so inveterate the evil habits which it generates, that it is not improbable it may be necessary to withdraw wholly, for the present, the society's settlements formed beyond the precincts of the colony of Sierra Leone." Subsequent accounts render it probable that this anticipation has been actually realized.

In addition to the facts already adduced to show the prevalence of French slave trade, a letter from Dominica, dated January 7, 1817, states, "that in the month of November, 1816, a Portuguese brig, the Elenora, of Lisbon, with 265 Africans, from Gaboon, arrived off St. Pierre's, in Martinique, and on the 25th of the same month landed them at Carlet, between St. Pierre's and Fort Royal, the brig afterwards returning to the former port." It was also known that two vessels had been fitted out and despatched from St. Pierre's to the coast of Africa for slaves, and that at the same time a fast-sailing schooner was about to depart for a similar purpose. "The impunity," it is added, "which these infractions of treaties meet with in the French colonies will no doubt increase the repetition of them to an unbounded degree." In a subsequent letter, dated Dominica, September 4, 1817, it is observed: "A few weeks ago a large ship arrived from the coast of Africa, and landed at Martinique more than five hundred slaves; they were disembarked some little distance from St. Pierre's, and marched in by twenties."

In addition to these instances of slave trading, I have to state that a gentleman who returned about a fortnight since from a voyage to the coast of Africa informed me that while he was lying (about three or four months ago) in the river Gambia two French vessels navigating under the white flag carried off openly from that river 350 slaves.

The following extract of a letter from Cape Coast Castle, March 5, 1817, shows that the Dutch functionaries in that quarter, notwithstanding the decrees of their Government, are actively engaged in the slave trade. "We deem it our duty to inform you of the conduct of the Governor of Elmina; we are well aware that a particular feature in the Dutch Government at this time is the desire of preventing the slave trade, which their representative in this country takes every opportunity of aiding and abetting. Portuguese vessels are furnished with canoes, and Spaniards supplied with water. The beginning of last month a Spanish ship was four days at anchor in Elmina, receiving water and bartering dollars for such goods as were suited for the purchase of slaves. This vessel proceeded a short distance to leeward, and came to anchor off Opam, a place about eight miles to the eastward of Tantum, where the master purchased to the number of 400 slaves, and carried them off to the coast; a Spanish schooner also took slaves off from the same neighborhood about three months ago."

I have the honor to be, &c.,

Z. MACAULEY.

Viscount Castlereagh, K. G., &c., &c., &c.

No. 3.

Protocol of the conference between the plenipotentiaries of the five powers of February 7, 1818.

Present: Baron De Humboldt, Lord Castlereagh, Count Lieven, Marquis D'Osmond, and Prince Esterhazy.

The protocol of the last conference being read, the plenipotentiaries approved and signed it.

Count Palmella having accepted the verbal invitation which, in conformity to what had been agreed upon at the conference of the 4th of February last, was made to him by the plenipotentiaries, Lord Castlereagh communicates to him the convention concluded between his Government and that of Spain on the 23d September, 1817, relative to the abolition of the slave trade, and invites him, in concert with the plenipotentiaries his colleagues, to add his efforts to theirs for the attainment of an object so interesting to humanity, and which can only be completed when his most faithful Majesty shall have adopted similar measures.

Count Palmella replied, that in accepting, by his note of the 17th February, 1817, the invitation which had been addressed to his predecessor to take part in the conferences held in pursuance of the additional article of the treaty of Paris of the 20th of November, 1815, he had, by order of his court, declared the conditions upon which he was authorized to assist at these conferences, and that he did not doubt, from the renewed invitation he had just received from the plenipotentiaries, but that those "bases" had been accepted, the more so as they were entirely grounded upon the most just principles.

Count Palmella added, that he would lose no time in transmitting to his court the communication of the treaty just concluded between the British and Spanish Governments for the abolition of the slave trade on the part of the subjects of his Catholic Majesty; and that his most faithful Majesty, according to the known principles professed by him individually, would doubtless behold with the most perfect satisfaction the advantages which would thereby result to the cause of humanity; which principles his plenipotentiaries had solemnly declared at the Congress of Vienna, and to which Count Palmella entirely referred himself, as also to the explanations given at the same period respecting the circumstances particularly affecting the Brazils.

Upon which the sitting was adjourned.

HUMBOLDT.
ESTERHAZY.
D'OSMOND.
LIEVEN.
CASTLEREAGH.

No. 4.

Protocol of the conference between the plenipotentiaries of the five powers of February 11, 1818.

Present: Lord Castlereagh, Count Lieven, Baron De Humboldt, Marquis D'Osmond, and Prince Esterhazy.

The protocol of the last conference of the 7th February being read, was approved and signed.

Count Palmella having declared himself, at the conference of the 7th of February, ready to receive and transmit to his court the communication of the convention concluded between Great Britain and Spain, under date of the 23d of September, 1817, the plenipotentiaries agree to inclose the same to him in a note, which is annexed to this protocol, *sub. lit.* A.

The plenipotentiaries do not consider themselves called upon to enter at present into discussion on the subject of the conditions stated in Count Palmella's official note of the 17th of February, 1817, and to which he alluded at the last conference, thinking it sufficient to refer, as to the principal object of their present proceeding, entirely to what is to be found in the protocols of the conferences held on this subject at the Congress of Vienna, as also to the solemn declaration of the powers, dated on the 8th of February, 1815, made at the said Congress.

Upon which the sitting was adjourned.

HUMBOLDT.
ESTERHAZY.
D'OSMOND.
LIEVEN.
CASTLEREAGH.

[Inclosure in No. 4.]

Annex A to the protocol of the conference of the 11th of February, 1818.

Note of the plenipotentiaries of the five powers to Count Palmella.

LONDON, *December* 11, 1817.

The undersigned, in reference to the communication made to Count Palmella at the conference of the 7th instant, lose no time in having the honor of transmitting herewith inclosed to his excellency the treaty concluded between his Britannic Majesty and his Catholic Majesty, which stipulates on the part of Spain the final abolition of the slave trade, and thus offers a very satisfactory result to the solicitude which their respective courts evince for the fulfilment of the engagements they have contracted by the additional article of the treaty of Paris of the 20th of November, 1815. The complete attainment of this interesting object, now solely depending on the abandonment by the court of Portugal of that part of the slave trade which she has still reserved to herself south of the line, the undersigned have the honor to invite Count Palmella to solicit from his court full powers to enable him to act in concert with them towards the accomplishment of so desirable an object.

They have at the same time the honor to add herewith extracts from the protocols of the two last conferences on this subject for his excellency's information, and they avail themselves of this opportunity to offer him the assurances of their distinguished consideration.

LIEVEN.
HUMBOLDT.
CASTLEREAGH.
D'OSMOND.
ESTERHAZY.

No. 5.

Extract of the protocol of the sitting of the 14th of February, 1818.

Present: The Marquis D'Osmond, Lord Castlereagh, Baron De Humboldt, Prince Esterhazy, and Count De Lieven.

The plenipotentiaries having approved the protocol of the last conference of the 11th of February, it is signed.

The answer of the Count de Palmella to the note which the plenipotentiaries addressed to him on the 11th of February is read and placed upon the present protocol, *sub. lit.* A.

[Inclosure in No. 5.]

Annex A to the protocol of the 14th of February, 1818.

LONDON, *February* 12, 1818.

The undersigned has received the note which. the plenipotentiaries of those courts who signed the additional article of the treaty of Paris of the 20th of November, 1815, have done him the honor to address to him under the date of yesterday.

He will take the earliest opportunity of conveying to the knowledge of his court the treaty concluded between his Britannic Majesty and his Catholic Majesty, which their excellencies have been pleased to communicate to him officially, together with the extracts of the protocols of their two last conferences on this subject.

The undersigned, being already furnished with the full powers and instructions necessary to enable him to assist at the conferences held by their excellencies, and to discuss in concert with them the means of attaining the desirable objects in question, does not think himself entitled to ask for new full powers unless the question should positively change its nature by a refusal (which the undersigned cannot possibly expect from the plenipotentiaries) to admit on their part the principles put forth in the first note which he had the honor to address to them. Whenever their excellencies shall think themselves called upon to enter into the discussion of those principles, they will see that they all evidently and immediately spring from the declaration of the Congress of Vienna of the 8th February, 1815, and from the treaty concluded at the period of the said Congress between his most faithful Majesty and his Britannic Majesty for the extinction of the slave trade to the north of the line.

The undersigned takes this opportunity of offering to their excellencies the assurance of his high consideration.

THE COUNT DE PALMELLA.

Memorandum.—The plenipotentiaries, having reason to understand that the instructions under which Count Palmella acted were not of a nature which would enable him to conclude any convention assigning any fixed period for the abolition on the part of Portugal without reference to his Government, did not think it expedient to enter, under such circumstances, into further discussions with Count Palmella, inasmuch as they conceived that such discussions could not have led to any satisfactory result.

UNITED STATES.

No. VI.

Letter from Viscount Castlereagh to Richard Rush, Esq., American minister in London, dated

FOREIGN OFFICE, *June* 20, 1818.

SIR: The distinguished share which the Government of the United States has, from the earliest period, borne in advancing the cause of the abolition of the slave trade, makes the British Government desirous of submitting to their favorable consideration whatever may appear to them calculated to bring about the final accomplishment of this great work of humanity. The laudable anxiety with which you personally interest yourself in whatever is passing upon this important subject will have led you to perceive that, with the exception of the crown of Portugal, all States have now either actually prohibited the traffic in slaves to their subjects or fixed an early period for its cessation, whilst Portugal has also renounced it to the north of the equator. From May, 1820, there will not be a flag which *can legally* cover this detested traffic to the north of the line, and there is reason to hope that the Portuguese may ere long be also prepared to abandon it to the south of the equator; but so long as some effectual concert is not established amongst the principal maritime powers for preventing their respective flags from being made a cover for any illicit slave trade, there is but too much reason to fear, whatever may be the state of the law on this subject, that the evil will continue to exist, and, in proportion as it assumes a contraband form, that it will be carried on under the most aggravated circumstances of cruelty and desolation. It is from a deep conviction of this truth, founded upon experience, that the British Government, in all its late negotiations upon this subject, has endeavored to combine a system of alliance for the suppression of this most abusive practice, with the engagements which it has succeeded in contracting with the Governments of Spain and Portugal for the total or partial abolition of the slave trade. I have now the honor to inclose to you copies of the treaties which have been happily concluded with those powers, together with the acts which have recently passed the legislature for carrying the same into execution.

I have also the satisfaction to transmit to you copies of a treaty which has been recently concluded with the King of the Netherlands for the like purpose, though at too late a period in the session to admit of its provisions receiving the sanction of Parliament. I am induced to call your attention more particularly to this convention, as it contains certain provisions which were calculated to limit in some respects the powers mutually conceded by the former treaties in a manner which, without essentially weakening their force, may render them acceptable to the contracting parties.

The intimate knowledge which you possess of this whole subject renders it unnecessary for me, in requesting you to bring these documents to the observation of your Government, to accompany them with any more detailed explanations. What I have earnestly to beg of you is, to bring them under the serious consideration of the President, intimating to him the earnest wish of the British Government, that the exertions of the two States may be combined upon a somewhat similar principle to put down this great moral disobedience wherever it may be committed to the laws of both countries. I am confident this cannot effectually be done except by mutually conceding to each other's ships-of-war a qualified right of search, with a power of detaining the vessels of either State with slaves actually on board. You will perceive in these conventions a studious and, I trust, a successful attempt to narrow and limit this power within due bounds, and to guard it against perversion.

If the American Government is disposed to enter into a similar concert, and can suggest any further regulations the better to obviate abuse, this Government will be most ready to listen to any suggestion of this nature; their only object being to contribute, by every effort in their power, to put an end to this disgraceful traffic.

I am, &c.,

CASTLEREAGH.

Richard Rush, Esq., &c.

No. VII.

Letter from Richard Rush, Esq., to Viscount Castlereagh, dated

London, *June* 23, 1818.

My Lord: I have been honored with your lordship's note of the 20th of this month, inclosing copies of treaties recently concluded between this Government and the Governments of Portugal, Spain, and the Netherlands, respectively, in relation to the slave trade, and designed to draw the attention of the Government of the United States to this subject, with a view to its co-operation, upon principles similar to those held out in these treaties, in measures that may tend to the more complete and universal abolition of the traffic.

The United States, from an early day of their history, have regarded with deep and uniform abhorrence the existence of a traffic attended by such complications of misery and guilt. Its transcendent evils roused throughout all ranks a corresponding zeal for their extirpation; one step followed another until humanity triumphed; and against its continuance, in any shape, by their own citizens, the most absolute prohibitions of their code have, for a period of more than ten years, been rigorously and, it is hoped, beneficially levelled. Your lordship will pardon me this allusion to the earnest efforts of the United States to put down the trade within their own limits; falling in, as it merely does, with the tribute which you have been pleased to pay to their early exertions in helping to dry up this prolific source of human woe.

Whether any causes may throw obstacles in the way of their uniting in that concert of external measures, in which Europe generally, and this nation in particular, are now so happily engaged, the more effectually to banish from the world this great enormity, I dare not, in the total absence of all instructions, presume to intimate, much less have I any opinion of my own to offer upon a subject so full of delicacy and interest; but it is still left for me to say, that I shall perform a duty peculiarly gratifying, in transmitting, by the earliest opportunities, copies of your lordship's note, with the documents which accompanied it, to my Government; and I sufficiently know the permanent sensibility which pervades all its councils upon this subject to promise that the overture which the former embraces will receive from the President the full and anxious consideration due to its importance, and, above all, to the enlarged philanthropy, on the part of this Government, by which it has been dictated.

I have, &c.,

RICHARD RUSH.

Viscount Castlereagh, K. G., &c.

No. VIII.

Note from Richard Rush, Esq., to Viscount Castlereagh, dated

London, *December* 21, 1818.

The undersigned, envoy extraordinary and minister plenipotentiary from the United States, has the honor to present his compliments to Lord Castlereagh.

In the note of the 23d of June, which the undersigned had the honor to address to his lordship, in answer to his lordship's communication of the 20th of the same month, relative to the slave trade, the undersigned had great pleasure in giving the assurance that he would transmit a copy of that communication to his Government, together with the documents which accompanied it, being copies of treaties entered into on the part of Great Britain with Spain, Portugal, and the Netherlands, for the more complete abolition of the odious traffic in slaves. He accordingly lost no time in fulfilling that duty, and has now the honor to inform his lordship of the instructions with which he has been furnished by his Government in reply.

He has been distinctly commanded, in the first place, to make known the sensibility of the President to the friendly spirit of confidence in which these treaties and the legislative measures of Parliament founded upon them, have been communicated to the United States; and to the invitation which has been given, that they would join in the same or similar arrangements, the more effectually to accomplish the beneficial objects to which they look. He is further commanded to give the strongest assurances that the solicitude of the United States for the universal extirpation of this traffic continues with all the earnestness which has so long and steadily distinguished the course of their policy in relation to it.

Of their general prohibitory law of 1807 it is unnecessary that the undersigned should speak, his lordship being already apprised of its provisions; amongst which the authority to employ the national force, as auxiliary to its execution, will not have escaped attention. But he has it in charge to make known, as a new pledge of their unremitting and active desire in the cause of abolition, that so lately as the month of April last another act of Congress was passed, by which not only are the citizens and vessels of the United States interdicted from carrying on or being in any way engaged in the trade, but in which also the best precautions that legislative enactments can devise, or their penalties enforce, are raised up against the introduction into their territories of slaves from abroad, under whatever pretext attempted, and especially from dominions which lie more immediately in their neighborhood. A copy of this act is herewith inclosed for the more particular information of his lordship.

That peculiarity in the eighth section which throws upon a defendant the labor of proof as the condition of acquittal, the undersigned persuades himself will be regarded as signally manifesting an anxiety to suppress the hateful offence, departing as it does from the analogy of criminal jurisprudence, which so generally requires the independent and positive establishment of guilt as the first step in every public prosecution. To measures of such a character, thus early adopted and sedulously pursued, the undersigned is further commanded to say that the Government of the United States, acting within the pale of its constitutional powers, will always be ready to superadd any others that experience may prove to be necessary for attaining the desirable end in view.

But on examining the provisions of the treaties which your lordship honored the undersigned by communicating, it has appeared to the President that their essential articles are of a character not adapted to the circumstances or to the institutions of the United States.

The powers agreed to be given to the ships-of-war of either party to search, capture, and carry into port for adjudication, the merchant vessels of the other, however qualified, is connected with the establishment, by each treaty, of mixed courts, one of which is to have its seat in the colonial possessions of the parties, respectively. The institution of such tribunals is necessarily regarded as fundamental to the whole arrangement, whilst their peculiar structure is doubtless intended, and would seem to be indispensable, towards imparting to it a just reciprocity. But to this part of the system the United States, having no colonies upon the coast of Africa, in the West Indies, or elsewhere, cannot give effect.

Moreover, the powers of government in the United States, whilst they can only be exercised within the grants, are also subject to the restrictions of the Federal Constitution. By the latter instrument all judicial power is to be vested in a Supreme Court, and in such other inferior courts as Congress may, from time to time, ordain and establish. It further provides that the judges of these courts shall hold their offices during good behavior, and be removable on impeachment and conviction of crimes and misdemeanors. There are serious doubts whether, obeying the spirit of these injunctions, the Government of the United States would be competent to appear as party to the institution of a court for carrying into execution their penal statutes in places out of their own territory; a court consisting partly of foreign judges, not liable to impeachment under the authority of the United States, and deciding upon their statutes without appeal.

Again, obstacles would exist towards giving validity to the disposal of the negroes found on board the slave trading vessels condemned by the sentence of the mixed courts. If they should be delivered over to the Government of the United States as freemen, they could not, but by their own consent, be employed as servants or free laborers. The condition of negroes, and other people of color, in the United States being regulated by the municipal laws of the separate States, the Government of the former could neither guaranty their liberty in the States where they could only be received as slaves, nor control them in the States where they would be recognized as free. The provisions of the fifth section of the act of Congress which the undersigned has the honor to inclose will be seen to point to this obstacle, and may be taken as still further explanatory of its nature.

These are some of the principal reasons which arrest the assent of the President to the very frank and friendly overture contained in your lordship's communication. Having their foundation in constitutional impediments the Government of his Britannic Majesty will know how to appreciate their force. It will be seen how compatible they are with the most earnest wishes, on the part of the United States, that the measures concerted by these treaties may bring about the total downfall of the traffic in human blood, and with their determination to co-operate, to the utmost extent of their constitutional power, towards this great consummation, so imperiously due at the hands of all nations to the past wrongs and sufferings of Africa.

The undersigned prays Lord Castlereagh to accept the assurances of his distinguished consideration.

RICHARD RUSH.

Viscount CASTLEREAGH, K. G., &c.

CONFERENCES AT AIX-LA-CHAPELLE.

No. IX.

Despatch from Viscount Castlereagh to Earl Bathurst, dated

AIX-LA-CHAPELLE, *November* 2, 1818.

MY LORD: In the conference of the 24th October I opened to the plenipotentiaries the existing state of the trade in slaves and the progress made by the plenipotentiaries in London in proposing further measures for accomplishing its final abolition.

As the further examination of this question required that the ministers should have time to peruse the voluminous documents connected with it, I gave notice that I should, on a future day, submit to them two propositions:

The first, for addressing a direct appeal on the part of the five courts to the King of Portugal, founded upon the declaration made in his Majesty's name by his plenipotentiary at Vienna, and urging his Majesty to give effect to that declaration at the period fixed by Spain for final abolition, viz, on the 20th May, 1820.

The second would be, that the powers there represented should accept the principle of a qualified right of mutual visit as adopted by the courts of Great Britain, Spain, Portugal, and the Netherlands, and should apply the same to the case of their respective flags as circumstances should point out.

It was impossible not to perceive in the short discussion which ensued that there was considerable hesitation, especially in the French plenipotentiary, with regard to the principle of the latter measure. Under these circumstances I thought it better to avoid a prolongation of the conversation. I had an interview with the Duke de Richelieu on the following day for the purpose of urging his excellency to a more favorable view of this important question. This led to a very full examination of the measure in all its bearings; and though I cannot say that I succeeded in shaking his grace's opinion, I flatter myself I reduced the weight and number of his objections, and that I brought his mind to feel the extreme inconvenience as well as moral objection to leaving the question where it is.

It is due to the Duke de Richelieu that I should state that I have found his excellency uniformly anxious to render the measures of his own Government effectual to its object; and that he has been cordially disposed to receive and follow up every information which I have laid before him concerning the malpractices of the subjects of France in this traffic; but he seems, as yet, under great apprehension of the effect in France of any concession of the nature above suggested.

The Duke, however, gave me every assurance of its being fully considered, and as a means of doing so, his excellency desired me to furnish him with a memorandum stating the substance of those explanations which I had given him of the question. I now have to transmit to your lordship a copy of this paper, and to assure you that I shall lose no opportunity, in conjunction with the Duke of Wellington, of following up with zeal and perseverance this important part of my instructions.

I have the honor, &c.,

CASTLEREAGH.

Earl BATHURST, &c., &c., &c.

[First inclosure in No. 9.]

Protocol of the conference between the five powers held at Aix-la-Chapelle October 24, 1818.

Lord Castlereagh makes known to the conference the result hitherto obtained by the measures adopted for the general abolition of the trade in slaves and of the actual state of things in regard to this interesting question, distinguishing between the legal and the illegal trade. His excellency observed, that since the convention of the 23d of September, 1817, by which Spain fixed the year 1820 for the final termination of this traffic, Portugal was the only power which had not explained itself as to the period of abolition. Lord Castlereagh added, that whilst there was a State whose laws authorized the trade, if it were but partially, and a flag which could protect it, it would scarcely be possible to prevent the continuation of this commerce by contraband means, the increase of which had been very considerable of late years; and that even when the slave trade should be prohibited by the laws of all civilized countries, an active and permanent *surveillance* could alone guaranty the execution of those laws.

After this representation, Lord Castlereagh communicated several papers relative to the question, referring to the details already submitted to the ministers assembled in London. He at the same time explained his ideas:

1st. Upon the means of prosecuting the application of the principle of the legal abolition of the trade.
2d. Upon the means of insuring the execution of the laws and conventions relating to it.

Relative to the first object, Lord Castlereagh proposed that a measure should be agreed upon to be taken with respect to the court of Rio de Janerio, in order to induce it to explain itself as to the period it intended to fix for the final abolition of the trade.

Relative to the second object, his excellency proposed to adopt generally and in an obligatory form the measures decreed by the last treaties between Great Britain, Spain, Portugal, and the kingdom of the Netherlands.

These propositions were taken *ad referendum*, and it was agreed to resume the deliberation in a subsequent sitting.

METTERNICH.
RICHELIEU.
CASTLEREAGH.
HARDENBERG.
BERNSTORFF.
NESSELRODE.
CAPO D'ISTRIA

[Second inclosure in No. 9.]

Note from Viscount Castlereagh to the Duke de Richelieu, dated

AIX-LA-CHAPELLE, *October* 27, 1818.

Lord Castlereagh has the honor to inclose to the Duke de Richelieu the memorandum which he yesterday promised to submit to his excellency's consideration.

Lord Castlereagh will be most happy to reply, without loss of time, to any queries which the Duke de Richelieu will have the goodness to put to him on this subject, or to procure for his excellency any information which may appear to him material, and which Lord Castlereagh may not have the means of immediately himself supplying.

Lord Castlereagh requests the Duke de Richelieu to accept the assurances of his distinguished consideration.

[Third inclosure in No. 9.]

MEMORANDUM. (A)

1. *As to Right of Visit.*

None of the three conventions signed by Great Britain with Spain, Portugal, and Holland, gives this right to King's ships indiscriminately. In all it is confined to King's ships having the *express instructions and authority*, as specified in the treaty.

The provision is, in all cases, reciprocal, but the treaty with the Netherlands restricts the exercise of this right to a specified number of ships of each power, not exceeding twelve in the whole. Each power, as soon as it grants these instructions to any of its ships-of-war, is bound to notify to the other the name of the vessel so authorized to visit.

2. *Right of Detention.*

No visit or detention can take place except by a commissioned officer having the instructions above referred to as his special authority for the same; nor can he detain and carry into port any vessel so visited except on the single and simple fact of *slaves found on board*. There is a saving clause to distinguish domestic slaves acting as servants or sailors from those strictly appertaining to the traffic. The powers mutually engage to make the officer personally responsible for any abusive exercise of authority, independent of the pecuniary indemnity to be paid, as hereafter stated, to the owner for the improper detention of his vessel.

3. *Adjudication.*

The visiting officer finding slaves on board, as he conceives, contrary to law, may carry the vessel into whichever of the two ports is the nearest where the mixed commission belonging to the capturing and captured vessels shall reside; but by doing so, he not only renders himself personally responsible to his own Government for the discretion of the act, but he also makes his Government answerable to the Government of the State to whom the vessel so detained belongs for the full compensation, in pecuniary damage, which the mixed commission may award to the owners for the detention, if unjustifiably made.

The mixed commission has no jurisdiction of a criminal character, and consequently can neither detain nor punish the persons found on board ships so detained for any offences they may, by such slave trading, have committed against the laws of their particular State. The mixed commission has no other authority than summarily to decide whether the ship has been properly detained or not for having slaves illicitly on board. If this is decided in the affirmative, the ship and cargo (if any on board) are forfeited, the proceeds to be equally divided between the *two States;* the slaves to be provided for by the State in whose territory the condemnation takes place.

If the mixed commission orders the vessel to be released, it is required at the same moment to award such pecuniary compensation to the owners for the detention as appears to them reasonable.

A table of demurrage is given in the treaties, and the Government of the detaining officer is bound to discharge the same so awarded, without appeal, within twelve months.

The mixed commission is composed of a commissary judge and a commissary arbitrator, of each nation, as provided in the convention signed between Great Britain and France, in 1815, for adjudicating the private claims.

4. *The Sphere of Operation.*

In the Spanish and Portuguese conventions there is no other restriction as to the limits within which detention as above may take place than what arose naturally out of the state of the laws, viz: That so long as either power might lawfully trade in slaves to the south of the equator, no detention should take place within those limits.

In the convention with Holland a line is drawn from the Straits of Gibraltar to a point in the United States, so as to except out of the operation what may be called the European seas.

In all these conventions the whole range of voyage from the coast of Africa to the opposite shores of both Americas, including the West Indies, is subjected to the regulated *surveillance* thus established.

Observations.

Upon the first head, it does not occur that any further restrictions than those provided in the Netherlands convention can be required; but this is always open to negotiation.

The same observation appears applicable to the second head.

The same observation applies also to the third head, with this distinction, that a State, such as Austria, for example, agreeing to the measure, but having little or no trade on that coast, instead of immediately going to the expense of constituting commissions, might reserve the power of doing so whenever she thought fit; or might be enabled, if she prefer it, to authorize the Commissioners of any other State to take cognizance in her name of any cases in which the property of Austrian subjects might be concerned.

The fourth head seems most susceptible of comment, as it admits the possibility of search over the whole surface of the Atlantic and in the West Indian seas, where the trading vessels of commercial States are more numerous than on the coast of Africa.

Great Britain was herself so fully satisfied that under the checks established abuse is so little to be presumed, that she did not hesitate to expose her own commerce in those seas, however extended, to this, as she conceives, imaginary inconvenience; considering that so urgent a claim upon her humanity would not only justify but impose upon her as a moral duty even a greater sacrifice.

But notwithstanding what Great Britain has already done in her treaties with the three powers with whom she has contracted, and is ready to do with all other civilized States, namely, to run some risk of inconvenience for so noble a purpose, there is a distinction which may reasonably be taken between giving effect to this system upon the coast of Africa, and for a certain distance, say two hundred leagues from that particular coast, and the extending the same over the entire of the Atlantic and West Indian seas. The latter, as the most effectual measure, Great Britain has preferred, with whatever of inconvenience it may be connected in its operation; but she would not be the less disposed to attach value to the more limited application of the principle.

It may be stated that so long as the laws of any one State shall permit a trade in slaves, or that any flag shall exist in the world which is not comprehended in this system of maritime police against the contraband slave trader, the evil will continue to exist. This reasoning, although plausible, should not discourage a common effort against the abuse committed, and upon close examination it will be found fallacious.

1st. The whole of the African coast north of the line is, at this moment, emancipated from the traffic by the laws of all the States having colonies.

2d. By the 20th May, 1820, no flag of any such State will be enabled legally to carry on the traffic anywhere to the north of the line on either side of the Atlantic, nor any flag other than the Portuguese be authorized to trade south of the line.

Supposing, for a moment, that Portugal should not abolish to the south of the line till the expiration of the eight years complete from the declaration of Vienna, viz, 1823, what an immense sphere, nevertheless, of salutary operation would not this conservative alliance have in the interval?

The other branch of the objection is not more solid. It is true that the ship and flag of the smallest power might, in legal theory, cover these transactions; but where the property is not belonging to a subject of that power, but of a State that has abolished, the flag of that power, so used in fraud, would be no cover, and the property thus masked would be condemned, whilst the sovereign whose flag was thus prostituted neither could nor would complain.

But so long as any of the great powers, such as France, having a considerable extent of commerce on those coasts, shall refuse to adopt the system, not only their example will discourage other States whose interest is merely nominal from taking a part, but it will furnish the illicit slave trader with a flag, not only so much to be respected in itself, but so presumable to be found on the coast for purposes of innocent commerce, that no commissioned officer will run the risk of looking into such a vessel at the hazard of involving himself and his Government in a question with a foreign power. The practical as well as the moral effects of the principal maritime States making common cause upon this subject is incalculable. In fact, it must be decisive; without it their flags must be made the instrument of reciprocally withdrawing the subject from the authority of the sovereign when committing this offence.

This latter point will appear clear when we consider the working of the system under the two alternatives: If all the great maritime States adopt the principle, their cruisers form but one squadron against the illicit slave traders, and none of their flags can be made to cover the fraudulent transaction; the immediate effect of which would be considerably to multiply the number of the cruisers, consequently the chance of captures, whilst it would reduce the number of the flags which the illicit slave traders could assume. Whereas, if France acts alone, the danger to the French illicit trade is reduced to the chance of what her own cruisers may be enabled to effect along the immensity of that coast; and even where a French armed ship falls in with a French slave trader, by hoisting English, Spanish, Portuguese, or Dutch colors, the French officer, supposing him anxious to do his duty, will be very cautious in hazarding a visit where there is so reasonable a presumption that the vessel may be what the flag announces.

But take the other supposition, that all the principal maritime powers shall act in concert, and that the vessel suspected of having slaves on board hoists the flag of any other State, suppose the Hanseatic flag, the presumption is so conclusive against a Hamburg vessel trading in slaves on her own account, that no officer would hesitate to search the vessel in order to detect the fraud.

It may be further confidently asserted, that if the powers having a real and local interest come to an understanding and act together, the other States will cheerfully come into the measure, so far as not to suffer their flags to be so monstrously perverted and abused. The omission of France is, above all others, important, from its station in Europe, and from its possessions in Africa; its separation from the common effort, more especially if imitated by Russia, Austria, and Prussia, will not only disappoint all the hopes which the world has been taught to form with respect to the labors of the conference established in London, under the third additional article of the treaty of November, 1815, but will introduce schism and murmur into the ranks of the friends of abolition. The States having abolished will no longer form one compact and unanimous body, laboring to affiliate the State which has yet to abolish to a common system, and to render their own acts efficacious; but they will compose two sects, one of States that have made the possible inconvenience of a restricted visit to their merchant ships bend to the greater claims of humanity, the other of States considering their former objection as so far paramount as not to admit of any qualification, even for the indisputable advantage of a cause to the importance of which they have at Vienna given a not less solemn sanction. This must materially retard the ultimate success of the measure, and it may in the interval keep alive an inconvenient degree of controversy and agitation upon a subject which has contributed above all others seriously to excite the moral and religious sentiments of all nations, but especially of the British people, by whom the question has long been regarded as one of the deepest interest.

No. X.

Despatch from Viscount Castlereagh to Earl Bathurst, dated

Aix-la-Chapelle, *November* 12, 1818.

My Lord: I have the honor to inclose to your lordship the protocol of the conferences of the allied ministers of the 4th instant.

This protocol details the further proceedings upon the slave trade, and has annexed to it the memorandum drawn up by me on the same subject, which was communicated to your lordship in my despatch of the 2d instant.

I have, &c.,

CASTLEREAGH.

Earl Bathurst, &c., &c.

[Inclosure in No. 10.]

Protocol of the conferences between the plenipotentiaries of the five powers held at Aix-la-Chapelle the 4th of November, 1818.

In reference to the communications made to the conference on the 24th of October, Lord Castlereagh this day developed his propositions relative to the abolition of the slave trade; propositions the object of which is, on the one hand, to complete and extend the measures already adopted for the attainment of the definite extinction of this traffic, and on the other hand to insert the execution and the efficacy of those measures. As to the first object, Lord Castlereagh proposed that some measure should be adopted towards his Majesty the King of Portugal and Brazil, and that a letter should be written in the name of the sovereigns, in the most pressing and at the same time the most affectionate terms, in order to engage his most faithful Majesty, reminding him of the part he had taken in the declaration of Vienna of the 8th of February, 1815, to fix without further delay the period for the definitive abolition of the slave trade throughout his possessions, a period which, after the engagements entered into by the plenipotentiaries of his said Majesty at Vienna, and inserted in the protocol of the 20th of November, 1815, should not extend beyond the year 1823, but which the allied sovereigns desire, from the interest they take in this great cause, to see coincide with that which his Majesty the King of Spain has adopted in fixing the 30th of May, 1820, as the final term of that traffic. This proposition was unanimously received.

Lord Castlereagh, in calling the attention of the conference to the declaration of the plenipotentiaries of his most faithful Majesty, made at Vienna on the 6th of February, 1815, "that they were forced to require, as an indispensable condition for the final abolition, that his Britannic Majesty should on his side consent to the changes which they had proposed in the commercial system between Portugal and Great Britain," renewed the assurance that his Majesty the King of Great Britain was ready to accede to all the reasonable modifications which should be proposed in the existing treaties of commerce with Portugal; which assurance he had repeatedly given to the Portuguese minister in London. Lord Castlereagh, above all, desired to call the attention of the conference to the expression *reasonable modifications*, which he made use of, because he could not suppose that the Portuguese ministers intended to demand, on the part of a single power, sacrifices which one State could not well expect of another as indispensable conditions of a general measure, having for its object the good of humanity alone.

As to the second object, Lord Castlereagh communicated a memorandum (A) containing explanations of the treaties concluded in 1817 between Great Britain, Spain, and Portugal, and the kingdom of the Netherlands, establishing the right of visit against the vessels evidently suspected of being engaged in the trade in direct contravention of the laws already existing or hereafter to be made by the different States. Persuaded that, after the explanations given and the modifications proposed in the said memorandum, such a measure might be adopted without any serious inconvenience, Lord Castlereagh invited the plenipotentiaries to take it into their consideration in the sense the most favorable to the success of the abolition, and to agree to it; or, if not, at least to substitute some counter projet effectually to prevent the abuse which the illicit trader will not fail to make of the flag of the powers who should refuse to concur in the above mentioned general measure. The memorandum of Lord Castlereagh was annexed to the protocol, *sub. lit.* A.

Lord Castlereagh added to these propositions that, according to the opinion of several persons whose authority was of great weight on this question, it would be useful and perhaps necessary to consider the trade in slaves as a crime against the law of nations, and to this effect to assimilate it to piracy as soon as, by the accession of Portugal, the abolition of the traffic shall have become an universal measure. He requested the plenipotentiaries to take this opinion into consideration without making at present a formal proposition upon it.

METTERNICH.
RICHELIEU.
CASTLEREAGH.
WELLINGTON.
HARDENBERG.
BERNSTORFF.
NESSELRODE.
CAPO D'ISTRIA.

No. 11.

Despatch from Viscount Castlereagh to Earl Bathurst, dated

AIX-LA-CHAPELLE, *November 23, 1818.*

MY LORD: I have the honor to transmit to your lordship the notes of the Russian, French, Austrian, and Prussian plenipotentiaries upon the two propositions which were brought forward by the British plenipotentiaries and earnestly pressed upon their attention, as stated in the protocol of the 24th ultimo.

The result of these notes being extremely discouraging to our hopes, it was determined to review the objections brought forward to the measure of mutually conceding the right of visit, especially by the plenipotentiary of France.

After presenting this review to the consideration of the conference in the memorandum B, (of which a copy is inclosed,) and in an audience with which I was honored by the Emperor of Russia, I took occasion to represent to his Imperial Majesty, in the strongest terms, the necessity of taking some effective measure of this nature without delay, and without waiting for the decree of final abolition on the part of Portugal.

His Imperial Majesty listened with his accustomed interest to my representations on this subject, and promised me to give directions to his ministers to propose that the consideration of the question should be reopened in London under fresh instructions.

The modification which I have finally urged of this measure, and I trust with considerable hope of success, is, that, in addition to the limitation of the right of visit to the coast of Africa and to a specific number of ships of each power, the duration of the convention should be for a limited number of years—

say seven; at the end of which period the several powers would again have it in their power to review their decision, after some experience of its convenience or inconvenience of its efficacy to the object, and of the necessity of its being renewed, regard being had to the then state of the illicit slave trade. This arrangement would sufficiently meet our most pressing wants, whilst it would go less permanently to disturb the acknowledged principles of maritime law as regulating the right of visit. By the aid of this latter expedient, I flatter myself that I have made a considerable impression in removing the strong repugnance which was at first felt to the measure.

A projet of the letters to be addressed by the sovereigns to the King of Portugal on this subject is also forwarded in this despatch; and I have to request that your lordship will receive the Prince Regent's pleasure as to making a similar appeal to his most faithful Majesty, on his royal highness' part, taking measures for forwarding the whole to the Brazils by the first packet.

 I have, &c.,

                CASTLEREAGH.

Earl BATHURST, &c.

[First inclosure in No. 11.]

Opinion of the Russian Cabinet upon the Slave Trade.

             AIX-LA-CHAPELLE, *November* 7, 1818.

The Russian cabinet has laid before the Emperor, and taken, in pursuance of his orders, into mature consideration, the different communications made to the conferences of Aix-la-Chapelle by the plenipotentiaries of his Britannic Majesty on the subject of the slave trade.

There is no object in which his Imperial Majesty takes a more lively interest, and which he has more at heart, than that the decision upon this question may be conformable to the precepts of the Christian religion, to the wishes of humanity, and to the rights and real interests of all the powers invited to assist therein.

Although it cannot be dissembled that the measures in which these indispensable conditions are to be united are attended with difficulty, his Imperial Majesty hopes, nevertheless, that the obstacles will not be insurmountable.

His Imperial Majesty entirely concurs in the proposition of the British cabinet to make an amicable representation to the court of Brazil for the purpose of engaging it to fix a final and early termination to the power which it has reserved to itself to exercise the trade. The force of the motives upon which the wishes of the allied sovereigns rest, and that of the example which they have already given, will doubtless be sufficient to influence the free determination which Portugal is invited to make. The cabinet of Russia has hastened to draw out, upon the invitation of the British plenipotentiaries, the project of a letter which may be addressed with this view to the King of Portugal. This projet is hereunto annexed.

The Emperor views with satisfaction the probable success of a measure which will complete the accession of all the Christian States to the entire and perpetual abolition of the trade.

It is only when this abolition shall have been thus solemnly declared in all countries, and without reserve, that the powers will be able to pronounce, without being checked by distressing and contradictory exceptions, the general principle which shall characterize the trade and place it in the rank of the deepest crimes.

Then, and taking this principle for a basis, may be put in practice the measures which shall serve for its application.

The cabinet of his Britannic Majesty has communicated those by which it has already begun to give effect to the principle of abolition—that is to say, the conventions with Portugal, Spain, and the Netherlands.

It is proposed to adopt generally among the maritime powers the rules laid down in these three conventions, and more particularly to establish, as a general principle, the reciprocal right of visit to be exercised by the respective cruisers.

The cabinet of Russia, in doing homage to the intentions which have dictated these dispositions, stipulated between the British Government and the three courts above mentioned, and, in appreciating their real efficacy on the supposition that they were universally adopted, has only to express its hopes that the special and most urgent interests which each of the maritime States must consult will not oppose the attainment of a general coalition. For inasmuch as it is true that the universal establishment of the reciprocal right of visit would contribute to this end, so it is equally incontestable that the measures in question must necessarily become illusory if a single maritime State only, of whatever rank it may be, finds it impossible to adhere to them. It is, therefore, with a view to produce this universal consent that the allied powers should use their efforts, having once agreed among themselves upon the principle of the right of visit, to obtain the free adherence of all the others to the same basis.

The ministers of his Majesty the Emperor of Russia regret not to be able to contemplate an accession so unanimous. It appears to them beyond a doubt that there are some States whom no consideration would induce to submit their navigation to a principle of such high importance. It cannot, then, be disguised that it is not in this principle that the solution of the difficulty is to be sought.

It has been asked if some other mode, equally sure in its effects, could not be proposed, and of which the general admission on the part of all the States might be more easily foreseen.

Without prejudging the result of the overture of the British cabinet, a mode is here submitted which, in the event of that not being adopted, is without exception in respect to the right of visit, and which will, perhaps, obtain the suffrage of all States, equally desirous of accomplishing a sacred duty, in putting an end to the horrors of the slave trade.

This expedient would consist in a special association between all the States, having for its end the destruction of the traffic in slaves.

It would pronounce, as a fundamental principle, a law characterizing this odious traffic as a description of piracy, and rendering it punishable as such.

It appears evident that the general promulgation of such a law could not take place until the abolition was universally pronounced—that is to say, until Portugal had totally and everywhere renounced the trade.

The execution of the law should be confided to an institution, the seat of which should be in a central point on the coast of Africa, and in the formation of which all the Christian States should take a part.

Declared forever neutral, to be estranged from all political and local interests, like the fraternal and Christian alliance, of which it would be a practical manifestation, this institution would follow the single object of strictly maintaining the execution of the law. It would consist of a maritime force, composed of a sufficient number of ships-of-war, appropriated to the service assigned to them.

Of a judicial power, which should judge all crimes relating to the trade, according to a legislation established upon the subject by the common law.

Of a supreme council, in which would reside the authority of the institution; which would regulate the operations of the maritime force, would revise the sentences of the tribunals, would put them in execution, would inspect all the details, and would render an account of its administration to the future European conferences.

The right of visit and of detention would be granted to this institution as the means of fulfilling its end; and perhaps no maritime nation would refuse to submit its flag to this police, exercised in a limited and clearly defined manner, and by a power too feeble to allow of vexations, too disinterested on all maritime and commercial questions, and above all, too widely combined in its elements not to observe a severe but impartial justice towards all.

Would it not be possible to compose this institution of such different elements as to give it no other tendency, as long as it remained united, but that of doing its duty?

The expense which it would occasion, divided amongst all the Christian States, could not be very burdensome, and its duration would be regulated according to the time required for the development of African civilization, which it would protect, and it might also bring about a happy change in the system of cultivation in the colonies.

In submitting these views to the wisdom of the allied cabinets, that of Russia reserves to itself the power, in case they desire to search into and examine them, of entering into more ample explanations upon the subject.

[Second inclosure in No. 2.]

Memoir of the French Government on the Slave Trade.

France has proved, in the most evident manner, that she desires to concur effectually in the complete abolition of the slave trade. Engaged by the declaration to which she has subscribed, of the 8th of February, 1815, at Vienna, with the powers who signed the treaty of the 30th of May, to employ for this purpose "all the means at her disposal, and to act in the employment of these means with all the zeal and perseverance due to such a great and noble cause," she flatters herself that she has complied with this engagement; and, in a few months after the declaration of Vienna, she renounced the stipulation of 1814, which had given her a delay of five years for effecting the cessation of the trade. She declared, the 30th of July, 1815, that from that day the trade should cease on her part everywhere and forever. The acts of her administration have been conformable to this declaration. The instructions given in the ports of France and in the colonies have preceded a special ordinance of the King prohibiting the trade.

This ordinance has been since confirmed by a law enacted in March, 1818, which pronounces against the violators of the dispositions agreed upon the most severe punishments which the laws of France can inflict.

Measures of *surveillance* have also been prescribed with a view to secure the execution of the law; and the King has ordered a naval force to cruise on the western coast of Africa, and visit all vessels which should be suspected of continuing a trade which has been prohibited.

Such are the acts of the French Government; they clearly prove that they have used "the means which they had at their disposal" to repress the trade.

They have displayed their zeal in creating the means which were wanting and in the adoption of a formal law.

Nevertheless, the Government of his Britannic Majesty, who, to secure the actual abolition of the trade, evince an ardor which cannot but add to the glory which the English nation have acquired in fostering whatever has for its object the good of humanity, have been informed that the end of their efforts and of those of the other powers is not yet attained; and that, in spite of the measures taken to prevent it, many slaves are still carried away from the coast of Africa by a contraband trade. And they have conceived that these violations of the laws evince the insufficiency of the dispositions to insure the execution of them. They believe that a system of measures combined between the principal powers already engaged, by a clause in the treaty of the 20th November, 1815, to concert means for this object, might finally eradicate the evil. They have proposed, among other measures, to visit rigorously the vessels which shall navigate upon the western coast of Africa; and, in order that this visit should have due effect, they have judged that it would be proper that each of the powers should grant to the others the right of exercising it upon all the ships carrying its flag. The creation of mixed commissions, charged to pronounce upon the legitimacy of the expeditions suspected of fraud, forms the second part of the English project.

It would be impossible not to acknowledge that in proposing such a measure the Government of his Britannic Majesty have done all that depended on them to accompany it with precautions to prevent its abuse.

With this view, the limitation of the number of ships-of-war authorized to visit, and of the places where the visit may be exercised, the rank of the officers who alone can perform this service, give assurance of their respect for the rights of each of the contracting parties.

Three powers, Spain, Portugal, and the kingdom of the Netherlands, have subscribed to these propositions.

The Government of his most Christian Majesty would eagerly follow such an example if, carrying their views exclusively to the object, they did not perceive in the means indicated for its attainment dangers which attach, perhaps, to their particular position, but which it is their duty to prevent.

It would be useless to discuss here, in regard to right, the question of visit at sea in profound peace.

The English Government have done homage to the principle which insures in this respect the independence of all flags, and it is only in limitation of the principle, not in denial of its existence, that they propose to grant to each power, respectively, the faculty of detaining ships carrying the flag of others, and of ascertaining the legality of the trade in which they are engaged.

But upon this first point the Government of his most Christian Majesty feel an invincible obstacle to the proposition of England.

France, by the reverses and misfortunes which she has lately experienced, and which, if they have not effaced, have at least obscured the glory which she had acquired, is bound to evince more jealousy of her own dignity than if fortune had not betrayed her. The nation, happy to be again under the rule of its legitimate sovereign, does not regret vain conquests, but she is more than ever alive to the feeling of national honor.

Without doubt a concession, accompanied by the necessary precautions, and with that clause of reciprocity which would save the dignity of each party, might be proposed without fear of wounding the vanity of any one. But it would still be a concession; and the opinion of a nation habituated to judge of the acts of her Government under the influence of a lively imagination would be alarmed to see them abandon, even with every possible modification, what she regards as one of her most precious rights. She would conceive that the honor of her flag was thereby endangered—a point of the utmost delicacy, and on which she has ever shown a quick susceptibility. She would see in the abandonment of this right a new sacrifice attached, as it were, as an indispensable condition of the evacuation of her territory and as a monument of the state of dependence in which she was for a moment placed. There is no doubt that in giving a generous example in submitting to the reciprocal right of visit which she regards as proper to attain the end proposed, England proves to the world that the visit is not incompatible with the honor of the flag. But placed in different circumstances, supported by the opinion of the English nation, which for twenty-five years has called for the abolition of the trade, Great Britain secures all her advantages even in appearing to abandon the absolute exercise of them, and she cannot fear that the idea of a compulsory sacrifice might attach to the concession.

But even should the Government of his most Christian Majesty feel themselves authorized to overlook such powerful considerations, and to adopt, notwithstanding the dangers which they perceive in theory, the projet relative to the visit, they would still see in its application serious cause of uneasiness.

It cannot be denied that there exists between the subjects of Great Britain and France, and, as it were, blended with the esteem which they mutually inspire, a sentiment of rivalry, which, heightened by numerous and unfortunate circumstances, has often assumed the character of animosity. It is unfortunately too probable that the mutual exercise of the right of visit at sea would furnish it with new excitements. Whatever precautions may be taken, however mildly it be exercised, the visit must necessarily be a source of disquiet and vexation. Can it be thought that the vessel which believes she can elude it will not seek to do so by every means? It will then be necessary that the visiting vessel exert force. This force may produce resistance. On the high seas, far from all control, the subjects of the two powers might be tempted to believe themselves no longer bound by the orders of their own sovereigns, and listening to the voice of a false point of honor, might take up arms in their defence. The most prudent enactments will be illusory. Will the captain of a ship-of-war charged with the visit consent to show his commission to the inconsiderable trader? If not, how is he to be constrained to do so, and what guaranty shall the detained vessel have that the visit is not an arbitrary act? How prevent, also, the possible infractions of the regulations agreed upon for rendering the visit less vexatious? The trader may, indeed, complain and demand punishment; but it is known by experience how difficult is the decision of these abuses. Will not the oppressed be often without the means of knowing what officer shall have abused in his case the right reserved to the cruisers, or shall have unduly arrogated it to himself? What proof do the incidents bring which pass far from all witnesses, and which each of the parties may represent under a different light? The English Government know that, when they have themselves wished to punish abuses committed by their ships upon the coast of France, or within the limits of her territorial jurisdiction, they have been prevented by the impossibility of procuring documents sufficiently positive to ascertain the guilty.

These inconveniences, which it would be imprudent to lose sight of, receive an additional importance from the probability that they would lead to mutual exasperation; and it is too well known that such sentiments among the people have often disturbed the peace of nations.

If such a misfortune were to follow, would not Europe have a right to demand of the powers a strict account of those measures which, concerted for the good of humanity, should have compromised the public tranquillity?

There is another consideration which would induce the Goverment of his most Christian Majesty to pause, even if they did not see the impossibility of admitting the proposition of the visit. This is, in reference to the mixed commissions which would be empowered to adjudge the questions of prize in the spirit of the regulations for restricting the trade.

The immediate consequence of such an institution would be to withdraw the subjects of his Majesty from their natural judges, and circumstances will not permit him to believe that he has the right to do so. Jurisdiction is, of all the rights of sovereignty, that which is the most essentially destined to the defence of the subject, and it may be said that it is the only one exclusively for the interest of the latter. There are circumstances in which the common law of Europe admits that the jurisdiction of the sovereign ceases of right, because he cannot in fact exercise it. It is when a subject commits upon a foreign territory a crime against the laws of the country upon which this territory depends. He is then liable to the application of those laws, and his sovereign, who cannot oppose, tolerates it.

But, except in these circumstances, the sovereign could not consent that his subject should pass under a foreign jurisdiction. In vain would it be alleged that the mixed commission does not exercise its jurisdiction in a criminal manner, and that it only pronounces "upon the legality of the seizure of the vessel having slaves illicitly on board."

To pronounce upon the legality of the seizure is to judge the question as much as it is possible to do it; it is to decide that the captured has or has not incurred the penalties attached to the crime which he has committed. His fate is thenceforward fixed.

It matters little that the penalties which he has or has not incurred be determined by the code of his country, or by that of another. When he has undergone the examination of the commission, it only remains to apply this code or to set him at liberty; he is then in reality judged, and that not by his natural judges. His most Christian Majesty, it is repeated, does not believe himself, in conscience, to have the right to sanction such a change in the legislation of his kingdom; and, should he think that this right might belong to him, it is out of all probability that the powers whose co-operation would be necessary to him in order to admit of this change would acknowledge it.

. It results, from the preceding observations, that France has done all that depended upon her to bring about the complete abolition of the slave trade; that she perceives in the projet proposed by England for suppressing all possible continuation of this odious commerce dangers which will not permit her to admit it; that, in a word, it appears to her that to attain one desirable end for the interest of a portion of mankind, the risk is run of compromising interests still more precious, since they relate to the maintenance of the peace and the repose of Europe.

She has given her opinion upon this subject with the more freedom in proportion to her anxiety to attain the objects to which her acts of legislation and administration have been directed. She has no separate views inconsistent with her declarations. The reports, indeed, which announce that the trade is still actively continued on the French territory are anterior to the establishment of a naval force upon the coast, and to the new instructions sent to Senegal for putting an end to all fraudulent trade. This is perhaps the place to remark, that implicit faith should not be given to the reports brought forward against the authorities of Senegal. The reports, which implicate them so seriously that the accusers ought to be called upon for their proofs, are in part prepared by persons who conceived themselves to have other grounds of complaint against these authorities.

France, moreover, would not feel that she had sufficiently proved her desire to co-operate in the measures of repression against the trade if she did not indicate, in her turn, new means of effecting it. Hitherto the dispositions made in this respect have been directed against the transport of slaves, since it is principally upon the manner of detaining at sea the vessels employed in this commerce that they have been concerted. The principle is good, since the length of the passage offers great probability that the illicit traffic may be intercepted. But, on the other hand, the uncertainty of the sea, and consequently the hope of escaping observation, as well as the enormous benefits it holds out, offer chances and an attraction sufficiently powerful for the slave merchants not to be totally discouraged. The measures which would tend to check the commerce of slaves, not in its middle passage, but at its birth and at its termination, that is to say, upon the points where the purchase and sale of the negroes are effected, might effectually contribute, when combined with the other arrangements, to accomplish the salutary work which is intended.

It is proposed, then, to establish in the comptoirs where the purchase of slaves is habitually made commissioners charged to notify the same to the Government, and empowered to prosecute the offending parties in the public tribunals. There might also be introduced into all colonies, where the proprietors are interested in recruiting slaves, regulations like those of the registry bill, to fix the number of blacks existing upon each plantation, and to ascertain, by periodical computations, that the law has not been eluded. The confiscation of the negroes upon each plantation, beyond the number previously declared, (saving those born on the spot,) and a heavy fine for each slave clandestinely introduced, might be the punishment inflicted upon the delinquents. These measures, which enter into the interior administration of each Government, might, however, be concerted between all; and, instead of mixed commissions, charged with pronouncing upon the culpability of the individuals who import the negroes, committees might be established, charged with the duty of watching the individuals who purchase them, and to make known to the superior authorities of the country the infractions which the inferior agents might show reluctance in prosecuting. These arrangements are in the nature of those which the Government of his most Christian Majesty might take, without fear to wound the rights of his subjects, and he is ready to come to an understanding in this respect with the powers who unite their efforts for bringing about the entire abolition of a trade odious in itself, and which has been stigmatized with general condemnation.

[Third Inclosure in No. 11.]

Opinion of the Austrian Cabinet upon the question of the Slave Trade.

Since the abolition of the slave trade has been the object of the common deliberations of the powers of Europe, the cabinet of Austria has not ceased to devote to this question all the interest which it merits in. its great relation with the good of humanity, as well as with the precepts of sound morality and religion. Faithful to the principles solemnly proclaimed in this respect at the period of the Congress of Vienna, and to the successive engagements founded upon those bases, Austria, although not able, from her geographical position, to co-operate directly for the success of so meritorious and noble an enterprise, has not less eagerly concurred in all which might advance and perfect it; and it has been with these unalterable sentiments that the minister of Austria has examined with the most serious attention the propositions made by the plenipotentiaries of his Britannic Majesty to the present conferences for completing and extending the system hitherto pursued for attaining the final extinction of the trade, and for insuring the execution and the efficacy of this system.

His Majesty the Emperor is ready to take part in the measures which the allied sovereigns are about to adopt with the cabinet of Rio de Janeiro, to engage it to fix as soon as possible the period of definitive abolition.

His Majesty cannot but feel that the sovereign of Brazil may meet in this transaction difficulties more real, perhaps, and stronger than any other power has had to surmount who has consented to this salutary measure. But he reckons too much upon the loyalty of this sovereign to admit that any obstacles whatever would prevent him from fulfilling a sacred engagement, such as that which he has contracted in the face of the world by the declaration of the 8th of February, 1815.

With respect to the measures proposed by the British plenipotentiaries to put an end to the illicit trade, as it appears admitted on all parts that a system of permanent *surveillance* cannot be effectually established until the abolition of the trade shall have been generally and definitively pronounced by all the powers, the Austrian cabinet is of opinion that, in adjourning to that period the ulterior discussion of the measures to be adopted for this purpose, the intermediate time might be usefully employed in reconciling and conciliating all opinions, persuaded, as it is, that provided the fundamental principle, that of arriving at the universal and effectual abolition of the trade, be never lost sight of, and that each power continues to second with its utmost efforts those which the British Government have hitherto used in so honorable a cause, they will ultimately agree upon the most effectual means for securing its full and complete accomplishment.

The Austrian cabinet also desire that the ministerial conference established in London for the consideration of this question may continue its work in the sense most conformable to the principles by which it has hitherto been guided.

[Fourth inclosure in No. 11.]

Opinion of the Prussian Cabinet on the Slave Trade question.

Invariably attached to the principles of morality and humanity, which for a long time have demanded the abolition of the slave trade, and faithful to the engagements which they have made to this effect, the Prussian Government is constantly ready to concur in everything that may contribute to the definitive accomplishment of this noble end.

In consequence, they do not hesitate to accede to the proposition of a combined representation to the court of Brazil in order to engage it to accelerate, as much as the circumstances and the necessities of its situation may permit, the entire abolition of the trade.

As to the measures of general police that may be adopted to prevent or put a stop to the illicit trade, the Prussian Government cannot dissemble the inseparable inconveniences of the concession of a right of visit exercised on the high seas; a concession which will become but too easily a source of abuse and misunderstanding, and which would subject peaceable and innocent traders to molestations of which the idea alone will indispose them perhaps still more than the real mischief.

The Prussian Government, in consequence, believe it to be their duty to give the preference to every measure of precaution and of *surveillance* which, being confined to the point of departure and to the point of arrival, that is, to the coast of Africa and the colonies interested in favoring these illicit enterprises, will admit of an execution more rigorous and more decisive.

[Fifth inclosure in No. 11.]

Memorandum. (B.)

The plenipotentiaries of Great Britain, after attentively perusing the votes given by the several cabinets on the measures brought forward on the part of the Prince Regent for effectuating the abolition of the slave trade, cannot dissemble their deep regret that the deliberations of the august assembly which is now about to terminate is not destined to be marked in the page of history by some more decisive interposition than is likely to take place in relief of the sufferings of Africa.

They had persuaded themselves that it was reserved for the plenipotentiaries assembled at Aix-la-Chapelle to have completed at once the work of peace in Europe, and to have laid a broad and lasting foundation on which the deliverance of another great quarter of the globe from a scourge far more severe than European warfare, in its most aggravated forms, might have been effectuated, by establishing an alliance which should forever deny to the fraudulent slave trader, of whatever nation, the cover of their respective flags for the purposes of his iniquitous traffic. Although disappointed in this hope, they will not despair of ultimately arriving at their object, whilst they have so powerful a cause to advocate, and whilst they can address themselves not less to the understandings than to the hearts of those sovereigns who, when assembled in Congress at Vienna, solemnly pronounced upon this question, and devoted their future exertions to the consummation of this work of peace.

They derive additional consolation from the perusal of the documents above referred to; for although they fail them for the present in their conclusion, they nevertheless bear in all their reasonings such homage to the principle, and in some of their details so fully evince the strong sense of duty which animates the august sovereigns in the prosecution of this measure, as to be regarded rather as the precursors of some decided effort for putting an end to this great moral evil, than as indicating on their part any abandonment of a cause which, in the face of mankind, they have taken under their especial protection. It has been the fate of this question, in every stage of its progress, to have difficulties represented as insurmountable, which in a little time have yielded to the perseverance and to the more matured impulses of humanity.

The language in every country has been at times discouraging, and yet the principles of truth and of justice have ultimately triumphed, so as to have left only one great blot in the civilized world at this day unremoved. Every nation, one only excepted, has secured itself from this pollution, and his most faithful Majesty has taken steps sufficiently decisive in the same direction to afford the most encouraging prospect of his determination to deliver his people, without loss of time, from a practice which must degrade them in the scale of enlightened policy, so long as it shall continue to be tolerated among them. It is against the fraudulent slave trader, for the welfare of Africa, that more decisive measures are urgently called for; were it not for his pestilential influence, more than half of that great continent would at this day have been consigned to peaceful habits and to the pursuits of industry and of innocent commerce. But they are his piratical practices on the coast of Africa, in breach of the laws of every civilized Government, which not only vex that extended portion of the globe but which have undone the work of many years of slow, but successful improvement.

It was the fraudulent slave trader who introduced anew on those coasts the traffic, with all its desolating influence on the interior of the country, and which, if not soon checked by measures of a decisive character, will banish not only every trace of improvement, but all commerce other than that of slaves.

On the eve of the departure of the illustrious sovereigns from this place, and after the ample deliberations which have already taken place on this subject, the British plenipotentiaries cannot flatter themselves with the hope of obtaining at this time a more favorable decision; but they could not satisfy their own sense of duty were they not to record their observations upon the objections which have been brought forward to the measures which they were directed to propose, humbly but confidently submitting them on the part of their court to the more matured consideration of the different cabinets. And as it is the species of measure best calculated to suppress this evil, upon which they are alone divided in sentiments, as all are agreed in the enormity of the offence, and all equally animated with a determination effectually to suppress it, they indulge the confident expectation that the subject may be resumed at no distant period in the conferences in London, and prosecuted under more favorable auspices to some decisive result.

And first, with respect to the memoir presented by the plenipotentiaries of Russia. The plenipotentiaries of Great Britain do homage to the sentiments of enlightened benevolence which on this, as on every other occasion, distinguish the elevated views of the august sovereign of Russia.

They only lament that the Russian cabinet, in the contemplation of other measures to be hereafter taken, should have been discouraged with respect to the great good which lay within their reach; and that his Imperial Majesty should thus have abstained for the present to throw into the scale of the proposed measure his illustrious and powerful example.

It appears that the Russian Government looks forward to the moment when Portugal shall have finally abolished the trade for founding a system upon the coast of Africa, which shall be authorized not merely to pronounce upon the property of the slave trader, but which shall be competent to proceed criminally against him as a pirate, and which, in addition to those high functions, shall have a naval force at its disposition, and be invested with a general right of visit of all flags, at least upon those coasts. That this institution should be composed of elements drawn from all civilized States; that it should have a directing council and a judicial system; in short, that it should form a body politic, neutral in its character, but exercising these high authorities over all States. The British Government will, no doubt, be most anxious to receive from the Russian cabinet the further development of this plan which is promised; but as the prospect of some institution of this nature may form a serious obstacle to the adoption of what appears to them the more pressing measure, the British plenipotentiaries cannot delay to express their doubts as to the practicability of founding, or preserving in activity, so novel and so complicated a system.

If the moment should have arrived when the traffic in slaves shall have been universally prohibited, and if, under those circumstances, the mode shall have been devised by which this offence shall be raised in the criminal code of all civilized nations to the standard of piracy, they conceive that this species of piracy, like any other act falling within the same legal principle, will, by the law of nations, be amenable to the ordinary tribunals of any or every particular State.

That the individuals charged with the piracy can plead no national character in bar of such jurisdiction, whether taken on the high seas or on the African coast.

If they be pirates, they are "*hostes humani generis.*" They are under the protection of no flag, and the verification of the fact of piracy by sufficient evidence brings them at once within the reach of the first criminal tribunal of competent authority before whom they may be brought.

It seems equally unnecessary to have recourse to so new a system for arriving at a qualified and guarded right of visit.

In this, as in the former instance, the simplest means will be found the best, and the simplest will generally be found to consist in some modification of what the established practice of nations has for ages sanctioned.

Right of visit is known and submitted to by all nations in time of war.

The belligerent is authorized to visit the neutral, and even to detain upon adequate cause.

If the right to visit be to exist at all, and that it must exist, at least upon the coast of Africa, in some shape or to some extent, seems to be fully admitted by the Russian memoir, it is infinitely better it should exist in the form of a conventional but mitigated regulation of the established practice of nations, for the due administration of which every Government is responsible, than that it should be confided to a new institution which, to be neutral, must be irresponsible, and whose very composition would place it wholly beyond the reach of control.

These observations apply to the period when all nations shall have abolished the trade; but why should the Russian, Austrian, and Prussian Governments unnecessarily postpone the taking some measure of this nature for an indefinite period, and until Portugal shall have universally abolished?

Have they not more than two-thirds of the whole coast of Africa, upon which it might at once operate, and as beneficially as if that much wished for era was arrived?

Has not Portugal herself given unanswerable proofs upon this point by conceding the right of visit north of the equator, where the abolition has been completed, as well by her as now by Spain and all other powers?

Perhaps it is because no instance can be quoted that any slave trader, under either the Russian, Austrian, or Prussian flags, has yet appeared on the coast of Africa, that these powers, from a sentiment of delicacy towards States more directly interested both in the local and maritime question, have felt some reluctance to take a lead in giving their sanction to this principle.

The Russian memoir seems expressly to withhold, or rather to delay its adherence until there is reason to presume that a general concurrence is attainable; but surely in all such cases the most certain mode of obtaining a general concurrence is to augment the ranks of the concurring parties.

The United States and France are probably alluded to as the dissenting powers; but even in those States how much might not the chances of success have been improved had the three powers in question followed the example of those that have already adopted this system; and how narrowed would have been the chance of fraud had the sphere of the alliance been thus extended by their accession? It is still to be hoped that their present doubts will yield to more mature reflection upon the nature of the proposition. The first instance in which any of their flags should be made the cover of abuse the British plenipotentiaries are satisfied would be the signal for their vindicating its character, by taking an immediate and decisive step on this subject; but, without waiting for such a stimulus, they trust that the minds of those illustrious sovereigns remain still open to every suggestion on this subject which can improve the chances of general success; and that the opinion hitherto given on the part of their respective cabinets will form no obstacle to the adoption on their part of that measure, whatever it may be, which, under all the circumstances of the case, shall appear to them most effectual to the suppression of the mischief.

In adverting to the memoir which has been presented to the conference by the plenipotentiaries of France, the British plenipotentiaries are ready to bear their testimony to the spirit of fairness with which the subject has been met, and to the auspicious protection which the cause of abolition has progressively received from his most Christian Majesty.

The French plenipotentiary has candidly conceded, 1. That the proposed measure cannot be considered as any infraction of the law of nations. That it confirms, on the contrary, that law, inasmuch as it seeks to obtain a new power as a conventional exception from the admitted principles of the general law.

2. That it can be regarded as no exclusive surrender of the maritime rights of any particular State, as its provisions are strictly reciprocal, and for an object in which all feel and avow that they have a common interest.

3. That the principle of reciprocity may be still further guarded by confining the right of visit, as in the treaty with Holland, to an equal and limited number of ships-of-war of each State.

4. That every endeavor has been made strictly to limit the exercise of the power to the immediate purpose for which it is granted, and by suitable regulations to guard it against abuse.

5. That in order still further to distinguish this system from the ordinary right of visit, which every belligerent is entitled to exercise in time of war, it has been proposed to confine its operations, if desired, to the coasts of Africa, and to a limited distance from those coasts.

The objections on the part of France are of a more general description, and such as, it is hoped, time will in itself serve to remove; and, first, as to the objection which seems to weigh so strongly, viz: that the measure, if now taken, might be falsely regarded by the French nation as a concession imposed upon their Government by the powers of Europe as the price of the evacuation of their territory. It is impossible to contend in argument against such a delusion; but it may be observed that, had the other powers been pressed to adopt the arrangement in concert with France, it does not seem possible that such an invidious interpretation could have been given to so general and so benevolent a measure; but this happily is one of those objections which a short time must serve to remove.

The second objection is, that there is, as it were, some moral incompetency in the French nation to conform themselves to this measure; that what is felt by the crowns of Spain and Portugal, and of the Netherlands, to be no disparagement of the honor of their flag, nor any inconvenient surrender of the commercial rights and interests of their people, would in France work nothing but a sense of humiliation and discontent.

With great deference to the authority upon which this conclusion is stated, the plenipotentiaries of Great Britain cannot refrain from indulging the hope that although in France there may at first sight exist prejudices against this measure when received in an exaggerated shape, and without the necessary explanations; that although there may be also a feeling with respect to possible inconveniences which, notwithstanding every exertion on the part of the respective governments, might occasionally attend it in the execution, yet they confidently persuade themselves that a people so enlightened would not fail cordially to answer to an appeal made by their Government to the generosity of their feelings upon such a point, and that the French nation would never shrink from a competition with the British or any other nation in promoting whatever might conduce to an end in which the great interests of humanity are involved. It is true that Great Britain and France have been regarded as rivals as well as neighboring nations; but if they have had occasionally the misfortune to contend against each other in arms, nothing has arisen in the result of those contests which should create a sense of inferiority on either side. Both nations have well sustained their national honor, and both have learned to respect each other. Why, then, should the French people feel that as derogatory to their dignity which is viewed by the British nation in so different a light? Let us rather hope that, after their long and common sufferings in war, both nations will feel the strong interest they have in drawing closer those ties of friendship which now happily unite them, and in cultivating those relations in peace which may render their intercourse useful to each other and to the world. What object more worthy of their common councils and efforts than to give peace to Africa; and could their rivalship take a more ennobling and auspicious character?

Should a doubt or murmur, at the first aspect, arise among the people of France, they may be told that four of the most considerable of the maritime powers of the world have cheerfully united their exertions in this system for the deliverance of Africa; they will learn that the British people, so sensitively alive as they are known to be to every circumstance that might impede their commercial pursuits or expose the national flag to an unusual interference, have betrayed no apprehension in the instance before us; not a single remonstrance has been heard either in Parliament or from any commercial body in the empire, not even from any individual merchant or navigator. If the doubt should turn upon the prejudice which such a measure might occasion to the French commercial interests on the coast of Africa, they will, on inquiry, find that if France wishes to preserve and to improve her legitimate commerce on that coast she cannot pursue a more effectual course than by uniting her efforts to those of other powers for putting down the illicit slave trader, who is now become an armed freebooter, combining the plunder of merchant vessels of whatever nation with his illegal speculations in slaves.

If the idea should occur that French merchant ships frequenting that coast may experience interruption and delays by such visits; that officers may possibly abuse their trust, and that disputes may occur between their subjects and those of foreign powers, let them reduce this objection calmly to its true value; let them estimate it according to the extent of trade on that coast, and the chances of such accidents occurring. Notwithstanding every precaution taken by the respective Governments, let them set this evil, taken at the highest computation, in competition with the great moral question whether a whole continent, in order to avoid these minor inconveniences, shall be suffered to groan under all the aggravated horrors of an illicit slave trade; and let the Government of his most Christian Majesty judge whether it is possible that the French Government would hesitate in the decision to which it would wish to come upon such an alternative.

If any instance of abuse should occur for a moment to occasion regret, it will be remembered that this is the price, and how inconsiderable a price, which an humane and enlightened people are deliberately willing to pay for the attainment of such an object; it will be looked at in contrast with the African villages that would have been plundered; with the wars that would have been waged in the interior of that unhappy continent; with the number of human victims that would have been sacrificed to the cupidity of the slave trader, if civilized nations had not combined their exertions for their protection.

The French memoir argues against the principle of subjecting the property of French subjects to any other jurisdiction than that of their own tribunals; but it will appear that this practice is by no means unusual in time of war, and for the security of the belligerent this is constantly the case.

The neutral is, in all cases, amenable for the alleged infractions of the rights of the belligerent in matters of blockade, contraband of war, &c., to the tribunals of the belligerent, not to his own or to any mixed tribunal.

If it is said that this is not a case of war, but a regulation introduced in peace, and for the first time, the obvious answer is, does the case warrant the innovation?

If it does, the novelty of the practice ought to form no decisive objection to its adoption; but it is by no means true that this is the first instance in time of peace where the property of the subject has been brought under a jurisdiction other than the ordinary tribunals of his own State. Claims both of a private and public nature have frequently, by conventional laws, been made the object of such a proceeding, which is made to operate as a species of arbitration. Can we quote a more decisive example than the two conventions which, in November, 1815, referred the private claims upon the French Government, immense as they were in amount, to the decision of a *mixed* commission similarly constituted?

It is also to be observed that the subject gains a singular advantage by having his case disposed of before such a commission, which he would not obtain were he to have to proceed either in his own courts or in that of the capturing power for the restitution of his property: namely, that the commission, in deciding upon his cause, not only has the power of pronouncing upon his wrongs, but can give him, by its decision, ample damages, for the discharge of which the State of the capturing ship is made answerable; whereas, in an ordinary case of capture, he would have a dilatory and expensive suit to carry on against, perhaps, an insolvent captor.

Having noticed the principal objections brought forward in the French memoir, which they venture to persuade themselves are not insurmountable, the British plenipotentiaries have observed with satisfaction the exertions which the French Government have made, and are still prepared to make, for combatting this evil, at least as far as it can be alleged to subsist within their own limits, and to be carried on by French subjects; but they feel persuaded that the Government of his most Christian Majesty will take a more enlarged view of their power of doing good, and that they will be disposed to extend the sphere of their activity to the suppression of the mischief wherever it can be reached by their exertions.

The British Government also does full justice to the manner in which the French Government has on all occasions sought from them such information as might enable them the better to enforce the law of abolition. They bear testimony with pleasure not only to the sincerity of their exertions but to the arrangements lately made by stationing a naval force on the coast of Africa for the more effectual suppression of the slave trade, so far as it is carried on by French ships and subjects. They also view, with the highest satisfaction, the determination now announced of introducing into all the French colonies a registry of slaves; all these beneficent arrangements may be expected to operate powerfully so far as the mischief has decidedly a French character, but until all the principal powers can agree to have, as against the illicit slave trader, *at least on the coast of Africa*, but one common flag and co-operating force, they will not have gone to the full extent of their means to effectuate their purpose in conformity to their declarations at Vienna. With these observations the British plenipotentiaries will conclude their statement, submitting it to the candid examination of the several cabinets.

It would be a great satisfaction to them to be assured that the representations which they have felt it their duty to make were likely to receive their earliest consideration, and that the ministers of the several powers in London might expect to receive such further instructions as might enable them, without loss of time, to resume their labors with effect. It being humbly submitted that the final act, which the sovereigns are about to solicit from his Majesty the King of Portugal, is not an indispensable preliminary towards establishing by common consent on the coast of Africa, at least north of the equator, some efficient system for the suppression of the illicit traffic in slaves, which is at this moment carried on to the most alarming extent and under the most aggravating circumstances, such as loudly to call for the special and authoritative interference of the illustrious sovereigns to whom these remarks are respectfully submitted.

[Sixth inclosure in No. 11.]

Projet of a letter to his Most Faithful Majesty.

SIR, MY BROTHER: At the period of the Congress of Vienna, the voice of religion and the groans of suffering humanity obtained the most consoling triumph. The world contemplated the near prospect of the termination of a scourge which has long desolated Africa; and your Majesty has justly acquired the right to the eternal gratitude of nations in proclaiming, in concert with your allies, the principle of universal abolition of the trade in slaves. Since then the acts concluded at Paris in 1815, and the happy issue of the several negotiations devoted to the progressive execution of this measure, have strengthened the generous hopes of the age, and have predicted the full accomplishment of the transaction which they have solemnly sanctioned.

If the result of the conference of Aix-la-Chapelle, which consummate the pacification and guaranty the prosperity of Europe, still leave a wish, it is that of seeing insured the final triumph of the declaration of the 8th of February, 1815, by means of an act decreeing the abolition of the slave trade in all parts and forever; that my allies and myself be not permitted to separate without turning our confident regards towards the powers to whom the Supreme Arbiter of the destinies of the earth has reserved the glory of putting an end to the afflictions of an unfortunate population.

This definitive success will be without doubt the fruit of your Majesty's intimate relations with the Government of Great Britain, because a concurrence of conciliating intentions and of reciprocal sacrifices, is alone of a nature to prosper a work equally meritorious before God and in the eyes of men.

It is only at the close of this negotiation that the measures of mutual inspection, decreed for the strict execution of a law become general, will crown the noble efforts of all the powers called to govern the different parts of the globe by the same sentiments of fraternity, of justice, and of religion.

&c., &c., &c.

No. 12.

Despatch from Viscount Castlereagh to Earl Bathurst, dated

AIX-LA-CHAPELLE, *November* 24, 1818.

MY LORD: I have the honor to transmit to your lordship the inclosed protocol of the conferences of the allied ministers of the 11th and 19th instant, containing the votes of the different powers on the subject of the slave trade, which I have already forwarded to your lordship.

I have the honor, &c.,

CASTLEREAGH.

Earl BATHURST, *&c., &c., &c.*

[First inclosure in No. 12.]

Protocol of the conference between the plenipotentiaries of the five powers held at Aix-la-Chapelle November 11, 1818.

The Duke de Richelieu read his observations upon the means proposed by the plenipotentiaries of Great Britain for inspecting and repressing the illicit slave trade. The observations of the Duke de Richelieu, as well as the opinion of the Austrian cabinet and that which the Prussian cabinet made known in a preceding sitting are annexed to the protocol.

METTERNICH.
RICHELIEU.
CASTLEREAGH.
WELLINGTON.
HARDENBERG.
BERNSTORFF.
NESSELRODE.
CAPO D'ISTRIA.

[Second inclosure in No. 12.]

Protocol of the conference between the plenipotentiaries of the five powers held at Aix-la-Chapelle November 19, 1818.

To resume the discussion of the ulterior measures to be adopted against the slave trade, Lord Castlereagh read a memorandum, in which he observed upon the different propositions which have occupied the preceding conferences, and expressed his sincere regret that the present reunion had not brought about a more decisive result for the final success of the abolition, nor, above all, some resolution directly applicable to the repression of the cruel abuses by which the fraudulent commerce has hitherto eluded and frustrated the measures already agreed upon, and the laws and regulations already in force in various States.

After having analyzed and discussed in detail the objections brought forward to combat the system of reciprocal visit of ships suspected of being engaged in the illicit trade, and especially those which were developed in the vote of the plenipotentiaries of France, as well as the means of execution proposed by the plenipotentiaries of Russia, Lord Castlereagh, in again calling the most serious attention of the powers to a cause so deserving of their interest, desired that the ministers of the courts taking part in the conferences in London should be enjoined to continue their deliberations upon this question without waiting the effect which the formal measure adopted towards his Majesty the King of Portugal and the Brazils might produce; particularly as the result of this step was not an indispensable preliminary to the resolutions to be adopted with common consent for effectually suppressing the illicit traffic on the coasts to the north of the line.

The memorandum of Lord Castlereagh was annexed to the protocol, and the plenipotentiaries agreed to instruct the ministers of the courts in London in the sense of this last proposition.

On the reading of this protocol, the plenipotentiaries of Russia added that, independent of the instruction agreed upon between the courts, the ambassador of his Majesty the Emperor, in London, would be informed of the desire of his Imperial Majesty to see the ministerial conference in London occupied not only with the general question relative to the basis of the system to be adopted against the illicit trade, but at the same time the practical question of the amount of force necessary to be provided for the execution of the general measures, his Majesty the Emperor of Russia being ready to furnish his contingent as soon as the regulations to be established for this purpose shall be agreed upon.

METTERNICH.
RICHELIEU.
CASTLEREAGH.
WELLINGTON.
HARDENBERG.
BERNSTORFF.
NESSELRODE.
CAPO D'ISTRIA.

No. 13.

Despatch from Viscount Castlereagh to Earl Bathurst, dated Paris, December 10, 1818.

MY LORD: Since I arrived here I have deemed it my duty to renew with the Duke de Richelieu the subject of the abolition, in order that I might be better enabled to judge as to the course it would be most advisable to pursue for resuming in London, under the protocol signed at Aix-la-Chapelle on the 19th November, the deliberations on this question.

In conference with his excellency, it was agreed that I should have an interview with the minister of the marine and colonies, the Count de Molé, and with the Count de Laisné, the minister of the interior, as the two departments in the Government the most competent to advise the King upon the propriety as well as upon the effect which those regulations might be expected to produce upon the public mind in France, which I had been directed, in conjunction with the Duke of Wellington, to press at Aix-la-Chapelle.

I had, accordingly, a conference with these ministers of nearly three hours, in which I was enabled to go through with them, in the utmost detail, the whole of this important subject; to all the bearings of which they appeared to me to give their utmost attention, and with a desire that the difficulties which they conceived, at least for the present, to stand in the way of their adopting the measure, might be found in the end not to be insurmountable.

It is unnecessary that I should attempt to report to your lordship the particulars of this extended conversation, as they would not vary in any essential point from the arguments brought forward by the Duke de Richelieu, and which are already so fully before the Prince Regent's Government; I have no reason to draw any more unfavorable inference from the manner in which these minister treated the subject, and they assured me of their disposition to render public in France every information which might tend to throw light on this interesting question and to strengthen it in the public favor.

Upon the whole, my lord, whilst I cannot give you hopes of any immediate progress, I venture, nevertheless, to indulge a sanguine expectation that if the object be pursued with the same persevering and conciliating temper on the part of Great Britain which has already achieved so much for the cause of abolition, the French Government may be brought, at no distant period, to unite their naval exertions with those of the other allied powers for the suppression of the illicit slave trade under the modified regulations submitted for this purpose to the plenipotentiaries assembled at Aix-la-Chapelle.

I have the honor to be, &c.,

CASTLEREAGH.

Earl BATHURST, &c., &c., &c.

16TH CONGRESS.]   No. 347.   [2D SESSION.

TREATY WITH SPAIN OF FEBRUARY 22, 1819, AS FINALLY RATIFIED.

COMMUNICATED TO THE HOUSE OF REPRESENTATIVES FEBRUARY 23, 1821.

To the Senate and House of Representatives of the United States:

The treaty of amity, settlement, and limits, between the United States and Spain, signed on the 22d of February, 1819, having been ratified by the contracting parties, and the ratifications having been exchanged, it is herewith communicated to Congress that such legislative measures may be taken as they shall judge proper for carrying the same into execution.

JAMES MONROE.

WASHINGTON, *February* 22, 1821.

BY THE PRESIDENT OF THE UNITED STATES.

A PROCLAMATION.

Whereas a treaty of amity, settlement, and limits, between the United States of America and his Catholic Majesty, was concluded and signed between their plenipotentiaries, in this city, on the twenty-second day of February, in the year of our Lord one thousand eight hundred and nineteen, which treaty, word for word, is as follows:

[Original.]

TREATY

Of amity, settlement, and limits, between the United States of America and his Catholic Majesty.

The United States of America and his Catholic Majesty, desiring to consolidate, on a permanent basis, the friendship and good correspondence which happily prevails between the two parties, have determined to settle and terminate all their differences and pretensions by a treaty, which shall

[Original:]

TRATADO

De Amistad, arreglo de diferencias, y Límites, entre S. M. Ca. y los Estados Unidos de America.

Deseando S. M. Católica y los Estados Unidos de America, consolidar de un modo permanente, la buena correspondencia y amistad que felizmente reyna entre ambas partes, han resuelto transigir y terminar todas sus diferencias y pretensiones por medio de un Tratado, que fixe con precision, los límites de

designate, with precision, the limits of their respective bordering territories in North America.

With this intention, the President of the United States has furnished with their full powers John Quincy Adams, Secretary of State of the United States, and his Catholic Majesty has appointed the most excellent Lord Don Luis De Onis, Gonsalez, Lepez y Vara, Lord of the town of Rayaces, perpetual Regidor of the corporation of the City of Salamanca, Knight Grand-Cross of the Royal American Order of Isabella the Catholic, decorated with the Lys of La Vendee, Knight Pensioner of the Royal and distinguished Spanish Order of Charles III, member of the Supreme Assembly of the said Royal Order, of the council of his Catholic Majesty, his Secretary, with Exercise of Decrees, and his Envoy Extraordinary and Minister Plenipotentiary near the United States of America.

And the said plenipotentiaries, after having exchanged their powers, have agreed upon and concluded the following articles:

ARTICLE 1. There shall be a firm and inviolable peace and sincere friendship between the United States and their citizens and his Catholic Majesty, his successors and subjects, without exception of persons or places.

ARTICLE 2. His Catholic Majesty cedes to the United States, in full property and sovereignty, all the territories which belong to him situated to the eastward of the Mississippi, known by the name of East and West Florida. The adjacent islands dependent on said provinces, all public lots and squares, vacant lands, public edifices, fortifications, barracks, and other buildings, which are not private property, archives and documents which relate directly to the property and sovereignty of said provinces, are included in this article. The said archives and documents shall be left in possession of the commissaries or officers of the United States duly authorized to receive them.

ARTICLE 3. The boundary line between the two countries west of the Mississippi shall begin on the Gulf of Mexico, at the mouth of the river Sabine, in the sea, continuing north, along the western bank of that river, to the 32d degree of latitude; thence, by a line due north, to the degree of latitude where it strikes the Rio Roxo of Natchitoches, or *Red River;* then, following the course of the Rio Roxo westward, to the degree of longitude 100 west from London, and 23 from Washington; then, crossing the said Red river, and running thence, by a line due north, to the river Arkansas; thence, following the course of the southern bank of the Arkansas, to its source, in latitude 42 north; and thence, by that parallel of latitude, to the South Sea—the whole being as laid down in Melish's map of the United States, published at Philadelphia, improved to the 1st of January, 1818. But if the source of the Arkansas river shall be found in north or south of latitude 42, then the line shall run from the said source due south or north, as the case may be, till it meets the said parallel of latitude 42, and thence, along the said parallel, to the South Sea—all the islands in the Sabine, and the said Red and Arkansas rivers, throughout the course thus described, to belong to the United States; but the use of the waters and the navigation of the Sabine to the sea, and of the said rivers Roxo and Arkansas, throughout the extent of the said boundary, on their respective banks, shall be common to the respective inhabitants of both nations.

The two high contracting parties agree to cede and renounce all their rights, claims, and pretensions, to the territories described by the said line: that is to say, "the United States hereby cede to his Catholic Majesty, and renounce forever, all their rights, claims, and pretensions to the territories lying west and south of the above described line; and, in like manner, his Catholic Majesty cedes to the said United States all his rights, claims, and

sus respectivos y confinantes territorios en la America septentrional.

Con esta mira han nombrado, Sa M. Ca. al Exmo. Sor. Dn. Luis De Onis, Gonsalez, Lopez y Vara, Señor de la Villa de Rayaces, Regidor perpetuo del ayuntamiento de la Ciudad de Salamanca, Caballero Gran Cruz de la Real orden; Americana de Isabel la Cotólica, y de la decoracion del Lis de la Vendéa, Caballero Pensionista de la Real y destinguida orden Española de Carlos III, Ministro Vocal de la Suprema Asamblea de dicha Rl. orden, de su consejo, su Secretario con exercicio de Decretos y su Enviado Extraordinario y Ministro Plenipotenciario cerca de los Estados Unidos de America: Y el Presidente de los Estados Unidos, à Don Juan Quincy Adams, Secretario de Estado de los mismos Estados Unidos.

Y ambos Plenipotenciarios, despues de haver cangeado sus Poderes, han ajustado y firmado los Articulos siguientes:

ARTICULO 1. Habrá una paz solida e inviolable, y una amistad sincera entre S. M. Ca. sus sucesores y subditos y los Estados Unidos y sus ciudadanos sin exception de personas ni lugares.

ARTICULO 2. S. M. Ca. cede à los Estados Unidos, en toda propiedad y soberania, todos los territorios que le pertenecen, situados al Este del Misisipi, conocidos bajo el nombre de Florida Occidental y Florida Oriental. Son comprehendidos en este articulo las yslas adyacentes dependientes de dichas dos provincias, los sitios, plazas publicas, terrenos valdios, edificios publicos, fortificaciones, casernas y otros edificios que no sean propiedad de algun individuo particular, los archivos y documentos directamente relativos á la propiedad y soberania de las mismas dos provincias. Dichos archivos y documentos se entregarán á los comisarios ú oficiales de los Estados Unidos debidamente autorizados para recibirlos.

ARTICULO 3. La Linea divisoria entre los dos paises al Occidente del Misisipi arrancará del Seno Mexicano en la embocadúra del Rio Sabina en el Mar, seguirá al Norte por la Orilla Occidental de este Rio hasta el grado 32 de latitud; desde alli por una linea recta al Norte hasta el grado de latitud en que entra en el Rio Roxo de Natchitochez (Red river), y continuará por el curso del Rio Roxo al Oeste hasta el grado 100 de longitud Occidental de Londres y 23 de Washington, en que cortará este Rio, y Seguirá por una linea recta al Norte por el mismo grado hasta el Rio Arkansas, cuya Orilla Meridional Seguirá hasta su nacimiento en el grado 42 de latitud Septentrional; y desde dicho punto se terará una linea recta por el mismo paralelo de latitud hasta el Mar del Sur. Todo segun el Mapa de los Estados Unidos de Melish, publicado en Philadelphia y perfecionado en 1818. Pero si el nacimiento del Rio Arkansas se hallase al Norte ó Sur de dicho grado 42 de latitud, seguirá la linea desde el origen de dicho Rio recta al Sur ó Norte, segun fuese necesario hasta que encuentre el expresado grado 42, de latitud, y desde alli por el mismo paralelo hasta el Mar del Sur. Pertenecerán á los Estados Unidos todas las Yslas de los Rios Sabina, Roxo de Natchitochez, y Arkansas, en la extension de todo el curso descrito; pero el uso de las aguas y la navegacion del Sabina hasta el Mar y de los expresados Rios Roxo y Arkansas en toda la extension de sus mencionados limites en sus respectivas Orillas, sera comun á los habitantes de las dos naciones.

Las dos altas partes contratantes convienen en ceder y renunciar todos sus derechos, reclamaciones, y pretensiones sobre los territorios que se describen en esta linea; á saber, S. M. Ca. renuncia y cede para siempre por si, y á nombre de sus herederos y sucesores todos los derechos que tiene sobre los territorios al Esté y al Norte de dicha linea; y los Estados Unidos en egual forma ceden á S. M. Ca. y renuncian para siempre todos sus derechos, reclamaciones y pre-

pretensions to any territories east and north of the said line, and for himself, his heirs, and successors, renounces all claim to the said territories forever.

ARTICLE 4. To fix this line with more precision, and to place the landmarks which shall designate exactly the limits of both nations, each of the contracting parties shall appoint a commissioner and a surveyor, who shall meet before the termination of one year from the date of the ratification of this treaty, at Natchitoches, on the Red river, and proceed to run and mark the said line from the mouth of the Sabine to the Red river, and from the Red river to the river Arkansas, and to ascertain the latitude of the source of the said river Arkansas in conformity to what is above agreed upon and stipulated, and the line of latitude 42 degrees to the South Sea; they shall make out plans and keep journals of their proceedings, and the result agreed upon by them shall be considered as part of this treaty, and shall have the same force as if it were inserted therein. The two Governments will amicably agree respecting the necessary articles to be furnished to those persons, and also as to their respective escorts, should such be deemed necessary.

ARTICLE 5. The inhabitants of the ceded territories shall be secured in the free exercise of their religion without any restriction, and all those who may desire to remove to the Spanish dominions shall be permitted to sell or export their effects at any time whatever, without being subject in either case to duties.

ARTICLE 6. The inhabitants of the territories which his Catholic Majesty cedes to the United States by this treaty shall be incorporated in the Union of the United States as soon as may be consistent with the principles of the Federal Constitution and admitted to the enjoyment of all the privileges, rights, and immunities of the citizens of the United States.

ARTICLE 7. The officers and troops of his Catholic Majesty in the territories hereby ceded by him to the United States shall be withdrawn, and possession of the places occupied by them shall be given within six months after the exchange of the ratifications of this treaty, or sooner, if possible, by the officers of his Catholic Majesty to the Commissioners or officers of the United States duly appointed to receive them, and the United States shall furnish the transports and escort necessary to convey the Spanish officers and troops and their baggage to the Havana.

ARTICLE 8. All the grants of land made before the 24th of January, 1818, by his Catholic Majesty or by his lawful authorities in the said territories ceded by his Majesty to the United States shall be ratified and confirmed to the persons in possession of the lands to the same extent that the same grants would be valid if the territories had remained under the dominion of his Catholic Majesty; but the owners in possession of such lands who, by reason of the recent circumstances of the Spanish nation and the revolutions in Europe, have been prevented from fulfilling all the conditions of their grants shall complete them within the terms limited in the same, respectively, from the date of this treaty, in default of which the said grants shall be null and void. All grants made since the said 24th of January, 1818, when the first proposal on the part of his Catholic Majesty for the cession of the Floridas was made, are hereby declared and agreed to be null and void.

ARTICLE 9. The two high contracting parties, animated with the most earnest desire of conciliation, and with the object of putting an end to all the differences which have existed between them, and of confirming the good understanding which they wish to be forever maintained between them, reciprocally renounce all claim for damages or injuries which they themselves as well as their respective citizens and subjects may have suffered until the time of signing this treaty.

tensiones á qualesquiera territorios situados al Oeste y al Sur de la misma linea arriba descrita.

ARTICULO 4. Para fixar está linea con mas precision y establecer los Mojones que señalen con exactitud los limites de ambas naciones, nombrará eada una de ellas un comisario y un geómetra que se junterán antés del termino de un año, contado desde la fecha de la ratificacion de este tratado, en Natchitochez, en las Orillas del Rio Roxo, y procederán á señalar y demarcar dicha linea, desde la embocadura del Sabina hasta el Rio Roxo, y de este hasta el Rio Arkansas, y á averiguar con certidumbre, el origen del expresado Rio Arkansas, y fixar segun queda estipulado y convenido en este Tratado, la linea que debe seguir, desde el grado 42, de latitud hasta el Mar Pacifico. Llevaran diários y levantarán planos de sus operaciones, y el resultado convenido por ellos se tendrá por parte de este Tratado, y tendrá la misma fuerza que si estuviese inserto en el; deviendo convenir amistosamente los dos Gobiernos en el arreglo de quanto necesiten estos individuos, y en la escolta respectiva que deban llevar, siempre que se crea necesario.

ARTICULO 5. A los habitantes de todos los territorios cedidos se les conservará el exercicio libre de su religion, sin restriccion alguna, y á todos los que quisieren trasladarse à los dominios Españoles se les permitirá la venta ó extraccion de sus efectos en qualquiera tiempo, sin que pueda exigirseles en uno ni otro casa derecho alguno.

ARTICULO 6. Los habitantes de los territorios que S. M. Ca. cede por este Tratado á los Estados Unidos seran incorporados en la Union de los mismos Estados, lo mas presto posible, segun los principios de la Constitucion Federal, y admitidos al goce de todos los privilegios, derechos é inmunidades de que disfrutan los ciudadanos de los demas Estados.

ARTICULO 7. Los oficiales y tropas de S. M. Ca. evacuarán los territorios cedidos à los Estados Unidos seis meses despues del cange de la ratificacion de este tratado, ó antes si fuese posible, y darán posesion de ellos à los oficiales, ó comisarios de los Estados Unidos debidamente autorizados para recibirlos : Y los Estados Unidos proveerán los transportes y escolta necesarios para llevar à la Habana los oficiales y tropas Españolas y sus equipages.

ARTICULO 8. Todas las concesiones de terrenos hechas por S. M. Ca. ó por sus legitimas autoridadès antes del 24 de Enero, de 1818, en los expresados territorios que S. M. cede à los Estados Unidos, quedaran ratificadas y reconocidas á las personas que lo esten en posesion de ellas, del mismo modo que lo serian si S. M. hubiese continuado en el dominio de estos territorios; pero los propietarios que por un efecto de las circunstancias en que se ha hallado la Nacion Española y por las revoluciones de Europa, no hubiesen podido llenar todas las obligaciones de las concesiones, seran obligados á cumplirlas segun las condiciones de sus respectivas concesiones desde la fecha de este tratado, en defecto de lo qual seran nulas y de ningun valor. Todas las concesiones posteriores al 24 de Enero, de 1818, en que fueron hechas las primeras proposiciones de parte de S. M. Ca. para la cesion de las dos Floridas, convienen y declaran las dos altas partes contratantes que quedan anuladas y de ningun valor.

ARTICULO 9. Las dos altas partes contratantes animadas de los mas vivos deseos de conciliacion y con el objeto de cortar de raiz todas las discusiones que han existido entre ellas y afianzar la buena armonia que desean mantener pepetuamente, renuncian una y otra reciprocamente á todas las reclamaciones de daños y perjuicios que asi ellas como sus respectivos subditos y ciudadanos hayan experimentado hasta el dia en que se firme este tratado.

The renunciation of the United States will extend to all the injuries mentioned in the convention of the 11th of August, 1802.

2. To all claims on account of prizes made by French privateers, and condemned by French consuls, within the territory and jurisdiction of Spain.

3. To all claims of indemnities on account of the suspension of the right of deposit at New Orleans in 1802.

4. To all claims of citizens of the United States upon the Government of Spain, arising from the unlawful seizures at sea, and in the ports and territories of Spain, or the Spanish colonies.

5. To all claims of citizens of the United States upon the Spanish Government, statements of which, soliciting the interposition of the Government of the United States, have been presented to the Department of State, or to the minister of the United States in Spain, since the date of the convention of 1802, and until the signature of this treaty.

The renunciation of his Catholic Majesty extends:

1. To all the injuries mentioned in the convention of the 11th of August, 1802.

2. To the sums which his Catholic Majesty advanced for the return of Captain Pike from the provincias internas.

3. To all injuries caused by the expedition of Miranda, that was fitted out and equipped at New York.

4. To all claims of Spanish subjects upon the Government of the United States, arising from unlawful seizures at sea, or within the ports and territorial jurisdiction of the United States.

Finally, to all the claims of subjects of his Catholic Majesty upon the Government of the United States, in which the interposition of his Catholic Majesty's Government has been solicited before the date of this treaty, and since the date of the convention of 1802, or which may have been made to the Department of Foreign Affairs of his Majesty, or to his minister in the United States.

And the high contracting parties, respectively, renounce all claim to indemnities for any of the recent events or transactions of their respective commanders and officers in the Floridas.

The United States will cause satisfaction to be made for the injuries, if any, which, by process of law, shall be established to have been suffered by the Spanish officers, and individual Spanish inhabitants, by the late operations of the American army in Florida.

ARTICLE 10. The convention entered into between the two Governments on the 11th of August, 1802, the ratifications of which were exchanged the 21st December, 1818, is annulled.

ARTICLE 11. The United States, exonerating Spain from all demands in future, on account of the claims of their citizens to which the renunciations herein contained extend, and considering them entirely cancelled, undertake to make satisfaction for the same to an amount not exceeding five millions of dollars. To ascertain the full amount and validity of those claims, a commission, to consist of three Commissioners, citizens of the United States, shall be appointed by the President, by and with the advice and consent of the Senate, which commission shall meet at the city of Washington and, within the space of three years from the time of their first meeting, shall receive, examine, and decide upon the amount and validity of all the claims included within the descriptions above mentioned. The said Commissioners shall take an oath or affirmation, to be entered on the record of their proceedings, for the faithful and diligent discharge of their duties; and, in case of the death, sickness, or necessary absence of any such Commissioner, his place may be supplied by the appointment as aforesaid, or by the President of the United States, during the recess of

La renuncia de los Estados Unidos se extiende á todos los perjuicios mencionados en el Convenio de 11 de Agosto de 1802.

2. A todas las reclamaciones de presas hechas por los corsarios Franceses, y cóndenadas por los consules Franceses dentro del territorio y jurisdiccion de España.

3. A todas las reclamaciones de indemnizaciones por la suspension del derecho de deposito en Nueva Orleans en 1802.

4. A todos las reclamaciones de los ciudadanos de los Estados Unidos contra el Gobierno Español procedentes de presas y confiscaciones injustas asi en la Mar como en los puertos y territorios de S. M. en España y sus colonias.

5. A todas las reclamaciones de los ciudadanos de los Estados Uniodos contra el Gobierno de España, en que se haya reclamado la interposicion del Gobierno de los Estados Unidos antes de la fecha dé este tratado, y desde la fecha del convenio de 1802, ó presentadas al Departamento de Estado de esta Republica, ó Ministro de los Estados Unidos en España.

La renuncia de S. M. Ca. se extiende:

1. A todos los perjuicios mencionados en el convenio de 11 de Agosto, 1802.

2. A las cantidades que suplió, para la vuelta del Capitan Pike, de las provincias internas.

3. A los perjuicios causados por la expedicion de Miranda, armada y equipada en Nueva York.

4. A todas las reclamaciones de los subditos de S. M. Ca. contra el Gobierno de los Estados Unidos procedentes de presas y confiscaciones injustas asi en la mar como en los puertos y territorios de los Estados Unidos.

5. A todas las reclamaciones de los subditos de S. M. Ca. contra el Gobierno de los Estados Unidos, en que se haya reclamado la interposicion del Gobierno de España antes de la fecha de este tratado, y desde la fecha del convenio de 1802, ó que hayan sido presentadas al Departamento de Estado de S. M ó á su Ministro en los Estados Unidos.

Las altas partes contratantes renuncian reciprocamente todos sus derechos á indemnizaciones por qualquiera de los ultimos; a contecimientos y transacciones de sus respectivos comandantes y oficiales en las Floridas.

Y los Estados Unidos satisfaran los perjuicios, si los hubiese habido, que los habitantes y oficiales Españoles justifiquen legalmente haber sufrido por las operaciones de Exercita Americano en ellas.

ARTICULO 10. Queda anulado el convenio hecho entre los dos Gobiernos en 11 de Agosto, de 1802, cuyas ratificaciones fueron cangeadas en 21 de Diciembre de 1818.

ARTICULO 11. Los Estados Unidos descargando á la España para lo sucesivo de tódas las reclamaciones de sus ciudadanos á que se extienden las renuncias hechas en este tratado, y dan dolas por enteramente canceladas, toman sobre si la satisfaccion ó pago de todas ellas hasta la cantidad de cinco millones de pesos fuertes. El Sor. Presidente nombrará, con consentimiento y aprobacion del Senado, una Comision compuesta de tres Comissionados, ciudadanos de los Estados Unidos, para ave riguar con certidumbre el importe total y justificacion de estas reclamaciones; la qual se reunirá en la ciudad de Washington, y en el espacio de tres años, desde su reunion primera, recibirá, examinará, y decidirá sobre el importe y justificacion de todas las reclamaciones arriba expresadas y descritas. Los dichos comisionados prestarán juramento, que se onatará en los quadernos de sus operaciones, para el desempeño fiel y eficaz de sus deberes, y en caso de muerte, enfermedad ó ausencia precisa de alguno de ellos, será re emplazado del mismo modo, ó por el Sor. Presidente de los Estados Unidos, en ausencia del Senado. Los dichos comisionados se hallaran autorizados para oir

the Senate, of another Commissioner in his stead. The said Commissioners shall be authorized to hear and examine, on oath, every question relative to the said claims, and to receive all suitable authentic testimony concerning the same. And the Spanish Government shall furnish all such documents and elucidations as may be in their possession, for the adjustment of the said claims according to the principles of justice, the laws of nations, and the stipulations of the treaty between the two parties of 27th October, 1795; the said documents to be specified when demanded at the instance of the said Commissioners.

The payment of such claims as may be admitted and adjusted by the said Commissioners, or the major part of them, to an amount not exceeding five millions of dollars, shall be made by the United States, either immediately at their Treasury or by the creation of stock bearing an interest of six per cent. per annum, payable from the proceeds of sales of public lands within the territories hereby ceded to the United States, or in such other manner as the Congress of the United States may prescribe by law.

The records of the proceedings of the said Commissioners, together with the vouchers and documents produced before them, relative to the claims to be adjusted and decided upon by them, shall, after the close of their transactions, be deposited in the Department of State of the United States, and copies of them, or any part of them, shall be furnished to the Spanish Government, if required, at the demand of the Spanish minister in the United States.

ARTICLE 12. The treaty of limits and navigation of 1795 remains confirmed in all and each one of its articles, excepting the 2d, 3d, 4th, 21st, and the second clause of the 22d article, which, having been altered by this treaty, or having received their entire execution, are no longer valid.

With respect to the 15th article of the same treaty of friendship, limits, and navigation, of 1795, in which it is stipulated that the flag shall cover the property, the two high contracting parties agree that this shall be so understood with respect to those powers who recognize this principle; but if either of the two contracting parties shall be at war with a third party, and the other neutral, the flag of the neutral shall cover the property of enemies whose Government acknowledge this principle, and not of others.

ARTICLE 13. Both contracting parties, wishing to favor their mutual commerce by affording in their ports every necessary assistance to their respective merchant vessels, have agreed that the sailors who shall desert from their vessels in the ports of the other shall be arrested and delivered up, at the instance of the consul, who shall prove, nevertheless, that the deserters belonged to the vessels that claim them, exhibiting the document that is customary in their nation; that is to say, the American consul in a Spanish port shall exhibit the document known by the name of articles, and the Spanish consul in American ports, the roll of the vessel; and if the name of the deserter or deserters who are claimed shall appear in the one or in the other, they shall be arrested, held in custody, and delivered to the vessel to which they shall belong.

ARTICLE 14. The United States hereby certify that they have not received any compensation from France for the injuries they suffered from her privateers, consuls, and tribunals, on the coasts and in the ports of Spain, for the satisfaction of which provision is made by this treaty; and they will present an authentic statement of the prizes made, and of their true value, that Spain may avail herself of the same in such manner as she may deem just and proper.

ARTICLE 15. The United States, to give to his Catholic Majesty a proof of their desire to cement the relations of amity subsisting between the two nations, and to favor the commerce of the subjects of his Catholic Majesty, agree that Spanish vessels, coming laden only with productions of Spanish growth

y examinar bajo juramento qualquiera demanda relativa á dichas reclamaciones, y para recibir los testimonios autenticos y convenientes relativos á ellas. El Gobierno Español subministrará á todos aquellos documentos y aclaraciones que esten en su poder para el ajuste las expresadas reclamaciones, segun los principios de justicia, el derecho de gentes, y las estipulaciones del tratado entre las dos partes de 27 de Octobre de 1795, cuyos documentos se especifica a quando se pidan á instancia de dichos comisionadns.

Los Estados Unidos pagarán aquellas reclamaciones que sean admitidas y ajustadas por los dichos comisionados, ó por la mayor parte de ellos, hasta la cantidad de cinco milliones de pesos fuertes, sea in mediatamente en su Tesoreria, ó por medio de uno creacion de fondos con el interés de un seis por ciento al año, pagaderos de los productus de las ventas de los torrenos valdios en los territorios aqui cedidos á los Estados Unidos, ó de qualquiera otra manera que el Congreso de los Estados Unidos ordene por ley.

Se depositarán, despues de concluidas sus transacciones, en el Departamento de Estado de los Estados Unidos, los quadernos de las operaciones de los dichos Comisionados, juntamente con los documentos que se les presenten relativos á las reclamaciones que de ben a justar y decidar; y se entregarán copias de ellos ó de parte de ellos al Gobierno Español, y á peticion de su Ministro en los Estados Unidos, si lo solicitase

ARTICULO 12. El tratado de limites y navegacion de 1795, queda confirmado en todos y cada uno de sus articulos, excepto los articulos 2, 3, 4, 21, y la segunda clausula del 22, que habiendo sido alterados por este tratado, ó cumplido enteramente no pueden tener valor alguno.

Con respecto al articulo 15 del mismo tratado de amistad, limites y navegacion de 1795, en que se estipula, que la bandera cubre la propiedad, han convenido las dos altas partes contratantes en que esto se entienda asi con respecto á aquellas potencias que reconozcan este principio; pero que si una de las dos partes contratantes estuviere en guerra con una tercera, y la otra neutral, la bandera de esta neutral cubrirá la propiedad de los enemigos, cuyo gobierno reconozca este principio, y no de otros.

ARTICULO 13. Deseando ambas potencias contratantes favorecer el comercio reciproco prestando cada una en sus puertos todos los auxilios convenientés á sus respectivos buques mercantes, han acordado en hacer prender y entregar los marineros qué desierten de sus buques en los puertos de la otra, á instancia del consul; quien sin embargo deberá probar que los desertores pertenecen á los buques que los reclaman, manifestando el documento de costumbre en su nacion; esto es, que el consul Español en puerto Americano exhibirá el rol del buqueₑ y el consul Americano en puerto Español, el documento conocido bajo el nombre de articles; y constando en uno ú otro el nombre ó nombres del desertor ó desertores que se reclaman, se procederá al arresto, custodia y entrega al buque á que correspondan.

ARTICULO 14. Los Estados Unidos certifican por el presente que no han recibido compensacion alguna de la Francia por los perjuicios que sufrieron de sus corsarios, consules y tribunales en las costas y puertos de España para cuya satisfaccion se proveé en este tratado, y presentarán una relacion justificada de las presas hechas, y de su verdadero valor, para que la España pueda servirse de ella en la manera que mas juzgue justo y conveniente.

ARTICULO 15. Los Estados Unidos para dar á S. M. Ca. una prueba de sus deseos de cimentar las reclamaciones de amistad que existen entre las dos naciones, y de favorecer el comercio de los subditos de S. M. Ca. convienen en que, los buques Españoles que vengan solo cargados de productos de sus

or manufactures, directly from the ports of Spain or of her colonies, shall be admitted, for the term of twelve years, to the ports of Pensacola and St. Augustine, in the Floridas, without paying other or higher duties on their cargoes or of tonnage than will be paid by the vessels of the United States. During the said term no other nation shall enjoy the same privileges within the ceded territories. The twelve years shall commence three months after the exchange of the ratifications of this treaty.

ARTICLE 16. The present treaty shall be ratified in due form by the contracting parties, and the ratifications shall be exchanged in six months from this time, or sooner, if possible.

In witness whereof, we, the underwritten plenipotentiaries of the United States of America and of his Catholic Majesty, have signed, by virtue of our powers, the present treaty of amity, settlement, and limits, and have thereunto affixed our seals respectively.

Done at Washington, this twenty-second day of February, one thousand eight hundred and nineteen.
JOHN QUINCY ADAMS. [L. S.]
LUIS DE ONIS. [L. S.]

frutos ó manufacturas directamente de los puertos de España ó de sus colonias, sean admitidos por el espacio de doce años en los puertos de Panzacola y San Augustin de las Floridas, sin pagar mas derechos por sus cargamentos, ni major derechos de tonelage, que el que paguen los buques de los Estados Unidos. Durante este tiempo ninguna nacion tendrá derecho á los mismos privilegios en los territorios cedidos. Los doce años empezaran á contarse tres meses despues de haberse cambiado las ratificaciones de este tratado.

ARTICULO 16. El presente tratado será ratificado en debida forma por las partes contratantes, y las ratificaciones se cangearán en el espacio de seis meses desde esta fecha; ó mas pronto si es posible.

En fé de lo qual nosotros los infrascritos plenipotenciarios de S. M. Ca., y de los Estados Unidos de America, hemos firmado en virtud de nuestros poderes el presente tratado de amistad, arreglo de diferencias y limites, y le hemos puesto nuestros sellos respectivos.

Hecho en Washington, á veinte y dos de Febrero de mil ochocientos diez y nueve.
LUIS DE ONIS. [L. S.]
JOHN QUINCY ADAMS. [L. S.]

And whereas his said Catholic Majesty did, on the twenty-fourth day of October, in the year of our Lord one thousand eight hundred and twenty, ratify and confirm the said treaty, which ratification is in the words and of the tenor following:

[Translation.]

"Ferdinand the Seventh, by the grace of God, and by the constitution of the Spanish monarchy, King of the Spains.

Whereas, on the twenty-second day of February, of the year one thousand eight hundred and nineteen last past, a treaty was concluded and signed in the city of Washington between Don Luis de Onis, my envoy extraordinary and minister plenipotentiary, and John Quincy Adams, esquire, Secretary of State of the United States of America, competently authorized by both parties, consisting of sixteen articles, which had for their object the arrangement of differences and of limits between both Governments and their respective territories; which are of the following form and literal tenor:"

[Original.]

"Dn. Fernando Septimo por la gracia de Dios, y por la constitucion de la Monarquia Española, Rey de las Españas.

Por cuanto en el dia veinte y dos de Febrero, del año proximo pasado de mil ochocientos diez y nueve, se concluyo y firmo en la ciudad de Washington entre Dn. Luis de Onis mi enviado extraordinario y ministro plenipotenciaria, y Dn. Juan Quincy Adams, Secretario de Estado de los Estados Unidos de America, autorizados competentemente por ambas partes, un tratado compuesto de diez y seis articulos, que tiene por objeto el arreglo de diferencias y de limites entre ambos Gobiernos y sus respectivos Territorios; cuya forma y tenor literal es el siguiente."

[Here follows the above treaty word for word.]

"Therefore, having seen and examined the sixteen articles aforesaid, and having first obtained the consent and authority of the General Cortes of the nation with respect to the cession mentioned and stipulated in the 2d and 3d articles, I approve and ratify all and every one of the articles referred to and the clauses which are contained in them; and in virtue of these presents I approve and ratify them; promising, on the faith and word of a King, to execute and observe them and cause them to be executed and observed entirely as if I myself had signed them; and that the circumstance of having exceeded the term of six months, fixed for the exchange of the ratifications in the 16th article may afford no obstacle in any manner, it is my deliberate will that the present ratification be as valid and firm and produce the same effects as if it had been done within the determined period. Desirous at the same time of avoiding any doubt or ambiguity concerning the meaning of the 8th article of the said treaty in respect to the date which is pointed out in it as the period for the confirmation of the grants of lands in the Floridas, made by me, or by the competent authorities in my royal name, which point of date was fixed in the positive understanding of the three grants of land made in favor of the Duke of Alagon, the Count of Punonrostro, and Don Pedro de Vargas, being annulled by its tenor, I think proper to declare that the said three grants have remained and do remain entirely annulled and invalid, and that neither the three individuals mentioned nor

"Por tanto, haviendo visto y examinado los referidos diez y seis articulos, y habiendo precedido la anuencia y autorizacion de las Cortes generales de la nacion por lo respectivo a la cesion que en los articulos 2° y 3° se menciona y estipula, he venido a aprobar y ratificar todos y cada uno de los referidos articulos y clausulas que en ellos se contiene; y en virtud de la presente los apruebo y ratifico; prometiendo en fé y palabra de Rey cumplirlos y observarlos, y hacer que se cumplan y observen enteramente como si Yo mismo los hubiese firmado: sin que sirva de obstaculo en manera alguna la circunstancia de haber transcurrido el termino de los seis meses prefijados para el cange de las ratificaciones en el articulo 16; pues mi deliberada voluntad es que la presente ratificacion sea tan valida y subsistente y produzca los mismos efectos que si huviese sido hecha dentro del termino prefijado. Yo deseando al mismo tiempo evitar qualquiera duda ó ambiguedad que pueda ofrecer el contenido del articulo 8° del referido tratado con motivo de la fecha que en el se señala como termino para la validacion de las concessiones de tierras en las Floridas, hechas por mi ó por las autoridades competentes en mi real nombre, a cuyo señalamiento de fecha se procedió en la positiva inteligencia de dejar anuladas por su tenor las tres concesiones de tierras hechas a favor del Duque de Alagon, Conde de Puñonrostro, y Dn. Pedro de Vargas, tengo a bien declarar que las referidas tres concesiones han quedado y quedan enteramente anuladas

those who may have title or interest through them can avail themselves of the said grants at any time or in any manner under which explicit declaration the said 8th article is to be understood as ratified. In the faith of all which I have commanded to despatch these presents. Signed by my hand, sealed with my secret seal, and countersigned by the underwritten my Secretary of Despatch of State. ·

Given at Madrid, the twenty-fourth of October, one thousand eight hundred and twenty.

[Signed,]　　　　　　　　　FERNANDO.
[Countersigned,]　　　EVARISTO PEREZ DE CASTRO."

è invalidadas; sin que los tres individuos referidos, ni los que de estos tengan titulo ó causa, puedan aprovecharse de dichas concesiones en tiempo ni manera alguna: bajo cuya explicita declaracion se ha de entender ratificado el referido articulo 8°. En fé de todo lo cual mandé despachar la presente firmada de mi mano, sellada con mi sello secreto y refrendada por el infrascrito mi secretario del despacho de Estado. Dada en Madrid a veinte y quatro de Octubre de mil ochocientos veinte.

[Sign.]　　　　　　　　　FERNANDO.
[Refren.]　　　EVARISTO PEREZ DE CASTRO."

And whereas the Senate of the United States did, on the nineteenth day of the present month, advise and consent to the ratification, on the part of these United States, of the said treaty, in the following words:

"IN SENATE OF THE UNITED STATES, *February* 19, 1821."

"*Resolved, two-thirds of the senators present concurring therein,* That the Senate, having examined the treaty of amity, settlement, and limits, between the United States of America and his Catholic Majesty, made and concluded on the twenty-second of February, one thousand eight hundred and nineteen, and seen and considered the ratification thereof made by his said Catholic Majesty on the twenty-fourth day of October, one thousand eight hundred and twenty, do consent to, and advise the President of the United States to ratify the same."

And whereas, in pursuance of the said advice and consent of the Senate of the United States, I have ratified and confirmed the said treaty, in the words following, viz:

"Now, therefore, I, James Monroe, President of the United States of America, having seen and considered the treaty above recited, together with the ratification of his Catholic Majesty thereof, do, in pursuance of the aforesaid advice and consent of the Senate of the United States, by these presents, accept, ratify, and confirm the said treaty, and every clause and article thereof, as the same are hereinbefore set forth.

"In faith whereof, I have caused the seal of the United States of America to be hereto affixed.

· "Given under my hand, at the city of Washington, this twenty-second day of February, in the year of our Lord one thousand eight hundred and twenty-one, and of the Independence of the United States the forty-fifth.

' JAMES' MONROE.

"By the President:
　"JOHN QUINCY ADAMS,
　　　"*Secretary of State.*"

And whereas the said ratifications, on the part of the United States and of his Catholic Majesty, have been this day duly exchanged, at Washington, by John Quincy Adams, Secretary of State of the United States, and by General Don Francisco Dionisio Vives, Envoy Extraordinary and Minister Plenipotentiary of his Catholic Majesty: Now, therefore, to the end that the said treaty may be observed and performed with good faith on the part of the United States, I have caused the premises to be made public; and I do hereby enjoin and require all persons bearing office, civil or military, within the United States, and all others, citizens or inhabitants thereof, or being within the same, faithfully to observe and fulfil the said treaty, and every clause and article thereof.

In testimony whereof, I have caused the seal of the United States to be affixed to these presents, and signed the same with my hand.

Done at the city of Washington, the twenty-second day of February, in the year of our Lord one [L. S.] thousand eight hundred and twenty-one, and of the sovereignty and Independence of the United States the forty-fifth.

JAMES MONROE.

By the President:
　JOHN QUINCY ADAMS,
　　　Secretary of State.

TREATY WITH ALGIERS.

· COMMUNICATED TO THE SENATE JANUARY 7, 1822.

To the Senate of the United States:

I transmit to the Senate a treaty of peace and amity concluded between the United States and the Dey and Regency of Algiers on the 23d of December, 1816.

This treaty is, in all respects, the same in its provisions with that which had been concluded on the 30th of June, 1815, and was ratified, by and with the advice and consent of the Senate, on the 26th of December of that year, with the exception of one additional and explanatory article.

The circumstances which have occasioned the delay in laying the present treaty before the Senate, for their advice and consent to its ratification, are, that having been received in the spring of the year 1817, during the recess of the Senate, in the interval between the time when the Department of State was vacated by its late Secretary and the entrance of his successor upon the duties of the office, and when a change also occurred of the chief clerk of the Department, it was not recollected by the officers of the Department that it remained without the constitutional sanction of the Senate until shortly before the commencement of the present session. The documents explanatory of the additional articles are likewise herewith transmitted.

JAMES MONROE.

DECEMBER 30, 1821.

Treaty of peace and amity concluded between the United States of America and the Dey and Regency of Algiers.

The President of the United States and the Dey of Algiers, being desirous to restore and maintain upon a stable and permanent footing the relations of peace and good understanding between the two powers, and for this purpose to renew the treaty of peace and amity which was concluded between the two States by William Shaler and Commodore Stephen Decatur, as Commissioners Plenipotentiary on the part of the United States, and his Highness Omar Pashaw, Dey of Algiers, on the 30th day of June, 1815.

The President of the United States having subsequently nominated and appointed by commission the above named William Shaler, and Isaac Chauncey, commodore and commander-in-chief of all the naval forces of the United States in the Mediterranean, Commissioners Plenipotentiary, to treat with his Highness the Dey of Algiers, for the renewal of the treaty aforesaid; and they have concluded, settled, and signed, the following articles:

ARTICLE I. There shall be, from the conclusion of this treaty, a firm, perpetual, inviolable, and universal peace and friendship between the President and citizens of the United States of America on the one part, and the Dey and subjects of the Regency of Algiers, in Barbary, on the other, made by the free consent of both parties, and on the terms of the most favored nations; and if either party shall hereafter grant to any other nation any particular favor or privilege in navigation or commerce it shall immediately become common to the other party, freely, when freely it is granted to such other nations; but when the grant is conditional, it shall be at the option of the contracting parties to accept, alter, or reject, such conditions in such manner as shall be most conducive to their respective interests.

ARTICLE II. It is distinctly understood between the contracting parties that no tribute, either as biennial presents, or under any other form or name whatever, shall be required by the Dey and Regency of Algiers from the United States of America, on any pretext whatever.

ARTICLE III. Relates to the mutual restitution of prisoners and subjects, and has been duly executed.

ARTICLE IV. Relates to the delivery into the hands of the consul general of a quantity of bales of cotton, &c., and has been duly executed.

ARTICLE V. If any goods belonging to any nation with which either of the parties are at war should be loaded on board vessels belonging to the other party, they shall pass free and unmolested, and no attempt shall be made to take or detain them.

ARTICLE VI. If any citizens or subjects belonging to either party shall be found on board a prize vessel taken from an enemy by the other party, such citizens or subjects shall be liberated immediately ; and in no case, or on any pretence whatever, shall any American citizen be kept in captivity or confinement, or the property of any American citizen, found on board of any vessel belonging to any nation with which Algiers may be at war, be detained from its lawful owners after the exhibition of sufficient proofs of American citizenship and American property by the consul of the United States residing at Algiers.

ARTICLE VII. Proper passports shall immediately be given to the vessels of both the contracting parties, on condition that the vessels-of-war belonging to the Regency of Algiers, on meeting with merchant vessels belonging to the citizens of the United States of America, shall not be permitted to visit them with more than two persons besides the rowers; these only shall be permitted to go on board without first obtaining leave from the commander of said vessel, who shall compare the passports and immediately permit said vessel to proceed on her voyage; and should any of the subjects of Algiers insult or molest the commander, or any other person on board a vessel so visited, or plunder any of the property contained in her, on complaint being made to the consul of the United States residing in Algiers, and on his producing sufficient proofs to substantiate the fact, the commander or rais of said Algerine ship or vessel-of-war, as well as the offenders, shall be punished in the most exemplary manner.

All vessels-of-war belonging to the United States of America, on meeting a cruiser belonging to the Regency of Algiers, on having seen her passports and certificates from the consul of the United States residing in Algiers, shall permit her to proceed on her cruise unmolested and without detention.

No passport shall be granted by either party to any vessels but such as are absolutely the property of citizens or subjects of the said contracting parties, on any pretence whatever.

ARTICLE VIII. A citizen or subject of either of the contracting parties having bought a prize vessel condemned by the other party, or by any other nation, the certificates of condemnation and bill of sale shall be a sufficient passport for such vessel for six months, which, considering the distance between the two countries, is no more than a reasonable time for her to procure passports.

ARTICLE IX. Vessels of either of the contracting parties putting into the ports of the other, and having need of provisions or other supplies, shall be furnished at the market price; and if any such vessel should so put in from a disaster at sea and have occasion to repair, she shall be at liberty to land and re-embark her cargo without paying any customs or duties whatever; but in no case shall be compelled to land her cargo.

ARTICLE X. Should a vessel of either of the contracting parties be cast on shore within the territories of the other, all proper assistance shall be given to her and her crew; no pillage shall be allowed. The property shall remain at the disposal of the owners, and if reshipped on board of any vessel for exportation no customs or duties whatever shall be required to be paid thereon, and the crew shall be protected and succored until they can be sent to their own country.

ARTICLE XI. If a vessel of either of the contracting parties shall be attacked by an enemy within cannon shot of the forts of the other, she shall be protected as much as is possible. If she be in port she shall not be seized or attacked when it is in the power of the other party to protect her; and when she proceeds to sea no enemy shall be permitted to pursue her from the same port within twenty-four hours after her departure.

ARTICLE XII. The commerce between the United States of America and the Regency of Algiers; the protections to be given to merchants, masters of vessels, and seamen; the reciprocal rights of establishing consuls in each country; the privileges, immunities, and jurisdictions to be enjoyed by such consuls, are declared to be on the same footing, in every respect, with the most favored nations, respectively.

ARTICLE XIII. The consul of the United States of America shall not be responsible for the debts contracted by the citizens of his own country unless he gives previously written obligations so to do.

ARTICLE XIV. On a vessel or vessels-of-war belonging to the United States anchoring before the city of Algiers the consul is to inform the Dey of her arrival, when she shall receive the salutes which are by treaty or custom given to the ships-of-war of the most favored nations on similar occasions, and which shall be returned gun for gun. And if after such arrival, so announced, any Christians whatever, captives in Algiers, make their escape and take refuge on board any of the said ships-of-war, they shall not be required back again, nor shall the consul of the United States, or commander of the said ship, be required to pay anything for the said Christians.

ARTICLE XV. As the Government of the United States has, in itself, no character of enmity against the laws, religion, or tranquillity of any nation, and as the said States have never entered into any voluntary war or act of hostility, except in defence of their just rights on the high seas, it is declared by the contracting parties that no pretext arising from religious opinions shall ever produce an interruption of the harmony between the two nations; and the consuls and agents of both nations shall have liberty to celebrate the rights of their respective religions in their own houses.

The consuls, respectively, shall have liberty and personal security given them to travel within the territories of each other, by land and sea, and shall not be prevented from going on board any vessel they may think proper to visit; they shall likewise have the liberty to appoint their own dragoman and broker.

ARTICLE XVI. In case of any dispute arising from the violation of any of the articles of this treaty, no appeal shall be made to arms, nor shall war be declared on any pretext whatever; but if the consul residing at the place where the dispute shall happen shall not be able to settle the same, the Government of that country shall state their grievance in writing, and transmit the same to the Government of the other, and the period of three months shall be allowed for answers to be returned, during which time no acts of hostility shall be permitted by either party; and in case the grievances are not redressed and a war should be the event, the consuls and citizens and subjects of both parties, respectively, shall be permitted to embark with their effects, unmolested, on board of what vessel or vessels they shall think proper, reasonable time being allowed for that purpose.

ARTICLE XVII. If, in the course of events, a war should break out between the two nations, the prisoners captured by either party shall not be made slaves; they shall not be forced to hard labor or other confinement than such as may be necessary to secure their safe keeping, and shall be exchanged rank for rank; and it is agreed that prisoners shall be exchanged in twelve months after their capture, and the exchange may be effected by any private individual legally authorized by either of the parties.

ARTICLE XVIII. If any of the Barbary Powers, or other States at war with the United States, shall capture any American vessel and send her into any port of the Regency of Algiers, they shall not be permitted to sell her, but shall be forced to depart the port on procuring the requisite supplies of provisions; but the vessels-of-war of the United States, with any prizes they may capture from their enemies, shall have liberty to frequent the ports of Algiers for refreshment of any kind, and to sell such prizes in the said ports, without paying any other customs or duties than such as are customary on ordinary commercial importations.

ARTICLE XIX. If any of the citizens of the United States, or any persons under their protection, shall have any disputes with each other, the consul shall decide between the parties; and whenever the consul shall require any aid or assistance from the Government of Algiers to enforce his decisions it shall be immediately granted to him. And if any disputes shall arise between any citizens of the United States and the citizens or subjects of any other nations having a consul or agent in Algiers, such disputes shall be settled by the consuls or agents of the respective nations; and any disputes or suits at law that may take place between any citizens of the United States and the subjects of the Regency of Algiers shall be decided by the Dey in person, and no other.

ARTICLE XX. If a citizen of the United States should kill, wound, or strike, a subject of Algiers, or, on the contrary, a subject of Algiers should kill, wound, or strike, a citizen of the United States, the law of the country shall take place and equal justice shall be rendered, the consul assisting at the trial; but the sentence of punishment against an American citizen shall not be greater or more severe than it would be against a Turk in the same predicament; and if any delinquent should make his escape, the consul shall not be responsible for him in any manner whatever.

ARTICLE XXI. The consul of the United States of America shall not be required to pay any customs or duties whatever on anything he imports from a foreign country for the use of his house and family.

ARTICLE XXII. Should any of the citizens of the United States of America die within the Regency of Algiers, the Dey and his subjects shall not interfere with the property of the deceased, but it shall be under the immediate direction of the consul, unless otherwise disposed of by will. Should there be no consul, the effects shall be deposited in the hands of some person worthy of trust until the party shall appear who has a right to demand them, when they shall render an account of the property; neither shall the Dey nor his subjects give hindrance in the execution of any will that may appear.

ARTICLE ADDITIONAL AND EXPLANATORY. The United States of America, in order to give to the Dey of Algiers a proof of their desire to maintain the relations of peace and amity between the two powers, upon a footing the most liberal, and in order to withdraw any obstacle which might embarrass him in his relations with other States, agree to annul so much of the eighteenth article of the foregoing treaty as gives to the United States any advantage in the ports of Algiers over the most favored nations having treaties with the Regency.

Done at the palace of the Government in Algiers, on the 22d day of December, 1816, which corresponds to the 3d of the Moon Safar, year of the Hegira, 1232.

Whereas, the undersigned William Shaler, a citizen of the State of New York, and Isaac Chauncey, commander-in-chief of the naval forces of the United States stationed in the Mediterranean, being duly appointed Commissioners, by letters patent, under the signature of the President and seal of the United States of America, bearing date at the City of Washington, the twenty-fourth day of August, A. D. 1816, for negotiating and concluding the renewal of a treaty of peace between the United States of America and the Dey and subjects of the Regency of Algiers:

We, therefore, William Shaler and Isaac Chauncey, Commissioners as aforesaid, do conclude the aforegoing treaty, and every article and clause therein contained, reserving the same, nevertheless, for the final ratification of the President of the United States of America, by and with the advice and consent of the Senate of the United States.

Done in the chancery of the Consulate General of the United States, in the city of Algiers, on the 23d day of December, in the year 1816, and of the Independence of the United States the forty-first.
[L. s.]   WM. SHALER.
[L. s.]   I. CHAUNCEY.

No. 349.

CLAIM ON THE FRENCH GOVERNMENT BY A. MACTIER, G. W. DASHIELL, AND A. STEWART, OF BALTIMORE.

COMMUNICATED TO THE HOUSE OF REPRESENTATIVES JANUARY 31, 1822.

Mr. RUSSELL, from the Committee on Foreign Affairs, to whom was referred the petition of Alexander Mactier, George W. Dashiell, and Archibald Stewart, in the State of Maryland, asking indemnity of the Government of the United States, as responsible for acts of injustice and violence committed by the Government of France, having duly considered the same, reported:

That during the first session of the seventh Congress a select committee made a report (see printed reports of that session) on the memorials and petitions of sundry citizens of the United States, complaining of the spoliations and depredations which, in the then late European war, their lawful commerce had sustained from French armed vessels, and praying for compensation from this Government; that this report fully set forth all the public acts of the French Government and of the Government of the United States, from the year 1778 to the year 1801, inclusive, which can affect the case of the ship Triumph, one of the subjects of the petition now under consideration. To that report, therefore, the committee take leave to refer in relation to the ship Triumph just mentioned, and to request that it may be taken and considered as a part of the present report.

Your committee, after the most serious deliberation, are of opinion that if the Government of the United States, in expunging the second article of our convention with France of the 30th September, 1800, and in consenting to renounce the respective pretensions which were the object of that article, impaired the just power of the petitioners to resort to the Government of France for redress, still, by so doing, the American Government could be rightfully considered as becoming liable for such redress *to the same extent only* as it would otherwise have actually been obtained from France. The American Government has incurred the obligation only to save the petitioners from injury, and to see that they did not specially suffer by an act of policy adopted with a view to the general good. The petitioners, therefore, can in equity ask only of the American Government a compensation or indemnity precisely commensurate with the injury thus sustained, or, in other words, that their claim should be entertained and treated precisely in the same manner by the American Government that it would have been entertained and treated by the Government of France in case the same article aforesaid had been duly ratified by the contracting parties. The manner in which this claim had been entertained and treated by the French Government from the year 1795, the time of the capture of the Triumph, to the year 1801, the time of the rejection of the second article of the convention aforesaid, could not have reasonably been considered by the petitioners themselves as authorizing a well-founded expectation of its being thereafter liquidated and allowed by that Government. The second article aforesaid—the rejection of which by the American Government is now made the basis of this claim on this Government—promised no such liquidation or allowance; but, on the contrary, after stating that the two parties had not been able to agree on the indemnities mutually due, merely added, "the parties will negotiate further on these subjects *at a convenient time.*"

Your committee are of opinion that the assent of the American Government to such an article was the result of a thorough conviction only that the claims which it embraced on the Government of France were, owing to the character and conduct of that Government, entirely hopeless, and that an empty promise to negotiate further on them, when it might suit the convenience of that Government, was, in effect, an indefinite postponement even of negotiation, and, according to the construction uniformly given in such cases by the usage of nations, equivalent to a virtual renunciation of those claims. The difference, in effect, between such a renunciation and the renunciation complained of by the petitioners your committee do not feel themselves qualified to estimate; nor can they appreciate, with precision, the degree of injury which would have been sustained by the extinction of a claim which the petitioners had already, with the sanction and support of their own Government, prosecuted in vain, and without the faintest expectation of success, against the Government of France for the long period of six years.

Your committee are not aware that a single claim of American citizens on the Government of France for indemnity for its violence and injustice has, during the last thirty years, ever been liquidated or allowed by that Government, saving those claims only which were approved and paid by the Commissioners appointed under the convention between the two Governments of the 30th April, 1803, and in conformity to the provisions of that convention. Without that convention, not a single claim of the description of the one now in question would, it is believed, have ever been admitted and settled by the French Government; and thence the act of the American Government complained of by the petitioners could have in no way impaired their interests. But whatever might have been the injury inflicted on the petitioners by the act just mentioned, it could have existed only in the suspension of their claim for the brief period of two years, to wit: from its renunciation aforesaid, in 1801, to its revival, under the convention, in 1803;

for the petitioners expressly acknowledge, not the revival only of this claim under that convention, but that it actually passed the Board of American Commissioners aforesaid at Paris. Your committee are, therefore, of opinion, that however just the claim of the petitioners might have been on the Government of France, the act of renouncing that claim, in 1801, could have rendered this Government responsible to the petitioners for a compensation only for the chance which they thereby lost in recovering it during the two years aforesaid of the Government of France—a chance which, under the then existing circumstances, promised an advantage too small for computation, and the loss of which has been more than indemnified by the opportunity so soon after afforded by another act of the American Government, which authorized the petitioners to prove and to obtain this claim, if just, under the convention of 1803, however they may have neglected to avail themselves of that opportunity. But had the American Government, in the present case, taken private property for public use and exercised its power for the general good, to the special injury of the petitioners, and thereby became liable to them for a just compensation, to be measured, not by the justice of the French Government, which was thus released, nor by the probable extent of the injury actually sustained from this release by the petitioners, but by the merits of the claim itself, your committee are of opinion that no compensation can be rightfully demanded of this Government.

If, as the petitioners allege, there was a recent order of the French Government, which does not appear, "that free ships made free goods," or if they relied on the stipulation to that effect in the treaty between the two Governments of 1778, still it appears by the act of adjudication that the ship Triumph had not only forfeited the power of imparting this impunity to her cargo, but became herself liable to confiscation by being navigated contrary to the ordinances of France then in full force.

This act of adjudication states "that according to rigorous principles only, the demand of the restoration of the vessel ought not to be received."

"The regulation of 1778, and many much anterior to it, pronounce the confiscation of foreign vessels on board which there shall be a supercargo, merchant, clerk, or superior officers of an enemy's country, and the crew of which shall be composed, beyond ·one-third, of sailors the subjects of the States of an enemy, or ·which shall not have on board a roll of equipage, attested by the public officers of the neutral places whence the vessel shall have departed."

"The captain, in a different case, ought to justify that he has been obliged to take the superior officers and sailors in the ports where he may have touched to replace those of the neutral country who may have died during the voyage."

"If for a cargo taken in a neutral country one is obliged to conform to this law, how much stronger is the reason that he ought to be subject to it when the cargo is taken in the country of an enemy and for account of an enemy."

"The Triumph departed from New England for Amsterdam with a roll of equipage of American sailors; he has affirmed in his answers that they had all deserted, and that he was obliged to take such as could be procured."

"The mate and the three sailors, who have been heard, speak the Dutch language only. They have said, but they have not proved, that they were, the one from Hamburgh and the others from Bergre or Bremen, countries which have preserved their neutrality in the present war. All the sailors, whom we have not believed it necessary to interrogate, speak the Dutch language only. We could, therefore, without fear of committing any injustice, reject the claim of the captain of the ship Triumph for the restoration of the ship."

"We might add, in support of our opinion, that there have been found on ·board near a quintal of gunpowder and a certain quantity of barrels of tar and pitch, but being unwilling to depart from the considerations which have governed us in our former judgments upon captures made of American vessels leaving Amsterdam for Surinam, we will still give a proof, on this occasion, that the French Republican pronounces against his allies only when the condemned himself can form no doubt of the justice of the judgment. We adhere with so much the more reason to this mode of thinking, that it may not even be suspected that the burning of the ship Triumph may have contributed to her condemnation, and therefore we do not pronounce it."

Thus it appears by the act of adjudication that notwithstanding the ship had become, by the act of the captain, liable to be condemned under the French regulations therein referred to, she was not so condemned; but had she not been accidentally burned, which catastrophe is imputed by the said act of adjudication mainly to the negligence of the captain, she would have been restored in relaxation of the rigor of the law; and her sails, which were saved from the fire, were actually so restored by the decree of the court.

The principal item of the claim of the petitioners is the charge (of $13,333 33) for this ship, thus exposed to capture and condemnation by the act of her captain, and thus destroyed by his imputed negligence. Besides, the articles of contraband which appear ·by the act of adjudication to have been on board were sufficient to justify the detention of that ship, under the treaty of 1778, had she in no other respect partaken, as she had done, her national, neutral, or conventional privileges.

The next article in amount of the claim of the petitioners on this Government is the charge (of $12,800) for a return freight from Surinam to Amsterdam. This appears to have been the gross amount of the freight said to have been stipulated at Amsterdam, but never earned, deducting port charges and seamen's wages only, but not deducting insurance, provisions, or any other charge or expense whatever. There is no proof exhibited to your committee of such a contract, nor any evidence that such a claim has been preferred to the Government of France. It appears, indeed, by the act of adjudication already cited, that there had been a demand made at Cayenne for damages and interest on account of the detention of the ship, but the ship having been liable to condemnation, and actually destroyed, from the causes and in the manner already stated, this demand was rejected as the necessary consequence of these facts.

Mention is nowhere made in the documents submitted to your committee of a specific demand for compensation for the loss of the benefit of this stipulated return freight being preferred to the Government of France, either ·before or since the rejection of the second article of the convention of 1800, or that it existed in a shape to be affected by that rejection.

Your committee are of opinion that in no event such a demand, without first being so preferred, could be rightfully exacted of the Government of the United States. Notwithstanding the assertion in the petition, "free ships make free goods," it does not appear that such a plea was ever urged before the French tribunals; but the act of adjudication, already cited, expressly states "that the captain did not deny in his answers that the cargo was good prize," and if the cargo was good prize, it appears necessarily to follow that the capture and detention of the ship were legal, and that no injury, either immediate or consequential, proceeding from such capture and detention, could form a legitimate claim for compensation. If, then, for the loss of the ship herself there could be no just claim for indemnity, there could be no such claim for the merely contingent or possible consequences of that loss in the benefit of an unearned freight.

The third item of the claim of the petitioners consists in a charge (of $4,848 89) for freight and primage, stipulated for the transportation of the cargo actually on board, from Amsterdam to Surinam.

Notwithstanding all the circumstances of the case, the act of adjudication of the French tribunal at Cayenne decreed, according to the specification in the bills of lading, the sum of twenty-one thousand eight hundred and twenty-six francs, to be paid to the captain in liquidation of this very item of freight and primage, not in a depreciated currency alone, as is asserted, but "either in bills of the Treasury at Cayenne, (bons de caisse,) the only money of that colony, or *in letters of exchange on the Treasury of France, at the election of the captain.*"

This offer, as appears by the documents submitted to your committee, was refused by that captain, not because the mode of payment was insufficient or unsatisfactory, but because he avowed his determination "*to receive nothing unless the ship was paid for;* and it is in consequence of this refusal and determination of the captain, and not of any act of the American Government, that this item is now claimed of this Government.

The last item of the claim in question is a charge (of $265 11) on account of the captain for his stores lost in the ship. Neither this claim nor any other, on the personal account of the captain, was, as appears by the act of adjudication already mentioned, presented to the French tribunal at Cayenne, nor has it ever, as far as your committee are informed, been since presented to the Government of France. In relation to this claim it may also be observed, that if the loss of the ship, as already stated, was occasioned to the owners by the misconduct of the captain, and thence not a subject for indemnity, the consequential loss of his private stores on his own account cannot well be entitled to be treated as such a subject.

The other claim for indemnity in this petition is founded on *a contract* made with the French constituted authorities of St. Domingo.

On this claim the rejection of the second article of the treaty of 1800, and the mutual renunciation by the contracting parties of the pretensions therein contained, could have had no effect, it being in no way connected with, or dependent on, that article. No act of the American Government, within the knowledge of your committee, has ever been exercised to the prejudice of this claim on the Government of France. On the contrary, notwithstanding there was nothing in the nature of this claim to take it from the exclusive jurisdiction of France and to bring it under the operation of international law, nor to impose on the Government of the United States any obligation to interfere for its recovery, yet has this Government, not only through its agents employed indirectly its good offices, but it has, directly, by the 5th article of the treaty of 1800, which article was duly ratified by the contracting parties, and again by the convention of 1803, stipulated with the Government of France in favor of this claim, and thus, as far as was in its power, provided for its liquidation. To demand, under these circumstances, compensation of the Government of the United States for the non-performance by the Government of France of the contract which constitutes the subject of this claim betrays, on the part of the petitioners, not only a strange misapprehension of their rights, but an ungracious forgetfulness of their obligations.

No citizen of the United States who voluntarily gives a credit to a foreign Government has a right to consider his own Government as bound to guaranty a debt, in contracting which it was neither concerned nor consulted, or become the gratuitous insurer of the creditor against the insolvency or bad faith of his debtor.

Upon mature deliberation, therefore, on the whole subject submitted to them, your committee are of opinion that it is inexpedient to grant the prayer of the petitioners, and recommend the following resolution:

Resolved, That the claims of Alexander Mactier, George W. Dashiell, and Archibald Stewart, ought not to be allowed.

17TH CONGRESS.]   No. 350.   [1ST SESSION.

BOUNDARY LINE UNDER FIFTH ARTICLE TREATY OF GHENT.

COMMUNICATED TO THE HOUSE OF REPRESENTATIVES FEBRUARY 7, 1822.

To the House of Representatives:

I transmit to the House of Representatives a report from the Secretary of State on the subject required by the resolution of that House of the 22d ultimo, with the documents which accompanied that report.   JAMES MONROE.

WASHINGTON, *February* 6, 1822.

DEPARTMENT OF STATE, *Washington, February* 5, 1822.

The Secretary of State, to whom has been referred the resolution of the House of Representatives requesting of the President of the United States such information as he may possess in relation to the progress made by the Commissioners under the fifth article of the treaty of Ghent in ascertaining and establishing that part of the boundary line between the United States and the British provinces which extends "from the source of the river St. Croix to the northwesternmost head of Connecticut river;" how much of the above mentioned line has been actually surveyed; whether a map, duly certified, has been returned of any survey made, and whether the Commissioners of the two Governments have had any meetings within a year past, has the honor of reporting to the President that those Commissioners have, in the course of the year, had meetings at New York from the 14th of May to the 9th of June; from the 1st to the 14th of August, and from the 20th of September to the 4th of October, at which last meeting a difference of opinion upon two points having occurred between the Commissioners they adjourned to meet again on the first Monday of April next.

Copies of the journals of the Board at their meetings and a part of the arguments of the agents of the two Governments on the questions submitted to the Commissioners have been received and are at this Department. No authenticated map has been returned, the reason of which is shown in a letter from the agent of the United States of the 14th of October last, and a letter from the Commissioner of 20th November, copies of which are herewith submitted, and which exhibit the progress of the commission until the time of their last adjournment.

JOHN QUINCY ADAMS.

Mr. Bradley, agent of the United States under the fifth article of the treaty of Ghent, to the Secretary of State.

WESTMINSTER, *October* 14, 1821.

SIR: I have the honor to inclose a copy of the journal of the proceedings of the Commissioners under the fifth article of the treaty of Ghent at their meeting, which I recently received from the secretary of the Board. I have also the honor to forward by mail the last argument of the British agent, in reply to my answer to his first argument, which completes the arguments growing out of the British claim.

The copy of the claim and first argument on the part of the United States has been heretofore forwarded. The answer of the British agent and my reply thereto are so voluminous that the secretary has not yet been able to furnish copies. The delay, however, is principally occasioned by the absolute necessity of making copies for the Commissioners, by whom they are required for the purpose of framing their opinions and reports as directed by the treaty.

Permit me to observe, that the copies which have been furnished to the Department of State are intended merely for the purposes of earlier information. The difference of opinion which has taken place between the Commissioners in respect to the northwest angle of Nova Scotia and the northwesternmost head of Connecticut river has rendered necessary fair duplicate copies of all the proceedings, arguments, and documents, and these are now making for each Government in a shape proper to be submitted to a foreign power. This is, of course, a work of much labor, as there are, in addition to the reports, proofs, and arguments, nearly forty maps made by the surveyors who have been employed under the commission, but they will be completed before the close of the session of Congress, and when delivered, together with the opinions of the Commissioners, to the respective agents agreeably to the eighth article of the treaty, I shall have the honor to place in your possession those belonging to the Government of the United States.

I have the honor to be, with the greatest respect, sir, your very obedient humble servant,

WILLIAM C. BRADLEY.

Hon. JOHN QUINCY ADAMS, *Secretary of State.*

Cornelius P. Van Ness, Commissioner under the fifth article of the treaty of Ghent, to the Secretary of State.

BURLINGTON, *November* 20, 1821.

SIR: The Commissioners under the fifth article of the treaty of Ghent have disagreed in opinion on the principal points submitted to them, and will make their separate reports to the two Governments, conformably to the provisions of the treaty. The documents, consisting of the reports and maps of the surveyors and the arguments of the agents, besides various other papers, copies of which are to accompany the reports of the Commissioners, are very voluminous, but the necessary copies are preparing with all practicable despatch, and will probably be ready in the month of March next.

The reports of the Commissioners, with the accompanying papers and documents, therefore, will be received at Washington about the 1st of April next, but at any rate during the approaching session of Congress. The agent of the United States, I presume, has furnished you with a more detailed statement of the situation of the business of the Commissioners.

I intend to proceed to Washington myself in April next for the purpose of closing my accounts, which cannot very well be done without my personal attendance, and which cannot be finally done until the papers are completed.

I have the honor to be, very respectfully, your obedient servant,

C. P. VAN NESS.

Hon. JOHN QUINCY ADAMS, *Secretary of State.*

SUPPRESSION OF THE SLAVE TRADE.

COMMUNICATED TO THE HOUSE OF REPRESENTATIVES APRIL 12, 1822.

Mr. GORHAM, from the Committee on the Suppression of the Slave Trade, to whom was referred a resolution of the House of Representatives of the 15th of January last, instructing them to inquire whether the laws of the United States prohibiting that traffic have been duly executed; also, into the general operation thereof; and if any defects exist in those laws, to suggest adequate remedies therefor; and to whom many memorials have been referred touching the same subject, having, according to order, had the said resolution and memorials under consideration, reported:

That under the just and liberal construction put by the Executive on the act of Congress of March 3, 1819, and that of the 15th May, 1820, inflicting the punishment of piracy on the American slave trade, a foundation has been laid for the most systematic and vigorous application of the power of the United States to the suppression of that iniquitous traffic. Its unhappy subjects, when captured, are restored to their country, agents are there appointed to receive them, and a colony, the offspring of private charity, is rising on its shores, in which such as cannot reach their native tribes will find the means of alleviating the calamities they may have endured before their liberation.

When these humane provisions are contrasted with the system which they superseded, there can be but one sentiment in favor of a steady adherence to its support. The document accompanying this report, and marked A, states the number of Africans seized or taken within or without the limits of the United States and brought there, and their present condition.

It does not appear to your committee that such of the naval force of the country as has been hitherto employed in the execution of the laws against this traffic could have been more effectually used for the interest and honor of the nation. The document marked B is a statement of the names of the vessels, and their commanders, ordered upon this service, with the dates of their departure, &c. The first vessel destined for this service arrived upon the coast of Africa in March, 1820, and in the few weeks she remained there sent in for adjudication four American vessels, all of which were condemned. The four which have been since employed in this service have made five visits, (the Alligator having made two cruises in the past summer,) the whole of which amounted to a service of about ten months, by a single vessel, within a period of near two years; and since the middle of last November, the commencement of the healthy season on that coast, no vessel has been nor, as your committee is informed, is under orders for that service.

The committee are thus particular on this branch of their inquiry, because unfounded rumors have been in circulation that other branches of the public service have suffered from the destination given to the inconsiderable force above stated, which, small as it has been, has in every instance been directed, both in its outward and homeward voyage, to cruise in the West India seas.

Before they quit this part of their inquiry, your committee feel it their duty to state that the loss of several of the prizes made in this service is imputable to the size of the ships engaged in it. The efficacy of this force, as well as the health and discipline of the officers and crews, conspire to recommend the employment of no smaller vessel than a corvette or sloop-of-war, to which it would be expedient to allow the largest possible complement of men, and, if possible, she should be accompanied by a tender, or vessel drawing less water. The vessels engaged in this service should be frequently relieved, but the coast should at no time be left without a vessel to watch and protect its shores.

Your committee find it impossible to measure with precision the effect produced upon the American branch of the slave trade by the laws above mentioned and the seizures under them. They are unable to state whether those American merchants, the American capital and seamen which heretofore aided in this traffic, have abandoned it altogether, or have sought shelter under the flags of other nations. It is ascertained, however, that the American flag, which heretofore covered so large a portion of the slave trade, has wholly disappeared from the coasts of Africa. The trade, notwithstanding, increases annually, under the flags of other nations. France has incurred the reproach of being the greatest adventurer in this traffic, prohibited by her laws; but it is to be presumed that this results not so much from the avidity of her subjects for this iniquitous gain, as from the safety which, in the absence of all hazard of capture, her flag affords to the greedy and unprincipled adventurers of all nations. It is neither candid nor just to impute to a gallant and high-minded people the exclusive commission of crimes, which the abandoned of all nations are alike capable of perpetrating, with the additional wrong to France herself of using her flag to cover and protect them. If the vigor of the American Navy has saved its banner from like reproach, it has done much to preserve, unsullied, its high reputation, and amply repaid the expense charged upon the public revenue by a system of laws to which it has given such honorable effect.

But the conclusion to which your committee has arrived, after consulting all the evidence within their reach, is, that the African slave trade now prevails to a great extent, and that its total suppression can never be effected by the separate and disunited efforts of one or more States; and as the resolution to which this report refers requires the suggestion of some remedy for the defects, if any exist, in the system of laws for the suppression of this traffic, your committee beg leave to call the attention of the House to the report and accompanying documents submitted to the last Congress by the Committee on the Slave Trade, and to make the same a part of this report. That report proposes, as a remedy for the existing evils of the system, the concurrence of the United States with one or all the maritime powers of Europe in a modified and reciprocal right of search on the African coast, with a view to the total suppression of the slave trade.

It is with great delicacy that the committee have approached this subject, because they are aware that the remedy which they have presumed to recommend to the consideration of the House requires the exercise of the power of another Department of this Government, and that objections to the exercise of this power, in the mode here proposed, have hitherto existed in that Department.

Your committee are confident, however, that these objections apply rather to a *particular proposition* for the exchange of the right of search than to that modification of it which presents itself to your committee. They contemplate the trial and condemnation of such American citizens as may be found engaged in this forbidden trade, not by mixed tribunals sitting in a foreign country, but by existing courts, of competent jurisdiction, in the United States; they propose the same disposition of the captured Africans now authorized by law, and least of all their detention in America.

They contemplate an exchange of this right, which shall be in all respects reciprocal; an exchange which, deriving its sole authority from treaty, would exclude the pretension, which no nation, however, has presumed to set up, that this right can be derived from the law of nations; and, further, they have limited it, in their conception of its application, not only to certain latitudes, and to a certain distance from the coast of Africa, but to a small number of vessels to be employed by each power, and to be previously designated. The visit and search thus restricted, it is believed, would insure the co-operation of one great maritime power in the proposed exchange, and guard it from the danger of abuse.

Your committee cannot doubt that the people of America have the intelligence to distinguish between the right of searching a neutral on the high seas, in time of war, claimed by some belligerents, and that mutual, restricted, and peaceful concession by treaty, suggested by your committee, and which is demanded in the name of suffering humanity.

In closing the report, they recommend to the House the adoption of the following resolution, viz:

. *Resolved*, That the President of the United States be requested to enter into such arrangements as he may deem suitable and proper, with one or more of the maritime powers of Europe, for the effectual abolition of the slave trade.

A.

Statement of the number of Africans seized or taken within and without the limits of the United States, and their present situation.

No.	Date of seizure.	Present situation, &c.
202	Captured by the revenue cutter Dallas, in the Gen. Ramirez	One hundred and eighty-four in the hands of the marshal of Georgia; eighteen liberated by decree of court, and ready to be sent to Africa.
37	....	In the hands of the Governor of Georgia. A warrant issued from court against these Africans, February 21, 1821; the marshal has been instructed not to proceed on this warrant to take the Africans, because they are in the hands of the Governor.
100	Captured in May and June, 1818	In the hands of the marshal of Alabama.
10	Seized in March, 1819, at Baltimore	In the custody of the marshal of Maryland, subject to the orders of the President of the United States.
4	Seized in Charleston, S. C., April 9, 1819...............	Sent to Norfolk, Va., and conveyed to Africa on board brig Nautilus, under the charge of J. B. Winn, esq., United States agent to Africa, in January, 1821.
220	Captured in the brig La Pensee, by the sloop-of-war Hornet, November 19, 1821	Sent into New Orleans, and delivered to the marshal.

B.

Statement showing the names and rates of the several vessels ordered to cruise on the coast of Africa for the suppression of the slave trade; the names of their several commanders; the time of their respective departures from the United States; arrivals on the coast of Africa and departures therefrom; and the number of their captures.

Vessels' names.	Rates.	Commanders' names.	Date of departure from the U. States.	Date of arrival on the coast of Africa.	Date of departure from the coast of Africa.	Number of captures.
	Guns.					
Ship Cyane,............	24	Edward Trenchard.....	Jan. —, 1820	Mar. —, 1820	....	Four schooners, viz: Endymion, Esperanza, Plattsburg, and Science, sent into New York.
Ship Hornet............	18	George C. Read........	June —, 1820	....	....	Brig Alexander, sent into Boston.
Ship John Adams.......	24	A. S. Wadsworth......	July 18, 1820	....	....	
Schooner Alligator......	12	R. F. Stockton........{	April 3, 1821 Oct. 4, 1821	May 6, 1821 Nov. —, 1821	July —, 1821 Dec. 17, 1821	{ Four schooners, viz: Jeune Eugene, Mathilde, Daphne, and Eliza; the Jeune Eugene sent into Boston, the rest recaptured.
Schooner Shark.........	12	M. C. Perry............	Aug. 7, 1821	Sept. —, 1821	Nov. —, 1821	None.

NOTE.—All the above vessels were ordered to pass through the West Indies on their return to the United States, for the protection of commerce against the depredations of pirates, as well as the suppression of the slave trade.

17TH CONGRESS.]   No. 352.   [2D SESSION.

MESSAGE OF THE PRESIDENT OF THE UNITED STATES AT THE COMMENCEMENT OF THE SECOND SESSION OF THE SEVENTEENTH CONGRESS—PROCLAMATION OF TREATY WITH FRANCE OF JUNE 24, 1822—PROCLAMATION OF THE OPENING OF THE TRADE TO THE BRITISH WEST INDIA COLONIES, AUGUST 24, 1822.

COMMUNICATED TO THE SENATE DECEMBER 3, 1822.

Fellow-citizens of the Senate and of the House of Representatives:

Many causes unite to make your present meeting peculiarly interesting to our constituents. The operation of our laws on the various subjects to which they apply, with the amendments which they occasionally require, imposes, annually, an important duty on the representatives of a free people. Our system has happily advanced to such maturity that I am not aware that your cares, in that respect, will be augmented. · Other causes exist which are highly interesting to the whole civilized world, and to no portion of it more so, in certain views, than to the United States. Of these causes, and of their bearing on the interests of our Union, I shall communicate the sentiments which I have formed with that freedom which a sense of duty dictates. It is proper, however, to invite your attention, in the first instance, to those concerns respecting which legislative provision is thought to be particularly urgent.

On the 24th of June last, a convention of navigation and commerce was concluded, in this city, between the United States and France, by ministers duly authorized for the purpose.· The sanction of the Executive having been given to this convention under a conviction that, taking all its stipulations into view, it rested essentially on a basis of reciprocal and equal advantage, I deemed it my duty, in compliance with the authority vested in the Executive by the second section of the act of the last session, of the 6th May, concerning navigation, to suspend, by proclamation, until the end of the next session of Congress, the operation of the act entitled " An act to impose a new tonnage duty on French ships and vessels, and for other purposes," and to suspend, likewise, all other duties on French vessels, or the goods imported in them, which exceeded the duties on American vessels, and on similar goods imported in them. I shall submit this convention forthwith to the Senate for its advice and consent as to the ratification.

Since your last session the prohibition which had been imposed on the commerce between the United States and the British colonies in the West Indies and on this continent has likewise been removed. Satisfactory evidence having been adduced that the ports of those colonies had been opened to the vessels of the United States by an act of the British Parliament, bearing date on the 24th of June last, on the conditions specified therein, I deemed it proper, in compliance with the provisions of the first section of the act of the last session above recited, to declare, by proclamation, bearing date on the 24th of August last, that the ports of the United States should thenceforward, and until the end of the next session of Congress, be open to the vessels of Great Britain employed in that trade, under the limitation specified in that proclamation.

A doubt was entertained whether the act of Congress applied to the British colonies on this continent as well as to those in the West Indies; but, as the act of Parliament opened the intercourse equally with both, and it was the manifest intention of Congress, as well as the obvious policy of the United States, that the provisions of the act of Parliament should be met, in equal extent, on the part of the United States, and as also the act of Congress was supposed to vest in the President some discretion in the execution of it, I thought it advisable to give it a corresponding construction.

Should the constitutional sanction of the Senate be given to the ratification of the convention with France, legislative provision will be necessary to carry it fully into effect, as it likewise will be to continue in force, on such conditions as may be deemed just and proper, the intercourse which has been opened between the United States and the British colonies. Every light in the possession of the Executive will in due time be communicated on both subjects.

Resting essentially on a basis of reciprocal and equal advantage, it has been the object of the Executive, in transactions with other powers, to meet the propositions of each with a liberal spirit, believing that thereby the interest of our country would be most effectually promoted. This course has been systematically pursued in the late occurrences with France and Great Britain, and in strict accord with the views of the Legislature. A confident hope is entertained that, by the arrangement thus commenced with each, all differences respecting navigation and commerce with the dominions in question will be adjusted, and a solid foundation be laid for an active and permanent intercourse, which will prove equally advantageous to both parties.

The decision of his Imperial Majesty the Emperor of Russia, on the question submitted to him by the United States and Great Britain, concerning the construction of the first article of the treaty of Ghent, has been received. A convention has since been concluded between the parties, under the mediation of his Imperial Majesty, to prescribe the mode by which that article shall be carried into effect, in conformity with that decision. I shall submit this convention to the Senate for its advice and consent as to the ratification, and, if obtained, shall immediately bring the subject before Congress for such provisions as may require the interposition of the Legislature.

In compliance with an act of the last session, a Territorial Government has been established in Florida, on the principles of our system. By this act the inhabitants are secured in the full enjoyment of their rights and liberties, and to admission into the Union, with equal participation in the Government with the original States, on the conditions heretofore prescribed to other Territories. By a clause in the ninth article of the treaty with Spain, by which that territory was ceded to the United States, it is stipulated that satisfaction shall be made for the injuries, if any, which, by process of law, shall be established to have been suffered, by the Spanish officers and individual Spanish inhabitants, by the late operations of our troops in Florida. No provision having yet been made to carry that stipulation into effect, it is submitted to the consideration of Congress, whether it will not be proper to vest the competent power in the District Court at Pensacola, or in some tribunal to be specially organized for that purpose.

The fiscal operations of the. year have been more successful than had been anticipated at the commencement of the last session of Congress.

The receipts into the Treasury during the first three quarters of the year have exceeded the sum of fourteen millions seven hundred and forty-five thousand dollars. The payments made at the Treasury during the same period have exceeded twelve millions two hundred and seventy-nine thousand dollars; leaving in the Treasury on the 30th day of September last (including one million one hundred and sixty-eight thousand five hundred and ninety-two dollars and twenty-four cents which were in the Treasury on the first day of January last). a sum exceeding four millions one hundred and twenty-eight thousand dollars.

Besides discharging all demands for the current service of the year, including the interest and reimbursement of the public debt, the six per cent. stock of 1796, amounting to eighty thousand dollars, has been redeemed. It is estimated that, after defraying the current expenses of the present quarter, and redeeming the two millions of six per cent. stock of 1820, there will remain in the Treasury, on the first day of January next, nearly three millions of dollars. It is estimated that the gross amount of duties which have been secured, from the first of January to the 30th of September last, has exceeded nineteen millions five hundred thousand dollars, and the amount for the whole year will probably not fall short of twenty-three millions of dollars.

Of the actual force in service under the present military establishment, the posts at which it is stationed, and the condition of each post, a report from the Secretary of War, which is now communicated, will give a distinct idea. By like reports the state of the Academy at West Point will be seen, as will be the progress which has been made on the fortifications along the coast and at the public armories and arsenals.

The position on the Red river, and that at the Sault of St. Marie, are the only new posts that have been taken. These posts, with those already occupied in the interior, are thought to be well adapted to the protection of our frontiers. All the force not placed in the garrisons and along the coasts and in the ordnance depots, and indispensably necessary there, is placed on the frontiers.

The organization of the several corps composing the Army is such as to admit its expansion to a great extent in case of emergency, the officers carrying with them all the light which they possess to the new corps to which they might be appointed.

With the organization of the staff there is equal cause to be satisfied. By the concentration of every branch, with its chief in this city, in the presence of the Department, and with a grade in the chief military station to keep alive and cherish a military spirit, the greatest promptitude in the execution of orders, with the greatest economy and efficiency, are secured. The same view is taken of the Military Academy. Good order is preserved in it, and the youths are well instructed in every science connected with the great objects of the institution. They are also well trained and disciplined in the practical parts of the profession. It has always been found difficult to control the ardor inseparable from that early age in such a manner as to give it a proper direction. The rights of manhood are too often claimed prematurely, in pressing which too far, the respect which is due to age and the obedience necessary to a course of study and instruction in every such institution are lost sight of. The great object to be accomplished is the restraint of that ardor by such wise regulations and government as, by directing all the energies of the youthful mind to the attainment of useful knowledge, will keep it within a just subordination, and at the same time elevate it to the highest purposes. This object seems to be essentially obtained in this institution, and with great advantage to the Union.

The Military Academy forms the basis, in regard to science, on which the military establishment rests. It furnishes annually, after due examination, and on the report of the academic staff, many well-informed youths to fill the vacancies which occur in the several corps of the Army, while others, who retire to private life, carry with them such attainments as, under the right reserved to the several States to appoint the officers and to train the militia, will enable them, by affording a wider field for selection, to promote the great object of the power vested in Congress, of providing for the organizing, arming, and disciplining the militia. Thus, by the mutual and harmonious co-operation of the two governments in the execution of a power divided between them, an object always to be cherished, the attainment of a great result, on which our liberties may depend, cannot fail to be secured. I have to add that, in proportion as our regular force is small, should the instruction and discipline of the militia, the great resources on which we rely, be pushed to the utmost extent that circumstances will admit.

A report from the Secretary of the Navy will communicate the progress which has been made in the construction of vessels-of-war, with other interesting details respecting the actual state of the affairs of that Department. It has been found necessary, for the protection of our commerce, to maintain the usual squadrons on the Mediterranean, the Pacific, and along the Atlantic coast, extending the cruises of the latter into the West Indies, where piracy, organized into a system, has preyed on the commerce of every country trading thither. A cruise has also been maintained on the coast of Africa, when the season would permit, for the suppression of the slave trade; and orders have been given to the commanders of all our public ships to seize our own vessels, should they find any engaged in that trade, and to bring them in for adjudication.

In the West Indies piracy is of recent date, which may explain the cause why other powers have not combined against it. By the documents communicated it will be seen that the efforts of the United States to suppress it have had a very salutary effect. The benevolent provision of the act, under which the protection has been extended alike to the commerce of other nations, cannot fail to be duly appreciated by them.

In compliance with the act of the last session entitled "An act to abolish the United States trading establishments," agents were immediately appointed and instructed, under the direction of the Secretary of the Treasury, to close the business of the trading houses among the Indian tribes, and to settle the accounts of the factors and sub-factors engaged in that trade, and to execute in all other respects the injunctions of that act in the mode prescribed therein. A final report of their proceedings shall be communicated to Congress as soon as it is received.

It is with great regret I have to state that a serious malady has deprived us of many valuable citizens at Pensacola and checked the progress of some of those arangements which are important to the Territory. This effect has been sensibly felt in respect to the Indians who inhabit that Territory, consisting of the remnants of several tribes who occupy the middle ground between St. Augustine and Pensacola, with extensive claims, but undefined boundaries. Although peace is preserved with those Indians, yet their positions and claims tend essentially to interrupt the intercourse between the eastern and western parts of the Territory, on which our inhabitant, are principally settled. It is essential to the growth and prosperity of the Territory, as well as to the interests of the Union, that these Indians should be removed, by special compact with them, to some other position, or concentrated within narrower limits where they are. With the limited means in the power of the Executive, instructions were given to the Governor to accomplish this object, so far as it might be practicable, which was prevented by the distressing malady referred to. To carry it fully into effect in either mode, additional funds will be necessary, to the provision of which the powers of Congress alone are competent. With a view to such provision as may be deemed proper, the subject is submitted to your consideration, and, in the interim, further proceedings are suspended.

It appearing that so much of the act entitled "An act regulating the staff of the Army," which passed on the 14th April, 1818, as relates to the commissariat, will expire in April next, and the practical operation of that Department having evinced its great utility, the propriety of its renewal is submitted to your consideration.

The view which has been taken of the probable productiveness of the lead mines, connected with the importance of the material to the public defence, makes it expedient that they should be managed with peculiar care. It is therefore suggested whether it will not comport with the public interest to provide by law for the appointment of an agent skilled in mineralogy, to superintend them, under the direction of the proper Department.

It is understood that the Cumberland road, which was constructed at a great expense, has already suffered from the want of that regular superintendence and of those repairs which are indispensable to the preservation of such a work. This road is of incalculable advantage in facilitating the intercourse between the Western and the Atlantic States. Through it, the whole country from the northern extremity of Lake Erie to the Mississippi, and from all the waters which empty into each, finds an easy and direct communication to the seat of Government, and thence to the Atlantic. The facility which it affords to all military and commercial operations, and also to those of the Post Office Department, cannot be estimated too highly. This great work is likewise an ornament and an honor to the nation. Believing that a competent power to adopt and execute a system of internal improvement has not been granted to Congress, but that such a power, confined to great national purposes, and with proper limitations, would be productive of eminent advantage to our Union, I have thought it advisable that an amendment of the Constitution to that effect should be recommended to the several States. A bill which assumed the right to adopt and execute such a system having been presented for my signature at the last session, I was compelled, from the view which I had taken of the powers of the General Government, to negative it, on which occasion I thought it proper to communicate the sentiments which I had formed, on mature consideration, on the whole subject. To that communication, in all the views in which the great interest to which it relates may be supposed to merit your attention, I have now to refer. Should Congress, however, deem it improper to recommend such an amendment, they have, according to my judgment, the right to keep the road in repair, by providing for the superintendence of it, and appropriating the money necessary for repairs. Surely, if they had the right to apppropriate money to make the road, they have a right to appropriate it to preserve the road from ruin. From the exercise of this power no danger is to be apprehended. Under our happy system, the people are the sole and exclusive fountain of power. Each Government originates from them, and to them alone, each to its proper constituents, are they respectively and solely responsible for the faithful discharge of their duty, within their constitutional limits. And that the people will confine their public agents, of every station, to the strict line of their constitutional duties, there is no cause to doubt. Having, however, communicated my sentiments to Congress, at the last session, fully in the document to which I have referred, respecting the right of appropriation, as distinct from the right of jurisdiction and sovereignty over the Territory in question, I deem it improper to enlarge on the subject here.

From the best information that I have been able to obtain, it appears that our manufactures, though depressed immediately after the peace, have considerably increased, and are still increasing, under the encouragement given them by the tariff of 1816 and by subsequent laws. Satisfied I am, whatever may be the abstract doctrine in favor of unrestricted commerce, provided all nations would concur in it, and it was not liable to be interrupted by war, which has never occurred, and cannot be expected, that there are other strong reasons applicable to our situation and relations with other countries, which impose on us the obligation to cherish and sustain our manufactures; satisfied, however, I likewise am that the interest of every part of our Union, even of those most benefitted by manufactures, requires that this subject should be touched with the greatest caution, and a critical knowledge of the effect to be produced by the slightest change, on full consideration of the subject, in all its relations, I am persuaded that a further augmentation may now be made of the duties on certain foreign articles in favor of our own, and without affecting injuriously any other interest. For more precise details I refer you to the communications which were made to Congress during the last session.

So great was the amount of accounts for moneys advanced during the late war, in addition to others of a previous date, which, in the regular operations of the Government, necessarily remained unsettled, that it required a considerable length of time for their adjustment. By a report from the First Comptroller of the Treasury it appears that on the 4th of March, 1817, the accounts then unsettled amounted to one hundred and three millions sixty-eight thousand eight hundred and seventy-six dollars and forty-one cents, of which, on the 30th of September of the present year, ninety-three millions one hundred and seventy-five thousand three hundred and ninety-six dollars and fifty-six cents had been settled; leaving on that day a balance unsettled of nine millions eight hundred and ninety-three thousand four hundred and seventy-nine dollars and eighty-five cents. That there have been drawn from the Treasury, in paying the public debt and sustaining the Government in all its operations and disbursements, since the 4th of March, 1817, one hundred and fifty-seven millions one hundred and ninety-nine thousand three hundred and eighty dollars and ninety-six cents, the accounts for which have been settled to the amount of one hundred and thirty-seven millions five hundred and one thousand four hundred and fifty-one dollars and twelve cents; leaving a balance unsettled of nineteen millions six hundred and ninety-seven thousand nine hundred and twenty-nine dollars and eighty-four cents. For precise details respecting each of these balances, I refer to the report of the Comptroller and the documents which accompany it.

From this view it appears that our commercial differences with France and Great Britain have been placed in a train of amicable arrangement, on conditions fair and honorable, in both instances, to each party; that our finances are in a very productive state, our revenue being at present fully competent to all the demands upon it; that our military force is well organized in all its branches, and capable of rendering the most important service, in case of emergency, that its number will admit of; that due progress has been made, under existing appropriations, in the construction of fortifications, and in the operations of the ordnance department; that due progress has in like manner been made in the construction of ships-of-war; that our Navy is in the best condition, felt and respected in every sea in which it is employed for the protection of our commerce; that our manufactures have augmented in amount and improved in quality; that great progress has been made in the settlement of accounts and in the recovery of the balances due by individuals; and that the utmost economy is secured and observed in every department of the administration.

Other objects will likewise claim your attention; because, from the station which the United States hold, as a member of the great community of nations, they have rights to maintain, duties to perform, and dangers to encounter.

A strong hope was entertained that peace would, ere this, have been concluded between Spain and the independent Governments south of the United States in this hemisphere. Long experience having evinced the competency of those Governments to maintain the independence which they had declared, it was presumed that the considerations which induced their recognition by the United States would have had equal weight with other powers, and that Spain herself, yielding to those magnanimous feelings of which her history furnishes so many examples, would have terminated, on that basis, a controversy so unavailing and at the same time so destructive. We still cherish the hope that this result will not long be postponed.

Sustaining our neutral position, and allowing to each party, while the war continues, equal rights, it is incumbent on the United States to claim of each, with equal rigor, the faithful observance of our rights according to the well-known law of nations. From each, therefore, a like co-operation is expected in the suppression of the piratical practice which has grown out of this war, and of blockades of extensive coasts on both seas, which, considering the small force employed to sustain them, have not the slightest foundation to rest on.

Europe is still unsettled, and, although the war long menaced between Russia and Turkey has not broken out, there is no certainty that the differences between those powers will be amicably adjusted. It is impossible to look to the oppressions of the country, respecting which those differences arose, without being deeply affected. The mention of Greece fills the mind with the most exalted sentiments and arouses in our bosoms the best feelings of which our nature is susceptible. Superior skill and refinement in the arts, heroic gallantry in action, disinterested patriotism, enthusiastic zeal and devotion in favor of public and personal liberty, are associated with our recollections of ancient Greece. That such a country should have been overwhelmed, and so long hidden, as it were, from the world under a gloomy despotism, has been a cause of unceasing and deep regret to generous minds for ages past. It was natural, therefore, that the re-appearance of those people in their original character, contending in favor of their liberties, should produce that great excitement and sympathy in their favor which have been so signally displayed throughout the United States. A strong hope is entertained that these people will recover their independence and resume their equal station among the nations of the earth.

A great effort has been made in Spain and Portugal to improve the condition of the people, and it must be very consoling to all benevolent minds to see the extraordinary moderation with which it has been conducted. That it may promote the happiness of both nations is the ardent wish of this whole people, to the expression of which we confine ourselves; for, whatever may be the feelings or sentiments which every individual under our Government has a right to indulge and express, it is nevertheless a sacred maxim, equally with the Government and people, that the destiny of every independent nation, in what relates to such improvements, of right belongs, and ought to be left, exclusively to themselves.

Whether we reason from the late wars or from those menacing symptoms which now appear in Europe, it is manifest that if a convulsion should take place in any of those counties, it will proceed from causes which have no existence and are utterly unknown in these States, in which there is but one order, that of the people, to whom the sovereignty exclusively belongs. Should war break out in any of those countries, who can foretell the extent to which it may be carried, or the desolation which it may spread? Exempt as we are from these causes, our internal tranquillity is secure; and distant as we are from the troubled scene, and faithful to just principles, in regard to other powers, we might reasonably presume that we should not be molested by them. This, however, ought not to be calculated on as certain. Unprovoked injuries are often inflicted, and even the peculiar felicity of our situation might, with some, be a cause for excitement and aggression. The history of the late wars in Europe furnishes a complete demonstration that no system of conduct, however correct in principle, can protect neutral powers from injury from any party; that a defenceless position and distinguished love of peace are the surest invitations to war; and that there is no way to avoid it other than by being always prepared and willing, for just cause, to meet it. If there be a people on earth whose more especial duty it is to be at all times prepared to defend the rights with which they are blessed, and to surpass all others in sustaining the necessary burdens, and in submitting to sacrifices to make such preparations, it is undoubtedly the people of these States.

When we see that a civil war of the most frightful character rages from the Adriatic to the Black Sea; that strong symptoms of war appear in other parts, proceeding from causes which, should it break out, may become general, and be of long duration; that the war still continues between Spain and the independent Governments, her late provinces, in this hemisphere; that it is likewise menaced between Portugal and Brazil, in consequence of the attempt of the latter to dismember itself from the former; and that a system of piracy, of great extent, is maintained in the neighboring seas, which will require equal vigilance and decision to suppress it, the reasons for sustaining the attitude which we now hold, and for pushing forward all our measures of defence with the utmost vigor, appear to me to acquire new force.

The United States owe to the world a great example, and, by means thereof, to the cause of liberty and humanity a generous support. They have so far succeeded to the satisfaction of the virtuous and enlightened of every country. There is no reason to doubt that their whole movement will be regulated by a sacred regard to principle, all our institutions being founded on that basis. The ability to support our own cause, under any trial to which it may be exposed, is the great point on which the public solicitude rests. It has been often charged against free Governments that they have neither the foresight nor the virtue to provide, at the proper season, for great emergencies; that their course is improvident and expensive; that war will always find them unprepared, and whatever may be its calamities, that its terrible warnings will be disregarded and forgotten as soon as peace returns. I have full confidence that this charge, so far as relates to the United States, will be shown to be utterly destitute of truth.

JAMES MONROE.

Washington, *December* 3, 1822.

BY THE PRESIDENT OF THE UNITED STATES.

A PROCLAMATION.

Whereas, by the second section of an act of Congress of the 6th of May last, entitled "An act in addition to the act concerning navigation, and also to authorize the appointment of deputy collectors," it is provided, that, in the event of the signature of any treaty or convention concerning the navigation or commerce between the United States and France, the President of the United States, if he should deem the same expedient, may suspend by proclamation, until the end of the next session of Congress, the operation of the act entitled "An act to impose a new tonnage duty on French ships and vessels, and for other purposes;" and also to suspend, as aforesaid, all other duties on French vessels, or the goods imported in the same, which may exceed the duties on American vessels, and on similar goods imported in the same: and whereas a convention of navigation and commerce between the United States of America and his Majesty the King of France and Navarre has this day been duly signed by John Quincy Adams, Secretary of State, on the part of the United States, and by the Baron Hyde de Neuville, Envoy Extraordinary and Minister Plenipotentiary from France, on the part of his most Christian Majesty, which convention is in the words following:

Convention de Navigation et de Commerce entre sa Majesté le Roi de France et de Navarre et les Etats Unis d'Amerique.	*Convention of Navigation and Commerce between the United States of America and his Majesty the King of France and Navarre.*

Sa Majesté le Roi de France et de Navarre et les Etats Unis d'Amerique, desirant régler les relations de navigation et de commerce entre leur nations respectives par un convention temporarié reciproquement avantageuse et satisfaisante, et arriver aussi a un arrangement plus etendu et durable, ont respectivement donne leur pleins-pouvoirs, savoir: Sa Majesté Trés Chretienne au Baron Hyde de Neuville, Chevalier de l'ordre Royal et Militarie de St. Louis, Commandeur de la Legion d'Honneur, Grand Croix de l'ordre Royal Americain d'Isabelle la Catholique, son Envoyé Extraordinare et Ministre Plenipotentiare près les Etats Unis; et le President des Etats Unis, à John Quincy Adams, leur Sécrétare d'Etat; lesquels, apres avoir échangé leur pleins-pouvoirs, sont convenus des articles suivans:

The United States of America and his Majesty the King of France and Navarre, being desirous of settling the relations of navigation and commerce between their respective nations by a temporary convention reciprocally beneficial and satisfactory, and thereby of leading to a more permanent and comprehensive arrangement, have respectfully furnished their full powers in manner following, that is to say: The President of the United States to John Quincy Adams, their Secretary of State, and his most Christian Majesty to the Baron Hyde de Neuville, Knight of the Royal and Military Order of St. Louis, Commander of the Legion of Honor, Grand Cross of the Royal American Order of Isabella the Catholic, his Envoy Extraordinary and Minister Plenipotentiary near the United States, who, after exchanging their full powers, have agreed on the following articles:

Article 1. Les produits naturels ou manufacturés des Etats Unis importés en France sur batimens des Etats Unis payeront un droit additionel qui n'excédera point vingt francs par tonneau de marchandise, en sus droits payés sur les mèmes produits naturels ou manufacturés des Etats Unis quand ils sont importés par navires Français.

Article 1. Articles of the growth, produce, or manufacture of the United States, imported into France in vessels of the United States, shall pay an additional duty, not exceeding twenty francs per ton of merchandise over and above the duties paid on the like articles, also of the growth, produce, or manufacture of the United States, when imported in French vessels.

Article 2. Les produits naturels ou manufacturés de France importés aux Etats Unis sur batimens Français payeront un droit additionel qui n' excedera point trois dollars, soixante-quinze cents par tonneau de marchandise, en sus des droits payés sur les mèmes produits naturels ou manufacturés de France quand ils sont importés par navires des Etats Unis.

Article 2. Articles of the growth, produce, or manufacture of France, imported into the United States in French vessels, shall pay an additional duty, not exceeding three dollars and seventy-five cents per ton of merchandise over and above the duties collected upon the like articles, also of the growth, produce, or manufacture of France, when imported in vessels of the United States.

Article 3. Aucun droit differentiel ne sera levé sur les produits du sol et de l'industrie de France qui seront importés par navires Français dans les ports des Etats Unis pour transit ou re-exportation; Il en sera de meme dans les ports de France pour les produits du sol et de l'industrie de l'Union qui seront importés pour transit ou re-exportation par navires des Etats Unis.

Article 3. No discriminating duty shall be levied upon the productions of the soil or industry of France, imported in French bottoms into the ports of the United States for transit or re-exportation; nor shall any such duties be levied upon the productions of the soil or industry of the United States, imported in vessels of the United States into the ports of France for transit or re-exportation.

Article 4. Les quantités suivantes seront considerées comme formant le tonneau de marchandise pour chacun des articles ci-apres spécifiés:

Vins: quatre barriques de 61 gallons chaque, ou 244 gallons de 231 pouces cubes (mésure Americaine.)

Eau de vie, et tous autres liquides: 244 gallons. Soieries et toutes autres marchandises séches ainsi que tous autres articles généralement soumis au mésurage: quarante deux pieds cubes, mésure Française en France; et cinquante pieds cubes, mésure Americaine, aux Etats Unis.

Cotons: 804 lbs. avoir du poids, ou 365 kilogrammes.
Tabacs: 1,600 lbs. avoir du poids, ou 725 kilogrammes.
Potasse et perlasse: 2,240 lbs. avoir du poids, ou 1,016 kilogrammes.
Riz: 1,600 lbs. avoir du poids, ou 725 kilogrammes. Et pour tous les articles non specifiés et qui se pésent, 2,240 lbs. avoir du poids ou 1,016 kilogrammes.

Article 4. The following quantities shall be considered as forming the ton of merchandise for each of the articles hereinafter specified:

Wines: Four 61 gallon hogsheads, or 244 gallons of 231 cubic inches, American measure.

Brandies, and all other liquids: 244 gallons. Silks and all other dry goods, and all other articles usually subject to measurement: forty-two cubic feet, French, in France, and fifty cubic feet American measure, in the United States.

Cotton: 804 lbs. avoirdupois, or 365 kilogrammes.
Tobacco: 1,600 lbs. avoirdupois, or 725 kilogrammes.
Ashes, pot and pearl: 2,240 lbs. avoirdupois, or 1,016 kilogrammes.
Rice: 1,600 lbs. avoirdupois, or 725 kilogrammes; and for all weighable articles, not specified, 2,240 lbs. avoirdupois, or 1,016 kilogrammes.

Article 5. Les droits de tonnage, de phare, de pilotage, droits de port, courtage et tous autres droits sur la navigation etrangere en sus de ceux payés respectivement par la navigation nationale dans les deux pays, autre que ceux specifiés dans les articles 1 et 2 de la presente convention, n'excederout pas, en France, pour les batimens des Etats Unis, cinq francs par tonneau d'apres le registre

Article 5. The duties of tonnage, light-money, pilotage, port charges, brokerage, and all other duties upon foreign shipping, over and above those paid by the national shipping in the two countries, respectively, other than those specified in articles 1 and 2 of the present convention, shall not exceed in France, for vessels of the United States, five francs per ton of the vessel's American register; nor

Américain du batiment, ni pour les batimens Français aux Etats Unis, quatre vingt quatorze cents par tonneau d'apres le passeport Français du batiment.

ARTICLE 6. Le parties contractantes desirant favoriser mutuellement leur commerce, en donnant dans leur ports toute assistance nécessaire a leurs batimens respectifs, sont convenues que les consuls et vice consuls pourront faire arrêter les matelôts faisant partie des équipages des batimens de leurs nations respectives qui auraient déserté des dits batimens pour les renvoyer et faire transporter hors du pays. Auquel effet les dits consuls et vice consuls s'adresseront aux tribunaux, juges et officiers compétens, et leur feront, par ecrit, la demande des dits déserteurs, en justifiant par l'exhibition des registres du batiment ou rôle d'equipage ou autres documens officiels que ces hommes faisaient partie des dits equipages. Et sur cette demande ainsi justifiée, sauf toutefois la preuve contraire, l'extradition ne pourra être refusée, et il sera donné toute aide et assistance aux dits consuls et vice consuls pour la recherche, saisie et arrestation des susdits deserteurs, lesquels seront même detenus et gardés dans les prisons du pays à leur réquisition, et à leurs frais, jusqu'à ce qu'ils ayent trouvé occasion de les renvoyer; mais s'ils n'etaient renvoye dans le delai de trois mois à compter du jour de leur arrêt, ils seront élargis et ne pourront plus étre arretés pour la même cause.

ARTICLE 7. La présente convention temporaire aura son plein effet pendant deux ans à partir du 1er. Octobre prochain, et même après l'expiration de ce terme, elle sera maintenue jusqu'à la conclusion d'un traité definitif, ou jusqu'à ce que l'une des parties ait déclaré à l'autre son intention d'y renoncer, laquelle déclaration devra être faite au moins six mois d'avance.

Et dans le cas où la presente convention viendrait à continuer, sans cette declaration par l'une ou l'autre partie, les droits extraordinaires specifiés dans les 1 et 2 articles, seront, a l'expiration des dites deux années, diminués de part et d'autre d'un quart de leur montant, et successivement d'un quart du dit montat d'année en année, aussi longtems qu' aucune des parties n'aura déclaré son intention d'y renoncer, ainsi qu'il est dit ci-dessus.

ARTICLE 8. La présente convention sera ratifiée de párt et d'autre, et les ratifications seront échangées dans l'eseace d'une année à compter de ce jour, ou plutôt si faire se peut; mais l'execution de la dite convention commencera dans le deux pays le premiere Octobre prochain, et aura son effet, dans le cas même de non-ratification, pour tous batimens partis *boná fide* pour les ports de l'une ou l'autre nation, dans la confiance qu'elle était en vigueur.

En foi de quoi, les plenipotentiares respectifs ont signé la presente convention, et y ont apposé leur sceaux, en la ville de Washington, ce 24me jour de Juin, de l'an de notre seigneur, 1822.

G. HYDE DE NEUVILLE. [L. S.]
JOHN QUINCY ADAMS. [L. S.]

ARTICLE SÉPARÉ. Les droits extraordinaires levés de part et d'autre jusqu'à ce jour, en vertu dé l'acte du Congrès du 15 Mai, 1820, et de l'ordonnance du 26 Juillet de la même année et autres la confirmant, qui n'ont point deja été remboursés, seront restitués. Signé et scellé comme ci-dessus ce 24me jour de Juin, 1822.

G. HYDE DE NEUVILLE. [L. S.]
JOHN QUINCY ADAMS. [L. S.]

ARTICLE SÉPARÉ. Il est convenu que les droits extraordinaires specifiés dans les 1 et 2 articles de cette convention, ne seront levés que sur l'excédant de la valeur de la marchandise importée, sur la valeur de la marchandise exportée par le même batiment dans le même voyage; en sorte que si la valeur des articles exportés égale ou surpasse celle

for vessels of France in the United States, ninety-four cents per ton of the vessel's French passport.

ARTICLE 6. The contracting parties, wishing to favor their mutual commerce by affording in their ports every necessary assistance to their respective vessels, have agreed that the consuls and vice consuls may cause to be arrested the sailors, being part of the crews of the vessels of their respective nations, who shall have deserted from the said vessels, in order to send them back and transport them out of the country. For which purpose the said consuls and vice consuls shall address themselves to the courts, judges, and officers competent, and shall demand the said deserters in writing, proving, by an exhibition of the registers of the vessel, or ship's roll, or other official documents, that those men were part of said crews; and on this demand so proved, (saving, however, where the contrary is proved,) the delivery shall not be refused; and there shall be given all aid and assistance to the said consuls and vice consuls for the search, seizure, and arrest of said deserters, who shall even be detained and kept in the prisons of the country, at their request and expense, until they shall have found an opportunity of sending them back. But if they be not sent back within three months, to be counted from the day of their arrest, they shall be set at liberty, and shall be no more arrested for the same cause.

ARTICLE 7. The present temporary convention shall be in force for two years from the first day of October next, and even after the expiration of that term, until the conclusion of a definitive treaty or until one of the parties shall have declared its intention to renounce it, which declaration shall be made at least six months beforehand.

And in case the present arrangement should remain without such declaration of its discontinuance by either party, the extra duties specified in the first and second articles shall, from the expiration of the said two years, be on both sides diminished by one-fourth of their whole amount, and afterwards by one-fourth of the said amount from year to year, so long as neither party shall have declared the intention of renouncing it as above stated.

ARTICLE 8. The present convention shall be ratified on both sides, and the ratifications shall be exchanged within one year from the date hereof, or sooner, if possible; but the execution of the said convention shall commence in both countries on the 1st of October next, and shall be effective, even in case of non-ratification, for all such vessels as may have sailed *bona fide* for the ports of either nation in the confidence of its being in force.

In faith whereof, the respective plenipotentiaries have signed the present convention, and have thereto affixed their seals, at the city of Washington, this 24th day of June, A. D. 1822.

JOHN QUINCY ADAMS. [L. S.]
G. HYDE DE NEUVILLE. [L. S.]

SEPARATE ARTICLE. The extra duties levied on either side before the present day, by virtue of the act of Congress of the 15th May, 1820, and of the ordonnance of 26th July of the same year, and others confirmative thereof, and which have not already been paid back, shall be refunded.

Signed and sealed as above, this 24th day of June, 1822.

JOHN QUINCY ADAMS. [L. S.]
G. HYDE DE NEUVILLE. [L. S.]

SEPARATE ARTICLE. It is agreed that the extra duties specified in the first and second articles of this convention shall be levied only upon the excess of value of the merchandise imported over the value of the merchandise exported in the same vessel upon the same voyage; so that if the value of the articles exported shall equal or exceed that of the articles

des articles importés par le même batiment(exceptant toutefois les articles importés pour transit ou re-exportation) aucun droit extraordinaire ne sera lévé; et si les articles exportés sont inférieurs en valeur à ceux importés, les droits extraordinaires ne seront levés que sur le montant de la difference de leur valeur. Cet article toutefois n'aura d'effet que dans le cas de ratification de part et d'autre, et seulement deux mois apres l'echange des ratifications; mais le refus de ratifier cet article d'une ou d'autre part, n'affectera et n'affaiblira en rien la ratification ou la validité des articles précedéns de cette convention.

Signé et scellé comme ci-dessus ce 24me jour de Juin, 1822.

G. HYDE DE NEUVILLE. [L. s.]
JOHN QUINCY ADAMS. [L. s.]

imported in the same vessel (not including, however, articles imported for transit or re-exportation) no such extra duties shall be levied; and if the articles exported are less in value than those imported, the extra duties shall be levied only upon the amount of the difference of their value. This article, however, shall take effect only in case of ratification on both sides, and not until two months after the exchange of the ratifications; but the refusal to ratify this article, on either side, shall in nowise affect or impair the ratification or the validity of the preceding articles of this convention.

Signed and sealed as above, this 24th day of June, 1822.

JOHN QUINCY ADAMS. [L. s.]
G. HYDE DE NEUVILLE. [L. s.]

Now, therefore, be it known that I, James Monroe, President of the United States, in pursuance of the authority aforesaid, do hereby suspend, from and after the first day of October next, until the end of the next session of Congress, the operation of the act aforesaid, entitled "An act to impose a new tonnage duty on French ships and vessels, and for other purposes; and also, all other duties on French vessels, and the goods, being the growth, produce, and manufacture of France, imported in the same, which may exceed the duties on American vessels, and on similar goods imported in the same, saving only discriminating duties payable on French vessels, and on articles of the growth, produce, and manufacture of France, imported in the same, stipulated by the said convention to be paid.

In testimony whereof, I have caused the seal of the United States to be affixed to these presents, and signed the same with my hand. Done at Washington, the twenty-fourth day of June, in the year of [L. s.] our Lord one thousand eight hundred and twenty-two, and of the Independence of the United States the forty-sixth.

JAMES MONROE.

By the President:
JOHN QUINCY ADAMS, *Secretary of State.*

BY THE PRESIDENT OF THE UNITED STATES.

A PROCLAMATION.

Whereas, by an act of the Congress of the United States, passed on the 6th day of May last, it was provided that, on satisfactory evidence being given to the President of the United States that the ports in the islands or colonies in the West Indies, under the dominion of Great Britain, have been opened to the vessels of the United States, the President should be, and thereby was, authorized to issue his proclamation, declaring that the ports of the United States should thereafter be opened to the vessels of Great Britain employed in the trade and intercourse between the United States and such islands or colonies, subject to such reciprocal rules and restrictions as the President of the United States might, by such proclamation, make and publish, anything in the laws entitled "An act concerning navigation," or an act entitled "An act supplementary to an act concerning navigation," to the contrary notwithstanding; and whereas satisfactory evidence has been given to the President of the United States that the ports hereinafter mentioned in the islands or colonies in the West Indies, under the dominion of Great Britain, have been opened to the vessels of the United States, that is to say:

The ports of Kingston, Savannah La Mar, Montego bay, Santa Lucia, Antonio, Saint Ann, Falmouth, Maria, and Morant bay, in Jamaica;
Saint George, Grenada;
Roseau, Dominica;
Saint John's, Antigua;
San Josef, Trinidad;
Scarborough, Tobago;
Road Harbor, Tortola;
Nassau, New Providence;
Pittstown, Crooked Island;
Kingston, St. Vincent;
Port St. George and Port Hamilton, Bermuda;

Any port where there is a custom-house, Bahamas;
Bridgetown, Barbadoes;
St. John's, St. Andrew's, New Brunswick;
Halifax, Nova Scotia;
Quebec, Canada;
St. John's, Newfoundland;
Georgetown, Demarara;
New Amsterdam, Berbice;
Castres, St. Lucia;
Basseterre, St. Kitts;
Charlestown, Nevis;
And Plymouth, Montserrat.

Now, therefore, I, James Monroe, President of the United States of America, do hereby declare and proclaim that the ports of the United States shall hereafter, and until the end of the next session of the Congress of the United States, be open to the vessels of Great Britain employed in the trade and intercourse between the United States and the islands and colonies hereinbefore named, anything in the laws entitled "An act concerning navigation," or an act supplementary to an act entitled "An act supplementary to an act concerning navigation," to the contrary notwithstanding, under the following reciprocal rules and restrictions, namely:

To vessels of Great Britain, *bona fide* British built, owned, and the master and three-fourths of the mariners of which at least shall belong to Great Britain, or any United States built ship or vessel which has been sold to, and become the property of, British subjects, such ship or vessel being also navigated with a master, and three-fourths of the mariners at least belonging to Great Britain; and provided always, that no articles shall be imported into the United States in any such British ship or vessel other than articles of the growth, produce, or manufacture of the British islands and colonies in the West Indies, when imported in British vessels coming from any such island or colony; and articles of the growth, pro-

duce, or manufacture of the British colonies in North America, or of the island of Newfoundland, in vessels coming from the port of St. John's, in that island, or from any of the aforesaid ports of the British colonies in North America.

Given under my hand, at the city of Washington, this twenty-fourth day of August, in the year [L. S.] of our Lord one thousand eight hundred and twenty-two, and in the forty-seventh year of the Independence of the United States.

JAMES MONROE.

By the President:
JOHN QUINCY ADAMS, *Secretary of State.*

17TH CONGRESS.]   No. 353.   [2D SESSION.

NEGOTIATIONS AND TREATY WITH FRANCE OF JUNE 24, 1822.

COMMUNICATED TO THE SENATE, IN EXECUTIVE SESSION, DECEMBER 10, 1822, AND THE INJUNCTION OF SECRECY SINCE REMOVED.

To the Senate of the United States:

The convention between the United States and France, concluded at Washington, on the 24th day of June last, is now transmitted to the Senate for their advice and consent with regard to its ratification, together with the documents relating to the negotiation, which may serve to elucidate the deliberations of the Senate concerning its objects and the purposes to which it was adapted.

JAMES MONROE.

WASHINGTON, *December 4, 1822.*

Convention de Navigation et de Commerce entre sa Majesté le Roi de France et de Navarre et les Etats Unis d'Amerique.

Sa Majesté le Roi de France et de Navarre et les Etats Unis d'Amerique, desirant régler les relations de navigation et de commerce entre leur nations respectives par un convention temporaire reciproquement avantageuse et satisfaisante, et arriver aussi a un arrangement plus etendu et durable, ont respectivement donne leur pleins-pouvoirs, savoir. Sa Majesté Très Chretienne au Baron Hyde de Neuville, Chevalier de l'ordre Royal et Militaire de St. Louis, Commandeur de la Legion d'Honneur, Grand Croix de l'ordre Royal Americain d'Isabelle la Catholique, son Envoye Extraordinaire et Ministre Plenipotentiaire près les Etats Unis; et le President des Etats Unis, à John Quincy Adams, leur Sécrétaire d'Etat; lesquels, apres avoir échangé leur pleins-pouvoirs, sont convenus des articles suivans :

ARTICLE 1. Les produits naturels ou manufacturés des Etats Unis importés en France sur batimens des Etats Unis payeront un droit additionel qui n'excédera point vingt francs par tonneau de marchandize, en sus droits produits naturels ou manufacturés des Etats Unis quad ils sont importés par navires Français.

ARTICLE 2. Les produits naturels ou manufacturés de France importés aux Etats Unis sur batimens Français payeront un droit additionel qui n' excédera point trois dollars, soixante-quinze cents par tonneau de marchandise, en sus des droits payés sur les mêmes produits naturels ou manufacturés de France quand ils sont importés par navires des Etats Unis.

ARTICLE 3. Aucun droit differentiel ne sera levé sur les produits du sol et de l'industrie de France qui seront importés par navires Français dans les ports des Etats Unis pour transit ou re-exportation; il en sera de meme dans les ports de France pour les produits du sol et de l'industrie de l'Union qui

Convention of Navigation and Commerce between the United States of America and his Majesty the King of France and Navarre.

The United States of America and his Majesty the King of France and Navarre, being desirous of settling the relations of navigation and commerce between their respective nations, by a temporary convention reciprocally beneficial and satisfactory, and thereby of leading to a more permanent and comprehensive arrangement, have respectively furnished their full powers in manner following, that is to say: The President of the United States to John Quincy Adams, their Secretary of State; and his most Christian Majesty, to the Baron Hyde de Neuville, Knight of the Royal and Military Order of St. Louis, Commander of the Legion of Honor, Grand Cross of the Royal American Order of Isabella the Catholic, his Envoy Extraordinary and Minister Plenipotentiary near the United States; who, after exchanging their full powers, have agreed on the following articles :

ARTICLE 1. Articles of the growth, produce, or manufacture of the United States, imported into France in vessels of the United States, shall pay an additional duty, not exceeding twenty francs per ton of merchandise over and above the duties paid on the like articles, also of the growth, produce, or manufacture of the United States, when imported in French vessels.

ARTICLE 2. Articles of the growth, produce, or manufacture of France, imported into the United States in French vessels, shall pay an additional duty, not exceeding three dollars and seventy-five cents per ton of merchandise over and above the duties collected upon the like articles, also of the growth, produce, or manufacture of France, when imported in vessels of the United States.

ARTICLE 3. No discriminating duty shall be levied upon the productions of the soil or industry of France, imported into the ports of the United States for transit or re-exportation; nor shall any such duties be levied upon the productions of the soil or industry of the United States,

seront importés pour transit ou re-exportation par navires des Etats Unis.

ARTICLE 4. Les quantités suivantes seront considerées comme formant le tonneau de marchandise pour chacun des articles ci-apres spécifiés:

Vins—quatre barriques de 61 gallons chaque, ou 244 gallons de 231 pouces cubes (mésure Americaine.)

Eaux de vie, et tous autres liquides, 244 gallons.

Soieries et toutes autres marchandises séches ainsi que tous autres articles généralement soumis au mésurage quarante deux pieds cubes, mésure Français en France; et cinquante pieds cubes, mésure Americaine, aux Etats Unis.

Cotons—804 lbs. avoir du poids ou 365 kilogrammes.

Tabacs—1600 lbs. avoir du poids ou 725 kilogrammes.

Potasse et perlasse 2240 lb. avoir du poids ou 1016 kilogrammes.

Riz—1600 lbs. avoir du poids ou 725 kil. Et pour tous les articles non specifiés et qui se pèsent 2240 lbs. avoir du poids ou 1016 kilogrammes.

ARTICLE 5. Les droits de tonnage, de phare, de pilotage, droits de port, courtage et tous autres droits sur la navigation etrangère en sus de ceux payés respectivement par la navigation nationale dans les deux Pays, autre que ceux spécifiés dans les articles 1 et 2 de la presente convention, n'excéderont pas, en France, pour les batimens des Etats Unis, cinq francs par tonneau d'apres le registre Américain du batiment, ni pour les batimens Français aux Etats Unis, quatre vingt quatorze cents per tonneau d'apres le passeport Français du batiment.

ARTICLE 6. Le parties contractantes désirant favoriser mutuellement leur commerce, en donnant dans leur ports toute assistance nécessaire a leurs batimens respectifs, sont convenues que les consuls et vice consuls pourront faire arréter les matelòts faisant partie des équipages des batimens de leurs nations respectives qui auraient déserté des dits batimens pour les renvoyer et faire transporter hors du pays. Auquel effet les dits consuls et vice consuls s'adresseront aux tribunaux, juges et officiers compétens, et leur feront, par ecrit, la demande des dits déserteurs, en justifiant par l'exhibition des registres du batiment ou ròle d'equipage ou autres documens officiels que ces hommes faisaient partie des dits equipages. Et sur cette demande ainsi justifiée, sauf toutefois la preuve contraire, l'extradition ne pourra étre refusée, et il sera donné toute aide et assistance aux dits consuls et vice consuls pour la recherche, saisie et arrestation des susdits deserteurs, lesquels seront méme detenus et gardés dans les prisons du pays à leur réquisition, et à leurs frais, jusqu'à ce qu'ils ayent trouvé occasion de les renvoyer; mais s'ils n'etaient renvoye dans le delai de trois mois à compter du jour de leur arrét, ils seront élargis et ne pourront plus étre arretés pour la méme cause.

ARTICLE 7. La présente convention temporaire aura son plein effet pendant deux ans à partir du 1er. Octobre prochain, et méme après.l'expiration de ce terme, elle sera maintenue jusqu'à la conclusion d'un traité définitif, ou jusqu'à ce que l'une des parties ait déclaré à l'autre son intention d'y renoncer, laquelle déclaration devra étre faite au moins six mois d'avance.

Et dans le cas où la présente convention viendrait à continuer, sans cette declaration par .l'une ou l'autre partie, les droits extraordinaires spécifiés dans les 1 et 2 articles, seront, a l'expiration des dites deux années, diminués de part et d'autre d'un quart de leur montant, et successivement d'un quart du dit montant d'année en année, aussi longtems qu' aucune des parties n'aura déclaré son intention d'y renoncer, ainsi qu'il est dit ci-dessus.

ARTICLE 8. La présente convention sera ratifiée de párt et d'autre, et les ratifications seront échangées dans l'espace d'une année à compter de ce jour, ou

imported in vessels of the United States into the ports of France for transit or re-exportation.

ARTICLE 4. The following quantities shall be considered as forming the ton of merchandise for each of the articles hereinafter specified:

Wines: Four 61 gallon hogsheads, or 244 gallons of 231 cubic inches, American measure.

Brandies, and all other liquids: 244 gallons.

Silks and all other dry goods, and all other articles usually subject to measurement: forty-two cubic feet, French, in France, and fifty cubic feet American measure, in the United States.

Cotton: 804 lbs. avoirdupois, or 365 kilogrammes.

Tobacco: 1,600 pounds avoirdupois, or 725 kilogrammes.

Ashes, pot and pearl: 2,240 lbs. avoirdupois, or 1,016 kilogrammes.

Rice: 1,600 lbs. avoirdupois, or 725 kilogrammes, and for all weighable articles not specified 2,240 lbs. avoirdupois, or 1,016 kilogrammes.

ARTICLE 5. The duties of tonnage, light-money, pilotage, port charges, brokerage, and all other duties upon foreign shipping, over and above those paid by the national shipping in the two countries respectively, other than those specified in articles 1 and 2 of the present convention, shall not exceed in France, for vessels of the United States, five francs per ton of the vessel's American register; nor for vessels of France in the United States ninety-four cents per ton of the vessel's French passport.

ARTICLE 6. The contracting parties, wishing to favor their mutual commerce by affording in their ports every necessary assistance to their respective vessels, have agreed that the consuls and vice consuls may cause to be arrested the sailors, being part of the crews of the vessels of their respective nations, who have deserted from the said vessels, in order to send them back and transport them out of the country; for which purpose the said consuls and vice consuls shall address themselves to the courts, judges, and officers competent, and shall demand the said deserters in writing, proving, by an exhibition of the registers of the vessel or ship's roll, or other official documents, that those men were part of said crews, and on this demand, so proved, (saving, however, where the contrary is proved,) the delivery shall not be refused; and there shall be given all aid and assistance to the said consuls and vice consuls for the search, seizure, and arrest of said deserters, who shall even be detained and kept in the prisons of the country, at their request and expense, until they shall have found an opportunity of sending them back. But if they be not sent back within three months, to be counted from the day of their arrest, they shall be set at liberty, and shall be. no more arrested for the same cause.

ARTICLE 7. The present temporary convention shall be in force for two years from the first day of October next, and even after the expiration of that term, until the conclusion of a definitive treaty, or until one of the parties shall have declared its intention to renounce it, which declaration shall be made at least six months beforehand.

And in case the present arrangement should remain without such declaration of its discontinuance by either party, the extra duties specified in the 1st and 2d articles shall, from the expiration of the said two years, be on both sides diminished by one-fourth of their whole amount, and afterwards by one-fourth of the said amount from year to year, so long as neither party shall have declared the intention of renouncing it as above stated.

ARTICLE 8. The present convention shall be ratified on both sides, and the ratifications shall be exchanged within one year from the date hereof, or

plutòt si faire se peut. Mais l'execution de la dite convention commencera dans le deux pays le premiere Octobre prochain, et aura son effet, dans le cas même de non-ratification, pour tous batimens partis *bonâ fide* pour les ports de l'une ou l'autre nation, dans la confiance qu'elle était en vigueur.

En foi de quoi, les plenipotentiares respectifs ont signé la presente convention, et y ont apposé leur sceaux, en la ville de Washington, ce 24me jour de Juin, de l'an de notre seigneur, 1822.

G. HYDE DE NEUVILLE. [L. S.]
JOHN QUINCY ADAMS. [L. S.]

ARTICLE SÉPARÉ. Les droits extraordinaires levés de part et d'autre jusqu'à ce jour, en vertu dé l'acte du Congres du 15 Mai, 1820, et de l'ordonnance du 26 Juillet de la même année et autres la confirmant, qui n'ont point deja été remboursés, seront restitués. Signé et scellé comme ci-dessus ce 24me jour de Juin, 1822.

G. HYDE DE NEUVILLE. [L. S.]
JOHN QUINCY ADAMS. [L. S.]

ARTICLE SÉPARÉ. Il est convenu que les droits extraordinaires specifiés dans les 1 et 2 articles de cette convention, ne seront levés que sur l'excédant de la valeur de la marchandise importée, sur la valeur de la marchandise exportée par le même batiment dans le même voyage: en sorte que si la valeur des articles exportés égale ou surpasse celle des articles importés par le même batiment (exceptant toutefois les articles importés pour transit ou re-exportation) aucun droit extraordinaire ne sera lévé; et, si les articles exportés sont inférieurs en valeur à ceux importés, les droits extraordinaires ne seront levés que sur le montant de la différence de leur valeur. Cet article toutefois n'aura d'effet que dans le cas de ratification de part et d'autre; et seulement deux mois apres l'echange des ratifications. Mais le refus de ratifier cet article d'une ou d'autre part, n'affectera ni n'affaiblira en rien la ratification ou la validité des articles précédens de cette convention. Signé et scellé come ci dessus ce 24me jour de Juin, 1822.

G. HYDE DE NEUVILLE. [L. S.]
JOHN QUINCY ADAMS. [L. S.]

sooner, if possible. But the execution of the said convention shall commence in both countries on the 1st of October next, and shall be effective, even in case of non-ratification, for all such vessels as may have sailed bona *fide* for the ports of either nation in the confidence of its being in force.

In faith whereof, the respective plenipotentiaries have signed the present convention, and have thereto affixed their seals, at the city of Washington, this 24th day of June, A. D. 1822.

JOHN QUINCY ADAMS. [L. S.]
G. HYDE DE NEUVILLE. [L. S.]

SEPARATE ARTICLE. The extra duties levied on either side before the present day, by virtue of the act of Congress of 15th May, 1820, and of the ordonnance of 26th July, of the same year, and others confirmative thereof, and which have not already been paid back, shall be refunded. Signed and sealed as above, this 24th day of June, 1822.

JOHN QUINCY ADAMS. [L. S.]
G. HYDE DE NEUVILLE. [L. S.]

SEPARATE ARTICLE. It is agreed that the extra duties specified in the first and second articles of this convention shall be levied only upon the excess of value of the merchandise imported over the value of the merchandise exported in the same vessel upon the same voyage; so that if the value of the articles exported shall equal or exceed that of the articles imported in the same vessel (not including, however, articles imported for transit or re-exportation) no such extra duties shall be levied; and if the articles exported are less in value than those imported, the extra duties shall be levied only upon the amount of the difference of their value. This article, however, shall take effect only in case of ratification on both sides, and not until two months after the exchange of the ratifications. But the refusal to ratify this article, on either side, shall in nowise affect or impair the ratification or the validity of the preceding articles of this convention. Signed and sealed as above, this 24th day of June, 1822.

JOHN QUINCY ADAMS. [L. S.]
G. HYDE DE NEUVILLE. [L. S.]

List of correspondence relating to the convention with France.

Mr. Adams to Baron de Neuville, August 20, 1821.
Baron de Neuville to Mr. Adams, October 15, 1821.
Same to same, March 11, 1822, and Facts.
Same to same, April 5, 1822.
Mr. Adams to Baron de Neuville, April 9, 1822.
Baron de Neuville to Mr. Adams, April 11, 1822.
Mr. Adams to Baron de Neuville, April 24, 1822.
Baron de Neuville to Mr. Adams, April 28, 1822.
Mr. Adams to Baron de Neuville, May 11, 1822.
Baron de Neuville to Mr. Adams, May 15, 1822.
Mr. Adams to Baron de Neuville, May 27, 1822.
Same to same, June 14, 1822.
Baron de Neuville to Mr. Adams, June 22, 1822.   Extract.

Baron de Neuville to the Secretary of State.

WASHINGTON, *December* 15, 1817.

SIR : The Envoy Extraordinary and Minister Plenipotentiary of his most Christian Majesty has received reiterated orders to ascertain the truth of the statement made by several masters of merchant ships, affirming that French vessels are not treated, in the ports of Louisiana, upon the footing of the most favored nations.

Upon investigation, it not only appears that such is actually the case, but the undersigned has even found that several protests had been lodged in vain with the local authorities against this manifest infraction of the 8th article of the Louisiana treaty.

He is well assured that this must have been the mere consequence of error or of incorrect interpretation, given on the spot, to a clause which is absolute and unconditional by its own terms, and which can neither be limited nor modified, being the essential unlimited condition of a contract of cession, can neither be subject to limitation nor to any modification whatever. The minister of H. M. C. M. persuades himself that it will suffice thus to call the attention of the Federal Government to this affair, in order to obtain from its justice the reparation of an injury so very prejudicial to French commerce.

He therefore requests of the Secretary of State that this, his representation, made by order of his court, be submitted, as soon as possible, to the President, in order that his Excellency may be pleased to issue orders to such effect that in future the 8th article of the treaty of 1803, between France and the United States, receive its entire execution, and the advantages granted to great Britain in all ports of the United States be secured to France in those of Louisiana.

The principle of justice here claimed cannot be denied, and must necessarily insure the reimbursement of the duties which have been unjustifiably levied upon French vessels in New Orleans.

The undersigned minister expects, with entire confidence, the decision of the President, of which he requests the Secretary of State will enable him to inform his court as soon as possible. The Government of his Majesty desires, as soon as possible, to quiet the commerce of France with regard to proceedings so contrary to its interests and the true spirit of the Louisiana treaty.

The undersigned has the honor, &c., &c.,

HYDE DE NEUVILLE.

Mr. Adams to Mr. De Neuville.

DEPARTMENT OF STATE, *December* 23, 1817.

The undersigned, Secretary of State, has received and laid before the President the note which he had the honor of receiving from the Envoy Extraordinary and Minister Plenipotentiary of France, complaining that French vessels are not, conformably to the eighth article of the treaty of cession of Louisiana, treated in the ports of that State upon the footing of the most favored nation, and claiming as a right, deducible from the same article, that French vessels should in future enjoy, in the ports of Louisiana, all the advantages granted to the English nation in all the ports of the Union.

The undersigned is instructed to say that the vessels of France are treated, in the ports of Louisiana, upon the footing of the most favored nation, and that neither the English nor any other foreign nation enjoys any gratuitous advantage there which is not equally enjoyed by France. But English vessels, by virtue of a conditional compact, are admitted into the ports of the United States, including those of Louisiana, upon payment of the same duties as the vessels of the United States. The condition upon which they enjoy this advantage is, that the vessels of the United States shall be admitted into the ports of Great Britain upon payment of the same duties as are there paid by British vessels.

The eighth article of the treaty of cession stipulates that the ships of France shall be treated upon the footing of the most favored nations in the ports of the ceded Territory; but it does not say, and cannot be understood to mean, that France should enjoy as a free gift that which is conceded to other nations for a full equivalent.

It is obvious that if French vessels should be admitted into ports of Louisiana upon the payment of the same duties as the vessels of the United States, they would be treated, not upon the footing of the most favored nation, according to the article in question, but upon a footing more favored than any other nation; since other nations, with the exception of England, pay higher tonnage duties, and the exemption of English vessels is not a free gift, but a purchase, at a fair and equal price.

It is true that the terms of the 8th article are positive and unconditional; but it will readily be perceived that the condition, though not expressed in the article, is inherent in the advantage claimed under it. If British vessels enjoyed, in the ports of Louisiana, any gratuitous favor, undoubtedly French vessels would, by the terms of the article, be entitled to the same.

A more extensive construction cannot be given to the article consistently with the Constitution of the United States, which declares, that "all duties, imposts, and excises, shall be uniform throughout the United States; and that no preference shall be given, by any regulation of commerce or revenue, to the the ports of one State over those of another."

It would be incompatible with other articles of the treaty of cession itself, one of which cedes the territory to the United States "*in full sovereignty;*" and another declares that its "inhabitants shall be incorporated in the Union of the United States, and admitted, as soon as possible, according to the principles of the Federal Constitution, to the enjoyment of all the rights, advantages, and immunities, of citizens of the United States." If France could claim, *forever,* advantages in the ports of Louisiana, which could be denied to her in the other ports of the United States, she would have ceded to the United States, not the full, but an imperfect, sovereignty; and if France could claim admission for her vessels, forever, into the ports of Louisiana, upon the payment of duties not uniform with those which they must pay in the other ports of the United States, it would have been impossible to have admitted the inhabitants of Louisiana, according to the principles of the Federal Constitution, to the enjoyment of all the rights, advantages, and immunities of citizens of the United States.

The undersigned is happy to be authorized, in concluding this note, to add that the Government of the United States is willing to extend to France, not only in the ports of Louisiana, but in those of all the United States, every advantage enjoyed by the vessels of Great Britain, upon the fair and just equivalent of reciprocity; and that, in the meantime, the vessels of France shall be treated, in all the ports of the United States, including Louisiana, on the footing of the most favored nation, enjoying, gratuitously, every favor indulged, gratuitously, to others, and every conditional favor, upon the reciprocation of the same to the vessels of the United States in France.

He prays the minister of France to accept the assurance of his very distinguished consideration.

JOHN QUINCY ADAMS.

M. HYDE DE NEUVILLE,
  Envoy Extraordinary, &c.

Mr. De Neuville to Mr. Adams.

WASHINGTON, *June* 16, 1818.

SIR: I have had the honor of receiving your note in answer to mine of the 15th December last, concerning the non-execution of the 8th article of the Louisiana treaty.

I took care duly to communicate the proposal made by the Federal Government to extend to France, not only in the ports of Louisiana, but even in all those of the United States, the advantages therein enjoyed by British vessels, on a footing of absolute reciprocity.

H. M. is ever disposed not to neglect anything that can tend to rivet the bonds of friendship of the two countries and to improve their commercial intercourse, and will, no doubt, examine this proposal with very particular attention.

In the meantime, as it would be neither just nor proper that the execution of the clauses of a contract already made and completely concluded should be dependent on an arrangement which, as yet, is only in contemplation, and as the enjoyment of a perpetual unconditional right should never, in any case, be blended with reciprocal advantages or concessions which time annuls, and which accidental causes may modify or destroy; as France claims nothing but what she knows is due to her, and as she is well persuaded that the Federal Government will never deny what it is conscious of owing, there is much reason to hope that the following observations will suffice to establish our right, and thus remove every obstacle to its free enjoyment.

I will add, that fresh orders from his Majesty make it my duty to neglect no means of obtaining, as soon as possible, this act, whose accomplishment must be expected, from mature deliberation on the question, and is warranted by the acknowledged equity of the Federal Government.

You have stated, sir, that *French vessels are treated in the ports of Louisiana upon the footing of the most favored nation, and that no foreign nation enjoys there any gratuitous advantage which is not equally enjoyed by France.* You add, sir, *that if British vessels are allowed in the ports of the United States certain advantages which American vessels likewise enjoy in the ports of Great Britain, it is by virtue of a conditional compact founded on reciprocity of advantages.*

Finally, after recalling the 8th article, which stipulates expressly that in future, and forever, French vessels shall be treated upon the footing of the most favored nations in the ports of the ceded territory, you observe, *that the article does not say, and that it could not be understood to mean, that France should enjoy, as a free gift, that which is conceded to other nations for a full equivalent.*

I shall, in the first place, have the honor to observe, that France asks not for a *free gift.* She claims the enjoyment of a right which it is not even necessary for her to acquire, since it proceeds from herself, being a right which, when she consented to dispose of Louisiana, she had power to reserve for the interest of her trade, and the actual reservation of which is established, not impliedly, but in the most precise and formal terms by the 8th article of the Louisiana treaty.

France, I repeat it, asks no free gift, since the territory ceded is the equivalent already paid by her for all the clauses, charges, and conditions, executed, or which remain to be fulfilled by the United States, and which principally consist in the 7th and 8th articles of the treaty, and 1st of the convention.

If the 8th article of the Louisiana treaty had no other object but that of securing to France a conditional advantage in the ports of Louisiana, if such had been the true spirit of this clause, and, finally, if the American negotiators had been firmly convinced that this reservation of the French Government was not absolute, but was merely one of those customary reciprocal concessions which occur in almost all treaties of amity and commerce, it is likely that no pains would have been taken to frame the article so as absolutely to contradict the intention of the contracting parties; and it stands to reason that, if such had been their views, the terms usually employed in other treaties would have been employed here also, instead of so precise a stipulation of an unconditional and perpetual advantage in favor of France.

In all the treaties between France and the United States the condition of reciprocity is positively mentioned. They all expressly say that the contracting parties shall reciprocally enjoy such favors as shall be conceded to other nations, *freely, if freely granted to other nations, or upon granting the same condition, if conditionally granted.*

How shall we account for the strange and unusual construction here adopted? Who would admit the possibility or likelihood of an omission on the part of negotiators, the object of whose mission was not to stipulate doubtful clauses, subject to discussion, but, on the contrary, as it is expressly stated in the treaty, "to remove all source *of misunderstanding* relative to objects of discussion, and to strengthen the union and friendship which, at the time of the said convention, was happily re-established between the two nations?"

And, furthermore, how shall we reconcile the silence observed by the Senate, in 1803, respecting this unconditional and unlimited favor secured to France with the positive refusal of the same House, in 1801, to ratify a convention founded on reciprocity of advantage, unless on the express condition that it should be limited to eight years?

The natural inference, the only explanation of all this, is, that in 1801 the question was on a convention or treaty of amity and commerce, while in 1803 it was on a contract of sale or cession; which instruments are of so different a nature as not to admit the application of similar principles and consequences, nor can it be supposed that the negotiators of the treaty of 1801 had forgotten to mention that the citizens of the two nations should reciprocally be treated each, in the ports of the other, upon the footing of the most favored nations, since this principle of reciprocity was not only the general basis, but was even, in almost every instance, the *sine qua non* of preceding commercial conventions.

But the negotiators of the treaty of 1803 knew full well that they were not commissioned to settle the commercial or navigating interests of the two countries, and were merely authorized to make a contract of sale or cession; which, however important from the value of the object ceded, was not the less subject, like every conveyance between individuals, to certain and invariable rules of construction and interpretation.

A contract of sale admits of no implication, (sous-entendu;) it is a plain, simple transaction, by which one party is bound to deliver a certain property, and the other party to receive it on certain charges and conditions, more or less rigorous.

Those clauses and conditions cannot be interpreted otherwise than according to the terms in which they are expressed in the contract; nor can they be annulled or modified, except by the consent of both parties. Their entire execution is, indeed, so rigorously binding that *it, alone,* may be said finally to seal the transaction. But the article would appear to you, sir, to be in this, its only natural construction, inconsistent with the Constitution, which declares that *all duties, imposts, and excises, shall be uniform throughout the United States.*

It would seem to me that this clause of the Constitution has no other reference than to the interior administration of the country, and that it cannot be proper to consider in the light of a mere tax or impost that which is an express condition of the sale or cession of a territory, and is one of the clauses of a treaty which, itself, becomes a law of the United States.

You express an opinion, sir, that the eighth article, if interpreted according to its grammatical and literal sense, *would be incompatible with another article of the same treaty, which cedes the territory to the United States in full sovereignty; arguing that if France could claim forever advantages in the ports of Louisiana which could be denied to her in the other ports of the United States, she would have ceded to the United States not the full, but an imperfect sovereignty.*

Allow me to observe that this last point of the argument is answered by your own decision, admitting that if *British vessels enjoyed in the ports of Louisiana any gratuitous favor, undoubtedly French vessels would, by the terms of the treaty, be entitled to the same.*

This admits the possibility of an imperfect sovereignty, and supposes an instance in which France might be entitled to claim in the ports of Louisiana a favor which could be denied her in the other ports of the United States.

Moreover, if the United States have, by the Constitution, a right to grant to other nations gratuitous favors in their ports, it follows, from your own interpretation of the perpetual reservation made by France, that, in order to deprive her of the right so reserved, and to avoid rendering thereby the sovereignty of this republic imperfect, the Federal Government must not grant to other nations any gratuitous concessions in the territory ceded by France, though it should be found expedient so to do, and advantageous to their commercial interest and policy. In other words, the Federal Government, by consenting to the eighth article, would have deprived itself of a real right of sovereignty.

In the preceding hypothesis the difficulty is merely eluded and not removed. The right is not the less unqualified and consented to *forever.*

But will it be said the Constitution allows no preferences among the different States? They are all, by the federal compact, subject to the same charges, and are to enjoy the same privileges. It would appear to me, sir, that this perfect uniformity is applicable only to a State when it has once become a State. The regulations made for the family cannot be meant to extend beyond its circle; and the law which establishes such regulations never can have blended the circumstances pre-existent to the admission of a new member (much less the very conditions of admission) with the rights, charges, and privileges which are the consequence springing therefrom. Thus did Congress judge. To them it appeared that the instrument of sale or cession of Louisiana had no analogy to a commercial regulation or to a distribution of taxes, and they admitted without discussion the seventh and eighth articles of the treaty, because, if the Constitution does not allow that a territory, when once admitted into this Union, be marked by any distinctive charges or advantages, it does not, on that account, prevent the fulfilment of clauses exacted and consented to as conditions of its admission. In all this there is neither exception nor preference; it is the mere and simple execution of a contract freely and lawfully entered into.

But the third article says that the inhabitants of the ceded territory shall be incorporated into the Union, and admitted as soon as *possible* to the enjoyment of all the advantages and immunities of citizens of the United States.

This is true, and such, no doubt, was the intention of the contracting parties. They expressly agreed that this admission should take place as soon as possible, but most assuredly it was meant that this should be done in conformity with the clauses and conditions mentioned in the treaty; and if the 8th article could have been considered as an obstacle to the execution of the 3d article, it would equally have been so thought of the 7th. This article was, however, never contested. It even received, during the twelve years of its duration, or should have received, its full and entire operation, by virtue of the regulating act of Congress of the 24th of February, 1804.

France and Spain still enjoyed, in 1815, in Louisiana, the rights and privileges secured by the 7th article, which rights, by the very terms of the treaty, never can be granted to any other nation.

France and Spain were in the full enjoyment of these exclusive rights and privileges in 1815, and yet in 1812 the stipulation of the 3d article was fulfilled, the Territory of Louisiana was admitted as a State into the federal body, and this new State was received, without restriction, on an equal footing with the original States in all respects whatever.

If, therefore, there were at this day any contradiction between the 3d and 8th articles, how could Congress, in 1812, surmount the objection arising from the much stronger inconsistency which, on this supposition, must have existed between the 3d and 7th articles?

When Congress made Louisiana a member of the Union, before the expiration of the twelve years it was judged that such a compliance with the conditions of a treaty was by no means incompatible with the exercise of the full and entire rights of sovereignty. Perhaps it may be answered that the 7th article granted only temporary privileges, and that the 8th article had no term fixed to it. To me it appears that the words *forever* change nothing but the duration of the privilege, without, in the least degree, altering the nature of the question. Under a constitutional system, nothing can be done, ordered, or consented to, that would infringe, even but for a limited term, the established laws of the country. All the transactions of Governments must be legal. If, therefore, the provisions of the constitution which regulate the existence of a State after its admission were applicable to the conditions on which it is to be admitted, it would, in such case, have been no less impossible in 1812 than at the present day to grant to the inhabitants of Louisiana the rights, privileges, and immunities of citizens of the United States. Since, on that supposition, they must, in common with the other States, have had a right to make France and Spain pay, in their ports, higher tonnage duties than those paid by the citizens of the United States; and since the Federal Government had no right at that time to grant, in the ports of the ceded territory, to other nations the privileges therein secured to France and Spain. France did intend to cede the Territory of Louisiana to the United States forever, and in full sovereignty; but sovereignty does not exist in the enjoyment of every right and privilege: it lies in the pre-eminent important authority to enforce their observance.

When the French Government ceded Louisiana it ceased to be the sovereign of the country, but it did not cease to hold property therein, since it reserved a right or privilege; for a privilege, acquired or reserved, is property as sacred as an annuity, as a rent charge, or any other.

France, therefore, claims only the enjoyment of what is her property. Giving her possession of this lawful right, far from rendering the sovereignty of the United States imperfect, would seem, in a measure, only to make it more complete, since it is certain that the right claimed by France is one of the essential conditions of the cession made by her of that sovereignty.

It may, perhaps, be answered that there is some difference between the contracts of nations with other nations and a sale made by one individual to another. I see very little, I confess, on the score of equity, the rules of interpretation being, in all cases, alike applicable to every human transaction.

By the law of nations it is an invariable rule that treaties or contracts, of whatsoever nature, should be understood according to the force and meaning of their expressions, and nothing, surely, can be more unconditional, or more clearly expressed, than the following clause:

"In future, and forever, after the expiration of the twelve years, French vessels shall be treated upon the footing of the most favored nations in the ports of the said Territory."

In future and forever, are expressions free from all ambiguity.

After the expiration of the twelve years: these words prove that the treatment or privilege secured by the eighth article is to follow, without condition or limitation of time, that of the seventh article.

French vessels shall be treated, does not mean *may be treated*, but that they shall undoubtedly and positively be treated upon the footing of the most favored nation.

And it makes no difference whether that treatment be the consequence of a gratuitous or of a conditional concession, the article has no restriction; it expressly states, French vessels shall be treated upon the footing of the favored nations. The consequence is, that French vessels are, without condition, to be treated in the ports of Louisiana upon the footing of the vessels of Great Britain, which is at this time the most favored nation.

I think I have proved, sir, that to demand an equivalent of France because England has given one would, in a measure, be requiring her to purchase what is already her own property, and obliging her to pay twice for the same thing.

I think I have also proved that the sovereignty of the United States is, and will still remain, entire and perfect, such as it was ceded by the treaty of 1803, although France be put into possession of that right which is secured to her *in future and forever*.

I could cite many examples of analogous privileges which never were considered as impairing the sovereignty of nations. But, it appears to me, that the best of all arguments that can be addressed to the equity and honest feelings of the American Government is, that France claims only her lawful due and right; that the title establishing it is worded in terms of such force and precision as must suffice to remove every doubt, and absolutely to solve the question. The claim which I have the honor to address to you, sir, being entirely dependent on the Executive authority, I cannot but hope I shall soon have to inform my court that the President has been pleased to issue such orders as will secure, in future, the execution of the eighth article of the Louisiana treaty, and the immediate reimbursement of the duties which have been unjustifiably levied to this day.

I have the honor to be, &c., &c.,

HYDE DE NEUVILLE.

The SECRETARY OF STATE.

Mr. De Neuville to the Secretary of State.

[Translation.]

WASHINGTON, *March* 29, 1819.

MR. SECRETARY OF STATE: The reclamations of the Chambers of Commerce, the repeated representations of the Minister of Marine, the just complaints of all the consular agents of his Majesty, in fine, the intolerable abuses which ensue from the present legislation of the States of the Union as to the desertion of foreign sailors, have induced my court to send me more positive orders than ever to make this state of things the object of strong and repeated remonstrances.

It is not to be doubted, sir, but that what passes daily in the United States must tend to nothing less than the entire exclusion of our navigation from their ports, if such abuse be not put a stop to.

But although the evil is great it may be remedied; and the amity and justice of the Federal Government assure me that it will eagerly adopt a remedy.

I shall not anew enter here, sir, into the recital of the disadvantages; they are too grievous not to be easily felt. I shall only repeat (which cannot be disputed) that the consuls of the United States enjoy in France all the rights of their office, and that their minister does not neglect carefully to demand them.

I know the institutions of the Union, and I accurately reckon upon the difficulties which they sometimes may oppose to the good will and even to the wish of the Executive.

Therefore, without discussing here the law of nations, or the principle of reciprocity, or other considerations, which are no less forcible in the United States than in Europe, I shall go, sir, straight to the point.

The abuse exists here, and does not exist in France. Here, as in France, they wish it remedied. In France, the laws and custom prevent its being practiced; here, the want of a law or political convention prevents its being equally repressed in all the States.

A law for that purpose was proposed to the last Congress. It was postponed. One of the principal causes of its postponement was, to know if the European States would offer a reciprocity to the United States.

The answer of my Government is, that it offers it, it guarantees it, and, to remove every difficulty, it is ready to conclude a convention upon this point.

I have the honor of acquainting you that I have received from my court sufficient authority as to this convention.

I therefore beg leave to request that you will be pleased to submit the preceding observations to the President as soon as possible. I have no doubt but that he, as well as you, sir, will appreciate the utility and the urgency of any measure repressive of a state of things as pernicious to the commerce as to the morality of nations.

Accept, Mr. Secretary of State, the renewed assurances of the high consideration with which I have the honor to be, &c.,

HYDE DE NEUVILLE.

Inclosure in M. De Neuville's letter of March 29, 1819.

[Translation.]

The convention should specify:

1. That the consuls and vice consuls should be enabled to procure the arrest of the captains, officers, mariners, sailors, and all other persons making part of the crews of vessels-of-war and of commerce of their respective nations, who may have deserted from said vessels.

2. The said consuls and vice consuls should be bound, in order to obtain the surrender, to prove that these men make a part of the above mentioned crews.

They should prove it by the exhibition of the register of said vessels, or rolls d'equipage.

The consuls or vice consuls should apply, for obtaining the surrender of deserters, to competent judges, and every aid and assistance should be given to them for arresting the above mentioned deserters, who should be carefully detained and guarded in the prisons of the country, at the expense of their Governments, till the consuls may find an opportunity of shipping them.

Nevertheless, a period should be fixed, after which the said detained deserter should be of right enlarged, and be afterwards free from arrest for the same cause.

The treatment which they should be allowed during their detention should be equally fixed, it being well understood that, in default of payment in advance, the deserter should be enlarged, and should enjoy the advantage above expressed.

Several formalities might be agreed upon as to the rolls d'equipage, which, without being troublesome to navigation and commerce, might become powerful and sufficient security for individual liberty.

What the Government of his Majesty desires is, that the abuse cease; but his Majesty wishes likewise that his subjects should be free, and that they should not, in any case, nor under any pretext, be oppressed. He wishes that the laws of his kingdom should be, in everything and every place, the protection of the weak against the strong; but to oblige a citizen to fulfil his contract is not, will never be, to oppress or to enslave. True liberty rests in all countries and under all Governments upon good faith, probity, and patriotism.

Mr. Adams to Mr. De Neuville.

DEPARTMENT OF STATE, *Washington, March* 31, 1819.

SIR: The proposal contained in your letter of the 29th instant of concluding a consular convention between the United States and France, for the purpose of stipulating the mutual restoration of seamen deserting from the armed or merchant vessels of either nation in the ports of the other, has been submitted to the President of the United States, by whose direction I have the honor of informing you that he thinks a partial arrangement of one particular subject of interest in the commercial relations between the two countries would be liable to inconvenience, and less satisfactory, than a general review of those relations with the view of coming to arrangements concerning them, which may be calculated to promote the interests of both, and to strengthen and perpetuate the friendship and good understanding subsisting between them.

Before your contemplated visit to France, I shall be happy to confer with you upon this subject, and of concerting with you some general preparatory ideas which that incident may furnish the means of maturing to the mutual satisfaction of both our Governments. In the meantime, it may contribute to the facility of removing, in another form, the inconvenience which you observe to be suffered by the French commerce in consequence of the desertion of seamen from French vessels in our ports, if you will have the goodness to direct that authentic statements of every particular case of that nature which may occur should be transmitted by your consuls to your legation, and through that to this Department.

I take this opportunity to acknowledge, also, the receipt of your note of the 20th instant, announcing your intention to avail yourself of a leave of absence from your sovereign to pay the visit to your country to which I have referred. I am directed by the President to assure you of the great satisfaction which he takes in bearing testimony to the propriety and friendliness of your conduct and deportment since you have resided here as the representative of France, and of his peculiar sensibility to the interest which, as the organ of your Government, you have taken in promoting a conciliatory adjustment of the long standing and complicated differences between the United States and Spain. The minister of the United States in France has been instructed to make known to your Government these sentiments of the President, to which I beg leave to add the assurance of my best wishes that your excursion may be prosperous and agreeable to you, and that at no distant day, if it suits your own views and those of your Government, we may again welcome your return to your station at this place.

I pray you, sir, to be assured of the sentiments of my very distinguished consideration.

JOHN QUINCY ADAMS.

Mr. HYDE DE NEUVILLE,
　Envoy Extraordinary and Minister Plenipotentiary from France.

Mr. De Neuville to the Secretary of State.

[Translation.]

WASHINGTON, *May* 23, 1819.

MR. SECRETARY OF STATE: In your letter of the 31st March last, in answer to mine of the 29th, by which I had the honor of informing you that I was authorized by my court to sign a convention relative to deserting sailors, you did me the honor to tell me that the President was of opinion that a partial arrangement would present several inconveniences, and that it would be more beneficial to adjust, by a general convention, all the points which could affect the commercial interests of the two countries. His Majesty the King, my master, will always receive with extreme pleasure all communications which may tend more and more to cement the harmony which happily subsists between the two nations and as no one has it more in his power than you, sir, to point out whatever may be useful or advisable for the best interest of the people of both nations, I presume to request that you will have the goodness, before my departure, which cannot fail to be soon, to communicate to me all your ideas. Here, sir, you have mine as to the consular convention. This communication, on my part, has and can have nothing official. It is a simple sketch which I thought fit to lay before you, and I shall be led to believe that my observations may be of some utility, if they shall receive, in whole or in part, your approbation.

It will afford me pleasure to be able, before leaving Washington, to lay with you, sir, the principal bases of the indissoluble union of our two countries; and, I confess, it would be with great alacrity that I would receive, on returning to the United States, the honor of a concurrence in consolidating them.

Accept, Mr. Secretary of State, the renewed assurances of my high consideration.

G. HYDE DE NEUVILLE,
　Envoy Extraordinary and Minister Plenipotentiary of H. M. C. M. to the United States.

Mr. De Neuville's observations on the Consular Convention of ——

[Translation.]

ARTICLE 1. In general, the expressions of *exequatur* are a great deal too vague. A convention may and ought to be precise, and the attributes of the treaty which may follow ought to be expressed in a manner the most clear; but ought not these attributes to be equally defined when there exists no consular convention?

For example, what does the Executive mean by these words?

" I do therefore recognize him, and declare him free to exercise and enjoy such functions, powers, and privileges as are allowed to the consuls of all friendly powers between whom and the United States there is no particular agreement for the regulation of the consular functions."

What is the real *status rerum?*

Does it rest upon the most equitable principle of the law of nations, reciprocity, or upon the common law, the usage of each State or of each place, or, in fine, is it left to the more or less arbitrary interpretation of the municipal authorities?

It will be perceived how important it would be, especially to the United States, that the *status rerum* be well defined. His Majesty's consuls are really thereby impeded in every step of the exercise of their functions. They are ignorant how far they can go, and, to speak the truth, having only to content themselves with the kindness of the local authorities as to what can regard them personally, they very generally receive from them only refusals, in the circumstances which most interest our commerce and our navigation. And yet their just remonstrances rest always upon the principle of *reciprocity.*

What, then, are the real privileges "of all friendly powers with whom there is no particular agreement for the regulation of the consular functions."

The *exequatur* ought, perhaps, to mention *the consular district,* in order to avoid *all* mistakes.

ARTICLE 2. Although the immunities of consular agents cannot be so extended as those of diplomatic agents, it would be, perhaps, useful to the two countries for avoiding certain incidents which might, without the knowledge and contrary to the will of the Executive power, produce real difficulties, or, at least, cause some slight suspicions to arise, which it is prudent in two friendly nations to prevent, it might, I say, be perhaps useful, that the privileges of consuls should be a little less restricted. For example, would it not be advisable that the immunity which they enjoy for their chanceries and their papers were extended to their persons, and that they should be independent of the criminal justice of the place where they reside, *atrocious crimes* excepted.

Would it not be equally wise, that in all cases where they may be subjected to the laws of the country as inhabitants, no action should be commenced against them but with the approbation of the Executive, who should not fail to inform the minister of the friendly power, and to concert with him the proper means of averting judiciary processes, without offending against justice? It will be perceived how this amicable method would be advantageous, and the abuses which it could produce do not appear many.

Could not the exemption also be extended to *all* duties on those objects or articles which the consular agents may import for their own use, as well as upon those which they bring with them to the country? This favor, thus limited, would not, I believe, present any inconvenience, and might add to the consideration of the consular agents in the place of their residence, which enters essentially into the interest of the two nations.

In place of "*they shall place upon the outer door,*" &c., it would appear better to say: "*They shall have the right of placing,*" &c.

It may be added to the preceding reflections that foreign consuls enjoy in France personal immunity in the extent above mentioned. The regulations of his Majesty say: "*They shall enjoy personal immunity except in the case of atrocious crime, and without prejudice to the actions which may be commenced against them for an act of commerce.*"

ARTICLE 3. The word *merchants* (negocians) ought to be suppressed. The consuls and vice consuls of his Majesty are not authorized to engage in commerce; it appears, therefore, advisable to leave them free to choose their agents without distinction amongst the merchants and other individuals, national or foreign.

The article may be terminated thus: *They shall confine themselves, respectively, to render to their respective national and commercial navigators and vessels all possible services, and to inform the consul or vice consul of their district, or, in case of urgency, any other agent of his Majesty nearer to them, of the wants of said national commercial navigators and vessels. The said agents shall have it in their power, also, if they are specially authorized by their commission, to terminate all differences, process, and discussions between those of their nation, and that, conformably to the 12th article of the present convention, without their being authorized otherwise to participate in the immunities and privileges granted to consuls and vice consuls, and without their having authority, upon any pretext whatever, to exact other duties than those which shall be received in the chanceries of the nation.*

The motives which induce the proposal of granting, in case of need, to the agents of the consuls the privileges mentioned in the 12th article will be shown hereafter, (see article 12.)

ARTICLES 4 and 5. (After the words *to pass,* it is proposed to add *and to deposit.*)

. This observation is so much more useful, as the consuls of France are not authorized to receive testaments but only to be depositaries of holograph wills.

(At the words " they shall proceed in it with the assistance," &c.)

It would be for the interest of the two nations that this right of the consuls should be extended to inventories of such of their fellow-citizens who, being naturalized in the country, should be found, like the first, to have neither testamentary executors, nor trustees or legitimate heirs upon the spot.

However, as this regulation might appear and be in fact an infringement of the rights of a citizen, defined and secured by the constitutional law of each State, it will be limited to a proposed addition to this article:

"That, in case of the decease of a naturalized Frenchman or American, and dying *intestate,* without heirs, or whose heirs are not all upon the spot, the authority which shall be competent to grant letters of administration shall be bound to inform the nearest consul of the nation by sending him a copy of all the deeds, titles, and papers, necessary to show the nature and value of the inheritance. It might even be stipulated, I believe, that in cases where all the heirs should be found foreigners, the administration of the estate should be granted to the consul unless where there was a real impediment, such as his distance, &c. The Federal Government can have no difficulty in granting the right of administration to consular agents on the estates of those of their nation, since the law of Congress of the 14th April, 1792, gives it to American consuls, if the power where they reside is willing to admit them to it.

This question of inheritance is so much more important, as in some States, such as that of Georgia, foreigners find themselves subjected even to the law of escheat, (droit d'aubaine.) The law of that State places in the hand of a trustee vacant estates, the property of deceased Frenchmen, without permitting any Frenchman having the right of succession, be it the known heir or creditor, to be capable of becoming administrator by giving security, which takes place among those of their nation. The consul has not the right of taking cognizance of the inheritance, nor of interfering, even for the purposes of preservation. It is only to the State that the executor named owes an account of his administration.

Civilization has demonstrated how far this law (right) of escheat (droit d'aubaine) *which allows a foreigner to live free, but die a slave,* is contrary to the principles of amity and of justice which ought to animate all nations. This scandalous abuse has been entirely removed by the French Legislature. It is to be hoped that it will be so in all nations. The knowledge and liberality of the American people will be a guaranty that, among them at least, it will be easily abolished, if it yet exist in any of the States. This right is so generally regarded as a monstrous exaction, which, in many countries where it still exists in principle, has nevertheless ceased to be exercised; I know not if I am mistaken, but I believe that it is thus in all the States of the Union.

ARTICLE 6. The law of Congress above cited confers upon American consuls the rights mentioned in this article; and they may enjoy it fully in France.

ARTICLE 7. This article cannot, I believe, cause the least objection; the observation annexed to the preceding article being applicable to this.

ARTICLE 8. (At the end.) It will be a matter of absolute necessity that it be inserted in the 8th or in the 9th article, or that this clause be made an additional article, that—

The sailors making part of the crews of their respective nations shall not be in any case, nor upon any pretext, arrested for debt.

The abuse which may take and has taken place, of withholding deserters and even criminals from justice by this means, shows the utility and even the high importance of this addition. It is not long since a wretch wished to use in one of the ports of the Union this method for saving a being of his species who had become guilty of crime, not only of insubordination, but of insurrection, on board a French vessel. And, truly, he would have completely succeeded if the judge of the place, indignant, and even shocked at the audacious effrontery of the pretended creditor, had not taken upon him to accept security for the debt, which afterwards, upon trial, was declared a fraud, and to deliver the guilty to the consul, who had it in his power to send him to France.

ARTICLE 9. (After roll d'equipage.) The registers or roll d'equipage ought always to follow the vessel; it is therefore proposed to add, in order to render the measure truly useful, (the deserters not having been seized before the departure of the vessel,) these words: *or upon a copy of said register or roll d'equipage, certified by the consul.*

(At the end.) This delay appears a little short.

Could not this part of the article, in order to reconcile at the same time justice, humanity, and the interest of navigation, be thus expressed?

But if they should not be sent back in the course of five months, reckoned from the day of their arrest, they shall be set at liberty, and shall not be liable to a second arrest for the same cause. This detention shall not exceed two months, if a vessel of their nation is going directly back from the port where they are found to be detained, except that from the physician of the prison it appear that they cannot be embarked on account of sickness.

It may further be added, that liberation shall equally take place in full right, in case the prisoner shall not receive very exactly the treatment allowed during his detention, and which may be agreed upon, that nothing may be left in the power of despotism.

In fine, the article should be so expressed as to insure protection to the weak against the strong. It is and ought to be the wish of every country, that every man, rich or poor, scrupulously fulfil his contract, when he has agreed to it freely, and when it is for the interest of society that he do so.

ARTICLE 10. A foreigner (especially a poor one) is more exposed than all others to suspicion and to calumny. Too much cannot, therefore, be done to insure to him protection and support in misfortune. The article, too, does not seem to be expressed as it ought to be: as long as a man is only amenable, there can be nothing against him but presumption. It ought not, therefore, to be said: *In the case where the respective subjects or citizens shall have committed;* but, *shall be accused or arraigned;* this remark will perhaps appear finical, the word *amenable* (justiciable) expressing sufficiently what is intended. But still it is better to express clearly what one wishes to say, especially when the liberty and the reputation of the citizens are in question.

It is proposed to terminate the article thus: *They shall be amenable to the judges of the country, who shall, however, give notice of the suits to the consul or vice consul of the district, in order that he may appear personally, or by his attorney, if he judge it proper, as the protector or defender of the accused, &c., &c.*

One of the first duties of consular agents is to defend those of their nation before foreign authorities, when either natural justice or treaties are violated in their regard; when either the dispositions, or the forms established by the law of the country, are deviated from to their detriment, in the case where they are subjected to this law; it is, in fine, their duty to protect and defend them, whenever they are or may become the victims of calumny or of error. It will therefore be supposed that it is useful, and even indispensable, that no criminal procedure should be pursued against them, unless the agent of their nation be at least informed of it. Foreigners, especially poor foreigners, ought always to be considered, in the eye of the law, as minors; the consul as their father; he ought, therefore, to be called to their aid, as being in some sort their official tutor.

ARTICLE 11. It is proposed to add to the 11th article:

The same interference shall take place, as often as an intimation ought to be made, on board the said vessels, and that for any cause whatever.

This addition appears necessary, the authority of the place being able to go, in the case of a surrender on board of a foreign vessel, for other causes than those mentioned in the opposite article. For, avoiding all refusals or difficulties on the part of captains or commanders, it might even be added, that, if the consul or vice consul judge that he ought not to go on board, he shall be bound immediately to give his declaration about it to the bearer of the order of the territorial judges, in order that this agent of the King may not be able, on any pretext, to plead ignorance.

A good many troublesome examples sufficiently prove the utility of this last precaution. The harmony between two powers ought not to be allowed to depend upon the humor or vulgarity of a captain, who, under the pretext of not knowing the soldiers, the constables, or the marshals, goes sometimes so far as to give himself up to fits of passion, which may become, between two Governments, serious subjects of discussion. *To prevent,* in order not *to punish,* ought to be the first care of all heads of families.

ARTICLE 12. Every convention, in order to be truly useful, ought to be easy, and, above all, susceptible of execution.

Now, it cannot be dissembled that the distances, especially in the United States, do not permit that the disputes and suits between those of the same nation there should all be terminated by the consuls or vice consuls. How, for example, could it be required that the French settled in Ohio or in the State of Illinois should be bound to present themselves before the consul of Philadelphia, and that the inhabitants of Tennessee should go to Charleston. Yet the bad faith of a Frenchman established in these countries might make him oppose to his fellow-countryman the article of the convention, and authorize him to refuse to appear otherwise than before the consul of the district. This consideration alone will make it perceivable how useful it is to grant to the agents of consuls and vice consuls the right demanded for them in the third article. This agent would be, in some sort, wherever there might be a certain number of French families established, a justice of the peace, or a conciliator. His Majesty's minister should be careful that no one be chosen in an inconsiderate manner, and the consequence of this latitude granted to the consular administration would be, that no part of those of his nation would find themselves abandoned and precluded from rights which might be secured to them by the convention. It ought not to be dissembled, that foreigners who possess nationality, who know that the eye and the benevolence of an esteemed fellow-countryman watches over them, are possessed of the more self-respect. They do not think themselves lost in the crowd; they conduct themselves with more prudence; and if they fall into misfortune, or if death is ready to inflict the mortal wound, they at least find near them a protector, a defender, a man who speaks their language, and who will convey their last words and last wishes to their families.

In order to render the article truly advantageous, and to prevent the benefit which is real to those of their nation who live near the consuls, from having, as to the others, the effect, in some sort, of a denial of justice, it should be provided—

1st. That the same facilities be granted, as explained in article 3, to the agents of consuls and vice consuls.

2d. That the distance of the consul or of his agent from those of his nation be determined, and that to the extent of that distance those of his nation be bound to present themselves before the territorial judges with all their suits and disputes; or, in case of the refusal of one of the parties, that party be obliged previously to give security, before the competent authority of the place, for all the costs and damages which the removal and the distance alone may occasion; and, as, in the two countries, a good many contracts, not only commercial, but of every other nature, between foreigners, may be attached to interests purely local, it might be enacted, that, in all cases and in every place, the parties should have the power, notwithstanding the twelfth article of the convention, to carry, by common consent, all the disputes in which they may find themselves interested before the territorial judges, who should not refuse to take cognizance of them.

It cannot be dissembled that the principle, generally enough acknowledged, *actor sequitur forum rei*, can only be productive, especially when persons beyond seas are in question, of grievous inconveniences. But it will be evident that the exceptions proposed, and which are found to be chiefly necessary between two nations very distant, and both sincerely friends, ought to be clearly explained; otherwise it would happen that, in spite of being bound by the letter of the convention, every territorial officer would refuse, in both countries, to take cognizance of an affair which might appear *to be* essentially the business of the consul. Both Governments are interested, that their respective citizens may be, everywhere, under the protection of a justice easy to be obtained.

ARTICLE 13. The Congress having determined by law in what manner commercial affairs between foreigners and citizens of the United States should be determined, it is proposed to word the article thus:

ARTICLE 13. *The subjects of his Majesty settled in the United States and the citizens of the United States 'settled in France shall be judged reciprocally for all the commercial disputes which may arise upon the spot between them and the inhabitants of the country or the citizens of another country residing there, by the tribunals instituted or appointed ad hoc, and according to the particular forms ordained by the law of the country. Solely, and with a view to facilitate as much as possible the commercial transactions between the two nations, and to prevent the delays often very pernicious to the interests of the foreigner, the two Governments agree that all commercial affairs between the trading citizens of France and those of the United States, and vice versa, shall be always taken up in preference to those of ordinary plaintiffs in courts of justice or tribunals of commerce of the two countries.*

No one is ignorant with what celerity the affairs of commerce are terminated in France. No one is ignorant how very prejudicial a delay may be to a foreigner, whom important affairs may call elsewhere, and who is, notwithstanding, detained by the idea that he will leave behind him, if he go to a distance, only lawyers, who, according to the candid expression of one of our great and ancient jurists, know, in every country, only *to extend their practice and spin out the cause.* One may be persuaded, therefore, after this consideration, that the advantage proposed in favor of the foreigner is very wise and very liberal. After all, the more foreign industry is protected in a country, the more it is extended, and the more are the ties which unite the two nations strengthened.

ARTICLE 14. For avoiding all discussion, and all abuse, it is not believed that this article should be so general. A stranger ought actually to be exempt from all personal service. At all times when the ordinary duties of a citizen are to be performed, he ought to be exempt from those to which the municipal law of all countries compel those of their nation; but there are obligations which hospitality imposes in all places, and it is not always sufficient. As I have been eager to agree, by letter of the 2d January, 1818, to the Secretary of State, for a stranger to live submissive to the law which protects him, he ought, on certain occasions, provided for by the general law of nations, to partake of the danger to which the citizens of the place where he lives may find themselves exposed.

"From a sense of gratitude for the protection granted him, and the other advantages he enjoys, the stranger ought not to confine himself to the respect due to the laws of the country; he ought to assist it upon occasion, and to contribute to its defence, &c., &c., &c. Nothing hinders his defending it against pirates or robbers; against the ravages of an inundation or the devastation of fire. Can he pretend to live under the protection of a State, and to participate in a multitude of advantages, without doing anything for its defence, and to be a tranquil spectator of the dangers to which the citizens are exposed?"

On this principle, which I admit as essentially moral, and as entering into the order of human societies, I will go so far as to avow, that if a stranger settled, or a proprietor, on the frontiers of the United States, has the right of retiring in an offensive or defensive war against the Indians, he cannot argue this privilege, if, without any declaration of war, some hordes of savages make an irruption into the country, this attack is only a wilful murder; and, in similar circumstances, *every man is, and ought to be, a citizen.* I should not then be far from thinking that it would be advisable even in granting to a stranger the rights which he ought to enjoy, to prevent, by a very explicit provision, all the shameful comments of selfishness. Good conventions between nations, as between individuals, are those which are founded, not upon general speculative ideas, but upon all local circumstances and necessities, as well as upon the possibilities from which they may be derived. I will add, that many examples, in time past, concur in demonstrating the utility of the preceding observations. Not to put them in execution would be perhaps for the advantage of the cause which I ought to defend; but no treaty is or can be solid, except it rest upon equity, conciliate all interests, foresee and prevent all difficulties.

ARTICLE 15. (After the words, "in the terms stipulated.")

In the terms stipulated, &c., &c. This end of the article to be suppressed, as being now useless.

ARTICLE 16. This period appears proper and sufficient. Nothing will hinder it from being supplied by additional articles; what may be judged necessary, and for the interest of the two countries, during the time of the convention.

NOTE.—Complaints appear to have been made (at least by the American consul at Havre) that the entry of vessels which arrive from the United States in our ports cannot be made but by the intervention of brokers. It has been demanded that the consuls of the nation should enjoy, jointly with the brokers of the port, this advantage. I know that the American consul does enjoy it. I see by the newspapers that they complain of having been a little after deprived of it; and I also see that, in consequence of the letter of the Minister of the Interior, which put a stop to the privilege, there has been held in Havre itself "a meeting of the masters of vessels, and that such meeting resulted in the adoption of a letter to Mr. Beasley, the American consul, remonstrating, in strong and dignified terms, against the unjust regulation."

Without examining here the irregularity of this kind of representations, which ought only to come through the ordinary channel of diplomatic agents; and without attending to the noise which the consul of the United States at Havre already has made, or been the means of making, at several times, through the medium of newspapers, I shall observe, that the letter of the Minister of the Interior says, "if foreign consuls should consider themselves injured by this regulation, it must become the subject of diplomatic arrangement." I think, therefore, that the difficulty which presents itself may be easily removed, if the American Government thinks it still of consequence to secure this privilege to their consular agents.

As to the duties of tonnage and of light-houses, it has been pretended, and very improperly, that they were higher in France than in the United States; it is quite contrary, and in that regard His Majesty's Government would be justified, I believe, in making some representations; but this question is unconnected with the subject of which I treat, I therefore do not wish to stop for it.

These observations are my own. I am only authorized by my court to sign a convention relative to deserting sailors; but if it should appear that all the bases, which I have only pointed out, ought to be agreed to, as I am persuaded that a similar convention could not but be advantageous to the two countries, and produce other arrangements no less useful, I shall make it my duty to insist with my court, as soon as I shall have obtained, confidentially or officially, some data a little more certain as to the dispositions of the Federal Government.

In submitting these observations to the Secretary of State, I seize this opportunity of requesting him to accept the renewed assurances of my high consideration.

G. HYDE DE NEUVILLE,
Minister of H. M. C. M. to the United States.

WASHINGTON, *May* 22, 1819.

M. De Neuville to the Secretary of State.

[Translation]

WASHINGTON, February 17, 1821.

MR. SECRETARY OF STATE: I have the honor to address to you a copy of the powers with which the King my master has been pleased to honor me. From what you have done me the honor to tell me, I presume that those of the President will be very soon drawn up; I shall, therefore, be ready, sir, to enter upon a conference on the day and at the hour which you shall think proper to point out.

You are not ignorant, sir, of the amicable views which have induced his Majesty the King my master to transfer the negotiation to Washington. He was of opinion that it would be the means of accelerating the conclusion of the affair, and, in that regard, the opinion of the minister of the United States has been in accordance with that of his Majesty.

I dare hope, sir, that it will be easy for us, when all the indispensable explanations have been given and received, to obviate the difficulties which may have arisen between our two countries. No real cause of collision exists between them ; but I perceive several of perfect and lasting harmony. I cannot, therefore, doubt of the happy result of a negotiation which can only have a tendency to conciliate mutual interests, and put a speedy termination to a state of affairs equally pernicious to the two nations.

I request you to accept, sir, of the renewed assurances of the high consideration with which I have the honor to be your most humble and obedient servant,

G. HYDE DE NEUVILLE.

Copy of Mr. De Neuville's full powers.

[Translation.]

Louis, by the grace of God, King of France and of Navarre, to all who shall see these present letters— health. Desirous to fix and regulate, in a manner respectively advantageous, the relations of commerce and navigation between France and the United States, for these causes we, having entire confidence in the capacity, prudence, and experience of our very dear and well beloved the Sieur Baron Hyde de Neuville, Knight of our Royal and Military Order of St. Louis, Officer of the Legion of Honor, Grand Cross of the Royal Order of Isabella the Catholic, and our Envoy Extraordinary and Minister Plenipotentiary at Washington, have named and appointed him, and by these presents signed with our hand, we name and appoint him our plenipotentiary, giving him full and absolute power, that, by uniting himself with the plenipotentiary or plenipotentiaries of the United States, equally furnished with full powers in proper form, he may negotiate, conclude, and sign in our name, with the same authority as we ourselves would or could do, such articles, conventions, and other acts, as he may judge fit for attaining the important end which we propose. Promising, on the faith and word of a King, to agree to, accomplish, and execute punctually, all that our said plenipotentiary shall have stipulated, promised, and signed in our name, and in virtue of these present full powers, without ever contravening, or permitting it to be contravened, directly or indirectly, for any cause or under any pretext whatsoever ; likewise, to give our letters of ratification in proper form, and to have them delivered, for exchange, within the periods which shall be agreed upon. In faith whereof, we have caused our seal to be put to these presents. Given at the Palace of the Tuilleries the twentieth day of the month of October, in the year of grace one thousand eight hundred and twenty, and in the twenty-sixth of our reign.

LOUIS.

By the King:
    Pasquier.

A TRUE COPY.

The Envoy Extraordinary and Minister Plenipotentiary of his most Christian Majesty, near the United States,

G. HYDE DE NEUVILLE.

[L. S.]

Department of State, Washington, February 19, 1821.

Sir: I have had the honor of receiving your letter of this day, with the copy of your full power. In inclosing to you a copy of that by which I am authorized to treat with you concerning the commercial relations between the United States and France, I add with pleasure the assurance of the President's earnest desire that this negotiation may terminate in the settlement of those relations upon a basis of entire reciprocity, satisfactory to both parties, and promotive of the most cordial harmony between them. It will give me pleasure to confer with you at 3 o'clock to-morrow, at the office of this Department.

I pray you, sir, to accept the tender of my most distinguished consideration.

JOHN QUINCY ADAMS.

His Excellency the Baron Hyde de Neuville,
    Envoy Extraordinary and Minister Plenipotentiary from France.

Inclosure in Mr. Adams' letter of February 19, 1821.

James Monroe, President of the United States of America, to all whom these presents shall concern, greeting:

Know ye that I have given and granted, and do hereby give and grant, to John Quincy Adams, Secretary of State of the United States, full power and authority, and also general and special command, to meet and confer with the Envoy Extraordinary and Minister Plenipotentiary of his most Christian Majesty the King of France and Navarre, residing in the United States, being furnished with the like full powers, of and concerning all matters relating to the commerce and navigation between the said United States and France, and to conclude a treaty or convention, touching the premises, for the final ratification of the President of the United States, by and with the advice and consent of the Senate thereof, if such advice and consent be given.

In testimony whereof, I have caused the seal of the United States to be hereunto affixed. Given [L. S.]   under my hand, at the city of Washington, the 19th day of February, A. D. 1821, and of the Independence of the United States the forty-fifth.

JAMES MONROE.

By the President:
    John Quincy Adams, Secretary of State.

Baron de Neuville to the Secretary of State.

[Translation.]

Washington, February 23, 1821.

Sir: As I am solicitous to accelerate, as much as possible, the progress of the negotiation, I now take the liberty to request an answer to the letter which I had the honor of addressing to your Government on the 16th of June, 1818, relative to the eighth article of the Louisiana treaty.

Should the Federal Government admit the interpretation given to this article, on the part of France, it would be unnecessary to discuss the subject any further ; but if, after thorough investigation, it should still adhere to a contrary opinion, you will think with me, sir, that it is material to both parties to know how far they disagree on this very important article of the treaty.

Both Governments having the same honest intentions, every point in dispute between them ought to be easily and promptly settled.

What, I would ask, sir, even in its most limited sense, is the right secured to France by the eighth article of the Louisiana treaty, and in what cases is our navigation to obtain its enjoyment?

It would appear to me that the negotiators, on either part, had but one and the same object in inserting the 7th and 8th articles ; their express intention was, to secure forever to French vessels, in the ports of the ceded territory, a real advantage over those of all other nations ; and, in my opinion, the very expressions of the article established, in the most positive terms, that intention of the negotiators.

There are two other affairs which must, of necessity, be settled before those which only affect our commercial interests. I shall, however, refrain from discussing, or even examining, them at present, and consider that in this I am giving an additional proof of my conciliatory disposition.

It is possible they may not be of as serious a nature as they seem (from newspaper reports) to have been considered in France; or, at all events, I persist in the opinion that nothing can prevent an accommodation when the respective parties are prepared to make such concessions as their mutual interest and friendly dispositions may require, and are willing to satisfy every consideration of propriety.

Accept, &c., &c.,

G. HYDE DE NEUVILLE.

The Secretary of State.

The Secretary of State to Baron de Neuville.

Department of State, *Washington, March 29, 1821.*

Sir: By the seventh article of the treaty of April 30, 1803, by which Louisiana was ceded to the United States, certain special privileges, within the ports of the ceded territory, were stipulated in favor of the ships of France and Spain for the term of twelve years, and, by the eighth article of the same treaty, it is further provided that, "in future, and forever, after the expiration of the twelve years, the *ships* of France shall be treated upon the footing of the *most favored nations in the ports above mentioned.*"

In your note of the 15th of December, 1817, you demanded, upon the allegation of this article, that the advantages conceded to the English nation, *in all the ports of the Union*, should be secured to France in those of Louisiana. The citation of the words of the article would, of itself, be an answer to the claim. The stipulation of the eighth article is, in its terms, limited to grants of favors *in the ports of Louisiana.* The seventh article had secured to French and Spanish vessels *in those ports* peculiar privileges, to the exclusion of the vessels of other nations; and the object of the eighth article was evidently to provide that, after the expiration of those twelve years, no such peculiar privileges should be granted, *in the same ports*, to the vessels of any other nation, to the exclusion of those of France. The whole scope of both the articles is, by their letter and spirit, limited to special favors and privileges granted in those particular ports.

The claim of France, therefore, is not, and cannot be, by *any* construction of the 8th article, to enjoy, in the ports of Louisiana, the advantages conceded to any other nation, *in all the ports of the Union*, but only that the *ships* of France should be entitled to the special advantages conceded to the ships of other nations in the ports of Louisiana.

Were it then even true that the English, or any other nation, enjoyed, by virtue of general stipulations of treaties, advantages in all the ports of this Union over other nations, inasmuch they would not be favors specially limited to the ports of Louisiana, granted with any special reference to them, they would, neither by the letter nor the spirit of the Louisiana treaty, give to France any just claim to the special participation, in those particular ports, of advantages there enjoyed only by general arrangements co-extensive with the whole Union.

But in the answer from this Department, of December 23, 1817, to the note of Mr. De Neuville, of the 15th of that month, it was averred, and is now repeated, that the ships of France are, and, since the expiration of the twelve years stipulated by the seventh article of the treaty, uniformly have been, treated upon the footing of the most favored nation in the ports of Louisiana. That they will continue to be so, France may be assured, not only from that sacred regard for the obligation of treaties, which is the undeviating principle of the American government, but from a maxim founded in that justice which is at once the highest glory and the soundest policy of nations—that every favor granted to one, ought equally to be extended to all.

It is no exception, but an exemplification of this principle, that the vessels of England, Prussia, the Netherlands, and the Hanseatic cities, pay in the ports of this Union, including those of Louisiana, no other or higher duties than the vessels of the United States. This is not a *favor*, but a *bargain*. It was offered to all nations by an act of Congress of March 3, 1815. Its only condition was *reciprocity*. It was always, and yet is, in the power of France to secure this advantage to her vessels. It always depended upon her will alone to abolish every discriminating duty operating against her ships in the United States. Great Britain, Prussia, the Netherlands, the Hanseatic cities, accepted the proffer and granted the equivalent. Had France seen fit also to accept it, the American Government would have hailed the acceptance, not as a favor, but as equal justice. They were far from anticipating that, instead of this, France would found, upon equal reciprocity, offered to all mankind, a claim to special privileges never granted to any. Special, indeed, would be the favor which should yield to a claim of free gift to one, of that which had been sold at a fair price to another. English vessels, therefore, enjoy, in the ports of Louisiana, no *favors* which are not equally enjoyed by the vessels of France; nor do they enjoy any reduction of duties which French vessels might not, at the option of their own Government, have enjoyed at any time since the 3d of *March*, 1815. That France did not think proper to accept the offer, is not mentioned with a view to reproach. France consulted what she thought her own interest, and instead of reciprocity, aggravated discriminating duties to prohibition. She exercised her rights. But if, in levying those prohibitory duties, there was no *disfavor* to the United States, surely as little can it be alleged that the extension of reciprocal advantages to all is a grant to any one of a *favor*.

It is observed in the reply of Mr. De Neuville, dated the 18th of June, 1818, to the letter from this Department of the 23d of December preceding, that France, by claiming *forever*, in the ports of Louisiana, the full enjoyment of every advantage enjoyed by any other nation in all the ports of the Union, as the price of equivalent advantages secured to the United States, still claims nothing gratuitous, inasmuch as the equivalent for this special advantage to France was already paid in the cession of Louisiana itself. This idea is not only contradicted by the whole tenor of the Louisiana treaty, and by the special and obvious purport of the seventh and eighth articles, but I hesitate not to aver, that if the American Government had believed those articles to be susceptible of such a construction, and had those articles *alone* been presented to them as the *whole* price for the cession of Louisiana, they never would have accepted it upon such terms; for such terms would not only have destroyed the effect of the cession of the province *in full sovereignty;* they would not only have been in direct violation of the Constitution of the United States, but they would have been a surrender of one of the highest attributes of the sovereignty of this whole nation; they would have disabled this nation forever from contracting with any power on earth but France for any advantage in navigation, however great, and however amply compensated; it would have been little short of a stipulation never to conclude a commercial treaty with any other nation than France; for what else are commercial treaties than the mutual concession of advantages for equivalents? And if every advantage obtained from others for equivalents were, by a retrospective obligation of this article, to be secured, as already paid for by France, they would have been secured to her, not only in the ports of Louisiana, but in those of the whole Union; such a treaty, far from being an acquisition of the full sovereignty of Louisiana, would have been, on the partof the United States, a formal abdication of their own.

From the obvious purport of the seventh and eighth articles, it is apparent that neither of them was considered in any respect as forming a part of the equivalent for the cession of Louisiana. The cession of Louisiana, and the equivalents paid for it, were not even included in the same treaty; the cession was in one treaty, and the equivalents in two separate conventions of the same date. The seventh and eighth articles referred to are in the treaty of cession, and not in the conventions of equivalents. The three instruments are, indeed, explicitly declared to be parts of one and the same transaction; but the very form of the arrangements adopted by the parties shows their common intention to regulate the cession by one compact, and the equivalent given for it by others.

Nor is the proof that these articles formed no part in the estimation of either of the parties of the equivalents for the cession confined to this tacit evidence in the forms of the negotiation. The seventh article bears upon its face the avowal of the motives by which it was dictated. Its introductory words, ' as it is reciprocally advantageous to the commerce of France and the United States to encourage the communication of both nations, for a limited time, in the country ceded by the present treaty, until general arrangements relative to the commerce of both nations may be agreed on." This is the motive specially assigned, by the article itself, for its subsequent stipulations; the reciprocal advantage to the commerce of France and the United States was the end; the encouragement of their communications, *for a limited time*, in the country ceded were the means; and the eighth article, following as a corollary from the seventh, merely stipulated that, after the twelve years of special and exclusive privilege, the ships of France should be treated upon the footing of the most favored nations. In neither of the articles can a single word be found importing that they were understood by either party as forming any portion of the equivalent for the cession.

In the note of Mr. Hyde de Neuville, of the 16th of June, 1818, this claim of France to enjoy, for nothing and forever, in the ports of Louisiana, every advantage which the United States may concede, for a full equivalent to any other nation, in all the ports of the Union, is supported by a supposed peculiarity in the phraseology of the article by virtue of which it is claimed. To support this pretension, it is asserted that "in *all* the treaties between France and the United States the condition of reciprocity is mentioned in the most formal manner; that they *all expressly* say that the two contracting parties shall reciprocally enjoy the favor granted to another nation, *gratuitously*, if the concession is gratuitous, *or by granting the same compensation* if the concession is conditional."

The mutual stipulation of being treated as the most favored nation is *not*, in all the treaties between France and the United States, accompanied by the *express* declaration that the favor granted to a third party shall be extended to France or the United States gratuitously if the grant is gratuitous, and upon granting the same compensation if it be conditional. This explanatory clause is expressed in terms only in one treaty between the United States and France, and that was the first treaty ever contracted between them, namely: the treaty of amity and commerce of February 6, 1778, in its second article. It has never been repeated in any of the subsequent treaties between the parties. It was alluded to, adopted and applied to consular pre-eminences, powers, authority, and privileges, by the 15th article of the consular convention of 14th November, 1788. But in vain will any such clause be sought for in the convention of 30th September, 1800, the words of the 6th article of which are as follows: "commerce between the parties shall be free; the vessels of the two nations, and their privateers, as well as their prizes, shall be treated in their respective ports as those of the nation the most favored; and, in general, the two parties shall enjoy, in the ports of each other, in regard to commerce and navigation, the privileges of the most favored nations." There is not a word in this article, nor in the whole convention, saying that these favors shall be enjoyed freely, if freely granted to others, or upon granting the same condition, if conditionally granted; yet who can doubt that this was implied in the article, though not expressed?

The fact, then, with regard to this argument, being directly the reverse of the statement in the note of Mr. de Neuville, of June 16, 1818, it cannot escape his attention how forcibly the argument recoils itself. If, from the uniform use of the explanatory clause in *all* the preceding treaties, stated in the note as a fact, its omission in the Louisiana treaty could have warranted the inference that no such qualification was intended by it, with much stronger reason may it be concluded that, as the parties had before repeatedly contracted the same engagements, at one time with, and at another time without, the explanatory clause, but always intending the same thing, this variety in the modes of expression was considered by them as altogether immaterial, and that, whether expressed or not, no claim to a favor enjoyed by others could justly be advanced by virtue of any such stipulation without granting the same equivalent with which the advantage had been purchased.

There is, therefore, no necessity for supposing any forgetfulness on the part of the negotiators of the treaty of cession, nor of recurring to any supposed distinctions between the construction applicable to a convention of commerce and to a treaty of sale. It has been proved that neither the 7th nor 8th article was ever understood by either party as forming any part of the equivalent for the cession. That the reciprocity of the 7th article is expressed upon its face, and that the 8th, as a consequence from it, only stipulated that after the period of special privilege, in those special ports, should have expired, no such privilege in those particular ports should be granted to other nations without being made common to the vessels of France. If it be admitted that, in a contract of sale, nothing can be undersood by implication, (*sous entendu,*) this principle would be no less fatal to the claim of France than every other admissible rule of reason; for what implication could be more violent and unnatural than, by a stipulation to treat the ships of France on the footing of those of the most favored nation *in the ports of Louisiana*, the United States had disabled themselves forever from purchasing a commercial advantage from any other nation without granting it particularly to France?

That the Senate, in 1803, did not formally object to the stipulations of these seventh and eighth articles must be ascribed to its never having entered into the imagination or conception of that body that such a claim as that now attempted to be raised from it by France was either expressed in or to be implied from them. Whether the special privileges granted for twelve years to the ships of France and Spain in those ports were compatible with the Constitution of the United States, or with the other article of the treaty by which the inhabitants of the ceded territory were to be incorporated into the Union, and admitted, according to the principles of that Constitution, to the enjoyment of all the rights, advantages, and immunities of citizens of the United States, might be and was a question to the Senate in deliberating upon the treaty. It was a question of construction upon a clause of the Constitution, and that construction prevailed with which the terms of the treaty were reconcilable to it and to themselves; but whether the claim now advanced by France is reconcilable with the Constitution of the United States is no question of construction or of implication. It is directly repugnant to the express provision that the regulations of commerce and revenue in the ports of all the *States* of the Union shall be the same.

The admission of the State of Louisiana, in the year 1812, *on an equal footing with the original States* in all respects whatever, does not impair the force of this reasoning, although the admission of French and Spanish vessels into their ports for a short remnant of time upon different regulations of commerce and revenue from those prescribed in the ports of all the other States in the Union, gave them a preference not sanctioned by the Constitution, and upon which the other States might, had they thought fit, have delayed the act of admission until the expiration of the twelve years; yet as this was a condition of which the other States might waive the benefit for the sake of admitting Louisiana, sooner even than rigorous obligation would have required, to the full enjoyment of all the rights of American citizens, this consent of the only interested party to anticipate the maturity of the adopted child of the Union can be considered in no other light than a friendly grant in advance of that which, in the lapse of three short years, might have been claimed as of undeniable right.

The Government of the United States have fulfilled, and will fulfil, the eighth article of the Louisiana treaty, according to its plain and obvious meaning. The ships of France are and will be treated in the ports of Louisiana on the footing of the most favored nation. The ships of no nation enjoy any special favor in the ports of Louisiana. The ships of all nations are, in the ports of Louisiana, on the same footing as in the ports of all the other States of the Union. The ships of all nations, in all the ports of the Union, enjoy the same advantages which the nation to which they belong concedes to the vessels of the United States in return. The favor, and the only favor they enjoy, is *reciprocity*. That favor the American Government extend to French vessels, and ask no better of France than to accept. But the American Government cannot grant as a gratuitous favor to France that which they have conceded for a valuable consideration to others; no such stipulation is expressed in the Louisiana treaty; no such stipulation can, from all or any of its articles, be justly inferred. In this, as in all their commercial relations with France, their most friendly cherished hope is mutual friendship; their most earnest desire, equal reciprocity.

I pray you, sir, to accept the assurance of my distinguished consideration.

JOHN QUINCY ADAMS.

His Excellency the Baron DE NEUVILLE, *Envoy Extraordinary, &c.*

Baron de Neuville to the Secretary of State.

[Translation.]

WASHINGTON, *March* 30, 1821.

SIR: I have received your letter, dated yesterday, in answer to mine of June 16, 1818, and 23d ultimo.

I shall have the honor to reply, and believe it will not be difficult for me to show that all my citations are correct. Not only all the treaties between France and this country, (those, it is well understood, which could admit of such a clause,) but *even all* the treaties and conventions between the United States and European Governments, or *nearly all*, express in positive or in equivalent terms what I have stated.

I will add, that the force of my argument would not be impaired even admitting the sense attributed by you to the paragraph which seems to have more particularly fixed your attention.

I shall return, in a future note, to the point of the discussion as well as to all the others, and shall draw my best arguments from the very acts of the Federal Government, and from the opinions of the most enlightened men in the country. A better source could not be resorted to.

Allow me, sir, in the mean time to make an observation suggested by the following passage of your letter:

"The Government of the United States have fulfilled, and will fulfil, the eighth article of the Louisiana treaty, according to its plain meaning. The ships of France *are* and will be treated in the ports of Louisiana on the footing of the most favored nation."

You had stated in your note of December, 1817: "It is true that the terms of the eighth article are positive and unconditional; but it will be readily perceived that the condition, though not expressed in the article, is inherent in the advantage claimed under it. If British vessels enjoyed in the ports of Louisiana any gratuitous favor, undoubtedly French vessels would, by the terms of the article, be entitled to the same."

In your letter of yesterday you say that, "from a maxim founded in that justice which is at once the highest glory and the soundest policy of nations, that every favor granted to one ought equally to be extended to all."

"It is no exception, but an exemplification of this principle, that the vessels of England, Prussia, the Netherlands, and the Hanseatic towns, pay in the ports of this Union, including those of Louisiana, no other or higher duties than the vessels of the United States. This is not a favor, but a bargain."

I cannot, I must confess, view those matters in the same light, nor especially can admit your conclusion. But even admitting that, in reality, the four instances above mentioned are mere excepted cases; allowing that England, Prussia, the Netherlands, and the Hanseatic towns enjoy no gratuitous privilege or right in the United States; that they are not favored nations, and that, as you assert, sir, *this is not a favor, but a bargain;*

Admitting even your doctrine that gratuitous concessions alone constitute what is called *favor*, whereby a nation becomes in the ports of another either a favored nation or the most favored nation;

Allowing all this, still how would it be possible to reconcile the interpretations which the difference between the duties now paid in *the ports of Louisiana* by French vessels, and those paid in the same ports by the vessels of such nations as have neither *convention* nor *treaty*, nor have made any bargain with this republic?

I am not apprised that Russians, Spaniards, Portuguese, or other nations having none but such like, relations with this country, have been made to pay a duty of eighteen dollars per ton in the ports of Louisiana; and yet this duty is frequently required of the vessels of that nation which, by virtue of an authentic instrument and of a positive contract, is entitled *to be treated in future and forever in the said ports* upon the footing of the most favored nation. Although nothing can be more clear or better established than the right of France, "this is not a favor, but a bargain."

It was not without nature that the chargé d'affaires of his Majesty took care to observe, in his letter of 18th July last, that this was not the case of *a favor refused*, but that of *a charge* imposed by one party on the other.

Such a state of things, whatever may be the interpretation given to the eighth article, is so injurious to the rights of France, and so very contrary to the equity and honesty of the Federal Government, that I cannot but flatter myself that the answer now solicited to this letter and to that of Mr. Roth of the 18th of July will be such as to give full satisfaction on this point.

And if France should not be made to enjoy immediately the right which I claim, most assuredly she cannot be denied in the mean time the enjoyment of that which is acknowledged.

I have the honor, &c.,

G. HYDE DE NEUVILLE.

P. S. *March 31.*—I have the honor to acknowledge the receipt of your letter of the 30th, with the accompanying documents.

The Secretary of State to Mr. Hyde de Neuville.

DEPARTMENT OF STATE, *Washington, April 6,* 1821.

SIR: I have submitted to the consideration of the President the confidential communication which I had the honor of receiving from you last evening, dated the 4th instant.

I am directed by him to assure you that, in the same confidential spirit with which it was made by you, he has given to its contents the most deliberate attention. As the result of this has been no variation of the sentiments which I have had the honor of expressing to you in my letter of the 30th of last month, it is submitted to your discretion to determine whether a further discussion between us at present of the particular point to which it relates would tend to that harmony and conciliation between our countries which is the avowed object and earnest desire of both.

He directs me, at the same time, to repeat to you the assurance given you in my letter of the 30th ultimo, that any proposals which you are authorized by your Government to make in relation to the commercial intercourse between the United States and France will be received, whenever you may think proper to make them, with immediate and the most friendly attention.

Be pleased to accept the renewed assurance of my distinguished consideration.

JOHN QUINCY ADAMS.

His Excellency HYDE DE NEUVILLE, *Envoy Extraordinary, &c.*

Discriminating Duties on Tonnage.

[Translation.]

1. The duties of entry upon the wines of France shall be reduced so as to pay no more to the United States (proportionally) than the wines of other countries.
[The calculation of it has been made, I believe, at the Treasury; it is, at all events, a point upon which exact data will be easily procured.]

2. There shall be upon the silks of India and of China an augmentation of ————— or a reduction of ————— in the duties of entry of our silks.

3. There shall be a consular convention between the two countries, based upon that of 1788.

4. The discriminating duties actually imposed on a foreign flag shall be reduced ————— in favor of French vessels laden with the natural productions and manufactures of France.

5. There shall be, in the same manner, a reduction of ————— in France upon cottons, potash, rice, and tobacco, coming from the United States, and imported by American vessels.

6. The duties of tonnage which the vessels of the two nations shall be bound to pay in their respective ports will be very easily understood, but it will be necessary to know, first, what the Federal Government may desire in that regard.

If all the points in litigation can be agreed upon, the convention may be definitive; otherwise, it can only be provisional, and, as one may say, an experiment.

The provisional arrangement should not cease before the term of —————, and even at the expiration of this period it should be continued till one of the two parties shall have declared to the other its intention of renouncing it; which declaration ought to be made at least ————— beforehand.

NOTE.—These preliminaries being agreed upon, there shall be no further question but of discussing, more or less, the reductions or augmentations.

Memorandum from Mr. Adams to Baron de Neuville.

APRIL 18, 1821.

1. The duties upon French wines shall be reduced to the extent proposed by the Baron de Neuville, to ten cents a gallon in casks, and twenty cents in bottles.

2. The duties upon silks imported from beyond the Cape of Good Hope shall be raised to thirty per cent.

3. A consular convention, upon the basis of that of 1788, shall be made with certain necessary alterations. If it should be found that the parties cannot agree upon these, an article shall be stipulated for the mutual restoration of seamen, deserters from their vessels.

4. The sale of tobacco from the United States shall be released from the monopoly of the *administration* and be made common, as all French articles are in the United States and all other American articles are in France.

5. All *discriminating* duties and *surcharges*, whether upon the *tonnage* of vessels or upon articles of merchandise, the produce or manufacture of either country, imported into the other, shall cease on both sides.

This article to be the same, in principle and substance, as the second article of the convention of July 3, 1815, between the United States and Great Britain.

The convention may be concluded to commence from and after the passage of an act of Congress for the stipulated increase and reduction of the duties.

Baron de Neuville to the Secretary of State.

[Translation.]

WASHINGTON, *April* 21, 1821.

Commercial concessions are only of secondary consideration, and may therefore be set aside, at least for the present.

The principal question is that which relates to the discriminating duties.

In my first interview with the Secretary of State, I stated the basis on which *alone* I was authorized to treat; I shall now repeat it, adding some remarks which have appeared important.

If the present state of things continue, matters must become worse.

If both parties sincerely wish to put a period to it, nothing appears to me more easy.

On my part, I shall comply with everything that can tend to reconcile, upon honorable terms, the views of the two countries; but for that purpose the two Governments must necessarily determine not to insist further upon such principles as are too absolute.

The friendship which has always prevailed between the two nations, their real interest and sound policy, appear to me to point out what should be done. *Both parties ought to make advances so as to meet halfway.*

His most Christian Majesty's Government does not hesitate to propose it, and to make a first advance. Should any one be pleased to estimate correctly to the present period the consequences of the law of the 15th of May and of the *ordonnances* of the 26th of July, he will readily be convinced that the French Government is less taken up with its commercial interest, than actuated by a constant desire of following the policy of Louis the XVI. towards the United States.

With this view, if it should be agreed upon to discuss first the question relative to the discriminating duties, I shall propose the adoption of the following bases:

1st. Those duties shall be reduced on both sides.

2d. They shall, for the future, be made sufficiently moderate to enable the shipping of both nations to be employed for importation, as well as exportation, in both countries.

If this principle be definitively adopted, it will only be necessary to come to an understanding upon the calculations proper to insure a desirable result, and upon the most simple and efficacious means of execution.

G. HYDE DE NEUVILLE.

Memorandum from Mr. Adams to Baron de Neuville.

DEPARTMENT OF STATE, *Washington, April* 26, 1821.

In the commercial regulations established merely by law, the basis upon which every nation proceeds is its own interest, without reference to that of other nations. But commerce being an interchange of commodities, in the disposal of which both parties are interested, it is just in itself, and conformable to the practice of nations, that the regulation of it should be by arrangements to which both parties consent, and in which due regard is paid to the interests of both.

The first principle, therefore, of all negotiation upon such interests is *reciprocity;* and wherever a collision of interests exists, it is apparent that they can be conciliated only by reciprocal concession.

In the subject upon which a collision of interest between the United States and France has arisen, the two parties have heretofore enacted, respectively, each with exclusive reference to its own interest, certain regulations, securing, so far as its power extended, certain advantages to its own shipping, by certain special charges within its jurisdiction, direct or indirect, upon the shipping of the other; the result of which *counteracting* legislation, on both sides, has been in a great measure the exclusion of the shipping of both parties from the carriage of the commerce between them.

This result is injurious to the interests of both parties; and the effort now made by both is to agree upon some arrangement, by which the conflicting interests of both parties may be conciliated. It is further to be observed that no concession, the effect of which would be to sacrifice the interest of either party more, or as much as it is sacrificed by the existing state of things, could either be durable or satisfactory to both parties.

The difference between the parties having originated altogether from the surcharges upon *shipping*, the natural and obvious principle of reciprocity, applicable to the case, would be that of repealing all discriminating duties and surcharges on both sides; and this is what has been repeatedly offered and urged on the part of the United States.

It is represented, on the part of France, that this principle is inadmissible; but for this refusal no reason has been assigned. No objection to it on the ground of natural justice or general policy has been or it is believed can be alleged. It has been assumed, without proof, that the effect of it would be to throw the whole commerce into the channel of American shipping, although it is notorious that all the outfits of navigation, and the wages of seamen, are much cheaper in France than in the United States.

Whatever disadvantages French navigation may labor under in competition with that of the United States are believed to be within the control of France to remove. Nevertheless, the opinion of the French Government of the subject being stated by the Baron de Neuville to be irrevocably fixed, the President has been willing to meet any supposed disadvantage to France in such an arrangement, by advantages, thought to be fully equivalent for them, to the agriculture, commerce, and manufactures of France. In the minutes of a projet first presented by the Baron de Neuville, the President welcomed what he thought countenanced the hope of such a compromise. The Baron suggested special accommodations to the principal exports from France to the United States, and other benefits to French interests, all which were assented to by the President to the extent proposed by the Baron himself. In return for these concessions, he had reason to expect some concession on the part of France; in which, however, he has as yet been disappointed. He thought that with such great advantages granted to the commerce and manufactures of France, the least that could be required in return was that reciprocity which should discard all discriminating duties upon the mere carriage of the trade.

In the second projet received from the Baron de Neuville, he proposes to set aside all questions of commercial advantage, as merely secondary objects, and to take that of the shipping interests alone. He proposes a reduction of the discriminating duties on both sides, on the basis of calculations which may be adapted to secure a share of the carriage of the trade to each party. To the admission of this principle the Government of the United States have constantly objected, upon the most substantial and cogent reasons. The President is not yet aware of any form in which it can be satisfactorily admitted. Nevertheless, in the earnestness of his desire to terminate the commercial conflict between the two countries, he will receive and consider with the utmost attention, any specific proposals which the Baron de Neuville may be authorized to make for the accomplishment of this desirable object. To abridge the negotiation, perhaps it may be most convenient that the Baron de Neuville should present his proposals in the form of an article for a convention.

The Baron de Neuville to the Secretary of State.

[Translation.]

APRIL 28; 1821.

France, in all her political and commercial relations with this Union, has always aimed at the conciliation of the interests of the two countries. She will never deviate from this rule. She wishes *that reciprocity* which, if well calculated, can *alone* be durable, viz., the *reciprocity of advantages.*

The Government of the King is, nevertheless, far from rejecting absolutely the proposals of the United States. It is more than probable that one day it may be enabled to accept it, even without any modification; it will then, as well as at this time, evince the spirit of moderation with which it is animated; for its object is not the triumph of any particular doctrine, and it is especially not with a friendly nation, that it would wish to render its commercial system exclusive; but it has calculated with attention the interests of its navigation, and with its usual good faith has made known that it could not for the present treat upon a basis of merely nominal reciprocity.

His Majesty's Government thinks that each nation is the best judge of what is favorable or unfavorable to itself; and, without examining too closely what motives could have excited the complaints of this republic, it is disposed to believe that there was some foundation for her remonstrances against a state of things considered as unfavorable to her navigation. If, however, both parties should come to assign their reasons, it would appear more easy to justify, in present circumstances, the pretensions of France than those of the United States.

In this regard facts speak. Dr. Seybert says:

"The extra duties imposed by the act of the 20th of July, 1790, constitute what are called *discriminating duties.* All foreign nations were affected by the system we had adopted. It seemed to operate like magic in favor of the ship owners of the United States.

"In the course of twenty years we raised our tonnage so as to be equal to that of Great Britain one century after they had passed the navigation act," &c., &c., &c.

Here now is a statement which cannot be disputed, and which proves that the encouragement given to our navigation is still far from operating like magic in its favor.

Statement showing the amount of American and French tonnage arriving in the ports of Boston, New York, Philadelphia, Baltimore, Norfolk, Charleston, Savannah, and New Orleans, from France and her dependencies, during the years 1817, 1818, and 1819:

	American tonnage.	French tonnage.
From the 1st January to the 31st December, 1817	71,738	15,105
From the 1st January to the 31st December, 1818	62,081	23,108
From the 1st January to the 31st December, 1819	54,277	25,945
Total tonnage	188,096	64,158

The comparison above is not made by way of reproach, neither is it meant to open a discussion, which it is thought would be of no use to either party. Both are sincere, each may hold more or less to its opinion, but they have an equal desire of arriving speedily at an amicable adjustment. This is the important point to be aimed at, but it was thought proper to answer the following passage of the note of the 26th instant:

"It is represented on the part of France that this principle is inadmissible, but for this refusal *no reason has been assigned.*"

The reasons are *facts,* before which all speculations, even the most seducing, must disappear.

His Majesty's Government is prepared, however, to make a sacrifice in order to give this Union a new evidence of its sincere friendship.

I say it is ready to make a sacrifice, because every reduction upon its discriminating duties will prove a loss, perhaps, more considerable than will have been calculated.

I have demanded some commercial concessions, and these are a consideration, and most assuredly will be received as such; but they cannot be a *compensation* in the present state of French navigation. Had they been asked as such, it would not have been sufficient to require such slight advantages.

In order to abridge the negotiation as much as possible, I shall, at the request of the Secretary of State, proceed to present, in general terms, some articles and considerations which may form part of the provisional convention.

The two contracting parties, equally animated with a desire of terminating a state of things as pernicious to the interests of the two countries as contrary to the ties of sincere friendship, which have not ceased to unite them; and until better informed about their individual interests, and about the connexion of those interests, (that they may agree upon a definitive arrangement of navigation and commerce,) have thought fit to adopt the following provisional articles:

ARTICLE I. The law of the 15th May and the *ordonnance* of 26th July, &c., are revoked.

ARTICLE II. The extraordinary duties collected in consequence of the two acts mentioned in the preceding article, from vessels both of France and America, shall be restored by the two parties.

ARTICLE III.—1. The extra duties actually imposed upon a foreign flag in the United States shall be reduced one-third in favor of French vessels laden with the natural or manufactured productions of France.

The duties upon the wines of France shall be reduced in the proportion mentioned in the note of Mr. Adams of the 18th instant.

ARTICLE III.—2. The extra duties actually imposed upon a foreign flag in the United States shall be reduced one-half in favor of French vessels laden with the natural or manufactured productions of France.

ARTICLE IV. The extra duties actually existing in France upon *cotton, potash, rice,* and *tobacco,* shall be reduced one-third for the said articles when the growth of the United States, and imported by American vessels.

ARTICLE V. The duties of tonnage and other collections, made by public authority upon the vessels in their respective ports, shall be regulated upon the footing of a perfect reciprocity, so that French vessels in America, and American vessels in France, do not pay more than —— per ton, (what shall be agreed upon.)

Other indispensable articles will be added, as also the consular convention, which shall be made with modifications which the Federal Government appears to judge necessary. If any difficulties should arise, the said consular convention may be postponed till the definitive arrangement between the two parties, and they may, for the present, only insert an article relative to deserting seamen, as the Secretary of State has proposed.

The Federal Government will have the choice of the two articles No. 3.

The first counterbalances, by a commercial concession and a smaller reduction of the discriminating duties, the advantage granted (Art. IV) by France. The second (Art. III) is the pure and simple reduction of the discriminating duties, but in a higher proportion.

It will be easy to explain why mention has been made in the fourth article only of cotton, rice, potash, and tobacco, and why it proposes an unequal reduction of the discriminating duties in case no commercial concession should be allowed.

France, in treating with this republic, in making to it some very substantial concessions, should not expose herself to certain —— which it is easy to foresee, and which she must at least guard against. Any one who will please to calculate with attention what she offers and what she demands, will remain convinced of her desire of conciliating, to the utmost of her power, the views and interests of the two countries.

There are other points in dispute, about which M. de N. believes an understanding may be equally had, but it is proper first to settle the question of which the present note treats.

As to the affair of the *Apollon,* it shall remain in suspense, as the Federal Government appears to desire; M. de Neuville presumes, nevertheless, to repeat that he sees with pain that all the difficulties will not be accommodated at the same time. In the mean time he sends to France all the papers concerning the *Eugene* and the *Apollon* collected by him, or which have been communicated to him by Mr. Adams, and earnestly wishes that the explanation already made, or which Mr. Gallatin shall make, may banish every serious subject from the discussions of the two countries.

M. de Neuville will be happy to have it in his power to transmit to his court intelligence sufficient to prove that there is greater reciprocity than ever in the dispositions of the two Governments.

His messenger will set out on Wednesday evening or Thursday morning, unless the despatches which Mr. Adams may have to entrust him with should not be ready. In such case, he shall await the orders of the Secretary of State.

G. HYDE DE NEUVILLE.

Mr. Adams to Baron de Neuville.

DEPARTMENT OF STATE, *Washington, May* 11, 1821.

In the communication from the Baron de Neuville, received on the 14th of April, an abstract was presented of six proposed articles for arranging by a convention the commercial intercourse between the United States and France.

Of these articles, the first, second, and third were adapted to secure, by concession on the part of the United States, important advantages to the commerce and navigation of France. They were articles, not of mutual operation, equally, or, at least, reciprocally beneficial to both parties, but of which the whole benefit would be for France, and the whole sacrifice or concessions on the part of the United States.

The fourth article was also exclusively for the benefit of France. It was a reduction of the discriminating duties of the United States in favor of French vessels laden with French productions or manufactures generally and without exception.

. The fifth article offered a reduction indefinite of the discriminating duties imposed in France upon four specific articles, and no more, of American produce, when imported from the United States into France in American vessels.

' ' The sixth article proposed to settle the tonnage duties on both sides on principles of reciprocity.

This project, therefore, consisted of one article of reciprocal benefit, one article of partial equivalent to the United States for a corresponding article of general benefit to France, and three articles exclusively for the advantage of France without any equivalent whatever.

In the memorandum transmitted on the 18th of April to the Baron de Neuville, as an answer to the above proposals, the offer was made to agree to the *three* articles, the operation of which would be exclusively favorable to France; the only equivalent asked for which was, that the sale of American tobacco in France should be released from the shackles of a monopoly and placed on the footing of all other articles of the traffic between the two countries.

And it was proposed that all discriminating duties and surcharges, whether of tonnage upon vessels or upon the articles of the traffic, should be abolished on both sides, and the principles of perfect reciprocity be substituted for them.

In the reply of the Baron de Neuville, dated the 21st of April, he observes that commercial concessions, being only of secondary consideration, may, for the present, be altogether set aside, and proposes to adjust the navigating question alone.

To which purpose he proposes a basis founded upon two principles; one, that the discriminating duties on both sides should be reduced; the other, that the reduction should be so modified that the vessels of both countries might share in the conveyance of the articles of trade between them.

. However reluctant the American Government must naturally feel at acceding to a basis, the avowed object of which was to burden the shipping of the United States for the benefit of the shipping of France, at consenting to deprive, by unequal incumbrances, their own navigation of advantages which it possessed, yet even this basis was not rejected. And in the note from this Department of 26th April, the Baron de Neuville was requested to specify, in the form of an article, what reduction of the discriminating duties on both sides he would consider as suitable to the views of France, and likely, upon the principle of mutual concession, to be just to the interests and satisfactory to the feelings of both countries.

It has not been without surprise and concern that, in the reply to this note, the President has seen, not the specification desired of a single article setting aside, as proposed by the Baron de Neuville himself, the commercial concessions as secondary, nor even a return to the project first presented, but a third project in five articles, not only blending again together the navigating and commercial concessions, but advancing new and additional claims of articles exclusively favorable to France, and suggesting that other *indispensable* articles must follow, without even an intimation of what the purport of those articles would be or to what they relate.

The objects of discussion, and suitable for adjustment between the two countries, are various and encumbered with difficulties in various degrees. But there is *one* which, in the present state of things, bears with peculiar hardship upon the interests of both countries, and must continue so to bear so long as it shall remain unadjusted. It is in the power of the two Governments, by an immediate agreement, to remove this altogether, and to restore the commercial intercourse between them, through the medium of their own navigation. Every day of delay to this adjustment adds to the injuries suffered from the present state of things by both parties. Not only commercial concessions, as remarked by the Baron de Neuville, but *all* the other subjects of negotiation between the two Governments, are secondary to this. It was, therefore, with much satisfaction that, in the Baron de Neuville's note of 21st April, the President perceived a proposal to arrange this interest first of all, and separately from all others. Pursuing this idea, I am authorized to propose that the discriminating duties, as at present existing, as well upon vessels as their cargoes, shall cease on both sides; that in their stead the tonnage duties and all charges upon the vessels shall be equalized, as proposed by the Baron de Neuville, and that the discriminating duties on articles of the growth, produce, or manufacture of the United States, imported in American vessels into France, or of the growth, produce, or manufacture of France, imported in French vessels into the United States, shall be respectively charged with an *additional* duty of —— per cent. on *the value of the article* at the place of lading, beyond the duty levied upon the same articles when imported in the vessels of the importing nation respectively.

Should the Baron de Neuville accept this *basis* of arrangement, it will only remain to agree upon the precise amount per centum on the value of all articles which shall constitute the surcharge; and it is believed there can be little difficulty in ascertaining an amount which, in its operation, will secure to the vessels of both nations a competent participation in the carriage of the trade.

The President believes that an agreement on this point, once concluded, would greatly facilitate a mutual good understanding upon every other. He is, nevertheless, willing to consider all the others suggested by the Baron de Neuville in concurrence with it. It is only to be remarked that reason and justice equally dictate the necessity of proceeding upon a basis of reciprocity. That either the commercial concessions must be set aside, as proposed in the Baron's note of 21st April, for after and separate consideration, or, if taken into the account, being all in favor of France, they must be compensated either by commercial concessions to the United States, or by *entire* reciprocity in the article relative to navigation.

With regard to the last claim of the Baron de Neuville, founded upon the 8th article of the Louisiana cession treaty, as set forth in his note of 30th March, and with regard to the cases of the Apollon and Eugene, as referred to in the Baron's notes of 4th and 23d April, with Captain Edon's report, distinct and explicit answers will at a suitable time be given. It may suffice, at present, to say, that after a deliberate reconsideration of the claim under the convention, this Government adheres to the opinion that the article has no more bearing upon the tonnage duty of eighteen dollars, than upon the previous discriminating duties, and that French vessels have, under the treaty and the existing laws of the Union, no claim to any privilege in the ports of Louisiana which they have not in all other ports of the United States.

As to the cases of the Apollon and Eugene, after repeating the remark heretofore made, that the tribunals of the nation are open to all persons interested in them, to obtain redress for any wrong sustained by them in property or person, if any has been sustained, it is only necessary now to add, that, if they are to be treated diplomatically with a view to arrangement by convention, it will be equally just and indispensable that the claims of citizens of the United States upon the Government of France should also be included in the negotiation.

M. de Neuville, to Mr. Adams.

WASHINGTON, *May* 15, 1821.

SIR: I have now the honor to answer your letter of the 29th of March last.

The terms of the 8th article of the Louisiana treaty are as follows:

"In future and forever, after the expiration of the twelve years, the ships of France shall be treated upon the footing of the most favored nations in the ports above mentioned;" meaning the ports of the territory ceded by France, Louisiana.

It evidently results, from the terms of this article, that the French nation is to be treated, *in future, and forever after,* upon the footing of the most favored nations, not in all the ports of the United States, but in those of Louisiana.

But what is meant, what can be understood, by the terms, *being treated upon the footing of the most favored nations?*

Is there but one way of obtaining the right to be so treated? or may it be held by more than one title?

Upon consulting the various treaties made between different nations, and particularly those which the United States have entered into with European powers, I find in almost all of them a definition of what is meant by *being treated upon the footing of the most favored nations,* and these definitions are so precise that I do not see how any controversy can arise on that point. In most cases relating to the rights and privileges of the most favored nations, the parties even go on to explain that the favor shall be free, if freely granted to another nation, or, upon granting the same compensation, if the concession be conditional; from which I conclude that the right to be treated upon the footing of the most favored nations may be enjoyed in two ways, either *gratuitously* or *conditionally.*

You, moreover, appear to me, sir, to admit this very material point; you even declare (and in this opinion I may readily acquiesce; I have, at least, no interest in opposing it,) that it is not necessary that the terms *gratuitously* or *conditionally* be expressed in the agreement; meaning, I suppose, where the condition of reciprocity is stipulated.

Alluding to the convention of the 30th of September, 1800, you say: "There is not a word in the whole convention saying that these favors shall be enjoyed freely, if freely granted, or upon granting the same condition, if conditionally granted; yet, who can doubt that this was implied in the article, though not expressed."

The article does, in my opinion, contain what I attributed to it, if not in express, at least in equivalent terms; but let us examine what you have stated in your answer.

In the article it is expressly said *that the two parties shall reciprocally enjoy, each, in the ports of the other, as far as regards commerce and navigation, the privileges of the most favored nations.*

It goes no further; it gives no explanation as to gratuitous or conditional favors, and perhaps it was unnecessary here. Yet, do you add, who can doubt *that this was implied in the article, though not expressed?* This admission determines the first point, viz: that there are two modes of being treated upon the footing of the most favored nations, and that the rights resulting therefrom may be enjoyed either *freely,* if freely granted, or *conditionally,* if granted upon condition to other nations.

We shall soon have to examine whether France has, or has not, from the very nature of the contract of 1803, a right to be treated, *in the ports of Louisiana, upon the footing of the most favored nations, unconditionally, and without further compensation on her part.*

This second question is of no less importance, but I think it right to detach it from that which here engages my attention, and the solution of which, must precede all further discussion.

Permit me, sir, here to suggest an observation which has struck me as being very forcible. If France, by virtue of the treaty of 1800, which secured her the rights and privileges of the most favored nation, has had a right to enjoy *every favor freely, if freely granted to other nations, or upon granting the same condition, if conditionally granted,* upon what principle, after the treaty of 1803, which secures the same treatment in a still more solemn manner, should she be reduced to the enjoyment of only such favors as are granted freely to other nations?

"If British vessels enjoyed in the ports of Louisiana any gratuitous favor, undoubtedly French vessels would, by the terms of the article, be entitled to the same."

It appears to me that, after your explanation just above cited, it would be equally allowable to say: 'If British vessels enjoyed in the ports of Louisiana any conditional favor, undoubtedly French vessels would, by the terms of the article, be entitled to the same."

Thus, sir, I hope you will admit, with me, the first question to be sufficiently settled.

France is to enjoy, *in future and forever, in the ports of the territory ceded by her, the privileges of the most favored nations;* and as the treatment or favor which a nation may receive is either free or conditional, it follows that France has a right to be treated in Louisiana upon the footing of the most favored nation, either freely or conditionally, unless it be proved that her contract is to form an exception; that she has already *paid for* the privilege which she claims, and has, therefore, a right to be treated, *without further compensation,* upon the footing of the most favored nation. This, sir, is what I think I can easily prove.

In the mean time it is evident, not only that French vessels do not enjoy in the ports of Louisiana the privileges reserved by France, but that they are even deprived of those which cannot be disputed.

I have already shown that, far from being treated upon the footing of the most favored nations, France, at this time, is, of all nations, that which is most unfavorably treated in Louisiana, which forms a striking contrast with the precise stipulations of the 8th article of the Louisiana treaty.

But what nations are (comparatively with France) treated upon the most favored footing in the ports of Louisiana?

All those, I answer, which enjoy in the said ports, whether freely or conditionally, by virtue of treaties or without stipulation to that effect, any rights, favors, or privileges denied to France. Hence, as it so happens, at this time, that the vessels of four different nations pay, in the ports of Louisiana, no other or higher duties than those paid by American vessels, I have surely a right to claim the same advantage for our navigation, by virtue of the 8th article of the Louisiana treaty.

You will observe, sir, that I do not speak of *all the ports of the United States.* Finding this last phrase repeated several times, and underlined, in your letter of the 29th, I have some fear not to have been rightly understood, or, rather, not to have used expressions sufficiently distinct.

France has nothing to ask; she claims nothing *in all the ports of the United States;* she has not to examine whether any or several nations indiscriminately enjoy, in these, any rights or privileges, nor on what condition such rights or privileges may have been granted; but as the ports of Louisiana are of the number of *all the ports of the United States,* and as France has a right to be treated in those upon the footing of the most favored nation, she claims that right as soon as it is found that the vessels of any other nation are treated there more favorably than hers.

But I find, sir, in your letter: "Were it even true that the English or any other nation enjoyed, by virtue of general stipulations of treaties, advantages in all the ports of this Union over other nations, inasmuch as they would not be favors specially limited to the ports of Louisiana, or granted with any special reference to them, they could neither by the letter nor the spirit of the Louisiana treaty give to France any just claim to the special participation, in those particular ports, of advantages there enjoyed only by general arrangements, co-extensive with the whole Union."

It seems to me that it would have been useless, and even perfectly idle, to make any *special mention* of the ports of Louisiana in the treaties and conventions, by which certain rights, favors, or privileges are granted in all the ports of the United States, since they are comprised within the denomination of the ports of the United States. Giving the whole is giving every component part, and in such cases the general term necessarily embraces every particular denomination: let us suppose a case. You make over to me conditionally the privilege of hunting on one of your estates, situated in a certain district; I am to enjoy this privilege if you grant it to others; soon after you sell or make over to one of my neighbors the privilege of hunting on all your estates you hold in the same district—it is clear that my right does not on that account extend to all your estates, but it certainly does include that which is specified in my contract or conveyance; the favor is *general* for my neighbor, but, as it regards me, is only *special;* for the general term, I repeat it, necessarily embraces every particular denomination.

Such matters it is not thought necessary to explain, because it is not expected that they can ever be subject to discussion.

But suppose, further, that the right which I so justly claim was not even granted by you; that I held it only in my own right; suppose it to be an express *reservation* which I had thought it proper to make on disposing, in your favor, of that estate which I had consented to sell merely to oblige you, and to suit your convenience. If I yielded to your instant and pressing solicitations; if, in order to persuade me to sell this estate, you had gone so far as to offer me not a mere conditional right *of chase, but that privilege free from all charges or conditions, to enjoy it with you to the same extent as yourself, and forever;* if I can prove this last assertion by your own documents, you will surely admit, sir, that this is an indisputable sacred right, rather in the nature of property vested in me, than a mere privilege over yours—*this is not a favor, but a bargain*

What may now appear a mere assertion shall hereafter be proved.

You do me the honor to state: "The stipulation of the eighth article is, in its terms, limited to grants of favors *in the ports of Louisiana.* The seventh article has secured to French and Spanish vessels, *in those ports,* peculiar privileges, to the exclusion of vessels of other nations; and the object of the eighth article was evidently to provide that, after the expiration of those twelve years, no such peculiar privilege should be granted, *in the same ports,* to the vessels of any other nation, to the exclusion of those of France. The whole scope of both articles is, by their letter and spirit, limited to special favors and privileges granted in those particular ports."

I must confess, sir, that, so often as I have read the eighth article, I cannot discover that it *evidently* states that, after the expiration of those twelve years, no such peculiar privilege should be granted *in the same ports* to the vessels of any other nation, to the exclusion of those of France. The article states, nothing can be more clear, *in future and forever after* the expiration of the twelve years, the ships of France shall be treated upon the footing of the most favored nations in the ports above mentioned. Nothing whatever is said about *peculiar favors granted in the same ports to the vessels of any other nation;* why, then, should we attribute to the article what it does not contain—I will add, what it could not express? and this I shall now proceed to prove. When France disposed of Louisiana she certainly was entitled to reserve any rights whatever in that province, whether *special, gratuitous, limited, or unconditional.* She sold her own property and had a right to fix its price, as the other party was free to accept or to decline the offer. The express reservation made by her, in the first place for twelve years, and then, on condition of certain events, *forever after,* was no more than a part of the price of the territory ceded, and by no means a favor granted by one party and received by the other.

"This stipulation was a part of the price of the territory; it was a condition which the party ceding had a right to require and to which we had a right to assent. The right to acquire involved the right to give the equivalent demanded."

I shall have occasion to revert to this opinion of one of the most distinguished men of this country, and which is so much in point.

But to proceed with my argument. It is easy to conceive that France was entitled, when disposing of her property, to reserve such rights as she pleased, *with or without reciprocity,* for a *limited time* or *forever.* "This was a part of the price of the territory." But if, as you observe, sir, *there is an express provision in the Constitution that the regulations of commerce and revenue in the ports of all the States of the Union shall be the same,* it evidently follows that no nation can acquire, by treaty or commercial convention, in the ports of Louisiana alone, the advantage which France enjoys there by a special title, by virtue of a bargain and sale; which instrument is singular from its very nature and cannot be repealed in favor of any nation, whatever may be its connexion or commercial interests with the United States, at least so far as respects the territory ceded by France. If, therefore, no other nation can acquire, in ports of *Louisiana alone,* whether *gratuitously* or *conditionally,* the special favor, or, *to speak more correctly,* the right which France has thought proper to reserve in those ports *"in future and forever after,"* surely I am authorized to maintain not only that the eighth article *does* not but even that it *could* not admit of the meaning which is attributed to it. Can it be supposed that the American negotiators had proposed to France to reserve an advantage or privilege which, according to the Federal Constitution, could never be realized? To give such an interpretation to this article would not be doing justice to their honesty. It surely must have some other meaning. Why not, then, adopt that which is most natural? *"We do not presume,"* says *Vattel,* *"that sensible persons had nothing in view in treating together,* or in forming any other serious agreement. The interpretation which renders a treaty null and without effect cannot then be admitted."* . .

"Every clause should be interpreted in such a manner as that it may have *its effect,* and not be found vain and illusive."* . . . .

Let us then leave to the eighth article its true sense. Its expressions are clear and distinct; and it is admitted that in the *interpretation of treaties, pacts, and promises, we ought not to deviate from the common use of the language;†* we also know that the first general maxim is, that *it is not allowable to interpret what has no need of interpretation;‡* and you allow, sir, in your letter of the 23d of December, 1817, that *the terms of the eighth article are positive and unconditional.*

It being admitted that the terms are positive and unconditional, and since, *in order to ascertain the true sense of a contract, attention ought to be paid principally to the words of him who promises;§* and since *on every occasion when a person has and ought to have shown his intention we take for true against him what he has sufficiently declared; ‖* what motive can there be for denying France a right established *in positive and unconditional terms,* more especially when the intention of the American negotiators, of *those who promised,* is sufficiently declared and perfectly manifest. On this subject it will soon be shown that the eighth article, which in itself is so precise as to require no corroboration, has withal, by way of corollary, a document calculated to remove every possible doubt, if any could still remain.

But, sir, you seem to think that the seventh and eighth articles have never been (in any respect) considered *"as forming part of the equivalents for the cession of Louisiana, and that the cession was in one treaty and the equivalents in two separate conventions of the same date;"* and finally, while admitting that the three instruments form but one whole, as it is expressly declared, you add, *"but the very form of the arrangements adopted by the parties shows their common intention to regulate the cession by one compact, and the equivalents given for it by others."* If we are ever to deal in conjectures, why should we not say, for there would seem to be more ground for the assertion, that the seventh and eighth articles of the convention are the *equivalents,* and the two subsequent instruments merely accessory and the *complement* of the bargain? We shall soon find that it is quite allowable to consider as a mere *accessory* what you, sir, regard not only as the principal part, but even as *the whole of the compensation.*

But let us set every commentary aside. The convention of 1803 cannot give rise to any mistake. The seventh and eighth articles establish, without the least ambiguity, the nature and conditions of the rights reserved by France. The ninth article coming next, because what is most important should be settled before points of minor consequence, sufficiently shows that the two supplementary instruments are only matters of execution. They, in fact, contain calculations of banking and exchange, and details of liquidation, which could not well have been comprised in the convention; and it is even, moreover, fully explained that those two instruments, signed on the same day, *"are to have their execution in the same manner as if they had been inserted in the principal treaty; that they be ratified in the same form, and in the same time, and jointly."*

The question, it appears to me, may be viewed in two different lights, and will still, in either case, equally resolve itself in favor of the claims of France.

In the first place, France may be considered as having reserved certain rights of property on disposing of her sovereignty in Louisiana, and this would appear the more correct view of the case; for, strictly speaking, the seventh and eighth articles are not the equivalents of the cession, according to the true sense of the treaty, as understood in 1803.

In the other supposition, considering the seventh and eighth articles as part of the equivalents, the rights and privileges therein secured to France will form, with the $15,000,000, the full and entire compensation for the territory ceded by her.

The privileges secured by the seventh and eighth articles are still, in either case, a right of property of the most sacred nature.

"This is not a favor, but a bargain." "This is not a free gift, but the fair price of that which has been sold."

But suffer me, sir, to observe, that it is entirely erroneous to suppose that *neither the seventh nor eighth article was ever understood by either party as forming a part of the equivalent for the cession.* Not only was it understood they did, and was so meant by the negotiators, but one of them, Mr. Livingston, while offering to the French Government the express reservation of the rights and privileges in question, as I shall hereafter prove, went so far as to say that, *by those means, France would enjoy all the advantages of the colony without incurring the expense of maintaining it.*

Let us now add to Mr. Livingston's expressions the formal opinion of Mr. Randolph, and it will be no longer possible to maintain that *neither the seventh nor eighth article was ever considered as forming part of the equivalent* for the territory ceded by France.

"I regard this stipulation only as a part of the price of the territory. It was a condition which the party ceding had a right to require, and to which we had a right to assent. The right to acquire involved the right to give the equivalent demanded."**

In your letter of the 29th of March last, as well as in your note of the 23d of December, 1817, you advance that, if France could claim *forever,* in the ports of Louisiana, a privilege which could be denied to her in the other ports of the United States, France would, in such case, have transferred only an *imperfect sovereignty* to this republic.

I have already endeavored to establish (letter of June 16, 1818) that *sovereignty* should ever be distinguished from *property;* in support of which I could cite many instances of transfers of a *full and entire sovereignty,* with the reservation of certain rights or privileges, in the nature of that which France holds in the ports of Louisiana. But the very terms of the article make it perfectly useless to discuss this point. The expression *forever* is sufficiently explicit. *In the ports of the territory ceded,* surely implies that France is entitled to the privilege claimed by her *in Louisiana only;* and it may, therefore, at all times, be denied her in the other ports of the United States, unless some other treaty or convention should intervene.

You persist, also, in believing that the right claimed by France is in contradiction with the Constitution of the United States, which declares that "all duties, imposts, and excises shall be uniform throughout

---

* Vattel, book 2, ch. xvii, sec. 283.　† Vattel, book 2, ch. xvii, sec. 272.　‡ Vattel, book 2, ch. xvii, sec. 263.　§ Vattel, book 2, ch. xvii, sec. 267.　‖ Vattel, book 2, ch. xvii, sec. 266. .

** Congress.—House of Representatives.—Mr. Randolph.—Debate of the Louisiana treaty, Tuesday, October 25, 1803.

the United States, and that no preference shall be given by any regulation of commerce or revenue to the ports of ·one State over those of *another*." I could add several very plausible arguments to those which I have already made against that supposed *inconsistency*. I might, perhaps, also contend, with some advantage, against the manner in which you explain the admission of the *State of Louisiana on an equal footing with the original States in all respects whatever*, in spite of the privilege which France and Spain still enjoyed in its ports. I think I should have some right to observe, that, in all *constitutional* questions, no modification is admissible, and nothing is to be assumed except according to the forms required by the Constitution itself; that representative governments scarcely admit of acts of mere courtesy; that they have the law alone in view; and that it is, therefore, to be presumed that Congress would not have emancipated, before its maturity, *the adopted child of the Union, nor have given him a preference not sanctioned by the Constitution*,* if, in fact, the measure could have been considered as illegal. But, sir, my Government *has nothing* to do with the question of constitutionality. It is therefore proper for me to decline discussing it; and I shall be satisfied with recalling some very respectable opinions which militate in favor of my positions or against what is objected to them, and destroy all idea of inconsistency between the seventh and eighth articles of the Louisiana treaty and the Federal Constitution.

† "Mr. RODNEY. It is contended that the United States have no right to purchase territory; ·that they have no right to admit the people of Louisiana to a participation of the rights derived from an admission into the Union; and that a peculiar favor is about being granted to the ports of New Orleans, in violation of the Constitution.

"In view of the Constitution, the Union was composed of two corporate bodies, of States and Territories. A recurrence to the Constitution will show that it is predicated on the principle of the United States acquiring territory either by war, treaty, or purchase. There was one part of that instrument, within whose capacious grasp all these modes of acquisition were embraced. By the Constitution, Congress have power to lay and collect taxes, duties, imposts, and excises, to pay the debts and provide for the common defence and general welfare of the United States."

"*To provide for the general welfare*: the import of these terms is very comprehensive indeed. If this general delegation of authority be not at variance with other particular powers specially granted, nor restricted by them; if it be not in any degree comprehended in those subsequently delegated, I cannot, said Mr. Rodney, perceive why, within the fair meaning of this general provision, is not included the power of increasing our territory, if necessary, for the *general welfare or common defence*. Suppose, for instance, that Great Britain should propose to cede to us the island of New Providence, so long the seat of pirates preying upon our commerce, and the hive from which they have swarmed, will any gentleman say that we ought not to embrace the opportunity presented as a defence against further depredations. Suppose the Cape of Good Hope, where our East Indiamen so generally stop, were offered to be ceded to us by the nation to which it belongs, and that nation should say, on our possessing it, you shall declare it a *free port!* Is there any member who hears me that would contend that we were not authorized to receive it, notwithstanding the great advantages it would insure to us?"

"There is another sound answer to the objection of gentlemen. *This is property ceded to us, by the power ceding it, with a particular reservation*."

‡ Mr. SMILIE. "If the prevailing opinion shall be that the inhabitants of the ceded territory cannot be admitted under the Constitution as it now stands, the people of the United States can, if they see fit, apply a remedy by amending the Constitution so as to authorize their admission."

§ Mr. CROWNINSHIELD. "It surely cannot be unconstitutional to receive the ships of *France or Spain* in the ports of the new territory upon any terms whatever; *it is a mere condition of the purchase*, and this House may or may not agree to it. Being a mere commercial regulation, we have the power to give our assent or dissent to the article in question; for I hold it to be correct doctrine, that this House, by the Constitution, have the power to regulate commerce with foreign nations, as well as with the Indian tribes, and that whenever the President and Senate make a treaty involving any commercial point, our consent is absolutely necessary to carry the treaty into effect.

"By giving our assent we do not injure the rights of the other ports in the Atlantic States, as the privilege is extended only to ports in the ceded territory. I consider the eastern or carrying States as particularly and deeply interested in the acquisition of Louisiana; it is true, their ·ships already visit almost every part, but under many restrictions, and I wish to see them sailing on the Mississippi without molestation or restraint.

"I am in favor of adopting these treaties, and they shall have my hearty support."

‖ Mr. RANDOLPH. "The unconstitutionality of this treaty is attempted to be shown by the following quotation from that instrument: 'No preference shall be given to the ports of one State over those of another State,' &c., &c.

"New Orleans, therefore, will enjoy an exemption. She is therefore a favored port, in contradiction to the express letter of ·the Constitution."

"To me, it appears that this argument has much more of ingenuity than of force in it—more of subtility than of substance. Let us suppose that the treaty, instead of admitting French and Spanish vessels on the terms proposed, merely covenanted to admit American vessels on equal terms with those of France and Spain. If we acquire this right, divested of the country, it would have been considered, and justly, as an important privilege. Annex the territory to it and you cannot accept it! You may, indeed, acquire either the commercial privilege or the territory without violating the Constitution, but take them both, and that instrument is infringed!!"

"I regard this stipulation only as a part of the price of the territory. It was a condition which the party ceding had a right to require, and to which we had a right to assent. The right to acquire involved the right to give the equivalent demanded.

"Mr. Randolph said, that he expected to hear it said, in the course of the debate, that the treaty in question might clash with the treaty of London in this particular. He would, therefore, take this opportunity of remarking, that the privilege granted to French and Spanish bottoms being *a part of the consideration for which we had obtained the country*, and the court of London being officially apprised of the

---

* It cannot, most assuredly, be correct to violate the principles of the Constitution *for a day.*—Mr. Griswold, House of Representatives, debate, October 25, 1803.
† Debate, House of Representatives, October 25, 1803.
‡ Debate on the Louisiana treaty, Tuesday, October 25, 1803.
§ Debate on the Louisiana treaty, Tuesday, October 25, 1803.
‖ Debate, October 25, 1803.

transaction and acquiescing in the arrangement, it would ill become any member of that House to bring forward such an objection."

*Mr. ADAMS. "But it has been argued that the bill ought not to pass, because the bill itself is an unconstitutional, or, to use the words of the gentleman from Connecticut, an extra-constitutional act. It is, therefore, say they, a nullity. We cannot fulfil our part of its conditions, and, on our failure in the perform-ance of any one stipulation, France may consider herself as absolved from the obligations of the whole treaty on hers. I do not conceive it necessary to enter into the merits of the treaty at this time. The proper occasion for that discussion is past. But, allowing even that this is a case for which the Constitution has not provided, it does not, in my mind, follow that the treaty is a nullity, or that its obligations, either on us or on France, must necessarily be cancelled. France never can have the right to come and say: I am dis-charged from the obligations of this treaty, because your President and Senate, in ratifying it, exceeded their powers; for this would be interfering in the internal arrangements of our Government. It would be intermeddling in questions with which she has no concern, and which must be settled entirely by ourselves. The only question for France is, whether she has contracted with the Department of our Government authorized to make treaties, and, this being clear, her only right is to require that the conditions stipulated in our name be punctually performed. I trust they will be so performed, and will cheerfully lend my hand to every act necessary for the purpose; *for I consider the object as of the highest advantage to us.*"

The opinions I have just cited have so much weight, that I shall not attempt to support them by further authority, and shall consider it as sufficiently established—

1st. That the rights reserved by France are, in fact, property vested in her, or, in other words, that the territory of Louisiana *is a property ceded with particular reservation.*

2d. That if, in 1803, the Louisiana treaty was deemed *unconstitutional* by some of the distinguished characters of the United States, the great majority of Congress declared itself in favor of a contrary doctrine.

3d. That the question of *constitutionality* is, and should be, foreign to France, and that her only right *is to require* that the conditions stipulated be *punctually* and *faithfully* performed. The French Government desires no more, and has, therefore, I think, a right to expect that a claim so well founded will cease to be disputed.

I read in your letter: "Nor is the proof that these articles formed no part, in the estimation of either of the parties, of the equivalents for the cession, confined to this tacit evidence in the forms of the negotia-tion. The seventh article bears upon its face the avowal of the motives by which it was dictated. Its in-troductory words are: "*As it is reciprocally advantageous to the commerce of France and the United States to encourage the communication of both nations for a limited time in the country ceded,*" &c. The reciprocal advantages to the commerce of France and the United States was the end; the encouragement of their communications *for a limited time,* in the country ceded, was the means. And the eighth article, following as a corollary from the seventh," &c.

I think I have already sufficiently shown that the two parties in the contract had but one and the same mode of understanding the seventh and eighth articles; but, even if I had not, in support of my opinion, those already cited, and that of Mr. Livingston, which I shall soon have occasion to produce, still would my position be incontrovertibly proved by the very terms of those articles.

You cite, sir, the introductory expressions of the seventh article. Allow me to invite you to examine its conclusion, which appears to me more explicit, and leaves no doubt as to the true intention of the nego-tiators. But, perhaps, it would be still better to cite the whole article. It speaks for itself, and suffi-ciently explains what induced the negotiators to fix the duration of the privilege conveyed by the seventh article, and to assign no limitation to the right of property secured by the eighth.

"As it is reciprocally advantageous to the commerce of France and of the United States to encourage the communication of both nations for a limited time, in the country ceded by the present treaty, until general arrangements relative to the commerce of both nations may be agreed on, it has been agreed between the contracting parties that the French ships, coming directly from France, or any of her colonies, loaded only with the produce or manufactures of France, or her said colonies, and the ships of Spain, coming directly from Spain, or any of her colonies, loaded only with the produce or manufactures of Spain, or her colonies, shall be admitted, during the space of twelve years, in the ports of New Orleans and in all other legal ports of entry within the ceded territory, in the same manner as the ships of the United States coming directly from France or Spain, or any of their colonies, without being subject to any other or greater duty on merchandise, or other or greater tonnage, than those paid by the citizens of the United States.

"During the space of time above mentioned, no other nation shall have a right to the same privileges in the ports of the ceded territory. The twelve years shall commence three months after the exchange of ratifications, if it shall take place in France, or three months after it shall have been notified at Paris to the French Government, if it shall take place in the United States. It is, however, well understood that the object of the above article is to favor the manufactures, commerce, freight, and navigation of France and of Spain, so far as relates to the importations that the French and Spanish shall make into the said ports of the United States without in any sort affecting the regulations that the United States may make con-cerning the exportation of the produce and merchandise of the United States, or any right they may have to make such regulations."

What appears most clearly deducible from the terms of this article is, that it was thought advan-tageous to the commerce of France and of the United States to encourage, in a *very special manner,* the communications of the two nations in the ports of the territory ceded; that the principal object was to favor the manufactures, the commerce, and the shipping of France and Spain. I can see no other advantage resulting from the seventh article for the United States, and it must be admitted that its stipulations are, in fact, advantageous only to France and to Spain. No reciprocity is granted to the United States either in the ports of France or in those of Spain. Their communications with France will, it is true, be more frequent, but *only in the ports of the ceded territory.*

Perhaps the article might have been worded with more care; but, after all, it expresses no more than I have stated. If the avowed object of the article was to favor, *in a special manner,* not only the commerce and navigation of France, but likewise the commerce and navigation of Spain, *without any reciprocal stipulation* for the United States, it is easy to discern what induced the American negotiators to demand that the privilege which France *was not alone* to enjoy in Louisiana *should be limited in its duration;* more especially as, during that time, *no other nation* could be admitted to enjoy the same favor. But where the privilege ceased to be common to Spain, the French Government, while consenting to modify it as by the eighth article, stipulated for the *perpetual* and unconditional enjoyment of the right of property thus reserved.

The eighth article does not, as did the seventh, stipulate that other nations shall not be treated as favorably as those of France in the ports of the territory ceded by her; such a condition could be imposed but for a limited time. But it was natural that, when yielding to the solicitations of the American negotiators, the French Government consented to cede Louisiana, it should secure to France the right *never* to be treated more unfavorably than any other nation in the ports of her former colony, whether those favors be purchased or not by such nations. That the transaction which, on the part of France, was at once a great sacrifice, and a striking proof of her friendship for these United States, should not, in the end, turn to her detriment, but should, at least, secure some lasting advantage to her commerce and navigation.

All this is not mere conjecture of my own. The facts are positive and clear, and every doubt must cease after attending to the following sentiments, not of the French negotiators, but of Mr. *Livingston* himself.

In the memorial addressed by him to the French Government on this question, "Is it advantageous for France to take possession of Louisiana?" he does not confine himself to proposing that France should reserve *forever, and without reciprocity for the United States*, the right stipulated in the eighth article, but even that which she subsequently held by the seventh article for twelve years only.

"Does France wish," says Mr. Livingston, "to introduce more easily her productions into the western country? Does she desire to accustom its inhabitants to her wines and manufactures, and to conquer the prejudices which the Americans entertain in favor of English goods?" &c.

"*All this can be accomplished only* by the cession of New Orleans to the United States, with the reserve of the right of entry, at all times, for the ships and merchandise of France, free from all other duties than those paid by American vessels. By those means American merchants established in New Orleans will be interested in her trade. Their capital, instead of being sent to England, will go to France, *who will thus enjoy all the advantages of the colony without incurring the expense requisite to support it*, and the specie which England, not enjoying the same advantages, and *paying higher duties*, could not furnish them at the same price."

This passage of the memorial of the minister from the United States is sufficiently clear, and we shall see that he furthermore takes care to corroborate its evident intention. Let us continue to follow the course of his argument.

"The possession of Louisiana," does he say, "is very important for France, if she draws from it the only advantage which sound policy would seem to indicate. I speak of Louisiana only, not including Florida, because I do not consider it as forming part of the territory ceded, as she may, by means of the cession, have a free trade on the Mississippi, if she knows how to avail herself of the circumstance by an understanding with the United States. She will find a market for a great variety of goods when she shall have accustomed the inhabitants of the western country to prefer them to English goods, which she can only accomplish by giving them at a lower price, and this she can obtain only by giving American merchants an interest in selling them, in employing there their capital, and by inducing the American Government to give them the preference. All this can only be accomplished by the cession of New Orleans to the United States, reserving the right of entry at all times free from all other duties than those paid by American vessels, together with the free navigation of the Mississippi.

"This will give her vessels *the advantage over those of all other nations*, and will not only retain, but increase the capital of the city of New Orleans; and hence, provisions for the islands will be purchased there at a lower rate, and French manufactures will be more easily introduced into the western country, which the United States will have no interest in preventing, every cause of rivalship between the two nations being completely removed.

"Thus will France command respect, without inspiring fear to the two nations whose friendship is most important to her commerce, and to the preservation of her colonies; and all these advantages will be secured without incurring the expense of establishments which ruin the public treasure and divert its capital from its true object."

What! Mr. Livingston, in order to induce France to cede the territory of Louisiana, offers her *more* from benevolent motives, established in the very treaty itself! She subsequently consents to accept or to reserve *less*, and even this shall be contested! and the article which secures this to her shall be said to have no meaning, and be supposed to have expressed a mere impossibility! I will here dwell upon an idea tending to explain how such doubts could have arisen. Mr. Livingston's memorial must have been lost sight of.

I shall now proceed to discuss, as briefly as possible, the error which you think you have discovered in the citation of my note of June 16, 1818.

On this subject I have already observed, in my letter of the 30th March last, that if even such an error had been committed, the strength of my argument would not thereby have been impaired.

But let us examine if, in fact, there be any such mistake:

There are but eight treaties, or contracts, between France and the United States; *four of these* are of such a nature as not to admit the clause in question; in *two others* it is *formally* expressed; in another it is mentioned in equivalent terms; the last, which is the Louisiana treaty, is alone *silent* in that respect; and this silence furnishes of itself an irresistible argument. I was, therefore, right in saying, that all the treaties, which could admit of that clause, mention *expressly* the condition of reciprocity. It is of no consequence that one of them should not positively use the words, *freely, if freely granted, or upon granting the same condition, if conditionally granted*. These words are mere accessory, irrelevant to the question, in the examination of which, you have alleged my quotation to be erroneous.

This question I shall now establish in its simplest form, and shall give it some extension, so as better to explain my opinion.

I say, that in all the treaties of the United States, not only with France, but with the other European nations, when mention is made therein of being treated upon the footing of the most favored nations, this condition of reciprocity is expressed, stipulating that the contracting parties shall enjoy the same privileges and advantages, each, in the ports of the other. One instrument, alone, is drawn in very different terms: it states, *in future, and forever after, the French nation shall be treated upon the footing of the most favored nations in the ports of the territory ceded by her.* The clause stops here. What are we to conclude? that, in fact, there was nothing *omitted, nothing implied*, by the negotiators, (sous intendu;) reciprocity was not due; and thus, therefore, no mention is made of it. It was not due, because the convention of 1803 had no analogy with mere commercial treaties of regulations; it was a sale, a bargain; the seventh and eighth articles are reservations of rights of property made by the vendor: *a mere condition of the purchase*, (Mr. Crowninshield,) *a part of the price of the territory*, (Mr. Randolph;) finally, because the territory of Louisiana *is a property ceded with a particular reservation*, (Mr. Rodney.)

Were it even a commercial treaty, still, since the condition of reciprocity is not mentioned, France would have a right to maintain that she owes it not, and she could allege in her favor a very respectable opinion in the following words of Mr. Madison:—(Speech on the British treaty.)

"The fifteenth article has another extraordinary feature, which I should imagine must strike every observer. In other treaties, which profess to put the parties on the footing of the most favored nations, it is stipulated that where new favors are granted to a particular nation, in return for favors received, the party claiming the new favor shall pay the price of it. This is just and proper where the footing of the most favored nation is established at all. But this article gives to Great Britain the full benefit of all privileges that may be granted to any other nation, without requiring from her the same or equivalent privileges with those granted by such nation. Hence it would happen that, if Spain, Portugal, or France, should open their colonial ports to the United States, in consideration of certain privileges in our trade, the same privileges would result *gratis* and *ipso facto* to Great Britain."

But we have not even to examine this question; that which occupies our attention is quite different, since it relates to a *sale, a bargain;* not a *favor, but a bargain.*

I think, sir, I have sufficiently proved, 1st, that there are two modes of being treated upon the footing of the most favored nations, either *gratuitously* or *conditionally.*

2d. That the ships of four nations enjoy at this time in the United States, and of course in the ports of Louisiana, the rights and privileges of the most favored nations.

3d. That France, according to the terms of the eighth article of the Louisiana treaty, has a right to be put in possession of the same privileges in these said ports, being part of those of the United States.

4th. That she owes, and can owe, no reciprocity, not only because no such condition is stipulated in the contract, but also because the privilege in question is a right of property reserved, or, if you prefer it so, is one of the equivalents of the bargain.

5th. That the intention of the negotiators cannot be doubtful, since the article, which in itself requires no explanation, has, as a corollary, an authentic document, which would irresistibly prove, by the very circumstances of the case, what was meant and intended if the treaty itself had not expressed it in the most explicit terms.

I therefore hope, sir, that after the preceding explanations the President will be pleased to order that in future, and forever, (unless in case of subsequent arrangements to the contrary between France and the United States,) the eighth article of the Louisiana treaty receive its full and entire execution, and that, by consequence, French vessels be immediately made to enjoy, in the ports of the ceded territory, all the rights, advantages, and privileges, granted to Great Britain and to other nations, by virtue of treaties, or in any other manner.

I have the honor, &c., &c., &c.,

H. DE NEUVILLE,
Minister Plenipotentiary and Envoy Extraordinary from H. M. C. M.

NOTE.—Is it likely that France can have intended to cede, for the mere consideration of a sum of fifteen millions of dollars, property which, even before the cession, was considered as having an incalculable value? which a distinguished member of Congress valued (debate October 25, 1803) at more than fifty millions, and which, in a well written article in the National Intelligencer of the 10th of October, 1803, was esteemed to be worth six hundred millions of dollars?

And it must not be said that France was ignorant of its value, since, before the cession, the American public prints took continual pains to inform her of it.

I shall here cite one of these articles, signed Columbus—National Intelligencer, September 2, 1803.

The writer complains that several of the public prints strive to take from the merit of Mr. Livingston's memorial; he expresses a fear that they should persuade France that it is contrary to her interests to cede Louisiana to this Republic. He cites the following passage of a paper published in Fredericktown, which would go to prove to the French minister in Washington that the First Consul would commit an act of great folly in consenting to abandon so vast a territory.

" The democrats cannot think the First Consul Bonaparte such a simpleton as to part with that country for any compensation we can make him."

Thus, adds Columbus, it is represented that nothing in our command is enough for those objects (Louisiana and New Orleans.)

Most certainly Bonaparte will never be regarded as a simpleton, nor will it be alleged that he had such affection for the inhabitants of these United States as to have had, in the cession of Louisiana, no other object but that of rendering them a service; surely he must, at the same time, have thought of his own country, and have intended, by reserving certain rights and privileges in favor of France, to secure, at least, a sort of compensation for the great sacrifice to which he was subjecting her.

In whatever light this subject is viewed, the cession of Louisiana must certainly be considered as one of the most inconsiderate and fatal measures of the usurper; but still, it is not allowable to suppose that he could, on this occasion, have entirely lost sight of the interests of France, and have consented to give up, for the mere consideration of fifteen millions of dollars, an immense territory, which will be a never-failing source of riches and prosperity to these United States, and which, to *France*, would have been worth all the colonies which she now possesses, or has possessed, in the two hemispheres.

The following opinion is such authority that I cannot better conclude than with citing it:

' I consider the object as of the highest advantage to us, and the gentleman from Kentucky, himself, who has displayed with so much eloquence the immense importance to this Union of the possession of the ceded country, cannot carry his ideas further on that subject than I do."*

* Sen. Deb., November 3, 1803.

Baron de Neuville to the Secretary of State.

[Translation.]

WASHINGTON, *May* 28, 1821.

All the relations of France with the United States, from the origin of the Republic, have been based upon a true and disinterested friendship the most complete.

This policy, so full of benevolence, is essentially that of his Majesty's Government, and the present negotiation attests it.

In the various propositions which Mr. de Neuville has had the honor of making to the Secretary of State, he has constantly aimed at the reconciliation of the views of the two Governments. He has endeavored to come, as near as possible, to an *equilibrium*, without, however, dissembling that, whatever arrangement may be made, the scale will always incline, more or less, to the side of the Union.

All that Mr. de Neuville advances above can be demonstrated by means of simple calculation and facts.

Mr. de Neuville has agreed to discuss at present only the question concerning the discriminating duties, but he does not mean to leave entirely the other points in question.

Mr. Adams' note of the 11th, treating of these different points, Mr. de Neuville thinks that he ought also to approach, in order that there may be no misunderstanding in the negotiation which ensues.

As to the 8th article, Mr. de Neuville will confine himself to saying that he flatters himself that his letter of the 15th May will have a more happy result than that of the 30th March. He therefore awaits with confidence the answer of the Secretary of State to that last communication, persuaded that it cannot fail of having an advantageous influence upon the combination of the definitive or provisional arrangement between the two countries.

The discussion relative to the *Apollo* and the *Eugene* has been suspended by common consent, and it has been agreed to await the result of the explanations which Mr. Gallatin has been instructed to give to the King's Government.

A despatch of February 22, which Mr. de Neuville has just received, orders him to reclaim against the acts of violence of which two French ships, the Eugene and the Neptune, have had to complain—violence committed without the jurisdiction of the United States by the armed vessels of the Republic.

In this same letter of the February 22, the Minister of Foreign Affairs refers to the instructions previously addressed to Mr. de Neuville concerning the Apollo.

These instructions have not yet reached the minister of France. He therefore requests the Secretary of State to be pleased to let him know if, posterior to the 22d February, the explanations have been made at Paris, and if they have had the consequence which Mr. Adams has always appeared to expect.

These documents are requested by Mr. de Neuville, in consequence of the extreme desire which he has and always will have of avoiding every discussion which might tend to involve the difficulties uselessly.

Let the question relative to navigation rest.

Mr. Adams has thought that he saw in all the propositions of Mr. de Neuville advantages for France *without sufficient reciprocity for the Union.* Mr. de Neuville judges otherwise, and he hopes that fresh calculations will prove to the Secretary of State that the Government of the King knows how to go as far as possible in the case of conciliation and concessions. As to the rest, Mr. de Neuville will make it hereafter appear that he is not afraid of taking a good deal upon himself in order to smooth the difficulties which ought never to have arisen between the two nations.

Ought they, at all events, to interrupt their relations *even for one instant?*

France had much to suffer in 1790 *from the additional duty* laid by the Union upon foreign vessels. This act was not only contrary to the interests of her navigation, but she considered it as a manifest violation of the treaty then existing between her and the United States.

Without recurring to this old question, let us stop at the following fact. It is, that from 1790 to 1791 the French tonnage was reduced to little more than half; yet what did the French Government in a similar occurrence? *He will confine himself to some representations.* What had it done formerly, on the occasion of certain extraordinary duties imposed by the northern States upon the French navigation? *It had remonstrated to Congress against this violation* of the treaty of 1778.

What has been its conduct during more than twenty-five years as to wines and other products of France, subjected to duties out of all proportion to their value? *It has remonstrated* and *only remonstrated.* What course has she pursued or does she pursue against a state of things as destructive to her navigation as to public morals—the desertion of her sailors? In short, to what means has she had recourse in other cases equally important and to this day uselessly repeated? *She remonstrates, she discusses, she waits.*

Mr. de Neuville is very far from wishing by the preceding recital to offer the slightest reproach, but he wishes to point out that the French nation knows how to be patient with her friends, and that she is always very repugnant to do herself justice by her own hand.

Mr. de Neuville will now examine the different propositions of Mr. Adams. He is convinced that the Secretary of State is no less desirous than he of the re-establishment of the direct relations between the two nations. It is therefore with frankness and confidence that, in this confidential note, he submits the observations which to him appear proper to produce this happy consequence.

For some commercial concessions, unimportant, and pointed out by Mr. de Neuville *only* as a sort of compensation for the sacrifice which France will make in consenting to any diminution whatever of her discriminating duties, the Secretary of State demands (memorandum of 18th April:)

1. That the discriminating duties be abolished on both sides.

2. That the law relative to the management of tobacco be repealed in favor of the Union.

The first of these two propositions, if it were acceded to, would be equivalent (at least for the present) to the total ruin of the French navigation.

The second would destroy all the economy of an interior administration; and can a foreign Government demand advantages which the Legislature of the country is obliged to deny *even to its inhabitants?*

By his last note (that of the 11th) Mr. Adams proposes to lay the additional duties upon the value of the merchandise, and consequently to abolish the surcharges which at present exist on both sides.

This proposition, which has never been made either at Paris or at Washington, could not be foreseen by the Government of the King. The instructions of Mr. de Neuville are therefore silent as to this basis.*

---

* Mr. de Neuville has had the honor to make known, verbally and by writing, the principal basis according to which he was authorized to treat.—(See the note sent on the 21st April.)

Nevertheless, as he would not hesitate to take upon himself to accept of everything which could evidently conduce to the same end, he has calculated and caused calculations to be carefully made of all the possible results of the proposition of the Secretary of State.

The results are such as induce Mr. de Neuville to believe that the error is on his side; otherwise, the proposition of Mr. Adams would evidently tend only to secure all the freight of importation and of exportation to the American navigation, and that without any advantage, even commercial, for France.

Mr. de Neuville must therefore be mistaken in his calculations; yet he doubts if in any case the proposition of Mr. Adams could produce the desirable effect, which is to establish as much as possible the equality of chances for the two flags in the participation of the commerce of freight. If, however, after a new examination of the projet, the Secretary of State wishes to pursue the discussion, Mr. de Neuville requests that he will be pleased to communicate to him the calculations and the proportion according to which the mean ulteriorly proposed could have been judged preferable to that, the basis of which appeared to be adopted by both parties, and the execution of which is in all respects the most easy, (the reduction of the existing surcharges in both countries.)

Besides, Mr. de Neuville is far from rejecting a proposition which submits to some modifications; as, for example, the laying the duty only on certain articles of importation and of exportation might perhaps produce sufficient combinations; but he believes he ought, nevertheless, to observe, that if it is decided on to abandon the first basis, it must be for one that presents itself more naturally than that which Mr. Adams points out. The question turns entirely on navigation. Now, would it not be more simple to make an additional duty, which might have only for its aim, to maintain a sort of equilibrium in the commerce of freight, fall upon the tonnage of the merchandise rather than its value.

But Mr. de Neuville thinks that, everything being seen and considered, the two Governments will find it better to abide by the first basis, and to apply the remedy to the present state of things, especially by an arrangement which ought to be but provisional. Mr. de Neuville says that the arrangement ought to be but provisional, since it appears to him almost demonstrated that sufficient data are wanting for establishing the individual interest of each State, and, especially, the connexion of their interests. In this case is it not prudence in the two Governments to commence by re-establishing between them, by an *amicable mean,* (*mezzo termine amical*,) the direct relations, safe to pursue the negotiation with the desire which both sides have, and ought to have, of attaining, by reason, by good faith, by the irresistible force of facts, the definitive arrangements of all the points in question?

A bargain too advantageous cannot be pretended on both sides without imprudence; here at least it would be bad policy. What ought to be wished, what ought to be desired, is, that the transaction be such as the prudent in both countries may applaud and wish to be lasting. What must be done for this purpose? The equality of chances must be established by prudent combinations; in a word, the conventions must be made to approach as much as possible to the only solid basis—*the reciprocity of advantages.*

Now, it must be agreed, there is here a point difficult enough to seize; it is that which experience alone can point out with precision.

Mr. de N. admits then this question is only a *trial;* only a provisional transaction, which will give time to both countries to develop their respective rights and wants; which will put it in their power to collect indispensable documents; (for after all, the very exact statements of the custom-houses, in one year alone, will resolve the question a great deal better than all the speculative calculations which could be made on both sides could do in ten.)

In fine, Mr. de N. admits that, without wishing to hold to an absolute principle, that without intending to sacrifice any rule or opinion too easily, each Government is still disposed amicably to subscribe to a sort of commercial armistice, in order to set bounds to a state of things which cannot be prolonged without grievous inconveniences to both nations; without, in some degree, relaxing the bonds of reciprocal amity and benevolence.

Therefore Mr. de N. will take upon himself—although it were easy for him to prove* evidently that already his propositions of 28th April are of advantage to the Union—to modify the third and fourth articles; in consequence, he will consent to render equal on both sides the reduction of the discriminating duties.

Mr. de N. had proposed that the reduction should be only brought to bear on the four articles which compose nearly all the productions of the United States, and to render the measure general for the products of France. This difference in the two terms of the stipulation would not injure the interest of the Republic. Mr. de N. could confine himself to the support of a pretension so just, to give weight to a very wise argument of Mr. Jefferson, in a case nearly similar—an argument which he will have occasion perhaps to produce hereafter. But Mr. de N. will still shorten the present difficulty by consenting to what the reduction bears indiscriminately upon the natural and manufactured products of the two countries.

Thus the propositions of Mr. de N. contained in his note of 28th April will rest upon a perfect reciprocity in the concessions. Will this reciprocity exist in the advantages? He is very far from believing it. But, in fine, his Majesty's Government will not be stopped by too rigid mercantile calculations, when the question is *of a trial,* the results of which will be perhaps eminently useful to both countries.

Now, what shall be the reduction of the extra duties? Every proposition of Mr. de N. could only be based upon the idea which he has, that, notwithstanding the encouragement granted to the French navigation, the balance has already been in favor of the Union.

The Secretary of State appears to be of a contrary opinion; it becomes useful, therefore, to verify this important point of the discussion; for, the reduction having for its object the establishment or maintenance *for the equilibrium* in the navigation of the two nations, it is but just that both sides should take into great, even very great consideration, the state of affairs before the 15th May.

Mr. de Neuville considers as a fact, without doubt, that in the year 1819, and the first six months of 1820, the navigation of France has participated in the freight of the importations and exportations still less than that of the United States. If it has been otherwise, if certain documents† can be produced in support of the assertion of the Secretary of State, Mr. de Neuville will be eager to prove that all that the Government of the King wishes is *a perfect equality in the advantages or at least in the chances;* Mr. de Neuville will, therefore, then consent to a more considerable reduction than he could at present accept, after the preceding considerations.

* It is a fact, demonstrable by the most simple calculation, that the least reduction will be a real advantage for the Union; that even a considerable reduction will be pretty nearly of the same effect for France.

† If these documents exist, Mr. Adams will much oblige Mr. de Neuville by communicating them to him.

Mr. de Neuville requests then that Mr. Adams will be pleased, if he adopt the last basis proposed, to point out the reduction of the discriminating duties which may appear to him advisable.

The answer of Mr. de N. will make known definitively if the two Governments can be reconciled. Mr. de N. earnestly desires it, and he believes he proves it by all the concessions which he takes upon himself to make.

Mr. Adams to the Baron de Neuville.

DEPARTMENT OF STATE, *Washington, June 15, 1821.*

SIR: In replying to the two letters which I have had the honor of receiving from you, the one bearing date the 29th of March last and the other the 15th of May, I find it necessary to restate, in its simplest terms, the question in discussion between us.

The seventh and eighth articles of the treaty by which Louisiana was ceded to the United States contain two distinct but obviously connected stipulations; that of the seventh article by which certain special privileges in the ports of the ceded territory are secured, for the term of twelve years, to the vessels of France and Spain, *to the exclusion of the vessels of all other nations;* and that of the eighth article, that after the expiration of this special privilege thus limited to the ports of the ceded territory, French vessels should be forever, in the ports of the ceded territory, on the footing of the most *favored nation in the same ports.*

Upon the terms of this article, by your note of the 15th December, 1817, you demanded, in the name and by order of your Government, and as in fulfilment of this article, that all the advantages yielded, *for ample equivalent,* to British vessels *in all the ports of this Union,* should be yielded, *without any equivalent,* to French vessels in the ports of Louisiana.

The answer which immediately presented itself on the first disclosure of this demand was, that the claim was, in two important particulars, broader than the stipulation upon which it was raised; first, inasmuch as upon the mere right to *equal favor* it required, gratuitously, that which was conceded to another for a just equivalent; and secondly, inasmuch as, upon a stipulation limited in all its parts to *the ports of Louisiana,* it required concessions yielded to others *in all the ports of the Union.*

As the claim was thus without support from the *letter* of the article, it was also apparently contradictory to its spirit and motives, as well as to the whole purpose of the treaty; and expressly incompatible with other articles of the treaty and with the Constitution of the United States. Such was the substance of the answer which, on the 23d of December, 1817, I had the honor of addressing to you in reference to this claim.

By your note of June 16, 1818, you replied with the allegation that France was entitled by this article to enjoy, *unconditionally,* in the ports of Louisiana, any advantage granted *upon* conditions to others in all the ports of the Union, because France was to be considered as having already given the equivalent by the cession of the territory; and especially, because you alleged that in *all* the other treaties between France and the United States it was expressly said that the two contracting parties should enjoy, reciprocally, any favor granted to others *gratuitously,* if the concession to others should be gratuitous, or by granting the same compensation if the concession should be conditional: and as no such distinction between *conditional* and *gratuitous* favor was formally expressed in the eighth article of the Louisiana cession treaty, you insisted, with great earnestness, that this variation in the phraseology of the article from that which had been universally used in all the preceding treaties between the parties, led irresistibly to the conclusion that no such distinction was intended, but the United States were bound forever to *give* to the vessels of France, in Louisiana, every advantage which, to the end of time, they might *sell for a price* to the vessels of other nations throughout the Union.

The great stress with which your note of the 16th June, 1818, dwelt upon this supposed departure from the universal language of the prior treaties made it necessary to observe that this only basis was an error in point of fact; that no such concurrence, in the form of language used in relation to the same principle, existed in the prior treaties; that the alternative reciprocity of *conditional* or *gratuitous* favor, far from being expressed in *all* the treaties between the parties, had in terms been expressed only in *one,* and that the first treaty ever made between them; and particularly that a treaty concluded with the same Government, as the Louisiana cession, and only three years before, contained such an article, stipulating mutually the advantages *of the most favored nation,* without any notice whatsoever of distinction between favors *gratuitous* and favors *conditional;* and that this variation in the prior treaties of stipulations, obviously intending the same thing, not only swept away the argument which you had drawn from the supposed universal coincidence of the former treaties, but made it recoil upon itself, and proved that the gratuitous or the conditional nature of *equal favor* was inherent in the terms themselves, and had only been expressly developed in the treaty of February 6, 1778, from the abundant caution of contracting parties new to each other, and above all, anxious to leave no possible question of their meaning thereafter to arise.

Your reply of 30th March last to my note of the preceding day insists that "all your citations in your preceding letters had been perfectly exact; that not only *all* the treaties between France and this Republic, (meaning the conventions which could be judged susceptible of the clause in question,) but also all, or nearly all the treaties or conventions between the United States and European Governments, say, in terms formal *or equivalent,* what you had understood, what you had read, what you had been bound to say."

Permit me to observe, that the simple question between us was, whether *all* the treaties between the United States and France, excepting only the Louisiana treaty, in stipulating the advantages of *the most favored nation,* had *expressly* added that the favor should be free, if freely granted to others, and upon the same condition, if conditionally granted. Your letter of June 16, 1818, in the most unqualified terms, asserted that they had; and from this position, connected with the omission of the same explanatory clause, in the stipulation of the Louisiana treaty, you had deduced and most earnestly pressed an argument, that this supposed solitary change in the reduction necessarily imported a different construction, and entitled France to enjoy, in the ports of Louisiana, *unconditionally,* every favor granted to others, whether with condition or without.

The demand upon a stipulation of *equal favor* to enjoy, without equivalent or condition, that which was conceded to others only for an equivalent or upon condition, was, in itself, so extraordinary, that it assuredly required something stronger than inferences and implications and equivalent terms for its support. The main argument upon which Mr. de Neuville's letter of June 16, 1818, had relied for this unexampled claim, was the omission, in the Louisiana cession treaty, of the *express* explanatory words alleged to be *in all the others*. But the fact being otherwise, the conclusion was more clearly the reverse.

It may now be added, that the only possible sense in which a stipulation for equal favor *can* be carried into effect, is by granting it freely, or for the equivalent, according as it is granted to others. For, if the same advantage should be granted to *France, without* return, which is conceded to others only for the return, who does not see that France, instead of being upon equal footing with the most favored nation, would herself be upon a footing *more* favored than any other?

In the latter part of your letter of March 30, without abandoning this demand of *exclusive* favor, built upon a simple engagement of equal favor, you seem to admit that the diminution of duties conceded to the vessels of several nations in the ports of this Union is not a favor, but a bargain; and you allege that, even upon this principle, French vessels should be exempted from the additional tonnage duty of the act of the 15th May, 1820, in the ports of Louisiana, because the vessels of Russia, Spain, Portugal, and other nations with whom the United States have no treaty, are not subject to it; and, repeating a remark which had been made by the chargé d'affaires of France, in August last, you say this is not merely a favor refused, but a burden imposed.

The vessels of nations with whom the United States have no treaties enjoy *no favors in the ports of Louisiana*. In the ports of Louisiana, the vessels of all nations are on the same footing as in those of all the other ports of the United States. There is no most favored nation in the ports of Louisiana, nor in any other port of the United States. During the twelve years while the vessels of France and Spain were admitted into the ports of Louisiana alone, upon terms more favorable than into the ports of the United States, and from which the vessels of other nations were excluded, they were the most favored nations *in the ports of Louisiana*. But the favors were confined both to the vessels of those nations and to the ports of Louisiana. They enjoyed this favor by virtue of the seventh article of the treaty; and the object and purport of the next article was to stipulate that, when this special and limited period of favor should expire, no such special and exclusive favor should be granted to any other nation *in the same ports*. Such is the engagement of the United States, and as such it has been and will continue to be fulfilled. No favor is now granted to any nation *in the ports of Louisiana;* and the eighth article of the treaty has no more application to the general commercial laws of the United States, operating alike in every part of the Union, than it has to the special bargains by which the vessels of some nations enjoy a reduction from the duties imposed by those general laws, *on the condition* of equivalent advantages to the vessels of the United States, in the countries to which they belong.

To the demand, therefore, that the vessels of France should pay no higher duties in the ports of Louisiana than the vessels of Russia, Spain, Denmark, or Portugal, pay in *all the ports of the Union*, the answer is the same as that given to your demand in terms by your letter of December 15, 1817, that the vessels of France should pay, in the ports of Louisiana, no higher duties than those paid by British vessels *in all the ports of the Union*. The claim is broader than the stipulation upon which it is founded. The stipulation is, both by its letter and spirit, confined to *special favors* in *special ports*. The claim is either to *general* favors, applied to special ports, or to *unrequited* favors, for conditional obligations. In every such case, and by either of the constructions for which you contend, the United States could not assent to your claim without favoring France, in the ports of Louisiana, *more* than any other nation. Instead of being upon the same footing as the most favored nation, she would herself be the most favored nation, and enjoy advantages conceded to none others. This is not the stipulation of the treaty.

In your letter of the 15th ultimo you remark, that the exemption of the vessels of other nations from the extraordinary tonnage duties levied upon those of France, inasmuch as it is enjoyed in all the ports of the Union, is enjoyed, also, *in the ports of Louisiana*, as a part of the Union, and, being enjoyed there, France has, by the engagement of the treaty, a right to claim the same exemption *in those ports*, although she is not entitled to claim it in the other ports of the Union. But it is this very generality, by virtue of which the vessels of other nations enjoy the exemption, which takes away from it all application of the eighth article of the treaty. Their exemption is not a *favor in the ports of Louisiana*, even when they enjoy the benefit of it in those ports. They enjoy no special favor there, and it is to such special favor only that the stipulation could give France an equal claim.

In your letter of the 15th ultimo it is observed that the question is, "What must be understood by being treated upon the footing of the most favored nation?" But this is not the question, because it does not cite the whole stipulation. The omission of the words "in the ports above mentioned," changes the state of the question from its special to a general character. The stipulation is, that "the ships of France shall be treated upon the footing of *the most favored nations in the ports above mentioned.*" The qualifying and special terms "in the ports above mentioned" apply both to the most favored nations and to the treatment of the ships of France; nor can France claim *any* favor in the ports of Louisiana, by this stipulation, without first showing that some other nation enjoys the same favor, as a special favor exclusively in those ports. There is no such favored nation in the ports of Louisiana. In the omission of those words, it is believed that their great importance to the question in discussion had escaped attention. Their restoration to the statement of the question will immediately show their leading to a different conclusion.

You observe, indeed, in another part of your letter, that you claim this favor in favor of France only *in the ports of Louisiana*, and you express your apprehension that I had misunderstood the purport of the demands in your preceding letters, because I had specially underscored the terms *in all the ports of the Union* when referring to the duties collected upon the vessels of other nations. I am well aware that you have demanded the special favor for France only in the ports of Louisiana; but you demand the special favor in the special ports, not as the stipulation of the article would warrant, if the case existed, because other nations enjoy the same special favor in the special ports, but because, by general laws applicable to the vessels of those foreign nations *in all the ports of the Union*, they pay in the ports of Louisiana less for tonnage duty than the vessels of France.

You observe that it would have been superfluous and even idle to make *special* mention of the ports of Louisiana in treaties granting certain rights, favors, or privileges, in all the ports of the Union, because in the ports of the Union are included those of Louisiana: that to give the whole is to give a part, as in such cases the generality necessarily includes the specialty. This observation, as applicable to treaties between the United States and other nations, is correct; but the inference to be drawn from the principle asserted is conclusive against the claim of France in the present case. For it is not to any such concession of a general nature, and which is enjoyed by others in the ports of Louisiana only because they are ports of the Union, that the stipulation of the eighth article of the Louisiana cession treaty applies. That stipulation, both in letter and spirit, is in all its parts special and not general. The whole transaction refers specially to Louisiana as distinct from and not as a part of this Union. The seventh article stipulates for special favors in its ports for a term of years, *to the exclusion of other nations*, and the eighth provides against the concession of similar special favors, after the expiration of the twelve years, to other nations, to the exclusion of those of France.

It is not, therefore, sufficient for France to say that the vessels of four other nations pay only one dollar a ton in the ports of Louisiana, while those of France are required to pay eighteen. For those vessels pay that dollar only, not because they are more *favored* than other nations *in those ports*, but because they pay the same in all the ports of the Union; because those nations have passed no laws excluding the vessels of the United States from carrying to their ports the productions of their own soil, by the excessive aggravations of surcharges.

There is no difference of opinion between us with regard to the principles which ought to apply in the construction of compacts, promises, and treaties. Admitting the correctness of all your citations from Vattel, I would specially invite your attention to that which forbids all constructive interpretation of that which speaks for itself. But I ask that, in stating the question upon the stipulation, none of its essential words should be omitted; that it should not be stated as a general question of "what is meant by being treated on the footing of the most favored nation," but as a special question of what is meant by being treated as *the most favored nation in the ports of Louisiana*. For when, upon a stipulation in these words, you raise a claim to be treated, in Louisiana, on the footing of *the most favored nations in the ports of the United States*, and when, to support this claim to special favor, in special places, resort is had to the argument that the whole includes all its parts, and that the generality embraces the specialty, what is this but interpreting that which has no need of interpretation? To us it appears not only so, but an interpretation as contrary to the manifest intention of the article, inferrible from its connexion with the article immediately preceding, as to its letter, which is special in all its parts.

Of the numerous extracts which you have taken the trouble of introducing in your letter of the 15th ultimo from the speeches of individual members of Congress, reported in the National Intelligencer as having been delivered at the debates on the passage of the laws for carrying the Louisiana treaties into execution, I regret not to have been able to discover *one* which has any bearing whatever upon the question between us, which is of the true import of the eighth article of the treaty. They *all* have reference to the seventh article; to the exclusive privileges which made France and Spain, for a limited term of twelve years, *the most favored nations in the ports above mentioned;* and the objection was strongly urged that this stipulation was incompatible with the provision in the Constitution which forbids any preference to be given, by any regulation of commerce or revenue, to the ports of one *State* over those of another. To this objection, the speeches from which you have cited passages were the answers; and they all distinctly assume the principle that the prohibitive injunction of the Constitution was not incompatible with the stipulation of the treaty, because Louisiana was acquired, not as a State, but as a Territory; so that, while she continued in the territorial or colonial condition, regulations of commerce different from those prescribed for the *States* of the Union might be established in her ports without contravening the Constitution. And there was not in any of those speeches the intimation of a doubt but that, when Louisiana should be admitted as a *State* into the Union, the regulations in her ports must be the same as in the ports of all her sister States.

But the third article of the treaty stipulated that "the inhabitants of the ceded territory should be incorporated into the Union of the United States, and admitted *as soon as possible, according to the principles of the Federal Constitution*, to the enjoyment of all the rights, advantages, and immunities of citizens of the United States." And as this article could be carried into execution only by their admission into the Union as a State or States, so, by their admission in that capacity, their ports became subject to that provision of the Constitution which interdicts all preference to one State over those of another. If the admission of a part of those inhabitants did in fact, by a short time, precede the termination of the period subject to the exclusive privileges of French and Spanish vessels in their ports, although the sentiment cited by the Baron de Neuville be perfectly correct, that the Constitution ought not to be violated for a single day; as no question appears to have arisen at the time of the admission of the State upon the application of this article, and as the privilege of French and Spanish vessels was never, in fact, denied them during the term for which they were entitled by the article to claim it; whatever transient and inadvertent departure, in favor of the inhabitants of Louisiana, from the principles of the Constitution, may have occurred, is, as the Baron de Neuville observes, a question of internal administration in this Government, from which France has received no wrong, and of which, therefore, she can have no motive to complain.

For the term of twelve years, therefore, from the time specified in the treaty, France and Spain enjoyed, by virtue of the seventh article, special *favors and privileges in the ports of Louisiana*. But it was not certain at the time when the treaty was concluded that the inhabitants could, within twelve, or twenty, or even fifty years, according to the principles of the Federal Constitution, be entitled to claim admission into the Union as a *State*. After the expiration of the twelve years there might be an indefinite interval of time, during which the special favors conceded to France and Spain, in the seventh article, might be transferred to other nations; and the eighth article was obviously intended to avert that contingency by stipulating that, after the twelve years special favor in the ports of Louisiana, the vessels of France should be on the footing of the *most favored nation in the ports aforementioned;* importing, by the proper meaning of the terms, and without any ambiguous inferences of specialties from generalities, or, as the Baron de Neuville's reasoning would require, of generalities from specialties, that no such special favor in the ports of Louisiana should, after the twelve years, ever be conceded to any other nation, to the exclusion of France. This is the plain and obvious meaning of the article; the only meaning deducible from its letter; the only meaning traceable to the intention of the parties, by its immediate connexion with the special and exclusive privilege of the article immediately preceding it, and of which it is the natural complement.

If the opinions cited by the Baron de Neuville from the speeches of individual members of Congress, *after* the conclusion of the treaty, as is now admitted, as bearing whatever upon the meaning of the article now in discussion, much less can it be expected that the proposals in a memoir addressed by Mr. Livingston to the French Government nine months *before* the negotiation of the treaty, and intended to show that it was not the interest of France to take possession of Louisiana at all, should have any reference to a treaty founded upon totally different principles.

The object of this memoir was to convince the French Government that it was for the interest of France, instead of taking *possession* of Louisiana, to put *the island of New Orleans* into the hands of the United States, reserving to herself the right of a free port there, paying no higher duties than American vessels, and securing also to France the navigation of the Mississippi. The memoir was written at a time when the project of establishing a military colony at New Orleans was contemplated by France; but even the treaty by which Louisiana was ceded to France by Spain had not then been concluded. There is an error in the citation from this memoir in the letter of the Baron de Neuville, (page 32,) of the 15th ultimo, where it is quoted as saying that "the *possession* of Louisiana was very important to France;" while in the memoir itself the expressions are, that "the *cession* of Louisiana is very important to France." The substitution of the term *possession* for that of *cession* is only noticed because it might give an erroneous idea of the whole scope of the memoir, which was to prove that the *possession* of Louisiana by France would be in a very high degree detrimental to the interest of France; but that she might render the cession useful to her by putting *New Orleans* in the possession of the United States, securing to herself the privilege in it of a free port, together with the navigation of the Mississippi. The memoir did not even propose that Louisiana should be *ceded* to the United States, but merely that New Orleans should be put in their *possession*, to be held by them, not as an independent and sovereign State of the Union, but on the same colonial condition as it was then held by Spain, and as it would have been held by France had she taken and retained possession of the province. Under such a project, embracing no other purpose of a change in the political condition of the inhabitants, the parties were competent to stipulate conditions like these without violating the Constitution of the United States, even though without limitation of time. But the compact actually made was of a totally different character. By the compact actually made, not only the island of New Orleans but the whole province of Louisiana was *ceded* in full sovereignty to the United States for a valuable consideration in money; an equivalent far more valuable to France than any benefit she would ever have derived from the possession of the province forever. The nature of that compact, however, made it necessary to provide for the future condition of the inhabitants of the country. Justice to them required that when thus ceded in full sovereignty to the United States, they should in due time be released from all the shackles of colonial bondage and assume their station as a free and equal portion of the Republic to which they were annexed. With this wise and just condition France could no longer claim to stipulate for the navigation of the Mississippi. She could no longer ask without limitation the privilege for her ships of exclusive favors in the ceded ports; both these conditions, perfectly compatible with a treaty upon the basis which had been proposed by the memoir of Mr. Livingston, in August, 1802, became quite inadmissible in a treaty founded on the basis finally adopted; the comparison, therefore, of the *proposals* in the memoir of Mr. Livingston, cited in the letter of the Baron de Neuville, with the actual stipulations in the third, seventh, and eighth articles of the treaty, affords itself a very conclusive argument against the present claim of France. The proposals are, that France should merely give *possession* to the United States of New Orleans, reserving to her own ships, without limitation of time, the privileges of paying there no higher duties than American vessels, and the navigation of the Mississippi. But not a word was said in them of a stipulation that the vessels of France should be upon the footing of the most favored nations in the same ports. The treaty is a cession in full and entire sovereignty of the whole province, but with no right reserved for navigating the Mississippi, and with the right of admission for French and Spanish vessels upon the same footing as American vessels limited to twelve years. Why these great and remarkable variations from the offers of the memorial? Why, but because they necessarily flowed from the principle of a cession in full sovereignty, and because all the rights and privileges of the Constitution of the United States were, by a new stipulation, secured to the inhabitants of the province? The cause and the effect are both palpable from every point of departure in the actual treaty from the proposals of the memoir. The limitation in the article of that which the proposals offered unbounded is the proof of its own necessity; and the substitute, in the eighth article, of equal favor *with the most favored of those ports*, after the expiration of the limitation, instead of the perpetuity of the special privilege, is illustrated both in its meaning and extent by the exposition of the unlimited offer in the memorial, of which it supplied the place.

Of the numerous citations in the letter of the Baron de Neuville, of the opinions of individual members of Congress, and even of anonymous publications in the American newspapers, one purpose appeared to be, to dwell with great earnestness on the supposed advantages of the Louisiana cession to the United States. Without referring to the estimates of nameless authorities, it is not necessary to inquire whether those of the members referred to were exaggerated or otherwise. It is, however, to be observed, first, that all those estimates were formed under impressions that the extent of the Louisiana cession was vastly more comprehensive than the subsequent declarations and efforts of the French government would have made it; and secondly, that probably all those persons, to whose anticipations the Baron de Neuville appeared with so much confidence, agreed as they were in the importance and value of Louisiana to the United States, would also have agreed in the opinion so forcibly urged in the memoir of Mr. Livingston, that the possession of the same country would have been worse than useless, highly detrimental and pernicious to France. Of this opinion, one at least of the individuals, whose sentiments the Baron de Neuville has been pleased to quote with very flattering deference, then was, and still is. He has no doubt that, in the possession of France, Louisiana would have continued to be, as it always has been, a burden, and not a benefit; and at the time when the cession was made, the only practical question to France was, whether Louisiana should pass into the hands of a friend, for ample compensation, or into the grasp of an enemy, for no compensation at all. Louisiana then was of great value to the United States, and of much less than no value to France; and the cession of it by France to the United States was one of those treaties which are the best and most useful of transactions between nations, a compact highly advantageous to both the contracting parties.

But, whether advantageous or otherwise, and whether to both or to neither of the parties, has no more bearing upon the present question between the two Governments than the speculative forecast of individual members of Congress or the lucubrations of newspaper *party* writers. The question is upon the true meaning of the eighth article of the treaty. That meaning is expressed in the words of the article. It is confirmed to demonstration by its immediate connexion with the preceding article. It is illustrated by its variation from the proposals in Mr. Livingston's memoir, cited by the Baron de Neuville himself. Nor has it been possible for the Baron, at any stage of the discussion, to state the present claim of France, in any shape, without essentially departing both from the words and from the spirit of the article upon which it would rely. When first advanced, he expressly demanded, upon a promise of *equal favor in the ports of Louisiana with the most favored in the ports of Louisiana*, a performance of equal favor in Louisiana with the most favored in *all the ports in the Union*. Upon a promise of equal favor, he demanded a grant, *without equivalent*, of that which had been conceded to others for an equivalent. In his letter of the 15th of May, he states the question to be *what is understood by being treated on the footing of the most favored nation?* omitting the words "in the ports above mentioned;" which words are part of the stipulation in the article, but the very insertion of which, in the statement of the question, would have been fatal to the present claim.

After the fullest consideration of the question in controversy, and the most deliberate examination of the arguments adduced by the Baron de Neuville in his several letters on this subject, I am instructed to say that this Government adheres to the opinion that the eighth article of the Louisiana treaty does in no respect authorize the present claim of France, inasmuch as, since the expiration of the twelve years specified in the seventh article, there has been no one nation *more favored than another in the ports of Louisiana.*

I avail myself with pleasure of this occasion of renewing to you the assurance of my distinguished consideration.

JOHN QUINCY ADAMS.

Mr. Adams to the Baron de Neuville.

DEPARTMENT OF STATE, *Washington, June 27, 1821.*

In the notes which have been received at this Department from the Baron de Neuville on the *navigation question*, the great and important point upon which the unequivocal interest of both countries seems most urgently to recommend to both an immediate adjustment, much is said of the friendly dispositions and conciliatory views of France towards the United States. To all general observations of this character the Government of the United States offers a return of the most cordial reciprocity. With this disposition thus mutually entertained the Government of the United States has been desirous of avoiding as much as possible all retrospection to acts on either part which, if not incompatible with it, have at least nothing of that friendly spirit in their effects. Yet, when such references are made, it becomes indispensably necessary to meet them by demonstrating either that the statement of them has resulted from erroneous impressions, or that they were the counterparts to measures of like character on the other side.

In the note from this Department of the 26th of April it was observed that, in declining the offer repeatedly made to France, by the United States, to abolish on both sides all discriminating duties upon the tonnage and upon the merchandise of the produce or manufacture of either nation in the traffic with the other, France *had assigned no reason for the refusal*. This circumstance was considered the more remarkable because it was of public notoriety that, in the competition for the carriage of the trade between the shipping of France and that of the United States, that of the former would have the decisive advantages of cheaper outfits and a lower rate of seamen's wages. When, therefore, it was proposed that the navigators of each nation should be put, in the ports of both, upon the same footing with the natives, the whole benefit of that arrangement, so far as it was the act of the two Governments, was in favor of the French shipping. It was, of all possible arrangements, that which, in its own nature, carried most into effect the demonstration of that mutually friendly disposition so earnestly professed by both Governments. Its tendency was to promote the same spirit of friendship between the individuals and especially between the navigators of the two countries; for all experience proves that as generous spirits are always willing to enter in the race of active enterprise and industry upon *equal* terms with their competitors, so nothing has so direct and unavoidable a tendency to produce discontent, irritation, and ill will, as exclusive privileges and partial favors to one of the competitors on the same field to the disadvantage of the other.

To the remark above alluded to, the Baron de Neuville, in his note of April 29, has replied by an extract from Dr. Seybert's statistical work, commenting upon the effect of the *discriminating duties* established by the laws of the United States in the year 1790, and by a statement of the American and French tonnage which arrived in the principal ports of the United States in the years 1817, 1818, and 1819; the former showing that the discriminating duties of 1790 had operated greatly to the advantage of American shipping, and the latter, that while, in the year 1817, the proportion of the American to the French tonnage arrived in the ports of the United States was nearly as five to one, it had, in the year 1819, diminished to little more than the double; still, however, exhibiting that proportion of superiority in the American tonnage.

It is not perceived that either this extract from Seybert or this comparative statement of French and American tonnage furnish a just or amicable *reason* for France to decline the fair and friendly proposal of the American Government to abolish the discriminating duties on both sides. The legitimate inference to be drawn from these facts could at most only be that, by the operation of a moderate discriminating duty in favor of the shipping of the United States, it had engrossed five-sixths of the tonnage employed in the trade between the two countries, and that by the counteracting effect of a very heavy discriminating duty imposed by France, her shipping had, in the space of two years, not recovered, even so, one-half of the carriage of the trade in her ships. But neither of these facts, nor yet both of them together, can lead to a correct conclusion of the effect which would arise from the extinction of *all* the discriminating duties.

In the Baron de Neuville's note of the 28th ultimo there is a recurrence again to the discriminating tonnage duties imposed by the act of Congress of July, 1790; to certain tonnage duties imposed by the northern States even before the existence of the Constitution of the United States; to duties formerly, but no longer, levied upon French wines; and even to the desertion of French seamen from their vessels. It is indeed observed that this *exposé* is not intended by way of reproach, but to show how patient, during the last thirty years, the French nation has been with its friends, and how unwilling to do itself justice by its own hands.

If the review of the treatment experienced during the last thirty years by the United States from the French nation, acting by their Government, the only action in which the *friendship* of the nation could have been usefully manifested, were calculated to elucidate the justice or the friendliness of her now reject-ing the proposal to abolish on both sides all discriminating duties, it would readily be undertaken. It is believed, however, that, as well from the situation of France and of the commerce between the two countries during the far greater portion of that period as from other considerations, this review would have no tendency to bring the parties to a more accordant view of the present subjects of discussion between them. It will, therefore, be waived; but with regard to the tonnage duties levied by the act of July, 1790, it is to be observed that they were imposed by Congress neither in a disposition unfriendly to France, nor from any interested propensity favorable to the principle of discriminating surcharges. These were reluctantly resorted to by Congress as a defensive measure necessary to counteract the operation of similar discriminations, as well of France as of other European powers. The principles of the American Government at that time are consigned in a report of the then Secretary of State, Mr. Jefferson, upon a message referred to him by the House of Representatives, "with instructions to report to Congress the nature and extent of the privileges and restrictions of the commercial intercourse of the United States with foreign nations, and the measures which he should think proper to be adopted for the improvement of the commerce and navigation of the same." .

The following is an extract from that report:

"Were the ocean, which is the common property of all, open to the industry of all, so that every person and vessel should be free to take employment wherever it could be found, *the United States would certainly not set the example of appropriating to themselves exclusively any portion of the common stock of occupation.* They would rely on the enterprise and activity of their citizens for a due participation of the benefits of the sea-faring business, and for keeping the marine class of citizens equal to their object. But if particular nations grasp at undue shares, and more especially if they seize on the means of the United States to convert them into aliment for their own strength, and withdraw them entirely from the support of those to whom they belong, *defensive and protecting measures become necessary* on the part of the nation whose marine resources are thus invaded, or it will be disarmed of its defence; its productions will be at the mercy of the nation which has possessed itself exclusively of the means of carrying them, and its politics may be influenced by those who command its commerce."

In the same report a view is taken of the regulations of France as they operated on the commerce and navigation of the United States, in which it is said:

"During their former Government our tobacco was under a monopoly, but paid no duties, and our ships were freely sold in their ports and converted into national bottoms. The first national assembly took from our ships this privilege. They emancipated tobacco from its monopoly, but subjected it to duties of eighteen livres fifteen sous the quintal carried in their own vessels, and twenty-five livres carried in ours; a difference more than equal to the freight of the articles."

At that time, cotton not being an article of exportation from the United States, the most important of their exports to France was tobacco. It is unnecessary to remind the Baron de Neuville that, in the present state of things, the monopoly of tobacco, which the first national assembly had abolished, has been restored, and yet that the discriminating duty between its importation in French or in American vessels is more than equal to the freight.

Such, then, were the discriminating duties imposed by the act of Congress of 1790. They were merely defensive; and even then the policy which the United States would have preferred would have been that of fair and equal competition. Such as it was, however, it is well known to the Baron de Neuville that their system could, but for a very short time, have any operation at all upon the navigation of France, since, from the year 1792 until 1815, if France had any commercial shipping at all, it was confined to a precarious and perilous coasting trade. And on the 3d of March, 1815, passed that act of Congress which offered to France, as well as all other nations, the abolition of all discriminating duties on the tonnage and merchandise of their country employed in the commerce with the other. There has been, therefore, no time since the establishment of the Constitution of the United States, no, not for a moment, when the United States would not have given a welcome assent to the proposal of putting their shipping upon a footing of the most perfect reciprocity, and of equal favor with that of the natives in both countries.

These observations were indispensable in reply to the statements in the two notes of the Baron de Neuville, from which, however intended, it could not but be inferred that the discriminating system had been begun by the United States, and that France had only counteracted it after a long endurance of its ill effects. The facts, as will be seen by this plain exposition, are directly the reverse.

With regard to the French and American tonnage, which, by the statement of the Baron de Neuville's note, entered the principal ports of the United States in the years 1817, 1818, and 1819, even that of the first of those years, that which appears in the comparison most disadvantageous to the shipping of France, exhibits a proportion of French tonnage employed in the trade three times greater than the proportional bulk of the articles of export from France, compared with that of the articles of import. By which it is meant to say, that if each nation had exclusively carried its own articles to the other the amount of French tonnage would have been three times less and that of the American tonnage would have been as much more than it appears to have been even in the year 1817. But it was in that year that the grievous discriminating duties upon American articles imported in American vessels in the ports of France were laid. This measure was taken, not only without notice given, but at the very moment when the American Government, at the instance of the Baron de Neuville, and as an earnest of their kindly disposition towards France, were reducing the duties which had existed upon French wines. It was a measure which operated upon the shipping interest of the United States in the most injurious manner possible. The American ship owners were taken by surprise. Going from the ports of the United States to France upon freights apparently equal to those of French vessels departing from the same American ports, they found, upon their arrival in France, the whole of that freight absorbed, and the adventure brought in debt by the surcharge of duty upon the cargo; while the French shipper upon a like adventure, from and to the same ports, upon the same freight, was making a most profitable voyage. The diminution of the American and increase of French tonnage, during the years 1818 and 1819, was accordingly gradual and permanent; but this was not the consequence the most unfavorable to the United States. The most pernicious mischief to them was, not the privation of profit to those of their merchants who withdrew from the trade, but the positive and heavy losses of those who persisted in it. A shipwreck was less fatal to an American shipper, under these circumstances, than a safe arrival; for against shipwreck he could be protected by insurance, but against these consuming duties there was neither defence nor remedy.

.This perseverance in a ruinous trade was the cause why, during the years 1818 and 1819, the diminution of the American and the corresponding increase of the French tonnage employed in the commerce between the two countries was so slow and gradual. It would have been far less injurious to the United States and their navigating interest if, from the establishment of these heavy surcharges in France, the *whole* trade had been carried in French vessels, for it would have saved the Americans from so much positive loss. How indeed could it be otherwise? The Baron de Neuville states, from Seybert, that a discriminating duty of only 44 cents per ton and an advance of only 10 per cent. on the amount of duties levied upon the articles of importation had, in 1790, been sufficient to turn the balance, before altogether on the side of France, entirely in favor of the American shipping. If so very slight an additional burden *operated like magic* upon the relative amount of shipping of the two countries engaged in the trade, how overwhelming must those duties have been which, upon *every* considerable article of the exports from the United States, amounting to more than a full freight, and which, by calculations exhibited last summer to the French Government by Mr. Gallatin, were proved by the lowest estimates to be equivalent to a surcharge upon the *average* of at least *twelve dollars* a ton. No shipping could possibly stand under it, and so enormous is the surcharge that any proposition to reduce it by one-third, or even by one-half, would have no effect whatever. It would still leave a prohibitory duty upon American navigation to the French ports. A duty of twelve or of twelve hundred dollars a ton could do no more.

By a statement, from the same source with those cited by the Baron de Neuville, of the comparative amount of French and American tonnage arrived in the principal ports of the United States in the first half year of 1820, it appears that the French exceeded in amount the American tonnage. This difference, compared with the statement of the preceding years, proves that the American shipping was in the last stage of evanescence, and that in the compass of another half year it would have been completely rooted out of the trade. For this and for other reasons, which it is not necessary now to enumerate, the result of the discussion has been to convince the President definitively that there is no prospect of an approximation to agreement between the parties upon any basis of *reducing* the duties on both sides as they now exist, and he thinks it would be useless to pursue the discussion upon that basis any further. It was proposed, in a late note from this Department, that a discriminating duty upon the value of the article at the place of exportation should be laid on both sides; and as the duty would be of the same per centum on both sides, its operation would, on the whole amount of tonnage employed, be advantageous to the shipping of France in proportion as the value of her imports from exceeds that of her exports to the United States. The Baron de Neuville, without rejecting this proposition, thinks that, from the result of all his calculations, its effect would be to deprive the French shipping of all share in the carriage of the trade. He proposes, therefore, that if the basis of mutual reduction should be departed from, that of a reciprocal duty upon the tonnage of the articles, rather than upon their value, should be assumed. This basis will, of course, be as much more favorable to France and disadvantageous to the United States than that which had been proposed from this Department, as the proportional bulk of the respective articles of export and import exceeds their proportional value. Nevertheless, from a disposition to make every possible effort to restore the direct commercial intercourse between the two countries, and with a view to a mere provisional arrangement, the effect of which may be experimentally tried by both, this basis is accepted, and the Baron de Neuville is invited to state the amount of the surcharge which he would propose on the tonnage of the articles.

Baron de Neuville to the Secretary of State.

[Translation.]

WASHINGTON, *June* 30, 1821.

., SIR: I have received the letter which you have done me the honor to write to me, dated the 15th of this month.

In my turn, I shall endeavor to re-establish the question which occupies our attention, and by removing some errors which it behooves me to rectify, I shall answer the new arguments which you have opposed to those advanced by me in the commencement of the discussion; from these I cannot depart, since nothing appears to me to weaken their force:

You do me the honor to state that "the eighth article stipulates that French ships shall be *forever, in the ports of the ceded territory,* upon the footing of the most favored nation *in the same ports.*"

Further, you add, "the qualifying and special terms in the ports above mentioned apply both to the most favored nation and to the treatment of the most favored nation."

Finally, you say, sir, that I have founded on the eighth article, which you cite, my remonstrance of the 15th December, 1817, tending to obtain for French vessels *in the ports of Louisiana* the advantages granted to the English nation *in all the ports of the Union.*"

I founded my demand upon the eighth article, *such as it is in the treaty of cession.*

I will here observe that, in my opinion, even though the article were expressed as you present it, my cause would still be no less founded. But it is prudent to make no concessions to so formidable an adversary. I shall, therefore, attack your principal argument in its basis, and shall endeavor to prove that it is erroneous, even in the point whereby you seek to establish that there is no question but of *special favors* to be granted specially and *exclusively* in the ports of the territory ceded by France.

Allow me, sir, in the first place, to make the following observation:

My claim is entirely grounded upon the article, such as it is in the treaty, as it should be understood *in the common usage of language;* and, in fact, it is always by modifying it, or, to speak with more propriety, by making it anew, that an attempt is made to oppose my arguments.

This eighth article, according to your note of the 29th of March, means, *evidently,* that, after the expiration of the twelve years, *no such peculiar privileges should be granted in the same ports to the vessels of any other nation to the exclusion of those of France.*

But the article appears to me, *evidently,* to stipulate quite the reverse. It has no relation to the *special right* which France reserved by the seventh article for Spain and for herself for the space of twelve years, but to all the rights, privileges, immunities, favors, which, after the twelve years, might be granted to other nations under any title whatever.

France is to be treated *in future and forever upon the footing of the most favored nation.* This is the whole question. If what you understand to be its import had really been meant, would it not have been more natural to have entirely suppressed the eighth article, and after the following clause of the seventh (*"during the space of time above mentioned no other nation shall be entitled to the same privileges in the ports of the ceded territory"*) to have added: "after the expiration of the twelve years aforesaid, if the same privileges are granted to any other nation in the same ports, they shall become common to France also?" But even these expressions, I perceive it, sir, would not come perfectly up to your idea, nor effectually overrule my opinion.

Why, then, was not the article worded in the following terms? they would naturally have occurred to the negotiators, if they had thought at that time of what you now conjecture:

"In future and forever France shall enjoy gratuitously, in the ports of the territory ceded by her, all the rights or privileges which may be granted *gratuitously* and *specially* in the said ports to any other nation."

The clause would then have been clear and precise, and I should, in such case, have perfectly conceived what you do me the honor to state in your note of the 23d of December, 1817.

"If British vessels enjoyed in the ports of Louisiana any *gratuitous favor,* undoubtedly French vessels would, by the terms of the article, be entitled to the same."

But, to be candid, how can it be asserted *now* that France is to enjoy only such favors as may be granted *gratuitously* to other nations, when we read in the eighth article:

"In future and forever, after the expiration of the twelve years, the ships of France shall be treated upon the footing of the most favored nations in the ports above mentioned?"

I therefore had reason to advance that it was essentially necessary first to define correctly what must be understood by the terms *most favored nations.* It makes but little difference whether we say the *most favored nation in the ports of Louisiana, or only the most favored nation;* since we have only to determine this first point of the difficulty, why should France enjoy in the said ports only such favors as should be conceded *gratuitously,* and not such as might be granted *conditionally.*

The eighth article says no such thing; why, therefore, by what law, by what rule, can it be positively established that "if British vessels enjoyed in the ports of Louisiana any gratuitous favor, undoubtedly French vessels would, by the terms of the article, be entitled to the same?"

Is there, then, but one mode of becoming, in any country whatever, *the most favored nation?* or, if the *conventional* law of nations admits, particularly in the United States, that this treatment may be obtained not only *gratuitously* but *conditionally;* if the Federal Government has been ever careful to have the clause inserted in its different treaties; if I find it in the conventions of 1778, 1783, 1785; if I find it again in the treaty with Prussia, negotiated by Mr. Adams himself, in 1799, how can the Secretary of State say now that "if British vessels enjoyed in the ports of Louisiana any *gratuitous favor,* undoubtedly French vessels would, by the terms of the treaty, be entitled to the same?"

France, I repeat it, has a right to enjoy in the ports of Louisiana the treatment of *the most favored nation,* whether this nation be favored *gratuitously* or *conditionally;* she has a right to enjoy it, inasmuch as the eighth article stipulates expressly that "*in future and forever French ships shall be treated upon the footing of the most favored nation in the ports of the territory ceded by France.*"

To pretend that she is to obtain this treatment in case only that it shall be conceded *gratuitously* to another nation, is subjecting the eighth article to an arbitrary interpretation; it is going in the face of a doctrine generally received; it is interpreting what requires no interpretation; it amounts, in fine, to the creation of a new conventional law of nations peculiar to the ports of Louisiana.

I now pass, sir, to the entirely new interpretation which you give in your letter of the 15th of this month to this same article. You make it express that, after the expiration of this special privilege, (that of the seventh article,) thus limited to the ports of the ceded territory, French vessels should be forever *in the ports of the ceded territory* on the footing of the most favored nation in the same ports.

If the question were only to new mould the article, nothing could be more easy, as I have already made appear, than to give it the sense which is now attempted to be ascribed to it; but we must adhere to its letter if we mean ever to come to an understanding.

It is certain that French vessels are to be treated upon the footing of the most favored nation: but where are they to be so treated? I answer, in the ports of the territory ceded by France, and this *ipso facto, gratis,* whatever be the title under which *the most favored nations* may enjoy the same treatment. Has it been meant by the article to say *the nation most favored in the said ports—exclusively in the said ports?* Finally, are we to read, as you now for the first time propose, *the most favored nation in the ports of the ceded territory?* Doubtless no. The last member of the period has no reference to *the most favored nation;* it can have no relation except to *the treatment of French vessels:* "*In future and forever French vessels shall be treated upon the footing of the most favored nation.*" Here the sense is complete with regard to the words *most favored nation.* All instruments found in public law clearly show what is meant by *the most favored nation.* There can therefore be no misconception in this repect. But this is not the case with the other member of the sentence. It is not sufficient to stipulate that French vessels shall, *in future and forever, be treated upon the footing of the most favored nation.* It is necessary, moreover, to specify *where* they shall be so treated; for otherwise the sense would be incomplete, and the article would have no meaning at all.

I shall avoid all grammatical discussion; but if the sense of the article did not evidently bear me out, and if I were under the necessity of showing by its construction that it cannot have the meaning which you attribute to it, I would cite, in favor of my assertion, several phrases of your last note, and would prove by their correctness that the eighth article, such as it has been drawn and worded in the treaty, cannot admit the argument made by you on the concluding words of the sentence.

It concerns not France to examine if any nation enjoys in the ports of the territory ceded by her any right or privilege *as a special favor exclusively in those ports.* She has only to inquire whether any nation is there treated upon the footing of the most favored nation, or, in other words, if the treatment she receives is more favorable than that of French vessels in the said ports. It is matter of small importance to her to know whether such nation, being the most favored in Louisiana, is at the same time the most favored in Baltimore, New York, or Boston, or to know by what title such favor is granted in the ports of Louisiana. The *fact* alone, when ascertained, is of itself sufficient ground for claiming, as her due, the fulfilment of the eighth article of the Louisiana treaty, which stipulates that *in future and forever, after the expiration of the twelve years, French vessels shall be treated upon the footing of the most favored nation in the ports above mentioned.*

Which, without gloss or comment, expressly means, "In future and forever, after the expiration of the twelve years aforesaid, French vessels shall be treated *in the ports above mentioned* (that is, in the ports of Louisiana territory ceded by France) upon the footing of the most favored nations."

It would be needless to add anything to this explanation, since the sense is complete; and it would be vain to seek, even in a forced wording (*redaction*) of the article, the *special favor exclusively* in those ports. The article neither expresses nor could express any such thing.

It does not express it, as has been just proved. It could not express it.

This, sir, you would constantly prove by objecting that, "according to the Constitution, no preference shall be given by any regulations of commerce or revenue to the ports of one State over those of another."

From this it clearly follows, in your own opinion, sir, that no nation can receive a *special favor in a special port*, and exclusively in that port.

What is not allowable at this time could not surely be done in 1803; and how can it be conceived that the only end of the American negotiators was to grant to France nothing but an illusive advantage, a privilege which she could *never be put in possession of* consistently with the Constitution?

How could the French negotiators have claimed or accepted such a favor? How is it possible to reconcile the idea of a clause which would amount to a mere *mockery* with expressions so solemn as these, *in future and forever?* It cannot, I repeat it, be presumed that discreet and sensible men, making a treaty and a solemn conveyance, have intended to make a mere nullity.

Let us examine what is proper to have taken place, what certainly did occur during the negotiation, and we shall find that it is not at all necessary to torture the expressions of the article in order to establish its true and positive meaning.

France was about to cede a vast territory in order to render air important service to a friendly nation; that territory was her property; she therefore had a right to settle the clauses and conditions of the contract.

This was not the case of a favor granted nor of a commercial regulation to be made by the United States; but, on the contrary, of a favor to be received, of a very important acquisition to be made by them.

This bargain could not but be very advantageous, in every respect, to the United States. France was not to gain as much by it. This she knew. But, although she willingly consented to make so great a sacrifice, was she entirely to neglect her own interests?

The French Government knew, at the same time, that difficulties had arisen already between the two countries; and the convention of 1800 testified that the parties had not been able to come to an understanding on the treaties of 1778. The provisional convention of 1800 was to remain in force only five years more; it might possibly be renewed; the parties might come to an understanding on the various points in dispute; but, at the same time, it was also possible that other discussions should produce injurious measures, impolitic steps, and lead to a state of things equally injurious to both nations.

Experience seems to have proved how prudent it was in them to foresee, and how wise to act in prevention.

Such being the state of things, how was it proper for France to act? I will answer, just as she did act; and this course was too obvious not to have been pursued.

She was about to cede an immense colony, the inhabitants of which spoke the French language, and were not likely to lose the French tastes or to abandon French fashions. It particularly behooved her to secure *forever* such a market for her productions.* Mr. Livingston *told her so;* policy and common sense told her to do so. It was, therefore, that the French Government, while ceding Louisiana, in order to give the United States a remarkable proof of friendship, and to do away every cause of rivalship between the two nations, reserved in the ports of the territory ceded a right or privilege, the full and entire enjoyment of which should be independent of all general arrangements of commerce or navigation existing at that time, or which might subsequently be made by the two nations. That the privilege should secure to French merchants the advantage of being *forever* treated in Louisiana upon the footing of the most favored nation, whatever might be the footing upon which they should be received in the other ports of the United States; therefore did France demand that, after the expiration of the twelve years, during which both Spain and herself were to enjoy an equal privilege, she, France, should have *alone*, in future and *forever*, a right to be treated, in the ports of Louisiana, upon the footing of the most favored nation; not of the nation most favored *exclusively* in the said ports, (which most assuredly the eighth article does not say,) but of the most favored nation, by whatever title, (which the article may be said to stipulate expressly, since no condition is annexed to the favor.)

It cannot, at all events, be asserted that this is a forced interpretation, since it agrees so perfectly with the text and letter of the article, which is, moreover, abundantly explained by antecedent facts, by the circumstances of the case, and by subsequent events.

It appeared to me, sir, that, in my letter of the 15th of May, I had clearly replaced upon its proper footing the question relating to a supposed error in that of the 16th of June, 1818. I thought it was proved that, whether there were or were not such an error in my letter, there would still remain the same force in the argument, which, alone it was material to attack. But since you have thought it proper, sir, again to return to this citation, which, I repeat it, even if erroneous, would not alter my argument in the least, let us again examine, with minute attention, if there really be any mistake on my part.

There are eight treaties, compacts, or conventions between France and the United States; four of these are of such a nature as not to admit the clause in question; the four others, being such as to allow its insertion, are:

The treaty of amity and commerce, of September, 1778.
The consular convention, of 9th November, 1778.
The commercial convention, of 1800.
And last, the Louisiana treaty, of 1803.

In the treaty of 1778, stipulating that both countries shall enjoy, each, in the ports of the other, the treatment of the most favored nation, the very same expression which I have used will be found in the 2d, 3d, and 4th articles.

The convention of 9th November refers to the 2d, 3d, and 4th articles of the said preceding treaty.

Two, therefore, out of these four treaties state precisely what I have attributed to them, viz: that each

* See the end of Mr. Livingston's memorial.

nation shall enjoy, in the ports of the other, the treatment of the most favored nation; *freely,* if freely granted, or conditionally, if the concession be *conditional.*

The third treaty (of 1800) stipulates expressly that the two nations shall reciprocally enjoy the treatment of the most favored nation, both as regards the rights and privileges of consular agents, (article 10,) and with respect to all privileges, immunities, liberties, and exemptions in trade, navigation, and commerce, and as to duties or imposts, of what nature soever they may be, or by what name soever called.

An attentive examination of these two articles will surely suffice to produce an absolute conviction that, when the condition of reciprocity is thus expressed, nations are reciprocally to enjoy the treatment of the most favored nations upon the conditions generally understood.

Thus, the convention of 1800 does state in *equivalent* terms what is stipulated expressly in the treaties of 1778. I, therefore, concur in your opinion, sir, on one point. In truth, *who can doubt that this was implied in the article?* But I cannot go on to say with you, *though not expressed,* since it does not appear to me possible to express anything more clearly in equivalent terms.

Last, remains the Louisiana treaty; and it is precisely because the treatment of the most favored nation is secured to France, *without reciprocity on her part,* that a discussion has arisen on these points. Where, then, have I committed any error? Perhaps it would have been more rigorously exact to have said the treaties, instead of *all the treaties,* since the reference was but to four treaties. But I would ask, sir, if that single word, *all,* was of such moment as to fix so repeatedly your attention?

Yes, I repeat it, all the treaties between France and the United States, (those, it is understood, which could admit of such a clause,) all the treaties between the United States and European nations, wherein the treatment of the most favored nation is mentioned, stipulate that it shall be *reciprocal.* And on examining the other compacts between nations, I find the same stipulation of reciprocal advantages in every case, except where, as in the Louisiana treaty, there is some charge imposed by one party on the other, or a privilege reserved.

Whence is it that one treaty, that of 1803, should alone mention, *without reciprocity,* the treatment of the most favored nation? The reason becomes obvious if we consider that it is the only treaty of the United States, *sui generis,* which does not relate to commercial arrangements. A commercial convention, grounded on expected contingencies, and stipulating mutual services and advantages which do not require any advances, has no sort of analogy with a *contract of sale,* a mere bargain. In this last case the vendor conveys his property to the vendee, who binds himself for the stipulated consideration, consisting in the other clauses, charges, and conditions of the bargain, as well as in the funds to be paid at hand, or by instalments. The right of the vendor, *his only right,* as you observed, sir, in 1803, *is to require that the conditions stipulated be punctually and faithfully performed.* This is all France desires. She has enjoyed, or might have enjoyed, during the space of twelve years, the right secured to her by the 7th article; and she now demands the fulfilment of the 8th article, which, as well as the 7th, is "*a part of the price of the territory, a mere condition of the purchase.*"

In your letter of the 15th you say:

"Of the numerous extracts which you have taken the trouble of introducing in your letter of the 15th ultimo from the speeches of individual members of Congress, reported in the *National Intelligencer* as having been delivered at the debates on the passage of the laws for carrying the Louisiana treaties into execution, I regret not to have been able to discover one, which has any bearing whatever upon the question between us, which is of the true import of the eighth article of the treaty; they all have reference to the seventh."

Suffer me, sir, to observe, that in thus taking the trouble to cite these very respectable opinions, my principal object was to answer the following passage of your letter of the 15th of March:

"From the obvious purport of the 7th and 8th articles, it is apparent that *neither* of them was considered, in any respect, as forming a part of the equivalent for the cession of Louisiana."

I was, therefore, right in not separating them, when my object was to prove that neither of them was considered, in any respect, as forming a part of the equivalents for the cession of Louisiana. And although the question of constitutionality cannot, in any case, concern France, it was proper that I should establish its having been completely settled in 1803, and that I was not alone of opinion that Louisiana was properly ceded, "*with particular reservation, with a condition which the party ceding had a right to require, and to which the United States had a right to assent.*" It makes but little difference what particular article of the treaty gave rise to the speeches cited, if they had a full bearing on the whole convention, and if every argument adduced on the seventh article is, *a fortiori,* applicable to the eighth.

The 7th and 8th articles are both *a part of the equivalents for the cession,* or, rather, they are reservations of rights of property.

France owed no reciprocity, and therefore it is that no reciprocity was stipulated on her part; it was no error or omission of the negotiators.

I read, sir, in your letter of the 15th: "In the latter part of your letter of the 30th of March, without abandoning this demand of *exclusive* favor, you *seem to admit* that the diminution of duties conceded to the vessels of several nations, in the ports of this Union, is not a favor, but a bargain." Now, sir, I admit nothing of the kind in my letter of the 30th; far from *seeming to admit,* my expressions in the very phrase cited by you, sir, are, *Je ne saurois admettre,* I cannot admit.

As to the question treated of in that letter, I shall confine myself to expressing again my surprise that France should be denied, in the ports of the territory ceded by her, even those advantages which are granted to nations having no treaty or convention with the United States. *Those nations, you say, sir, have passed no laws excluding the vessels of the United States from carrying to their ports the productions of their own soil by the excessive aggravation of surcharges.* To this I shall answer, that France has done no such thing, and that her discriminating duties are far from having* *operated like magic in favor of the ship owners* of France, and have not even secured to her navigation a due share in the carrying trade. And, after all, where is it stipulated that France shall be treated, in Louisiana, upon the footing of the most favored nations, (as by the 8th article,) only in case she shall make no regulations on navigation injurious to the interest of the United States, or which might be supposed contrary thereto? Is not every nation free to regulate her own commerce and navigation as she sees fit? If her laws amount to prohibitions, if they appear unjust, if they are deemed injurious, it is, no doubt, allowable to adopt similar countervailing

---

*These extra charges were sufficient to drive from our ports the greatest proportion of the foreign tonnage; all foreign nations were affected by the system we had adopted; it seemed to operate like magic in favor of the ship owners of the United States.—*Dr. Seybert on the American discriminating duties.*

measures. But such measures on her part cannot make it justifiable to lose sight of the respect due to a sacred right of property which is absolute in its nature, and is independent of all regulations of commerce and navigation.

Observe, moreover, sir, that French vessels are not treated in the ports of Louisiana either *upon the footing of the most favored nations, nor upon that of nations having no treaty or convention with the United States,** nor even upon the footing of those in whose ports the vessels of the United States are not ordinarily permitted to go and trade.* This requires no comment.

You have stated, sir, that all the speeches cited by me tend to prove that there was no inconsistency between the Federal Constitution and certain conditions of the treaty of cession, "because Louisiana was acquired not as a State, but as a Territory; so that while she continued in the territorial or colonial condition, regulations of commerce different from those prescribed for the States of the Union might be established in their ports without contravening the Constitution."

I have already answered this argument by stating the fact that the seventh article which, in your opinion, was judged to be compatible with the Constitution so long only as Louisiana should continue to be a colony, received its full execution *during three years after Louisiana had become a State.*

To this you reply, that in this there was in truth a violation of the Constitution, "from which France has received no wrong, and of which she can have no motive to complain;" but if we have adopted in Europe, as a monarchial principle, that *the King can do no wrong,* we also expressly admit, with Mr. Griswold, that the Legislature *cannot violate the Constitution even for a day.* I look upon it as certain and indubitable that Congress had not the desire, as it had not the power, to violate *intentionally* the Constitution for *a day, nor even for an hour.* Besides, how can it be considered as a *transient, inadvertent departure* from the Constitution, that the unconstitutional execution of the seventh article should have place, not for a day, but for three years, while all the discussion which the speeches referred to had tended only to establish that in such case there would, in fact, be a violation of the Constitution?

You add, sir, "there was not, in any one of those speeches, the intimation of a doubt but that when Louisiana should be admitted as a *State* into the Union, the regulations in her ports must be the same as in the ports of all her sister States."

And, in another part of your letter, you again repeat "that, by the admission of Louisiana into the Union, her ports became subject to that provision of the Constitution which interdicts all preference to the ports of one State over those of another."

I think I have shown that this article of the Constitution is not in any case applicable to the express stipulations of a sale and conveyance of property, and that it did not belong to France to examine the question. I could, perhaps, prove also that the two last assertions are not, in every point, rigorously correct. You will find, sir, that in those very speeches it has been questioned whether *all* the ports of the United States were, at that time, subject to the same commercial regulations.

"But, turning to our statute books, (says Mr. Randolph,) it will be perceived that at present there are some ports entitled to benefits which other ports do not enjoy." He shows, in another place, referring to a treaty between the United States and Great Britain, "that several ports of the State of New York have a system of customs and duties peculiar to themselves, and in this, (he says,) gentlemen could not avail themselves of the distinction taken between a Territory and State, even if they were so disposed, since the ports in question were *ports of a State.* †

We see, besides, that Mr. Rodney's principal argument is grounded, not on the article of the Constitution mentioned by you, but on that which gives to Congress the power to *provide for the general welfare.*

Let us conclude, from the various instances, that the question of constitutionality is foreign to that which we now discuss; that it is of little moment to know whether a State may or may not modify its administration of customs and duties; that even this point was discussed in 1803; that, whether questioned or not, the right of France remains still the same, because it is a right of property, *not a favor, but a bargain;* and, finally, that the least doubtful point in all human transactions is the necessity of fulfilling, *punctually* and *faithfully,* all their conditions and stipulations.

As to the memoir of Mr. Livingston, its object, in your opinion, sir, was to convince the French Government that it was its interest, instead of taking possession of Louisiana, to put New Orleans into the hands of the United States.

In the first place, I shall ask, what would then have become of the terrritory? and whether, in such case, Mr. Livingston's object, which was to prevent every collision, to remove every motive of rivalship between the two nations, would have been fully accomplished? But every discussion on that subject would, I think, be quite useless, the perusal of the memoir being sufficient alone to remove every doubt.

Its very basis is this question: "Is it the interest of France to take possession *of Louisiana?*"

It runs from beginning to end on that subject, and no other.

If in one paragraph it proposes to put the United States in possession of New Orleans, it is palpable from that very paragraph, and from the following, that the *memoir* refers not to New Orleans alone, but to the whole of Louisiana.

Let us cite some passages:

"Who then will be willing to cultivate *Louisiana* with slaves?"

"*Louisiana* is surrounded by an immense wilderness."

"What advantage can France derive from settling that colony?"

"The productions of *Louisiana* being the same with those of the Antilles, &c., &c., it grows to evidence that, with respect to commerce, the settling (colonization) of Louisiana, would be prejudicial to France, since it would deprive her other colonies of capitals which might be more usefully employed there."

"The possession of *Louisiana* is, however, very important to France if she applies it to the only use which sound policy would seem to approve. I speak of *Louisiana* only, and in this I do not mean to comprehend the Floridas, because I think they are no part of the cession; as she can acquire by this cession the right to carry on the Mississippi a free trade, &c., &c."

Further, after having taken pains to explain all the advantages which France is to derive from the cession of *Louisiana* to the United States, Mr. Livingston adds:

---

* American tonnage law, article 1st.

† Mr. Randolph said he did not mean to affirm that this exemption made by the treaty of London was constitutional. To solve that question was not his object. He would, however, observe, that France had a view, in signing the treaty, to ascertain whether all its articles were constitutional or not, since here, as well as elsewhere, the most enlightened men frequently disagree on certain points of legislation.

"All this can take place only by the cession of New Orleans to the United States, with the reserve of the right of entry at all times, free from all other duties than those paid by American vessels, together with the right of navigation on the Mississippi."

It becomes evident that he means the cession of the whole of *Louisiana*, since he advises France to secure to herself the navigation on the Mississippi; for how could this stipulation have been necessary if she were to have retained possession of the western shore?

In what case does Mr. Livingston mention New Orleans only? It is to her he speaks of a free port, and of securing a free access to French vessels and merchandise. And in these particulars it is plain that he could not express himself otherwise, New Orleans being at that time the only port in Louisiana.

But what is the object of all the arguments of the minister of the United States?

To dissuade France from taking possession of *Louisiana;* to prove that under her government, *Louisiana* never would, nor ever could flourish; that not only in relation to commerce, but also with respect to policy, the settling of Louisiana could not be profitable to her; that she would find greater advantages in securing to herself the solid friendship of the United States, than in the acquisition of a Territory which would become a source of *rivalship;* that she ought not to change a natural ally from a warm friend into a suspicious and jealous neighbor, &c.

What is Mr. Livingston's conclusion? That, by adopting this opinion, France would easily be able to introduce into the western country the products of her manufactures, which the United States would have no interest to prevent, every cause of *rivalship* between the two nations being thus removed.

What more, I ask, can be wanting to prove that the memoir relates not to the cession of New Orleans alone, but to that of the whole Territory of Louisiana?

You observe that Mr. Livingston proposes to France to cede New Orleans to the United States, to be taken possession of by them, not as an independent and sovereign State, but *merely* on the same colonial condition it was held in by Spain, and as it would have been held by France, had she taken and retained possession of the province.

To this I can make no other answer than that I have not been able, even on the closest examination, to discover any such thing expressed in the memoir; the word *merely* is not to be seen there any more than the word *exclusively* in the eighth article of the treaty. There is nothing in the memorial that could suggest the idea of Louisiana continuing under the colonial condition, when belonging to the United States.

You do me the honor to state, sir, that Mr. Livingston's memoir was presented to the French Government in August, 1802; and yet I read in another part of your letter that it was written at a time when even the treaty ceding Louisiana *to France* was not concluded. In this there is error of date, since the treaty of St. Ildephonso, by which Spain ceded the colony or province of Louisiana to France, was signed on the 1st of October, 1800, as is stated in the convention of 1803, and in all the other documents of that period, which gives it a date more than twenty months anterior to Mr. Livingston's memoir.

The error which you think you have found in the citation of page 32 of my letter of the 15th May does not exist. I have now the honor to send you a copy of the original memoir, addressed, in Mr. Livingston's own handwriting, to the French Government; you will there find the word *possession*, and not *cession* of Louisiana, in the paragraph alluded to.

In my letter of the 15th of May I called to mind what, even at the time of the cession, was the acknowledged value of the territory ceded by France, and cited not only the opinions of various writers, but also those of several distinguished members of Congress. To this you reply that, "all those estimates were formed under impressions that the extent of the Louisiana cession was vastly more comprehensive than the subsequent declarations and efforts of the French Government would have made it."

I do not know to what subsequent declarations you allude.

In the first article of the treaty it is expressly stated that the French Government cedes Louisiana, "*in order to give the United States a remarkable proof of friendship.*" In all their subsequent declarations I find expressions of the same good will and friendly dispositions, combined with a sense of justice, from which even friendship should never depart. As to the *efforts of the French Government*, as you do not specify them nor indicate of what description they were, I wish to persuade myself, sir, that you thereby allude to those efforts which, on more than one important occasion within the last forty-three years, France has taken a pleasure in making to promote the prosperity of these United States.

What were the real motives which induced the French Government not to retain Louisiana? I see no other, nor can discover any, but those expressed in the treaty, and, therefore, shall not discuss this point. I can, however, assert that France has, at all times, proved that she could do much for her friends, and had little fear of her enemies. For this reason, "the opinion *so forcibly urged in the memoir of Mr. Livingston*" has made but little impression on my mind; and if such a question were not irrelevant to the present subject of discussion, I believe that I could easily show that France could have retained her Territory of Louisiana, as well in war as in peace.

I cannot conclude better than by citing, in support of my cause, the words of a celebrated statesman, whose opinions I have already had occasion to quote, and must be received as authority everywhere and on every occasion.

Opinion of Mr. Madison in 1794.

"The fifteenth article, Mr. Chairman, has another extraordinary feature, which, I should imagine, must strike every observer. In the treaties which profess to put us on the footing of the most favored nation, it is stipulated that, where new favors are granted to a particular nation, in return for favors received, the party claiming the new favor shall pay the price of it. This is just and proper, where the footing of the most favored nation is established at all. But this article gives to Great Britain the full benefit of all privileges that may be granted to any other nation, without requiring from her the same equivalent privileges with those granted by such nation. Hence it would happen, that, if Spain, Portugal, or France, should open their colonial ports to the United States, in consideration of certain privileges in our trade, the same privileges would result *gratis* and *ipso facto* to Great Britain."[*]

The present claim of France is the same, or, rather, it is better, since it grows not out of a commercial convention, but out of a contract of sale; and since France has, in fact, already paid for her privilege, while England, in the instance cited, would have given no consideration. Still, however, Mr. Madison says that England must, by the terms of the article, obtain, *gratis* and *ipso facto*, every right or privilege granted to any other nation, whether *gratuitously* or for an *equivalent;* from all which I conclude,

---

[*]Mr. Madison's speech, British treaty, April 15, 1792.

sir, that France has a right to enjoy *gratis* and *ipso facto* the privilege reserved to her by the eighth article of the Louisiana. treaty.

When so able an advocate as Mr. Madison has taken up my defence, I need say no more.

I have the honor, &c., &c.,.

G. HYDE DE NEUVILLE.

N. B. Mr. de Neuville is far from desiring to protract the discussion to an indefinite length. In case, therefore, Mr. Adams should persist in the opinion expressed in the conclusion of his letter, (15th of May,) and it should be possible to come to an understanding on the other points in dispute, Mr. de Neuville would propose a provisional arrangement to the following effect:

The right accruing to France from the eighth article of the Louisiana treaty shall be settled in a special negotiation, which the two Governments shall enter into without delay.

Mr. de Neuville to the Secretary of State.

[Translation.]

WASHINGTON, *July* 3, 1821.

M. de Neuville has received Mr. Adams' note of the 27th June, and will have the honor to answer it hereafter ; at present he thinks it proper merely to observe, that he has never proposed but one and the same basis, namely : *the reduction of the discriminating duties.*

Besides, without accepting, without rejecting any proposition, and well convinced of its being, in more than one respect, urgent to close the discussion, Mr. de Neuville is prepared to make or to receive a definitive proposal. He will willingly make the offer if the Federal Government desire it. He will state, upon every point, how far his Government is willing to go; and it will thus be known at once, by both parties, if there be any chance of conciliation, or of coming to an understanding. Mr. de Neuville, still believes it to be not only possible, but easy. Both loyalty and a sense of duty require of him, however, from the nature of his late instructions, to request Mr. Adams, as a previous step, to inform him of the President's decision in relation to the ships *Apollon, Eugene,* and *Neptune.*

From what Mr. Adams stated to Mr. de Neuville on the 30th of May, he has every reason to believe that the accommodation of these three matters will not be attended with any difficulty, and that it will be as honorable to the two countries as satisfactory to his Majesty's Government; but he cannot any longer defer informing his court of the determination of the Federal Government upon this subject. Mr. Roth, secretary of his Majesty's legation, will take his departure for France in ten or twelve days. Mr. de Neuville still flatters himself that it will be in his power to announce to his court, that all the difficulties which have arisen between the two nations have been removed, definitively or provisionally.

Mr. de Neuville sees nothing, absolutely nothing, that can form a serious obstacle, and flatters himself with the idea that he is not alone of this opinion.

DEPARTMENT OF STATE, *Washington, July* 5, 1821.

The Secretary of State has submitted to the consideration of the President of the United States the note which he had the honor of receiving from the Baron de Neuville, dated the 3d instant; and, by direction of the President, he informs the Baron de Neuville that he is ready to receive any proposition which his excellency may think proper to make, as well with regard to the commercial negotiation as to the cases of the *Apollon,* the *Neptune,* and the *Eugene.* He is happy to add the assurance that, whatever the propositions may be, they will be received with the most earnest and anxious desire that they may lead to an adjustment honorable and satisfactory to both parties.

Mr. Adams to the Baron de Neuville.

DEPARTMENT OF STATE, *Washington, August* 13, 1821.

SIR: Your letter of the 3d instant has been laid before the President of the United States, and has received his most deliberate consideration. He thinks the present state of the commerce and navigation between the United States and France a subject of importance to both countries; so important, especially to the United States, that he not only believes its adjustment will be most easily effected by separating it from the consideration of all others, but that the settlement of any other interest will best be promoted by postponing it to that.

I am, therefore, directed to waive, for the present, any reply to your note of 30th June last, relating to the claim under the 8th article of the Louisiana treaty, with the assurance that, although the opinion maintained on the part of the United States concerning it remains unshaken, yet the discussion will hereafter be resumed, and a reply given to the above mentioned note of 30th June last, whenever it may be desired by you or your Government.

I am also directed to abstain from any present reply to your remarks on the note which I had the honor of addressing to you on the 28th of last month, relating to the case of the Apollon. If, after the explanations already given in the correspondence with you, and those which it appears, by a despatch from Mr. Gallatin of 23d June, the substance of which I had the honor of communicating to you, he was preparing to make directly to your Government, it shall hereafter be judged necessary to resume the discussion, I shall ever be ready to give any further explanations which the subject may require.

In the mean time I am instructed to say, with reference to your proposal on the question of navigation, that the opinion heretofore expressed, of the inefficacy of *any* proportional reduction of the discriminating duties imposed in France and in the United States, respectively, upon merchandise imported into one of those countries, in the vessels of the other, is yet retained. It is believed that a duty of 1½ per cent. on the value of the article at the place of exportation, to be levied in the United States upon articles imported from France, additional to the duties upon the same article when imported in vessels of the United States; and in France, upon importations from the United States, in American vessels, beyond those collected upon the same articles when imported in French vessels, would, in its operation, place the vessels of the two nations in fair and equal competition for the carriage of the trade.

Or, if you prefer it, I am ready to agree to a similar discriminating duty upon the bulk of the article, and propose that the additional duty be of $1 50 upon every American ton measure of French articles imported here in French vessels; and of nine francs upon every ton, French measure, of American merchandise, imported into France in American vessels; and no other discriminating duty or surcharge to be allowed on either side. Should you agree to either of these proposals, and will have the goodness to signify it to me, I will immediately communicate to you the draught of an article of a convention for carrying it into effect. An article for the restoration of deserting seamen would also be consented to. If these offers meet your approbation, I should be happy to sign with you, in the course of this present week, a convention to be confined to these two articles, and to the term of two years. This arrangement, experimental on both sides, would restore the direct commercial intercourse between the two countries, now unhappily interrupted, and would give time to both to mature, before the expiration of the term, a system which may be satisfactory to both.

I have the honor of inclosing a copy of the document from the Treasury, referred to in one of my former notes, and request you, sir, to accept the renewed assurance of my distinguished consideration.

JOHN QUINCY ADAMS.

His Excellency Mr. HYDE DE NEUVILLE,
　　Envoy Extraordinary, &c.

Baron de Neuville to the Secretary of State.

[Translation.]

WASHINGTON, *August* 15, 1821.

SIR: I have received your letter of the 13th instant, and now hasten to answer it.

From the nature of my instructions I cannot conclude any commercial arrangement without having previously settled the three affairs in which our national honor is interested.

Being, however, informed that the principal question (relative to the Apollon) is under treaty in Paris, I consider myself as justified in taking upon myself to lay it aside for the moment.

This course is prescribed by my respect for this Government and for my own, and it accords with the spirit of conciliation which has never ceased to influence me in the course of the negotiation which his Majesty has been pleased to commit to my charge. I am therefore prepared, as already stated in my letter of the 3d instant, to settle, conditionally, the commercial question.

My instructions do not allow me to detach entirely the *Louisiana* question from that which relates to commerce and navigation. At the same time my Government, with its usual spirit of propriety and justice, has considered that, in case the two negotiators should not come to an understanding on the *Louisiana* question, it would be the interest of both countries not to make this an insurmountable obstacle in the general course of the negotiation.

It is believed that in such case neither party can have a right to claim the exclusive privilege of interpreting the clause in question, whence it becomes proper to leave the settlement of this difficulty to a future negotiation to be established for that express purpose.

This is the only footing upon which I can admit the separation of the two aforementioned affairs.

It is not in my power, sir, to accept your proposal; my instructions positively forbid it, and I do not hesitate to assure you that either arrangement would prove the utter ruin of French shipping, so far, at least, as regards its relations with this country. I am persuaded the Federal Government desires no such thing, and therefore flatter myself that, after a thorough investigation of the business, it will remain satisfied that his Majesty's Government cannot negotiate upon such terms without abandoning all hope of reviving the shipping of France. Both the King and the nation design to re-establish it upon a proper footing, nor can this Government have a contrary desire.

France, in all this, does no more than what has been done by England, at all times, and by the United States from the 20th of July, 1789. She strives to encourage her navigation, and to revive her shipping, which had sustained great losses in the last thirty years; but, far from pretending to attain this desirable end at the expense of other nations, she offers to them all a *reciprocity of advantages.* Can anything more be expected?

To conclude, I shall now, without further discussion, propose the substance of a temporary arrangement which I would undertake to sign, under the express reservation mentioned in my letter of the 3d instant.

In case it should not be accepted, I shall consider myself bound to await further instructions from my Government.

1. The law of the 15th of May, and the royal ordonnance of the 26th of July, shall be revoked.

2. The Louisiana question shall be the subject of a future negotiation, to be established for that express purpose.

3. The consuls of both nations shall be invested with proper authority over deserting seamen.

4. The duties of tonnage, and all other collections made by public authority upon vessels in the respective ports, shall be regulated upon the footing of a perfect reciprocity.

5. The extra duties imposed at present upon a foreign flag shall, in both countries, suffer the following reduction, viz: Of *one-third,* if the convention remain in force from *two* to five years; of one-

half, if the arrangement be only temporary, and last only for *eighteen months* or *two years*, at the option of the Federal Government.

6. The extraordinary duties collected in consequence of the law of the 15th of May, and of the ordonnance of July 26, shall be returned.*

Having stated above *what I should take upon myself*, I now deem it necessary (even for my own responsibility) to add the following explanation:

If I considered nothing but the commercial intérests of France, I certainly should not consent to a reduction of more than a third part of the duties; for I am convinced that, in the present state of our shipping, such a reduction would be more than sufficient to maintain an equal balance *and a reciprocity of advantages;* but I am influenced in this business by other considerations important to both countries. It is my opinion, that, if the arrangement should not be concluded at once, it must, of necessity, be postponed to the next year, and perhaps much longer; and it is to be feared that difficulties will increase, and both countries must suffer a great loss from a state of things from which other nations would reap great profits, without any ultimate advantage either to France or to the United States.

For this reason I have made up my mind to assume much upon my own responsibility, and to propose an *experiment*, from which the shipping of France will not, in all probability, derive any advantage. I should, however, be happy to have proposed it, if it should lead the two Governments to a general accommodation upon all points, and if it should bring them to a mutual understanding concerning their respective interests, whether considered separately or connectedly.

Accept, sir, &c., &c., &c.,

G. HYDE DE NEUVILLE.

P. S. It would be laying me under obligation to inform me, as soon as possible, of the decision of the President.

Mr. Adams to the Baron de Neuville.

DEPARTMENT OF STATE, *Washington, August 20, 1821.*

SIR: I have had the honor of receiving your letter of the 15th instant, which has been submitted to the consideration of the President of the United States, and to which, by his directions, I now reply.

With regard to the cases of the Apollon, the Neptune, and the Eugene, I shall be ready to resume the discussion by further explanations, in reply to your last note on the subject, should you deem it desirable, after receiving the further instructions of your Government.

The same observation is made with reference to the claim to special privileges in Louisiana. Although the opinion of this Government has been fully made up upon this subject, on great consideration, and has remained unchanged, notwithstanding the frequent examinations which have been given of it, yet I shall always receive any communications which your Government may think proper to make on it, and to bestow on them all the attention which has been invariably shown and is due to the friendly relations existing between our countries.

The first, third, and fourth, of your propositions will be readily agreed to, and also the sixth, if you persist in desiring it. Not, however, with a view to the advantage of the United States, as we should prefer the convention without it.

To the fifth we cannot accede. The extreme of the reduction which you propose, a reduction of the discriminating duties on both sides by one half, would leave a surcharge upon the vessels of the United States of from six to ten dollars a ton, according to the various articles with which they might be laden. This would be a *prohibitory* duty, as effectual as that which now exists, or would lead the shippers of the United States, under the appearance of an equal compact, into the same ruinous expeditions which occasioned the necessity of the act of Congress of 15th May, 1820.

It is deeply regretted that the view which your Government takes of this subject is so widely different from that which is entertained by the Government of the United States. In the communication of this view we have acted with the utmost sincerity and candor. In the whole correspondence between us, as well as in that of Mr. Gallatin, which had preceded it, ours have been unfolded in a very explicit manner. The calculations of Mr. Gallatin, particularly, which accompanied his letter and note of 7th and 8th of July, 1820, to Baron Pasquier, and the accuracy of which has not been questioned, show to demonstration that a diminution of one half the surcharges on American vessels in France would still leave a discrimination against them nearly equal to the entire freight.

I infer, from the communication which you have made me of the nature of your powers, that it will be necessary for you to wait further instructions from your Government before we can make any arrangement of these important interests. I mention this to assure you that, should such recurrence to your Government be necessary, I shall be happy to resume the discussion whenever it may suit your convenience.

I pray you to accept the assurance of my distinguished consideration.

JOHN QUINCY ADAMS.

Mr. HYDE DE NEUVILLE,
 Envoy Extraordinary and Minister Plenipotentiary from France.

Baron de Neuville to the Secretary of State.

[Translation.] .

WASHINGTON, *October 15, 1821.*

SIR: I have received fresh instructions from my Government, requiring me to insist upon the execution of the eighth article of the Louisiana treaty, or to demand, at least, that in the mean time our

----

* This last article may be omitted if desired, but it would seem, in all respects, to be very proper, and, on one account it would be more advantageous to this Government than to France.

shipping be made to enjoy, in the ports of the territory ceded by France, all the privileges and advantages which are granted in the same ports to such nations as have no treaty or convention with the United States.

On this subject I must again refer to my letter of the 30th of March last.

Considering, however, that at the date of these instructions my Government was not informed of the present state of the negotiation, and being solicitous to make all possible exertions for the removal of every difficulty to the negotiation, I have the honor again to propose, (in case you should persist in your opinion on the Louisiana question, as I adhere to mine,) that we enter into the agreement suggested in my letters of June 30 and August 3.

Accept, &c.,

G. HYDE DE NEUVILLE.

Baron de Neuville to the Secretary of State.

[Translation.]

WASHINGTON, *March* 11, 1822.

SIR: I have the honor of inclosing some observations which I must request you will have the goodness of submitting to the consideration of the President.

If that *exposé* shall be found to be incorrect, I shall thankfully accept the communication of whatever can contribute to rectify any mistake I may have fallen into; for truth is my only object, and my sole desire is to conciliate the interests of the two countries.

But if my calculations be correct; if I can adduce in support of them the most authentic documents and past experience, may I not hope that undeniable facts will have more weight than mere conjectures, especially in regard to *an experiment*—a merely temporary arrangement between the two countries?

"I hope still," said Mr. Gallatin in his letter to Baron Pasquier, October 15, "that a compromise, at least a provisional one, will be acceded to."

And I also shall repeat, (what I have never ceased to say,) let us come at least to a provisional compromise; our two nations should be united.

I have the honor, sir, to inform you that, in pursuance of the instructions of my court, I am ready to resume the negotiation as soon as the President shall deem it proper. I believe that it may be concluded, upon all points, both *speedily* and *upon proper terms*. It is also my opinion that it must soon come, in one way or other, to a conclusion.

I earnestly and very sincerely desire that the present state of things may be put an end to before the close of the present session, were it even necessary therefor that France should make real sacrifices, for it has already lasted too long. I shall only take the liberty of repeating that even a temporary arrangement must, in order to lead to a more lasting settlement, approximate as much as possible to an equality of advantages.

Accept, &c.,

G. HYDE DE NEUVILLE.

FACTS.

1. In the years 1789 and 1790 the Government of the United States thought proper to establish discriminating duties for the purpose of encouraging their rising navigation.(*a*)

(*a*) On the discrimination between the duty on the tonnage of foreign and American bottoms a great degree of sensibility was discovered, there not being a sufficient number of vessels owned by the citizens of the United States to export all the produce of the country. It was said that the increased tonnage on foreign bottoms operated as a tax on agriculture and a premium to navigation. This discrimination, it was therefore contended, ought to be very small.—(*Marshall's Life of Washington.*)

In answer to these arguments Mr. Madison said: If it is expedient for America to have vessels employed in commerce at all, it will be proper that she have enough to answer all the purposes intended; to form a school for seamen; to lay the foundation of a Navy, &c. I consider an acquisition of maritime strength essential to this country; *granting a* preference to *our own* navigation will insensibly bring it forward to that perfection so essential to American safety.—(*Madison's Speech on Discriminating Duties.*)

Congress, very soon after the organization of the present Government, adopted measures to secure for the citizens of the United States the advantages which would arise from a *monopoly* of the tonnage required for their commerce.—(*Seybert, page* 292.)

The acts of the American Government alarmed the shipping interest in Great Britain. In 1791 the merchants and ship owners in Glasgow predicted that the discriminations adopted in the United States would, in time, give a decided superiority to the American shipping. *In a few years* it was demonstrated that their anticipations were well founded.—(*Seybert, page* 293.)

Before the discriminating duties the American tonnage was not sufficient for the conveyance of the produce of the United States. In a short time it proved more than adequate for that purpose.—(*Marshall's Life of Washington.*)

FACTS.

1. In 1816 France judged it expedient to follow this example in order to repair the losses sustained by her navigation during twenty-five years of revolution.(*a*)

(*a*) Whilst the late political storms were almost desolating the civilized world, the vessels belonging to *France*, Holland, and Spain *were swept* from the ocean; in proportion as the tonnage of these nations diminished, that of other States was augmented, and none in a greater degree than *our own*. Foreign nations will make every effort to *regain* the navigation that the last wars had taken from them. We must anticipate a *reduction* on our part.—(*Seybert, page* 305.)

Here it is proper to observe that our discriminating duties were consequential to the system first established by the United States and which was not adopted by France *until many years after.*—(*Extract—General Council of Commerce, Paris, November* 23, 1819.)

France, therefore, was not influenced by any hostile views; she did no more than follow the example first set by the United States, and she could not do otherwise without abandoning completely the interests of her navigation.

The present state of the shipping of France is attributable to the long continued interruption of her maritime operations and to the losses sustained in consequence thereof, both in men and in all the materials necessary to the building and equipment of vessels.—(*Extract from the Memorial of the Chamber of Commerce of Nantes.*) The commercial shipping of several nations had obtained a prodigious increase, while that of France was prostrate. It became, therefore, the indispensable duty of her Government, on the re-establishment of peace, to protect its weakness by *granting* every proper encouragement.

It is proper to observe here, with respect to the United States of America, that in all this France did no more than what had been long before practiced in that country to the injury of the shipping of France.

2. In the year 1789, out of 224 vessels sent from the United States to France, there were 43 English, 163 Americans, and but 13 French.

In 1790 the statements drawn from custom-house accounts were nearly to the same effect.

In 1791, in consequence of the discriminating duties established by Congress, France had lost, in the course of a single year, one-half of their proportion of the tonnage employed in the trade with the United States.(a)

3. In 1789 and 1790 the United States enjoyed several gratuitous advantages (b) granted to this Republic by his Majesty Louis XVI; there could not, therefore, be any call for *defensive measures*, so far, at least, as regarded France.(c)

4. On the 20th July, 1789, Congress established an extra duty upon all foreign bottoms entering into the ports of the United States.

On the 20th July, 1790, that duty was doubled.

On the 10th of August, 1790, an extra duty of 10 per cent. additional on all the rates of duty imposed on merchandises imported in American vessels was imposed on foreign vessels. (Those acts constitute what are usually called the discriminating duties of the United States.)

It is, therefore, clear that in 1789 and 1790 the United States set the example of imposing dis-

2. In 1816, before our law of the 28th April was enacted, the tonnage of France employed in the trade between the two countries was reduced nearly to nothing.

In 1820, after our surtax had been four years established, the tonnage of the United States employed in the trade was still superior to ours.(a)

3. In 1816, and preceding years, France was not only without any gratuitous favor from the United States, but she moreover had paid, during nearly twenty-six years, very heavy duties upon the productions of her soil and industry, besides a surtax which had almost entirely excluded her shipping from the carriage of her principal articles. (b)

4. In 1789 and 1790, and the following years, the Government of France made representations (as will be seen hereafter) against the acts of Congress of July 20, 1789, and July 20, 1790, as being contrary to the text, the spirit, and the very object of the treaty of the 6th of February, 1788.

France might, from that time, have followed the example of the United States; and perhaps she ought to have done so for the protection of her commercial shipping.

The merchants of France repeatedly desired it to be done. The agents of the King, in the United

---

All foreign nations were affected by the system we had adopted; it seemed to operate *like magic* in favor of the ship owners in the United States.—(*Seybert, page* 294.)

Mr. Randolph said, on the subject of the Louisiana treaty, that that province might, in the end, obtain the enjoyment of the advantages secured to the other States by the discriminating duties.—(*Debate of October* 25, 1803.)

"We now have the sovereignty of it, and only stipulate that for twelve years France and Spain should be admitted, not on an equal footing with us, but that their vessels, laden with their own produce, not otherwise, should pay no higher duties than our own. At the expiration of that period we can give a decided preponderance to our own trade by discriminating duties."

Mr. R. Griswold says, on the same day:

"If, however, it is really intended in this sideway manner to bring about a repeal of the discriminating duties, I hope it may, at this time, be so understood. The commerce of this country, and particularly that of the northern States, has long flourished under these protecting duties, and it would be extraordinary, indeed, if a treaty should be formed laying the Government under an obligation to repeal laws so essential to our commercial prosperity."

It is, therefore, obvious that the discriminating duties were ever considered in the United States as the best means of encouraging navigation. It is true that those discriminating duties did not alone raise the shipping of the United States to that extraordinary degree of prosperity which it has at this day attained. Events fatal to humanity, and which might have been foreseen in 1790, must have contributed to that state of things which is really out of all proportion; but, even with the revolution in France, what would have been the condition of the navigation of the United States without the aid of the discriminating duties established in 1790?

(a) From 13,435 tons, the tonnage of France employed in the trade fell down to 7,523.

The tonnage duties collected upon foreign bottoms from September to the 31st of December of the last year had risen to $50,000, while those levied upon American vessels did not amount to more than $11,000. Even this proportion, from five to one, did not appear sufficient to the merchants and shippers of the northern States; those of Portsmouth, New Hampshire, made a memorial asking Congress to double the existing duty of fifty cents per ton upon foreign bottoms.— (*Extract from a note of Mr. Otto, dated May* 20, 1790.)

It is well known that, notwithstanding this great difference of five to one, the duty was, in fact, doubled on the 20th of July following.

(b) *Vide* the treaties and conventions of 1778, 1782; letter from Mr. de Calonne to Marquis La Fayette, January 9, 1784; the same to Mr. Jefferson, October 22, 1786; decree of the council, 1788.

These various documents prove how much his Majesty was disposed to favor the commerce and navigation of the United States.

(c) It has been stated that the discriminating duties had been established by Congress as a mere defensive measure, necessary to counteract the operation of similar discrimina-

(a) *Extract—General Council of Commerce, Paris, June* 30, 1820.—President, Baron Hottinguer. Present: Messrs. Odrier, Outequin, Duvergier de Hauraune, Simon de la Roche, Pillet, Will, Dellessert, Perrier, Balguerie, Stuttenberg, Cottier, Terneaux, Rossean, Guiarud, Leillieres, Lefebvre. A particular statement of the arrival of cotton at Havre, from the United States, in American and French bottoms, during the years 1818, 1819, and the first five months of 1820, shows a much greater number of American than of French arrivals; and that the quantity of cotton by them brought is also much greater than that imported in French bottoms; and although the proportions of French arrivals had increased in 1819 and 1820, yet the difference (with respect to the number of bales imported) had still remained in favor of American vessels. Besides those cottons, the Americans have imported a considerable quantity of sugar, nankeens, coffee, tea, pepper, potash, &c., while the cargoes of the French vessels, whose tonnage is in general much less, consisted principally in cotton. We have, therefore, ground to conclude that our system of duties on foreign shipping does not operate as much to the disadvantage of the United States, as has by them been asserted, as a justification of their last measures.

Statement showing the amount of American and French tonnage arriving in the ports of Boston, New York, Philadelphia, Baltimore, Norfolk, Charleston, Savannah, and New Orleans, from France and her dependencies, during the years 1817, 1818, *and* 1819.

	American tonnage.	French tonnage.
From January 1 to December 31, 1817	71,738	15,105
From January 1 to December 31, 1818	62,081	23,108
From January 1 to December 31, 1819	54,277	25,945
Total tons	188,096	64,158

TREASURY DEPARTMENT, *Register's Office, May* 26, 1820.

JOSEPH NOURSE.

(b) The following is an extract from a note written by a merchant in this country experienced in such matters:

"The additional tenth collected upon foreign bottoms amounts to a prohibition in the United States in regard to the principal articles; for brandies pay, per gallon, 4 cts. 80-100.

"The customary freight is from $12 to $15 per ton, which, per gallon, gives, say at most 6.

"A French vessel could not, therefore, obtain any share in the carriage except for a freight equal to the difference, amounting only to, per gallon, 1 ct. 20-100.

"On silks and other articles of our manufacture the case is still worse; for setting the duty upon the average at 20 per cent. of their value, the additional tenth would amount to 2 per cent:

"And in order to make this difference equal, at this rate, to the usual freight of $15 per ton, each ton of such manufactured goods must be valued only at $750, including the tenth generally added; whereas, it would be absurd to give so low a value even to the more bulky of those articles, such as crapes, fancy goods," &c., &c.

criminating duties for the encouragement of their shipping.

These discriminating duties, which in the course of twenty years raised the tonnage of the Union so as to be equal to that of Great Britain,[a] one century after they had passed the navigation act, were supported in 1789 and 1790 by the most enlightened and influential men in the United States; no one pretended, at that time, to deny the right of every nation to encourage its navigation and commerce by discriminating duties, provided they apply to all nations.

"We shall not think it unfriendly in you to lay a like duty on coasters, because it will be no more than we have done ourselves. You are free, also, to lay that or any other duty on vessels coming from foreign ports, provided they apply to all other nations, even the most favored. We are free to do the same *under the same restriction.*"—(*Extract of a letter from Mr. Jefferson, Secretary of State, to Mr. Otto, Chargé d'Affaires of France, dated March 29, 1791.*)

5. The 1st of July, 1812, an additional duty, amounting to one dollar and fifty cents per ton, was laid by Congress upon all foreign vessels entered in the ports of the United States.

6. The 3d of July, 1815, Congress repealed "so much of the acts heretofore passed imposing a discriminating duty on goods imported, and on tonnage in favor of vessels of the United States, so far as the same respects the produce or manufacture of the nation to which such foreign vessels may belong. Such repeal to take effect in favor of any nation whenever the President shall be satisfied that the discriminating or countervailing duties of such foreign nation, so far as they operate to the disadvantage of the United States, have been abolished."—(*Extract from a note on the subject, from Mr. Gallatin, July,* 7, 1820.)

The United States have concluded treaties upon this principle with Great Britain and Sweden, and have made arrangements of the same nature with the Netherlands, Prussia, and the Hanseatic towns, in consequence of the mutual repeal of all surtaxes.

The trade of the United States with Russia, Spain, Portugal, and Italy, being entirely passive

tions, *as well of France* as of other powers.--(*Vide Mr. Adams' note of June* 27, 1821.)

This is manifestly an error, at least with regard to *France.* All the documents of that period, and the speeches delivered in Congress in 1790, preclude all doubt on the subject.

It was repeatedly proposed to exempt France from the surtax, and motives of *justice* and *gratitude* were alleged in support of the proposition; it was opposed on the principles of the general interests of the State—of those in particular of its navigation—and the difficulty of raising a sufficient revenue. But *no one* made even the most distant allusion *to defensive measures.*

"We feel every disposition on our part to make considerable sacrifices where they could result to the sole benefit of your nation, but where they would excite from other nations corresponding claims it becomes necessary to proceed with caution."—(*Extract from a letter of Mr. Jefferson, March* 29, 1791.)

It remains evident that in 1790 there was no idea of resorting to *defensive measures* against France.

Two acts of the National Assembly of France have been cited as injurious to the interests of this Republic.

These two laws, relating, the one to tobacco, the other to the sale of foreign vessels in France, had no particular relation to the United States and nothing that could excite complaint. At all events, it will be observed that they were not enacted *until March,* 1791, and therefore could not have been taken into consideration by Congress in 1789 and 1790.

See likewise Mr. Jefferson's letter to Mr. Otto, dated December 29, 1790.

(a) In 1788 the tonnage of Great Britain and Ireland amounted to 1,359,752 tons. In 1809 the tonnage of the United States amounted to 1,350,281 tons.—(*See M'Pherson's Annals of Commerce, vol.* 4.) (*See Seybert, page* 294.)

States, proposed it; and complaints against the discriminating duties imposed by the United States were, from all parts, addressed to the French Government.[a]

The interests of the country called for such a measure.[b] His Majesty's Government consulted, however, and would consider nothing but the situation of a friendly power requiring her to encourage her navigation. It refused to enact any countervailing measures, and the United States continued to enjoy in our ports the same favors and privileges before granted to them by his Majesty.

5. Thus France paid, in the ports of the United States, an extra duty of $1 50, besides the ordinary duties, and she did not on that account increase hers.

The tonnage duty paid by American vessels on their arrival in France did not amount (before the law of May 15 and July 26, 1820) to more than 3f. 75c. and with the additional decime 4f. 12½c. ($0 77.)

6. To the opposite paragraph France will answer: Every nation acts, and should act, with a view to its particular local or accidental situation.

Some have no Navy, or do not care to have any; others, whose Navy is in a settled state of prosperity, may, for the purpose of securing a great commercial advantage, submit, in point of navigation, to a sacrifice unimportant to them. Such countries must have very different views on the subject from a nation which feels the want of a naval force and which has the intention and the means of creating one corresponding with the extent of her power.

If, as Mr. Madison observes, "it is expedient for her to have vessels employed in commerce at all, it will be proper that she have enough to answer all the purposes intended to form a school for seamen," &c. &c.

To which it may be added, in the words of Mr. Jefferson:

"This nation is free to lay any duty on vessels

(a) See Mr. Otto's letter to Mr. Jefferson, January 8, 1791.

(b) A senator admitted (in July, 1790) that if France exacted, by way of reprisals, the same duty from American bottoms, these would have to pay six times more than French vessels did to the United States; but added, that he did not doubt but France would take into consideration the motives of urgent necessity which called for the measure.

as regards those different countries, the United States were not interested in taking measures to obtain the same object from them. France remained the only nation with which it was important to have such an understanding.

7. In 1790 France expostulated against the extra duty imposed in the United States upon foreign bottoms, and which was by her considered as contrary to the very object of her treaty with this Republic. Since that time she has not ceased complaining of the enormous duties collected upon the productions of her soil and industry; but after all, France has at all times done nothing more than remonstrate.(a)

8. On the 15th of May, 1820, Congress opposed the French law of April, 1816, (which was *common* to all nations,) by an extra tonnage duty imposed upon *French vessels alone.*

"Each party remains free to lower or raise its tonnage, *provided* the change operates on all nations." (Mr. Jefferson's note to Mr. Otto, March 29, 1791.)

The law of the 15th May excludes (such at least is its consequence) French bottoms from the ports of the United States.

The law of the 15th of May was accompanied by a retroactive provision both unjust and ruinous to those who had sailed *bona fide* from France.(b)

(a)Extract of a letter written on the 10th of July, 1790, by Mr. de Montmorin, the Minister of Foreign Affairs, to Mr. Otto, Chargé d'Affaires in the United States:

"It results from these remarks, that the United States had no right to impose any duty on freights upon our vessels. Such a treatment would justify us in treating them in the same manner; but the King has judged it more consistent with propriety, and more in accordance with the relations existing between his Majesty and the United States, to remonstrate with Congress and to ask the repeal of those regulations so far as they operate against us. You will therefore please, sir, to take all necessary steps to accomplish the King's intentions. His Majesty does not doubt but Congress will acknowledge the justice of his reclamation."

Extract of a letter from Mr. Jefferson to Mr. Otto, dated March 29, 1791:

"SIR: The note of December 13, which you did me the honor to address to me on the acts of Congress of the 20th of July, 1789 and 1790, fixing the tonnage payable by foreign vessels arriving from a foreign port, *without excepting those of France*, has been submitted to the Government of his most Christian Majesty in making this the subject of fair discussion and explanation as a new proof of his justice and friendship, and they have entered on the consideration with all the *respect* due to whatever comes from his Majesty or his ministers."

NOTE.—It is not my intention here to bring into view the justice of the reclamation from the French Government made in 1790, and I recall what took place at that period for the sole purpose of completely justifying what was done in 1816. It will be seen that France remonstrated against the surtax imposed in 1790, not merely because she exempted American vessels from such a duty; not because she had, by several regulations very favorable to the shipping of the United States, given a greater extension to the advantages secured to the United States by the treaty of 1778, but because she considered herself as *of right* excepted, by the provisions of that very treaty, from the surtax imposed by Congress in July, 1789, upon foreign bottoms, and renewed on the 20th of July following, 1790. France had, therefore, more than one motive to remonstrate, and yet she was content with making amicable representations.

(b) Such vessels as were compelled to enter into the ports of the United States have been subjected to the full rigor of the law and forced to pay *in cash* the entire duty of $18 per ton, and were thereby under the necessity of borrowing at a very high interest. Others steered off from the coast, not knowing whither to carry their cargoes; three or four went to Florida. It is well known that they were prevented from anchoring in the territory of Spain. It is also known what has been the fate of the ship *Apollon*, which had anchored in the river *Bell.*

coming from foreign ports *provided they apply to all nations*," and France has never done more.

Great Britain acted according to what she thought her interest when she accepted under modifications the offer of the Federal Government; she no doubt had foreseen what would be the consequence.*(a)*

France also calculates what would inevitably happen if she accepted a nominal reciprocity as the basis of a treaty of commerce with the United States; she knows that such a treaty would operate to the entire exclusion of her shipping from the trade with the United States. She therefore proposes a reciprocity of advantages, which equity and, it may be added, both sound policy and reason seem obviously to point out as the only basis calculated to give a durable existence to conventions between nations.

7. In 1820 France was about to consent (this may be asserted) to a reduction of her discriminating duties, although she considered the claim of the American merchants as being unfounded, or at least premature, when intelligence was received in Paris of the act of May 15, attended with circumstances not calculated, it may be well said, to mitigate the real or apparent harshness of that measure.*(b)*

8. On the 26th of July, 1820, his most Christian Majesty, without, however, using his right of reprisals to a full extent, ordained measures which the act of Congress had rendered necessary, and an extra tonnage duty was therefore established upon American bottoms equal to that which had been imposed in the United States upon French vessels.

The ordinance of the 26th July exempts from the extraordinary duty such American vessels as come in ballast into the ports of France.

The ordinance of the 26th of July did not operate until the Government of his Majesty had acquired a certainty that the law of the 15th of May could not fail to be known in all the ports of the United States.

It appeared to the Government of his Majesty that, as soon as the citizens would be informed of the measure taken by their Government, it would readily occur to them that their vessels would be treated in like manner in our ports, and it was therefore decided that a rigorous measure, intended merely as defensive, and adopted with regret, should not affect such vessels as had sailed *bona fide* from the United States.*(c)*

(a) It is well known that the United States have at this day the seven-eighths of the tonnage employed in their trade with Great Britain. (See the last general statement showing the quantity of American and foreign tonnage presented to Congress by the Treasury Department.)

(b) Extract of a letter from Mr. Gallatin to the Secretary of State, dated Paris, January 20, 1820:

"I have now the honor to inclose the copy of Mr. Pasquier's long promised answer on the subject of our commercial relations, which was not received till after I had closed my last despatch to you. I am confirmed in the opinion that nothing will be done here until *we shall have done justice to ourselves by our own measures.*"

Extract of the above mentioned letter from Mr. Pasquier to Mr. Gallatin, January 14, 1820:

"As soon, therefore, as the various points of information indispensably necessary to guide the decision of his Majesty's Government, as well in relation to the two stipulations proposed in your note as to the other clauses which it may be found expedient to insert in the intended convention, shall have been collected, *I will lose no time* in entering with you into more particular discussions, and I have every reason to believe that I may be enabled to do so speedily."

(c) The ordinance was modified in favor of such vessels as *had entered bona fide*; they were admitted to give bonds of security; such as left the coast of France found many neighboring countries to which they could carry and sell their cargoes; such as placed themselves on the very limits of our law were not molested, and to this day we still receive the productions of the United States through Nice and other places very near to France, from which the ordinance of July operates very differently from the act of the 15th of May.

France and the United States considered in their relations of navigation and commerce since the law of France of April 28, 1816, until the passage of the act of Congress of May 15, 1820.

9. In the United States the discriminating duties were of one-tenth paid by French vessels over and above the duties paid by American vessels upon all goods, wares, and merchandise, without distinction. That duty is paid in the United States since the 10th of August, 1790.

10. The discriminating duties established by Congress in 1790 have never ceased to secure to the vessels of the United States an almost exclusive preference with respect to all cargoes shipped from France to the United States, so that French vessels were always obliged, before the act of the 15th of May, to come in ballast to the United States.

11. The Americans enjoyed in France the resources derived from the *transit*, and as, in such cases, they paid no discriminating duty and could load their vessels for a *lower freight*, they were always preferred, even by French merchants, for the carriage of goods destined to be sent to Switzerland and Germany.

The Americans brought freely to France the productions of the East and West Indies, and those of several other countries. They could likewise re-export, free of duty, the foreign productions brought into the deposits (entrepots established in France.)

12. *Freight.*—It has been asserted that the Americans ruined themselves in taking cotton to France at a freight of 1½ cent per pound, while French shippers received 2½ and 3 cents per pound.

It is added that, in one year more, French vessels would have obtained an entire monopoly of that branch of trade.—(Mr. Gallatin's note of the 7th July, 1820.)

13. *Tonnage Duty.*—It has been stated that the tonnage duty, brokers' fees, and other local charges paid in France by foreign vessels might be valued at about eight francs per ton, ($1 50,) and that therefore exceeded by three francs (56 cents) the extra tonnage duty paid by French vessels in the United States before the act of the 15th of May.*(a)*

14. It has been stated that the law of the 15th of May was enacted for the purpose of re-establishing a just balance, or at least to prevent an inequality which could not fail to take place.

Because it is said if the state of things existing before had continued, the shippers, who were ruined by their trade with France, would soon have been left with only one-fifth of the carrying trade.—(Mr. Gallatin's note of the 7th of July, 1820.)

9. In France the discriminating duties are fixed, individually, for each article, and are calculated according to the bulk, the value, and the importance of each; so that if some articles pay more, others pay less, and others pay no discriminating duty at all. It must be admitted that the duty could not rest upon a better basis, nor one more consistent with the true principles of a good system of the revenue.

The discriminating duties were first established in France on the 28th of April, 1816.

10. The discriminating duties established in France on the 28th of April, 1816, had not availed to secure to French vessels even one-half of the *freights* from the United States to France.

Before the act of the 15th of May, American vessels always came to France with full cargoes.

11. The commerce and navigation of France enjoyed nothing in the United States to compensate the very important advantages granted to the Americans in France, as mentioned in the opposite paragraph.

"It is well known that there is no allowance of the drawback of duties for the amount of the additional duties on goods imported in foreign bottoms."

12. *Freight.*—The difference was, in fact, of only one cent, and it may be said there was really none, except on freights for cotton.

If there was any difference as to tobacco, it never exceeded one half cent. This it is easy to prove; and even though the shippers of France had taken no freight at all on the exportation of the productions of its soil and industry, the monopoly in that branch of trade would have still remained to the Americans.*(a)*

Besides, if one year more would have sufficed to justify the measure adopted by the United States on the 15th of May, 1820, why did they not wait? France had given, for a long time, the example of moderation and patience.

13. *Tonnage Duty.*—The statement cited in the opposite paragraph is manifestly erroneous.*(b)* The various duties there mentioned have constantly been higher in the United States than in France, and the difference in their different ports has often been exorbitant.

After all, by way of removing all difficulty on this point, France has proposed to fix the tonnage duty in both countries, including all local charges, at a particular sum.

It is also offered to fix such specific duty (including all charges) on the American basis, and not on that of France—*id est*, the average of what foreign bottoms pay in the United States.

14. To this it is answered, as before stated, that the injury was only anticipated, and that there was therefore no harm in waiting.

It may be added, even admitting that French shipping would, in the end, have obtained an advantage in the carrying trade from the United States to France, it is not perceived how such an advantage could give it the four-fifths of the carrying trade between the two countries. Most as-

---

(a) The United States consuls have made much ado, even in the newspapers, in order to obtain the right of brokerage.

The consuls of France, who are not allowed to trade, have been content with addressing their complaints, accompanied with statements, to their Government.

The consequence is, that credit has been given here to the clamors of the first, while the silence of the last has been misconstrued.

(a) See note by a merchant, page 117, ante.

(b) It would be easy to furnish custom-house reports proving this beyond all doubt.

15. It is, however, admitted that the act of the 15th of May was not sufficiently matured; that, though the principle upon which it was enacted be indisputable, there were some errors in the calculations then made that the duty of $18 per ton, superadded to the former surtax of an additional tenth upon all articles imported in French ships, amounts to more than the surtax collected in France upon American vessels.

It is calculated that the balance in France against American shipping amounted, before the 15th of May, 1820, to 46 francs 50 centimes per ton, French measure. It is allowed that the act of the 15th of May raises the balance in the United States against French vessels to 40 francs 8 centimes per ton, American measure, or 37 francs per ton, French measure; and, finally, it is added:

Although French merchants have been justly alarmed at the consequence of the act of the 15th of May, and although the Government of his Majesty has had cause to regret that since the United States only contended for reciprocity, they had not been satisfied with equalizing the duties, still, however, there is nothing offensive or hostile to be found in that measure.—(Mr. Gallatin's note of the 7th July, 1820.)

suredly, the shippers of the United States would still have continued to engross all the freights between France and the United States, and, also, that of such foreign productions as they were at liberty to import into France.

This last and immense advantage was not, perhaps, sufficiently appreciated when the act of May 15 was passed.

15. It results, at least, from the calculations cited in the opposite paragraph, that the merchants of France may have been justly alarmed, and that the Government of the King may have had cause of complaint against the act of the 15th of May.

To which it is added, that, even admitting the difference of freights to have been (before the act of the 15th of May, 1820,) of 46f. against American vessels, it is not perceived upon what principle it can have appeared proper to place the first ally and constant friend of the United States upon a worse footing than such nations as go so far as to exclude the vessels of the United States from their ports.

Extract from "the act supplementary to an act to regulate the duties of import and tonnage;"

"SEC. 2. And be it further enacted, That on all foreign ships or vessels which shall be entered in the United States before the 30th day of June next from any foreign port or place to and with which vessels of the United States are not ordinarily permitted to go and trade, there shall be paid a duty at the rate of $2 per ton."—January 14, 1819.

It will, furthermore, be asked, for what reason, when the extra duty of $18 per ton was laid upon French vessels, it was not provided, at least, that they should be exempted therefrom in all the ports of the territory ceded by France, (Louisiana?)

It is known that, according to the terms of the treaty of cession, the vessels of France are, in future and forever, to be treated in Louisiana upon the footing of the most favored nation, and, a fortiori, they must never be there upon the footing of the nation least favored or treated worse.

But, after all, his Majesty's Government has perceived nothing hostile in the measure of the 15th of May; it has caused both surprise and regret, and, if measures of reprisals have been taken, they are extremely moderate, and France has not discontinued to evince, as before, her friendly dispositions and her sincere desire of coming to an arrangement upon the basis of a perfect reciprocity of advantages.

Calculations will now be opposed to those of the opposite paragraph.

But what are calculations compared with facts? (a)

(a) The following statement is from a merchant of New York. It is submitted without alteration, as coming from one who is experienced in such matters, who is friendly to both countries, and understands perfectly well their commercial relations. It is, however, believed that the question might be presented in a light more favorable to the interests of France:

"As it is very probable that the actual state of our commercial relations with France will be one of the first subjects of discussion in Congress, it is doubtless desirable that the basis of the controversy should be well understood by the public at large.

This appears to me so much the more important, as I have not seen anywhere the calculations that may have led that respectable body to pass the law imposing a duty of eighteen dollars per ton on all French vessels entering the ports of these States, and in trying myself to discover the grounds on which that law might have been enacted, I find a very different result.

From a number of statements made in France, it appears that an American vessel will upon an average carry—
750 pounds French weight per measurement ton.
Deduct 45 pounds French tare allowed by the custom-house, at 6 per cent.
————
705 pounds net, paying duty per American vessel, at the rate of 19 francs, 25 cents, including the additional tenth, per 100 half kilogrammes, is ------------------------ francs. 135 71
On per French vessel, at francs 11------do. 77 55
————
The difference for each measurement ton is, therefore, on cotton ---------------------- francs. 58 16
====

And as, by a late comparison of the present American and French gold and silver coins, the average relative value of the American dollar is found to be francs 5 449-1000, we will say, francs 58 16 is -------------------------------- $10 67

Pot ashes pay, in French bottoms, 66 francs per ton less than in American vessels, and, supposing the ton in weight being equal to the measurement ton, is $12 11.

Tobacco, by French vessels, is free of duty, and pays by American vessels 11 francs per 100 kilogrammes.

If we value, therefore, the measurement ton at 1,200 half kilogrammes, the duty is $12 11 per ton.

Both these articles pay more duty than cotton ; but it is well known that the quantity of American tobacco imported from this country direct, which is sold for consumption in France, is very inconsiderable ; and the consumption of pot ashes has also, within a few years, been considerably reduced by the use of artificial salts.

Against this must be set off the immense quantity of produce of the East and West Indies, and other foreign produce, imported into France in American vessels, and sold there for exportation, free of duty.

This quantity we may safely set down at one-fourth of the whole quantity of goods imported into France; and of the other three-fourths it may not be unreasonable to calculate that cotton constitutes the nine-tenths and tobacco and pot ashes one-tenth—then,

25 parts of a ton pay-------------------------- 0 00
67½ parts of a ton pay, in cotton, at $10 67 per ton.. $7 20
7½ parts of a ton pay, in tobacco and pot ashes, at $12 11 per ton-------- ----------------- 0 91

The whole difference is, therefore, per ton, equal to.. 8 11

THE DUTIES.

Considered, first, with respect to commerce; second, with regard to navigation.

Every nation has a right to raise or lower its duties as it may deem expedient for its revenue or for the encouragement of its national industry; for the same reason every nation has a right to favor its own navigation, and to impose, for that purpose, an extra or discriminating duty upon foreign navigation, *provided the charge operate on all nations.* But if the United States had any right to complain of the discriminating duties imposed by France in 1816, when theirs, laid in 1790, were so injurious to the navigation of France, it is at least allowable to compare the duties respectively imposed by either party upon the productions of the soil and industry of the other. We shall therefore proceed to state the principal articles of exportation of both countries, (excluding the discriminating duties,) and, to be more distinct, in the simplest form.

Commercial interests.

This question is easy to solve.

If an American planter or merchant send to France, in a French vessel, $2,000 worth of cotton and tobacco, he will have to pay for the $1,000 worth of cotton from $95 to $100—say $100.

For the $1,000 worth of tobacco—nothing.

If a French grower or merchant send to the United States, in an American vessel, $2,000 worth of brandies and wines, he will pay for the $1,000 worth of brandies from $800 to $850—say $800; for the $1,000 worth of wines from $500 to $600—say $550; $1,350.

Likewise, if a French merchant send to the United States, in an American vessel, an equal proportion, say $2,000 worth of silk and fancy goods, the duties thereon will amount, in the United States, to 15 per cent. on silks, 30 per cent. on the fancy goods—say $450.

We have given, in this statement, the principal articles of exportation and importation, and will observe—

1st. Pot ashes and rice are but of secondary importance in the amount of exports from the United States to France, though next in rank after cotton and tobacco.

2d. Rice pays but a low duty when imported in French bottoms, and "has seldom been subject to this duty; but, on the contrary, the shippers (as it has been already stated) have received several times from the Government a bounty for importing it, even in American bottoms."

3d. The Americans have the markets of all Europe for the sale of their productions, since they are allowed in France (without paying any duty) either to re-export them or to send them to Germany and Switzerland.

4th. The French, on the contrary, are under the necessity of selling in the United States, at any price, the articles which they send there, because they cannot re-export them without paying the drawback duty, and have, besides, no ports at hand to send them to.

5th. The different articles exported by France for the United States (fancy goods for example) pay such heavy duties, and are so liable to damages and to fluctuations in value, that those who deal in them frequently suffer considerable losses, and are ruined, in the end, by the trade.

6th. There is, therefore, no possible comparison between the positive advantages resulting to the American and to the French merchants from the commercial relations of the two countries.

Navigation.

The discriminating duties have originated in both countries from the same motive, the *interest of navigation.*

I make no mention of rice or flour, because since the French tariff is in execution they have seldom been subject to the duty, and several times, on the contrary, the shippers have received from the Government a bounty for importing them in American bottoms. And if we reflect that a certain proportion of the cotton and ashes imported in French ports, particularly those of Bordeaux and Marseilles, sell there in bonds, we may overlook the difference of duty on the small quantity of other articles that may sell for consumption.

From this calculation it would, therefore, appear that a tonnage duty of *eight dollars* on French vessels would have been amply sufficient to compensate for the extra duty paid in France on goods imported in American vessels; but, at the same time, the law which imposes an additional tenth on the duties paid by goods of all kinds imported in French vessels ought to have been repealed; for that tenth being about equal to the price of freight of almost all articles imported from France, French vessels can never come to the United States with a cargo, and are therefore deprived of a very great advantage enjoyed solely by American vessels.

NOTE FROM THE SAME.

"I stated, in consequence of my first calculation, that the favor secured in France to French bottoms was equal to $8 per ton.

I shall now proceed, on the other hand, to state the advantages enjoyed by the Americans:

1. *The freights on return cargoes.*—Suppose they employ one-fourth of the tonnage in the trade, and estimating the amount of freight to be $12, or less, this would still give to the Americans an advantage equal to $3 per ton.

2. *The importation of goods for the transit.*—It would be necessary, in order to calculate this advantage, to have a statement

of the productions of the United States, and of those of other countries, imported by them into France, and then reported. It has not been in my power to obtain it.

From this it is clear that if a duty of $5 per ton were imposed in the United States upon French bottoms, the Americans would still have over French vessels the benefit of the transit, as well as other advantages easy to discover.

Supposing, after all, that matters should remain as they were before the discussion began, French vessels could not enter into competition unless they paid less than that duty of $5 per ton, or, what comes to the same thing, unless the difference between the duties paid by the Americans at Havre upon the productions brought by them should be equivalent to the duty of $5 per ton, and moreover to the benefit of the transit and other advantages not enumerated here."

NOTE.—To the above calculations the following remarks are made:

1. That the return cargoes from France employed more than one-fourth of the whole American tonnage in the trade.

2. That the freight upon exports from France to the United States is generally above $12.

3. That the foreign productions carried by the Americans to France amounted to more than one-fourth of their exports to that country.

4. That the right of *transit* and of re-exporting free of duty such goods as are carried into the (entrepots) deposits established in France were very considerable advantages to the Americans.

From which the difference against the Americans was reduced to much less than stated in the above note. The merchant of New York probably meant to be *liberal* in his calculations, in order to give more weight to his opinions and conclusions.

They cannot, therefore, be considered in any other light, since it is evident that the merchants or owners may, on both sides, avoid them by employing for the carriage of their goods or productions the vessels of the country for which they are destined.

In point of equity and reciprocity, it must be allowed that the United States have no right to complain, since France did no more in 1816 than follow the example which they themselves had set in 1790.

Let us now examine whether France has done more for the encouragement of her navigation than the United States had done for theirs.

It would appear necessary, first, to come to an understanding respecting the quantity of pounds or kilogrammes which form a ton of each species of goods. The Chambers of Commerce of France, England, and of the United States differ on this point, and so do the merchants of those different countries; even when residents of the same town they generally disagree.

It will be observed, by the way, that this difficulty, which has been the cause of so much misunderstanding, might be easily raised by fixing a precise quantity of pounds and of kilogrammes for the ton of each of the principal articles of the trade of the two countries.

The same might be done for the measurement of vessels; for much complaint has been made, as well in France as in the United States, against the arbitrary manner in which vessels are gauged in either country. Nothing can be easier than to come to some agreement on this point.

Taking, however, the average of the different calculations collected from different quarters on this question, we find the ton of cotton in France to be from 351 to 352 kilogrammes, net weight.(a.)

We say net weight on account of the deduction of six per cent. allowed at the custom-house, viz: three per cent. for tar, and three per cent. for "boussoids" or "tombre de balance."

The surtax on cotton imported in foreign vessels (including the additional decime) amounts to .16f. 50c. per hundred kilogrammes, making 58f. 8c. or $10 89 per ton.

Brandies (4th proof) which are imported in greatest quantity from France into the United States, pay 4 8-10 cents per gallon. The ton, containing from 240 to 250 gallons, pays upon an average $11 78.

From this it results that France has, for a long time, paid upon the principal article of exportation into the United States (when brought in her own vessels) a surtax much more considerable than that which is paid by the United States, (and only since the year 1816,) upon the principal article of their importations into France in their vessels.

Tobacco is, after cotton, the most important article of exportation of the United States. The surtax paid in France upon this article is 11f. per hundred kilogrammes, making 66f. or $12 37 per ton.

But it must be observed that this surtax of $12 37 cents was merely nominal with regard to the navigation of the United States; for the difference of freights received by French vessels over those received by American vessels never amounted to more than $6 per ton; most generally it has been much less, and owing to the privileges of transit and re-exportation there was often no difference at all.

We shall, however, state this difference at six dollars. Mercantile men well know that even this is too high.

The surtax upon French wines has, indeed, been diminished by the act of March, 1818; but can that be considered as an advantage conceded to France which was a mere act of justice, obtained after a lapse of many years, after repeated remonstrances, and which, besides, is still inadequate?

As to the other productions of the soil and industry of France, it is obvious that the surtax in the United States is tantamount to a sort of prohibition against French vessels, while there was none of the productions of the United States which could not be imported, and was not, in fact, imported into France in American bottoms before the ordinance of the 26th of July.

It must, moreover, be observed that several of the productions which the Americans are at liberty to carry to France (as staves, for example,) pay no discriminating duty at all.

From all the information which has been obtained from France, and in the various seaports of the United States, the following facts may be asserted as beyond all doubt:

1st. Since 1816 there has never been any material difference between the freights received by American vessels and those given to French vessels for the carriage of rioc and pot ashes.

2d. On tobacco, this difference has not exceeded six dollars per ton, and has often been as small as three dollars per ton.

3d. On cotton, it cannot be valued at more than eight dollars per ton.

4th. The produce of the East and West Indies, and of other foreign countries, imported into France in American vessels, and sold there for exportation, free of duty, composed more than one-quarter of the whole quantity of goods imported by them into France.

5th. The return cargoes employed at least one-third of the tonnage engaged in the trade with France.

Upon these data, and estimating the importations of foreign productions only for two-sevenths of all the articles imported into France in American bottoms, we shall say:

Two-sevenths of a ton pay... $0 00
One-seventh of tobacco, at $6 per ton..   86
Four-sevenths of cotton, &c., at $8 per ton... 4 57

The whole difference of these calculations would therefore be................................ 5 43
And supposing that the return cargoes, which we think compose one-third of the American tonnage
    employed in the trade, should in fact be only one-fourth, and estimating at $12 the freights
    from the United States to France, (while in fact they have always been from $12 to $15,) we
    shall have to deduct from the above $5 43.. 3 00

The balance against the Americans will only be $2 43, and they will still have the privilege of
    transit and other advantages already enumerated.. 2 43

It is therefore evident that calculations may easily be opposed to calculations, but it is not so easy to do away the positive results of conclusive facts, and the fact is—

(a) The ton of cotton is generally valued at from 375 to 400 kilogrammes; at 400 kilogrammes gross, it would be 376 kilogrammes net weight. But, in our opinion, that is too high an estimation, and it has appeared more correct to take the average of the different opinions obtained on the subject. The same has been done in regard to tobacco. But, at all events, nothing can be easier than to fix a standard for both countries as proposed above, which would resolve all difficulties on that score.

That France has done no more than follow the example first set by the United States; that in doing this she observed much moderation.

That, in spite of the discriminating duties, the United States had still, before the act of the 15th of May, more than half of the tonnage employed in the trade between the United States and France.

And, that the navigation of France has no share whatever in the freights of the exports from France to the United States.

To sum up, we shall say:

1st. That the tonnage of foreign nations, employed in their trade with the United States, stood thus in 1821—

Tonnage entered into the United States..	81,226
Tonnage departing from the United States...	83,073
Total foreign tonnage in 1821.......................................	164,299

2dly. And the tonnage of the United States in 1821—

Tonnage entered into the United States...	765,098
Tonnage departing from the United States...	804,947
Total amount of tonnage in 1821....................................	1,570,045

The United States ought to be satisfied with the unparalleled progress of their navigation, and the evident effects of their discriminating duties, since their entire tonnage, of every description, only amounted, in 1789, to 201,562.

France is far from expecting the same happy results; all she wishes is to re-establish her mercantile shipping, so as to be able to place her Navy upon its proper respectable footing. France cannot, therefore, without sacrificing her navigation, consent to what is proposed by the United States. She cannot revoke her discriminating duties; she offers to reduce them, this is all she can do.

If that offer, which has been assented to by the Federal Government, should again be adopted as a basis, it would be possible to conclude an arrangement between the two countries. Such are the conciliatory dispositions which the Government of his Majesty has never ceased to evince, that it is not perceived what obstacle could prevent it from being concluded as soon as the points in which the national honor is interested shall be settled in a proper manner.

There remain, therefore, three courses to be pursued:

1st. The mutual repeal of the acts in consequence of which the direct commercial relations of the two countries have been interrupted.

2d. The mutual reduction of their respective discriminating duties in a proportion of, say ——, or a surtax upon every ton of merchandise, equal in both countries.

3d. To break off the negotiation, and wait until that of the two parties which may be in error shall have been informed through the salutary influence of time and experience.

The first is the most simple and, it may be added, the most consistent with the friendly dispositions of the two nations; it would give their Governments leisure to come to a better understanding on what is required by their interests, whether viewed separately or in their reciprocal connexion.

The second would be a sort of *mezzo termine*—a provisional arrangement—or rather an experiment which would probably lead to the same result, but by a course which, it must be allowed, would not be as eligible as the first; for in all transactions, as well between nations as between private individuals, liberality and courtesy always prove most satisfactory in the end.

The third might possibly lead to an unhappy state of things; France would probably be under the necessity of completing the ordinance of the 26th of July to the full extent of the principle of reprisals; the United States would, in all probability, reciprocate measures of the same nature, which would lead to an almost entire interruption of their commercial relations: even indirect trade would find a different channel.

Those who calculated amiss, whether designedly or through ignorance, (and it must be allowed that in both countries there are men who are ill informed, and some who have no great inclination to promote the union of the two countries,) such men would unite to foment ill will, to awake feelings of national pride, and would seek to prove that such a state of things affected but slightly the commercial interests of the parties; they might perhaps, by their clamors and false representations, contrive to make the Governments persevere in the most injudicious and unwise course of policy they could possibly adopt; for after all, if neither party can sacrifice the interests of its navigation, they both have a real, and, it may be well said, paramount interest *in being united*. With this opinion the enlightened and prudent men of both nations are fully impressed. Let them, therefore, unite their efforts to remove difficulties which, in fact, must be considered as having but a secondary importance when weighed in the scale of great political interests.

NOTE.—Much has been said about certain regulations, supposed to be injurious to the progress of French navigators.

To this it might be answered, that complaints are constantly made in the United States against the imprudence of American seamen, as it appears from several articles inserted in the public prints, and particularly in the National Intelligencer.

It might be, moreover, observed, that every nation has a right to establish such regulations as it may think proper for its navigation, and to adopt such measures of safety and precaution as it may deem necessary.

Admitting, however, that, everything well calculated, it might, perhaps, be better to leave individuals to act for themselves whenever they alone are to be exposed, we would observe that even though the regulations established in France should, in their nature, be injurious to navigation, they cannot, in fact, have had any such effect, since the greater part of them are not enforced; and the Baron Portal, their Minister of the Navy, completely defeated this great objection in our presence, before several members of the general council of commerce.

The English, who are so knowing in navigation, have probably established bad maritime regulations, at least since their commercial treaty with the United States; for it appears by the public documents of this year that the United States have more than seven-eighths of the tonnage employed in the trade of the two nations.*

The English must have become very bad seamen, or it must be admitted that several real causes, which are quite independent of the art of navigation, combine to give to the American the immense advantages they have obtained over the English in the carrying trade of the two countries.

England, we must again repeat it, has calculated that if she lost on one point she would secure a profit on another; and what would France gain by consenting to the entire sacrifice of her share of the carrying trade with the United States?

Let the Americans deal with France as she does with them; she takes much of their bulky articles; let them take a corresponding quantity of wines and brandies; and there will be then something like a reciprocity in the mutual relations of the two countries.

But how, in the present state of their commercial relations, can it be expected that France will consent to adopt the basis of a nominal reciprocity?

It is certain that, under the influence of her discriminating duties, France had already succeeded in reviving in some degree her commercial shipping. It is even probable that, before two or three years, she might have obtained one-half of the carrying trade between the two countries if matters had remained in the same state as before the act of the 15th of May, 1820.

France, although she had not yet one-half of the carrying trade between the two countries has, however, from a disposition to conciliate, thought proper to propose an equal reduction by both parties of their respective discriminating duties, taken as they existed in the United States since 1790, and in France since 1816.

Without examining here the proper proportion of such reduction, we may state, without fearing to be mistaken, that if the reduction be of one-quarter, the navigation of France may (in the course of time) obtain nearly an equal share in the carrying trade.

If it be of one-third, France will have hardly one-third of the carrying trade.

And if the reduction be of one-half, France will scarcely obtain one-fourth.

Leaving it to more experienced speculators to present, if they can, the question under a more favorable aspect, we give the solution as we apprehend it, and conclude by again stating *that no convention is good but such as can be lasting.*

There still remains another question; it is of a delicate nature, but we shall treat it with candor, esteeming it ever best so to do.

Are the cottons of the United States (for in these lie all the difficulties) indispensable to France?

Have the Americans a right to expect that, by adhering to their basis of a nominal reciprocity, they will bring his Majesty's Government to consent to it in the end?

France wants the different productions of this Republic, but she cares much more for bonds of friendship which should keep the two countries ever united.

No union can be permanent beween nations except when consistent with the *interests* of both parties, and especially with *their national independence.* One of the interests of France is the prosperity of her navigation.

Her independence requires that those of her wants which she cannot satisfy with the production of her own soil should never become indispensably necessary.

If, therefore, any foreign production, and more especially the growth of a country beyond the seas, should happen to be deemed indispensable to France, it is probable, we shall say it is indubitable, that, so soon as this is perceived, patriotism and good sense will unite to make her citizens break off such anti-national habits. A great and powerful nation should never place any branch of its national industry under the absolute dependence of a foreign power, and still less under that of uncertain events.

But this is not the case with France; and we are well persuaded that sensible and well informed men in the United States judge perfectly well her situation, her resources, and the means she possesses of securing the prosperity of her manufactures, without sacrificing her navigation.

Nothing can be indispensable to France; and, we still like to repeat it, what she principally desires of the United States is their friendship.

The union of the two countries will ever be more valuable to them than a mere nominal reciprocity; they will find in this wise policy what is their real interest: "A reciprocity of advantages."

Baron de Neuville to the Secretary of State.

[Translation.]

WASHINGTON, *April* 5, 1822.

SIR: I have just received the report of the Committee on Commerce of the House of Representatives.

As that document did not come to me through any official channel, I shall refrain from noticing some grave errors relating to France; and without discussing or commenting upon the principal fact stated by the committee, viz: "That, before the act of the 15th of May, 1820, the discriminating duties paid in our ports by American vessels amounted to eighteen dollars per ton of merchandise." I have now the honor to propose, taking that statement for a basis, to reduce the surtax of France, not to one-half, nor to one-third, but even to *one-fourth* of that sum, and to apply that discriminating duty indistinctly to all the productions of the United States imported into France in American bottoms.

I propose this arrangement, sir, for the space of eighteen months; and in case no treaty of commerce has been concluded between the two countries before the expiration of that period, I even consent, for the following year, to retrench one-eighth from the surtax already reduced to one-fourth. As also, that the same reduction be made, from year to year, so long as neither of the two Governments shall have declared, at least six months beforehand, that it cannot continue upon the same footing.

It is, of course, understood, as a fair reciprocity, that no higher duties shall be imposed in the United

_____

a Tonnage entered into the United States from England and dependencies, in 1821: American, 387,110 tons; tonnage departed from the United States: American, 305,418 tons; total, 692,528 tons.

Tonnage entered into the United States from England and dependencies, in 1821: English, 49,781 tons; tonnage departed from the United States: English, 31,136 tons; total, 80,917 tons.

States upon the productions of France, imported in French vessels, and that an equal reduction shall likewise be made thereon from year to year.

I have not received from the Viscount de Montmorency the instructions announced by Mr. Gallatin in his despatches, of which you were pleased to give me communication; and my opinion still remains unaltered as to the reduction which it would have been expedient to adopt for the real interest of both countries; and I therefore yield at this time to a consideration which must outweigh all others in the eye of a sincere friend to both countries, I mean the urgency for them both of re-establishing, immediately, their direct commercial relations.

In the course of one year, or of eighteen months, Mr. Sanford's law will accomplish the rest; it will establish incontrovertible facts, and thus put an end to all conjectural calculations.

I make no mention, sir, of the other points that remain to be settled, so much do I like to persuade myself that we shall readily come to an understanding upon them all.

As I mean to despatch Count d'Apremont on the 10th of this month, I must request, sir, that you will be pleased to inform me as soon as possible of the decision of the President.

Accept, &c., &c.,

G. HYDE DE NEUVILLE.

Hon. J. Q. ADAMS, &c., &c., &c.

Mr. Adams to Mr. de Neuville.

DEPARTMENT OF STATE, *Washington, April 9, 1822.*

SIR: Your letters of the 11th of March and of the 5th instant, together with the statement of facts received with the former, have been submitted to the consideration of the President of the United States.

He has thought that a further discussion of the principal topics embraced by the statement of facts not being likely to result in the object most desirable to the two countries—the restoration of the direct commercial intercourse between them—might with propriety be postponed for the present. The *right* of France and of the United States, respectively, to enact laws for the advantage of their own shipping interests has not been contested by us; and as the proposal and desire of the United States have been to establish the *future* intercourse between the two nations upon the most entire and perfect reciprocity; as this disposition was manifested by the act of Congress of March 3, 1815, more than a year before the heavy discriminating duties with which France charged the principal articles of the produce and manufacture of the United States imported in American vessels, it is useless to inquire whether, twenty-five years before, France or the United States had been the first to pass laws for the advantage of their own navigation, or what the effect of those laws had been during the long protracted convulsions of the intervening period.

I come, therefore, immediately to the proposal in your letter of the 5th instant, which is understood to be, that, in lieu of all the discriminating duties now existing in France upon American vessels and the produce of the United States imported in them, a duty of surcharge of $4 50 upon the *American* ton of laden merchandise shall be levied upon condition that, reciprocally, no higher duties of discrimination shall be levied in the United States upon the productions of France imported in French vessels in the United States; and that this surcharge shall, at the end of eighteen months, be yet further reduced by one-eighth every year until notice shall be given by either party to the other.

In my letter of the 18th of August last, I had the honor of proposing a duty of nine francs surcharge upon the tonnage of importations of American vessels into France. As far as an estimate can be formed, your proposal is of a similar duty, from 25 to 30 francs per French ton, with a reciprocal duty of about six dollars here on the American ton of French merchandise imported in French vessels.

I am authorized to state that, with a view to meet this offer as nearly as possible, I am prepared to agree to an article of the following purport:

That all other discriminating duties, as well of tonnage as of surcharge, upon merchandise and port charges be repealed, and in lieu thereof, on American productions imported into France, there shall be paid on the French ton space of merchandise 12 francs; and that, on all French importations into the United States, a similar duty of $2 50 per ton, of American measurement, shall be levied; this extra tonnage to be reduced by one-eighth on both sides every year after the expiration of eighteen months till either party shall give six months' notice to the other that it cannot continue on the same footing.

I pray you, sir, to accept the assurance of my distinguished consideration.

JOHN QUINCY ADAMS.

His Excellency the Baron HYDE DE NEUVILLE,
　Envoy Extraordinary and Minister Plenipotentiary from France.

Mr. de Neuville to the Secretary of State.

[Translation.]

WASHINGTON, *April 11, 1822.*

SIR: Yesterday evening I had the honor of receiving your letter of the 9th, which I now answer.

I esteem it of no use to discuss facts. Yet still I ought to set those in a proper point of view which have been misunderstood.

I confess, sir, I do not see how a surcharge of only *four dollars and fifty cents* a ton can be equivalent to a duty of from twenty-five to thirty francs on one side and of about *six dollars* on the other.

I confess, also, that I cannot conceive how our discriminating duties previous to the act of May 15 were equal to a surcharge of $18 a ton, according to Mr. Newton, whilst, according to the calculation of Mr. Gallatin, (see his note of 7th July, 1820,) the difference against the American tonnage was 46 francs 55 centimes a ton, United States measure, or about 42 francs a ton, French measure, $7 87; and by the second calculation of the same, (see errors corrected in the note of July 7, 1820,) of 50 francs 90 centimes a ton, United States measure, or about 46 francs 50 centimes a ton, French measure, was $8 72.

It is evident that between the calculation of Mr. Newton.................................... $18 00
And the corrected one of Mr. Gallatin...   8 72
                                                                                     ————
There is a difference of...   9 28

This difference is enormous, it must be allowed. Now, it is at least allowable to conclude, from the discordance of the two able calculators, that figures are not always *facts*, and that facts can be clearly proved without figures.

I am also obliged to confess that I cannot conceive how (in case of our agreeing) you now propose to me, sir, 12 francs for $2 50, when your offer of the month of August was 9 francs for $1 50.

Permit me to remark to you that there is a loss to me of 20 per cent. in your proposition of the day before yesterday, and, that it may correspond with the other, it ought to be at least 15 francs for $2 50.

Let us add, sir, that I ought to be as much surprised to see that there is no question but of 12 *francs*, (and that when the business is of our coming nearer,) when one of your propositions in the month of August last (I lay aside the calculation of the Baron Pasquier, and only speak of that of Mr. Gallatin) is found to be equivalent to 13 *francs* a ton.

I will, moreover, sir, endeavor to explain better, if I can, my proposition of the fifth instant. It is simple and its execution easy.

My proposition is:

1. To substitute a surcharge of ———— upon each ton of merchandise, in lieu of the discriminating duties which existed in the two countries of the 15th of May.

2. To apply it in the two countries, so as that in France no more shall be paid upon the products of the soil and of the industry of the Union imported in vessels of the Republic, of other duties than those which shall be paid in the United States upon the products of the soil and of the industry of France imported in French ships. It is of no moment whether this surcharge be regulated *in dollars* or *in francs*.

The proportion of the two moneys is known. At all events, the ratio can be fixed for the whole duration of the convention.

The difficulty which might result from the difference between the French and the American pound may be also obviated, nothing being more easy, as I had the honor of proposing to you, sir, verbally and by writing, than to agree (at least with regard to the principal articles of commerce between the two countries) *upon the quantities* which, with respect to the different species of merchandise, shall be considered as forming the ton.

Two merchants will arrange these details in less than an hour, if my data are found to be a little different from yours; but, really, I believe that in this respect we will easily come to an understanding.

Thus, then, I have proposed (taking the calculation of the Committee of Commerce of the House) to reduce by *three-fourths* the discriminating duties which existed in France upon the products of the Union, in general, previous to the act of the 15th of May.

There would remain, consequently, $4 50, and nothing but $4 50, which would be equivalent to 23 to 24 francs, say 23 francs, cutting off by half the existing difference, according to Mr. Gallatin, between our respective propositions of the month of August last.*

Now, sir, the arrangement which I proposed in my letter of the 5th is evidently equivalent to the reduction on the part of France of its discriminating duties, viz: of three-fourths according to the calculation of Mr. Newton, and thirteen-twentieths according to that of Mr. Gallatin.

In conscience, sir, animated as the Government of his Majesty is with the spirit of conciliation, determined as it is to make a real and even considerable sacrifice that it may thereby come to a trial, to a temporary arrangement, can it think of going further?

Ought it even, in the well calculated interest of its navigation, to go so far? I think it ought not; and I confess I will abide firmly by my opinion as long as nothing shall demonstrate to me that my observations, which, as to myself and many others, are *facts*, are only mistakes or hypotheses.

The observations added to my letter of March 11 prove, sir, that my personal opinion is that, in the present state of her navigation, France ought hardly to go so far in the reduction as one-half.

But Mr. Gallatin's letter of the 15th of October to the Baron Pasquier seems to announce that, in order to close it, the Government of the King is disposed to overcome this obstruction.

I have not yet received the instructions of the Viscount Montmorency.

The Congress draws to a close.

The question is only about a temporary arrangement.

This arrangement would re-establish the direct relations between the two countries.

I am acquainted with the Sanford law.

I am convinced that in eighteen months or two years the data will be such on both sides that it will be finally possible to build upon solid foundations and to arrive at a proper and lasting arrangement.

I am therefore ready, sir, and shall be so, as long as I shall not receive instructions to the contrary, to agree (with respect to the point of which I have just been treating) to the foregoing clauses and conditions, referring myself, as to other points, to my letter of the 15th of August last, and to that of the 5th instant.

Accept, sir, the renewed assurances of my high consideration.

G. HYDE DE NEUVILLE,
Envoy Extraordinary, &c., &c.

Hon. J. Q. Adams, &c., &c.

* Extract of Mr. Gallatin's letter to the Baron Pasquier of October 15, 1821:

"I understood that your excellency considered the substitution of a duty of 1½ per cent. on the value, in lieu of the existing discriminating duties, as equivalent to a surcharge of 16 francs 50 centimes per ton on cotton, or nearly to one-fourth part of its present rate. The difference between the two Governments is, according to that calculation, about equal to that between one-half and one-fourth of the French surcharge, and equivalent to about 15 or 17 francs per ton, as it applies to cotton alone, or to all the American products. But I believe that Mr. Adams' proposal is less unfavorable to the United States; that, in the calculation made here, the prime cost of cotton in America has been rated too high; and that, according to the average prices at this moment, the rate of duty proposed by my Government is not equivalent to more than 13 francs per ton. I consider, therefore, the difference between the proposals respectively made to be equal to that between one-half and one-fifth of the French discriminating duty, and equivalent to about 18 or 20 francs per ton; and I think this difference to be the true point at issue between the two Governments."

Mr. Adams to the Baron de Neuville.

DEPARTMENT OF STATE, *Washington, April* 24, 1822.

SIR: Your letter of the 11th instant has been submitted to the consideration of the President of the United States.

The proposition made in my letter of the 9th was offered with a view to avoid a continuance of long and fruitless discussions. It was distinct and specific, without reference to calculations of various persons, all founded upon estimates composed of different elements. It was not deemed necessary to account for the difference between these estimates, as calculated by Mr. Gallatin, and as presented by a committee of the House of Representatives, nor to inquire upon what principle, after having stated, among the *facts* of your memoir of February 15, that the discriminating duties against American tonnage in France, before the act of Congress of May 15, 1820, were equivalent only to two dollars and forty-three cents, you now proposed, as a *reduction* of that amount, a discriminating tonnage duty of four and a half dollars.

If protracted discussion is to be substituted for specific proposal, with a view to the arrangement of the commercial intercourse between our countries, there are many things in your memoir of the 15th of February which will require examination. In the mean time, I must observe, that the propositions in my letter to you of (13th) August last, were *specific*, and that neither the estimates of Mr. Gallatin nor of Baron Pasquier, of what they were *equivalent to*, can be assumed as foundations for making them other than what they were.

One of them was a duty of nine francs per ton of merchandise, and the other a duty of one and a half per cent. on the value of merchandise. The latter is that which Baron Pasquier appears to have estimated as *equivalent* (applied only to the article of cotton) to a duty of sixteen and a half francs per ton, and Mr. Gallatin, as equivalent to thirteen francs. It is sufficient to say that when offered here it was considered as equivalent to the alternative proposal made at the same time with it, and that, in offering now to agree to a duty of twelve francs in its stead, we propose an increase of one-third to the advantage of France upon the former proposal.

Assuming, however, the estimate of Baron Pasquier as correct, and that one and a half per cent. on the *value* of merchandise was equivalent to a discriminating duty of 16.50 francs, in favor of France, I am now authorized to extend the offer to a reciprocal discriminating duty of two per cent. on the value of the merchandise, which, according to the calculation of Baron Pasquier, is equivalent to a tonnage duty of 22 francs, and, by your own calculation, within one franc of that which you propose.

This proposal has a double advantage of a reciprocity, not dependent upon the proportions of value between dollars and francs, or those of bulk between the French and American ton. But, if an arrangement, subject to these proportions, is to be made, and this Government consents to increase the duty against American merchandise in France, from nine to twelve francs a French ton, it will be necessary to restore the reciprocity of value in the amount of duties to be levied upon French merchandise, in the United States, by increasing the duty from $1\frac{1}{2}$ to $2\frac{1}{2}$ dollars on the American ton. It is true that this increase will be rather more on the merchandise of France in the United States than upon that of the United States in France; but the difference will only be sufficient to restore the equality of the duty on both sides. In offering to admit a duty of nine francs upon the French ton, for $1\frac{1}{2}$ dollar on the American ton, even the principle of a reciprocal duty of the same value, upon the same bulk of merchandise, was in some degree impaired, and in the small amount of the difference was found the only motive for the admission of the principle. If, therefore, the amount is to be increased, the balance must be restored.

The proposal in your note of the 5th instant was, that the discriminating duties of France, existing before the act of Congress of May 15, 1820, should be reduced to one-fourth. Assuming as correct the report of the Committee on Commerce, that they had been equivalent to eighteen dollars the ton, but as the duty will, of course, in France be levied in francs, and upon the French ton, in my letter of the 9th instant it was estimated that a duty of $4\frac{1}{2}$ dollars upon the American ton of merchandise would, when applied to the French measure and the French currency, range from 25 to 30 francs upon the French ton. By the convention of the 30th of April, 1803, the relative value of the moneys of the two countries was of $5\frac{333}{1000}$ francs to the dollar, by which $4\frac{1}{2}$ dollars are equal to 24 francs. The difference between the French and American ton, arising from different rules of admeasurement, is more or less, as applied to different vessels. In double decked vessels, such as must be all those navigating between the two countries, the American ton exceeds in capacity that of France, from one-tenth to one-fourth; that is, a vessel of 300 tons cleared out from the United States would be required in France to pay for from 330 to 360 tons; and if a duty of 24 francs per ton should be levied upon her cargo, arriving at Havre or Marseilles, it would be equivalent to a duty of between five and six dollars the American ton. Suppose, then, a French vessel of 350 tons, French measure, arriving in the United States, she pays a duty of $4\frac{1}{2}$ dollars a ton; measuring only 300 tons by the American measure, she pays 1,350 dollars surcharge. But an American vessel of the same capacity, paying 24 francs a ton upon 350 tons, will pay 8,400 francs or 1,575 dollars surcharge. She pays, therefore, 225 dollars more of surcharge in France than a French vessel of the same capacity will have paid in the United States, and the discriminating duty of 24 francs a ton, French measurement, will be equal to a duty of about six dollars a ton, levied upon the same vessel in the United States, and according to the American measure.

The offer that a surcharge of 12 francs on the French ton levied in France shall countervail a similar duty of $2\frac{1}{2}$ dollars on the American ton in the United States, assumes that the average difference between the two measurements is of one-tenth, or ten per cent. Thus, a French vessel of 300 tons, fully laden, would pay, in the United States, an extra duty of $2\frac{1}{2}$ dollars a ton upon 270 tons, or 675 dollars. An American vessel of the same capacity would pay in France 12 francs a ton upon 300 tons, or 3,600 francs, equal to the same sum of 675 dollars. This average agrees with the calculation of Mr. Gallatin, in the note B to his letter of July 7, 1820, to Baron Pasquier; a calculation very precisely founded upon a mean proportional between the French and the American rules of gauging for merchant vessels. It is more advantageous to France than the average drawn in his note of the next day, from the two American vessels, the Phœnix and the Solon, which were of $754\frac{24}{95}$ tons American, but paid in France, for 907 tons French tonnage, a difference of five to six.

A duty of two per cent. on the value of the merchandise, with more simplicity, would avoid the necessity of all these calculations.

I pray you, sir, to accept the assurance of my distinguished consideration.

JOHN QUINCY ADAMS.

Baron Hyde de Neuville, .
    Envoy Extraordinary, &c.

Baron de Neuville to the Secretary of State.

[Translation.]

Washington, *April* 28, 1822. ,

Sir: I now have the honor of replying to your letter of the 24th instant.

All my propositions are likewise offered with a view to avoid the continuance of long and fruitless discussions; they are precise and distinct; and the various calculations referred to by me are rather corollaries than the basis of my propositions.

But, after all, it is of but little importance to determine whether the calculations of the committee of the House of Representatives, of those of Mr. Gallatin, of Mr. Pasquier, whether yours, sir, or mine, be rigorously correct or not.

I have proposed $4 50 cents on either side, which, according to the calculations of the committee of the House, would be reducing the discriminating duties by three-fourths.

I have said 23 francs, thus dividing the difference between one-half and one-fifth; difference, which, according to Mr. Gallatin, is the real point of difficulty between the two Governments. (Mr. Gallatin rates the fifth at 13 francs.)

It is obvious that, if Mr. Gallatin has calculated right, my proposition tends to reduce the discriminating duties by $\frac{4}{4}$ths. But whether the above calculations be correct or not, my propositions are not, on that account, less distinct, viz: $4 50 cents in the first case; 23 francs in the second; both resulting upon the same principle, that, these various calculations being imperfect and uncertain, it is necessary to come to some positive point.

I accept, sir, the two per cent. on the value of merchandise, if that basis is to produce 22 francs per ton, or thereabouts; and, to avoid all misunderstanding on that score, all mistakes and errors, I propose to fix the maximum and minimum of the surtax, with regard to the principal articles of importation and exportation, and to agree that the discriminating duties be superseded on both sides by a duty of two per cent. on the value of merchandise, on condition, however, that this surtax shall never amount to less than 21 francs or more than 26 francs per ton on the articles hereafter specified.

Imported from the United States to France, cotton, tobacco, rice, pot ashes.

Imported from France to the United States, brandy, wine, silks, dry goods.

If you agree, sir, to this modification, which, in my opinion, is founded on a principle of justice, and which partly corresponds with Mr. Gallatin's views, (see his letter of the 15th October, 1821,) there will only remain for us to determine the respective quantities (pounds or kilogrammes) which, for the future, shall be considered as a ton, and to fix a rate of exchange for the continuation of the convention.

It cannot be necessary to observe, sir, that the minimum would be for France and the maximum for the United States; and that my proposition would not, by any means, be founded on a perfect reciprocity of advantages; but we have it now in view to make an experiment; and, to conclude, I am not afraid of being liberal, nay, even very liberal.

With this view, in case it should appear that the above arrangement is attended with difficulties, (and, I confess, sir, there seem to me to be many resulting from that mode of collection,) I again propose to resort to a discriminating duty on the ton of merchandise, which appears to me to be the easiest mode of coming to a temporary transaction. ,

I had spoken, sir, of 23 francs; you, sir, according to your last offer, calculate on 22; let us say 20, as a last word.

I will add, that in order to prove more clearly the sincerity of my propositions, and my candid desire of conciliating the real interests of the two countries, I am ready to sign the following clause:

"The discriminating duty of 20 francs per ton of merchandise shall be paid by each vessel in the respective ports, only upon the difference in value between its imported and exported cargo."

By reading again my observations of the 15th of February, and my subsequent letters, you will convince yourself, sir, that I never intended to reduce a duty of $4 50 to one only equivalent to $2 43. I did say, and I here repeat it, that, everything well considered, I only found a difference of $2 43 between the discriminating duties levied in the United States upon the productions of the soil and industry of France and the duties collected in France upon those of the United States; not taking even then to account certain advantages which the navigation of the United States has not ceased to enjoy in France, without any such being reciprocally granted to French shipping in the United States.

I did, therefore, propose, in lieu of the discriminating duties which exist in the United States since 1790, and of those imposed in France since 1790, which Mr. Gallatin considers as equivalent to 65 francs per ton, to substitute a surtax, which, being equal on both sides, would leave no room for disputes about reciprocity.

My propositions of this day are founded upon the same considerations.

Referring to my letters of the 5th and 11th of this month, as to the other points which remain to be settled,

    I have the honor, &c.,

G. HYDE DE NEUVILLE.

Hon. J. Q. Adams, *&c.*

Mr. Adams to Mr. de Neuville.

DEPARTMENT OF STATE, *Washington, May* 11, 1822.

SIR: In order to bring the discussion between us to a precise point, I have the honor of inclosing, herewith, a projet of a convention for your consideration; to the substance of which I am authorized by the President of the United States to agree.

In consenting to so heavy a discriminating duty as four dollars upon every ton of laden merchandise, for the first year of that arrangement, which is considered on both sides only as an experiment to restore the direct commercial intercourse between the two countries, so earnestly desired by the United States, a principal motive has been the suggestion, in some of your communications, of a gradual reduction, till the principle for which the United States have constantly and earnestly insisted—the principle of absolute reciprocity and mutual abandonment of all discriminating duties—shall be found, in the judgment of France herself, the system of intercourse most advantageous to her interests, as well as to those of the United States.

It is, therefore, proposed that the convention should be limited to four years' duration, and that, beginning with a discriminating duty of four dollars the laden ton in the United States, and of 20 francs the *tonneau* in France, it should be diminished by one-fourth every year on both sides.

I shall be happy to receive your observations on this projet, either in personal conference, or in writing, or by a counter-projet, as may be most agreeable and convenient to yourself.

I pray you, sir, to accept the assurance of my distinguished consideration.

JOHN QUINCY ADAMS.

His Excellency HYDE DE NEUVILLE,
  Envoy Extraordinary, &c.

Projet of a convention between the United States and France, communicated to the Baron Hyde de Neuville, with Mr. Adams' letter of May 11, 1822.

The United States of America and his most Christian Majesty, desirous, by a temporary agreement, to regulate the commerce and navigation between their respective Territories and people in such manner as to render the same reciprocally beneficial and satisfactory, and thereby lead to a more permanent and comprehensive arrangement, by treaty, of their commercial intercourse, have, respectively, furnished their full powers, in manner following—that is to say: the President of the United States, to John Quincy Adams, their Secretary of State; and his most Christian Majesty, to the Baron Hyde de Neuville, who after producing and showing to each other their said full powers, and exchanging copies of the same, have agreed on and concluded the following articles:

ARTICLE 1. There shall be no other or higher duties levied on the importation into the United States of any articles, the growth, produce, or manufacture of France, when imported in French vessels, than when in the vessels of the United States, excepting as follows: Upon all such articles so imported in French vessels, unless for transit or re-exportation, there shall be levied an additional duty of four dollars for every ton of merchandise laden in the vessels, according to the measurement of the United States, over and above the duty which shall be levied on articles of the same kind and of the same growth, produce, or manufacture, when imported in the vessels of the United States.

ARTICLE 2. And, in like manner, there shall be levied upon articles of the growth, produce, or manufacture of the United States, imported into France, (with the exception of articles imported for transit or re-exportation,) when in vessels of the United States, an additional duty of twenty francs for every ton of merchandise laden in the vessel, according to the measurement of French tonnage, over and above the duty which shall be levied on articles of the same kind and of the same growth, produce, or manufacture, when imported in French vessels.

ARTICLE 3. No other or higher duties of tonnage, light-money, port charges, pilotage, brokerage, or other charges upon shipping, shall be levied upon vessels of the United States, in the ports of France, than upon French vessels; nor upon French vessels, in the ports of the United States, than upon vessels of the United States.

ARTICLE 4. This convention shall be subject to the ratification of the President, by and with the advice and consent of the Senate of the United States, and to that of his most Christian Majesty. But it shall take effect for all vessels of the United States which shall arrive in France, and for all French vessels which shall arrive in the United States, from and after the 30th day of June next. It shall be in force for the term of four years from that day; but the duty of discrimination or surcharge upon articles of the growth, produce, or manufacture of France, imported into the United States in French vessels, shall be reduced one dollar for every laden ton each year during the said four years; and, in like manner, the duty of discrimination or surcharge upon articles of the growth, produce, or manufacture of the United States, imported into France in vessels of the United States, shall be reduced five francs for every laden ton each year during the said four years; so that the duty of surcharge upon the lading of French vessels in the United States shall, from and after the 30th day of June, 1823, for one year, be three dollars; the succeeding year, two dollars; and the last year, one dollar, for each laden ton; and, in like manner, the surcharge upon merchandise imported into France in vessels of the United States shall, from and after the 30th day of June, 1823, be, for one year, fifteen francs; for the next year, ten francs; and for the last year, five francs, for each laden ton.

ARTICLE 5. The ratifications of this convention shall be exchanged at Washington within one year from the date hereof, or sooner, if possible.

In witness whereof, we have hereunto set our hands and seals, this convention being drawn up and executed as original, in our respective languages, at the city of Washington, this —— day of May, in the year of our Lord 1822.

Baron Hyde de Neuville to the Secretary of State.

[Translation.]

WASHINGTON, *May* 15, 1822.

Mr. de Neuville requests Mr. Adams to excuse him for not waiting upon him at the Department of State, as he has been three days confined by indisposition. He has the honor to send to Mr. Adams the substance of a contre-projet. The articles are not duly arranged; but, in drawing up the convention, each clause shall be placed in order, and everything useless shall be expunged.

Mr. de Neuville is in hopes that the time desired by both countries has arrived, and prays Mr. Adams to accept the renewed assurances of his high consideration.

G. HYDE DE NEUVILLE.

Hon. J. Q. ADAMS.

Substance of a temporary arrangement between France and the United States, communicated to Mr. Adams May 15, 1822.

ARTICLE 1. The law of the 15th of May, 1820, and the ordinance of the 26th of July, same year, shall be repealed.

2. The extra duties levied on either side in consequence of said law and ordinance shall be refunded.

(3.) Mr. de Neuville thinks that it would perhaps be better to sign immediately a consular convention on the basis of that of 1788, with such modifications as might be deemed necessary.

He will refer on this subject to his letters of 31st of March, and 23d of May, 1819.

3. The consuls and vice consuls may cause to be arrested the captains, officers, mariners, sailors, and all other persons, being part of the crews of the vessels of their respective nations, who shall have deserted from the said vessels, in order to send them back and transport them out of the country; for which purpose the said consuls and vice consuls shall address themselves to the courts, judges, and officers competent, and shall demand the said deserters in writing, proving, by an exhibition of the registers of the vessels, or ship's roll, or of a copy of said document, certified by them, that those men were part of the said crews, and on this demand so proved (saving, however, where the contrary is proved) the delivery shall not be refused; and there shall be given all aid and assistance to the said consuls and vice consuls for the search, seizure, and arrest of the said deserters, who shall even be detained and kept in the prisons of the country at their request and expense until they shall have found an opportunity of sending them back. But if they be not sent back within three months, to be counted from the day of arrest, they shall be set at liberty, and shall be no more arrested for the same cause.

(4.) The clause relating to transit and re-exportation offers no great advantage except to the United States. Mr. de Neuville is nevertheless willing to insert it, such as proposed by Mr. Adams, articles 1 and 2 of his projet.

4. The discriminating duties levied in France upon foreign vessels shall be reduced, with regard to vessels of the United States laden with the productions of the soil or industry of the United States, to 20 francs per ton of merchandise.

5. The same surtax of 20 francs, corresponding to three dollars and seventy-five cents, shall be imposed in the United States per ton of merchandise imported in French vessels laden with productions of the soil or industry of France.

(6.) As soon as the basis shall have been adopted, Mr. de Neuville will have the honor to propose a table of the quantities which, with respect to each of the various species of merchandise mentioned in the adjoining article, shall be considered as forming a ton.

There can, at all events, be no difficulty on this point, since the question is as to the average of the rates generally received in trade.

6. In order that the amount of said duties be not left subject to the variation of arbitrary valuations, there shall be an understanding between the parties as to the amount per ton of each of the principal articles of imports and exports, viz:

Cotton, tobacco, rice, potash, wines, brandies, oil, silks, dry goods, &c.

The articles not thus specified shall be subjected to an equal rule of calculation according to their weight or bulk.

It is proposed to adopt as the basis of this valuation—

1st. The American pound (avoirdupois.)

2d. The American ton weight (20 cwt.)

3d. The American measurement ton (40 American cubic feet.)

On the whole, it is hereby intended to propose an equal rule for both countries, so as to render the surtax perfectly equal.

(7.) Mr. Gallatin has asserted that these duties amounted to eight francs in France and did not exceed five francs in the United States. This second sum is proposed here for both coutries. If any discussion should arise out of this proposal, Mr. de Neuville thinks it would be easy for him to prove that fixing the amount of these various duties would be the best means of preventing the future recurrence of those petty vexations of which foreigners have not ceased to complain in all countries, whether with or without sufficient ground. It must, moreover, be considered that, if France consents to so important a deviation from her general revenue laws, she cannot in any case consent to change to such an extent her port regulations.

(8.) The delay of two years is more than sufficient to answer the end proposed by the two Governments.

As their object is to make an experiment, it should be so established as not to press too heavily upon whichever of the two parties may, on experience; be found to have erred in the calculation.

Besides, the proposal of Mr. de Neuville is in perfect accordance with that made by Mr. Gallatin to his Majesty's Government, (vide letter of October 15, 1821.)

"Each of the two Governments," says Mr. Gallatin, "shall expressly reserve the right of annulling the arrangement whenever it shall please, by giving sufficient reasons to the other contracting party."

Most assuredly, if it be possible to make any further reduction after the two years; if, in three or four years, it should be possible to annul the entire surtax without injuring the navigation of the country, his Majesty's Government will cheerfully consent to do so. It desires only what is just, what is consistent with the real interest of both countries.

7. The tonnage duties and other collections levied upon vessels under public authority in the respective ports shall be regulated, as Mr. de Neuville has always proposed, upon a footing of perfect reciprocity, so that French vessels coming directly from France to the United States and American vessels coming directly from the United States to France shall not pay more than five francs per ton.

8. The present temporary arrangement shall be for two years; and even after the expiration of that term, it shall endure until the conclusion of a definitive convention, or until one of the parties shall have declared to the other its intention to abondon it; which declaration shall be made at least six months beforehand.

Mr. de Neuville would willingly agree, that if, after two years, the arrangement should continue without reclamation of either party, the surtax shall, in such case, be reciprocally reduced by one-eighth from year to year.

9. The present convention shall be ratified on either side, and the ratification shall be exchanged in the course of one year, or sooner if practicable. Nevertheless, its execution shall commence in the ports of both countries on the 25th of August next, and shall continue (in case the ratification shall not be had) for all such vessels as may have sailed bona fide from the ports of either nation.

Mr. de Neuville proposes to insert the following clause in this present temporary arrangement:

10. In order to favor commerce on both sides, it is agreed that the surtax imposed per ton of merchandise in the respective ports shall be levied only upon the difference in value between the imports and exports.

This clause shall take effect on the exchange of the ratifications, and either Government shall remain at liberty to retrench said clause if it should think proper so to do; which suppression shall not in any manner affect the validity of the other articles of the convention, which, in such case, shall continue to be executed as if said clause had never been inserted.

(10.) Example.—He that will import a cargo amounting to $10,000, and export to the amount of $6,000, will have a surtax of 20 francs, if in France, or three dollars and seventy-five cents, if in the United States, on such a number of tons of merchandise, selected at his option, upon his invoice, as will amount to the balance of $4,000.

If he exports a cargo equal or superior in value to his import cargo, he will have nothing to pay.

If the calculations of Mr. Gallatin on the gauging of vessels be correct, they only prove how necessary it is for both Governments to adopt, at least on the conclusion of a definitive convention, an equal rule of measurement; for Mr. de Neuville has found in the United States the same result that Mr. Gallatin found in France. He has before him at this time a statement relating to a French vessel from Havre (the Hirondella) which gauged in France from 182 to 183 tons, and paid in Savannah for 205 63-95 tons. He could produce many other statements of the same nature. This proves, at least, that the same inconveniences exist on both sides.

DEPARTMENT OF STATE, *May* 27, 1822.

Observations on the "substance of a temporary arrangement between France and the United States," communicated by his Excellency the Baron Hyde de Neuville, Envoy Extraordinary and Minister Plenipotentiary from France, May 15, 1822.

Articles 1 and 2 inadmissible. The arrangement will be most effectually made without retrospective reference to former acts on either side. It will, in effect, repeal the laws mentioned, and leave a formal repeal of them quite unnecessary. The duties levied within a reasonable time of notice of their existence have already been refunded by both countries. It is not necessary for either country to retrace its steps.

Article 3 belongs to a consular convention. We are willing to enter upon a negotiation for that purpose, but it will require much time to settle its details. For a temporary arrangement, we desire, first of all, *to restore the direct intercourse between the two countries;* that is, to adjust the discrimination duties *alone.* When this shall have been done, the parties will, on both sides, be more amicably disposed and better qualified to discuss the general questions interesting to their commercial relations.

The 4th and 5th articles proposed by the Baron de Neuville are not reciprocal either in form or substance. By the 4th it is proposed merely to *reduce,* in France, the existing extra duties on merchandise imported in vessels of the United States; while in the 5th it is proposed that new duties should be imposed on merchandise imported in French vessels into the United States. On the part of France, it offers a mere modification of existing laws; on that of the United States, a change of the basis of legislation itself is required. If the United States abandon the basis of their revenue legislation for this arrangement, France must do the same. To proceed upon the plan of *reduction* on both sides is impracticable, since even the reduction on the side of France, which the Baron proposes, must be met by *increase* of the duties in the United States. It is therefore desirable that the present arrangement should be made on a basis having no reference to the existing legislation of either country; saying that, instead of all extra duties heretofore levied on either side, there shall in future be levied so much upon importations in French vessels in the United States and upon importations in vessels of the United States into France.

Article 6. It is believed that a more accurate proportion than of 20 francs upon the French ton and of four dollars upon the American ton could not be devised, and that it would, in the result, be to the advantage of France. A new table of tonnage, fixing different quantities of each specific article to be taken as between the parties for a ton, would render more complex instead of simplifying the question of measurement, and create additional embarrassments to the navigators and merchants of both nations.

Article 7. This article may be admitted, but it must be made specific in form; that is, it must be explained what is meant by *other collections* levied upon vessels under public authority. It would be far more simple, and answer more effectually the object desired, of *perfect reciprocity,* to say of *all* such duties that there shall be levied no more on the vessels of either nation than upon those of the other in either country.

Article 8. Agreed to, with the reduction of the discriminating duties, after two years, by one-eighth from year to year.

Article 9. Agreed to, substituting the 1st of September for the 25th of August.

Article 10. Agreed to, with the proviso admitted by the Baron, that articles imported for transit or exportation are not to be charged with any extra duties.

The Secretary of State sent to the Baron de Neuville the draught of a convention in formal articles. He invites the Baron to discuss those articles by *admission, proposed alteration, or rejection;* or to send him a counter-projet, also in formal articles, to be discussed in that manner. This is obviously the mode of bringing the negotiation most speedily to a termination.

DEPARTMENT OF STATE, *Washington, June 14, 1822.*

SIR: I have the honor of inclosing herewith the draught of a convention which I am authorized on the part of the United States to sign. It is in most respects conformable to the projet which I had the honor of last receiving from you. I shall be happy to confer with you upon the particulars in which it differs therefrom at 3 o'clock this day, or at the same hour to-morrow, should that better suit your convenience.

I pray you, sir, to accept the assurance of my distinguished consideration.

His Excellency the BARON HYDE DE NEUVILLE,
  Envoy Extraordinary, &c.

Convention of Navigation and Commerce between the United States of America and his Majesty the King of France and Navarre.

The United States of America and his Majesty the King of France and Navarre, being desirous of settling the relations of navigation and commerce between their respective nations by a temporary convention reciprocally beneficial and satisfactory, and thereby of leading to a more permanent and comprehensive arrangement, have, respectively, furnished their full powers in manner following—that is to say: The President of the United States, to John Quincy Adams, their Secretary of State; and his Most Christian Majesty the King of France and Navarre, to the Baron Hyde de Neuville, Knight of the Royal and Military Order of St. Louis, Commander of the Legion of Honor, Grand Cross of the Royal American Order of Isabella the Catholic, his Envoy Extraordinary and Minister Plenipotentiary near the United States, who, after exchanging their full powers, have agreed on the following articles:

ARTICLE 1. Articles of the growth, produce, or manufacture of the United States, imported into France in vessels of the United States, shall pay an additional duty, not exceeding twenty francs per ton of merchandise, over and above the duties paid on the like articles, also of the growth, produce, or manufacture of the United States, when imported in French vessels.

ARTICLE 2. Articles of the growth, produce, or manufacture of France, imported into the United States in French vessels, shall pay an additional duty, not exceeding three dollars and seventy-five cents per ton of merchandise, over and above the duties collected upon the like articles, also of the growth, produce, or manufacture of France, when imported in vessels of the United States.

ARTICLE 3. The above extra duties shall not be levied, either in France or in the United States, upon articles imported for transit or re-exportation; but such articles, and the vessels importing them, of either nation, shall continue to enjoy, in the United States and in France, the same advantages of transit and re-exportation for all articles, as heretofore, and on the same terms.

ARTICLE 4. The following quantities shall be considered as forming the ton of merchandise for each of the articles hereinafter specified:

Wines, four 58 gallon hogsheads, or 232 gallons, of 231 cubic inches, American measure.

Brandies, and all other liquids, 232 gallons.

Silks, and all other dry goods, and all other articles usually subject to measurement, forty-two cubic feet, French, in France, and fifty cubic feet, American measure, in the United States.

Cotton, 882 lbs. avoirdupois weight, or 400 kilogrammes.

Tobacco, 1680 lbs. avoirdupois weight, or 762 kilogrammes.

Ashes, pot and pearl, 2240 lbs. avoirdupois, or 1016 kilogrammes.

Rice, 1792 lbs. gross avoirdupois, or 812 kilogrammes.

And for all weighable articles not specified, 2240 lbs. avoirdupois, or 1016 kilogrammes.

ARTICLE 5. The duties of tonnage, light-money, port-charges, brokerage, and other duties upon foreign shipping, over and above those paid by the national shipping in the two countries, respectively, other than those specified in articles 1 and 2 of the present convention, shall not exceed, in France, five francs per ton of the vessel's American register, nor 94 cents, in the United States, per ton, of the vessel's French passport, for vessels of the United States in France, nor for vessels of France in the United States.

ARTICLE 6. The contracting parties, wishing to favor their mutual commerce by affording in their ports every necessary assistance to their respective vessels, have agreed that the sailors, who shall desert from their vessels in the ports of the other, shall be arrested and delivered up at the demand, in writing, of the consul or vice consul, who shall nevertheless be held to prove that the deserters belonged to the vessels claiming them, and shall exhibit the shipping paper, roll of the equipage, or other document, officially showing the list of the crew; and if the name of the deserter or deserters claimed shall appear therein, and not be otherwise disproved, they shall be arrested, held in custody, and delivered to the vessel to which they belong.

ARTICLE 7. The present temporary convention shall be in force for two years, from the first day of September next, and after the expiration of that term until the conclusion of the definitive treaty, or until one of the parties shall have declared its intention to renounce it; which declaration shall be made at least six months beforehand. And in case the present arrangement should remain without such declaration of its discontinuance by either party, the extra duties specified in the first and second articles shall, from the expiration of the said two years, be on both sides diminished by one-fourth of their whole amount, and afterwards by one-fourth of the said amount from year to year, so long as neither party shall have declared the intention of renouncing it, as above stated.

ARTICLE 8. The present convention shall be ratified on both sides, and the ratifications shall be exchanged at Washington, within one year from the date hereof, or sooner if possible; but the execution of the said convention shall commence in both countries on the first of September next, and shall be effective, even in case of non-ratification, for all such vessels as may have sailed *bona fide* for the ports of either nation in the confidence of its being in force.

In faith whereof, the respective plenipotentiaries have signed the present convention, original in both the languages of the United States and of France, and have thereto affixed their seals, at the city of Washington, this — day of June, in the year of our Lord one thousand eight hundred and twenty-two.

SEPARATE ARTICLES.

ARTICLE 1. It is agreed that the extra duties specified in the first and second articles of this convention shall be levied only upon the excess of value of the merchandise imported over the value of the merchandise exported in the same vessel upon the same voyage; so that if the value of the articles exported shall equal or exceed that of the articles imported in the same vessel, (not including, however, articles imported for transit or re-exportation,) no such extra duties shall be levied; and if the articles exported are less in value than those imported, the extra duties shall be levied only upon the amount of the difference of their value. This article, however, shall take effect only in case of ratification on both sides, and not until two months after the exchange of the ratifications; but the refusal to ratify this article on either side shall in nowise affect or impair the ratification or the validity of the preceding articles of this convention.

ARTICLE 2. The extra duties levied on either side, by virtue of the act of Congress of the 15th May, 1820, and of the ordinances of July 26, of the same year, and others confirmative thereof, and which have not already been paid back, shall be refunded.

Signed and sealed as above, this — day of June, 1822.

Extract of a letter from the Baron Hyde de Neuville to the Secretary of State, dated at

WASHINGTON, *June* 22, 1822.

"We have agreed, sir, to leave for subsequent discussion the affairs which have not as yet been settled. I have, therefore, the honor to inform you that I shall attend at the Department of State at the hour appointed, on Monday next, for the purpose of signing the temporary convention of navigation and commerce, the various articles of which have been agreed upon."

CONVENTION WITH GREAT BRITAIN UNDER THE MEDIATION OF RUSSIA, EXPLANATORY OF THE FIRST ARTICLE OF THE TREATY OF GHENT, CONCERNING INDEMNITY FOR SLAVES CARRIED FROM THE UNITED STATES BY THE BRITISH FORCES IN 1812-'14.

COMMUNICATED TO THE HOUSE OF REPRESENTATIVES JANUARY 25, 1823.

To the Speaker of the House of Representatives of the United States:
The convention concluded and signed at St. Petersburg, on the 12th day of July last, under the mediation of his Imperial Majesty the Emperor of all the Russias, having been ratified by the three powers parties thereto, and the ratifications of the same having been duly exchanged, copies of it are now communicated to Congress, to the end that the measures for carrying it, on the part of the United States, into execution may obtain the co-operation of the Legislature necessary to the accomplishment of some of its provisions. A translation is subjoined of the three explanatory documents, in the French language, referred to in the fourth article of the convention, and annexed to it. The agreement executed at the exchange of the ratifications is likewise communicated.

JAMES MONROE.

WASHINGTON, *January* 16, 1823.

BY THE PRESIDENT OF THE UNITED STATES.

A PROCLAMATION.

Whereas a convention between the United States of America and his Britannic Majesty was concluded and signed at St. Petersburg, under the mediation of the Emperor of all the Russias, on the twelfth day of July last, by the respective plenipotentiaries of the three powers: And whereas the said convention has been by them duly ratified, and the respective ratifications of the same were exchanged at Washington, on the tenth day of the present month, by John Quincy Adams, Secretary of State of the United States, the Right Honorable Stratford Canning, Envoy Extraordinary and Minister Plenipotentiary of his Britannic Majesty, and Mr. George Ellisen, Chargé d'Affaires of his Imperial Majesty the Emperor of all the Russias, on the part of their several Governments: which convention is in the words following, to wit:

In the name of the most holy and indivisible Trinity.

The President of the United States of America and his Majesty the King of the United Kingdom of Great Britain and Ireland, having agreed, in pursuance of the fifth article of the convention concluded at London on the 20th day of October, 1818, to refer the differences which had arisen between the two Governments upon the true construction and meaning of the first article of the treaty of peace and amity, concluded at Ghent on the 24th day of December, 1814, to the friendly arbitration of His Majesty the Emperor of all the Russias, mutually engaging to consider his decision as final and conclusive: And his said Imperial Majesty having, after due consideration, given his decision upon these differences in the following terms, to wit:

"That the United States of America are entitled to claim from Great Britain a just indemnification for all private property which the British forces may have carried away; and as the question relates to slaves more especially, for all the slaves that the British forces may have carried away from places and territories, of which the treaty stipulates the restitution, in quitting these same places and territories."

"That the United States are entitled to consider as having been so carried away all such slaves as may have been transferred from the above mentioned territories to British vessels within the waters of the said territories, and who for this reason may not have been restored."

"But that, if there should be any American slaves who were carried away from territories of which the first article of the treaty of Ghent has not stipulated the restitution to the United States, the United States are *not* entitled to claim an indemnification for the said slaves."

Now, for the purpose of carrying into effect this award of his Imperial Majesty, as arbitrator, his good offices have been further invoked to assist in framing such convention or articles of agreement between the United States of America and his Bri-

Au nom de la très-sainte et indivisible Trinité.

Le Président des Etats-Unis d'Amérique, et Sa Majesté le Roi du Royaume uni de la Grande Bretagne et de l'Irlande, ayant décidé d'un commun accord en conséquence de l'article V. de la convention conclue à Londres le 20 Octobre, 1818, que les différends qui se sont élevés entre les deux Gouvernemens sur la construction et le vrai sens du 1r article du traité de paix et d'amitié, conclu à Gand le 24 Décembre, 1814, seraient déférés à l'arbitrage amical de Sa Majesté l'Empereur de toutes les Russies; s'etant en outre engagés réciproquement à regarder sa décision comme finale et définitive : et sa Majesté Impériale après mûre considération, ayant émis cette décision dans les termes, suivans:

" Que les Etats-Unis d'Amérique sont en droit de réclamer de la Grand Bretagne une juste indemnité pour toutes les propriétés particulieres que les forces Britanniques auroient emportées; et comme il s'agit plus spécialement d'esclaves, pour tous les esclaves que les forces Britanniques auroient emmenés des lieux et territoires dont le traité stipule la restitution, en quittant ces mêmes lieux et territoires."

' Que les Etats-Unis sont en droit de regarder comme emmenés tous ceux de ces esclaves qui, des territoires indiqués cidessus auroient été transportés à bord de vaisseaux Britanniques mouillés dans les eaux des dits territoires, et qui par ce motif n'auroient pas été restitués."

"Mais que s'il y a des esclaves Américains emmenés de territoires dont l'article 1r du traité de Gand n'a pas stipulé la restitution aux Etats Unis, les Etats Unis ne sont pas en droit de réclamer une indemnité pour les dits esclaves:"

Comme il s'agit à présent de mettre cette sentence arbitrale à exécution, les bons offices de Sa Majesté Impériale ont été encor invoqués, afin qu'une convention arrêtée entre les Etats-Unis et Sa Majesté Britannique stipulât les articles d'une accord propre

tannic Majesty, as shall provide the mode of ascertaining and determining the value of slaves and of other private property which may have been carried away in contravention of the treaty of Ghent, and for which indemnification is to be made to the citizens of the United States, in virtue of His Imperial Majesty's said award, and shall secure compensation to the sufferers for their losses so ascertained and determined; and his Imperial Majesty has consented to lend his mediation for the above purpose, and has constituted and appointed CHARLES ROBERT COUNT NESSELRODE, his Imperial Majesty's Privy Counsellor, member of the Council of State, Secretary of State directing the Imperial Department of Foreign Affairs, Chamberlain, Knight of the order of Saint Alexander Nevsky, Grand Cross of the order of Saint Vladimir of the first class, Knight of that of the White Eagle of Poland, Grand Cross of the order of St. Stephen of Hungary, of the Black and of the Red Eagle of Prussia, of the Legion of Honor of France, of Charles III of Spain, of St. Ferdinand and of Merit of Naples, of the Annunciation of Sardinia, of the Polar Star of Sweden, of the Elephant of Denmark, of the Golden Eagle of Wirtemberg, of Fidelity of Baden, of St. Constantine of Parma, and of Guelph of Hanover; and JOHN COUNT CAPODISTRIAS, his Imperial Majesty's Privy Counsellor and Secretary of State, Knight of the order of St. Alexander Nevsky, Grand Cross of the order of Saint Vladimir of the first class, Knight of that of the White Eagle of Poland, Grand Cross of the order of St. Stephen of Hungary, of the Black and of the Red Eagle of Prussia, of the Legion of Honor of France, of Charles III of Spain, of St. Ferdinand and of Merit of Naples, of St. Maurice and of St. Lazarus of Sardinia, of the Elephant of Denmark, of Fidelity and of the Lion of Zähringen of Baden, Burgher of the canton of Vaud, and also of the canton and of the Republic of Geneva, as his plenipotentiaries to treat, adjust, and conclude such articles of agreement as may tend to the attainment of the above mentioned end with the plenipotentiaries of the United States and of his Britannic Majesty; that is to say, on the part of the President of the United States, with the advice and consent of the Senate thereof, HENRY MIDDLETON, a citizen of the said United States, and their Envoy Extraordinary and Minister Plenipotentiary to his Majesty the Emperor of all the Russias; and on the part of his Majesty the King of the United Kingdom of Great Britain and Ireland, the Right Honorable Sir CHARLES BAGOT, one of his Majesty's most honorable Privy Council, Knight Grand Cross of the most honorable order of the Bath, and his Majesty's Ambassador Extraordinary and Plenipotentiary to his Majesty the Emperor of all the Russias; and the said plenipotentiaries, after a reciprocal communication of their respective full powers, found in good and due form, have agreed upon the following articles:

ARTICLE I. For the purpose of ascertaining and determining the amount of indemnification which may be due to citizens of the United States under the decision of his Imperial Majesty, two Commissioners and two arbitrators shall be appointed in the manner following, that is to say: one Commissioner and one arbitrator shall be nominated and appointed by the President of the United States of America, by and with the advice and consent of the Senate thereof, and one Commissioner and one arbitrator shall be appointed by his Britannic Majesty; and the two Commissioners and two arbitrators thus appointed shall meet and hold their sittings as a Board in the city of Washington. They shall have power to appoint a secretary, and before proceeding to the other business of the commission they shall, respectively, take the following oath (or affirmation) in the presence of each other; which oath or affirmation, being so taken and duly attested, shall be entered on the record of their proceedings, that is to

à établir d'une part, le mode à suivre pour fixer et déterminer la valeur des esclaves ou autres propriétés privées qui auroient été emmenés en contravention au traité de Gand, et pour lesquels les citoyens des Etats-Unis auraient droit de réclamer une indemnité en vertu de la décision cidessus mentionnée de sa Majesté Impériale; de l'autre à assurer un dédommagement aux individus qui ont supporté les pertes qu'il s'agit de vérifier et d'évaluer. Sa Majesté Impériale a consenti à prêter sa mediation pour le dit objet, et a fondé et nommé le Sieur CHARLES ROBERT COMTE DE NESSELRODE, son Conseiller privé, membre du Conseil d'Etat, Secrétaire d'Etat dirigeant le Ministère des Affaires Etrangères, Chambellan actuel, Chevalier de l'ordre de St. Alexandre Nevsky, Grand Croix de l'ordre de St.Wladimir de la 1re classe, Chevalier de celui de l'Aigle Blanc de Pologne, Grand Croix de l'ordre de St. Etienne de Hongrie, de l'Aigle Noir et de l'Aigle Rouge de Prusse, de la Légion d'Honneur de France, de Charles III d'Espagne, de St. Ferdinand et du Mérite de Naples, de l'Annonciade de Sardaigne, de l'Etoile Polaire de Suède, de l'Eléphant de Dannemare, de l'Aigle d'or de Würtemberg, de la Fidélité de Bade, de St. Constantin de Parme, et des Guelfes de Hanovre; et le Sieur JEAN COMPTE DE CAPODISTRIAS, son Conseiller privé et Secrétaire d'Etat, Chevalier de l'ordre de St. Alexandre Nevsky, Grand Croix de l'ordre de St. Wladimir de la 1re crosse, Chevalier de celui de l'Aigle Blanc de Pologne, Grand Croix de l'ordre de St. Etienne de Hongrie, de l'Aigle Noir et de l'Aigle Rouge de Prusse, de la Légion d'Honneur de France, de Charles III d'Espagne, de St. Ferdinand et du Mérite de Naples, des Sts. Maurice et Lazare de Sardaigne, de l'Eléphant de Dannemare, de la Fidélité et du Lion de Zähringen de Bade, Bourgeois du Canton de Vaud, ainsi que du Canton et de la République de Genève, pour ses plénipotentiaires à l'effet de négocier, régler et conclure tels articles d'un accord qui pourraient faire atteindre la fin indiquée plus haut, conjointement avec les plénipotentiaires des E'tats-Unis et de sa Majesté Britannique, savoir de la part du Président des Etats Unis, de l'avis et du consentement de leur Sénat, le Sieur HENRY MIDDLETON, citoyen des dits Etats-Unis et leur Envoyé Extraordinaire et Ministre Plénipotentiaire près sa Majesté Impériale, et de la part de sa Majesté le Roi du Royaume Uni de la Grande Bretagne et de l'Irlande, le très honorable Sir CHARLES BAGOT, l'un des membres du très honorable Conseil privé de sa Majesté, Chevalier Grand Croix du très honorable ordre du Bain et son Ambassadeur Extraordinaire et Plénipotentiaire près sa Majesté Impériale; lesquels plénipotentiaires, après s'être réciproquement communiqué leurs pleinpouvoirs respectifs, trouvés en bonne et due forme, sont convenus des articles suivants:

ARTICLE I. Pour vérifier et déterminer le montant de l'indemnité qui pourra être dûe aux citoyens des Etats-Unis par suite de la décision de sa Majesté Impériale, deux commissaires et deux arbitres seront nommés de la manière suivante, savoir: un commissaire et un arbitre seront nommés et accrédités par le Président des Etats-Unis, de l'avis et du consentement de leur Sénat; l'autre commissaire et l'autre arbitre seront nommés par sa Majesté Britannique. Les deux commissaires et les deux arbitres ainsi nommés se réuniront en Conseil, et tiendront leurs séances dans la ville de Washington. Ils auront le pouvoir de choisir un secrétaire, et avant de procéder au travail de la commission, ils devront prêter respectivement et en présence les uns des autres, le serment ou l'affirmation qui suit, et ce serment ou affirmation prêté et formellement attesté fera partie du protocole de leurs actes et sera conçu ainsi qu'il suit: "Moi, A B, l'un des commissaires (ou arbitres, suivant le cas,) nommés en exécution de la convention conclue à St. Pe-

say: "I, A. B, one of the Commissioners (or arbitrators, as the case may be,) appointed in pursuance of the convention concluded at St. Petersburg on the 30th day of June, (12th July,) one thousand eight hundred and twenty-two, between his Majesty the Emperor of all the Russias, the United States of America, and his Britannic Majesty, do solemnly swear (or affirm) that I will diligently, impartially, and carefully examine, and, to the best of my judgment, according to justice and equity, decide all matters submitted to me as Commissioner (or arbitrator, as the case may be,) under the said convention."

All vacancies occurring by death or otherwise shall be filled up in the manner of the original appointment, and the new Commissioners or arbitrators shall take the same oath or affirmation, and perform the same duties.

ARTICLE II. If, at the first meeting of this Board, the Governments of the United States and of Great Britain shall not have agreed upon an average value to be allowed as compensation for each slave for whom indemnification may be due, then, and in that case, the Commissioners and arbitrators shall conjointly proceed to examine the testimony which shall be produced under the authority of the President of the United States, together with such other competent testimony as they may see cause to require or allow, going to prove the true value of slaves at the period of the exchange of the ratifications of the treaty of Ghent; and upon the evidence so obtained, they shall agree upon and fix the average value. But in case that a majority of the Board of Commissioners and arbitrators should not be able to agree respecting such average value, then, and in that case, recourse shall be had to the arbitration of the minister or other agent of the mediating power, accredited to the Government of the United States. A statement of the evidence produced, and of the proceedings of the Board thereupon, shall be communicated to the said minister or agent, and his decision, founded upon such evidence and proceedings, shall be final and conclusive. And the said average value, when fixed and determined by either of the three before mentioned methods, shall in all cases serve as a rule for the compensation to be awarded for each and every slave for whom it may afterwards be found that indemnification is due.

ARTICLE III. When the average value of slaves shall have been ascertained and fixed, the two Commissioners shall constitute a Board for the examination of the claims which are to be submitted to them, and they shall notify to the Secretary of State of the United States that they are ready to receive a definitive list of the slaves and other private property for which the citizens of the United States claim indemnification; it being understood and hereby agreed that the commission shall not take cognizance of, nor receive, and that his Britannic Majesty shall not be required to make compensation for any claims for private property under the first article of the treaty of Ghent not contained in the said list. And His Britannic Majesty hereby engages to cause to be produced before the commission, as material towards ascertaining facts, all the evidence of which His Majesty's Government may be in possession, by returns from His Majesty's officers or otherwise, of the number of slaves carried away. But the evidence so produced, or its defectiveness, shall not go in bar of any claim or claims which shall be otherwise satisfactorily authenticated.

ARTICLE IV. The two Commissioners are hereby empowered and required to go into an examination of all the claims submitted, through the above mentioned list, by the owners of slaves or other property, or by their lawful attorneys or representatives, and to determine the same, respectively, according to the merits of the several cases, under the rule of the imperial decision herein above recited, and having

tersburg, le 30 Juin, (12 Juillet,) mil-huit-cent-vingt et deux, entre sa Majesté l'Empereur de toutes les Russies, les Etats Unis d'Amérique, et sa Majesté Britannique jure ou affirme solennellement que j'examinerai avec diligence, impartialité et sollicitude, et que je déciderai d'après mon meilleur entendement et en toute justice et équité, toutes les réclamations qui me seront déférées en ma qualité de commissaire (ou d'arbitre, suivant le cas,) à la suite de la dite convention."

Les vacances causées par la mort ou autrement, seront remplies de la même manière qu'au moment de la nomination primitive, et les nouveaux commissaires ou arbitres devront prêter le même serment ou affirmation, et s'acquitter des mêmes devoirs.

ARTICLE II. Si lors de la première réunion de ce conseil, le Gouvernement des Etats-Unis et celui de la Grande Bretagne ne sont point parvenus à déterminer d'un commun accord la valeur moyenne qui devra être assignée comme compensation pour chaque esclave, pour lequel il sera dû une indemnité, dans ce cas les commissaires et les arbitres procèderont conjointement à l'examen de tous les témoignages qui leur seront présentés par ordre du Président des Etats-Unis, ainsi que de tous les autres témoignages valables qu'ils croiront devoir requérir ou admettre dans la vue d'arrêter la véritable valeur des esclaves à l'époque de l'échange des ratifications du traité de Gand; et d'après les preuves qu'ils auront ainsi obtenues, ils établiront et fixeront la susdite valeur moyenne. Dans le cas où la majorité du conseil des commissaires et arbitres ne pourroit pas s'accorder sur cette valeur proportionnelle, alors on aura recours à l'arbitrage du ministre ou autre agent de la puissance mediatrice accrédité auprès du Gouvernement des Etats-Unis. Toutes les preuves produites et tous les actes des opérations du conseil à ce sujet, lui seront communiqués et la décision de ce ministre ou agent, basée, comme il vient d'être dit, sur ces preuves et sur les actes de ces opérations, sera regardée comme finale et définitive. C'est sur la valeur moyenne fixée par un des trois modes mentionnés ci-dessus, que devra être règlée en tout état de cause la compensation qui sera accordée pour chaque esclave pour lequel on reconnoitra par la suite, qu'une indemnité est dée.

ARTICLE III. Lorsque le prorata aura été ainsi arrêté, les deux commissaires se constitueront en conseil pour l'examen des réclamations qui leur seront soumises, et ils notifieront au Secrétaire d'Etat des Etats-Unis, qu'ils sont prêts à recevoir la liste définitive des esclaves et autres propriétés privées pour lesquels les citoyens des Etats-Unis réclament une indemnité. Il est entendu que les commissaires ne sauroient examiner ni recevoir, et que Sa Majesté Britannique ne sauroit, en vertu des clauses de l'article 1ᵉʳ. du traité de Gand, bonifier aucune prétention, qui ne seroit pas portée sur la dite liste. Sa Majesté Britannique s'engage d'autre part à ordonner, que tous les témoignages que son Gouvernement peut avoir acquis par les rapports des officiers de sa dite Majesté ou par tout autre canal sur le nombre des esclaves emmenés, soyent mis sous les yeux des commissaires, afin de contribuer à la vérification des faits. Mais soit que ces témoignages viennent à être produits, soit qu'ils manquent, cette circonstance ne pourra porter préjudice à une réclamation ou aux réclamations qui par une autre voie seront légitimées d'une manière satisfaisante.

ARTICLE IV. Les deux Commissaires sont autorisés et chargés d'entrer dans l'examen de toutes les réclamations qui leur seront soumises au moyen de la liste ci-dessus mentionnée, par les propriétaires d'esclaves ou les possesseurs d'autres propriétés, ou par les procureurs ou mandataires de ceux-ci, et à prononcer sur ces réclamations suivant le degré de leur mérite, la lettre de la décision Imperiale citée plus

reference, if need there be, to the explanatory documents hereunto annexed, marked A and B. And, in considering such claims, the Commissioners are empowered and required to examine, on oath or affirmation, all such persons as shall come before them, touching the real number of the slaves, or value of other property, for which indemnity is claimed; and also to receive in evidence, according as they may think consistent with equity and justice, written depositions or papers; such depositions or papers being duly authenticated, either according to existing legal forms, or in such other manner as the said Commissioners shall see cause to require or allow.

ARTICLE V. In the event of the two Commissioners not agreeing in any particular case under examination, or of their disagreement upon any question which may result from the stipulations of this convention, then, and in that case, they shall draw by lot the name of one of the two arbitrators, who, after having given due consideration to the matter contested, shall consult with the Commissioners and a final decision shall be given, conformably to the opinion of the majority of the two Commissioners, and of the arbitrator so drawn by lot. And the arbitrator, when so acting with the two Commissioners, shall be bound in all respects by the rules of proceeding enjoined by the fourth article of this convention upon the Commissioners, and shall be vested with the same powers and be deemed, for that case, a Commissioner.

ARTICLE VI. The decision of the two Commissioners, or of the majority of the Board, as constituted by the preceding article, shall, in all cases, be final and conclusive, whether as to number, the value, or the ownership of the slaves, or other property, for which indemnification is to be made. And his Britannic Majesty engages to cause the sum awarded to each and every owner in lieu of his slave or slaves, or other property, to be paid in specie, without deduction, at such time or times, and at such place or places, as shall be awarded by the said Commissioners, and on condition of such releases or assignments to be given as they shall direct: provided, that no such payments shall be fixed to take place sooner than twelve months from the day of the exchange of the ratifications of this convention.

ARTICLE VII. It is further agreed, that the Commissioners and arbitrators shall be respectively paid in such manner as shall be settled between the Governments of the United States and Great Britain at the time of the exchange of the ratification of this convention. And all other expenses attending the execution of the commission shall be defrayed jointly by the United States and his Britannic Majesty, the same being previously ascertained and allowed by the majority of the Board.

ARTICLE VIII. A certified copy of this convention, when duly ratified by his Majesty the Emperor of all the Russias, by the President of the United States, by and with the advice and consent of their Senate, and by his Britannic Majesty, shall be delivered by each of the contracting parties, respectively, to the minister or other agent of the mediating power, accredited to the Government of the United States, as soon as may be after the ratifications shall have been exchanged, which last shall be effected at Washington in six months from the date hereof, or sooner if possible.

In faith whereof, the respective plenipotentiaries have signed this convention, drawn up in two languages, and have hereunto affixed their seals.

Done in triplicate, at St. Petersburg, this thirtieth (twelfth) day of June, (July,) one thousand eight hundred and twenty-two.

haut, et en cas de besoin la teneur des documens ci-annexés et cotés A et B. En considérant les dites réclamations, les Commissaires sont autorisés à interpeler sous serment ou affirmation telle personne qui se présenterait à eux, concernant le véritable nombre des esclaves ou la valeur de toute autre propriété pour laquelle il serait réclamé une indemnité; ils sont autorisés de même à recevoir autant qu' ils le jugeront conforme à l'equité et à la justice, toutes les dépositions écrites, qui seraient duement legitimees soit d'après les formes existantes, voulues par la loi, soit dans tout autre mode que les dits Commissaires auraient lieu d'exiger on d'admettre.

ARTICLE V. Si les deux Commissaires ne parviennent pas à s'accorder sur une des réclamations qui seront soumises à leur examen, ou s'ils different d'opinion sur une question résultant de la présente convention, alors ils tireront au sort le nom d'un des deux arbitres, lequel après avoir pris enmure délibération l'objet en litige, le discutera avec les Commissaires. La décision finale sera prise conformément à l'opinion de la majorité des deux Commissaires et de l'arbitre tiré au sort. Dans des cas semblables, l'arbitre sera tenu de procéder à tous égards d'après les regles prescrites aux Commissaires par le 4me article de la présente convention. Il sera investi des même pouvoirs et censé pour le moment faire les mêmes fonctions.

ARTICLE VI. La décision des deux Commissaires ou celle de la majorité du conseil formé ainsi qu'il à été dit en l'article précédent, sera dans tous les cas finale et définitive, soit relativement au nombre et à la valeur, soit pour la vérification de la propriété, des esclaves ou de tout autre bien meuble privé, pour lequel il sera réclamé une indemnité. Et Sa Majesté Britannique prend l'engagement que la somme adjugée à chaque proprietaire en place de son esclave ou de ses esclaves, ou de toute autre propriété, sera payée en espéces sans déduction, à tel tems ou à tels termes, et dans tel lieu ou tels endroits, que l'auront prononcé les dits Commissaires et sous clause de telles exemptions ou assignations, qu'ils l'auront arrété: pourvu seulement qu'il ne soit pas fixé pour ces payemens de terme plus rapproché que celui de douze mois à partir du jour de l'échange des ratifications de la présente convention.

ARTICLE VII. Il est convenu en outre, que les Commissaires et arbitres recevront de part et d'autre un traitement, dont les Gouvernemens des Etats-Unis et de Sa Majesté Britannique se réservent de déterminer le montant et le mode à l'epoque de l'échange des ratifications de la présente convention. Toutes les autres depenses qui accompagneront les travaux de la commission seront supportées conjointement par les Etats-Unis et par Sa Majesté Britannique. Ces dépenses devront d'ailleurs être au préalable vérifiées et admises par la majorité du conseil.

ARTICLE VIII. Lorsque la présente convention aura été duement ratifiée par Sa Majesté Impériale, par le President des Etats-Unis de l'avis et du consentement de leur Sénat, et par Sa Majesté Britannique, une copie vidimée en sera délivrée par chacune des parties contractantes au ministre ou autre agent de la puissance médiatrice, accrédité près le Gouvernement des Etats-Unis, et cela le plutôt que faire se pourra, après que les ratifications auront été échangées: çette dernière formalité sera remplie à Washington, dans l'espace de six mois, de la date cidessous, ou plutôt s'il est possible.

En foi de quoi, les plenipotentiaires, respectifs ont signé la présente convention et y ont apposé respectivement le cachet de leurs armes.

Fait triple à St. Pétersbourg, 30 Juin, (12 Juillet,) dè l'anneé mil-huitcent-vingt et deux.

NESSELRODE.	[L. S.]
CAPO D'ISTRIAS.	[L. S.]
HENRY MIDDLETON.	[L. S.]
CHARLES BAGOT.	[L. S.]

A.

Lé Soussigné Secrétaire d'Etat Dirigeant le Ministère Impériale des affaires étrangeres a l'honneur de communiquer à Monsieur de Middleton, Envoyé Extraordinaire et Ministre Plénipotentiaire des Etats Unis d'Amérique, l'opinion que l'Empereur, Son Maitre, a cru devoir exprimer sur l'objet des différends qui se sont élevés entre les Etats-Unis et la Grande Bretagne, relativement à l'interprétation de l'Article premier du Traité de Gand.

Monsieur de Middleton est invité à considérer cette opinion comme la décision arbitrale demandeé à l'Empereur par les deux Puissances.

Il se rappellera sans doute, qu'aussi bien que le Plenipotentiaire de S. M. Britannique, il a dans tous ses mémoires principalement insisté sur le sens grammatical de l'Arf. I. du Traité de Gand, et que même dans sa note du 4 (16) Novembre, 1821, il a formellement déclaré que c'étoit sur la *signification des mots dans le texte de l'article tel qu'il existe*, que devoit se fonder la décision de Sa Majesté Impériale.

La même déclaration étant consignée dans la note du Plenipotentiaire Britannique en date du 8 (20) Octobre, 1821, L'Empereur n'a fait que de se conformer aux vœux énoncés par les deux parties, en vouant toute son attention à l'examen de la question grammaticale.

L'opinion ci-dessus mentionnée fera connoitre la maniére dont Sa Majesté Impériale juge cette question, et afin que le cabinet de Washington connoisse également les motifs sur lesquels se fonde le jugement de L'Empereur, le Soussigné joint à la présente, un extrait de quelques observations, sur le sens littéral de l'Article premier du Traité de Gand.

Sous ce rapport, L'Empereur c'est borné à suivre les régles de la langue employée dans la rédaction de l'acte, par lequel les deux Puissances ont réclamé son arbitrage, et défini l'objet de leur differend.

C'est uniquement à l'autorité de ces régles, que Sa Majesté Impériale a cru devoir obéir et Son Avis ne pouvoit qu'en être la conséquence rigoureuse et nécessaire.

Le Soussigné saisit avec empressement cette occasion, pour réitérer à Monsieur de Middleton les assurances de sa considération trés-distinguée.

St. Petersbourg, *le 22 Avril,* 1822.

NESSELRODE.

À Monsieur de Middleton, &c.

A.

Opinion de Sa Majesté Impériale.

Invité par les Etats-Unis d'Amérique et par la Grande Bretagne à émettre une opinion, comme arbitre dans les différends qui se sont élevés entre ces deux Puissances, au sujet de l'interprétation de l'article premier du Traité qu'elles ont conclu à Gand, le 24 Décembre, 1814, l'Empereur a pris connoissance de tous les actes, mémoires et notes où les plénipotentiaires respectifs ont exposé à son ministère des affaires étrangéres, les argumens que chacune des parties en litige fait valoir à l'appui de l'interprétation qu' élle donne au dit article.

Aprés avoir murement pesé les observations développées de part et d'autre: considérant que le plénipotentiaire Américain et le plénipotentiaire Britannique ont demandé que la discussion fût close, considérant que le premier dans sa note du 4–16 Novembre, 1821, et le second dans sa note du 8–20 Octobre, de la même année, ont déclaré que c'est *sur la construction du texte de l'article, tel qu'il existe*, que la décision arbitrale doit se fonder, et que l'un et l'autre n'ont invoqué que comme moyens subsidiaires les principes génèraux de droit des gens et de droit maritime.

L'Empereur est d'avis, "que ce n'est que d'aprés le sens littéral et grammatical de l'article I, du traité de Gand que la question peut être décidée."

Quant au sens littéral et grammatical de l'article 1, du traité de Gand.

Considérant   que la période sur la signification de la quelle il s'éléve des doutes, est construite ainsi qu'il

"Tous les territoires, lieux et possessions quelconques, pris par l'une des parties sur l'autre, durant la guerre, ou qui pourroient être pris aprés la signature du présent traité, à l'exception seulement des isles ci-dessous mentionées, seront rendons sans délai et sans faire détruire ou emporter aucune partie de l'artillerie ou autre pritété publique *originairement prise dans les dits forts et lieux et qui s'y trouvera au moment de l'échange des ratifications du traité*, ou aucuns esclaves ou autres propriétés privées. Et tous archives, registres, actes et papiers, soit d'une nature publique ou appartenans à des particuliéres, qui dans le cours de la guerre peuvent être tombés entre les mains des officiers de l'une ou de l'autre partie, seront de suite, en tant qu'il sera praticable, restitués et délivrés aux autorités propres et personnes auxquelles ils appartiennent respectivement; considérant que dans cette période, les mots: *originairement prise et qui s'y trouvera au moment de l'échange des ratifications*, forment une phrase incidente, laquelle ne peut se rapporter *grammaticalement* qu'aux substantifs ou sujets qui précèdent.

Qu'ainsi l'article 1 du traité de Gand, ne défend aux parties contractantes d'emporter des lieux dont il stipule la restitution, que les seules propriétés publiques *qui y auroient été originairement prises et qui s'y trouveroient au moment de l'échange des ratifications*, mais qu'il défend d'emporter de ces mêmes lieux, *aucune propriété particulière quelconque.*

Que d'un autre coté, ces deux défenses ne sont applicables qu'uniquement aux lieux dont l'article stipule la restitution.

L'Empereur est d'avis:

"Que les Etats-Unis d'Amérique, sont en droit de réclamer de la Grande Bretagne une juste indemnité, pour toutes les propriétés particuliéres que les forces Britanniques auroient emportées, et comme il s'agit plus spécialement d'esclaves, pour tous les esclaves que les forces Britanniques auroient emmenés des lieux et territoires dont le traité stipule la restitution, en quittant ces mêmes lieux et territoires.

"Que les Etats-Unis sont en droit de regarder comme emmenés, tous ceux de ces esclaves qui, des territoires indiqués cidessus, auroient été transportés à bord de vaisseaux Britanniques mouillés dans les eaux des dits territoires, et qui par ce motif n'auroient pas été restitués."

"Mais que s'il y a des esclaves Américains emmenés de territoires dont l'article 1, du traité de Gand n'a pas stipulé la restitution aux Etats-Unis, les Etats-Unis ne sont pas en droit de réclamer une indemnité, pour les dits esclaves."

L'Empereur déclare en outre, qu'il est prêt à exercer l'office de médiateur qui lui a été défére d'avance, par les deux Etats, dans les negociations que doit amener entre eux, la décision arbitrale qu'ils ont demandée.

Fait à St. Pétersbourg, le 22 Avril, 1822.

B.

Le Soussigné Secrétaire d'Etat, dirigeant le Ministére Impérial des affaires étrangeres, s'ets empressé de porter à la cofioissance de l'Empereur son maitre, les explications dans lesquelles Mr. l'Ambassadeur de S. M. Britannique est entré avec le Ministére Imperial, à la suite de la communication préalable et confidentielle qui a été faite à Monsieur de Middleton ainsi qu'à Mr. le Chevalier Bagot de l'opinion exprimée par l'Empereur, sur le vrai sens de l'art. 1er du Traité de Gand.

Mr. le Chevalier Bagot entend qu'en vertu dela décision de Sa Majesté Impériale, "S. M. Britannique n'est pas tenue à indemniser les Etats-Unis d'aucuns esclaves qui, venant des endroits qui n'ont jamais été occupés par ses troupes, se sont volontairement réunis aux forces Britanniques, ou en conséquence de l'encourgement que les officiers de S. M. leur avoit offert, ou se dérober au pouvoir de leur maitre, ces esclaves n'ayant pas été emmenés des lieux ou territoires pris par S. M. Britannique durant la guerre, et conséquemment n'ayant pas été emmenés des lieux dont l'article stipule la restitution."

Eé réponse à cette observation, le soussigné est chargé par Sa Majesta Imperiale, de communiquer ce qui suit à Monsieur le ministre des Etats-Unis d'Amerique.

L'Empereur ayant, du consentement mutuel des deux plenipotentiares, émis une opinion fondée uniquement sur le sens qui résulte *du texte de l'article* en litige, ne se croit appelé à décider ici aucune question relative à ce que les loix de la guerre permettent ou défendent aux parties belligérantes, mais toujours fidéle à l'interpretation grammaticale de l'art. 1er du traité de Gand, Sa Majesté Imperiale déclare une seconde fois qu'il lui semble, d'aprés cette interpretation.

"Qu'en quittant les lieux et territoires dont le traité de Gand stipule la restitution aux Etats-Unis, les forces de S. M. Britannique n'avoient le droit d'emmener de ces mémes lieux et territoires, absolument aucun esclave, par quelque moyen quil fût tombe ou venu se remettre en leur pouvoir."

"Mais que si, durant la guerre, des esclaves Américains avoient été emmenés par les forces Anglaises, d'autres lieux que ceux dont le traité de Gand stipule la restitution, sur territoire ou à bord de vaisseaux Britanniques, la Grande Bretagne ne seroit pas tenue d'indemniser les Etats-Unis de la perte de ces esclaves, par quelque moyen qu'ils fussent tombés ou venus se remettre au pouvoir de ces officiers."

Quoique convaincu, par les explications préalables dont il a été question plus haut, que tel est aussi le sens que Mr. le Chevalier Bagot attache à son observation, le soussigné n'en a pas moins reçu de Sa Majesté Impériale, l'ordre d'adresser aux plénipotentiaires respectifls, la présente note, qui leur prouvera, que pour mieux répondre à la confiance des deux gouvernemens, l'Empereur n'a pas voulu qu'il pût s'élever le plus leger doute sur les conséquences de son opinion.

Le Soussigné saisit avec empressement cette occasion de réitérer à Monsieur de Middleton, l'assurance de sa considération trés distinguée.

NESSELRODE.

St. Petersbourg, *le 22 Avril*, 1822.

Now, therefore, be it known that I, James Monroe, President of the United States, have caused the said convention to be made public, to the end that the same, and every clause and article thereof, may be observed and fulfilled with good faith by the United States and the citizens thereof.

In witness whereof, I have hereunto set my hand and caused the seal of the United States to be affixed.

[L. S.] Done at the city of Washington, this eleventh day of January, in the year of our Lord one thousand eight hundred and twenty-three, and of the Independence of the United States the forty-seventh.

JAMES MONROE.

By the President:

John Quincy Adams, *Secretary of State.*

A.

Count Nesselrode to Mr. Middleton.

[Translation.]

The undersigned Secretary of State, directing the Imperial administration of Foreign Affairs, has the honor to communicate to Mr. Middleton, Envoy Extraordinary and Minister Plenipotentiary of the United States of America, the opinion which the Emperor, his master, has thought it his duty to express upon the object of the differences which have arisen between the United States and Great Britain, relative to the interpretation of the first article of the treaty of Ghent.

Mr. Middleton is requested to consider this opinion as the award required of the Emperor by the two powers.

He will doubtless recollect that he, as well as the plenipotentiary of his Britannic Majesty, in all his memorials has principally insisted on the grammatical sense of the first article of the treaty of Ghent, and that even in his note of November 4, [16,] 1821, he has formally declared that it was on the *significa-*

tion of the words in the text of the article as it now is that the decision of his Imperial Majesty should be founded.

The same declaration being made in the note of the British plenipotentiary, dated October 8, [20,] 1821, the Emperor had only to conform to the wishes expressed by the two parties by devoting all his attention to the examination of the grammatical question.

. The above mentioned opinion will show the manner in which his Imperial Majesty judges of this question; and in order that the cabinet of Washington may also know the motives upon which the Emperor's judgment is founded, the undersigned has hereto subjoined an extract of some observations upon the literal sense of the first article of the treaty of Ghent.

In this respect the Emperor has confined himself to following the rules of the language employed in drawing up the act, by which the two powers have required his arbitration and defined the object of their difference.

His Imperial Majesty has thought it his duty, exclusively, to obey the authority of these rules, and his opinion could not but be the rigorous and necessary consequence thereof.

The undersigned eagerly embraces this occasion to renew to Mr. Middleton the assurances of his most distinguished consideration.

NESSELRODE.

St. Petersburg, *April 22*, 1822.

A.

His Imperial Majesty's Award.

[Translation.]

Invited by the United States of America and by Great Britain to give an opinion as arbitrator in the differences which have arisen between these two powers on the subject of the interpretation of the first article of the treaty which they concluded at Ghent, on the 24th December, 1814, the Emperor has taken cognizance of all the acts, memorials, and notes, in which the respective plenipotentiaries have set forth to his administration of foreign affairs the arguments upon which each of the litigant parties depends in support of the interpretation given by it to the said article.

After having maturely weighed the observations exhibited on both sides:

Considering that the American plenipotentiary and the plenipotentiary of Britain have desired that the discussion should be closed;

Considering that the former, in his note of November 4, (16,) 1821, and the latter, in his note of October 8, (20,) of the same year, have declared that it is *upon the construction of the text of the article as it stands* that the arbitrator's decision should be founded, and that both have appealed only as subsidiary means to the general principles of the law of nations and of maritime law;

The Emperor is of opinion "that the question can only be decided according to the literal and grammatical sense of the first article of the treaty of Ghent."

As to the literal and grammatical sense of the first article of the treaty of Ghent:

Considering that the period upon the signification of which doubts have arisen is expressed as follows:

"All territory, places, and possessions, whatsoever, taken by either party from the other during the war, or which may be taken after the signing of this treaty, excepting only the islands hereinafter mentioned, shall be restored without delay and without causing any destruction or carrying away any of the artillery or other public property *originally captured in the said forts or places, and which shall remain therein upon the exchange of the ratifications of this treaty*, or any slaves or other private property; and all archives, records, deeds, and papers, either of a public nature or belonging to private persons, which, in the course of the war, may have fallen into the hands of the officers of either party, shall be, as far as may be practicable, forthwith restored and delivered to the proper authorities and persons to whom they respectively belong."

Considering that, in this period, the words *originally captured, and which shall remain therein upon the exchange of the ratifications,* form an incidental phrase which can have respect, *grammatically*, only to the substantives or subjects which precede;

That the first article of the treaty of Ghent thus prohibits the contracting parties from carrying away from the places of which it stipulates the restitution only the public property *which might have been originally captured there, and which should remain therein upon the exchange of the ratifications,* but that it prohibits the carrying away from these same places *any private property* whatever;

That, on the other hand, these two prohibitions are solely applicable to the places of which the article stipulates the restitution:

The Emperor is of opinion:

' That the United States of America are entitled to a just indemnification from Great Britain for all private property carried away by the British forces; and, as the question regards slaves more especially, for all such slaves as were carried away by the British forces from the places and territories of which the restitution was stipulated by the treaty, in quitting the said places and territories.

"That the United States are entitled to consider as having been so carried away all such slaves as may have been transported from the above mentioned territories on board the British vessels within the waters of the said territories, and who, for this reason, have not been restored.

"But that, if there should be any American slaves who were carried away from territories of which the first article of the treaty of Ghent has not stipulated the restitution to the United States, the United States are not to claim an indemnification for the said slaves."

. The Emperor declares, besides, that he is ready to exercise the office of mediator, which has been conferred on him beforehand by the two States, in the negotiations which must ensue between them in consequence of the award which they have demanded.

Done at St. Petersburg, April 22, 1822.

B.

Count Nesselrode to Mr. Middleton.

[Translation.]

The undersigned Secretary of State, directing the Imperial administration of foreign affairs, has, without delay, laid before the Emperor, his master, the explanations into which the ambassador of his Britannic Majesty has entered with the Imperial ministry, in consequence of the preceding and confidential communication which was made to Mr. Middleton, as well as to Sir Charles Bagot, of the opinion expressed by the Emperor upon the true sense of the 1st article of the treaty of Ghent.

Sir Charles Bagot understands, that, in virtue of the decision of his Imperial Majesty, "his Britannic Majesty is not bound to indemnify the United States for any slaves who, coming from places which have never been occupied by his troops, voluntarily joined the British forces, either in consequence of the encouragement which his Majesty's officers had offered to them, or to free themselves from the power of their master—these slaves not having been carried away from places or territories captured by his Britannic Majesty during the war, and, consequently, not having been carried away from places of which the article stipulated the restitution."

In answer to this observation, the undersigned is charged by his Imperial Majesty to communicate what follows to the minister of the United States of America.

The Emperor, having, by the mutual consent of the two plenipotentiaries, given an opinion, founded solely upon the sense which results *from the text of the article* in dispute, does not think himself called upon to decide here any question relative to what the laws of war permit or forbid to the belligerents; but, always faithful to the grammatical interpretation of the 1st article of the treaty of Ghent, his Imperial Majesty declares a second time that it appears to him according to this interpretation:

"That in quitting the places and territories of which the treaty of Ghent stipulates the restitution to the United States, his Britannic Majesty's forces had no right to carry away from these same places and territories absolutely any slave, by whatever means he had fallen or come into their power.

"But that if, during the war, American slaves had been carried away by the English forces from other places than those of which the treaty of Ghent stipulates the restitution upon the territory, or on board British vessels, Great Britain should not be bound to indemnify the United States for the loss of these slaves, by whatever means they might have fallen or come into the power of her officers."

Although convinced, by the previous explanation above mentioned, that such is also the sense which Sir Charles Bagot attached to his observation, the undersigned has nevertheless received from his Imperial Majesty orders to address the present note to the respective plenipotentiaries, which will prove to them that, in order the better to justify the confidence of the two Governments, the Emperor has been unwilling that the slightest doubt should arise regarding the consequences of his opinion.

The undersigned eagerly embraces this occasion of repeating to Mr. Middleton the assurance of his most distinguished consideration.

NESSELRODE.

St. Petersburg, *April 22, 1822.*

We, the undersigned, having this day met in the City of Washington to exchange the ratifications of the convention concluded and signed at St. Petersburg on the 30th day of June, (12th day of July,) 1822, by the respective plenipotentiaries of the United States of America, his Majesty the King of the United Kingdom of Great Britain and Ireland, and his Majesty the Emperor of all the Russias, do hereby certify that, at the time of exchanging the said ratifications, it was agreed by us, for our respective Governments, conformably to the seventh article of the above mentioned convention, that the salary or compensation of the Commissioners and arbitrators mentioned therein shall be at the rate of one thousand pounds sterling, or four thousand four hundred and forty-four dollars, to each Commissioner, and of seven hundred and fifty pounds sterling, or three thousand three hundred and thirty-three dollars, to each arbitrator, per annum, from the time of the first meeting of the Commissioners at Washington until the final dissolution of the Board, to be paid quarterly; with an additional allowance, to be paid with the first quarter's salary, of six hundred pounds sterling to the Commissioners, and of the same sum to the arbitrator, to be appointed on the part of his Britannic Majesty, in consideration of their being called upon to exercise their functions at a distance from their country, and of a sum of five hundred pounds sterling to each of them at the close of their commission for their return home.

It was also agreed by us that the compensation of the secretary of the said Board of Commissioners shall be at the rate of four hundred and fifty pounds sterling, or two thousand dollars, a year, to commence from the period of his appointment, until the final dissolution of the Board.

And it was lastly agreed by us that the said salaries and additional allowances shall, like the contingent expenses of the commission, be defrayed jointly by the United States and his Britannic Majesty, the said expenses to be laid before the Board at the end of each quarter, and, after being ascertained and allowed by a majority of the Board, to be divided, including salary and allowance, as above, into two moieties, for each of which the Commissioners on either side shall draw, respectively, on the proper departments of their own Governments.

In witness whereof, we have hereunto set our hands and affixed our seals, at Washington, this tenth day of January, one thousand eight hundred and twenty-three.

JOHN QUINCY ADAMS. [L. s.]
STRATFORD CANNING. [L. s.]

TREATY WITH FRANCE OF JUNE 24, 1822, AS RATIFIED.

COMMUNICATED TO THE HOUSE OF REPRESENTATIVES FEBRUARY 20, 1823.

To the Speaker of the House of Representatives of the United States:

The Convention of Navigation and Commerce, between the United States of America and his Majesty the King of France and Navarre, concluded and signed at Washington on the 24th of June, 1822, with the first separate article thereto annexed, having been ratified by the two parties, and the ratifications of the same having been duly exchanged, copies of it, and of the separate articles referred to, are now communicated to the two Houses of Congress, to the end that the necessary measures for carrying it into execution, on the part of the United States, may be adopted by the Legislature.

JAMES MONROE.

Washington, *February 18, 1823.*

BY THE PRESIDENT OF THE UNITED STATES.

A PROCLAMATION.

Whereas a Convention of Navigation and Commerce between the United States of America and his Majesty the King of France and Navarre, together with two separate articles annexed to the same, was concluded and signed at Washington, on the twenty-fourth day of June last past, by the respective plenipotentiaries of the two powers; and whereas the said convention, and the first separate article annexed to the same, have been duly and respectively ratified by me and by his Majesty the King of France and Navarre, and the ratifications of the same have this day and year been exchanged at the city of Washington, by John Quincy Adams, Secretary of State, and the Count Julius de Menou, Chargé d'Affaires of France; which convention and the first separate article annexed to the same are in the words following, to wit:

Convention de Navigation et de Commerce entre sa Majesté le Roi de France et de Navarre et les Etats Unis d'Amerique.

Sa Majesté le Roi de France et de Navarre et les Etats Unis d'Amerique, desirant regler les relations de navigation et de commerce entre leur nations respectives par une convention temporaire reciproquement avantageuse et satisfaisante, et arriver ainsi à un arrangement plus étendu et durable, ont respectivement donne leur pleine-pouvoirs, savoir. Sa Majesté Tres Chretienne au Baron Hyde de Neuville, Chevalier de l'ordre Royal et Militaire de St. Louis, Commandeur de la Legion d'Honneur, Grand Croix de l'ordre Royal Americain d'Isabelle la Catholique, son Envoye Extraordinaire et Ministre Plenipotentiaire prés les Etats Unis; et le Présidente des Etats Unis, à John Quincy Adams, leur Secretaire d'Etat; lesquels, apres avoir echangé leur pleins-pouvoirs, sont convenus des articles suivans:

ARTICLE 1. Les produits naturels on manufacturés des Etats Unis importés en France sur batimens des Etats Unis payeront un droit additionel qui n'excédera point vingt francs par tonneau de marchandise, en sus des droits payés sur les mémes produits naturels ou manufacturés des Etats Unis quand ils sont importés par navires Français.

ARTICLE 2. Les produits naturels ou manufacturés de France importés aux Etats Unis sur batimens Français payeront un droit additionel qui n'excédera point trois dollars, soixante-quinze cents par tonneau de marchandise, en sus des droits payés sur les mémes produits naturels ou manufacturés de France quand ils sont importés par navires des Etats Unis.

ARTICLE 3. Aucun droit differentiel ne sera levé sur les produits du sol et de l'industrie de France qui seront importés par navires Français dans les ports des Etats Unis pour transit ou re-exportation: il en sera de même dans les ports de France pour les produits du sol et de l'industrie de l'Union qui seront importes pour transit ou re-exportation par navires des Etats Unis.

Convention of Navigation and Commerce between the United States of America and his Majesty the King of France and Navarre.

The United States of America and his Majesty the King of France and Navarre, being desirous of settling the relations of navigation and commerce between their respective nations, by a temporary convention reciprocally beneficial and satisfactory, and thereby of leading to a more permanent and comprehensive arrangement, have respectively furnished their full powers in manner following, that is to say: The President of the United States to John Quincy Adams, their Secretary of State, and his most Christian Majesty to the Baron Hyde de Neuville, Knight of the Royal and Military Order of St. Louis, Commander of the Legion of Honor, Grand Cross of the Royal American Order of Isabella the Catholic, his Envoy Extraordinary and Minister Plenipotentiary near the United States; who, after exchanging their full powers, have agreed on the following articles:

ARTICLE 1. Articles of the growth, produce, or manufacture of the United States, imported into France in vessels of the United States, shall pay an additional duty not exceeding twenty francs per ton of merchandise over and above the duties paid on the like articles, also of the growth, produce, or manufacture of the United States, when imported in French vessels.

ARTICLE 2. Articles of the growth, produce, or manufacture of France, imported into the United States in French vessels, shall pay an additional duty not exceeding three dollars and seventy-five cents per ton of merchandise over and above the duties collected upon the like articles, also of the growth, produce, or manufacture of France, when imported in vessels of the United States.

ARTICLE 3. No discriminating duty shall be levied upon the productions of the soil or industry of France, imported in French bottoms into the ports of the United States for transit or re-exportation; nor shall any such duties be levied upon the productions of the soil or industry of the United States, imported in vessels of the United States into the ports of France for transit or re-exportation.

ARTICLE 4. Les quantitiés suivantes seront considerées comme formant le tonneau de marchandise pour chacun des articles ci-après spécifiés:

Vins—quatre barriques de 61 gallons chaque ou 244 gallons de 231 pouces cubes (mésure Americaine.)

Eaux de vie et tous autres liquides 244 gallons.

Soieries et toutes autres marchandises séches ainsi que tous autres articles généralement soumis au mésurage quarante deux pieds cubes, mésure Française en France; et cinquante pieds cubes mésure Américaine, aux Etats Unis.

Cotons—804 lb. avoir du poids ou 365 kilogrammes.

Tabacs—1600 lb. avoir du poids ou 725 kilogrammes.

Potasse et perlasse 2240 lb. avoir du poids ou 1016 kilogrammes.

Riz—1600 lb. avoir du poids ou 725 kilog: Et pour tous les articles non specifiés et qui se pésent 2240 lb. avoir du poids ou 1016 kilogrammes.

ARTICLE 5. Les droits de tonnage, de phare, de pilotage, droits de port, courtage et tous autres droits sur la navigation etrangère en sus de ceux payés respectivement par la navigation nationale dans les deux pays, autre que ceux spécifiés dans les articles 1 et 2 de la presente convention, n'excéderout pas, en France, pour les batimens des Etats Unis, cinq francs par tonneau d'après le registre Américain du batiment, ni pour les batimens Français aux Etats Unis, quatre vingt quatorze cents par tonneau d'après le passeport Français du bâtiment.

ARTICLE 6. Le parties contractantes désirant favoriser mutuellement leur commerce, en donnant dans leurs ports toute assistance nécessaire à leurs batimens respectifs, sont convenues que les consuls et vice consuls pourront faire arrêter les matelôts faisant partie des équipages des batimens de leurs nationes respectives qui auraient déserté des dits batimens pour les renvoyer et faire transporter hors du pays. Auquel effet les dits consuls et vice consuls s'adresseront aux tribunaux, juges et officiers compétens, et leur feront, par cerit, la demande des dits déserteurs, en justifiant par l'exhibition des registres du batiment ou rôle d'equipage ou autres documens officiels que ces hommes faisaient partie des dits equipages. Et sur cette demande ainsi justifiée, sauf toute fois lapreuve contraire, l'extradition ne pourra être refusée, et il sera donne toute aide et assistance aux dits consuls et vice consuls pour la recherche, saisie et arrestation des susdits déserteurs, lesquels seront même detenus et gardés dans les prisons du pays à leur réquisition, et à leurs frais, jusqu'a ce qu'ils ayent trouvé occasion de les renvoyer; mais s'ils n'etaient renvoye dans le delai de trois mois à compter du jour de leur arrêt, ils seront élargis et ne pourront plus être arretés pour la même cause.

ARTICLE 7. La presente convention temporaire aura son plein effet pendant deux ans à partir du 1er. Octobre prochain, et même après l'expiration de ce terme, elle sera maintenue jusqu'à la conclusion d'un traité définitif, ou jusqu'à ce que l'une des parties ait déclaré à l'autre son intention d'y renoncer, laquelle declaration devra être faite au moins six mois d'avance.

Et dans le cas où la presente convention viendrait à continuer, sans cette declaration par l'une ou l'autre parte, des droits extraordinaires specifiés dans les 1 et 2 articles, seront, a l'expiration des dites deux années, diminués de part et d'autre d'un quart de leur montant, et successivement d'un quart du dit montant d'année en année, aussi longtems qu' aucune des parties n'aura déclaré son intention d'y renoncer, ainsi qu'il est dit ci dessus.

ARTICLE 8. La presente convention sera ratifiée de párt et d'autre, et les ratifications seront échangées dans l'espace d'une année à compter de ce jour, ou plutot si faire se peut. Mais l'execution de la dite

ARTICLE 4. The following quantities shall be considered as forming the ton of merchandise for each of the articles hereinafter specified:

Wines—four 61 gallon hogsheads, or 244 gallons of 231 cubic inches, American measure.

Brandies and all other liquids, 244 gallons.

Silks and all other dry goods, and all other articles usually subject to measurement, forty-two cubic feet, French, in France, and fifty cubic feet, American measure, in the United States.

Cotton—804 lbs. avoirdupois, or 365 kilogrammes.

Tobacco—1,600 pounds avoirdupois, or 725 kilogrammes.

Ashes, pot and pearl, 2,240 lbs. avoirdupois, or 1,016 kilogrammes.

Rice—1,600 lbs. avoirdupois, or 725 kilogrammes; and for all weighable articles not specified 2,240 lbs. avoirdupois, or 1,016 kilogrammes.

ARTICLE 5. The duties of tonnage, light-money, pilotage, port charges, brokerage, and all other duties upon foreign shipping, over and above those paid by the national shipping in the two countries respectively, other than those specified in articles 1 and 2 of the present convention, shall not exceed in France, for vessels of the United States, five francs per ton of the vessel's American register; nor for vessels of France in the United States ninety-four cents per ton of the vessel's French passport.

ARTICLE 6. The contracting parties, wishing to favor their mutual commerce by affording in their ports every necessary assistance to their respective vessels, have agreed that the consuls and vice consuls may cause to be arrested the sailors, being part of the crews of the vessels of their respective nations, who shall have deserted from the said vessels, in order to send them back and transport them out of the country; for which purpose the said consuls and vice consuls shall address themselves to the courts, judges, and officers competent, and shall demand the said deserters in writing, proving by an exhibition of the registers of the vessel or ship's roll, or other official documents, that those men were part of said crews, and on this demand so proved (saving, however, where the contrary is proved) the delivery shall not be refused; and there shall be given all aid and assistance to the said consuls and vice consuls for the search, seizure, and arrest of said deserters, who shall even be detained and kept in the prisons of the country, at their request and expense, until they shall have found an opportunity of sending them back. But if they be not sent back within three months, to be counted from the day of their arrest, shall be set at liberty, and shall be no more arrested for the same cause.

ARTICLE 7. The present temporary convention shall be in force for two years from the first day of October next, and even after the expiration of that term until the conclusion of a definitive treaty, or until one of the parties shall have declared its intention to renounce it, which declaration shall be made at least six months beforehand.

And in case the present arrangement should remain without such declaration of its discontinuance by either party, the extra duties specified in the first and second articles shall, from the expiration of the said two years, be, on both sides, diminished by one-fourth of their whole amount; and afterwards, by one-fourth of the said amount from year to year, so long as neither party shall have declared the intention of renouncing it, as above stated.

ARTICLE 8. The present convention shall be ratified on both sides, and the ratifications shall be exchanged within one year from the date hereof, or sooner, if possible. But the execution of the said

convention commencera dans la deux pays le premiere Octobre prochain, et aura son effet, dans le
cas même de non-ratification, pour tous batimens
partis *bonâ fide* pour les ports de l'une ou l'autre
nation, dans la confiance qu'lle était en vigueur.

En foi de quoi, les plenipotentiaires respectifs ont
signé la presente convention, et y ont apposé leur
sceaux, en la ville de Washington, ce 24me jour de
Juin, de l'an de notre seigneur, 1822.

G. HYDE DE NEUVILLE. [L. s.]
JOHN QUINCY ADAMS. [L. s.]

ARTICLE SÉPARÉ. Les droits extraordinaires levés
de part et d'autre jusqu'à ce jour, en vertu dé l'acte
du Congrés du 15 Mai, 1820, et de l'ordonnance du
26 Juillet de la même année et autres la confirmant,
qui n'ont point deja été remboursés, seront restitues.
Signé et scellé comme ci-dessus ce 24me jour de
Juin, 1822.

G. HYDE DE NEUVILLE. [L. s.]
JOHN QUINCY ADAMS. [L. s.]

convention shall commence in both countries on the
1st of October next, and shall be effective, even in
case of non-ratification, for all such vessels as may
have sailed *bona fide* for the ports of either nation,
in the confidence of its being in force.

In faith whereof, the respective plenipotentiaries
have signed the present convention, and have thereunto affixed their seals, at the city of Washington,
this 24th day of June, A. D. 1822.

JOHN QUINCY ADAMS. [L. s.]
G. HYDE DE NEUVILLE. [L. s.]

SEPARATE ARTICLE. The extra duties levied on either
side before the present day, by virtue of the act of
Congress of May 15, 1820, and of the ordinance
of July 26 of the same year, and others confirmative thereof, and which have not already been paid
back, shall be refunded.

Signed and sealed as above, this 24th day of June,
1822.

JOHN QUINCY ADAMS. [L. s.]
G. HYDE DE NEUVILLE. [L. s.]

Now, therefore, be it known that I, James Monroe, President of the United States, have caused the
said convention and first separate article to be made public, to the end that the same, and every clause
and article thereof, may be observed and fulfilled with good faith by the United States and the citizens
thereof.

In witness whereof, I have hereunto set my hand and caused the seal of the United States to be
affixed. Done at the city of Washington, this twelfth day of February, in the year of our Lord
[L. s.] one thousand eight hundred and twenty-three, and of the Independence of the United States the
forty-seventh.

JAMES MONROE.

By the President:
　JOHN QUINCY ADAMS, *Secretary of State.*

TRADE WITH THE BRITISH NORTH AMERICAN AND WEST INDIA COLONIES.

COMMUNICATED TO THE HOUSE OF REPRESENTATIVES JANUARY 21, 1823.

Mr. RUSSELL, from the Committee on Foreign Affairs, to whom was referred a resolution instructing them to
inquire whether the provisions of an act of the Parliament of Great Britain passed the 5th of August,
1822, violate any of the rights of the United States or are detrimental to their interests, having, in
pursuance of instructions, inquired into the several matters referred, reported:

That the provisions of the act of Parliament above mentioned are not, in their opinion, repugnant to
rights secured to the citizens of the United States by existing treaties or to national law. That act of
Parliament, so far as it regards the United States, permits to be imported therefrom, by land or water, to
any port or place of entry in Upper or Lower Canada, at which there is, or may hereafter be, lawfully
established, a custom-house, the goods, wares, and commodities, the growth, produce, and manufacture of
the United States, enumerated in a schedule annexed to that act, marked A, on paying the duties specified
in another schedule, also annexed to that act, marked B.

There is no provision of that act which imposes duties on the merchandise of citizens of the United States
passing into Lower Canada or down the river St. Lawrence with a view to exportation, and whatever
might, heretofore, have been our right to such a passage for such a purpose, it has not been impaired by
any provision of that act, as no reference to it whatever is to be found therein. Your committee are not
aware that the citizens of the United States ever enjoyed the right to export their merchandise in their
own vessels from the Canadas, or that they were permitted to navigate the river St. Lawrence, with their
vessels and merchandise, below the port of Quebec, until that port was placed, by the British act of
Parliament of the 24th of June, 1822, among the ports thereby declared to be open to American commerce.

Although the British act of Parliament of the 5th of August, 1822, does not, in the opinion of your
committee, violate any conventional or perfect national right of the United States, yet your committee
cannot but regard that act as highly detrimental to the interests of that portion of our citizens which it
immediately affects.

It was a measure, indeed, not only unexpected, but certainly inconsistent with that liberal spirit
which has recently been avowed by both Governments in relation to their general commercial intercourse
with each other, and repugnant to the course of conduct which both had tacitly pursued in relation to
that particular commercial intercourse which this measure is intended specially to regulate.

Since the cessation of all treaty stipulations on the subject, and until the enactment of this statute,
both Governments had allowed this particular intercourse between the United States and the Canadas

to be as freely enjoyed by both parties, as it was, or of right could have been enjoyed, while those stipulations continued to be in force.   The inhabitants of the United States have still been permitted to import into the two Canadas *all goods and merchandise,* the importation of which was not entirely prohibited, subject to the payment of *no higher or other duties* than would be payable by British subjects, on the importation of the *same from Europe* into the said territories.   But now, by the act of Parliament under consideration, not only are our citizens, without any cause therefor being given on our part, prohibited from importing into those territories all goods and merchandise which are not the growth, produce, or manufacture of the United States, but many important articles which are the growth, produce, or manufacture of said States, and even the articles which are not so prohibited are subjected to the payment of a duty so exorbitant as, in some instances, to be equivalent to a prohibition.

As this act, while it thus seriously injures a portion of our citizens, is highly dissatisfactory to those British subjects on whom it immediately operates, your committee are of opinion that, before resorting to any legislative measure to redress ourselves or to counteract the evils to which our citizens are exposed under the act of Parliament aforesaid, an attempt should be made to obtain, by amicable negotiation, an arrangement on this subject as shall accord with the friendly and liberal views professed by both Governments, and be perfectly satisfactory to the now suffering citizens or subjects of both.

Your committee, therefore, submit the following resolution:

Resolved, That the subject be referred to the President of the United States, and that he be requested to obtain, by negotiation with the Government of Great Britain, such modifications of the act of Parliament of the 5th of August, 1822, as may remove all just cause of complaint.

An act to regulate the trade of the provinces of Lower and Upper Canada, and for other purposes, relating to the said provinces.—[*August* 5, 1822.]

Whereas it is expedient to make further regulations respecting the trade of the provinces of Upper and Lower Canada, in North America :

Be it therefore enacted by the King's most excellent Majesty, by and with the advice and consent of the Lords Spiritual and Temporal and Commons in this present Parliament assembled, and by the authority of the same, That, from and after the passing of this act, it shall be lawful to import, by land or inland navigation, in any British or American vessel or vessels, boat or boats, carriage or carriages, the goods, wares, and commodities, the growth, produce, or manufacture of the United States of America, enumerated in the schedule or table annexed to this act, marked (A), from any port or place in the United States of America, into any port or place of entry at which a custom-house now is, or hereafter may be, lawfully established, in either of the provinces of Upper and Lower Canada: *Provided always, nevertheless,* That it shall and may be lawful for the Governor, Lieutenant Governor, or person administering the Government of either of the said provinces, respectively, by and with the advice and consent of the Executive Council thereof, for the time being, from time to time, to diminish or increase, by proclamation, the number of ports or places which are, or hereafter may be, appointed in such province, for the entry of goods, wares, and commodities, imported from the United States of America.

II. *And be it further enacted,* That, from and after the passing of this act, there shall be raised, levied, collected, and paid unto his Majesty, his heirs and successors, for and upon such of the goods, wares, and commodities which shall be so imported as are enumerated in the schedule or table annexed to this act, marked (B,) the several duties of customs, as the same are respectively inserted or described and set forth, in figures, in the said schedule.

III. *Provided always, and be it further enacted,* That if, upon the importation of any article charged with duty by this act, the said article shall also be liable to the payment of duty under the authority of any colonial law, equal to, or exceeding in amount, the duty charged by this act, then, and in such case, the duty charged upon such article by this act shall not be demanded or paid upon the importation of such article: *Provided, also,* That if the duty payable under such colonial law shall be less in amount than the duty payable by this act, then, and in such case, the difference only between the amount of the duty payable by this act and the duty payable under the authority of such colonial laws shall be deemed to be the duty payable by this act; and the same shall be collected and paid in such and the like manner, and appropriated and applied to such and the like uses as the duties specified in the said schedule annexed to this act, marked (B,) are directed to be collected, paid, appropriated, and applied.

IV. *And be it further enacted,* That the same tonnage duties shall be paid upon all American vessels or boats importing any goods into either of the said provinces as are, or may be, for the time being, payable in the United States of America on British vessels or boats entering the harbors of the State from whence such goods shall have been imported.

V. *And be it further enacted,* That in all cases in which the duties imposed by this act upon the importation of articles into the said provinces, or either of them, are charged not according to the weight, gauge, or measure, but according to the value thereof, such value shall be ascertained in the mode prescribed by an act passed in this present session of Parliament, intituled "An act to regulate the trade between his Majesty's possessions in America and the West Indies and other places in America and the West Indies."

VI. *And be it further enacted,* That if the importer or proprietor of such articles shall refuse to pay the duties hereby imposed thereon, it shall and may be lawful for the collector, or other chief officer of the customs, where such articles shall be imported, and he is hereby respectively required to take and secure the same, with the casks or other package thereof, and to cause the same to be publicly sold within the space of twenty days, at the most, after such refusal made, and at such time and place as such officer shall, by four or more days' public notice, appoint for that purpose; which articles shall be sold to the highest bidder; and the money arising from the sale thereof shall be applied to the payment of the said duties, together with the charges which shall have been occasioned by the said sale; and the overplus (if any) shall be paid to such importer, or any other person authorized to receive the same.

VII. And whereas a certain act, made and passed in the twenty-eighth year of the reign of his late Majesty King George the Third, entitled "An act to allow the importation of rum and other spirits from his

Majesty's colonies or plantations in the West Indies into the province of Quebec without payment of duty, under certain conditions and restrictions," has been repealed during the present session of Parliament; and whereas doubts may be entertained whether a certain act, passed in the forty-ninth year of his said late Majesty's reign, intituled " An act to allow the importation of rum and other spirits from the island of Bermuda into the province of Lower Canada without payment of duty, on the same terms and conditions as such importation may be made directly from his Majesty's sugar colonies in the West Indies," might not still remain in force, notwithstanding the repeal of the said first mentioned act: *Be it therefore enacted and declared,* That the said last mentioned act shall be, and the same is hereby, repealed.

VIII. And whereas it is expedient to afford protection to the trade between the said colonies and plantations and the province of Lower Canada, by imposing the same duty upon rum or other spirits, the produce or manufacture of the said colonies, imported from Great Britain into the said province, as is now payable upon the same articles when imported from his Majesty's said colonies or plantations in the West Indies: *Be it further enacted,* That, from and after the passing of this act, there shall be raised, levied, collected, and paid unto his Majesty, his heirs and successors, for and upon every gallon of rum or other spirits, the produce or manufacture of any of his Majesty's islands, colonies, or plantations in the West Indies, which shall be imported or brought into any port of the said province of Lower Canada from Great Britain or Ireland, or any of the British dominions in Europe, the sum of sixpence over and above all other duties now or hereafter to be made payable thereon in the said province.

IX. *And be it further enacted,* That the rates and duties chargeable by this act shall be deemed and are hereby declared to be sterling money of Great Britain, and shall be collected, recovered, and paid to the amount of the value which such nominal sums bear in Great Britain; and that such sums may be received and taken according to the proportion and value of five shillings and sixpence to the ounce in silver; and that the said duties hereinbefore granted shall be received, levied, collected, paid, and recovered in the same manner and form, and by such rules, ways, and means, and under such penalties and forfeitures, as any other duties payable to his Majesty upon goods imported into the said provinces of Upper Canada and Lower Canada, are or shall be raised, levied, collected, paid, and recovered by any act or acts of Parliament, as fully and effectually, to all intents and purposes, as if the several clauses, powers, directions, penalties, and forfeitures relating thereto were particularly repealed and again enacted in the body of this act; and that all the moneys which shall arise by the said duties (except the necessary charges of raising, collecting, levying, recovering, answering, paying, and accounting for the same) shall be paid by the collector of his Majesty's customs into the hands of his Majesty's Receiver General in the said provinces, respectively, for the time being, and shall be applied to and for the use of the provinces of Upper and Lower Canada, respectively, in such manner only as shall be directed by any law or laws which may be made by his Majesty, his heirs, or successors, by and with the advice and consent of the Legislative Council and Assembly of each of the said provinces, respectively.

X. *And be it further enacted,* That it shall be lawful to export in any British or American vessel or vessels, boat or boats, carriage or carriages, from any of the ports or places of entry now or hereafter to be established in the said provinces, to any port or place in the United States of America, any article of the growth, produce, or manufacture of any of his Majesty's dominions, or any other article legally imported into the said provinces: *Provided always,* That nothing herein contained shall be construed to permit or allow the exportation of any arms or naval stores, unless a license shall have been obtained for that purpose from his Majesty's Secretary of State; and in case any such articles shall be shipped or waterborne, for the purpose of being exported contrary to this act, the same shall be forfeited, and shall and may be seized and prosecuted as hereinafter directed.

XI. *And be it further enacted,* That nothing in this act contained shall be construed to interfere with or repeal, as respects the inland navigation of the said provinces, any of the provisions contained in a certain act passed in the seventh and eighth years of the reign of King William, intituled "An act for preventing frauds and regulating abuses in the plantation trade," except in so far as the same are altered or repealed by this act.

XII. *And be it further enacted,* That all penalties and forfeitures incurred in either of the said provinces under this act (except where it is otherwise provided) shall and may be sued for and prosecuted in any court having competent jurisdiction within such province, respectively; and the same shall and may be recovered, divided, and accounted for in the same manner and form, and by the same rules and regulations in all respects as other penalties and forfeitures for offences against the laws relating to the customs and trade of the said provinces, respectively, shall or may, by any act or acts of the Legislatures of such provinces, be directed to be sued for, prosecuted, recovered, divided, and accounted for within the same, respectively.

XIII. And whereas it is expedient to encourage the trade between Newfoundland, Nova Scotia, New Brunswick, and Prince Edward's Island, by enabling the merchants and traders of Newfoundland to export from thence into Canada rum and other spirits the produce of the British West India islands, or any of his Majesty's colonies on the continent of South America, free of any duty which may have been imposed upon its importation from any of the places last aforesaid, and for which purpose to allow, upon the export of such rum or other spirits, a drawback of the full duties paid upon the importation thereof: *Be it therefore enacted,* That, from and after the passing of this act, there shall be paid and allowed, upon the exportation from any or either of the said colonies of Newfoundland, Nova Scotia, New Brunswick, or Prince Edward's Island, into Canada of rum or other spirits, being the produce of the British West India islands, or any of his Majesty's colonies on the continent of South America, a drawback of the full duties of customs which may have been paid upon the importation thereof from any of the places last aforesaid into any or either of the said colonies of Newfoundland, Nova Scotia, New Brunswick, or Prince Edward's Island, upon a certificate being produced, under the hands and seals of the collector and comptroller of his Majesty's customs at Quebec, certifying that the said rum or other spirits have been duly landed in Canada.

XIV. *And be it further enacted,* That no entry shall pass nor any drawback be paid or allowed upon the exportation of rum or other spirits from any or either of the said colonies of Newfoundland, Nova Scotia, New Brunswick, or Prince Edward's Island, into Canada, unless such entry may be made in the name of the real owner or owners, proprietor or proprietors, of the said goods; and that before such owner or owners, proprietor or proprietors, shall receive the said drawback so allowed as aforesaid, one or more of them shall verify upon oath, upon the debenture to be made out for the payment of such drawback, that he or they is or are the real owner or owners of the said goods; nor unless proof, on oath, shall be made to the satisfaction of the collector and comptroller of his Majesty's customs at the port from whence the said goods shall be so imported into Canada that the full duties due upon the importation of the said goods at the said port had been paid and discharged: *Provided always*, That, in case where the owners of the said goods are resident in any other part of the British dominions, it shall be lawful for their known and established agents in the colonies from whence the said goods shall be so imported into Canada to take the necessary oaths on behalf of the said owners.

XV. *And be it further enacted*, That the said drawbacks shall be paid by the collector of his Majesty's customs at the port from whence the said goods shall be so imported into Canada, with the consent of the comptroller there, out of any moneys in his hands arising from the duties of customs.

XVI. *And be it further enacted*, That no drawback shall be paid and allowed as aforesaid unless the said rum or other spirits shall be duly entered for exportation with the proper officers of the customs, and actually shipped on board the ship or vessel in which the said goods are intended to be exported, within the space of one year from the time such rum or other spirits were originally imported into the colony from whence it is intended to export them to Canada, nor unless such drawback shall be claimed within one year after the goods are so shipped for exportation.

XVII. And whereas, since the division of the province of Quebec into the provinces of Lower and Upper Canada, divers regulations have from time to time been made, by agreements concluded under the authority of acts passed by the Legislature of the said two provinces, respectively, concerning the imposing of duties upon articles imported into the province of Lower Canada and the payment of drawbacks of such duties to the province of Upper Canada, on account of the proportion of goods so imported into Lower Canada, and passing from thence into the said province of Upper Canada, and consumed therein; the last of which agreements expired on the first day of July, one thousand eight hundred and nineteen: And whereas it appears, by the report of the Commissioners last appointed for the purposes aforesaid, that the province of Upper Canada claims certain arrearages from the province of Lower Canada on account of such drawbacks, which claims are not admitted on the part of the province of Lower Canada; and it further appears by the report of the said Commissioners, appointed on behalf of both provinces for the purpose aforesaid, that they have failed to establish any regulation for the period beyond the first day of July, one thousand eight hundred and nineteen, by reason that they could not agree upon the proportion of duties to be paid to Upper Canada by way of drawbacks: For remedy of the inconvenience occasioned by the suspension of the said agreement, and for the satisfactory investigation and adjustment of the said claims: *Be it enacted*, That it shall and may be lawful for the Governor, Lieutenant Governor, or person administering the Government of each of the said provinces of Upper and Lower Canada, so soon as conveniently may be after the passing of this act, to appoint, by commission under the great seal of his respective province, one arbitrator, and that the said arbitrator so appointed shall have power, by an instrument under their hands and seals, to appoint a third arbitrator; and, in case of their not agreeing in such appointment within one month from the date of the appointment of the arbitrators so directed to be made on the part of the respective provinces, or the last thereof, if the said appointments shall not be made on the same day, his Majesty, his heirs or successors, shall have power, by an instrument under his sign manual, to appoint such third arbitrator, who (if appointed in manner last mentioned) shall not be an inhabitant of either of the said provinces; and that the three arbitrators, so appointed as aforesaid, shall have power to hear and determine all claims of the province of Upper Canada upon the province of Lower Canada on account of drawbacks or proportion of duties under agreements made and ratified by the authority of the Legislatures of the said two provinces according to the fair understanding and construction of the said agreements; and also to hear any claim which may be advanced on the part of the province of Upper Canada to a proportion of duties heretofore levied in Lower Canada under British acts of Parliament, the division of which duties shall not have been embraced within the terms of any provincial agreement, and to report the particulars of any such claim, with the evidence thereupon, to the Lords Commissioners of his Majesty's Treasury for the time being; and if it shall appear to the Commissioners of his Majesty's Treasury that any sum is justly due from the province of Lower Canada to the province of Upper Canada, on account of such last mentioned claim, they shall signify the same, together with the amount, to the Governor or person administering the Government of the province of Lower Canada for the time being, who shall thereupon issue his warrant upon the Receiver General of Lower Canada to pay such amount to the Receiver General of Upper Canada, in full discharge of any such claims.

XVIII. *And be it further enacted*, That the said arbitrators shall have power to send for and examine such persons, papers, and records as they shall judge necessary for their information in the matters referred to them; and that if any person or persons shall refuse or neglect to attend the said arbitrators, or to produce before them any papers or documents, having been duly served in either province with reasonable notice in writing for that purpose, he, she, or they, shall forfeit and pay the sum of fifty pounds, to be recovered by bill, plaint, or information, in any court having competent jurisdiction within the province in which such person usually resides, to be applied towards the support of the civil Government of the said province, and to be accounted for to his Majesty, through the Lords Commissioners of his Majesty's Treasury for the time being, in such manner and form as it shall please his Majesty to direct.

XIX. *And be it further enacted*, That the witnesses to be produced before the said arbitrators, if it is desired by either of the said arbitrators, shall and may be sworn before any of his Majesty's justices of the peace within either of the said provinces, or before any one of the said arbitrators, who are hereby empowered jointly or severally to administer such oath; and that if any person shall, in any such oath so taken as aforesaid, wilfully forswear himself, he shall be deemed guilty of wilful and corrupt perjury.

XX. *And be it further enacted*, That in case of the death, removal, or incapacity of either of the said arbitrators before making an award, or in case the third arbitrator, chosen or appointed as aforesaid, shall refuse to act, another shall be appointed in his stead, in the same manner as such arbitrator so dead, removed, or become incapable or refusing to act, as aforesaid, was originally appointed; and that in case a third arbitrator shall be appointed by his Majesty, as hereinbefore mentioned, it shall be lawful for the Governor-in-chief in and over the said provinces to determine the amount of remuneration to be paid to such arbitrator, which amount shall be defrayed in equal proportions by each province, and shall be paid by warrants to be issued for that purpose by the Governor, Lieutenant Governor, or person administering the Government of each province, upon the Receiver General thereof, respectively.

XXI. *And be it further enacted*, That the award of the majority of the said arbitrators, so far as the same shall be authorized by this act, shall be final and conclusive as to all matters therein contained; and that if either of the arbitrators nominated by the Governor, Lieutenant Governor, or persons administering the Government of either of the said provinces, shall refuse or neglect to attend, on due notice being given, the two remaining arbitrators may proceed to hear and determine the matters referred to them, in the same manner as if he were present.

XXII. *And be it further enacted*, That the said arbitrators, or a majority of them, as herein before mentioned, shall certify the award to be made by them in the premises, under their hands and seals, to the Commissioners of his Majesty's Treasury of the United Kingdom of Great Britain and Ireland, and to the Governor, Lieutenant Governor, or person administering the Government of each of the said provinces; and that if any sum be directed by the said award to be paid to the province of Upper Canada by the province of Lower Canada, it shall and may be lawful for the Governor, Lieutenant Governor, or person administering the Government of the said province of Lower Canada, and he is hereby required, to issue his warrant upon the Receiver General of the province of Lower Canada, in favor of the Receiver General of the province of Upper Canada, for the sum so awarded, which sum shall be accordingly paid by the Receiver General of Lower Canada in discharge of such warrant, and shall be accounted for by him to the Lords Commissioners of his Majesty's Treasury for the time being, in such manner and form as his Majesty, his heirs, and successors, shall be graciously pleased to direct.

XXIII. *And be it further enacted*, That the arbitrators to be appointed under this act shall have power to hear and determine any claim which may be advanced on the part of the province of Lower Canada upon the province of Upper Canada, being of the same description as those which, by this act, may be preferred to the same arbitrators on the part of Upper Canada ; and that their award thereupon shall be final and conclusive, and shall be carried into effect, if the same be made in favor of the province of Lower Canada, ·in the same manner as is herein directed with respect to any award which may be made in favor of the province of Upper Canada.

XXIV. *And be it further enacted*, That, of all duties which have been levied in the province of Lower Canada since the first day of July, one thousand eight hundred and nineteen, under any act passed in the said province, upon any goods, wares, merchandise, or commodities imported by sea into the province of ·Lower Canada, and also of all duties which, after the passing of this act and before the first day of July, one thousand eight hundred and twenty-four, shall be levied in the province of Lower Canada, under any act passed in the said province, upon any goods, wares, merchandise, or commodities imported by sea into the said province of Lower Canada, the province of Upper Canada shall be entitled to have and receive one-fifth part, as the proportion of duties arising and due to the said province of Upper Canada upon such importations; and that the Governor, Lieutenant Governor, or person administering the Government of the province of Lower Canada, shall and. may issue his warrant forthwith upon the Receiver General of Lower Canada, in favor of the Receiver General of the province of Upper Canada, for such proportion of the duties as shall have been received in the province of Lower Canada before the passing of this act; and shall and may, on the first day of January and the first day of July, in each and every year thereafter, issue his warrant upon the Receiver General of Lower Canada, in like manner, for the payment to the Receiver General of Upper Canada of such sum as may be then ascertained to be due on account of the said proportion, according to the provisions of this act.

XXV. *And be it further enacted*, That, immediately after the said first day of July, one thousand eight hundred and twenty-four, the proportion to be paid to Upper-Canada, for the four years next succeeding, of duties levied in the province of Lower Canada, under the authority of any act or acts passed, or to be passed therein, upon goods, wares, and commodities imported therein by sea, shall and may be ascertained by the award of arbitrators, to be appointed in the same manner, and with the same powers, as herein-before provided, with respect to the arbitrators to whom the question of arrears is to be referred, and that arbitrators shall, in like manner, be appointed, and an award made once after every four years there-after, for the purpose of establishing such proportion from time to time ; and all and every the provisions contained in this act respecting the appointment, powers, and remuneration of the arbitrators to be first appointed after the passing thereof, and regarding the execution of their duty, shall apply and extend to the arbitrators to be appointed for the purposes last herein mentioned.

XXVI. *And be it further enacted*, That, after the said first day of July, one thousand eight hundred and twenty-four, and until a new proportion of duties to be paid to Upper Canada shall be established, as hereinbefore provided, and also, at all times hereafter, in default of any such proportion being appointed, the proportion of duties last assigned to be paid to Upper Canada, under the authority of this act, shall continue to be paid by the province of Lower Canada, and warrants shall issue for the payment of the same, in the same manner as for the period before the same first day of July, one thousand eight hundred and twenty-four: *Provided always*, That it shall be in the power of the arbitrators, nevertheless, by their subsequent award, to alter such proportion from the period for which it was last established, if it shall appear to them·just so to do.

XXVII. And whereas, by a certain act of the Parliament of Great Britain, passed in the fourteenth year of his late Majesty's reign, intituled "An act to establish a fund towards further defraying the charges of the administration of justice and support of the civil Government within the province of Quebec, in America," certain duties were imposed upon goods and commodities imported into the said province, which duties are, by the said act, directed to be applied, under the authority of the Lord High Treasurer, or Commissioners of his· Majesty's Treasury, in making a more certain and adequate provision towards defraying the expense of the administration of justice and the support of. the civil Government of the said province of Quebec; and, since the division of the said province of Quebec into the provinces of Upper and Lower Canada, it has been contended, on behalf of the said provinces, that the proceeds of such duties should be distributed between the said two provinces in proportion to the amount of expenses defrayed by each, respectively, towards the administration of justice and the support of its civil Government, and not in proportion to the estimated consumption within either province of the articles upon which such duties shall have been paid: *Be it therefore enacted*, That it shall be lawful for the arbitrators, to be appointed from time to time, for the purpose of establishing the proportion which shall be paid to Upper Canada of such duties as now are or hereafter may be imposed by acts passed in the province of Lower.Canada, to receive the claims in behalf of each province, with respect to its proportion of duties levied under the said act, passed in the fourteenth year of his said late Majesty's reign, since the expiration of the last provisional agreement, heretofore ratified between the said two provinces, or·which may hereafter be levied under the authority of the said act, upon goods and commodities imported into Lower Canada, and to report the same, with the evidence thereon, to the Lords Commissioners of his Majesty's Treasury for the United Kingdom of Great Britain and Ireland for the time being, in order that they may make such order respecting the proportion in which the same shall be expended within each of the said provinces, respectively, for the purposes mentioned in the said act, as to them shall seem meet:

Provided always, nevertheless, That, until such order shall be made by the Lords Commissioners of his Majesty's Treasury, as aforesaid, the proceeds of such duties shall be distributed in the same proportion between the said two provinces as the duties levied under the provincial acts of the province of Lower Canada within the same period; subject, nevertheless, to be increased or diminished, as respects either of the said provinces, by any subsequent order of the said Lords Commissioners, extended to the period for which no such order had before been made.

XXVIII. And whereas the division of the province of Quebec into the two provinces of Upper and Lower Canada was intended for the common benefit of his Majesty's subjects residing within both of the newly constituted provinces, and not in any manner to obstruct the intercourse or prejudice the trade to be carried on by the inhabitants of any part of the said late province of Quebec with Great Britain, or with other countries; and it has accordingly been made a subject of mutual stipulation between the said two provinces, in the several agreements which have heretofore subsisted, that the province of Upper Canada should not impose any duties upon articles imported from Lower Canada, but would permit and allow the province of Lower Canada to impose such duties as they might think fit upon articles imported into the said province of Lower Canada, of which duties a certain proportion was by the said agreements appointed to be paid to the province of Upper Canada; and whereas, in consequence of the inconveniences arising from the cessation of such agreements as above recited, it has been found expedient to remedy the evils now experienced in the province of Upper Canada, and to guard against such as might in future arise from the exercise of an exclusive control, by the Legislature of Lower Canada, over the imports and exports into and out of the port of Quebec; and it is further expedient, in order to enable the said province of Upper Canada to meet the necessary charges upon its ordinary revenue and to provide with sufficient certainty for the support of its civil Government, to establish such control as may prevent the evils which have arisen or may arise, from the Legislature of Lower Canada suffering to expire unexpectedly, or repealing suddenly, and without affording to Upper Canada an opportunity of remonstrance, existing duties upon which the principal part of its revenue and the necessary maintenance of its Government may depend: *Be it therefore enacted,* That all and every the duties which, at the time of the expiration of the last agreement between the said provinces of Upper and Lower Canada, were payable, under any act or acts of the province of Lower Canada, on the importation of any goods, wares, or commodities, into the said province of Lower Canada, (except such as may have been imposed for the regulation of the trade by land or inland navigation, between the said province and the United States of America,) shall be payable and shall be levied according to the provisions contained in any such acts until any such act or acts for repealing or altering the said duties, or any part thereof, respectively, shall be passed by the Legislative Council and Assembly of the said province of Lower Canada, and until such act or acts, repealing or altering such duties, shall, after a copy thereof has been transmitted to the Governor, Lieutenant Governor, or person administering the Government of the province of Upper Canada, be laid before both Houses of the Imperial Parliament, according to the forms and provisions contained in a certain act of the Parliament of Great Britain, passed in the thirty-first year of the reign of his said late Majesty, intituled "An act to repeal certain parts of an act passed in the fourteenth year of his Majesty's reign, intituled 'An act for making more effectual provision for the Government of the province of Quebec, in North America,' and to make further provision for the Government of the said province," and the royal assent thereto proclaimed within the province of Lower Canada, according to the provisions of the said last mentioned act.

XXIX. *And be it further enacted,* That, from and after the passing of this act, no act of the Legislature of the province of Lower Canada whereby any additional or other duties shall or may be imposed on articles imported by sea into the said province of Lower Canada, and whereby the province of Upper Canada shall or may in any respect be directly or indirectly affected, shall have the force of law until the same shall have been laid before the Imperial Parliament, as provided in certain cases by the said act, passed in the thirty-first year of his said late Majesty's reign, and the royal assent thereto published by proclamation in the said province of Lower Canada, a copy of such act having, within one month from the time of presenting the same for the royal assent in the said province, been transmitted by the Governor, Lieutenant Governor, or person administering the Government of the province of Lower Canada, to the Governor, Lieutenant Governor, or person administering the Government of the province of Upper Canada: *Provided always, nevertheless,* That it shall not be necessary to transmit any such act to be laid before the Imperial Parliament, if, before the same shall have been presented for the royal assent within the said province of Lower Canada, the Legislative Council and House of Assembly of the said province of Upper Canada shall, by address to the Governor, Lieutenant Governor, or person administering the Government of the said province of Upper Canada, pray that their concurrence in the imposition of the duties intended to be imposed by such act may be signified to the Governor, Lieutenant Governor, or person administering the Government of the said province of Lower Canada.

.XXX. And whereas it is expedient that the productions of the province of Upper Canada should be permitted to be exported, without being made subject by any act of the province of Lower Canada, either directly or indirectly, to duties or impositions on their arrival in that province, or in passing through the waters thereof: *Be it enacted,* That, from and after the passing of this act, all and every the boats, scows, rafts, cribs, and other craft, belonging to any of his Majesty's subjects, and coming from the province of Upper Canada into the province of Lower Canada, not laden with the productions of any foreign country, shall be allowed freely to pass into and through the said province, and shall not be subject to any rate, tax, duty, or imposition, other than any charge which may now exist for pilotage, or which may now be established for toll at any lock or other work now actually erected on the navigable waters thereof, any law, statute, or usage, of the province of Lower Canada to the contrary notwithstanding; and that the expense of improving the navigation of the waters of the river St. Lawrence shall in future be defrayed by such measures and in such proportions as the arbitrators to be appointed under the provisions of this act shall determine, upon the prayer of either province: *Provided always,* That no such determination shall be carried into effect until sanctioned and enacted by the Legislatures of both the said provinces.

XXXI. And whereas doubts have been entertained whether the tenures of lands within the said provinces of Upper and Lower Canada, holden in fief and seigniory, can legally be changed; and whereas it may materially tend to the improvement of such lands, and to the general advantage of the said provinces, that such tenures may henceforth be changed in the manner hereinafter mentioned: *Be it therefore further enacted and declared,* That if any person or persons holding any lands in the said provinces of Lower and Upper Canada, or either of them, in fief and seigniory, and having legal power and authority to alienate the same, shall, at any time, from and after the commencement of this act, surrender the same into the hands of his Majesty, his heirs or successors, and shall, by petition to his Majesty, or to the Governor, Lieutenant Governor, or person administering the Government of the province in which the lands so holden shall be situated, set forth that he, she, or they, is or are desirous of holding the same in free and common soccage, such Governor, Lieutenant Governor, or person administering the Government of such province as aforesaid, in pursuance of his Majesty's instructions, transmitted through his principal Secretary of State for Colonial Affairs, and by and with the advice and consent of the Executive Council of such province, shall cause a fresh grant to be made to such person or persons of such lands to be holden in free and common soccage, in like manner as lands are now holden in free and common soccage in that part of Great Britain called England; subject, nevertheless, to payment to his Majesty, by such grantee or grantees, of such sum or sums of money as for a commutation for the fines and other dues which would have been payable to his Majesty under the original tenures, and to such conditions as to his Majesty, or to the said Governor, Lieutentant Governor, or person administering the Government aforesaid, shall seem just and reasonable: *Provided always*, That, on any such fresh grant being made as aforesaid, no allotment or appropriation of lands for the support and maintenance of a Protestant clergy shall be necessary; but every such fresh grant shall be valid and effectual without any specification of lands for the purpose aforesaid, any law or statute to the contrary thereof in anywise notwithstanding.

XXXII. *And be it further enacted*, That it shall and may be lawful for his Majesty, his heirs and successors, to commute with any person holding lands at Cens et Rentes in any censive or fief of his Majesty, within either of the said provinces, and such person may obtain a release from his Majesty of all feudal rights arising by reason of such tenure, and receive a grant from his Majesty, his heirs or successors, in free and common soccage, upon payment to his Majesty of such sum of money as his Majesty, his heirs or successors, may deem to be just and reasonable, by reason of the release and grant aforesaid; and all such sums of money as shall be paid upon any commutations made by virtue of this act shall be applied towards the administration of justice and the support of the civil Government of the said province.

XXXIII. *And be it further enacted*, That if any person or persons shall be sued or prosecuted for anything done or to be done in pursuance of this act, such person or persons may plead the general issue, and give this act and the special matter in evidence; and if the plaintiff or plaintiffs, prosecutor or prosecutors, shall become nonsuit, or forbear the prosecution, or discontinue his, her, or their action, or if a verdict shall pass against him, her, or them, the defendants shall have treble costs, and shall have the like remedy for the same as in cases where costs are by law given to defendants.

Schedules to which this act refers.

SCHEDULE (A.)

Asses,	Diamonds and precious stones,
Barley,	Flax,
Beans,	Fruit and vegetables,
Biscuit,	Fustic, and all sorts of wood for dyers' use,
Bread,	Flour,
Beaver, and all sorts of fur,	Grain of any sort,
Bowsprits,	Garden seeds,
Calavances,	Hemp,
Cocoa,	Heading boards,
Cattle,	Horses,
Cochineal,	Hogs,
Coin and bullion,	Hides,
Cotton wool,	Hay,
Drugs of all sorts,	Rye,
Hoops,	Rice,
Hardwood, or mill timber,	Staves,
Indigo,	Skins,
Live stock of any sort,	Shingles,
Lumber,	Sheep,
Logwood,	Tar,
Mahogany, and other wood for cabinet wares,	Tallow,
Masts,	Tobacco,
Mules,	Turpentine,
Neat cattle,	Timber,
Oats,	Tortoise shell,
Peas,	Wool,
Potatoes,	Wheat,
Poultry,	Yards.
Pitch,	

SCHEDULE (B.)

	Sterling. £. s. d.
Barrel of wheat flour, not weighing more than 196 lbs. net weight..........................	0 5 0
Barrel of biscuit, not weighing more than 196 lbs. net weight.............................	0 2 6
For every cwt. of biscuit...	0 1 6
For every 100 lbs. of bread, made from wheat or other grain, imported in bags or packages...	0 2 6
For every barrel of flour, not weighing more than 196 lbs. made from rye, peas, or beans.....	0 2 6
For every bushel of peas, beans, rye, or calavances...................................	0 0 7
Rice, for every 100 lbs. net weight...	0 2 6
For every 1,000 shingles, called Boston chips, not more than 12 inches in length...........	0 7 0

	Sterling.		
	£.	s.	d.
For every 1,000 shingles, being more than 12 inches in length...........................	0	14	0
For every 1,000 red oak staves...	1	1	0
For every 1,000 white oak staves or headings...	0	15	0
For every 1,000 feet of white or yellow pine lumber, of one inch thick.....	1	1	0
For every 1,000 feet of pitch pine lumber...	1	1	0
Other kinds of wood and lumber, per 1,000 feet.......................................	1	8	0
For every 1,000 wood hoops...	0	5	3
Horses, for every £100 of the value thereof..	10	0	0
Neat cattle, for every £100 of the value thereof.......................................	10	0	0
All other live stock, for every £100 of the value thereof................................	10	0	0

An act to regulate the trade between his Majesty's possessions in America and the West Indies, and other places in America and the West Indies.—[*June* 24, 1822.]

Whereas divers acts of Parliament have been from time to time passed for regulating the importation and exportation of certain articles into and from certain territories, islands and ports, under the dominion of his Majesty in America and the West Indies, and it is expedient that the said several acts should be repealed and other provisions made in lieu thereof:

Be it therefore enacted by the King's most excellent Majesty, by and with the advice and consent of the Lords Spiritual and Temporal and Commons in this present Parliament assembled, and by the authority of the same, That, from and after the passing of this act, an act passed in the twenty-eighth year of the reign of his late Majesty King George the Third, intituled "An act for regulating the trade between the subjects of his Majesty's colonies and plantations in North America and in the West India islands and the countries belonging to the United States of America, and between his Majesty's said subjects and the foreign islands in the West Indies;" also, an act passed in the twenty-eighth year of the reign of his late Majesty King George the Third, intituled "An act to allow the importation of rum and other spirits from his Majesty's colonies or plantations in the West Indies into the province of Quebec without payment of duty, under certain conditions and restrictions;" also, an act passed in the twenty-ninth year of the reign of his said late Majesty, intituled "An act to enable his Majesty to authorize, in case of necessity, the importation of bread, flour, Indian corn, and live stock, from any of the territories belonging to the United States of America, into the province of Quebec and all the countries bordering on the Gulf of Saint Lawrence, and the islands within the said Gulf and to the coast of Labrador;" also, another act passed in the twenty-ninth year of the reign of his said late Majesty, intituled "An act for explaining and amending an act passed in the last session of Parliament, intituled 'An act to regulate the trade between the subjects of his Majesty's colonies and plantations in North America and in the West India islands and the countries belonging to the United States of America, and between his Majesty's said subjects and the foreign islands in the West Indies;'" also, an act passed in the thirtieth year of the reign of his said late Majesty, intituled "An act to amend two acts made in the twenty-eighth year of the reign of his present Majesty, the one intituled 'An act for regulating the trade between the subjects of his Majesty's colonies and plantations in North America and in the West India islands and the countries belonging to the United States of America, and between his Majesty's said subjects and the foreign islands in the West Indies,' and the other intituled 'An act to allow the importation of rum or other spirits from his Majesty's colonies or plantations in the West Indies into the province of Quebec, without payment of duty, under certain conditions and restrictions;'" also, an act passed in the thirty-first year of the reign of his said late Majesty, intituled "An act to amend an act made in the twenty-eighth year of his present Majesty's reign for regulating the trade between the subjects of his Majesty's colonies and plantations in North America and in the West India islands and the countries belonging to the United States of America, and between his Majesty's said subjects and the foreign islands in the West Indies;" and also, an act made in the twenty-seventh year of his present Majesty's reign for allowing the importation and exportation of certain goods, wares and merchandise, in the ports of Kingston, Savannah la Mar, Montego Bay, and Santa Lucia, in the island of Jamaica, in the port of Saint George, in the island of Grenada, in the port of Rosseau, in the island of Dominica, and in the port of Nassau, in the island of New Providence, one of the Bahama islands, under certain regulations and restrictions;" also, an act passed in the thirty-third year of the reign of his said late Majesty, intituled "An act to amend an act passed in the twenty-seventh year of his present Majesty's reign, for allowing the importation and exportation of certain goods, wares, and merchandise, in foreign ships, into and from certain ports and places in the West Indies;" and for amending so much of an act made in the thirty-second year of the reign of his present Majesty as relates to permitting the importation of sugar in the Bahama and Bermuda islands in foreign ships; and so much of two acts made in the twenty-eighth and thirty-first years of his present Majesty's reign as prohibits the importation of timber into any island under the dominion of his Majesty in the West Indies, from any foreign colony or plantation in the West Indies or South America; and so much of the said act made in the twenty-eighth year of his present Majesty's reign as prohibits the importation of pitch, tar, and turpentine, into Nova Scotia or New Brunswick, from any country belonging to the United States of America;" also, an act passed in the forty-fourth year of the reign of his said late Majesty, intituled "An act for permitting until the first day of August, one thousand eight hundred and seven, the exportation of salt from the port of Nassau, in the island of New Providence, the port of Exuma, and the port of Crooked Island, in the Bahama islands, in ships belonging to the inhabitants of the United States of America and coming in ballast;" also, an act passed in the forty-fifth year of the reign of his said late Majesty, intituled "An act to consolidate and extend the several laws now in force for allowing the importation and exportation of certain goods and merchandise into and from certain ports in the West Indies;" also, an act passed in the forty-sixth year of the reign of his said late Majesty, intituled "An act for enabling his Majesty to permit the importation and exportation of certain goods and commodities into and from the port of Road Harbor, in the island of Tortola;" also, an act passed in the forty-eighth year of the reign of his said late Majesty, intituled "An act to permit the importation of rice, flour, and grain, from any foreign colonies on the continent of America into certain ports in the West Indies, and to allow certain articles to be imported from the United States of America into the British provinces in North America for the purpose of exportation to the British islands in the West Indies;" also, an act passed in the forty-ninth year of the reign of his said late Majesty, intituled "An act for allowing the importation and exportation of certain goods and commodities into and from the port of Falmouth, in the island of Jamaica;" also, an act passed in the fifty-second year of the reign of his said late Majesty, intituled "An act to allow British plantation sugar and coffee imported into Bermuda in British ships to be exported to the territories of the United States of America in foreign ships or vessels, and to permit articles the production of the said United States to be imported into the said island in foreign ships or vessels;" also, another act passed in the said fifty-second year of the reign of his said late Majesty, intituled "An act for allowing certain articles to be imported into the Bahama islands, and exported therefrom in foreign vessels, and for encouraging the exportation of salt from the said islands;" also, an act passed in the fifty-third year of the reign of his said late Majesty, intituled "An act to amend an act of the twenty-eighth year of his present Majesty, for allowing the importation of rum or other spirits from his Majesty's colonies or plantations in the West Indies into the province of Quebec without payment of duty;" also, another act passed in the fifty-third year of the reign of his said late Majesty, intituled "An act for further allowing the importation and exportation of certain articles at the island of Bermuda;" also, an act passed in the fifty-fourth year of the reign of his said late Majesty, intituled "An act to revive and make perpetual certain acts for consolidating and extending the several laws in force for allowing the importation and exportation of certain articles into and from certain ports in the West Indies;" also, an act passed in the fifty-seventh year of the reign of his said late Majesty, intituled "An act to extend the powers of two acts for allowing British plantation sugar and coffee and other articles imported into Bermuda in British ships to be exported to America in foreign vessels, and to permit articles the produce of America to be imported into the said island in foreign ships, to certain other articles;" also, another act passed in the said fifty-seventh year of the reign of his said late Majesty, intituled "An act to extend several acts for allowing the importation and exportation of certain goods and merchandise to Porta Maria, in the island of Jamaica, and to the port of Bridge Town, in the island of Barbadoes;" also, an act passed in the fifty-eighth year of the reign of his said late Majesty, intituled "An act to allow, for three years, and until six weeks after the commencement of the then next session of Parliament, the importation into ports specially appointed by his Majesty within the provinces of Nova Scotia and New Brunswick of the articles therein enumerated, and the re-exportation thereof from such ports;" also, an act passed in the said fifty-eighth year of the reign of his said late Majesty, intituled "An act to permit the importation of certain articles into his Majesty's colonies or plantations in the West Indies, or on the continent of South America, and also certain articles into certain ports in the West Indies;" also, an act passed in the fifty-ninth year of the reign of his said late Majesty, intituled "An act to make perpetual an act of the forty-fourth year of his present Majesty, for permitting the exportation of salt from the port of Nassau, in the island of New Providence, the port of Exuma, and the port of Crooked Island, in the Bahama islands, in American ships coming in ballast;" also, an act passed in the fifty-ninth year of the reign of his said late Majesty, intituled "An act to extend the provisions of three acts of the fifty-second, fifty-third, and fifty-seventh years of his present Majesty, for allowing British plantation sugar and coffee and other articles imported into Bermuda in British ships, to be exported to America in foreign vessels, and to permit articles the produce of America to be imported into Bermuda in foreign ships, to certain other articles;" also, an act passed in the first year of the reign of his present Majesty, intituled "An act to extend several acts for allowing the importation and exportation of certain goods and merchandises to Morant Bay, in the island of Jamaica;" also, another act passed in the first year of his present Majesty's reign, intituled "An act to permit the importation of coffee from any foreign colony or plantation in America into the port of Bridge Town, in Barbadoes;" also, an act passed in the first and second years of the reign of his present Majesty, intituled "An act to make perpetual an act of the fifty-eighth year of his late Majesty, to allow the importation into certain ports in Nova Scotia and New Brunswick of certain enumerated articles, and the re-exportation thereof from such ports;" shall be, and the same are hereby, repealed.

II. *Provided also, and be it further enacted,* That nothing in this act contained shall extend, or be deemed or construed to extend, to release or discharge any seizure of goods, wares, or merchandise, or of any ship or vessel, or to release or discharge any forfeiture or penalty incurred on or before the passing of this act; but that the same may be prosecuted, sued for, recovered, and divided in such and the like manner as any such seizure, forfeiture, or penalty might have been prosecuted, sued for, recovered, and divided, if this act had not been made.

III. *And be it further enacted,* That, from and after the passing of this act, it shall be lawful to import into any of the ports enumerated in the schedule annexed to this act, marked (A,) from any foreign country on the continent of North or South America, or from any foreign island in the West Indies, whether such country or island, as aforesaid, shall be under the dominion of any foreign European sovereign or State, or otherwise, the articles enumerated in the schedule annexed to this act, marked (B,) either in British built ships, or vessels owned and navigated according to law, or in any ship or vessel *bona fide* the built of and owned by the inhabitants of any country or place belonging to or under the dominion of the sovereign or State of which the said articles are the growth, produce, or manufacture, such ship or vessel being navigated with a master and three-fourths of the mariners, at least, belonging to such country or place; or in any British built ship or vessel which has been sold to and become the property of the subjects of any such sovereign or State, such ship or vessel last mentioned being also navigated with a master and three-fourths of the mariners, at least, belonging to such country or place: *Provided always,* That no articles enumerated in the said schedule shall be imported in any foreign ship or vessel, or in any British built ship or vessel so sold as aforesaid, unless shipped and brought directly from the country or place of which they are the growth, produce, or manufacture.

IV. *And be it further enacted,* That it shall be lawful to export in any British built ship or vessel owned and navigated according to law, or in any foreign ship or vessel as aforesaid, or in any British built ship or vessel so sold as aforesaid, from any of the ports enumerated in the schedule annexed to this act, marked (A,) any article of the growth, produce, or manufacture of any of his Majesty's dominions, or any other article legally imported into the said ports, provided that the said articles, when exported in any such foreign ship or vessel, or in any British built ship or vessel so sold as aforesaid, shall be exported direct to the country or State in America or the West Indies to which such ship or vessel belongs as aforesaid; and before the shipment thereof security by bond shall be given to his Majesty, his heirs and successors, in a penalty equal to half the value of the said articles; such bond to be entered into by the master and exporter before the collector or other chief officer of the customs of such colony, plantation, or island, for the due landing of the said articles at the port or ports for which entered, and for producing a certificate thereof within twelve months from the date of such bond, under the hand and seal of the British consul or vice consul resident at the port or place where the said articles shall have been landed; but in case there shall not be any such consul or vice consul there resident, such certificate to be under the hand and seal of the chief magistrate, or under the hand and seal of two known British merchants residing at such port or place; but such bond may be discharged by proof, on oath, by credible persons, that the said articles were taken by enemies or perished in the seas: *Provided always,* That nothing herein contained shall be construed to permit or allow the exportation of any arms or naval stores unless a license shall have been obtained for that purpose from his Majesty's Secretary of State; and in case any such articles shall be shipped or waterborne for the purpose of being exported contrary to this act, the same shall be forfeited, and shall and may be seized and prosecuted as hereinafter directed.

V. *Provided always, and be it further enacted,* That for ten years after the passing of this act, nothing in this act contained shall extend, or be construed to extend, to exclude from the trade allowed by this act any foreign ship or vessel which, previous to the passing of this act, may have been engaged in lawful trade with his Majesty's said colonies, islands, or plantations, on account of such ship or vessel not being of the build of the country to which such ship or vessel may belong.

VI. *And be it further enacted,* That in case any doubt shall arise whether any goods, wares, or merchandise, intended to be exported in any foreign ship or vessel under the authority of this act, had been legally imported into such port, the legality of such importation shall be made to appear to the satisfaction of the Collector or Comptroller, or other principal officer of the customs of such port, before such goods, wares, and merchandise shall be suffered to be shipped for exportation.

VII. *And be it further enacted,* That, from and after the passing of this act, there shall be raised, levied, collected, and paid unto his Majesty, his heirs and successors, upon the several articles enumerated or described in the said schedule marked (C,) imported or brought into any of the ports enumerated in the schedule marked (A) from any such foreign island, State, or country, under the authority of this act, the several duties or customs as the same are respectively inserted or described and set forth in figures in the said schedule annexed to this act, marked (C,) and the same shall be under the management of the Commissioners of the Customs in England, and shall be raised, levied, collected, paid, and recovered in such and the like manner and form, and by such and the like rules, ways, means, and methods, respectively, and under such penalties and forfeitures, as any duties now payable to his Majesty on goods imported into any of the islands, plantations, colonies, or territories belonging to, or under the dominion of his Majesty, in America or the West Indies, are or may be raised, levied, collected, paid, and recovered by any act or acts of Parliament now in force as fully and effectually, to all intents and purposes, as if the several clauses, powers, directions, penalties, and forfeitures relating thereto were particularly repeated and again enacted in the body of this act; and the produce of such duties shall be paid by the Collector of the Customs to the Treasurer or Receiver General of the colony, province, or plantation in which the same shall be respectively levied, to be applied to such uses and purposes as may be directed by the authority of the respective general courts or general assemblies of such colonies, provinces, or plantations.

VIII. *And be it further enacted,* That in case there shall be no general courts or general assemblies in the colony, province, or plantation in which the said duties shall have been levied and collected under the authority of this act, the net proceeds of such duties shall then be applied and appropriated in such and the like manner, and to such uses as any other duties levied and collected in any of his Majesty's colonies, provinces, or plantations in America or the West Indies, not having general courts or general assemblies, may now, by any act or acts of Parliament passed in Great Britain or the United Kingdom of Great Britain and Ireland, or by any order of his Majesty in council, or by any proclamation issued in his Majesty's name, be appropriated and applied.

IX. *And be it further enacted,* That in all cases where, by the schedule marked (C,) the duties imposed upon the importation of articles into his Majesty's colonies, plantations, or islands in America or the West Indies, are charged, not according to the weight, gauge, or measure, but according to the value thereof, such value shall be ascertained by the declaration of the importer or proprietor of such articles, or his known agent or factor, in manner and form following, that is to say:

"I, A B, do hereby declare that the articles mentioned in the entry, and contained in the packages, [here specifying the several packages, and describing the several marks and numbers, as the case may be,] are of the value of ———. Witness my hand the ——— day of ———. A B."

"The above declaration, signed the ——— day of ———, in the presence of C D, Collector, or other principal officer."

Which declaration shall be written on the warrant of entry of such articles, and shall be subscribed with the hand of the importer or proprietor thereof, or his known agent or factor, in the presence of the Collector or other principal officer of the customs at the port of importation: *Provided,* That if, upon view and examination of such articles by the proper officer of the customs, it shall appear to him that the said articles are not valued according to the true price or value thereof, and according to the true intent and meaning of this act, then and in such case the importer or proprietor, or his known agent or factor, shall be required to declare, on oath, before the Collector or chief officer of the customs at the port of importation (which oath he is hereby authorized and required to administer) what is the invoice price of such articles, and that he verily believes such invoice price is the current value of the articles at the place from whence the said articles were imported; and such invoice price, with the addition of ten pounds per centum thereon, shall be deemed and taken to be the value of the articles in such colony, plantation, or island, as aforesaid, in lieu of the value so declared by the importer or proprietor, or his known agent or factor, and upon which the duties specified in the said schedule shall be charged and paid: *Provided, also,* That if it shall appear to the Collector or other chief officer of the customs that such articles have been invoiced below the real and true value thereof at the place from whence the same were imported, or if the invoice price is not known, the articles shall, in such case, be examined by two competent persons, to be nominated and appointed by the Governor or commander-in-chief of the colony, plantation, or island into which the said articles are imported; and such persons shall declare, on oath, before the Collector or chief officer of the customs, what is the true and real value of such articles in such colony, plantation, or island; and the value so declared on the oaths of such persons shall be deemed to be the true and real value of such articles, and upon which the duties specified in the said schedule, marked (C,) shall be charged and paid.

X. *And be it further enacted,* That if the importer or proprietor of such articles shall refuse to pay the duties hereby imposed thereon, it shall and may be lawful for the Collector or other chief officer of the customs where such articles shall be imported, and he is hereby, respectively, required, to take and secure the same, with the casks or other package thereof, and to cause the same to be publicly sold, within the space of twenty days, at the most, after such refusal made, and at such time and place as such officer shall, by four or more days' public notice, appoint for that purpose, which articles shall be sold to the best bidder; and the money arising by the sale thereof shall be applied, in the first place, in payment of the said duties, together with the charges that shall have been occasioned by the said sale, and the overplus, if any, shall be paid to such importer or proprietor, or any other person authorized to receive the same.

XI. *And be it further enacted,* That whenever any foreign article is liable to duty by this act on the importation thereof into any of his Majesty's colonies, plantations, or islands in America or the West Indies, under the provisions of this act, the like duty shall be payable upon any such foreign article when imported into any such colonies, plantations, or islands direct from any part of the United Kingdom of Great Britain and Ireland; and such duty shall be raised, levied, collected, and paid in such and the like manner, and be appropriated and applied to such and the like uses as the duty payable upon the like article imported from any other place, under the provisions of this act, is, by this act, directed to be raised and applied.

XII. *Provided always, and be it further enacted,* That if, upon the importation of any article charged with duty by this act, the said articles shall also be liable to the payment of duty under the authority of any colonial law equal to or exceeding in amount the duty charged by this act, then, and in such case, the duty charged upon such article by this act shall not be demanded or paid upon the importation of such article: *Provided, also,* That if the duty payable under such colonial law shall be less in amount than the duty payable by this act, then, and in such case, the difference only in the amount of the duty payable by this act and the duty payable under the authority of such colonial law shall be deemed to be the duty payable by this act; and the same shall be collected and paid in such and the like manner, and appropriated and applied to such and the like uses, as the duties specified in the said schedule annexed to this act, marked (C,) are directed to be collected, paid, appropriated, and applied.

XIII. *And be it further enacted,* That all sums of money granted and imposed by this act as duties shall be deemed, and are hereby declared to be, sterling money of Great Britain, and shall be collected, recovered, and paid to the amount of the value which such nominal sums bear in Great Britain, and that such moneys may be received and taken according to the proportion and value of five shillings and sixpence the ounce in silver.

XIV. *And be it further enacted,* That any article enumerated in the schedule (B) legally imported, as aforesaid, under the authority of this act, shall be allowed to be exported in any British ship or vessel, owned and navigated according to law, to any other British island, colony, or plantation in America or the West Indies: *Provided,* That upon the importation thereof into any such other British island, colony, or plantation, proof shall be produced that the said duties due to his Majesty have been first paid in the colony or plantation into which the said articles shall have been first imported; and any article so imported in any ship or vessel as aforesaid shall be allowed to be exported to any part of the United Kingdom of Great Britain and Ireland under the rules, regulations, restrictions, securities, penalties, and forfeitures, particularly mentioned and provided in an act of Parliament made in the twelfth year of the reign of King Charles the Second, intituled "An act for the encouraging and increasing of shipping and navigation;" and in another act of Parliament, made in the twenty-second and twenty-third years of the reign of King Charles the Second, intituled "An act to prevent the planting of tobacco in England, and for regulating the plantation trade;" and in another act of Parliament, made in the twentieth year of his late Majesty's reign, intituled "An act to allow the trade between Ireland and the British colonies in America and the West Indies, and the British settlements on the coast of Africa, to be carried on in like manner as it is now carried on between Great Britain and the said colonies and settlements," or in any of the said acts with respect to the goods, wares, or merchandise therein enumerated or described.

XV. And whereas it is the intention and meaning of this act that the privileges hereby granted to foreign ships and vessels shall be confined to the ships and vessels of such countries only as give the like privileges to British ships and vessels in their ports in America and the West Indies: *Be it therefore enacted,* That it shall be lawful for his Majesty, his heirs and successors, by order in council, from time to time, when and as often as the same shall be judged expedient, to prohibit trade and intercourse, under the authority of this act, with any country or island in America or the West Indies, if it shall appear to his Majesty that the privileges granted by this act to foreign ships and vessels are not allowed to British ships and vessels trading to and from any such country or island under the provisions of this act; and in case such order of his Majesty in council shall be issued, then, during the time that such order in council shall be in force, none of the provisions of this act, either as respects the laws herein repealed or to any other provisions of this act, shall apply, or be taken to apply, to any country or State the trade with which, under the provisions of this act, shall be prohibited by any such order of his Majesty in council; and if any goods whatever shall be imported from, or shipped for the purpose of being exported to, any such country or island in America or the West Indies, in any foreign ship or vessel, after trade and intercourse therewith shall have been prohibited by any such order of his Majesty in council, issued under the authority of this act, all such goods, together with the ship or vessel in which the same shall have been imported or in which the same shall have been shipped for the purpose of being exported as aforesaid, shall be forfeited, with all her guns, furniture, ammunition, tackle, and apparel; and in every such case the same shall and may be seized by any officer of his Majesty's customs or Navy authorized or empowered to make seizures in cases of forfeiture, and shall and may be prosecuted in manner as hereinafter directed.

XVI. *And be it further enacted,* That if his Majesty shall deem it expedient to extend the provisions of this act to any port or ports not enumerated in the schedule marked (A,) it shall be lawful for his Majesty, by order in council, to extend the provisions of this act to such port or ports, and from and after such order in council, all the privileges and advantages of this act and all the provisions, penalties, and forfeitures therein contained shall extend, and be deemed and construed to extend, to any such port or ports, respectively, as fully as if the same had been inserted and enumerated in the said schedule at the time of passing this act.

XVII. *And be it further enacted,* That no articles, except such as are enumerated in the schedule marked (B,) shall be imported in any such British built ship or vessel, or in any such foreign ship or vessel, or in any British built ship or vessel so sold as aforesaid, from any foreign country or State on the continent of America or island in the West Indies, into any of the ports enumerated in the schedule marked (A,) or into any port which may be added to the schedule marked (A) by virtue of any order in council, as aforesaid, on any pretence whatever, on pain of forfeiting such articles, together with the ship or vessel in which the same shall have been imported, and the guns, tackle, apparel, and furniture of such ship or vessel; and in every such case the same shall and may be seized by any officer or officers of his Majesty's customs or Navy who are or shall be authorized and empowered to make seizures in cases of forfeiture, and shall and may be prosecuted in such manner as hereinafter directed.

XVIII. *And be it further enacted,* That no articles whatever shall be imported or exported, either in a British built ship or vessel or in any such foreign ship or vessel as aforesaid, from or to any foreign country on the continent of North or South America, or from or to any foreign island in the West Indies, into or from any port of any British colony, plantation, or island in America or the West Indies, not enumerated in the schedule annexed to this act, marked (A,) on any pretence whatever, on forfeiture of such articles, as also the ship or vessel in which the same shall be imported, with all her guns, furniture, ammunition, tackle, and apparel.

XIX. *Provided always, and be it further enacted,* That nothing in this act contained shall affect, or be construed to affect, the right which British subjects or others may enjoy under any law in force at the passing of this act of exporting in British ships from ports not enumerated in the said schedule marked (A) the produce of the fisheries carried on from any of his Majesty's said colonies, plantations, or islands.

XX. *And be it further enacted,* That all penalties and forfeitures imposed by this act shall and may be, respectively, prosecuted, sued for, and recovered, and divided in Great Britain, Guernsey, Jersey, or the Isle of Man, or in any of his Majesty's colonies or islands in America, in the same manner and form, and by the same rules and regulations, in all respects, in so far as the same are applicable, as any other penalties and forfeitures imposed by any act or acts of Parliament made for the security of the revenue of the customs, or for the regulation or improvement thereof, or for the regulation of trade or navigation, and which were in force immediately before the passing of this act, may be, respectively, prosecuted, sued for, recovered, and divided in Great Britain, Guernsey, Jersey, or the Isle of Man, or in any of his Majesty's colonies or islands in America.

Schedules to which this act refers.

SCHEDULE (A.)

List of free ports.

Kingston, Savannah Le Mar, Montego Bay, Santa Lucia, Antonio, Saint Ann, Falmouth, Maria, Morant Bay, Jamaica.
Saint George, Grenada.
Rosseau, Dominica.
Saint John's, Antigua.
San Josef, Trinidad.
Scarborough, Tobago.
Road Harbor, Tortola.
Nassau, New Providence.
Pitt's Town, Crooked Island.
Kingston, Saint Vincent.
Port St. George and Port Hamilton, Bermuda.

Any port where there is a custom-house, Bahamas.
Bridgetown, Barbadoes.
St. John's, St. Andrew's, New Brunswick.
Halifax, Nova Scotia.
Quebec, Canada.
St. John's, Newfoundland.
Georgetown, Demarara.
New Amsterdam, Berbice.
Castries, St. Lucia.
Basseterre, St. Kitts.
Charlestown, Nevis.
Plymouth, Montserrat.

SCHEDULE (B.)

Asses,
Barley,
Beans,
Biscuit,
Bread,
Beaver, and all sorts of fur,
Bowsprits,
Calavances,
Cocoa,
Cattle,
Cochineal,
Coin and bullion,
Cotton wool,
Drugs of all sorts,
Diamonds and precious stones,
Flax,
Fruit and vegetables,
Fustic, and all sorts of wood for dyers' use,
Flour,
Grain of any sort,
Garden seeds,
Hay,
Hemp,
Heading boards,
Horses,
Hogs,
Hides,
Hoops,
Hardwood or mill timber,

Indian corn meal,
Indigo,
Live stock of any sort,
Lumber,
Logwood,
Mahogany, and other wood for cabinet wares,
Masts,
Mules,
Neat cattle,
Oats,
Peas,
Potatoes,
Poultry,
Pitch,
Rye,
Rice,
Staves,
Skins,
Shingles,
Sheep,
Tar,
Tallow,
Tobacco,
Turpentine,
Timber,
Tortoise shell,
Wool,
Wheat,
Yards.

SCHEDULE (C.)

A schedule of duties payable on articles imported into his Majesty's possessions in America and the West Indies, from other places in America and the West Indies, the duties following, that is to say:

	Sterling.		
	£	s.	d.
Barrel of wheat flour, not weighing more than 196 pounds net weight..................	0	5	0
Barrel of biscuit, not weighing more than 196 pounds net weight......................	0	2	6
For every hundred weight of biscuit..	0	1	6
For every 100 pounds of bread, made from wheat or other grain, imported in bags or packages	0	2	6
For every barrel of flour, not weighing more than 196 pounds, made from rye, peas, or beans..	0	2	6
For every bushel of peas, beans, rye, or calavances	0	0	7
Rice, for every 100 pounds net weight	0	2	6
For every 1,000 shingles, called Boston chips, not more than 12 inches in length............	0	7	0
For every 1,000 shingles, being more than 12 inches in length.........................	0	14	0
For every 1,000 red oak staves...	1	1	0
For every 1,000 white oak staves or headings	0	15	0
For every 1,000 feet of white or yellow pine lumber, of one inch thick	1	1	0
For every 1,000 feet of pitch pine lumber	1	1	0
Other kinds of wood and lumber, per 1,000 feet.....................................	1	3	0
For every 1,000 wood hoops	0	5	3
Horses, for every £100 of the value thereof..	10	0	0
Neat cattle, for every £100 of the value thereof	10	0	0
All other live stock, for every £100 of the value thereof..............................	10	0	0

An act to regulate the trade between his Majesty's possessions in America and the West Indies and other parts of the world.—[June 24, 1822.]

Whereas it is expedient to allow greater freedom of trade and intercourse between the colonies, plantations, and islands belonging to his Majesty in America and in the West Indies and other parts of the world, and to repeal certain acts now in force relating to the trade and intercourse hitherto allowed to be carried on between his Majesty's colonies, plantations, islands, and places in Europe, south of Cape Finisterre, and to make further provision for encouraging and extending the same:

Be it therefore enacted by the King's most excellent Majesty, by and with the advice and consent of the Lords Spiritual and Temporal and Commons in this present Parliament assembled, and by the authority of the same, That so much of an act passed in the twenty-fifth year of the reign of King Charles the Second entitled "An act for the encouragement of the Greenland and Eastland trades and for the better securing the plantation trade, as imposes a duty upon the exportation of sugar, tobacco, cotton wool, indigo, ginger, logwood, fustic, dyeing wood, and cocoa nuts, from any of his Majesty's plantations in America, Asia, or Africa;" also, an act passed in the fifty-first year of the reign of his late Majesty King George the Third entitled "An act to regulate the trade between places in Europe, south of Cape Finisterre, and certain ports in the British colonies in North America;" also, an act passed in the fifty-second year of the reign of his said late Majesty entitled "An act to permit sugar, coffee, and cocoa to be exported from his Majesty's colonies and plantations to any port in Europe, to the south of Cape Finisterre, and corn to be imported from any such port, and from the coast of Africa into the said colonies and plantations, under licenses granted by the Collectors and Comptrollers of the Customs;" also, so much of an act passed in the fifty-fifth year of the reign of his said late Majesty entitled "An act to regulate the trade between Malta and its dependencies and his Majesty's colonies and plantations in America, and also, between Malta and the United Kingdom, as relates to the trade allowed to be carried on between the island of Malta and the dependencies thereof, and his Majesty's colonies and plantations in America;" also, an act passed in the fifth-seventh year of the reign of his said late Majesty entitled "An act to extend the privileges of trade of Malta to the port of Gibraltar;" also, another act passed in the fifty-seventh year of the reign of his said late Majesty entitled "An act to allow the importation of oranges and lemons from the Azores and the Madeiras into the British colonies in North America," shall be, and the same are hereby, repealed, save and except as to the recovery of any forfeiture or penalty incurred on or before the passing of this act: *Provided, nevertheless,* That all acts expressly repealed by any of the said acts shall be deemed and taken to be, and shall remain, repealed.

II. *And be it further enacted,* That it shall be lawful to export from any of his Majesty's said colonies, plantations and islands, in any British built ship or vessel, owned and navigated according to law, any articles the growth, produce, or manufacture of any such colony, plantation, or island, and any articles which have been legally imported into any such colony, plantation, or island, direct to any foreign port in Europe, or in Africa, or to Gibraltar, the island of Malta, or the dependencies thereof, or the islands of Guernsey, Jersey, Aldernay, or Sark, anything contained in an act made in England in the twelfth year of the reign of his Majesty King Charles the Second, entitled "An act for the encouraging and increasing of shipping and navigation," or of any other act or acts in force in the United Kingdom or in Great Britain or Ireland, respectively, to the contrary notwithstanding.

III. *And be it further enacted,* That before any such articles shall be laden or put on board any ship or vessel in the said colonies, plantations, or islands, the exporter shall make a regular entry thereof with the Collector and Comptroller of his Majesty's customs, on which entry shall be endorsed the marks and numbers of the packages with the proper denomination of the goods contained therein, and also the place, quay, or wharf where the goods are intended to be laden: *Provided,* That no goods shall be laden at any place, quay, or wharf which shall not be situate within the limits of a port where a custom-house is established, and at which place, quay, or wharf an officer shall be appointed to attend the lading and shipping of such goods, or at such place or places as shall be mentioned in a sufferance or warrant to be taken out from the Collector and Comptroller of the Customs for that purpose: *Provided always,* That nothing in this act contained shall extend or be construed to extend to alter the existing regulations for lading and shipping the produce of the fisheries of the said colonies, plantations, or islands.

IV. *And be it further enacted,* That if upon examination of any goods allowed to be exported from any of the said colonies, plantations, or islands under the authority of this act, either before or after the shipment, it shall be found that the weight or quantity thereof, or the number of the casks or packages, shall be greater than shall have been endorsed upon the entry, or if any articles are laden and put on board any ship or vessel for the purpose of being exported to any part of Europe or in Africa as aforesaid without entry thereof being made with the proper officer of the customs, or shall be brought to any place, quay, or wharf, or put into any hoy, boat, or other vessel for the purpose of being shipped on board any such ship or vessel for exportation to such foreign port of Europe or in Africa previous to such entry being made, or if any goods shall be put on board or attempted to be put on board any ship or vessel intending to proceed to any such port of Europe or Africa in any manner contrary to the directions of this act, all such goods in every such case shall be forfeited, together with the hoy, boat, or other vessel, or carriage whatever employed in shipping or attempting to ship such goods, and also the ship or vessel in which the same shall be laden; and all such goods, vessels, boats, and carriages, may be seized by any officer or officers of the customs, and the owner thereof shall forfeit double the value of such goods.

V. *And be it further enacted,* That in case any ship or vessel clearing out from the said colonies, plantations, or islands, under the authority of this act, shall take on board in any of the said colonies, plantations, or islands, any other articles than such as are allowed to be on board and exported by virtue of this act, all such articles so taken or laden on board such ship or vessel shall be forfeited and lost, and shall and may be seized by the commander or commanders of any of his Majesty's ships or vessels-of-war, or any commissioned, warrant, or petty officer specially authorized by him or them, or by any officer or officers of the customs; and the master and shipper of any such goods shall severally forfeit double the value of the goods so laden or taken on board contrary to the directions of this act.

VI. *And be it further enacted,* That the person exporting fish from any British colony or plantation in North America to any port or place, as aforesaid, under the authority of this act, shall make oath at the port of shipment before the chief officer of the customs at such port, or if there be no such chief officer of the customs then before a magistrate, or if there be no magistrate then before two respectable persons being at such port or ports, (which oath such officer of the customs, or magistrate, or such respectable persons as aforesaid are hereby authorized to administer,) that the said fish is the produce of the British fisheries, really and *bona fide* taken and cured by his Majesty's subjects carrying on the said fisheries from some of the British colonies or plantations in North America.

VII. *And be it further enacted,* That before the shipment of any pickled fish or dry fish for the purpose of exportation from Canada to any port or place, as aforesaid, under the authority of this act, the person in whose possession the same shall have continued, from the time of its being landed from the British fishing vessel employed in the taking it until the same shall be so shipped for exportation, shall make oath before the chief officer of the customs at Quebec (who is hereby authorized to administer such oath) that the same is the produce of the British American fisheries, really and *bona fide* taken and cured by his Majesty's subjects carrying on the said fisheries from some of the said colonies or plantations.

VIII. *And be it further enacted,* That it shall be lawful to export in any British ship or vessel owned and navigated according to law, from any foreign port in Europe or in Africa, or from Gibraltar, the island of Malta, or the dependencies thereof, or the islands of Guernsey, Jersey, Aldernay, or Sark, to any of his Majesty's colonies, plantations, or islands in America or the West Indies, the articles enumerated or described in the schedule hereunto annexed, marked A, anything contained in an act made in England in the fifteenth year of the reign of his Majesty King Charles the Second, intituled "An act for the encouragement of trade," or any other act or acts in force in the United Kingdom or in Great Britain or Ireland, respectively, to the contrary notwithstanding.

IX. *And be it further enacted,* That from and after the passing of this act there shall be raised, levied, collected, and paid unto his Majesty, his heirs and successors, upon the importation of the several articles enumerated or described in the schedule hereunto annexed, marked B, into any of his Majesty's colonies, plantations, or islands in America or the West Indies, under the authority of this act, from any port or place in Europe or Africa as aforesaid, the several duties of customs as the same are respectively inserted or described and set forth in figures in the said schedule marked, B; and the same shall be raised, levied, collected, paid, and received under the management of the Commissioners of the Customs in England in such and in like manner and form, and by such and the like rules, ways, means, and methods, respectively, and under such penalties and forfeitures as any other duties now payable to his Majesty on goods imported into any of the islands, plantations, colonies, or territories belonging to or under the dominion of his Majesty, in America or the West Indies, are or may be raised, levied, collected, paid, and recovered by any act or acts of Parliament now in force, as fully and effectually, to all intents and purposes, as if the several clauses, powers, directions, penalties, and forfeitures relating thereto were particularly repeated and again enacted in the body of this act; and the produce of such duties shall be paid by the Collector of the Customs to the Treasurer or Receiver General of the colony, province, or plantation in which the same shall be respectively levied, to be applied to such uses and purposes as may be directed by the authority of the respective general courts or general assemblies of such colonies, provinces, or plantations.

X. *And be it further enacted,* That in case there shall be no general courts or general assemblies in the colonies, province, or plantation in which the said duties shall have been levied under the authority of this act, the net proceeds of such duties shall be applied and appropriated in such and the like manner, and to such uses, as any other duties levied and collected in any of his Majesty's colonies, provinces, or plantations in America or the West Indies, not having general courts or general assemblies, may now, by any act or acts of Parliament, passed in Great Britain or the United Kingdom of Great Britain and Ireland, or by any order of his Majesty in council, or by any proclamation issued in his Majesty's name, be appropriated and applied.

XI. *And be it further enacted,* That in all cases where, by the schedule marked B, the duties imposed on the importation of articles into his Majesty's colonies, plantations, or islands in America or the West Indies, are charged, not according to the weight, gauge, tale or measure, but according to the value thereof, such value shall be ascertained by the declaration of the importer or proprietor of such articles, or his known agent or factor, in manner and form following, that is to say:

"I, A B, do hereby declare, that the articles mentioned in the entry and contained in the packages [here specifying the several packages and describing the several marks and numbers, as the case may be] are of the value of ———. Witness my hand the ——— day of ———.   A B."

"The above declaration, signed the ——— day of ———, in the presence of ———. C A. ———, Collector, or other principal officer."

Which declaration shall be written on the warrant of entry of such articles, and shall be subscribed with the hand of the importer or proprietor thereof, or his known agent or factor, in the presence of the Collector or other principal officer of the customs at the port of importation: *Provided,* That if, upon view and examination of such articles by the proper officer of the customs, it shall appear to him that the said articles are not valued according to the price and value thereof, and according to the true intent and meaning of this act, then, and in such case, the importer or proprietor, or his known agent or factor, shall be required to declare on oath, before the Collector or chief officer of the customs at the port of importation, (which oath he is hereby authorized to administer,) what is the invoice price of such articles, and that he verily believes such invoice price is the current value of the articles at the place from whence the said articles were imported; and such invoice price, with the addition of ten pounds per centum thereon, shall be deemed and taken to be the value of such articles in such colony, plantation, or island, as aforesaid, in lieu of the value so declared by the importer or proprietor, or his agent or factor, and upon which the duties specified in the said table shall be charged and paid: *Provided, also,* That if it shall appear to the Collector or other chief officer of the customs that such articles have been invoiced below the real and true value thereof at the place from whence the same were imported, or if the invoice price is not known, the articles shall, in such case, be examined by two competent persons, to be nominated and appointed by the Governor or commander-in-chief of the colony, plantation, or island into which the said articles are imported; and such persons shall declare on oath, before the Collector or other chief officer of the customs, which oath such Collector or other chief officer of the customs is hereby authorized to administer, what is the true and real value of such articles in such colony, plantation, or island; and the value so declared on the oaths of such persons shall be deemed to be the true and real value of such articles, and upon which the duties specified in the said schedule, marked B, shall be charged and paid.

XII. *And be it further enacted,* That if the importer or proprietor of such articles shall refuse to pay the duties hereby imposed thereon, it shall and may be lawful for the Collector or other chief officer of the customs where such articles shall be imposed, and he is hereby, respectively, required, to take and secure the same, with the casks or other packages thereof, and to cause the same to be publicly sold, within the space of twenty days, at the most, after such refusal made, and at such time and place as such officer shall, by four or more days, public notice, appoint for that purpose, which articles shall be sold to the highest bidder; and the money arising from the sale thereof shall be applied to the payment of the said duties, together with the charges which shall have been occasioned by the said sale, and the overplus (if any) shall be paid to such importer, proprietor, or any other person authorized to receive the same.

XIII. *Provided always, and be it further enacted,* That if, upon the importation of any article charged with duty by this act, the said article shall also be liable to the payment of duty under the authority of any colonial law equal to or exceeding in amount the duty charged upon such article by this act, then, and in such case, the duty charged upon such article by this act shall not be demanded or paid upon the importation of such article: *Provided, also,* That if the duty payable under such colonial law shall be less in amount than the duty payable by this act, then, and in such case, the difference only in the amount of the duty payable by this act and the duty payable under the authority of such colonial law shall be deemed to be the duty payable by this act; and the same shall be collected and paid in such and the like manner, and appropriated and applied to such and the like uses as the duties specified in the said schedule annexed to this act, marked B, are directed to be collected, paid, appropriated, and applied.

XIV. *And be it further enacted,* That all sums of money granted and imposed by this act, either as duties, penalties, or forfeitures, shall be deemed, and are hereby declared to be, sterling money of Great Britain, and shall be collected, recovered, and paid to the amount of the value which such nominal sums bear in Great Britain; and that such moneys may be received and taken according to the proportion and value of five shillings and sixpence the ounce in silver.

XV. *And be it further enacted,* That all and every the goods or commodities, and all ships or vessels forfeited by this act, shall and may be seized by the commander or commanders of any of his Majesty's ships or vessels-of-war, or any commissioned, warrant, or petty officer specially authorized by him or them, or by any officer or officers of his Majesty's customs; and that every forfeiture and penalty incurred by this act shall and may respectively be sued for, prosecuted, and recovered, in such courts, and by such and the like ways, means and methods, and the produce thereof, respectively disposed of and applied in such and the like manner, and to such and the like uses and purposes, as any forfeiture or penalty incurred by any law respecting the revenue of the customs may now be sued for, prosecuted, or recovered, disposed of and applied, either in this kingdom, or in any of his Majesty's dominions in America or the West Indies, respectively, as the case may happen to be.

XVI. *And be it further enacted,* That if any person or persons shall be sued or prosecuted for anything done or to be done in pursuance of this act, such person or persons may plead the general issue, and give this act and the special matter in evidence; and if the plaintiff or plaintiffs, prosecutor or prosecutors, shall become nonsuit or forbear the prosecution, or discontinue his, her, or their action, or if a verdict shall pass against him, her, or them, the defendant shall have treble costs, and shall have the like remedy for the same as in cases where costs are by law given to defendants.

Schedules to which this act refers.

SCHEDULE A.

A schedule of articles allowed to be exported from ports in Europe or in Africa to any of his Majesty's colonies, plantations, or islands in America or the West Indies.

Anchovies,	Anniseed,
Argol,	Amber,
Alabaster, rough and worked,	Almonds,

Biscuit,
Brandy,
Bullion,
Brimstone,
Boxwood,
Beans,
Botargo,
Cattle,
Currants,
Capers,
Cantharides,
Corn,
Cummin seed,
Coral,
Cork,
Cinnabar,
Cascasoo,
Caviar,
Dates,
Essence of bergamot,
Essence of citron,
Essence of lemon,
Essence of orange,
Essence of lavender,
Essence of roses,
Essence of rosemary,
Emery stone,
Flour,
Fruit,
Fruit, dry and wet,
Fruit preserved in brandy and sugar,
Fruit preserved in jars and bottles,
Figs,
Garden seeds,
Gum arabic,
Gum mastic,
Gum myrrh,
Gum sicily,
Gum ammoniac,
Grain,
Honey,
Jalap,
Incense,
Juniper berries,
Lava and Malta stone for buildings,
Lentils,
Lumber,

Manna,
Mosaic works,
Medals,
Musk,
Meal,
Marble, rough and worked,
Mill timber,
Maccaroni,
Mules,
Nuts of all kinds,
Oil of olives,
Oil of almonds,
Opium,
Orris root,
Ostrich feathers,
Ochres,
Orange buds and peel,
Olives,
Pickles in jars and bottles,
Paintings and prints,
Pozzolano,
Precious stones,
Pearls,
Punck,
Pumice stone,
Peas,
Parmesan cheese,
Quicksilver,
Raisins,
Rhubarb,
Rice,
Salt,
Sausages,
Senna,
Scammony,
Sarsaparilla,
Saffron,
Safflower,
Shingles,
Sponges,
Staves,
Sheep,
Vermillion,
Vermicelli,
Whetstones,
Wine,
Wood hoops.

SCHEDULE B.

A schedule of duties payable on articles imported into his Majesty's colonies, plantations, or islands in America or the West Indies from ports in Europe or Africa under the authority of this act.

	Sterling.		
	£	s.	d.
Wine imported in bottles, viz:			
French wine, the tun of 252 gallons	10	10	0
Madeira wine, the tun of 252 gallons	7	7	0
Portugal wine, the tun of 252 gallons	7	7	0
Rhenish, Germany, and Hungary wine, the tun of 252 gallons	9	9	9
Spanish wine and wine not otherwise enumerated, the tun of 252 gallons	7	7	0
And in addition to the specified duties, hereby imposed upon such wines, respectively, a further duty for every £100 of the true and real value thereof	7	10	0
And for every dozen of foreign quart bottles, in which such wine may be imported	0	8	0
Corn, flour, grain, meal, peas, beans, for every £100 of the true and real value thereof	12	0	0
Headings, for every 1,000	1	1	0
Lumber, viz: Yellow or white pine per 1,000 feet	1	1	0
All other descriptions	1	8	0
Mill timber, the like	10	0	0
Shingles, for every 1,000, not exceeding 12 inches in length	0	7	C
Shingles, for every 1,000, exceeding 12 inches in length	0	14	0
Staves, oak, red or white, for every 1,000	1	1	0
Wood hoops, for every 1,000	0	5	0

Alabaster, anchovies, argol, anniseed, amber, almonds, brandy, brimstone, botargo, boxwood, currants, capers, cascasoo, cantharides, cummin seed, coral, cork, cinnabar, dates, essence of bergamot, essence of lemon, essence of roses, essence of citron, essence of orange, essence of lavender, essence of rosemary, emery stone; fruit, viz: dry and preserved in sugar; wet, preserved in brandy; figs; gum arabic, gum mastic, gum myrrh, gum sicily, gum ammoniac; honey, jalap, juniper berries, incense of frankincense, lava and Malta stone, (for building,) lentils, manna, marble, (rough and worked,) mosaic work, medals, musks, maccaroni, nuts of all kinds, oil of olives; oil of almonds, opium, orris root, ostrich feathers, ochres, orange buds and peel, olives, pickles in jars and bottles, paintings, pozzolano, pumice stone, punck, Parmesan cheese, pickles, prints, pearls, precious stones, (except diamonds,) quicksilver, raisins, rhubarb, rice, sausages, senna, scammony, sarsaparilla, saffron, safflower, sponges, vermillion, vermicelli, wine not in bottles, (except wine imported into Newfoundland,) whetstones, for every £100 of the true and real value thereof..

Sterling.
£   s.   d.
7   10   0

No. 357.

POLITICAL CONDITION OF ST. DOMINGO.

COMMUNICATED TO THE SENATE IN EXECUTIVE SESSION FEBRUARY 26, 1823, AND THE INJUNCTION OF SECRECY SINCE REMOVED.

To the Senate of the United States:

By a resolution of the 27th of December last the President of the United States was requested to communicate to the Senate such information as he might possess respecting the political state of the island of St. Domingo; whether the government thereof was claimed by any European nation; what our commercial relations with the Government of the island were, and whether any further commercial relations with that Government would be consistent with the interest and safety of the United States.

From the import of the resolution it is inferred that the Senate was fully aware of the delicate and interesting nature of the subject embraced by it in all its branches. The call supposes something peculiar in the nature of the Government of that island, and in the character of its population, to which attention is due. Impressed always with an anxious desire to meet every call of either House for information, I most willingly comply in this instance, and with a view to the particular circumstances alluded to.

In adverting to the political state of St. Domingo, I have to observe that the whole island is now united under one Government, under a constitution which retains the sovereignty in the hands of the people of color, and with provisions which prohibit the employment in the Government of all white persons who have emigrated there since 1816, or who may hereafter emigrate there, and which prohibit also the acquisition by such persons of the right of citizenship or to real estate in the island. In the exercise of this sovereignty the Government has not been molested by any European power. No invasion of the island has been made or attempted by any power. It is, however, understood that the relations between the Government of France and the island have not been adjusted; that its independence has not been recognized by France, nor has peace been formally established between the parties.

The establishment of a Government of people of color in the island, on the principles above stated, evinces distinctly the idea of a separate interest and a distrust of other nations. Had that jealousy been confined to the inhabitants of the parent country it would have been less an object of attention; but by extending it to the inhabitants of other countries, with whom no difference ever existed, the policy assumes a character which does not admit of a like explanation. To what extent that spirit may be indulged or to what purposes applied our experience has yet been too limited to enable us to form a just estimate. These are inquiries more peculiarly interesting to the neighboring islands. They nevertheless deserve the attention of the United States.

Between the United States and this island a commercial intercourse exists, and it will continue to be the object of this Government to promote it. Our commerce there has been subjected to higher duties than have been imposed on like articles from some other nations. It has, nevertheless, been extensive, proceeding from the wants of the respective parties and the enterprise of our citizens. Of this discrimination to our injury we had a right to complain and have complained. It is expected that our commercial intercourse with the island will be placed on the footing of the most favored nation. No preference is sought in our favor, nor ought any to be given to others. Regarding the high interest of our happy Union, and looking to every circumstance which may, by any possibility, affect the tranquillity of any part, however remotely, and guarding against such injury by suitable precautions, it is the duty of this Government to promote, by all the means in its power and by a fair and honorable policy, the best interest of every other part and thereby of the whole. Feeling profoundly the force of this obligation, I shall continue to exert, with unwearied zeal, my best faculties to give it effect.

JAMES MONROE.

FEBRUARY 25, 1823.

ILLEGAL BLOCKADE OF THE PORTS OF THE SPANISH MAIN AND CAPTURES BY PRIVA-
TEERS FROM PORTO RICO OF AMERICAN VESSELS.

COMMUNICATED TO THE HOUSE OF REPRESENTATIVES MARCH 1, 1823.

To the House of Representatives of the United States:

In compliance with a resolution of the House of Representatives, of this day, requesting information of the measures taken with regard to the illegal blockade of the ports of the Spanish Main and to depredations of privateers fitted out from Porto Rico and other Spanish islands upon the commerce of the United States, I transmit to the House a report from the Secretary of State containing the information required by the resolution.

JAMES MONROE.

WASHINGTON, *March* 1, 1823.

DEPARTMENT OF STATE, *Washington, March* 1, 1823.

The Secretary of State, to whom has been referred the resolution of the House of Representatives of the United States, of this day, requesting the President of the United States to communicate to that House, as far as the public interest will permit, what measures have been taken to remove or annul the illegal and pretended blockade of the ports of the Spanish Main; to obtain restitution of vessels of the United States captured by privateers fitted out in Porto Rico and other Spanish islands under pretext of breach of the said blockade, and to prevent such illegal and unwarrantable captures hereafter, has the honor of reporting to the President that the measures taken for the purposes described in the resolution of the House have consisted, first, of instructions to the commanders of the armed vessels of the United States successively stationed in the West India seas, and, secondly, of instructions to the minister of the United States in Spain to make suitable representations on these subjects to the Spanish Government. The direct communications between the naval officers in command of the vessels of the United States employed in that service and the Governors of Cuba and Porto Rico have been frequent and successful in obtaining the restitution of some captured vessels. Some of the vessels notorious for outrages committed by them on the commerce of the United States have been captured and sent into the United States, and are now upon trial before the judicial tribunals. No answers have yet been received to the representations directly ordered to be made to the Government of Spain.

All which is respectfully submitted.

JOHN QUINCY ADAMS.

PROCEEDINGS OF THE COMMISSIONERS UNDER THE SIXTH AND SEVENTH ARTICLES
OF THE TREATY OF GHENT WITH GREAT BRITAIN, AND MEASURES TAKEN UNDER
THE FOURTH ARTICLE OF THE TREATY WITH SPAIN OF FEBRUARY 22, 1819, FOR
FIXING BOUNDARY LINE.

COMMUNICATED TO THE HOUSE OF REPRESENTATIVES MARCH 1, 1823.

To the House of Representatives of the United States:

I transmit to the House of Representatives, in pursuance of a resolution of that House, on the 30th of January last, a report from the Secretary of State containing the information required in relation to the transactions of the Commissioners under the 6th and 7th articles of the treaty of Ghent; and, also, as to the measures which have been taken under the 4th article of the treaty with Spain of February 22, 1819, for fixing the boundary line described in the third article of the last mentioned treaty.

JAMES MONROE.

WASHINGTON, *February* 26, 1823.

DEPARTMENT OF STATE, *Washington, February* 25, 1823.

The Secretary of State, to whom has been referred a resolution of the House of Representatives of the United States, of the 30th of January last, requesting the President of the United States to lay before the House information, not previously communicated to Congress, in relation to the transactions of the Commissioners under the 6th and 7th articles of the treaty of Ghent; and, also, to inform the House whether any, and what, measures have been taken under the 4th article of the treaty with Spain of the 22d February,

1819, for fixing the boundary line described in the 3d article of the last mentioned treaty, and whether any part of the said line has been fixed and designated, has the honor of reporting to the President—

..That the Commissioners aforesaid, under the 6th and 7th articles of the treaty of Ghent, have had several meetings in the course of the last year, and that at a meeting held by them at Utica, in the State of·New York, on the 18th of June last, they agreed upon and executed an instrument containing their decision of the questions submitted to them under the 6th article of the treaty of Ghent, a copy of which decision is herewith respectfully reported. And with the same decision there have been returned to this Department a series of twenty-three maps, upon which the boundary line is delineated in conformity with it.

That, at the same meeting, the secretary and assistant secretary were directed to furnish the agents and the principal surveyors, respectively, with a copy of instructions relative to the survey under the 7th article.

A copy of these instructions is herewith submitted, together with extracts of letters from the agent of the United States under this commission, dated the 24th of July and 24th of September last, showing the progress made by the commission in reference to the 7th article, and the prospects with regard to the time when the duties of said Commissioners may probably be completed.

With regard to the boundary line referred to in the 4th article of the treaty with Spain of 22d February, 1819, it was stipulated by the said article that Commissioners and surveyors should be appointed by the contracting parties, who should meet at Natchitoches, on the Red river, before the termination of one year from the date of the ratification of the treaty, and proceed to run and mark the line. The Spanish Government, although repeatedly pressed, on the part of the United States, to appoint those officers on their part, so that they might have met those of the United States within the limited time, postponed the appointment, so that notice of it was not given until after the year had elapsed.

Under a misapprehension that the difference of opinion between the two Houses of Congress at their last session, with regard to the appropriation for running this line, had resulted in the omission to make it, a communication to that effect was made to the minister of Spain, in this country, shortly after the close of the session. But the error having been a few days after discovered, he was informed, by a letter of 29th May last, from this Department, that the appropriation had been made, and that this Government was then ready to proceed to the execution of the article.

He was also requested to state at what time the Commissioner and surveyor on the part of Spain would be at Natchitoches, and was assured that the Commissioner and surveyor on the part of the United States would be instructed to meet them at that place, and at the time which he should designate as that when the Commissioner and surveyor of Spain would be there.

By a communication from Mr. Anduaga, dated the 1st of June last, he stated that, having immediately forwarded to his Government the previous notice received from this Department, he could not say at what time the Spanish Commissioners would repair to Natchitoches; but his Majesty the King of Spain would take the most speedy and efficacious measures for carrying into effect, on his part, the stipulations of the treaty.

The minister of the United States in Spain was shortly afterwards instructed that, if the Spanish Government should be desirous of postponing the meeting of the Commissioners to run the line, we should not be disposed to urge them to it; but that we should be ready to attend to it at their convenience. No further determination from the Spanish Government concerning it has since been received.

All which is respectfully submitted.

JOHN QUINCY ADAMS.

Papers sent.

Decision of the Commissioners, June 18, 1822.
Extract from the minutes of the proceedings of the Board of Commissioners under the 6th article of the treaty of Ghent, June 18, 1822.
Extract of a letter from Mr. Delafield to the Secretary of State, July 24, 1822.
Extract of a letter from same to same, September 24, 1822.

DECISION OF THE COMMISSIONERS.

The undersigned, Commissioners appointed, sworn, and authorized, in virtue of the sixth article of the treaty of peace and amity between his Britannic Majesty and the United States of America, concluded at Ghent on the 24th·of December, 1814, impartially to examine and, by a report or declaration under their hands and seals, to designate that portion of the boundary of the United States "from the point where the 45th degree of north latitude strikes the river Iroquois, or Cataraqui, along the middle of said river into Lake Ontario; through the middle of said lake until it strikes the communication by water between that lake and Lake Erie; thence along the middle of said communication into Lake Erie; through the middle of said lake until it arrives at the water communication into Lake Huron; thence through the middle of said water communication into Lake Huron; thence through the middle of said lake to the water communication between that lake and Lake Superior;" and to "decide to which of the two contracting parties the several islands lying within the said rivers, lakes, and water communications do respectively belong, in conformity with the true intent of the treaty of 1783," do decide and declare that the following described line (which is more clearly indicated on a series of maps accompanying this report, exhibiting correct surveys and delineations of all the rivers, lakes, water communications, and islands, embraced by the sixth article of the treaty of Ghent, by a black line, shaded on the British side with red and on the American side with blue, and each sheet of which series of maps is identified by a certificate subscribed by the Commissioners and by the two principal surveyors employed by them) is the true boundary intended by the two before mentioned treaties; that is to say:

Beginning at a stone monument erected by Andrew Ellicott, esq., in the year 1817, on the south bank or shore of the said river Iroquois, or Cataraqui, (now called the St. Lawrence,) which monument bears south seventy-four degrees forty-five minutes west, and is eighteen hundred and forty yards distant from the stone church in the Indian village of St. Regis, and indicates the point at which the 45th parallel of north latitude strikes the said river; thence running north thirty-five degrees forty-five minutes west into the river, on a line at right angles with the southern shore, to a point one hundred yards south of the opposite island, called Cornwall island; thence turning westerly and passing around the southern and western sides of said island, keeping 100 yards distant therefrom, and following the curvatures of its shores, to a point opposite to the northwest corner or angle of said island; thence to and along the middle of the main river until it approaches the eastern extremity of Barnhart's island; thence northerly along the channel which divides the last mentioned island from the Canada shore, keeping one hundred yards distant from the island, until it approaches Sheik's island; thence along the middle of the strait which divides Barnhart's and Sheik's islands, to the channel called the Long Sault, which separates the two last mentioned islands from the lower Long Sault island; thence westerly (crossing the centre of the last mentioned channel) until it approaches within one hundred yards of the north shore of the Lower Sault island; thence up the north branch of the river, keeping to the north of and near the Lower Sault island, and also north of and near the Upper Sault (sometimes called Baxter's) island, and south of the two small islands, marked on the map A and B, to the western extremity of the Upper Sault, or Baxter's island; thence, passing between the two islands called the Cats, to the middle of the river above; thence along the middle of the river, keeping to the north of the small islands marked C and D, and north also of Chrystler's island, and of the small island next above it, marked E, until it approaches the northeast angle of Goose Neck island; thence along the passage which divides the last mentioned island from the Canada shore, keeping one hundred yards from the island, to the upper end of the same; thence south of and near the two small islands called the Nut islands; thence north of and near the island marked F, and also of the island called Dry, or Smuggler's island; thence, passing between the islands marked G and H, to the north of the island called Isle au Rapid Plat; thence along the north side of the last mentioned island, keeping one hundred yards from the shore, to the upper end thereof; thence along the middle of the river, keeping to the south of and near the islands called Cousson (or Tussiu) and Presque isle; thence up the river, keeping north of and near the several Gallop isles, numbered on the map 1, 2, 3, 4, 5, 6, 7, 8, 9, and 10, and also of Tick, Tibbet's, and Chimney islands, and south of and near the Gallop isles numbered 11, 12, and 13, and also of Duck, Drummond, and Sheep islands; thence along the middle of the river, passing north of island number 14, south of 15 and 16, north of 17, south of 18, 19, 20, 21, 22, 23, 24, 25, and 28, and north of 26 and 27; thence along the middle of the river, north of Gull island and of the islands numbered 29, 32, 33, 34, 35, Bluff island, and numbers 39, 44, and 45, and to the south of numbers 30, 31, 36, Grenadier island, and numbers 37, 38, 40, 41, 42, 43, 46, 47, and 48, until it approaches the east end of Well's island; thence to the north of Well's island and along the strait which divides it from Rowe's island, keeping to the north of the small islands numbered 51, 52, 54, 58, 59, and 61, and to the south of the small islands numbered and marked 49, 50, 53, 55, 57, 60, and X, until it approaches the northeast point of Grindstone island; thence to the north of Grindstone island, and keeping to the north also of the small islands numbered 63, 65, 67, 68, 70, 72, 73, 74, 75, 76, 77, and 78, and to the south of numbers 62, 64, 66, 69, and 71, until it approaches the southern point of Hickory island; thence passing to the south of Hickory island and of the two small islands lying near its southern extremity, numbered 79 and 80; thence to the south of Grand or Long island, keeping near its southern shore, and passing to the north of Carlton island, until it arrives opposite to the southwestern point of said Grand island, in Lake Ontario; thence passing to the north of Grenadier, Fox, Stoney, and the Gallop islands, in Lake Ontario, and to the south of and near the islands called the Ducks, to the middle of said lake; thence westerly along the middle of said lake to a point opposite to the mouth of the Niagara river; thence, to and up the middle of the said river, to the Great Falls; thence up the falls, through the point of the Horse Shoe, keeping to the west of Iris or Goat island, and of the group of small islands at its head, and following the bends of the river so as to enter the strait between Navy and Grand islands; thence along the middle of said strait to the head of Navy island; thence to the west and south of and near to Grand and Beaver islands, and to the west of Strawberry, Squaw, and Bird islands, to Lake Erie; thence southerly and westerly along the middle of Lake Erie, in a direction to enter the passage immediately south of Middle island, being one of the easternmost of the group of islands lying in the western part of said lake; thence along the said passage, proceeding to the north of Cunningham's island, of the three Bass islands, and of the Western Sister, and to the south of the islands called the Hen and Chikens, and of the Eastern and Middle Sisters; thence to the middle of the mouth of the Detroit river, in a direction to enter the channel which divides Bois Blanc and Sugar islands; thence, up the said channel, to the west of Bois Blanc island, and to the east of Sugar, Fox, and Stoney islands, until it approaches Fighting or Great Turkey island; thence along the western side, and near the shore of said last mentioned island, to the middle of the river above the same; thence along the middle of said river, keeping to the southeast of and near Hog island, and to the northwest of and near the island called Isle a la Pêche, to Lake St. Clair; thence through the middle of said lake, in a direction to enter that mouth or channel of the river St. Clair which is usually denominated the old ship channel; thence along the middle of said channel, between Squirrel island, on the southeast, and Herson's island on the northwest, to the upper end of the last mentioned island, which is nearly opposite to Point aux Chéneson, on the American shore; thence along the middle of the river St. Clair, keeping to the west of and near the islands called Belle Riviere isle, and Isle aux Cerfs, to Lake Huron; thence through the middle of Lake Huron, in a direction to enter the strait or passage between Drummond's island on the west and the Little Manitou island on the east; thence through the middle of the passage which divides the two last mentioned islands; thence turning northerly and westerly around the eastern and northern shores of Drummond's island, and proceeding in a direction to enter the passage between the island of St. Joseph's and the American shore, passing to the north of the intermediate islands No. 61, 11, 10, 12, 9, 6, 4, and 2, and to the south of those numbered 15, 13, 5, and 1; thence up the said last mentioned passage, keeping near to the island of St. Joseph's, and passing to the north and east of thé Isle a la Crosse, and of the small islands numbered 16, 17, 18, 19, and 20, and to the south and west of those numbered 21, 22, and 23, until it strikes a line (drawn on the map with black ink, and shaded on one side of the point of intersection with blue, and on the other with red) passing across the river at the head of St. Joseph's island, and at the foot of the Neebish Rapids, which line denotes the termination of the boundary directed to be run by the 6th article of the treaty of Ghent.

And the said Commissioners do further decide and declare that all the islands lying in the rivers, lakes, and water communications between the before described boundary line and the adjacent shores of Upper Canada do, and each of them does, belong to his Britannic Majesty; and that all the islands lying in the rivers, lakes, and water communications between the said boundary line and the adjacent shores of the United States, or their Territories, do, and each of them does, belong to the United States of America, in conformity with the true intent of the second article of the said treaty of 1783, and of the 6th article of the treaty of Ghent.

In faith whereof, we, the Commissioners aforesaid, have signed this declaration, and thereunto affixed our seals.

Done in quadruplicate, at Utica, in the State of New York, in the United States of America, this eighteenth day of June, in the year of our Lord one thousand eight hundred and twenty-two.

PETER B. PORTER. [L. S.]
ANTH. BARCLAY. [L. S.]

Extract from the minutes of the proceedings of the Board of Commissioners, under the sixth article of the Treaty of Ghent, held at Utica, in the State of New York, on the 18th June, 1822.

The secretary and assistant secretary are directed to furnish the agents and the principal surveyors, respectively, with a copy of the following instructions relative to the survey under the 7th article.

The Commissioners have deemed it proper to prepare the following written instructions for the guidance of the agents and principal surveyors in ascertaining the course of the boundary, &c., under the 7th article of the treaty, comporting with the verbal directions given to the surveyors at the commencement of the present season.

It is required that the direction which the true line intended by the treaty shall take be ascertained from the point where the boundary, under the 6th article, terminated, near the head of St. Joseph's island, below the Neebish Rapids, proceeding "through Lake Superior, northward of the Isles Royal and Philipeaux, to the Long lake; thence, through the middle of said Long lake and the water communication between it and the Lake of the Woods, to the Lake of the Woods; thence, through the said lake, to the most northwestern point thereof."

In your operations to effect this object, the Commissioners do not require you to commence at the nearest end of the contemplated line, nor to conduct your survey in continuity; but they confide in your discretion to proceed in such manner, relatively to the several parts thereof, as the convenience or necessities of the seasons and other causes may, in your judgment, render most proper.

In ascertaining the boundary under the 7th article, you are aware that it is not our intention to pursue the course of a trigonometrical survey, observed under the 6th. It will, however, be desirable that we have a survey of the shores and islands between the foot of the Neebish Rapids and Lake Superior. It will also be desirable to have the latitude and longitude of some point at the gorge of Lake Superior.

In proceeding through Lake Superior to the northward of the Isles Royal and Philipeaux, (if there be any of the last name,) examine whether any islands lie so near the boundary line described in the treaty as to render it doubtful on which side of the said line they may be situated; and if any such be found, ascertain, by the most easy and expeditious means, the shape and extent of them, as well as of the Isles Royal and Philipeaux, and also their geographical position, either by astronomical observations, or by triangles connecting them with the main shore or other islands, whose position is known.

After passing Lake Superior, ascertain the position of the Long lake, or (if no lake of that name is to be found) the chain of waters supposed to be referred to in the treaty by that designation. Should you discover (as you probably will) that these waters do not communicate with Lake Superior, ascertain what rivers or waters, divided by a height of land, and emptying, one into Lake Superior and the other into the Lake of the Woods, approximate most nearly. Fix the latitude and longitude of their points of approximation, and perambulate these waters downwards, observing their courses and distances, and also the islands in them, their situation and extent. Fix the latitudes and longitudes at which these rivers communicate with the respective lakes.

As to the Lake of the Woods, make such rapid surveys of its shores and islands as, upon examination thereof, you may deem necessary to a fair designation of the boundary. In fixing the latitude and longitude of "the most northwestern point of the Lake of the Woods," great care and accuracy must be observed. As regards the other geographical points mentioned in these instructions, you will determine them with ordinary certainty. You are desired to report to the Commissioners, severally, and from time to time, such matters as relate to your then past transactions, and such discoveries as you may have made, and which, in your opinion, may influence your future progress in the duties with which you are charged.

After perambulating and ascertaining the approximating waters between Lake Superior and the Lake of the Woods, if any doubt should be entertained by you as to the direction which the boundary ought to take, we wish to be advised of it as early as practicable, in order that we may proceed, if necessary, to that place to determine such difficulty.

It is expected of the agents that they will be prompt and vigilant in supplying all the wants of the surveyors and of their parties, and that they will, at all times, whether present or absent, assist them with their advice.

Extract of a letter from Mr. Joseph Delafield, agent under the 6th and 7th articles of the treaty of Ghent, to the Secretary of State.

"WASHINGTON, July 24, 1822.

"In respect to the seventh article of the treaty, great pains has been taken by the Commissioners to effect its speedy execution. The American party now employed consists of a principal surveyor and one assistant, who is also the draughtsman, with a few batteau-men to conduct their boats and provisions.

"I accompanied our party to Lake Superior, in which neighborhood they had commenced their work, and before I left them every arrangement was made to subsist them during the present, and the summer of the next year, in the Northwest Territory. With the supplies afforded and contemplated, together with the provisional arrangements I was enabled to effect through the kindness of the agent of the American Fur Company (in case of accidents) at all their trading posts, I do not doubt the maintenance of this party in the Indian country for the time specified; and should the British surveyors render an equal service, and, together with our own, prove successful in the performance of the duty expected of them, there is a well founded belief that the surveys and all essential observations and information will be obtained previous to their return.

"The passage from Lake Superior to Long lake, mentioned in the treaty, (which probably means Rainy lake,) may demand more time and labor to explore than has been apprehended. The old Grand Portage route has of late been abandoned by the British traders, and a more northern route assumed. Whether the one or the other of these routes, or an intermediate one, is to be the boundary line, can only be ascertained by explorations of much hardship and labor, on account of the formation of the country which divides the waters that flow into lake Superior from those that flow toward and into the Lake of the Woods. The southern or Fond du Lac route does not seem to be in question, although it has, by some persons, been improvidently suggested. From the Rainy lake to the Lake of the Woods the water communication is said to be direct, and the greatest task to encounter there will be to produce, in a summary way, a chart of the latter lake sufficiently accurate to designate the line through the numerous islands it contains. The exact but laborious trigonometrical survey heretofore conducted it has been determined to abandon, and the surveyors are instructed to ascertain the desired information by a more rapid method (as described in the journal) with sufficient certainty for the just purposes of the commission. Besides these requisitions of the surveyors, there will be several points of latitude and longitude to be determined, and some of them with great care and accuracy, particularly that of the northwest point of the Lake of the Woods.

"I have mentioned these several objects to show that although there is a reasonable prospect that the work may be perfected in another season, yet that there may be obstacles which our imperfect knowledge of the country must keep concealed until our own investigations shall disclose them. From the line of trading posts, but little can be learned that is satisfactory of this part of the Northwest Territory; and as it will sometimes occur that the surveyors must explore a section that is unknown and even untrod but by the hunter, I think there has already been made the best prediction of the time it may consume."

Extract of a letter from Joseph Delafield, agent under the 6th and 7th articles of the Treaty of Ghent, to the Secretary of State, dated

"BOSTON, *September* 24, 1822.

"Since I had last the honor to address you, I have made known to the American Commissioner that the Long lake, mentioned in the treaty of 1783, (which lake is unknown at the present day by that name,) is a sheet of water or passage near the old Grand Portage from Lake Superior, and is so laid down and described upon the map used for the purposes of that treaty, as appears by the same in your office.

"I have also communicated this fact to our surveyor employed in the northwest.

"My last accounts from him state that he should be at Lac la Pline by the middle of August last, and that in his way there he should take the old Grand Portage route, which is the Long lake route, as now properly understood. The British party were to proceed by the same route. I am much gratified to have it in my power to give these particulars, because there is no longer any serious question open as to the general course that the line is intended to be run, and because it is now more certain that upon the return of the surveyors the next season the Board will be possessed of all necessary information to determine the doubts, under the 7th article of the treaty, and designate the line."

MESSAGE OF THE PRESIDENT OF THE UNITED STATES, AT THE COMMENCEMENT OF THE FIRST SESSION OF THE EIGHTEENTH CONGRESS.

COMMUNICATED TO THE SENATE DECEMBER 2, 1823.

Fellow-citizens of the Senate and House of Representatives:

Many important subjects will claim your attention during the present session, of which I shall endeavor to give, in aid of your deliberations, a just idea in this communication. I undertake this duty with diffidence, from the vast extent of the interests on which I have to treat, and of their great importance to every portion of our Union. I enter on it with zeal, from thorough conviction that there never was a period since the establishment of our Revolution when, regarding the condition of the civilized world and its bearing on us, there was greater necessity for devotion in the public servants to their respective duties, or for virtue, patriotism, and union in our constituents.

Meeting in you a new Congress, I deem it proper to present this view of public affairs in greater detail than might otherwise be necessary. I do it, however, with peculiar satisfaction, from a knowledge that in this respect I shall comply more fully with the sound principles of our Government. · The people being with us exclusively the sovereign, it is indispensable that full information be laid before them on all important subjects to enable them to exercise that high power with complete effect. If kept in the dark, they must be incompetent to it. We are all liable to error, and those who are engaged in the management of public affairs are more subject to excitement, and to be led astray by their particular interests and passions than the great body of our constituents, who, being at home in the pursuit of their ordinary avocations, are calm but deeply interested spectators of events, and of the conduct of those who are parties to them. To the people, every department of the Government and every individual in each are responsible, and the more full their information the better they can judge of the wisdom of the policy pursued, and of the conduct of each in regard to it. From their dispassionate judgment much aid may always be obtained, while their approbation will form the greatest incentive and most gratifying reward for virtuous actions, and the dread of their censure the best security against the abuse of their confidence. Their interests in all vital questions are the same, and the bond by sentiment as well as by interest will be proportionably strengthened as they are better informed of the real state of public affairs, especially in difficult conjunctures. It is by such knowledge that local prejudices and jealousies are surmounted, and that a national policy, extending its fostering care and protection to all the great interests of our Union, is formed and steadily adhered to.

A precise knowledge of our relations with foreign powers, as respects our negotiations and transactions with each, is thought to be particularly necessary. Equally necessary is it that we should form a just estimate of our resources, revenue, and progress in every kind of improvement connected with the national prosperity and public defence. It is by rendering justice to other nations that we may expect it from them. It is by our ability to resent injuries and redress wrongs that we may avoid them.

The Commissioners under the fifth article of the treaty of Ghent, having disagreed in their opinions respecting that portion of the boundary between the Territories of the United States and of Great Britain, the establishment of which had been submitted to them, have made their respective reports, in compliance with that article, that the same might be referred to the decision of a friendly power. It being manifest, however, that it would be difficult, if not impossible, for any power to perform that office without great delay and much inconvenience to itself, a proposal has been made by this Government, and acceded to by that of Great Britain, to endeavor to establish that boundary by amicable negotiation. It appearing, from long experience, that no satisfactory arrangement could be formed of the commercial intercourse between the United States and the British colonies in this hemisphere by legislative acts, while each party pursued its own course without agreement or concert with the other, a proposal has been made to the British Government to regulate this commerce by treaty, as it has been to arrange in like manner the just claim of the citizens of the United States inhabiting the States and Territories bordering on the lakes and rivers which empty into the St. Lawrence to the navigation of that river to the ocean. For these and other objects of high importance to the interests of both parties, a negotiation has been opened with the British Government which, it is hoped, will have a satisfactory result.

The Commissioners under the sixth and seventh articles of the treaty of Ghent, having successfully closed their labors in relation to the sixth, have proceeded to the discharge of those relating to the seventh. Their progress in the extensive survey, required for the performance of their duties, justifies the presumption that it will be completed in the ensuing year.

The negotiation which had been long depending with the French Government on several important subjects, and particularly for a just indemnity for losses sustained in the late wars by the citizens of the United States, under unjustifiable seizures and confiscations of their property, has not as yet had the desired effect. As this claim rests on the same principle with others which have been admitted by the French Government, it is not perceived on what just grounds it can be rejected. A minister will be immediately appointed to proceed to France and resume the negotiation on this and other subjects which may arise between the two nations.

At the proposal of the Russian Imperial Government, made through the minister of the Emperor residing here, a full power and instructions have been transmitted to the minister of the United States at St. Petersburg, to arrange, by amicable negotiation, the respective rights and interests of the two nations on the northwest coast of this continent. A similar proposal has been made by his Imperial Majesty to the Government of Great Britain, which has likewise been acceded to. The Government of the United States has been desirous, by this friendly proceeding, of manifesting the great value which they have invariably attached to the friendship of the Emperor, and their solicitude to cultivate the best understanding with his Government. In the discussions to which this interest has given rise, and in the arrangements by which they may terminate, the occasion has been judged proper for asserting as a principle in which the rights and interests of the United States are involved, that the American continents, by the free and independent condition which they have assumed and maintain, are henceforth not to be considered as subjects for future colonization by any European powers.

Since the close of the last session of Congress, the Commissioners and arbitrators for ascertaining and determining the amount of indemnification which may be due to citizens of the United States under the decision of his Imperial Majesty the Emperor of Russia, in conformity to the convention concluded at St. Petersburg, on the twelfth of July, one thousand eight hundred and twenty-two, have assembled in this city and organized themselves as a Board for the performance of the duties assigned to them by that treaty. The commission constituted under the eleventh article of the treaty of twenty-second February, one thousand eight hundred and nineteen, between the United States and Spain, is also in session here; and as the term of three years limited by the treaty for the execution of the trust will expire before the period of the next regular meeting of Congress, the attention of the Legislature will be drawn to the measures which may be necessary to accomplish the objects for which the commission was instituted.

In compliance with a resolution of the House of Representatives, adopted at their last session, instructions have been given to all the ministers of the United States accredited to the powers of Europe and America to propose the proscription of the African slave trade by classing it under the denomination, and inflicting on its perpetrators the punishment, of piracy. Should this proposal be acceded to, it is not doubted that this odious and criminal practice will be promptly and entirely suppressed. It is earnestly hoped that it will be acceded to from a firm belief that it is the most effectual expedient that can be adopted for the purpose.

At the commencement of the recent war between France and Spain it was declared by the French Government that it would grant no commissions to privateers, and that neither the commerce of Spain herself nor of neutral nations should be molested by the naval force of France, except in the breach of a lawful blockade. This declaration, which appears to have been faithfully carried into effect, concurring with principles proclaimed and cherished by the United States from the first establishment of their independence, suggested the hope that the time had arrived when the proposal for adopting it as a permanent and invariable rule in all future maritime wars might meet the favorable consideration of the great European powers. Instructions have accordingly been given to our ministers with France, Russia, and Great Britain, to make those proposals to their respective Governments; and when the friends of humanity reflect on the essential amelioration to the condition of the human race which would result from the abolition of private war on the sea, and on the great facility by which it might be accomplished, requiring only the consent of a few sovereigns, an earnest hope is indulged that these overtures will meet with an attention animated by the spirit in which they were made, and that they will ultimately be successful.

The ministers who were appointed to the republics of Colombia and Buenos Ayres during the last session of Congress proceeded, shortly afterwards, to their destinations. Of their arrival there official intelligence has not yet been received. The minister appointed to the republic of Chili will sail in a few days. An early appointment will also be made to Mexico. A minister has been received from Colombia, and the other Governments have been informed that ministers, or diplomatic agents of inferior grade, would be received from each accordingly as they might prefer the one or the other.

The minister appointed to Spain proceeded, soon after his appointment, for Cadiz, the residence of the sovereign to whom he was accredited. In approaching that port, the frigate which conveyed him was warned off by the commander of the French squadron by which it was blockaded, and not permitted to enter, although apprised by the captain of the frigate of the public character of the person whom he had on board, the landing of whom was the sole object of his proposed entry. This act, being considered an infringement of the rights of ambassadors and of nations, will form a just cause of complaint to the Government of France against the officer by whom it was committed.

The actual condition of the public finances more than realizes the favorable anticipations that were entertained of it at the opening of the last session of Congress. On the first of January there was a balance in the Treasury of four millions two hundred and thirty-seven thousand four hundred and twenty-seven dollars and fifty-five cents. From that time to the thirtieth of September the receipts amounted to upwards of sixteen millions one hundred thousand dollars, and the expenditures to eleven millions four hundred thousand dollars. During the fourth quarter of the year it is estimated that the receipts will at least equal the expenditures, and that there will remain in the Treasury on the first day of January next a surplus of nearly nine millions of dollars.

On the first of January, eighteen hundred and twenty-five, a large amount of the war debt and a part of the revolutionary debt will become redeemable. Additional portions of the former will continue to become redeemable annually until the year eighteen hundred and thirty-five. It is believed, however, that, if the United States remain at peace, the whole of that debt may be redeemed by the ordinary revenue of those years, during that period, under the provision of the act of March third, eighteen hundred and seventeen, creating the sinking fund; and in that case, the only part of the debt that will remain after the year eighteen hundred and thirty-five will be the seven millions of five per cent. stock subscribed to the Bank of the United States, and the three per cent. revolutionary debt, amounting to thirteen millions two hundred and ninety-six thousand and ninety-nine dollars and six cents, both of which are redeemable at the pleasure of the Government.

The state of the Army and its organization and discipline has been gradually improving for several years, and has now attained a high degree of perfection. The military disbursements have been regularly made, and the accounts regularly and promptly rendered for settlement. The supplies of various descriptions have been of good quality, and regularly issued at all of the posts. A system of economy and accountability has been introduced into every branch of the service which admits of little additional improvement. This desirable state has been attained by the act reorganizing the staff of the Army, passed on the fourteenth of April, eighteen hundred and eighteen.

The moneys appropriated for fortifications have been regularly and economically applied, and all the works advanced as rapidly as the amount appropriated would admit. Three important works will be completed in the course of this year: that is, Fort Washington, Fort Delaware, and the fort at the Rigolets, in Louisiana.

The Board of Engineers and the Topographical Corps have been in constant and active service, in surveying the coast, and projecting the works necessary for its defence.

The Military Academy has attained a degree of perfection in its dicipline and instruction equal, as is believed, to any institution of its kind in any country.

The money appropriated for the use of the Ordnance Department has been regularly and economically applied. The fabrication of arms at the national armories, and by contract with the Department, has been gradually improving in quality and cheapness. It is believed that their quality is now such as to admit of but little improvement.

The completion of the fortifications renders it necessary that there should be a suitable appropriation for the purpose of fabricating the cannon and carriages necessary for those works.

Under the appropriation of five thousand dollars for exploring the western waters for the location of a site for a western armory, a commission was constituted, consisting of Colonel McRee, Colonel Lee, and Captain Talcott, who have been engaged in exploring the country. They have not yet reported the result of their labors, but it is believed that they will be prepared to do it at an early part of the session of Congress.

During the month of June last, General Ashley and his party, who were trading under a license from the Government, were attacked by the Ricarees while peaceably trading with the Indians at their request. Several of the party were killed or wounded and their property taken or destroyed.

Colonel Leavenworth, who commanded Fort Atkinson, at the Council Bluffs, the most western post, apprehending that the hostile spirit of the Ricarees would extend to other tribes in that quarter, and that thereby the lives of the traders on the Missouri and the peace of the frontier would be endangered, took immediate measures to check the evil.

With a detachment of the regiment stationed at the Bluffs, he successfully attacked the Ricaree village, and it is hoped that such an impression has been made on them, as well as on the other tribes on the Missouri, as will prevent a recurrence of future hostility.

The report of the Secretary of War, which is herewith transmitted, will exhibit in greater detail the condition of the Department in its various branches, and the progress which has been made in its administration during the first three quarters of the year.

I transmit a return of the militia of the several States, according to the last reports which have been made by the proper officers in each to the Department of War. By reference to this return, it will be seen that it is not complete, although great exertions have been made to make it so. As the defence, and even the liberties of the country must depend, in times of imminent danger, on the militia, it is of the highest importance that it be well organized, armed, and disciplined, throughout the Union. The report of the Secretary of War shows the progress made during the first three quarters of the present year, by the application of the fund appropriated for arming the militia. Much difficulty is found in distributing the arms according to the act of Congress providing for it, from the failure of the proper Departments in many of the States to make regular returns. The act of May the twelfth, one thousand eight hundred and twenty, provides that the system of tactics and regulations of the various corps in the regular army shall be extended to the militia. This act has been very imperfectly executed, from the want of uniformity in the organization of the militia, proceeding from the defects of the system itself, and especially in its application to that main arm of the public defence. It is thought that this important subject, in all its branches, merits the attention of Congress.

The report of the Secretary of the Navy, which is now communicated, furnishes an account of the administration of that Department for the first three quarters of the present year, with the progress made in augmenting the Navy, and the manner in which the vessels in commission have been employed.

The usual force has been maintained in the Mediterranean Sea, the Pacific Ocean, and along the Atlantic coast, and has afforded the necessary protection to our commerce in those seas.

In the West Indies and the Gulf of Mexico our naval force has been augmented by the addition of several small vessels, provided for by the " act authorizing an additional naval force for the suppression of piracy," passed by Congress at their last session. That armament has been eminently successful in the accomplishment of its object. The piracies by which our commerce in the neighborhood of the island of Cuba had been afflicted have been repressed, and the confidence of our merchants, in a great measure, restored.

The patriotic zeal and enterprise of Commodore Porter, to whom the command of the expedition was confided, has been fully seconded by the officers and men under his command ; and, in reflecting with high satisfaction on the honorable manner in which they have sustained the reputation of their country and its Navy, the sentiment is alloyed only by a concern that, in the fulfilment of that arduous service, the diseases incident to the season and to the climate in which it was discharged have deprived the nation of many useful lives, and among them of several officers of great promise.

In the month of August a very malignant fever made its appearance at Thompson's island, which threatened the destruction of our station there. Many perished, and the commanding officer was severely attacked. Uncertain as to his fate, and knowing that most of the medical officers had been rendered incapable of discharging their duties, it was thought expedient to send to that post an officer of rank and experience, with several skilful surgeons, to ascertain the origin of the fever, and the probability of its recurrence there in future seasons; to furnish every assistance to those who were suffering, and, if practicable, to avoid the necessity of abandoning so important a station. Commodore Rodgers, with a promptitude which did him honor, cheerfully accepted that trust, and has discharged it in the manner anticipated from his skill and patriotism. Before his arrival, Commodore Porter, with the greater part of the squadron, had removed from the island, and returned to the United States, in consequence of the prevailing sickness. Much useful information has, however, been obtained as to the state of the island, and great relief afforded to those who had been necessarily left there. .

Although our expedition, co-operating with an invigorated administration of the Government of the island of Cuba, and with the corresponding active exertions of a British naval force in the same seas, have almost entirely destroyed the unlicensed piracies from that island, the success of our exertions has not been equally effectual to suppress the same crime, under other pretences and colors, in the neighboring island of Porto Rico. They have been committed there under the abusive issue of Spanish commissions. At an early period of the present year remonstrances were made to the Governor of that island by an agent, who was sent for the purpose, against those outrages on the peaceful commerce of the United States, of which many had occurred. That officer, professing his own want of authority to make satisfaction for our just complaints, answered only by a reference of them to the Government of Spain. The minister of the United States to that court was specially instructed to urge the necessity of the immediate and effectual interposition of that Government, directing restitution and indemnity for wrongs already committed, and interdicting the repetition of them. The minister, as has been seen, was debarred access to the Spanish Government, and, in the meantime, several new cases of flagrant outrage have occurred, and citizens of the United States in the island of Porto Rico have suffered, and others been threatened with assassination, for asserting their unquestionable rights, even before the lawful tribunals of the country.

The usual orders have been given to all our public ships to seize American vessels engaged in the slave trade, and bring them in for adjudication ; and I have the gratification to state that not one so employed has been discovered, and there is good reason to believe that our flag is now seldom, if at all, disgraced by that traffic.

It is a source of great satisfaction that we are always enabled to recur to the conduct of our Navy with pride and commendation. As a means of national defence, it enjoys the public confidence, and is steadily assuming additional importance. It is submitted, whether a more efficient and equally economical organization of it might not, in several respects, be effected. It is supposed that higher grades than now exist by law would be useful. They would afford well merited rewards to those who have long and faithfully served their country; present the best incentives to good conduct, and the best means of insuring a proper discipline ; destroy the inequality in that respect between the military and naval services, and relieve our officers from many inconveniences and mortifications which occur when our vessels meet those of other nations—ours being the only service in which such grades do not exist.

A report of the Postmaster General, which accompanies this communication, will show the present state of the Post Office Department, and its general operations for some years past.

There is established by law eighty-eight thousand six hundred miles of post roads, on which the mail is now transported eighty-five thousand seven hundred miles; and contracts have been made for its transportation on all the established routes, with one or two exceptions. There are five thousand two hundred and forty post offices in the Union, and as many postmasters. The gross amount of postage which accrued from the first of July, one thousand eight hundred and twenty-two, to the first of July, one thousand eight hundred and twenty-three, was one million one hundred and fourteen thousand three hundred and forty-five dollars and. twelve cents. During the same period, the expenditures of the Post Office Department amounted to one million one hundred and sixty-nine thousand eight hundred and eighty-five dollars and fifty-one cents, and consisted of the following items: compensation to postmasters, three hundred and fifty three thousand nine hundred and ninety-five dollars and ninety-eight cents; incidental expenses, thirty thousand eight hundred and sixty-six dollars and thirty-seven cents; transportation of the mail, seven hundred and eighty-four thousand six hundred dollars and eight cents; payments into the Treasury, four hundred and twenty-three thousand dollars and eight cents. On the first of July last there was due to the Department, from postmasters, one hundred and thirty-five thousand two hundred and forty-five dollars and twenty-eight cents; from late postmasters and contractors, two hundred and fifty-six thousand seven hundred and forty-nine dollars and thirty-one cents; making a total amount of balances due to the Department of three hundred and ninety-one thousand nine hundred and ninety-four dollars and fifty-nine cents. These balances embrace all delinquencies of postmasters and contractors which have taken place since the organization of the Department. There was due by the Department to contractors, on the first day of July last, twenty-six thousand five hundred and forty-eight dollars and sixty-four cents.

The transportation of the mail within five years past has been greatly extended, and the expenditures of the Department proportionably increased. Although the postage which has accrued within the last three years has fallen short of the expenditures two hundred and sixty-two thousand eight hundred and twenty-one dollars and forty-six cents, it appears that collections have been made from the outstanding balances to meet the principal part of the current demands.

It is estimated that not more than two hundred and fifty thousand dollars of the above balances can be collected, and that a considerable part of this sum can only be realized by a resort to legal process. Some improvements in the receipts for postage is expected. A prompt attention to the collection of moneys received by postmasters, it is believed, will enable the Department to continue its operations without aid from the Treasury, unless the expenditure shall be increased by the establishment of new mail-routes.

A revision of some parts of the post office law may be necessary; and it is submitted whether it would not be proper to provide for the appointment of postmasters, where the compensation exceeds a certain amount, by nomination to the Senate, as other officers of the General Government are appointed.

Having communicated my views to Congress at the commencement of the last session respecting the encouragement which ought to be given to our manufactures, and the principle on which it should be founded, I have only to add that those views remain unchanged, and that the present state of those countries with which we have the most immediate political relations and greatest commercial intercourse tends to confirm them. Under this impression, I recommend a review of the tariff, for the purpose of affording such additional protection to those articles which we are prepared to manufacture, or which are more immediately connected with the defence and independence of the country.

The actual state of the public accounts furnishes additional evidence of the efficiency of the present system of accountability in relation to the public expenditure. Of the money drawn from the Treasury since the fourth of March, one thousand eight hundred and seventeen, the sum remaining unaccounted for on the thirtieth of September last is more than a million and a half of dollars less than on the thirtieth of September preceding; and during the same period a reduction of nearly a million of dollars has been made in the amount of the unsettled accounts for moneys advanced previously to the fourth of March, one thousand eight hundred and seventeen. It will be obvious that, in proportion as the mass of accounts of the latter description is diminished by settlement, the difficulty of settling the residue is increased from the consideration that, in many instances, it can be obtained only by legal process. For more precise details on this subject, I refer to a report from the First Comptroller of the Treasury.

The sum which was appropriated at the last session for the repair of the Cumberland road has been applied with good effect to that object. A final report has not yet been received from the agent who was appointed to superintend it. As soon as it is received, it shall be communicated to Congress.

Many patriotic and enlightened citizens, who have made the subject an object of particular investigation, have suggested an improvement of still greater importance. They are of opinion that the waters of the Chesapeake and Ohio may be connected together by one continued canal, and at an expense far short of the value and importance of the object to be obtained. If this could be accomplished, it is impossible to calculate the beneficial consequences which would result from it. A great portion of the produce of the very fertile country through which it would pass would find a market through that channel. Troops might be moved with great facility in war, with cannon, and every kind of munition, and in either direction. Connecting the Atlantic with the western country, in a line passing through the seat of the national Government, it would contribute essentially to strengthen the bond of Union itself. Believing, as I do, that Congress possess the right to appropriate money for such a national object, (the jurisdiction remaining to the States through which the canal would pass,) I submit it to your consideration whether it may not be advisable to authorize, by an adequate appropriation, the employment of a suitable number of the officers of the Corps of Engineers to examine the unexplored ground during the next season, and to report their opinion thereon. It will likewise be proper to extend their examination to the several routes through which the waters of the Ohio may be connected, by canal, with those of Lake Erie.

As the Cumberland road will require annual repair, and Congress have not thought it expedient to recommend to the States an amendment to the Constitution, for the purpose of vesting in the United States a power to adopt and execute a system of internal improvement, it is also submitted to your consideration whether it may not be expedient to authorize the Executive to enter into an arrangement with the several States through which the road passes to establish tolls each within its limits, for the purpose of defraying the expense of future repairs, and of providing also, by suitable penalties, for its protection against future injuries.

The act of Congress of the seventh of May, one thousand eight hundred and twenty-two, appropriated the sum of twenty-two thousand seven hundred dollars for the purpose of erecting two piers as a shelter for vessels from ice near Cape Henlopen, Delaware Bay. To effect the object of the act, the officers of the Board of Engineers, with Commodore Bainbridge, were directed to prepare plans and estimates of piers sufficient to answer the purpose intended by the act. It appears by their report, which accompanies the documents from the War Department, that the appropriation is not adequate to the purpose intended; and as the piers would be of great service, both to the navigation of the Delaware Bay and the protection of vessels on the adjacent parts of the coast, I submit for the consideration of Congress whether additional and sufficient appropriation should not be made.

The Board of Engineers were also directed to examine and survey the entrance of the harbor of the port of Presque Isle, in Pennsylvania, in order to make an estimate of the expense of removing the obstructions to the entrance, with a plan of the best mode of effecting the same, under the appropriation for that purpose by act of Congress passed third March last. The report of the Board accompanies the papers from the War Department, and is submitted for the consideration of Congress.

A strong hope has been long entertained, founded on the heroic struggle of the Greeks, that they would succeed in their contest, and resume their equal station among the nations of the earth. It is believed that the whole civilized world takes a deep interest in their welfare. Although no power has declared in their favor, yet none, according to our information, has taken part against them. Their cause and their name have protected them from dangers which might ere this have overwhelmed any other people. The ordinary calculations of interest and of acquisition, with a view to aggrandisement, which mingle so much in the transactions of nations, seem to have had no effect in regard to them. From the facts which have come to our knowledge, there is good cause to believe that their enemy has lost forever all dominion over them; that Greece will become again an independent nation. That she may obtain that rank is the object of our most ardent wishes.

It was stated at the commencement of the last session that a great effort was then making in Spain and Portugal to improve the condition of the people of those countries, and that it appeared to be conducted with extraordinary moderation. It need scarcely be remarked that the result has been, so far, very different from what was then anticipated. Of events in that quarter of the globe with which we have so much intercourse, and from which we derive our origin, we have always been anxious and interested spectators. The citizens of the United States cherish sentiments the most friendly in favor of the liberty and happiness of their fellow-men on that side of the Atlantic. In the wars of the European powers in matters relating to themselves we have never taken any part, nor does it comport with our policy so to do. It is only when our rights are invaded or seriously menaced that we resent injuries or make preparation for our defence. With the movements in this hemisphere we are, of necessity, more immediately connected, and by causes which must be obvious to all enlightened and impartial observers. The political system of the allied powers is essentially different in this respect from that of America. This difference proceeds from that which exists in their respective Governments. And to the defence of our own, which has been achieved by the loss of so much blood and treasure, and matured by the wisdom of their most enlightened citizens, and under which we have enjoyed unexampled felicity, this whole nation is devoted. We owe it, therefore, to candor, and to the amicable relations existing between the United States and those powers, to declare that we should consider any attempt on their part to extend their system to any portion of this hemisphere as dangerous to our peace and safety. With the existing colonies or dependencies of any European power we have not interfered and shall not interfere. But with the Governments who have declared their independence, and maintained it, and whose independence we have, on great consideration and on just principles, acknowledged, we could not view any interposition for the purpose of oppressing them, or controlling in any other manner their destiny, by any European power, in any other light than as the manifestation of an unfriendly disposition towards the United States. In the war between these new Governments and Spain we declared our neutrality at the time of their recognition, and to this we have adhered and shall continue to adhere, provided no change shall occur which, in the judgment of the competent authorities of this Government, shall make a corresponding change on the part of the United States indispensable to their security.

The late events in Spain and Portugal show that Europe is still unsettled. Of this important fact no stronger proof can be adduced than that the allied powers should have thought it proper, on any principle satisfactory to themselves, to have interposed, by force, in the internal concerns of Spain. To what extent such interposition may be carried, on the same principle, is a question in which all independent powers whose Governments differ from theirs are interested, even those most remote, and surely none more so than the United States. Our policy in regard to Europe, which was adopted at an early stage of the wars which have so long agitated that quarter of the globe, nevertheless remains the same, which is, not to interfere in the internal concerns of any of its powers; to consider the Government de facto as the legitimate Government for us; to cultivate friendly relations with it, and to preserve those relations by a frank, firm, and manly policy, meeting, in all instances, the just claims of every power; submitting to injuries from none. But in regard to these continents, circumstances are eminently and conspicuously different. It is impossible that the allied powers should extend their political system to any portion of either continent without endangering our peace and happiness; nor can any one believe that our southern brethren, if left to themselves, would adopt it of their own accord. It is equally impossible, therefore, that we should behold such interposition, in any form, with indifference. If we look to the comparative strength and resources of Spain and those new Governments, and their distance from each other, it must be obvious that she can never subdue them. It is still the true policy of the United States to leave the parties to themselves, in the hope that other powers will pursue the same course.

If we compare the present condition of our Union with its actual state at the close of our Revolution, the history of the world furnishes no example of a progress in improvement in all the important circumstances which constitute the happiness of a nation which bears any resemblance to it. At the first epoch our population did not exceed three millions. By the last census it amounted to about ten millions, and, what is more extraordinary, it is almost altogether native, for the emigration from other countries has been inconsiderable. At the first epoch half the territory within our acknowledged limits was uninhabited and a wilderness. Since then new territory has been acquired of vast extent, comprising within it many rivers, particularly the Mississippi, the navigation of which to the ocean was of the highest importance to the original States. Over this territory our population has expanded in every direction, and new States have been established almost equal in number to those which formed the first bond of our Union. This expansion of our population and accession of new States to our Union have had the happiest effect on all its highest interests. That it has eminently augmented our resources and added to our strength and respectability as a power is admitted by all. But it is not in these important circumstances only that this happy effect is felt. It is manifest that, by enlarging the basis of our system and increasing the number of States, the system itself has been greatly strengthened in both its branches. Consolidation and disunion have thereby been rendered equally impracticable. Each Government, confiding in its own strength, has less to apprehend from the other; and in consequence, each enjoying a greater freedom of action, is rendered more efficient for all the purposes for which it was instituted. It is unnecessary to treat here of the vast improvement made in the system itself by the adoption of this Constitution, and of its happy effect in elevating the character and in protecting the rights of the nation as well as of individuals. To what, then, do we owe these blessings? It is known to all that we derive them from the excellence of our institutions. Ought we not, then, to adopt every measure which may be necessary to perpetuate them?

WASHINGTON, *December* 2, 1823.   JAMES MONROE.

No. 361.

SPOLIATIONS BY A SPANISH CRUISER.

COMMUNICATED TO THE SENATE DECEMBER 18, 1823.

Mr. LLOYD, of Massachusetts, from the Committee on Naval Affairs, to whom was referred the petition of William Gray and Henry Gray, praying the interposition of the Government of the United States in the case of the brig Otter, captured by a Spanish cruiser from Porto Rico, and carried into that island, and condemned by the judicial authorities thereof, reported:

That they have attended to the duty assigned them, and that it has appeared from the documents and testimony submitted to them that the brig Otter was an American vessel built at Somerset, in Massachusetts, in the year 1821; that she was owned by Henry Gray, and fitted on a trading voyage from the port of Boston, with a cargo of lawful merchandise for Laguira, by William Gray and Henry Gray, highly respectable merchants of said Boston, and that both the vessel and cargo were exclusively the property of the said Henry and William Gray, and were placed for their account under the sole charge and direction of Oliver Keating, of Boston, master of the said brig; that with the said cargo, and none other, the vessel sailed from Boston aforesaid on the said voyage on the 26th May, 1823; that on the 22d of June following, when within about eight leagues distance from the port of Laguira, she was forcibly taken possession of and captured by the Spanish Porto Rico privateer, or armed brig, Scipio, mounting fourteen guns, and commanded by Captain Romayne Torres, under a royal commission from Ferdinand the Seventh; that a prize crew were put on board the Otter, who, notwithstanding the exhibition of the regular and sufficient documentary papers from the custom-house at Boston, the innocent nature alike of the voyage and the cargo, and the reiterated protest and remonstrance of the master, carried the said brig into the port of Mayaguez, in Porto Rico, where pretences the most frivolous were set up, and practices the most iniquitous attempted, fraudulently to furnish ostensible causes in justification of the condemnation of the property, and which, notwithstanding such false and scandalous allegations were rebutted, was condemned by the courts of that island, an appeal granted, and a delivery of the property decreed to the captor, on condition that they should give bond with sufficient sureties to respond therefor; but, regardless of such condition, the said property was delivered to the captors, as the said master believes, without sufficient security, and was immediately thereafter publicly sold at a great sacrifice, and the proceeds received by the said captors, who are supposed to be irresponsible for the amount thereof; thus leaving the sufferers, as they contend, even in the event of a final judgment on an appeal in their favor, wholly without other redress than that to be derived from the Spanish Government, through the effective interposition of that of their own country. And seeing that remonstrances have been already made, and negotiations are now pending between the United States and Spain relative to wrongs and depredations of a similar character, the committee recommend that the petition aforesaid be referred to the Department of State, in order that such measures may be taken thereon as the rights of the citizens of the United States and the interests and dignity of the Government may to the Executive appear to require.

No. 362.

SYMPATHY FOR THE GREEKS.

COMMUNICATED TO THE HOUSE OF REPRESENTATIVES DECEMBER 29, 1823.

To the Congress of the United States:

The memorial of the committee appointed at a numerous and respectable meeting of the citizens of New York, assembled to take into consideration the situation of the Greeks, respectfully showeth:

That the citizens whom they represent have, in common with their fellow-citizens throughout the United States, witnessed with lively sensibility the heroic efforts of the Greeks to rescue themselves from Turkish bondage. It appeared to them that the Greek cause was not only entitled to the good wishes of this country, but, as far as might be done consistently with the views of Government, to every possible assistance. In the opinion of the meeting the independence of the Greek nation was a subject of the highest concern to the interests of the human race, and recommended itself to the approbation of every civilized people by the most powerful considerations that could possibly be addressed either to the judgment or to the sympathy of mankind.

Your memorialists have accordingly been instructed to apply to Congress with the request that the independence of the Greek nation might be recognized by the Government of this country. In undertaking to comply with this instruction, the committee conceive that they will have discharged their trust when they make known to Congress the anxious desire of the citizens of New York, either that the independence of the Greeks may be speedily and formally recognized, or such steps preparatory thereto taken as may, in the opinion of Government, be consistent with its interests, its policy, and its honor. The suitable time for the exercise of such a prerogative of the Government must always rest in its sound discretion, and your memorialists repose with entire confidence in the wisdom of the application of that discretion. They would, however, respectfully suggest that, in the opinion of their fellow-citizens, as far as they have hitherto thought proper to declare it, the Greeks have proved themselves competent to maintain their independence, and that by their union, their political system, their organization, their strength, their successes, their intelligence, and their determined spirit, they have sufficiently vindicated their title to assume a separate and equal station among the nations of the world.

How far the case of the South American Governments, whose national existence was admitted by the United States some time since, may be deemed analogous is respectfully submitted to the superior judgment of those to whom this application is addressed. It has, however, been supposed that there are peculiar circumstances connected with the cause of the Greeks which ought to awaken the most active concern for their welfare, and which require the application of every just precedent in support of their independence.

Your memorialists would deem it improper on this occasion to enlarge on this subject or to do more than merely allude to the consideration of the barbarous dominion of the Turks, equally fatal to liberty, learning and taste, and under which the Greeks have been most cruelly oppressed for ages; to the spirit of the Mahometan superstition, presenting an insurmountable obstacle to the progress of civilization; to the ingenious, enterprising, free and commercial character of the Greeks; to their language, their literature, their religion, and their eventful history, exciting the deepest interest in their favor and endearing them to the Christian world by recollections of their past sufferings and of their ancient glory.

And your memorialists will ever pray, &c.

MARINUS WILLETT,	SAM'L BOYD,
JNO. P. ROMEYN,	S. JONES,
HENRY D. SEWALL,	M. CLARKSON,
FELIX PASCALIS,	ISAAC LAWRENCE,
HIRAM KETCHUM,	STEPHEN ALLEN,
CADWALLADER D. COLDEN,	J. MORTON,
J. R. HURD,	ALEX'R M'LEOD,
GEO. DEMAREST,	J. G. SWIFT,
JON. GOODHUE,	WM. JOHNSON,
NATH'L F. MOORE,	R. SEDGWICK,
JNO. TRUMBULL,	JOHN G. COSTER,
PHILIP HONE,	CHARLES KING,
WM. BAYARD,	ROBERT M'QUEEN,
JAMES KENT,	JOS. OGDEN HOFFMAN,
RICHARD VARICK,	THOMAS H. MERRY,
LYNDE CATLIN,	WILLIAM PAULDING, JR.,
HENRY RUTGERS,	WM. JOHNSON,
HENRY WHEATON,	RUSSELL H. NEVINS.
JOHN PINTARD,	

18TH CONGRESS.]   **No. 363.**   [1ST SESSION.

PRESENT CONDITION AND FUTURE PROSPECTS OF THE GREEKS.

COMMUNICATED TO THE HOUSE OF REPRESENTATIVES DECEMBER 31, 1823.

To the House of Representatives of the United States:

I transmit to the House of Representatives a report from the Secretary of State, with accompanying documents, containing the information requested by the resolution of the House of the 19th instant relating to the condition and future prospects of the Greeks.

JAMES MONROE.

WASHINGTON, *December* 31, 1823.

DEPARTMENT OF STATE, *Washington, December* 31, 1823.

The Secretary of State, to whom has been referred the resolution of the House of Representatives of the United States of the 19th instant, requesting the President of the United States to lay before the House any information he may have received, and which he may not deem it improper to communicate, relating to the condition and future prospects of the Greeks, has the honor of reporting to the President the papers in the possession of this Department containing the information requested by the resolution of the House.

JOHN QUINCY ADAMS.

List of papers sent.

Extract of a letter from Mr. Forsyth to Mr. Adams, dated December 13, 1822, with—
Note, dated Corinth, April 8, [20] 1822. Translation.
Note, Mr. Luriottis to Don Evaristo San Miguel, dated November 21, 1822. Translation.
Mr. Rush to Mr. Adams, February 24, 1823. Copy.
Mr. Luriottis to same, February 20, 1823. Copy.
Mr. Adams to Mr. Rush, August 18, 1823. Copy.
Same to Mr. Luriottis, August 18, 1823. Copy.
Extract of a letter to Secretary of State, dated Marseilles, August 6, 1823.
Extract of a letter to Secretary of State, dated Marseilles, August 27, 1823.
Statistical table of Greece. Translation. Original copy received from Mr. Middleton.

Extract of a letter from Mr Forsyth to the Secretary of State, dated Madrid, December 13, 1822.

"The Greeks have an agent in this Peninsula, (Larioty.) He was here a fortnight, asking aid of money, which he did not receive. Indeed, he left this, disgusted with the coldness with which he was treated by San Miguel. He has gone to Lisbon with sanguine hopes of meeting, if not aid, at least kinder treatment. I inclose to you copies Nos. 1 and 2 of an official statement, made for him in April last by his Government, of the state of their affairs, and of his letter to the Spanish Government. We have favorable news from the Greeks from various sources. The Albanians are now their allies; they have again been successful by sea against the Turks, and the best hopes of their ultimate and complete triumph are entertained."

[Translation.]

Department of Foreign Affairs—No. 66 of the Protocol.

VIEW OF THE PRESENT STATE OF GREECE.

The most cruel of tyrannies, of exactions without number, induced the Greeks to a just revolt. Their first operations were attended with some successes, which were of very little consequence, owing to the want of union among themselves. Some particular Governments were established, but they did not answer the purpose which was intended. Then the deputies of the nation were called together at Epidamus for the purpose of establishing an organic law. This assembly, of which Prince Marrocordato was President, after a month of deliberations, fixed the mode of a provisional Government, the duration of which was to be one year.

After the dissolution of this assembly, the Government which had been formed in it was proclaimed and recognized in the islands, the Peloponnesus, and the continent. The people, being satisfied, submitted with joy to its decisions, and order and justice succeeded to violence and anarchy.

The authority of this Government acquires every day new strength, and it may be hoped that soon Greece, regenerated by the benefits of a wise and paternal administration, will show herself worthy of its independence.

By the efforts of its defenders, the Peloponnesus will be no more polluted by the presence of its oppressors. Four fortresses, Patras, Coron, Modon, Napoli de Romani, only remain in the power of the Turks, and the hour of their fall approaches. Napoli de Romani is about to follow the example of Corinth, which surrendered at discretion, and the other places are about to be entirely deprived of provisions and munitions by the flight of the Turkish fleet. This fleet, having left the Dardanelles in the month of February, was favored by the winds, which prevented their passage of the Archipelago from being disputed. But at Navarino the Greeks, seconded by the ability of General Lenormand and by the courage of some European officers who were shut up there, rendered the projects upon that place abortive; this doubtless compelled it to go against Patras, and there effect the landing of the troops which it had on board. It was after this operation that it was encountered by the naval forces of the Greeks. The Turkish fleet, beaten, pursued, and entirely dispersed, was obliged to seek refuge towards the coasts of Egypt, where it was surprised by a tempest, in which it lost four frigates and two brigs. All the crews of these ships and the commander of the squadron, Ismael Gibraltar, were drowned. It was also obliged to abandon, on our coasts, several transports loaded with provisions destined for the army which came to be landed.

This army, composed of four thousand men, weakened every day by the diseases and dissensions which have sway in it, takes refuge under the cannon of the fortress of Patras, into which entrance has been refused it. There, blockaded on one side by a Greek squadron, and on the other harassed night and day by the troops of General Colocotroni, it will prove, by its total annihilation, that every effort will always be vain against a people which wishes for its liberty, cost what it will.

In Attica the fortress of Athens alone is in the power of the Turks, and the bombardment of it, to which a fortunate issue is expected, commenced several days ago.

Bœotia, Phocis, and Locris have driven out the enemies of their beautiful provinces. The Government is very seriously occupied with the means of possessing itself of Zitonny, where there is still a body of the Turkish army, in order to enable it to cause the troops in Thessaly to advance simultaneously with the general movement of the inhabitants of Mount Olympus, a bold and warlike people, and render the position of the enemy more critical.

The defiles of Pindus being in our possession, all communication between the rest of Turkey and Thessaly, and all retreat for the enemy's army that shall then be in this province, will be immediately, from that time, impossible. All Etolia, Epirus, and almost all Arcania are in the power of the Government, with the exception of some places which are under a rigorous blockade.

I have now to speak of Albania. What will be its relations with us? The future alone can resolve this important question, and the well known character of this people does not permit the calculation of events from probabilities; sometimes neuter and sometimes partisans, by turns our allies and our enemies, which they have practised to the present time, passing in appearance from one party to another without really serving the interests of that which they had adopted. The death of Ali Pacha has produced little effect. The Turks, proud of this success, which they owe only to the treachery of the very soldiers of this Pacha, have appeared to take courage; but, being repulsed at Wonizza, they appeared to have almost abandoned their attempts. Such is the situation of affairs in the Peloponnesus and on the continent.

Almost all the islands, being free, have submitted to the Government, and cause the Greek flag to be respected in the Archipelago. At Chios six thousand Samiotes have landed to favor the independence of that island and have shut up the Turks in the fortress. Mitylene in a short time will have shaken off its yoke, and Candia still combats with advantage against superior forces; but the known valor of its inhabitants, and the justice of their cause, will make up for number.

At the moment I am writing the news of the victory obtained over the Turks at Riguassa comes to be communicated to the Government. Four hundred of the enemy remain upon the field of battle, and the rest of their army has been put to flight. The Suliotes, by their accustomed bravery, have covered themselves with glory.

More recent news comes to inform us of more new successes. Colonel Ulysses, with fifteen hundred men, landed on the first of April at Helisa. After an obstinate battle against forces superior in number he became master of that village, as also of the port of St. Marine, pursued the enemy to Zitonni, killed three hundred men and made some prisoners. General Niketa, commander of the Peloponnesian troops, joined his operations to those of Colonel Ulysses, and, from everything, it is believed they have already entered Zitonni. Colonels Mitzi, Kondojanni, and Skalzodini advance upon Patradjik, and have gained some advantages. Of the body of the Greek army, composed of ten thousand men, who act from this side to the centre, commanded by Colonel Panvurja, supported by Miezatis, the right wing is formed by the troops of General Eritika and of Colonel Ulysses, and its left wing by those of Colonels Kondojanni and Skalzodini.

A new fleet is just gone from Constantinople. It is composed of vessels of different sizes. It has attempted a landing on the island of Chios, but, repulsed with loss at that point, it has retired.

TH. NEGRIS, *Secretary of State and Minister of Foreign Affairs.*
V. GALLIVA, *Secretary General.*

CORINTH, *April* 8, [20,] 1822.

[Translation.]

Note of Mr. Luriottis, Agent of the Greeks at Madrid, to his Excellency Evaristo San Miguelo, Secretary of the Despatch of State of his Catholic Majesty.

MAY IT PLEASE YOUR EXCELLENCY: If there is a time when the principles ought to be revived which an unfortunate but very celebrated philosopher of France published in 1793, "That the men of all countries are brothers, and the different nations ought mutually to assist each other according to their power, as citizens of the same State;

"That those who make war on a people for the purpose of arresting the progress of liberty and destroying the rights of man ought to be everywhere pursued, not as ordinary enemies, but as assassins and rebellious robbers;

"That tyrants, whoever they may be, are slaves revolted against mankind, the sovereign of the earth, and against nature, the legislator of the universe;"

And if there is a nation in whose favor these principles ought to be applied, it is, doubtless, Greece at the present time. It is not intended here to press the rights which the Greeks have to the being recognized by the civilized nations of Europe for the lights which their ancestors have given them in liberal sciences, arts, legislations, and in true models of men, illustrious for their love of country; and still less the most evident rights which they will now have to shake off the Mussulman yoke with which any of the despotisms against which the other nations of Europe contend could not be compared. It will be sufficient only to remark that Greece, victorious and free, is the most certain security of the liberties of the Spanish peninsula.

Because, from the certain liberty in Greece necessarily flows that of Italy, which is enslaved, if I may be allowed the expression, between the peninsula and the new Grecian States;

Because, the establishment of a free State, raised in Greece upon the ruins of the legitimate Ottoman power at the time when open war has been declared between the people and the despots, as between the principles of light and the principles of darkness, ought to result in the annihilation of this empire of the crescent, and, consequently, that of its accessories, Tunis, Tripoli, and Algiers; and, the Greeks being once masters of the Ægean sea, these three pirates will be no more able to recruit their bands of assassins in Albania, at Smyrna, and at Constantinople; and they will there lose their forces, which have been always restless, and even now, Spain, and the increase of this moral fire, which the legitimates call pest, which ought to deliver Germany from despotism and encourage the French to resume their ancient post in the career of liberty; and because, in fine, this will only be after the accomplishment of these prophecies that this peninsula will be left sufficiently tranquil at home and abroad to be able to reckon upon the consolidation of its liberty, which has cost and does every day cost it so many sacrifices of every kind.

Spain has no real need of succor from any other nation for maintaining itself a State free and independent,

The courage, the heroism of her children are in every respect a proof; but the despotism, to succeed in its liberticidal projects, does not always please to excite, to irritate this valor. It is sure of its triumph, provided that it should succeed in keeping alive the fire of civil discord. Even the most courageous people feel themselves fatigued of so trifling yet continued a war, and often, after the torments of despotism, they have recourse to this as to a guardian angel, preferring the future, but little felt, evil to the present, and tranquillity, although cadaverous, to a struggle which leaves them no repose. At this very moment Spain makes trial of a part of this sad truth. The insulating, therefore, of a nation which wishes to be free is, in the times wherein we live, the most impolitic measure which she can adopt.

Despotism has formed and published its alliance, and has, if I may be allowed the expression, hurled a formal defiance at the nations that wish to establish, or to recover their liberties. It insults them all because it is conscious of its power to vanquish them, either by the force of hireling bayonets with which it inundates them, or by the silent manœuvres which organize civil war—the division and quarrels of parties with which it harasses them. It is therefore necessary to oppose to this alliance of tyrants that of the nations who have achieved their liberty.

If for a nation to be free the will of being so were sufficient; if what gives the disposition insured equally success; if, in fine, the valor of a people were a sure guaranty of success, Greece and the Greeks would not this day doubt of their triumph. The modern Greeks have already, in more than one engagement with the Turks, shown themselves worthy successors of the Greeks of Marathon, of Thermopylæ, of Salamis, of Strimon, of Cnidus, &c., but they want men; for frightful despotism capriciously destroyed them, and of it population has never been an accompaniment. They want money, because it would have been the price of their head to have been rich. They want arms, powder, lead, because no despotic

Government leaves these at the mercy of slaves, and because the struggle which the Greeks have so long maintained has consumed the provisions which their bravery and the small succors brought by the foreigner had procured them. Yet they still continue, in more than one place, to fight and defend themselves against the Turks with inferior weapons.

They have abundance of lands and national property: for three-fifths of the territory belonged to the Mussulmans as the price of confiscations made after cutting off the heads of opulent Greeks, but these lands, this property, are nothing at the present moment, when the Greeks ought to handle the musket instead of the plough, when money is wanting, and when the public credit is not yet established.

The Greeks will never return under the Ottoman yoke; but in continuing a struggle so unequal, without other support, without other succor, they will all perish. What is the use of liberty in the tomb? What the advantages which Spain, Italy, and Europe, panting after liberty, can expect from a triumph over the Greeks?

The United States of America, after having sustained with equal courage and at equal sacrifices their cause of independence against a despotism much less dreadful, owed their triumph to the protection of a European power. Why should not Greece rely upon some protector among the free States of that same part of the world to which she belongs? By what fatality is she persecuted by the Government of England, which ought to be the father of free nations, and forgotten by those Governments which profess the same principles which she has just proclaimed?

The Greeks have till now been flattered by a number of private associations who came to their aid, but no Government has as yet partaken of this generous enthusiasm, and yet the succors, as well moral as physical, which are necessary for them cannot be afforded them but by Governments.

There is some reason to believe that the Government of Corinth has opened some negotiation with the said United States of America. May these States pay in favor of Greece the tribute of recognition which they owe to Europe for the liberty which they know so well how to enjoy.

The same Government, which leaves nothing untried which may conduce to the triumph of the holy cause which it directs, cannot forget to address itself to magnanimous Spain—to a nation which, more than every other, shows to the universe that she feels all the value of liberty and independence to a Government; which each day ought to be more persuaded that the allied despotism aims and will aim, more or less openly but always obstinately enough, at the consolidation of its present system. As to politics, the before cited Wigueford says that the infallible means of vanquishing one's rivals in diplomacy is to be frank, because he is sure of not meeting them in his way.

If, then, Spain can believe it to be to her advantage to recognize and to protect and to succor the Government of Corinth, what measure, what conduct, has she to pursue towards the other Governments which have never openly pronounced against the Hellenic revolution?

The undersigned is not authorized to speak upon this article. He is only commissioned in general to solicit every species of succor which the Spaniards can send to the Greeks, either in money or arms, powder, lead, men, ships, frigates, brigs, &c., of war.

But he knows how far, among the generous succors, the article of a like moral aid would preponderate. Interested for his country, he confines himself to the making the rough draught and to offer up prayers that the Spanish Government would be pleased to send some one to Greece to treat upon this important subject, and upon all the others which might be necessary and of great utility to Spain.

In the meantime, upon the point of physical succor, the undersigned has the honor to observe to your excellency that the question is not respecting a donation, but only respecting a loan, and that the responsibility of a free Government in Greece is beyond all the wants and those which it will have to fulfil to arrive at its consolidation.

That small succors are also useful to the Greeks in their present situation, because every little thing becomes a great deal to one who is pressed by want.

That the manner of carrying them into Greece and securing the reimbursement is left to the will of the Spanish Government.

That the greatest secrecy ought to be observed in all that Spain wishes to do as a Government in favor of the Greeks, in order that the diplomatic spies may not try to perplex it, and may not succeed in rendering it abortive.

That, finally, in the absence of the persons to whom the undersigned had letters to deliver here at Madrid, on the part of Prince Marrocordato, of the Minister of Foreign Affairs, Negri, and of the Bishop Ignatius of Pisa, that they would be pleased to support their requests, as well before the Government as before the brave Spanish patriots, it was doubtless a happiness for the undersigned to have met here a ministry so eminently well affected, and a minister of foreign relations so liberal as your excellency, to whom he can directly address himself in the two-fold aim mentioned and in the accomplishment of his mission.

Your excellency's most obedient and most humble servant,

LURIOTTIS.

Madrid, *November* 21, 1822.

Extract of a letter from Mr. Rush to Mr. Adams, dated

London, *February* 24, 1823.

"I received the day before yesterday a paper, of which a copy is inclosed, addressed to you by Andreas Luriottis, an agent or deputy from Corinth on behalf of the cause of the Greeks.

"It will be perceived that, after describing the general nature of the revolution now going on in Greece, the object of the paper is to solicit aid of the United States and the establishment of diplomatic connexions with them.

"This gentleman, who has recently arrived in London, brought me a letter of introduction from General Dearborn, at Lisbon, and I received him in a manner due to the interesting character which he bears. I assured him that the fortunes of his country were dear to the people of the United States, who, cherishing the freedom which they themselves inherited and enjoyed, looked with the warmest sympathy upon the struggle of the Greeks for their national liberties, and that the Government of the United States participated in this feeling. Of the latter, I considered the late mention of the subject by the President, in his message to Congress at the opening of the session, as the authentic proof.

"To the inquiries of Mr. Luriottis, whether my Government would open political or diplomatic relations with his at the present day, I replied that this formed a point on which I was wholly uninformed and could not undertake to give my opinion; that it involved considerations of expediency as applicable to the United States, as well as of advantage or otherwise as applicable to the Greek cause itself, that would be maturely weighed at Washington before any decision could be pronounced. All that I could say was to reiterate the assurance of the friendly interest that was felt amongst us for the success of the cause in which his country was embarked; and I adverted to the part which my Government had acted in relation to the South American struggle—a part so much in advance of that of any other Government—as a sure indication that it could feel no backwardness in welcoming, when the proper day arrived, the new-born freedom of Greece into the family of nations. In the end I informed him that I would gladly become the organ of transmitting to my Government whatever distinctive overtures or communication he might determine to make to it—a request which, in the course of our conversation, he had himself made of me. These overtures he has set forth in the paper inclosed.

"Mr. Luriottis dwelt with confidence upon the advances which his country has made in the career of her independence—advances the more solid and encouraging as they have been won amidst formidable difficulties by the mere unassisted efforts of her own valor and constancy. Since the capture of Napoli de Romania, the strongest fortress which the Turks had in the Morea, he seemed to consider that the cause of independence was placed upon a sure basis. The Greeks since this event have removed the seat of their Government from Corinth, where it was fixed at first, to Napoli."

Andreas Luriottis, Envoy of the Provisional Government of Greece, to the Honorable John Quincy Adams, Secretary of State to the United States of America.

SIR: I feel no slight emotion while, in behalf of Greece, my country struggling for independence and liberty, I address myself to the United States of America.

The independence for which we combat, you have achieved. The liberty to which we look with anxious solicitude, you have obtained and consolidated in peace and in glory.

Yet Greece, old Greece, the seat of early civilization and freedom, stretches out her hands imploringly to a land which sprung into being, as it were, ages after her own lustre had been extinguished; and ventures to hope that the young and most vigorous sons of liberty will regard with no common sympathy the efforts of the descendants of the heir and elder born, whose precepts and whose example have served, though insufficient hitherto for our complete regeneration, to regenerate half a world.

I know, sir, that the sympathies of the generous people of the United States have been extensively directed towards us; and since I have reached this country, an interview with their minister, Mr. Rush, has served to convince me more strongly how great their claim is on our gratitude and our affection. May I hope that some means may be found to communicate these our feelings of which I am so proud to be the organ? We still venture to rely on their friendship; we would look to their individual if not to their national co-operation. Every, the slightest, assistance under present circumstances will aid the progress of the great work of liberty; and if, standing, as we have stood, alone and unsupported, with everything opposed to us, and nothing to encourage us but patriotism, enthusiasm, and sometimes even despair; if thus we have gone forward, liberating our provinces, one after another, and subduing every force which has been directed against us, what may we not do with the assistance for which we venture to appeal to the generous and the free?

Precipitated by circumstances into that struggle for independence which, ever since the domination of our cruel and reckless tyrants, had never ceased to be the object of our vows and prayers, we have, by the blessing of God, freed a considerable part of Greece from the ruthless invaders. The Peloponnesus, Etolia, Carmania, Attica, Phocida, Bœotia, and the islands of the Archipelago and Candia, are nearly free. The armies and the fleets which have been sent against us have been subdued by the valor of our troops and our marine. Meanwhile, we have organized a Government founded upon popular suffrages; and you will probably have seen how closely our organic law assimilates to that Constitution under which your nation so happily and so securely lives.

I have been sent hither by the Government of Greece to obtain assistance in our determined enterprise, on which we, like you, have staked our lives, our fortunes, and our sacred honor; and I believe my journey has not been wholly without success. I should have been wanting to my duty had I not addressed you, supplicating the earliest display of your amicable purposes; entreating that diplomatic relations may be established between us; communicating the most earnest desire of my Government, that we may be allowed to call you allies as well as friends; and stating that we shall rejoice to enter upon discussions which may lead to immediate and advantageous treaties, and to receive as to expedite diplomatic agents without delay. Both at Madrid and at Lisbon I have been received with great kindness by the American representative, and am pleased to record the expression of my gratitude.

Though fortunately you are so far removed and raised so much above the narrow politics of Europe as to be little influenced by the vicissitudes, I venture to believe that Mr. Rush will explain to you the changes which have taken place, and are still in action around us, in our favor; and I conclude rejoicing in the hope that North America and Greece may be united in the bonds of long-enduring and unbroken concord, and have the honor to be,

With every sentiment of respect, your obedient humble servant,

AND. LURIOTTIS.

LONDON, *February* 20, 1823.

Mr. Adams to Mr. Rush.

DEPARTMENT OF STATE, *Washington, August* 18, 1823.

SIR: I have the honor of inclosing herewith an answer to the letter from Mr. Luriottis, the agent of the Greeks, addressed to me, and a copy of which was transmitted with your despatch, No. 295.

If upon the receipt of this letter Mr. Luriottis should still be in London, it will be desirable that you should deliver it to him in person, accompanied with such remarks and explanations as may satisfy him and those whom he represents, that, in declining the proposal of giving active aid to the cause of Grecian emancipation, the Executive Government of the United States has been governed, not by its inclinations or a sentiment of indifference to the cause, but by its constitutional duties, clear and unequivocal.

The United States could give assistance to the Greeks only by the application of some portion of their public force or of their public revenue in their favor, and it would constitute them in a state of war with the Ottoman Porte, and perhaps with all the Barbary powers. To make this disposal either of force or treasure, you are aware, is, by our Constitution, not within the competency of the Executive. It could be determined only by an act of Congress, which would assuredly not be adopted, should it even be recommended by the Executive.

The policy of the United States with reference to foreign nations has always been founded upon the moral principle of natural law—*peace* with all mankind. From whatever cause war between other nations, whether foreign or domestic, has arisen, the unvarying law of the United States has been *peace* with both belligerents. From the first war of the French Revolution to the recent invasion of Spain, there has been a succession of wars, national and civil, in almost every one of which *one* of the parties was contending for liberty or independence. To the first revolutionary war a strong impulse of feeling urged the people of the United States to take side with the party which, at its commencement, was *contending*, apparently at least, for both. Had the policy of the United States not been essentially pacific, a stronger case to claim their interference could scarcely have been presented. They nevertheless declared themselves neutral, and the principle then deliberately settled has been invariably adhered to ever since.

With regard to the recognition of sovereign States, and the establishment with them of a diplomatic intercourse, the experience of the last thirty years has served also to ascertain the limits proper for the application of principles in which every nation must exercise some latitude of discretion. Precluded by their neutral position from interfering in the question of right, the United States have recognized the *fact* of foreign sovereignty only when it was undisputed, or disputed without any rational prospect of success. In this manner the successive changes of government in many of the European States, and the revolutionary Governments of South America, have been acknowledged. The condition of the Greeks is not yet such as will admit of the recognition upon these principles.

Yet as we cherish the most friendly feelings towards them, and are sincerely disposed to render them any service which may be compatible with our neutrality, it will give us pleasure to learn from time to time the actual state of their cause, political and military. Should Mr. Luriottis be enabled and disposed to furnish this information, it may always be communicated through you, and will be received with satisfaction here. The public accounts from that quarter have been of late very scanty, and we shall be glad to obtain any authentic particulars which may come to your knowledge from this or through any other channel.

I am, with great respect, sir, your very humble and obedient servant,

JOHN QUINCY ADAMS.

RICHARD RUSH, *Envoy, &c., at London.*

Mr. Adams to Mr. Luriottis.

DEPARTMENT OF STATE, *Washington, August* 18, 1823.

SIR: A copy of the letter which you did me the honor of addressing to me on the 20th of February last has been transmitted to me by the minister of the United States at London, and has received the deliberate consideration of the President of the United States.

The sentiments with which he has witnessed the struggles of your countrymen for their national emancipation and independence had been made manifest to the world in a public message to the Congress of the United States. They are cordially felt by the people of this Union, who, sympathizing with the cause of freedom and independence wherever its standard is unfurled, behold with peculiar interest the display of Grecian energy in defence of Grecian liberties, and the association of heroic exertions at the present time with the proudest glories of former ages in the land of Epaminondas and of Philopœmen.

But, while cheering with their best wishes the cause of the Greeks, the United States are forbidden by the duties of their situation from taking part in the war, to which their relation is that of neutrality. At peace themselves with all the world, their established policy and the obligations of the laws of nations preclude them from becoming voluntary auxiliaries to a cause which would involve them in *war*.

If, in the progress of events, the Greeks should be enabled to establish and organize themselves as an independent nation, the United States will be among the first to welcome them in that capacity into the general family, to establish diplomatic and commercial relations with them suited to the mutual interests of the two countries, and to recognize with special satisfaction their constituted state in the character of a sister Republic.

I have the honor to be, with distinguished consideration, sir, your very humble and obedient servant,

JOHN QUINCY ADAMS.

ANDREAS LURIOTTIS, *Envoy of the Provisional Government of the Greeks, London.*

Extract of a letter to the Secretary of State, dated

MARSEILLES, *August* 6, 1823.

"I have endeavored to obtain accurate information relative to the actual state of the struggle between the Greeks and the Ottomans. The following particulars, I think, may be relied on. The Porte is making great preparations by land to bring the war to a successful conclusion. The Turkish fleet has succeeded in provisioning for a year the garrisons of Carysto, in Negropont, Canée, the capital of Candia, (or Crete,) and also *Coron*, Modon, *Patras*, and Corinth, in the Morea. The two last places have been repeatedly and incorrectly represented in the American newspapers as having long since surrendered. The Porte has offered the Greeks, through the mediation of Lord Strangford, to place the Morea on the same footing as the provinces of Wallachia and Moldavia; that is, to place it under the government of a Greek prince, who should have the entire administration of the affairs of the province, and who should annually pay a certain portion of its revenues into the treasury of the Porte. The British ambassador, in order to induce the Greeks to accept these terms, has dispersed among them a declaration that they are not to expect aid from any of the European sovereigns. On the other hand, the Greeks do not seem as yet disposed to peace, but are making preparations to resist, as they may, the forces which are approaching them on all sides. Such was the state of things by the last advices."

Extract of a letter to the Secretary of State, dated,

MARSEILLES, *August* 27, 1823.

"There is no certain intelligence from Greece later than that contained in a letter I had the honor to forward to you a fortnight since. The Turkish admiral was, fifteen days ago, in the neighborhood of Patras, where he had landed five thousand men. The Smyrna Gazette reports that the main Turkish army, 60,000 strong, had obtained, after some hard fighting, possession of the defiles of Thermopylæ; but this, as yet, is not confirmed."

[Translation.]

Statistical table of Greece, according to the work of Mr. Pouqueville. Original received from Mr. Middleton, Envoy Extraordinary and Minister Plenipotentiary of the United States at St. Petersburg.

Greece may be apportioned into three grand divisions: continental Greece,† the Isthmus of Peloponnesus,* and the Islands.

Continental Greece.—It contains seven provinces, which are: Epirus,† Macedonia,† Thessaly,† Acarnania,* Etolia,* Locris,* Phocis,* comprehending Lividia.†

Epirus† has an extent of 1,100 square leagues of 2,500 toises. The population is estimated at 373,000 souls. Its principal cities are Janina, Zagori, Conitza, Prémithy, Cleissoura, Condessi, Canina, Tebelin, Aulone, (a port,) Bérat, (a fortress,) Elbassan, Durazzo, (a fort,) Argyro Castron, Liboro, Delvino, (fortified,) Conispolis, Paramythia, Gomenitza, (a port,) Margariti, Parga, (a fort,) Regniassa, (a fort,)* Preresa, (a port and fort,) Souli, (fort,)* Arta, (a fort and seaport,) Calarites,* Metzowo,* Syraco, &c.

The rivers which pass through Epirus in different ways are the Voioussa or Aoüs, the Calamas or Thyamis, the Glykys or Acheron.

The country generally is mountainous, intersected with large valleys; its aspect is various, and may be said to present an abridgment of all the climates; it abounds in cattle and in rich pastures. The articles of exportation consist of grain, of sheep and goats, of building timber, cotton, wool, pitch, wax, tobacco; and some mountains of Epirus contain mines, which the Government neglect to explore, and which the Christian inhabitants dare not discover, fearful of being themselves buried in these mines to gratify the cupidity of their masters.)a)

The principal seaports of Epirus are: L'Arta, Aulone, Prevesa, Vonitza, Port Palarme, Porto Raguzeo, Gomenitza, Durazzo. The value of wares and foreign productions imported by these ports was, in the year 1812, 6,590,902 piastres; the exportation during the same year was 7,804,063 piastres. The Epirotes are, in general, warlike and of a robust constitution, impatient of the yoke and proud, in spite of the dependence in which they live; shepherds rather than agriculturists, they almost all carry arms, and prefer to inhabit the mountains and the situations most difficult of access. Divided into colonies, and long governed by the feudal administration of the Beys, they have seen, too late, all these partial tyrannies united into one only, and the most monstrous of all, that of Ali Pacha of Janina. In the midst of the chaos of the administration of this Vizier, it may be calculated that Epirus paid annually to the Grand Seignor a tribute of two millions(b) of piastres, and that Ali received for himself ten other millions, without including the revenues of his sons, the advances and spoliations of every kind to which this province was exposed.

Macedonia,† divided into Illyrian and Cisaxian, has an extent of 1,692 square leagues. Its population may approximate to 436,000 inhabitants. Its most remarkable cities and towns are: Bitolia or Monastir, Prilipé, Cojani, Delvendos, Flourina, Cailary, Castoria, Greveno, Lepsini, Bichlistas, Croupitcha, Piassa, Gheortelia, Staria, Prespa, Critchowa, Ochrida, Chiatista, Veria,* or Karaveria, Jenidgé, Salonica.

The rivers which water Macedonia are: the Vardar, or Axius, and the Bichlista, or Haliæmon. This province abounds in small cattle, corn, wines, cotton, and tobacco.

The Macedonians are agriculturists and merchants. The merchants of Bitolia, of Castoria, of Chatista, and of Salonica, have frequent correspondence with the commercial places of Europe; they send caravans to Bosnia and Hungary. The Macedonians, as well as the other nations of Greece, partake of their Hellenic origin; they are brave and considerate(c). Numerous Bulgarian and Albanian colonies are established

N. B.   * This mark indicates the cities and provinces freed since 1821, and at present in submission to the National Congress of Corinth.
† Indicates the countries in insurrection.
‡ Indicates the cities and forts besieged by the Turks.
(a) Vid. Tom. 1, p. 279.   Tom. 2, p. 247.   (b) Vid. Tom. 3, p. 432.   (c) Vid. Tom. 4, p. 405.

in this province, actually divided into cantons, and subject to the destructive administration of the Pachas of Romelia and their subordinates.

Thessaly† contains, within an extent of 516 square leagues, 275,000 inhabitants; there are reckoned 962 villages and the following cities: Tricala, (the chief place, and residence of a Pacha,) Klinoro, Stagous, Pharsalia, Larissa, Alasson, Rapchana, Tournovo, Platamon, (a fort,) Caterin, Agia, Velestina,. Dechani,.Volo, (a port,) Armyros, Thaumaco. Thessaly, watered by the Peneus, and by several other rivers, tributaries of that river, is one of the most fertile countries of European Turkey; it produces corn, silk, cotton, tobacco, and, until the year 1810, the manufactories of Tournovo, of Ambelakia, and of Agia, sent abroad dyed cottons, stuffs, and woolens, to the amount of several millions;(a) the Greek merchants of these cities had factories in Germany. The seaport of Volo, situated on the gulf of the same name, favored the exportation of the grain which the sailors of Idra and of other islands came there to load. The natives of Thessaly vary in their character and their occupations according to the places which they inhabit; industrious and submissive in the cities, laborious and peaceful husbandmen in the country, intrepid sailors in the cantons situated near the sea, they are bold and independent in the mountainous regions. Numerous bands of these mountaineers go from Olympus, from Ossa, and from Mount Pelion, and having at their head enterprising chiefs, sometimes contend with the forces of the Pacha of Epirus and of Romelia;(b) they have even possessed themselves of several cities of Thessaly and defended them for years. Worn out with efforts, disappointed in their hopes, and deprived of their brave chiefs, they retired to their mountains, where they still form a population warlike and independent.

Acarnania* has an extent of 92 square leagues, and 8,635 inhabitants; the remains of a population formerly flourishing. There are still reckoned there sixteen cities and villages, the most remarkable of which are, Vonitza, Catona, Dragomestre, and Catochi, (a seaport.) This province, which made a part of the Government of Ali Pacha, and which has undergone all the torments of his administration, presents only ruins and solitude. It, nevertheless, carries on a feeble commerce with the Ionian islands and the Ambracian or Artan Gulf; its inhabitants keep up the fisheries in the same gulf, as well as on the numerous lakes in the interior of the country.

In this province, as in all the continent of Greece, there are found, in the declivities of mountains,(c) hamlets and villages inhabited by men who, flying from oppression, and striving to insulate themselves wherever they find a savage nature. Masters of the defiles which form the passage between Epirus and the southern provinces of Greece, the mountaineers of Acarnania can interrupt the communication between these two provinces, and oppose with success the movements of an army which might try to advance from this side towards Etolia and the Morea. Some cantons of .this province are at. this day entirely uncultivated and depeopled; others are covered with forests and barren grounds, which only want strength to be converted into productive lands. ·

Etolia,* separated from Acarnania by the river Aspropotamos or Acheloüs, contains, in its present subdivisions, four cantons and 83,455 inhabitants, distributed among 236 towns and villages; the principal of which are: Vrachori, Carpenitze, Agrapha, Missolongi, (a port,) Lepante,‡ or Naupacte, (a fort, and residence of a Pacha.) This province produces grain, rice, oil, silk, and wine. These productions, added to the revenue of the fisheries and customs, give an annual produce of 3,293,700 piastres.(d)

The cantons of Etolia, annexed, according to the register of the Ottoman Government, to the Pachalik of Negropont, had been successively seized upon by Ali Pacha, who entrusted the administration of them to his lieutenants. The pure blood of the ancient Etolians, their carelessness, their contempt of death, is still found among the colonies of Agrapha and of Carpenitze.(e) Animated with the energy which the vital air of the mountains of these cantons gives them, they are always induced to repel the attacks of the tyranny. In this part of Etolia the league of the armatolis was formed. These bands, reinforced by all the discontented of Greece, have sometimes opposed force to force, fanaticism to fanaticism, and have caused the satraps of Thessaly and of Epirus to make satisfaction for the unjust enterprises formed against their liberty.

. .. The country comprehending Locris,* Phocis,* Livadia,‡ and Attica, contains, by an approximating calculation, 450 square leagues, and a population of about 140,000 souls. Salone, Thebes, Livadia, and Athens,‡ are the principal cities of this country; the face and resources of which are, with some variations, nearly the same as in the countries which have been just above delineated in the table. It may be affirmed that, in all these provinces, forming continental Greece, the number of Christian inhabitants is to that of Mahometans in the proportion of five to one;(f) which would give to all this region a total of 1,316,080 inhabitants, of which there are more than a million of Christians, dispersed over an extent of country which could abundantly contain and support upwards of thrice that population.

Peloponnesus.

Peloponnesus,* or the Morea, has a surface of 840 square leagues. Its population is 240,000 Christian inhabitants, distributed in 1,421 villages, towns, and cities, the principal of which are: Corinth, (a fort,) Argos, Naupli, (a fort and port,)‡ St. Pierre, Mistra, or Sparta, Monembossie, (a fort,) Calamate, Androussa, Coron, (a fort and road for shipping,)‡ Modon, (a fort and road,)‡ Navarin, (a fort and port,) Arcadia, Gastonni, Lala, Patras, (a fort and port,)‡ Vostitza, Calavryta, Tripolitza, (a fort,) Caritène, Leondari.

Its rivers are the Rofia, or the Alpheus, the Vossili-Potamos, or the Eurotas, and several others of a shorter course. The mountains of Arcadia, those of Lala, or the ancient Pholöe, Mount Olenos, and the Taygete, connect the country in different ways. Notwithstanding the catastrophes which the Peloponnesus has experienced, and notwithstanding the ruinous administration of the Pachas, this province still preserves immense resources, owing to its fertility as well as to its topographical situation; its agricultural productions are numerous and various, and, according to a calculation made upon the places, the different cantons of the Peloponnesus produce, one year with another, 820,000 kilos. of corn, (wheat,) which fetches 6,560,000 piastres, reckoning the kilo. at 8 piastres, the selling price upon the places; 1,169,000 kilos. of maize, barley, and dry vegetables, making 7,402,000 piastres, according to the ordinary sale price; 63,000 barrels of oil, making 2,790,200 piastres, reckoning the barrel at from 40 to 45 piastres; 227,550 pounds of silk, making 3,738,500 piastres; 278,000 quintals of cotton and raw wool, making 1,388,800 piastres. The other revenues of agriculture and of industry, such as wine, cheese, butter, cattle, currants, honey, cotton, thread, and fish, produce, annually, in cash, the sum of 8,818,500 piastres, which gives a total of 30,698,000.(g) The different imposts and ground rents of the province amounted, in the year

(a) Vid. Tom. 3, p. 49.　　(b) Vid. Tom. 3, p. 16.　　(c) Vid. Tom. 3, p. 159.　　(d) Vid. Tom. 3, pp. 183, 202, 217.　　(e) Vid. Tom. 3, p. 233.　　(f) Vid. Tom. 3, p. 441.　　(g) Vid. tom. 5, p. 176.

1814, to 12,816,241 piastres, which left in favor of the managers a difference of 17,881,759 piastres. With this excess, of which the seventeenth went into the treasuries of the Beys, the Agas, and the great proprietors, the inhabitants pay their individual expenses, and the cantons buy in the markets of the province the provisions of the first necessity which they do not grow, and the articles coming from abroad.

In the above extract of revenues and of ground rents of the Peninsula the country of Magna,* or ancient Laconia, is not included. This canton, placed upon the declivities of Mount Taygete from the city Calamata to Cape Matapan, is divided into twelve captaincies, and forms a particular species of government, subject to the authority of a native Bey or Prince, held of the grand admiral of the Porte. The Magnates, poor, and naturally ferocious, know no other business but that of arms and piracy; in 1813 there were reckoned 10,000 men capable of bearing arms, in a population of 30,000 inhabitants, Christians and aborigines, who depended only nominally on the Ottoman Porte.

Islands of Greece. (a)

The islands of Greece, according to their geographical order from south to north, and from ——— are:

Candia,(†) or Crete. It is sixty leagues long and twenty broad. The ports are: the city of Candia,(‡) Rethymo,(*) Canca,(‡) Kissamos. Its population is two hundred and forty thousand inhabitants.

Milo,(*) or Melos, twelve leagues in circuit, and seven thousand inhabitants.

Santorin,(*) nine leagues in circuit; twelve thousand inhabitants.

Siphanto, or Syphnos,(*) nine leagues long and two broad; seven thousand inhabitants.

Nio, or Ios,(*) twelve leagues in circuit; two thousand seven hundred inhabitants. It has a good harbor.

Amargos,(*) twelve leagues in circuit; six thousand inhabitants, and a good harbor.

Paros(*) four leagues long and three broad; two thousand inhabitants.

Naxos,(*) thirty leagues in circuit; ten thousand inhabitants.

Serpho,(*) four leagues long and two broad, with a good harbor and two thousand inhabitants.

Thermia, or Cythnos,(*) five leagues long and two broad, with a good harbor and four thousand inhabitants.

Engia, or Egyne,(*) near the Morea, five leagues long and three broad; five thousand inhabitants.

Coloury, or Salamine,(*) twenty leagues in circuit, with a good harbor and eight thousand inhabitants.

Zea, or Ceos,(*) six leagues long and three broad; six thousand inhabitants.

Syra, or Syros,(*) fifteen leagues in circuit, with a harbor and five thousand inhabitants.

Dili, or Delos, not inhabited.

Myconi,(*) twelve leagues in circuit, with a good harbor and four thousand inhabitants.

Tine, or Tenos,(*) seven leagues long and three broad, and nine thousand inhabitants.

Andros,(*) thirty leagues in circuit, a harbor, and twelve thousand inhabitants.

Negropont, or Eubea,(†) four leagues long and ten broad; twenty-five thousand inhabitants.

Skiros, six leagues long and three broad; six thousand inhabitants.

Scopelos, eight leagues long and four broad; seven thousand inhabitants.

Thassos, thirty leagues in circuit, with a good harbor and eight thousand inhabitants.

Samandraky, or Samothrace, eight leagues in circuit, and two thousand inhabitants.

Imbros, ten leagues in circuit, with a fortified harbor and three thousand inhabitants.

Stalimène, or Lemnos,(*) ten leagues long and eight broad, with a fortified harbor and twenty thousand inhabitants.

Tenedos, fifteen leagues in circuit, with a fortified harbor and five thousand inhabitants.

Mitylene or Lesbos, twenty leagues long and fifteen broad, with a fortified harbor and eighteen thousand inhabitants.

Chio,(†) fifteen leagues in circuit [long] and five broad, with a large and good harbor and sixty thousand inhabitants.

Samos,(*) twelve leagues long and six broad, with two harbors and twelve thousand inhabitants.

Nicari, or Icaria,(*) eight leagues long and three broad; two thousand inhabitants.

Patmos,(*) few inhabitants.

Leros,(*) with a large harbor and few inhabitants.

Calimne, or Claros,(*) six leagues in circuit, with a good harbor and three thousand inhabitants.

Stanco, or Cos,(*) ten leagues long and four broad, with a fortified harbor and five thousand inhabitants.

Stimpalie, or Astipaloe,(*) seven leagues long and three broad, with a good harbor, and six thousand inhabitants.

Carpathos,(*) twelve leagues in circuit, with a harbor and four thousand inhabitants.

Rhodes, twenty-five leagues long and twenty broad; one hundred and fifty thousand inhabitants. The city of Rhodes is fortified; it has a large and good harbor.

Cyprus, one hundred and thirty leagues long and sixty at its greatest breadth; its population is eighty-three thousand. The cities are: Nicosia, Cerina, (a large harbor,) Paphos, Limassal, Famagouste, and Lamaca.

The islands of Idra,(*) Spetzia,(*) and Ipsara,(*) very important for their marine, reckon a population of fifty-eight thousand souls, or thereby.

The sum total of the population of the islands of Greece may be estimated at eight hundred and thirty thousand inhabitants, among which are included about one hundred and sixty thousand Mahometans, and seven hundred and seventy thousand Christians. Add two hundred and seventy thousand for the Morea, and one million for continental Greece, and there is two million and forty thousand for the Greek population of these countries.

The Greek inhabitants of Thrace, of Bulgaria, of Constantinople, of Smyrna, and of all Asia Minor, are not included in this number.

According to a detailed table, digested in the year 1813, the Greek marine of the islands and of different ports of Greece amounted to six hundred and fifteen merchant vessels, five thousand eight hundred and seventy-eight cannons, and seventeen thousand five hundred and twenty-six sailors; of which two hundred and forty vessels, four thousand three hundred and twenty cannons, and nine thousand nine hundred sailors belong to the three islands alone of Idra, Spetzia, and Ipsara.—(Vide Pouqueville, t. 5, page 68.)

(a) Vid. Abridgment of Geography, by l'Anglois, t. 2, pp. 24, 320.

SYMPATHY FOR THE GREEKS.

COMMUNICATED TO THE HOUSE OF REPRESENTATIVES JANUARY 2, 1824.

STATE OF SOUTH CAROLINA.

In the Senate, *December* 19, 1823.

Resolved, That the State of South Carolina regards with deep interest the noble and patriotic struggle of the modern Greeks to rescue from the foot of the infidel and barbarian the hallowed land of Leonidas and Socrates, and would hail with pleasure the recognition by the American Government of the independence of Greece.

Resolved, That a copy of this resolution be transmitted to our senators and representatives at Washington.

Ordered, That the resolutions be sent to the house of representatives for concurrence.

By order of the senate.

WM. D. MARTIN, *C. S.*

In the House of Representatives, *December* 20, 1823.

Resolved, That the house do concur in the resolutions.

Ordered, That they be returned to the senate.

By order of the house.

R. ANDERSON, *C. H. R.*

I certify that the above is a true copy of the original forwarded to me by the proper officers, and which I have presented to the senate.

ROB. Y. HAYNE.

SYMPATHY FOR THE GREEKS.

COMMUNICATED TO THE HOUSE OF REPRESENTATIVES JANUARY 5, 1824.

MEMORIAL.

To the Honorable the Senate and House of Representatives of the United States in Congress assembled:

The undersigned, a committee appointed for this purpose by a large number of the citizens of Boston and its vicinity, convened by public notification on the 19th instant, beg leave most respectfully to represent:

That they feel a deep interest in the political situation of the people of Greece, and rejoice in the information recently communicated by the Chief Magistrate of the United States, "that there is good reason to believe Greece will become again an independent nation."

That the contest of an oppressed and enslaved people for the invaluable blessings of self-government, and of a Christian people for the enjoyment of religious liberty, has a claim to the best wishes of this nation for its eventual success, and to whatever aid and encouragement, consistently with the primary duty of self-preservation, it may have the ability to afford.

No one who has duly reflected upon the consequences which have resulted from our own successful struggle in the cause of civil liberty, not as respects the interests of our nation only, but as it has affected also the condition of the whole civilized world, can hesitate to admit that the question of the erection of a new independent Christian State is the most momentous that can occur in the progress of human affairs, and especially deserving the attention of the representatives of a free people.

Centuries, whose annals are filled with the common succession of wars and conquests, may pass away, without being attended with any important result to the great cause of civilization and humanity; but the emancipation from a barbarous despotism of a gallant and enterprising and intelligent people must be followed by the most propitious consequences, and cannot fail to add to the security of all free Governments, by increasing the number of those who are devoted to their common defence.

The extermination of the Turkish despotism on the coasts and islands of the Mediterranean sea has justly been regarded as a more worthy object of concert and coalition among civilized powers than any which ever engaged their united attention. The existence of that despotism has reduced to a state of desolation several of the most fertile countries on the globe, and annihilated the commerce that might otherwise have been maintained. It has been attended with the grossest insults and outrages on the dignity of States and the liberty of their citizens. The maintaining of a powerful marine force, expensive consular establishments, disgraceful tribute, slavery and war, have successively been among the evils to which this lawless domination has subjected the civilized world, and from which our own country has not been exempted.

It is, then, quite obvious that the erection of a new and free State in the Mediterranean, possessing not only the coasts of Southern Greece, but the islands, particularly of Candia and Cyprus, would form a powerful check upon the barbarous dependencies of the Porte in those seas, and give facility to that commercial enterprise which now finds its way only to one port of European or Asiatic Turkey.

Your memorialists would not presume to make any suggestion as to the course which it may become the American Government to pursue at this interesting crisis. They feel, in common with their fellow-citizens generally, the just weight and obligation of that policy which hitherto has prohibited an interference with the internal concerns of any of the powers of Europe, and content themselves, therefore, with expressing their assurance, that if the peculiar and unprecedented condition of the Greeks should, in the opinion of the Government of the United States, form a case of exception to that rule of policy, the measures which may be adopted shall receive their cordial support. ...

But your memorialists, at any rate, cannot refrain from the expression of their earnest wish that the indignation and abhorrence which they are satisfied is universal throughout the United States at the mode in which the Turkish Government is carrying on the war against Greece should be distinctly avowed in the face of the world, and that other civilized and Christian nations should be invited to join in a solemn remonstrance against such barbarous and inhuman depravity.

The sale of forty thousand Christian women and children, (after the massacre of their husbands and fathers,) in open market, in the presence of Christian Europe, and without one word of remonstrance from the surrounding nations, is a circumstance discreditable to the age in which we live. If older and nearer nations are silent on such a subject, there is the greater reason and the more honor in giving utterance to the feelings which are excited on this side the Atlantic, and of endeavoring to obtain the interference and combining the sentiment of all civilized nations to put an end to such horrible scenes.

The just indignation of the world has recently been manifested by a simultaneous effort to humble and restrain the Barbary powers. Every year has witnessed some new exertion among Christian nations to abolish the horrible traffic in African slaves; an amelioration of the ancient laws of war with regard to private property has recently been propounded as a subject worthy the consideration of the nations; and yet no remonstrance has been made in behalf of Christian brotherhood and suffering humanity.

Your memorialists do therefore most earnestly commend to the constitutional representatives of the American people an attentive consideration of the aforegoing interesting and important subjects.

All which is most respectfully submitted, &c.

> THOMAS L. WINTHROP,
> GEORGE BLAKE,
> H. A. S. DEARBORN,
> SAMUEL F. JARVIS,
> JAMES T. AUSTIN,
> SAMUEL D. HARRIS,
> HENRY ORNE,
> S. ADAMS WELLS,..-.
> EDWARD EVERETT,
> JOHN C. WARREN,
> WARREN DUTTON.

SPOLIATIONS BY A SPANISH PRIVATEER.

COMMUNICATED TO THE HOUSE OF REPRESENTATIVES JANUARY 12, 1824.

Mr. FORSYTH, from the Committee on Foreign Relations, to whom was referred the petition of Henry Cotheal, David Cotheal, and Abraham S. Hallet, reported:

That it appears by the documents accompanying the petition that the schooner Mosquito, Captain Teft, loaded with a cargo the property of the petitioners, citizens of the United States, was captured on a voyage from St. Andrew's to New York by the Spanish privateer Fortuna, Captain Antonio Peyro, of Porto Rico. The schooner was carried first into Aquadilla, a port of the island of Porto Rico, where a portion of the cargo was plundered by the prize crew, and from thence, with the residue of the cargo, she was carried to St. John's, in the same island, and there condemned as lawful prize to the captors. From this decision an appeal to the superior tribunal of the island of Cuba has been made.

The conduct of the captain and crew of the privateer seems to have been both wanton and fraudulent. The captain of the schooner was grossly ill-treated; compelled by threats to sign a declaration written on board the privateer in the Spanish language, of which he is ignorant, and without receiving such an explanation of its contents as enabled him to understand it. After his signature was fixed to this paper, of the contents of which he is still ignorant, the first occasion that offered was taken to separate him from the property under his care. He was put on board a vessel bound to Curaçoa.

The mate, who, in the captain's absence, was the guardian of the rights of the owners of the vessel and cargo, was detained on board the schooner from the 17th of August, the day she reached St. John's, until the 23d of the same month, and not permitted during that time to have communication with the shore.

The grounds upon which the vessel and cargo were condemned the committee cannot state accurately to the House, copies of the documents in the cause not having been furnished by the petitioners, as they allege, because copies could not be procured from the Spanish authorities in Porto Rico; but as far as they are informed there was no justifiable cause of condemnation. The condemnation is stated to have been founded upon two circumstances—that the schooner had no clearance from St. Andrew's, and had a gun on board not mentioned in her papers. The first was inevitable, as there is said to be no custom-house at St. Andrew's, and the second, admitting the fact, which is denied by the owners, was susceptible of satisfactory explanation: the gun was carried as a defence against the pirates infesting the seas she was navigating. As the expectation that the superior tribunal of Cuba will speedily do justice to the owners of the vessel and cargo may be rationally indulged, the committee are of opinion that it is not expedient to act further on the subject. They propose, therefore, the following resolution:

Resolved, That the Committee on Foreign Relations be discharged from the further consideration of the petition of Henry Cotheal, David Cotheal, and Abraham S. Hallett, and that the petitioners have leave to withdraw their petition and the documents presented with it.

18TH CONGRESS.]   No. 367.   [1ST SESSION.

EUROPEAN SYMPATHY FOR SPAIN IN THE SUBJUGATION OF HER AMERICAN COLONIES

COMMUNICATED TO THE HOUSE OF REPRESENTATIVES JANUARY 12, 1824.

To the House of Representatives of the United States:

In answer to a resolution of the House of Representatives of December 24, requesting the President of the United States to lay before the House such information as he may possess, and which may be disclosed without injury to the public good, relative to the determination of any sovereign, or combination of sovereigns, to assist Spain in the subjugation of her late colonies on the American continent, and whether any Government of Europe is disposed or determined to oppose any aid or assistance which such sovereign or combination of sovereigns may afford to Spain for the subjugation of her late colonies above mentioned, I have to state that I possess no information on that subject not known to Congress which can be disclosed without injury to the public good.

JAMES MONROE.

WASHINGTON, *January* 12, 1824.

18TH CONGRESS.]   No. 368.   [1ST SESSION.

CORRESPONDENCE WITH SPAIN RELATIVE TO THE CESSION OF THE FLORIDAS.

COMMUNICATED TO THE HOUSE OF REPRESENTATIVES FEBRUARY 2, 1824.

To the House of Representatives of the United States:

In compliance with a resolution of the House of Representatives of the 11th of December last, requesting the President of the United States to communicate to the House all such parts of the correspondence with the Government of Spain, relating to the Florida treaty, to the period of its final ratification, not heretofore communicated, which, in his opinion, it might not be inconsistent with the public interest to communicate, I herewith transmit a report from the Secretary of State, with copies of the documents requested.

JAMES MONROE.

WASHINGTON, *February* 2, 1824.

DEPARTMENT OF STATE, *Washington, January* 26, 1824.

The Secretary of State, to whom the resolution of the House of Representatives of the United States of the 11th of last month has been referred, requesting the President to communicate to the House all such parts of the correspondence with the Government of Spain, touching the Florida treaty, to the period of its final ratification, which have not yet been communicated, and which, in his opinion, it may not be inconsistent with the public interest to communicate, has the honor of reporting to the President copies of the papers desired by that resolution.

JOHN QUINCY ADAMS.

List of papers sent to the President of the United States, with a report from the Department of State, January 26, 1824.

1. Mr. Forsyth to Mr. Adams, August 22, 1819. Marked private.
2. Same to same, January 28, 1820. Marked extracts.
3. Same to same, February 15, 1820. No. 12; extract.
4. Same to the Duke of San Fernando and Quiroga, January 27, 1820.
5. Same to Mr. Adams, March 30, 1820. No. 15.
6. Mr. T. L. L. Brent, acting as Chargé d'Affaires at Madrid, to Mr. Adams, detailing the substance of a conversation with Mr. Jabat, April 27, 1820. Extract.
7. Mr. Forsyth to Mr. Adams, May 20, 1820. No. 18; extract.
8. Same to same, July 13, 1820. No. 19; extract.
9. Same to same, July 30, 1820. Marked private; extract.
10. Same to same, August 27, 1820. Marked private; extracts.
11. Same to same, September 21, 1820. No. 20; extract.
12. Same to Don Evaristo Peres de Castro, Secretary of the Despatch of State, &c., July 21, 1820.
13. Mr. de Castro to Mr. Forsyth, July 25, 1820. Translation.
14. Mr. Forsyth to Mr. Adams, September 21, 1820. Marked private.
15. Same to same, October 5, 1820. Marked private.
16. Same to same, October 11, 1820. No. 21.
17. Mr. de Castro to Mr. Forsyth, October 6, 1820. Translation.
18. Mr. Forsyth to Mr. de Castro, October 7, 1820.
19. Mr. de Castro to Mr. Forsyth, October 9, 1820. Translation.
20. Mr. Forsyth to Mr. de Castro, October 10, 1820.
21. Mr. de Castro to Mr. Forsyth, October 11, 1820. Translation.
22. Mr. Forsyth to Mr. de Castro, October 11, 1820.
23. Same to Mr. Adams, October 12, 1820. Marked private.
24. Same to same, October 15, 1820. Marked private.
25. The Spanish Minister to the Chargé d'Affaires of Russia at Madrid, October 15, 1820. Translation.
26. Mr. Forsyth to Mr. Adams, October 24, 1820. No. 22; extract.
27. Same to Mr. de Castro, October 17, 1820.
28. The Minister of Spain to Mr. Forsyth, October 24, 1820. Translation.
29. Order of the King of Spain for the delivery of the Floridas, October 24, 1820. Translation.
30. Mr. Adams to General Vives, February 28, 1821.

Extracts of a letter from Mr. Forsyth, marked private, to Mr. Adams, dated Madrid, August 22, 1819.

"The duplicates of my despatches by the Hornet not having been forwarded before this, I deem it unnecessary to send you the extract of that part of my private journal, a copy of which was transmitted with my former letters. To the information contained in my official letter of this day's date I have little to add of much importance. The most interesting fact I am able to communicate is, that the affair of the grants is not the sole or the principal difficulty with this Government. After receiving Mr. Salmon's note of the 10th instant, and ascertaining from Duke Laval, that this Government expected me to insist on the King's agreeing to receive Mr. Onis' declaration, or to make one of his own, I gave information to the duke, with the expectation and belief that he would communicate to the Government and to the parties interested that this was a mistake. I had no instructions to insist upon either. We expected the King might offer it; but, if he did not, the treaty was already ratified by the United States, and the act could not be recalled. To produce a good effect, I said, also, that the mistake about the grants must be corrected, if the business should be (what was altogether improbable) settled amicably in the United States. The only hope of the grantees was, to have the exchange of ratifications before made here. Relying upon the correctness of the information received here, of the date of Punon Rostro's and Alagon's grant, and the opinion that the cedula was the first valid act of the concession, and, of course, the date of the grant must be the date of the cedula, I intimated to Mr. Salmon that the difficulty in regard to the donations could be obviated here. His reply was, that there were other points upon which the King wished explanations. What these are, I have collected from other sources. The first and great object in view is to procure an assurance that we will not recognize Buenos Ayres, &c. The extreme pertinacity and anxiety on this subject has its origin in the disclosure made by Great Britain of the conversations between Mr. Rush and Lord Castlereagh, on the contemplated reception of a consul general, to reside officially in the United States, from the provinces of La Plata. This disclosure has done us no good. Sir Henry Wellesley, to whom, on his stating that he was endeavoring to promote our objects here, I remarked that I considered much of the difficulty of our affair was imputable to this cause, gave a very plausible answer; of its truth I am skeptical. He said the object was to show to Spain the absolute necessity of a settlement of our differences with her. Whatever was the motive, the effect has not been happy. The instructions to Onis were given before this disclosure was made; it was not useful in producing those instructions; and it is equally clear, from the conduct of Spain, that it has not had the effect of inducing her to ratify what her minister, under these instructions, promised in her name. Sir Henry Wellesley has at all times held very reasonable language, and friendly, in relation to this affair; and since the above conversation, he has certainly taken some pains to promote our wishes. He tells me that he sent a message, by a confidential agent, to the Duke of Infantado, who had urged the argument, that Great Britain ought not to be irritated by the cession of Florida to us; that he was entirely mistaken in supposing Great Britain adverse to the ratification of the convention, and that he had directions from the British ministry to press the ratification. He told Salmon that Spain would hazard much by refusing it, and that the object she had in view could be better accomplished by ratifying immediately. After the determination of this Government was known—and it was known immediately—he conversed with me, and wished me to believe that it was all imputable to the dispute about the grants. I said this could not be, as the Government must know that the King, having it in his power to accept or reject Onis' declaration, could throw upon us the burden refusing the exchange of ratifications. He then asked if the affair of the grants could be got over here. For the reasons stated in the first part of this letter for my disclosures to Laval and Salmon, and believing myself justified by my instructions, after the receipt of the letter of the 10th of August, I replied I was confident they could be. He proposed to me to permit him to engage Tatischeff, the Russian minister, whose influence and means of communicating with the Government are said to be superior to all the rest of the corps diplomatique, to have this suggestion communicated to the King. To this I consented; but as I thought it would be better, if Tatischeff did anything, to procure his good offices by an immediate application, I apprised him of this conversation. He was very friendly in his expressions, personally believed the ratification necessary and proper for Spain, and, certainly, the policy of Europe required it to be done. Sir Henry and Tatischeff had a similar conversation, and the suggestion was made. The next time I saw the Russian minister he said, if you can give assurances that there will be no recognition of the South American Governments the treaty will be ratified. I replied, if that is the case there will be no ratification. I had previously furnished Duke Laval with a memorandum on this topic, which, after keeping twenty-four hours, and, I have no doubt, showing it to Lozano Torres, who is supreme here, he returned it to me. The substance of it was, that the system of the Government was an impartial neutrality; it had been adhered to when we had, in our differences with Spain, the most powerful inducements to abandon it; that when these differences were settled there could be no inducement to change it. If Spain desired us to remain stationary in the dispute with her colonies, the first step to secure her object was to ratify our treaty, then to consult our wishes, and to shape her policy as to inspire a sentiment of good will, powerful enough to counteract the prepossessions naturally entertained for the people of South America by the people of the United States. This was the rational mode and, in fact, the only mode of reaching her point. To refuse our treaty, and ask, as a condition of it, that we would not recognize, was the certain way to disappoint their wishes. The Government would not consider such a proposition. This memorandum I showed to Tatischeff. He said what it contained was true and just, but there was no reasoning with ignorance and presumption. I did not hold any of these conversations until after the note of the 10th was received; and I was careful to express the desire that these gentlemen should do what was done, not with a view to our interest, but to prevent Spain from injuring herself and endangering what is termed the pacific policy of Europe.

"On the whole, I am impressed with a belief that they will propose to exchange ratifications in Washington, with the insertion of a promise not to recognize the patriot Governments and to preserve the grants. The latter will be as a dernier resort, given up as the price of the first. Without this, or something equivalent, we may do ourselves justice; they will not."

Extracts of a letter from Mr. Forsyth, marked private, to Mr. Adams, dated January 28, 1820.

"General Vives left this place on the 25th for Paris, on his way to Washington. He went post to France, and I am informed is directed to remain as short a time as possible in Paris. He goes to England to embark for the United States. The alteration in his mode of travelling, and the directions he has received not to delay, give me some hope that he will arrive in America time enough to prevent the necessity of doing that without the consent of Spain which the American Government prefers to do with her consent."

"I send this by the way of Gibraltar, that the earliest notice may be had of General V.'s movements. In the course of the coming week I shall write officially, and inclose a copy of my answer to the Duke of S. Fernando's last note, written to inform me of General Vive's appointment."

Extract of a letter from Mr. Forsyth, (No. 12,) Minister Plenipotentiary of the United States in Spain, to Mr. Adams, Secretary of State, dated Madrid, February 15, 1820.

"By the return of Lieutenant Weaver, who came to this place yesterday with a letter from Captain Stewart, I have a convenient opportunity of sending, inclosed, a copy of my last note to the Duke of San Fernando, No. 1, dated the day after General Vives left Madrid. It was written in conformity to what I believe, from the message at the opening of Congress, to be the wishes of the President. If in this I should unhappily be mistaken, the affair stands in such a state that I can at any moment correct the error. Having informed this Government that I only *detain the remonstrance*, I can at any moment present it, if directed so to do, or if I shall be satisfied that the King has not given such authority to General Vives as will render unnecessary a recurrence to this disgraceful business."

Mr. Forsyth to the Duke of San Fernando and Quiroga, First Minister of State, January 27, 1820.

MADRID, *January* 27, 1820.

SIR: I have had the honor to receive your excellency's officio of the 16th December, giving me notice of the appointment of the Marriscal de Campo Don Francisco Dionisio Vives as Minister Plenipotentiary of the United States. According to the request of your excellency I communicated, by the first convenient opportunity that occurred, a copy of your note to the American Government.

The appointment of the Minister Plenipotentiary has been so long delayed, his departure so much procrastinated, his route to the United States is so circuitous, and his movements are so deliberate, that I very much apprehend he will find on his arrival the determination before now taken by the American Government executed. His Catholic Majesty may be assured by your excellency that should this be the case the American Government will, nevertheless, governed by that temper of conciliation which has at all times marked its policy, give any explanations which may, in the spirit of amity, be asked in the name of the King.

Your excellency views it as superfluous to continue discussions here of the points of the transaction with which his Majesty's minister goes charged, and as likely to embarrass the course of the direct negotiation. As to the future, I have to inform your excellency that I have no directions to discuss any of those points; and certainly I have received here very slender encouragement voluntarily to encounter them. My duty in regard to the convention was terminated when I had the honor to send you the remonstrance of the 18th of October, which has given rise to an unpleasant question between us. From circumstances *well known to your excellency*, I understand that the observations quoted have reference, also, to that question. With this understanding, I give you the strongest proof in my power of my anxious desire to promote harmony between the two nations by taking upon myself the responsibility of having so long withheld the return of the remonstrance, and in determining still longer to retain it in my hands. I do this with the confident expectation that the justice of his Catholic Majesty has, in the powers given to General Vives, rendered a further recurrence to that unhappy affair altogether unnecessary. While I give to your excellency this proof of my wishes to conciliate, I must repeat that I hold it as *unquestionably my right* to have that paper, or any other. I may deem it necessary to send, laid before your excellency's royal master for his perusal and consideration; holding myself responsible to my own Government only for the language in which it may be expressed, or the sentiments it may contain.

I renew to your excellency the assurances of my profound consideration.

.JOHN FORSYTH.

His Excellency the Duke of San Fernando and Quiroga, *First Minister of State, &c.*

Extract of a letter from Mr. Forsyth to Mr. Adams, (No. 15,) March 30, 1820.

"Soon after the change of Government was officially made known to me, I determined to see the Duke of San Fernando respecting our affairs, to learn if the powers given to Vives were such that no bad effect would be produced by the recent events upon the relations of Spain with the United States, and to endeavor to procure, in this season of generous feelings, the release of the Americans in confinement. Waiting a few days for the first bustle to be over, the Duke was removed from office and a further delay unexpectedly occurred. As the new Secretary was not expected for some time, on the 27th I asked by written note for an interview with Mr. Jabat, who had charge of the office. It was appointed for the 29th. I saw him at the time fixed, and had a very long conversation with him. I stated the objects I had in view. He answered with great frankness. The substance of what I learned from him is, that General Vives did not carry the treaty ratified by the United States; that the King, having taken the oath to observe the Constitution, could not now ratify; that instructions had been just prepared for General Vives to apprise him of the change that had taken place, and of the want of power in the King to act further in the business; the whole matter would be laid before the Cortes, and the minister had no doubt it would be arranged to the mutual satisfaction of the two Governments, as the Cortes would probably be composed of the most liberal and enlightened men of the nation; men who had the disposition, the ability, and the courage to give and to act upon good counsel. He spoke of the resemblance of the institutions of the two nations and of his anxious wish to see them on the best terms. Of the American prisoners he professed a desire to do what would be agreeable to us, and would bring the subject before the King. For this object, it was agreed upon between us that I should address him an official note. A copy of it, marked No. 6, is inclosed. It was prepared immediately after the interview and sent on the 30th. Mr. Jabat asked me, in turn, what would be the determination of our Government in this new state of things? I replied, that I was exceedingly disappointed to learn that General Vives had not the ratified treaty to exchange in the United States; that I apprehended his going without it would produce a very bad effect, and that I had no doubt there would be an immediate occupation of Florida, as recommended by the President to Congress; that we had always the strongest desire to be friendly with Spain, a desire which recent circumstances would increase. I was perfectly aware that the King had now no power to ratify, and trusted, with him, that everything would be arranged satisfactorily when the Cortes assembled. In the meantime I hoped that no unpropitious effect on the dispositions of this Government would be produced by the measures we should have been reluctantly compelled to take. I expressed the greatest satisfaction at the prospect of a favorable answer to the application in favor of the confined Americans, and assured him it would be considered as a conclusive proof on the part of Spain of a desire to do us justice and kindness in all things. The revolution will produce the best effects for us, if a judgment is to be formed from the language of the people in office and of those out of office. The Government of the United States is considered, with reason, more friendly to them than any other. The European Governments, without exception, see in the change which has been produced here a dangerous example to their people, and speculate with dread upon its probable effect. I had supposed that the influence of Great Britain would be very great under the new order of things. At present there is a very wholesome jealousy and prejudice against that Government existing among the people, and carefully cherished by the ruling men. It is to be traced, in part, to the conduct of the English on the return of the King from his captivity. They were supposed to have had some agency in preventing, at that time, the King's acceptance of the Constitution. The language used here is, there are but two free nations—the Spaniards and the people of the United States. The English were free, but have been recently enslaved by their ministry and Parliament. I hope that, before General Vives receives and communicates to the President the change in the Government, Florida will be occupied by us, or, at least, that Congress will have passed a law in such terms as to render it obligatory upon the President to take it. Delaying to take it until the news is received of the establishment of a free Government and liberal institutions here might be injurious. At present everybody here expects it will be seized, and the event will have no bad effect, unless it can, by misrepresentation, be made to appear the consequence of the recent events in Spain. It is important that Florida should be in our possession when the Cortes deliberate on the treaty. The defect of granted authority in that body to cede territory was not adverted to by Mr. Jabat, and has probably escaped notice. The general assertion that the sovereignty resides essentially in the nation, which is represented by the Cortes, would no doubt be considered sufficient when the territory was held by us; it might admit of dispute if it was not. You will perceive that two deputies from Cuba and the Floridas are to be in the Cortes. Before July I hope to receive from you particular and special instructions on this and all other subjects connected with our interests. During the Cortes would be the most favorable time for a commercial arrangement, if one is to be made here, and I indulge the belief that should, as is probable, the business of Florida be amicably arranged, an advantageous commercial treaty may be formed. I look with anxiety for directions from you, formed upon the deter. mination Congress may have made."

Extract of a letter from Mr. Thomas L. L. Brent, acting as Chargé d'Affaires at Madrid, containing the substance of a conversation between him and Mr. Jabat, April 27, 1820, to Mr. Adams.

"He (Mr. Jabat) then adverted to the bill reported by the Committee of Foreign Relations to the House of Representatives, for the occupation of Florida, and asked me if I had received instructions to give any explanations on the subject. He intimated that if we did not extend our views further than its occupation every effort would be made to preserve amicable relations with the United States, every sacrifice consistent with a due self-respect; but that the United States ought not to expect Spain would go any further. Now that this had become a representative Government, they would be under the neces. sity of examining, with more scrupulous attention than ever, every act of theirs which could in any degree compromit the just pride and dignity of the nation. I told Mr. Jabat that I had no instructions on the subject. I only knew, I said, from the public papers, that such a bill was before Congress, and consequently did not feel authorized to give any explanations. That, as soon as I received, I would make them known to him. I begged him to tranquilize himself. I said I hoped that with such dispositions as were manifested by the *new* Government, and the corresponding sentiments of mine, that everything would finally be amicably arranged; and that matters might be so managed as that the steps which the United States may have thought it necessary to take for the assertion of their rights might be made reconcileable with the pride of his Government; steps which they will have been compelled to resort to, from the conduct of the former administration of his Government and the measures of the old system. It may be proper to notice that this minister was evidently under an apprehension that the United States might not limit themselves to the occupation of the territory of Florida alone. In the course of the conversation Mr. Jabat said that, as there would be opposition, blood might be spilt in the occupation of Florida; and the idea of it seemed to give him great pain. Mr. Jabat's manner during the whole of this interview was mild and friendly, and mine corresponded to his."

Extracts of a letter from Mr. Forsyth to Mr. Adams, (No. 18,) dated May 20, 1820.

"By the Gibraltar mail of the — instant I received the duplicate of your No. 11. You will herewith receive copies of Mr. Jabat's letter, giving notice of the birth and title of the son of the Infante Don Francisco de Paula, and my answer."

"On the 12th I paid the minister a visit at the office of state, and, as I expected, he inquired if I had any recent advices from America. I stated to him very frankly that I had received nothing but the permission from our Government to return to the United States, which, from a belief that it would be most agreeable to the President, I should not use until after the celebration of the Cortes. He professed to be much gratified by this determination, which he thought was calculated to promote that good understanding between our respective Governments, to secure which was the object of our mutual wishes. From this the conversation naturally turned to the unofficial notices from the United States, and particularly to the report of the committee on the affairs of Florida. He did not appear to apprehend that we should do more than occupy the territory; but he expressed a great deal of dread lest there should be blood shed in effecting that object and carrying into effect the act proposed by the committee. As I had been told, as stated in my No. 17, that some uneasiness was felt on the first point, I thought it prudent to show him that, with the dispositions now entertained in Spain, there was no reason to fear that we should be disposed to go beyond the limits of the treaty of February, 1819. He would recollect that the only motives we could have were to procure satisfaction for the injury sustained by the delay of Spain to ratify the treaty, and compensation for any deficiency in the fund for the payment of our citizens, occasioned by the mistake of Mr. Onis, about the date of the large grants. On the first, I was sure a reasonable explanation would be deemed sufficient; on the second, there could be no difficulty, as the abandonment of all pretension in favor of the grantees was more necessary to the character of Spain than it was important to the interests of the United States."

"I did not suppose there was much ground for the fears he seemed to entertain of a formidable resistance to the occupation of Florida; nevertheless, as he was seriously apprehensive, I suggested that the President would no doubt employ a force so powerful that resistance would be hopeless, and I presumed the good sense of the Spanish authorities would prevent them from making a useless sacrifice of the lives of the soldiers committed to their care. It was obvious, from the conversation of Mr. Jabat, that the seizure of the territory was anticipated, and that the only fear really entertained was that the mode of occupation would impose an obligation on the present rulers to make a noise about it. The interview terminated by a renewal of the assurances formerly given of the desire of the Government to establish a permanent friendship with us, and with the hope, reciprocally expressed, that nothing might occur to render it difficult. On the 15th I received a note from Mr. Jabat (copy inclosed) inviting me to see him the next day at eleven. I saw him at the hour appointed, and his first question was, Have you anything from Washington? To my reply in the negative, he said, then I shall have the pleasure of giving you very recent advices from that place. He showed me a despatch from Mr. Serna, of the 28th of March, inclosing copies of the President's message to the House of Representatives of the 27th, and of the documents accompanying it. Mr. Jabat was highly gratified; said nothing could have occurred more favorable to the future amity of the two nations; that he had shown these papers to the King, who was pleased both with the measure proposed and the reasons offered for it by the President. Mr. Jabat did not omit to suggest, *what I knew perfectly well, that the accomplishment of the expectations of the President would have to be imputed to the recent revolution in Spain.* He explained to me what I did not understand in our previous conversation—the foundation of his fears of a formidable resistance in Florida. It seems the ports of the territory had been reinforced from Cuba, and the Governor-General of that island had given official notice of it to the Secretary of State. Joining with the Spanish secretary in his expressions of satisfaction, I suggested the hope that General Vives would not arrive until after the adjournment of Congress, as it was impossible to foresee what might be the effect produced by his arrival without competent power to meet the just expectations of the American Government. I did not fear any ill consequences if news of the revolution in Spain should reach Washington before a determination was taken. I was confident that, irritating as this want of authority might be, the President would be disposed to give to the King of the Spains proofs of the moderation and good will which had distinguished the conduct of the United States to the King of Spain. Taking the time at which Congress has usually adjourned as the criterion, I supposed that General Vives would scarcely see Washington before the adjournment of the legislative body. I have since learned from our newspapers that Congress would have continued its session until the beginning of this month, and that General Vives reached New York on the 5th of April. I now hope that Mr. Hackley, who carried my despatches of the 9th of March, and who left the Straits of Gibraltar about the 27th of March, will be in the United States within a short time after the arrival of the Spanish minister. In the present state of things nothing could be more auspicious than the proposed delay of acting against Florida, although the President will have perceived, from your first communications with General Vives, that, but for recent events we should have given another proof of useless forbearance, if the utility of forbearance was to be estimated by the good effect it would have produced on the Government of Spain. Mr. Jabat proposed to me to see the King at the circle that day—a ceremony I have not thought it necessary to observe since the postponement of the ratification of the treaty; always, however, replying politely to the notes sent on particular occasions, and once calling at the palace when the King was ill, I had resolved to renew these visits of ceremony immediately after the liberation of the Americans, prisoners in Spain, and therefore the more readily acceded to this proposal. I attended the circle with the diplomatic body, and was received, as I had been taught to expect, perfectly well, and as if there had been no interruption in my visits to it."

Extract of a letter from the same to the same, (No. 19,) dated July 13, 1820.

" A few days after the arrival of the Minister of State, Perez de Castro, I called at his office to see him on our affairs. I stated that the time for the meeting of the Cortes was near at hand, and I was desirous to know what was proposed by this Government to be done. He declared himself to be unable to converse on the subject of the negotiation with the United States. He was not master of the correspondence, and that his numerous and pressing engagements had rendered it impossible for him as yet to become so. He was examining and hoped to speak advisedly on it in a short time. I gave him a translation of the remonstrance of the 18th of October, to apprise him of the state of the dispute in relation to the 8th article of the treaty, not officially, but as a document for his own examination, telling him that I did not conceive it necessary, from the disposition manifested since the revolution, to make an official representation on this subject. He received it very willingly. He had seen, as he stated, in the foreign newspapers that it was asserted by the American Government that the treaty was obligatory upon Spain, although not ratified; this position he could not consider as founded either in the opinion of the best authorities or in the usages of nations. I explained to him that we considered the treaty obligatory *in justice and in honor* as if ratified by Spain. As no satisfactory reason had been or, as we believed, could be given for the refusal to ratify, there could be no question as to our right to resort to any measure we deemed proper to obtain satisfaction. The least we could do was to execute the treaty; and when we gave to Spain all the advantages she could derive from it, we should take from her all just cause even to complain of the course pursued. He spoke a good deal at large of the charge of bad faith which was urged against Spain, and said she had no motive of avarice or ambition to gratify in her negotiation with us; and if her policy required her to procrastinate, this was no reason to charge her with ill faith. To all this I answered that the systematic procrastination, although at all times vexatious, had never been urged as a proof of bad faith; it was the non-compliance with engagements actually made by persons duly authorized and empowered by this Government. That, if the avarice or ambition of the Government was not known in the negotiation, that of individuals who had possessed influence in Spain was but too visible. I saw him again after ten days. He had run over the whole correspondence; talked of the treaty of 1802; the proposals of Mr. Pinckney; the guaranty of the Spanish American dominions, as an inducement to cede Florida; in short, of all that had passed prior to the convention of 1819; of the losses Spain had sustained, and of our gains. I listened patiently to all he had to advance; when he had finished, I replied that we had gained nothing from Spain; if her arrangement with another power was matter of regret, it was not our fault. What we had obtained was purchased and paid for. That I had no instructions from the President since August, 1819, and therefore could not speak certainly of what might be the wish of my Government; but that it appeared to me it would be better for Spain at the present juncture not to look beyond the treaty of 1819, but to consider what obligations were imposed upon her by it, and by her as yet unexplained refusal to ratify it. He did not seem unwilling to adopt this idea, and entered into a short examination of the conduct of the United States in the dispute between the colonies and Spain; the expeditions fitted out by Miranda, Mina, &c., &c.; of the patriot privateers, &c., &c. I replied that we had done all Spain had a right to expect from us; that, determining to be neutral between the contending parties, we had taken every means necessary to preserve that neutrality. If the law of the United States had been sometimes violated with impunity, it was what occurred, and would occur in all nations, by the escape of persons who had committed offences. That all reclamations founded upon them by causes of complaint were removed by the convention, &c. Previous to this conversation I had seen in the English newspapers the President's message to Congress, of the 9th of April, headed by a sort of abstract of your correspondence with General Vives, in which it was stated that this Government had not asked explanations of me relative to the treaty, because of my intemperate conduct. I remarked to the minister that this was not the fact. Explanations were not asked of me, because, anticipating what would be required, I had given the ministry to understand that upon the subject of the dispute with the colonies I had no explanations to give, and that it was informally made known to me, before the 22d of August, that I could have the convention if I was authorized to promise that the Government of the United States would not recognize the independence of any of 'the patriot Governments. He said he had read the note I had given him, and those previously written, and that there were expressions stronger than he had ever met with in diplomatic correspondence, but he supposed they were written when I was a little warm. I questioned whether he had ever met with a similar case in the history of diplomacy, and that I was not a little warm, but indignant, at seeing the character of a great nation, and its peace, and that of my own country, put in jeopardy for the sake of and by the intrigues of selfish individuals. As the minister had not seen the message, I promised to procure and send it to him. He was not prepared to say what course would be recommended to the Cortes, upon whom everything depended. I pressed upon him the necessity of doing what was done promptly. He was satisfied of the importance of doing so, and promised to let me know the determination of the ministry as soon as it was made. At parting, he referred to the assistance received from Spain during our revolutionary war, which he said we ought not to forget. The reply was, we never forget when you permit us to remember it. I met the Secretary of State at dinner on the same day, at the English ambassador's. He told me he had received that morning from General Vives despatches, the President's message, and the correspondence sent with it to Congress. He had not yet had time to read them attentively, but appeared to be pleased with what he had seen in glancing over the papers. On the 4th of July, Mr. de Castro dined at my house, and brought with him a copy of the message and correspondence, which he left with me, to be returned, as he had but the one copy. On the 6th, the Cortes was installed; Espiga chosen President, a priest, but one of the most liberal; and Quiroga Vice President. I was in the tribune prepared for the diplomatic corps during the votation, and went from it to the office of Mr. de Castro to restore to him the documents he had loaned me. He was just going to the King, and had but a few moments to converse with me. In these few he said he thought that the President did not look beyond the ratification of the convention, the grants being set aside, and there could be no difficulty about them. It was his opinion that this should be done. I do not say, he continued, it will be done; that depends on another body; but it is my opinion that it will be. What say you, he asked; will this be satisfactory? I reminded him that I had no instructions; hoped to receive them. I could give him only an opinion in turn. Judging from the correspondence and message, I saw no sufficient reason to change the opinion already given to Mr. Jabat, that the ratification of the treaty, accompanied by satisfaction for the injury caused by the delay, would be accepted by the United States. I was present at the session of the Cortes on the 9th. The oath required by the Constitution was taken by the King, in due form, and an address made to him by the President. The King said a few words in reply, and then read his speech. Copies furnished by the Department of State are inclosed, as also copies of the answer of the Cortes prepared by a select committee appointed for that purpose. The answer to that part of the King's speech which refers to the dispute with the United States is marked by the introduction of a very emphatic word. The King says 'although the complication of various circumstances has not permitted as yet the adjustment of those differences (with the United States and Portugal) I hope that the justice and moderation of the principles which direct our diplomatic operations will produce a result decorous to the nation and agreeable to the pacific system, &c., of Europe.' The answer is, the 'Cortes only regret that there exists differences with the United States and his most faithful Majesty, but the principles of moderation that will direct now our diplomatic negotiations give hope to the Cortes that they will conclude in terms which, being a termination decorous to the nation, may not interrupt the pacific system, &c., of Europe.'

"On the 11th the Minister of State read his report to the Cortes and gave them an account of the state of the dispute with the United States. I was not present; a very imperfect account of it is published in the newspapers. I hope to procure it to send with this despatch; as also a very interesting report of the minister for the Government of the Peninsula, Augustin Arguelles."

Extract of a letter from the same to the same, marked private, July 30, 1820.

" On the 22d I wrote to Mr. de Castro, to say to him that the President would accept the treaty of 1819, subject to the advice and consent of the Senate, if immediately ratified by Spain. Had the Secretary of State been in Madrid, after what has occurred in our conversations, I should only have stated to him verbally what I had been instructed to say; but as the time of his stay at Sacedon was uncertain, I thought it better to write than to ask an interview at that place, as the latter might be imputed to an anxiety on the subject I was instructed not to discover. His answer is of the 25th, and is perfectly satisfactory. He has the commands of the King- ' to bring the business of the negotiation immediately before the Cortes, and is using all exertions to do so.' Mr. Jabat called on me the 27th to say that, in consequence of this correspondence, the King would shorten his stay at Sacedon, would come to Madrid on the 10th of August, and that the negotiation would be by the 12th before the Cortes. There is therefore every reason to hope that all will be finished by the 20th. As so little time is to elapse before I shall have it in my power to say what has been done, I write hastily, intending, immediately after the determination of the Cortes, to forward copies of the correspondence and a more formal statement of what has occurred and may occur."

Extracts of a letter from the same to the same, marked private, August 27, 1820.

"My hopes of seeing the business of the Florida treaty definitively arranged by the 20th of this month have been disappointed. The King did not come from Sacedon until the 12th. I was taught to expect an immediate movement in our affairs, but it was not made. Early last week I had an accidental interview with one of the ministers, Mr. Jabat, who told me the necessary papers were prepared and would be before the Cortes during' the week. Yesterday morning, as nothing had been done, I called at the office of Mr. de Castro to know what was the motive for delaying to present the subject to the Cortes. Mr. de Castro imputed it entirely to the press of important matters at home. He had just sent to ask the Cortes to designate the day and hour when he could lay before'them, in the name of the King, the business of the treaty for the cession of Florida. Before I left the office the Secretary of State was informed that the Cortes would receive him immediately. At one o'clock yesterday the Cortes had a secret session, and no doubt the proper communication was made. I still refrain, therefore, from sending you copies of the previous correspondence with this Government, believing that within a few days I shall be able to give you the result of the deliberations of the National Cortes.

"With the expectation of giving you in a very short time the final resolution of this Government on the affairs of the treaty,

I am, dear sir, respectfully, your most obedient servant."

Extract of a letter from the same to the same, (No. 20,) September 21, 1820.

"In a postscript, dated July 20, to my despatch of No. 19, I had the honor to acknowledge your No. 12 of the 25th of May. On the 21st I wrote to Mr. de Castro, who was at Sacedon with the King, a note, (copy marked No. 1.) His answer, (copy marked No. 2,) dated the 25th, was received on the 26th of July. On the 27th I had a visit from Mr. Jabat, who called by the desire of Mr. de Castro. Mr. Jabat informed me that the King would shorten his stay at Sacedon; would be in Madrid on the 10th of August; that all the documents relating to the treaty of cession and the late correspondence would be presented by the 12th to the Cortes, and he hoped all would be despatched before the 20th. For the reasons explained in my private letter of the 27th of August, the necessary communication was not made to the Cortes until the 26th. The subject was referred to the Political Commission, who have not yet given to the Cortes the result of their examination of it. Mr. de Castro has uniformly assured me of his anxiety to have an immediate decision. He solicited a speedy decision when he presented the papers to the Cortes. Although I look daily for further information of the movements of 'that body, I am without the means to know certainly when they will be made."

Mr. Forsyth to Don Evaristo Perez de Castro, Secretary of the Despatch of State, &c.

MADRID, *July 21, 1820.*

SIR: In the several conversations I have had with your excellency on the relations of our respective Governments, arising from the convention of 1819, I have expressed my conviction that, notwithstanding what has occurred, a prompt ratification of that instrument by Spain, accompanied by satisfaction for the injuries sustained by the United States, in consequence of its being heretofore withheld, would be accepted by my Government. I have now the instructions of the President, and am authorized to assure you that the immediate ratification by Spain of the convention of February, 1819, will be accepted by the President, subject to the advice and consent of the Senate of the United States.

Relying implicitly upon the assurances received, of the desire of this Government to terminate at once, and in the most amicable manner, the dispute with the United States, I with pleasure avoid the unpleasant task of remarking upon the disagreeable occurrences connected with this subject, since my residence near the person of his Catholic Majesty, or upon the surprise and disappointment felt in the United States, on the discovery of the object of the mission of General Vives, and the limited power granted to him. Your excellency is already apprised that the Government of my country has been induced to delay acting decisively against Spain, by the extraordinary change in the Constitution of this monarchy; a revolution without example in the history of the world, the admiration of the present, as it will be of every future age. The expectation that all differences between Spain and the United States would be speedily and satisfactorily adjusted as soon as this Government was completely organized on the principles of the change which had taken place was the cause of this delay. The moment has arrived which will see this expectation realized or disappointed. His Catholic Majesty now sees in his capital the representatives of the people. The Cortes are in the full and tranquil exercise of the high and important duties confided to them by the Constitution of the Spanish monarchy. I refrain from indulging the free expression of my congratulation to the King and to the nation at the interesting events of which I have been the witness. Were I to use the only language I am accustomed to use, that which truly expresses my sentiments, my motives might be misunderstood, or I should be accused of substituting the effusions of enthusiasm for the offerings of diplomatic respect. I content myself, therefore, with the simple expression of my satisfaction at the situation in which this Government finds itself, as it affords the opportunity of bringing to its close the long protracted negotiation with my own country. The attention of the Cortes has been already called to this subject, and they have been informed by his Majesty that their intervention will be, under the present system, necessary to its final settlement. This intervention cannot be too prompt, considering either the effect to be produced on the future relations between the two countries, or the time which has elapsed, not only since the signature of the convention, but since the expiration of the period at which the ratifications of it were by express stipulation to have been exchanged. The only questions presented for decision are of a character that demand but little consideration. The principles which must regulate this decision are so well known as scarcely to admit a difference of opinion respecting them.

What are the obligations imposed upon Spain by the signature of the treaty and the subsequent failure to ratify it? The obligation to ratify is the inevitable result of the formation of a treaty, and can only be avoided by showing what in this case has never been asserted, that the negotiator who signed it stipulated in the name of his Government what he was not authorized to stipulate. Upon the principles universally recognized by the law of nations, it is beyond dispute that the faith of the nation, once pledged by its monarch having competent power, no change in the internal Government can release it.

The promise of the King once given to a foreign Government, no subsequent engagement with his own subjects or with other nations can impair its strength. If these principles are true, the obligations consequent upon the failure to ratify are unquestionable. The first of these is the prompt ratification of the instrument; the second, an explanation of the causes justifying the *postponement* to this time of the ratification, or an atonement for the injuries resulting from it. In urging an immediate decision, I am specially instructed to add, that it is not the intention of the President to avail himself of the incidents of this negotiation, and of the principles of the laws of nations applicable to them, to fasten a hard and unequal bargain upon Spain. He has always considered and still views the treaty as highly advantageous to Spain, and would not now desire its ratification if, in the *just* and reasonable estimation of Spain herself, it could be viewed in any other light.

The causes which have heretofore delayed this ratification here present themselves for examination; but for the reason already indicated, and from a desire to avoid all unpleasant and useless recollections, I shall not dwell upon them; it is enough that, however satisfactory they may have been made to appear to his Catholic Majesty, they do not justify, in the eyes of the United States, the course that has been pursued. But even these causes, so far as the judgment of his Majesty's minister in the United States can be relied upon, no longer present obstacles to the immediate and final decision of this affair. But, while the Government of the United States is far from considering the delay which has taken place as justifiable, I am not instructed by the President to insist upon or even to ask satisfaction for the injuries occasioned by it. That this satisfaction has not been claimed by the United States is to be imputed not to any doubt of their right to demand, or of the obligation of Spain to afford it, but has sprung from the desire to manifest more clearly the principles of forbearance and moderation that have governed their march in this negotiation.

That it is not asked now arises from sentiments towards the Spanish nation no one more truly than your excellency can understand and appreciate.

What follows will, I trust, be found to be altogether unnecessary; nevertheless, it is incumbent upon me to say to your excellency that if the determination of Spain to ratify the convention of February, 1819, is not immediate, the claim to further satisfaction will be no longer waived; that upon any future adjustment the United States will insist upon an indemnity; that an additional provision will be indispensable for the existing claims of their citizens upon the Spanish Government; and that the right of the United States to the western boundary of the Rio del Norte will be re-asserted and never again relinquished.

I renew to your excellency, whom may God preserve, the assurances of my perfect respect.

JOHN FORSYTH.

His Excellency Don Evaristo Perez de Castro,
　　Secretary of the Despatch of State, &c., &c.

Extract of a letter from Mr. Forsyth to Mr. Adams, marked private, September 21, 1820.

"Apprehensive that the decision of the Cortes on the business of Florida will not be made in time to enable me to give you notice of it before the meeting of Congress, I have thought it prudent to forward to you my despatch of this day's date. You will see the grounds I had for believing that a speedy decision would be made, and that the decision would be what was desired by the President. Although the delay is apparently without motive, I have no reason to doubt that the decision, when made, will be what we have a right to expect. I saw Martinez de la Rosa, appointed to the political commission in place of Count Toreno, who was elected President of the Cortes, three days since. He told me the Secretary of State had pressed them to make an early determination, and that the report of the commission would be soon prepared. He acknowledged at the same time that he did not know the state of the business. Mr. de Castro, on Tuesday, expressed the greatest anxiety to have the affair arranged before the meeting of Congress; had directed General Vives to give you every assurance of the wish of the Government to satisfy us. It is true that the change in the head of the political commission accounts for a portion of this delay, and that the Cortes have been occupied by the consideration of questions apparently more pressing, as they related to the affairs of the Peninsula and were connected with the public tranquillity; still, however, there has been ample time for the adjustment of this business.

"Mr. Onis has published a memoir on the negotiation between the United States and Spain, with a statistical notice of our country; a work that does little credit to his penetration or candor. He accuses us of ambition and avarice, and yet endeavors to show that the treaty of cession of Florida ought to be considered as a treaty of exchange of Florida for Texas—a country more extensive, fertile, and valuable. I send you an extract from that part of the work which relates to the correspondence on the subject of the grants after the treaty was signed. In another part of the work he imputes the refusal to ratify prior to August, 1819, to a belief that England would make use of the cession of Florida to us as a pretext to seize the island of Cuba, and to a belief that we would occupy the territory by force, and by this means secure the donations to Alagon, Punon-Rostro, and Vargas."

Don Evaristo Perez de Castro to Mr. Forsyth.

[Translation.]

Sir: I have lost no time in laying before the King, my august master, the contents of your excellency's note of the 22d instant. His Majesty has received with the greatest interest and satisfaction the information contained in the communication which you were pleased to make to me concerning the instructions which you had received from your Government, and which are conformable to what has been communicated by the minister of Spain at Washington. You may be firmly persuaded that the desires of this cabinet to see a prompt termination of the business left pending by the non-ratification of the treaty of February, 1819, on the part of the King, are as lively and sincere as its will is decided; and it is full of hope that the decision of this subject will be satisfactory for both States, and apt to be found upon unalterable bases, the friendship which his Majesty is desirous of preserving with the United States.

It being indispensable to hear the Cortes of the Kingdom before the King, my master, can take the final step which the President desires, and with which his Majesty flatters himself to see the present dispute happily terminated, he has been pleased to command me to put this business in a state of being presented to the National Congress so speedily as that it may experience no more delay than may be absolutely indispensable to accomplish it. I have received this order with singular pleasure, as being so agreeable to my personal sentiments; and overcoming, by dint of activity, every impediment which might oppose the desired ready despatch of this important subject through my recent entrance into this ministry and the imperious necessity of my informing myself of its former and present state. I have the honor to assure you that I hasten, and, if I may be allowed the expression, count the moments, to present myself before the Cortes with this business; it being by solicitude to give every activity to its resolution and not to delay an instant the desired conclusion of the whole. In the mean time his Majesty has seen with satisfaction the sentiments which animate the President of the United States, an estimable proof that he has confidence in those of the King, my august master, and in the punctuality and good faith of the nation happily regenerated by the new institutions, which cannot fail to designate in the acts of the Government that firm and loyal march of which the noble Spanish character and the wisdom of their representatives are the guarantees.

I avail myself of this occasion to reiterate to you the demonstrations of my great consideration; and I pray God to preserve you many years.

                    Your most obedient servant,

                                                    EVARISTO PEREZ DE CASTRO.

SACEDON, July 25, 1820.

Mr. Forsyth to Mr. Adams, marked private, October 5, 1820.

DEAR SIR: Three days since the political commission made a report to the Cortes, and this day, in secret session, that body advised the King to cede the Floridas to the United States. They have also declared null and void the cessions of land to Alagon, &c., although the treaty of February, 1819, should not be ratified. I presume I shall receive from the Minister of State early information of the King's ratification of the treaty.

I am, dear sir, sincerely and respectfully, your obedient servant,

                                                    JOHN FORSYTH.

JOHN QUINCY ADAMS, *Secretary of State.*

Mr. Forsyth to Mr. Adams, (No. 21,) dated Madrid, October 11, 1820.

SIR: On the 5th I had the honor to inform you that the Cortes had authorized the King to cede the Floridas to the United States, according to the convention of February 22, 1819. On the 6th I received from Mr. de Castro an official notice of the determination of the Cortes, and a request to be informed of the wishes of the American Government in regard to the 8th article, as I supposed, with a view to have the ratification of the King in such terms as to prevent the necessity of anything but the mere delivery of the treaty at Washington, when the ratifications are to be exchanged. A copy of his note is inclosed, marked No. 1. I replied on the 7th; a copy of my answer is marked No. 2. This answer I carried with me to the palace, it being court day. In the Secretary of State's office I received a message from Mr. de Castro, who was confined to his bed at home, requesting me to visit him. I went immediately, and carried with me my answer to his note. As he reads English with difficulty, he opened, but did not read it. His object appeared to be to ascertain if I was authorized to make any stipulations about the 8th article of the treaty; or if there was a probability of obtaining any stipulations in Washington, favorable to Spanish claimants, for injuries suffered from the United States. He said the Cortes had given the King authority to execute the treaty and to set aside the grants of Alagon and Punon-Rostro; that of Vargas was out of the question, being subsequent to the 24th of January, 1818. He spoke of the cession of Vargas as a fund for the payment of American claims on Spain; said the treaty was clearly in favor of Alagon and Punon-Rostro. The 24th of January was not assumed as an arbitrary date, but fixed upon on principle, by Mr. Onis, who, in his letter to Mr. Adams of the 10th of March, stated, after acknowledging he believed them to be posterior to the 24th of January, that he would have insisted on their being admitted as valid had he known them to be anterior. Mr. de Castro had no desire to procure anything for such people as Alagon and Punon-Rostro, but thought it equitable that the United States should set apart a portion of this fund, increased by Spain's abandoning the literal import of the treaty, for the benefit of Spanish subjects. To all this I answered what was contained in my letter: I had no authority to make any stipulations. So far as regarded the Government of the United States, the question was considered as settled. I begged him not to think of asking anything at Washington; it could not be granted; might do injury; could not produce any good result. I reminded him that the offer made in October, 1819, to the Duke of San Fernando and Quiroga, the admission of the American declaration against the grant, was a condition upon which alone the ratification of the treaty by Spain could be admitted; and also of the declaration of General Vives, that upon the subject of the grants he was satisfied with the explanations given to, and received from, Mr. Adams, at Washington; and that these donations were never insurmountable obstacles to the ratification of the treaty on the part of Spain. He replied that this admission was on the supposition that the other explanations would be satisfactory. Satisfaction not having been received on the last and most important, the others might again be brought into view. He talked of the guaranty offered by Mr. Pinckney; of there being no provision in the treaty for Spanish claimants, as there was in that of 1802, and how desirable it would be if something could be procured for them on the adjustment of this difficulty in the convention, an adjustment in which Spain gave up what was clearly secured to some of her subjects. I remarked to him that the offer made by the instructions of the President, in July last, was made on the admission of General Vives that there would be no demur respecting the grants. If these were brought again into question, my Government was not bound by the offer then made. He said it appeared somewhat unequitable and hard to insist upon the alteration or modification of the treaty without any equivalent. To this I answered, that all he had urged might have been plausible if urged before the 22d of August, 1819, but after the delays which had occurred and the incidents of the negotiation, we thought we exercised a degree of unexampled moderation, agreeing to take the ratification on the terms originally agreed upon and understood between the two negotiators. We had some conversation on the mode of ratification by the King, to obviate all difficulty at Washington. I stated to him that this, of course, was a matter in which we would do whatever was agreeable to the Spanish Government. The American declaration of the force of the 8th article might be received by Spain; a declaration might be made by the King, declaring the sense in which his Majesty understood it, or a joint declaration might be made. He proposed seeing me again on the following day, at twelve, in company with a confidential person, at the office, if he was able to go out, or in his room, if he was not; to which I consented. At parting, I pointed out to him in the published documents relating to the treaty, which I carried for the purpose, the declaration I was directed to present by my first instructions; the instructions relating to it; the subsequent instructions modified, which came to me by the Hornet; and my offer to the Duke of San Fernando and Quiroga, made in conformity with them. He said he would examine the papers; sketch something to show me in our next interview; would despatch everything with the greatest possible expedition, and send off a messenger to Washington.

On the 8th I saw him again, at his house, at twelve. He had with him the elder Heredia. The conversation was a repetition of that of yesterday. The only new idea expressed was, that it was important to the new Government to gain credit by procuring some advantage in arranging the business of the treaty, and a suggestion that Mr. Onis would not have made the treaty in any terms but those in which the 8th article is expressed. To the first I replied that the new Government would deserve and receive all praise for saving the country from the consequences of the impolitic steps of the old, and preserve the honor of the nation by abandoning pretensions which injured its character. To the last, that this suggestion was altogether at variance with the declaration of Mr. Pizarro, with Mr. Onis' expressed willingness to give up the donations, and to the remark made to me by Mr. Casa Yrujo, "that he regretted that the grants had not been executed by name." Heredia urged, in the conversation, that the United States had in the treaty admitted it to be necessary to the King's honor that the grants prior to the 24th January, 1818, should be preserved. This conclusion I positively denied: In allowing Mr. Onis to shape the 8th article, we did not become parties to the correctness or propriety of his opinions; on the contrary, in our opinion, the honor of the King was concerned to make void all donations made subsequent to the date of his full power to his negotiator to cede the Floridas. The conversation concluded by a formal request from Mr. de Castro to know what my impressions were on this point, and whether they could calculate on my good offices with my Government to procure some advantage to Spain, in consideration of its desire to gratify us in this business, and of the similarity of the institutions of the two Governments. I gave him my thoughts without reserve, "that the ground which must be taken was altogether untenable; that it would injure, could not benefit the Spanish Government; that the United States would receive any intimation on this point with surprise and regret. As for myself, with the strongest desire to do everything to gratify this Government, I could not say anything to my own in favor of pretensions I believed to be altogether unreasonable." Mr. de Castro said that, in presenting the subject, it would be done in such a way as to prevent any bad effect; turning to Heredia, he remarked that it must be attempted at Washington. He concluded by saying that he should pass to me a note embodying what had been urged in our conversation, which he hoped I would answer in the shortest convenient time, as he was anxious to send off a messenger to the United States. This I promised, stating to him, at the same time, the necessity of despatching his messenger at the earliest hour possible, as Congress would be in session before he could possibly arrive.

On recollection, I find I have omitted a remark made by both Heredia and de Castro, that, according to my first instructions, as contained in the printed documents, I was authorized to exchange the ratifications without insisting upon the declaration of the import of the 8th article being received, that this exchange would have secured the claimants the large grants which they might have recovered in the courts of the United States. To this I answered that such were my instructions; but they were founded upon the belief that the notice given to the Spanish Government, through Mr. Onis, rendered the declaration unimportant. That, certainly, if the treaty had been ratified by Spain, the question of the grants would have become a judicial, in place of a political one. But supposing, what I could not admit, that the tribunals of the United States could have decided in favor of the claimants, this decision would have been the foundation of a demand on Spain for an equivalent, or satisfaction. This conversation endured two hours. In this, as well as in that of the 7th, I am unable to give anything but the substance, without regarding the order of what was said. My impressions are, that, after making all exertions to obtain some advantage, and failing, they will proceed on the business as they ought to have done without having made any exertion. What is most unpleasant is, to perceive that the opinions of Mr. Onis, as expressed in his book, have weight with this Government, and that what is done is rather a sacrifice to policy than founded on a conviction of the justice and equity of our demands, or on a proper sense of our moderation and forbearance.

Late at night, on the 9th, I received Mr. de Castro's letter of that day's date, the copy of which is marked No. 3, to which I replied on the day succeeding. The copy of the answer is marked No. 4. This reference to the affair of the grants is disagreeable, and will be altogether unexpected. After what has occurred, I cannot suppose the Spanish ministry can hope to succeed in procuring anything more at our hands. Perhaps the sole object is, to enhance the value of the ratification on their part. I am endeavoring to procure accurate information of all that occurred in the Cortes. My private letter of the 5th is almost a literal translation of a note from one of the deputies; and I have been since informed that the Cortes would not hear a petition from Punon Rostro in relation to his claim, considering the whole affair at an end by their previous decision on the treaty.

Shortly after the publication of Mr. Onis' book, I conceived that some of its statements were so injurious to us as to require examination, and proposed to publish a review of it, to be distributed among the members of the Cortes. The affair of the treaty came so soon under the consideration of that body, after I procured a copy of the book, that it was impossible to do more than to make a few hasty remarks upon it, and to have distributed five or six copies of a translation of them among the principal members. A copy of this translation is sent to you, marked No. 5. No. 6 is the copy of an original paper received from _____ _____, an extract from which, in cypher, was forwarded to you some time ago.

The Cortes have resolved, according to the constitutional provision, to continue their session until November.

At night.—At five this afternoon I received Mr. de Castro's letter, of this day's date, which I answered immediately. The copies of the letter and answer are marked Nos. 7 and 8.

This last letter confirms the conjecture I have made, that the object is to enhance the value of what will be called the concession of Spain to the American construction of the 8th article of the treaty. I regret extremely that anything has been said by the ministers of this Government on this topic, as it will have the effect of weakening, in some degree, the confidence, not so much as the uprightness of their intentions, as in the frankness of their mode of proceeding. No doubt something will be said by General Vives on this point, or at least he will formally communicate the letter of Mr. de Castro of the 9th. I shall send triplicates of this communication, one by Bordeaux, one by Gibraltar, and one by the Spanish courier who carries the ratified treaty to the Spanish minister at Washington.

As soon as he is fairly out of Madrid, I shall think of using the permission of the President to return to the United States. Before I leave this, however, I shall have occasion to write to you again.

I am, sir, very respectfully, your humble servant,

JOHN FORSYTH.

JOHN Q. ADAMS, *Secretary of State.*

Mr. de Castro, Minister of Foreign Despatch, to Mr. Forsyth, Minister Plenipotentiary of the United States of America at Madrid, (October 6, 1820.)

[Translation.]

SIR: I have the honor to acquaint your excellency that the Cortes of the nation, in secret session, have authorized his Majesty's Government to ratify the cession of the territory situated east of the Mississippi, which is known by the name of East and West Florida, to the United States, and that consequently there is no inconvenience in proceeding, on the part of the King, to the ratification of the treaty concluded at Washington on the 22d day of February, 1819.

His Majesty would have immediately proceeded to command the ratification of the treaty to be extended, had it not been for the interference of the circumstance that your excellency's Government, after confirming and ratifying, on its part, the said instrument, as the plenipotentiaries duly authorized by the high contracting parties had extended it, manifested its desire to have some explanations or modifications in the text of the 8th article, which relates to the property of certain unoccupied and royal lands in both Floridas. This incident, or proposal of modification made by the Government of the United States, which has contributed in a great part to the delay and difficulties which have occurred, might have rendered improper, at that time, and an event little agreeable to the American Government, a ratification extended in the usual form, which, relapsing upon the said instrument, with all and each of its clauses and articles, would consequently embrace those of the 8th article, referred to in the form in which it had been conceived. This being the case, and his Majesty being desirous, conformably to the intention of the Cortes, that the ratification of the treaty should terminate at once all the differences which have for so many years existed between two Governments whose interest, in a reciprocal good understanding, had been increased by the nature of their political institutions, has thought it necessary that, for extending the ratification, an explanation should precede, limited and circumscribed to the point of the modifications which your excellency's Government requires to be in the text of the 8th article, since all the other articles present no difficulty, nor need any further explanation in order to be ratified on the part of his Majesty, according to their literal tenor. Your excellency's Government has indicated a desire of having a modification in the context of said article; and as for determining what ought to be, and what is, agreeable to the interest of both countries, it may be necessary to proceed, by common consent, I am desirous of knowing if your excellency is authorized to point out the modification and explanation, as I also am by his Majesty, for the same purpose. If your excellency be so, we might, in a very few days, have this point settled in a manner reciprocally satisfactory; and in case of your not being so, I could desire at least that we had a conference for the purpose of agreeing on the means by which this only obstacle may be removed, which might present itself to the exchange of the ratifications in Washington, if it should be remitted by his Majesty, extended in the usual form, embracing all and each of the clauses of the 16 articles of the treaty confirmed at Washington on the 22d of February of the past year, 1819.

I therefore renew to your excellency the assurances of my distinguished esteem, and pray God that you may live many years.

I am, your excellency's most obedient faithful servant,

EVARISTO PEREZ DE CASTRO.

At the PALACE, *October 6, 1820.*

Mr. Forsyth to Mr. de Castro, dated Madrid, October 7, 1820.

SIR: I had the honor to receive yesterday your excellency's officio, announcing to me that the Cortes had authorized the Government of his Majesty to ratify the cession of the Floridas to the United States. In reply to the inquiry contained in it, I must refer your excellency to my letter of the 21st of July, in which I stated, by the instructions of the President, that under the Constitution of the United States it would be necessary that the advice and consent of the Senate should again be given before the exchange of ratifications of the treaty of the 22d February, 1819, could take place, inasmuch as the six months within which it should have been made had expired. I am not, therefore, authorized to do more than has already been done. Perfectly possessed, however, of the opinions and wishes of my Government in relation to the 8th article of the treaty, I can give your excellency all the information that can be desired to prevent the possibility of any difficulty in the exchange of ratifications at Washington. In my official communication of the 2d of October, 1819, to the Duke of San Fernando and Quiroga, accompanied by the copy of a declaration to be delivered on the exchange of ratifications, should it be made, your excellency will probably find all that it may be important to know. If these should not be sufficient, it will give me pleasure to confer with your excellency at any hour it may be convenient for you to appoint. In expressing to your excellency the very great satisfaction I have received from the near prospect of a most friendly termination of the disputes which have so long unhappily agitated our respective Governments, I must take leave to add that the United States have never desired to change or modify any part of the treaty of 1819. Their sole object has been, and still is, to have it ratified upon the well known terms, and according to the acknowledged intentions, of the respective negotiators of it.

I renew to your excellency, whom may God preserve, the assurances of my most respectful consideration.

JOHN FORSYTH.

His Excellency Don Perez de Castro,
       Secretary of the Despatch of State, &c., &c., &c.

[Translation.]

M. de Castro, Minister of Foreign Despatch, to Mr. Forsyth, Minister Plenipotentiary of the United States of America, dated at

Madrid, *October* 9, 1820.

Sir: On the 6th current I had the honor to communicate to your excellency that the Cortes had authorized his Majesty's Government to cede the Floridas to the United States; and that, in consequence of that act, no other obstacle presented itself against proceeding, on the part of the King, to the ratification of the treaty confirmed at Washington, the 22d February, 1819, except that which arose from the modification or explanation of the 8th article of the same treaty, solicited by the American Government after the confirmation, and even the ratification on its part, of the said agreement; adding that, if your excellency were authorized, we could proceed to make the desired explanation with regard to the object of said 8th article in terms agreeable to the interest of both countries, that we could terminate this business very soon, and that, by all means, I was desirous of a conference between us, in order to the removal of this only obstacle which could oppose the exchange of the ratifications in Washington. Your excellency has had the goodness to reply to me, dated the 7th, complimenting me on the proximity of an order that went to terminate the differences that had existed for so long a time between the two Governments, but manifesting to me at the same time, that, in consequence of the period fixed for the ratification of the treaty by that instrument having been overrun, it ought again to be presented to the Senate of the United States, agreeably to the Constitution; by which circumstance your excellency had not powers to act in the negotiation further than you had done, although, being perfectly instructed in the intentions of your Government upon the said article of the treaty, you could furnish me with the necessary dates in regard to them in the conference which we might have, and which we actually had on that day.

Both yesterday and before, I had the honor to point out to your excellency the difficulties which opposed the explanation or modification demanded by the American Government of the context of the 8th article, since, according to the literal and very explicit tenor of it, every donation or grant of lands in the Floridas made by authority of his Majesty prior to the 24th January, 1818, was declared valid or firm at the same time that every grant made after the said 24th of January was annulled. It appeared, at the same time, that the determining of that date was not a casual occurrence, unpremeditated and directed solely to mark one day or epoch. Since then nothing could have been more obvious and natural than to have designated the first day of the same month of January, 1818, which was the beginning of the year; and it was distinctly considered that the intention of the plenipotentiaries was to establish a principle legal and justly expressed in the text of the same article, in continuance from the date which it was to give for a foundation, that his Majesty's plenipotentiaries on that day solemnly offered the cession of the Floridas to the United States, in order to denote that it was then, and not before, when his Majesty, by said offer, tied up his hands from making innovations in those Territories, and when, by the same offer, the indisputable right which, without that, enabled him to dispose the absolute property of any lands belonging to his crown was suspended. The tenor of this article was already not only admitted and confirmed by the plenipotentiaries, but also ratified by the American Government, jointly with all the other articles which the treaty embraced, when the Secretary of State, Mr. Adams, thought fit to ask of Mr. Onis an explanation about the grants of land made by his Majesty at the end of the year 1817, the validity of which appeared to have been recognized by the letter of the treaty, they being anterior to the 24th January, 1818, and upon which both plenipotentiaries were supposed to have proceeded with a certain equivocation of the fact, having believed them posterior to the epoch mentioned. Mr. Onis, notwithstanding that all his functions and powers upon the subject had expired with the conclusion and confirmation of the treaty, did not refuse to give a firm proof of the good faith of his Government, and of his own, by frankly confessing that, in fact, he had understood that the grants of land referred to were posterior to the 24th January, 1818; but added, at the same time, a circumstance worthy of notice and perfectly conformable to the tenor of the 8th article, and it was, that, as the fixing of that epoch had been founded upon the principle that the 24th of January, and not before, was the day on which, by means of the solemn offer of the Floridas, the indisputable power which his Majesty before had of disposing of those lands remained suspended, if he had known that all or any of said grants was anterior to the 24th of January he would have insisted upon the acknowledgment of such as were so, and would not have consented to their being annulled. Taking the first part of this declaration of Mr. Onis as a foundation, and feigning ignorance of the second, the American Government solicited, by means of your excellency, at this court, that, to the ratification of the treaty on the part of his Majesty, an explanation should be added, which was fundamentally a real revocation of the literal context of the 8th article. The scrupulous good faith of his Majesty's Government restrained it from entering upon a question about what wrong the equivocation or, to speak more properly, the want of exact knowledge of a fact authentic, solemn, and of more than a year's notoriety and publicity in a supreme council and chancery of the nation, could do to one who had had the means and, in a certain degree, the necessity of being informed of it with evidence; but two essential points did not cease to call the attention of his Majesty: 1st. That, if any equivocation could have happened about the date of the grants, in order to their being a pure deed, it never could have been, nor was it in the recognition of the principle which served as a basis and was the real foundation of the 8th article, that is, that the Spanish Government did not consider itself bound, nor did the American Government consider it bound, in the use of its right as absolute lord of the lands of Florida, unless by means of the offer made on the 24th of January, 1818, and only from that epoch. That an essential equivocation could have been in this date, it was necessary to prove that it was not that of the said solemn offer, since that was the module or symbol to which all the dates of the grants ought to be adjusted, and with which they ought to be compared, in order to decide upon their validity or nullity, and not to pretend, as had been pretended, to accommodate it to the others by altering that date inversely. 2d. That if the American Government availed itself of, and founded its desires of an explanation upon, the former part of Mr. Onis' declaration which in any way favored it, neither could it, in honor and good faith, reject the second part of that declaration, to constitute the whole one self-same act and a single document. If Mr. Onis confessed the equivocation about the date of the grants, he also confessed that he would not have, for his part, subscribed to annul that which had taken place anterior to the 24th of January. What will be inferred, then, in reality and sound logic, from that declaration, taken conjointly? Will it be an accident which had expressed the real or, at least, the intentional connivance of both the plenipotentiaries concerning the annulling of the grants referred to which were anterior to the 24th of January, as the American Government pretends. An interpretation like this is diametrically opposite, not only to the second part of the declaration of Mr. Onis, but even to the legal principle established in the same 8th article. All that can be inferred, at most, was, and is, that the error into which both parties had run about the substance of the 8th article had rendered it null, invalid, and baseless; and that it was necessary to remodel it and agree upon something to the point by a new mutual agreement, and not by the way of a declaration or explanation which its context did not admit.

The question accidentally presented in this humble view would not have been offered, nor given an opportunity for the many difficulties which have occurred. The grants made to Don Pedro de Vargas could have been immediately separated, and, as being posterior to the 24th January, 1818, might have been declared the property of the United States, according to the letter and spirit of the article; and with regard to the other two, anterior to the said day, upon which grants the equivocation had relapsed, the liberal medium might have been adopted, which is generally used in doubtful cases, by yielding to each one a part of his claims, in compliance with a good understanding. But as this was not solicited by your excellency, and if the text of the 8th article, whose letter and the principle which supported it favored Spain, might yet receive an interpretation diametrically opposite to the said letter, being founded for that purpose on a declaration of Mr. Onis, the second part of which evidently resisted a similar interpretation, difficulties seemed easily to arise from hence, which, with more or less foundation, might be likewise converted into suspicions concerning the stability of the other articles of the treaty, on seeing the readiness with which doubts had arisen also concerning one, the literal tenor of which seemed less ambiguous. This disposition of the thoughts brought to recollection the offer of a guarantee of the Spanish possessions in North America, made by his excellency Mr. Pinckney on the 7th of February, 1802, in the name of the United States, in case the Spanish Government would consent to cede the Floridas to the United States for a sum to be stipulated—a guarantee which was not asked by the Government of Spain, and yet offered in the name of that of the United States, but to which my Government gave so much importance that, if his offer had been renewed, it would have ceded, in compensation, any right over the grants of land which remained by the 8th article of the treaty. From these principles flowed, no doubt, the new mission of General Vives to the United States, and all the other incidents of which your excellency is informed.

The changes which happened a little afterwards in the Government of Spain, and the re-union of the national representation, have been the cause that the Government of his Majesty, complying with the provision of the Constitution of the State, should offer to the consideration of the Cortes all that has occurred in this long and complicated negotiation, for the purpose of obtaining their consent, as well as that the dismemberment of the Spanish territory in America might be discussed. It must have been a sensible grief to the representatives of the nation, in the first steps of their august functions, to be obliged to authorize a dismemberment of the territory. They have been solely guided by the consideration that this sacrifice may be conducive to cement, upon a solid basis, the relations of friendship and harmony between Spain and the United States, by avoiding the causes of future discords, and establishing a fixed and permanent dividing line, which prevents all ambiguity and indecision for the future. Besides the reciprocal interests which ought always to unite the Governments of both countries, the great analogy which now actually exists between their political institutions, after the change that has occurred in those of Spain, appears to have given greater weight to that interest, and to have increased the importance of a good understanding. These, at least, are the dispositions which have produced the resolution I have mentioned, of the representatives of the Spanish nation. May they be answered with similar and reciprocal dispositions on the part of the Government and people of the United States for the well-being of both nations! But at the same time that the Cortes and his Majesty's Government have rendered easy even the most serious difficulty which the subject could present, they could not but direct their attentions to the reflections made known to your excellency, which have been expressed above, on the explanation which the American Government desired to give to the 8th article diametrically opposite to its literal tenor, and to the principle or rule which is established in the same article. The Spanish Government does not pretend that it may not be firm and be executed as it is printed; its delicacy does not permit it to pretend ignorance of the equivocation committed, which the declaration of Mr. Onis lays open sufficiently in its first part; but this equivocation does not destroy the principle which serves as the basis for the formation of the article, to which the second part of the declaration of the same Mr. Onis is evidently referred. It cannot be agreeable to the honor and the good faith of the American Government to take advantage of that part of the declaration of the said minister, or of any act or instrument which it may find useful, in order to tie it down and quote it in its favor, and to pretend not to understand that which does not favor it in the same instrument. No impartial person who examines the 8th article, and the declarations of Mr. Adams and Mr. Onis, will see in the whole of it anything else but that, by the involuntary error which has intervened, there has not been a real contract or agreement upon the point of the waste lands; and that, if there is anything existing in the article, it is the rule or principle of leaving untouched what the King did when his hands were not bound by means of the offer of the 24th of January, 1818.

In this case, then, it appears that harmony, the desire of peace, the honor of both Governments, and the necessity of repairing an equivocation that had passed their plenipotentiaries, dictate that middle path which is proper in doubtful cases and questions of this nature. The grants made to Don Pedro de Vargas may remain immediately in favor of the United States, because inasmuch as they are posterior to the 24th of January, 1818, they are excluded by the letter and by the spirit of the 8th article; and those, respectively, to Alagon and Punon Rostro, which, as anterior to the 24th of January, 1818, constitute the real point of the doubt, may be divided by equal parts, or by the mode which may be agreed upon by the Spanish and American Governments. His Majesty, agreeably to the intention of the Cortes, is desirous of being able to make a better exchange of property by applying one part of this fund to the redress and indemnification of the Spaniards injured and comprehended in the agreement of 1802, whose indemnification was at the charge of the American Government even whilst the treaty was not ratified, and whose lot was entirely unattended to by the plenipotentiaries of 1819. The American Government and Congress, so jealous of the interests of their fellow-citizens, can do no less than applaud these correct intentions of the King and the representatives of the Spanish people towards their own people. On the other hand, it would appear very indecorous that the Cortes, in the commencement of their august functions, should not only have to authorize the dismemberment of the territory, but also to assent that a doubtful act, which was in favor of Spain, (the letter of the article and the foundation on which it is supported,) should be explained in a sense diametrically opposite to its tenor, and that upon the basis of a declaration of the Spanish minister, truncated and disregarded in its second part.

If the means hinted had not been thought admissible, there still remained another, equally conformable to the spirit and to the letter of the treaty. All the waste lands of the Floridas, including the three grants of Vargas, Alagon, and Punon Rostro, may be valued according to the prices of lands of their class in the bordering territories of the United States; the amount of five millions of dollars may be deducted from their value, in which the same treaty adjusts, and with which the American Government obliges itself to satisfy the amount of the claims; and the surplus may be declared to belong to Spain, because it can liquidate the indemnifications of its subjects, for which the United States are responsible, by the agreement of 1802, which continues in force whilst the treaty is not ratified. It may be objected that the claims exceed the sum agreed upon; but it ought also to be considered that, even to this day, an examination and liquidation of such claims has not taken place; and that, if the agreement of 1802, and the mixed tribunal established by it, had been carried into effect, perhaps the claims admitted and approved of by the mixed Spanish and American tribunal might not have amounted to said sum, especially if the fifth commissary chosen by lot had been of the nation which was bound to pay them; so that, on the whole, five millions of dollars being the sum which the treaty fixes, and there having been, even to this day, no examination or liquidation of individual claims, this sum, and no other, is that which legally represents the amount of said indemnifications.

Such have been the reflections and observations which I have had the honor of making to your excellency in our two conferences, by order of his Majesty, in regard to the intentions of the Cortes. By these, and by all besides, which I have had the honor to point out by word, your excellency will have come to the knowledge of his Majesty's resolution to terminate entirely the subjects pending, by means of a prompt exchange of the ratifications of the treaty. I have been very sensible that your excellency has not been authorized to agree to the explanation which the 8th article requires, but I am assured of the candor, good faith, and spirit of conciliation which animate your excellency, that you will present to your Government the observations referred to, in regard to the only point upon which an explanation is desired by both parties, that at, the time of Gen. Vives' presenting the ratification of the treaty on the part of his Majesty's Government, which it is about to send, an explanation may be presented and submitted, of the sense of the 8th article, in the terms of equity and reciprocal satisfaction which I have hinted, or others equivalent, such as the good faith and the honor of both Governments dictate. The King and the representatives of the Spanish nation see, in this honorable and impartial explanation, the beginning of a new order of political relations, which, by tightening the bonds of friendship between both nations, present the most secure guaranty of their union and prosperity in future.

I renew to your excellency the assurances of my most exalted and distinguished consideration, and pray God that your excellency may live many years.

Your obedient humble servant,

EVARISTO PEREZ DE CASTRO.

At the PALACE, *October 9,* 1820.

Mr. Forsyth to Mr. de Castro.

MADRID, *October 10,* 1820.

SIR: I had the honor, late last night, to receive your excellency's officio of the 9th. From our two conversations, previously held, and from your letter, embodying the substance of what was suggested and urged in those conversations, I learned, with concern, that I had mistaken the object and intention of the note of the 6th instant. I supposed it intended merely to enable your excellency to determine on the most convenient mode for the ratification of the convention of February, 1819, by his Catholic Majesty, to prevent any discussion or delay preceding the exchange of the ratifications at Washington. It was with unfeigned surprise and great regret that I discovered that the object was to bring again into view what is considered by the Government of the United States as no longer a subject of discussion with that of his Majesty. In the verbal communications I have made in our two conversations, my intention was, solely, to prevent, if possible, any further attempts to discuss this matter, satisfied that no advantage could be derived from a reference to a topic of such an unpleasant character. As I have had the misfortune not to produce this desired effect, I do not think myself authorized to enter into any further investigation of the subject. I shall communicate to my Government the notes received from his Majesty, and such replies will be given to Gen. Vives as the case may require. But I cannot take leave of the subject without stating, explicitly, that the official communication made to your excellency on the 21st July was framed and bottomed upon the admission of Gen. Vives that he was satisfied with the explanations given at Washington on the subject of the 8th article of the treaty, and that it was the determination of his Government to assent to the total nullity of the large grants. If this admission was unauthorized, the offer of the President I had the honor to communicate to his Majesty, through your excellency, is not obligatory upon the United States; the whole ground of dispute is open for re-examination; and the original claims and pretensions of my Government will be re-asserted and maintained.

Although beyond my duty, I cannot forbear to remark to your excellency that a great error is committed in supposing the construction put on the 8th article by the United States is founded altogether upon the declaration given by Mr. Onis after the signature of the treaty. This construction is taken from the instrument itself, explained and elucidated, as all instruments must be, by the intention of the parties and the nature of the subject-matter of it. Mr. Onis' letter of the 10th October is no further of importance than as a simple evidence to all nations and to his Catholic Majesty of the act and intention of his minister to annul the large grants, and the express recognition by him of the correctness of the assertion of the American negotiator that the phrases supposed to be equivocal were admitted *only upon the condition* that the annulment of those grants was not affected by the use of those favorite phrases. The qualifying addition to Mr. Onis' frank declaration of what he believed and understood amounts to nothing more than an assertion that the treaty would not have been agreed to without a recognition of such of the large grants as were of a date prior to January 24, 1818, an assertion altogether at variance with the declarations of Mr. Pizarro to Mr. Erving, that these donations would not be obstacles to the treaty, contradicted by Mr. Onis' perfect readiness to annul them, and by the reasons he assigned for it, "that the essential conditions of them had not been complied with," and altogether irreconcileable to a remark made to me in person by the Marquis of Casa-Yrujo, when Minister of State *ad interim*, "that he regretted the large grants had not been particularly named in the treaty, and their annulment expressly stipulated."

From an anxious desire to see, buried in oblivion all recollections unfavorable to the perfect harmony between Spain and the United States, in closing this note I would entreat his Majesty's Government to re-examine this whole subject before it is again pressed; to reflect that all that has occurred has arisen from a reliance on the information and good faith of the minister and confidence in the purity of the Government of Spain. The Duke of San Fernando stated that the American Government wished to change the 8th article by a declaration, a copy of which I had inclosed to him. Your excellency now tells me the wish of the American Government is diametrically opposed to the literal text of the treaty, inasmuch as Alagon's and Punon Rostro's grants are of a date prior to the date fixed in the 8th article. The Duke of San Fernando refused, as inconsistent with the honor of the King, to order me copies of those donations. What would your excellency think were I to say to you, "Sir, I do not know that your assertion is true; show me the donations!" If the Duke of San Fernando and Quiroga thought his general assertion, that the declaration changed the treaty, was so full that further information could not be asked without reflecting upon his Majesty's honor, what would be the reply to a doubt of the correctness of your excellency's unqualified, deliberate, and explicit assertion? Yet, in relying upon the information and the word of Mr. Onis, the United States had the same reason to confide as they now have in the assertion made by your excellency, unless it should be supposed that there is a difference in the degree of confidence due to the representative of Spain at home and abroad. I feel, however, that I am treading upon the yet warm ashes of a previous unprofitable controversy, and exceeding the limits to which, at the outset, I proposed to confine myself.

I hasten, therefore, to assure your excellency that the United States wish nothing but what they believe to be just and equitable; what is equally honorable to Spain and to the United States; nothing inconsistent with the decorum and glory of his Catholic Majesty, or with the duties and obligations of the Cortes, by whose advice and authority the treaty of February, 1819, is to be ratified.

I renew to your excellency, whom may God preserve many years, the assurance of my perfect respect.

JOHN FORSYTH.

His Excellency Don EVARISTO PEREZ DE CASTRO, *Secretary of the Despatch of State, &c.*

Mr. de Castro, Minister of Foreign Despatch, to Mr. Forsyth, Minister Plenipotentiary of the United States of America, at Madrid, October 11, 1820.

[Translation.]

SIR: I have received your excellency's note of yesterday's date, in which you seem to agree with mine of the 9th. In said note I proposed to myself to recapitulate and send to you all the essentials of the controversies which we had on the two antecedent days, not with the view which your excellency appears to have apprehended, of commencing new discussions incompatible with the desire which animates his Majesty of seeing all the points which have been the object of the treaty speedily terminated, but with that of agreeing here with your excellency upon the proper terms of extending the explanation or declaration of the 8th article in a mode satisfactory, and such as that the exchange of the ratifications might not experience any obstacle or inconvenience at Washington.

On a view, therefore, of what your excellency had the goodness to express in the said conferences, and of what you manifested in your said note of yesterday, I confine myself to secure that which was contended for in the ratification on the part of this Government, which will be sent back to the United States in terms which will be, no doubt, satisfactory to the American Government, and which avoid the discussions which your excellency seems to fear, to ascertain that neither the tenor of our conferences nor that of my said note are intended for this object which inspires your fear.

If your excellency should please, in order to forward despatches to your Government, to avail yourself of the opportunity of a courier, who must be despatched as soon as possible, with the ratifications and packets for General Vives, you may begin to prepare them immediately, in expectation of which, I shall again give you information some hours before the departure of the courier.

I renew to your excellency the assurances of my high consideration, and pray God that you may live many years.

I am, your obedient and humble servant,

EVARISTO PEREZ DE CASTRO.

At the PALACE, *October 11, 1820.*

Mr. Forsyth to Mr. de Castro.

MADRID, *October* 11, 1820.

SIR: I have received with great satisfaction your excellency's note of this day's date. If I have misapprehended the object in our conferences and the tenor of the note of the 9th, your excellency must do me the justice to impute it to my imperfect knowledge of the Spanish language and to my anxiety to comply with your excellency's request to give an immediate [answer] to the note.

I shall with pleasure use the occasion you have offered to me of sending despatches to my Government by the Spanish courier. A messenger will go from this legation to the United States the close of the present week; should your excellency have anything to send to General Vives, it will gratify me to forward it by this opportunity.

I renew to your excellency, whom may God preserve many years, the assurance of my most distinguished consideration.

JOHN FORSYTH.

His Excellency Don EVARISTO PEREZ DE CASTRO,
    Secretary of the Despatch of State, &c.

Mr. Forsyth to Mr. Adams, marked "private."

[Extract.]

MADRID, *October* 12, 1820.

DEAR SIR: "I have this moment learned that the Cortes, in authorizing, by an almost unanimous vote, the ratification of the treaty, and annulling the donations, at the same time recommended to the ministers to *endeavor* to procure some advantages to the nation on account of the difficulty about the 8th article. With this recommendation the ministers must comply, even although they may be satisfied the effort will be useless. The attempt once made, and failing, the affair will proceed to its proper conclusion without further trouble."

I am, dear sir, very sincerely, your obedient servant,

JOHN FORSYTH.

Hon. JOHN QUINCY ADAMS, *Washington.*

Mr. Forsyth to Mr. Adams, marked "private," dated

MADRID, *October* 15, 1820.

DEAR SIR: In great haste I send you a rough copy of a note from Mr. de Castro to Count Bulgary, of this day's date. I believe the Count Bulgary has inclosed, in the accompanying letter to Mr. Poletica, a copy of the same paper.

I had on the 4th a short conversation with the Spanish minister, which served to confirm the opinion expressed in my private letter of the 12th instant.

I am, dear sir, respectfully, your obedient servant,

JOHN FORSYTH.

Hon. J. Q. ADAMS,
    Secretary of State.

The Spanish Minister to the Chargé d'Affaires of Russia.

[Translation.]

MADRID, *October* 15, 1820.

SIR: His Majesty's Government having given information to the Cortes of the nation concerning the existing differences with the United States of America, resulting from the treaty entered into between Spain and that power on the 22d of February, 1819, and not ratified by the King, in order that the legislative power might authorize his Majesty to cede the two Floridas, as is stipulated in one of the articles of said treaty, and grant power to proceed, consequently, to the ratification of it, which his Majesty has thought fit to do; and the Cortes having resolved to give to the Government the authority required, carries into effect the ratification.

His Catholic Majesty, to whom are evident the good offices of his Majesty the Emperor of all the Russias, at several stages of the negotiation with the American Government, proving his august and friendly solicitude in favor of Spain, discharges the grateful task of communicating to the cabinet of his Imperial Majesty the flattering state in which this affair is, and the resolution of his Majesty to ratify the treaty mentioned, which will produce the re-establishing of that perfect harmony between Spain and the United States, which it is of so great importance to both powers to maintain without the least shadow of discord.

With this motive, the King rejoices to repeat to his august friend, the Emperor of all the Russias, the esteem and gratitude with which, on all occasions, he has seen his Imperial Majesty take the most distinguished interest in the prosperity of his Majesty and that of his people, &c.

(Signed by the Spanish Minister and addressed to the Chargé d'Affaires of Russia.)

Extract of a letter (No. 22) from Mr. Forsyth to Mr. Adams.

MADRID, *October* 24, 1820.

"The delay of the departure of the Spanish messenger enables me to give you copies of my correspondence with Mr. de Castro, subsequent to the decision of the Cortes on the cession of Florida, in regard to the execution of the convention of February 22, 1819. No. 1 is a copy of my note calling the attention of the Spanish minister to the provisions of the first and seventh articles of the treaty. I saw Mr. de Castro on Saturday. He had received my letter; the propriety of issuing the order suggested in my note had not escaped him, and he would send, as I requested, a copy of it as soon as it was made. To-day I received his answer, with a copy of the order to which it refers. Copies are marked Nos. 2 and 3."

Mr. Forsyth to Mr. de Castro.

MADRID, *October* 17, 1820.

SIR: By the seventh article of the convention of the 22d February, 1819, the ratification of which is preparing on the part of his Catholic Majesty to be sent to General Vives at Washington, it is stipulated that the officers and troops of his Majesty shall evacuate the Floridas within six months after the exchange of ratifications, or sooner if possible, and shall give possession of them to the officers or Commissioners of the United States who may be properly authorized to receive them. Calculating on a speedy exchange of ratifications, I would suggest, if it has not already occurred to your excellency, that it would be extremely convenient if the order of his Majesty for the evacuation and delivery of the territory, as also the archives and documents relating to the sovereignty and property of the same, should go to General Vives with the ratified treaty, to be forwarded to the property authority on the exchange of ratifications; as by these means the United States would have timely notice to prepare the escort and transports to carry the officers and troops of his Majesty, and their equipage to the Havana, in conformity with the obligation of the said article. I should be pleased to be enabled, by the politeness of your excellency, to furnish to my Government a copy of this order, if his Majesty's Government should send it to General Vives.

I seize with avidity every occasion to offer to your excellency, whom may God preserve, the assurance of my distinguished respect.

JOHN FORSYTH.

The Minister of Spain to Mr. Forsyth.

[Translation.]

SIR: I have received your esteemed note of the 17th current, in which you say that you have taken the liberty of suggesting to me, in case it should not have already occurred to his Majesty's Government, that it would be extremely convenient, if the order of his Majesty for the evacuation and delivery of the Floridas, and of the archives and documents relating to the sovereignty and property of those provinces, should go to General Vives with the ratification of the treaty, that it should be sent at the same time to the proper authorities, in order to be transmitted after the exchange of the ratifications; and that it would be very agreeable to your excellency to have it in your power to send a copy of said order to your Government, if his Majesty should transmit it to General Vives, and should find no inconvenience in granting it.

The idea had occurred to his Majesty's Government, as it could not fail to do, of transmitting General Vives the proper order for the delivery of the Floridas and whatever else is stipulated in the seventh article of the treaty of the 22d February, 1819, in order to be forwarded to the proper authorities after the exchange of the ratifications. Estimating, as it deserves, your excellency's suggestion, produced, no doubt, from desire of connecting more closely the relations of amity and good understanding between Spain and the United States by removing every obstacle or distant incident which might retard so desirable an object; and cheerfully acceding to the desire which your excellency has manifested to me of obtaining a copy of the order which may be sent to the proper authority for carrying into effect the seventh article of the treaty, I have the honor of enclosing to you a copy of that which is addressed to the Captain General of the island of Cuba, through the medium of General Vives, in order that he may make use of it immediately after the exchange of the ratifications has been certified.

In all to-morrow an extraordinary courier will go to convey the despatches of the Government to his Majesty's minister in the United States, and I have the satisfaction of giving your excellency this advice beforehand that you may, if you please, forward any packets to your Government by this opportunity, in which case I hope you will have the kindness to send me them by two in the afternoon of to-morrow, the 25th current.

I renew to your excellency the assurances of my distinguished consideration, and pray God that you may live many years.

Your most humble and obedient servant,

EVARISTO DE CASTRO.

PALACE, *October* 24, 1820.

Translation of the royal order of the King of Spain to the Captain General and Governor of the island of Cuba and of the Floridas.

OCTOBER 24, 1820.

Ferdinand the Seventh, by the grace of God and by the Constitution of the Spanish monarchy King of the Spains, to you the Captain General and Governor of the island of Cuba and of the Floridas: Know you, that by a treaty concluded in the city of Washington on the twenty-second of February of the last year, one thousand eight hundred and nineteen, by plenipotentiaries duly authorized for the purpose of arranging the differences which have existed between the Government of Spain and that of the United States of America and the limits of their respective territories, there was stipulated on the part of Spain the cession to the United States of all the country situated east of the Mississippi, known by the name of East and West Florida, the adjacent islands dependent upon the two Floridas being comprehended in said cession, together with all public lots and squares, vacant lands, public edifices, fortifications, barracks, and other buildings which are not private property, with the archives and documents which relate directly to the property and sovereignty of said provinces, it being provided at the same time that the inhabitants of the territories so ceded shall be secured in the free exercise of their religion without any restriction, and that all those who may desire to remove to the Spanish dominions shall be permitted to sell or export their effects at any time whatever, in order that they may better effect their purpose, without being subject, in either case, to duties, and that those who prefer remaining in the Floridas shall be admitted, as soon as possible, to the enjoyment of all the rights of citizens of the United States, it being added by another article of the same treaty that the Spanish officers and troops shall evacuate the said territories ceded to the United States six months after the exchange of the ratification of the same treaty, or sooner if possible, and shall give possession of them to the officers or commissaries of the United States duly authorized to receive them, and that the United States shall provide the transports and escort necessary to convey the Spanish officers and troops and their baggage to the Havana. And I, having considered and examined the tenor of the articles of the treaty, after having obtained the consent and authority of the general Cortes of the nation with respect to the said cession, have thought proper to approve and ratify the treaty referred to, the ratification of which must be exchanged at Washington with that which was formed by the President of the United States, with the advice and consent of the Senate of the same, after which exchange the said treaty will begin to be obligatory on both Governments and their respective citizens: therefore I command you and ordain that, after the information which shall be seasonably given you by my Minister Plenipotentiary and Envoy Extraordinary at Washington of the ratifications having been exchanged, you proceed on your part to make the proper dispositions, in order that, at the end of six months, counting from the date of the exchange of the ratifications, or sooner if possible, the Spanish officers and troops may evacuate the territories of both Floridas, and that possession of them be given to the officers or commissaries of the United States duly authorized to receive them, in the understanding that the United States shall provide the transports and escort necessary to convey the Spanish officers and troops and their baggage to the Havana. You shall arrange in proper time the delivery of the islands adjacent and dependent upon the Floridas, and the public lots and squares, vacant lands, public edifices, fortifications, barracks, and other buildings which are not private property, as also the archives and documents which relate directly to the property and sovereignty of the same two provinces by placing them at the disposal of the commissaries or officers of the United States duly authorized to receive them, and all the other papers and the effects which belong to the nation and which have not been comprehended and mentioned in the expressed clauses of the cession you shall have conveyed and transported to another part of the Spanish possessions which may be most convenient for the public service; as, also, you shall take care that, previous to the delivery, it may be made known by edicts to all the present inhabitants of the Floridas that they have power to remove to the Spanish territories and dominions, the sale or exportation of their effects being permitted to them by the United States at any time whatever, without being subject to duties; and also the advantages stipulated in favor of those who shall prefer to remain in the Floridas, to whom I have wished to give this last proof of the protection and affection which they have always experienced under the Spanish Government. Of the delivery which you may make or may be made by your delegation, in the form which has been expressed, you shall make or cause to be made a corresponding receipt, duly authenticated, for your discharge; and in order that you may proceed with entire knowledge in the execution of this commission, there shall be likewise sent to you, by my Minister Plenipotentiary at Washington, an authentic copy of the treaty referred to of the twenty-second of February, one thousand eight hundred and nineteen, with the insertion of the ratifications of both parties and of the certificate relative to the exchange of the same, of which documents and of this my royal order you shall send a copy, in authentic form, to the Governors of both the Floridas and to the person or persons who may have in your name the accomplishing of the delivery, if it have not been made by yourself.

All which you shall well and completely execute, in the form which I have prescribed to you, agreeably to the public service, advising me of your having executed it through my under-written Secretary of Despatch of State.

Given at Madrid, the twenty-fourth of October, one thousand eight hundred and twenty.

Mr. Adams to General Vives.

DEPARTMENT OF STATE, *Washington, February 28, 1821.*

SIR: I have submitted to the consideration of the President of the United States the observations which, in conformity to the instructions of your Government, were verbally made by you in the conference which I had the honor of holding with you, when you notified me of your readiness to exchange the ratifications of the treaty of February 22, 1819, between the United States and Spain.

With regard to the omission, on the part of the Spanish negotiator of the treaty, to insist upon some provision of indemnity in behalf of Spanish claimants, to whom a pledge of such indemnity had been stipulated by the previously ratified convention of 1802, an omission stated by you to have been peculiarly dissatisfactory to the Cortes, I am directed to observe that, as in all other cases of the adjustment of differences between nations, this treaty must be considered as a compact of mutual concessions, in which each party abandoned to the other some of its pretensions. These concessions on the part of the United States were great; nor could it be expected by the Spanish nation that they would be obtained without equivalent. Probably the Spanish negotiator considered the claims of Spanish subjects embraced by that convention as so small in amount as scarcely to be worthy of inflexible adherence to them. He certainly considered the whole treaty as highly advantageous to Spain—a sentiment in which the Government of the United States always entirely participated and still concurs.

This also furnishes the reply which most readily presents itself to the proposition which you have also been instructed to make, that some compensation should be allowed by the United States for the benefit of the grantees of lands recognized by the treaty to have been null and void. While appreciating in all its force the sense of justice by which, after the maturest deliberation and the fullest examination, the Cortes have declared that those grants were, so as, at the signature of the treaty, they had been clearly, explicitly, and unequivocally understood to be by both the plenipotentiaries who signed it, the President deems it unnecessary to press the remark which must naturally present itself that, to grantees whose titles were in fact null and void, and by all parties to the negotiation were known to be null and void, no indemnity can be due, because no injury was done. While appreciating

Nor can it be admitted that this is one of the cases of misunderstanding from which the grantees could be entitled to the benefit of a doubtful construction. The construction of the article was in nowise doubtful. For any construction which would have admitted the validity of the grants would have rendered impossible the fulfilment of other most important stipulations of the treaty.

The discussion of this subject, having already been a subject of correspondence between the Minister of Foreign Affairs of your Government and Mr. Forsyth, could now be continued to no profitable purpose. I take much more satisfaction in assuring you of the pleasure with which the President has accepted the ratification of the treaty, as an earnest of that cordial harmony which it is among his most ardent desires to cultivate between the United States and Spain. This disposition, he cherishes the hope, will be further promoted by the community of principle upon which the liberal institutions of both nations are founded, and by the justice, moderation, and love of order, which they combine with the love and the enjoyment of freedom.

I pray you, sir, to accept the assurance of my distinguished consideration.

JOHN QUINCY ADAMS.

General Don FRANCISCO DIONISIO VIVES,
    Envoy Extraordinary and Minister Plenipotentiary from Spain.

18TH CONGRESS.]   No. 369.   [1ST SESSION.

SPOLIATIONS BY FRANCE ON THE COMMERCE OF THE UNITED STATES.

COMMUNICATED TO THE HOUSE OF REPRESENTATIVES FEBRUARY 5, 1824.

To the Speaker of the House of Representatives of the United States:

I transmit to the House of Representatives a report from the Secretary of State, agreeably to a resolution of that House of the 11th of December last, with the papers which accompanied that report.

JAMES MONROE.

WASHINGTON, *February* 2, 1824.

DEPARTMENT OF STATE, *Washington, February* 2, 1824.

The Secretary of State, to whom has been referred the resolution of the House of Representatives of the 11th of December last, "requesting the President of the United States to communicate to that House copies of such parts of the correspondence of the late minister of the United States at the court of France with the French Government, and such parts of the correspondence of said minister with the Secretary of State, relative to claims of citizens of the United States for spoliations upon our lawful commerce, as in his opinion may not be inconsistent with the public interest," has the honor of submitting to the President the papers required by that resolution.

JOHN QUINCY ADAMS.

List of papers transmitted.

Secretary of State to Mr. Gallatin, (general instructions,) April 15, 1816. Extracts.
Secretary of State to Mr. Gallatin, May 7, 1816. Copy.
Mr. Gallatin to Secretary of State, No. 10, November 11, 1816. Extract.
Mr. Gallatin to Duke de Richelieu, November 9, 1816. Original.
Mr. Gallatin to the Secretary of State, No. 19, January 20, 1817. Extracts.

Mr. Gallatin to Duke de Richelieu, December 26, 1816. Copy.
Duke de Richelieu to Mr. Gallatin, January 16, 1817. Translation.
Mr. Gallatin to Secretary of State, No. 27, April 23, 1817. Extracts.
Mr. Gallatin to the Duke de Richelieu, April 22, 1817. Copy.
Mr. Gallatin to the Secretary of State, No. 37, July 12, 1817. Extracts.
Mr. Gallatin to the Secretary of State, No. 55, January 2, 1818. Extract.
Mr. Gallatin to the Secretary of State, No. 67, April 27, 1818. Extract.
Mr. Gallatin to the Duke de Richelieu, April 3, 1818. Copy.
Duke de Richelieu to Mr. Gallatin, April 7, 1818. Translation.
Secretary of State to Mr. Gallatin, December 31, 1818. Extracts.
Mr. Gallatin to Marquis Dessolle, February 11, 1819. Copy.
Mr. Gallatin to Secretary of State, No. 113, July 3, 1819. Extracts.
Minister of Finance to Mr. Parish, May 22, 1819. Translation.
Mr. Gallatin to Secretary of State, No. 140, March 16, 1820. Original.
Mr. Gallatin to Duke de Richelieu, June 9, 1818. Original.
Decree of Council of State, (with translation,) December 23, 1819. In original.
Mr. Gallatin to Baron Pasquier, March 15, 1820. Original.
Mr. Gallatin to Secretary of State, No. 143, April 27, 1820. Extract.
Mr. Gallatin to Secretary of State, No. 147, June 9, 1820. Extract.
Mr. Gallatin to Baron Pasquier, May 9, 1820. Original.
Secretary of State to Mr. Gallatin, March 31, 1821. Extract.
Secretary of State to Mr. Gallatin, June 29, 1821. Copy.
Mr. Gallatin to Secretary of State, No. 193, November 15, 1821. Extract.
Mr. Gallatin to Baron Pasquier, October 31, 1821. Translation.
Mr. Gallatin to Secretary of State, No. 200, January 14, 1822. Extract.
Mr. Gallatin to Viscount de Montmorency, (with translations,) January 10, 1822. Original.
Mr. Gallatin to Secretary of State, No. 203, January 28, 1822. Extract.
Mr. Gallatin to Secretary of State, No. 208, April 23, 1822. Extract.
Mr. Gallatin to Secretary of State, No. 212, May 13, 1822. Copy.
Mr. Gallatin to Viscount de Montmorency, May 3, 1822. Copy.
Mr. Gallatin to Secretary of State, No. 216, June 13, 1822. Extracts.
Viscount de Montmorency to Mr. Gallatin, June 1, 1822. Translation.
Mr. Gallatin to Viscount de Montmorency, June 13, 1822. Original.
Mr. Gallatin to Secretary of State, No. 230, June 8, 1822. Extract.
Mr. Gallatin to Viscount de Montmorency, August 17, 1822. Original.
Mr. Gallatin to Mr. de Villèle, August 31, 1822. , Translation, extract.
Mr. de Villèle to Mr. Gallatin, September 3, 1822. Translation.
Mr. Gallatin to Secretary of State, No. 233, September 24, 1822. Extract.
Mr. Gallatin to Secretary of State, No. 236, November 13, 1822. Extract.
Mr. de Villèle to Mr. Gallatin, November 6, 1822. Translation.
Mr. Gallatin to Mr. de Villèle, November 12, 1822. Original.
Mr. Gallatin to Secretary of State, No. 237, November 19, 1822. Copy.
Mr. de Villèle to Mr. Gallatin, November 15, 1822. Translation.
Mr. Gallatin to Secretary of State, No. 250, February 27, 1823. Extract.
Mr. Gallatin to Viscount de Chateaubriand, February 27, 1823. Original.

CORRESPONDENCE, &c.

Extracts from the general instructions of Mr. Monroe, Secretary of State, to Mr. Gallatin, Envoy Extraordinary and Minister Plenipotentiary of the United States to France, dated

DEPARTMENT OF STATE, *Washington, April 15, 1816.*

" It has at all times since our Revolution been the sincere desire of this Government to cultivate a good intelligence with France. The changes which have taken place in her Government have never produced any change in this disposition. The United States have looked to the French nation, and to the existing Government as its proper organ, deeming it unjustifiable to interfere with its interior concerns. The existing Government has, in consequence, been invariably recognized here as soon as known. Should you find that unfounded prejudices are entertained on this subject, which a frank explanation may remove, you are authorized to make it.

" Cherishing these sentiments towards the French nation, under all the Governments which have existed there, it has not been less a cause of surprise than of regret that a corresponding disposition has not at all times been reciprocated by the French Government towards the United States. The history of the last ten years is replete with wrongs received from that Government, for which no justifiable pretext can be assigned. The property wrested in that space of time from our citizens is of great value, for which reparation has not been obtained. These injuries were received under the administration of the late Emperor of France, on whom the demand of indemnity was incessantly made while he remained in power. Under the sensibility thereby excited, and the failure to obtain justice, the relations of the two countries were much affected. The disorder which has of late existed in France has prevented a repetition of this demand; but now that the Government appears to be settled, it is due to our citizens who were so unjustly plundered to present their claim anew to the French Government."

" A gross sum will be received in satisfaction of the whole claim, if the liquidation and payment of every claim founded on just principles, to be established, cannot be obtained.

" The management of this important interest is committed to your discretion, as to the moment and manner of bringing it under consideration, in which the prospect of obtaining a satisfactory reparation will necessarily have its due weight. You will be furnished with a letter of instruction, authorizing you to provide for it by convention, should that mode be preferred."

The Secretary of State to Mr. Gallatin.

DEPARTMENT OF STATE, *Washington, May* 7, 1816.

SIR : On the presumption that his most Christian Majesty may be disposed to provide by special convention for the just claims of the citizens of the United States against France, as also for the like claims of French subjects against the United States, this letter is given to you, by direction of the President, as an authority and instruction to negotiate a convention for that purpose with such person or persons as may have a like authority from his most Christian Majesty.

I have the honor to be, &c.,

JAMES MONROE.

Extract of a letter, No. 10, *from Mr. Gallatin, Envoy Extraordinary and Minister Plenipotentiary to France, to Mr. Monroe, Secretary of State, dated*

PARIS, *November* 11, 1816.

"I have the honor to inclose the copy of my note of the 9th instant to the Duke de Richelieu, on the subject of indemnities due to citizens of the United States, on account of the illegal and irregular sequestrations and condemnations made under the authority of the former Government of France. I had some difficulty in collecting, from scattered documents, the information necessary to present a correct view of the subject, and adapted to existing circumstances."

PARIS, *November* 9, 1816.

MONSIEUR LE DUC: I had already the honor, in some preliminary conversations, to present to your excellency a general view of the losses sustained by American citizens, under various illegal acts of the former Government of France, and for which the United States claim an indemnity from the justice of his most Christian Majesty.

The right to an indemnity being founded on the law of nations extends to all cases where there has been an evident infraction of that law, such as it is recognized by civilized nations.

Of the acts of the former French Government openly violating that law, those issued on the 21st November, 1806, at Berlin, and on the 17th December, 1807, at Milan, were promulgated in the shape of public decrees, applicable, at least, nominally, to other nations as well as the United States. Other acts were, exclusively, directed against America; appearing, also, sometimes under the form of decrees, as that of Bayonne, of April 17, 1808, and that of Rambouillet, of March 23, 1810; and at times being only special orders for seizing or selling certain American vessels and cargoes. To these various acts must be added the wanton destruction, at different times, of American vessels on the high seas.

That the Berlin and Milan decrees, so far as they declared liable to capture and condemnation neutral vessels pursuing an innocent commerce, and contravening no municipal laws, were an evident violation of the law of nations has not been and cannot be denied. The plea of retaliation, grounded on a supposed acquiescence of neutral powers in certain acts of Great Britain, and urged in justification of those decrees, was unjust in its principle and altogether inadmissible when affecting a neutral instead of an enemy. And even that pretence for plundering a friendly power was abandoned when the two belligerent Governments, whilst continuing to capture the vessels of the neutral trading with their respective enemy, permitted a direct commerce by means of licenses. But that plea was, in point of fact, destitute of foundation with respect to the United States. That they had uniformly opposed the aggressions of Great Britain on their neutral rights is notorious. It is not less true, and appears from all their public acts and from the tenor of their negotiations with both belligerents, that it was solely owing to the acts of France, to the Berlin and Milan decrees, that still more decisive measures of resistance were not early adopted against Great Britain. So long as France and England equally continued to violate the neutral rights of America she could not have selected either of those nations for an enemy without tamely submitting to the aggressions of the other, and without deviating from that impartial course which it was her constant endeavor to pursue. And when, at last, the French decrees had been revoked, so far as America was concerned, the perseverance of England in continuing her unlawful orders and in violating the rights of the United States produced a declaration of war, on their part, against that country.

Notwithstanding the intrinsic justice of the claim of the United States for losses sustained by their citizens under the Berlin and Milan decrees, it was intimated by your excellency that those decrees, having been of a general nature, other nations that had also experienced losses by their operation would have had an equal right to an indemnity, and that those acts not having been enumerated in the last treaties and conventions between France and other European powers amongst those for which a compensation should be made by France, the United States ought not to expect to be placed on a better footing than other nations.

It would be preposterous to suppose, and it cannot have been intended to suggest, that the United States can in any case be bound by treaties to which they were not parties, and in which no attention whatever could have been paid to their interest. Nor can, by any correct analogy, the principles therein adopted be applied to America.

The allied powers naturally sought to obtain indemnity in those cases in which they were most interested. Almost all, if not all, of them had been during the late European wars either at war or in alliance with France, whilst the United States had never stood in either of those relations towards her. Hence, it necessarily followed that the injuries sustained by the subjects of those powers differed essentially from those inflicted by France on American citizens. The Berlin and Milan decrees, so far as they extended beyond prohibitory municipal regulations, although nominally general, applied, in fact, almost exclusively to the United States. If there was any exception, it was in amount too small, and applied to nations whose weight was too inconsiderable, to be taken into consideration. Of the other powers, many had no interest that indemnities should be obtained on that account, whilst several of them, namely, England, Spain, Holland, Denmark, and Naples, had a direct interest that the principle should not be admitted. It will, of course, appear that, by the convention between France and Great Britain, compensation is to be made by France for all the property of English subjects confiscated or sequestered, not only during the last war, but also during that which preceded the treaty of Amiens, and including even the loss arising from the reduction of the public debt of France to one-third of its nominal amount, with the exception of the seizures and confiscations made in consequence of the laws of war, and of the prohibitory laws. And the exception precisely embraces the principal classes of injuries for which the United States are entitled to indemnity, since their grounds of complaint against France are the abuse on her part of belligerent rights and the unlawful extension of prohibitory laws beyond their legitimate sphere.

Not only were the Berlin and Milan decrees an evident and acknowledged violation of the law of nations; not only the plea of retaliation against England, and of a presumed acquiescence in her aggressions, was unfounded with respect to the United States; not only neither the treaties between France and the allied powers are binding on America, nor the principles adopted in those treaties applicable to the relations in which she stood towards France; but those decrees were also an open infraction of the treaties subsisting between the two countries, namely, of the 12th, 13th, and 14th articles of the convention of September 30, 1800, which did not expire till July 31, 1809. For it was therein stipulated that the citizens of either country might sail with their ships and merchandise (contraband goods excepted) from any port whatever to any port of the enemy of the other, and from a port of such enemy, either to a neutral port or to another port of the enemy, unless such port should be *actually* blockaded; that a vessel sailing for an enemy's port without knowing that the same was blockaded should be turned away, but neither be detained nor her cargo be confiscated; that implements and ammunition of war should alone be considered contraband of war; and that free ships should make free goods, extending that freedom even to an enemy's property, on board the ships belonging to the citizens of either country. The French decrees, in violation of those stipulations, after having declared the British islands and possessions in a state of blockade, although they were not pretended to be actually blockaded, made liable to capture and condemnation all American (as well as other neutral) vessels sailing on the high seas from or to an English porort, even which might have been visited by an English vessel, as well as every species of merchandise belonging to English subjects or of English origin.

It is true that, in answer to the American minister who had applied for explanations respecting the construction intended to be given to the Berlin decree, assurances were at first given that it would produce no change in the previous regulations respecting neutral navigators, nor in the convention with the United States. This construction, which gave to that decree the character only of a prohibitory municipal law, was adhered to during the ten first months which followed its promulgation; and it was only in September, 1807, that merchandise found on board of neutral vessels at sea was declared liable to condemnation, merely on account of its being of British growth or manufacture. This fact is here stated for the purpose of observing that the assurances which had thus been given, and the practical construction thus first put on the Berlin decree, prevented the early opposition which otherwise the United States would have made to it; and that this supposed acquiescence on their part served as a pretence for the British orders in council of November, 1807, which were immediately followed by the French decree of Milan.

The decrees and orders of the French Government which applied exclusively to the United States will now be noticed.

Assailed by the simultaneous aggressions of the two belligerent powers, the first step of the American Government was to withdraw the commerce of the United States from the depredations to which it was everywhere exposed. An embargo was laid, in the latter end of the year 1807, on all their vessels, and notwithstanding the extraordinary privations and the great loss of revenue which were incurred, that measure was persevered in during fifteen months. In the meanwhile strong remonstrances were made to the French and English Governments on the subject of their unlawful acts. Not only was the appeal to their justice fruitless, but it appears that by an order said to have been issued at Bayonne on the 17th of April, 1808, all American vessels then in the ports of France, or which might thereafter come into them, were directed to be seized on the pretence that no vessel of the United States could then navigate without infringing a law of the United States, as if the infraction of a municipal law could be lawfully punished by a foreign power; as if it had not been notorious that a number of American vessels, which were abroad when the embargo became known to them, remained in foreign seas and countries in order to avoid the effect of that law.

The pressure of the embargo on the agriculture and commerce of the United States became such that Congress found it proper to modify that measure. By a law of the 1st March, 1809, the act laying an embargo was repealed with respect to all countries, England and France only excepted, and the vessels and merchandise of both countries were excluded from the United States after the 20th of May following; with the proviso, that, in case either France or Great Britain should so revoke or modify their edicts as that they should cease to violate the neutral commerce of the United States, the commercial intercourse of the United States should be renewed with the nation so doing. This law in its nature was entirely municipal and pacific; and its object was to avoid immediate hostilities and to give further time for negotiations; to withdraw, as far as practicable, the navigation of the United States from the operation of the unlawful acts of both France and England, and to give to both sufficient inducements for repealing their edicts, by the actual privation of the benefits derived from the American commerce, and by the prospect that, in case of such repeal by either nation, she would again enjoy those advantages of which her enemy would continue to be deprived.

The act was officially communicated on the 29th of April, 1809, by the American minister to the French Government; it was not at that time treated as hostile; and if it produced no favorable change, no remonstrance was made against it. But towards the end of the same year orders were given to seize all the American vessels in France or in the countries occupied by her arms; and after a great number had been thus seized, principally in Spain and in Holland, an imperial decree was, on the 23d March, 1810, issued at Rambouillet, ordering or rather confirming that seizure, extending it to all American vessels which had entered France or those countries since the 20th May, 1809, and directing that the product of the sales should be deposited in the caisse d'amortissement. The act of Congress of March 1, 1809, was alleged as the motive for that outrageous measure. In point of fact, it is not believed that any vessel the property of French subjects had been forfeited for a violation of that act. At least it is not recollected that any application was made for the remission of such forfeiture to the Treasury Department, which by the law was authorized to grant such remissions, and would certainly have done it in any case where the law might not have been within the knowledge of the parties. But it cannot be necessary seriously to discuss a plea which was evidently but a pretence for plunder. It will be sufficient to observe that the gross injustice of the Rambouillet decree consists in its retrospective operation; and that if the French Government had promulgated an order excluding American vessels from the ports of France and of the countries occupied by her arms, and pronouncing the penalty of confiscation after due notice of that order, American citizens who might have voluntarily and knowingly violated the provisions of what was only a municipal law would have been justly liable to its penalties.

The American property seized or captured by virtue either of those four general decrees, or of special orders, which are but partially known to the Government of the United States, may, in reference to its present situation, be classed under two general heads, viz: that which has never been condemned, and that which has been actually confiscated.

The first class embraces the vessels and cargoes burnt at sea and those which have been sequestered.

It is not necessary to make any observations on the destruction of vessels at sea, your excellency having already intimated that the Government of France was disposed to make compensation for acts of that nature.

The vessels and cargoes sequestered and not condemned consist principally of those seized at St. Sebastian and other places in the latter end of the year 1809 and in the beginning of 1810, and sold by virtue of the decree of Rambouillet. Fourteen vessels which, during that winter, had been driven into Holland, and which, by a particular agreement between the Government of that country and that of France, bearing date, it is said, the 16th of March, 1810, were put at the disposal of France, are of the same description. And, exclusively of other special orders of the same nature, which may not be known to me, the cargoes of seven vessels arrived at Antwerp in the beginning of the year 1807, and which were permitted to be landed there, were also sequestered and finally sold, by virtue of an order of Government, dated the 4th of May, 1810. In all these cases there has been no condemnation, no final decision. The vessels and cargoes were only seized and sold by order of Government, and the proceeds of sales *deposited* in the caisse d'amortissement, or in some other public chest.

The right to demand and obtain a decision on all those suspended cases is undeniable. Either the proceeds of sales will be restored to the lawful owners by virtue of that decision, or the present Government of France must go beyond what had been done by the former Government, and decree the final confiscation of property which even that Government had been unwilling to condemn. I will not permit myself for a moment to suppose that there can be any hesitation on that question.

With respect to property actually condemned, without intending to impair the indisputable right of the United States to an indemnity for every condemnation made by virtue of decrees, violating the acknowledged law of nations, I will beg leave to add some observations on the manner in which those decrees were executed, for the purpose of showing that an investigation and revision of those condemnations ought to take place, even if it was admitted that France had a right to issue the Berlin and Milan decrees, and to condemn vessels contravening their tenor. The time necessary to obtain information in that respect has occasioned the delay which has taken place in making this communication since the last conference I had the honor to hold with your excellency.

1. These condemnations have, as has already been stated, been made in contravention of an existing treaty; so far, at least, as relates to property seized or captured prior to the 31st of July, 1809.

2. Several of the condemnations, or rather acts of confiscation, were made by what has been called "imperial decisions," meaning thereby not those cases where an appeal may have been made from the council of prizes to the council of State, but those instances where the order of condemnation issued from that council, or from Napoleon himself, without any previous regular trial and condemnation by the council of prizes. Such proceedings must be considered as irregular and arbitrary acts, contravening the usages and law of nations. It is sufficiently hard for the neutral that his property should be tried exclusively by the tribunals of the belligerent, where a natural bias exists in favor of the captors. It is at least necessary that the decisions should be made by a regular and permanent tribunal, acting according to fixed rules, and affording every security of which such an institution is susceptible. But the United States have a right to demand that those imperial decisions should be annulled not only as contravening the usages and law of nations, but as violating also an existing treaty. It had been stipulated by the 22d article of the convention of the 30th of September, 1800, "that in all cases the established courts for prize causes in the country to which the prizes might be conducted should alone take cognizance of them." Of 27 vessels and cargoes, (captured or seized prior to the 1st of November, 1810,) which, as appears by a list now before me, were condemned by imperial decisions, eighteen had been seized or captured prior to the 31st of July, 1809, the day on which the convention expired.

3. I have been assured that upon investigation it will be found that some of the decisions of the council of prizes itself have taken place without observing the forms prescribed by law; without giving an opportunity to the parties of bringing their proofs; without an examination of the ship papers, and, in fact, in obedience to an imperial order. A decision of the council, dated September 10, 1811, and by which six ships and cargoes were at once condemned, is particularly mentioned.

4. The retrospective operation of the Rambouillet decree has already been mentioned. It will also be found that in several instances the Milan decree has received a similar construction, and that vessels have been condemned for having contravened that decree which could not have known its existence, having sailed from American ports either before or a short time after it had been issued, and the alleged infraction of the decree itself having at least in one instance taken place prior to its date.

5. It might have been expected that when the Berlin and Milan decrees were declared to be revoked from and after the 1st of November, 1810, no further condemnations would take place with respect to cases not yet decided at that time; notwithstanding which, it appears that forty-eight ships and cargoes, previously seized or captured, were condemned subsequent to that day, namely, by the council of prizes, eighteen before, and ten after the 28th of April, 1811; and by imperial decisions, eleven before, and nine after the last mentioned day. Yet the decree of that day (28th of April, 1811,) enacts and declares that the Berlin and Milan decrees are, from and after the 1st of November, 1810, definitively considered, as if they had not existed *(comme non avenus)* with respect to American vessels.

6. Several condemnations were made for frivolous pretences of vessels captured after the 1st November, 1810, or in other cases which the general decrees could not reach, such as alleged irregularities in the certificates of origin or in other ship papers, presumed navigation under British convoy, mutiny on board, intention to remit the proceeds of sales through England.

It appears from the preceding statement that, independent of the illegality of the Berlin and Milan decrees, there is sufficient cause for the revision of the condemnations which have taken place. Nor is there anything novel in that course. A number of unlawful captures of American vessels having been made by Great Britain during the commencement of her war with France, particularly by virtue of certain British orders in council of the 6th November, 1793, it was agreed by the seventh article of the treaty of November, 1794, between the United States and England, that full and complete compensation should be made by the British Government for the losses and damage sustained by citizens of the United States by reason of *irregular or illegal captures or condemnations* of their vessels and other property under color of authority or commissions from his Britannic Majesty, and a sum exceeding twelve hundred thousand pounds sterling in specie was actually paid to American citizens by the decision of the joint commission appointed in conformity with the said treaty.

From this view of the subject, I have the honor to propose to your excellency an arrangement founded on the following basis, in which, without abandoning the just rights of the citizens of the United States, a positive stipulation is avoided, which would, at this time, bind the Government of France to make compensation generally for all the condemnations under the Berlin and Milan decrees.

First. That the Government of France will engage to make compensation to the citizens of the United States: 1. For all vessels and cargoes captured, seized, or sequestered, which have not been definitively condemned by the council of prizes and the proceeds of which were placed either in the public treasury, in the *caisse d'amortissement*, or in any other public chest, and also for all vessels and cargoes destroyed at sea and likewise not condemned by the council of prizes. 2. For the losses sustained by reason of such other irregular or unlawful seizures, captures, or condemnations as will be decreed by a joint commission to have been made contrary to public law and justice or in contravention of existing treaties.

Second. That a joint commission (or commissions) shall be established with power, 1. To liquidate the amount due for property either destroyed at sea or sequestered and not definitively condemned as aforesaid; 2. To decide in what other cases of irregular or unlawful seizures, captures, or condemnations the Government of France is justly bound to make also compensation, and to what amount.

The manner in which the commission or commissions should be appointed and organized may, it is presumed, be easily arranged, and every reasonable stipulation will be admitted which may be necessary to limit exclusively the right to compensation to cases of *bona fide* American property.

I cannot end this communication without saying that the present situation of France is known and felt by the Government of the United States. It is evidently the interest of America that France should be prosperous and powerful. It is the sincere wish of the Government of America that the present Government of France may soon be relieved from the difficulties which the lamentable event of March, 1815, has occasioned. It is, therefore, with reluctance and only in obedience to a sacred duty that a demand is made at this time which may have a tendency to increase those difficulties, and every disposition exists to accede to such time and mode of payment as, without being inconsistent with the just rights of the citizens of the United States, may be least inconvenient to France.

Permit me to request your excellency to take the subject into early consideration, and to communicate to me as soon as may be practicable the determination of his Majesty's Government.

I have the honor to be, with the highest consideration, your excellency's most obedient servant,

ALBERT GALLATIN.

His Excellency the DUKE DE RICHELIEU,
Minister Secretary of State for the Department of Foreign Affairs, &c.

Extracts of a letter, No. 19, *from Mr. Gallatin, Envoy Extraordinary and Minister Plenipotentiary to France, to Mr. Monroe, Secretary of State, dated*

PARIS, *January* 20, 1817.

"Having received no answer from the Duke de Richelieu to my letter of the 9th of November last, I addressed to him, on the 26th of December, a short note, of which and of his answer, dated the 16th instant, copies are inclosed.

"In the interview which accordingly took place to-day, I requested that he would proceed to state what he had concluded to offer in answer to the basis proposed in my note of the 9th of November. He said that his offer would fall very short of our demands; that he would not go beyond an indemnity for vessels burnt at sea, and for those the proceeds of which had been only sequestered and deposited in the caisse d'amortissement. He added that he would make his proposal in writing, and that this would not be attended with much delay. I then said that I could not give any opinion on his proposal until I had received his note, but that I wished him to understand that if the Government of the United States thought it proper (which I could not at present promise) to accept an indemnity for certain classes only of our claims, this never would be purchased by a relinquishment of the other just demands of our citizens."

Mr. Gallatin to the Duke de Richelieu.

PARIS, *December* 26, 1816.

The undersigned, sensible of the important business which at the opening of the two Chambers, must have engrossed the attention of his most Christian Majesty's Government, has heretofore avoided to urge the consideration of the subject-matter of the letter which he had the honor to address, on the 9th of November last, to his excellency the Duke de Richelieu. It has, however, become necessary that he should be able to communicate to his own Government the result of his application. He therefore requests an interview as early as will suit the convenience of the Duke de Richelieu.

The undersigned embraces with pleasure this opportunity of presenting to his excellency the Duke de Richelieu the reiterated assurance of his most distinguished consideration.

ALBERT GALLATIN.

The Duke de Richelieu to Mr. Gallatin.

[Translation.]

PARIS, *January* 16, 1817.

The Duke de Richelieu cannot but deeply regret that his weighty and multiplied avocations have compelled him to put off until this moment the time he had promised himself to receive Mr. Gallatin, and now fixes the time for Monday morning, the 20th of the present month, at noon, if that day meets his convenience.

He prays him to accept, meanwhile, the renewed assurance of his most distinguished consideration.

Extract of a letter, No. 27, from Mr. Gallatin to the Secretary of State, dated Paris, April 28, 1817.

"I had an interview on the 13th instant with the Duke de Richelieu, in which he announced to me that he had concluded not to give a written answer to my note of the 9th of November last, on the subject of American claims. The claims of the subjects of European powers which France was, by the convention of 1815, bound to pay, had been estimated at a sum not exceeding, at most, one hundred and fifty millions of francs, or an annuity of seven and a half millions. But it was now found that the terms thus imposed were much harsher than the French Government had expected or than the allies themselves had intended. The reclamations, under the convention with Great Britain, did not indeed exceed the sum of fifty millions, at which they had been estimated; but those of the subjects of continental powers, filed with the commission appointed for that purpose, exceeded twelve hundred millions, without including a portion of the Spanish claims, the time for presenting which had not yet expired. Many of those demands would undoubtedly be rejected or reduced by the commission. Still, the probable amount which might be declared justly due so far exceeded every previous calculation, and was so much beyond the ability of France to pay, that he (the Duke) was now employed in seeking some means of obtaining modifications which might bring the payments in some measure within the resources of the country. Under such circumstances, and whilst unable to face the engagements which superior force had imposed on them, it was, he said, utterly impossible for his Majesty's Government to contract voluntarily new obligations. They were not willing to reject absolutely and definitively our reclamations *in toto;* they could not at this time admit them. What he had now verbally communicated could not, for many reasons, become the ground of an official answer to my note. He had therefore concluded that a silent postponement of the subject was the least objectionable course, since, having now made our demand for indemnity in an official manner, the question would be left entire for discussion at some more favorable time, after France was in some degree disentangled from her present difficulties. He added, that if there was any apparent inconsistency between the language he had formerly held and what he was now compelled to say, it must be ascribed to the circumstances he had stated, to the extraordinary and frightful amount to which he had lately found other foreign claims to have swelled.

"After some remarks on the disappointment which, after what had passed in our first conversations, this unexpected determination must produce, I replied that the payment by France of exaggerated and doubtful claims to the subjects of every other foreign power did but increase the injustice of refusing to admit the moderate and unexceptionable demands of the American citizens. The present embarrassments of France, however, increased by the magnitude of those foreign private claims, could form no solid objection to the recognition and liquidation, although they might impede the immediate discharge of our reclamations. It was with this view of the subject that I had, from the first outset, expressed the disposition of the Government of the United States to accommodate that of France, as to the time and manner of making compensation to the claimants. I added, that his declining to answer my note in writing would, exclusively of other objections, leave no trace of the ground on which he placed the postponement of the subject.

"The Duke, without answering my observations in a direct way, gave me to understand that, after the great sacrifices to which the King's ministers had been compelled to give a reluctant assent, and the magnitude of which would soon be known, they would not dare to take the responsibility of acknowledging a new debt, although made payable at a distant period.

"On my mentioning that his Majesty's Government had voluntarily recognized all the engagements previously contracted with French subjects, and which constituted what was called the *arrieré,* and suggesting that the sequestrations of American property might be considered as coming under that description, which would prevent the necessity of asking a specific credit for that object from the legislative body, he answered that the law would not justify such a construction.

"Having exhausted every argument which the occasion suggested, I ended the conference, by saying, that as I could not compel him to give me a written answer, I would reflect on the course which it behooved me to pursue, and that probably I would refer the case to my Government. He said that he intended to write to Mr. de Neuville to make to you a communication similar to that which he now had made to me."

"I addressed to him yesterday the letter of which a copy is inclosed. Its principal object, as you will perceive, is to put on record the ground on which he had himself placed the postponement of the subject, and to leave the door open to further representations respecting cases of property not condemned, in case you should think it best not to urge further at present the demand for indemnity in all cases."

Mr. Gallatin to the Duke de Richelieu.

PARIS, *April* 22, 1817.

MONSIEUR LE DUC: In the interview which I had the honor to have with your excellency on the 13th instant, you intimated that the increased magnitude of the claims made upon France by subjects of European powers, under the conventions of the year 1815, rendered it necessary to postpone to a more favorable time the discussion of the American claims which were the subject of my note of the 9th of November last. Without repeating here the unavailing arguments which I urged against this indefinite and unexpected delay, I will only say that I am not authorized to accede to it, and that it cannot be viewed favorably by the Government of the United States, after the assurances which had been given of its disposition to concur in any reasonable arrangement which might be proposed, with respect to the time and manner of making compensation to the claimants.

I presume, however, that the postponement is intended to apply only to those claims which, though founded on strict justice, were found by his Majesty's Government in a situation that seemed to render a convention necessary for their proper adjustment. The demands for property burnt at sea, or seized and sequestered without having ever been condemned or even brought to a trial before any tribunal whatever, are not of that description. They are, to all intents and purposes, an *arriere*, or unliquidated debt, for property seized, which, if not condemned, must be paid for, and the settlement of which does not require a specific convention. It cannot be supposed that, after his Majesty's Government has not only agreed to pay various foreign claims, of a different nature, but has recognized all those of French subjects arising from the acts of the former Governments of France, the citizens of the United States should alone be excepted from the operation of those measures dictated by justice and sound policy which, under most arduous circumstances, have so eminently contributed to surmount every difficulty and to restore public credit. If any distinction was, indeed, attempted to be made, it should be in favor of the citizens of a foreign nation at peace, whose property was forcibly arrested from them, rather than in favor of subjects who voluntarily advanced theirs, and in many instances with a view to an expected profit. But no such distinction is claimed; and I only trust that, whilst the communication made to me compels me to wait for further orders from my Government on the subject of American claims generally, those of the description last mentioned shall not remain suspended, and that orders shall be given to the proper authorities for their speedy liquidation and for discharging them in a manner as favorable, at least, as that which has been provided for the claims of French subjects known by the name of *arriere*.

I request your excellency to accept the assurances of the distinguished consideration with which I have the honor to be your most obedient servant,

ALBERT GALLATIN.

Extract of a letter from Mr. Gallatin, (No. 37,) detailing the substance of a conversation with the Duke de Richelieu, to the Secretary of State, dated

PARIS, *July* 12, 1817.

"He (the Duke de Richelieu) then said that he wished it to be clearly understood that the postponement of our claims for spoliations was not a rejection; that a portion of them was considered as founded in justice; that he was not authorized to commit his Majesty's Government by any positive promise; but that it was their intention to make an arrangement for the discharge of our just demands as soon as they were extricated from their present embarrassments. He still persisted, however, in his former ground, that they could not, at present, recognize the debt or adjust its amount."

Extract of a letter from the same, (No. 55,) to Mr. Adams, Secretary of State, dated

PARIS, *January* 2, 1818.

"Fifteen millions are spoken of, which, with the five millions already paid, and the three allotted to British subjects, will make an aggregate of four hundred and sixty millions, in five per cent. stock, paid by France for European private claims. Ours, in the mean while, remain in the same situation; and I wait for an answer to my despatch, No. 27, (of the 23d of April last,) before I take any new steps on the subject."

Extract of a letter from the same, (No. 67,) to the same, dated

PARIS, *April* 27, 1818.

"I had, in my letter of the 2d of January last, mentioned that I would wait for an answer from your Department to my despatch of the 23d April, 1817, before I took any new steps on the subject of our own claims; and I had no expectation that a new application would at this moment prove successful. Yet it appeared that, to remain altogether silent, at the moment when an arrangement for the claims of the subjects of every other nation was on the eve of being concluded, might, in some degree, be injurious to the rights of our citizens. It was also apprehended that, in their public communications, the ministers of the King, wishing to render the new convention as palatable as possible, might announce to the nation, in general terms, that all the foreign claims of individuals were now satisfied. These considerations induced me to address to the Duke de Richelieu the note of the 3d instant, of which I have the honor to inclose a copy, as well as of that by which he acknowledged the receipt of mine. You will perceive that, in his communication to the Chambers, (which has been inserted correctly in no other newspaper than the Moniteur,) that he has expressed himself in the following terms: 'France (by this payment) is liberated, both as to principal and interest, from all the debts contracted towards the subjects of the other *European* powers, prior to the 20th November, 1815.' The consideration of our claims is not, therefore, barred by anything which has taken place; but there is not yet any disposition to take up the subject."

Mr. Gallatin to the Duke de Richelieu.

PARIS, *April* 3, 1818.

MONSIEUR LE DUC: I have not had the honor to address your excellency on the subject of American claims since my letter of the 22d of April last. The disposition of the Government of the United States never to abandon the just rights of their citizens, and, at the same time, to pay every due regard to the unfavorable circumstances under which France has been placed, is sufficiently known to your excellency. It is, however, notorious that negotiations are now carried on for the amicable liquidation of all the private claims of the subjects of European powers against France; and it is generally believed that the negotiations are on the eve of being terminated, and that the sum to be paid on that account will be definitively settled. The magnitude of those claims, and the uncertain result of the liquidations contemplated by the former conventions with the allied powers, had been alleged, in April last, as reasons which rendered it necessary to postpone, at that time, the consideration of American reclamations. It has therefore become my duty to bring these once more to your excellency's recollection.

It is not my intention to renew, at this moment, the discussion of the justice of our demands. In this stage of the business, I could only refer to the facts and observations contained in former notes, which still remain unanswered. But I must say that further delays in the adjustment of American claims, when those of the subjects of other nations are settled, could not be viewed favorably by the Government of the United States; whilst, on the other hand, a simultaneous and definitive arrangement of all foreign demands arising from the injustice of the former Government of France seems most consistent with sound policy, and could not fail to have a beneficial effect on public credit.

Whatever course may be pursued, I feel satisfied that the result of the late negotiations with the European powers will not be considered or announced by his Majesty's Government as a total liberation of all the foreign claims of individuals; for, however unsuccessful my endeavors may heretofore have been, I have uniformly ascribed that result to the untoward situation of France; and I know that my Government has never ceased to place a firm reliance on the spirit of justice and good faith which animates his Majesty's councils.

I request your excellency to accept the assurance of the distinguished consideration with which I have the honor to be your excellency's most obedient servant,

ALBERT GALLATIN.

Duke de Richelieu to Mr. Gallatin.

[Translation.]

PARIS, *April* 7, 1818.

SIR: You have done me the honor to address to me, on the 3d of this month, some new observations on the American claims which I shall take care to lay before his Majesty.

Accept, sir, the assurances of the high consideration with which I have the honor to be your very humble and obedient servant,

RICHELIEU.

Extracts of a letter from the Secretary of State to Mr. Gallatin, dated

DEPARTMENT OF STATE, *Washington, December* 31, 1818.

"No communication from you since your return to France has yet been received; but it is hoped that since the foreign troops have been withdrawn from that country, and an adjustment has been made by the French Government of the claims of the subjects of European powers, there will be time and a disposition to make a suitable provision for those of citizens of the United States."

"Meanwhile, you have herewith inclosed a copy of a statement made to this Department of a claim of Archibald Gracie & Sons, which appears to stand upon grounds so peculiar and unexceptionable that we cannot but hope the French Government will give immediate satisfaction upon it, without waiting for the discussion or delay which may be thought necessary for others, and without prejudice or disparagement to them."

Mr. Gallatin to the Marquis Dessolle, Minister of Foreign Affairs.

PARIS, *February* 11, 1819.

MONSIEUR LE MARQUIS: I have the honor to transmit to your excellency a memorial addressed by Mr. Parish, a citizen of the United States, to his excellency the Minister of Finance, on the subject of a claim which it appears has been laid before that Department.

Having been confined for the last three weeks by indisposition, I have been prevented from asking an interview of your excellency, with which I was desirous of being favored before I presented to you this memorial and renewed my application for the settlement of the American claims in general. But having recently received very special orders from my Government, accompanied by a particular recommendation of Mr. Parish's claim, I am no longer at liberty to defer the discussion of this interesting concern.

I have, therefore, to request your excellency to have the goodness to examine the official notes which I had the honor to address to the Duke of Richelieu upon the subject of these claims and to which I have yet received no answer. I shall not now enlarge upon the view presented in my note of November 9, 1816. By that of April 22, 1817, it will be seen that the negotiations on that subject were suspended solely in consideration of the trying situation in which France was then placed, and especially of the embarrassments of the administration by the enormous and unexpected mass of claims brought forward by the subjects of allied powers. These obstacles are now happily removed; every demand of all the European powers and their subjects has been amicably adjusted and settled. The rights, so legitimate, of the citizens of the United States alone remain unsatisfied. My Government, preserving an unshaken confidence in his Majesty, cannot doubt that the time has at length arrived when ample justice will be rendered to its claims.

With respect to that of Mr. Parish, it may be remarked that it is very simple and is susceptible of being adjusted without waiting the result of or in the least interfering with a general settlement. In fact, the cargoes in question were never condemned, but were only sold for the joint benefit of all, and the proceeds deposited provisionally in the Sinking Fund. It is further important to remark, that by an order of the French Government permission was granted to the consignees of cargoes sequestered at that period, at Antwerp, to take possession and dispose of them on their giving an obligation to become responsible for the amount to the public treasury, in the event of a decision pronouncing their confiscation. The house of Mr. Ridgway, consul of the United States, together with that of Mr. Parish, refused their assent to a condition which implied an admission of the legality of the seizure. The European consignees, with whom this consideration had no weight, received and sold their goods; and their obligations were subsequently returned to them. Thus, by refunding to the houses of Ridgway and Parish the proceeds of the cargoes consigned to them, the decision which was virtually carried into effect in the case of all others similarly situated will only receive its due application as it regards them.

I have to observe that, although the claims of both these houses are perfectly similar to each other, that of Mr. Parish is the only one which appears to have been taken into consideration by the Department of Finance.

In the hope that my health may soon permit me to confer personally with your excellency, I have the honor to be, &c., &c.,

ALBERT GALLATIN.

Extracts of a letter from Mr. Gallatin to the Secretary of State, dated

PARIS, *July* 3, 1819.

"I transmitted, in my despatch No. 100, the copy of the letter which I had addressed to Marquis Dessolle, on the 11th of February last, on the subject of American claims in general, and more particularly of that of Messrs. Gracie and Parish.

"On the 23d of March, in transmitting to the same minister a letter from Mr. Hyde de Neuville, in behalf of Mr. Gracie, I reminded him of my preceding note, and requested that a report which the Director General of the Douanes was shortly to make on the claim might be communicated to me before the Minister of Finances should decide upon it. This was the more important, as the Director was known to be decidedly hostile to the claim, and to the restitution of any sum which had, in any shape, found its way to the public treasury.

"My request was not complied with; but Mr. Parish still thought that the affair had taken a favorable turn, and, not expecting an immediate decision, left this city for Antwerp, and went thence on some business to England. From this last country he wrote to me a few days ago, and transmitted the inclosed copy of a letter addressed to him by the Minister of Finances, and by which he is informed that his claim is inadmissible.

"The minister's letter is not less incorrect as to facts than weak in argument. The order to sell and to pay into the treasury the proceeds of the sales of sequestered property is not and was not, by the then existing Government, considered as a condemnation. When the vessels in question arrived at Antwerp, the only penalty to which they were liable for having touched in England was to be refused admission, and the only question was whether this exclusion should be enforced, or whether the consignees should be permitted to sell the cargoes. It was not at all by giving a retrospective effect to the Milan decree that the cargoes were sold. The sale took place about the same time that the property seized at St. Sebastian was sold. It was done by virtue of an order from Government, distinct from the Rambouillet decree, and for which no motive was assigned. I have requested Mr. Parish's lawyer to procure copies of the order of sale, and of that by which the money was paid into the public treasury, instead of the *caisse d'amortissement;* for, although the substance of the orders is known, the text has not been communicated.

"But, however easy it might be to answer the minister's letter, there would be some inconvenience in pursuing that course, or in prosecuting further Mr. Parish's claim distinct from others of the same nature."

"The decision of the Minister of Finances, founded on the assumed principle that no redress remains when the money has been paid into the treasury and been expended, would apply with equal force to all the American claims. If it becomes necessary to combat seriously that doctrine, it will be better to do it generally, and in a direct correspondence with the Minister of Foreign Affairs, than by answering a letter which is not addressed to me, and applying my arguments to a single case."

"In the present state of things I will try, until I am positively instructed to keep the negotiation alive, but without urging a decision, unless I can ascertain that a favorable result will be thus obtained."

The Minister of Finance to Mr. Parish.

[Translation.]

PARIS, *May* 22, 1819.

SIR: You have applied, in behalf of Mr. Archibald Gracie, of New York, for the restitution of the value of the cargoes of three American ships—the Perseverance, the Hiram, and the Mary—sequestered by the Imperial Government in 1807, and the proceeds of which were afterwards confiscated by it.

Having had a detailed statement laid before me of the circumstances connected with this transaction, the documents exhibited established the following facts:

By a decree issued at Berlin, November 21, 1806, the British islands were placed in a state of block‑ade. By articles 7 and 8 of this decree, every vessel coming directly from England, or from the English colonies, or having been there since the publication of the said decree, was refused admission into any port; and every vessel attempting to contravene that clause, by means of a false declaration, was, together with the cargo, subject to seizure and confiscation, as if they were English property. It was while these legislative measures were in force that the three ships in question arrived at Antwerp, to your address. They had put into England—a circumstance which was, however, not considered by the custom-house as an irremissible cause of confiscation, there being reason to presume that it was through stress of weather.

In the interval of time previous to the decision which was to be made by the chief of the State, a proposal was made to you to dispose, conditionally, of the cargoes of these vessels, on your engaging to refund the proceeds, in the event of their final confiscation. You refused your assent to this offer, and, at a subsequent period, claimed its execution; but things had then changed, the legislative measures having become more rigorous.

By a decree of 23d November, 1807, it was declared:

"ARTICLE 1. That all vessels which, after touching in England, from any cause whatsoever, shall enter the ports of France, shall be seized and confiscated, together with their cargoes, without exception or distinction, of goods and merchandise."

By a retrospective effect, which I am certainly very far from wishing to justify, but to which it is proper to advert, because it forms one of the striking features of the case, this decree of November 23 was enforced as to these three vessels. It was ineffectually that the Director General of the Customs repre‑ sented to the head of the Government that the English had no interest whatever in these three vessels, and that they were solely and *bona fide* American property, an immediate sale of their cargoes having been ordered by the supreme authority on the 4th of May, 1810. This order was carried into execution on the 15th of June following, and the proceeds, at first deposited in the Sinking Fund, were subsequently withdrawn, in conformity, also, with the same superior orders, and placed in the public treasury, as having definitively become the property of the State.

I admit with you, sir, the iniquity of these measures, and with you I deplore their effects, but to repair them is not within the compass of my power. If the cargoes in question still existed in the custom-house stores, they should be immediately restored to you, but they were sold, and their proceeds no longer exist. The whole transaction was terminated, irrevocably terminated, four years prior to the restoration, and it is not within the power of his Majesty's Government to revive an obsolete claim, to renew a discussion on rights which are extinct, or to repair individual losses by an augmentation of the public burdens.

With the expression of my regrets, be pleased, sir, to accept the assurance of my perfect consideration.

BARON LOUIS,
The Minister of Finance and Secretary of State.

No. 140.

PARIS, *March* 16, 1820.

SIR: I had, on the 9th of June, 1818, addressed a letter to the Duke de Richelieu in relation to the American vessels "Dolly" and "Telegraph," burnt at sea by two French frigates in the latter end of the year 1811. Mr. Lagrange, the lawyer of the owners, communicated to me, a short time ago, the decision of the Council of State in that case, copy of which, as well as of my letter to the Duke de Richelieu, is herewith inclosed. You will thereby perceive that the application for indemnity has been rejected, principally on the ground that the French captains must have been ignorant of the revocation of the Berlin and Milan decrees, since the decree of April 28, 1811, was not published till the 8th of May, 1812.

It appeared to me essential not only to remonstrate against this flagrant injustice, but also to refute at large the doctrine thus attempted to be established in violation of the solemn engagements of the French Government. The effect the decision might have on our claims in general, and the ground which had been uniformly assumed by the Government of the United States in its discussions with that of Great Britain, and in all the public reports made on that subject, are considerations too obvious to require any comment on my part.

I have the honor to inclose a copy of the letter which I have addressed to Mr. Pasquier on the occasion, and am, with great respect, sir, your obedient servant,

ALBERT GALLATIN.

Hon. JOHN QUINCY ADAMS, *Secretary of State, Washington.*

PARIS, *June* 9, 1818.

MONSIEUR LE DUC: I had heretofore abstained from addressing your excellency on the subject of special American claims for spoliations committed on our commerce by the French authorities. A general decision had appeared, and still seems to be, the most eligible mode of coming to a satisfactory arrange- ment. Being, however, informed that some cases are still pending before the Council of State, it becomes my duty to depart in these instances from the line of conduct I had adopted.

I have, therefore, the honor to transmit to your excellency a memoir, addressed to the King in council, in behalf of the owners of the ships and cargoes of the American vessels *Dolly* and *Telegraph*, burnt at sea in November and December, 1811, by the French frigates *la Méduse* and *la Nymphe*.

It is certainly preposterous to suppose that his Majesty's council will, at this time, condemn American vessels for any presumed contravention to the iniquitous decrees of Berlin and Milan. But a discussion of that point is not even necessary in these cases. It is evident that those vessels were destroyed several months, at least, after the solemn revocation of those decrees, so far as respected the United States. It is equally evident that neither the presumed fact that the captors were ignorant of that revocation nor the omission of formalities, to use no stronger language, on their part, can be plead against the American owners. It seems unnecessary, in a case so plain, to enforce those arguments or to anticipate objections. In simply recommending it to your excellency's attention, I feel a perfect confidence that the parties will obtain from his Majesty's council that decision in their favor which has been too long protracted and to which they are so justly entitled.

I pray your excellency to accept, &c.,

ALBERT GALLATIN

His Excellency the DUKE DE RICHELIEU,
 Minister of Foreign Affairs, &c.

CONSEIL D'ETAT.

Extrait du Registre des Délibérations, Séance du 23 Décembre, 1819.

Louis, par la Grace de Dieu, Roi de France et de Navarre, sur le rapport du Comité du Contentieux.

Vû la requête à nous présenté au nom des propriétaires et chargeurs des navires Américains le *Dolly*, et le *Télégraphe*, capturés le 29 Novembre et 6 Décembre, 1811, par les frégates Françaises la *Méduse* et la *Nymphe*, et brutés en mer par les orders du Sieur Raoul, capitaine de la frégate la Méduse et commandant la dite division; la dite requête enregistrée au Secrétariat Général de notre Conseil d'Etate, le 11 Juin, 1818, et tendant à ce qu'il nous plaise—

1. Declarer les dites captures nulles et illegales;
2. Ordonner que les propriétaires des dits navires et de leur chargements seroient indemnisés des pertes et dommages que le brulement leur a occasionne;
  3. Les renvoyer devant qui de droit pour la liquidation des dites indemnités, sous la reserve de tous moyens et exceptions, notamment d'agir et de conclure, ainsi qu'il appartiendra, contre les auteurs ou complices des soustractions qu'ils pretendent avoir été commises à bord des deux navires, et généralement sous toutes les réserves de droit;

Vû les procès-verbaux de la prise et du brulement des navires Américains le *Dolly* et le *Télégraphe*, rédigés en mer les 29 Novembre et 6 December, 1811, signés des capitaine, lieutenant, enseignes de vaisseau et agent comptable composant l'équipage de la frégate la *Méduse;*

Vû les actes de protêt et déclaration faits par devant le consul des Etats-Unis à L'Orient, savoir par le Sieur Stephen Bayard, capitaine du navire le *Télégraphe*, le 11 Janvier, 1812, et par le Sr. Guillaume Friat, passager à bord du *Dolly*, et se disant propriétaire de diverses marchandises embarquées à bord du dit batiment, en date du 29 Décembre, 1811;

Vû les connaisemens et actes d'affirmation annexés à ces déclaration;

Vû les conclusions, en date du 31 Octobre, 1814, du Procureur Géneral prés le Conseil des Prises, à qui ces réclamations avoient été soumises;

Vû la décision prise par se conseil le même jour, 31 Octobre, 1814, par laquelle il étoit ordonné qu'avant faire droit, les personnes composant les équipages des frégates le *Méduse* et la *Nymphe* seroient interrogées sur les diverses circonstances des dites prises;

Vû les procès-verbaux des interrogatoires subis le 13 Janvier, 1815, par le Sr. Raoul, capitaine de la frégate la *Méduse*, et le Sr. Crom, alors contre maitre sur la même frégate desquels il resulte que ses prises et brulemens ont en lieu en suite de ses instructions, qui lui prescrivoient l'éxécution des decrets de Berlin et de Milan;

Vû les décrets datés de Berlin, du 21 Novembre, 1806, et de Milan, des 23 Novembre et 17 Décembre, 1807;

Considérant qu'il est constant que le navire le *Dolly*, chargé de merchandises à la destination de la Havane sortoit de Liverpool, port de la domination Anglaise, et que le navire le *Télégraphe*, charge de farine à Philadelphia, étoit destiné pour Lisbonne, occupé à cette époque par les troupes Anglaises; et que dés lors ces batimens naviguoient en contravention aux décrets de Berlin et de Milan;

Considérant que la première notification publique qui ait été donnée du décret de révocation des dits décrets à l'égard des Américains, n'a lieu que les notes insérées dans le Moniteur du huit Mai, 1812, plusieurs mois après la prise des dits batimens, et que des lors des capitains de la Méduse et de la Nymphe ne pouvoient en avoir connoisance, et qu'il paroit même d'après la note en date du 12 Mars, 1812, attribuée par les requérans au ministre plénipotentiaire des Etats-Unis, qu'à cette époque ce ministre lui même ne la conpoissoit pas—

Notre Conseil d'Etat entendu, nous avons ordonné et ordonnons, ce qui suit:

ART. 1er. La requête des propriétaires et chargeurs des navires le *Télégraphe* et le *Dolly* est rejettée, sans rien préjuger sur les réservés insérées dans leurs conclusions.

ART. 2me. Notre Garde. des Sceaux. Ministre le Secrétaire d'Etat au Département de la Justice, et notre Ministre Secrétaire d'Etat au Departement de la Marine et des Colonies, sont chargés, chacun en ce qui le concerne, de l'exécution de la présente ordonnance.

Apprové le 29 Decembre, 1819.

LOUIS.

Le Garde des Sceaux, Ministre de la Justice,
 Par le Roi, H. DE SERRE.

Pour expédition conforme à la minute enregistrée à Paris, le 6 Janvier, 1820, par Billard, qui a reçu 29. 50c. subvention comprise.

Le Secrétaire Général du Conseil d'Etat,
 HOCHET.

Translation of the foregoing decree.

COUNCIL OF STATE.

Extract from the Register of Deliberations, session of December 23, 1819.

Louis, by the grace of God King of France and Navarre, upon the report of the Board of Questions:

Having seen the petition presented to us in the name of the proprietors and owners of the American ships the *Dolly* and the *Telegraph*, captured on the 29th November and 6th December, 1811, by the French frigates the *Méduse* and the *Nymphe*, and burnt at sea by the orders of Mr. Raoul, captain of the frigate Meduse, and commander of said division, the said petition being registered at the Secretary General's Office of our Council of State the 11th June, 1818, and that it would be our pleasure—

1st. To declare the said captures null and illegal;

2d. To ordain that the proprietors of said ships, and of their lading, should be indemnified for the losses which the burning them has occasioned;

/ 3d. To remit them to the legal tribunal for the liquidation of said indemnities, under the reservation of all means and exceptions; especially to proceed and conclude as shall be proper against the authors or accomplices of the abstractions which they pretend to have been committed on board of the two ships, and generally under all the reservations of right;

Having seen the procès-verbal of the capture and of the burning of the American ships *Dolly* and *Telegraph*, which occurred at sea on the 29th November and 6th December, 1811, signed by the captain, lieutenant, ensigns de vaisseau, (second lieutenants,) and purser, (agent comptable,) composing the crew of the frigate *la Meduse;*

Having seen the acts of protest and declaration made before the consul of the United States at L'Orient, to wit, by Mr. Stephen Bayard, captain of the ship *Dolly*, on the 11th January, 1812, and by Mr. William Friat, passenger on board the *Dolly*, and calling himself proprietor of divers merchandise embarked on board of said vessel, dated 29th December, 1811;

Having seen the bills of lading and affidavits annexed to these declarations;

Having seen the conclusions, dated 31st October, 1814, of the Attorney General before the council of prizes, to whom these claims had been submitted;

Having seen the decision made by this council, on the same 31st October, 1814, by which it was ordained that, before a decree, the persons composing the crews of the frigates *la Méduse* and *la Nymphe* should be interrogated upon the different circumstances of said captures;

Having seen the procès-verbal of the interrogatories undergone on the 13th January, 1815, by Mr. Raoul, captain of the frigate *la Méduse*, and Mr. Crom, at that time boatswain's mate in the same frigate, from which it results that these captures and burnings took place in consequence of their instructions, which prescribed to them the execution of the Berlin and Milan decrees;

Having seen the decrees, dated, that of Berlin on the 21st November, 1806, and that of Milan on the 23d November and 17th December, 1807;

Considering that it is evident that the ship the *Dolly*, laden with merchandise for Havana, sailed from Liverpool, a port of the English dominion, and that the ship the *Telegraph*, laden with flour at Philadelphia, was destined for Lisbon, at that time occupied by the English troops, and that since that time these vessels sailed in contravention of the Berlin and Milan decrees;

Considering that the first public notification which was given of the revocation of said decrees, with respect to the Americans, took place only by the notes inserted in the Moniteur of the 8th of May, 1812, several months after the capture of said vessel, and that from that time the captains of the *la Méduse* and *la Nymphe* could not know it; and that it even appears, according to the note dated 12th March, 1812, imputed by the petitioners to the Minister Plenipotentiary of the United States, that at that time this minister himself did not know it;

Having heard our Council of State, we have ordained and do ordain as follows:

ARTICLE 1. The petition of the proprietors and owners of the ships *Telegraph* and *Dolly* is rejected, without prejudging anything of the reservations inserted in their conclusions.

ARTICLE 2. Our Keeper of the Seals, Minister Secretary of State of the Department of Justice, and our Minister Secretary of State of the Department of the Marine and of the Colonies, are charged, each in what concerns him, with the execution of the present ordinance.

Approved the 29th December, 1819.

LOUIS.

By the King: The Keeper of the Seals, Minister of Justice,

H. DE SERRE.

Copy conform to the minute registered at Paris the 6th January, 1820, by Billard, who has received 29f. 50c., duty included.

The Secretary General of the Council of State,

HOCHET.

Mr. Gallatin to Baron Pasquier.

PARIS, *March* 15, 1820.

SIR: The American brig "Dolly," bound from Liverpool to Havana and New Orleans with a valuable cargo, was captured and burned at sea on the 29th of November, 1811, by the French frigates "Méduse" and "Nymphe." On the 6th of December following the same frigates also captured and burned the American ship "Telegraph," bound from New York to Lisbon with a cargo consisting principally of flour. Mr. Barlow, then minister of the United States at Paris, addressed, on the 12th of March, 1812, a strong remonstrance on the subject to the Duke of Bassano, then Minister of Exterior Relations. The death of the American consul, with whom the captains of the vessels destroyed had left their powers, and the interruption in the communications occasioned by the war which took place in 1812 between the United States and Great Britain, created a delay in the regular application of the parties, and prevented an immediate decision. The affair in the meanwhile took the usual course, and was transferred, in 1815, from the council of prizes to a committee of the Council of State. On the application of the parties, I had the honor, on the 9th of June, 1818, to transmit their *memoire* to his excellency the Duke de Richelieu, and added such short observations as the case seemed to require.

It was with equal astonishment and regret that I received, a few days ago, the information that the application of the parties for indemnity had been rejected by a decision of the Council of State of the 23d of December, 1819, on the following grounds:

"Considérant qu'il est constant que le navire le *Dolly* chargé de marchandises à la destination de la Havane, sortôit de Liverpool, port de la domination Anglaise, et que le navire le *Télégraphe*, chargé de farine à Philadelphie, etoit destiné pour Lisbonne, occupé à cette époque par les troupes Anglaises; et que, dès lors, ces batimens naviguoient en contravention aux décrets de Berlin et de Milan:

"Considérant que la première notification publique qui ait été donnée du décret de revocation des dits décrets à l'egard des Américains n'a eu lieu que par les notes insérés dans le Moniteur du huit Mai, 1812, plusieurs mois après la prise des dits batimens, et que, dès lors, les capitaines de la Méduse et de la Nymphe ne pourroient, en avoir connoissance, et qu'il paroit même, d'après la note en date du 12 Mars, 1812, attribuée par les réquérans au Ministre Plénipotentiaire des Etats Unis, qu'à cette époque lui-même ne la connoissoit pas.

"Notre Conseil d'Etat entendu, &c."

I must, in the first place, enter my most solemn protest against this decision, so far as it seems to sanction the Berlin and Milan decrees. These acts were in flagrant violation of the law of nations and of common justice. The United States never acquiesced in them, and have never ceased to claim the indemnity justly due to American citizens for the injuries and losses they suffered by reason of those illegal enactments. But it is unnecessary on this occasion to discuss that question. The owners of the *Dolly* and *Telegraph* claimed indemnity solely on the ground of the previous revocation of the decrees so far as they applied to the American commerce; and it is to that point alone that I beg leave to call your excellency's attention.

I am at a loss to understand whether by the decision of the Council of State it was intended to assert that the ignorance on the part of the French captains of the revocation of the decrees deprives the parties of their right to an indemnity, or to suggest that the revocation was to take effect only from the date of its publication in the Moniteur. Both positions are equally untenable.

The Council of State seems to have been unacquainted with the circumstances which attended the revocation of the decrees, and to have supposed that that revocation depended only on the decree of the 28th of April, 1811, and to have considered this last decree not as the result of a solemn engagement but as a mere municipal law, or at least as a gratuitous concession to the United States. It is difficult, even on that supposition, to understand how they could omit altogether to take notice of the clause which gives to the decree a restrospective effect. But it is not on that decree as an insulated act that the United States found their demand for indemnity. A recapitulation of the facts connected with the revocation will place the question on its true ground. Permit me first to take notice of an error in the statement of the council.

This error consists in supposing that the minister of the United States, when writing his letter of the 12th of March, 1812, to the Duke of Bassano, was not aware of the revocation of the Berlin and Milan decrees. His ignorance in that respect, had it been real, would not have affected the rights of the claimants; but the supposition on the part of the Council of State that he was unacquainted with it, is an evident proof that their own decision is founded in error, and must be solely ascribed to the facts not having been properly laid before them. If, in his letter to the Minister of External Relations, Mr. Barlow did not mention by name the revocation of the illegal decrees, it was because he considered the burning at sea of two American vessels as a wanton outrage not at all connected with those decrees, which, indeed, did not authorize any such proceeding. It was, perhaps, also because the revocation was so well known both to him and to the Duke of Bassano that it had become unnecessary to refer to it on every occasion. That it was thus known is sufficiently proven by all the correspondence between them, as it stands in the archives of the department over which your excellency presides. It will be sufficient for me to quote Mr. Barlow's letter to the Duke of Bassano of the 6th of February, 1812, and written, therefore, about a month prior to the time at which he is supposed to have been ignorant of the revocation. In that letter (of the 6th of February, 1812) Mr. Barlow complains that the brig *Belisarius*, of New York, was about to be confiscated as liable to the decree of Milan, and then says: "I know positively that this American vessel left New York *the 17th of June*, 1811, *seven months after the revocation of the decrees of Milan and Berlin.*" He concludes by ascribing the decision to an error of date, by which the year 1810 may have been taken for the year 1811, and asking for a revision of the affair. The Duke of Bassano, in his answer dated the 16th of March, 1812, informs Mr. Barlow that the difficulty in that case arose from some irregularity in the ship papers respecting the ownership, which was a formal contravention of the rules of navigation *generally adopted and established at all times;* that the vessel and the part of the cargo of which the ownership *(pour compte)* was proven would be given up, and time allowed to establish the fact that the residue of the cargo was American property *conformably to the ancient rules.*

All the facts relative to the revocation of the decrees are, indeed, so perfectly known to the French Department of Foreign Affairs, that I thought it unnecessary, in my letter of the 9th of June, 1818, to his excellency the Duke de Richelieu, to say anything more on the subject, but barely to refer to it. I had presumed that every explanation on that point which the Council of State might require would be, of course, supplied by that Department; and the following statement of facts is intended for that body, and not for the purpose of giving any new information to your excellency.

It is well known that the Government of the United States attempted, by various successive measures of the most moderate and conciliatory nature, to avert the injuries inflicted on the commerce of their citizens by the unlawful decrees of France and Great Britain, to obtain redress for those injuries, and, above all, to induce both powers to rescind those decrees and to adopt a course consistent with justice and with the acknowledged law of nations.

An embargo of fifteen months' duration was succeeded by the act of Congress of the 1st of March, 1809, which prohibited the introduction of British and French merchandise into the United States, and interdicted their ports to vessels of both nations. To this temporary act, which expired on the 1st of May, 1810, another was substituted, of the same date, by which it was enacted: 1. That the ports of the United

States should be interdicted to the armed vessels of France, and Great Britain. 2. That if either of those two powers should, prior to the 3d of March, 1811, revoke its unlawful edicts, (which fact the President of the United States should declare by proclamation,) the interdiction thus imposed on armed vessels should cease in relation to such power. 3. That if the other nation should not, in that case, revoke her unlawful edicts within three months thereafter, the restrictions imposed by the act of the 1st of March, 1809, that is to say, the prohibition to import merchandise and the interdiction of all vessels, should, at the expiration of three months after the proclamation aforesaid, be revived, in relation to the nation thus refusing to revoke her edicts.

This last act of Congress of the 1st of May, 1810, having been communicated both to the French and to the British Government, the Duke de Cadore, then Minister of External Relations, addressed on the 5th of August, 1810, a letter to Mr. Armstrong, then minister of the United States, at Paris, in which, after having commented on the various acts of Congress, he says: "In this new state of things I am authorized to declare to you that the decrees of Berlin and Milan *are revoked*, and that *after the first of November* they will cease to have effect; it being understood that in consequence of this declaration the English shall revoke their orders in council and renounce the new principles of blockade which they have wished to establish, *or that the United States, conformably to the act you have just communicated, shall cause their rights to be respected by the English.*"

The execution of this revocation depended then on the alternative of two conditions, one of which was not under the control of the United States; but the other was only that they should act conformably to what they had already announced to be their determination.

The President of the United States did accordingly, by his proclamation of the 2d of November, 1810, declare that the decrees of France, in question, had been revoked, so far as they had ceased to have effect on the 1st day of that month, and that all the restrictions imposed by the act of Congress of the 1st of May, 1810, were henceforth to cease in relation to France.

On the same day, the 2d of November, 1810, the Secretary of the Treasury Department of the United States transmitted the President's proclamation to the several Collectors of Customs, and gave them instructions for the immediate admission of French armed vessels in the ports of the United States, and for the exclusion of all British vessels, and the prohibition of all British merchandise after the 2d of February, 1811, that is to say, three months from the date of the President's proclamation, in case they, the said Collectors, should not before that day be officially notified by the Treasury Department that Great Britain had revoked her unlawful edicts.

Although both those documents were at the time officially communicated to the French Government, copies are again herewith inclosed.

Great Britain not having revoked her edicts, the interdiction of her vessels and merchandise accordingly took place on the 2d of February, 1811. It received an additional sanction by the act of Congress of the 2d of March following, and continued in force till the month of June, 1812, when, in addition to that measure, Great Britain still persevering in her refusal, the United States found themselves at last obliged to declare war against her.

The United States having thus, with perfect good faith, fulfilled the engagement contracted by their act of the 1st of May, 1810, and on which the execution of the revocation of the Berlin and Milan decrees was made to depend, it follows that the right to demand the complete execution of that revocation from the 1st of November, 1810, and an indemnity in every case where injuries were sustained subsequent to that day by American citizens, under color of those decrees, is fully established as the result of a positive compact, and is altogether independent of any subsequent act of the French Government. That right would remain entire even if that Government had departed from their engagement and had attempted to revive the Berlin and Milan decrees with respect to the United States. This, however, was not the case.

On the 25th of December, 1810, two letters were addressed, one by the Duke of Massa, Minister of Justice, to the President of the Council of Prizes, the other by the Duke of Gaëte, Minister of Finance, to the Director General of the Customs. Both letters recapitulate the paragraph already quoted, of the Duke of Cadore's letter of the 5th of August, 1810, to Mr. Armstrong, and the substance of the proclamation of the President of the United States, and of the circular letter of the Secretary of their Treasury Department of the 2d of November, 1810. The Director General of the Customs is accordingly informed that the Berlin and Milan decrees must not be applied to any American vessels that have entered French ports since the 1st of November, or may enter in future. By the letter of the Grand Judge, Minister of Justice, it is ordered that "in consequence of the engagement entered into by the United States (the President's proclamation and the circular of the Secretary of the Treasury) all the causes that may be pending in the Council of Prizes of captures of American vessels, made after the 1st of November, *and those that may in future be brought before it, shall not be judged according to the principles of the decrees of Berlin and Milan,* but that they shall remain suspended; the vessels captured or seized to remain only in a state of sequestration, and the rights of the proprietors being reserved for them until the 2d of February next, the period at which, the United States having fulfilled the engagement to cause their rights to be respected, *the said captures shall be declared null by the Council,* and the American vessels restored, together with their cargoes, to their proprietors."

It is not irrelevant to observe that these two letters were immediately made public in France. They appeared even in a Bordeaux newspaper as early as the 30th of December.

Accordingly, as soon as the restrictions on British vessels and on British merchandise, as announced by the previous acts of the American Government, had actually been carried into effect, on the 2d of February, 1811, and an account of it had been received by the French Government, the American vessels were admitted to entry in the French ports, although they might have been in contravention to the Berlin and Milan decrees; and the vessels which had been captured subsequent to the 1st of November, 1810, by virtue of those decrees, were released in all cases where some other objection unconnected with those decrees, such as the question of ownership in the case of the *Belisarius,* did not occur.

It was with reference to all these circumstances that his excellency the Minister of Marine, in a letter of the 30th of November, 1813, to the Council of State, stated that the revocation of the Berlin and Milan decrees had been *definitively pronounced* only on the 2d of February, 1811. His expressions are, "que le Capitaine Raoul, commandant les deux frégates, parti de la rivière de Nantes le 28 Decembre, 1810, n'a pas pû avoir connoissance de la revocation des décrets de Berlin et de Milan, à l'egard des Americains, revocation qui n'a été définitivement prononcée que le 2 Fevrier suivant." Without admitting the correctness of that statement in all its parts, it is at least evident that the minister knew, and that the Council of State might have seen by that letter, that there was some other act besides, and previous to the decree of the 28th of April, 1811, by which the revocation had been already definitively pronounced.

The general admission of American vessels to entry was announced to Mr. Russel, Chargé d'Affaires of the United States, by a letter of the Duke of Bassano, of the 4th of May, 1811. To prove that no distinction was made with respect to vessels, in contravention to the Berlin and Milan decrees, it will be sufficient, in addition to the case of the *Belisarius*, to mention that of the *New Orleans Packet*.

That vessel arrived from Gibraltar at Bordeaux the 3d of December, 1810, and had, besides, been boarded by two public British vessels. She was immediately, for these express causes, seized by the Director of Customs, as having violated the Milan decree. On the representation of the American Chargé d'Affaires, and in conformity with the letter of the Minister of Finances, of the 25th of December, 1810, which has already been quoted, the vessel and cargo were restored to the consignees, on giving bond to pay the estimated value, should it definitively be so decided. And, according to orders given to that effect, the bond was cancelled shortly after the date of the Duke of Bassano's letter of the 4th of May, 1811.

With respect to vessels *captured* subsequent to the 1st of November, 1810, I can appeal to the records of the court of prizes for proof that not a single one was condemned for a contravention to the Berlin and Milan decrees. The archives of this legation, though necessarily defective in that respect, enable me to mention the following vessels, viz: the *Two Brothers*, *Good Intent*, *Star*, *Neptune*, and *Acastus*, all of which, having been captured and brought into port for having contravened those decrees, were acquitted and released in consequence of their revocation. Whether, besides the *Dolly* and the *Telegraph*, there might not be some other case which remained undecided in April, 1814, I cannot positively assert. There is none within my knowledge.

It is material to add, that all the vessels which I have mentioned were released *before the 8th of May*, 1812, the day on which the decree of the 28th of April, 1811, is stated by the Council of State to have been published in the Moniteur. And your excellency may have perceived that in the preceding statement of facts I have not alluded to that decree. Indeed, if the Council of State, instead of suggesting that the revocation of the Berlin and Milan decrees was unknown to the minister of the United States at the time when he wrote his letter of the 12th of March, 1812, had only said that he was unacquainted with the decree of the 28th April, 1811, I would, whilst showing, as I have done, that his ignorance in that respect was irrelevant to the question, have acknowledged the fact to be true. That decree was first communicated to him on the 10th of May, 1812, and did not reach the Government of the United States till the 13th of July following, that is to say, one month after war had been declared against England. It therefore had no effect on any of their acts, or any part of their conduct. The compact was complete without it, and rested on the official declarations of the Minister of Foreign Relations, and on the execution of the engagement on the part of the French Government. In what manner that Government chose to announce the revocation to its officers and subjects was immaterial to the United States. The only point in which they were concerned was, that that revocation should, according to the engagement, be faithfully carried into effect. And this is the reason why I thought it necessary to show in what manner it was executed in France. Why the publication of the decree of 28th April, 1811, was delayed is not known to the United States, and they have no interest in knowing it. The delay cannot affect them, since their rights, founded on compact, are independent of the decree, and would be precisely the same if it had never been enacted.

Had all these facts been brought within the view of the Council of State; had that body been aware that the revocation of the Berlin and Milan decrees had been the result of an engagement taken by the French Government, on a condition which had been faithfully fulfilled by that of the United States; had they been informed that it was thus considered by the former Government of France, and that every decision which had heretofore taken place in relation to American vessels was consistent with the principle that those decrees had ceased to have effect with respect to American commerce from the first of November, 1810, it is impossible to suppose that the presumed ignorance of that revocation on the part of the captains of two French frigates could have been alleged as a reason why the owners of the *Dolly* and *Telegraph* should not be indemnified for the destruction of their vessels and cargoes more than one year after that date.

The ignorance on the part of the captains may be accepted as a sufficient justification for every part of their conduct, so far as respects their responsibility towards their own Government, if that Government thinks it proper. That is a point in which the United States have no concern. But that circumstance cannot release the Government of France from their engagement with that of America, that the decrees should have no effect after the first of November, 1810, nor from the obligation of indemnifying the American citizens who may, in contravention of that engagement, have sustained losses by the erroneous application of those decrees subsequent to that day.

The Government of France, having once entered into that engagement, became responsible for its faithful and complete execution. The solemn promise was made on the 5th of August, 1810, and it became irrevocable, provided the condition attached to it was fulfilled. In postponing the execution till the first of November—an epoch fixed by the French Government itself—time was taken, sufficient in its own opinion, to give the necessary orders and to insure the performance of the promise. It became the duty of that Government to give instructions to that effect to their tribunals and officers; and they are bound to indemnify if, through neglect, or any other cause, some of their naval officers were not duly instructed, and American citizens have suffered any injury on that account. The condition annexed to the revocation, as announced on the 5th of August, 1810, was only that the United States should act in conformity with the act of Congress of the first of May preceding. As there was, of course, the strongest probability that that condition would be fulfilled, and that the revocation would, as in fact it did, take effect on the first of November following, orders ought to have been immediately issued to prevent, after that day, any act violating the engagement. It may be added, without attaching much importance to the fact, that the President's proclamation and the Treasury circular of the 2d of November, 1810, were communicated by Mr. Russell to the Duke of Cadore on the 17th of December following, that is to say, eleven days prior to the sailing of the *Medusa*.

In the case of the *Dolly* and *Telegraph*, there are two distinct acts committed by the captains of the French frigates,—the capture of the American vessels, and afterwards their destruction. In all cases of capture the United States have a right to demand a trial by a competent tribunal. According to the present jurisprudence of France, that tribunal appears to be the Committee of the Council of State, known by the name of "Comité du Contentieux." The first question they had to decide was, whether the capture was legal or not? On that question there could not have been any hesitation. The series of the acts connected with the revocation, the decree itself, of the 28th of April, 1811, all the former precedents, all the decisions of the council of prizes, left not the smallest doubt that the Berlin and Milan decrees had ceased to have effect on the first of November, 1810, and that any subsequent capture, founded on those decrees, was illegal and null. Indeed, there would have been no difficulty if the captains of the frigates, ignorant of the revocation, had only captured the *Dolly* and *Telegraph* and sent them into port for adjudication. Those two vessels would have been acquitted and restored, as were all the other American vessels that were brought into French ports under similar circumstances. Instead of pursuing this course, the French captains plundered and burnt the ships. This act renders the restoration impracticable; but, the capture being illegal, it does not, at least, release the French Government from its responsibility.

A belligerent has a right to capture, and, at his discretion, to destroy, the vessels of the enemy. With respect to neutrals, he can only capture and send in for adjudication the vessels pursuing a trade contrary to the duties imposed on neutrals by the law of nations. It is already sufficiently hard on them that the decision should be made by a tribunal of the belligerent power. But the benefit of such a trial was never denied to them; not even by the Berlin and Milan decrees. Those decrees declared, in violation of the law of nations, neutral vessels liable to capture and condemnation for pursuing a legitimate commerce; but they did not change the course of proceedings with respect to the mode of decision. A trial and condemnation, by a competent tribunal, were still necessary. Navy officers, by the law of nations, never are, and even by those decrees were not, authorized, in any case, to burn at sea the vessels of a nation at peace. Such an act is a wanton outrage, wholly unjustifiable, and for which, if at any time committed, even under a plea of necessity, the nation is always responsible. The most aggravating circumstance of the whole case cannot, in any view of the subject, be adduced as a reason to defeat the right of the parties to an indemnity. That indemnity is equally due by the Government of France; that Government is equally responsible for the outrage committed by the officers of its Navy, whether the act be owing to neglect in not issuing in time the necessary orders, to improper or unauthorized conduct on the part of the officers, or to any other cause.

Having laid before your excellency what, I trust, will be considered a conclusive statement of facts, it grieves me to be compelled to say, that the decision of the Council of State of the 19th of December last is the first positive act by which the Government of France seems to have considered itself as released from the solemn obligation contracted with the United States, "That the Berlin and Milan decrees were to cease to have effect after the first of November, 1810." And it has afforded me great relief to find, on the face of that ordinance, irrefragable proofs that it must be ascribed to an unintentional error, arising from the council not having been put in possession of all the material facts connected with the case.

I apply, therefore, to your excellency, with perfect confidence in the justice of his Majesty's Government, and have the honor to request, first, that you will be pleased to lay the subject before his Majesty, in order that the ordinance of the 23d of December last may be rescinded and a revision of the affair ordered; secondly, that when brought again before the Council of State you will have the goodness to have all the facts relative to the revocation of the Berlin and Milan decrees fairly laid before that body, in order that the owners of the Dolly and Telegraph may receive the indemnity justly due to them for such a wanton and unjustifiable outrage as the destruction of their vessels and cargoes.

I request your excellency to accept the assurances, &c.,

ALBERT GALLATIN.

His Excellency BARON PASQUIER,
    Minister of Foreign Affairs, &c., &c., &c.

No. 143.

Extract of a letter from Mr. Gallatin, Envoy Extraordinary and Minister Plenipotentiary of the United States to France, to Mr. Adams, Secretary of State, dated

PARIS, *April* 27, 1820.

"Mr. Pasquier has also informed me that he had referred to the Minister of Justice my remonstrance, of the 15th of March last, against the decision of the Council of State in the case of the *Dolly* and *Telegraph*. This is a very unusual course in an affair where our rights are founded on a positive agreement between the two countries—an agreement entirely political, and in which the Minister of Foreign Affairs was the organ of the French Government."

No. 147.

Extract of a letter from Mr. Gallatin, Envoy Extraordinary and Minister Plenipotentiary of the United States to France, to Mr. Adams, Secretary of State, dated

PARIS, *June* 9, 1820.

"Being yet without instructions on the subject of our claims for indemnity, I acquiesced in Mr. Parish's wish to lay the Antwerp cases before the Department of Foreign Affairs, and have the honor to inclose the copy of a letter which I wrote to Mr. Pasquier on that subject."

In duplicate of Mr. Gallatin's No. 147.

PARIS, *May 9, 1820.*

SIR: I had the honor, on the 11th of February, 1819, to transmit to his excellency General Dessolle a memorial of Mr. David Parish to his excellency the Minister of Finances, relative to certain American vessels and cargoes sequestered at Antwerp in the beginning of the year 1807; and I now beg leave to transmit a new application of that gentleman, addressed to your excellency. Permit me to add a few observations to those contained in those memorials and in my letter of the 11th of February, 1819, to General Dessolle.

The only extraordinary French decree in force when those vessels arrived at Antwerp was that of Berlin, dated the 21st of November, 1806. Some of its enactments were unjust and contrary to the law of nations; yet it made merchandise liable to confiscation only in case of its being British property, or of the manufacture or produce of Great Britain or her colonies. With respect to vessels coming from England, it was by that decree only declared that they should not be received in French ports; and such vessels were, with their cargoes, made liable to confiscation only in case they should have contravened that provision by means of a false declaration. It was not until the 17th of December, 1807, that, by the still more arbitrary decree of Milan, neutral vessels which might have been searched by an English ship or sent to England were declared to be denationalized and good prize.

The vessels in question were bound from the United States to France; but had on their passage been sent forcibly to England, and were afterwards released. They do not seem to have come in any shape within the purview of the Berlin decree. But even if considered as coming from England, within the meaning of the act, as they had not concealed the fact by any false declaration, the utmost penalty to which they were liable by that or any other existing decree was not to be received in a French port. Their being, nevertheless, admitted and sequestered, instead of being sent off, was the act of the French Government. They were detained, as will immediately be shown, only in order to ascertain whether there was not some other contravention of the decree; whether the cargo, or some part of it, was not British property. Unless this can be established, or that they had made a false declaration, the simple fact of their having arrived at Antwerp from an English port, did not make them liable to confiscation.

By an imperial decision of July 2, 1808, the cargoes, being of a perishable nature, were ordered to be sold and the proceeds to be placed as a deposit in the *casse d' amortissement;* and in inquiry was directed to be made in order to ascertain whether the property was not British. H. E. Baron Louis, to whom, as Minister of Finances, the memorial of Mr. Parish above mentioned had been addressed, wrote to him on the 22d of May, 1819, that the proceeds of the sales had been withdrawn by superior orders from the *caisse d' amortissement* and paid into the public treasury; and he adds that they were thereby definitively acquired by the state. He has communicated neither the date nor the tenor of those orders. That he should have considered them as precluding him, on his own authority and without the sanction of Government, from ordering the money to be repaid to the American owners may be understood; and it is presumed that this was his meaning. He cannot have intended either to pronounce on the merits of the case or to maintain the untenable position that the transmission of the money from one public chest to another could have affected the rights of the parties. Its being expended for public purposes instead of remaining as a deposit is a proof of the wants of Bonaparte, but is not a decision on the case. A definitive confiscation, even under the imperial *regime*, could only take place with the usual forms, and by virtue of a direct and positive act to that effect. All that was done by that Government with respect to this property was the order of sale, the order to place the proceeds in some public chest, and the inquiry relative to the ownership. No final decision, no condemnation has ever taken place.

It happens even that, with the exception of these vessels and of four others consigned to Mr. Ridgeway, the American consul at Antwerp, all the other cargoes sequestered in that port under similar circumstances were delivered to the owners, and that the conditional bonds they had given were returned to them. The principle has thus been decided in favor of the claimants, and nothing remains but to apply it to their special case.

Having received special instructions from my Government in regard to this claim, it is in its name that I beg leave to call your excellency's attention to Mr. Parish's memorial, and that I ask for that decision which justice requires, and which has been but too long protracted.

Your Excellency will perceive that this decision does not depend on the question of the legality or illegality of the Berlin and Milan decree, and that I have argued as if those acts had been valid. Although they cannot certainly be admitted as such by the Government of the United States, it is a question unconnected with the present case and which is reserved for a future discussion.

I request your excellency to accept the assurances, &c.,

ALBERT GALLATIN.

His Excellency Baron PASQUIER,
    Minister of Foreign Affairs, &c., &c., &c.

Extract of a letter from Mr. Adams to Mr. Gallatin, dated

DEPARTMENT OF STATE, *Washington, March 31, 1821.*

"Mr. Archibald Gracie has again solicited some special interposition of this Government to press that of France for the adjustment of his claim. He considered it as standing upon grounds so clear and incontrovertible, that the French Government cannot ultimately resist the equitable obligation of providing for it.

"The Government of the United States cannot undertake to discriminate between the comparative merits of the claims of their citizens upon the Government of France. It asks justice for them all; it asks no more than justice for any. More than two years since the claims of Mr. Gracie, and all the Antwerp cases, were recommended to your special attention, in the presumption that, standing on ground peculiarly imposing on the French Government, it would not be able to resist them, and that success in those cases would pave the way for it in all others. It is in this view, that is, by pressing this and the

Antwerp cases generally, the other cases would not only not be injured but benefitted, that your attention to them is suggested. The force of example, added to the other powerful considerations in their favor, might do much. But that is left altogether to your judgment, aided as you are by all the lights belonging to the subject; and unless you shall be satisfied that the proposed pressure will have the good effect contemplated, it is expected that you will, of course, decline it."

Mr. Adams to Mr. Gallatin.

DEPARTMENT OF STATE, *Washington, June 29, 1821.*

SIR: I have the honor of inclosing herewith a copy of a letter received at this Department, some time since, from Mr. Connel, as agent for sundry insurance companies in Philadelphia having claims upon the French Government, upon which I would refer you to the letter which I lately wrote you concerning the case of Mr. Gracie's claim. These gentlemen appear to have received recent information, upon which they place some reliance, indicating on the part of the French Government a disposition more favorable to claimants upon their justice than had been previously manifested. Should any prospect of that nature be perceived by you, your own disposition to make it available for the benefit of the sufferers will, itself, serve the purpose of a standing instruction.

I am, with great respect, sir, your very humble and obedient servant,

· JOHN QUINCY ADAMS.

No. 193.

Extract of a letter from Mr. Gallatin, Envoy Extraordinary and Minister Plenipotentiary of the United States to France, to Mr. Adams, Secretary of State, dated

PARIS, *November 15, 1821.*

"Mr. De la Grange, the lawyer generally employed in American cases, having requested me to transmit to the Minister of Foreign Affairs a copy of his memoir in the appeal of Richard Faxon, now pending before the Council of State, for indemnity on account of a seizure made at Santander, in the year 1812, I addressed to Mr. Pasquier, on the 31st ultimo, a note on the subject, copy of which, as well as of the said memoir, I have the honor to inclose. You will perceive that I took that opportunity of reminding the minister of the case of the 'Dolly' and 'Telegraph,' on which it does not seem that the Minister of Justice has yet made any report."

Mr. Gallatin to Baron Pasquier.

[Translation.]

PARIS, *October 31, 1821.*

SIR: I have the honor to transmit to your excellency, under this cover, a memorial addressed to the King, in his Council of State, for Richard Faxon, a citizen of the United States, who complains of a judgment of the Board of Finances, approved by his excellency the minister of the same department.

The question is of a seizure made by the French customs in 1812, at Santander, in the stores of Joachim Munios, of a quantity of sugars belonging to said Faxon. The Board of Finances seems to have dismissed his claim from supposed presumption that he was not the proprietor, and your excellency, by glancing over the memorial, will be convinced that there can be no doubt in this regard.

But the Board has, if I may be allowed the expression, reserved a subsidiary question, that of knowing if a citizen of the United States could pretend to any indemnity for having suffered, in this part of Spain, the application of the laws of France, which then aimed at colonial goods. Ignorant of what laws the Board speaks, I can only observe, generally, that none could ever give the right of seizing, without indemnity, upon the known property of a citizen of the United States deposited for three years, without having been there molested, in the stores of his correspondent.

As it is, however, possible that the laws in question may be no other than the Berlin and Milan decrees, and the different imperial or administrative decrees which have been the consequence of them, I pray your excellency to be pleased to lay before the Council of State the correspondence between the ministers of the Government, from that time, and those of the United States, as well as the other documents, which prove that these decrees had been repealed, in regard of the United States, long before the seizure of the sugars of Mr. Faxon.

I ought also to remind your excellency of another affair, more important for the principles which apply to it, but which depends, likewise, upon the date of the repeal of these two celebrated decrees. I had the honor to address to you, under date of March 15, 1820, a very long note on the subject of the decision of the Council of State, by which the claim of the proprietors of the vessels *Dolly* and *Telegraph*, burned on the open sea by two French frigates in November and December, 1811, was rejected. This decision could only have taken place because the documents proving the date of the repeal had not been laid before the Council. But it is supported by considerations which can only produce the most troublesome effects. I can assure your excellency that the revision is of high importance, and I hope that you will judge that a delay, which is already upwards of twenty months, ought to be no further prolonged.

I pray your excellency to accept the assurance, &c.,

ALBERT GALLATIN.

No. 200.

Extract of a letter from Mr. Gallatin to the Secretary of State, dated

PARIS, *January* 14, 1822.

"I have the honor to inclose the copy of a note which I wrote on the 10th instant to the Minister of Foreign Affairs, on the subject of the Antwerp claims."

PARIS, *January* 10, 1822.

SIR: I had the honor, on the 9th of May, 1820, to transmit to your excellency's predecessor a memorial of Mr. David Parish, relative to the American cargoes sequestered at Antwerp in the beginning of the year 1807, and to add some observations in support of the claim. Twenty months having since elapsed, a time amply sufficient to make every inquiry respecting the merits of the case, I have been instructed by my Government to renew the application, and to call, in the most forcible manner, the earnest attention of his Majesty's ministers to that subject.

In urging a decision on this reclamation, separately from others, there is not the most distant intention of abandoning the other claims of citizens of the United States for the indemnities so justly due to them. But it is time, after so many delays, to obtain at last a decisive answer, and to ascertain the determination of the Government of France in that respect. And this claim has been selected because it is altogether free of any of the objections, however unfounded these may be, which have been suggested in regard to other cases.

It is not, in the first place, necessary in this instance to discuss questions connected with the illegality of any of the decrees contravening the law of nations, which were issued by Bonaparte. The vessels in question had not violated any of those decrees; their cargoes were not liable to confiscation by virtue of any provision contained in any edict in force at the time of their seizure.

And, secondly, not only is the case entire, with not only that there been no trial or condemnation of the cargoes, but the principal that they were not liable to confiscation has been settled by the decisions of Government in analogous cases, and even with respect to portions of the identical property for which indemnity is now claimed.

I trust that I will be able to establish both these positions to your excellency's satisfaction.

The only extraordinary decree of the French Government affecting the navigation of neutral nations, in force at the time of the arrival of the vessels alluded to in a French port, was that issued at Berlin, the 21st of November, 1806.

It was by that decree, amongst other provisions, declared: 1st, that merchandise belonging to a British subject, or being the produce or the manufactures of colonies of Great Britain, should be condemned as good prize, (Art. 5 and 6;) 2d, that no vessel coming directly from England or from her colonies, or going there (qui s'y rendra) after the known publication of the decree, should be permitted to enter any French port, (Art. 8;) 3d, that every vessel contravening the decree by a false declaration should be seized and her cargo confiscated as British property, (Art. 9.)

During the first months subsequent to that decree a number of American vessels arrived in France, coming from the United States, but having on their passage been compelled to stop in England, either by British cruisers or by stress of weather. The question arose whether it was intended by the 8th article of the decree to exclude only vessels which had gone voluntarily to an English port, or whether it included even those which had been compelled to do it by what is called *relâche forcée.* The words used in the article, *venant directement* and *qui s'y rendra,* seemed to favor the first construction; and it was clear that if the last was adopted, British cruisers had nothing to do but to stop for a few days every neutral vessel bound to France in order to destroy her external commerce. These, however, were questions for the French authorities exclusively to decide. It was altogether in their power to have decided that the vessels in question were embraced by the decree, and to have refused to admit them in any port. The Minister of Finances, impelled by what was evidently for the interest of the French commerce, allowed the cargoes to be provisionally landed and deposited in the public stores until the decision of Bonaparte on the question was known, and permitted, also, that they should be delivered to the consignees on their giving an obligation to pay to the custom-house the estimated value thereof if so ordered by that decision. It was, therefore, by the act of the French Government that the vessels landed their cargoes instead of being ordered off. And that provisional construction continued in force till the 4th of September, 1807, when the Director General of the Douanes announced, by a circular, "That the Emperor had decided that the 8th and 9th articles must have their full and entire execution, and that no vessel which had touched in England, or been conducted there, could be admitted." "Thus," added the Director, "the immediate retrogradation of those vessels shall be required, whatever be the alleged causes of superior force and the documents produced in proof thereof. Those which, by a false declaration, may conceal the fact of having touched in England and succeed in thus entering our ports, shall be seized, and the vessels and their cargoes shall be proceeded against in the form prescribed by the decree in relation to English property." In conformity with this decision, several American vessels bound to Antwerp were sent away, amongst which may be mentioned the "Dragon" and the "Two Brothers," and also the Orozimbo, belonging to one of the owners of the cargoes for which indemnity is now claimed, although her cargo had already been actually landed. It would have been fortunate for the owners of the merchandise, which is the object of this reclamation, that this decision should have been made from the first, or that when made it should have been applied to their property.

Amongst the American vessels arrived from the United States in French ports in the year 1807, prior to the decision of September 4, and which had been compelled to touch in England, seven came to Antwerp, consigned to two American houses, the Bordeaux Packet, Helena, North America, and Diamond, to that of Mr. Ridgway, and the Perseverance, Hiram, and Mary, to that of Mr. Parish. The consignees declined availing themselves of the option offered by the French authorities to receive the cargoes, on giving bond for their value, to abide by the final decision of Bonaparte. *(a.)* They preferred that the cargoes should remain in the custom-house stores subject to that decision. Their motive was obvious.

It was only by the subsequent decree of Milan of November 23, 1807, that it was enacted, "That all vessels which, after having touched at England, might, from any motive whatever, enter the ports of France, should be seized and confiscated as well as their cargoes, without exception or distinction of produce or merchandise." The only causes of confiscation by the Berlin decree were concealment of the fact of having touched in England, and the merchandise being either British property or the produce of England or of her colonies. It was known to the consignees, had already been acknowledged, and was further substantiated by a subsequent inquiry, that every part of the cargoes belonged to American citizens, and that no part was the produce of Great Britain or of her colonies. It was equally known, and has never been denied, that the captains of all the seven vessels had, on their first arrival, made no concealment; that they had all made true declarations of the compulsory touching in England, *(relâche forcée.)* The expected imperial decision could, therefore, only apply to the doubtful question whether the vessels and cargoes in that predicament were embraced or not by the article of the decree which forbade, in general terms, the admission of vessels that had touched in England, whether the cargoes in question should be admitted or sent away. In case the decision should be that the vessels were, notwithstanding the *relâche forcée,* included in the article of the decree, and that the cargoes were inadmissible, they might, by remaining in the public stores in their original state, be sent out of France, and the decision be strictly complied with. But if, instead of that, those cargoes were sold, (and the consignees could have had no object in receiving them but that of selling them,) the exportation could not have taken place in conformity with the decision; and the consignees, unable to comply with it, might have been compelled to pay the amount of the bond, which would have been tantamount to a confiscation of the property.

The decision of September 4, 1807, being made only prospective, the consignees at first hoped that the cargoes of the seven vessels previously arrived would be admitted to be sold for home consumption, and accordingly delivered to them. But when they found themselves disappointed in that respect, adhering to the same line of conduct which they had pursued, not to depart from the enactments of the Berlin decree, they applied on the 22d of March, 1808, to the Director General of the Douanes, and on the 7th of April ensuing renewed the application, both to him and to the Minister of Finances, stating that, the steps they had taken to obtain the definitive admission of that merchandise having been fruitless, and the goods, especially the potash, rice, brown sugar, and cochineal, becoming gradually damaged in the entrepôt, they now asked the permission to export the merchandise to a foreign country, and that in conformity with the decree of November 21, 1806.

In answer to that petition, Bonaparte ordered, by a decision of July 2, 1808, that the cargoes should be sold and the proceeds deposited in the caisse d'amortissement, and that an inquiry should be made on each of the vessels which had brought in the cargoes in order to ascertain whether the owners were not British. On this decision it is only necessary to observe that it corroborates what has already been stated, and was, indeed, evident, that no concealment having been made by the captains of their *relâche forcée* in England, no other cause or pretence for confiscation could be or was alleged than the apprehension that the property was British or of British origin.

To the sale of the cargoes for the purpose intended the consignees did of course object; and they succeeded in preventing it for two years. But to that part of the decision which ordered an inquiry they cheerfully submitted, and communicated all the documents, papers, and letters connected with the vessels and their cargoes. A severe scrutiny took place, the result of which was altogether favorable, it being proven in the clearest manner that the cargoes were exclusively owned by American citizens. Of their origin there does not appear to have ever existed any doubt.

The merchandise, notwithstanding the result of this inquiry, was not restored to the consignees. By a decree dated at Ebersdorf, May 29, 1809, 780 barrels of potash and pearlash, making part of the cargoes of the Perseverance and Mary, were put at the disposal of the Minister of War, and the estimated value directed to be paid by him in the caisse d'amortissement. That portion of the cargoes was accordingly taken from the enterpôt and delivered to that department, having previously been valued at near 450,000 francs, notwithstanding a deduction made on account of the damages arising from the long detention in the public stores. Finally, the whole of the residue of the cargoes was sold in June, 1810, by virtue of an imperial decision of May 4, of that year. It is asserted that by virtue of an order subsequent to the sales, which has never been published nor communicated, the proceeds of those sales were ultimately paid, in whole or in part, into the public treasury.

Your excellency must agree with me that, from the preceding statement of facts, it evidently follows, 1st, That, as I had stated in the beginning of this letter, there has been in this case no violation of any existing decree that the cargoes were not liable to confiscation by virtue of any provision contained in any edict then in force; 2d, That the consignees uniformly took those decrees as the basis of their conduct, and committed no act which might impair the rights of the owners of the property; 3d, That, by allowing the cargoes to be deposited in the public stores until the decision of Bonaparte was known, whether the vessels were or were not embraced by the article of the decree which forbade the admission of those which had gone to England, a formal engagement had been contracted on the part of Government to permit the exportation of the merchandise in conformity with the decree, in case the decision was against its being admitted for home consumption; 4th, That, although nothing could be further from the views of the Minister of Finances, yet it was solely owing to the doubts he entertained respecting the construction of the Berlin decree that the cargoes fell in the possession of the custom-house; that it was the unforeseen consequence of his act, which was that of the proper French authority in that case, that, the above mentioned engagement not having been fulfilled, the owners have, by a flagrant injustice, been to this day deprived of the merchandise and of its proceeds.

The fact that there has been no trial or condemnation of the property is notorious, and I would at once proceed to the decisions made in analogous cases, was it not necessary to take, in the first place, notice of a most extraordinary and unfounded inference drawn from a fact immaterial in itself, and which, although not officially communicated, has been made known to me by the parties.

Among the several applications for indemnity made at different times and in various shapes by the consignees, a memorial had been addressed to the Minister of Finances by Mr. Parish, which, at his

---

(a) To this there were two exceptions, the consignees having subscribed obligations, first, for a small quantity of potash, (about 15,000 francs in value,) received and sold by them on the first arrival of the vessel; secondly, for the value of some of those vessels, in order to enable them to leave the port. The others were permitted to depart without the bond being required.

request, I transmitted on the 11th of February, 1819, to Marquis Dessolle. I wrote again to that minister on the same subject on the 23d of March following, and had requested that a report intended to be made by the direction of the Douanes to the Minister of Finances might be communicated to me. This was not done; but H. E. Baron Louis wrote to Mr. Parish on the 22d of May of the same year that the proceeds of the sales had been withdrawn by superior orders from the caisse d'amortissement, and paid into the public treasury; and he added that they were thereby definitively acquired by the State. This inference appeared so preposterous that, when alluding to it in my letter of the 9th of May, 1820, to H. E. Baron Pasquier, I said that I presumed the meaning of the Minister of Finances to have simply been that he considered the orders in question as precluding him on his own authority, and without the sanction of Government from ordering the money to be repaid to the American owners.

The assertion having, however, been made in that broad way, I am compelled to refute it. But I beg your excellency to be persuaded that I do it only in a hypothetical way, and in discharge of my responsibility, and that I do not suppose or mean to insinuate that it ever has been or can be the intention of his Majesty's ministers seriously to resort to such an untenable pretence for the purpose of avoiding the payment of a just debt. I consider the objection as being the work of a subordinate agent, whose duty it may have been to collect whatever might be suggested against claims on the public treasury, and the communication to Mr. Parish as only intended to afford him the means of knowing and repelling every such suggestion. For that purpose the following observations will, it is hoped, be deemed conclusive:

1. It was declared by the 22d article of the convention between France and the United States of the 30th September, 1800, (a) which was in full force when the vessels in question arrived at Antwerp, that the established courts for prize causes should alone take cognizance of them; that whenever such tribunal of either of the parties should pronounce judgment against any vessel, or goods, or property, claimed by the citizens of the other party, the sentence or decree should mention the reasons or motives on which the same should have been founded; and that an authenticated copy of the sentence or decree, and of all the proceedings in the case, should, if demanded, be delivered to the commander or agent of the said vessel. By the 10th article of the Berlin decree, the Council of Prizes at Paris was accordingly charged to decide on all cases arising under the said decree in the following words: "Notre Conseil des Prises à Paris est chargé de décider de toutes contestations qui pourront s'élever au sujet des prises qui en vertu du present decret pourront être faites, tant dans notre empire que dans les pays occupés par nos troupes." There having never been any trial in the cases in question before the Council of Prizes, there can have been no condemnation of the property, in conformity either with the solemn obligations of the treaty or with the provisions of the only decree in force at the time, and applicable to those cases. (b)

2. Independent of any consideration drawn from treaty obligations, or from the provisions of the decree itself, it is equally repugnant to the principles of the law of nations, as generally recognized by the civilized world, and to those of the municipal laws of any civilized nation, to consider the order in question as implying the condemnation of the property of the parties, or as in the smallest degree affecting their rights. There was not in this case even the form of a trial—no hearing of the parties—no notice given to them of any alleged ground for condemnation, or even of any intention to bring them to a trial. Nor was the order alluded to communicated to them or made public either in the bulletin of laws or in any other manner. On those topics it is unnecessary to dwell; it is sufficient to have stated them. I will only observe that, without publicity in laws or decrees, there would be no guaranty for the rights of individuals; that publication has, therefore, by the laws of every well ordered country, of France as well as of every other, always been made a necessary ingredient of any judgment or decree affecting such rights; and that the fact of the order in this case not having been published, or at least communicated, is alone a conclusive proof that it was a mere administrative order binding on the public functionaries to whom it was directed, and in no shape impairing or affecting the ultimate rights of the parties.

3. The official reports and acts of Government, since the restoration, are in direct contradiction with the inference attempted to be drawn, that the payment (versement) into the treasury, or the application to public purposes of funds before deposited there, is tantamount to a definitive acquisition to the state of such funds, and releases it from the obligation of repaying the same. This will be fully demonstrated by the following quotations from the report of the Minister of Finances, (Baron Louis himself,) of July 4, 1814:

"La caisse d'amortissement avoit été instituée dépositaire des fonds des cautionnemens . . . . ; les consignations judiciaires et plusieurs dépots particuliers lui avoient été confiés à la charge de les restituer. Tous ces fonds ont été depuis long tems, par les ordres du chef du Gouvernement, employés aux dépenses de l'Etat; les fonds déposés à la caisse d'amortissement sont les cautionnemens, ils s'élèvent à la somme de . . . . (dont elle) n'a actuellement reçu qu'une somme de . . . . Le surplus a été versé et est resté au trésor pour 88,675,000 francs, &c. Les consignations judiciaires déposés à la caisse d'amortissement s'élèvent à 11,814,000. Les autres fonds en dépôt sont . . . . total 7,358,000. Les remboursemens sur ces fonds ont été continués, &c.

"Les fonds dèposés à la caisse de service montent à 43,000,000. Les remboursemens des fonds déposés ont été fidèlement continués, quoiqú ils eussent été consommés, &c.

"La nécessité des anticipations les a introduites dès le commencement de chaque exercice, et bientôt elles se sont étendues à tous les fonds que ce ministére (des finances) a pû atteindre, et elles ont dévoré les fonds déposés, &c. . . . . L'arriéré du ministere des finances, au 1er Avril, se compose des dépots consommés, &c." *

(a) The convention was to be in force for eight years from the date of the exchange of the ratifications, which took place at Paris on the 31st of July, 1801.

(b) This provision appears to have been omitted in the Milan decrees of the 23d of November and 17th of December, 1807. But even then condemnations took place only by virtue of special and positive imperial decisions to that effect, and were not inferred from an order to pay in the treasury. Thus, in the case of the Sally, condemned under those decrees, the Minister of Finances wrote on the 6th of November, 1810, to the Director General of the Douanes: "J'ai l'honneur de vous informer que par decision du 30 Octobre dernier, Sa Majeste a ordonne la confiscation du navire Americain la Sally, Cap. M. Brown, ainsi que de sa cargaison, pour cause de deux relaches en Angleterre."

[Translation.]

a : "The caisse d'amortissement was instituted as a depository of the funds of securities; the judiciary deposits and several individual deposits were entrusted to it on a provision of restitution. All these funds were, for a long time, by the orders of the chief of the Government, employed for the expenses of the State; ——. The funds, deposited in the caisse d'amortissement, are the securities—they amount —— to the sum of ——, (of which it) has only actually received a sum of ——. The surplus has been paid over and remains in the treasury, for 88,675,000 francs, &c. The judiciary deposits, placed in the caisse

I must here beg leave to observe that I do not mean to say that H. E. Baron Louis was inconsistent with himself with respect to the question relative to the proceeds of the Antwerp cargoes. The transaction was probably unknown to him, or not attended to at the date of the report alluded to; or he may, at that time, have already been told that they made no part of those deposits (*dépots consommés*) which Government was bound to reimburse. All that concerns me is to refute the inference as made in his letter to Mr. Parish, that such deposits were acquired to the State merely because they had, by superior orders, been withdrawn from a certain *caisse*, and paid (versés) in the treasury. And it follows, irresistibly, from the quotations I have made, that it was the general habit of the head of the Government, at that time, to apply to the expenses of the State, whenever exigencies required it, every species of deposited funds without regard to their origin, or to the particular chest in which they were deposited; that the proceeds of the Antwerp cargoes would not have been any more respected had they been nominally left in the caisse d'amortissement instead of being transferred (versé) into the treasury; that the funds originally deposited, although withdrawn and expended, (consommés) continued to be faithfully reimbursed by Government, and especially that the payment (versement) in the treasury did not, as is clearly proven in the instance of the cautionnemens, operate as a release from the obligation of reimbursing the funds thus diverted and expended. I will add that, although those cautionnemens are not, from their nature, generally considered as a debt, the payment of which may be required, (cette exigible) yet a very considerable portion has actually been reimbursed to the functionaries or persons belonging to territories formerly annexed to France, which make no longer part of it. ·

4. The Council of State has decided, in an analogous case, that the payment in the treasury was not tantamount to a condemnation. In January, 1810, the American vessel *Eagle* had been captured, within five leagues of the shore, by a French privateer, and conducted to the port of Passage. The captured and captors made a compromise on the subject; but the vessel and cargo were seized, sequestered, sold, and the proceeds paid in the treasury by virtue of the decrees passed at that time by Bonaparte, under color of reprisals. The case was brought before the Council of State, who, on the 20th of April, 1820, ratified the compromise above mentioned, notwithstanding the opposition, both of the captured and of the general direction of the Douanes. The first reason assigned for this decision is in the following words: "Considérant qu'il n'existe dans l'espece aucun acte qui ait prononcé la confiscation du navire l'Aigle au profit du Gouvernement François." This case and that of the Antwerp vessels may differ in many other respects; but the Eagle was included in the general, arbitrary and unjustifiable seizures, known by the name of the St. Sebastian sequestration; and the vessels and cargoes, thus sequestered, are, so far as relates to the particular question now under discussion, precisely in the same predicament as the Antwerp cargoes. They were equally sold, nearly at the same time, and the proceeds were equally, by a similar order, paid in the treasury and applied to public purposes. Indeed, from the comparison of dates and other information obtained, I may assert, that the identical order by which the proceeds of the Antwerp cargoes were directed to be paid in the treasury included all the others which had been sequestered, and among them the St. Sebastian and Passage vessels and cargoes, including the Eagle. The fact, at all events, of the proceeds of sales in this last case having, like those of the Antwerp cargoes, been paid into the treasury, is not only notorious, but was within the full knowledge and view of the Council of State when the above decision was made. For, in the observations laid before it by the direction of the Douanes, in opposition to the claim of the captors, it is expressly stated, "*que c'est en vertu d'ordres émanés de S. M.* et ayant pour base le droit de représailles, que le sequestre avoit été mis, la vente effectuée, et *le produit versé au trésor.*" In declaring, therefore, that there existed no act which had pronounced the confiscation of the vessel *Eagle* to the profit of the French Government, the Council of State has explicitly and directly decided, that an order issued from Bonaparte, directing the sale of a vessel and cargo, and that the proceeds should be paid in the treasury, was not an act pronouncing the confiscation of such vessel and cargo, or of their proceeds.

Your excellency will probably think that it was superfluous on my part to have accumulated such an overwhelming mass of proofs for the purpose of crushing a mere shadow, which may be dissipated without recurring to any extraneous consideration. In taking for granted the order alluded to by Baron Louis, it must be assumed such as he had stated it, that is to say, as simply directing the withdrawing of the proceeds of sales from a certain chest, and their being paid into the treasury. Indeed, had there been anything further affecting the question in that document, he would not have failed to mention it in support of the inference attempted to be drawn. Such a decree, from its nature, must be strictly construed; it cannot be extended beyond what appears on the face of it, beyond its positive enactments, and be made to say what is not contained in it. Had it been intended not only to make use of the property for immediate exigencies, but to pronounce its definitive condemnation, there could have been no motive, since the decree was not to be published, for not inserting in it a positive clause to that effect, as was done in the other cases where condemnation was the object. But whatever may have been the intention, the omission of such a clause is of itself and alone conclusive against the gratuitous and unjustifiable assertion that the order is tantamount to a condemnation. · The order in question does not confiscate the property, because it contains no clause to that effect.

The acts and decisions of the Government directly supporting or recognizing the justice of the claim will now be stated.

All the vessels which arrived under similar circumstances with those whose cargoes were sequestered at Antwerp subsequent to the decision of the 4th of September, 1807, and prior to the Milan decree of the 23d of November ensuing, instead of being detained, were refused admittance and sent off. One of them, at least—the Orozimbo—was within the power of the Government, and her cargo, which, as has already been stated, was actually landed on account of repairs wanted by the vessel, might certainly have been seized. On the same principle on which she was suffered to depart with that cargo, those of the seven vessels previously detained should have been allowed to be exported. To admit that she was not liable to seizure was an acknowledgment that there was no right to sequester and sell those of the other vessels. But there are other cases still more in point.

d'amortissement, amount to 11,814,000. The other funds in deposit are ——— total 7,358,000. *The reimbursements* on these funds have been continued, &c.

"The funds deposited in the caisse de service amount ——— total 43,000,000. The reimbursements of the funds deposited have been faithfully continued, *although they had been expended, &c.*

· "The necessity of anticipations introduced them from the commencement of each duty, and they have often been extended to all the funds which this minister (of finances) could obtain, and they have *devoured the funds deposited, &c.* The arrearage of the Minister of Finances, on the 1st of April, is composed *of deposits expended, &c.*

It was only in the instance of the seven vessels in question that it was agreed that the cargoes should be deposited in the public stores until the final decision respecting the construction of the Berlin decree was known. The consignees of all the other numerous vessels which arrived during the same period, and under the same circumstances, in the other ports of France, preferred to avail themselves of the option given by the Minister of Finances to receive the cargoes and to give bond for the estimated value thereof. The obligations (soumissions) subscribed by the consignees were in the following form:

Etat des marchandises venues en ce port par le navire ——, que nous réclamons du sequestre de la Douane, où elles sont déposées par ordre, &c.
(Ici suit l'énumeration et l'évaluation des marchandises.)
"Laquelle somme de —— ——; nous nous soumettons, avec notre caution solidaire ——, représenter au receveur des Douanes de ——, si la décision de S. M. J. l'ordonne, pour cause de la relâche forcée en Angleterre du dit navire ——, nous réservant au besoin recours sur que de droit. Fait à ——, le ——."
(Signé) "Les consignataires et leur caution."*

The number of cases in which obligations of this kind were given is known to the French Government, though not to me, but it embraces, as already stated, all the vessels, the seven which came to Antwerp only excepted, which, having been compelled to touch in England, arrived in French ports from the publication of the Berlin decree in the latter end of 1806 until the decision of the 4th of September took place.

In no instance whatever has the payment of any one of these obligations been enforced. In every other instance but that of the Antwerp cargoes those of vessels precisely in the same predicament have been sold for the use of the owners, no steps taken to recover the estimated value for which the obligations were given, and, in some instances at least, those obligations have been positively annulled. Notwithstanding the difficulty of obtaining information on the last point, the parties interested in the Antwerp claims have been able to furnish me with the following extracts of two decisions:

"Du 20th Septembre, 1809.

"Napoleon, &c.
"La soumission souscrite à la Douane de Marseille par M. M. Autran Bellier, pour répondre de la valeur de la cargaison du navire Américain l'Elisa, qui avoit été remise à leur disposition, est annullée."

"Du 16 Novembre, 1809.

"Même decrete en faveur de M. Hottinguer, pour la cargaison du navire Americain l'Ann, arrivé à Cherbourg."†

Whatever may have been the motive of Government for not enforcing the payment of those obligations, the omission of doing it in any case whatever is an absolute recognition on its part that there was no ground for confiscation, and the two instances quoted are sufficient to establish the fact of positive decisions in cases perfectly similar to that which is the object of the present reclamation.

The same principle has been applied even to a portion of the identical property sequestered at Antwerp, the payment of similar obligations which, as already stated, had been subscribed, not only for some of the vessels but also for a small part of the cargo of one of them, having never been enforced.

Finally, indemnity has actually been paid since the restoration for a considerable portion of one of the cargoes.

The house of Mr. Parish had, a short time after the arrival of the vessels, sold to Messrs. Fillietaz & Co., of Antwerp, 256 bales of cotton, part of the cargo of the ship Hiram. It being then confidently expected that the merchandise would be delivered to the parties, the sale was absolute and at the risk of Mr. Fillietaz. He paid the purchase-money, received a proper bill of sale, and became thus vested with all the rights of the original shipper, but without recourse against him or the consignees. He was disappointed in his expectation of receiving the merchandise thus purchased. His cotton shared the fate of the rest, and was sold in the same manner and at the same time for a sum exceeding 400,000 francs. The proceeds, undistinguished from those of the other cargoes, were, in the same manner and under the same order, paid in the treasury. He applied for indemnity, as a subject or resident of Belgium, to the mixed commission appointed under the treaties and conventions of Paris. His claim was allowed and placed in the first class, that of *cautionnemens* and deposits,‡ and he has received in payment an inscription of five per cent. consolidated French stock, amounting in principal to 495,760 francs, bearing interest from the 22d of March, 1819, together with 10,726 francs in specie for arrears of interest, after deducting the commission expenses or charges.

It has now been fully demonstrated, not only that the claim is founded in strict justice; not only that

---

* [Translation.]
State of the merchandise brought into this port by the ship ——, which we claim from the sequestration of the custom-house, where they are deposited by order, &c.
[Here follows the enumeration and valuation of the merchandise.]
"Which sum of —— —— we submit, with our security for the whole debt ——, to represent to the Receiver of the Customs of ——, if the decision of his Imperial Majesty ordain it, on account of the forced visit in England of said ship ——, we reserving, in need, recourse to the legal tribunal. Done at ——, the ——.
(Signed) "The trustees and their security."

† [Translation.]
"September 20, 1809.
"Napoleon, &c.
"The underwritten recognizance to the custom-house of Marseilles, by M. M. Autran Bellier, to answer for the value of the cargo of the American ship Elisa, which was remitted to their disposal, is annulled."

"November 16, 1809.
"The same decrees in favor of M. Hottinguer, for the cargo of the American ship Ann, arrived at Cherbourg."

‡ Mr. Mertens, of Brussels, formerly a partner in the house of Mr. Ridgway, presented a claim to the same commission for the whole amount which had been consigned to that house. His application was rejected on correct grounds, because, although himself a subject of Belgium, his house was American, and because they were only consignees and not owners of the cargoes, the right to which, with the exception of the sale to Mr. Fillietaz, has remained the property of American citizens."

the property was never confiscated, and that there never was any decision to that effect, either in that or similar cases; not only that, on the contrary, there have been positive decisions recognizing the validity of the claim, but also that other foreigners, who had become owners of part of it, have been indemnified by virtue of the treaties concluded between his Majesty's Government and foreign powers. Permit me to add, that France has received and continues to enjoy the benefit of the money arising from the sales of the cargoes.

That money was paid in the treasury and applied towards defraying the public expenses of the State. Had it been restored to the legitimate owners and not thus applied, those expenses would have been exactly the same. The only difference would have been that the large *arriéré* left unpaid by Bonaparte would have been still further increased precisely by the sum thus detained from the American citizens. With what good faith the whole of that *arriéré*, without even excepting the expenses of the hundred days, has been liquidated and paid by his Majesty's Government is well known. In fact, unless France sets up two measures, one for her own subjects and all other foreigners, and another for the citizens of the United States, it is impossible that she can refuse discharging this just debt.

I beg leave to apply, not only for that payment, but also for a speedy decision. The United States had, from the most friendly motives, yielded to the reluctance to take up the subject of American claims which was evinced in the year 1817. The objection arising from the state of the finances and from the enormous amount of the demands pressing at that time on the resources of France has now happily ceased to exist. Time amply sufficient has in the meanwhile been taken for every possible investigation of this claim. The parties have already experienced most grievous losses from the long detention of so large an amount of property. They should not be tortured by further vexatious delays. Justice, when too tardy, often fails in its object. When it is known, as in this case, that such is the nature of the claim that it will ultimately be paid, intriguing speculators are never wanting who will try to take advantage of the distance and of the necessities of the claimants to purchase their rights at a depreciated rate. Such attempts, which, even when not actually tainted, never can avoid the suspicion of corruption, it has been my duty to repel, and heretofore with success. I have told the parties to listen to no proposals, to reject every indirect interference, that their claim was indisputable and must necessarily be allowed. We employ, to attain that object, no other but direct means; no weapons but those of argument. I trust that they will not have been used in vain when the appeal is made to your known loyalty, to his Majesty's high sense of justice, to those principles of good faith in discharging the obligations of the State which in every instance but that of the American claims have uniformly distinguished his Government.

I request your excellency to accept the reiterated assurances of the distinguished consideration with which I have the honor to be, &c., &c.,

ALBERT GALLATIN.

His Excellency Viscount DE MONTMORENCY,
   Minister of Foreign Affairs, &c., &c., &c.

No. 203.

Extract of a letter from Mr. Gallatin, Envoy Extraordinary and Minister Plenipotentiary of the United States to France, to Mr. Adams, Secretary of State, dated

PARIS, *January 28,* 1822.

' I had yesterday a conference with the Minister of Foreign Affairs on the subject of the Antwerp claims. In the course of it I referred him to my letters to one of his predecessors of November 9, 1816, and of April 22, 1817; to the first, in order that he might have a general view of the nature and extent of our claims; to the other, for the purpose of showing both the cause of the delay which had taken place on that subject, and that we had always considered the reclamations for property sequestered and not condemned to be of such nature that the claims ought to be liquidated and paid in the ordinary course of business, and did not require any diplomatic transaction. I then stated, that although our commercial difficulties might justly claim the more immediate attention of the two Governments, yet there was this difference between the two subjects, that the last was only one of mutual convenience, each party being, after all, at liberty, though at the risk of encountering countervailing measures, to regulate his own commerce as he pleased; whilst the question of indemnity for injuries sustained was one of right. In this case we demanded justice, and I was sorry to be obliged to say, that, notwithstanding my repeated applications during a period of near six years, I had not been able to obtain redress in one single instance for my fellow-citizens; an observation which applied not only to cases which had arisen under the former Government of France, but also to wrongs sustained under that of his Majesty. Such result could not escape the notice of my Government, and had accordingly been complained of in the most pointed manner in the instructions I had from time to time received. There was, indeed, an aggravating and most extraordinary circumstance with respect to the applications relative to injuries sustained under Bonaparte's Government. Not only had I failed in obtaining redress, but I had not even been honored with an answer. It could not be concealed that such a course of proceeding on the part of France had a tendency to impair the friendly relations between the two countries, and might have an unfavorable effect even in the discussion of other subjects. I therefore earnestly requested that he would immediately attend to the reclamation now before him, and no longer delay the decision which we had a right to expect."

"Viscount Montmorency at once answered that he had read the papers relative to the Antwerp sequestrations, and that he was struck with the justice of the claim. He regretted, he added, that the settlement of this reclamation should have fallen on the present ministry; that a decision had not taken place in the year 1819; that such an objection as that complained of had at that time been raised by the Minister of Finances. This candid declaration was made, he said, in full confidence that I would understand it as an opinion formed on a first impression and as being only his individual opinion; he had not yet conferred on the subject with the Minister of Finances or his other colleagues, which he promised to do without delay, and to lay the subject before the King as soon as possible. Speaking of our claims generally, he alluded to the hardship that the King's Government should be made responsible for all the misdeeds of Bonaparte; an observation to which I did not think necessary to answer, as he spoke only of the hardship of the case, and did not assert that the obligation did not exist."

No. 208.

Extract of a letter from Mr. Gallatin to Mr. Adams, dated

Paris, *April* 23, 1822.

"In several conversations I had with Viscount de Montmorency on the subject of the Antwerp cases he always evinced a sense of the justice of the claim and a disposition that indemnity should be made, but I have not yet been able to obtain an official answer; and finding that objections, which were not distinctly stated, were still made by the Department of Finances, I asked Mr. Montmorency's permission to confer on the subject with Mr. de Villèle, in order that I might clearly understand what prospect there was of obtaining justice. This was readily assented to, and I had accordingly an interview yesterday with that minister.

"I found that Mr. de Villèle had only a general knowledge of the subject, and had not read my note of 10th January last, to which I referred him, and which he promised to peruse with attention. It appeared, however, to me that, although he was cautious not to commit himself, he was already satisfied, from the inspection of the papers in his Department, and without having seen my argument, that the claim was just, and that the ground assumed by Baron Louis in his letter to Mr. Parish was untenable.

"His objections to a payment of the claim at this time, supposing that on a thorough investigation it proved to be just, were the following:

"1st. There were no funds at his disposal from which the payment could be made, and it was absolutely necessary that an application should be made to the Chambers for that purpose—a demand which would be very ill received, as it had been generally supposed that France was relieved from every foreign claim of that description.

"2d. Such was the amount of wrongs committed by Bonaparte, and the acknowledged impossibility that France could repair them all, that all the European powers, although with arms in their hands, and occupying a part of the country, had consented· to receive, as a payment in full, a stipulated sum which fell very short of the amount of their claims. The payments thus made by France had, therefore, been, in every instance, the result of an agreement (d'une transaction) founded on equitable principles and on an abandonment on the part of the foreign powers of a considerable part of their claims. It appeared to him impossible that an application for funds could be made to the Chambers for the purpose of satisfying American claims, unless it was also the result of a *transaction* of a similar nature.

"3d. Even in that case, the engagement to pay any sum at this time for that object would, for the reasons already stated, and for many others arising from the change of Government, appear extremely hard. The only way to render it palatable was, that it should be accompanied by the grateful information that our commercial difficulties were arranged in a satisfactory manner. He regretted, therefore, extremely, that the discussion of the two subjects had been separated, one being treated in the United States and the other here, and he asked whether it was probable that the result of the negotiation at Washington would be known at Paris before the next session of the Chambers, which is to take place in June next.

"I must say that these observations did not appear to be made with an intention of throwing new obstacles in the way of an adjustment of our claims, but for the purpose of stating the difficulties which the Government would have to encounter in any attempt to effect that object. It was not the less necessary to reply to the suggestions thus made, and I observed, with respect to the delays which had taken place, that they were to be ascribed solely to the French Government. It was in consequence of the determination of the Duke of Richelieu, and I referred to my letter to him of the 22d of April, 1817; it was against my opinion, and notwithstanding my strong remonstrances, that the subject had been postponed, and that provision was not made for our claims at the same time as for those of subjects of the European powers. But I had taken care to remind the Duke of Richelieu, when the communication for the last object was made to the legislative body, that the American claims were not included in the settlement, and he had accordingly expressly stated in that communication that the sum to be voted would discharge France from all demands on the part of the subjects of the European powers. This was so well understood that a subsequent grant of seven millions had been voted for the purpose of discharging the Algerine claims. Ours alone remained unsettled, and the Chambers must have expected, and could not therefore be astonished, that an application for that object should also be made to them.

"As to the propriety of a convention for the general adjustment of the claims of American citizens, I informed Mr. de Villèle that this was precisely what the United States had asked, and. I referred him to my note of the 9th of November, 1816, which to this day remained unanswered. The extraordinary silence of the French Government was at least a proof of its reluctance to adopt that mode of settlement, and there was an intrinsic difficulty in what he called a transaction. The United States could have no objection to a partial admission and reimbursement of the claims of their citizens, but they would not, in order to obtain that object, sacrifice other reclamations equally just, and give that general release which France was desirous to obtain in consideration of that partial payment. Under these circumstances, it was a natural, and perhaps the most practicable, course, to press a settlement of those claims which it might be presumed she intended ultimately to pay. To repel this, on a plea that a convention embracing the whole was a preferable mode, was an untenable position, so long as our overture having the last object in view remained unanswered.

"After having expressed my sincere wishes that an arrangement of our commercial difficulties might soon be effected, and having shown from a recapitulation of what had taken place at the time that the transfer of the negotiations for that object to Washington was owing to the French Government, I stated that there was no connexion whatever between that and the subject of our claims, and that even when discussed at the same place they had always been treated distinctly. Our reclamations were of much older date, and, not to speak of the former government of this country, they had, since the restoration, been pending near four years before any discussion of our commercial relations had commenced. I was ready to acknowledge that it would be at any time an unpleasant duty for his Majesty's ministers to be obliged to ask funds for the purpose of repairing the injuries sustained during a former period by the citizens of a foreign nation, and I was sensible that the task would be more easy after the settlement than during the existence of other difficulties. But justice and our perseverance, on which he might rely, required that the duty, however unpleasant, should at some time be performed; and I was the less disposed to acquiesce in new and vexatious delays on the ground alluded to, because the result of the negotiations was very uncertain. The delay in that respect was solely due to the French Government; they had thrown great obstacles in the way of an arrangement by blending other subjects with that immediately to be attended to; afterwards they became sensible, in the latter end of September last, that it was necessary to send new instructions to Mr. de Neuville. I had, in the month of October, made every representation and given all the explanations which could be necessary; yet the instructions to Mr. de Neuville were not, as I understood, sent till late in January, and had not yet, I believed, been received on the 12th of March. The success of the negotiations depended on the nature of those instructions, with which I was not acquainted. If they produced no favorable result, the consequence would only be, that the commerce between the two countries would be lessened, and flow through indirect channels; probably to our mutual loss, and to the profit of the British manufacturers and navigation. But, however this might be lamented, it was only a question of policy; each of the two nations had a right to regulate her commerce as in her opinion best suited her interest. But, with respect to our claims, it was a question of right, the consideration of which ought not and could not be abandoned or postponed, even if the commercial relations should continue to be less extensive and less advantageous than they had formerly been or might again become, in case a satisfactory arrangement respecting the discriminating duties was made; whether the result of the negotiation would be known here in June, it was, of course, impossible for me to say.

"Mr. de Villèle, having taken a memoranda, and promised to read the notes to which I had alluded, asked me whether there was any difference between Mr. Parish's claim (meaning the three vessels consigned to his house) and that for the four other Antwerp ships? to which I answered, most decidedly, in the negative. He then, having the decree of July 22, 1810, before him, inquired in what consisted the difference between the Antwerp claims and those for other property sequestered and embraced by the same decree, viz: the St. Sebastian seizures and the vessels given up by Holland. I answered, none, whatever, in substance, and that the reason why a specific application was made for the Antwerp claims alone, in my letter of the 10th January last, was, that, having already demanded indemnity for all the claims, particularly in my note of the 9th of November, 1816, the claimants, who relied on the exertions of their Government to obtain redress, had generally thought it unnecessary to make separate applications. Mr. Parish, however, being on the spot, had urged a special decision in his case; and my Government having, for the reasons already stated, acquiesced in that course, the Antwerp claims were, in that manner, first presented to the consideration of that of France. But I had expressly stated in my note that this was not in any way to be construed as an abandonment of their claims, equally just, although their features might not in every respect be precisely the same. Between the Antwerp and the other claims for property sequestered and not condemned, I knew none but merely nominal differences. The St. Sebastian vessels and cargoes had been seized and sold under an untenable and frivolous pretence—that of retaliation—to which a retrospective effect had been given. The Antwerp cargoes had been seized and sold without any pretence whatever being assigned for it. In neither cases had a condemnation taken place. In both cases we had always claimed restitution or trial before the ordinary competent tribunal. The right to ask for such trial was, in both cases, derived from the law of nations, and it was for the Antwerp cargoes, also founded on positive treaty stipulations."

Mr. Gallatin to the Secretary of State, No. 112.

PARIS, *May* 13, 1822.

SIR: I have the honor to inclose the copy of a letter I wrote on the 3d instant to Viscount Montmorency on the subject of the Antwerp claims. He has promised an answer; but as he spoke, though in vague terms, of objections which it would be better to prevent rather than to answer, I asked him an interview, which is to take place on Saturday next.

I have the honor to be, with great respect, sir, your most obedient servant,

ALBERT GALLATIN.

Mr. Gallatin to the Viscount Montmorency.

PARIS, *May* 3, 1822.

SIR: I had the honor on the 10th of January last to address to your excellency a note relative to the American cargoes sequestered at Antwerp. But, although the conversations I had since the honor to have with your excellency on that subject had led me to hope that there was a disposition to render a tardy justice to the claimants, the note still remains unanswered.

It is my duty to remind also your excellency that all the former notes which I had the honor to address to his Majesty's ministers, either with respect to that reclamation, or generally on the subject of the American claims, and particularly the note of the 9th November, 1816, have shared the same fate. That, on a subject so important, no official answer should for such length of time have been given to the earnest and repeated applications of a friendly power; that, where favors are not asked, but justice is demanded, there should have been such a tacit perseverance in avoiding even to discuss the question, must.be allowed a most uncommon proceeding in the intercourse between independent nations.

To these considerations I beg leave to add, that two American citizens, with powers from the owners of the greater part of the Antwerp cargoes, have been here for a length of time, one of them a year, for the sole purpose of pursuing and liquidating that claim; and that they both unite in requesting that they may be no longer detained, and that, at all events, a decision may be made in that case.

Permit me, therefore, most earnestly to request from your excellency that no further delays may take place, and to ask that official answer, which, I have never doubted, would, when made, prove satisfactory to the just expectation of the parties interested.

I request your excellency to accept the renewed assurance of the distinguished consideration with which, &c.

ALBERT GALLATIN.

Extracts of a letter from Mr. Gallatin to the Secretary of State, No. 216, dated

PARIS, *June* 13, 1822.

'The conference I had on the 18th ultimo with Viscount de Montmorency, on the subject of the American claims, turned principally on the difficulties which this Government would find in effecting an arrangement with us. The result of a free conversation on what was practicable seemed to be, that a definitive agreement was preferable to a partial payment, and that the choice must, in that respect, be between the two following modes: either the payment of a stipulated sum, in full discharge of the demands of the United States for spoliations, and to be distributed by their Government; or, the reference of the whole case to a joint commission, which, in case of disagreement, would refer the disputed points to a Sovereign chosen by the two Governments."

"Although Mr. de Montmorency appeared to continue to be personally well disposed, he did not conceal that there were objections in the Council of Ministers; and he stated, a few days after, that they were inclined to postpone the subject until the result of the negotiation at Washington was ascertained. I concluded, nevertheless, to insist for an answer to my last note, being satisfied that it would not amount to a rejection, which would have committed hereafter this Government, and that there would be some advantage in obtaining, at least, something more than verbal from them. The answer of the first instant, was accordingly received, copy of which is herewith inclosed. We had so many accounts of a near prospect of an arrangement being on the eve of being concluded between you and Mr. De Neuville, that I waited a few days before I made a reply; but having now heard of the adjournment of Congress, without any convention having been made, I this day have made the answer, of which I have the honor to inclose a copy."

Viscount Montmorency to Mr. Gallatin.

[Translation.]

PARIS, *June* 1, 1822.

SIR: I have received the letter which you did me the honor to write me on the 3d of May, relative to the American cargoes sequestered in the port of Anvers, and to the other claims which you have already heretofore laid before the ministers of the King.

I could have wished, sir, to have been able to answer you sooner, and, especially, to have been able to welcome your demands; but I was under the necessity of first submitting them to the King, who is engaged in council; his Majesty having nothing more at heart than to see adjusted, in a proper and satisfactory manner, the affairs of mutual interest for both countries, and thus to multiply between them useful and amicable relations.

The object of your claims is, without doubt, interesting to a great number of individuals; and we have, also, individual claims to make, which are likewise of great interest to the subjects of the King, whom they concern. I would be the first to wish that the Government could be engaged with them; but you are not ignorant, sir, that there is at this moment at Washington a negotiation which embraces general interests of the highest importance to the navigation of France and of America.

The King's council has judged that it was better to put off the examination of the individual claims until the negotiation upon the general interests was concluded; and as soon as that shall take place, I shall hasten, sir, to move in the King's council the examination of the claims which form the object of your letter of the 3d of May.

I have the honor to renew to you, sir, the assurance of my high consideration,

MONTMORENCY.

PARIS, *June* 13, 1822.

SIR: I had the honor to receive your excellency's letter of the 1st instant, in answer to mine of the 3d of May, relative to the American reclamations.

It is satisfactory to find that the unfavorable suggestions heretofore made on that subject are no longer alluded to, and that the only reason assigned for its postponement is foreign to the merits of the claim. I had expected no less from the justice of his Majesty's Government. But this new delay is as vexatious as unexpected, and the grounds on which it is placed appear altogether untenable.

It will appear, by my letter of the 22d of April, 1817, to his excellency the Duke of Richelieu, that the magnitude of the claims made upon France by subjects of European powers was the reason alleged at that time for postponing to a more favorable moment the discussion of the American claims in question. The Government of the United States, from the most friendly motives, though with great reluctance, acquiesced so far in that delay as to have abstained from pressing again the subject until the European claims had been arranged in a satisfactory manner. I made at that time, as will appear by my letter to the Duke of Richelieu of the 3d of April, 1818, an unavailing effort to obtain a simultaneous and definitive arrangement of the American claims as most consistent both with common justice and sound policy. And now, when the original cause of the postponement has ceased to exist, when the prosperous situation of the finances of France leaves no ground for the primitive objection, a new cause for delay is sought in circumstances of a subsequent, date, and which are wholly unconnected with the subject in question. The consideration of the American claims was adjourned on a presumed plea of temporary inability, or inconvenience, early in 1817; and the commercial difficulties, which it is the object of the negotiation pending at Washington to arrange, did not arise till the year 1819. That the question of indemnity ought not to be made to depend on the fate of that negotiation is equally evident.

An arrangement which will restore to the navigation of America and France those advantages now enjoyed, to, the exclusion of both, by foreign vessels, and which will have a tendency to extend the commercial and friendly relations between the two countries, is undoubtedly a most desirable object and of the highest importance. But it is, after all, not of right, but policy. Either of the two Governments may, on that subject, take an erroneous determination; but each of them, should they not, unfortunately, be able to agree on that point, has ultimately the right to make its own commercial regulations, exposing itself, without doubt, to countervailing measures, but without giving thereby any just ground of complaint, or disturbing, in other respects, the harmony subsisting between the two nations. In fact, that state of things exists to a much greater extent between France and many European powers, particularly with Great Britain. The commerce between America and France, and which may be estimated to amount in value to about eighty millions of francs a year, may still be carried on in foreign vessels or through indirect channels. Neither country has prohibited the importation of the products of the soil and industry of the other. The only question under discussion, and on which they may happen not to agree, is that of the navigation, that is to say, of the freight of the articles of exchange, which may, in the whole, be worth about three millions a year. But, from the respective prohibitions existing in France and England, it is not merely the navigation, but the commerce itself, between the two countries, which is so nearly annihilated as not to exceed twelve or fifteen millions a year. It has certainly, in this case, never been suggested, that, because each Government follows, in that respect, its own views, the other questions of right or general policy should on that account be suspended; that because a treaty of commerce may appear injurious to either of them, the other would, for that reason, be justified in refusing to do justice in other respects. The question of the indemnity claimed by the United States is one not merely of policy, but of right. It will again revert, and with the same force, in case there should be no arrangement of the commercial difficulties. The foundation on which the demand rests cannot be affected by that result. France must still acknowledge or deny the justice of the claim. She is bound, in the first case, to grant the indemnity; in the other, to adduce satisfactory reasons for her denial.

I must beg leave to observe, that the object of these reclamations cannot be, and is not, considered by the Government of the United States as only affecting the interests of private individuals, but as an important subject of public concern. It is not for private contracts voluntarily entered into, or other claims of a similar nature: it is for numerous spoliations committed, not only contrary to every principle of common justice, but in violation of the acknowledged law of nations, and of positive treaty stipulations; it is for the most flagrant and continued infractions of their rights as a neutral and independent nation that the United States demand that at least a satisfactory indemnity should be made to her citizens for the losses thus suffered. The whole series of their public acts, at home and abroad, when those outrageous proceedings took place, and the peculiar circumstances, (arising from simultaneous aggressions on the part of England,) which alone prevented a resort to war, are facts of such notoriety as to render it difficult to conceive how the subject can be viewed as of an inferior importance and as only affecting private interests. If any further proof was required, in that respect, the 10th article of the treaty of the 16th of March, 1810, between France and Holland, might be quoted. Certain American cargoes, which make part of our reclamations, were, by that treaty, put at the disposal of France; "in order," according to the said article, "that the same may be dealt with according to circumstances, and to the political relations between France and the United States."

Not knowing to what reclamations by subjects of France against the United States your excellency alludes, I can only observe, that if there are any, respecting which a stipulation should be deemed necessary, it must, of course, be understood that every such stipulation will in every respect be reciprocal, and embrace, on both sides, all reclamations of a similar nature, and for the same period of time.

I request your excellency to accept the assurances, &c.,

ALBERT GALLATIN.

His Excellency Viscount DE MONTMORENCY,
   Minister of Foreign Affairs, &c., &c., &c.

No. 230.

Extract of a letter from Mr. Gallatin to the Secretary of State, dated

PARIS, *September* 8, 1822.

' I had, on the 17th ultimo, written to Viscount Montmorency, and again on the 31st to Mr. de Villèle, on the subject of our reclamations, only to remind them that the late convention had removed the sole cause assigned for delay. I received last night Mr. de Villèle's note of the 3d, of which copy is inclosed."

Mr. Gallatin to Mr. de Montmorency, dated August 17, 1822.

I beg leave to call again your excellency's attention to the American claims for sequestrations and spoliations. The cause assigned by your excellency, in your letter of the first of June last, for suspending their consideration, being happily removed by the late commercial arrangement, I trust that no further delay will take place, and that, in conformity with the tenor of that letter, your excellency will be pleased to bring that important subject before the King's council.

I request your excellency to accept, &c.

[Translation.]

Extract of a letter from Mr. Gallatin to Mr. de Villèle, dated

PARIS, *August* 31, 1822.

"Permit me to remind your excellency that the three last letters which I had the honor of addressing to his excellency the Viscount de Montmorency are still unanswered. The first, under the date of the

17th current, had for its object the different claims of citizens of the United States. The second, on the 20th, contained my observations on the project of an ordinance necessary that the execution of the convention of June 24 may commence on the first of October next. The last, of the 27th, remonstrated against the conduct pursued by the local authorities in regard to the American vessel the General Hamilton, thrown upon the coast near Montreuil, on the sea."

"I eagerly seize this occasion to beg your excellency to be pleased to accept the assurance, &c."

Mr. de Villèle to Mr. Gallatin, dated September 3, 1822.

[Translation.]

You did me the honor, on the 31st of August last, to remind me of several American claims, of which you had formerly apprised the Viscount de Montmorency. It is necessary for me to collect some documents respecting this affair, in order to judge of what consequences they may be susceptible. Be pleased to believe, sir, that I shall attend to them with a good deal of interest and attention.

Accept, sir, the assurances, &c.

No. 233.

Extract of a letter from Mr. Gallatin, Envoy Extraordinary and Minister Plenipotentiary to France, to Mr. Adams, Secretary of State, dated

PARIS, *September 24, 1822.*

"I had yesterday a conference with Mr. Villèle on the subject of our claims. He expressed his wish that a general arrangement might take place, embracing all the subjects of discussion between the two countries; stated those to be, the reclamations of the United States for spoliations on their trade, those of France on account of Beaumarchais's claim, and of the vessels captured on the coast of Africa, and the question arising under the Louisiana treaty; and asked whether I was prepared to negotiate upon all those points? I answered that I was ready to discuss them all, but that I must object to uniting the Louisiana question to that of claims for indemnity, as they were essentially distinct; and as I thought that after all that had passed, we had a right to expect that no further obstacle should be thrown in the discussion of our claims by connecting it with subjects foreign to them."

No. 236.

Extract of a letter from Mr. Gallatin, Envoy Extraordinary and Minister Plenipotentiary to France, to Mr. Adams, Secretary of State, dated

PARIS, *November 13, 1822.*

"I received on the 8th instant a letter of Mr. de Villèle of the 6th, copy of which is inclosed, together with that of my answer of the 12th."

Mr. de Villèle to Mr. Gallatin.

[Translation.]

PARIS, *November 6, 1822.*

SIR: The convention concluded at Washington on the 24th of June last has removed the obstacles which have, momentarily, impeded the relations of commerce between France and the United States. Although this convention is only temporary, it holds out the expectation of a treaty more extensive and more durable. It has left leisure proper for discussing and establishing this treaty upon bases the most conformable to the interest of the two States. Already the communications are re-opened, on both sides, on the most amicable footing ; his Majesty has seen with satisfaction this happy effect of the arrangement concluded in his name and in that of the United States.

If any partial difficulties still remain to be removed, they will be easily arranged between two powers who sincerely wish to establish their relations upon the most perfect equity.

In this spirit of reciprocal justice I have received the claims which you have done me the honor to transmit to me, and without prejudging anything in their regard, I must, first of all, sir, remark to you, that France has also claims pending, or to be produced to the Government of the United States. It would appear agreeable to the interest of the two parties, and to the reciprocity of justice, and of protection, to which the subjects of the two States have equally a right, that these affairs should be examined and arranged, unanimously, by way of negotiation.

His Majesty's intention would be, that these claims and the other points in dispute, upon which the convention of June 24 has not been able to pronounce, should be the object of this negotiation, in order to terminate simultaneously, and in a definitive manner, every dispute between the two States, especially in what concerns the duties received in Louisiana on the French commerce, contrary to the tenor of the 8th article of the treaty of cession.

You will only perceive, sir, in this intention of his Majesty the most firm desire of leaving in future no cause or pretext of misunderstanding or of complaints between the two States, and on the part of their respective subjects.

If you are authorized, sir, to follow this march, I pray you let me know, and I will hasten to demand of the King the necessary powers to a negotiator charged with treating with you.

If you were also authorized to sign a consular convention, the same plenipotentiary would receive powers, *ad hoc*, for also pursuing the negotiation.

Accept, sir, the assurance of the high consideration, &c.

JH. DE VILLELE,
The Minister of Finance, charged, ad interim, with the Port Folio of Foreign Affairs.

PARIS, *November* 12, 1822.

SIR: I had the honor to receive your excellency's letter of the 6th instant.

I have special powers to negotiate a convention providing for the just claims of citizens of the United States against France; as also for the like claims of French subjects against the United States, with such person or persons as may have a like authority from his Most Christian Majesty.

As minister of the United States, I am authorized to discuss the question respecting the construction of the 8th article of the Louisiana treaty, and to give and receive explanations on that subject. But the negotiation on that point having been transferred to Washington, no special powers in that respect have been transmitted to me. I had understood, in the course of the conference I had the honor to have with your excellency on the 23d of September, and had accordingly written to my Government, that it was not intended to insist that that subject should be blended with that of private claims. It is, indeed, obvious that it would be utterly unjust to make the admission of these to depend on the result of a negotiation on a subject with which they have no connexion whatever, and the difficulties respecting which are of a date posterior to that of the claims.

All the representations which his Majesty's Government has made to that of the United States, whether on private or on public subjects, have uniformly been taken into consideration, and received that attention to which they were so justly entitled. In no instance has the Government of the United States declined to open a discussion on any subject thus offered to their consideration by France, or made it a preliminary condition that the discussion should also embrace some other subject in which they might happen to take a greater interest. The question respecting the 8th article of the Louisiana treaty has, in particular, been the subject of a voluminous correspondence, in the course of which the arguments in support of the construction insisted on by each party, respectively, were made known to the other. I have, in the meanwhile, for six years, made unceasing applications to his Majesty's Government for the settlement of claims to a vast amount, affecting the interest of numerous individuals, and arising from flagrant violations of the law of nations and of the rights of the United States, without having ever been able to obtain to this day satisfaction in a single instance, or even that the subject should be taken into consideration and discussed. After so many vexatious delays, for which different causes have at different times been assigned, it cannot now be intended again to postpone the investigation of that subject by insisting that it should be treated in connexion with one foreign to it, and which has already been discussed. The United States have at least the right to ask that their demands should also be examined and discussed, and I trust that, since I am authorized to treat, as well concerning the claims of French subjects against the United States as respecting those of American citizens against France, a distinct negotiation to that effect will be opened without any further delay.

Permit me, at the same time, to renew to your excellency the assurances that the United States have the most earnest desire that every subject of difference between the two countries should be amicably arranged, and their commercial and political relations placed on the most friendly and solid footing. They will be ready to open again negotiations on the subject of the 8th article of the Louisiana treaty, and on every other which remains to be adjusted, and will have no objection that the seat of those negotiations should be transferred from Washington to this place.

Although my powers to treat respecting every subject connected with the commerce of the two countries may embrace that of a consular convention, yet, as this had not been contemplated by my Government, I am not at this time prepared to conclude an arrangement for that purpose.

I request your excellency to accept the assurances, &c.

ALBERT GALLATIN.

His Excellency Count DE VILLELE,
Charged with the Department of Foreign Affairs, &c.

No. 237.

Mr. Gallatin to the Secretary of State.

PARIS, *November* 19, 1822.

SIR: I received last night and have the honor to inclose a copy of Mr. de Villèle's answer (dated 15th instant) to my letter of the 12th. You will perceive that, without taking any notice of the reasons I had urged why a distinct negotiation should be immediately opened on the subject of the claims against both Governments, he insists that this shall be treated in connexion with the question respecting the construction of the 8th article of the Louisiana treaty. The object is too obvious to require any comments on my part, and this final decision leaves me no other course than to refer the whole to my Government.

I have the honor to be, with great respect, sir, your most obedient servant,

ALBERT GALLATIN.

Mr. de Villèle to Mr. Gallatin.

[Translation.]

PARIS, *November* 15, 1822.

SIR: You did me the honor to announce to me, on the 12th of this month, that you were authorized to negotiate a convention relative to the claims of Americans against France, and to those of France against the United States, but that you had no power to enter upon a negotiation concerning the interpretation of the 8th article of the Louisiana treaty.

The discussions which have arisen upon this last point between your Government and the King's Minister Plenipotentiary to the United States having had no result, and this question being thus left undecided, it is both proper and just to resume the examination of it; it touches upon too great interests not to be treated of with renewed attention, or to be abandoned.

If a new arrangement takes place for the claims which are still in controversy, it ought to comprehend the whole, and the desire of the King's Government is not to leave any difficulty, any indecision remaining in the relations of the two countries.

It is for the same reason, sir, that I demanded, in the letter which I had the honor to address to you on the sixth of this month, that the negotiation to be opened on the respective claims should also include a consular convention.

If your powers for discussing these difficult points should not appear to you sufficiently extensive to make it the object of a negotiation, I think, sir, that you will deem it fit to ask of your Government supplementary authority to come at an arrangement which cannot be of the utility proposed by the two Governments, unless it shall embrace all the questions and the claims which are still in dispute.

I can only refer, sir, on this subject, to the communications which I had the honor to make to you on the 6th of this month, and with which you have doubtless acquainted your Government.

Accept, sir, the assurance of my high consideration,

JH. DE VILLELE,
The Minister of Finances, charged, ad interim, with the Port Folio of Foreign Affairs.

No. 250.

Extract of a letter from Mr. Gallatin, Envoy Extraordinary and Minister Plenipotentiary to France, to Mr. Adams, Secretary of State, dated

PARIS, *February* 27, 1823.

' The more I have reflected upon the ground assumed by this Government on the subject of our claims, and on the attempt to connect their discussion with the question arising under the 8th article of the Louisiana treaty, the more I have felt satisfied that it was impossible that the United States should depart from the true construction of that article, and acquiesce in that contended for by France, and that a renewed discussion on that subject would be unprofitable, and lead to no result whatever. As a last, but, I believed, unavailing effort, I have concluded to express that conviction to the French Government, and have accordingly addressed, this day, to Mr. Chateaubriand, the letter of which I have the honor to inclose a copy."

PARIS, *February* 27, 1823.

SIR: I had the honor to receive his excellency Count de Villèle's letter of the 15th of November last, by which, notwithstanding the remonstrances contained in mine of the 12th, his excellency, being at that time charged with the Department of Foreign Affairs, still insisted that the discussion of the claims of individuals of both nations upon the two Governments, respectively, should not take place unless it was connected with a renewed negotiation on the 8th article of the Louisiana treaty.

A conversation I had the honor to have with his excellency the Duke de Montmorency, after his return from Verona, induced me to hope, although he did not encourage any expectations of a different result, that he would, however, again lay the subject before his Majesty's Council of Ministers. This circumstance, the subsequent change in the Department of Foreign Affairs, and the objects of primary importance which have heretofore necessarily engrossed your excellency's attention, have prevented an earlier official answer to his excellency Count de Villèle's letter.

It has, together with the others on the same subject, as he had naturally anticipated, been of course transmitted to my Government. But on a review of the correspondence of Mr. Adams with Mr. Hyde de Neuville, and with myself, I must express my perfect conviction that the subject having been maturely examined and thoroughly discussed, there cannot be the least expectation that the United States will alter their view of it, or acquiesce in the construction put by his Majesty's minister on the 8th article of the Louisiana treaty.

It is not my intention, at this moment, to renew a discussion which seems to have been already exhausted; but I will beg leave simply to state the question to your excellency.

It was agreed by the article above mentioned that the ships of France should forever be treated upon the footing of the most favored nation in the ports of Louisiana.

Vessels of certain foreign nations being now treated in the ports of the United States (including those of Louisiana) on the same footing with American vessels, in consideration of the American vessels being treated in the ports of those nations on the same footing with their own vessels, France has required that French vessels should, by virtue of the said article, be treated in the ports of Louisiana on the same footing with the vessels of those nations, without allowing on her part the consideration or reciprocal condition by virtue of which those vessels are thus treated.

The United States contend that the right to be treated upon the footing of the most favored nation, when not otherwise defined, and when expressed only in those words, is that, and can only be that, of being entitled to that treatment gratuitously, if such nation enjoys it gratuitously, and on paying the same equivalent, if it has been granted in consideration of an equivalent. Setting aside every collateral matter and subsidiary argument, they say that the article in question, expressed as it is, can have no other meaning, is susceptible of no other construction, for this plain and incontrovertible reason: that if the French vessels were allowed to receive gratuitously the same treatment which those of certain other nations receive only in consideration of an equivalent, they would not be treated as the most favored nation, but more favorably than any other nation. And, since the article must necessarily have the meaning contended for by the United States, and no other, the omission or insertion of words to define it is wholly immaterial, a definition being necessary only when the expressions used are of doubtful import, and the insertion of words to that effect in some other treaties, belonging to that class of explanatory but superfluous phrases, of which instances are to be found in so many treaties.

It might, indeed, have, perhaps, been sufficient to say, that, in point of fact, there was no most favored nation in the United States; the right enjoyed by the vessels of certain foreign nations to be treated in the ports of the United States as American vessels, in consideration of American vessels receiving a similar treatment in the ports of those nations, not being a favor, but a mere act of reciprocity.

Let me also observe, that the pretension of France would, if admitted, leave no alternative to the United States than either to suffer the whole commerce between France and Louisiana to be carried exclusively in French vessels, or to renounce the right of making arrangements with other nations deemed essential to our prosperity, and having for its object not to lay restrictions on commerce, but to remove them. If the meaning of the 8th article of the Louisiana treaty was such, indeed, as has been contended for on the part of France, the United States, bound to fulfil their engagements, must submit to the consequences, whatever these might be; but this having been proven not to be the case, the observation is made only to show that the United States never can, either for the sake of obtaining indemnities for their citizens, or from their anxious desire to settle by conciliatory arrangements all their differences with France, be brought to acquiesce in the erroneous construction put upon the article in question.

The proposal made by his excellency Mr. de Villèle in his letter of the 6th of November, and reiterated in that of the 15th, can, therefore, have no other effect than to produce unnecessary delays, and would, if persisted in, be tantamount to an indefinite postponement of the examination and settlement of the claims of the citizens of the United States. It will remain for his Majesty's Government to decide whether this determination be consistent with justice, whether the reclamations of private individuals should be thus adjourned, because the two Governments happen to differ in opinion on a subject altogether foreign to those claims. Having nothing to add to my reiterated and unavailing applications on that subject, my only object at this moment has been to show that I cannot expect any instructions from my Government that will alter the state of the question.

I request your excellency to accept the assurance, &c.,

ALBERT GALLATIN.

His Excellency Viscount DE CHATEAUBRIAND,
    Minister of Foreign Affairs, &c., &c., &c.

18TH CONGRESS.]   No. 370.   [1ST SESSION.

SPOLIATIONS BY FRANCE FROM 1793 TO 1800.

COMMUNICATED TO THE HOUSE OF REPRESENTATIVES MARCH 25, 1824.

Mr. FORSYTH, from the Committee on Foreign Relations, to whom were referred the petitions of Hadrianus Van Noorden, William and Nathaniel Hooper, Daniel Henshaw, several merchants and underwriters of Salem, several merchants of Gloucester, several merchants and underwriters of Alexandria, District of Columbia, several merchants of Washington, North Carolina, Henry Clark and others, of Kennebunk, and several others, merchants, in Maine, reported:

That no evidence accompanies either of the petitions, all of which, except the first, are literally the same, having been apparently prepared by concert among the claimants to be presented to Congress. To discriminate between them is not practicable, if it were desirable. The committee are compelled to present, in general terms, the nature of these claims as set forth by the parties interested, and to examine as briefly as possible the grounds upon which relief is asked from the Government of the United States. The claims are founded upon spoliations committed by the private and public armed vessels of France between the years 1793 and 1800.

The petitioners allege that the French Government, to the date of the ratification of the treaty of 1800, always considered the recognition of their claims as due to its honor, and attached them as a charge upon its national character.

That the Government of the United States, which had volunteered its agency for the recovery of them from France, exercised its power and authority to prevent the petitioners from obtaining indemnity; that the Government of the United States received from France a full and fair equivalent for these claims, in the discharge from its liabilities under the treaties with France and the abrogation of these treaties.

Similar applications, if not by the same persons, have been frequently made to Congress, and reports upon them are to be found in the records of the House of Representatives and of the Senate; none of these applications have been successful. Without attempting even to enumerate the failures to obtain a sanction to their statements and to their claims, the committee refer the House to a detailed report of the various acts of the Government of the United States, and of France, from 1793 and 1800, made by a select committee on the 22d of April, 1802, to which applications like the present were referred. Governed by that report, the Committee on Foreign Relations are not satisfied that the French Government ever admitted the justice of the claims of the petitioners, or ever intended to pay them; that the Government of the United States used every effort, even to war itself, to rescue the property of American merchants from the lawless violence of France; that its efforts to procure payment for the spoliations committed by the French cruisers were not discontinued until it was obvious that there was no hope of success. That this Government *never* received from France any equivalent for the claims of Americans upon France. The war of aggression was commenced by France, and every act of the United States was a just retaliation for previous injury. The treaties with France were annulled by an act of Congress in 1798, in consequence of the utter disregard of the stipulations of them by that power.

In short, to justify their claims upon the United States, the petitioners assume that France was right and their own Government wrong; that France was prepared to make a just reparation for the outrages committed under her own laws until released from her obligations by the United States, who were faithless to their trust in the first instance, and have been regardless of the obligations of justice ever since; assumptions not consistent with truth, nor creditable to the patriotism of those who make them. The committee recommend to the House to adopt the following resolution:

Resolved, That petitions of the several persons who ask indemnity for spoliations committed by French cruisers on their property, between the years 1793 and 1800, be rejected.

18TH CONGRESS.]   No. 371.   [1ST SESSION.

SUPPRESSION OF THE SLAVE TRADE.

COMMUNICATED TO THE SENATE IN EXECUTIVE SESSION APRIL 30, 1824, AND THE INJUNCTION OF SECRECY SINCE REMOVED.

To the Senate of the United States:

I transmit to the Senate, for their constitutional advice with regard to its ratification, a convention for the suppression of the African slave trade, signed at London, on the 13th ultimo, by the minister of the United States, residing there, on their part, with the plenipotentiaries of the British Government, on the part of that nation, together with the correspondence relating thereto; part of which is included in a communication made to the House of Representatives on the 19th ultimo, a printed copy of which is among the documents herewith sent.

Motives of accommodation to the wishes of the British Government render it desirable that the Senate should act definitively upon this convention as speedily as may be found convenient.

JAMES MONROE.

WASHINGTON, *April* 30, 1824.

List of papers sent.

Mr. Rush to Mr. Adams, January 23, 1824. No. 1.
Same to same, March 15, 1824. No. 2.
Convention signed March 13, 1824. Copy.
Counter-projet and protocols.
Printed copy of message of the President to the House of Representatives, March 19, 1824.

No. 1.

LONDON, *January* 23, 1824.

SIR: I received, on the evening of the 20th instant, a note from Mr. Secretary Canning, requesting me to call on the following day at the Foreign Office, for the purpose of meeting there Mr. Huskisson and Mr. Stratford Canning, by which I at once understood that the negotiation which the President has confided to me was now about to have its regular commencement. I went at the time appointed, when, meeting these gentlemen, I was informed by them that their instructions, as well as full powers as the plenipotentiaries of this Government, were made out, and that all things were ready on their side for opening the negotiation. I replied that I, too, was ready on the part of the United States, upon which the 23d was fixed upon for our first meeting.

The negotiation has accordingly been opened this day, in due form, at the Office of the Board of Trade. At the wish of Mr. Secretary Canning, specially expressed at the Foreign Office the day before yesterday, the subject of the slave trade is that upon which we have first entered. Our introductory conferences upon it occupied a couple of hours, when an adjournment took place until Thursday next, the 29th instant. It was agreed that the same subject should then be resumed, and, without discussing others, proceeded with until it should be finished.

In making my reports to you of this negotiation, for the information of the President, my intention is not to make them from meeting to meeting, a course that might often prove unsatisfactory and unavailing, but to wait the issue of the whole, or, at any rate, the completion of some one subject, before I proceed to write about it. This was the plan pursued at the joint negotiation with this court in 1818, in which I bore a share, and I hope will be approved. I will take care to deviate from it whenever circumstances may seem to render a deviation necessary and proper. As, moreover, I must, simultaneously with this negotiation, attend to the business of the legation, it has occurred to me, that, as often as I may find it necessary to write to you respecting the latter, whilst the negotiation is in progress, I will go on with the regular series in numbering my despatches, treating those that I shall write on the negotiation as distinct, and so numbering them.

I cannot flatter myself with the expectation that the work of the negotiation will be very soon done. The subjects are many and complicated. The session of Parliament is at hand, and will, when it arrives, make heavy calls upon the time of one of the British plenipotentiaries; added to which, the daily interruptions to which my own time is liable—always the lot of the permanent incumbent of this mission—will be too liable to increase the unavoidable obstacles to frequent and rapid conferences. I can only repeat, that my best endeavors shall not be spared, and I presume to hope that my past conduct in this trust will be accepted as the pledge of my future diligence. Although there have been delays in bringing on the negotiation, all my preliminary correspondence in relation to it will, I trust, have not arisen through my instrumentality.

The standing of one of the British plenipotentiaries is so well known with us that I need not speak of it. The other, Mr. Huskisson, (first named in the commission,) is of the Cabinet, a distinguished member of the House of Commons, the president of the Board of Trade, and Treasurer of the Navy. Besides his reputation for talents, which is high, he seems to be no less generally regarded as a man of liberal principles and conciliating temper.

I have the honor to remain, with very great respect, your obedient servant,

RICHARD RUSH.

Hon. John Quincy Adams, *Secretary of State.*

No. 2.

London, *March* 15, 1824.

Sir: I have the honor to inform you that I concluded and signed, on behalf of the United States, the day before yesterday, a convention with this Government for the suppression of the slave trade, which instrument I herewith transmit to your hands, to be laid before the President.

In my despatch, No. 355, written previously to the commencement of the negotiation, I mentioned that Mr. Secretary Canning had expressed a wish that the subject of the slave trade should be treated separately from all others on which I had received the instructions of my Government, and that I had not thought it necessary to object to this course. In pursuance of it, this subject was accordingly taken up separately; and was the first upon which we entered, as you have already been informed in my despatch, which announced the formal opening of the negotiation. The only deviation from the course indicated in my latter despatch has been, that other subjects have since been gone into, though none, as yet, finished, a mode of proceeding that was found eligible.

With the convention, I also transmit the protocols of the several conferences at which its provisions were discussed and settled; and, for the better understanding of the whole subject, I proceed to give you a more full account of the nature and progress of the discussions than can be afforded by the protocols.

I offered, in the first instance, to the British plenipotentiaries, and without any alteration, the projet that came inclosed to me in your despatch, No. 65, of the 24th of June, explaining and recommending its provisions by such considerations as were to be drawn from your despatch, and others that seemed apposite. They remarked, that they hoped it would be borne in mind that the plan offered was not of the choice of Great Britain, her preference having been distinctly made known to Europe, as well as to the United States, for a different plan; nor was it, they said, necessary towards the more effectual abolition of the traffic by her own subjects, her home statutes and prohibitions being already adequate to that end. As regarded the latter intimation, I replied, that the United States stood upon at least equal ground with Great Britain, their existing laws against the slave trade being marked by even a higher tone of severity, and the consequent exclusion of their citizens from all participation in the trade being, as was believed, so far as the virtue of municipal laws could avail, not less effectual. As to the preference of Great Britain for a different plan, I contented myself with alluding, without more of retrospect, to the uniform objections that had been made to it by the leading powers of Europe, especially by France and Russia, as well as by the United States; and with remarking, that my Government had charged me with the duty of presenting the projet in question, under the two-fold view of bringing forward, according to the wish of Great Britain, a substitute for the plan that had been rejected, and to carry into effect a resolution which had passed the House of Representatives of the United States upon this subject at the close of the last session of Congress. I added, that it was the sincere belief of my Government, rendering, at the same time, full justice to all the past efforts of Great Britain in the cause of abolition, that if she could see her way to the acceptance of the plan now offered, combining, as it did, the great principle of denouncing the slave trade as piracy, with a system of international co-operation for its suppression, the evil would be more effectually extirpated, and at a day not distant, than by any other modes that had heretofore been devised. The British plenipotentiaries replied, that they would give it a candid examination, esteeming themselves fortunate, considering the great moral interests at stake, and which both nations had alike at heart, if they could reconcile its acceptance with the opinions and convictions which had hitherto guided the conduct of their Government on this subject. They gave their unhesitating assent to the principle of denouncing the traffic as piracy by the laws of Great Britain, provided we could arrive at a common mind on all other parts of the plan proposed.

After they had had the plan a proper time under consideration, they expressed their fears that parts of it would prove ineffectual, unless with modifications and additions, which they would proceed to enumerate. These were principally as follows: They said that as soon as the two powers, by their mutual laws, had rendered all participation in the slave trade piracy, and, by a formal convention, agreed to unite their naval efforts for its suppression, it might be expected that the subjects and citizens of each who meditated a commission of the offence would no longer venture to assume the proper flag of either country, but seek to shroud their guilt under that of some third power not yet a party to the convention. British subjects or American citizens might, for example, readily charter a Danish, a Swedish, or a Russian vessel, and, under cover of either of these flags, with simulated papers and other fraudulent contrivances, pursue the traffic, whilst the true owner of the vessel remained in ignorance of the real and guilty transaction. Were such transgressors, the British plenipotentiaries asked, to be screened from all detection and punishment, though the vessel should be afterwards restored? I answered, that I presumed not, and that the words of the second article of the projet, *or for the account of their subjects or citizens.* were, as I supposed, intended to meet such a case, or other similar attempts to get rid, by evasive pretexts, of the penalties created by the convention. They agreed in ascribing to them this meaning, but thought that some more distinctive provision would be necessary to prevent such evasions. They further asked, suppose a British subject or an American citizen to be taken whilst engaged in the slave trade on board of a vessel not belonging to either power, or navigated on account of the subjects or citizens of either, and brought into Great Britain or her dominions, or into the United States, ought he not to be tried indiscriminately in either country, since the laws of each would alike brand him as a pirate? This inquiry, if answered in the affirmative, involving a conflict with one of the primary provisions of the plan, the British plenipotentiaries did not press, but, on the contrary, willingly withdrew it. They proposed, in lieu of it, that the subjects or citizens of either party, taken under such circumstances, should be sent home for trial before the tribunals of their own country; and to the proposition, as altered in this essential particular, I said that there would, probably, be no exception taken, for it might happen that British subjects thus offending would be found within the jurisdiction of the United States; and if their own citizens were ever justly captured whilst so offending, as a law of Congress already subjected them when in this predicament to the doom of pirates, I did not anticipate from my Government any objection to their being sent home for trial in our own courts, under whatever circumstances or by whatever country they might be lawfully seized.

Would not serious or fatal embarrassments, they also asked, arise in regard to evidence, under the criminal prosecution against the crew of the slave trading vessel for the act of piracy, as provided by the eighth article of the projet? If the libel against the vessel took place first, as was supposed would be the case, how could the captain or crew be examined on interrogatories, since the fact of the condemnation of the vessel would draw after it their own guilt? Their answers, consequently, might bring them into jeopardy. I replied, that the commander or boarding officer, and other persons belonging to the capturing vessel, being sent in as witnesses against the accused vessel, might, perhaps, under a convention of a character like the present, supersede, in some degree, the necessity of examining the crew, as was usual in admiralty causes; but that if this would not be proper as a general rule, it might hold good, to some extent, in cases where the interior arrangements and structure of the vessel, and, above all, the actual presence of slaves, combined to establish more unequivocally, to the very eye, the iniquity of the voyage. At all events, the objection, if valid, which was not admitted, could go no further than to except from the criminal prosecution those of the crew, supposed to be few in number, who might be selected as witnesses on the part of the State or Crown, leaving the rest open to all the penal inflictions of the convention. The British plenipotentiaries ultimately agreed that the objection was unfounded, on learning from their law officers that the right of a witness not to answer, where a confession of guilt might be involved, was merely a general shield thrown over him, to be used or not, according to circumstances and the opinion of the court, without otherwise affecting the action at law or public prosecution, in the course of which the right might be claimed. It was an independent right that stood upon its own basis, the existence and knowledge of which was not previously to foreclose the institution of this or any other prosecution any more than it would the institution of a suit in a court of chancery or before any other judicial tribunal.

They next drew my attention to the fifth article, which provides that no person shall be taken out of the captured vessel; a point that I had declared would be considered by my Government as indispensable. What, then, they asked, might sometimes be the lot of the slaves? Suppose an hundred of them, or even more, on board the captured vessel, and that vessel perhaps a small one; suppose them all crowded together under such circumstances of cruelty, that disease was among them, and death daily thinning their numbers; a supposition not exaggerated under all the recollections of this afflicting traffic, but too likely to be often realized as long as it was continued; what, in such a case, was to be done? I replied, that I did not, for myself, understand the word *person* as applicable in this sense to the slaves, but to the crew of the vessel. Nor did I regard the term *cargo*, against which a prohibition of removal alike indispensable existed, as descriptive, under this convention, of the slaves. Hence, when the removal of the latter, or of any portion of them, should be found obviously necessary from imperious motives of humanity, I saw no sufficient reason for questioning the propriety of allowing, under suitable regulations, such removal to take place.

As no person belonging to the crew was to be taken out, the British plenipotentiaries, continuing their remarks upon the fifth article, next said that a power on the part of the capturing ship to confine the crew below, or otherwise restrain them, would be absolutely necessary, in contingencies to be fairly imagined, to give full effect to the principles which the projet intended to secure. The delinquent vessel, as often happened, might be powerfully manned. These men rendered fierce, not to add desperate, by their vocation, and the perils to which by capture they would become exposed, could not want the desire and would naturally watch the opportunity of overcoming the captors in whose custody they were placed. Ought not, therefore, the captors to be furnished with adequate means of keeping the mastery over them until the captured vessel was safely conveyed to her destination?

Such were the principal amendments or suggestions which the British plenipotentiaries at an early stage put forward, and they were discussed between us in a temper frank and amicable. They declared that they did not offer them in the spirit of objection, but under sincere wishes to secure for the plan at all points the recommendations and potency which it must be supposed each nation equally aimed at imparting to it. It was designed to act upon a stubborn as well as malignant class of offenders, whose cunning was not behind their depravity, and who had hitherto put to scorn the efforts of good men in all countries to check the stupendous enormity of their deeds. They concluded with saying that they would present to my consideration a counter-projet, on the part of Great Britain, embracing what they deemed to be the necessary provisions upon the whole subject. I replied, that the articles of the plan which I had submitted had not been drawn up to the exclusion of others that Great Britain might, in turn, have to propose; nor were they all to be insisted upon in the shape in which they first stood. There were, indeed, cardinal principles in them that could on no account be departed from; but there were others, as well as much of detail, open to whatever alterations or additions both parties might be able to agree in thinking proper and useful. This was the spirit in which I knew it to be the desire of my Government that the negotiation should be conducted.

The essential principles of our plan, as gathered from my best attention to it, in connexion with your instructions, I considered to be: 1st. That this nation was to declare the slave trade piracy by act of Parliament. 2d. That the captured vessel was to be sent to her own country for trial before its own tribunals, and never before those of the capturing power. 3d. That no individual belonging to the crew was ever to be taken out of the accused vessel. 4th. That the capturing officer should be laid under the most effective responsibility for his conduct, in all respects. 5th. That no merchant vessel under the protection or in the presence of a ship-of-war of her own nation was ever to be visited by a ship-of-war of the other nation. I informed the British plenipotentiaries, unreservedly, that I could consent to nothing that did not give full security to each and all of the above principles. I knew that some of them bespoke a great change in pre-existing principles and usages under the maritime code of the world; but the change was not for light but high objects, and was believed by my Government to be the only means by which they could be adequately and permanently secured.

At the fourth conference their counter-projet was brought forward. I was happy to find that it acceded to all the principles that are above recapitulated, adopting, too, and largely, the language in which our own articles had been framed. To its first article, however, or rather to that passage in it which relates to convoy, I took strong exception, owing to the manner in which it was worded and the import that it might bear. I also objected as strongly to the phraseology of so much of its tenth article as purported to save to both parties all their existing rights; upon both these passages; upon their second article, bringing under the cognizance of the convention the subjects or citizens of either power surreptitiously chartering the flag of a third power; upon that part of their seventh article, also, bringing within the pale of the convention the subjects or citizens of either power found on board the slave trading vessel of a third power, though not chartered or owned by them; and upon those parts of their fourth article which make provision for restraining the crew of the captured vessel and removing the slaves, full discussions followed at the fourth, the fifth, and the sixth conferences. More than once I was not without apprehensions that the whole work would fall through. More than once it rested upon a difficult balance, awakening solicitude for its fate. To their passage on convoy I objected, on full consideration, absolutely, and urged the reinsertion of our own article on this subject in its very words, as being simple, intelligible, and appropriate. They as strenuously resisted its reinsertion, not, as they repeatedly and unequivocally declared, from any desire ever to exercise the power which it interdicted, and which would, therefore, render the reinsertion superfluous, but because they objected to the word convoy and to the whole formality of our article, which would be embarrassing in its comparison with the arrangements settled on this point in the treaty between Great Britain and the Netherlands of May, 1818. Finally, as I could not give up the principle, but was not tenacious of the word, I agreed to drop it on having any other words, however few, that would carry the principle, but not more than the principle. Their own words, viz: except when in the presence of a ship-of-war of its own nation, would, I said, satisfy me, provided all that followed were expunged; and to this they assented. To the part expunged I had many objections, and, amongst others, that it approximated closely to the article in their treaty with the Netherlands, if, indeed, constructively, it might not have become identical with it, though the British plenipotentiaries protested against intending to give it any such character or meaning. It implied, also, I thought, the indecorum of presupposing that the naval officers of either power could be lax in the execution of their own duty.

The words of their tenth article, designed to save existing rights, I also struck out, declaring that those which formed the concluding passage of our own ninth article must be received as the substitute for them. Why, I asked, mention existing rights at all? By the universal rule of interpretation, applicable to treaties, they would remain unchanged. The treaty or convention that we were forming was special in its objects; special in its powers; special in its concessions. All other rights, whatever they might be, on either side, that did not range within the peculiar orbit of this convention, as novel as beneficent in its grand intention, were necessarily left just as they were before. But they continued to insist upon the exclusion of my words and the retention of their own until the close of the sixth conference, when they agreed to allow mine to stand, and to abandon theirs, in the parts from which I did not feel authorized to withdraw my opposition. The last member of the sentence upon this point, in the article as it now stands in the convention, viz: *nor be taken to affect in any other way the existing rights of either of the high contracting parties*, is that with which, in the end, they became satisfied. It will be seen how essentially it varies from the parallel passage as first submitted in their counter-projet.

To the sending home of our citizens for trial if taken in the act of piracy under the flag of a third power, as provided in their seventh article, I objected, on more consideration, as not likely to bring with it the due practicable reciprocity when the convention went into operation. Great Britain had the right under existing treaties to seize the slave trading vessels of Portugal, of Spain, and of the Netherlands; whereas the United States, as yet, had no such correlative right. But the British plenipotentiaries earnestly pressed its adoption, with a view to the more full attainment of all the objects of the convention now and hereafter. In the face of our own act of Congress of the 15th of May, 1820, which already subjects to death as a pirate any citizen of the United States convicted of being of the crew or ship's company of any foreign vessel engaged in the slave trade; in the face, too, of the general rule of public law, which has heretofore authorized the punishment of pirates by the courts of whatever nation they may be brought before, I did not feel called upon to persist in my opposition. I could scarcely continue to urge as very objectionable the being furnished with the means (should the occasion arise) of executing our own laws upon our own citizens, by whomsoever they might be detected and secured, whilst in the act of violating them. The British plenipotentiaries, moreover, remarked that the whole convention exhibited a preponderance of concession on the side of Great Britain in accommodation to the principles and views of the United States. At our instance she was about, by a new statute of her realm, to make the slave trade piracy; at our instance she agreed that the captured vessel and crew should be sent to their own country for trial, a course also new to all her past maritime doctrines and experience; and as regarded all the incidental consequences flowing from these two fundamental concessions, she still, at our instance, gave up or modified many of her former national and jurisprudential practices and predilections. They said, too, that the preponderance of burden under the convention would lie with Great Britain, both in the greater number of public ships that she would employ in the suppression of the traffic, and in the fact of the United States not having colonial dependencies, as Britain had, to serve as ready depots for those detected in it. I was far from lending my concurrence to these sentiments, which were to be taken with their just qualifications. The occasion, I remarked, was one where, instead of each nation pushing adverse rights, or striving for superior advantages, it ought rather to be considered that *each* was equally and spontaneously surrendering up a portion of its anterior system; each moving under one and the same impulse, towards one and the same object; each proposing to itself no other interests than those of benevolence and justice; no other gain (yet how great the gain!) than that of protecting the innocent, and laying prostrate the guilty. It was a negotiation with this distinguishing feature, that it looked *exclusively* to the benefit of a third party, assuming reciprocal duties and burdens for its sake, and flinging aside, as alien to the benign spirit in which it was conceived and undertaken, every selfish end or feeling. To the obligations, no less elevated than interesting, that sprung from such a negotiation, it was believed that neither party was insensible, and that both stood alike anxious to hail its favorable results. In mentioning the sentiments which the British plenipotentiaries expressed it must not be understood that I report them as having been uttered in complaint; and it would be an omission inexcusable in me were I not to add that they cordially and zealously responded to the enlarged and animating objects of the international compact which we were endeavoring to adjust.

To their second article, bringing under the penalties of the compact the subjects or citizens of either power, chartering the vessel of a third power for the purpose of carrying on the trade, I assented, believing that it did no more than effectuate the intention of our own second article, under words more full. To the provision in their fourth article, giving a power for laying the crew of the captured vessel under such restraints as might become indispensable for their detention and safe delivery, I also consented; varying its language to such as it will now be seen in the convention. I considered, in fact, such a power as only analogous, under one view, to that which is familiar to all jurisprudence, of securing an accused party between the time of arrest and of trial; and as doubly called for in this instance, in that it went to the necessary safeguard and protection of those who were constituted, by the convention, its incipient ministers of justice. With a like variation in the language, I consented to the passage, in the same article, which gives power for removing the slaves. The preservation of their lives, or other urgent motive of humanity, is made the condition of their removal, and a stipulation is superadded that they are to be accounted for to the Government of the country to which the captured vessel belongs, and be disposed of according to its laws.

I have thus indicated all the changes appearing to me to be important between the projet which you committed to me and the convention as it has been signed. A few other deviations, verbal, or in arrangement, will be perceived, but have not struck me as sufficiently material to call for particular notice or elucidation. The less so as I write under the pressure of other duties, arising out of the general negotiation, and with a desire to secure for the convention as early an arrival at Washington as possible; considerations which, I trust, will account for and excuse my omitting to trace, by minute marginal parallels, the whole of the alterations superinduced upon the counter-projet before the work was terminated. It is only left for me to hope that this despatch, with its inclosures, will render the progress of the negotiation intelligible. It may be needless in me to say that I have done all in my power to make the result satisfactory. The motive for using all practicable expedition in making up my despatch is, that should the convention be approved by the President, the option may not be lost of submitting it to the consideration of the Senate before the present session of Congress reaches its close. Should it, looked at as a whole, meet acceptance in the eyes of my Government, and become, happily, the era of a new and saving spirit introduced into the laws of nations for the relief of Africa, her redeemed and grateful children will have cause to pour out the fervent thanksgiving of their hearts towards those Christian powers that have at length been enabled, and rejoice that they have been enabled, to arrest the portentous desolation that for long ages has swept over their land, filling it with the concentration of every human woe. Then, at last, may we all hope, and not in vain, to see their tears dried up, their sufferings turned to joy, their groans to songs of benediction.

The inclosures of this despatch are: 1st. The convention. 2d. The British counter-projet, marked C. 3d. Copies of the first, second, fourth, fifth, sixth, and seventh protocols. I have ventured to omit sending a copy of our own projet, marked B; it having been submitted in the precise state in which I had it from you. Nor do I employ a special messenger for conveying the convention; not having done so when I forwarded the treaty of 1818, a course that was not disapproved. I shall now, as then, commit it to the care of our consul at Liverpool, with a request that he will get it on shipboard with all speed, and under the best auspices he can command.

I have the honor to remain, with very great respect, your obedient servant,

RICHARD RUSH.

Hon. JOHN QUINCY ADAMS,
    Secretary of State.

CONVENTION.

The United States of America and his Majesty the King of the United Kingdom of Great Britain and Ireland, being desirous to co-operate for the complete suppression of the African slave trade, by making the law of piracy, as applied to that traffic under the statutes of their respective Legislatures, immediately and reciprocally operative on the vessels and subjects or citizens of each other, have, respectively, appointed their plenipotentiaries to negotiate and conclude a convention for that purpose, that is to say: on the part of the United States of America, Richard Rush, Envoy Extraordinary and Minister Plenipotentiary from those States to the court of his Majesty; and, on the part of his Britannic Majesty, the Right Honorable William Huskisson, a member of his Majesty's most honorable Privy Council, President of the Committee of Privy Council, for Affairs of Trade and Foreign Plantations, Treasurer of his Majesty's Navy, and a member of the Parliament of the United Kingdom; and the Right Honorable Stratford Canning, a member of his said Majesty's most honorable Privy Council, and his Envoy Extraordinary and Minister Plenipotentiary to the United States of America; which plenipotentiaries, after duly communicating to each other their respective full powers, found to be in proper form, have agreed upon and concluded the following articles:

ARTICLE I. The commanders and commissioned officers of each of the two high contracting parties, duly authorized under the regulations and instructions of their respective Governments, to cruise on the coasts of Africa, of America, and of the West Indies, for the suppression of the slave trade, shall be empowered under the conditions, limitations, and restrictions hereinafter specified, to detain, examine, capture, and deliver over for trial and adjudication by some competent tribunal of whichever of the two countries it shall be found on examination to belong to, any ship or vessel concerned in the illicit traffic of slaves, and carrying the flag of the other, or owned by any subjects or citizens of either of the two contracting parties, except when in the presence of a ship-of-war of its own nation; and, it is further agreed that any such ship or vessel, so captured, shall be either carried or sent by the capturing officer, to some port of the country to which it belongs, and there given up to the competent authorities, or be delivered up for the same purpose to any duly commissioned officer of the other party; it being the intention of the high contracting powers that any ship or vessel within the purview of this convention, and seized on that account, shall be tried and adjudged by the tribunals of the captured party, and not by those of the captor.

ARTICLE II. In the case of any ship or vessel detained under this convention, by the cruisers of either of the two contracting parties, on suspicion of carrying on the slave trade, being found, on due examination by the boarding officer, to be chartered on account of any of the subjects or citizens of the other party, although not actually bearing the flag of that party, nor owned by the individuals on whose account she is chartered, or by any other citizens or subjects of the same nation, it is hereby agreed that, in such case also, upon the delivery of the said vessel to the tribunals of that country to which the persons on whose account she is chartered belong, the vessel, cargo, and crew, shall be proceeded against in like manner as any other vessel, cargo, and crew, within the purview of this convention, in so far as the general practice under the law of nations will allow.

ARTICLE III. Whenever any naval commander or commissioned officer of either of the two contracting powers shall, on the high seas, or anywhere not within the exclusive jurisdiction of either party, board, or cause to be boarded, any merchant vessel bearing the flag of the other power, and visit the same as a slave trader, or on suspicion of her being concerned in the slave trade; in every such case, whether the vessel so visited shall or shall not be captured and delivered over, or sent into the ports of her own country for trial and adjudication, the boarding officer shall deliver to the master or commander of the visited vessel a certificate in writing, signed by the said boarding officer, and specifying his rank in the Navy of his country, together with the names of the commander by whose orders he is acting, and of the national vessel commanded by him; and the said certificate shall further contain a declaration purporting that the only object of the visit is to ascertain whether the merchant vessel in question is engaged in the slave trade, or not; and, if found to be so engaged, to take and deliver her to the officers or tribunals of her own country, being that of one of the two contracting parties, for trial and adjudication.

In all such cases, the commander of the national vessel, whether belonging to Great Britain or to the United States, shall, when he makes delivery of his capture, either to the officers or to the tribunals of the other power, deliver all the papers found on board the captured vessel, indicating her national character, and the objects of her voyage, and; together with them, a certificate, as above, of the visit, signed with his name, and specifying his rank in the Navy of his country, as well as the name of the vessel commanded by him, together with the name and professional rank of the boarding officer by whom the said visit has been made.

This certificate shall also contain a list of all the papers received from the master of the vessel detained or visited, as well as those found on board the said vessel; it shall also contain an exact description of the state in which the vessel was found when detained, and the statement of the changes, if any, which have taken place in it, and of the number of slaves, if any, found on board at the moment of detention.

ARTICLE IV. Whenever any merchant vessel of either nation shall be visited under this convention, on suspicion of such vessel being engaged in the slave trade, no search shall in any such case be made on board the said vessel, except what is necessary for ascertaining, by due and sufficient proofs, whether she is or is not engaged in that illicit traffic. No person shall be taken out of the vessel so visited (though. such reasonable restraints as may be indispensable for the detention and safe delivery of the vessel may be used against the crew) by the commanding officer of the visiting vessel, or under his orders; nor shall any part of the cargo of the visiting vessel be taken out of her till after her delivery to the officers or tribunals of her own nation; excepting only when the removal of all or a part of the slaves, if any, found on board the visited vessel shall be indispensable, either for the preservation of their lives, or from any other urgent consideration of humanity, or for the safety of the persons charged with the navigation of the said vessel after her capture. And any of the slaves so removed shall be duly accounted for to the Government of that country to which the visited vessel belongs, and shall be disposed of according to the laws of the country into which they are carried; the regular bounty, or head-money, allowed by law, being in each instance secured to the captors, for their use and benefit, by the receiving Government.

ARTICLE V. Whenever any merchant vessel, of either nation, shall be captured under this convention, it shall be the duty of the commander of any ship belonging to the public service of the other, charged with the instructions of his Government for carrying into execution the provisions of this convention, at the requisition of the commander of the capturing vessel, to receive into his custody the vessel so captured, and to carry or send the same for trial and adjudication into some port of his own country, or of its dependencies. In every such case, at the time of the delivery of the vessel, an authentic declaration shall be drawn up in triplicate, and signed by the commanders both of the delivering and receiving vessels; one copy, signed by both, to be kept by each of them, stating the circumstances of the delivery, the condition of the captured vessel at the time of delivery, including the names of her master or commander, and of every other person, not a slave, on board at that time, and exhibiting the number of the slaves, if any, then on board of her, and a list of all the papers received or found on board at the time of capture, and delivered over with her. The third copy of the said declaration shall be left in the captured vessel, with the papers found on board, to be produced before the tribunal charged with the adjudication of the capture.

And the commander of the capturing vessel shall be authorized to send any one of the officers under his command, and one or two of his crew, with the captured vessel, to appear before the competent tribunal as witnesses of the facts regarding her detention and capture; the reasonable expenses of which witnesses in proceeding to the place of trial, during their detention there, and for their return to their own country, or to their station in its service, shall be allowed by the court of adjudication, and defrayed, in the event of the vessel being condemned, out of the proceeds of its sale; in case of the acquittal of the vessel, the expenses, as above specified, of these witnesses, shall be defrayed by the Government of the capturing officer.

ARTICLE VI. Whenever any capture shall be made under this convention by the officers of either of the contracting parties, and no national vessel of that country to which the captured vessel belongs is cruising on the same station where the capture takes place, the commander of the capturing vessel shall, in such case, either carry or send his prize to some convenient port of its own country, or of any of its dependencies, where a court of vice admiralty has jurisdiction, and there give it up to competent authorities for trial and adjudication.

The captured vessel shall then be libelled according to the practice of the court taking cognizance of the case; and, if condemned, the proceeds of the sale thereof, and of its cargo, if also condemned, shall be paid to the commander of the capturing vessel, for the benefit of the captors, to be distributed among them according to the rules of their service respecting prize money.

ARTICLE VII. The commander and crew of any vessel captured under this convention and sent in for trial shall be proceeded against, conformably to the laws of the country whereinto they shall be brought, as pirates engaged in the African slave trade; and it is further agreed that any individual, being a citizen or subject of either of the two contracting parties, who shall be found on board any vessel not carrying the flag of the other party, nor belonging to the subjects or citizens of either, but engaged in the illicit traffic of slaves, and lawfully seized on that account by the cruisers of the other party, or condemned under circumstances which, by involving such individual in the guilt of slave trading, would subject him to the penalties of piracy, he shall be sent for trial before the competent court in the country to which he belongs, and the reasonable expenses of any witnesses belonging to the capturing vessel, in proceeding to the place of trial, during their detention there, and for their return to their own country, or to their station in its service, shall, in every such case, be allowed by the court and defrayed by the country in which the trial takes place; but every witness belonging to the capturing vessel shall, upon the criminal trial for piracy, be liable to be challenged by the accused person and set aside as incompetent, unless he shall release his claim to any part of the prize money upon the condemnation of the vessel and cargo.

ARTICLE VIII. The right reciprocally conceded by the two contracting parties of visiting, capturing, and delivering over for trial the merchant vessels of the other engaged in the traffic of slaves shall be exercised only by such commissioned officers of their respective navies as shall be furnished with instructions for executing the laws of their respective countries against the slave trade.

For every vexatious and abusive exercise of this right, the boarding officer and the commander of the capturing or searching vessel shall, in each case, be personally liable in costs and damages to the master and owners of any merchant vessel delivered over, detained, or visited by them under the provisions of this convention.

Whatever court of admiralty shall have cognizance of the cause, as regards the captured vessel, in each case the same court shall be competent to hear the complaint of the master or owners, or of any person or persons on board the said vessel or interested in the property of her cargo at the time of her detention, and, on due and sufficient proof being given to the court of any vexation and abuse having been practiced during the search or detention of the said vessel, contrary to the provisions and meaning of this convention, to award reasonable costs and damages to the sufferers, to be paid by the commanding or boarding officer convicted of such misconduct.

The Government of the party thus cast in damages and costs shall cause the amount of the same to be paid, in each instance, agreeably to the judgment of the court, within twelve months from the date thereof.

In case of any such vexation and abuse occurring in the detention or search of a vessel detained under this convention, and not afterwards delivered over for trial, the persons aggrieved, being such as are specified above, or any of them, shall be heard by any court of admiralty of the country of the captors before which they make complaint thereof, and the commanding and boarding officer of the detaining vessel shall, in such instance, be liable, as above, in costs and damages to the complainant, according to the judgment of the court, and their Government shall equally cause payment of the same to be made within twelve months from the time when such judgment shall have been pronounced.

ARTICLE IX. Copies of this convention and of the laws of both countries actually in force for the prohibition and suppression of the African slave trade shall be furnished to every commander of the national vessels of either party charged with the execution of those laws; and in case any such commanding officer shall be accused by either of the two Governments of having deviated, in any respect, from the provisions of this convention and the instructions of his own Government in conformity thereto, the Government to which such complaint shall be addressed agrees hereby to make inquiry into the circumstances of the case, and to inflict on the officer complained of, in the event of his appearing to deserve it, a punishment adequate to his transgression.

ARTICLE X. The high contracting parties declare that the right which in the foregoing articles they have each reciprocally conceded of detaining, visiting, capturing, and delivering over for trial the merchant vessels of the other engaged in the African slave trade, is wholly and exclusively grounded on the consideration of their having made that traffic piracy by their respective laws; and further, that the reciprocal concession of the said right, as guarded, limited, and regulated by this convention, shall not be so construed as to authorize the detention or search of the merchant vessels of either nation by the officers of the Navy of the other, except vessels engaged or suspected of being engaged in the African slave trade, or for any other purpose whatever than that of seizing and delivering up the persons and vessels concerned in that traffic for trial and adjudication by the tribunals and laws of their own country, nor be taken to affect in any other way the existing rights of either of the high contracting parties.

And they do also hereby agree and engage to use their influence, respectively, with other maritime and civilized powers, to the end that the African slave trade may be declared to be piracy under the law of nations.

ARTICLE XI. The present convention, consisting of eleven articles, shall be ratified, and the ratifications exchanged at London, within the term of twelve months, or as much sooner as possible.

In witness whereof, the respective plenipotentiaries have signed the same, and have affixed thereunto the seals of their arms.

Done at London, the thirteenth day of March, in the year of our Lord one thousand eight hundred and twenty-four.

RICHARD RUSH.   [L. S.]
W. HUSKISSON.   [L. S.]
STRATFORD CANNING. [L. S.]

[With Mr. Rush's No. 2, of March 15, 1824.]

C.

PREAMBLE.

His Majesty the King of the United Kingdom of Great Britain and Ireland, and the United States of North America, being desirous to co-operate for the complete suppression of the African slave trade, by making the law of piracy, as applied to that traffic under the statutes of their respective Legislatures, immediately and reciprocally operative on the vessels and subjects or citizens of each other, have, respectively, appointed their plenipotentiaries to negotiate and conclude a convention for that purpose: that is to say, on the part of his Britannic Majesty, the Right Honorable William Huskisson, &c., &c., and the Right Honorable Stratford Canning, &c., &c., and on the part of the United States, Richard Rush, Envoy Extraordinary and Minister Plenipotentiary from those States to the court of his Majesty; which plenipotentiaries, after duly communicating to each other their respective full powers, found to be in proper form, have agreed upon and concluded the following articles:

I. The commanding and commissioned officers of each of the two high contracting parties, duly authorized under the regulations and instructions of their respective Governments to cruise on the coasts of Africa, of America, and of the West Indies, for the suppression of the slave trade, shall be empowered, under the conditions, limitations, and restrictions hereinafter specified, to detain, examine, capture, and deliver over for trial and adjudication by some competent tribunal of whichever of the two countries it shall be found on examination to belong to, any ship or vessel concerned in the illicit traffic of slaves, and carrying the flag of the other, or owned by any subjects or citizens of either of the two contracting parties, except when in presence of a ship-of-war of its own nation; in which case the commanding officer of the other party, instead of ordering the detention or search of the suspected vessel himself, shall give information of his suspicions to the commander of the said ship-of-war, and invite him to cause the suspected vessel to be searched and detained under his exclusive authority; provided, however, that the delay required for this purpose be not such, from peculiar and unavoidable circumstances, as to enable the suspected vessel to escape.

It is further agreed that any such ship or vessel, so captured, shall either be carried or sent by the capturing officer to some port of the country to which it belongs, and there given up to the competent authorities, or be delivered up for the same purpose to any duly commissioned officer of the other party; it being the intention of the high contracting powers that any ship or vessel within the purview of this convention, and seized on that account, shall be tried and adjudged by the tribunals of the captured party, and not by those of the captor.

II. In the case of any ship or vessel detained by the cruisers of either of the two contracting parties on suspicion of carrying on the slave trade being found, on due examination by the boarding officer, to be chartered on account of any of the subjects or citizens of the other party, although not actually bearing the flag of that party, nor owned by the individuals on whose account she is chartered, or by any other citizens or subjects of the same nation, it is hereby agreed that in such case also, upon the delivery of the said vessel to the tribunals of that country to which the persons on whose account she is chartered belong, the vessel, cargo, and crew shall be proceeded against in like manner as any other vessel, cargo, and crew within the purview of this convention, in so far as the general practice under the law of nations will allow.

III. Whenever any naval commander or commissioned officer of either of the two contracting powers shall, on the high seas, or anywhere not within the exclusive jurisdiction of either party, board or cause to be boarded any merchant vessel bearing the flag of the other power, and visit the same as a slave trader, or on suspicion of her being concerned in the slave trade, in every such case, whether the vessel so visited shall or shall not be captured and delivered over or sent into the ports of her own country for trial and adjudication, the boarding officer shall deliver to the master or commander of the visited vessel a certificate in writing, signed by the said boarding officer, and specifying his rank in the Navy of his country, together with the names of the commander by whose orders he is acting, and of the national vessel commanded by him; and the said certificate shall further contain a declaration purporting that the only object of the visit is to ascertain whether the merchant vessel in question is engaged in the slave trade or not, and if found to be so engaged, to take and deliver her to the officers or tribunals of her own country, being that of one of the two contracting parties, for trial and adjudication.

In all such cases, the commander of the national vessel, whether belonging to Great Britain or to the United States, shall, when he makes delivery of his capture either to the officers or to the tribunals of the other power, deliver all the papers found on board the captured vessel indicating her national character and the objects of her voyage, and, together with these, a certificate, as above, of the visit, signed by his name, and specifying his rank in the Navy of his country, as well as the name of the vessel commanded by him, together with the name and professional rank of the boarding officer by whom the said visit has been made.

This certificate shall also contain a list of all the papers received from the master of the vessel detained or visited, as well as those found on board the said vessel. It shall also contain an exact description of the state in which the vessel was found when detained, and a statement of the changes, if any, which have taken place in it, and of the number of slaves, if any, found on board at the moment of detention.

IV. Whenever any merchant vessel of either nation shall be visited, under this convention, on suspicion of such vessel being engaged in the slave trade, no search shall in any such case be made on board the said vessel, except what is necessary for ascertaining by positive and sufficient proofs whether she is or is not engaged in that illicit traffic. No person shall be taken out of the vessel so visited, though measures of restraint and personal coercion, necessary for the detention and safe delivery of the vessel, may be employed against its crew by the commanding officer of the visiting vessel or under his orders; nor shall any part of the cargo of the visited vessel be taken out of her till after her delivery to the officers or tribunals of her own nation, excepting only when the immediate removal of all or a part of the slaves, if any, found on board the visited vessel shall be necessary, either for the preservation of their lives or for the safety of the persons charged with the navigation of the said vessel after her capture. And any of the slaves so removed shall be duly accounted for to the Government of that country to which the visited vessel belongs, and shall be disposed of according to the laws of the country into which they are carried, the regular bounty or head-money allowed by law being, in each instance, secured to the captors for their use and benefit by the receiving Government.

V. Whenever any merchant vessel of either nation shall be captured under this convention, it shall be the duty of the commander of any ship belonging to the public service of the other, charged with the instructions of his Government for carrying into execution the provisions of this convention on the coast of Africa, of America, or of the West Indies, at the requisition of the commander of the capturing vessel, to receive into his custody the vessel so captured, and to carry or send the same for trial and adjudication into some port of his own country. In every such case, at the time of the delivery of the vessel, an authentic declaration shall be drawn up *in triplicate* and signed by the commander, both of the delivering and receiving vessel, one copy signed by both to be kept by each of them, stating the circumstances of the delivery, the condition of the captured vessel at the time of delivery, including the names of her master or commander, and of every other person, not a slave, on board at that time, and exhibiting the number of the slaves, if any, then on board her, and a list of all the papers received or found on board at the time of capture and delivered over with her. The third copy of the said declaration shall be left in the captured vessel, with the papers found on board, to be produced before the tribunal charged with the adjudication of the capture.

And the commander of the capturing vessel shall be authorized to send any one of the officers under his command, and one or two of his crew, with the captured vessel, to appear before the competent tribunal as witnesses of the facts regarding her detention and capture; the reasonable expenses of which witnesses in proceeding to the place of trial, during their detention there, and for their return to their own country, or to their station in its service, shall be allowed by the court of adjudication and defrayed, in the event of the vessel being condemned, out of the proceeds of its sale. In case of the acquittal of the vessel, the expenses, as above specified, of these witnesses shall be defrayed by the Government of the capturing officer.

VI. Whenever any capture shall be made under this convention by the officers of either of the contracting parties, and no national vessel of that country to which the captured vessel belongs is cruising on the same station where the capture takes place, the commander of the capturing vessel shall, in such case, either carry or send his prize to some convenient port of its own country, or of any of its dependencies where a court of vice admiralty has jurisdiction, and there give it up to the competent authorities for trial and adjudication. The captured vessel shall then be libelled according to the practice of the court taking cognizance of the case; and in case of its being condemned, the proceeds of the sale thereof and of its cargo, if also condemned, shall be paid to the commander of the capturing vessel for the benefit of the captors, to be distributed among them according to the rules of their service respecting prize money.

VII. The commander and crew of any vessel captured under this convention, and sent in for trial, shall be proceeded against, conformably to the laws of the country whereinto they shall be brought, as pirates engaged in the African slave trade; and it is further agreed that any individual, being a citizen or subject of either of the two contracting parties, who shall be found on board any vessel not carrying the flag of the other party, nor belonging to the subjects or citizens of either, but engaged in the illicit traffic of slaves, and seized or condemned on that account by the cruisers of the other party under circumstances which, by involving such individual in the guilt of slave trading, would subject him to the penalties of piracy, he shall be sent for trial before the competent court in the country to which he belongs, and the reasonable expenses of any witnesses belonging to the capturing vessel in proceeding to the place of trial, during their detention there, and for their return to their own country, or to their station in its service, shall, in every such case, be allowed by the court, and defrayed by the country in which the trial takes place.

VIII. The right, reciprocally conceded by the two contracting powers, of visiting, capturing, and delivering over for trial the merchant vessels of the other engaged in the traffic of slaves, shall be exercised only by such commissioned officers of their respective navies as shall be furnished with instructions for executing the laws of their respective countries against the slave trade.

For every vexatious and abusive exercise of this right, the boarding officer and the commander of the capturing or searching vessel shall, in each case, be liable in costs and damages to the master and owners of any merchant vessel delivered over, detained, or visited by them, under the provisions of this convention.

Whatever court of admiralty shall have cognizance of the cause, as regards the captured vessel, in each case the same court shall be competent to hear the complaint of the master, or of any person on board, or interested in the property of her cargo, at the time of her detention; and on clear, indubitable proof being given to the court of any vexation and abuse having been practiced during the search or detention of the said vessel, contrary to the provisions and meaning of this convention, to award reasonable costs and damages to the sufferers, to be paid by the commanding or boarding officer convicted of such misconduct.

The Government of the party thus cast in damages and costs shall cause the amount of the same to be paid, in each instance, agreeably to the judgment of the court, within twelve months from and after the date thereof.

In case of any such vexation and abuse occurring in the detention or search of a vessel detained under this convention, and not afterwards delivered over for trial, the persons aggrieved, being such as are specified above, or any of them, shall be heard by any court of admiralty of the country of the captors before which they make complaint thereof, and the commander and boarding officer of the detaining vessel shall, in each instance, be liable, as above, in costs and damages to the complainants, according to the judgment of the court, and their Government shall equally cause payment of the same to be made within twelve months from the time when such judgment shall have been pronounced.

IX. Copies of this convention and of the laws of both countries, actually in force, for the prohibition and suppression of the African slave trade, shall be furnished to every commander of the national vessels of either party charged with the execution of those laws; and in case any such commanding officer shall be accused by either of the two Governments of having deviated in any respect from the provisions of this convention, and the instructions of his own Government in conformity thereto, the Government to which such complaint shall be addressed agrees hereby to make inquiry into the circumstances of the case, and to inflict on the officer complained of, in the event of his appearing to deserve it, a punishment adequate to his transgression.

X. The high contracting parties declare that the right which, in the foregoing articles, they have each reciprocally conceded, of detaining, visiting, capturing, and delivering over for trial the merchant vessels of the other engaged in the African slave trade, is wholly and exclusively grounded on the consideration of their having made that traffic piracy by their respective laws; and, further, that the concession of the said right, as guarded, limited, and regulated by this convention, is meant and understood by them neither to extend to nor in any way to affect any other existing or eventual right of search or of capture at sea, in like manner as the mode of delivery and adjudication stipulated in this convention is not intended by them to affect in any way the ordinary modes of proceeding against vessels captured on the high seas under the law of nations; and they do also hereby agree and engage to use their influence, respectively, with other maritime and civilized powers to the end that the African slave trade may be generally declared to be piracy under the law of nations.

[With Mr. Rush's No. 2, of March 15, 1824.]

Protocol of the first conference of the American and British Plenipotentiaries, held at the Board of Trade on the 23d of January, 1824.

Present: Mr. Rush, Mr. Huskisson, Mr. Stratford Canning.

It was agreed, after the communication and exchange of the respective full powers, that the negotiation should be carried on by conference and protocol, with the right on both sides of annexing to the protocol any written statement which either party might consider necessary, as matter either of record or of explanation.

It was further agreed that the slave trade should be made the first subject of discussion, and that any articles on that head which the parties might agree in drawing up should be formed into a separate convention, to be submitted for ratification to the respective Governments immediately on its conclusion, and without reference to the state of the negotiation on other matters.

The British plenipotentiaries intimated their expectation to receive from Mr. Rush, in the first instance, a full communication of the proposals intended to be brought forward successively by his Government, under the heads of the several questions for the adjustment of which the negotiation had been opened, in conformity with the annexed memorandum previously communicated by him, (marked A.)

In pursuance of this intimation, Mr. Rush, after some introductory remarks explanatory of the views of his Government upon this subject, communicated *in extenso* the projet of a convention (marked B) for effecting a system of co-operation between the United States and Great Britain, with a view to the complete suppression of the slave trade.

The British plenipotentiaries, in receiving this projet, observed that they could not be expected to express any opinion as to its admissibility, either in whole or in part, on a first perusal; to which observation the American plenipotentiary assented; and it was agreed that the next conference should take place on Monday, the 2d of February.

RICHARD RUSH.
W. HUSKISSON.
STRATFORD CANNING.

A.

Memorandum referred to in the first conference.

1. Commercial intercourse between the United States and the colonial possessions of Great Britain in America and the West Indies, and the claim of the United States to the navigation of the river St. Lawrence.

2. Suppression of the slave trade.

3. Boundary line under the fifth article of the treaty of Ghent.

4. Admission of consuls of the United States in the colonial ports of Great Britain.

5. Newfoundland fishery.

6. Ukase of his Imperial Majesty the Emperor of Russia, of September, 1821, with a view to an adjustment of the boundaries between the United States and Great Britain on the Northwest Coast of America.

7. Questions of maritime law heretofore in discussion between the two nations, and also that of abolishing privateering as between them.

Protocol of the second conference of the American and British Plenipotentiaries, assembled at the Board of Trade, on the 2d of February, 1824.

Present: Mr. Rush, Mr. Huskisson, Mr. Stratford Canning.

The protocol of the preceding conference was read over and signed.

The British plenipotentiaries stated that, after mature consideration of the projet given in by Mr. Rush at the former conference, they were disposed to consent to the general principle on which it rested, but that there were serious difficulties in the mode of carrying that principle into effect, which they wished to point out and discuss with Mr. Rush, in the hope of arriving, with his assistance, at some solution satisfactory to both parties.

The discussion which ensued, with a view to the removal or modification of such provisions in the projet as were thought likely to render the proposed convention more or less ineffectual, terminated in an agreement on the part of the American plenipotentiary, after he had stated his first impressions on the subject, to reconsider, more at leisure, the points of his projet which appeared objectionable to the British plenipotentiaries, and on their part to ascertain, by reference to the proper law officers, how far it might be practicable to obviate the legal difficulties on their side.

It was agreed to meet again on the 5th instant, and, in case of any further causes of delay arising in the consideration of the slave trade projet, to proceed at once with the next subject of negotiation until these causes should be removed.

RICHARD RUSH.
W. HUSKISSON.
STRATFORD CANNING.

Protocol of the fourth conference of the American and British Plenipotentiaries, held at the Board of Trade, February 16, 1824.

Present: Mr. Rush, Mr. Huskisson, Mr. Stratford Canning.

The protocol of the preceding conference was read over and signed.

Several points connected with the propositions brought forward by the American plenipotentiary in the previous conferences were informally discussed with a view to explanation and, if possible, to the removal of difficulties on both sides.

The British plenipotentiaries communicated a counter-projet, (marked C,) comprising the principal alterations which they proposed to introduce into the articles on the slave trade, presented by Mr. Rush and annexed to the protocol of the first conference.

After discussing these alterations in a general way, it was agreed that a formal consideration of the articles on this subject, as produced on both sides, should take place at the next conference, to be fixed at as early a period as possible, with a view to the conclusion of a convention satisfactory to each of the contracting parties.

Adjourned.

RICHARD RUSH.
W. HUSKISSON.
STRATFORD CANNING.

Protocol of the fifth conference of the American and British Plenipotentiaries, held at the Board of Trade, March 9, 1824.

Present: Mr. Rush, Mr. Huskisson, Mr. Stratford Canning.

The protocol of the preceding conference was read over and signed.

The discussion which had taken place at the last conference upon the subject of the slave trade was renewed, principally with reference to the first and tenth articles of the counter-projet of the British plenipotentiaries.

No satisfactory adjustment of the points at issue being arrived at, it was agreed to meet again on the 11th instant for their further consideration.

RICHARD RUSH.
W. HUSKISSON.
STRATFORD CANNING.

Protocol of the sixth conference of the American and British Plenipotentiaries, held at the Board of Trade, March 11, 1824.

Present: Mr. Rush, Mr. Huskisson, Mr. Stratford Canning.

The protocol of the preceding conference was read over and signed.

The points on the subject of the slave trade which had been left undetermined at the last conference were again brought under discussion, and being at length satisfactorily adjusted, it was determined that at the next meeting, to be held on the 13th instant, the business should be completed by the signature of the convention as agreed on.

RICHARD RUSH.
W. HUSKISSON.
STRATFORD CANNING.

Protocol of the seventh conference of the American and British Plenipotentiaries, held at the Board of Trade, March 13, 1824.

Present: Mr. Rush, Mr. Huskisson, Mr. Stratford Canning.
The protocol of the preceding conference was read over and signed.
In pursuance of the agreement entered into at the last conference, the convention on the subject of the slave trade was produced, and, being found on perusal to be in all respects satisfactory to the plenipotentiaries on both sides, received their respective signatures.
The protocol of the present conference was also read over and signed.

RICHARD RUSH,
W. HUSKISSON.
STRATFORD CANNING.

[The following are the message and documents to the House of Representatives that were communicated to the Senate in executive session, with the preceding message of the President of April 30, 1842.]

Message from the President of the United States, transmitting the information required by a resolution of the House of Representatives of 27th February last, in relation to the suppression of the African slave trade.

To the House of Representatives:

I transmit herewith to the House of Representatives a report from the Secretary of State, with the papers therein referred to, in compliance with a resolution of that House of the 27th of January last.

JAMES MONROE.

WASHINGTON, *March* 19, 1824.

DEPARTMENT OF STATE, *Washington, March 18, 1824.*

The Secretary of State, to whom has been referred a resolution of the House of Representatives of the 27th of January last, requesting the President to communicate to that House such part as he may not deem inexpedient to divulge of any correspondence or negotiation which he may have instituted with any foreign Government since the 28th of February, 1823, in compliance with a request contained in a resolution of the same House of that date relative to the denunciation of the African slave trade as piracy, has the honor to submit to the President copies of the correspondence requested.

JOHN QUINCY ADAMS.

List of papers sent.

1. Mr. Canning to Mr. Adams, January 29, 1823.
2. Mr. Adams to Mr. Canning, March 81, 1823.
3. Mr. Canning to Mr. Adams, April 8, 1823.
4. Mr. Adams to Mr. Canning, June 24, 1823.
5. Same to Mr. Nelson, April 28, 1823. Extract.
6. Same to Mr. Rodney, May 17, 1823. Extract.
7. Same to Mr. Anderson, May 27, 1823. Extract.
8. Same to Mr. Rush, with one inclosure; convention slave trade, June 24, 1823. Extract.
9. Same to Mr. Middleton, July 28, 1823. Copy.
10. Same to Mr. Everett, August 8, 1823. Copy.
11. Same to General Dearborn, August 14, 1823. Extract.
12. Mr. Rush to Mr. Adams, October 9, 1823. Extracts.
13. Mr. Sheldon to Mr. Adams, October 16, 1823. Extracts.
14. Same to Same, with two inclosures; correspondence with Viscount Chateaubriand, November 5, 1823. Extracts.
15. Mr. Everett to Mr. Adams, with two inclosures; correspondence with Baron Nagell, November 20, 1823. Extracts.

Mr. Canning to Mr. Adams.

WASHINGTON, *January* 29, 1823.

SIR: To the complete abolition of the African slave trade, Great Britain, as you are well aware, has long devoted her anxious and unremitting exertions; she availed herself, during war, of her belligerent rights, and extended dominion in the colonies to put down the inhuman traffic; in peace, she has spared no labor and shrunk from no sacrifice to supply, by a general co-operation of the maritime powers, whatever has been withdrawn from her peculiar control by the cessation of hostilities and the colonial arrangements consequent on that event. It is matter of deep regret to his Majesty's Government that the result of their exertions is far from corresponding either to the cause which demands or to the zeal which sustains them. The pest, which they have pledged themselves to destroy, if it be in human power to destroy it, not only survives, to the disgrace and affliction of the age, but seems to acquire a fresh capacity for existence with every endeavor for its destruction.

To whatever fatality it may be owing, that, while the obligation of adopting and enforcing measures for the extermination of the slave trade is solemnly acknowledged by the civilized world, this great object seems rather to elude the grasp than to approach its consummation. Great Britain perceives, in the postponement of her hopes, however mortifying for the moment, no reason either to relax from her efforts or to abandon the expectation of final success. Impelled by the noblest motives to persevere in the cause of abolition, and mindful by what slow, laborious steps the present point has been attained, she looks forward, through surrounding obstacles, to the triumphant accomplishment of her purpose, the benefit and glory of which will only be rendered more signal by the difficulties attending on its progress.

In calling on Europe and America to join with them in the discharge of this sacred duty, his Majesty and his ministers have appealed, sir, with the more confidence, to your Government, as the United States have long proclaimed their decided hostility to the slave trade, and are surpassed by no country in the vigor of their legislative enactment for its repression. The identity of principle existing on this subject between the two Governments is distinctly recorded in the treaty of peace; and, in answer to every proposal which has since, by his Majesty's command, been addressed to your cabinet for redeeming that pledge by a broad and effectual application of the principle, a fresh assurance has been given of the unceasing interest with which the United States continue to promote the cause of abolition. When to this accord, in principle and sentiment, is added the conviction, avowed by both parties, that, in spite of laws and treaties, the accursed traffic still thrives, under the eyes of an indignant world, it would seem impossible that the two powers should be long prevented from concerting a joint system of measures against the common object of their abhorrence and just proscription. Whatever circumstances, views, or impressions may have hitherto defeated this expectation, his Majesty's ministers are still unwilling to despair of finding the United States at length prepared either to close with the system of concert already offered to their acceptance, or to suggest a plan of equal efficiency in its place. The alternative embraces a duty, for the performance of which both countries are responsible before God and man.

A deep sense of this duty, and a reliance, by no means relinquished, on the general disposition of the United States, have prompted the several communications on this question which have been addressed to you at successive periods, either through me or by means of the American envoy in London. You will readily call to mind, sir, that in the course of last summer I apprised you of the intention of his Majesty's ministers to press for an early reconsideration of the subject, submitting whether it might not prove agreeable to the American cabinet to anticipate that intended recurrence to it on the part of Great Britain, by some efficient proposal, originating with itself. I took occasion, in repeated conversations, to urge anew those various arguments which support and justify the opinion of his Majesty's Government; and I also placed in your hands the official papers, then recently printed by order of Parliament, in further evidence of the extent to which the traffic in human beings was still carried on from Africa, under circumstances of aggravated cruelty. In declaring, as on former occasions, the readiness of his Majesty's ministers to examine, with respect and candor, whatever scheme of concert, if any, the American cabinet might think proper to bring forward, as a substitute for theirs, you will remember how strongly I expressed my belief that the only effectual measure devised or likely to be devised, was a mutual concession of the right of search. In the exercise of that right, under such guards and with such limitations as may serve to tranquillize the most apprehensive and scrupulous minds, it is still conceived that the best and only cure for this intolerable mischief is to be found. You assured me, at a subsequent conference, that my representations had been duly submitted to the President. I wish it were in my power to add that the cause which I pleaded had prevailed.

From the printed documents which I had the honor of communicating to you, it appears that the French flag is more particularly employed to cover the illicit trade on the coast of Africa. It would, perhaps, be unfair to conclude that French property and French subjects are concerned to the full proportion in which the colors of that nation are used; but it is manifest that both are engaged in this commerce of blood, to an extent which reflects discredit, if not on the motives of the French administration, at least on the efficiency of its measures, and makes it imperative on those Governments which are pledged to each other for the suppression of the slave trade to declare their reprobation of what is at best a culpable remissness, and to omit nothing that may rouse the French cabinet to a more active exercise of its authority.

It was a part of my instructions to bring this point under your immediate consideration, and to intimate that the remonstrances of his Majesty's ambassador at Paris might be attended with more effect if the American envoy at that court were directed to concur with his excellency in a joint representation on the subject. It would be idle at present to repeat the arguments adduced in executing this instruction. The answer which you returned in the name of the President was unfavorable to the step I had suggested; and such was the result which it became my duty to announce to his Majesty's Secretary of State. But no doubt was started with respect to the grounds on which my application rested; and of those notorious facts to which I referred, as calling for a joint and impressive appeal to the good faith and good feelings of the French Government, you seemed to be equally convinced with myself.

The reasons, indeed, which you allege for declining at that time to comply with a proposal no less simple in its nature than useful in its object, I understood to be rather of a temporary character; and under this impression I cannot but hope that the period is now arrived when they will no longer be found to stand in opposition to the great considerations involved in this question.

In repeating, therefore, the invitation which I have already had the honor to convey to you on the part of his Majesty's Government, it only remains for me to request an early communication of the intentions at present entertained on this head by the Government of the United States.

I beg, sir, that you will accept the assurance of my distinguished consideration,

STRATFORD CANNING.

Hon. JOHN QUINCY ADAMS, *Secretary of State, &c.*

Mr. Adams to Mr. Canning.

DEPARTMENT OF STATE, *Washington, March* 31, 1823.

SIR: Your letter of the 29th of January was, immediately after being received, submitted to the consideration of the President of the United States. The delay which has hitherto procrastinated a reply to it has been occasioned, not by any abatement of the interest on the part of the Government of the United States with which it regards every effort and proposal for the full and final suppression of the African slave trade, nor by any hesitation with regard to the decision which had already been formed and declared respecting the proposal of submitting the vessels and citizens of the United States to the search of foreign officers upon the high seas, but by an expectation that measures contemplated by the national House of Representatives might, before the close of the session of Congress, indicate to the Executive Government of this country views upon which it would be enabled to substitute a proposal for accomplishing a total abolition of the traffic, more effectual to its purpose, and less liable to objections on other accounts, than that, to which the United States cannot be reconciled, of granting the right of search. These measures were matured in the branch of the Legislature where they originated, only at the very termination of the session, and the Senate had not the opportunity of pronouncing its opinion upon them. There is, however, no doubt on the mind of the President that they would have obtained their sanction; and he has, therefore, no hesitation in acting so far upon the expressed and almost unanimous sense of the House, as to declare the willingness of this Union to join with other nations in the common engagement to pursue and to punish those who shall continue to practice this crime, so reprobated by the just and humane of every country as enemies of the human race, and to fix them irrevocably in the class and under the denomination of pirates.

I have the honor of inclosing herewith a copy of the 4th and 5th sections of a law of the United States, passed on the 15th of May, 1820, by which it will be seen that any citizen of the United States being of the crew or ship's company of any *foreign* ship or vessel engaged in the slave trade, or any person *whatever* being of the crew or ship's company of *any* ship or vessel owned in the whole or part, or navigated for or in behalf of any citizen or citizens of the United States participating in the slave trade, is declared to have incurred the penalties of piracy, and made liable to atone for the crime with his life. The legislation of a single nation can go no further to mark its abhorrence of this traffic, or to deter the people subject to its laws from contamination by the practice of others.

If the inference in your letter of the 29th of January, from the documents to which it refers, be correct, that the French flag is more particularly employed to cover the illicit trade on the coast of Africa; and the conjecture likewise suggested in it, that this flag is used to cover the property and the persons of individuals bound to other allegiances, be well founded, this statute makes every citizen of the United States concerned in such covered traffic liable, if detected in it, to suffer an ignominious death. The code of Great Britain herself has hitherto no provision of equal severity in the pursuit of her subjects, even under the shelter of foreign banners, and to the covert of simulated papers and property.

I am directed by the President of the United States to propose on their part the adoption, by Great Britain, of the *principle* of this act, and to offer a mutual stipulation to annex the penalties of *piracy* to the offence of participating in the slave trade by the citizens or subjects of the respective parties. This proposal is made as a substitute for that of conceding a mutual right of search, and of a trial by mixed commissions which would be rendered useless by it. Should it meet the approbation of your Government, it may be separately urged upon the adoption of France, and upon the other maritime powers of Europe in the manner most conducive to its ultimate success.

I have the honor of tendering to you the renewed assurance of my distinguished consideration,

JOHN QUINCY ADAMS.

The Right Hon. STRATFORD CANNING,
 Envoy Extraordinary and Minister Plenipotentiary from Great Britain.

Mr. Canning to Mr. Adams.

WASHINGTON, *April* 8, 1823.

SIR: I have received your official letter dated the 31st ultimo, in answer to that which I had the honor of addressing to you on the 29th of January, and, together with it, a transcript of the 4th and 5th sections of an act of Congress approved the 15th of May, 1820.

From this communication I learn that the Government of the United States is willing to join with other powers in declaring slave trade piracy, under the law of nations, and treating the perpetrators of this crime as enemies of the human race; that the American Government is further prepared to enter into a formal engagement with Great Britain, to the effect of carrying the principle just specified into immediate operation, reciprocally, as to their respective subjects or citizens; and, finally, that as soon as this proposal shall be accepted by the British Government, the United States will be ready to concur in pressing its adoption on the court of France and other maritime powers in such manner as may afford the fairest prospect of success.

In whatever degree his Majesty's Government may be disposed to receive this offer as an acknowledgment that measures more efficient than any now generally in force are indispensable for the suppression of the slave trade, it is not difficult to foresee that fresh sentiments of regret will be excited by the unfavorable view which the American administration continues to take of the principal measure suggested on the part of his Majesty. That measure, you are well aware, sir, is a mutual limited concession of the right of search; and though, as I have frequently stated, his Majesty's Government, in adopting it by treaty with several of the maritime powers, and in recommending it with earnestness to the acceptance of others, particularly of the United States, have never opposed the consideration of any other plan brought forward as equally effective; yet, having from the first regarded it in conscience as the only true and practical cure for the evil in question, they are naturally anxious, from a deep sense of duty, to place it in its proper light, and to guard it as far as possible from prejudice or misconception. I therefore deem it of importance on this occasion to bring into one point of view the several limitations under which it is conceived that the right of search might be so exercised as to clear it of every imaginable difficulty. To give the intended limitations their just value, it is requisite to bear in mind the particular objections which have been urged against the interchange of a right of search; and for these, in their full extent, I can hardly be wrong in referring to your previous correspondence, since the last communication which I have received from you on this subject, though it describes the impressions of the American Government as remaining unaltered, does not exhibit any argument in support of their opinion.

In answer to that class of objections which relate to the mixed commissions established by treaty between his Majesty and the courts of Lisbon, Brussels, and Madrid, it may suffice to remind you of the intimation conveyed through Mr. Rush, in the early part of last year, which I had subsequently the honor of confirming at the Department of State. It might be expected that any arrangement for the adjudication of vessels engaged in the slave trade, independent of those tribunals, would either leave the detained vessels to be disposed of in the ordinary way, by the sentence of a court of admiralty in the country of the captor, or place them under the jurisdiction of a similar court in the country to which they belonged. On the former supposition it is not to be anticipated that the United States could hesitate to admit the jurisdiction of a foreign court of admiralty, when sanctioned by mutual agreement, over the persons and property of citizens abandoned to a pursuit so flagrantly iniquitous as to be classed by the Legislature of their country with crimes of the most heinous description, and which the American Government has declared its willingness to treat as piracy, under the law of nations. Great Britain, for her part, desires no other than that any of her subjects, who so far defy the laws and dishonor the character of their country as to engage in a trade of blood, proscribed not more by the acts of the Legislature than by the national feeling, should be detected and brought to justice even by foreign hands and from under the protection of her flag. In either of the supposed cases it is clear that all impediments connected with the forms of proceeding and peculiar construction of the mixed commissions would be completely avoided; and with respect to any embarrassment attending the disposal of condemned vessels and liberated slaves, it has already been suggested by a committee of the House of Representatives that the provisions of the act of Congress, passed the 3d of March, 1819, might be applied to them without difficulty or inconvenience.

The question being thus relieved from all connexion with the mixed commissions, every constitutional objection arising out of their alleged incompatibility with the institutions of the United States is at once removed from consideration. The remaining obstacles may be reduced under the following heads : the unpopularity of the right of search in this country; its tendency, if mutually employed, to produce an unfriendly collision between the two nations; and a certain supposed inequality which would attend its exercise.

With respect to any doubt of its utility, created by a persuasion that very few vessels under American colors have been discovered, for some time past, on the coast of Africa, it requires but little reflection to prove that no conclusive inference can be drawn from that circumstance. Not to dwell upon the extent and nature of the slave coast, peculiarly favorable to the concealment of trading vessels, it must be remembered that the United States have maintained at no time a greater number of cruisers than two, rarely more than one, and latterly, during several months together, no ship-of-war whatever on the African station. As late as the 14th of January, 1822, it was stated officially by the Governor of Sierra Leone, "that the fine rivers Nunez and Pongas were entirely under the control of renegado European and American slave traders."

But, if it were even manifest that the active and judicious exertions of your naval officers in that quarter had really effected a total disuse of the American flag in slave trading, the right of search would still be most highly desirable, in order to secure and extend so important an advantage. As an example, indeed, to other powers, particularly to France, whose subjects, encouraged by the loose and equivocal measures of their Government, are convicted, by a mass of evidence too strong to be resisted, of being concerned to a deplorable degree in this atrocious commerce, the concurrence of the United States in a system of which the very first result is to augment considerably the means of bringing offenders to justice, can hardly be rated at too high a value. The example which they are called upon to give is not merely due to the claims of humanity; Great Britain and the United States are not only pledged to put down the slave trade within the limits of their immediate jurisdiction, they are also bound by solemn obligations to employ their utmost endeavors for its complete and universal extermination. They have both succeeded in their benevolent object, so far as the rigor of legislative enactments is capable of counteracting the temptation of enormous profit, which stimulates the unprincipled avarice of the slave merchant. It is the facility of escaping detection, and not any want of severity in the punishment attached to a violation of their laws, which, so far as they are concerned, requires a more decisive remedy; and a remedy adequate to the evil can only be found in such measures as will strip the illicit trader of every disguise, and throw the chances entirely on the side of failure in his inhuman speculations. In the case of search at sea, the means unavoidably employed in the commission of this crime are fortunately, it may be said providentially, of such a nature as in general to furnish a plain substantial body of proof for the conviction of the criminal.

For the satisfaction of those who seriously apprehend that the friendly relations subsisting between the two countries would be endangered by the admission of a practice which, in their opinion, must necessarily produce a vexatious exercise of authority on the part of the searching officer, and frequent complaints on that of the merchant whose vessel is subjected to search, with the supposed aggravation of an unequal pressure on one of the contracting parties, his Majesty's Government would doubtless agree to confine the right of visit to a fixed number of cruisers on each side, restricted in the performance of this duty to certain specified parts of the ocean, and acting under regulations prepared by mutual consent, for the purpose of preventing abuses. To these important limitations, if not deemed sufficient, others might easily be added; the arrangement, for example, might be temporary; adopted in the first instance for a short period, and only to be continued in the event of its being found on trial to operate in a satisfactory manner. With this understanding a speedy termination would, at least, be insured to any objectionable result attending its operation; and for the sake of interests as dear to humanity, an experiment, of which the advantage as to its main object is certain and complete, the inconvenience, contingent and momentary, might surely be reconciled with a due regard to considerations exclusively national.

Supposing that inconvenience should be found in practice to press unequally on the two parties, Great Britain, and not the United States, is most likely to have cause of complaint, inasmuch as the greater extent of her trade, especially on the coast of Africa, must naturally expose her in a greater degree to any injurious consequences of the agreement. Great Britain, however, is less disposed to shrink from any sacrifice by which she can materially advance the sacred cause of abolition, than to lament, and, if possible, to dispel those mistaken notions and unfounded jealousies which deprive her exertions of their full effect, and serve, but too successfully, to protract the existence of a mischief which all unite in deploring. In point of principle, the honor of neither flag would be tarnished by having its protection withdrawn for a season from those who perpetrate the atrocities of the slave trade; and permit me, sir, to add, that what Great Britain is ready to allow in a matter so vital to her pride and to her power may surely be allowed, reciprocally, by any other nation, however scrupulous in the maintenance of its maritime independence.

That an agreement between our respective cabinets, founded on a mutual right of search, thus guarded and explained, would fail to obtain the consent of the American Senate, or that a nation so inquiring and enlightened as the United States would confound the proposed measures with that practice which afforded matter of painful contention during the last wars in Europe, is what I am extremely unwilling to anticipate. The two objects are, in fact, so totally distinct from each other in principle, purpose, and mode of execution, that the proposal of the British Government need only be presented to the examination, I will not say of a select and experienced assembly, but of the people at large, in order to be seen in its true bearings.

So far is the British proposal from tending to commit the American Government on the long disputed question of the belligerent right of search, that if it may be supposed to touch that question at all, it appears rather to operate in the sense of the United States, than unfavorably for their view of the subject.

The officers intrusted on either side with the duty of examining suspected vessels would necessarily act under instructions calculated to insure a perfect harmony between the principle and the application of this conceded right, nor is it to be feared that they would presume, in any case, to extend the visit thus authorized at sea beyond the particular and specified object to which it is meant to be confined.

I have the honor to request, sir, that you will again accept the assurance of my highest consideration.

STRATFORD CANNING.

Hon. John Quincy Adams, *Secretary of State, &c.*

Mr. Adams to Mr. Canning.

DEPARTMENT OF STATE, *Washington, June 24, 1823.*

SIR: In the letter which I had the honor of addressing you on the 31st of March last a proposal was made, to be submitted to the consideration of your Government, that the *principle* assumed in an act of the Congress of the United States of May 15, 1820, of considering and punishing the African slave trade as *piracy*, should be adopted as the basis of a stipulation by treaty between the United States and Great Britain, and to be urged separately upon the adoption of France and upon the other maritime nations of Europe, in the manner most conducive to its ultimate success. It was observed that this offer was presented as a substitute for that of conceding a mutual right of search and a trial by mixed commissions, to which the United States could not be reconciled, and which would be rendered useless by it.

Your letter of the 8th of April, to which I have now the honor to reply, intimates that his Majesty's Government will be disposed to receive this offer only as an acknowledgment that measures more efficient than any now generally in force are indispensable for the suppression of the slave trade; and that, although they have never opposed the consideration of any other plan, brought forward as equally effective, yet, having from the first regarded a mutual limited concession of the right of search as the *only* true and practical cure for the evil, their prevailing sentiment will be of regret at the unfavorable view still taken of it by the Government of the United States. Your letter, therefore, urges a reconsideration of the proposal for the mutual concession of the right of search, and by presenting important modifications of the proposal heretofore made removes some of the objections which had been taken to it as insuperable, while it offers argumentative answers to the others which had been disclosed in my previous communications on this subject to you.

In the treaties of Great Britain with Spain, Portugal, and the Netherlands, for the suppression of the slave trade, heretofore communicated, with the invitation to the United States to enter into similar engagements, three principles were involved, to neither of which the Government of the United States felt itself at liberty to accede. The first was the mutual concession of the right of search and capture, in time of peace, over merchant vessels on the coast of Africa. The second was the exercise of that right even over vessels under *convoy* of the public officers of their own nation; and the third was the trial of the captured vessels by mixed commissions in colonial settlements under no subordination to the ordinary judicial tribunals of the country to which the party brought before them for trial should belong. In the course of the correspondence relating to these proposals it has been suggested that a substitute for the trial by mixed commissions might be agreed to, and in your letter of the 8th April an *expectation* is authorized that an arrangement for the adjudication of the vessels detained might leave them to be disposed of in the ordinary way, by the sentence of a court of admiralty in the country of the captor, or place them under the jurisdiction of a similar court in the country to which they belonged; to the former alternative of which you anticipate the unhesitating admission of the United States, in consideration of the aggravated nature of the crime, as acknowledged by their laws, which would be thus submitted to a *foreign* jurisdiction. But it was precisely because the jurisdiction was *foreign* that the objection was taken to the trial by mixed commissions; and if it transcended the constitutional authority of the Government of the United States to subject the persons, property, and reputation of their citizens to the decisions of a court partly composed of their own countrymen, it might seem needless to remark that the constitutional objection could not diminish in proportion as its cause should increase, or that the power incompetent to make American citizens amenable to a court consisting one-half of foreigners should be adequate to place their liberty, their fortune, and their fame at the disposal of tribunals entirely *foreign*. I would further remark that the sentence of a court of admiralty in the country of the captor is not the *ordinary way* by which the merchant vessels of one nation, taken on the high seas by the officers of another, are tried in time of peace. There is, in the ordinary way, no right whatever existing to take, to search, or even to board them; and I take this occasion to express the great satisfaction with which we have seen this principle solemnly recognized by the decision of a British court of admiralty. Nor is the aggravation of the crime for the trial of which a tribunal may be instituted a cogent motive for assenting to the principle of subjecting American citizens, their rights, and interests, to the decision of foreign courts; for, although Great Britain, as you remark, may be willing to abandon those of her subjects who defy the laws and tarnish the character of their country by participating in this trade to the dispensation of justice even by foreign hands, the United States are bound to remember that the power which enables a court to try the guilty authorizes them also to pronounce upon the fate of the innocent, and that the very question of *guilt* or innocence is that which the protecting care of their Constitution has reserved for the citizens of this Union to the exclusive decision of their own countrymen. This principle has not been departed from by the statute which has branded the slave trader with the name, and doomed him to the punishment, of a pirate. The distinction between piracy by the law of nations and piracy by statute is well known and understood in Great Britain; and while the former subjects the transgressor guilty of it to the jurisdiction of any and every country into which he may be brought, or wherein he may be taken, the latter forms a part of the municipal criminal code of the country where it is enacted, and can be tried only by its own courts.

There remains the suggestion, that the slave trader, captured under the mutual concession of the power to make the capture, might be delivered over to the jurisdiction of his own country. This arrangement would not be liable to the constitutional objection, which must ever apply to the jurisdiction of the mixed commission, or of the admiralty courts of the captor; and if your note is to be understood as presenting it in the character of an alternative, to which your Government is disposed to accede, I am authorized to say that the President considers it as sufficient to remove the insuperable obstacle which had precluded the assent of the United States to the former proposals of your Government, resulting from the character and composition of the tribunals to whom the question of guilt or innocence was to be committed.

The objections to the right of search, as incident to the right of detention and capture, are also, in a very considerable degree, removed by the introduction of the principle that neither of them should be exercised but under the responsibility of the captor to the tribunals of the captured party in damages and costs. This guard against the abuses of a power so liable to abuse would be indispensable; but if the provisions necessary for securing effectually its practical operation would reduce the right itself to power merely nominal, the stipulation of it in a treaty would serve rather to mark the sacrifice of a great and precious principle than to attain the end for which it would be given up.

In the objections heretofore disclosed to the concession desired of the mutual and qualified right of search, the principal stress was laid upon the repugnance which such a concession would meet in the public feeling of this country, and of those to whom its interests are intrusted in the department of its Government, the sanction of which is required for the ratification of treaties. The irritating tendency of the practice of search, and the inequalities of its probable operation, were slightly noticed, and have been contested in argument, or met by propositions of possible palliatives, or remedies for anticipated abuses, in your letter. But the source and foundation of all these objections was, in our former correspondence, scarcely mentioned, and never discussed. They consist in the nature of the right of search at sea, which, as recognized or tolerated by the usage of nations, is a right exclusively of *war*, never exercised but by an outrage upon the rights of *peace*. It is an act analogous to that of searching the dwelling-houses of individuals on the land. The vessel of the navigator is his dwelling-house, and like that, in the sentiment of every people that cherishes the blessings of personal liberty and security, ought to be a sanctuary inviolable to the hand of power, unless upon the most unequivocal public necessity, and under the most rigorous personal responsibility of the intruder. Search at sea, as recognized by all maritime nations, is confined to the single object of finding and taking contraband of war. By the law of nature, when two nations conflict together in war, a third, remaining neutral, retains all its rights of peace and friendly intercourse with both. Each belligerent, indeed, acquires by war the right of preventing a third party from administering to his enemy the direct and immediate materials of war; and, as incidental to this right, that of searching the merchant vessels of the neutral on the high seas to find them. Even thus limited, it is an act of power which nothing but necessity can justify, inasmuch as it cannot be exercised but by carrying the evils of war into the abodes of peace, and by visiting the innocent with some of the penalties of guilt. Among the modern maritime nations, an *usage* has crept in, not founded upon the law of nature, never universally admitted, often successfully resisted, and against which all have occasionally borne testimony by renouncing it in treaties, of extending this practice of search and seizure to *all* the property of the enemy in the vessel of the friend. This practice was, in its origin, evidently an abusive and wrongful extension of the search for contraband: effected by the belligerent, because he was armed; submitted to by the neutral, because he was defenceless; and acquiesced in by his sovereign for the sake of preserving a remnant of peace, rather than become himself a party to the war. Having thus, occasionally, been practiced by all as belligerents, and submitted to by all as neutrals, it has acquired the force of an usage which, at the occurrence of every war, the belligerent may enforce or relinquish, and which the neutral may suffer or resist, at their respective options.

This search for and seizure of the property of an enemy in the vessel of a friend is a relic of the barbarous warfare of barbarous ages—the cruel and, for the most part, now exploded system of *private* war. As it concerns the enemy himself, it is inconsistent with that mitigated usage of modern wars which respects the private property of individuals on the land. As relates to the neutral, it is a violation of his natural right to pursue, unmolested, his peaceful commercial intercourse with his friend. Invidious as is its character in both these aspects, it has other essential characteristics equally obnoxious. It is an uncontrolled exercise of authority by a man in arms over a man without defence—by an officer of one nation over the citizen of another—by a man intent upon the annoyance of his enemy, responsible for the act of search to no tribunal, and always prompted to balance the disappointment of a fruitless search by the abusive exercise of his power, and to punish the neutral for the very clearness of his neutrality. It has, in short, all the features of unbridled power, stimulated by hostile and unsocial passions.

I forbear to enlarge upon the further extension of this practice by referring to injuries which the United States experienced when neutral in a case of vital importance; because, in digesting a plan for the attainment of an object which both nations have equally at heart, it is desirable to avoid every topic which may excite painful sensations on either side. I have adverted to the interest in question from necessity, it being one which could not be lost sight of in the present discussion.

Such being the view taken of the right of search, as recognized by the law of nations and exercised by belligerent powers, it is due to candor to state that my Government has an insuperable objection to its extension by treaty, in any manner whatever, lest it might lead to consequences still more injurious to the United States, and especially in the circumstance alluded to. That the proposed extension will operate in time of peace and derive its sanction from compact present no inducements to its adoption. On the contrary, they form strong objections to it. Every extension of the right of search on the principles of that right is disapproved. If the freedom of the sea is abridged by compact for any new purpose, the example may lead to other changes. And if its operation is extended to a time of peace, as well as of war, a new system will be commenced for the dominion of the sea, which may eventually, especially by the abuses into which it may lead, confound all distinction of time and circumstances, of peace and of war, and of rights applicable to each state.

The United States have, on great consideration, thought it most advisable to consider this trade as piracy, and to treat it as such. They have thought that the trade itself might, with great propriety, be placed in that class of offences; and that by placing it there we should more effectually accomplish the great object of suppressing the trade than by any other measure which we could adopt.

To this measure none of the objections which have been urged against the extension of the right of search appear to be applicable. Piracy being an offence against the human race, has its well known incidents of capture and punishment by death by the people and tribunals of every country. By making this trade piratical, it is the nature of the crime which draws after it the necessary consequences of capture and punishment. The United States have done this, by an act of Congress, in relation to themselves. They have also evinced their willingness and expressed their desire that the change should become general by the consent of every other power, whereby it would be made the law of nations. Till then, they are bound by the injunctions of their Constitution to execute it, so far as respects the punishment of their own citizens by their own tribunals. They consider themselves, however, at liberty until that consent is obtained to co-operate to a certain extent with other powers to insure a more complete effect to their respective acts; they placing themselves severally on the same ground by legislative provisions. It is in this spirit, and for this purpose, that I have made to you the proposition under consideration.

By making the slave trade piratical, and attaching to it the punishment as well as the odium incident to that crime, it is believed that much has been done by the United States to suppress it in their vessels and by their citizens. If your Government would unite in this policy, it is not doubted that the happiest consequences would result from it. The example of Great Britain in a manner so decisive could not fail to attract the attention and command the respect of all her European neighbors. It is the opinion of the United States that no measure short of that proposed will accomplish the object so much desired, and it is the earnest desire of my Government that the Government of his Britannic Majesty may co-operate in carrying it into effect.

I pray you, sir, to accept the renewed assurances of my distinguished consideration.

JOHN QUINCY ADAMS.

The Right Hon. STRATFORD CANNING,
Envoy Extraordinary and Minister Plenipotentiary from Great Britain.

Extract of a letter from Mr. Adams to Mr. Nelson, dated

DEPARTMENT OF STATE, *Washington, April 28, 1823.*

"A resolution of the House of Representatives, at the last session of Congress, requests the President to enter upon and to prosecute, from time to time, such negotiations with the several maritime powers of Europe and America as he may deem expedient for the effectual abolition of the African slave trade, and its ultimate denunciation as piracy under the law of nations, by the consent of the civilized world. You will take an early opportunity to make known this disposition to the Spanish Government; communicating to them copies of the fourth and fifth sections of the act of 3d March, 1819, which declares this traffic piratical when pursued by citizens of the United States; and you will express the willingness of the American Government to enter into negotiations for the purpose of declaring it so by the common consent of nations."

Extract of a letter from Mr. Adams to Mr. Rodney, dated.

DEPARTMENT OF STATE, *Washington, May 17, 1823.*

"A resolution of the House of Representatives, at the late session of Congress, requests the President of the United States to enter upon and prosecute, from time to time, such negotiations with the several maritime powers of Europe and America as he may deem expedient for the effectual abolition of the African slave trade, and its ultimate denunciation as piracy under the law of nations, by the consent of the civilized world.

"In pursuance of the object proposed by this resolution, you will communicate to the Government of Buenos-Ayres copies of the several acts of Congress for the suppression of the slave trade, of April 20, 1818, (U. S. Laws, vol. 6, page 325;) March 3, 1819, (page 435;) and of May 15, 1820, (page 529;) pointing their attention particularly to the fourth and fifth sections of the last, which subject to the penalties of piracy every citizen of the United States guilty of active participation in the African slave trade. The adoption of this principle in the legislative code of all the maritime nations would, of itself, probably, suffice for the suppression of the trade. But as it would yet not authorize the armed vessels of any one nation to capture those of another engaged in the trade, a stipulation to that effect might be agreed to by treaty, conditioned that the captor shall deliver over the captured party to the tribunals of his own country for trial; to which should be added some guard of responsibility upon the capturing officer, to prevent the abusive exercise of his power."

Extract from the General Instructions to Richard C. Anderson, appointed Minister Plenipotentiary to the
Republic of Colombia, dated

DEPARTMENT OF STATE, *Washington, May* 27, 1824.

"A resolution of the House of Representatives, at the late session of Congress, requests the President of the United States to enter upon and to prosecute, from time to time, such negotiations with the several maritime powers of Europe and America as he may deem expedient for the effectual abolition of the African slave trade, and its ultimate denunciation as *piracy* under the law of nations, by the consent of the civilized world.

"In pursuance of this object, you will communicate to the Colombian Government copies of the several acts of our Congress for the suppression of the slave trade, of April 20, 1818, (U. S. Laws, vol. vi, p. 325;) of March 3, 1819, (p. 435;) and of May 15, 1820, (p. 529;) pointing their attention particularly to the fourth and fifth sections of the last, which subject to the penalties of piracy every citizen of the United States guilty of active participation in the African slave trade. The adoption of this principle in the legislative code of all the maritime nations would, of itself, probably, suffice for the suppression of the trade; but as it would yet not authorize the armed vessels of any one nation to capture those of another engaged in the trade, a stipulation to that effect may be agreed to by the treaty, conditioned that the captor shall deliver over the captured party to the tribunals of his own country for trial; to which should be added some guard of responsibility upon the capturing officer, to prevent the abusive exercise of his powers."

Extract of a letter from Mr. Adams to Mr. Rush, dated

DEPARTMENT OF STATE, *Washington, June* 24, 1823.

"A resolution of the House of Representatives, almost unanimously adopted at the close of the last session of Congress, requested 'the President of the United States to enter upon and to prosecute, from time to time, such negotiations with the several maritime powers of Europe and America as he may deem expedient for the effectual abolition of the African slave trade, and its ultimate denunciation as piracy under the law of nations, by the consent of the civilized world.'

"At the two preceding sessions of Congress, committees of the House had proposed a resolution, expressed in more general terms, that 'the President of the United States be requested to enter into such arrangements as he may deem suitable and proper, with one or more of the maritime powers of Europe, for the effectual abolition of the African slave trade;' and this resolution had, in each case, been the conclusion of a report, recommending that the United States should accede to the proposal of a mutual and qualified concession of the right of search. The sentiments of the committee were, in this respect, different from those which had been expressed by the Executive Department of the Government in its previous correspondence with that of Great Britain. No decision by the House of Representatives was made upon these resolutions, proposed at the preceding sessions; but, upon the adoption of that which did pass at the last session, it was well ascertained that the sentiments of the House in regard to the right of search coincided with those of the Executive, for they explicitly rejected an amendment which was moved to the resolution, and which would have expressed an opinion of the House favorable to the mutual concession of that right.

"You have been fully informed of the correspondence between the Governments of the United States and of Great Britain concerning the suppression of the slave trade heretofore, and have been, from time to time, effectually instrumental to it yourself. You are aware of the grounds upon which the proposals on the part of Great Britain, that the United States should accede to the stipulations similar to those which she had succeeded in obtaining from Spain, Portugal, and the Netherlands, were on our part declined.

"The subject was resumed by the British minister residing here, Mr. S. Canning, a short time before the decease of the Marquis of Londonderry. It was suggested that, since the total disappearance of the British and American flags, as well as of those of the nations which had consented to put the execution of their laws against the trade under the superintendence of British naval officers, it continued to flourish under that of France; that her laws, though in word and appearance equally severe in proscribing the traffic, were so remiss in the essential point of execution that their effect was rather to encourage than to suppress it; and the American Government was urged to join in friendly representations to that of France by instructing the minister of the United States at Paris to concur in those which the British ambassador at that court had been charged with making to insure a more vigilant fulfilment of the prohibitory laws. This invitation, at that time given only in oral conference, was also declined, from an impression that such a concurrence might give umbrage to the French Government and tend rather to irritation than to the accomplishment of the object for which it was desired. Mr. Gallatin was, nevertheless, instructed separately to bring the subject to the notice of the French Government, and did so by a note communicating to them copies of the recent laws of the United States for the suppression of the slave trade, and particularly of that by which it has subjected every citizen of the United States who, after the passage of the law, should be polluted with it to the penalties of piracy.

"On the 29th of January last, Mr. Canning, in a letter to this Department, repeated the invitation of a joint and concurrent remonstrance to be made by the British ambassador and our minister in France; and, at the same time, called with great earnestness upon the Government of the United States either to accede to the principle of the mutual and qualified right of search, emphatically pronounced, in his belief, to be the *only* effectual measure devised or likely to be devised 'for the accomplishment of the end, or to bring forward some *other* scheme of concert,' which it again declared the readiness of his Majesty's minister to examine with respect and candor, as a substitute for that of the British cabinet.

"However discouraging this call for an alternative might be, thus coupled, as it was, with so decisive a declaration of belief that no effectual alternative had been or was likely to be devised, an opportunity was offered, in pursuance of the resolution of the House of Representatives, adopted at the close of the late session of Congress, for proposing a substitute, in our belief, more effectual than the right of search could be for the total and final suppression of this nefarious trade, and less liable either to objections of principle or to abuses of practice.

"This proposition was accordingly made in my letter to Mr. Canning of 31st of March last, to which his letter of the 8th of April was the answer. In this answer, Mr. Canning barely notices our proposition to express an opinion that his Government will see in it nothing but an acknowledgment of the necessity of further and more effectual measures, and then proceeds with an elaborate review of all the objections which, in the previous correspondence between the two Governments, had been taken on our part to the British connected proposal of a mutual right of search and a trial by mixed commissions. Our objection had been of two kinds: first, to the mixed commissions, as inconsistent with our Constitution; and secondly, to the right of search, as a dangerous precedent, liable to abuse and odious to the feelings and recollections of our country.

"In this letter of Mr. Canning the proposal of trial by mixed commissions is formally withdrawn, and an alternative presented as practicable, one side of which only, and that the inadmissible side, is distinctly offered, namely, of trial by the courts of the *captor*. The other side of the alternative would, indeed, remove our constitutional objection, and with it might furnish the means of removing the principal *inherent* objection to the concession of the right of search, that by which the searching officer is under no responsible control for that act.

"But in our previous correspondence our strong repugnance to the right of search had been adverted to merely as matter of fact, without tracing it to its source or referring to its causes. The object of this forbearance had been to avoid all unnecessary collision with feelings and opinions which were not the same on the part of Great Britain and upon ours. They had been willingly left undiscussed. This letter of Mr. Canning, however, professedly reviewing all the previous correspondence for the removal or avoidance of our objections, and contesting the analogy between the right of search, as it had been found obnoxious to us, and as now proposed for our adoption by formal compact, I have been under the absolute necessity of pointing out the analogies really existing between them, and of showing that, as right of search, independent of the right of *capture*, and irresponsible or responsible only to the tribunals of the captor, it is, as proposed, essentially liable to the same objections as it had been when exercised as a belligerent right. Its *encroaching* character, founded in its nature as an irresponsible exercise of force, and exemplified in its extension from search for contraband of war to search for enemies' property, and thence to search for *men* of the searcher's own nation, was thus necessarily brought into view, and connected the exhibition of the evils inherent in the practice with that of the abuses which have been found inseparable from it.

"We have declared the slave trade, so far as it may be pursued by citizens of the United States, piracy; and, as such, made it punishable with death. The resolution of the House of Representatives recommends negotiation to obtain the consent of the civilized world to recognize it as piracy under the law of nations. One of the properties of that description of piracies is, that those who are guilty of it may be taken upon the high seas and tried by the courts of every nation. But by the prevailing *customary* law they are tried only by the tribunals of the nation to which the vessel belongs in which the piracy was committed. The crime itself has been, however, in modern times, of so rare occurrence that there is no uniformity in the laws of the European nations with regard to this point, of which we have had remarkable and decisive proof within these five years in the case of piracy and murder committed on board the schooner Plattsburg, a merchant vessel of the United States. Nearly the whole of her crew were implicated in the crime, which was committed on the high seas. They carried the vessel into Christiansand, Norway, there abandoned her and dispersed. Three of them were taken up in Denmark; one in Sweden; one at Dantzig, in Prussia; and one in France. Those taken up in Denmark and in Sweden were delivered up to officers of the United States, brought to this country, tried, convicted, and executed. The man taken at Dantzig was, by the consent of the Prussian Government, sent to Elsineur, and there confronted with those taken in Denmark. The evidence against him on the examination was decisive; but as he persisted in the refusal to *confess* his guilt, the Prussian Government, bound by an established maxim of their municipal law, declined either to deliver him up or to try him themselves, but sent him back to Dantzig, there to remain imprisoned for life. The French Government, upon advisement of the highest judicial authority of the kingdom, declined also either to try the man taken up there or to deliver him up, unless upon proof of his guilt being produced against him at the place where he was confined; with which condition it not having been in our power to comply, the man remained there also in prison presumably for life. From these incidents it is apparent that there is no uniformity in the modes of trial to which piracy, by the law of nations, is subjected in different European countries; but that the trial itself is considered as the right and the duty only of the nation to which the vessel belongs on board of which the piracy was committed. This was, however, a piracy committed on board of a vessel by its own crew. External piracies, or piracies committed by and from one vessel against another, may be tried by the courts of any country, but are more usually tried by those of the country whose vessels have been the sufferers of the piracy, as many of the Cuba pirates have been tried in the British West India islands, and some of them in our courts.

"This principle we should wish to introduce into the sytem, by which the slave trade should be recognized as piracy under the law of nations, namely: that, although seizable by the officers and authorities of every nation, they should be triable only by the tribunals of the country of the slave trading vessel. This provision is indispensable to guard the innocent navigator against vexatious detentions and all the evils of arbitrary search. In committing to foreign officers the power, even in a case of conventional piracy, of arresting, confining, and delivering over for trial a citizen of the United States, we feel the necessity of guarding his rights from all abuses, and from the application of any laws of a country other than his own.

"The draught of a convention is herewith inclosed, which, if the British Government should agree to treat upon this subject on the basis of a legislative prohibition of the slave trade by both parties under the penalties of piracy, you are authorized to propose and to conclude. These articles, however, are not offered to the exclusion of others which may be proposed on the part of the British Government, nor is any one of them, excepting the first, to be insisted on as indispensable, if others equally adapted to answer their purposes should be proposed. It is only from the consideration of the crime in the character of piracy that we can admit the visitation of our merchant vessels by foreign officers for any purpose whatever, and in that case only under the most effective responsibility of the officer for the act of visitation itself, and for everything done under it.

"If the sentiments of the British Government should be averse to the principle of declaring the trade itself, by a legislative act, piratical, you will not propose or communicate to them the inclosed project of convention. Its objects, you will distinctly understand, are two-fold—to carry into effect the resolution of the House of Representatives, and to meet, explicitly and fully, the call so earnestly urged by the British Government, that in declining the proposals pressed by them upon us of conceding a mutual and qualified right of search we should offer a substitute for their consideration. The substitute, by declaring the crime piracy, carries with it the right of search for the pirates existing in the very nature of the crime. But to the concession of the right of search, distinct from the denomination of the crime, our objections remain in all their original force.

"It has been intimated by Mr. S. Canning that the suggestion itself to the British Government of the propriety of their passing a legislative act might excite in them some repugnancy to it. We should regret the excitement of this feeling, which the very nature of the negotiation seems to foreclose. Besides the legislative enactments which have virtually been pressed upon us by all the invitations to concede the right of search and to subject our citizens to trial for violations of our own laws by foreign tribunals, Great Britain, in almost all her slave trade treaties, has required and obtained express stipulations for the enactment of prohibitory laws by France, Spain, Portugal, and the Netherlands. It was not expected that she would receive with reluctance herself a mere invitation to that which she had freely and expressly required from others. Still, if the sentiment should exist, we would forbear pressing it to the point of irritation by importunity. You will, in the first instance, simply state that, if the British Government is prepared to proclaim the slave trade piracy by statute, you are authorized to propose and to conclude a convention by which the mutual co-operation of the naval force of Great Britain and of the United States may be secured for carrying into effect the law which, on that contingency, will be common to both. Should the obstacle to the preliminary prove insuperable, you will refer the objections on the part of the British cabinet to this Government for consideration.

"By the loose information hitherto communicated in the public journals it would seem that the proposition for recognizing the slave trade as piracy, by the law of nations, was discussed at the Congress of Verona. We are expecting the communication of the papers relating to this subject, promised by Lord Liverpool to be laid before Parliament. Heretofore, although the United States have been much solicited and urged to concur in the measures of Great Britain and her allies for the suppression of the trade, they have been always communicated to us as purposes consummated to which the *accession* of the United States was desired. From the general policy of avoiding to intermeddle in European affairs, we have acquiesced in this course of proceeding; but, to carry fully into effect the late resolution of the House of Representatives, and to pursue the discussions hereafter with Great Britain herself, whether upon her proposals or upon ours, it is obviously proper that communication should be made to us of the progress of European negotiation for accomplishing the common purpose while it is in deliberation. If we are to co-operate in the result, it is just that we should be consulted, at least with regard to the means which we are invited to adopt."

DRAFT OF A CONVENTION FOR THE SUPPRESSION OF THE SLAVE TRADE, REFERRED TO IN MR. ADAMS'
NOTE OF JUNE 24, 1823.

A convention for the suppression of piracy committed by the African slave trade.

ARTICLE 1. The two high contracting powers, having each separately, by its own laws, subjected their subjects and citizens who may be convicted of carrying on illicit traffic in slaves on the coast of Africa to the penalties of piracy, do hereby agree to use their influence, respectively, with the other maritime and civilized nations of the world, to the end that the said African slave trade may be recognized and declared to be piracy under the law of nations.

ARTICLE 2. It is agreed by the two high contracting parties that the commanders and commissioned officers of either nation, duly authorized, under the regulations and instructions of their respective Governments, to cruise on the coasts of Africa, of America, or of the West Indies, for the suppression of the slave trade, shall be authorized, under the conditions, limitations, and restrictions hereinafter mentioned, to capture, and deliver over to the duly authorized and commissioned officers of the other, *any ship or vessel carrying on such illicit traffic in slaves under the flag of the said other nation, or for the account of their subjects or citizens, to be sent in for trial and adjudication by the tribunals of the country to which such slave ship or vessel shall belong.* And the said commanders and commissioned officers shall be further authorized to carry or send in any such slave-trading ship, so by them captured, into the ports of the country to which such slave-trading ship shall belong, for trial by the tribunals and conformably to the laws of the said country. But the slave ship so captured shall not be sent into the ports or tried by the tribunals of the captor.

ARTICLE 3. If any naval commander or commissioned officer of the United States of America shall, on the high seas, or anywhere without the territorial jurisdiction of the said States, board, or cause to be boarded, any merchant vessel of Great Britain, and visit the same as a slave trader, or on suspicion of her being engaged in carrying on the illicit traffic in slaves, in every case, whether the said visited vessel shall be captured and delivered over or sent into the ports of her own country for trial and adjudication or not, the boarding officer shall deliver to the master or commander of the visited vessel a certificate in writing, signed by the said boarding officer with his name and the addition of his rank in the service of the United States, and the name of the public vessel of the United States and of her commander by whose order the said visit shall have been ordered; and the said certificate shall declare that the only object of the said visit is to ascertain whether the said British merchant vessel is engaged in the slave trade or not; and if found to be so engaged, to take and deliver her over to the officers or the tribunals of her own nation for trial and adjudication. And the commander of the said public vessel of the United States shall, when he delivers her over to the officers or tribunals of Great Britain, deliver all the papers found on board of the captured vessel, indicating her national character and the objects of her voyage, and with them a like certificate of visitation in writing, signed by his name, with the addition of his rank in the Navy of the United States and the name of the public vessel commanded by him, together with the name and rank of the boarding officer by whom the said visit was made. This certificate shall also specify all the papers received from the master of the vessel detained or visited, or found on board the vessel, and shall contain an authentic declaration exhibiting the state in which be found the vessel detained and the changes, if any, which have taken place in it, and the number of slaves, if any, found on board at the moment of detention. And the same duties, herein described, shall devolve upon every commander or commissioned officer of the Royal Navy of Great Britain by whom, or by whose order, any merchant vessel of the United States, or navigating under their flag, shall be visited for the said purposes, and upon the boarding officer by whom the visit shall be effected, on the high seas, or anywhere without the territorial jurisdiction of Great Britain.

ARTICLE 4. No merchant vessel of either of the contracting parties under the convoy of a public vessel of her own nation shall, under any circumstances whatever, be captured or visited by or from any public vessel of the other nation as being engaged, or on suspicion of being engaged, in the slave trade.

ARTICLE 5. No search shall be made by or under the orders of the commander or boarding officer of any public vessel of either party visiting any merchant vessel of the other as being engaged, or under suspicion of being engaged, in the slave trade, excepting such as may be necessary to ascertain if there be slaves on board for the purposes of the said traffic, or other proof that the said vessel is so engaged. No person shall be taken out of the said visited or captured merchant vessel of either nation by the commanding officer of the visiting vessel, or under his order. Nor shall any part of the cargo of the said visited vessel be removed out of her until delivered over to the officers or tribunals of her own nation.

ARTICLE 6. When a merchant vessel of either nation shall be captured as being engaged in the slave trade by any commander or commissioned officer of the Navy of the other nation, it shall be the duty of the commander of any public ship of the Navy of the nation to which the captured vessel shall belong, upon the offer thereof being made to him by the commander of the capturing vessel, to receive into his custody the vessel so captured, and to carry or send the same into the ports of his own country for trial and adjudication; and at the time of the delivery of the said vessel an authentic declaration shall be drawn up in triplicates, signed by both the commanders of the delivering and of the receiving vessels, one copy of which shall be kept by each of them, stating the circumstances of the delivery, the condition of the vessel captured at the time of the delivery, the number of slaves, if any, on board of her, a list of all the papers received or found on board of her at the time of capture and delivered over with her, and the names of the master or commander of the captured vessel, and of every person on board of her other than the slaves at the said time of delivery; and the third copy of the said declaration shall be transmitted, with the said captured vessel and the papers found on board of her, to one of the ports of the country to which the said captured vessel shall belong, to be produced before the tribunal appointed or authorized to decide upon the said capture; and the commander of the said capturing vessel shall be authorized to send the boarding officer and one or two of his crew with the said captured vessel to appear as witnesses of the facts in relation to her capture and detention before the said tribunal; the reasonable expenses of which witnesses, in proceeding to the place of trial, during their necessary detention there, and for their return to their own country, or to rejoin their station in its service, shall be allowed by the tribunal of trial, and in case of the condemnation of the captured vessel, be defrayed from the proceeds of the sale thereof; and in case of the acquittal of the said vessel, they shall be paid by the Government of the capturing officer.

ARTICLE 7. The commander or commissioned officer of the Navy of either of the contracting parties having captured a merchant vessel of the other as being engaged in the slave trade, if there be no public vessel of the nation to which the said captured vessel belongs cruising upon the same station, to the commander of whom the said captured vessel may be delivered over as stipulated in the preceding article, shall carry or send the said captured vessel to some convenient port of her own country, there to be delivered up to the competent tribunal for trial and adjudication. And the said captured vessel shall there be libelled in the name and behalf of the captors; and in case of the condemnation of the said vessel, the proceeds of the sale thereof and of her cargo, if also condemned, shall be paid to the commander of the said capturing vessel for the benefit of the captors, to be distributed according to the established rules of the service of the nation to which such capturing vessel shall belong for the distribution of prize money.

ARTICLE 8. The captain or commander and crew of the said vessel so captured and sent in for trial and adjudication shall be proceeded against conformably to the laws of the country whereinto they shall be so brought upon the charge of piracy, by being engaged in the African slave trade; and the captain or commander, the boarding officer, and other persons belonging to the capturing vessel, shall be competent witnesses to the facts relating to the said charge and to the capture of the said vessel, to which they shall be personally knowing. But every such witness upon the criminal trial for piracy shall be liable to be challenged by the person accused, and set aside as incompetent, unless he shall release and renounce all his individual claim to any part of the prize money upon the condemnation of the vessel and cargo.

ARTICLE 9. It is agreed between the high contracting parties that the right of visiting, capturing, and delivering over for trial, the vessels engaged in the African slave trade, and assuming their respective flags, is mutually conceded to the officers of their respective navies, on the consideration that they have, by their respective laws, declared their citizens and subjects actively participating in the said traffic guilty of the crime of piracy.

That no part of this convention shall be so construed as to authorize the detention, search, or visitation of the merchant vessels of either nation, by the public officers of the Navy of the other, except vessels engaged in the African slave trade, or for any other purpose whatever than that of seizing and delivering up the persons and vessels concerned in that traffic for trial and adjudication by the tribunals and laws of their own country.

ARTICLE 10. It is further agreed that this right of visiting, detaining, and delivering over for trial, vessels engaged in the slave trade, shall be exercised only by the commissioned officers of the Navy of the parties, respectively, furnished with instructions from their respective Governments for the execution of their respective laws for the suppression of the slave trade. That the boarding officer, and the captain or commander, of the vessel exercising these rights, or either of them, shall be personally responsible in damages and costs to the master and owners of every merchant vessel, so by them delivered over, detained, or visited, for every vexatious or abusive exercise of the right. In the case of every vessel delivered over, as herein stipulated, for trial, the tribunal shall be competent to receive the complaint of the master, owner, or owners, or of any person on board of such captured vessel, or interested in the property of her cargo at the time of her detention, and, on suitable proof of such vexatious or abusive detention or visitation, to award reasonable damages and costs to the sufferers, to be paid by the said commanding or boarding officer, or either of them, so charged with vexatious or abusive detention or visit. And the high contracting parties agree that their respective Governments shall, in every such case, cause payment to be made of all such damages and costs so awarded to the persons so entitled to receive them within twelve months from the date of such award. And if any case of such vexatious or abusive detention or visit should occur, in which the vessel detained or visited shall not be delivered over for trial and adjudication, as herein provided, the commander and boarding officer by whom such vexatious and abusive detention or visit shall have been made, shall also be responsible in costs and damages to the sufferers, upon complaint before the competent admiralty court of the country of the said commander and boarding officer. And the respective Governments shall, in like manner, cause payment to be made of any damages and costs awarded by said court within twelve months from the date of the award.

ARTICLE 11. A copy of this convention, and of the laws of the two countries actually in force for the prohibition and suppression of the African slave trade, shall be furnished to every commander of the public vessels instructed to carry into effect such prohibition. And in case any such commanding officer of the Navy of the United States or of Great Britain shall deviate in any respect from the dispositions of this treaty, and from the instructions of his Government conformable to it, the Government which shall conceive itself to be wronged by such conduct shall be entitled to demand reparation; and in such case the Government of the nation, to the service of which he may belong, binds itself to cause inquiry to be made into the subject of the complaint, and to inflict upon him, if he be found to have deserved it, a punishment proportioned to the transgression which may have been committed.

ARTICLE 12. The present treaty, consisting of ——— articles, shall be ratified, and the ratifications exchanged within one year from this date, or sooner if possible.

In witness whereof, the respective plenipotentiaries have signed the same, and thereunto affixed their seals.

Done at ———, the ——— day of ———, in the year of our Lord ———.

Mr. Adams to Mr. Middleton, No. 17.

DEPARTMENT OF STATE, *Washington, July* 28, 1823.

SIR: At the close of the last session of Congress a resolution was adopted by the House of Representatives, almost unanimously, requesting "the President of the United States to enter upon, and to prosecute from time to time, such negotiations with the several maritime powers of Europe and America as he may deem expedient for the effectual abolition of the African slave trade, and its ultimate denunciation as piracy, under the law of nations, by the consent of the civilized world."

In pursuance of this resolution, instructions for carrying it into effect have been given to the ministers of the United States destined to the Republics of Colombia and of Buenos Ayres, and to the minister who has recently departed for Spain. But, as a negotiation for co-operation to effect the suppression of the African slave trade had already been commenced with Great Britain, a special instruction upon the subject was forwarded to Mr. Rush, together with a full power, and a draft of a convention, to be proposed, in substance, to that Government, and which he has been authorized to conclude.

A copy of that instruction and draft are herewith inclosed; the general terms of which you will communicate, at such time and in such manner, to the Imperial Russian Government, as you shall think proper.

You will also communicate to them the purport of the resolution of the House of Representatives, above cited, and copies of the laws of the United States prohibiting the slave trade. You will particularly invite their attention to the two sections of the act of the 15th May, 1820, by which this offence, when committed by citizens of the United States, is subjected to the penalties of piracy.

The proposal that this principle should be recognized by the general consent of civilized nations, recommended by the resolution of the House of Representatives, appears to be substantially the same with that made by Great Britain at the Congress of Verona. It was not acceded to by any one of the other powers there assembled, and the conferences on this subject terminated there by a mere renewal of the joint declaration against the traffic, of the Congress at Vienna. So long as the trade shall not be recognized as piracy by the law of nations, we cannot, according to our Constitution, subject our citizens to trial for being engaged in it by any tribunal other than those of the United States.

The admission of the crime as piracy by the law of nations would seem necessarily to subject the perpetrators of it to *capture* by the armed force of every nation. And this might endanger the lawful commerce of the maritime nations, by subjecting them to the abuses of vexatious searches, without some special provision to guard against them.

This is the object of the stipulations proposed in the draft herewith transmitted; requiring that all vessels of one nation which may be captured, as slave traders, by the cruisers of another, should be delivered over for trial to the tribunals of their *own* country.

You will see that Mr. Rush is instructed to correspond with you upon this subject. If the draft of the articles inclosed should lead to the conclusion of a convention between the United States and Great Britain, a communication of it to the Russian Government will be made as soon as possible, and we shall propose that his Imperial Majesty's accession to it, if agreeable to him, shall be invited.

In the meantime you will informally suggest to his ministry that it will be the desire of the Government of the United States to proceed in this matter in perfect good understanding and harmony with them; and you will further intimate that, as this has now become a general concern of the whole civilized world, and as Great Britain is negotiating *jointly* and *severally* with each and every of her allies in Europe, apart, and again with them all together, while she is also separately treating with us, we wish it to be considered whether it would not be expedient on all sides that communication should be made to us of all the jointly concerted measures while they are mere proposals, and not that the knowledge of them should be withheld from us until they are matured into positive treaties.

I am, with great respect, sir, your very humble and obedient servant,

JOHN QUINCY ADAMS.

Hon. HENRY MIDDLETON, *Envoy Extraordinary and Minister Plenipotentiary*
of the United States, at St. Petersburg.

Mr. Adams to Mr. Everett, No. 10.

DEPARTMENT OF STATE, *Washington, August* 8, 1823.

SIR: At the close of the last session of Congress a resolution was adopted, almost unanimously, by the House of Representatives, "that the President of the United States be requested to enter upon, and to prosecute from time to time, such negotiations with the several maritime powers of Europe and America as he may been expedient for the effectual abolition of the African slave trade, and its ultimate denunciation as piracy, under the law of nations, by the consent of the civilized world."

In pursuance of this resolution, instructions for carrying it into effect have been given to the ministers of the United States destined to the Republics of Colombia and of Buenos Ayres, and to the several ministers of the United States in Europe.

As a negotiation for co-operation to effect the suppression of the African slave trade had already been commenced with Great Britain, a special instruction upon the subject has been forwarded to Mr. Rush, together with a full power, and a draft of a convention, to be proposed, in substance, to the British Government, and which he is authorized to conclude.

A necessary preliminary to the conclusion of this proposed convention, should it meet the assent of the British Government, will be the enactment of a statute declaring the crime of African slave trading piracy by the British law. In that event, it is proposed, by proper co-operation, that the influence of the two powers should be exerted to obtain the consent of other nations to the general outlawry of this traffic as piracy. In the meantime, to give at once effect to the concert of both nations, it is proposed that the armed vessels of both, duly authorized and *instructed*, shall have power to *capture* the slave-trading vessels which may assume the flag of *either*, and, if not of their own nation, to deliver over the captured slave trader to the officers or tribunals of his own country for trial and adjudication.

This principle is essential, as connected with that of constituting the traffic piracy by the law of nations. So long as the offence was considered as of inferior magnitude, the Constitution of the United States forbade the submission of it, when charged upon their citizens, to any foreign tribunal; and when the crime and the punishment are aggravated to involve the life of the accused, it affords but a more imperative inducement for securing to him the benefit of a trial by his countrymen and his peers.

It appears that, at the conferences of Verona, the proposition was made by the British Government that the slave trade should be recognized and proclaimed as piracy by the law of nations. We have, therefore, reason to hope that the proposal now made to them on the part of the United States will be favorably considered by them. In that case, further communications on the subject with other Governments will ensue.

In the meantime, to fulfil the intentions of the House of Representatives in relation to the Netherlands, you will communicate to their Government a copy of the resolution, together with copies of the laws of the United States prohibiting the slave trade, with particular notice of the two sections of the act of 15th May, 1820, by which the crime of being concerned in the African slave trade, when committed by citizens of the United States, is declared to be and is made punishable as for piracy. And you will announce the readiness of the American Government, should it suit the views of his Majesty the King of the Netherlands, to enter upon a negotiation for the purpose of carrying into effect the object of the resolution of the House of Representatives, namely, the denunciation of the African slave trade as piracy by the law of nations.

I am, with great respect, sir, your very humble and obedient servant,

JOHN QUINCY ADAMS.

Hon. ALEXANDER H. EVERETT, *Chargé d'Affaires United States to the Netherlands.*

Extracts of a letter, No. 6, *from Mr. Adams to General Dearborn, Envoy Extraordinary and Minister Plenipotentiary of the United States at Lisbon, dated*

DEPARTMENT OF STATE, *Washington, August* 14, 1823.

"At the close of the last session of Congress a resolution was adopted, almost unanimously, by the House of Representatives—

"'That the President of the United States be requested to enter upon, and to prosecute from time to time, such negotiations with the several maritime powers of Europe and America as he may deem expedient for the effectual abolition of the African slave trade, and its ultimate denunciation as piracy, under the law of nations, by the consent of the civilized world.'

"A negotiation for concerting measures of co-operation to effect the suppression of the African slave trade had already for several years been pending with Great Britain, for which reason a special instruction has been transmitted to Mr. Rush, together with a full power, and a draft of a convention, to be proposed, in substance, to the British Government, which he is authorized to conclude.

"Should this proposal meet the assent of the British Government, a necessary preliminary to the conclusion of the convention will be the passage of an act of Parliament declaring the crime of African slave trading, when committed by British subjects, piracy. An act of Congress to that effect, as relates to citizens of the United States, has been in force, as you are aware, these three years. When the crime shall have been constituted piracy by the statute law of both countries, each with reference to its own citizens or subjects, the principle offered by the projected convention is, that the armed vessels of each, specially empowered and instructed to that end, shall be authorized to *capture* slave-trading vessels assuming the flag of the other, and to deliver over the captured vessels to the public cruisers, or to the tribunals of their own country, for trial. This plan is offered as a substitute for that which was offered to us by Great Britain, which was predicated on the treaties already concluded between that power and Spain, Portugal, and the Netherlands. The leading principle of these treaties was the mutual concession of the right of maritime search, in time of peace, to the armed vessels of both cruising for slave traders, and a mixed court of commissioners and arbitrators, sitting in colonial possessions of the parties, for the trial of the delinquents. . To this system the United States have steadily declined to accede, for two reasons: one, because they had an invincible repugnance to subject their merchant vessels to the maritime search of foreign officers in time of peace; and the other, because they could not subject their citizens to the jurisdiction of foreign tribunals, upon trials for offences against their laws.

"At the conferences of Verona, the British Government appears to have proposed that the African slave trade should be declared piracy by the law of nations. This is the same proposition recommended by the resolution of the House of Representatives of the United States. The ultimate object of the United States and of Great Britain, therefore, is the same."

"The negotiations suggested by the resolution of the House must depend materially for their character and progress, with reference to other powers, upon the event of that which is thus pending with Great Britain. The instructions to the ministers of the United States in other countries have therefore been only of a general character."

"Portugal is the only maritime power of Europe which has not yet declared the African slave trade, without exception, unlawful. Her own internal situation has, perhaps, recently tended to diminish the influence of those interests which have heretofore prevailed to delay and postpone her acquiescence in the principle of total proscription upon that trade. It is hoped that she will not much longer resist the predominating spirit of the age, calling so loudly upon the rulers of mankind effectually to put down the crying sin of that abominable traffic."

"In communicating to the Portuguese Government copies of the resolution of the House of Representatives, and of the laws of the United States prohibiting the slave trade, you will state that the Government of the United States will be ready to enter at any time, when it may suit the views of that of Portugal, upon the negotiation contemplated by the resolution."

Mr. Rush to Mr. Adams, giving him the substance of a conversation with Mr. Canning.

[Extracts.]

LONDON, *October 9*, 1823.

"This latter subject" (the slave trade) "he said it was his wish to take in hand with me himself, and thus keep it detached from the general negotiation."

"Whilst we were speaking of the mode of taking up the question of the slave trade, I did not scruple to intimate, even at this early stage, that unless this Government was prepared to say that it would cause a statute to be passed declaring the trade by its own subjects to be piracy, and rendering it punishable as such, in manner as had been done by the United States, that I was not authorized to make any proposals upon the subject; that this, in fact, was the only basis upon which it fell within the intentions of my Government to attempt any arrangement of the subject whatever. I was happy to hear Mr. Canning say, in reply, that he did not, speaking from his first impressions, see any insurmountable obstacle upon this score to our proceeding with the subject."

Extract from No. 11 of Mr. Sheldon, Chargé d'Affaires of the United States at Paris, to the Secretary of State.

PARIS, *October 16*, 1823.

"In the same conference I also informed Mr. de Chateaubriand of the resolution of the House of Representatives respecting the slave trade, which made the subject of your despatch, No. 2, of the 14th of August. He repeated, in substance, what he had before stated to Mr. Gallatin in conversation, viz: that the French Government were sincerely desirous of putting an end to that trade, and were taking all the measures in their power to effect it by pursuing offenders and executing rigidly the laws now in existence; but that the public opinion generally in France, and more especially in the Chambers, was against it, owing not only to the prevalence of the colonial interest in the question, but particularly to the circumstances under which their stipulations with England upon this subject had been made; so tender were they upon this point that the proposition of adding new rigors to their laws would be taken as a new concession to that power, and, instead of being adopted in the Chambers, would be more likely to provoke an attempt to repeal the prohibitory measures already established, in order to rid themselves in that way of one of the charges imposed upon them by the foreign occupation; that time was necessary to wear away these impressions; and until that should have arrived, no minister in France could be strong enough upon this point to do more than to watch over the execution of the laws already in force, which they were now disposed to do fully and faithfully, and which, if not entirely efficient, at least made the prosecution of the trade under the French flag hazardous and difficult.

"At present, therefore, it is not probable that France will consent to the proposal of the President to enter upon the negotiation contemplated by the resolution of the House of Representatives. I have, however, made the proposal in obedience to your directions, and have the honor to inclose a copy of the letter to Viscount de Chateaubriand, in which I have communicated to him that resolution."

Extracts from No. 14 of Mr. Sheldon, Chargé d'Affaires, to the Secretary of State, dated

PARIS, *November 5*, 1823.

"I have received answers from Viscount de Chateaubriand on the subject of the new and more effective measures proposed against the slave trade."

"On the subject of the slave trade, the answer manifests a disposition to adopt such new provisions as may be found necessary for its more effectual suppression, and this disposition really exists; but after what Mr. de Chateaubriand had stated in conversation, and which I have already communicated, these new and more rigorous legislative provisions can only be introduced gradually, and some time will be required for effecting that purpose."

Mr. Sheldon to the Viscount de Chateaubriand.

Paris, *October* 15, 1823.

Sir: The minister of the United States to this court had, some time before he left Paris, transmitted to your excellency copies of the laws successively adopted by the United States for the suppression of the slave trade. This communication was intended for the special purpose of making the French Government acquainted with the fact that, so far as the United States were concerned, their legislation upon this subject had been ineffectual; that their laws had been violated and the trade had continued until they had denounced against it the highest punishment that a human tribunal can inflict. Since it has been declared to be piracy, and punishable with death, the American flag has no longer been soiled with it.

At the last session of Congress that body, desirous that the co-operation of the maritime powers might be obtained in measures which we had found to be so effectual, formally requested the President to enter upon and prosecute negotiations with those powers to that end. I have the honor to inclose a copy of the resolution adopted with great unanimity by the House of Representatives upon that subject, and I am directed to declare that the President is ready to enter upon the negotiation contemplated by it with France whenever it may be agreeable to her. Instructions to the same effect have been given to all the ministers of the United States accredited to foreign powers, and the favorable results which are hoped from them will be made known at the earliest opportunities to the French Government. It may be expected that a co-operation in measures equally effectual with those heretofore brought forward for the suppression of this trade, and not open to similar objections, will be generally and readily afforded.

I beg to offer to your excellency the renewed assurances, &c.

D. SHELDON.

Viscount de Chateaubriand to Mr. Sheldon.

[Translation.]

Paris, *October* 29, 1823.

Sir: You did me the honor of writing me on the 15th of this month that the Government of the United States had only attained the effectual suppression of the slave trade by making it piracy, and by rendering those guilty of it liable to the same punishment. You have at the same time informed me that that Government was disposed to co-operate with the other powers, by negotiations, to attain by the same means the complete and general abolition of this traffic.

The communication which you did me the honor to address to me cannot but deserve great consideration. I have requested the Keeper of the Seals to review with great care the laws and ordinances which have been made in France for obtaining the abolition of the trade; to certify, after this examination, in what points they may be insufficient, and to propose for completing them, in case of need, all the new dispositions which might accord with the independence and rights of the flag, and which might appear most proper to assure, in France, in an efficacious manner, the absolute cessation of a traffic so contrary to the rights of humanity.

Accept, sir, the assurances, &c.

CHATEAUBRIAND.

Extract of a letter from Mr. Everett, Chargé d'Affaires, to the Secretary of State, dated

Brussels, *November* 20, 1823.

"I have received from the Baron de Nagell a preliminary answer to my note of the 7th upon the slave trade, of which I have the honor to inclose a copy."

Mr. Everett to Baron de Nagell.

[Translation.]

Brussels, *November* 7, 1823.

Sir: I have the honor to subjoin to your excellency, by order of my Government, a printed copy of the laws of the United States which forbid their citizens to pursue the slave trade; also a copy of the resolution of the House of Representatives of the 8th of February, 1823, by which the President is requested to concert with the maritime powers of Europe and of America the measures which may be most proper to effect the abolition of that trade, and to make it, by the universal consent of the civilized world, equivalent to the crime of piracy.

Your excellency will remark that it is already viewed in this light by the laws of the United States. The act of March 15, 1820, declares (sections 4 and 5) that the persons subject to the jurisdiction of the Republic who shall be engaged in the slave trade, either by seizing these unfortunates by force or fraud and carrying them on board their vessels, or by keeping them there, and making them an object of traffic, shall be deemed pirates, and punished with death.

In fact, this pretended commerce bears all the characteristics of piracy—that is, of felony committed on the sea; and as it has been denounced as a crime by the greater part of civilized nations, it ought to fall into the particular class of crimes to which it naturally belongs, and undergo the penalties which the usage and the law of nations impose upon them. An unanimous declaration of the Christian powers to this effect would inevitably produce the entire cessation of the trade. The public ships of each power would then be authorized by the law of nations to cruise against the persons who might be engaged in it, without regard to the color of the flag with which they might pretend to be sheltered; whilst, if the trade is only regarded in each country as an offence against the municipal laws, it would be lawful for any one nation alone, by permitting it, to afford an asylum under its flag to the pirates of all the others.

The known character of the King, and the zeal which his Majesty has already displayed in his efforts to bring about the abolition of this infamous commerce, furnish a presumption to the Government of the United States that that of the Low Countries will voluntarily co-operate with it to that effect. In communicating to your excellency the subjoined papers, and in praying that you will be pleased to lay them before the King, I am charged to announce to him the desire of the President of the United States to obtain the co-operation of his Majesty in this work of justice and to establish a concert between the two powers in the measures which they may pursue, in common, to render the slave trade equivalent to the crime of piracy by the universal consent of the Christian world.

I eagerly embrace this occasion to renew to your excellency the homage of my most distinguished consideration.

A. H. EVERETT.

Baron de Nagell to Mr. Everett.

[Translation.]

BRUSSELS, November 13, 1823.

SIR: I have the honor to acknowledge the receipt of your note of the 7th of this month, containing some propositions in regard to the slave trade, and to inform you that without delay I laid this paper and its inclosures before the King.

I shall hasten to impart to you the determination of his Majesty as soon as I shall have been informed of it; and, in the meantime, I seize this opportunity to renew the assurance of my distinguished consideration.

A. W. C. DE NAGELL.

18TH CONGRESS.]　　　　　　　　　No. 372.　　　　　　　　　[1ST SESSION.

SUPPRESSION OF THE SLAVE TRADE.

COMMUNICATED TO THE SENATE, IN EXECUTIVE SESSION, MAY 8, 1824, AND THE INJUNCTION OF SECRECY SINCE REMOVED.

To the Senate of the United States:

I communicate to the Senate copies of additional documents, relating to the convention for the suppression of the African slave trade, which have this day been received at the Department of State.

JAMES MONROE.

WASHINGTON, *May* 7, 1824.

List of papers.

Letter from Mr. Rush to the Secretary of State, April 1, 1824.
Letter from Mr. Huskisson to Mr. Rush, March 31, 1824.
Letter from the British Secretary of Foreign Affairs to Mr. Addington, communicated by Mr. Addington.
Act of Parliament of March 31, 1824, declaring the African slave trade piracy.

Mr. Rush to Mr. Adams.

LONDON, *April* 1, 1824.

SIR: I have now the honor to transmit, in the shape in which it has received the royal assent, a copy of the British act of Parliament making the slave trade piracy. It was sent to me to-day by Mr. Huskisson, with a note, of which a copy is inclosed. It passed the House of Lords the day before yesterday by an unanimous vote.

In addition to the explanation which Mr. Huskisson afforded me of the clause at the end of the act, both himself and Mr. Secretary Canning have since stated to me that a further reason for it was, that a consolidation of this act with all the other British slave trade laws and regulations is in contemplation, perhaps in the course of the present session of Parliament, with a view to give to the British naval officers one comprehensive code of instructions under them.

I have the honor to be, with very great respect, your obedient servant,

RICHARD RUSH.

Hon. JOHN QUINCY ADAMS, *Secretary of State.*

Mr. Huskisson to Mr. Rush.

BOARD OF TRADE, *April* 1, 1824.

MY DEAR SIR: I have the satisfaction to transmit to you three copies of the bill which received the royal assent yesterday, for declaring slave trading to be piracy.

These copies are the bill as printed for the House of Lords, in which shape, as no amendment was made in that House, it received the royal assent; but some few days will elapse before it can be published in the usual form among the laws of the present session.

I have the honor to be, dear sir, your very faithful, obedient servant,

W. HUSKISSON.

Hon. RICHARD RUSH, &c., &c.

Mr. Canning to Mr. Addington.

FOREIGN OFFICE, *April* 2, 1824.

SIR: I herewith inclose to you several copies of the bill which has now passed into a law, affixing to the crime of carrying on the slave trade by British subjects the pains and penalties attached to piracy.

You will lose no time in calling on Mr. Adams, and in communicating this act of Parliament to him, in proof of the anxiety of his Majesty to carry into early and effectual execution the convention lately concluded on this subject by the United States; and with reference to that clause in the act which provides for possible alteration in the course of the session, you will explain to the American minister that this clause has in view no change in the act, but merely its consolidation with all the other slave trade regulations in one general act, (which is intended to be brought in before the close of this session of Parliament,) in order that British officers may be furnished with one comprehensive code of instruction on this subject.

I have the honor to be, &c., &c.,

GEORGE CANNING.

Hon. HENRY UNWIN ADDINGTON, &c.

An act for the more effectual Suppression of the African Slave Trade.

MARCH 31, 1824.

Whereas it is expedient to make further provision for the suppression of the African slave trade, by enacting that persons committing the offences hereinafter specified shall be deemed and adjudged to be guilty of piracy:

Be it therefore enacted by the King's most excellent Majesty, by and with the advice and consent of the Lords Spiritual and Temporal, and Commons, in this present Parliament assembled, and by the authority of the same, That if any subject or subjects of his Majesty, or any person or persons residing or being within any of the dominions, forts, settlements, factories, or territories now or hereafter belonging to his Majesty, or being in his Majesty's occupation or possession, or under the Government of the United Company of Merchants of England trading to the East Indies, shall, except in such cases as are in and by the laws now in force permitted, after the first day of January, one thousand eight hundred and twenty-five, upon the high seas, or in any haven, river, creek, or place, where the Admiral has jurisdiction, knowingly and wilfully carry away, convey, or remove, or aid or assist in carrying away, conveying, or removing any person or persons as a slave or slaves, or for the purpose of his, her, or their being imported or brought as a slave or slaves into any island, colony, country, territory, or place whatsoever, or for the purpose of his, her, or their being sold, transferred, used or dealt with as a slave or slaves; or shall, after the said first day of January, one thousand eight hundred and twenty-five, except in such cases as are in and by the laws now in force permitted, upon the high seas, or within the jurisdiction aforesaid, knowingly and wilfully ship, embark, receive, detain, or confine, or assist in shipping, embarking, receiving, detaining, or confining on board any ship, vessel, or boat, any person or persons, for the purpose of his, her, or their being carried away, conveyed, or removed, as a slave or slaves, or for the purpose of his, her, or their being imported or brought as a slave or slaves into any island, colony, country, territory, or place whatsoever, or for the purpose of his, her, or their being sold, transferred, used, or dealt with as a slave or slaves, then, and in every such case, the person or persons so offending shall be deemed and adjudged guilty of piracy, felony, and robbery, and being convicted thereof, shall suffer death, without benefit of clergy, and loss of lands, goods, and chattels, as pirates, felons, and robbers upon the seas, ought to suffer.

II. *Provided always, and it is hereby further enacted and declared*, That nothing in this act contained, making and declaring the aforesaid offences to be piracies, felonies, and robberies, shall be construed to repeal, annul, or alter the provisions and enactments of any other act or acts contained, imposing forfeitures and penalties, or either of them, upon the same offences, or to repeal, annul, or alter the remedies given for the recovery thereof; but that the said provisions and remedies shall, in all respects, be deemed and taken to be and remain in full force, as they existed immediately before the passing of this act: *Provided, also*, That nothing herein contained shall be construed to repeal, annul, or alter any of the enactments or provisions contained in an act passed in the fifty-first year of his late Majesty, intituled "An act for rendering more effectual an act made in the forty-seventh year of his Majesty's reign, intituled 'An act for the abolition of the slave trade,'" except so far as such enactments or provisions are altered or varied by this act, but that the said act shall, in all other respects, remain in full force and effect.

III. *And be it further enacted and declared*, That all and every the offences hereinbefore specified shall and may be inquired of, either according to the ordinary course of law and the provisions of an act passed in the twenty-eighth year of the reign of King Henry the Eighth, intituled "An act for pirates," or according to the provisions of an act passed in the forty-sixth year of the reign of his late Majesty King George the Third, intituled "An act for the more speedy trial of offences committed in distant parts upon the high seas."

IV. *And be it further enacted*, That this act may be amended, altered, or repealed, by any act or acts to be passed in this present session of Parliament.

18TH CONGRESS.]   No. 373.   [1ST SESSION.

SUPPRESSION OF PIRACIES IN THE WEST INDIES.

COMMUNICATED TO THE HOUSE OF REPRESENTATIVES MAY 19, 1824.

Mr. POINSETT, from the Committee on Foreign Relations, to whom was referred so much of the President's message as relates to the "piracies by which our commerce in the neighborhood of the island of Cuba has been afflicted;" and "to the depredations which have been committed on the lawful commerce of the United States, under other pretences and other color, in the neighboring island of Porto Rico," reported:

That the prompt and energetic measures adopted by Congress at the commencement of their last session, seconded by the zeal and enterprise of the officers entrusted with the command of the light squadron destined to suppress piracy in the West Indies and the Gulf of Mexico, have succeeded in putting a stop to the piracies by which our commerce had been afflicted in the neighborhood of the island of Cuba, as far as a foreign force, unaided by the public authorities of the island, could succeed in accomplishing this object.

These piracies had been continued for years under the immediate observation of the Government of the island of Cuba, which, as well as the Spanish Government, has been repeatedly and ineffectually required to suppress them. Many of them have been committed by boats which remained concealed in the harbors and under the headland until they discovered their prey, which they captured, plundered and destroyed upon the shores of the island. When pursued by a superior force the pirates have escaped to the shore, and our commanders have been refused permission to land in pursuit of them, even on the desert and uninhabited parts of the island.

It appears, from the most respectable testimony, that these atrocious robberies were committed by persons well known in Havana and in Regla, where they were organized into a band, and that the traffic in their plunder was carried on openly; that they were sometimes committed by vessels equipped at Havana and at Regla; and that they cautiously avoided molesting Spanish vessels, but attacked without discrimination the defenceless vessels of all other nations.

The present Captain General of the island of Cuba has acted with great courtesy towards our commander and officers engaged on this service, and has co-operated with them by arresting the pirates who had escaped to the shore, nor has he complained when our officers have found it necessary to pursue them, and to break up their haunts on the desert and unfrequented keys that surround the island. In no case, however, within our knowledge, where pirates have been seized by the authorities of the island, have they been brought to that punishment their crimes merited; and those who are well known to have fitted out piratical cruisers and to have sold their plunder with the utmost notoriety, are suffered to remain in Havana and Regla in the unmolested enjoyment of the fruits of their crimes. Under these circumstances the British and American squadrons in those seas may repress piracy, so long as they continue cruising in the neighborhood of the island; but there is reason to apprehend that, on their removal, similar outrages on our commerce will be renewed. In the opinion of your committee, piracy can only be effectually suppressed by the Government of Spain and by the authorities of the island taking the necessary measures to prevent piratical vessels or boats from being equipped or sailing from any part of the island, and to apprehend and punish every description of outlaws, as well those who actually commit acts of piracy as those who receive and traffic in goods plundered on the high seas.

The commerce of the United States with the island of Cuba, superior to that with Spain and all its other dependencies, and fully equal to that with France, claims in a peculiar manner the protection of Government. The safety of that commerce requires that the Government of Spain should be urged to adopt prompt and vigorous measures effectually to suppress piracy in the neighborhood of the island, and to co-operate with the maritime powers most interested in effecting this object: and your committee are of opinion, that, for the protection of this important commerce, and of the persons and property of our fellow-citizens, when in the ports of the island, the residence of consuls or authorized commercial agents of the United States at these places is absolutely necessary, and ought to be insisted upon.

Privateers, distinguished from pirates only by commissions of most equivocal character from Spanish officers whose authority to issue them has never been shown, have been equipped in the island of Porto Rico, and have committed outrages and depredations upon the persons and property of the citizens of the United States; outrages which no commission could divest of their piratical character. With no other naval force than a frigate, a brig and a schooner, they presumed to declare a blockade of more than twelve hundred miles of coast. To this violation of all the rights of neutrality they added the absurd pretension of interdicting the peaceable commerce of other nations with *all* the ports of the Spanish main, upon the pretence that it had heretofore been forbidden by the Spanish colonial laws; and, on the strength of these two inadmissible principles, they issued commissions in the island of Porto Rico to a swarm of privateers, which have committed extensive and ruinous depredations upon the lawful commerce of the United States. Frequent remonstrances have been made, both to Spain and to the authorities of the island, by the Executive, without producing any effect. During the last summer a special agent was sent to Porto Rico to obtain the restitution of American vessels captured by the privateers of that island, and to collect documentary evidence of the trials and condemnation of others. To the first demand the political chief referred the agent to the Government of Spain, declaring that he could not, without an open infraction of fundamental laws, take cognizance of causes legally determined; that the officers of that province could not proceed but by the express orders of the Supreme Government, and to that the United States, after the example of Great Britain, must have recourse.

It appears by the testimony collected by this gentleman that it had been the practice of these privateers not to send in their prizes to the large and frequented ports where impartial judges could determine on the validity of the capture, and where the captured could have the means of fairly defending their rights; but to send them into distant and obscure seaports where the courts are notoriously corrupt, and where the captains and owners were deprived of the means of making even statements of their cases. There are many instances of vessels condemned most unjustly; and even where they have had the rare good fortune to escape condemnation, their owners have been subjected to ruinous costs and charges; and in some cases, before the vessels have reached the port, the cargoes and property have been plundered, and the officers and crew treated in a cruel and barbarous manner.

In San Juan, the principal town of the island of Porto Rico, attempts have been made to assassinate the commercial agent of the United States and the master of a merchant vessel in order, as they believe, to prevent them from taking legal measures to recover property unlawfully captured. Your committee deem it unnecessary to enumerate the vessels that have been captured and condemned without the color of justice, or to recapitulate each particular case of barbarous outrage committed upon the persons and property of the citizens of the United States by privateers fitted out in the ports of Porto Rico; outrages which, in their opinion, would justify reprisals and a rigorous blockade of the ports of that island. Your committee forbear to recommend the immediate adoption of those measures only because the minister of the United States at Madrid has been instructed to remonstrate with his Catholic Majesty on the culpable neglect of the Spanish authorities in the island of Porto Rico, and to require indemnity for the losses sustained by the citizens of the United States from the lawless conduct of the commanders of privateers bearing his Majesty's commission. That this remonstrance and demand were not made earlier arose from circumstances beyond the control of Government. The former minister had left Madrid before his instructions on this subject reached that place, and the subsequent invasion of Spain by France, and the conduct of the French commander of the blockading squadron off Cadiz, retarded the arrival of our present minister. While the committee advise that Government wait the result of the negotiation now pending at Madrid, or, at all events, the answer to the remonstrance of our minister at that court, before a resort is had to reprisals and blockade, they earnestly recommend that two or more small cruisers should be constantly kept off the ports of San Juan, and in the Moro Passage so as to protect our commerce and intercept at the entrance of San Juan, Aguadilla, Mayaguez, Cape Roco, and Ponce, American vessels unlawfully captured by Spanish privateers; and that the commanders of the United States vessels-of-war be instructed to capture and send into a port of the United States for trial any privateer that commits an outrage on the persons or plunders the property of citizens of the United States on the high seas, whenever good and sufficient testimony of such piratical act can be obtained.

SUPPRESSION OF THE SLAVE TRADE.

COMMUNICATED TO THE SENATE, IN EXECUTIVE SESSION, MAY 21, 1824; AND THE INJUNCTION OF SECRECY SINCE REMOVED.

To the Senate of the United States:

Apprehending, from the delay in the decision, that some difficulty exists with the Senate respecting the ratification of the convention lately concluded with the British Government for the suppression of the slave trade, by making it piratical, I deem it proper to communicate, for your consideration, such views as appear to me to merit attention. ·Charged, as the Executive is, and as I have long been, with maintaining the political relations between the United States and other nations, I consider it my duty, in submitting for your advice and consent, as to the ratification, any treaty or convention which has been agreed on with another power, to explain, when the occasion requires it, all the reasons which induced the measure. It is by such full and frank explanation, only, that the Senate can be enabled to discharge the high trust reposed in them with advantage to their country. Having the instrument before them, with the views which guided the Executive in forming it, the Senate will possess all the light necessary to a sound decision. . . . ' . . . ' . . .   · · · · · ·

By an act of Congress of May 15, 1820, the slave trade, as described by that act, was made piratical, and all such of our citizens as might be found engaged in that trade were subjected, on conviction thereof by the circuit courts of the United States, to capital punishment. To communicate more distinctly the import of that act, I refer to its fourth and fifth sections, which are in the following words:

" SEC. 4. *And be it further enacted*, That if any citizen of the United States, being of the crew or ship's company of any foreign ship or vessel engaged in the slave trade, or any person whatever, being of the crew or ship's company of any ship or vessel, owned in the whole or part, or navigated for or in behalf of any citizen or citizens of the United States, shall land from any such ship or vessel, and on any foreign shore, seize any negro or mulatto, not held to service or labor by the laws of either of the States or Territories of the United States, with intent to make such negro or mulatto a slave, or shall decoy or forcibly bring or carry, or shall receive such negro or mulatto on board any such ship or vessel, with intent as aforesaid, such citizen or person shall be adjudged a pirate; and on conviction thereof, before the circuit court of the United States for the district wherein he may be brought or found, shall suffer death."

" SEC. 5. *And be it further enacted*, That if any citizen of the United States, being of the crew or ship's company of any foreign ship or vessel engaged in the slave trade, or any person whatever, being of the crew or ship's company of any ship or vessel, owned wholly or in part, or navigated for or in behalf of any citizen or citizens of the United States, shall forcibly confine or detain, or aid and abet in forcibly confining or detaining on board such ship or vessel any negro or mulatto, not held to service by the laws of either of the States or Territories of the United States, with intent to make such negro or mulatto a slave, or shall, on board any such ship or vessel, offer or attempt to sell, as a slave, any negro or mulatto not held to service as aforesaid, or shall, on the high seas, or anywhere on tide water, transfer or deliver over to any other ship or vessel any negro or mulatto, not held to service as aforesaid, with intent to make such negro or mulatto a slave, or shall land or deliver on shore from on board any such ship or vessel any such negro or mulatto, with intent to make sale of, or having previously sold such negro or mulatto as a slave, such citizen or person shall be adjudged a pirate; and on conviction thereof, before the circuit court of the United States for the district wherein he may be brought or found, shall suffer death."

And on the 28th February, 1823, the House of Representatives, by a vote of 131 to 9, passed a resolution to the following effect:

" *Resolved*, That the President of the United States be requested to enter upon, and prosecute from time to time, such negotiations with the several maritime powers of Europe and America as he may deem expedient for the effectual abolition of the African slave trade, and its ultimate denunciation as piracy, under the law of nations, by the consent of the civilized world."

By the act of Congress above referred to, whereby the most effectual means that could be devised were adopted for the extirpation of the slave trade, the wish of the United States was explicitly declared that all nations might concur in a similar policy. It could only be by such concurrence that the great object could be accomplished; and it was by negotiation and treaty alone that such concurrence could be obtained, commencing with one power and extending it to others. The course, therefore, which the Executive, who had concurred in the act, had to pursue, was distinctly marked out for it. Had there, however, been any doubt respecting it, the resolution of the House of Representatives, the branch which might with strict propriety express its opinion, could not fail to have removed it.

By the tenth article of the treaty of peace between the United States and Great Britain, concluded at Ghent, it was stipulated that both parties should use their best endeavors to accomplish the abolition of the African slave trade. This object has been, accordingly, pursued by both Governments with great earnestness, by separate acts of legislation, and by negotiation almost uninterrupted, with the purpose of establishing a concert between them in some measure which might secure its accomplishment.

Great Britain, in her negotiations with other powers, had concluded treaties with Spain, Portugal, and the Netherlands, in which, without constituting the crime as piracy or classing it with crimes of that denomination, the parties had conceded to the naval officers of each other the right of search and capture of the vessels of either that might be engaged in the slave trade, and had instituted courts, consisting of judges, subjects of both parties, for the trial of the vessels so captured.

In the negotiations with the United States, Great Britain had earnestly and repeatedly pressed on them the adoption of similar provisions. They had been resisted by the Executive on two grounds: one, that the constitution of mixed tribunals was incompatible with their Constitution; and the other, that the concession of the right of search in time of peace for an offence not piratical would be repugnant to the feelings of the nation and of dangerous tendency. The right of search is the right of war of the belligerent towards the neutral. To extend it in time of peace to any object whatever might establish a precedent which might lead to others with some powers, and which, even if confined to the instance specified, might be subject to great abuse. . .

Animated by an ardent desire to suppress this trade, the United States took stronger ground, by making it, by the act above referred to, piratical—a measure more adequate to the end, and free from many of the objections applicable to the plan which had been proposed to them. It is this alternative which the Executive, under the sanctions and injunctions above stated, offered to the British Government, and which that Government has accepted. By making the crime piracy, the right of search attaches to the crime, and which, when adopted by all nations, will be common to all; and that it will be so adopted may fairly be presumed, if steadily persevered in by the parties to the present convention. In the meantime, and with a view to a fair experiment, the obvious course seems to be to carry into effect with every power such treaty as may be made with each in succession.

In presenting this alternative to the British Government, it was made an indispensable condition that the trade should be made piratical by act of Parliament, as it had been by an act of Congress. This was provided for in the convention, and has since been complied with. In this respect, therefore, the two nations rest on the same ground. Suitable provisions have also been adopted to protect each party from the abuse of the power granted to the public ships of the other. Instead of subjecting the persons detected in the slave trade to trial by the courts of the captors, as would be the case if such trade was piracy by the law of nations, it is stipulated that, until that event, they shall be tried by the courts of their own country only. Hence there could be no motive for an abuse of the right of search, since such abuse could not fail to terminate to the injury of the captor.

Should this convention be adopted, there is every reason to believe that it will be the commencement of a system destined to accomplish the entire abolition of the slave trade. Great Britain, by making it her own, confessedly adopted at the suggestion of the United States, and being pledged to propose and urge its adoption by other nations in concert with the United States, will find it for her interest to abandon the less effective system of her previous treaties with Spain, Portugal, and the Netherlands, and to urge on those and other powers their accession to this. The crime will then be universally proscribed as piracy, and the traffic be suppressed forever.

Other considerations of high importance urge the adoption of this convention. We have, at this moment, pending with Great Britain, sundry other negotiations intimately connected with the welfare and even with the peace of our Union. In one of them, nearly a third part of the territory of the State of Maine is in contestation. In another, the navigation of the St. Lawrence, the admission of consuls into the British islands, and a system of commercial intercourse between the United States and all the British possessions in this hemisphere, are subjects of discussion. In a third, our territorial and other rights upon the Northwest Coast are to be adjusted; while a negotiation on the same interest is opened with Russia. In a fourth, all the most important controvertible points of maritime law in time of war are brought under consideration; and in the fifth, the whole system of South American concerns, connected with a general recognition of South American independence, may again, from hour to hour, become, as it has already been, an object of concerted operations of the highest interest to both nations, and to the peace of the world.

It cannot be disguised that the rejection of this convention could not fail to have a very injurious influence on the good understanding between the two Governments on all these points. That it would place the Executive administration under embarrassment, and subject it, the Congress and the nation, to the charge of insincerity respecting the great result of the final suppression of the slave trade; and that its first and indispensable consequence will be to constrain the Executive to suspend all further negotiation with every European and American power to which overtures have been made in compliance with the resolution of the House of Representatives of February 28, 1823, must be obvious. To invite all nations, with the statute of piracy in our hands, to adopt its principles as the law of nations, and yet to deny to all the common rights of search for the pirate, whom it would be impossible to detect without entering and searching the vessel, would expose us not simply to the charge of inconsistency.

It must be obvious that the restriction of search for pirates on the African coast is incompatible with the idea of such a crime. It is not doubted, also, if the convention is adopted, that no example of the commission of that crime by the citizens or subjects of either power will ever occur again. It is believed, therefore, that this right, as applicable to piracy, would not only extirpate the trade, but prove altogether innocent in its operation.

In further illustration of the views of Congress on this subject, I transmit to the Senate extracts from two resolutions of the House of Representatives—one of February 9, 1821, the other of April, 12, 1822. I transmit also a letter from the Chargé d'Affaires of the British Government, which shows the deep interest which that Government takes in the ratification of the treaty.

JAMES MONROE.

WASHINGTON, *May* 21, 1824.

Extract of a report of the 9th February, 1821, to the House of Representatives by the Committee to whom had been referred so much of the President's message as relates to the slave trade, and to whom were referred the two messages of the President, transmitting, in pursuance of the resolution of the House of Representatives of the 4th of December, a report of the Secretary of State, and inclosed documents relating to the negotiation for the suppression of the slave trade.

"The detestable crime of kidnapping the unoffending inhabitants of one country, and chaining them to slavery in another, is marked with all the atrociousness of piracy; and, as such, it is stigmatized and punishable by our own laws.

"To efface this reproachful stain from the character of civilized mankind would be the proudest triumph that could be achieved in the cause of humanity. On this subject, the United States, having led the way, owe it to themselves to give their influence and cordial co-operation to any measure that will accomplish the great and good purpose; but this happy result, experience has demonstrated, cannot be realized by any system except a concession by the maritime powers to each other's ships-of-war of a qualified right of search. If this object was generally attained, it is confidently believed that the active exertions of even a few nations, would be sufficient entirely to suppress the slave trade."

Extract from a report made April 12, 1822, by the Committee on the suppression of the slave trade, to whom had been referred a resolution of the House of Representatives, of the 15th January preceding, instructing them to inquire whether the laws of the United States prohibiting that traffic have been duly executed; also, into the general operation thereof; and, if any defects exist in those laws, to suggest adequate remedies therefor; and to whom many memorials had been referred touching the same subject.

"But the conclusion to which your committee have arrived, after consulting all the evidence within their reach, is, that the African slave trade now prevails to a great extent, and that its total suppression can never be effected by the separate and disunited efforts of one or more States; and as the resolution to which this report refers requires the suggestion of some remedy for the defects, if any exist, in the system of laws for the suppression of this traffic, your committee beg leave to call the attention of the House to the report and accompanying documents submitted to the last Congress by the committee on the slave trade, and to make the same a part of this report. That report proposes, as a remedy for the existing evils of the system. the concurrence of the United States with one or all the maritime powers of

Europe in a modified and reciprocal right of search on the African coast, with a view to the total suppression of the slave trade.

"It is with great delicacy that the committee have approached this subject; because they are aware that the remedy, which they have presumed to recommend to the consideration of the House, requires the exercise of a power of another Department of this Government, and that objections to the exercise of this power, in the mode here proposed, have hitherto existed in that Department.

"Your committee are confident, however, that these objections apply rather to a *particular proposition* for the exchange of the right of search than to that modification of it which presents itself to your committee. They contemplate the trial and condemnation of such American citizens as may be found engaged in this forbidden trade, not by mixed tribunals sitting in a foreign country, but by existing courts, of competent jurisdiction, in the United States; they propose the same disposition of the captured Africans now authorized by law; and least of all their detention in America.

"They contemplate an exchange of this right, which shall be in all respects reciprocal; an exchange, which, deriving its sole authority from treaty, would exclude the pretension, which no nation, however, has presumed to set up, that this right can be derived from the law of nations; and further, they have limited it, in their conception of its application, not only to certain latitudes and to a certain distance from the coast of Africa, but to a small number of vessels to be employed by each power, and to be previously designated. The visit and search thus restricted, it is believed, would insure the co-operation of one great maritime power in the proposed exchange, and guard it from the danger of abuse.

"Your committee cannot doubt that the people of America have the intelligence to distinguish between the right of searching a neutral on the high seas, in time of war, claimed by some belligerents, and that mutual, restricted, and peaceful concession by treaty suggested by your committee, and which is demanded in the name of suffering humanity."

Mr. Addington to the Secretary of State.

WASHINGTON, *May* 16, 1824.

SIR: Nearly three weeks have now elapsed since I had the honor of making my first communication to you on the subject of the convention, concluded on the 13th of March last, between the British Government and the American envoy in London.

At that time, in pursuance of instructions conveyed to me from his Majesty's Secretary of State for Foreign Affairs I made known to you the earnest desire of the British Government, that no time should be lost by that of the United States in proceeding to the ratification of that instrument, in order that it might be returned to England in time to have it submitted to Parliament prior to its prorogation, which was expected to take place at an early period.

I flattered myself, sir, that the wish thus anxiously expressed by me on behalf of his Majesty's Government would meet with a corresponding ardor on the part of all the authorities to whom it was addressed, especially considering that the project of the convention originated with this Government, at the instigation of the House of Representatives; and that his Majesty's ministers had not hesitated an instant to comply with the preliminary act desired by the President, of procuring the passage of a bill through Parliament denouncing as piracy by statute the African slave trade when exercised by British subjects.

This consideration, sir, necessarily precludes my entertaining a doubt as to the eventual ratification of the convention by this Government, and I, therefore, attribute the delay which has hitherto occurred to the pressure of other business which it would have been found inconvenient to postpone.

I think it my duty, however, to press once more and in the most earnest manner upon your attention the anxiety of the British Government on this subject. Of this anxiety, a most convincing proof may be found in the circumstance of an extra packet having been despatched by them for the sole purpose of conveying to this country the act of Parliament, declaring slave trade piracy, immediately after its passage through both Houses, in order that the want of that document might not oppose any obstacle to the sanction of the convention by this Government.

Perhaps, sir, you will allow me to add, that I now detain that same packet for the express purpose of reconveying the instrument in question, as soon as ratified, with utmost possible celerity to England.

I have the honor to be, with distinguished consideration, sir, your most obedient, humble servant,
H. U. ADDINGTON.

Hon. JOHN Q. ADAMS, *Secretary of State.*

18TH CONGRESS.]   No. 375.   [1ST SESSION.

ON COUNTERVAILING DUTIES AFFECTING THE COMMERCE AND TONNAGE BETWEEN GREAT BRITAIN AND THE UNITED STATES—DUTIES ON ROLLED IRON, ETC.

COMMUNICATED TO THE HOUSE OF REPRESENTATIVES MAY 22, 1824.

Mr. NEWTON, from the Committee on Commerce, to whom has been referred a resolution "instructing them to report to this House whether any law exists in contravention of the provisions of the convention of the 3d of July, 1815, made between this country and Great Britain; also to inquire into the expediency of countervailing by law any duties or port charges on American commerce and tonnage which Great Britain may lay thereon in her colonies or elsewhere," reported:

That, having bestowed on the first part of the resolution the consideration due to its importance, take leave to state to the House that no law has been passed by Congress which contravenes or violates any provision of the convention subsisting between the United States and Great Britain. They regret, however, to find that an opinion is entertained by the British Government that the act of Congress passed the 27th of April, 1816, entitled "An act to regulate the duties on imports and tonnage," in imposing a higher duty on iron manufactured by rolling than on hammered iron, contravenes the provisions of that convention on the ground that the duty operates exclusively on iron manufactured by that mode in Great Britain. Were the facts on which this opinion rests established, the committee do not think they would, giving to the convention either a strict or liberal construction, warrant the inference.

From the views taken of this subject by the committee, they are much gratified in being relieved from the necessity of going into a long and elaborate argument on that point by stating that the facts set forth and relied on by the British Government to support the position taken by it will not enable it to maintain successfully that position, as will satisfactorily appear by reference to the report of the Secretary of the Treasury of the 11th of February, 1824, stating the imports into and exports from the United States. That report informs the committee that iron manufactured by rolling is an import into the United States not only from Great Britain, but also from Sweden, Russia, and other countries. During the last fiscal year, ending the 30th of September, 1823, 27,700 cwt. of iron manufactured by rolling was imported from Sweden, and 2,003 cwt. from Russia, which iron was subjected to the payment of one dollar and fifty cents per hundred weight.

These facts, therefore, evidently and conclusively show that iron manufactured by rolling is not, according to the position taken by the British Government, a manufacture exclusively British. One among many reasons which influence Congress to impose a higher duty on rolled than on hammered iron was the inferiority of the former to the latter in use and quality. Mr. Stratford Canning, in his letter to Mr. Adams, Secretary of State, November 26, 1821, says: "Any difference of use or quality resulting from the mode of manufacture may, indeed, constitute a fair ground of distinction; but there is every reason to believe that no such difference exists in the present instance." That a difference in use and quality does exist, which Mr. Canning admits to be a fair ground of distinction, is known to every blacksmith, and to every man who has used it. Every man of judgment gives the preference to hammered iron, because it is freer from dross or impurities than the rolled, and because, whatever articles are made of the former are not only better, but more durable. The allusion made by Mr. Canning to Mr. Whitney's saw gin, and his comparison of that machine to the machinery employed in rolling iron, is an ingenious effort to get over puzzling difficulty by attempting to make things similar which have in them nothing common to each other on which to found a similitude. It is known, and it not unfrequently happens, that the importance of the interest threatened to be attacked produces a solicitude for its security which often occasions its advocates, more zealous to preserve it from injury than judicious in their defence of it, to surrender unwarily the vantage ground. Aware of this, the committee have given to the suggestion or allusion of Mr. Canning all the consideration it merits, and have satisfied themselves, on investigating it, that it does not support him in the argument he founds on it. The machinery employed in rolling or manufacturing iron requires, to use it properly, expert and skilful workmen, disciplined in that business, and also the constant and vigilant attention of an intelligent superintendent to make that mode of manufacturing iron succeed. But Mr. Whitney's saw gin, how happy soever the invention may be, or how much credit soever it may reflect on his genius, is so simple in its construction, so easily worked and managed, that negroes in the Southern States are employed to work it, and the effect of its operation is not to produce a change in the use or quality of the cotton by that mode of separating the cotton from the seed; for, after the process is completed, the cotton is as much a raw material as iron ore is when taken from the mine.

The ports of the United States have been open generally to the introduction of British manufactures, before and since the convention, on principles of amity and liberality; and the committee are not a little surprised to find that the Government of the United States should be charged with giving to the convention an astuteness of construction incompatible with its provisions, especially when the ports of his Britannic Majesty in Europe are closed against the introduction of the staple articles of the Eastern and Middle States. Will the Government of Great Britain allow the importation into Great Britain of cotton and wool cards and cut nails, manufactures of the United States, on the ground that those articles are manufactured exclusively in the United States by machines the invention of ingenious citizens? Or does it allow, on any terms, the importation of those articles into Great Britain? The statutes of that kingdom will give the answer and the commentary. In short, on which side soever the committee look, they see the industry and enterprise of the citizens of the United States subjected by British policy to prohibitions or restrictions that are not retorted by the Government of the United States on the industry and enterprise of British subjects. From the views which the committee have taken of this subject, they cannot recommend to the House any alteration or modification of the act of Congress imposing a higher duty on iron manufactured by rolling than on that prepared by the hammer.

As to the second part of the resolution, the committee respectfully state that, although the commerce and navigation of these United States with the British West India islands experience many embarrassments, and are subjected to high duties and charges to which the commerce and navigation of those islands are not liable in the United States, yet the committee forbear at this time to recommend the adoption of any countervailing measure, as the points of difference in relation to this subject are in negotiation between the two Governments.

The committee, having performed the duty assigned them, respectfully submit to the House the following resolution:

Resolved, That the committee be discharged from the further consideration of the resolution referred to them.

Mr. Canning to Mr. Adams.

WASHINGTON, *November* 25, 1822.

SIR: The approach of another session of Congress induces me to remind you of the correspondence which I had the honor of addressing to you last year, by the express commands of my Government, on the subject of the unequal duties levied on rolled and hammered iron, according to the tariff which is now in force. Being aware that the correspondence in question has been communicated officially to Congress, and that the consideration of it by that assembly has been deferred only in consequence of the great pressure of business at the close of the last session, I confine myself at present to requesting your good offices that, as far as depends upon the Executive Government, this matter may be brought, in the course of the ensuing session, to a just and satisfactory conclusion.

I beg, sir, that you will accept the assurance of my perfect consideration.

STRATFORD CANNING.

Hon. JOHN Q. ADAMS, &c.

Mr. Canning to Mr. Adams.

WASHINGTON, *March* 17, 1823.

SIR: Not having the honor to hear from you during the late session of Congress, or since its close, respecting the equalization of the duties on British rolled and hammered iron imported into the United States, on which subject I have frequently had occasion to address you, it becomes my duty to request a communication of the intentions of the American Government on this point, for the information of his Majesty's ministers. The message which was sent down to Congress last year by the President of the United States, together with the correspondence relative to the duties on rolled and hammered iron, afforded a reasonable expectation that the many strong facts and arguments repeatedly urged against the existing discrimination in the duties on those articles had at length produced their just effect, and that the American Legislature would hasten to pass an act for placing the duties in question on a footing consistent with a fair and equitable construction of the commercial treaty.

In ignorance of the circumstances, if any, which may have prevented this expectation from being realized, I cannot but hope, sir, that your occupations will admit of my being honored with an early answer to this letter.

I avail myself of the opportunity to repeat to you the assurance of my most distinguished consideration.

STRATFORD CANNING.

Mr. Addington to Mr. Adams.

WASHINGTON, *November* 20, 1823.

SIR: It is now seven years since, in pursuance of instructions from his Majesty's Secretary of State, the first representation was submitted by the British minister, resident in this capital, to the Government of the United States, against the unequal and unjust duties laid on British rolled iron imported into the United States.

Since that time the subject has been repeatedly brought under their consideration, as well as under that of the supreme legislative body.

It has been presented in so many lights, and all the arguments in support of the claim advanced by the British traders to be exonerated from those duties have been so often and so unanswerably pressed, that it would be presumption in me to attempt to add anything in support of a cause advocated by persons so much more capable by their weight and ability of doing justice to it than myself.

I feel, therefore, sir, that, as far as regards the discussion of the merits of the question, I cannot do better than refer you to Mr. Stratford Canning's letter to yourself, dated November 26, 1821, in which the subject is handled with a clearness and soundness of logic difficult to surpass, and which must carry conviction to every candid and unprejudiced mind.

Setting aside, then, all further argumentation of the question, I shall content myself with appealing, which I do with confidence, to the feelings of integrity and justice which animate the Government of this country, for the exertion of its powerful influence with the Legislature, in order to procure the revision of an act passed under an erroneous impression, or rather total misapprehension of the subject.

That act is manifestly contrary to the spirit, indeed to the letter of the convention, concluded in 1815, between Great Britain and the United States, in which it is stipulated, that *like* duties shall be reciprocally leviable upon *like* articles. No mention is therein made of the specific mode of manufacturing those articles.

By imposing an extra duty on rolled iron, between which and that produced by hammering it is now proved that, if there exist any difference in quality, that difference is in favor of the former, a shackle is placed on the hands of genius and invention, and a premium offered for the discouragement of science. But surely, sir, this war against useful invention and improvement is altogether unworthy of a nation distinguished by its love of novelty, by its rapid progress in the arts, and by the native vigor and inventiveness of mind of its inhabitants.

If Great Britain, instead of allowing in her own markets to the manufactures of the United States a fair and free competition with those of other nations, were, by a forced construction of the terms of her conventions, to burden with oppressive duties such of the articles of the former as, being the produce of the creative talents of their citizens, evinced in the superiority of their machinery, enjoy thereby an advantage over "the like" wares of other countries, would she not render herself justly obnoxious to the imputation of injustice, and illiberality? And yet, sir, this is but the course which the United States have adopted with regard to the iron manufactures of Great Britain.

But I am persuaded that this course is not accordant with the genuine feelings of the country; that the duties in question were originally imposed by Congress under a misapprehension of the real merits of the case; that those merits being once well known and duly appreciated, as they must now be, the appeal made to the candor of a body so distinguished by integrity and liberality of sentiment as the Congress of the United States will not be urged in vain; and that the inventive genius of Great Britain will be allowed to secure to her manufacturers those honest profits to which they are so justly entitled.

I have only to add, sir, the expression of my hope that you will lose no time in submitting to Congress, as shortly after its convocation as may be expedient, the application now made in behalf of the British iron merchants, and that you will lend it the powerful aid of a recommendation from the Government that the subject may be taken by that body into their immediate consideration.

I have the honor to be, with the highest respect, sir, your most obedient, humble servant,

H. U. ADDINGTON.

Hon. JOHN QUINCY ADAMS, *Secretary of State, &c., &c.*

Mr. Addington to Mr. Adams.

WASHINGTON, *March 4, 1824.*

SIR: I take the liberty of calling your attention to a letter which I had occasion to address to you on the 20th of November last, (to which I have not as yet had the honor of receiving an answer,) in which I requested the interposition of the Executive Government with the House of Congress, for the purpose of procuring an equalization of the duties on British iron.

In a conversation which, posterior to the date of that letter, I had the honor of holding with you, I received an assurance, that although no step in furtherance of the above object had at that time been taken by the Government, yet, as soon as the question of the tariff should be brought under the consideration of the Legislature, my wishes should be attended to.

It was with no small mortification that I learnt yesterday that the subject of the duties on iron had been already brought to an issue unfavorable to the just demands of the British Government; and *that,* without any formal intervention in favor of those demands having taken place on the part of this Government with the House of Representatives. I have also been assured that, had such an intervention taken place at the proper time, the point desired would, in all probability, have been carried.

I have now, therefore, the honor of addressing you once more upon this subject, and of submitting a request, in the name of his Majesty's Government, that the President will be pleased to recommend to the Senate the consideration of this matter, in order that, according to the express terms of the commercial treaties existing between the two countries, the iron manufactures of Great Britain may be placed upon a footing of strict equality with those of the nations which, in the existing state of things, enjoy an undue advantage over the former.

I have the honor to be, with distinguished consideration, sir, your most obedient, humble servant,

H. U. ADDINGTON.

Hon. JOHN Q. ADAMS, *&c., &c.*

Mr. Addington to Mr. Adams.

WASHINGTON, *May 5, 1824.*

SIR: Agreeably to your desire, as expressed to me yesterday, I have the honor to transmit to you, herewith, the copy of a despatch which I have recently received from his Majesty's Secretary of State for Foreign Affairs, relative to the unequal duties levied in this country upon rolled iron, the manufacture of Great Britain.

In this despatch you will perceive, sir, that I am instructed to press this subject once more, and in the most earnest manner, upon the attention of the American Government, and to represent to them that, in case a claim founded upon the clearest grounds of right and equity be still disregarded by the Legislature of the United States, it must become a question for the consideration of his Majesty's Government whether, in justice to the interest of Great Britain, it may not be expedient *to act upon the principles laid down by the United States themselves,* by considering their cotton, which stands in precisely the same relation to that of other countries as the iron of Great Britain to foreign iron as a manufactured article, and subjecting it, as such, to a higher rate of duty than is charged on other cotton which has not been cleansed by machinery.

I trust, sir, that the Legislature of the United States, by candidly admitting the validity of the claim advanced by Great Britain, will spare his Majesty's Government the pain of taking a measure which, however just, would not be resorted to by them without unfeigned reluctance, and as a step called for by an imperious sense of justice to the interests of his Majesty's subjects.

The equalization of duties desired by the British Government is of comparatively trifling importance to this country, but of very serious moment to the interests of Great Britain, inasmuch as those duties directly affect one of her staple commodities; and surely, sir, it were much to be regretted that, by persevering in a course by which, independent of its injustice, the United States in general are so little benefitted, the Legislature of this country should hazard any diminution of the friendly feelings and good correspondence which subsist between the two nations, by forcing Great Britain (for it would be a matter of positive compulsion) into the adoption of measures which, however undeniably equitable, might yet tend to create in the United States sentiments of a character opposite to those which at present so happily animate both people in their relations with each other, and which it is the earnest desire of his Majesty's Government to perpetuate by every legitimate means.

I have the honor to be, with distinguished consideration, sir, your most obedient, humble servant,

H. U. ADDINGTON.

Mr. Canning to Mr. Addington.

FOREIGN OFFICE, *March* 13, 1824.

SIR: In consequence of renewed applications from the persons engaged in the iron trade of this kingdom, his Majesty's Government have again had under their consideration the difference of duty levied in the United States on rolled and hammered iron the produce of Great Britain.

The British Government had hoped that the message sent by the President of the United States to the Congress in the year 1822, and the very strong facts and arguments repeatedly used by Sir Charles Bagot and Mr. Stratford Canning, during their several missions in America, against the existing discrimination in the duties on these articles, would have produced their just effect; but as this, unfortunately, does not appear to have been the case, I have to instruct you to bring this business again before the American Government, and to represent to them the injury to which the iron trade of this country continues to be exposed by this measure, and the injustice of withholding that relief to which they, in effect, admitted our claim by the message of the President above referred to.

You will observe, that, if the principle which appears to have led the Congress to delay the repeal of this discriminating duty were admitted, it might with equal justice be applied by his Majesty's Government to the article of American cotton, imported into this country, as compared with that brought from the East Indies or South America; for the cotton of the United States, being cleaned and separated from the seeds and husks by a process requiring the aid of machinery, becomes, (if this principle is to be acted upon to its fullest extent,) by parity of reasoning, as much, in truth, as the rolled iron, a manufactured article, when compared with the cotton of the other countries above mentioned; this last article being imported nearly in the state in which it is gathered, without undergoing any process for the purpose of cleaning or separating it from the seeds, &c.

In pressing, therefore, the American Government to come to a conclusion on this subject, in conformity with the repeated representations addressed to them from hence, I have to request that, in addition to the very able reasoning contained in the notes of your predecessor to the American Government, of the 31st March and the 26th November, 1821, on this subject, you will urge this argument also, and that you will apprise them that if, contrary to our just expectation, the existing inequality of duty on rolled and hammered iron be not removed, it must become a question for the consideration of his Majesty's Government whether, in justice to the interests of this country, it may not be expedient to act on the principle laid down by the United States themselves, by considering their cotton as a manufactured article, and subjecting it, as such, to a higher rate of duty than is charged on other cotton which has not been cleaned by machinery.

I am, &c.,

GEORGE CANNING.

SPOLIATIONS BY FRANCE.

COMMUNICATED TO THE HOUSE OF REPRESENTATIVES MAY 24, 1824.

Mr. FORSYTH, from the Committee on Foreign Relations, on the several petitions of Archibald Gracie, Ezra Davis, Matthew, Thomas S. and Levinus Clarkson, William Gray, and others, of the merchants and insurance companies of Philadelphia, of the merchants and underwriters of Baltimore, referred to them by the House, reported:

That the petitioners ask the intervention of Congress for the recovery of their just claims against France for spoliations committed and property seized or destroyed under different pretexts since the year 1806. These claims are alluded to by the President in his message at the opening of the present session of Congress as resting upon the same principle with other claims which have been admitted by the French Government, and are the subject of the correspondence of the minister of the United States with the French Government, communicated to the House of Representatives on the 5th of February last. To this correspondence the attention of the House is invited for a full and fair understanding of the claims of the present petitioners and of the other citizens of the United States having similar demands against France, but who have not joined in this application for redress.

The committee have seen with surprise that, although the attention of the present Government of France was especially invited to this subject in 1816, and has been repeatedly recalled to it since that time, France has not yet thought proper to enter upon the discussion of it. No other answers have yet been given to various official communications of the minister of the United States than those required by the mere obligations of international courtesy.

The committee are of opinion that measures ought to be taken to impress upon France the necessity of an early and definite adjustment of this subject, and they would offer such measures to the consideration of the House if the hope was not entertained that the Government of France would be found, during the ensuing summer, prepared to investigate it.

The committee are confident that a fair examination, entered into with a disposition to do full justice, will be followed by an arrangement satisfactory to all parties.

The claims of our citizens may be divided into four classes:

1. For property sequestered.

2. For property condemned, regularly, under the Berlin and Milan decrees.

3. For property irregularly [condemned under the same decrees, including that condemned by imperial mandate without the intervention of any judicial tribunal.

4. For property burnt or destroyed at sea; a portion of it after the] decrees authorizing such destruction had been repealed.

The first class includes, in addition to other property not acted upon by the judicial tribunals, the seizures at Antwerp in 1807, at St. Sebastian in 1809–'10, in Holland in 1810, under a secret article of the treaty incorporating Holland with France. The right of the claimants to an immediate and full indemnity for all property sequestered and never condemned cannot be plausibly contested. It was put under sequestration by an imperial decree, on suspicion that it was English property, merely to give time to ascertain whether it was English or not. That it was not English is now well known to the Government of France. Had it been English it must have been given up or paid for under the 4th article of the additional articles of the treaty of the 30th of May, 1814, between that power and Great Britain. By that article the parties stipulate to release all property put under sequestration since 1793. If the property of our citizens seized at Antwerp, St. Sebastian, and in Holland, had been what it was, without the shadow of reason, alleged to be, payment would be due for it to English owners. A singular spectacle will be exhibited if payment is denied when the motive for the seizure is shown to have been false, or should any doctrine of France place the property of a neutral in a worse situation than if it had belonged, as was suspected, to an enemy. Such doctrine cannot be advanced by France unless she intends to instruct other powers that, in all future wars in which she may be engaged with a formidable rival, it will be more prudent to be her enemy than her friend.

Nor can the committee anticipate any grounds upon which a decision unfavorable to the other claims embraced in the other three enumerated classes can be justly made, resting as they obviously do upon the immutable bases of justice and national law.

A due regard to those relations of amity that have ever united this Government with France, to the stipulations of her treaty with us, to her character for liberal justice to foreign claimants, will doubtless induce the Government of that country to adjust those claims whenever they are fairly considered.

Under the hope and expectation that attention will be given to this interesting subject by France, prior to the next session of Congress, the committee, without asking to be discharged from the further consideration of the several petitions referred to them, recommend to the House the following resolution:

Resolved, That the President of the United States be requested to lay before the House at the next session, as early as the public interest will permit, the correspondence which may be held with the Government of France, prior to that time, on the subject of injuries sustained by citizens of the United States since the year 1806.

18TH CONGRESS.]

No. 377.

[1ST SESSION.

SPOLIATIONS BY FRANCE FROM 1793 TO 1800.

COMMUNICATED TO THE HOUSE OF REPRESENTATIVES MAY 25, 1824.

To the House of Representatives of the United States:

I transmit to the House of Representatives a report from the Secretary of State concerning a resolution of that House of the 20th of April last, which was referred to him.

JAMES MONROE.

WASHINGTON CITY, *May* 25, 1824.

DEPARTMENT OF STATE, *Washington, May* 25, 1824.

The Secretary of State, to whom was referred a resolution of the House of Representatives of the 20th of April last, requesting the President to communicate to that House the correspondence between this Government and France relating to spoliations committed on American commerce between the years 1793 and 1800; and also relating to the claims of France upon this Government for not complying with the treaties of alliance and commerce of February 6, 1778, has the honor of informing the President that the documents and information required by the said resolution are to be selected from a mass of correspondence so voluminous that it has been found impracticable to prepare them before the close of the present session of Congress, but will be ready for communication to the House at their next annual meeting.

JOHN QUINCY ADAMS.

MESSAGE OF THE PRESIDENT OF THE UNITED STATES AT THE COMMENCEMENT OF THE SESSION.

COMMUNICATED TO CONGRESS DECEMBER 7, 1824.

Fellow-citizens of the Senate and of the House of Representatives:

. The view which I have now to present to you of our affairs, foreign and domestic, realizes the most sanguine anticipations which have been entertained of the public prosperity. If we look to the whole, our growth as a nation continues to be rapid beyond example; if to the States which compose it, the same gratifying spectacle is exhibited. Our expansion over the vast territory within our limits has been great, without indicating any decline in those sections from which the emigration has been most conspicuous. We have daily gained strength by a native population in every quarter—a population devoted to our happy system of Government, and cherishing the bond of union with fraternal affection. Experience has already shown that the difference of climate and of industry proceeding from that cause, inseparable from such vast domains, and which under other systems might have a repulsive tendency, cannot fail to produce with us, under wise regulations, the opposite effect. What one portion wants the other may supply, and this will be most sensibly felt by the parts most distant from each other, forming thereby a domestic market and an active intercourse between the extremes and throughout every portion of our Union. Thus, by a happy distribution of power between the national and State Governments, Governments which rest exclusively on the sovereignty of the people and are fully adequate to the great purposes for which they were respectively instituted, causes which might otherwise lead to dismemberment operate powerfully to draw us closer together. In every other circumstance a correct view of the actual state of our Union must be equally gratifying to our constituents. Our relations with foreign powers are of a friendly character, although certain interesting differences remain unsettled with some. Our revenue, under the mild system of impost and tonnage, continues to be adequate to all the purposes of the Government. Our agriculture, commerce, manufactures, and navigation flourish. Our fortifications are advancing in the degree authorized by existing appropriations to maturity, and due progress is made in the augmentation of the Navy to the limit prescribed for it by law. For these blessings, we owe to Almighty God, from whom we derive them, and with profound reverence, our most grateful and unceasing acknowledgments.

In adverting to our relations with foreign powers, which are always an object of the highest importance, I have to remark, that, of the subjects which have been brought into discussion with them during the present administration, some have been satisfactorily terminated; others have been suspended, to be resumed hereafter under circumstances more favorable to success; and others are still in negotiation, with the hope that they may be adjusted with mutual accommodation to the interests and to the satisfaction of the respective parties. It has been the invariable object of this Government to cherish the most friendly relations with every power, and on principles and conditions which might make them permanent. A systematic effort has been made to place our commerce with each power on a footing of perfect reciprocity, to settle with each in a spirit of candor and liberality all existing differences, and to anticipate and remove, so far as might be practicable, all causes of future variance.

It having been stipulated by the 7th article of the convention of navigation and commerce, which was concluded on the twenty-fourth of June, one thousand eight hundred and twenty-two, between the United States and France, that the said convention should continue in force for two years from the first of October of that year, and for an indefinite term afterwards, unless one of the parties should declare its intention to renounce it, in which event it should cease to operate at the end of six months from such declaration; and no such intention having been announced, the convention having been found advantageous to both parties, it has since remained, and still remains in force. At the time when that convention was concluded many interesting subjects were left unsettled, and particularly our claim to indemnity for spoliations which were committed on our commerce in the late wars. For these interests and claims it was in the contemplation of the parties to make provision at a subsequent day by a more comprehensive and definitive treaty. The object has been duly attended to since by the Executive, but as yet it has not been accomplished. It is hoped that a favorable opportunity will present itself for opening a negotiation which may embrace and arrange all existing differences, and every other concern in which they have a common interest, upon the accession of the present King of France, an event which has occurred since the close of the last session of Congress.

With Great Britain our commercial intercourse rests on the same footing that it did at the last session. By the convention of one thousand eight hundred and fifteen the commerce between the United States and the British dominions in Europe and the East Indies was arranged on a principle of reciprocity. That convention was confirmed and continued in force, with slight exceptions, by a subsequent treaty for the term of ten years from the twentieth of October, one thousand eight hundred and eighteen, the date of the latter. The trade with the British colonies in the West Indies has not as yet been arranged by treaty, or otherwise, to our satisfaction. An approach to that result has been made by legislative acts, whereby many serious impediments which had been raised by the parties in defence of their respective claims were removed. An earnest desire exists, and has been manifested on the part of this Government, to place the commerce with the colonies likewise on a footing of reciprocal advantage, and it is hoped the British Government, seeing the justice of the proposal and its importance to the colonies, will ere long accede to it.

. The Commissioners who were appointed for the adjustment of the boundary between the Territories of the United States and those of Great Britain, specified in the fifth article of the treaty of Ghent, having disagreed in their decision, and both Governments having agreed to establish that boundary by amicable negotiation between them, it is hoped that it may be satisfactorily adjusted in that mode. The boundary specified by the sixth article has been established by the decision of the Commissioners. From the progress made in that provided for by the seventh, according to a report recently received, there is good cause to presume that it will be settled in the course of the ensuing year.

· It is a cause of serious regret that no arrangement has yet been finally concluded between the two

Governments to secure, by joint co-operation, the suppression of the slave trade. It was the object of the British Government, in the early stages of the negotiation, to adopt a plan for the suppression which should include the concession of the mutual right of search by the ships-of-war of each party of the vessels of the other for suspected offenders. This was objected to by this Government, on the principle that, as the right of search was a right of war of a belligerent towards a neutral power, it might have an ill effect to extend it by treaty, to an offence which had been made comparatively mild, to a time of peace. Anxious, however, for the suppression of this trade, it was thought advisable, in compliance with a resolution of the House of Representatives, founded on an act of Congress, to propose to the British Government an expedient which should be free from that objection, and more effectual for the object, by making it piratical. In that mode the enormity of the crime would place the offenders out of the protection of their Government, and involve no question of search, or other question, between the parties, touching their respective rights. It was believed, also, that it would completely suppress the trade in the vessels of both parties, and, by their respective citizens and subjects, in those of other powers with whom, it was hoped, that the odium which would thereby be attached to it would produce a corresponding arrangement, and, by means thereof, its entire extirpation forever. A convention to this effect was concluded and signed in London, on the thirteenth day of March, one thousand eight hundred and twenty-four, by plenipotentiaries duly authorized by both Governments, to the ratification of which, certain obstacles have arisen which are not yet entirely removed. The difference between the parties still remaining has been reduced to a point not of sufficient magnitude, as is presumed, to be permitted to defeat an object so near to the heart of both nations, and so desirable to the friends of humanity throughout the world. As objections, however, to the principle recommended by the House of Representatives, or at least to the consequences inseparable from it, and which are understood to apply to the law, have been raised, which may deserve a reconsideration of the whole subject, I have thought it proper to suspend the conclusion of a new convention until the definitive sentiments of Congress may be ascertained. The documents relating to the negotiation are, with that intent, submitted to your consideration.

Our commerce with Sweden has been placed on a footing of perfect reciprocity by treaty, and with Russia, the Netherlands, Prussia, the free Hanseatic Cities, the Dukedoms of Oldenburg and Sardinia, by internal regulations on each side, founded on mutual agreement between the respective Governments.

The principles upon which the commercial policy of the United States is founded are to be traced to an early period. They are essentially connected with those upon which their independence was declared, and owe their origin to the enlightened men who took the lead in our affairs at that important epoch. They are developed in their first treaty of commerce with France of sixth of February, one thousand seven hundred and seventy-eight, and by a formal commission which was instituted immediately after the conclusion of their revolutionary struggle for the purpose of negotiating treaties of commerce with every European power. The first treaty of the United States with Prussia, which was negotiated by that commission, affords a signal illustration of those principles. The act of Congress of the third March, one thousand eight hundred and fifteen, adopted immediately after the return of a general peace, was a new overture to foreign nations to establish our commercial relations with them on the basis of free and equal reciprocity. That principle has pervaded all the acts of Congress and all the negotiations of the Executive on the subject since.

A convention for the settlement of important questions in relation to the Northwest Coast of this continent, and its adjoining seas, was concluded and signed at St. Petersburg, on the fifth day of April last, by the minister plenipotentiary of the United States and plenipotentiaries of the Imperial Government of Russia. It will immediately be laid before the Senate for the exercise of the constitutional authority of that body with reference to its ratification. It is proper to add, that the manner in which this negotiation was invited and conducted on the part of the Emperor has been very satisfactory.

The great and extraordinary changes which have happened in the Governments of Spain and Portugal within the last two years, without seriously affecting the friendly relations which, under all of them, have been maintained with those powers by the United States, have been obstacles to the adjustment of the particular subjects of discussion which have arisen with each. A resolution of the Senate, adopted at their last session, called for information as to the effect produced upon our relations with Spain by the recognition, on the part of the United States, of the independent South American Governments. The papers containing that information are now communicated to Congress.

A chargé d'affaires has been received from the independent Government of Brazil. That country heretofore a colonial possession of Portugal, had, some years since, been proclaimed by the sovereign of Portugal himself an independent kingdom. Since his return to Lisbon a revolution in Brazil has established a new Government there, with an Imperial title, at the head of which is placed the prince, in whom the Regency had been vested by the King at the time of his departure. There is reason to expect that, by amicable negotiation, the independence of Brazil will ere long be recognized by Portugal herself.

With the remaining powers of Europe, with those on the coast of Barbary, and with all the new South American States, our relations are of a friendly character. We have ministers plenipotentiary residing with the Republics of Colombia and Chili, and have received ministers of the same rank from Colombia, Guatemala, Buenos Ayres, and Mexico. Our commercial relations with all those States are mutually beneficial and increasing. With the Republic of Colombia a treaty of commerce has been formed, of which a copy is received, and the original daily expected. A negotiation for a like treaty would have been commenced with Buenos Ayres, had it not been prevented by the indisposition and lamented decease of Mr. Rodney, our minister there, and to whose memory the most respectful attention has been shown by the Government of that Republic. An advantageous alteration in our treaty with Tunis has been obtained by our Consular Agent residing there, the official document of which, when received, will be laid before the Senate.

The attention of the Government has been drawn with great solicitude to other subjects, and particularly to that relating to a state of maritime war, involving the relative rights of neutral and belligerent in such wars. Most of the difficulties which we have experienced, and of the losses which we have sustained since the establishment of our independence, have proceeded from the unsettled state of those rights, and the extent to which the belligerent claim has been carried against the neutral party. It is impossible to look back on the occurrences of the late wars in Europe, and to behold the disregard which was paid to our rights as a neutral power, and the waste which was made of our commerce by the parties to those wars by various acts of their respective Governments, and under the pretext by each that the other had set the example, without great mortification, and a fixed purpose never to submit to the like in future. An attempt to remove those causes of possible variance by friendly negotiation and on just principles, which should be applicable to all parties, could, it was presumed, be viewed by none other than as a proof of an earnest desire to preserve those relations with every power. In the late war between France and Spain, a crisis occurred, in which it seemed probable that all the controvertible principles involved in such wars might be brought into discussion, and settled to the satisfaction of all parties. Propositions having this object in view have been made to the Governments of Great Britain, France, Russia, and of other powers, which have been received in a friendly manner by all, but as yet no treaty has been formed with either for its accomplishment. The policy will, it is presumed, be persevered in, and in the hope that it may be successful.

It will always be recollected that with one of the parties to those wars, and from whom we received those injuries, we sought redress by war. From the other, by whose then reigning Government our vessels were seized in port as well as at sea, and their cargoes confiscated, indemnity has been expected, but has not yet been rendered. It was under the influence of the latter that our vessels were likewise seized by the Governments of Spain, Holland, Denmark, Sweden, and Naples, and from whom indemnity has been claimed and is still expected, with the exception of Spain, by whom it has been rendered. With both parties we had abundant cause of war, but we had no alternative but to resist that which was most powerful at sea and pressed us nearest at home. With this all differences were settled by a treaty founded on conditions fair and honorable to both, and which has been so far executed with perfect good faith. It has been earnestly hoped that the other would, of its own accord, and from a sentiment of justice and conciliation, make to our citizens the indemnity to which they are entitled, and thereby remove from our relations any just cause of discontent on our side.

It is estimated that the receipts into the Treasury during the current year, exclusive of loans, will exceed eighteen million five hundred thousand dollars, which, with the sum remaining in the Treasury at the end of the last year, amounting to nine million four hundred and sixty-three thousand nine hundred and twenty-two dollars and eighty-one cents, will, after discharging the current disbursements of the year, the interest on the public debt, and upwards of eleven million six hundred and thirty-three thousand dollars of the principal, leave a balance of more than three million dollars in the Treasury on the 1st day of January next.

A larger amount of the debt contracted during the late war, bearing an interest of six per cent., becoming redeemable in the course of the ensuing year than could be discharged by the ordinary revenue, the act of the 26th of May authorized a loan of five million dollars, at four and a half per cent., to meet the same. By this arrangement an annual saving will accrue to the public of seventy-five thousand dollars.

Under the act of the 24th of May last a loan of five million dollars was authorized, in order to meet the awards under the Florida treaty, which was negotiated at par with the Bank of the United States at four and a half per cent., the limit of interest fixed by the act. By this provision the claims of our citizens who had sustained so great a loss by spoliations, and from whom indemnity had been so long withheld, were promptly paid. For these advances the public will be amply repaid, at no distant day, by the sale of the lands in Florida. Of the great advantage resulting from the acquisition of the territory in other respects too high an estimate cannot be formed.

It is estimated that the receipts into the Treasury during the year one thousand eight hundred and twenty-five will be sufficient to meet the disbursements of the year, including the sum of ten million dollars, which is annually appropriated, by the act constituting the Sinking Fund, to the payment of the principal and interest of the public debt.

The whole amount of the public debt on the first of January next may be estimated at eighty-six million dollars, inclusive of two millions five hundred thousand dollars of the loan authorized by the act of the twenty-sixth of May last. In this estimate is included a stock of seven million dollars issued for the purchase of that amount of the capital stock of the Bank of the United States, and which, as the stock of the Bank still held by the Government will at least be fully equal to its reimbursement, ought not to be considered as constituting a part of the public debt. Estimating, then, the whole amount of the public debt at seventy-nine million dollars, and regarding the annual receipts and expenditures of the Government, a well-founded hope may be entertained that, should no unexpected event occur, the whole public debt may be discharged in the course of ten years, and the Government be left at liberty thereafter to apply such portion of the revenue as may not be necessary for current expenses to such other objects as may be most conducive to the public security and welfare. That the sum applicable to these objects will be very considerable may be fairly concluded when it is recollected that a large amount of the public revenue has been applied since the late war to the construction of the public buildings in this city; to the erection of fortifications along the coast, and of arsenals in different parts of the Union; to the augmentation of the Navy; to the extinguishment of the Indian title to large tracts of fertile territory; to the acquisition of Florida; to pensions to revolutionary officers and soldiers, and to invalids of the late war. On many of these objects the expense will annually be diminished, and cease at no distant period on most of them. On the first of January, one thousand eight hundred and seventeen, the public debt amounted to one hundred and twenty-three million four hundred and ninety-one thousand nine hundred and sixty-five dollars and sixteen cents; and notwithstanding the large sums which have been applied to these objects, it has been reduced since that period thirty-seven million four hundred and forty-six thousand nine hundred and sixty-one dollars and seventy-eight cents. The last portion of the public debt will be redeemable on the first of January, one thousand eight hundred and thirty-five; and while there is the best reason to believe that the resources of the Government will be continually adequate to such portions of it as may become due in the interval, it is recommended to Congress to seize every opportunity which may present itself to reduce the rate of interest on every part thereof. The high state of the public credit and the great abundance of money are at this time very favorable to such a result. It must be very gratifying to our fellow-citizens to witness this flourishing state of the public finances, when it is recollected that no burden whatever is imposed upon them.

The military establishment in all its branches, in the performance of the various duties assigned to each, justifies the favorable view which was presented of the efficiency of its organization at the last session. All the appropriations have been regularly applied to the objects intended by Congress; and, so far as the disbursements have been made, the accounts have been rendered and settled without loss to the public. The condition of the Army itself, as relates to the officers and men in science and discipline, is highly respectable. The Military Academy, on which the Army essentially rests, and to which it is much indebted for this state of improvement, has attained, in comparison with any other institution of a like kind, a high degree of perfection. Experience, however, has shown that the dispersed condition of the corps of artillery is unfavorable to the discipline of that important branch of the military establishment. To remedy this inconvenience eleven companies have been assembled at the fortification erected at Old Point Comfort, as a school for artillery instruction, with intention, as they shall be perfected in the various duties of that service, to order them to other posts, and to supply their places with other companies for instruction in like manner. In this mode a complete knowledge of the science and duties of this arm will be extended throughout the whole corps of artillery. But to carry this object fully into effect will require the aid of Congress, to obtain which the subject is now submitted to your consideration.

Of the progress which has been made in the construction of fortifications for the permanent defence of our maritime frontier, according to the plan decided on and to the extent of the existing appropriations, the report of the Secretary of War, which is herewith communicated, will give a detailed account. Their final completion cannot fail to give great additional security to that frontier, and to diminish, proportionably, the expense of defending it in the event of war.

The provisions in the several acts of Congress of the last session for the improvement of the navigation of the Mississippi and the Ohio, of the harbor of Presque isle, on Lake Erie, and the repair of the Plymouth beach, are in the course of regular execution, and there is reason to believe that the appropriation, in each instance, will be adequate to the object. To carry these improvements fully into effect, the superintendence of them has been assigned to officers of the Corps of Engineers.

Under the act of thirtieth April last, authorizing the President to cause a survey to be made, with the necessary plans and estimates, of such roads and canals as he might deem of national importance in a commercial or military point of view, or for the transportation of the mail, a Board has been instituted, consisting of two distinguished officers of the Corps of Engineers and a distinguished civil engineer, with assistants, who have been actively employed in carrying into effect the object of the act. They have carefully examined the route between the Potomac and the Ohio rivers; between the latter and Lake Erie; between the Alleghany and the Susquehanna, and the routes between the Delaware and the Raritan, Barnstable and Buzzard's bay, and between Boston harbor and Narraganset bay. Such portion of the Corps of Topographical Engineers as could be spared from the survey of the coast has been employed in surveying the very important route between the Potomac and the Ohio. Considerable progress has been made in it, but the survey cannot be completed until the next season. It is gratifying to add, from the view already taken, that there is good cause to believe that this great national object may be fully accomplished.

It is contemplated to commence early in the next season the execution of the other branch of the act, that which relates to roads, and with the survey of a route from this city, through the Southern States, to New Orleans, the importance of which cannot be too highly estimated. All the officers of both the Corps of Engineers who could be spared from other services have been employed in exploring and surveying the routes for canals. To digest a plan for both objects, for the great purposes specified, will require a thorough knowledge of every part of our Union, and of the relation of each part to the others, and of all to the seat of the General Government. For such a digest it will be necessary that the information be full, minute, and precise. With a view to these important objects, I submit to the consideration of Congress the propriety of enlarging both the Corps of Engineers, the military and topographical. It need scarcely be remarked, that the more extensively these corps are engaged in the improvement of their country, in the execution of the powers of Congress, and in aid of the States in such improvements as lie beyond that limit, when such aid is desired, the happier the effect will be in many views of which the subject is susceptible. By profiting of their science, the works will always be well executed; and, by giving to the officers such employment, our Union will derive all the advantage, in peace as well as in war, from their talents and services, which they can afford. In this mode, also, the military will be incorporated with the civil, and unfounded and injurious distinctions and prejudices of every kind be done away. To the corps themselves, this service cannot fail to be equally useful, since, by the knowledge they would thus acquire, they would be eminently better qualified, in the event of war, for the great purposes for which they were instituted.

Our relations with the Indian tribes within our limits have not been materially changed during the year. The hostile disposition evinced by certain tribes on the Missouri during the last year still continues, and has extended in some degree to those on the Upper Mississippi and the upper lakes. Several parties of our citizens have been plundered and murdered by those tribes. In order to establish relations of friendship with them, Congress at the last session made an appropriation for treaties with them, and for the employment of a suitable military escort to accompany and attend the Commissioners at the places appointed for the negotiations. This object has not been effected. The season was too far advanced when the appropriation was made, and the distance too great to permit it, but measures have been taken, and all the preparations will be completed, to accomplish it at an early period in the next season.

Believing that the hostility of the tribes, particularly on the Upper Mississippi and the lakes, is in no small degree owing to the wars which are carried on between the tribes residing in that quarter, measures have been taken to bring about a general peace among them, which, if successful, will not only tend to the security of our citizens, but be of great advantage to the Indians themselves.

With the exception of the tribes referred to, our relations with all the others are on the same friendly footing, and it affords me great satisfaction to add, that they are making steady advances in civilization and the improvement of their condition. Many of the tribes have already made great progress in the arts of civilized life. This desirable result has been brought about by the humane and persevering policy of the Government, and particularly by means of the appropriation for the civilization of the Indians. There have been established under the provisions of this act thirty-two schools, containing nine hundred and sixteen scholars, who are well instructed in several branches of literature, and likewise in agriculture and the ordinary arts of life.

Under the appropriation to authorize treaties with the Creeks and Quapaw Indians, Commissioners have been appointed, and negotiations are now pending, but the result is not yet known.

For more full information respecting the principle which has been adopted for carrying into effect the act of Congress authorizing surveys, with plans and estimates for canals and roads, and on every other branch of duty incident to the Department of War, I refer you to the report of the Secretary.

The squadron in the Mediterranean has been maintained in the extent which was proposed in the report of the Secretary of the Navy of the last year, and has afforded to our commerce the necessary protection in that sea. Apprehending, however, that the unfriendly relations which have existed between Algiers and some of the powers of Europe might be extended to us, it has been thought expedient to augment the force there, and, in consequence, the "North Carolina," a ship of the line, has been prepared, and will sail in a few days to join it.

The force employed in the Gulf of Mexico and in the neighboring seas for the suppression of piracy has likewise been preserved essentially in the state in which it was during the last year. A persevering effort has been made for the accomplishment of that object, and much protection has thereby been afforded to our commerce; but still the practice is far from being suppressed. From every view which has been taken of the subject, it is thought that it will be necessary rather to augment than to diminish our force in that quarter. There is reason to believe that the piracies now complained of are committed by bands of robbers who inhabit the land, and who, by preserving good intelligence with the towns, and seizing favorable opportunities, rush forth and fall on unprotected merchant vessels, of which they make an easy prey. The pillage thus taken they carry to their lurking places and dispose of afterwards at prices tending to seduce the neighboring population. This combination is understood to be of great extent, and is the more to be deprecated because the crime of piracy is often attended with the murder of the crews, these robbers knowing, if any survived, their lurking places would be exposed and they be caught and punished. That this atrocious practice should be carried to such extent is cause of equal surprise and regret. It is presumed that it must be attributed to the relaxed and feeble state of the local Government, since it is not doubted, from the high character of the Governor of Cuba, who is well known and much respected here, that if he had the power he would promptly suppress it. Whether those robbers should be pursued on the land, the local authorities be made responsible for these atrocities, or any other measure be resorted to to suppress them, is submitted to the consideration of Congress.

In execution of the laws for the suppression of the slave trade, a vessel has been occasionally sent from that squadron to the coast of Africa, with orders to return thence by the usual track of the slave ships, and to seize any of our vessels which might be engaged in that trade. None have been found, and it is believed that none are thus employed. It is well known, however, that the trade still exists under other flags.

The health of our squadron while at Thompson's island has been much better during the present than it was the last season. Some improvements have been made and others are contemplated there which, it is believed, will have a very salutary effect.

On the Pacific our commerce has much increased, and on that coast as well as on that sea the United States have many important interests which require attention and protection. It is thought that all the considerations which suggested the expediency of placing a squadron on that sea operate with augmented force for maintaining it there, at least in equal extent.

For detailed information respecting the state of our maritime force on each sea, the improvement necessary to be made on either, in the organization of the naval establishment generally, and of the laws for its better government, I refer you to the report of the Secretary of the Navy, which is herewith communicated.

The revenue of the Post Office Department has received a considerable augmentation in the present year. The current receipts will exceed the expenditures, although the transportation of the mail within the year has been much increased. A report of the Postmaster General, which is transmitted, will furnish in detail the necessary information respecting the administration and present state of this Department.

In conformity with a resolution of Congress of the last session, an invitation was given to General Lafayette to visit the United States, with an assurance that a ship-of-war should attend at any port of France which he might designate, to receive and convey him across the Atlantic, whenever it might be convenient for him to sail. He declined the offer of the public ship from motives of delicacy, but assured me that he had long intended and would certainly visit our Union in the course of the present year. In August last he arrived at New York, where he was received with the warmth of affection and gratitude to which his very important and disinterested services and sacrifices in our revolutionary struggle so eminently entitled him. A corresponding sentiment has since been manifested in his favor throughout every portion of our Union, and affectionate invitations have been given him to extend his visits to them. To these he has yielded all the accommodation in his power. At every designated point of rendezvous the whole population of the neighboring country has been assembled to greet him, among whom it has excited in a peculiar manner the sensibility of all to behold the surviving members of our Revolutionary contest, civil and military, who had shared with him in the toils and dangers of the war, many of them in a decrepid state. A more interesting spectacle, it is believed, was never witnessed, because none could be founded on purer principles—none proceed from higher or more disinterested motives. That the feelings of those who had fought and bled with him in a common cause should have been much excited was natural. There are, however, circumstances attending these interviews which pervaded the whole community and touched the breasts of every age, even the youngest among us. There was not an individual present who had not some relative who had not partaken in those scenes, nor an infant who had not heard the relation of them. But the circumstance which was most sensibly felt and which his presence brought forcibly to the recollection of all was the great cause in which we were engaged, and the blessings which we have derived from our success in it. The struggle was for independence and liberty, public and personal, and in this we succeeded. The meeting with one who had borne so distinguished a part in that great struggle, and from such lofty and disinterested motives, could not fail to affect profoundly every individual and of every age. It is natural that we should all take a deep interest in his future welfare, as we do. His high claims on our Union are felt, and the sentiment universal that they should be met in a generous spirit. Under these impressions I invite your attention to the subject with a view that, regarding his very important services, losses, and sacrifices, a provision may be made and tendered to him which shall correspond with the sentiments and be worthy the character of the American people.

In turning our attention to the condition of the civilized world, in which the United States have always taken a deep interest, it is gratifying to see how large a portion of it is blessed with peace. The only wars which now exist within that limit are those between Turkey and Greece, in Europe, and between Spain and the new Governments, our neighbors, in this hemisphere. In both these wars the cause of independence, of liberty, and humanity, continues to prevail. The success of Greece, when the relative population of the contending parties is considered, commands our admiration and applause, and that it has had a similar effect with the neighboring powers is obvious. The feeling of the whole civilized world is excited in a high degree in their favor. May we not hope that these sentiments, winning on the hearts of their respective Governments, may lead to a more decisive result? that they may produce an accord among them to replace Greece on the ground which she formerly held, and to which her heroic exertions at this day so eminently entitle her?

With respect to the contest to which our neighbors are a party, it is evident that Spain, as a power, is scarcely felt in it. These new States had completely achieved their independence before it was acknowledged by the United States, and they have since maintained it with little foreign pressure. The disturbances which have appeared in certain portions of that vast territory have proceeded from internal causes, which had their origin in their former Governments, and have not yet been thoroughly removed. It is manifest that these causes are daily losing their effect, and that these new States are settling down under Governments elective and representative in every branch similar to our own. In this course we ardently wish them to persevere, under a firm conviction that it will promote their happiness. In this their career, however, we have not interfered, believing that every people have a right to institute for themselves the Government which, in their judgment, may suit them best. Our example is before them, of the good effect of which, being our neighbors, they are competent judges, and to their judgment we leave it, in the expectation that other powers will pursue the same policy. The deep interest which we take in their independence, which we have acknowledged, and in their enjoyment of all the rights incident thereto, especially in the very important one of instituting their own Governments, has been declared and is known to the world. Separated, as we are, from Europe by the great Atlantic Ocean, we can have no concern in the wars of the European Governments, nor in the causes which produce them. The balance of power between them, into which ever scale it may turn, in its various vibrations, cannot affect us. It is the interest of the United States to preserve the most friendly relations with every power, and on conditions fair, equal, and applicable to all. But in regard to our neighbors our situation is different. It is impossible for the European Governments to interfere in their concerns, especially in those alluded to, which are vital, without affecting us; indeed, the motive which might induce such interference in the present state of the war between the parties, if a war it may be called, would appear to be equally applicable to us. It is gratifying to know that some of the powers with whom we enjoy a very friendly intercourse, and to whom these views have been communicated, have appeared to acquiesce in them.

The augmentation of our population, with the expansion of our Union, and increased number of States, have produced effects in certain branches of our system which merit the attention of Congress. Some of our arrangements, and particularly of the Judiciary Establishment, were made with a view to the original thirteen States only. Since then the United States have acquired a vast extent of territory; eleven new States have been admitted into the Union, and Territories have been laid off for three others, which will likewise be admitted at no distant day. An organization of the Supreme Court, which assigns to the judges any portion of the duties which belong to the inferior, requiring their passage over so vast a space, under any distribution of the States that may now be made, if not impracticable in the execution, must render it impossible for them to discharge the duties of either branch with advantage to the Union. The duties of the Supreme Court would be of great importance if its decisions were confined to the ordinary limits of other tribunals; but when it is considered that this court decides, and in the last resort, on all the great questions which arise under our Constitution, involving those between the United States individually, between the States and the United States, and between the latter and foreign powers, too high an estimate of their importance cannot be formed. The great interests of the nation seem to require that the judges of the Supreme Court should be exempted from every other duty than those which are incident to that high trust. The organization of the inferior courts would, of course, be adapted to circumstances. It is presumed that such a one might be formed as would secure an able and faithful discharge of their duties, and without any material augmentation of expense.

The condition of the aborigines within our limits, and especially those who are within the limits of any of the States, merits likewise particular attention. Experience has shown that, unless the tribes be civilized, they can never be incorporated into our system, in any form whatever. It has likewise shown that, in the regular augmentation of our population, with the extension of our settlements, their situation will become deplorable, if their extinction is not menaced. Some well digested plan, which will rescue them from such calamities, is due to their rights, to the rights of humanity, and to the honor of the nation. Their civilization is indispensable to their safety, and this can be accomplished only by degrees. The process must commence with the infant state, through whom some effect may be wrought on the parental. Difficulties of the most serious character present themselves to the attainment of this very desirable result on the territory on which they now reside. To remove them from it by force, even with a view to their own security and happiness, would be revolting to humanity, and utterly unjustifiable. Between the limits of our present States and Territories, and the Rocky mountains and Mexico, there is a vast territory to which they might be invited, with inducements which might be successful. It is thought if that territory should be divided into districts, by previous agreement with the tribes now residing there, and civil Governments be established in each, with schools for every branch of instruction in literature and the arts of civilized life, that all the tribes now within our limits might gradually be drawn there. The execution of this would necessarily be attended with expense, and that not inconsiderable; but it is doubted whether any other can be devised which would be less liable to that objection or more likely to succeed.

In looking to the interests which the United States have on the Pacific Ocean and on the Western Coast of this continent, the propriety of establishing a military post at the mouth of Columbia river, or at some other point in that quarter within our acknowledged limits, is submitted to the consideration of Congress. Our commerce and fisheries on that sea and along the coast have much increased and are increasing. It is thought that a military post to which our ships-of-war might resort would afford protection to every interest, and have a tendency to conciliate the tribes to the Northwest, with whom our trade is extensive. It is thought, also, that, by the establishment of such a post, the intercourse between our Western States and Territories and the Pacific and our trade with the tribes residing in the interior, on each side of the Rocky mountains, would be essentially promoted. To carry this object into effect, the appropriation of an adequate sum to authorize the employment of a frigate, with an officer of the Corps of Engineers, to explore the mouth of the Columbia river and the coast contiguous thereto, to enable the Executive to make such establishment at the most suitable point, is recommended to Congress.

It is thought that attention is also due to the improvement of this city. The communication between the public buildings and in various other parts and the grounds around those buildings require it. It is presumed, also, that the completion of the canal, from the Tiber to the Eastern Branch, would have a very salutary effect. Great exertions have been made and expenses incurred by the citizens in improvements of various kinds; but those which are suggested belong exclusively to the Government, or are of a nature to require expenditures beyond their resources. The public lots which are still for sale would, it is not doubted, be more than adequate to these purposes.

From the view above presented, it is manifest that the situation of the United States is, in the highest degree, prosperous and happy. There is no object which, as a people, we can desire which we do not possess, or which is not within our reach. Blessed with Governments the happiest which the world ever knew, with no distinct orders in society or divided interests in any portion of the vast territory over which their dominion extends, we have every motive to cling together which can animate a virtuous and enlightened people. The great object is to preserve these blessings and to hand them down to the latest posterity. Our experience ought to satisfy us that our progress, under the most correct and provident policy, will not be exempt from danger. Our institutions form an important epoch in the history of the civilized world. On their preservation, and in their utmost purity, everything will depend. Extending, as our interests do, to every part of the inhabited globe, and to every sea, to which our citizens are carried by their industry and enterprise, to which they are invited by the wants of others, and have a right to go, we must either protect them in the enjoyment of their rights, or abandon them, in certain events, to waste and desolation. Our attitude is highly interesting as relates to other powers, and particularly to our Southern neighbors. We have duties to perform with respect to all to which we must be faithful. To every kind of danger we should pay the most vigilant and unceasing attention, remove the cause where it may be practicable, and be prepared to meet it when inevitable.

Against foreign danger the policy of the Government seems to be already settled. The events of the late war admonished us to make our maritime frontier impregnable by a well-digested chain of fortifications, and to give efficient protection to our commerce by augmenting our Navy to a certain extent, which has been steadily pursued, and which it is incumbent upon us to complete as soon as circumstances will permit. In the event of war, it is on the maritime frontier that we shall be assailed. It is in that quarter, therefore, that we should be prepared to meet the attack. It is there that our whole force will be called into action to prevent the destruction of our towns, and the desolation and pillage of the interior. To give full effect to this policy, great improvements will be indispensable. Access to those works by every practicable communication should be made easy, and in every direction. The intercourse, also, between every part of our Union should be promoted and facilitated by the exercise of those powers which may comport with a faithful regard to the great principles of our Constitution. With respect to internal causes, those great principles point out with equal certainty the policy to be pursued. Resting on the people, as our Governments do, State and National, with well-defined powers, it is of the highest importance that they severally keep within the limits prescribed to them. Fulfilling that sacred duty, it is of equal importance that the movement between them be harmonious; and, in case of any disagreement, should any such occur, a calm appeal be made to the people, and their voice be heard and promptly obeyed. Both Governments being instituted for the common good, we cannot fail to prosper, while those who made them are attentive to the conduct of their representatives and control their measures. In the pursuit of these great objects, let a generous spirit and national views and feelings be indulged, and let every part recollect that by cherishing that spirit, and improving the condition of the others in what relates to their welfare, the general interest will not only be promoted, but the local advantage be reciprocated.

I cannot conclude this communication, the last of the kind which I shall have to make, without recolleeting, with great sensibility and heartfelt gratitude, the many instances of the public confidence, and the generous support which I have received from my fellow-citizens in the various trusts with which I have been honored. Having commenced my service in early youth, and continued it since with few and short intervals, I have witnessed the great difficulties to which our Union has been exposed, and admired the virtue and courage with which they were surmounted. From the present prosperous and happy state I derive a gratification which I cannot express. That these blessings may be preserved and perpetuated will be the object of my fervent and unceasing prayers to the Supreme Ruler of the Universe.

JAMES MONROE.

WASHINGTON, *December* 7, 1824.

18TH CONGRESS.] <u>No. 379.</u> [2D SESSION.

CORRESPONDENCE WITH GREAT BRITAIN RELATIVE TO THE SUPPRESSION OF THE SLAVE TRADE.

COMMUNICATED TO CONGRESS WITH THE MESSAGE OF THE PRESIDENT, DECEMBER 7, 1824.

[See No. 378.]

DOCUMENTS FROM THE DEPARTMENT OF STATE.

Papers in relation to the convention between the United States and Great Britain for the suppression of the slave trade, communicated with the President's message to Congress, December 7, 1824.

1. Proceedings of the Senate at its last session, with copies of the messages, convention, and other papers communicated to that House.
2. Mr. Adams to Mr. Rush, May 29, 1824.
3. Mr. Rush to Mr. Adams, June 28, 1824. Extract.
4. Same to same, July 5, 1824. Extract.
5. Same to same, August 9, 1824. Extract.
6. Same to same, August 30, 1824. Copy.
6. *a.* Mr. George Canning to Mr. Rush, August 27, 1824. Copy.
6. *b.* Mr. Rush to Mr. George Canning, August 30, 1824. Copy.
7. Mr. Adams to Mr. Rush, November 12, 1824. Copy.
8. Mr. Addington to Mr. Adams, November 6, 1824. Copy.
9. Mr. Adams to Mr. Addington, December 4, 1824. Copy.

No. 1.

Message from the President of the United States, transmitting a convention between the United States and Great Britain for the suppression of the slave trade.

,IN SENATE, *Friday, April 30, 1824.*

The following written message was received from the President of the United States by Mr. Everett, his Secretary:

[For this message and documents see No. 379.|

IN SENATE, SATURDAY, *May 8, 1824.*

Mr. Barbour, from the Committee on Foreign Relations, to whom was referred, on the 30th April, the message of the President of the United States of that date, together with the convention with Great Britain, reported the same without amendment. The said convention was read the second time.

WEDNESDAY, *May 12, 1824.*

The Senate proceeded to consider, as in Committee of the Whole, the convention with Great Britain, concluded at London the 13th of March, 1824; and, *Ordered,* That it lie on the table.

TUESDAY, *May 13, 1824.*

The Senate resumed, as in Committee of the Whole, the consideration of the convention between the United States and Great Britain, and Mr. Barbour proposed the following amendment thereto; which was read:

"Article XII. This convention shall continue in force until one of the parties shall have declared its intention to renounce it; which declaration shall be made at least six months beforehand."

MONDAY, *May 17, 1824.*

The Senate resumed, as in Committee of the Whole, the consideration of the convention with Great Britain, together with the amendment proposed on the 13th instant; and, on motion, *Ordered,* That the further consideration thereof be postponed to and made the order of the day for Wednesday next.

IN SENATE OF THE UNITED STATES, MAY 21, 1824.

Message from the President of the United States.

[For this message see No. 374.]

Extract of a report of the 9th of February, 1821, to the House of Representatives, by the Committee to whom had been referred so much of the President's message as relates to the slave trade, and to whom were referred the two messages of the President, transmitting, in pursuance of the resolution of the House of Representatives of the 4th of December, a report of the Secretary of State and inclosed documents relating to the negotiation for the suppression of the slave trade.

[For this report see No. 346.]

Extract from a report made April 12, 1822, by the Committee on the suppression of the slave trade, to whom had been referred a resolution of the House of Representatives of the 15th of January preceding, instructing them to inquire whether the laws of the United States prohibiting that traffic have been duly executed; also, into the general operation thereof; and, if any defects exist in those laws, to suggest adequate remedies therefor, and to whom many memorials have been referred touching the same subject.

[For this report see No. 351.]

Mr. Addington to the Secretary of State.

WASHINGTON, *May 16, 1824.*

[For this letter see No. 374.]

IN SENATE, FRIDAY, *May* 21, 1824.

Agreeably to the order of the day, the Senate resumed, as in Committee of the Whole, the considera. tion of the convention with Great Britain, together with the amendment proposed on the 13th instant; and the amendment having been modified, as follows:

Provided, That an article be added, whereby it shall be free to either of the parties, at any time, to renounce the said convention, giving six months' notice beforehand:

On the question to agree thereto, it was determined in the affirmative, yeas 36, nays 2.

Those who voted in the affirmative are Messrs. Barbour, Barton, Bell, Benton, Branch, Brown, Clayton, Eaton, Edwards, Elliott, Findlay, Gaillard, Hayne, Holmes, of Maine, Holmes, of Mississippi, Jackson, Johnson, of Kentucky, Henry Johnson, Josiah S. Johnston, Kelly, King, of Alabama, King, of New York, Knight, Lloyd, of Massachusetts, Lowrie, McIlvaine, Macon, Mills, Palmer, Parrott, Ruggles, Seymour, Taylor, of Virginia, Thomas, Van Dyke, and Williams.

Those who voted in the negative are Messrs. Chandler and D'Wolf.

And no further amendment having been made, the convention was reported to the Senate.

On the question to concur in the amendment made in Committee of the Whole, to wit:

Insert at the end of the resolution for the ratification of the convention—

Provided, That an article be added, whereby it shall be free to either of the parties, at any time, to renounce the said convention, giving six months' notice beforehand,

It was determined in the affirmative, yeas 34, nays 2.

Those who voted in the affirmative are Messrs. Barbour, Barton, Bell, Benton, Branch, Brown, Clayton, Eaton, Edwards, Elliott, Findlay, Gaillard, Hayne, Holmes, of Mississippi, Jackson, Johnson, of Kentucky, Josiah S. Johnston, Kelly, King, of Alabama, King, of New York, Knight, Lloyd, of Massachusetts, Lowrie, McIlvaine, Macon, Mills, Parrott, Ruggles, Seymour, Taylor, of Virginia, Thomas, Van Dyke, and Williams.

Those who voted in the negative are Messrs. Chandler and D'Wolf.

Ordered, That the convention pass to a third reading.

SATURDAY, *May* 22, 1824.

The convention with Great Britain was read the third time. Whereupon Mr. Barbour submitted the following motion for consideration, which was read:

Resolved, Two-thirds of the senators present concurring therein, That the Senate do advise and consent to the ratification of the convention made and concluded at London the thirteenth day of March, one thousand eight hundred and twenty-four, between the United States of America and the King of the United Kingdom of Great Britain and Ireland: *Provided*, That an article be added, whereby it shall be free to either of the parties, at any time, to renounce the said convention, giving six months' notice beforehand.

On motion by Mr. Macon, to postpone the further consideration of the convention to the first Monday in December next, it was determined in the negative, yeas 16, nays 26. The yeas and nays being desired by one-fifth of the senators present—

Those who voted in the affirmative are Messrs. Bell, Brown, Chandler, D'Wolf, Dickerson, Elliott, Gaillard, Holmes, of Maine, Knight, Lowrie, Macon, Ruggles, Smith, Thomas, Van Buren, and Ware.

Those who voted in the negative are Messrs. Barbour, Barton, Benton, Branch, Clayton, Eaton, Edwards, Findlay, Hayne, Holmes, of Mississippi, Jackson, Johnson, of Kentucky, Henry Johnson, Josiah S. Johnston, Kelly, King, of New York, Lloyd, of Massachusetts, McIlvaine, Mills, Noble, Parrott, Seymour, Taylor, of Indiana, Taylor, of Virginia, Van Dyke, and Williams.

On motion by Mr. Josiah S. Johnston, to strike out of the convention, article 1, line 1, the words "of America," on the question, "Shall these words stand as part of the article?" it was determined in the negative, yeas 23, nays 20.

Those who voted in the affirmative are Messrs. Barbour, Barton, Clayton, Eaton, Edwards, Findlay, Hayne, Holmes, of Mississippi, Jackson, Johnson, of Kentucky, Henry Johnson, Kelly, King, of New York, Lloyd, of Massachusetts, McIlvaine, Mills, Noble, Parrott, Seymour, Taylor, of Indiana, Taylor, of Virginia, Van Dyke, and Williams.

Those who voted in the negative are Messrs. Bell, Benton, Branch, Brown, Chandler, D'Wolf, Dickerson, Elliott, Gaillard, Holmes, of Maine, Josiah S. Johnston, King, of Alabama, Knight, Lowrie, Macon, Ruggles, Smith, Thomas, Van Buren, and Ware.

On motion by Mr. Josiah S. Johnston, to strike out, article 1, line 5, the words "and of the West Indies"—

On the question, "Shall these words stand as part of the article?" it was determined in the affirmative, yeas 29, nays 14.

Those who voted in the affirmative are Messrs. Barbour, Barton, Benton, Brown, Clayton, Eaton, Edwards, Findlay, Hayne, Holmes, of Mississippi, Jackson, Johnson, of Kentucky, Henry Johnson, Kelly, King, of New York, Knight, Lloyd, of Massachusetts, Lowrie, McIlvaine, Macon, Mills, Noble, Parrott, Ruggles, Seymour, Taylor, of Indiana, Taylor, of Virginia, Van Dyke, and Williams.

Those who voted in the negative are Messrs. Bell, Branch, Chandler, D'Wolf, Dickerson, Elliott, Gaillard, Holmes, of Maine, Josiah S. Johnston, Smith, Thomas, Van Buren, and Ware.

A motion was made by Mr. Josiah S. Johnston to strike out the second article, and on the question, "Will the Senate advise and consent to the ratification of this article?" it was determined in the negative, yeas 27, nays 16.

Those who voted in the affirmative are Messrs. Barbour, Barton, Benton, Branch, Clayton, Eaton, Edwards, Findlay, Hayne, Holmes, of Mississippi, Jackson, Johnson, of Kentucky, Henry Johnson, Kelly, King, of New York, Knight, Lloyd, of Massachusetts, M'Ilvaine, Mills, Noble, Parrott, Ruggles, Seymour, Taylor, of Indiana, Taylor, of Virginia, Van Dyke, and Williams.

Those who voted in the negative are Messrs. Bell, Brown, Chandler, D'Wolf, Dickerson, Elliott, Gaillard, Holmes, of Maine, J. S. Johnston, King, of Alabama, Lowrie, Macon, Smith, Thomas, Van Buren, and Ware.

On motion to strike out of the 7th article the following words:

"And it is further agreed that any individual, being a citizen or subject of either of the two contracting parties, who shall be found on board any vessel not carrying the flag of the other party, nor belonging to the subjects or citizens of either, but engaged in the illicit traffic of slaves, and seized or condemned on that account by the cruisers of the other party, under circumstances which, by involving such individual in the guilt of slave trading, would subject him to the penalties of piracy,.he shall be sent for trial before the competent court in the country to which he belongs, and the reasonable expenses of any witnesses belonging to the captured vessel, in proceeding to the place of trial, during their detention there, and for their return to their own country, or to their station in its service, shall, in every such case be allowed by the court and defrayed by the country in which the trial takes place:"

On the question, "Shall these words stand as part of the article?" it was determined in the negative, yeas 22; nays 21.

Those who voted in the affirmative are Messrs. Barton, Benton, Clayton, Eaton, Edwards, Findlay, Hayne, Holmes, of Mississippi, Jackson, Johnson, of Kentucky, Henry Johnson, Kelly, King, of New York, Knight, M'Ilvaine, Mills, Noble, Parrott, Seymour, Taylor, of Virginia, Van Dyke, and Williams.

Those who voted in the negative are Messrs. Barbour, Bell, Branch, Brown, Chandler, D'Wolf, Dickerson, Elliott, Gaillard, Holmes, of Maine, Josiah S. Johnston, King, of Alabama, Lloyd, of Massachusetts, Lowrie, Macon, Ruggles, Smith, Taylor, of Indiana, Thomas, Van Buren, and Ware.

On the question to agree to the resolution, amended accordingly, for the ratification of the convention, it was determined in the affirmative, yeas 29, nays 13.

Those who voted in the affirmative are Messrs. Barbour, Barton, Benton, Branch, Brown, Clayton, Eaton, Edwards, Findlay, Hayne, Holmes, of Mississippi, Jackson, Johnson, of Kentucky, Henry Johnson, Josiah S. Johnston, Kelly, King, of Alabama, King, of New York, Knight, Lloyd, of Massachusetts, Lowrie, M'Ilvaine, Mills, Parrott, Seymour, Taylor, of Indiana, Taylor, of Virginia, Van Dyke, and Williams.

Those who voted in the negative are Messrs. Bell, Chandler, D'Wolf, Dickerson, Elliott, Gaillard, Holmes, of Maine, Macon, Ruggles, Smith, Thomas, Van Buren, and Ware.

So it was resolved, two-thirds of the senators present concurring therein, That the Senate do advise and consent to the ratification of the convention made and concluded at London the thirteenth day of March, one thousand eight hundred and twenty-four, between the United States of America and the King of the United Kingdom of Great Britain and Ireland, with the exception of the words "of America," in line four of the first article, with the exception of the second article, and of the following words in the seventh article: "And it is further agreed that any individual, being a citizen or subject of either of the two contracting parties, who shall be found on board any vessel not carrying the flag of the other party, nor belonging to the subjects or citizens of either, but engaged in the illicit traffic of slaves, and seized or condemned on that account by the cruisers of the other party, under circumstances which, by involving such individual in the guilt of slave trading, would subject him to the penalties of piracy, he shall be sent for trial before the competent court in the country to which he belongs, and the reasonable expenses of any witnesses belonging to the captured vessel, in proceeding to the place of trial, during their detention there, and for their return to their own country, or to their station in its service, shall, in every such case, be allowed by the court and defrayed by the country in which the trial takes place:" *Provided,* That an article be added, whereby it shall be free to either of the parties, at any time, to renounce the said convention, giving six months' notice beforehand.

No. 2.

Mr. Adams to Mr. Rush.

DEPARTMENT OF STATE, *Washington, May 29,* 1824.

SIR: The convention between the United States and Great Britain for the suppression of the African slave trade is herewith transmitted to you, with the ratification on the part of the United States, under certain modifications and exceptions, annexed as conditions to the advice and consent of the Senate to its ratification.

The participation of the Senate of the United States in the final conclusion of all treaties, to which they are parties, is already well known to the British Government; and the novelty of the principles established by the convention, as well as their importance, and the requisite assent of two-thirds of the senators present to the final conclusion of every part of the ratified treaty, will explain the causes of its ratification under this form. It will be seen that the great and essential principles which form the basis of the compact are admitted, to their full extent, in the ratified part of the convention. The second article, and the portion of the seventh which it is proposed to expunge, are unessential to the plan, and were not included in the project of convention transmitted to you from hence. They appear, indeed, to be, so far as concerned the United States, altogether inoperative, since they could not confer the power of capturing slave traders under the flag of a third party,—a power not claimed either by the United States or Great Britain, unless by treaty, and the United States having no such treaty with any other power. It is presumed that the bearing of those articles was exclusively upon the flags of those other nations with which Great Britain has already treaties for the suppression of the slave trade, and that, while they give an effective power to the officers of Great Britain, they conferred none upon those of the United States.

The exception of the coast of America from the seas upon which the mutual power of capturing the vessels under the flag of either party may be exercised had reference, in the views of the Senate, doubtless, to the coast of the United States. On no part of that coast, unless within the Gulf of Mexico, is there any probability that slave-trading vessels will ever be found. The necessity for the exercise of the authority to capture is, therefore, no greater than it would be upon the coast of Europe. In South America, the only coast to which slave traders may be hereafter expected to resort, is. that of Brazil, from which it is to be hoped they will shortly be expelled by the laws of the country.

The limitation by which each party is left at liberty to renounce the convention, by six months' notice to the other, may, perhaps, be useful in reconciling other nations to the adoption of its provisions. If the principles of the convention are to be permanently maintained, this limitation must .undoubtedly be abandoned; and when the public mind shall have been familiarized to the practical operation of the system, it is not doubted that this reservation will, on all sides, be readily given up.

In giving these explanations to the British Government, you will state that the President was fully prepared to have ratified the convention without alteration as it had been signed by you. He is aware that the conditional ratification leaves the British Government at liberty to concur therein or to decline the ratification altogether, but he will not disguise the wish that, such as it is, it may receive the sanction of Great Britain and be carried into effect. When the concurrence of both Governments has been at length obtained, by exertions so long and so anxiously continued, to principles so important and for purposes of so high and honorable a character, it would prove a severe disappointment to the friends of freedom and of humanity if all prospect of effective concert between the two nations for the extirpation of this disgrace to civilized man should be lost by differences of sentiment, in all probability transient, upon unessential details.

Should the convention, as ratified on the part of the United States, be likewise ratified on the part of Great Britain, you will exchange the ratifications and forthwith transmit the British ratified copy to this place. On exchanging the ratifications, a certificate of that act is usually executed under the hand and seal of the persons performing it and mutually delivered. A copy of the form of that used in exchanging the ratifications of the convention of 20th October, 1818, is herewith inclosed, and it appears to be the form generally used on such occasions by the British Government. You will transmit the certificate exchanged with the British ratification. To complete the documents belonging to the negotiation, a copy of the full power of the British plenipotentiaries and of the protocol of the third conference are yet to be forwarded to us.

By the ninth article of the convention it is provided that copies of it "and of the laws of both countries, actually in force, for the prohibition and suppression of the slave trade shall be furnished to every commander of the national vessels of either party charged with the execution of those laws." The fulfilment of this article will require the continued and particular attention of both Governments. I inclose, herewith, a printed pamphlet containing all the laws of the United States on this subject now in force. It is stated in your despatches to have been the intention of the British Government to consolidate into one act, during the present session of Parliament, all the British laws relating to the subject; and perhaps Congress, at their next session, may deem it expedient to do the same here. At all events, you will not fail to forward to me a copy of all the laws in force which come within the purview of the convention; and although not expressly stipulated in that instrument, you will suggest to the British Government that copies of the *instructions* relating to this object, given by each of the parties to its own naval officers, should be communicated to the other and furnished to all the officers, on either side, intrusted with the execution of the laws made by this convention common to both. Lists of the vessels of either party, and of their commanders, thus instructed, might also facilitate the accomplishment of the great purposes of both, and harmonize the practical operation of a system not less important by the magnanimous end to be obtained than by the novelty of the means adopted for its accomplishment.

The conclusion of this convention has been highly satisfactory to the President, whose entire approbation of the course pursued by you in the negotiation of it I am instructed to make known to you. He indulges the hope that it will, even as now modified, contribute largely to two objects of high importance: to the friendly relations between the two countries, and to the general interests of humanity. He sees in it, with much pleasure, that spirit of mutual accommodation so essential to the continuance and promotion of their harmony and good understanding, and welcomes it as an earnest of the same spirit in accomplishing the adjustment of the other interesting objects in negotiation between the two parties.

I am, with great respect, sir, your very humble and obedient servant,

JOHN QUINCY ADAMS.

Hon. Richard Rush, *Envoy Extraordinary and Minister Plenipotentiary United States, London.*

No. 3.

Extract of a letter from Mr. Rush to Mr. Adams, dated

London, *June* 28, 1824.

"I have this day had the honor to receive your despatch, No. 79, of the 29th of May, with the convention for the suppression of the slave trade, as ratified on the part of the United States, under certain modifications and exceptions, annexed as conditions to the advice and consent of the Senate to its ratification.

"I shall proceed immediately to lay the convention, as thus ratified, before this Government, and endeavor to recommend to its acceptance the modifications and exceptions, now a part of the instrument, by all the suggestions and arguments with which your despatch has supplied me."

No. 4.

Extract of a letter from Mr. Rush to Mr. Adams, dated

London, *July* 5, 1824.

"I have had one interview with Mr. Secretary Canning since the 28th of last month on the business of the convention for the suppression of the slave trade, but as yet am not able to communicate any of the sentiments of this Government in relation to it. You shall hear them from me at the earliest moment after I am myself apprised of them."

No. 5.

Extracts of a letter from Mr. Rush to Mr. Adams, dated

LONDON, *August* 9, 1824.

"I have the honor to inform you that Mr. Secretary Canning has given me to understand, in an interview which I have this day had with him, that this Government finds itself unable to accede to the convention for the suppression of the slave trade, with the alterations and modifications that have been annexed to its ratification on the part of the United States. He said that none of these alterations or modifications would have formed insuperable bars to the consent of Great Britain, except that which had expunged the word America from the first article, but that this was considered insuperable."

"The reasons which Mr. Canning assigned for this determination on the part of Great Britain I forbear to state, as he has promised to address a communication in writing to me upon the subject, where they will be seen more accurately and at large; but to guard against any delay in my receiving that communication, I have thought it right not to lose any time in thus apprising you, for the President's information, of the result."

No. 6.

No. 11.]   *Mr. Rush to Mr. Adams.*

LONDON, *August* 30, 1824.

SIR: I had the honor to apprise you in my letter of the 9th instant that Mr. Secretary Canning had informed me, in an interview that I had with him on that day, that this Government would decline acceding to the convention for the suppression of the slave trade as ratified on the part of the United States, and that he promised to address me an official note upon this subject. This note I received on Saturday the 28th instant, the delay having arisen from an attack of fever under which he has been laboring. A copy of it is herewith inclosed.

I lost no time after receiving your instructions of the 29th of May in laying the matter of them before Mr. Canning, having, on the 30th of June, written him a note to request an interview for the purpose of executing this duty, which he granted me at the Foreign Office, on the first of July. It was in that interview that I laid fully before him all the considerations and arguments for the adoption of the treaty as ratified at Washington, with which your above instructions had charged me, omitting no part of them. He gave no opinion at that time on the course which this Government would be likely to pursue, but afterwards, on the 9th of August, informed me, as I have heretofore mentioned, that the omission of the words "and America," from the first article of the treaty, was considered by Great Britain as an insuperable objection to its acceptance on her part, and to this effect is the note which I now transmit from him. A copy of my answer to it, dated to-day, is inclosed.

It may be proper for me to state, that, whilst Mr. Canning, in the interview I had with him on the ninth of August, was assigning the reasons of this Government, as they will now be seen in his note, for not acceding to the treaty, took occasion to remark that Great Britain would be willing to give to the omitted words a meaning that would restrict their operation to the southern portion of North America as proximate to the British West Indies, excluding the range of coast which comprehended the middle and northern States, if I thought that such a plan would be acceptable to my Government. I immediately and most decidedly discountenanced such a proposition as objectionable under every view. He replied, that, having no other object in making the intimation than that of preventing the treaty from falling through, and not knowing himself in what light it might be received, he had, of course, nothing more to say, after learning from me that it would be objectionable.

I avail myself of this opportunity to forward to you a copy of the act of the last session of Parliament for consolidating the laws of this realm for the abolition of the slave trade, as requested in your communication of the 29th of May.

I have the honor to remain, &c.,

RICHARD RUSH.

Hon. JOHN QUINCY ADAMS, *Secretary of State.*

No. 6, (*a.*)

Mr. George Canning to Mr. Rush.

FOREIGN OFFICE, *August* 27, 1824.

SIR: In pursuance of what I stated to you in our late conference, I have now the honor to address you on the subject of the qualified ratification, on the part of your Government, of the treaty for the more effectual suppression of the slave trade, which was concluded and signed in the month of March last by you and his Majesty's plenipotentiaries.

His Majesty's Government have given the most anxious and deliberate consideration to this subject, and if the result of that consideration has been to decide that they cannot advise his Majesty to accept the American ratification, (notwithstanding the arguments alleged by you, in the name of your Government, in favor of such acceptance,) I entreat you to believe it is not from any diminished sense of the importance of the matter to which that treaty relates.

Nor do they at all underrate the desire which, as you have assured me, and as they really believe, was felt by the President of the United States to adopt the provisions of the treaty, such as it was transmitted to America. But the result is not the less inconvenient.

A treaty of which the basis was laid in propositions framed by the American Government was considered here as so little likely to be made a subject of renewed discussion in America that not a moment was lost in ratifying it, on the part of his Majesty; and his Majesty's ratification was ready to be exchanged against that of the United States when the treaty came back; not as it had been sent to America, but with material variations: variations not confined to those stipulations or parts of stipulations which had been engrafted upon the original projet, but extending to that part of the original projet itself which had passed unchanged through the negotiation.

The knowledge that the Constitution of the United States renders all their diplomatic compacts liable to this sort of revision undoubtedly precludes the possibility of taking exception at any particular instance in which that revision is exercised; but the repetition of such instances does not serve to reconcile to the practice the feelings of the other contracting party whose solemn ratification is thus rendered of no avail, and whose concessions in negotiation having been made (as all such concessions must be understood to be made) conditionally, are thus accepted as positive and absolute, while what may have been the stipulated price of those concessions is withdrawn.

In the instance before us the question is not one merely of form. A substantial change is made in the treaty, and, as I have said, on a point originally proposed by yourself, sir, as the American plenipotentiary, and understood to be proposed by the special direction of your Government.

The right of visiting vessels suspected of slave trading, when extended alike to the West Indies and *to the coast of America*, implied an equality of vigilance, and did not necessarily imply the existence of grounds of suspicion on either side.

The removal of this right as to the coast of America, and its continuance to the West Indies, cannot but appear to imply the existence on one side and not on the other of a just ground either of suspicion of misconduct, or for apprehension of an abuse of authority.

To such an equality, leading to such an inference, his Majesty's Government can never advise his Majesty to consent. It would have been rejected if proposed in the course of negotiation. It can still less be admitted as a new demand after the conclusion of the treaty.

With the exception of this proposed omission, there is nothing in the alterations made by the Senate of the United States in the treaty (better satisfied, as his Majesty's Government undoubtedly would have been if they had not been made,) which his Majesty's Government would not rather agree to adopt than suffer the hope of good to which this arrangement had given rise to be disappointed.

Upon this omission they trust the Senate of the United States will, on another consideration of the subject, see that it is not equitable to insist.

A full power will therefore be sent to Mr. Addington, his Majesty's Chargé d'Affaires at Washington, to conclude and sign, with any plenipotentiary to be appointed by the American Government, a treaty *verbatim* the same as the returned treaty would be with all the alterations introduced into it by the Senate, excepting only the proposed omission of the words "and America," in the first article; which treaty, if transmitted to England with the ratification of the Government of the United States, his Majesty will be ready to ratify.

But I am to apprise you, sir, that his Majesty will not be advised to appoint plenipotentiaries to conclude and sign the like treaty *here*, to be, as before, ratified by his Majesty and to be again subjected, after ratification by his Majesty, to alterations by the Senate of the United States.

I am confident that you will see in this distinction nothing more than a reasonable safeguard for his Majesty's dignity and a just desire to ascertain, before his Majesty again ratifies a diplomatic instrument, to what conditions that ratification is affixed.

I have the honor to be, with the highest consideration, sir, your most obedient servant,

GEORGE CANNING.

Hon. RICHARD RUSH, &c.

No. 6, *(b.)*

Mr. Rush to Mr. G. Canning.

LONDON, *August* 30, 1824.

SIR; I had the honor to receive, on the 28th instant, your note of the 2d of this month, giving me information that his Britannic Majesty's Government have declined, for the reasons you have enumerated, advising his Majesty to accept the ratification by the President and Senate of the United States of the treaty for the suppression of the slave trade, lately signed on behalf of the two powers, in manner and form as that ratification had been made known by me to his Majesty's Government.

Having already, sir, had the honor to lay before you all the reasons that operated with my Government for giving way to the desire and the hope that his Majesty's Government might have felt able to accept the treaty with the alterations introduced by the Senate as conditions of its ratification, I have only to express my regret at the disappointment of this hope.

All power over the instrument on my part, as the plenipotentiary of the United States at his Majesty's court, ceasing by this decision, it only remains for me to say that I will, with promptitude, transmit to my Government a copy of your note, at which source it will receive, I am sure, all the attention due to the high interests of which it treats.

I have the honor to be, with distinguished consideration, sir, your most obedient servant,

RICHARD RUSH.

The Right Honorable GEORGE CANNING,
  His Majesty's Principal Secretary of State for Foreign Affairs.

No. 7.

No. 82.]   *Mr. Adams to Mr. Rush.*

DEPARTMENT OF STATE, *Washington, November* 12, 1824.

SIR: Your despatches to Nos. 395 and 12, inclusive, have been received. The proposal for the negotiation of a new convention for the suppression of the slave trade will receive the deliberate consideration of the President.

It is observed with regret that the reasons assigned in Mr. Secretary Canning's letter of August 27 to you, as having induced the British Government to decline the ratification of that which you had signed, as modified by the advice and consent of the Senate of the United States, appear to have arisen from impressions altogether erroneous. It is stated that, under the expectation that the treaty would not be made a subject of renewed discussion in the United States, it had actually been ratified on the part of the British Government as at first concluded; and hence an argument of inconvenience is deduced that a second and qualified ratification could not be given without impairing the dignity of the Government, by the implication that the former ratification had been an act of the sovereign performed in vain.

To give weight to this reasoning, it would seem an essential part of the facts that the ratification alluded to had been transmitted to the United States, or at least that it was known to have taken place by the Government of the United States at the time when the convention came under the consideration of the Senate. This, however, was not the case. That it had been ratified in Great Britain was neither known nor believed. It appears to have been an act altogether voluntary, and in nowise referring to that which was expected on the part of the United States. The argument, therefore, rests upon facts other than those which were really applicable to the subject.

While admitting that the knowledge of those provisions of our Constitution which reserve to the Senate the right of revising all treaties with foreign powers, before they can obtain the force of law, precludes the possibility of taking exception to any particular instance in which that revision is exercised, Mr. Canning urges that this part of our system operates unfavorably upon the feelings of the other contracting party, whose solemn ratification, he says, is thus rendered of no avail, and whose concessions in negotiation, having been made (as all such concessions must be understood to be made) conditionally, are thus accepted as positive and absolute, while what may have been the stipulated price of those concessions is withdrawn.

It may be replied, that, in all cases of a treaty thus negotiated, the other contracting party being under no obligation to ratify the compact before it shall have been ascertained whether and in what manner it has been disposed of in the United States, its ratification can in no case be rendered unavailing by the proceedings of the Government of the United States upon the treaty; and that every Government contracting with the United States, and with a full knowledge that all their treaties, until sanctioned by the constitutional majority of their Senate are, and must be, considered as merely inchoate and not consummated compacts, is entirely free to withhold its own ratification until it shall have knowledge of the ratification on their part. In the full powers of European Governments to their ministers, the sovereign usually *promises* to ratify that which his minister shall conclude in his name; and yet, if the minister transcends his instructions, though not known to the other party, the sovereign is not held bound to ratify his engagements. Of this principle Great Britain has once availed herself in her negotiations with the United States. But the full powers of our ministers abroad are necessarily modified by the provisions of our Constitution, and promise the ratification of treaties signed by them only in the event of their receiving the constitutional sanction of our own Government.

If this arrangement does in some instances operate as a slight inconvenience to other Governments, by interposing an obstacle to the *facility* of negotiation, it is, on the other hand, essential to guard against evils of the deepest import to our own nation utterly incompatible with the genius of our institutions; and it is supported by considerations to which the equitable sense of other nations cannot fail to subscribe.

The treaties of the United States are, together with their Constitution, the supreme law of the land. The power of contracting them is, in the first instance, given to the President, a single individual. If negotiated abroad, it must be by a minister or ministers under his appointment; and if in Europe, with powers largely discretionary—the distances seldom permitting opportunities to the minister of consulting his Government for instructions during the progress of negotiation. Were there no other check or control over this power, and were there an obligation, even of delicacy, requiring the unqualified sanction of every treaty so negotiated, the result would be an authority possessed by every minister of the United States entrusted with a full power for negotiating a treaty to change the laws of this Union upon objects of the first magnitude to the interests of the nation.

In their negotiations with each other, the European nations are generally so near, and the communications between them are so easy and regular, that a negotiator can seldom have a justifiable occasion to agree to any important stipulation without having an opportunity of asking and receiving the instructions of his Government; a practice always and peculiarly resorted to by British plenipotentiaries. With an intervening ocean, this is seldom possible; and it is, therefore, just and proper that the right of judgment upon all the stipulations agreed to by a minister should be reserved in the most unqualified manner to *both* Governments parties to the treaty, and that every compact so negotiated should be understood to be signed by the minister *remote* from his own country only *sub spe rati;* not conclusive upon his nation until its Government shall have passed sentence of approbation upon it.

These general observations are submitted in order that you may make such use of them as you shall deem expedient to satisfy the British Government that in this established principle of our Constitution there is nothing to which any foreign Government can justly take exception, and that it only reserves to our Government a power of supervision necessary for our own safety which the European Governments effectively reserve to themselves, and none more cautiously than Great Britain.

I am, with great respect, sir, your very humble and obedient servant,

JOHN QUINCY ADAMS.

Hon. R. RUSH, *Envoy, &c., London.*

No. 8.

Mr. Addington to Mr. Adams.

WASHINGTON, *November* 6, 1824.

SIR: You have already been apprised of the circumstance of his Majesty, my sovereign, having declined affixing his ratification to the convention concluded in London on the 13th of March last, between the British and American plenipotentiaries, for the more effectual suppression of the slave trade, amended and qualified as that instrument had been by the Senate of the United States.

In lieu of that convention, however, his Majesty proposes to the American Government to substitute another, *verbatim* the same as the amended instrument, one point alone excepted. That exception is the erasure of the word "America," in the first article, a word which stood in the original projet of the article as proposed by the President to the British Government, but which the United States thought fit, after the mutual acquiescence of both parties in it, to expunge.

In announcing to you the fact of my having been furnished with full powers to conclude and sign with the American Government a new treaty, such as I have above described, it will be unnecessary for me to enter at length into the motives which have actuated his Majesty in coming to this decision, as you have already been made acquainted with those motives through the medium of an official letter addressed on the 27th of August last by his Majesty's Secretary of State to the American Envoy in London, in which all the grounds of that determination are fully expounded.

A few observations on my part, however, in brief allusion to one or two points connected with this subject, may here be not misplaced.

In the acquiescence of his Majesty in all the alterations, with one only exception, effected by the Senate in a treaty originally projected by this Government at the spontaneous recommendation of the House of Representatives, the President will, I doubt not, see the clearest manifestation of the earnest desire of his Majesty's Government to carry into effect the important and salutary object for which that treaty was designed, however they may have deemed the original form in which the treaty was presented for the ratification of this Government the best calculated to attain that object.

To the amendment which would exempt the shores of America from that vigilance which is to be employed on those of the British West Indies, thereby destroying that equality which is the prevailing principle of the provisions of the treaty, and which cannot be withdrawn on the one side or on the other consistently with the mutual respect and confidence which subsist between the two contracting parties, his Majesty has found himself unable to accede; and I doubt not that, upon a fair and unbiassed reconsideration of that point, the American Government will see and acknowledge the justice of his Majesty's views, and will not hesitate to prove that acknowledgment by consenting to re-admit the expunged word "America" into the treaty.

It will not fail, sir, to occur to you that the condition required of Great Britain prior to the signature of the treaty by the American plenipotentiary, namely, the denunciation as piracy by the British Parliament of the slave trade, when exercised by British subjects, has already been fulfilled.

On the justice of accepting the value already paid for a stipulated act, and withholding the performance of that act, I leave it with confidence to your own sense of honor and equity to determine.

The sanction of this Government of the *original* provisions of the treaty in *full* was the equivalent to be received by his Majesty for his performance of the condition required of him, namely, his sanction of an act of Parliament declaring the slave trade piracy. Those provisions have been in part rejected, in part modified by this Government, and yet his Majesty is still willing to abide by his original agreement, provided this Government will recede from one alone of the various amendments made by them in the treaty.

I might here cite as a proof, if proof were necessary, of the unlimited confidence which his Majesty reposed in the good faith of the Government of this republic, and their sincerity in wishing to execute the treaty signed by their plenipotentiary in London—a treaty, I repeat, projected in conformity with the express recommendation of the House of Representatives, that his Majesty affixed without delay his own ratification to the treaty, in the full security of that instrument being equally invested with that of this Government. No shadow of a suspicion ever entered, ever *could* enter, his Majesty's mind that that ratification could be withheld in whole or in part.

Under all the circumstances of the case, sir, I cannot but feel an entire conviction that the sense of justice and the right feelings which animate the American Government will lead them to accede without hesitation to the proposition now submitted to them on the part of his Majesty, and that the President will find no difficulty in sanctioning the conclusion of a treaty the provisions of which must eventually result in such incalculable benefits to a most oppressed and afflicted portion of the human race.

With this conviction I need not assure you, sir, of my readiness to wait upon you at any time which you may think fit to appoint, in order to give effect to the instructions which I have received from his Majesty's Secretary of State, by affixing my signature to the convention as newly modelled.

I beg, sir, that you will receive the assurances of my distinguished consideration.

H. U. ADDINGTON

No. 9.

Secretary of State to Mr. Addington.

DEPARTMENT OF STATE, *Washington, December* 4, 1824.

SIR: Your note of the 6th ultimo has been submitted to the consideration of the President of the United States. While regretting that it has not been found conformable to the views of his Britannic Majesty's Government to concur in the ratification of the convention for the suppression of the slave trade, as recommended by the advice and consent of the Senate of the United States, he has thought it most advisable, with reference to the success of the object common to both Governments, and in which both take the warmest interest, to refer the whole subject to the deliberate advisement of Congress. In postponing, therefore, a definitive answer to the proposal set forth in your note, I have only to renew the assurance of the unabated earnestness with which the Government of the United States looks to the accomplishment of the common purpose, the entire extinction of that odious traffic, and to the concert of effective measures to that end between the United States and Great Britain.

I pray you, sir, to accept the assurance of my distinguished consideration.

JOHN QUINCY ADAMS.

CORRESPONDENCE WITH SPAIN RELATIVE TO AFFAIRS UNDER DISCUSSION WITH THAT COUNTRY.

COMMUNICATED TO CONGRESS WITH THE MESSAGE OF THE PRESIDENT OF DECEMBER 7, 1824.

[See No. 378.]

List of papers sent.

No. 1. Mr. Adams to Mr. Forsyth, (No. 16,) June 13, 1821, (copy.)
No. 2. Same to same, (No. 17,) June 16, 1821, (copy.)
No. 3. Same to same, (No. 18,) June 18, 1821, (copy.)
No. 4. Same to same, (No. 20,) June 20, 1821, (copy.)
No. 5. Mr. Brent to same, September 25, 1821, (copy.)
No. 6. Mr. Adams to same, (No. 21,) March 9, 1822, (copy.)
No. 7. Mr. Forsyth to Mr. Adams, (No. 38,) May 2, 1822, (extract.)
No. 8. Same to same, (No. 39,) May 20, 1822, (extract.)
No. 8, a. Mr. De la Rosa to Mr. Forsyth, May 15, 1822, (translation.)
No. 9, Mr. Adams to Mr. Forsyth, (No. 24,) June 19, 1822, (copy.)
No. 10. Mr. Forsyth to Mr. Adams, (No. 40,) June 23, 1822, (extract.)
No. 10, a. Mr. De la Rosa to Mr. Forsyth, June 21, 1822, (translation.)
No. 10, b. Mr. Forsyth to Mr. De la Rosa, June 22, 1822, (copy.)
No. 10, c. Manifesto to the courts of Europe, (translation.)
No. 11. Mr. Forsyth to Mr. Adams, (No. 41,) June 28, 1822, (extract.)
No. 12. Same to same, (No. 44,) August 26, 1822, (extract.)
No. 13. Mr. Adams to Mr. Forsyth, (No. 26,) October 23, 1822, (copy.)
No. 14. Same to same, (No. 27,) December 16, 1822, (copy.)
No. 15. Same to same, (No. 30,) January 3, 1823, (copy.)
No. 16. Mr. Appleton to Mr. Adams, March 20, 1823, (extract.)
No. 17. Mr. Anduaga to same, March 9, 1822, (translation.)
No. 18. Mr. Adams to Mr. Anduaga, April 6, 1822, (copy.)
No. 19. Mr. Anduaga to Mr. Adams, April 11, 1822, (translation.)
No. 20. Same to same, April 24, 1822, (translation.)
No. 21. Same to same, October 11, 1822, (translation.)
No. 22. Same to Mr. Meade, October 16, 1822, (translation.)
No. 23. Same to Mr. Adams, December 11, 1822, (translation.)
No. 24. Same to same, December 14, 1822, (translation.)
No. 25. Mr. Anduaga to Mr. Adams, January 6, 1823, (translation.)
No. 25, a. Note of the Secretary of Despatch of State to Mr. Forsyth, September 3, 1822, (translation.)
No. 26. Mr. Anduaga to Mr. Adams, February 23, 1823, (translation.)
No. 26, a. Mr. Daunes to Mr Anduaga, February 12, 1823, (translation.)
No. 27. Mr. Anduaga to Mr. Adams, March 6, 1823, (translation.)
No. 28. Same to same, March 7, 1823, (translation.)
No. 29. Mr. Salmon to Mr. Adams, April 15, 1823, (translation.)
No. 30. Same to same, April 28, 1823, (translation.)
No. 30, a. Testimony in the case of the Ninfa Catalana, (translation.)
No. 31. Mr. Adams to Mr. Salmon, April 29, 1823, (copy.)
No. 32. Mr. Brent to same, September 22, 1824, (copy.)
No. 33. Mr. Salmon to Mr. Brent, September 29, 1824, (translation.)
No. 33, a. Paper communicated with the above, September 19, 1824, (copy.)
No. 34. Mr. Adams to Mr. Nelson, general instructions, April 28, 1823, (extract.)
No. 35. Mr. Nelson to Mr. Adams, (No. 4,) January 15, 1824, (extract.)
No. 35, a. Same to Count Ofalia, January 10, 1821, (copy.)
No. 36. Same to Mr. Adams, (No. 35,) July 15, 1824, (extracts.)
No. 37. Same to same, (No. 39,) September 11, 1824, (extracts.)
No. 37, a. Same to Mr. de Salazar, September 7, 1824, (copy.)
No. 38. Same to Mr. Adams, (No. 42,) October 4, 1824, (extract.)
No. 39. Same to same, (No. 43,) October 12, 1824, (extract.)
No. 39, a. Same to Mr. Bermudez, October 6, 1824, (copy.)
No. 39, b. Mr. Bermudez to Mr. Nelson, October 8, 1824, (translation.)
No. 39, c. Mr. Nelson to Mr. Bermudez, October 9, 1824, (copy.)
No. 39, d. Same to same, October 12, 1824, (copy.)

No. 1.

Mr. Adams to Mr. Forsyth, No. 16.

DEPARTMENT OF STATE, *Washington, June* 13, 1821.

SIR: The hope had been entertained, after the ratification by both parties of the treaty of February 22, 1819, between the United States and Spain, that all our relations with that country would, thenceforth, have been of the most amicable character, signalized only by the interchange of good offices. It is painful to be obliged, on the return to your station at Madrid, to charge you with representations to be made to the Government of Spain relative to the unwarrantable delays by the Governor and Captain General of the island of Cuba, in taking the measures incumbent upon him for carrying the treaty into execution.

By the seventh article of the treaty the Spanish troops were to be withdrawn from the ceded territories, and possession of them was to be given of the places occupied by them within six months after the exchange of the ratifications, *or sooner if possible.* And the United States were to furnish the transports and escort necessary to convey the Spanish officers and troops, and their baggage, to the Havana.

As soon as was practicable after the exchange of the ratifications arrangements were made on the part of this Government with the view of carrying into effect these stipulations. The royal order from the King of Spain to the Captain General of the island of Cuba for the delivery of the ceded territories, and of the archives belonging to them, to the Commissioner of the United States authorized to receive them, had been transmitted with the Spanish ratification of the treaty to the minister of Spain residing here, to be delivered by him after the exchange of the ratifications. It was accordingly delivered by him. Colonel James Grant Forbes was appointed by the President to carry it to the Governor of Cuba, and commissioned to receive the orders to the Governors or commanding officers of the places within the territories for their delivery, and also the archives which were to be given up. The United States ship Hornet was despatched to the Havana with Colonel Forbes, who was instructed, on receiving them, to proceed with them, forthwith, to Pensacola, taking suitable measures for transmitting the order to the Governor of East Florida, at St. Augustine. A letter from the Spanish minister here to the Governor of Cuba was also furnished to Colonel Forbes, announcing him as the officer authorized to receive the order for delivery and the archives. General Jackson was appointed by the President Governor of East and West Florida, and was instructed to proceed immediately to Montpelier, the post within the United States nearest to Pensacola, there to await the arrival of Colonel Forbes with the necessary orders; upon which the General was directed to receive possession for the United States, and to provide for the transportation of the Spanish officers and troops, and their baggage, to the Havana; and by a liberal construction of that article of the treaty the provisions necessary for the subsistence of these officers and troops on their passage was considered as concluded within its obligation.

General Jackson reached the post of his destination on the 30th of April. On the 22d of the same month Colonel Forbes had arrived in the Hornet at the Havana; and had he been despatched without delay might have arrived at Pensacola in season for the reception of General Jackson without any unnecessary detention. The letters received at this Department from Colonel Forbes, copies of which are herewith inclosed, exhibit a series of delays on the part of the Governor for which no adequate reason is assigned, but which have already produced great public inconvenience to the United States, and which, if longer continued, will give them the most serious grounds of complaint. The last letter received from Colonel Forbes bears date the 23d of May, when his detention had already been protracted more than a month, in the interval of which the re-appearance of the disease incident to the climate excited strong apprehensions for the health of the captain and crew of the Hornet, as well as of Colonel Forbes himself. There is too much reason for the alarm with regard to Captain Reid, who is stated, by accounts of dates more recent than those officially received, to have been on the 28th of May still at the Havana, and very dangerously ill.

General Jackson, desirous of ascertaining the number of men for whom it would be necessary to procure transports and provisions, as well as to make arrangements for the supplies necessary to the troops of the United States who were to take their place, sent, on the 1st of May, Dr. Bronaugh and Judge Brackenridge to Pensacola, with a communication to Don José Callava, Governor of West Florida, to communicate to him the commission and authority with which he was clothed, and to ask of him such information as would be necessary for the arrangements adapted to the evacuation of the territory by the troops of Spain, and to the taking of possession on the part of the United States. Governor Callava declined making any such communication, declaring himself subordinate altogether to the Governor General of Cuba, and that he did not feel authorized to act at all in regard to the execution of the treaty until duly instructed to that effect by his superior officer. The letters, copies of which are inclosed, contain intimations from various sources that all these dilatory proceedings have too much connexion with private purposes and dishonorable pecuniary speculations. It is yet wished that this awkward and unpleasant state of things may, before this, have terminated; but the unreasonable delays of the Governor General of Cuba, inconsistent no less with good faith than with the good harmony which we are so desirous of cultivating with Spain, cannot be suffered to pass without animadversion. You will take the earliest opportunity after your arrival at Madrid to make suitable representations on this subject to the Spanish Government, and to state that whatever unpleasant or injurious consequences may result from this unwarrantable conduct of the Governor of Cuba must be attributed altogether to him.

By the fourth article of the treaty each of the contracting parties engages to appoint a Commissioner and surveyor, to meet, before the termination of one year from the ratification of the treaty, at Natchitoches, on the Red river, to run and mark the boundary line. Colonel McRae has been appointed the Commissioner on the part of the United States, and will be ready to proceed on the important duties of the commission as soon as the appointment of the Spanish Commissioner and surveyor shall be notified to us. It is further stipulated that the two Governments will amicably agree respecting the necessary articles to be furnished to those persons, and to their escorts, if necessary. At the time of the exchange of the ratifications, General Vives, at my request, promised to remind his Government of the necessity of an immediate appointment of the Commissioner and surveyor on their part. It is presumed this will have been done before you reach Madrid. Your attention to the subject is, nevertheless, requested, in case anything should yet remain to be done to put in train the execution of this article. As the necessary supplies for the Commissioners will be naturally best known on the scene of their operations, it is presumed the Spanish Government will authorize its minister here to agree for them to such arrangements, in this particular, as may be found necessary.

I am, with much respect, sir, your very humble and obedient servant,

JOHN QUINCY ADAMS.

Hon. John Forsyth, *Minister Plenipotentiary of the United States to Spain.*

No. 2.

Mr. Adams to Mr. Forsyth, No. 17.

DEPARTMENT OF STATE, *Washington, June 16, 1821.*

SIR: Since my letter of the 13th instant, a letter of the 28th ultimo, with inclosures, has been received from Colonel James G. Forbes, copies of which will be forwarded to you next week. By a letter of the 5th instant from Mr. Warner, our commercial agent at the Havana, we are informed that Colonel Forbes, in the Hornet, sailed for Pensacola on the 30th ultimo, and the Nonsuch for St. Augustine on the 1st instant.

It is hoped that, on the arrival of these vessels at their respective places of destination, no further vexations and unwarrantable delays will occur in the execution of the seventh article of the treaty. But Colonel Forbes has been obliged to depart without the archives and public documents which were stipulated by the treaty, and directed by the royal order to the Governor and Captain General of Cuba to be delivered over to us.

As Colonel Forbes thus appears to have been *at last* despatched, the uncertainty as to the extent of time during which this measure might be protracted has ceased, and the representation which, by my letter of the 13th instant, you were requested to make to the Spanish Government, will properly be accommodated to the circumstances as now known to us, with the complaints of delays, without the assignment of any reasonable cause, which it will yet be proper that you should prefer; a firmer confidence in the expectation that no further unnecessary postponements will occur may be expressed, but our disappointment at the detention of the archives will also require to be more explicitly signified; and it will be very desirable that you should obtain a new and peremptory order to the Governor and Captain General for the delivery of *all* the archives and documents to which we are entitled by the treaty, which will leave him no apology or pretence for either denial or procrastination.

I am, with much respect, sir, your very humble and obedient servant,

JOHN QUINCY ADAMS.

Hon. John Forsyth, *Minister Plenipotentiary of the United States to Spain.*

No. 3.

Mr. Adams to Mr. Forsyth, No. 18.

DEPARTMENT OF STATE, *Washington, June 18, 1821.*

SIR: Herewith are inclosed copies of a letter from Captain Downes, commander of the United States frigate Macedonian, to the Secretary of the Navy, together with correspondence between him and the Vice Roy of Peru, relating to certain transactions in which several persons belonging to the Macedonian lost their lives, and others were wounded; and much injury was suffered by the American schooner Rampart, for which some responsibility seems to attach to the officers and troops of Spain, if not personally to the Vice Roy.

These papers are transmitted to you that you may be in possession of the facts, and that you should make such representation of them to the Spanish Government as may be warranted by circumstances. Much of the injuries suffered by our people in this case is perhaps irreparable; but, in communicating the facts and the correspondence to the Spanish Government, without any specific or formal demand of reparation, you will avoid any form of statement which might foreclose any such demand which, upon further and more special information, may hereafter be found necessary or proper.

I am, with much respect, sir, your very humble and obedient servant,

JOHN QUINCY ADAMS.

Hon. John Forsyth, *Minister Plenipotentiary of the United States to Spain.*

No. 4.

Mr. Adams to Mr. Forsyth, No. 20.

DEPARTMENT OF STATE, *Washington, June 20, 1821.*

SIR: In a despatch received from Mr. Brent, at Madrid, dated the 23d of March last, it is observed that, as by the 20th article of the decree of the Spanish Cortes of the 6th of October last, the same tonnage duty and other charges are to be exacted from American vessels in the ports of Spain as are paid by Spanish vessels in those of the United States, he suggests the propriety of transmitting a note of the charges upon Spanish vessels here that it may be officially communicated to that Government.

The duties paid by Spanish vessels in the ports of the United States are fifty cents a ton for tonnage, and the same sum for light money. They pay none others, to which vessels of the United States are not equally subjected; but an advance of ten per cent. on the amount of duties levied upon articles the produce or manufacture of Spain, imported from Spain in vessels of the United States, is paid when they are imported in Spanish vessels.

By an act of Congress of March 3, 1815, since limited in its operation to the 1st day of January, 1824, all these discriminating duties are repealed, the repeal to take effect in favor of any foreign nation whenever the President shall be satisfied that the countervailing or discriminating duties of such foreign nation so far as they operate to the disadvantage of the United States, have been abolished.

Upon this act, if the 20th article of the decree of the Cortes of 6th of October last had stood alone the President would have issued his proclamation declaring the repeal to have taken effect from that date in favor of the vessels and produce or manufactures of Spain.

But, from your despatch of the 22d of November last, it appears that the duties payable on goods imported into Spain in foreign vessels are regulated by the decree of November 6, 1820, referring to a former regulation by which they pay one-third or 33⅓ per cent. more than in Spanish vessels—a discriminating duty more than three times heavier than ours, and under which the act of Congress of March 3, 1815, cannot take effect.

The act of March 3, 1815, being an offer made to all commercial and navigating nations, is a manifestation of the liberal spirit of Congress, which, it is hoped, when understood, the Cortes will duly appreciate. You will take a proper occasion of suggesting to the Spanish Government that, in the operation of their two decrees upon their commercial relations with us, there is an inconsistency of principle between the 20th article of the decree of the 6th of October and the 5th article of that of the 6th of November; since, while the former places the direct duty upon shipping on the fair and equitable principle of perfect reciprocity, the latter lays a heavy indirect charge upon all foreign shipping, which totally destroys the balance so accurately poised in the other. You will add that, if the Cortes will extend the principle of reciprocity to the indirect charge of one-third upon the merchandise the produce or manufacture of the two countries, respectively, the President will readily issue his proclamation, conformably to the act of March 3, 1815, and thenceforward Spanish vessels and Spanish produce or manufactures imported in them will pay no more than the vessels of the United States on the same article imported in them.

Mr. Brent has, during your absence, urged the admission of consuls of the United States in the ultra marine ports of Spain without obtaining a definitive answer. You will resume the subject immediately after your return. There appears to be no doubt that a Russian consul has been formally recognized at Manila. At the Havana our intercourse has become so great that the agency of a consul is as necessary to the convenience of the Colonial Government as to our citizens. Numbers of seamen frequent that port, who, in illness or distress, will become burdensome to the local Government itself, unless provided for by an acknowledged agent of our own.

In general, I beg leave to recommend to your particular attention our commercial relations, both with Spain and all her possessions. The effect of the recent changes by the Cortes will come more immediately under your observation than ours, and you will lose no opportunity which may present itself of removing any obstructions, or of promoting any facility or advantages to our commerce.

You will not fail to avail yourself of any opportunity which may be accessible to obtain copies of records which may throw light on the titles to possessions in the newly ceded territories, and particularly which may tend to screen the public from the imposture of false, illegal, or forfeited concessions. You are authorized to employ Mr. Rich in this service, if you think it expedient, and to charge in your accounts any reasonable expense which it may occasion.

I am, with much respect, sir, your very obedient servant,

JOHN QUINCY ADAMS.

Hon. John Forsyth, *Minister Plenipotentiary of the United States to Spain.*

No. 5.

Mr. Daniel Brent to Mr. Forsyth.

Washington, *September 25, 1821.*

Sir: I received a letter from Mr. Adams, at Boston, a few days ago, directing me to forward to you the copy inclosed, of one which he has written to General Vives upon the subject of the cannon attached to the fortifications in the Floridas, and the provisions furnished for the transportation of the Spanish garrisons, &c., to the Havana. I am sorry that I cannot send at the same time a copy of the letter of General Vives, to which this is a reply; that letter being in the hands of Mr. Adams, who is still at Boston.

You will find in the public prints which accompany this the statement of a very unpleasant occurrence at Pensacola, in the arrest and imprisonment of the ex-Governor, Callava, by the order of Governor Jackson, for refusing to deliver up some papers supposed to be interesting to individuals at Pensacola, and which were regularly demanded of him at the instance and upon the representation of the alcalde of the court, Brackenridge. Governor Jackson himself has furnished this Department with a full and particular account of the transaction, in which he states the motives and the grounds of his proceeding in it, and of that which grew out of it in relation to Judge Fromentin, which is not materially different from that taken from the Floridian, except in the exposition of the motives and grounds of his conduct. The Secretary, upon his return to this place, will probably have occasion to give you special instructions on this subject; and you will then, I presume, be furnished with the copies of all the papers connected with it.

I have the honor to be, very respectfully, sir, your obedient and humble servant,

DANIEL BRENT.

Hon. John Forsyth, *Minister Plenipotentiary of the United States, at Madrid.*

No. 6.

Mr. Adams to Mr. Forsyth, No. 21.

DEPARTMENT OF STATE, *Washington, March* 9, 1822.

SIR: Your despatches from No. 26 to No. 31, inclusive, with their inclosures, have been received.

I have now barely time to inclose with this letter the communications made by the President to Congress, during their present session, relating to our affairs with Spain. The message yesterday sent in, and which you will find in the National Intelligencer of this morning, may, perhaps, excite the attention of the Spanish Government; and should any manifestation of it be made to you, its purport will enable you to give every necessary explanation concerning it, and, particularly, that it resulted from a disposition in nowise unfriendly to Spain.

With this letter you will also receive a letter from the President to his Catholic Majesty on the recall of General Vives, which you are requested to present in the usual form.

I am, with much respect, sir, your very humble and obedient servant,

JOHN QUINCY ADAMS.

Hon. JOHN FORSYTH, *Minister Plenipotentiary of the United States, at Madrid.*

No. 7.

Extract of a letter (No. 38) from Mr. Forsyth to the Secretary of State, dated

MADRID, *May* 2, 1822.

"The President's message to Congress of the 8th of March, carried to Liverpool by the March packet from New York, was brought to this Government by a special messenger from Mr. Onis. The message was published in the French and English papers that arrived here on Monday week. On the afternoon of that day I had a casual conversation with Don F. M. de la Rosa. I asked him if he knew such a message had been sent to Congress; he replied that he had seen it in the French papers of that morning. From his mode of expressing these few words, and his suddenly shifting the conversation to an indifferent subject, I saw that this event was not expected by the ministers here, and has created great sensibility.

"You will find in the Madrid Gazette of the 29th ultimo, herewith inclosed, a circular of the Minister of War on the subject of the Spanish officers who have left the ultramarine army to return to this Peninsula. It is interesting, as, joined to other circumstances, it tends to show the determination of this Government to continue the war with some, at least, of their former provinces."

No. 8.

Extract of a letter (No. 39) from Mr. Forsyth to the Secretary of State, dated

MADRID, *May* 20, 1822.

' The King and royal family went down to Aranjuez shortly after the meeting of the Cortes; the diplomatic body made the ordinary complimentary visit on the Queen's day, and it was understood among us that we were to pay no more visits until the anniversary of the King's entrance into Madrid, on his return from France, on the 13th of this month, and St. Ferdinand's day, the 30th. Notes were written by the Secretary of State, on the 4th of April, inviting us to be present at the time of the delivery of the wife of Don Carlos; (a copy of that to me is inclosed, No. 1.) I had determined not to go; but a second note, on the 30th, (copy No. 2,) and the knowledge that all the other ministers had gone down to Aranjuez, induced me to change this determination; being unwilling, especially at this juncture, to give any room for complaint from a failure to comply with the customs of the court. I went to Aranjuez on the 5th instant. On the 7th I received a note (copy marked No. 3) to attend at the expected delivery of Don Francisco's wife. The wife of Don Francisco gave birth, on the 13th instant, to a prince. Although I had been so long at Aranjuez I received no notice to attend when the event took place. Under ordinary circumstances I should have taken it for granted that the omission was accidental, but in the present state of the relations of Spain and the United States I thought it necessary to ascertain that it was not an intended slight. I wrote, therefore, on the 13th, a note to M. de la Rosa, (copy No. 4,) to which I received a satisfactory reply, (copy No. 5.) On the 16th the other princess was delivered of a second son. I had notice, but not early enough to get to the apartment adjoining that of the princess, to witness the exhibition of the new-born babe, at which I very heartily rejoiced.

' "On the 14th instant I received your No. 21, inclosing the President's answer to the King's letter of recall of General Vives. Copies of my note to the Secretary of State and of his reply, on the subject of that letter, are inclosed, (Nos. 6 and 7.) I remained in Aranjuez until the 17th, and, agreeably to the King's wish, as communicated to me by the Secretary of State, I delivered the letter on that day.

"Nos. 8 and 9 are copies of the Secretary of State's answers to the application for a continuance of the privilege of depositing, free of duty, naval stores, &c., for the exclusive use of our squadron in the Mediterranean, at Mahon, and to that for an order in favor of American vessels coming loaded with prohibited goods to St. Sebastian's. The refusal to continue longer the privilege of deposit at Mahon was altogether unexpected, and shows that this Government is determined to prove to us its displeasure at the message of the 8th of March. It is the more remarkable, as the Cortes, in their session of the 6th of April, approved a report of the Committee of Hacienda, recommending that this privilege should be continued. A statement of this determination of the Cortes, translated from the Government Gazette, is as follows:

"'The Committee of Hacienda, in view of the application of the minister of the United States for the continuance, for an indefinite period, of the permission to introduce, free of duties, into the port of Mahon, the naval stores for the use of the American squadron cruising in the Mediterranean, is of opinion that the request should be acceded to, taking the necessary precautions to avoid abuses. Approved.'

"I had previously understood from the English Secretary of Embassy, Mr. Harvey, resident minister since Sir H. Wellesly's departure, that M. de la Rosa had spoken of the President's message of the 8th of March as hostile towards the Spains, and the report of the committee of the House of Representatives as an attack upon legitimacy. On my return to Madrid, on the 18th, I saw M. de la Rosa, and, as instructed by your No. 21, assured him that the message 'resulted from a disposition in nowise unfriendly to Spain.' He spoke with a great deal of warmth on the subject; said it was what, from the friendly conduct of the Spains to the United States, they could not have expected; in no state of circumstances could it have a friendly effect on the interests of this Government; that it appeared from the message itself that, not satisfied with taking this step ourselves, we had been, and still were, instigating on other Governments to do so likewise, and that the measure was adopted upon information incorrect in itself and derived from sources of doubtful authority. As it regarded Mexico and Peru, especially, there was absolutely no authentic information communicated to Congress with the message, as was proved by a copy of the published documents in his office. He considered it particularly injurious to Spain at this moment when they were about setting on foot a negotiation with the different parts of Spanish America. He concluded by expressing an opinion that the Spanish Americans were unequal to self-government, and that their independence, instead of being accelerated, would be retarded by this act of our Government. I replied, that the message itself explained the ground upon which the step was taken; that the intentions of the President were not unfriendly to Spain. As to the effect of the measure, it would, or it would not, be injurious, according to the views of this Government. If they were disposed to yield to circumstances and act prudently·it could do them no injury. I made no reply to his remarks on the published documents as I had not seen them. As to the communications made to other foreign Governments, instead of being unfriendly, they had, in reality, proceeded from a contrary disposition—from a desire, on our part, that other powers, more remotely concerned in the question, should express an opinion on it at the same time with ourselves, with a view to its effects on the policy of this Government. That this step was taken in entire ignorance of the negotiation to which he alluded. The Cortes Extraordinary had authorized the Government to enter upon this negotiation *only in February last*. The only information possessed by the Government of the United States of conciliatory attempts on the part of Spain was the knowledge of the mission to Buenos Ayres in 1820, and of the negotiation begun here with the Commissioners of Venezuela in 1821. The first had totally failed, the Commissioners of Spain not being permitted to land; and the second had been interrupted by an order from the Government to the Commissioners of Colombia to leave the kingdom. It might be convenient to Spain to delay; but circumstances did not permit other Governments to imitate her dilatory policy. That 'the Spanish Americans were unequal to self-government,' I thought an unfortunate observation, as it proved, if true, that they were not fit to live under the Spanish constitution. We should regret very much that a measure intended to be useful should prove injurious to either of the parties, but should not be satisfied that such would be the effect until experience had proved it. The conversation terminated by a remark on his part, that what was intended to be done by the President was yet uncertain, and that they would *wait* to know how far the Government of the United States would go."

"There has been a Council of State on this act of ours. A protest was recommended; the minister of Spain with to withdrawn from the United States, *at least for the present*, and the preparation of the necessary force to act efficiently in Ultramar, as formerly advised by the same council. This advice, it is said, has been sent to the Cortes, and is before the Commission of Ultramar; of this I have no certain information, but it is altogether probable.

"The proposed admission of the flags of the Spanish American Governments into English ports is said to be as vexatious as our determination to recognize their independence. Of herself, Spain can do nothing but negotiate with the Spanish American Governments. Nor has she the means to procure the assistance of other powers which she is willing to give and they willing to accept. M. de la Rosa has spoken to some of the foreign ministers here of the proposed recognition as a violation of treaty stipulations; referring, I conjecture, to the treaty of Utrecht, and of the Holy Alliance, with which we have as little concern as with the compact between Rome and Carthage. Constitutional Spain is no favorite with the Holy Alliance, and the revolution of 1820, glorious as it was for this country, settled the question between the Spanish Old and New World. The use of force to be sent from Europe, since March of that year, has not been seriously thought of. The liberal Government adopted here, and the equality of rights and privileges offered to the Spanish Americans, were supposed to be means sufficient to restore at least a portion of revolted Spanish America and assure the fidelity of the parts still connected with Spain to the empire. The appeal of M. de la Rosa to the principles of the Holy Alliance is a proof of mental weakness I did not expect from him.

"If a successor is appointed, with directions to come to Spain about that time, all the necessary instructions will, of course, be given to him; if not, you will be so good as to communicate to me what disposition the President desires to have made of the affairs of the legation, when I am about to leave Spain, and, in either case, to furnish me with the necessary documents to enable me to take leave here with decorum."

No. 8, (a.)

Don Francisco Martinez de la Rosa to Mr. Forsyth.

[Translation.]

MADRID, *May* 15, 1822.

SIR : I acknowledged to you in proper time the receipt of your note of the 18th of September last, in which you requested that his Majesty would extend, for an indefinite or a limited time, the privilege which he was pleased to grant on February 26, 1821, to admit into Mahon, for the term of six months, naval stores and provisions sent from the United States for the exclusive use of the American squadron cruising in the Mediterranean.

Having submitted a translated copy of the above note of yours to the Secretary of Hacienda, he replied to me that his Majesty was not disposed at present to grant the extension for which you applied.

I renew to you the assurances of my most distinguished consideration, and pray God to preserve you many years.

Your very obedient servant,

FRANCISCO MARTINEZ DE LA ROSA.

Mr. John Forsyth.

No. 9.

Mr. Adams to Mr. Forsyth, No. 24.

DEPARTMENT OF STATE, Washington, June 19, 1822.

SIR: Since I had the honor of writing you on the 30th ultimo, I have received your letter, No. 36, of the 15th April, inclosing your accounts.

A letter, of which a translation is now inclosed, has also been received from the Spanish minister, Anduaga.

If the Spanish Government are desirous of postponing the meeting of the Commissioners to run the line, we are not disposed to urge them to it. You will, accordingly, not press the subject upon them; and if they address you concerning it, will manifest our readiness to attend to it at their convenience.

I am, with great respect, sir, your very humble and obedient servant,

JOHN QUINCY ADAMS.

Hon. John Forsyth, *Minister Plenipotentiary of the United States, Madrid.*

No. 10.

Extract of a letter (No. 40) from Mr. Forsyth to the Secretary of State, dated

MADRID, June 23, 1822.

"Mr. de Barras arrived here twenty days since with Mr. Anduaga's protest against the message of the 8th March, and your reply. On the 21st I received from the Secretary of State two copies of a manifesto passed by order of the King to the different courts of Europe. One of them is inclosed with this despatch, with a copy of the note received with it, and of my acknowledgment of their receipt. This manifesto was prepared in obedience to the resolutions of the Extraordinary Cortes, a translation of which was sent to you with my No. 34. *When* it was written I do not know; but my belief is, that it has been prepared *since* a copy of the President's message of 8th March was received by this Government. I wait with some anxiety to receive instructions subsequent to the close of your correspondence with Mr. Anduaga on this subject. I cannot anticipate exactly what this Government will do. The probability is, that they will not do more than break off their diplomatic intercourse with us. If this is done by merely recalling their minister from the United States, I shall not feel at ease until I know the wishes of the President.

"The 'informé' of the Commission of Ultramar, on the memoir of the Minister of Ultramar, which you will receive herewith, is an interesting document; although the question between the Spanish American Government and Spain is not considered under the new shape it assumed after the President's message of the 8th March, the 'informé' will serve to put you in possession of the views of a respectable committee of the Cortes after the message was known to have been sent to Congress. The idea of establishing neutral ports in Spanish America, and a neutral flag *only*, for the Peninsular and American Spaniards, *is new.* The only propositions that promise any practical good are those made by Sanchez, already alluded to, and those with which Sbarra, a member of the Commission of Ultramar, concludes his particular vote. Everything which has been done on this subject proves, conclusively, that the Cortes and the Government are satisfied that they are without the power to produce a reunion of Spanish America with the Peninsula *by force;* yet, with this conviction, there exists a perverse determination not to adopt the only measure which promises to be advantageous to Spain. The Cortes will close its session in a few days; they will probably do something before they rise. I expect, however, nothing of a decisive character. There have been lately several secret sessions, with what object, as yet, I know not."

No. 10, (a.)

Don Francisco Martinez de la Rosa to Mr. Forsyth.

[Translation.]

Don Francisco Martinez de la Rosa presents his respects to the minister of the United States of America, and has the honor to inclose to him two copies of the manifesto which the ministers and chargés d'affaires of Spain have passed to the courts of Europe, by order of his Majesty.

PALACE, June 21, 1822.

No. 10, (b.)

Mr. John Forsyth to his Excellency the Secretary of Despatch of State.

To his excellency the Secretary of Despatch of State Mr. John Forsyth presents his respects, and has had the honor to receive the two copies of the manifesto passed, by order of his Catholic Majesty, to the courts of Europe, inclosed with his excellency's note of the 21st instant.
JUNE, 22, 1822.

No. 10, (c.)

Manifesto that, by order of his Majesty, the Ministers and Chargé d'Affaires of Spain have passed to the courts of Europe.

[Translation.]

His Catholic Majesty, in calling the attention of his august allies towards the dissident Spanish provinces of America, judges it not only useless, but unseasonable, to examine the causes which produced in those countries a desire to separate from the mother country; it is sufficient to his Catholic Majesty to have the consolation that it was not the abuse of power nor the weight of oppression which originated so serious an event; and that only extraordinary circumstances, and the terrible crisis in which Spain saw herself compromised, to free her throne and her dignity from the imminent risk of a foreign usurpation, could occasion a disunion so fatal between the members of one and the same family.

Since that epoch, as glorious as unfortunate, various have been the political aspects which the different provinces of Ultramar have presented; military events have succeeded each other with alternate success; the cause of the dissidents has taken a different direction in each one of the principal parts of that immense continent, and his Majesty sees with the most profound grief those interesting regions suffering all the ills and exposed to all the dangers which are the inevitable consequences of a revolution.

For the same reason his Catholic Majesty desires ardently to put an end to a situation so painful of anxiety and of uncertainty; and, carrying into execution the beneficent resolutions of the *Cortes,* has named the respective Commissioners to proceed to the dissident provinces of Ultramar, hear their propositions, transmit them to the Spanish Government, and open a frank and sincere correspondence, which may have for object and the good of those countries and that of the nation in general.

H. C. M. does not present himself to those provinces as a resentful monarch before his misled subjects, but as a pacific mediator in the discords of his children. He casts a veil over the past, in order to see the present without any kind of prejudice, and contemplates the actual situation under all the relations which unite it with the future. The common good of the provinces of both hemispheres; this is the only end of the negotiations; this, its only basis; this, the common centre where all its combinations must be directed.

Never has a more important transaction presented itself; but neither is it possible for a Government to prepare to commence it with greater loyalty and good faith. H. C. M. cannot persuade himself that the interest of the provinces of Ultramar can be found in opposition to that of European Spain; and this sentiment, so worthy of his heart, stimulates him to look for the means of reconciling their common advantages, and offers him a consolatory confidence that it will not be impossible to find it. H. C. M. gratifies himself with the flattering hope that this frank and generous confidence will spare those regions whole ages of misery and destruction; prevent civil war and anarchy from retarding the progress of civilization and improvement; avoid the depopulation, poverty and immorality which attend great political oscillations, and which condemn to disgrace and misery one generation without securing the repose or the felicity of the following.

H. C. M. believes, at the same time, that the greatest good he can procure to Peninsular Spain is to put an end to a desolating and fratricide war; and that, placed between brothers united by the ties of blood and of religion, of language, of customs, and even of convenience itself, his voice cannot fail to be heard with benefit to one and the other.

But H. C. M. extends his views to a more extensive horizon, and considers this great question as an European question. A long time passed before the prodigious effects of the discovery of the New World were perceived in this continent; nobody could foresee them, much less calculate them; it was an unknown, immense career, without any barriers to confine it within its space. The same, H. M. judges, may be said of the great events which are agitating America, and whose effects must influence necessarily, and in a very rapid manner, the lot of Europe. It is not possible to determine the degrees of this influence, nor the alterations which it must produce in the reciprocal relations of the one and the other hemisphere; but H. C. M. hesitates not to affirm that the transaction which fixes the lot of the Spanish provinces of America, and puts an end to the blind and impetuous course of its revolution, will be one of the benefits the most memorable for the civilized world.

Necessities, commerce, habit, communications of every species, have united with multiplied bonds the two hemispheres; and it is easy to conceive that an entire continent, delivered to the struggle of the passions, and made the theatre of a durable revolution, cannot fail to influence perniciously the political and moral relations of Europe, when it has scarcely begun to recover from the agitations and disturbances it has labored under for the space of thirty years.

There will be, perhaps, superficial spirits who will see a solid and established Government and a constituted nation in each province which may have declared its independence; and who, without attending to obstacles of any kind, nor to the principles of public right, nor to the best known maxims of the law of nations, will believe that the mere fact of the separation of a province from the state of which it formed a part legitimates its existence! insulated and independent! and gives it the right to be recognized as such by other powers.

But Governments fortunately know, by a sad experience, the effects which are produced by a similar overthrow of principle; they foresee the consequences of its propagation, not less fatal to legitimate Governments than to the integrity of nations; and are well aware of the consequence to Europe of sanctioning in America, as some pretend, the undefined right of insurrection.

Thus it is that H. C. M. believes not only interested in this question those nations who possess colonies and establishments in Ultramar, to which the same theory could be applied, that it is now intended to legitimate with respect to the Spanish provinces of America; but that he also considers this business as intimately connected with those conservatory principles that offer securities to all Governments and guarantees to society.

Before this great and capital object all other considerations disappear by their smallness, and therefore H. C. M. does not recur to those subaltern reasons which, in ordinary times and circumstances, are employed by policy in support and defence of justice.

Although the question is viewed under this other aspect, Spain presents in all her relations new and powerful motives, which ought to excite in her favor profound sentiments of the most severe impartiality. Without any kind of ambitious pretension, placed with respect to all nations in an inoffensive situation, and dedicated exclusively to affirm and consolidate her interior felicity, she can neither provoke jealousies nor rivalries, nor cause to be desired the violent dismemberment of the various parts of the monarchy with the object of debilitating it. Spain, however powerful she may be, cannot threaten the repose nor the security of other nations; and Spain, rich and powerful, could advantageously influence the preservation of the equilibrium of power. An instinct of honor and of loyalty reunited the unknown elements of her strength, and engaged in the most unequal struggle, gave time to the continent to rise up against the common enemy and destroy his oppressive yoke. This fact alone renders unnecessary all reflections and commentaries. It alone inspires interest in favor of the magnanimous nation, and announces what ought to be its destiny, always beneficent, and never offensive; nature and policy designate it this advantageous position on the map of nations.

This grand political view was not hidden from the European cabinets when they saw destroyed the colossal and exaggerated power which Spain, alarming Europe, had exercised for the space of two centuries.

After a long struggle, it was determined at last to fix the lot of Spain, considering it inwoven with the federal European system, and, at the same moment, was foreseen the advantage of affirming her power, securing it in America a point of support that might augment its weight in the political balance to obtain the equilibrium of Europe.

To such a point was given importance to this consideration of general interest, that Spain obliged herself not to transfer or dispose of, in any manner, any portion of her territory in America; and, in order to make its possession more secure and inviolable, and to remove even the motives for suspicion and want of confidence, she deprived herself even of the liberty of conceding to other nations, by any means or under any pretext, the commerce and trade with those countries.

Time, notwithstanding, has produced a very important alteration in this point and a more enlightened policy; the change in the mercantile relations, the rectification of economical principles, and a multitude of other combined causes, have convinced Spain that it will be as prejudicial to her peninsular interests, as injurious to the provinces of Ultramar, to aspire to the preservation of a commercial monopoly formerly viewed as the bond of union between the two great moieties of the monarchy.

H. C. M. judges, on the contrary, that those ties only are durable which are founded on the common interest, and that peninsular Spain may obtain commercial advantages favorable to her industry and navigation without aspiring to a privilege so exclusive; that new necessities and new desires, arising from the progress of civilization and of wealth, make necessary a more frank and liberal system for the provinces of Ultramar; and that, in place of struggling uselessly with the mercantile spirit, which has so much influence in the political system of modern nations, the true interests of Spain consist in conciliating it, instead of provoking it as an irreconcilable enemy.

Proposing to itself such important objects, all the laws, all the dispositions given since the restoration of the constitution, have a tendency beneficent, generous, and to the colonization of strangers in Spanish America, and to the freedom of commerce in those regions; and the experiment made in the island of Cuba has been sufficient to demonstrate practically that the general interest of all nations, the interest of the provinces of America and that of European Spain, all coincide in one same point.

By this simple and natural mean, H. C. M. has found absolutely removed the only obstacle that might prevent the most perfect union between the policy of Spain and that of the other cabinets. A solid, stable, and recognized Government, a faithful observer of its treaties, prepares to treat with the dissident provinces of America, and offers to the other powers the greatest commercial advantages; it would not be possible to designate (even when the question should be reduced to the simple calculation of lucrative interest) an object which might serve as a counterpoise in the opposite extreme.

The civil wars and the anarchy that frequently succeed revolutions, and especially when their elements are so heterogeneous and contradictory as in America, are surely not calculated to augment the exchangeable products of a country, nor to invite strangers with the effective and persuasive security which is the soul of commerce, nor can precarious and uncertain governments, without any guarantee, secure themselves the advantages which they may offer. It is now twelve years since Buenos Ayres, delivered to its own fortune, has toiled in vain to consolidate a Government, and the misery and depopulation suffered by the provinces of Costa-firma have retarded, instead of accelerating their wealth and prosperity. In matters of this class, when facts come in support of reason, it is useless to oppose to certain and known results vague and indefinite hopes.

But it appears only as if a new calamity has taken place, in confirmation of the evils which should have been foreseen; the insurrection of the American continent has given color and support to the piracy of the seas, and commerce in general begins to suffer from the insecurity and dangers of this immoral and barbarous war, which knows no law but that of sordid interest, and which treats and despoils as enemies the industrious individuals of all nations, indiscriminately.

Hence, and by an admirable concatenation, everything concurs to establish the utility and urgency of a definitive arrangement of a business of such vast and profound ramifications, and everything contributes to stimulate the Spanish Government not to retard, by any secondary motive, a transaction so important.

H. C. M. flatters himself with the greatest satisfaction that, about to establish with the dissident provinces this ample and friendly communication, he will find in the other Governments that circumspect and deliberate conduct that justice prescribes, and that policy recommends, and that sentiments of impartiality and benevolence inspire.

The Spanish nation, treating to put an end to a domestic discord, the same inviolable respect which it professes to the rights of other nations inspires it with the just confidence of being treated reciprocally with the same considerations, not being able to suspect, even on the part of the nations who desire to continue in friendship and harmony with her, any hazarded step which might suppose already resolved the question which the Spanish nation is about to decide as its own, in use of its legitimate acknowledged rights, and which it has never in any manner renounced.

In which state the same means made use of to excite Government to the recognition of the indepen- dence of the dissident Spanish provinces of America will offer, on the contrary, a notorious and solemn occasion to sanction the fundamental principles upon which the integrity and tranquillity of nations and the public morality of Governments repose.

The tenor and spirit of treaties, the good faith which ought to reign between friendly powers, the conviction of an obligation supported equally by an enlightened and foreseeing policy, the real welfare itself of the dissident provinces, and even the general utility of all the potentates, offer an equal number of securities to his Catholic Majesty that his laudable desires will find in his august allies the most favorable and friendly reception.

MADRID, *June* 28, 1822.

No. 11.

Extract of a letter (No 41) from Mr. Forsyth to the Secretary of State, dated

MADRID, *June* 28, 1822.

"I have not been able to ascertain if anything has been said or proposed in the Cortes during their secret sessions with regard to the United States. There is one striking circumstance that renders it probable that there has. In the discussion of the business of Ultramar not even the most remote allusion has been made to the resolution of our Government to recognize the Spanish American Governments. The message of the 8th of March, your subsequent correspondence with Anduaga, and the determination of the Council of State when consulted by the ministers, are certainly known to the Cortes, if not, as is more probable, formally communicated to them. I can hardly conceive it possible that a reference to this step of ours should not have been made, if it had not been studiously avoided, and I see no sufficient motive for a studious avoidance of it if the subject had not been under consideration in a different shape. This is mere conjecture; you will give to it its due importance, as you are made acquainted with the foundation of it."

No. 12.

Extract of a letter (No. 44) from Mr, Forsyth to Mr. Adams, dated

MADRID, *August* 26, 1822.

"The late events have had a favorable effect for us. The danger so near home has drawn their attention from American affairs and blunted the sensibility excited by our recognition of the Governments established in our hemisphere. Every one feels, too, that, among the Governments, the Spanish constitution has no friends but the United States, and perhaps England. Every one is sensible that Spain has no power to compel Spanish America to unite with the Peninsula, and that no assistance is to be procured from the European powers without a sacrifice of the free institutions now established here. The adminis- tration has passed into the hands of a party at all times more reasonable and less prejudiced on this subject than those who have heretofore administered the Government."

No. 13.

Mr. Adams to Mr. Forsyth, No. 26.

DEPARTMENT OF STATE, *Washington, October* 23, 1822.

SIR: By an act passed at the last session of Congress, (May 8, 1822,) for ascertaining claims and titles to land within the Territory of Florida, a commission was established, to consist of three Commis- sioners, for the adjudication of claims at Pensacola and St. Augustine, under certain rules, regulations, and conditions prescribed in the act. James P. Preston, Nathaniel A. Ware, and Samuel R. Overton were appointed the Commissioners.

I have the honor of inclosing herewith copies of letters from two of them, Mr. Ware and Mr. Overton, in session as a Board at Pensacola, and from Joseph W. White, their secretary, from which you not only perceive conclusive proof of the indispensable necessity, for the purposes of public justice, that the documents and archives transmitted to the Havana should be delivered up, conformably to the express stipulation of the treaty, but, what is still more extraordinary, that *copies* have been produced before the Board, certified by the Captain General himself at the Havana, of documents which could not consistently with good faith be withheld.

By the decease of the Captain General, Mahy, the duties of his office have passed into other hands. The President hopes and trusts that it will afford an opportunity, of which the Spanish Government will readily avail itself, to redeem the pledge of their express and positive engagements. He desires you therefore to renew, in an earnest though friendly and conciliatory manner, the application for the most explicit orders to the commanding officer at the Havana for the delivery to the United States of all the archives and documents relating to the sovereignty and property of Florida which, conformably to the treaty, should have been surrendered. They include, of course, all documents relating to land titles in the province, since the province itself is the only place where they can be useful or necessary to establish the right of any one to property there, and since such rights can, in most cases, be established there only by them.

Should the Spanish Government accede to this demand, due to its own good faith no less than to justice, you will request that a duplicate of the order to the Captain General or commanding officer at the Havana for the delivery of the archives should be furnished to you to be transmitted hither, that it may be forwarded hence by a person duly authorized by the Government of the United States to receive them.

I am, with great respect, sir, your very humble and obedient servant,

JOHN QUINCY ADAMS.

Hon. JOHN FORSYTH, *Minister, &c.*

No. 14.

Mr. Adams to Mr. Forsyth, No. 27.

DEPARTMENT OF STATE, *Washington, December 16, 1822.*

SIR: I have had the honor of receiving your despatches to No. 48, inclusive, with their inclosures.

Copies of a late correspondence between the Spanish minister, Auduaga, and this Department, relating to the capture of the Spanish privateer brig Palmyra by the United States schooner Grampus, are herewith transmitted; and in the printed documents and papers now forwarded you will see the multiplied outrages and depredations to which the commerce of the United States has been and continues to be exposed, from pirates issuing chiefly from the islands of Porto Rico and Cuba. To the distressing catalogue of injuries which we have thereby sustained is now added the loss of several lives of our seamen; and among them, that of Lieutenant Allen, commander of the Alligator, who perished in the act of re-capturing five valuable vessels which were in possession of the pirates.

This evil has been long growing to a magnitude which is no longer supportable nor remediable but by measures of promptitude and vigor. These atrocious robberies are committed by men issuing from the ports of those islands in shoal waters and under the protection of the very shores in many cases, with small boats unapproachable by vessels of force adequate to subdue them. When closely pursued they abandon their boats and escape to the shores; and, when successful, the fruits of their lawless plunder are exposed in the public marts of the island with an indecency little creditable to the authorities of the island themselves, which have hitherto made little more than ostensible exertion to suppress them.

In this state of things a plan has been laid before Congress for their consideration, for the organization of a force specially adapted to the extirpation of this cluster of banditti, a force adapted to pursue them into the shallow waters, where they have hitherto often found a too effectual refuge. To its complete success it may occasionally be necessary for our officers and men to follow them even to and upon the shores of the island; of this necessity the President wishes you to apprise the Spanish Government, and to obtain their immediate consent thereto. You will state that the urgency of the case will not admit of delay, and that he trusts it will be assented to by Spain without hesitation. You will, at the same time, press upon the Spanish Government the propriety of instructions being given forthwith to their commanding officers in those islands to co-operate by the most effective means with our naval force for the suppression of these common enemies of the human kind, and of affording to our officers every facility in their power in aid of their operations. An agent will be shortly despatched to the Havana for the purpose of concerting with the authorities in Cuba the measures which may be most effectual to this end, and of giving effect, by communication with the officers commanding our armament, to their proceedings. He will, also, be charged with authority to receive the archives and documents relating to Florida, which have been so long withheld, and for the delivery of which by your despatch, No. 48, it appears that a new and positive order has been promised.

I am, with great respect, sir, your very obedient and humble servant,

JOHN QUINCY ADAMS.

Hon. JOHN FORSYTH, *Minister Plenipotentiary United States, Madrid.*

No. 15.

Mr. Adams to Mr. Forsyth, No. 30.

DEPARTMENT OF STATE, *Washington, January 3, 1823.*

SIR: Mr. Edward Wyer, the bearer, is despatched as a confidential messenger with the letters and documents, which he will deliver to you. The unpleasant incidents which occurred in the course of the last summer at Algiers are doubtless known to you. If the misunderstanding should be known to you to be still subsisting upon Mr. Wyer's arrival at Madrid, he is instructed to proceed thence with a despatch to our Consul General, Mr. Shaler, wherever he may be.

It is hoped, however, that ere this an amicable explanation may have removed the difficulties which had arisen, and that Mr. Shaler will have returned to Algiers and resumed his consular functions there. In that case, Mr. Wyer will transmit the despatch for Mr. Shaler with which he is charged by any safe and ordinary mode of conveyance, and will return here with any despatches which you may intrust to him; waiting, as long as you may think advisable, for the answer to the demand of permission to pursue the pirates of Cuba on the shores of the island.

Besides the correspondence with Mr. Anduaga, copies of which are herewith transmitted, I have received several very long and earnest communications from that minister, the replies to which have been and yet are delayed, in the hope that they may be received by him in a disposition more calm and temperate than that which is manifested by his notes. He appears to think it material to the interest of his Government to maintain the attitude of loud complaint in regard to transactions with respect to which the primary cause of complaint is on our side. The only exception to this remark relates to a miserable attempt at an expedition against the island of Porto Rico, headed by a foreign officer named Decoudray de Holstein, but on board of which were some misguided citizens of the United States. One of the vessels appears to have been fitted out at Philadelphia and one at New York, but the first intimation of these facts, received by this Government, was long after they had sailed, and from the island of St. Bartholomew's.

We have since learned that the masters of the vessels were deceived with regard to their destination, and that when it was discovered by them they positively refused to proceed upon it, and insisted upon going into the island of Curaçoa, where the chief and others of the expedition were arrested. You will make this known to the Spanish Government, and assure them that this Government knew nothing of this expedition before the departure of the vessels from the United States. This will not be surprising when it is known that it escaped equally the vigilance of Mr. Anduaga himself, who divides his residence between New York and Philadelphia, and of all the other Spanish official agents and consuls at those places.

Mr. Anduaga has taken this occasion to renew, with much sensibility, all his own complaints and those of his predecessors against armaments in our ports in behalf of the South American patriots, and even against that commerce which our citizens, in common with the subjects of all the maritime nations of Europe, have for many years maintained with the people of the emancipated colonies. These complaints have been so fully and repeatedly answered that there is some difficulty in accounting for Mr. Anduaga's recurrence to them with the feelings which mark his notes concerning them. Should the occasion present itself, you will give it distinctly to be understood, that, if some of those notes remain long, and may even finally remain unanswered, it is from a principle of forbearance to him and of unequivocal good will towards his Government and his country.

I am, with much respect, sir, your very humble and obedient servant,

JOHN QUINCY ADAMS.

Hon. John Forsyth,
   Minister Plenipotentiary United States, Madrid.

No. 16.

Extract of a letter from Mr. Appleton to Mr. Adams, giving the substance of a conversation with the Secretary of State for Foreign Affairs, dated

Madrid, *March* 20, 1823.

"I determined to improve the first opportunity of sounding Mr. San Miguel. This opportunity was presented on the 13th, when he informed me that he had resisted the demand of England to be permitted to land on the island in pursuit of pirates. I said that if it was true, as circulated, that the British had landed 500 men at Matanzas, they had not been satisfied with his answer. To this Mr. San Miguel replied that he did not believe the report, as the only pretext which the English could allege for landing had been abandoned by them, on being assured that the Governor of Cuba would readily co-operate with their fleet for the destruction of the pirates."

No. 17.

Don Joaquin de Anduaga to the Secretary of State.

[Translation.]

Washington, *March* 9, 1822.

Sir: In the National Intelligencer of this day I have seen the message sent by the President to the House of Representatives, in which he proposes the recognition by the United States of the insurgent Government of Spanish America. How great my surprise was may be easily judged by any one acquainted with the conduct of Spain towards this Republic, and who knows the immense sacrifices which she has made to preserve her friendship. In fact, who could think that, in return for the cession of her most important provinces in this hemisphere; for the forgetting of the plunder of her commerce by American citizens; for the privileges granted to this Navy, and for as great proofs of friendship as one nation can give another, this Executive would propose that the insurrection of the ultramarine possessions of Spain should be recognized. And, moreover, will not his astonishment be augmented to see that this power is desirous to give the destructive example of sanctioning the rebellion of provinces which have received no offence from the mother country, to those to whom she has granted a participation of a free constitution, and to whom she has extended all the rights and prerogatives of Spanish citizens? In vain will a parallel be attempted to be drawn between the emancipation of this Republic and that which the Spanish rebels attempt, and history is sufficient to prove that if a harassed and persecuted province has a right to break its chains, others loaded with benefits, elevated to the high rank of freemen, ought only to bless and embrace more closely the protecting country which has bestowed such favors upon them.

But, even admitting that morality ought to yield to policy, what is the present state of Spanish America, and what are its Governments to entitle them to recognition? Buenos Ayres is sunk in the most complete anarchy, and each day sees new despots produced who disappear the next. Peru, conquered by a rebel army, has near the gates of its capital another Spanish army, aided by part of the inhabitants. In Chili, an individual suppresses the sentiments of the inhabitants, and his violence presages a sudden change; on the coast of Firma, also, the Spanish banners wave, and the insurgent generals are occupied in quarrelling with their own compatriots, who prefer taking the part of a free power to that of being the slave of an adventurer. In Mexico, too, there is no Government, and the result of the questions which the chiefs commanding there have put to Spain is not known. Where, then, are those Governments which ought to be recognized? where the pledges of their stability? where the proof that those provinces will not return to a union with Spain when so many of their inhabitants desire it? and, in fine, where the right of the United States to sanction and declare legitimate a rebellion without cause, and the event of which is not even decided?

I do not think it necessary to prove that, if the state of Spanish America were such as it is represented in the message; that if the existence of its Governments were certain and established; that if the impossibility of its reunion with Spain were so indisputable; and that if the justice of its recognition were so evident, the powers of Europe, interested in gaining the friendship of countries so important for their commerce, would have been negligent in fulfilling it. But seeing how distant the prospect is of even this result, and faithful to the ties which unite them with Spain, they await the issue of the contest, and abstain from doing a gratuitous injury to a friendly Government, the advantages of which are doubtful and the odium certain. Such will be that which Spain will receive from the United States in case the recognition proposed in the message should take effect. And posterity will be no less liable to wonder that the power which has received the most proofs of the friendship of Spain should be the one delighted with being the first to take a step which could have only been expected from another that had been injured.

Although I could enlarge upon this disagreeable subject, I think it useless to do so, because the sentiments which the message ought to excite in the breast of every Spaniard can be no secret to you. Those which the King of Spain will experience at receiving a notification so unexpected will be, doubtless, very disagreeable, and at the same time that I hasten to communicate it to his Majesty, I think *it my duty to protest, as I do solemnly protest, against the recognition of the Governments mentioned of the insurgent Spanish provinces of America by the United States; declaring that it can in no way now, or at any time, lessen or invalidate in the least the right of Spain to the said provinces, or to employ whatever means may be in her power to reunite them to the rest of her dominions.*

I pray you, sir, to be pleased to lay this protest before the President, and I flatter myself that, convinced of the solid reasons which have dictated it, he will suspend the measure which he has proposed to Congress, and that he will give to his Catholic Majesty this proof of his friendship and of his justice.

I remain, with the most distinguished consideration, praying God to guard your life many years, your most obedient, humble servant,

JOAQUIN DE ANDUAGA.

No. 18.

Mr. Adams to Mr. Anduaga.

DEPARTMENT OF STATE, *Washington, April 6, 1822.*

SIR: Your letter of the 9th of March was, immediately after I had the honor of receiving it, laid before the President of the United States, by whom it has been deliberately considered, and by whose direction I am, in replying to it, to assure you of the earnestness and sincerity with which this Government desires to entertain and to cultivate the most friendly relations with that of Spain.

This disposition has been manifested not only by the uniform course of the United States in their direct political and commercial intercourse with Spain, but by the friendly interest which they have felt in the welfare of the Spanish nation, and by the cordial sympathy with which they have witnessed their spirit and energy, exerted in maintaining their independence of all foreign control and their right of self-government.

In every question relating to the independence of a nation two principles are involved—one of *right* and the other of *fact;* the former exclusively depending upon the determination of the nation itself, and the latter resulting from the successful execution of that determination. This right has been recently exercised, as well by the Spanish nation in Europe as by several of those countries in the American hemisphere which had for two or three centuries been connected as colonies with Spain. In the conflicts which have attended these revolutions the United States have carefully abstained from taking any part respecting the right of nations concerned in them to maintain or newly organize their own political constitutions, and observing, whenever it was a contest by arms, the most impartial neutrality. But the civil war in which Spain was for some years involved with the inhabitants of the colonies in America has, in substance, ceased to exist. Treaties equivalent to an acknowledgment of independence have been concluded by the commanders and Vice Roys of Spain herself with the Republic of Colombia, with Mexico, and with Peru, while in the province of La Plata and in Chili no Spanish force has, for several years, existed to dispute the independence which the inhabitants of those countries had declared.

Under these circumstances the Government of the United States, far from consulting the dictates of a policy questionable in its morality, yielded to an obligation of duty of the highest order by recognizing as independent States nations which, after deliberately asserting their right to that character, have maintained and established it against all the resistance which had been or could be brought to oppose it. This recognition is neither intended to invalidate any right of Spain nor to affect the employment of any means which she may yet be disposed or enabled to use, with the view of reuniting those provinces to the rest of her dominions. It is the mere acknowledgment of existing facts, with a view to the regular establishment with the nations newly formed of those relations, political and commercial, which it is the moral obligation of civilized and Christian nations to entertain reciprocally with one another. It will not be necessary to discuss with you a detail of facts, upon which your information appears to be materially different from that which has been communicated to this Government, and is of public notoriety, nor the propriety of the denominations which you have attributed to the inhabitants of the South American provinces. It is not doubted that other and more correct views of the whole subject will very shortly be taken by your Government, and that it will, as well as the other European Governments, show that deference to the example of the United States which you urge it as the duty or policy of the United States to show to theirs. The effect of the example of one independent nation upon the counsels and measures of another can be just only so far as it is voluntary; and as the United States desire that their example should be followed, so it is their intention to follow that of others upon no other principle. They confidently rely that the time is at hand when all the Governments of Europe friendly to Spain, and Spain herself, will not only concur in the acknowledgment of the independence of the American nations, but in the sentiment that nothing will tend more effectually to the welfare and happiness of Spain than the universal concurrence in that recognition.

I pray you, sir, to accept the assurances of my distinguished consideration.

JOHN QUINCY ADAMS.

Don JOAQUIN DE ANDUAGA, *Envoy Extraordinary and Minister Plenipotentiary from Spain.*

No. 19.

Don Joaquin de Anduaga to the Secretary of State.

[Translation.]

PHILADELPHIA, *April* 11, 1822.

SIR: I had the honor of receiving your note of the 6th instant, in which you were pleased to inform me that this Government has recognized the independence of the insurgent provinces of Spanish America. I despatched immediately to Spain one of the secretaries of this legation to carry to his Majesty news as important as unexpected; and, until I receive his royal orders upon the subject, I have only to refer to my protest of the 9th of March last, still insisting upon its contents as if its substance were repeated in the present note.

With the greatest respect, I renew the assurance of my distinguished consideration.

JOAQUIN DE ANDUAGA.

No. 20.

Don Joaquin de Anduaga to the Secretary of State.

[Translation.]

PHILADELPHIA, *April* 24, 1822.

SIR: As soon as the news was received in Madrid of the recent occurrences in New Spain, after the arrival at Vera Cruz of the Captain General and Supreme Political Chief, appointed for those provinces, Don Juan O'Donoju, and some papers were seen relative to those same transactions, it was feared that, for forming the treaty concluded in Cordova, on the 24th of August last, between the said general and the traitor, Colonel Don Augustin Iturbide, it had been falsely supposed that the former had power from his Catholic Majesty for that act, and in a little time the correctness of those suspicions was found, as, among other things, the said O'Donoju, when, on the 26th of the same August, he sent this treaty to the Governor of Vera Cruz, notifying him of its prompt and punctual observance, he told him that, at his sailing from the Peninsula, preparation for the independence of Mexico was already thought of, and that its bases were approved of by the Government and by a commission of the Cortes. His Majesty, on sight of this, and of the fatal impression which so great an imposture had produced in some ultramarine provinces, and what must, without difficulty, be the consequence among the rest, thought proper to order that, by means of a circular to all the chiefs and corporations beyond seas, this atrocious falsehood should be disbelieved; and now he has deigned to command me to make it known to the Government of the United States that it is false as far as General O'Donoju published beyond his instructions, by pointing out to it that he never could have been furnished with other instructions than those conformable to constitutional principles.

In compliance with this order of his Majesty, I can do no less than observe to you, sir, how unfounded one of the reasons is, in your note of the 6th instant, for the recognition by this Government of those of the insurgent provinces of Spanish America; that it was founded on the treaty made by O'Donoju with Iturbide, since, not having had that power, nor instruction to conclude it, it is clearly null and of no value.

I repeat to you, sir, the sentiments of my distinguished consideration, and pray God that you may live many years.

JOAQUIN DE ANDUAGA.

No. 21.

Don Joaquin de Anduaga to the Secretary of State.

[Translation]

PHILADELPHIA, *October* 11, 1822.

SIR: I have the honor to transmit to you a copy of a despatch which has been sent to me by the Political Chief of the island of Porto Rico relative the capture of the Spanish privateer Panchita, *alias* Palmyra, by the United States vessel-of-war the Grampus, and another of the declaration delivered to the Spanish vice consul in Charleston by the captain of the said privateer. Both documents, notwithstanding their having been dictated by persons and in places far apart, are so consistent in the facts to which they refer that there can be no doubt of their certainty.

The circumstances of the capture of the Panchita are as follows: Having approached the Grampus to deliver an official letter to her captain, having the Spanish flag and pendant flying, and, moreover, the parliamentary white flag at the foretop, the Grampus poured into her a discharge of her artillery with such effect that the Panchita was continually in danger of sinking, and had to surrender. The attack, the discharge, the assassination of a Spanish mariner, the wounds of others, and the destruction of the Palmyra, was all the work of an instant, without any preceding altercation or dispute, and as scarcely could have been done if the two nations had been at war, because in this case the commander of the Grampus, before the attack, would have demanded a surrender. The succeeding conduct was agreeable to such a beginning. He caused to be put in chains and irons one part of the crew and Spanish officers, guarding the rest with sentinels in view. He first carried his prize and prisoners to St. Thomas, where he celebrated his victory with feasting and drinking; from thence he sent the wounded to Porto Rico, and eventually he carried the privateer and the rest of the crew to Charleston, where they were put into the public prison, being conducted thither in a manner the most insulting and ignominious.

This is the purport of the subjoined documents, but, not satisfied with the evidence which appears from them, I endeavored to procure information from the various publications which have been made in the newspapers of this Republic upon this subject, of the motive which had impelled the commander of the Grampus to commit so unheard of an outrage; and at last, in the National Gazette of this city, of the 7th instant, I saw the opinion given by Judge Johnson, in this case, the result of which was, that the aforesaid commander, when in St. Thomas, received a complaint from the captain of an American merchant vessel, the Coquette, of having been robbed of some effects by the mariners of a boat which had been sent to examine her by a privateer, the name of which he did not know, and gave him her marks; that Captain Gregory was persuaded that they were those of the Palmyra, and that this was the reason he had for attacking her. It does not appear that he stopped to insaetigate the truth of the complaint; and, upon the simple word of an individual, he hurried to attack a vessel belonging to a nation in friendship with his own, and to sacrifice the lives and property of Spanish citizens. Besides, by the subjoined declaration of Captain Escurra, you will see that the accusation made by the captain of the Coquette was false; and that if the individuals in the boat came to examine his vessel committed any trifling excess, they were restrained in the act, and the guilty reserved for future punishment. . But yet, admitting the truth of the complaint, the same Judge Johnson, in his opinion, says that those only who had committed the crime ought to be punished, and by no means the officers and the rest of the crew to which they belonged. Yet Captain Gregory, with his impetuosity, sacrificed the lives of those who were not yet accused, and the property of the owners of the privateer who never could be so. Very clear is the conduct which the captain of the Coquette and of the Grampus ought to have observed, if they believed the offence made out, to have demanded of the captain of the Palmyra the punishment of the guilty, and if that had been refused, to give information to this Government, to which that of Spain would have had the pleasure of giving the most prompt and complete satisfaction. Far from this, the Spanish flag has been insulted and attacked, Spanish citizens killed and wounded, Spanish property plundered and carried away on the high seas. Such atrocities call for a prompt and severe punishment, and I believe the informing you of them, sir, sufficient to persuade me that the President, pursuing the principles of justice which characterize him, will be pleased to give the most prompt and determined orders that the Palmyra be immediately restored and delivered to her captain, her crew set at liberty, satisfaction made for the immense damages caused to the owners of the privateer; and that, to give to Spain the satisfaction which is due to her for the outrage which has been committed on her in this circumstance, he will order an inquiry, in the competent tribunal, into the conduct of Captain Gregory, that he may be punished as those deserve who so scandalously violate the general laws of civilized nations and the treaties and particular connexion of two friendly powers.

I await your orders, sir, and renew the assurance of my high consideration.

JOAQUIN DE ANDUAGA.

No. 22.

Don Joaquin de Anduaga to Mr. Meade.

[Translation.]

PHILADELPHIA, *October* 16, 1822.

SIR: I have received your letter of the 10th of the present month, in which you are pleased to communicate to me that the commission established at Washington in fulfilment of the treaty of February 22, 1819, had judicially declared, on the 17th of June last, its intention of considering as null the liquidation made by the Spanish Government of the claims which you had against it, and of demanding other proofs of their validity and justice, concluding with asking me if you can be certain of the intervention of Spain in your favor, and that, in case of necessity, the documents, proceedings, and evidence, to which you alluded in the letter which you addressed to me in April of this year, would be presented.

What you communicate to me upon the resolution of the commission has surprised me above measure, and I am persuaded that it will not persist in it when it reflects on the injustice which it contains and the notable injury which it does to my Government.

The obligation and the desires of the commission in the examination of your claim can be no other than that of being convinced of its justice, in order to adjudge to you its amount. For this purpose, they ought to demand of you the most authentic and credible documents that are known in the country in which your claims took place; and if you exhibit them and prove that they have the greatest character of authenticity, and that they are authorized by the tribunals established for that purpose in said country, and by the persons to whom, being at the head of the Government, entire credit should be given, there being neither corporations nor individuals more elevated, and in whom greater confidence may be placed, it is clear that the commission cannot ask for more satisfactory evidence. Yet the liquidation which was made to you by the Spanish Government took place at the instances of the minister of the United States at Madrid; was not the work of subjects chosen by the ministry, but of the most respectable tribunals of Spain; was not examined by one only, but by various commissions, composed of persons of the greatest probity, high rank, and little disposed to favor you; and at last, after the most minute proceedings, received the sanction of the King. It is worthy of notice, that, when all this was done, there was no probability that the United States would be obliged to pay this debt, and that when the liquidation which was made to you was communicated to the minister of the United States at Madrid by the Minister of State he not only made no difficulty, but he returned thanks, in the name of his Government, and appeared very much satisfied with it. This liquidation, thus sanctioned by his Catholic Majesty, admitted and approved by the minister of the United States, is what you presented to the commission; and what document more convincing can be given by any Government? Will the commission give more credit to the signature of a notary, of a merchant, than to the testimony of the Council of Finance, of the great tribunal of accounts, of the Treasurer General, Minister of Finance, and, in one word, of the King himself? Will the commission refuse its credit to the monarch and authority to their constituents, the President of the United States? Can it be doubted that Spain made, with the most scrupulous exactness, a liquidation which, in the time of her greatest fiscal distresses, she thought herself bound to satisfy?

Although I am persuaded that you have made these reflections, I thought it my duty to point them out, in order to observe to you the natural consequence to be deduced from them, that the Spanish Government will consider it as a grievous insult to see the testimony considered as null which in Spain is acknowledged as the most sacred and respectable; that she will never consent that the legality and integrity with which your liquidation was made should be placed in doubt, which has all the characters of authenticity which could be given to it; and, in fine, that, although it were practicable to collect again the documents which served to make the aforesaid liquidation, his Catholic Majesty knows too well what is due to his high dignity, to the reputation of his ministers, and to the integrity of his tribunals, to admit that a foreign commission should think itself authorized to revise his decrees. As to the rest, you may be assured that I am ready to render you what good offices you may think necessary with this Government.

God preserve you many years.

JOAQUIN DE ANDUAGA.

No. 23.

Don Joaquin de Anduaga to the Secretary of State.

[Translation.]

NEW YORK, *December* 11, 1822.

SIR: The vice consul of Spain at Charleston has informed me, under date of the 28th of November last, that a certain Pereyra, a native of the Havana, detained in that prison, had been condemned as a pirate.

Inclosed I have the honor to send you an original, a judicial information, taken at the Havana, in which the innocence of the Pereyras of the crime of piracy is not only proved, but that they were forcibly torn from their firesides by the crew of an American vessel-of-war, and their property destroyed, in consequence of a violation of the Spanish territory, which produced the ruin of said family. In these circumstances, I pray you, sir, as the pressure of the case requires, to be pleased to obtain from the President an order for the suspension of the sentence fulminated against Pereyra, in order that his cause may be reconsidered with the presence of the subjoined document; and that, if the truth of its contents be proved, Pereyra may be set at liberty, and the violators of his Catholic Majesty's territory may be punished, and the damages and injuries originating from this crime be repaired.

I repeat my respects to you, sir, assuring you of my high consideration.

JOAQUIN DE ANDUAGA.

No. 24.

Don Joaquin de Anduaga to the Secretary of State.

[Translation.]

NEW YORK, *December* 14, 1822.

SIR: The expedition formed in the ports of this Republic, and which sailed from thence in the month of August last, to conquer the island of Porto Rico and to separate it from Spain, has fixed the attention of all Europe. The effect which this extraordinary event has produced on the citizens of the United States proves, to a demonstration, the sentiments of virtue and probity which animate an immense majority of them, and that the attempts which unfortunately so frequently stain the meritorious reputation of these inhabitants are the work of a small number, and are felt and detested by the mass of the nation. The publications made on this noisy subject, in all the newspapers of the Union, clearly display this truth; and, at the same time that I admire and respect the virtues and sensibilities of the American people, I can do no less than give them the tribute of my sincere gratitude for the indignation they have shown at seeing their laws so scandalously trampled upon, and a nation, their friend, and from which they have received such great proofs of esteem and regard, so perfidiously dealt by.

The nature of the aforesaid expedition, the manner in which it has been framed, the publicity which it had before its sailing, the criminality or negligence which has appeared in the officers of the United States, are so odious, and so clearly is it the interest of the Government to show to the whole world, for its own reputation, that, far from approving such excesses, it hastens to repress them, and to punish them, as soon as they come to their knowledge, that I flatter myself that the bare mention which I have made to you, sir, of this event in my former notes was sufficient for the President to have taken those means dictated by his justice that the delinquents should suffer the punishment which they deserved; that the conduct observed on this occasion by the officers of the customs should be examined, and to the end that, by means of some communication, I should have been enabled to calm the uneasiness and concern which have been caused to his Catholic Majesty by an event so opposite to the friendship which unites him with this Republic and to the laws of all nations.

I will not do the President the injustice to doubt for a moment that he has taken the measures which public vengeance and the honor of this Republic demand; but I must express how much I am hurt that in so long a time you have not had the goodness to give me any explanation on so important a subject, and the means of fully acquainting his Catholic Majesty with the object I have just mentioned.

Such is the publicity of the aforesaid expedition, of its authors, of those who are parties to it, and of its event, that I think I may dispense with distracting your attention with the particulars, except that I ought to fix it upon the circumstance, of which I am assured, of Mr. Irvine, one of the chiefs of it, having been claimed by the captain of the United States corvette the Cyane from the governor of Curaçoa, who had arrested him upon the petition of Spanish officers. If this circumstance should be certain, it would give rise to consequences which it is impossible to admit, and I am persuaded that the President will reprove the conduct observed in this case by the commander of the Cyane, contrary, no doubt, to the instructions and intentions of his Government.

Although I anticipate the communication the President will be pleased to order me relative to the said expedition, which can be no other than that which the honor of this Republic and justice imperiously claim, I take the liberty of asking you, sir, to have the goodness to transmit it to me as soon as possible; my object in this request being to be able to dissipate, without more delay, the anxiety and uncertainty with which the silence of this Government upon a case so public and scandalous cannot fail to inspire his Catholic Majesty and all the Spaniards.

I repeat, sir, that I am at your disposal, assuring you of my very high consideration.

JOAQUIN DE ANDUAGA.

No. 25.

Don Joaquin de Anduaga to the Secretary of State.

[Translation.]

NEW YORK, *January* 6, 1823.

SIR: I have the honor to transmit to you a copy of a note which, under date of the 3d of September last, his excellency Don Evaristo San Miguel sent to the Minister Plenipotentiary of the United States near his Catholic Majesty. By that you will be pleased to observe that his Majesty has not thought himself bound to accede to the broad and free interpretation which the President has given to the articles two and seven of the treaty of 1819, concerning the artillery and munitions of war in the Floridas at the time of the delivery of those provinces, inasmuch as that interpretation would be injurious to Spain; and that he demanded, according to the literal tenor of the second article, the delivery of said artillery and other effects, his Majesty relinquishing the claim which he thought he had upon this Government to furnish provisions for the Spanish troops which were transported from the said provinces, and binding himself to reimburse the amount of the rations which were furnished as soon as the proper account of them should be presented and the orders for the delivery of the artillery, &c., should be furnished.

His Majesty does not doubt that the President, convinced of the justice and solidity of the reasons which have produced this determination, will not delay a moment in giving orders for the delivery of the artillery and other effects, and he has thought proper to command me to request it, as well as an account of the rations which were furnished to our troops by this Government. He has, moreover, authorized me, in case this Government should wish to purchase the whole or any part of the effects which ought to be delivered to us, to listen to its propositions of purchase, and to transmit them to his Majesty, observing to you, sir, that, if it shall be preferred that a valuation be made by experienced persons nominated by both parties, the one on our side will be pointed out when his Majesty is informed of the wishes of the President in this particular.

It being urgent for my Government to know as soon as possible the intentions of the President relative to this business, it has been pleased to order me to pray of you, sir, to have the goodness to communicate them to me as soon as may be possible; and, persuaded that you will cheerfully comply with my wishes, I confine myself to renew to you the assurances of my high consideration.

JOAQUIN DE ANDUAGA.

No. 25, (a.)

[Translation.]

Copy of a note transmitted on the 3d of September, 1822, by his excellency the Secretary of Despatch of State to the Minister Plenipotentiary of the United States at Madrid.

SIR: The minister at Washington duly informed his Majesty of the disputes between the Spanish and American Commissioners charged with the delivery of the Floridas relative to the interpretation which was attempted to be given to the 2d article of the treaty, by pretending that in the word *fortifications* the artillery and munitions of war ought to be considered as included. This point being discussed by the respective Commissioners, they came to a provisional agreement, by which it was stipulated that the effects should remain in deposit until their Governments decided upon the business in question.

The principal reason which the Commissioners of your Government alleged for supposing that the artillery and munitions should be considered as included in the cession of the fortifications consisted in this: that the transportation of those effects not having been promised in the 6th article, it must be under. stood to have been the intention of the negotiator that they should be comprehended in the word fortifi. cations. His Majesty's minister, in the note which he sent to Mr. Adams on the 27th July, 1821, showed that the artillery and munitions could not be comprehended in the fortifications, which consist of works built to defend a point in the way; that in the word *barracks*, the utensils which are in them for the service of the troops are not comprehended. These and other reasons being alleged by the minister, to show that the cession referred to the buildings, and in nowise to the movable effects which they might contain, he requested that, in fulfilment of the 2d article of the treaty, the artillery, munitions, and instruments of war in both the provinces at the time of the delivery should be given over to the Spanish Commissioners, that they might provide for their transportation agreeably to the orders which they had received.

In the answer which Mr. Adams gave on the 13th of August, 1821, to his Majesty's minister, he informs him of the correspondence which had taken place upon the subject between the respective Commissioners, and shows that the conduct of those of his Government had been approved of, as being conformable to the instructions which had been communicated to them. Mr. Adams added, that it was certain that in the 2d article of the treaty the cession of the artillery, &c., was not comprehended, because it was not expressed in precise terms; but that it was no less certain that, by the 7th article, the United States were not obliged to furnish provisions for the transportation of the Spanish troops, inasmuch as it was not expressly mentioned; that this being the strict and literal sense of each of the articles, the President had given a broad and free interpretation to their tenor by ordering that the necessary provisions should be furnished for the transportation of the Spanish troops, although they were not expressly mentioned in the 7th article, and considering the artillery and munitions of war in the fortifications as ceded, although not expressly mentioned in the 2d article; and, lastly, that the President was persuaded that the Spanish Government would not insist that the 2d article should be interpreted rigorously and the 7th literally, but that it would agree to give a liberal sense to both, knowing that that interpretation emanated from the same principle, and that if in one case it was favorable to the United States, in the other it was so to Spain.

The King's minister made it appear, in his answer to Mr. Adams on the 23d of August, that there was not between the 2d and 7th articles the analogy which was supposed, because, setting aside that the Spanish negotiator was no doubt well apprised that, in the transportation of the Spanish troops, it was understood the provisions should be furnished at the expense of the United States, as the transports were, there was not and could not be the pretended equality in the interpretation of both articles, because Spain would have ceded for a small number of rations the value of an artillery and munitions of great consideration, and the said minister concluded his note by showing that he would inform his Government of the correspondence which had passed upon the subject, that it might settle this point by a common agreement with that of the United States.

In the reply of Mr. Adams of the 25th of September, he brings forward the same arguments as in his former, insists upon the mutual convenience of the liberal interpretation of the articles, and leaves this point to the decision of both Governments.

These are the proceedings which have taken place in this business and the state in which it is left. His Majesty considers it as superfluous, after the discussion which has been had upon this point, to give new reasons in support of those given by his minister at Washington, to show that the artillery, munitions, and instruments of war are not comprehended in the cession of the fortifications. Both yourself, sir, and your Government have in your possession a copy of the cedula, order, which his Majesty addressed to the Captain General of the island of Cuba, under date of the 24th of October, 1820, and in that he tells him, "that the *papers* and *effects* which might belong to the nation, and might not be *comprehended* and *mentioned* in the expressed clauses of the cession, he should cause to be carried and transported to another point of the Spanish possessions."

Your Government cautiously examined the contents of the order, and never avowed pretensions to the artillery, although the phrase, *the other papers and the effects which may belong to the nation*, could not and ought not to be understood as having reference except to the papers not comprehended in the cession, and to *the artillery and munitions of war*; the movable effects are not comprehended in the cession of the *immovable* unless *express mention* of it is made, and the 2d article of the treaty speaks of fortifications and public buildings, and does *not name* the artillery nor the effects which they might contain. Your Government, sir, knows the irresistible force of these reasons, and hence it is that it has had no recurrence to an *allegation of right*, but to *interpretations* which it supposes reciprocally advantageous. It is evident that the pretended utility which the President supposes would result to both nations from the liberal interpretation of the 2d and 7th articles of the treaty, being admitted on the part of the Spanish Government, would cause injury of great consideration to Spain, because, in virtue of it, the United States would receive all the artillery, munitions, and instruments of war in both Floridas, the value of which is nearly about a hundred thousand dollars; and Spain, for a pretended equivalent, the provisions which were furnished to the transported troops, which, to judge by those given in West Florida, would not exceed the sum of $2,500.

It being demonstrated that the supposed reciprocity in the interpretation of the articles does not exist, his Majesty omits giving reasons sufficiently well founded, without having recourse to interpretations, to make it appear that the provisions for the Spanish troops ought to have been at the expense of your Government; since the 7th article, being extended by the Spanish negotiator, appears to raise a doubt, lest he wished to include the rations in the word *transports*, and that he made no particular expression of them from supposing that no doubt could arise upon the matter, because, in the *transports* for an expedition, speaking in a military manner, the provisions are included.

The King does not wish to make a merit of these and other reasons to show that the provisions ought to be at the expense of your Government, and, adhering scrupulously to the literal text of the articles, he yields the right, which he believes he has by the 7th article, to the furnishing by the United States of the provisions for the transportation of the Spanish troops, and demands that delivery be made agreeably to the 2d article, of the artillery, munitions, and instruments of war, &c., which were in the magazines and fortifications of both Floridas at the time when those provinces were delivered up to your Government. In virtue of this mode of conciliating the interests of both powers, in conformity with the literal tenor of the treaty, his Majesty's Government is ready to make good to yours the sum which has been paid for furnishing the Spanish troops with provisions in their passage to the island of Cuba, as soon as the corresponding account of its amount is presented, and the proper orders have been despatched for placing the artillery and other effects at the disposal of the Spanish Government.

His Majesty, being of opinion that many of the articles which ought to be delivered over to Spain may be an accommodation to your Government, orders me to acquaint you, for the information of your Government, that it would not be inconvenient to sell the effects which might be of use to the United States, hearing their propositions, and making, in case of necessity, a valuation of them by skilful men appointed by both Governments.

The King promises himself that, by this means, agreeably to the literal tenor of the treaty, this business will be definitively concluded, which could have, been terminated, at first, in the United States, between your Government and his Majesty's minister, without having given occasion to the disagreements, raised by this subject, between the Commissioners of both Governments; disagreements which your Government foresaw would occur, as the result of the instructions communicated by Mr. Adams to General Jackson, under date of the 23d of March, 1821. It has been a matter of great grief to the King that the American Government, which extended its foreknowledge to understand that, from the artillery not being delivered to the Spanish Commissioner, disgusts would originate, should not have, in obedience to justice and to the desire which has been manifested to avoid every cause of complaint between the two powers, hindered this compromise between the two Commissioners of both Governments, who, with contradictory orders, could not agree among themselves. To this and other acts, which might have been avoided, his Majesty attributes the disagreements which have taken place between the Commissioners of both powers; and that an operation so simple as the delivery of the Floridas has been accompanied with violent steps and insults offered to the Spanish Governors; and it is as certain that when the minds are exasperated in the commencement of a business, although it be for a cause of little import, it is not easy to bring it to a conclusion with a calmness, good faith, and cordiality which are necessary for its amicable and happy conclusion.

I hope, sir, that you will communicate this note to your Government, and I do the same on my part to his Majesty's minister at Washington, that an agreement may take place with the Federal Government upon the points of which it treats.

I renew to you, sir, the assurances of my most distinguished consideration, and pray God that you may live many years.

JOAQUIN DE ANDUAGA.

No. 26.

Don Joaquin de Anduaga to the Secretary of State.

[Translation.]

NEW YORK, *February* 23, 1823.

SIR: In the month of January last, the United States brig-of-war Spark being in the port of Havana, Captain Howell, of the American ship Nancy Elenora, presented himself to her commander, and informed him that a schooner which had robbed him two months before was then in the very port of Havana. The vessel accused was the Spanish merchantman named the Catalan Nymph. It appears that the commander of the Spark was with Captain Howell and two of his sailors, at the house of the commercial agent of the United States, Mr. Warner, and caused some declarations to be extended which said that the robbery had been committed in October last, near Honduras. Afterwards, without making the least representations to the authorities of the Havana, the Spark set sail, convoying the Nancy, at the same time that the Catalan Nymph sailed for Campeachy, and scarcely was she out of port when she was captured by the Spark and sent to Baltimore for adjudication for the pretended crime; into which port not having been able to enter for the ice, she has been carried to Norfolk. This is what Captain Howell and individuals of the Spark have published.

According to the official information which I have received from Norfolk, it turns out that the schooner Catalan Nymph, Captain Don Pablo Daunes, is a merchant vessel, sailing between the Havana and Campeachy, and carries one cannon and some muskets to defend herself against the pirates which infest the coast, her crew consisting of ten men; that on the present occasion she had sailed from the Havana with a cargo of brandy, wine, liquors, coffee, fruits, cloths, and other articles belonging to various individuals, and twelve passengers; that upon her sailing from the Havana, about three miles from the Moro, the Spark began to give chase to the Nymph; that the Captain, wondering at this, tried to return to the Havana, but the Spark cut off her retreat, and her commander made him come on board of him with his papers; that he afterwards ordered an officer with Captain Howell to go to the schooner, who did not recognize any individual, until at last Howell said that he recognized the boatswain as one of the pirates of whom he made a declaration; that Captain Daunes represented to the commander of the Spark that he should examine his papers and he would see that his vessel was a merchantman, or that he should carry her to the Havana, where he could deliver her to the authorities; that the said commander refused everything; that upon the arrival of the Nymph at Norfolk the captain and the ten sailors of the Nymph were publicly carried to prison, escorted by a troop of marines, the latter handcuffed; that the Spanish consul, having had recourse to the competent authority, obtained by the law of habeas corpus that the captain and crew should be set at liberty, except the boatswain, Nicholas Gargoy; and that two of the sailors, in consequence of such atrocities, were dangerously ill.

I have the honor to inclose to you copies of the declaration of Captain Howell, and of the representation which Captain Daunes has made to me; it appearing by this and other documents that on the 16th of October, when the robbery was said to have been committed, the Catalan Nymph was at Sisal, loading for Havana.

From this relation it results—

1. That the United States brig-of-war Spark being in the port of Havana, her commander received from the captain of another merchant vessel of the same nation a declaration that he had been plundered at sea by a schooner which at that time was in the very port of Havana.

2. That the said commander took before the commercial agent of the United States in the s i city a declaration of the aforesaid Captain Howell upon his complaint.

3. That without further examination he resolved to capture the Nymph as soon as she should sail from the port.

4. That he did not make the least attempt with the competent authorities to investigate the foundation of the accusation, nor to punish the guilty, if it should be certain.

5. That he carried his intention into effect by actually capturing the Nymph in sight of the port.

6. That he refused to examine the papers of Captain Daunes and the just representations which he made to him.

7. That, by sending the Catalan Nymph to Norfolk, the proprietors and freighters of the vessel have suffered immense losses, and Spanish citizens have been treated in a manner the most unworthy, and two of them have been rendered so ill as to endanger their lives. And, in a word, that the commander of the Spark, in union with Mr. Warner, have erected in the port of Havana a tribunal to try Spaniards in the said city, to condemn them without a hearing, and to carry their sentence into execution in a manner so vile and treacherous that only a few examples of similar conduct can be met with among the pirates, whom the commander of the Spark has orders to pursue, and not to imitate.

I think it needless to observe that the commander aforesaid has covered with ignominy, upon this occasion, the uniform which he wears, and that the outrage which he has committed upon Spain is such as no doubt the Government of the United States will not delay a moment in punishing as a crime no less injurious to Spain than degrading to this Republic—in this manner proving to Europe that it wishes to preserve with his Catholic Majesty the ties which unite both nations. This provision is so much the more urgent, inasmuch as, if it should be tardy in the execution, it is impossible to calculate the effect which this delay will have in the Spanish dominions, into the ports of which the ships-of-war of the United States cannot be admitted with safety, after so scandalous an example. Thus, then, in compliance with the orders which I have from his Majesty to promote with all my power the means which may draw more close the friendship which he wishes to maintain with this Republic, and to remove what may be capable of relaxing it, I pray you, sir, be pleased to lay what I have explained before the President, and obtain from his justice the due punishment of the commander of the Spark, the restitution of the schooner Catalan Nymph, the liberty of the boatswain, and security for the immense losses and damages which the owners and shippers of the said vessel have sustained.

The importance of this business, and my anxiety to avoid the deplorable consequences which may ensue in the island of Cuba to the trade between the Spaniards and Americans, oblige me to request that you will be pleased to answer this note as soon as possible.

I repeat to you, sir, the assurances of my most distinguished consideration.

                                                  JOAQUIN DE ANDUAGA.

No. 26, (a.)

Don Pablo Daunes to Don Joaquin de Anduaga.

[Translation.]

                                                  NORFOLK, *February* 12, 1823.

YOUR EXCELLENCY: Don Pablo Daunes, captain of the Spanish schooner named the Catalan Nymph, the property of Don Bartolomé Yglesias, Don José Calvet, Don Domingo Zubira, and Don Gregoria Garcia, passengers in said schooner and owners of some part of her cargo, all Spaniards, in their name and in that of the others interested, with the greatest respect, explains to your excellency that the said schooner having sailed from Havana on the 26th of January last, cleared by that custom-house and the respective authorities, bound to Campeachy, were detained on their voyage by the brig-of-war of the United States named the Spark, her commander, Wilkinson, under pretext of a declaration which it appears an American captain made to him in the Havana that the said schooner had plundered him. Having made Captain Daunes come on board of him, he caused the said American captain, with two sailors, to appear, whom he ordered, with his boat armed, on board the Nymph. They caused all the crew to appear, and the American captain referred to, after having hesitated some time, at last said he recognized her to be the same schooner which had plundered him, and pointed to one of the individuals, (who is the boatswain, Nicholas Gargoy,) saying that he likewise recognized him, which, being heard by his two sailors, although doubtful, they agreed in the same. At the same moment, the commander, Wilkinson, captured her as a pirate, put the crew in irons, and a prize captain and crew to conduct her to the United States. Captain Daunes presented to him the papers that he might see they were in due form, and represented to him that, carrying a cargo of value belonging to various individuals, he should carry her to the Havana, and that there he would be assured that he was not a pirate, and that neither the schooner nor that individual had plundered any vessel; and, on the contrary, she was a vessel of such credit that all the merchants preferred her for a cargo, and she always made voyages from Havana to Campeachy and Sisal with valuable cargoes. The commander, Wilkinson, would attend to nothing, nor look at the papers, wherefore Captain Daunes told him that he protested against the losses and damages which might result to the interested from an act so violent. Conducted to this port by a prize officer and crew, she arrived on the 8th current, and on the 9th, in the morning, they publicly conducted to the prison, escorted by troops, Captain Daunes and the crew (the latter in irons) and told the three passengers they might go where they pleased. These proceedings would have been just if they really were pirates, but being all persons of good credit in the Havana for their conduct, to whom interests of consideration were intrusted, Captain Wilkinson should have examined the papers, and, in case of suspicion, have carried them to the Havana, reflecting that a vessel, with a cargo of so great a value which he himself saw sail, and which had not a crew sufficient for committing piracies, was a scandalous, arbitrary act, contrary to the good understanding which subsists between the United States and Spain. The losses and damages which the owners of the schooner and cargo sustain are incalculable; the expenses of the exponents in this country considerable, in virtue of her being a Spanish merchant vessel, with her papers in due form, not pirates, as Captain Wilkinson supposes, and the robbery which he attributes to her being also a supposition, as, upon the 16th of October last, which appears evident in the declaration, the robbery was committed near the Honduras, it can be easily proved, and even here, by letters which are in the possession of Captain Daunes, that at that time the schooner was in Sisal loading for the Havana, and that she had never gone so far as those points. The invariable rules of justice and of the good understanding used by nations, and chiefly between the United States and Spain, imperiously demand that the Government of the United States immediately order the restoration of the schooner and cargo to their owners, with security for all the losses, damages, and deteriorations, which may be the result of the said capture, inasmuch as it has been committed by one of their vessels and officers without its being deserved, and contrary to every rule of justice, as also indemnification to the individuals of the crew of the stigma of pirates and ill treatment which they have suffered; to which their refined conduct never caused them to be subjected: Therefore the exponents entreat your excellency, with the utmost submission, as their only protector, to be pleased to claim of the Government of the United States the restoration of the vessel and cargo, security for losses and damages, and indemnification which they solicit, which they hope from your accredited zeal, and whose life, &c. ,

PABLO DAUNES.
DOMINGO ZUBIRA.
GREGORIO GARCIA.
JOSÉ CALBETE.

His Excellency Don JOAQUIN DE ANDUAGA,
    Minister Plenipotentiary of his Catholic Majesty near the United States.

No. 27.

Don Joaquin de Anduaga to the Secretary of State.

[Translation.]

NEW YORK, *March* 6, 1823.

SIR: Under date of the 14th of December of last year I had the honor to address you a note, requesting explanations on the expedition from these ports for the conquest of the island of Porto Rico, and the disapprobation of the conduct of the captain of the United States corvette Cyane, in the claim which he was said to have made to the Governor of Curaçoa in favor of Mr. Irvine, one of the chiefs of that expedition. Lately I have received official letters from my Government, in which is energetically expressed the surprise of his Catholic Majesty at seeing the possessions of Spain attacked in a manner so public and scandalous by the citizens of a power to which so great and so costly proofs have been given of its friendship; and although it has appeared to him extraordinary that the President should have been ignorant of preparations made with so little secrecy, and that a collection of men and of ships, laden with munitions of war, in the ports nearest to the capital, should have been able to be concealed from him; nevertheless, judging by his own sentiments of those which he believed animated the President, he did not doubt that it was so, and that this Government, the instant it should have notice of such an event, would hasten to take the most vigorous measures for the punishment of the delinquents and for preventing such excesses in future; and, above all, that to prove to his Majesty and to all Europe the indignation produced to it by this attempt, it would have been gratified in giving to the cabinet of Spain the satisfaction and explanations which so odious a breach of the laws of nations and of the friendship which unites this Republic with Spain so imperiously demanded. This persuasion was so natural that it is very easy to calculate what effect it would have on the mind of his Majesty, and on that of all the Spaniards, to know that this Government not only has thought proper not to give a spontaneous explanation on an event injurious to Spain, and which in so shameful manner stains the good faith and reputation of this Republic, but that an answer has been withheld for so many months to the notes which I have had the honor to address to it on this subject. The consequence which should be drawn from this cannot escape your penetration. It is very clear that if, from the ports of Spain, an expedition should depart for the attack and conquest of a province of the United States, and that his Catholic Majesty should not only not give at the time explanations of his ignorance and disapprobation of it, but that he should neglect the representations of the American minister at Madrid, the President would have a right to believe that that hostile measure had been carried into execution, if not with the consent of the Spanish Government, at least with its connivance. But if the conviction which I have of the equity of the President, and of his desire to maintain with Spain the amity which happily subsists, prevents me from drawing, in the case whereof I treat, that consequence, evident as it may appear, I cannot help seeing in your silence a singular indifference to the feelings of his Catholic Majesty, in respect to the attacks which his possessions and subjects receive on the part of the Americans. I know how painful this will be to my Government, and how grievous not to see its friendship towards this Republic answered in a correspondent manner, nor the proofs which it has given of it; and anxious to tranquilize it, I take the liberty of requesting you to be pleased to answer my note of the 14th of December last, not doubting but that it will be such as will calm the inquietude and uneasiness which must be caused in the mind of his Catholic Majesty by the expedition referred to, and by having left my notes unanswered.

I renew to you, sir, therefore, the assurance of my high consideration.

JOAQUIN DE ANDUAGA.

No. 28.

Don Joaquin de Anduaga to the Secretary of State.

[Translation.]

NEW YORK, *March* 7, 1823.

SIR: I have the honor to send you inclosed copies of the protest made in Pensacola by Don Jacinta Correa, captain of the Spanish schooner called the Carman, alias Galliga the Third, and of a judicial declaration made by the same before the consul of Spain in New Orleans.

In both documents are set forth the capture of the said schooner by the United States ship-of-war Peacock and the oppression and robbery committed by her crew, all which has been confirmed to me by the Captain General of the Havana, and by the consul of Spain in New Orleans. As the circumstances of these crimes are expressed in the inclosed documents I avoid repeating them in this note, and shall rest content with calling your attention to three of the principal, which are, the Peacock having made the capture with the *Spanish flag*, the violation of the public correspondence between two provinces of his Catholic Majesty, and the malicious contrivance of Captain Cassin in sending the crew of the Carman to Pensacola and the vessel to New Orleans, that there might be no one to defend her there. Such violations of all public law, and such refined perfidy, are so evident and odious that I think it unnecessary to insist upon them, since it would be doing an injury to the sense and justice of this Government. Notwithstanding the insidious precaution of Captain Cassin, scarcely had the courts of Pensacola and New Orleans examined the case, when the former declared the crew innocent and set them at liberty, and the other ordered the restitution of the vessel, which saves me the trouble of proving the illegality of the capture; and it only remains with me to request that the President would be pleased to order satisfaction to the owners of the schooner Carman for the losses and damages which they have sustained, and that the money and effects of which they have been plundered be restored to the crew. This is what it concerns me to ask in favor of said individuals; but the just satisfaction of my Government, the assurance in future of due respect to the Spanish flag and the lives and property of Spanish citizens, imposes upon me the obligation of speaking to you with that frankness which ought to subsist between two friendly powers whose interest it is to maintain the greatest harmony.

The injuries done by this country to his Catholic Majesty and to his subjects are not confined to expeditions of individuals for the conquest of his provinces, to hostilities under the insurgent flag, to building armed ships for the enemies of Spain, to furnish these men with munitions of war, &c.; but they have gone to attack publicly the vessels of Spain by ships-of-war of the United States, and to trample upon Spanish citizens by American officers; the excess being carried to such a pitch that his Catholic Majesty's territory is violated, and if a speedy check be not put to it the Spanish commerce must be in dread of the ships-of-war of a nation which is said to be friendly as it would of another with which it was in a complete state of rupture.

The violations of neutrality and of friendship between two nations, committed by individuals, always give room to the offended power to believe that they have taken place without the knowledge and against the will of the Government of the aggressors, and that it will grant a competent satisfaction; but when this is not only refused, and not even private citizens but the ships and officers of that Government give the insult and commit hostilities with its approbation, since it neither punishes them nor prevents them from continuing their aggressions, the illusion must cease, and, alarmed for the intentions of said Government, the imperious obligation which it is under of protecting its subjects lays it under the necessity of demanding a frank explanation of them, and indispensable provisions for the putting a stop to the scandal of acts which continue could only be followed by consequences which his Catholic Majesty has a lively desire of avoiding, it being his most sincere wish to preserve inviolate the friendship which he professes towards this Republic.

Vain have been my repeated remonstrances to obtain satisfaction for the insults offered to my Government and fellow-citizens by the American officers. And if, in the courts of the United States, the Spaniards have found justice, the Government has not only refused my petitions, but has not even given an answer to the greater part of my notes. The very sentences of the courts prove the justice of my complaints against the said officers; and when it is seen that this Government, in spite of these complaints and the opinion of the most eminent and just judges of this Republic, refuses to his Catholic Majesty the satisfaction which is his due, does not answer the representations of his minister, and continues its protection and favor to the officers accused, the suspicion is allowed that its friendly sentiments towards Spain have undergone an alteration. This doubt will be extremely painful to his Catholic Majesty, wherefore I spend more time in requesting you to be pleased to clear it up, and this can be done in no other way than by giving to his Majesty the satisfaction which he has demanded for so great injuries, with the punishment of the officers who have committed them, and especially of Captain Cassin, and giving the most peremptory orders that they be not repeated.

The multiplied proofs of friendship which his Majesty has given to this Republic, the sacrifices which he has made in its favor, and the utility which results to both nations in the continuance of a good understanding between both, are to me a sure guaranty that the President, deigning to take into consideration the important contents of this note, will be pleased to order such an answer to it as will at once dissipate the disagreeable impressions which the acts of the American officers have made, and assure his Catholic Majesty that his desires for the continuance of the strictest friendship with this Republic will be fulfilled.

I repeat my devotion to you, sir, and pray you to accept the assurance of my high consideration.

JOAQUIN DE ANDUAGA.

No. 29.

Don Hilario de Rivas y Salmon to the Secretary of State, April 15, 1823.

[Translation.]

SIR: Don Richard Meade, a citizen of the United States, addressed two letters to my predecessor, his excellency Don Joaquin de Anduaga, dated April 4 and October 10, 1822, inclosing your correspondence with the Commissioners appointed in virtue of the 11th article of the treaty of the 22d of February, 1819, ratified by his Catholic Majesty and exchanged in February, 1821, relative to the admission of certain claims which are therein mentioned. The said gentleman sent these documents to my Government, along with the answer which he made to Mr. Meade, on the 16th of October, 1822, copy of which I have the honor to inclose to you.

His Majesty has been pleased to approve and sanction the said answer to Mr. Meade, and commands me to support his claims, and to represent to you, in the most friendly terms, but, at the same time, in the most energetic and solemn manner, against all opposition which may be attempted to be made, that the particular credit which said Meade had against the Spanish nation is not satisfied, but that, in virtue of the last treaty, the Government of the United States has taken it upon itself.

This credit is, in truth, the only one which has been solemnly acknowledged by his Catholic Majesty. It was executed at the pressing instances of the minister of the United States at Madrid, and its acknowledgment and final liquidation took place at a time and in circumstances which do not admit the least doubt to ensue as to its legitimacy and import.

The value of the credit was represented to both Governments during the negotiation. Its liquidation could be effected only by the parties interested in the contracts and in the damages and injuries by which an indemnification was claimed, and the investigation, with precision of the exact sum which was due, appeared to be a point of equal interest to both Governments. This was at least shown and insisted on with vigor by the Government of the United States before and after the date of the treaty; and his Catholic Majesty, when he acceded to its anxiety, desirous of shunning new causes of complaint, chose four of his counsellors, from different tribunals, and commanded them to examine, scrupulously and in detail, all the circumstances regarding an account so complicated, and which required all the possible knowledge and intelligence of the laws of Spain and commercial regulations of the nation to be able to form a just conception of all the transaction. No subject of this nature has been ever considered so cautiously and with so much matureness, not only by the Commissioners appointed for that purpose, but, latterly, by the Treasurer General, by the greater accountant's office, by the Minister of Finance, and, lastly, it received the sanction of his Majesty.

In these circumstances, his Majesty thinks that he ought not to see with indifference, nor remain undisturbed, when an attempt is made to invalidate an act so solemn. The Spanish nation was certainly responsible for the total amount of the acknowledged debt. The Government of the United States, by the latter ratification of the treaty, took upon itself this debt, in virtue of the fifth renunciation of the 11th (9th) article, and with a full knowledge of its amount, which had been communicated long before the conclusion of the treaty to the minister of the United States at Madrid by his Majesty's Secretary of State for the information of the American Government. Certainly, after all that has passed, it was not to be expected that a new investigation of the business should be judged necessary.

There cannot be a doubt that if the treaty of the 22d of February had not been concluded, Mr. Meade would have received from the Spanish nation the total amount of his debt; and his Majesty cannot comprehend the justice of the Commissioners in having attempted, in the first place, to reject entirely this debt as not being comprehended in the treaty, and much less could his Majesty be persuaded that so solemn an act of his Government, an act which was in a great degree founded upon the interposition of the American cabinet, and which was done in good faith, would have been afterwards placed in doubt by their agents.

The slight which the commission of claims has endeavored to throw upon the most respectable authorities of Spain, and upon his Majesty himself, and consequently on the whole nation, has caused his Majesty great pain.

I have, therefore, the order of my Government to inform you that it cannot keep silence when an act so incontestable is placed in doubt, and I beforehand protest solemnly and respectfully against any decision of the Commissioners appointed in virtue of the treaty which invalidates, in any manner, the acknowledgment made by my Government of the total debt of Mr. Meade, agreeably to the certificate which they sent to him in consequence and which is in their possession.

I have the honor to repeat to you, sir, the testimony of my distinguished and high consideration.

HILARIO DE RIVAS Y SALMON.

No. 30.

Mr. Salmon to the Secretary of State.

[Translation.]

APRIL 28, 1823.

SIR: I recommend very forcibly to your attention the letter of Dr. Pablo Chacon, a copy of which I have the honor to inclose, respecting the business of the Spanish schooner the Ninfa Catalana. My predecessor sent you two notes, dated the 23d and 28th of February last, concerning the unjust detention of this vessel and the scandalous insulting of her crew without any motive or cause whatever. His excellency accompanied this sad truth with sufficient proofs, but, for the greater abundance, I now inclose other testimony, which I have just received from the Havana, of the process raised there by the consignee of the said vessel. You will find that it is in accordance with the other proofs, and forms, with them, one whole. But what more evident proof can be required of the innocence of the whole crew and of the atrocious injustice of the captors than that the whole individuals of it being set free in virtue of the *habeas corpus* in their favor?

Permit me, sir, to repeat with efficacy the representations of his excellency on this business, and I pray you to obtain from your Government a decision prompt and satisfactory to his Majesty and the subjects of Spain, so grievously injured in their reputation and interests.

I renew to you, sir, the assurance of my respect and high consideration.

HILARIO DE RIVAS Y SALMON.

Don Sebn. Kindelan to Mr. Anduaga.

[Translation.]

MARCH 4, 1823.

In consequence of what I mentioned to your excellency in my official letter of the 17th of February last, relative to the decree by the Junta of Government of this national consulship, on the event which took place to the Spanish schooner named Ninfa Catalana on her sailing from this port with the American brig-of-war Spark, I now send to your excellency a copy of the memorial which Don Pedro Lopez, a merchant here, has presented to me, as consignee of the vessel, inclosing at the same time testimony of the process which has been raised upon the business, in order that your excellency may be pleased to make the representations which you may think best, as well in regard to the vessel as of the rest which is mentioned. I recommend very particularly to your excellency this business, in which the national honor and the interests of this trade are concerned.

God preserve your excellency many years.

SEBN. KINDELAN.

Memorial of Don Pedro Lopez.

[Translation.]

HAVANA, *March* 4, 1823.

SEÑOR SUPERIOR POLITICAL CHIEF: Don Pedro Lopez, merchant of this city, and consignee of the Spanish schooner called the Ninfa, with due respect represents: That all the documents relative to the unfortunate business of the said schooner Ninfa being collected as they are, he accompanies them with legalized testimony, in order that you may be pleased to make suitable use of it; and for this purpose entreats you will be pleased to have the goodness to order the aforesaid documents to be laid before the Minister Plenipotentiary of our Spanish nation resident in the United States of America, with all the recommendations and energy which a case so extraordinary requires, in order that the offended honor of the Spanish flag may be repaired, the individuals harassed and maltreated, and the interests detained with the damages, costs, expenses, and losses which have been incurred may be recovered, because it belongs to strict justice, and will be the favor which he hopes to merit from you.

PEDRO LOPEZ.

A true copy.

ANTONIO M. DE LA TORRE Y CARDENAS.

No. 30, (*a.*)

Testimony in the case of the Ninfa Catalana.

[Translation.]

HAVANA, *January* 31, 1823.

PETITION.

SEÑOR SUPERIOR POLITICAL CHIEF: Don Pedro Lopez, merchant of this city, and consignee of the Spanish schooner Ninfa Catalana, Captain Don Pablo Daunes, with the usual respect says: That being charged with the despatch of said vessel for the port of Campeachy, she sailed for that destination on the twenty-sixth of the present month, under the formal and circumspect order which our laws prescribe; and when I thought that she was pursuing the course of her voyage, yesterday a letter from her captain was delivered to me, informing me of his having been detained, or rather captured and maltreated, by the United States brig-of-war called the Spark; I being obliged, in such a case, to make the protest, which I duly present in testimony. By said document you will see at first that the only pretext for such a proceeding is that a merchant captain, also an American, complained to the commander of the Spark that the boatswain and the schooner Ninfa herself, coming from Cadiz, had robbed him; and when delicacy, the law of nations, that of reciprocal alliance and friendship, the laws of the territory, and the consideration just and due to its authorities legally constituted, might have dictated that he should have had recourse to the judicial power of this capital, in order that the accuser and accused might be heard in form, and the matter be determined as civilized nations are accustomed to do, the commander of the Spark feigned not to understand at all; he remained until the sailing of the schooner Ninfa to perpetrate the offence which produces the protest which I am about to make. From such a proceeding you will infer that the navigation, the commerce, and the property of the Spaniards are subject to the caprice of a malicious man, who, without any appearance of justice, may wish to destroy at once the most sacred rights of men in society; that the laws and authorities of the Spaniards are of so little value and importance that the simple will of one man renders them not only insignificant, but also insecure and so despised that, with an unheard-of freedom, the said brig Spark has returned to enter this port yesterday, bringing several passengers of the Ninfa with her. In virtue of this, and with a reservation of the rights of others who act with me, I entreat you that, receiving as presented the protest which I now produce, you will be pleased to take into your superior consideration an act so scandalous, that the true spirit of general law and of the common laws may be put in force; what is necessary may be done, that this occurrence may not remain unpunished to prevent its progress; that the entire losses and damages may be made good; that the guilty be punished; that it may not be concealed from the respective Governments, and that we may be Spaniards in reality and not in theory. All which in justice I implore from you.

PEDRO LOPEZ.

DECREE ON THE MARGIN.

HAVANA, *January* 31, 1823.

Pass it to the Acting Auditor of War.

KINDELAN.

DICTAMEN ON THE MARGIN.

HAVANA, *February* 1, 1823.

SOR. CAPTAIN GENERAL: I think, in the first place, that the information should be received, on the facts of which this process treats, the petitioner producing the witnesses of the case, and with his merit he will supply what may be more conformable, saving always, &c.

FRAN. DEL CRISTO.

DECREE ON THE MARGIN.

HAVANA, *February* 1, 1823.

I agree with the foregoing dictamen, and order that it may be fulfilled; and in virtue of it the information may be received which the Auditor of War suggests as before.

KINDELAN.
MAL. DE LA TORRE.

HAVANA.·

On the said day it was made known to Don Pedro Lopez.
Attest: TORRE.

TESTIMONY OF PROTEST.

HAVANA, *January* 31, 1823.

In the always faithful city of the Havana, on the thirtieth of January, one thousand eight hundred and twenty-three, before me, the public notary, and the witnesses, appeared Don Pedro Lopez, an inhabitant and merchant here, to whom I give credit and whom I know, and said, that about half-past one in the afternoon of this day the American brig-of-war called the Spark entered this port, and there was delivered to him, as he says, a letter by Don Ignatio Lopez, dated at sea, the 26th of the current month, subscribed by Don Pablo Daunes, the tenor of which is literally as follows:

"*AT SEA, January* 26, 1823.

"SIR: The brig of Don Pedro Martinez having this morning made the signal for getting under way, I weighed and went out, the American brig-of-war named the Spark having gone before, and being about pistol shot from her, he ordered me to launch the boat, which I obeyed, and he told me that I was accused of having robbed the American schooner, which had this day sailed from this port of the Havana, called or named the Elenora, Captain Howell; and said Howell having gone on board to recognize the men, said that it is the boatswain, Nicholas Gongoll, very old in this vessel, as you and the house of Sogas know; said Howell also said that the schooner Ninfa Catalana was the same that had robbed him; and thus I have endeavored to show you the whole truth, as all the merchants of the Havana, it appears to me, know me and the vessel; that we have never been guilty of any crime, either the vessel, myself, or the crew. They command us to follow, it appears, to Baltimore or Charleston, and I have charged the commander with the losses which may take place. I desire you to pass and send it to your friend Pablo Daunes. Do not fail to write me, and to speak with some one who has knowledge of these matters, or others whom I mention, how we may conduct ourselves, and write to Iglesias.

"Senor Don PEDRO LOPEZ."

It is conformable to said letter which I, the notary, corrected and compared, and have returned sealed to the same Don Pedro Lopez, to whom I refer, who pursues, saying, that having been informed by the same D. Ignacio Lopez, D. Juan Pastor, D. Juan Alvarez, D. Salvador Fernandez, and others, who may be named in time and form, passengers and shippers, interested in the Spanish schooner Ninfa Catalana; that in fact, being on board said vessel, within cannon shot of the Moro Castle of this port, the aforesaid schooner Ninfa Catalana was detained, seized, and manned by the crew of the American brig-of-war Spark, by the order and will of her commander, manning her with eighteen of the crew of the said brig, with two marine guards, leaving on board of the same Ninfa her armament, putting manacles on the boatswain and irons on his feet, and leaving the captain, D. Pablo Daunes, and three passengers free; in which state it was determined, as the said witnesses understood and will agree with their signatures as proof, and likewise mentioned in the letter which has just been produced, that they directed the said schooner to the port of Charleston, or of Baltimore, observing that the before mentioned American brig-of-war sailed from this port on the same twenty-sixth day of the current month, half an hour before the schooner Ninfa Catalana: so that the attack was premeditated, in violation of the laws of justice and of nations, of the local authorities of the territory, of a friendly flag, and of the reciprocal respect which civilized nations insure to commerce and the nation. Wherefore, there being no example of a similar crime, leaving safe all the resources which may be favorable to him and the laws allow him, he protests, once, twice, thrice, and four times, if it be necessary, and the laws authorize him, against the commander, crew and vessel of the said American brig-of-war Spark, of the United States of America, for the detention, seizure, losses, damages, injuries, demurrage, consequent damage, and profit ceasing, expenses and charges which such a proceeding may occasion, that they may be refunded to those who may be lawfully interested in the before mentioned Spanish schooner Ninfa Catalana, hull, keel, and other appurtenances, as well to those who may be her shippers, as whatever else may be necessary of her hull.

In testimony whereof, thus he said, agreed, and signed, at half-past five in the afternoon of this day, with the other individuals referred to as witnesses, D. José Segundo, D. Calletano Covisor, and D. Francisco Valerio, inhabitants and present. Pedro Lopez, Salvador Hernandez, at the request of D. Ignacio Lopez, and D. Juan Alvarez, who in the act declared that they knew not how to sign; Francisco Valerio, Juan Pastor, José de Salinas. Agreeable to the original, which remains in the archive of this notarial office under my charge, to which I refer, and upon the petition of Don Pedro Lopez I give these presents in duplicate.

JOSÉ SALINAS.

PETITION.

To the Acting Captain General:

D. Pedro Lopez, an inhabitant and merchant of this city, and consignee of the Spanish schooner Ninfa Catalana, Captain D. Pablo Daunes, with due respect explains to you that, by the former decree which provides that competent information be received before the Auditor of War which may establish the truth of the facts to which he confines himself in his former process, and to fulfil it, it is proper for him that you will be pleased to order that those to whom he refers in his said memorial should say, under the solemnity of an oath, and declare, respecting the following particulars, 1st. If they know Don Bartolomé Iglesias, owner and captain of the said schooner, D. Pablo Daunes, second captain, and accidentally first, he (Iglesias) having been left sick in Campeachy, and Nicolas Gongall, boatswain in the present voyage, formerly a sailor in her, incapable from their known honor of having committed hostility or injury upon any vessel of a friendly or allied power, it being impossible, from the said circumstances, that they could have tolerated any other individual belonging to the said schooner to have perpetrated the crime of which the commander of the American brig-of-war Spark accuses them. That they say, as they know and is evident to them, that from the 26th of November of the year 1818, when the aforesaid Iglesias purchased the said schooner Ninfa Catalana of D. Martin de Zavala, to the present time, he has made no other voyage than to Campeachy, Sisal, or other port of the Gulf of Mexico, without ever having seen or heard of this vessel having been destined to other places than those mentioned. In the same manner, say how Don Ignacio Lopez, or any other of the witnesses to whom it may be known, say how he knows that the accusation which the American schooner made of the Ninfa Catalana, to the commander of the brig already cited, arises from the resentment of a sailor of the former against one of the latter, who shall certainly be the boatswain of her, for not having permitted him to make fast a rope to the Ninfa when he came alongside of the former at the wharf, for which reason the American threatened that he would pay him, and this was the cause of the false accusation already related; wherefore I entreat you to be pleased to accede to this request agreeably to justice.

PEDRO LOPEZ.

HAVANA, *February* 3, 1823.

DECREE.

Havana, February 3, 1823. As he requests—two dashes.

MANUEL DE LA TORRE.

NOTIFICATION.

In the Havana, on the said day, I notify it to Don Pedro Lopez.
Attest:

TORRE.

DECLARATION.

In the ever faithful city of the Havana, on the 3d of February, 1823, before the Acting Auditor of War, appeared Don Ignacio Lopez, a native of the Kingdom of Galicia, an inhabitant of Campeachy, and at present a resident here, a married man, and by profession a merchant, who made oath in due form of law, under which he offered to speak the truth; and being examined by the particulars of the foregoing interrogatory and memorial of the former page, said, after being informed of the said memorial and of the protest which accompanies it, that the passage is certain and true which the last relates, in which appears copied the letter which the captain of the schooner Ninfa Catalana directed to Don Pedro Lopez, his consignee, which fact took place at the distance of a cannot shot from the Moro, loading the boatswain of the schooner Ninfa and the sailors with chains; and answers, being interrogated on the first particular, he said: That he knows the individuals to whom the interrogatory refers, whom he takes and has taken for honest men, and of regular conduct, not having ever heard it said that the said individuals could have committed the crime of which they have been accused by the captain of the schooner which was said to be robbed, conceiving at the same time that such an imputation is a falsehood; and answers to the second, that it is certain that, from the date which is cited, the voyages which the said schooner has made have been to the ports which the interrogatory mentions, in the Gulf of Mexico, without having heard it said that she had been destined to other points than those related; to the third and last, that it is certain that the accusation which the captain of the American schooner made has no other origin than that which is related as having passed in the terms written; and answers that what he has declared is the truth, in virtue of the oath which he has taken; that he is forty years of age. It was read to him, and he declared it to be correct; that he is not comprehended in the general principles of the law; does not sign from not knowing how; which I attest. Before me,

MANUEL DE LA TORRE.

DECLARATION.

In the ever faithful city of the Havana, the same day, month and year, before the same Sör Auditor, appeared Don Salvador Fernandez, a native of Galicia, a married man, and by profession a merchant, to whom an oath was administered, which he made with due form of law, under which he promised to speak the truth; and being examined as to the foregoing, said, that the event is certain and true, described in the memorial of the first page and the protest, which is added in testimony, as it happened accordingly and as this document relates it, which is evident to him in consequence of his being on board the schooner Ninfa Catalana on the day mentioned, as he had taken his passage in her for Campeachy, to which port she was bound and proceeded about a cannon shot's distance from the Moro; and answers, being interrogated by the first particular of the preceding interrogatory, said, that he has been in the habit of sailing upwards of two years in the said schooner, for the purchase and sale of his merchandise, for which reason he knows and is acquainted with the persons whom the interrogatory indicates, whom he has considered, and still considers as men of honorable proceedings, who are incapable of committing hostilities, or allowing them to be committed, or causing damage to any vessel belonging to nations our allies; and answers to the second, that, by what he has related in his former answer, he knows that the schooner Ninfa Catalana has not directed her voyages to other ports than those mentioned. To the third and last, that it is certain the declarant was present, and also one of the sailors of the schooner Ninfa, who had been brought by the orders of the American brig Spark; and answers that what he has declared is the truth, in virtue of his oath; that he is twenty-seven years of age; it was read to him and he declared it to be correct and signed it, declaring that he is not comprehended in the general principles of the law. The Auditor did it, which I attest.

SALVADOR FERNANDEZ.

Before me, MANUEL DE LA TORRE.

DECLARATION.

In continuance of the act, appeared before his lordship D. José Ferrer, a native of Catalonia, a married man, domiciliated in Campeachy, and by profession a merchant, to whom was administered the oath in the form prescribed by law, under which he promised to speak the truth; and being examined by the memorial of the first page, which was read to him, as also the protest, which is added in testimony, said, that the fact is certain and true which the memorial and protest mention as having happened on the date and in the terms which the letter inserted in the protest indicates, the schooner Ninfa Catalana being distant about a cannon shot from the Moro; and answers, being interrogated by the first particular of the preceding interrogatory, said, that from having made voyages in the schooner Ninfa Catalana, as a passenger, he knows the persons mentioned, whom he has considered and considers as men of all honor, incapable, from their good qualities, of committing hostilities or causing damage to any vessel belonging to nations our allies, or of permitting a sailor belonging to her to commit it; and answers to the second, for the reason already given, he is equally certain that the said schooner has made no other voyages than to the points which the interrogatory indicates; and answers to the third and last, that he is ignorant of it, although he has heard it said in the same vessel, for which reason he does not assert it; and answers that what he has declared is the truth, in virtue of his oath; that he is of the age of thirty-five years; that it was read to him, and he declared it to be correct; he did not sign from not knowing how; the Auditor did it, which I attest.

Before me,

MANUEL DE LA TORRE.

DECLARATION.

In the ever faithful city of the Havana, on the fourth of February, one thousand eight hundred and twenty-three, before acting Auditor of War, appeared Don Juan Pastor, a native of Tarragona, in the principality of Catalonia, and an inhabitant of Merida, in Yucatan, a widower, and professionally a merchant, whose oath was taken by God and the Holy Cross, under which he promised to speak the truth; and being examined by the preceding representations and the protest, which is added in testimony, being read to him, he said that the said protest attests the truth of the facts, for which purpose he subscribed it, the said first memorial being also agreeable to it. Being examined by the contents of the second, he said that he knows the persons who are mentioned, and has sailed with them, and by the same he can say, with all safety, that they are honorable men, of irreproachable conduct, and thus he considers them incapable of having committed any hostility on vessels belonging to a friendly nation, esteeming whatever may be said to the contrary as a calumny; he can do no less than represent, that, having requested the captain of the American brig-of-war to mark the point at which the schooner Ninfa Catalana had caused the damage, as she had been in the trade from Campeachy to the Havana about four years, the declarant being the consignee in Sisal, and he answered in his language, and by an interpreter, that he did not know. To the second, that all that is related in the interrogatory is certain, and answers that what he has declared is the truth, in virtue of his oath; that he is advanced in age. It was read to him, and he declared it to be correct, and signed it with his lordship, which I attest—one dash.

JUAN PASTOR.

Before me, MANUEL DE LA TORRE.

DECLARATION.

In continuation, appeared before his lordship Don Juan Alvarez de Castro, a native of Galicia, and inhabitant of this city, a bachelor, and his business that of a merchant, who made oath, in due form of law, under which he promised to speak the truth; and being examined by the memorial of the first page, which was read to him, as well as the protest, which accompanies it in testimony, said: That what both documents express is certain and true, because, as a passenger of the schooner Ninfa Catalana, he was present at the whole and assisted in forming the protest; and being examined by the other representations, said: To the first, that he knows all the persons who are named, whom he considers as men of honorable conduct, and does not believe capable of having committed the crime which the commander of the American brig-of-war Spark, belonging to an allied nation, attributes to them. To the second, that, as far as the interrogatory expresses is well known to him, and answers that what he has declared is the truth by the oath which he has taken; that he is forty-six years of age. It was read to him, and he declared it to be correct. He did not sign, as he said he did not know how, which was done for him, which I attest.

Before me,   MANUEL DE LA TORRE.

DECLARATION.

In continuation, before his lordship appeared Don José Anet, a native of Catalonia, and inhabitant of this city, a married man, and merchant, to whom was administered the oath, in due form of law, under which he promised to speak the truth; and being examined by the memorial of the first page, and the protest, which accompanies it, being read to him, said: That the contents of the memorial and protest, which were read to him, agree with the declarations which Don Pedro Lopez has made to him; and being examined by the particulars of the last representation produced by this man, said: To the first, that he knows the persons who are mentioned as belonging to the schooner Ninfa Catalana, always esteeming them honest men, as having heard nothing to the contrary, and therefore does not presume that they can have committed any hostility, and especially upon vessels belonging to an allied nation. To the second, that what the interrogatory expresses is known to him, except the date when the schooner was purchased, and answers that what he has declared is the truth by his oath; that he is thirty-one years of age. It was read to him, and he declared it to be correct, and signed with his lordship, which I attest.

                                                                                            JOSÉ ANET.
Before me, MANUEL DE LA TORRE.

DECREE.

                                                                HAVANA, *February* 4, 1823.

The informatory evidence having been furnished, which was provided in the decree of the first current, let these proceedings be delivered to D. Pedro Lopez, that he may advance that part of it which he thinks proper.

                                                                                            KINDELAN.
MANUEL DE LA TORRE.

NOTIFICATION.

In the Havana, on the said day, I notified it to Don Pedro Lopez.

Attest: TORRE.

PETITION.

To the Acting Captain General:

Don Pedro Lopez, an inhabitant and merchant here, consignee of the Spanish schooner Ninfa Catalana, in the proceedings which he has instituted in this Captaincy General, with the usual respect says: That for the better clearing up the information which he has brought forward, and to give it all the force necessary for that purpose, has requested his excellency the Commander General of the Marine that the Captain of the Port, having examined the books under his charge, will certify, as is true, that the said vessel had directed her voyages only to the ports of the Gulf of Mexico and never to that of Cadiz; and his excellency was pleased to accede to the request, the Captain of the Port certifying in consequence; which documents he accompanies with the ceremonial of style, in order that they may produce the proper effects: Wherefore he entreats you to be pleased, they being presented, to order that they be added to the process, that it may have the proper effects, which is justice. Havana, February the fifth, one thousand eight hundred and twenty-three.

                                                                                            PEDRO LOPEZ.

DECREE.

                                                                HAVANA, *February* 5, 1823.

Let the presented papers which accompany be added to the proceedings of the business, that it may have the effect which may happen.

                                                                                            KINDELAN.
MANUEL DE LA TORRE.

NOTIFICATION.

In the Havana, the said day, I notified it to Don Pedro Lopez.

Attest: TORRE.

PETITION.

His Excellency the Commander General of Marine:

Don Pedro Lopez, an inhabitant and merchant of this city, as consignee of the private Spanish schooner called the Ninfa Catalana, respectfully says to your excellency that it is agreeable to his right that the Captain of the Port, upon examination of the rolls which he has despatched to said schooner from the twenty-sixth of November, one thousand eight hundred and eighteen, when his consigner, Don Bartolomé Iglesias, purchased her, according to the testimony of writing which duly accompanies. Certify in continuation, if from any of them it appear that she had at any time been despatched to the port of Cadiz; and, as is the truth, that from the said date to the present time she has performed no other voyages than to the Gulf of Mexico and almost constantly to Campeachy; as also that the said Iglesias has constantly commanded her, whose conduct has been irreprehensible in his command of captain and master of her; therefore he entreats your excellency to be pleased to order that the certificate which he solicits by the principal be proved to him by the said office, and the act be delivered to him, to serve him as a proof in what he intends doing respecting the false accusation which the captain of an American merchant vessel made against said schooner to the commander of the brig-of-war which took her and is now in the port; which is justice, and which he expects from your excellency's equity.

PEDRO LOPEZ.

HAVANA, *February* 1, 1823.

DECREE ON THE MARGIN.

HAVANA, *February* 3, 1823.

To the Captain of the Port for what is requested.

GASTON.

TESTIMONY.

Be it known that I, Don Martin Zavala, an inhabitant and merchant of this place, by these presents agree to sell, really, in favor of Don Bartolomé Iglesias, an inhabitant of the city of Campeachy, residing in this, of the Havana, a Spanish merchant schooner, my property, named *Sircasiana*, of the burden of one hundred and sixteen and a half tons; the same which I had and purchased of a citizen of the United States of America, Patrick Ayres, for himself, and as attorney of William Wood, merchant, of Philadelphia, as appears from the writing lodged in this very archive, and before the present notary, on the eleventh of September of the past year, one thousand eight hundred and sixteen, at which date she was naturalized and matriculated in this province, with the formalities of the ordinance, being placed in the roll of the register at folio one thousand four hundred and eighty-two of the lists of smaller vessels; and she was sold, moored, and anchored in this port with all her masts, sails, anchors, rigging, rudder, bowsprit, yards, binnacle, launch or boat, and other necessaries, as appear from her inventory, with which the purchaser was furnished free from all demands, claims, and obstacles, from which, in sufficient form, I insure and make her good for the price and clear sum of one thousand five hundred and fifty dollars, which I have received of the aforesaid in current money in hand and admit as paid to my satisfaction. I renounce the proof, laws of delivery, specie, fraud, and other things of the case, of which I acknowledge the formal receipt, by which I declare that the just price and value of the said schooner Circaciana, at the time of her last bidding at the public vendue of Don Mariano Canelas on the twenty-fourth current, is that of those who know, one thousand five hundred and fifty dollars, for which the highest bid was made; but if somewhat more is or may be the value of the excess, whatever it may be, I make a gift and donation to the purchaser, mere, pure, perfect, and irrevocable, the assignable right and title, (titula intervivos,) with all the clauses, entails, requisites, and stabilities necessary for its validity. In virtue of which, I abandon and desist from the right, property, possession, use, dominion, and other actions, real and personal, which I held or had to the said schooner, and all her advantages; I give up and transfer the whole to the purchaser and his lawful representative, that, as his own property, he may possess, sell, or alienate her at his pleasure, in virtue of this writing, which I acknowledge in his favor, in token of the real delivery with which he is seen to have acquired his possession and dominion, without the necessity of other proof, from which I exonerate him, and bind myself to the security and guarantee of this sale with my property, present and future, in sufficient form of right and as may be most proper, in favor of the purchaser, who, being present, received in his favor this writing; by it he receives the purchase of the said schooner, which, by his order, has since been named the *Ninfa Catalana;* and for her being delivered to his satisfaction he renounces the proof, laws of delivery, fraud, and other things of the case, of which he acknowledges the formal receipt. In testimony whereof, it is dated in the ever faithful city of the Havana, the 26th of November, 1818. I, the Notary of War Marine, attest, know the person granting, that thus they said, granted, and signed. Witnesses: Don Carlos Alvarez, Don Manuel Lopez, and Don José Poso, inhabitants, and present.

MARTIN DE ZABALA.
BARTOLOMÉ IGLESIAS.

Before me, JOSÉ MIGUEL ISQUIERDO.

It is agreeable to its original, which remains in the archive under my charge, to which I refer; and from the petition, by order, I extract the present. Havana, February 1, 1823.

JOSÉ MIGUEL ISQUIERDO.

CERTIFICATION.

I, Don José de Alcala y Guerra, knight with the cross and insignia of the royal and military order of St. Hermenegild, post captain advanced from the national fleet, and acting of this port, certify: That the Spanish schooner called Ninfa Catalana, of this register, and the property of Don Bartolomé Iglesias, enrolled in folio 1482 of the list of vessels enrolled in this capital, never has been cleared for the port of Cadiz; and from the month of November, 1818, that the said Iglesias purchased her, he has always sailed with her, in the situation of captain and pilot, to the ports of Vera Cruz, Sisal, and Campeachy, until the 13th of December, last year, when the said vessel entered this port under the command of a new captain, D. Pablo Daunes, from the said Iglesias having been left sick in the said port of Campeachy, as the whole is plain by the rolls of said vessel in this office. And that it is evident, I give the present, in consequence of the provision of this date of his excellency the Commander General of the Marine of this station, returned in the instance presented by D. Pedro Lopez, merchant and inhabitant here. Captaincy of the port of Havana, February 3, 1823.

JOSÉ DE ALCALA.

The Acting Captain General: D. Pedro Lopez, merchant here, with the usual respect, says: That, by the decree of the 4th current, the proceedings were ordered to be delivered to him, which he has brought forward, respecting the schooner Ninfa Catalana, in order to have the information finished, that the decree of the first of the same ordered him to receive them, that convenience may be promoted. In their state, nothing else is wanting but that you will be pleased to communicate to him your approbation, to give them all necessary force. In virtue whereof, he entreats you to be pleased, in virtue of your decree, to communicate to him the competent approbation, and order the originals to be returned to him, with the testimonies which he shall ask, authorized in public form.

                                                                    PEDRO LOPEZ.
Havana, *February* 6, 1823.

Havana, February 6, 1823.   Let it be done—two dashes.
                                                              MANUEL DE LA TORRE.

At the Havana, on the said day, I make known the preceding decree to D. Pedro Lopez.
        Attest: TORRE.

                                                        Havana, *February* 7, 1823.
On examination, as far as belongs to right, the information furnished by D. Pedro Lopez, in concordance with what was ordered by the decree of the 1st current, is approved; and for its greater validity and firmness his lordship interposes his authority and judicial decree. Consequently, let the originals be delivered to the promoter, that he may have the use of them which may be suitable; and let him be provided with the testimonials which he shall ask respecting them, corrected and authorized in due form. Let the costs be valued and paid by the said Lopez, with forty-eight reals of assessment.
                                                                    KINDELAN.
Manuel de la Torre.

At the Havana, on said day, I notified it to Don Pedro Lopez.
        Attest: TORRE.

                                                        Havana, *February* 5, 1823.
We send to you a certified copy of the representation which Don Pedro Lopez, a merchant here, has addressed to the Junta of Government of this consulate, showing the incident which happened to the Spanish schooner named Ninfa Catalana, on her leaving this port, with the American brig-of-war Spark, that you may be pleased to take into consideration the contents of the memorial, and support the opinion of the Junta manifested in their resolution at the foot of said copy.
        God preserve you many years.
                                                    JOSÉ MARIA PERNALVER.
                                                    JOSE JOAQUIN DE AISPURNA,
                                                        The Acting Superior Political Chief.

                                                        Havana, *February* 6, 1823.
Pass it to the deliberation of the Acting Auditor of War.
                                                                    KINDELAN.

Señor Captain General: Don Pedro Lopez, merchant here, consignee in this place of the Spanish schooner named Ninfa Catalana, which sailed from Campeachy on the twenty-sixth last, has represented to the economical Junta of the consulate the hostile insult which this vessel has suffered from the United States brig-of-war Spark under the guns of the Moro Castle, with the rest which is read in his memorial, of which, as well as from the resolution of the Junta held on the third current, a copy has been sent to you, signifying to you the gravity of the case, and the transcendency of such conduct, with the observations which appeared to them proper; and, having taken charge of the whole, have agreed by common consent, and from hence immediately, and without loss of time, this Government should proceed as the Junta proposes, laying before his Majesty a copy of these papers, and of any others which the party interested may propose, that the claims may be better instructed and founded, until, if it is possible, the incident present itself with the conviction which renders the whole charge undeniable, and leaves no responsibility, before it supports the justice of the charges, and any other means; but with your superior information you will determine what you think most proper.
                                                                FRAN. DEL CRISTO.
Havana, *February* 7, 1823.

                                                        Havana, *February* 7, 1823.
I agree with the preceding dictamen, and let everything be done as is expressed in it, giving an account of it to his Majesty for his royal determination.
                                                                    KINDELAN.

Mr. President, and Members of the Economical and Administrative Junta of the Consulate:

Don Pedro Lopez, an inhabitant and merchant here, with due respect represents to you, that on account of his being in this port, consignee of the Spanish schooner named Ninfa Catalana, Captain Don Pablo Daunes, he loaded and despatched her for that of Campeachy, and she set sail on the twenty-sixth of the current month; and when he was calculating on the issue of his navigation, he yesterday received a letter from said captain, informing him of the capture which he had undergone by the United States brig-of-war called the Spark; in consequence of which he immediately set about forming the protest which followed, and which, in testimony, duly accompanies. The preliminary step of the protest being finished, the exponent endeavored to be informed of the case, and was informed that, the said brig Spark being at anchor in this port, it was announced to her commander by an American captain that the schooner Ninfa and her boatswain had robbed him on her voyage from Cadiz. This being so, it appears that the order of things dictated that the said commander should have addressed himself to the tribunals of this country; but, crime in every point of view scandalous! he waited for the day in which the Ninfa Catalana was to set sail; he weighed before the said schooner, waited for her in the mouth of the harbor, and detained her within cannon shot of the castle, manned her with sixteen men and two marine guards, put handcuffs upon her crew, and, in addition, put a pair of irons upon the boatswain; he left on board the captain and three passengers, transferred to his own ship six passengers, commanded the vessel to go to Charleston or Baltimore, and, having perpetrated this deed, returned to enter into this port yesterday, scandalizing this commerce and its bay in a manner which, from its results, tends to compromise the public tranquillity, retard it from entering, at the time of one of his boats endeavoring to come alongside the wharf of Cabal-laria. An occurrence of such magnitude sufficiently calls the attention: the exponent has had recourse to the Superior Political Chief, that, as the superior authority of the territory, he may know of an act which may produce very fatal consequences; to his excellency the Commander General of Marine, as Military Naval Chief, and an aggression committed on his coasts; and to you, gentlemen, as the protectors of the navigation, the commerce, and the agriculture of this island. You, gentlemen, will sufficiently know that the law of nations has been violated; that the laws and authorities of the territory have been trampled upon; that the fortress of the Moro has been despised; that the navigation and the commerce are ruined at once; that the least dissimulation of a similar crime places the Spaniards in the most deplorable state; that thus public securities are destroyed; and, lastly, nothing proves with more evidence the contempt and want of consideration with which we are treated than the very brig Spark having returned to enter this port after having committed such an offence. It is not possible, Mr. President and members, that such an act can be authorized by the Government of the United States; but so it is, that, in the meantime, it is notorious that their vessels respect the independent flags, whilst they attack and detain ours, as happened with the schooner Gallega the Third, carried to New Orleans; the brig seized near Porto Rico; the permitting to arm in their ports the greater part of the privateers which have ruined and destroy our navigation and commerce, carrying our vessels captured to their own ports, and planting the courts in their own country. The crews of the independents are, comparatively speaking, citizens of the United States, and, in a word, they have already thrown off the mask, and their own ships-of-war attack with impunity Spanish ships upon our coasts and under our batteries; and what will the Government of the United States say? It is content with disapproving the conduct of the commander who perpetrates a crime as the Spark, and reserves the right against him. And is this capable of giving satisfaction or securing any person? Every individual privateer has a security, which guarantees the bad use which she may make of her patent. And what security do the commanders of American vessels-of-war produce? They are authorized to make what depredations their commanders desire; but they resent, and suppose our authorities indifferent to, the crimes which are committed, to their great sorrow, upon these coasts by foreign subjects, for the most part, of their nation; and they determine, notwithstanding, on a naval armament to cruise upon the seas of this island, which may, God grant it, be not the artful covering of their intentions. In the time of the meritorious intendant, D. Alexandro Ramirez, an expedition of the captured vessels was formed, which were in pursuit of this trade, and this very expedition sufficiently proved the disasters which the United States of America have caused to the Spanish navigation. At this very time privateers of force, which persecute and ruin us, are supplied in their ports; in the Old Channel, at opening that of Bahama, at the Capes of San Antonio, and Corrientes, and even in the mouth of the Straits of Gibraltar, are vessels cruising at the present moment which, although under the flag of Colombia, are Americans of the United States. And is our Government criticized? After all this exposition, what will be the lot of the boatswain of the schooner Ninfa, fettered and manacled, and what that of her crew? What losses have not been caused to her proprietors and shippers? Who will repair these losses? We cannot even appeal to the principal sufferers, or those unable; we cannot expect that the individuals can claim some rights which, although their own, already interest the whole nation and, very particularly, the island of Cuba, which object may be the resort of these scandalous intrigues; and that, if the legitimate authorities do not reclaim in time with energy, and take such measures as may produce order, the excesses which may at such a time be committed as reprisals ought not to be wondered at, which may produce consequences that cannot be remedied when it is thought necessary. On an idea of all that can be explained, I entreat you, gentlemen, that, having as presented the testimony of protest which I produce, you will be pleased to grant what appears most just and agreeable to the enlightened penetration of the Junta; now may it render its desires uniform with the Superior Political Chief; now with his excellency the Commander General of Marine; now being addressed, in an official letter, to the Government of the United States; and now, lastly, to the legislative and executive of our monarchy, that the evil, damages, and vexations caused to the schooner Ninfa by the commander and brig Spark may be reported, and dictating such means as may correct, radically, like abuses, and put entirely to rest the Spaniards from other new ones, as interesting to this country and the bodies which you, gentlemen, represent.

HAVANA, *January* 31, 1823.

Besides, by the interest and urgency of this business, he entreats you to be pleased to convoke the extraordinary Junta to grant what it may think fit, before the brig Spark weigh from this port, which is to be done in the state of this business; (date as above.) Besides, to have recourse, in case of necessity on my part, to the supreme Government of the nation, I entreat you to be pleased to order that I may be provided, by the Secretary of the consulate, with a copy, certified in form, of this proceeding and all its determinations or resolutions, (date as above.)

PEDRO LOPEZ.

RESOLUTION OF THE CONSULATE.

In Junta of Government of the consulate, of the 3d of February, 1823, the President being the second consul, D. Antonio Toso, a representation was seen of Don Pedro Lopez, merchant here, in which he relates the scandalous fact that the commander of the American brig-of-war Spark, anchored in this port, had gone to sea, and, in sight of our forts, had captured the schooner Ninfa Catalana, of his consignment, sending her to Charleston, and making prisoners the captain and crew, under the pretext that he was informed, by the captain of an American vessel, that the boatswain of the schooner had robbed him, on the high sea, on another voyage; and, after the commission of this act and violence, the brig Spark had returned to enter the port without having brought the complaint before the Spanish authorities, which was in order, if he wished the boatswain to be punished agreeably to the laws. In virtue of this exposition, Lopez solicited that, by the consulate, as a corporation charged with the protection of the interests of this commerce, what was proper should be granted to him; and the Junta, taking into consideration some facts which, by their notoriety, have called the attention of this public, and conceiving the necessity that suitable measures be taken by the Anglo-American Government, as well in respect to the fault committed by the commander of the brig Spark as to avoid, on the part of their naval officers, the repetition of such acts, which can in no manner be authorized by that Government, bound to ours in terms of friendship by a solemn treaty, and this consulate desires, at the same time, to favor the just solicitude of the individuals injured, has granted it in the case to which allusion is made, that by the prior and consuls, a certified copy of the representation of Lopez be transmitted to the Captain General, Acting Superior Political Chief, that the indemnification to which he is in justice entitled may be obtained in that Government, and that, in the same manner, he may make the proper complaints to its high representation, in order to avoid similar injuries to our navigation and insults to our flag. And, finally, that our supreme Government may take, at convenience, the measures which the protection of the national flag requires; the same Superior Political Chief will be pleased to lay the document before his Majesty, with a recommendation of its importance. Lastly, that a certified copy of this resolution be given to Lopez, for the effects which may take place.

ANTONIO TOSO.
JOSE JOAQUIN DE AISPURNA.
WINCELAO DE VILLA VRRUTIA.

A true copy.

WINCELAO DE VILLA VRRUTIA.

It is agreeable to the original acts, formed on the false accusation which the captain of the American schooner called the Eleonora made to the commander of the brig-of-war, also American, the Spark; whence resulted the capture of the Spanish merchant schooner Ninfa Catalana, to which I refer; and, in fulfilment of command, I write these presents.

MANL. DE LA TORRE.

(Signed with a flourish.)
HAVANA, *March* 6, 1823.

We certify and attest that Don Manuel de la Torre, who, by authority, attests the preceding, is a notary, national, and, ad interim, of war, as he is styled, faithful, loyal and confidential; he uses and practices his profession with general approbation, and, to his equals, he has always given and gives entire faith and credit in both offices.

HAVANA, date as above.
(Signed with three separate flourishes.)

PHILIP ALVAREZ.
JPH. FRANO. RODRIGUEZ.
FRANCO. AYALA.

No. 31.

Mr. Adams to Mr. Salmon.

DEPARTMENT OF STATE, *Washington, April* 29, 1823.

SIR: I have had the honor of receiving your letter of the 15th instant, inclosing a copy of one bearing date the 16th of October, 1822, from Don Joaquin de Anduaga to Mr. Meade.

By the 5th specific renunciation, in the ninth article of the treaty between the United States and Spain, *signed* on the 22d of February, 1819, but ratified by his Catholic Majesty only on the 24th of October, 1820, it was provided, that the renunciation, on the part of the United States, of all claims for damages or injuries sustained by themselves or their citizens from Spain, stipulated by the preceding part of the same article, should extend—

"To all claims of citizens of the United States upon the Spanish Government, statements of which, soliciting the interposition of the Government of the United States, have been presented to the Department of State or to the minister of the United States in Spain, since the date of the convention of 1802, and until the *signature* of this treaty."

You will observe that the time of the *signature*, and not that of the ratification by either party, nor that of the exchange of ratifications, is expressly agreed upon as the *time*, until which the claim and the *statements* of them to the Department of State or to the minister of the United States in Spain had been received, which claims were, on the part of the United States, renounced.

The reason for fixing upon this particular *time* for the period at which the obligation of the United States to assume the payment of these claims should *terminate* is *obvious*. It was neither proper nor could it be the intention of the parties that they should renounce claims or admit *statements* of them not known to the party assuming the obligation at the time of contracting it. Whatever claims might arise or whatever *statements* of them might be made after the *signature* of the treaty, were not, therefore, and could not, with propriety, be provided for by it.

By the eleventh article of the same treaty it was stipulated that—

"The United States, exonerating Spain from all demands *in future* on account of the claims of their citizens, to which .the renunciations herein contained extend, and considering them entirely cancelled, undertake to make satisfaction for the same to an amount not exceeding five millions of dollars. That—

. "To *ascertain* the full *amount* and validity of these claims, a commission, to consist of three Commissioners, citizens of the United States, shall be appointed by the President, by and with the advice and consent of the Senate, which commission shall meet at the city of Washington, and within the space of three years from the time of their first meeting shall *receive, examine*, and *decide* upon the *amount* and *validity* of all claims included within the descriptions above mentioned." That "The said Commissioners shall take an *oath* or affirmation, to be entered on the record of their proceedings, for the *faithful* and diligent *discharge of their duties;*" and that "the said Commissioners shall be authorized to hear and examine, on oath, every question relative to the said claims, and to receive all suitable authentic testimony concerning the same. And the Spanish Government shall furnish all such *documents* and elucidations as may be in their possession *for the adjustment* of the said claims according to the principles of justice, the laws of nations, and the stipulations of the treaty between the two parties of October 27, 1795, the said documents to be specified, when demanded, at the instance of the said Commissioners."

It has been necessary to set forth, in the terms of the treaty itself, the engagements respectively contracted by the parties to it in these articles, in order to show with clearness their bearing upon the question now brought into discussion by your letter and that of Mr. Anduaga, which it inclosed.

The claims, payment of which to a fixed and limited amount was assumed by the United States, were claims not only existing, but *statements* of which had been exhibited at the Department of State or to the minister of the United States in Spain *before the signature* of the treaty.

To *ascertain* the full *amount* and *validity* of those claims, Commissioners were to be appointed, to act under oath, and charged with the duty to receive, examine, and *decide upon the amount and validity of* all the claims.

And the Spanish Government solemnly bound itself to furnish all such *documents* and *elucidations* as might be in their possession for the *adjustment* of the said claims.

If anything in human intention can be made clear by human language, it is that the claims provided for by the above stipulation were in the condition as they had been exhibited at the time of the *signature* of the treaty; that the authority and the trust of examining, ascertaining, and *deciding* their *amount* and *validity* was *solely* and *exclusively* committed to the Commissioners, and that the Spanish Government was and is bound to furnish them, at their demand, all documents and *elucidations* in possession of the said Government for the *adjustment* of the claims.   .

No transaction between any of the claimants and the Spanish Government, subsequent to the signature of the treaty, could be evidence to the Commissioners of the condition of the claim at the time of that signature. No appeal from the decision of the Commissioners, either to the Government of the United States or of Spain, was reserved. By the transfer to the United States of the obligation of making payment, conformably to the treaty, of those claims, Spain deliberately and with full knowledge transferred also the right of examining and deciding their amount and validity. It is to little purpose, therefore, that Mr. Anduaga's letter descants so largely upon the variety and respectability of the Spanish commissions and tribunals, which, many months *after the signature* of the treaty, undertook to liquidate, that is, to decide upon, the amount and validity of Mr. Meade's claim upon the Spanish Government. Neither the number nor the character of those courts is at all questioned, but from the day of the *signature* of the treaty they had no jurisdiction to try or decide upon any of the claims, the payment of which was assumed by the United States. Whatever jurisdiction they did exercise, however obligatory it might be upon his Catholic Majesty's Government, could have no effect whatever to charge the United States, or, so far as they were concerned, to change the condition of the claim, as it had been exhibited to the Government of the United States or to their minister at Madrid, before the signature of the treaty. It had been exhibited as an unsettled and unliquidated claim; if comprised at all within the provisions of the treaty, it was as an unsettled and unliquidated claim, upon which, as upon all the rest, the commission instituted under the treaty was, by the express engagement of both parties, exclusively to decide.

It is alleged by Mr. Anduaga, and repeated in substance by you, that the decision by the Spanish tribunals upon the amount and *validity* of Mr. Meade's claim, made many months after the signature of the treaty, many months even after his Catholic Majesty was bound to have ratified the same, and after its ratifications ought to have been exchanged, was given at the earnest instance of the minister of the United States in Spain, and that he, as well as the Government of the United States, expressed their satisfaction at the event. The answer to this argument is, however, furnished by Mr. Anduaga and by you. Mr. Anduaga says: "When all this was done, there was no probability that the United States would be obliged to pay this debt;" that is to say, there was no probability that his Catholic Majesty would perform the express and solemn promise that he had made to ratify the treaty. Undoubtedly, when there was no probability that the United States would be charged with the payment of the debt, their Government and their minister did earnestly press the Spanish Government to do justice at least to Mr. Meade. What that justice was, what was the amount and validity of his claim upon the Spanish Government, the United States neither had nor claimed the right to decide. So far as it was an obligation to be paid by Spain, and by which no other interests of the United States or of their citizens could be affected, the right to decide upon it was exclusively of the resort of Spanish tribunals; and the American Government and minister naturally expressed their satisfaction at the adjustment, by the Spanish Government, of a claim of *one* of their citizens, in whose favor they had taken a deep and generous interest, it being always understood by them that this interest did not conflict with their duties to the people of the United States and to all their other fellow-citizens, also claimants upon Spain, and in whose favor their Government was bound to take an interest as earnest and generous as in that of Mr. Meade.

. While there was no probability that the treaty would be ratified by Spain, the adjustment by Spanish tribunals, binding only upon Spain, could in nowise affect any other right or interest of the people of the United States, or of other American citizens claimants upon Spain. That adjustment could in nowise charge the United States. It was an obligation of Spain, contracted *after* the signature of the treaty, and was thereby excluded, by the express terms of the treaty itself, from the number of those which the United

States had by the treaty engaged to assume upon themselves. The cognizance taken at the time by the Spanish tribunals of this claim, and the acknowledgment of the amount and validity of this one alone as you affirm, among many hundreds of other claims of American citizens, many of much longer standing and all equally entitled to adjustment and liquidation, are, indeed, powerful arguments to prove that Mr. Meade's claim was not one of those for which Spain had intended to provide by the treaty. And this argument is strongly fortified by another, which Mr. Meade himself and his learned counsel in this country have urged with great force, namely: that the claims of Mr. Meade upon Spain were of a nature which, by the laws of nations and of justice, Spain could not discharge and the United States could not renounce by any treaty or compact between themselves. The conclusion from these arguments, if correct, undoubtedly is, that Mr. Meade's claims upon Spain were not intended to be, and even could not be, provided for by the treaty, and were, therefore, not included in it. If, then, the Commissioners under the treaty did, in the first instance, entertain very serious doubts whether the claim of Mr. Meade was among those provided for, or intended to be provided for by the treaty, it was to these proceedings of the Spanish Government after the signature of the treaty, and to the argument of Mr. Meade and his counsel against the *right* of the contracting parties to the treaty to dispose of Mr. Meade's claim, that these doubts must be ascribed. It was assuredly never the intention of the Government of the United States, in that treaty, either to renounce any claim which they had not the right to assume, nor to assume any claim which they had not the right to renounce. As far was it, doubtless, from the intention of Spain to discharge any just claim of Mr. Meade's upon her by the attempt to transfer it to a third party without his consent. Nothing can be more clear than that Spain remains at this hour bound to satisfy, to the last real, every claim acknowledged by herself to be just, and which she had not the right to transfer to a third party without the consent of the claimant.

The treaty, by its express terms, made provision only for unsettled and *unliquidated* claims. The United States assumed them as they existed and had been exhibited at the signature of that instrument, the 22d of February, 1819. In assuming the duty of Spain to discharge those claims, the United States acquired the right, and it was in express words secured to them by the treaty, of ascertaining and deciding, exclusively by a commission of their own citizens, the *amount* and *validity* of each claim assumed. At the same moment when the obligation to discharge the claim attached to the United States, this exclusive right of the commission to examine and decide its amount and validity attached with it. From that moment the Spanish tribunals had no more right to examine or pass, in any manner, upon the claims than the tribunals of the United States had to examine and pass upon them before the signature of the treaty. This provision imported no distrust in the justice or integrity of the Spanish tribunals. It followed, as an indispensable consequence, from the engagement contracted by the United States to pay the claims.

By the treaty itself, and by the full power of Don Luis de Onis, its negotiator on the part of Spain, his Catholic Majesty was bound to ratify the treaty so that the ratifications should be exchanged within six months from the day of its signature. Had this engagement been performed, Mr. Meade's claims would have remained in the same state in which they had been on the day of the signature of the treaty, unsettled and unliquidated. Mr. Meade's claims were not provided for by name, nor had any mention of them been made in the course of the negotiation. The Spanish Government was at that time so far from admitting that Mr. Meade had any just claim upon them that they had but very recently, at the earnest and peremptory interposition of the Government of the United States, released him from imprisonment as a defaulter to them.

The treaty remaining unratified by his Catholic Majesty, and, as Mr. Anduaga affirms, there being no probability that it would be ratified, long after the period had expired when he had promised, on his royal word, that it should be ratified, the minister of the United States at Madrid, at the earnest and repeated solicitations of Mr. Meade, certainly did urge the Spanish Government to adjust, liquidate, and satisfy his claims. From the nature of these claims, his learned counsel in this country have since drawn it in question whether the Government of the United States had any right to interpose with that of Spain in relation to them at all; and upon this question depends the other, before noticed, whether Spain could, by treaty, transfer to the United States her own obligation to pay those claims. They were claims which Mr. Meade had acquired, not in his neutral character as a citizen of the United States, but as a voluntary contractor with the Spanish Government, while residing in their territory and living under their allegiance. They were therefore, unquestionably, much less entitled to the interference of the American Government than the great mass of the claims provided for by the treaty—claims for wrongs suffered by citizens of the United States in their genuine character as such—for wrongs, in the origin of which there was no voluntary agency of their own, no forfeiture of their neutral rights, no resort but to the perfect obligation of their own Government to support them. Had the Spanish Government, at the time when the minister of the United States interposed in behalf of this claim, taken the ground of argument since assumed by Mr. Meade and his counsel—had they said this is a claim in which the Government of the United States have no right to interfere—a question upon contracts between Mr. Meade and us, while living in our territories and amenable to our laws—undoubtedly, by the principles of the rights and duties of nations, universally recognized, Mr. Meade and the American Government must fain have put up with this answer as conclusive, and Mr. Meade's claim could never have been pretended to be included in the provisions of the treaty.

But no such ground was then taken either by the Spanish Government or by Mr. Meade; so little was his reliance upon the justice of the Government with which he had contracted, and under whose protection he dwelt, without the effectual interposition in his favor of the Government under which he had been born, that his entreaties for the interposition of the American minister and Government, in favor of his claims, were urgent and unceasing. To this interposition the Spanish Government did not object. Mr. Meade *desired* that provision for his claim should be made in the treaty which was then negotiating, and made known this desire to the Government of the United States. He was informed, in answer, that, if the treaty should be concluded, his claims would be considered and attended to, as far as might be practicable, in *common with the others;* and to this arrangement he never suggested an objection till after the ratification of the treaty by Spain, nor until just at the moment before its second ratification by the United States. He *then*, to be sure, and then, for the first time, addressed the President and Senate of the United States, calling upon them to refuse the ratification of a treaty in which the only possible indemnity of many hundreds of their fellow-citizens for their losses, to the amount of five millions of dollars, was secured; or to make the ratification conditional, that another article should be added, by which *his* claim, not as *existing* at the time of the signature of the treaty, but as many months *after* that compact ought to have been ratified by Spain, liquidated by Spanish officers before the Spanish ratification of the treaty, should be paid to the full amount as acknowledged by them, and without being subject, like all the other claims, to the honest investigation and scrutiny of the American Commissioners; and the principal argument urged by Mr. Meade's counsel in support of this demand, that the American Government should sacrifice the acquisition of the Floridas, and five millions of dollars of indemnities justly due to their citizens, whose right to the effectual support of their country was perfect, was, that his claim was of a nature that the American Government had no right to interpose with Spain in its favor at all.

If the claims of Mr. Meade upon Spain were included among those provided for by the treaty, it was in common with all the others, to be treated like all the others, and to abide the same issue with the others. Such was the clear, unequivocal intention of both parties to the treaty; nor could the American Government, in equal justice to all the claimants, have negotiated upon any other principle. The amount of claims exhibited to them to be provided for by the treaty, as stated by the claimants themselves, was nearly ten times the five millions which they agreed that the people of the United States should pay, from the proceeds of the Florida lands, to discharge them. But it was well understood that many of the claims were not even valid against Spain; that most of them were swollen by the statements far beyond what, upon a fair examination, would be found to be due; that equitable deductions from equitable claims would reduce almost all of them within very contracted dimensions; and that, for the whole mass of them, the *only* hope of the claimants was in the munificence of the treaty. They were all, by the terms of the treaty, unsettled claims. Their just amount could then be only judged of by an *estimate*, in many respects conjectural, but it was believed, upon considerations duly weighed, that, when stripped of all their appendages to naked justice, five millions of dollars would be sufficient to cover them all. As they were to be paid by the people of the United States, it was the duty of the Government to allow no larger sum than would be sufficient, in rigorous justice, to discharge them. It might happen that even the just and indisputable claims would amount to something more. In that case, the claimants must consider it as a composition of their claims, the best that their Government has been able to obtain for them; and it was not doubted that they who had been from one to twenty years waiting, with very little probability of ever obtaining *anything* for their claims, would be more than contented to receive so nearly all that they could have asked, and to abandon to their country the small remainder for the salvage of the rest. But to render this principle compatible with justice to all parties, it was indispensable that all the claims should be placed upon the same footing; that all should be subjected to the close, vigilant, and rigorous scrutiny and investigation of an upright and intelligent commission of American citizens; that all should be alike submitted to their examination and decision, and that no transaction between the Spanish Government and any one of the claimants, subsequent to the *signature*, but before the ratification of the treaty, should alter the character of his claim, and give him an advantage at the expense of the people of the United States, and of *all* the other claimants under the treaty. If the American Government could have admitted any discrimination between the claims, and that any one should have been privileged above the rest, Mr. Meade's claim, if the present argument of his learned counsel is sound, would have been the very lowest on the list and the least entitled to favor; since most, if not all the rest, were claims which the American Government had been, from the beginning, bound, by the duty of protection to the rights of their own citizens, to support and maintain even, if necessary, to the issuing of reprisals, while that of Mr. Meade, incurred voluntary by himself while domiciliated in Spain, and by transactions of no neutral character, was of a nature to leave it doubtful whether the American Government had ever possessed the right of interposing in its behalf at all.

The interest taken, therefore, by the American minister at Madrid in Mr. Meade's favor, by urging on the Spanish Government the settlement of his claims; the satisfaction that he expressed after the liquidation had been obtained; the letter of congratulation from the American Secretary of State to Mr. Meade upon the event when informed of it by him, have not the slightest bearing upon this argument. The answer to all this is furnished by Mr. Anduaga when he says: "There was, then, *no probability* that the treaty would be ratified by Spain." The American minister and Secretary of State expected that what the Spanish tribunals had liquidated and settled the Spanish Government would pay. They knew perfectly well that no interests of the people of the United States, or of the other claimants upon Spain, could be injuriously affected by this Spanish liquidation of Mr. Meade's claims. If the treaty should be ratified, and Mr. Meade should be receivable as a claimant under it, they knew that his claims could be admitted only as provided for by the treaty, and that no intermediate transaction between him and the Spanish Government could be evidence of his claims, as they had existed and been exhibited at the *signature* of the treaty. That no decision of a Spanish tribunal could settle that which the treaty in express terms reserved to the exclusive decision of the American commission. If the treaty should *not* be ratified, they rejoiced that their exertions in *his* favor had been so far successful; that he had a nearer prospect of obtaining satisfaction from the Spanish Government itself. Their pleasure was that of a benevolent and friendly feeling towards Mr. Meade. But the American Government had duties of a more imperious nature to others: to the people of the United States and to all their fellow-citizens, the *other* claimants upon Spain. To them it was due that, if the treaty should be ratified and Mr. Meade be a claimant under it, his claim should stand on the same foundation and pass through the same ordeal with the rest. The American Government knew that it was so stipulated in the treaty, and they little expected the pretension that, by this separate transaction between him and the Spanish Government, the treaty being yet unratified, the nature of the engagements of the United States in it was changed if it ever should be ratified; that they would be bound to receive as settled claims which they had engaged to receive as unsettled, and to take the dictum of a Spanish tribunal as the decision which the treaty had trusted exclusively to an American commission.

Mr. Meade himself, and the learned counsel whom he has employed in this country, know better. They were the first to doubt whether his claims were provided for by the treaty at all. They clearly saw that, if provided for, it was only upon the same terms and upon the same conditions with all the rest. His memorial to the President of the United States, objecting to the ratification of the treaty, was on the avowed and only ground that it had not provided for the satisfaction of *his* claims. He demanded that the ratification of the treaty should be refused, or given upon a condition that a new article should be added providing for the payment, in full, of his claims; that the Floridas should be sacrificed, and the only hopes of many hundreds of other claimants *blasted*, that *he* might be sure to receive, at the expense of the United States, payment, to the last maravedi, of what a Spanish tribunal had, since the treaty was concluded, awarded him as a debt due to him from Spain. His memorial insisted that neither Spain nor the United States had ever possessed the *right* of making between themselves a composition of his claims; and without being aware or mindful that, if this position was true, the irresistible conclusion from it was, that they were not included in the treaty at all, and remained in full force against Spain as if the treaty had never been made, he yet required that the United States should make the ratification of this treaty *conditional* upon the assent of Spain to *another*, by which *his* claims should be distinguished from all the rest; admitted without asking questions, and paid without the deduction of a *mille*. And the principal argument for this moderate proposal was, that *his* claims upon Spain were such that the American Government has never possessed the right of interfering to support them against Spain at all.

Thus Mr. Meade himself, and his learned counsel, first raised the question whether his claims were included among those provided for by the treaty; and if they failed of convincing the President and Senate of the United States of the propriety of withholding the ratification of the treaty which they had made to exact the consent of Spain to another which they had *not* made, they conclusively proved that the United States had never been under obligations of negotiating with Spain concerning them at all, and gave plausible color, at least, to the belief that his claims, not being embraced by the provisions of the treaty, remained in all their force, acknowledged and unimpaired, to be paid, without deduction or compromise, from the treasury of Spain.

But after the ratifications of the treaty had been exchanged, and after the commission instituted under it was organized, Mr. Meade produced before them his claims as being among those provided for by the treaty; and when the Commissioners, in the discharge of their duty to their country and to all the other claimants whose rights and interests were involved in the decision—when the Commissioners, yielding to the force of arguments which had been most strenuously urged by Mr. Meade himself and counsel—when the Commissioners, seeing in the treaty, which was their law, no mention of Mr. Meade's claim by name, and no description of claims within which it *could*, as a settled and liquidated claim, be embraced—when the Commissioners, men of high and irreproachable character, with the oath of God upon their souls, with no evidence before them but such as the treaty must exclude, and no argument but that of Mr. Meade and of his counsel, excluding his claim from the treaty—when these Commissioners but intimated an opinion that Mr. Meade's claims were not among those submitted by the treaty to their decision, the basest and most inflammatory anonymous newspaper publications issued from a prostituted press, for the apparent purpose of intimidating by defamation the members of a judicial tribunal from the discharge of their trust according to the conviction of their consciences.

Mr. Meade then, too, resorted to the Spanish minister in this country for his testimony to prove that it *had* been the intention of the Spanish Government to include his claim among those which were provided for by the treaty. That Spanish minister was not the negotiator of the treaty, nor could he more than any other person testify to the intention of the Spanish Government any otherwise than as appeared on the face of the treaty itself. It has already been said, that during the negotiation of the treaty neither the name nor the claim of Mr. Meade had ever been mentioned between the negotiators, and that when it was signed the Spanish Government had never admitted that he had a valid claim upon them for so much as a dollar. Mr. Anduaga did, however, furnish Mr. Meade with his *opinion* that Mr. Meade's claim was embraced by the treaty, and that opinion was laid before the Commissioners. Other claims were also presented to them involving the same question, whether *contracts* of the Spanish Government had been among the cases provided for by the treaty; and at the application of one of the suitors they addressed a letter to the Secretary of State, suggesting their impressions that claims of that description, which the American Government had never been under any obligation to enforce, and in favor of which even their *right* to interfere might be questioned, were not included in the treaty, the main and obvious object of which was to obtain indemnity for the wrongs of American citizens entitled beyond all question to the full protection of their Government. This letter was laid before the President of the United States, by whose direction the answer was returned, which was conformable to the truth of the facts, and this formed the correspondence which you state to have been communicated by Mr. Meade to Mr. Anduaga, and by him to your Government.

In concluding the treaty, the American Government was well aware, and the Spanish Government could not be ignorant, that by the laws of eternal justice a nation has no more than an individual the *right* of discharging itself from the obligation of its *contracts* by the agreement of a third party to assume them, without the consent, express or implied, of the party (whether nation or individual) with whom the contract was made.

The parties to the treaty well knew, also, that *contracts* and liquidated acknowledged debts are not in their nature subjects of negotiation; especially not of negotiation between one of the parties with a third party not privy to the contract. The duty of a nation bound by such a contract is not negotiation, but performance.

They likewise knew that with regard to the contracts of an individual born in one country with the Government of another, most especially when the individual contracting is domiciliated in the country with whose Government he contracts, and formed the contract voluntarily, for his own private emolument and without the privity of the nation under whose protection he had been born, he has no claim whatsoever to call upon the Government of his nativity to espouse his claim, this Government having no right to compel that with which he voluntarily contracted to the performance of that contract.

But unacknowledged, unsettled, unliquidated claims form the natural subject of negotiation; and of all negotiation, the necessary and essential character is compromise. Of such claims, whether originating in contract or in wrong, the very application of an individual to one Government to assist him in the enforcement of his claims upon another, imports of itself the consciousness that he cannot obtain his claims without that assistance, and makes them at once a subject of negotiation and compromise.

For such unliquidated claims, alone, provision was made by the 5th renunciation of the United States in the ninth article of the treaty of 22d February, 1819, which, by its terms, is limited to claims of citizens of the United States upon the Spanish Government, *statements of which, soliciting the interposition of the Government of the United States,* had been exhibited since the convention of 1802, and until the signature of the treaty.

Mr. Meade was a citizen of the United States, who, since the convention of 1802, and before the signature of the treaty, had *solicited* the interposition of the Government of the United States and had presented some general statement of part of his claims. He had specially desired that they should be included in the negotiation of the treaty, and had been informed of the only terms upon which they would or could be considered in that negotiation in *common* with the other claims for which it was to provide. They were and could be known to the American Government only as unsettled and disputed claims, and the *right* to negotiate a compromise for them in common with the rest, founded upon his own *solicitation* and the acquiescence of Spain, was not for a moment questioned; but as an acknowledged claim, the amount and validity of which was known and admitted, and about which the United States and Spain had no right to negotiate between themselves a compromise not sanctioned by him, it certainly was not included nor ever intended to be included in the treaty. From the moment that Spain considers it as such, she contracts the obligation of discharging it herself as a contract, the compromise of which neither she nor the United States could rightfully negotiate between themselves without the privity of Mr. Meade, and which, not having been so negotiated, she, Spain, is bound in honor and in justice to him to discharge to the last farthing from her own Treasury.

This is what Spain can perform without injustice to others. But you will perceive at a glance that the Government of the United States could not, without the grossest injustice to their nation, and to all the other claimants under the treaty, admit that a transaction between Spanish tribunals and Mr. Meade, between the signature and ratification of the treaty, should change the nature of the compact between the United States and Spain, control the express terms of the treaty itself, and bind the Commissioners charged with the duty of ascertaining and deciding the amount and validity of unliquidated claims to take an acknowledgment in 1820 as evidence of the condition of a claim in 1819. The sum stipulated for payment by the United States of *all* the claims assumed was limited to five millions of dollars. The amount due upon the whole mass might ultimately be found less, or it might exceed that sum. If it should prove less, the balance would be so much less of debt to be paid by the people of the United States. If more, a proportional deduction from the sum awarded to every claimant must be made, each of whom must make this small sacrifice to the adjustment of all these long standing, perplexed, disputed, and I may safely say, otherwise *desperate* demands. Those of Mr. Meade, in February, 1819, were assuredly not less desperate than the rest. To allow that a Spanish tribunal, long after the treaty ought to have been ratified, and while Spain retained the power of ratifying or rejecting it, should select this claim of Mr. Meade from all the rest, to invest it with the exclusive and invidious exemption from the scrutiny to which all others must be subjected; that it should be taken out of the treaty for examination and settlement and cast back upon the treaty for payment in full; that it should be screened from all investigation and privileged from all proportionable deduction; that the people of the United States, and the fund devoted to the just indemnity of many hundred claimants, should be doubly ransomed to satisfy the plenitude of that claim, and in reverence to the dignity of tribunals, which under the treaty had no right to pass upon it at all, would be as wide from all the duties of the American Government as from the dictates of justice, and as far from its present intentions as from those of either party to the treaty at the time of its conclusion.

It was intended by the Government of the United States that Mr. Meade's claims, as then exhibited to them, unsettled, disputed claims of a mixed character for contracts; for losses upon exchange; for depreciation of Spanish Government paper; for interest and for damages, all, except the first, of most uncertain amount and validity, should, in common with the other claims provided for, have the benefit of the treaty. But no stipulation of special favor to the claims of Mr. Meade, at the expense of other claimants, was or could be intended by the Government of the United States. The claim presented by Mr. Meade to the Commissioners is for an acknowledged *debt* from the Spanish Government to him, dated May, 1820, and directed to be paid *out of the funds of the royal finance department*, with *interest*. To say that this is not the claim which, in February, 1819, the United States had renounced and agreed to compound, would be to say that daylight is not darkness. Mr. Meade might, with as much propriety, have purchased in the market at its current price any other order upon the *funds of the royal finance department*, and brought it before the Commissioners as a claim provided for by the treaty, as he could this order—a part of the sum constituting which was for interest *accrued after the treaty had been signed.*

Of the obligation of the *Spanish* Government to pay Mr. Meade, *with interest*, the whole amount of this sum, acknowledged by its own tribunals to be due, there can be no doubt. But it is equally clear that it is *not* the debt which, in February, 1819, the United States had agreed to assume, to consider as cancelled, and to discharge. It was not the claim which had been exhibited, or had even existed in February, 1819. It was a claim of a totally distinct and different character. It was a new obligation of Spain, for which no provision had been made by the treaty, and with which the United States could not, without injustice to themselves and to all the other claimants, be charged.

By the intention of including Mr. Meade's claims among those provided for by the treaty at the time of its negotiation, the American Government had shown its kindness towards him to the utmost verge of its compatibility with their duties to others. Mr. Meade's claims, as then existing, however meritorious as against Spain, were far from being against the United States as deserving as many others with which they were to share the benefit of the treaty. They were claims, part of which were for supplies to support the *ally* of Spain, then, or very shortly after, the enemy of the United States; supplies to maintain a cause to which, so far as concerned Spain, the United States were neutral, but which, by its inseparable connexion with Great Britain, was the cause of that nation against Mr. Meade's country. There was no one point of view in which those claims could be considered that gave them a title to the special favor or support of the *American* Government or nation; and by extending to them the advantages of a composition which they were enabled to effect with Spain of numerous other and far more meritorious claims, in meaning to do equal justice to all, they perhaps did more than justice to Mr. Meade.

While, therefore, your position that the Spanish nation was certainly responsible to Mr. Meade for the *total* amount of the acknowledged debt is indisputable, his Catholic Majesty will find, by further examination of the treaty, that the Government of the United States *did not* take upon itself *by the latter ratification of the treaty*, nor ever in any other manner, *this debt*. The fifth renunciation of the ninth article of the treaty neither did, nor could, nor was ever intended to include this debt. And the latter ratification of the United States neither did, nor could, in the slightest degree, alter the character of the obligation which the United States had contracted on the face of the treaty on the 22d of February, 1819. The fifth renunciation, upon its face and by its terms, was limited to claims stated but unsettled of uncertain amount and validity, as existing at the *signature* of the treaty. The ratification of the United States could no more change the import of this renunciation than it could change the *words* in which it was expressed. The fourth article of the treaty reserves the examination and decision of the *amount* and *validity* of *all* the claims assumed by the United States for the *exclusive* cognizance of a commission of American citizens; and whoever appears before them as a claimant under the treaty must abide by their decision conformably to the treaty. For all subsequent engagements, contracts, and *debts* of the Spanish Government, whether with Mr. Meade or with any other claimants, Spain, and not the United States, is chargeable. If Mr. Meade claims the benefit of the treaty by the treaty, must he submit to be judged; and according to the terms of the treaty must he receive his indemnity. If he means to resort to engagements or *debts* subsequently contracted, or to the decisions of Spanish tribunals, to Spain alone must he have recourse for satisfaction.

This conclusion cannot be departed from by the Government of the United States. It is due to the plain intent and unequivocal language of the treaty; it is due to the rights and interests of the people of the United States; it is due to those of many hundreds of their citizens, whose demands upon the justice of Spain were at least as strong and clear, and whose right to the support and protection of their country was at least more perfect and unequivocal than those of Mr. Meade. Special, unstipulated *favor* to him would be flagrant injustice to them.

When, therefore, in the conclusion of your letter, you beforehand solemnly and respectfully protest against any decision of the Commissioners appointed in virtue of the treaty which *invalidates*, in any manner, the *acknowledgment* made by your Government of the *total* debt of Mr. Meade, agreeably to the certificate which they sent to him in consequence, and which you state to be in possession of the commissioners, I am directed to say in answer: 1. That the Government of the United States have no more than the Government of Spain the right or authority to dictate or control the decisions of the Commissioners appointed by virtue of the treaty of February 22, 1819; and that as the United States will not assume themselves, so they will not suffer from Spain the exercise of any such dictation or control, alike repugnant to the principles of impartial justice and to that judicial independence which constitutes the excellence and the glory of the institutions, both of this country and of Spain; and 2. That there neither has been nor is there reason to expect any decision of the Commissioners, to *invalidate*, in any manner, any *acknowledgment* by your Government of the total debt to Mr. Meade; the *validity* of any such acknowledgment being, like the obligation which it imports, for the exclusive cognizance of the Spanish Government itself, and importing neither obligation nor authority for which the United States is answerable or the charge of which they have ever consented to assume.

I pray you, sir, to accept the assurance of my distinguished consideration.

JOHN QUINCY ADAMS.

Don HILARIO DE RIVAS Y SALMON, *Chargé d'Affaires from Spain.*

No. 32.

Mr. Brent to Mr. Salmon.

DEPARTMENT OF STATE, *Washington, September 22, 1824.*

SIR: I was directed by the Secretary of State, before his late departure from this city, to furnish the Attorney of the United States for the eastern district of Pennsylvania with an extract from your letter to him of the 16th of August, and, at the same time, to request that officer to adopt such measures as might be deemed advisable to the preservation of the neutrality of the United States and the vindication of their laws, in reference to certain armaments which you state to have been already prepared, and to others which are now preparing in the port of Philadelphia, for the use and on account of some of the South American States in the contest in which they are engaged with Spain; and I lost no time in complying with the Secretary's instructions.

I have the honor now, sir, to transmit to you a copy of Mr. Ingersoll, the District Attorney's letter, in answer to the one which I addressed to him in pursuance of the Secretary's instructions, including a short correspondence between himself and the Collector of Customs at Philadelphia, which I flatter myself will prove abundantly satisfactory as to the armaments in question, already sent forth from the port of Philadelphia, and entirely remove any apprehensions which you may entertain with regard to those which are in a train of preparation at the same port.

I pray you, sir, to accept the assurance of my very distinguished consideration.

DANIEL BRENT.

Don HILARIO DE RIVAS Y SALMON, *Chargé d'Affaires from Spain.*

No. 33.

Don Hilario de Rivas y Salmon to Mr. Brent.

[Translation.]

LEGATION OF SPAIN, *Philadelphia, September 29, 1824.*

SIR: I have had the honor of receiving your note, in absence of Mr. Adams, in answer to mine of the 16th of August last, relative to the illegal armaments which have been made in this port on account of the separated Governments of Spanish America.

I shall, as soon as possible, transmit its contents to my Government, but I cannot say that it will be so satisfactory as you flatter yourself, as, at the very time that you were writing that note, three of the *twelve gun-boats* which I said were building on account of the Colombian Government were dropping down the river, and two more have sailed since, all despatched in the name of a Mr. H. Somers, scarcely known in this place. It is true, as I have been informed, the custom-house did not permit them to take on board the armament which they had prepared close by the very arsenal of the United States; but this is of little moment, because they can easily send this armament in another vessel as ballast. They run no risk in doing this, as they have done it before on many occasions. I do not understand, however, that the custom-house has used more rigor with these Colombian vessels than with those despatched by Mr. Meade to Mexico, because, if by chance there was any difference in the force or armament between these vessels and the former, they were stronger than those just sailed; and if the custom-house do not consider cannon of *very large calibre, and upon pivots,* as an armament, but as mere *signal* guns, as it appears the guns which these vessels ought to carry will be signal guns, as those were which the others carried, and, in this case, it will be cruelty to prevent those that sail now from carrying them as well as the others, *mounted on deck,* that they may be ready in case of need. But you will be pleased to observe that if said artillery were embarked for the sole purpose of *signals,* there could be no necessity for each boat carrying *two* pieces, nor for their being of so large a calibre as from 24 to 32-pounders, much less for any of them being on pivots, because for making signals it is not necessary to take aim, which is the only intention of a pivot gun. It is to be observed that the Fiscal (or Attorney General) of the United States for this district was unable to obtain the legal proofs which he sought from the different persons employed by the custom-house, whose information it was easy to anticipate, because it is to be supposed that if they had considered said armaments as illegal they would not have been wanting to their duty in permitting them to sail with them. Upon the whole, it appears by their correspondence with the said Fiscal that they were not entirely ignorant by whom and for whom these gun-boats were building. Neither are they fit for trade, nor can it be presumed that either Mr. Meade or Mr. Barry, who have retired from business, would make use of them. This alone, in my opinion, ought to have infused a suspicion founded on the real object which they had, and was a just cause for detaining them to investigate the case with certainty. The *ten gun-boats* which Mr. Meade despatched in this port are not the only vessels which he has got built in the United States on account of the Government of Mexico. According to information which I have, very worthy of credit, he has caused some more to be built in Baltimore, although there his name has not been mentioned. One of them, now called the Yguala, detains vessels of the United States themselves which go to the ports of Mexico, as I have lately seen in the newspapers. Another, called Anahuæ, a most beautiful schooner of 238 tons, came here before going to Mexico, carrying the armament in the hold, which consisted of twelve cannons, 18-pounders, with their carriages, besides other arms and oars, &c. She was despatched from hence with some cargo by Mr. R. Adams, under the command of one Whigman, and at present is in New York, now with the Mexican flag. Her present captain, *Cochrane*, is a native of that port, where likewise his family resides.

The Colombian privateer, the General Santander, of which I made mention in the note which you answer, a little after came into Norfolk with a crew of 250 men, who only speak English, and although he who at present commands her is not now *Chase*, but one NORTHRUP, likewise a citizen of the United States, a native of Connecticut. In that port he recruited men and augmented his force with *four officers* and the crew of another Colombian privateer that was in Baltimore and belongs to Daniels, of whom I also spoke at that time. Being thus supplied, he sailed to cruise off New York, where there is a Spanish vessel which cannot sail without great risk of falling into his power. Thus it may be said that Spanish vessels seem blockaded in the ports of the United States themselves through the agency of their citizens. The consul of Spain gave information of this to the competent authorities that they might put a stop to it, but all excused themselves, saying they could not do it; that the laws upon this point were not sufficiently positive and clear. The same thing was told to the acting vice consul of Spain in Charleston on another occasion by the *marshal* of the United States in that district, (whose original letter I have in my possession,) and *Mr. Ingersoll* gives the same understanding in his correspondence which you now inclose to me. But, as I have already said before, his Catholic Majesty has nothing to do with the peculiar laws of this country. They, such as they are, are the exclusive work of the United States, and Spain, in this point only, ought to attend to the treaties.

But how do the United States fulfil these treaties with Spain? If his Majesty's representative may have recourse to the Federal Government, to prevent the armaments which the citizens of the United States fit out, to commit hostilities upon the Spanish commerce under insurgent banners, he is told that there are *laws* which have respect to the treaties, and *tribunals* which put them in force, and that it is necessary to apply to them. When, in virtue of this, his Majesty's consuls apply to those *tribunals*, requesting the punishment of such citizens as have applied for and accepted commissions from Governments enemies of his Catholic Majesty, they declare that they have no jurisdiction for it. When they request of the custom-houses (or other authorities) the detention of vessels built, armed, and manned in this country on account of those Governments, or of individuals who attempt hostilities against Spain, they answer that the *laws* are not sufficiently clear, and that they have not sufficient authority. If said vessels carry the armament in the hold, it is called *ballast*. If the artillery is mounted on deck, it is to make signals *only*. The consequence is, that these vessels and armaments and citizens of the United States sail publicly, and without any risk, and that they continue making innumerable prizes, and cause immense losses to the Spanish nation.

Permit me, sir, to make another important observation. A learned man so eminent as Mr. *Ingersoll*, charged with the execution of the laws of the United States, ought not to be ignorant of them; and when he says that he does not know in the present case another law applicable to it but the act of Congress of the 20th of April, 1818, it is to be believed that there is no other. But if, in effect, there be no more law than this for preventing the armaments which are made here, and punishing the citizens of the United States, who, with commissions of foreign States or Governments, make war on his Catholic Majesty, the irresistible consequence is, that the laws of the United States contradict one another. Because here we have one law, which is the present act, which prescribes to the courts an *arbitrary* punishment, to the decision of the judges, of only *fine and imprisonment* to the citizens, for instance, who accept and make use of commissions of any State or Government at war with a power at peace with the United States; whilst there is another, sanctioned at the same time also by Congress, which are the treaties with Spain, which point out a *determinate* punishment against those delinquents, and it is that of *death*, because they are called *pirates*. To which of these two laws, differing upon the same case, ought the tribunals to have recourse? They cannot depart from the letter of the law, nor impose *the punishment of death*, if they hold to the former, which prescribes only *fine and imprisonment*. I will not conceal from you, sir, that if, in the United States, there is no other law than the act cited by Mr. *Ingersoll* respecting illegal armaments, I have few hopes that the Federal Government can, with it alone, duly fulfil the existing treaties with Spain, although it should recommend the greatest vigilance to the local authorities. Besides, such an act appears to me little serviceable and insufficient for the effect. The officers of the custom-house *may*, in virtue of this act, detain a vessel which they know or suspect to carry an illegal armament; but what responsibility have they if they do not? I see none. What obligation have they to inquire into these armaments? None. They are not ordered to take this trouble. Who will come to inform them of what is passing? No citizen of the United States has an interest in doing it; rather the contrary. What, then, signifies this act, which appears so completely to defeat the intention of *the 14th article* of the treaty of 1795, with Spain? Can it be said that Congress, at the passing of said act, did not bear the treaties in mind? or will it be said (and may be even much worse) that it knew it, but that still it addressed the tribunals in other words, the following for example:

"The treaties which we have with Spain call such of our citizens *pirates* as, with foreign commissions, make war upon her; and consequently, they incur thereupon the *penalty of death*. But we declare by this that you ought not to fulfil this part of the treaty. The *Government* of the United States, who concurred with Spain in imposing upon them a punishment so severe, atrocious, and disproportioned to the offence, was wanting to its duty and to the confidence of the nation which it governs. The *Senate*, which approved the treaty at that time, was not worthy of us, who, as being more illustrious, establish other laws more rational and humane. His Catholic Majesty will be very well satisfied with imposing upon these delinquents *a fine and imprisonment*, at your pleasure. To *diminish* the punishment is not *to change the treaty.*"

The consequences of such a doctrine would be fatal. What would succeed if other nations should follow this example? England has just made a convention with the United States, as appears, relative to the abolition of *the slave trade.* If any of the two contracting parties should *afterwards* alter the punishment of those who are declared *pirates*, would not this be to change the essence of their stipulations, and in fact to annul such convention? It would be utterly to destroy the treaties which bind nations, if it were permitted to alter them in this manner by the particular legislation of each. Thus, then, it is not possible to expect this immoral and Machiavelian language from any Government of the civilized world; and it would be doing the greatest injury to the respectable and august Congress of the United States to believe that it would on any occasion alter intentionally the literal sense of the treaties, in the religious fulfilment of which its own honor is concerned. Whatever may be the defect which may be observed in the act of the 20th of April, (and what human law has not defects?) I am well persuaded that the intention was not *to alter*, as appears at first view, but, on the contrary, *to enforce* the fulfilment of the stipulations of the treaty referred to with Spain, although experience has proved that that noble object has not been realized, as we see by the infractions which still continue to be committed in spite of it; and that the officers of the United States themselves do not hit upon the proper means of fulfilling it, and interpret it in different ways to the incalculable loss of Spain.

I have just received a letter from Charleston, an extract of which I have the honor to inclose, which will give you some idea how considerable these losses and damages must be. You will be pleased to remark that that port was one of those which the privateers of which I complain frequented less till now; but the evil is spreading and augments in an extraordinary degree every day, doubtless because they see how little they have to fear in this country the consequences of their shameful intrigues. The privateer named the "*Padilla*," of which it speaks, was last in the same port of Charleston, commanded apparently by a Frenchman called *Daverac*, but the true captain was (and when she sailed commanded her) one *Bradford*, a native of the United States, (as well as, also, were a great part of the crew which she carried,) and, having there surreptitiously augmented their number, returned to cruise against the Spaniards. Only since I sent my last note to *Mr. Adams*, two more Spanish *prizes* have entered, which I know, into the ports of this Union. One is the brig "*Cazador*," of which the inclosed letter speaks, and another is the schooner "*Tereza*," which has gone into Savannah to the care of one *Bureil*, a prize of the same privateer, the "*Polly Hampton*." Such privateers, availing themselves of various pretexts and subterfuges, easily dispose of their robberies here. This is public and notorious, and there is no cause to conceal it if they see that it can be done with impunity. And, in truth, how can they cease to see this, if even the newspapers of the same United States publish and *celebrate* the part which they take against Spain in the war with the revolted Governments of her America, not as if it were some private and obscure citizen of the United States, but even men of the greatest distinction for their talents and ranks in society and *officers* of the very *Government*. The inclosed newspaper, which came to my hands a little after having sent my last note to *Mr. Adams*, is an undeniable proof of this. By it you will see, sir, that a *Consul General* of the United States, putting himself at the head of a body of insurgents in South America, has been probably the cause of his Catholic Majesty losing one of his best kingdoms.

I have been more diffuse in my thoughts, with the view of letting you know how little good has been produced by the means hitherto taken by the Federal Government to prevent the armaments of which I complain, and you supposed there was no reason to fear in future, whilst they were still continuing to carry them on. I will conclude by requesting that you will be pleased to inform the President of it, in order that if he sees fit he may adopt other means more efficacious and satisfactory to his Catholic Majesty. I should be very happy if on this occasion I could assure his Majesty that the correct intentions of the President would in future be realized, and that he had no reason to fear the sailing of more armaments from the ports of the United States against the Spanish trade.

In the meantime I have much satisfaction in the honor of offering to you the assurances of my respect and attentive consideration.

HILARIO DE RIVAS Y SALMON.

No. 33, (a.)

Copy communicated with Mr. Salmon's letter to Mr. Daniel Brent, of September 29, 1824.

CHARLESTON, *September 19, 1824.*

" One vessel had been fitted out of this port to cruise against the property of Spaniards; she was a sloop called '*Amelia.*' Said vessel was captured by the Spanish.

" Several vessels arrived in this port under the insurgent flag have augmented their force in arms and men. This may be ascertained by some persons who shipped them; one, however, who was very instrumental in this business, died a few days ago of the yellow fever.

" There have and continue to arrive prizes taken by vessels under the insurgent flags, who come in and pretend distress, and get liberty to sell a sufficient quantity to defray expenses, or repairs, &c., under which permission they generally sell the greater part of their plunder. This is the general impression.

" Yesterday arrived the *Spanish brig* '*Cazador*,' *Williams*, with sugar, leather, corn, &c., prize to the Colombian armed schooner '*Polly Hampton*,' *Captain Natty*, captured four weeks since off Havana, in distress, leaky, bound to Cumana, Spanish Main, having sprung a leak on the 14th instant. This is a very likely story.

" Ought to be taken into consideration Mr. Ortega's application to the district judge for process to have the property taken by the '*Padilla*' restored, she having made captures contrary to the law of nations, which he refused hearing.

"One of the prizes of the ' *Centella*' being run ashore at Key West, with an understanding of a certain *Captain Appleby*, part of the cargo was sent here to Mr. Street & Co., say, value about $15,000 sugar, cigars, cochineal, indigo, &c.; the remainder was sold by the Captain of the schooner at public auction; with which circumstances I believe you are acquainted."

No. 34.

Extract of the General Instructions, No. 1, from Mr. Adams, Secretary of State, to Mr. Nelson, Minister Plenipotentiary to Spain, dated

DEPARTMENT OF STATE, *Washington, April 28*, 1823.

The critical and convulsed condition of Spain may indeed bring forth many incidents now unforeseen, and upon which the President relies upon your own judgment for the course which, under them, you will find it prudent to pursue. But with regard to the ordinary relations between the two countries there are various objects upon which I now proceed to request your attention.

The renewal of the war in Venezuela has been signalized on the part of the Spanish commanders by proclamations of blockade unwarranted by the laws of nations, and by decrees regardless of those of humanity. With no other naval force than a single frigate, a brig, and a schooner, employed in transporting supplies from Curaçoa to Porto Cabello, they have presumed to declare a blockade of more than twelve hundred miles of coast. To this outrage upon all the rights of neutrality they have added the absurd pretension of interdicting the peaceable commerce of other nations with *all* the ports of the Spanish Main, upon the pretence that it had heretofore been forbidden by the Spanish colonial laws; and on the strength of these two inadmissible principles they have issued commissions, at Porto Cabello and in the island of Porto Rico, to a swarm of privateers, which have committed extensive and ruinous depredations upon the lawful commerce of the United States as well as upon that of other nations, and particularly of Great Britain.

It was impossible that neutral nations should submit to such a system; the execution of which has been as strongly marked with violence and cruelty as was its origin with injustice. Repeated remonstrances against it have been made to the Spanish Government, and it became necessary to give the protection of our naval force to the commerce of the United States exposed to these depredations.

By the act of Congress, of March 3, 1819, "to protect the commerce of the United States and punish the crime of piracy," the President was authorized to instruct the commanders of the public armed vessels of the United States to *take* any armed vessel "which shall have attempted or committed any piratical aggression, search, restraint, depredation, or seizure upon any vessel of the United States, or of the citizens thereof, *or upon any other vessel;* and, also, to retake any vessel of the United States, or its citizens, which may have been *unlawfully* captured upon the high seas."

A copy of this act and of the instructions from the Navy Department to the officers who have been charged with the execution of it are herewith furnished you. The instructions will enable you to show how cautiously this Government, while affording the protection due to the lawful commerce of the nation, has guarded against the infringement of the rights of all others.

The privateers from Porto Rico and Porto Cabello have been, by their conduct, distinguishable from pirates only by commissions of most equivocal character, from Spanish officers, whose authority to issue them has never been shown; and they have committed outrages and depredations which no commission could divest of the piratical character. During the same period swarms of pirates and of piratical vessels, without pretence or color of commission, have issued from the island of Cuba and the immediate neighborhood of the Havana, differing so little in the composition of their crews and their conduct from the privateers of Porto Cabello and Porto Rico as to leave little distinction other than that of being *disavowed* between them. These piracies have now been for years continued, under the immediate observation of the Government of the island of Cuba, which, as well as the Spanish Government, has been repeatedly and ineffectually required to suppress them. Many of them have been committed by boats within the very harbors and close upon the shores of the island. When pursued by superior force the pirates have escaped to the shores; and twelve months have elapsed since the late Captain General Mahy refused to Captain Biddle the permission to land even upon the desert and uninhabited parts of the island where they should seek refuge from his pursuit. Governor Mahy at the same time declared that *he had* taken the necessary measures to defend his territorial jurisdiction and for the apprehension of every description of outlaws.

Governor Mahy is since deceased; but neither the measures which he had then taken nor any since adopted by the Government of the island have proved effectual to suppress or in any manner even to restrain the pirates. From the most respectable testimony we are informed that these atrocious robberies are committed by persons well known, and that the traffic in their plunder is carried on with the utmost notoriety. They are sometimes committed by vessels equipped as merchant vessels, and which clear out as such from the Havana. It has also been remarked that they cautiously avoid molesting Spanish vessels, but attack without discrimination the defenceless vessels of all other nations. You will see by a letter from Lieutenant Gregory to the Secretary of the Navy (p. 64 of the printed documents) that a large portion of the crews of the Porto Rico privateers consist of these same pirates from Cuba.

In November last, a gallant officer of the Navy, Lieutenant Allen, lost his life in a conflict with some of these pirates; and an armament was immediately afterwards fitted out, and is now on the spot under the command of Commodore Porter, for the defence and protection of our commerce against them. Notice was despatched of this movement to Mr. Forsyth, by a special messenger, in January last, with instructions to him to require of the Spanish Government the permission to land in case of necessity in pursuit of the robbers. Copies of the instructions from the Secretary of the Navy are herewith furnished. From this statement of facts it is apparent that the naval officers of the United States who have been instructed to protect our commerce in that quarter have been brought in conflict with two descriptions of *unlawful* captors of our merchant vessels, the acknowledged and disavowed pirates of Cuba, and the ostensibly commissioned privateers from Porto Rico and Porto Cabello; and that in both cases the actual depredators have been of the same class of Spanish subjects and often probably the same persons. The consequence has been that several of the commissioned privateers have been taken by our cruisers, and that in one instance a merchant vessel, belonging to the Havana, but charged upon oath of two persons as having been the vessel from which a vessel of the United States had been robbed, has been brought into port and is now at Norfolk to be tried at the next session of the District Court of the United States. In all these cases the Spanish minister, Anduaga, has addressed to this Department complaints and remonstrances in language so exceptionable that it precluded the possibility of an amicable discussion of the subject with him. In some of the cases explanations have been transmitted to Mr. Forsyth to be given in a spirit of amity and conciliation to the Spanish Government. But as your mission affords a favorable opportunity for a full and candid exposition of them all, copies of the correspondence with Mr. Anduaga, relating to them, are annexed to these instructions, to which I add upon each case of complaint the following remarks:

1. The first is the case of a man named Escandell, prize master of a Dutch vessel called the Neptune, taken by a privateer in Porto Cabello, called the Virgin del Carmen, and retaken by the United States armed brig Spark, then commanded by Captain John H. Elton, since deceased. From the report of Captain Elton it appears: 1st. That the Dutch vessel had been taken within the territorial jurisdiction of the Dutch island of Curaçoa. 2d. That he, Captain Elton, delivered her up to the Governor of the island of Aruba. 3d. That he retook her as a vessel piratically captured; the prize master, Escandell, having produced to him no papers whatsoever. He therefore brought him and the prize crew to Charleston, South Carolina, where they were prosecuted as pirates.

Mr. Anduaga's first letter to me on this case was dated the 24th of July, 1822, inclosing a copy of a letter from Escandell to the Spanish vice consul at Charleston, invoking his protection; Escandell being then in prison, and under an indictment for piracy. He solicits the interposition of the vice consul, that he may obtain, from the Captain General of the Havana and the commanding officer at Porto Cabello, documents to prove that he was lawfully commissioned; and he alleges that the captain of the privateer had furnished him with a *document* to carry the prize into Porto Cabello; that he did deliver this document to Captain Elton, who *concealed* it from the court at Charleston; that Elton and his officers well knew that he, Escandell, was commissioned by the King of Spain, and had assisted at the disembarking of General la Torre with the privateer and the prize, but that Elton had withheld his knowledge of these facts from the grand jury. Mr. Anduaga's letter to me noticed this contradiction between the statement of Captain Elton and the declaration of Escandell, and requested that the trial at Charleston might be postponed till he could receive answers from the Captain General of the Havana and the commandant of Porto Cabello, to whom he had written to obtain the documents necessary to prove the legality of the capture. This was accordingly done.

This letter of Mr. Anduaga was unexceptionable in its purport; but, on the 17th of October, he addressed me a second, inclosing the papers which he had received from Porto Cabello, and assuming a style of vituperation not only against Captain Elton, then very recently dead, but against the Navy in general, the Government, and even the people of the United States, which required the exertion of some forbearance to avoid sending it back to him as unsuitable to be received at this Department from a foreign minister.

It was the more unwarrantable, because, while assuming, as proved, against an officer of the United States, no longer living to justify himself, that he had *concealed* documents furnished him by Escandell, he declares it "evident that not the public service but avarice, and the atrocious desire of sacrificing upon a gibbet the lives of some innocent citizens of a friendly power, were the moving principles of this commander's conduct." To those who personally knew Captain Elton, what language could reply in terms of indignation adequate to the unworthiness of this charge? And how shall I now express a suitable sense of it, when I say that it was advanced without a shadow of proof, upon the mere original assertion of Escandell, made in the most suspicious manner, and which the very documents from Porto Cabello tended rather to disprove than to sustain.

It was made, I say, in the most suspicious manner; for, in his affidavit before the clerk of the United States court at Charleston, made on the 8th of June, 1822, where he might have been confronted by Captain Elton and the officers of the Spark, Escandell had not even hinted at this concealment of his papers by Captain Elton, or pretended that he had produced any to him. But *after* he had been arraigned upon the indictment, and after the court had, at the motion of his counsel, postponed his trial to the next term, for the express purpose of giving him time to obtain proof that he had been commissioned, in a secret letter to Castro, the owner of the privateer, at Porto Cabello, and in another to the Spanish vice consul at Charleston, he makes these scandalous allegations against Captain Elton at times and places where he could not be present to refute them. That the documents from Porto Cabello, transmitted to Mr. Anduaga, tended rather to disprove than to sustain them, you will perceive by an examination of the translations of them herewith furnished you. The only documents among them showing the authority under which Escandell, when captured by Captain Elton, had possession of the Neptune, is a copy of the commission of the privateer Virgin del Carmen, which had taken the Neptune, and a declaration by the captain of the privateer, Lorenzo Puyol, that, on capturing the Neptune, he had put Escandell, as prize master, and six men, on board of her, ordering her into the port of Cabello, and furnishing Escandell *with the documents necessary for his voyage.* No copy of these documents is produced; and the declaration of this Captain Puyol himself is signed only with a cross, he not knowing how to write his name.

It is conceived that the only admissible evidence of Escandell's regular authority as prize master of a captured vessel would have been an authenticated copy of the document itself, furnished him by Puyol. The extreme ignorance of this man, whoa ppears, on the face of his own declaration, unable to write his own name, raises more than a presumption that he knew as little what could be a regular document for a prize master, and is by no means calculated to give confidence to his declaration as a substitute for the authentic copy of the document itself. The absurdity of the imputation of avaricious motives to Captain Elton is demonstrated by the fact that he delivered up the prize, which was a Dutch vessel, to the Governor of Aruba, and not her original captain; and as to that of his having concealed Escandell's papers to bring him and six innocent seamen to a gibbet, I can even now notice it only to leave to the candor of the Spanish Government whether it ought ever to be answered.

Copies are herewith furnished of Captain Elton's report of this transaction to the Secretary of the Navy; of the agreement by which the Neptune was by him delivered up to the Dutch commandant, at the island of Aruba, Thielen; and of the receipt given by her original captain, Reinar Romer, to whom she was restored. In these documents you will see it expressly stipulated both by the Dutch commandant and by Captain Romer that the "vessel and cargo, or the value thereof, should be returned to any legal authority of the United States of America, or to the Spanish Government, or prize claimants, *in due course of the laws of nations.*" You will find, also, that in the document signed by Captain Romer he expressly declares that the persons by whom he had been captured *purported* to belong to a Spanish felucca privateer, but *not having any credentials or authority* to cruise upon the high seas with them *he supposes them to have been pirates.*

This declaration of Romer himself is directly contradictory to the assertion which Escandell, in his affidavit at Charleston, on the 8th of June, 1822, pretends that Captain Romer made to the boarding officer from the Spark, in answer to his inquiries whether Escandell and his men were pirates. Escandell says that Romer answered they were *not;* Romer himself says that he supposes they were.

You will remark that, in the copy of Escandell's affidavit, transmitted by Mr. Anduaga to the Department of State, the name of the Dutch captain of the Neptune is written Reinas Buman, apparently by mistake in the copy. The name, as signed by himself, is Reinar Romer.

On a review of the whole transaction, as demonstrated by these documents, it will be seen that the conduct of Captain Elton was fair, honorable, cautiously regardful of the possible rights of the captors and Spanish Government, and eminently disinterested. He retook the Neptune, a Dutch vessel, at the request of an officer of the Dutch Government. He had already known and protected her as a neutral before. He restored her to her captain without claiming salvage, and upon the sole condition that the Dutch Governor should restore to their owners, citizens of the United States, the proceeds of a vessel and cargo also wrongfully captured by a Spanish privateer, and which had been brought within his jurisdiction. And he provided that if the capture of the Neptune should eventually prove to have been lawfully made, the Dutch commandant and the captain of the Neptune himself should be responsible to the Spanish and American Governments and to the captors for the result.

I have entered into this detail of the evidence in this case not only to give you the means of satisfying the Spanish Government that the complaints of Mr. Anduaga against Captain Elton were as groundless in substance as they were unjust to him and disrespectful to this Government and nation in form, but to vindicate from unmerited reproach the memory of a gallant officer, of whose faithful and valuable services his country had been deprived by death only twenty days before these dishonorable imputations were cast upon him by Mr. Anduaga.

The harshness and precipitation of that minister's judgment, in preferring this complaint, is the more remarkable, inasmuch as he avows in that very note the opinion that the bare word, without proof, of a *merchant* captain is not evidence sufficient to furnish even a *pretext* to the naval officers of the United States to attack the armed vessel by which he had been plundered. If the word of the captain of a merchant vessel, supported by his oath, were of such trivial account, of what weight in the scale of testimony is the bare word of a captain of a privateer who cannot write his name, to prove the existence and authority of a written or printed document pretended to have been given by himself?

If the capture of the Neptune by Puyol had been lawful, her owners would at this day possess the means of recovering indemnity for their loss by the recapture, in the written engagements of the Dutch commandant, Thieleman, and of Captain Romer. But it was not lawful. By the documents transmitted by Mr. Anduaga it appears that a part of the cargo of the Neptune, after her capture by the Virgin del Carmen, had been transhipped to another vessel, and that at Porto Cabello it was condemned by Captain Lavorde, commander of the Spanish frigate Ligera, who had issued the privateer's commission, and then sat as judge of the admiralty court upon the prize. And the sole ground of condemnation assigned is the breach of the pretended blockade by the Neptune and her *trading* with the Independent Patriots. You will remark the great irregularity and incompatibility with the principles of general justice as well as of the Spanish Constitution, that one and the same person should be acting at once in the capacity of a naval officer, of a magistrate issuing commissions to privateers, and of a judge to decide upon the prizes taken by them.

But the whole foundation of his decision is a nullity. The blockade was a public wrong. The interdiction of all trade was an outrage upon the rights of *all* neutral nations, and the resort to two expedients bears on its face the demonstration that they who assumed them both had no reliance upon the justice of either; for if the interdiction of *all* neutral trade with the Independents were lawful, there was neither use nor necessity for the blockade; and if the blockade were lawful, there could be as little occasion or pretence for the interdiction of the trade. The correctness of this reasoning can no longer be contested by the Spanish Government itself. The blockade and interdiction of trade have, from the first notice of them, not only been denounced and protested against by the Government and officers of the United States, but by those of Great Britain, even when the ally of Spain, and who has not yet acknowledged the independence of the revolted colonies. The consequences of these pretensions have been still more serious to Spain, since they terminated in a formal notification by the British Government that they had issued orders of reprisal to their squadrons in the West Indies to capture all Spanish vessels until satisfaction should be made for the property of all British subjects taken or detained under color of this preposterous blockade and interdiction. And Spain has formally pledged herself to make this demanded reparation.

2. The second cause of complaint by Mr. Anduaga, upon which I have to animadvert, is that of the capture of the Porto Rico privateer Palmyra by the United States armed schooner Grampus, Lieutenant Gregory, commander.

With his letter of the 11th of October, 1822, Mr. Anduaga transmitted copies of a letter from the captain of the privateer Escurra to the Spanish consul at Charleston, dated the 16th of September, 1822, and of sundry depositions taken at Porto Rico from seamen who had belonged to her relating to the capture. The account of the transaction given by Lieutenant Gregory is among the documents transmitted to Congress with the President's message at the commencement of the last session, pages 62, 63, and 64, to which I refer. The subject is yet before the competent judicial tribunal of this country. The captain and seamen of the Palmyra, with the exception of those charged with the robbery of the Coquette, were discharged by a decree of the District Court of the United States at Charleston, and the vessel was restored to her captain; but the judge, (Drayton, since deceased,) in giving this decree, declared that Lieutenant Gregory had been fully justified in the capture. By a decree of the Circuit Court of the same district heavy damages were awarded against Lieutenant Gregory, from which sentence there is an appeal pending before the Supreme Judicial Court of the United States. Whatever their final decision may be, the character of the court is a sure warrant that it will be given with every regard due to the rights and interests of all the parties concerned, and the most perfect reliance may be placed upon its justice, impartiality, and independence. The decision of the Circuit Court, indeed, would imply some censure upon the conduct of Lieutenant Gregory, and may be represented as giving support to the complaints of the Spanish minister against him. But it is the opinion of a single judge, in direct opposition to that of his colleague on the same bench, and liable to the revisal and correction of the supreme tribunal. It is marked with two principles, upon which it may be fairly presumed the judgment of the Supreme Court will be more in accord with that of the district. The justification of Lieutenant Gregory for taking and sending in the Palmyra rests upon two important facts: First, the robbery committed by part of her crew, sworn to by Captain Souther, of the schooner Coquette, and confirmed by the oaths of her mate and two of her seamen; and secondly, that at the time of her capture she had commenced the firing upon the Grampus by a full volley from small arms and cannon. But as the *fact* of the robbery from the Coquette was not in rigorously judicial evidence before the Circuit Court, the judge declared that, although he had no doubt the fact was true, yet, in the absence of the evidence to prove it, he must *officially* decide that it was false; and as to the circumstance of the first fire, as the Spanish and American testimony were in contradiction to each other, he should set them both aside and form his decision upon other principles. If, indeed, Lieutenant Gregory is ultimately to be deprived of the benefit of these two facts, he will be left *judicially* without justification. But, considered with reference to the discharge of his duty as an officer of the United States, if the declaration of Captain Souther, taken upon oath, confirmed by those of his mate and two of his men, was not competent testimony upon which he was bound to act, upon what evidence could an officer of the Navy ever dare to execute his instructions and the law by rescuing or protecting from the robbers of the sea the property of his fellow-citizens?

The robbery of the Coquette by the boat's crew from the Palmyra is assuredly sufficiently proved for all other than judicial purposes by the fact, which was in evidence before the District Court, that the memorandum book, sworn by John Peabody, junior, mate of the Coquette, to have been taken from him, together with clothing, was actually found in a bag with clothing on board the Palmyra.

In answering Mr. Anduaga's letter of October 11, I transmitted to him a copy of the printed decree of Judge Drayton, in which the most material facts relating to the case, and the principles applicable to it upon which his decision was given, are set forth. Some additional facts are disclosed in a statement published by Lieutenant Gregory, highly important to *this* discussion, inasmuch as they identify a portion of the crew of the Palmyra with a gang of the Cape Antonio pirates, and with an establishment of the same character which had before been broken up by that officer.

In a long and elaborate reply to my letter, dated the 11th of December, 1822, Mr. Anduaga, without contesting the fact that the Coquette had been robbed by the boarding crew from the Palmyra, objects to the decision of Judge Drayton, as if, by detaining for trial the individual seamen belonging to the Palmyra charged with the robbery, it assumed a jurisdiction disclaimed by the very acknowledgment that the privateer was lawfully commissioned, and sanctioned the right of search, so long and so strenuously resisted by the American Government.

In this reply, too, Mr. Anduaga attempts, by laborious argument, to maintain, to the fullest and most unqualified extent, the right of the Spanish privateers to capture, and of the Spanish prize courts to condemn, all vessels of every other nation trading with any of the ports of the Independent Patriots of South America, because, under the old colonial laws of Spain, that trade had been prohibited. And with the consistency of candor, at least, he explicitly says that the decrees issued by the Spanish commanders on the Main, under the name of blockades, were not properly so called, but were mere enforcements of the antediluvian colonial exclusions; and such were the instructions under which the Palmyra, and all the other privateers from Port Rico and Port Cabello, have been cruising. Is it surprising that the final answer of Great Britain to this pretension was an order of *reprisals?* or that, under the laws of the United States, it has brought their naval officers in conflict of actual hostility with privateers so commissioned and so instructed? The Spanish Government have for many years had notice, both from Great Britain and from the United States, that they considered as rightful the peaceful commerce of their people with the ports in possession of the Independent Patriots. Spain herself has opened most of those of which her forces have been able to retain or to recover the possession. The blockades proclaimed by General Morillo, in 1815, were coupled with this same absurd pretension; they were formally protested against by the Government of the United States; and wherever Morillo obtained possession, he himself immediately opened the port to foreign and neutral commerce.

Mr. Anduaga seems to have had much confidence in the conclusiveness of his reasoning in this letter of December 11; for, without considering the character of our institutions which have committed to the Executive authority all communications with the ministers of foreign powers, he permitted himself the request that the President would communicate it to Congress; without having the apology for this indiscretion, which, on a prior occasion, he had alleged for a like request, namely, that it was in answer to letters from this Department which had been communicated to the Legislature. In the former case he was indulged by compliance with his request. In the latter it was passed over without notice. But Mr. Anduaga was determined that his argument should come before the public, and sent a copy of it to the Havana, where it was published in the newspapers, whence it has been translated, and inserted in some of our public journals.

The British order of reprisals; the appropriation by the Cortes of forty millions of reals for reparation to British subjects of damages sustained by them, in part from capture and condemnation of their property, under this absurd pretension; and the formal revocation by the King of Spain of these unlawful blockades, will, it is presumed, supersede the necessity of a serious argument in reply to that of Mr. Anduaga upon this point. It is in vain for Spain to pretend that, during the existence of a civil war, in which, by the universal law of nations, both parties have equal rights, with reference to foreign nations, she can enforce against all neutrals, by the seizure and condemnation of their property, the laws of colonial monopoly and prohibitions, by which they had been excluded from commercial intercourse with the colonies before the existence of the war, and when her possession and authority were alike undisputed. And if, at any stage of the war, this pretension could have been advanced with any color of reason, it was pre-eminently nugatory on the renewal of the war, after the formal treaty between Morillo and Bolivar, and the express stipulation which it contained, that, if the war should be renewed, it should be conducted on the principles applicable to wars between independent nations, and not on the disgusting and sanguinary doctrine of suppressing rebellion.

As little foundation is there for the inference drawn by Mr. Anduaga from the decree of the district judge, admitting the Palmyra to have been lawfully commissioned as a privateer, but detaining for trial the portion of her crew charged with the robbery from the Coquette, that it sanctions the right of search, against which the United States have so long and so constantly protested: for, in the first place, the

United States have never disputed the belligerent right of search as recognized and universally practiced, conformably to the laws of nations. They have disputed the right of belligerents, under color of the right of search for contraband of war, to seize and cary away men, at the discretion of the boarding officer, without trial and without appeal; men, not as contraband of war, or belonging to the enemy, but as subjects, real or pretended, of the belligerent himself, and to be used by him against his enemy. It is the fraudulent abuse of the right of search, for purposes never recognized or admitted by the laws of nations; purposes, in their practical operation, of the deepest oppression, and most crying injustice, that the United States have resisted and will resist, and which warns them against assenting to the extension, in time of peace, of a right which experience has shown to be liable to such gross perversion in time of war. And secondly, the Palmyra was taken for acts of *piratical* aggression and *depredation* upon a vessel of the United States, and upon the property of their citizens. Acts of *piratical* aggression and depredation may be committed by vessels having lawful commissions as privateers, and many such had been committed by the Palmyra. The act of robbery from the Coquette was, in every respect piratical; for it was committed while the privateer was under the Venezuelan flag, and under that flag she had fired upon the Coquette, and brought her to. It was piratical, therefore, not only as depredation of the property by the boat's crew who took it away, but as aggression under the sanction of the captain of the privateer who was exercising belligerent rights under false colors. To combat under any other flag than that of the nation by which she is commissioned, by the laws of nations subjects a vessel, though lawfully commissioned, to seizure and condemnation as a pirate.—(See Valin's Ordonnance de la Marine, vol. 2., p. 239.) And although the decree of the district judge ordered the restitution of the vessel to her captain, because it held him to have been lawfully commissioned; neither did the law of nations require, nor would the law of the United States permit, that men brought within the jurisdiction of the court, and charged with piratical depredations upon citizens of the United States, should be discharged and turned over to a foreign tribunal for trial, as was demanded by Mr. Anduaga. They had been brought within the jurisdiction of the court, not by the exercise of any right of search, but as part of the crew of a vessel which had committed piratical depredations and aggressions upon vessels and citizens of the United States. The District Court, adjudging the commission of the privateer to have been lawful, and considering the gun fired under the Venezuelan flag, to bring the Coquette to, though wrongful and unwarrantable, as not amounting rigorously to that *combat*, which would have been complete piracy, discharged the captain and portion of the crew which had not been guilty of the robbery of the Coquette, but reserved for trial the individuals charged with that act.

The conduct of the Palmyra for months before her capture had been notoriously and flagrantly piratical. She had, in company with an other privateer, named the *Boves*, both commanded by the same captain, Pablo Slanger, fired upon the United States schooner Porpoise, Captain Ramage, who abstained from returning the fire. For this act of unequivocal hostility, Captain Slanger's only apology to Captain Ramage was, that he had taken the Porpoise for a Patriot cruiser.—(See documents with the President's message of December, 1822, p. 65.) Numbers of neutral vessels, of different nations, had been plundered by her; and among the affidavits made to Lieutenant Gregory, at St. Thomas, was one of the master and mate of a French schooner, that she had been robbed by a boat's crew from her of a barrel of beef and a barrel of rice. In the letter from Captain Escurra to the Spanish consul at Charleston, he admits the taking of these provisions, alleging that the master of the French vessel gave them to him at his request. The affidavit of the French master and mate shows what sort of a *gift* it was, and is more coincident with all the other transactions of this privateer.

In the same letter of December 11, Mr. Anduaga, with more ingenuity than candor, attempts at once to raise a wall of separation between the pirates of Porto Rico and the privateersmen of Porto Rico and Porto Cabello, and to identify the pirates, not only with all those who at a prior period had abused the several independent flags of South America, but with the adventurers from the United States who at different times have engaged in the Patriot service; and be endeavors to blend them all with the foolish expedition of last summer against Porto Rico. While indulging his propensity to complain, he revives all the long exploded and groundless charges of his predecessors in former years, and does not scruple to insinuate that the Cuba pirates themselves are North Americans from the United States. It is easy to discern and point out the fallacy of these endeavors to blend together things totally distinct, and to discriminate between things that are identical. It is in proof before our tribunals, in the case of the Palmyra itself, that some of the pirates of Cuba and of the Porto Rico privateersmen are the same. Among the Cuba pirates that have been taken, as well by the vessels of the United States as by British cruisers, *not one* North American has been found. A number of those pirates have been executed at the Bahama islands, and ten from one vessel at the island of Jamaica, all Spanish subjects, and from the Spanish islands. Not a shadow of evidence has been seen that, among the Cuba pirates, a single citizen of the United States was to be found.

As to the complaints of Mr. Anduaga's predecessors, meaning those of Don Luis de Onis, it might have been expected that we should hear no more of them after the ratification of the treaty of 1819. Whatever had been the merits of those complaints, full satisfaction for them all had been made by that treaty to Spain, and was acknowledged by the ratification of the Spanish Government in October, 1820. Since that time no complaints had been made by Mr. Anduaga's predecessors. It was reserved for him as well to call up those phantoms from the dead, as to conjure new ones from the living. That supplies of every kind, including arms and other implements of war, have been, in the way of lawful commerce, procured within the United States for the account of the South American Independents, and at their expense and hazard exported to them, is doubtless true. And Spain has enjoyed and availed herself of the same advantages.

The neutrality of the United States has, throughout this contest between Spain and South America, been cautiously and faithfully observed by their Government. But the complaints of Mr. Anduaga as well as those of his predecessor, Mr. Onis, are founded upon erroneous views and mistaken principles of neutrality. They assume that all *commerce*, even the most peaceful commerce of other nations, with the South Americans, is a violation of neutrality. And while they assert this in principle, the Spanish commanders, in the few places where they yet hold authority, attempt to carry it into effect in a spirit worthy of itself. The decree of General Morales, of the 15th of September, 1822, as in perfect accord with the argument of Mr. Anduaga, on the 11th of December of the same year. The unconcerted but concurring solemn protests against the former, of the Dutch Governor of Curaçoa, Cantzlaar, of the British Admiral Rowley, and of our own Captain Spence were but the chorus of all human feeling revolting at the acts of which Mr. Anduaga's reasoning was the attempted justification.

3. The next case of complaint by Mr. Anduaga is in a letter of the 23d of February last, against

Lieutenant Wilkinson, commander of the United States schooner Spark, for capturing off the Havana a vessel called the Ninfa Catalana or the Santissima Trinidad, Nicholas Garyole master, and sending her into Norfolk. As there are reasons for believing that in this case Lieutenant Wilkinson acted upon erroneous information, a court of inquiry has been ordered upon his conduct, the result of which will be communicated to you. The Ninfa Catalana remains for trial at the District Court to be held in the eastern district of Virginia in the course of the next month. Immediately after receiving Mr. Anduaga's letter on the subject, I wrote to the attorney of the United States for the district, instructing him to obtain, if possible, an extraordinary session of the court, that the cause might be decided without delay. but the judge declined appointing such session unless all the witnesses summoned to the court upon the case could be notified of it, which not being practicable, the short delay till the meeting of the regular session of the court has been unavoidable. You will assure the Spanish Government that the most impartial justice will be rendered to all the parties concerned, as well by the adjudication of the admiralty court as by the military inquiry on the conduct of Lieutenant Wilkinson. I ought to add, that no evidence hitherto has come to the knowledge of the Government which has implicated the correctness of Lieutenant Wilkinson's intentions, or manifested any other motive than that of discharging his duty and protecting the property of his fellow-citizens. .

4. The capture of the Spanish schooner Carmen, alias Gallega the Third, by the United States sloop. of-war Peacock, Captain Cassin, has furnished the fourth occasion for this class of Mr. Anduaga's remonstrances.

There are two declarations, or depositions, made by the captain and persons who were on board of this vessel at the time of her capture: one at Pensacola, and the other at New Orleans. The first, before the notary, José Escaro, by Jacinto Correa, captain of the Gallega, the pilot, Ramon Echavarria, boatswain, Manuel Agacio, three sailors, and Juan Martin Ferreyro, a passenger. All the witnesses, after the first, only confirm, in general and unqualified terms, *all* his statements, although many of the circumstances, asserted by him as facts, could not have been personally known to them, and others could not have been known to himself but by hearing from some of them. The protest, for example, avers that, when first captured by the Peacock, Captain Correa, with his steward and cook, were taken on board that vessel, and, while they were there, he represents various disorders to have been committed on board of his own vessel by the boarding officer from the Peacock, though, by his own showing, he was not present to witness them. His whole narrative is composed of alleged occurrences on board of three vessels, the Peacock, the Louisiana cutter, and the Gallega, and no discrimination is made between those of his own knowledge and those which he had heard from others. The second declaration was made before Antonio Argote Villalobos, Spanish consul at New Orleans, only by Captain Correa and Echavarria, the mate, and gives an account of several *other* Spanish vessels captured by the Peacock while they were on board of that vessel as prisoners. A very inadequate reason is assigned by Captain Correa for not having made it at the same time with the first at Pensacola; and the whole purport of it is, to represent those *other* vessels which he had seen captured as inoffensive, unarmed vessels, and the capture of them by the Peacock as itself piratical.

Copies of the proceedings of the courts at Pensacola and at New Orleans upon these cases are expected at this Department, and the substance of them will be duly communicated to you.

In the meantime, the reports of Captain Cassin, of the Peacock, and of Captain Jackson, commander of the revenue cutter Louisiana, to the Navy Department, will give you a very different and, doubtless, more correct account of these transactions.

There is a strong reason for believing that the Gallega did actually belong to the gang of pirates of which those who pretended inoffensive and unarmed vessels certainly formed a part; that Correa and Echavarria were testifying in behalf of their accomplices; and their warm sympathy with those convicted pirates is much more indicative of their own guilt than of their belief in the innocence of the others.

That the *other* vessels were piratical is no longer a subject of question or dispute. Two of them were carried by Captain Cassin to the Havana, where one of them, a schooner of nine guns, was claimed by a lady, widow of a merchant in that city, as her property, and, at her application, supported by that of the Captain General, was restored to her upon payment of $1,000 salvage. The part of the cargo which had been saved was sold in like manner with the approbation of the Captain General. The vessel had been taken by the pirates but a few days before, and, in retaking and restoring her to the owner, Captain Cassin had not only rendered an important service to a Spanish subject, but taken from the pirates the means of committing more extensive and atrocious depredations.

Among the articles found on board of these vessels were some of female apparel, rent and blood-stained; and many other traces to deeds of horror with which these desperate wretches are known to be familiar. The pirates had, when close pursued, abandoned their vessels and escaped to the shore. They were pursued, but not discovered. The coffee was found hidden in the woods, and, with the vessel brought into New Orleans, has been regularly condemned by the sentence of the court. And these are the characters, and this the description of people, whom Captain Correa and his mate, Echavarria, represent, in their declaration before the Spanish consul at New Orleans as innocent Spanish subjects, piratically plundered of their lawful property by Captain Cassin. And upon such testimony as this has Mr. Anduaga suffered himself to be instigated to a style of invective and reproach, not only against that officer, but against the officers of our Navy generally, against the Government and people of this country, upon which, while pointing it out and marking its contrast with the real facts of the case, I forbear all further comment.

Let it be admitted that the Catalan Nymph and the Gallega were lawful traders, and that, in capturing them as pirates, Lieutenant Wilkinson and Captain Cassin have been mistaken; that they had probable cause, sufficient for their justification, I cannot doubt, and am persuaded will, upon a full investigation of the cases, be made apparent.

In the impartial consideration of this subject, it is necessary to advert to the *character* of these pirates, and to the circumstances which have made it so difficult to distinguish between lawfully commissioned and registered Spanish vessels and the pirates.

The first of these has been the unlawful extent given to the commissions and instructions of the privateers, avowed by the Spanish Government—an authority to take all commercial vessels bound to any of the ports in possession of the Patriots. The very assumption of this principle, and the countenance given to it by the adjudications of the courts, was enough to kindle all the passions of lawless rapine in the maritime population of the islands. It was holding out to them the whole commerce of the neutral world as lawful prey. The next is the impunity with which those robberies have been committed in the very port of the Havana, and under the eye of the local Government. It is represented, and believed to be true, that many inhabitants of the city, merchants of respectable standing in society, are actively concerned in these transactions. That of the village of Regla, opposite the city, almost all the inhabitants are, with public notoriety, concerned in them. That some of the deepest criminals are known and pointed at—while the vigilance or energy of the Government is so deficient that there is an open market for the sale of those fruits of robbery; and that threats of vengeance are heard from the most abandoned of the culprits against all who molest them in their nefarious and bloody career.

The third is, that many of the piracies have been committed by merchant vessels laden with cargoes. The Spanish vessels of that description in the islands are all armed, and when taken by the pirates, are immediately converted to their own purposes. The schooner of nine guns, taken by Captain Cassin, and restored to its owner in the Havana, affords one proof of this fact; and one of the most atrocious piracies committed upon citizens of the United States was that upon the Ladies' Delight, by the Zaragosana, a vessel regularly cleared at the Havana as a merchant vessel.

There are herewith furnished you copies of the general instructions, from the Secretary of the Navy, given to all our naval officers, successively stationed in those seas, for the protection of our commerce and for carrying into effect the laws against piracy and the slave trade, together with printed copies of those laws. They will enable you to present to the Spanish Government the most conclusive proof of the friendly sentiments towards Spain, and of the undeviating regard to her rights which have constantly animated this Government, and effectually to counteract any representations of a different character, which may be made by Mr. Anduaga.

In reflecting upon the conduct of this minister, during his residence in the United States, it has been impossible to avoid the suspicion that it has been instigated by a disposition, not more friendly to the existing liberal institutions of his own country than to the harmonious intercourse, to which they were so well calculated to contribute, between the United States and Spain.

From the time of the re-establishment in Spain of a constitutional Government the sympathies of this country have been warm, earnest, and unanimous in favor of her freedom and independence. The principles which she asserts and maintains are emphatically ours, and, in the conflict with which she is now threatened for supporting them, a cordial good understanding with us was as obviously the dictate of her policy as it was the leading principle of ours. This national sentiment has not been silent or unobserved. It was embodied and expressed in the most public and solemn manner in the message to Congress at the commencement of their last session, as will be within your recollection. The conduct of the Government has been invariably conformable to it. The recognition of the South American Governments, flowing from the same principle which enlisted all our feelings in the cause of Spain, has been, in its effects, a mere formality. It has in nowise changed our actual relations, either with them or with Spain. All the European powers, even those which have hitherto most strenuously denied the recognition in *form*, have treated and will treat the South Americans as independent in fact. By his protest, against the formal acknowledgment, Mr. Anduaga had fulfilled his duties to his own Government, nor has any one circumstance arisen from that event which could require of him to recur to it, as a subject of difference between us and Spain, again. We have not been disposed to complain of his protest, nor even of his permanent residence at a distance from the seat of Government. But the avidity with which he has seized upon every incident which could cause unpleasant feelings between the two countries; the bitterness with which his continual notes have endeavored to exasperate and envenom; the misrepresentations of others, which he has so precipitously assumed as undeniable facts; and the language in which he has vented his reproaches upon the fair and honorable characters of our naval officers, upon the Government, and even the people of this Union; and, above all, the artifice by which he suffered the absurd and ridiculous expedition of De Coudray Holstein to obtain some paltry supplies of men and arms in this country, without giving notice of it to this Government, when they might have effectually broken it up, leaving it unknown to us till after its inevitable failure, when he could trump it up as a premeditated hostility of ours against Spain, and a profligate project of invasion of her possessions, are indications of a temper which we can trace to no source, either of friendly feeling towards our country or of patriotic devotion to his own. It has the aspect of a deliberate purpose to stir up and inflame dissentions between the United States and Spain; to produce and cherish every means of alienation and distrust between them, with ultimate views to the counteraction of these differences, upon the internal administration and Government of his own nation.

It is hoped that he will, in no event, be permitted to return hither; and, in the full and just explanations which you will be enabled to give upon every complaint exhibited by him while here, the Spanish Government will be satisfied with the justice, and convinced of the friendly disposition towards Spain, which have governed all our conduct. With the same spirit, and the just expectation that it will be met with a reciprocal return, you will represent to them the claim of all the citizens of the United States, whose vessels and other property have been captured by the privateers from Porto Rico and Porto Cabello, and condemned by the courts of those places for supposed breaches of the pretended blockade, or for *trading* with the South American Independents. Restitution or indemnity is due to them all; and is immediately due by the Spanish Government, inasmuch as these injuries, having been sanctioned by the local authorities, military and civil, the sufferers in most of the cases can have no resort to the individuals by whom the captures were made. A list of all the cases which have come yet to the knowledge of this Department is now inclosed. There are probably many others. An agent will be shortly sent to collect at the respective places, the evidence in all the cases not already known, and to obtain, as far as may be practicable, restitution by the local authorities. Whatever may be restored by them will diminish by so much the amount of claim upon the Spanish Government; which will be the more indisputable, as they have already admitted the justice and made provision for the satisfaction of claims of British subjects which sprung from the same cause.

Of the formal revocation by the Spanish Government of the nominal blockade the Governor of Porto Rico has given express notice to Commodore Porter. As a consequence of this, it is hoped that no commissions for privateers will be issued. The revocation did, indeed, come at a critical time; for it cannot be too strongly impressed upon the Spanish Government that all the causes of complaint, both by Spanish subjects against the Navy officers of the United States, and by the citizens of the United States, with which you are now charged, proceeded directly, or as a consequence, from those spurious blockades. They were in violation of the laws of nations. They were in conflict with the law of Congress for protecting the commerce of the United States. It was impossible that ships-of-war of the United States with commanders instructed to carry that law into execution, and Spanish privateers commissioned and instructed to carry into effect the atrocious decree of General Morales, should meet and fulfil their respective instructions without hostile collision. The decree of General Morales constituted all those Spanish subjects who acted under it in a state of war *de facto* with all neutral nations; and on the sea it was a war of extermination against all neutral commerce. It is to the responsibility of her own officers therefore, that Spain must look for indemnity to the wrongs endured by her own subjects as necessary consequences of their official acts, as well as for the source of her obligation to indemnify all the innocent sufferers under them who are entitled to the protection of other nations. You will take an immediate opportunity, after your reception, to urge upon the Spanish Government the absolute necessity of a more vigorous and energetic exercise of the local authorities in the island of Cuba for the suppression of the piracies by which it is yet infested. Their professions of co-operation with the naval force of the United States to this object have not been followed up by corresponding action. As long since as last May Captain Biddle, then commanding the Macedonian frigate, represented to the Captain General, Mahy, the necessity that would frequently arise of pursuing them from their boats to the shores on the desert and uninhabited parts of the island, and requested permission to land for such purpose, which was explicitly refused. Mr. Forsyth has been instructed to renew the demand of this permission to the Spanish Government itself. And, as there are cases in which the necessity will constitute the right of anticipating that permission, Commodore Porter has been instructed accordingly. From a recent debate in the British Parliament it appears that similar instructions have been given to the commanders of the British squadrons despatched for the protection of the commerce of that nation, and that when notified to the Spanish Government, although at first resisted by them, they finally obtained their acquiescence. These circumstances will serve for answer to one of the most aggravated complaints of Mr. Anduaga against Captain Cassin. That officer did land; and although not successful in overtaking the pirates themselves, he did break up one of the deposits of their lawless plunder, burned several of their boats, and took from them two of their armed vessels. Mr. Anduaga sees in all this nothing but *a violation of his Catholic Majesty's territory;* a sentiment, on such an occasion, which would be more suitable for an accessory to the pirates than for the officer of a Government deeply and earnestly intent upon their suppression.

From the highly esteemed and honorable character of General Vives, who has, probably, before this, arrived at the Havana as Governor and Captain General of the island, we hope for more effectual co-operation to this most desirable event. There has been, according to every account, a laxity and remissness on that subject in the Executive authority of that port which we hope will no longer be seen. The boldness and notoriety with which crimes of such desperate die are committed in the very face of authority is, of itself, irrefragable proof of its own imbecility or weakness. Spain must be sensible that she is answerable to the world for the suppression of crimes committed within her jurisdiction, and of which the people of other nations are almost exclusively the victims. The pirates have generally, though not universally, abstained from annoying Spanish subjects and from the robbery of Spanish property. It is surely within the competency of the Government of Cuba to put down that open market of the pirates which has so long been denounced at the Havana. It appears that masters of American vessels which had been robbed have seen their own property openly exposed to sale in that city, but have been dissuaded from reclaiming it by the warning that it would expose them to the danger of assassination. One instance, at least, has occurred of unpunished murder of a citizen of the United States for the indiscreet expression of his expectation that the arrival of Commodore Porter's squadron would secure more respect to the persons and property of American citizens; and other cases have happened of outrages upon citizens of the United States in which the protecting power of the Government has been deficient, at least, in promptitude and vigor.

To the irritation between the people of the two nations, produced by the consequences of the abominable decree of General Morales, must be attributed that base and dastardly spirit of revenge which recently actuated a Spanish subaltern officer at Porto Rico, by which Lieutenant Cocke lost his life. Copies of the correspondence between Commodore Porter and the Governor of Porto Rico on that occasion are among the inclosed papers. They will show that the act of firing upon the Fox was utterly wanton and inexcusable; and the President desires that you would expressly demand that the officer, by whom it was ordered, should be brought to trial and punishment for having ordered it.

There are several subjects connected with the execution of the treaty of February 22, 1819, to which it may be proper to advert as being likely to claim your attention. On the delivery of the two provinces of the Floridas to the United States, by virtue of stipulations of that treaty, a question arose whether, under the term *fortifications* which were to be delivered over with them, was included the artillery, without which they could not, with propriety, bear the name. By another article of the treaty it was agreed that the United States should furnish *transports* for the conveyance of the Spanish officers and troops to the Havana. Under this engagement, the Spanish officers understood it was *implied* that the *provisions* necessary, for the passage should also be furnished at the expense of the United States. In this liberal construction of that article this Government acquiesced, insisting, however, that on that same principle that provisions for the passage would be understood as implied in an engagement to supply the passage itself, the ordnance, which constituted the essential part of the fortifications, must be considered as embraced by the word, and that the United States were entitled to claim its delivery with the buildings which, without it, would substantially be no fortifications at all. The Spanish officers at Pensacola and St. Augustine objected to this liberal construction of the article which imposed an obligation upon Spain, while they insisted upon it with regard to the article in her favor. It was therefore agreed, both at Pensacola and St. Augustine, that the artillery in the forts should be left there, receipts for it being given by General Jackson and Colonel Butler, leaving the question as to the property in them to the determination of the two Governments. A correspondence ensued between this Department and the Spanish Legation here, and between the Ministers of Foreign Affairs and our Legation at Madrid, the last document of which is a note of September 3, 1822, from Don Evaristo San Miguel to Mr. Forsyth, from whom, as well as from Mr. Anduaga, separate copies of it have been transmitted to this Department. This note announces his Catholic Majesty's final determination to abide by the *strict* construction of both the articles in question, on the acknowledged ground that the value of the cannon is more than the cost of the provisions. It therefore proposes that the cannon should be restored to Spain, and offers to repay the expense incurred by the United States for the provisions; or it offers to receive proposals for the purchase, by the United States, of the cannon, and, if necessary, to sell them at a fair appraisement, by competent persons to be appointed by the two Governments; and after deducting the amount paid by the United States for the provisions, to receive the balance.

In the compacts between nations, as in the bargains of individuals, the most essential requisites are candor and fair dealing. The comparative *value* of the cannon in the forts, and of the provisions for the passage of the Spanish troops, formed no part of the considerations upon which the artillery was claimed by the United States, together with the walls of which they formed the defence. It was to the *principle* alone that our attention was turned. The officers of Spain, under a stipulation for *passage*, claimed a supply of provisions. Acquiescing in that liberal construction of our engagement which would warrant them in the claim, we thought it, in fairness and reciprocity, applicable to another article, the benefit of which would enure to the United States. In the course of this discussion no distinction has been shown on the part of Spain that could justify a different rule of construction for the two articles. In both cases the *incident* was so essential to the main object of the stipulation as to be inseparable from its existence and accomplishment. The passage without provisions was impracticable. The walls, without their artillery, were no fortifications. If in one case the implication was just, it was indispensable in the other. But we do not wish to press the controversy further. You are authorized to signify to the Spanish Government the acceptance of the proposal contained in Mr. San Miguel's note, and that, on the repayment by the Spanish Government of the money paid by the United States for provisions for the Spanish officers and troops from the Floridas to the Havana, the ordnance left behind, and receipted for by General Jackson and Colonel Butler, will be delivered up to the order of the Governor of Cuba, or to any officer duly authorized to receive it.

There is in the note of Mr. San Miguel a complaint, somewhat gratuitous, that the American Government had not, in the first instance, adjusted this question with the Spanish Minister at Washington, or afterwards prevented the compromise between the Commissioners of the two Governments at the delivery of the provinces. The Government of the United States was not informed that the Spanish Minister here had any authority to discuss the mode of execution with regard to the delivery of the territory. It was not to him, but to the Governor and Captain General of the island of Cuba, that the royal order for the delivery was addressed; nor was it supposed that he had, or could have, any instructions authorizing him to settle any question of construction which might arise in the details of the execution. That a question might arise, both with regard to the provisions and to the artillery, was foreseen, but there was no necessity for anticipating it, by a reference to the Spanish Minister, when it might not arise at all, and who, if it should, had no power to settle it. The suggestion of it, as a question *to him*, could, in all probability, tend only to *delay* the delivery itself of the Floridas; for if his views of the construction of the article concerning the fortifications should differ from those of this Government, he could only refer it to his own, and, in the meantime, the delivery of the country must be postponed, or accepted by the United States, subject to the construction of the Spanish envoy. The American Government had no motive for starting questions which might be turned to purposes of delay. It was sufficient for them to proceed upon principles fair and equitable in themselves, and to foresee questions of construction only so far as to preclude the admission of one rule, when its operation would be against the United States, and of another, when its effect would be in their favor. When the question between the Commissioners had arisen, it was not more in the power of this Government to prevent the compromise upon which they agreed than it was in that of Spain. A reference of it prior to the delivery might have been made to Madrid in little more time than to Washington. And the intimation of Mr. San Miguel, that the unfortunate disputes in which the ex-Governors of St. Augustine and Pensacola were involved, and which issued in occurrences personally unpleasant to them, originated in this compromise concerning the artillery, is founded upon erroneous impressions. Those incidents, much and sincerely lamented by us, arose from the non-delivery, deliberate, concerted, and systematic, by the late Captain General Mahy, and by both the Governors of St. Augustine and Pensacola, of the *archives* and *documents*, which they were required by an express stipulation of the treaty and an explicit order from the King of Spain to deliver up. The Governor of Cuba, after informing Colonel Forbes, who was commissioned to receive that portion of those archives and documents which were at the Havana, that twenty boxes of documents had been sent there from Pensacola, relating to West Florida, and that all those relating to East Florida were at St. Augustine; and after detaining Colonel Forbes at the Havana nearly six weeks, in the daily protracted expectation of delivering them, finally obliged him, with exhausted patience, to depart without the former, and with an explicit assurance that he had instructed the Governor of St. Augustine to deliver the latter. Yet the Governor of St. Augustine refused to deliver them, on the allegation of doubts whether the engagement of the treaty extended to the delivery of *any* public documents or archives relating to individual property. This extraordinary effort to withhold and to carry away all the records of land titles of both the provinces has been the fruitful source of all those subsequent misunderstandings and painful occurrences to which Mr. San Miguel's note alludes; and it commenced on the part of the Governor of Cuba long before any question relating to the delivery of the artillery had occurred.

Mr. Thomas Randall is now about to proceed to the Havana, charged with a new commission, to demand and receive the archives and documents yet remaining there, and of which, as Mr. Forsyth was informed, a new royal order has been expedited to command the delivery. There are also many at Madrid, in the office of the Ultramarine Department, which Mr. Forsyth has taken measures, at different times, to obtain, hitherto without success. You will learn the state of this concern upon your arrival, and, as occasions may present themselves, will give it all the attention it may require.

By the fourth article of the treaty of February 22, 1819, provision was made for the appointment of Commissioners and surveyors to run the boundary line between the United States and the then adjoining Spanish provinces, from the mouth of the Sabine river to the South sea. They were to meet at Natchitoches within one year from the ratification of the treaty. But the appointment of the Spanish Commissioner and surveyor, though repeatedly urged by Mr. Forsyth upon the Spanish Government, was not made in seasonable time, and the revolution in Mexico having soon after demolished the Spanish dominion in that country, it became doubtful whether that article of the treaty could be carried into execution.

There was some hesitation in Congress, and different votes between the two Houses, with regard to making the appropriation for that purpose. The appropriation was, however, made, and the appointment of the Commissioner and surveyor on the part of the United States was made known to Mr. Anduaga, and also, through Mr. Forsyth, to the Spanish Government, with notice that we were ready to proceed in the measures agreed upon for carrying the article into execution.

No further notice of the subject has been taken by the Spanish Government, nor have we been informed who were the Commissioner and surveyor appointed by them. It will not be necessary for you to revive the subject by any communication to that Government, unless it should be brought up on their part. The new Government of Mexico, since the revolution there, has made known its assent to the boundary as marked out by the treaty, and it is probable that Spain will, henceforth, have no interest in the settlement of the line. It may form a subject of further arrangement between us and our immediate neighbors hereafter. Of the other subjects of discussion with Spain, which may require your official notice, you will be informed by Mr. John James Appleton, remaining there, charged with the affairs of the legation after the departure of Mr. Forsyth, and by the archives of the legation which he will deliver over to you. The laws relating to commerce, since the restoration of the Cortes, have been rather restrictive than favorable to the relations between the United States and Spain. You will be specially attentive to all negotiations, whether commercial or political, in which Spain may be concerned, during the continuance of your mission; transmit to this Department two copies of every treaty printed by authority immediately after its publication, and copies, by duplicate, of all conventions, treaties, separate articles, or other diplomatic communications of which you may acquire the knowledge, and which you can obtain without expense or charge.

An object of considerable importance will be to obtain the admission of *consuls* from the United States in the ports of the colonies; specially in the islands of Cuba and of Porto Rico. It was incidental to the old colonial system of Spain, which excluded all commerce of foreign nations with their colonies, to admit in their ports no foreign consuls. The special duties and functions of those officers consisting in the protection of the commerce, navigation, and seamen of their respective countries, in the ports where they reside, it was a natural and necessary consequence of the exclusive colonial principle that, where no commerce was allowed to foreign nations, there could be no duties for a foreign consul to perform, and no occasion for the acknowledgment of such an officer; but when the colonial ports were opened to foreign trade, all the *reasons* which recommend, and all the necessities which urge the appointment and admission of foreign consuls to reside in them, apply as forcibly to those ports as to any others. The commerce between the United States and the Havana is of greater amount and value than with all the Spanish dominions in Europe. The number of American vessels which enter there is, annually, several hundreds. Their seamen, from the unhealthiness of the climate, are peculiarly exposed to need there the assistance which it is a primary purpose of the consular office to supply; nor is there any conceivable motive for continuing to maintain the pretension to exclude them, and to refuse the formal acknowledgment of consuls. Informal commercial agents have, in many of the ports, been allowed to reside, and partially to perform the consular duties; but as they are thus left much dependent on the will of the local Government, and subject to control at its pleasure, they have neither the dignity nor authority which properly belongs to the office. There has already been much correspondence between Mr. Forsyth and the Spanish Department of Foreign Affairs on this subject. You will follow it up, as there may be opportunity, till a definitive answer shall be obtained.

A letter from the Spanish chargé d'affaires, Mr. Salmon, dated the 15th of April, has been received at this Department, inclosing a copy of one from Mr. Anduaga to Mr. R. W. Meade, of October 16, 1822, relating to his claim, pending before the Commissioners under the Florida treaty. Translations of these papers, and a copy of my answer to Mr. Salmon's letter, are herewith inclosed. The claim of Mr. Meade, as presented to the Commissioners, was palpably not, and could not be, embraced by the treaty, as, [by] an order for payment of it by the Spanish Department of Finance, Spain was undoubtedly bound to the payment of it in full; and so she was for the payment of all the certificates of her public debt, which were purchasable in the market at thirty or forty per cent. of their nominal value. All the claims provided for by the treaty were unsettled claims, the proper subjects of compromise, and the avowed and unequivocal principle of the treaty was to make such compromise. This was well known to Mr. Meade as well as to the Spanish Government. The first report of the Spanish Junta of four counsellors, in favor of Mr. Meade's claims, was made on the 30th of September, 1819, *after* the termination of the period when the treaty should have been ratified by Spain. The certificate delivered to Mr. Meade in May, 1820, directed that the sum which had been found due to him should be paid *out of the funds of the Royal Finance Department, with interest*. The treaty, though not ratified by Spain, was then public in Europe and America. It had twice been communicated by the President of the United States to Congress; first in February, 1819, immediately after it was signed, and again in December of the same year, when it was published with the documents at the commencement of that session. It was well known to Mr. Meade that it did not provide for his claim, thus liquidated and acknowledged. If he then expected that it should ever be chargeable upon the United States, that was the time for him to have so declared to the Spanish Government. The nature of his claim was entirely changed by the liquidation, but it made and could make no corresponding change in the stipulation of the *treaty*. It was not for an order on the funds of the Royal Finance Department of Spain for near half a million of dollars, with interest from May, 1820, that the United States had undertaken to provide; and the real effect of the liquidation and certificate was to take the case entirely out of the treaty.

That Mr. Meade was fully sensible of this is proved by his subsequent memorial to the President of the United States, soliciting, *on their part*, a conditional ratification, either acknowledging his claim as finally liquidated by Spain, to be paid in full, or excepting specifically the renunciation which included his claim, as it had existed when the treaty was signed, or the claim itself by name as afterwards settled. His whole memorial, indeed, is an unanswerable argument to prove that his *settled* claim was *not* included in the treaty, nor was it possible that it should be. The treaty was signed in February, 1819, and professed to provide for none but unsettled claims, prescribing the manner in which they should all be settled alike. Mr. Meade's claim was liquidated in May, 1820, the treaty being then as if it had never been made. It is a strange use to make of the warm interest and ardent solicitation of the American minister in Spain, in Mr. Meade's favor, to obtain a settlement by Spain of his claims, and of the friendly congratulation of the American Secretary of State, after it had been obtained, *when the treaty had no existence*, to contend that these manifestations of kindness to him bound the United States to payment in full of his demand upon Spain, if that treaty should ever be ratified. It is very evident that the liquidation of Mr. Meade's claims in Spain was made on principles which, however fair and laudable as between him and the Spanish Government, would not be proper for the liquidation to be made by the American Commissioners conformably to the treaty. The principle of the treaty is a compromise of unadjusted claims. The principle of the liquidation was payment in full, with profuse allowances for interest and damages; these, very suitably for Spain to make in acknowledgment of great services of the claimant to her, were in nowise proper for the United States, being under no such obligation to assume, nor could they assume them without wrong to other claimants more entitled to favor from *them*, though less from Spain, than Mr. Meade. In that liquidation it is abundantly shown by Mr. Meade himself that the Spanish tribunals intended to discharge a debt of Spanish gratitude as well as of justice; to remunerate services as well as to fulfil engagements. It is doubtful whether any others of the claimants under the treaty will obtain any allowance for *interest*, even simple interest, upon the clearest and most inveterate of their demands. Mr. Meade's liquidated claim calls for interest upon interest on a debt of half a million of dollars; compound interest accruing after the treaty was signed, and accumulating by the act of Spain herself in withholding the stipulated ratification of the treaty. Other claimants besides Mr. Meade had been wrongfully and far more rigorously imprisoned by authority of the Spanish Government. Should they be paid at the rate of nearly forty thousand dollars a year for such detention, the five millions of dollars allotted to the settlement of the claims, five times doubled, would scarcely suffice for their satisfaction. To complete the demonstration that Mr. Meade's liquidated claim was not included in the treaty, let it be supposed that the order which, in May, 1820, he received *upon the funds of the Royal Finance Department* had been immediately paid, and that the Spanish Government had afterwards ratified the treaty as it did, Mr. Meade would assuredly then have had no claim under the treaty; and as little could the Spanish Government have claimed repayment by the United States of the money paid to Mr. Meade.

And why was not the order upon the Royal Finance Department immediately paid? Mr. Meade himself has answered that it was owing to the embarrassments of the new Revolution. He petitioned the Cortes for immediate payment, and to designate the mode of payment. But he could obtain no definitive resolution from the Cortes till the 5th of October, 1820, the day they decided in favor of ratifying the Florida treaty. Upon which occasion, says Mr. Meade, "they ordered that my memorial should be united with the papers relative to the treaty, and submitted to the King, in order to have it *ascertained* whether the American Government had consented to the introduction of *my individual claim* into the negotiations of the treaty, and, if so, that the American Government had distinctly assumed upon itself the payment of my claim, and had wholly exonerated Spain from it; but if it should be found that my case had not been taken into view by the negotiators, *and was not distinctly understood as embraced* in the treaty stipulations, they in that case decreed the immediate payment of the debt by the Spanish Government. Upon this reference from the Cortes the Spanish Minister of State pronounced an unequivocal opinion that the debt had been *distinctly and specifically* assumed by the United States in exoneration of Spain; *or would be so* upon the exchange of the ratifications." Here we see that the Cortes, when advising to the ratification of the treaty, before them, considered the assumption by the United States of Mr. Meade's claim as entirely depending on the question whether it had *individually, distinctly* and *specifically* been treated for in the negotiation between Mr. Onis and the American Secretary of State. This the Cortes did not know, with the treaty and all the documents of the negotiation before them. As little did the minister to whom they referred it know; for he only pronounced an opinion that the debt had been *distinctly* and *specifically* assumed by the United States in exoneration of Spain, *or would be so upon the exchange of the ratifications.*

Mr. Meade proceeds in his memorial to say, "the opinion of the minister was founded (as I was informed from *high authority*) upon facts *said* to have been notorious to the negotiators of the treaty, and verified, *as it was said*, by the official communications of Mr. Onis to the Spanish Government, to wit, that my claim had been introduced by name into the discussion between Mr. Adams and Mr. Onis, who finally agreed in their *verbal conferences* that it should be assumed and paid by the United States; that Mr. Onis proposed the insertion of my name and a specific stipulation to that effect in the treaty; but that Mr. Adams thought it unnecessary to do so, though he agreed to the insertion of a clause intended to comprehend my case, without naming it, and to exonerate Spain from the debt, with the understanding, nevertheless, that it was to be specifically assumed and paid by the United States." I shall not inquire how it happened that the Cortes, with this fable, *said* to have been verified by the official communications of Mr. Onis to the Spanish Government, before them, *could* have referred it to the King to ascertain whether Mr. Meade's claim had been assumed by the United States or not; nor how the minister of State, to whom it was again referred, should have been so uncertain with regard to the fact as merely to give an *opinion* that the claim had been specifically assumed by the United States, *or would be so upon the exchange of the ratifications.* Neither shall I ask how it happened that Mr. Meade, at Madrid, in October, 1820, with his claim liquidated and acknowledged, and demanding immediate payment, when put off with these uncertainties of the Cortes and the minister, should have contented himself with this information from *high authority* of facts *said* to have been notorious, and said to have been verified by official communications of Mr. Onis to his Government, without demanding, as under those circumstances he had the unquestionable right and the deepest interest to do, authenticated copies of these official communications of Mr. Onis to produce them before the American Government: how it happened that for this *only* document which could have given Mr. Meade the shadow of a claim upon the American Government for specific satisfaction of his liquidated claim, he took at Madrid this information from *high authority* of things *said to have been said*, and then came to the United States and called upon their President and Senate to palm upon the people of this Union the payment of half a million of dollars, with interest, to him, or to annul by a conditional ratification the Florida treaty, with this hearsay of hearsay for the only color of his demand. That it was from beginning to end a fable is certain. Mr. Meade's claim, far from being specifically provided for by name, was never even mentioned by Mr. Onis during the negotiation of the treaty. No individual claim was never mentioned, nor would the American Government have stipulated for the benefit of any claimant a favor which could not be extended equally to all the rest.

But the facility with which Mr. Meade received upon trust this information from *high authority* of an official document, which would have been the only admissible voucher for his new claim upon the United States, is not the only surprising part of this allegation in his memorial to the President. He says that the Spanish Minister of State pronounced an unequivocal opinion that the debt had been distinctly and specifically assumed by the United States, in exoneration of Spain, *or would be so upon the exchange of the ratifications.* That it had not been is now shown beyond all power of reply, nor was it at the exchange of the ratifications. Mr. Meade, after failing in the attempt to stay the ratification of the United States, did apply to the Spanish minister then here, General Vives, to make some such specific reference to his individual claim, which General Vives explicitly declined. There was, indeed, no pretence upon which it could have been made, and the tale which Mr. Meade had received from *high authority* appears to be no other than a device to elude his importunities for payment, and only proves the consciousness, of necessity for resorting to fiction to give a show of coloring to Mr. Meade's liquidated claim as chargeable to the United States.

It may be said that, if the claims of Mr. Meade, as existing in February, 1819, are admitted to have been included within the provisions of the treaty, the United States cannot justly avail themselves of the liquidation subsequently effected at the instances of their own minister, to recharge upon Spain the paymen.

of the whole sums from which she would have been exonerated but for the intermediate liquidation between the signature and the final ratification of the treaty. Neither is this the desire of the American Government. The Commissioners, whose doubt, whether Mr. Meade was receivable at all as a claimant under the treaty, arose, first, from the certainty that his claim, as presented by himself, was not included in the treaty, and, secondly, from his own argument that it was of a character that the United States and Spain had no *right* to dispose of it by negotiation, on application to the Secretary of State, were informed that the intention of the treaty on the part of the United States had been to include within its provisions all *unsettled* and *unliquidated* claims of citizens of the United States upon Spain for which the interposition of the Government of the United States had been *solicited* by the claimants themselves, until the *signature* of the treaty. Mr. Meade's claim, at the time of the signature of the treaty, was of that description, and the Commissioners have received him as a claimant under the treaty.

The subsequent liquidation and acknowledgment of the Spanish tribunals gave Mr. Meade a new, entirely distinct claim upon Spain. It was an order upon the Spanish treasury for a specific sum of money, with interest from May, 1820. The effect of this transaction was to take the claims of Mr. Meade entirely out of the treaty; and Spain, by the subsequent ratification of the treaty without noticing in any manner this claim or its liquidation, gave the United States some reason for insisting, were they so disposed, that no provision for any part of it had been made by the treaty at all.

But the rule of equity applicable to this case, and by which substantial justice may be done to all parties, is this: Mr. Meade's claims, as existing and exhibited before the signature of the treaty, are included in its provisions. Their *amount* and *validity* must be proved to the Commissioners, conformably to the provisions of the treaty. The allowance or rejection of every item in them must be determined on principles applied by the Commissioners to all other claims of a similar description before them. The sum finally awarded to him must be subject to all the other provisions of the treaty. To charge the United States in the exact proportion stipulated by the treaty, and to suffer deduction from their admitted account, in common with all the other claims, as they may be finally admitted. So far have they been assumed by the United States, and so far has Spain been exonerated from them. For the balance of the sum which Mr. Meade may thus receive from the United States, to equalize in amount the specific sum, with interest from May, 1820, awarded him by the Spanish liquidation, his claim remains unimpaired *upon the Spanish treasury*. It was never assumed or renounced by the United States; it was never cancelled by Spain. For the decisions of her own tribunals, subsequent to the signature of the treaty, Spain alone must be responsible. The treaty alone must be the standard to which the decisions of the American Commissioners and the obligations of the United States must conform.

By the fifteenth article of the treaty of October 27, 1795, it was stipulated that, in times of war, the flag should cover the property, and free ships make free goods. By the twelfth article of the treaty of February 22, 1819, it is agreed that this shall be so understood with respect to those powers who recognize this principle; but if either of the two contracting parties shall be at war with a third, and the other neutral, the flag of the neutral shall cover the property of enemies whose Government acknowledge this principle, and not of others.

In the impending war between Spain and France you may, perhaps, have occasion to require the exact observance of this engagement. In all the treaties between the United States and France the principle that free ships make free goods is established and recognized. It is presumed that it will yet be recognized by France, and it is hoped there will be no cause to complain of its infringement by Spain.

A resolution of the House of Representatives at the last session of Congress requests the President to enter upon, and to prosecute from time to time, such negotiations with the several maritime powers of Europe and America as he may deem expedient for the effectual abolition of the African slave trade, and its ultimate denunciation as piracy, under the law of nations, by the consent of the civilized world. You will take an early opportunity to make known this disposition to the Spanish Government, communicating to them copies of the fourth and fifth sections of the act of March 3, 1819, which declares this traffic piratical when pursued by citizens of the United States; and you will express the willingness of the American Government to enter into negotiations for the purpose of declaring it so by the common consent of nations.

No. 35.

Extract of a letter (No. 4) from Mr. Nelson to Mr. Adams, dated

MADRID, *January* 15, 1824.

"I herewith inclose another note which I addressed to the Spanish Government on the 10th instant. In this I have presented the views of our Government on two of the important subjects with which I was entrusted—the piracies on our commerce in the West Indies, with a requisition on the Spanish Government for immediate orders to their provincial officers to suppress these outrages; and the offence of the Spanish officer by whose order the life of Lieutenant Cocke was sacrificed, with a demand upon his Catholic Majesty's Government for a satisfactory atonement for this unparalleled aggression. In a few days I shall present to this Government another note, embracing the remaining interesting topics of my instructions, with a demand for the appropriate redress for the respective wrongs sustained by our citizens."

No. 35, (a.)

Mr. Nelson to the Count of Ofalia.

MADRID, *January* 10, 1824.

The undersigned, the Minister Plenipotentiary of the United States of America, has the honor, through his excellency, to assure his Catholic Majesty of the unfeigned desire of the President of the United States to preserve inviolate the friendly relations subsisting between the two Governments. This harmony, sometimes menaced with interruption by the great convulsions which the world has witnessed at the termination of the last century and in the progress of the present, has fortunately never experienced a total rupture. Events have occurred which seemed to threaten a collision between nations long united in the strongest bonds of friendship; measures deemed necessary to maintain the security of some who were engaged in the conflict of arms, or to preserve the neutrality of others who were so fortunate as to escape its ravages, may have sometimes, in their tendency, borne with severe pressure on those against whom they were not intended to operate injuriously; a sensibility, bordering on a degree of jealousy, may have been excited by erroneous views of the policy and measures of the American Government; and the councils of Spain may have received impressions calculated to produce suspicions incompatible with the frank and mutual confidence necessary to sustain the cordial intercourse of friendly nations. The policy of the American Government, founded in justice and truth, has never led to the adoption of any measure towards a foreign nation which it would not cheerfully acquiesce in if, under similar circumstances, adopted towards itself; nor has it ever asked an act of justice from a foreign power which it would not have equally conceded to the demand of such foreign power, in a parallel condition, appealing for justice to the American Government. This onward course of candid and disinterested policy ever leads it to expect a reciprocal return from the foreign powers to whom it appeals, at any time, for the fulfilment of those obligations which are imposed by the principles of justice and reciprocity. These are expected with confidence from his Catholic Majesty; and whilst, on the one hand, the undersigned is authorized to give full assurance of the earnest wish of the American Government to cherish and perpetuate its friendly relations with Spain, on the other he is directed to ask of the Government of Spain the fulfilment of those obligations which a sense of honor and of justice and a reciprocal desire to preserve inviolate the friendly and harmonious intercourse between the two countries will impose upon the Government of his Catholic Majesty. Actuated by feelings congenial to those which he is instructed to avow and manifest by his Government towards the Government of Spain, the undersigned begs to call the attention of his excellency to cases of aggravated injury and wrong which the citizens of the United States have suffered from the subjects of his Catholic Majesty, and in some instances from those who had been distinguished by his royal commissions.

It had been heretofore made known to his Catholic Majesty's Government by his predecessor, that, in the great agitations which, of late years, have been experienced in a portion of the Western World, swarms of pirates, issuing from the island of Cuba, had infested the West Indian seas, desolating, wherever they could encounter it, the peaceful commerce of the neighboring nations. In their ruthless fury after rapine and destruction, sweeping from that ocean the peaceful and defenceless navigators, they have not spared even the subjects of Spain herself. The nations exercising commerce in these seas have been compelled to arm for its protection, and to send their ships into that region to defend their citizens in their persons and their property from these insatiate plunderers. The United States, in common with others, have been forced to send naval armaments into these regions, and have always, in a spirit of harmony and friendship, given ample notice to the local authorities of the Spanish islands of the object and destination of these equipments. Time after time have they called upon the Spanish authorities in Cuba to suppress these hordes of banditti. Often has the assurance been given that the local authorities would, and had taken all the necessary measures to suppress them. Yet, in defiance of these repeated assurances, the ocean teemed with these freebooters; and so fearless and undaunted were these scourges of the ocean, that the city of Havana itself has witnessed piracies committed at the verge of its harbor. Armament after armament has been equipped and despatched from the United States, instructed to co-operate with the local authorities in their suppression; and always with the fullest and most positive instructions to pay the utmost respect to the rights and interests of Spain. Her rights have always been respected by the commanders of the American squadrons; nor has a single instance, it is believed by the American Government, occurred, wherein there has been a wanton violation of that respect which, as a friendly nation, the United States owed to the rights and interests of Spain. But, although such has been the scrupulous regard which the United States have, on all occasions, manifested to these obligations which their friendly relations to Spain imposed, they have not found any relief to their commerce against these piracies, either from the reiterated assurance given by the Spanish local authorities of their determination to suppress, or of their adoption of the "necessary measures to defend their territorial jurisdiction, and for the apprehension of every description of outlaw." On the contrary, the American Government has had too much reason to believe that, however the local authorities might be inclined to apprehend these outlaws, yet from want of power, or from some other cause, adequate measures were not adopted for their suppression, but that these sea robbers, acquiring boldness from the inaction of the Government of the Captain General, not only displayed their successful cruisers, laden with their spoils, in the port of the Havana, but fearlessly exposed to sale in the streets of the city, in the very teeth of the Government, unawed and unrestrained, the unhallowed fruits of their piracies and plunder. Instances have occurred in which the American citizen has beheld exposed to sale, in open market, in the streets of Havana, the property plundered from him by these ferocious miscreants, from reclaiming which he has been restrained by the admonition of others, warned that he would find no protection from the Government, and that he would only draw down upon his own head the infernal malice of the secret assassin. Nor has a case been wanting in which one of the citizens of the United States, excited by this shameless disregard of all laws, human and divine, having declared that, on the arrival of the American naval commander, who was then expected in those seas, more respect would be shown to the rights of persons and property, met, as the reward of his temerity, the deadly stroke of the poniard from the midnight murderer. These pirates have their establishments and places of asylum in the bays and harbors on the coast of the uninhabited parts of the island of Cuba. Thence they sally forth in quest of plunder in vessels adapted to a shoal water navigation, bringing ruin and desolation on the defenceless commercial vessels they can find, and if, perchance, they encounter a foe, competent by his armament to subdue them, they fly for refuge to these shoals and bays, whither the pursuer cannot come, through fear of being wrecked if rashly he rush on; or if, perchance, the commander of some lighter vessel pursue them to the margin of the shore, they instantly abandon their vessel, and, concealing themselves in places of retreat previously marked out and prepared for this purpose, they elude their pursuers, and escape by the sacrifice of some mean, worthless vessel, and save their persons from seizure and detection.

The American Government beheld with regret this unfortunate state of things in that region; anxious to treat with due respect the rights and interests of Spain; bound to protect their citizens in their persons and their property; wishing to believe that the local authorities were thus inactive only because they were unable to re ress these pirates; and never for a moment entertaining any other opinion of his Catholic Majesty's Government than that it deplored, equally with the American Government, the calamities to which the commerce of these seas was subjected by the diabolical passions of the most abandoned and nefarious ruffians of the human race, has felt most sensibly the delicacy and difficulty of its situation when summoned, by a sense of duty, to adopt measures of energy to insure protection t those who were entitled to demand it from their Government. Believing that, in the adoption of such measures as the necessity of the case imposed, they would equally consult the interest and honor of Spain, as of the whole civilized world, in destroying a horde of monsters who were leagued and combined against the fair and legitimate trade of all nations using these seas, they gave instructions to the predecessor of the undersigned to make known to his Catholic Majesty's Government that it would be indispensable for the American cruisers, in pursuing these banditti to their places of shelter and retreat in the uninhabited parts of the island, to land some portion of their crews in those places in which the power of the local authorities was not exercised to suppress them, to execute the purpose of arresting and bringing to justice these freebooters and marauders. Conscious of the purity of their designs, and convinced that Spain would equally benefit with all the world in the extirpation of this stock of buccaniers, they did not hesitate to instruct their naval commanders, in case of indispensable necessity, and of that only, to land in these desert and uninhabited places for the sole purpose of pursuing and arresting the pirates; and as soon as that service was performed, to embark immediately in their vessels again, withdrawing from the territory of Spain.

Presuming that, in a case of such imperious necessity, when the rights and interests of humanity were so deeply involved as in the extirpation of these outlaw freebooters; in a case where the object and design of the American Government were so open and notorious, and, with great propriety it may be added, were so laudable, as being aimed at the suppression of those who, by common consent, are denom. inated the enemies of all mankind; in a case where, as no contempt of the authority of Spain was or could be intended, so none could be inferred, the American Government hoped and believed that Spain would sanction a measure fraught with so much benefit to all the maritime nations of the earth, although it might not so strictly accord with those little observances of scrupulous punctilio which nations so fastidi. ously exact in their intercourse with each other. The measure was free from all design of wounding the feelings or of offering contempt to Spain. It was called for by the irresistible necessity of the case, and was scarcely less than justified by the omission of the local authorities, through weakness or through want of inclination, to adopt measures for their suppression, which had been often promised and too rarely fulfilled. The scrupulous delicacy of the American Government towards the rights and interests of Spain are displayed in the orders to their naval commanders, of which copies accompany this note. In their efforts to attain the desirable object of expelling from the ocean these lawless buccaniers, the United States have had to deplore the loss of one of their most gallant and distinguished naval officers, Lieutenant Allen, who fell by the hands of one of these pirates whilst he was nobly attempting to subdue a nest of them in arms against the honest commerce of the civilized world. The undersigned is directed by the President of the United States to urge upon the Government of Spain the absolute necessity of its ordering the local authorities of the island of Cuba to adopt the most energetic and efficacious measures for controlling and suppressing these pirates, and of asking that these authorities may be instructed to use every possible means of co-operation with the naval armaments of the United States which may be sent into the West Indian seas for the purpose of suppressing an evil under which the American commerce has too long suffered.

Connected with the facts detailed in the foregoing part of this note is another case of a most malignant character, on which I am directed to ask of his Catholic Majesty's Government a prompt and vigorous redress of an unparalleled injury which the American Government has sustained at the hands of an officer having the commission of his Catholic Majesty. The United States, under the increasing urgency of afford-ing protection against the pirates in the West Indian seas, have sent out their naval armaments to afford this protection. But even with these exertions they have not been able to afford entire security to their commerce. The local authorities, with an indifference to the sufferings of commerce and an incredible tolerance to this system of plundering, have almost uniformly refused all co-operation in this just and holy object. They have denied to the fleets and naval armaments of the United States those courtesies and civilities which common hospitality would enjoin even in the case of entire strangers, but which, to a nation in the strictest bond of friendship, and engaged in the holy and beneficent object of extirpating a nest of pirates, all laws, human and divine, would imperiously command them to administer; they have denied those facilities and accommodations to the American Navy, whilst they have permitted them to be enjoyed by the lawless freebooters of the ocean. Nor have markets, open and shameless, been wanting in the most conspicuous places in the islands for the sale of the plunder piratically obtained by them. When the American Government has sent their ships into these seas, the most rigid orders have been given to their commanders to respect, in the fullest possible extent, the rights of Spain. When, in the beginning of the last year, a necessity arose from the continued and increased depredations on the commerce of the American merchants to augment the United States naval armament in these seas, the same scrupulous regard to the rights of Spain was observed. Due notice was given to the Spanish authorities, both in the mother country and in the islands, of the object and design of this equipment. The proceedings of the American Legislature, open and unconcealed, announced and proclaimed to the whole world, through the medium of the press, the object and destination of this augmented armament. And the officer command-ing this squadron, Commodore Porter, on his arrival in the West Indies, gave notice to the Spanish authorities of Porto Rico, when he approached that island, of the object and design of the expedition under his command. He found, on his arrival near St. John's, in that island, the ships-of-war of England enjoying freely and uninterruptedly the facilities and accommodations of that port. Before attempting to enter with his ships, he sent into the port of St. John's one of the smallest vessels of the squadron, whose commander bore a letter to the Governor of the island, assuring him of the friendly object of his visit to these seas. This vessel was permitted to enter and anchor in the port, and the officer to land and hold intercourse with the commandant in the fort, in the absence of the Governor, who was out of town; whilst the commodore, with the residue of his fleet, lay off a few miles distant from the port, but in full view of the forts, with the American flag displayed at their masthead, giving assurance of the real character of the fleet which had recently arrived. The officer despatched to bear the letter to the Governor of the island had with him a copy of that letter, which he was authorized to show to the second in command, should the case occur of the temporary absence of the Governor. This copy was shown and its contents made known to the second in command, the Governor being absent. (A copy of it is herewith furnished.)

The American commodore, finding the vessel delayed in port some days, and much longer than he had expected, still forbearing to attempt to enter with his fleet, despatched another of the smaller vessels of his squadron to bear an order to the officer commanding the vessel which lay at anchor in the port. Lieutenant Cocke, a young and gallant officer, commanding this latter vessel, in obedience of the orders of his commander, sailing into port, unsuspicious of hostility from the forts, under pressure of a strong breeze and a very high sea, was treacherously and perfidiously fired upon from the fort by order of the second in command in the port of St. John's. The wind blowing with great violence and the sea breaking most dangerously around the vessel, Lieutenant Cocke was unable to hear if anything was said, or to comprehend, by the firing of the gun, what was the object of the officer commanding in the fort. His vessel, driven on by the force of the wind and the irresistible power of the waves, pursued her course towards the harbor, when the firing was repeatedly reiterated, until this gallant officer, in the act of endeavoring by hailing to learn the object of the firing, was almost literally torn in pieces by a ball from a forty-two pounder, discharged from this fort. This vessel, thus treacherously and wantonly fired upon, carried three guns and was of little more than forty tons; the fort mounted nearly five hundred guns from thirty-two to forty-two pounders. This vessel was then compelled, at the hazard of its own destruction and the loss of the whole crew, to anchor in the billows of a sea running continually over her. Her boat was despatched with a midshipman and crew, at whom a large gun was pointed as soon as he reached the shore, and he was ordered not to move on pain of being fired on; and, as if to add insult to injury, he was then put under guard, conducted like a criminal and delivered to the officer of the fort who had so wantonly murdered his gallant commander. In this case of the murder of Lieutenant Cocke, the undersigned is directed by the President of the United States to demand of his Catholic Majesty's Government that the officer by whose order this act was done should be brought to trial and punished for a deed so flagrant, wanton, and unprovoked. On this occasion the undersigned rests assured that the indignant feelings of his Catholic Majesty will correspond with those of the President of the United States, and that justice will not be delayed in an instance which so imperiously requires it.

The undersigned tenders to his excellency the Count of Ofalia, holding ad interim the office of first Secretary of State and of the Despatch, his distinguished consideration, and subscribes himself his excellency's very humble and obedient servant,

HUGH NELSON.

No. 36.

Extract of a letter from Mr. Nelson (No. 35) to Mr. Adams, dated

MADRID, *July* 15, 1824.

"The change in the cabinet of his Catholic Majesty, in the removal of the Count of Ofalia from his office of first Secretary of State, occurred two days since, and is disclosed in the annexed document, dated the 13th instant, which announced this alteration. This place is filled 'ad interim' by Salazar, the Minister of Marine; but the permanent appointment is conferred on Zea Bermudez, the minister of Spain to England, who is at present not in the Kingdom. This constant changing the minister at the head of their foreign affairs is extremely embarrassing to the intercourse which other nations are constrained to hold with this Government. It will be fortunate for Spain if foreigners alone feel the evil consequences of this perpetual vacillation. The Count of Ofalia is not only deprived of his office, but is banished from Madrid, and ordered to retire to his estates in Grenada. This removal is regretted by most of the diplomatic corps, who found the Count ready in his duties, accessible in his deportment, and easy and polite in his intercourse with them."

"I have now had the honor to present my respects to four of these different gentlemen in about six months. It produces a necessity of beginning 'ab ovo' with each new Secretary on all matters of consequence, on which one may have discoursed and corresponded repeatedly, and in which the hope may have been indulged that an approach was making to the consummation of some desired object."

No. 37.

Extracts of a letter (No. 39) from Mr. Nelson to the Secretary of State, dated

MADRID, *September* 11, 1824.

"In pursuance of my intention expressed in a late despatch, I have prepared and presented to the Spanish Government a note concisely recapitulating the communications on the most important subject of my correspondence with it. These are the murder of Lieutenant Cocke, the piracies by the vessels from Cuba, and the captures by the privateers from Porto Rico and Porto Cabello. The tone of this note is somewhat higher than the orginal communications on these subjects. To this I was led by the last newspapers received from the Department, in one of which was contained the report of the Committee of Foreign Relations on piracies. Long convinced that we should derive more advantage from communicating with this Government in a higher pitch than we had used in the previous applications, I seized with pleasure the style of this document, which I was willing to consider as an index of the national feeling as of that of the Government, and notified the Secretary that respectful delicacy for his Catholic Majesty, and the expectation that the remonstrances of the American minister at Madrid would meet the prompt attention of this Government, alone restrained the recommendation of a system of reprisals. That the legislative councils would again shortly convene, when it might be anticipated that these measures would speedily follow, unless prevented by the measures adopted by this Government. In order to prevent all apology for delay in taking up this communication, it was translated into Spanish by Mr. Appleton, and the translation furnished with the original. A copy of this note is inclosed.

"I send also a copy of another note which I have found it necessary to present to this Government, on account of their conduct to American vessels coming into Spanish ports.

"On the 4th of July the King issued a royal order, requiring that all foreign vessels entering his ports with goods in transit for foreign countries should be compelled to give bond, with good security, for producing the certificate of the Spanish consul residing at the foreign port to which they were represented to be destined, that they were actually delivered at such port. This royal order had never been published in the papers of Madrid, but had been sent to the seaports, and there communicated to foreign consuls by the local authorities. My first information of it was derived from our consul, Mr. Sterling, at Barcelona. Nothing occurring under it for some time,' I had not made it a subject of communication until, within a few days, I received information from the same consul that the authorities of Tarragona had proceeded to enforce it against an American vessel in that port, where the vice consul had obtained the release of the vessel by executing bond with the captain for the fulfilment of this condition. I instantly addressed a remonstrance to the Secretary of State, urging the repeal of this order and the cancelling of the bonds which should be executed under it.

"This remonstrance was succeeded by another application, of which a copy is also inclosed, produced by an incident of a most unpleasant nature. A man, asserting that he is an American citizen, was captured with a band of insurgents, who made an unsuccessful assault, in August, on the town of Almeria, on the Mediterranean coast. They approached in an armed brig the batteries of the place, and attempted to force its surrender by a cannonade; they were repulsed in this onset. Thirty of the crew afterwards landed, and being joined by a number of the inhabitants of the neighborhood, they attempted to storm the place by attacking it at several points. They were baffled in these, and most of those who landed from the brig were either killed or captured. Among the latter was this unfortunate man. Under a royal decree, issued immediately after the affair of Tariffa, the sentence of death was promptly pronounced against all these prisoners. The vice consul appointed at that place by Mr. Barrell, of Malaga, learning that a seaman claiming to be an American was included in this sentence, promptly interfered, and, by his exertions, suspended, as to this man, for a time, the execution which was forthwith carried into effect against the others, including foreigners as well as Spaniards. Mr. Spencer, the vice consul, made his report to Mr. Barrell, who directly transmitted the documents to me. I lost no time in laying these, accompanied by my note, before the Secretary of State. They were presented last night at eleven o'clock by Mr. Appleton, who explained the subject fully, and urged the interference of the proper authority immediately to suspend all proceedings until the pleasure of the King could be understood in this case. This man, very young, had only been twenty-four hours in the Bay of Gibraltar, when he was inveigled into this expedition by the means of intoxication and the flattering promises held out to him. To the solicitation for his pardon, I have added, in case of failure on this point, the assertion of the just claim to a fair trial under the right secured by the stipulations of the treaty of 1795."

"SEPTEMBER 13.

"With a promptitude very unusual in this Government, and which does them honor on this occasion, we last night received the inclosed answer to the last application. The King has consented to spare the life of the man, and orders that he shall be sent out of this Kingdom, under a prohibition never to return. I also inclose my note, written in acknowledgment of this concession of his Majesty, in which I have ventured, without instructions, to state the estimate which the American Government would place on an act of this character."

"It is said here that all the agents of France, who have been sent out to the new Governments of South America, have gone with the sanction of the Government of Spain, and that they are furnished with credentials from this Government, to be used by them if occasions should make it necessary. From what we have learned, I think we are justified in believing that the English Government have resolved on some new measure for the protection of their commerce in the West Indies. I am not certain if it extend to making of reprisals, but the chargé d'affaires who is left here since Sir William A'Court departed, acknowledged that measures had been adopted for the effectual suppression of the pirates, from whom their commerce had suffered greatly."

No. 37, (a.)

Mr. Nelson to Mr. Salazar.

MADRID, *September* 7, 1824.

The undersigned, the Minister Plenipotentiary of the United States of America, begs leave to call the attention of his Catholic Majesty's Government to certain subjects of the deepest interest to the United States, on which the applications heretofore made by the undersigned have failed to rouse the attention, or to obtain the slightest mark of regard from his Catholic Majesty. The undersigned, from delicacy to the Sovereign of Spain, whom he found, on his presentation, occupied in the re-establishment of the affairs of the Kingdom, just emerging from the confusion incident to a state of war, has forborne to urge, with the vehement pressure which his instructions from his Government would seem to require, the decisions of Spain on the several reclamations which were a long time since presented by the undersigned to his Catholic Majesty's Secretary of State.

On the 10th day of January last the undersigned had the honor to address to the Secretary of State of his Catholic Majesty a reclamation on the part of his Government in behalf of its citizens injured by the illegal and piratical conduct of the subjects of his Catholic Majesty in the West Indian seas. It was represented that property to a very large amount had been captured and sent into the ports of his Catholic Majesty, in his American possessions, in many instances against all law and justice, by pirates, who, after committing the most atrocious and nefarious deeds, sought and found shelter and asylum in the islands, and often in the most conspicuous ports and harbors, with the fruits and profits of their inhuman outrages. In many instances these atrocities were perpetrated not less in defiance of right and justice by persons pretending to act under the color of authority, but whose authority has never been justified; and which, if justified, would never sanction these transactions, marked by a character of piracy and rapacity which no commission could justify. In the cases of robberies committed by the Spanish vessels acting as pirates, the American property thus plundered was often carried into the ports of Cuba, and especially of the Havana, and there, in the most open and daring manner, exposed to sale, in the view of the local authorities, unrestrained and unchecked by their slightest interference. American citizens have s n their property, thus violently and feloniously taken from them, offered for sale in open market, without the protection of the local Government in the assertion of their rights, and deterred from the vindication of their just claims by the fullest conviction that they would find no support in the Government of the island, but would meet, in all probability, as the requital of their temerity, the fiend-like vengeance of the murderous assassin. In other instances, where the property of the American citizen has been captured under color of authority in the vessel making the capture, the conduct of the captors has been scarcely less flagrant than that prácticed by the pirates. Oftentimes has the booty found in the American vessel been partitioned among the plunderers without going into port, and distributed, without legal adjudication, by these lawless robbers; and when carried, occasionally, into port, a secret, unknown, and unfrequented port has been resorted to, where law and justice were disregarded, and where every means of obtaining right was denied to the parties concerned—unapprised of the proceedings—and not permitted to avail themselves of the customary means of vindication.. In the prosecution of these felonious practices, American citizens have been seized and thrown into prison, and there cruelly detained, often in a horrible state of suffering, almost without the indispensable necessaries for human subsistence. In some instances, their property, which the merciless captors had spared and sent into port, has been wasted and embezzled to such an extent that, when the mock trial to which it had been subjected had terminated, even in their favor, the subject of controversy could no longer be found. Thus has every species of abuse of the rights of person and of property of American citizens been practiced in these regions. The local authorities have been appealed to in vain; the Government of Spain has been appealed to, as yet, without effect; the reclamations are again renewed; the patience of the American Government is tried to its fullest extent of sufferance; and the day is probably not very distant when the necessity of warding off these reiterated and aggravated injuries, and the obligation of doing justice to its citizens, may compel the Government of the United States to resort to measures of a more efficient character for prevention of injury and the redress of wrongs. This interesting subject has already claimed the attention of the legislative councils of the nation. They have hitherto forborne to recommend the adoption of measures of reprisals from a desire to manifest their friendly dispositions to his Catholic Majesty, and from the hope that the reclamations, long since presented by their minister near this court, would speedily receive attention, and be followed with his Majesty's answer and determination on these important questions. At no very distant period their councils will, in the regular course of their proceedings, be again assembled at the seat of the National Government, when, doubtless, this subject will again be revived by them, and such measures as the existing evils and the disregard, on the part of his Majesty, of the demands hitherto presented by the American minister, will form with them irrefragable arguments for the adoption of a more efficient system of energetic policy. The undersigned has presented, in different appeals to the Government of his Catholic Majesty, the various subjects of complaint which have arisen from the misconduct of his Majesty's officers and subjects in his ultramarine possessions. One of the most prominent and aggravated was the sacrifice of a gallant officer of the American Navy, whilst peaceably entering the port of St. John's, in Porto Rico, who was most wantonly and treacherously murdered by a gun from the fort, fired by the order of the officer at that time in command, in the absence of the Governor. In this instance, the American Government demands that this subject shall be rigorously investigated, and an adequate punishment inflicted on the officer by whose command this outrage was perpetrated.

An appeal has likewise been made to his Catholic Majesty's Government on the subject of the multiplied piracies which have been committed on the peaceable American commerce in the West Indian seas by vessels equipped and sailing from the ports of his Majesty's possessions in these regions, on which reiterated complaints have been made to the local authorities without effect, and on which the interference of his Majesty has been required to compel those authorities to fulfil their duty in this regard by effectual measures for the suppression of the pirates, and by co-operating with the squadron of the United States, sent into these seas for the extirpation of this scourge to the honest and lawful commerce of the whole civilized world.

Another demand upon his Majesty's Government has been made for indemnification against the enormous losses sustained by the American citizens, from the captures made by vessels pretending to act under commissions issued by agents alleging to be authorized by his Catholic Majesty.

The authority to issue these commissions has never been proved; the right to issue them, on the principles avowed, of a paper blockade, without adequate force, of an interdiction of all neutral commerce with the ports of the Spanish Main, on the alleged ancient rights of Spain over that country, has always been resisted and protested against by all neutral nations, and especially by the United States, and relinquished by his Majesty's officers in that region, and finally renounced or abandoned by his Majesty himself, in his decree of December last, opening the commerce of these countries to all the world. On this subject the undersigned, in obedience to instructions of his Government, demanded that a just indemnification should be made to all the American citizens who had suffered any loss in consequence of these illegal acts, done under color and pretence of his Majesty's authority, but really perpetrated in violation of all laws and justice, whose obligation is acknowledged by all the civilized nations of the world. The release of all citizens, and surrender of all American property whose condition had not been changed, but was unjustifiably and illegally detained, was also required.

The undersigned begs leave to present to his excellency this rapid and cursory sketch of the most important subjects of complaint, which he was instructed to press upon the Government of his Catholic Majesty. He begs to refer his excellency to the different notes presented by him, dated the 10th and 23d of January, and the 3d of February last, in which these grievances are more minutely and specially detailed, and where the appropriate and specific redress demanded is more explicitly and at large stated than the undersigned has considered it necessary at this time to recapitulate.

The undersigned begs leave to urge upon his excellency the necessity of an early answer to these applications that his Government may learn how far the spirit and disposition of an harmonious intercourse is reciprocated towards the United States by his Catholic Majesty; that they may be confirmed in that opinion which they have ever entertained, that an appeal to his Majesty's honor is only necessary to obtain the redress of grievances inflicted without his sanction and authority; and that the United States may be relieved from the painful necessity of deciding that an appeal to a more energetic policy, totally at variance with their ardent desire to preserve harmony, and avoid collision, is at length become absolutely and indispensably necessary.

The undersigned tenders to his excellency his most distinguished consideration, and subscribes himself his excellency's very humble and obedient servant,

HUGH NELSON.

His Excellency D. LOUIS MARIA DE SALAZAR,
    First Secretary of State and of the Despatch, ad interim.

No. 38.

Extract of a letter from Mr. Nelson (No. 42) to Mr. Adams, dated

MADRID, *October* 4, 1824.

"I waited upon Mr. Zea yesterday, and had an opportunity of conversing with him on that subject, as also upon others of importance. He assured me that in a very few days I should receive an answer on the subject of this debt which he did not doubt would be perfectly satisfactory. That there was every disposition on the part of his Majesty's Government to afford the aid requested, and that everything that could be done would be complied with to effectuate the object. I then stated to him the subject of the claims of American citizens for spoliations on their commerce in the West Indies, by vessels pretending to act under commissions which had never been legalized; and which, if legalized, would never sanction the piratical acts which they had perpetrated under pretext of these commissions. He assured me that he would forthwith undertake the examination of the correspondence on this subject. He would not content himself with assuring me that he would devote the first leisure he should have to this object, but that he would enter upon it promptly, and avail himself of every occasion to obtain an acquaintance with the whole matter. I urged upon him the necessity of enabling me to communicate immediately to the American Government the views of Spain on this interesting subject; that the attention of Congress would doubtless be turned to it at a very early period of their session; that it had been reviewed by them at their late session, and they had forborne to adopt some measure of energy for the relief of the American commerce, simply from deference to their wish to maintain the friendly relations with Spain inviolate, and from a hope that the appeals made by the American minister at Madrid to his Catholic Majesty's Government would meet with a proper attention, and produce the desired effect of a friendly adjustment of all existing differences. I assured him of the earnest desire of the Executive of the United States to maintain, unimpaired the friendship between the two Governments, but that I would not assure him how far the influence of this feeling might operate with the Legislature to control the adoption of energetic measures, even to the extent of making reprisals on the commerce of Spain, unless Spain should manifest a disposition to pay a due regard to the reclamations which had been presented upon this subject. I stated that the Count of Ofalia had assured me that the new minister to the United States should be instructed and empowered to treat upon this matter at Washington, as being most convenient to the place where these transactions had occurred, and more convenient for obtaining the necessary testimony. He then remarked on the death of the Chevalier Isnardi, and said that he had not yet had leisure to designate a fit person for this mission, but that this would soon be done. He was informed that Congress would meet in the beginning of December, before which the American Government ought to receive the answer of Spain to the communications made on this subject. He reciprocated the anxious wish of his Majesty to preserve the harmony between Spain and the United States, and that he personally felt the influence of the same consideration."

No. 39.

Extract of a letter from Mr. Nelson to the Secretary of State, (No. 43,) dated

MADRID, *October* 12, 1824.

"The despatch, No. 39, has presented the correspondence with this Government, in the case of John B. Pechut, an American citizen, taken with the band of insurgents at Almeria, in the Kingdom of Grenada. From that you will have learned that the King had consented to his pardon, on condition of his being sent out of his dominions, never to return to them. Whilst I was in the daily expectation of receiving intelligence of the happy release of Pechut under this act of clemency, I had the mortification to receive communications from Mr. Barrell, and his vice consul, Mr. Spencer, acting at Almeria, and who was so prompt and active as to obtain from the local authorities the suspension of Pechut's execution, giving the melancholy news of the execution of this unfortunate man under a positive order from the Captain General of Grenada—this same ruffian Quesada, who had been sent from Madrid for conniving at the assassination of some of the French soldiers. I learn that the Military Governor of Almeria, on the application of Mr. Spencer, claiming this man as an American citizen, and informing the Governor that the case would be sent to the American minister, to be presented to his Majesty, had suspended the sentence until the pleasure of the King should be known. The Military Governor made a report to the Captain General Quesada, stating the fact that the case had been suspended on the claim made of the American citizen, and that an appeal was in progress to his Majesty for his directions in reference to the prisoner. Yet, notwithstanding this full knowledge, Quesada immediately replied to the Military Governor's report with a peremptory order for the prompt execution of Pechut. The subordinate officer conceived himself bound to obey the command of the superior, and the execution was effected upon this poor man on the 10th of September. Instantly on receiving the information of the facts I addressed a note to the Secretary of State, couched in the terms which my feelings dictated, and as strong as the proper decorum would justify. The Secretary replied immediately, asking information in regard to dates. To his note I replied forthwith, much in the spirit of the first communication. The copies of this correspondence accompany this despatch. I have nothing further from this Government on this subject.

"I also send a copy of a note addressed to the Secretary, dated of this day, written with the design of obtaining some answer in relation to our demands on the subject of the spoliations on our commerce in the West Indies, in the hope of getting something in time to enable the President to show to Congress the state of this question between the two Governments. It must come very soon to be in time. I have talked and written continually on this subject, without effect. If this terror of reprisals on their commerce do not bring forth something, I shall despair of vanquishing Spanish apathy, and shall think the energy of the Committee on Foreign Relations will not be excessive, even if it should extend to the recommendation of doing justice to our citizens, by something more effectual than negotiation.

"If I might presume to advise, I should at least think it prudent to forbear for a reasonable portion of the session; giving Spain time to answer, so as not to lose the occasion of acting upon this subject during the session. Some allowance must be made for the perpetual change in their councils, and some respect may be due to Count Ofalia's promise given, to authorize the new minister who should go to the United States to treat upon this important question."

No. 39, (a.)

Mr. Nelson to Mr. Bermudez.

MADRID, *October 6, 1824.*

The undersigned, the Minister Plenipotentiary of the United States of America, has the honor to communicate to his excellency that he has this day experienced the deepest mortification in learning from the American consul at Malaga and the vice consul at Almeria that the inexorable rigor of the Captain General of Grenada has cruelly defeated the benignant clemency of his Majesty, which, on the application of the undersigned, had been graciously extended to an American citizen, John Baptist Pechut, seduced, through ignorance, into a combination with others, charged with an attempt to disturb the repose of his Majesty's dominions. This unfortunate young man, just arrived in the port of Gibraltar, in less than twenty-four hours after his reaching this port was beguiled by the artifice and seductions of subtile and insidious men to engage in an enterprise, the object of which, as disclosed to him, was in no manner levelled against the safety or power of his Catholic Majesty. The undersigned had the honor to address to his excellency, the then acting Secretary of State, on the 9th ultimo, his appeal to his Majesty's clemency for the exercise of his most glorious and divine-like attribute of mercy to the unfortunate; this appeal was promptly answered by the assurance that his Majesty, actuated by that clemency which it is his Majesty's highest delight to practice on all just occasions, and by a wish to manifest his feelings of respect and friendship to the representative of the American Government, had granted a pardon to this unfortunate, deluded young man; and by the communication of the information that an order to that effect had been immediately transmitted to his Majesty's Secretary for the Department of War, with instructions that Pechut should be placed at the disposal of the undersigned; to be sent out of his Majesty's dominions, and to incur the sentence of perpetual banishment from them. The undersigned, under the influence of those feelings which this act of clemency was calculated to inspire, lost no time in making to his Majesty the proper return of the acknowledgments of his Government and of his own personal sensibility for this distinguished mark of liberality. The undersigned immediately communicated to his Government this act of clemency on the part of his Catholic Majesty, as a new evidence of his Majesty's disposition to cherish and fortify the harmony and friendship happily subsisting between the two Governments. His excellency cannot fail to appreciate the indignant sensibility with which the undersigned must receive the report from the American consul, that the unrelenting severity of one of his Majesty's officers has baffled the gracious purposes of his royal clemency, and set at nought the sacred obligations of existing treaties which, at least, pretend to assure to the citizens or subjects of either in the jurisdiction of the other *a just* and fair trial for alleged offences or crimes against their laws. But the undersigned must experience still deeper regret, when, in the execution of his duties to his own Government, it shall devolve upon him to announce to it that the highly-lauded humanity of his Majesty has been counteracted by the infuriated vengeance of an arbitrary Governor of a province, and that his Majesty's design of according to the representative of a friendly power a new evidence of his sincere wish to cultivate their good will has been converted into an instrument of discord and irritation by a blind surrender to the most vindictive feelings.

The undersigned feels constrained to ask of his excellency that the officer whose conduct has produced this unhappy disappointment may be called upon to answer for this unjustifiable act; and that, henceforward, should any American citizen be unhappy placed in a situation subjecting him to be proceeded against judicially in Spain, to demand that the rights secured to them by treaty shall be most scrupulously administered in all cases by the tribunals of his Catholic Majesty.

The undersigned has the honor to tender to his excellency the consideration of his most distinguished regard, and to subscribe himself his excellency's very humble and obedient servant,

HUGH NELSON.

His Excellency Don FRANCISCO ZEA BERMUDEZ,
    His Catholic Majesty's First Secretary of State, &c.

No. 39, (b.)

Don Francisco de Zea Bermudez to Mr. Nelson.

[Translation.]

SAN LORENZO, *October 8, 1824.*

SIR: The sad communication which you were pleased to make to me in your note of the 6th current, which came to my hands at half-past 8 o'clock this morning, referring to the pardon which the King, my august master, with his natural clemency, judged good to grant to John Pechut, in whose favor, as an American subject, you were pleased to interest yourself, not having had the desired fulfilment, has caused to me the most lively grief. I am certain that his Majesty, to whom I shall hasten to give an account of this unfortunate occurrence, will learn, with the most sincere sorrow, that his beneficent disposition, intended to prove more and more his friendly sentiments to your Government, has not been realized. Anticipating his royal orders, I have not lost a moment in communicating the proper orders, that all the circumstances relative to the trial and sentence of the unfortunate Pechut may be investigated with scrupulous exactness, including the fixed times of the despatch and arrival of the royal orders communicated in this business, which were sent from this chief office, under my charge, without the least delay, on the 11th of last month, as I had the honor of informing you on the same day. You need not doubt, sir, that the known rectitude of his Majesty will severely punish any fault, omission, or disobedience to his royal commands, if any such have taken place in this affair; and, in the whole case, I shall consider it as a duty, sir, to inform you, circumstantially, of the result of the investigations ordered, and of the consequent resolution of his Majesty, for your information and satisfaction. In the meantime, and to elucidate further this painful event, I request you will have the goodness to transmit to me, with due precision and punctuality, all the data relative to it which may have come to your knowledge; resting assured that, on my part, I shall omit no means within the compass of my power to evince to you the distinguished value which his Majesty's Government sets upon their friendly relations with yours, and of their constant exactitude in observing justice and treaties.

I embrace, with pleasure, this occasion of renewing to you, sir, the sentiments of my most distinguished consideration. God preserve you many years.

FRANCISCO DE ZEA BERMUDEZ.

No. 39, (c.)

Mr. Nelson to Mr. Bermudez.

MADRID, *October 9, 1824.*

The undersigned, the Minister Plenipotentiary of the United States of America, has the honor to acknowledge the receipt of his excellency's note of the 8th instant, which was received this morning, and to state, in reply, that he is informed, by letters from the vice consul at Almeria, that, on the 25th of August last, on his urgent solicitation, the Military Governor and Junta of Almeria suspended the execution of Pechut, who had been previously, with others, made a prisoner; and that they gave an assurance to the American vice consul, on his representation that this subject would be immediately laid before his Majesty's Government; that his sentence should be respited until his Majesty's pleasure should be known. The American vice consul proceeded to correspond with the consul at Malaga, who transmitted the documents to the American minister at Madrid, who, immediately on their receipt, addressed the Secretary of State on the subject, who promptly returned the assurance of his Majesty's pardon. The further correspondence of the American vice consul at Almeria informs the undersigned that the Military Governor of that place, on the 29th of August last, suspending the execution of Pechut, on the vice consul's representations of the case being in a course to be submitted to his Majesty's pleasure, presented the subject to his excellency the Captain General of the Kingdom of Grenada, stating the reasons which induced the suspension of Pechut's execution, being those which the American vice consul offered at the time that the declaration of the said Pechut was made before the Military Governor of Almeria, and the Junta associated with him. This declaration accompanied the first note of the undersigned to the Secretary of State on this subject. The Captain General of the Kingdom of Grenada, in defiance of the knowledge conveyed to him by the Military Governor of Almeria, that this case of an American citizen, claimed by the American representative, was in course of submission to his Catholic Majesty, on the 6th of September proceeded to order the execution of Pechut, and enjoined upon the authorities implicit obedience to this command. The Military Governor of Almeria, having received this peremptory command from his superior, who was fully informed of all the facts of the case, and especially made to know that an appeal to his Majesty's clemency was in progress for the pardon of this unfortunate young man, conceived himself bound to execute this sanguinary order; nor could the remonstrances, protests, and appeals of the American vice consul produce any effect in mitigating or suspending this inexorable sentence, which the undersigned learns was cruelly fulfilled on the evening of the 10th of September. The undersigned presents this case to his excellency, not as one of complaint against the Captain General for disregard of his Majesty's command, which would be an affair entirely between his Majesty and the officer, with which a foreign Government could have no right to interfere, but as a complaint against this officer for a total disregard of the rights of a foreign power, secured by the sacred obligations of a treaty, which the Military Governor and Junta of Almeria, not less zealous in the service of his Majesty than the Captain General himself, deemed of sufficient force to induce them, in the first instance, to suspend Pechut's execution; as a complaint against the Captain General of Grenada, for presuming to decide a question between a foreign Government and his Catholic Majesty, wresting the authority from the higher tribunals, by a decision not to be reversed from the unhappy condition of the unfortunate victim, outraging the rights of a foreign nation, presumptuously anticipating the judgment of his Majesty, and defeating the humane and benevolent designs of his Majesty in extending his clemency to a deluded and ignorant victim, uninfluenced by any sentiment of hostility to the sacred rights of his Catholic Majesty; a complaint that this officer remained inexorable to an appeal which aroused the sympathies of the tribunal which first investigated the case, and which, at the first blush, met in the clemency of his Majesty a sympathizing sentiment sufficient to produce an immediate order for the pardon of the unfortunate Pechut. The undersigned closes this with feelings of the deepest regret, and laments that an officer in his Majesty's service, high and distinguished by his confidence, should be found manifesting an overweening zeal, by the perpetration of acts from which humanity revolts, and from which the benignant clemency of his Majesty's heart must recoil with the deepest abhorrence. The undersigned begs to repeat his earnest appeal to his Majesty to cause the subsisting treaties between Spain and the United States to be fulfilled, should any cases occur wherein American citizens may be so unfortunate as to be involved in criminal prosecutions in Spain, and to renew to his excellency the tender, &c., &c.

HUGH NELSON.

His Excellency Don FRANCISCO DE ZEA BERMUDEZ,
  His Catholic Majesty's First Secretary of State and of Despatch.

No. 39, (d.)

Mr. Nelson to the Secretary of State and of Despatch.

MADRID, *October* 12, 1824.

The undersigned, the Minister Plenipotentiary of the United States of America, salutes his excellency, and asks to call his attention to the topics on which they conversed when last the undersigned had the honor of an interview with his excellency; but especially to that which concerned the claims of the American citizens for spoliations on their commerce in the West India seas, committed by Spanish cruisers, in violation of the laws of nations and the peaceful relations subsisting between Spain and the United States. The undersigned is led to recall this subject to his excellency's recollection from an apprehension that the great pressure of important business, at this time occupying his excellency's attention, may have diminished the force of his recollection in regard to communications made in a personal conference, and not in writing; and from an earnest desire to prevent, by all means, the chance of the friendly and harmonious relations between the two countries being brought into the hazard of collision. The undersigned had the honor to state that this subject had been presented to his Majesty's Government on the 10th of January last; that it had been continually recalled since, both in writing and in conversation, at intervals, to its recollection; that it had been presented to the Secretary of State *ad interim* who had preceded his excellency; and was, lastly, presented to his excellency, accompanied by the information that the maintenance of the friendship and good feelings between the United States and Spain seemed to make it highly important that Spain would turn her attention to the subject as soon as possible, and give an answer to those repeated remonstrances, which the undersigned might communicate to the Government of the United States as the evidence that Spain was not wholly inattentive to a subject to which the United States attached so much importance. The undersigned had the honor to urge upon his excellency the necessity of a speedy reply, because of the approaching session of the American Congress, before whom there was great reason to believe the President of the United States would consider it necessary to lay some report in reference to this subject, so interesting to a large class of the American community; and, also, because the Congress of the United States had, at their last session, turned their attention to this subject, but had forborne to recommend measures of energy, by possibility extending to measures of reprisal on the commerce of Spain, purely from deference to their anxious desire to maintain, unimpaired, their friendly relations with Spain, and from the hope which they entertained that a strong sense of justice on the part of Spain would induce her to give a just attention to the remonstrances on the subject presented by the American minister near his Catholic Majesty. The undersigned had the honor to state that he was authorized to say, that the Executive of the United States felt an anxious wish to preserve undisturbed the harmonious relations and the friendly sentiments between the two Governments; that he, the undersigned, personally felt the influence of the same strong feelings; but that he did not feel justified in expressing the opinion that the same influence might operate with the National Legislature to the extent of protracted forbearance, after the lapse of twelve months, expended in fruitless efforts on the part of the American minister to induce the councils of his Majesty to turn their attention to the appeals of a friendly nation, bound to protect its citizens and to obtain justice for them, aggrieved by the misconduct of the officers of another nation. The undersigned begs leave to inform his excellency that the Congress of the United States will commence its session on the sixth day of December ensuing; at which time it would, doubtless, be highly agreeable to the American Government to be informed of the disposition of his Catholic Majesty to meet their reclamations in the most amicable manner, and of his Majesty's determination to adopt such a plan of accommodation of these matters of difference between the two Governments as shall comport with the great principles of justice and with the just obligations of a friendly nation to indemnify others injured by the misconduct of its officers in a manner satisfactory to the nation whose citizens have sustained the injuries.

The undersigned has the honor to renew to his excellency the tender of his most distinguished consideration, and subscribes himself his excellency's very humble and obedient servant,

HUGH NELSON.

His Excellency Don FRANCISCO DE ZEA BERMUDEZ,
 His Catholic Majesty's First Secretary of State and of Despatch.

PIRACIES ON THE COMMERCE OF THE UNITED STATES IN THE WEST INDIES.

COMMUNICATED TO THE HOUSE OF REPRESENTATIVES DECEMBER 13, 1824.

To the Senate and House of Representatives of the United States in Congress assembled:

The citizens of New York solicit the attention of your honorable body to a subject of the deepest interest, affecting equally the commerce and revenue of the nation, the lives of our citizens, and the prosperity of a most respectable class of merchants.

The trade to the island of Cuba has for many years been increasing, and has now become one of the most valuable branches of our foreign commerce. In its importance to the Union it is not inferior to our trade with France and all her colonies. It is a most advantageous market for our produce and manufactures; furnishes us with many useful articles of consumption; employs a vast amount of American tonnage; is a nursery for our seamen, and yields a large revenue to our Treasury. This trade was prosecuted until within a few years past with 'but little interruption; but in consequence of wars in the different Spanish provinces, which have had the effect greatly to weaken the sense of moral obligation, and from a partial suppression of the Spanish slave trade, many ferocious spirits have been put out of employment, and a class of men have arisen and located themselves in different parts of that island who seem, by their robberies and their cruelties, to emulate the buccaniers of former times.

The piracies of these men were confined for a time principally to plundering our vessels and maltreating our seamen. By the exertions of the naval force under Commodore Porter their atrocities were rendered less frequent, and a hope was entertained that they would be entirely discontinued, but this hope has proved delusive. The necessary withdrawal of our ships-of-war during the sickly season, the supineness or connivance of the local authorities of Cuba, and the imbecility of the Spanish Government, have conspired to renew the piratical system with increased activity and horror. Whole crews have been recently murdered, their vessels burnt, and their cargoes plundered, and, in some instances, openly sold at the Matanzas or the Havana.

Without some protection to this trade more efficient than any which has yet been afforded, and better adapted to repel the attacks of these abandoned men, we are apprehensive that this great branch of our foreign commerce, and the revenues arising from it, will be materially diminished. It is a lawful commerce, and our citizens have the right to claim the protection of Government in its pursuit.

The system adopted by these bands of pirates is to go out from their places of concealment in small open boats, attack unarmed vessels, and, by indiscriminate slaughter, to remove all chance of detection. A commerce liable to such risks cannot be prosecuted; merchants will be unwilling to expose their property, and seamen will not be willing to jeopardize their lives.

We have thus briefly stated the evils which threaten not only our direct trade to Cuba, but also our commerce to every part of the Gulf of Mexico. It is not too much to say that they are too great to be endured; and, confiding in the wisdom and justice of your honorable body, we pray that suitable and effectual measures may be speedily devised to remove them.

We would respectfully submit to the consideration of Congress whether it would not be expedient that a law should be passed authorizing merchant vessels to arm for their own protection, under such regulations and with such rules for their government as may appear necessary, and which may avoid the danger of committing the peace of the nation to the discretion of individuals; and that the squadron on the Cuba station should be reinforced; that decoy vessels should be employed, and that the ships-of-war be furnished with additional launches and boats calculated to pursue the pirates into their retreats and fastnesses.

We would further respectfully suggest that the President of the United States be requested to make suitable remonstrances to the Government of Spain and to the authorities of Cuba relative to the piracies committed on American vessels and the murder of their crews by persons issuing from the shores of that island, and to state most explicitly that, if the evils are not removed, they will be held liable for the consequences.

Should such remonstrances be made, and should they be ineffectual, the citizens of New York pledge themselves to support their Government in any ulterior measures which may be necessary, even if they extend to the blockade of every part of that island.

And your memorialists, as in duty bound, will ever pray, &c.

A true copy of a memorial unanimously adopted at a meeting of merchants and citizens of the city of New York, held at the Tontine Coffee House on the 2d day of December, 1824.

WM. BAYARD, Chairman.

Attest:
  ·STEPHEN ALLEN, Secretary.

CLAIM OF PELATIAH FITCH, ON ACCOUNT OF FRENCH SPOLIATIONS.

COMMUNICATED TO THE HOUSE OF REPRESENTATIVES DECEMBER 14, 1824.

To the House of Representatives of the United States:

The SECRETARY OF STATE, to whom, by a resolution of the 9th of January, 1822, was referred the petition, with the accompanying documents, of Pelatiah Fitch, of Athens, in the county of Greene, in the State of New York, and who, by a resolution of this House of the 24th of May last, was directed to report, at this session of Congress, his opinion upon the claim of the said Fitch, has the honor, in compliance therewith, of submitting the following report:

The petition sets forth that a vessel, called the Hiram, sailed from New York in December, 1796, bound to Jamaica, and was captured and condemned by the French in the year 1797; that the Hiram was valued at *five thousand dollars* and upwards, the whole claim to which has devolved upon the petitioner; and that the portion of the cargo belonging to him at the time of its shipment was worth *three thousand dollars* or more.

That the petitioner was advised and believed that he had a valid claim upon David Ross and John Baptist Loir for the value of the vessel; that proceedings were commenced against them in Pennsylvania, prosecuted with great trouble and expense through the courts of law and equity, and *recently* resulted in a total failure.

That it was his confidence of succeeding against said Ross and Loir, and his wish to save the United States the expense, that prevented him from interposing his claim under the Louisiana treaty.

That he hopes, therefore, should all the funds growing out of the cession of Louisiana to the United States and set apart for liquidáting claims for French spoliations be exhausted, that Congress will take into consideration the justice and hardship of his case and grant him compensation, either in money or in lands, or in such other way as shall be deemed right.

By a document accompanying the petition it appears that the Hiram and her cargo were condemned by the French Commissioners, Santhonax and Raimond, in the island of St. Domingo, about the first of February, 1797, under the authority of a decree of the Executive Directory of France, and upon the sole ground that the vessel was cleared out for, and bound to, the island of Jamaica.

From this decision no appeal was taken in behalf of the owners of the Hiram, nor was any claim of indemnity interposed in their behalf upon the subsequent negotiation for indemnities at the cession of Louisiana. Whether the funds, therefore, set apart for liquidating claims provided for by that negotiation are or are not exhausted, no part of them could, under any circumstances, be applied to indemnify the petitioner for this loss.

The only question remaining, then, is, whether Congress, in consideration of the justice and hardship of his case, will grant him compensation from other public funds. The reasons assigned by the petitioner for his omission to interpose his claim under the Louisiana treaty are, his wish to save expense to the United States and his confidence of succeeding in a claim against David Ross and John Baptist Loir for recovering, by process of law in their country, the property which had thus come into their possession.

These persons, it appears, had purchased the vessel at the time when she was condemned by the French Commissioners in St. Domingo in 1797. She was immediately sent to the United States, entered at the port of Philadelphia on the 27th of April, 1797, and again on the first of September following. On the 5th of September, 1797, she was registered at Philadelphia as the property of David Ross, and on the 4th day of October of the same year again as the property of John Baptist Loir, Joseph Henry Chevalier, and David Ross.

The petitioner and Rufus Bacchus, then joint owner with him of the Hiram, sued out, in the Circuit Court of the United States at the October session of the said court, at Philadelphia, a writ of replevin for the said vessel, upon which was returned by William Nickols, then marshal of the Pennsylvania district, "Replevied and delivered;" which return the petitioner states to have been contrary to the fact, though not known to him to have been so until after the death of the said Nickols. On this suit, however, judgment for the plaintiff was rendered by the court in October, 1800.

Ten years after that time a bill in chancery was filed in the Circuit Court of the United States for the district of Delaware by the same complainants, Pelatiah Fitch and Rufus Bacchus, against the same defendants, David Ross and John Baptist Loir, setting forth the facts above stated and others, showing that the complainants had, notwithstanding the above cited return of the marshal upon the writ of replevin and judgment of the court in their favor, never received restitution of their property or indemnity for the loss of it, and praying a subpœna to the defendants, commanding them to appear and answer the said bill, and to abide the order and decree of the court upon the premises.

To this bill David Ross, one of the defendants, by his counsel, filed a demurrer, which, upon full argument, was sustained by the court, and in October, 1812, the bill of complaint was dismissed, but without costs.

Without inquiry into the causes of the petitioner's failure to obtain the restitution of his vessel or indemnity for his loss, through the channel in which he voluntarily sought his remedy, the tribunals of his own country, it is apparent that they have given him no claim to indemnity from the United States. The omission to press the claim upon the Government of France at the time when it might have been provided for was altogether of the petitioner's own option; and patriotic as one of his motives for this forbearance was, and disappointed as he has been in the expectation which suggested the other, they can, neither separately nor united, constitute any obligation upon the United States to take upon themselves the burden of an injury, in the infliction of which they had no participation, and for the reparation of which their interposition was not even requested by the petitioner.

All which is respectfully submitted.

JOHN QUINCY ADAMS.

DEPARTMENT OF STATE, *Washington, December 13, 1824.*

CONVENTION WITH THE BEY OF TUNIS.

COMMUNICATED TO THE SENATE, IN EXECUTIVE SESSION, DECEMBER 15, 1824, AND THE INJUNCTION OF SECRECY SINCE
REMOVED.

To the President of the Senate pro tempore:

I transmit to the Senate a convention negotiated and signed by Samuel D. Heap, Acting Consul of the United States, on the part of the United States, and Mahmoud Bashaw, Bey of Tunis, on the 24th day of February last, together with copies of Mr. Heap's correspondence appertaining to the negotiation of the same, for the constitutional consideration of the Senate with regard to its ratification.

JAMES MONROE.

WASHINGTON, *December 13, 1824.*

CONVENTION BETWEEN THE UNITED STATES AND THE BEY OF TUNIS.

Whereas sundry articles of the treaty of peace and friendship concluded between the United States of America and Hamuda Bashaw, of happy memory, in the month of Rebia Elul, in the year of the Hegira 1212, corresponding with the month of August of the Christian year 1797, have, by experience, been found to require alteration and amendment; in order, therefore, that the United States should be placed on the same footing with the most favored nations having treaties with Tunis, as well as to manifest a respect for the American Government, and a desire to continue, unimpaired, the friendly relations which have always existed between the two nations, it is hereby agreed and concluded between his Highness Mahmoud Bashaw, Bey of Tunis, and S. D. Heap, Chargé d'Affaires of the United States of America, that alteration be made in the sixth, eleventh, twelfth, and fourteenth articles of said treaty; and that the said articles shall be altered and amended in the treaty to read as follows:

ARTICLE VI. If a Tunisian corsair shall meet with an American vessel, and shall visit it with her boat, two men only shall be allowed to go on board, peaceably to satisfy themselves of its being American; who, as well as any passengers of other nations they may have on board, shall go free, both them and their goods; and the said two men shall not exact anything on pain of being severely punished. In case a slave escapes and takes refuge on board an American vessel-of-war, he shall be free, and no demand shall be made either for his restoration or for payment.

ARTICLE XI. When a vessel-of-war of the United States shall enter the port of the Goletta, she shall be saluted with twenty-one guns, which salute the vessel-of-war shall return gun for gun only; and no powder will be given as mentioned in the ancient eleventh article of this treaty, which is hereby annulled.

ARTICLE XII. When citizens of the United States shall come within the dependencies of Tunis to carry on commerce there, the same respect shall be paid to them which the merchants of other nations enjoy; and if they wish to establish themselves within our ports, no opposition shall be made thereto; and they shall be free to avail themselves of such interpreters as they may judge necessary, without any obstruction, in conformity with the usages of other nations; and if a Tunisian subject shall go to establish himself within the dependencies of the United States, he shall be treated in like manner. If any Tunisian subject shall freight an American vessel, or load her with merchandise, and shall afterwards want to unload and ship them on board of another vessel, we shall not permit him until the matter is determined by a reference of merchants, who shall decide upon the case, and after the decision the determination shall be conformed to.

No captain shall be detained in port against his consent, except when our ports are shut for the vessels of all other nations, which may take place with respect to merchant vessels, but not to those of war. The subjects and citizens of the two nations, respectively, Tunisians and Americans, shall be protected in the places where they may be, by the officers of the Government there existing; but on failure of such protection and for redress of every injury, the party may resort to the chief authority in each country, by whom adequate protection and complete justice shall be rendered. In case the Government of Tunis shall have need of an American vessel for its service, such vessel being within the Regency, and not previously engaged, the Government shall have the preference, on its paying the same freight as other merchants usually pay for the same service, or at the like rate, if the service be without a customary precedent.

ARTICLE XIV. All vessels belonging to the citizens and inhabitants of the United States shall be permitted to enter the ports of the Kingdom of Tunis, and freely trade with the subjects and inhabitants thereof, on paying the usual duties which are paid by other most favored nations at peace with the Regency. In like manner all vessels belonging to the subjects and inhabitants of the Kingdom of Tunis shall be permitted to enter the different ports of the United States, and freely trade with the citizens and inhabitants thereof, on paying the usual duties which are paid by other favored nations at peace with the United States.

Concluded, signed, and sealed, at the palace of Bardo, near Tunis, the 24th day of the moon Jumed-teni, in the year of the Hegira 1239, corresponding to the 24th of February, 1824, of the Christian year; and the 48th year of the Independence of the United States; reserving the same, nevertheless, for the final ratification of the President of the United States, by and with the advice and consent of the Senate.

S. D. HEAP,
Chargé d'Affaires of the United States of America, at Tunis.

[*Seal of Mahmoud Bashaw.*]

[*Seal of Hassan Bey.*]

Extract of a letter from S. D. Heap, acting as Consul of the United States at Tunis, to the Secretary of State, dated January 24, 1824.

"I have now the honor to inform you that all the consuls waited on the Bey this morning, on the occasion of his return to Bardo from the Baths, where he had spent some weeks for the restoration of his health. After we had withdrawn, I was informed his Highness wished to see me, when he expressed the most friendly disposition towards the United States, and wished to know why American vessels never visited his ports; I replied, that his Highness must be well aware of the cause; that, so long as the present treaty existed, he must not expect to see an American merchantman enter his ports. I also observed, that the commerce of the United States in the Mediterranean was very considerable, and annually increasing; that I had reason to believe, if such changes were made in the treaty as would place us in the situation of the most favored nation, he would soon see our enterprising citizens engage in a commerce which would prove highly beneficial to his Government and subjects. I further observed, that many years' experience must have convinced his Highness of the truth of my remark, and that he must have become sensible, by this time, that the objectionable articles in the treaty had ceased to be of much consequence to us, but that they operated greatly to his disadvantage. I then briefly stated to him all the objectionable articles which it would be necessary to expunge or alter in order to produce the desired effect. The Bey, with the utmost apparent candor, assented to the truth of my observations, and charged me to inform my Government of his willingness to expunge or alter the objectionable articles. He moreover requested me to inform the commander of the first American vessel-of-war which should arrive in this bay that he would salute him, and that in future no demand would be made for powder, nor should any claim be made for any slave who might escape in a United States vessel hereafter."

S. D. Heap, Esq., to the Secretary of State.

UNITED STATES CONSULATE, *Tunis, March 4, 1824.*

SIR: I had the honor of informing you, in my communications of January 20 and 24 and February 10, that his Highness the Bey had evinced the most friendly disposition towards the United States, and had agreed to expunge and remodel certain articles of our treaty which have always been considered as disgraceful, and have not unfrequently been a source of litigation and trouble.

I thought it advisable to avail myself of the present favorable disposition of the Bey to effect such a change as could not but be agreeable to my Government, more especially as it has been effected without expense, or the slightest intimation that presents of any description would be expected.

I inclose a copy of the treaty; the original will be forwarded by the first vessel-of-war of the United States which may visit this port.

In this affair, I trust I shall not be considered by the honorable the Secretary of State to have acted with precipitation; if, however, such should, unfortunately for me, be the case, I hope it will be attributed to my zeal to be of service to my country.

With great respect, I have the honor to be your obedient servant,

S. D. HEAP,
Chargé d'Affaires.

Hon. JOHN QUINCY ADAMS,
Secretary of State of the United States.

18TH CONGRESS.]   No. 384.   [2D SESSION.

CORRESPONDENCE AND CONVENTION WITH RUSSIA RELATIVE TO NAVIGATION AND TRADE ON THE NORTHWEST COAST OF AMERICA.

COMMUNICATED TO THE SENATE, IN EXECUTIVE SESSION, DECEMBER 15, 1824, AND THE INJUNCTION OF SECRECY SINCE REMOVED.

To the President of the Senate of the United States pro tempore:

I transmit to the Senate the convention signed by the plenipotentiaries of the United States and of his Imperial Majesty the Emperor of Russia, at St. Petersburg, on the 5th (17th) of April last, referred to in my message to both Houses of Congress, together with the documents appertaining to the negotiation of the same, for the constitutional consideration of the Senate with regard to its ratification.

JAMES MONROE.

WASHINGTON, *December 13, 1824.*

CONVENTION.

Au nom de la très Sainte et Indivisible Trinité: Le President des Etats Unis d'Amérique, et sa Majesté l'Empereur de toutes les Russies, voulant cimenter les liens d'amitié qui les unissent, et assurer entre eux le maintien invariable d'un parfait accord, moyennant la présente Convention, ont nommé pour leurs Plenipotentiaires à cet effet, savoir: le President des Etats Unis d'Amérique, le sieur HENRY MIDDLETON, citoyen des dits Etats et leur Envoyé Extraordinaire et Ministère Plénipotentiaire près sa Majesté Impèriale, et sa Majesté l'Empereur de toutes les Russies, ses amés et féaux les sieurs CHARLES ROBERT Comte de NESSELRODE, Conseiller Privé actuel, Membre du Conseil d'Etat, Sécretaire d'Etat Dirigeant le Ministère des Affaires Etrangères, Chambellan actuel, Chevalier de l'ordre de St. Alexandre Nevsky, Grand Croix de l'ordre de St. Wladimir de la premiere classe, Chevalier de celui de l'Aigle Blanc de Pologne, Grand Croix de l'ordre de St. Etienne d'Hongrie, Chevalier des ordres du St. Esprit et de St. Michel, et Grand Croix de celui de la Legion d'Honneur de France, Chevalier Grand Croix des ordres de l'Aigle Noir et de l'Aigle Rouge de Prusse, de l'Annonciade de Sardaigne, de Charles III. d'Espagne, de St. Ferdinand, et du Mérite de Naples, de l'Eléphant de Danemarc, de l'Etoile Polaire de Suède, de la Couronne de Würtemburg, des Gnelphes de Hanovre, du Lion Belge, de la Fidélité de Bade, et de St. Constantin de Parme, et PIERRE DE POLETICA, Conseiller d'Etat actuel, Chevalier de l'ordre de St. Anne de la premiere classe, et Grand Croix de l'ordre de St. Wladimir de la second; lesquels, apres avoir échangé leurs pleins pouvoirs, troûvés en bonne et due forme, ont arrêté et signé les stipulations suivantes:

ARTICLE PREMIERE. Il est convenu que dans aucune partie du grand océan, appelé communèment

Océan Pacific ou Mer du Sud les citoyens ou sujets respectifs des hautes puissances contractantes ne seront ni troubles, ni gênés soit dans la navigation, soit dans l'exploitation de la pêche, soit dans la faculté d'aborder aux côtes sur des points qui ne seroient pas déjà occupés, à fin d'y faire le commerce avec les indigènes, sauf toutefois les restrictions et conditions determinées par les articles qui suivent.

ARTICLE DEUXIEME. Dans la vue d'empêcher que les droits de navigation et de pêche exercés sur le grand océan par les citoyens et sujets des hautes Puissances contractantes ne deviennent le prétexte d'un commerce illicite, il est convenu, que les citoyens des Etats Unis n'aborderont à aucun point où il se trouve un etablissement Russe, sans la permission du gouverneur ou commandant; et que réciproquement les sujets Russes ne pourront aborder sans permission à aucun etablissement des Etats Unis sur la côte nord-ouest.

ARTICLE TROISIEME. Il est convenu en outre, que dorénavant il ne pourra être formé par les citoyens des Etats Unis, ou sous l'autorité des dits Etats, aucun etablissement sur la côte nord ouest d'Amérique, ni dans aucune des îles adjacentes *au nord* du cinquante quatriéme degrè et quarante minutes de latitude septentrionale; et que de même il n'en pourra être formée aucun par des sujets Russes, ou sous l'autorité de la Russie *au sud* de la même parallèle.

ARTICLE QUATRIEME. Il est neanmoins entendu que pendant un terme de dix années, à compter de la signature de la présente convention, les vaisseaux des deux puissances, ou qui appartiendroient à leurs citoyens ou sujets respectifs, pourront réciproquement fréquenter, sans entrave quelconque, les mers intérieures, les golfes, hâvres, et criques sur la côte mentionée dans l'article précédent, afin d'y faire la pêche et le commerce avec les naturels du pays.

ARTICLE CINQUIEME. Sont toutefois exceptées de ce même commerce, accordé par l'article précédent, toutes les liqueurs spiritueuses, les armes à feu, armes blanches, poudre, et munition de guerre de toute espéce, que les deux puissances s'engagent réciproquement à ne pas vendre, ni laisser vendre aux indigénes par leur citoyens et sujets respectifs, ni par aucun individu, que se trouveroit sous leur autorité. Il est également stipulé, que cette restriction ne pourra jamais servir de pretexte, ni être alléguée, dans aucun cas, pour autoriser soit la visite ou la detention des vaisseaux, soit la saisie de la merchandise, soit enfin des mesures quelconques de contrainte envers les armateurs ou les equipages qui feroient ce commerce, les hautes puissances contractantes s'etant réciproquement reservé de statuer sur les peines à encourir, et d'infliger les amendes encourües en cas de contravention à cet article, par leur citoyens ou sujets respectifs.

ARTICLE SIXIEME. Lorsque cette convention aura été duement ratifiée par le President des Etats Unis de l'avis et du consentement du Sénat, d'une part, et de l'autre, par sa Majesté l'Empereur de toutes les Russies, les ratifications en seront échangées à Washington dans le délai de dix mois de la date ci-dessous, ou plutôt si faire se peut. En foi de quoi les plenipotentiaires respectifs l'ont signée, et y ont fait apposer les cachets de leurs armes.

Fait à St. Petersbourg le 5th (17th) Avril, de l'an de grâce mil huit cent vingt quatre.

LE COMTE CHARLES DE NESSELRODE. [L. S.]
HENRY MIDDLETON. [L. S.]
PIERRE DE POLETICA. [L. S.]

[Translation.]

Convention between the United States and Russia.

In the name of the most Holy and Indivisible Trinity:

The President of the United States of America and his Majesty the Emperor of all the Russias wishing to cement the bonds of amity which unite them, and to secure between them the invariable maintenance of a perfect concord, by means of the present convention, have named as their plenipotentiaries to this effect, to wit: The President of the United States of America, HENRY MIDDLETON, a citizen of said States, and their Envoy Extraordinary and Minister Plenipotentiary near his Imperial Majesty; and his Majesty the Emperor of all the Russias, his beloved and faithful CHARLES ROBERT, Count of NESSELRODE, Actual Privy Counsellor, member of the Council of State, Secretary of State, directing the administration of Foreign Affairs, Actual Chamberlain, Knight of the order of St. Alexander Nevsky, Grand Cross of the order of St. Wladimir of the first class, Knight of that of the White Eagle of Poland, Grand Cross of the order of St. Stephen of Hungary, Knight of the orders of the Holy Ghost and of St. Michael, and Grand Cross of the Legion of Honor of France, Knight Grand Cross of the orders of the Black and of the Red Eagle of Prussia, of the Annunciation of Sardinia, of Charles III, of Spain, of St. Ferdinand and of Merit of Naples, of the Elephant of Denmark, of the Polar Star of Sweden, of the Crown of Wirtemberg, of the Guelphs of Hanover, of the Belgic Lion, of Fidelity of Baden, and of St. Constantine of Parma; and PIERRE DE POLETICA, Actual Counsellor of State, Knight of the order of St. Anna of the first class, and Grand Cross of the order of St. Wladimir of the second; who, after having exchanged their full powers, found in good and due form, have agreed upon and signed the following stipulations:

ARTICLE 1. It is agreed that in any part of the great ocean, commonly called the Pacific Ocean, or South Sea, the respective citizens or subjects of the high contracting powers shall be neither disturbed nor restrained either in navigation, or in fishing, or in the power of resorting to the coasts upon points which may not already be occupied, for the purpose of trading with the natives, saving always the restrictions and conditions determined by the following articles.

ARTICLE 2. With the view of preventing the rights of navigation and of fishing exercised upon the great ocean by the citizens and subjects of the high contracting powers from becoming the pretext for an illicit trade, it is agreed that the citizens of the United States shall not resort to any point where there is a Russian establishment without the permission of the Governor or commander; and that, reciprocally, the subjects of Russia shall not resort without permission to any establishment of the United States upon the Northwest Coast.

ARTICLE 3. It is moreover agreed that hereafter there shall not be formed by the citizens of the United States, or under the authority of the said States, any establishment upon the Northwest Coast of America, nor in any of the islands adjacent *to the north* of fifty-four degrees and forty minutes of north latitude; and that in the same manner there shall be none formed by Russian subjects or under the authority of Russia *south* of the same parallel

ARTICLE 4. It is, nevertheless, understood that during a term of ten years, counting from the signature of the present convention, the ships of both powers, or which belong to their citizens or subjects, respectively, may reciprocally frequent, without any hindrance whatever, the interior seas, gulfs, harbors, and creeks upon the coast mentioned in the preceding article for the purpose of fishing and trading with the natives of the country.

ARTICLE 5. All spirituous liquors, fire-arms, other arms, powder, and munitions of war of every kind, are always excepted from this same commerce permitted by the preceding article; and the two powers engage reciprocally neither to sell nor suffer them to be sold to the natives by their respective citizens and subjects, nor by any person who may be under their authority. It is likewise stipulated that this restriction shall never afford a pretext nor be advanced in any case to authorize either search or detention of the vessels, seizure of the merchandise, or, in fine, any measures of constraint whatever towards the merchants or the crews who may carry on this commerce; the high contracting powers reciprocally reserving to themselves to determine upon the penalties to be incurred and to inflict the punishments in case of the contravention of this article by their respective citizens or subjects.

ARTICLE 6. When this convention shall have been duly ratified by the President of the United States, with the advice and consent of the Senate, on the one part, and on the other by his Majesty the Emperor of all the Russias, the ratifications shall be exchanged at Washington, in the space of ten months from the date below, or sooner, if possible. In faith whereof, the respective plenipotentiaries have signed this convention and thereto affixed the seals of their arms.

Done at St. Petersburg the 5th (17th) of April, of the year of grace one thousand eight hundred and twenty-four.

> LE COMPTE CHARLES DE NESSELRODE. [L. S.]
> HENRY MIDDLETON. [L. S.]
> PIERRE DE POLETICA. . [L. S.]

List of papers sent with the President's Message to the Senate of December 13, 1824, relative to the Convention with Russia.

No. 1. Baron Tuyll to the Secretary of State, April 12, (24,) 1823, (translation.)
No. 2. Mr. Adams to Baron Tuyll, May 7, 1823.
No. 3. Same to Mr. Middleton, (No. 16, instructions,) July 22, 1823.
No. 3, *a.* Full power to Mr. Middleton.
No. 3, *b.* Mr. Daschkoff to Mr. Smith, January 4, 1810, (translation.)
No. 3, *c.* Count Romanzoff to Mr. Harris, May 17, 1808, (translation.)
No. 3, *d.* Mr. Smith to Mr. Adams, May 5, 1810, (copy.)
No. 3, *e.* Mr. Daschkoff to Mr. Smith, April 24, 1810, (copy.)
Translation of the above.
No. 3, *f.* Mr. Smith to Mr. Daschkoff, May 5, 1810, (copy.)
No. 3, *g.* Mr. Adams to Mr. Smith, (No. 23,) September 5, 1810, (extract.)
No. 3, *h.* Same to same, (No. 25,) September 30, 1810, (extract.)
No. 3, *i.* Same to same, (No. 27,) October 12, 1810, (extract.)
No. 3, *k.* Observations on the claim of Russia, &c.
No. 4. Mr. Adams to Mr. Rush, (No. 70,) July 22, 1823, (copy.)
No. 5. Mr. Middleton to Mr. Adams, (No. 29,) September 7, (19,) 1823, (copy.)
No. 5, *a.* Count Nesselrode to Mr. Middleton, August 22, 1823, (translation.)
No. 6. Mr. Middleton to Mr. Adams, (No. 31,) October 5, (17,) 1823, (copy.)
No. 7. Same to same, (No. 32,) November 1, (13,) 1823, (extract.)
No. 8. Same to same, (No. 33,) December 1, (13,) 1823, (extract.)
No. 8, *a.* Confidential memorial, with notes, from *a* to *g*, (translation.)
No. 9. Mr. Middleton to Mr. Adams, (No. 34,) February 5, (17,) 1824, (extracts.)
No. 10. Same to same, (No. 35,) April 7, (19,) 1824, (copy.)
No. 10, *a.* Convention with Russia, April 5, (17,) 1824, (original.)
No. 10, *a.* Same, for printers, (copy.)
No. 10, *a.* Same, (translation.)
No. 10, *b.* Full power to Sir Charles Bagot; and other papers, from *b* to *v*, inclusive.
No. 11. Mr. Rush to Mr. Adams, (No. 353,) December 19, 1823, (copy.)
No. 12. Same to same, (No. 358,) January 19, 1824, (copy.)

No. 1.

Baron Tuyll to Mr. Adams.

Le soussigné, Envoy Extraordinaire et Ministère Plenipotentiare de sa Majesté l'Empereur des toutes les Russies, près les Etats Unis d'Amerique, a eù l'honneur de témoigner à Monsieur Adams, Secrétaire d'Etat, que l'Empereur, son maitre, constamment animé d'une amitié sincere envers le Gouvernement des Etats Unis, desire de voir terminer, au moyen d'une negociation amicale, les discussions, qui se sont elevées entre le cabinet de St. Petersbourg et celui de Washington, à l'occasion de quelques unes des dispositions comprises dans l'oukaze du 4, (16,) Septembre, 1821, concernant les possessions Russes sur la côte nord-ouest d'Amerique.

Ces vûes de sa Majesté Impérialé coincident avec le voeu expremé, il y a quelque tems, de la part des Etats Unis, relativement à une fixation de limites sur la dite côte.

Le ministère de l'Empereur ayant engagé le ministère Britanique à munir Sir Charles Bagot, Ambas-sadeur de S. M. le Roi d'Angleterre, prés sa Majesté Impériale, des plein pouvoirs requis pour la négotiation, que va séntamer dans le but d'applanir à l'amiable les difficultés nées entre les deux cours, au sujet de la côte nord-ouest, le Gouvernement Anglais s'est empressé d'accéder à cette invitation.

Le soussigné a reçu l'ordre de temoigner à Monsieur le Sécrétaire d'Etat Adams, au nom de son auguste maitre, et comme une nouvelle preuve de sentimens que sa Majesté Impériale porte a Monsieur le President des Etats Unis, et au Gouvernement Americain, l'expression du désir, que Mons. Middleton soit, de même, muni des pouvoirs nécéssaires pour terminer avec le cabinet Impériale, par une arrangement fondé sur le principe des convenances mutuelles, toutes les discussions, qui se sont élevées entre la Russie et les Etats Unis, à la suite du réglement publié le 4 (16) Septembre, 1821.

Le soussigné croit pouvoir espérer, que le cabinet de Washington accueillera, avec plaisir, une proposition tendante à faciliter la conclusion d'un arrangement basé sur les sentimens d'une bienveillance réciproque, et de nature, à concilier les intérets de deux pays.

Il profite de cette occasion pour réitérer à Monsieur Adams, l'assurance de sa haute considération.

TUYLL.

WASHINGTON, *ce* 12 (24) *Avril*, 1823.

No. 1.

Baron Tuyll to the Secretary of State.

[Translation.]

WASHINGTON, *April* 12, (24,) 1823.

The undersigned, Envoy Extraordinary and Minister Plenipotentiary of his Majesty the Emperor of all the Russias near the United States of America, has had the honor to express to Mr. Adams, Secretary of State, the desire of the Emperor, his master, who is ever animated by a sincere friendship towards the United States, to see the discussions that have arisen between the cabinets of St. Petersburg and Washington, upon some provisions contained in the ukase of the 4th (16th) of September, 1821, relative to the Russian possessions on the Northwest Coast of America, terminated by means of a friendly negotiation.

These views of his Imperial Majesty coincide with the wish expressed some time since on the part of the United States in regard to a settlement of limits on the said coast.

The ministry of the Emperor, having induced the British ministry to furnish Sir Charles Bagot, ambassador of his Majesty the King of England near his Imperial Majesty, with full powers necessary for the negotiation about to be set on foot for reconciling the difficulties existing between the two courts on the subject of the Northwest Coast, the English Government is desirous of acceding to that invitation.

The undersigned has been directed to communicate to Mr. Adams, Secretary of State, in the name of his august master, and as an additional proof of the sentiments entertained by his Imperial Majesty towards the President of the United States and the American Government, the expression of his desire that Mr. Middleton be also furnished with the necessary powers to terminate with the Imperial cabinet, by an arrangement founded on the principle of mutual convenience, all the differences that have arisen between Russia and the United States in consequence of the law published September 4, (16,) 1821.

The undersigned thinks he may hope that the cabinet of Washington will, with pleasure, accede to a proposition tending to facilitate the completion of an arrangement based upon sentiments of mutual good will and of a nature to secure the interests of both countries.

He profits of this occasion to renew to Mr. Adams the assurance of his high consideration.

TUYLL.

Mr. ADAMS, *Secretary of State, &c., &c.*

No. 2.

Mr. Adams to the Baron de Tuyll.

DEPARTMENT OF STATE, *Washington, May* 7, 1823.

The undersigned, Secretary of State of the United States, has submitted to the consideration of the President the note which he had the honor of receiving from the Baron de Tuyll, Envoy Extraordinary and Minister Plenipotentiary from his Imperial Majesty the Emperor of all the Russias, dated the 12th (24th) of the last month.

The undersigned has been directed, in answer to that note, to assure the Baron de Tuyll of the warm satisfaction with which the President receives and appreciates the friendly dispositions of his Imperial Majesty towards the United States; dispositions which it has been, and is, the earnest desire of the American Government to meet with corresponding returns, and which have been long cemented by the invariable friendship and cordiality which have subsisted between the United States and his Imperial Majesty.

Penetrated with these sentiments, and anxiously seeking to promote their perpetuation, the President readily accedes to the proposal that the minister of the United States at the court of his Imperial Majesty should be furnished with powers for negotiating, upon principles adapted to those sentiments, the adjustment of the interests and rights which have been brought into collision upon the Northwest Coast of America, and which have heretofore formed a subject of correspondence between the two Governments, as well at Washington as at St. Petersburg.

The undersigned is further commanded to add that, in pursuing, for the adjustment of the interests in question, this course, equally congenial to the friendly feelings of this nation towards Russia and to their reliance upon the justice and magnanimity of his Imperial Majesty, the President of the United States confides that the arrangements of the cabinet of St. Petersburg will have suspended the possibility of any consequences resulting from the ukase to which the Baron de Tuyll's note refers which could affect the just rights and the lawful commerce of the United States during the amicable discussion of the subject between the Governments respectively interested in it.

The undersigned requests the Baron de Tuyll to accept the assurance of his distinguished consideration.

JOHN QUINCY ADAMS.

The BARON DE TUYLL,
    Envoy Extraordinary and Minister Plenipotentiary from Russia.

No. 3.

Mr. Adams to Mr. Middleton, No. 16.

INSTRUCTIONS.

DEPARTMENT OF STATE, *Washington, July* 22, 1823.

SIR: I have the honor of inclosing, herewith, copies of a note from Baron de Tuyll, the Russian minister, recently arrived, proposing, on the part of his Majesty the Emperor of Russia, that a power should be transmitted to you to enter upon a negotiation with the ministers of his Government concerning the differences which have arisen from the imperial ukase of 4th (16th) September, 1821, relative to the Northwest Coast of America, and of the answer from this Department acceding to this proposal. A full power is accordingly inclosed, and you will consider this letter as communicating to you the President's instructions for the conduct of the negotiation.

From the tenor of the ukase, the pretensions of the Imperial Government extend to an exclusive territorial jurisdiction from the forty-fifth degree of north latitude, on the Asiatic coast, to the latitude of fifty-one north on the western coast of the American continent; and they assume the right of interdicting the *navigation* and the fishery of all other nations to the extent of one hundred miles from the whole of that coast.

The United States can admit no part of these claims. Their right of navigation and of fishing is perfect, and has been in constant exercise from the earliest times, after the peace of 1783, throughout the whole extent of the Southern Ocean, subject only to the ordinary exceptions and exclusions of the territorial jurisdictions, which, so far as Russian rights are concerned, are confined to certain *islands* north of the fifty-fifth degree of latitude, and have no existence on the continent of America.

The correspondence between Mr. Poletica and this Department contained no discussion of the principles or of the facts upon which he attempted the justification of the Imperial ukase. This was purposely avoided on our part, under the expectation that the Imperial Government could not fail, upon a review of the measure, to revoke it altogether. It did, however, excite much public animadversion in this country, as the ukase itself had already done in England. I inclose herewith the North American Review for October, 1822, No. 37, which contains an article (p. 370) written by a person fully master of the subject; and for the view of it taken in England, I refer you to the 52d number of the Quarterly Review, the article upon Lieutenant Kotzebue's voyages. From the article in the North American Review it will be seen that the rights of discovery, of occupancy, and of uncontested possession, alleged by Mr. Poletica, are all without foundation in fact.

It does not appear that there ever has been a permanent Russian settlement on this continent, south of latitude 59; that of New Archangel, cited by Mr. Poletica, in latitude 57° 30', being upon an island. So far as prior *discovery* can constitute a foundation of right, the papers which I have referred to prove that it belongs to the United States as far as 59° north, by the transfer to them of the rights of Spain. There is, however, no part of the globe where the mere fact of discovery could be held to give weaker claims than on the Northwest Coast. "The great sinuosity," says Humboldt, "formed by the coast between the 55th and 60th parallels of latitude embraces discoveries made by Gali, Behring and Tchivikoff, Quadra, Cook, La Perouse, Malespier and Vancouver. No European nation has yet formed an establishment upon the immense extent of coast from Cape Mendosino to the 59th degree of latitude. Beyond that limit the Russian factories commence, most of which are scattered and distant from each other, like the factories established by the European nations for the last three centuries on the coast of Africa. Most of these little Russian colonies communicate with each other only by sea, and the new denominations of Russian America, or Russian possessions in the new continent, must not lead us to believe that the coast of Behring's bay, the peninsula of Alaska, or the country of the Ischugatschi, have become Russian *provinces* in the same sense given to the word when speaking of the Spanish provinces of Sonora, or New Biscay."—(Humboldt's New Spain, vol. 2d, book 3d, ch. 8, p. 496.)

In Mr. Poletica's letter of 28th February, 1822, to me, he says that when the Emperor Paul I granted to the present American Company its first charter in 1799, he gave it the *exclusive possession* of the Northwest Coast of America, which belonged to Russia, from the 55th degree of north latitude, to Behring's Strait.

In his letter of 2d of April, 1822, he says that the charter to the Russian American Company, in 1799, was merely conceding to them a part of the sovereignty, or *rather certain exclusive privileges of commerce.*

This is the most correct view of the subject. The Emperor Paul granted to the Russian American Company certain exclusive privileges of commerce—exclusive with reference to other Russian subjects; but Russia had never before *asserted* a right of sovereignty over any part of the North American continent; and in 1799 the people of the United States had been at least for twelve years in the constant and uninterrupted enjoyment of a profitable trade with the natives of that very coast, of which the ukase of the Emperor Paul could not deprive them.

It was in this same year, 1799, that the Russian settlement at Sitka was first made, and it was destroyed in 1802 by the natives of the country. There were, it seems, at the time of its destruction three American seamen, who perished with the rest, and a new settlement at the same place was made in 1804.

In 1808, Count Romanzoff, being then Minister of Foreign Affairs and of Commerce, addressed to Mr. Harris, consul of the United States at St. Petersburg, a letter, complaining of the traffic carried on by citizens of the United States with the native islanders of the Northwest Coast, *instead* of trading with the Russian possessions in America. The Count stated that the Russian Company had represented this traffic as *clandestine*, by which means the savage *islanders*, in exchange for otter skins, had been furnished with fire-arms and powder, with which they had destroyed a Russian fort, with the loss of several lives. He expressly disclaimed, however, any disposition on the part of Russia to abridge this traffic of the citizens of the United States, but proposed a convention to be carried on *exclusively* with the agents of the Russian American Company at Kodiack, a small island near the promontory of Alaska, at least 700 miles distant from the other settlement at Sitka.

On the 4th of January, 1810, Mr. Daschkoff, Chargé d'Affaires and Consul General from Russia, renewed this proposal of a convention, and requested, as an alternative, that the United States should, by a legislative act, prohibit the trade of their citizens with the natives of the Northwest Coast of America, as *unlawful and irregular*, and thereby induce them to carry on the trade exclusively with the agents of the Russian American Company. The answer of the Secretary of State, dated the 5th of May, 1810, declines those proposals for reasons which were then satisfactory to the Russian Government, or to which, at least, no reply on their part was made. Copies of these papers, and of those containing the instructions to the minister of the United States then at St. Petersburg, and the relation of his conferences with the chancellor of the empire, Count Romanzoff, on this subject, are herewith inclosed. By them it will be seen that the Russian Government at that time explicitly declined the assertion of *any* boundary line upon the Northwest Coast, and that the proposal of measures for confining the trade of the citizens of the United States exclusively to the Russian settlement at Kodiack, and with the agents of the Russian American Company, had been made by Count Romanzoff, under the impression that they would be as advantageous to the interests of the United States as to those of Russia.

It is necessary now to say that this impression was erroneous. That the traffic of the citizens of the United States with the natives of the Northwest Coast was neither *clandestine* nor unlawful nor irregular. That it had been enjoyed many years before the Russian American Company existed, and that it interfered with no lawful right or claim of Russia.

This trade has been shared, also, by the English, French, and Portuguese. In the prosecution of it, the English settlement of Nootka Sound was made, which occasioned the differences between Great Britain and Spain in 1789 and 1790, ten years before the Russian American Company was first chartered.

It was in the prosecution of this trade that the American settlement at the mouth of the Columbia river was made in 1811, which was taken by the British during the late war, and formally restored to them on the 6th of October, 1818. By the treaty of the 22d of February, 1819, with Spain, the United States acquired all the rights of Spain north of latitude 42°; and by the third article of the convention between the United States and Great Britain, of the 20th of October, 1818, it was agreed that any country that might be claimed by either party on the Northwest Coast of America, westward of the Stony mountains, should, together with its harbors, bays, and creeks, and the navigation of all rivers within the same, be free and open, for the term of ten years from that date, to the vessels, citizens, and subjects of the two powers, without prejudice to the claims of either party or of any other State.

You are authorized to propose an article of the same import for a term of ten years from the signature of a joint convention between the United States, Great Britain, and Russia.

The right of the United States from the forty-second to the forty-ninth parallel of latitude on the Pacific Ocean we consider as unquestionable, being founded, first, on the acquisition by the treaty of February 22, 1819, of all the rights of Spain; second, by the discovery of the Columbia river, first from sea, at its mouth, and then by land by Lewis and Clarke; and third, by the settlement at its mouth in 1811. This territory is to the United States of an importance which no possession in North America can be of to any European nation, not only as it is but the continuity of their possessions from the Atlantic to the Pacific Ocean, but as it offers their inhabitants the means of establishing hereafter water communications from the one to the other.

It is not conceivable that any possession upon the continent of North America should be of use or importance to Russia for any other purpose than that of traffic with the natives. This was, in fact, the inducement to the formation of the Russian American Company and to the charter granted them by the Emperor Paul. It was the inducement to the ukase of the Emperor Alexander. By offering free and equal access for a term of years to navigation and intercourse with the natives to Russia, within the limits to which our claims are indisputable, we concede much more than we obtain. It is not to be doubted that, long before the expiration of that time, our settlement at the mouth of the Columbia river will become so considerable as to offer means of useful commercial intercourse with the Russian settlements on the islands of the Northwest Coast.

With regard to the territorial claim, separate from the right of traffic with the natives and from any system of colonial exclusions, we are willing to agree to the boundary line within which the Emperor Paul had granted exclusive privileges to the Russian American Company, that is to say, latitude 55°.

If the Russian Government apprehend serious inconvenience from the illicit traffic of foreigners with their settlements on the Northwest Coast, it may be effectually guarded against by stipulations similar to those, a draft of which is herewith subjoined, and to which you are authorized, on the part of the United States, to agree.

As the British ambassador at St. Petersburg is authorized and instructed to negotiate likewise upon this subject, it may be proper to adjust the interests and claims of the three powers by a joint convention. Your full power is prepared accordingly.

Instructions conformable to these will be forwarded to Mr. Rush at London, with authority to communicate with the British Government in relation to this interest, and to correspond with you concerning it, with a view to the maintenance of the rights of the United States.

I am, &c.,

JOHN QUINCY ADAMS.

HENRY MIDDLETON,
   Envoy Extraordinary and Minister Plenipotentiary of the United States, St. Petersburg.

ARTICLE 1. In order to strengthen the bonds of friendship, and to preserve, in future, a perfect harmony and good understanding between the contracting parties, it is agreed that their respective citizens and subjects shall not be disturbed or molested, either in navigating or in carrying on their fisheries in the Pacific Ocean or in the South Seas, or in landing on the coasts of those seas in places not already occupied, for the purpose of carrying on their commerce with the natives of the country; subject, nevertheless, to the restrictions and provisions specified in the two following articles.

ARTICLE 2. To the end that the navigation and fishery of the citizens and subjects of the contracting parties, respectively, in the Pacific Ocean or in the South Seas, may not be made a pretext for illicit trade with their respective settlements, it is agreed that the citizens of the United States shall not land on any part of the coast actually occupied by Russian settlements, unless by permission of the Governor or commander thereof, and that Russian subjects shall, in like manner, be interdicted from landing without permission at any settlement of the United States on the said Northwest Coast.

ARTICLE 3. It is agreed that no settlement shall be made hereafter on the Northwest Coast of America by citizens of the United States or under their authority, nor by Russian subjects, or under the authority of Russia, south of the fifty-fifth degree of north latitude.

No. 3, (a.)

JAMES MONROE,

PRESIDENT OF THE UNITED STATES OF AMERICA,

To all to whom these presents may come, greeting:

KNOW YE, That, reposing special trust and confidence in the integrity, prudence, and abilities of Henry Middleton, Envoy Extraordinary and Minister Plenipotentiary of the United States at the court of his Imperial Majesty the Emperor of all the Russias, I have invested him with full and all manner of power, for and in the name of the United States, to meet and confer with any person or persons furnished with like powers on the part of his said Imperial Majesty, and with him or them to negotiate and conclude a convention or conventions, treaty or treaties, of and concerning the commerce and navigation of the two countries; of and concerning their respective rights and claims in respect to navigation, fishery, and commerce, on the Northwest Coast of America and the ocean and islands thereto adjoining or appertaining; of and concerning the abolition of the African slave trade; and of and concerning the principles of maritime war and neutrality. And I do further invest him with full power, also, to meet and confer on the said subjects with any person or persons furnished with like powers on the part of his Majesty the King of the United Kingdom of Great Britain and Ireland; and with the said Russian and British plenipotentiaries jointly to conclude a treaty or treaties, convention or conventions, in relation to the respective rights and claims of the three powers in and to the said navigation, fishery, commerce, and territorial possessions on the said Northwest Coast of America and adjoining ocean and islands; or in relation to the abolition of the African slave trade; or in relation to the principles of maritime war and neutrality; he, the said Henry Middleton, transmitting any and every such convention or treaty, whether concluded jointly with British and Russian, or severally with Russian plenipotentiaries, to the President of the United States, for his ratification, by and with the advice and consent of the Senate of the United States, if the same shall be given.

In testimony whereof, I have caused the seal of the United States to be hereunto affixed. Given under [L. S.] my hand, at the city of Washington, the twenty-ninth day of July, anno Domini 1823, and of the Independence of the United States of America the forty-eighth.

JAMES MONROE.

By the President:
JOHN QUINCY ADAMS,
    Secretary of State.

No. 3, (b.)

Mr. Daschkoff to Mr. Smith.

[Translation.]

The undersigned, Chargé d'Affaires and Consul General of his Majesty the Emperor of all the Russias, in conformity with the orders of his Government, has the honor to address to the Secretary of State of the United States the copy of the note of his excellency the Count de Romanzoff, Minister of Foreign Affairs and Commerce of his Imperial Majesty, to Mr. Levett Harris, Consul General of the United States at St. Petersburg, under date of the 17th of May, 1808, and that of Mr. Harris' reply to the Russian minister, relative to the illicit trade carried on by vessels of the United States with the natives of his Imperial Majesty's possessions on the Northwest Coast of America.

The Secretary of State will there perceive that his Majesty the Emperor, ever anxious for the happiness of his people, could not but learn with regret the injurious effects attending the illicit trade of some Americans with the natives of the said possessions of his Imperial Majesty, upon that portion of his subjects who, by their proximity to the United States, might cultivate relations of commerce with their citizens with reciprocal and increasing advantage, if they were properly regulated, and in accordance with the principles of equity and the law of nations.

The undersigned, therefore, prays the Secretary of State to communicate to his excellency the President of the United States the subject of the above note of the minister of his Imperial Majesty. The

Russian Government, persuaded of the friendship existing between both States, and assured of their mutual desire to strengthen this connexion, believes that the Government of the United States will not refuse to terminate, by proper and sufficient means, the illicit trade of some American speculators on the Northwest Coast of America and the adjacent islands, by which the security of the subjects of the said possessions of his Imperial Majesty is not only endangered, but has been violated, as also that of many citizens of the United States.

In exhibiting the dangerous consequences of the trade which some Americans carry on in articles contraband of war with the natives of said countries, who, from their savage character, are frequently excited to insurrection, and make use thereof to destroy the establishments and commerce of his Imperial Majesty's subjects, the undersigned cannot refrain from mentioning to the Secretary of State the opinion entertained by the Russian Government in regard to the commercial relations of the United States and the possessions of his Imperial Majesty on the Northwest Coast of America, an opinion which he has frequently found among American merchants.

It consists in the important advantages that might be derived from a law of the Government of the United States which, in drawing off its citizens from an illicit and irregular trade with the natives of the Northwest Coast of America, prejudicial to both nations, would induce them to trade in those countries exclusively with the factory or agents of the Russian Company. The utility of it would be real and reciprocal. By suppressing in this way a small number of adventurers, who, by a trade without regularity, without calculation, with operations committed to chance, may obstruct the progress of mutual relations, and destroy rather than strengthen this rising branch of commerce, it might be expected that these relations would daily become firmer and more extensive, whilst subjected to a certain judicious and prudent regulation.

If his excellency the President should also be of opinion that the idea suggested by the minister of his Imperial Majesty to the Consul General of the United States, of stipulating, by a convention, the above arrangement of commerce between the United States and the Russian establishments on the Northwest Coast of America, may be carried into effect, as the most proper means of preventing all future complaint, and of strengthening the connexions of amity and good feeling that subsist between the two States, the undersigned has the honor to inform the Secretary of State that he is clothed with the necessary powers for entering upon that negotiation.

The undersigned, requesting the Secretary of State to communicate to him his views of the subject before mentioned, seizes this occasion to renew to the Secretary of State the assurance of his high esteem and distinguished consideration.

ANDRE DE DASCHKOFF.

PHILADELPHIA, *January* 4, 1810.

·No. 3, (c.)

Count Romanzoff to Mr. Harris.

[Translation.]

The commercial establishment here, under the name of the American Company, has repeatedly represented to the undersigned, Minister of Foreign Affairs and of Commerce, that the ships of the United States, instead of trading with the Russian possessions in America, have there carried on a clandestine trade with the savages, to whom, in exchange for otter skins, they furnish fire-arms and powder, the use of which, till then unknown to these islanders, has been in their hands very prejudicial to the subjects of his Imperial Majesty.

By means of these arms a Russian fort has been destroyed and a number of persons have lost their lives.

Some citizens of the United States, themselves deceived by an unfortunate carelessness for the offensive means of these savages, have become the victims of the imprudent speculation of their countrymen.

Pursuant to these established facts, the undersigned has been charged by the Emperor, his august master, to communicate them to Mr. Harris, Consul General of the United States, requesting him to make them known to his Government, and to call their serious attention thereto. The care which they take to show the scrupulous connexion of their interests with those of other powers and their respect for the principles of the law of nations induce the hope that this illicit traffic will meet with their disapprobation, and that positive orders will put a stop to it.

Very far, however, from wishing to obstruct the commercial relations between the two nations in the said Russian possessions, his Imperial Majesty, on the contrary, would behold with satisfaction their increase; but, to avoid the pernicious consequences of a clandestine trade with the savages, he would wish that a commerce of exchange were established exclusively at Kodiack, and with the agents of the company. For this purpose, the undersigned, believing that it would be mutually useful to stipulate the above mentioned object by a convention, has the honor to propose the matter to Mr. Harris, as the most proper to remove every successive complaint and to strengthen the bonds of amity and of good understanding which subsist between the two countries; the undersigned anxiously believing that Mr. Harris will do full justice to the personal dispositions which he has uniformly shown, on his part, in either administration, in favor of the commerce of the citizens of the United States.

Requesting, therefore, the Consul General to communicate to him his ideas upon the subject above expressed, the undersigned seizes with pleasure this occasion of renewing to him the assurance of his most distinguished consideration.

THE COUNT ROMANZOFF.

ST. PETERSBURG, *May* 17, 1808.
    Copy conformable to the original.
        ANDRE DASCHKOFF.

No. 3, (d.)

Mr. Smith to Mr. Adams.

DEPARTMENT OF STATE, *May* 5, 1810.

SIR: You will herewith receive copies of a letter from Mr. Daschkoff, and of my answer. They relate, as you will perceive, to a subject of a very delicate character. The Russian Government, it would seem, considers the United States bound to restrain their citizens from trading in warlike articles with the Indians connected with the Russian establishments on the Northwestern Coast of America. This is manifestly an error. If the Indians be under the Russian jurisdiction, the United States are bound only to leave their citizens to the penalties operating within the territorial limits. If the Indians are to be considered as independent tribes inhabiting an independent territory, Russia cannot of right prohibit other nations from trading with them, unless it be in contraband of war, during a state of war, in which case she may enforce the prohibition on the high seas. If the Indians should fall under the character of rebels or insurgents against Russian authority, the same rule may be applicable.

In this view of the subject, the United States being under no legal obligation to comply with the demand of Russia, they cannot otherwise be brought under such obligation than by compact, and whatever disposition they may feel to seek for a foundation for such a compact, in consideration of reciprocity and of friendship, it would be difficult to attain the end in that mode without maintaining a right which this nation has not yet asserted, in opposition to the Spanish claim to the Western Coast of America south of that of Russia, and consequently without a contest unseasonable and premature, at least with the Spaniards.

The United States might, indeed, by a gratuitous regulation, yield to the wishes of the Emperor on this subject, and certainly it would be very agreeable to them to give proofs, on every occasion, of their friendship for his Imperial Majesty. But such a measure is not within the authority of the Executive, and could not well be formally proposed to the Legislature without the usual basis of mutual stipulations.

These remarks may assist you in placing the subject before the Russian Government in a light best fitted to satisfy them. It may be added that, as Russia has the means of enforcing its own rights against those who intrude on the coast possessed by her, or who are carrying implements of war to be used in hostility against her, it cannot be essential that any foreign power should co-operate with her for the purpose.

In explaining the sentiments of the United States on this occasion, it will be advisable for you to bring into view the hopes of the United States that it will be found consistent with the liberal policy of the Emperor to favor a commerce of the Americans in innocent articles, both with the Russians and Indians in that quarter, and even their intercession in the trade between the Russian establishments and China.

As it does not appear how far the Russians stretch their claim southwardly, along the coast, it is material that some latitude be fixed as the limit, and it is desirable, as the coast south of it will enter into the plan of Indian trade likely to be embraced by our citizens, that the limit should be as little advanced southwardly as may be. It appears, from what passed between Spain and Great Britain, in the affair of Nootka Sound, in the year 1790, that the claim of the former extended to the 60th degree of latitude.

I have the honor to be, &c.,

R. SMITH.

JOHN Q. ADAMS, Esq., *St. Petersburg.*

No. 3, (e.)

Mr. Daschkoff to Mr. Smith.

PHILADELPHIA, *le* 24 *Avril*, 1810.

A mon depart de Washington vous avez paru desirer de savoir le tems où j'expederai mon rapport au Ministère Imperial concernant la negociation que j'ai eu l'honneur d'entamer avec vous, a fin d'envoyer à la même epoque des instructions relatives à cette affaire à votre ministère, près de ma cour, dans le cas qu'elle puisse se terminer à St. Petersbourg.

Je me fais un plaisir de vous informer, monsieur, qu'ayant rencontré, à la fin, un passager d'un batiment destiné pour la Russie, à qui je peux confier mes depéches, et qui doit partir la sémaine prochaine, je vais profiter de cette occassion favorable. Si vous desirez que les votres parviennent à Monsieur Adams par la même voie, je me charge de les lui faire parvenir avec autant de sùreté, que je peux compter pour les miennes.

J'ai mandé a mon Governement que ma negociation, rélative au trafic des Americains des articles de contrebande de guerre avec les naturels dans nos establissemens, a été remise; que Monsieur le President ayant appris que je n'etois pas authorisé de fixer une latitude, au sud de nos establissemens, pour servir de ligne de dimarcation au batimens Americains que feroient le commerce de ces côtes, trouve de la difficulté de passer une loi precise par la quelle le trafic de la contrebande doit être prohibé au dé la d'un certain degré; que son excellence n'a pas cru les inconveniens obviés, par la proposition, que j'ai eu l'honneur de vous faire ensuite, de substituer à une latitude nommée la fixation de quelque degres au dessous de nôtre demier etablissement, situé au sud-est, jusqu'à ce qu'on aura des nouvelles exactes sur sa situation geographique. J'ai aussi informé mon Governement, que Monsieur le President n'a pas jugé d'entrer dans des détails ulterieurs de ma negociation, avant que je ne reçoive des pouvoir plus étendus, ou que mon Gouvernement ne choisisse de la terminer avec vôtre ministère prés de sa Majesté Imperiale. Il m'a été très agreable de rendre compte en même tems, au Ministère Imperiale, des assurances reiterées que vous m'avez données des dispositions favorables de son excellence aux desirs de mon Gouvernement.

Je saisis avec empressement cette occasion de vous communiquer, Monsieur, un paragraphe d'une dépéche, datée du 12 Novembre, du Ministère des Affaires Etrangeres de sa Majesté Imperiale, qui m'est parvenue depuis peu. Je suis persuadé, qu'il ne manquera pas de vous être très agreable.

"L'accueil qu'a fait l'Empereur à Mr. Adams, a dû le convaincre que si sa destination etoit agreable à sa Majesté la choix de sa personne n'y contribuait pas moins. Recommendable par le nom qu'il porte, ainsi que par ses qualités personelles, ces titres ont été justement appreciés par sa Majesté Imperiale." Je ne doute pas, Monsieur que son Excellence le President des Etats Unis n'en réssente une satisfaction personelle de l'attention de sa Majesté l'Empereur à son choix.

Je vous prie de me croire, &c., &c.

ANDRE DE DASCHKOFF.

ROBERT SMITH, Esq., *Secretary of State of the United States.*

No. 3, *(e.)*

Mr. Daschkoff to Mr. Smith, Secretary of State.

[Translation]

PHILADELPHIA, *April* 24, 1810.

At my departure from Washington you appeared desirous of knowing the time when I was to send my report to the Imperial Ministry concerning the negotiation which I had the honor of commencing with you, in order to send, at the same time, instructions relative to that affair to your minister near my court, in case it could be terminated at St. Petersburg.

I am happy to inform you, sir, that having at last met with a passenger of a ship bound for Russia to whom I can entrust my despatches, and who must depart the ensuing week, I shall take advantage of this favorable opportunity. If you wish to forward yours to Mr. Adams by the same way, I undertake for their reaching him with as much safety as I can reckon on for my own.

I have written to my Government that my negotiation relative to the trade of the Americans in articles of contraband of war with the natives in our establishments has been suspended; that the President, having learned that I was not authorized to fix a latitude to the south of our establishments to serve as a line of demarkation to the American ships which trade on these coasts, finds difficulty in passing a precise law by which the traffic of contraband should be prohibited beyond a certain degree; that his excellency did not think the inconveniences obviated by the proposition which I had afterwards the honor of making to you, of substituting a latitude named, as a boundary, some degrees below our last establishment situated to the southeast, until there should be exact accounts of its geographical situation. I have also informed my Government that the President had determined not to enter into any further details of my negotiations until I should receive more extended powers, or my Government should choose to terminate it with your minister near his Imperial Majesty. I have had very great pleasure in stating, at the same time, to the Imperial Ministry the repeated assurances which you have given me of the favorable dispositions of his excellency to the desires of my Government.

I embrace, with pleasure, sir, this opportunity of communicating to you a paragraph of a despatch, dated November 10, (22,) from the Minister of Foreign Affairs of his Imperial Majesty, which has come to my hand lately. I am persuaded that it will not fail of being very agreeable to you. "The reception which the Emperor has given to Mr. Adams ought to convince him that, if his appointment was agreeable to his Majesty, the choice of his person contributed no less to his pleasure. Commendable by the name which he bears, as well as by his personal qualities, these titles have been justly appreciated by his Imperial Majesty." I doubt not, sir, that his excellency the President of the United States has received personal satisfaction from the attention of his Majesty the Emperor to his choice.

I pray you to believe me, &c., &c.,

ANDRE DE DASCHKOFF.

No. 3, *(f.)*

Mr. Smith to Mr. Daschkoff.

DEPARTMENT OF STATE, *May* 5, 1810.

SIR: Your letter of the 24th ultimo, which I have had the honor of receiving, has been laid before the President of the United States. Sincerely anxious to foster the friendly relations existing between Russia and the United States, the President will have great satisfaction in any equitable arrangement relative to the traffic of Americans with the natives of the Russian establishments. Your instructions not having authorized you to fix a precise line of demarkation, no definitive adjustment could, therefore, be possibly made. But, had this difficulty been removed, others of a very delicate character would have occurred. These I will now present to your view.

If the Indians be under the Russian jurisdiction the United States are bound only to leave their citizens to the penalties operating within the territorial limits. If the Indians are to be considered as independent tribes, inhabiting an independent territory, Russia cannot, of right, prohibit other nations from trading with them, unless it be in contraband of war in a state of war, in which case she may enforce the prohibition on the high seas. If the Indians should fall under the character of rebels, or insurgents, against Russian authority, the same rule may be applicable. In this view of the subject, the United States being under no legal obligation to comply with the demand of Russia, they cannot otherwise be brought under such obligation than by compact, and whatever disposition they may feel to seek for a foundation for such a compact in consideration of reciprocity and of friendship, it would be difficult to attain the end in that mode without maintaining a right which this nation has not yet asserted, in opposition to the Spanish claim to the Western Coast of America, south of that of Russia, and, consequently, without a contest, unseasonable and premature, at least with the Spaniards. The United States might, indeed, by a gratuitous regulation, yield to the wishes of the Emperor on this subject, and certainly it would be very agreeable to them to give proofs on every occasion of their friendship for his Imperial Majesty. But such a measure is not within the authority of the Executive, and could not well be formally proposed to the Legislature, without the usual basis of mutual stipulations.

The paragraph of the despatch from the Minister of Foreign Affairs of his Imperial Majesty, which you have done me the honor of communicating to me, has afforded the President great satisfaction, as will every circumstance of an aspect auspicious to the lasting good understanding between the two countries.

I have the honor to be, &c.,

R. SMITH.

Mr. DASCHKOFF, &c., &c.

No. 3, (g.)

Extract of a letter from Mr. Adams (No. 23) to Mr. Robert Smith, Secretary of State, dated

ST. PETERSBURG, *September* 5, 1810.

" The day after I had the honor of receiving the duplicate of your despatches, dated 5th May and 5th June last, I had a conference with the chancellor, Count Romanzoff, in which I mentioned to him that I received those despatches, observing, however, that I was referred by them to other documents which I have not yet received. He said that he had also received despatches from Mr. Daschkoff, stating that his application had been favorably received by the Government of the United States. That this Government had a growing settlement on the Northwest Coast of America, from which a very profitable trade might be carried on to China. They had sent two public ships there, under the command of Captain Krusenstern, which had proceeded from thence to Canton, in China. Canton was a port open to all the nations of Europe; but the Russians, who were specially favored by the Chinese Government, had an exclusive trade with them, carried on at a place called Kiachta. The Chinese had refused to admit Captain Krusenstern, under the cunning pretext, that, as the Russian trade with them had long been carried on overland, with exclusive privileges at Kiachta, they supposed that if the Russians had meant to change the channels of trade they would have given them notice of it. And as they had heard nothing about such vessels coming to Canton beforehand, although they gave themselves out for Russians, the Chinese Government could not tell whether they were such or not, and therefore had refused to receive them. There had been, the Count said, some *sheets* passed between the two Governments since on the subject, but the convulsed state of Europe, and other objects of so much greater magnitude, had so much absorbed his attention that they had not yet come to any arrangement with them for the admission of Russian vessels at Canton. He had therefore wished that the trade from the Russian settlements on the Northwest Coast of America to China might be carried on by the Americans. And as the settlement itself was in the neighborhood of Indians who were sometimes troublesome and dangerous neighbors to it, he had thought an arrangement might be concerted with the United States under which the Americans might have the trade of the settlement, subject to a restriction not to furnish warlike weapons and materials to the neighboring Indians.

" I told him that I collected from the papers which I had received that Mr. Daschkoff was not specifically instructed as to the limits within which it was wished that this restriction should be extended, and asked him whether he could point them out to me. He said that it would require some consideration, but that their maps included the whole of Nootka Sound and down to the mouth of Columbia river as a part of the Russian possessions. It will be unnecessary for me to say anything further to the Count upon this subject until I shall have received your original despatch, inclosing the copy of Mr. Daschkoff's letter to you containing the proposal on the part of Russia. I do not imagine that it is the Count's serious intention to claim to the mouth of the Columbia river; but perhaps the fixing upon a boundary may present difficulties to the proposed convention which had not been anticipated. In the meantime, the Count manifested no objection to the carrying on of the trade between the settlements by American vessels. And as Russian vessels are not admitted at Canton, it is much for the interest of the settlement that vessels which have access there should come and take their peltries to carry there. This can be done so conveniently and, probably, so cheaply by no others as by the Americans."

No. 3, (h.)

Extract of a letter (No. 25) from Mr. Adams to Mr. Smith, Secretary of State, dated,

ST. PETERSBURG, *September* 30, 1810.

" In the course of a few days I purpose to ask a conference with the chancellor, Count Romanzoff, on the subject referred to in Mr. Daschkoff's letter. The difficulty of fixing upon a boundary within which a prohibition of trade could be stipulated, I suppose, will not easily be removed. I know not whether it had been contemplated when the proposition was first made, but the necessity of fixing upon a line is obvious. Mr. Harris has communicated to me copies of his correspondence with Count Romanzoff and the memorials of the Russian American Company relative to this object. I find by them that the Russian claim, even then, was asserted to the mouth of the Columbia river."

No. 3, *(i.)*

Extract of a letter (No. 27.) from Mr. Adams to Mr. Smith, Secretary of State, giving an account of a conference with Count Romanzoff, dated

St. Petersburg, *October* 12, 1810.

"The Count requested me to call upon him, on the 9th instant, at eleven in the forenoon, which I accordingly did. I told him that I had now received from the United States the despatches respecting the proposition which had been made by Mr. Daschkoff, in relation to the trade with the Indians on the Northwest Coast of America; that I was instructed, in the first instance, to declare the sincere and earnest desire of the President of the United States to concur in any measure which might be useful to the Russian dominions, and agreeable to his Imperial Majesty; that some difficulties had occurred to the American Government with regard to the nature of the stipulation which had been suggested as desirable by Mr. Daschkoff. The people of the United States were so extensively engaged in commercial navigation to all parts of the world that the traffic with the Indians on the Northwest Coast could not be prevented, unless by special prohibitions of law—prohibitions which it would seem almost, if not altogether, impracticable to carry fully into execution. The Russians were a nation not so much addicted to navigation as my countrymen, and yet he, the Count, was well aware how ineffectual the prohibitions to send vessels to particular foreign countries were to prevent them from going thither, in fact.

"If such was the experience of this Government, the difficulties must be obviously much greater in preventing a trade so distant with wandering savages, scattered along a coast over several degrees of latitude, having no ports or custom-houses, not even permanent dwelling places, from which it would be possible to collect evidence of any transgression of the law. That even were a convention concluded to prohibit this traffic, the Indians would probably still get their supplies, if not from our vessels, yet from the English, either by water or by land, from the English settlements north of us. And although nothing could be easier than to draw an article of a convention to prohibit the trade, it would indicate a want of frankness and candor in the United States to contract such engagements, and then find them not executed. For, although it should arise from a state of things not within their control, it would be manifest that such a state of things ought to have been considered before the contract was formed. I was, however, instructed to inquire what would be the boundary line within which it was the wish of this Government to extend the prohibition?—a question which I had intimated in a former conference, immediately after receiving your despatches, which first came to hand on this subject.

"The Count answered me that he would render to the Emperor an exact report of the observations I had now made to him; that it was an object concerning which they had no great solicitude. Their first idea had been that this trade with the Indians, especially as to the article of fire-arms, might be as detrimental to the United States themselves as to the Russian settlement, and more so. That in that point of view the United States might find it expedient to issue the prohibition, provided it were compatible with our constitutions. He did not think it possible for those supplies of arms to be furnished to those Indians from the British settlements by land. The distance and the wilderness between them were too wide. A voyage by an American vessel round Cape Horn was much easier, and it was, in fact, by that means that the savages had been furnished with the weapons which they had used against the Russian settlement. He must do the English the justice to say, although they were at war with Russia, he had not received any complaint that the Indians had ever received any supplies from them.

"I told him it was what they were in the constant habit of doing, even when at peace with us, to the Indians within our boundaries, and the Spaniards had formerly done the same.

"With regard to a mutual stipulation, the Count said he must candidly confess there was no basis for it. To engage that the Russians should not thus trade would be nugatory, as no Russian vessels traded there, and there was no privilege which could be granted for trade with the Russian settlement but which now existed *de facto*. What might be done at a future period, if the settlement should become an object of important consideration, he could not say; but now the trade of all nations there was perfectly free. As to the fixing of a boundary, it would be most advisable to defer that to some future time, for the sake of avoiding all possible collision, and even every pretext for uneasiness or jealousy. In the present state of the world, the first and strongest wish of his heart was to bring all the civilized nations to pacific dispositions, and most carefully to avoid everything which could strike out a single new spark of discord among them. At any rate, I might be assured of the continuance of the Emperor's amicable dispositions towards the United States."

No. 3, *(k.)*

Observations on the claim of Russia to territorial possessions on the continent of North America, communicated with Mr. Adam's letter to Mr. Middleton of July 22, 1823.

It is assumed as an indisputable fact, that, before the third and last voyage of Captain Cook, no European settlement had been formed on the Northwest Coast of the American continent north of Cape Mendocino, or of the fortieth degree of north latitude.

The account of that voyage was published under the direction of the British Government in 1784. In the introduction to it, written by Dr. Douglass, Bishop of Salisbury, among the advantages enumerated as derivable to all mankind from the discoveries which had been made in the progress of that undertaking, was the opening of a valuable trade in furs from the Northwest Coast of America, and particularly from King George's or Nootka Sound to China.

This advantage was also pointed out in various passages of the work itself, both by Captain Cook, in the two volumes written by him, and by Captain King, the author of the third and concluding volume.

The only place on the Northwestern American Coast where Captain Cook found a Russian settlement was at Onalashka, one of the Aleutian islands; the principal person of which settlement, *Ismaeloff*, and the other Russians whom he met there, "affirmed that they *knew nothing* of the continent of America to the northward."

The *first* Russian settlement, at Kodiack, was made by Shelekoff, in the winter of 1748.—*(Coxe's Russian Discoveries, p. 215.)* In 1786, the first English trading voyage between the Northwest Coast of America and China was undertaken, and was prosecuted under the command and direction of Lieutenant Meares.

A similar expedition was undertaken in 1787, at Boston, in the United States, whence two vessels, the *Washington* and *Columbia,* were despatched. It was by the commander of one of these vessels that the great river of the west was discovered, and from her received its name. Until that time the only European nation which *pretended* to an *exclusive* right on the Western Coast of the American continent was SPAIN.

These commercial expeditions, as well as the Russian *attempts* to make settlements at the northern extremity of the American continent, excited the jealousy of the Spanish Government, and produced the seizure, in May, 1789, of two English vessels at Nootka Sound, by Don Estevan Joseph Martinez, commander of two Spanish vessels-of-war despatched by the Viceroy of Mexico from the port of San Blas, to which place they were taken, but where they were released by order of the Viceroy.

At the time of this seizure the American vessels, the Washington and Columbia, were likewise in the harbor of Nootka Sound, but were not molested by the Spanish commander, Martinez. This difference of treatment between the British and American vessels was alleged to be because the former appeared to be there for the purposes of trade and settlement, while it appeared from the papers of the latter that they were driven there by distress, and only came in to refit.

This transaction gave rise to the remarkable Nootka Sound dispute between Spain and Great Britain, which for some time threatened an immediate war between those two nations.

Martinez had taken possession of the lands at Nootka Sound, upon which Lieutenant Meares had built a temporary habitation, "pulled down the British flag and hoisted the standard of Spain thereon, with such ceremonies as are usual upon such occasions;" declaring at the same time "that all the lands comprised between Cape Horn and the sixtieth degree of north latitude did belong to his Catholic Majesty." This claim was asserted by Spain in all the diplomatic papers of that controversy, the following passages from which prove how erroneous the assertions of Mr. Poletica, in his letter of February 28, 1822, were, that the Spanish Government at that time acknowledged that its possessions ought not to extend beyond the latitude of 42° 50' north. They will also give a very sufficient reason why Martinez gave no disturbance to the Russian colonies and navigators, none of which had then reached within ten degrees of latitude from Nootka Sound.

Extracts from the memorial of the Court of Spain, delivered June 13, 1790, to Mr. Fitzherbert, the British Ambassador at Madrid.—(Annual Register, 1790, p. 294, State Papers.)

"The vast extent of the Spanish territories, navigation, and dominion, on the continent of America, isles and seas, contiguous to the South Sea, are clearly laid down and authenticated by a variety of documents, laws, and formal acts of possession, in the reign of King Charles II. It is also clearly ascertained that, notwithstanding the repeated attempts made by adventurers and pirates on the Spanish coasts of the South Sea and adjacent islands, Spain has still preserved her possessions entire, and opposed with success those usurpations by constantly sending her ships and vessels to take possession of such settlements. By these measures and reiterated acts of possession Spain has preserved her dominion, which she has extended to the borders of the Russian establishments in that part of the world.

"The Viceroys of Peru and New Spain having been informed that these seas had been for some years past more frequented than formerly; that smuggling had increased; that several usurpations prejudicial to Spain and the general tranquillity had been suffered to be made, they gave orders that the Western Coasts of Spanish America and islands and seas adjacent should be more frequently navigated and explored.

"They were also informed that several Russian vessels were upon the point of making commercial establishments upon that coast. At the time that Spain demonstrated to Russia the inconveniences attendant upon such encroachments, she entered upon the negotiation with Russia, upon the supposition that the Russian navigators of the Pacific Ocean had no orders to make establishments within the limits of Spanish America, of which the Spaniards were the first possessors, (limits situated within Prince William's Strait,) purposely to avoid all dissensions, and in order to maintain the harmony and amity which Spain wished to preserve.

"The court of Russia replied, it had already given orders that its subjects should make no settlements in places belonging to other powers, and that if those orders had been violated, and any had been made in Spanish America, they desired the King would put a stop to them in a friendly manner. To this pacific language on the part of Russia, Spain observed that she could not be answerable for what her officers might do at that distance, whose general orders and instructions were not to permit any settlements to be made by other nations on the continent of Spanish America."

Extract from Count Florida Blanca's reply to Mr. Fitzherbert, June 18, 1790.—(Annual Register, page 299, State Papers.)

"You will pardon me, sir, that I cannot give my assent to the principles laid down in your last letter, as Spain maintains, on the most solid grounds, that the detention of the vessels was made in a port, upon a coast, or in a bay of Spanish America, the commerce and navigation of which belonged, exclusively, to Spain, by treaties with all nations, even England herself. The principles laid down cannot be adapted to the case. The vessels detained attempted to make an establishment at a port where they found a nation actually settled, the Spanish commander at Nootka having, previous to their detention, made the most amicable representations to the aggressors to desist from their purpose."

Extract from the letter of Count Fernan Nunez to Mr. Montmorin, Secretary of the Foreign Department of France, Paris, June 16, 1790.—(Annual Register, page 301, State Papers.)

"I have the honor to address you with this a faithful extract of all the transactions which have hitherto passed between my court and that of London, on the subject of the detention of two English vessels which were seized in the bay of St. Lawrence or Nootka, situated in the fiftieth degree to the north of California, and which were afterwards taken to the port of San Blas.

"You will observe by this relation—

"1. That, by the treaties, demarkations, takings of possession, and the most decided acts of sove_reignty, exercised by the Spaniards in these stations from the reign of Charles II, and authorized by that monarch in 1692, the original vouchers for which shall be brought forward in the course of the negotiation, *all the coast to the north of the western America, on the side of the South Sea, as far as beyond what is called Prince William's Sound, which is in the sixty-first degree, is acknowledged to belong exclusively to Spain.*

"2. That the court of Russia, having been informed of this extent of our boundary, assured the King, my master, without the least delay, of the purity of its intentions in this respect, and added, 'That it was extremely sorry that the repeated orders issued to prevent the subjects of Russia from violating, in the smallest degree, the territory belonging to another power, should have been disobeyed.'"

By these papers it is demonstrated—

That, at that time, the claim of Spain to exclusive possession of the Northwest Coast extended *beyond* Prince William's Sound, in latitude 61.

That the court of Russia had been informed of this extent of the Spanish boundary; had disclaimed any intention of interfering with it, and added expressions of its sorrow that its repeated orders to prevent the subjects of Russia from violating the territory belonging to another power had been disobeyed.

So far was Russia, in 1790, from asserting any claim whatsoever to territory on the continent of North America.

The ground assumed by Great Britain in the Nootka Sound controversy was, that British subjects ' had been forcibly interrupted in a trade which they had carried on for years, without molestation, in parts of America where they had an incontrovertible right of trading, and in places to which *no country* could claim an exclusive right of commerce and navigation;" that "the court of Madrid had advanced a claim to the exclusive right of navigation in those seas that was unfounded and exorbitant, indefinite in its consequences, aiming destruction to the valuable fisheries (of the British subjects) in the southern ocean, and tending to the annihilation of a commerce in its infancy, just beginning to be carried on to the profit of Britain, in hitherto unfrequented parts of the globe."—(*Annual Register for* 1790, *p.* 96.)

The result of the contest was, that Spain receded from her claim of exclusive right to navigation, commerce, or territory north of those parts already occupied by Spain, but that wherever settlements, either British or Spanish, had been made since April, 1789, or wherever they should thereafter be made, the subjects of the other party should have free access and should carry on their trade without any disturbance or molestation.

By the convention of October 28, 1790, it was agreed that the buildings and tracts of land situated on the Northwest Coast of the continent of North America, or on the islands adjacent to that continent, of which the subjects of his Britannic Majesty were dispossessed about the month of April, 1789, by a Spanish officer, shall be restored to the said British subjects.

In June, 1794, this restitution was partially effected, but not completely, in consequence of a disagreement between the Spanish officer, Quadra, and Captain Vancouver, as to the *extent* of the order of restitution in the letter from Count Florida Blanca.

At *that* time it was ascertained by Captain Vancouver that the extremest eastern Russian settlement on the Northwest Coast was at Port Etches, on Hinchinbrook island, latitude 60, in Prince William's Sound.

In 1799 the settlement at New Archangel was first made.

The Spanish settlement at Nootka Sound was undoubtedly made with the view to maintain the claim of that nation to the exclusive *possession* of the whole Northwest Coast. Its abandonment in 1794 was reluctant, and with pretensions, still retained, that the exclusive right of Spain, recognized in the 5th article of the convention of the 28th of October, 1790, extended to the immediate vicinity of that spot. Vancouver refused to receive the restoration upon the terms on which it was offered. He received it as a *Spanish* settlement, and it was abandoned by both nations.

The first purchases of lands from the native inhabitants of the Northwest Coast were made by the adventurers in the Washington and Columbia. They were made at Nootka, and from the chief, Maqninna.

The principle upon which the convention between Great Britain and Spain of October 28, 1790, was concluded was, that the Northwest Coast of America, north of the Spanish settlements actually made, could not be considered as the exclusive property of *any* European nation. It has been seen that Russia, so far from claiming any such exclusive property at that time, had just before, in substance, *admitted* that of Spain to beyond Prince William's Sound, in latitude sixty-one.

The only object of present interest, for which all these settlements on the Northwest Coast have been made, whether by Russians, English, or Americans, has been the traffic with the native inhabitants in furs, for the Chinese market. This trade has, in point of fact, not only been enjoyed by the citizens of the United States, but has been prosecuted by them to a greater extent than by all the others together. It has been combined with a trade in sandal wood from the Sandwich Islands to China; and during the long wars in which Europe was involved, from 1790 to 1815, it was left almost entirely to them.

In 1816 a Russian settlement was made at Atooi, one of the Sandwich Islands, and another near the coast of California, within a few leagues of San Francisco, the most northern Spanish settlement. If the motive of these establishments was to lay the foundation for an exclusive territorial claim of Russia to the Northwest Coast, down to the very borders of California, and, founded thereon, to assert exclusive rights of trading with the natives of the Northwest Coast, and to navigation and fishery in the Pacific Ocean, it is time for the nations whose rights and interests are affected by this project effectually to interpose.

There can, perhaps, be no better time for saying, frankly and explicitly, to the Russian Government, that the future peace of the world, and the interest of Russia herself, cannot be promoted by Russian settlements upon any part of the American Continent. With the exception of the British establishments north of the United States, the remainder of both the American continents must henceforth be left to the management of American hands. It cannot possibly be the purpose of Russia to form extensive *colonial* establishments in America. The new American Republics will be as impatient of a Russian neighbor as the United States; and the claim of Russia to territorial possession, extending to the 51st degree of north latitude, is equally incompatible with the British pretensions.

These observations, thus supported by reference to indisputable documents, are made with a view to the following conclusion:

That the United States can in nowise admit the right of Russia to exclusive territorial possession on any part of the continent of North America south of the 60th degree of north latitude.

That they will maintain the right of their citizens, enjoyed without interruption since the establishment of their independence, of free trade with the original natives of the Northwest Coast throughout its whole extent.

That the right of navigation and of fishing in the Pacific Ocean, even upon the Asiatic coast, north of latitude forty-five, can as little be interdicted to them as that of traffic with the natives of North America.

No. 4.

Mr. Adams to Mr. Rush, No. 70.

DEPARTMENT OF STATE, Washington, July 22, 1823.

SIR: Among the subjects of negotiation with Great Britain which are pressing upon the attention of this Government is the present condition of the Northwest Coast of this Continent. This interest is connected, in a manner becoming from day to day more important, with our territorial rights; with the whole system of our intercourse with the Indian tribes; with the boundary relations between us and the British North American dominions; with the fur trade; the fisheries in the Pacific Ocean; the commerce with the Sandwich Islands and China; with our boundary upon Mexico; and, lastly, with our political standing and intercourse with the Russian empire.

By the third article of the convention between the United States and Great Britain of October 20, 1818, it is agreed that any "country that may be claimed by either party on the Northwest Coast of America, westward of the Stony mountains, shall, together with its harbors, bays, and creeks, and the navigation of all rivers within the same, be free and open, for the term of ten years from the date of the signature of the convention, to the vessels, citizens and subjects of the two powers: it being well understood that this agreement is not to be construed to the prejudice of any claims which either of the two high contracting parties may have to any part of the said country, nor shall it be taken to affect the claims of any other power or State to any part of the said country, the only object of the high contracting parties in that respect being to prevent disputes and differences amongst themselves."

On the 6th of October, 1818, fourteen days before the signature of this convention, the settlement at the mouth of Columbia river had been formally restored to the United States by order of the British Government.—(Message of the President of the United States to the House of Representatives, April 15, 1822, page 13. Letter of Mr. Prevost to the Secretary of State of November 11, 1818.)

By the treaty of amity, settlement and limits between the United States and Spain, of February 22, 1819, the boundary line between them was fixed at the forty-second degree of latitude, from the source of the Arkansas river to the South Sea. By which treaty the United States acquired all the rights of Spain north of that parallel.

The right of the United States to the Columbia river, and to the interior territory washed by its waters, rests upon its discovery from the sea and nomination by a citizen of the United States; upon its exploration to the sea by Captains Lewis and Clarke; upon the settlement of Astoria, made under the protection of the United States, and thus restored to them in 1818; and upon this subsequent acquisition of all the rights of Spain, the only European power who, prior to the discovery of the river, had any pretensions to territorial rights on the Northwest Coast of America.

The waters of the Columbia river extend by the Multnomah to the forty-second degree of latitude, where its source approaches within a few miles of those of the Platte and Arkansas, and by Clarke's river to the fiftieth or fifty-first degree of latitude; thence, descending southward, till its sources almost intersect those of the Missouri.

To the territory thus watered, and immediately contiguous to the original possessions of the United States, as first bounded by the Mississippi, they consider their right to be now established by all the principles which have ever been applied to European settlements upon the American hemisphere.

By the ukase of the Emperor Alexander, of the 4th (16th) of September, 1821, an exclusive territorial right on the Northwest Coast of America is asserted as belonging to Russia, and as extending from the northern extremity of the continent to latitude 51°, and the navigation and fishery of all other nations are interdicted by the same ukase to the extent of one hundred Italian miles from the coast.

When Mr. Poletica, the late Russian minister here, was called upon to set forth the grounds of right conformable to the laws of nations which authorized the issuing of this decree, he answered in his letters of February 28 and April 2, 1822, by alleging, first, discovery, occupancy, and uninterrupted possession.

It appears, upon examination, that these claims have no foundation in fact. The right of discovery, on this continent, claimable by Russia, is reduced to the probability that, in 1741, Captain Tchirikoff saw from the sea the mountain called St. Elias, in about the 59th degree of north latitude. The Spanish navigators, as early as 1582, had discovered as far north as 57° 30'.

As to occupancy, Captain Cook, in 1779, has the express declaration of Mr. Ismaeloff, the chief of the Russian settlement at Onalashka, that they knew nothing of the continent in America; and in the Nootka Sound controversy between Spain and Great Britain it is explicitly stated in the Spanish documents that Russia had disclaimed all pretension to interfere with the Spanish exclusive rights to beyond Prince William's Sound, latitude 61°. No evidence has been exhibited of any Russian settlement on this continent south and east of Prince William's Sound to this day, with the exception of that in California, made in 1816.

It never has been admitted by the various European nations which have formed settlements in this hemisphere that the occupation of an island gave any claim whatever to territorial possessions on the continent to which it was adjoining. The recognized principle has rather been the reverse, as, by the law of nature, islands must be rather considered as appendages to continents than continents to islands.

The only color of claim alleged by Mr. Poletica which has an appearance of plausibility is that which he asserts as an authentic fact: "that in 1789 the Spanish packet St. Charles, commanded by Captain Haro, found in the latitude 48° and 49° Russian settlements, to the number of eight, consisting, in the whole, of twenty families and 462 individuals." But, more than twenty years since, Heurien had shown, in his introduction to the voyage of Marchaud, that in this statement there was a mistake of at least ten degrees of latitude, and that, instead of 48° and 49°, it should read 58° and 59°. This is probably not the only mistake in the account. It rests altogether upon the credit of two private letters—one written from San Blas, and the other from the city of Mexico, to Spain—there communicated to a French consul in one of the Spanish ports, and by him to the French Minister of Marine. They were written in October, 1788, and August, 1789. We have seen that in 1790 Russia explicitly disclaimed interfering with the exclusive rights of Spain to *beyond* Prince William's Sound in latitude 61°; and Vancouver, in 1794, was informed by the Russians on the spot that their most *eastern* settlement there was on Hitchin-brook island, at Port Etches, which *had been established in the course of the preceding summer*, and that the adjacent continent was *a sterile and uninhabited country*.

Until the Nootka Sound contest Great Britain had never advanced any claim to territory upon the Northwest Coast of America by right of occupation. Under the treaty of 1763 her territorial rights were bounded by the Mississippi.

On the 22d of July, 1793, McKenzie reached the shores of the Pacific by land from Canada, in latitude 52° 21′ north, longitude 128° 2′ west of Greenwich.

It is stated in the 52d number of the Quarterly Review, in the article upon Kotzebue's voyage, "that the whole country, from latitude 56° 30′ to the boundary of the United States, in latitude 48°, or thereabouts, is now and has long been in the actual possession of the British Northwest Company;" that this company have a post on the borders of a river in latitude 54° 30′ north, longitude 125° west, and that, in latitude 55° 15′ north, longitude 129° 44′ west, "by this time (March, 1822) the United Company of the Northwest and Hudson's Bay have, in all probability, formed an establishment."

It is not imaginable that, in the present condition of the world, *any* European nation should entertain the project of settling a *colony* on the Northwest Coast of America. That the United States should form establishments there, with views of absolute territorial right and inland communication, is not only to be expected, but is pointed out by the finger of nature, and has been for many years a subject of serious deliberation in Congress. A plan has, for several sessions, been before them for establishing a Territorial Government on the borders of the Columbia river. It will undoubtedly be resumed at their next session, and even if then again postponed there cannot be a doubt that, in the course of a very few years, it must be carried into effect.

As yet, however, the only useful purpose to which the Northwest Coast of America has been or can be made subservient to the settlements of civilized men are the fisheries on its adjoining seas and trade with the aboriginal inhabitants of the country. These have, hitherto, been enjoyed in common by the people of the United States, and by the British and Russian nations. The Spanish, Portuguese and French nations have also participated in them hitherto, without other annoyance than that which resulted from the exclusive territorial claims of Spain, so long as they were insisted on by her.

The United States and Great Britain have both protested against the Russian Imperial ukase of September 4, (16,) 1821. At the proposal of the Russian Government, a full power and instructions are now transmitted to Mr. Middleton, for the adjustment, by amicable negotiation, of the conflicting claims of the parties on this subject.

We have been informed by the Baron de Tuyll that a similar authority has been given on the part of the British Government to Sir Charles Bagot.

Previous to the restoration of the settlement at the mouth of Columbia river in 1818, and again upon the first introduction in Congress of the plan for constituting a Territorial Government there, some disposition was manifested by Sir Charles Bagot and by Mr. Canning to dispute the *right* of the United States to that establishment, and some vague intimation was given of British claims on the Northwest Coast. The restoration of the place and the convention of 1818 were considered as a final disposal of Mr. Bagot's objections, and Mr. Canning declined committing to paper those which he had intimated in conversation.

The discussion of the Russian pretensions in the negotiation now proposed necessarily involves the interests of the three powers, and renders it manifestly proper that the United States and Great Britain should come to a mutual understanding with respect to *their* respective pretensions, as well as upon those their joint views with reference to those of Russia. Copies of the instructions to Mr. Middleton are, therefore, herewith transmitted to you, and the President wishes you to confer freely with the British Government on the subject.

The principles settled by the Nootka Sound convention of October 28, 1790, were—

1st. That the rights of fishery in the South Seas, of trading with the natives of the Northwest Coast of America, and of making settlements on the coast itself for the purposes of that trade, north of the *actual* settlements of Spain, were common to all the European nations, and of course to the United States.

2d. That so far as the actual settlements of Spain had extended, she possessed the exclusive rights, territorial, and of navigation and fishery, extending to the distance of ten miles from the coasts so *actually occupied*.

3d. That on the coasts of *South America*, and the adjacent islands *south* of the parts already occupied by Spain, no settlement should thereafter be made either by British or Spanish subjects, but on both sides should be retained the liberty of landing, and of erecting temporary buildings for the purposes of the fishery. These rights were, also, of course, enjoyed by the people of the United States.

The exclusive rights of Spain to any part of the American continents have ceased. That portion of the convention, therefore, which recognizes the exclusive colonial rights of Spain on these continents, though confirmed as between Great Britain and Spain, by the first additional article to the treaty of the 5th of July, 1814, has been extinguished by the fact of the independence of the South American nation and of Mexico. Those independent nations will possess the rights incident to that condition, and their territories, will, of course, be subject to no *exclusive* right of navigation in their vicinity, or of access to them by any foreign nation.

A necessary consequence of this state of things will be, that the American continents, henceforth, will no longer be subjects of colonization. Occupied by civilized independent nations, they will be accessible to Europeans and to each other on that footing alone, and the Pacific Ocean in every part of it will remain open to the navigation of all nations, in like manner with the Atlantic.

Incidental to the condition of national independence and sovereignty, the rights of anterior navigation of their rivers will belong to each of the American nations within its own territories.

The application of colonial principles of exclusion, therefore, cannot be admitted by the United States as lawful upon any part of the Northwest Coast of America, or as belonging to any European nation. Their own settlements there, when organized as Territorial Governments, will be adapted to the freedom of their own institutions, and, as constituent parts of the Union, be subject to the principles and provisions of their constitution.

The right of carrying on trade with the nations throughout the Northwest Coast they cannot renounce. With the Russian settlements at Kodiack, or at New Archangel, they may fairly claim the advantage of a free trade, having so long enjoyed it unmolested, and because it has been and would continue to be as advantageous at least to those settlements as to them. But they will not contest the right of Russia to prohibit the traffic, as strictly confined to the Russian settlement itself, and not extending to the original natives of the coast.

If the British Northwest and Hudson's Bay Companies have any posts on the coast, as suggested in the article of the Quarterly Review above cited, the third article of the convention of October 20, 1818, is applicable to them. Mr. Middleton is authorized by his instructions to propose an article of similar import, to be inserted in a joint convention between the United States, Great Britain, and Russia, for a term of ten years from its signature. You are authorized to make the same proposal to the British Government, and, with a view to draw a definite line of demarkation for the future, to stipulate that no settlement shall hereafter be made on the Northwest Coast or on any of the islands thereto adjoining by Russian subjects south of latitude 55°, by citizens of the United States north of latitude 51°, or by British subjects either south of 51° or north of 55°. I mention the latitude of 51°, as the bound within which we are willing to limit the future settlement of the United States, because it is not to be doubted that the Columbia river branches as far north as 51°, although it is most probably not the Taconesche Tesse of Mackenzie. As, however, the line already runs in latitude 49° to the Stony mountains, should it be earnestly insisted upon by Great Britain, we will consent to carry it in continuance on the same parallel to the sea. Copies of this instruction will likewise be forwarded to Mr. Middleton, with whom you will freely, but cautiously, correspond on this subject, as well as in relation to your negotiation respecting the suppression of the slave trade.

I have the honor to be, with great respect, sir, your very humble obedient servant,

JOHN QUINCY ADAMS.

Hon. RICHARD RUSH, *Envoy Extraordinary and*
Minister Plenipotentiary of the United States, London.

No. 5.

Mr. Middleton to the Secretary of State, No. 29.

St. PETERSBURG, *September* 19, 1823.

SIR: I have the honor to acquaint you that Count Nesselrode, on the morning of the day in which he left St. Petersburg for Odessa, addressed me the note of which copy is herewith sent. He mentioned to me some days previously having had advices from Baron Tuyll, intimating that the negotiation upon the subject of the ukase of September, 4, (16,) 1821, would be transferred to this place.

Sir Charles Bagot likewise has communicated to me instructions he has received from his Government, in which a *joint* negotiation appears to be in contemplation of the British minister. Sir Charles at the same time informed me that Mr. Canning eagerly caught at the proposition of Mr. Rush going to that effect; and that instructions from you, correlative to those of the British Government, would undoubtedly be sent me. I have told him that I do not as yet know anything of the intentions of my Government upon that head, having received no despatch from the Department of State later than that brought by Mr. Pinkney. Upon Sir Charles's expressing his wish to be informed respecting the actual state of the *northwest* question between the United States and Russia, so far as it might be known to me, I saw no objection to making a *confidential* communication to him of the note of Count Nesselrode, dated August 1, 1822, by which, in fact, staying the execution of the ukase above mentioned, Russia has virtually abandoned the pretensions therein advanced. I learned in this conversation with the British ambassador that up to that time he had done nothing upon the subject further than telling Count Nesselrode that Great Britain would probably, at some future day, feel obliged to object to some of the provisions of this ukase. The reply made to him was, that in such case the matter must be made the subject of a negotiation.

I am in daily expectation of learning what arrangements the President may have been pleased to direct. Mr. Poletica, who is charged by the Imperial Government with the laboring oar upon this occasion, is not unfrequently inquiring whether there are yet any instructions received which might authorize the conferences invited by Count Nesselrode.

I have the honor to be, sir, very faithfully, your obedient servant,

HENRY MIDDLETON.

No. 5, *(a.)*

Count Nesselrode to Mr. Middleton.

[Translation.]

St. PETERSBURG; *August* 22, 1823.

SIR: On quitting St. Petersburg, the Emperor charged me to announce to you that, as he had given me orders to follow him on his journey, he had authorized Mr. Poletica, Actual Counsellor of State, to begin with you, sir, the conferences relative to the differences which have arisen between Russia and the United States, in consequence of the new regulation given to the Russian American Company by the ukase of his Imperial Majesty, dated September 4, (16,) 1821.

These conferences will have for their aim to prepare the way for the definitive adjustment of these differences, and I doubt not they will facilitate this result so eagerly desired by the Emperor.

I seize with pleasure the occasion which is offered to me of repeating to you, sir, the assurance of my most distinguished consideration.

NESSELRODE.

No. 6.

Mr. Middleton (No. 31) to the Secretary of State.

St. Petersburg, *October 5, (17,) 1823.*

Sir: I avail myself of the sailing of the last American vessel in port to send a duplicate of my last despatch, and to acknowledge the receipt of yours, numbered 15, 16, and 17, brought to hand yesterday, in the afternoon, by Mr. Hughes, who has been detained much beyond his original calculation by his own account. The delay, however, is not much to be regretted, as nothing important can be done here during the absence of the Emperor from this residence, where he cannot be expected to return before November.

I have only to add, that the different subjects embraced in these despatches shall receive my best attention, and that no endeavor shall be wanting on my part to carry into effect the intentions of the President.

I have the honor to be, sir, very faithfully, your obedient servant,

HY. MIDDLETON.

No. 7.

Extract of a letter (No. 32) from Mr. Middleton to Mr. Adams, dated

St. Petersburg, *November 1, (15,) 1823.*

" Shortly after the receipt of the instructions contained in No. 16 I had several conferences with Mr. Poletica, as well as with Sir Charles Bagot, upon the subject referred to in that despatch. I found that the first named of these gentlemen had no powers to *conclude* anything, and that he was merely authorized to hold *des pour parlers*, in other words, to discuss the matter. I very soon discovered, too, that a very great divergence of opinion between him and me upon all points relative to the Northwest question must render fruitless all attempts at coming to an understanding *with him.* I was not sorry, therefore, when an incident enabled me to decline further conference until it could be renewed with a better prospect of success. Sir Charles, upon referring to his full power, of which a copy is herewith sent,* discovered that it had only relation to the maritime question. It became necessary, then, to remedy this before he could proceed in the business; and accordingly a special messenger was despatched by him for the purpose of obtaining the requisite full powers. I availed myself of the circumstances to decline further conference with Mr. de Poletica, and all proceedings remain suspended until an answer to Sir Charles' despatches can be received, which may be expected about the middle of December. I am hopeful, from the conversations I have had with him, that a perfect understanding respecting the common objects desirable to be attained by the two countries in this negotiation will be effected through him. In the meantime I have prepared a confidential memoir upon the Northwest question, to be ready against the return of the Emperor."

No. 8.

Extract of a letter (No. 33) from Mr. Middleton to Mr. Adams, dated

St. Petersburg, *December 1, (13,) 1823.*

" I have prepared, and shall deliver in on the first fit occasion, for his Imperial Majesty's inspection, a confidential memoir on the Northwest question; and I now forward a copy of it, marked *(a.)* The subject must be trite to you; but I have found here that it is indispensable to make some statement of facts and principles in this case, before I can proceed further in the negotiation. I hope you will approve of the course I am pursuing, and that you will find that I have stated correctly both facts and principles. I felt it to be necessary to broach the subject in this mode, knowing the erroneous impressions which prevail. I have now great hopes, notwithstanding the unfavorable appearances which this affair has worn for a few weeks past, that it may take a new turn, and that I may yet be enabled to succeed in attaining the main objects of the negotiation.

"Sir Charles Bagot is now daily expecting the return of his messenger with new powers and instructions respecting the same matters. I mentioned in my last, and I now repeat, that I have a reasonable expectation that he will be instructed to pursue the course of policy so obviously pointed out by the true interests of England and suggested by a sense of the propriety of *being consistent*, and of persevering in the principles which marked the Nootka Sound contestation. Neither he nor I foresee any difficulty in reconciling and adjusting the interests of our respective countries upon this question."

No. 8, (a.)

[Translation.]

CONFIDENTIAL MEMORIAL.

" Great men never fear the truth, and wish nothing to be concealed from them."—(*Montesquieu.*)

Observations upon the rights and claims of Spain, of Russia, of England, and of the United States, relative to the West Coast of North America; and upon the Ukase of September 4, (16,) 1821.

The part of the New World situated towards the north of the great ocean has been explored and known very much later than any other portion of the same continent in the torrid and temperate zones,

* See document marked 10, *b.*

by reason of its greater distance from Europe, whose navigators can only arrive thither by doubling Cape Horn or that of the Good Hope.

Yet Spain, about the end of the sixteenth century and in the course of the seventeenth, had pushed her discoveries even in these remote regions; and already, in 1692, claimed the exclusive property of the coasts which she had there discovered, in virtue of grants made by an authority respected at the time, and which continued to be so until she acquired the right of prescription over these possessions.

About this last time, but a little later, in 1697, the Russians penetrated by Siberia as far as Kamtschatka; and from thence, embarking at the ports of Okhotsk and Avatcha, between the years 1710 and 1741, they pushed their discoveries in the northern latitudes of the great ocean. From these discoveries Russia derives her rights to that long chain of islands intervening between the western and the eastern continents, and even to a very considerable portion of the continent of America—rights which have never been contested.

Although the navigators of England, from Drake, in 1578, to Cook and Vancouver, that is, for more than two centuries, had frequently visited these coasts, either to make discoveries there or for trade, yet she never announced having any pretensions there whatever until in the year 1790, when a very sharp dispute broke out with Spain relative to Nootka Sound.

The summary of what passed between the courts of England, Spain and Russia at the time of the discussion of that question may serve to throw light upon the respective pretensions of these powers.

This difference arose from the seizure of an English vessel from Macao to trade for peltries. After the discoveries of Cook, in 1778, Nootka began to be considered as the principal market for furs of the Northwest Coast of America, and the enormous profits of this trade had, after some time, brought thither a great number of European and American navigators.

The court of Madrid, fearing lest the English or Russians should attempt to fix themselves at Nootka, had given order to form an establishment there. Mr. Martinez, charged with that order, arrived in this port on the 5th of May, 1789. He found there, in fact, one English ship, one Portuguese and two American. He seized all four. Two months after the English ship Argonaut arrived, under the command of Captain Colnet. He imparted to the Spanish commander the order of his Government, of which he was the bearer, to establish a factory at that place, and there to build a frigate and a schooner, in order henceforth to prevent every other European nation from taking part in the fur trade.

Martinez represented in vain that, long before Cook, Perez had first anchored in this port. The dispute grew warm between the two officers, and Martinez, to make good his title of priority, caused to be arrested Colnet, and sent him prisoner to San Blas.

It is unnecessary to the object of these observations to pursue the discussion which took place between the courts of London and Madrid in consequence of the act of Martinez. It will be sufficient to refer to note (a) for some particulars of this subject, and to cite here the letter of Count Fernan Nunez to M. de Montmorin, Secretary of the Department of Foreign Affairs of France, under date of June 15, 1790:

"I have the honor of addressing to you below a faithful extract of all the transactions between my court and that of London, on the subject of the detention of two English ships, which were seized in the bay of St. Lawrence or Nootka, situated to the north of California, under the 50th degree of latitude.

"By this relation you will be enabled to judge: 1st, That, by treaties, boundary lines, taking possession, and by all the most decided acts of sovereignty exercised by the Spaniards upon these regions, from the reign of Charles II, and authorized by that monarch in 1692, the proofs of which will be produced in the course of this negotiation, all the Northwest Coast of America on the side of the Pacific Ocean, as far as to the other side of what is called Prince William's Sound, under the 61st degree of latitude, is recognized as belonging exclusively to Spain. 2dly, That the court of Russia, having had knowledge of this extent of our limits, did not hesitate to give assurances to the King, my master, of the purity of his intentions on this subject; and added, that he regretted exceedingly that the repeated orders given to prevent the violation of the territory of a foreign power by the subjects of Russia had been disobeyed."

It is proved by the pieces produced in this discussion that the claims of Spain extended to the other side of Prince William's Sound, situated in the 61st degree of north latitude; and that the court of Russia, having had information of the extent of these limits, has declared that she had no intention of opposing it; that she had even added expressions of regret that her repeated orders to prevent the violation of the territory of Spain by Russian subjects should have been disobeyed.

It is then demonstrated that Russia, in the year 1790, was far from forming any territorial claim for herself upon the continent of North America, on this side of the 61st degree of north latitude.

The principle upon which England insists is, that the Northwest Coast of America, north of the actual establishments of Spain, ought not to be deemed to belong exclusively to any European.

Thus England did not, like Russia, admit the exclusive claims of Spain as far as the 61st degree; and it appears that, in consequence, she took for the basis of her stipulations in the treaty of the 28th of October, 1790, the principle that the rights of freely navigating and fishing in the Pacific Ocean, and of trading with the natives of the coasts, by landing in the unoccupied places where there making establishments, are common to all nations. The 5th article, moreover, stipulates that in all parts of the Northwest Coast of North America, or of the adjacent islands, situated to the north of the parts of said coast occupied by the Spaniards before the month of April, 1789, as well as in the places restored as in those where the subjects of one of the two powers shall come to form establishments, the subjects of the other shall have free access, and shall carry on their trade without trouble or molestation. Besides, several other articles of immediate interest to the two nations, but which involve no general principle, were agreed on.

From what precedes, it will be readily perceived what was the relative position of the three powers in their claims upon the Northwest Coast of America in the year 1790. Russia confined herself on the other side of the 60th degree of north latitude, whilst Spain and England had conventionally fixed their respective rights in all the parts of the Northwest Coast situated from the last establishments of Spain to the south of Cape Mendocino, to the 60th degree, inclusive.

Nine years after, the Emperor Paul granted to the Russian American Company (see note b) certain exclusive privileges of commerce on these coasts as far as the 55th degree of north latitude, (see note c,) exclusive, it must be believed, in respect to other Russian subjects simply; for Russia had never claimed sovereignty of the part of this coast situated on this side of the 60th degree, to which, on the contrary, she had recognized the rights of Spain; and in the year 1799 several nations, and especially the United States of America, for more than twelve years had pursued a free and uninterrupted trade with the natives of this coast, from which, consequently, the ukase of that State neither ought nor could exclude them.

It is difficult to be convinced of the fact that such was the intention of the ukase when attention is paid to the declaration of Russia (known to all Europe) of which we have made mention before.

Yet, to be enabled to judge if the claim of having exclusive rights upon all the coast, even to the 55th degree, could be justified by facts, it may be useful to take a hasty review of the discoveries of Russia in the *Eastern* Ocean as to them, and, for this purpose, let us refer to note *d*, partly extracted from the work of M. Levesque.

It appears by this extract that Behring and Tschirikoff are the only Russian navigators who touched at the continent of America, on this side of the 60th degree, previous to the year 1790; and it is even on this sole circumstance that a foundation was made for forming a claim to the discovery and the possession of this coast. It is alleged "that in 1789 the Spanish packet San Carlos, commanded by Captain de Haro, found, in latitude 48° to 49°, Russian establishments to the number of eight, making in all twenty families, or 468 individuals." But it may be answered, that it is more than twenty years since M. de Fleurieu demonstrated, in the learned historical introduction to the voyage of Captain Marchaud, that there must be in this recital an error of ten degrees of latitude at least, and that, instead of 48° to 49°, it ought to read 58° to 59°. It is even very probable that that is not the only error which is in the relation, for that story originates from two private letters, the one written from San Blas, the other from Mexico, communicated to a French consul in one of the ports of Spain, and by him to the Minister of Marine in France. The dates are, October, 1788, and August, 1789. Now, we have just seen that in the following year Russia confirmed the rights of Spain as far as the other side of Prince William's Sound, in the latitude 61 degrees. It can scarcely, then, be necessary to lay more stress upon the trifling importance of the alleged circumstance.

It appears that Tschirikoff never landed, but having approached the coast without knowing if it were the continent or an island, and having successively sent his long-boat, and then his canoe, he lost both, together with the men who were in them, whom he believed to be massacred by the natives of the country, and then he returned to Kamtschatka. Behring, on his part, discovered and examined the bay (strait) which bears his name.

Captain Vancouver learned, in 1794, from the Russians themselves, upon the spot, that their most easterly establishment was then at port Eches, in *Hinchin Brook* island, (*Tchatcha* island of the Russians, and *Magdalena* of the Spaniards, in latitude 60° 25') where they were established the preceding summer; and that *the continent* in the vicinity of that place was barren and *uninhabited*.

From these facts, incontestibly proved by historical documents, an irresistible conclusion follows, which agrees with the declaration of Russia in 1790; and it ought to appear definitive that she had no right to claim, either under the title of discovery or of possession, *on the continent* east or south of Behring's Strait, about the 60th degree of north latitude.

Moreover, the note (*e*) on the diplomatic communications between the Government of the United States and Russia, on this subject, will make known what were the ideas of the Imperial Minister during the year 1810. It will be perceived, by the recital of what passed in the conferences of September and October of that.year, that the Imperial Government was then undecided what side it should have taken definitively, for foreign commerce, on the Northwest Coast, either Russian or Spanish, of North America. It will also be remarked, that the Government of the United States had, till then, principally insisted on the difficulty of pronouncing in a case where Spain ought to have claims. This scruple proves, at least, how attentive it was not to do prejudice to the right of a third.

In expectation of the decision which thus remained in suspense, the commerce of the United States increased very considerably in these latitudes. It is easy to prove, even by the authority of Russian voyagers, what the extent of this commerce was. Among others, Mr. Lisianski had remarked, from the year 1804, that the Russians could collect as many as eight thousand otters' skins annually, in the bay of Sitka, if they had the means of excluding the Americans from this trade;.whilst at that time they only took from thence about three thousand.—(See page 236, English edition.). It will be sufficient to add, that in the last years there has been sent from the ports of the United States, in the season for trade on the Northwest Coast, as many as seventeen merchant vessels, which are for the most part in the habit of trading in China with the cargoes which they obtain on this coast, and in the islands of the Pacific Ocean.

It is now time to consider what can be the foundations of the territorial claims of the United States of America upon the Northwest Coast of their continent. Their bordering position to one part of that coast gives them a much greater importance for themselves than for any of the powers of Europe. The territory situated west of the ancient provinces of the United States presents to them contiguity of possessions from the Atlantic to the Pacific Ocean, and will afford their inhabitants the means of establishing communications of internal navigation from the one sea to the other.

The two ships which had been seized by Martinez were released by him, to continue the navigation which they had attempted round the globe. During this voyage the sloop.Columbia anchored the first in a great river, which had been but imperfectly discovered by Quadra, and which Vancouver was unable to find again, but which is since known under the name of Columbia. An establishment has been since formed at its mouth, under the protection of the United States, whose Government has also sent by land, for the same destination, a military expedition under the command of Captains Lewis and Clarke. These officers have visited and explored the country surrounding this river and its tributaries, and have published a chorographical account of it.

During the last war between the United States and Great Britain the fort situated at the mouth of the river was given up to the English, but they afterwards restored it to the United States, under the stipulation of the first article of the treaty of peace.

To the rights acquired by that possession, situated on the coast of the continent under 46° 15' of north latitude, and contiguous to their ancient territory, the United States have joined those which they derive from the treaty of limits with Spain, signed at Washington, February 22, 1819. By the third article of this treaty his Catholic Majesty cedes to the United States all his rights, claims, and pretensions to the territories situated to the north of the 42d parallel of latitude, from the source of the river Arkansas to the great ocean.

It may be useful to remark here that the establishment at Nootka has been abandoned both by Spain and by England; and that it appears probable that these two nations have not now any possession upon the Northwest Coast between the 42d and the 60th degrees of north latitude.

The Russians have an establishment upon the *island of Sitka*,[*] in latitude 57° 50'. This fort, built in 1799, was destroyed three years after by the natives of the country, and re-established in 1804, by Mr. Lisianski, who called it New Archangel. Russia cannot, however, avail herself of the circumstance of that possession to form a foundation for rights *upon the continent*, the usage of nations never having established that the occupation of an island could give rights upon the neighboring continent. The principle is, rather, that the islands ought to be considered as dependent upon the continent, than the inverse of the proposition.

·It appears, then, that the position of Russia, relative to her rights upon the Northwest Coast of America, had not at all changed since 1790. The Russian American Company had enjoyed its exclusive rights granted by the Emperor Paul. It had prospered and formed an establishment in the limits marked out by the ukase of 1799. It had, however, never pretended to exclude other nations from a commerce shared with them for so long a time; but it saw with jealousy its profits diminished by this rivalship. In fine, it took a violent part, and at length obtained by its solicitations the ukase of 4th (16th) September, 1821.

In speaking of this measure, we shall make it our business to say nothing but what appears strictly necessary to set it in its true light, convinced, as we are, that the enlightened Government from whence it emanates will listen with good will to observations conceived with the intention of obtaining nothing but what is just in itself and useful to all interested.

The ukase, by its first three articles, under the form of a grant to a private association, presupposes the existence of exclusive territorial rights (a pretension unknown till now) on a great extent of continent, with the intervening islands and seas, and it forbids all foreign nations from approaching nearer them than one hundred Italian miles to these coasts. The ukase even goes to the shutting up of a strait which has never been till now shut up, and which is at present the principal object of discoveries interesting and useful to the sciences.

The very terms of the ukase bear that this pretension has now been made known for the first time.

The following sections relate to the seizure of vessels, and to the proceedings before the tribunals against those who infringe the regulation, and might furnish remarks worthy of attention as to the right of visit against ships in times of peace, permitted even to merchant vessels, as well as upon other points. But it is thought better to pass over these matters, as simply accessories to the principal point. Nothing is intended but first to know if the vast territory contained in the limits marked out by the ukase is, in fact, incorporated with the empire of Russia upon admissible principles.

All jurists are agreed upon the principle that real occupation only can give the rights to the property and to the sovereignty of an unoccupied country, newly discovered.—(See note *f*.)

With all the respect which we owe to the declared intention and to the determination indicated by the ukase, it is necessary to examine the two points of fact: 1st, If the country to the south and east of Behring's Strait, as far as the 51st degree of north latitude, is found strictly unoccupied? 2d, If there has been, latterly, a real occupation of this vast territory?

We have already seen, in the summary of the dispute between England and Spain, what was the decision of Russia upon the first point. It cannot be necessary for us to repeat it.

As to what regards the real occupation, one may be convinced, on having recourse to the charts officially published by the Russian Government, that the only establishment on this side of the 60th degree is that which is found on the island of Sitka, situated under 57° 30' of latitude, and consequently more than six degrees from the southern limit fixed by the ukase.

· The conclusion which must necessarily result from these facts does not appear to establish that the territory in question had been legitimately incorporated with the Russian empire.

The extension of territorial rights to the distance of a hundred miles from the coasts upon two opposite continents, and the prohibition of approaching to the same distance from these coasts, or from those of all the intervening islands, are innovations in the law of nations, and measures unexampled. It must thus be imagined that this prohibition, bearing the pains of confiscation, applies to a long line of coasts, with the intermediate islands, situated in vast seas, where the navigation is subject to innumerable and unknown difficulties, and where the chief employment, which is the whale fishery, cannot be compatible with a regulated and well determined course.—(See note *g*.)

The right cannot be denied of shutting a port, a sea, or even an entire country, against foreign commerce in some particular cases. But the exercise of such a right, unless in the case of a colonial system already established, or for some other special object, would be exposed to an unfavorable interpretation, as being contrary to the liberal spirit of modern times, wherein we look for the bonds of amity and of reciprocal commerce among all nations being more closely cemented.

Universal usage, which has obtained the force of law, has established for all the coasts an accessory limit of a moderate distance, which is sufficient for the security of the country and for the convenience of its inhabitants, but which lays no restraint upon the universal rights of nations, nor upon the freedom of commerce and of navigation.—(See Vattel, B. I, chap. 23, sec. 289.)

In the case where this territorial limit would be insufficient, it is always allowable to make to it the augmentations which may be desired, by the way of diplomacy, in concluding treaties with the nations that might be found interested in it, the only means of reconciling them to the species of constraint which must necessarily result in this case to the maritime powers.

The only object of these observations is to induce a reconsideration of all this question, in general, on the part of the Russian Government, whose just and reasonable disposition cannot be doubted, and to prevail upon it to adopt the measures which its wisdom shall point out to it as most proper to mitigate the inconveniences which arise to foreign nations from the decree on the privileges of the Russian American Company.

----

[*] The Tchinkitane of the Indians in the *Bay of Guadalupe* of the Spaniards in 1775, and the *Norfolk bay* of the English of 1787.

NOTE (*a.*)

Dispute between the Courts of Madrid and of London.

The court of Madrid hastened to give to that of London the news of what had passed at Nootka, by demanding that the Government of Great Britain should give orders that the coasts occupied by subjects of Spain should be no more visited by the English; and it announces that, in consideration of the ignorance in which the captains of English ships had been of the rights of Spain, and out of regard to the nation to which they belonged, the Viceroy of Mexico had released the vessels.

The memorial of June 4, signed by the Count of Florida Blanca, declares that "the vast extent of the Spanish territories, navigation, and dominion, on the continent of America, isles and seas contiguous to the South Sea, are clearly laid down, and authenticated by a variety of documents, laws, and formal acts of possession in the reign of King Charles II. It is also clearly ascertained that, notwithstanding the repeated attempts made by adventurers and pirates on the Spanish coasts of the South Sea and adjacent islands, Spain has still preserved her possessions entire, and opposed with success those usurpations, by constantly sending her ships and vessels to take possession of such settlements. By these measures and reiterated acts of possession Spain has preserved her dominion, which she has extended to the borders of the Russian establishments in that part of the world.

"The Viceroys of Peru and Mexico having been informed that these seas had been for some years past more frequented than formerly; that smuggling had increased; that several usurpations prejudicial to Spain and the general tranquillity had been suffered to be made, they gave orders that the western coasts of Spanish America, and islands and seas adjacent, should be more frequently navigated and explored.

"They were also informed that several Russian vessels were upon the point of making commercial establishments upon that coast. At the time that Spain demonstrated to Russia the inconveniences attendant upon such encroachments, she entered upon the negotiation with Russia, upon the supposition that the Russian navigators of the Pacific Ocean had no orders to make establishments within the limits of Spanish America, of which the Spaniards were the first possessors, (limits situated within Prince William's Straits,) purposely to avoid all dissensions, and in order to maintain the harmony and amity which Spain wished to preserve.

"The court of Russia replied, it had already given orders that its subjects should make no settlements in places belonging to other powers, and that if those orders had been violated, and any had been made in Spanish America, they desired the King would put a stop to them in a friendly manner. To this pacific language on the part of Russia, Spain observed that she could not be answerable for what her officers might do at that distance, whose general orders and instructions were, not to permit any settlements to be made by other nations on the continent of Spanish America."

Mr. Pitt, then Prime Minister in England, in his speech to Parliament on this subject, declared, "That the subjects of his Britannic Majesty had been forcibly interrupted in a trade which they had carried on for years without molestation, in parts of America where they had an incontrovertible right of trading, and in places *to which no country could claim an exclusive right of commerce and navigation;* that the court of Madrid had advanced a claim to the exclusive right of navigation in those seas that was unfounded and exorbitant, indefinite in its consequences, aiming destruction to the valuable fisheries established by the English in the South Seas; in fine, that it was necessary to adopt such measures as might in future prevent any such disputes."—(See Annual Register for 1790, p. 96.)

Suffice it to say, that they could not agree upon the question of right, and that after a negotiation, supported by immense preparations for war on both sides, the court of Madrid determined to accept the ultimatum which arrived with an order to the English ambassador to leave Madrid if it was not agreed to.

The first and second articles of the convention signed at the Escurial, October 28, 1790, stipulate the damages to be paid by Spain for the ships seized and restored. The third and fourth articles determine that the respective subjects may freely navigate and fish in the Pacific Ocean or South Sea, landing on the coasts in the places unoccupied, and the fifth article bears that all the parts of the Northwest Coast of North America (situated to the north of the parts of this coast already occupied by Spain previous to the month of April, 1789) the respective subjects shall have free access everywhere where the subjects of either power shall have formed, after the same date, or may by consequence form, establishments. In fine, that the respective subjects shall not form any establishment upon the parts of these coasts situated to the south of the parts already occcupied by Spain.

NOTE (*b.*)

The Russian American Company.

Chilikoff may be considered as the founder of the American Company. After the discoveries of Behring and Tchirikoff, of the islands between Asia and America, the Russian merchants made voyages thither to procure peltries, which they traded with great profit upon the frontiers of China; for all furs, and especially the beautiful skins of the sea otter, are an indispensable article for the effeminate Chinese. They change their dress upon the least variation of air, and in winter wear pelisses even at Canton, which is situated under the tropic. As many as twenty ships depart annually from the ports of Okhotsk and Avatchka; each ship equipped for the chase of animals for furs had its different proprietors, who, without pity either for the inhabitants of the Aleutian Islands, whom they treated barbarously, or for the animals which they hunted beyond measure, without any providence for the future, only thought of promptly completing their cargo and returning as soon as possible to Okhotsk. From hence, so great a destruction of these precious animals took place, that there was soon room to believe that this trade would cease entirely.

Convinced of the necessity of putting a stop to these devastations, Chilikoff made the greatest efforts to unite in one company all those interested in this trade, that it might in future be conducted with prudence, according to a plan which he had laid down. The brothers Golikoff joined the association in

1785. Their united capitals enabled them even to fit out several ships, which the enterprising Chilikoff commanded himself. They formed an establishment upon the island of Kodiac, which still serves as a depot for the trade of America. Placed at an equal distance from the Aleutian Isles, and from Kamtschatka on the west, and from the coast of America on the east, no situation is, in fact, more convenient. This trade, thus conducted, produced great riches. The good success of this association induced several merchants to join it. From this came the present company of America.

On almost all the Aleutian Isles factories were formed, protected by small forts. The principal seat of the company was fixed at Irkutsk. Yet the company appeared rather simply tolerated than formally authorized by the Government; so that its existence was always precarious enough. The irregular manner in which this sort of trade had been carried on, the unjust and cruel conduct of the Russian merchants towards the unhappy inhabitants of the isles of America, complaints of which had even come to the capital, had raised up so great and so powerful enemies that Paul the First resolved to abolish the company, in order to put an end to a traffic so revolting. This resolution would certainly have been carried into effect but for the interposition of M. de Resanoff, who was afterwards sent to Japan as ambassador. He had married the daughter of Chilikoff, who had brought him in dowry a very great number of bills of the company, the value of which depended upon gains or losses of the trade. By his knowledge and authority he happened to render the Emperor so favorable to the company that he rejected all the representations which were addressed to him against it, confirmed it formally in 1799, and granted to it great privileges. Then the principal residence of the company. was transferred from Irkutsk to St. Petersburg, and its trade began to acquire great importance.

As soon as the Emperor Alexander mounted the throne he took a lively interest in the company; he himself took shares in it, and thus induced many of the nobility of the empire to imitate him. Assured by that of a lasting protection, the company labored with zeal, under the direction of the Count Romanzoff, to give to its trade, so long neglected, a form entirely new.—*(Voyage of M. de Krusenstern, vol. 1, p. 14, and the following pages.)*

NOTE (c.)

Extract from M. de Humboldt's Essay on New Spain, Book III, chapter 8, page 344.

" If the puerile ceremonies which the Europeans name acts of possession, if the astronomical observations made upon a coast recently discovered, could give rights of property, this portion of the new continent would be singularly parcelled out and subdivided among the Spaniards, the English, the Russians, the French, and the Americans of the United States. Even a small island would sometimes have to be divided among two or three nations at once, because each one could prove its having discovered a different cape of it. The great sinuosity of *the coast between the parallels of* 55 *and* 60 *degrees embraces the discoveries made successively* by Gali, Behring, and Tchirikoff, Quadra, Cook, La Perouse, Malaspina, and Vancouver.

"As far as this no European nation has formed a lasting establishment upon the immense extent of coasts which reach from Cape Mendocino to the 59th degree of latitude. *Beyond this limit* the Russian factories commence, the greatest part of which are scattered and distant from one another as the factories which the Europeans have established for the last three centuries on the coasts of Africa. The greater part of these small Russian colonies only communicate with each other by sea, and the new denominations of *Russian America*, or *the Russian possessions in the new continent*, ought not to induce us to believe that the coast of *Behring's Basin*, the peninsula *Alashka*, or the countries of *Tschugatschi*, are become *Russian provinces* in the sense given to this word, when speaking of the *Spanish provinces* of Sonora, or New Biscay."

NOTE (d.)

A view of the discoveries of the Russians on the coast of America.

It was only towards the year 1710, when a Japanese ship was wrecked on the coasts of Kamtschatka, that it began to be supposed that Japan was not far distant from that peninsula. Some Cossack adventurers consequently made the discovery of several of the Kurile islands, and Peter the First, in the latter part of his life, thought of the project of ordering an expedition for resolving the doubts which existed respecting the separation or contiguity of Asia and America. He died without having had time to put his design in execution; but his successors, the Empresses, Catherine I, Anne, and Elizabeth, successively resumed it, and in 1728 Behring made his first expedition, penetrated the strait which bears his name by coasting along Asia, but returned to Kamtschatka without having seen the coasts of America. On his return he was assured that, from the high coasts of Kamtschatka, one might see, in a clear day, the neighboring land, which encouraged him to undertake, in the following year, a new voyage, which had no better success, for, having sailed fifty leagues from the coast without seeing anything, he changed his course, landed at Okhotsk, and returned afterwards to St. Petersburg.

The attention of the Russian Government having been attracted anew to the eastern coasts of their empire by another shipwreck of a Japanese vessel in 1732, Behring proposed to attempt new discoveries in a sea still so little known. In fine, on the 4th of June, 1741, two vessels, built at Okhotsk, set sail from the port of Avatcha, (which was on that occasion named Petro Parloskoi,) the one commanded by Behring, the other by his Lieutenant, Tchirikoff.

The vessels having been separated by a severe storm and thick fogs, the commodore saw the continent of America on the 18th of July, and three days before Tchirikoff had gained the same coast. In rectifying their estimate for the longitude, the learned Muller thinks that the first had seen the land at 58° 28' of latitude, and at 236° of longitude, and the second at 56° of latitude and 241° of longitude. Tchirikoff having had the misfortune of sending to the land his long-boat and his canoe, from whence they did not return, lost them, with several of his companions and took the route for Kamtschatka. Behring, on his part, trying to obtain a knowledge of the coast which he had seen, anchored, on the 20th of July, a short distance from the continent. He named a cape, which advanced into the sea, *St. Elias*, and another cape, west of the former, *St. Hermogenes*, between which there is a gulf known afterwards by the name of Behring's bay. He remained a long time in sight of the rocks which line it. At length he bent his course south, and soon found himself in a safe sea. On the 30th of July they discovered an island which was named *Toumanoi*, or Foggy island.

It would be useless to recount the misfortunes which pursued the commodore during the rest of this voyage. Attacked by the scurvy, which broke out among the crew, he soon became incapable of fulfilling the duties of his station. The advanced season made him resolve, in the month of September, to endeavor to return to Kamtschatka. A group of islands was discovered, which received the names of St. Macaire, St. Theodore, and St. Abraham. In fine, on the 30th of October, they saw two other islands which they had the misfortune to take for the most northerly of the Kuriles; this fatal error made them call those islands by the name of *Seduction*. They are nearly at the same elevation of the pole, but they are distant from them nearly eight degrees of longitude east. They thought they were not more than two days' sail from Avatcha; they steered west, but they saw no point of coast, and the season being too much advanced left no more hope of gaining the port. They then went back, and after several days of a horrible navigation their vessel run upon an island, where the commodore and a great part of the crew perished of disease and fatigue, and which afterwards received his name. In the spring his companions constructed a small vessel with one mast, in which they returned to the port of Avatcha in the month of August, 1742.

This voyage, by informing the Russians of the relative situation of Asia and America, opened to them the path for the successive discovery of this long archipelago of islands known under the collective names of Aleutian Islands, Fox Islands, Audreanorski Islands, and of that part of the coast of America which is spread under the parallel of sixty degrees, with a great number of islands situated to the south of the main land; in short, of the peninsula of Alashka and of the lands situated to the north of this peninsula as far as the 70th degree. Such were the discoveries made successively, either by adventurers at the expense of owners of Kamtschatka, or by the officers of the imperial marine at the expense of the Russian Government. The voyage of Miche, Navodtsikoff, in 1745, that of Emelien Yagoff, of 1750, Cholodiloff, Serebranikoff, and Krassilnickoff, of 1756, Demetrius Paikoff, Pushkareff, Pierre Wasintinskoi, and Maxime Lazaroff, of 1758 to 1760, Drusinin, Medredeff, Korovin, and Etienne Glotoff, of 1762, Solovioff and Lieutenant Synd, of 1764, Aphanassei Otcheredin, of 1766, and that of Captain Krenitzin and Lieutenant Levasheff, in 1768 to 1769.—*(See Russian Discoveries by Coxe.)*

The voyages of Billings, of 1789 to 1793, of Krusenstern, of 1803 to 1806, and of Kotzbue, who all sailed upon the tracks of Cook, De la Perouse, and of so many other modern navigators, do not enter into the consideration of the present question.

NOTE (*e.*)

Abstract of diplomatic communications between the United States and Russia on the subject of the trade of the Northwest Coast.

Count Romanzoff, Minister of Foreign Affairs and of Commerce, acquainted the chargé d'affaires of the United States at St. Petersburg, in the year 1808, "that the American Company had represented to him that the ships of the United States, instead of trading with the Russian possessions in America, went thither to carry on a clandestine traffic with the savages, to whom they furnished, in exchange for otters' skins, fire-arms and powder, the use of which, till then unknown to these *islanders*, had been in their hands very hurtful to the subjects of his Imperial Majesty; and that the citizens of the United States had become themselves the victims of the imprudent speculation of their countrymen." (His excellency doubtless meant to speak of the destruction of the Russian fort at Sitka, in 1801, of which Mr. Lisianski gives the account in his voyage from 1803 to 1806.) His excellency requests the chargé d'affaires to make known these *established facts* to his Government and to call its serious attention to them, adding "that the care it takes of becoming distinguished by the scrupulous combination of its interests with those of other powers, and its respect for the law of nations, excite the hope that this *illicit* traffic will meet with its disapprobation, and that rigid orders will put a stop to it."

The chargé d'affaires of America, in acknowledging the receipt of this note, promised to convey information of the reclamation to his Government.

Mr. Daschkoff, chargé d'affaires of his Imperial Majesty, renewed, under date of January 4, 1810, the same representation to the Government of the United States at Washington; and he proposed as a remedy the medium of a regulation of the Government of the United States, which should forbid to their citizens all commerce with the natives of the Northwest Coast of America, and which should confine them to trade with the Russian factories in the said latitudes; in a word, he solicited a law of the United States, or a convention between the two Governments, to declare all commerce with the natives of the country to be contraband. This negotiation was put off to another time, Mr. Daschkoff not being authorized to fix a latitude which might serve as a line of demarkation to American vessels that might trade on these coasts; and it appears by his letter of April 24, 1810, that he "was under the necessity of waiting as long as he could to receive correct information of the *geographical situation* of the Russian establishments."

The Government of the United States answered him, under date of May 5, 1810, that it would afford the President the utmost satisfaction to come to an equitable arrangement for the commerce of the United States with the natives in the Russian establishments; but that, the instructions of Mr. Daschkoff not having authorized him to fix a precise line of demarkation, the definitive arrangement of this question was not at present possible; but that if this obstacle were even removed by the full powers of his Government, others of a very delicate nature would present themselves to it.

That on the supposition that the natives of the country should be found under the jurisdiction of Russia, the United States would have only to abandon their merchants to the penalties incurred by those who carry on a contraband trade in a foreign jurisdiction; that if, on the contrary, the natives ought to be regarded as independent tribes, Russia could not prohibit foreigners from trading with them unless in contraband of war and in time of war; in which case she can herself put in execution the prohibition on the open sea.

The same rule may be applicable if the natives are considered as rebels or insurgents against the authority of Russia. Considering the subject in this point of view, it would be difficult for the United States, notwithstanding their constant desire of giving proofs of their friendship and of their respect towards his Imperial Majesty, to receive this proposition by recognizing such a state of things, since, in pronouncing upon opposite pretensions, they might expose themselves with Spain, whose rights upon the Northwest Coast of America extended to the south of the establishments of Russia. And, in fine, that if such an arrangement should be proposed to Congress it would still want there the basis of reciprocity. In expressing the sentiments of the Government of the United States, the Secretary of State added the expression of the desire that it might be found conformable to the benevolent and magnanimous intentions of his Imperial Majesty to favor the commerce of the United States, as well with the natives of the country as with the Russian establishments in these latitudes, in all the objects which may not be of a nature to be prejudicial to either.

In the month of September, 1810, his excellency Count Romanzoff, in a conference with Mr. Adams, minister of the United States at St. Petersburg, explained to him his ideas on the commerce of the Northwest Coast of America. His excellency observed that Russia had establisments on this coast from which a very advantageous trade with China might be carried on. That the Imperial Government had sent thither two ships, under the command of Captain Krusenstern, who had proceeded from thence to China; that, although the port of Canton be open to all the European nations, the Chinese had refused to admit the ship of Captain Krusenstern, under the pretext that the Russians had for a long time enjoyed the advantage of an exclusive privilege of trade by land at Kiachta, and that they were persuaded that if the Russians had had the intention of changing the route of their trade they would have mentioned it beforehand. Count Romanzoff wished, for these reasons, that the trade of the Russian establishments in these parts with China might be carried on by the intervention of American ships: and as these establishments were in the vicinity of the natives of the country, a race of men ferocious and dangerous, he thought an arrangement possible with the United States by which they might enjoy the trade of the establishments, under the restriction of not furnishing arms and munitions of war to the natives in the neighborhood of these establishments.

Upon Mr. Adams observing that he would wish to know what were the limits in which the restriction would operate, his excellency replied that this point required deliberation, but that the Russian charts represented the whole coast to the mouth of Columbia river as comprehended in their possessions.

In a second conference, in the month of October following, Mr. Adams mentioned in detail the difficulties which opposed an arrangement of the nature of that which his excellency the Minister of Trade wished, who finally appeared to agree that reciprocity, at least, was wanting to the restrictions which were demanded; and as to what regards the privilege granted for them, namely, the trade with the Russian establishments, it was evident that it did, in fact, already exist; (and it may be added, by way of parenthesis, that it was a trade without which the very existence of the Russian colonies had been often exposed.)

Besides, his excellency has not raised objections to the continuation of the trade of American vessels with the coasts in the neighborhood of the Russian establishments; he had even declared that this commerce was open to all friendly nations; he had only insisted on the inconveniences which resulted from their having furnished fire-arms and powder to the natives. In fine, his excellency observed, that, as to what regarded the fixing of a limit to the Russian territories, the measure presented great difficulties at the moment, and that it would be better to defer this fixing to a future time, in order to avoid possible collisions and every pretext of discontent and jealousy. For, in the present state of the world, the most ardent wish of his heart was to bring all the civilized nations to pacific dispositions, and to avoid everything which might be capable of sowing discord.

Mr. Adams saw, about the same time, the memorials of the Russian American Company, in which a territorial claim was advanced as far as the mouth of Columbia river.

NOTE (f.)

Vattel's Law of Nations, book 1, chapter 18, section 207. "All mankind have an equal right to the things that have not yet fallen into the possession of any one; and these things belong to the first possessor. When, therefore, a nation finds a country uninhabited, and without a master, it may lawfully take possession of it; and after it has sufficiently made known its will in this respect, it cannot be deprived of it by another. Thus navigators going on the discovery, furnished with a commission from their sovereign, and meeting with islands or other desert countries, have taken possession of them in the name of their nation; and this title has been commonly respected, *provided it was soon after followed by a real possession.*"

SEC. 208. "But it is questioned whether a nation may thus appropriate to itself, by merely taking possession of a country which it does not really occupy, and in this manner reserve to itself much more than it is able to people or cultivate. It is not difficult to determine that such a pretension would be absolutely contrary to the law, and opposite to the views of nature, who, appointing all the earth to supply the wants of man in general, gave to no nation the right of appropriating to itself a country but for the use it makes of it, and not to hinder others from improving it. *The law of nations then only acknowledges the property and sovereignty of a nation over uninhabited countries, of which they shall really, and in fact, take possession,* in which they shall form settlements, or of which they shall make actual use."

NOTE (g.)

Vattel's Law of Nations, book 1, chap. 23, section 282. "The right of navigating and fishing in the open sea being then a right common to all men, the nation who attempts to exclude another from that advantage does it an injury, and gives a sufficient cause for war; nature authorizing a nation to repel an injury, that is, to make use of force against whoever would deprive it of its rights."

SEC. 283. "We may moreover say that a nation which, without a title, would arrogate to itself an exclusive right to the sea, and support it by force, does an injury to all nations, whose common right it violates; and all are at liberty to unite against it, in order to repress such an attempt. Nations have the greatest interest in causing the law of nations, which is the basis of their tranquillity, to be universally respected. If any one openly tramples it under foot, all may and ought to rise up against them, and, by uniting their forces to chastise the common enemy, they will discharge their duty towards themselves and towards human society, of which they are members."—(Prelim. sec. 22.)

No. 9.

Extracts of a letter (No. 34) from Mr. Middleton to Mr. Adams, dated February 5, (17,) 1824.

"Sir Charles Bagot not having received any instructions from his court in relation to the Northwest question up to the middle of December last, I was unwilling to lose any further time, and took occasion, (as I informed you in my last it was my intention to do,) from Count Nesselrode having expressed an opinion to me, " qu'il y avoit beaucoup de vague dans toute cette question," to assure him that it was far otherwise, and to request him to receive for his own and for the Emperor's perusal the *Confidential Memorial*, of which I forwarded you the first sketch with my number 33. This was put into his hand on the 17th December, and will have changed, I hope, some of the views entertained up to that time. I think it must appear clearly to all who examine the subject that the acts of this Government in relation to the Northwest Coast have originated in errors of fact and of theory."

"I have within these few days past been notified by Sir Charles Bagot that it is the intention of Great Britain to proceed separately in relation to this interest. I shall abstain from making any remark at present upon this very unexpected turn in the affair, but I am hopeful that the Imperial Government will now proceed in the negotiation without further delay, as it has always professed its readiness to do."

No. 10.

Mr. Middleton to Mr. Adams, No. 35

ST. PETERSBURG, *April* 7, (19,) 1824.

SIR: I am here to have the honor of endeavoring to give you a connected though cursory narrative of the proceedings which have taken place, during several months past, in relation to the negotiation upon the Northwest Coast question, which has at length terminated in the conclusion of a convention, signed with the Russian plenipotentiaries, upon the 5th (17th) of this month, and now to be forwarded by Mr. Lucius Bull, who is to proceed hence for Washington as special messenger.

You are already apprised of the proceedings upon this question having been suspended, in the expectation that Great Britain would proceed jointly with the United States in the measures to be taken in relation to this interest. That such an expectation was not altogether groundless will appear from the following extracts of a note I made at the time from two despatches addressed by Mr. Secretary Canning to Sir Charles Bagot, and read by him to me just after receiving them:

"Upon the subject of the ukase I have delayed sending you further and more precise instructions, in consequence of an intimation from the Government of the United States, through our minister in America, that they were desirous of combining with ours their representations and negotiations on the subject."

Another despatch, extracts of which were read to me, stated, "That a copy of a despatch from his Majesty's minister in America upon the subject of the Russian ukase was forwarded for his excellency the ambassador's information. It is therein stated that the Government of the United States are desirous to join with that of his Majesty in bringing forward some proposition for the definitive settlement of this question with Russia."

"But we have no specific information as to the views of the American Government, Mr. Rush not having yet received any instructions upon the subject."

"It seems probable, however, that the part of the question in which the American Government is peculiarly desirous of establishing a concert with this country is that which concerns the extravagant assumption of maritime jurisdiction. Upon this point, such a concert as the United States are understood to desire might be peculiarly advantageous."—Dated July 12, 1823.

With these extracts before me, and frequent opportunities of observing how anxious Sir C. Bagot was to have our co-operation, it is not surprising that I should be fully under the impression that England would willingly adopt a joint negotiation. It may be very well understood why, then, when I discovered that the full power sent over to Sir Charles had relation to the *maritime question alone,* (see the paper lettered A,) and when, too, I perceived that Mr. Poletica, who was left in the absence of the Emperor and of Count Nesselrode to *"hold conferences,"* it may well be understood *why* I was well pleased to avail myself of Sir Charles' want of powers, to decline continuing a negotiation which could conclude nothing. I then waited patiently until the return of the Emperor; but finding, in the middle of December, that Sir Charles' instructions were not yet forthcoming, and being unwilling to lose any further time, I took occasion, from Count Nesselrode's telling me in conversation upon the subject of the Northwest Coast question, * * * * to beg to offer to his perusal and that of the Emperor a confidential memoir I had drawn up, a copy of which (in the form in which it was presented) I now forward.—(See book lettered A.) I then waited anxiously the news we were to have from London. Great, indeed, was my surprise when, on the 9th of February, (N. S.,) I received Mr. Rush's letter, dated January 9.—(See papers lettered *b* and *c*.) Mr. Rush therein states that Mr. Canning had intimated to him that Sir Charles Bagot had only *paused under my suggestions.* Mr. Rush might have contradicted this, for he must have known that the fact was otherwise. The first intimations from our Government of its desire to concert measures with England had been conveyed through Mr. Stratford Canning.

My first act, upon receiving the notification that England would treat separately from the United States, was, to acquaint both the Russian Secretary and the British Ambassador that if any attempt was made to negotiate upon the territorial question without our participation it would become my duty to protest in the strongest terms. I represented to Sir Charles, 1st. That Great Britain having no establishment or possession upon any part of the Northwest *Coast* of America, she can have no right or pretension, except such as may result from her convention with Spain, concluded October 28, 1790; and, of course, she can convey to a third power no rights, claims, or pretensions, except such as she herself may have derived from her convention with Spain. 2d. That the United States, in virtue of their convention concluded with Spain February 22, 1819, have acquired all the rights, claims, and pretensions whatsoever of that power upon the same coast, north of the 42d parallel of latitude; and that, consequently, the said States have concurrent rights, claims, and pretensions with Great Britain, to whatever point hers may be considered to extend. 3d. That, therefore, any convention or agreement which might be made between Russia and Great Britain, without the participation of the United States, must be nugatory and null as regards them, and cannot divest the said States of the rights they enjoy upon that coast.

To Count Nesselrode I stated that the benefit to Russia, at least of a convention with England from which we should be excluded, must be small indeed. They seemed willing to assume that the territorial question regarded exclusively Russia and England as "limitrophes" upon this coast. This I denied, and contended that the rights of the United States, to say the least, were *concurrent* with those of England; and to show how little any agreement to which we were not parties would avail them, I used the argument of which a condensed statement follows in the language we used:

" That supposing that England, for herself, renounced the rights which the community of the waters which wash these shores gives her, this renunciation can in no way prejudice the rights of others. Thus, in spite of her renunciation, these seas would remain free to all other nations. For a convention between two nations which stipulate their interests according to their own good pleasure, cannot have any effect either on the principles of the law of nations, or on the rights of other nations. It will be found, then, that when our citizens go to traffic in the latitudes of the great Northern Ocean, the Russians cannot oppose to them, *in a valid manner*, the convention concluded with Great Britain. The compact with this power would only prove that there had been a dispute, and that the two contracting powers had made an arrangement in this regard," &c., &c.

Such was the general reasoning I used; and shortly after the circumstance of England having determined to treat separately was known here, I received permission to see Count Nesselrode officially, and he invited me by note, under date of February 6, (O. S.,) stating the fact as communicated to him by the British ambassador, of his Government having determined to act *separately*, and inviting any communication I might think proper to make. At my solicitation he appointed the Saturday following for our first meeting upon the Northwest question. I was happy to find at this meeting that the Russian Government was as well disposed to treat with us as ever. Various conferences have since taken place, from my notes of all which, (as, in general, no protocol was drawn up,) I shall endeavor to make a short statement in the following sheets.

FIRST CONFERENCE.

Count Nesselrode received me by appointment, at his own house, on Saturday, February 9, at eight o'clock in the evening. He opened the business of the Northwest Coast negotiation by declaring that he believed it would be best for us to waive all discussion upon abstract principles of *right* and upon the actual state of *facts*, and that we must endeavor to settle the difference which had arisen between our Governments "on the basis which might be found most conformable to our *mutual interests*." In answer, I stated that I was perfectly ready to accede to the course proposed by him, although I felt confident that the United States had nothing to apprehend from the strictest examination into their claims and pretensions, but that I must reserve to myself the right, which he would also of course retain on his part, of invoking, occasionally, such principles of national law and of alleging such facts as we might, respectively, deem necessary to the defence of the rights and interests of either party.

He then inquired whether I had prepared any *projet* of convention for the settlement of the disputed points in this question? I placed under his eye the two *drafts* of which the copies herewith sent are lettered D and E.—(See the documents.) He promised that these papers should be submitted to the Emperor at an early day, and we parted with an understanding that he would give me notice when I could again [see] him upon the same business.

SECOND CONFERENCE.

Having received an invitation from Count Nesselrode, I waited on him on Wednesday, February 20, at one o'clock p. m. I found Mr. Poletica with the Count, and a *rescript* from the Emperor to these gentlemen was exhibited to me, empowering them to treat and adjust a settlement of the differences which had arisen in consequence of his Majesty's ukase of September 4, (16,) 1821.—(See paper lettered *f*.) I exhibited to them my power from the President of the United States, to the same effect, and we exchanged copies of the same. Some 'informal talk then arose respecting the general merits of the question we had in hand. I shall give a very short statement upon this head, because, according to previous understanding with Count Nesselrode, who took no part in it, all discussion of this nature was *private* and *extra official*. I shall use the language in which we spoke.

M. de Poletica, among other things, has affirmed that the pretended declaration of Russia, in the dispute between Spain and England on the subject of Nootka, is only a gratuitous assertion on the part of Spain. It was answered that this assertion, made in the face of Europe, had not been denied at the time by Russia, and that from that it is to be concluded to be well founded, until the proofs of the contrary were produced.

M. de Poletica has also pretended that the convention of 1819 only cedes to the United States the rights and pretensions of Spain to the territories *to the east* and *to the north* of the boundary line, (which would, in effect, be the position of the greatest part of the Northwest Coast of America,) so that, according to him, a perpendicular line ought to be drawn from the point where the forty-second parallel touches the Pacific Ocean, that is to say, that it ought to follow the *parallel of longitude* from this point towards the North Pole for finding the western limits of the United States. But, it has been answered to him, can M. de Poletica be ignorant that the forty-second parallel of north latitude actually reaches across the great ocean, and that the coasts of the northwest are necessarily found *all to the north* of this parallel? Besides, these coasts having been included in the pretensions of Spain, in the year 1790, as far as Prince William's Sound, *all this territory* ought actually to be comprised in the cession of the rights of Spain to the United States. Otherwise, it cannot be denied that, in the case of the cession not having been made to the United States, then the possession must necessarily still belong to Spain, and can in no manner be claimed by Russia, &c., &c.

After some further desultory conversation upon the same topics, the Count put into my hand a *contre-projet*, consisting of a translation into French of the projet I had offered, with some insertions, alterations, and additions, (see paper lettered *g*.) I observed, that the insertion in the second article was utterly inadmissible, as repugnant to the stipulations of the former article, and that, instead of the admission of American vessels solely to New Archangel, in the third article, I should propose the commercial principle adopted by the United States and England upon the same coast, (indiscriminate admission, &c., for a limited period.) That I must now frankly tell them that my instructions required that I should obtain two points as necessary conditions to the third object contemplated by the projet of convention. First, the revocation, either spontaneous or by convention, of the maritime provisions of the ukase of September 4, (16,) 1821. Secondly, the adoption of the commercial principle (or something similar) agreed upon between the United States and Great Britain, in their convention of 1818, in relation to these coasts. Thirdly, that, these preliminaries being settled, a *territorial delimitation for settlements* at fifty-five degrees might be agreed upon.

Upon this Mr. Poletica assured me, with a strong asseveration, that *he* would never be brought to sign an instrument containing the principle of free admission for *our ships to their coasts*, whatever *the Count* might think proper to do. He continued to argue warmly against anything of the kind. I replied somewhat at length, and concluded by saying that, unless he could be brought to change his mind upon this point, it was more than probable *we* should be able to do nothing. Russia must then be content to *keep her ukase*, and other nations would only have to see what means they may possess of carrying on the northwest trade *in spite of it*. The Count took no share in this *a-parte* discussion, and when it concluded I told him that I should take his contre-projet home with me to consider it and make such further propositions as reflection should suggest. We agreed to meet again in three days.

THIRD CONFERENCE.

We met again at 8 o'clock in the evening of Saturday, February 23, when I presented my counter-projet, (see paper lettered *h*,) accepting the first article, and the second, with the omission of what they had inserted upon my first projet. With regard to the third article, I observed that the proposal of inserting 54° 40' instead of 55°, with a view, as they explained it, of preserving to Russia two points of the island in which the port, called *Bucarelli* by the Spaniards, is situate, might [not] be absolutely inadmissible, although I should exceed my instructions in agreeing to it; but that at all events I must restore the phraseology I had used in the commencement of the article, as we could not admit for them or claim for ourselves *possessions*, except where there are actual establishments. Count Nesselrode stated that he had intentionally introduced the alteration in the phraseology, meaning thereby to secure their settlement near Bodeja (which lies *south* of the line of delimitation) against all possible objection, if, indeed, they should hereafter consider it to be worth their while to continue it, and, provided also, that neither *Spain* nor *Mexico* should object to it. He would now, however, consent to adopt my phraseology, since it should seem that what lies *south* of Cape Mendocino cannot be correctly considered as being any part of the Northwest Coast. Coming to the latter part of the article as proposed by me, which substitutes, in lieu of admission to our vessels at the port of Archangel, a provision for their free admission *to all parts* of that coast, including a free trade with the natives, he appeared to consider this to be utterly inadmissible. Upon my persisting, however, to aver that nothing could be done without it, he consented, at least, to take the proposition *ad referendum*. I stated I had yet an alternative to offer, which, leaving the line of delimitation undecided, might settle all difficulties on our part; and I proposed to let the third article run as set forth in the paper lettered *(d.)* It was not difficult to perceive that the utmost reluctance was felt in admitting the principle of free trade in any form. I thought it probable that this proposition would lead them to appreciate the advantage they might derive from delimitation, and prepare them to be willing to pay the price of it.

FOURTH CONFERENCE.

After a fortnight's interruption, I met his Majesty's plenipotentiaries on Saturday, March 8, at 8 o'clock in the evening. Count Nesselrode stated that my last projet had been considered, and that there remained very little to be done to bring our projets together. That there were but two lines to be *omitted* and *one word* to be *altered*. [See lines *in italic*, in paper *(h,)* viz: the words *"and the trade with the natives of the country,"* to be omitted; and the word *"ten"* to be exchanged for *"five."*] I observed that, as the article would in that case remain, it would amount to a stipulation that we should enjoy for a very limited period, and as a privilege, what we are now entitled to by the law of nature, in common with all the independent nations, to wit: *the fisheries* upon an *unoccupied* coast; less infinitely than is permitted by this same projet upon all the other shores of the great ocean; where, by the preceding articles, as well as by common right, we may land and trade in unoccupied places. I therefore must at once declare the positive inadmissibility of that proposition. With regard to shortening the term for which a free trade was reciprocally to be granted, I could have no idea that it would be seriously pressed, being in itself so small an object. I then begged leave to place under his eye a short statement of principles and facts, which might have some weight in relation to the subject under consideration, and which I considered to be incontrovertible.

See paper lettered *(k.)* Having read this with attention, he exclaimed, "Well, *here is a convention*. We must see if 'tis not possible to come to an arrangement." He then stated that there could, however, now remain only one mean of accommodating the existing difference. This he would state hypothetically, (supposing the possibility of the Emperor's permitting the stipulation of a free trade for ten years to be agreed to.) It was a proposition which, *perhaps*, would be made to me at a future meeting. It would he intended to prohibit the trade in fire-arms and ammunition. He went into a recapitulation of the complaints of Mr. Daschkoff and Count Pahlen, on account of the injuries arising from the fire-arms furnished to the natives by our citizens. I took occasion here to declare that all these proceedings of the Russian Government were founded in *erroneous* impressions, and arose from their having improperly conceived that they had *a right* to regulate our commerce upon a coast which, being unoccupied, was free and open to all nations. It was clear that they had no right to demand any regulation of the kind. He replied; they did not now, of course, expect any arrangement which should not be marked by *reciprocity*. I remarked, that any restriction of the kind would be in many respects liable to objections. That the first which presented itself to my mind was, that such a regulation could not be carried into effect without admitting a right of search, which was wholly inadmissible in time of peace. He replied, they had no intention of proposing anything of the kind, for that they would be satisfied with the right of *making representations* to our Government, in case of the infraction of the regulation which should be adopted by our traders. I remarked, that if the restriction could be carried into effect, as regards our vessels and their own, that it would be giving a premium to the traders of other nations; for example, to the English or to the Dutch, who have considerable possessions west of the Pacific, or to the Portuguese of Macao, or to the Mexicans, since Mexico may now be considered as a State; all of whom would enjoy the faculty of carrying on a trade, voluntarily relinquished by ourselves, in arms and ammunition, articles which appear to be much coveted by the natives of those coasts. I was answered, that the English were ready to give up, altogether, the right of trading to the coasts, which would accrue to Russia by the arrangements about to be made, (a circumstance, by way of parenthesis, which was fully confirmed to me by Sir Charles Bagot, in a subsequent conversation,) and that Russia has the means of influencing all other nations to abstain from a trade which would be no longer open, except in the form she should please to give it. I still objected to the *impracticability* of the project, and intimated my apprehensions that it would only be a pretext for vexations; stating, however, that the question was new to me, and entirely unprovided for in my instructions; but that I was bound, at least, to consider any proposition they might think proper to offer. We then parted, the Count promising to notify me when I could have another meeting with him.

SUBSEQUENT CONFERENCES.

Considerable delay occurred after the conference of the 8th March, occasioned partly, as I understood, by the indisposition of the Emperor, and partly, too, as I supposed, to give time for consultation with the Directors of the Russian American Company. At length, on the morning of the 22d March, Mr. Poletica called upon me, and stated that he had now a projet to offer on the part of his Government, (see paper lettered *l*,) and that he would leave it with me for consideration. Among other things, he observed that the prohibition of a trade in arms and ammunition would be a *sine qua non*, and that the Emperor wished, in views of benevolence, to add thereto all kinds of spirituous liquors. This was confirmed to me by Count Nesselrode's note of 20th March, (see paper lettered *m*.) Mr. Poletica stated that Count Nesselrode proposed to receive me on Monday, the 24th instant, at his house, at one o'clock p. m.

Accordingly I attended on Monday, the 24th March, and offered the projet, (lettered *n*.) The argument this day turned generally upon the restrictions proposed to be imposed upon the trade. The sale of arms to savages, whose blind passions are unrestrained by any moral tie, must be equally pernicious to themselves and all who come within their reach. The greatest objection to this prohibition appeared to me to be, that the restriction may be converted into a pretext for vexations upon our commerce, if seizure or confiscation were permitted; and, on the other hand, it seemed likely that all other modes of carrying the prohibition into effect would prove nugatory. I had been told, however, that they would be satisfied with its interdiction under such penalties as we might think proper to impose; that in case of infraction they would content themselves with *representations* to the Government; but that, finally, the measure was a *sine qua non*. In order to meet this proposition, I had drawn up the article as it stands in the projet, as, upon the whole, I concluded that our Government will probably consider the proposal as less objectionable than at a former period, from considerations, at least, of *reciprocity, now* that we have an acknowledged territory upon the western coast, and when, too, it might perhaps be unavailing to attempt to resist the claims of Russia, likely so soon to be fully acknowledged by Great Britain.

On the 28th Mr. Poletica brought me the projet lettered *(o.)* It now appeared to me that the latter part of the fourth article, "that the reciprocal right shall cease," &c., had still too much the appearance of a substantive stipulation, although I had changed it from an entire article in their projet of the 22d of March, so as to stand as an accessory to the preceding stipulation of an open trade. In the fifth article, their expression "of arbitrary measures" did not appear to me to be sufficiently precise, as it left them at liberty to adopt *regulations* and to carry them into effect, because it could not be said that such regulations were arbitrary. For these reasons, I proposed at our meeting on the 31st that the fourth and fifth article should stand as set forth in the projet lettered *(p.)*

The fourth article became the subject of warm debate during the three meetings upon the 31st of March and the 1st and 2d of April; at the last of which they proposed that I should sign a protocol of the tenor of that lettered *(q.)* This was refused by me as asserting what was evidently untrue, to wit: that the two forms specified therein *meant the same thing;* but I consented to sign another protocol, of which one of the originals is forwarded herewith, lettered *(r.)* The protocol of signature is lettered *(s,)* and the convention *(t.)*

Such is the sum and substance of what passed in our conferences, as extracted from the short notes I made directly after each meeting. If it should appear to be meagre and desultory, this must be accounted for from the circumstance that we had set out disclaiming all *regular discussion* of right or of fact; and if anything approaching to it was resorted to, it was only when I deemed some statement absolutely necessary to support our pretensions; but in general everything of the nature of *discussion* appeared to be carefully avoided by the adversary.

I now beg leave to add a few observations on the convention as concluded.

In order to judge equitably the merits of this convention, (or indeed of any other,) it may be necessary to make some allowance for the circumstances in which it was negotiated.

In the very outset of this negotiation the *defection* of England was a circumstance of a character likely to throw great difficulties in the way of it. *This* was occasioned, as I am well informed, partly by a conviction that *our* interests were different from if not directly opposed to *hers*, and partly, too, by the notion that *the doctrine* of the President's message *respecting colonization upon the American continent* must be peculiarly displeasing to Russia, and such as would render the negotiation much more difficult for the

United States than for Great Britain. The latter power appears to have given over all thoughts of *keeping open* the trade upon the Northwest Coast of America. Her object in this negotiation seems to be to obtain an abandonment of the extravagant maritime pretension set up by Russia, and at the same time to acquire for herself territorial rights over such portion of the shores of the American continent as may secure her free egress from her interior possessions, lying towards the east, into the Pacific Ocean. Whenever these rights shall have been acknowledged, she will probably use her accessorial maritime domain for the purpose of excluding other nations from trading within her jurisdiction. With these prospects we must not indulge in the expectation of her renewing the trading privilege we now enjoy within her limits, unless it be made the price of our acknowledgment of a line of delimitation.

From the commercial activity which prevails universally at this day it is not to be expected that any coasts upon which valuable articles of trade are obtained can long continue unappropriated. That this should have been the case up to the present time upon the Northwest Coasts of America can be only accounted for from the circumstance of those regions being of extreme difficult access to all the inhabitants of Europe by reason of their remoteness from that part of the globe; while at the same time the wars which have generally absorbed the attention of the whole civilized portion of mankind almost continually since the discoveries of Captain Cook have prevented their importance being duly appreciated. In the short period of peace which intervened between the first American war and those of the French revolution, several expeditions were undertaken, which indicate that the general opinion of that importance had begun to prevail. That of M. de la Perouse, and that of Marchaud, by the French; those of Vancouver, and other English navigators; several voyages undertaken by enterprising citizens of the United States; and lastly, the affair of Nootka Sound, all go to prove how general an opinion prevailed of the value of the trade in furs, above all, with reference to the China market. During a length of time the Russians had enjoyed the benefit of supplying that market with furs obtained either in their Asiatic possessions or in the American islands, although they are obliged to transport them from Okhotsk by land carriage to Kiachta, thence to introduce them by Malmaichin, the only *port of entry* for all the borders between Russia and China. They have been anxious, on account of the delay and expense attendant upon this route, to establish a right of admission for their vessels into Canton, where all European flags are admitted; but they have been hitherto prevented from doing so by some strange caprice of the Chinese.

The confusion prevailing in Europe in 1799 permitted Russia (who alone seems to have kept her attention fixed upon this interest during that period) to take a decided step towards the monopoly of this trade, by the ukase of that date, which trespassed upon the acknowledged rights of Spain; but at that moment the Emperor Paul had declared war against that country as being an ally of France. This ukase, which is, in its *form*, an act purely domestic, was never notified to any foreign State with injunction to respect its provisions. Accordingly it appears to have been passed over unobserved by foreign powers, and it remained without execution in so far as it militated against their rights. The partial success of this measure seems, however, to have encouraged the yet more bold assumptions of the ukase of September, 1821. It may easily be imagined how much a *fancied* but equally *unquestioned* (either by themselves or others) *possession* during upwards of twenty years must have strengthened the opinion the Russians had of their own rights. I have reason to know that even in the Emperor's mind this conviction had taken strong hold. When urged both by England and America to recede from his territorial pretensions, he expressed himself ready to undo his own act, but declared that the act of his father must be maintained. The fifty-fifth degree was therefore a barrier not to be broken through; and a further small addition was required because the point of an island was cut off by that parallel. In consequence of this, it was urgently pressed by the Russian plenipotentiaries to make the line of delimitation run upon the parallel of 54° 40', a small deviation from the instructions I had received. To this I thought I could, without impropriety, accede. To show how much importance they attach to the parallel of 54° 40', it may now be mentioned that it is only upon this point that the negotiation with Great Britain has been broken off. England had agreed to accept this delimitation *upon the islands*, but insisted upon carrying her territorial claim *upon the continent* up to 56° and some minutes, in order to retain the mouth and course of a river which disembogues about that latitude, and as being necessary to the convenience of certain posts established in that neighborhood by the Northwest and Hudson's Bay Companies; but Russia has decidedly refused to accede to that delimitation, and Sir Charles has sent for further instructions.

It may, perhaps, be thought that, as certain restrictions upon our trade were insisted upon, which were not provided for in any instructions, I ought to have deferred the signature of the convention, and to have sent home for further instructions. Such would have been my course had I not apprehended that the question of delimitation between England and Russia must certainly, long before I could have any answer, be settled one way or other without our participation, and that we should then have no equivalent to offer for the trade we covet upon their shores, as neither of these nations seem disposed to consider as valuable any like advantage we may have it in our power to grant.

It may possibly, too, be objected, upon a superficial view of the convention, that it surrenders a permanent *right* to a community of trade upon the Northwest Coast in exchange for a *privilege* which is to expire in ten years. In answer to this objection, I submit that this right must always have been held subject to extinguishment whenever the maritime domain, incident to actual occupation and settlement, shall be acquired by any nation upon those coasts; and I beg leave further to remark upon the same point, that I kept it always in recollection that when the stipulation of the fourth article, for liberty of trading with the natives, shall have expired by its own limitation, these coasts, in so far as they may then remain unoccupied, will fall into the general category of *unoccupied places upon the coasts of the great ocean.*

The Russian plenipotentiaries had been all along particularly anxious to introduce into the convention a *substantive* stipulation, that the privilege to trade upon these coasts should absolutely *cease* after ten years. An example of this may be seen in their projet of March 22, in which it formed the subject of the fifth article. Such a stipulation I perseveringly resisted in all shapes, declaring that we retained a hope that our trade would become valuable and indispensable to their settlements before the expiration of the period specified, and that I was not authorized to enter into any stipulation of that nature. After three conferences, in which this point was the principal subject of contest, they consented to adopt my projet of a fourth article, with the explanation to be seen in the protocol of the 2d of April, "that *the reciprocal right* to trade *granted by this stipulation* cannot be extended beyond said term but by mutual consent." This appeared to them, although it can by no means change the nature or character of the article, and only admits that the *privilege granted by the article* must cease by its own limitation—a proposition sufficiently evident from the terms of the article itself, and which cannot affect the stipulations of other articles. As to the *mutual consent* necessary to the prolongation of the faculty granted by the article, it must be self-evident that if *that* were not necessary to *its existence in the form* allowed by the article, the article itself would have been altogether without an object. But with regard to *the trade in unoccupied places*, as permitted by the permanent articles, I am confident in the opinion that *all the shores of the great ocean* upon which the parties to this contract have any claim will continue open to them, respectively, for its pursuit under these stipulations.

The specific and particular privileges granted by the article (which, upon examination, will be found to contain an *extension* of the general privileges embraced by the preceding articles,) will, of course, cease after ten years, unless renewed by mutual consent.

The entire article was offered in conformity to the spirit of the instruction, although the tripartite convention anticipated by the instruction had not been concluded, because the agreement for an open trade upon that portion of the coast claimed by England has yet five years to run.

Such are my views of this subject. I have only to hope that I may not have mistaken those of my Government. If I have erred in concluding this convention, which may, indeed, in some degree disappoint just expectation, I shall console myself, knowing that I have done so under the impression that I was bound to take upon myself the responsibility of this act, rather than to suffer, through a fear of incurring a disavowal of it, that the public interest should risk a loss by my letting pass an opportunity of securing advantages which can never again offer.

You will be aware, sir, how anxiously I must expect your answer, by which I shall be enabled to ascertain how far the President will approve of what I have done.

I have the honor to be, sir, most faithfully, your obedient servant,

HENRY MIDDLETON.

P. S. In stating the communication made to me by the British ambassador, respecting the determination of his court to treat separately from the United States with Russia, I omitted to mention that he at the same time informed me that he was instructed, in case he should form a convention with Russia, without our being admitted to treat, to insert in it a saving clause for the rights of other States, similar to that contained in our convention of October 20, 1818. Since the conclusion of the negotiation on our part, the British ambassador has furnished me with a copy of his instruction *ad hoc.* (See paper lettered *v.*)

H. M.

The SECRETARY OF STATE *of the United States, &c.*

No. 10, *b.*—35 (*a.*)

G. R. *(manu regià.)*

George the Fourth, by the Grace of God King of the United Kingdom of Great Britain and Ireland, Defender of the Faith, King of Hanover, &c., &c., to all and singular to whom these presents shall come, greeting:

Whereas an imperial edict was promulgated at St. Petersburg, on the fourth day of September, in the year of our Lord one thousand eight hundred and twenty-one, prohibiting, under pain of confiscation, all foreign vessels from approaching within one hundred Italian miles of the Northwestern Coast of America, the Aleutian and Kurile Isles, and the eastern coasts of Siberia; and whereas differences have, in consequence, arisen respecting the right of commerce and navigation in those seas, and we, being desirous that the said differences should be amicably adjusted, have thought proper to name some person of approved fidelity, ability, and zeal, for this salutary purpose: Know ye, therefore, that we, reposing especial trust and confidence in our right trusty and well-beloved counsellor Sir Charles Bagot, Knight Grand Cross of the most honorable order of the Bath, and our Ambassador Extraodinary and Plenipotentiary to our good brother the Emperor of all the Russias, have named, made, constituted, and appointed, as we do by these presents name, make, constitute, and appoint him our undoubted Commissioner, Procurator, and Plenipotentiary; giving unto him all and all manner of power and authority to treat, adjust, and conclude, with such minister or ministers as may be vested with similar power and authority on the part of our good brother the Emperor of all the Russias, any articles or agreement that may promote the above mentioned end, and to sign for us and in our name everything so agreed upon and concluded, and to do and transact all such matters in as ample manner and form, and with equal force and efficacy, as we ourself could do if personally present; engaging and promising, upon our royal word, that whatever things shall be so transacted and concluded by our said Commissioner, Procurator, and Plenipotentiary, shall be agreed upon, acknowledged and accepted by us in the fullest manner, and that we will never suffer any person whatsoever to infringe the same or act contrary thereto. In witness whereof, we have caused the great seal of our United Kingdom of Great Britain and Ireland to be affixed to these presents, which we have signed with our royal hand.

Given at our court at Brighthelmstone, the twentieth day of February, in the year of our Lord one [L. S.] thousand eight hundred and twenty-three, and in the fourth of our reign.

No. 35, (*b.*)

Extract of a letter from Mr. Rush, dated

LONDON, *December* 22, 1823.

"In an interview that I had with Mr. Canning last week I made known to him, as preparatory to the negotiation, the views of our Government relative to the Northwest Coast of America. These, as you know, are:

"First, That, as regards the country westward of the Rocky mountains, the three powers, viz: Great Britain, the United States, and Russia, should jointly agree to a convention, to be in force ten years, similar in its nature to the third article of the convention of October, 1818, now subsisting between the two former powers; and secondly, that the United States would stipulate not to make any settlements on that coast north of the fifty-first degree of latitude, provided Great Britain would stipulate not to make any south of 51° or *north of fifty-five;* and Russia not to make any south of 55°.

"Mr. Canning expressed no opinion on the above propositions further than to hint, under his first impressions, strong objections to the one which goes to limit Great Britain northwards to 55°. His object in wishing to learn from me our propositions at this point of time was, as I understood, that he might the better write to Sir Charles Bagot on the whole subject to which they relate."

Extract of a letter from Mr. Rush, dated

LONDON, *December* 6, 1823.

"I received, in the course of the past summer, instructions from our Government to open negotiations with this Government upon a great variety of subjects interesting to the two countries; and amongst others, on that of the Russian ukase of September, 1821, relative to the Northwest Coast of America. As you are in possession of a copy of the Secretary of State's letter to me of the second [22d] of July, on this last subject, I need say nothing at present respecting it. I write on this occasion barely to inform you that, as yet, the negotiations have not commenced on any one of the subjects which I have in charge, and of course, therefore, this of the Russian ukase remains also untouched. As I am instructed to correspond with you upon this subject, as well as upon that relating to the suppression of the slave trade, I will take care to do so as events may render it necessary and proper after the negotiations shall have been entered upon. I have announced to this Government my entire readiness to commence them, but am still unable to say at what precise time a beginning will be made.

"I will also apprise you in due time of the results that may attend my discussions upon all the other subjects."

No. 35, (c.)

Extract of a letter from Mr. Rush, dated

LONDON, *January* 9, 1824.

"I have heretofore written to you on the 6th and 22d of December, and have now to inform you that from interviews which I have had with Mr. Canning since the present month set in, I find that he will decline sending instructions to Sir Charles Bagot to proceed jointly with our Government and that of Russia in the negotiation relative to the Northwest Coast of America; but that he will be merely informed that it is now the intention of Great Britain to proceed separately.

"Mr. Canning intimated to me that to proceed separately was the original intention of this Government, to which effect Sir Charles Bagot had been instructed, and never to any other; and that Sir Charles had only paused under your suggestions to him of its being the desire of our Government that the three powers should move in concert at St. Petersburg upon this subject.

"The resumption of its original course by this Government has arisen chiefly from the principle which our Government has adopted, of not considering the American continents as subjects for future colonization by *any* of the European powers—a principle to which Great Britain does not accede.

"I have informed the Secretary of State of the above intention of this Government. It will produce no alteration in my endeavors to obtain in negotiation here a settlement of the points as between the United States and Great Britain, respecting the Northwest Coast, in manner as my instructions lay them down to me."

No. 35, *(d.)*

State of the Question.

The United States, by their discovery of the mouth of the Columbia river, and by their subsequent *real occupation* and continued possession of a district on the same part of the Northwest Coast of America, have perfected their right of sovereignty to that territory.

By the third article of a convention with Great Britain, concluded October 20, 1818, they stipulated "that any country that might be claimed by either party on the Northwest Coast of America westward of the Stony mountains should, together with its harbors, bays, and creeks, and the navigation of all rivers within the same, be free and open, for the term of ten years from that date, to all vessels, citizens, and subjects, of the two powers, without prejudice to the claims of either party or of any other State."

By a convention with Spain of February 20, 1819, the United States acquired all the rights, claims, and pretensions, of that power to all the Northwest Coast lying north of the 42d parallel of latitude. The claims of Spain appear to have rested on *prior discovery,* as far as the 59th degree north. So far, then, as prior discovery can constitute a foundation of right, the Northwest Coast as far as the 59th degree north belongs to the United States by the transfer of the rights of Spain.

Great Britain has no establishment or possession on any part of the Northwest Coast. She has, therefore, no right, claim, or pretension to any portion thereof, except such as may result from the convention with Spain concluded October 28, 1790. It is, then, evident that her claim is concurrent with those of the United States, and can only reach to whatever point these last may be considered to extend.

It appears, then, that Russia and England cannot make a definitive arrangement without the participation of the United States, or at least going to their exclusion. Any agreement which these two powers may make will be binding upon themselves, but cannot affect the rights of a third power.

The United States offer to Russia an article of the same import with that of October, 1818, with Great Britain, to be in force for the term of ten years. By offering free and equal access to navigation and intercourse within the limits to which their claims are indisputable, they concede much more than they obtain.

With regard to territorial claim, separate from any system of exclusion, they are willing to agree to the boundary line within which the Emperor Paul had granted exclusive privileges to the Russian Company, that is to say, latitude 55°.

If the Russian Government apprehends serious inconvenience from *illicit traffic* with their settlements, it may be guarded against by stipulations similar to those in the annexed projet.

No. 35, *(e.)*

Projet of the United States of February 8.

ARTICLE I. In order to strengthen the bonds of friendship and to preserve in future a perfect harmony and good understanding between the high contracting parties, it is agreed that their respective citizens and subjects shall not be disturbed or molested, either in navigating or in carrying on their fisheries in any part of the great ocean vulgarly called the Pacific or South Sea, or in landing on the coasts thereof in places not already occupied, for the purpose of carrying on their commerce with the natives of the country, subject nevertheless to the restrictions and provisions specified in the following articles.

ARTICLE II. To the end that the navigation and fisheries in the great ocean carried on by citizens and subjects of the high contracting parties may not be made a pretext for illicit trade with their respective settlements, it is agreed that the citizens of the United States shall not land on any part of the coast actually occupied by Russian settlements, unless by permission of the Governor or commandant thereof; and that Russian subjects shall, in like manner, be interdicted from landing without permission at any settlement of the United States on the Northwest Coast.

ARTICLE III. It is further agreed that no settlement shall be made hereafter on the Northwest Coast of America, or on any of the islands adjacent thereto, *north* of the 55th degree of north latitude, by citizens of the United States, or under their authority, nor by Russian subjects or under the authority of Russia, *south* of the same parallel of latitude.

Full power of the Emperor of all the Russias.

[Translation]—*(f.)*

We, Alexander the First, by the Grace of God Emperor and Autocrat of all the Russias, of Muscovy, Kiovia, Wladimiria, Novogorod, Czar of Kazan, Czar of Astracan, Czar of Poland, Czar of Siberia, Czar of the Crimea, Lord of Plescon, and Grand Duke of Smolensko, Lithuania, Volhynia, Podolia, and Finland; Duke of Esthonia, Livonia, Cowland, and Semigall, of Samogitia, Bialostok, Carelia, Twez, Yargoria, Permia, Wiatka, Bulgaria, and others; Lord and Grand Duke of Lower Novogorod, of Czernigovia, Rezan, Polock, Rostow, Yaroslau, Belovseria, Udoria, Obdoria, Condinia, Witepsk, Mstislau; Lord of all the North Coast; Lord of Iveria, Cartalinia, Georgia, and Cabardia; hereditary Prince and Sovereign of the Princes of Circassia, Gorsky, and others; successor of Norway, Duke of Schleswick Holstein, Stormaria, Dithmarsen, and Oldenburg, &c., &c., &c., make known that, certain disputes having arisen between our Government, that of his Majesty the King of the United Kingdom of Great Britain, and that of the United States of America, in consequence of our ukase, dated September 4, (16,) 1821, and having considered the necessity of terminating these disputes by means of an amicable negotiation, we have resolved to appoint, and do appoint, for our plenipotentiaries in the said negotiation, our beloved and faithful CHARLES ROBERT, Count of Nesselrode, our Actual Privy Counsellor, member of the Council of State, Secretary of State directing the administration of Foreign Affairs, Actual Chamberlain, Knight of the order of St. Alexander Nevsky, Grand Cross of the order of St. Wladimir of the first class, Knight of that of the White Eagle of Poland, Grand Cross of the order of St. Stephen of Hungary, of the Black and of the Red Eagle of Prussia, of the Legion of Honor of France; of Charles III of Spain, of St. Ferdinand and of Merit of Naples, of the Annunciation of Sardinia, of the Polar Star of Sweden, of the Elephant of Denmark, the Golden Eagle of Wirtemburg, of Fidelity of Baden, of St. Constantine of Parma, and of the Guelphs of Hanover; and PIERRE POLETICA, our Actual Counsellor of State, Knight of the order of St. Anne of the first class, and Grand Cross of the order of St. Wladimir of the second class; promising, on our imperial word, to make good and ratify all the arrangements which the said plenipotentiaries shall conclude and sign in regard to the objects above pointed out, with the plenipotentiaries duly authorized to that effect by his Majesty the King of the United Kingdom of Great Britain, and by the United States of America.

In faith whereof, we have signed the present full powers, and have hereto caused to be affixed the seal of our empire.

Done at St. Petersburg, the 12th of February, in the year of Grace one thousand eight hundred and twenty-four, and of our reign the twenty-third year.

[L. S.]

(Countersigned,)
By translation agreeable to the original.
THE COUNT OF NESSELRODE.

ALEXANDER.
COUNT NESSELRODE,
Secretary of State.

Counter Projet of Russia of February 20.

[Translation]—(*g.*)

ARTICLE 1. To cement the bonds of amity, and to secure, for the future, a good understanding and a perfect concord between the high contracting powers, it is agreed that, in any part of the great ocean, commonly called the Pacific Ocean, or South Sea, the respective citizens or subjects shall be neither disturbed nor restrained, either in navigation or in fishing, or in the power of resorting to the coasts upon points which may not already be occupied, for the purpose of trading with the natives; saving, always, the restrictions and conditions determined by the following articles.

ARTICLE 2. With the view of preventing the rights of navigation and of fishing, exercised upon the great ocean by the citizens and subjects of the high contracting powers, from becoming the pretext for an illicit trade with their respective establishments, it is agreed that the citizens of the United States shall not resort to any part of the coasts already occupied by Russian establishments, *or belonging to Russia, from the line of demarkation pointed out in the article below,* without the permission of the governor or commander of said establishments ; and that, reciprocally, the subjects of Russia shall not resort; without permission, to any establishment of the United States upon the Northwest Coast, *from the same line of demarkation.*

 · ARTICLE 3. It is, moreover, agreed that, in the respective possessions of the two high powers on the Northwest Coast of America, or in any of the adjacent islands, there shall not be formed by the citizens of the United States, or under the authority of the said States, any establishment to the north of 54° 40′ of north latitude; and that, in the same manner, there shall be none formed by Russian subjects, or under the authority of Russia, to the south of the same parallel.

[With admission of American vessels to New Archangel.]

Counter Projet of the United States of February 23.

[Translation.]—(A.)

ARTICLE 1. The article proposed by the projet of February 20 is accepted.

ARTICLE 2. Same, with the omission of these words, "*or belonging to Russia from the line of demarkation pointed out in the article below,*" words repugnant to the stipulation expressed in the preceding article, which grants the power of resorting to points not occupied. The words which terminate this article, "*from the same line of demarkation,*" ought also to be erased.

ARTICLE 3. The modification of the article which proposes for a line of demarkation *fifty-four degrees forty minutes* instead of 55° may be accepted, provided the article be conceived in the following manner:

It is, moreover, agreed that, hereafter, there shall not be formed any establishment upon the Northwest Coast of America, nor in any of the islands adjacent *to the north* of 54° 40′ of north latitude, by the citizens of the United States, or under the authority of said States; and on the other side there shall be none formed by Russian subjects, or under the authority of Russia, to the south of the same parallel. It is at the same time agreed, however, that the vessels of the two powers, or belonging to their citizens and subjects, may, reciprocally, frequent all the interior seas, gulfs, harbors, and creeks of the said coast, in order to carry on fishing [*and trade with the natives of the country*]* without any hindrance or molestation whatever, during ten [*five*] years, to be counted from the date of signing the present convention.

(i.)

Second Counter Projet of the United States of February 23.

ARTICLE 3. The high contracting parties being unable at this time to adjust, to their mutual satisfaction, a line of demarkation for their respective possessions upon the Northwestern Coast of America, it is hereby agreed that all the said coast to which they respectively lay claim, together with all interior seas, bays, and creeks of the same, shall remain free and open to the vessels, citizens, and subjects of the two nations, reciprocally, without prejudice to the claims of either party, or of any other State, to the full end and term of ten years from the signature of this convention, or until the high contracting parties shall have come to some agreement respecting the aforesaid limitation of their possessions.

[Translation.]—(*k.*)

FOURTH CONFERENCE.

The dominion cannot be acquired but by a *real* occupation and possession, and an *intention* (animus) to establish it is by no means sufficient.

Now, it is clear, *according to the facts established,* that neither Russia nor any other European power has the right of dominion upon the continent of America between the 50th and 60th degrees of north latitude.

 ° Words erased by the plenipotentiaries of Russia at the conference of March 8.

Still less has she the dominion of the adjacent maritime territory, or of the sea which washes these coasts, a dominion which is only accessory to the territorial dominion.

Therefore, she has not the right *of exclusion or of admission* on these coasts, nor in these seas, which are free seas.

The right of navigating all the free seas belongs, by natural law, to every independent nation, and even constitutes an essential part of this independence.

The United States have exercised navigation in the seas, and commerce upon the coasts, above mentioned, from the time of their independence; and they have a *perfect* right to this navigation and to this commerce, and they can only be deprived of it by their own act or by a convention.

Projet of a Convention offered by Russia on Saturday, March 22.

[Translation.]—(*l.*)

His Majesty the Emperor of all the Russias and the Government of the United States of America, wishing to cement the bonds of amity which unite them, and to secure between them the invariable maintenance of a perfect concord, by means of the present convention, have named as their plenipotentiaries to this effect, to wit: his Majesty the Emperor of all the Russias, his beloved and faithful Charles Robert, Count of Nesselrode, &c., and Pierre de Poletica, &c., and the Government of the United States of America, Henry Middleton, esquire, &c.; who, after having exchanged their full powers, found in good and due form, have agreed upon and signed the following stipulations:

ARTICLE I. It is agreed that in any part of the great ocean, commonly called the Pacific Ocean, or South Sea, the respective citizens and subjects of the high contracting parties shall be neither disturbed nor restrained either in navigation or in fishing, or in the power of resorting to the coasts upon points which may not already be occupied for the purpose of trading with the natives, saving always the restrictions and conditions determined by the following articles.

ARTICLE II. With the view of preventing the rights of navigation and of fishing, exercised upon the great ocean by the citizens and subjects of the high contracting parties, from becoming the pretext for an illicit trade, it is agreed that the citizens of the United States shall not resort to any point of the coasts already occupied by Russian establishments, without the permission of the governor or commander of said establishments; and that, reciprocally, the subjects of Russia shall not resort, without permission, to any establishment of the United States upon the Northwest Coast.

ARTICLE III. It is moreover agreed *that, in the respective possessions* of the two high powers upon the Northwest Coast of America or in any of the adjacent islands, there shall not be formed by the citizens of the United States, or under the authority of said States, any establishment to the north of 54° 40' of north latitude; and that, in the same manner, there shall be none formed by Russian subjects, or under the authority of Russia, to the south of the same parallel.

ARTICLE IV. It is, nevertheless, understood that the vessels of the two powers, or which belong to their respective citizens or subjects, may reciprocally frequent, without any hindrance whatever, the interior seas, gulfs, harbors and creeks in the possessions of Russia and of the United States of America on the Northwest Coast, for the purpose of fishing and trading with the natives of the country.

ARTICLE V. This reciprocal right of fishing and of trade is only granted for a term of ten years from the date of the signing of the present convention, at the end of which term it shall cease on both sides.

ARTICLE VI. From this time, fire-arms, other arms, powder, and munitions of war of every kind, are always excepted from this same commerce, which the two powers engage not to sell nor allow to be sold to the natives by their respective citizens and subjects, nor by any person who may be under their authority.

ARTICLE VII. The present convention shall be ratified, and the ratifications thereof shall be exchanged at St. Petersburg in the space of ———.

In faith whereof, the respective plenipotentiaries have signed it, and thereto affixed the seal of their arms.

Done at ——— the ——— of the year of Grace 1824.

Count Nesselrode to Mr. Middleton.

[Translation.]—No. 35, (*m.*)

The undersigned, Actual Privy Counsellor, Secretary of State directing the administration of Foreign Affairs, has had the honor to mention to Mr. Middleton, Envoy Extraordinary and Minister Plenipotentiary of the United States of America, the desire which the Emperor had of seeing arms, munitions, and spirituous liquors excepted from the articles of which the reciprocal trade might be declared free during ten years with the natives of the Northwest Coast of America, by the convention which Russia and the United States are upon the point of concluding.

The undersigned hastens to assure Mr. Middleton, by writing, that the immediate prohibition of the trade in arms and munitions with the natives is a condition to which his Imperial Majesty attaches the highest importance, a condition the absence of which would not permit him to give his assent to the rest of the treaty.

As to the prohibition of the trade in spirituous liquors the Emperor eagerly desires that it should be pronounced, and he does not doubt that Mr. Middleton and the Government of the United States [will] receive in the most favorable manner this wish, dictated by motives of humanity and morality.

The undersigned embraces with pleasure this occasion of repeating to Mr. Middleton the assurance of his most distinguished consideration.

                                                            NESSELRODE

ST. PETERSBURG, *March 20, 1824.*

Projet of the United States of March 24.

[Translation.]—(n.)

His Majesty the Emperor of all the Russias and the President of the United States of America, wishing to cement the bonds of amity which unite them, and to secure between them the invariable maintenance of a perfect concord, by means of the present convention, have named as their plenipoten- tiaries to this effect, to. wit: his Majesty the Emperor of all the Russias, his beloved and faithful Charles Robert, Count of Nesselrode, &c., &c., and Pierre de Poletica, &c., &c., and the President of the United States of America, Henry Middleton, a citizen of said States, and their Envoy Extraordinary and Minister Plenipotentiary near his Imperial Majesty; who, after having exchanged their full powers, found in good and due form, have agreed upon and signed the following stipulations:

ARTICLE I. It is agreed that in any part of the great ocean, commonly called the Pacific Ocean, or South Sea, the respective citizens and subjects of the high contracting parties shall be neither disturbed nor restrained either in navigation or in fishing, or in the power of resorting to the coasts upon points which may not already be occupied for the purpose of trading with the natives, saving always the restrictions and conditions determined by the following articles.

ARTICLE II. With the view of preventing the rights of navigation and of fishing, exercised upon the great ocean by the citizens and subjects of the high contracting powers, from becoming the pretext for an illicit trade, it is agreed that the citizens of the United States shall not resort *to any point where there is a Russian establishment*, without the permission of the governor or commander; and that, reciprocally, the subjects of Russia shall not resort, without permission, to any establishment of the United States upon the Northwest Coast.

ARTICLE III. It is moreover agreed that, hereafter, there shall not be formed by the citizens of the United States, or under the authority of the said States, any establishment upon the Northwest Coast of America, nor in any of the islands adjacent, to the north of 54° 40' of north latitude; and that, in the same manner, there shall be none formed by Russian subjects, or under the authority of Russia, to the south of the same parallel.

ARTICLE IV. It is, nevertheless, understood that the vessels of the two powers, or which belong to their citizens or subjects, respectively, may reciprocally frequent, without any hindrance whatever, the interior seas, gulfs, harbors, and creeks upon the said coast, for the purpose of fishing and of trading with the natives of the country. But the reciprocal right *granted by this article* shall cease, on both sides, after the term of ten years, to be counted from the signing of the present convention.

ARTICLE V. Fire-arms, other arms, powder, and munitions of war of every kind, are always excepted from this same commerce permitted by the preceding article; and the two powers engage, reciprocally, neither to sell, nor suffer them to be sold, to the natives, by their respective citizens and subjects, nor by any person who may be under their authority. It being well understood that, in any case, this restriction shall not be considered to authorize, under the pretext of a contravention of this article, the visit, or the detention of vessels, or the seizure of the merchandise, or, in fine, any vexations whatever, exercised towards the owners or the crews employed in this commerce; the high contracting powers, reciprocally, reserving to themselves to determine upon the penalties to be incurred, and to inflict the punishments due, in case of the contravention of this article by their respective citizens and subjects.

ARTICLE VI. When this convention shall have been duly ratified by his Majesty the Emperor of all the Russias, on one part, and on the other by the President of the United States, with the advice and consent of the Senate, the ratifications thereof shall be exchanged at Washington in the space of ten months from the date below, or sooner, if possible.

In faith whereof, the respective plenipotentiaries have signed this convention, and thereto affixed the seals of their arms.

Done at —— the —— of the year of Grace 1824.

Contre Projet of Russia, March 28.

[Translation.]—(o.)

His Majesty the Emperor of all the Russias and the President of the United States of America, wishing to cement the bonds of amity which unite them, and to secure between them the invariable maintenance of a perfect concord, by means of the present convention, have named as their plenipoten- tiaries to this effect, to wit: his Majesty the Emperor of all the Russias, his beloved and faithful Charles Robert, Count of Nesselrode, &c., &c., and Pierre de Poletica, &c., &c., and the President of the United States of America, Mr. Henry Middleton, a citizen of said States, and their Envoy Extraordinary and Minister Plenipotentiary near his Imperial Majesty; who, after having exchanged their full powers, found in good and due form, have agreed upon and signed the following stipulations:

ARTICLE 1. It is agreed that in any part of the great ocean, commonly called the Pacific ocean, or South Sea, the respective citizens or subjects of the high contracting powers shall be neither disturbed nor restrained either in navigation or in fishing, or in the power of resorting to the coasts upon points which may not already be occupied for the purpose of trading with the natives, saving always the restrictions and conditions determined by the following articles.

ARTICLE 2. With the view of preventing the rights of navigation and of fishing, exercised upon the great ocean by the citizens and subjects of the high contracting powers, from becoming the pretext for an illicit trade, it is agreed that the citizens of the United States shall not resort to any point where there is a Russian establishment, without the permission of the governor or commander; and that, reciprocally, the subjects of Russia shall not resort, without permission, to any establishment of the United States upon the Northwest Coast.

ARTICLE 3. It is moreover agreed that, hereafter, there shall not be formed by the citizens of the

United States, or under the authority of said States, any establishment upon the Northwest Coast of America, nor in any of the islands adjacent, *to the north* of 54° 40′ of north latitude; and that, in the same manner, there shall be none formed by Russian subjects, or under the authority of Russia, *to the south* of the same parallel.

ARTICLE 4. It is, nevertheless, understood that the vessels of the two powers, or which belong to their respective citizens or subjects, may reciprocally frequent, without any hindrance whatever, the interior seas, gulfs, harbors, and creeks upon the said coasts, for the purpose of fishing and trading with the natives of the country. But the reciprocal right granted by this article shall cease, on both sides, after the term of ten years, to be counted from the signing of the present convention.

ARTICLE 5. Fire-arms, other arms, powder, and munitions of war of every kind, are always excepted from this same commerce permitted by the preceding article; and the two powers engage, reciprocally, neither to sell, nor suffer them to be sold, to the natives by their respective citizens and subjects, nor by any person who may be under their authority. It is stipulated always that this restriction shall never be deemed to authorize, under the pretext of a contravention of the present article, the visit or the detention of vessels, or the seizure of the merchandise, or, in fine, any arbitrary measures whatsoever exercised towards the owners or the crews employed in this commerce; the high contracting powers, reciprocally, reserving to themselves to determine upon the penalties to be incurred, and to inflict the punishments due, in case of the contravention of this article by their respective citizens or subjects.

ARTICLE 6. When this convention shall have been duly ratified by his Majesty the Emperor of all the Russias, on one part, and on the other by the President of the United States, with the advice and consent of the Senate, the ratifications thereof shall be exchanged at Washington in the space of ten months from the date below, or sooner, if possible. In faith whereof, the respective plenipotentiaries have signed this convention, and thereto affixed the seal of their arms.

Done at —— the —— of the year of Grace 1824.

Projet of the United States, March 31.

[Translation.]—(*p.*)

ARTICLE 4. It is, nevertheless, understood that, during a term of ten years, to be counted from the signing of the present convention, the ships of the two powers, or which belong to their citizens or subjects, respectively, may reciprocally frequent, without any hindrance whatever, the interior seas, gulfs, harbors, and creeks upon the coast mentioned in the preceding article, for the purpose of fishing and trading with the natives of the country.

ARTICLE 5. All spirituous liquors, fire-arms, other arms, powder, and munitions of war of every kind, are always excepted from the commerce permitted by the preceding article; and the two powers engage, reciprocally, neither to sell, nor suffer them to be sold, to the natives by their respective citizens and subjects, nor by any person who may be under their authority. It is likewise stipulated that this restriction shall never serve for a pretext, nor be alleged, in any case, to authorize either the search or detention of vessels, or the seizure of the merchandise, or, in fine, any measures of constraint whatever towards the merchants or the crews who may carry on this commerce; the high contracting powers, reciprocally, reserving to themselves to determine upon the penalties to be incurred, and to inflict the punishments due, in case of a contravention of this article by their respective citizens or subjects.

Projet of Protocol.

[Translation.]—(*g.*)

The undersigned, after having discussed in several conferences a projet of convention proposed for removing all the differences which have arisen between Russia and the United States of America, in consequence of a regulation published by the former of these powers, on the 4th (16th) September, 1821, definitively drew up the different articles of which this convention is composed, added to them their sign manual, and mutually engaged to sign them as they are found annexed to the present protocol.

In drawing up the 4th of these articles, the plenipotentiaries of Russia recollected that they had proposed to the plenipotentiary of the United States to arrange the said article in the following terms:

ARTICLE 4. "It is, nevertheless, understood that the ships of the two powers, or which belong to their citizens or subjects, respectively, may mutually frequent, without any hindrance whatever, the interior seas, gulfs, harbors, and creeks upon the said coast, for the purpose of there fishing and trading with the natives of the country. But the reciprocal right granted by this article shall cease, on both sides, after a term of ten years, to be counted from the signing of the present convention."

* ARTICLE 4. "*It is, nevertheless, understood that, during a term of ten years, to be counted from the signing of the present convention, the ships of the two powers, or which belong to their citizens or subjects, respectively, may mutually frequent, without any hindrance whatever, the interior seas, gulfs, harbors, and creeks upon the said coast, for the purpose of there fishing and trading with the natives of the country.*"

. The plenipotentiaries of Russia added, that, after agreeing to this arrangement, the plenipotentiary of the United States had afterwards invited them to change the ending of this very article, and to agree to it as it is transcribed opposite,* observing that this second arrangement, more conformable to the letter of the instructions which he had received, in no way altered the sense of that which had been proposed by the plenipotentiaries of Russia.

The plenipotentiary of the United States having repeated this observation, the article in question was signed with the modification which he had demanded to be there introduced.

After which, all the other articles were also signed, and it was resolved to proceed to the signature of the convention itself the —— following. Done at St. Petersburg, the ——, 1824.

All this in italics rejected, and filled up as stands in the protocol (r.)

PROTOCOL.

[Translation.]—(r)

The undersigned, after having discussed in several conferences a projet of a convention proposed for settling all the differences which arose between the United States of America and Russia, in consequence of a regulation published by the latter of these powers, on the 4th (16th) September, 1821, definitively drew up the different articles of which this convention is composed, added to them their sign manual, and mutually engaged to sign them as they are found annexed to the present protocol.

In drawing up the 4th of these articles, the plenipotentiaries of Russia recollected that they proposed to the plenipotentiary of the United States to arrange the said article in the following terms:

ARTICLE 4. "It is, nevertheless, understood that the ships of the two powers, or which belong to their citizens or subjects, respectively, may mutually frequent, without any hindrance whatever, the interior seas, gulfs, harbors, and creeks upon the said coast, for the purpose of there fishing and trading with the natives of the country. But the reciprocal right granted by this article shall cease, on both sides, after a term of ten years, to be counted from the signing of the present convention."

The plenipotentiaries of Russia added, that, after agreeing to this arrangement, the plenipotentiary of the United States had afterwards invited them to change the ending of this very article, and agree to it as it is found signed in the convention, observing that this second arrangement, more conformable to the letter of the instructions which he received, is the only one which he thinks himself authorized to sign; but, moreover, that this arrangement does not essentially alter the sense of that which had been proposed by the plenipotentiaries of Russia, because, at the end of the term mentioned, the stipulation ceasing equally by the two arrangements, the reciprocal power of trading granted by that stipulation cannot be prolonged beyond the said term but by mutual agreement.

Under these observations the article in question has been signed, with the modification which the plenipotentiary of the United States had demanded to be there introduced.

After which, all the other articles were also signed respectively, and it was resolved to proceed to the signature of the convention itself on the fifth following.

Done at St. Petersburg, April 2, (14,) 1824.

> HENRY MIDDLETON.
> NESSELRODE.
> POLETICA.

PROTOCOL.

[Translation.]—(s.)

The undersigned, having engaged by the protocol of their last conference to sign on the 5th April of the present year the convention of which they signed all the articles, assembled this day at two o'clock in the afternoon, at the hotel inhabited by Count Nesselrode, and after having duly collated with the said articles the two copies of the convention which they had caused to be prepared, they have attached to both their respective signatures and the seal of their arms.

Done at St. Petersburg, April 5, (17,) 1824.

> HENRY MIDDLETON.
> NESSELRODE.
> P. POLETICA.

(v.)

Extract from a despatch from Mr. Canning to Sir Charles Bagot, upon the Northwest business.

"The only point of view in which the United States can now desire to take cognizance of the negotiation between us and Russia would be in order to see that the pretensions on the Northwest Coast of America, derived to the United States from Spain through the treaty of 1819, were not prejudiced by our separate agreement. That object cannot be more effectually provided for than by inserting into our convention with Russia, as a protection for the claims of the United States, that part of the third article of the convention concluded by us with the United States in 1818 which was inserted in that convention for the protection of the claims of Spain herself, in the rights which she had not then ceded. By that article it is stipulated 'that the agreement between the two contracting parties should not be taken to affect the claims of any other power or State in any part of the said country.'

"Such a clause your excellency will voluntarily propose to insert in the convention which you are to conclude with Count Nesselrode, and you will apprise Mr. Middleton of your intention to propose that insertion."

No. 11.

Mr. Rush to Mr. Adams, (*No.* 353.)

London, *December* 19, 1823.

SIR: Since I last wrote, Mr. Canning has been confined to his house by a sharp attack of gout; nevertheless, he wrote me a note the day before yesterday inviting me to call upon him on that day, for the purpose of having our proposed conference on the topic of the Northwest Coast. I went accordingly, and was received by him in his chamber.

He repeated his wish to learn from me our general grounds upon this subject, preparatory to his sending off instructions to Sir Charles Bagot.

I at once unfolded them to him by stating that the proposals of my Government were, 1st. That as regarded the country lying between the Stony mountains and the Pacific Ocean, Great Britain, the United States, and Russia, should jointly enter into a convention, similar in its nature to the third article of the convention of the 20th of October, 1818, now existing between the two former powers, by which the whole of that country westward of the Stony mountains and all its waters would be free and open to the citizens and subjects of the three powers as long as the joint convention remained in force. This my Government proposed should be for the term of ten years.

And 2d. That the United States were willing to stipulate to make no settlements north of the 51st degree of north latitude on that coast, provided Great Britain stipulated to make none south of 51° or north of 55°, and Russia to make none south of 55°.

These, I said, were the principal points which I had to put forward upon this subject. The map was spread out before us, and, in stating the points, I endeavored to explain and recommend them by such appropriate remarks as your instructions supplied me with, going as far as seemed fitted to a discussion regarded only as preparatory and informal.

Mr. Canning repeated that he had not invited me to call upon him with any view to discussion at present, but only to obtain from me a statement of the points, in anticipation of the opening of the negotiation, from the motive that he had mentioned of writing to Mr. Bagot. Yet my statement naturally led to further conversation. He expressed no opinion on any of the points, but his inquiries and remarks under that which proposes to confine the British settlements within 51° and 55° were evidently of a nature to indicate strong objections on his side, though he professed to speak only from his first impressions. It is more proper, I should say, that his objections were directed to our proposal of not letting Great Britain go above 55° north, with her settlements, whilst we allowed Russia to come down to that line with hers. In treating of this coast, he had supposed that Britain had her northern question with Russia, as her southern with the United States. He could see a motive for the United States desiring to stop the settlements of Great Britain southward; but he had not before known of their desire to stop them northward, and, above all, over limits conceded to Russia. It was to this effect that his suggestions went. He threw out no dissent to the plan of joint usufruction between the three powers of the country westward of the Stony mountains for the period of time proposed.

In the course of my remarks I said that the United States no longer regarded any part of that coast as open to European colonization, but only to be used for purposes of traffic with the natives, and for fishing in the neighboring seas; that we did not know that Great Britain had ever advanced any claim whatever to territory there founded on occupation, prior to the Nootka Sound controversy; that under the treaties of 1763 her territorial rights in America were bounded westward by the Mississippi; that if the Northwest and Hudson's Bay Companies now had settlements as high up as 54° or 55° we suppose it to be as much as could be shown, and were not aware how Great Britain could make good her claims any further; that Spain, on the contrary, had much larger claims on that coast, by right of discovery, and that to the whole extent of these the United States had succeeded by the Florida treaty; that they were willing, however, waiving for the present the full advantage of these claims, to forbear all settlements north of 51°, as that limit might be sufficient to give them the benefit of all the waters of the Columbia river; but that they would expect Great Britain to abstain from coming south of that limit, or going above 55°, the latter parallel being taken as that beyond which it was not imagined that she had any actual settlements. The same parallel was proposed for the southern limit of Russia, as the boundary within which the Emperor Paul had granted certain commercial privileges to his Russian American Company in 1799; but that, in fixing upon this line as regarded Russia, it was not the intention of the United States to deprive themselves of the right of traffic with the natives above it, and still less to concede to that power any system of colonial exclusion above it.

Such was the general character of my remarks which Mr. Canning said he would take into due consideration. In conclusion, I said to him that I should reserve myself for the negotiation itself, for such further elucidations of the subject as might tend to show the justice and reasonableness of our propositions.

I have the honor to be, &c., &c., &c.,

RICHARD RUSH.

Hon. JOHN QUINCY ADAMS, *Secretary of State.*

No. 12.

Mr. Rush to Mr. Adams, (*No.* 358.)

London, *January* 19, 1824.

SIR: It was an omission in me not to have stated in my communication of the 6th instant what are to be the claims of Great Britain on the Northwest Coast of America, though as yet Mr. Canning has not made them known to me formally.

She will claim, I understand, to a point northwards above 55°, though how much above it I am not able to say, and southwards as low down as 49°. Whether she designs to push a claim to the whole of this space with earnestness I am also unable as yet to say, but wait the more full and accurate disclosure of her views. To a portion of it she will certainly assert her title with great confidence, and she will be chiefly tenacious of the right which she will allege to settle or colonize, after her own plans, now or in future, all such parts of that coast, out of the admitted boundaries of other nations, as she can make good her title to.

She will regard as alike open (standing upon the question of right) to her future settlements or colonization any part of the North American continent, however minute, on the eastern coast, northern coast, or elsewhere undiscovered and unsettled by other powers, and which she has recently explored, or may for the future explore and settle, through her expeditions under Parry and Franklin, or others that she may fit out by land or water.

I need scarcely subjoin that I shall resist her claims under the lights that your instructions afford me and such others as I may be able to command; that I shall allege and endeavor to prove, from treaties and other sources, that the true sovereignty over the whole of that coast from the 42d to the 61st or 60th degree of north latitude is now vested in the United States; and that, consequently, if the United States are willing to leave to Great Britain her present actual settlements there between 55° and 51°, it is as much as the latter power can reasonably ask.

Nevertheless, if the President should think that, as connected with any part of this subject, further instructions might prove useful to me, I beg to repeat that I should be thankful to receive them from you, taking the chance of their still getting to hand before the negotiation, not yet begun, shall finally close.

I have the honor to remain, &c., &c., &c.,

RICHARD RUSH.

Hon. John Quincy Adams, *Secretary of State.*

PIRACIES ON THE COMMERCE OF THE UNITED STATES IN THE WEST INDIES.

COMMUNICATED TO THE HOUSE OF REPRESENTATIVES DECEMBER 16, 1824.

*To the honorable the Senate and the honorable the House of Representatives
of the United States of America in Congress assembled:*

The subscribers, a committee selected for the purpose by the merchants of the town of Portland, in the State of Maine, beg leave respectfully to represent, that for many years the trade to Cuba and the other islands and ports in the West India seas has occupied the principal part of the tonnage of this collection district; that of late this trade has been much annoyed by a set of pirates, who have constantly watched every opportunity to commit the most lawless depredations. At first, they were content to plunder and maltreat the crews of our vessels, without proceeding to actual murder. Of late, however, they have not stopped short of the most brutal and inhuman outrages. In some instances whole crews, humble and unoffending, have fallen victims to their barbarous and unrelenting fury.

We are in nowise unmindful of the efforts of our own Government, made with a view to the suppression of these intolerable practices, and we are moreover aware that these efforts have, in some measure, been crowned with success. It can but be observed, nevertheless, that the effect has been, at the same time, to add to the desperation and fury of these freebooters. They seem now to consider themselves as engaged with the people of the United States in a war of extermination as well as of plunder. To this they have been led by motives of revenge, and a hope thereby to avoid the means of detection.

These enemies of the human race are found almost wholly in the vicinity of Spanish territory and Spanish population, and are themselves generally Spaniards, and uniformly come from and fly to Spanish territory for succor and protection; and the goods plundered are unblushingly exposed to sale, not unfrequently, in the most public marts of the Spanish West Indies, and in such a manner and under such circumstances as clearly to evince the connivance, if not of the officers of Government themselves, certainly of a portion of their citizens. It is not even too much to infer, from what has currently taken place, that a very considerable part of the population of the Spanish islands are concerned, directly or indirectly, in these piratical expeditions; and, furthermore, that if the Spanish authorities are not actually implicated in these atrocities, they are at least overawed by those who are.

Your memorialists would not, without manifest reason, depart from that comity which is ordinarily due from one nation to another, and would not on any occasion entertain jealousies and suspicions without adequate foundation. But such has been the frequency and publicity of these acts of piracy, especially on the coasts of Cuba; so formidable and imposing have been their numbers and their armaments; and so long have they been tolerated there, with scarcely the color of an effort on the part of the Spanish authorities to suppress them, that none but the most infatuated or the most wilfully blind can hope for any voluntary exertions on the part of the Spaniards or their Government to afford redress.

Your memorialists cannot hesitate to believe that the time has arrived when it is incumbent on the United States to assume such an attitude, in relation to the Governments of these islands, as shall induce them to consider that we shall hold them responsible for these hostilities of their own people. Have we not already made Spain responsible for spoliations committed upon our commerce in those very seas? And do we not hold all nations answerable for the acts of their people?

It will be replied, perhaps, that Spain constantly disavows and disapproves of these lawless acts; that she professes to abhor piracy, and considers pirates as outlaws, and as her enemies, as well as the enemies of the human race. If so, let her acts correspond with her professions, and sincerity will be accorded to her. Till then, and while she continues a forbearance nothing short in its effect of direct encouragement, we must and ought to hold her identified with the pirates themselves, and answerable for their depredations.

The trade from this part of the country to the West Indies is carried on almost wholly by the shipment of lumber, great portions of which are necessarily carried on deck, perhaps to the amount of one-third, at least. Hence we cannot arm in our defence. And, besides, these lumber cargoes are of small comparative value, and would by no means admit of such an expense. We have, therefore, but one resource: a reliance upon the arm of the Government for protection—a Government, we trust, that will not be duped by empty profession, and that will not with impunity see its peaceful and unoffending citizens wantonly butchered by the desperadoes of any nation.

We do not stop to calculate the value, although inestimable, of our trade to Cuba or to the West Indies. It should suffice that we have a right to a free and uninterrupted navigation of those seas. When whole crews of our fellow-citizens, in the pursuit of a lawful commerce, are seized and unrelentingly butchered, shall we coolly set ourselves down to a calculation of profit and loss before we determine to seek redress? The means are in our power to secure protection to our suffering fellow-citizens, and it is not to be apprehended that we shall be backward in using them.

Your memorialists would respectfully suggest that the class of small cruisers heretofore destined to this service should be increased, and kept constantly upon the alert in those seas; and particularly upon the coasts of Cuba and Porto Rico; and that during the summer and sickly season they should never be allowed to enter any of the ports in that climate but from necessity or in pursuit of pirates; by which means our commerce would be effectually guarded, and the health of our brave seamen effectually secured. Whether a system of convoying can be established in the vicinity of Cuba is also respectfully submitted to the wisdom of Congress. And, as in duty bound, &c.

EZEKIEL WHITMAN,
ASA CLAPP,
ALBERT NEWHALL,
WM. SWANN,
CHARLES FOX,
Committee.

PORTLAND, *December* 9, 1824.

CORRESPONDENCE WITH GREAT BRITAIN RELATIVE TO A LIGHT ON THE BAHAMA BANKS.

COMMUNICATED TO THE HOUSE OF REPRESENTATIVES DECEMBER 27, 1824.

DEPARTMENT OF STATE, *December* 23, 1824.

The Secretary of State, in compliance with a resolution of the House of Representatives of the 23d of December last, directing him to "ascertain and report to that House whether the rocks called the Double Headed Shot Keys, or any other of the rocks or desert isles near the Bahama Banks, but separated therefrom by a deep channel, and on which the security of navigation of the Gulf of Florida requires that lighthouses or beacons should be placed, are within the dominion of any, and what, foreign Kingdom or State, or whether they are not now subject to be appropriated by the right of occupancy," has the honor to submit to the House copies of the correspondence upon that subject, containing the information obtained, conformably to the resolution of the House.

JOHN QUINCY ADAMS.

Papers sent.

The Secretary of State to the Secretary of the Navy, January 1, 1824.	Copy.
Secretary of the Navy to Secretary of State, July 17, 1824.	do.
Commodore Porter to the Secretary of the Navy, May 28, 1824.	do.
Same to the Duke of Manchester, March 29, 1824.	do.
Duke of Manchester to Commodore Porter, April 7, 1824.	do.
Commodore Porter to Governor Grant, April 15, 1824.	do.
Governor Grant to Commodore Porter, April 24, 1824.	do.
Memorandum inclosed in the above.	
Commodore Porter to Governor Vives, May 12, 1824.	Copy.
Governor Vives to Commodore Porter, May 15, 1824.	Translation.

The Secretary of State to the Secretary of the Navy.

DEPARTMENT OF STATE, *Washington, January 1*, 1824.

SIR: I have the honor of inclosing herewith two resolutions of the House of Representatives of the United States, adopted on the 23d of last month, and of requesting that instructions may be given to Captain David Porter to endeavor to obtain and transmit such information as may enable me to report to the House, as required by one of the resolutions, whether the rocks called the Double Headed Shot Keys, or any other of the rocks or desert isles near the Bahama Banks, but separated therefrom by a deep channel, and on which the security of the navigation of the Gulf of Florida requires that light-houses or beacons should be placed, are within the dominion of any, and what, foreign Kingdom or State, or whether they are not now subject to be appropriated by the right of occupancy. And, secondly, to specify what portion of the island of Abaco, at or near the Hole in the Wall, and what other places within the acknowledged dominions of Great Britain, on the islands, keys, or shoals, on the Bahama Banks, may be necessary for the erection and support of light-houses, beacons, or buoys, or floating lights, for the security of navigation over and near the said Banks. The description of the place should be made with sufficient precision with regard to the topography to be inserted in the articles of cession, if the consent of Great Britain to make it should be obtained.

I am, with great respect, sir, your very humble and obedient servant,

JOHN QUINCY ADAMS.

Hon. SAMUEL L. SOUTHARD, *Secretary of the Navy.*

Secretary of the Navy to the Secretary of State.

NAVY DEPARTMENT, *July* 17, 1824.

SIR: I have the honor to inclose copies of several communications received from Commodore David Porter, numbered 1 to 9, inclusively, relating to two resolutions of Congress of December 23, 1823.

I am, very respectfully, your most obedient servant,

SAMUEL L. SOUTHARD.

Hon. JOHN QUINCY ADAMS, *Secretary of State.*

Commodore Porter to Mr. Southard, Secretary of the Navy.

UNITED STATES STEAM GALLIOT SEA GULL, *Matanzas, May* 28, 1824.

SIR: I have the honor to submit you copies of my correspondence with the Duke of Manchester, Governor of Jamaica, the Governor of the Bahamas, and the Captain General of Cuba, on the subject confided to me by your instructions of the ——.

As the interests of the Government of the Bahamas will be much lessened by the building of light-houses on Abaco and the neighboring keys, it deriving its principal revenue from wrecked goods, it is reasonable to apprehend that some obstacles will be opposed to the benevolent project of our Government from that quarter; but should this be the case, the efforts of the Duke of Manchester, and those of the Captain General of Cuba, in favor of it, will more than counterbalance them.

I have the honor to be, &c.,

D. PORTER.

P. S. Not having your instructions at hand, cannot state the date of them.

Hon. SAMUEL L. SOUTHARD, *Secretary of the Navy.*

Commodore Porter to the Duke of Manchester, Governor of Jamaica, &c.

UNITED STATES SHIP JOHN ADAMS, *Port Royal Harbor, March* 29, 1824.

MY LORD: In reference to the conversation I had with your grace on the 26th instant, relative to the two resolutions of the Congress of the United States, copies of which I have the honor to inclose to you, the subjects of which have been confided to me by the Government of the United States, in order that the necessary information for the proper Department may be obtained; and your grace having been pleased to signify to me that a reference to his Britannic Majesty's Government is indispensable, I have the honor to request that your grace will, by such reference, obtain and furnish me with the information required, in order that the measures contemplated by the resolutions, and so desirable to the commercial world, may be promptly and speedily effected.

I have the honor to be, &c.,

D. PORTER,
Commanding United States Naval Forces, &c.

His Grace the DUKE OF MANCHESTER.

Duke of Manchester to Commodore Porter.

KING'S HOUSE, *Jamaica, April* 7, 1824.

SIR: I have the honor to acknowledge the receipt of your communication of the 29th ultimo, inclosing copies of two resolutions of the House of Representatives in Congress, bearing date 23d day of December last, and to acquaint you that I shall forward them to his Majesty's principal Secretary of State for the Colonies by the first opportunity.

I have the honor to be, &c.,

MANCHESTER.

Commodore PORTER, *&c., &c., &c.*

Commodore Porter to Governor Grant.

UNITED STATES SHIP JOHN ADAMS, *Thompson's Island, April* 15, 1824.

YOUR EXCELLENCY: I have the honor to transmit you copies of two resolutions of the Congress of the United States, in the House of Representatives, adopted on the 23d of December last, requiring that the Secretary of State be directed to ascertain and report to that House "whether the rocks called the Double Headed Shot Keys, or any other of the rocks or desert isles near the Bahama Banks, but separated therefrom by a deep channel, and in which the security of the navigation of the Gulf of Florida requires that light-houses or beacons should be placed, are within the dominion of any, and what, foreign Kingdom or State, or whether they are not now subject to be appropriated by the right of occupancy;" and, secondly, "that the President of the United States be requested to negotiate with the Government of Great Britain for a cession of so much land on the island of Abaco, at or near the Hole in the Wall, and on such other places within the acknowledged dominion of that power, on the islands, keys, and shoals, on the Bahama Banks, as may be necessary for the erection and support of light-houses, beacons, buoys, or floating lights, for the security of navigation over and near the said Banks, and to be used solely for such purposes."

In consequence of these resolutions, and a call made by the Secretary of State on the Secretary of the Navy, the whole subject has been referred to me, with instructions to obtain the necessary information thereon, to be laid before the Government; and I have the honor to solicit of your excellency the information called for, with your opinion as to what portion of the island of Abaco, near the Hole in the Wall, and what other places within the acknowledged dominion of Great Britain, on the islands, keys, and shoals, as described in the resolutions, may be necessary for the purposes therein mentioned.

The description of the places should be made with sufficient precision in regard to topography to be inserted in the articles of cession, if the consent of Great Britain to make it should be obtained.

Such information as your excellency may be enabled to furnish, without reference to his Britannic Majesty's Government, I shall be glad to have as early as convenient; and where reference is necessary, when the information may be obtained, I beg that I may be enabled to lay it before the Government of the United States with as little loss of time as possible, in order that an object so desirable to the commercial world may be promptly undertaken and speedily executed.

I had hoped to have had it in my power to have done myself the honor to make this application in person, but circumstances connected with my public duties here will deprive me of the pleasure I had anticipated.

With the highest respect, &c.,

D. PORTER,
Commanding United States Naval Forces, &c., &c.

His Excellency Major General LEWIS GRANT,
Governor of the Bahamas.

Governor Grant to Commodore Porter.

GOVERNMENT HOUSE, *Bahama, April* 24, 1824.

SIR: I have had the honor of receiving from Lieutenant Commander McIntosh your excellency's communication of the 16th instant, containing two inclosures. Connected with the subject-matter of your excellency's despatch, and in part reply thereunto, I have to mention that, very early last year, I received from our minister at Washington, Mr. Canning, a letter, stating to me that, in the course of occasional conversation, not altogether official, with the authorities at Washington, the subject of facilitating and rendering less dangerous the navigation in the vicinity of the Gulf of Florida, by means of light-houses and buoys, had been repeatedly brought forward, and that he had been applied to for information whether the British Government would be inclined to establish light-houses on certain points of the Bahama islands, and to buoy a part of the channel for the benefit of trade passing in that direction, in return for the light-houses which were contemplated to be built, under acts of Congress, on certain other points on the opposite shores of the United States.

Accompanying Mr. Canning's letter, a memorandum came to me, of which the inclosed is a copy. My reply to Mr. Canning was to the effect that, in the event of the British Government adopting its proposed portion of the undertaking, the information which I had obtained here was in favor of the Hole in the Wall, the Binvinis, (in preference to the Great Isaacs,) and the Double Headed Shot Keys, as the fit situations for light-houses, and that the placing of buoys might serve to mark the course between Stirrup Key and Orange Key. I think I may venture to suppose it must be a mistake in that part of the memorandum which speaks of placing buoys between the Hole in the Wall and the Great Isaacs. It does not appear to me that there is much necessity for placing buoys all the way across the Bank from Stirrup Keys to Orange Keys; but that it might be sufficient to mark distinctly and conspicuously the NE· and S. points of the extensive shoal lying halfway between them. Notwithstanding the general opinion being in favor of the Hole in the Wall as the most eligible site for a light-house in that quarter, I cannot say that I am completely brought over to think that it is entitled to a preference over some point of Abaco, more to the east and north, about Cheesic Sound. This, however, is only a suggestion, and by no means an attempt to put an opinion of mine in competition with that of a professional person.

My letter to Mr. Canning went from hence about the middle of March, 1823, and, as he seemed to be earnest on the subject, I have little doubt but he, early after its receipt, made it part of his correspondence with his Government; nothing further, however, relative to the matter has as yet reached me.

Having now, from a desire to facilitate the inquiry which your excellency has been directed to make, freely communicated all the circumstances of information I was in possession of in any way connected with the subject of your despatch, previous to my receiving it, I have to state, in continuation, and in more direct reply to your excellency's letter, and in reference to the two resolutions of the House of Representatives which accompanied it, that I have not hitherto been put in possession by my Government of any authority to enter upon the discussion of the subject of ceding any portion of the island of Abaco, or other place, within the Government of Bahamas; and in respect to the Double Headed Shot Keys, your excellency will perceive, on inspection of the charts, that their locality constitutes them an appendage to that portion of the Bahama Government which lies on Key Sal Bank, and therefore not subject to be appropriated by the right of occupancy by any other Government.

I shall embrace the earliest opportunity which offers to transmit to my Government the contents of your excellency's despatch, in order to place the subject in view, although I have no doubt that Mr. Canning has already done this sufficiently, if ever it became an official topic of discussion, while he was at Washington.

I should have had very much pleasure in welcoming your excellency here had it been convenient for you to have paid this place a visit; or if on a future occasion this should be the case, it will afford me very great satisfaction. I purpose soon going towards the Turk's islands, if I can conveniently do so, on the arrival of our European mail. I shall return early in June, and should regret to be absent if your excellency was coming this way.

I have the honor to be, &c.,

LEWIS GRANT, M. G.,
Governor of Bahamas.

D. PORTER, Esq., &c., &c.

Original inclosed in Governor Grant's letter to Commodore Porter.

Copy of memorandum in Mr. Canning's letter.

Light-houses are wanted at the Hole in the Wall (or rock) at the Double Headed Shot Keys, and at Great Isaac island.

Buoys are wanted in the channel across the Bank from the Hole in the Wall (or rock) to Great Isaacs, nearly in a straight direction.

In the United States a sum of money has already been appropriated by Congress for light-houses at Tortugas islands and Key Largo. It is expected that a further sum will be appropriated during the present session for erecting another light-house either at Cape Carnaveral or at some point between that cape and Key Largo.

L. GRANT.

Commodore Porter to Governor Vives.

HAVANA, *May* 12, 1824.

YOUR EXCELLENCY: In the conversation had with you yesterday respecting the benevolent object of the Government of the United States in erecting light-houses for the purpose of rendering the navigation of the Gulf channel more secure, it afforded me sincere pleasure to perceive that your excellency fully appreciated the motives which prompted the measure and the importance of the object, either as regards the preservation of the lives of those engaged in navigation, or its effects in increasing the commerce of Cuba and the Gulf of Mexico, by lessening the risks which now attend it.

It afforded me no less pleasure to hear your excellency declare that the sovereignty of the Double Headed Shot Keys belonged exclusively to Spain, and that you would use your efforts to further the views of the Government of the United States by such measures towards the Government of Spain as would be calculated to produce the cession of one of the said keys for the sole purpose of erecting a light-house in the event of Spain not being disposed to erect and maintain one at her own expense.

The cause of my satisfaction on this subject is, that, in a correspondence had with the Governor of Bahamas, he claims the Double Headed Shot Keys as part of the Government of Bahamas, not subject to be appropriated to the use of any foreign nation by right of occupancy, and without giving any assurance corresponding with that given by your excellency.

I have now the honor to transmit the two resolutions on which I have been instructed to act. Your excellency will perceive that only one of them has relation to the Double Headed Shot Keys, which lie on the Key Sal Bank, (the key from which the bank takes its name being now in the occupancy of Spain,) and are separated from the Bank of Bahama by the deep channel of Santareen; the other relates to islands and keys under, it is presumed, the exclusive jurisdiction of the British Government. I have, however, laid both resolutions before your excellency that you may be enabled to bring the subject more fully before the Government of Spain, and make it the better acquainted with the object and the extent of the views of the Government of the United States, taken in connexion with the erection of light-houses and placing of beacons on the capes, islands, and shoals of the coast of Florida, and within its acknowledged jurisdiction.

It will be the cause of great satisfaction to the Government of the United States, and it will be of great utility, if your excellency will express your own views as regards the most eligible situations for light-houses for the Gulf channel generally; and in fixing on that for the Double Headed Shot Keys, it is very desirable that the description of the place should be made with sufficient precision, in regard to the topography, to be inserted in the articles of cession, if the consent of Spain to make it should be obtained.

I have the honor to be, &c.,

D. PORTER.

His Excellency the CAPTAIN GENERAL OF CUBA, *and its dependencies.*

Governor Vives to Commodore Porter.

[Translation.]

HAVANA, *May* 15, 1824.

I have had the pleasure to receive your letter of the 12th instant, inclosing two resolutions of the Congress of the United States, respecting the erection of light-houses in this Gulf, for the better security of the vessels navigating the Bahama channel; all of which, according to the assurances I gave you in our conversation on the subject, I shall submit to his Majesty, that, as far as depends on me, so benevolent an object may be speedily effected.

Receive assurances of my high consideration. God protect you many years.

F. D. VIVES.

Commodore DAVID PORTER.

No. 387.

FRENCH SPOLIATIONS SINCE 1806.

COMMUNICATED TO THE HOUSE OF REPRESENTATIVES DECEMBER 27, 1824.

To the House of Representatives of the United States:

I transmit, herewith, to the House a report from the Secretary of State, with copies of the correspondence with the Government of France, requested by the resolution of the House of the 26th of May last.

JAMES MONROE.

WASHINGTON, *December* 23, 1824.

DEPARTMENT OF STATE, *Washington, December* 23, 1824.

The Secretary of State, to whom has been referred a resolution of the House of Representatives of the 26th of May last, requesting that the President of the United States would lay before that House, at the then next session, as early as the public interest would permit, the correspondence which might be held with the Government of France, prior to that time, on the subject of injuries sustained by citizens of the United States since the year 1806, has the honor of reporting to the President copies of the documents requested by that resolution.

JOHN QUINCY ADAMS.

Correspondence sent.

1. Mr. Adams to Mr. Sheldon, No. 1, August 13, 1823. Extract.
1, *a.* Count de Menou to Mr. Adams, July 11, 1823. Translation.
1, *b.* Mr. Adams to Count de Menou, August 12, 1823. Copy.
2. Mr. Sheldon to Mr. Adams, No. 11, October 16, 1823. Extract.
2, *a.* Same to Viscount de Chateaubriand, October 11, 1823. Copy.
3. Mr. Adams to Mr. Brown, (general instructions,) December 23, 1823. Extracts.
4. Mr. Brown to Mr. Adams, No. 2, April 28, 1824. Extract.
4, *a.* Same to Viscount de Chateaubriand, April 28, 1824. Copy.
5. Same to Mr. Adams, No. 3, May 11, 1824. Extract.

5, *a.* Viscount de Chateaubriand to Mr. Brown, May 7, 1824.   Translation.
6. Mr. Adams to Mr. Brown, No. 4, August 14, 1824.   Extracts.
7. Mr. Brown to Mr. Adams, No. 12, August 12, 1824.   Copy.
8. Same to same, No. 14, September 28, 1824.   Copy.
9. Same to same, No. 16, October 23, 1824.   Extract.
9, *a.* Same to Baron de Damas, October 22, 1824.   Copy.

No. 1.

Extract of a letter from Mr. Adams (No. 1) to Mr. Sheldon, dated

DEPARTMENT OF STATE, *Washington, August* 13, 1823.

"I have had the honor of receiving your despatches Nos. 1 and 2; the latter dated the 10th of June. Mr. Gallatin arrived, with his family, at New York on the 24th of that month.

"I inclose, herewith, copies of the recent correspondence between the Count de Menou, the Chargé d'Affaires of France, and this Department, on various subjects, highly interesting to the relations between the two countries.

"With regard to the Count's note of the 11th of July, the President received, with great satisfaction, the testimonial of the Viscount de Chateaubriand to the candor and ability with which Mr. Gallatin has performed the duties of his official station in France. The proposal to renew the negotiation in behalf of the well-founded claims of our citizens upon the French Government, in *connexion* with a claim, on the part of France, to special privileges in the ports of Louisiana, which, after a full discussion, had, in the views of this Government, been proved utterly groundless, could neither be accepted nor considered as evidence of the same conciliatory spirit. The claims of our citizens are for mere justice. They are for reparation of unquestionable wrongs; for indemnity or restitution of property taken from them, or destroyed, without shadow or color of right. The claim under the 8th article of the Louisiana convention has nothing to rest upon but a forced construction of the terms of the stipulation, which the American Government considered, and have invariably considered, as totally without foundation. These are elements not to be coupled together in the same negotiation; and while we yet trust to the final sense of justice in France for the adjustment of the righteous claims of our citizens, we still hope that their unquestionable character will ultimately secure to them a consideration unincumbered with other discussions. You will, respectfully, make this representation to the Viscount de Chateaubriand, with the assurance of the readiness of this Government to discuss the question upon the Louisiana convention further, if desired by France, but of our final conviction that it is not to be blended with the claims of our citizens for mere justice."

No. 1, (*a.*)

Count de Menou to Mr. Adams.

[Translation.]

LEGATION OF FRANCE TO THE UNITED STATES, *Washington, July* 11, 1823.

His excellency the Viscount de Chateaubriand, in announcing to me that Mr. Gallatin was about to leave France, expresses his regret at his departure in such terms that I should do him injustice were I not to use his own expressions. "My correspondence with this minister," he remarks to me, "has caused me to appreciate his talents, his ability, and his attachment to the system of friendship that unites the two powers. It is with regret that I suspend my communications with him."

I esteem myself happy, sir, in conveying to you such sentiments towards the representative of the United States in France, and I should have thought that I had but imperfectly apprehended the design of the Viscount de Chateaubriand had I neglected to communicate them to the Federal Government.

The Minister for Foreign Affairs reminds me also, on this occasion, that Mr. Gallatin having frequently laid before him claims of Americans against the French Government, he had shown himself disposed to enter upon a general negotiation, in which they should be comprehended with the claims of French citizens against the Federal Government, at the same time with the arrangement relative to the execution of the 8th article of the treaty of Louisiana. The object of his excellency was to arrive at a speedy and friendly disposition of all difficulties that might subsist between the two powers, well assured that France and the United States would be found to have the same views of justice and conciliation.

His excellency regrets that Mr. Gallatin, who, he says, "has convinced him how pleasing and advantageous it is to negotiate with a statesman who exhibits candor and ability in his discussions," did not receive from his Government during his stay in France the necessary powers for this double negotiation. But he informs me that the Government of his Majesty remains always disposed to open it, either with Mr. Gallatin, should he return with these powers, or with Mr. Sheldon, if the Federal Government should think proper to confer them on him.

I greatly desire, sir, to see these propositions acceded to by the Federal Government, and to be able to reply to his excellency, as he expresses his wish that an arrangement, putting an end to every subject of discussion, might soon be expected.

I pray the Secretary of State to receive the renewed assurance of my high consideration.

MENOU,
Chargé d'Affaires of France near the United States.

The Hon. SECRETARY OF STATE.

No. 1, (b.)

Mr. Adams to Count de Menou.

DEPARTMENT OF STATE, *Washington, August* 12, 1823.

SIR: Your letter of the 11th of last month has been submitted to the consideration of the President of the United States, by whom I am directed to express the high satisfaction that he has felt at the manner in which his excellency the Viscount de Chateaubriand has noticed in his correspondence with you in the temporary absence of Mr. Gallatin from France, and the terms of regard and esteem with which he notices the character and conduct of that minister. The anxious desire of the President for the promotion of the good understanding between the United States and France could not be more gratified than by the testimonial of his most Christian Majesty's Government to the good faith and ability with which the minister of the United States at his court has performed his official duties.

With regard to the assurance of his excellency the Viscount de Chateaubriand's disposition to enter upon a negotiation with Mr. Gallatin, in the event of his return to France, or with Mr. Sheldon during his absence, concerning the claims of citizens of the United States on the Government of France, in connexion with an arrangement concerning the 8th article of the Louisiana treaty, I am directed to observe that those subjects rest upon grounds so totally different that the Government of the United States cannot consent to connect them together in negotiation.

The claims of the citizens of the United States upon the French Government have been of many years standing, often represented by successive ministers of the United States, and particularly by Mr. Gallatin, during a residence of seven years, with a perspicuity of statement and a force of evidence which could leave to the Government of the United States no desire but that they should have been received with friendly attention, and no regret but that they should have proved ineffectual. The justice of these claims has never been denied by France; and while the United States are still compelled to wait for their adjustment, similar and less forceful claims of the subjects of other nations have been freely admitted and liquidated.

A long and protracted discussion has already taken place between the two Governments in relation to the claim of France under the 8th article of the Louisiana convention, the result of which has been a thorough conviction on the part of the American Government that the claim has no foundation in the treaty whatever. The reasons for this conviction have been so fully set forth in the discussion that it was not anticipated a further examination of it would be thought desirable. As a subject of discussion, however, the American Government are willing to resume it whenever it may suit the views of France to present further considerations relating to it; but, while convinced that the claim is entirely without foundation, they cannot place it on a footing of concurrent negotiation with claims of their citizens, the justice of which is so unequivocal that they have not even been made the subject of denial.

From the attention which his Excellency the Viscount de Chateaubriand has intimated his willingness to give to the consideration of these claims, the President indulges the hope that they will be taken into view upon their own merits; and in that hope the representative of the United States at Paris will, at an early day, be instructed to present them again to the undivided and unconditional sense of the justice of France.

I pray you, sir, to accept the renewed assurance of my distinguished consideration.

JOHN QUINCY ADAMS.

The Count DE MENOU, *Chargé d'Affaires from France.*

No. 2.

Extract of a letter from Mr. Sheldon (No. 11) to Mr. Adams, dated

PARIS, *October* 16, 1823.

"I took an early occasion, after the receipt of your despatch, No. 1, of the 10th of August, to communicate the subjects of it in a conversation I had with Viscount de Chateaubriand. His observations in relation to that of the claims, as connected with the pretensions of France under the Louisiana treaty, were of a very general nature, and amounted to little more than a repetition of his readiness to enter upon the consideration of whatever subjects of discussion might exist between the two countries, and the expression of his satisfaction at the prospect of being soon relieved from the labor which the affairs of Spain had thrown upon him, and having thus more time to devote to those of the United States and others not of the same pressing nature. He avoided any intimation of a disposition to take up the claims by themselves, and it can hardly be expected that the French Government will, at this time, relax from the ground they have so lately taken upon that point. I informed him that I should communicate, in writing, an answer to the overture made by Count de Menou, at Washington, for uniting in a new negotiation this subject with that of the Louisiana treaty, in substance the same as that gentleman had already received there, and should again press upon the French Government the consideration of the claims by themselves; to which he replied that any communication I might make would be received and treated with all the attention to which it was entitled on his part."

No. 2, (a.)

Mr. Sheldon to the Viscount de Chateaubriand.

PARIS, *October* 11, 1823.

SIR: Mr. Gallatin, during his residence as minister of the United States in France, had, upon various occasions, called the attention of his Majesty's Government to the claims of our citizens for the reparation of wrongs sustained by them from the unjust seizure, detention, and confiscation of their property by officers and agents acting under authority of the Government of France. During the past year his Majesty's ministers had consented to enter upon the consideration of these claims, but they proposed to couple with it another subject, having no connexion with those claims, either in its nature, its origin, or the principles on which it depended—a question of the disputed construction of one of the articles of the treaty of cession of Louisiana, by virtue of which France claimed certain commercial privileges in the ports of that province. Mr. Gallatin had not received from his Government any authority to connect these two dissimilar subjects in the same negotiation, or indeed to treat upon the latter, which had already been very amply discussed at Washington, between the Secretary of State of the United States and his Majesty's minister at that place, without producing any result, except a conviction on the part of the Government of the United States that the privileges for French vessels, as claimed by the minister of France, never could have been, and were not in fact, conceded by the treaty in question. A stop was then put to the negotiations already commenced in relation to the claims, and with which had been united on the proposition of the French Government, and as being naturally connected with it, the consideration of certain claims of French citizens on the Government of the United States.

The Chargé d'Affaires of France at Washington has lately, on behalf of his Government, expressed to that of the United States a wish that this double negotiation might be resumed, and that a definitive arrangement might be made, as well in relation to the disputed article of the Louisiana treaty, as of the subject of the claims upon one side and upon the other. The Government of the United States has nothing more at heart than to remove, by friendly arrangements, every subject of difference which may exist between the two countries, and to examine, with the greatest impartiality and good faith, as well the nature and extent of the stipulations into which they have entered, as the appeals to their justice made by individuals claiming reparation for wrongs supposed to have been sustained at their hands.

But these two subjects are essentially dissimilar; there are no points of connexion between them; the principles upon which they depend are totally different; they have no bearing upon each other, and the justice which is due to individuals ought not to be delayed or made dependent upon the right or the wrong interpretation, by one or the other party, of a treaty having for its object the regulation of entirely distinct and different interests.

The reclamations of American citizens upon the Government of France are for mere justice; for the reparation of unquestionable wrongs, indemnity, or restitution of property taken from them, or destroyed forcibly and without right. They are of ancient date, and justice has been long and anxiously waited for; they have been often represented to the Government of France, and their validity is not disputed. Similar reclamations, without greater merit or stronger titles to admission, presented by citizens of other nations, have been favorably received, examined, and liquidated; and it seems to have been hitherto reserved to those of the United States alone to meet with impediments at every juncture, and to seek in vain the moment in which the Government of France could consent to enter upon their consideration.

Although the question arising under the 8th article of the Louisiana treaty has already been fully examined, the Government of the United States is ready, if it is desired by France, and if it is thought that any new light can be thrown upon it, to discuss the subject further, whenever it shall be presented anew by France to their consideration. But they are convinced that, by blending it with the claims, not only will no progress be made towards its solution, but that these last, standing upon their own unquestionable character, ought not to be trammelled with a subject to which they are wholly foreign.

I am instructed to bring them anew before your excellency, and to express the hope of the President that his Majesty's Government will not continue to insist upon connecting together two subjects of so different a nature, but that the claims may be taken up, on their own merits, and receive the consideration which they deserve, unincumbered with other discussions.

I request your excellency to accept the assurance, &c.

D. SHELDON.

No. 3.

Extracts of a letter from the Secretary of State to Mr. Brown, dated

WASHINGTON, *December* 23, 1823.

"You will immediately, after your reception, earnestly call the attention of the French Government to the claims of our citizens for indemnity."

"You will at the same time explicitly make known that this Government cannot consent to connect this discussion with that of the pretension raised by France, on the construction given by her to the 8th article of the Louisiana cession treaty. The difference in the nature and character of the two interests is such that they cannot, with propriety, be blended together. The claims are of reparation to individuals for their property, taken from them by manifest and undisputed wrong. The question upon the Louisiana treaty is a question of *right*, upon the meaning of a contract. It has been fully, deliberately, and thoroughly investigated, and the Government of the United States are under the entire and solemn conviction that the pretension of France is utterly unfounded. We are, nevertheless, willing to resume the discussion, if desired by France; but to refuse justice to individuals, unless the United States will accede to the construction of an article in a treaty, contrary to what they believe to be its real meaning, would be not only incompatible with the principles of equity, but submitting to a species of compulsion derogatory to the honor of the nation."

No. 4.

Extract of a letter (No. 2) from James Brown, Envoy Extraordinary and Minister Plenipotentiary of the United States, dated

"APRIL 28, 1824.

"I have, in a letter to M. de Chateaubriand, copy of which I have now the honor to send, made an effort to separate the claims of our citizens from the Louisiana question."

No. 4, (a.)

Mr. Brown to M. de Chateaubriand.

PARIS, *April* 28, 1824.

SIR: In the conference with which your excellency honored me a few days ago I mentioned a subject deeply interesting to many citizens of the United States, on which I have been instructed to address your excellency, and to which I earnestly wish to call your immediate attention.

It is well known to your excellency that my predecessor, Mr. Gallatin, during several years, made repeated and urgent applications to his Majesty's Government for the adjustment of claims, to a very large amount, affecting the interests of American citizens, and originating in gross violations of the law of nations and of the rights of the United States, and that he never could obtain from France either a settlement of those claims or even an examination and discussion of their validity. To numerous letters addressed by him to his Majesty's ministers on that subject, either no answers were given, or answers which had for their only object to postpone the investigation of the subject. Whilst, however, he indulged the hope that these delays would be abandoned, and that the rights of our citizens, which had been urged for so many years, would at length be taken up for examination, he learned with surprise and regret that his Majesty's Government had determined to insist that they should be discussed in connexion with the question of the construction of the 8th article of the Louisiana treaty of cession. Against this determination he strongly but ineffectually remonstrated in a letter to Mr. de Villele, dated the 12th November, 1822.

It is notorious that the Government of the United States, whenever requested by that of his Majesty, have uniformly agreed to discuss any subject presented for their consideration, whether the object has been to obtain the redress of public or private injuries. Acting upon this principle, the question of the 8th article of the Louisiana treaty was, upon the suggestion of the minister of France, made the subject of a voluminous correspondence, in the course of which all the arguments of the parties respectively were fully made known to each other and examined. The result of this discussion has been a thorough conviction on the part of the Government of the United States that the construction of that article of the treaty contended for by France is destitute of any solid foundation and wholly inadmissible. After a discussion so full as to exhaust every argument on that question, the attempt to renew it in connexion with the question of the claims of our citizens appeared to the Government of the United States to be a measure so contrary to the fair and regular course of examining controverted points between nations, that they instructed Mr. Sheldon, their Chargé d'Affaires, to prepare and present a note explaining their views of the proceeding, which he delivered on the 11th of October, 1823. To this note no answer has ever been received.

I have the express instructions of the Government again to call the attention of that of his Majesty to this subject, and to insist that the claims of our citizens may continue to be discussed as a distinct question, without connecting it in any way with the construction of the Louisiana treaty. The two subjects are in every respect dissimilar. The difference in the nature and character of the two interests is such as to prevent them from being blended in the same discussion. The claims against France are of reparation to individuals for their property taken from them by undisputed wrong and injustice. The claim of France under the treaty is that of a right founded on a contract. In the examination of these questions the one can impart no light to the other: they are wholly unconnected, and ought on every principle to undergo a distinct and separate examination. To involve in the same investigation the indisputable rights of American citizens to indemnity for losses and the doubtful construction of a treaty, can have no other effect than to occasion an indefinite postponement of the reparation due to individuals, or a sacrifice on the part of the Government of the United States of a treaty stipulation in order to obtain that reparation. The United States would hope that such an alternative will not be pressed upon them by the Government of his Majesty.

Whilst I indulge a hope that the course to which I have objected will no longer be insisted on by his Majesty's ministers, permit me to renew to your excellency the sincere assurance that the United States earnestly desire that every subject of difference between the two countries should be amicably adjusted, and all their relations placed upon the most friendly footing. Although they believe that any further discussion of the 8th article of the Louisiana treaty would be wholly unprofitable, they will be at all times ready to renew the discussion of that article or to examine any question which may remain to be adjusted between them and France.

I request your excellency to accept, &c.

JAMES BROWN.

His Excellency VISCOUNT DE CHATEAUBRIAND,
    Minister of Foreign Affairs, &c.

No. 5.

Extract of a letter (No. 3) from James Brown to the Secretary of State, dated

PARIS, *May* 11, 1824.

"I have the honor to inclose a copy of the answer of the Minister of Foreign Affairs to the letter which I addressed to him on the 28th ultimo upon the subject of the claims of our citizens against the French Government. You will perceive that no change has been made in the determination expressed to Mr. Gallatin, of connecting in the same discussion the question on the 8th article of the Louisiana treaty of cession, and the claims of the citizens of the United States against France. In expressing this resolution it has not been considered necessary even to notice the arguments made use of to induce them to adopt a different opinion."

No. 5, (a.)

Viscount Chateaubriand to Mr. Brown.

[Translation.]

PARIS, *May* 7, 1824.

SIR: The object of the letter which you did me the honor to address me on the 28th of April is to recall the affair of American claims, already repeatedly called up by your predecessors, that they may be regulated by an arrangement between the two powers, and that in this negotiation the examination of the difficulties which were raised about the execution of the 8th article of the Louisiana treaty should not be included.

Although the claims made by France upon this last point be of a different nature from those of the Americans, yet no less attention ought to be paid to arrange both in a just and amicable manner.

Our claims upon the 8th article had already been laid before the Federal Government by his Majesty's Minister Plenipotentiary when he was negotiating the commercial convention of June 24, 1822.

The negotiators, not agreeing upon a subject so important, the King's Government did not wish this difficulty to suspend any longer the conclusion of an arrangement which might give more activity to commerce, and multiply relations equally useful to the two powers. It reserves to itself the power of comprehending this object in another negotiation, and it does not renounce in any manner the claim which it urged.

It is for this reason, sir, that my predecessors and myself have constantly insisted that the arrangements to be made upon the 8th article of the Louisiana treaty should be made a part of those which your Government were desirous of making upon other questions still at issue.

It is the intention of his Majesty not to leave unsettled any subject of grave discussion between the two States; and the King is too well convinced of the friendly sentiments of your Government not to believe that the United States will be disposed to agree with France on all the points.

His Majesty authorizes me, sir, to declare to you that a negotiation will be opened with you upon the American claims, if this negotiation should also include the French claims, and particularly the arrangements to be concluded concerning the execution of the 8th article of the Louisiana treaty.

Accept, sir, the assurances of the very distinguished consideration with which I have the honor to be, &c.

CHATEAUBRIAND.

No. 6.

Extracts of a letter (No. 4) from the Secretary of State to Mr. Brown, dated

DEPARTMENT OF STATE, *Washington, August* 14, 1824.

"The subject which has first claimed the attention of the President has been the result of your correspondence with the Viscount de Chateaubriand in relation to the claims of numerous citizens of the United States upon the justice of the French Government.

"I inclose, herewith, a copy of the report of the Committee on Foreign Relations of the House of Representatives upon several petitions addressed to that body at their last session by some of those claimants, and of a resolution of the House adopted thereupon."

"The President has deliberately considered the purport of Mr. de Chateaubriand's answer to your note of April 28 upon this subject; and he desires that you would renew with earnestness the application for indemnity to our citizens for claims notoriously just, and resting upon the same principle with others which have been admitted and adjusted by the Government of France."

"In the note of the Viscount de Chateaubriand to you of May 7 it is said that he is authorized to declare, a negotiation will be opened with you upon the American claims, if this negotiation should also include French claims, and particularly the arrangements to be concluded concerning the execution of the eighth article of the Louisiana treaty."

"You are authorized, in reply, to declare that any just claims which subjects of France may have upon the Government of the United States will readily be included in the negotiation; and to stipulate any suitable provision for the examination, adjustment, and satisfaction of them."

"But the question relating to the eighth article of the Louisiana treaty is not only of a different character, it cannot be blended with that of indemnity for individual claims without a sacrifice on the part of the United States of a principle of right. The negotiation for indemnity presupposes that wrong has been done; that indemnity ought to be made; and the object of any treaty stipulation concerning it can only be to ascertain what is justly due, and to make provision for the payment of it. By consenting to connect with such a negotiation that relating to the eighth article of the Louisiana convention the United States would abandon the *principle* upon which the whole discussion concerning it depends. The situation of the parties to the negotiation would be unequal. The United States, asking reparation for admitted wrong, are told that France will not discuss it with them, unless they will first renounce their own sense of right to admit and discuss with it a claim the *justice* of which they have constantly denied."

"The Government of the United States is prepared to renew the discussion with that of France, relating to the eighth article of the Louisiana treaty, in any manner which may be desired, and by which they shall not be understood to admit that France has *any* claim under it whatever."

No. 7.

Mr. Brown to Mr. Adams, No. 12.

PARIS, *August* 12, 1824.

SIR: Some very unimportant changes have taken place in the composition of the ministry. The Baron de Damas, late Minister of War, is now Minister of Foreign Affairs; the Marquis de Clermont Tonese is appointed to the Department of War; and the Count Chabrol de Crousal to that of the Marine.

These appointments are believed to correspond with the wishes of the President of the Council of Ministers, and do not inspire a hope that our claims will be more favorably attended to than they have been under the former administrations. The interpretation of the eighth article of the Louisiana treaty contended for by France will, I apprehend, be persisted in, and all indemnity refused until it shall have been discussed and decided. After the correspondence which has already passed upon that article, it would appear that any further discussion upon it would be wholly unprofitable. With a view, however, of ascertaining the opinions of the Minister of Foreign Affairs, I shall, at an early day, solicit a conference with him, and inform you of the result.

I have had the honor of receiving your letter recommending the claim of Mr. Kingston to my attention. The difficulties which that claim must experience from its antiquity, and from the operation of the treaty of 1803, cannot have escaped your observation. It has also to encounter, in common with all our claims, the obstacle presented by the eighth article, which is found broad enough to be used as a shield to protect France, in the opinion of ministers, from the examination and adjustment of any claim which we can present.

I have the honor to be, with great respect, sir, your most obedient and humble servant,

JAMES BROWN.

No. 8.

Mr. Brown to Mr. Adams, No. 14.

PARIS, *September* 28, 1824.

SIR: Little has occurred of importance during the present month except the death of the King. This event had been anticipated for nearly a year; he had declined gradually, and the affairs of the Government have been for some time almost wholly directed by Monsieur, who, on his accession to the throne, has declared that his reign would be only a continuation of that of the late King. No change in the policy of the Government is expected, and probably none in the composition of the ministry. The present King is satisfied with Mr. de Villèle, who is at its head, and if any of its members should be changed, the spirit in which public affairs are directed will not, it is believed, be affected by that circumstance.

The ceremonies attending the change of the crown have principally occupied the public attention for the last fortnight. It will, I presume, be officially announced by the French minister at Washington, and, according to the forms observed here, will, I understand, require fresh letters of credence for all foreign ministers at this court, addressed to the new King.

My health has not permitted me (having been confined for some weeks to the bed by a rheumatic affection) to confer with the Baron de Damas on our affairs, since his appointment as Minister of the Foreign Department. I should regret this the more if I were not satisfied that the same impulse will direct the decisions of the Government upon these points now, as before he had this Department in charge, and that no favorable change in those decisions can be expected from any personal influence which might be exerted by the new minister. I shall, however, take the earliest opportunity that my health will allow to mention the subject to him and ascertain what his views of it are.

I have the honor to be, with great respect, sir, your most obedient and humble servant,

JAMES BROWN.

No. 9.

Extracts of a letter from Mr. James Brown to Mr. Adams, No. 16.

PARIS, *October* 23, 1824.

"The packet ship which sailed from New York on the 1st of September brought me the letter which you did me the honor to address to me on the 14th of August."

"In conformity with the instructions contained in that letter, I have addressed one to the Baron de Damas, Minister of Foreign Affairs, a copy of which I now inclose. I expect to receive his answer in time to be sent by the packet which will sail from Havre on the 1st of next month, in which event it may probably reach Washington about the 15th of December."

"The recent changes which have been made in the ministry, of which I have already informed you, do not justify any very strong expectation that a change of measures in relation to our affairs at this court will follow. The same individuals fill different places in the ministry from those which they formerly held, but in all probability adhere to their former opinions in relation to the subjects of discussion between the United States and France. On the point to which my letter to the Baron de Damas particularly relates, the Count de Villèle has already given his deliberate views in his letters to Mr. Gallatin, dated the 6th and 15th of November, 1822, and I have every reason to believe that they remain unchanged. Having bestowed much attention on the subject, it is probable his opinion will be, in a great measure, decisive as to the answer which shall be given to my letter. It is the opinion of many well informed men that, in the course of a few months, important changes will be made in the composition of the ministry. As these changes, however, will proceed from causes wholly unconnected with foreign affairs, I am by no means sanguine in my expectations that, under any new composition of the ministry, we may hope for a change of policy as it relates to our claims. The 8th article of the Louisiana treaty will be continually put forward as a bar to our claims, and its adjustment urged as often as we renew our claim for indemnity."

"The Journal des Debats of this morning states that at a superior Council of Commerce and of the Colonies, at which his Majesty yesterday presided, Mr. de St. Cricq, President of the Bureau de Commerce, made a report on the commercial convention of June 24, 1822, between the United States and France."

No. 9, (a.)

Mr. Brown to Baron de Damas.

PARIS, *October* 22, 1824.

SIR: I availed myself of the earliest opportunity to transmit to my Government a copy of the letter which I had the honor to address to the Viscount de Chateaubriand on the 28th day of April last, together with a copy of his answer to that letter, dated the 7th of May.

After a candid and deliberate consideration of the subject of that correspondence, my Government has sent me recent instructions to renew with earnestness the application, already so frequently and so ineffectually made, for indemnity to our citizens for claims notoriously just, and resting on the same principles with others which have been admitted and adjusted by the Government of France.

In reply to that part of the Viscount de Chateaubriand's letter in which he offers to open with me a negotiation upon American claims, if that negotiation should also include French claims, and particularly the arrangements to be concluded concerning the 8th article of the Louisiana treaty, I have been instructed to declare that any just claims which the subjects of France may have upon the Government of the United States will readily be embraced in the negotiation, and that I am authorized to stipulate any suitable provision for the examination, adjustment, and satisfaction of them.

The question relating to the 8th article of the Louisiana treaty is viewed by my Government as one of a very different character. It cannot be blended with that of indemnity for individual claims without a sacrifice on the part of the United States of a principle of right. Every negotiation for indemnity necessarily presupposes that some wrong has been done, and that indemnity ought to be made; and the object of every treaty stipulation respecting it can only be to ascertain the extent of the injury and to make provision for its adequate reparation. This is precisely the nature of the negotiation for American claims which has been for so many years the subject of discussion between the Governments of the United States and of France. The wrongs done to our citizens have never been denied, whilst their right to indemnity has been established by acts done by the French Government in cases depending upon the same principles under which they derive their claim. By consenting to connect with such a negotiation that relating to the 8th article of the Louisiana treaty the United States would abandon the principle upon which the whole discussion depends. When asking for reparation for acknowledged wrong, the United States have been told that France will not discuss it with them, unless they will first renounce their own sense of right, and admit and discuss in connexion with it a claim the justice of which they have hitherto constantly denied. In any negotiation commenced under such circumstances the situation of the parties would be unequal. By consenting to connect the pretensions of France under the 8th article of the Louisiana treaty with claims for indemnity for acknowledged injustice and injury, the United States would be understood as admitting that those pretensions were well founded; that wrong had been done to France, for which reparation ought to be made. The Government of the United States, not having yet been convinced that this is the case, cannot consent to any arrangement which shall imply an admission so contrary to their deliberate sense of right.

I am authorized and prepared, on behalf of the United States, to enter upon a further discussion of the 8th article of the Louisiana treaty in any manner which may be desired, and by which they shall not be understood previously to admit that the construction of that article claimed by France is well founded, and also to renew the separate negotiation for American claims, embracing at the same time all just claims which French subjects may have upon the Government of the United States.

The change which has lately taken place in his Majesty's Department of Foreign Affairs encourages the hope that this important subject will be candidly reconsidered; that the obstacles which have arrested the progress of the negotiation may be removed, and that the subjects of contestation between the two Governments may be ultimately adjusted upon such principles as may perpetuate the good understanding and harmony which have so long subsisted between the United States and France.

Should I, however, be disappointed in the result of this application, it is to be seriously apprehended that, as the United States have not hitherto seen in the course of the discussion any just claim of France arising from the 8th article of the Louisiana treaty, so, in the persevering refusal of the French Government to discuss and adjust the well founded claims of citizens of the United States to indemnity for wrongs, unless in connexion with one which they are satisfied is unfounded, the United States will ultimately perceive only a determination to deny justice to the claimants.

Permit me respectfully to request that, at as early a day as your convenience will allow, your excellency will favor me with an answer to this letter.

I embrace with pleasure this occasion to offer to your excellency the renewed assurance, &c.

JAMES BROWN.

His Excellency BARON DE DAMAS, *Minister of Foreign Affairs, &c.*

CORRESPONDENCE WITH GREAT BRITAIN RELATIVE TO CESSION OF LAND ON ISLAND
OF ABACO, ONE OF THE BAHAMAS, FOR A LIGHT-HOUSE ESTABLISHMENT.

COMMUNICATED TO THE HOUSE OF REPRESENTATIVES DECEMBER 27, 1824.

To the Speaker of the House of Representatives:

In compliance with a resolution of the House of Representatives of the 23d of December, 1823,
requesting that a negotiation should be opened with the British Government "for the cession of so much
land on the island of Abaco, at or near the Hole in the Wall, and on such other places within the
acknowledged dominion of that power, on the islands, keys, or shoals, on the Bahama Banks, as may be
necessary for the erection and support of light-houses, beacons, buoys, or floating lights, for the security of
navigation over and near the said Banks, and to be used solely for such purposes," directions were given to
the minister of the United States at London, on the 1st of January, 1824, to communicate the purport of
that resolution to the Government of Great Britain, with a view to their acceding to the wish of this; and
I now transmit to the House copies of Mr. Rush's correspondence upon this subject, communicating the
result of his application to the British Government.

JAMES MONROE.

Washington, *December 24, 1824.*

Inclosures.

Mr. Adams to Mr. Rush, January 1, 1824.
Mr. Rush to Mr. Adams, No. 360, February 6, 1824.
Same to Mr. Canning, February 6, 1824.
Same to Mr. Adams, No. 379, May 17, 1824.   Extract.
Same to same, No. 397, September 16, 1824.   Copy.

Mr. Adams to Mr. Rush.

Department of State, *Washington, January 1, 1824.*

Sir: I have the honor of inclosing herewith a copy of a resolution of the House of Representatives of
the United States, adopted on the 23d of last month, the purport of which you will communicate to the
Government of Great Britain. The object is of a nature to authorize the expectation that it will be
readily acceded to by them, and, if the proposal should meet their acceptance, measures will be taken for
ascertaining and fixing upon the sites specially adapted to the attainment of the objects of the resolution.

I am, with great respect, sir, your very humble and obedient servant,

JOHN QUINCY ADAMS.

Hon. Richard Rush, *Envoy Extraordinary and*
      Minister Plenipotentiary of the United States, London.

Mr. Rush to Mr. Adams, No. 360.

London, *February 6, 1824.*

Sir: I received on the 1st instant your despatch (No. 78) of the 1st of January, covering a resolution
of the House of Representatives, passed on the 23d of December, relative to the establishment of lights on
the island of Abaco, &c., for the security of navigation over and near the Bahama Banks; and, in fulfilment
of your instructions upon this subject, I have this day addressed a note to Mr. Secretary Canning, of which
a copy is inclosed.

I have the honor to remain, &c.,

RICHARD RUSH.

Hon. John Quincy Adams, *Secretary of State.*

Mr. Rush to Mr. Canning.

London, *February 6, 1824.*

The undersigned, Envoy Extraordinary and Minister Plenipotentiary from the United States, has the
honor to inclose to Mr. Secretary Canning a copy of a resolution of the House of Representatives of the

United States, passed on the 23d of December, the purport of which will be seen to be to request the President to negotiate with his Majesty's Government for a cession of so much land on the Island of Abaco, at or near the Hole in the Wall, and on such other places within the acknowledged dominion of Great Britain, on the islands, keys, or shoals, on the Bahama Banks, as may be necessary for the erection and support of light-houses, beacons, buoys, or floating lights, for the security of navigation over and near the said Banks, and to be used solely for such purposes.

The object of the foregoing resolution is so distinctly stated in the resolution itself, that the under_ signed deems it unnecessary at this time to enlarge upon it. It appears to be of a nature to authorize the hope that no objection will be seen to it; and the undersigned has been instructed by his Government to say that, should the proposal which the resolution embraces meet the acceptance of his Majesty's Government, measures will be taken for ascertaining and fixing upon the sites specially adapted to the attainment of the objects in view.

The undersigned is happy to avail himself of this opportunity of tendering to Mr. Canning the assurances of his distinguished consideration.

RICHARD RUSH.

Extract of a letter (No. 379) from Mr. Rush to Mr. Adams, dated

LONDON, May 17, 1824.

"I have lately had some conversation with Mr. Huskisson on my application to this Government respecting the establishment of lights on the island of Abaco, and hope, before long, to have some communication to make upon this subject."

Mr. Rush to Mr. Adams, No. 397.

LONDON, September 16, 1824.

SIR: I had the honor to mention, in my despatch of May 17, that I had had some conversation with Mr. Huskisson on the application which I made to this Government respecting the establishment of lights on the island of Abaco, and that I expected, soon after that conversation, to have had it in my power to make some communication to you upon the subject of it.

On the twenty-second of July I had, at Mr. Huskisson's instance, a special interview with him, and with Lord Melville, upon the above subject at the Admiralty. It seems that my note to Mr. Secretary Canning of the 6th of February had been referred to the Admiralty, and I was given to understand, at the above interview, both by Lord Melville and Mr. Huskisson, that Great Britain could not accede to the principle contained in my note. She could not accede to the principle of negotiating with the United States with a view to the cession of any part of the island of Abaco, or other islands in the Bahamas, for the purpose of setting up beacons, buoys, or lights, for the benefit of navigation.

But his lordship and Mr. Huskisson proceeded to say that, if the United States would designate the proper sites, Great Britain herself would not be indisposed to the erection and establishment of these aids to navigation upon those islands, provided the United States would pay the necessary fees towards keeping them up, in all cases where their vessels derived benefit from them, whilst making voyages in that direction.

I immediately remarked upon what appeared to me the objectionable character of such a proposition. I asked how light money, charged upon vessels of the United States, was to be levied and paid over to the British treasury. They replied, that Britain would willingly leave that operation to the custom-houses of the United States, assisted by some agency on the part of her consuls in the ports of the United States, under any arrangements that the two countries might deem satisfactory.

I said that the whole plan appeared to me to be anomalous. The very principle of raising a revenue for any purpose, and however small, presupposed the right of enforcing it, and here was a plan for raising a revenue for one country in the heart of another.

They replied, that several of the lights on the British coast were in the hands of private individuals, or corporate bodies, but that the Government, nevertheless, received, under proper arrangements, a portion of the proceeds; to which I rejoined, that, however this might be as between a Government and its own subjects, the case, to my mind, appeared to be altogether different, as between one foreign nation and another.

The interview terminated by a declaration on my part, that, as the proposal was entirely new to me, and had not been within the contemplation of my instructions, all that I could do would be to transmit it to my Government, to which end I added, that I should be happy to receive it in writing. This was promised to me, and I have since been in expectation of receiving it. As it has not yet come, I have thought it best to impart to you, as above, without waiting longer, what may be regarded as the substantial decision of this Government upon the subject, though it will be more satisfactory to me to convey that decision to you hereafter, as I trust I shall be enabled to do, in the more accurate form of a written communication from Mr. Secretary Canning.

I have the honor to remain, with very great respect, your obedient servant,

RICHARD RUSH.

Hon. JOHN QUINCY ADAMS, *Secretary of State.*

CLAIM OF REUBEN SHAPLEY UNDER SECOND ARTICLE OF TREATY OF PEACE WITH
GREAT BRITAIN FOR A VESSEL AND CARGO.

COMMUNICATED TO THE HOUSE OF REPRESENTATIVES JANUARY 5, 1825.

To the honorable the Senate and House of Representatives of the United States in Congress assembled:

The petition of Reuben Shapley, of Portsmouth, in the State of New Hampshire, merchant, most respectfully represents, that the schooner John, and cargo, belonging to your petitioner, was captured by his Britannic Majesty's ship-of-war Talbot, in latitude 31° 40′ and longitude 78° 10′ west. The time was March 5, 1815, which, with the place where, brought the capture within the stipulation of the second article of the treaty of peace for the restoration of such property.

That, seven days after, said schooner, under conduct of a prize master and crew, went ashore on the island of Cuba, and, with her cargo, was totally lost.

That it appeared by the protest of the schooner's officers that she was lost by the negligence or misconduct on the part of the captors.

That, on application by this Government to the British for indemnification, the British minister, with the advice of the King's law officers, proposed that your petitioner should apply to the Court of Admiralty, to which the minister sent the papers in the case, a court which it appeared had liberated a prize or prizes taken after the peace.

That, by advice of his friends in England, your petitioner made such application at much expense, and the result has been a judgment, that a case of negligence was not made out against the capturing officers on reasons alleged, which your petitioner has the utmost confidence that he can show to be insufficient, on which point he begs leave to refer to the annexed statement of his case.

A subsequent application to the British Government has been made for indemnity by the American minister, but that Government, relying on a judicial decision in the Court of Admiralty, refuses compensation, as the captor was ignorant of the peace, and chargeable with no fault, as is alleged in regard to the subsequent loss of the vessel.

This takes several things for granted: 1st. That the United States are bound to prove that there was no impossibility of restoring the vessel, except from the fault of the captors; whereas the proof of an impossibility, not caused by negligence or fault, is on the other side. 2d. That Britain, by its own court, can decide and has decided a national question; neither of which propositions are true. 3d. That, if a clear case of loss by fault of the captors is not made out, the British Government is not obliged to compensate or indemnify the owners; a position that can be easily disproved.

It is agreed that the vessel was lost, and admitted on both sides that, if the loss happened through any fault or negligence of *any agent* of the British Government, compensation must be made. And the freeing the captor, the commander, an individual, from blame in a proceeding against him, does not exculpate inferior agents for whom the Government may be responsible, nor touch the claim against the other party, viz: the Government itself.

The great question divides itself into two parts: 1st. Is the British Government bound to make compensation if the vessel was lost through negligence of its agents, who take it by force into their custody? And both parties admit her liability in such a case. And your petitioner is confident that he can establish this by proof, deemed sufficient in courts, whether of common or civil law; in regard to these proofs, he begs leave to refer to his statement, only remarking that the Admiralty had decreed restoration as directed by the treaty, and he took that course as recommended, and as being the readiest, not doubting compensation would be obtained in another course, if it failed in that—not entertaining a suspicion that he could be doomed to relinquish any right, or that this recommended course would be interpreted against his claim.

The other branch of the great question is this: Is not the British Government bound by the treaty to make compensation, even on the unadmitted supposition of the loss of the property by inevitable accident? And your petitioner is humbly of opinion that the affirmative is true, and may be clearly supported. It is evident from the common, easy, and familiar words of the treaty, from the apparent words of the contracting parties from making this its own interpreter, from the rules of interpretation laid down by high authority for the construction of treaties. All this your petitioner has endeavored to evince in his statement of the case. He conceives, further, that this Government has put this construction on the treaty, and would have made compensation in a like case; and he understands that it has made compensation in a case which, though in many features not similar to this, yet, if he understands it, goes to show that where actual restoration was rendered impossible by a taking out and distributing captured goods, compensation was made for them instead of restoration; and he further understands that the captor had not *authentic information* of the peace, so might be legally ignorant, notwithstanding rumors.

Your petitioner, with all due deference, submits it whether it is not of great national importance that treaties should be so constructed, that tacit conditions or restrictions should not be supposed where none are expressed, whereby words creating rights are changed in meaning, and that the faith of treaties be considered as inviolable. He feels that the question that has arisen is deeply interesting and of very serious import to himself, and cannot admit a doubt of its receiving all due attention from the great council of the nation.

He looks up with strong and most respectful confidence to this high guardian of citizens' rights that he shall receive indemnity for his loss, humbly conceiving that it belongs to our nation to enforce the compact another has made with it, and to render justice to individual citizens.

He therefore prays that his petition, statement, and documents, may be examined by a committee or otherwise, and relief from so heavy a loss sustained from the injury of others, and no fault of his own, granted him, in such manner as to your wisdom and equity shall seem meet.

And he, as in duty bound, will ever pray.

REUBEN SHAPLEY.

Statement of the proofs in support of the petition of Reuben Shapley to Congress.

The great question respecting responsibility by the treaty of peace divides itself into two parts: First, was the captured vessel lost through the fault or negligence of the captors?

Secondly, is not the British Government responsible, by the terms and spirit of the treaty, if the fact of negligence were doubtful, or even if the loss occurred by inevitable accident?

Two kinds of proof may be adduced on the first question equally pertinent: first, such as show that the loss arose from the negligence or faulty mistakes of the capturing commander; or, secondly, from those of some subordinate agent having custody of the property.

The proofs of the first kind are, the testimony of the master and mate of the captured vessel, distinctly stated in their protest. This is the usual, natural, and proper evidence, together with the daily register, styled the log-book, of occurrences at sea. These narratives, having internal marks of fairness and truth, are, and must be, received as proofs for the security of maritime property removed from the ordinary protection of municipal law. Protests are so established by commercial usage that the want of them is set down as a defect of expected and often indispensable proof. Those who make them are, from the trust reposed in them, respectable. They are not only the proper but the only witnesses the case admits of, and must always be deemed credible, unless their characters or the testimony itself be in some way discredited.

By two such witnesses (whose characters are capable of honorable support were it needful) the negligence of the capturing commander is proved, not by a general declaration that there was negligence, which would be only opinion, and might arise from mistake or ignorance, but a clear, distinct relation of facts, which they could not be mistaken in, and which, if true, undeniably proves negligence, though they never use the word. The master of the schooner, being applied to, assured the commander that the land in sight was not the key called the Hogsties, which, having been up it, he described, and positively said that the land in sight made very differently. But the captain disregarded the information of one declaring his judgment founded on personal knowledge, and whose personal safety was concerned in judging right. And the fact confirmed his judgment, and the ignorance of the captain, who, shaping his course for the windward passage, confident of seeing Jamaica the next day, that very night got his prize wrecked about 180 miles east of that passage, not driven on a lee shore by a tempest, but in good weather, under full sail for Jamaica, stranded on Cuba. After seeing land, and warned as he was, the captain ought not to have run in the night, as he did for about nine hours, among keys which might be mistaken one for another, or lest he might strike Cuba instead of the passage, as he did in fact. Again, he ought not to have trusted a prize master, an inferior officer, to keep a lookout in the night for both vessels. The prize should not have been suffered to be ahead of the ship, and then she would not have run on shore, nor does it appear she would had she or the ship kept a good lookout, as they ought to have done. Certainly not; had they laid to, or kept off, lest they should strike land in the night, such negligent conduct would have freed insurers from bearing the loss. Again, it is the duty of a commander, unless in particular cases restrained by orders, to send a prize to a near port instead of a distant one, other things being equal; and had he, instead of ordering this prize (for his own convenience probably) for Jamaica, ordered her to New Providence, about half as far distant, she had never been wrecked on the island of Cuba; or, had she been sent to Bermuda, through an open sea, and safe, though longer navigation, she would not have blundered and missed her way among dangerous keys, so as finally to get on shore far from her proper course to Jamaica, and the deviation not owing to winds, but to ignorance of the way. If the point of capture be marked on the chart, it will appear that the schooner had passed the danger of shores and shoals, and, well advanced, was pursuing her course in a safe and open sea, with a fair prospect of soon reaching her port, and ought not, without necessity, in a time of peace, to have entangled among shoals in a dangerous sea, where, if lost, no insurance, except that of the treaty, could relieve the suffering owners, and a comparison of the protest with the chart will tend greatly to confirm the former.

But an attempt has been made to take off the force of the strong, clear testimony of the protest. It appears from the Proctor's letter that the Judge of Admiralty said that a case of negligence in the loss of the vessel was not made out; the master, in his protest and letter written at Jamaica on his arrival there, made no charge of negligence, and it is not until his arrival in America that he, in his protest made there, mentioned any mistake or neglect in the navigation of the vessel after capture. He added, that he did not decide whether the Government was or was not responsible, under the stipulations of the treaty, as the proceeding was against the captor.

This implies, first, that a protest, unless invalidated, is proper and good evidence. 2d. That the second protest is not proof in this case, because negligence is not stated in the first, seeming to intimate that it was a story made up afterwards. But here an inference is drawn not warranted by the premises. The omission is perfectly accounted for. The master wrote the commander that his owner would seek indemnity, and required his log-book and papers. They were refused and suppressed. Had he only protested against this, and left all matters out until his return home, he would have acted correctly. He who unjustly withholds the materials of a protest must not object to its insufficiency. The master had a right to complete the log-book by the insertion of after occurrences. This right, against all reason and justice, was denied him, and then advantage is sought to be taken from this injurious conduct. His letter intimated plainly enough the pursuing the claim for indemnity, and the want and demand of the documents for that very purpose, and this might be the cause of the detention. No good reason can be presumed, and, just out of prison, it surely was not for him to provoke a powerful captor by writing to him that his ignorance and blunders had caused the loss of the vessel. But there is another reason for the omission, of itself sufficient, and confirmed by oath, namely: at making his protest he was told by the notary or justice, or both, that there was no need of inserting the particulars. They might wish to favor the captors; at any rate, such advice of men in office, and supposed to know what was proper, was suited to have weight, and was submitted to. The master might naturally think that his having certified this purpose of claiming by letter was sufficient there, or that he could not so safely and fully have the facts appear, where his opponent had interest and he had none, and it is no uncommon thing to uote a protest in due time at one port, and extend it, by an enumeration of circumstances in detail, at another. Under all these circumstances, there is no ground for the inference that the protest should be set aside as an after-made story. Thus, the objections being done away, the competent testimony remains in its full force, making out a case of negligence against the captor.

It might be the interest of the British Government to have a decision of the question respecting negligence; and the effect of the sentence pronounced would doubtless be to acquit the capturing officer, so that his Government could not throw the loss of the vessel on him; yet that Government might be, and is, responsible; the same question being still open as ever between it and the United States, for one power cannot decide a question between itself and another power. The sentence of a British court is as inoperative in such a question as the opinion of the Attorney General. But the court has declared that it has decided no national question.

The great principle that negligence clearly implies liability is the same wherever the negligence was found. If a prize was burnt or run ashore by the negligence of the prize master, or a sailor, the capturing commander would be free from blame, but the Government would be liable, whether it could or could not get satisfaction of its faulty agent; and in this case, if the prize master got ahead of the ship, contrary to orders, the loss occurred by his negligence, at least as one cause.

The burden of proof lies wholly on the other side. The law of nations speak of a *legitimate excuse*, founded on a real and insurmountable obstacle making it forever impossible to perform the stipulated act, as laid down in Vattel, 506. This imports impossibility not arising from the fault of the non-performing party, and that it lies on the party making the excuse to make proof.

But, supposing, without granting, that no negligence appears in the case, in answer to the second question, it may be affirmed that the British Government is bound, by the treaty of peace, to compensate the loss sustained.

There is not the least ambiguity in the second article. The act to be done could not have been more clearly and simply described. The word *restore* is not less easy and of less common use than the words pay or deliver; and the circumstance that the obligation is not less clear, *capture* in time and place distinctly described. To such a case is applicable the maxim of national law on treaties, that it is not permitted to interpret what has no need of interpretation.—(*Vattel*, 310.) But although plain words cannot be made plainer by other or explanatory words, yet the same meaning may be indicated by other sentences or clauses in the instrument.

It is stipulated in the beginning of the second article that orders shall be sent to the armies, squadrons, &c. To what end? Evidently to save to unoffending individuals their property, lawfully employed on the ocean, from loss by means of capture; and if this should not prevent it, they were to be reinstated, or placed, as nearly as possible, in their former state, by being entitled to re-possession where the intended prevention was impossible.

The stipulation to restore to that purpose follows, and is introduced or prefaced by these significant expressions " to prevent all causes of complaint which might arise, it is agreed," &c.

The owners of vessels captured after peace are here brought to view, as the persons who might have cause to make complaint. And it would be that theirs was a case of peculiar hardship; an event for the general good produced their calamity. Their property was their living, and while lawfully employed for their own and the public good, it was to them lost, taken by friends, in a time of peace. This just cause of complaint the parties undertake to prevent or remove. The property *shall be restored;* if this be not literally done, or an equivalent given where it is not, individuals would be left to complain of loss which might be their ruin.

It is laid down that, by the law of nature, he who has made a promise to any one has conferred upon him a true right to acquire the thing promised.—(*Vattel*, 260.)

What is the thing in this case promised?

The property forcibly taken away.

Again, as the engagements of a treaty impose, on the one hand, a perfect obligation, they produce, on the other, a perfect right, which to violate is to do an injury.—(*Vattel*, 261.)

Here, then, is a perfect right to the thing promised. When an act is stipulated to be done, and the circumstances that raise the obligation are clearly expressed, no tacit conditions, restrictions, or provisos, can limit the act. It must be performed, or the natural legal consequences of non-performance suffered, that is, making good the damage sustained by it. Most especially, if on one part of an agreement to restore property a restriction is mentioned, and in another part, speaking of another property, there is no mention of any restriction, which is the present case. By the first article of the treaty, certain property is to be restored conditionally, so far as practicable. By the second, certain captured vessels are to be restored, and no limiting restriction is inserted, which shows a distinction intended. The treaty thus explains itself.

The treaty was intended to give relief to suffering individuals. And national law gives ' to every disposition the full extent properly implied in the terms, if it appears that the author had in his view everything properly comprehended in them."—(*Vattel*, 314.)

The terms import *restoration* when the subject of the promise was a vessel supposed to be at sea. It was impossible that it should not have been in view that it was liable to perish on seas or shores, and in such could not be restored; yet no proviso is inserted for explanation in such a case, though it was contemplated.

The law of nations raises an obligation to restore what should be captured, by misfortune, without authentic information, after peace was concluded. It must, says that law, be certainly restored. The only alteration made by the treaty is, substituting, in different places, another day for that of conclusion, after which the effect must be precisely the same *certain restoration.*

In the treaty each party speaks to the other in a promise, and whether in the same sentence in the plural number, or in different clauses in the singular, binding itself to the other, is of no manner of consequence, the binding is the same. The language on the part of Britain to these States, who use the same, is, we will restore; on our part this language is understood to be without restriction. The British say, we meant to restore conditionally, provided the property should not be lost by accident while in our possession. But where is this condition now for the first time mentioned? It cannot now be created, annexed, and made part of the agreement; for there is nothing in national law more clear than this, " If he who can and ought to have explained himself clearly and plainly has not done it, it is worse for him; he cannot be allowed to introduce subsequent restrictions which he has not expressed."—(*Vattel*, 311.)

Britain would probably have most vessels to be restored, (to avoid all questions on general law,) a clear article for restoration would be therefore for her interest; and, if so, she may be presumed to be the progressor, and then another plain rule in that law would apply on a question being made.

" In case of doubt, the interpretation goes against him who gave law in the treaty; for it was in some sort dictated by him. He is in fault in neglecting to express himself more clearly; therefore, in extending or restricting the signification of the terms within the meaning the least favorable to him, no injury is done him, or, at least, only that to which he has willingly exposed himself."—(*Vattel*.)

But, although the promise to perform a certain act be absolute, unqualified by condition or hint of any exception, yet a question is made as to the effects of non-performance, and is said, in this case, that the vessel, the subject, having perished, and restoration become, by an invincible obstacle, impossible, the promise is vacated and the promisor perfectly excusable; because it is a maxim that there can be no obligation to an impossibility. It is admitted that this maxim is founded in reason. If the act stipulated is, by unavoidable accident, become impossible, he who promised is not bound to perform *that* act, but reason and law require compensation or indemnification if the case admits of it. Some cases do, and some do not. In these last only is the promise vacated. Conventional law is clear on this head. It states, speaking of insurmountable obstacles, "that if the impediment be real, time must be allowed, for there can be no obligation to an impossibility; and, for the same reason, if an insurmountable obstacle should render the execution of the article not only impracticable for the present, but forever impossible, he who engaged for it is guilty of no fault, and the other party cannot make his inability a reason for breaking the treaty, but is to accept of indemnification if the case be of such a nature, and (or that) indemnification be practicable."—(*Vattel*, 515.)

Nothing can be plainer than that, in the case last mentioned, indemnification must be made, for the reason that the subject admits of it.

Again it is stated, "a legitimate excuse, founded on a real insurmountable obstacle, is to be admitted, nobody being bound to impossibilities. The obstacle, when the promise (or promisor) is not in fault, vacates a promise which cannot be made good by an equivalent, nor the performance of it be deferred to another time," &c.—(*Ibid.*, 116.)

This shows clearly that no promise is vacated by insurmountable accident, but one that cannot be made good by an equivalent. The promise to restore, then, has not been vacated by impossibility.

This law, thus distinguishing, is grounded on reason; some things have, from their nature, an adequate perfect equivalent in specie as a common measure of value; some things cannot be so valued, have no equivalent, admit of no price. Of the first sort are chattels, even slaves, where slavery is permitted. Of the last sort are free, intelligent beings. An engagement to restore prisoners of war must be understood to mean living persons. If they die by the act of God merely, before the time of re-delivery, the party promising is perfectly freed from his obligation; the promise is vacated. But a ship or a puncheon of rum has, by universal consent, a capacity of being represented by a definite quantity of gold or silver; and the person, whether public or private, who promises to deliver, re-deliver, or restore a specific chattel, is bound, on failure, to pay such equivalent, which, with incidental damages, is all that is required or recovered in such cases, the legal substitute standing for the article itself. And the promisor is not excused from compensation by the circumstance that the article has perished, for the value has not, and by that the engagement may, and ought to be, substantially made good to the promissee. There being no invincible obstacle in this case to be made a legitimate excuse for non-performance, the party entitled by the promise can have the effect of it, as being, to every reasonable purpose, performed.

18TH CONGRESS.]   No. 390.   2D SESSION.]

AFFAIRS WITH SPAIN RELATIVE TO PIRACIES IN THE WEST INDIES.

COMMUNICATED TO THE SENATE JANUARY 10, 1825.

The Committee on Foreign Relations submit a Report on so much of the President's Message as relates to Piracies.

That our commerce for years has been harassed and the lives of our citizens destroyed by pirates, issuing from the colonies of Spain in the West Indies, is a fact derived not only from the message of the President, but is of universal notoriety. These outrages have been so long and so often repeated, and marked with such atrocious circumstances, that a detail of the particular cases would be as impracticable as unnecessary. Our Government, with a view to protect our citizens, has resorted to the means within their power by stationing a naval force near the places where the pirates resort; a measure also pursued by other powers. Every effort, heretofore, has been unavailing to put an end to these atrocities. These desperadoes, acquiring confidence from impunity, becoming more ferocious from habit, and multiplying by recruits from the most abandoned of other nations, threaten the most disastrous mischiefs, justly alarming to that highly valuable and most respectable portion of our fellow-citizens whose pursuits are on the high seas. It is manifest, as well from facts derived from other sources as from the message of the President, that the continuance of this evil is ascribable to the asylum afforded the banditti in the colonies of Spain. The Government of the United States, cherishing the most amicable disposition towards Spain, has presented the subject with great earnestness to the Spanish Government, demanding reparation for the past and security for the future. To these reiterated remonstrances no answer was returned till very recently, and to this day all that has been obtained is a *promise* of a satisfactory answer to the applications of the Government of the United States; although Spain has been solemnly warned that if she did not promptly acquit herself of her obligations to us on this subject, our Government would be constrained, from the nature of the outrages, to become its own avenger, and, availing itself of its own resources, protect the commerce and lives of the American citizens from destruction. In the same spirit of concilia᷒ tion an appeal has been made to the local authorities, accompanied with a request that if, from weakness, they were unable to exterminate the hordes of banditti who took shelter from pursuit within their territories, that permission might be given our forces to pursue them on land. This has been denied on the vain punctilio of national dignity. The posture in which Spain now stands is that of connivance in these injuries, or incapacity to prevent them. "A sovereign who refuses to cause reparation to be made of the damage caused by his subject, or to punish the guilty, or, in short, to deliver him up, renders himself an accomplice in the injury, and becomes responsible for it." If the committee were of opinion that the refusal on the part of Spain was wilful, and not the result of inability, they would, with a full view of all the consequences which the measure involves, at once recommend an appeal to the last resort of nations against Spain and all her dependencies; but believing, as they do, that courtesy requires that her refusal to do us justice should be placed on the ground of inability—an inability resulting from causes which the committee intentionally forbear to enumerate—they content themselves with recommending only such measures as are believed to be indispensable effectually to reach the mischief. And hence they beg leave to present a bill with suitable provisions for the end designed.

18th Congress.]   No. 391.   [2d Session.

MESSAGE AND DOCUMENTS RELATIVE TO PIRACIES NEAR THE SPANISH WEST INDIA ISLANDS.

COMMUNICATED TO THE SENATE JANUARY 13, 1825.

To the Senate of the United States:

In compliance with two resolutions of the Senate—the first of the 21st, and the second of the 23d December last—requesting information respecting the injuries which have been sustained by our citizens by piratical depredations, and other details connected therewith; and requesting, also, information of the measures which have been adopted for the suppression of piracy; and whether, in the opinion of the Executive, it will not be necessary to adopt other means for the accomplishment of the object; and, in that event, what other means it will be most advisable to recur to, I herewith transmit a report from the Secretary of State, and likewise a report from the Secretary of the Navy, with the documents referred to in each.

On the very important question submitted to the Executive, as to the necessity of recurring to other more effectual means for the suppression of a practice so destructive of the lives and property of our citizens, I have to observe that three expedients occur: one, by the pursuit of the offenders to the settled as well as the unsettled parts of the island from whence they issue; another, by reprisal on the property of the inhabitants; and a third, by the blockade of the ports of those islands. It will be obvious that neither of these measures can be resorted to, in a spirit of amity with Spain, otherwise than in a firm belief that neither the Government of Spain nor the Government of either of the islands has the power to suppress that atrocious practice, and that the United States interpose their aid for the accomplishment of an object which is of equal importance to them as well as to us. Acting on this principle, the facts which justify the proceeding being universally known and felt by all engaged in commerce in that sea, it may fairly be presumed that neither will the Government of Spain nor the Government of either of those islands complain of a resort to either of those measures, or to all of them, should such resort be necessary. It is therefore suggested that a power commensurate with either resource be granted to the Executive, to be exercised according to his discretion, and as circumstances may imperiously require. It is hoped that the manifestation of a policy so decisive will produce the happiest result; that it will rid these seas and this hemisphere of this practice. This hope is strengthened by the belief that the Government of Spain and the Governments of the islands, particularly of Cuba, whose chief is known here, will faithfully co-operate in such measures as may be necessary for the accomplishment of this very important object. To secure such co-operation will be the earnest desire and, of course, the zealous and persevering effort of the Executive.

                                                            JAMES MONROE.
Washington, *January* 13, 1825.

DEPARTMENT OF STATE, *Washington, January* 11, 1825.

The Secretary of State, to whom have been referred the resolutions of the Senate of the 21st and 23d of December last, requesting that the President would cause to be communicated to that body correspondence and information relative to the piracies referred to in his message; the means adopted by the Executive for their suppression; and the additional means necessary and expedient to be entrusted to the Executive for the suppression of the same; and also the number of merchant vessels belonging to the citizens of the United States, with their names, owners, and value of merchandise, which have been captured or plundered, and of injuries inflicted on citizens of the United States by the pirates since the first of December, eighteen hundred and twenty-three; and the number of pirates and piratical vessels, with the names of the said vessels, that have been taken by our naval force since that period of time, has the honor of reporting to the President copies of documents received at this Department in relation to the subject of those resolutions, which, together with those already communicated to Congress, contain the information required by the resolutions, so far as it is within the competency of this Department to furnish it.

                                                     JOHN QUINCY ADAMS.

List of papers transmitted to the Senate with the report of the Secretary of State of January 11, 1825.

    1. Extract of a letter of instructions from the Secretary of State to Mr. Thomas Randall, agent for commerce and seamen at Porto Rico and Cuba, dated April 21, 1823.
    2. Mr. Randall to the Secretary of State, July 1, 1824. (Extract.)
    3. Same to same, July 5, 1824. (Copy.)
    4. Same to same, July 14, 1824. (Extract.)
    5. Same to same, September 6, 1824. (Extract.)
    6. Same to same, September 15, 1824. (Extract.)
    7. Same to same, October 31, 1824. (Extract.)
    8. Mr. Mountain, vice consul, to Mr. Warner, consul, July 5, 1824. (Copy.)
    9. Same to same, October 30, 1824. (Extract.)
    10. Same to same, October 30, 1824. (Copy.)
    11. Same to same, November 25, 1824. (Extract.)
    12. Hugh Nelson, esq., to the Secretary of State, with a note to Mr. Salazar, Minister of State, &c., of September 7, 1824.

No. 1.

Extract of a Letter of Instructions from the Secretary of State to Mr. Thomas Randall, appointed Agent of Commerce and Seamen at Porto Rico and Cuba, dated April 21, 1823.

    " You will also obtain and communicate to this Department any information which it may be useful to possess relating to the pirates and piracies which have so long infested the coasts of Cuba. And if it may prove useful to the public service, you will, with due discretion, correspond with any of the naval officers of the United States stationed in those seas for the suppression of the slave trade and of piracies."

No. 2.

Extract of a letter from Mr. Randall to Mr. Adams, dated

HAVANA, *July* 1, 1824.

    " Mr. Mountain, vice consul of the United States at this port, has just been informed by a respectable merchant of this place that there are some *piratical* boats or vessels lying off Matanzas, by which the sailing of a number of merchant vessels, now ready for sea, is prevented. The information is brought by a letter from Matanzas, which also contains a request from one of the persons interested that Mr. Mountain would advise some American man-of-war of the fact, that relief might be afforded them. Unfortunately, there is no vessel-of-war of the United States now here, but the intelligence will not be neglected."

No. 3.

Mr. Randall to the Secretary of State.

HAVANA, *July* 5, 1824.

    SIR: The last letter which I had the honor to address to you was dated the 1st instant, and despatched, *via* Charleston, by the brig Trader, which sailed the ensuing day. In that letter I advised you that information had been received at this place of the re-appearance of the pirates off the port of Matanzas, by which the sailing of a number of merchant vessels had been prevented. Recent captures made by those pirates off that port confirm the truth of the above report.
    Two American vessels are certainly known to have been captured and plundered, and there are reports of the capture of three others. Of the former, the brig Castor, of Portland, Capt. Hood, has arrived at this port. This vessel was captured entering the bay of Matanzas by seven men in an open boat, was taken thence to port "Escondido," in the neighborhood, where the pirates were joined by a large party from the shore with boats and horses, with the assistance of which the brig was plundered of everything portable or valuable, including all the clothes of the captain and his crew. The cargo being principally lumber, the amount taken from the brig was by no means considerable. The captain and his men were, as usual, most severely and cruelly beaten. This boat had previously captured, on the same morning, the brig Betsy, Done, of Newport; and after plundering the vessel and casting off her boats they set her on fire in several places and abandoned her. The crew succeeded in extinguishing the fire, and thus preserved themselves from the horrid death designed for them by their merciless captors.
    It is reported here that a brig called the John, from an eastern port of the United States; a ship, the name and description of which are not stated; and a schooner from New York, with a valuable cargo of dry goods, have also been captured within a few days by the pirates. I have not yet been able to arrive at any direct and certain authority for this last report, which is, however, generally credited here. I thought it my duty to give you the earliest intelligence of those depredations, however imperfect in its details.

The temporary absence of the United States cruisers from their usual station has emboldened those men to renew their piracies. The necessity which has caused this very short and casual absence of the whole American squadron from the neighborhood of Matanzas and this port is much to be regretted. Very great alarm prevails in this place among the masters of vessels, several of whom are fearful of putting to sea without convoy. A British cutter, the Grecian, has just arrived at this port. Mr. Mountain, our vice consul, solicited her commander to make a short cruise to Matanzas in pursuit of those pirates. He promised to sail this evening with that object.

This letter will be sent by the steamship Robert Fulton, which will sail for New York early to-morrow morning. I regret that the short stay of this vessel prevents me from enlarging my letter on this very interesting topic, as I had designed. I have been endeavoring to collect all the facts I could arrive at in relation to the piracies committed from this island, and shall take occasion to write more fully upon the subject by the earliest safe conveyance.

I have the honor to be, with the greatest consideration and respect, sir, your obedient servant,

THOMAS RANDALL.

Hon. JOHN QUINCY ADAMS.

No. 4.

Extract of a letter from Mr. Randall to Mr. Adams, dated

HAVANA, *July 14, 1824.*

"I had the honor to write to you last by the steamship Robert Fulton, *via* New York, of the date of the 5th instant. In this letter I gave information of the capture of the brig Castor, of Portland, and of the Betsy, Done, of Newport, by the pirates, off Matanzas, and of the reported capture of several other American vessels. Since that date we have certain intelligence of the capture of the schooner Mercator by a piratical vessel off Port Escondido. It is derived from a passenger (a Spaniard) who, as far as we yet know, is the only person who has been permitted to escape from the hands of the captors. He calls himself Don Joseph Manuel Rey, and on the 9th instant made a deposition before the vice consul of the United States at this port, of which the following extract is the substance:

"'That he was a passenger on board the schooner Mercator, Henry Allen master, from New York, bound to this port, Havana; that on the 3d day of this present month the said vessel was boarded, when near the port of Escondido, on this coast, by a sharp built foretopsail schooner, with about forty armed men, who took possession of said Mercator, confined this deponent in the cabin, (after first suspending him by the thumbs and then by the neck, to extort information where the money was to be found on board,) for three days, when they sent this deponent on shore, alone, near Camrioca, to the windward of Matanzas; for the three days this deponent was confined he had no communication with any one, and knows not what was done with Captain Allen and his crew.'

"It is greatly to be feared that these unfortunate men have all been destroyed by the pirates, a fate from which the above named passenger was only saved by being a Spaniard.

"From further information derived from this passenger, I apprehend there was on board the Mercator both public and private letters for me, sent from the Department of State, through the Collector's office of New York. I mention this that, should the fact be so, and the communications of importance, duplicates may be despatched to me.

"The United States brig Grampus, Commandant Sloat, arrived off this port on the 7th, and sent in her boat with an officer. The Grampus is from the coast of Mexico, and is bound to New York. The consul wrote to Captain Sloat, informing him of the appearance of the pirates off Matanzas, and advising him to proceed to that place. I urged the same in a message by the lieutenant who was sent on shore. The Grampus sailed the same night, and I take it for granted has proceeded to the scene of those depredations.

"It will thus be seen to what a fearful head so short an interval of the absence of our vessels-of-war has enabled this horrible system of piracy again to swell, demonstrating conclusively that, though rendered inert for a time by the pressure of external force, it has continued to exist in full vitality, and ready to be exerted the moment that pressure was removed. Such, it is feared, will ever be the case until measures of greater severity on the part of the United States shall be resorted to. I hope the importance of the subject will serve as an excuse for me if I attempt, somewhat at large, to explain the nature and extent of this evil, and respectfully to suggest the only remedy which appears to me to be effectual and adequate to its entire suppression.

"It may be now assumed as an undoubted fact that the crime of piracy is not limited to the mariners who are the active agents in its perpetration, but has advocates and partisans in a very numerous class of the inhabitants of this island. Of the latter class, many have a direct concern in the equipment and arming of those vessels and a participation in their plunder. Others amongst the planters on the coast and the merchants are indirectly concerned in the great profit derived from purchasing the property plundered by them. Besides those persons thus concerned, the Spaniards of this island, generally, observe with perfect apathy, and some even with pleasure, those depredations against the commerce of the United States, for it is not a little extraordinary that one may hear in the streets of Matanzas, and even of this city, this most odious crime warmly defended, on principle, by men of property, and deemed respectable here. They urge in its defence that it is but a retaliation for the conduct of citizens of the United States in capturing, under the insurgent flag, the property of Spaniards. They say that the conduct of the people of Regla and Matanzas, and other places from which the pirates issue, is no worse than that pursued in certain places in the United States which they name. Many of the Spanish merchants have sustained immense losses from captures made by Colombian and other vessels-of-war, and privateers, commanded and partly manned by citizens of the United States; and they assert that the conduct of our Government and its citizens, in this particular, is no less reprehensible than that which is charged against the Spaniards in respect to piracy. I shall not stop to show the utter absence of truth in the charge made against the Government of the United States; and although I entirely disapprove of the conduct of those Americans who, for the sake of plunder, have engaged in the war between Spain and her colonies, I do not think it necessary to point out the great difference of turpitude in the respective practices. I merely mention the opinions of those Spaniards to give semblance and probability to the sentiments they utter, which would, otherwise, from their extreme perversity and immorality, be scarcely credited. The moment a prize to the pirates arrives on the coast, persons from the interior throng to the spot to share in or purchase the plunder, as in the late case of the brig Castor. The property soon finds its way into the cities and tempts cupidity by the advantages of the traffic. But four days past, the anchor and cable of the brig Castor, plundered about the beginning of this month, was found on board an American vessel in this port, the captain of which purchased it from the *Patron* of a droger or coaster of this island. Two years ago it was common for persons to cross the harbor to Regla publicly to buy property from the pirates. Allegations of this kind have been repeatedly made in the United States, and generally credited, and it is believed that the records of your Department contain sufficient proof of their truth. Here they are matters of notoriety, and generally credited.

"A publication appeared in the Charleston Courier, in or about September, 1823, in relation to this subject, containing a detail of the transactions at Regla. A suit was brought in the court of Carolina, by a Spaniard of Regla, against the editor of the Courier, for a libel, in charging him with being concerned with the pirates. A commission has been sent to this place to examine witnesses in behalf of the defendant in justification of the publication, and the commission is now open. The subject is much talked of, and I have been told by some of the commissioners, and by many of the most respectable merchants of this place, that every allegation in the piece charged as libellous is unquestionably true, and susceptible of full proof if witnesses dare to declare the whole truth. But such is the fear of the prosecutor and his associates, that it will be difficult to find a witness hardy enough to expose himself to the vengeance of those men, by disclosing, at this place, what he knows of their practices. The publication is said here to be a true but faint and imperfect sketch of the horrible transactions of the period to which it alludes. For that reason I mention it that it may be referred to for further information. I beg leave, for further confirmation of the opinions above advanced, to mention one other fact, which I have received from a gentleman of unquestionable veracity.

"A representation was made to the Captain General, about the period of the greatest activity amongst the pirates, that a large sum of money in doubloons, which had been plundered from a Boston vessel, had been traced to Regla, and could there be found and identified. Information had been given by one of the pirates concerned in the capture. After instituting an examination, the Captain General sent for the claimant, and informed him, 'that he feared all Regla would be found to be implicated in the robbery; and that, in the present disturbed and critical condition of the island, he dared not push the investigation further;' and so the affair rested.

"While, then, those practices, so far from finding a corrective or check in the moral feeling of this community, are rather countenanced and aided by it, it is obvious that a Government of even greater energy and virtue than that of this island would be scarcely adequate to their suppression. But with the exception of the present chief of this Government, and a very few of its highest officers, it is more than suspected that the great majority of these public agents are either indifferent, or feel an interest adverse to its suppression. Participating in the general prejudices of their countrymen, they have also a pecuniary interest in occasionally conniving at those robberies, and in protecting their perpetrators from the hands of justice. I should not have credited those charges but upon the most undoubted testimony. Various facts have been mentioned to me by resident merchants, of the highest respectability, of this place, as being known to them personally, where the officers of the customs and others have got possession of property known to have been captured by pirates, and have applied the whole or the greater part to their own use, preventing the legal owners from all chance of identifying and recovering their property; where they have, for large rewards, suffered persons known to be pirates to escape from justice. The case of the cargo of the Jamaica coffee, brought to this place, which is referred to in the Charleston Courier, above mentioned, was told to me as an undoubted fact before I had read it in that paper. Even where a few of the pirates have had the singular ill fortune to be arrested and confined in prison, they either manage to escape by bribery, or they are confined without trial until their names and offences have been forgotten, and their crimes no longer susceptible of proof.

"In aid of those moral causes, there exist others of a local and physical character, furnishing those marauders the means both of annoyance and protection. The numerous ports of this island, only partially visited by and known to strangers, afford them every facility to secrete their plunder and evade the most rigorous pursuit.

"Whatever disposition, then, the present Governor may evince to suppress this crime, (and from information I have received he has used every exertion,) his efforts, unaided by the executive officers, by the tribunals, and by public opinion, will be powerless and ineffectual; nor can more satisfactory results be anticipated from the application of the most active system of mere external preventive measures, such as have been heretofore resorted to by the United States. If experience had not conclusively settled the question, the facts and reasons above stated would seem sufficient to demonstrate, *a priori*, the inefficacy of those measures of prevention.

"Notwithstanding the large armament maintained by the United States on this coast, attended with a profuse waste of treasure, and with the sacrifice of the healths and lives of so many of their gallant crews, the only result has been the temporary and partial interruption of the practice, while the source and cause of the mischief have not been reached.

"This naturally brings me to an inquiry as to the means adequate to its suppression; and the obvious result, from what has been stated, is, that the remedy, to be effectual, must be applied directly to the origin and seat of the evil. Public opinion in this island must be changed; and as this cannot be effected by reason, or the voice of justice, it must be corrected by force. The authorities must be stimulated by counter-motives of interest or fear to the exercise of greater vigilance, and to measures of more rigor and severity against delinquents. Those salutary changes, in my opinion, can only be produced by a rigid system of reprisals and hostilities, on the part of the United States, against Spanish property, and particularly that belonging to this island. This plan is by no means new, but has been often suggested, and (I am informed) by the Committee of "Foreign Relations," at the last session of Congress. I have not read the report, but am told the committee forbear to recommend its immediate adoption, but advise the awaiting the result of an application to the supreme Government of Spain. If the views above presented, of the causes and extent of the evil, be correct, it is to be feared that, as at present circumstanced, Spain can do but little to remedy it. It is not believed that she is able or willing to spare an adequate force to effect the object. New orders may be issued to the authorities here, enjoining greater vigilance and energy, but it cannot be conceived that any greater sanction or obligation can be thereby superadded to those which ought already to exist. Those, however, have been insufficient so far.

"I am not unaware that the Executive, without the sanction of Congress, is incompetent to apply the above remedy. The remarks are made to impress the principle I wish to inculcate, and which I hope will be concurred in; that this remedy must in all probability be eventually resorted to, and thus to induce corresponding preparations.

"The reprisals should not be confined to the capturing of the foreign commerce of the island and its coasting trade, but should also extend to the levying of contributions on all places and towns on the coast (wherever assailable) at which piratical vessels are fitted out or received. The advantages of this would be, that every part of the community would partake of the distress caused by those retaliatory measures. Those participating, directly or indirectly, would be detected and exposed by their exasperated countrymen and be made to disgorge their plunder. Those merely indifferent or favorable to the crimes of those pirates would, through interest and fear, be incited to discountenance them. The planters would suffer by the capture of their produce in the coasting vessels; the merchants and others by the contributions levied on their property, and by the capture and interruption of their commerce. The authorities would be incited to redoubled vigilance and vigor, and, receiving the co-operation of the inhabitants, would in a short time render the pursuit of this practice hazardous and fruitless. For when it shall have been seen that for every capture made by pirates from this island strict and full retribution will be exacted from the inhabitants, there can be no doubt that the great mass of the community will combine to rid themselves of the cause of this infliction. That thus combined their efforts would be adequate to its extinction, no reasonable doubt can be entertained. If a rigorous blockade of the ports of this island was at the same time established, the distress produced, as well to individuals as to the Government, in cutting off its only source of supply and ordinary revenue, would soon bring all parties to a proper sense of their true interest and duty.

"It would be unnecessary and presumptuous in me to offer, seriously, to prove that such a course on the part of the United States would be fully justified by every principle of reason and of international law applicable to the subject. The facts of the case prove that a large part of the people of this island are engaged in hostilities of the most cruel and oppressive character against the property and lives of citizens of the United States, without the inclination or ability on the part of the supreme Government of Spain or the local authorities to put a stop to it. Nothing short of this remedy can afford a corrective, which is, therefore, justified on the great principles of humanity and self-defence.

"As to the amount of force adequate to effect those objects, it is believed that a ship of the line, a frigate, or two sloops-of-war, with some smaller vessels, armed with the requisite powers to make reprisals, would, in the course of a few months, give an entire check to it. Upon this subject, however, the President can doubtless be better informed by the naval officers of the United States.

"It is with feelings of more than mere diffidence that I have ventured, from a sense of duty, to submit with freedom these ideas to the Government. I claim for them no originality, for they are common to all the intelligent men with whom I have conversed within the transactions of this island for the last few years; and I shall be better satisfied if they are found to coincide with the opinions already formed by the Executive of the United States on this interesting subject.

"I have just been informed by Captain Paine, of the United States schooner Weasel, (arrived yesterday,) that he visited Port Escondido and its vicinity since the period of the captures made off that place, but could find no pirates. From the evidences of their practices existing there he will be induced to repeat his visit. This shows with what facility the pirates are enabled to dispose of their prizes and evade pursuit. The United States ship John Adams, Captain Dallas, arrived in this port the 12th instant from the Bay of Mexico, and will leave it for Philadelphia this day or to-morrow. I hasten to close this letter to be despatched by that ship."

No. 5.

Extracts of a letter from Mr. Randall to the Secretary of State, dated

Havana, *September* 6, 1824.

"The Government will have learned from my letter of the 14th July, by the John Adams, and from other accounts, of the renewal of the *piracies* at this island in their most atrocious and sanguinary form. In that letter I mentioned the cases of the Mercator, the Castor, and others. While at Matanzas I was informed that several other captures had occurred near that city, but, from the destruction of the vessels and crews, no particulars were known. At the same time the brig Industry, of Baltimore, when in the harbor of Matanzas, and only a few miles from the city, was attacked by five piratical boats, which were beaten off. The firing was distinctly heard in Matanzas. A Spanish brig-of-war lay in the port, but no efforts were made to capture the boats."

"While at Matanzas and in its neighborhood I heard much of the nature and extent of the piracies committed there, and of the extensive participation in it by persons of the city and country. The facts are truly appalling, and far exceed in degree and turpitude the views of it presented in my letter of the 14th July. Large quantities of their plunder are known to have been introduced by the pirates into Matanzas, and are vending there at prices which alone betray the nature of the property. Many articles of a peculiar fabric, and known not to have been regularly introduced, are seen there constantly, such as French hats, of the newest fashion, on the heads of vulgar ruffians. The retailers of goods are seen travelling to the coast with pack-horses, for the known purpose of making purchases from the pirates. A respectable Englishman, who keeps the ferry near the city, informed me that the returns from his ferry give certain indications when prizes are on the coast, from the number of persons who resort from Matanzas to their rendezvous. No effectual measures are taken to stop this traffic. If, occasionally, goods are seized in the attempt to smuggle them into the city, the affair terminates by their condemnation, or being taken by the officers of the customs, and nothing more is heard of it. Persons known to be pirates walk the streets unmolested, no one being willing to incur the risk of denouncing them.

"But very recently a scene of piracy has been exposed in another quarter, which must have been acting for several months, and which, for the extent of its depredations and their atrocity, transcends all that have been known for several years. They have taken place at Baya Honda, to the leeward of this place, near Cape San Antonio, the old scene of similar crimes. Information having been given to Captain Graham, of the British sloop-of-war Icarus, an expedition was fitted out in his boats, which proceeded to Baya Honda on the 21st ultimo, and succeeded in capturing two pirate vessels and in killing several of the pirates. On the approach of the boats the pirates, about forty in number, fled into the bushes. On board one of the pirate vessels were confined the captain and crew of the brig Henry, of Hartford, Connecticut, who were most seasonably released. The Henry was captured on the 16th ultimo, bound from a port in Mexico to Matanzas, with a cargo of mules. The captain and his crew were treated with the accustomed cruelty of those ruffians, and were designed to be killed the next day, after they had assisted in landing the mules. The Henry was dismasted and stripped.

"In the bay were found the wrecks of twelve vessels recently destroyed by the pirates, the crews of all of which are supposed to have been murdered. Some of the vessels were very large, and the British officers computed that their crews could not have consisted of a less number than one hundred and twenty persons. Of this horde of villains nothing had been previously heard, and they had been no doubt carrying on their depredations for a considerable time without interruption. Some of the crew of the Henry were told by the pirates that all those vessels, twelve in number, had been captured and destroyed by them; and upon being asked what had been done with their crews, they very significantly shrugged their shoulders, but gave no answer. This part of the coast has been but little observed of late by men-of-war, from an idea that the pirates had entirely deserted it, and it is still believed to be very imperfectly explored and known. The place is represented as having many secret harbors, difficult of detection without a very strict scrutiny with boats. The pirates run their prizes into those small harbors or inlets, cut away their masts, and to vessels merely cruising in the bay they are then invisible. It is further stated by the crew of the Henry that the pirates had sold to persons on shore the mules on board that vessel, which they were about landing when surprised by the boats of the Icarus. It is impossible that such extensive operations could have been carried on without the full knowledge and participation of the adjacent country.

"Captain Graham made a representation to the authorities of the island, but, I am told, complains much of the apathy evinced by them on the occasion. He has, however, been promised that measures should be taken to discover and punish the delinquents, to which purpose orders would be sent to the captain of the 'partido' or district where the affair occurred. To Captain Graham, his officers, and men, the greatest praise is due for their promptness in equipping the force, the gallantry and spirit with which it was conducted, and not less for their humanity to our unfortunate seamen, whom they relieved in the very crisis of their fate. This officer was before advantageously known for his good conduct and success against the pirates, in killing the noted chief, Pépé, and destroying his establishment at the Isle of Pines. Captain Graham states that the Governor of the Isle of Pines had, a short time before, presented to this notorious pirate an elegant pair of pistols. On the destruction of his party by the English, this same Governor claimed great merit for the aid he afforded. I have also been told, and have reason to believe, that the Spanish brig-of-war 'El Marte,' Don José Apodaca commander, a few days since fell in with and boarded a pirate vessel, the consort of those destroyed by the boats of the Icarus. The visit terminated, however, in mutual civilities. The officers of the man-of-war received various presents from the pirate and let him pass, although his character was well known to all on board. The pirate urged that he only cruised against the enemies of Spain. The account is given by a seaman who was on board the 'Marte,' and visited the pirate.

"I report these facts, out of many similar ones which occur, to satisfy the Government that the whole body of the State is infected and tainted with this dreadful crime, and as a justification for any extremity of treatment which the United States may find it necessary to apply. I must add my increased conviction, arising from more varied information, that nothing short of a system of strict reprisals against this island, its trade, and property, will afford an effectual remedy. I took the liberty, in my letter sent by the John Adams, to offer some remarks in recommendation of this measure. In the meantime, to check and restrain it partially, a large and active force must be constantly kept up on this coast. It is also, in my opinion, necessary that the force employed should be always present, with an undivided view and attention to this business. Their occasional absence on other duties materially impairs their efficacy. Their operations against the pirates should be consecutive and unremitting. It has been found that occasional visits to suspected places, by different vessels, and at long intervals, produce no serious impression on the pirates. They serve, it is true, to afford convoy and a momentary protection, but the intervals of their absence are occupied by the pirates in renewed depredations. It is considered by all intelligent persons at Matanzas to be indispensable that a vessel of at least the force of one of our largest schooners should be constantly lying in the entrance of that harbor. The advantage of such a measure has been before evinced. While on this subject, I think it my duty to state that much dissatisfaction and complaint exists amongst the merchants and traders here, citizens of the United States, because of the great diminution of our naval force in this quarter during the past summer. They allege the summer months to be much more fraught with danger to vessels, because of the calms which prevail, and which, while they permit the smallest species of piratical boats to keep the sea, expose the merchant vessels much more to their attacks. In the more boisterous months many of those boats cannot cruise, and the vessels approaching rapidly to the coast, and running at once into port, are much less liable to capture. I have endeavored to silence their complaints (which will probably be heard in the United States) and to convince them that every possible care has been taken to afford them protection. I cannot but lament, however, the causes (sufficient no doubt) which have induced the withdrawing of so large a portion of the force. Recent events here have proved, that if this was induced by the supposition that piracy was effectually put down, or that the force left was adequate to restrain it, the opinion was erroneous and its consequences deplorable."

No. 6.

Extract of a letter from Mr. Randall to the Secretary of State, dated

HAVANA, *September 15, 1824.*

"The pirates at Key Sal and to the windward have lately received an increase of numbers, which threatens to give more extension to their ravages. Several slave vessels and others were captured by a Colombian privateer, and their crews, to the number of 140 men, sent into Matanzas. A large number of those desperadoes stole boats and left that place avowedly to join the pirates. The vessels to which they belonged were under convoy of a French brig-of-war, which, however, did not attempt to afford them any protection. This conduct of the French commander has much exasperated the Spaniards, and they are now as much incensed against the French as they were before against the Americans and English. Some of the owners of those vessels openly threaten reprisals, and say they will respect no flag; in other words, that they will turn pirates and make up their losses.

"Some persons have been lately arrested at or near Baya-Honda and sent in custody to this city, charged with being concerned in the late piracies committed in that quarter. Some of them belong to Regla, a village in this harbor which has ever been the *headquarters* of the pirates. The authorities of this island have, at length, made a serious effort against the pirates. An expedition of launches and boats was prepared and actually sailed on the night of the 12th instant on this service. To conceal the design from the pirates, an embargo was, on the 11th, laid upon all vessels and boats in this harbor, which was not raised until the 14th. But, as much time was consumed by their tardy preparations, and no other precautions taken to prevent its being known, it is not to be doubted that the pirates have received, from their fellows here, timely intelligence of the movement. This new-born zeal of the authorities has excited some surprise and speculation in this city. It is supposed to have [been] excited by the affair of the brig Marte, mentioned in my last letter. The commandant of that vessel has himself reported to the Government his having fallen in with the pirates off 'Cayo Comfites,' or Sugar Key, and that he had treated with them *under a flag of truce*, not feeling strong enough to attack them. This disgraceful affair has thrown such contempt on the flag of Spain and its authorities that Government is now incited to attempt something effectual. The present expedition is, however, the subject of derision in this city, and from its composition promises nothing but failure and disgrace. I anticipate better results from two other expeditions which will be on the same service about the same time. The one in his British Majesty's brig Thracian, which sailed the 13th to the windward, on a cruise against the pirates. The other has been fitting out at Key West for some days past, and has ere this, I hope, fallen in with the party at Sugar Key."

No. 7.

Extracts of a letter from Mr. Randall to the Secretary of State, dated

HAVANA, *October 1, 1824.*

"My former letters contain all the cases of piracy which have come to my knowledge since my residence at this place, and I regret I have to add to the black catalogue some recent instances, marked with a degree of cruelty so wanton and atrocious as to be peculiar even in the annals of this most barbarous warfare. Several American vessels were captured about the 20th instant, near Matanzas, by a large launch from Regla, their crews all murdered, with the exception of one seaman, and the vessels burnt. Two of the vessels are known, viz: the Laura Ann and the Morning Star, both of New York, the latter supposed to have been bound to New Orleans, with passengers. From the first named vessel one seaman escaped, by secreting himself under the cargo, when his companions were murdered. The pirates, after setting fire to the vessel, deserted her, when this seaman escaped by swimming to the shore. He reached Matanzas, and has there given a detail of the horrid affair. A piratical boat, belonging to Regla, was, the next day, captured by the boats of the United States schooner Porpoise, and is the same which made the above captures. Her crew, unfortunately, escaped to the shore at ——.

"The boat and the articles which it contained gave bloody evidences of the tragical scenes which had been acted by its crew. Many suits of clothes were found on board, bloody, and pierced with holes, through which their unfortunate wearers had been stabbed. Some of them, partly worn, belonged to females.

"The pirates are known to have remained together, and to have slept the ensuing night in a house on the shore, near ——, without molestation, although the blaze of the vessel which they burnt, and the pursuit of their vessel by the boats of the Porpoise, were all distinctly seen by the people on the shore, in whose view the pirates landed. Those facts I have just heard from a respectable person from Matanzas, and Mr. Mountain has received a letter from Matanzas of the same tenor. This letter has been sent to the Captain·General, on his application.

"A full detail of the affair has, no doubt, been sent to the United States by the naval officers and the consular agents on that station. Other vessels are missing, and are supposed to have shared the same fate. From the evidence of the seaman of the Laura Ann, above referred to, it appears that the pirates were not content with simply putting to death the crew of that vessel, which made no resistance and offered nothing to excite their cupidity, but perpetrated it with the most refined and cruel tortures they could invent. It is an important fact, also, in this case, that the fate of the Laura Ann was known at this place, through the means of the pirates themselves, more than twenty-four hours before any regular communications had or could have been received from the scene of action through any other medium. The first account came from Regla, and when inquiries were made by me as to its authority, I was answered, 'that it was undoubtedly true, for it came from Regla, and might, therefore, be relied upon as official.' One other circumstance convinces me that the first account must have been communicated by the pirates themselves to their confederates in Regla. It is this: it was first reported here that every man on board had been put to death. This the pirates certainly must have believed to be the case, from the care they took to effect it, and that the burning of the vessel had sealed the fate of all on board, and thus they reported it. The escape of the seaman was not known until the arrival of the steamboat from Matanzas brought the first authentic and certain intelligence on the subject.

"It will thus be seen that this horrible crime continues to be perpetrated to an extent, and with a savage ferocity, never before equalled. Of the numerous captures, the particulars of which are known, the indiscriminate murder of all on board appears to be the settled purpose of those remorseless villains. It is painful to reflect upon the numbers who may have fallen victims to the same fate, but whose tragical history may be buried in the ocean with their mangled bodies. It is now obvious that piracy has found so congenial a soil, has grown to so fearful an extent, and is so deeply rooted in this island, as to require the efforts of all commercial nations to eradicate it. Piracy, with the slave trade, (the prolific parent of this and many other crimes,) now reign in full licentiousness, and defy as well the sanction of law as the impotent arm of Government. These crimes have become the settled, inveterate habit and occupation of a large portion of the people of this island. The thirst for illicit gain has displaced all desire for fair and legitimate acquisitions, and familiarity with scenes of blood and carnage has stifled the voice of humanity and remorse. It has now become a cause in which not only individual property and lives, to a fearful aggregate, are jeopardized, but even the honor of nations and the cause of civilization are at stake. It cannot be endured, that this band of remorseless wretches should be suffered longer to cumber the earth. The robberies and cruelties of the Barbary States, which have so often roused all Christendom to arms, were trifling in extent and ferocity, compared with those of the pirates of Cuba. It is in vain for commercial nations to rely for security upon mere preventive measures at sea, or upon the efforts of the authorities and people of this island to extirpate it. The authorities cannot restrain it if they would. Even the present Governor, characterized as he is for firmness and moral courage, feels his honor too precarious, at this crisis, to venture upon the measures of rigor and severity essential to its suppression. The ridiculous issue of the late expedition from this port has only served to display in full relief the weakness of the Government, and to afford another argument of security to the pirates. The unprincipled and wicked have obtained the complete ascendency, and the honest few dare not denounce or pursue the criminals. In such a state of things the pirates m$_{ust}$ be pursued by foreign forces into their retreats on land, and this community coerced by a severe and just retribution to aid in ejecting those miscreants from its bosom. The cause of justice and humanity will require that parts of this island be occupied by a foreign force, and that the sword of justice be wrested from the hands of those who have proved themselves unworthy or too weak to wield it. Pardon me, sir, if on this subject I suffer my feelings to lead me into too great a warmth of expression or importunity of zeal. To be here on the spot, to witness these horrid scenes of devastation and murder upon the unarmed citizens of friendly nations; to know that these savage acts are participated in and countenanced by numbers, and viewed with a frigid indifference by the whole community; to find the Government of this island shamefully remiss in measures of prevention and punishment, cannot but excite the most lively indignation at the past, and the most intense anxiety for the future.

"On this subject, I beg leave to refer you to a publication in the National Gazette, of Philadelphia, of the 17th September last, which I have just read, and which presents a most lively and faithful picture of this crime in Cuba. This piece has excited much sensation at this place, and the entire accuracy of its details, and the profound and just views which it exhibits of the causes, nature, and extent of this crime, are borne testimony to by every intelligent man with whom I have conversed upon the subject. I beg leave to refer to this account (the writer of which I know not) as developing fully, and more ably than I could myself do, my views upon this subject.

"I take the liberty to add some remarks on the disposition and conduct of the naval forces of the United States on this station, which were designed to be employed in the suppression of piracy. It is here a matter of common observation and complaint, that the anti-piratical squadron has effected nothing against the pirates, commensurate with its numbers and force, during the last six months. This has not been owing to the want of zeal, of enterprise, or courage on the part of our officers and seamen actually engaged in this pursuit, but to their diversion to other objects incompatible with the efficient performance of this highly important service. Since the spring the vessels have been dispersed on various services remote from this island, which they have merely made a touching point 'in transitu,' without remaining long enough to make any permanent impression on the system. For a considerable time the most exposed part of this coast, at the most dangerous season, was not visited by a single vessel of war, and, for a still longer time, by none but the smallest and most inefficient.

The temporary cessation of piracies some time before, caused by the presence of a large force on the coast, seems to have induced a delusive and fatal opinion that the evil was extinguished, and to have led to the diversion of too large a portion of the force to objects of infinitely less pecuniary, and of scarcely any material importance. I allude to the carrying of specie for our merchants in vessels of war, the whole effect of which is to give a trifling premium of insurance to one class of the community which would otherwise be paid to another class. In denouncing this practice as detrimental to the best interests of the nation, I but repeat the common sentiment of every man who has witnessed its effects during the past summer. If the benefit to commerce by this medium for the transportation of specie be of sufficient importance, it may be effected by vessels especially designated for that purpose. But experience shows that the suppression of piracy and the transportation of specie on the late system are incompatible. The first alone is more than sufficient to occupy all the time and energies of any force we can detach for that service. It must be evident that officers arriving here, their vessels freighted with large sums of money deliverable in the United States or elsewhere, for which they have signed bills of lading, and on which insurance has been effected by all parties for their respective interests, have contracted obligations, always embarrassing and frequently directly adverse to the performance of some important service. Such has been the predicament of many vessels of the United States, designed to protect our trade against the pirates, which have merely touched at this island, in their voyages to and from other islands out of the sphere of piracy, and the ports of the Gulf of Mexico, the usual termini of those cruises. They stop at the larger ports of this island barely time enough to take in water, and other supplies, to land or receive specie, and then, after a long cruise, return to the United States, their usefulness limited to the convoying of a few vessels from the coast. I trust the notoriety of the practice here, its effects upon the character of the Navy and the nation, and more especially upon the property and lives of our citizens, will be sufficient to justify these suggestions. I am aware that it is a delicate subject, and not lightly or rashly to be touched; but I should illy discharge my duty as an American citizen, and as an officer of the Government, if, from an ill-timed or fastidious delicacy, I omitted to denounce a practice so pregnant with mischief.

"I am happy to add, that Captain Kennedy and the officers now on this station discountenance this practice, and that both their conduct and proceedings are entirely conformable to the most rigid dictates of duty. The Hornet, the Porpoise, and some of the smaller vessels, are actively engaged in the pursuit of the pirates."

No. 8.

John Mountain, Esq., acting as Consul, to John Warner, Esq., Consul of the United States, dated

HAVANA, *July* 5, 1824.

MY DEAR SIR: I am sorry to inform you that, in consequence of the absence of our squadron in this quarter, the pirates have again commenced their diabolical depredations on our commerce on this side of the island.

The brig Castor, of Portland, Captain Hood, from thence bound to Matanzas, was on the 1st instant, in the bay of Matanzas, boarded by a boat with seven men armed with muskets, carbines, swords, pistols and knives, who ordered the captain to take the vessel out; when, after beating the master most cruelly and driving the crew below, brought the vessel to anchor in the port of Escondido, where they robbed her of everything portable on board; the captain arrived here on the next day.

The brig John, of Portland, has arrived at Matanzas, after having been robbed of everything, except the lumber on board, by those marauders; the master and crew have been all treated in a very cruel manner. The pirates now boast that they have nothing to fear, as the United States squadron has left the station.

A number of American vessels are loaded and ready for sea at Matanzas, but dare not prosecute their voyage, fearful of being overtaken by those worst of enemies.

Several vessels in this port are ready for sea, but are fearful of the consequences of going out to sea; they prefer waiting a few days, hoping that some one of the squadron may come in to afford them protection. What has become of the squadron, and whether it is employed as directed by the act of Congress, appears to be the general inquiry. Indeed, I am unable to give a distinct answer to these questions. I have only to join in the general lamentations that this coast is entirely neglected, unprotected, and our commerce and citizens left completely at the mercy and entire control of a set of cut-throats, who boast and rejoice at the favorable opportunity of enriching themselves by plundering the Americans.

The Betsy, Done, a brig bound to Matanzas, has also been robbed, near Matanzas, of all that part of her cargo consisting of provisions, clothes, sails, rigging, boat, oars, &c.

Some two or three others are reported to be in the possession of the pirates at this time, but of this I have no certain information. I mention it as rumor, but am fearful it may be true.

I am, my dear sir, your very obedient servant,

JOHN MOUNTAIN.

No. 9.

Extract of a letter from Mr. Mountain to Mr. Warner.

HAVANA, *October* 30, 1824.

' Herewith accompanying I have given you a long extract of a letter from Mr. Lattin, of Matanzas. It is a lamentable fact that, unless some efficient measures are taken by our Government to put a stop to the pirates, our poor countrymen must suffer; it is too true our trade has not been protected on this side of Cuba since early last spring; our men-of-war have, it is certain, occasionally been here, and off here on their way to or from the ports in the bay of Mexico, carrying freight. A thirst for making money prevails with others as well as those in the island of Cuba."

No. 10.

Mr. Mountain, acting Consul of the United States at Havana, to Mr. Warner, the Consul.

HAVANA, *October* 30, 1824.

MY DEAR SIR: Herewith I have the pleasure to hand you the latest weekly report.

Piracies have again commenced on or near the shores of Cuba to an alarming degree. The following is an extract of a letter from Mr. Lattin, with whom you are acquainted, dated

"MATANZAS, *October* 27, 1824.

"I am sorry to say the pirates have committed the most horrid depredations last Thursday and Friday between this and your port. The Laura Ann, of New York, belonging to Griswold, of that place, from Montevideo, with a cargo of jerked beef, was taken, all the crew except one hung, the vessel set on fire, when Jack, who had hid away amongst the beef, crawled out, jumped overboard, and got ashore; he presented himself here on Monday morning, in a state of nudity, not able to walk. He states that they first hung the captain, then the second mate, laid them on the quarter deck, talked as if they did not intend to injure the sailors, but drove them into the forecastle, and were taken up one by one, and he had proof of their experiencing the same fate, which induced him to hide himself amongst the beef, they searched for him with a light, some saying *todos* had been hung, and others declaring *uno mas*. The fact is, they were determined, if not hung, he should be roasted; accordingly, set fire abaft to the vessel; after ascending on deck, he could see the dead bodies lying amongst the flames on the quarter deck; took his station on the bowsprit, and fell to praying; they having thrown beef overboard, the sharks were in abundance, which held poor Jack mighty uneasy; he preferred the risk of the watery enemy to the flames, and let himself down by a rope, when two sharks took him under their protection, swimming along side of him, so as occasionally to be in his way; so soon as he got to the rocks, they tacked ship and left him. Jack has some confidence in prayers; this took place just at dark; the burning of the brig gave light to see his companions on his way ashore, which was about 20 rods; after resting awhile, he looked out for a hole to pass the night; he found one with sundry goods in it, which induced him to clear out, and proceed from the scene of horror; he represents having fell in with several deposits of goods. Last evening the Ferret arrived, and has gone out, taking Jack to survey the premises; I hope they may succeed in getting some of the plunder. Jack says a brig was taken on Friday morning, and a schooner in the afternoon, by the same party; the boat is a schooner of about 25 to 30 hogsheads; was taken on Friday by the boats of the Porpoise off Camarioca, loaded with clothing, &c.; three American colors, six compasses, five quadrants, &c.; the crew all escaped on shore. Mr. Smith, from Camarioca, came in last night; was with all the English families on the beach; heard the firing, and afterwards that thirteen armed men had gone to a small estate and demanded food; the captain of the Partido got out his forces, but none were taken. We judge upwards of thirty lives were sacrificed from the three vessels taken; the letter bag of the brig Morning Star, of New York, was on board the piratical boat. If some efficient measures are not taken by foreign nations, we may say, shake hands Algiers, and acknowledge the buccaniers of Cuba to be your superiors in barbarity. The subject of this is an insult on our Government, and if Commodore Porter does not be prevailed on to believe the coasts of Cuba are not quite cleared of pirates, we may expect to hear of many tragical cases shortly."

The foregoing account, I have no doubt, is strictly true.

His excellency sent for and obtained Mr. Lattin's letter twice yesterday and this day for his perusal.

We have some assassinations and a few cases of fever, yet the subject of piracy occupies the attention of most people here with whom I mingle.

JOHN MOUNTAIN.

JOHN WARNER, *Consul of the United States at Cuba, now in Baltimore.*

No. 11.

Extract of a letter from Mr. Mountain, Consular Agent of the United States at Havana, dated November 25, 1824, to Mr. Randall, at Washington.

"Piracies are not at an end; we learn, *via* Nassau, that the brig Edward, of New York, Dillingham master, from France, has been taken by the pirates, on the 15th day of October, off Cape Maise, by four boats, manned by Spaniards. The captain and crew were murdered, except the supercargo and three men, who made their escape in an open boat, and, after fifteen days' exposure, landed in a small key near Turk's Island; and from thence were taken to Nassau, New Providence."

No. 12.

Extract of a letter from Mr. Nelson, Minister Plenipotentiary of the United States at Madrid, to the Secretary of State, dated

MADRID, *September* 11, 1824.

"In pursuance of my intention, expressed in a late despatch, I have prepared and presented to the Spanish Government a note, concisely recapitulating the communications on the most important subjects of my correspondence with it. These are, the murder of Lieutenant Cocke; the piracies by the vessels from Cuba; and the captures by the privateers from Porto Rico and Porto Cabello."

Copy of a letter from Mr. Nelson, Minister Plenipotentiary of the United States at Madrid, to Mr. Salazar, Secretary of State, dated

MADRID, *September* 7, 1824.

The undersigned, the Minister Plenipotentiary of the United States of America, begs leave to call the attention of his Catholic Majesty's Government to certain subjects of the deepest interest to the United States, on which the applications heretofore made by the undersigned have failed to arouse the attention or to obtain the slightest mark of regard from his Catholic Majesty. The undersigned, from delicacy to the Sovereign of Spain, whom he found, on his presentation, occupied in the re-establishment of the affairs of the Kingdom, just emerging from the confusion incident to a state of war, has forborne to urge, with the vehement pressure which his instructions from his Government would seem to require, the decisions of Spain on the several reclamations which were a long time since presented by the undersigned to his Catholic Majesty's Secretary of State.

On the 10th day of January last the undersigned had the honor to address to the Secretary of State of his Catholic Majesty a reclamation on the part of his Government, in behalf of its citizens injured by the illegal and piratical conduct of the subjects of his Catholic Majesty in the West Indian seas. It was represented that property to a very large amount had been captured and sent into the ports of his Catholic Majesty in his American possessions, in many instances against all law and justice, by pirates, who, after committing the most atrocious and nefarious deeds, sought and found shelter and an asylum in the islands; and often in the most conspicuous ports and harbors, with the fruits and profits of their inhuman outrages. In many instances these atrocities were perpetrated, not less in defiance of right and justice, by persons pretending to act under color of authority, but whose authority has never been justified; and which, if justified, could never sanction these transactions, marked by a character of piracy and rapacity which no commission could justify. In the cases of robberies committed by the Spanish vessels acting as pirates, the American property thus plundered was often carried into the ports of Cuba, and especially of the Havana, and there, in the most open and daring manner, exposed to sale in the view of the local authorities, unrestrained and unchecked by their slightest interference. American citizens have seen their property, thus violently and feloniously taken from them, offered to sale in open market, without the protection of the local Government in the assertion of their rights, and deterred from the vindication of their just claims by the fullest conviction that they would find no support in the Government of the island, but would meet, in all probability, as the requital of their temerity, the fiend-like vengeance of the murderous assassin. In other instances, where the property of the American citizen has been captured under color of authority in the vessel making the capture, the conduct of the captors has been scarcely less flagrant than that practiced by the pirates. Oftentimes has the booty found in the American vessel been partitioned among the plunderers without going into port, and distributed without legal adjudication by these lawless robbers; and when carried occasionally into port, a secret, unknown, and unfrequented port has been resorted to where law and justice were disregarded, and where every means of obtaining right was denied to the 'parties concerned—unapprised of the proceedings, and not permitted to avail themselves of the customary means of vindication. In the prosecution of these felonious practices American citizens have been seized and thrown into prison, and there cruelly detained, often in a horrible state of suffering, almost without the indispensable necessaries for human subsistence. In some instances, their property, which the merciless captors had spared and sent into port, has been wasted and embezzled to such an extent, that, when the mock trial to which it had been subjected had terminated even in their favor, the subject of controversy could no longer be found. Thus has every species of abuse of the rights of person and of property of American citizens been practiced in these regions. The local authorities have been appealed to in vain. The Government of Spain has been appealed to, as yet, without effect. The reclamations are again renewed—the patience of the American Government is tried to its fullest extent of sufferance—and the day is probably not very distant when the necessity of warding off these reiterated and aggravated injuries, and the obligation of doing justice to its citizens, may compel the Government of the United States to resort to measures of a more efficient character, for prevention of injury and the redress of wrongs. This interesting subject has already claimed the attention of the legislative councils of the nation. They have hitherto forborne to recommend the adoption of measures of reprisals, from a desire to manifest their friendly dispositions to his Catholic Majesty, and from the hope that the reclamations long since presented by their minister near this court would speedily receive attention, and be followed with his Majesty's answer and determination on these important questions. At no very distant period these councils will, in the regular course of their proceedings, be again assembled at the seat of the National Government, when, doubtless, this subject will again be revived by them; and such measures as the existing evils, and the disregard on the part of his Majesty of the demands hitherto presented by the American minister, will form with them irrefragable arguments for the adoption of a more efficient system of energetic policy. The undersigned has presented, in different appeals to the Government of his Catholic Majesty, the various subjects of complaint which have arisen from the misconduct of his Majesty's officers and subjects in his ultramarine possessions. One of the most prominent and aggravated was the sacrifice of a gallant officer of the American Navy, whilst peaceably entering the port of St. John, in Porto Rico, who was most wantonly and treacherously murdered by a gun from the fort, fired by the order of the officer at that time in command, in the absence of the Governor. In this instance, the American Government demands that this subject shall be rigorously investigated, and an adequate punishment inflicted on the officer by whose command this outrage was perpetrated.

An appeal has likewise been made to his Catholic Majesty's Government on the subject of the multiplied piracies which have been committed on the peaceable American commerce in the West Indian seas by vessels equipped and sailing from the ports of his Majesty's possessions in these regions, on which reiterated complaints have been made to the local authorities without effect; and on which the interference of his Majesty has been required to compel those authorities to fulfil their duty in this regard by effectual measures for the suppression of the pirates, and by co-operating with the squadron of the United States, sent into these seas for the extirpation of this scourge to the honest and lawful commerce of the whole civilized world.

Another demand upon his Majesty's Government has been made for indemnification against the enormous losses sustained by the American citizens from the captures made by vessels pretending to act under commissions issued by agents alleging to be authorized by his Catholic Majesty.

The authority to issue these commissions has never been proved; the right to issue them, on the principles avowed, of a paper blockade, without adequate force, of an interdiction of all neutral commerce with the ports of the Spanish Main, or the alleged ancient rights of Spain over that country, has always been resisted and protested against by all neutral nations, and especially by the United States, and relinquished by his Majesty's officers in that region, and finally renounced or abandoned by his Majesty himself in his decree of December last, opening the commerce of these countries to all the world. On this subject, the undersigned, in obedience to instructions of his Government, demanded that a just indemnification should be made to all the American citizens who had suffered any loss in consequence of these illegal acts, done under color and pretence of his Majesty's authority, but really perpetrated in violation of all laws and justice, whose obligation is acknowledged by all the civilized nations of the world.

The release of all citizens and surrender of all American property, whose condition had not been changed, but was unjustifiably and illegally detained, was also required.

The undersigned begs leave to present to his excellency this rapid and cursory sketch of the most important subjects of complaint which he was instructed to press upon the Government of his Catholic Majesty; he begs leave to refer his excellency to the different notes presented by him, dated the 10th and 23d of January, and the 3d of February last, in which these grievances are more minutely and specially detailed, and where the appropriate and specific redress demanded is more explicitly and at large stated than the undersigned has considered it necessary at this time to recapitulate.

The undersigned begs leave to urge upon his excellency the necessity of an early answer to these applications, that his Government may learn how far the spirit and disposition of an harmonious intercourse is reciprocated towards the United States by his Catholic Majesty, that they may be confirmed in that opinion, which they have ever entertained, that an appeal to his Majesty's honor is only necessary to obtain the redress of grievances inflicted without his sanction and authority, and that the United States may be relieved from the painful necessity of deciding that an appeal to a more energetic policy, totally at variance with their ardent desire to preserve harmony and avoid collision, is at length become absolutely and indispensably necessary.

The undersigned tenders to his excellency his most distinguished consideration, and subscribes himself his excellency's very humble and obedient servant,

                                                            HUGH NELSON.

His Excellency Don LUIS MARIA DE SALAZAR,
    First Secretary of State and of the Despatch, ad interim.

REPORT FROM THE NAVY DEPARTMENT.

                                        NAVY DEPARTMENT, January 12, 1825.

The Secretary of the Navy has the honor to present the following report, in answer to two resolutions of the Senate of the United States, on the subject of piracies; one of which was passed on December 21, 1824, and the other on the 23d of the same month.

Immediately after the passage of the law of December 20, 1822, "authorizing an additional naval force for the suppression of piracy," the vessels contemplated in that act were purchased and prepared for sea, and, with others, placed under the command of Captain David Porter. They consisted of the sloops John Adams and Hornet; the brig Spark; the schooners Porpoise, Grampus, Alligator, and Shark; the Sea Gull, and eight small schooners; five barges, and one transport ship; in all, seventeen vessels of different sizes, besides the barges.

On February 14, 1823, Captain Porter sailed from the United States, under orders dated February 1, 1823, a copy of which is annexed to this report, and marked A.

The manner in which Captain Porter has performed the duty assigned him, and the "information" received from him, will be seen by the reports from this Department to the President of the United States, and communicated by him with his message at the last and present sessions of Congress; and by paper marked B, which was unintentionally omitted in the report from this Department on the first of December last.

All the vessels above enumerated, except four, have been uniformly employed in the object, so far as their size and the necessity of occasional returns into port for stores and repairs would permit. Of the four vessels above alluded to, the Alligator and Wild Cat have been lost, and the Greyhound and Jackal were sold, "being so much out of repair that it was not for the interest of the United States to repair the same."

There are now employed in the West Indies and Gulf of Mexico thirteen vessels and five barges; and the frigate Constellation will join the squadron in a few days, her crew being nearly completed. The disposition of the force has been left principally to the commanding officer, who, being in the region where its services were required, was best able to judge of the positions in which the vessels should be placed, and the particular duties each should perform.

The papers herewith transmitted, marked C and D, having been written in answer to letters from the Chairman of the Committee on Naval Affairs of the Senate and House of Representatives of the United States, it appears to be proper to communicate them as part of the report from this Department.

                                                            SAM. L. SOUTHARD.

The PRESIDENT of the United States.

A.

                                        NAVY DEPARTMENT, February 1, 1823.

SIR: You have been appointed to the command of a squadron, fitted out under an act of Congress of the 20th of December last, to cruise in the West Indian seas and Gulf of Mexico for the purpose of suppressing piracy and affording effectual protection to the citizens and commerce of the United States. Your attention will also be extended to the suppression of the slave trade, according to the provisions of the several acts of Congress on that subject; copies of which, and of the instructions heretofore given to our naval commanders thereon, are herewith sent to you. While it is your duty to protect our commerce against all unlawful interruption, and to guard the rights both of person and property of the citizens of the United States wherever it shall become necessary, you will observe the utmost caution not to encroach upon the rights of others; and should you at any time be brought into discussion or collision with any foreign power in relation to such rights, it will be expedient and proper that the same should be conducted with as much moderation and forbearance as is consistent with the honor of your country and the just claims of its citizens. Should you, in your cruise, fall in with any foreign naval force engaged in the suppression of piracy, it is desirable that harmony and a good understanding should be cultivated between you; and you will do everything on your part that accords with the honor of the American flag to promote this object. So soon as the vessels at Norfolk shall be ready for sea, you will proceed to the West Indies by such route as you shall judge best for the purpose of effecting the object of your cruise. You will establish at Thompson's Island, usually called Key West, a depot, and land the ordnance and marines to protect the stores and provisions; if, however, you shall find any important objection to this place, and a more suitable and convenient one can be found, you are at liberty to select it as a depot.

You will announce your arrival and object to the authorities, civil and military, of the island of Cuba, and endeavor to obtain as far as shall be practicable their co-operation, or at least their favorable and friendly support, giving them the most unequivocal assurance that your sole object is the destruction of pirates. The system of piracy which has grown up in the West Indies has obviously arisen from the war between Spain and the new Governments, her late provinces in this hemisphere, and from the limited force in the islands and their sparse population, many portions of each being entirely uninhabited and desolate, to which the active authority of the Government does not extend. It is understood that establishments have been made by parties of those banditti in those uninhabited parts, to which they carry their plunder, and retreat in time of danger. It cannot be presumed that the Government of any island will afford any protection or countenance to such robbers. It may, on the contrary, confidently be believed that all Governments, and particularly those most exposed, will afford all means in their power for their suppression.

Pirates are considered, by the law of nations, the enemies of the human race. It is the duty of all nations to put them down; and none who respect their own character or interest will refuse to do it, much less afford them an asylum and protection. The nation that makes the greatest exertions to suppress such banditti has the greatest merit. In making such exertions, it has a right to the aid of every other power to the extent of its means, and to the enjoyment, under its sanction, of all its rights in the pursuit of the object.

In the case of belligerents, where the army of one party enters the territory of a neutral power, the army of the other has a right to follow it there. In the case of pirates, the right of the armed force of one power to follow them into the territory of another is more complete. In regard to pirates, there is no neutral party, they being the enemies of the human race; all nations are parties against them, and may be considered as allies. The object and intention of our Government is to respect the feelings as well as the rights of others, both in substance and in form, in all the measures which may be adopted to accomplish the end in view. Should, therefore, the crews of any vessels which you have seen engaged in acts of piracy, or which you have just cause to suspect of being of that character, retreat into the ports, harbors, or settled parts of the island, you may enter, in pursuit of them, such ports, harbors, and settled parts of the country, for the purpose of aiding the local authorities or people, as the case may be, to seize and bring the offenders to justice, previously giving notice that this is your sole object.

Where a Government exists and is felt, you will in all instances respect the local authorities, and only act in aid of and co-operation with them, it being the exclusive purpose of the United States to suppress piracy, an object in which all nations are equally interested, and in the accomplishment of which the Spanish authorities and people will, it is presumed, cordially co-operate with you. If, in the pursuit of pirates, found at sea, they shall retreat into the unsettled parts of the islands or foreign territory, you are at liberty to pursue them so long only as there is reasonable prospect of being able to apprehend them; and in no case are you at liberty to pursue and apprehend any one after having been forbidden so to do by competent authority of the local Government. And should you, on such pursuit, apprehend any pirates upon land, you will deliver them over to the proper authority to be dealt with according to law, and you will furnish such evidence as shall be in your power to prove the offence alleged against them. Should the local authorities refuse to receive and prosecute such persons so apprehended, on your furnishing them with reasonable evidence of their guilt, you will then keep them safely and securely on board some of the vessels under your command, and report without delay to this Department the particular circumstances of such cases. Great complaints are made of the interruption and injury to our commerce by privateers fitted out from Spanish ports. You will endeavor to obtain from the Spanish authorities a list of the vessels so commissioned, and ascertain how far they have been instructed to intercept our trade with Mexico and the Colombian Republic, impressing upon them that, according to the well-settled rule of the law of nations, the United States will not consider any portion of coast upon the Gulf of Mexico as legally blockaded, except where a naval force is stationed sufficient to carry into effect the blockading order or decree; and that this Government does not admit the right or authority of Spain to interdict or interrupt our commerce with any portion of the coast included within the Colombian Republic or Mexican Government not actually blockaded by a competent force.

All the United States ships and vessels-of-war in the West Indies, of which a list is herewith inclosed, are placed under your command; and you will distribute them to such stations as shall appear to you best calculated to afford complete protection to our commerce, in which you will embrace the object of protecting the convoy of specie from Vera Cruz, and the Mexican coast generally, to the United States. Keep one vessel, at least, upon this service, to be at or near Vera Cruz during the healthy season of the year, and to be relieved as occasion shall require, both for the convoy of trade and to bring specie to the United States, confining the transportation to the United States only. You will be particularly watchful to preserve the health of the officers and crews under your command, and to guard, in every possible manner, against the unhealthiness of the climate, not permitting any intercourse with the shore where the yellow fever prevails, except in cases of absolute necessity.

Wishing you good health and a successful cruise, I am, very respectfully, your obedient servant,

SMITH THOMPSON.

Com. DAVID PORTER, *Commanding United States Naval Force, West Indies.*

B.

Copy of a letter from Lieutenant C. W. Skinner, commander of the United States schooner Porpoise, inclosing copies of the correspondence referred to in the letter.

UNITED STATES SCHOONER PORPOISE, *Matanzas, October 24, 1824.*

SIR: I have the honor to inform you that, after leaving the convoy from Havana, I stretched in for this port, where I anchored on the evening of the 18th. On inquiry, I was informed no piracies had been recently committed in this vicinity. I, however, determined to despatch the boats secretly from the harbor, and examine the adjacent bays and inlets. On the night of the 19th, I placed them under command of Lieut. Hunter and acting Lieut. Johnson, with orders to examine about Point Yeacos, Sewappa bay, and Camrioca, places long notorious as a retreat for pirates. On the evening of the 22d, Lieut. Hunter returned with a piratical schooner of one carriage gun, one new American cutter, and two other boats; one, having three men on board, he captured in Sewappa bay. Every appearance justified the suspicion of piracy. The persons informed Lieut. Hunter their vessel had been taken by armed men; the boat they were in given in exchange, with a promise of returning in a few days and restoring their vessel. The next day, off Camrioca, Lieut. Hunter discovered a suspicious schooner standing to sea, in chase of a vessel in sight. On his approach, the schooner tacked, and made for the shore, closely pursued by the boats. The crew abandoned the vessel and fled to the wood, where they were sought for in vain; she proved to be a pirate, mounting one gun, and small-arms. From the number of nautical instruments, trunks of clothing, rigging, and sails, with three sets of American colors, found on board, she must have robbed several vessels. From stains of blood on the clothes, and other articles on board, I fear the unfortunate persons to whom they belonged must have been murdered. No papers were discovered which could lead to the name of the vessel or vessels captured; several articles of clothing were marked "Captain Shaw," a number with the initials "A. S." A bag on board was lettered "Brig Morning Star's letter bag." One waistcoat contained in the pocket a printed card, "Mr. M. Loris' boarding-house, Charleston, South Carolina," and appeared to have been newly printed. A medicine chest on board was put up in New York. I have delivered the prisoners to the Governor of Matanzas, and shall furnish him all the testimony in my power which can throw light on their character. The schooner I sent out last night, under command of acting Lieut. Brown, in hopes of decoying some of her former comrades. I sail with convoy to-morrow, and after joining the prize at sea, shall proceed to Thompson's Island for supplies, and return to the protection of commerce on this coast. I trust, sir, should the prize be sufficiently fortunate to meet with pirates, I shall have the pleasure to give a satisfactory account of them.

I do myself the honor to inclose the correspondence relative to the capture of the vessels and prisoners.

I have the honor to be, respectfully, sir, your obedient servant,

CH. W. SKINNER.

Hon. SAMUEL L. SOUTHARD, *Secretary of the Navy, Washington City.*

UNITED STATES SCHOONER PORPOISE, *Matanzas, October 23, 1824.*

I deliver to your excellency three men, captured by a detachment of my boats, a few days since, under circumstances justifying a belief of their having committed piracy. An armed schooner was also captured, which the prisoners claim as their property, alleging, in explanation, that their vessel had been forcibly seized by armed men, and, in exchange, they had received from the pirate his vessel, with a promise to return in a few days, and restore their original property; under this expectation they were anxiously awaiting her arrival. Fortunately for humanity, my boats encountered her; from the quantity of clothing, goods, and nautical instruments found on board, she must have robbed several vessels, and, from stains of blood on clothes, &c., most probably murdered the unfortunate people who fell into their hands. We found on board, also, three sets of American colors. These enormities call loudly for punishment. It affords me pleasure to deliver these people to your excellency, as I am well persuaded, from your well known regard to justice, they will meet the punishment due their crimes.

If your excellency will inform me when you will receive them, they shall be landed under an escort.

I inclose to your excellency the papers found on board; and have the honor to be, respectfully, your excellency's obedient servant,

C. W. SKINNER,

His Excellency Don CECELIO AYILLOR, *Governor of Matanzas.*

I have just received your statement of this day, relative to the capture of a small vessel, whose crew ran to the sea shore, suspected, with much reason, to be pirates, not only on account of their flight and equipment, but of some crimes committed by them; in consequence thereof, I will give my orders to receive on the wharf, at four o'clock in the afternoon, the three men which you captured, and that you promised to remit me. I hope that to-morrow, between ten and eleven, you will have the kindness to send to this Government the officer and marine guards that joined in the capture of the vessel, to hear their respective informations, as the beginning of the summary. I hope, also, that, for their examination, you will please send the clothes stained with blood, and other articles and arms, all of which will serve for the inquiry or search, and which will be returned whenever you require it, after the matter is finished.

I now put you in mind that the papers that you mention in your statement have not come to hand.

I declare to you that your recommendable services to the cause of humanity, and in favor of our commercial relations, will be worthy of praise to the Superior Government; and for my part, I promise you, with all the justice of the laws, and my firmness to observe them, that I will contribute to the most to the extermination of these wicked men.

With the greatest regard, I am, dear sir, &c.,

CECELIO AYILLOR.

The COMMANDER *of the American Schooner-of-war Porpoise.*

UNITED STATES SCHOONER PORPOISE, *Matanzas, October* 24, 1824.

I had the honor to receive your excellency's reply to my communication in relation to the prisoners made by this vessel, and have delivered them agreeably to your wishes. The papers which I neglected to send I forwarded immediately on discovering the omission. The clothes stained with blood, and many other articles, were in a condition so filthy, I caused them to be thrown into the sea; for a corroboration of the testimony which you will receive this day, I beg leave to refer your excellency to the Spanish officer and his interpreter, who came on board the moment of arrival, and to whom the articles alluded to were exhibited.

I have the honor to be, your excellency's obedient servant,

C. W. SKINNER.

His Excellency Don CECELIO AYILLOR, *Governor of Matanzas.*

C.

Copy of a letter addressed to the honorable Benjamin W. Crowninshield, Chairman of the Naval Committee in the House of Representatives.

NAVY DEPARTMENT, *December* 21, 1824.

SIR: I have the honor to acknowledge the receipt of your letter of the 14th instant, making certain inquiries respecting the suppression of piracy, to which I submit the following answer:

The nature and extent of the force required must necessarily be regulated by the nature and extent of the evil to be repressed. The views of the Department on this latter point are contained in the annual report made to the President of the United States, and communicated by him to Congress with his message, and to which I beg leave to refer you.

There have lately been very few, if any, vessels of a large size engaged in piratical depredations at a distance from the land. The naval force which has been employed, and which is stated in the report referred to, has succeeded in driving away or destroying vessels of that description, and has thus effected the immediate object for which it was created. But the evil has assumed another shape, for which this force does not seem to be well fitted. Our vessels, even the smallest, cannot follow the pirates into many of the creeks and inlets to which they resort—this must always be done in boats, which cannot be carried by them in sufficient numbers to be effectual; nor can the greater part of them, on account of their size and the want of accommodations for water and stores, remain long at sea, so as permanently and effectually to watch even the most suspected places.

I would, therefore, respectfully recommend three or more frigates, or sloops-of-war, as an addition to the force now in the West Indies and Gulf of Mexico, or as a substitute for the small vessels. The sloops would be as competent to the object as the frigates, and would be much less expensive. We cannot, however, detach that or even a less number from the stations where they now are without weakening our squadrons too much.

It will be necessary to build them, which can be done in less time, and at less expense, than would require to repair and fit for sea the same number of frigates. Two, or perhaps three, might be finished in four or five months. These vessels would be able to lie or cruise steadily, and for long periods, where their presence was most needed, and, being well provided with boats, could pursue into any waters where escape was attempted.

In addition to this provision, our officers should be authorized to pursue the pirates wherever they may fly. The authority which has heretofore been given on this point will be seen by the extracts from the orders to Commodore Porter, hereunto annexed, and marked A. The right to follow should be extended to the settled as well as the unsettled parts of the islands; and should this prove ineffectual, a resort will be necessary to such a general and rigorous blockade as will make both the local Governments and their subjects feel that their interest, as well as their honor, requires a respect for our rights and the rights of humanity. For such an extremity, the proposed sloops-of-war will be indispensable. What warnings should be given, or demands made upon Spain, or what negotiations had with other Governments, before this course be adopted, it is not my province to suggest. But, as these pirates are, essentially, robbers, living upon the land, and not upon the ocean, if the local Governments cannot, or will not, prevent them from inflicting such serious injuries upon us, we must seek them where they are to be found, and so punish them as to prevent a repetition of their crimes.

Should the foregoing suggestions be adopted, a law would be necessary authorizing the building of the sloops-of-war, with an appropriation of $85,000 for the cost of each, and $61,086 50 for the annual support of each; or the sums mentioned may be added to the estimates for the support of the Navy; the amount for building, under the head of building and repairs of vessels; and the other under those of—

Pay and subsistence	$31,391 50
Provisions	15,695 00
Repairs, including wear and tear	12,000 00
Hospital stores and medicine	2,000 00
	$61,086 50

In answer to your inquiry on the subject, I would suggest that it is not believed to be proper to designate, in any act of Congress, the disposition of the force, the only effect of which would be to apprise the pirates more fully of the mode and place of attack, and thus enable them more surely to escape.

It is proper to remark, that any naval force which we can apply to this object will not be sufficiently extensive to cover, at all times, every part of the shores of the islands and Gulf of Mexico; and that some merchant vessels may, and probably will, be caught, without other protection than that which their own strength affords. Hence, the suggestion of arming them is very obvious, and has been frequently made. The evils to be apprehended from it, however, are equally obvious. No sufficient pledge can be given that some of them, if armed, and feeling their power, would not abuse it, and, in the present situation of the West Indies and countries south of us, endanger our friendly relations, and commit acts almost as much to be deprecated as those against which we are attempting to guard. The natural state of merchant vessels is the peaceful and unarmed state; and although permission to arm might, in this instance, free them from some of the evils to which they would be exposed without such authority, yet it is believed that few whose only object is fair commerce would avail themselves of the legal privilege. The expense and inconvenience of arming is great, and would be illy borne by a large part of the commerce now carried on in that quarter in American vessels. The danger does not seem to be considered so urgent as to compel them to do it. Convoy has been often declined rather than submit to slight delays or changes in the course of the vessel; and it is understood that insurance is unusually low, and that the offices add little, if anything, on account of this risk. It may be effected to the West Indies at one per cent. on the outward, and one on the homeward voyage, and, in some instances, at one and a half, embracing both, which is below the actual expense of arming.

It has been sometimes proposed that the expense should be met by the Government, and protection afforded by placing on board each vessel a number of marines or soldiers; but this plan will at once be perceived to be impracticable, when the number of our merchant vessels is considered, with the different routes which they pursue, and the times at which they sail. The remedy must be extremely partial or the expense enormous. The whole marine corps would, probably, not equal one-fifth of what would be required for a sufficient and equal distribution among all.

It has also been proposed to furnish convoy at stated periods. This could be done at periods of fifteen or twenty days, from some position on our coast to some point which is considered beyond the danger. But to this there are also obvious objections. It would employ all our force in the Atlantic, and prevent attention to other objects; an evil of too serious a magnitude to be encountered. It would be impossible to extend the convoy throughout the whole cruise; and stopping at a given point, the pirates would immediately transfer and renew their attacks beyond that point, where the vessels would, in that case, be more unprotected than they now are. It would also destroy competition of enterprise among our merchants, and confine them all to the same times and course of navigation—an evil which they well know how to estimate. They would not accept your protection at such a price.

I do not, then, perceive in any of the suggestions which have been presented to my mind so cheap, efficient, and certain a remedy for the evil as that which I have preferred; and if it be adopted, we shall, after the proposed vessels are prepared, be enabled to dispose of the small schooners now employed in the West Indies and Gulf of Mexico—a force which has been found exceedingly expensive and injurious to the discipline and efficiency of the service.

I am, very respectfully, sir, your most obedient servant,

SAM'L L. SOUTHARD.

D.

Extracts of a letter to the Honorable James Lloyd, Chairman of the Committee on Naval Affairs, of the Senate, dated December 29, 1824.

"I have the honor to state that there are no 'cases of piratical depredations,' or other information on the subject, in the possession of the Department, which are not referred to in the report accompanying the President's message to Congress."

"No reports of cases have been received, except those made by naval officers of such as have come, in some way, under their own observation. No memorandum has been kept of the cases detailed in the public journals, but some of them have occasionally been inclosed to the commanding officer of the station to afford him information in the discharge of his duties."

"The 'additional means' alluded to as proper to be intrusted to the Executive, if an efficient co-operation of the local Governments could not be obtained, were three or four frigates or sloops-of-war, with boats for pursuit of the pirates; authority to pursue them wherever they might attempt to escape, and authority to enforce a rigorous blockade if other efforts should prove ineffectual."

"I have not supposed that it would be expedient to authorize, by law, our merchant vessels to arm. Should Congress entertain a different opinion on this point, and pass a law on the subject, it should embrace 'provisions and restrictions' similar to those contained in the 3d and 4th sections of the 'Act to authorize the defence of the merchant vessels of the United States against French depredations,' passed June 25, 1798."

CLAIM OF SAMUEL G. PERKINS ON THE FRENCH GOVERNMENT FOR SEQUESTRATIONS IN HOLLAND.

COMMUNICATED TO THE HOUSE OF REPRESENTATIVES JANUARY 17, 1825.

To the honorable the House of Representatives in Congress assembled:

The memorial of Samuel G. Perkins, of Boston, Massachusetts, is respectfully submitted.

Your memorialist, having seen by the message of the President of the United States to the representatives of the nation that the Government contemplate taking some measures in relation to the property seized and sequestered on the continent of Europe by the French and other Governments submitting to their control, respectfully begs leave to lay before your honorable body a statement of facts in relation to the ship Governor Strong and her cargo, and the brig Sally and her cargo, belonging to the memorialist and other American citizens; parts of which cargoes were sequestered in Holland in the years 1809 and 1810 by the Dutch Government, and by them transferred to the French authorities, under whose orders the same were sold either at Antwerp or Paris, and the net proceeds paid into the caisse d'amortissement, or into the public treasury at Paris for the use of the French Government, in violation of the neutral rights of citizens of these United States, and without even a pretence that the said vessels or their crews had violated any law or decree of either of the said Governments.

The American ship Governor Strong, Robert Lord, master, belonging exclusively to citizens of the United States, was laden at Boston, State of Massachusetts, in May, 1809, with a cargo of sugar, coffee, cotton, potashes, tobacco, logwood, and elephants' teeth, and sailed on the 24th of said month for Rotterdam. On the 20th June she arrived at Helvoet Sluice, without having met with anything worth notice during the passage.

Here the ship was detained until the 7th July, when she was ordered to proceed up to Gravendeel. On her way there and *at* Gravendeel her cargo was taken out of her into lighters, under the orders of the Commissary General, and deposited in the Government stores, against the will and remonstrance of the master of the said ship.

A portion of the cargo having been subsequently delivered over to the consignees by the Government, will serve to show that no illicit act on our part had been the cause of the seizure; but the greater part of the cargo was detained until March, 1810, when it was transferred, without condemnation, and even without trial, to France, by an article of a secret treaty made between the French and Dutch Governments then existing; and the same was delivered over to the French authorities in conformity "by orders from his Majesty the Emperor and King," as appears by a certificate of the Director General of the Dutch Customs, dated October 11, 1810.

The portion of this cargo which was made over to the French Government by the Dutch nation was sold at auction at Antwerp, in October and November, 1810, under the direction of the collector of the customs at that place, for the sum of.. Fs. 1,605,805 71
or about $320,000; out of which the French customs took for duties

the sum of... Fs. 795,689 95
And the officers of the Government, for the expenses of the sale, took 36,561 19
                                                                          ——————
                                                                          832,251 14

Leaving for account of the American owners.................................... 773,554 57
or about $150,000; which sum was deposited or paid into the French treasury, and employed for the current expenses of that Government, or went to pay off a portion of its debts.

The brig Sally, Cotton, master, belonging exclusively to citizens of the United States, sailed from Boston in June, 1809, bound for the north of Europe, with a cargo of coffee, sugar, and cotton, and arrived at the Texel, July 15, and was there detained by the Dutch authorities, and her cargo taken out and deposited in the King's stores. The cotton was subsequently given up to the consignees, but the rest of the cargo was, like that of the Governor Strong, delivered over to the French Government and sent to Paris, where it was sold, and the net proceeds, amounting to between fifty and sixty thousand dollars, paid into the treasury and used for the public service.

These two cases form a part of a considerable class which may be denominated the *Dutch claims*, in contradistinction to the Antwerp, St. Sebastian, and other designated claims, which have been so ably and manfully advocated by our late minister (Mr. Gallatin) at the court of St. Cloud, in his excellent memorial of January 10, 1822.

Of this class of Dutch cases your memorialist has now before him the catalogues of sixteen cargoes which were sequestered in Holland, delivered over to the French Government, and sold, either in Antwerp or Paris, in the fall of 1810, and the net proceeds applied to the use of the French nation.

These cases are all known to the Government of the United States, and have received the greatest attention, from their chargé d'affaires (Mr. Everett) at the Hague; through whom a most able and interesting correspondence has been carried on with that Government upon this subject. As that correspondence will probably be laid before the honorable the House of Representatives, your memorialist need not enter upon the reasons which justice and good faith present in favor of these claims. Neither is it necessary for him at present to inquire against which nation our claim lies. If the Dutch nation found it for her interest to take the property of the citizens of a neutral State without condemnation, or even without the forms of a trial, and present it to France to appease her wrath or to conciliate her favor, or as an offset for pecuniary claims, she certainly has assumed a responsibility which it appears impossible she should disclaim; for she has, in fact, received the value of that property in some shape or other from France, or she never would have consented to the measure; and as the French nation have set Holland an example of justice, in having fully compensated one of her citizens belonging to Brabant for a large property seized and sequestered at Antwerp, under similar circumstances, by paying him the full of the net proceeds of the articles sold, with interest up to the time of payment, as stated by Mr. Gallatin in his memorial, it is to be hoped that she will not continue to resist claims so evidently just, when she sees that our Government is determined not to relinquish them, and that the Executive is supported in his demands by the represent-atives of the nation at large.

The positive and severe deprivations and sufferings which many of our citizens are now laboring under, in consequence of these sequestrations, are respectfully submitted to your consideration, in the hope that some means may be found by the Government to induce the Dutch or French nation to discharge this debt.

SAMUEL G. PERKINS.

Boston, *January* 6, 1825.

18TH CONGRESS.]   No. 393.   [2D SESSION.

WESTERN BOUNDARY OF THE UNITED STATES UNDER THE TREATY WITH SPAIN.

COMMUNICATED TO THE HOUSE OF REPRESENTATIVES JANUARY 17, 1825.

To the House of Representatives of the United States:

I transmit herewith to the House a report from the Secretary of State, containing the information required by the resolution of the House of the 16th ultimo, relating to the western boundary of the United States.

JAMES MONROE.

Washington, *January* 17, 1825.

DEPARTMENT OF STATE, *Washington, January* 15, 1825.

The Secretary of State, to whom has been referred the resolution of the House of Representatives of the United States, of the 16th of December last, requesting information from the President, if not incompatible with the public welfare, of the causes which have prevented the execution of the fourth article of the treaty of the 22d of February, 1819, between the United States of America and the Kingdom of Spain, so far as the same relates to the surveying of the western boundary of the United States, and if the same has been prevented by the actual situation of the Government of Mexico in respect to the Kingdom of Spain and this country as connected with the said boundary; and whether any measures have been taken to call the attention of the Government of Mexico to the final establishment of a boundary between that country and the United States, has the honor of reporting to the President that the causes suggested in the resolution have prevented the execution, by the joint operation of the United States and of Spain, of the article referred to, as was contemplated by the treaty. That, soon after the change of Government in Mexico to the republican form, and before the adoption of the recent constitution, a communication was received from the supreme authority then existing that they assented to the boundary as established by the treaty, and would readily co-operate in the measures necessary for carrying that article into execution in concert with the United States. The postponements of the mission to Mexico have delayed the proposal of definitive arrangements with that Government upon the subject.

All which is respectfully submitted.

JOHN QUINCY ADAMS.

18TH CONGRESS.]   No. 394.   [2D SESSION.

CLAIM OF JOHN F. DUMAS ON THE FRENCH OR SPANISH GOVERNMENT FOR SEQUESTRATIONS IN SPAIN.

COMMUNICATED TO THE SENATE JANUARY 19, 1825.

The Committee on Foreign Relations, to whom were referred the petitions of John F. Dumas and William Manson, reported:

That these petitioners claim relief from the Government of the United States for spoliations on their vessels and cargoes committed by Spaniards, or by Frenchmen in Spanish ports, previous to the Florida treaty, for which they urge they were entitled to indemnity under that treaty. But that the commissioners erroneously rejected their claims, and hence they ask relief from the Government.

The committee, independently of the high and unshaken confidence in the capacity and integrity of the citizens constituting the board whose decision is the subject of complaint, think, on principle, their decision should be conclusive, and that it would be a precedent fraught with much mischief should Congress again open for investigation that whole mass of cases which have been the subject of arbitration. They, therefore, recommend the following resolution:

Resolved, That the petitions of John F. Dumas and William Manson be rejected.

To the honorable the Senate and House of Representatives of the United States of America in Congress assembled:

The memorial of the undersigned citizen of the United States, and resident merchant of the city of Philadelphia, respectfully showeth:

That during the months of November and December, in the year 1809, your memorialist, confiding in the relations of peace and amity subsisting between the United States and France, and relying upon the faith of the law of nations, made shipment of a considerable amount of property (cotton, the produce of the United States,) on board of vessels solely owned by citizens of the United States, destined for the port of St. Sebastian, in Spain.

That at the departure of the said vessels from the United States there existed no decree or edict prohibiting American vessels entering the said port of St. Sebastian, but, on the contrary, American vessels entering the said port of St. Sebastian had been permitted to enter and depart at pleasure.

The vessels, having on board the goods so shipped by your memorialist, arrived safe at the port of their destination, on which a premium of insurance, in one instance, was paid at the rate of twenty-five per cent., free from any seizure in port, so little danger did your memorialist apprehend on the score of seizure; but, contrary to the common rules of justice, on the arrival of the said vessels they were seized by authority of the French Government, with their respective cargoes on board, and afterwards the latter were transported to Bayonne, and there sold at public auction, and the proceeds ordered to be deposited in the caisse d'amortissement.

The decree ordering the sequestration of this property took place about the latter end of March, 1810, but was only made public on the 13th of May following, when the same appeared in the newspapers.

The property thus situated was never considered by the late Government of France but as neutral property, for which it considered itself bound to restore, as the same was never condemned, but was only sold and the proceeds deposited in the caisse d'amortissement, to wait the issue of political events between the United States and France.

Property of a nature similarly detained has been restored by the late French Government, and your memorialist, with great deference, will cite the case of the brig Mary Torrens, belonging to the port of Philadelphia, bound also to the port of St. Sebastian, which was wrecked on the coast, near the port of St. John de Luz, in the month of November, 1809; the greater part of the cargo was saved, and was also sequestrated; the same was sold by order of the French Government, and the funds deposited also in the caisse d'amortissement. After one or two years the property was finally restored to its lawful owners, which demonstrates that the then Government of France never did consider the property thus sequestrated as the property of the Government.

There is also a number of other cases where property had been sequestrated, nearly at the same time, by the late Government of France, and restored by the present Government. Among others, your memorialist will only mention the case of the ship Eagle, of the port of Philadelphia, which, having been captured by a French privateer and brought into the port of St Sebastian, was also sequestrated by the late Government; and as it was a case of capture, a compromise took place between the captors and original owners, and the same has been restored by an order of the Council of Prizes, and sanctioned by the late Sovereign in council, and the proceeds of the sales ordered to be paid to the owners and captors, agreeable to the compromise entered into between them.

Your memorialist, deprived of his property for such length of time, has not failed to avail himself of all the circumstances that could have had a tendency to the restoration of his property, and has consequently sent his power of attorney to France, in order to claim and recover the same. His correspondents have presented petitions to the French Government on that subject, but the same has been without effect.

Under such circumstances your memorialist conceives that the private claims of an individual to that Government becomes abortive; he therefore, with all deference, begs leave to lay his claim before Congress, that they will please take the same under their consideration and grant such relief as in your wisdom you may deem proper.

JOHN F. DUMAS.

PHILADELPHIA, *December* 1, 1824.

To the honorable the Senate and House of Representatives in Congress of the United States:

William Manson, late of the State of Massachusetts, humbly showeth that he was captain of a certain vessel, viz: the brig Neptune, of Baltimore, and that on the 9th day of December, 1803, his vessel was captured by the Spaniards and carried into St. Jago de Cuba; and that he presented his claim to the Spanish commissioners under the late treaty, for loss and damage sustained on that account, as appears by the schedule annexed, and that said claim was rejected by the commissioners on the ground that the said vessel touched at St. Domingo, when, in fact, she only touched there in distress, for the purpose of obtaining water, which fact the claimant is ready to verify.

WM. MANSON,

William Manson, formerly master and one-quarter part owner of the brig Neptune, of Baltimore, claims, on his own account, for loss and damage sustained by him in consequence of said brig being captured by the Spaniards and carried into St. Jago de Cuba, December 9, 1803, viz:

50 barrels superfine flour, cost in Baltimore, on board	$341 09
80 coffee bags	40 00
Freight of 56 barrels out and home, shipped by Alexander Beard and Henry Bride, consigned to me, which freight I was to receive in consequence of my not filling up my quarter of the brig, per barrel $1 75	98 00
One-quarter of a draft, drawn by me in favor of Maurice Rogers, for $250, to enable him to get home, $250	62 50
One-quarter of brig Neptune and outfit, valued at $6,000	1,500 00
My wages from October 13 to December 9, 3 months and 20 days	131 66
Carried forward	2,173 25

		Brought forward...........	2,173	25
Wages of 2 apprentices, from October 13 to December 9, 3 months and 20 days...........			59	70
			2,232	95
Interest on $2,232 95 from December 9, 1803, to July 9, 1821, 17 years and 7 months, at 6 per cent..			2,355	75
			4,588	70
The above 50 barrels flour would have sold for $23 per barrel, agreeably to the deposition of Captain Greenwell.......................................	$1,150	00		
From which deduct 20 per cent. duty.......................................	230	00		
	920	00		
	341	09		
Say...	578	91		
Interest on the same for 17 years and 7 months.............................	610	74		
			1,189	65
			5,778	35
Credited.—By cash received by me of what was recovered in Philadelphia December, 1804......................................	401	04		
Interest on the same for 16 years and 7 months...........................	399	00		
			800	04
			4,978	31

LIMERICK, COUNTY OF YORK, STATE OF MAINE, *July* 9, 1821.

I, William Manson, do hereby solemnly declare and say that the annexed account, by me signed, is a true statement of my loss in consequence of the capture of the brig Neptune, formerly of Baltimore, by the Spaniards, as set forth in my protest; and that the amount thereof, and of every part thereof, if allowed, does now, and at the time when the said claim arose did, belong solely and absolutely to me, and that I have never received any sum of money or other equivalent or indemnification for said loss other than is set forth in said account; and I further declare that I am a citizen of the United States, was born in the town of Gorham, in the county of Cumberland, State of Maine. That at the time of my capture I belonged to Baltimore, since which I have chiefly resided in the town of Limerick, county of York, State of Maine, where myself and family now live.

WILLIAM MANSON.

YORK, STATE OF MAINE, *November* 18, 1824.

Sworn to before

J. HOLMES, *Justice of the Peace.*

18TH CONGRESS.]　　　　　　　　　No. 395.　　　　　　　　　[2D SESSION.

RELATIVE TO THE ESTABLISHMENT OF A LIGHT-HOUSE ON THE BRITISH ISLAND OF ABACO, ONE OF THE BAHAMA ISLANDS.

COMMUNICATED TO THE HOUSE OF REPRESENTATIVES JANUARY 20, 1825.

The Committee on Foreign Affairs, to whom the message of the President relative to the island of Abaco, &c., was referred, reported:

That the President, complying with the request of the House contained in the resolution adopted at the last session of Congress, instructed our minister near the court of Great Britain to negotiate for a cession of so much land on the island of Abaco, at or near the Hole in the Wall, and in such other places within the acknowledged dominion of that power, on the islands, keys, or shoals, on the Bahama Banks, as may be necessary for the erection and support of light-houses, beacons, buoys, or floating lights, for the security of navigation over and near the said Banks. Obeying these instructions, an official application was made to the British Government on the 6th of February last. To this application no formal answer has been given; but an official conversation was held on the subject with Mr. Rush, in July. From this conversation it appears that Great Britain cannot accede to the wishes of our Government in the manner proposed, but has a desire to accomplish the object in view in some other form. Great Britain will not cede any part of the island of Abaco, or other islands, &c., on the Bahama Banks, for the purpose of setting up light-houses, &c., for the benefit of navigation; but is not indisposed, if the United States will designate the proper sites, to erect and establish these aids to navigation among those islands: *Provided*, the United States will pay the necessary fees for keeping them up where their vessels derive benefit from them while making voyages in that direction. On the propriety of acceding to this arrangement, no difficulty would be felt if it was a question of cost merely; the cession is desired with the single motive to incur the expense of erecting and preserving the proposed safeguards to the vessels and crews of all nations frequenting those seas. Interesting as the object is, it is not, however, of sufficient importance to justify the admission of any new principle or practice in the intercourse of nations. The rule of the United States (and the committee are not aware that any nation has a different rule) is, that all vessels shall enjoy the benefit of·lights, beacons, and buoys, on their coast, without charge, unless they enter some port of the United States. All Europe partake of the benefits of the expenditure on these objects on our extensive coast, as we, in like manner, partake of the advantages of the beacons of Europe. The plan suggested by Great Britain is impracticable, independent of the insurmountable objections to the collection of a revenue for a foreign Government in the United States. It must be obvious that it would be impossible to ascertain with accuracy what proportion of our commerce would be benefitted by the beacons and buoys proposed to be erected, and which ought to bear the expense incident to their erection. Although just in theory that the commerce benefitted by the erection of a light-house should pay the charge of preserving it, yet the establishment of it as a rule among nations would, in practice, be followed by innumerable inconveniencies, and give birth to a thousand perplexing and disagreeable controversies, not justified by the value in dispute, and unworthy of the character of the objects of it. Policy dictates to all commercial nations a generous competition in the multiplication of every species of security to the life and property exposed to the hazard of navigation, without regard to immediate expense, or contingent reimbursement. The committee are confident, from what has been disclosed by the British Government, that the interesting object of the resolution of the last session may be soon, if not immediately, accomplished by negotiation with Great Britain. That Government has shown too much anxiety on the subject of increasing the security of commerce and navigation, to be indifferent to any proposition having that object only in view. When two nations honestly and cordially desire to effect the same end, means are easily discovered.

The committee forbear to bring into view any of the modes that have occurred to them as most likely to effect the object in the least objectionable form, as they do not consider it the province of the House of Representatives to make suggestions to the Executive of what ought to be done by treaty with a foreign power on any subject, and as they are aware that no suggestion which they could make would bind the representatives of the people hereafter to approve what might be done by the President and Senate. It is obvious, from the communication of Mr. Rush, that a proper caution is observed; that if the object is accomplished, it will be obtained without a change in the rule at present governing commercial nations, without fixing upon the United States an obligation to collect within their ports revenue for a foreign nation, or to pay a specific tax upon a portion of our commerce for the common security afforded by light-houses, beacons, &c., upon a desert shore. Satisfied that there is no call for the expression of an opinion of the House to prevent the Executive from entering into an engagement the representatives of the people could not approve, they ask leave to be discharged from the further consideration of the subject.

18TH CONGRESS.]   No. 396.   [2D SESSION.

CORRESPONDENCE WITH GREAT BRITAIN ON THE VARIOUS TOPICS OF DISCUSSION BETWEEN THE UNITED STATES AND THAT GOVERNMENT, VIZ:

1. Commercial intercourse with the British Colonies of the West Indies and Canada.
2. Boundary under the fifth article of the treaty of Ghent, and the navigation of the St. Lawrence river.
3. Admission of consuls of the United States into British colonial ports.
4. The Newfoundland fishery.
5. Maritime questions.
6. Northwest Coast of America.

COMMUNICATED TO THE SENATE, IN EXECUTIVE SESSION, JANUARY 20, 1825, AND THE INJUNCTION OF SECRECY SINCE REMOVED.

To the Senate of the United States:

I transmit herewith to the Senate a report from the Secretary of State, with the documents desired by their resolution of the 13th instant. In requesting that the originals may eventually be returned, it may be unnecessary to add that the negotiations being, by common consent, to be hereafter resumed, it is important that this communication should be regarded by the Senate as strictly confidential.

                                                                JAMES MONROE.
WASHINGTON, *January* 19, 1825.

DEPARTMENT OF STATE, *Washington, January* 19, 1825.

The Secretary of State, to whom has been referred the resolution of the Senate of the 13th instant, requesting that the President would cause to be laid before the Senate, in confidence, the instructions to Mr. Rush, and his correspondence on the various topics of discussion between the United States and Great Britain, has the honor of reporting to the President copies of the instructions referred to and the original despatches from Mr. Rush, containing his reports of the negotiation. The latter are transmitted to avoid the loss of time which must necessarily have ensued in making out copies of them, but it is desirable that they should ultimately be returned to this Department. It is proper that the Senate should likewise be apprised that the negotiation, although now suspended, is, at the instance of the British Government, to be resumed at an early day.

The instructions and despatches relating to the negotiations concerning the Northwest Coast and the suppression of the slave trade, having been heretofore made known to the Senate, are not included in this communication.

                                                                JOHN QUINCY ADAMS.

List of papers with the President's Message to the Senate, in compliance with their resolution of January 13, 1825, communicated confidentially.

Mr. Adams to Mr. Rush, No. 64, June 23, 1823.
Mr. Canning to Mr. Adams, March 27, 1823.
Mr. Adams to Mr. Canning, April 8, 1823.
Mr. Canning to Mr. Adams, April 10, 1823.
Mr. Adams to Mr. Canning, May 14, 1823.
Mr. Canning to Mr. Adams, May 17, 1823.
Mr. Adams to Mr. Rush, No. 66, June 25, 1823.
Same to same, No. 67, June 26, 1823.
Same to same, No. 68, June 27, 1823.
Same to same, No. 71, July 28, 1823.
Mr. Rush to Mr. Adams, No. 5, May 20, 1824.
Same to same, No. 8, August 2, 1824.
Same to same, No. 10, August 12, 1824.
Protocol of the third conference of the American and British plenipotentiaries, and
Protocols of subsequent conferences of the same plenipotentiaries, from the 8th to the 26th, inclusive.
Copy of the full power of British plenipotentiaries.
A. Paper annexed to the third protocol.
W. On the commercial intercourse question, from the British plenipotentiaries.
Act of Parliament on reciprocity of duties, and commercial treaty between Great Britain and Prussia.
L. British counter projet on commercial intercourse.
B. American paper on the navigation of the St. Lawrence.
N. British paper on the navigation of the St. Lawrence.
D. American paper on the boundary line under the fifth article of the treaty of Ghent.
E. American paper on the Newfoundland fishery.
Note, May 3, 1824, to Mr. Secretary Canning, on the Newfoundland fishery.
M. British articles on general miscellaneous points, annexed to protocol of the 22d conference.
F. American paper on the Northwest Coast of America.
P. British paper on the Northwest Coast of America, 23d protocol.

Mr. Adams to Mr. Rush, No. 64.

DEPARTMENT OF STATE, *Washington, June 23, 1823.*

SIR: I have the honor of inclosing herewith copies of the correspondence between the British minister residing here, Mr. Stratford Canning, and this Department, since the close of the last session of Congress, relating to the act of March 1, 1823, "to regulate the commercial intercourse between the United States and certain British colonial ports."

This act was intended as a corresponding measure on the part of the United States to the act of Parliament of June 24, 1822, (3 Geo. IV, ch. 44.) On the 24th of August, 1822, immediately after this act of Parliament was received here, the President of the United States issued the proclamation, a copy of which was transmitted to you with my despatch No. 59, of the 27th of the same month.

That proclamation was issued in conformity with an act passed at the preceding session of Congress, (U. S. Laws, 17th Cong., 1st session, p. 49,) which had provided that, on satisfactory evidence being given to the President of the United States that *the ports* in the islands or colonies in *the West Indies* under the dominion of Great Britain *had been opened* to the vessels of the United States, the President should be authorized to issue his proclamation declaring that the *ports of the United States* should thereafter *be open* to the vessels of Great Britain employed in the trade and intercourse between the United States and *such islands or colonies,* subject to such *reciprocal* rules and restrictions as the President might, by such proclamation, make and publish, anything in the laws entitled "An act concerning navigation" or an act entitled "An act supplementary to an act concerning navigation" to the contrary notwithstanding.

The proclamation of the President was necessarily limited by the authority given in the law, and the law was enacted in anticipation of measures known to be then depending in Parliament, *one* of the objects of which was the opening of the British colonial ports to foreign vessels, including those of the United States. When the act of Congress passed (May 6, 1822,) it was not known what colonial ports would be opened by the expected act of Parliament, nor under what rules and restrictions. It was therefore expressed in general and indefinite terms, looking to the opening of *the* ports in the British West Indies generally, and manifesting the disposition to meet the British Government forthwith in *any* plan for opening the ports to the navigation of both countries upon terms of *reciprocity,* the laws of both countries having at that time interdicted the trade between the United States and those colonies in the vessels of either nation.

This interdiction on the part of the United States had been effected by the two laws referred to in the act of May 6, 1822, the act concerning navigation, bearing date the 18th of April, 1818, (United States Laws, vol. 6, p. 296,) and the supplementary act of the 15th of May, 1820, (p. 534.)

These laws had been enacted as counteractive to those of a like character, long before existing on the part of Great Britain, interdicting the trade in vessels of the United States. They had been resorted to after the failure of repeated attempts to settle by amicable negotiation the manner in which the trade might be regulated upon principles of reciprocity—attempts which were renewed immediately after the passage of the first of them, and upon the abortive issue of which the second received the sanction of Congress.

This intermediate negotiation, between the 18th of April, 1818, and the 15th of May, 1820, must be constantly borne in mind in all discussion of the measures adopted on the part of the United States, predicated upon the act of Parliament of June 24, 1822, opening the colonial ports. The whole subject of it is familiar to your memory as one of the negotiators of the convention of October 20, 1818, and as the sole subsequent negotiator, concerning the article referred by the plenipotentiaries of the United States who concluded that convention to their Government.

By the convention of July 3, 1815, the commercial intercourse between the United States and the British territories *in Europe* was placed, in relation to navigation and revenue, on the following footing:

1. No other or higher duties of *importation* are to be imposed in either country on any articles *the growth, produce, or manufacture of the other*, than are payable on *the like articles* being the growth, produce, or manufacture of any other *foreign* country.

2. No higher or other *duties* or *charges* of *exportation* are to be imposed on any articles exported to the two countries, respectively, than are payable on the exportation of the like articles *to* any other foreign country.

3. No *prohibition*, of exportation or importation, of articles the growth, produce, or manufacture of either country to the other, which shall not equally extend to all other nations.

4. No higher or other *duties* or *charges* to be imposed in the ports of either party upon the *vessels* of the other than upon its own.

5. The *same* duties to be paid on the importation of articles the growth produce, or manufacture of either country into the ports of the other, whether imported in the vessels of the United States or of Great Britain.

6. The same *duties* to be paid and the same *bounties* allowed on *exportation* of articles the growth, produce, or manufacture of either country to the other, whether exported in British vessels or in vessels of the United States.

7. In cases of *drawbacks* allowed upon re-exportation of any goods, the growth produce, or manufacture of either country to the other, respectively, the amount of drawback to be the same whether the goods re-exported were *originally imported* in a British or an American vessel.

8. But when the re-exportation is to any other foreign country the parties reserve to themselves, respectively, the right of regulating or diminishing the drawback.

9. And lastly, the intercourse between the United States and the British West Indies and on the continent of North America was not to be affected by any of these provisions, but each party was to remain in complete possession of its rights with respect to such an intercourse.

The system of reciprocity with regard to navigation established by this article between the United States and the British possessions in Europe was substantially the acceptance of a proposal made to all the nations with which the United States have commercial intercourse by the act of Congress of March 3, 1815, conditionally repealing our discriminating duties.—(United States Laws, volume 4, page 824.) But it was expressly limited to the British possessions *in Europe*, and while accepting it thus far, the British Government reverted to the system of interdiction to the admission of our vessels into her American colonial ports.

The direct trade between the United States and Great Britain was so interwoven with and dependent upon that between the United States and the colonies, that this convention would have been worse than nugatory to the United States, if, while the European part of this intercourse was placed upon a footing of entire reciprocity, that between the United States and the colonies had been exclusively monopolized by British navigators. This was practically felt from the moment that the convention took effect, and in the year 1816 several efforts were made to induce the British Government to adjust this collision of interests by amicable negotiation.—(See message of the President of the United States of February 13, 1823, pp. 37, 39, 49; also documents of the 15th Congress, 1st session, (87,) report of committee of House of Representatives of the United States of February 9, 1818, document marked F.)

In March, 1817, a draft of four articles was communicated by Lord Castlereagh through your predecessor to the Government of the United States, which were stated to embrace all that could then be assented to by Great Britain towards admitting the United States to a participation in the trade between them and the colonies.

The first of these articles extended to the United States the provisions of the free port acts of Parliament of June 27, 1805, and of June 30, 1808, authorizing a certain trade in certain enumerated articles with certain enumerated ports of British West India islands, to the colonial inhabitants of foreign *European* possessions, in vessels of one deck. The island of Bermuda was included in the provisions of this act.

The second article made a special and additional provision for the trade between the United States and the island of Bermuda—allowing a longer list of articles both of import and export, and without limitation as to the size or form of the vessels to be employed in the trade.

The third article proposed to allow access to vessels of the United States to Turk's Island for salt, and to import tobacco and cotton wool, produce of the United States.

The fourth proposed to regulate the intercourse between the United States and the British territories adjoining them on the continent of North America.

After a full and deliberate consideration these articles were considered by the Government of the United States as not acceptable, and the act of Congress of April 18, 1818, concerning navigation, was passed.

The negotiation of the convention of October 20, 1818, immediately afterwards ensued, with regard to which you are referred to—

The letter from this Department to you, dated May 21, 1818, (message of February 13, 1823, p. 59.)
The letter from this Department to Mr. Gallatin, dated May 22, 1818, (p. 62.)
Your letter to this Department, dated July 25, 1818, (pp. 68, 69, 70.)
Instructions from this Department to Messrs. Gallatin and Rush, dated July 28, 1818, (pp. 71, 72.)
Letter from Messrs. Gallatin and Rush to this Department, dated October 20, 1818, (pp. 107, 108, 109, 110, 111.)
Protocol of 3d conference, article C, and another proposed by American plenipotentiaries, (p. 115, 118.)
Protocol of 5th conference, article D, proposed by British plenipotentiaries, (p. 133.)
Protocol of 8th conference, article F, proposed by British plenipotentiaries and taken by the American plenipotentiaries for reference to their Government, (p. 150.)
And subsequently to the conclusion of the convention to—
Letter from this Department to you, dated December 1, 1818, (p. 89.)
Letter from this Department to you, dated May 7, 1819, and two articles proposed, (pp. 91, 97.)

Your letter to this Department, dated June 14, 1819, (p. 97.)
Your letter to this Department, dated September 17, 1819, (p. 99.)
Letter from this Department to you, dated May 27, 1820, transmitting the act of Congress of May 15, 1820, (p. 101.)

By the act of Congress of April 15, 1818, concerning navigation, the ports of the United States were, from the 30th of September of that year, closed against British vessels coming from any British colony, by *the ordinary laws of navigation and trade*, closed against vessels of the United States; and British vessels sailing with cargoes from ports of the United States were laid under bonds to land their cargoes in some port or place other than in a colony closed against vessels of the United States.

It was a non-intercourse in *British* vessels with ports closed by British laws against the vessels of the United States.

By the supplementary act of May 15, 1820, the ports of the United States were, from the 30th of September of that year, closed against British vessels coming or arriving by sea from *any* British colonial ports in the West Indies, or American British vessels from ports of the United States were laid under bonds to land their cargoes in some place other than any British American colony; and articles of British West Indian or North American produce were allowed to be imported into the United States only direct from the province, colony, plantation, island, possession, or place of which they were *wholly* the growth, produce, or manufacture. It was a non-intercourse in *British vessels* with all the British American colonies, and a prohibition of all articles the produce of those colonies, except the produce of each colony imported directly from itself.

In the meantime an act of Parliament of May 8, 1818, (58 Geo. III, ch. 19,) and an order of council of May 27, 1818, founded thereon, opened the ports of Halifax, in Nova Scotia, and of St. John, in New Brunswick, to the vessels of all foreign nations in amity with Great Britain, for importation of certain enumerated articles, and for exportation to the country to which the foreign vessel should belong. This act was limited in its duration to three years and six weeks after the commencement of the then next session of Parliament, but the order of council specifying the ports to which it should be extended was *revocable at pleasure.*

This act of Parliament and order in council were construed in the United States not to affect in any manner the provisions of the act of Congress of April 15, 1818. The ports of Halifax and St. John remained closed against vessels of the United States, *by the ordinary laws of navigation and trade,* although opened for a limited time by an order of council, revocable at pleasure. Their real condition, therefore, in October, 1818, was that of being open to the vessels of the United States, while the ports of the United States were closed against British vessels coming from them.

It was on October 6, 1818, that the British plenipotentiaries, at the negotiation of the convention of the 20th of that month, proposed the article D, relating to the intercourse between the United States and the provinces of Nova Scotia and New Brunswick, which article they on the 19th declared was, together with the one offered in March, 1817, relating to Bermuda, a *sine qua non* of *any* article to be signed by them relating to the direct intercourse between the United States and the British colonies in the West Indies.

And the article D contained precisely the same list of articles importable and the same limitations with regard to export in vessels of the United States as were already contained in the act of Parliament of the 8th and in the order in council of May 27, 1818; and the article further proposed an equalization of duties of impost and tonnage on the vessels and articles employed in the trade, whether British or American.

So that the proposition really was, that the United States should open to the British a free and equal participation of the intercourse between the United States and the provinces of Nova Scotia and New Brunswick, then by the counteracting regulations of the two countries exclusively enjoyed by the United States themselves.

The article relating to the intercourse between the United States and Bermuda was yet more remarkable. By an act of Parliament of July 1, 1812, (52 Geo. III, ch.,) sugar and coffee, the produce of any British colony or plantation in the West Indies, imported into the island of Bermuda in British ships, was allowed to be exported from the port of St. George to the United States in any foreign ship above 60 tons burden, belonging to any country in amity with Great Britain, and a list of articles enumerated was allowed to be imported from the United States to the said port in any foreign ship belonging to any country in amity with Great Britain; and this list contained, besides every article enumerated in the proposal of the British plenipotentiaries, horses, neat cattle, sheep, hogs, poultry, and live stock of any sort, which in the British proposal were excluded from the Bermuda list, and transferred to that of Nova Scotia and New Brunswick. To the articles of sugar and coffee, exportable by the act of Parliament, the proposal added molasses, cocoa nuts, ginger and pimento.

These two articles, therefore, were to be considered as the equivalents asked of the United States for the admission proposed of their vessels to any British ports in the West Indies which should be open to the vessels of any other foreign power or State.

The following parallel lists of articles proposed to be admitted for importation and exportation in the intercourse between the United States, on one part, and Nova Scotia, with New Brunswick, Bermuda, and the West Indies, on the other, by the three connected and inseparable articles proposed by the British plenipotentiaries, may serve further to elucidate the character of the proposal:

Articles of importation proposed to be admitted in vessels of the United States.

To Nova Scotia and New Brunswick.—Tobacco, pitch, tar, turpentine, scantling, staves, heading-boards, planks, shingles, hoops, horses, neat cattle, sheep, hogs, poultry, live stock of any sort, fruits, seeds, bread, biscuit, flour, pease, beans, potatoes, wheat, rice, oats, barley, grain of any sort.

To Bermuda.—Tobacco, pitch, tar, turpentine, hemp, flax, masts, yards, bowsprits, staves, heading-boards, plank, timber, shingles, lumber of any sort, bread, biscuit, flour, pease, beans, potatoes, wheat, rice, oats, barley, grain of any sort.

To the West Indies.—Tobacco, pitch, tar, turpentine, staves, headings, shingles, horses, mules, poultry, live stock, provisions of all sorts except salted, provisions of any description, whether meat, fish, or butter.

Exports.

From Nova Scotia and New Brunswick.—Gypsum, grindstones, any articles of the growth of the province or of British dominions.

From Bermuda.—Any goods exportable to any foreign country, sugar, molasses, coffee, cocoa nuts, ginger, pimento, any British goods.

From the West Indies.—Rum, molasses, salt, and other articles exportable in foreign vessels to any other foreign country.

By another act of Parliament of May 23, 1818, the articles of tobacco, rice, grain, pease, beans, and flour were allowed to be imported in *British* vessels into *any* British colony in the West Indies or on the continent of South America from any foreign European colony in America, and pease and beans were allowed to be imported into the enumerated ports of the British West Indies from foreign *European* possessions in the West Indies and on the continent of America in foreign single-decked vessels. In the letter from this Department to you of May 7, 1819, a comparative view was taken between the articles which had been proposed at the third conference by the American plenipotentiaries, at the negotiation of the convention, and the articles proposed at the fifth and eighth conferences by the British plenipotentiaries, and then received by the American plenipotentiaries for reference to their Government, and a draft of two articles was inclosed with the latter, forming a compromise between the two proposals reviewed, and which you were authorized to offer as a final proposal on the part of this Government in relation to the subject. These articles, acceding to a limited and enumerated list of ports of importation in the British colonies, and to a limited and enumerated list of articles importable in them, adhered only to two principles: First, that the list of importable articles should be the same for the West Indies, for Bermuda, and for the North American provinces; and second, that *all* the duties and charges imposable upon them should be equalized, and particularly that no other or higher duties should be charged upon them than upon similar articles when imported from *any other country or place* whatsoever. Your letter of June 14, 1819, announced that a copy of this draft had been submitted by you to the consideration of the British Government, and your letter of September 17, 1819, that they had declined accepting it. At the conference between you and Lord Castlereagh, when he informed you of this determination, he stated the special objections to the project upon which it had been founded, and you repeated to him the views of the Government of the United States on which the offer had been made. The supplementary navigation act of Congress was approved on the 15th of May, 1820.

This, then, was the relative state of the intercourse between the United States and, first, the provinces of Nova Scotia and New Brunswick; second, the island of Bermuda; and, third, the British colonies in the West Indies, from September 30, 1820, till the passage of the act of Parliament of June 24, 1822.

By the acts of Parliament of 3 Geo. IV, ch. 42 and 43, the navigation act of 12 Charles II, ch. 18, was repealed so far as related to the *importation* of goods and merchandise into Great Britain. But the American trade acts, and the acts relating to importations from the British colonies in America and the West Indies were left in full force.

The act of 3 Geo. IV, ch. 44, purports to be an act to regulate the trade between his Majesty's possessions in America and the West Indies and *other places* in America and the West Indies:

It leaves the principle of the navigation act of Charles II untouched, but by its first section repeals the whole series of what were called American trade acts; that is, acts regulating the trade between the United States of America and the British American and West India colonies, since the independence of this country, beginning with the act of 28 Geo. III, ch. 39, and ending with 1 and 2 Geo. IV, ch. 7, twenty-five statutes, for which it substitutes the following system:

1. By the third section it provides that from and after the passing of the act *a certain list of enumerated articles* shall be importable *into a certain list of enumerated ports* in the British American colonies, insular or continental, in British vessels or in foreign vessels, *bona fide* the build of and owned by the inhabitants of the country of which the said articles are the growth, produce, or manufacture; or British built vessels become their property and navigated with a master and three-fourths of the mariners, at least, belonging to such country or place: *Provided*, that in the *foreign* vessels the articles shall only be brought directly from the country or place of which they are the growth, produce, or manufacture.

2. By the fourth section it allows the *exportation* from the enumerated ports, in British vessels or in *any foreign ship or vessel as aforesaid*, of any article of the growth, produce, or manufacture of any of the British dominions, or any other article legally imported into the said ports, (arms and naval stores excepted, unless by license from his Majesty's Secretary of State,) provided that in *foreign* ships they shall be exportable only *direct* to the country or State in America or the West Indies to which the vessel belongs; and export bonds are to be given, in a penalty equal to half the value of the articles, that they shall be landed at the port or ports for which entered, and certificate of the landing to be produced within twelve months.

By the 7th section it is provided that upon a certain portion, enumerated in schedule C, of the articles enumerated as importable in schedule B, certain duties shall be levied and collected when imported from any *foreign* island, State, or country, under the authority of the act.

The 11th section enacts that the same duties upon the *foreign* articles shall also be levied, if imported direct from any port of Great Britain and Ireland.

The 14th section authorizes the exportation in *British* vessels of the articles enumerated in schedule B to any other British colony or plantation in America or the West Indies, or to any port of Great Britain and Ireland subject to the provisions of the navigation act of 12 Charles II, ch. 18, and of 22 and 23 Charles II, ch. 26, and 20 Geo. III, ch. 10.

The 15th section authorizes the King, by order in council, to prohibit trade and intercourse with any country or island in America or the West Indies, if it shall appear to his Majesty that the privileges *granted by this act* to foreign ships and vessels are not allowed to British ships and vessels trading to and from any such country under the provisions of the act; and in case such order in council shall be issued, then, during the time of its being in force, none of the provisions of the act shall apply to any country or State the trade with which, under the provisions of the act, shall be prohibited by the order in council.

The 17th section prohibits, on penalty of the forfeiture of vessel and cargo, the importation into the enumerated ports, from any foreign country on the continent of America or any island in the West Indies, of any articles except those enumerated in the schedule B.

And the 18th section prohibits, upon like penalty, the importation or exportation of any articles whatever from or to any foreign country on the continents of North or South America, or any foreign island in the West Indies, into or *from any port* of any British colony, plantation, or island in America or the West Indies, not enumerated in the schedule A.

If the object of this act of Parliament was to open the ports of the British colonies in the West Indies and in America to the vessels of the United States upon terms of *reciprocity*, it was not well adapted to its purpose.

In the 15th section it is declared to be the intention and meaning of the act that the privileges granted by it to foreign ships and vessels shall be confined to the ships and vessels of such countries only as give *the like privileges* to British ships and vessels in their ports in America and the West Indies; and the King is authorized to issue his order in council *prohibiting trade and intercourse* under the authority of the act, if it shall appear to him that *the privileges granted by this act* to foreign ships and vessels are not *allowed* to British vessels trading to and from any such country or island under the provisions of this act.

Now, what are the *privileges granted by this act* to the vessels of the United States? That they may bring *directly*, and not otherwise, from some port of the United States, to certain colonial ports named in the act of Parliament, *and none others*, certain articles of merchandise specifically named, *and none others*. That upon their arrival, of all the articles which they are permitted to bring, they shall pay enormous duties upon that portion which consists of the productions of the United States, consumable in the colonies themselves; and the only portion which in the results of the trade would be to the United States profitable export, and to one part of the colonies necessary import; and these duties are to be paid while the British vessels, enjoying *all the privileges granted by this act*, possess the additional and exclusive privilege of carrying to the same West India ports, directly or indirectly, the same articles thus heavily charged when coming from the United States, but free from all duty when carried from the colony in North America to the colony in the West Indies.

Again: the vessel of the United States admitted to the above privilege, has the further privilege, if she can procure a cargo, to return *directly*, and not otherwise, to the United States, and to give bond, upon penalty equal to half the value of said cargo, for the landing it at the port or ports for which entered, and for producing a certificate whereof within twelve months. But there is a charge not indeed *imposed by this act*, but from which this act has not relieved them—that of paying a colonial export duty of four or five per cent. ad valorem upon this return cargo. To this charge British vessels may also be liable if their owners choose to incur it; but if they prefer exporting their cargoes without paying any export duty, they are free to go to any port of the British dominions in Europe or America. They are not required to give the export bond for the landing of the articles at the port or ports for which entered, and for producing a certificate within twelve months a certificate thereof.

By the letter of the act of Parliament, if the privileges *granted by it* to the vessels of the United States should appear to the King not *to be allowed* to British vessels trading under the provisions of the act, he may, by an order in council, at his discretion, *prohibit trade and intercourse* under the authority of the act.

The words ."the privileges granted by this act" are explained by the context of the section to mean *like* privileges, to be allowed by the laws of the United States to British vessels employed in the same trade.

If an act of Congress had passed admitting British vessels, coming from colonial British ports in America and the West Indies, to enter a certain specified list of ports in the United States, selected at the pleasure of Congress, *and no others;* if it had allowed them to bring in those vessels an enumerated list of articles (from which rum and molasses, for example, should be excluded,) and no others; if it had included, for example, sugar and coffee among the admissible articles, but burdened them with duties equivalent to ten per cent. ad valorem *more* than would be paid upon the same articles imported from elsewhere; if it had compelled the British vessels, so admitted, if they took a return cargo, to give bonds for landing it at the port or ports in the British colonies for which the vessel should clear out, and if not by the act of Congress but by some law of the State from which this privileged British vessel should depart, an export duty of four or five per cent. ad valorem should be levied upon this her return cargo, then British vessels in the ports of the United States would have been allowed *like* privileges with those granted by the act of Parliament to vessels of the United States in the colonial ports; and so exactly *like* would they have been, that, under such an act of Congress and such a grant of privileges to British vessels, the conditional authority given by the 15th section of the act of Parliament to the King, of prohibiting the trade and intercourse, would not have attached according to the letter of the act, although it might have appeared to his Majesty that "*the privileges granted by this act*" were not allowed to British vessels trading to and from the United States under its provisions.

The privileges granted by this act could, of course, be allowed only by the same authority from which it emanated—that is, by the British Parliament. *Like* privileges would have been such as I have now described; that is, privileges subject to like limitations and restrictions, which, as the bare exposition of them here will show, would have been found to be no privileges at all.

The act of Parliament opened certain colonial ports upon certain very onerous conditions to vessels of the United States. If the United States had opened their ports to British vessels from the colonies without condition or limitation, the privileges of British vessels in our ports would have been in nowise *like* those of the vessels of the United States in the colonial ports. In point of fact, the privilege of the British vessels would have been *exclusive*, and that of the American vessels *exclusion*.

Immediately after receiving the act of Parliament which opened certain ports of the British colonies in the West Indies and in America to the vessels of the United States, the President, exercising the authority given him by anticipation in the act of Congress of May 6, 1822, issued his proclamation opening the ports of the United States generally to British vessels coming from any of the ports enumerated in the act of Parliament. And in this proclamation he gave the most liberal construction for the benefit of British vessels to the act of Congress on which it was founded. For, by the laws of the United States, when the act of Congress passed, and until the proclamation issued, the ports of the United States were closed against British vessels from *any* of the British colonies in the West Indies or in America; while by the British laws the ports of St. John and Halifax, in New Brunswick and Nova Scotia, those of Port St. George and Hamilton, in the island of Bermuda, and the ports of the Bahama islands, were opened to vessels of the United States. These ports, therefore, the act of Parliament did not open to our vessels; and the proclamation, by opening the ports of the United States to vessels coming from them, was much more extensive in its operation than the act of Parliament itself.

As *reciprocal* to the rules and restrictions under which the trade was permitted by the act of Parliament, the President's proclamation provided that no articles should be imported into the United States in British vessels coming from the West Indies, other than articles of the growth, produce, or manufacture of the British West India colonies, and none other than articles of the growth, produce, or manufacture of the British colonies in North America or Newfoundland, in British vessels coming respectively from that island, or from the North America colonies; and by the existing revenue laws of the United States all British vessels and their cargoes, coming from any of the colonies, remained subject to the *foreign* tonnage and impost duties. In my letter to you of August 27, 1822, inclosing a copy of this proclamation, I suggested to you the opinion that some further understanding between the two Governments would be necessary for regulating this trade in a manner advantageous to the interests of both parties, and the readiness of this Government to enter upon arrangements for that purpose with the British Government.

On the 25th of October, 1822, the British minister residing here addressed a note to this Department, containing representations against the rules and restrictions provided in the proclamation, as not being *specific counterparts* to those of the act of Parliament, and also claiming exemption from the *foreign* tonnage and impost duties for British vessels and their cargoes coming from the colonies; because the act of Parliament subjected British and foreign vessels engaged in this trade only to the same duties and charges, and if there were in the colonies any discriminating charges against foreign vessels, they *did not appear in the act of Parliament.*

I have shown you above what would have been a *specific counterpart* to the rules and restrictions of the act of Parliament, and to the colonial export duty coexisting with it. Had the President possessed the power of prescribing them by his proclamation, they would have been, in effect, equivalent to a total prohibition of the intercourse in British vessels, and appeared little better than a mockery. But the President had no such power. He could neither select an exclusive list of ports of admission, nor levy an export duty, nor repeal the foreign tonnage and impost.

Mr. Canning's note was answered and he replied. There was also much discussion of the subject between us at personal interviews, in which, as well as in his note, he kept me constantly reminded of the authority given by the act of Parliament to the King to prohibit the intercourse by an order in council, *if the privileges granted by this act* should not be allowed to British vessels, and of the necessity; there would be for countervailing discriminations, if those of the proclamation and the foreign tonnage and impost duty should remain.

In the course of this correspondence and of these conferences, which continued through the whole of the late session of Congress, Mr. Canning, with great earnestness, pressed the claim of admission for British vessels from the colonies, free from *all* discriminating duties and charges, on the *argument* that there were no discriminating duties or charges operating against vessels of the United States in the colonies. On the 13th of January, 1823, he addressed to this Department a note, claiming distinctly the withdrawal of all the discriminating duties, and particularly the application to British vessels coming from the colonies of the fair and full operation of such acts of Congress, *including that of March* 3, 1815, as appear to have an immediate application to the case.

In support of his *argument*, that there were no discriminating duties operating against us in the colonies, he then, and at other times, communicated copies of documents from a few of the enumerated ports, certifying that British and American vessels paid the same fees, or that by the *act of Parliament* they paid the same duties, or that they paid the same *custom-house expenses;* and he constantly urged that these were sufficient to establish the fact that our vessels and their cargoes paid in the colonies no other or higher fees, duties, or charges, than British vessels, and, consequently, the claim that British vessels from the colonies should pay no higher or other duties, fees, or charges, than our own; but he invariably declined pledging himself or his Government to any declaration that there were no discriminating duties in the enumerated ports; and we have now satisfactory information that in some of them there were and still are discriminations to our disadvantage, besides those of the act of Parliament.

The act of Congress of March 1, 1823, "to regulate the commercial intercourse between the United States and certain British colonial ports," was introduced into the Senate by their Committee on Foreign Relations at an early period of their late session. In maturing it they had before them the act of Parliament of June 24, 1822, the President's proclamation, and the correspondence between Mr. Canning and this Department concerning it. While it was in discussion before the committee of the Senate, Mr. Canning, to whom a copy of the bill had been communicated, made some written remarks upon it, which were immediately submitted to the consideration of the committee. The full import of the term *elsewhere,* in the second, third, and fifth sections of the act, which formed the principal subject of these remarks, was deliberately examined and settled, as well in Senate as upon a consultation by the President with the members of the administration, and was explicitly made known to Mr. Canning.

The principle assumed by the act was not the *repeal,* but the suspension, during the continuance of the admission of our vessels into the colonial ports by the act of Parliament, of our two navigation acts. In return for the opening of the colonial ports to our vessels by the act of Parliament, we opened our ports to British vessels from the same colonial ports; but as a power was left to the King, by an order in council, to prohibit the trade and intercourse, it was necessary to be prepared for that contingency, if it should occur, by making the revival of our acts of navigation also contingent upon the same event.

As by the act of Parliament the intercourse in our vessels was limited to *direct* voyages both to and from the United States and the enumerated ports, the same limitation was prescribed for the intercourse in British vessels by the act of Congress; one of Mr. Canning's remarks was, that the condition in the 5th section of our act, which limits the permission to export in British vessels to such as *have previously come directly* from any of the enumerated ports, did not appear to have any *counterpart* in the British act of Parliament. This is true. The counterpart was not in that act of Parliament, but in the old navigation act of 12 Charles II. By that act no vessel of the United States could *enter* any of the enumerated ports, coming from any other part of the world, and the act of June 24, 1822, admitted them only *direct* from the United States; no vessel of ours, therefore, other than such as have previously come direct from the United States to the enumerated ports, can export anything from them, because no other are admitted into the enumerated ports at all. Now, we could not exclude British vessels from coming to the United States from every other part of the world except the enumerated ports, which would be the full counterpart to the exclusion of the old navigation act of Charles II, still in force against us; but we could and did exclude those coming from elsewhere from bringing with them merchandise from the enumerated ports, and those coming from the enumerated ports from bringing with them merchandise from elsewhere. The result was strictly reciprocal, though our act, in granting the like privilege to that of the act of Parliament of June 24, 1822, annexed to it the *like* restriction to that of the old British navigation act of Charles II.

The principal objection of Mr. Canning was to the import of the term elsewhere; he was distinctly informed that the construction of which he observes in his remarks it appears to be susceptible was the construction which it was intended to bear, and would receive; but that it would put the question of the discriminating duties on a footing irreconcilable with the fair and natural view "of the subject' we can by no means admit. As little do we admit that, having reference to the conclusion of the negotiation in 1819, it ought to have been unexpected. It has been seen that the United States then explicitly declined acceding to an article which would have opened the colonial ports, *because* it would have reserved to Great Britain the right of laying in the colonial ports higher duties upon articles of the growth, produce, or manufacture of the United States, than upon the like articles of the growth, produce, or manufacture of Great Britain or her own colonies. The act of Parliament (3 George IV, chapter 44) of June 24, 1822, opened the colonial ports with a threat to close them again (or rather to prohibit all trade and intercourse with them) if it should not be acceded to in all its parts of *privilege*, without regard to its conditions of restriction, or to the other restrictions under which the privileges must be, if at all, accepted. It undertook to do, by British laws, that, the reserved right to do which we had unequivocally refused to accede to by compact. In the course of the conference with Mr. Canning I proved this to him by reading to him the parts of the joint letter from Messrs. Gallatin and Rush to this Department of October 20, 1818, relating to the subject, and the extracts from your letters of June 14 and September 17, 1819, connected with it. The duties in the schedule C of the act of Parliament are *all* upon articles of the first necessity to the West India colonies—articles which *can* be furnished them only from the United States or from the adjoining North American British colonies, and articles constituting almost all the valuable exports allowed by the act of Parliament, and consumable in the colonies. They are all upon *breadstuffs, live stock, and lumber*, and the whole of them are equivalent to an average of at least ten per cent. upon the value of the articles. Of these articles, the live stock and the lumber could be exported only from the northern parts of the United States; could it possibly be supposed that, while from the ports of the State of Maine such articles imported into Jamaica, St. Kitts, or Antigua, should be burdened with a duty of ten per cent. upon their value, the same articles from the province of New Brunswick being admitted duty free, there could be any competition sustainable between the vessels of the two countries in which they should on such unequal terms be introduced? And if we add to this that, after disposing of her cargo, the vessel from New Brunswick might take a return cargo, also duty free, or might trade from colony to colony without restraint, while the vessel from Maine must depart in ballast, or return to the United States laden with an export duty upon her cargo, what feature of reciprocity would there be upon which the very idea of competition could escape the charge of absurdity?

The act of Congress, therefore, opens the ports of the United States to British vessels from the colonial ports enumerated in the act of Parliament, but not upon the identical terms prescribed in it.

The restrictions of the act of Congress are counterparts not only to the restrictions of that particular act of Parliament, but to the others to which the American trade to the colonies is subject, whether by colonial laws or by the navigation act of Charles II; and as some of those British restrictions were of a character which we could not meet by *specific* counterparts, we meet them by analogical restrictions productive of the same result. This was insisted on by our plenipotentiaries at the discussion during the negotiation of the convention of 1818, and Great Britain could not justly expect that discriminating surcharges, the reserved right of levying which we unequivocally refused to sanction with our consent as a *bargain*, we should be ready to accept as a dispensation of British law. For an enumerated list of ports, part only of which are opened by the act of Parliament, we open *all* our ports in return; for an enumerated and very scanty list of importable articles, we agreed to receive in return all the valuable exportable articles of all the opened British colonies; for a duty of ten per cent. import, and of four or five per cent. on exports, upon the *value of the articles* of the trade, we retain a foreign tonnage duty of ninety-four cents per ton on British vessels employed in the trade, and ten per cent. additional (not upon the value of the article, but upon the import duty otherwise charged upon it) upon the articles imported in them.

It is doubtful whether these countervailing restrictions on our part will prove sufficient to enable our vessels to pursue the trade in equal competition with the British. Still more doubtful whether, under the double system of restrictions, the trade itself can be pursued in a manner which will relieve the British West India colonies from the distress which was rapidly hurrying them to ruin under the preceding restrictions of the navigation act of Charles II. Surely the British Government must be aware that profit is the *sine qua non* of trade; and that if they load with enormous duties the articles indispensable to the existence of their colonies, those duties must be paid by the colonies themselves, or they will smother the trade itself. If the object of the act of Parliament was merely to balance the advantages of our proximity to the West Indies, their duties of import are at least five-fold too heavy; and as to the export duty, how could it possibly be paid upon articles to be brought into our market in competition with the like articles, partly of our own produce, and most largely from Cuba, St. Domingo, and other West India islands, where no export duty exists. The result must be, and has already proved to be, that our vessels admitted to the British colonial ports can take no return cargoes, and must come away in ballast. So that if they could sell their outward cargoes at a profit upon which the trade could *live*, it must be paid in *specie* by the colonists, leaving their staple commodities to rot upon their plantations, or to the old monopoly of the market at *home*.

The request of explanation as to the extent of the meaning of the term *elsewhere* in the act of Congress in Mr. Canning's correspondence with this Department since the close of the session has not arisen from any doubt which he could entertain in his own mind of the construction which would be given to it here. This was fully discussed during the passage of the act and well understood by him; but the eagerness of the British merchants in Nova Scotia and New Brunswick, and in some of our cities, to have the trade entirely to themselves, prompted them to expect that a different construction would be given to the act—a construction which would have left the word *elsewhere* without any effect or meaning at all. Mr. Chipman, acting as Governor of New Brunswick, issued a proclamation declaring that in that province no other or higher duties of tonnage or impost, and no other charges of any kind, are levied or exacted on vessels of the United States than upon British vessels, or upon the like goods, wares, and merchandise imported therein from *elsewhere;* but in this *elsewhere* the British territories in Europe and the West Indies were not included. They, according to him, were not *elsewhere* with reference to the *ports of the United States*, or, in other words, were ports of the United States. The Lieutenant Governor of Nova Scotia was more cautious. He transmitted to Mr. Canning statements from the officers of the customs showing that by the act of Parliament no other duties of impost or of tonnage were levied upon vessels of the United States at Halifax than upon *British* vessels; but even this, according to a document accompanying these statements, did not include vessels of the province itself. They, by a colonial law, are entitled to a deduction of two pence per ton from the tonnage duty payable by *British* vessels, according to which doctrine they are not British vessels themselves.

I have explicitly assured Mr. Canning that the proclamation of the President, authorized by the third section of the act of Congress of March 1, 1823, cannot be issued without a declaration pledging the faith of the British Government that, upon the vessels of the United States admitted into *all and every one of* the enumerated ports, and upon any goods, wares, or merchandise imported therein, in the said vessels, no other or higher duties of tonnage or impost, and no other charges of any kind, are levied or exacted than upon all British vessels, (including all vessels of the colonies themselves,) or upon the like goods, wares, or merchandise imported into the said colonial ports from *anywhere,* including Great Britain and the other British colonies themselves; and that, until such proof shall be given, British vessels and their cargoes coming from the colonies to the U_{nit}e_d States must continue to pay our foreign tonnage and ten per cent. additional impost duties. Notice of this has been given by Mr. Canning to the British consuls in a letter which has been published, and which you will find in one of the newspapers herewith sent— (National Intelligencer of May 29, 1823.)

By the respective regulations of the two countries the present condition of the trade is as follows:

The intercourse between the ports of the United States and the enumerated colonial ports is open to the vessels of both parties.

By the British regulations—

American vessels are admitted into the enumerated ports only *direct* from the United States. They are allowed to import only certain enumerated articles.

Upon all the important articles of this list a duty equivalent to ten per cent. ad valorem is imposed.

If they take return cargoes, they must give export bonds for landing them in the port or ports of the United States, for which *only* they can clear out.

And in most, if not all, of the West India colonies they pay an export duty of from four to five per cent. ad valorem.

British vessels are admitted into the enumerated ports and others without restriction. They may enter direct from the United States or from any other part of America, or from the British possessions in Europe.

They are allowed to import not only the enumerated articles but all others not entirely prohibited; and among the articles the exclusive carriage of which is reserved to them are articles of the first necessity to the colonies, and staple exports from the United States; on the important articles which, in common with the vessels of the United States, they may import direct from the United States, if they *do so* import them, the ten per cent. duty ad valorem must be paid. But they may import the like articles from Great Britain, or from the North American to the West India colonies, *duty free;* they are liable to no export bond; may trade between colony and colony; may export cargoes for any port of the British dominions in Europe or America, and pay no export duty, unless they choose to return to the United States.

By the American regulations—

British vessels from the enumerated ports are admitted, if laden, into the United States only with cargoes of colonial produce.

They are allowed to take return cargoes only *direct* to the enumerated ports.

They pay the foreign tonnage duty of ninety-four cents per ton, and the foreign ten per cent. additional impost on their cargoes.

American vessels may bring from the enumerated ports any articles the exportation of which from those ports is permitted by the British laws.

They are in no case compelled to return to the enumerated ports.

They are exempt from the foreign tonnage and additional impost duties.

It is impossible to take this comparative view of the respective exemptions and restrictions operating on the vessels of the two countries employed in the same trade without perceiving that the balance of advantage is highly in favor of the British and against the American navigation; and that the United States could not consent to equalize the tonnage and impost duties without surrendering the whole trade to the British shipping and defeating the object for which both our navigation acts of 1818 and 1820 were provided.

The act of Parliament (3 Geo. IV, ch. 44) of June 24, 1822, must also be considered in connexion with the act of August 5, 1822, (3 Geo. IV, ch., 119,) or Canada trade act. I inclose herewith a copy of a memorial to the President, from a committee of the freeholders and inhabitants of the county of Franklin and State of New York, exhibiting the severe pressure of this act upon the people of a very large portion of our Union. A similar memorial was presented to the House of Representatives at the late session of Congress, and a report thereon was made to the House by their Committee on Foreign. Relations, a copy of which is likewise inclosed.—(Document 96, House of Representatives United States, reports of committees, 17th Congress, 2d session.) The resolution recommended by the committee at the close of the report, requesting the President of the United States to obtain by negotiation with the Government of Great Britain such modifications of the act of Parliament of August 5, 1822, as may remove all just cause of complaint was adopted by the House.

The report of the committee discountenances the claim of the memorialists to the privileges to which they had supposed themselves to be entitled by the third article of the treaty of 1794; and it admits that there is in the act of Parliament nothing in their opinion repugnant to national law. But the committee remark that the act is highly detrimental to the interests of that portion of our citizens which it immediately affects—a measure *unexpected* and certainly inconsistent with that liberal spirit recently avowed by both Governments, in relation to their general commercial intercourse with each other, as well as repugnant to the course of conduct which both had tacitly pursued in relation to that particular commercial interest which it is intended specially to regulate.

You will see in the report of the committee a comparative view of the existing state of the trade before and until the act of Parliament of August 5, 1822, with that under which it now labors, and which so seriously affects the *immediate* interest of the people of six among the largest and most populous States of our Union and one Territory.

With regard to the *right* of that portion of our people to navigate the river St. Lawrence to and from the ocean, it has never yet been discussed between us and the British Government. I have little doubt that it may be established upon the sound and general principles of the law of nature; and if it has not been distinctly and explicitly asserted in negotiation with the British Government hitherto, it is because the benefits of it have been, as the committee remark, *tacitly* conceded, or because the *interest*, now become so great, and daily acquiring additional moment, has, it may almost be said, originated since the acknowledgment of our independence by the treaty of 1783.

The memorial from the committee of the inhabitants of Franklin county, New York, is perfectly correct when it asserts this right upon the principles asserted at the period when our right to the navigation of the Mississippi was in question; and so far as the right *by the law of nature* was maintained on the part of the United States in that case, so far is the Government of the United States bound to maintain for the people of the Territory of Michigan, and of the States of Illinois, Indiana, Ohio, Pennsylvania, New York, and Vermont, the natural right of communicating with the ocean by the only outlet provided by nature from the waters bordering upon their shores.

We know that the possession of both the shores of a river at its mouth has heretofore been held to give the right of obstructing or interdicting the navigation of it to the people of other nations inhabiting the banks of the river above the boundary of that in possession of its mouth. But the exclusive right of jurisdiction over a river originates in the social compact and is a right of sovereignty. The right of navigating the river is a right of nature preceding it in point of time, and which the sovereign right of one nation cannot annihilate as belonging to the people of another.

This principle has been substantially recognized by all the parties to the European alliance, and particularly by Great Britain at the negotiation of the Vienna Congress treaties. It is recognized by the stipulations of those treaties which declare the navigation of the Rhine, the Necker, the Mayne, the Moselle, the Maes, and the Scheldt, free to all nations. The object of those stipulations undoubtedly was to make the navigation of those rivers effectually free to all the people dwelling upon their banks, and to abolish all those unnatural and unjust restrictions by which the people of the interior of Germany had before that time been deprived of their natural outlet to the sea, by the abuse of that right of sovereignty which imputed an exclusive jurisdiction and property over a river to the State possessing both shores at its mouth. There is no principle of national law upon which those articles of the Vienna Congress treaties could be founded which will not apply to sustain the right of the people of this Union to navigate the St. Lawrence river to the ocean.

These ideas are suggested to you to be used, first, in conference with the British Minister of Foreign Affairs, and afterwards, if necessary, in correspondence with him. The manner and the time of presenting them will be best judged of by your discretion. By the two acts of Parliament of 3 Geo. IV, ch. 44 and 119, the navigation of the St. Lawrence from our territories to the ocean is, in fact, conceded to us; by the first, from the ocean to Quebec; and by the second, from any part of our territories to the same port. But a discretionary power is given to the colonial Governments in Canada to withdraw the latter of these concessions, by excepting any of the Canadian ports from those to which our vessels are, by the act, made admissible; and the duties imposed by the act upon all those of our exports which could render the trade profitable are *prohibitory*.

Throughout the whole course of these modifications of the old British navigation act of Charles II, offered us by the acts of Parliament of June 24 and August 5, 1822, the admission of our vessels to the British *West India* colonies has been presented to us, not only upon conditions excessively burdensome, but under a direct *menace* that, if we should not accept it upon the identical terms offered in those acts, *all* commercial intercourse between us and *all* the British colonies in this hemisphere would be prohibited by an order in council; and we have received frequent intimations that this power, reserved to the King by the act of June 24, would be exercised, if we should not immediately exempt British vessels employed in the trade from the foreign tonnage and additional impost duties, and place them in these respects on the same footing with our own. We have been, therefore, under the necessity of deciding upon our course of policy relating to this interest, upon a calculation of probability that the power would be exercised, and that the order of council would issue; and from a full and deliberate view of the subject, we have come to the conclusion that, however injurious that measure, if resorted to, would prove to us, it would still be less mischievous than the total abandonment of our defensive system of counteraction, established by our navigation acts of 1818 and 1820. We are also perfectly convinced that this would be the effect of our acceptance, unconditional, of the intercourse as prescribed by the act of Parliament of June 24, 1822, and particularly of releasing the British shipping employed in the trade from the foreign tonnage and impost duties. The act of Congress has provided that, if the British order prohibiting the trade and intercourse in our vessels with any of the enumerated ports, under the authority of the act of Parliament, should be issued, from the day of the date of the order in council, or from the time of its commencing to be in operation, our two navigation acts should revive and be in full force. This measure, on our part, is merely defensive; but we think we have some reason to complain, if not of harshness, at least of a proceeding somewhat peremptory in the *mode* of opening to us the West India colonial ports. They are opened to us, as I have shown, upon terms which we had effectually rejected in negotiation, and which we could not possibly accept without surrendering the whole navigation interest for which we have so long contended. They are opened to us, subject to a total interdiction of the commerce, at the discretion of the King, by an order in council, without an hour's notice to those of our citizens whose interest may be affected by it. There is also some obscurity in the phraseology of the 15th section of the act of Parliament of June 24, 1822, leaving us in doubt what the condition of our intercourse would be with any colony concerning which the prohibitory order in council might issue.

It says that, on the contingency prescribed, it shall be lawful for the King, by order in council, *to prohibit trade and intercourse under the authority of this act* with any country, &c.; and that if such order in council shall issue, "then, during the time that such order in council shall be in force, *none* of the provisions of *this act*, either as *respects* the laws herein *repealed* or TO any other provisions of this act, shall apply or be taken to apply to any country or State the trade with which, under the provisions of this act, shall be prohibited by any such order of his Majesty in council." But the provisions of this act, *as respects* the laws *repealed* in it, are no other than the *repeal* of them itself; and if by virtue of the prohibitory order in council *none* of the provisions of this act, *as respects* the laws *repealed* in it, shall apply, or be taken to apply, the conclusion would seem to be that those laws would not be repealed, that is, that they would again revive and be in force with regard to the country the trade with which, "under the authority of this act," should be prohibited by the order in council. But some of these laws repealed are laws *authorizing* trade and intercourse, in vessels of the United States, with the colonies of Nova Scotia, New Brunswick, Bermuda, and the Bahama islands; and if by the prohibitory order in council the provisions as respect those laws, in the act of 3 Geo. IV, ch. 44, should cease to apply, it would follow that the trade and intercourse under *them* would again be authorized, and its condition would be precisely the same as if that act of Parliament had not been made. All this would be very clear and unequivocal but for the remaining part of the paragraph in the same 15th section of the act, which says that, "if any goods whatever shall be imported from or shipped for the purpose of being exported to any such country or island in America or the West Indies, in any foreign ship or vessel, after trade and intercourse therewith shall have been prohibited by any such order of his Majesty in council, issued under the authority of this act," all such goods, with the ship or vessel, &c., shall be forfeited. Thus the provisions of the section appear to be contradictory to themselves, and leave us in doubt whether it was meant that the prohibitory order in council would revive and reinforce the free port acts repealed by the act of Parliament, or would operate as a total interdiction of trade and intercourse in our vessels with the interdicted colony.

You are authorized to renew to the British Government the proposal of continuing this intercourse in other respects on the footing upon which it is placed by the acts of Parliament and the act of Congress, but with a removal of the discriminating duties on both sides, and particularly that the duties in the schedule C of the act of Parliament of 3 Geo. IV, ch. 44, and in the schedule B of the act of 3 Geo. IV, ch. 119, on the part of Great Britain, and the foreign tonnage duty and additional impost upon British vessels from the enumerated ports, on the part of the United States, should be mutually repealed. If this proposal should be accepted, it may be carried into effect by an act of Parliament, upon the passage of which the President's proclamation would immediately be issued; or it may be agreed upon by a convention, which you are hereby authorized to sign and to transmit for ratification. A new full power is inclosed, to be used if required. The act of Parliament or the convention should be explicit in the removal of all discriminating duties and charges, whether imposed by Parliament or by colonial laws, and it should apply to *all* the enumerated ports. Should the offer be declined, you will receive any proposition which may be made in its stead, for reference to this Government.

I am, with great respect, sir, your most obedient servant,

JOHN QUINCY ADAMS.

Hon. RICHARD RUSH, *Envoy Extraordinary and Minister Plenipotentiary of the United States, London.*

Mr. Stratford Canning to Mr. Adams.

WASHINGTON, *March* 27, 1823.

The undersigned, his Britannic Majesty's Envoy Extraordinary and Minister Plenipotentiary, referring to the third section of an act of Congress approved March 1, 1823, and entitled "An act to regulate the commercial intercourse between the United States and certain British colonial ports," requests the American Secretary of State will do him the honor to afford him information of the exact *nature* and *scope* of the "proof" which is thereby required to enable the President to issue his proclamation for the repeal of the discriminating duties still levied on British vessels entering from such ports of his Majesty's colonies as are enumerated in the first section of the act.

The undersigned conceives that in his previous communications on this subject he has already furnished abundant and satisfactory evidence of the intention of his Majesty's Government, long since carried into effect, to place American vessels on the same footing with British in respect to the duties on import and tonnage under the expectation of a strict reciprocity on the part of the United States; but learning, from the printed circular addressed, on the 17th instant, to the Collectors by the Comptroller of the Treasury in explanation of the act approved on the 1st, and but recently brought to his knowledge, that no authority has yet been given to dispense with the collection of alien duties on British vessels arriving from his Majesty's colonies, the undersigned is desirous of knowing whether any, and what, further communication may be expected by the President under the act now in force as necessary to the execution of the third section, to the end that he may either at once remove any obstacle which it depends on him to remove, or have it in his power to apprise his Government of the real state of the case in this particular.

The undersigned requests the Secretary of State to accept the assurance of his high consideration.

STRATFORD CANNING.

Hon. JOHN QUINCY ADAMS, *Secretary of State.*

Mr. Adams to Mr. S. Canning.

DEPARTMENT OF STATE, *Washington, April* 8, 1823.

SIR: In answer to your note of the 27th ultimo, I have the honor of stating that any authentic declaration from your Government, communicated either through the minister of the United States in England, or through his Britannic Majesty's minister residing here, "that upon the vessels of the United States admitted into the enumerated British colonial ports, and upon any goods, wares, or merchandise imported therein in the said vessels, no other or higher duties of tonnage or impost, and no other charges of any kind are levied or exacted than upon British vessels or upon the like goods, wares, and merchandise imported into the said colonial ports from *elsewhere*," will be received by the President of the United States as the satisfactory proof required by the act to authorize him to issue his proclamation extending the reciprocal privileges offered in the same third section to British vessels and their cargoes coming from the enumerated ports to the United States.

In the communications hitherto received from you on this subject, although *"the intention* of his Majesty's Government to place American *vessels* on the same footing with British in respect to the *duties* on impost and tonnage" has been sufficiently manifested, they have fallen short of the proof required by the section of the act of Congress now referred to, inasmuch as they have not averred either that no other or higher duties are levied in the enumerated ports upon the goods, wares, or merchandise imported therein in American vessels than upon the like articles imported from *elsewhere*, or that no other *charges* of any kind are levied upon the vessels of the United States and their cargoes than upon British vessels and their cargoes; or finally, that the *intention* of your Government, even in its most limited purport, has been *long since carried into effect* in all the enumerated ports.

The act of Congress requires that the reciprocity of *burdens* and *exemptions* should extend not only to the vessels but to the articles imported in them. This has not hitherto been affirmed by you to be the intention of your Government. It is not doubted that their intention has been to equalize the charges, but it appears that in some of the enumerated ports discriminating duties have continued to be levied to a very recent date; and express information has but a few days since been received at this Department that a tonnage duty of two shillings and sixpence sterling, imposed by act of Parliament of 28 George III, continued to be levied upon all vessels of the United States, at Turk's Island, until the 23d of December last, several months after your communications claiming, even before the meeting of Congress, a total removal of discriminating duties upon British vessels from the enumerated ports, on the ground that American vessels were admitted upon the same terms with British vessels into them.

The act of Parliament of 3 George IV, chapter 44, appears to have given rise in several of the enumerated ports to questions with regard to its construction, and not to have received in all the same solution. As an experiment, to open an intercourse before interdicted by the laws both of Great Britain and the United States, its *intention* was received by this Government with a cordial welcome and a sincere disposition to meet it in the spirit of conciliation and of real reciprocity. But for the regulation of the intercourse, as the consent of both parties was indispensable, so it was just and necessary that the interests of both parties, as understood by themselves, should be consulted. It seems obvious that this could not be accomplished by mere legislation of either party. An arrangement by mutual understanding and concert was proposed by this Government immediately after the act of Parliament of June 24 was made known here. Whatever is yet known of the operation of that act, and of the system of which it forms a part, has contributed to fortify this impression. An act of Parliament of August 5, 1822, (3 George IV, chapter 119,) in particular, already bears upon the intercourse between an important portion of this Union and the contiguous British provinces with a pressure which has excited the attention of Congress, and which a resolution of the House of Representatives at their last session recommends to the Executive of the Union as a subject for immediate negotiation with Great Britain. I am directed by the President of the United States to make the proposal, and to request that you would make your Government acquainted with it. Should it prove acceptable, I shall be happy to confer with you upon it, with the view to the conclusion of a convention; or if your Government should prefer to treat of it in England, the powers and instructions necessary for the purpose may be transmitted to the minister of the United States at London.

I pray you, sir, to accept the assurance of my distinguished consideration.

JOHN QUINCY ADAMS.

Right Hon. STRATFORD CANNING,
    Envoy Extraordinary and Minister Plenipotentiary from Great Britain.

Mr. Stratford Canning to Mr. Adams.

WASHINGTON, *April* 10, 1823.

SIR: The declaration which you describe in your letter of the 8th instant as requisite to authorize the President of the United States to issue his proclamation for the removal of all alien charges at present exacted on British vessels and their cargoes, arriving from his Majesty's colonies, I am ready to give, in so far as regards the corresponding condition of the act of Congress, an extract of the third section of which you have done me the honor to communicate. British and American vessels entering the colonial ports, under the act of Parliament passed June 24, are subject to equal charges on every article imported under that act, whether in American or in British vessels, the same if any and no other charges are levied. With respect to the succeeding clause of the same section, cited in your letter, relative to duties levied "upon the like goods, wares, and merchandise imported into the said colonial ports *from elsewhere*," I must request that you will have the goodness to inform me of the precise meaning attached to the expression which I have underlined, as, in strictness of construction, these words seem capable of bearing a sense completely at variance with a principal provision of the above mentioned act of Parliament, and one which it is therefore wholly out of my power to include in the proposed declaration. I might, perhaps, presume that the term *elsewhere* was only meant to signify other places not belonging to Great Britain in America and the West Indies; but the bare possibility of a more comprehensive signification being attached to it makes me desirous of ascertaining from you, in the first instance, whether I am right in giving it exclusively that interpretation; or, if not, in what more ample sense it is to be understood.

In answer to my previous representations on this subject, whether addressed to you before or during the late session of Congress, you informed me that the President was not at liberty to withdraw the discriminating duties on imports and tonnage, to which alone I adverted, in consequence of his not having received from Congress the authority necessary for that purpose. In proof, however, that the intention of his Majesty's Government, long since communicated to you, has also been long since carried into effect, I have only to mention that a circular instruction, a copy of which is at this moment before me, was issued as early as the third of July from the custom-house in London to the Collectors and Comptrollers of the Customs in his Majesty's colonial ports, directing them "not to charge any higher fees whatever, in respect of the trade allowed by the said act to be carried on in foreign vessels, than are now payable thereon in British vessels,"

By what authority the tonnage duty of two shillings and sixpence, mentioned in your last letter, can possibly have been collected at Turk's Island so late as December 23 I am wholly at a loss to conceive, as, besides the operation of the custom-house circular, the act of Parliament under which you state that duty to have been levied was expressly repealed during the last session.

The remaining part of your letter must necessarily be left to the consideration of his Majesty's Government. It only occurs to me at this moment to submit whether some more definite statement of the points on which you have expressed the President's desire to negotiate might not be attended with the advantage of leading to an earlier and more satisfactory decision respecting that proposal.

I avail myself of this opportunity to repeat to you, sir, the assurance of my perfect consideration.

STRATFORD CANNING.

Hon. JOHN QUINCY ADAMS, *Secretary of State.*

Mr. Adams to Mr. S. Canning.

DEPARTMENT OF STATE, *Washington, May* 14, 1823.

SIR: I have the honor of informing you that, by the third section of the act of Congress of the 1st of March last "to regulate the commercial intercourse between the United States and certain British colonial ports," the term *elsewhere* is understood to be of meaning equivalent to *anywhere else*, and, of course, to include all places other than those from which the importations into those ports may be made in vessels of the United States.

The views of this Government with regard to a regulation of this intercourse in future by a convention, or by further concert between the two Governments, will, at an early day, be transmitted by the instructions to the minister of the United States at London.

In the meantime, it is to be observed that the circular instructions, referred to in your letter of the 10th of last month as having issued on the 3d of July last from the custom-house in London to the Collectors and Comptrollers of the Customs in his Majesty's colonial ports, directing them "not to charge any higher *fees* whatever, in respect of the trade allowed by the said act to be carried on in foreign vessels, than are now payable thereon in British vessels," did not, as, by the import of the terms it would seem that they could not, remove any existing discriminating duties or charges other than the mere *fees* of the officers to whom they were addressed.

That other charges and even *duties* discriminating to the disadvantage of the vessels of the United States have continued to be levied in several of the enumerated ports until a late period has been already shown; and, by the papers which you had the goodness to submit to my inspection only three days since, it appears that a discriminating tonnage duty is still levied upon the vessels of the United States in the ports of Nova Scotia equal to two-thirds of the whole tonnage duty which is paid in our ports by those British vessels which are admitted upon the same footing with our own.

I pray you, sir, to accept the assurance of my distinguished consideration.

JOHN QUINCY ADAMS.

Right Hon. STRATFORD CANNING,
    Envoy Extraordinary and Minister Plenipotentiary from Great Britain.

Mr. S. Canning to Mr. Adams.

WASHINGTON, *May* 17, 1823.

SIR: In acknowledging your letter of the 14th instant, which I had the honor to receive the day before yesterday, I must be allowed to express my regret at finding that the declaration expected by the American Government as a condition of the removal on their part of alien charges from British vessels entering the ports of the United States from certain of his Majesty's possessions in North America and the West Indies is meant to extend beyond the cessation of corresponding charges, as they affect the vessels of the United States in the open ports of the British colonies, the term *elsewhere*, in the third section of the act of Congress to which you refer, being intended, as I understood from your letter, to include even the British territories.

Such being the intention of the act, it is vain, for the present, to enter upon any discussion of the question which it involves, and it is altogether unnecessary to dwell upon the other points to which you have adverted, as this alone precludes, and necessarily precludes, my giving in a declaration such as would prove satisfactory to the President.

Suffice it on this occasion to observe, that the discriminating tonnage duty, which you described as being still levied on the vessels of the United States in harbors of Nova Scotia, appears, from the papers which you cite, to be levied on the vessels of Great Britain also; and, further, that the limited acceptation in which you seem to understand the circular instruction issued from the custom-house in London, under date of the 3d of July last, is completely at variance with the statement which I had the honor to communicate to you as long ago as the 18th of December, on the authority of a letter dated the 21st of October, from the Collector of the Customs at Kingston, in Jamaica.

I request, sir, that you will again accept the assurance of my high consideration.

STRATFORD CANNING.

No. 66.

Mr. Adams to Mr. Rush.

DEPARTMENT OF STATE, *Washington, June* 25, 1823.

SIR: Next to the colonial intercourse and the suppression of the slave trade, the subject upon which I am to invite your attention is the disagreement between the Commissioners under the 5th article of the treaty of Ghent. The authority and duty of that commission was—

1. To ascertain the northwest angle of Nova Scotia.

2. To ascertain the northwesternmost head of Connecticut river.

3. To survey the boundary line from the source of the river St. Croix directly north to the northwest angle of Nova Scotia; thence along the highlands which divide those rivers that empty themselves into the river *St. Lawrence* from those which fall into the *Atlantic Ocean* to the northwesternmost head of Connecticut river; thence down along the middle of that river to the 45th degree of north latitude; thence by a line due west on said latitude until it strikes the river Iroquois or Cataraguy.

4. To make a map of the said boundary, and annex to it a declaration under their hands and seals, certify it to be the true map of the said boundary, and particularizing the latitude and longitude of the northwest angle of Nova Scotia, of the northwesternmost head of Connecticut river, and of such other points of the said boundary as they might deem proper. And both parties to the treaty agreed to consider such map and declaration as finally and conclusively fixing the said boundary.

The treaty of Ghent further provided, that, in the event of the two Commissioners differing upon *all* or *any* of the matters so referred to them, they shall make, jointly or separately, report or reports to the two Governments, stating in detail the points on which they differ, and the grounds upon which their respective opinions have been formed. And the parties to the treaty agreed to *refer the report or reports* of the said Commissioners to some friendly sovereign to be then named for that purpose, and *who shall be requested to decide on the differences which may be stated in the said report or reports.* And his Britannic Majesty and the Government of the United States engaged to consider the decision of such friendly sovereign or State to be final and conclusive on all the matters so referred.

The two Commissioners, both sworn to examine and decide *impartially* upon all the points referred to them, after six years of meetings, examinations, and surveys, assisted by able surveyors, geographers, astronomers, and agents of both parties, have differed—

1. Upon the point where the northwest angle of Nova Scotia is.

2. Upon what is the northwesternmost head of Connecticut river.

3. Upon the meaning of the words "along the highlands which divide those rivers that empty themselves into the *river St. Lawrence* from those which fall into the Atlantic Ocean."

4. Upon the admission of the general maps respectively presented by the agents of the two Governments, each objecting to the correctness of that presented by the other, and pressing for the reception of his own.

5. Upon a proposal by the British Commissioner to send out surveyors to ascertain the correctness of the former surveys in regard to the points objected to in the maps presented by the agents.

6. Upon a demand made by the British agent to examine upon oath the surveyors who made the maps, with regard to their correctness.

7. Upon the reception and entering upon the journals of a memorial of the British agent, containing a statement of one of the British surveyors relating to the maps presented by the agents.

8. Upon the reception of a written motion by the British agent, requesting leave to exhibit a memorial containing statements of the British surveyors relating to the maps, and that the same might be entered on the journals.

There is, therefore, no *map* of the said boundary, under the hands and seals of the Commissioners certifying it to be the true map, and particularizing the latitude and longitude of the northwest angle of Nova Scotia, or of the northwesternmost head of Connecticut river. The essential object of the commission was to ascertain those two points; and the only object of interest to the two nations which could possibly be obtained by the reference to a friendly sovereign to decide on the differences stated in the reports of the Commissioners would be to ascertain them by his decision.

The Commissioners differed upon other points, and from their reports, separately made, there appears to be less of harmony and concert in their operations than was to have been desired. There is a tone of mutual dissatisfaction and complaints in the reports, and some imputations of uncandid attempts in the surveyors and agents on both sides to overreach each other in the surveys and projection of the maps.

The difference between the Commissioners with regard to the northwest angle of Nova Scotia is of more than one hundred miles, and embraces a territory of more than ten thousand square miles. As the Commissioners could not agree upon either of the two points to be ascertained, it became impossible for them to agree upon the map and declaration which it was stipulated by the treaty should finally and conclusively fix the boundary. There is no such map, and the general map produced by each side is totally discredited by the other.

There was an astronomical survey of the 45th parallel of north latitude from the Connecticut river to the river Iroquois or Cataraguy, (viz: the St. Lawrence.) Of the accuracy of the survey itself there are some doubts; but its effect has been to *unsettle* a boundary which had been already fixed upon surveys made, by order of the British Government, just before the commencement of the American Revolution. The difference between the two lines is trifling in extent, but it cuts off a point of considerable importance to the State of New York, at Lake Champlain, and expensive fortifications erected upon it.

The principal astronomers on both sides who made this survey were both foreigners, both natives of Switzerland, countrymen and friends. Mr. Hasler, who was employed by the American Government, expressed an opinion that the survey of the 45th parallel of latitude should be made with allowance for the elliptical figure of the earth; or, as he terms it, the geocentric latitude. The agent of the United States presents this as a question for the consideration of the commissioners: *If the ancient established line is to be unsettled?* Upon which the British agent makes large extracts from *Vattel* about *mental reservations, gross quibbles*, a *real* piece of *knavery*, a *real perfidy*, and the like, all which the British Commissioner details at full length in his report; while, on the other hand, this very British agent himself labors under a heavy imputation of having filed a falsified copy of Mitchell's map to aid him in another point of his argument—a procedure which the British Commissioner thinks quite uncensurable, inasmuch as when this error was detected the agent obtained leave to file another and more correct copy of the map.

The American Commissioner did not think it necessary to give an opinion upon this survey, the reason assigned by him for which is, that as there was a disagreement about the two main points of the whole boundary line, the surveys became useless as to the purpose of fixing it. But the British Commissioner gives his opinion upon the whole line, refers to the map of the British surveyors as if it were admitted to to be correct, and adopts all the arguments of the British agent as conclusive. Under this state of things it became a serious question for the two governments, *What is there to refer* to the decision of a friendly sovereign, conformably to the stipulation of the treaty? and, subordinate to it, the questions further arise, *how* and to *whom* it shall be referred?

The contingent reference to a friendly sovereign of this and of other questions was an experiment first proposed at the negotiation of the Ghent treaty by the plenipotentiaries on the part of Great Britain, instead of a commission of *three* members, which had been proposed on the part of the United States, the decision of a *majority* of which that proposal had intended should be final. The British substitute was accepted as an alternative, to the execution of which no immediate objection presented itself, and was agreed to without discussion. A question, which afterwards arose upon the construction of a few words in the first article of that treaty, has already been referred to the decision of a friendly sovereign, and the result of that reference is yet to be awaited.

From the moment when it became necessary to give practical effect to this new expedient for adjusting differences of national interest and importance, difficulties arose which had not been anticipated in the distant contemplation of a project, the broad and principal idea of which was, that of reference to an impartial arbitrator. It became obvious that if a question of no greater compass than the grammatical meaning of a few words in an article of a treaty might be referred to the personal decision of a foreign sovereign, without too severely taxing his patience or his friendship, it would scarcely be within the bounds of respectful decency to *ask a foreign* sovereign to pronounce between two such nations as Great Britain and the United States, upon differences between them involving a boundary line of at least six hundred miles extent, through a half discovered region, the topography of which was unknown, and which Commissioners of their own, aided by surveyors, geographers, astronomers, and agents, after years upon years of labor and investigation devoted entirely to that object, had not been able to settle. My impressions upon this subject were communicated to you, even at the threshold of the negotiation for the convention of October 20, 1818; and if nothing else had occurred to confirm them, the incident which has brought us to the necessity of acting upon the *disagreement* between the Commissioners under this 5th article of the treaty would have sufficed. What have we now to refer for decision? We are to ask a foreign sovereign to decide—

1. Where is the northwest angle of *Nova Scotia?*
2. What is the northwesternmost head of Connecticut river?
3. Where is the range of highlands that divide the rivers that flow into the St. Lawrence from those that flow into the Atlantic Ocean?
4. What point upon Connecticut river is the forty-fifth degree of north latitude?
5. Where a line due west from that point will strike the St. Lawrence river?

Incidental to these questions are others, embracing the construction of ancient charters, treaties, and royal proclamations—controversies between France and England before the cession of Canada to Great Britain—questions of theoretical geography and astronomy; and, finally, a choice between two maps, each discredited by one of the Commissioners under whose directions they were taken. The arbitrator must, in the first place, assume one of these maps, to the exclusion of the other. Upon the map assumed he must trace the boundary line of at least six hundred miles extent. He must mark upon it the points in dispute: the northwest angle of Nova Scotia, the range of highlands, the northwesternmost head of Connecticut river, and the 45th parallel of latitude between the Connecticut and St. Lawrence rivers. The decision will, after all, be only upon the map, and not upon the territory; and the map of each party being declared by the other utterly incorrect, if the map on which the boundary must be drawn should prove so, will it not leave the question between the two countries more unsettled than ever?

It cannot be the desire of the parties, nor cannot be imagined, without disrespect to the arbitrator, that he would decide all these questions without understanding their merits. There are upwards of thirty folio volumes of manuscripts, all in the English language, containing the journals of the Commissioners, the proceedings of the surveyors and geographers, the observations and calculations of the astronomers, and the arguments of the agents. The *report* of the British Commissioner is a volume of about five hundred pages, closely written, and there are three atlases or collections of maps, filed before the Commissioners during the discussion, besides the two general maps not admitted by the Commissioners, but upon one of which, if the arbitrator decides at all, he must trace the boundary line in question.

Is there a sovereign upon earth of whom it could be reasonably requested that he would devote the time and take upon him the labor indispensable to inform himself of the merits of all those disputed questions; and if there be, is it not morally certain that upon examining them, as presented by the reports of the two Commissioners, questions must arise in his own mind which could be resolved only by evidence not before him, or upon discussion by the parties? No man worthy of being selected by two nations as the umpire of a difference between them would consent to assume the office without a deep sense of the duties which it would impose upon him; and if, at the first presentation of this reference, the sovereign to whom it would be made should not immediately perceive the laborious examination which it would require of him, he could not fail to be made sensible of it upon entering into the inquiries necessary for the performance of the duty; the result of which, I apprehend, must necessarily be that he would decline a task to the performance of which he must be conscious of his own incompetency.

It was on these and the like considerations that, when the disagreement between the Commissioners under the fifth article of the treaty of Ghent was first known, a proposition was made, by direction of the President, to the British Government, that, before resorting to the reference stipulated by that article, an effort should be made by direct communication between the two Governments to adjust it between themselves. By your despatch of February 11, 1822, we were informed that this proposition had been offered by you to the late Marquis of Londonderry, and by that of April 6, 1822, you announced that it had been formally acceded to. From that time we had been in expectation that the British minister residing here would have been empowered to treat upon the subject with us; but the decease of Lord Londonderry having happened soon after, and a consequent change in the British Department of Foreign Affairs, we had supposed that those circumstances had occasioned a delay in the transmission of the powers until

Mr. S. Canning recently gave us notice that he had received instructions to propose an immediate reference of the case for the decision of a friendly sovereign, according to the stipulation of the treaty, and called upon us to nominate the sovereign to whom we should incline to make the reference. There has been much conversation between us on the subject, in which the difficulties necessarily incident to such a reference have again been adverted to, and the proposal itself, as now presented, has been noticed as unexpected. Mr. S. Canning appears to entertain the idea that the British Government, by acceding to the proposals of attempting an adjustment by direct communications, did not intend to pledge themselves to negotiate, but merely to receive from us and consider a direct and specific offer of a boundary line by compromise—a measure for which, had there been no other obstacles in the way, we could not be prepared, on account of the disagreement respecting the maps and surveys, and for which, from that and other causes, we are yet unprepared. Mr. Canning, however, now on the point of departure under a leave of absence, supposed that his Government, upon being reminded of their agreement, as notified in your despatch of April 6, 1822, will still consent either to treat for a boundary by compromise, or to receive and consider a distinct proposal of a line to be offered by us. I have admitted that, if they should agree to treat, we should be expected to propose a line, but have objected to make the proposal, under the uncertainty whether it would be received on the principle of negotiating, or merely as an offer to be accepted or rejected at the option of Great Britain. The President directs that, on receiving this despatch, you shall candidly communicate to the British Government his desire that the further prosecution of this affair should be by direct negotiation between the parties without reference to any foreign sovereign, and that an article to that effect should be introduced into the convention which you are to propose. You will fairly exhibit the reasons, founded upon the nature of the questions to be determined, and upon the state in which they are presented, by the reports of the Commissioners and the record of their proceedings under the commission, for the belief that it would be *impossible for any* foreign arbitrator, on the documents which could now be laid before him, to decide them. The extent of his power and of his office would be to fix a boundary line in various directions, and of six hundred miles extent, upon the surface of the earth, by delineating it upon a map; and the parties who ask him to do this for them furnish him a library of books and documents and three atlases of maps to examine and study, but among them not one map upon which he could, with any safety to his own judgment, or any chance of giving satisfaction to the parties, draw the delineation. You will add, that the Government of the United States feel some repugnance, in which repugnance they trust to the delicacy of sentiment of the British Government for taking their own share, at the idea of submitting such questions, in such a state, to the decision of a third party; or, in other words, of uncovering their common nakedness to the eyes of a common friend. Mutual imputations of bad faith, of falsification of documents, of *knavery*, and of *perfidy*, between the persons upon whose testimony the arbitrator must decide—in fact, the whole of that testimony—could scarcely fail of communicating their infection to the decision itself. If the British Secretary of State, after giving a full examination to the reports of the two Commissioners, with their necessary references to the maps, will undertake to prepare a *statement of the case to be submitted to the arbitrator*, it is not to be doubted that he will be sensible of the difficulties here suggested. If the British Cabinet should agree to negotiate, you will observe that the difficulty with regard to the map upon which the line shall be delineated presents an obstacle to be removed before a specific proposal of a line can be made. The Commissioners made no map, as by the commission they were required to do; and, without entering upon the inquiry upon whom the blame should fall for having left this part of their commission unexecuted, or whether blame attach to it at all, the result is, that neither the parties nor the contingent arbitrator can, in the present state of things, have a map upon which to delineate the boundary. Neither of the two general maps used by the agents for the illustration of their respective arguments is recognized by the Commissioners. They are both *ex parte* documents, acknowledged on both sides to be very incorrect, and each too obviously projected with more direct reference to the *claims* of the parties than to the territory of which they should be the portraiture.

The first thing which would seem to be indispensable to the settlement of this difference is the *verification* of the maps, or rather their correspondence with the territory upon which the line is to be drawn. Should the British Government entertain a different opinion, you will inquire *what* map they propose to use, either for fixing the line by agreement, or for the submission of it to the arbitrator? We cannot acquiesce in the use of the map offered by the British agent, for the account of the manner in which it was taken, given by Mr. Odell himself, who made it, is sufficient to destroy all our confidence in it. Yet the decision of the British Commissioner refers directly and explicitly to this map, which is not even part of the *evidence* reported by the commission. If the British Government are willing that both the maps should be received as if they had both been reported without objection by the commission, we are willing to waive all objections to them, and to propose a line, which, referring to local positions known and ascertained on the territory, shall be traceable on both the maps without danger of impairing the rights of the parties upon the land itself by the fictitious features of its picture upon paper. But either the two maps must be admitted as of equal authority, or we must insist on the objection to the use of either in forming the final decision upon the question, or in drawing the definitive boundary line. For the purposes of compromise, both the maps may be used without danger of error or injustice. For decision by an arbitration, neither of them would be admissible.

Should negotiation be agreed to, it is desirable that it should be transacted in this country; and you will propose that the British Government should furnish their minister here, or such other person as they may think proper to charge with the trust, with a power adequate to the purpose. The reasons for this are, that all the documents and maps reported by the commission are here, and could not, without some risk of loss, be transported beyond sea. Another copy of them is, indeed, in England, and might, with the assent of the British Government, be used by you in the management of the business there; but the territory upon which the line is to be settled is in this country, and all the interests immediately affected by it are here. It concerns the territorial rights and possessions of five or six States of this Union, whose inhabitants and authorities must so far be consulted as to insure the ratification, by and with the advice and consent of the Senate of the United States, of the arrangement which may be concluded. This could be effected here with much less difficulty and loss of time than if the negotiation should be pursued in England. If, however, the British Government should decline negotiation, and insist upon resorting to the arbitration stipulated by the treaty, there remains the question, *to whom* and *in what manner* the case shall be submitted? I have already named to Mr. Canning the Emperor of Russia, as the sovereign whom we shall, on that contingency, propose; and you are authorized to repeat the nomination. Mr. Canning appeared to believe there might be some inconvenience in this, from the pendency of a prior reference to the same sovereign and an unwillingness to overburden him with the solicitation of a second friendly office, for the mere accommodation of the parties, and in which his own empire has no interest. He adverted to the fact that this had already been suggested on our part; and it really formed one of our motives for a preference of negotiation rather than a recurrence to any arbitrator. Mr. Canning, without naming any, has given me to understand that the King of the Netherlands would be agreeable to his Government. But the relations of that prince with great Britain are so intimate, and his obligations to the British Government so great, that, with whatever impartiality he might form his decision, it would, if favorable to Great Britain, be attributed, in the public opinion here, to a pre-existing bias, and give as much dissatisfaction as if the decision should be left to Great Britain herself. Excepting the Emperor of Russia, the only European sovereign who, by his general position, appears to be independent, and so disconnected otherwise with the parties as to promise entire impartiality, is the King of Prussia; and to him, if he should be proposed, you are authorized ultimately to assent.

The *manner* of submitting the case to the arbitrator, if that should be insisted on, is lastly to be considered. From the nature and the number of the questions to be determined, it cannot be expected that *any* sovereign would undertake personally to examine and investigate them in the detail necessary for coming to a decision upon their merits. In the case of the former reference to the Emperor of Russia, you will recollect, there was a *statement of the case*, drawn up by agreement between Mr. Middleton and Lord Castlereagh, and presented concurrently in memorials by Sir Charles Bagot and Mr. Middleton to the Russian ministry. A question of more simplicity could scarcely be presented for solution than that. But now, if the reference is to be made, you will request that a *statement of the case*, such as the British Government will agree to exhibit to the referee or arbitrator, should be drawn up and presented to us for consideration. I would readily send you such a *statement* as we could agree to, were it not from a conviction that we *could* draw none up to which the British Government would agree. To take the first and most important question : The location of the *northwest angle of Nova Scotia*. It is described in the treaty of 1783 as "that angle which is formed by a line drawn due north from the source of St. Croix river to the highlands; along the said highlands, which divide those rivers that empty themselves into the river St. Lawrence from those which fall into the Atlantic Ocean, to the northwesternmost head of Connecticut river." The map used by the negotiators of the treaty of 1783 was one which, in the year 1755, had been published under the authority of the British Government and the direction of Governor Pownall. From the name of the publisher, it is called Mitchell's map. The northwest angle of Nova Scotia and the range of highlands described in the article of the treaty are very distinctly laid down upon this map; and the boundary line itself is marked on the copy of it used by the negotiators of the treaty now in our possession. Yet the report of the British Commissioner decides this angle and range of highlands to be upwards of one hundred miles distant from their location upon Mitchell's map, and in directions where, until this commission, it is believed there was never suspected to be any range of highlands at all. In support of this decision, the Commissioner refers to an *ex parte* map used by the British agent in support of his argument, but not admitted to be filed nor reported by the commission. The range of highlands delineated on this map is believed by the American Commissioner to have no existence in nature; and the same opinion appears to be entertained by the British Commissioner of the range delineated on the map exhibited by the American agent, which, however, is at least countenanced by Mitchell's map.

In drawing up the statement to which we should be willing to agree, we should necessarily refer either to the general map, exhibited by the agent of the United States before the Commissioners, or to Mitchell's map, the same that was used by the negotiators of the treaty of 1783. But will the British Government be willing to acquiesce in a statement of the case, for the decision of the arbitrator, which shall refer to either of them? The British Commissioner refused to admit upon the files the map exhibited by our agent, and certainly with sufficient reason, according to his views; for the bare inspection of it would have shown the absurdity of his report. But the same objection would exist against the very map used by the negotiators of the treaty of 1783, and with reference to which the boundary line in question was by them described. I have therefore thought it would be altogether useless to prepare a statement, which would probably not be accepted; and in desiring that the specific proposal of the statement to be submitted should come from Great Britain, I would exclude the consideration of nothing which should admit of reference to *all* the maps, though we can in nowise consent to a submission which should refer specially to the British map not reported by the commission.

The question concerning the northwesternmost head of Connecticut river, and the forty-fifth parallel of latitude from the Connecticut to the St. Lawrence, do not depend so much upon the accuracy of the maps. But, besides the scientific question of the geocentric latitude, the survey of the line itself was not made in a satisfactory manner; and whether that survey shall be taken into consideration at all, or whether the old line of the survey of 1772 shall not be adhered to as definitive, is one of the points to be decided by the arbitrator. The appalling mass of argument and discussion upon all these topics, contained in the many volumes of documents reported by the Commissioners, and constantly referred to in their reports, carries with it a moral certainty that no sovereign would undertake the investigation of them in person. We think it could not even respectfully be *proposed* to any one that he should. This investigation must be made, if at all, by delegated authority; by a person or persons *commissioned* by the arbitrator sovereign to report to him a decision founded upon a deliberate examination of facts and arguments, and explanatory comments from the parties, to which decision the sovereign would be required only to give his approbation and sanction. The simplest course we can imagine would be, that the minister of the arbitrator residing here should be charged by him to make such a report, and you will accordingly make the proposal, in the event that the reference should still be claimed by the British Government as a right. But whatever arrangement is finally determined upon, the difficulty respecting the maps must first be removed. We are, on our part, exceedingly anxious to bring this difference to a termination; but the effect of the commission has unfortunately been to make it infinitely more difficult to settle than it was before. The report of the British Commissioner is a labored attempt to support a system of the British agent, in which ingenuity maintains an endless argument against common sense. They have removed mountains from their position upon the earth, to locate them where it suited their purposes that they should stand, and the result, if submitted to by us, would be to take off from the State of Maine one-third part of its territory. By objecting to the general map exhibited by our agent, the British Commissioner compelled ours to take the same objection against that exhibited by the British agent, and the consequence is, that the *only* evidence, without which no decision can be made, is excluded from the report. Whether this was the design of the British Commissioner or not, to him alone must it be imputed; and the manner in which he took the exception, as well as the absence of all substantial reason for his refusal to submit for the decision of the arbitrator evidence of the validity of which the arbitrator would have been the judge, while he insisted on the exclusive submission of the *ex parte* map produced by the agent of his own Government manifests an eagerness for advantages in the submission which we cannot consent to indulge. We do not mean to complain of his conduct; but we must ask the British Government to inform us how they propose to supply the chasm in the evidence, essential to the decision of the dispute, occasioned by the exclusion of both the general maps which were exhibited to the commission ?

We cannot but hope that the British Government will consent to settle the affair by direct negotiation, and that at all events they will admit the use of *all* the maps, without insisting upon any exclusive privilege for their own.

I am, with great respect, sir, your most obedient servant,

JOHN QUINCY ADAMS.

Hon. RICHARD RUSH. *Envoy Extraordinary and*
    Minister Plenipotentiary of the United States to Great Britain.

No. 67.

Mr. Adams to Mr. Rush.

DEPARTMENT OF STATE, *Washington, June 26, 1823.*

SIR: Upon the subject of the admission of consuls of the United States into the ports of the British colonies which have been opened by the British acts of Parliament of June 24, 1822, to a commercial intercourse with the United States in the vessels of the latter, it appears by the note of Mr. S. Canning to you, 29th November last, a copy of which was transmitted with your despatch No. 281, that the British Government have consented to receive consuls at one port of the island of Jamaica, at one of the Leeward Islands, to be designated by the Government of the United States, and at one port in the North American colonies, with an assurance that the British Government will reconsider the proposition which had been made by you, that consuls should be admissible at *all* the ports opened to the intercourse, if any practical inconvenience should be shown on the part of the United States to the limitation of the number of their consuls to three for all the ports opened by the act of Parliament.

During the last session of Congress, consuls were appointed, by and with the advice and consent of the Senate, for the islands of Jamaica and of St. Christopher, and for the colony of Demarara. The commissions for the consuls at St. Christopher and at Demarara are the only ones that have yet been issued. It was perfectly proper that your note claiming the admission of consuls into the enumerated ports should extend the claim equally to them all; but in advancing this claim it was not the intention nor is it the desire of this Government to make appointments for them all. Our consular system, as you are aware, allows no salaries to those officers, and their only emoluments arise from fees, levied upon actual trade, in the port where they reside. No appointment will, therefore, be made at any port where the services of the officer will not be needed. The person appointed as consul at Jamaica has declined accepting the office, and another appointment will shortly be made for that island. A certificate of consular commercial agency has been given to John M. Kankey for the island of Barbadoes. At the next session of Congress the President proposes to nominate the same or another person to the Senate as *consul* for that island, which is one of those where there will probably be the most occasion for the office. You will give notice of these circumstances to the British Government, and request that instructions may be sent to the Governor of Barbadoes to allow the exercise of the ordinary consular functions to Mr. Kankey until the regular appointment of a consul; and that when a person so appointed shall present himself, with a commission, the Governor be authorized to recognize him in that capacity. The suggestion in Mr. Canning's note, that the admission of consuls of the United States into the colonial ports is not considered by the British Government as a matter of mere reciprocity, because American consuls are received in all ports of Great Britain, and the United States have no colonies of their own, where a practical reciprocity could be exercised, as you have observed, admits of an easy answer. The essential object of the consular office is the protection of the commerce, merchants, and mariners, of one nation in the ports of another. Wherever the commercial intercourse exists, the services of the consular office may be required; and if British merchants and mariners, coming from the colonies in the prosecution of the trade open to both nations, can avail themselves of the services of the British consuls in the ports to which they come, we think it would be an entire denial of reciprocity to say that our merchants and seamen pursuing the same trade, and going to the ports of the same colonies, should be refused the benefit of like protection from consuls of their own country there. If a British trader from Jamaica can claim and receive protection from a British consul at New York, it is needless to say there would be no reciprocity to the American trader to Jamaica who should there be told that he might claim the protection of the American consul at Liverpool.

It is presumed there will be no occasion for *discussing* this point with the British Government, and I have made the above remarks only to guard against the inference that our claim to the admission of consuls into the opened colonial ports rests upon other grounds than *mere reciprocity.* But in the negotiation of a convention it may be proper to propose, at least, an article prescribing the *manner* in which the exequatur shall be furnished to consuls generally. That they shall be delivered to them *gratis* we have a right of strict reciprocity to claim, because they are so delivered to all British consuls in the United States. With this addition, you are authorized to propose the sixteenth article of the treaty of November 19, 1794, as a model for one to be inserted in the convention. But as it reserves to the parties the right of excepting from the residence of consuls such *particular places* as each party shall judge proper to be so excepted, it may be necessary, if that clause should be retained, to reserve all the reciprocal right of excluding from the protection of the respective consuls all merchants, mariners, and vessels of their country coming from ports from which consuls of the other nation are excluded.

We are not, indeed, tenacious of the insertion of *any* article relating to consuls into the convention; but, whether by convention or otherwise, you will not fail to insist upon the claim of admission for our consuls into all the opened ports whence British vessels, merchants, and mariners, coming to our ports, may claim the protection of British consuls here, and where, from the state of the trade, we may deem it useful to our citizens that a consul of the United States should reside; and also that the exequaturs of all our consuls in the British dominions should henceforth be delivered without any charge or expense to them whatever.

The British Government may be assured that we shall use the power of appointing consuls to *any* of the opened ports for no improper purpose; but the right to consular protection is one of the ordinary advantages of trade in foreign ports which ought not to be denied to our countrymen, in ports where they are admitted, on the principles of reciprocal trade. The want of a consul of the United States at the island of Barbadoes, for instance, has been exemplified in a circumstance which has recently come to our knowledge. That island was one of those from which Mr. S. Canning received and communicated to me a declaratory certificate that vessels of the United States were liable to no other or higher duties and fees than British vessels coming from the United States. We are now informed that a citizen of the United States, who went to Barbadoes with a cargo of flour, was compelled, in December last, to pay a duty of two per cent. on the proceeds of the sales of his cargo, under the denomination of a transient tax, which no British subject would have been required to pay. We understand that the American himself would have escaped this tax if his cargo had been consigned to an established commercial house in the island. But it is one of the many modes of levying discriminating duties, which cannot comport with the principle of real reciprocity. If a tax of two per cent. is exacted from the foreign trader for the privilege of transacting his own business, which the native trader enjoys gratuitously, they are not upon terms of equal competition. It is presumed that had there been at that time a consul of the United States in the island, this tax would have been remitted upon his representations—at least, he would have given notice to this Government of its existence. This circumstance, as well as the other fact recently disclosed, and noticed in my letter of the 23d instant, that in Nova Scotia there is a deduction in favor of *the vessels of the province* from the tonnage duty paid by *British* vessels, proves at once the necessity that we should have consuls in the opened colonial ports, and that of the most vigilant caution, in abandoning on our part all discriminating duties favorable to our own navigation in this trade. Whether this subject is to be regulated hereafter by convention, or by corresponding acts of Parliament and of Congress, we are to understand explicitly, that, according to our view of removing all discriminations, the system must embrace the colonial as well as the parliamentary legislation; and if in any one colony the vessels or people of the colony have advantages or preferences secured to them over other *British* vessels and subjects, it cannot be satisfactory to us to be placed on the same footing with the British not of the province. If the Provincial enjoys at home a discriminating advantage over the *Briton*, we cannot admit him here *as a Briton*, unless our vessels are also admitted into the colony with the provincial privileges. All this is essential to real reciprocity, and to the removal of our foreign tonnage and impost duty upon British vessels and cargoes coming from the opened colonial ports for trade with the United States.

I am, with great respect, sir, your very humble and obedient servant,

JOHN QUINCY ADAMS.

Hon. RICHARD RUSH, *Envoy Extraordinary and*
Minister Plenipotentiary of the United States, London.

P. S.—The person appointed consul for St. Christopher and Antigua is Robert M. Harrison, and that for Demarara, Edmund Roberts.

No. 68.

DEPARTMENT OF STATE, *Washington, June 27, 1823.*

SIR: Your despatches Nos. 265 and 275, inclosing copies of your correspondence with Mr. Gallatin concerning the question which has arisen with France in regard to the right of fishing on a certain part of the coast of Newfoundland, have been duly received.

The transactions which gave rise to this controversy occurred in the years 1820 and 1821, when several fishing vessels of the United States, on the coast and within the strictest territorial jurisdiction of the island of Newfoundland, were ordered away by the commanders of French armed vessels upon the pain of seizure and confiscation. Two distinct questions arose from these incidents: one, upon the pretension of France to the *exclusive* right of fishing on that part of the coast of Newfoundland; and the other, upon the right of French armed vessels to order away vessels of the United States from places within the exclusive jurisdiction of Great Britain. In both these questions Great Britain had an interest and concern not less important than that of the United States; but the President, in the first instance, determined to address the complaint which the occasion required to the French Government alone. The motives for this forbearance were, to give the French Government the opportunity of disowning these acts of its officers, and of disclaiming any pretensions to the exclusive fishing right at the place where they had occurred, without implicating Great Britain at all in the transaction. This course of proceeding was thought to be most consistent with delicacy towards both those Governments, by avoiding towards France the appearance of recurring upon a question between her and us to the interposition of a third power, and by abstaining towards Great Britain from calling for her interference with France in a difference which might be adjusted without needing the aid of her influence. This was the reason upon which the instructions to make representations on this subject were forwarded only to Mr. Gallatin, and that until now it has never been mentioned in the instructions from this Department to you.

But the complaint to France has hitherto proved ineffectual, excepting to demonstrate that the pretensions of France to an exclusive right of fishing at the place referred to are without solid foundation, and that her intention of resorting to force to maintain this inadmissible pretension, though not yet unequivocally asserted, has been so far ascertained as to remove all scruple of delicacy with regard to the propriety of stating the case to the British Government, and calling upon them to maintain at once the faith of their treaty with us and the efficacy of their own territorial jurisdiction, violated by the exercise of force against the fishing vessels of the United States engaged in their lawful occupation under its protection.

The untenable character of the French claim and pretension has been so satisfactorily proved, as well in the correspondence between you and Mr. Gallatin as in that of Mr. Gallatin with the French Government, that it is altogether unnecessary for me to enter upon the discussion. I am not aware of anything that has escaped your attention in the development of our right to the free participation in the fisheries at the controverted points, and from the result of your oral communications with Mr. Robinson, in the course of your inquiries relating to this affair, it is not to be doubted that the whole contest will continue to be seen in its true light by Great Britain.

Copies are herewith transmitted to you of the correspondence between Mr. Gallatin, in the execution of his instructions, with the Viscount de Chateaubriand, in which you will find all the argument that France has been able to adduce in support of her claims to the *exclusive* right of fishery. It completes the demonstration that the pretension cannot be supported. But you will see that Mr. de Chateaubriand, in his letter of the 5th of April last, while evading or abandoning the attempt of reply to Mr. Gallatin, with regard to the claim of *exclusive* fishery, says that he had *some time since* instructed the chargé d'affaires of France at this place to enter upon explanations with the Government of the United States concerning this object, and that he was then writing to him again about it. With regard to the exercise of force within the British jurisdiction the Viscount has given Mr. Gallatin no answer whatever; but Mr. Gallatin, in his letter to this Department of 17th April, states that in a conversation with the Minister of Marine, to whom he knew the subject had been referred, that minister "gave it as his opinion, in explicit terms, that France, being in possession of the exclusive right of fishing on the coast in question, inasmuch as she had not before the last occurrence been disturbed in it by the fishermen either of England or America, she had the right to retain such possession, and ought to continue to exercise that right by expelling any vessels that should attempt to participate in the fisheries." Mr. Gallatin had not ascertained whether the Viscount de Chateaubriand and the other minister concurred in this opinion of the Minister of Marine, the candor and explicitness of which must be acknowledged, but the chargé d'affaires of France here declares that he has received no instructions from his Government to give the explanations promised by the letter of Mr. Chateaubriand to Mr. Gallatin, and we should no longer be excusable for refraining from a representation of the whole case to the Government of Great Britain. The question concerning the jurisdiction belongs peculiarly to her. The documents cited by you, in your correspondence with Mr. Gallatin, show that the premises of the French Marine Minister, upon which he relies for the basis of his opinion, are as incorrect in point of fact as his conclusion is extraordinary in point of principle. The deliberate pretension to exercise force within purely British waters was unexpected on the part of France. We shall not, for the present, employ force to meet force, although that result was properly presented by Mr. Gallatin to the French Government as a consequence to be anticipated from the perseverance of their armed vessels in disturbing our fishermen. We respect the territorial jurisdiction of Great Britain in resorting to her for the effectual exercise of it to carry into execution her engagements with us.

The President desires that, in your conferences with the British Secretary of State, you will give him information of the present state of this concern between us and France. You will be careful to present it in the aspect the most favorable and friendly towards France that can be compatible with the effective maintenance of our own rights. It is probable that there may be no such interruption to our fishermen during the present season; and the occasion appears to be highly favorable for an adjustment of it to our satisfaction. Perhaps a mutual explanation and understanding between the British and French Governments concerning it, at this time, may render any resort to other measures unnecessary. But if, on discussion of the subject between them, France should not explicitly desist from both the pretensions to the exclusive fishery and to the exercise of force within British waters to secure it, you will claim that which the British Government cannot fail to perceive is due, the unmolested execution of the treaty stipulation contained in the convention of October 20, 1818; and if the British Government admits the claim of France to *exclusive* fishery on the western coast of Newfoundland from Cape Bay to the Quirpon Islands, they will necessarily see the obligation of indemnifying the United States by an equivalent for the loss of that portion of the fishery, expressly conceded to them by the convention, which, in the supposed hypothesis, must have been granted by great Britain under an erroneous impression that it was yet in her power to grant.

I am, with great respect, sir, your very humble and obedient servant,

JOHN QUINCY ADAMS.

Hon. R. Rush, *Envoy Extraordinary and*
  Minister Plenipotentiary of the United States, London.

No. 71.

Mr. Adams to Mr. Rush.

DEPARTMENT OF STATE, *Washington, July 28, 1823.*

SIR: Among the subjects of negotiation which you have been authorized to propose to the British Government, included in the full power recently transmitted to you, and with regard to which you have been informed that further instructions would be given you, are several points relating to the rights of maritime neutrality in time of war.

By the pervading principle of the treaty known under the denomination of the Holy Alliance, and by the persevering efforts of Great Britain for the suppression of the African slave trade, the principal powers of Europe have solemnly pledged themselves to the principle that it is among the most indispensable duties of the rulers of mankind to combine their exertions for the general amelioration of the condition of man.

This principle is entirely congenial to the political system of the United States, and has formed one of the maxims of their external policy from the period of the establishment of their independence. Among the benefits which the Christian religion has secured to the human race, and particularly to those nations by which it has been adopted as a rule of faith and of conduct, none has been more conspicuous than its influence in mitigating the laws and usages of *war*. It is impossible, indeed, to examine the system of Christianity, as contained in its sacred books, without coming to the conclusion that its main object was ultimately to abolish war upon earth altogether; and it is equally clear that if its precepts were universally adopted and practiced among men, *war* upon earth would cease by the fact itself. The history of the human race since the introduction of Christianity has not encouraged the expectation that this object can, for many ages yet, be fully accomplished; but if this must be conceded, the same appeal to history will justify the assertion that the influence of Christianity has been marked in a signal manner by the gradual establishment of rules in the hostile conflicts of nations tending to assuage the evils of war.

It is the prevalence of pacific and benevolent sentiment which has successively expunged from the laws of nations, as practiced among Christians, that absolute control over the *life* of the vanquished in war, upon which the customary right of reducing him to slavery was founded; all the rights of war over the person of an enemy are now, by the usages of Christian nations, reduced to that of holding him, if taken as a combatant, in prison; and even the usage is the disposal of officers upon parole. The same relenting spirit has extended to the disposal of *property*, and, without requiring the stipulation of treaties, it has become a law of war among Christian nations to exempt from violation the private property of individuals.

These great and cheering indications of progressive amelioration in the condition of man, effected by the influence of Christianity, have been set forth with much force and ingenuity by the English historian of the laws of nations, *Ward*. In the introduction and establishment of these mitigations to the rigor of war, Great Britain herself, to her never-fading honor, has more than once taken the lead. That the feelings in which these improvements upon the ancient laws of nations originated are strong in the breasts of her statesmen of the present age is proved, not only by the spirit and perseverance with which they are pursuing the abolition of the African slave trade, but by the stipulations in the tenth and twenty-sixth articles of her treaty of November 19, 1794, with the United States. To these principles and feelings, therefore, it is believed that an earnest and confident appeal may be made, as the foundation of the proposals which you will now be instructed to make.

In the conversation with Mr. S. Canning, before he left this city, in which a general idea was given of the negotiation which it was intended to propose to the British Government, the remark was made that, with the exception of the arrangement respecting colonial intercourse and the suppression of the slave trade, all the other subjects, concerning which instructions would be furnished to you, might be connected with the negotiation, or omitted from it, at the option of Great Britain. Your instructions would direct that you should express the earnest wish of the President that they should all be discussed between the two Governments, from a strong conviction that the adjustment of them would have an auspicious effect upon the future peace and harmony of the two nations, and from a belief that the present is a period peculiarly favorable for a strong exertion to obtain that adjustment. With regard especially to the debatable points of maritime law, and the relative rights of belligerent and neutral nations, I observed that we should not be discouraged by the failure of our endeavors and offers at the negotiation of Ghent, and of the convention of 1818. We saw that even since the latest of these dates the political aspect of Europe and of America had undergone a total change. The European Alliance, so far as Great Britain was a party to it, might be considered as virtually dissolved. She and the great continental powers, parties to that alliance, were now publicly pledged to principles hardly reconcilable together, and their policy was as much at variance as their principles. With regard to the war which appeared to be opening between France and Spain, the principles and the policy of the United States coincided with those of Great Britain, and not with those of the European continental allies. They disapproved a war made for the avowed purpose of dictating to a foreign nation the terms of her internal constitution. They disapproved especially a war declared upon the avowed principle, by a King of France, that Spain could receive a legitimate constitution only from the hands of her King. The general maxim, however, of abstaining from interference in the quarrels of other nations would still govern the policy of the United States on this occasion; their relation to the war would be like that of Great Britain, *neutrality*. The condition of every part of America, the United States excepted, had also changed since the conclusion of the convention of October, 1818. The independence of all Spanish America on these continents was no longer problematical. It had been formally acknowledged by the United States, and so far by Great Britain that she had maintained, to the extent of issuing reprisals, the right of her subjects to trade with the emancipated colonies. To the war between Spain and them the United States and Great Britain were also both neutral. The general *interests* of Great Britain, therefore, in all parts of the world, were interests of *neutrality*. Those of the United States were the same. From many recent indications of the policy of the British Cabinet we had seen cause to hope that the *rights* of neutrality were more favorably viewed by them than heretofore; and we thought it probable they would not be unwilling to review the doctrines heretofore held by them with a disposition more favorable to neutral interests. There was much in the general state of the world which we thought admonished the statesmen both of the United States and of Great Britain to cultivate and cherish the sentiments, and to avail themselves of the events which tended to conciliation and harmony between the two nations; and we, on our part, were so convinced of the importance to them both of a mutual good understanding, that we seized with eagerness every opportunity offered by the course of events for promoting it. But I observed our desire to discuss these collisions of neutral and belligerent right essentially reposed on the assumption that the views of Great Britain concerning them were not exactly the same that they had been when we had discussed them with her heretofore. If we were mistaken in that; if she would enter upon the negotiation only to adhere to the doctrines which she had maintained heretofore, we should prefer postponing again the discussion to a future period.

On this foundation you will broach that part of the subject to the British Secretary for Foreign Affairs. If the great changes in the political aspects of Europe and of America, since October, 1818, have left Great Britain unshaken in all her belligerent pretensions, we candidly say the time has not yet come when a hope may be entertained that we can agree with her concerning any of them; and we rather wish she would say so distinctly, and decline negotiation on these points, than that she should consent to enter upon the negotiation under the expectation that we are disposed to depart from any of the principles upon which we have heretofore insisted with regard to the rights of neutrality. Mr. S. Canning, to whom I made this explicit avowal, thought there might be some objection to the sacrifice of self-respect, which might be implied in the consent to open a negotiation upon such a basis, but he intimated that it would rather be an objection of form than of substance; that his Government could, of course, not accede to a negotiation from the outset of which they should acknowledge themselves to have been heretofore in the wrong. But he admitted that some of the principal collisions between us and Great Britain, in the late European wars, had arisen from measures which Great Britain had resorted to, not as legitimate by the ordinary laws of nations, but as retaliatory upon preceding excesses of her enemy. I disclaimed, of course, all disposition on the part of this Government to ask Great Britain any disavowal, expressed or implied, of her former acts. Our object is not retrospection of the past, but forecast for the future.

The world in which we both moved is no longer the same. Her great national interests are no longer the same. They were belligerent; they are now neutral. Maritime war itself, and all the questions connected with it, *must* be affected by the downfall of the colonial system. Of what use, for example, will her too celebrated rule of the war of 1756 ever again be to her, when all the ex-colonies of Europe and the colonies yet existing, her own included, are open to foreign commerce and shipping *in time of peace?* Let her next maritime war break out with whom it will, she can no longer seize and confiscate neutral commerce with the colonies of her enemy, on the pretence that it was not allowed *in time of peace.* We press no disavowal upon her; but we think the present time eminently auspicious for urging upon her, *and upon others,* an object which has long been dear to the hearts and ardent in the aspirations of the benevolent and the wise; an object essentially congenial to the true spirit of Christianity, and, therefore, peculiarly fitting for the support of nations intent, in the same spirit, upon the final and total suppression of the slave trade, and of sovereigns who have given public pledges to the world of their determination to administer imperial dominion upon the genuine precepts of Christianity.

The object to which I allude is the abolition of private war upon the sea.

It has been remarked that, by the usages of modern war, the private property of an enemy is protected from seizure or confiscation as such, and private war itself has been almost universally exploded *upon the land.* By an exception, the reason of which it is not easy to perceive, the private property of an enemy *upon the sea* has not so fully received the benefit of the same principle. Private war, banished by the tacit and general consent of Christian nations from their territories, has taken its last refuge upon the ocean, and there continues to disgrace and afflict them by a system of licensed robbery, bearing all the most atrocious characters of piracy. To a Government intent, from motives of general benevolence and humanity, upon the final and total suppression of the slave trade, it cannot be unreasonable to claim her aid and co-operation to the abolition of private war upon the sea.

From the time when the United States took their place among the nations of the earth this has been one of their favorite objects. "It is time," said Dr. Franklin, (in a letter of March 14, 1785,) "It is high time, for the sake of humanity, that a stop were put to this enormity. The United States of America, though better situated than any European nation to make profit by privateering, are, as far as in them lies, endeavoring to abolish the practice by offering in all their treaties with other powers an article engaging solemnly that, in case of future war, no privateer shall be commissioned on either side, and that unarmed merchant ships, on both sides, shall pursue their voyages unmolested. This will be a happy improvement of the law of nations. The humane and the just cannot but wish general success to the proposition."

It is well known that, in the same year that this letter was written, a treaty between the United States and the King of Prussia was concluded, by the twenty-third article of which this principle was solemnly sanctioned in the form of a national compact. The twenty-sixth article of the treaty between the United States and Great Britain of 19th November, 1794, carries it, in some respects, still further, though in others falling short of it. The articles of the inclosed draft combine the special stipulations of both those articles, and in proposing them you will express the earnest desire of the President that they may prove acceptable to the British Government.

You will, at the same time, propose the restipulation of the tenth article of the treaty of November 19, 1794. It is, indeed, apparently the intention of that article to bind the parties to it in perpetuity, and, although the remainder of that treaty has been extinguished by the late war, and expired by its own limitation, neither of the parties now, or at any future time, could make the seizure or confiscation forbidden by it without a breach of their faith thus pledged against *any event of war,* as well as of natural justice. But a renewal of the engagement, even if unnecessary to its continued validity, will be useful and honorable to the parties, as pledging again their sanction to the principle of justice and humanity to which it appeals. So far as it could affect the *interest* of the parties, its operation, at the time when it was first agreed to, was almost entirely to the advantage of Great Britain. It will yet be so. But in protecting, by a pledge of faith, justice and humanity against the exasperated passions and undistinguishing rapacity of war, if some sacrifice of selfish interest must be made, it can but set in clearer light the sincerity of those who consent to make it.

The *stipulation* in the tenth article of the treaty of November, 1794, was inserted in our treaty with France of 30th September, 1800; but the reason assigned for the engagement in the former was omitted in the latter. In proposing the renewal of the article, it is desirable that the reason should be repeated with the promise, not only because it is such as does honor to the contracting parties, but because it is applicable, with equal force, to the other article which we wish now to introduce. *It is* unjust and impolitic that the *debts* of individuals, their shares and moneys in public funds or in banks, should be destroyed or impaired by national authority, on account of national differences and discontents. But it is *equally* unjust and impolitic that *any* private property of individuals should ever be destroyed or impaired by national authority for national quarrels. The right of *property* is, in moral principle, equally sacred, whether it consist in debts or stocks, or in ships or houses; whether in a crop growing upon the soil, gathered in the garner, or shipped for the market; or whether in the manufacture of human industry and skill. The injustice consists in the spoliation of private property for public disputes; and the violation of confidence between individuals, committed by the confiscation of their debts, is merely an incident of aggravation to the general wrong of wreaking the public vengeance upon the property of individuals.

We wish this consideration to be pressed with earnestness upon the moral sense of the British Government. We are aware that, in the abolition of *private* war upon the sea, that nation, while yielding homage to the principle of general justice, must abandon the use of a weapon of offence against others which she has heretofore used much to their annoyance. But we are firmly convinced that it will ultimately prove as beneficial to her interest as to that of others; and the magnanimity displayed by her in contracting an engagement so consonant to eternal right, though partially affecting a temporary interest of her own, cannot fail to give energy to her solicitations when urging upon others the sacrifice of their special interests for the purpose of consummating the triumph of justice and humanity.

The other articles of the inclosed draft, adapted to the contingency of a war between the parties, are all dictated by the same spirit of mitigating the unnecessary rigors of hostility; they are all congenial to the temper and founded upon the reasoning of the first; all sanctioned by the main argument for the general concurrence to the suppression of the slave trade, and by the principle proclaimed as the foundation of the Holy Alliance, the application of the benevolent precepts of Christianity to the public intercourse of sovereign States.

The subsequent articles of the draft, from the seventh to the eighteenth, inclusive, are adapted to the contingency of a war in which one of the parties should be belligerent and the other neutral. Many of their provisions would become useless and inapplicable if the war should be between parties both acceding to the principle of abstaining from private war against each other upon the sea. The result of the abolition of private maritime war would be the coincident abolition of maritime neutrality. By this, the *neutral* nations would be the principal losers; and sensible as we are of this, we are still anxious, from higher motives than of mere commercial gain, that the principle should be universally adopted. We are willing that the world, in common with ourselves, should gain in peace whatever we may lose in profit.

But if the British Government should decline acceding to this proposal, or either of the parties should hereafter be engaged in war with a third party not bound by a similar engagement, the articles of the inclosed draft, from the seventh to the eighteenth, are intended to regulate the relations between the belligerent and the neutral party upon the points of collision which have heretofore arisen from that state of things.

The seventh is adopted from a provision already stipulated in the eighteenth article of the treaty of 19th November, 1794, with a definition of blockade, which was acceded to by the British plenipotentiaries at the negotiation of the convention of October, 1818.

The eighth is an article existing in several of our treaties with other powers. As a principle warranted by the law of nations, independent of compact, it appears to have been recognized to its full extent by the British Government in their late controversy with Spain relating to the capture of the Lord Collingwood, and in their order of reprisals issued to enforce the right of British subjects to trade with the South Americans. For, if she considers these as still *de jure* Spanish colonies, her subjects would still be excluded from trading with them as neutrals by her own rule of the war of 1756. But considering them as a people in a state of civil war with Spain, it is only under the principle of this article that she can maintain her right as a neutral of trading with them. A reference to the engagements of her treaty of 5th July, 1814, with Spain, will set this in a yet clearer light.

The ninth article contains the usual list of contraband of war, omitting the articles used in the construction or equipment of vessels. These articles are not included in the *principle* upon which contraband of war was originally founded. They are all important articles of commerce in time of peace and for purposes of commerce. Several of them are articles of ordinary export from the United States, and the produce of their soil and industry. Others are articles equally important to the commerce of other nations, particularly Russia, whose interests would be unfavorably affected by embracing them in the contraband list. The first effect of including them in a list of contraband with one nation, while they are excluded from the same list in treaties with others, is, that the belligerent with whom they have been stipulated as contraband acquires, so far as the treaties are observed, an exclusive market for the acquisition of the articles of which the other belligerent is deprived. The next consequence is, that the other belligerent, suffering under the double injury of this contradictory rule, breaks through the obligation of her own treaty, and seizes and confiscates upon the principle of *retaliation* upon the enemy. This observation applies to every other point of maritime law in which the neutral interest is sacrificed to the belligerent interest with one power, while the reverse is stipulated with the other. The uniform and painful experience which we have had of this should operate as a warning to the Government of the United States to introduce the harmony of one congenial system into their federative relations with foreign powers; and never to concede as maritime right to one power a principle the reverse of which they have stipulated with others.

The tenth article of the draft proposes the adoption of the principle that free ships make free goods and persons; and, also, that neutral property shall be free, though laden in a vessel of the enemy. The Government of the United States wish, for the universal establishment of this principle, as a step towards the attainment of the other, the total abolition of private maritime war. This question of free ships making free goods has been much and long debated, and, as a question of the law of nations, remains to this day unsettled. By the law of nature, undoubtedly, the *right* as well as the equity and *humanity* of the controversy is on the *neutral* side. By the *customary law* of nations it has been, with several remarkable exceptions, the practice for some ages to take enemy's property found in the vessel of a friend. To the many efforts which have been made for restoring the original pacific principle of natural law we wish now to add another. Great Britain, by the treaties of Utrecht and 1786 with France, did assent to the principle that free ships should make free goods; and in the twelfth article of the treaty with the United States of November, 1794, did promise to negotiate with them two years after the termination of the war in which she was engaged, and to endeavor to agree with them "whether in any, and in what, cases neutral vessels should protect enemy's property."

Two years after that war Great Britain was engaged in another, and the promised endeavor to agree never took effect. But the engagement itself implied that, in time of peace, Great Britain might be disposed to stipulate more favorably to neutral rights and pretensions than she would at that time; and as she has now been eight years at peace, and is at this time neutral to a maritime war between other States, there could scarcely be foreseen a more favorable time for giving substantial execution to that pledge of faith.

The 11th article of the draft is taken with a modification from the 17th article of the treaty of 1794.

The 12th and 13th articles are intended to abolish forever the practice of impressment from our merchant vessels upon the high seas, and to remove henceforth all cause and pretext for resorting to it hereafter. By the stipulation now offered of excluding, *in the event of a war*, and from its commencement, all natural born subjects or citizens of the belligerent party, unless naturalized by some authentic public act before the commencement of the war, from the naval service, public and private, of the neutral party, a security is given to Great Britain against the employment of her seamen in our service at the only time when it could be prejudicial to her; a security which, if not stipulated while peace continues, we shall not be able to give after the war shall have broken out. We believe it impossible that the practice of impressing men from our vessels at sea should be renewed without producing war—an event which we deeply deprecate. You are authorized even to extend the exclusion of persons who may be naturalized after the exchange of the ratifications of the treaty, which, if the peace should continue a very few years longer, will be equivalent to an exclusion of all natural born subjects. But we are not willing to make of this a temporary arrangement, as was proposed at the negotiation of 1818, nor to agree to the mutual exclusions from the respective services in time of peace.

The 14th article is from the treaty of 1794, and is chiefly valuable by fixing the sum for which bonds shall be required of privateers.

The 15th, 16th, 17th, and 18th articles are also borrowed from the treaty of 1794, with some modifications, the object of which is more effectually to secure the rights and to fulfil the obligations of neutrality, and·to·place·the belligerent parties on precisely the same footing of favor and of restriction in the neutral ports.

The 19th, 20th, and 21st articles are provisions against pirates; the 20th including cases of re-capture of a neutral by a belligerent in time of war.

The great object of the whole convention, as proposed, is to take the first step towards the eventual abolition by the law of nations of *private war upon the sea*, an improvement entirely congenial to that of the final and total abolition of the slave trade; and entirely coincident, or, it may rather be said, necessarily deducible from the *principles* declared in the autographic alliance between the sovereigns of Russia, Austria, and Prussia. In communicating the draft of these articles to the British Government, (should they agree to negotiate on the subject,) you will declare the readiness of this Government to accede to any modification of them, or addition to them, which may be promotive of the purpose and desirable to Great Britain. You will add, that we have been encouraged to present this plan for a great improvement in the law of nations and amelioration of the condition of human kind, by the proposal deliberately made by the French Government to establish the principle during their present war with Spain. That we make the first proposal to Great Britain as to the power most competent to secure its ultimate success, and to the nation which we sincerely believe would finally derive the greatest share of the blessing which its universal establishment would bestow upon the family of man. And you will observe that, as it is the intention of the President to present the same plan to the other principal maritime powers of Europe, particularly to France and Russia, it would be peculiarly agreeable to him to offer it to them in concert with Great Britain, supported by the weight of her powerful influence.

I am, sir, with great respect, your obedient and very humble servant,

JOHN QUINCY ADAMS.

Hon. Richard Rush, *Envoy Extraordinary and*
    Minister Plenipotentiary of the United States, London.

No. 5.

London, *May* 20, 1824.

Sir: It is more than a month since I have had a meeting with the British plenipotentiaries, the last having been held on the thirteenth of April. The Easter holidays led to the first part of this interval, since which Mr. Huskisson's parliamentary and other engagements, added to an attack of illness which has confined him to his bed, have created the further delay. We hope now to resume our labors in the course of next week, and the British plenipotentiaries have given me reason to think that we shall make rapid progress towards a conclusion when we do resume them. Nothing whatever has yet been settled on any one point since the convention on the slave trade.

I have the honor to remain, with very great respect, your obedient servant,

RICHARD RUSH.

Hon. John Quincy Adams, *Secretary of State.*

No. 8.

London, *August* 2, 1824.

Sir: The negotiations in which I have been engaged with this Government have at length reached their close without any treaty or arrangement whatever having been concluded upon any one of the many subjects that I had in charge. The last meeting of the plenipotentiaries took place on the 28th of last month. My report to you of all that has passed shall be made without any delay that I can avoid; yet from circumstances, with a detail of which I need not trouble you, I am forced to add that it will not be done as soon as I could wish. I shall hope, however, to draw it up in the course of the present month if my health allows me.

I am still without any communication from this Government as to its intentions respecting the slave trade convention. It may be superfluous for me to add, that I have fully laid before Mr. Secretary Canning all the considerations and arguments derived from your instructions of the 29th May on this subject.

I have the honor to remain, with great respect, your obedient servant,

RICHARD RUSH.

Hon. John·Quincy Adams, *Secretary of State.*

No. 10.

London, *August* 12, 1824.

Sir: My letter of the second of this month will have informed you that the negotiations in which I had so long been engaged with this Government had come to a close, but without any treaty or other arrangement having been concluded on any of the subjects which had been given in charge to me. This is a result which I should lament the more did I not endeavor to reconcile myself to it by the reflection that I have earnestly, though fruitlessly, striven to render it more auspicious, and by the consideration— far more important—that as several of the subjects discussed have been both of novelty and magnitude between the two nations, my Government will have the opportunity of being put in more full possession of the sentiments of this Government, prior to the conclusion, or to the proposal anew, of any definite or final stipulations.

The task of reporting to you, for the information of the President, the whole progress of the negotiation now devolves upon me. I enter upon it in the anxious hope that, whilst shunning a prolixity that might fatigue, I may nevertheless omit nothing necessary to a full understanding of all that has passed. I console myself with the recollection that the protocols and other papers that will be transmitted to you will mainly delineate every material occurrence. From these may be learned all the formal proposals that have been made on the one side or on the other; but the grounds of them, the discussions by which they were sustained or opposed, together with various explanations which the written memorials of the negotiation, wearing for the most part the character of abstracts only, do not indicate; these it becomes my duty to make you also acquainted with in every essential particular. It must be my purpose to fulfil this duty in the course of the present despatch.

It was my first intention to have made my report to you in the shape of separate communications, allotting a distinct one to each subject, that I might be able to follow, in this respect, the example of your instructions to me. But, after the discussions were opened, it was often found impracticable to keep the subjects distinct. More than one subject, or branches of more than one, would sometimes engage our conferences on the same day, superinducing the necessity of mixing them up in one and the same protocol. For this reason, and because also the British plenipotentiaries in some instances established a connexion between subjects where, as I thought, none regularly had place, and so treated them in our records in the manner I shall have occasion to describe, it has appeared to me most conducive to good order to present the whole under one view. If this unity in my report would not appear at first sight to be suggested by a view of the diversity as well as number of its subjects, it has seemed to me, upon the whole, to adapt itself best to the course which the negotiation actually took, both in the oral discussions and in the entries upon the protocols; and that it will become most intelligible, whether in its incidents or its general spirit, when exhibited as a whole. In the hope that this mode of making up my report may meet your approbation, I proceed, without more of introduction, to its proper business.

After the slave trade question had been disposed of, the subject upon which we next entered was that of the commercial intercourse between the United States and the British colonial ports in the West Indies and North America. Copious as this subject was found to be when examined in all its details, its mere discussion—I mean the strictly commercial part—was perhaps attended with less difficulty than that of some others. It had been familiar to the past, and even recent, discussions of the two Governments—so much so, that upon almost every point connected with it opinions had been formerly expressed by both. When, at an early stage, the British plenipotentiaries said that, after the opening of this trade to the vessels of the United States by the act of Parliament of the 24th of June, 1822, it had not been expected by Great Britain that our foreign tonnage duty and additional impost would have been continued to be levied upon their vessels, I naturally replied that to whatever other observations the policy of the United States might be open in this respect, it could scarcely be said to have been unexpected, as upon at least two occasions since I had been their organ at this court they had expressly declined acceding by compact to the very terms in regard to this trade that were afterwards moulded into the act of Parliament. Your instructions being precise and full upon this head, I caused them to be well understood. I recapitulated the history of the negotiations that led to the convention of the 20th of October, 1818, in all those parts of it which had relation to the question of commercial intercourse. I presented the review of all the legislative acts or other measures affecting this intercourse, as well prior as subsequent to that convention; on the side of Great Britain, the act of Parliament of July, 1812, the draft of the four articles submitted by Lord Castlereagh in 1817, the act of Parliament of May, 1818, and the order of council which followed it on the twenty-seventh of the same month; on the side of the United States, the act of Congress of the 3d of March, 1815, (the legislative basis of their system of reciprocity,) the two acts, original and supplementary, of April 18, 1818, and May 15, 1820, concerning navigation, the act of May 6, 1822, with the President's proclamation of the 24th of August founded upon that act. To all these I referred, in connexion also with the second negotiation of June and September, 1819, when the proposals again made by the United States for regulating this intercourse by treaty were again rejected by Great Britain. The deduction, I maintained, from the whole was, that the United States had, with uniform consistency and steadiness, pursued a course in regard to this trade which aimed at placing it upon a footing of entire reciprocity; that they asked nothing more, but, in justice to their citizens, could be satisfied with nothing less.

To work out this reciprocity seemed, however, not to be an easy task, I remarked, on the side of Great Britain, whatever had been her desire. Her commercial system was of long standing, and, from its great extent, often in no slight degree complicated and intricate. It was marked out not only by a diversity in its operation upon her home and colonial empire, but by subdivided diversities in its application to her colonies. In some of her West India islands, for example, there were export duties; in others none. Some had port charges and various other local charges operating upon vessels or their cargoes not recognized in others; but what was more important than all, her ancient navigation acts still remained substantially in force, mingling their fetters with all her modern legislation upon the same subject. Her commercial and navigating system, whatever other recommendations it might possess in her eyes, had been rendered by time and her past policy deficient in the uniformity and simplicity calculated to place it, in these respects at least, upon a par with the commercial and navigating system of the United States. This broad distinction between the two countries was always necessary to be kept in mind, I said, in their commercial dealings, and whatever explanation or excuse it might furnish to Great Britain for continuing the pursuit of a course which still moved in many points in subordination to her ancient policy, it afforded to the United States neither motive nor justification for giving up their claim to the principle of an absolute and perfect equality in all their regulations of trade with Great Britain.

This brought me to the true nature of the act of Parliament of the 24th of June, 1822. I explained to the British plenipotentiaries that this statute had not, whatever might have been its intention, opened the ports of the British colonies in the West Indies and America to the vessels of the United States upon the same terms as were enjoyed by British vessels. The privileges granted by it to vessels of the United States were, that they might carry directly, but in no other way, from some port of the United States to certain specified colonial ports, certain specified articles of merchandise, whilst very high duties were to be paid on all such of those articles as could alone be the subjects of a profitable trade. British vessels, on the other hand, possessed the additional and exclusive privilege of carrying the same articles to the same colonial ports, directly or indirectly, and free from all duty whatever when carried from a British colony in North America to a British colony in the West Indies. Moreover, I observed the vessels of the United States admitted only as above to the colonial ports were obliged, supposing they obtained a cargo, to return directly to the United States, and to give bond, under a heavy penalty, for landing it at the port for which it was entered, with the additional burden, not imposed by the act of Parliament, but existing in fact, of paying a colonial export duty of four or five per cent. upon the value of this return cargo. This burden did not fall equally upon British vessels, as they might avoid it by going, which they were free to do, to any port of the British dominions either in Europe or America, a range not allowed to the vessels of the United States. Nor were the British vessels required to give any export bond for landing the articles at the port for which entered, and producing within twelve months a cer_ tificate of this fact, a condition which was also attached to American vessels. It was evident, I insisted, from the foregoing recapitulation, that vessels of the United States had not the same privilege under this act of Parliament with British vessels, and that the former were also subject to restrictions, imposed by the act or otherwise existing, from which the latter were exempt.

I reminded the British plenipotentiaries, however, that no sooner had the knowledge of this act of Parliament reached the United States than the President, exercising, without the least delay, the authority with which by anticipation he had been invested, issued his proclamation of the twenty-fourth of August, 1822, opening the ports of the United States *generally* to British vessels coming from any of the ports *enumerated* in the British act—an exercise of authority in a high degree liberal, considering the relative state of the statutes of the two countries, then in force, for the regulation of this trade. In other respects, the proclamation of the President had done nothing more, I said, than lay British vessels coming from the colonies to the United States under the same restrictions, in regard to their cargoes, to which vessels of the United States were subject when going to the colonies. This, in necessary justice to the United States, it was obliged to do, and, by the permanent laws of the Union, British vessels continued liable to the charge of foreign tonnage and import duties. I explained to the British plenipotentiaries that, if neither the proclamation nor the permanent laws of the Union imposed burdens upon British vessels and their cargoes, which were the specific counterparts of those imposed by the act of Parliament of the 24th of June, 1822, upon American vessels, they were, nevertheless, the necessary counterparts of the burdens which did, in point of fact, exist as against American vessels. To their owners it mattered not whence these burdens originated, so long as they continued to press unequally in the competition of American with British vessels. It was to complete the intention of meeting these burdens upon a basis of reciprocity, at all points, that the act of Congress of the first of March, 1823, was finally and on full deliberation passed. Its express object I described to be to countervail all restrictions, of whatever kind they might be, in actual operation against vessels of the United States, whether enacted by the act of the 24th of June, 1822, in force under the old navigation act of Charles the Second, or recognized and permitted by colonial ordinances or local regulations in any of the British ports that had been opened. As this act of Congress could not effectuate its just object by applying to British vessels restrictions which were of the precise and corresponding nature with those operating against the vessels of the United States, it adopted, I said, such as were analogous to them, without, however, in any instance, going beyond the measure of a necessary retaliation, but rather keeping within than exceeding this limit. The act of Parliament had, it was true, proceeded upon the hypothesis of extending like privileges to American as to British vessels, but here it had stopped, without imposing upon the latter the same restrictions which had previously existed against the former. The act of Congress went further, and, in according the like privileges with the British act, imposed also restrictions equivalent to those that were really and injuriously in force against the vessels of the United States.

It was in this manner that I fully opened to the British plenipotentiaries the principles and views of my Government in relation to this interest. If I am not more minute in recounting all that I said, it is merely because I abstain from swelling this communication by a repetition of the principles, the facts, and the arguments contained in your despatch to me of the twenty-third of June, 1823. With the various matter of this despatch I had made myself familiar by frequent perusals of it, and it was alike my duty and my endeavor to exhibit it all to the British plenipotentiaries in the most perspicuous and impressive ways in my power. I went on to remark that it seemed plain, notwithstanding our countervailing restrictions, that we were still left at a disadvantage in the competition, for that, for an enumerated list of ports open to our vessels, only part of which, too, had been opened by the act of Parliament of the 24th of June, 1822, we had opened all of our ports in return to British vessels. For an enumerated list of articles which we were alone allowed to export to the colonies, we received in return all articles which the colonies found it most to their interest to send to us; and for a duty of ten per cent. on our articles imported into the West Indies, and of four or five per cent. on those that we brought away, our laws did nothing more than retain a foreign tonnage duty of less than a dollar per ton on British vessels, and of ten per cent. on the duty otherwise chargeable on the articles brought to the United States in them. It was even doubtful, I said, whether, under these circumstances, our vessels would be able to continue the trade, and it was perhaps quite as much so whether the double system of restrictions, upon which it stood, would not deprive it of all value to both countries. I used, under this branch of the subject, all the topics of illustration with which your despatch had supplied me.

The British order in council of the seventeenth of July, 1823, laying a duty of four shillings and three pence sterling per ton on our vessels going to the colonial ports, to countervail, as Mr. Secretary Canning informed me in October last, our foreign tonnage duty, having been subsequent in date to your instructions to me, no remarks upon it were, consequently, embraced in them. But I considered the duty imposed by this order open to the same animadversions as all the other burdens falling upon our vessels. If we had grounds for complaint before this measure, they were but increased by it. If we were deprived of the opportunity of fair competition in the absence of this new duty, its imposition could not but augment the inequality. If we were carrying on the trade under every prospect of disadvantage without it, a more positive and certain loss to us must be the result if it were continued. Hence, I did not scruple to say to the British plenipotentiaries that it must be considered as giving additional force to all our other objections to their regulations. I had not, I admitted, and from the cause stated, received your instruc- tions upon the subject of it; but as our foreign tonnage duty and the additional impost had been kept up against British vessels, in necessary self-defence against all the anterior restrictions upon our vessels, and duties upon their cargoes, I took it for granted that this new British duty, if not abrogated, would, on the same principles and from the same necessity, be met by some measure of counteraction on our side. In offering such comments as these upon it, I trust that they will be thought conformable to the true nature and objects of your instructions, though not in words pointed out by them.

In the end, I offered for the entire and satisfactory regulation of this trade a draft of the two articles (marked A) annexed to the protocol of the third conference. The first of these articles, after reciting the restrictions upon the trade that existed on each side, and the desire and intention that prevailed of removing them, goes on to provide that, upon the vessels of the United States admitted by law into the colonial ports, and upon the merchandise imported in them, no other duties or charges of any kind should be levied than upon British vessels, *including all vessels of the colonies themselves*, or upon the like merchandise imported into the colonial ports from any other port or place, *including Great Britain and the colonial ports themselves;* and, reciprocally, that upon the vessels of Great Britain admitted by law into the ports of the United States, and upon the merchandise imported in them, no other duties or charges of any kind should be levied than upon vessels of the United States, *including vessels of each and every one of the States*, or upon the like merchandise imported into the United States from any other port or place whatever. The words last underscored were inserted only for the greater satisfaction of the British plenipotentiaries, it being explained by me, and so understood by them, that they could carry no new meaning, there being no such thing under our system with foreign nations as a vessel of any one of the States distinct from a vessel of the United States. It followed that the passage would have had the same meaning without these words. The second article provided, in fulfilment of the intentions of the first, that the trade should continue upon the footing on which it had been placed by the laws of the two countries, with the exception of the removal by Great Britain of the duties specified in the schedule C of the act of Parliament of the 24th of June, 1822, and those specified in schedule B of the act of the fifth of August of the same year; and of the removal by the United States of the foreign tonnage duty and additional impost complained of by Great Britain. The article concluded with a mutual pledge for the removal of all discriminating duties on either side, of whatever kind they might be, from the desire which operated with the parties of placing the trade, in all respects, upon a footing of perfect equality. Such was the nature of my proposals, for the more exact terms of which I beg to refer to the paper which contained them.

The British plenipotentiaries made immediate and the most decided objections to the part of these proposals which went to the abolition of the duties in the two schedules indicated. They declared that, under no circumstances, could they accede to such a principle; and they proceeded to assail it under every form. The fundamental error of their reasoning, as always heretofore upon the same point, appeared to me to lie in considering their colonial possessions as part of the entire British dominion at one time, yet treating them as separate countries at another. For her own purposes, Britain could look upon these colonies as of one and the same country with herself; for the purposes of trade with foreign States, she felt herself at liberty to consider them as detached from herself and forming a new and distinct country; as moving, in that, within a commercial orbit wholly of their own. It was to this that her rule, resolved into its true principles, came at last. However such a rule might be met and its application admitted, as between foreign States mutually possessing colonies, and therefore mutually able in their commercial intercourse with each other to act upon it, its application was manifestly unequal and incongruous towards the United States. Possessing no colonies themselves, the United States neither legislated nor acted upon a principle of subdividing their empire for any purpose of commercial advantage, or, above all, monopoly, with other nations, but held out indiscriminately to all one integral and undivided system. In strict justice, it would, hence, not be unreasonable in them to expect that all nations with which they entered into commercial stipulations should look upon their colonies, if they had any, only in the light of an extension of the territories and jurisdiction of the parent State, since this was, in effect, the aspect which the United States presented throughout the whole extent of their territories and jurisdiction to all foreign nations. The productions of Massachusetts, for example, which entered into the articles of international traffic, were, as compared with those of Louisiana, scarcely less different in their nature than were those of Britain from those of Jamaica; yet one commercial code spread itself over the whole of the United States, of which foreign nations, and Britain amongst them, had the benefit, whilst different commercial codes, and entangling commercial practices under them, were seen to exist on the part of Britain. This resulted from the mere fact—important it might be to Britain, but indifferent to the United States—of these codes and these practices being applicable to the Government of different portions of the British empire, some of which fell under the denomination of her home dominion, and some of her colonial dominion.

It was to no effective purpose, however, that I enlarged upon and endeavored to enforce, by placing in other lights, the foregoing distinctions. The British plenipotentiaries continued to combat my positions, and to insist upon their right to lay whatever duties they deemed expedient upon our productions going to their islands, in protection of the like articles exported to them from any part of their own dominions. They said that they could never part with this right, for which we offered them no equivalent concession. They likened our request for its surrender, by an analogy the force of which I could never see, to a request on the side of Great Britain, should she prefer such a request, to be admitted into a participation of our coasting trade. They alleged, also, that in laying these duties they had aimed only at making them a necessary protection to their own subjects in their North American colonies; and that they were scarcely up to this point, was shown by the fact, which they also alleged, of their subjects in those colonies not having yet been able, since the trade was opened, to obtain a proportionate share of it.

I had more than once occasion to remark, that it was not the *right* of either party to model its own laws as it thought proper that we were discussing; it was the *terms* upon which it would be best to do so that we ought rather to be desirous of settling. Here were certain colonies belonging to Great Britain on the continent of North America. It happened that some of them were in the immediate neighborhood of the United States. Their course of industry was the same, their productions the same. If the live stock and lumber from one of these colonies—from that of New Brunswick, for example—were allowed to be imported into Antigua or St. Christopher duty free, whilst similar articles from the State of Maine, bordering upon New Brunswick, labored under a duty of ten per cent. on their importation into the same islands, was not, I asked, all just competition at an end? Still more was this the case, I remarked, if, after disposing of their cargoes, the vessel from New Brunswick could take in a return cargo absolved from an export duty, and was, moreover, left at liberty to take advantage of circumstances by trading from colony to colony, whilst the vessel from Maine was obliged to depart in ballast, or, if she took in a cargo, do so subject to the export duty. How, too, under the weight of this latter duty, were the articles upon which it was charged to bear up, in the markets of the United States, against the competition of similar articles found in their markets, partly of their own produce and partly derived from islands in the West Indies, other than those belonging to Great Britain? It was thus that I endeavored to establish the reasonableness of our complaints, and to recommend our proposals to adoption. I admitted the general right which every nation had to foster the industry of its own subjects preferably to that of strangers, but controverted its justice or expediency as applicable to this trade—a trade that was anomalous in many points, and to be judged of and regulated, not so much on any general theory as under an impartial view of all the peculiarities that belonged to it. As to the expression "from elsewhere," introduced into the act of Congress of the first of March, 1823, I insisted upon the propriety of giving it a construction that would include the British colonies themselves as well as foreign countries—the only construction that could ever satisfy the United States, because the only one that could ever be equitable. Without it, a reciprocity in words might exist, but there would be none in fact. There was obviously no foreign nation except the United States that supplied the British West Indies with the articles in which a traffic had been opened. To say, therefore, that they should be imported into the British islands subject to no higher duties than were levied on articles of the same kind coming from any other foreign country would be altogether unmeaning. The field of competition was exclusively in the North American colonies of Britain. These, by their position and all their local peculiarities, were fairly to be considered as another country in the estimate of this trade, though they were, it was true, in political subjection to Great Britain. Their being dependencies altered not those physical and geographical characteristics in them which made them the rivals in this intercourse, and the only rivals, of the United States.

The British plenipotentiaries yielded to none of this reasoning. They admitted that there were many difficulties in the way of a satisfactory adjustment of the shipping question, and of this intercourse generally, between Great Britain and the United States. These difficulties were partly colonial, partly the result of their old navigation laws, and partly springing from the nature of the British North American trade, which bore so close an affinity to some portion of the trade of the United States. But they continued to declare their determination not to admit the productions of the United States into their islands upon the same footing with the like productions from other colonies of their own; and they reiterated their allegations that, even under the present duties cu cur productions, the trade was in our favor. They argued, hence, that the amount of the duties, instead of being too high, seemed insufficient thus far, taken on a general scale, to balance the advantage of our proximity to the West Indies, and of the greater extent and productiveness of our soil. On this head they gave me details. They said that, by their latest accounts, full two-thirds of the flour and lumber sent to their islands from North America were ascertained to have been of the produce of the United States, and that perhaps seven-eighths of this quantity were conveyed in vessels of the United States. On the return trade, also, they declared that our vessels had a share not much below the same proportion. To these statements I could only reply, that my impressions were different; that it was true I was in possession of no returns subsequent to June, 1823, but that, up to that period, my information justified me in believing that the trade had not yielded a fair proportion of gain to our merchants. The British plenipotentiaries dwelt emphatically upon the circumstance of our vessels taking away specie from their islands in place of a return cargo in the produce of the islands as indicative of the trade being against the islands, since it left upon their hands their rum and molasses—articles which they were chiefly anxious should find a market in the United States. If it were the export duty that produced this necessity in our vessels to take payment in money for their cargoes rather than in the produce of the islands, the plenipotentiaries said that they could not repeal it, because it applied equally to British vessels. It was a duty of four and a half per cent. existing on the exportation of produce, not in all of the islands, but in some of them, viz: in Antigua, St. Christopher, Montserat, Barbadoes, Nevis, and the Virgin Islands. In the latter it was granted for the benefit of the Crown, in 1774. In most or all of the others it had existed, for the same purpose, as far back as 1668. British vessels paid it, they said, when going from these islands, whether their destination was the mother country or any foreign country; but I did not understand them to say that it was paid if they went only from colony to colony.

To the objection of only a limited number of ports being open to our vessels, they said that they admitted them wherever custom-houses were established, and that the privilege reserved to British vessels of going from colony to colony was only the privilege of letting them enjoy their own coasting trade. They seemed to forget that, by whatever name this privilege went, it was still one which operated against the competition of vessels of the United States. On the non-admission into their islands of articles that we desired to send—as, for example, salt fish, beef, pork—these, they said, were also excluded from the direct trade between Great Britain and the United States, including all other foreign countries. Here, too, they seemed to throw out of mind that this very exclusion, in whatever principle it originated, still operated against the commerce of the United States, for that a system of positive exclusion formed no part of the regular or permanent system of the United States, and was, therefore, one of which, as long as they dealt out a different measure of commercial benefit to other nations, they had good grounds to complain.

I am saved the necessity of recapitulating any further the remarks of the British plenipotentiaries upon our proposals from their having furnished me with a summary of them in writing. This was not in the regular course of our proceedings, and, the paper not being considered as an official one, was not annexed to any protocol, or referred to in any. It was merely given to me as an informal memorandum, in which light I was willing and glad to receive it, as it protects me from all risk of not doing justice in my report to their representations. It will be found among the inclosures, marked W.

After all that I have said, it may be almost superfluous to state that this Government will decline abrogating the tonnage duty of four shillings and three pence sterling imposed upon our vessels by the order in council of July, 1823. Mr. Huskisson expressly brought this subject before the House of Commons, in the course of the last session of Parliament, with a view to give full validity to that order, doubts having arisen how far it was justified by the provisions of the act of Parliament of the preceding session, on which it was founded. By this act a general power had been given to the King in council to impose counter-vailing duties on the cargoes of foreign vessels, but not upon their tonnage. It was under this act that the order of July, 1823, affecting the tonnage of our vessels, passed, and Mr. Huskisson obtained at the last session a new act for indemnifying all persons concerned in executing this order, which, though out of the words, was conceived to be within the objects of the first act. A copy of the last act is inclosed. The two acts taken together now give to the King and council a permanent power to meet other nations on the ground of reciprocity in duties, both as to vessels and cargoes. To this ground Russia has acceded by a treaty concluded with this Government in April last, a printed copy of which I inclose that its terms may be seen. Denmark has done the same, by a treaty concluded in June. The latter is not published as yet, but I have reason to know that its terms are the same as those of the treaty with Prussia. It does not include the colonies of Denmark nor, of course, those of Britain, standing, in this respect, upon the footing of our commercial convention with Britain of 1815. Prussia having no colonies, her treaty, as far as there will be room for its operation at all, necessarily stands upon the same footing. Among the colonies of Denmark are comprehended Greenland, Iceland, and the Faroe Islands, which are enumerated as such in the treaty. It is understood that Sweden has shown a disposition to come into this reciprocity, and that there are pending negotiations between this Government and that of the Netherlands to the same effect.

After the British plenipotentiaries had finished all their remarks upon our proposals, I thought it best, seeing that they had not proved acceptable, to invite others from them in turn, to be taken for reference to my Government. These they afforded me, and they are annexed, marked L, to the protocol of the sixteenth conference. The first article, after reciting the desire of both parties to abolish, reciprocally, all discriminating duties in this trade, proceeds to effect this purpose after the British understanding of it. It pledges Great Britain to lay no higher duties on our produce than upon produce of the same kind imported, not from *elsewhere*, or from any other country, but from any other *foreign* country; using here the very term to which, in both the former negotiations, we had objected at large. The same term has place in the part of the article intended to operate against Great Britain, as she only claims, in sending her colonial produce to the United States, that it shall be received subject to the same duties as are paid on articles of the same kind when imported into the United States from any other *foreign* country. To this correlative provision the British plenipotentiaries referred as illustrative of the true idea of reciprocity. I again insisted upon its manifesting the very reverse. It was palpable that the term had a real substantive meaning in the one case, but might as well be omitted in the other. Like produce with that sent to the British islands from the United States the islands obtained, as we had seen, from no other foreign country, but only from the British possessions in North America; whereas, the United States *did* receive from Cuba, from St. Domingo, and from other foreign islands and countries, the same kind of produce as that yielded in the British islands. Surely, then, Great Britain would be benefitted by the operation of the term, whilst to the United States it must be nugatory. There was a visible sphere within which it would act in the one case, whilst in the other there was no shadow of foundation upon which it could rest. But I was always unsuccessful in obtaining from the British plenipotentiaries the admissions due to us on this cardinal principle. Their second article provides for the actual abolition, subject, of course, to the foregoing reservation, of all discriminating duties or charges of every kind, whether on the vessels or cargoes of the two powers. The third contains a stipulation that, in case the trade should prove, on trial, unduly advantageous to one of the parties, the other will examine in a proper spirit the complaint, and, on its being substantiated, adopt measures in unison with the true principles on which the parties intended to fix it. The fourth provides, that whatever advantages Great Britain may in future extend to any friendly State in Europe or America with respect to this trade shall be common to the United States; and that the United States shall extend to Great Britain whatever advantages they may at any time grant to the most favored State in any trade carried on between the possessions of such State in the West Indies or America, and the United States. The fifth and last article provides, *in consideration of the foregoing arrangements,* that consuls shall be admitted from the United States into the open colonial ports, and received on the same conditions as are stipulated in the fourth article of the convention of July, 1815. Upon this last article I shall have occasion to remark in another part of my communication. The others I leave, including the fourth, upon the remarks already made. The fourth, it is evident, still keeps to the British principle of considering their colonies as equivalent of themselves to the whole of the United States in the arrangements of this trade.

During the pendency of the negotiation I received a letter, which seemed to me to be of importance, from Mr. Kankey, our consular commercial agent at the island of Barbadoes. He informed me that, under directions which had been recently given to the Collector and Comptroller of the Customs of that island by the Lords Commissioners of the Treasury, vessels of the United States were permitted to land there a portion of their cargoes, and to carry the remainder elsewhere, if entered for exportation, paying the import duty only on so much as was landed. This regulation, he added, would be of service to our trade, provided the necessity of paying the tonnage money of four shillings and three pence sterling per ton at more than one of the colonial ports during the same voyage could be avoided, and he appealed to me to have this effected. I immediately brought the subject before the British plenipotentiaries, urging the right of our vessels to an exemption from all such double payments, on the ground of British vessels never being subject to double payments of tonnage duty in the United States during the same voyage, though they did proceed from port to port. I was asked if I had any instructions from my Government upon this point. I replied that I had not, but that I was confident in my belief that, under our laws, the fact could not be otherwise than as I had stated it. Mr. Huskisson then said that he would obtain the sanction of this Government for placing our vessels in the West Indies upon the same footing in this respect upon which British vessels were placed in the United States, and would undertake, in his official capacity of President of the Board of Trade, to see that the necessary orders were forthwith issued for the accomplishment of this object.

Mr. Kankey made another representation to me, which I also brought before the British plenipotentiaries as pertinent to the business in which we were engaged. He stated that an improper duty was charged at Barbadoes on the article of biscuit when imported in barrels from the United States, a repeal of which he had not been able to effect by remonstrating with the Collector. This article, when intended for a foreign market, is packed in barrels, such as are used to hold flour, and seldom contain, it appears, more than eighty pounds weight. But, without any reference to the weight, the Collector was in the habit of demanding on every such barrel of biscuit (the cracker) landed at Barbadoes a duty of two shillings and six pence sterling, when, by the true construction of the act of Parliament of the 24th of June, 1822, under which the duty arose, it was believed that only *one* shilling and six pence *per hundred weight* ought ever to be charged. Of this heavy overcharge on a single article, which the exporters of the Middle States were constantly sending to the British islands, I complained in the terms that Mr. Kankey's representation to me warranted. Mr. Huskisson gave me an immediate assurance that my complaint should be attended to. He subsequently informed me that, in consequence, of it the officers of the customs generally in the islands had been directed, in all cases where such biscuit was imported from the United States in barrels weighing less than one hundred and ninety six pounds, to charge the duty by the weight, and at the rate of not more than one shilling and six pence sterling per hundred weight. I am happy to think that in at least these two instances some portion of immediate relief is likely to be extended to our trade in that quarter.

From Mr. Monroe Harrison, the consul of the United States at Antigua, I also received a communication whilst our proceedings were going on, of which I apprised the plenipotentiaries of this Government.

He informed me that our citizens trading to that island, being often compelled to sell their cargoes on a credit, payable in produce when the crops came in, found it convenient, if not sometimes necessary, to make another voyage to the West Indies, in order to recover the proceeds of their cargoes so disposed of. The markets in the French and other islands being often better than in the British islands, our citizens in the predicament stated would find it, Mr. Harrison remarked, to their advantage to be able to resort to the former islands in the first instance. But this object they were precluded from coupling with that of afterwards calling at the British islands for the collection of their debts in the produce of them, since, should they only touch at the British islands, having on board any article other than of the produce of the United States, their vessels became liable to seizure. I did not receive from the British plenipotentiaries the same attention to this representation that was shown in the other cases, nor, under my present lights, did I feel altogether warranted in pressing it upon the same grounds. They informed me, in the course of our conversation upon it, that there was no objection, under the British regulations, to a vessel of the United States, bound from one of our ports to any island in the West Indies other than British, afterwards proceeding from such other island to a British island with the whole or part of her cargo, provided it had not been landed at any intermediate port, and that there had been no change in the property during the voyage. I presume that those of our citizens who are interested in knowing it are acquainted with this construction of the British laws, which, however, does not present itself to my mind in the light of any important boon.

The act of Parliament of August 5, 1822, having immediate relation to the commercial intercourse between the United States and the British continental possessions in their neighborhood, I naturally regarded it, as your instructions to me had done, in connexion with the act of June 24, 1822. This brought under consideration our claim to the navigation of the river St. Lawrence. Between this question and the questions of commercial intercourse under the act of June, 1822, the British plenipotentiaries were constantly unwilling to acknowledge any connexion; nevertheless, looking to your instructions, and as well to the reason of them as to their authority, I treated the two questions as belonging to one and the same general subject. They asked whether, taking the two acts of Parliament together, the United States did not already enjoy the navigation of this river. I said that they did; by the act of June 24, 1822, they enjoyed it from the ocean to Quebec, and by that of August 5, 1822, from any part of the territories of the United States to Quebec; but from the fact of the colonial Governments in Canada being invested with a discretionary power to withdraw the latter of these concessions, by excepting any of the Canadian ports from those to which our vessels were made admissible, it followed that our enjoyment of the navigation of this river was rendered contingent upon British permission. This was a tenure not reconcilable, in the opinion of the Government of the United States, with the growing and permanent wants of their citizens in that portion of the Union, or with the rights of the nation. It was due to both these considerations that it should stand upon a different tenure, and the time had arrived when it was desirable that the two nations should come to an understanding upon a question of so much importance.

The British plenipotentiaries next asked whether any question was about to be raised on the right of Great Britain to exclude altogether vessels of the United States from trading with British ports situated upon the St. Lawrence, or elsewhere in Canada. I replied, that I was not prepared absolutely to deny such a right in Great Britain to whatever considerations its exercise might be open. I remarked, also, that it seemed already to have been substantially exercised by this act of August 5, 1822; for, by its provisions, only certain enumerated articles were allowed to be exported from the United States into Canadian ports, and duties were laid upon these articles which might be said to amount to a prohibition. I added that, although the foregoing act had not laid any duty on the merchandise of the United States descending the St. Lawrence with a view to exportation by sea, yet that an act of the preceding year did, viz: upon their timber and lumber, which made it highly expedient that the relative rights of the parties to the use of the waters of this great stream should be ascertained. I here went into a review of the footing upon which the trade between the United States and the Canadas stood, under the stipulations of the treaty of 1794. The memorial from the inhabitants of Franklin county, in the State of New York, and the report of the committee of the House of Representatives upon that document, furnished me with the necessary lights for executing this duty, as well as for pointing out the injurious and burdensome operation of the act of August 5, 1822. The latter act had superseded all the former conditions of this intercourse. With these conditions the citizens of the United States had been, I said, content, and it was believed that they had been found, on experience, satisfactory on both sides. The treaty stipulations of 1794 were among the articles of that instrument declared, when it was made, to be permanent; and so mutually beneficial had appeared to be their operation that both parties continued, in practice, to make them the rule of their conduct for some years after the war of 1812, until, by the acts of Parliament just recited, Great Britain chose to consider the intervention of that war as putting an end to their validity. This state of things, by remitting each party to their anterior and original rights, rendered it manifestly incumbent upon the Government of the United States now to attempt to settle by convention, or in some other manner, with Great Britain, the true nature of the tenure by which they held the navigation of this stream. Such was the character of the remarks by which I illustrated the propriety of adding to the two articles which I had offered for the regulation of the commercial intercourse between the United States and the British colonies, whether continental or insular, a third article relating exclusively to the navigation of the St. Lawrence. A third article will be found, accordingly, in this connexion as part of our projet, already referred to as annexed to the protocol of the third conference. Its stipulations were, that the navigation of the St. Lawrence, in its whole length and breadth to and from the sea, should be at all times equally free to the citizens and subjects of both countries, and that the vessels belonging to either party should never be subject to any molestation whatever by the other, or to the payment of any duty for this right of navigation. After this unequivocal provision, it concluded with a clause that, regarding such reasonable and moderate tolls as either side might claim and appear to be entitled to, the contracting parties would treat at a future day, in order that the principles regulating such tolls might be adjusted to mutual satisfaction.

I deemed it most advisable to ingraft upon the article this principle respecting tolls, although it was not particularly mentioned in your despatch. In pursuing into their details some of the general principles which you had laid down, I was left under the impression that our title to navigate this river, independently of the consent of Great Britain, would be made out with more complete and decisive strength, under the qualified admission of the claim to toll. The writers on public law had generally so treated the subject, and in some of the modern treaties of high authority in our favor on the general question the admission was also to be seen. I refer particularly to the fifth article of the treaty of peace of the thirteenth of May, 1814, between the allied powers and France, where, after providing for the free navigation of the Rhine to all persons, it is agreed that principles should be laid down at a future Congress for the collection of the duties by the States on its banks, in the manner most equal and favorable to the commerce of all nations. In adverting to the claim of toll as a question only for future discussion, and one that might be of like interest to both parties, (the British navigation of this river being obliged in some parts to pass close to our bank,) and, moreover, where the claim, if advanced on either side, was to be made dependent on sufficient cause being shown for it, I did not believe that I was losing sight of any principle of value to the United States in this controversy. The clause, I hope, will be found to have been too guarded in its terms to be open to such a risk.

There was another point on which I felt more uncertainty. The navigation of this stream, although I believed it could be demonstrated to be the just right of the people of the United States, could not draw after it all its benefits to them without a concurrent right of stopping at some point or port where both of its banks fell within the colonial territory of Great Britain. Upon what footing was I to treat this latter and subordinate question? Your instructions had not dealt with it, and I felt myself at a loss. It could scarcely be doubted but that our right to navigate the river being established, Britain would, as matter of international comity, and as an arrangement advantageous also to herself, allow us a place of entry for our vessels, and deposit for our produce somewhere on its shores. She has so largely, of late years, been extending the warehousing system to all other nations for their convenience and her own, that it might well be presumed she would not exclude the United States from a participation in it at Quebec, or elsewhere at a suitable port in Canada. Yet I felt it to be a point of some delicacy, and therefore thought that it would be most judicious to leave it wholly untouched in my proposal. Another reason operated with me for this silence. As far as I was able to carry my investigations into the point, I found much ground for supposing that the right to the navigation of a river, under the strong circumstances which marked that of the United States to the navigation of the St. Lawrence, would involve as an incident the right of innocent stoppage somewhere on the shores, an incident indispensable to the beneficial enjoyment of the right itself. By the seventh article of the treaty of Paris, of 1763, the free navigation of the Mississippi was granted to Great Britain, but without any clause securing to British vessels the privilege of stopping at New Orleans, then a French port, or at any other port or place on any part of the shores. Yet the historical fact appears to have been that Britain did use New Orleans as a place for her vessels to stop at, and this without any subsequent arrangement with France upon the subject. The case becomes still stronger if, afterwards, when New Orleans fell into the hands of Spain, the British continued to use it for the same purpose, contrary, at first, to the remonstrances of the Spanish Governor of that town, which is also believed to have been the fact. I abstained, however, from asserting in this negotiation the subordinate right in question.

On the principal question of our equal right with the British to the entire and unobstructed navigation of this river I dwelt with all the emphasis demanded by its magnitude. I spoke of it as a question intimately connected with the present interests of the United States, and which assumed an aspect yet more commanding in its bearing upon their future population and destinies. Already the immense regions which bordered upon the lakes and northern rivers of the United States were rapidly filling up with inhabitants, and soon the dense millions who would cover them would point to the paramount and irresistible necessity for the use of this great stream as their only natural highway to the ocean. Nor was the question one of magnitude to this part of the Union alone. The whole nation felt their stake in it, the middle and the north more immediately, but all the rest by the multiplied ties and connexions which bound up their wants, their interests, and their sympathies with the middle and the north. It was under such a view of the immediate and prospective value of this navigation to us that I first presented it to the notice of the British plenipotentiaries as a question of right. I told them that they must understand this to be the sense in which I had drawn up the article upon the subject, and that it was the sense in which I felt myself bound, as the plenipotentiary of the United States, to urge its adoption.

I approach an interesting part of this negotiation when I come to make known in what manner the British plenipotentiaries received this disclosure. They said that on principles of accommodation they were willing to treat of this claim with the United States in a spirit of entire amity; that is, as they explained, to treat of it as a concession on the part of Great Britain, for which the United States must be prepared to offer a full equivalent. This was the only light in which they could entertain the question. As to the claim of right, they hoped that it would not even be advanced; persisted in, they were willing to persuade themselves, it would never be. It was equally novel and extraordinary. They could not repress their strong feelings of surprise at its bare intimation. Great Britain possessed the absolute sovereignty over this river in all parts where both its banks were of her territorial dominion. Her right, hence, to exclude a foreign nation from navigating it was not to be doubted, scarcely to be discussed. This was the manner in which it was at first received. They opposed to the claim an immediate, positive, unqualified resistance.

I said that our claim was neither novel nor extraordinary. It was one that had been well considered by my Government, and was believed to be maintainable on the soundest principles of public law. The question had been familiar to the past discussions of the United States, as their State papers, which were before the world, would show. It had been asserted, and successfully asserted, in relation to another great river of the American continent flowing to the south, the Mississippi, at a time when both of its lower banks were under the dominion of a foreign power. The essential principles that had governed the one case were now applicable to the other.

My reply was not satisfactory to the British plenipotentiaries. They combatted the claim with increased earnestness, declaring that it was altogether untenable, and of a nature to be totally and unequivocally rejected. Instead of having the sanction of public law, the law and the practice of nations equally disclaimed it. Could I show where was to be found in either the least warrant for its assertion? Was it not a claim plainly inconsistent with the paramount authority and exclusive possession of Great Britain? Could she for one moment listen to it?

I remarked that the claim had been put forward by the United States because of the great national interests involved in it; yet that this consideration, high as it was, would never be looked at but in connexion with the just rights of Great Britain. For this course of proceeding both the principles and practice of my Government might well be taken as the guaranty. The claim was, therefore, far from being put forward in any unfriendly spirit, and would be subject to a frank and full interchange of sentiments between the two Governments. I was obviously bound, I admitted, to make known on behalf of mine the grounds on which the claim was advanced—a duty which I would not fail to perform. I stated that we considered our right to the navigation of this river as strictly a *natural right*. This was the firm foundation on which it would be placed. This was the light in which it was defensible on the highest authorities, no less than on the soundest principles. If, indeed, it had ever heretofore been supposed that the possession of both the shores of a river below had conferred the right of interdicting the navigation of it to the people of other nations inhabiting its upper banks, the examination of such a principle would at once disclose the objections to it. The exclusive right of jurisdiction over a river could only originate in the social compact, and be claimed as a right of sovereignty. The right of navigating the river was a right of nature, preceding in point of time, and which the mere sovereign right of one nation could not annihilate as belonging to the people of another. It was a right essential to the condition and wants of human society, and conformable to the voice of mankind in all ages and countries. The principle on which it rested challenged such universal assent, that wherever it had not been allowed it might be imputed to the triumph of power or injustice over right. Its recovery and exercise had still been objects precious among nations, and it was happily acquiring fresh sanction from the highest examples of modern times. The parties to the European alliance had, in the treaties of Vienna, declared that the navigation of the Rhine, the Necker, the Mayne, the Moselle, the Maes, and the Scheldt, should be free to all nations. The object of these stipulations was as evident as praiseworthy. It could have been no other than to render the navigation of those rivers free to all the people dwelling upon their banks; thus abolishing those unjust restrictions by which the people of the interior of Germany had been too often deprived of their natural outlet to the sea by an abuse of that right of sovereignty which claimed for a State happening to possess both the shores of a river at its mouth the exclusive property over it. There was no principle of national law upon which the stipulations of the above treaties could be founded which did not equally apply to the case of the St. Lawrence. It was thus that I opened our general doctrine. It was from such principles that I deduced our right to navigate this river, independent of the mere favor or concession of Great Britain, and, consequently, independent of any claim on her side to an equivalent.

I abstain from any further recapitulation to you of the principles which I invoked, or of the authorities to which I referred, for a reason to be now mentioned. It will be seen by the first protocol that our agreement had been to carry on the negotiation by conference and protocol. This, the more usual mode at all times, was conceived to be peculiarly appropriate where the subjects to be handled were so various, and their details in some instances so extensive. It was recommended, also, and this was of higher sway with me, by the example of the negotiation of 1818, in the course of which some of the same subjects had been discussed with this Government. Nevertheless, each party had reserved, under this agreement, the right of annexing to the protocol any written statement that might be considered necessary as matter either of record or of explanation. In your instructions to me respecting this claim to the navigation of the St. Lawrence—a question wholly new as between the two nations—you had adverted to my presenting it in writing, if necessary, and I determined, under all the circumstances, that I should not properly come up to my duty unless by adopting this mode. The question was not only new, but of the greatest moment. I saw, also, from the beginning, that it would encounter the most decided opposition from Great Britain. In proportion as her plenipotentiaries became explicit and peremptory in denying it, did it occur to me that it would be proper on my part to be unequivocal in its assertion. This could be best done upon paper. This would carry the claim distinctly to the archives of this Government, rather than trust it to foundations more uncertain and fugitive. It would explain, as well as record, the sense in which it was inserted in the protocol. Another motive with me for this course, and scarcely a secondary one, was, that it would serve to draw from Great Britain in the same form a precise and full avowal of the grounds on which she designed to oppose the claim. On a question so large, and which, from all that I perceived to mark its first opening between the two Governments, could hardly fail to come under discussion again hereafter, it appeared to me that it would be more acceptable to my Government to be in possession of a written document which should embody the opinions of this Government, than to take the report of them from me under any form less exact or authentic.

I accordingly drew up a paper upon the subject, which, under the right reserved, I annexed (marked B) to the protocol of the eighteenth conference, and so it stands amongst the papers of the negotiation. The British plenipotentiaries continued to urge their animated protests against this proceeding on my part, not that they could divest me of my privilege of recording my sentiments in the shape of this written statement, but that they earnestly pressed the propriety of my abandoning altogether any claim to the navigation of this river as a claim of right which shut them out from treating of it upon other bases. But, having taken my determination under other estimates of my duty, I did not depart from it.

The paper which I drew up aimed at presenting a broad but intelligible outline of the principal reasons in support of our claim. These were such as you had set before me, and as I judged to be immediately deducible from them. Under the latter I included the argument on the Mississippi question used by an illustrious individual, then the organ of our Government in its intercourse with foreign States. I considered this argument as virtually comprehended in your instructions by the reference which they contained to it; the questions in both cases, so far as each drew support from the deep foundations of the law of nature, being the same. Of this luminous State paper I followed the track, adopting its own language wherever this could be done as the safest, the most approved, the most national.' The only view of the subject not elicited on that occasion which I ventured to take up was one pointed out by the locality of the St. Lawrence. I will briefly explain it.

The exclusive right possessed by Great Britain over both banks of this river was won for her by the co-operation of the people who now form the United States. Their exertions, their treasure, their blood, were profusely employed in every campaign of the old French war. It was under this name that the recollection of that war still lived in the United States; a war which, but for the aid of New England, New York, and Pennsylvania, if of no more of the States, would probably not have terminated when it did in the conquest of Canada from France. If these States were at that epoch a part of the colonial empire of Britain, it was, nevertheless, impossible to obliterate the recollection of historical facts, or exclude the inferences that would attach to them. The predecessors of the present inhabitants of those States had borne a constant and heavy burden in that war, and had acquired, simultaneously with the then parent State, the right of descending this stream, on the hypothesis, assumed for the moment, of their not having possessed it before; a right of peculiar importance to them from their local position and necessities. It was to this effect that I noticed a title by *joint acquisition*, as also susceptible of being adduced for the United States to the navigation of this river. There was, at least, a strong national equity in it which would come home to the people of the United States, impressing them with new convictions of the hardship of now refusing them the use of this stream as an innocent pathway to the ocean. But as I had not your elucidations of this view of the subject, I was careful to use it only in subordination to the argument of natural right. The latter I treated as sufficient in itself to make out our title, and repudiated the necessity of resorting to any other. I will own, however, that my disposition to confide in the argument founded upon joint acquisition was increased by the analogy which it appeared to me to bear to the course of reasoning pursued with Great Britain, by my predecessor in this mission in relation to the fisheries. If our title to a full participation with Britain in the fisheries, though they were within the acknowledged limits and jurisdiction of the coasts of British America, was strengthened by the fact of the early inhabitants of the United States having been among the foremost to explore and use the fishing grounds, why was the analogous fact of their having assisted to expel the French from the lower shores of the St. Lawrence to be of no avail? I had believed in the application and force of the argument in the one instance, and could not deny it all the consideration that it merited in the other.

  The necessity of my recounting to you the British argument in answer to our claim is superseded by my being able to transmit it to you in their own words upon paper. It is sufficiently elaborate, and was drawn up with great deliberation. It is annexed (marked N) to the protocol of the twenty-fourth conference. The intention avowed by the British plenipotentiaries at the nineteenth conference of obtaining for its doctrines, before it was delivered to me, the full sanction of their highest professional authorities on matters relating to the law of nations, may serve to show the "gravity and importance," to repeat their own expression, which the question had assumed in their eyes. I have otherwise reasons for knowing that their argument was prepared under the advice and assistance of five of the most eminent publicists of England. With all the respect due to a paper matured under such auspices, I am not able to look upon it as impugning the argument which, under your direction, and following the course of others before me, I had become the organ of making known on behalf of the United States.

In several instances the British paper has appealed to the same authorities that are to be found in mine. It is in the application of them only that the difference is seen. In other parts the difference is made to turn upon words rather than substance. But an error that runs throughout nearly the whole of their paper consists in attributing to mine a meaning which does not belong to it. This applies especially to the particular description of right which we claim; how far it is one of mere innocent utility, how far a right necessary to us and not injurious to Britain, how far a right which, if not falling under the technical designation of absolute, is nevertheless one that cannot be withheld—these are all qualifications that were not overlooked in my exposition of the doctrine, a light, however, in which the British paper does not appear to have regarded it. But as each document is now of record, and will be judged by the terms which it has used, and the construction that justly attaches to them, I will not enlarge upon this head.

The British paper deals with our claim as standing upon equal footing with a claim to the use of the roads, canals, or other artificial ways of a country, forgetting that the case in dispute is that of a natural stream forming the only natural outlet to the ocean—the stream itself being common by nature to both countries. Commenting upon the acquired title of the United States, which I had put forward under the restriction described, their paper argues that the same ground would justify a co-relative claim by Great Britain to the use of the navigable rivers and all other public possessions of the United States which existed when both countries were united under a common Government! By a like misapplication of obvious principles it argues that our claim would also justify Britain in asking a passage down the Mississippi, or the Hudson, though neither the one nor the other touch any portion of the British territories; or that it might equally justify a claim on her side to *ascend* with British vessels the principal rivers of the United States as far as their draught of water would admit, instead of depositing their cargoes at the appointed ports of entry from the sea. On doctrines such as these I could only say to the British plenipotentiaries that I was wholly unable to perceive their application to the argument, unless the United States had been advancing a claim to the navigation of the river Thames in England.

Their argument also assumes that the treaty stipulations of 1794 exclude all idea of a right on our side to the navigation of this river, forgetting that if under those stipulations vessels of the United States were interdicted the navigation of British rivers between their mouths and the highest port of entry from the sea, so, on the other hand, British vessels were interdicted the navigation of the rivers of the United States beyond the highest ports of entry from the sea, and also that the whole terms of the international intercourse in that quarter were, by this compact, such as at the time satisfied both parties without impairing the rights which either possessed independent of the compact, and which only remained in suspense during its existence. This observation suggests another to which their argument is open in parts which they press as of decisive weight. It alleges that because, by the general treaty of Vienna, the powers whose States were crossed by the same navigable rivers, engaged to regulate by common consent all that regarded their navigation; because Russia held by treaty the navigation of the Black Sea, and because of the many instances capable of being cited where the navigation of rivers or straits that separated or flowed through the territories of different countries was expressly provided for by treaty— that because of these facts the inference was irresistible that the right of navigation under such circumstances depended upon *common consent*, and could only be claimed *by treaty*. Here, too, it seems to have been forgotten that it is allowable in treaties, as well as oftentimes expedient for greater safety and precision, to enter into stipulations for the *enjoyment* or *regulation* of pre-existing rights; that treaties are, in fact, expressly declared by the writers upon the laws of nations to be of two general kinds: those which turn on things to which we are already bound by the law of nature, and those by which we engage to do something more. In their quotation, also, of the note from the first volume of the Laws of Congress, containing an intimation that the United States could not be expected to yield the navigation of the Mississippi without an equivalent, they seem wholly to have overlooked, besides the other points of that note, that it was made at a period when it was well known that no part of that river touched the territories of a foreign power, and when, therefore, its exclusive navigation belonged to the United States as much so as the Delaware or the Potomac.

The foregoing are some of the remarks upon the British paper which I submitted at the conference after receiving it. The first impressions that I had of my duty in regard to it, and consequently my first determination, was to reply to it at large in writing, annexing my reply to the protocol. But, on more reflection, I deemed it most proper to abstain, at present, from this step. As a view of the whole subject, given out under the immediate eye and authority of this Government, and with extraordinary care, it appeared to me that the British paper ought to come under the knowledge of my own Government before receiving a formal or full answer from any source less high. If it be thought to require such an answer, a short delay would be nothing to the advantage of its being afforded, either through me or my successor in this mission, under the light of further instructions from home. The pause seemed the more due, not only from the newness of the discussion between the two Governments, but because I may not, at this moment, be sufficiently apprised of all the modifications under which mine may desire it to be presented in a second and more full argument.   I hope that this forbearance on my part will be approved as having been, under the exigency, the most circumspect and becoming course.   I gave the British plenipo‑ tentiaries to understand that the written argument on the side of the United States must not be considered as closed, but, on the contrary, only as opened. .

Finally, in coming to a conclusion on the general subject of our commercial intercourse with the British West Indies and their North American colonies, whether by the way of the ocean or the St. Lawrence, it may be proper in me to recapitulate what I take to be the determinations of this Government in regard to it at all points.

1. They will not give up the duty of four shillings and three pence sterling per ton imposed upon our vessels by the order in council of July, 1823.

2. They will enter into no convention or arrangement with us that does not recognize the principle embraced in the first article of their counter project annexed to the sixteenth protocol: I mean that which goes to place our produce imported into their islands upon the same footing in respect of duties as the like produce imported into them from any other *foreign* country. ˙This term they adhere to on the avowed principle of protecting and encouraging the produce of their own colonial possessions in North America.

3. They will not abolish the duties specified in schedule C of the act of Parliament of June 24, 1822, or those specified in schedule B of the act of August 5, 1822.

4. They totally deny our right to the navigation of the St. Lawrence, declaring that they cannot treat of the subject upon such a basis.

5. They will be willing to repeal entirely, if not already done, all duties or charges whatever, whether imposed by act of Parliament, growing out of colonial laws or usages, or in whatsoever manner existing, which go to subject vessels of the United States to any burden not common to British vessels—the repeal to extend to all the enumerated ports, without exception.

6. Though stating that they are not satisfied with the trade on its present footing, they are willing that it should have a further experiment; that is, to let it go on, the United States retaining their foreign tonnage duty and additional impost of ten per centum, and Great Britain retaining her tonnage duty of July, 1823, and also an additional impost of ten per centum.

The protocols which have reference to the different branches of this whole subject are the third, the ninth, the fifteenth, the sixteenth, the seventeenth, the eighteenth, the nineteenth, the twenty-fourth, and the twenty-fifth.   I pass to another subject.

II. BOUNDARY LINE UNDER THE FIFTH ARTICLE OF THE TREATY OF GHENT.

This subject was, throughout, coupled by the British plenipotentiaries with the one the descriptions respecting which I have just been detailing, viz: the navigation of the St. Lawrence.   Their reasons for this course will be seen presently, though I did not acquiesce in their validity.   I brought the subject before them by stating from the treaty of Ghent the duties which under its fifth article were to have been performed by the Commissioners of the two countries in relation to this long-unsettled boundary.   I brought into view from your instructions of June 25, 1823, the many and essential points upon which the Commissioners had differed: 1. Upon where the northwest angle of Nova Scotia was situated? 2. Upon what was the northwesternmost head of the Connecticut river? 3. Upon the meaning of the words in the old treaty of 1783, "along the highlands which divide those rivers that empty themselves into the river St. Lawrence from those which fall into the Atlantic Ocean." 4. Upon the admission of the general maps respectively presented by the agents of the two Governments, each objecting to the correctness of that presented by the other, and pressing for the reception of his own.   5. Upon a proposal by the British Commissioner to send out surveyors to ascertain the correctness of the former surveys in regard to the points objected to in the maps presented by the agents. 6. Upon a demand made by the British agent to examine upon oath the surveyors who made the maps, with regard to their correctness.   7. Upon the reception and entering upon the journals of a memorial of the British agent containing a statement of one of the British surveyors relating to the maps presented by the agents. 8. Upon the reception of a written motion by the British agent, requesting leave to exhibit a memorial containing statements of the British surveyors relating to the maps, and that the same might be entered on the journals.   There were still other points upon which the Commissioners had differed, but the foregoing, as it was plain to see, embraced the chief ones.   Neither of the two points, viz., the latitude and longitutde of the northwest angle of Nova Scotia, or the northwesternmost head of the Connecticut river, the ascertaining of which had been the great object of the commission, having been fixed, it had become impossible, I remarked, for the Commissioners to agree upon the map and declaration which, by the stipulations of the treaty of Ghent, were conclusively to have determined the boundary, and that, consequently, there was now no such map, whilst to aggravate this difficulty the general map produced by each side had been totally discredited by the other.

I then recited those parts of the fifth article of the treaty of Ghent under which, in conjunction with the corresponding clauses of the fourth article, provision is made for carrying the differences of the Commissioners, in case they failed to arrange this boundary, before some friendly sovereign for his decision; but added, that the Government of the United States, instead of adopting this course, desired to attempt a settlement of these differences by direct negotiation between the two countries, as heretofore proposed by the United States and acceded to by Great Britain.   Having thus opened our plan, I proceeded to expatiate on the topics enlarged upon in your despatch towards its elucidation and support.   I pointed to the formidable embarrassments which surrounded the subject on all sides in its present actual state, regarded as one to be settled by an umpirage; to the necessity which would be devolved upon the sovereign of deciding upon a boundary of at least six hundred miles in extent, through a half-discovered country, which the parties themselves, after six years of laborious investigation, had altogether failed to fix, assisted, too, as they had been, by able surveyors, geographers, astronomers, and agents; to the various questions of construction of ancient charters, treaties, and proclamations, into which he would have to travel; to the controversies between France and England prior to the cession of Canada to the latter, with which he must become familiar; and to the immense volume of documents produced by the labors, scientific, argumentative, or practical, of the Commissioners, and those who acted in co-operation with them, which he would have to peruse.   I forbear to go further with a recapitulation of the difficulties, as I omitted none that your despatch had laid before me, and, above all, did not omit to state that, to the appalling train of them would be added that of the sovereign having to choose between maps that had alike been discredited by both parties. It was to avoid all these difficulties, and the uncertain results that might and probably would hang upon them if the differences were carried before an arbitrator, that my Government had charged me, I said, with the duty of now submitting, in a distinct and formal manner, the proposal for settling them by direct negotiation. This proposal I accordingly offered in the shape of a written article, (marked D,) annexed to the protocol of the ninth conference. The article, after reciting that the Commissioners under the fifth article of the treaty of Ghent for ascertaining the latitude and longitude of the northwest angle of Nova Scotia and the northwesternmost head of Connecticut river, and for surveying that part of the boundary line between the dominions of the two powers which extends from the source of the river St. Croix directly north to the above northwest angle of Nova Scotia, (and so on, pursuing the words of the treaty,) had not been able to agree, and also reciting that it was the desire of the parties, instead of referring their differences to the arbitration of a sovereign, as provided by the treaty, to endeavor to settle them by negotiation between themselves, went on to stipulate that the parties would accordingly negotiate on them at Washington; and further, that in the course of such negotiation they would receive, if necessary, the maps that had been respectively submitted and used by the Commissioners of each nation, but that none that had been used on the one side should be received or used to the exclusion of those used on the other. Such were the terms of my proposal, which, I trust, will be thought to have embodied with sufficient care your directions in relation to this subject.

The British plenipotentiaries, after hearing my proposal, and the reasons that had been given in its support, though not accepting it, did not object to the principle of compromise. They declared, however, that if ever they did enter into any regular agreement to settle the question by negotiation or compromise, it must, in their view, contain a clause that, this mode of settlement failing, that by arbitration, under the treaty, was still to be retained as the right of the parties. They expressed their concurrence in opinion as to the difficulty which there might be in submitting differences of such scope and complication to the arbitration of a sovereign, and wished, if practicable, to avoid resorting to this plan. What they desired, under present circumstances, was, that Great Britain should be allowed to settle the several disputed points which had arisen under the fifth article of the treaty of Ghent, by going into them on principles of mutual concession, *in connexion with the claim of the United States to the navigation of the St. Lawrence.* They distinctly submitted this proposal to me, which, however, was not given in writing, further than as it will be seen in the seventeenth and eighteenth protocols.

To this proposal I made immediate objections, as both new and unexpected. I admitted no connexion between the two subjects. How could I consent to treat of them conjointly, on the basis of mutual concession, when the United States expressly claimed the right of navigating this river, independent of all concession. The subjects were distinct, and would not, I expressed a hope, be coupled by the intervention of a principle wholly alien to the one, and not admitted by my Government to have any application to the other.

The British plenipotentiaries, always renewing their pointed denials of our right to the navigation of the St. Lawrence, said that they had coupled these subjects, because of their affinity, under the general head of boundary, some of the disputed points under the fifth article of the treaty of Ghent being, as to locality, contiguous to that part of the St. Lawrence which flows through the British territories: This was one of their reasons. Another and stronger one was, that they were prepared to make offers which they would describe as founded upon a most liberal and comprehensive view of the wishes and interests of the United States in relation to the differences under the fifth article of the treaty of Ghent, in connexion with offers of the same character in relation to the navigation of the St. Lawrence, provided we were prepared to treat of the latter on the footing of concession by Great Britain. By having both of the questions under our hands at the same time, they urged the greater probability of our being able to settle both, and expressed their belief that, by thus multiplying the materials of compromise, we might arrive at a speedy and satisfactory arrangement on both subjects. They therefore hoped that I would accede to their wish of coupling these two subjects together in the manner that they proposed.

I repeated my objections to their proposal, declaring that my instructions did not permit me to hesitate a moment in rejecting it. The boundary question was one that stood upon its own foundation. No other had been coupled with it by my Government, and I could not consent to treat of it with any other, where the connexion was confessedly to impair the equal ground of the United States as soon as the principle of compromise was admitted. The boundary question, too, besides being detached and independent, was, in its nature, peculiarly ample. The materials of compromise existed within its own limits, rendering it unnecessary, therefore, to seek in a new subject what was already at hand. The association of another subject with it, and that subject the navigation of the St. Lawrence, would be open to the danger of producing further collisions, full as much, perhaps, as any enhanced prospect of an easy arrangement. Besides, I remarked, was the agreement heretofore signified by Great Britain to attempt the settlement of this question of boundary by direct negotiation between the two Governments, without the association of any other with it being at that period so much as thought of—was this to be overlooked? Here I recalled to the British plenipotentiaries what had passed between Lord Londonderry and me upon this question, and at a subsequent conference I read to them those parts of my despatches of February 11 and April 6, 1822, which detailed it to you. It was in this manner that I met the proposal of joining the two subjects upon the terms intimated.

The British plenipotentiaries, repeating their opinion that the junction would be likely to accomplish results satisfactory to both sides, said that they had neither the desire nor intention of overlooking any past agreement upon this subject with which their Government might be chargeable. They then asked whether, in case they were willing to go at once into the boundary question as one by itself, I was prepared to make to them any specific offers for a settlement. I replied that I was not. My Government had not looked to a settlement of the question here, at the present moment, by any offers to be made through me. Nor had it at any time contemplated the submission of offers merely to be accepted or rejected by this Government, but only to be received on the principle of negotiating, and it was to secure a negotiation upon the entire subject that I had drawn up the article that had been given to them. I had occasion to perceive that the British plenipotentiaries reverted to the same construction of their acceptance heretofore of our proposal of attempting an adjustment by direct communication, as that suggested to you by the British minister in Washington. They did not appear to consider that it charged this Government with the obligation of a regular and formal negotiation upon the point, but only with that of receiving from us, and considering an offer of a boundary line by compromise, which they still professed their readiness to do. I said that the United States were not prepared at present to make this offer, to say nothing of their objections to making it at all, under the uncertainty of whether or not it would be received on the principle of negotiating, and I labored to show the latter to have been the true spirit of the past agreement. Certainly it was that, I said, in which it had been understood on our side. But, under the turn which the question of the St. Lawrence had taken, I found the British plenipotentiaries unwilling to give to their past agreement any larger meaning than that to which they considered themselves pledged by their own understanding of its terms; and although I continued to the last to press upon them the acceptance of my proposal in the form annexed to the ninth protocol, I was not able to succeed.

They asked whether, in case *they* were to submit to me an offer of a boundary by compromise, I was prepared to conclude anything under such an offer. To this, too, I replied that I was not. They next inquired whether I was prepared to conclude arrangements with them which, in their opinion, must accompany any mere agreement to settle the disputed points by compromise. I answered, that this would depend upon the particular nature of the arrangements. I had already myself put forward a formal proposal intended to effectuate, through negotiation, this end. If this proposal had proved objectionable in any points where the option of modification might rest with me, I would willingly take into consideration counter proposals having in view the same end. Understanding, however, that any counter proposals from them, if submitted at this juncture, would contain at least some allusions to the question of the St. Lawrence, I said that I would decline the conclusion of any previous arrangement upon the subject.

It will be seen from all that I have said how constant and earnest a desire was manifested by the British plenipotentiaries to blend these two questions, and how constantly I felt it my duty under every aspect to keep them asunder. I have stated also, that, on the supposition of their being joined together - as elements of accommodation, the British plenipotentiaries remarked that they were prepared to make offers founded (I use their own words) "on a most liberal and comprehensive view of the wishes and interests of the United States" in relation to both. Such a declaration could not fail to excite my attention. I was aware, indeed, that Britain might make offers which she would doubtless believe to wear this character of benefit to the United States, without the United States being laid under the same convictions—so different an estimate might each party form of what was its due. Yet the expressions were strong; and although I felt that I could accede to nothing whatever myself, coupled with the principle of compromise that had been avowed, I nevertheless thought that there might be some propriety in knowing, for the information of my Government, the nature of the offers which professed, and in terms so awakening, to bear upon the interests and wishes of the United States. I therefore said to the British plenipotentiaries that I should be glad to be made acquainted with them, not in a way pledging this Government to any ulterior step, but merely as offers that would have been made in case I had expressed a willingness to receive them upon the condition from which they were not to be severed. They asked, what progress I supposed would be made towards a settlement by a compliance on their part with my request. I replied, none at present, but that I would transmit their offers to my Government in the light of an incidental fact evolved in the course of the negotiation; and, so far, it might be proper and possibly useful that I should know them. They next asked whether I could undertake to give them any reasonable assurance that my Government, on receiving them, and finding them satisfactory and advantageous, would be disposed to take them into consideration under their essential condition of our claim to the navigation of the St. Lawrence, as a right, being waived. I replied that I was wholly unauthorized to give them the slightest assurance to that effect. This closed my endeavors to obtain a knowledge of their offers, which, as will be inferred, were in the end not communicated to me. In the course of the remarks to which these endeavors led, I did not scruple to express the belief I entertained that my Government looked forward with a well grounded and even confident hope to the negotiation on the boundary question alone terminating, on a principle of compromise, in a manner satisfactory to both nations.

All attempts under present circumstances to put the case into an effective train of settlement, either by direct offers of compromise or by an agreement to negotiate on that principle, having thus failed, the plan of arbitration next presented itself for consideration. I thought at one time that the British plenipotentiaries designed to press an immediate resort to this plan. I informed them, in reply to their own inquiry, that I was prepared, if they insisted upon it, to enter upon the necessary steps for the selection of a sovereign as arbitrator. I again dwelt, however, upon the extreme difficulty, not to say impossibility, which, in the opinion of my Government, there would be, under existing circumstances, in going on with an arbitration. How, I asked, was it ever to be begun? Was this Government prepared to furnish with a statement of the case proper to be laid before the arbitrator, and which would at the same time invite the concurrence of the United States? In regard to the first idea, I reminded the British plenipotentiaries of the mutual complaints and recriminations, often sharp and angry, which, it was alike to be admitted and lamented, were too profusely to be found among the elaborate journals and other proceedings of the commission, and over which it might be supposed that each nation would rather desire to draw a veil than publish more largely to the world. This feature in the complicated transaction formed, indeed, one of the many reasons for not resorting to an umpirage at all, and so I had been instructed to declare. But, this objection removed, how, I asked, in the second place, would Britain prepare her statement in a manner to be acceptable to the United States? Upon what maps would it be founded? Not upon those used by the United States; for to these Britain objected; not upon her own, for to these the United States objected; and there was no common map which could reconcile these discordant opinions. My own Government, I added, would have performed the task of drawing up a statement but for this difficulty about the map, not the only one, however, but a difficulty common to both parties, and which met them at the very threshold. It was thus that I addressed the British plenipotentiaries when we spoke of arbitration.

I perceived, to my surprise, that they were under an impression, at first, that no statement at all was necessary, and, perhaps, under the treaty of Ghent, might not even be admissible. They quoted the words of the fourth article that run as follows, viz: "That, in the event of the two Commissioners differing upon all or any of the matters so referred to them, or in the event of both or either of the said Commissioners refusing or declining, or wilfully omitting, to act as such, they shall make, jointly or separately, a report or reports, as well to the Government of his Britannic Majesty as to that of the United States, stating in detail the points on which they differ and the grounds on which their respective opinions have been formed, or the grounds upon which they, or either of them, have so refused, declined, or omitted to act. And his Britannic Majesty and the Government of the United States hereby agree to refer the *report* or *reports* of the said Commissioners to some friendly sovereign or State, to be then named for that purpose, and who shall be requested to decide on the differences which may be stated in the said *report* or *reports*, or upon the report of one Commissioner, together with the grounds upon which the other Commissioner shall have refused, declined, or omitted to act." From the tenor of the article, as thus quoted, the British plenipotentiaries said that they rather inferred it to be the intention of the treaty that it was the *report* itself, as the authentic and official document, and not a statement framed out of the report, that was to be laid before the arbitrator. It was to the source itself that he was to look for his information, not to anything derivative.

I replied that I considered this by no means the true, certainly not as the imperative, construction of the treaty. The statement indicated by my Government as proper upon the occasion was to be nothing more than an abstract, to be made, by consent of both parties, from the report, presenting in a succinct and intelligible form to the arbitrator the points on which he was to decide, and drawing his attention to such parts of the report as might especially call for his investigation. It was not to supersede the report, but to be something in addition to it. The parties were surely competent to adopt, by mutual agreement, such a measure. It would be obviously a convenient if not an indispensable form by which to secure to their case a ready and advantageous hearing. I admitted that I would not advert to the precedent of the statement prepared when the slave question was submitted to the Emperor of Russia as governing in this instance, for, in that case, the arbitration had not taken place under any provision in the treaty; but I insisted that the cases were analogous in reason, the measure being designed chiefly, and in this light imperiously due, to smooth the labors, difficult as they must needs be with every mitigation, of the umpire.

The British plenipotentiaries, without pushing the argument on this point further, now inquired whether, if they were disposed to waive whatever right they might have under the treaty to object to the necessity of a statement, and prepare one after their own understanding of what it should contain, I was empowered to accede to it, without any reference home to my Government. Here, again, I could only give them a reply in the negative. My Government, I said, had not anticipated such a step by me. I had been fully written to on the whole subject, but was not now in possession of the multitude of documents that belonged to it. I could not, therefore, be supposed to be armed with the means of fitly judging of their statement. My sole duty respecting it would be to transmit it to my Government; and I subjoined that how far it would prove acceptable to my Government must depend, in a great degree, on the map that was used in drawing it up. Upon this point, important as it is, I was not able to obtain from the British plenipotentiaries any explicit declaration of their intentions, nor did they incline to take any steps with me towards the concurrent selection of an arbitrator. They admitted that difficulties would lie in the way of their furnishing me with any statement, at this juncture, that would be likely to be satisfactory to my Government, and thought that no time would be lost by their forbearing at present to offer one.

In the course of our conversations on the mode of carrying the arbitration into effect, I always, as I have already mentioned, held up in the strongest lights in my power the numerous, the intrinsic, the insuperable obstacles presenting themselves on every side to a practical resort to this mode of adjustment. Your despatch had abundantly supplied me with matter for doing so, and I was not sparing in the use of it. Amongst other topics which I advanced was that of the full belief of my Government that the case, from its great bulk and entanglement, would be altogether beyond the compass of the personal attention of any arbitrator. Towards deciding upon this extensive boundary in unsettled regions, and on all the points of difference involved in it, it would become, I said, a part of his duty to examine thirty folio volumes of manuscripts, at the least, made up of conflicting statements, conflicting arguments, conflicting opinions. He would have, besides, to hunt for the lines of his award, if ever he should arrive at one, by the light of three collections of conflicting maps. Would it be proper, I asked, to approach any sovereign with an enumeration of these details of duty for his own immediate personal occupation, or could his compliance, on such terms, be in candor expected? Hence the suggestion of my Government was, that the investigation, if gone into at all by an umpire, must be by delegated authority; by a person or persons commissioned by the umpire to report to him a decision founded upon a full examination of the whole case, to which decision it would be enough that the umpire annexed his formal sanction. I added that, as the simplest way of carrying this suggestion into effect, it had occurred to my Government that the minister plenipotentiary of the sovereign arbitrator, residing at Washington, should be charged with this delegated trust in such manner as would render its execution effectual. The British plenipotentiaries made immediate objections to this course. They said that if a settlement by umpirage was finally forced upon the parties, their opinion was, that it should take place at the court of the sovereign arbitrator, leaving him to seek there all such instrumentality and assistance in the case as might be proper towards its investigation and decision. From the tone in which they urged this opinion I am left under the belief that it is one from which their Government would not depart.

It will be perceived from my foregoing report that this Government has manifested a reluctance, which I was incapable of overcoming, at entering into any distinctive agreement at present upon any one of the preliminary points which you had given me in charge relative to this question. The ground of their reluctance is obviously to be sought in their disappointment at my not consenting to connect it with the question of the St. Lawrence. As they not only declined coming into all agreement for settling the former question by compromise, but also coming into any of the previous arrangements indispensable for ripening it into a state for arbitration, what, I inquired, was to be done? Was the case to stand still? Was it never to be settled? I knew of no mode by which it could be brought to a close except the two preceding. The British plenipotentiaries replied that they must not be understood as finally declining a resort to either mode of settlement; but they did not withhold an expression of their strong desire that the case should rest where it is until my Government had become apprised of the discussions relative to the St. Lawrence, the nature of which, from their being until now new between the two nations, could not as yet be known. They wanted my Government at least to be made acquainted, before proceeding any further, with their desire to treat of the two subjects in conjunction, and upon the terms which they had explained. I would not, of myself, have consented to this course, not feeling at all at liberty, but was not able to prevent it. I reconcile myself to it under the reflection that possibly something may be thought due, all the circumstances considered, to this desire of Great Britain, and under the hope that the slight additional loss of time thus incurred may bring with it no peculiar inconvenience over a question that has already been pending since the Revolution. Having put you in possession of all the discussions which passed on it, and shown you the predicament in which it now stands, unsatisfactory I must own, I go on to the consideration of another subject. The protocols relating to it are the ninth, the seventeenth, the eighteenth, and the nineteenth.

My report upon this subject will be shortened by the communications which I have already had the honor to address to you at former periods in relation to it. I allude more particularly to my despatches, number 343 and 352, of November and December, 1823, and to my official note to Mr. Secretary Canning, of the 17th of November, 1823. In that note, written after I had received your despatch of the 26th of June, 1823, I found it necessary to execute in a great degree the instructions which your despatch contained. This Government, during the negotiation, as well as when the correspondence above alluded to took place, always considered the subject of appointing consuls to reside in their colonies as connected with that of the commercial intercourse generally; and here I agreed that the connexion was a natural one. It was evident that, but for the opening of the colonial ports to our trade, we should not have asked for the privilege of appointing consuls to reside at them; and if by any circumstances they were again to be closed, it was equally evident that our claim to consular representation would be at an end.

The consular appointments made by the President, for Jamaica, St. Christopher and Antigua, Demarara, and Barbadoes, had been sufficiently explained and justified to this Government in the course of my communications above mentioned, in conjunction also with my number 349, which covered another official note from me to Mr. Canning upon the same subject. Nevertheless, I did not omit to bring before the British plenipotentiaries all the circumstances of this correspondence. They were particularly pertinent to our discussions on the question of commercial intercourse, which had hinged so entirely on the point of reciprocity, and throughout the whole course of which it had been the aim of each party to exonerate itself from any charge of deficiency in this important point, if not to fix that charge upon the other. I remarked upon the fact of our trade to the opened colonial ports having now continued for two years without a single consul on the part of the United States having, to this day, been recognized in any one of them, though at least three of those who had gone there and presented themselves for recognition had been appointed under the previous and express consent of his Majesty's Government; whilst, on the other hand, during the whole of this period, the British trade from those ports had been receiving full consular protection from the consuls of Great Britain in the ports of the United States. In this, at least, it must be admitted, there was no reciprocity. Nor was the absence of it cause of mere nominal complaint on the part of the United States; and here I brought into view, from your despatch of the 26th of June, 1823, the practical inconveniences, especially in the island of Barbadoes, to which our trade had been subjected in the opened ports on occasions which probably would not have occurred had consuls from the United States been residing there. The British plenipotentiaries met this complaint in the manner their Government had formerly done. They said that when their consent had been given for appointing consuls at three of the colonial ports, it had been given under an expectation by Great Britain that the United States would carry on the trade on terms that were reciprocal; but that afterwards, finding the terms to be such as Great Britain did not consider reciprocal, she forbore to perfect the appointments until the issue could be known, apprehending that the effect of new retaliating measures on either side would soon be, to put an end to the trade altogether. I rejoined, that whatever motive deemed by herself sufficient, though not so regarded by the United States, Britain might allege for her course of conduct in this particular, it did not destroy the broad fact, or lessen the evils arising from it, of Britain having enjoyed the advantage, during the two years of this trade, of full consular representation in the ports of the United States, whilst the United States had enjoyed none in the British ports.

On the principal question of the claim of the United States to appoint consuls for the colonial ports, I took the ground which you had laid before me and heretofore maintained in my note to Mr. Secretary Canning of November 17, 1823, as well as in the one which I first of all addressed to him on this subject on the 17th of October, 1822, namely: that our claim extended, not to any specified number of the colonial ports, but to all, without exception, that had been opened by the act of Parliament of the 24th of June, 1822. This was the ground which I pressed upon the attention of the British plenipotentiaries. It was the only ground, I said, which, in the true sense of reciprocity, and therefore in the true sense of justice, could be supposed to be satisfactory to the United States; as they gave all, so it was reasonable that they should ask all. The United States excepted none of their ports to which the British colonial vessels resorted from the residence of British consuls, and had a fair right to expect that none of the colonial ports to which American vessels resorted would be excepted from the residence of American consuls. Consular protection was an incident of trade which the United States did not feel at liberty to forego in behalf of their citizens, so long as they allowed it to be enjoyed in their ports, without limit or exception, by the subjects of Britain. It satisfied neither the real nor even the verbal meaning of the term reciprocity in this discussion to say that the residence of British consuls in the ports of the United States was matched by the residence of American consuls in the ports of Great Britain, in Europe. It was palpable that, if a British ship, whether arriving from Liverpool or Barbadoes, received consular protection at New York, and an American ship received it at Liverpool but not at Barbadoes, there was no reciprocity in fact, whatever artificial reasons might justify Britain to herself in distinguishing in this respect, too, her colonial from her home dominion. The only true match to the privilege on the one side would be the extension of it to all the ports that were open, whether home or colonial, on the other.

The United States, I continued, in claiming to appoint consuls for all the colonial ports, meant not to make an unreasonable use of the privilege, and so I was instructed to declare. But the privilege of selecting the ports must rest, I said, exclusively with the United States. Their consular system did not recognize any fixed emoluments as the standard of remuneration for their consuls, but left it to depend upon the fees produced by trade. Hence, in the ports to which trade flowed consuls were necessary, and to those where there was none it was not to be supposed they would be sent, or so much as consent to go. But as the channels of trade were liable to shift, there was a manifest convenience and propriety, on this and all other accounts, in leaving the selection of the ports to the sound discretion of the appointing power. Such were my remarks upon this subject, in addition to those that I formerly made orally and in writing to Mr. Canning. I did not, in conclusion, offer any formal article in relation to it; first, because I thought it unnecessary after the aspect which the negotiation had assumed on the primary question of the commercial intercourse itself; and, secondly, because I had been informed in your instructions that the President was not tenacious of any article relating to consuls being inserted in a commercial convention, if one had been formed. But I gave the British plenipotentiaries fully to understand the true nature of our claim, and that it could not in anywise fall short of the privilege of appointing for all the opened ports.

They consented, substantially, to this principle, as will be seen by the protocol of the twenty-fourth conference. Their expression in it that they saw no objection to the admission of our consuls into their colonies, "subject to the usual exceptions and reservations," means that both parties were to be considered as reserving to themselves the privilege of excepting from the residence of consuls such particular places as they might think proper. This they explained to be their meaning. The same reservation had place in the sixteenth article of the treaty of the 19th of November, 1794, which was pointed out to me by you as the model of an article on the present occasion, had one been framed. It also exists in the fourth article of the commercial convention of the 3d of July, 1815, which article is indicated by the British plenipotentiaries as the model in the fifth article of their own counter projet annexed to the protocol of the sixteenth conference. The two articles on this subject in the treaty of 1794 and in that of 1815 are so much alike that they might be adopted indiscriminately as models; the latter being a copy, with only slight variations, from the former. In my note to Mr. Canning of the 17th of November, 1823, I had reminded him that, in case Great Britain excluded American consuls from the ports of the colonies, the United States would have to reserve the right of excluding from consular benefit in their ports all British vessels and seamen arriving from the colonies. So, also, I reminded the British plenipotentiaries that the United States would have to protect themselves by a similar reservation, to an extent coequal with that to which Britain might use her option, of excepting from the residence of our consuls particular places in her colonies, there being no other appropriate mode by which we could countervail on our side this right of exception on hers, so far as regarded her colonies.

It will be seen from the twenty-fourth protocol that Britain continues to decline for the present receiving our consuls in any of her colonial ports. She acts, in this respect, under an impression that there is danger of the intercourse between these ports and the United States being soon wholly interrupted. She waits the disappearance of this danger before she recognizes our consuls, as its reality would, according to her way of reasoning, render their recognition of little value. It was in vain that I urged the justice of recognizing ours at once, so that we might be upon a par with Britain *until* ulterior events were known. * * * * * * If her tonnage duty of four shillings and three pence sterling per ton on our vessels entering her colonial ports, and her additional impost of ten per cent., be met by countervailing duties on our side—as I was forced, for the reasons given in another part of this despatch, to intimate my belief that they would be—her plenipotentiaries have informed me that it will lead to fresh measures of the same character on her side, thus bringing on a state of things that can only terminate in rendering the trade no longer worth the pursuit of either country. If, on the other hand, the trade remains as at present regulated, without any alteration by either party, although Britain, as I have had occasion to remark before, alleges that she is dissatisfied with it, she will let it have a further trial, and in this event will receive our consuls on the terms mentioned in the twenty-fourth protocol. This she will do, as I understand her intentions, notwithstanding the tenor of the fifth article of her counter projet above mentioned, which would seem to make her consent to the reception of our consuls dependent upon our acceptance of her four preceding articles. I believe, moreover, that she would raise no obstacle on the score of expense, but grant to our consuls exequaturs free of all charge, as we grant exequaturs to hers. This point I mentioned to the British plenipotentiaries, and to its obvious justice they took no exception. There remains nothing further for me to impart to you on this subject. The protocols that relate to it are the twenty-third and twenty-fourth.

IV. NEWFOUNDLAND FISHERY.

This subject was thrown out of the negotiation altogether. I was not the less mindful, however, of your instructions upon it. I brought it under the notice of the British plenipotentiaries at the tenth conference. I gave them a full history of the question from its origin. I stated the grounds of complaint which the United States had against France, as shown by the bare statement of the relative rights and pretensions of the two nations to the fishery in dispute. I stated the past unwillingness of France to do us justice, and the obligations hence arising to Great Britain to interpose her friendly and efficacious offices, to the end that justice should be rendered to us. From your despatch of the 27th of June, 1823, I also stated the motives which had restrained the President until the present epoch from laying this case before the British Government—motives that I felt sure would be appreciated, and that would increase the claims which it now had to attention. The case being wholly new until now, in any formal shape, to this Government, and being one which involved also the duties and the rights of a third power, I thought that it would be most proper not to content myself with a verbal explanation of it merely. Having, therefore, gone through with this, under the lights that your instructions and my own past investigations of the subject had afforded, I finished by delivering to the British plenipotentiaries a paper embracing a written summary of its merits, and one which might serve as a memorandum to Great Britain of the true nature of our claim. This paper consists of a synopsis of the question which I had formerly made out from Mr. Gallatin's letter to me of August the third, 1822, together with a reference to the correspondence subsequently carried on by the United States and France in relation to it. It is amongst the papers of the negotiation, marked E, and annexed to the protocol of the tenth conference. It commences with references to the different treaties—that of Utrecht in 1713, of Aix-la-Chapelle in 1748, of Paris in 1763, our own with Britain in 1783, that between Britain and France of the same year, and the treaty of Paris of 1814, also between Britain and France—all of which go to show that whilst France possessed the right of taking fish on the western coast of the island of Newfoundland, she did not possess it, as she now claims it, exclusively, but that Great Britain, the undoubted sovereign of the island, held it in common with her. It next recites the first article of the convention of the 20th of October, 1818, between the United States and Great Britain, by which the people of the United States are expressly allowed to take fish on the western coast (and on other parts) of this island, in common with the subjects of Great Britain. It then states the fact of the cruisers of France having, in the years 1820 and 1821, ordered American fishing vessels away from this coast even whilst they were within the acknowledged jurisdiction of the island, threatening them with confiscation if they refused. Finally, it concludes with pointing to the three-fold duty which devolved upon Great Britain under the emergency described: first, to make good the title of the United States to take fish on the coast in question, as stipulated by the convention of 1818; but, second, if she could not do that, to give the United States an equivalent for the loss of so valuable a right; and, third, to vindicate her own sovereignty over this island, already impaired and further threatened by the conduct of the French cruisers towards the fishing vessels of the United States within its jurisdiction. The paper subjoined copies of all the official notes that passed between Mr. Gallatin and Viscount

Chateaubriand in January, February, and April, 1823, on the respective rights of the two nations to the fishery in controversy.

The British plenipotentiaries, after having this paper in their possession, and consulting, as they informed me, their Government respecting it, entered upon the matter of it at the next succeeding conference. They said that it was not their intention to controvert the title of the United States to participate with Great Britain in certain fishing liberties described in the first article of the convention of 1818. They said, too, that the United States might require a declaration of the extent of those liberties as enjoyed by British subjects under any limitations prescribed by treaty with other powers. The United States might also ask from Britain, as sovereign of the island of Newfoundland, support in the enjoyment of the liberties as so limited; but the plenipotentiaries went on to remark, that the nature of the question seemed, in their opinion, to be varied, by France having, as seen in the notes of Viscount Chateaubriand to Mr. Gallatin, placed her claim to exclude the United States from the fishery in dispute on engagements contracted by the United States with France prior to the convention of 1818, and also on the fact of the United States having opened discussions upon the whole subject with France. They further remarked, that they had understood from one of their own negotiators of the convention of 1818 that the American negotiators had been apprised at that period by Great Britain of the French right to fish on this coast. At all events, they said that, as the subject stood, they must decline entertaining it as one susceptible of being handled in any effective way at present in this negotiation. Whatever rights or remedies the United States were entitled to from Great Britain upon the occasion could be brought into view, if thought necessary, by a direct application to the British Government, in the usual form. With this intimation they would consider the subject, for so they concluded with saying, as no longer upon the list of those which it was the object of our endeavors to mould into a general treaty or convention between the two States.

I said to the British plenipotentiaries, in reply, that I had certainly not anticipated all the above avowals. I did not admit that the fact of the United States having opened a correspondence upon this subject with France could diminish in any degree their right to resort to Great Britain, remarking that it could scarcely have been expected that a forbearance on their part to hasten to this resort in the first instance, from considerations of delicacy both towards Britain and France, was now to be turned against them. Forbearance had been due to France, at first, to avoid the appearance of recurring, on a question between her and the United States, to the aid of a third power; and to Great Britain it had been due, as it was hoped that the case might have been settled without putting her upon her duty of interfering. As little did I admit * * * * the allegation of the French Government, that the United States were excluded from this fishery by their previous engagements to France, was entitled to any weight. These engagements, I said, had been taken under treaties long since expired, and the provisions of which were otherwise nugatory as to any just bearing upon this controversy. Here I adverted to * * * * the argument used by Mr. Gallatin in reply to the notes of the Viscount Chateaubriand relative to the operation of the tenth article of the treaty with France of 1778, and of the twenty-seventh article of the convention with her of 1800, arguments which completed the demonstration, as you had remarked in your despatch, that the pretension of France to an exclusive fishery was not to be supported. I admitted, as one of the American negotiators of the convention of 1818, that we had heard of the French right at that time, but never that it was exclusive. Such an inference was contradicted not only by the plain meaning of the article in the convention of 1818, but by the whole course and spirit of the negotiation, which, it was well known, had been drawn out into anxious and protracted discussions upon the fishery question. As regarded the arguments of Viscount Chateaubriand, I reminded the British plenipotentiaries that whilst part of them labored to give to obsolete treaties, as against the United States, a validity and extent greater than they ever could have had whilst existing, the remainder went to assert a pre-existing and exclusive right in France to fish on this coast as against all the world, and, of course, as against Great Britain. Was Britain, I asked, prepared to acquiesce in this branch of the argument? for, undoubtedly, it was that which it most concerned France to establish, and without which the other branch would be of little avail to her.

The British plenipotentiaries peremptorily asserted a right in Great Britain to participate in the fishery on the coast, and denied, in this same tone, that the French right was exclusive. But having concluded to consider the subject as no longer amongst those embraced in our negotiations, they declined pursuing any further the discussion of it, leaving me to pursue such other course as I might judge applicable and expedient. My great duty having been to place the subject explicitly before this Government with a view as well to our rights as our remedies, I said to the British plenipotentiaries that the form in which I did so was not material, and that I should therefore adopt, without delay, that of addressing an official representation in regard to the whole subject to his Majesty's principal Secretary of State for Foreign Affairs. I accordingly prepared such a note to Mr. Canning, a copy of which will be found amongst the papers which I transmit, under date of the 3d of May. I do not recapitulate its contents, as they are to the same general effect with the paper which I had previously caused to be annexed to the protocol of the tenth conference. I was careful, in pursuance of your directions, to give it an aspect as friendly towards France as was compatible with duly making known the rights of the United States. I recollect nothing further that I have to communicate in explanation of this subject. The protocols in which it is mentioned are the tenth and the fourteenth. My note to Mr. Canning, considered in the light of a first formal application to this Government, is designed to bring on explanations respecting our claim between the Governments of Britain and France. These I must hope will take place, and eventuate in a manner satisfactory to the United States. I mentioned to the British plenipotentiaries the strong intimation given to Mr. Gallatin by the French Minister of Marine, that as France had, according to her own judgment, the exclusive rights of fishery on the coast in dispute, so she ought to expel from it the fishing vessels of any nation. But I abstained from inserting this intimation in my note to Mr. Canning. I did no more than advert to the menace of seizure directed by France against our vessels.

V. MARITIME QUESTIONS.

I entered upon this subject with all the anxiousness that belongs to its deep and permanent connexion with the interests and character of the United States, with all the recollections that their past history calls up, and all the anticipations that every view of the future must awaken when it is mentioned. It was at the thirteenth conference that I brought it forward. I laid before the British plenipotentiaries the opinions and the hopes which my Government had formed upon this great branch of the relations between the two countries, and strove to do justice to the principles upon which these opinions and these hopes were founded. I said that the United States were not behind any of the powers of Europe in wishes, and, moving in their proper sphere, would never be behind them in endeavors to bring about a general melioration in the condition of mankind. That such a principle was eminently congenial to their political institutions, and had always been a maxim of their policy in the whole system of their external relations. Peace, I said, was their invariable desire, as well as policy; but war taking place, it had been as invariably their desire and their effort to do homage to those beneficent principles which serve as well to shorten its duration as mitigate its evils. I instanced, as pertinent to a negotiation with Great Britain, the stipulations of the tenth and the twenty-sixth articles of the treaty of the 19th of November, 1794, when both countries successfully engaged in the work of sacrificing to these principles belligerent rights which both in strictness might otherwise have claimed and exercised.

But in the wide maritime field, whether occupied by the belligerent or the neutral, there were, I continued, questions of the highest moment to the United States and Great Britain, which they had heretofore ineffectually endeavored to arrange. These questions the United States again desired to approach, animated by the hope that better auspices might shed themselves over another attempt to come to a satisfactory and harmonious understanding respecting them. My Government, I remarked, was not discouraged from this attempt by the failure to adjust them during the negotiations at Ghent, nor by the more recent failure at London in 1818. Even since the latest of these periods the most material changes had been witnessed in the political aspect of Europe and of America. The European alliance had been impaired by a variance in the principles or in the policy of some of its chief members, and the whole of that part of the continent of America lately dependent upon Europe had assumed a new character in itself, and was hastening to new relations with the rest of the world. The most extensive alterations, if not an entire revolution in the colonial system, would, in all probability, follow in the train of the latter of these changes. These would probably superinduce the necessity of corresponding ones in maritime. interests and claims, once regarded by Great Britain as essential to her welfare. I remarked, too, that the circumstance of Britain having held towards this struggle in America an attitude of neutrality, as she had also done towards the recent war in the Spanish peninsula, had served to strengthen the belief that she might, perhaps, at the present period, be disposed to view neutral doctrines in different and more favorable lights than formerly, under circumstances so opposite. It was under the combined force of these considerations that the United States again came forward to her with an offer to negotiate on them. But if Britain still viewed them as hitherto—if she still felt herself restrained from treating of them but on her former maritime principles, my Government would prefer being so informed with candor in the outset, it being alike due to candor to say that the principles of the United States remained the same, there having been no equipollent changes in their political, commercial, or maritime position in the world. It was thus that I opened this part of the subject to the British plenipotentiaries, discouraging our entering upon any discussion of these questions upon terms that could not be productive of any beneficial results.

I then proceeded to the paramount part of your instructions of the 28th of July, 1823. I said that there was yet another object, new to all the past discussions between the two Governments, but of pre-eminent interest in the eyes of mine, by its connexion with the cause of civilization and the peace of the world, which it desired to propose to Great Britain. This object was that of totally abolishing all private war upon the ocean.

The United States, I said, from an early period of their history, aimed at bringing about among nations this great consummation of benevolence and humanity. Once they had secured it by a treaty with one of the powers of Europe—with Prussia—and now they desired to offer it to the consideration of Great Britain. They hoped that she would go hand in hand with them in giving validity and extent to the benign consequences which its general adoption must introduce into the world. The question, though of novelty between the two Governments, was one of too much magnitude, under considerations of a moral as well as political nature, to be discarded on that account. In proceeding to develop the reasoning by which you had directed me to recommend this object to the favor and acceptance of the British Government, it may be sufficient for me to say that I omitted no part of it, resorting, under this delicate head of my instructions, to the very language of them as the most appropriate and effectual for imparting the sentiments which they embodied. I need not, therefore, repeat any more at large the manner in which I executed this portion of my duty. I finished by expressing, in the name of my Government, a hope that Great Britain might be able to see her way towards a concurrence in this object, the more so as it was also to be proposed by the United States to other European nations, with whom the example of Great Britain might be of powerful, perhaps decisive influence.

The British plenipotentiaries promised to take my whole exposition of the subject into consideration, and consult their Government before giving me an answer as to the course which it might become their duty to adopt.

In speaking of the maritime questions heretofore in discussion between the two countries, I had mentioned that of impressment as of leading importance. A question was then put to me by the British plenipotentiaries which, with my answer, it is proper that I should at once state. They asked whether I would be willing to treat of the above class of questions generally, supposing impressment not to be included among the number ? I had anticipated such question, and was prepared with an answer. Your instructions not having supplied me with one, it was only left for me to act upon my own discretion. I therefore declined such a course, saying that I was unwilling to enter at all upon the other points of maritime law, unless the question of impressment was received by Great Britain as part of the negotiation. It will be understood that I spoke independently of the question of abolishing private war upon the ocean.

My reasons for this determination were derived, first, from the extraordinary importance of the question of impressment, transcending, as in my judgment it did, not only the importance of any other, but the collective importance of them all. I knew of no other so closely linked in with the rights, the sovereignty, and the peace of the Republic. There was always a rational hope that the harmony of the two countries might remain undisturbed in the absence of conventional arrangements upon the other questions; but, that of impressment always carried with it the seed of dissention, was always difficult, always threatening. The question of blockade, of contraband, of the right of the neutral carrier to protect the property of an enemy, and all the maritime questions, were ones, to be sure, which it would be desirable to settle; but, upon some of them the two Governments had not always been widely asunder in their negotiations, and the whole were distinguished by this feature, that each party, when differences arose under them, could more readily appeal to the standard of principles and usages to which other nations appealed. Impressment, on the contrary, springing from a claim by Great Britain to enforce her common law upon the high seas, was not so much distinguished by its international as its exclusive character. It was a question in a great measure sui generis; peculiar in its practical operation to the two nations, remarkable for the earnestness and perseverance with which the point of right was asserted to exist on the one side, and the explicitness with which it had ever been pronounced a positive and insupportable wrong upon the other. I did not, therefore, believe that any treaty on maritime questions, admitting that one had been concluded, would have been acceptable to my Government, of which an adjustment of this subject of perpetual animosity and collision did not make a part. Another reason was, that I followed in this respect the precedent, or at least the analogy, of the negotiation of 1818. It will be recollected that in that negotiation the plenipotentiaries of the United States were instructed not to entertain the discussion of maritime topics, unless that of impressment was also brought forward, and by Great Britain. I trust that these reasons for the course which I pursued may be approved. It is alike proper for me to mention, that whilst I declined going into the field of maritime discussion, impressment being left out of it, I avowed my perfect readiness to take up impressment by itself. Its absorbing interest justified also, in my eyes, this course.

The British plenipotentiaries, on hearing this last opinion from me, immediately inquired if I had any new securities to propose on behalf of my Government against the employment of British subjects in the merchant vessels of the United States? I replied that I had none that differed essentially from those brought forward in former negotiations.

After an interval of deliberation, that was not over until the twenty-first conference, the British plenipotentiaries communicated to me the decision of their Government upon the topics which I had unfolded to them. First they spoke of impressment. They said that Great Britain anxiously desired to reconcile the exercise of this established right with the convenience and feelings of other nations; that this desire had ever actuated her heretofore, and ever would in future. It was her duty to obey its impulse, and her interest no less than her duty. But the right was, nevertheless, one essential to her highest interests, and deemed by her as incontrovertible as it was ancient. It was a right interwoven with the frame of her laws, and precious to her by its connexion with principles to which she trusted for her strength and her safety at conjunctures when both might be at stake. She could never abandon such a right; it was impossible. Nor would her duty allow her to waive it with respect to the United States, but upon conditions the most satisfactory. She could only forego it in their favor, on receiving what she could deem ample security that the objects for which it was exercised might be attained by other means. They added, that having been informed by me that I had no proposals to make on this head essentially differing from those that my Government had submitted in former negotiations, they felt themselves forced to abstain in this from entering into the subject. The sentiments of their Government with respect to the impressment of British subjects in time of war out of the merchant vessels of whatever nation, upon the high seas, remained unchanged, and they could therefore indulge no hope of any good results from a fresh discussion on only the same grounds which Great Britain had, on full deliberation, adjudged to be inadequate in all former discussions. It was to this effect that the British plenipotentiaries spoke. It was in this manner that they disposed of the question of impressment.

With regard to the other maritime questions, affecting the relations of neutral and belligerent powers, the plenipotentiaries remarked, that as I was not prepared to enter into stipulations respecting them, but in conjunction with the question of impressment, which was excluded for the reason given, the discussion of the others, in any way, could be to no useful purpose; it would therefore be declined by them.

Thus it was that the whole of this subject fell to the ground. The decision upon it will be found recorded in the protocol of the twenty-first conference.

I next said to the British plenipotentiaries that the question of abolishing privateering, and the capture of private property at sea, whether by national ships or by privateers, was one that I considered as standing apart from those on which their decision had been given to me. Upon this question, therefore, I desired them to understand that I was ready to treat as of one occupying ground wholly of its own.

They replied that they were not prepared to adopt this course. All other questions of a maritime nature having been shut out from the negotiation, there would be, they said, manifest inconvenience in going into that for abolishing private war upon the ocean. They considered it a question belonging to the same class with maritime questions, and one which, besides being totally new, as between the two Governments, contemplated a most extensive change in the principles and practice of maritime war as hitherto sanctioned by all nations. Such was their answer.

This answer was given in the terms that I state, and so entered upon the protocol. But it is proper for me to remark, that no sentiment dropped from the British plenipotentiaries authorizing the belief that they would have concurred in the object if we had proceeded to the consideration of it. My own opinion unequivocally is, that Great Britain is not prepared to accede, under any circumstances, to the proposition for abolishing private war upon the ocean.

By the preceding decisions of the British Government, in conjunction with the restrictions under which I had laid myself, discussions the most interesting, and which it might have been anticipated would have been the most ample, have been altogether precluded. My report, by necessary consequence, under this division of your instructions, becomes proportionably abridged. From your despatch of the 28th of July, 1823, I understood that I was to make no communication to the British Government of the draft of the articles which it inclosed, unless they first agreed to negotiate respecting them. As they declined doing so upon the terms which, taking into view the whole spirit of your instructions, I had deemed the only admissible ones, it follows, that I withheld altogether any offer of the draft. The negotiation on the maritime questions fell through ostensibly, and, according to my best judgment, with sufficient reason, on the point of impressment. But here, too, I have to remark, that the British plenipotentiaries said nothing to warrant the opinion of any change in the doctrines of their Government on the other points of maritime law, any more than upon that of impressment. My own opinion is, that no such change has taken place. If the altered political and commercial circumstances of the times should hereafter serve to make her rule of 1756 an exception, it will probably be found the only exception. Nor will this be a rule abandoned by her, so much as lapsed; nor even wholly lapsed, if, according to indications contained in earlier parts of this communication, there be any likelihood of her returning to her own colonial system in the West Indies, rather than of her making larger departures from it. I am aware that she would probably denominate it a coerced return; whilst all the facts would present to the United States a view of the subject so very different.

The British plenipotentiaries, after all negotiation on the maritime questions had been foreclosed, informed me that they were willing to treat of other points which, though not immediately falling under this class, were connected with the friendly intercourse between the two countries, and would aim at its improvement. I replied that I was not prepared to enter into any stipulations with them of this description, detached from all other subjects, but that I would receive and transmit to my Government whatever proposals they might have to offer of the nature stated. They accordingly gave me, at the twenty-second conference, the substance of nine articles, which are inclosed, (marked M,) as belonging to the protocol of that conference. They were not put into a formal shape, being rather the heads of subjects, than as designed to be expressed in full language.

The first of these articles relates to the mutual delivery of criminals, the subjects or citizens of either party, taking refuge in the dominions of the other, analogous to the twenty-seventh article of the treaty of November, 1794, so far as murder and forgery were concerned. The second proposes arrangements for settling the claims made by the subjects or citizens of either party to lands situated within the territories of the other in America, and arising out of grants heretofore made by authorities competent at the time to make them. The following is the explanation of this article: At the opening of the negotiation the British plenipotentiaries inquired whether I was empowered to treat of certain claims of British subjects to lands in Florida. I replied that my instructions embraced no allusion whatever to such a subject, and that if brought forward by Great Britain, all that I could do would be to refer it to my Government. It was the first mention of it that I had heard, and it was not mentioned afterwards. It is to this subject that the above article points. The third article has reference to the non-confiscation of private debts in case of war between the two countries, as the fifth has to the protection of the merchants on each side found within the dominions of the other on the breaking out of a war, as under the tenth and twenty-sixth articles of the treaty of 1794. Though fully aware of the importance attached to the principle of these articles under your instructions, I did not feel myself at liberty to conclude engagements concerning them in a detached way. After the question of impressment had been expunged, and all the other maritime questions, together with that for the abolition of private war upon the ocean, which I could not but regard as the chief question contemplated under your despatch of the 28th of July, 1823, it did not seem to me either necessary or judicious that a treaty should be entered into for the sake of these two articles alone. I was the more swayed to this opinion from the hope that may reasonably be cherished that neither nation will hereafter be disposed to depart from the principles which these articles sanctify, though not now confirmed by a new treaty, since both nations have formerly agreed to them in this manner, and are both seen at this day substantially ready to propose them again to each other's acceptance.

The remainder of their articles, as a brief recapitulation of them will show, are only of subordinate interest. The fourth provides for a previous statement of grievances and demand of redress before a resort to reprisals by either party, like the twenty-second article of the treaty of '94. The sixth relates to wrecks and salvage, as is common in treaties between commercial nations. The seventh extends hospitality to vessels of either party forced by stress of weather into ports of the other to which they would not, under other circumstances, be admissible, as is also common, and as has place in the treaty of '94. The eighth contains a provision respecting merchant vessels rescued from pirates; and the ninth, and last, a provision for mutually exempting the consuls of each nation within the territories of the other from personal service and the operation of direct taxes. It must be confessed that, under this last provision, it would be the consuls of the United States who would derive the most benefit.

On my declining, for the reasons I have given, to conclude any arrangement at present on the foregoing articles, the British plenipotentiaries lamented that whilst they made the inability to treat of impressment no obstacle to entering into stipulations concerning them, I did. To this I replied by remarking upon the obviously different ground on which the two nations stood in this particular. To the United States, the question of impressment was vital; to Great Britain, it was of little concern, further than as it might be supposed that she was desirous of rendering to the United States justice in regard to it. The British plenipotentiaries here repeated the unfeigned regret which they said they felt at our preliminary terms having precluded them from arranging, at so favorable a season of peace, this question, which they desired I would understand that they, too, considered as one of great moment. Whilst they held their right to resort to the practice of impressment to be fully sanctioned by the general voice of nations, under that maxim which entitled every nation to command the allegiance and services of its own subjects, they were not unaware that the practice itself, from peculiar and insurmountable causes, pressed heavily upon the people of the United States. Hence, they had been most anxious to come to some arrangement by which an end might have been put to this source of contention; and they declared that they would have accounted it amongst the happiest and proudest incidents of their lives had they been able to sign with me a treaty by which so imposing a bar to the harmony of our respective countries could have been effectually and permanently removed. As things had eventuated, all that they could say was, and this they desired to say in a spirit the most sincere and earnest, that whenever in future the practice might be resorted to, it would be in a manner to give the least possible inconvenience to the United States, and none that could ever be avoided consistently with what was imperiously due to the essential rights and interests of Great Britain.

I joined in the regrets expressed by the British plenipotentiaries, and, I will presume to add, in a spirit not less sincere. I lamented our failure to come to an understanding upon this formidable question— one upon which, perhaps, the peace of two powerful nations hung. I spoke of the past offers of the United States for its settlement; how far they had gone, how far they would still go, in an accommodation to the British views. They had offered to abstain from employing British seamen on board of their vessels, for they did not want them there, having seamen enough of their own; and to effect this exclusion, they offered the highest enactments and sanctions of their laws, pledges which they deemed sufficient, and which they could never help thinking might be accepted as sufficient. It was to be considered, I said, that impressment was a question in which were bound up the highest rights and interests of the United States no less than of Great Britain. The United States admitted not the doctrine of perpetual allegiance. As the rule of nations, ancient or modern, they denied its existence. It had no place in their own code; and if it had in that of Britain, it was but as a municipal rule, to be executed at home, not upon the high seas, and on board the vessels of an independent and sovereign State. The latter carried with it the assumption of a right of search *for men*. This, whether as a right direct or incidental, was denied by the United States to have the least sanction in public law. The bare claim was affronting to the United States in the dearest attributes of their national sovereignty. I declared that I, too, would have hailed it as the most auspicious act of my life to have been able to mark the last days of my official residence at his Majesty's court by putting my name with theirs to stipulations that would have closed up forever this fruitful and bitter source of strife between our countries. As it was, it was only left for me to deplore results under which so high and solid a satisfaction had vanished from me. By an interchange of remarks such as these, neither side had proposed to itself any discussion or review of a question already dropped from our discussions, but barely to give expression to sentiments which both sides have such good cause for feeling at the abortive issue of this new endeavor to get rid of the evils of impressment.

Before leaving this part of the subject entirely, I feel impelled to one or two extraneous observations. The practice of seizing men by force for the supply of the Navy, even as a lawful exercise of municipal authority in Britain, is one that carries with it such a disregard of the liberty of the subject, and involves such an aggravation of individual horrors, that the propriety, the humanity, and the very policy of its total relinquishment, even in her own dominions, has not escaped the thoughts of some of her considerate and enlightened men. On my first arrival in this country I had occasion to notice, and not unfrequently, evidences of the existence of this feeling, both in private life and in the discussions of the press, and was willing to give way to the hope of its further, and at no very distant day, efficient progress. I lament to say that this cheering hope has been put back by a recent and too authentic indication, the relevancy of which to the subject-matter of this part of my report will be sufficient, I trust, to excuse my allusion to it. At the late session of Parliament, and only in the month of June, Mr. Hume, an active member of the House of Commons, from Scotland, introduced into the House a motion expressly upon the subject of impressment. The purport of it was, that "the House, being well aware of the difficulty of manning the Navy in time of war, and of the evils of forcibly impressing men for that purpose, and considering that a time of profound peace would best admit of the fullest and fairest examination of that most important subject, would, early in the next session of Parliament, take it into their serious consideration, with a view to the adoption of such regulations as might prevent those evils in future, consistently with the efficiency of the Navy and, the best interests of the British Empire." In giving his notice of this motion, he declared, as one motive for its claims upon the attention of the House, that it would be a part of his duty in discussing it to show that, in the event of a new war between Great Britain and any of the European powers, it would be impossible for her to continue the practice of impressment, without adding the United States to the list of her enemies. It is a fact that would be deplored in the United States, that even such a motion as this, a motion that proposed nothing more than a future and guarded consideration of a subject so full of international importance, (the light alone in which it is of any concern to the United States,) should have been scarcely listened to by a British House of Commons. It was debated to comparatively empty benches, and thrown out by a vote of one hundred and eight to thirty-eight. The most impressive part of this public fact remains to be disclosed. This motion, which, in my mere capacity as an American spectator of the deliberations of the British Parliament, I cannot hesitate to think the most momentous by far in its bearing upon the foreign relations of the country of any that has offered itself to that body during my residence of six years in England; this motion, so far as I know, was not deemed worthy to engage the attention of a single minister of the Crown. It is certain that not one of them spoke upon it. In the House of Commons, in this alleged sanctuary of knowledge, patriotism, and statesmanship, in Britain, a question implicating the highest interests of two whole nations, and most essentially their future peace, passed away with less of discussion and excitement than might have been given to a bill for laying off a new road or inclosing a sterile heath. It was a spectacle calculated to fill with pain the mind of an American citizen, and I have adverted to it in no other spirit than that of unmingled sorrow at the greater distance to which, in conjunction with the failure of my negotiation, it seems to have removed all hope of arriving at a settlement of this ever perilous and exasperating topic of international hostility.

Having nothing more to say, at present, on the maritime questions, I leave them. The protocols in which they are noticed are the thirteenth, the twenty-first, and the twenty-second.

VI. NORTHWEST COAST OF AMERICA.

I now come to the last of the subjects that the President confided to me—that contained in your instructions of the second of July, 1823, relative to the Northwest Coast of America. Although no arrangement was concluded on this subject, it is not the less incumbent upon me carefully to apprise you of the discussions by which it was marked. They will probably be found not without interest.

In one of my preliminary communications respecting the negotiation, viz: my number 356, I informed you that I had thought it necessary, yielding to events that transpired after your instructions were received, to treat of this subject of the Northwest Coast with this Government alone, without considering the negotiation as common also to Russia, as had been contemplated by your instructions. For this deviation from your instructions I assigned my reasons, which, as they weighed strongly with me at the time, and do not appear, from any lights that I possess, to have lost any of their force since, I must hope will have been approved. My duty, therefore, will now be confined to informing you of the discussions that took place in my hands with Britain, and as limited to the interests of the United States and Britain. These are the only discussions, I may add, with which I have any acquaintance, not having heard from Mr. Middleton of the nature of those that were carried on at St. Petersburg, though, through the kindness of the Russian ambassador at this court, I have very recently been apprised of their result. It is probable that it has been through some accident that I have not heard from Mr. Middleton, having apprised him of the course that I had felt myself compelled to adopt. In obedience to your instructions, I also wrote to him on the subject of the slave trade, transmitting him a copy of the convention with this Government as soon as I had signed it.

In another of my communications, written before the negotiation opened, viz: my number 358, I gave you a general intimation of what I then supposed would be the terms upon which this Government would be disposed to arrange with us the questions of boundary upon the Northwest Coast. At that time, however, I had been put in possession of nothing distinctive or final upon the subject, and was to wait the arrival of the negotiation itself for the full and authentic statement of the British claims. I am the more particular in referring back to this latter communication, as it appears that I was under important misapprehensions in it, in regard to the true nature of the British claims. They proved, on formally and accurately disclosing themselves, to be far more extensive than I had believed, and were advanced in a manner more confident than I had even then anticipated.

I opened this subject to the British plenipotentiaries at the eleventh conference. I remarked that although it had been understood in my preparatory conversations with the proper organ of his Majesty's Government that the respective territorial or other claims of the United States and Russia, as well as of Great Britain and Russia, regarding the country westward of the Rocky mountains, were to be matter of separate discussion at St. Petersburgh, yet that those of the United States and Britain were now, according to the understanding in the same conversations, to be taken up for formal discussion in London. My Government was aware that the convention of October, 1818, between the United States and Great Britain, one article of which contained a temporary regulation of this interest, had still four years to run; but the President, nevertheless, was of opinion that the present was not an unsuitable moment for attempting a new and more definite adjustment of the respective claims of the two powers to the country in question. It was a country daily assuming an aspect, political, commercial, and territorial, of more and more interest to the United States. It bore upon their relations with other States, upon their fisheries as well as their commerce in the Pacific, upon their fur trade, and the whole system of their intercourse with vast tribes of the Indians. I reminded the British plenipotentiaries that, by the third article of the treaty of Washington, of February 22, 1819, between the United States and Spain, the boundary line between the two countries was fixed, in part, along the southern bank of the Arkansas, to its source in latitude 42° north, and thence by that parallel of latitude to the South Sea; and that Spain had also renounced to the United States, by the same article, all her rights north of that parallel. I then made known at this and other conferences (for from the extent of the subject I was unable even to open it all at one conference) what I understood to be the nature of the title of the United States to the whole of the country north of the parallel stated. I said, that, apart from all the right as thus acquired from Spain, which, however, was regarded by my Government as surpassing the right of all other European powers on that coast, the United States claimed in their own right, and as their absolute and exclusive sovereignty and dominion, the whole of the country west of the Rocky mountains, from the 42d to at least as far up as the 51st degree of north latitude. This claim they rested upon their first discovery of the river Columbia, followed up by an effective settlement at its mouth, a settlement which was reduced by the arms of Britain during the late war, but formally surrendered up to the United States at the return of peace. Their right by first discovery they deemed peculiarly strong, having been made not only from the sea by Captain Gray, who first discovered its sources and explored its whole inland course to the Pacific Ocean. It had been ascertained that the Columbia extended, by the river Multnomah, to as low as 42° north, and by Clarke's river to a point as high up as 51°, if not beyond that point, and to this entire range of country contiguous to the original dominion of the United States, and made a part of it by the almost intermingling waters of each; the United States, I said, considered their title as established by all the principles that had ever been applied on this subject by the powers of Europe to settlements in the American hemisphere. I asserted that a nation discovering a country by entering the mouth of its principal river at the seacoast, must necessarily be allowed to claim and hold as great an extent of the interior country as was described by the course of such principal river and its tributary streams, and that the claim to this extent became doubly strong where, as in the present instance, the same river had also been discovered and explored from its very mountain springs to the sea. Such a union of titles, imparting validity to each other, did not often exist. I remarked that it was scarcely to be presumed that any European nation would henceforth project any colonial establishment on any part of the Northwest Coast of America, which, as yet, had never been used to any other useful purpose than that of trading with the aboriginal inhabitants or fishing in the neighboring seas; but that the United States should contemplate, and at one day form, permanent establishments there was naturally to be expected, as proximate to their own possessions and falling under their immediate jurisdiction. Speaking of the powers of Europe who had ever advanced claims to any part of this coast, I referred to the principles that had been settled by the Nootka Sound convention of 1790, and remarked that Spain had now lost all her exclusive colonial rights that were recognized under that convention, first, by the fact of the independence of the South American States and of Mexico, and next by her express renunciation of all her rights, of whatever kind, above the 42d degree of north latitude to the United States. Those new States would themselves now possess the rights incident to their condition of political independence; and the claims of the United States above the 42d parallel as high up as 60°, claims as well in their own right as by their succession to the title of Spain, would henceforth necessarily preclude other nations from forming colonial establishments upon any part of the American continents. I was, therefore, instructed to say that my Government no longer considered any part of those continents as open to further colonization by any of the powers of Europe, and that this was a principle upon which I should insist in the course of the negotiation.

It was in this manner that I first laid down, for the information of this Government, the principles contained in your despatch, or flowing from them. I combined with what you had written to me the contents of the message of the President to Congress, of the second of December last, a document which I could not but regard as of the highest solemnity towards marking out my duty. I added, that the United States did not desire to interfere with the actual settlements of other nations on the Northwest Coast of America, and that in regard to those which Great Britain might have formed above the 51st degree of latitude, they would remain, with all such rights of trade with the natives, and rights of fishery, as those settlements had enjoyed hitherto. As regarded future settlements by either of the parties, I said that it was the wish of my Government to regulate these upon principles that might be mutually satisfactory and tend to prevent all collision. I was, therefore, instructed to propose, first, the extension to a further term of ten years of the third article of the convention of October, 1818; and, secondly, that Britain should stipulate during the like term that no settlement should be made by any of her subjects on the Northwest Coast of America, or the islands adjoining, either south of the fifty-first degree of latitude, or north of the fifty-fifth degree, the United States stipulating that none should be made by their citizens north of the fifty-first degree. This proposal I drew up in form and annexed it (marked F) to the protocol of the twelfth conference. I said that these limits were supposed to be sufficient to secure to Great Britain all the benefit to be derived from the settlements of her Northwest and Hudson's Bay Companies on that Coast, and were indicated with that view.

The insertion of a limit of ten years, which I introduced as applicable to the above restriction upon future settlements, may require explanation. In your despatch to me, as I understood it, there was no such limit of time specified. But in your instructions to Mr. Middleton, of July 22, 1823, which you inclosed to me, I perceived that there was this limit introduced, and that it was under this limit the proposal was described to him as the one which I was to submit to the British Government. I concluded that it would be erring on the safe side to take, in this particular, the instructions to Mr. Middleton as my guide, and I did so accordingly.

It is proper now, as on the question of the St. Lawrence, that I should give you faithful information of the manner in which the British plenipotentiaries received my proposal, and the principles under which I had introduced it. I may set out by saying, in a word, that they totally declined the one, and totally denied the other. They said that Great Britain considered the whole of the unoccupied parts of America as being open to her future settlements in like manner as heretofore. They included within these parts as well that portion of the Northwest Coast lying between the forty-second and the fifty first degrees of latitude as any other parts. The principle of colonization on that coast, or elsewhere on any portion of those continents not yet occupied, Great Britain was not prepared to relinquish. Neither was she prepared to accede to the exclusive claim of the United States. She had not by her convention with Spain in 1790, or at any other period, conceded to that power any exclusive rights on that coast where actual settlements had not been formed. She considered the same principles applicable to it now as then. She could not concede to the United States, who held the Spanish title, claims which she had felt herself obliged to resist when advanced by Spain, and on her resistance to which the credit of Great Britain had been thought to depend.

Nor could Great Britain at all admit, the plenipotentiaries said, the claim of the United States as founded on their own first discovery. It had been objectionable with her in the negotiation of 1818, and had not been admitted since. Her surrender to the United States of the port at Columbia river after the late war was in fulfilment of the provisions of the first article of the treaty of Ghent, without affecting questions of right on either side. Britain did not admit the validity of the discovery by Captain Gray. He had only been on an enterprise of his own as an individual, and the British Government was yet to be informed under what principles or usage among the nations of Europe his having first entered or discovered the mouth of the river Columbia, admitting this to have been the fact, was to carry after it such a portion of the interior country as was alleged. Great Britain entered her dissent to such a claim, and least of all did she admit that the circumstance of a merchant vessel of the United States having penetrated the coast of that continent at Columbia river was to be taken to extend a claim in favor of the United States along the same coast, both above and below that river, over latitudes that had previously been discovered and explored by Great Britain herself, in expeditions fitted out under the authority and with the resources of the nation. This had been done by Captain Cook, to speak of no others, whose voyage was at least prior to that of Captain Gray. On the coast, only a few degrees south of the Columbia, Britain had made purchases of territory from the natives before the United States were an independent power, and upon that river itself, or upon rivers that flowed into it west of the Rocky mountains, her subjects had formed settlements coeval with, if not prior to, the settlement by American citizens at its mouth.

Such is a summary of the grounds taken at the very outset by the British plenipotentiaries in opposition to our claims. On my remarking immediately, and before proceeding to any discussion of them, that I had not before been aware of the extent and character of all these objections, they replied that it was also for the first time that they had been apprised, in any authentic and full way, of the nature of the claims, as I had now stated them, on behalf of the United States; claims which they said they were bound to declare at once that Great Britain was wholly unprepared to admit, and especially that which aimed at interdicting her from the right of future colonization in America.

Resuming the subject, I said that it was unknown to my Government that Great Britain had ever even advanced any claim to territory on the Northwest Coast of America, by right of occupation, before the Nootka Sound controversy. It was clear that, by the treaty of Paris of 1763, her territorial rights in America were bounded westward by the Mississippi. The claim of the United States, under the discovery by Captain Gray, was, therefore, at all events, sufficient to overreach, in point of time, any that Great Britain could allege along that coast, on the ground of prior occupation or settlement. As to any alleged settlements by her subjects on the Columbia, or on rivers falling into it, earlier or as early as the one formed by American citizens at Astoria, I knew not of them, and was not prepared to admit the fact. As to the discovery itself of Captain Gray, it was not for a moment to be drawn into question. It was a fact before the whole world. The very geographers of Britain had adopted the name which he had given to this river. Vancouver himself, undoubtedly the first British navigator who had ever entered it, admitted that he found Captain Gray there, and the very instructions to this British officer, drawn up in March, 1791, and to be seen among the records of the British Admiralty, expressly referred by name to the previous expedition in that quarter of the American sloop the Washington. Was this, I asked, to be accounted nothing? Did it lie with a foreign power, whose own archives might supply her with the essential incontestible fact of the first discovery by the vessel of another power of a vast river whose waters from their source to the ocean had remained until then totally unknown to all civilized nations—did it lie with such foreign power to say that the discovery was not made by a national ship or under national authority? The United States, I said, could admit no such distinction; could never surrender under it, or upon any ground, their claim to this discovery. The ship of Captain Gray, whether fitted out by the Government of the United States or not, was a national ship. If she was not so in a technical sense of the word, she was in the full sense of it applicable to such an occasion. She bore at her stern the flag of the nation, sailed forth under the protection of the nation, and was to be identified with the rights of the nation. The extent of interior country attaching to this discovery was founded, I said, upon a principle at once reasonable and moderate; reasonable, because, as discovery was not to be limited to the local spot of a first landing place, there must be a rule both for enlarging and circumscribing its range, and none more proper than that of taking the water courses which nature had laid down both as the fair limits of the country and as indispensable to its use and value ; moderate, because the nations of Europe had often, under their rights of discovery, carried their claims much further. Here I instanced, as sufficient for my purpose and pertinent to it, the terms in which many of the royal charters and letters patent had been granted by the Crown in England to individuals proceeding to the discovery or settlement of new countries on the American continent: among others, those from Elizabeth, 1578, to Sir Humphrey Gilbert, and in 1584 to Sir Walter Raleigh; those from James I to Sir Thomas Gates, in 1606 and 1607, and the Georgia charter of 1732. All these, extracts from which I produced, comprehended a range of country fully justifying my remark. By the words of the last a grant is passed to all territories along the seacoast from the river Savannah to the most southern stream "of another great river called the Altamaha, and westward *from the heads of the said rivers* in a direct line to the South Seas." To show that Britain was not the only European nation who, in her territorial claims on this continent, had had an eye to the rule of assuming water courses to be the fittest boundaries, I also cited the charter of Louis XIV to Crozat, by which "all the country *drained by the waters emptying directly or indirectly into the Mississippi*" is declared to be comprehended under the name and within the limits of Louisiana.

If Britain had put forth no claims on the Northwest Coast, founded on prior occupation, before the Nootka sound contest, still less could she ever have established any, I remarked, at any period, founded on prior discovery. Claims of the latter class belonged wholly to Spain, and now, consequently, to the United States. The superior title of Spain on this ground, as well as others, was, indeed, capable of demonstration. Russia had acknowledged it in 1790, as the State papers of the Nootka Sound controversy would show. The memorial of the Spanish court to the British minister on that occasion expressly asserted that, notwithstanding all the attempted encroachments upon the Spanish coasts of the Pacific Ocean, Spain had preserved her possessions there entire—possessions which she had constantly, and before all Europe, on that and other occasions, declared to extend to as high at least as the 60th degree of north latitude. The very first article of the Nootka Sound convention attested, I said, the superiority of her title; for whilst by it the nations of Europe generally were allowed to make settlements on that coast, it was only for purpose of trade with the natives, thereby excluding the right of any exclusive or colonial establishments for other purposes. As to any claim on the part of Britain under the voyage of Captain Cook, I remarked that this was sufficiently superseded (passing by everything else) by the journal of the Spanish expedition from San Blas in 1775, kept by Don Antonio Maurelle, for an account of which I referred the British plenipotentiaries to the work of Daines Barrington, a British author. In that expedition, consisting of a frigate and a schooner, fitted out by the Viceroy of Mexico, the Northwest Coast was visited in latitude 45°, 47°, 49°, 53°, 55°, 56°, 57°, and 58°, not one of which points, there was good reason for believing, had ever been explored, or as much as seen, up to that day by any navigator of Great Britain. There was, too, I said, the voyage of Juan Peres, prior to 1775; that of Aguilar in 1601, who explored that coast in latitude 45°; that of De Fuca in 1592, who explored it in latitude 48°, giving the name, which they still bear, to the straits in that latitude, without going through a much longer list of other early Spanish navigators in that sea, whose discoveries were confessedly of a nature to put out of view those of all other nations. I finished by saying that, in the opinion of my Government, the title of the United States to the whole of that coast, from latitude 42° to as far north as latitude 60°, was, therefore, superior to that of Britain or any other power; first, through the proper claim of the United States by discovery and settlement; and, secondly, as now standing in the place of Spain and holding in their hands all her title.

Neither my remarks nor my authorities, of which I have endeavored to present an outline, made the impression upon the British plenipotentiaries which I was desirous that they should have produced. They repeated their animated denials of the title of the United States as alleged to have been acquired by themselves, enlarging and insisting upon their objections to it, as I have already stated them. Nor were they less decided in their renewed impeachments of the title of Spain. They said that it was well known to them what had formerly been the pretensions of Spain to absolute sovereignty and dominion in the South Seas, and over all the shores of America which they washed; but that these were pretensions which Britain had never admitted. On the contrary, she had strenuously resisted them. They referred to the note of the British minister to the court of Spain of May 16, 1790, in which Britain had not only asserted a full right to an uninterrupted commerce and navigation in the Pacific, but also that of forming, with the consent of the natives, whatever establishments she thought proper on the Northwest Coast, in parts not already occupied by other nations. This had always been the doctrine of Great Britain, and from it nothing that was due in her estimation to other powers now called upon her in any degree to depart. As to the alleged prior discoveries of Spain all along that coast, Britain did not admit them, but with great qualification. She could never admit that the mere fact of Spanish navigators having first seen the coast at particular points, even where this was capable of being substantiated as the fact, without any subsequent or efficient acts of sovereignty or settlement following on the part of Spain, was sufficient to exclude all other nations from that portion of the globe. Besides, they said, even on the score of prior discovery on that coast, at least as far up as the 48th degree of north latitude, Britain herself had a claim over all other nations. Here they referred to Drake's expedition in 1578, who, as they said, explored that coast on the part of England from 37° to 48° north, making formal claim to these limits in the name of Elizabeth, and giving the name of New Albion to all the country which they comprehended. Was this, they asked, to be reputed nothing in the comparison of prior discoveries, and did it not even take in a large part of the very coast now claimed by the United States as of prior discovery on their side? Such was the character of their remarks on this part of the title. In connexion with them, they called my attention to the report of a select committee of the House of Representatives, in April last, on the subject of the Columbia river. There is a letter from General Jesup in this report, adopted by the committee as part of the report, and which, as the British plenipotentiaries said, had acquired importance in the eyes of their Government from that fact. They commented upon several passages of this letter, a newspaper copy of which they held in their hands, but chiefly on that part which contains an intimation that a removal from our territory of all British subjects now allowed to trade on the waters of the Columbia might become a necessary measure on the part of the United States as soon as the convention of 1818 had expired. Of this intimation the British plenipotentiaries complained, as one calculated to put Great Britain especially upon her guard, arriving as the document did at a moment when a friendly negotiation was pending between the two powers for the adjustment of their relative and conflicting claims to that entire district of country. Had I any knowledge, they asked, of this document?

I replied that I had not, as communicated to me by my Government. All that I could say of it was, and this I would say confidently, that it was sure it had been conceived in no unfriendly spirit towards Great Britain, yet, I was bound unequivocally to re-assert, and so I requested the British plenipotentiaries would consider me as doing, the full and exclusive sovereignty of the United States over the whole of the territory beyond the Rocky mountains, washed by the river Columbia, in manner and extent as I had stated, subject, of course, to whatever existing conventional arrangements they may have formed in regard to it with other powers. Their title to this whole country they considered as not to be shaken. It had often been proclaimed in the legislative discussions of the nation, and was otherwise public before the world. Its broad and stable foundations were laid in the first uncontradicted discovery of that river, both at its mouth and at its source, followed up by an effective settlement, and that settlement the earliest ever made upon its banks. If a title in the United States thus transcendent needed confirmation, it might be sought in their now uniting to it the title of Spain. It was not the intention of the United States, I remarked, to repose upon any of the extreme pretensions of that power to speculative dominion in those seas which grew up in less enlightened ages, however countenanced in those ages, nor had I, as their plenipotentiary, sought any aid from such pretensions; but to the extent of the just claims of Spain, grounded upon her fair enterprise and resources at periods when her renown for both filled all Europe, the United States had succeeded, and upon claims of this character it had therefore become as well their right as their duty to insist. I asserted again the incontestible priority of Spanish discoveries on the coast in question. I referred to the voyage of Cortes, who, in 1537, discovered California; to those of

Alarçon and Coronado, in 1540; to that of Cabrillo, in 1542, all of whom were prior to Drake; and the last of whom made the coast, by all the accounts that are given, as high up as latitude 44°. As to Drake, I said, that although Fleurieu, in his introduction to Marchaud, did assert that he got as far north as 48°, yet Hakluyt, who wrote almost at the time that Drake flourished, informs us that he got no higher than 43°, having put back at that point from "the extreme cold." All the later authors or compilers also who spoke of his voyage, however they might differ as to the degree of latitude to which he went, adopted from Hakluyt this fact of his having turned back from the intensity of the weather. The preponderance of probability, therefore, I alleged, as well as of authority, was, that Drake did not get beyond 43° along that coast. At all events, it was certain that he had made no settlements there, and the absence of these would, under the doctrine of Great Britain as applied by her to Spain, prevent any title whatever attaching to his supposed discoveries. They were moreover put out of view by the treaty of 1763, by which Britain agreed to consider the Mississippi as her western boundary upon that continent.

Our discussions, which grew into length, and only a condensed view of which I have aimed at presenting to you, terminated without any change of opinion on either side. Having stated the principal points which marked them, my duty seems to be drawing to a close, without the necessity of setting before you all the amplifications and details into which, on topics so copious, they would sometimes run. They were ended on the side of Great Britain by her plenipotentiaries repeating that they found it altogether impossible to accede either to the proposal of the United States or to the reasoning invoked in its support. That, nevertheless, they desired to lay a foundation of harmony between the two countries in that part of the globe—to close, not leave open, sources of future disagreement which time might multiply and aggravate. That with this view, and setting aside the discordant principles of the two Governments in the hope of promoting it, they had to propose: First, that the third article of the convention of October, 1818, should now be considered as at an end. Secondly, that instead of it, the boundary line between the territories respectively claimed by the two powers westward of the Rocky mountains should be drawn due west along the 49th parallel of latitude to *the point where it strikes the northeasternmost branch of the Columbia, and thence down along the middle of the Columbia* to *the Pacific Ocean*, the navigation of this river to be forever free to the subjects and citizens of both nations; and further, that the subjects or citizens of either should not in future be allowed to form settlements within the limits to be thus assigned to the other, with a saving in favor of settlements already formed within the prohibited limits, the proprietors or occupants of which, on both sides, should be allowed to remain ten years longer.

This proposal they annexed in form (marked P) to the protocol of the twenty-third conference. They remarked, that in submitting it they considered Great Britain as departing largely from the full extent of her right, and that if accepted by the United States it would impose upon her the necessity, ultimately, of breaking up four or five settlements formed by her subjects within the limits that would become prohibited, and that they had formed under the belief of their full right as British subjects to settle there. But their Government was willing, they said, to make these surrenders, for so they considered them, in a spirit of compromise on points where the two nations stood so divided.

I instantly declared to the British plenipotentiaries my utter inability to accept such a boundary as they had proposed. I added, at the same time, that I knew how the spirit of just accommodation also animated the Government of the United States upon this occasion. That in compliance with this spirit, and in order to meet Great Britain on ground that might be deemed middle, I would consent so far to vary the terms of my own proposal annexed to the twelfth protocol as to shift its *southern* line as low as 49°, in place of 51°. I desired it to be understood that this was the extreme limit to which I was authorized to go, and that, in being willing to make this change, I, too, considered the United States as abating their rights, in the hope of being able to put an end to all conflict of claims between the two nations to the coast and country in dispute.

The British plenipotentiaries, after having this modification of my first proposal a fortnight under consideration, rejected it, and they made me no new proposal in return. They did not, in terms, enter their rejection of this my second proposal on the protocol, and I did not urge it, thinking that their abstinence, as far as it could have any effect, might tend to leave the door somewhat less permanently closed against re-consideration, should the second proposal as so modified by me ever be again made. But it is right for me to state that they more than once declared, at the closing hours of the negotiation, that the boundary marked out in their own written proposal was one from which the Government of the United States must not expect Great Britain to depart.

I have to add, that their proposal was first made to me, verbally, at the twentieth conference, and that it then embraced an alternative of leaving the third article of the convention of 1818 to its natural course and limit. But this they afterwards controlled by their more formal and final proposition in writing, annexed, as before described, to the protocol of the twenty-third conference.

Having made you acquainted with all that transpired on this subject, I close it by referring to the protocols in which it is mentioned. These are the eleventh, the twelfth, the nineteenth, the twentieth, and the twenty-third.

I have now gone through all the subjects, and feel it time to come to a conclusion. I have made no omissions that are material, of which at present I have any consciousness. If, on reviewing at full leisure, the private journals from which I have selected the materials of this official despatch, I discover omissions, I will take care that they shall be supplied by a supplemental communication. I have laid before you a faithful, I would hope an intelligible, account of the progress, the character, and the results of the whole negotiation. The importance, to use the appropriate words of your own despatch to me of the 29th of July, 1823, of most of its subjects; the complicated character of the considerations involved in them, and their momentous bearings in present and future ages upon the interests, the welfare, and the honor of the United States, I have felt, deeply felt, throughout the protracted period allotted to their investigation and discussion. A load of responsibility and solicitude has weighed unceasingly upon my mind. A just, I will add a painful, sense of the great duty that was confided to me has never been absent from my thoughts. If it had pleased the President to have assigned me a colleague in its exercise, I should have felt thankful, having, as I took the liberty to say before it came on, entertained an unfeigned distrust in my own unassisted endeavors. For a proper estimate of what was due from me, for zeal, for good intentions, for diligence, I must humbly hope that the confidence reposed in me has not been misplaced. For the rest I cannot answer. Now that the negotiation is over, I cannot presume to hope that the manner in which I have conducted it, under all the many aspects which it assumed—aspects unforeseen, and to me often as difficult as unforeseen—will be deemed to have been always above exception. Constantly as I looked to the guiding light of your instructions, and ample as was the light shed by them over my general path, there were, there must have been, in the progress of voluminous discussions—where not the just desires of one nation, but the clashing interests of two, were at stake—points for which they did not provide. Reposing, upon all these occasions, on their general spirit, I must seek solace in the consciousness that, however unsuccessful the issue of my endeavors, they were always well meant, and in the hope that, regarded in their general character and tendency, they will be looked at with an indulgence proportioned to the anxious desire for my country's good, in which I feel sure it will be believed they ever originated. Of the questions that it fell to my lot to discuss with this nation, those that were old were full of difficulty, and had proved baffling in hands more skilful than mine in times that are passed; those that were new were found to be encompassed with difficulties not less formidable and intrinsic. Nor will it, I hope, be reputed out of place with my duty, or with the solemnity of this communication, to close it finally by the remark that the negotiation of which it has aimed at exhibiting an authentic history has been conducted with a nation not only mighty in her power, but unbending in her pretensions. The deliberate determinations to which she appears to have come in this negotiation I have felt it an imperious duty to report, without, in any instance, abating the force of any of the considerations by which I understood her plenipotentiaries to expound and maintain them.

I have the honor to remain, with very great respect, your obedient servant,

RICHARD RUSH.

Hon. John Quincy Adams, *Secretary of State.*

List of papers sent with despatch No. 10 of August 12, 1824.

1. All the protocols of the negotiation, being twenty-six in number, with the exception of the first, the second, the fourth, the fifth, the sixth, and the seventh, which were forwarded with the convention for the suppression of the slave trade.
2. Copy of the full power of the British plenipotentiaries, dated the 29th of November, 1823. (This instrument contains an inaccurate description of the constitutional mode of appointment, applicable to the plenipotentiary of the United States. It was pointed out to the British plenipotentiaries, but they did not correct it, and the plenipotentiary of the United States did not deem the error to be of a nature to impair the validity of the instrument.)
3. Draft of three articles for the regulation of commercial intercourse and the navigation of the St. Lawrence, submitted by the American plenipotentiary, and annexed to the protocol of the third conference, (marked A.)
4. Informal paper from the British plenipotentiaries on the commercial intercourse question, (marked W.)
5. Printed copy of an act of Parliament of the session of 1824, for establishing reciprocity of duties.
6. Printed copy of the commercial treaty between Great Britain and Prussia, for establishing reciprocity of duties, dated April, 1824.
7. British counter projet on commercial intercourse, annexed to the protocol of the sixteenth conference, (marked L.)
8. Paper on the navigation of the St. Lawrence, submitted by the American plenipotentiary, and annexed to the protocol of the eighteenth conference, (marked B.)
9. British paper on the above subject, annexed to the protocol of the twenty-fourth conference, (marked N.)
10. Paper submitted by the American plenipotentiary for settling the boundary line, under the fifth article of the treaty of Ghent, annexed to the protocol of the ninth conference, (marked D.)
11. Paper submitted by the American plenipotentiary on the Newfoundland fishery, and annexed to the protocol of the tenth conference, (marked E.)
12. Copy of an official note from the American plenipotentiary to Mr. Secretary Canning upon the above subject, dated May 3, 1824.
13. British articles on several miscellaneous points annexed to the protocol of the twenty-second conference, (marked M.)
14. Paper submitted by the American plenipotentiary relative to the Northwest Coast of America, and annexed to the protocol of the twelfth conference, (marked F.)
15. British paper on the above subject, annexed to the protocol of the twenty-third conference, (marked P.)

R. R.

London, *August 12, 1824.*

Protocol of the third conference of the American and British plenipotentiaries, held at the Board of Trade, February 5, 1824.

Present: Mr. Rush, Mr. Huskisson, and Mr. Stratford Canning.

The protocol of the preceding conference was read over and signed.

In pursuance of previous agreement, Mr. Rush brought forward the propositions of his Government respecting the trade between the British colonies in North America and the West Indies and the United States, including the navigation of the St. Lawrence by vessels of the United States.

On concluding the statement with which Mr. Rush introduced these proposals, in explanation of the views and antecedent proceedings of his Government, he gave in the three articles which are hereunto annexed, (marked A.)

The British plenipotentiaries, in receiving the articles thus presented to them for consideration, confined themselves to stating their first impressions as to the scope and extent of the American proposals, and the extreme difficulty resulting therefrom, observing on such parts of the American plenipotentiary's statement as appeared to them to call for immediate objection, or to admit of satisfactory explanation.

Adjourned to Monday, the 16th instant, at two o'clock.

RICHARD RUSH.
W. HUSKISSON.
STRATFORD CANNING.

Protocol of the eighth conference of the American and British plenipotentiaries, held at the Board of Trade,
March 18, 1824.

Present: Mr. Rush, Mr. Huskisson, and Mr. Stratford Canning.
Another original copy of the convention on the subject of the slave trade, having been prepared at
the request of the American plenipotentiary, with the view of enabling him to transmit that instrument
in duplicate to his Government, was read over, and, upon its proving to be perfectly correct, was signed
by the plenipotentiaries on both sides.

RICHARD RUSH.
W. HUSKISSON.
STRATFORD CANNING.

Protocol of the ninth conference of the American and British plenipotentiaries, held at the Board of Trade,
March 25, 1824.

Present: Mr. Rush, Mr. Huskisson, and Mr. Stratford Canning.
The protocol of the preceding conference was read over and signed.
The British plenipotentiaries stated that, not being yet at liberty, from circumstances already
explained, to make a full communication with respect to the three articles proposed by Mr. Rush at the
third conference, while, they were disposed, in the spirit of that perfect amity and good will which
subsisted between the respective Governments, to treat of the free navigation of the river St. Lawrence
by American vessels, on the principle of accommodation and mutual concession, they thought it desirable
that the American plenipotentiary should at once bring forward the proposals of his Government on the
several questions already submitted by him for negotiation.
The American plenipotentiary readily acquiesced in the expediency of this course, on the obvious
understanding that the views of the British Government would be, in turn, communicated to him. He
consequently gave in the paper (D) annexed hereto, as containing the proposal of his Government for
endeavoring to adjust, by compromise, the differences arising under the 5th article of the treaty of Ghent.
Mr. Rush remarked at the same time on the extreme difficulties attending an arbitration as prescribed
by that treaty, and stated his conviction that his Majesty's late Secretary of State for Foreign Affairs
had signified to him the assent of the British Government to his proposal of endeavoring to settle the
points at issue by direct communication between the two Governments.
In reply to a question from the British plenipotentiaries, Mr. Rush informed them that he was not
prepared, in case of his proposal being finally accepted, to submit any particular terms of compromise for
settling the disputed boundary, though he was persuaded that his Government, in proposing a negotiation on that principle, looked with confidence to its issuing in an agreement satisfactory to both parties;
and also that, in the event of an arbitration being insisted on, his present instructions would enable him
to proceed at once to the concurrent selection of an arbitrator, agreeably to the treaty of Ghent.
It was agreed that the next conference should be held on Monday next, the 29th instant, when the
American plenipotentiary would be prepared to continue his communication of the proposals of his
Government.

RICHARD RUSH.
W. HUSKISSON.
STRATFORD CANNING.

Protocol of the tenth conference of the American and British plenipotentiaries, held at the Board of Trade,
March 29, 1824.

Present: Mr. Rush, Mr. Huskisson, and Mr. Stratford Canning.
The protocol of the preceding conference was read over and signed.
The American plenipotentiary entered upon the subject of the Newfoundland fishery. He stated at
length the circumstances constituting the case which his Government thought it advisable to bring under
the view of the British Government, and concluded by giving in as a memorandum of his statement the
paper marked E, annexed to the present protocol.
The British plenipotentiaries, after making such inquiries of Mr. Rush as they deemed conducive to
a thorough understanding of the points in question, agreed to meet him again in conference on Thursday,
the 1st of April.

RICHARD RUSH.
W. HUSKISSON.
STRATFORD CANNING.

Protocol of the eleventh conference of the American and British plenipotentiaries, held at the Board of Trade,
April 1, 1824.

Present: Mr. Rush, Mr. Huskisson, and Mr. Stratford Canning.
The protocol of the preceding conference was read over and signed.
The American plenipotentiary opened the subject of territorial claims on the Northwest Coast of
America westward of the Rocky mountains. It having been understood that the pretension which had
been put forward by the cabinet of St. Petersburg, respecting its jurisdiction in that quarter, was to be

matter of separate discussion between the respective parties, he observed that, notwithstanding this circumstance, and although the convention of October, 1818, one article of which contained a temporary regulation with respect to the above mentioned claims, had still four years to continue, his Government was of opinion that the present was not an unsuitable moment for attempting a settlement of the boundary on the Northwest Coast of America westward of the Rocky mountains, and he therefore proceeded to explain the nature of the claims which his Government thought itself entitled to advance.

His statement not being completed in the present conference, Mr. Rush undertook to resume it on the following day.

RICHARD RUSH.
W. HUSKISSON.
STRATFORD CANNING.

Protocol of the twelfth conference of the American and British plenipotentiaries, held at the Board of Trade, April 2, 1824.

Present: Mr. Rush, Mr. Huskisson, and Mr. Stratford Canning.
The protocol of the preceding conference was read over and signed.
The American plenipotentiary resumed the communication which he had commenced in that conference on the subject of the territorial claims on the Northwest Coast of America westward of the Rocky mountains, and concluded by giving in the paper marked F, annexed hereto, as containing the proposal of his Government on that head.
Adjourned to Monday, the 5th of April.

RICHARD RUSH.
W. HUSKISSON.
STRATFORD CANNING.

Protocol of the thirteenth conference of the American and British plenipotentiaries, held at the Board of Trade, April 5, 1824.

Present: Mr. Rush, Mr. Huskisson, and Mr. Stratford Canning.
The protocol of the preceding conference was read over and signed.
The American plenipotentiary stated that, in addition to the questions submitted for negotiation at the preceding conferences, he was instructed to treat with Great Britain on various subjects of maritime law heretofore in discussion between the two countries, and also on that of the abolition of privateering and the exemption from all capture of private property in merchant ships at sea. Amongst the former subjects he mentioned that of impressment as of leading importance.

He added that, as he was not authorized to assent to anything new in principle on such of these points as had been discussed on former occasions, it was right for him to premise that, unless the British Government were ready to negotiate with the understanding that the views which they had heretofore entertained on them were essentially changed, or likely, in the course of negotiation, to be materially modified, the Government of the United States would prefer, on the whole, not bringing these questions under discussion at the present time.

After stating the general political considerations which had induced his Government to make this overture, he informed the British plenipotentiaries, in reply to an inquiry on their part, that, although he was willing to treat of impressment alone, he should not feel inclined to enter on the other points of maritime law unless the question of impressment was at the same time received by his Majesty's ministers as part of that negotiation.

The British plenipotentiaries having further asked whether any additional securities would be proposed or admitted by the American Government against the employment of British natural born subjects in the merchant vessels of the United States, the American plenipotentiary replied that he had none to offer essentially differing from those brought forward in former negotiations.

RICHARD RUSH.
W. HUSKISSON.
STRATFORD CANNING.

Protocol of the fourteenth conference of the American and British plenipotentiaries, held at the Board of Trade, April 13, 1824.

Present: Mr. Rush, Mr. Huskisson, and Mr. Stratford Canning.
After the protocol of the preceding conference had been agreed to and signed, the British plenipotentiaries stated that they had invited Mr. Rush to an interview in order to inform him that, in consequence of the inquiries which they had made as to the right of fishing on the Western Coast of Newfoundland, they conceived that the case, as previously described by him, was hardly of a nature to be entertained among the subjects of the present negotiation.

The citizens of the United States were clearly entitled, under the convention of October, 1818, to a participation with his Majesty's subjects in certain fishing liberties on the coasts of Newfoundland; the Government of the United States might, therefore, require a declaration of the extent of those liberties as enjoyed by British subjects under any limitations prescribed by treaty with other powers, and protection in the exercise of the liberties so limited, in common with British subjects, within the jurisdiction of his

Majesty as sovereign of the island of Newfoundland; that such declaration and protection, if necessary, might be applied for in the regular diplomatic course; but that it was to be observed that the question appeared to have been in some degree varied, first, by the line of argument pursued in the correspondence between Mr. Gallatin and Viscount Chateaubriand, the latter having rested his claim to the right of exclud ing the United States from the fisheries on those parts of the coast of Newfoundland to which the above mentioned correspondence applied, upon engagements contracted by the American Government towards that of France long before October, 1818, according to his construction of which engagements the United States had virtually rendered their exercise of the liberty of fishing between Cape Ray and the Quirpon islands, conceded by Great Britain, dependent on the compliance of his most Christian Majesty; and, secondly, by the consent of the American Government to open discussions on this subject, at Washington, with the French chargé d'affaires.

The American plenipotentiary, protesting wholly against the grounds assumed by France as impairing in any degree the fishing rights of the United States, held under the convention of October 20, 1818, and not admitting that any correspondence which had taken place between the Governments of the United States and France upon this subject could affect any of those rights, remarked that his main object being to bring the question which had arisen between the United States and France fully under the notice of the Government of his Britannic Majesty, with a view to the objects stated in his paper, marked E, (annexed to the protocol of the tenth conference,) he should adopt the course of addressing an official representation upon the whole subject to his Majesty's principal Secretary of State for Foreign Affairs.

RICHARD RUSH.
W. HUSKISSON.
STRATFORD CANNING.

Protocol of the fifteenth conference of the American and British plenipotentiaries, held at the Board of Trade, June 4, 1824.

Present: Mr. Rush, Mr. Huskisson, and Mr. Stratford Canning.

The protocol of the preceding conference was read over and signed.

The British plenipotentiaries stated that, having received the instructions of their Government on the various important and extensive questions submitted for negotiation, they were now prepared to communicate fully and definitively thereon with the American plenipotentiary.

Beginning with the articles of colonial intercourse proposed by him at the third conference, they explained at large the sentiments of their Government, showing what insuperable objections, alike in principle as in practice, precluded Great Britain, in their estimation, from acceding to the articles in question, except with the omission of such parts as stipulated, in reference to that intercourse, for a complete assimilation of the duties on imports from the United States into the colonies, to those levied on like imported articles the produce of his Britannic Majesty's possessions.

The American plenipotentiary stated that he was not authorized to sign the proposed articles without a full stipulation to the preceding effect; but that he was instructed to invite the British plenipotentiaries, in case of the terms which he had offered not being accepted, to bring forward counter proposals which he should be ready to transmit, together with any explanations for consideration, to his Government.

Adjourned to Tuesday, the 8th instant.

RICHARD RUSH.
W. HUSKISSON.
STRATFORD CANNING.

Protocol of the sixteenth conference of the American and British plenipotentiaries, held at the Board of Trade, June 8, 1824.

Present: Mr. Rush, Mr. Huskisson, and Mr. Stratford Canning.

The protocol of the preceding conference was read over and signed.

The British plenipotentiaries, after further discussion in relation to commercial intercourse between the United States and certain of the British colonies, gave in the annexed counter projet on that subject, in reference to what had passed at the preceding conference, observing at the same time that the first two articles of the proposal communicated by the American plenipotentiary in their third conference with him had, in their opinion, no necessary connexion with the third, relating to the navigation of the river St. Lawrence, and that they conceived it would be more convenient to treat of them separately.

Adjourned to Tuesday, the 15th instant

RICHARD RUSH.
W. HUSKISSON.
STRATFORD CANNING.

Protocol of the seventeenth conference of the American and British plenipotentiaries, held at the Board of Trade, June 15, 1824.

Present: Mr. Rush, Mr. Huskisson, and Mr. Stratford Canning.

The protocol of the preceding conference was read over and signed.

The British plenipotentiaries stated that, in pursuance of the proposals of the American Government, they were ready to enter into stipulations for settling by compromise the several questions which had arisen under the 5th article of the treaty of Ghent; and that, agreeably to the disposition which they had expressed in a former conference to treat of the navigation of the river St. Lawrence by vessels of the United States on principles of accommodation and mutual concession, they now proposed to negotiate on that subject in connexion with the said questions which affect the boundary of the British and American territories throughout the region contiguous to that part of the St. Lawrence which flows exclusively through his Majesty's dominions. They intimated, at the same time, that the .course which they proposed in this manner to pursue was founded on the understanding that the navigation of the St. Lawrence throughout his Majesty's territories was not to be claimed by the United States as a right; and this intimation they accompanied with an exposition of the very decided opinion entertained by their Government against such an absolute, independent claim.

The American plenipotentiary said that he was not able to go into the proposed negotiation, as relating to the St. Lawrence, on the principle of concession, but, on the contrary, that his instructions imposed upon him the obligation of pressing the claim of the United States to the entire navigation of that river expressly on the ground of independent right, and that he conceived it would be his duty, in asserting that claim, to enter it so grounded on the protocol of the conferences.

It was agreed, however, that it would be convenient, on the whole, to postpone any decided step thereupon until the ensuing conference.

Adjourned.

RICHARD RUSH.
W. HUSKISSON.
STRATFORD CANNING.

Protocol of the eighteenth conference of the American and British plenipotentiaries, held at the Board of Trade, June 19, 1824.

Present: Mr. Rush, Mr. Huskisson, and Mr. Stratford Canning.

The protocol of the preceding conference was read over and signed.

The American plenipotentiary, referring to that conference, stated that he felt himself bound to present the claim of the United States to a concurrent enjoyment of the navigation of the river St. Lawrence from its source to the sea, on the express ground of independent right. He said that he had, indeed, been left at liberty to exercise his judgment as to the time and manner of presenting that claim, but he was positively instructed to urge it in the course of the negotiations in the above decided sense of right; that otherwise, he should have been obliged to prefer the same claim by direct application to the Foreign Department. It was in discharge of the duty thus imposed upon him that he gave in the annexed paper, (marked B,) containing a distinct exposition of the views and principles on which the above mentioned claim of the American Government was sustained.

The British plenipotentiaries, on receiving this declaration and written argument from Mr. Rush, observed that it became their duty to deny, and they did therefore deny, in explicit terms, the right so claimed on behalf of the United States to navigate, in common with British subjects, that part of the river St. Lawrence which flows exclusively through his Majesty's territories. They added, that they could not conceal the surprise which they felt at learning that such a right was to be asserted by the American Government, especially as it must necessarily have the effect of tying up their hands with respect to the instructions which they had received from their Government on a very different apprehension of the subject, and which they had no hesitation in describing as founded on a most liberal and comprehensive view of the wishes and interests of the United States, with respect to the disputed points of the boundary line under the 5th article of the treaty of Ghént, no less than as touching the navigation of the St. Lawrence, which they had considered, on the principle of accommodation and mutual concession, as supplying additional means for the satisfactory adjustment of those disputed points by negotiation and compromise.

The American plenipotentiary, in supporting the claim of his Government, averred that it was not put forward in any unfriendly spirit, but with reference to such of the national interests as were immediately concerned in the question, and that it was subject, of course, to the operation of further discussion between the two Governments, and a frank communication of their respective sentiments.

Adjourned.

RICHARD RUSH.
W. HUSKISSON.
STRATFORD CANNING.

Protocol of the nineteenth conference of the American and British plenipotentiaries, held at the Board of Trade, June 26, 1824.

Present: Mr. Rush, Mr. Huskisson, and Mr. Stratford Canning.

The protocol of the preceding conference was read over and signed.

The British plenipotentiaries stated that, having considered the declaration made by Mr. Rush in that conference concerning the independent right of the United States to the entire navigation of the river St. Lawrence, and the written argument which he had annexed to the protocol in support of that right, they felt themselves called upon to communicate, in a manner equally explicit and formal, the ground on which their Government denied a right of the description asserted on the part of the United States. They added that, although the opinions which they had already declared on that point were unchanged, they thought it due to the gravity and importance of the question not to give in their reply to the American argument until it had received the full sanction of the highest professional authorities in the country on matters relating to the law of nations. For the accomplishment of this object, an interval of some days was obviously requisite, and therefore, to delay as little as possible the progress of the negotiations, they proposed to pass on, for the present, to the questions of boundary on the Northwest Coast of America.

The American plenipotentiary said that any delay, as to the question of the St. Lawrence, did not, in his opinion, affect the points to be adjusted under the fifth article of the treaty of Ghent, and that he desired to proceed at once to the conclusion of an agreement by which those points should be referred to a direct negotiation between the two Governments, as before proposed by him. But, as it appeared, on discussing these matters, that Mr. Rush was authorized only to take *ad referendum* any counter proposals of the British Government on the above mentioned points, (whether those counter proposals conveyed any positive terms of compromise, or only such arrangements as the British plenipotentiaries conceived must necessarily accompany the mere agreement to settle the points at issue by compromise,) and that his instructions would not allow of his *concluding* anything at present with the British plenipo. tentiaries as to the various preparatory steps indispensable for carrying the disputed points of the fifth article of the treaty of Ghent before an arbitrator, if arbitration should be found, after all, to be inevitable, it was finally agreed that the plenipotentiaries should meet again on the 29th instant, in order to communicate definitively on the subject of the northwest boundary.
  Adjourned.

RICHARD RUSH.
W. HUSKISSON.
STRATFORD CANNING.

Protocol of the twentieth conference of the American and British plenipotentiaries, held at the Board of Trade, June 29, 1824.

  Present: Mr. Rush, Mr. Huskisson, and Mr. Stratford Canning.
  The protocol of the preceding conference was read over and signed.
  The British plenipotentiaries stated and explained at length the sentiments of their Government with respect to the conflicting claims of Great Britain and the United States to the territories in North America lying between the Rocky mountains and the Pacific Ocean. They declined the proposal made on this subject by the American plenipotentiary, and annexed to the twelfth protocol, because it would substantially have the effect of limiting the claims of their Government to a degree inconsistent, as they thought, with the credit and just interests of the nation. After much discussion and mutual explanation of the claims on each side, when taken in their full extent, it was agreed that, following the example given by the American plenipotentiary in his proposal, it would be advisable to attempt a settlement on terms of mutual convenience, setting aside for that purpose the discordant principles on which the respective claims were founded. Whereupon the British plenipotentiaries stated, in general terms, that they were ready either to agree on a boundary line, to be drawn due west from the Rocky mountains along the 49th parallel of latitude to the northeasternmost branch of the Columbia or Oregon river, and thence down the middle of that river to the ocean, or to leave the third article of the convention of 1818 to its natural course. The American plenipotentiary, in remarking upon this boundary, declared his utter inability to accede to it, but, finding that the line offered in his former proposal was considered wholly inadmissible by the British plenipotentiaries, said that, in the hope of adjusting the question, he would so far vary his former line *to the south* as to consent that it should be the forty-ninth instead of the fifty-first degree of north latitude.
  In the course of the conference the American plenipotentiary stated that he was instructed to insist on the principle that no part of the American continent was henceforward to be open to colonization from Europe. To explain this principle, he stated that the independence of the late Spanish provinces precluded any new settlement within the limits of their respective jurisdictions; that the United States claimed the exclusive sovereignty of all the territory within the parallels of latitude which include as well the mouth of the Columbia as the heads of that river and of all its tributary streams; and that with respect to the whole of the remainder of that continent not actually occupied, the powers of Europe were debarred from making new settlements by the claim of the United States as derived under their title from Spain.
  The British plenipotentiaries asserted, in utter denial of the above principle, that they considered the unoccupied parts of America just as much open as heretofore to colonization by Great Britain, as well as by other European powers, agreeably to the convention of 1790 between the British and Spanish Governments, and that the United States would have no right whatever to take umbrage at the establishment of new colonies from Europe in any such parts of the American continent.
  The British plenipotentiaries added, that they felt themselves more particularly called upon to express their distinct denial of the principle and claims thus set forth by the American plenipotentiary, as his claim respecting the territory watered by the river Columbia and its tributary streams, besides being essentially objectionable in its general bearing, had the effect of interfering directly with the actual rights of Great Britain, derived from use, occupancy, and settlement.

RICHARD RUSH.
W. HUSKISSON.
STRATFORD CANNING.

Protocol of the twenty-first conference of the American and British plenipotentiaries, held at the Board of Trade, July 3, 1824.

  Present: Mr. Rush, Mr. Huskisson, and Mr. Stratford Canning.
  The protocol of the preceding conference was read over and signed.
  The questions of maritime law were taken up. The British plenipotentiaries stated, with reference to Mr. Rush's communication on this head, as recorded in the protocol of the thirteenth conference, that the sentiments of their Government respecting the impressment of British seamen in time of war were

unchanged; and that however anxious they were to reconcile the eventual exercise of that right on the high seas with the convenience and feelings of other nations, they could not, consistently with their duty, agree to waive it with respect to the vessels of the United States, except on receiving a full and efficient security that the end for which it was occasionally resorted to should be substantially attained by other satisfactory means; that having been informed by the American plenipotentiary that he had to propose no measures for effecting this important object essentially differing from those which in former negotiations had been found inadequate, they could not but concur with him in the opinion that any discussion of the question at the present moment of general tranquillity would be altogether unadvisable.

With regard to the other maritime questions affecting the relations of neutral and belligerent powers, the British plenipotentiaries observed that, as the American plenipotentiary was not prepared to enter into stipulations respecting them, except in conjunction with the subject of impressment, which subject was not to be entered into for the reasons above stated, the discussion of these questions, under the present circumstances, would obviously be attended with no practical utility.

They expressed themselves willing, at the same time, to treat on other points not falling under this head, but connected with the improvement of friendly intercourse and good neighborhood already subsisting between the two countries, if the American plenipotentiary felt himself at liberty to entertain proposals founded on this principle.

The American plenipotentiary expressed his readiness to receive and transmit to his Government any suggestions of this description, but stated that he was not prepared to propose or definitively accept any stipulations of such a nature, except in conjunction with an arrangement as to the maritime questions.

Adjourned.

RICHARD RUSH.
W. HUSKISSON.
STRATFORD CANNING.

Protocol of the twenty-second conference of the American and British plenipotentiaries, held at the Board of Trade, July 9, 1824.

Present: Mr. Rush, Mr. Huskisson, and Mr. Stratford Canning.

The protocol of the preceding conference was read over, and, after some discussion, signed.

The American plenipotentiary stated that the question of abolishing private war, and all capture of private property at sea, was considered by him as standing apart from the other questions of maritime law, which had been heretofore discussed between the two Governments, inasmuch as it was perfectly new, and had been proposed by his Government to other European powers as well as to Great Britain; and he wished it to be understood that he was ready to treat on that question alone, notwithstanding the decision already taken upon the other questions of maritime war.

The British plenipotentiaries said, in reply to this statement, that under the circumstances which prevented any present discussion of the questions of maritime law discussed in former negotiations, there would be manifest inconvenience in now going into a question of the same class, which, besides being totally new as an object of discussion, involved a most extensive change in the principles and practice of maritime war as hitherto sanctioned by the usage of all nations.

The British plenipotentiaries, adverting to the other points not falling under the head of maritime law, but connected with the improvement of friendly intercourse and good neighborhood between the two nations, on which, in the preceding conference, they had offered to treat independently, communicated the substance of nine articles which they had been prepared to give in if the American plenipotentiary had felt himself at liberty to conclude an arrangement on them, and on which they declared themselves still ready to enter into stipulations with the Government of the United States.

RICHARD RUSH.
W. HUSKISSON.
STRATFORD CANNING.

Protocol of the twenty-third conference of the American and British plenipotentiaries, held at the Board of Trade, July 13, 1824.

Present: Mr. Rush, Mr. Huskisson, and Mr. Stratford Canning.

The protocol of the preceding conference was read over and signed.

The British plenipotentiaries, in more complete explanation of the statement made by them in the twentieth conference, gave in an article comprising the counter proposals of their Government as to the northwest boundary in America from the Rocky mountains to the Pacific Ocean. They observed, at the same time, that, if their article were accepted in substance by the American Government, it would be necessary, on framing it into a convention, to give its details and accompanying arrangements a more distinct and expanded shape. They added that, in making the annexed proposal, they had departed considerably from the full extent of the British right, agreeably to the readiness which they had before expressed to settle the northwest boundary on grounds of fair compromise and mutual accommodation.

The American plenipotentiary, in receiving the above article from the British plenipotentiaries, remarked, that he wished it also to be understood that, in proposing a modification of the article originally submitted by him on this subject, he had been governed by the same view.

The American plenipotentiary introduced the question of allowing United States consuls to reside in the British colonial ports, and requesting to be made acquainted with the sentiments of the British Government thereon.

The British plenipotentiaries referred, in reply, to the counter proposals which they had already given in on the subject of colonial intercourse, of which proposals the reception of American consuls formed a distinct part.

Mr. Rush observed that the residence of foreign consuls in any country did not appear so much to depend on any particular set of commercial regulations as to belong essentially to trade, under whatever form it might be carried on; and he supported this observation by arguments connected with the protection of merchants trading under any lawful circumstances with a foreign country.

The British plenipotentiaries agreed to take this suggestion into consideration before the next conference.

Adjourned.

RICHARD RUSH.
W. HUSKISSON.
STRATFORD CANNING.

Protocol of the twenty-fourth conference of the American and British plenipotentiaries, held at the Board of Trade, July 19, 1824.

Present: Mr. Rush, Mr. Huskisson, and Mr. Canning.

The protocol of the preceding conference was read over and signed.

The British plenipotentiaries gave in the annexed paper in reply to the argument relating to the free navigation of the river St. Lawrence, given in by the American plenipotentiary at a preceding conference, and, in like manner, annexed by him to the protocol.

The British plenipotentiaries, referring to what had passed at the preceding conference on the subject of receiving United States consuls in his Majesty's open colonial ports, stated that, although they saw no objection to the admission into those colonies of foreign consuls, subject to the usual exceptions and reservations, while foreign vessels were in the practice of carrying on a lawful trade with the colonial ports, they conceived that there would be inconvenience in actually recognizing such appointments there so long as it was uncertain, not only whether the proposals which they had given in on the subject of colonial intercourse would be accepted by the American Government, but even whether the trade now carried on between the United States and his Majesty's colonies would not be so clogged with additional burdens as to lead to its total interruption.

Adjourned.

RICHARD RUSH.
W. HUSKISSON.
STRATFORD CANNING.

Protocol of the twenty-fifth conference of the American and British plenipotentiaries, held at the Board of Trade, July 22, 1824.

Present: Mr. Rush, Mr. Huskisson, and Mr. Stratford Canning.

The protocol of the preceding conference was read over and signed.

The American plenipotentiary, referring to the reply given in by the British plenipotentiaries to his argument on the navigation of the river St. Lawrence, and annexed to the protocol of the preceding conference, made observations tending, in his opinion, to sustain the view which he had before presented of that subject.

It was agreed, in consideration of the numerous and complicated questions on which the conferences had turned, that the plenipotentiaries should meet again and communicate with each other prior to sending in to the respective Governments their final reports of the present state of the negotiations, suspended by the necessity of referring to Washington on some of the subjects which had been presented for discussion.

Adjourned.

RICHARD RUSH.
W. HUSKISSON.
STRATFORD CANNING.

Protocol of the twenty-sixth conference of the American and British plenipotentiaries, held at the Board of Trade, July 28, 1824.

Present: Mr. Rush, Mr. Huskisson, and Mr. Stratford Canning.

The protocol of the preceding conference was read over and signed.

The plenipotentiaries, after communicating with each other in pursuance of the agreement taken at the preceding conference, and persuaded that they had sufficiently developed the sentiments of their respective Governments on the various subjects of their conferences, separated under the circumstances which necessarily prevented, for the present, any further progress in the negotiations.

RICHARD RUSH.
W. HUSKISSON.
STRATFORD CANNING.

GEORGE R:

George the Fourth, by the Grace of God King of the United Kingdom of Great Britain and Ireland, Defender of the Faith, King of Hanover, &c., &c., &c.: To all and singular to whom these presents shall come greeting: Whereas, for the better treating of and arranging certain matters now in discussion between us and our good friends, the United States of America, the President of the United States, with the consent and by the authority of the Senate and House of Representatives of the said United States, has nominated, constituted, and appointed Richard Rush, Esq., Envoy Extraordinary and Minister Plenipotentiary of the said United States at our court, to be their Commissioner to conduct the said discussion on their behalf; and we, reposing especial trust and confidence in the wisdom, loyalty, diligence, and circumspection of our right trusty and well-beloved councillor, William Huskisson, a member of our Imperial Parliament, President of the Committee of our Privy Council for Affairs of Trade and Foreign Plantations, and Treasurer of our Navy, and of our right trusty and well-beloved councillor, Stratford Canning, our Envoy Extraordinary and Minister Plenipotentiary to our said good friends, the United States of America, have nominated, constituted, and appointed, and by these presents do nominate, constitute, and appoint them our true, certain, and undoubted Commissioners, Procurators, and Plenipotentiaries, giving to them all and all manner of faculty, power, and authority, together with general as well as special orders (so as the general do not derogate from the special, nor on the contrary) for us and in our name to meet, confer, treat, and conclude with the said Richard Rush, Esq., being duly furnished with sufficient powers on the part of our said good friends, the United States of America, of and concerning all such matters and things as may be requisite and necessary for accomplishing and completing the several ends and purposes hereinbefore adverted to, and of and concerning all such matters and things as may tend to the mutual interests and advantage of our subjects or dominions, and of those of our said good friends, and to the promoting and maintaining a mutual friendship, good understanding, and intercourse between our subjects or dominions, and those of our said good friends, and for us and in our name, to sign all such article or articles, or other instruments whatsoever, as may be agreed upon between the said plenipotentiaries, and mutually to deliver and receive the same in exchange, and to do and perform all such other acts, matters, and things as may be in anywise proper and conducive to the purposes above adverted to, in as full and ample manner, and with the like validity and effect as we ourself, if we were present, could do and perform the same, engaging and promising, on our royal word, that we will accept, ratify, and confirm all such acts, matters, and things as shall be so transacted and concluded by our aforesaid Commissioners, Procurators, and Plenipotentiaries, and that we will never suffer any person to violate the same in the whole, or in part, to act contrary thereto. In testimony and confirmation of all which, we have caused the great seal of our United Kingdom of Great Britain and Ireland to be affixed to these presents, which we have signed with our royal hand. Given at our court, at Carlton House, the twenty-ninth day of November, in the year of our Lord one thousand eight hundred and twenty-three, and in the fourth year of our reign.

[L. S.]

A true copy:
W. HUSKISSON.
STRATFORD CANNING.

A.

I. Whereas, by the trade as it now exists under the respective laws and regulations of the two high contracting parties between certain enumerated ports of his Britannic Majesty's colonies in America and the West Indies and the ports of the United States, discriminating duties and charges are reciprocally imposed and levied upon the vessels and cargoes of each nation in the ports of the other as aforesaid; and whereas it is the desire of the contracting parties, for the reciprocal advantage of their subjects and citizens, to abolish all such discriminating duties and charges: it is therefore agreed that, upon the vessels of the United States admitted by law into all and every one of his Britannic Majesty's colonial ports as aforesaid, and upon any goods, wares, and merchandise lawfully imported therein in the said vessels, no other or higher duties of tonnage or impost, and no other charges of any kind shall be levied or exacted, than upon British vessels, including all vessels of the colonies themselves, or upon the like goods, wares, or merchandise imported into the said colonial ports from any other port or place whatever, including Great Britain and the colonial ports themselves. And that upon the vessels of Great Britain admitted by law into all and every one of the ports of the United States, and upon any goods, wares, and merchandise lawfully imported therein in the said vessels, no other or higher duties of tonnage or impost, and no other charges of any kind shall be levied or exacted than upon vessels of the United States, including vessels of each and every one of the said States, or upon the like goods, wares, or merchandise imported into the United States from any other port or place whatever.

II. For the more perfect fulfilment of the intentions of the high contracting parties, as expressed in the foregoing article, it is agreed that the trade to which it has reference shall continue on the footing upon which it now stands by the laws and regulations of the two countries, respectively, with the exception of the removal by Great Britain of the duties specified in the schedule C of the act of Parliament passed on the twenty-fourth day of June, one thousand eight hundred and twenty-two, in the third year of his present Majesty's reign, chapter forty-four, and those specified in schedule B of the act of Parliament passed on the fifth day of August, in the same year and reign, chapter one hundred and nineteen; and of the removal by the United States of all additional duties of tonnage in the light of foreign tonnage duty, and of all additional duties of impost in the light of foreign impost, existing against British vessels and merchandise coming to the United States from any of the colonial ports aforesaid. And the high contracting parties pledge themselves to remove reciprocally the duties herein recapitulated, as well as all other discriminating duties and charges of whatever kind they may be, intended by this and the foregoing article to be removed, it being the desire and intention of the parties to place the aforesaid trade upon a footing of perfect equality in all respects.

III. It is agreed by the high contracting parties that the navigation of the river St. Lawrence shall be at all times free to the citizens of the United States as to the subjects of Great Britain, in its whole breadth and length to and from the sea, and that the vessels belonging to either party shall not be stopped, visited, or subjected to any let, impediment, or hindrance whatsoever by the other; nor shall they be liable to the payment of any duty whatever for this right of passage on the said river. But respecting such moderate and reasonable tolls as either party may claim and appear entitled to, the high contracting parties agree to treat at a future day, that the principles regulating the same may be adjusted to mutual satisfaction.

W.

Paper on the Commercial Intercourse Question, from the British plenipotentiaries.

The British plenipotentiaries present the following remarks on the articles of colonial intercourse, proposed by the American plenipotentiary at his third conference with them:

The first two articles have no necessary connexion with the third, which relates to the navigation of the river St. Lawrence; and the British plenipotentiaries are of opinion that it is more convenient to treat of them separately.

The proposal contained in the two articles on colonial intercourse is, in substance, as follows: The trade between the United States and his Majesty's colonies in North America and the West Indies to continue, as at present, regulated by the respective acts of Parliament and Congress, except that all discriminating charges on alien vessels and their cargoes concerned in that trade should be withdrawn on both sides; and further, that all articles of United States produce should be admitted into the colonies exactly on the same terms as the like productions of the colonies themselves or of the mother country.

To all but the last clause of this proposal the British Goverment are willing to consent. To that condition they decidedly object.

The objectionable condition amounts to no less than a stipulation that Great Britain shall renounce, in favor of the United States, and without a return on their side, the power of protecting the staples of her own subjects by levying import duties on the like productions of a foreign country.

In *principle* such a proposition is evidently inadmissible. It could not be entertained with credit by any power on which it was calculated to operate exclusively. It is directly at variance with the practice of all commercial, of all civilized States. It has no precedent in the commercial relations subsisting between the British dominions in Europe and the United States.

The *specific* grounds alleged in support of it by the American plenipotentiary are, in the opinion of the British Government, wholly insufficient for that purpose.

They are understood to be, in effect: First. That American vessels are subject to an export duty in the British West Indies to which British vessels are not equally liable. Second. That, while all the ports of the United States are open to British vessels, only certain enumerated ports of the British colonies are open to vessels of the United States. Third. That American vessels are confined to a direct trade between the place of export and the place of import, while British vessels labor under no such restriction. Fourth. That the British vessels, though confined to the same enumerated articles as the American in the direct trade, are not so confined in trading from colony to colony or with the ports of the mother country. Fifth. That while all articles of British colonial produce are admitted into the United States, many important articles of American produce are excluded from the British West Indies; and Sixth. That on these articles of American produce which are admitted into the British colonies import duties are levied, or, at least, that higher import duties are levied than on the like articles produced in his Majesty's dominions.

These several allegations are met in detail by the following specific statements:

First. The export duty complained of is a duty of 4½ per cent. levied in some of the Leeward Islands on the produce of those islands, whether exported in British or in American vessels, and equally whether exported to Great Britain or to foreign countries.

Second. The colonial ports opened by act of Parliament to foreign vessels from America are all those in which custom-houses are established.

Third. The American Congress has passed an act confining British vessels to a direct trade under bond, in the very same manner as American vessels are restricted by the British act of Parliament, and even to a greater degree.

Fourth. The liberty of trading between colony and colony, as well as within the mother country, enjoyed exclusively by British vessels in this trade, is no other than a part of the coasting trade, which every Government secures to its own subjects. The Americans enjoy a like advantage on their side; and the British are not allowed, on the same principle, to carry on trade between the several ports and States of the American Union.

Fifth. The exclusion of certain articles of American produce, such as salt fish, from the West India market, is no other than what already exists in the trade between Great Britain and the United States, comprising other foreign countries. It is by no means peculiar to the colonial intercourse. The rum and molasses of the British West Indies are, *in point of fact*, but barely admitted to the market of the United States.

Sixth. The protecting duties levied in the British West Indies on the flour, lumber, &c., of the United States are absolutely necessary to afford the inhabitants of his Majesty's North American provinces a chance of sending their superfluous produce to market on equal terms with the citizens of the United States. These latter enjoy great natural advantages over their northern competitors by reason of the open climate and comparative vicinity of their country to the West India Islands. The sugar of the British West Indies, their principal export, has, besides, to pay in the United States an import duty proportionally higher than the duty levied on American flour in the ports of the British colonies.

On the specific grounds, then, alleged by the American plenipotentiary, the above mentioned stipulation cannot be accepted by Great Britain without injustice to her own subjects, any more than it can be accepted by her on general principles, without prejudice to her character as an independent commercial power. Much as the British Government are disposed to cherish and improve their relations of commerce and good neighborhood with the United States, such sacrifices cannot, in fairness, be expected, even for the sake of those objects.

Still less are they to be expected, when the statements of the British Government, in answer to those of the American, are fully borne out by the state, as hitherto ascertained, of the trade carried on under the respective laws of the two countries.

There is reason to suppose that about two-thirds of the flour and lumber received from North America by the British West Indies are produced by the United States; and it is not too much to say that even seven-eighths of that quantity are conveyed to the market in American vessels, while even upon the return trade it appears that American vessels enjoy a share not greatly inferior to that proportion.

Under these circumstances the British plenipotentiaries can only accept the articles on commercial intercourse tendered to them by the American plenipotentiary, with the omission of the stipulation already specified.

With every disposition to remove unnecessary obstructions from the trade, and to keep the protecting duties within fair and moderate bounds, no difference whatever being made in point of duties and charges between American and British vessels, whether belonging to the colonies or to Great Britain, it is impossible for the British Government to admit a condition which would expose their North American provinces to a total exclusion from the West India market, and that, as they conceive, without any equivalent concession being proposed on the part of the United States.

The British plenipotentiaries are ready, at the same time, to enter into stipulations, not only for removing all alien charges whatever from the vessels and their cargoes, as such, of both parties, in the United States on one side, and in the enumerated British colonies on the other, but also for extending to the United States, eventually, and in consideration of a fair return from them, any further advantages in that trade which, in the progress of events, Great Britain may find it safe or desirable to concede to any other foreign nation or State in the trade between her colonies and its possessions. In making this contingent agreement, it would be the intention of the British Government to apply, in proportion as circumstances might allow, to the trade between his Majesty's open colonies and the United States the same principle already adopted in the convention of 1815, namely, of placing each party, with respect to imports and exports, on the footing of the most favored nation; and, in the same spirit, there would be no objection to giving a suitable extension to the fourth article of the commercial convention respecting consuls.

Act of Parliament on reciprocity of duties and commercial treaty between Great Britain and Prussia.

ANNO QUINTO GEORGII IV. REGIS.

CAP. I. An act to indemnify all persons concerned in advising, issuing, or acting under a certain order in council for regulating the tonnage duties on certain foreign vessels, and to amend an act of the last session of Parliament for authorizing his Majesty, under certain circumstances, to regulate the duties and drawbacks on goods imported or exported in any foreign vessels.
. MARCH 5, 1824.

Whereas, by an act passed in the last session of Parliament, intituled *An act to authorize his Majesty, under certain circumstances, to regulate the duties and drawbacks on goods imported or exported* 4 G. 4. c. 77. *in foreign vessels, and to exempt certain vessels from pilotage,* his Majesty is authorized, by and with the advice of his privy council, or by his Majesty's order or orders in council, whenever it shall be deemed expedient, and under the provisions in the said act contained, to levy and charge any additional duty or duties of customs upon any goods, wares, or merchandise imported into the United Kingdom, or into any of his Majesty's dominions, in vessels belonging to any foreign country, in which higher duties shall have been levied upon goods, wares, or merchandise when imported into such foreign country in *British* vessels, than are levied or granted upon similar goods, wares, or merchandise when imported in vessels of such country; provided that such additional duties shall not be of greater amount than may be deemed fairly to countervail the difference of duty paid or granted on goods, wares, or merchandise imported into or exported from such foreign country in *British* vessels, more than the duties there charged upon similar goods, wares, or merchandise imported into or exported from such foreign country in vessels of such country; and whereas his Majesty, by and with the advice of his privy council, since the passing of the said recited act, has been pleased to order that there should be charged on all vessels of the United States of *America* which should enter any of the ports of his Majesty's possessions in *America* or the *West Indies* with articles of the growth, production, or manufacture of the said States, a tonnage duty equal (as nearly as may be) to the difference between the tonnage duty payable by vessels of the United States, and the higher tonnage duty payable by *British* vessels entering any of the ports of the said United States from any ports of his Majesty's dominions in *America* or the *West Indies*; and by the said order in council the Lords Commissioners of his Majesty's Treasury of the United Kingdom of *Great Britain* and *Ireland* were required to give the necessary directions accordingly: and whereas such tonnage duty hath been and may be levied and paid upon and in respect of such vessels accordingly: and whereas doubts have arisen how far the provisions of the said recited act extend to the levying, by the authority of the said order in council, additional tonnage duties upon the vessels aforesaid; and it is expedient that all proceedings under the said order in council should be sanctioned by Parliament; and that all persons concerned in advising, issuing, or carrying the same into execution should be respectively indemnified:

Order in coun- *Be it therefore enacted by the King's most excellent Majesty, by and with the advice and consent of the* cil for regulat- *Lords, Spiritual and Temporal, and Commons, in this present Parliament assembled, and by the* ing certain ton- *authority of the same,* That such order in council, and any directions or warrants of the said nage duties de- Commissioners of his Majesty's Treasury accordingly, shall be deemed and taken to be good clared valid, and valid in law, to all intents and purposes whatever, as if the same had been specifically and persons in- authorized by the said recited act; and that all persons concerned in advising, issuing, or demnified for carrying into execution such order in council, or in issuing, giving, or advising any such acting under the directions or warrants, and also all persons having acted, or who may act under or in same. pursuance of, or in obedience to any such order, direction, or warrant, shall be, and they are hereby, respectively indemnified for and on account of the same, and of any act or thing done . in pursuance of, or in obedience to, or in conformity with any such order, direction, or warrant as aforesaid, as fully and effectually, to all intents and purposes whatsoever, as if any such order, direction, or warrant had been given, and such acts, matters, and things had been done, in pursuance of any act or acts of Parliament; anything in the said recited act, or in any other act or acts of Parliament, to the contrary thereof in anywise notwithstanding.

II. *And be it further enacted,* That if any action, suit, or prosecution hath been or shall Actions to be commenced against any person or persons for any act, matter, or thing advised or done stayed. under such order in council, or under any such directions or warrants as aforesaid, it shall and may be lawful for the defendants or defenders in such actions, suits, or prosecutions, respectively, in whatever courts such actions, suits, or prosecutions shall have been commenced, to apply to such court or courts, respectively, to stay all proceedings therein respectively, by motion, in a summary way; and such court or courts are hereby required to make order for that purpose accordingly; and the court or courts making such order shall award and allow to the defendant or defenders, respectively, double costs of suit, for which they shall respectively have the like remedy as in cases where costs are by law given to defendants or defenders.

III. *And be it further enacted,* That from and after the passing of this act it shall and His Majesty, by may be lawful to and for his Majesty, by and with the advice of his Privy Council, or by his order in coun-Majesty's order or orders in council, to be published from time to time in the *London* cil, may direct Gazette, (whenever it shall be deemed expedient,) to levy and charge any additional or additional ton-countervailing duty or duties of tonnage upon or in respect of any vessels which shall enter be levied on any of the ports in the United Kingdom of *Great Britain* and *Ireland,* or in any of his vessels belong. Majesty's dominions, and which shall belong to any foreign country in which any duties of ing to countries tonnage shall have been or shall be levied upon or in respect of *British* vessels entering the where higher ports of such country higher or greater than are levied or granted upon or in respect of the tonnage duties vessels of such country: *Provided always,* That such additional or countervailing tonnage British vessels duties, so to be levied and charged as aforesaid, shall not be of greater amount than may be than on vessels deemed fairly to countervail the difference of duty paid in such foreign country upon of in of such coun-respect of the tonnage of *British* vessels more than the duty there charged or granted upon tries. or in respect of the vessels of such country.

IV. *And be it further enacted,* That from and after the passing of this act it shall and may be His Majesty, by lawful to and for his Majesty, by and with the advice of his Privy Council, or by his Majesty's order in coun-order or orders in council, to be published from time to time in the *London* Gazette, to cil, may autho-permit and authorize the entry into any port or ports of the United Kingdom of *Great Britain* rize the entry and *Ireland,* or of any other of his Majesty's dominions, of any foreign vessels, upon sels, on pay-payment of such and the like duties of tonnage only as are or may be charged or granted ment of like upon or in respect of similar *British* vessels: *Provided always,* That before any such order tonnage duties or orders shall be issued, satisfactory proof shall have been laid before his Majesty and his as on British Privy Council that vessels of the foreign country in whose favor such permission shall be tain proof. granted are charged with no other or higher tonnage duties on their entrance into the ports of such foreign country than are levied on the entry into such ports upon the vessels of such country.

V. *And be it further enacted,* That such additional or countervailing tonnage duties shall Duties to be le-be levied, recovered, and applied in such and the like manner as any duties of customs are vied as duties of now by law levied, recovered, and applied. customs.

VI. *And be it further enacted,* That his Majesty, by and with the advice of his Privy Duties may be Council, or by any order or orders in council, as aforesaid, is hereby empowered to remove removed, or or again to impose any such additional or countervailing tonnage duties whenever it shall again imposed. be deemed expedient so to do.

VII. *Provided always, and be it enacted,* That this act may be altered, varied, or repealed Act may be al-by any act or acts of this present session of Parliament. tered this session.

Convention of Commerce between his Britannic Majesty and the King of Prussia.

His Majesty the King of the United Kingdom of Great Britain and Ireland and his Majesty the King of Prussia, being equally desirous of extending and increasing the commercial intercourse between their respective States, and of affording every facility and encouragement to their subjects engaged in such intercourse, and being of opinion that nothing will more contribute to the attainment of their mutual wishes in this respect than a reciprocal abrogation of all discriminating and countervailing duties which are now demanded and levied upon the ships or productions of either nation in the ports of the other, have appointed their plenipotentiaries to conclude a convention for that purpose, that is to say: His Majesty the King of the United Kingdom of Great Britain and Ireland, the Right Honorable George Canning, a member of his said Majesty's most honorable Privy Council, a member of Parliament, and his said Majesty's principal Secretary of State for Foreign Affairs; and the Right Honorable William Huskisson, a member of his said Majesty's most honorable Privy Council, a member of Parliament, President of the Committee of Privy Council for Affairs of Trade and Foreign Plantations, and Treasurer of his said Majesty's Navy; and his Majesty the King of Prussia, the Baron de Werther, his said Majesty's Chamberlain, and his Envoy Extraordinary and Minister Plenipotentiary at the Court of his Britannic Majesty; who, after having communicated to each other their respective full powers, found to be in due and proper form, have agreed upon and concluded the following articles:

ARTICLE 1. From and after the 1st day of May next Prussian vessels, entering or departing from the ports of the United Kingdom of Great Britain and Ireland, and British vessels, entering or departing from the ports of his Prussian Majesty's dominions, shall not be subject to any other or higher duties or charges whatever than are or shall be levied on national vessels entering or departing from such ports, respectively.

ARTICLE 2. All articles of the growth, produce, or manufacture of either of the dominions of either of the high contracting parties which are or shall be permitted to be imported into, or exported from, the ports of the United Kingdom and of Prussia, respectively, in vessels of the one country, shall, in like manner, be permitted to be imported into, and exported from, those ports in vessels of the other.

ARTICLE 3. All articles not of the growth, produce, or manufacture of the dominions of his Britannic

Majesty, which can legally be imported from the United Kingdom of Great Britain and Ireland into the ports of Prussia in British ships, shall be subject only to the same duties as are payable upon the like articles if imported in Prussian ships; and the same reciprocity shall be observed in the ports of the United Kingdom in respect to all articles not the growth, produce, or manufacture of the dominions of his Prussian Majesty which can legally be imported into the ports of the United Kingdom in Prussian ships.

ARTICLE 4. All goods, wares, and merchandise which can legally be imported into the ports of either country shall be admitted at the same rate of duty, whether imported in vessels of the other country or in national vessels; and all goods, wares, or merchandise which can be legally exported from the ports of either country shall be entitled to the same bounties, drawbacks, and allowances, whether exported in vessels of the other country or in national vessels.

ARTICLE 5. No priority or preference shall be given, directly or indirectly, by the Government of either country, or by any company, corporation, or agent, acting on its behalf, or under its authority, in the purchase of any article the growth, produce, or manufacture of either country, imported into the other, on account of, or in reference to, the character of the vessel in which such article was imported, it being the true intent and meaning of the high contracting parties that no distinction or difference whatever shall be made in this respect.

ARTICLE 6. The present convention shall be in force for the term of ten years from the date hereof; and further, until the end of twelve months after either of the high contracting parties shall have given notice to the other of its intention to terminate the same, each of the high contracting parties reserving to itself the right of giving such notice to the other at the end of the said term of ten years; and it is hereby agreed between them that, at the expiration of twelve months after such notice shall have been received by either party from the other, this convention and all the provisions thereof shall altogether cease and determine.

ARTICLE 7. The present convention shall be ratified, and the ratifications shall be exchanged at London within one month from the date hereof, or sooner, if possible.

In witness whereof, the respective plenipotentiaries have signed the same, and have affixed thereto the seals of their arms. Done at London, the second day of April, in the year of our Lord one thousand eight hundred and twenty-four.

GEORGE CANNING. [L. S.]
W. HUSKISSON. [L. S.]

L.

British counter projet on Commercial Intercourse, (Sixteenth Protocol.)

His Britannic Majesty and the United States of America, being desirous to regulate, by mutual agreement, and on principles of just reciprocity, the trade now open under their respective laws between the United States and the British colonies in North America and the West Indies, have appointed plenipotentiaries to negotiate and conclude a convention for that purpose: that is to say, on the part of his Britannic Majesty ——— ———, and on the part of the United States of America ——— ———; which plenipotentiaries, after duly communicating to each other their respective full powers, found to be in proper form, have agreed upon and concluded the following articles:

ARTICLE I. The subjects of his Britannic Majesty and the citizens of the United States shall continue to have liberty to trade between the ports of those States and the open ports of his Majesty's possessions in North America and the West Indies under the existing laws and regulations of the high contracting parties.

And whereas it is considered mutually advantageous to the subjects and citizens of both parties that all discriminating duties and charges reciprocally imposed and levied on the vessels of each nation and their cargoes in the ports of the other, as aforesaid, should be withdrawn and altogether abolished, it is hereby agreed that upon the vessels of the United States admitted by law into all and every one of his Britannic Majesty's colonial ports, as aforesaid, and upon any goods, wares, or merchandise lawfully imported therein in the said vessels, no other or higher duties of tonnage or impost, and no other charges of any kind, shall be levied or exacted than upon British vessels, including all vessels of the colonies themselves, or upon the like goods, wares, or merchandise imported into the said colonial ports from any other foreign port or place whatever; and likewise, that upon the vessels of Great Britain and of her colonies admitted by law into all and every one of the ports of the United States, and upon any goods, wares, or merchandise lawfully imported therein in the said vessels, no other or higher duties of tonnage or impost, and no other charges of any kind, shall be levied or exacted than upon vessels of the United States, including all vessels of each and every one of the said States, or upon the like goods, wares, or merchandise imported into the United States from any other foreign port or place whatever.

ARTICLE II. For the more perfect fulfilment of the intentions of the high contracting parties, they pledge themselves hereby to remove, with as little delay as possible, his Britannic Majesty on his side, and the United States on their side, all additional duties of tonnage in the light of foreign tonnage duty, and all additional duties of import in the light of duties on goods imported in foreign vessels, at present existing, either against the vessels of the United States and their cargoes, admitted by law into any of the British colonial ports as aforesaid, or against British vessels and their cargoes, admitted by law into the ports of the United States, as well as all other discriminating duties and charges of whatever kind they may be, intended by this and the foregoing article to be removed and altogether abolished.

ARTICLE III. It being the desire and intention of the high contracting parties to place the trade in question on a footing of just reciprocity, they further agree that, in case of any of the existing enactments on either side regulating the navigation in this trade shall, contrary to expectation, be found, on further experience, to operate partially, and in such manner as to give to the subjects or citizens of the one party engaged therein a clear and decided advantage, to the manifest prejudice of the subjects or citizens of the other, in opposition to the intention above declared, each of the two Governments shall, in such case, and according as the case may be, receive and examine the representations made to it thereon by the other, and, the complaints being fairly substantiated, shall lose no time in adopting such additional laws and regulations as may correct the grievance complained of, in conformity with the principle herein laid down.

ARTICLE IV. The high contracting parties being further desirous to promote and extend this trade in proportion as circumstances may from time to time allow, his Britannic Majesty, on his part, engages that whatever facility or advantage may hereafter be granted to any friendly State, either in Europe or in America, with respect to any commerce, direct or circuitous, to be carried on between such State and his Majesty's colonies in the West Indies or America, shall be in like manner granted to the citizens of the United States; and the United States, on their part, engage that, under this contingency, the subjects of his Majesty shall enjoy whatever facilities or advantages may at any time be granted by them to the subjects or citizens of the most favored State in any trade carried on between the possessions of that State in the West Indies or America and the United States.

ARTICLE V. In consideration of the foregoing arrangements, his Britannic Majesty consents that the Government of the United States shall be at liberty to appoint consuls in his Majesty's open colonial ports in North America and the West Indies, and that consuls so appointed on their behalf shall be received under the same conditions as those which are stipulated in the fourth article of the convention of commerce concluded in London on the 3d July, 1815.

ARTICLE VI. The ratifications of this convention, &c., &c.

B.

American paper on the Navigation of the St. Lawrence, (Eighteenth Protocol.)

The right of the people of the United States to navigate the river St. Lawrence to and from the sea has never yet been discussed between the Governments of the United States and Great Britain. If it has not been distinctly asserted by the former in negotiation hitherto, it is because the benefits of it have been tacitly enjoyed, and because the interest, now become so great and daily acquiring fresh magnitude, has, it may almost be said, originated since the acknowledgment of the independence of the United States in 1783. This river is the only outlet provided by nature for the inhabitants of several among the largest and most populous States of the American Union. Their right to use it as a medium of communication with the ocean rests upon the same ground of natural right and obvious necessity heretofore asserted by the Government in behalf of the people of other portions of the United States in relation to the river Mississippi. It has sometimes been said that the possession by one nation of both the shores of a river at its mouth gives the right of obstructing the navigation of it to the people of other nations living on the banks above; but it remains to be shown upon what satisfactory grounds the assumption by the nation below, of exclusive jurisdiction over a river thus situated, can be placed. The common right to navigate it is, on the other hand, a right of nature. This is a principle which, it is conceived, will be found to have the sanction of the most revered authorities of ancient and modern times; and if there have been temporary occasions when it has been questioned, it is not known that the reasons upon which it rests, as developed in the most approved works upon public law, have ever been impugned. As a general principle it stands unshaken. The dispute relative to the Schelde, in 1784, is perhaps the occasion when the argument drawn from natural right was most attempted to be impeached. Here the circumstances were altogether peculiar. Amongst others, it is known to have been alleged by the Dutch that the whole course of the two branches of this river, which passed within the dominions of Holland, was *entirely artificial;* that it owed its existence to the skill and labor of Dutchmen; that its banks had been reared up at immense cost, and were in like manner maintained. Hence, probably, the motive for that stipulation in the treaty of Munster, which had continued for more than a century, that the Lower Schelde, with the canals of Sas and Swin, and other mouths of the sea bordering upon them, should be kept *closed* on the side belonging to the States. But the case of the St. Lawrence is totally different. Special, also, as seemed the grounds which the Dutch took as against the Emperor of Germany in this case of the Schelde, and although they also stood upon a specific and positive compact of long duration, it is nevertheless known that the public voice of Europe on this part of the dispute preponderated against them. It may well have done so, since there is no sentiment more deeply and universally felt than that the ocean is free to all men, and the waters that flow into it to those whose home is upon their shores. In nearly every part of the world we find this natural right acknowledged by laying navigable rivers open to all the inhabitants of their banks; and wherever the stream, entering the limits of another society or nation, has been interdicted to the upper inhabitants, it has been an act of *force* by a stronger against a weaker party, and condemned by the judgment of mankind. The right of the upper inhabitants to the full use of the stream rests upon the same imperious wants as that of the lower—upon the same intrinsic necessity of participating in the benefits of this flowing element. Rivers were given for the use of all persons living in the country of which they make a part, and a primary use of navigable ones is that of external commerce. The public good of nations is the object of the law of nations, as that of individuals is of municipal law. The interest of a part gives way to that of the whole; the particular to the general. The former is subordinate; the latter paramount. This is the principle pervading every code, national or municipal, whose basis is laid in moral right, and whose aim is the universal good. All that can be required under a principle so incontestable, so wise, and, in its permanent results upon the great fabric of human society, so beneficent, is, that reasonable compensation be made whenever the general good calls for partial sacrifices, whether from individuals in a local jurisdiction, or from one nation considered as an integral part of the family of nations. This is accordingly done in the case of roads and the right of way in single communities, and is admitted to be just in the form of moderate tolls where a foreign passage takes place through a natural current kept in repair by the nation holding its shores below. The latter predicament is not supposed to be that of the St. Lawrence at this day, since it is not known that any artificial constructions, looking simply to its navigation, have yet been employed either upon its banks or in keeping the channel clear. This has been the case, in connexion with other facilities and protection afforded to navigation, with the Elbe, the Maese, the Weser, the Oder, and various other rivers of Europe that might be named, and the incidental right of toll has followed.

It may be mentioned, however, as a fact, under this head, that the prevailing disposition of Europe defeated an attempt once made by Denmark to exact a toll at the mouth of the Elbe, by means of a fort on the Holstein side, which commanded it. The Sound dues have been admitted in favor of Denmark, but not always without scrutiny, and only under well established rules. We know that, under some circumstances, and with due precautions, a right is even allowed to armies to pass through a neutral territory for the destructive purposes of war. How much stronger and more unqualified the right to seek a passage through a natural stream for the useful and innocent purposes of commerce and subsistence? A most authentic and unequivocal confirmation of this doctrine has been afforded at a recent epoch by the parties to the European alliance, and largely, as is believed, through the enlightened instrumentality of Great Britain at the negotiation of the treaties at the Congress of Vienna. It has been stipulated in these treaties that the Rhine, the Neckar, the Mayne, the Moselle, the Maese, and the Schelde, are to be free to all nations. The object of these stipulations undoubtedly has been to lay the navigation of these rivers effectively open to all the people dwelling upon their banks or within their neighborhood, and to abolish those unnatural and unjust restrictions by which the inhabitants of the interior of Germany have been too often deprived of their outlet to the sea by an abuse of that sovereignty rather than its right, which would impute an exclusive dominion over a river to any one State not holding all its shores. These stipulations may be considered as an indication of the present judgment of Europe upon the point, and would seem to supersede further reference to the case of other rivers, and, from their recent as well as high authority, further illustration of any kind. They imply a substantial recognition of the principle that, whatever may sometimes have been the claim to an exclusive right by one nation over a river, under the circumstances in question, the claim (if founded in an alleged right of sovereignty) could at best only be supposed to spring from the social compact; whereas the right of navigating the river is a right of nature, pre-existent in point of time, not necessary to have been surrendered up for any purpose of the common good, and unsusceptible of annihilation. There is no principle of national law and universal justice upon which the provisions of the Vienna treaties are founded that does not apply to sustain the right of the people of the United States to navigate the St. Lawrence. The relations between the soil and the water, and those of man to both, form the eternal basis of this right. These relations are too intimate and powerful to be separated. A nation deprived of the use of the water flowing through its soil would see itself stripped of many of the most beneficial uses of the soil itself; so that its right to use the water, and freely to pass over it, becomes an indispensable adjunct to its territorial rights. It is a means so interwoven with the end, that to disjoin them would be to destroy the end. Why should the water impart its fertility to the earth if the products of the latter are to be left to perish upon the shores?

It may be proper to advert to the footing in point of fact upon which the navigation of this river stands at present between the two countries, so far as the regulations of Great Britain are concerned. The act of Parliament of 3 Geo. IV, chapter 119, August 5, 1822, has permitted the importation from the United States, by land or water, into any port of entry in either of the Canadas at which there is a custom-house, of certain articles of the United States enumerated in a schedule, subject to the duties which are specified in another schedule. Under the former schedule many of the most important articles of the United States are excluded, and under the latter the duties are so high as to be equivalent to a prohibition of some that are nominally admitted. The foregoing act lays no impositions on the merchandise of the United States descending the St. Lawrence with a view to exportation on the ocean; but an act of Parliament of 1821 does, viz: upon the timber and lumber of the United States. Such, in general terms, is the footing upon which the intercourse is placed by the British acts, and it may be alike proper, in connexion with this reference to it, to mention the conditions of intercourse which it has superseded. To whatever observations the duties imposed on the products of the United States imported for sale into the ports of Canada may otherwise be liable, as well as the exclusion of some of them altogether, it will be understood that it is only the unobstructed passage of the river, considered as a common highway, that is claimed as a right. By the treaty stipulations of November, 1794, between the two countries, the United States were allowed to import into the two Canadas all articles of merchandise, the importation of which was not entirely prohibited, subject to no other duties than were payable by British subjects on the importation of the same articles from Europe into the Canadas. The same latitude of importation was allowed into the United States from the Canadas, subject to no other duties than were payable on the importation of the same articles into the Atlantic ports of the United States. Peltries were made free on both sides. All tolls and rates of ferriage were to be the same upon the inhabitants of both countries. No transit duties at portages or carrying places were to be levied on either side. These provisions were declared in the treaty to be designed to secure to both parties the local advantages common to both, and to promote a disposition favorable to friendship and good neighborhood. The waters on each side were made free, with the exception reciprocally at that time of vessels of the United States going to the seaports of the British territories, or navigating their rivers between their mouths and the highest port of entry from the sea, and of British vessels navigating the rivers of the United States beyond the highest ports of entry from the sea. These treaty regulations are found among the articles declared, when the instrument was made, to be permanent. Both countries continued to abide by them until Great Britain passed the acts above recited, by which it appears that she has considered the intervening war of 1812 as abrogating the whole of the treaty of November, 1794. The United States have continued to allow, up to the present time, its provisions regulating this intercourse to operate in favor of the Canadas. By the act of Parliament of 3 Geo. IV, chapter 44, taken in conjunction with the act of the same year, chapter 119, above mentioned, the right of the vessels of the United States to the whole navigation of the St. Lawrence appears to be taken for granted: by the first, from the ocean to Quebec; and by the second, from any part of the territories of the United States to Quebec. But a discretionary power is given to the colonial Governments in Canada to do away the effect of the latter permission by excepting any of the Canadian ports from those to which the vessels of the United States are by the act made admissible, whilst the duties which it imposes upon such of the exports of the United States as could alone render the trade profitable are prohibitory. But it is the right of navigating this river upon a basis of certainty, without obstruction or hindrance of any kind, or the hazard of it in future, that the United States claim for their citizens.

The importance of this claim may be estimated when it is considered that the people of at least as many of the States as Illinois, Indiana, Ohio, Pennsylvania, New York, Vermont, Maine, New Hampshire, and the Territory of Michigan, have an immediate interest in it, not to dwell upon the prospective derivative interest which is attached to it in other portions of the Union. The parts of the United States connected directly or remotely with this river and the inland seas through which it communicates with the ocean, form, indeed, an extent of territory, and comprise, even at this day, an aggregate of population, which bespeak the interest at stake to be of the very highest nature, and one which, after every deduction suggested by the artificial channels which may be substituted for the natural one of this great stream, make it emphatically an object of national concernment and attention. Having seen the grounds of necessity and reason upon which the right of so great and growing a population to seek its only natural pathway to the ocean rests, it may be expected that they should be supported by the established principles of international law. This shall be done by the citation of passages from the writings of the most eminent publicists, always bearing in mind that the right under discussion becomes strong in proportion to the extent which the country of the upper inhabitants, in its connexion with the stream, bears to the country of the lower inhabitants. Vattel, in book 2, chapter 9, section 127, lays down the following as a general position: "Nature, who designs her gifts for the common advantage of men, does not allow of their being kept from their use when they can be furnished with them without any prejudice to the proprietor, and by leaving still untouched all the utility and advantages he is capable of receiving from his rights." The same author, same book, chapter 10, section 132, says: "Property cannot deprive nations of the general right of travelling over the earth, in order to have a communication with each other, for carrying on trade, and other just reasons. The master of a country may only refuse the passage on particular occasions where he finds it is prejudicial or dangerous." In section 134, he adds: "A passage ought also to be granted for merchandise, and, as this may in common be done without inconvenience, to refuse it without just reason is injuring a nation and endeavoring to deprive it of the means of carrying on a trade with other States; if the passage occasions any inconvenience, any expense for the preservation of canals and highways, it may be recompensed by the rights of toll." Again, in book 1, chapter 22, section 266, we are told that if "neither the one nor the other of the two nations near a river can prove that it settled first, it is to be supposed that they both came there at the same time, since neither can give any reason of preference; and in this case the dominion of each will be extended to the middle of the river." This is a principle too relevant to the doctrine under consideration to be passed over without remark. It relates, as will be seen, to *dominion*, and not to right of passage simply. Now, if simultaneous settlement confers coequality of dominion, by even stronger reason will simultaneous *acquisition* confer coequality of *passage*. Without inquiring into the state of the navigation of the St. Lawrence as between Great Britain and France prior to the peace of 1763, it is sufficient that in the war of 1756-'63, which preceded that peace, the people of the United States, in their capacity of English subjects, contributed jointly with the parent State (and largely, it may be added with historical truth) towards gaining the Canadas from France. The right of passage, therefore, of this river, admitting that it did not exist before, was, in point of fact, opened to the early inhabitants of New York and Pennsylvania at an epoch at least as soon as to British subjects living afterwards in the newly conquered possessions. A title thus derived is not invoked as resting upon the same ground with the title derived from natural right; but it serves to strengthen it, and is of pertinent application, as against Great Britain in this instance. Let it be looked at under either of the following alternatives which present themselves. If Great Britain possessed the navigation of this river prior to 1763, so did the people of the United States as part, at that time, of her own empire. If she did not, but only first acquired it when the Canadas were acquired, the people of the United States, acting in common with her, acquired it in common, and at as early a date. It will not be said that the right which necessarily inured to the colonies, as part of the British empire, was lost by their subsequently taking the character of a distinct nation, since it is the purpose of this paper to show that the right of passage may, as a natural right, be claimed by one foreign nation against another, without any reference whatever to antecedent circumstances. But the latter, when they exist, make up part of the case, and are not to be left out of view. The peculiar and common origin of the title of both parties, as seen above, is calculated to illustrate more fully the principle of common right applicable to both now. The antecedent circumstances show that the natural right, always appertaining to the early inhabitants of the shores of this river above the Canadian line, to navigate it has once been fortified by joint conquest, and by subsequent joint usufruction. One other quotation is all that will be given from the same author. It relates to a strait and not a river; but the reasoning from analogy is not the less striking and appropriate. "It must be remarked," he says, "with regard to straits, that when they serve for a communication between two seas, the navigation of which is common to all or many nations, he who possesses the strait cannot refuse others a passage through it, provided that passage be innocent and attended with no danger to the State. Such a refusal, without just reason, would deprive these nations of an advantage granted them by nature; and, indeed, the right of such a passage is a remainder of the primitive liberty enjoyed in common." If we consult Grotius, we shall find that he is equally or more explicit in sanctioning, in the largest extent, the principle contended for. He even goes so far as to say, after laying down generally the right of passage, that "the fears which any power entertains from a multitude, in arms, passing through its territories, do not form such an exception as can do away the rule, it not being proper or reasonable that the fears of one party should destroy the rights of another."— (Book 2, chapter 2, section 13.) In the course of the same section he declares, that upon "this foundation of common right a free passage through countries, *rivers*, or over any part of the sea, which belong to some particular people, ought to be allowed to those who require it for the necessary occasions of life, whether these occasions be in quest of settlements after being driven from their own country, *or to trade with a remote nation*." The reasons which Grotius himself gives, or which he adopts from writers more ancient, for this right of innocent passage, (and he is full of authorities and examples as well from sacred as profane history,) are of peculiar force. He denominates it "*a right interwoven with the very frame of human society*." "Property," he says, "was originally introduced with a reservation of that use which might be of general benefit, and not prejudicial to the interest of the owner." He concludes the section in the following manner: "A free passage ought to be allowed not only to persons but to merchandise, for no power has a right to prevent one nation trading with another at a remote distance, a permission which, for the interest of society, should be maintained; nor can it be said that any one is injured by it, for though he may thereby be deprived of an *exclusive* gain, yet the loss of what is not his due *as a matter of right* can never be considered as a damage or the violation of a claim." After authorities of such immediate bearing on the point under consideration, further quotation will be forborne. The question of right is conceived to be made out, and if its denomination will be found to be sometimes that of an imperfect in contradistinction to an absolute right, the denial of it is nevertheless agreed to be an injury, of which the party deprived may justly complain. The sentiments taken from these two writers, (and they are not the only ones capable of being adduced,) though deemed sufficient, have the full support of coincident passages in Puffendorf, book 3, chapter 3, sections 4, 5, 6, and in Wolfius, section 310.

Finally, the United States feel justified in claiming the navigation of this river on the ground of paramount interest and necessity to their citizens; on that of *natural right* founded on this necessity, and felt and acknowledged in the practice of mankind, and under the sanction of the best expounders of the laws of nations. Their claim is to its full and free navigation from its source to the sea, without impediment or obstruction of any kind. It was thus that Great Britain claimed and had the navigation of the Mississippi, by the seventh article of the treaty of Paris of 1763, when the mouth and lower shores of that river were held by another power. The claim, while necessary to the United States, is not injurious to Great Britain, nor can it violate any of her just rights. They confidently appeal to her justice for its enjoyment and security; to her enlightened sense of good neighborhood; to her past claims upon others for the enjoyment of a similar right; and to her presumed desire for the advantageous intercourse of trade and all good offices, now and henceforth, between the citizens of the United States and her own subjects bordering upon each other in that portion of her dominions.

N.

British paper on the Navigation of the St. Lawrence, (Twenty-fourth Protocol.)

The claim of the United States to the free navigation of the river St. Lawrence wears a character of peculiar importance when urged as an independent right.

The American plenipotentiary must be aware that a demand rested upon this principle necessarily precludes those considerations of good neighborhood and mutual accommodation with which the Government of Great Britain would otherwise have been anxious to enter upon the adjustment of this part of the negotiation.

A right claimed without qualification on the one side affords no room for friendly concession on the other. Total admission or total rejection is the only alternative which it presents.

On looking to the objects embraced by the American claim, we find them to be of no ordinary magnitude. The United States pretend to no less than the perpetual enjoyment of a free, uninterrupted passage, independent of the territorial sovereign, through a large and very important part of the British possessions in North America. They demand, as their necessary inherent right, the liberty of navigating the St. Lawrence from its source to the sea, though in the latter part of its course, which lies entirely within the British dominions, and comprises a space of nearly six hundred miles, that river traverses the finest settlements of Canada; communicates by the Sorell with Lake Champlain, and washes the quays of Montreal and Quebec.

A pretension which thus goes to establish a perpetual thoroughfare for the inhabitants, vessels, and productions of a foreign country through the heart of a British colony, and under the walls of its principal fortress, has need to be substantiated on the clearest and most indisputable grounds. It requires, indeed, an enlarged view of what is owed in courtesy by one nation to another to justify the British Government in entering at this late period on the discussion of so novel and extensive a claim.

There will, however, be little difficulty in showing that the claim asserted by the American plenipotentiary rests, as to any foundation of *natural* right, on an incorrect application of the authorities which he has consulted. With respect to the claim derived from an *acquired* title, which he has also alleged, that ground of claim will remain to be examined hereafter; but it may be observed, in the outset, that the natural and acquired title depend on principles essentially distinct; that the one cannot be used to make good any defect in the other, and, although they may be possessed independently by the same claimant, that they can in no degree contribute to each other's validity.

Proceeding to consider how far the claim of the United States may be established on either of these titles, it is first necessary to inquire what must be intended by the assertion that their claim is founded on *natural* right. "The right of navigating this river," says the American plenipotentiary, "is a right of nature, pre-existent in point of time, not necessary to have been surrendered up for any purpose of common good, and unsusceptible of annihilation." The right here described can be of no other than of that kind which is generally designated in the law of nations a *perfect* right. Now, a perfect right is that which exists independent of treaty, which necessarily arises from the law of nature, which is common, or may, under similar circumstances, be common to all independent nations, and can never be denied or infringed by any State without a breach of the law of nations. Such is the right to navigate the ocean, without molestation, in time of peace.

Upon these principles, now universally received, it is contended for the United States that a nation possessing both shores of a navigable river at its mouth has no right to refuse the passage of it to another possessing a part of its upper banks, and standing in need of it as a convenient channel of commercial communication with the sea. Applying the same principles to the case of the St. Lawrence, the American Government maintain that Great Britain would be no more justified in controlling American navigation on that river than in assuming to itself a similar right of interference on the high seas.

To this extent must the assumption of a *perfect* right be carried, or such claim is no longer to be considered in that character; but, falling under the denomination of an *imperfect* right, it becomes subject to considerations essentially and entirely different.

The first question, therefore, to be resolved is, whether a perfect right to the free navigation of the river St. Lawrence can be maintained according to the principles and practice of the law of nations.

Referring to the most eminent writers on that subject, we find that any liberty of passage to be enjoyed by one nation through the dominions of another is treated by them as a qualified occasional exception to the paramount rights of property. "The right of 'passage,'" says Vattel, "is also a remainder of the primitive communion in which the entire earth was common to men, and the passage was everywhere free according to their necessities." Grotius, in like manner, describes mankind as having, in their primitive state, enjoyed the earth and its various productions in common until after the introduction of property, together with its laws; by a division or gradual occupation of the general domain. Among the natural rights, which he describes as having, in part, survived this new order of things, are those of necessity and of innocent utility, under the latter of which he classes the right of passage. Following his principle, this natural right of passage between nation and nation may be compared to the right of highway, as it exists in particular communities, between the public at large and the individual proprietors of the soil, but with this important difference, that, in the former case, commanding and indispensable considerations of national safety, national welfare, and national honor and interest, must be taken especially into the account.

It is clear that on this principle there is no distinction between the right of passage by a river flowing from the possessions of one nation through those of another to the ocean, and the same right to be enjoyed by means of any highway, whether land or of water, generally accessible to the inhabitants of the earth. "Rivers," says Grotius, "are subject to property, though neither where they rise nor where they discharge themselves be within our territory." The right to exclusive sovereignty over rivers is also distinctly asserted by Bynkershoek in the ninth chapter of his treatise "On the Dominion of the Sea." Nor is this by any means the full latitude to which the principle, if applied at all, must in fairness be extended. "All nations," says Vattel, "have a general right to the innocent use of the things which are under any one's domain." "Property," says the same author, "cannot deprive nations of the general right of travelling over the earth, in order to have communication with each other, for carrying on trade, and other just reasons." The nature of these *other just reasons* is explained by Grotius in the following sentence: "A passage ought to be granted to persons, whenever just occasion shall require, over any lands and rivers or such parts of the sea as belong to any nation: as, for instance, if, being expelled from their own country, they want to settle in some uninhabited land, or if they are going to traffic with some distant people, or to recover by a just war what is their own right and due."

For other purposes, then, besides those of trade, for objects of war as well as for objects of peace, for all nations no less than for any nation in particular, does the right of passage hold good under those authorities to which the American plenipotentiary has appealed. It has already been shown that, with reference to this right, no distinction is drawn by them between land and water, and still less between one sort of river and another. It further appears from Vattel that the right in question, particularly for the conveyance of merchandise, is attached to artificial as well as to natural highways. "If this passage," he observes, "occasion any inconvenience, any expense for the preservation of *canals* and *highways*, it may be recompensed by rights of toll."

Is it, then, to be imagined that the American Government can mean to insist on a demand involving such consequences, without being prepared to apply, by reciprocity, the principle on which it rests in favor of Great Britain? Though the sources of the Mississippi are now ascertained to lie within the territory of the United States, the day cannot be distant when the inhabitants of Upper Canada will find convenience in exporting their superfluous produce by means of the channel of that river to the ocean. A few miles of transport over land are of little consequence when leading to a navigable river of such extent. Even at the present time, a glance upon the map is sufficient to show that the course of the Hudson, connected as it now is with the waters of the St. Lawrence, would afford a very commodious outlet for the produce of the Canadian provinces. The comparative shortness of this passage, especially with reference to the West Indies, would amply compensate for any fair expense of tolls.

It would also be, in some instances, convenient and profitable for British vessels to ascend the principal rivers of the United States as far as their draught of water would admit, instead of depositing their merchandise, as now, at the appointed ports of entry from the sea. Nor is it probable that other nations would be more backward than the British in pressing their claim to a full participation in this advantage. The general principle which they would invoke, in pursuance of the example given by America, and a partial application of such principles, no country can have a right to expect from another, is clearly of a nature to authorize the most extraordinary and unheard of demands: as for the right of passage from sea to sea across any intervening isthmus, such, for instance, as that of Corinth, or of Suez, and more especially from the Atlantic to the Pacific by the Isthmus of Panama; that right of passage follows as immediately from this principle as any such right claimed from one tract of land to another, or to the ocean by water communication.

The exercise of a right which thus goes the length of opening a way for foreigners into the bosom of every country must necessarily be attended with inconvenience, and sometimes with alarm and peril, to the State whose territories are to be traversed. This consequence has not been overlooked by writers on the law of nations. They have felt the necessity of controlling the operation of so dangerous a principle by restricting the right of transit to purposes of *innocent* utility, and by attributing to the local sovereign the exclusive power of judging under what circumstances the passage through his dominions is or is not to be regarded as *innocent*. In other words, the right which they have described is, at best, only an *imperfect* right.

It is under the head of *innocent utility* that Grotius has classed the right of passage, as before laid down in his own expressions.

"Innocent utility," he adds, "is when I only seek my own advantage *without damaging* any one else." In treating of the same right, Vattel remarks that "since the introduction of domain and property, we can no otherwise make use of it than by respecting the proper rights of others." "The effect," he adds, "of property is to make the advantage of the proprietor prevail over that of all others."

The same author defines the *right of innocent use or innocent utility* to be "the right we have to that use which may be drawn from things belonging to another without causing him either loss or inconvenience." He goes on to say that "this right of *innocent use* is not a perfect right, like that of *necessity;* for it belongs to the master to judge if the use we would make of a thing that belongs to him will be attended with no damage or inconvenience."

With respect to the assertion of Grotius, as quoted by the American plenipotentiary, "that the mere apprehension of receiving injury from the exercise of this right is not a sufficient reason for denying it." The author, it must be observed, is addressing himself to the conscience of the sovereign through whose territories a passage may be demanded, impressing upon his mind that he cannot fully discharge his moral obligations in giving such refusal, unless he be well convinced that his fears originate in just causes. But it would be absurd, and contrary to the general tenor of his argument, to suppose that a well-founded apprehension was not to have its due effect, or that the advantage or even necessity of a foreign nation could be justly recognized by him as paramount, in the one case, to the leading interests, in the other, to the safety, of his own.

It is further to be observed that Grotius, in the argument referred to, had clearly in view an *occasional* liberty of passage, not of that *perpetual* uninterrupted kind, which the regular activity of modern commerce requires. But the doctrine of Grotius, applied to merchandise, and taken in the sense ascribed to it by the American plenipotentiary, is distinctly contradicted by other eminent writers on the law of nations. Puffendorf, for instance, in his great work on that subject, expresses himself as follows: "We may have good reasons for stopping foreign merchandise as well by land as on a river, or on an arm of the sea within our dependence. For, besides that a too great affluence of foreigners is sometimes prejudicial or suspicious to a State, why should not a sovereign secure to his own subjects the profit made by foreigners under favor of the passage which he allows them?" "I admit that, in allowing foreigners to carry their merchandise elsewhere, even without paying for the passage, we do not sustain any damage, and that they do us no wrong in pretending to an advantage of which we might have possessed ourselves before them. But, at the same time, as they have no right to exclude us from it, why should we not try to draw it to ourselves? Why should we not prefer our interest to theirs?"

The same author observes, in the next section of his work, "that a State may fairly lay a duty on foreign goods conveyed through its territory *by way of compensation for what its subjects lose by admitting a new competitor into the market.*"

To appreciate the full force of these opinions, it must be borne in mind that Puffendorf appears to speak of a foreign nation so situated as to depend exclusively on the passage in question for the sale of its superfluous produce and the importation of supplies from abroad. This part of the subject may be closed with the following decisive words of Barleyrac, in his notes on Grotius: "It necessarily follows from the right of property that the proprietor may refuse another the use of his goods. Humanity, indeed, requires that he should grant that use to those who stand in need of it when it can be done without any considerable inconvenience to himself; and if he even then refuses it, though he transgresses his duty, he doth them no *wrong*, properly so called, except they are in extreme necessity, which is superior to all ordinary rules."

But the American plenipotentiary maintains that the right of passage, as understood by him in opposition to his own authorities, that is, independent of the sovereign's consent, and applied to the single predicament of the St. Lawrence, has been substantially recognized by the powers of Europe in the treaties of general pacification concluded at Paris in 1814, and in the following year at Vienna.

It is true that in the solemn engagements then contracted by them the sovereigns of the leading States of Europe manifested a disposition to facilitate commercial intercourse between their respective countries by opening the navigation of such of the principal rivers as separated or traversed the territories of several powers. This policy was applied more particularly to the Rhine, the Neckar, the Mayne, the Moselle, the Maese, and the Scheldt. But neither in the general nor in these special stipulations relating to the free navigation of rivers is there anything to countenance the principle of a natural independent right, as asserted by the American plenipotentiary. We find, on the contrary, that in the treaty concluded at Paris, between France and the allied powers, the Rhine was the only river at once thrown open to general navigation. With respect to the other rivers, it was merely stipulated that the means of extending that arrangement to them should be determined by the Congress about to assemble at Vienna. In the instance of the Rhine, it was natural for France, in giving up possessions which she had for some time enjoyed on the banks of that river, to stipulate a reserve of the navigation. The stipulations relating to river navigation in the general treaty of Vienna commence in the following manner: "The powers whose States are separated or crossed by the same navigable river *engage* to regulate, by *common consent*, all that regards its navigation." They close with an agreement that the regulations once adopted shall not be changed *except with the consent of all the powers bordering on the same river.*

It is evident, therefore, that the allied Governments, in concurring to favor the circulation of trade through the great water communications of continental Europe, did not lose sight of what was due to the sovereignty of particular States; and that when they referred the common enjoyment of certain navigable rivers to voluntary compact between the parties more immediately concerned, they virtually acknowledged the right of any one of those parties till bound by its own engagements to withhold the passage through its dominions from foreign merchant vessels. As freedom of navigation in favor of all nations, and not merely of those which border on the rivers thus opened by treaty, was the immediate object of the above mentioned stipulations, it must be presumed that the powers assembled in Congress, if they had felt themselves borne out by the practice or general opinion of Europe, would not have hesitated to proclaim the measure which they adopted as one of natural independent right. Their silence alone on this point might have been taken as strongly indicative of their belief that the prevailing usage of Europe would authorize no such declaration. But the principle of mutual consent is surely irreconcilable with the contrary supposition, and must at least be understood to give a special character to the engagements contracted under it, confining them to the rivers enumerated in the treaty, and, however laudable, as an example to other States whose circumstances may allow of their imitating it without danger or detriment, expressive of no obligation beyond the occasion for which the treaty was framed.

It would take up too much time to demonstrate by a detailed investigation of every case to which the American argument applies the negative proposition that no nation exercises the liberty of navigating a river through the territories of another except by permission or express concession under treaty. It is rather for the American Government to present a single instance in which the liberty claimed for the United States is exercised explicitly as a natural independent right.

The case of the Scheldt, though referred to by the American plenipotentiary, is certainly not one of this kind. The leading circumstances relating to that river were, first, that its mouths, including the canals of Sas and Swin, lay within the Dutch territory, while parts of its upper channel were situate within the Flemish provinces; secondly, that the treaty of Westphalia had confirmed the right of the Dutch to close the mouths of the river; thirdly, that the exercise of this right was disputed after a lapse of more than a hundred years by the Emperor of Germany; and, fourthly, that the dispute between that monarch and the Dutch Republic terminated in 1785 by leaving the Dutch in possession of the right which had been disputed. It is true that at the latter period the Dutch founded their claim, in part, on the expense and labor which they had undergone in improving the river; but it is true, at the same time, that they also grounded it on the general law of nations. Above all, they rested it on the treaty of Westphalia. But if the right of the Dutch Republic had been countenanced by the law and practice of nations, why, it may be asked, should it have been thought necessary to confirm that right by the treaty of Westphalia? The reply is obvious. That confirmation was the resort of the weak against the strong, of the former dependants of Spain against the encroachments of a haughty power, still sovereign of Antwerp and the neighboring provinces, and not having yet renounced its claim of sovereignty over Holland itself. It was natural for the Dutch, under such circumstances, to fortify their right by the general sarction of Europe, but it was not natural for the principal parties in the pacification of Munster to lend their sanction to a measure in direct contradiction to acknowledged principles; or if their scruples as to the admission of such a measure had been removed by special motives, it is strange that they should not have taken the obvious precaution of recording those motives. During the discussions about the Scheldt, in 1785, the Empress of Russia was the only sovereign who officially declared an opinion in favor of the House of Austria. But the United States can derive no great advantage from a declaration couched in such terms as these: "Nature herself hath granted to the Austrian low countries the use and advantage of the river in dispute; Austria alone, by virtue of the law of nature and nations, is entitled to an *exclusive* right to the use of the river in question. So that the equity and disinterestedness of Joseph II can only impart this right to other people, it belonging *exclusively* to his States."

The opinions proclaimed on this subject by the Russian Government are the more remarkable, as there is no country which has a greater interest than Russia in the disputed question. It is well known that the only approach to the Russian ports in the Black Sea, from the Mediterranean and Atlantic, is by the passages of the Dardanelles and Bosphorus. These canals are, in fact, salt water straits, communicating from sea to sea, passing, it is true, between the Turkish territories in Europe and Asia, but with no great length of course, and leading to a vast expanse of inland water, the shores of which are occupied by no less than three independent powers.

There is manifestly a wide difference between such a case and that of the St. Lawrence, nor can the marked difference in principle between rivers and straits be overlooked; and yet, as matter of fact, the navigation of the Black Sea, and the adjacent canals, is enjoyed by Russia—by that power which has so often dictated its own conditions to the Porte, in virtue of a treaty founded, like other treaties, on the mutual convenience and mutual advantage of the parties.

Even the navigation of the Danube downwards to the ocean was first accorded to Austria by the Turkish Government as a specific concession, made at a juncture when the Porte, involved in a quarrel with the most formidable of its neighbors, was compelled to propitiate the good will of other Christian powers.

The case of the Mississippi is far from presenting an exception to this view of the subject. The treaty of 1763, which opened the navigation of that river to British subjects, was concluded after a war in which Great Britain had been eminently successful. The same motives that prevailed with France to cede Canada must have restrained her from hazarding a continuance of hostilities for such an object as the exclusive navigation of the Mississippi. The agreement respecting that river makes part of the general provisions as to the western boundary of the British possessions in America, by which the whole left side of the Mississippi was ceded to Great Britain, with the exception of the town and island of New Orleans. This reservation was admitted on the express condition that the navigation of the whole channel should be open to British subjects. The very fact of its having been thought necessary to insert this stipulation in the treaty, in consequence of France having retained possession of both banks of the river at a single spot, leads irresistibly to an inference the very reverse of what is maintained by the American plenipotentiaries.

At a later period the navigation of the Mississippi became a subject of arrangement between Spain and the United States. By the fourth article of their treaty of boundary and navigation, concluded in 1795, a similar agreement to that which had before subsisted between France and Great Britain was effected between those powers, with this remarkable difference, that the liberty of navigating the river was expressly confined to the parties themselves, unless the King of Spain, to use the words of the treaty, "should extend this *privilege* to the subjects of other powers by *special convention.*"

It must not be overlooked that when the clause which is here quoted, and the exclusive stipulation immediately preceding it, were drawn up, the sources of the Mississippi were still supposed to be within the British territory, and, at the same time, there was in force a treaty between Great Britain and the United States declaring that "the navigation of the river Mississippi, from its source to the ocean, should *forever* remain free and open to the subjects of Great Britain."

Some additional light may, perhaps, be thrown on the object of the present discussion by the quotation of a note on the fourth article of the Spanish treaty, which is printed in the collection of the United States Laws, *arranged and published under the authority of an act of Congress.* It is as follows:

"Whatsoever right his Catholic Majesty had to interdict the free navigation of the Mississippi to any nation at the date of the treaty of San Lorenzo el Real, (the 27th of October, 1795,) that right was wholly transferred to the United States, in virtue of the cession of Louisiana from France, by the treaty of April 30, 1803. And as the definitive treaty of peace was concluded previously to the transfer to the United States of the right of Spain to the dominion of the river Mississippi, and, of course, prior to the United States possessing the Spanish right, it would seem that the stipulation contained in the 8th article of the definitive treaty with Great Britain could not have included any greater latitude of navigation on the Mississippi than that which the United States were authorized to grant on the 3d of September, 1783.

"The additional right of sovereignty which was acquired over the river by the cession of Louisiana was *paid for* by the American Government; and, therefore, any extension of it to a foreign power could scarcely be expected *without an equivalent.*"

The natural right asserted by the American plenipotentiary being thus examined, in respect both to the principles which it involves and to the general practice of nations, the *acquired* title, as distinct from the *natural*, stands next for consideration.

This title is described in the American argument as originating in circumstances which either preceded or attended the acquisition of the Canadas by Great Britain. It is said "that if Great Britain possessed the navigation of the St. Lawrence before the conclusion of peace in 1763, so did the people of the United States, as forming, at that time, a part of the British empire; but if Great Britain only first acquired it, together with the Canadas, then did the people of the United States acquire it in common with her at the same period." In both the supposed cases it is taken for granted that whatever liberty to navigate the St. Lawrence, in the whole length of its course, the inhabitants of the United States enjoyed when those States were part of the British empire, continued to belong to them after their separation from the mother country. Now, if this were so, it would also be true, and in a far stronger degree, that the subjects of Great Britain have an equal right to enjoy, in common with American citizens, the use of the navigable rivers, and other public possessions of the United States, which existed when both countries were united under the same Government. For the acquired title, be it remembered, does not affect the St. Lawrence, as a river flowing from the territories of one power through those of another to the sea, but is manifestly grounded on the supposition that an object, which had been possessed in common by the people of both countries up to the time of their separation, continues to belong, in point of use, to both, after they have ceased to be parts of the same community. If it be true that the inhabitants of the United States contributed, as British subjects, to effect the conquest of Canada, it cannot, at the same time, be denied that the United States, before their separation from Great Britain, were frequently indebted to the counsels and exertions of the parent country for protection against their unquiet and encroaching neighbors. Specifically did they owe to Great Britain their first enjoyment of the waters of the Mississippi—conquered, in part, from France by the very same efforts which transformed Canada from a French settlement into a British colony. The pretension of the American Government, as grounded on the simultaneous acquisition of the St. Lawrence, as well by the inhabitants of the adjacent, and, at that time, British provinces, as by those of the countries originally composing the British monarchy, must, therefore, if admitted even for the sake of argument, be applied reciprocally in favor of Great Britain.

The fact, however, is, that no such pretension can be allowed to have survived the treaty by which the independence of the United States was first acknowledged by Great Britain. By that treaty a perpetual line of demarkation was drawn between the two powers, no longer connected by any other ties than those of amity and conventional agreement.

No portion of the sovereignty of the British empire, exclusive to the actual territory of the United States, as acknowledged by that treaty, could possibly devolve upon the people of the United States, separated from Great Britain.

By the same instrument, the territorial boundary of the States, as recognized by their former sovereign, was carefully defined, for the express purpose of avoiding disputes in future; and the articles stipulating for a concurrent enjoyment of the North American fisheries, and of the navigation of the river Mississippi, prove that equal care was taken to determine, in the general act of pacification and acknowledgment, those objects, of which the usufruct in common was either retained or conceded by Great Britain.

Is it conceivable, under these circumstances, that the treaty of 1783 should have made no mention of the concurrent navigation of the St. Lawrence, if the claim now raised by the United States had rested on any tenable grounds?

But the commercial treaty of 1794 would afford additional proof, if it were wanted, that the channel of the St. Lawrence, from the sea to the 45th parallel of latitude, was never for a moment considered as forming any exception to the territorial possessions of Great Britain.

The third article of the commercial treaty shows most clearly that the power of excluding foreign vessels from those parts of the river which flow entirely within the British dominions was deemed to belong of right to the British Government. The leading purpose of that article is to establish a free commercial intercourse between the two parties throughout their respective territories in North America.

The same article contains a limitation of this privilege, with respect to a considerable portion of the St. Lawrence, to which it was declared that American vessels were not to have access; and the corresponding restriction against Great Britain was an exclusion of British vessels from such parts of the rivers of the United States as lie above the highest ports of entry for foreign shipping from the sea.

It necessarily results from the nature of the two clauses, thus viewed with reference to each other, that the authority of Great Britain over the part of the St. Lawrence interdicted to American vessels was no less completely exclusive than that of the United States over such parts of their interior waters as were in like manner interdicted to the shipping of Great Britain.

The former limitation is, besides, of itself inconsistent with the notion of a right to a free, uninterrupted passage for American vessels by the St. Lawrence to the ocean.

Nor is it the less conclusive as to the merits of the case when coupled with the declaration contained in the very same article, that the navigation of the Mississippi was to be enjoyed in common by both parties, notwithstanding that a subsequent article of the same treaty expresses the uncertainty which already prevailed with respect to the sources of that river being actually situated within the British frontier.

With these facts in view, it is difficult to conceive how a tacit enjoyment of the navigation, now claimed, can be stated by the American plenipotentiary to account for the silence maintained on this subject by his Government from the establishment of its independence to the present negotiation.

In the course of forty years, during which no mention whatever has been made of this claim, there has been no want of opportunities fit for its assertion and discussion. To say nothing of periods anterior to the rupture of 1812, it is strange that an interest of such vast importance should have been wholly neglected, as well on the renewal of peace in 1815 as during the negotiation of the commercial treaty which took place in the close of that year. This long continued silence is the more remarkable, as the mere apprehension of an eventual change in the regulations, under which a part of the St. Lawrence is actually navigated by foreign vessels, has been alleged by the American Government as their reason for now raising the discussion.

The regions contiguous to the upper waters of the St. Lawrence are doubtless more extensively settled than they were before the late war, and the inhabitants of those regions might at times find it advantageous to export their lumber and flour by the channel of that river. But mere convenience and the profits of trade cannot be deemed to constitute that case of extreme necessity, under the law of nations, to which the rights of property may perhaps be occasionally required to give way. It has already been shown that such interests can, at most, amount to an imperfect right of innocent utility, the exercise of which is entirely dependent on the will and discretion of the local sovereign. Of this description are the rights and accompanying duties of nations to trade with each other, and to permit the access of foreigners to their respective waters in time of peace; but will any one at the same time call in question the co-existing right of every State not only to regulate and to limit its commercial intercourse with others, but even, as occasion may require, to suspend or to withhold it altogether?

If ever there was a case which particularly imposed on a sovereign the indispensable duty of maintaining this right unimpaired, even with every disposition to consult the convenience and fair advantage of friendly nations, it is the present unqualified demand of the United States.

It cannot be necessary to enumerate the various circumstances which make this claim peculiarly objectionable; but there is no concealing that, besides the ordinary considerations of territorial protection, those of commercial interest and colonial policy are alike involved in the demand of a free, gratuitous, unlimited right of passage for American citizens, with their vessels and merchandise, from one end of Canada to the other.

Interests of such high national importance are not to be put in competition with the claims of justice; but when justice is clearly on their side, they have a right to be heard, and cannot be denied their full weight. That the right is, in this instance, undoubtedly on the side of Great Britain, a moment's reflection on the preceding argument will suffice to establish.

It has been shown that the independent right asserted by the United States is inconsistent with the dominion, paramount sovereignty, and exclusive possession of Great Britain.

It has been proved, by reference to the most esteemed authorities on the law of nations, with respect as well to the general principle as to the opinions distinctly given on this point, that the right of sovereignty and exclusive possession extends over rivers in common with the territory through which they flow.

The same principles and the same opinions have been cited to prove that those parts of the river St. Lawrence which flow exclusively through the British dominions form no exception to the general doctrine so applied to rivers.

The existence of any necessity calculated to give the United States in this case a special right, in contradiction to the general rule, has been distinctly denied, and the denial conclusively supported by a reference to known facts.

With no disposition to contest such imperfect claims and moral obligations as are consistent with the paramount rights of sovereignty and exclusive possession, it has been proved from the authorities already quoted that of those imperfect claims and moral obligations the territorial sovereign is the judge.

The title of the United States, as derived from previous enjoyment at the time when they formed part of the British Empire, has been shown to have ceased with the conclusion of that treaty by which Great Britain recognized them in the new character of an independent nation.

It has also been shown that while the American Government acknowledge that their claim is now brought forward for the first time, not only have they had, since their independence, no enjoyment under treaty of the navigation now claimed, but that the provisions of the commercial treaty concluded in 1794, and described as having been till lately in force, are in direct contradiction with their present demand.

It has finally been made to appear that the treaties concluded by European powers as to the navigation of rivers, far from invalidating the rights of sovereignty in that particular, tend, on the contrary, to establish those rights; and that the general principle of protection, essential to sovereignty, dominion, and property, applies with peculiar force to the present case of the river St. Lawrence.

D.

American paper on the Boundary Line, under the 5th article of the treaty of Ghent, (Ninth Protocol.)

Whereas the Commissioners appointed by the high contracting parties, under the fifth article of the treaty of Ghent, for ascertaining the latitude and longitude of the northwest angle of Nova Scotia and the northwesternmost head of Connecticut river, and for surveying that part of the boundary line, between the dominions of the two powers, which extends from the source of the river St. Croix directly north to the above mentioned northwest angle of Nova Scotia; thence along the highlands which divide those rivers that empty themselves into the river St. Lawrence from those which fall into the Atlantic Ocean to the northwesternmost head of Connecticut river; thence down along the middle of that river to the forty-fifth degree of north latitude; thence by a line due west on the said latitude until it strikes the river Iroquois or Cataraguy, have not been able, after long and earnest endeavors, to come to an agreement; and whereas it is the desire of the contracting parties, instead of referring their differences to the arbitration of a friendly sovereign in manner as provided by the said treaty of Ghent, to endeavor to settle them by negotiation between themselves: It is therefore agreed, accordingly, that they will negotiate on these differences, at Washington, in the hope of bringing them to a satisfactory adjustment. And they also agree, that in the course of such negotiation they will receive, should they deem it necessary, the maps that were respectively submitted and used by the Commissioners as aforesaid on the side of each nation; but it is distinctly understood and agreed that the map or maps used on the one side shall not be received or used to the exclusion of that or those used on the other side.

E.

American paper on the Newfoundland Fishery, (Tenth Protocol.)

By the thirteenth article of the treaty of Utrecht of 1713 the sovereignty of the island of Newfoundland was ceded by France to Great Britain, France being allowed the right of fishing, and of drying fish, from Cape Bonavista, on the eastern coast, to the northern extremity of the island, and thence along the western coast to the place called Pointe Riche, but on no other parts.

The provisions of this treaty were renewed and confirmed by that of Aix-la-Chapelle of 1748, and also, as far as relates to Newfoundland and the French fisheries on its coast, by the treaty of Paris of 1763.

By the treaty of peace between the United States and Great Britain of September 3, 1783, article third, it is stipulated that "the inhabitants of the United States shall have liberty to *take* fish of every kind on such part of the coast of Newfoundland *as British fishermen shall use,* but not to dry or cure the same on that island."

By the treaty of the same date between Great Britain and France, articles fourth and fifth, the right of Great Britain to this island was confirmed, (the small adjacent islands of St. Pierre and Miquelon being excepted,) and the right of the French to fish on a certain part of the eastern coast, as above recited, was exchanged for that of fishing on the remainder of the eastern and on the whole of the western coast, as far down from the north as Cape Ray. See also the declaration and counter declaration of the plenipotentiaries of the two Governments annexed to this treaty, which are material as respects fishing rights.

By the treaty of Paris of 1814, between Great Britain and France, the former restores to the latter the colonies, fisheries, factories, and establishments of every kind which France possessed on the first of January, 1792, in the seas, or on the continents of America, Asia, and Africa, with the exception of Tobago, St. Lucie, and the Isle of France. By the nineteenth article of this treaty it is declared that, "as to the French right of fishery on the grand bank of Newfoundland, on the coasts of the island of that name, and the adjacent islands, and in the Gulf of St. Lawrence, everything shall be restored to the same footing as in 1792."

Finally, by the convention of October 20, 1818, between the United States and Great Britain, it is provided, article first, that "the inhabitants of the said United States shall have forever, *in common with the subjects of his Britannic Majesty*, the liberty to take fish of every kind on that part of the southern coast of Newfoundland which extends from Cape Ray to the Rameau islands, and on the *western and northern* coast from the said Cape Ray to the Quirpon islands." By the same convention the United States are allowed to *dry* and *cure* fish on the southern part of the coast of this island, as above described, but not on the western coast.

From the preceding statement, it follows that the French have the right of taking and drying fish on the western coast of the island of Newfoundland. The United States claim for their citizens the right of *taking* fish on the same coast. But this France denies, saying that the right both of taking and drying belongs to her EXCLUSIVELY. Her cruisers have, accordingly, in 1820 and 1821, ordered off the American fishing vessels whilst within the acknowledged jurisdiction of the coast, threatening them with seizure and confiscation in case of refusal.

It may be that France will allege in support of her doctrine that by her treaty of September 3, 1783, with Great Britain, which gave her the right of fishing and drying fish on the western coast of this island, it was intended that the right should be exclusive; that the words of the treaty, and, above all, those of the declaration annexed to it, show this to have been the meaning, as France obtained the western coast in exchange for a part of the eastern coast with a view to prevent quarrels between the French and British fishermen. To this end, as it may perhaps be also alleged, the words of the declaration provide that British subjects were not to interrupt the French fishery on this coast (the western) by their competition "in any manner;" and further provide that the "fixed settlements" which had been formed there (by British subjects it is presumed) should be removed.

The United States insist, on the other hand, that Great Britain never could have intended by her treaty of 1783 with France to grant a right of fishing, and of drying and curing fish, on the western coast of the island to French fishermen exclusively, but that the right of British subjects to resort there *in common* must necessarily be implied. That a contrary construction of the instrument cannot be received, the sovereignty of the whole island, without any exception, having been fully vested in Great Britain, and even confirmed by this very treaty. That it can never be presumed that she intended so far to renounce or in anywise diminish this sovereignty as to exclude her own subjects from any part of the coast. That no positive grant to this effect is to be found in the treaty, any more than in the treaty of Utrecht, and that the claim of France to an exclusive right, a claim so totally repugnant to the sovereign rights of Great Britain, can rest on nothing less strong than a positive grant. That all that the words contained in the *declaration* to the treaty of 1783 can be construed to mean is, that British subjects should never, whilst exercising their right, improperly or injuriously "interrupt by their competition" the *enjoyment* of the French right. Furthermore, the United States cannot suppose that Great Britain, by the convention of October, 1818, above recited, would ever have agreed that the inhabitants of the United States should have (for a just equivalent contained in the convention) the right or the liberty to take fish on the very coast in question in common with British subjects but under the conviction that British subjects had the liberty of resorting there; and if they had, the claim of France to drive away the fishing vessels of the United States cannot stand.

The above summary may serve to present the general nature of the question which has arisen between the United States and France respecting fishing rights, and which Great Britain will doubtless desire to see settled in a manner satisfactory to the United States. It is obvious that, if Great Britain cannot make good the title which the United States hold under her to *take* fish on the western coast of Newfoundland, it will rest with her to indemnify them for the loss. Another question which it is supposed will also be for her consideration is, how far she will deem it proper that France should be allowed to drive or order away the fishermen of the United States from a coast that is clearly within the jurisdiction and sovereignty of Great Britain.

AUGUST, 1822.

Since the foregoing was drawn up, and which, as will be seen, was in part hypothetical, a correspondence has taken place between the minister of the United States at Paris and the French Government, that will serve to show more distinctly the grounds upon which France claims to evict the United States from so essential a portion of their fishing rights on the coast of this island. The correspondence consists of four letters from Mr. Gallatin to Viscount Chateaubriand, dated January 22, March 14, April 2, and April 15, 1823, and two from Viscount Chateaubriand to Mr. Gallatin, dated February 28 and April 5, 1823. Copies of these letters are annexed. For the articles of the treaties (no longer, however, in force) between the United States and France, to which Viscount Chateaubriand alludes, see volume 1, of the Laws of the United States, edition of 1814, pages 80 and 131.

MARCH, 1824.

Note to Mr. Secretary Canning on the Newfoundland Fishery.

LONDON, *May 3, 1824.*

The undersigned, Envoy Extraordinary and Minister Plenipotentiary from the United States, has received the instructions of his Government to lay before Mr. Canning, his Majesty's principal Secretary of State for Foreign Affairs, the following case;

By the first article of the convention between the United States and Great Britain, concluded at London on the 20th of October, 1818, it is, amongst other things, provided that the "inhabitants of the said States shall have forever, in common with the subjects of his Britannic Majesty, the liberty to take fish of every kind on that part of the southern coast of Newfoundland which extends from Cape Ray to the Rameau islands, on the western and northern coast of Newfoundland, from the said Cape Ray to the Quirpon islands, on the shores of the Magdalen islands, and also on the coasts, bays, harbors, and creeks from Mount Joly, on the southern coast of Labrador, to and through the straits of Belleisle, and thence northwardly, indefinitely, along the coast."

After the ratification of the above convention, the fishermen of the United States proceeded, according to its stipulations, to take fish on the western and northern coast of Newfoundland, between the limits of Cape Ray and the Quirpon islands, as aforesaid; but, in the course of the years 1820 and 1821, whilst pursuing in a regular manner their right to fish within these limits, and being also within the strictest territorial jurisdiction of the island, these fishermen found themselves ordered away by the commanders of the armed vessels of France, on pain of seizure and confiscation of their fishing vessels.

This measure was afterwards ascertained to rest upon a claim set up by France to an *exclusive* fishery upon that part of the coast of the island—a claim conceived by the Government of the United States to be without just foundation, and in violation of the rights of the citizens of the United States; as settled by the foregoing article of the convention of 1818.

The Government of the United States forbore, at first, to make any representation of the above occurrence, so injurious to the interests as well as rights of their citizens, to the Government of his Britannic Majesty, cherishing the hope that the difficulty which appeared to have arisen would be removed on a fit representation to the court of France. A correspondence accordingly took place upon the subject between the American plenipotentiary at Paris and the Minister of Foreign Affairs of his most Christian Majesty, which, however, has not terminated in a manner satisfactory to the Government of the United States, it appearing from it that France distinctly asserts an exclusive right of fishery within the limits in question. Copies of this correspondence, consisting of four letters from Mr. Gallatin, dated the 22d of January, the 14th of March, the 2d of April, and the 15th of April, 1823, and of two letters from Viscount Chateaubriand, dated February the 28th and April the 5th, of the same year, the undersigned has the honor to inclose for the more full information of Mr. Canning. It will be seen that the United States claim for their citizens the right to *take* fish only, not to cure and dry the same, within the limits from which France would interdict them, and that their claim is in common with the subjects and fishermen of his Britannic Majesty. The undersigned has not been furnished with any affidavits or other formal proofs to substantiate the fact of the fishing vessels of the United States having been ordered away by French vessels-of-war, as above mentioned, since it will be seen, by the notes of the French Minister of State, that no question is raised upon that point, but that the fact itself is justified under a claim of right, thereby rendering superfluous all extrinsic evidence of its existence. The grounds of justification assumed by France are believed, by the Government of the United States, to be satisfactorily refuted by their plenipotentiary in the correspondence inclosed; and although France rests her claim as against the United States upon the footing of treaties once subsisting between the two powers, it will not fail to be perceived that she also asserts, in the most unqualified manner, her anterior, unlimited, and exclusive right to the fishery in question under the treaties of Utrecht and of Paris; consequently, as pre-existent to her former treaties with the United States, and paramount to all title in any other power. In the note of Viscount Chateaubriand, of the 5th of April, it is stated that the Chargé d'Affaires of France at Washington had been instructed to enter upon explanations with the Government of the United States concerning this interest, and was then about to be written to again on the same head; yet it becomes the duty of the undersigned to say that no adjustment of the subject has taken place, and that the fishing vessels of the United States still remain under the interdiction put upon them by the cruisers of France.

The undersigned, in fulfilling the orders of his Government to bring under the official notice of Mr. Secretary Canning the circumstances of the above case, does so in full reliance that, through the friendly dispositions of his Majesty's Government, the whole subject will receive such attention as it will be seen to merit. The United States seek only the fair and unmolested enjoyment of the fishing rights which they hold at the hands of Great Britain under the convention of 1818, satisfied that Great Britain, whether as regards the guarantee of these rights, or the maintenance of her own sovereign jurisdiction over this island and its immediate waters, will take such steps as the occasion calls for, and above all, as are appropriate to the just and amicable intentions which it may be so confidently supposed will animate the Government of his most Christian Majesty, as well as that of his Britannic Majesty, towards the United States, touching the full rights of the latter under the convention aforesaid.

The undersigned prays Mr. Canning to accept the assurances of his perfect consideration.
R. R.

Right Hon. George Canning,
   His Majesty's principal Secretary of State for Foreign Affairs.

M.

British articles annexed to Twenty-second Protocol.

1. Mutual delivery of criminals, the subjects or citizens of either party, taking refuge within the dominions of the other.

2. Arrangement for the adoption of measures to facilitate and complete, in an equitable and satisfactory manner, the settlement of claims made by the subjects or citizens of either of the two parties, to lands situated within the territories of the other in America, and arising out of grants heretofore made by authorities competent at the time to make such grants.

3. Agreement that on neither side shall debts due from individuals of the one nation to those of the other, or moneys which they may have in the public funds, or in public or private banks, ever be confiscated

or sequestered in case of war or differences between the two countries; and, also, that every facility be mutually afforded for the recovery of debts.

4. Further, that no act of reprisal shall be ordered by the one party against the other on complaint of injuries or damages till after a statement of grievances shall have been given in and the redress demanded either refused or unreasonably delayed.

5. Further, that in case of rupture at any time between the two nations, the merchants of either party shall be allowed to remain and carry on their trade within the dominions of the other so long as they behave peaceably and lawfully; and in case of their being sent away for misconduct, they shall have a reasonable time allowed before removal for the settlement of their affairs and necessary preparations.

6. Further, that in case of any vessel belonging to the Government or individuals of one nation being wrecked on the coasts of the other, any property belonging to them recovered therefrom shall be restored, all practicable assistance rendered, and no more salvage claimed than in like cases from natives.

7. Further, that vessels of either party forced by distress into any port of the other, not being an open port, shall, nevertheless, be hospitably received, and allowed, if necessary, to victual, repair, unlade its cargo, and dispose of a part thereof under proper regulations.

8. Further, that ships and merchandise belonging to either party, when rescued from pirates by the other, shall be restored to the original owners on payment of salvage, no higher than would be claimed in like case from the subjects or citizens of the rescuing party.

9. Finally, that the consuls and vice consuls of either party having an *exequatur*, in due form, shall be exempt from the payment of direct taxes, and from personal service of every kind, respectively, within the territories of the other.

F.

American paper on the Northwest Coast of America, (Twelfth Protocol.)

Whereas, by the third article of the convention between the United States and his Britannic Majesty, signed at London on the twentieth of October, 1818, it was agreed that any country that might be claimed by either party on the Northwest Coast of America, westward of the Stony mountains, should, together with its harbors, bays, and creeks, and the navigation of all rivers within the same, be free and open, for the term of ten years from the date of the said convention, to the vessels, citizens, and subjects of the two powers; it having been understood that such agreement was not to be construed to the prejudice of any claim which either of the parties might have to any part of the said country, or taken to affect the claims of any other power, but only to prevent disputes and differences between the parties themselves; and whereas it is desirable that the provisions of the said article should be continued for a longer term than as therein specified: It is therefore agreed by the high contracting parties that the same shall continue in force for the full term of ten years from the signature of the present convention. The high contracting parties further agree that, during the like term, no settlement shall be made on the Northwest Coast of America, or on any of the islands thereunto adjoining, by citizens of the United States, north of the fifty-first degree of north latitude, or by British subjects either south of the said fifty-first degree or north of the fifty-fifth degree of north latitude.

P.

British paper on the Northwest Coast of America, (Twenty-third Protocol.)

It is agreed that the third article of the convention concluded at London on the 20th of October, 1818, between his Britannic Majesty and the United States of America, shall cease and determine from the date hereof; and instead of the stipulations contained in that article, it is further agreed that the boundary line between the territories claimed by his Britannic Majesty and those claimed by the United States, to the west, in both cases, of the Rocky mountains, shall be drawn due west along the 49th parallel of north latitude, to the point where that parallel strikes the great northeasternmost branch of the Oregon or Columbia river, marked in the maps as McGillivray's river, thence down along the middle of the Oregon or Columbia, to its junction with the Pacific Ocean; the navigation of the whole channel being perpetually free to the subjects and citizens of both parties, the said subjects and citizens being also reciprocally at liberty, during the term of ten years from the date hereof, to pass and repass by land and by water, and to navigate with their vessels and merchandise all the rivers, bays, harbors, and creeks, as heretofore, on either side of the above mentioned line, and to trade with all and any of the nations free of duty or impost of any kind; subject only to such local regulations as, in other respects, either of the two contracting parties may find it necessary to enforce within its own limits, and prohibited from furnishing the natives with fire-arms and other exceptionable articles to be hereafter enumerated: and it is further especially agreed that neither of the high contracing parties, their respective subjects or citizens, shall henceforward form any settlements within the limits assigned hereby to the other, west of the Rocky mountains, it being at the same time understood that any settlements already formed by the British to the south and east of the boundary line above described, or by citizens of the United States to the north and west of the same line, shall continue to be occupied and enjoyed at the pleasure of the present proprietors or occupants, without let or hindrance of any kind, until the expiration of the above mentioned term of ten years from the date hereof.

RATIFIED CONVENTION WITH RUSSIA OF APRIL 5, 1824.

COMMUNICATED TO THE HOUSE OF REPRESENTATIVES JANUARY 21, 1825.

To the House of Representatives of the United States:

I communicate herewith to both Houses of Congress copies of the convention between the United States and his Majesty the Emperor of all the Russias, concluded at St. Petersburg on the 5th (17th) of April last; which has been duly ratified on both sides, and the ratifications of which were exchanged on the eleventh instant.

WASHINGTON, *January* 18, 1825.

JAMES MONROE.

BY THE PRESIDENT OF THE UNITED STATES OF AMERICA.

A PROCLAMATION.

Whereas a convention between the United States of America and his Majesty the Emperor of all the Russias was concluded and signed at St. Petersburg on the 5th (17th) day of April, in the year of our Lord one thousand eigh thundred and twenty-four; which convention, being in the French language, is, word for word, as follows, a translation of the same being hereto annexed:

[Original.]	[Translation.]
Au nom de la très Sainte et Indivisible Trinité :	*In the name of the most Holy and Indivisible Trinity :*

Le Président des Etats Unis d'Amérique et Sa Majesté l'Empereur de toutes les Russies, voulant cimenter les liens d'amitié qui les unissent, et assurer entre eux le maintien invariable d'un parfait accord, moyennant la présente convention, ont nommé pour leurs plénipotentiaires à cet effet, savoir: Le Président des Etats Unis d'Amérique, le Sieur HENRY MIDDLETON, citoyen des dits Etats, et leur Envoyé Extraordinaire et Ministre Plénipotentiaire près Sa Majesté Impériale; et Sa Majesté l'Empereur de toutes les Russies, ses amés et féaux les Sieurs CHARLES ROBERT Comte de NESSELRODE, Conseiller Privé actuel, Membre du Conseil d'Etat, Secrétaire d'Etat Dirigeant le Ministère des affaires étrangères, Chambellan actuel, Chevalier de l'ordre de St. Alexandre Nevsky, Grand Croix de l'ordre de St. Wladimir de la 1re classe, Chevalier de celui de l'aigle blanc de Polonge, Grand Croix de l'ordre de St. Etienne d'Hongrie, Chevalier des ordres du St. Esprit et de St. Michel, et Grand Croix de celui de la Legion d'Honneur de France, Chevalier Grand Croix des ordres de l'aigle noir et de l'aigle rouge de Prusse, de l'Annonciade de Sardaigne, de Charles III d'Espagne, de St. Ferdinand et du mérite de Naples, de l'Eléphant de Danemarc, de l'Etoile Polaire de Suède, de la Couronne de Wurtemberg, des Guelphes de Hanovre, du Lion Belge, de la Fidelité de Bade, et de St. Constantin de Parme; et PIERRE de POLETICA, Conseiller d'Etat actuel, Chevalier de l'ordre de St. Anne de la 1re classe, et Grand Croix de l'ordre de St. Wladimir de la seconde; lesquels après avoir échangé leurs pleins-pouvoirs, trouvés en bonne et due forme, ont arrêté et signé les stipulations suivantes:

ARTICLE PREMIER.—Il est convenu que dans aucune partie du grand océan, appelé communément Océan Pacifique ou Mer du Sud, les citoyens ou sujets respectifs des hautes puissances contractantes ne seront ni troublés, ni gênés, soit dans la navigation, soit dans l'exploitation de la pêche, soit dans la faculté d'aborder aux côtes sur des points qui ne seroient pas déjà occupés, afin d'y faire le commerce avec les indigènes, sauf toutefois les restrictions et conditions déterminées par les articles qui suivent:

ARTICLE DEUXIEME.—Dans la vue d'empêcher que les droits de navigation et de pêche exercés sur le grand océan par les citoyens et sujets des hautes puissances

The President of the United States of America and his Majesty the Emperor of all the Russias, wishing to cement the bonds of amity which unite them, and to secure between them the invariable maintenance of a perfect concord, by means of the present convention, have named as their plenipotentiaries, to this effect, to wit: The President of the United States of America, HENRY MIDDLETON, a citizen of said States, and their Envoy Extraordinary and Minister Plenipotentiary near his Imperial Majesty; and his Majesty the Emperor of all the Russias, his beloved and faithful CHARLES ROBERT Count of NESSELRODE, actual Privy Counsellor, Member of the Council of State, Secretary of State directing the administration of Foreign Affairs, actual Chamberlain, Knight of the order of St. Alexander Nevsky, Grand Cross of the order of St. Wladimir of the first class, Knight of that of the White Eagle of Poland, Grand Cross of the order of St. Stephen of Hungary, Knight of the orders of the Holy Ghost and of St. Michael, and Grand Cross of the Legion of Honor of France, Knight Grand Cross of the orders of the Black and of the Red Eagle of Prussia, of the Annunciation of Sardinia, of Charles III of Spain, of St. Ferdinand and Merit of Naples, of the Elephant of Denmark, of the Polar Star of Sweden, of the Crown of Wirtemberg, of the Guelphs of Hanover, of the Belgic Lion, of Fidelity of Baden, and of St. Constantine of Parma; and PIERRE de POLETICA, actual Counsellor of State, Knight of the order of St. Anne of the first class, and Grand Cross of the order of St. Wladimir of the second; who, after having exchanged their full powers, found in good and due form, have agreed upon and signed the following stipulations:

ARTICLE FIRST.—It is agreed that in any part of the great ocean, commonly called the Pacific Ocean or South Sea, the respective citizens or subjects of the high contracting powers shall be neither disturbed nor restrained, either in navigation or in fishing, or in the power of resorting to the coasts upon points which may not already have been occupied, for the purpose of trading with the natives, saving always the restrictions and conditions determined by the following articles:

ARTICLE SECOND.—With the view of preventing the rights of navigation and of fishing, exercised upon the great ocean by the citizens and subjects of the

contractantes ne deviennent le prétexte d'un commerce illicite, il est convenu, que les citoyens des Etats Unis n'aborderont à aucun point où il se trouve un établissement Russe, sans la permission du Gouverneur ou Commandant; et que réciproquement les sujets Russes ne pourront aborder sans permission à aucun établissement des Etats Unis sur la cote nord ouest.

ARTICLE TROISIEME.—Il est convenu en outre, que dorénavant il ne pourra être formé par les citoyens des Etats Unis, ou sous l'autorité des dits Etats, aucun établissement sur la Côte nord ouest d'Amérique, ni dans aucune des îles adjacentes *au nord* du cinquante quatrième degré et quarante minutes de latitude septentrionale; et que de même il n'en pourra être formé aucun par des sujets Russes, ou sous l'autorité de la Russie, *au sud* de la même parallèle.

ARTICLE QUATRIEME.—Il est, néanmoins entendu que pendant un terme de dix années à compter de la signature de la présente convention, les vaisseaux de deux puissances, ou qui appartiendroient à leurs citoyens ou sujets respectifs, pourront réciproquement frequenter, sans entrave quelconque, les mers interieurs, les golfes, hâvres et criques sur la côte mentionée dans l'article précédent, afin d'y faire la pêche et le commerce avec les naturels du pays.

ARTICLE CINQUIEME.—Sont toutefois exceptées de ce même commerce accordé par l'article précédent, toutes les liqueurs spiritueuses, les armes à feu, armes blanches, poudre et munitions de guerre de toute espèce, que les deux puissances s'engagent réciproquement à ne pas vendre, ni laisser vendre aux Indigénes par leurs citoyens et sujets respectifs, ni par aucun individu qui se trouveroit sous leur autorité. Il est également stipulé que cette restriction ne pourra jamais servir de prétexte, ni être alleguée dans aucun cas, pour autoriser soit la visite ou la détention des vaisseaux, soit la saisie de la marchandise, soit en fin des mesures quelconques de contrainte envers les armateurs ou les equipages qui feroient ce commerce; les hautes puissances contractantes s'etant réciproquement reservé de statuer sur les peines à encourir, et d'infliger les amendes encourues en cas de contravention à cet article, par leurs citoyens ou sujets respectifs.

ARTICLE SIXIEME.—Lorsque cette convention aura été duement ratifiée par le Président des Etats Unis de l'avis et du consentement du Sénat, d'une part, et de l'autre par sa Majesté l'Empereur de toutes les Russies, les ratifications en seront échangées à Washington dans le délai de dix mois de la date ci-dessous ou plutôt si faire se peut. En foi de quoi les plénipotentiaires respectifs l'ont signée, et y ont fait apposer les cachets de leurs armes.

Fait à St. Petersbourg, Avril 17, (5,) de l'an de Grâce mil huit cent vingt quatre.

HENRY MIDDLETON, [L. S.]
LE COMTE C. DE NESSELRODE. [L. S.]
PIERRE DE POLETICA. [L. S.]

high contracting powers, from becoming the pretext for an illicit trade, it is agreed that the citizens of the United States shall not resort to any point where there is a Russian establishment, without the permission of the governor or commander; and that, reciprocally, the subjects of Russia shall not resort, without permission, to any establishment of the United States upon the Northwest Coast.

ARTICLE THIRD.—It is moreover agreed, that, hereafter, there shall not be formed by the citizens of the United States, or under the authority of the said States, any establishment upon the Northwest Coast of America, nor in any of the islands adjacent, *to the north* of fifty-four degrees and forty minutes of north latitude; and that, in the same manner, there shall be none formed by Russian subjects, or under the authority of Russia, *south* of the same parallel.

ARTICLE FOURTH.—It is, nevertheless, understood that during a term of ten years, counting from the signature of the present convention, the ships of both powers or which belong to their citizens or subjects, respectively, may reciprocally frequent, without any hindrance whatever, the interior seas, gulfs, harbors, and creeks upon the coast mentioned in the preceding article, for the purpose of fishing and trading with the natives of the country.

ARTICLE FIFTH.—All spirituous liquors, fire-arms, other arms, powder, and munitions of war of every kind, are always excepted from this same commerce permitted by the preceding article; and the two powers engage, reciprocally, neither to sell nor suffer them to be sold to the natives by their respective citizens and subjects, nor by any person who may be under their authority. It is likewise stipulated that this restriction shall never afford a pretext, nor be advanced in any case, to authorize either search or detention of the vessels, seizure of the merchandise, or, in fine, any measures of constraint whatever towards the merchants or the crews who may carry on this commerce; the high contracting powers reciprocally reserving to themselves to determine upon the penalties to be incurred and to inflict the punishments, in case of the contravention of this article by their respective citizens or subjects.

ARTICLE SIXTH.—When this convention shall have been duly ratified by the President of the United States, with the advice and consent of the Senate, on the one part, and on the other by his Majesty the Emperor of all the Russias, the ratifications shall be exchanged at Washington in the space of ten months from the date below, or sooner, if possible. In faith whereof, the respective plenipotentiaries have signed this convention, and thereto affixed the seals of their arms.

Done at St. Petersburg, April 17, (5,) of the year of Grace one thousand eight hundred and twenty-four.

HENRY MIDDLETON.
LE COMTE C. DE NESSELRODE.
PIERRE DE POLETICA.

And whereas the said convention has been duly ratified on both parts, and the respective ratifications of the same were exchanged at Washington, on the eleventh day of the present month, by John Quincy Adams, Secretary of State of the United States, and the Baron de Tuyll, Envoy Extraordinary and Minister Plenipotentiary of his Imperial Majesty, on the part of their respective Governments:

Now, therefore, be it known that I, James Monroe, President of the United States, have caused the said convention to be made public, to the end that the same, and every clause and article thereof, may be observed and fulfilled with good faith by the United States and the citizens thereof.

In witness whereof, I have hereunto set my hand and caused the seal of the United States to be affixed. Done at the city of Washington, this twelfth day of January, in the year of our Lord [L. S.] one thousand eight hundred and twenty-five, and of the independence of the United States the forty-ninth.

JAMES MONROE.

By the President:
JOHN QUINCY ADAMS,
Secretary of State.

PIRACY AND OUTRAGE ON COMMERCE OF THE UNITED STATES BY SPANISH PRIVATEERS.

COMMUNICATED TO THE HOUSE OF REPRESENTATIVES JANUARY 31, 1825.

Mr. FORSYTH, from the Committee on Foreign Relations, to whom was referred so much of the President's message to Congress, at the opening of the present session, as relates to piracy and the outrages committed upon our commerce by vessels bearing Spanish commissions, and the memorials from different quarters of the Union on the same subjects, availing themselves of the documents accompanying the President's message to the Senate, of the 13th of January, which have been printed by order of that body, present to the House the result of their deliberations upon the subject submitted to them:

From the commencement of the revolution which has terminated in the separation of Spanish continental America from Old Spain, the commerce of the United States, in common with that of all other nations, has suffered frequent outrages from the vessels of the adverse parties duly commissioned, with doubtful commissions, and from pirates who sought to conceal their true character by the use of the flag of some one of the belligerents. Constant efforts have been made by this Government to redress injuries suffered and to prevent future outrage. Congress has at all times been prepared to give, and has afforded, all the means necessary for these purposes within its province.

The act of the third of March, 1819, was passed specially to protect the commerce of the United States and punish the crime of piracy. It gave to the President power (a power, however, which the President possesses without an act of Congress) to employ the public armed vessels of the United States to protect our merchant vessels and their crews from piratical aggression and depredation; to authorize the detention, capture, and trial of any armed vessels which attempted any piratical depredation, search, seizure, or restraint of an American vessel. It authorized our merchant vessels to capture armed ships not commissioned by a friendly power, and to recapture vessels taken by them, and it directed the condemnation of the vessels so captured or recaptured; it provided for the punishment of the pirates, when convicted by the competent tribunals. This act was limited to one year, but was continued in force by the act of May 15, 1820, for two years, and the first four sections made perpetual by the act of the 30th January, 1823.

The re-establishment of the constitutional Government in Old Spain, in March, 1820, inspired the strongest hope that the contest between Spain and Spanish continental America would be soon amicably terminated in a manner satisfactory to the parties at war, to the commercial and civilized world, and to all the lovers of humanity, justice, and liberty. The first movements of the regenerated government promised a speedy realization of this hope.

The Cortes of Spain directed negotiations to be opened with Spanish America; Commissioners were appointed, but the contending parties did not take the same view of the great questions between them. Old Spain would not admit the recognition of the independence of the Spanish American Governments as the basis of negotiation; and the Spanish American Governments would not negotiate without that preliminary recognition. While these abortive attempts at negotiation were made, there was a temporary cessation of hostilities in Venezuela. The war, however, was renewed in Venezuela before the negotiations were broken off. Fortune favored the Americans, and the European Spaniards were driven from the continent. During this desperate contest, General Morales, the commander of the Spanish forces, issued his extraordinary proclamation declaring a coast of twelve hundred miles in a state of blockade, and interdicting all foreign commerce with the Spanish Main as inconsistent with the colonial law of Old Spain. This proclamation has been the fruitful source of most of the evils since suffered by all commercial nations in the West Indies and in the Gulf of Mexico. Numerous pirates and swarms of privateersmen (subsequently degenerated into pirates) have preyed upon all neutral commerce. Protection to that of the United States should have been, if it has not been, afforded against pirates by the use of all the necessary means under the control of the Executive; by a vigorous exertion of the naval power; by incessant watchfulness on the seas, and on the coasts infested by them; rigorous examination of all suspected vessels of every size; ardent pursuit of the persons found *flagrante delicto*, wherever they sought refuge; careful prosecution before the competent tribunals of all the accused who were taken; unrelenting severity in inflicting punishment, where guilt was judicially established, against privateersmen; by appeals to the Government of Spain, requiring immediate redress for the past and security for the future; if made in vain, application should have been made to Congress to authorize reprisals, or to declare war, as the extent of the injury and a due regard to the condition of the Spanish Government should have required. A further reference, however, to the past would not be useful. For the present and for the future, if legislative provisions are necessary, they should be made.

Piracy at present exists in the same form as in the year 1822, when a species of naval force, supposed to be particularly adapted to suppress it, was placed at the disposal of the Executive. This force was believed to have answered the expectations entertained of it, as the President at the opening of the last session of Congress announced that "it had been eminently successful in the accomplishment of its objects." If further experience has shown that this species of force is inadequate to the accomplishment of the object, and that another may be advantageously substituted, there can be no doubt of the propriety of the substitution. This is a point, however, that the committee do not consider it their duty to examine; it belongs properly to another committee, the result of whose deliberations on it has been already presented to the House. The merchants of the United States who have, with the exception of our seamen, the deepest interest in this subject, suggests the propriety of suffering the owners of vessels to arm for their own defence. There is no law forbidding such defensive armament, nor is any law required to justify it. It is, however, asserted that the restraints upon the armament of merchant vessels are inconvenient and oppressive, and that they ought to be removed. The only provision on this subject is that which requires bond and security to be given to prevent an unlawful use of the armed vessel; a provision which should not be changed—an adherence to which the best interest of commerce requires.

The propriety of authorizing by law the pursuit of the pirates on land has also been a subject of consideration. The committee do not deem an act of Congress for this purpose necessary. The rule of international law is, that fugitives from the justice of one nation are to be considered in another as strangers entitled to protection, and having a right of residence, on the common principle that no nation has a right to punish a person who has not offended itself, nor is it bound to assist its neighbor in the execution of its criminal laws. Pirates are criminals against all nations, punishable in every tribunal; the common enemies of mankind; the duty of all nations and every man is, to hunt them down, that they may be delivered up to offended justice. Fresh pursuit of enemies into the territory of a common friend is not universally admitted to be a right of war. Powerful nations never permit feeble neighbors to enter their territory for this purpose, but enter without scruple in pursuit of their enemies the territory of such neighbors, unless restrained by the apprehension that the mutual friend seeks a fair occasion to become an ally against them in war. Practically, the question is one not of right, but of relative power. The pursuit of a mutual enemy into the territory of a friendly or allied power is a right of war; it cannot be deemed a violation of the sovereignty of that power; it confers a favor, and imposes upon him an obligation of gratitude.

The common enemy cannot avail himself of the protection of the territory of the third power but by surrendering himself as prisoner of war, and in that event, if the force of the pursuer was the cause of the surrender, the pursuer might rightfully claim the benefit of the surrender. Under this rule the pursuit and capture of pirates anywhere and everywhere may be justified. The Executive has acted upon it. Instructions have been given to our naval commanders to pursue and capture on Spanish territory pirates who seek refuge or concealment there. The Government of Spain has been duly warned of the existence of these orders; it knows that they will be obeyed. No remonstrance has been made by it; no objections have, as far as the committee have been informed, been urged. The acquiescence of Spain is all that should be desired. A distinction is supposed to exist between pursuit of pirates on lands uninhabited and those inhabited; and it is imagined that the authority of Congress is necessary to justify pursuit in the latter case, while in the former the power of the Executive alone is sufficient. The committee do not admit the correctness of this distinction. Fresh pursuit is justifiable in either case, if necessary to the capture of the pirate. There is greater danger of collision with the friendly power when the object of pursuit flies into a settled country, and greater care is requisite to avoid giving offence; but the same principles apply to either case, and it is just as necessary that Congress should legislate to justify the capture of pirates as to authorize the pursuit of them into any place of refuge inhabited or unsettled.

From an attentive examination of the letters of the agent who was sent to Cuba to obtain information relative to pirates who have long infested the coast of that island, it would seem that no fresh pursuit on land will eradicate the evil. Authority must exist to search in the suspected settlements for persons believed to be guilty of piracy, and for the evidence of their guilt, and to bring them before our tribunals for trial and punishment. This authority Congress cannot give without making war upon Spain. It cannot be used without wresting from Spain her municipal jurisdiction. The evil lies too deep to be reached by any ordinary measures which foreign powers can apply to it.

The Government of Spain must give to the local authority what it is said to want—sufficient strength to prevent and to punish crimes; it must perform its duties, or those who suffer from its neglect or weakness will be driven by the necessity of the case to apply the corrective. The committee would bring more distinctly into view the only efficient remedy, and recommend a resort to it, if they believed sufficient time had elapsed since remonstrances were made by our Government to Spain to prove incontestably that she wanted either the power or the will to do her duty, although they are aware that the conduct of any Government in applying that remedy without previous concert with other nations alike interested in the question would be liable to misconception, and excite well founded jealousies. The committee cannot doubt that the Executive, applying all proper means to prevent, to detect, and to punish the crime of piracy, and pressing upon Spain and her local authorities that the honor and the interest of Spain requires their best exertions for the same purpose, will not fail to confer with the great commercial nations on the extraordinary measures to be used, if the object is not speedily accomplished by the faithful exertion of the powers of Spain.

The danger to which our commerce is exposed, and the injuries it has suffered from privateers acting under regular or irregular commissions, are of a different character, and require a different remedy. The committee understand that outrages of this kind have almost, if not entirely, ceased; for those which have been inflicted, or which may hereafter be inflicted, Spain is directly responsible. Reparation must be had, by negotiation or by the exercise of such powers as may, for that purpose, be vested in the Executive by Congress.

To guard against future injury, the safest resource is to enforce, promptly, ample redress for that which has been suffered. The committee have already referred to the injuries suffered in consequence of the proclamation of Morales. Those injuries are not yet redressed. The Government of Spain has not attempted to justify a proclamation declaring, with a naval force insufficient to shut up the smallest port on the coast, a seacoast of twelve hundred miles in a state of blockade, nor the absurd pretension that the property of all neutral nations is, under the colonial law of Spain, liable to confiscation if taken on its way to Spanish America; but the property of American citizens captured by privateers from the islands of Porto Rico and Cuba, and from Porto Cabello, is now withheld under these pretensions. The Spanish Government, having formally revoked the blockade, gives to the tribunals of Spain an excuse for the condemnation of all property seized prior to that revocation; an excuse of which they do not hesitate to avail themselves. Acting under instructions from the President, of the 28th April, 1823, the minister of the United States at the court of Spain demanded satisfaction in January, 1824, from that Government for the outrages committed from Porto Cabello and the islands of Porto Rico, and Cuba upon the commerce of the United States, and for the wanton murder of one of our gallant officers in the harbor of St. John, by the officer commanding the fort at its entrance. In September of the same year Spain was again called upon to indemnify those who had suffered in person or property under the proclamation of blockade, or from the interdiction of neutral commerce to the Spanish Main. In October the just reclamations of our Government were, for the third time, formally made to the Government of Spain. No satisfaction has been given; no indemnity has been promised; nor has there been even a satisfactory excuse given for the delay to answer the just demands of the minister of the United States.

The character of the injury sustained, its origin, the period elapsed since it was inflicted, the formal and fruitless demand for reparation for more than twelve months, justify reprisals. An anxious desire not to act harshly to a Government embarrassed by internal difficulties and enfeebled by recent revolutions, the distance of the seat of the Spanish Government from the places in which the evils complained of originated, the death of the minister appointed by the Spanish Government on the eve of his departure to this country, and the recent selection of another minister, whose appointment and intended departure for the United States has been communicated in an official letter, a translation of which is herewith presented to the House, induce the committee not to propose any legislative enactment, under the firm conviction that this forbearance will give to Spain a new motive to make speedily ample reparation for the injuries sustained, and that, if it does not produce this desired effect, it will justify, in the eyes of all nations, any and every step Congress may hereafter be compelled to take.

DEPARTMENT OF STATE, Washington, January 24, 1825.

SIR: I have the honor of inclosing herewith a translation of the only answer yet received from the Spanish Government to Mr. Nelson's notes on the subject of piracy and outrages on our commerce. It has been received since the communications to Congress of the previous documents were made.

I am, with great respect, sir, your very humble and obedient servant,

JOHN QUINCY ADAMS.

Hon. JOHN FORSYTH,
Chairman of the Committee of Foreign Relations, H. R. U. S.

Mr. Zea Bermudez to Mr. Nelson.

[Translation.]

SAN LORENZO, November 19, 1824.

SIR: From the middle of September last, when I took possession of the appointment which the kindness of the King, my august master, deigned to entrust to me, I dedicated, by order of his Majesty, my attention to the different notes presented by you relative to the claims of the American subjects who thought themselves entitled to be indemnified by Spain for the losses which they have suffered in the seas of America. A business so complicated, in which considerable interests are involved, presented so much more difficulty, by how much there were intermingled with it other interests and other claims of Spanish subjects against the Government and subjects of the United States.

His Majesty, desirous of preserving the friendship and good harmony which happily subsists between both nations, and that, in faithful observance of existing treaties, both Governments should terminate, in a friendly manner, this delicate question, the legitimate rights and just pretensions of both being mutually conciliated, has thought that the most proper means for gaining this desired end is to send immediately a minister plenipotentiary to reside near the American Government, who, by his information, prudence, and practical knowledge of the relations between both countries, may be, at the same time, the interpreter and the executor of the just intentions of the King. In consequence, his Majesty has been pleased to appoint Don José de Heredia his Envoy Extraordinary and Minister Plenipotentiary in the United States of America. He will set out for his new destination as soon as possible.

I hasten to inform you of this, that you may be pleased to lay it before your Government; and I avail myself of this occasion to repeat to you the assurances of my most distinguished consideration. God preserve you many years.

Your most obedient servant,

FRANCISCO DE ZEA BERMUDEZ.

<table>
<tr><td>18TH CONGRESS.]</td><td style="text-align:center">No. 399.</td><td>[2D SESSION.</td></tr>
</table>

RATIFIED TREATY WITH TUNIS.

COMMUNICATED TO THE SENATE FEBRUARY 4, 1825.

To the Senate of the United States:

I communicate, herewith, to both Houses of Congress, copies of the alterations in the treaty of peace and friendship of August, 1797, between the United States and the Bashaw Bey of Tunis, concluded at the palace of Bardo, near Tunis, on the 24th of February last, and of treaties* between the United States and the Sac and Fox tribes of Indians, and the Iowa tribe of Indians, concluded at the city of Washington, on the 4th of August last, which have been duly ratified.

JAMES MONROE.

WASHINGTON, *February 2, 1825.*

* These treaties will be found in Class of Indian Affairs.

A PROCLAMATION.

Whereas certain alterations in the treaty of peace and friendship of August, 1797, between the United States and the Bashaw Bey of Tunis were agreed upon and concluded between his Highness Sidi Mahmoud, the Bey, and S. D. Heap, chargé d'affaires of the United States at Tunis, on the twenty-fourth day of February, one thousand eight hundred and twenty-four, by the articles in the words following, to which are annexed the altered articles as they were in the treaty before the alterations:

Whereas sundry articles of the treaty of peace and friendship concluded between the United States of America and Hamuda Bashaw, of happy memory, in the month of Rebia Elul, in the year of the Hegira, 1212, corresponding with the month of August, of the Christian year 1797, have, by experience, been found to require alteration and amendment; in order, therefore, that the United States should be placed on the same footing with the most favored nations having treaties with Tunis, as well as to manifest a respect for the American Government, and a desire to continue, unimpaired, the friendly relations which have always existed between the two nations, it is hereby agreed and concluded between his Highness Sidi Mahmoud Bashaw, Bey of Tunis, and S. D. Heap, esq., chargé d'affaires of the United States of America, that alteration be made in the sixth, eleventh, twelfth, and fourteenth articles of said treaty, and that the said articles shall be altered and amended in the treaty to read as follows:

ARTICLE VI—*As it now is.*

If a Tunisian corsair shall meet with an American vessel, and shall visit it with her boat, two men only shall be allowed to go on board, peaceably, to satisfy themselves of its being an American, who, as well as any passengers of other nations they may have on board, shall go free, both them and their goods; and the said two men shall not exact anything, on pain of being severely punished. In case a slave escapes, and takes refuge on board of an American vessel of war, he shall be free, and no demand shall be made either for his restoration or for payment.

ARTICLE VI—*As it was.*

If a Tunisian corsair shall meet with an American merchant vessel, and shall visit it with her boat, she shall not exact anything, under pain of being severely punished; and, in like manner, if a vessel-of-war of the United States shall meet with a Tunisian merchant vessel, she shall observe the same rule. In case a slave shall take refuge on board of an American vessel-of-war, the consul shall be required to cause him to be restored; and if any of their prisoners shall escape on board of the Tunisian vessels, they shall be restored; but if any slave shall take refuge in any American merchant vessel, and it shall be proved that the vessel has departed with the said slave, then he shall be returned, or his ransom shall be paid.

ARTICLE XI—*As it now is.*

When a vessel-of-war of the United States shall enter the port of the Gouletta, she shall be saluted with twenty-one guns, which salute the vessel-of-war shall return gun for gun only, and no powder will be given, as mentioned in the ancient eleventh article of this treaty, which is hereby annulled.

ARTICLE XI—*As it was,*

When a vessel-of-war of the United States of America shall enter the port of Tunis, and the consul shall request that the castle may salute her, the number of guns shall be fired which he may request; and if the said consul does not want a salute, there shall be no question about it. But, in case he shall desire the salute, and the number of guns shall be fired which he may have requested, they shall be counted, and returned by the vessel in as many barrels of cannon powder.

The same shall be done with respect to the Tunisian corsairs when they shall enter any port of the United States.

ARTICLE XII—*As it now is.*

When citizens of the United States shall come within the dependencies of Tunis to carry on commerce there, the same respect shall be paid to them which the merchants of other nations enjoy; and if they wish to establish themselves within our ports no opposition shall be made thereto, and they shall be free to avail themselves of such interpreters as they may judge necessary, without any obstruction, in conformity with the usages of other nations; and if a Tunisian subject shall go to establish himself within the dependencies of the United States he shall be treated in like manner. If any Tunisian subject shall freight an American vessel and load her with merchandise, and shall afterwards want to unload or ship them on board of another vessel, we shall not permit him until the matter is determined by a reference of merchants, who shall decide upon the case, and, after the decision, the determination shall be conformed to.

No captain shall be detained in port against his consent, except when our ports are shut for the vessels of all other nations, which may take place with respect to merchant vessels, but not to those of war.

ARTICLE XII—*As it was.*

When citizens of the United States shall come within the dependencies of Tunis to carry on commerce there, the same respect shall be paid to them which the merchants of other nations enjoy; and if they wish to establish themselves within our ports no opposition shall be made thereto, and they shall be free to avail themselves of such interpreters as they may judge necessary, without any obstruction, in conformity with the usages of other nations; and if a Tunisian subject shall go to establish himself within the dependencies of the United States he shall be treated in like manner. If any Tunisian subject shall freight an American vessel and load her with merchandise, and shall afterwards want to unlade or ship them on board of another vessel, we will not permit them until the matter is determined by a reference of merchants, who shall decide upon the case, and, after the decision, the determination shall be conformed to.

No captain shall be detained in port against his consent, except when our ports are shut for the vessels of all other nations, which may take place with respect to merchant vessels, but not to those of war.

The subjects and citizens of the two nations, respectively, Tunisians and Americans, shall be protected in the places where they may be, by the officers of the Government there existing; but, on failure of such protection, and for redress of every injury, the party may resort to the chief authority in each country, by whom adequate protection and complete justice shall be rendered. In case the Government of Tunis shall have need of an American vessel for its service, such vessel being within the Regency, and not previously engaged, the Government shall have the preference, on its paying the same freight as other merchants usually pay for the same service, or at the like rate, if the service be without a customary precedent.

The subjects of the two contracting powers shall be under the protection of the Prince, and under the jurisdiction of the chief of the place where they may be, and no other person shall have authority over them. If the commandant of the place does not conduct himself agreeably to justice, a representation of it shall be made to us.

In case the Government shall have need of an American merchant vessel, it shall cause it to be freighted, and then a suitable freight shall be paid to the captain, agreeably to the intention of the Government, and the captain shall not refuse it.

ARTICLE XIV—*As it now is.*

All vessels belonging to the citizens and inhabitants of the United States shall be permitted to enter the ports of the Kingdom of Tunis and freely trade with the subjects and inhabitants thereof, on paying the usual duties which are paid by other most favored nations at peace with the Regency. In like manner, all vessels belonging to the subjects and inhabitants of the Kingdom of Tunis shall be permitted to enter the different ports of the United States, and freely trade with the citizens and inhabitants thereof, on paying the usual duties which are paid by other most favored nations at peace with the United States.

ARTICLE XIV—*As it was.*

A Tunisian merchant, who may go to America with a vessel of any nation soever, loaded with merchandise which is the production of the Kingdom of Tunis, shall pay duty (small as it is) like the merchants of other nations; and the American merchants shall equally pay for the merchandise of their country which they may bring to Tunis, under their flag, the same duty as the Tunisians pay in America. But if an American merchant, or a merchant of any other nation, shall bring American merchandise under any other flag, he shall pay six per cent. duty; in like manner, if a foreign merchant shall bring the merchandise of his country under the American flag, he shall also pay six per cent.

Concluded, signed, and sealed at the Palace of Bardo, near Tunis, the 24th day of the moon Jumed-teni, in the year of the Hegira, 1239, corresponding to the 24th of February, 1824, of the Christian year, and the forty-eighth year of the Independence of the United States, reserving the same, nevertheless, for the final ratification of the President of the United States, by and with the advice and consent of the Senate.

S. D. HEAP, *Chargé d'Affaires.*   [L. S.]
SIDI MAHMOUD'S   signature and   [L. S.]

And whereas the Senate of the United States did, on the 13th of January instant, two-thirds of the senators present concurring therein, advise and consent to the ratification of the convention containing the said alterations; and whereas, in pursuance of the said advice and consent, I have ratified, on the part of the United States, the said articles:

Now, therefore, I do hereby proclaim the same, and have caused the said articles to be made public, to the end that they and every clause thereof, as they now are, may be observed and fulfilled with good faith by the United States and their citizens.

In witness whereof, I have hereunto set my hand, and caused the seal of the United States to be affixed. Done at the city of Washington, this twenty-first day of January, in the year of our Lord [L. S.] one thousand eight hundred and twenty-five, and of the Independence of the United States the forty-ninth.

JAMES MONROE.

By the President:
JOHN QUINCY ADAMS,
Secretary of State.

PIRATES IN THE ISLAND OF CUBA.

COMMUNICATED TO THE HOUSE OF REPRESENTATIVES FEBRUARY 11, 1825.

Extract of a letter from Francis Adams, Commercial Agent of the United States at Matanzas, to Mr. Adams, dated December 30, 1824.

"Those piratical bands, who have become the disgrace and scourge of the island, are for the present restrained by the number and vigilance of the forces sent by the United States and Great Britain for their suppression, but that they are only *restrained* and not extirpated is certain, from the fact that few or none have been captured, and that depredations have recently been committed on land, by bodies of fifteen to twenty persons, by which, the foreign settlers, on the coast have been the sufferers. Their migratory course of life, and the various points of the coast which afford fine harbors, and are at the same time distant from any military post, or even inhabited district, renders their extirpation by the authorities of the island difficult, if not impossible; and the arming of merchant vessels to resist the attacks of small boats, and the constant presence of a naval force sufficient to prevent the egress of larger vessels, appears to be the only means of securing our trade from their depredations, until the hopelessness of their employment, or the revival of Spanish commerce, shall have induced an abandonment of their desperate course of life."

　　　　　　　No. 401.　　　　　　　

COMMERCIAL RELATIONS WITH THE NETHERLANDS.

COMMUNICATED TO THE HOUSE OF REPRESENTATIVES FEBRUARY 11, 1825.

Department of State, *Washington, February* 10, 1825.

The Secretary of State, in obedience to a resolution of the House of Representatives of the 21st of January last, directing him to communicate to that House any information he may have in this Department "showing whether the duties levied on the tonnage of the vessels of the United States entering the ports of the Kingdom of the Netherlands, and on the merchandise with which they may be loaded, exceed those paid by the vessels belonging to the said Kingdom," has the honor to submit to the House of Representatives copies of the correspondence in this Department having relation to that subject.

Respectfully submitted.

JOHN QUINCY ADAMS.

List of papers.

No. 1. Mr. Everett to Mr. Adams, (No. 102,) March 17, 1823. (Extracts.)
No. 2. Same to Baron de Nagell, March 7, 1823. (Copy.)
No. 3. Same to Mr. Adams, (No 105,) June 1, 1823. (Extract.)
No. 4. Baron de Nagell to Mr. Everett, March 10 1823. (Translation.)
No. 5. Same to same, May 27, 1823. (Translation.)
No. 6. Mr. Everett to Baron de Nagell, May 31, 1823. (Copy.)
No. 7. Mr. Adams to Mr. Everett, August 9, 1823. (Copy.)
No. 8. Mr. Everett to Mr. Adams, (No 107,) November 11, 1823. (Copy.)
No. 9. Same to Baron de Nagell, November 5, 1823. (Copy.)
No. 10. Same to Mr. Adams, (No. 110,) February 21, 1824. (Copy.)
No. 11. Same to Chevalier Reinhold, February 20, 1824. (Copy.)
No. 12. Chevalier Reinhold to Mr. Everett, February 20, 1824. (Translation.)
No. 13. Mr. Everett to Mr. Adams, (No. 111,) March 23, 1824. (Extract.)
No. 14. Same to Chevalier Reinhold, March 22, 1824. (Copy.)

No. 1.

Extracts of a letter (No. 102) from Mr. Everett to Mr. Adams, dated

Brussels, *March* 17, 1823.

"I have the honor to inclose copies of two notes which I have lately had occasion to address to Baron de Nagell, and of his answer to them."

"The reply to my application in regard to the difference in the duties imposed upon goods imported in national and foreign vessels is merely an acknowledgment of the receipt of the note. As the principal object of the new financial system is to encourage the commerce and navigation of this country, it is perhaps hardly to be expected that the exception which I have suggested in favor of the United States will be admitted. If it is not, a partial repeal of the law of the 20th of April, 1818, will probably be thought necessary. But as this measure cannot be taken till the meeting of the next Congress, there will be ample time in the interval to receive the definitive answer of this Government."

"A separate discriminating duty in favor of national vessels has also been imposed since the commencement of this year upon the importation of coffee from Batavia, which is to be in force until the end of 1824."

No. 2.

Mr. Everett to the Baron de Nagell.

BRUSSELS, *March* 7, 1823.

SIR: The new tariff which has recently gone into operation contains several articles affecting the commercial relations between this country and the United States. I think it my duty to invite your excellency's attention to these articles, and to point out the manner in which they will operate upon the American trade.

Your excellency will recollect that the Government of the United States, by the law of the 20th of April, 1818, extended to the ships of the Netherlands arriving in the ports of the Republic nearly the same privileges that are enjoyed by our own. They pay the same tonnage duty, and also the same duties on their cargoes, as far as these consist of articles being the growth or manufacture of the Netherlands, or of such neighboring countries as usually ship their products from the Dutch ports. These privileges were granted to the commerce of the Netherlands in consequence of the adoption, in this Kingdom, of the law of October 3, 1816, which abolished the discriminating tonnage duty, and of the understanding that there was no other discriminating duties in force. If any change were to take place in the laws of this Kingdom, in either of these respects, the natural consequence would be a corresponding change in those of the United States.

I regret to find that the new financial system appears to contemplate some important alterations of this description. Several articles of the tariff establish a difference of duties in favor of goods imported in Dutch vessels; and the law of the 26th of August, 1822, creates, in the form of a drawback, a general discrimination to the same effect; the tenth article being as follows: *One-tenth of the duties paid upon the importation or exportation of all goods shall be returned when the same are imported or exported in Dutch vessels, excepting those articles of which the importation and exportation in Dutch vessels are otherwise specifically favored by the tariff.*

It has always been the wish of the Government of the United States to lend its aid in placing the commerce of the world upon the most liberal footing. With this view, it was proposed to all the powers of Europe, soon after the close of the late wars, to abolish, mutually, all discriminating duties on tonnage; and the proposition having been, in substance, accepted by the Government of the Netherlands, the arrangement took effect between the two countries. As it was also understood that no other discriminating duties existed, a similar regulation was established in favor of goods imported in Dutch vessels into the United States. It is obvious, however, that these privileges cannot be continued upon any other principle than that of reciprocity. It would not suit either with the honor or interest of the United States that the merchants of the Netherlands should enjoy in our ports the same advantages with native citizens, while our merchants were subjected in this country to unfavorable discriminations. If this Government is resolved to abandon the equalizing system, which led to the enaction of our law of April 20, 1818, the immediate and necessary consequence will be the repeal of that law, as far as it applies to the vessels of the Netherlands.

I must, therefore, take the liberty of requesting your excellency to inform me whether it is the intention of the Government of this country that the new principles introduced by the late tariff shall be applied to the American trade. The Government of the United States has no wish to interpose, in any way, with the policy of the Netherlands, and has never sought or accepted exclusive or onerous commercial advantages in the ports of any nation. The liberal system which has lately prevailed in the intercourse between the two countries was regarded as mutually beneficial, and as conformable to the general spirit of the administration of both. I assure your excellency that my Government would regret to find itself compelled to depart from this system, and I venture to hope that you will furnish me with such explanations as may show that a measure of that kind will not be necessary.

I have the honor to be, with high respect, sir, your excellency's obedient servant,

A. H. EVERETT.

No. 3.

Extract of a letter (No. 105) from Mr. Everett to Mr. Adams, dated

BRUSSELS, *June* 1, 1823.

"I transmit herewith copies of an answer from Baron de Nagell to my note of the 7th of March, respecting the discriminating duty established by the new provincial system, and of my reply."

No. 4.

Baron de Nagell to Mr. Everett.

[Translation.]

The undersigned, Minister of Foreign Affairs, being eager to lay before the King the note which Mr. Everett, chargé d'affaires of the United States of America, sent him, of the 7th of this month, has the honor of informing him that the observations which it contains on the new system of imposts of the Kingdom of the Netherlands, as far as it applies to the commerce of the United States, shall immediately be taken into grave consideration.

The undersigned flatters himself with being shortly enabled to give to Mr. Everett the desired explanations on this subject, and embraces this occasion to renew to him the assurance of his distinguished consideration.

A. W. C. DE NAGELL.

BRUSSELS, *March* 10, 1823.

No. 5.

Baron de Nagell to Mr. Everett.

[Translation.]

The new system of duties introduced in the Kingdom of the Netherlands having naturally appeared to the Government of the United States of America to produce a change in the commercial relations between the two countries, Mr. Everett had thought it his duty to demand, by the note which he had done him the honor of addressing to the undersigned Minister of Foreign Affairs, on the 7th of March last, explanations proper to tranquilize in this regard the Government of the United States, or to direct its future conduct.

The King has just authorized the undersigned to give here the explanations desired.

The 10th article of the law which precedes the new tariff of duties of entry and clearance is the argument upon which Mr. Everett founds his representations. This article grants a drawback of ten per cent. of the duties on merchandise imported or exported by the vessels of the Netherlands; now, as by an act of Congress of the United States, of April 20, 1818, all difference of treatment between the ships of the Netherlands and America has been abolished, founded upon this, that in the Kingdom of the Netherlands the flag of the United States enjoyed the same advantages as the national flag, the new disposition of the tariff appears to Mr. Everett to be in opposition to the principle of reciprocity.

The answer is found in the aim of this disposition, which does not appear to have been well understood.

By the laws of 12th June, 1821, and 10th August last, the duties remain, without distinction, the same for foreign ships and for national. This restitution of a tenth for the merchandise imported by the ships of the Netherlands, has done no more (as the 11th article of the law of the 12th July, 1821, expresses it) than to give encouragement and proper aid to the works of the nation. This restitution, therefore, supplies the place of the premiums of encouragement which the Government might have granted to every ship built in the Netherlands; a disposition which certainly never could have given room to the American Government to complain of an inequality of treatment in respect to the ships. If the Government of the United States had found it good to grant a similar premium to the American ships, surely the King could have found in that no cause of remonstrance. His Majesty would have only seen in it a bounty intended to encourage or to favor the manufactures of the nation.

Although the Government of the Netherlands might confine itself to this explanation, the undersigned has, nevertheless, been charged to take advantage of this occasion to examine the question more thoroughly. In approaching it with frankness, it will be easy to find in the conduct of the United States the justification of what is charged upon the Government of the Netherlands.

After the negotiations begun at the Hague by the respective Commissioners, for a treaty of commerce, were interrupted, the act of Congress of April 20, 1818, was passed. In the course of these negotiations, observation was made to the American Commissioners of the liberality of the Government of the Netherlands in its relations with America, and an attempt was made to convince them that at all times the American flag had been more favored here than the flag of the Netherlands had been in America.

Such are apparently the reports of the American plenipotentiaries, as well as the representations of the chargé d'affaires of his Majesty at Washington, which produced this act of April 20, 1818, by which that of March 3, 1815, concerning the general, but conditional abolition of *discriminating* duties, has been rendered applicable, and even amplified, to the flag of the Netherlands. As long as this state of things exists, the explanations demanded in the official letter of Mr. Everett may appear proper.

But can Mr. Everett be ignorant that his Government is upon the point of revoking the prolongation of these advantages; and that an act of the 3d of March, 1819, decrees that the two acts before cited (that of March 3, 1815, and of April 20, 1818) shall cease to be in force at the date of January 1, 1824; and that, in consequence, the equalization of duties of entry and clearance, and the duties of tonnage of vessels under the flag of the Netherlands, in the different ports of the United States, will no more continue after that time? His note would cause the presumption that he had no knowledge of it; otherwise, we may be allowed to believe that he would not have addressed it. It is, doubtless, a matter of surprise that he has not been informed of a disposition which so essentially changes the state of affairs; but, although it does not belong to this article, it is sufficient that it is impossible for the Government of the Netherlands to call in question the existence of this revocation for having a ground upon which the commercial relations with the United States are to be found, and to know which of the two Governments has made the commencement.

The discussion of the causes which can have determined the American Government to revoke, from the beginning of the following session of Congress, the act of April 20, 1818, is unknown to the Government of the Netherlands. No conjecture will be permitted if the measure, in place of being specially directed against the commerce of the Netherlands, do not rather announce a complete alteration of system.

The deliberations of Congress in the fall will resolve this problem; but, in the meantime, the certain prospect of losing the advantages assured by the act before mentioned to our commerce or to our navigation alone serves as a sufficient cause for preventing the Government of the Netherlands from establishing any exception in the new tariff in favor of the American flag.

The undersigned has the honor to renew to Mr. Everett the assurance of his distinguished consideration.

A. W. C. DE NAGELL.

BRUSSELS, *May* 27, 1823.

No. 6.

Mr. Everett to the Baron de Nagell.

BRUSSELS, *May* 31, 1823.

SIR: I have just received your excellency's answer to the note which I had the honor of addressing to you on the 7th March, upon the subject of some of the provisions of the new tariff, and learn, with regret, from this communication, that it is the King's intention to enforce these provisions against the commerce of the United States. I shall immediately transmit your reply to my Government, who will judge how far the new policy of this country is justified by the arguments you allege in its favor, and what measure it may be expedient for them to adopt under the circumstances of the case.

Without pretending to anticipate the decision of the President and Congress of the United States upon this subject, I think it my duty to add here a few short remarks, relating chiefly to the latter part of your excellency's note, in which you dwell upon the effect of the act of March 3, 1819. You appear to consider this act as a definitive repeal of the two former laws on the same subject, and looking at it from this point of view you naturally conclude that it forms of itself a complete reply to the reasoning in my note, and that, because I did not mention it, I could not be aware of its existence. The act is a document of public notoriety, and is printed in the collection of the Laws of the United States, with the other laws which I had occasion to quote. It produced no material effect upon the relations between the countries, and did not, therefore, require to be mentioned in the course of my remarks upon the subject. I rather regret, however, that I had not attended to it, and explained its operation, inasmuch as the construction given to it by your excellency, though erroneous, was natural enough in a foreigner unacquainted with the forms of our legislation, and seems to have had an unfavorable influence upon the whole tenor of your reply.

The object of this act, which wears the shape of a repeal of the two former ones, was to fix a time when the subject should be taken up again in Congress. A limitation of this sort is, with us, annexed to almost all new laws of much importance, and often makes a part of them. It furnishes, therefore, in this case, no proof of an intention to change the system; and as the laws and negotiations of the United States, subsequent to its adoption, prove, on the contrary, their disposition to adhere to it, there is little or no reason to doubt that the result of a reconsideration of the subject will be to re-enact the law, with such alterations as may appear expedient. Among these alterations will probably be the repeal of the privileges granted by the act to any powers which may have subsequently withdrawn the corresponding privileges formerly allowed by them to the citizens of the United States. Hence, the only effect of this act upon the relations between those States and the Netherlands will be to fix the time when the American Government will probably remodel their system in conformity to that which may be in force here; and if the King is really desirous to continue those relations upon their present footing, the act of March 3, 1819, instead of operating as an objection to the allowance of an exemption to American vessels from the effect of the new tariff, would serve, on the contrary, as a reason for taking such a measure with the least possible delay.

Such are the remarks which I have thought it my duty to communicate to your excellency in relation to the act of March 3, 1819. The other part of your answer, which treats more directly the points in question, would also admit of some objections. You intimate that, provided the duties levied upon foreigners and native citizens are nominally the same, a Government may allow a drawback in favor of the latter, without subjecting itself to the charge of partiality. This distinction seems, however, to be more formal than real; and if the foreigner actually pays in any way ten per cent. more than the citizen, it would be rather difficult to prove that they are placed upon an equal footing; or, in other words, that they pay the same. Your excellency also remarks, that the discrimination established by the new law, in favor of the subjects of the Netherlands, is justifiable on account of its object, which was to encourage the navigation of the country. In regard to this point, I must take the liberty to suggest that the end, supposing it to justify the means, does not change their character, nor, in this instance, prove that a discrimination in favor of citizens is consistent with perfect impartiality between citizens and foreigners. The American Government had in view the same object, viz: the encouragement of the navigation of their country, in establishing a discriminating tonnage duty in favor of our own vessels; but they certainly never thought of maintaining that the foreigners, against whom this discrimination operates, are as favorably treated in our ports as the citizens of the United States, or of claiming, under this pretence, an impartial treatment for the latter in the ports of such foreigners.

I must, however, beg your excellency, in conclusion, not to consider these new remarks as intended for the purpose of urging very strenuously upon the Government of the Netherlands a compliance with the proposition contained in my note of the 7th of March. My principal object has been to explain one or two points in that communication, which you seem to have misunderstood. The people of the United States are too well satisfied with the goodly heritage which the bounty of Providence has alloted to them, and too abundantly supplied from their own territories with the best products of almost all climates, to solicit very anxiously of any foreign power the concession of favors, commercial or political. In proposing to other nations to open to them, on a footing of equality, the immense and various resources of our vast Republic, they conceived themselves to be acting for the good of those nations and of humanity, as well as for their own. If the King does not deem it expedient for himself or his subjects to accept this offer, the Government of the United States, without complaining of his refusal, and without suffering much from it, will doubtless regret that the views of so enlightened a monarch upon a great question in political economy should be different from their own.

I have the honor to be, with the highest respect, sir, your excellency's very obedient servant,

A. H. EVERETT.

No. 7.

Copy of a letter from the Secretary of State to Mr. Everett, Chargé d'Affaires of the United States to the Netherlands.

DEPARTMENT OF STATE, *August 9, 1823.*

SIR: Your despatches, to No. 105, inclusive, have been received, and your letters marked private, to No. 27.

The object requiring most immediate attention is your correspondence with the Baron de Nagell, concerning the law of the Netherlands, of the 26th of August, 1822, establishing a *drawback* of one-tenth of the duties upon merchandise exported or imported in national vessels, and referring to other *favors* to the national flag, in the general law, and in the tariff.

The view you have taken of both parts of the agreement, in the Baron de Nagell's note of the 27th of May, is approved, and leaves me little to say in addition to it. From the strenuous manner in which the Baron urges the act of Congress of the 3d March, 1819, in justification of the new discriminations in the law of the Netherlands, it is apparent that he places little reliance upon the other part of his note. The object of *all* discriminating duties is to favor the national shipping and ship-building interest; and whether in the shape of additional impost, of tonnage, of drawback, or of bounty, they are alike felt in the competition of navigation, and alike incompatible with the principle of equal privilege and burden. It will be proper, therefore, explicitly to state that the case, hypothetically stated by the Baron de Nagell, of a bounty upon ship-building, is considered by this Government as much within the principle of discriminating duties as a direct tonnage duty, and equally at variance with the system of equalization established with a mutual understanding between the United States and the Netherlands, by reciprocal acts of legislation.

The limitation prescribed by the act of Congress of March 3, 1819, was, as you have observed, no intimation of an intention on their part to abandon the system. The act of March 3, 1815, was an experimental offer, made to all the maritime nations. It was, in the course of the same year, accepted by Great Britain, confirmed in the form of a convention. A similar effort was made with the Netherlands in 1817, but without success; but the principle of equalization was established by corresponding legislative acts. The Hanseatic cities and Prussia successively acceded to the same system, and, as well as the Netherlands, required an extension of the equalizing principle offered by the act of Congress of March 3, 1815, to merchandise of the growth, produce, or manufacture of countries other than that to which the vessel should belong, but usually first exported from thence. In conceding this extension of their first offer to the cities of Hamburg and Bremen and to Prussia, after having yielded it to the Netherlands, Congress thought proper to fix a time for a deliberate revision of the whole system, and, therefore, limited the duration of all the laws relating to it to the 1st of January, 1824. But neither Congress nor the Executive Government have manifested any intention to abandon the system. The President has, on the contrary, more than once expressed the favorable view in which it is considered by him, and particularly in his message to Congress, at the opening of the session, on the 3d December, 1821.

The whole subject will undoubtedly be one of the first objects of deliberation at the ensuing session of Congress. There is no reason to doubt that the existing equalization with regard to the Netherlands would be continued, but for the change which has been made on their part. A declaration from that Government that the discriminations against which you have made representations have not been and will not be applicable to the United States so long as the vessels of the Netherlands in the ports of the United States shall continue to enjoy the equalization secured to them by the act of Congress of March 3, 1815, and April 20, 1818, will supersede, without doubt, all change of the existing regulations here favorable to the navigation of that country. It is very desirable that you should obtain such a declaration in time to forward it, so that it may be received here by the first Monday in December, when the session of Congress will commence, or as soon after as possible. The act of Congress on the revision of the system will probably pass in the course of that month.

In the Baron de Nagell's note mention is made of three laws of the Netherlands in relation to this subject, of 12th of June and 12th of July, 1821, and of the 10th of August, 1822. I will thank you to send me copies of all these acts in French, and also of the law of the 26th of August, 1822, and of the new tariff.

I am, with great respect, sir, your very humble and obedient servant,

JOHN QUINCY ADAMS.

Hon. ALEXANDER H. EVERETT.
    Chargé d'Affaires of the United States to the Netherlands.

No. 8.

Mr. Everett to Mr. Adams, No. 107.

BRUSSELS, *November, 11, 1823.*

SIR: Your despatches of the 8th and 9th of August, which came under the same cover, were received on the first of November. Agreeably to your instructions, I immediately addressed notes to the Baron de Nagell upon the subjects of both, copies of which are inclosed. I have requested an early answer respecting the discriminating duty, but there is very little chance of obtaining it in time for it to be known at Washington before the new law is passed.

The laws of July 12, 1821, and August 26, 1822, are the only ones quoted by the Baron de Nagell in his note of May 27. The appearance of a different date in one of the passages in which they are alluded to arose from an accidental error of the clerk in the original note, which, it seems, was retained, in the hurry of writing, in my copies. The beginning of the fifth paragraph should read, *D'après les loix du 12*

Juillet, 1821, *et* 26 *Août dernier, instead of D'après les loix du* 12 *Juin,* 1821, *et* 10 *Août dernier.* The law of the 12th of July and the tariff of the 26th of August were transmitted to the Department about the time of their adoption, viz: the former with my despatch No. 80, and the latter with my letter, marked "private No. 18." The general law of the 26th of August was not sent with the tariff, not being then in print. I have now the honor of sending you copies of both, bound together in a volume. I have made inquiry for the law of July 12, but have not yet been able to procure it; and the copy I have on hand is bound up in a volume with several other documents, which would be useless at the Department. As soon as I can obtain a copy I shall certainly transmit it to you. In the meantime, if you should have occasion to consult this law, you may perhaps find upon the files the copy which was sent before It is, however, a mere statement of general principles, preliminary to the laws of August 26, 1822, and contains no regulations whatever intended for immediate practical effect.

You will observe that, besides the general drawback of ten per cent. in favor of national vessels, there are discriminations to a similar effect upon several separate articles. The principal of these are tea, coffee, and sugar. The duty on teas is raised by the present tariff; but the discrimination has existed since the year 1817, and does not appear to have been considered as inconsistent with the equalizing system, probably because the article is not of the growth of the United States. The discrimination in regard to coffee, established by the general law, article 5, section 9, is new; but being in favor of the national colonial trade, is not, perhaps, a fair subject of complaint. The additional duty on sugar, imported in foreign vessels, is however, a direct violation of the equalizing system; as are also those upon one or two other articles of less importance, such as salt, molasses, and wood for building, which, with the three mentioned above, are the only ones in which I have noticed any special discrimination.

A decree has lately been published, offering a bounty of eight florins per ton on all ships of above three hundred tons burden built within the country for three years to come. This regulation, which is intended to encourage the building of national ships, and not the trade in such ships after they are built, is, of course, no violation of the equalizing system. I have thought, since this decree made its appearance, that a bounty of this kind must have been intended by the Baron de Nagell, in his note of May 27, as the distinction between the effect of a bounty on transportation in national ships and a formal discrimination in the duties seems to be really too absurd to be taken in earnest by any man of common sense. If the Baron meant by his *prime d'encouragement* a bounty on ship building, it is true, as he says, that such a bounty would form no subject of complaint; but this fact does not strengthen his argument, because such a bounty has no analogy whatever to the drawback on goods imported in national ships. I should, perhaps, have introduced this idea in my note of the 5th, but I had written and transmitted it before the decree was in print.

I have the honor to be, with high respect, sir, your most obedient, and very humble servant,

A. H. EVERETT.

Hon. JOHN QUINCY ADAMS, *Secretary of State.*

No. 9.

Mr. Everett to the Baron de Nagell.

BRUSSELS, *November* 5, 1823.

SIR: I have the honor to inform your excellency that I have just received the instructions of my Government in regard to the subjects treated of in my note of the 7th of last March. I am directed to communicate to you, for the information of his Majesty, the President's views respecting that affair.

My object in the note just mentioned was to remonstrate against certain parts of the new financial law, which appeared to me to infringe the system of impartiality that has formed, for some time past, the basis of the commercial relations between the United States and the Netherlands; and I specified particularly the tenth article of the law of the 20th of August, 1822, which establishes a drawback of ten per cent. of the whole amount of duties in favor of goods imported in Dutch vessels. Your excellency did me the honor to state, in your note of the 27th of May, that these distinctions were justifiable on the ground of their patriotic design, which was no other than to afford a suitable encouragement to the shipping of the country. You remarked, that a drawback in favor of the citizen was not equivalent in principle to a formal discrimination against foreigners, but rather to a bounty—a measure not inconsistent, in the view of his Majesty's Government, with a system of perfect impartiality between citizens and foreigners; and you added, in conclusion, that, supposing the article in question to be really inconsistent with such a system, the Government of the United States would still possess no right to demand their repeal, inasmuch as they had already, by their act of March 3, 1819, revoked their own former laws in favor of the commerce of the Netherlands.

As your excellency insisted a good deal upon this last point, and expressed some surprise that I had not alluded in my note to this act of 1819, I thought it my duty to inform you at the time, by my answer of May 31, that the law in question was intended merely to determine the period at which the subject should be taken up again in Congress, and that the Government of the United States had no design of abandoning the established system. I added, that the distinction pointed out by your excellency between the different modes of favoring the shipping of a country did not appear to me to be strictly just, and that, if foreigners really paid ten per cent. more than subjects, it was of little importance to them whether they did it in one form or another. Confining myself to these remarks, I referred the matter to my Government for decision, and transmitted to Washington the correspondence that had passed.

I have now the honor of informing your excellency, by direction of the President, that he has learned with much regret the intention of his Majesty's Government to alter the liberal system which has been in force for some time past, and which was considered as beneficial to both parties, and conformable to their general principles of administration.

As to the reasoning by which your excellency justifies this change in your note of the 27th of March, my Government confirms, in general, the remarks which I had made in reply to it in my communication of the 31st of the same month. The President cannot admit the correctness of the distinction between the effect of a bounty or a drawback and that of a formal discrimination. He thinks, on the contrary, that impartiality is at an end whenever the foreigner finds himself in any way less advantageously situated than the native, and is rather surprised that the Government of the Netherlands should question a principle which appears so perfectly evident. And, as your excellency seems to have taken it for granted that the Government of the United States would not have considered a bounty on the transportation of goods in Dutch vessels as any violation of the equalizing system, I am authorized to assure you explicitly that, in the view of the American Government, such a measure would be entirely inadmissible, being equivalent in principle, as it is in effect, to a formal discrimination.

The patriotic intention of his Majesty's Government in adopting these measures is highly honorable to the character of the King and his ministers, but cannot certainly be understood to reconcile contraries, or to prove that discriminations in favor of native citizens are consistent with a system of impartiality between citizen and foreigner. The encouragement of the national industry is, doubtless, with enlightened Governments, the principal object of all commercial regulations; and in seeking to effect this object each Government adopts the policy which appears to suit best with its particular position. Some nations attempt to include the competition of foreigners by [placing] them higher than citizens, and by granting bounties to the latter; while others, on the contrary, endeavor to make their dominion the marts of general commerce, and hold out every possible inducement to foreigners to frequent their ports. This latter policy was formerly preferred in the Netherlands, at the time when Bourges, Antwerp, and Amsterdam figured, in succession, with so much brilliancy, at the head of the industry and commerce in Europe; and it seems, in fact, to agree very well with the situation of a country of limited extent and dense population, watered by numerous rivers that connect it with the more productive parts of Europe, and embosomed in seas that afford an easy intercourse with all the rest of the world. Both these systems, however, have their peculiar advantages; and each supposes alike, on the part of the administration, the intention to encourage national industry and promote the public good. But, were it even admitted that the exclusive policy were more advantageous, and, consequently, more patriotic than the liberal one, it would still be not the less certain that the two are essentially different, and that partial measures, however patriotic they may be, can never be impartial. Your excellency remarks, in your note of the 27th of May, that the bounties and drawbacks allowed to the subjects of the Netherlands furnish the American Government with no just ground of complaint, *because these measures are intended to protect and encourage the shipping of the country.* But however just and laudable this design may be in itself, the partial measures adopted in pursuance of it are, unquestionably, fair subjects of complaint with any foreign nation which has a valid claim to be treated on a footing of impartiality.

Having submitted to your excellency, by order of my Government, these additional observations upon the first part of your note of the 27th of May, I am directed to remark further, that the President is disposed to believe and to hope that the change of system which has taken place has been owing chiefly to a misunderstanding of the act of March 3, 1819. In regard to this point, I am now authorized to assure you explicitly, in the name of my Government, as I have done before in my own, that the object of the act was simply to fix a time when the subject should be reconsidered in Congress, and that the Government has no intention whatever to abandon the system. The acts and negotiations that have taken place since its adoption, and the messages addressed by the President to Congress, in particular that of December, 1821, attest the steady disposition of the administration, in all its branches, to maintain this course. The laws which expire at the end of the year will be doubtless re-enacted with such modifications as may appear expedient; and if one of these modifications should be the omission of the name of the Netherlands from the list of privileged nations, the change will be owing entirely to the new regulations contained in the Dutch law of August 26, 1822.

The American Government is, however, inclined to hope that this retaliatory measure will not be necessary; and that, if the act of March 5, 1819, has been explained to the satisfaction of his Majesty, he will reconsider the provisional decision, announced in your excellency's note of the 31st of May, and restore to the American trade the privileges which it has heretofore enjoyed. Should this be the case, I will thank your excellency to give me as early information of the fact as may be convenient, that I may transmit it immediately to Washington. The subject will probably be taken up in Congress before the close of the year, and it is desirable that the King's final decision should be known previous to the passage of the new law.

Your excellency will permit me to remark, in conclusion, that the privilege enjoyed by the Dutch flag, of covering the products of Germany and Switzerland, has also been extended to the flags of Prussia and the Hanse Towns. As the ports of the Netherlands are more conveniently situated for shipping these products to the United States, it is believed that the greater part of this commerce now takes that direction. If, however, the privilege in question should be revoked, as respects the Netherlands, and continued to the other above mentioned powers, there would be an advantage of ten per cent. in conveying the products of the interior of Europe to the United States, through the ports of Prussia and the Hanse Towns, rather than those of this country; and this difference in the present state of commerce would decide the preference. The subjects of the Netherlands will therefore lose, by the effects of the new system, not only a considerable advantage in the carriage of their own products, but the profits of a pretty important and lucrative branch of trade which they must now nearly monopolize.

I have the honor to be, with high respect, sir, your excellency's very obedient servant,

A. H. EVERETT.

No. 10.

Mr. Everett to Mr. Adams, No. 110.

BRUSSELS, *February 21, 1824.*

SIR: I learn from the public papers that a new law has been enacted on the subject of the discriminating duties, and presume that I shall receive a copy of it from you, with instructions to communicate it to this Government. But as the time of my departure is now pretty near, I thought it advisable, in order to give them an opportunity to deliberate upon the matter before I go, not to wait for this, but to address a note at once to the Minister of Foreign Affairs. I have accordingly sent one, of which I have the honor to inclose a copy. If I should hereafter receive any orders from you upon the subject, I shall give them, of course, the most punctual attention, and take any further measures that they may prescribe.

I have the honor to be, with high respect, sir, your very obedient, humble servant,

A. H. EVERETT.

Hon. John Quincy Adams, *Secretary of State.*

FEBRUARY 24.

Postscript.—Since writing the above, I have received from Mr. Reinhold a preliminary answer to my note, of which I have the honor to add a copy.

No. 11.

Mr. Everett to the Chevalier de Reinhold.

BRUSSELS, *February 20*, 1824.

SIR: I have the honor to inform your excellency that the privileges granted to the Dutch flag in the ports of the United States, by the act of the 20th of April, 1818, which expired at the close of the last year, have been renewed by the late law of January 9. As soon as I receive an authentic copy of the new act I shall take the liberty of sending it to you. You will find in the Brussels Journal of the 16th instant a French translation, which appears to be correct.

The passage of this law confirms the assurances which I gave to your predecessor, the Baron de Nagell, that the act of March 3, 1819, repealing that of April 20, 1818, was merely formal, and that the Government had no intention to abandon the system. The new act extends the privileges granted by the former one to all such foreign powers as may allow the same privileges to us in their ports, and for the same length of time. If any foreign power shall revoke these privileges, our law will cease to have its effect in regard to such power. Hence, if the Government of the Netherlands shall so modify its new regulations as to make them inapplicable to the American trade, they will thereby retain the advantages they now enjoy in the ports of the Republic. If, on the contrary, they persist in putting these regulations in force against us, the President of the United States is authorized by the law to withdraw these privileges immediately, and to place the Dutch flag upon the footing of that of the least favored nations, by subjecting it to the additional duties that are levied upon foreigners.

As the principal cause which appears to have occasioned the application of the new rules to the trade of the United States no longer exists, the American Government have, perhaps, some right to flatter themselves that the effect will cease with it, and that the King will be disposed to continue, or rather to restore, the equalizing system. Without entering now into the train of reasoning upon this subject which I have already pursued at sufficient length in my former notes, I shall content myself upon the present occasion with remarking, that the answer which I may carry to my Government, upon my return to the United States, will probably be regarded as final, and that it would give me great pleasure to be the bearer of one that should tend, by its character, to strengthen the bonds of amity and good understanding that now so happily unite the two countries.

I have the honor to be, with high respect, sir, your excellency's very obedient servant,

A. H. EVERETT.

No. 12.

Mr. J. G. Reinhold to Mr. Everett.

[Translation.]

HAGUE, *February 20*, 1824.

SIR: I have taken care to communicate without delay to the Department of Public Industry the note which you did me the honor to address to me on the 20th of this month, on the subject of the law of the 7th January, by which the Government of the United States has renewed the principal dispositions in favor of the commerce of the Netherlands, from that of the 20th April, 1818, expired on the 31st December last, except the modification, in what concerns the navigation of the Republic, of articles of the new system of impositions in the Netherlands which establish discriminations against strangers.

I have likewise informed his Majesty as well of the course which you are about to pursue as of the consequence which I have provisionally given to it, and I shall not fail, sir, to inform you of the determination which shall be taken in that regard, as soon as I shall be informed of it.

In the meantime, I take this occasion, sir, to renew to you the assurance of my very distinguished consideration.

J. G. REINHOLD.

No. 13.

Extract of a letter from Mr. Everett to Mr. Adams, (*No.* 111,) *dated*

BRUSSELS, *March 23*, 1824.

"A file of the Intelligencer came to hand a few days ago, which contained the new law respecting the discriminating duties. I immediately transmitted a copy of it to the Minister of Foreign Affairs, accompanied by a short note, of which I have the honor to inclose a copy."

No. 14.

Mr. Everett to the Chevalier de Reinhold.

BRUSSELS, *March* 22, 1824.

SIR: I have the honor to transmit, herewith, to your excellency a copy of the new law mentioned in my note of the 20th of February. You will perceive that it secures all the privileges granted to the Dutch flag by the act of April 20, 1818, and particularly that of transporting to the United States, upon a footing of equality, the products of the interior of Europe. This provision was, I believe, omitted in the French translation of the act published by the Brussels Journal.

I have had occasion, in several preceding notes, to offer to the consideration of his Majesty's Government such remarks as I thought would place the subject in its proper light, and I deem it unnecessary to renew the discussion at present. Requesting your excellency to communicate the inclosed law to his Majesty the King,

I have the honor to be, with high respect, sir, your excellency's very obedient servant,
A. H. EVERETT.

18TH CONGRESS.]   No. 402.   [2D SESSION.

CLAIMS OF CITIZENS OF THE UNITED STATES UPON THE GOVERNMENT OF THE NETHERLANDS.

COMMUNICATED TO THE HOUSE OF REPRESENTATIVES FEBRUARY 15, 1825.

To the House of Representatives of the United States:

I transmit, herewith, to the House a report from the Secretary of State, with copies of the correspondence relating to the claims of the citizens of the United States upon the Government of the Netherlands, requested by a resolution of the House of the 18th of January last.

JAMES MONROE.

WASHINGTON, *February* 7, 1825.

DEPARTMENT OF STATE, *Washington, February* 7, 1825.

The Secretary of State, to whom has been referred a resolution of the House of Representatives of the 18th of January last, requesting the President "to communicate to that House any correspondence which may have taken place between the United States or their agents and the Government of the Netherlands, relative to the claims of the citizens of the United States on that Government, so far as such information may be deemed by him not injurious to the public interests," has the honor respectfully to submit, herewith, to the President the correspondence requested.

JOHN QUINCY ADAMS.

List of papers sent.

No. 1. Mr. Monroe to Mr. Eustis, May 9, 1815. (Extract.)
No. 2. Mr. Eustis to Mr. Monroe, October 31, 1815. (Copy.)
No. 2, *a.* Baron de Nagell to Dr. Eustis, October 17, 1815. (Translation.)
No. 2, *b.* Mr. Eustis to Baron de Nagell, August 22, 1815. (Copy.)
No. 3. Mr. Eustis to Baron de Nagell, October 29, 1815. (Copy.)
No. 4. Mr. Monroe to Mr. Eustis, May 20, 1816. (Extract.)
No. 5. Mr. Eustis to Mr. Monroe, August 5, 1816. (Extract.)
No. 5, *a.* Same to Baron de Nagell, July 4, 1816. (Copy.)
No. 6. Same to Mr. Monroe, October 6, 1816. (Extract.)
No. 6, *a.* Baron de Nagell to Mr. Eustis, August 14, 1816. (Translation.)
No. 6, *b.* Mr. Eustis to Baron de Nagell, September 25, 1816. (Copy.)
No. 7. Mr. Adams to Mr. Everett, August 10, 1818. (Extract.)
No. 8. Mr. Everett to Mr. Adams, February 25, 1819. (Extract.)
No. 8, *a.* Same to Baron de Nagell, February 22, 1819. (Copy.)
No. 9. Same to Mr. Adams, June 21, 1819. (Extract.)
No. 9, *a.* Baron de Nagell to Mr. Everett, June 14, 1819. (Translation.)
No. 10. Mr. Everett to Mr. Adams, July 18, 1819. (Extract.)
No. 10, *a.* Same to Baron de Nagell, July 15, 1819. (Copy.)
No. 11. Same to Mr. Adams, November 8, 1819. (Extract.)
No. 11, *a.* Baron de Nagell to Mr. Everett, November 4, 1819. (Translation.)
No. 12. Mr. Everett to Mr. Adams, November 16, 1819. (Extract.)

No. 12, *a*. Same to Baron de Nagell, November 10, 1819. (Copy.)
No. 13. Baron de Nagell to Mr. Everett, December 9, 1819. (Translation.)
No. 14. Mr. Everett to Mr. Adams, January 25, 1820. (Extract.)
No. 14, *a*. Same to Baron de Nagell, without date.
No. 15. Mr. Adams to Mr. Everett, May 26, 1820. (Extract.)

No. 1.

Extract of a letter from Mr. Monroe to Mr. Eustis, dated

MAY 9, 1815.

"In the late European war the United States suffered great injury in Holland by the unwarrantable seizure, detention, and even confiscation of the property of their citizens, by the existing Government. For those acts there were, in many instances, not the slightest pretext, and in most, if not in all, no justifiable cause. A nation is, in strictness, answerable for the acts of its Government. This ought not to be pressed, though the idea may be brought into view and the claim kept open. In all instances in which the property has not been disposed of, it cannot be doubted that it will be delivered up. You will endeavor to obtain for our citizens the justice to which they are entitled for all the losses thus sustained."

No. 2.

Mr. Eustis to the Secretary of State.

HAGUE, *October* 31, 1815.

SIR: I have the honor herewith to inclose the answer of the Baron de Nagell, Minister of State for Foreign Relations, to the note presented on the 22d of August, on the subject of certain claims of American citizens for property taken from them, and confiscated by the Government of this country in the year 1809, by which it appears that the present Government declines making restitution.

To the note of the Baron de Nagell I thought it proper to make a reply (a copy of which is also herewith transmitted) with the view of correcting the misrepresentations of my note, of preserving to the claim its proper ground, and of leaving it open to such future representation as may be judged expedient. In the meantime, and until otherwise instructed, I shall not press the subject.

I have the honor to be, with perfect respect, your obedient servant,

WILLIAM EUSTIS.

Hon. JAMES MONROE, *Secretary of State.*

No. 2, (*a.*)

Baron de Nagell to Dr. Eustis.

[Translation.]

HAGUE, *October* 17, 1815.

The undersigned, Minister of Foreign Affairs, has the honor of receiving the note which Mr. Eustis, Envoy Extraordinary and Minister Plenipotentiary of the United States of America, addressed to him on the 22d of August, respecting certain claims made by the citizens of the United States upon the Government of his Majesty the King of the Netherlands.

The claim is founded upon this, that the measures which will dispose of the cargoes, the fate of which was the object of the note, were an act of violence which the French Government forced upon the Dutch Government; and, upon the principle *that nations are bound by the acts of their Governments, and that this obligation always exists without diminution, whatever be the changes which otherwise take place in the Republic.*

The undersigned has orders to make known that the King finds in each of these reasons causes for remaining an absolute stranger to this affair.

In fact, if the ancient Dutch Government itself could not equitably be made responsible for having yielded to an irresistible power at that time, for a stronger reason it could not be charged with its conduct, and reparation be demanded of it on the part of a Government which did not enter there for nothing.

And if the principle invoked (which the undersigned cannot forbear believing inadmissible in general, and certainly when it is applied to acts of the nature of that in question,) could be adopted in the present case, it would then be upon the Government which succeeded that which exacted the measure, that those interested should press their rights. That is to say, upon the French Government, and not upon that of the King, who, far from homologating the measures forced upon the Government which is just abolished, has constantly announced his disavowal of these systems and of these acts which have brought ruin upon so many individuals and raised up all civilized nations against them.

The undersigned seizes this occasion to have the honor of offering to Mr. Eustis the assurances of his high consideration.

A. W. C. DE NAGELL.

No. 2, (b.)

Mr. Eustis to the Baron de Nagell.

HAGUE, *August* 22, 1815.

The undersigned, Envoy Extraordinary and Minister Plenipotentiary of the United States of America, is instructed by his Government to invite the attention of his excellency the Secretary of State for Foreign Affairs to the subject of certain claims of citizens of the United States upon his Majesty's Government; the facts are as follows:

In the course of the year 1809 a number of American vessels arrived in the ports of Holland with cargoes, consisting of articles partly the growth of the United States and partly that of the colonies. The latter portion, being the more considerable, was seized by the Government, at that time in the hands of the ci-devant.King of Holland, Louis Bonaparte, and detained in the royal warehouses. In the month of March of the next year a treaty was concluded at Paris between the ex-King of Holland and the ex-Emperor of the French, by virtue of which the property so detained was made over to the latter. It was soon after conveyed into France, and sold for the benefit of the French treasury; the whole amounting to about one million of dollars.

This act of iniquity, which had not the slightest pretence or shadow of right to justify it, by which many individuals have been injured and ruined, the undersigned has no doubt will be considered with just disapprobation by a Government so enlightened and upright as that of his Majesty the King, nor can it be necessary to urge that nations are responsible for the acts of their rulers, and that changes of Government cannot diminish the force of obligations and contracts.

With these impressions, the undersigned feels a confidence that the claims in question will meet with early attention and prompt redress. He has contented himself for the present with making a general statement of the case, the principal features of which, as he presumes, are not unknown to his excellency the Secretary of State for Foreign Affairs. He will be happy to avail himself of any opportunity that may be afforded him to furnish such further details and evidence as may be necessary to a final settlement.

The undersigned takes advantage of this opportunity to offer to his excellency the Secretary of State for Foreign Affairs the assurances of his high consideration.

WILLIAM EUSTIS.

His Excellency Baron DE NAGELL,
Minister of State for Foreign Affairs.

No. 3.

Mr. Eustis to Baron de Nagell.

HAGUE, *October* 29, 1815.

The undersigned has had the honor of receiving the note which his excellency the Minister for Foreign Affairs addressed to him on the 17th instant, informing him that his Majesty declines taking any measures respecting the claims which formed the subject of the note presented by the undersigned on the 22d of August.

As the ground of fact on which the claims in question were represented to rest appears to have been misconceived by his excellency the Minister, the undersigned takes the liberty to remark that he certainly would not have meant to found his claim on the fact, that the measures which decided the fate of the cargoes in question were an act of violence, extorted by the French Government from that of Holland; for he neither knew, nor had he any means of knowing, the motive of those measures. He relied on the fact that the seizure and confiscation were the act and deed of the Government of Holland; whether the proceeds were converted to the immediate use of that Government, or transferred, for any consideration whatever, to another power, it was not for the claimants to inquire. The Government of Holland had taken their property, and to the Government of Holland they looked for redress. Still less could they inquire into the motives which induced this act of violence on their property. If the sacrifice of this property saved the nation from a greater evil, and this is necessarily included in the supposition of compulsion, the claim to indemnity is, in that case, strengthened.

If this view of the subject be correct, and the Government of the time was bound in justice to restore or make compensation for the property, the argument grounded by his excellency the Minister on the supposition of the contrary loses its force, and the only remaining question will be, whether the present Government, in succeeding to the former, succeeded also to this obligation.

The undersigned cannot permit himself to believe that his excellency the Minister intended to question very seriously the correctness of the general principle that nations are bound by the acts of their Governments. This principle has been too long established and acted upon, and is, moreover, too consonant with equity, to admit of doubt. It is rather presumed that the Baron de Nagell intended to rest the force of his observation on the idea contained in the latter part of the sentence, namely: that the principle, however generally correct, could not be applied to acts of violence, like the one in question.

The exemption from responsibility would then be founded on the nature of the act of violence. With respect to this, the undersigned begs leave to add that, if the principle before mentioned is admitted, and the present Government succeeds to the obligations of the former, with the right to claim indemnity for injuries done to the nation under that Government, and with the obligation to repair injuries done to the subjects or citizens of foreign nations by that Government, he is unable to discern, in the nature or circumstances of the present case, a just ground of exception.

The undersigned avails himself of this opportunity to assure his excellency the Minister of his perfect consideration and respect.

WILLIAM EUSTIS.

His Excellency the Baron DE NAGELL,
Minister for Foreign Affairs.

No. 4.

Extract of a letter from Mr. Monroe, Secretary of State, to Mr. William Eustis, Minister Plenipotentiary of the United States at the Hague, dated May 20, 1816.

"From the measures taken with other powers you will see the ropriety of renewing your applie;tion to the Government of the Low Countries for a similar indemnity.p The claim is founded on princir'les universally recognized, and which have existed through all ages. The Government of Holland, by which the seizures and confiscations of which we complain were made, was in full possession of the sovereignty of the nation, and exercised all the rights appertaining to it; it was acknowledged by other powers, to many of whom it sent ministers, and from whom it received others in return. The Government *de facto* of any country is the competent Government for all public purposes. These facts being well known, and the principle of unquestionable authority, it is hoped and presumed that the Government which is now established there will admit the justice and see the propriety of making the reparation which is claimed. You will bring the subject again before the Government of the Low Countries in a friendly manner, indicating the reliance which is placed in a satisfactory decision, as well from the high character of the present sovereign as the justice of the claim. Should your demand not be acceded to, it will be proper to leave the affair open for further discussion. It gives me pleasure to state that the judicious manner in which you have already treated the subject has been very satisfactory to the President."

No. 5.

Extract of a letter from Mr. Eustis to the Secretary of State, dated at the Hague, August 5, 1816.

"Conformably to the instructions contained in your letter of the 21st of May, I have renewed to this Government the claims of the American merchants for the cargoes seized and confiscated by the Government of Holland, in the year 1809–'10, stating two cases which appeared to me to have peculiar merit. I inclose herewith a copy of the note presented on the occasion, and as soon as an answer shall be received I shall have the honor of transmitting it."

No. 5, (a.)

Mr. Eustis to the Baron de Nagell.

LEGATION OF THE UNITED STATES OF AMERICA AT THE HAGUE, *July* 4, 1816.

The undersigned has the honor to inform his excellency the Baron de Nagell that, having communicated to his Government the correspondence which has taken place in relation to the claims of certain American citizens for property seized and confiscated by the Government of Holland in 1809 and 1810, he has received instructions again to present that subject to the consideration of his Majesty's Government.

The claims in question are considered, as the undersigned has had the honor to state in a former note, to be founded on principles universally recognized, and which have existed through all ages. The Government of Holland, by which the seizure and confiscation were made, was *de facto* the Government of the nation, in full possession of its sovereignty, exercising all the rights appertaining to it, and acknowledged by other powers with whom it had its diplomatic relations established.

These facts being verified, and the principle being of indisputable authority, the undersigned has reason to hope and expect, from the justice of the claim, and from the well known character of his Majesty, that the subject will be again taken into consideration, and that the result of the inquiry (or examination) will be more satisfactory.

The annexed cases (the particulars of which have been transmitted to the undersigned, with full confidence of indemnification on the part of the owners,) are stated to show that, in one instance, the cargo was landed in consequence of shipwreck, and, in the other, on the advice of one of the most respectable mercantile houses in Amsterdam, and by express permission of the constituted authority of the country.

"The ship *Bacchus*, being authorized by previous regulations, after having eluded the British blockading squadron, arrived at Amsterdam in the year 1809, with a cargo of tobacco, amounting, by appraisement, to one hundred thousand dollars. She was ordered to depart from this port, although, in so doing, she was exposed to almost certain capture. In endeavoring to get out she was wrecked. Her cargo was saved and put in store, and subsequently delivered over by the Government of Holland to the French Government."

"In the spring of 1809 the brig *Baltimore*, with a cargo consisting chiefly of colonial produce, amounting to upwards of forty-two thousand dollars, was ordered for Amsterdam, with instructions to the captain, on her arrival on the coast, to lay to, and send in by the pilot a letter to the consignees, Messrs. Hope & Co., to learn the state of the market, and whether the property would be safe in case he should enter. The vessel remained off the coast several days, when letters were received from the consignees, informing of the state of the market, and that, if the cargo should in the first instance be put in the King's store, it would, on being examined as to its origin, (of which satisfactory evidence accompanied it,) be delivered to the proprietors. The captain, in one of his letters, suggested his apprehension of danger of French privateers hovering about the coast. In answer to this, Messrs. Hope & Co. sent him off a protection and a license to enter, from the King of Holland. On receiving this letter, the captain proceeded through the Vlie passage to Harlingen, where the cargo was landed and put in the King's stores. After several months, that part of the cargo which was the growth of the United States was delivered to the consignees. In the month of August, 1810, the residue of the cargo was sent to Antwerp, and there sold and disposed of, with other American property, by virtue of an order from the King of Holland."

The undersigned avails himself of this occasion to present to the Baron de Nagell renewed assurance of his high consideration.

WILLIAM EUSTIS.

No. 6.

Extract of a letter from Mr. Eustis to the Secretary of State, dated

The Hague, *October* 6, 1816.

"By the Harmony, for Baltimore, whose sailing on Tuesday is announced to me this morning, I have only time to inform you that, with my letter of the 5th of August, I had the honor to inclose to you a copy of the note on the subject of the claims of certain American citizens, presented on the 4th of July, in conformity with my instructions; and to transmit a copy of the answer of the Baron de Nagell, with my reply."

No. 6, (a.)

Baron de Nagell to Mr. Eustis.

[Translation.]

In the note which Mr. Eustis, Envoy Extraordinary and Minister Plenipotentiary of the United States of America, has done him the honor of addressing, on the 4th of July, to the undersigned Minister of Foreign Affairs, he submits anew, by order of his Government, to the consideration of the King the claims of certain American citizens, respecting certain confiscations made in 1809 and in 1810 by the Government of Holland.

These claims are there represented as founded on general acknowledged principles, and Mr. Eustis therein refers, in that regard, to a preceding note.

But far from admitting these principles in all their generality, the undersigned has constantly, in his answers, attached to them and adduced divers restrictions.

These restrictions are not discussed in the new official letter; he even approaches the question under another aspect, and confines himself to maintaining that the Government of Holland, in 1809 and in 1810, was, *incontestably, de facto.*

But, besides that, even on this hypothesis, the modifications brought to the principles claimed should preserve all their force, the characters which the note mentions should lead to a conclusion entirely opposite; since, with the exception of the proof, so insignificant in these latter times, of the recognizing of a Government by some other powers, that of Holland, at that time, could not present any of the traits which the note gives as proofs of the sovereignty. For, admitting the correctness of the exposition transmitted by the claimants, two American ships having discharged their cargoes in Holland, without the guaranty of a formal permission and *protection* from the constituted authority, the ex-Emperor of the French, notwithstanding, ordered their transportation to France and their confiscation.

The history of these two seizures would be then sufficient, alone, to authorize the maintenance that the Government of Holland was not then more *de facto* than *de jure;* and that, if the absolute possession of the sovereignty, and the exercise of rights of which she is in possession, form the *criterium* of it, it was that of France which was *de facto.* It was also on this consideration that the undersigned had orders to send the claimants to the French Government for the reparation of an act of violence and power, for which the Government of Holland had never been responsible.

But the assertion that the French Government was, in 1809 and in 1810, the sole Government *de facto,* is supported by still stronger proofs, and the nullity of that of Holland was repeated so publicly in the face of Europe that, in fine, they obliged a phantom of a King to abdicate a ridiculous authority.

In 1809 a message to the French legislative body announced that Holland was, in reality, only a part of France, and that it was time to make her return to the natural order. An official note gave information that she was only a company of merchants, and that the ex-Emperor did not consider her as a nation. The Moniteur stated that her ports and her coasts were about to be occupied by French troops and custom-house officers, as they had been after the conquest in 1794, and that all the means for regulating the administration were about to be employed. These troops and these custom-house officers actually came, and General Oudinot took possession, in a military manner, of the country.

By a formal treaty of March 26, 1810, the weak delegate of Napoleon was obliged to consent to it. French *licenses* were alone declared valid; the ex-Emperor alone pronounced upon the ships in contravention; the evacuation and the independence of Holland would not be granted but when England should have withdrawn the orders in council of 1807; the tenth article decreed that all merchandise coming in American ships, entered in the ports of Holland, after the 1st of January, 1809, should be sequestered and belong to France, to be disposed of as she should judge proper; and that every store-house (magazine) of prohibited articles should be seized in their territory. A shadow of independence still existed—the French troops did not occupy the capital; the last shadow must disappear, and the troops entered Amsterdam.

The undersigned ought, therefore, to make known to Mr. Eustis that the objections opposed to the pretensions of the claimants not having been removed, and the exposition transmitted in his last note still supporting these objections; besides, that the two seizures, of which mention is therein made, took place after the term of the 1st of January, 1809, and the last even the 10th of August, 1810, that is, after the union with France, the King can only continue to regard these claims as absolutely foreign to the present Government of the Netherlands.

The undersigned has the honor to renew to Mr. Eustis the assurances of his high consideration.

A. W. C. DE NAGELL.

HAGUE, *August* 14, 1816.

———

No. 6, (*b*.)

Mr. Eustis to the Baron de Nagell.

HAGUE, *September* 25, 1816.

The undersigned, Envoy Extraordinary and Minister Plenipotentiary of the United States of America, has the honor to acknowledge the receipt of the note of his excellency the Baron de Nagell, Minister of State for Foreign Affairs, dated the 4th of August, wherein it is maintained that the person exercising the supreme authority by which the property of certain American citizens was seized and confiscated, in the years 1809 and 1810, was not *de facto* the sovereign of this nation.

In stating in his last note (what he had not believed would have been contested) that Louis Napoleon was, at the time, sovereign *de facto*, the undersigned conceived himself fully justified by the circumstance of his exercise of all the functions of sovereignty for several years, in the face of all Europe; his reception and acknowledgment by the States General and the other constituted authorities of the nation, civil, military and ecclesiastic; and by his official intercourse with them from the time of his arrival in the country to that of his abdication.

His diplomatic relations with other nations were adduced as corroborating the evidence of his sovereignty; and it is still believed that an interchange of public ministers with Russia, France, Denmark, Prussia, Austria, Spain, and other powers, is not considered by the most respectable nations in Europe an insignificant evidence of sovereignty, even " in these modern times."

The treaty of March, 1810, which transferred the property in question to the French Government, appears in itself to have been an act of sovereignty not bearing any evidence of violence; and if it should be alleged that it was coerced by the power or influence of France, the rights of the claimants, whose property had been antecedently seized, ought not, it is contested, to be affected by an act over which they had no control.

The message to the French legislature in 1809, announcing " that it was time to embody Holland with the mother country;" the publication in the Moniteur, stating " that her ports and stores were to be occupied by French troops," &c.; the military possession of the capital by General Oudinot, as stated in the note of his excellency the Baron de Nagell, are not at variance with the well known facts, that the abdication of Louis Napoleon, the annexation of Holland to France, and the military occupancy of the capital by General Oudinot, all took place in July, 1810; whereas the order for depositing the property in the public stores was issued by the then King of Holland in the spring of 1809. The cargoes were generally so deposited in the course of that year—two of them in the winter or spring of 1810—and the whole of them (including that mentioned by the claimant as having been removed to Antwerp as late as August, 1810,) were transferred to France by virtue of the treaty of March, 1810. Whence it follows that the annexation of Holland to France, with the other circumstances cited in the note of his excellency, cannot be construed to affect the claims.

With respect to the limitations or restrictions attached by his excellency to the principles on which the claims are founded, the undersigned has had the honor to state, in a former note, that he was unable to discover in this case a just ground of exception to those principles, and must persist in objecting to the admission of any limitations or restrictions tending to impair them.

Availing himself of this occasion, the undersigned has the honor to present to his excellency the Baron de Nagell the assurance of his high consideration.

WILLIAM EUSTIS.

———

No. 7.

Extract of a letter from Mr. Adams to Mr. Alexander H. Everett, Chargé d'Affaires at the Hague, August 10, 1824.

"No principle of international law can be more clearly established than this: That the *rights* and the *obligations* of a nation, in regard to other States, are independent of its internal revolutions of government. It extends even to the case of conquest. The conqueror who reduces a nation to his subjection receives it subject to all its engagements and duties towards others, the fulfilment of which then becomes his own duty. However frequent the instances of departure from this principle may be in point of fact, it cannot with any color of reason be contested on the ground of right. On what other ground is it, indeed, that both the Governments of the Netherlands and of the United States now admit that they are still reciprocally bound by the engagements and entitled to claim from each other the benefits of the treaty between the United States and the United Provinces of 1782 ? If the nations are respectively bound to the stipulations of that treaty now, they were equally bound to them in 1810, when the depredations, for which indemnity is now claimed, were committed; and when the present King of the Netherlands came tō the sovereignty of the country, he assumed with it the obligation of repairing the injustices against other nations, which had been committed by his predecessors, however free from all participation in them he had been himself.

"It is fully understood that the European allied powers have acted upon this principle in their support of the claims of indemnities of their subjects upon the present Government of France; and France, on her part, claims from the United States not only the advantage of every stipulation contracted by the United States with the Government of Napoleon, but, by a latitude of construction of her own, privileges which were not intended to be conceded by them.

..... "With regard to the facts upon which the claims of indemnity of our citizens upon the Government of the Netherlands are founded, it is supposed they are of a nature not to be contested. They are generally cases of seizure and confiscation, by decrees and orders of the Government, of the most arbitrary and unjustifiable character. Some of them were doubtless attended with circumstances of more aggravation than others. That of the St. Michael, as represented in the pamphlet herewith forwarded, is particularly recommended to your attention. In using every proper exertion in your power to obtain from the Dutch Government a recognition of the justice of these claims, and provision for them, you will carefully avoid, both in the manner and substance of your applications, every appearance of useless importunity, and every expression of an irritating or offensive character. They must understand that, although pursued with moderation and forbearance, the claims will not be abandoned or renounced."

<hr>

No. 8.

Extract of a letter (marked No. 9) from Mr. Everett to the Secretary of State, dated Brussels, February 25, 1819.

"Sir: I have the honor to inclose a copy of the note which I have just written to Baron de Nagell, upon the subject of the confiscations of 1809–'10. I delayed writing it longer than I otherwise should have done, after my arrival here, in hopes of obtaining some further information upon the circumstances of the transaction from the consular agent at Amsterdam, to whom I wrote for that purpose, but without success. I have no documents here, besides those which I brought out, and the former correspondence. As the question, however, is at present upon the acknowledgment of a general principle, the details are of less consequence, and I fear very much that there will be no immediate necessity for entering upon them. I shall transmit to you the answer of this Government to the application as soon as I receive it."

<hr>

No. 8, (a.)

Mr. Everett to the Baron de Nagell.

Brussels, *February* 22, 1819.

The undersigned, chargé d'affaires of the United States, has the honor to inform his excellency Baron de Nagell, Minister of Foreign Affairs, that he is instructed to lay before his Majesty's Government once more the claims of those American citizens whose property was taken and confiscated in 1809–'10 by the arbitrary act of the late Government of Holland. The Government of the United States entertain a hope that, although his Majesty was not satisfied of the justice of the claim at the time when it was presented to him before, he will be induced, upon a further consideration of the subject, to adopt a different opinion, and to render that satisfaction to the claimants which, in the opinion of the American Government, they are strictly entitled to demand.

It is, perhaps, unnecessary to recapitulate in detail the various circumstances attending the several seizures that occurred under the acts in question. The undersigned will mention only one or two cases, which were marked by more than ordinary hardship, and which will show that the Government of Holland of that day not only violated the duties of hospitality and justice, but exhibited a total want of those sentiments of self-respect and common humanity that may often be found among the most barbarous nations. For example, no ruler of any people, civilized or uncivilized, is so utterly destitute of a sense of honor as to violate his own safe conduct, and employ the sacred pledge of his word as an instrument of mischief to a friendly power. If such instances have occurred once or twice in the history of modern Europe, they have been marked as an indelible stain on the character of their authors and of the age. Such, however, was the conduct of the Government of Holland, in the case of the brig Baltimore, which arrived at Amsterdam with a cargo of colonial produce, consigned to Messrs. Hope & Co., in the spring of 1809. Before she ventured to enter the port, she sent in to obtain information whether it would be safe to land her cargo, and received from her consignees a protection and license from the Government. Notwithstanding this, her cargo was deposited, as soon as landed, in the King's stores, and the greater part of it afterwards confiscated.

Two of the cases in question are even stronger than this. They are those of the Bacchus and the St. Michaels, which were driven by stress of weather and the accidents of the sea upon the Dutch coast. The former had been destined for Amsterdam, but on her arrival off that port was informed by her consignees that it was not safe to enter. On her way out she was wrecked. Her cargo, which was saved from the violence of the elements, was immediately seized, and subsequently confiscated by the Government. The St. Michaels was bound for Tonningen, and put into the Texel in distress, not being able to keep the sea. Will it be believed that, under these circumstances, the Government of Holland took possession of her by military force, and seized and confiscated her cargo? Thus, at the present day, and on the territory of one of the first maritime nations of Europe, the wrecks of friendly vessels were plundered under the public authority of the country. A description of violence not unknown, perhaps, to the piratical inhabitants of the northern coasts of Europe in the dark ages, but altogether unheard of as the act of a civilized community.

It is understood by the Government of the United States that the facts upon which these claims are founded are not disputed, but that the objection made to the liquidation of them arises from doubts that are entertained whether the present Government is bound, by the law of nations, to make compensation for injuries done by the former; and whether, even admitting this as a general principle, the claimants ought not rather, under the circumstances of the present case, to resort for redress to the Government of France, than to that of the Netherlands. In the expectation that the claim may be objected to on these grounds, the undersigned will take the liberty of adding a few remarks in confirmation of the view taken by the American Government of the principles of the law of nations as they apply to this case.

.It is regarded by the Government of the United States as a settled and unquestionable principle of public law, that the rights and obligations of nations are in no way affected by their internal revolutions in government. Political forms may be altered; different persons or families may be called to the administration; but, under every change that occurs, the new Government succeeds to all the obligations, as it does to all the rights, of the old one; or, in other words, the nation, though it has changed its rulers, continues to be bound by its own acts. If this were not the case, a nation, by changing its rulers or its form of government, could at any time release itself from all its engagements—a supposition too absurd to be refuted. Hence, the Dutch nation, having, through the agency of its public functionaries, confiscated the property of the American merchants, is bound to make reparation for this act of violence through the medium of the same rulers that committed it, while their functions continue, or of any other Government that may succeed them, since no act of the nation can discharge it from this duty except the fulfilment of it.

These principles are recognized by the great writers on national law. Grotius observes, that the debts contracted by a nation under one form of Government are binding upon it under another, and it is evident that the same reasoning applies to the reparation of an injury. The nation, he adds, cannot escape from the obligations of common honesty, however the form of Government may be altered. Whether it prefers a monarchy, an aristocracy, or a democracy, it is still bound to pay its debts. Puffendorf expresses the same opinions, in nearly the same words, and supports them at greater length: "Public debts," says he, "are not extinguished by the political changes that occur in a State. Those who maintain the contrary, have asserted that, as the State can only be bound by its own acts, it is not obliged to fulfil the engagements of an absolute monarch or an oligarchy whose authority reposes on force alone, and not on considerations of public good. But this reasoning is undoubtedly false, (*sans contredit frivole.*) The acts of the rulers of the State, whatever may be the source and tenure of their authority, are supposed to be the acts of the State itself."

A nation, therefore, cannot claim to be exempted from holding itself responsible for the acts of a former Government under the pretence that that Government was founded in usurpation. To do this, would be to suppose that nations possess the means and the right to decide upon each other's internal policy—a supposition which is not true in fact, and which no people that values its independence could for a moment admit. The actual rulers of every people must be received by all others as the rightful ones, and it would be not less presumptuous than injurious in foreigners to pretend to examine their title.

Accordingly, the writer last quoted extends his remarks further, to a state of things agreeing precisely with the view supposed to be taken by his Majesty's Government of the circumstances of the present claim. If the rightful sovereign succeeds in dethroning a usurper and recovering his authority, what course is to be taken in regard to the obligations contracted by the usurper during his reign? With the unerring instinct of an honest mind he decides this inquiry on principles too obviously just to be disputed. The sovereign may exercise his discretion in regard to general laws and political dispositions; but he is bound by all those acts and contracts of the usurper in which the rights of innocent third persons are concerned. Hence, on the view which is probably taken of this subject by his Majesty's Government, upon which the undersigned, as the agent of a foreign nation, is not at liberty to express an opinion, however he might otherwise be disposed to consider it as correct. His Majesty's Government is still responsible, in reason and justice, and according to the opinion of distinguished publicists, for those acts of the late Government by which the American merchants acquired a right to compensation—just as much as if the late Government were acknowledged by his Majesty to have been a legitimate one.

The undersigned will not multiply citations from written or public law to this effect. It is well known to his excellency that those which have already been quoted are the leading authorities upon these subjects. In confirmation of what has been advanced, he will, however, observe that it is believed by the American Government that the practice of nations is entirely conformable to the principles which have now been stated. On this point the undersigned begs leave to request the attention of his excellency to the following considerations:

1. In the practice of civilized nations, the stability of treaties, and other public acts of the Government, is never affected by revolutions or changes of dynasty. If this were not the case, the whole fabric of society would be unsettled at every political movement, and all the titles of private property rendered uncertain. Hence, the present Government of France has maintained, in general, the acts of the preceding one, and, amongst others, the sale of the national domains, though strongly urged by an opposite interest to the contrary; and though one of the German princes adopted a different principle, in this particular, his conduct has been publicly disapproved by the Diet of the German Confederation, which has thus given a solemn and most respectable sanction to the rule, that succeeding governments are bound by the acts of their predecessors in all cases where private interest is concerned. On this principle, the treaty concluded in 1782 between the United States of America and the United Provinces of the Netherlands is admitted by the American Government, and, it is presumed, by that of his Majesty, to be still in force. If this be the case, it was also in force in 1810, when the confiscations took place. These acts of violence were, therefore, breaches of a solemn and positive contract, as well as of justice, hospitality, and common humanity; and the present Government, with the obligation to observe the treaty which descended to them from the former one, inherited also the obligation to repair it where it had been broken.

2. It is evident that the obligation to redress a wrong is, at least, as strong, if not still more binding and positive than the obligation to pay a debt. Now, there is no rule of national conduct more firmly established and universally practised upon in Europe than that the debts of the nation shall be held sacred, whatever changes may occur in the Government. All the countries in Europe in which, by the late occurrences, the former sovereigns have been restored to their authority, furnish instances directly in point in support of this position. Among the rest, the Government of his Majesty has complied, in this particular, with the dictates of justice and the general usage. The present Government of France has not only assumed the public debt as it stood at the period of the King's return, but has stipulated, in a convention with Great Britain, to restore to their full original value those debts due British subjects which had been reduced to one-third by the revolutionary Governments. If the pecuniary obligations of a preceding Government, founded on contract, are thus maintained without dispute by the successor, what good reason can be given why pecuniary obligations of at least an equally imperious character, because created against the will of the party injured, should be disregarded?

3. The instances just mentioned, of public acts and public debts, are analogous to the case of the present claim, and may serve to illustrate the principles upon which it is founded. But the late transac-

tions between the present Government of France and the other nations of Europe furnish a series of cases still more nearly resembling that of the present claim, and some of a character precisely parallel. By the 19th article of the treaty of Paris of May 30, 1814, the present Government of France undertakes to liquidate private debts of various kinds due by the former Government to subjects of all the Governments that are parties to that treaty, and, it is believed, makes itself responsible for all demands that could have been made, agreeably to the law of nations, upon the former Government. It is hardly possible to imagine a more imposing authority in favor of the principle for which the American Government contends than this great transaction, to which the principal States in Europe were parties. All these powers undoubtedly considered Napoleon as a usurper, and were disposed to extend every indulgence to the present Government of France. Notwithstanding this, they gave their sanction to the arrangement by which that Government became responsible for his public and private contracts. It is presumed that the subjects of his Majesty, among the rest, enjoy at present the benefit of this arrangement, and have received payment from the present French Government of debts, to a large amount, that were due to them by the last. It would seem not unreasonable, therefore, that they should extend to other nations the same measure of justice of which they have obtained the advantage themselves.

It may be urged, however, that this arrangement cannot be brought as a precedent in the present case, because it makes no provision for spoliations and acts of violence committed by Napoleon and his agents. But this circumstance was owing to the peculiar situation of the contracting parties. They were just emerging from a state of mutual hostility. The acts of violence of which they severally had to complain were committed in time of war by declared enemies; and on that account, by the acknowledged law of nations, no satisfaction could be demanded for them, because no satisfaction could have been demanded of the party that committed them. This was the reason assigned for their exclusion, and is recorded as such by Mr. Von Schoell, the historian of these treaties. The French Government, however, went even further than this in regard to British subjects, and made reparation for confiscations and spoliations committed during the war; thus assuming a responsibility that did not properly belong, by the law of nations, to Napoleon himself. Acts of violence that did not come within the description of damages of war were provided for in these arrangements. In proof of this, the undersigned, to avoid prolixity, will mention only two remarkable instances, those of the Bank of Hamburg, and of the confiscations in the Duchy of Berg.

In May, 1813, Marshal Davoust took possession of the city of Hamburg, and imposed upon the inhabitants a contribution of forty-eight millions, which they considered it impossible to raise, and declined to pay. Disappointed in this, he placed his seals upon the bank of that place, and threatened, unless his demand was complied with, to remove the funds, and apply them to his own use. This threat he afterwards executed, and took from the bank an amount of more than fifteen millions, a great part of which was the property of foreigners and neutrals. A claim for compensation was made by the Senate of Hamburg upon the present French Government, and in 1816 a convention was concluded, by which this Government undertakes to repair the injury done by the former one, and appropriates a capital of ten millions to be applied to this purpose.

A private claim, founded on the confiscations in the Grand Duchy of Berg, is recognized by the fourth article of the convention of November, 1815, between France and the allies. A quantity of cotton and other colonial goods had been seized and confiscated in that Duchy by the agents of Napoleon, under his own immediate orders. Substitute the name of Louis Bonaparte for that of Napoleon, and this is an exact description of the case of the present claimants. What then was the course pursued by the French Government? "As soon as the allied armies had delivered France from Bonaparte and his agents," says Mr. Schoell, in his account of this transaction, "the owners claimed compensation for the damage they had sustained. The Chamber of Commerce of Cologne sent a distinguished counsellor to Paris to solicit justice from Louis XVIII. The Provisional Government, established by the allies at Dupeldorf, promised to present the claim to the Congress at Vienna, if it proved unsuccessful at Paris. It was unnecessary, however, to take this step; the cause of the claimants was too just not to be recognized by a legitimate Government. A full indemnity was granted them by France for the losses they had sustained, and interest at the rate of twelve per cent. from the date of the decree of seizure."

The undersigned indulges a hope that the authorities and examples now adduced will satisfy his Majesty's Government of the correctness of the principle upon which the present claim is founded. It is understood, however, that if this principle were admitted, the further objection will remain, that, under all the circumstances of the case, recourse should rather be had by the claimants to the Government of France than to that of the Netherlands. An opinion of this kind is supposed to be entertained by his Majesty's Government, founded on the presumption that the money resulting from the confiscations in question was finally transferred by Louis Bonaparte to Napoleon, in pursuance of an article in a secret treaty between the brothers of March, 1810, since made public.

The undersigned can hardly imagine, however, that his Majesty's Government will insist very seriously upon this objection. It is a principle too trivial even to admit of argument, that the sufferer must resort for redress to the person or power that did the wrong, and is not bound to follow his property through the several transfers that may have been made of it subsequently to the original confiscation. The Government of Holland deprived these claimants of their property, and to the Government of Holland they look for satisfaction. Whether these identical articles, or the value of them, was afterwards transferred to France for a sufficient consideration, or extorted from Holland by force, are questions upon which the claimants have no information, and do not even feel themselves at liberty to inquire. They have neither the pretension nor the right to interfere in the international concerns of the Governments of Europe.

With these remarks, the undersigned submits the claim to the justice and good faith of his Majesty's Government, and cannot but hope that, upon a consideration of it, they will be induced to regard it in the light in which it appears to the Government of the United States. That Government is so fully satisfied of the intrinsic justice of the demand that they feel it a duty to the sufferers to use all their influence with his Majesty's Government to procure them redress; and the undersigned is instructed to observe that the claim, though pursued with moderation and forbearance, can never be abandoned or relinquished.

The undersigned avails himself of this occasion to offer to his excellency Baron de Nagell the renewed assurance of his perfect respect.

A. H. EVERETT.

No. 9.

Extract of a letter (No. 20) from Mr. Everett to Mr. Adams, dated

BRUSSELS, *June* 21, 1819.

"I have the honor to inclose a translation of the answer of this Government to my note on the claims. It is, as I feared it would be, unfavorable. I shall immediately prepare a reply to it, and will, therefore, not trouble you at present with any remarks upon the import."

No. 9, *(a.)*

The Baron de Nagell to Mr. Everett.

[Translation.]

BRUSSELS, *June* 14, 1819.

The King entertained a confident expectation that the Government of the United States would be satisfied with the answers given to the applications of Mr. Eustis, respecting the American property sequestered in Holland in 1809 and 1810, and confiscated by the French Government, and would refrain from pressing this claim any further; but it appears, from the last note of Mr. Eustis, and from the memoir which the undersigned Minister of Foreign Affairs had the honor of receiving from Mr. Everett, chargé d'affaires of the United States of America, last February, that this is not their intention.

As this note and the memoir contain a statement of the same principles and arguments with the preceding notes, only more in detail, the Government of the Netherlands might have contented itself with a simple repetition of the former answers; but, in order to give a new proof of respect for the American Government, and also of impartiality and justice, the King directed that the facts should be examined anew with the greatest attention, and that the reasoning on which the claim is founded should be analyzed in all its parts. These two heads will form the leading divisions of the present answer.

In order to have a clear view of the facts, it is necessary to recur to the state of things at the time when they happened.

The continental system was then in full vigor in Holland, as in all the countries where Bonaparte exercised his supremacy. Some attempts of King Louis to mitigate the severity of it only ended in provoking his imperious brother to still more rigorous measures. Thus, upon the remonstrance, to use no harsher term, of the French minister and his agents, King Louis was obliged to annul his decrees of March 31 and June 30, 1809, by that of July 29 of the same year; to revoke the slight modifications which they had effected in the general system; and to decree that every American vessel which did [not] exactly comply with the existing orders should be sent back without being allowed to enter the Dutch ports. By a subsequent decree of February 1, 1810, American vessels were prohibited from entering at all, and this decree was communicated to the American consul at Amsterdam.

This state of things, the dependence of King Louis upon his brother, his inability to resist his brother's orders, and the consequent danger of arriving in this country, were well known by sad experience to all the nations that still ventured to maintain any commercial relations with Holland.

After this preamble, which serves to place the facts in their true point of view, the undersigned will proceed to correct the statements by which the parties interested have permitted themselves to disfigure these facts and to surprise the religion of their Government.

On the 24th of July, 1809, and not in the spring of that year, the Baltimore, Captain J. Philips, arrived at Amsterdam. According to some of her papers, she was bound for Tonningen. Thirty bales of cotton, and the staves which formed a part of her cargo, and which were provided with a certificate from the French consul at Baltimore, were delivered to the consignees. The rest of the cargo was stored, according to law, in the King's warehouses, and afterwards delivered to the French authorities in consequence of the treaty of March 6, 1810, and not, as was represented to Mr. Eustis, carried to Antwerp and sold there, with other American property, under order from the King of Holland. The license, or pretended protection, obtained by the captain for his free entry, was not a safe conduct, but was intended merely to protect him, if possible, against the French privateers. It made no alteration in the laws of blockade, to which this ship, as well as every other, was subject.

The Bacchus, Captain R. Johnson, arrived at Amsterdam January 11, 1810. The certificates of origin of her cargo appeared suspicious, and, until further information could be obtained, her cargo was deposited in the public warehouses, where it remained till the 10th of the following February, when an order came to send the ship and cargo back to sea, according to the above mentioned decree of February 1. The ship was wrecked in going out, and the cargo saved with difficulty. It was then sequestered until, by virtue of the treaty of 1810, it was given up to the authorities of France.

The St. Michael, Captain J. Dowson, bound ostensibly to Tonningen, put into the Texel in April, 1810, but was refused an entry. The captain declined obeying the order to go to sea again, under pretence of the bad state of his ship. He was permitted to take refuge in port till it could be ascertained whether the ship was able to keep the sea or not. Although the ship arrived after the conclusion of the treaty of 1810, by the tenth article of which it was provided that "the cargoes of all American vessels entering the ports of Holland after the 1st of January, 1809, should be sequestered, and should belong to France, to be disposed of according to circumstances and the political relations with the United States," the Government of Holland ascribed the entry of the St. Michael to necessity, and interpreted the article as merely authorizing the sequester of the cargo, instead of the delivery of it to the French authorities. The cargo was placed upon the list of American cargoes still in controversy, and it was not until after the union with France that it was delivered to the director of the French customs.

Mr. Eustis was therefore misinformed when he was led to suppose that these several cargoes had been confiscated by order of the Dutch Government. It is more probable, on the contrary, from the manifest intentions of that Government, which contributed very much to hasten its fall, that the confiscation would not have taken place unless the owners or consignees had been proved by legal process to have contravened the existing and publicly notorious system of blockade which placed all cargoes under a kind of sequester, and only permitted the entry of American vessels on that condition. And, properly speaking, it was not the treaty of 1810, but the union of Holland to France, that placed these cargoes in the power of the French. This union was effected soon after the conclusion of the treaty, and abrogated it. But at this epoch the greatest part of the American cargoes were still in the public warehouses. The political existence of Holland was then terminated. The country passed under the Government of France, and the sequestered property was sold by order and for account of the "Imperial Treasury," as Mr. Eustis observes, and the proceeds were accordingly placed there. The confiscation cannot, therefore, be equitably imputed to a government which had constantly attempted to prevent it; nor can indemnity be claimed of this Government, which had already ceased to exist when the confiscation was effected under the authority and for the profit of France. More than this, among the cargoes, ostensibly American, delivered to France, there were several undoubtedly owned in Holland, and others upon which claims existed in Holland for advances made upon them to the captains. While Louis was still nominally King, the Dutch owners and creditors were, nevertheless, obliged to address themselves to the French Government with their claims of restitution and indemnity. And there is even reason to suppose that the United States themselves made application, at the time, to Bonaparte, in favor of the American owners, so natural and just did it appear to demand compensation from the Government which had taken possession of the property.

These details have been drawn from authentic sources; but even if the seizures had been made in the manner described by the parties interested, in their statements to the American Government, they would lead to a conclusion diametrically opposite to the one that has been drawn by that Government.

For, in fact, if these seizures had (to use the expressions of the memoir) borne all the marks of "a revolting breach of the first duties of hospitality and justice; a total want of those sentiments of self-respect and common humanity to be found among the most barbarous nations; the perfidious violation of a safe conduct for the purpose of doing mischief to a friendly power; the plunder of a wreck, and acts of violence of a description known only to the piratical inhabitants of the northern coasts of Europe in the dark ages," what other consequence would follow, but that Holland at this period had no Government that deserved the name; that this was a time of anarchy, when all social ties, and all the principles of the law of nations were trampled under foot; a blank in the moral existence of a people otherwise so celebrated for its hospitality, its justice, its humanity, its respect for the law of nations? And, were it even possible to admit that a legitimate Government is responsible for the acts of the usurping Government which it overthrew, it would still be necessary to except from the rule such acts as these; for it would be evidently confounding words and ideas to apply to such a period, and to such proceedings, the names and relations of Government, of social order, and of the law of nations.

But, without pushing to exaggeration the circumstances which preceded and attended the confiscation of the American property, it may easily be shown that Holland had ceased for a long time to form an independent State, under a Government acting for itself and responsible for its conduct. Vattel decides that a people which has passed under the dominion of another people no longer constitutes a State, and that the law of nations is not applicable to it. "Such," says he, "were the nations and kingdoms subdued by the Romans. Most of those even whom they honored with the name of friends and allies were not real States. They were governed within by their own laws and magistrates, but without they were compelled to obey in everything the orders of Rome." Certainly, in 1809 and 1810, Holland was obliged, not less at home than abroad, to obey in everything the orders of France.

Having thus corrected the statement of facts, the undersigned will proceed to examine the argumentative part of the memoir.

It has been somewhat difficult to discover the passages cited from the two ancient writers, which are simply quoted without reference to the places where they are found. A single observation is sufficient to destroy the force of those remarks of Grotius and Puffendorf which appear to be intended, and that is, that they relate to a matter entirely different from the one in question. Hence, it was necessary to recur to induction and analogy to make them apply. The undersigned has sought in vain for any direct decisions on the principle in controversy; and, as it may be presumed that they would not have escaped the observation of the writer of the memoir, it is fair to conclude that none exist. The quotation from Grotius appears to be taken from chapter ix, book 2, of his Treatise on the Law of Peace and War. It is sufficient to transcribe it to show that it is foreign to the question.

After quoting an obscure passage from Aristotle upon the point whether the debts of the State ought or ought not to be paid when the form of government has been changed, which, from the expressions of the philosopher, he appears to have considered doubtful, Grotius adds: "The debts contracted by a free people are not extinguished when they give themselves a King; for the people is still the same, and remains in possession of what belongs to it as a people. It even retains the sovereignty within itself," &c. But first, this chapter, with Barbeyrac's notes, clearly shows that the ancient publicists were not agreed upon this point. Besides, it is one thing to discuss whether a free people which voluntarily gives itself a King, and which still remains in possession of its property, and retains the sovereignty within itself, &c., ought to pay the public debts and perform the engagements which it acknowledges; and another, to determine whether a Government which has liberated a people that had been forced to renounce its form of government and all the attributes of independence, and to receive a King from the hands of a foreign usurper, is bound to repair all the injuries of which this people was only the involuntary instrument, and to be responsible for all the acts of the mock government which it came to destroy.

To apply to this case the reasoning of Grotius in regard to debts and contracts, acknowledged by treaties and special conventions, would be to take for granted the point in dispute. The indemnity now claimed does not belong to the class of acknowledged debts and contracts. On the contrary, the Government of the Netherlands does not admit, and has never admitted, that it was due. The memoir assumes, therefore, precisely the point in controversy, which is the existence of the obligation.

Puffendorf repeats the opinion of Grotius nearly in the same words, and admits, of course, the same answers. But, besides that, he confessed that there are differences of opinion upon the subject, and that the passage, like that of Grotius, refers to the obligation which a nation is under, notwithstanding the changes in the form of government to adhere to its treaties, contracts, and financial engagements. The argument he uses favors the opinion of the Government of the Netherlands, it being that the people still possess the property to which the debt is attached. But at the union of Holland and France the American cargoes were carried away and confiscated, so that Holland no longer possesses the property to which the debt, if it be one, is attached.

But every one knows that inductions and analogies drawn from the principles of the law of nations lead naturally to endless discussion, since it is always easy to oppose authority to authority, and citation to citation.

In proof of this remark, it would be sufficient to mention the qualifications with which the two writers who have been quoted, express their opinion even in regard to obligations apparently so evident, as those of fulfilling contracts and paying public debts. Grotius, nevertheless, declares plainly that neither the nation nor the legitimate King are bound to perform the engagements of a usurper.

Puffendorf repeats the same decision, and declares, that the legitimate sovereign, on recovering his rights, may annul the acts of the usurper, if he judges it for the public good; and he applies this remark not only to laws, but to other measures prejudicial to the State.

Martens, generally so severe in regard to the observation of treaties, acknowledges that the question whether a treaty is obligatory or not depends upon the justice or injustice of the means employed to obtain it. On the principles of the memoir, indemnities, compensations, debts, and treaties, are here synonymous categories. Let us, then, apply to them the principles by which publicists limit the obligations of the law of nations, and these restrictions will finish the answer of the Government of the Netherlands.

If it were thought proper to enlarge upon all the assertions in the memoir, it would be easy to show, by citations from the last of these writers, (whose opinions have the more authority from his being one of our cotemporaries,) under what restrictions it is necessary to receive the statement in the memoir, that the actual rulers of every country must be received by all others as the rightful ones, and that it would be not less injurious than presumptuous in foreigners to pretend to question this title. The history of almost all the great diplomatic transactions and the causes of many modern wars attest the contrary.

But, instead of entering upon this incidental discussion, the undersigned will rather proceed to examine the further arguments contained in the memoir.

The first of these is taken from the usage of civilized nations, and it is alleged that, according to this usage, the stability of treaties is never affected by revolutions or change of dynasty. But, besides that it would be easy to cite many treaties that have been abolished by revolutions, this question does not relate to treaties and stipulations; and, consequently, the remainder of the paragraph falls of itself.

The indemnities to which France was obliged to consent by the late treaties appear to the author another argument in his favor.

But if the duty of legitimate Governments, upon their restoration, to redress the wrongs and repair the injuries occasioned by the illegitimate Governments which have abolished and succeeded, were founded upon the broad and universally acknowledged principles supposed in the memoir, the allies would not have failed to appeal to these principles in the preambles of the treaties, or special conventions, by which they thought proper to stipulate the partial restitutions here alleged as examples. These stipulations would then have been superfluous. Their introduction is, therefore, an indirect proof that the contracting parties did not consider these indemnities as incontestably due by the law of nations.

The objects of these stipulations are also worthy of remark. That of the convention with Great Britain was the payment, in their full original value, of debts due to the subjects of his Britannic Majesty, reduced (tiercés) by the French revolutionary Government.

Why did not the other nations who were equally injured by this reduction obtain the same restitution? The answer is to be found in the particular circumstances that attended the conventions. In proof of this, it is only necessary to compare the treaty of Paris of 1814 with that of 1815. So far was France from considering the indemnities demanded of her as the natural and ordinary result of the common principles of the law of nations, that the Duke de Richelieu avowed the contrary. In communicating to the House of Deputies the treaties and conventions that France had just contracted, he did not hesitate to declare publicly (and he has not been contradicted by the other contracting parties) that these stipulations were the result of extraordinary circumstances in which France found herself placed by the fatality of events. In a different position, he adds, and at other times, we should have to present to the House only one of those acts which compose the historical collection of the public law of nations, and resemble each other so nearly in character. But it is not so with the transaction we have now to lay before you. It bears—it must necessarily bear—the marks of the situation in which the contracting parties were respectively placed, as also of the interests and considerations resulting from a state of things unheard of in history, unique in its nature, and which will be so, of course, in its consequences. The nation has been obliged to satisfy not only the pretensions, but the alarms of Europe. Without the power to deny or resist the incontestable superiority which demanded painful sacrifices, it has seen in those sacrifices the only means of obtaining peace. France finds herself, by a combination of circumstances, compelled to answer for all the sacrifices that have been made, and all the losses and injuries that have been sustained. The severity of this principle might have been softened in its application by the equity and magnanimity of the sovereigns; but particular considerations influenced their decision, and the recollection of the violence and oppression by which they had suffered led the sovereigns, as it were, involuntarily to adopt measures repugnant to their private feelings, so that their determinations are marked by passions which their personal generosity disapproves.

If, then, the treaties and conventions with France furnish no precedent in this case, the other examples mentioned in the memoir are also inapplicable, because they are not at all parallel to the claim in question.

By the 19th article of the treaty of March 30, 1814, the French Government merely engaged to liquidate the debts which it should be found to owe in foreign countries, by virtue of contracts and other formal engagements, passed between individuals or private establishments and the French authorities, as well for supplies as for lawful debts; but, far from thinking, with the memoir, that it is scarcely possible to imagine a more imposing authority in favor of the principle maintained by the American Government, the Government of the Netherlands is perfectly satisfied that this article was not intended to operate in nearly so extensive a way as is supposed in this paragraph. Considering that France had received all the resources of Holland for the first ten months of the year 1813, this Government thought it just that France should pay to Holland, out of those receipts, the interest on the debt that accrued within that period. It was agreed to refer the decision of the principle to arbitrators chosen from neutral powers. The decision was in the negative.

If, according to the remark of Mr. Schoell, historian of the treaties of Paris, no satisfaction could be demanded for those who had to complain of acts of violence committed during the war, because no satisfaction could have been demanded of the party that committed them; still less can this satisfaction be demanded of a party which not only did not commit them, but which endeavored, by all means in its power, to prevent them; and has derived no advantage from them.   If any Government was bound to make this satisfaction, it was the French Government, and that alone.

Mr. Everett appears, however, to find it difficult to suppose that the Government of the Netherlands will insist seriously on the propriety of appealing for redress to the French Government, it being, according to him, a principle too well known to require proof, that the suffering party must resort for redress to the author of the wrong; and that the Government of Holland having deprived the claimants of their property, it is to that Government they are to resort for satisfaction.

The undersigned has already proved, by facts, that it was not the Government of Holland, but that of France, which committed the spoliation.   And he will permit himself, in his turn, to state a comparison, the application of which is too obvious to require to be pointed out.   Certain turbulent neighbors compel the head of a family to quit his house, and place an intruder there.   Certain strangers, notwithstanding the prohibitions and warnings of this intruder, are imprudent enough to frequent the house, and are forced to leave the property there.   Soon after, the same neighbors eject the intruder, and take possession of everything they find in the house.   The head of the family succeeds at length in recovering possession.   Is it from him, or from the neighbors, that the strangers are to demand satisfaction?

It remains to examine two other instances—those of the Bank of Hamburg and of the Grand Duchy of Berg.   But, in order to make the first of these support the principles of the memoir, it would be necessary (supposing the greater part of the money given up to Marshal Davoust really belonged to foreigners and neutrals) that these foreigners and neutrals should have addressed their claims, not to the French Government, but to the magistrates of Hamburg, who succeeded the magistrates that permitted the bank to be plundered.

The influence of the events of 1815 was the sole inducement with France to consent to a special convention on this subject, on which nothing had been stipulated in the treaty of 1814.   The same force which compelled the Senate at Hamburg to permit money to be taken from the bank, had compelled the Government of Holland to permit the seizure of the American cargoes.   In both cases, the French Government was the author of the spoliation.

The claim on account of the spoliations in the Grand Duchy of Berg proceeded on different grounds. Agreeably to an order of May 8, 1813, a seizure was made of colonial goods in possession of several individuals, a part of which had even been purchased of the French Government.   They had been compelled to pay, a second time, duties and double duties of impost, although they had paid, at the proper time, what was lawfully due.   (Treaty of 1815, Art. 4.)   The petitioners demanded restitution, not of the Government which succeeded that of the Grand Duchy of Berg, but of the French Government; and it is not astonishing that so just a claim was admitted.

To conclude: The undersigned has proved that it was not the Government of Holland that deprived the claimants of their property, but that of France.   Had it even been the former, the principle that the present Government of the Netherlands is responsible for all the acts of the preceding Governments, from 1795 to 1813, is one which the King cannot admit without restriction.   If it might be admitted in regard to a succession of legitimate Governments, it could not be in regard to a Government established by violence, and which was not itself responsible for the acts to which it was forced by the tyranny of a foreign usurper; that the political nullity of this Government had long been a matter of public notoriety; and that if, notwithstanding daily warnings and known prohibitions, foreign merchants or navigators exposed themselves to suffer by it, and neglected to claim satisfaction at the time, in the proper quarter, they can no longer demand it from the Government of the Netherlands, which had no part in the measures imposed upon the former Governments of Holland, and derived no advantage from them.

The undersigned has the honor to renew to Mr. Everett the assurance of his distinguished consideration.

A. W. C. de NAGELL.

No: 10.

Extract of a letter from Mr. Everett to the Secretary of State, dated

BRUSSELS, *July* 18, 1819.

"I have the honor to transmit, inclosed, a copy of my reply to Baron de Nagell's note of the 14th ultimo, on the subject of the claims."

No. 10, (a.)

Mr. Everett to Baron de Nagell, dated

BRUSSELS, *July* 15, 1819.

In the several notes that have been presented on the part of the American Government to that of the Netherlands, on the subject of the American property sequestered and confiscated in the ports of Holland, in 1809 and 1810, it has been assumed as an acknowledged fact, that the acts by which the owners were deprived of their property were performed under the authority of the Government of Holland.   In the note dated June 14, which the undersigned, chargé d'affaires of the United States of America, has had the honor to receive from his excellency the Minister of Foreign Affairs, in answer to his note upon this subject of February 22, it is stated, as one of the grounds upon which his Majesty's Government decline to admit this claim, "that it was not the Government of Holland that deprived the claimants of their property, but that of France."

This objection is preliminary in its nature to every other, and, if well founded, is of course decisive. The undersigned apprehends, however, that the difference between the views of the two Governments upon this point is more apparent than real, and that no disagreement can possibly exist respecting the material facts, since they are all matters of public notoriety. These facts are no other than that the several decrees of March, June, and July, 1809, mentioned in the answer, were promulgated by authority of King Louis; that the sequestration of the American property was effected by his officers, and that the treaty of March 16, 1810, by which this property was conveyed to France, was concluded by his minister and executed by his agents. They are all admitted in the answer, and might be proved, if necessary, by official documents. Upon these facts a question may indeed be made, whether the Government of Holland was influenced, in the adoption of these measures, by that of France in such a way as to make the responsibility for them properly devolve upon the latter; and where it is asserted in the answer that the property was in fact confiscated by France, nothing more seems to be meant than to assert the existence of such an influence. But this question, as far as it affects the case, is a question of right alone.

It is observed, indeed, in the answer, that, "properly speaking, it was not the treaty of March 16, 1810, but the union of Holland to France, which placed these cargoes in the power of the French, for that the greater part of them were still in the public warehouses at the time of the union." But as it is repeatedly admitted that these cargoes were given up to the French in consequence of the treaty, and while Louis was still King, (eut encore le nom de regne,) the former remark can only be supposed to refer to their remaining in the public warehouses, after they had been delivered to the French authorities—a circumstance which, if true, has no connexion with the merits of the case.

The material facts being agreed between the parties, the only objections made to the claim by the Government of the Netherlands are the two following: First. That the French Government was properly responsible, in the first instance, for this confiscation; and, secondly, that, supposing the Dutch Government of that day to have been responsible, the present Government has not succeeded to the obligation. Both these objections were anticipated by the undersigned in his note, and it will be his object, at present, to support the views there taken of them against the arguments contained in the answer. He will first, however, briefly notice some other points of less importance in that part of the answer which is termed a correction of the statement of facts contained in the note.

The three cases of the Baltimore, the Bacchus, and the St. Michael, mentioned in the note, were, of course, intended merely as examples of the character of the transactions upon which the claim is founded. Any errors that might have occurred in the statement of either of these cases would not, therefore, have affected the general principles of the claim. But, upon comparing the account given of them in the answer with that of the note, the undersigned is unable to perceive any considerable variation, much less any correction of such importance as to warrant the charge made upon the sufferers, of permitting themselves to "disfigure facts, and surprise the religion of their Government."

After a commentary upon these cases mentioned in the note, it is observed in the answer, that "Mr. Eustis was mistaken in supposing that these several cargoes had been confiscated by order of the Dutch Government." Of the three cases, two only had been mentioned by Mr. Eustis; and of both of these, it is expressly observed in the answer that they were delivered to the French authorities by virtue of the treaty of March 16. This was what the American Government and Mr. Eustis mean by confiscation. Again: Mr. Eustis is said to have been misinformed as to the fact, that the cargo of the Baltimore was carried to Antwerp and sold there under authority from the King of Holland. But this inaccuracy, which occurred in Mr. Eustis' note of July 4, 1816, is corrected by himself in his subsequent note of September 25, of the same year, (the one referred to in the beginning of the answer,) where he observes, that "the cargoes in general *(including that mentioned by the claimants as having been removed to Antwerp as late as August,* 1810,) were transferred to France by virtue of the treaty of March, 1810."

The cargo of the St. Michael, it is observed in the answer, was not subjected to the full operation of the treaty of 1810, but was regarded as a doubtful case, and not delivered to the French till after the union. In this respect, there is certainly a difference in the information given to the two Governments, since it is asserted in a statement of this case, drawn up under the direction of the sufferers, by a counsellor of New York, that the cargo was transferred to France by virtue of the treaty. But the variation, even here, is not material. The seizure of a vessel which put into port in distress, to obtain assistance, was not authorized under any pretence by the existing system or the law of nations, and, from the time it took place, gave the sufferers a just claim to restoration or indemnity, not to be affected by any subsequent transaction; so that, in this case, the mere act of seizure amounted to confiscation.

With regard to the protection granted to the captain of the Baltimore, there is no variation, in fact, between the statements in the answer and the note. The undersigned was aware that it was intended as a protection against French privateers; nor did the parties interested claim, in consequence of it, any exemption from the system established at the time the vessel arrived. Had any deficiency or irregularity been found in the ship's papers, the parties would have submitted to confiscation without complaint. But, having been furnished by the King with a special pass to protect them from dangers attending the entry, they had a right to consider the faith as well as the justice of the Government, pledged to allow them a fair trial.

The date of the arrival of the Baltimore is said, in the answer, to have been on the 24th of July, 1809, and not in the spring of that year, as stated in the note. This variation arose from an accidental substitution in the note of the time of the ship's departure from America for the time of her arrival, and is, obviously, immaterial.

These are all the differences which the undersigned has been able to discover between the two accounts. It will be seen that, without adverting to an immaterial date, the supposed errors are three in number, two of which are attributed to Mr. Eustis; that one of these had already been corrected by Mr. Eustis, and that, in regard to the other, the writer of the answer is himself mistaken by his own admission. The remaining error, attributed to the undersigned, if real, is also immaterial; were it otherwise, it would afford but little foundation for so serious a charge.

The undersigned will now proceed to consider the arguments by which the two principal objections are supported in the answer.

The first of these objections, that the Government of France, and not that of Holland, was properly responsible at the time of the confiscation, and, consequently, is so at present, is maintained on the broad grounds that, without taking into view the particular circumstances of this affair, the Dutch nation was not, at that time, responsible for any of its actions, from the state of political dependence in which it stood with regard to France. This objection is supported by the authority of Vattel, who observes, that "when a people has passed under the Government of another people, it no longer constitutes a State, and is not at liberty to make use *(se servir)* of the law of nations." The applicability of this principle to the present claim depends upon the time when Holland passed under the Government of France; and this point is decided in the answer, which asserts, after mentioning the epoch of the union of Holland to France, "at that time Holland passed under the Government of France." Now, the confiscations were made before this period. Holland, therefore, at the time of the confiscation, had not, by the admission of the answer, passed under the Government of France, and the remark of Vattel is consequently inapplicable.

But, without taking advantage of this admission, let us grant, with Vattel, that States nominally independent, but substantially subject, like the allies of ancient Rome, are not at liberty to make use of the law of nations. They have no right then to claim the title and privileges appertaining to independent States. Have they, therefore, a right to exemptions and privileges which independent States never pretended to claim? Have they a right to plunder individuals, and plead their insignificance in justification? Such pretensions are as much at variance with the doctrine of Vattel as with common sense; for his object is clearly to restrain, rather than enlarge, the privileges of this class of States. It may safely be asserted as a general principle, that whatever people claims the title and exercises the powers of an independent State, shall be responsible as such for its conduct. Where, on any other supposition, is the line to be drawn between dependence and independence? There are always two or three powerful States in Europe which form the central points of the political system, and influence, in a greater or less degree, the movements of all the rest. Are these, then, to be the only responsible Governments? Even if this doctrine were admitted—if it were allowed that a people might sustain, at once, the double character of an independent nation and a subject province, it would be impossible to establish the fact that this state of things really existed in Holland at the time in question. It is well known, on the contrary, that Holland was, by no means, the least independent of the different powers whose policy was then directed by that of France; and that the reign of King Louis exhibited a continual struggle between him and his brother; that all intercourse between the two countries was prohibited during the greater part of it by the decrees of both, and that the final union of Holland to France was, probably, produced by the repugnance of Louis to carry into effect the Napoleon system.

Whether we look at the general relations existing at the time between France and Holland, or at the particular circumstances of the transaction in question, it is equally evident that the Government of Holland was immediately answerable for the confiscated property. If Holland was compelled by unjust means to agree to the stipulation in the tenth article of the treaty of 1810—if, in other words, the amount of property confiscated was at that time forcibly extorted from Holland by France, Holland, no doubt, had a good claim on France for restoration; and that claim and its corresponding obligation have descended to the respective Governments now established in the two countries, and are still in force. But this circumstance can in no way affect the claim of the sufferers, whose property was taken by the Dutch Government.

Hence, there is no hardship in the responsibility which devolves upon the Government of the Netherlands, supposing even that the property passed immediately into the hands of France, and that the Dutch Government derived no benefit from the transaction. The Dutch Government and the claimants were alike, on that supposition, the innocent victims of coercion, and the claim of each for redress is good when prosecuted in the proper quarter. The claimants have a right to demand restitution from Holland, and Holland, in her turn, may require it from France. In this way complete justice will be done to both. But if justice is denied to the sufferers by the Government of the Netherlands, they have no means whatever of obtaining redress. They can have no claim on the Government of France, since the property was not taken by France from them, but from Holland. If it were admitted even that they were at liberty to follow their property through the hands of the Dutch Government, and demand restitution of it at those of France, they want the necessary means of proving their claim, because they have no knowledge of the conditions upon which this property was transferred to France. There is no privity between them and the French Government. They only know that their property was seized by Holland. They have, indeed, seen the treaty of 1810 since it was published; but neither the American Government, nor the sufferers, nor anybody but the Government of the Netherlands, possesses the information which would authorize a resort to the Government of France for redress on the ground of that treaty. If the Government of the Netherlands are entitled to make such a claim, they are able to show it; and it would be a reflection on the justice of the French Government, and the vigor of that of his Majesty, to suppose that it would not receive due attention.

Is it true, however, that the Government of Holland derived no benefit from making this seizure? Was it, then, an act of wanton and useless injustice, committed without aid or motive, for the profit of France? More probably a regard for what he thought the public good induced King Louis to agree to this measure as a less evil, rather than expose himself to a greater. He appropriated to the public service a certain amount of property belonging to individuals, to avoid some important mischief with which the body politic was threatened in the event of his refusal.

Perhaps the existence of the nation could only have been preserved on this condition. This, then, was private property taken for the public service, and this is one of the cases in which the obligation of indemnity is most strongly insisted on by the writers on public law. Admit that the policy of Louis was questionable—that he would have done better to sacrifice a precarious and degraded existence, which lasted only three months longer, rather than stain the national character by an act of such signal violence. Still, the innocent sufferers are not responsible for his political errors, and the Dutch Government, far from deriving no benefit from the transaction, were indebted to it, on this supposition, for the very being of the nation.

It follows from these remarks that the influence exercised by France in this affair has no effect on the claim; and that the French Government, if responsible at all, is responsible to the Government of the Netherlands, and not to the sufferers. The undersigned has already examined the assertion which is made in the answer in support of this objection, that the property was, in fact, confiscated by the Government of France, and not of Holland, and has shown that the contrary is repeatedly admitted in the answer itself. He does not think it necessary to notice particularly the comparison of the head of a family, expelled from his house, by which his excellency has thought proper to illustrate his views. It has no effect on the argument, since, like most other comparisons, it takes for granted the point in dispute. It would be easy to meet it by another, in which the point in controversy should, in like manner, be assumed in favor of the United States; but as this would add nothing, in reality, to the strength of the case, the undersigned will rather proceed at once to the second objection.

The responsibility of the Dutch nation at the time being established, its responsibility at present follows, of course, on the plainest principles of public law. A nation is a moral person, and responsible as such for its actions; this obligation is attached to its existence as a nation, and not to the person of its rulers. It is applicable to all the acts of the nation. It is not affected by changes of magistracy or Government, and can only be destroyed by the destruction of the body politic.

These principles appear to be admitted in the answer under certain restrictions. A distinction is attempted, in the first place, between "undisputed debts and engagements acknowledged by treaties and conventions," and those of a different character. It is denied that the passages quoted from Grotius and Puffendorf refer to any obligations but those of the former class; and the undersigned is said to have begged the question in applying them to the present claim.

This distinction, however, is entirely unsupported, both by the language of these writers and the reason of the case. It is evident that the existence of an obligation does not depend, in any degree, upon its being acknowledged, or upon the form of its acknowledgment. If the debtor, by refusing to acknowledge his debt, could release himself from the obligation to pay it, the situation of the creditor would be precarious indeed. There is no foundation in the language of these writers for this dangerous distinction. On the contrary, both their expressions, and the reasons upon which they found the obligation, apply equally to all just debts. "The people," says Grotius, "remains the same." Moral obligation is attached to national, as it is to personal identity; and is no more affected by a change in the rulers of the people, than in the agents of an individual. Nor is it correct, as stated in the answer, that this obligation is attached by Puffendorf to the possession of the identical articles of which restitution is claimed. The passage has been misunderstood by the writer of the answer. It is as follows: "The nation is not a debtor precisely in its quality of body politic, but as a holder of common property, so that the debt is attached to the possession of this property and passes with it." The property meant is the general stock of the nation. In the course of his remarks upon this subject, Puffendorf considers the case of a usurper, who has confiscated the property of individuals and transferred it to foreigners; and decides that the transaction is valid, and that the sufferers cannot follow the property through his hands, and reclaim it of the actual holders. He thus determines, expressly, that the obligation to restore is not attached to the possession of the thing taken.

Thus, both the letter and spirit of these passages are directly applicable to the present claim. Other passages may also be produced in which the doctrine of national responsibility is laid down in a still more extensive way, so as to preclude the possibility of this distinction. Vattel remarks, (book 2, chapter 18,) that "a nation is obliged to repair the damage it may have occasioned and the injuries it may have committed;" and in book 1, chapter 4, "The sovereign being invested with the public authority, and with all that constitutes the moral personality of the nation, is bound by all its obligations, and possessed of all its rights." The obligation is attached to the nation, without reference to the person of the reigning sovereign, who is, on the contrary, expressly subjected to all the obligations of the nation. These ideas are repeated in various other passages of the same writer; and authority is given to the party injured to demand reparation, and to pursue it, if necessary, by violence. Grotius, (book 3, chapter 17, section 1,) applies this principle to the particular kind of injury inflicted in this case. Nations at war are not to deprive neutrals of their property; and if they do, they are to make compensation. No reference is made to the person of the reigning sovereign. These passages contain a general statement of the principle of national responsibility, the application of which, in the particular case of a succession in the Government, and a change in its form, is made in those quoted before.

A second distinction is attempted on the ground that this obligation was contracted under the reign of a usurper, and that such obligations are not binding. Whatever may be thought of the general correctness of this principle, it cannot be applied to the present claim, because the Government under which it arose was for that purpose, at least, legitimate. Every established Government is legitimate as far as foreign nations are concerned. In such cases, therefore, there is no room for the question how far the obligations of a usurper are binding. The independence of a nation consists in its right to exclude all foreign interference in its Government, in other words, in the obligation which all foreign nations are under to recognize as legitimate the established system. Foreigners being bound to admit the legitimacy of the established system in the interest of the nation, the nation is, of course, bound to admit it in the interest of foreigners. The great diplomatic transactions, and the modern wars referred to in the answer, far from contradicting this principle, afford the strongest confirmation of it. These wars were made and these treaties concluded professedly for the express purpose of securing the exercise of the right of self-government, and are never defended on any other ground. The distinction, then, is radically vicious, or at least entirely foreign to the present claim.

These principles were advanced in a note, and supported by some authorities, particularly that of Puffendorf. It was, therefore, with some surprise that the undersigned perceived the name of this writer cited in the answer in favor of this objection. Puffendorf certainly refutes the objection at considerable length, and applies to it, as was observed in the note, the epithet "sans contredit frivoli." He lays down the principle above mentioned, that the acts of a Government, whatever may be its title, are legitimate and binding as far as they regard foreign nations. It is true, as the answer remarks, that he supposes a case in which the lawful sovereign may annul the acts of a usurper. This is nothing more than the converse of his former principle, and is stated in the following terms: "As to the acts of a usurper, *whose operation is wholly interior*, the lawful sovereign may annul them upon his return," &c. It is only necessary to cite the passage, in order to show that, taken in connexion with the preceding remarks, it favors, instead of opposes, the views of the American Government.—(See *Puf. lib., chap.* 12, *sect.* 2.)

Grotius, says the answer, declares plainly that neither the people nor the legitimate sovereign is bound to keep the engagement of a usurper. It has already been shown that this question is foreign to the claim, and Grotius confirms this opinion by the qualification annexed to the above remark: "The King and people are bound to make restitution of what has come to their use."—(*Grotius, lib.* 2, *chap.* 14, *section* 14.)

The passage from Martens respecting treaties extorted by force is not applicable to the present claim. The analogy, as far as any exists, is favorable to the claimants. If treaties extorted by force are not binding, property extorted by force ought to be restored.

The views taken by the American Government of the law of nations, as applied to this claim, were supported in every point by the examples of national usage mentioned in the note. These examples were taken from the history of the latest times and the most important events. They were examples of a great nation, with the sanction of most of the other great nations of Europe, in particular of the Netherlands, making itself responsible for contracts made and spoliations committed under a foreign Government declared to be founded in usurpation. The undersigned will conclude this reply by a few remarks upon the objections made in the answer to the applicability of these examples.

The example of the indemnities granted to foreign nations by France in the late treaties of Paris is objected to on the ground that the principle of indemnity was not acknowledged by France, but that the allied powers took advantage of their situation to force upon her an arrangement which was in itself unjust, and which affords no rule for the conduct of other nations. When it is considered that the Government of the Netherlands, if not an immediate party to these treaties, was intimately allied to the powers that concluded them, and has participated largely in the pecuniary benefits resulting from this particular provision, the objection appears somewhat extraordinary. It is stated by Schoell that this Government has received from France sixty millions of francs, to be employed in the construction of fortresses, an equivalent for twenty-two millions granted as indemnity, and more than eighty millions in satisfaction of pecuniary debts contracted by the former authorities. The responsibility of the present French Government for the acts of the former one is, of course, supposed in all these payments; and the Government of the Netherlands could not possibly have consented to accept these sums, unless it had approved the principle upon which they were paid. Whatever opinion might be formed by indifferent persons of the character of these transactions, it is evident that they may safely be alleged as authority against the parties concerned, or those that derived a profit from them.

But, without insisting on this point, it may easily be shown that the principle of indemnity was, in fact, admitted by France herself. It is even admitted in the passage cited in the answer from a speech of the Duke de Richelieu in the French House of Deputies. The Duke complains, indeed, that the principle was enforced with too much severity. The rigor of it might have been alleviated by the equity and magnanimity of the sovereigns. What is this but saying that the principle in itself is just? Again, the recollections retained by the sovereigns of the violence that had been exercised by France within their territories, prevented them from giving way to those generous sentiments which they might otherwise have indulged. Was this violence, then, the act of Louis XVIII? Unless the French nation under Louis XVIII is responsible for the conduct of the French nation under Napoleon, upon what ground could the violent proceedings of the latter have irritated the sovereigns against his peaceful successor?

But the principle of indemnity is formally admitted by France in a document much more authentic than the reported speech of a minister to the House of Deputies, namely: in the official note of the French plenipotentiaries of September 21, 1815, written in answer to the note of the day preceding from the ministers of the four allied powers. It is there distinctly stated that the King admits in principle the payment of an indemnity; and in the reply of the allied ministers of the 22d they observed, "the French plenipotentiaries admit the principle of indemnity."

With regard to the 19th article of the treaty of March, 1814, to which the undersigned is said to have given too extensive a signification, he will only observe, that, under this article, claims to the amount of thirteen hundred millions of francs were presented to the French Government; that, by an amicable arrangement, a gross sum of about four hundred millions was allowed in satisfaction of the whole, and that, of this sum, as has been already observed, the Government of the Netherlands is said to have received more than eighty millions. A transaction of this kind is perhaps sufficiently extensive to warrant any language applied to it in the note. The undersigned does not perceive, however, that the principle of responsibility, supposed in the article, is affected in any degree by the extent of its application. He must be permitted to express his surprise that the principle upon which a certain class of private claims was excluded from this arrangement, namely, that they arose from damages committed by enemies in time of war, should have been considered applicable to the present claim. It can hardly be necessary to remind his excellency that the United States and Holland were not at war at the time of these confiscations.

The examples of the Bank of Hamburg and the Grand Duchy of Berg are objected to on the ground that, in order to make them support the principle of the note, satisfaction should have been demanded of the Governments of Berg and Hamburg, rather than France. Had the acts in question been performed by those Governments, the objection would be well founded. But, at the time of the spoliations at Hamburg, that city was a part of the French Empire; of course no Government of Hamburg existed; and in the Duchy of Berg the seizures were made by the French Government. It is not maintained in the note that a Government is responsible for all the acts of violence committed on its territory, but that it is responsible for its own actions.

The paragraph in which the usage of nations, in regard to treaties and other public acts, is alleged in confirmation of the claim, is said, in the answer, to "fall of itself," because this is not a question of treaties and stipulations. It was the opinion of the undersigned that the usage of nations, in this particular, was susceptible of a double application to this case; direct, because the confiscations were a breach of an existing treaty between the two countries; and indirect, because, if this had not been the case, no cause can be shown why a nation is not equally responsible for its other acts as for its treaties and stipulations. The conclusion would therefore follow, immediately, from the obligation in one case to the obligation in the other.

The claim of Holland on France, for the payment of a certain term of interest on the public debt, was not rejected on the ground that the present Government of France is not responsible for the acts of the former one, but on the ground that the treaties of Paris were a definitive arrangement of all the claims of the allies on France, and that this had not been provided for. The rejection of it by the arbitrators is, therefore, no argument in favor of the Government of the Netherlands in the present case; on the contrary, the making of it by that Government, as it supposes the principle of responsibility, may fairly be urged by the American Government as an authority in their favor.

The undersigned has thus examined, in detail, the several objections made by his excellency to the principles and authorities advanced in support of this claim, and has attempted to show that the views taken by the American Government are not affected by them. The demand made by the Government of the Netherlands, in the present case, to be relieved from the operation of the acknowledged principles of justice, to be excused from making satisfaction for an admitted injury, from paying a sum of money, the value of which has actually been received, is a pretension that derogates from common right, and, before it can be allowed, the grounds of exceptions must be established in the strictest manner. The undersigned has endeavored to prove, in confirmation of what has been advanced in his former note, that neither of those taken by the Government of the Netherlands is tenable; that the French Government, if responsible at all, is responsible to this country, and not to the United States; and that the question whether the acts of a usurper are binding on the people is foreign to the claim. If these points have been made out to the satisfaction of his Majesty's Government, it is presumed that the claim will still be considered valid, and the sufferers admitted to prove their losses and receive compensation.

The undersigned has the honor to assure his excellency Baron de Nagell of his high respect.

A. H. EVERETT.

No. 11.

Mr. Everett (No. 34) to the Secretary of State, dated

THE HAGUE, *November* 8, 1819.

I have the honor to transmit the reply of this Government to my note of July 15, on the subject of the claims. From the tenor of this communication, as well as of the former ones, there is very little appearance of a favorable result. It would be improper, I conceive, notwithstanding, to permit the correspondence to finish abruptly with this reply, and I shall, therefore, immediately prepare an answer.

I have the honor to be, with much respect, sir, your very obedient humble servant,

A. H. EVERETT.

No. 11, (a.)

[Translation.]

Baron de Nagell to Mr. Everett, dated

THE HAGUE, *November* 4, 1819.

In the reply which the undersigned had the honor to make, on the 14th of June last, to the note of Mr. Everett of the 22d of February preceding, the Government of the Netherlands thought itself justified in supposing that the reasons already assigned in the replies upon the subject of the American property confiscated by the French Government would have been sufficient to have brought that matter to a conclusion; it indulged a greater confidence of this, after the arguments used in the last note of the undersigned.

The reply transmitted by Mr. Everett, on the 15th of July last, again imposes on the undersigned the ever painful task of opposing, to the opinions reproduced in that reply, others entirely different. He proceeds to perform it with every disposition to admit what the evidence requires, and with all the candor of Mr. Everett's reply.

The Government of the Netherlands has always maintained the double position, that it was not the Government of Holland, which, at the period of the acts complained of, did not exist *in fact*, more than *in right*, but that of France, which was responsible for these acts; and that, even supposing this responsibility rested on the former, it could not fall upon the present Government of the Netherlands.

The reply admits that if the first objection be valid, it is decisive against the claims, but endeavors to profit of some admissions of the answer to refute it.

Although the undersigned is persuaded that it would be easy to show, since the *material facts*, and not appearances, are considered, that there should be on this point no difference of opinion, yet, to avoid repetitions, and not to anticipate his intended remarks, he will here confine himself to observe that his intention was not simply to assert that, under King *Louis, Holland* was influenced by *France*, (this, too, seemed to be the sentiment of the reply,) but, also, that in 1809 and 1810 she was governed so despotically by the latter that the name of King was merely an object of derision; that *Bonaparte* had not a regard even for appearances; and that, at the period when the American cargoes, particularly of the vessels mentioned in the answer, were conveyed to France, the Government of Holland did [not] exist even in *name*. This is why he said, in terms, *that it was not the treaty of* 1810, *but the union with France, properly speaking, which placed the cargoes of these vessels in the power of the French,* and that, therefore, the Government of Holland should not be held responsible for a confiscation made *by* and *for the profit of* France, and which would not have happened, had not the Government ceased to exist; that the words, "although King Louis had still the name of reigning," relate to a circumstance omitted in the reply, which is, that King Louis, though he still retained the title, held it so entirely under the authority of a King, that he was compelled to convey to the French Government cargoes belonging to his own subjects, as owners or creditors, but reputed to be American. But, as his object is to remove all doubt, he now declares that he intended to say, by the citations of the answer, that, in general, the cargoes sequestered, and especially those of the *Baltimore*, the *Bacchus*, and the *St. Michael*, were not confiscated by the French *till after the abdication of King Louis and the union of Holland with France.* The remark consequently applies, not to their continuance in the warehouses *after*, but *before* they were delivered to the French authorities.

Before the question of the responsibility of the Government of Holland is considered, the reply first examines a point which is regarded as of the least importance.

If, by those corrections, the undersigned has rectified the incorrect statement of the claims, the relative importance of those corrections seems to him still greater. It will not be difficult to assign the reasons for this opinion. According to the reply, "any errors that might have occurred in the statement of either of these cases would not affect the general claim." If by the *general principles* is understood the obligation to repair the injuries, it is evident that it is necessary, in the first place, to ascertain if the injury have been committed. For, even if the present Government of the Netherlands could admit that it is responsible for the violence, injustice, and spoliations, of which the Government of Holland is accused, it should then closely examine each claim to see if its merits will allow it to be embraced by the principle. And the undersigned hesitates not to say that no one of the cases in question should have this right, because they do not sustain the description under which the claimants have represented them, that they might interest the Government in favor of their complaints.

This assertion is very strong, and the reply says that but three variations are discovered between the statement and the correction. The first is an error in date, which is pronounced to be unimportant; the second relates to the time and authority which ordered the sale and transportation of one of the cargoes to Antwerp, (which is said to have been indirectly acknowledged and corrected by Mr. Eustis;) and lastly, a third one, in which the undersigned, *from his own acknowledgment*, must be deceived.

Notwithstanding his close examination to discover upon what this assertion is founded, he declares it to have been impossible to perceive it.

Let us again recur to facts. The Government of the United States claims of that of the Netherlands for the arbitrary acts of the former Government of Holland. Persuaded that this claim could not be sustained, but under the circumstances that accompanied the execution of the existing laws in 1809, till July, 1810, and not under the laws themselves; for, upon the supposition of the United States, the Government of Holland, enjoying the rights of independent States, had unquestionably that of prohibiting entry into its ports, as the United States did in their non-intercourse act, (Schoell, I, ix, p. 429, *et seq.*,) and even much more, as it was merely in retaliation of the acts of exclusion of the latter Government that Bonaparte ordered the same measure to be adopted, not only in the ports of France, but also in those of Holland, Spain, Italy, and the Kingdom of Naples; and the right of proceeding even to confiscation (supposing this may be attributed to King Louis) could no longer be denied to him, since the United States had frequently renewed similar orders of confiscation and sequestration.

The claims, it must be repeated, could only be sustained upon the accessory circumstances, and not upon the measure itself.

The notes having, in preference, denounced three cases, as particularly marked by arbitrary, unjust, and even perfidious circumstances, the Government of the Netherlands, in consequence, ordered an inquest of them to be instituted, so as to be able to judge of the subject understandingly; and as it is very common for complaints to impose upon the Government by exaggerated statements, if the cases selected and produced as those most loudly calling for justice should be found not to merit the imputations, that the rest might be decided upon more readily.

The first case is that of the Baltimore, represented to have been deceived by a license, safe conduct, or special passport, under guaranty of the sacred word of King Louis, and induced to go into Holland, where the greater part of her cargo was immediately seized and subsequently confiscated.

The examination has shown that this vessel *was bound for Holland;* that she arrived there on the 24th of July, 1809, and not in the spring of that year, which was consequently at a time when the exclusion laws were operative in America, for Consul Bourne had received official communication of it; that the paper solicited by her consignees, of King Louis, was *not* a special license, (although the claimants have persevered, strenuously, in maintaining it,) nor indeed could it be, for it is known that *Bonaparte* reserved to himself, exclusively, the grant of them; nor was it even a protection, properly speaking, *to exempt the vessel from the operation of the laws of blockade and sequestration,* but merely a means made use of at that time to enable vessels at their entry to elude the French privateers, and by which they might not, at least, be captured in our ports, before they could be assured whether their cargoes fell within the terms of the law or not.

Examination being made, that part of the cargo of the Baltimore not subject to the prohibitions was immediately returned, and the rest, according to the same laws, deposited in the warehouses.

This is, then, what the claimants are allowed to pronounce as a *violation of the rights of hospitality and justice, and as exhibiting a total want of those sentiments of self-respect and common humanity to be found among the most barbarous nations; for no people, civilized or uncivilized, are so utterly destitute of honor as to violate their own safe conduct, and employ the sacred pledge of their word as an instrument of mischief against a friendly power.*

By these declamations the undersigned will not say how much the claimants have committed their advocates.

The two other cases have been represented as still stronger.

To avoid repetitions, the undersigned will return to the details of his last note; they show that those two vessels received the same treatment they would have received anywhere else; that every assistance was rendered them which could have been expected by vessels in similar circumstances; that, so far from having merited the charge of the pretended pillage, at the order of the constituted authority, and of cruelties unknown to pirates, the Government of Holland sought for a pretext to relieve these vessels, and especially the *St. Michael,* from the severity of the stipulations of the treaty of 1810, although her entry was after its conclusion.

To these observations, made in his preceding note, the undersigned will add some particulars brought to light by the late examination. Although the present Government has assuredly no interest in making an apology for a state of things from which it considers itself perfectly estranged, justice and equity demand this testimony to be rendered to King Louis, that, if the tyranny of his brother forced upon him measures prejudicial to American merchants, his known wishes and constant efforts to prevent, as much as possible, their effects, demand for him the acknowledgment of the Government of the United States. There exist numerous proofs that, till the moment of his abdication, Louis was solicitously engaged in devising means for securing American cargoes to their owners. Respectable mercantile houses were also consulted on the subject. They confessed that, from every view of the case, under existing circumstances, sequestration was the best precaution. The veil will not be raised, but it is known that a violent letter was received by Louis from his brother, reproaching him with the emptiness of his warehouses.

The archives of 1809 and 1810 are filled with complaints and threats from the ambassador of France upon the manner in which Louis eluded the designs of Bonaparte and favored American vessels. Direct charges on this subject induced the Minister for Foreign Affairs repeatedly to solicit his dismission.

Lastly, a circumstance of the greatest importance has been established by authentic documents. It is, that, in consequence of the precautions of King Louis, *almost all the cargoes, especially those of the three vessels before mentioned, were found entire in the warehouses after the period of the abdication of Louis, and that they were not conveyed into France and confiscated by order of Bonaparte till, by the incorporation of Holland, the independence and the Government of Holland no longer existed even in name.* Supposing, therefore, that the Government which succeeded to that of Louis could be rendered responsible, it is plain that this would be the Government of France, and not that of the present King of the Netherlands, who did not assuredly succeed to the ex-Emperor.

These observations might suffice, but the same reasons that induced the undersigned to follow the note of the 22d February, in all its details, operate similarly in regard to the reply.

The important remarks which the undersigned has just made, as to the time when the cargoes fell into the power of the French, answer the objection made in the reply to the application of a remarkable passage of Vattel by the undersigned.

The *reply* pretends that the propriety of that application depends on the *time* when Holland passed under the Government of France, and that this point has been decided by the undersigned himself, who fixes it at the period of the union with France; and that, as the *confiscations were made previously, the remark of Vattel is therefore inapplicable.*

The reasoning of the undersigned has not been preserved in the reply. After having observed that the independence of Holland ceased unquestionably at the period of the union, the undersigned, in *another paragraph,* showed that, for a long time *before that period,* Holland was in the condition wherein, according to *Vattel,* a State ceases to be independent and responsible. He still contends, that the more the citation is compared with what preceded and followed the union, its application will appear more perfect.

After this, it is easy to answer the many questions of the reply. They all depend on the representations which the claimants are allowed to paint in such dark colors; but this representation has been shown to be imaginary.

Have States, nominally independent, but really subject, the right to pillage individuals? It is proved that the pillage, if there ever was any, was not committed by Holland. *Is not every people that claims the title, and exercises the powers of an independent State, responsible as such for its conduct?* Vattel informs us that this title may be fallacious, and that, while preserving certain attributes of an independent State, it may not be so in fact; the difficulty is, moreover, here solved: Was it from the full and free will of Holland that, when bending under foreign usurpation, she exercised the functions and pursued the measures complained of? The reply itself remarks, that the design of *Vattel* is rather to restrict than enlarge the attributes in like circumstances. *What is the line of distinction,* it is asked, *between dependence and independence?* Vattel, in the passage cited, has drawn it. The parallel between the influence always exercised, more or less, by some powerful States cannot form a comparison with the imperious tyranny, open and irresistible, that was exercised by Bonaparte over all the States where the troops and agents of France had penetrated. Far from its being impossible to establish that Holland, even before its incorporation, whether a Republic or a Kingdom, was, in fact, but a province of France, the undersigned appeals to the judgment of Europe for the correctness of what is advanced by a modern publicist, whose authority, he presumes to say, will not be questioned—Schoell.

In 1805, Holland, that till then was obliged to preserve a *certain independence in its relations with France,* received a prince and a master at the hands of the master of France, but Louis was merely the instrument of a foreign usurper. Nothing characterized the dependence of Holland more than the right assumed by Bonaparte to grant licenses to its inhabitants. The convention concluded on the 16th of March, 1810, terminated the series of treaties between France and Holland, if the *capitulations* imposed by a conqueror upon the people whom *he has reduced to live under his laws* may be always so termed. Louis could not obtain any modifications thereto; those which he proposed, to moderate the measures against the United States, were rejected as imperiously as the rest. He signed the treaty as it had been dictated by the tyrant. It will be difficult to think that, after having been degraded to this point of humiliation, Louis could hope to preserve the least degree of independence. He, at least, soon proved how vain such hope would be. Bonaparte soon after abolished the Kingdom of Holland, which he himself had erected, and united it to France, by a decree of the 9th of July, 1810; thus passed away that *shadow of independence* under which the United Provinces had existed for fifteen years.

It is, finally, *France* that is accused by England, in the face of Europe, of "the perfidious seizure of all the American vessels and their cargoes, in every port subjected to French arms."

How can the assertions, that it would be impossible to establish by facts that Holland, with the name of independence, was not in reality a subject province, nor one of those States whose acts were governed despotically by France, be reconciled with the opinions so generally entertained and drawn from the history of Holland? Did not the efforts made by Louis to release himself from this despotism terminate in his disgrace; and did it not serve to give greater weight to the yoke of Holland and hasten its ruin?

Inquiry into the motives that actuated or rather propelled Louis in all this transaction, or as to the conduct he should have maintained, is foreign to the present Government, and the reply is compelled to conjecture them.

But as to the assertion that Holland has ever derived the least advantage from that transaction, it is denied in its *fullest extent.*

It has already been seen that the *confiscation* was made by France, *after* the extinction of the Kingdom of Holland, and, of course, was made by the French. Mr. Eustis himself has acknowledged that the product was conveyed to the Imperial Treasury. And the undersigned will add, what is notorious, that Bonaparte, putting an end to the confiscation of which his brother had used a subterfuge in regard to the American cargoes, so as to gain time and wrest from him his prey, put aside all other measures, and issued the decree of incorporation.

If, then, it was unjust to claim of the Government of Holland for an injury in which that Government had but a passive part, and from which it only derived subjection and the ruin of the national fortunes, a just and reasonable Government could not insist upon making the present Government of the Netherlands responsible, since the true state of things has been represented, and because it had nothing in common with the usurper who forced Holland to be both the witness and the victim of his decrees.

But, *even supposing that the confiscations in question can be imputed to King Louis, the losses that were thereby occasioned to the owners cannot be claimed of the present Government of the Netherlands;* this constitutes the second objection which the reply endeavors to confute.

The principle advanced in the notes of Messrs. Eustis and Everett, that every Government should be responsible for all the acts of the preceding, is one whose nature and consequences will not allow the Government of the Netherlands to admit it, without restrictions.

After having read with attention the remarks of the reply in this part of the last note, and the interpretation it persists in giving to the citations whose application it denies, the undersigned may be permitted to say candidly, that, notwithstanding the novel considerations advanced, those authorities appear to him to relate to a different matter; and it is only by recurring to induction and analogy, which are ever uncertain, (as he remarks,) that they can be made to apply. In a word, that the civilians cited do not furnish any direct decision upon the principles in point. But, to avoid repetitions, and that this discussion may not degenerate into a literary dispute upon the sense of controverted passages, he will select one; and as the authority of Puffendorf is regarded by the reply as most favorable to the claim, the undersigned will again analyze that passage of this author, esteemed to be so conclusive by the reply as to induce the expression of surprise that an attempt should ever have been made to use it against the principle in question.

The passage is found at chapter 12, liber 8, which treats of the changes and the decline of States.

In section 1 Puffendorf maintains that a people does not cease to be the same, although the form of its government may have been changed: *thus*, says he, *when a free people is conquered they never cease to be the same people, provided the conqueror that has become master governs them afterwards as a* SEPARATE KINGDOM, AND NOT AS A PROVINCE ANNEXED TO HIS FORMER STATES.

In section 2 Puffendorf discusses the question whether, when a people passes from the absolute Government of a monarch, or an oligarchy, to a popular Government, the State, thus become free, should observe the treaties, contracts, and other acts of the King or aristocrats under whom they formerly existed. It is on this occasion, while combatting those who maintained the negative, on the ground that *the State did not properly constitute one when these obligations were contracted*, that he used the phrase on which the reply rests, that *it is certainly a frivolous reason*. This positive decision he sustains by the aid of a comparison; a mode of argument which it seems ought not to have great force, as the reply contends it has the defect of supposing what is required to be proved.

The section concludes with this sentence: *"When a people is reduced to the form of a province, and is not consequently of the body of the State, they are by no means on this account liberated"*—from what? From observing all the engagements of the Government abolished, and making indemnity for all the losses it may have caused to foreign nations? No: *but from paying what it may have previously borrowed; for it did not become a debtor necessarily as a part of a State, but because certain goods were possessed in common, so that the debt is attached to the property, into whatever hands it may pass.* And Puffendorf adds immediately after, section 3, in the margin, *how far are the acts and engagements of a usurper valid after he has been expelled;* and in the text, *the subject, in my opinion, presents no difficulty* IN REGARD TO DEBTS CONTRACTED FOR THE NECESSITIES OF THE STATE. *"But it is more difficult to decide, if this be generally correct, in regard to all the acts and engagements of an expelled usurper."* This appears to me to be the most reasonable. *If he who has invaded a State make an alliance with other States against a common enemy, and afterwards gives them a part of the booty to be sold, the alliance, gift, and the sale, exist even after the expulsion of the usurper. For, by virtue of these acts, the other States have acquired a valid right, since they treated with the usurper as with the chief of the State, the Government of which was in his possession,* AND BECAUSE THESE ACTS TENDED TO THE ADVANTAGE OF THE PEOPLE, *without implying any crime capable of annulling them.*

But if the usurper have sold to another State goods extorted by means unjust to the oppressed citizens, shall they afterwards be claimed, when the time may permit? Considering the notions and customs of people, I cannot perceive by what right those WHO HAVE BEEN DEPRIVED *of their goods can demand them of the purchasers. For, inasmuch as the usurper sustains himself only by force, he is esteemed as an enemy of the State, and therefore that part of his booty which has been conveyed to another State from the one he has despoiled cannot be reclaimed any more than the movable articles acquired by right of war. If the Government of the usurper is become legitimate, by consent of the citizens submitting to it, either tacitly or expressly, foreigners may then consider the goods of which he may deprive the citizens as legitimately confiscated.*

It is now easy to determine if this passage, which is but the amplification of a parallel one in Grotius, favors the reply.

It is wished to use it in proof of the position that a nation is not affected by the changes of the Government, and cannot be destroyed but by the dissolution of the body politic.

Puffendorf plainly excepts the case of a State that has become the *mere province of another*, and this case is precisely that of Holland by its incorporation with France.

It is wished to use it in proof of the position that every Government which succeeds another, even that of an usurper, is responsible for all the acts of the preceding Government.

Puffendorf confines this obligation to the *public debts contracted for the necessities of the State;* and suggests, as to the rest, what appeared to him NOT OBLIGATORY but REASONABLE.

It is wished to prove from it that a people is bound to repair injuries done to strangers.

The first case proposed by Puffendorf is that where a people may keep what has been taken, bought from, or bestowed by an usurper.

Lastly, it is wished to prove by it that a people is bound to restore what has been pillaged, even if the articles have passed into the hands of others.

Puffendorf, without approaching the second question, whether the obligation to restore be attached to the possession of the thing taken, decides that, according to the ideas and usages of people, if even citizens (and not, as the vague translation, *individuals*)—oppressed citizens, be unjustly deprived of their goods by an usurper, they have not the right to claim these goods.

All that this passage, therefore, proves is the distinction drawn by the undersigned between public debts, the obligation and justice of which cannot be denied, and engagements whose validity remains doubtful.

The reply contends against the distinction, and condemns the doctrine as dangerous. What doctrine? That the validity of an obligation of a *just debt* (an important correction made by the reply a few lines below) depends on its acknowledgment, or the form of this acknowledgment? The undersigned never intended to maintain it; and without proposing difficulties as to the degrees of influence that the *form* of acknowledgment, or the titles of creditors, frequently have upon the validity of a claim, he will confess that the condition of *creditors* in that case would be as precarious as the condition of *supposed debtors*, were it sufficient to declare, claim, and sue for a debt, to establish its existence and justice, and the obligation to pay it. He has not wished to affect this common obligation, but merely to show that neither the letter nor the spirit of the passage adduced is applicable to the present claim.

This may be said of that passage of Grotius, (Lib. III, chap. 17,) as to the conduct towards neutrals and their reciprocal duties.

It is only necessary to read the examples drawn from Moses, John the Baptist, the Goths, Greeks, Romans, Huns, Allains, &c., on which this publicist has endeavored to establish his principles, to be persuaded how inapplicable they are to the present state of things, and especially to the point in question.

The reply again asserts, that the question whether a legitimate Government be bound by the acts of an usurper is *foriegn to the case;* and 'resolves the difficulty by affirming that the Government of Holland was legitimate in regard to the object in question; for every established Government is legitimate as far as foreign nations are concerned. The undersigned, in his note, dwelled on this point as only accessory to the principal question whether a legitimate Government be responsible for all the acts of the Government it has overthrown. This was supported by some authorities, to which the reply opposed assertions which seemed to the undersigned by no means conformable with the just sense of the passages cited or the principles adopted at the time.

Before he proceeds to prove his positions, the undersigned will not deny that there may be on this subject a great incongruity between the theory and the practice.

Notwithstanding the theories which inculcate that the moral of nations is the same with that of individuals, and that the laws which regulate the conduct of an honest man should also direct the actions of a people, it is not the less true that a private person will dishonor himself in the opinion of the public, and risk his reputation and fortune by an association with villains and knaves, yet history teaches us how often interest induces nations to disregard scruples of delicacy and to contract friendly relations with usurpers and tyrants. But it is also true that the codes of the laws of nations oppose the doctrine of the reply, and that political disregard of restrictions and examples which are more operative upon the world.

Martens employs the third book of his Law of Modern Nations to exhibit and prove the reciprocal rights of States relatively to their constitutions; and he remarks (as the undersigned has said) that for centuries, and especially since the adoption of the system of the balance of power, the most of the disputes of succession have been determined by these rights.

The remarks of this publicist cannot be reconciled with the assertion that modern wars and treaties have been made from motives of asserting the right of self-government. The motives assigned by Martens are rather directed to the *maintaining* or *re-establishing of legitimate Governments.*

The undersigned, therefore, cannot but still consider the distinction established in his answer as both just and applicable to the present claim. He has already shown the true meaning of the passage of Puffendorf, (Lib. 8, chap. 12.) That which he has given to the passage of Grotius, (Lib. 2, chap. 14,) cannot be disproved by a mere assertion; and even if this author does add, that the King and the people are bound to restore what has been used to their *profit,* (this is the very term he uses,) this modification cannot render inappropriate the application of the passage adduced, since Mr. Eustis himself acknowledges that the product of the cargoes confiscated by the French was deposited in the Imperial Treasury; and the undersigned has, moreover, proved that all this transaction tended not to the *profit* but the *ruin* of Holland. The same thing may be said of the passage of Martens; it would be easy to apply it to the question, but difficult to discover wherein analogy renders it favorable to the claimants, at least against the present Government of the Netherlands. Is it because treaties concluded by force are not obligatory, that property taken by force should be restored? Be it so; but by whom? ·Undoubtedly by him who has extorted them; that is, in the present case, by the French Government.

Finally, the undersigned thinks he may safely affirm that the system now prevailing in Europe does not admit the full recognition of every Government whatsoever.

The undersigned will not pursue these reflections further. As it has been shown that the confiscations were made by Bonaparte, the question whether or not his Government was legitimate for this object, and whether foreigners are bound to admit the legality of his system, is not for the present Government of the Netherlands to decide, and has, moreover, been settled by the late treaties.

The reply next commences a more important reasoning, and supposes that proofs of its arguments are found in the late treaties and the history of modern times.

"There is here seen a great nation which, under the sanction, for the most part, of the other great nations of Europe, particularly of the Netherlands, makes itself responsible for the engagements entered into, and the spoliations committed, under a preceding Government, declared to be founded on usurpation."

The undersigned, in his last note, showed that these treaties and examples cited could not govern in the present case, because the principle advanced in the memoir did not influence the sovereigns thereto, especially the King of the Netherlands; and it would not have been recognized by France had not particular circumstances operated on the conventions and produced the treaties of Paris in 1814 and 1815. Far from having, however, the least intention of insinuating (as seen with surprise in the reply) that the allies availed themselves of their posture to impose on France an arrangement *unjust in itself,* neither this sentiment nor language are found in the answer.

As the discussion of this subject is more interesting than an inquiry into the opinions or theories of civilians, who had in view events that have no connexion with a state of things the possibility of which they could not even have foreseen, the undersigned will proceed carefully to examine this last species of argument. With this view he will consider the argument adduced by the reply, and that which the Government of the Netherlands opposes to it.

The position taken by the reply is, *that the large sums which France was bound to pay by virtue of the treaties of Paris were the indemnifications which she ought to have paid, according to the principles of the law of nations, for the violations and spoliations of the preceding Government; for every succeeding Government is responsible for all the acts of the preceding, whether legitimate or usurped.*

The position of the Government of the Netherlands, on the contrary, is, *that the late treaties of Paris did not furnish any argument in favor of this doctrine.*

The arguments of the reply reduce themselves to the following: *That the responsibility of the French Government is properly supposed in all these payments; that the Duke de Richelieu indirectly recognized the principle in his speech to the deputies, and that it had been distinctly recognized by France in a document much more authentic than a speech—an official note of the French plenipotentiaries; that the Government of the Netherlands would not have accepted the large sums assigned to it had it not approved the principle in virtue of which they were paid; and unless the French nation under Louis XVIII be made responsible for the French nation under Napoleon, upon what principle could France and Louis XVIII be made to suffer for the violence of Bonaparte.*

The undersigned will oppose to them the decisions of an impartial judge, whose authority will not be questioned by the author of the reply—Schoell.

First. *Is the responsibility of the present French Government, or, in other words, the principle that every succeeding Government, whether the preceding be legitimate or usurped, naturally supposed in the late treaties of Paris?*

Entirely to the contrary, if it is to be understood thereby that Louis XVIII was responsible for the acts of the preceding Government. The negotiations could not be difficult. But what was done in France twenty years ago was not by the Bourbons; they neither ordered nor approved the injuries inflicted on different people. Even they themselves were the victims of the revolutionary power.—(*Schoell, Hist. Ab. of the Treaties of Paris, I, X, et* 81.)

Was not the principle of the responsibility recognized, indirectly, by the Duke de Richelieu in his speech, laid down formally by the contracting powers, and admitted by the French plenipotentiaries themselves in an official note?

One explanation will suffice to refute this assertion.

"In the conference of the 2d of October, 1815, the principal bases were agreed upon. The principle of the cessions (territorial) that France was to make was here determined, as also the sum of indemnity to be paid by her for the expenses of the LATE ARMAMENTS."

This indemnity was only in reference to *these* LATTER, proofs of which abound in the details of the negotiation.

The Duke de Richelieu had acknowledged "that all the products of agriculture, the articles of commerce, and all sorts of property, were sacrificed by every people, alarmed at the return of Bonaparte; and more than a million of soldiers were precipitated upon the frontiers of France."

Let us consult the commentary of Mr. Schoell upon this text.

If the facility with which the inhabitants of France armed themselves against these nations gave them a right to demand a *guaranty*, the sacrifices they made authorizes them to claim an indemnity.

"But even this title was not without objection. After the principle was admitted that no provinces should be demanded of France under the title of *guaranty*, much less could such cession be demanded under title of *indemnity* for the *expenses of the wars*. The only means which then remained for the *reimbursement of these expenses* was the payment of a CONTRIBUTION."

This is also what the French plenipotentiaries acceded to in their note of the 21st of September, 1815.

It was, then, for the *expenses of the late armaments that a contribution was paid under the title of indemnity.* If there were still another proof wanting, on the sixth of November the plenipotentiaries of the four powers again drew up a representation to the Convention upon the principles by which the seven hundred millions of contribution to be paid by France should be divided. Nothing is found in that to support the hypothesis of the reply; but the partition was, on the contrary, proportioned to the part that each interested State had taken in the last campaign, considering their contingencies. It was on this account that Sweden was excluded from the partition, having from the commencement declined all active co-operation.

This is the reply to the objection that the King of the Netherlands would not have consented to receive the large sums assigned to him had he not approved the principle of responsibility, in virtue of which they were paid to him. It has been proved that this principle did not *at all* operate in the *partition*.

But unless the French nation under Louis XVIII be made responsible for the conduct of the French nation under Napoleon, upon what principle can Louis XVIII be held responsible for the outrages of Bonaparte?

Reply: "The King having been so unfortunately situated as to require the assistance of the allies, and they being obliged of themselves to terminate their enterprise, it belonged to them alone to deliberate upon what they might judge necessary to avoid like sacrifices in future."

"Will it be objected that the allies, in taking up arms against *Bonaparte and his adherents*, did not consider France as *an enemy's country, and, consequently, could not exercise over her the right of conquest?* Certainly that war should not have been one of conquest, and the allies would have acted against their principles, had they attempted to aggrandize themselves at the expense of France by profiting of her misfortunes. But it is not the less true that the conquest existed in fact; and if the powers, by declaring that they made war only upon Bonaparte and his adherents, wished to draw off the nation from the usurper, the nation having the right to claim this declaration should have separated itself from him in fact, and not favored his project either by a culpable indifference, or by bearing arms in his support."

But, what! could the pacific Louis XVIII admit these principles?

"When the alliance of March 25 was concluded he had already become a stranger to this war. Did he not also accede to that treaty by a *formal act,* as the other Governments did? But a simple adhesion was only required of his ministers."

The two answers made by the reply to the parts of the note that relate to examples of the Bank of Hamburg and the Grand Duchy of Berg are favorable to the principles maintained by the Government of the Netherlands. At the period of the confiscation Holland also made a *part of the French empire.* The modification that a Government is not responsible for all the acts of violence committed within its territory has always been held by the undersigned as a principle.

Has not the reasoning that follows the defect of proving too much? An obligation in one case to be applied by inference to another is too great an extension.

We have shown that the civilians cited in the reply have confined the obligations of a Government succeeding that of an expelled usurper to an entirely different object.

Finally, the rejection of the claim of Holland on France, a claim founded on a different basis from that of *responsibility,* as understood here, supports the assertion made before, that *forms* often determine the recognition of the most legitimate claims.—(*Vide Schoell, I, XI, p.* 538.)

These explanations, with those that have already been given in the preceding note, will, doubtless, place the claim in a different point of view from that under which they had been represented to the Government of the United States.

In conclusion, the undersigned will remark, that, to release the claim from the recognized principles of justice would not only be derogatory to the maxims of *common law,* but the mere supposition that the Government of the Netherlands would so act is what, from a sentiment of dignity, the undersigned must pass by in silence. There is no wrong acknowledged, consequently no satisfaction is due. It is of those who have received the money that a claim of restoration is to be made. It is, however, difficult to think that an ordinary tribunal would order restoration if a creditor had only the arguments of the claimants to urge, of which the reply has had the condescension to be the organ.

The Government of the Netherlands, therefore, must persist in its answer, and refer the claimants to the French Government. Have they so applied? In this case their course is plain. Have they failed to apply, and suffered the proper time to pass by? This is perhaps a tacit proof that the United States have admitted that no claim can be sustained against the result of measures which they themselves adopted.

The undersigned seizes this occasion to renew to Mr. Everett the assurance of his distinguished consideration,

A. W. C. DE NAGELL.

No. 12.

Extract of a letter from Mr. Everett to Mr. Adams, dated.

THE HAGUE, *November* 16, 1810.

"I received your despatch No. 4. Nos. 1 and 2 have never come to hand.

"I have the honor to inclose a copy of a note which I addressed to Baron de Nagell on the 10th, in reply to a part of his note of the 4th, on the claims. The basis of his whole argument in this long production is a loose and incorrect statement of the facts at the commencement, upon which he founds the assertion that the confiscations complained of were the acts of the French Government. This objection, if true, is of course conclusive of itself against the claim; and, although he professes to waive it in entering upon the discussion of principles, he still introduces it as an answer at every point where the argument presses. The objection was stated in his former note; but, as he admitted, notwithstanding, in detail, all the facts necessary to establish the claim, I thought myself at liberty to conclude that his general assertion was not meant to be taken in so exact a sense as to preclude all further argument. He now retracts these admissions, and states the same objection again, and again accompanies it with new admissions in detail of all the necessary facts. Under these circumstances I have thought it best to confine the discussion at present to this part of the subject, and to endeavor to come to some explicit understanding with M. de Nagell upon the facts from which it will be impossible for him to withdraw. If this can be effected, the discussion of the principles may be resumed with advantage. Should there be much delay in replying to this note, I shall converse with the Baron upon the subject, and endeavor to obtain from him verbally the necessary explanations."

No. 12, (a.)

Mr. Everett to Baron de Nagell:

THE HAGUE, *November* 10, 1819.

In the note which the undersigned, chargé d'affaires of the United States of America, had the honor of receiving from his excellency the Minister of Foreign Affairs, on the 4th instant, the position is still maintained that the property for the loss of which the American Government claims compensation was confiscated by the Government of France, and not by that of Holland. This objection, as was observed by the undersigned in his last note, is preliminary in its nature to the others, and with a view to avoid, as far as possible, any unnecessary discussion, he will confine his remarks at present to this part of the subject.

The facts which are considered by the American Government as necessary to the establishment of this claim are few in number and matters of public notoriety. They are no other than the seizure of the property in question by the Government of Holland, under the acts authorizing a sequester, and the transfer of this property to France by the treaty of March 16, 1810, which is itself the act of confiscation. The transfer is made in the following terms: *Toute marchandise venant seur des batimens Americaines, entres dans les ports de la Hollande depuis le 1 Janvier, 1809, sera mise sur le sequestre et appartiendra à la France pour en disposer selon les circonstances et les relations politiques avec les Etats Unis.*

It is not considered by the American Government as material whether the property thus transferred was delivered to France before or after the union. The act of transfer was the act of confiscation, and the one which justifies the claim. Whether the property was delivered before or after the union, it was still delivered by virtue of the treaty.

This view of the subject appears to be sanctioned by the authority of M. de Nagell himself. In his note of the 4th, he observes that the cargoes of the three ships which have been particularly mentioned "*were still in the magazines after the epoch of the King's abdication,*" and were not delivered to the French till after the union; and in his note of June 14 he remarks, that "*the cargo of the Baltimore was delivered to the French authorities by virtue of the treaty,*" and that "*the cargo of the Bacchus was sequestered till, in consequence of the treaty, it was delivered to the French authorities.*"

The conclusion appears irresistible that the cargoes of the Bacchus and the Baltimore and the others placed in similar circumstances, and not delivered till after the union, were still delivered by virtue of the treaty.

Should the propriety of this conclusion be denied by his excellency, there will still remain the cargoes which were actually delivered to the French before the union, concerning which there can be no dispute, that all the acts attending that seizure and confiscation were performed by the Dutch Government.

The undersigned thought himself at liberty to conclude, from several passages in Baron de Nagell's note of June 14, that this portion of the property in question was admitted to be very considerable; and the following remark in particular appeared to the undersigned to determine the time of the delivery of the cargoes in general to some period while Louis retained the name of King. *Among the cargoes reputed American delivered to France* (says M. de Nagell) *there were some which were wholly or in part Dutch property. Though Louis had still the name of reigning, the parties interested were not the less obliged to address themselves to the French Government, &c.*

It appears, however, from his excellency's last note, that the undersigned was mistaken in the construction of this passage, and that M. de Nagell did not intend to admit by this remark that *the cargoes were delivered to France while Louis had the name of reigning,* and the undersigned is disposed to acquiesce with great readiness in any construction which his excellency may choose to put upon his own language.

But, though M. de Nagell thus declines to admit that the cargoes in question were delivered before the union, it appears to follow, from several passages in both his notes, that at least a certain part of the property was in this situation. Thus, in his note of June 14 he remarks: *A l'epoque de la reunion la plus*

grande partie des cargaisons Américaines ètoit encore dans les magazins de l'Etat; and in that of November 4, *La presque totalité des cargaisons se trouvait encore dans les magazins aprés l'epoque de l'abdication.*
In both these remarks it seems to be implied that a certain portion of the cargoes had been delivered to the French before the union.
As the undersigned has had the misfortune to misunderstand, in a former case, the remarks of his excellency, he takes the liberty of requesting to be informed, in order to avoid the possibility of a similar error, whether he is correct in both or either of the above conclusions; that is, in supposing his excellency to admit that the cargoes of the Bacchus and the Baltimore and the others placed in similar circumstances, and not delivered till after the union, were still delivered by virtue of the treaty, and that a certain portion of the cargoes was delivered to the French before the union.
As the view of the undersigned, in making this request, is to avoid unnecessary discussion, he presumes that Baron de Nagell will readily comply with it, and avails himself of this occasion to offer to his excellency the assurance of his high respect.

A. H. EVERETT.

No. 13.

Baron de Nagell to Mr. Everett.

[Translation.]

THE HAGUE, December 9, 1819.

In making a detailed reply to all the arguments contained in the notes of Messrs. Eustis and Everett, especially of the latter, in favor of American property confiscated in Holland, the undersigned was assured that he entered into the views of his Government; which, supposing that these replies would be submitted to the Government of the United States, confidently believed that they would be appreciated by a Government that doubtless prefers equity to every other consideration.
The short interval between the last note of the undersigned, of the 4th of November, and that which he had the honor to receive of Mr. Everett, on the 11th of the same month, indicates that this course has not been pursued on the present occasion. This last note begins and ends by saying that, to avoid unnecessary discussions and questions, the inquiry will be confined to one object, whether the property was confiscated by Holland or by France.
This notice ought to have caused some surprise. The discussions and the questions here determined to be useless were not provoked by the Government of the Netherlands, but the repetitions of them being confined to two, in the official notes they should have been presumed to be considered as important by those who advanced them, although it will not be denied that some of them seemed to deserve the character here given of them. For example, they adduced the opinions of some ancient publicists in regard to a state of things of which they could never have had any idea; yet the undersigned thinks he should remark that this character should not be understood without reserve, and that, although the note of Mr. Everett only discusses the subject before mentioned, the Government of the Netherlands still regards a second position as no less important, which he will state, that his silence may [not] be construed as a tacit acquiescence; it is that, even if the responsibility of the Government of Holland could be established as to the confiscations of American property, the responsibility of the present Government of the Netherlands could not still be admitted.
In considering the first point as one of the most important, the undersigned, in his last notes, endeavored to establish the assertion that, from the moment appearances were disregarded, (which, for a greater part of the time, were not respected by Bonaparte,) his brother Louis no longer continued to be King in fact, more than in right; that all his measures were dictated to him imperiously; that the seques-tration which he had been forced to impose on the American cargoes could not justly be confounded with the act of confiscation, since he had changed it into a measure of preservation; that the confiscations (especially of the Baltimore, the Bacchus, and the St. Michael, the three cases specified) were not made till after his abdication, and, of course, were made by the French Government; that the treaty of 1810, the clause in which relating to these cargoes he had vainly endeavored to soften in its effects, and which seemed to have been imposed as a punishment for his conduct and to force him to abdicate, was, in the opinion of Europe, but a capitulation imposed by a despot, for which he alone was responsible, but which was, in fact, abrogated by the reduction of Holland to a province of the French Empire.
No one of these arguments has been refuted in the note. It merely renews the assertion that the act of sequestration was equivalent to confiscation, and that it is indifferent whether this latter took place before or after the union to France. It also endeavors to profit of such an act as the treaty of 1811.
This tenacity of opinion would authorize the Government of the Netherlands to persist in what it maintains; and the undersigned might here terminate his answer if, besides a motive of regard, of which he is always pleased to give new proofs, he did not feel it to be his duty to undeceive Mr. Everett, who seems to have inferred from some parts of the answers that the subject was considered in the same light as he viewed it.
Before he examines the quotations to that effect, the undersigned will make two remarks.
The first is, that, originally, the Government of the Netherlands had great difficulty in ascertaining the injuries upon which the claims were founded, but has had the satisfaction of reducing to order this chaos, which was a necessary result of the events of 1810. The design of this observation is to furnish a reason for some slight shades of difference which Mr. Everett may have discovered in the successive replies of the undersigned. Thus, after having said in one note that at the period of the union with France the *greater part* of the cargoes were still in the State warehouses, owing to the precautions and delays of King Louis, he remarked, in a subsequent one, that *almost the whole* of them were in this condition; and so of some other phrases.
The second remark is, that it ought not to be surprising if, in such minute replies, some expressions or facts should have needed correction when more knowledge had been obtained on the subject. This privilege of correction the undersigned thought himself at liberty to use after the precedent established by Mr. Eustis.

The object of this remark is to give greater weight to the assurance that, in reperusing his various notes with impartiality, he has not found occasion to use it in the whole course of his remarks.

Mr. Everett, however, does not disguise that he thinks he has discovered some passages of a doubtful sense, not to say contradictory; and, among others, the following one in the note of the 14th of June.

Among the cargoes, originally American, delivered to France, there were some decidedly the property of Holland, and others on which the inhabitants of Holland had a lien; and, although Louis had still the name of reigning, the proprietors and creditors were not the less obliged to address themselves to the French Government.

From this passage it is thought the inference may be drawn *that considerable parts of the cargoes were delivered by King Louis to France.* But if the quotation, which relates to an incidental circumstance, could of itself admit any doubt as to its just signification, the notes in which it is found, and the object for which it was made, render this commentary improper, (inadmissible.)

The notes maintain the position that the *greater part, almost the whole,* of the cargoes was not confiscated till after the abdication of King Louis and the union with France. How, then, could it be said of the undersigned that he had imprudently furnished arms against himself, by making known a fact before unknown, and, what is worse, by making it follow immediately after the place where it is said *that Holland had ceased to exist when the confiscation was made by and for the profit of France.*

It was, moreover, designed to show how dependent Louis was at that time. But if he himself delivered the cargoes in question to France, it was but natural that his subjects should be referred to the French Government. It was, indeed, in this case, the only step that could be taken. The explanation demanded can then be readily given.

In producing the proofs of the absolute nullity of the Government, there can be no difficulty, except in the selection of them. Thus, the privateers that captured all vessels indifferently, notwithstanding the precautions and certificates of King Louis, were French. The cargoes which King Louis was forced to restore to the French privateers which had captured them within his ports, and despite the resistance of his *guardes cotes,* belonged to Holland. Finally, the cargoes whose sequestration King Louis dared not raise were reputed to be American, but belonged to Holland. He had been taught, by much censure, not to commit himself further; and, by a public knowledge of dependence, referred the claimants to the French Government.

This last example was considered, at the most, as *ad rem.*

The sense of the citation then presents itself naturally; and, indeed, the only interpretation that can be admitted is this:

"Among the many cargoes delivered to France, *after the union,* there were some which belonged to citizens of Holland, and which had been all included in the sequestration as the property of Americans;" that, although Louis had still the name of King, he retained so little of the power as not to dare the raising of his own sequestration, but was obliged to refer his subjects to the French Government.

The conviction of the inutility of addressing themselves to Louis appeared to be felt by the American owners also, (which was insinuated at the same place.) The presumptions of this have been strengthened by discoveries that may be used at a proper time and place.

Mr. Everett, lastly, recapitulates his citations, and concludes his note by requesting the undersigned to answer these two questions: 1st. Whether he does not admit that the cargoes of the Bacchus, the Baltimore, and the others placed in *similar circumstances,* and which were not conveyed to France till after the union, were not delivered in virtue of the treaty? 2d. Whether a certain part of these cargoes was not delivered to France *before* the union.

As the replies to these questions would be official, as coming from the undersigned, he must excuse himself from making them.

In relation to the first, it would be impossible for him to answer officially, for a presumptive reason. The cargoes of the Baltimore and the Bacchus (to which he will add the St. Michael, but he is not certain there were any more in the same condition) were not delivered to France till after the Government of Holland had ceased to exist.

At this period the official information ceased. All the information that was afterwards collected on the subject of these vessels was procured after that which the undersigned had transmitted. But to know how, and if, the French Government did avail itself, after the abolition of the Kingdom of Holland, of a treaty concluded with this Kingdom, is a question to which the French authorities alone, who made the confiscation, are prepared to answer.

As to the *second,* the undersigned will observe that his answer was given, as far as his object required, when he declared that the cargoes of the three named vessels were not delivered till after the union. But if the design of Mr. Everett were to acquire new information and further arguments on which to found other suits, it should not be required of the Government of the Netherlands to make any investigation of the subject. To do this, would be in direct opposition to the principle that the Government which is wished to be made responsible is estranged from the whole course of conduct pursued in regard to the matter in question.

The undersigned seizes this occasion to renew to Mr. Everett the assurance of his distinguished consideration.

A. W. C. DE NAGELL.

No. 14.

Extract from a letter (No. 40) from Mr. Everett to the Secretary of State, dated

THE HAGUE, *January 25, 1820.*

" I mentioned in a late letter that I intended to address a note to the Minister of Foreign Affairs here, resuming the whole argument on the subject of the claims. On further reflection, I have thought it expedient to take a different course. From several phrases in both the last notes of Baron de Nagell, it appears to be the wish of this Government that the objection, founded on the fact that the greater part of the property was not delivered to the French till after the union, should be particularly submitted to the President's consideration. As there is no motive for pressing the correspondence with extraordinary rapidity, this circumstance has induced me to refrain from any further instances till I shall have the honor of receiving instructions from you respecting this point. I had prepared a considerable part of the note inclosed with the intention of presenting it at once, and I now transmit it to you as a report upon the present state of the correspondence, and an examination of the last communications from this Government.

The Minister of Foreign Affairs has contented himself with stating the simple fact, on which he founds the objection alluded to, without entering into the reasons which make it, in his opinion, a sufficient answer to the claim. The strongest form in which it can be presented seems to me to be the following: "The treaty of March, 1810, was an act extorted by force from the Government of Holland. It is, however, in form, the act of the Government, and the nation is, of course, responsible for its consequences, in fact. But it could not confer any rights on France; and as the Government of Holland had ceased to exist at the time when the French took possession of the property, they must be regarded as having exercised an act of direct violence upon it, for which they are directly responsible; whereas, had it been done before the union, in the form of a transfer from Holland, it would have been an act of indirect violence through the medium of Holland, for which Holland is immediately responsible, and France to her."

It may be urged, however, in answer to this, that if the property, by the operation of the treaty, was taken out of the course of judicial process and placed at the disposal of the French, the Government of Holland occasioned the loss, and is therefore the party responsible. The mere fact of sequester, though made in legal form, makes the Government accountable for the property. If it is lost, they must, at least, show that it was without their fault; and a mere detention, other than what would happen in the due course of law, would make them responsible.

The President will decide how far the objection is admissible. If considered sufficient, the effect of it would be to transfer the claim, for the part of the property affected by it, from Holland to France. In this case, it would probably be thought necessary for this Government to substantiate their assertion by such evidence as could be laid before the French Government. A claim would remain against the Netherlands for the part of the property not affected by this objection, and for all the property to which the existing decrees of sequester were illegally applied. Such, for example, was the case of the St. Michael. The law of nations does not permit the application of such decrees to vessels bound to a different country, and driven into port in distress. Many other cases would, probably, in different ways, be found to come within that predicament. An illegal sequester would, of course, make the Government responsible for the loss, however it may have happened.

Should the objection appear insufficient, the claim will still remain against this Government for all the property. In either case, the denial of the responsibility is a further and paramount objection. It does not appear to me to be maintained in the argument, but this Government is evidently resolved to persist in it, and it is, of course, conclusive against every part of the claim. The President will judge whether it is expedient to continue the correspondence any further on this point; whether, if it be continued, it might not be proper to accompany the next communication with a proposition similar to the one stated at the end of the inclosed note; and whether, if it be the intention of the Government to adopt ultimately any more vigorous measures for the recovery of the claim, on the failure of mere argument, it would be advantageous to give notice of them as an alternative at the same time that this proposition is presented.

No. 14 (a.)

Mr. Everett to the Baron de Nagell.

The undersigned, chargé d'affaires of the United States of America, has the honor to acknowledge the receipt of the note addressed to him by his excellency Baron de Nagell, Minister of Foreign Affairs, on the 9th of December. The undersigned has already observed, in a former note, that the denial of the fact of confiscation was a preliminary objection in its nature to any other, and, if well founded, necessarily decisive. The assertion upon which this denial rests does not, however, extend to all the property confiscated. It is only stated by Baron de Nagell that the greater part of the property (presque totaleté,) and not that the whole, was in the King's magazines at the time of the union. It was the principal object of the undersigned, in his last note, to point out this defect in the objection to Baron de Nagell, and to ascertain whether the Government of the Netherlands intended to admit, by making the assertion in this form, that a part of the property was delivered before the union, or whether, (as the general terms in which the objection founded on this assertion is conceived would seem to intimate,) they were ready to give such an explanation of it as would make it extend, in form, to all the property. In the latter case, it was the wish of the undersigned to avoid any further discussion of the principle of responsibility until the previous objection of fact could be removed. His views in making this request, which was clearly as much in the interest of one party as the other, seem to have been misunderstood by his excellency, and he declines to give any explanation upon the subject. The objection of fact remains, of course, insufficient in form as an answer to the whole claim; and the undersigned is compelled, in order to make a complete reply to the note of November, to resume again the whole discussion.

The system of defence adopted by the Government of the Netherlands consists of two parts: a denial of the fact that the property in question was confiscated by the Government of Holland, and a denial of the responsibility of the present Government for such confiscation, supposing it to be proved.

To establish the first of these points, it is asserted by M. de Nagell that the greater part of the property was in the King's warehouses at the time of the union of Holland to France, and was not delivered to the French until after that period.

The first remark, in answer to this objection, is obvious that it relates only to a part of the property, and cannot afford a foundation for a general answer in regard to the whole. The undersigned had the honor, in his last note, of pointing out this objection to M. de Nagell, and of requesting an explanation of his views respecting it, which his excellency, in his answer, declines to give. The objection, therefore, remains unanswered.

The second answer to this assertion is, that the property in question was ceded to the French Government by that of Holland several months before the union; that this cession deprived the owners of their property, and is the act upon which the claim is founded; and that the French, in taking possession of this property, only took possession of what belonged to them by a solemn treaty, ratified and executed in the usual forms. The undersigned had the honor of stating this answer, as well as the former one, in his last note, and supported it by passages from M. de Nagell's own notes, in which particular cargoes are said to have been delivered to the French by virtue of the treaty. M. de Nagell, without explaining these passages, observes, in his reply, that the Government have no official information upon this point. This accidental circumstance does not diminish the certainty of the fact, which is still confirmed by M. de Nagell's own testimony, and is too notorious to be called in question. The undersigned has in his possession several of the answers given at the time by the authorities of the country to the parties interested, in all of which it is directly implied, and in some explicitly stated, that the property was delivered to the French by virtue of the treaty; as in that of which he has the honor to transmit a copy annexed.

Thus the single assertion upon which the first part of the defence is founded is liable to two objections, either of which is sufficient to destroy its force, and neither of which has yet been attacked.

The second part of the defence maintains that the Government of this country is not responsible for the confiscation, supposing it to be proved. In this part of the argument, therefore, the fact of the confiscation is supposed, and this supposition is absolutely necessary, since, if the fact never happened, it is useless to reason upon its consequences. The undersigned will find occasion to recur to this preliminary observation in the course of his remarks, and will only add here that it was in this view, alone, that the discussion of the principle of responsibility was denominated unnecessary in his last note.

At the commencement of his argument on this principle, in his note of November, Baron de Nagell endeavors to prove that the King of Holland was not responsible for his own actions, on account of the dependence in which he was held by his brother Napoleon. He asserts that, in the opinion of Europe, the Government of France exercised at that time over that of Holland an influence inconsistent with national independence, and quotes, in support of this remark, as impartial expressions of the opinion of Europe, a passage from Mr. Schoell's abridged history of treaties, and a passage from a declaration of the British Government directed against that of the United States, in a time of war between the two countries. It is enough to mention the source from whence the latter of these passages is taken, to show that it is entirely inadmissible as authority on any subject against the United States. Mr. Schoell is certainly a respectable compiler, but has not been quoted by the undersigned as an authority in matters of opinion on the duties of nations, or as a sufficient organ of the sentiments of Europe. It is not necessary, however, to contest the remarks here cited from this writer, because it does not enter into the system of the American Government to deny that France exercised at this time a very great influence over Holland. The precise extent and character of this influence can, of course, be correctly known only to the Government of these two nations. But, in the view of the American Government, the existence of such an influence, however great it may have been, has no effect upon the claim, and the only operation of it would be to establish a corresponding claim of the Government of the Netherlands upon that of France. This idea has been already stated and developed several times in the notes of the undersigned, and he will not repeat here what he has before alleged in relation to it. He regrets that it has hitherto escaped the notice of M. de Nagell, because it is intended as an answer to one of the principal objections that have been urged against the claim.

With regard to the profit which Holland may be supposed to have derived from this transaction, the undersigned considers the remarks upon this point, in his note of July, as unaffected by those of Baron de Nagell in reply, and even as confirmed by the very forcible manner in which his excellency insists upon the friendly disposition of Louis towards the Americans. But this inquiry, like the one last considered, is immaterial, since a Government is not the less bound to make restitution of property acquired by violence, because it may have been in its turn deprived of the property so acquired by accident, as the greater violence of a stronger neighbor. An accidental remark of Mr. Eustis, that the proceeds of the property confiscated were ultimately deposited in the Imperial Treasury, has been repeatedly quoted by M. de Nagell, and seems to be regarded as an important admission. The undersigned does not see by what means this character can be attached to it. The fact upon which the claim is founded by the American Government is the cession of this property by Holland to France, and it is not surely very extraordinary that the proceeds of such a cession should be deposited in the French Treasury.

"But supposing King Louis to have been responsible for the seizure of the property, the responsibility does not devolve upon the present Government, because King Louis was a usurper."

How is this objection supported?

The undersigned has already stated, in regard to this point, a principle which appeared to him too clear to require proof, that established Governments are legitimate in the view of foreign nations. The Government of Louis was an established Government, in the fullest sense of the word. His title was never questioned in the Netherlands, from the time of his coronation to that of his abdication. The first posts of the administration were occupied in part by the same persons who now enjoy the confidence of his Majesty, and are employed in the Government; and the citizens in general acquiesced in his authority in various ways, express and implied. According to Puffendorf, in the passage cited by M. de Nagell, the acquiescence of the citizens, either tacit or express, makes the Government of a usurper legitimate, that is, binding on the citizens themselves. Surely, then, foreign nations have a right to consider it legitimate, since they are not bound to be more delicate for the citizens than they are for themselves. If, to use the strong language of Baron de Nagell, citizens who would consider themselves dishonored by associating in private life with rogues and robbers think proper to acquiesce in the Government of usurpers and tyrants, it is not for other nations to question their taste any further than their own safety may make it necessary.

What principles are opposed by Baron de Nagell to these plain propositions? The doctrine of Martens, which establishes the exception founded on the principle of self-defence—that is, with nations, the principle of self-government. The exception, instead of contradicting the rule, as usual, proves it, because they are only different developments of the same principle. The authority of Martens is, therefore, as the undersigned remarked in a former note, in favor of the American Government. As applied to the present case, his principle is as follows: "The United States would have had a right to interfere in the Government of Holland, had it been necessary for their own safety." Does this prove that they had no right to consider the established Government legitimate, when it was not necessary for their safety to interfere? Does it not suppose, on the contrary, that they had not only the right, but were bound, in general, to regard established Governments as legitimate? In like manner, on the same principle, the Netherlands have a right to interfere in the election of the President of the United States, if it should be necessary for their safety. Does this prove that they have no right to consider as legitimate the Government established in the United States? Does it not suppose, on the contrary, that they have not only the right, but are bound, in general, to regard it as legitimate?

The exception established by Martens, which, as has been shown, supposes the principle maintained by the United States is the only authority cited by Baron de Nagell in opposition to this principle, nor does he advance any arguments against it. He observes, however, that it is incompatible with the practice of the present day. What says the Government of Austria, in the late Presidential address to the German Diet, an address which has received the adhesion of Mr. de Martens, the author preferred by M. de Nagell, and a member of the Diet, as well as of the representative of this Government in that assembly? They are careful not to intrench upon the *right belonging to every State of the Confederacy to regulate its internal concerns according to its wants and its lights;* and yet the States of the Confederacy enjoy only a qualified sovereignty. How much more, then, does this right belong to States completely independent! The invasion of France by the allies in 1815 is the most remarkable instance in modern history of the exercise of the right of interference. How was it justified by the allies? They published a special declaration, stating that they were obliged, on the principle of self-defence, to make a united attack upon Napoleon Bonaparte, but disclaiming the intention of imposing a Government upon France. To this alliance the Government of the Netherlands acceded, and this is, therefore, their own interpretation of the right of interference. And what is the principle of this *legitimacy* which Baron de Nagell seems to oppose to the doctrine of the American Government? Is it not the very principle upon which the claim is founded, pushed to a much greater extent than is necessary to support it? The legitimacy of the Bourbons, for example: does it consist in having derived an undoubted title to the French crown from the founder of their race, who was himself a usurper, without the shadow of a title, or in the length of the time for which their Government had been established, and the quiet acquiescence of the French nation in it for a series of centuries? Is it not the European principle, that established Governments are not only legitimate, but that they are the only legitimate ones? That they are legitimate to the exclusion of others that might seem more conformable to the theory of political justice? This, if the undersigned is not deceived, is the European doctrine of legitimacy. The United States have no occasion, in the present case, to assert the principle to this extent. They only acknowledge the duty, and claim the right of regarding as legitimate, for the purpose of its foreign relations, a Government which was quietly established, and had received the acquiescence of the people.

Had the Government of the United States, after the establishment of the present Constitution, refused to pay the public debt contracted in the Netherlands, during the American war, on the ground that the form of government had been changed; that the debt was contracted under the old confederation; that they could not be responsible for what had been done by former Governments; that the Government was at that time illegitimate, founded in rebellion and usurpation, and not sanctified till some years after, by the acknowledgment of the mother country; and that the contracts of an illegitimate Government were not binding: the Government of the Netherlands would, probably, have replied, with great justice, that whatever might have been the character of the Government, in the opinion of the mother country, it was acknowledged as legitimate at the time by the citizens of the United States of America and the Netherlands, then in alliance, and that it was too late now to urge, in exemption from an obligation then contracted, that the title of the Government was, in theory, defective. They would have said that nations have a right to regulate their own Governments, but that the Government that they may establish, or in which they may acquiesce, is their legal representative, and that they are bound by its acts in their intercourse with foreign nations.

On these principles the Government of King Louis was a legitimate Government for the purposes of foreign relations. But grant that King Louis was a usurper, that is, that his title was defective, though the nation acquiesced in it. The doubts and distinctions expressed by Grotius and Puffendorf as to the obligation of the acts of a usurper arise altogether from the variety of senses in which the term may be understood. A usurper, in the proper sense of the term, is a pretender to the Government, whose claims have not been acquiesced in by the people. He is considered by the publicists as at war with the nation; and the nation, by opposing and making war upon him, enters a perpetual protest against his authority. Still, he exercises the Government, and therefore, for certain purposes, in fact, represents the nation. Distinctions may, perhaps, in such a case, be reasonably taken in regard to the degree in which his acts are binding. The publicists are, evidently, much disposed, even under these circumstances, to make them obligatory. Puffendorf says that there is no doubt that all the public debts are binding; that the obligation of the other acts is less clear, but that, in his opinion, they are obligatory. He considers the precise case of the present claim a valid and legitimate transaction: of course, the nation is responsible. The remark of Grotius is less favorable to the obligation of these acts, but, if it were more developed, would probably amount to the same thing, as he expressly enjoins in the same sentence the duty of restitution—a duty which, it would seem almost needless to add, cannot be affected by any accident or violence that may have happened to the property to be restored. The case of the Emperor Napoleon, during the hundred days, is one of the strongest cases of usurpation that can be imagined. And yet the French nation, under another Government, is made responsible, not only for public debts, but for the remote consequences of his actions during these hundred days to the amount of seven hundred millions of francs. Such are the opinions of the publicists and the practice of Europe in regard to the obligation of the acts of a usurper, taking the term in a strict and proper sense. They are, evidently, not unfavorable to the claim. But taking the claim in the only sense in which it can be applied to King Louis, a sovereign whose title is defective, but has received the acquiescence of the nation, and there is not a passage in any of the publicists which throws the least doubt upon the obligation of all his acts. The whole tenor of their writings shows that they regard such a Government as legitimate, not only for its foreign relations, but for all purposes whatsoever; and Puffendorf states this doctrine expressly in the very passage cited by Baron de Nagell.

The undersigned does not think it necessary to engage in a general defence of the ancient publicists against the repeated attacks of Baron de Nagell. The defects in their manner belonged to the age in which they wrote. Their merits are sufficiently proved by the use which has constantly been made of them up to the present day in the parliamentary, diplomatic, and judicial discussions of Europe and

America. The name of Grotius is regarded by foreigners as one of the titles of glory of which the Netherlands have to boast. Besides, the general principle of responsibility, in support of which they were quoted by the undersigned in his first note, is not denied by the Baron de Nagell. Consequently, the degree of weight which may properly be attached to their authority is, in this case, the less material. Notwithstanding these considerations, his excellency has employed a large part of his note of November in citing from Puffendorf the passage which relates to this subject, and accompanying it by a commentary. The undersigned, from a real respect for any reasoning that is sanctioned by the authority of his Majesty's Government, will take the passage as cited, although some parts of it favorable to the United States are omitted, and will examine in detail the commentary that accompanies it. After quoting the passage, M. de Nagell annexes the following remarks:

1. "This being the passage in question, and it is only an exemplification of a parallel passage in Grotius, we can now judge how far it favors the reply. It is said to prove that a nation is not affected by changes in its form of government, and can only be destroyed by the destruction of the body politic; while Puffendorf formally excepts the case in which a State becomes a simple province of another State, and this was precisely the case of Holland by its incorporation with France."

Answer. This remark denies the fact of the confiscation by the Government of Holland, which is here supposed. If the property was confiscated by the French after the union, the French are, of course, responsible. The question is here, whether the present Government is responsible, provided the property was confiscated before the union by King Louis; or in M. de Nagell's own language, "on the supposition that the confiscation may be fairly attributed to Louis." The remark of Puffendorf establishes the doctrine of the United States to a greater extent than is necessary to support this claim, and refutes all the reasoning of Baron de Nagell from the supposed supremacy exercised by France over Holland during the reign of Louis. Puffendorf states, that if one nation becomes a province of another in name and in reality, provided the province is governed in a separate form, the responsibility continues. It cannot be denied that Holland was separate in form and independent in name.

2. "The passage is said to prove that every Government which succeeds another, were the latter even founded in usurpation, is responsible for all the acts of the preceding Government; and Puffendorf confines the obligation expressly to the public debts contracted for the wants of the State, and contents himself with pointing out what appears to him *not obligatory* but *reasonable* with regard to the rest.

Answer. Puffendorf, as cited by M. de Nagell, declares, in general, that the *treaties, contracts,* and *other acts* of Governments, are binding on their successors. He adds, that, in the case of a usurper who had been dispossessed, and whose title has not been acquiesced in by the nation, (which is, of course, not the present case,) some have doubted whether any other engagements than public debts are binding, but that, in his opinion, *it is reasonable to consider them all obligatory.* The undersigned has repeatedly stated that, in the view of his Government, it is not necessary to examine, in this case, whether the acts of a usurper are binding on the successor; as far as he has considered this question, it has only been hypothetically.

3. "The passage is said to show that a people is bound to repair the injury done to foreigners; and the first case proposed by Puffendorf is, whether a people can keep what has been taken, bought, or given by a usurper."

Answer. The case proposed by Puffendorf is, whether a people ought to restore what has been taken by a foreign usurper from a third party, in time of war, and given or sold to them. The present case is, whether a people ought to restore what has been taken by itself, under a former Government, from a friendly power. It is easy to see that they are not the same.

4. "Finally, it is said to prove that a people is held to restore what it has plundered, although the plunder may have passed into other hands; and Puffendorf, without examining at all, in this second case, whether the duty of restitution is attached or not to the possession of the thing to be restored, decides that, according to general usage and the common opinion, if even *citizens* are not, as the reply vaguely translates the word, *individuals,* but oppressed citizens, have been unjustly plundered by a usurper, they have no right to reclaim their property."

Answer. Of whom does Puffendorf decide that they have no right to reclaim it? Of the usurper or his representatives? Just the contrary. They have no right to reclaim it of a third party, to whom the usurper has conveyed it—that is, in the present case, the Americans have no right to reclaim their property of France. This is the view taken of the subject by the American Government in bringing the claim against the Netherlands. As to the translation of the word *citoyens,* it is well known that the rights of friendly foreigners and citizens to the protection of Government are the same. To avoid an explanation, the undersigned translated the term at once by a word including the former.

5. "The only point, therefore, which the passage proves, is the distinction established by the undersigned (Baron de Nagell) between public debts, of which the acknowledgment and obligation cannot be contested, and engagements whose validity remains hypothetical."

Answer. It has been shown, in the answer to the second of these remarks, what foundation there is in Puffendorf for this distinction. Besides, the only difference between public debts and other engagements is, that the former are acknowledged in a particular form; and M. de Nagell admits, in his note of November, that this circumstance makes no difference in the obligation. Hence, the distinction, if really taken by Puffendorf, has been formally disavowed by his excellency. In general, any distinction that may be made between the degrees of obligation of various kinds of debts must be founded on different considerations from those of right. Policy may dictate a preference of public debts over other engagements, but in principle there is no medium between what is due and what is not due.

The undersigned perceives with pleasure that Baron de Nagell is disposed to regard with some attention the reasoning in favor of the claim from the parallel cases which occurred in France under the treaties of 1815. These examples are also considered by the American Government as among the strongest arguments in their behalf; and the more as they refute the objection of usurpation. The Government of Bonaparte, during the hundred days, independently of any supposed defects in his title. having no pretensions to the character of an established Government, may, perhaps, be fairly considered as strong an instance of usurpation as any on record; and yet, as has been already observed, it was for the result of the acts of the French nation during this period that they were made responsible under Louis XVIII.

M. de Nagell has accumulated, in his note of November, a considerable number of passages from Schoell and others, for the purpose of proving that the payments required of France were intended as an indemnity for the expense of the last preceding armaments. The undersigned never doubted this proposition, and if he had, the slightest inspection of the treaties, and of the tables of distribution of the money paid, would have satisfied him of his error; but he must beg leave to express his opinion that it does not destroy, in any degree, the application of the example. The acts of the French nation during ·the· hundred days subjected the allies, in their opinion, to a great expense, and this expense the French nation, under the succeeding Government of Louis XVIII, is required to pay. "In these payments," says M. de Nagell, "the principle of responsibility had no part." All that the American Government demand of the Government of the Netherlands is to be indemnified for losses occasioned by the acts of the former Government. As the cases are evidently parallel, it is unnecessary to reason upon the propriety of words. The undersigned must, however, be permitted to observe that, in his opinion, to say that the French nation was required to indemnify the allies for expenses occasioned by the acts of Bonaparte, is only to say, in other terms, that the French nation was made responsible for the acts of Bonaparte.

It is true that M. de Nagell has cited a passage from Schoell, in which that writer seems to intimate, in rather a vague way, that the payments in question were to be considered, in part, as a contribution imposed by right of conquest; in other words, as an act of arbitrary violence independent of any principle. The undersigned has shown, in a former note, that the principle of indemnity or responsibility, which is the same thing, is recognized by the plenipotentiaries of both parties, in their official correspondence, as the foundation of these payments. This idea of Schoell, therefore, (if, as may be doubted, he intended to convey the idea,) falls of itself; and it is too injurious to the allies to be insisted on by M. de Nagell. But, to remove all doubt upon this point, it is sufficient to add, that the allies themselves, in the negotiations upon this subject, expressly disclaim any pretensions of this description. Their plenipotentiaries observe, in their note of September 22, 1815, " none of the propositions which have been made by order of the sovereigns, to regulate the present and future relations of Europe, have been founded on the right of conquest, and they have carefully avoided, in their communications, everything that could lead to a discussion of this right."

The remark of M. de Nagell, in his note of November, upon the case of the Bank of Hamburg, involves a denial of the fact of confiscation by King Louis which is here supposed by both parties. The principle maintained by the undersigned in a former note in regard to the confiscations in the Duchy of Berg was this: that nations are responsible for the acts of violence committed by their Governments, but not for all those committed upon their territory. Baron de Nagell will judge for himself whether this is the principle he wishes to establish, recollecting, as has just been observed, that the act of confiscation is here supposed by both parties to be the act of King Louis.

The undersigned will not enter in detail into the particulars of the three cases of the Baltimore, the Bacchus, and the St. Michael, which Baron de Nagell has again introduced at the commencement of his note of November. No essential error has been pointed out in the statement of the undersigned respecting them. M. de Nagell again attributes to the undersigned an opinion respecting the protection granted to the Baltimore which it was never his intention to express and which he formally disavowed in his note of July. The variation in the date of the arrival of this vessel might have been important had the claim been founded on the sequester; but, as it is founded on the confiscation of the property, it is evidently immaterial. Baron de Nagell charged Mr. Eustis with error in stating that the cargoes of the Baltimore and the Bacchus were confiscated by order of the Dutch Government, while, in the same note, he observed himself, of these two cargoes, that they were delivered to the French by virtue of the treaty of March, 1810, which was the act of confiscation intended by Mr. Eustis. This was the particular variation concerning which the undersigned took the liberty of observing that Baron de Nagell was himself in error by his own admission.

His excellency has thought proper to quote a second time certain expressions applied by the undersigned, in his note of February, to the confiscation of shipwrecked property, with the remark, that, by these expressions, "the claimants have committed their protectors." The sense of this remark is not apparent, and the undersigned is, therefore, unable to judge of its propriety. He can only observe that, in his opinion, the confiscation of the property of a friendly nation, thrown into the power of the Government by shipwreck and stress of weather, or invited by facilities held out by itself, is an act of violence which, whether it is to be attributed to France or Holland, is deserving of the strongest terms of disapprobation that language can afford. As the two Governments look at the facts from different points of view, it is not singular that they should form different judgments of the moral character of the proceedings of the Government of Holland, according as they attribute to it a more or less immediate agency in the confiscation, and each may be right on its own supposition of fact. The undersigned must, however, be allowed to add, that he finds it impossible to reconcile with the facts, even as viewed by the Government of the Netherlands, the assertion of Baron de Nagell in regard to the St. Michael. The St. Michael was a ship bound to a different port and driven into the Texel by stress of weather, seeking only the hospitality of the shore and leave to depart. By the admission of M. de Nagell her cargo was sequestered by the Government of Holland, and yet he adds that she was treated as she would be anywhere else. The undersigned is not acquainted with any civilized nation where it is the practice to sequester the property of citizens of a friendly power driven into port by stress of weather.

The undersigned has now examined the several parts of M. de Nagell's last notes, and replied to them in a manner which appears to him to be satisfactory. He is aware, however, that, from the different views of the two Governments with regard to this subject, many of the considerations here adduced will be thought less forcible by his excellency; and that, in general, the effect of a discussion so long protracted as this is rather to confirm the respective opinions of the parties than to change them. He is, therefore, compelled, though reluctantly, to anticipate the failure of this attempt, as well as of the others which he has already made, to bring this claim to the conclusion desired by his Government. In this event it would be unreasonable to calculate upon a favorable result from any further proceedings in the way of direct negotiation; and, as the United States are not less unwilling to abandon the claim than the Netherlands are to allow it, it will become necessary, on the failure of this method, to adopt some other way of bringing the controversy to an amicable conclusion. For this purpose the undersigned has the honor of submitting to the consideration of his excellency the following propositions as likely, if adopted, to produce a result which, in either event, shall be satisfactory to both parties.

1. It is proposed that an impartial commission should be instituted by the two Governments in concert, to make a preliminary examination of the facts, as far as they affect the question of responsibility, and agree upon a statement of them to be reported to the Governments.

2. If, upon this statement of facts, the two Governments should still differ upon the question of

responsibility, it is proposed that this point should be referred to the decision of some friendly sovereign, to be agreed upon between them.

As the Government of the Netherlands appear to rest their defence, in a considerable degree, upon a denial of the facts which were supposed by the American Government, in the first instance, to be admitted, it seems absolutely necessary that this part of the subject should be submitted to an inquiry of the kind contemplated in the first of these propositions. The American Government is ready to substantiate by evidence the facts which they consider necessary to the establishment of the claim; and it is presumed that the Government of the Netherlands is also prepared to support, in the same way, those which they regard as contradictory to it. It is obvious that an examination of this kind cannot be conveniently conducted in the way of diplomatic correspondence, but must be referred to a commission constituted in such a way that both parties may be able to rely upon its decision.

The result of such an inquiry having defined with precision the basis of fact upon which the question of responsibility is raised, this question would, probably, be brought within much narrower limits; but, should the two Governments finally disagree respecting it, the mode of reference to a friendly sovereign seems to be an unexceptionable way of bringing it to a decision.

No. 15.

Extract of a letter from Mr. Adams to Mr. Everett, Chargé d'Affaires at the Hague, May 26, 1820.

' Your despatches to No. 43, inclusive, dated March 13, have been received. Your discussion of the claims of our citizens upon the Government of the Netherlands has been entirely satisfactory to the President, who regrets that its just reasoning and forcible appeals to well established facts has not been attended with success in producing the conviction, on the part of the Government of the Netherlands, that it was in justice incumbent on them to make provision for indemnifying the sufferers interested in them. On taking leave, the Viscount de Quabeck, under instructions from his Government, intimated verbally to me their wish that this discussion should not be further pressed; and, although he was distinctly informed that the rights of our citizens to indemnity for injuries so unjustifiable and flagrant could not be abandoned, the President believes that it may be expedient to forbear renewing applications in their behalf for the present. Your last note, therefore, of which you have forwarded to me the draft, may be reserved until you hear further from this Department on the subject."

18TH CONGRESS.]   No. 403.   [2D SESSION.

SUPPRESSION OF THE AFRICAN SLAVE TRADE.

COMMUNICATED TO THE HOUSE OF REPRESENTATIVES FEBRUARY 16, 1825.

Mr. GOVAN, from the Committee on the Suppression of the Slave Trade, to whom was referred so much of the President's message of the 7th of December last as relates to that subject, having, according to order, had the same under consideration, reported:

That, pursuant to the almost unanimous request of the House of Representatives, expressed by their resolution of February 28, 1823, the President of the United States concluded a convention with Great Britain on the 13th of March, in the following year, by which the African slave trade was denounced to be piracy under the laws of both countries; the United States having so declared it by their antecedent act of May 15, 1820, and it being understood between the contracting parties, as a preliminary to the ratification of the convention by the United States, that Great Britain should, by an act of her Parliament, concur in a similar declaration.

With great promptitude, and in accordance with this agreement, such an act was passed, declaring the African slave trade to be piracy, and annexing to it the penalty denounced against this crime by the common law of nations. A copy of this act was transmitted by the British Government to the Executive of the United States, and the convention submitted by the President to the Senate for their advice and consent.

The convention was approved by the Senate, with certain qualifications, to all of which, except one, Great Britain, *sub modo*, acceded; her Government having instructed its minister in Washington to tender to the acceptance of the United States a treaty agreeing in every particular, except one, with the terms approved by the Senate. This exception the message of the President to the House of Representatives presumes "not to be of sufficient magnitude to defeat an object so near to the heart of both nations" as the abolition of the African slave trade, "and so desirable to the friends of humanity throughout the world." But the President further adds, "that, as objections to the principle recommended by the House of Representatives, or at least to the consequences inseparable from it, and which are understood to apply to the law, have been raised, which may deserve a reconsideration of the whole subject, he has thought proper to suspend the conclusion of a new convention until the definitive sentiments of Congress can be ascertained."

Your committee are therefore required to review the grounds of the law of 1820 and the resolution of 1823, to which the rejected, or, as they rather hope, the suspended convention referred. The former was the joint act of both branches of Congress, approved by the President; the latter, although adopted with extraordinary unanimity, was the single act of the House of Representatives.

Upon the *principle* or *intention* of the act of Congress of 1820, making the slave trade punishable as piracy, the history of the act may reflect some light.

A bill from the Senate, entitled "An act to continue in force the act to protect the commerce of the United States and punish the crime of piracy, and also to make further provision to punish the crime of piracy," came to the House of Representatives on .the 27th of April, 1820, and was, on the same day, referred to a Committee of the Whole, to which had been referred a bill of similar purport and title that had originated in the House of Representatives.

Upon the 8th of May following, the Committee on the Suppression of the Slave Trade reported an amendment of two additional sections to the Senate's bill; also, a bill to incorporate the American Society for Colonizing the Free People of Color of the United States, and three joint resolutions, two of which related to the objects of that society, but the first of which, in behalf of both Houses of Congress, requested the President to "consult and negotiate with all the Governments where ministers of the United States are or shall be accredited, on the means of effecting an entire and immediate abolition of the African slave trade." The amendatory sections denounced the guilt and penalty of piracy against any citizen of the United States, of the crew or company of any foreign vessel, and any person whatever of the crew or company of any American vessel who should be engaged in this traffic.

The amendments, bill, and resolutions, along with the explanatory report which accompanied them, were referred to the Committee of the Whole above mentioned, and on the 11th of the same month the House proceeded to consider them. After a discussion in the committee, the piracy bill and its amendments, having been adopted, were reported, and both were concurred in by the House. The following day the bill, as amended, being then on its passage, a motion was debated and *negatived* to recommit the bill to a select committee, with an instruction to strike out the last section of the amendment. The bill then passed, and was ordered to be returned, as amended, to the Senate.

On the same day a motion prevailed to discharge the Committee of the Whole from the further consideration of the bill and the resolutions which accompanied the report; and the particular resolution already recited being under consideration, to try the sense of the House on its merits, it was moved to lay it on the table. The yeas and nays having been ordered on this motion, it was rejected by a majority of seventy-eight to thirty-five members. It having been again proposed to postpone the resolution till the ensuing or second session of the same Congress, and this proposal being also determined in the negative, the resolution was engrossed, read the third time, passed, and ordered to be transmitted to the Senate on the same day with the piracy bill.

The amendments of this bill underwent like scrutiny and debate in the Senate, and were finally concurred in the day after they were received from the House of Representatives without any division apparent on the journal of that House.

The resolution, which had been received by the Senate at a different hour of the same day, was read a second time on the 15th of May, was further taken up and considered, as in Committee of the Whole, reported to the House without amendment, and ordered, after debate, to pass to a third reading. But, this being the last day of the session of Congress, and a single member objecting "that it was against one of the rules of the Senate to read it the third time on the same day, without unanimous consent," it remained on the table of that body, on its final adjournment, after an ineffectual effort to suspend one of their rules, against which many of the friends of the resolution felt themselves compelled, by their invariable usage, to vote, in union with its enemies.

One of the objections to the resolution in the Senate was founded upon the peculiar relation of that branch of the National Legislature to the Executive in the ratification of treaties, which seemed, in the opinion of those who urged this argument, to interdict their concurrence in a request of the President to institute any negotiation whatever.

A cotemporary exposition of the object of the amendments of the piracy bill and the resolution, which the House of Representatives adopted by so large a majority, will be found in the report, which accompanied them, from the Committee on the Suppression of the Slave Trade, and which is hereto annexed, (A.) Those objects, it will be seen, were in perfect accordance with each other. They were designed to introduce, by treaty, into the code of international law a principle deemed by the committee essential to the abolition of the African slave trade, that it should be denounced and treated as piracy by the civilized world.

The resolution being joint, and having failed in the Senate, for the reason already stated, the subject of it was revived in the House of Representatives at a very early period of the succeeding session of Congress, by a call for information from the Executive, which, being received, was referred to a committee of the same title with the last. Their report, after reviewing all the antecedent measures of the United States for the suppression of the slave trade, urgently recommended the co-operation of the American and British Navy against this traffic, under the guarded provisions of a common treaty authorizing the practice of a qualified and reciprocal right of search.

This report, which is also annexed, closed with a resolution requesting "the President of the United States to enter into such arrangements as he might deem suitable and proper, with one or more of the maritime powers of Europe, for the effectual abolition of the African slave trade." (B)

The United States had, by the treaty of Ghent, entered into a formal stipulation with Great Britain, "that both the contracting parties shall use their best endeavors to accomplish the entire abolition of this traffic."

The failure of the only joint attempt which had been made by England and America, at the date of this report, to give effect to this provision being ascribable, in part, to a jealousy of the views of the former, corroborated by the language and conduct of one of the principal maritime powers of Europe in relation to the same topic, the committee referred to the decision of Sir William Scott in the case of the French ship Le Louis, to demonstrate that Great Britain claimed no right of search in peace but such as the consent of other nations should accord to her by treaty, and sought it by a fair exchange, in this tranquil mode, for the beneficent purpose of an enlarged humanity.

Certain facts disclosed by the diplomatic correspondence of France and England, during the pendency of that case in the British Court of Admiralty, were calculated to guard the sympathies of America from being misguided by the language of the former power.

. The painful truth was elicited that France had evaded the execution of her promise at Vienna to

Europe and mankind; that she had, long after the date of that promise, tolerated, if she had not cherished, several branches of a traffic which she had concurred in denouncing to be the opprobrium of Christendom, and which she had subsequently bound herself by the higher obligations of a solemn treaty to abolish, as inconsistent with the laws of God and Nature.

Succeeding events in the councils of the French nation have not impaired the force of this testimony. What authority can be accorded to the moral influence of a Government which insults the humanity of a generous and gallant people by pleading, in apology for the breach of its plighted faith, that its subjects required the indulgence of this guilty traffic?

The Emperor Napoleon, who re-established this commerce on the ruins of the French Republic, also abolished it again, when he sought to conciliate the people of France during that transient reign which immediately preceded his final overthrow.

Congress adjourned without acting on this report.

By an instruction to the Committee on the Suppression of the Slave Trade, of the 15th of January, 1822, the same subject was a third time brought directly before the House of Representatives. The instruction called the attention of the committee to the present condition of the African slave trade, to the defects of any of the existing laws for its suppression, and to their appropriate remedies. In the report made in obedience to this instruction, on the 12th of April, 1822, the committee state that, after having consulted all the evidence within their reach, they are brought to the mournful conclusion that the traffic prevailed to a greater extent than ever, and with increased malignity; that its total suppression, or even sensible diminution, cannot be expected from the separate and disunited efforts of one or more States, so long as a single flag remains to cover it from detection and punishment. They renew, therefore, as the only practicable and efficient remedy, the concurrence of the United States with the maritime powers of Europe in a modified and reciprocal exercise of the right of search.

In closing their report, the committee add, in effect, that they "cannot doubt that the people of America have the intelligence to distinguish between the right of searching a neutral on the high seas, in time of war, claimed by some belligerents, and that mutual, restricted, and peaceful concession, by treaty, suggested by the committee, and which is demanded in the name of suffering humanity." The committee had before intimated that the remedy which they recommended to the House of Representatives presupposed the exercise of the authority of another Department of the Government, and that objections to the exercise of this authority, in the mode which they had presumed to suggest, had hitherto existed in that Department. Their report, also annexed, closed with a resolution differing in no other respect from that of the preceding session than that it did not require the concurrence of the Senate, for the reason already suggested. (C.)

The report and resolution were referred to a Committee of the Whole, and never further considered.

After a delay till the 20th of the succeeding February a resolution was submitted to the House, which was evidently a part of the same system of measures, for the suppression of the slave trade, which had been begun by the act of the 3d of March, 1819, and followed up by the connected series of reports and resolutions which the committee have reviewed, and which breathe the same spirit.

This resolution, in proposing to make the slave trade piracy, by the consent of mankind, sought to supplant, by a measure of greater rigor, the qualified international exchange of the right of search for the apprehension of the African slave dealer, and the British system of mixed tribunals created for his trial and punishment; a system of which experience, and the recent extension of the traffic that it sought to limit, had disclosed the entire inefficacy.

The United States had already established the true denomination and grade of this offence by a municipal law. The resolution contemplated, as did the report which accompanied and expounded that law, the extension of its principle, by negotiation, to the code of all nations.

It denounced the authors of this stupendous iniquity as the enemies of the human race, and armed all men with authority to detect, pursue, arrest, and punish them.

Such a measure, to succeed to its fullest extent, must have a beginning somewhere. Commencing with the consent of any two States, to regard it as binding on themselves only, it would, by the gradual accession of others, enlarge the sphere of its operation until it embraced, as the resolution contemplated, all the maritime powers of the civilized world.

While it involved of necessity the visit and search of piratical vessels, as *belligerent rights* against the common enemies of man, it avoided all complexity, difficulty, and delay in the seizure, condemnation, and punishment of the pirate himself. It made no distinction in favor of those pirates who prey upon the property, against those who seize, torture, and kill, or consign to interminable and hereditary slavery, the persons of their enemies.

Your committee are at a loss for the foundation of any such discrimination. It is believed that the most ancient piracies consisted in converting innocent captives into slaves; and those were not attended with the destruction of one-third of their victims by loathsome confinement and mortal disease.

While the modern, therefore, accords with the ancient denomination of this crime, its punishment is not disproportionate to its guilt. It has robbery and murder for its mere accessories, and moistens one continent with blood and tears, in order to curse another by slow, consuming ruin, physical and moral.

One high consolation attends upon the new remedy for this frightful and prolific evil. If once successful, it will forever remain so, until, being unexerted, its very application will be found in history alone.

Can it be doubted that if ever legitimate commerce shall supplant the source of this evil in Africa, and a reliance on other supplies of labor its use elsewhere, a revival of the slave trade will be as impracticable as a reversion to barbarism? that after the lapse of a century from its extinction, except where the consequences of the crime shall survive, the stories of the African slave trade will become as improbable, among the unlearned, as the expeditions of the heroes of Homer?

The principle of the law of 1820, making the slave trade a statutory piracy, and of the resolution of the House of Representatives of May, 1823, which sought to render this denunciation of that offence universal, cannot, therefore, be misunderstood.

It was not misconceived by the House of Representatives, when ratified with almost unprecedented unanimity.

An unfounded suggestion has been heard that the abortive attempt to amend the resolution indicated that it was not considered as involving the right of search. The opposite conclusion is the more rational, if not, indeed, irresistible: that having, by the denomination of the crime, provided for the detection, trial, and punishment of the criminal, an amendment, designing to add what was already included in the main proposition, would be superfluous, if not absurd. But no such amendment *was* rejected. The House of

Representatives, very near the close of the session of 1823, desirous of economizing time threatened to be consumed by a protracted debate, entertained *the previous question* while an amendment—the only one offered to the resolution—was depending. The effect of the previous question was to bring on an immediate decision upon the resolution itself, which was adopted by a vote of 131 members to 9.

It is alike untrue that the resolution was regarded with indifference. The House had been prepared to pass it without debate, by a series of measures having their origin in 1839, and steadily advancing to maturity.

Before the resolution *did* pass, two motions had been submitted—to lay it on the table, and to postpone it to a future day. The former was resisted by an ascertained majority of 104 to 25; the latter, without a division.

Is the House now ready to retrace its steps?

The committee believe not. Neither the people of America nor their representatives will sully the glory they have earned by their early labor and steady perseverance in sustaining by their Federal and State Governments the cause of humanity at home and abroad.

The calamity inflicted upon them by the introduction of slavery in a form and to an extent forbidding its hasty alleviation by intemperate zeal is imputable to a foreign cause, for which the past is responsible to the present age. They will not deny to themselves and to mankind a generous co-operation in the only efficient measure of retributive justice to an insulted and afflicted continent, and to an injured and degraded race.

In the independence of Spanish and Portugese America the committee behold a speedy termination of the few remaining obstacles to the extension of the policy of the resolution of May, 1823.

Brazil cannot intend to resist the voice of the residue of the continent of America; and Portugal, deprived of her great market for slaves, will no longer have a motive to resist the common feelings of Europe. And yet, while from the Rio de la Plata to the Amazon and through the American archipelago the importation of slaves covertly continues, if it be not openly countenanced, the impolicy is obvious of denying to the American shore the protective vigilance of the only adequate check upon this traffic.

Your committee forbear to enter upon an investigation of the particular provisions of a depending negotiation, nor do they consider the message referred to them as inviting any such inquiry.

They will not regard a negotiation to be dissolved which has approached so near a consummation, nor a convention as absolutely void which has been executed by one party, and which the United States, having first tendered, should be the last to reject.

A.

Report of the Committee to whom was referred, at the commencement of the present session of Congress, so much of the President's message as relates to the slave trade, accompanied with a bill to incorporate the American Society for Colonizing the Free People of Color of the United States.

The Committee on the Slave Trade, to whom was referred the memorial of the President and Board of Managers of the American Society for Colonizing the Free People of Color of the United States, having, according to order, had under consideration the several subjects therein embraced, reported:

That the American Society was instituted in the city of Washington, on the 28th of December, 1816, for the benevolent purpose of affording to the free people of color of the United States the means of establishing one or more independent colonies on the western coast of Africa. After ascertaining, by a mission to that continent and other preliminary inquiries, that their object is practicable, the society request of the Congress of the United States a charter of incorporation and such other legislative aid as their enterprise may be thought to merit and require.

The memorialists anticipate from its success consequences the most beneficial to the free people of color themselves, to the several States in which they at present reside, and to that continent which is to be the seat of their future establishment. Passing by the foundation of these anticipations, which will be seen in the annual reports of the society and their former memorials, the attention of the committee has been particularly drawn to the connexion which the memorialists have traced between their purpose and the policy of the recent act of Congress for the more effectual abolition of the African slave trade.

Experience has demonstrated that this detestable traffic can be nowhere so successfully assailed as on the coast upon which it originates. Not only does the collection and embarkation of its unnatural cargoes consume more time than their subsequent distribution and sale in the market for which they are destined, but the African coast, frequented by the slave ships, is indented with so few commodious or accessible harbors that, notwithstanding its great extent, it could be guarded by the vigilance of a few active cruisers. If to these be added colonies of civilized blacks, planted in commanding situations along that coast, no slave ship could possibly escape detection; and thus the security as well as the enhanced profit which now cherishes this illicit trade would be effectually counteracted. Such colonies, by diffusing a taste for legitimate commerce among the native tribes of that fruitful continent, would gradually destroy among them, also, the only incentive of a traffic which has hitherto rendered all African labor insecure, and spread desolation over one of the most beautiful regions of the globe. The colonies and the armed vessels employed in watching the African coast, while they co-operated alike in the cause of humanity, would afford to each other mutual succor.

There is a single consideration, however, added to the preceding view of this subject, which appears to your committee, of itself, conclusive of the tendency of the views of the memorialists to further the operation of the act of the third of March, 1819. That act not only revokes the authority antecedently given to the several State and Territorial Governments to dispose, as they pleased, of those African captives who might be liberated by the tribunals of the United States, but authorizes and requires the President to restore them to their native country. The unavoidable consequence of this just and humane provision is, to require some preparation to be made for their temporary succor, on being relanded upon the African shore. And no preparation can prove so congenial to its own object, or so economical, as regards the Government charged with this charitable duty, as that which would be found in a colony of the free people of color of the United States. Sustained by the recommendations of numerous societies in every part of the United States, and the approving voice of the legislative assemblies of several States, without inquiring into any other tendency of the object of the memorialists, your committee do not hesitate to pronounce it deserving of the countenance and support of the General Government. The extent to which these shall be carried is a question not so easily determined.

The memorialists do not ask the Government to assume the jurisdiction of the Territory, or to become in any degree whatever responsible for the future safety or tranquillity of the contemplated colony. They have prudently thought that its external peace and security would be most effectually guarded by an appeal in its behalf to the philanthrophy of the civilized world, and to that sentiment of retributive justice, with which all Christendom is at present animated towards a much injured continent.

Of the constitutional power of the General Government to grant the limited aid contemplated by the accompanying bill and resolutions your committee presume there can exist no shadow of doubt; and they leave it to a period of greater national prosperity to determine how far the authority of Congress, the resources of the National Government, and the welfare and happiness of the United States, will warrant or require its extension.

Your committee are solemnly enjoined by the peculiar object of their trust, and invited by the suggestion of the memorialists, to inquire into the defects of the existing laws against the African slave trade. So long as it is in the power of the United States to provide additional restraints upon this odious traffic they cannot be withheld, consistently with justice and the honor of the nation.

Congress has heretofore marked, with decided reprobation, the authors and abettors of this iniquitous commerce in every form which it assumes; from the inception of its unrighteous purpose in America, through all the subsequent stages of its progress to its final consummation; the outward voyage, the cruel seizure and forcible abduction of the unfortunate African from his native home, and the fraudulent transfer of the property thus acquired. It may, however, be questioned if a proper discrimination of their relative guilt has entered into the measure of punishment annexed to these criminal acts.

Your committee cannot perceive wherein the offence of kidnapping an unoffending inhabitant of a foreign country; of chaining him down for a series of days, weeks, and months, amidst the dying and the dead, to the pestilential hold of a slave ship; of consigning him, if he chance to live out the voyage, to perpetual slavery in a remote and unknown land, differs in malignity from piracy, or why a milder punishment should follow the one than the other crime.

On the other hand, the purchase of the unfortunate African, after his enlargement from the floating dungeon which wafts him to the foreign market, however criminal in itself, and yet more in its tendency to encourage this abominable traffic, yields in atrocity to the violent seizure of his person, his sudden and unprepared separation from his family, his kindred, his friends, and his country, followed by all the horrors of the middle passage. Are there not united in this offence all that is most iniquitous in theft, most daring in robbery, and cruel in murder? Its consequences to the victim, if he survives, to the country which receives him, and to that from which he is torn, are alike disastrous. If the internal wars of Africa, and their desolating effect, may be imputed to the slave trade, and that the greater part of them must cannot now be questioned, this crime, considered in its remote as well as its proximate consequences, is the very darkest in the whole catalogue of human iniquities; and its authors should be regarded as *hostes humani generis.*

In proposing to the House of Representatives to make such part of this offence as occurs upon the ocean piracy, your committee are animated, not by the desire of manifesting to the world the horror with which it is viewed by the American people, but by the confident expectation of promoting, by this example, its more certain punishment by all nations, and its absolute and final extinction.

May it not be believed that, when the whole civilized world shall have denounced the slave trade as piracy, it will become as unfrequent as any other species of that offence against the law of nations? Is it unreasonable to suppose that negotiation will, with greater facility, introduce into that law such a provision as is here proposed, when it shall have been already incorporated in the separate code of each State?

The maritime powers of the Christian world have at length concurred in pronouncing sentence of condemnation against this traffic. The United States, having led the way in forming this decree, owe it to themselves not to *follow* the rest of mankind in promoting its vigorous execution.

If it should be objected that the legislation of Congress would be partial, and its benefit, for a time at least, local, it may be replied that the constitutional power of the Government has already been exercised in defining the crime of piracy, in accordance with similar analogies to that which the committee have sought to trace between this general offence against the peace of nations and the slave trade.

In some of the foreign treaties, as well as in the laws of the United States, examples are to be found of piracies which are not cognizable as such by the tribunals of all nations. Such is the unavoidable consequence of any exercise of the authority of Congress to define and punish this crime. The definition and the punishment can bind the United States alone.

A bill from the Senate, making further provision for the exercise of this constitutional power, being now before the House of Representatives, your committee beg leave to offer such an amendment of its provisions as shall attain the last object which they have presumed to recommend.

B.

Report of the Committee to whom was referred so much of the President's message as relates to the slave trade.

The Committee to whom was referred so much of the President's message as relates to the slave trade, and to whom were referred the two messages of the President transmitting, in pursuance of the resolution of the House of Representatives of the 4th of December, a report of the Secretary of State, and inclosed documents, relating to the negotiation for the suppression of the slave trade, reported:

That the committee have deemed it advisable, previous to entering into a consideration of the proposed co-operation to exterminate the slave trade, to take a summary review of the Constitution and laws of the United States relating to this subject. It will disclose the earnestness and zeal with which this nation has been actuated, and the laudable ambition that has animated her councils to take a lead in the reformation of a disgraceful practice, and one which is productive of so much human misery; it will, by displaying the constant anxiety of this nation to suppress the African slave trade, afford ample testimony that she will be the last to persevere in measures wisely digested to effectuate this great and most desirable object, whenever such measures can be adopted in consistency with the leading principles of her local institutions.

In consequence of the existence of slavery in many of the States, when British colonies, the habits and means of carrying on industry could not be suddenly changed; and the Constitution of the United States yielded to the provision that the migration or importation of such persons as any of the States now existing shall think proper to admit shall not be prohibited by the Congress prior to the year 1808.

But long antecedent to this period Congress legislated on the subject wherever its power extended; and endeavored, by a system of rigorous penalties, to suppress this unnatural trade.

The act of Congress of the 22d of March, 1794, contains provisions that no citizen or citizens of the United States, or foreigner; or any other person coming into or residing within the same, shall, for himself or any other person whatsoever, either as master, factor, or owner, build, fit, equip, load, or otherwise prepare, any ship or vessel within any port or place of the United States, nor shall cause any ship or vessel to sail from any port or place within the same, for the purpose of carrying on any trade or traffic in slaves to any foreign country; or for the purpose of procuring from any foreign Kingdom, place, or country, the inhabitants of such Kingdom, place, or country, to be transported to any foreign country, port, or place, whatever, to be sold or disposed of as slaves, under the penalty of the forfeiture of any such vessel, and of the payment of large sums of money by the persons offending against the directions of the act.

By an act of the 3d of April, 1798, in relation to the Mississippi Territory, to which the constitutional provision did not extend, the introduction of slaves, under severe penalties, was forbidden, and every slave imported contrary to the act was to be entitled to freedom.

By an act of the 10th of May, 1800, the citizens or residents of this country were prohibited from holding any right or property in vessels employed in transporting slaves from one foreign country to another, on pain of forfeiting their right of property, and also double the value of that right in money, and double the value of their interest in the slaves; nor were they allowed to serve on board of vessels of the United States employed in the transportation of slaves from one country to another, under the punishment of fine and imprisonment; nor were they permitted to serve on board foreign ships employed in the slave trade. By this act, also, the commissioned vessels of the United States were authorized to seize vessels and crews employed contrary to the act.

By an act of the 28th of February, 1803, masters of vessels were not allowed to bring into any port (where the laws of the State prohibited the importation) any negro, mulatto, or other person of color, not being a native, a citizen, or registered seaman of the United States, under severe penalties; and no vessel having on board persons of the above description was to be admitted to an entry; and if any such person should be landed from on board of any vessel, the same was to be forfeited.

By an act of the 2d of March, 1807, the importation of slaves into any port of the United States was to be prohibited after the first of January, 1808, the time prescribed by the constitutional provision. This act contains many severe provisions against any interference or participation in the slave trade, such as heavy fines, long imprisonments, and the forfeiture of vessels; the President was also authorized to employ armed vessels to cruise on any part of the coast where he might judge attempts would be made to violate the act, and to instruct the commanders of armed vessels to seize and bring in vessels found on the high seas contravening the provisions of the act.

By an act of the 20th of April, 1818, the laws in prohibition of the slave trade were further improved; this act is characterized with a peculiarity of legislative precaution, especially in the eighth section, which throws the labor of proof upon the defendant, that the colored persons brought into the United States by him had not been brought in contrary to the laws.

By an act of the 3d of March, 1819, the power is continued in the President to employ the armed ships of the United States to seize and bring into port any vessel engaged in the slave trade by citizens or residents of the United States, and such vessels, together with the goods and effects on board, are to be forfeited and sold, and the proceeds to be distributed, in like manner as is provided by law for the distribution of prizes taken from an enemy; and the officers and crew are to undergo the punishments inflicted by previous acts. The President by this act is authorized to make such regulations and arrangements as he may deem expedient for the safe keeping, support, and removal beyond the limits of the United States of all such negroes, mulattoes, or persons of color, as may have been brought within its jurisdiction, and to appoint a proper person or persons residing on the coast of Africa as agent or agents for receiving the negroes, mulattoes, or persons of color, delivered from on board of vessels seized in the prosecution of the slave trade.

And in addition to all the aforesaid laws, the present Congress, on the 15th of May, 1820, believing that the then existing provisions would not be sufficiently available, enacted, that, if any citizen of the United States, being of the crew or ship's company of any vessel engaged in the slave trade, or any person whatever, being of the crew or ship's company of any ship or vessel owned in the whole or in part, or navigated for or in behalf of any citizen or citizens of the United States, shall land from any such ship or vessel, and on foreign shore seize any negro or mulatto, not held to service or labor by the laws either of the States or Territories of the United States, with intent to make such negro or mulatto a slave, or shall decoy, or forcibly bring or carry, or shall receive such negro or mulatto on board any such ship or vessel with intent as aforesaid, such citizen or person shall be adjudged a pirate, and on conviction *shall suffer death.*

The immoral and pernicious practice of the slave trade has attracted much public attention in Europe within the last few years, and in a Congress at Vienna, on the 8th of February, 1815, five of the principal powers made a solemn engagement in the face of mankind that this traffic should be made to cease; in pursuance of which, these powers have enacted municipal laws to suppress the trade. Spain, although not a party to the original engagement, did soon after, in her treaty with England, stipulate for the immediate abolition of the Spanish slave trade to the north of the equator, and for its final and universal abolition on the 30th of May, 1820.

Portugal likewise, in her treaty in 1817, stipulated that the Portuguese slave trade on the coast of Africa should entirely cease to the northward of the equator, and engaged that it should be unlawful for her subjects to purchase or trade in slaves except to the southward of the line; the precise period at which the entire abolition is to take place in Portugal does not appear to be finally fixed, but the Portuguese ambassador, in the presence of the congress at Vienna, declared that Portugal, faithful to her principles, would not refuse to adopt the term of eight years, which term will expire in the year 1823.

At this time, among the European States, there is not a flag which can legally cover this inhuman traffic to the north of the line; nevertheless, experience has proved the inefficacy of the various and rigorous laws which have been made in Europe and in this country; it being a lamentable fact that the disgraceful practice is even now carried on to a surprising extent. During the last year Captain Trenchard, the commander of the United States sloop-of-war the Cyane, found that part of the coast of Africa which he visited lined with vessels engaged, as it is presumed, in this forbidden traffic; of these he examined many, and five, which appeared to be fitted out on American account, he sent into the jurisdic_tion of the United States for adjudication; each of them, it is believed, has been condemned, and the commanders of two of them have been sentenced to the punishment prescribed by the laws of the United States.

The testimony recently published, with the opinion of the presiding judge of the United States court of the southern district in the State of New York, in the case of the schooner Plattsburg, lays open a scene of the grossest fraud that could be practiced to deceive the officers of Government and conceal the unlawful transaction.

The extension of the trade for the last twenty-five or thirty years must, in a degree, be conjectural, but the best information that can be obtained on the subject furnishes good foundation to believe that during that period the number of slaves withdrawn from western Africa amounted to upwards of a million and a half; the annual average would be a mean somewhere between fifty and eighty thousand.

The trade appears to be lucrative in proportion to its heinousness; and as it is generally inhibited, the unfeeling slave dealers, in order to elude the laws, increase its horrors; the innocent Africans, who are mercilessly forced from their native homes in irons, are crowded in vessels and situations which are not adapted for the transportation of human beings, and this cruelty is frequently succeeded during the voyage of their destination with dreadful mortality. Further information on this subject will appear in a letter from the Secretary of the Navy, inclosing two other letters, marked 1 and 2, and also by the extract of a letter from an officer of the Cyane, dated April 10, 1820, which are annexed to this report. While the slave trade exists, there can be no prospect of civilization in Africa.

However well disposed the European powers may be to effect a practical abolition of the trade, it seems generally acknowledged that, for the attainment of this object, it is necessary to agree upon some concerted plan of co-operation; but, unhappily, no arrangement has as yet obtained universal consent.

England has recently engaged in treaties with Spain, Portugal, and the Netherlands, in which the mutual right of visitation and search is exchanged; this right is of a special and limited character, as well in relation to the number and description of vessels as to space; and, to avoid possible inconveniences, no suspicious circumstances are to warrant the detention of a vessel; this right is restricted to the simple fact of slaves being on board.

These treaties contemplate the establishment of mixed courts, formed of an equal number of individuals of the two contracting nations—the one to reside in a possession belonging to his Britannic Majesty, the other within the territory of the other respective power; when a vessel is visited and detained it is to be taken to the nearest court, and if condemned, the vessel is to be declared a lawful prize, as well as the cargo, and are to be sold for the profit of the two nations; the slaves are to receive a certificate of emancipation, and to be delivered over to the Government on whose territory the court is which passes the sentence, to be employed as servants or free laborers; each of the Governments binds itself to guaranty the liberty of such portion of these individuals as may be respectively assigned to it. Particular provisions are made for remuneration in case vessels are not condemned after trial, and special instructions are stipulated to be furnished to commanders of vessels possessing the qualified right of visitation and search.

These powers entertain the opinion that nothing short of the concession of a qualified right of visitation and search can practically suppress the slave trade; an association of armed ships is contemplated, to form a species of naval police, to be stationed principally in the African seas, where the commanders of the ships will be enabled to co-operate in harmony and concert.

The United States have been earnestly invited by the principal Secretary of State for Foreign Affairs of the British Government to join in the same or similar arrangements, and this invitation has been sanctioned and enforced by a unanimous vote, of the House of Lords and Commons in a manner that precludes all doubts as to the sincerity and benevolence of their design.

In answer to this invitation, the President of the United States has expressed his regret that the stipulations in the treaties communicated are of a character to which the peculiar situation and institutions of the United States do not permit them to accede.

The objections made are contained in an extract of a letter from the Secretary of State under date of the 2d of November, 1818, in which it is observed that, "in examining the provisions of the treaties communicated by Lord Castlereagh, all the essential articles appear to be of a character not adaptable to the institutions or to the circumstances of the United States. The powers agreed to be reciprocally given to the officers of the ships-of-war of either party to enter, search, capture, and carry into port for adjudication, the merchant vessels of the other, however qualified and restricted, is most essentially connected with the institution by each treaty of two mixed courts, one of which to reside in the external or colonial possession of each of the two parties respectively. This part of the system is indispensable to give it that character of reciprocity, without which the right granted to the armed ships of one nation to search the merchant vessels of another would be rather a mark of vassalage than of independence. But to this part of the system the United States, having no colonies either on the coast of Africa or in the West Indies, cannot give effect. That by the Constitution of the United States it is provided that the judicial power of the United States shall be vested in a Supreme Court and in such inferior courts as the Congress may, from time to time, ordain and establish. It provides that judges of these courts shall hold their offices during good behavior, and that they shall be removable by impeachment, on conviction of crimes and misdemeanors. There may be doubts whether the power of the Government of the United States is competent to institute a court for carrying into execution their penal statutes beyond the territories of the United States—a court consisting partly of foreign judges, not amenable to impeachment for corruption, and deciding upon statutes of the United States without appeal.

"That the disposal of the negroes found on board of the slave trading vessels which might be condemned by the sentence of these mixed courts cannot be carried into effect by the United States; for if the slaves of vessels condemned by the mixed courts should be delivered over to the Government of the United States as freemen, they could not, but by their own consent, be employed as servants or free laborers. The condition of the blacks being, in this Union, regulated by the municipal laws of the separate States, the Government of the United States can neither guaranty their liberty in the States where they could only be received as slaves, nor control them in the States where they would be recognized as free. That the admission of a right in the officers of foreign ships-of-war to enter and search the vessels of the United States in time of peace, under any circumstances whatever, would meet with universal repugnance in the public opinion of this country, and that there would be no prospect of a ratification, by advice and consent of the Senate, to any stipulation of that nature; that the search by foreign officers, even in time of war, is so obnoxious to the feelings and recollections of this country that nothing could reconcile them to the extension of it, however qualified or restricted, to a time of peace; and that it would be viewed in a still more aggravated light if, as in the treaty with the Netherlands, connected with a formal admission that even vessels under convoy of ships-of-war of their own nation should be liable to search by the ships-of-war of another."

The committee will observe, in the first instance, that a mutual right of search appears to be indispensable to the great object of abolition; for, while flags remain as a cover for this traffic against the right of search by any vessels except of the same nation, the chance of detection will be much less than it would be if the right of search was extended to vessels of other powers; and as soon as any one nation should cease to be vigilant in the discovery of infractions practiced on its own code, the slave dealers would avail themselves of a system of obtaining fraudulent papers and concealing the real ownership under the cover of such flags, which would be carried on with such address as to render it easy for the citizens or subjects of one State to evade their own municipal laws; but if a concerted system existed, and a qualified right of mutual search was granted, the apprehension of these piratical offenders would be reduced to a much greater certainty; and the very knowledge of the existence of an active and vigorous system of co-operation would divert many from this traffic, as the unlawful trade would become too hazardous for profitable speculation.

In relation to any inconveniences that might result from such an arrangement, the commerce of the United States is so limited on the African coast that it could not be much affected by it; and as it regards economy, the expense of stationing a few vessels on that coast would not be much greater than to maintain them at any other place.

The committee have briefly noticed the practical results of a reciprocal right of search as it bears on the slave trade; but the objection as to the propriety of ceding this right remains. It is with deference that the committee undertake to make any remarks upon it. They bear in recollection the opinions entertained in this country on the practice of searching neutral vessels in time of war; but they cannot perceive that the right under discussion is, in principle, allied in any degree to the general question of search. It can involve no commitment, nor is it susceptible of any unfavorable inference on that subject; and even if there were any affinity between the cases, the necessity of a special agreement would be inconsistent with the idea of existing rights; the proposal itself, in the manner made, is a total abandonment on the part of England of any claim to visit and search vessels in a time of peace, and this question has been unequivocally decided in the negative in her admiralty courts.

Although it is not among the objections that the desired arrangement would give any color to a claim or right of search in time of peace, yet, lest the case in this respect may be prejudiced in the minds of any, the committee will observe that the right of search in time of peace is one that is not claimed by any power as a part of the law of nations. No nation pretends that it can exercise the right of visitation and search upon the common and unappropriated parts of the sea, except upon the belligerent claim. A recent decision in the British admiralty court, in the case of the French slave ship Le Louis, is clear and decisive on this point. The case is annexed to this report.

In regard, then, to the reciprocal right wished to be ceded, it is reduced to the simple inquiry whether, in practice, it will be beneficial to the contracting nations. Its exercise, so far as it relates to the detention of vessels, as it is confined to the fact of slaves being actually on board, precludes almost the possibility of accident or much inconvenience.

In relation also to the disposal of the vessels and slaves detained, an arrangement perhaps could be effected, so as to deliver them up to the vessels of the nation to which the detained vessel should belong. Under such an understanding, the vessels and slaves delivered to the jurisdiction of the United States might be disposed of in conformity with the provisions of our own act of the 3d of March, 1819, and an arrangement of this kind would be free from any of the other objections.

An exchange of the right of search, limited in duration, or to continue at pleasure, for the sake of experiment, might, it is anxiously hoped, be so restricted to vessels and seas, and with such civil and harmonious stipulations, as not to be unacceptable.

The feelings of this country on the general question of search have often been roused to a degree of excitement that evince their unchangeable character; but the American people will readily see the distinction between the cases; the one, in its exercise to the extent claimed, will ever produce irritation, and excite a patriotic spirit of resistance; the other is amicable and charitable. The justness and nobleness of the undertaking are worthy of the combined concern of Christian nations.

The detestable crime of kidnapping the unoffending inhabitants of one country, and chaining them to slavery in another, is marked with all the atrociousness of piracy, and, as such, it is stigmatized and punishable by our own laws.

To efface this reproachful stain from the character of civilized mankind would be the proudest triumph that could be achieved in the cause of humanity. On this subject the United States, having led the way, owe it to themselves to give their influence and cordial co-operation to any measure that will accomplish the great and good purpose; but this happy result, experience has demonstrated, cannot be realized by any system, except a concession by the maritime powers to each other's ships-of-war of a qualified right of search. If this object was generally attained, it is confidently believed that the active exertions of even a few nations would be sufficient entirely to suppress the slave trade.

The slave dealers could be successfully assailed on the coast upon which the trade originates, as they must necessarily consume more time in the collection and embarkation of their cargoes than in the subsequent distribution in the markets for which they are destined; this renders that coast the most advantageous position for their apprehension; and, besides, the African coast frequented by the slave ships is indented with so few commodious or accessible harbors, that notwithstanding its great extent, it could be guarded by the vigilance of a small number of cruisers. But if the slave ships are permitted to escape from the African coast, and to be dispersed to different parts of the world, their capture would be rendered uncertain and hopeless.

The committee, after much reflection, offer the following resolution:

Resolved by the Senate and House of Representatives of the United States of America in Congress assembled, That the President of the United States be requested to enter into such arrangements as he may deem suitable and proper, with one or more of the maritime powers of Europe, for the effectual abolition of the African slave trade.

Case of the French slave ship Le Louis, extracted from the twelfth annual report of the African Institution, printed in 1818.

This vessel sailed from Martinique on the 30th of January, 1816, on a slave trading voyage to the coast of Africa, and was captured near Cape Mesurado by the Sierra Leone colonial vessel-of-war Queen Charlotte, after a severe engagement which followed an attempt to escape, in which eight men were killed and twelve wounded of the British; and proceedings having been instituted against Le Louis in the Vice Admiralty Court of Sierra Leone, as belonging to French subjects, and as fitted out, manned, and navigated for the purpose of carrying on the slave trade, after the trade had been abolished both by the internal laws of France and by the treaty between that country and Great Britain, the ship and cargo were condemned as forfeited to his Majesty.

From this sentence an appeal having been made to the High Court of Admiralty, the cause came on for hearing, when the court reversed the judgment of the inferior court, and ordered the restitution of the property to the claimants.

The judgment of Sir William Scott was given at great length. The directors will advert to such points of it as are immediately connected with their present subject. "No doubt," he said, "could exist that this was a French ship intentionally engaged in the slave trade." But as these were facts which were ascertained in consequence of its seizure, before the seizer could avail himself of this discovery, it was necessary to inquire whether he possessed any right of visitation and search; because, if the discovery was unlawfully produced, he could not be allowed to take advantage of the consequences of his own wrong.

The learned judge then discussed, at considerable length, the question, whether the right of search exists in time of peace? and he decided it without hesitation in the negative. "I can find," he says, "no authority that gives the right of interruption to the navigation of States in amity upon the high seas, excepting that which the rights of war give to both belligerents against neutrals. No nation can exercise a right of visitation and search upon the common and unappropriated parts of the sea, save only on the belligerent claim." He admits, indeed, and with just concern, that if this right be not conceded in time of peace, it will be extremely difficult to suppress the traffic in slaves.

"The great object, therefore, ought to be to obtain the concurrence of other nations by application, by remonstrance, by example, by every peaceable instrument which men can employ to attract the consent of men. But a nation is not justified in assuming rights that do not belong to her, merely because she means to apply them to a laudable purpose."

"If this right," he adds, "is imported into a state of peace, it must be done by convention; and it will then be for the prudence of States to regulate by such convention the exercise of the right, with all the softenings of which it is susceptible."

The judgment of Sir William Scott would have been equally conclusive against the legality of this seizure, even if it could have been established in evidence that France had previously prohibited the slave trade by her municipal laws. For the sake of argument, however, he assumes that the view he has taken of the subject might in such a case be controverted. He proceeds, therefore, to inquire how far the French law had actually abolished the slave trade at the time of this adventure. The actual state of the matter, as collected from the documents before the court, he observes, is this:

"On the 27th of July, 1815, the British minister at Paris writes a note to Prince Talleyrand, then minister to the King of France, expressing a desire on the part of his court to be informed whether, under the law of France as it then stood, it was prohibited to French subjects to carry on the slave trade. The French minister informs him, in answer, on the 30th of July, that the law of the Usurper on that subject was null and void, (as were all his decrees,) but that his most Christian Majesty had issued directions that, on the part of France, "the traffic should cease from the present time everywhere and forever."

"In what form these directions were issued or to whom addressed does not appear, but upon such authority it must be presumed that they were actually issued. It is, however, no violation of the respect due to that authority to inquire what was the result or effect of those directions so given—what followed in obedience to them in any public and binding form? And I fear that I am compelled to say, that nothing of the kind followed, and that the directions must have slept in the portfolio of the office to which they were addressed; for it is, I think, impossible that, if any public and authoritative ordinance had followed, it could have escaped the sleepless attention of many persons in our own country to all public foreign proceedings upon this interesting subject. Still less would it have escaped the notice of the British resident minister, who, at the distance of a year and a half, is compelled, on the part of his own court, to express a curiosity to know what laws, ordinances, instructions, and other public and ostensible acts, had passed for the abolition of the slave trade.

"On the 30th of November, in the same year, (1815,) the additional article of the definitive treaty, a very solemn instrument, most undoubtedly, is formally and publicly executed, and it is in these terms: 'The high contracting parties, sincerely desiring to give effect to the measures on which they deliberated at the Congress of Vienna, for the complete and universal abolition of the slave trade, and having each, in their respective dominions, prohibited, without restriction, their colonies and subjects from taking any part whatever in this traffic, engage to renew, conjointly, their efforts, with a view to insure final success to the principle which they proclaimed in the declaration of the 8th of February, 1815, and to concert, without loss of time, by their ministers at the court of London, the most effectual measures for the entire and definitive abolition of the traffic so odious and so highly reproved by the laws of religion and nature.'

"Now, what are the effects of this treaty? According to the view I take of it, they are two, and two only: one declaratory of a fact, the other promissory of future measures. It is to be observed that the treaty itself does not abolish the slave trade; it does not inform the subjects that that trade is *hereby* abolished, and that, by virtue of the prohibitions therein contained, its subjects shall not, in future, carry on the trade; but the contracting parties mutually inform each other of the fact that they have, in their respective dominions, abolished the slave trade, without stating at all the mode in which that abolition had taken place."

"It next engages to take future measures for the universal abolition.

"That, with respect to both the declaratory and promissory parts, Great Britain has acted with the *optima fides*, is known to the whole world, which has witnessed its domestic laws, as well as its foreign negotiations.

"I am very far from intimating that the Government of this country did not act with perfect propriety in accepting the assurance that the French Government had actually abolished the slave trade, as a sufficient proof of the fact; but the fact is now denied by a person who has a right to deny it; for, though a French subject, he is not bound to acknowledge the existence of any law which has not publicly appeared; and the other party having taken upon himself the burden of proving it in the course of a legal inquiry, the court is compelled to demand and expect the ordinary evidence of such a disputed fact. It was not till the 15th of January, in the present year, (1817,) that the British resident minister applies for the communication I have described, of all laws, instructions, ordinances, and so on; he receives in return what is delivered by the French minister as *the* ordinance, bearing date only one week before the requested communication, namely, the 8th of January. It has been asserted, in argument, that no such ordinance has yet, up to this very hour, even, appeared in any printed or public form, however much it might import both French subjects and the subjects of foreign States so to receive it.

"How the fact may be, I cannot say; but I observe it appears before me in a manuscript form; and by inquiry at the Secretary of State's office, I find it exists there in no other plight or condition.

"In transmitting this to the British Government, the British minister observes, it is not the document he had reason to expect, and, certainly, with much propriety; for how does the document answer his requisition? His requisition is for all laws, ordinances, instructions, and so forth. How does this, a simple ordinance, professing to have passed only a week before, realize the assurance given on the 30th of July, 1815, that the traffic 'should cease, from the present time, everywhere and forever?' or how does this realize the promise made in November, that measures should be taken, without loss of time, to prohibit not only French colonists but French subjects likewise from taking any part whatever in this traffic? What is this regulation in substance? Why, it is a mere prospective colonial regulation, prohibiting the importation of slaves into the French colonies from the 8th of January, 1817.

"Consistently with this declaration, even if it does exist in the form and with the force of a law, French subjects may be yet the common carriers of slaves to any foreign settlement that will admit them, and may devote their capital and their industry, unmolested by law, to the supply of any such markets.

"Supposing, however, the regulations to contain the fullest and most entire fulfilment of the engagement of France, both in time and in substance, what possible application can a prospective regulation of January, 1817, have to a transaction of March, 1816?

"Nobody is now to be told that a modern edict which does not appear cannot be presumed, and that no penal law of any State can bind the conduct of its subjects, unless it is conveyed to their attention in a way which excludes the possibility of honest ignorance. The very production of a law professing to be enacted in the beginning of 1817 is a satisfactory proof that no such law existed in 1816, the year of this transaction. In short, the seizer has entirely failed in the task he has undertaken, in proving the existence of a prohibitory law, enacted by the legal Government of France, which can be applied to the present transaction."

C.

Report of the Committee on the Suppression of the Slave Trade, made in the House of Representatives April 12, 1822.

The Committee on the Suppression of the Slave Trade, to whom was referred a resolution of the House of Representatives of the 15th of January last, instructing them to inquire whether the laws of the United States prohibiting that traffic have been duly executed; also, into the general operation thereof; and if any defects exist in those laws, to suggest adequate remedies therefor; and to whom many memorials have been referred touching the same subject, having, according to order, had the said resolution and memorials under consideration, reported:

That, under the just and liberal construction put by the Executive on the act of Congress of March 3, 1819, and that of May 15, 1820, inflicting the punishment of piracy on the African slave trade, a foundation has been laid for the most systematic and vigorous application of the power of the United States to the suppression of that iniquitous traffic. Its unhappy subjects, when captured, are restored to their country; agents are there appointed to receive them, and a colony, the offspring of private charity, is rising on its shores, in which such as cannot reach their native tribes will find the means of alleviating the calamities they may have endured before their liberation.

When these humane provisions are contrasted with the system which they supersede, there can be but one sentiment in favor of a steady adherence to their support. The document accompanying this report, and marked A, states the number of Africans seized within or without the limits of the United States and brought there, and their present condition.

It does not appear to your committee that such part of the naval force of the country as has been hitherto employed in the execution of the laws against this traffic could have been more effectually used for the interest and honor of the nation. The document marked B is a statement of the names of the vessels and their commanders ordered upon this service, with the dates of their departure, &c. The first vessel destined for this service arrived upon the coast of Africa in March, 1820; and in the few weeks she remained there sent in for adjudication four American vessels, all of which were condemned. The four which have been since employed in this service have made five visits, (the Alligator having made two cruises in the past summer,) the whole of which have amounted to a service of about ten months by a single vessel within a period of near two years; and since the middle of last November, the commence. ment of the healthy season on that coast, no vessel has been, nor, as your committee is informed, is under orders for that service.

The committee are thus particular on this branch of their inquiry, because unfounded rumors have been in circulation that other branches of the public service have suffered from the destination given to the inconsiderable force above stated, which, small as it has been, has in every instance been directed, both in its outward and homeward voyage, to cruise in the West India seas.

Before they quit this part of their inquiry, your committee feel it their duty to state that the loss of several of the prizes made in this service is imputable to the size of the ships engaged in it. The efficacy of this force, as well as the health and discipline of the officers and crews, conspire to recommend the employment of no smaller vessel than a corvette or a sloop-of-war, to which it would be expedient to allow the largest possible complement of men; and, if possible, she should be accompanied by a tender, or vessel drawing less water. The vessels engaged in this service should be frequently relieved, but the coast should at no time be left without a vessel to watch and protect its shores.

Your committee find it impossible to measure with precision the effect produced upon the American branch of the slave trade by the laws above mentioned, and the seizures under them. They are unable to state whether those American merchants, the American capital and seamen, which heretofore aided in this traffic, have abandoned it altogether, or have sought shelter under the flags of other nations. It is ascertained, however, that the American flag, which heretofore covered so large a portion of the slave trade, has wholly disappeared from the coasts of Africa. The trade, notwithstanding, increases annually under the flags of other nations. France has incurred the reproach of being the greatest adventurer in this traffic prohibited by her laws; but it is to be presumed that this results not so much from the avidity of her subjects for this iniquitous gain, as from the safety which, in the absence of all hazard of capture, her flag affords to the greedy and unprincipled adventurers of all nations. It is neither candid nor just to impute to a gallant and high-minded people the exclusive commission of crimes which the abandoned of all nations are alike capable of perpetrating, with the additional wrong to France herself of using her flag to cover and protect them. If the vigor of the American Navy has saved its banner from like reproach, it has done much to preserve unsullied its high reputation, and amply repaid the expense charged upon the public revenue by a system of laws to which it has given such honorable effect.

But the conclusion to which your committee has arrived, after consulting all the evidence within their reach, is, that the African slave trade now prevails to a great extent, and that its total suppression can never be effected by the separate and disunited efforts of one or more States; and as the resolution to which this report refers requires the suggestion of some remedy for the defects, if any exist, in the system of laws for the suppression of this traffic, your committee beg leave to call the attention of the House to the report and accompanying documents submitted to the last Congress by the Committee on the Slave Trade, and to make the same a part of this report. That report proposes, as a remedy for the existing evils of the system, the concurrence of the United States with one or all the maritime powers of Europe in a modified and reciprocal right of search on the African coast, with a view to the total suppression of the slave trade.

It is with great delicacy that the committee have approached this subject, because they are aware that the remedy which they have presumed to recommend to the consideration of the House requires the exercise of the power of another Department of this Government, and that objections to the exercise of this power, in the mode here proposed, have hitherto existed in that Department.

Your committee are confident, however, that these objections apply rather to a *particular proposition* for the exchange of the right of search, than to that modification of it which presents itself to your committee. They contemplate the trial and condemnation of such American citizens as may be found engaged in this forbidden trade, not by mixed tribunals sitting in a foreign country, but by existing courts, of competent jurisdiction, in the United States; they propose the same disposition of the captured Africans now authorized by law; and least of all, their detention in America.

They contemplate an exchange of this right, which shall be in all respects reciprocal; an exchange which, deriving its sole authority from treaty, would exclude the pretension which no nation, however, has presumed to set up, that this right can be derived from the law of nations; and further, they have limited it, in their conception of its application, not only to certain latitudes and to a certain distance from the coast of Africa, but to a small number of vessels to be employed by each power, and to be previously designated. The visit and search, thus restricted, it is believed would insure the co-operation of one great maritime power in the proposed exchange, and guard it from the danger of abuse.

Your committee cannot doubt that the people of America have the intelligence to distinguish between the right of searching a neutral on the high seas in time of war, claimed by some belligerents, and that mutual, restricted, and peaceful concession by treaty suggested by your committee, and which is demanded in the name of suffering humanity.

In closing this report, they recommend to the House the adoption of the following resolution, viz:

Resolved, That the President of the United States be requested to enter into such arrangements as he may deem suitable and proper with one or more of the maritime powers of Europe for the effectual abolition of the slave trade.

The following resolution was submitted to the House of Representatives on the 10th February, 1823, and adopted the 28th of the same month:

Resolved, That the President of the United States be requested to enter upon and to prosecute, from time to time, such negotiations with the several maritime powers of Europe and America as he may deem expedient for the effectual abolition of the African slave trade, and its ultimate denunciation as piracy, under the law of nations, by the consent of the civilized world.

No. 404.

CORRESPONDENCE WITH THE FRENCH GOVERNMENT RELATIVE TO THE INTERPRETA-
TION OF THE EIGHTH ARTICLE OF THE TREATY FOR THE CESSION OF LOUISIANA,
CONCERNING FRENCH COMMERCE IN THE UNITED STATES.

COMMUNICATED TO THE HOUSE OF REPRESENTATIVES FEBRUARY 17, 1825.

To the House of Representatives of the United States:

I transmit herewith to the House a report from the Secretary of State, with copies of the correspondence with the Government of France, requested by the resolution of the House of the 25th of
January last.

JAMES MONROE.

Washington, *February* 17, 1825.

Department of State, *Washington, February* 16, 1825.

The Secretary of State, to whom has been referred a resolution of the House of Representatives of
the 25th of January, requesting that the President would "communicate to that House any correspondence
in his possession which he may not deem it improper to disclose, which has taken place between the
Government of the United States and that of France, touching the interpretation of the 8th article of the
treaty of the cession of Louisiana," has the honor of reporting to the President copies of the documents
requested by that resolution.

JOHN QUINCY ADAMS.

List of papers sent.

No. 1. Mr. de Neuville to Mr. Adams, December 15, 1817, (translation.)
No. 2. Mr. Adams to Mr. de Neuville, December 23, 1817, (copy.)
No. 3. Mr. de Neuville to Mr. Adams, June 16, 1818, (translation.)
No. 4. Mr. Roth to same, July 19, 1820, (translation.)
No. 5. Mr. Gallatin to same, (No. 155,) July 31, 1820, (extract.)
No. 6. Mr. Roth to same, August 8, 1820, (extract.)
No. 7. Mr. Gallatin to Mr. Pasquier, August 15, 1820, (extract.)
No. 8. Mr. Adams to Mr. Gallatin, (No. 24,) August 24, 1820, (extract.)
No. 9. Mr. Gallatin to Mr. Adams, (No. 161,) September 19, 1820, (extract.)
No. 9, a. Baron Pasquier to Mr. Gallatin, September 13, 1820, (translation.)
No. 9, b. Mr. Gallatin to Mr. Pasquier, September 15, 1820, (copy.)
No. 10. Mr. Gallatin to Mr. Adams, (No. 163,) October 19, 1820, (extract.)
No. 11. Same to same, (No. 164,) October 23, 1820, (extract.)
No. 11, a. Same to Baron Pasquier, October 22, 1820, (copy.)
No. 12. Same to Mr. Adams, (No. 172,) February 1, 1821, (extract.)
No. 13. Baron de Neuville to same, February 23, 1821, (extract.)
No. 14. Mr. Gallatin to same, (No. 174,) March 29, 1821, (extract.)
No. 15. Mr. Adams to Baron de Neuville, March 29, 1821, (copy.)
No. 16. Baron de Neuville to Mr. Adams, March 30, 1821, (translation.)
No. 17. Same to same, May 15, 1821, (translation.)
No. 18. Mr. Adams to Baron de Neuville, June 15, 1821, (copy.)
No. 19. Baron de Neuville to Mr. Adams, June 30, 1821, (translation.)
No. 20. Same to same, October 15, 1821, (translation.)
No. 21. Mr. Gallatin to same, (No. 233,) September 24, 1822, (extract.)
No. 22. Same to same, (No. 236,) November 13, 1822, (extract.)
No. 22, a. M. de Villèle to Mr. Gallatin, November 6, 1822, (translation.)
No. 22, b. Mr. Gallatin to M. de Villèle, November 12, 1822, (copy.)
No. 23. Same to Mr. Adams, (No. 237,) November 19, 1822, (copy.)
No. 23, a. M. de Villèle to Mr. Gallatin, November 15, 1822, (translation.)
No. 24. Mr. Gallatin to Mr. Adams (No. 241,) January 5, 1823, (copy.)
No. 25. Same to same, (No. 250,) February 27, 1823, (copy.)
No. 25, a. Same to Viscount de Chateaubriand, February 27, 1823, (copy.)
No. 26. Mr. Brown to Mr. Adams, (No. 17,) November 29, 1824, (copy.)

No. 1.

Mr. Hyde de Neuville to Mr. Adams, dated December 15, 1817.

[Translation.]

Sir: The Envoy Extraordinary and Minister Plenipotentiary of his most Christian Majesty has
received reiterated orders to ascertain the truth of the statement made by several masters of merchant

ships, affirming that French vessels are not treated, in the ports of Louisiana, upon the footing of the most favored nations. Upon investigation, it not only appears that such is actually the case, but the undersigned has even found that several protests had been lodged in vain with the local authorities against this manifest infraction of the 8th article of the Louisiana treaty. He is well assured that this must have been the mere consequence of error, or of incorrect interpretation given on the spot to a clause which is absolute and unconditional by its own terms, and which can neither be limited nor modified, being the essential unlimited condition of a contract of cession, can neither be subject to limitation nor to any modification whatever. The minister of his most Christian Majesty persuades himself that it will suffice thus to call the attention of the Federal Government to this affair, in order to obtain from its justice the reparation of an injury so very prejudicial to French commerce. He, therefore, requests of the Secretary of State that this his representation, made by order of his court, be submitted as soon as possible to the President, in order that his excellency may be pleased to issue orders to such effect that in future the 8th article of the treaty of 1803, between France and the United States, receive its entire execution, and that the advantages granted to Great Britain in all the ports of the United States be secured to France in those of Louisiana. The principle of justice here claimed cannot be denied, and must necessarily insure the reimbursement of the duties which have been unjustifiably levied upon French vessels in New Orleans. The undersigned minister expects, with entire confidence, the decision of the President, of which he requests the Secretary of State will enable him to inform his court as soon as possible. The Government of His Majesty desires, as soon as possible, to quiet the commerce of France with regard to proceedings so contrary to its interests and to the true spirit of the Louisiana treaty.

The undersigned has the honor, &c.

G. HYDE de NEUVILLE.

No. 2.

Mr. Adams to Mr. Hyde de Neuville.

DEPARTMENT OF STATE, *December* 23, 1817.

The undersigned, Secretary of State, has received and laid before the President the note which he had the honor of receiving from the Envoy Extraordinary and Minister Plenipotentiary of France, complaining that French vessels are not, conformably to the 8th article of the treaty of cession of Louisiana, treated in the ports of that State upon the footing of the most favored nation; and claiming as a right, deducible from the same article, that French vessels should in future enjoy, in the ports of Louisiana, all the advantages granted to the English nation in all the ports of the Union.

The undersigned is instructed to say that the vessels of France are treated in the ports of Louisiana upon the footing of the most favored nation; and that neither the English nor any other foreign nation enjoys gratuitous advantage there which is not equally enjoyed by France. But English vessels, by virtue of a conditional compact, are admitted into the ports of the United States, including those of Louisiana, upon payment of the same duties as the vessels of the United States. The condition upon which they enjoy this advantage is, that the vessels of the United States shall be admitted into the ports of Great Britain upon payment of the same duties as are there paid by British vessels.

The 8th article of the treaty of cession stipulates that the ships of France shall be treated upon the footing of the most favored nations in the ports of the ceded territory; but it does not say, and cannot be understood to mean, that France should enjoy as a free gift that which is conceded to other nations for a full equivalent.

It is obvious, that, if French vessels should be admitted into the ports of Louisiana upon payment of the same duties as the vessels of the United States, they would be treated, not upon the footing of the most favored nation, according to the article in question, but upon a footing more favored than any other nation; since other nations, with the exception of England, pay higher tonnage duties, and the exemption of English vessels is not a free gift, but a purchase at a fair and equal price.

It is true that the terms of the 8th article are positive and unconditional; but it will readily be perceived that the condition, though not expressed in the article, is inherent in the advantage claimed under it. If British vessels enjoyed in the ports of Louisiana any gratuitous favor, undoubtedly French vessels would, by the terms of the article, be entitled to the same.

A more extensive construction cannot be given to the article, consistently with the Constitution of the United States, which declares that "all duties, imposts, and excises shall be uniform throughout the United States; and that no preference shall be given by any regulation of commerce or revenue to the ports of one State over those of another."

It would be incompatible with other articles of the treaty of cession itself, one of which cedes the territory to the United States "*in full sovereignty*," and another declares that its "inhabitants shall be incorporated in the Union of the United States, and be admitted as soon as possible, according to the principles of the Federal Constitution, to the enjoyment of all the rights, advantages, and immunities of citizens of the United States." If France could claim *forever* advantages in the ports of Louisiana which could be denied to her in the other ports of the United States, she would have ceded to the United States not the full, but an imperfect sovereignty; and if France could claim admission for her vessels forever into the ports of Louisiana, upon the payment of duties not uniform with those which they must pay in the other ports of the United States, it would have been impossible to have admitted the inhabitants of Louisiana, according to the principles of the Federal Constitution, to the enjoyment of all the rights, advantages, and immunities of citizens of the United States.

The undersigned is happy to be authorized, in concluding this note, to add, that the Government of the United States is willing to extend to France, not only in the ports of Louisiana, but in those of all the United States, every advantage enjoyed by the vessels of Great Britain, upon the fair and just equivalent of reciprocity; and that, in the meantime, the vessels of France shall be treated in all the ports of the United States, including Louisiana, on the footing of the most favored nation, enjoying gratuitously every favor indulged gratuitously to others, and every conditional favor, upon the reciprocation of the same to vessels of the United States in France.

He prays the minister of France to accept the assurances of his very distinguished consideration.

JOHN QUINCY ADAMS.

No. 3.

Mr. de Neuville to Mr. Adams.

[Translation]

Washington, *June* 16, 1818.

Sir: I have had the honor of receiving your note, in answer to mine of the 15th December last, concerning the non-execution of the 8th article of the Louisiana treaty.

I took care duly to communicate the proposal made by the Federal Government to extend to France, not only in the ports of Louisiana, but even in all those of the United States, the advantages therein enjoyed by British vessels on a footing of absolute reciprocity. His Majesty is ever disposed not to neglect anything that can tend to rivet the bonds of friendship of the two countries, and to improve their commercial intercourse, and will, no doubt, examine this proposal with very particular attention.

In the meantime, as it would be neither just nor proper that the execution of the clauses of a contract already made and completely concluded should be dependent on an arrangement which, as yet, is only in contemplation; and as the enjoyment of a perpetual unconditional right should never in any case be blended with reciprocal advantages or concessions which time annuls, and which accidental causes may modify or destroy; as France claims nothing but what she knows is due to her, and as she is well persuaded that the Federal Government will never deny what it is conscious of owing, there is much reason to hope that the following observations will suffice to establish our right, and thus remove every obstacle to its free enjoyment. I will add, that fresh orders from his Majesty make it my duty to neglect no means of obtaining, as soon as possible, this act, whose accomplishment must be expected from mature deliberation on the question, and is warranted by the acknowledged equity of the Federal Government.

You have stated, sir, that *French vessels are treated in the ports of Louisiana upon the footing of the most favored nation, and that no foreign nation enjoys there any gratuitous advantage which is not equally enjoyed by France.* You add, sir, *that if British vessels are allowed in the ports of the United States certain advantages which American vessels likewise enjoy in the ports of Great Britain, it is by virtue of a conditional compact founded on reciprocity of advantages.*

Finally, after expressly recalling the 8th article, which stipulates expressly that, in future, and forever, French vessels shall be treated upon the footing of the most favored nation in the ports of the ceded territory, you observe *that the article does not say, and that it could not be understood to mean, that France should enjoy as a free gift that which is conceded to other nations* for a full equivalent.

I shall, in the first place, have the honor to observe, that France asks not for a *free gift;* she claims the enjoyment of a right which it is not even necessary for her to acquire, since it proceeds from herself, being a right which, when she consented to dispose of Louisiana, she had power to reserve for the interest of her trade, and the actual reservation of which is established, not implicitly, but in the most precise and formal terms, by the 8th article of the Louisiana treaty.

France, I repeat it, asks no free gifts, since the territory ceded is the equivalent already paid by her for all the clauses, charges, and conditions, executed, or which remain to be fulfilled by the United States, and which principally consist in the 7th and 8th articles of the treaty, and 1st of the convention.

If the 8th article of the Louisiana treaty had no other object but that of securing to France a conditional advantage in the ports of Louisiana; if such had been the true spirit of this clause, and, finally, if the American negotiators had been firmly convinced that this reservation of the French Government was not absolute, but was merely one of those customary reciprocal concessions which occur in almost all treaties of amity and commerce, it is likely that no pains would have been taken to frame the article so as absolutely to contradict the intention of the contracting parties; and it stands to reason that, if such had been their views, the terms usually employed in other treaties would have been employed here also, instead of so precise a stipulation of an unconditional and perpetual advantage in favor of France. In all the treaties between France and the United States the condition of reciprocity is positively mentioned; they all expressly say that the contracting parties shall reciprocally enjoy such favors as shall be conceded to other nations, *freely, if freely granted to other nations, or, upon granting the same condition, if conditionally granted.* How shall we account for the strange and unusual construction here adopted? Who would admit the possibility or likelihood of an omission on the part of negotiators, the object of whose mission was not to stipulate doubtful clauses, subject to discussion, but, on the contrary, as it is expressly stated in the treaty, "to remove all sources of *misunderstanding* relative to objects of discussion, and to strengthen the union and friendship which, at the time of the said convention, was happily re-established between the two nations?"

And, furthermore, how shall we reconcile the silence observed by the Senate, in 1803, respecting this unconditional and unlimited favor secured to France, with the positive refusal of the same House, in 1801, to ratify a convention founded on reciprocity of advantage, unless on the express condition that it should be limited to eight years?

The natural inference, the only explanation of all this, is, that in 1801 the question was on a convention or treaty of amity and commerce, while in 1803 it was on a contract of sale or cession, which instruments are of so different a nature as not to admit the application of similar principles and consequences; nor can it be supposed that the negotiators of the treaty of 1801 had forgotten to mention that the citizens of the two nations should, reciprocally, be treated, each in the ports of the other, upon the footing of the most favored nations, since this principle of reciprocity was not only the general basis, but was even, in almost every instance, the *sine qua non* of preceding commercial conventions.

But the negotiators of the treaty of 1803 knew full well that they were not commissioned to settle the commercial or navigating interests of the two countries, and were merely authorized to make a contract of sale or cession, which, however important from the value of the object ceded, was not the less subject, like every conveyance between individuals, to certain and invariable rules of construction and interpretation. A contract of sale admits of no implication, (sous entendu;) it is a plain simple transaction, by which one party is bound to deliver a certain property, and the other party to receive it, on certain charges and conditions more or less rigorous.

Those clauses and conditions cannot be interpreted otherwise than according to the terms in which they are expressed in the contract, nor can they be annulled or modified except by the consent of both parties. Their entire execution is, indeed, so rigorously binding, that it alone may be said finally to seal the transaction. But the article would appear to you, sir, to be in this, its only-natural construction, inconsistent with the Constitution, which declares that all *duties, imposts*, and *excises* shall *be uniform throughout the United States.*

It would seem to me that this clause of the Constitution has no other reference than to the interior administration of the country, and that it cannot be proper to consider in the light of a mere tax or impost that which is an express condition of the sale or cession of a territory, and is one of the clauses of a treaty which itself becomes a law of the United States.

You express an opinion, sir, that the eighth article, if interpreted according to its grammatical and literal sense, *would be incompatible with another article of the same treaty, which cedes the territory to the United States in full sovereignty,* arguing that, *if France could claim forever advantages in the ports of Louisiana which could be denied to her in the other ports of the United States, she would have ceded to the United States not the full, but an imperfect sovereignty.*

Allow me to observe that this last point of the argument is answered by your own decision, admitting that, *if British vessels enjoyed in the ports of Louisiana any gratuitous favor, undoubtedly French vessels would, by the terms of the treaty, be entitled to the same.*

This admits the possibility of an imperfect sovereignty, and supposes an instance in which France might be entitled to claim, in the ports of Louisiana, a favor which could be denied her in the other ports of the United States.

Moreover, if the United States have, by the Constitution, a right to grant to other nations gratuitous favors in their ports, it follows, from your own interpretation of the perpetual reservation made by France, that, in order to deprive her of the right so reserved, and to avoid rendering thereby the sovereignty of this Republic imperfect, the Federal Government must not grant to other nations any gratuitous concessions in the territory ceded by France, though it should be found expedient so to do, and advantageous to their commercial interest and policy. In other words, the Federal Government, by consenting to the eighth article, would have deprived itself of a real right of sovereignty. In the preceding hypothesis the difficulty is merely eluded and not removed. The right is not the less unqualified and consented to *forever.*

But will it be said the Constitution allows no preferences among the different States; they are all, by the Federal compact, subject to the same charges and to enjoy the same privileges. It would appear to me, sir, that this perfect uniformity is applicable only to a State when it has once become a State. The regulations made for the family cannot be meant to extend beyond its circle; and the law which established such regulations never can have blended the circumstances pre-existent to the admission of a new member (much less the very conditions of admission) with the rights, charges, and privileges, which are the consequences springing therefrom. Thus did Congress judge; to them it appeared that the instrument of sale or cession of Louisiana had no analogy to a commercial regulation, or to a distribution of taxes; and they admitted, without discussion, the seventh and eighth articles of the treaty, because, if the Constitution does not allow that a Territory, when once admitted into this Union, be marked by any distinct charges or advantages, it does not, on that account, prevent the fulfilment of clauses exacted and consented to as conditions of its admission. In all this there is neither exception nor preference; it is the mere and simple execution of a contract freely and lawfully entered into. But the third article says that the inhabitants of the ceded territory shall be incorporated into the Union, and admitted, as soon as *possible,* to the enjoyment of all the advantages and immunities of citizens of the United States.

This is true, and such, no doubt, was the intention of the contracting parties. They expressly agreed that this admission should take place as soon as possible; but most assuredly it was meant that this should be done in conformity with the clauses and conditions mentioned in the treaty; and if the eighth article could have been considered as an obstacle to the execution of the third article, it would equally have been so thought of the seventh; this article was, however, never contested; it even received during the twelve years of its duration, or should have received, its full and entire operation by virtue of the regulating act of Congress of the 24th of February, 1804.

France and Spain still enjoyed in 1815, in Louisiana, the rights and privileges secured by the seventh article, which rights, by the very terms of the treaty, never can be granted to any other nation. France and Spain were in the full enjoyment of these exclusive rights and privileges in 1815; and yet, in 1812, the stipulations of the third article were fulfilled, the Territory of Louisiana was admitted as a State into the Federal body, and this new State was received, without restriction, on an equal footing with the original States in all respects whatever.

If, therefore, there were at this day any contradiction between the third and eighth articles, how could Congress, in 1812, surmount the objection arising from the much stronger inconsistency, which, on this supposition, must have existed between the third and seventh articles?

When Congress made Louisiana a member of the Union, before the expiration of the twelve years, it was judged that such a compliance with the conditions of a treaty was by no means incompatible with the exercise of the full and entire rights of sovereignty. Perhaps it may be answered that the seventh article granted only temporary privileges, and that the eighth article has no term fixed to it. To me, it appears that the word *forever* changes nothing but the duration of the privilege, without, in the least degree, altering the nature of the question. Under a constitutional system, nothing can be done, ordered, or consented to, that would infringe, *even* but for a limited term, the established laws of the country. All the transactions of Governments must be legal. If, therefore, the provisions of the Constitution which regulate the existence of a State after its admission were applicable to the conditions on which it is to be admitted, it would, in such case, have been no less impossible in 1812 than at the present day to grant to the inhabitants of Louisiana the rights, privileges, and immunities of citizens of the United States, since, on that supposition, they must, in common with the other States, have had a right to make France and Spain pay in their ports higher tonnage duties than those paid by the citizens of the United States; and since the Federal Government had no right, at that time, to grant, in the ports of the ceded territory, to other nations the privileges therein secured to France and to Spain. France did intend to cede the territory of Louisiana to the United States forever, and in full sovereignty; but sovereignty does not consist in the enjoyment of every right and privilege: it lies in the pre-eminent important authority to enforce their observance. When the French Government ceded Louisiana, it ceased to be the sovereign of the country, but it did not cease to hold property therein, since it reserved a right or privilege; for a privilege acquired or reserved, is property as sacred as an annuity, as a rent charge, or any other.

France, therefore, claims only the enjoyment of what is her property; giving her possession of this lawful right, far from rendering the sovereignty of the United States imperfect, would seem, in a measure, only to make it more complete, since it is certain that the right claimed by France is one of the essential conditions of the céssion made by her of that sovereignty. It may, perhaps, be answered that there is some difference between the contracts of nations with other nations and a sale made by one individual to another. I see very little, I confess, on the score of equity, the rules of interpretation being in all cases alike applicable to every human transaction. By the law of nations, it is an invariable rule that treaties or contracts, of whatsoever nature, should be understood according to the force and meaning of their expressions; and nothing surely can be more unconditional or more clearly expressed than the following clause: "In future, and forever, after the expiration of the twelve years, French vessels shall be treated upon the footing of the most favored nations in the ports of the said territory." *In future and forever* are expressions free from all ambiguity. *After the expiration of the twelve years*, these words prove that the treatment or privilege secured by the eighth article is to follow without condition or limitation of time. That of the seventh article, *French vessels shall be treated*, does not mean *may be treated*, but that they shall undoubtedly and positively be treated upon the footing of the most favored nation. And it makes no difference whether that treatment be the consequence of a gratuitous or of a conditional concession; the article has no restriction; it expressly states, French vessels shall be treated upon the footing of the [most] favored nations. The consequence is, that French vessels are, without condition, to be treated, in the ports of Louisiana, upon the footing of the vessels of Great Britain, which is at this time the most favored nation. I think I have proved, that to demand an equivalent of France, because England has given one, would, in a measure, be requiring her to purchase what is already her own property, and obliging her to pay twice for the same thing.

I think I have also proved that the sovereignty of the United States is, and will still remain, entire and perfect, such as it was ceded by the treaty of 1803, although France be put into possession of that right which is secured to her *in future and forever*. I could cite many examples of analogous privileges, which never were considered as impairing the sovereignty of nations. But it appears to me that the best of all arguments that can be addressed to the equity and honest feelings of the American Government is, that France claims only her lawful due and right; that the title establishing it is worded in terms of such force and precision as must suffice to remove every doubt, and absolutely to solve the question.

The claim which I have the honor to address to you, sir, being entirely dependent on the Executive authority, I cannot but hope I shall soon have to inform my court that the President has been pleased to issue such orders as will secure in future the execution of the eighth article of the Louisiana treaty, and the immediate reimbursement of the duties which have been unjustifiably levied to this day.

I have the honor to be, &c.

G. HYDE DE NEUVILLE.

No. 4.

Mr. Roth, Chargé d'Affaires of France, to the Secretary of State.

[Translation.]

LEGATION OF FRANCE TO THE UNITED STATES, *Washington, July 19, 1820.*

SIR: I learn by a letter from his Majesty's consul at New Orleans, dated June 13, the time when the law establishing a new duty of tonnage upon French ships came to be known in that city, that the officers of the custom-house there appeared to be of opinion that this law ought to be put into execution in Louisiana, as well as in the other parts of the Union, because it made no exception; and that these agents of the public revenue made their dispositions accordingly. The law of May 15, in question, does, in fact, point out no exception, and even has these words, "any act to the contrary notwithstanding."

But this disposition, implying an abrogation of anterior laws belonging to the duty of the State, cannot be applied to treaties and contracts of nation with nation, which are without the reach of interior legislation, and form another distinct law, which can only be modified by mutual consent by new treaties between the contracting parties.

This is predetermined and understood in all the private acts of nations.

The treaty of cession of Louisiana says, postively, article 8, "in future and forever, after the expiration of the twelve years, the ships of France shall be treated upon the footing of the most favored nations in the ports above mentioned."

Passing by the existing discussions upon this article, and in what manner the word favor is understood, there can be no doubt of the sense which it expresses for the present case.

The new duty of tonnage established on French ships, exclusively, places them in a state of grievous inequality in regard to the ships of other nations; even here there is no question of a favor refused, but of a charge imposed. What regards Louisiana is exactly contrary to what is guarantied forever and ever by the 8th article.

Relative to this state of inequality, in which the law of May 15 has placed French navigation in the ports of Louisiana, I shall observe, in passing, that there is a grave error in the reasonings which have been employed in Congress, and in the printed correspondence of Mr. Gallatin, to justify this measure.

It is pretended that its aim is to counterbalance the discriminating duties established in France. But these duties are applied in common to all foreign nations, and do not place the navigation of the United States in our ports upon any footing of inferiority with regard to other nations; whilst the new duty of tonnage imposed in America solely upon French ships places the navigation of France, with regard to other nations, in such a state of inferiority, that it is equivalent, if the law continued, to a real exclusion of our ships from the ports of the United States. This is anything but a compensation based upon reciprocity. Another disposition of this law, which would give it a character difficult to conceive if it were not supposed to arise from inadvertence, is the short time assigned for its execution. In America, a law made on the 15th of May, against a power in Europe, cannot be put into execution on the 1st of July, that is only forty-five days from the date, without injuring the security granted to commerce; and it is not from a power eminently commercial that an example so dangerous, given with deliberation, ought to be apprehended. It must be believed that the peculiarity arises solely from the considerable lapse of time between the presenting of the bill and its adoption. But it is nevertheless a tort with which our commerce by sea is threatened, and I expect strong remonstrances on the next arrivals of French ships, unless instructions, agreeably to received usages in this regard, are given to the officers of the customs, for ships that have sailed before the promulgation of the law, in the place whence they have departed.

It is not my intention, sir, to pursue at present the observations already contained in the letter of his Majesty's minister, dated May 24, upon this question in general, nor upon the discussion previously raised concerning the treaty of cession of Louisiana. I shall await, upon these two subjects, for your answer, and such instructions as may be directly addressed to me by my Government. But, as to the particular subject which I have the honor of submitting to you, the execution of the law of tonnage in the ports of Louisiana, notwithstanding an express stipulation of a treaty which this law cannot touch, this makes a part of my natural duties, and wants no special instructions for requiring my interference. The new law had only arrived in Louisiana at the moment I was written to. I must think that there was a mistake, or a want of sufficient instructions in the opinion then expressed by the officers of the customs. Before answering his Majesty's consul upon the conduct which he ought to pursue, I have the honor of praying you to be pleased to inform me on a point of such importance in the relations and ties existing between France and the United States.

I have the honor to offer you, sir, the respectful assurance of my high consideration.

ROTH,
Chargé d'Affaires, ad interim.

No. 5.

Extract of a letter (No. 155) from Mr. Gallatin (communicating the substance of a conversation with M. Pasquier) to Mr. Adams, dated July 31, 1820.

"An allusion was made, in the course of the conference, to the claim of the French, to be treated, without any equivalent, at New Orleans, in the same manner as the British now are. I did not know of this difficulty till it was occasionally mentioned in conversation by Mr. Pasquier. The pretension appears to me altogether untenable; but I would have wished to know what answer has been given at Washington to the reclamations of the French minister, and what are the President's intentions on that subject."

No. 6.

Extract of a letter from Mr. Roth, Chargé d'Affaires of France, to the Secretary of State, dated August 8, 1820.

[Translation.]

'The letter which I had the honor of addressing to you on the 18th of last month was intended to represent that the law of May 15, 1820, which established upon French ships in the ports of the United States a tonnage duty different from that which is levied upon other foreign ships, could not be applicable to French vessels in the ports of Louisiana, agreeably to the 8th article of the treaty of cession, which runs thus :

"'ARTICLE 8. In future, and forever, after the expiration of the twelve years, French ships shall be treated upon the footing of the most favored nation in the ports above mentioned.'

"I ought to confine myself to the citation of the text upon a condition so clearly, so positively expressed in a special clause of a treaty of cession, of which all the conditions together, and each of them in particular, are equally obligatory and necessary to the validity of a contract. I have not had the honor of being informed of the measures which the Federal Government has taken to enforce, in this point, the execution of the treaty of cession, agreeably to the obligations contracted by the treaty itself, notwithstanding every law to the contrary. This care of protection belongs to the power which has made the engagement. As regards the King's legation, I have done what was its duty, for the preservation of rights, by demanding that these measures should be taken, and by prescribing to his Majesty's consul at New Orleans, who expected an answer, to protest against every exaction which might be made by the custom-house from French vessels beyond what is received from ships belonging to the most favored nations; but not to go on, if his protest remain without effect, till it had been referred to the authority which signs and maintains the treaties. In this I have only conformed to the instructions formerly addressed in a similar case concerning the same 8th article of the treaty of cession of Louisiana."

No. 7.

Extract of a letter from Mr. Gallatin to Mr. Pasquier, dated August 15, 1820.

"I have, in this letter, confined myself to that subject which, from the present situation of the commercial relations of the two countries, requires the most immediate attention. But I must at once state that, having no other knowledge of the difficulties in the execution of the 8th article of the Louisiana convention than what is derived from your excellency, and having received no communication whatever on that subject from my Government, it is not in my power to discuss it at this time."

No. 8.

Extract of a letter (No. 24) from Mr. Adams to Mr. Gallatin, dated August 24, 1820.

"I had the honor of receiving, yesterday, your despatches, Nos. 148, 149 and 150, with their inclosures. The preceding numbers had been received before. The last of your letters being dated the 6th of July, I am in hopes that Mr. Hyde de Neuville, who sailed from Annapolis on the 1st or 2d of June, must have arrived in France within a very few days afterwards. He was the bearer of my letter to you, (No. 20,) and, by his personal observation, was aware of the friendly disposition towards France with which the act of Congress of the 15th of May was passed. The President will much regret the circumstance if it should be viewed by the French Government with a different spirit. The duty of 100 francs per ton upon American vessels, if laid, will probably not have very extensive effects, shipments to France in American vessels having already in a great measure ceased.

"It is sincerely hoped by the President that this counteracting and countervailing system will give way to the disposition for an amicable arrangement, in a conciliatory spirit, and with a view to the interests of both parties.

"The temper which has been manifested in France, not only on this occasion, but in relation to *all* the just claims of citizens of the United States upon the French Government, could not possibly terminate without coming to a crisis; and, at the same time that a positive rejection of the most indisputable demands of our citizens for indemnity was returned for answer to every note which you presented in their behalf, upon the untenable pretence that the Government of the Bourbons cannot be responsible for the outrages of its immediate predecessors, claims equally untenable were advanced, and reiterated with the most tenacious perseverance, of privileges, contrary to our Constitution, in the ports of Louisiana, founded on an inadmissible construction of an article in the treaty for the cession of Louisiana.

"If the construction contended for of that article by France were even correct, how can the present Government claim any advantage from a compact made with Napoleon, after an explicit declaration that they hold themselves absolved from all obligations of indemnities due to the United States and their citizens for his acts? I mention this now, because Mr. Roth informs me that he has directed the French consul at New Orleans to *protest* against the execution of the act of the 15th of May, 1820, specially in the ports of Louisiana. There was a long and elaborate note from Mr. de Neuville on this subject, to which a distinct and explicit answer was given by me. That minister replied; but as there was nothing new in the shape of argument in his second note, a second answer from me was postponed merely for the purpose of avoiding altercation, where it could be no possible object to us to have the last word. The pretence is, that, by the eighth article of the Louisiana treaty, French vessels are to be forever treated in that province on the footing of the most favored nation; and, on the strength of this, they claim to be admitted *there* paying no higher duties than English vessels. Our answer is, that English vessels pay there no higher or other duties than our own; not by *favor*, but by bargain. England gives us an equivalent for this privilege; and a merchant might as well claim of another, on the score of equal favor, that he should *give* a bag of cotton or a hogshead of tobacco to *him*, because he had *sold* the same articles to a third, as France can claim as a gratuitous favor to her that which has been granted for valuable consideration to Great Britain. The claim to which we admit that France is entitled under that article is to the same privilege enjoyed by England, upon her allowing the same equivalent. That is completely and exclusively our treatment of the most favored nation, and to that we are not only willing but desirous of admitting France. But even to that she can have no pretence while she refuses to be responsible for the deeds of Napoleon. If she claims the benefit of his treaties, she must recognize the obligation of his duties and discharge them."

No. 9.

Extract of a letter (No. 161) from Mr. Gallatin to Mr. Adams, dated September 19, 1820.

"On the 12th instant Mr. Pasquier invited me to a conference for the same day, in which, to my great astonishment, he stated that the King's Government considered the discussion of the eighth article of the treaty of the 30th of April, 1803, as inseparable from that of the discriminating duties, since France claimed under that article an exemption in Louisiana from our new tonnage duty, and generally from all those to the payment of which any other nation was not liable. I expressed my surprise at this determination, which, since I was not instructed on that subject, must, for the present, put an end to the negotiation. I said that what rendered it more extraordinary that a question which had heretofore been treated apart from all others should now be made an obstacle to the adjustment of other difficulties affecting all the commercial relations of the two countries was the silence which had at first been preserved by France on that point. The first convention between the United States and Great Britain, made in pursuance of the act of Congress of March, 1815, and by which the discriminating duties were reciprocally abolished on both sides, would have expired in 1819. It was renewed for ten years in the year 1818, without our Government having had any notice of this claim on the part of France, although the first convention had then been in force for more than two years and a half. I added, that if, according to my former suggestion, the negotiation should be now transferred to Washington, I thought it my duty to express my conviction that the Government of the United States would certainly consider the construction of the article for which France contended as altogether inadmissible. Mr. Pasquier accounted for the delay in claiming the privileges to which France thought herself entitled, by the peculiar situation in which she was placed during the period to which I alluded, and which had prevented her Government from attending to any other than her internal affairs or her European concerns. As he intimated that the determination not to separate the discussion of the article in question from that of discriminating duties was taken, I requested him to communicate it in writing, by answering my letter of the 15th of August. This he promised to do, and I have the honor to inclose copies of the letter which he accordingly wrote to me on the 13th, and of my answer of the 15th instant. You will perceive that the object of this answer is to impress on his Government the necessity of desisting from this preposterous claim, if they intend to bring the negotiation to a favorable result, either here or at Washington.

"Mr. Hyde de Neuville called on me on the evening of the 15th, and expressed his regret that I had not succeeded in concluding, at least, a provisional arrangement, and the reluctance he felt to be obliged to leave France at this time. I told him that he must be sensible that the failure could not be ascribed to me. Whatever might be my view of the subject, however disposed to listen to the arguments which might be adduced by the French Government, it was evident that a discussion of the 8th article was useless, since it was evident that I could not, without special instructions, accede to the construction assumed by France. It was, therefore, equally fair, and calculated to avoid unnecessary delays, to have declared at once, what was the fact, that, not being instructed on the subject, I could not discuss it. I would add, that this was the only reason why I had avoided the discussion, that the pretension set up by his Government appeared to me altogether untenable, and that little more seemed necessary to repel it than merely to state the question. This led to a desultory conversation on the nature of that claim, of which I will attempt to give the substance, although I am aware that I may not have fully understood his reasoning, and that, having already discussed the question with him, it must be more familiar to you than to me.

"Mr. de Neuville's arguments appeared to me to be drawn less from the natural and obvious meaning of the article than from collateral circumstances. He appealed to the intentions of the negotiators of the treaty of 1803, which he considered as susceptible of proof, and said that the condition stipulated in the 8th article was the essential compensation made to France, and, in fact, the real price paid by the United States for Louisiana; and that the eighty millions of francs were but an accessory. He mentioned the insertion in some other treaty of expressions limiting a similar provision to the sense for which we contended, and insisted that their omission in the article in question was fatal to our construction of it. He alluded to a supposed inconsistency of the article with the Constitution of the United States, which, if it rendered it impossible for us to comply with that provision of the treaty, made it necessary that we should, in lieu of it, make some other concession or compensation acceptable to France.

"This last argument was not perfectly intelligible to me, and it might have been inferred from it that the claim was set up only for the purpose of obtaining concessions in other respects. I observed, that any difficulty arising from a supposed inconsistency between our Constitution and the Louisiana treaty was a concern of our own; that I did not perceive any, as the Constitution of the United States became applicable to Louisiana, subject to any exception to be found in the instrument by which we had acquired that territory; and that, in point 'of fact, the 7th article of the treaty had, during twelve years, been carried into effect without any difficulty, although it gave to France and Spain privileges at New Orleans which they enjoyed in no other port of the United States. We could not at this time make a new treaty to that effect. I saw nothing that prevented the execution of that of 1803, according to its strict construction, which the United States could not at present, even if they were so disposed, enlarge in favor of France.

"Being unacquainted with the facts from which Mr. Hyde de Neuville inferred the intentions of the negotiators, I could form no opinion on that point; but I insisted that, whatever they might have been, it was not by these that the treaty must be construed; and that the two nations were bound by the expressions, and only by the expressions, used in the several articles, such as they had been ratified by the supreme authorities on both sides. As to any explanatory words which might have been used in some other treaty, whatever their effect might be on that treaty, their omission could not alter the obvious meaning of the 8th article of that by which the United States had acquired Louisiana; and the only question was, what was that meaning? The article simply provided that French vessels should forever be treated upon the footing of the most favored nations in the ports of Louisiana. Now, there were not, properly speaking, any *most favored nations* in the United States.

"Congress had, by a general law, proposed to all the nations with whom they had any commerce a *mutual* repeal of the discriminating duties. Every nation might have accepted that proposal, and it was in the power of France to avail herself of it whenever she pleased.

"The plan had been carried into effect with several powers, either by treaty stipulations, as was the case with Great Britain and Sweden, or only by an understanding, or mere municipal regulations, as in the case of the Netherlands and of the free towns of Germany. In every case the repeal was mutual, and the consequence of the general offer made by the United States. In every case the vessels of the nation which France now considered as more favored than herself were put in all the ports of the United States, including those of Louisiana, on the same footing as American vessels, on the express and reciprocal condition that American vessels should, in the ports of that nation, be treated on the same footing as indigenous vessels. What France claimed was, to enjoy the privilege without fulfilling the condition on which it was granted; that her vessels should be treated in Louisiana on the same footing as American vessels, whilst American vessels coming from Louisiana should, in her ports, continue to be subject to any discriminating duties she might be pleased to impose. She asked, in fact, to be treated, not as favorably, but more favorably than the nations she called most favored. The stipulation to place a country on the footing of the most favored nations necessarily meant that if a privilege was granted to a third nation for an equivalent, that equivalent must be given by the country which claimed the same privilege by virtue of such stipulation. A different construction implied a contradiction with the terms of the stipulation.

"It was true, I allowed, that there were cases in which a difficulty might arise; that is to say, if a privilege was granted by the United States to a third nation, in exchange for some favor or equivalent of a different nature from the privilege granted, and which France could specifically give. But this was not the present case. Not only France could give the equivalent, but this equivalent was of the same nature with the privilege granted, and both were so intimately connected that one could not be separated from the other. The moment an American vessel should cease to be treated in the ports of Great Britain or of the Netherlands as a British or Dutch vessel, the British or Dutch vessels, as the case might be, would at once cease to be treated as American vessels in the ports of the United States. I have found, since my conversation with Mr. Hyde de Neuville, that the treaty to which he alluded was that of commerce between the United States and France of the 6th of February, 1778; by the second article of which it is agreed that neither of the contracting parties shall grant any particular favor to other nations, in respect of commerce and navigation, which shall not become common to the other party, *who shall enjoy the same favor gratuitously if the concession was gratuitous, or on allowing the same compensation if the concession was conditional*. These last words, inserted for greater caution, define what was meant by that stipulation; and if any inference was to be drawn from them, it would be, that the two nations had in their first treaty thought proper to state explicitly what they intended by the .clause. of being placed on the footing of other (or most favored) nations; and that this explanation having once been given, the same construction must ever after be given to clauses of a similar nature, without its being necessary to repeat these explanatory words. And they have been accordingly omitted in every subsequent commercial arrangement between the two countries, as well in the 6th article of the convention of the 30th of September, 1800, as in the 8th article of the Louisiana treaty. But these words are mere surplusage. The clause would have precisely the same meaning without as with them; and their omission in an article of a subsequent treaty cannot, as I had observed to Mr. de Neuville, alter the only construction of which that article is susceptible.

"In answer to the objection that the article would, according our construction, be of no value to France, I answered generally that it would fulfil its avowed object, which was to enable her to trade at all times to New Orleans on terms not more but as advantageous as any other nation. It might be our interest to agree to a mutual repeal of discriminating duties, or to any other mutual commercial privilege with England or some other nation, and not with France; but if we had made such an agreement, France had a right, on fulfilling the reciprocal condition, to claim the same privilege in Louisiana, however inconvenient that might be to us. We might be compelled, by an unsuccessful war, or induced by political considerations, to grant some gratuitous favor to a third nation; and France would, in that case, immediately participate gratuitously in Louisiana in the same favor, although we had no motive for granting it to her. The article did confer substantial and permanent advantages on her, without recurring to the construction for which she contended."

No. 9, (a.)

Baron Pasquier to Mr. Gallatin.

[Translation.]

Paris, September 13, 1820.

Sir: I have submitted to the King the letter which you did me the honor to write to me on the fifteenth of last month, in answer to my note of the thirty-first of the month preceding. I have since recounted to his Majesty the conference which I had with you upon the object of that correspondence. His Majesty being informed, sir, of the impossibility of your entering upon an explanation of the difficulty which exists in America relative to the execution of the eighth article of the treaty of the 30th of April, 1803, and judging that the settlement of that difficulty cannot be separated from the negotiation of an arrangement of the respective navigation of the two States, considering that the article above mentioned secures special advantages to the French flag in the ports of Louisiana, is resolved to send, with the greatest possible promptitude, to America, his minister, to be near the Federal Government. He has thought—and his opinion in that has been in accordance with your own—that it was a means of accelerating the negotiation; a thing the more desirable because the present state can only, by being prolonged, be injurious to the well known interests of both countries.

I regret, sir, that this circumstance deprives me of the advantage of pursuing, directly, with you, an affair of that importance in which I am happy to believe that your superior information and your spirit of conciliation would have afforded all desirable facilities.

Accept the assurances of the high consideration with which I have the honor to be, sir, your most humble and most obedient servant.

PASQUIER.

No. 9, (b.)

Mr. Gallatin to Mr. Pasquier.

Paris, September 15, 1820.

Sir: I had the honor to receive your excellency's letter of the 13th instant, by which you inform me that, since I am without instructions respecting the 8th article of the treaty of the 30th of April, 1803, it has been determined that his Majesty's minister to the United States should depart as soon as possible for America.

Although I believe that a transfer of the negotiation to America may, under existing circumstances, accelerate a definitive result, your excellency will be pleased to recollect that, so far from having in any manner countenanced an expectation that the Government of the United States would accede to the construction put by that of France on the 8th article of the Louisiana treaty, I have expressed a contrary opinion.

I have not been led to that conclusion merely because I consider that construction as altogether untenable. Your excellency has informed me that the subject had already been discussed, in writing, at Washington, between his Majesty's minister and the Secretary of State of the United States, who had argued against the construction contended for in France.

Notwithstanding this discussion, the Secretary of State has not even alluded to that subject in the instructions which he has subsequently given to me in relation to an arrangement of the commercial relations of the two countries, and to an adjustment of the difficulties which have arisen in that respect. I am thence irresistibly led to infer that, after a thorough investigation, the view taken of the article by the Government of the United States essentially differs from that in which it is considered by his Majesty's Government.

These observations were necessary, on account of my own responsibility; but I pray your excellency to ascribe them principally to my earnest desire that the negotiation in which I have not been fortunate enough to succeed may, at Washington, be attended with a favorable result.

I request your excellency to accept, &c,

ALBERT GALLATIN.

No. 10.

Extract of a letter (No. 163) from Mr. Gallatin to Mr. Adams, dated October 19, 1820.

" From conversations with him (Mr. de Neuville) and with the Duke of Richelieu, I am induced to believe that this Government refused to separate in the negotiation the question relative to the Louisiana treaty from that of discriminating duties, less with a view to insist on their construction of the treaty than from the hope that the United States would make concessions in some other respect, in order to obtain from France a relinquishment of her pretensions under the article in question."

No. 11.

Extract of a letter (No. 164) from Mr. Gallatin to Mr. Adams, dated October 23, 1820.

" I had the honor, on the 20th instant, to receive your despatch No. 24, and addressed, on the 22d, to Mr. Pasquier, the letter of which a copy is inclosed. Its object—Mr. Hyde de Neuville not having left Paris—was to induce this Government to give him rational instructions. I had, the same evening, a short conversation with Mr. Pasquier, in which he used conciliatory language, but said that it appeared absolutely necessary to have some explanation on the 8th article of the Louisiana treaty, and drew a distinction between our old discriminating and our new tonnage duty, with reference to the privileges granted to France by that article. I have thought, upon reflection, that there might have been some foundation for that distinction, so far at least as our new tonnage duty exceeded that which it was intended to countervail. But the objection was not at all made on the receipt of the act of Congress. It was thought more eligible to retaliate than to discuss; and France, after having laid her one hundred francs duty, has at least now no right to complain.

" Mr. de Neuville called on me since the receipt of your despatch. Nothing very interesting occurred in the course of the conversation. I discovered, however, that when he had spoken of the privileges granted to France by the Louisiana treaty as being inconsistent with the Constitution of the United States, he alluded to an argument which you had used. I cannot help thinking that there has been in that respect some misconception on his part. It is very clear that the United States could not make, now that Louisiana is a State, a treaty containing conditions similar to those in question; but I do not perceive that the Constitution prevented them from acquiring on those terms Louisiana, when a foreign colony; still less that they could, without a compensation, be relieved from any obligation on the ground that the Constitution did not permit its performance. In your despatch to me you consider as contrary to our Constitution those privileges only claimed by France, which are founded on an inadmissible construction of the treaty. And the only argument which, it seems to me, can be drawn from the Constitution is, that the article must remain as it is, and that the Government of the United States cannot, even if so disposed, give to it a more extensive construction in favor of France than its literal and natural sense will admit."

No. 11, (a.)

Mr. Gallatin to Baron Pasquier.

PARIS, *October 22, 1820.*

SIR: I had the honor, in my letter of the 15th of September last, to state to your excellency the reasons which induced me to believe that the view taken by my Government of the eighth article of the Louisiana treaty essentially differed from that in which it seems to have been considered by his Majesty's Government. A despatch lately received from the Department of State at Washington leaves no doubt on that point.

The Secretary of State alludes in it to the correspondence between him and Mr. Hyde de Neuville—not for the purpose of giving me any instruction in that respect, for he does not seem to have presumed that this subject would be blended with that of the discriminating duties, or be discussed here—but in reference to a protest intended to be made by his Majesty's consul at New Orleans against the execution of the act of Congress of the 15th of May last. And he informs me, in the most explicit terms, that the construction put on the article in question by Mr. Hyde de Neuville is considered as inadmissible by the Government of the United States.

I have thought it my duty to make this communication to your excellency, because it thence appears extremely improbable that those difficulties which have produced a state of things so injurious to the commercial relations of the two countries can be adjusted at Washington, if his Majesty's Government shall insist on not separating that subject from the discussion of the article in question, and shall adhere to that construction of the article which had heretofore been contended for.

I request your excellency to accept, &c.

ALBERT GALLATIN.

No. 12.

Extract of a letter (No. 172) from Mr. Gallatin to Mr. Adams, dated February 1, 1821.

"You will have seen by my despatch (No. 164) that I had an opportunity, before Mr. de Neuville's final departure, to make use of your letters relating to the eighth article of the Louisiana treaty, and that this Government ought not to entertain any expectation of obtaining any concessions on our part in that respect."

No. 13.

Extract of a letter from Baron de Neuville to Mr. Adams, dated February 23, 1821.

" As I am solicitous to accelerate as much as possible the progress of the negotiation, I now take the liberty of requesting an answer to the letter which I had the honor of addressing to your Department on the 16th of June, 1818, relative to the eighth article of the Louisiana treaty. Should the Federal Government admit the interpretation given to this article on the part of France, it would be unnecessary to discuss the subject any further; but if, after a thorough investigation, it should still adhere to a contrary opinion, you will think with me, sir, that it is material to both parties to know how far they disagree on this very important article of the treaty. Both Governments having the same honest intentions, every point in dispute ought to be easily and speedily settled. What I ask, sir, even in its most limited sense, is the right secured to France by the eighth article of the Louisiana treaty, and in what cases is our navigation to obtain its enjoyment. It would appear to me that the negotiators on either part had but one a...d the same object in inserting the seventh and eighth articles, which express intention was to secure forever to French vessels in the ports of the ceded territory a real advantage over those of all other nations, and in my opinion the very expressions of the article establish in the most positive terms that intention of the negotiators."

No. 14.

Extract of a letter (No. 174) from Mr. Gallatin to Mr. Adams, dated March 29, 1821.

"In a conversation with one of the ministers, whom I have reason to believe to be desirous that an arrangement should take place, he suggested a prolongation for a limited time of the privileges which had, by the Louisiana treaty, been secured during twelve years to the French commerce in that quarter, as a substitute to the provision which allows permanent advantages to it, and as a mode of conciliating the difference of opinion of the two Governments on that subject. Another person of great respectability, and very friendly to the United States, alluded to the necessity of some concession on our part, which might enable this Government to come to an arrangement without abandoning altogether the ground they had taken."

No. 15.

Mr. Adams to Baron Hyde de Neuville.

DEPARTMENT OF STATE, *Washington, March 29, 1821.*

SIR: By the 7th article of the treaty of April 30, 1803, by which Louisiana was ceded to the United States, certain special privileges within the ports of the ceded territory were stipulated in favor of the ships of France and Spain for the term of twelve years; and by the eighth article of the same treaty it is further provided, that "in future and forever after the expiration of the twelve years, *the ships* of France shall be treated upon the footing of the *most favored nations in the ports above mentioned.*"

In your note of December 15, 1817, you demanded, upon the allegation of this article, that the advantages conceded to the English nation *in all the ports of the Union* should be secured to France in those of Louisiana. The citation of the words of the article would of itself be an answer to the claim. The stipulation of the eighth article is in its terms limited to grants of favors *in the ports of Louisiana.* The seventh article had secured to French and Spanish vessels *in those ports* peculiar privileges, to the exclusion of the vessels of other nations; and the object of the eighth article was evidently to provide that, after the expiration of those twelve years, no such peculiar privileges should be granted *in the same ports* to the vessels of any other nation, to the exclusion of those of France. The whole scope of both the articles is, by their letter and spirit, limited to special favors and privileges granted in those particular ports.

The claim of France, therefore, is not, and cannot be, by *any* construction of the eighth article, to enjoy in the ports of Louisiana the advantages conceded to any other nation *in all the ports of the Union,* but only that the *ships* of France should be entitled to the special advantages conceded to the ships of other nations in the ports of Louisiana.

Were, it then, even true that the English or any other nation enjoyed, by virtue of general stipulations' of treaties, advantages in all the ports of this Union over other nations, inasmuch as they would not be favors specially limited to the ports of Louisiana, or granted with any special reference to them, they could neither by the letter nor the spirit of the Louisiana treaty give to France any just claim to the special participation in those particular ports of advantages there enjoyed only by general arrangements co-extensive with the whole Union.

But in the answer from this Department of December 23, 1817, to the note of Mr. de Neuville, cf the 15th of that month, it was averred, and it is now repeated, that the ships of France at the expiration of the twelve years stipulated by the seventh article of the treaty, uniformly have been treated upon the same footing of the most favored nation in the ports of Louisiana. That they will continue to be so France may be assured, not only from that sacred regard for the obligation of treaties, which is the undeviating principle of the American Government, but from a maxim founded in that justice which is at once the highest glory and the soundest policy of nations, that every favor granted to one ought equally to be extended to all.

It is no exception, but an exemplification of this principle, that the vessels of England, Prussia, the Netherlands, and the Hanseatic cities, pay in the ports of this Union, including those of Louisiana, no other or higher duties than the vessels of the United States. This is not a *favor*, but a *bargain*. It was offered to all nations by an act of Congress of March 3, 1815. Its only condition was *reciprocity*. It was always, and yet is, in the power of France to secure this advantage to her vessels. It always depended upon her will alone to abolish every discriminating duty operating against her ships in the United States. Great Britain, Prussia, the Netherlands, the Hanseatic cities, accepted the proffer and granted the equiva. lent. Had France seen fit also to accept it, the American Government would have hailed the acceptance, not as a favor, but as equal justice. They were far from anticipating that, instead of this, France would found, upon equal reciprocity offered to all mankind, a claim to special privileges never granted to any. Special, indeed, would be the favor which should yield to a claim of free gift to one, of that which has been sold at a fair price to another.

English vessels, therefore, enjoy in the ports of Louisiana no *favors* which are not equally enjoyed by the vessels of France, nor do they enjoy any reduction of duties which French vessels might not, at the option of their own Government, have enjoyed at any time since the 3d of March, 1815. That France did not think proper to accept the offer is not mentioned with a view to reproach. France consulted what she thought to be her own interest, and, instead of reciprocity, aggravated discriminating duties to prohibition. She exercised her rights. But if, in levying those prohibitory duties, there was *disfavor* to the United States, surely as little can it be alleged that the extension of reciprocal advantages to all is a grant to any one of a *favor*.

It is observed in the reply of Mr. de Neuville, dated June 18, 1818, to the letter from this Department of the 23d of December preceding, that France, by claiming *forever* in the ports of Louisiana the full enjoyment of every advantage enjoyed by any other nation, in all the ports of the Union, as the price of equivalent advantages secured to the United States, still claims nothing gratuitous, inasmuch as the equivalent for this special advantage to France was already paid in the cession of Louisiana itself. This idea is not only contradicted by the whole tenor of the Louisiana treaty and by the special and obvious purport of the seventh and eighth articles, but I hesitate not to aver that if the American Government had believed those articles to be susceptible of such a construction, and had those articles *alone* been presented to them as the *whole* price of the cession of Louisiana, they never would have accepted it upon such terms. For such terms would not only have destroyed the effect of the cession of the province in *full sovereignty;* they would not only have been in direct violation of the Constitution of the United States, but they would have been a surrender of one of the highest attributes of the sovereignty of this whole nation. They would have disabled this nation forever from contracting with any power on earth but France for any advantage in navigation, however great, and however amply compensated. It would have been little short of a stipulation never to conclude a commercial treaty with any other nation than France. For what else are commercial treaties than the mutual concession of advantages for equivalents? And if every advantage obtained from others for equivalents were, by a retrospective obligation of this article, to be secured as already paid for by France, they would have been secured to her not only in the ports of Louisiana but in those of the whole Union. Such a treaty, far from being an acquisition of the full sovereignty of Louisiana, would have been on the part of the United States a formal abdication of their own.

From the obvious purport of the seventh and eighth articles, it is apparent that neither of them was considered in any respect as forming a part of the equivalent for the cession of Louisiana. The cession of Louisiana, and the equivalents paid for it, were not even included in the same treaty. The cession was in one treaty, and the equivalents in two separate conventions of the same date. The seventh and eighth articles referred to are in the treaty of cession, and not in the conventions of equivalents. The three instruments are, indeed, explicitly declared to be parts of one and the same transaction; but the very form of the arrangements adopted by the parties shows their common intention to regulate the cession by one compact, and the equivalents given for it by others.

Nor is the proof that these articles formed no part, in the estimation of either of the parties, of the equivalents for the cession confined to this tacit evidence in the forms of the negotiation. The seventh article bears upon its face the avowal of the motives by which it was dictated. Its introductory words are: "As it is reciprocally advantageous to the commerce of France and the United States to encourage the communication of both nations for a limited time in the country ceded by the present treaty until general arrangements relative to the commerce of both nations may be agreed on." This is the motive specially assigned by the article itself for its subsequent stipulations. The reciprocal advantage to the commerce of France and the United States was the end; the encouragement of their communications *for a limited time* in the country ceded were the means. And the eighth article, following as a corollary from the seventh, merely stipulated that, after the twelve years of special and exclusive privilege, the ships of France should be treated upon the footing of the most favored nations. In neither of the articles can a single word be found importing that they were understood by either party as forming any portion of the equivalent for the cession.

In the note of Mr. Hyde de Neuville, of the 16th of June, 1818, this claim of France to enjoy for nothing and forever, in the ports of Louisiana, every advantage which the United States may concede for a full equivalent to any other nation in all the ports of the Union is supported by a supposed peculiarity in the phraseology of the article by virtue of which it is claimed. To support this pretension, it is asserted that "in *all* the treaties between France and the United States the condition of reciprocity is mentioned in the most formal manner; that they *all expressly* say that the two contracting parties shall reciprocally enjoy the favor granted to another nation *gratuitously*, if the concession is gratuitous, *or by granting the same compensation, if the concession is conditional.*"

The mutual stipulations of being treated as the most favored nation is *not*, in all the treaties between France and the United States, accompanied by the *express* declaration that the favor granted to a third party shall be extended to France or the United States gratuitously, if the grant is gratuitous, and upon granting the same compensation, if it be conditional. This explanatory clause is expressed in terms only in one treaty between the United States and France, and that was the first treaty ever contracted between them, namely, the treaty of amity and commerce of February 6, 1778, in its second article. It has never been repeated in any of the subsequent treaties between the parties. It was alluded to, adopted, and applied to consular pre-eminences, powers, authorities, and privileges, by the 15th article of the consular convention of November 14, 1788. But in vain will any such clause be sought for in the convention of September 30, 1800, the words of the 6th article of which are as follows: "Commerce between the parties shall be free. The vessels of the two nations, and their privateers as well as their prizes, shall be treated in their respective ports as those of the nation the most favored, and, in general, the two parties shall enjoy, in the ports of each other, in regard to commerce and navigation, the privileges of the most favored nation." There is not a word in this article, nor in the whole convention, saying that these favors shall be enjoyed freely, if freely granted to others, or upon granting the same condition, if conditionally granted; yet who can doubt that this was implied in the article, though not expressed?

The fact, then, in regard to this argument, being directly the reverse of the statement in the note of Mr. de Neuville, of June 16, 1818, it cannot escape his attention how forcibly the argument recoils upon itself. If, from the uniform use of the explanatory clause in *all* the preceding treaties stated in the note as a fact, its omission in the Louisiana treaty could have warranted the inference that no such qualification was intended by it, with much stronger reason may it be concluded that, as the parties had before repeatedly contracted the same engagement, at one time with, and at another without, the explanatory clause, but always intending the same thing, this variety in the modes of expression was considered by them as altogether immaterial, and that, whether expressed or not, no claim to a favor enjoyed by others could justly be advanced by virtue of any such stipulation, without granting the same equivalent with which the advantage had been purchased.

There is, therefore, no necessity for supposing any forgetfulness on the part of the negotiators of the treaty of cession, nor of recurring to any supposed distinction between the construction applicable to a convention of commerce and to a treaty of sale. It has been proved that neither the seventh nor eighth article was ever understood by either party as forming any part of the equivalent for the cession; that the reciprocity of the 7th article is expressed upon its face; and that the 8th, as a consequence from it, only stipulated that after the period of special privilege in those special ports should have expired, no such privilege in those particular ports should be granted to other nations without being made common to the vessels of France. If it be admitted that, in a contract of sale, nothing can be understood by implication, (sous entendu,) this principle could be no less fatal to the claim of France than every other admissible rule of reason; for what implication could be more violent and unnatural than that, by a stipulation to treat the ships of France on the footing of those of the most favored nation *in the ports of Louisiana*, the United States had disabled themselves forever from purchasing a commercial advantage from any other nation, without granting it gratuitously to France?

That the Senate, in 1803, did not formally object to the stipulations of these 7th and 8th articles, must be ascribed to its never having entered into the imagination or conception of that body that such a claim as that now attempted to be raised from it by France was either expressed in or to be implied from them. Whether the special privileges granted for twelve years to the ships of France and Spain in those ports were compatible with the Constitution of the United States or with the other article of the treaty by which the inhabitants of the ceded territory were to be incorporated into the Union, and admitted, according to the principles of that Constitution, to the enjoyment of all the rights, advantages, and immunities of citizens of the United States, might be and was a question for the Senate in deliberating upon the treaty. It was a question of construction upon a clause of the Constitution; and that construction prevailed with which the terms of the treaty were reconcilable to it and to themselves. But whether the claim now advanced by France is reconcilable with the Constitution of the United States is no question of construction or of implication. It is directly repugnant to the express provision that the regulations of commerce and revenue in the ports of all the *States* of the Union shall be the same.

The admission of the State of Louisiana, in the year 1812, *on an equal footing with the original States in all respects whatsoever*, does not impair the force of this reasoning. Although the admission of French and Spanish vessels into their ports, for a short remnant of time, upon different regulations of commerce and revenue from those prescribed in the ports of all the other States in the Union, gave them a preference not sanctioned by the Constitution, and upon which the other States might, had they thought fit, have delayed the act of admission until the expiration of the twelve years; yet, as this was a condition of which the other States might waive the benefit, for the sake of admitting Louisiana, sooner even than rigorous obligation would have required, to the full enjoyment of all the rights of American citizens, this consent of the only interested party to anticipate the maturity of the adopted child of the Union can be considered in no other light than a friendly grant in advance of that which, in the lapse of three short years, might have been claimed as of undeniable right.

The Government of the United States have fulfilled, and will fulfil, the eighth article of the Louisiana treaty according to its plain and obvious meaning. The ships of France are and will be treated, in the ports of Louisiana, on the footing of the most favored nation. The ships of no nation enjoy any special favor in the ports of Louisiana. The ships of all nations are in the ports of Louisiana on the same footing as in the ports of all the other States in the Union. The ships of all nations in all the ports of the Union enjoy the same advantages which the nations to which they belong concede to the vessels of the United States in return. The favor and the only favor they enjoy is reciprocity. That favor the American Government extends to French vessels, and asks no better of France than to accept. But the American Government cannot grant as a gratuitous favor to France that which it has conceded for a valuable consideration to others. No such stipulation is *expressed* in the Louisiana treaty; no such stipulation can from all or any of its articles be justly inferred. In this, as in all their commercial relations with France, their most fondly cherished hope is mutual friendship, their most earnest desire equal *reciprocity*.

I pray you, sir, to accept the assurance of my distinguished consideration.

JOHN QUINCY ADAMS.

No. 16.

Baron de Neuville to Mr. Adams.

[Translation.]

MARCH 30, 1821.

SIR: I have received your letter dated yesterday, in answer to mine of June 16, 1818, and 23d ultimo. I shall have the honor to reply, and believe it will not be difficult for me to show that all my citations are correct. Not only all the treaties between France and this country, (those, it is well understood, which could admit of such a clause,) but *even all* the treaties and conventions between the United States and European Governments, or *nearly all*, express in positive or in equivalent terms what I have stated.

I will add, that the force of my argument would not be impaired, even admitting the sense attributed by you to the paragraph which seems to have more particularly fixed your attention. I shall return in a future note to this point of the discussion, as well as to all the others, and shall draw my best arguments from the very acts of the Federal Government, and from the opinions of the most enlightened men in the country. A better source could not be resorted to.

Allow me, sir, in the meantime, to make an observation, suggested by the following passage of your letter: "The Government of the United States have fulfilled, and will fulfil, the eighth article of the Louisiana treaty according to its plain meaning. The ships of France *are* and will be treated, in the ports of Louisiana, on the footing of the most favored nation." You had stated in your note of December, 1817: "It is true that the terms of the eighth article are positive and unconditional; but it will be readily perceived that the condition, though not expressed in the article, is inherent in the advantage claimed under it. If British vessels enjoyed in the ports of Louisiana any gratuitous favor, undoubtedly French vessels would, by the terms of the article, be entitled to the same."

In your letter of yesterday you say that "from a maxim founded in that justice which is at once the highest glory and the soundest policy of nations, that every favor granted to one ought equally to be extended to all."

"It is no exception, but an exemplification of this principle, that the vessels of England, Prussia, the Netherlands, and the Hanseatic Towns pay in the ports of this Union, including those of Louisiana, no other or higher duties than the vessels of the United States. This is not a favor, but a bargain." I cannot, I must confess, view those matters in the same light, nor, especially, can admit your conclusion. But even admitting that, in reality, the four instances above mentioned are mere excepted cases; allowing that England, Prussia, the Netherlands, and the Hanseatic Towns enjoy no gratuitous privilege or right in the United States; that they are not favored nations, and that, as you assert, sir, *this is not a favor, but a bargain;* admitting even your doctrine that gratuitous concessions alone constitute what is called a *favor*, whereby a nation becomes, in the ports of another, either a favored nation, or the most favored nation; allowing all this, still, how would it be possible to reconcile the interpretation which the difference between the duties now paid in *the ports of Louisiana* by French vessels and those paid in the same ports by the vessels of such nations as have neither *convention* nor *treaty*, nor have made any bargain with this Republic?

I am not apprised that Russians, Spaniards, Portuguese, or other nations, having none but such like relations with this country, have been made to pay a duty of eighteen dollars per ton in the ports of Louisiana; and yet this duty is frequently required of the vessels of that nation which, by virtue of an authentic instrument and of a positive contract, is entitled *to be treated in future and forever in the said ports* upon the footing of the most favored nation. Although nothing can be more clear or better established than the right of France, "this is not a favor, but a bargain." It was not without motive that the chargé d'affaires of his Majesty took care to observe, in his letter of the 18th of July last, that this was not the case of *a favor refused*, but that of a *charge* imposed by one party on the other.

Such a state of things, whatever may be the interpretation given to the eighth article, is so injurious to the rights of France, and so very contrary to the equity and honesty of the Federal Government, that I cannot but flatter myself that the answer now solicited to this letter, and to that of Mr. Roth of the 18th of July, will be such as to give full satisfaction on this point. And if France should not be made to enjoy immediately the right which I claim, most assuredly she cannot be denied, in the meantime, the enjoyment of that which is acknowledged.

I have the honor to be, sir, &c.,

G. HYDE DE NEUVILLE.

No. 17.

Baron de Neuville to Mr. Adams, dated May 15, 1821.

SIR: I have now the honor to answer your letter of the 29th of March last.

The terms of the eighth article of the Louisiana treaty are as follows: "In future and forever, after the expiration of the twelve years, the ships of France shall be treated upon the footing of the most favored nations in the ports above mentioned;" meaning the ports of the territory ceded by France, Louisiana. It evidently results from the terms of this article that the French nation is to be treated, *in future and forever after*, upon the footing of the most favored nations, not in all the ports of the United States, but in those of Louisiana.

But what is meant, what can be understood, by the terms *being treated upon the footing of the most favored nations?*

Is there but one way of obtaining the right to be so treated? or, may it be held by more than one title? Upon consulting the various treaties made between different nations, and particularly those which the United States have entered into with European powers, I find in almost all of them a definition of what is meant by being *treated upon the footing of the most favored nations,* and these definitions are so precise that I do not see how any controversy can arise on that point. In most cases relating to the rights and privileges of the most favored nations, the parties even go on to explain that the favor shall be free, if freely granted to another nation; or upon granting the same compensation if upon concession be conditional; from which I conclude that the right to be treated upon the footing of the most favored nations may be enjoyed in two ways, either *gratuitously* or *conditionally.*

You, moreover, appear to me, sir, to admit this very material point; you even declare (and in this opinion I may readily acquiesce, I have at least no interest in opposing it) that it is not necessary that the terms *gratuitously* or *conditionally* be expressed in the agreement; meaning, I suppose, where the condition of reciprocity is stipulated. Alluding to the convention of the 30th of September, 1800, you say: "There is not a word in the whole convention saying that these favors shall be enjoyed freely, if freely granted, or upon granting the same condition, if conditionally granted. Yet, who can doubt that this was implied in the article, though not expressed?" The article does, in my opinion, contain what I attributed to it, if not in express at least in equivalent terms; but let us examine what you have stated in your answer. In the article it is expressly said *that the two parties shall reciprocally enjoy, each in the ports of the other, as far as regards commerce and navigation, the privileges of the most favored nations.* It goes no further; it gives an explanation as to gratuitous or conditional favors, and perhaps it was unnecessary here. Yet, do you add, who can doubt *that this was implied in the article, though not expressed?* This admission determines the first point, viz: that there are two modes of being treated upon the footing of the most favored nations; and that the rights resulting therefrom may be enjoyed either *freely,* if freely granted, or conditionally, if granted upon condition to other nations.

We shall soon have to examine whether France has or has not, from the very nature of the contract of 1803, a right to be treated *in the ports of Louisiana upon the footing of the most favored nations, unconditionally, and without further compensation on her part.* This second question is of no less importance; but I think it right to detach it from that which now engages my attention, and the solution of which must precede all further discussion. Permit me, sir, here to suggest an observation which has struck me as being very forcible. If France, by virtue of the treaty of 1803, which secured her the rights and privileges of the most favored nations, has had a right to *enjoy every favor freely, if freely granted to other nations, or upon granting the same condition, if conditionally granted,* upon what principle, after the treaty of 1803, which secures the same treatment in a still more solemn manner, should she be reduced to the enjoyment of only such favors as are granted freely to other nations? *If* British vessels enjoyed in the ports of Louisiana any gratuitous favor, undoubtedly French vessels would, by the terms of the article, be entitled to the same." It appears to me that, after your explanation just above cited, it would be equally allowable to say, "if British vessels enjoyed in the ports of Louisiana any conditional favor, undoubtedly French vessels would, by the terms of the article, be entitled to the same."

Thus, sir, I hope you will admit, with me, the first question to be sufficiently settled. France is to enjoy, *in future and forever, in the ports of the territory ceded by her, the privileges of the most favored nations;* and as the treatment or favor which a nation may receive is either free or conditional, it follows that France has a right to be treated in Louisiana upon the footing of the most favored nation, either freely or conditionally, unless it be proved that her contract is to form an exception; that she has already *paid for* the privilege which she claims, and has, therefore, a right to be treated, *without further compensation,* upon the footing of the most favored nation. This, sir, is what I think I can easily prove.

In the meantime, it is evident not only that French vessels do not enjoy in the ports of Louisiana the privileges reserved by France, but that they are even deprived of those which cannot be disputed.

I have already shown that, far from being treated upon the footing of the most favored nations, France at this time is of all nations that which is most unfavorably treated in Louisiana, which forms a striking contrast with the precise stipulations of the 8th article of the Louisiana treaty.

But what nations are (comparatively with France) treated upon the most favored footing in the ports of Louisiana? All those, I answer, which enjoy in the said ports, whether freely or conditionally, by virtue of treaties or without stipulation to that effect, any rights, favors, or privileges denied to France. Hence, as it so happens at this time that vessels of four different nations pay in the ports of Louisiana no other or higher duties than those paid by American vessels, I have surely a right to claim the same advantage for our navigation by virtue of the 8th article of the Louisiana treaty.

You will observe, sir, that I do not speak of *all the ports of the United States.* Finding this last phrase repeated several times, and underlined in your letter of the 29th, I have some fear not to have been rightly understood, or rather not to have used expressions sufficiently distinct. France has nothing to ask, she claims nothing, *in all the ports of the United States.* She has not to examine whether any or several nations indiscriminately enjoy in these any rights or privileges, nor on what conditions such rights or privileges may have been granted. But as the ports of Louisiana are of the number of *all the ports of the United States,* and as France has a right to be treated in those upon the footing of the most favored nations, she claims that right as soon as it is found that the vessels of any other nation are treated there more favorably than hers. But I find, sir, in your letter: "Were it even true that the English or any other nation enjoyed, by virtue of general stipulations of treaties, advantages 'in all the ports of this Union over other nations, inasmuch as they would not be favors specially limited to the ports of Louisiana, or granted with any special reference to them, they could neither by the letter nor the spirit of the Louisiana treaty give to France any just claim to the special participation in those particular ports of advantages there enjoyed only by general arrangements co-extensive with the whole Union." It seems to me that it would have been useless and even perfectly idle to make any *special mention* of the ports of Louisiana, in the treaties and conventions, by which certain rights, favors, or privileges are granted in all the ports of the United States, since they are comprised within the denomination of the ports of the United States. Giving the whole is giving every component part; and in such cases the general term necessarily embraces every particular denomination. Let us suppose a case. You make over to me conditionally the privilege of hunting on one of your estates, situated in a certain district; I am to enjoy this privilege if you grant it to others. Soon after, you sell or make over to one of my neighbors the privilege of hunting on all your estates you hold in the same district. It is clear that my right does not on that account extend to all your estates, but it certainly does not include that which is specified in my contract or conveyance. The favor is *general* for my neighbors, but as it regards me is only *special;* for the general term, I repeat it, necessarily embraces every particular denomination. Such matters it is not thought necessary to explain, because it is not expected that they can ever be subject to discussion. But suppose, further, that the right which I so justly claim was not even granted by you; that

I held it only in my own right; suppose it to be an express *reservation* which I h$_{ad}$ thought it proper to make on disposing in your favor of that estate, which I had consented to sell merely to oblige you and to suit your convenience; if I yielded to your instant and pressing solicitations, if, in order to persuade me to sell this estate, you had gone so far as to offer me, not a mere conditional right *of chase, but that Privilege, free from all charges or conditions, to enjoy it with you to the same extent as yourself and forever;* if I can prove this last assertion by your own documents, you will surely admit, sir, that this is an indisputable, sacred right, rather in the nature of property vested in me than a mere privilege over yours. *This is not a favor, but a bargain.*

What may now appear a mere assertion shall hereafter be proved. "You do me the honor to state" "The stipulation of the eighth article is in its terms limited to grants of favors *in the ports of Louisiana.* The 7th article has secured to French and Spanish vessels *in those ports* peculiar privileges, to the exclusion of the vessels of other nations; and the object of the 8th article was evidently to provide that, after the expiration of those twelve years, no such peculiar privileges should be granted *in the same ports to* the vessels of any other nation, to the exclusion of those of France; the whole scope of both articles is by their letter and spirit limited to special favors and privileges granted in those particular ports." I must confess, sir, that, so often as I have read the 8th article, I cannot discover that it *evidently* states that, after the expiration of those twelve years, no such peculiar privileges should be granted *in the same ports to* the vessels of any other nation, to the exclusion of those of France. The article states—nothing can be more clear—*in future and forever, after* the expiration of the twelve years, the ships of France shall be treated upon the foot$_{ing}$ of the most favored nations in the ports above mentioned. Nothing whatever is said about *peculiar favors granted in the same ports to the vessels of any other nation;* why, then, should we attribute to the article what it does not contain—I will add, what it could not express? And this I shall now proceed to prove. When France disposed of Louisiana, she certainly was entitled to reserve any rights whatever in that province, whether *special, gratuitous, limited,* or *unconditional;* she sold her own property, and had a right to fix its price, as the other party was free to accept or to decline the offer. The express reservation made by her in the first place for twelve years, and then, on condition of certain events, *forever after,* was no more than a part of the price of the territory ceded; and by no means a favor granted by one party and received by the other.

"This stipulation was a part of the price of the territory; it was a condition which the party ceding had a right to require, and to which we had a right to assent; the right to acquire involved the right to give the equivalent demanded." I shall have occasion to revert to this opinion of one of the most distinguished men of the country, and which is so much in point. But to proceed with my argument: it is easy to conceive that France was entitled, when disposing of her property, to reserve such rights as she pleased, *with or without reciprocity,* for a *limited time or forever;* "this was a part of the price of the territory;" but if, as you observe, sir, *there is an express provision in the Constitution that the regulations of commerce and revenue in the ports of all the States of the Union shall be the same,* it evidently follows that no nation can acquire by treaty or commercial convention, in the ports of Louisiana alone, the advantage which France enjoys there by special title, by virtue of a bargain and sale; which instrument is singular from its very nature, and cannot be repeated in favor of any nation, whatever may be its connexion or commercial interests with the United States, at least so far as respects the territory ceded by France. If, therefore, no other nation can acquire in the ports of *Louisiana alone,* whether *gratuitously* or *conditionally,* the special favor, or, *to speak more correctly,* the right which France has thought proper to reserve in those ports "*in future and forever after,*" surely I am authorized to maintain, not only that the 8th article *does* not, but even that it *could* not, admit of the meaning which is attributed to it. Can it be supposed that the American negotiators had proposed to France to reserve an advantage or privilege which, according to the Federal Constitution, could never be realized? To give such an interpretation to this article would not be doing justice to their honesty; it surely must have some other meaning; why not then adopt that which is most natural? * *We do not presume,* says Vattel, *that sensible persons had nothing in view* in treating together, or in forming any other serious agreement. The interpretation which renders a treaty null and without effect cannot then be admitted.

"Every clause should be interpreted in such a manner as that it may have *its effect,* and not be found vain and illusive."* Let us, then, leave to the eighth article its true sense; its expressions are clear and distinct; and it is admitted that, *in the interpretation of treaties, pacts, and promises, we ought not to deviate from the common use of the language;*† we also know that the first general maxim is, that *it is not allowable to interpret what has no need of interpretation;*‡ and you allow, sir, in your letter of the 23d of December, 1817, that *the terms of the eighth article are positive and unconditional.* It being admitted that the terms are positive and unconditional, and since, *in order to ascertain the true sense of a contract, attention ought to be paid* §*principally to the words of him who promises; and since, on every occasion when a person has and ought to have shown his intention, we take for true against him what he has sufficiently declared,‖* what motive can there be for denying France a right established *in positive and unconditional terms,* more especially when the intention of the American negotiators, of *those who promised,* is sufficiently declared and perfectly manifest? On this subject it will soon be shown that the eighth article, which, in itself, is so precise as to require no corroboration, has, withal, by way of corollary, a document calculated to remove every possible doubt, if any could still remain. But, sir, you seem to think that the seventh and eighth articles have never been, in any respect, considered "*as forming part of the equivalents for the cession of Louisiana, and that the cession was in one treaty, and the equivalents in two separate conventions of the same date;*" and finally, while admitting that the three instruments form but one whole, as it is expressly declared, you add, "*but the very form of the arrangements adopted by the parties shows their common intention to regulate the cession by one compact, and the equivalents given for it by others.*" If we are ever to deal in conjectures, why should we not say, for there would seem to be more ground for the assertion, that the 7th and 8th articles of the convention are the *equivalents,* and the two subsequent instruments merely accessory, and the *compliment of* the bargain? We shall soon find that it is quite allowable to consider as a mere *accessory* what you, sir, regard not only as the principal part, but even as *the whole of the compensation.* But let us set every commentary aside, the convention of 1803 cannot give rise to any mistake. The 7th and 8th articles established, without the least ambiguity, the nature and conditions of the rights reserved by France; the 9th article coming next, because what is most important should be settled before points of

* Vattell, B. II. ch. xvii, § 283.
† Vattell, B. II. ch. xvii, §272.
‡ Vattell, B. II, ch. xvii, 263.

§ Vattell, B. II, ch. xvii, 267.
‖ Vattell, B. II, ch. xvii, 266.

minor consequence, sufficiently shows that the two supplementary instruments are only matters of execution. They, in fact, contain calculations of banking and exchange and details of liquidation which could not well have been comprised in the convention; and it is even, moreover, fully explained that those two instruments, signed on the same day, "*are to have their execution in the same manner as if they had been inserted in the principal treaty; that they be ratified in the same form, and in the same time and jointly.*"

The question, it appears to me, may be viewed in two different lights, and will still, in either case, equally resolve itself in favor of the claims of France. In the first place, France may be considered as having reserved certain rights of property on disposing of her sovereignty in Louisiana, and this would appear the more correct view of the case; for, strictly speaking, the 7th and 8th articles are not the equivalents of the cession according to the true sense of the treaty as understood in 1803. In the other supposition, considering the 7th and 8th articles as part of the equivalents, the rights and privileges therein secured to France will form, with the fifteen million dollars, the full and entire compensation for the territory ceded by her. The privileges secured by the 7th and 8th articles are still, in either case, a right of property of the most sacred nature.

"*This is not a favor, but a bargain. This is not a free gift, but the fair price of that which has been sold.*" But suffer me, sir, to observe that it is entirely erroneous to suppose that *neither the seventh nor eighth article was ever understood as forming a part of the equivalent for the cession.*" Not only it was understood they did, and was so meant by the negotiators, but one of them, Mr. Livingston, while offering to the French Government the express reservation of the rights and privileges in question, as I shall hereafter prove, went so far as to say that, *by those means, France would enjoy all the advantages of the colony, without incurring the expense of maintaining it.* Let us now add to Mr. Livingston's expressions the formal opinion of Mr. Randolph, and it will be no longer possible to maintain that *neither the 7th nor 8th article was ever considered as forming part of the equivalent* for the territory ceded by France. "I regard this stipulation only as a part of the price of the territory; it was a condition which the party ceding had a right to require, and to which we had a right to assent. The right to acquire involved the right to give the equivalent demanded."[*] In your letter of the 29th of March last, as well as in your note of the 23d of December, 1817, you advance that, if France could claim *forever* in the ports of Louisiana a privilege which could be denied to her in other ports of the United States, France would, in such case, have transferred only an *imperfect sovereignty* to this Republic. I have already endeavored to establish (letter of June 16, 1818,) that *sovereignty* should ever be distinguished from *property;* in support of which, I could cite many instances of transfers of a *full and entire sovereignty*, with the reservation of certain rights or privileges, in the nature of that which France holds in the ports of Louisiana. But the very terms of the article make it perfectly useless to discuss this point. The expression *forever* is sufficiently explicit. *In the ports of the territory ceded*, surely implies that France is entitled to the privilege claimed by her *in Louisiana* only, and it may therefore, at all times, be denied her in the other ports of the United States, unless some other treaty or convention should intervene. You persist, also, in believing that the right claimed by France is in contradiction with the Constitution of the United States, which declares that "all duties, imposts, and excises shall be uniform throughout the United States, and that no preference shall be given by any regulation of commerce or revenue to the ports of one State over those of *another*. I could add several very plausible arguments to those which I have already made against that supposed *inconsistency;* I might, perhaps, also contend with some advantage against the manner in which you explain the admission of the *State of Louisiana on an equal footing with the original States, in all respects whatever*, in spite of the privilege which France and Spain still enjoyed in its ports. I think I should have some right to observe that, in all *constitutional* questions no modification is admissible, and nothing is to be assumed, except according to the forms required by the Constitution itself; that representative Governments scarcely admit of acts of mere courtesy; that they have the law alone in view, and that it is therefore to be presumed that Congress would not have emancipated, before its maturity, *the adopted child of the Union, nor have given him a preference not sanctioned by the Constitution,*[†] if, in fact, the measure could have been considered as illegal. But, sir, my Government *has nothing* to do with the question of constitutionality; it is, therefore, proper for me to decline discussing it, and I shall be satisfied with recalling some very respectable opinions which militate in favor of my positions, or against what is objected to them, and destroy all idea of inconsistency between the 7th and 8th articles of the Louisiana treaty and the Federal Constitution.

‡ Mr. Rodney.—"It is contended that the United States have no right to purchase territory; that they have no right to admit the people of Louisiana to a participation of the rights derived from an admission into the Union; and that a peculiar favor is about being granted to the ports of New Orleans, in violation of the Constitution. In the view of the Constitution, the Union was composed of two corporate bodies, of States and Territories. A recurrence to the Constitution will show that it is predicated on the principles of the United States acquiring territory either by war, treaty, or purchase. There was one part of that instrument within whose capacious grasp all these modes of acquisition were embraced. By the Constitution, Congress has power to lay and collect taxes, duties, imposts, and excises, to pay the debts and provide for the common defence and general welfare of the United States. To provide for the general welfare; the import of these terms is very comprehensive indeed. If this general delegation of authority be not at variance with other particular powers specially granted, nor restricted by them; if it be not in any degree comprehended in those subsequently delegated, I cannot," said Mr. Rodney, "perceive why, within the fair meaning of this general provision, is not included the power of increasing our territory, if necessary, for the *general welfare* or *common defence*. Suppose, for instance, that Great Britain should propose to cede to us the island of New Providence, so long the seat of pirates preying upon our commerce, and the hive from which they have swarmed: will any gentlemen say that we ought not to embrace the opportunity presented as a defence against further depredations? Suppose the Cape of Good Hope, where our East Indiamen so generally stop, were offered to be ceded to us by the nation to which it belongs, and that nation should say, on our possessing it, you shall declare it a *free port:* is there any member who hears me that would contend that we were not authorized to receive it, notwithstanding the great advantages it would insure to us."

"There is another sound answer to the objection of gentlemen: *this is property ceded to us by the power ceding it with a particular reservation.*"

---

[*] Congress, House of Representatives. Mr. Randolph's debate of the Louisiana treaty, Tuesday, October 25, 1803.

[†] It cannot, most assuredly, be correct to violate the principles of the Constitution *for a day*.—Mr. Griswold, House of Representatives, debate October 25, 1803.

[‡] Debate, October 25, 1803, House of Representatives.

*Mr. Smilie.—"If the prevailing opinion shall be that the inhabitants of the ceded territory cannot be admitted under the Constitution, as it now stands, the people of the United States can, if they see fit, apply a remedy by amending the Constitution so as to authorize the admission."

* Mr. Crowninshield.—"It surely cannot be unconstitutional to receive the ships of *France* or *Spain* in the ports of the new territory, upon any terms whatever. *It is a mere condition of* the purchase, and this House may or may not agree to it. Being a mere commercial regulation, we have the power to give our assent or dissent to the article in question; for I hold it to be a correct doctrine that this House, by the Constitution, has the power to regulate commerce with foreign nations as well as with the Indian tribes, and that, whenever the President and Senate make a treaty involving any commercial points, our consent is absolutely necessary to carry the treaty into effect. By giving our assent, we do not injure the right of the other ports in the Atlantic States, as the privilege is extended only to ports in the ceded territory. I consider the eastern or carrying States as particularly and deeply interested in the acquisition of Louisiana. It is true, their ships already visit almost every part, but under many restrictions, and I wish to see them sailing on the Mississippi without molestation or restraint."

"I am in favor of adopting these treaties, and they shall have my hearty support."

* Mr. Randolph.—"The unconstitutionality of this treaty is attempted to be shown by the following quotation from that instrument: 'No preference shall be given to the ports of one State over those of another State,' &c., &c. New Orleans, therefore, will enjoy an exemption. She is, therefore, a favored port, in contradiction to the express letter of the Constitution. To me it appears that this argument has much more of ingenuity than of force in it; more of subtlety than of substance. Let us suppose that the treaty, instead of admitting French and Spanish vessels on the terms proposed, merely covenanted to admit American vessels on equal terms with those of France and Spain. If we acquired this right, divested of the country, it would have been considered, and justly, as an important privilege. Annex the territory to it, and you cannot accept it! You may, indeed, acquire either the commercial privilege or the territory without violating the Constitution, but take them both and that instrument is infringed.

"I regard this stipulation only as a part of the price of the territory. It was a condition which the party ceding had a right to require, and to which we had a right to assent. The right to acquire involved the right to give the equivalent demanded. Mr. Randolph said that he expected to hear it said in the course of the debate that the treaty in question might clash with the treaty of London in this particular; he would, therefore, take this opportunity in remarking that the privilege granted to French and Spanish bottoms being *a part of the consideration for which we had obtained the country,* and the Court of London being officially apprised of the transaction, and acquiescing in the arrangement, it would ill become any member of that House to bring forward such an objection."

†Mr. Adams.—"But it has been argued that the bill ought not to pass, because the bill itself is an unconstitutional, or, to use the words of the gentleman from Connecticut, an extra constitutional act. It is, therefore, say they, a nullity. We cannot fulfil our part of its conditions, and, on our failure in the performance of any one stipulation, France may consider herself as absolved from the obligations of the whole treaty on hers. I do not conceive it necessary to enter into the merits of the treaty at this time. The proper occasion for that discussion is past; but, allowing even that this is a case for which the Constitution has not provided, it does not, in my mind, follow that the treaty is a nullity or that its obligations either on us or on France must necessarily be cancelled. France never can have the right to come and say, I am discharged from the obligations of this treaty because your President and Senate, in ratifying it, exceeded their powers; for this would be interfering in the internal arrangements of our Government. It would be intermeddling in questions with which she has no concern, and which must be settled entirely by ourselves. The only question for France is, whether she has contracted with the department of our Government authorized to make treaties; and this being clear, her only right is to require that the conditions stipulated in our name be punctually performed. I trust they will be so performed, and will cheerfully lend my hand to every act necessary for the purpose, *for I consider the object as of the highest advantage to us.*"

The opinions I have just cited have so much weight that I shall not attempt to support them by further authority, and shall consider it as sufficiently established—

1. That the rights reserved by France are, in fact, properly vested in her; or, in other words, that the territory of Louisiana *is a property ceded with particular reservation.*

2. That if, in 1803, the Louisiana treaty was deemed *unconstitutional* by some of the distinguished characters of the United States, the great majority of Congress declared itself in favor of a contrary doctrine.

3. That the question of *constitutionality* is, and should be, foreign to France, and that her only right is to *require* that the conditions stipulated be *punctually* and *faithfully* performed.

The French Government desires no more, and has, therefore, I think, a right to expect that a claim so well founded will cease to be disputed.

I read in your letter, "nor is the proof that these articles formed no part, in the estimation of either of the parties, of the equivalents for the cession, confined to this tacit evidence in the forms of the negotiation. The seventh article bears upon its face the avowal of the motives by which it was dictated. Its introductory words are: '*As it is reciprocally advantageous to the commerce of France and the United States to encourage the communication of both nations, for a limited time, in the country ceded,*' &c., &c. The reciprocal advantages to the commerce of France and the United States was the end; the encouragement of their communications *for a limited time* in the country ceded were the means; and the eighth article, following as a corollary from the seventh," &c., &c., &c.

I think I have already sufficiently shown that the two parties in the contract had but one and the same mode of understanding the 7th and 8th articles; but even if I had not, in support of my opinion, those already cited, and that of Mr. Livingston, which I shall soon have occasion to produce, still would my position be incontrovertibly proved by the very terms of those articles.

You cite, sir, the introductory expressions of the seventh article. Allow me to invite you to examine its conclusion, which appears to me more explicit, and leaves no doubt as to the true intention of the negotiators.

But perhaps it would be still better to cite the whole article. It speaks for itself, and sufficiently

---

* Debate on the Louisiana treaty, Tuesday, October 25, 1803.　　　† Senate debate, November 3, 1803.

explains what induced the negotiators to fix the duration of the privilege conveyed by the seventh article, and to assign no limitation to the right of property secured by the eighth.

"As it is reciprocally advantageous to the commerce of France and the United States to encourage the communication of both nations, for a limited time, in the country ceded by the present treaty, until general arrangements relative to the commerce of both nations may be agreed on, it has been agreed between the contracting parties that the French ships coming directly from France or any of her colonies, loaded only with the produce or manufactures of France or her said colonies, and the ships of Spain, coming directly from Spain or any of her colonies, loaded only with the produce and manufactures of Spain or her colonies, shall be admitted, during the space of twelve years, in the ports of New Orleans, and in all other legal ports of entry within the ceded territory, in the same manner as the ships of the United States coming directly from France or Spain or any of their colonies, without being subject to any other or greater duty on merchandise, or other or greater tonnage, than those paid by the citizens of the United States. During the space of time above mentioned no other nation shall have a right to the same privileges in the ports of the ceded territory. The twelve years shall commence three months after the exchange of ratifications, if it shall take place in France, or three months after it shall have been notified at Paris to the French Government, if it shall take place in the United States. It is, however, well understood that the object of the above article is to favor the manufactures, commerce, freight, and navigation, of France and of Spain, so far as relates to the importations that the French and Spanish shall make into the said ports of the United States, without in any sort affecting the regulations that the United States may make concerning the exportation of the produce and merchandise of the United States, or any right they may have to make such regulations."

What appears most clearly deducible from the terms of this article is, that it was thought advantageous to the commerce of France and of the United States to encourage, in a *very special manner*, the communications of the two nations in the ports of the territory ceded; that the principal object was to favor the manufactures, the commerce, and the shipping of France and Spain. I can see no other advantage resulting from the seventh article for the United States, and it must be admitted that its stipulations are, in fact, advantageous only to France and to Spain. No reciprocity is granted to the United States either in the ports of France or in those of Spain. Their communication with France will, it is true, be more frequent, but *only in the ports of the ceded territory.* Perhaps the article might have been worded with more care, but, after all, it expresses no more than I have stated. If the avowed object of the article was to favor, *in a special manner*, not only the commerce and navigation of France, but likewise the commerce and navigation of Spain, *without any reciprocal stipulation* for the United States, it is easy to discern what induced the American negotiators to demand that the privilege which France *was not alone to enjoy in Louisiana should be limited in its duration;* more especially as, during that time, *no other nation* could be admitted to enjoy the same favor. But where the privilege ceased to be common to Spain, the French Government, while consenting to modify it as by the eighth article stipulated for the *perpetual* and unconditional enjoyment of the right of property thus reserved, the eighth article does not, as did the seventh, stipulate that other nations shall not be treated as favorably as those of France in the ports of the territory ceded by her; such a condition could be imposed but for a limited time. But it was natural that, when yielding to the solicitations of the American negotiators the French Government consented to cede Louisiana, it should secure to France the right *never* to be treated more unfavorably than any other nation in the ports of her former colony, whether those favors be purchased or not by such nations; that the transaction which, on the part of France, was at once a great sacrifice and a striking proof of her friendship for these United States, should not, in the end, turn to her detriment, but should, at least, secure some lasting advantage to her commerce and navigation. All this is not mere conjecture of my own; the facts are positive and clear; and every doubt must cease after attending to the following sentiments, not of the French negotiators, not of Mr. *Livingston* himself, in the memorial addressed by him to the French Government on this question: Is it advantageous for France to take possession of Louisiana? He does not confine himself to proposing that France should reserve *forever, and without reciprocity for the United States*, the right stipulated in the eighth article, but even that which she subsequently held by the seventh article for twelve years only. "Does France wish," says Mr. Livingston, "to introduce more easily her productions into the western country; does she desire to accustom its inhabitants to her wines and manufactures, and to conquer the prejudices which the Americans entertain in favor of English goods, &c., &c., &c. *All this can be accomplished only* by the cession of New Orleans to the United States, with the reserve of the right of entry, at all times, for the ships and merchandises of France, free from all other duties than those paid by American vessels. By those means American merchants established in New Orleans will be interested in her trade; their capital, instead of being sent to England, will go to France, *who will thus enjoy all the advantages of the colony, without incurring the expense requisite to support it*, and the money which America, by her industry, has drawn from Spain will be restored to France, which England, not enjoying the same advantages and *paying higher duties*, could not furnish them at the same price." This passage of the memorial of the minister from the United States is sufficiently clear, and we shall see that he, furthermore, takes care to corroborate its evident intention. Let us continue to follow the course of his argument. "The possession of Louisiana," does he say, "is very important for France, if she draws from it the only advantage which sound policy would seem to indicate. I speak of Louisiana only, not including Florida, because I do not consider it as forming part of the territory ceded, as she may, by means of the cession, have a free trade on the Mississippi, if she knows how to avail herself of the circumstance by an understanding with the United States. She will find a market for a great variety of goods when she shall have accustomed the inhabitants of the western country to prefer them to English goods, which she can only accomplish by giving them at a lower price, and this she can obtain only by giving American merchants an interest in selling them, in employing there their capital, and by inducing the American Government to give them the preference. All this can only be accomplished by the cession of New Orleans to the United States, reserving the right of entry at all times free from all other duties than those paid by American vessels, together with the free navigation of the Mississippi. This will give her vessels *the advantage over those of all other nations*, and will not only retain but increase the capital of the city of New Orleans, and hence provisions for the islands will be purchased there at a lower rate, and French manufactures will be more easily introduced into the western country, which the United States will have no interest in preventing, every cause of rivalship between the two nations being completely removed. Thus will France command respect without inspiring fear to the two nations whose friendship is most important to her commerce and to the preservation of her colonies; and all these advantages will be secured without incurring the expense of establishments which ruin the public treasure and divert its capital from its true object." What! Mr. Livingston, in order to induce France to cede the territory of Louisiana offers her *more!* From benevolent motives, established in the very treaty itself, she subsequently consents to accept or to reserve *less*, and even this shall be contested! The article which secures this to her shall be said to have no meaning, and be supposed to have expressed a mere impossibility! I will here dwell upon an idea tending to explain how such doubts could have arisen. Mr. Livingston's memorial must have been lost sight of. I shall now proceed to discuss, as briefly as possible, the error which you think you have discovered in the citation of my note of June 16, 1818. On this subject I have already observed, in my letter of the 30th March last, that even if such an error had been committed, the strength of my argument would not thereby have been impaired. But let us examine if, in fact, there be any such mistake. There are but eight treaties or contracts between France and the United States. *Four of these* are of such a nature as not to admit of the clause in question; in *two others* it is *formally* expressed; in another it is mentioned in equivalent terms; the last, which is the *Louisiana* treaty, is alone *silent* in that respect, and this silence furnishes of itself an irresistible argument. I was therefore right in saying that all the treaties which could admit of that clause mention *expressly* the condition of reciprocity. It is of no consequence that one of them should not positively use the words *freely, if freely granted, or upon granting the same condition, if conditionally granted.* These words are a mere accessory, irrelevant to the question, in the examination of which you have alleged my quotation to be erroneous. This question I shall now establish in its simplest form, and shall give it some extension so as better to explain my opinion. I say that in all the treaties of the United States, not only with France but with the other European nations, when mention is made therein of being treated upon the footing of the most favored nations, this condition of reciprocity is expressed, stipulating that the contracting parties shall enjoy the same privileges and advantages each in the ports of the other. One instrument alone is drawn in very different terms; it states, *in future and forever after, the French nation shall be treated upon the footing of the most favored nations in the ports of the territory ceded by her.* The clause stops here. What are we to conclude?' that, in fact, there was nothing *omitted, nothing implied* by the negotiators, (sous entendu;) reciprocity was not due, and therefore no mention is made of it. It was not due, because the convention of 1803 had no analogy with mere commercial treaties or regulations; it was a sale, a bargain. The seventh and eighth articles are reservations of rights of property made by the vendor; *a mere condition of the purchase*, (Mr. Crowninshield;) *a part of the price of the territory*, (Mr. Randolph;) finally, because the territory of Louisiana *is a property ceded with a particular reservation*, (Mr. Rodney.) Were it even a commercial treaty, still, since the condition of reciprocity is not mentioned, France would have a right to maintain that she owes it not, and she could allege in her favor a very respectable opinion in the following words of Mr. Madison, (speech on the British treaty:) " The fifteenth article has another extraordinary feature, which, I should imagine, must strike every observer. In other treaties which profess to put the parties on the footing of the most favored nations it is stipulated that, where new favors are granted to a particular nation in return for favors received, the party claiming the new favor shall pay the price of it. This is just and proper where the footing of the most favored nations is established at all. But this article gives to Great Britain the full benefit of all privileges that may be granted to any other nation, without requiring from her the same or equivalent privileges with those granted by such nation; hence it would happen that, if Spain, Portugal, or France should open their colonial ports to the United States, in consideration of certain privileges in our trade, the same privileges would result *gratis* and *ipso facto* to Great Britain."

But we have not even to examine this question; that which occupies our attention is quite different, since it relates to a *sale*, a *bargain;* not a *favor, but a bargain.*

I think, sir, I have sufficiently proved—

1st. That there are two modes of being treated upon the footing of the most favored nations, either *gratuitously* or *conditionally.*

2dly. That the ships of four nations enjoy at this time, in the United States, and, of course, in the ports of Louisiana, the rights and privileges of the most favored nations.

3dly. That France, according to the terms of the eighth article of the Louisiana treaty, has a right to be put in possession of the same privileges in these said ports, being part of those of the United States.

4thly. That she owes and can owe no reciprocity, not only because no such condition is stipulated in the contract, but also because the privilege in question is a right of property reserved, or, if you prefer it so, is one of the equivalents of the bargain.

5thly. That the intention of the negotiators cannot be doubtful, since the article, which in itself requires no explanation, has, as a corollary, an authentic document which would irresistibly prove, by the very circumstances of the case, what was meant and intended, if the treaty itself had not expressed it in the most explicit terms.

I therefore hope, sir, that, after the preceding explanation, the President will be pleased to order that, in future and forever, (unless in case of subsequent arrangements to the contrary between France and the United States,) the eighth article of the Louisiana treaty receive its full and entire execution, and that, by consequence, French vessels be immediately made to enjoy, in the ports of the ceded territory, all the rights, advantages, and privileges granted to Great Britain, and to other nations, by virtue of treaties, or in any other manner.

I have the honor to be, sir, your most humble and obedient servant,

　　　　　　　　　　　　　　　G. HYDE de NEUVILLE.

NOTE.—Is it likely that France can have intended to cede, for the mere consideration of the sum of fifteen millions of dollars, property which, even before the cession, was considered as having an incalculable value, which a distinguished member of Congress valued (Deb. October 25, 1803,) at more than fifty millions, and which, in a well written article of the National Intelligencer, of October 10, 1803, was esteemed to be worth six hundred millions of dollars? And it must not be said that France was ignorant of its value, since, before the cession, the American public prints took continual pains to inform her of it. I shall here cite one of these articles, signed Columbus, (National Intelligencer, September 2, 1803.) The writer complains that several of the public prints strive to take from the merit of Mr. Livingston's memorial; he expresses a fear that they should persuade France that it is contrary to her interests to cede Louisiana to this Republic. He cites the following passage of a paper published in Fredericktown, which would go to prove to the French minister in Washington that the first consul would commit an act of great folly in consenting to abandon so vast a territory.

"The democrats cannot think the first consul, Bonaparte, such a simpleton as to part with that country for any compensation we can make him." Thus, adds Columbus, it is represented that nothing in our command is enough for those objects, (Louisiana and New Orleans.)

Most certainly Bonaparte will never be regarded as a simpleton; nor will it be alleged that he had such affection for the inhabitants of these United States as to have had, in the cession of Louisiana, no other object but that of rendering them a service. Surely he must, at the same time, have thought of his own country, and have intended, by reserving certain rights and privileges in favor of France, to secure, at least, a sort of compensation for the great sacrifice to which he was subjecting her.

In whatever light this subject is viewed, the cession of Louisiana must certainly be considered as one of the most inconsiderate and fatal measures of the Usurper; but still it is not allowable to suppose that he could on this occasion have entirely lost sight of the interests of France, and have consented to give up, for the mere consideration of fifteen millions of dollars, an immense territory, which will be a never-failing source of riches and prosperity to these United States, and which, to *France*, would have been worth all the colonies which she now possesses or has possessed in the two hemispheres.

The following opinion is such authority that I cannot better conclude than with citing it:

"I consider the object as of the highest advantage to us; and the gentleman from Kentucky himself, who has displayed with so much eloquence the immense importance to this Union of the possession of the ceded country, cannot carry his ideas further on that subject than I do."—(Senate debates, November 3, 1803.)

Mr. Adams to Baron Hyde de Neuville.

DEPARTMENT OF STATE, *Washington, June* 15, 1821.

SIR: In replying to the two letters which I have had the honor of receiving from you, the one bearing date the 29th of March last, and the other the 15th of May, I find it necessary to re-state, in its simplest terms, the question in discussion between us.

The seventh and eighth articles of the treaty by which Louisiana was ceded to the United States contain two distinct but obviously connected stipulations; that of the seventh article, by which certain special privileges in the ports of the ceded territory are secured, for the term of twelve years, to the vessels of France and Spain, *to the exclusion of the vessels of all other nations;* and that of the eighth article, that after the expiration of this special privilege, thus limited to the ports of the ceded territory, French vessels should be forever, in the ports of the ceded territory, on the footing of the most *favored nation in the same ports.*

Upon the terms of this article, by your note of the 15th of December, 1817, you demanded, in the name and by order of your Government, and in fulfilment of this article, that all the advantages yielded *for ample equivalent* to British vessels, *in all the ports of this Union*, should be yielded, *without any equivalent*, to French vessels in the ports of Louisiana.

The answer which immediately presented itself, on the first disclosure of this demand, was, that the claim was, in two important particulars, broader than the stipulation upon which it was raised; first, inasmuch as, upon the mere right to *equal favor*, it required gratuitously that which was conceded to another for a just equivalent; and, secondly, inasmuch as, upon a stipulation limited in all its parts to *the ports of Louisiana*, it required concessions yielded to others *in all the ports of the Union.*

As the claim was thus without support from the *letter* of the article, it was also apparently contradictory to its spirit and motives, as well as to the whole purpose of the treaty, and expressly incompatible with other articles of the treaty and with the Constitution of the United States. Such was the substance of the answer which, on the 23d of December, 1817, I had the honor of addressing to you in reference to this claim.

By your note of June 16, 1818, you replied with the allegation that France was entitled by this article to enjoy, *unconditionally*, in the ports of Louisiana, any advantage granted *upon* conditions to others in all the ports of the Union, because France was to be considered as having already given the equivalent by the cession of the territory; and, especially, because you alleged that in *all* the other treaties between France and the United States it was expressly said that the two contracting parties should enjoy, reciprocally, any favor granted to others *gratuitously*, if the concession to others should be gratuitous, or by granting the same compensation if the concession should be conditional; and as no such distinction between *conditional* and gratuitous favor was formally expressed in the eighth article of the Louisiana cession treaty, you insisted with great earnestness that this variation in the phraseology of the article from that which had been universally used in all the preceding treaties between the parties, led, irresistibly, to the conclusion that no such distinction was intended; but that the United States were bound forever to give to the vessels of France, in Louisiana, every advantage which, to the end of time, they might *sell for a price* to the vessels of other nations throughout the Union.

The great stress with which your note of June 16, 1818, dwelt upon this supposed departure from the universal language of the prior treaties, made it necessary to observe that its only basis was an error in point of fact; that no such concurrence in the form of language used in relation to the same principle existed in the prior treaties; that the alternative reciprocity of *conditional* or *gratuitous* favor, far from being expressed in all the treaties between the parties, had in terms been expressed only in one, and that the first treaty ever made between them; and particularly that a treaty concluded with the same Government, as the Louisiana cession, and only three years before, contained such an article, stipulating, mutually, the advantages *of the most favored nation*, without any notice whatsoever of distinction between favors *gratuitous* and favors *conditional;* and that this variation in the prior treaties, of stipulations obviously intending the same thing, not only swept away the argument which you had drawn from the supposed universal coincidence of the former treaties, but made it recoil upon itself, and proved that gratuitous or the conditional nature of *equal favor* was inherent in the terms themselves, and had only been expressly developed in the treaty of the 6th February, 1778, from the abundant caution of contracting parties new to each other, and, above all, anxious to leave no possible question of their meaning thereafter to arise.

Your reply of the 30th of March last to my note of the preceding day insists that "all your citations in your preceding letters had been perfectly exact; that not only *all* the treaties between France and this

Republic, (meaning the conventions which could be judged susceptible of the clause in question,) but also all, or nearly all, the treaties or conventions between the United States and European Governments, say, in terms formal or equivalent what you had understood, what you had read, what you had been bound to say."

Permit me to observe that the simple question between us was, whether *all* the treaties between the United States and France, excepting only the Louisiana treaty, in stipulating the advantages *of the most* favored nation, had *expressly* added that the favor sho ld be free, if freely granted to others, and upon the same condition, if conditionally granted. Your letter of the 16th of June, 1818, in the most unqualified terms asserted that they had; and from this position, connected with the omission of the same explanatory clause in the stipulation of the Louisiana treaty, you had deduced and most earnestly pressed an argument that this supposed solitary change in the reduction necessarily imported a different construction, and entitled France to enjoy in the ports of Louisiana, *unconditionally*, every favor granted to others, whether with condition or without.

The demand upon a stipulation of *equal favor* to enjoy, without equivalent or condition, that which was conceded to others only for an equivalent or upon condition, was in itself so ext aordinary that it assuredly required something stronger than inferences and implications and equivalent terms for its support. The main argument upon which Mr. de Neuville's letter of the 16th of June, 1818, had relied for this unexampled claim was the omission in the Louisiana cession treaty of the *express* explanatory words alleged to be *in all the others*. But the fact being otherwise, the conclusion was more clearly the reverse.

It may now be added, that the only possible sense in which a stipulation for equal favor *can* be carried into effect is by granting it freely or for the equivalent, according as it is granted to others. For if the same advantage should be granted to *France, without return*, which is conceded to others only for the return, who does not see that France, instead of being upon equal footing with the most favored nation, would herself be upon a footing *more* favored than any other ?

In the latter part of your letter of the 30th of March, without abandoning this demand of *exclusive* favor, built upon a simple engagement of *equal* favor, you seem to admit that the diminution of duties conceded to the vessels of several nations in the ports of this Union is not a favor, but a bargain; and you alleged that, even upon this principle, French vessels should be exempted from the additional tonnage duty of the act of the 15th of May, 1820, in the ports of Louisiana, because the vessels of Russia, Spain, Portugal, and other nations with whom the United States have no treaty, are not subject to it; and, repeating a remark which had been made by the chargé d'affaires of France in August last, you say this is not merely a favor refused, but a burden imposed.

The vessels of nations with whom the United States have no trea ie enjoy no favors *in the ports of* Louisiana. In the ports of Louisiana the vessels of all nations are tons the same footing as in those of all the other ports of the United States. There is no most favored nation in the ports of Louisiana, nor in any other port of the United States. During the twelve years while the vessels of France and Spain were admitted into the ports of Louisiana alone upon terms more favorable than into the ports of the United States, and from which the vessels of other nations were excluded, they w re the most favored nations *in the ports of Louisiana*; but the favors were confined both to the vessels of those nations and to the ports of Louisiana. They enjoyed this favor by virtue of the seventh article of the treaty; and the object and purport of the next article was to stipulate that when this special and limited period of favor should expire no such special and exclusive favor should be granted to any other nation *in the same ports*. Such is the engagement of the United States; and as such it has been, and will continue to be, fulfilled. No favor is now granted to any nation *in the ports of Louisiana*, and the eighth article of the treaty has no more application to the general commercial laws of the United States, operating alike in every part of the Union, than it has to the special bargains by which the vessels of some nations enjoy a reduction from the duties imposed by those general laws *on the condition* of equivalent advantages to the vessels of the United States in the countries to which they belong.

To the demand, therefore, that the vessels of France should pay no higher duties in the ports of Louisiana than the vessels of Russia, Spain, Denmark, or Portugal pay in *all the ports of the Union*, the answer is the same as that given to your demand in terms by you letter of D cember 15, 1817, that the vessels of France should pay in e ports of Louisiana no higher duties than those paid by British vessels *in all the ports of the Union*. The claim is broader than the stipulation upon which it is founded. This stipulation is, both by its letter and spirit, confined to *special favors in special p rts*. The claim is either to *general* favors applied to special ports, or to *unrequited* favors for conditional obligations. In every such case, and by either of the constructions for which you contend, the United States could not assent to your claim without favoring France in the ports of Louisiana *more* than any other nation. Instead of being upon the same footing of the most favored nation, she would herself be the most favored nation, and enjoy advantages conceded to no others. This is not the stipulation of the treaty.

In your letter of the 15th ultimo you remark that the exemption of the vessels of other nations from the extraordinary tonnage duties levied upon those of France, inasmuch as it is enjoyed in all the ports of the Union, is enjoyed, also, *in the ports of Louisiana* as a part of the Union; and being enjoyed there, France has, by the engagement of the , a right to claim the same exemption *in those ports*, although she is not entitled to claim it in the other ports of the Union. But it is this very generality, by virtue of which the vessels of other nations enjoy the exemption, which takes away from it all application of the eighth article of the treaty. Their exem tion is not a *favor in the ports of Louisiana*; even when they enjoy the benefit of it in those ports they enjoy no special favor there; and it is to such special favor only that the stipulation could give France an equal claim.

In your letter of the 15th ultimo it is observed that the question is "What must be understood by being treated upon the footing of the most favored nation?" But this is not the question, because it does not cite the whole stipulation; the omission of the words "in the ports above mentioned" changes the state of the question from its special to a general character. The stipulation is, that "the ships of France shall be treated on the footing of *the most favored nations in the ports above mentioned*." The qualifying and special terms "in the ports above mentioned" apply both to the most favored nations and to the treatment of the ships of France; nor can France claim *any* favor in the ports of Louisiana by this stipulation, without first showing that some other nation enjoys the same favor as a special favor exclusively in those ports. There is no such favored nation in the Ports of Louisiana. In the omission of those words it is believed that their great importance to the question in discussion had escaped attention. Their restoration to the statement of the question will immediately show their leading to a different conclusion.

You observe, indeed, in another part of your letter, that you claim this favor in favor of France only *in the ports of Louisiana;* and you express your apprehension that I had misunderstood the purport of the demands in your preceding letters, because I had specially underscored the terms *in all the ports of the Union* when referring to the duties collected upon the vessels of other nations. I am well aware that you have demanded the special favor for France only in the ports of Louisiana; but you demand the special favor in the special ports, not as the stipulation of the article would warrant if the case existed, because other nations enjoy the same special favor in the special ports, but because, by general laws applicable to the vessels of those foreign nations *in all the ports of the Union,* they pay in the ports of Louisiana less for tonnage duty than the vessels of France.

You observe that it would have been superfluous and even idle to make *special* mention of the ports of Louisiana in treaties granting certain rights, favors, or privileges, in all the ports of the Union, because in the ports of the Union are included those of Louisiana; that to give the whole is to give a part; as in such cases the generality necessarily includes the specialty. This observation, as applicable to treaties between the United States and other nations, is correct; but the inference to be drawn from the principle asserted is conclusive against the claim of France in the present case. For it is not to any such concession of a general nature, and which is enjoyed by others in the ports of Louisiana only because they are ports of the Union, that the stipulation of the eighth article of the Louisiana cession treaty applies. That stipulation, both in letter and spirit, is, in all its parts, special and not general. The whole transaction refers specially to Louisiana as distinct from and not as a part of the Union. The seventh article stipulates for special favors in its ports for a term of years, *to the exclusion of other nations;* and the eighth provides against the concession of similar special favors after the expiration of twelve years to other nations, to the exclusion of those of France.

It is not, therefore, sufficient for France to say that the vessels of four other nations pay only one dollar a ton in the ports of Louisiana, while those of France are required to pay eighteen. For those vessels pay that dollar only, not because they are more *favored* than other nations *in those ports,* but because they pay the same in all the ports of the Union; because those nations have passed no laws excluding the vessels of the United States from carrying to their ports the productions of their own soil by the excessive aggravations of surcharges.

There is no difference of opinion between us with regard to the principles which ought to apply in the construction of compacts, promises, and treaties. Admitting the correctness of all your citations from Vattel, I would specially invite your attention to that which forbids all constructive interpretation of that which speaks for itself. But I ask that, in stating the question upon the stipulation, none of its essential words should be omitted; that it should not be stated as a general question of "what is meant by being treated on the footing of the most favored nation," but as a special question of what is meant by being treated as *the most favored nation in the ports of Louisiana;* for when upon a stipulation in these words you raise a claim to be treated in Louisiana on the footing of *the most favored nation in the ports of the United States,* and when, to support this claim to special favor in special places, resort is had to the argument that the whole includes all its parts, and that the generality embraces the specialty, what is this but interpreting that which has no need of interpretation? To us it appears not only so, but an interpretation as contrary to the manifest intention of the article, inferrible from its connexion with the article immediately preceding it, as to its letter, which is special in all its parts.

Of the numerous extracts which you have taken the trouble of introducing in your letter of the 15th ultimo from the speeches of individual members of Congress, reported in the National Intelligencer, as having been delivered at the debates on the passage of the laws for carrying the Louisiana treaties into execution, I regret not to have been able to discover *one* which has any bearing whatever upon the question between us, which is of the true import of the eighth article of the treaty; they all have reference to the seventh article—to the exclusive privileges which made France and Spain, for a limited term of twelve years, *the most favored nations in the ports above mentioned;* and the objection was strongly urged that this stipulation was incompatible with the provision in the Constitution which forbids any preference to be given, by any regulation of commerce or revenue, to the ports of one State over those of another. To this objection the speeches from which you have cited passages were the answers; and they all distinctly assume the principle that the prohibitive injunction of the Constitution was not incompatible with the stipulation of the treaty, because Louisiana was acquired, not as a State but as a Territory; so that while she continued in the territorial or colonial condition, regulations of commerce different from those prescribed for the *States* of the Union might be established in her ports without contravening the Constitution; and there was not in any one of those speeches the intimation of a doubt but that when Louisiana should be admitted as a *State* into the Union the regulations in her ports must be the same as in the ports of all her sister States. But the third article of the treaty stipulated that "the inhabitants of the ceded territory should be incorporated in the Union of the United States, and admitted *as soon as possible,* according to the principles of the Federal Constitution, to the enjoyment of all the rights, advantages, and immunities, of citizens of the United States;" and, as this article could be carried into execution only by their admission into the Union as a State or States, so by their admission in that capacity their ports became subject to that provision of the Constitution which interdicts all preference to the ports of one State over those of another. If the admission of a part of those inhabitants did, in fact, by a short time, precede the termination of the period subject to the exclusive privileges of French and Spanish vessels in their ports, although the sentiment cited by the Baron de Neuville be perfectly correct that the Constitution ought not to be violated for a single day, as no question appears to have arisen at the time of the admission of the State, upon the application of this article, and as the privilege of the French and Spanish vessels was never, in fact, denied them during the term for which they were entitled by the article to claim it, whatever transient and inadvertent departure in favor of the inhabitants of Louisiana from the principle of the Constitution may have occurred is, as the Baron de Neuville observes, a question of internal administration in this Government, from which France has received no wrong, and of which, therefore, she can have no motive to complain.

For the term of twelve years, therefore, from the time specified in the treaty, France and Spain enjoyed, by virtue of the seventh article, special *favors and privileges in the ports of Louisiana.* But it was not certain at the time when the treaty was concluded that the inhabitants could, within twelve, or twenty, or even fifty years, according to the principles of the Federal Constitution, be entitled to claim admission into the Union as a *State.* After the expiration of twelve years, there might be an indefinite interval of time, during which the special favors conceded to France and Spain in the seventh article might be transferred to other nations; and the eighth article was obviously intended to avert that contingency by stipulating that, after the twelve years of special favor in the ports of Louisiana, the vessels of France should be on the footing of *the most favored nations in the ports aforementioned*—importing, by the proper meaning of the terms, and without any ambiguous inferences of specialties from generalities, or, as the Baron de Neuville's reasoning would require, of generalities from specialties, that no such special favor in the ports of Louisiana should, after the twelve years, ever be conceded to any other nation, to the exclusion of France. This is the plain and obvious meaning of the article—the only meaning deducible from its letter—the only meaning traceable to the intention of the parties, by its immediate connexion with the special and exclusive privilege of the article immediately preceding it, and of which it is the natural complement.

If the opinions cited by the Baron de Neuville from the speeches of individual members of Congress, *after* the conclusion of the treaty, have, as is now maintained, no bearing whatever upon the meaning of the article now in discussion, much less can it be expected that the proposals in a memoir addressed by Mr. Livingston to the French Government, nine months *before* the negotiation of the treaty, and intended to show that it was not the interest of France to take possession of Louisiana at all, should have any referen to a treaty founded upon totally different principles.

The object of this memoir was to convince the French Government that it was for the interest of France, instead of taking *possession* of Louisiana, to put *the island of New Orleans* into the hands of the United States, reserving to herself the right of a free port there, paying no higher duties than American vessels, and securing also to France the navigation of the Mississippi. The memoir was written at a time when the project of establishing a military colony at New Orleans was contemplated by France; but even the treaty by which Louisiana was ceded to France by Spain had not then been concluded. There is an error in the citation from this memoir in the letter to Baron de Neuville, (page 32,) of the 15th ultimo, where it is quoted as the saying, that "the *possession* of Louisiana was very important to F ," while in the memoir itself the expressions are that "the *cession* of Louisiana is very important to France."

The substitution of the term *possession* for that of *cession* is only noticed because it might give an erroneous idea of the whole scope of the memoir, which was to prove that the *possession* of Louisiana by France would be in a very high degree detrimental to the interest of France, but that she might render the cession useful to her by putting *New Orleans* in the possession of the United States, securing to herself the privilege in it of a free port, together with the navigation of the Mississippi. The memoir did not even that Louisiana should be *ceded* to the United States, but merely that New Orleans should be put into their *possession*, to be held by them, not as an independent and sovereign State of the Union, but on the same colonial condition as it was then held by Spain, and as it would have been held by France had she taken and retained possession of the province. Under such a project, embracing no purpose of a change in the political condition of the inhabitants, the parties were competent to stipulate condition like these without violating the Constitution of the United States, even thoug without limitations of time. But the compact actually made was of a totally different character. By the compact actually made, not only the island of New Orleans but the whole province of Lousiana was *ceded* in full sovereignty to the United States for a valuable consideration in money, an equivalent far more valuable to France than any benefit she would ever have derived from the possession of the province forever. The nature of that compact, however, made it necessary to provide for the future condition of the inhabitants of the country. Justice to them required that when thus ceded in full sovereignty to the United States they should in due time be released from all the shackles of colonial bondage, and assume their station as a free and equal portion of the Republic to which they were annexed. With this wise and just condition, France could no longer claim to stipulate for the navigation of the Mississippi; she could no longer ask, without limitation, the privilege for her ships of exclusive favors in the ceded ports. Both these conditions, perfectly compatible with a treaty upon the basis which had been proposed by the memoir of Mr. Livingston, in August, 1802, became quite inadmissible in a treaty founded on the basis finally adopted. The comparison, therefore, of the *proposals* in the memoir of Mr. Livingston, cited in the letter of the Baron de Neuville, with the actual stipulations in the 3d, 7th, and 8th articles of the treaty, affords itself a very conclusive argument against the present claim of France. The proposals are, that France should merely give *possession* to the United States of New Orleans, reserving to her own ships, without li tation of time, the privileges of paying there no higher duties than American vessels, and the navigation of the Mississippi. But not a word was said in them of a stipulation that the vessels of France should be upon the footing of the most favored nations in the same ports. The treaty is a cession in full and entire sovereignty of the whole province, but with n right reserved of navigating the Mississippi, and with the right of admission for French and Spanish vessels, upon the same footing as American vessels, limited to twelve years. Why these great and remarkable variations from the offers of the memorial? Why, but because they necessarily flowed from the principle of a cession in full sovereignty, and because all the rights and privileges of the Constitution of the United States were, by a new stipulation, secured to the inhabitants of the province! The cause and the effect are both palpable, from every point of departure in the actual treaty from the proposals of the memoir. The limitation in the article, of that which the proposal offered unbounded, is the proof of its own necessity; and the substitute in the 8th article, of equal favor *with the most favored in those ports*, after the expiration of the limitation, instead of the perpetuity of the special privilege, is illustrated both in its meaning and extent by the exposition in the memorial of which it supplied the place.

Of the numerous citations in the letter of the Baron de Neuville of the opinions of individual members of Congress, and even of anonymous publications in the American newspapers, one purpose appears to be to dwell with great earnestness on the supposed advantages of the Louisiana cession to the United States. Without referring to the estimates of nameless authorities, it is not necessary to inquire whether those of the members referred to were exaggerated or otherwise. It is however to be observed, first, that all those estimates were formed under impressions that the extent of the Louisiana cession was vastly more comprehensive than the subsequent declarations and efforts of the French Government would have made it; and secondly, that probably all those persons to whose anticipations the Baron de Neuville appeals with so much confidence, agreed as they were in the importance and value of Louisiana to the United States, would also have agreed in the opinion so forcibly urged in the memoir of Mr. Livingston, that the possession of the same country would have been worse than useless, highly detrimental, and pernicious to France. Of this opinion one at least of the individuals whose sentiments the B de Neuville has been pleased to quote with very flattering deference then was and still is, H had no doubt that in the possession of France Louisiana would have continued to be, as it always had been, a burden and not a benefit; and at the time when the cession was made the only practical question to France was, whether Louisiana should pass into the hands of a friend for ample compensation, or into the grasp of an enemy for no compensation at all. Louisiana then was of great value to the United States, and of much less than no value to France; and the cession of it by France to the United States was one of those treaties which are the best and most useful of transactions between nations, a compact highly advantageous to both the contracting parties.

But whether advantageous or otherwise, and whether to both or to neither of the parties, has no more bearing upon the present question between the two Governments than the speculative forecast of individual members of Congress, or the lucubrations of newspaper party writers. The question is upon the true meaning of the eighth article of the treaty; that meaning is expressed in the words of the article; it is confirmed to demonstration by its immediate connexion with the preceding article; it is illustrated by its variation from the proposals in Mr. Livingston's memoir, cited by the Baron de Neuville himself; nor has it been possible for the Baron, at any stage of the discussion, to state the present claim of France in any shape, without essentially departing both from the words and from the spirit of the article upon which it would rely. When first advanced, he expressly demanded, upon a promise of *equal favor in the ports of Louisiana with the most favored in the ports of Louisiana,* a performance of equal favor in Louisiana with the most favored in *all the ports of the Union.* Upon a promise of equal favor, he demanded a grant, *without* equivalent, of that which had been conceded to others for an equivalent. In his letters of the 15th of May he states the question to be, *what is understood by being treated on the footing of the most favored nation?* omitting the words "in the ports above mentioned," which words are part of the stipulation in the article, but the very insertion of which, in the statement of the question, would have been fatal to the present claim.

After the fullest consideration of the question in controversy, and the most deliberate examination of the arguments adduced by the Baron de Neuville in his several letters on this subject, I am instructed to say that this Government adheres to the opinion that the eighth article of the Louisiana treaty does in no respect authorize the present claim of France, inasmuch as, since the expiration of the twelve years specified in the seventh article, there has been no nation *more favored than another in the ports of Louisiana.*

I avail myself with pleasure of this occasion of renewing to you the assurance of my distinguished consideration.

JOHN QUINCY ADAMS.

No. 19.

Baron de Neuville to the Secretary of State.

[Translation.]

WASHINGTON, *June* 30, 1821.

SIR: I have received the letter which you have done me the honor to write to me, dated the 15th of this month.

In my turn I shall endeavor to re-establish the question which occupies our attention; and by removing some errors which it behooves me to rectify, I shall answer the new arguments which you have opposed to those advanced by me in the commencement of the discussion; from these I cannot depart, since nothing appears to me to weaken their force.

You do me the honor to state that "the eighth article stipulates that French ships shall be *forever in the ports of the ceded territory* upon the footing of the most favored nation *in the same ports.*"

Further, you add, "the qualifying and special terms in the ports above mentioned apply both to the most favored nation and to the treatment of the most favored nations."

Finally, you say, sir, that I have founded on the 8th article, which you cite, my remonstrance of the 15th of December, 1817, tending "to obtain for French vessels *in the ports of Louisiana* the advantages granted to the English nation in *all the ports of the Union.*"

I founded my demand upon the 8th article, *such as it is in the treaty of cession.*

I will here observe that, in my opinion, even though the article were expressed as you present it, my cause would still be no less founded; but it is prudent to make no concessions to so formidable an adversary. I shall, therefore, attack your principal argument in its basis, and shall endeavor to prove it is erroneous, even in the point whereby you seek to establish that there is no question but of *special favors* to be granted—specially and *exclusively* in the ports of the territory ceded by France. Allow me, sir, in the first place, to make the following observation: My claim is entirely grounded upon the article such as it is in the treaty, as it should be understood *in the common usage of language;* and, in fact, it is always by modifying it, or, to speak with more propriety, by making it anew, that an attempt is made to oppose my arguments.

This eighth article, according to your note of the 29th of March, means *evidently* that, after the expiration of the twelve years, *no such peculiar privileges should be granted in the same ports to the vessels of any other nation to the exclusion of those of France.*

But the article appears to me *evidently* to stipulate quite the reverse. It has no relation to the *special right* which France reserved by the seventh article for Spain and for herself for the space of twelve years, but all the rights, privileges, immunities, favors, which, after the twelve years, might be granted to other nations under any title whatever.

France is to be treated, *in future and forever, upon the footing of the most favored nation.* This is the whole question. If what you understand to be its import had really been meant, would it not have been more natural to have entirely suppressed the eighth article, and, after the following clause of the seventh, ("*during the space of time above mentioned no other nation shall be entitled to the same privileges in the ports of the ceded territory,*") to have added, "after the expiration of the twelve years aforesaid, if the same privileges are granted to any other nation in the same ports, they shall become common to France also."

But even these expressions, I perceive it, sir, would not come perfectly up to your idea, nor effectually overrule my opinion.

Why, then, was not the article worded in the following terms—they would naturally have occurred to the negotiators if they had thought at that time of what you now conjecture:

"In future and forever France shall enjoy gratuitously, in the ports of the territory ceded by her, all the rights or privileges which may be granted *gratuitously* and specially in the said ports to any other nation." The clause would then have been clear and precise, and I should, in such case have perfectly conceived what you do me the honor to state in your note of the 23d December, 1817: "If British vessels enjoyed in the ports of Louisiana any *gratuitous favor*, undoubtedly French vessels would, by the terms of the article, be entitled to the same."

But, to be candid, how can it be asserted *now* that France is to enjoy only such favors as may be granted *gratuitously* to other nations, when we read in the 8th article, "In future and forever, after the expiration of the twelve years, the ships of France shall be treated upon the footing of the most favored nations in the ports above mentioned?" I, therefore, had reason to advance that it was essentially necessary first to define correctly what must be understood by the terms *most favored nations*. It makes but little difference whether we say the *most favored nations in the ports of Louisiana*, or only the most *favored nation*, since we have only to determine this first point of the difficulty.

Why should France enjoy in the said ports only such favors as should be conceded *gratuitously*, and not such as might be granted conditionally? The 8th article says no such thing; why, therefore—by what law, by what rule, can it be positively established, that "if British vessels enjoyed in the ports of Louisiana any gratuitous favor, undoubtedly French vessels would, by the terms of the article, be entitled to the same?" Is there, then, but one mode of becoming, in any country whatever, the most favored nation? Or, if the conventional law of nations admits, particularly in the United States, that this treatment may be obtained, not only *gratuitously* but *conditionally;* if the Federal Government has been ever careful to have this clause inserted in its different treaties; if I find it in the conventions of 1778, 1783, 1785; if I find it again in the treaty with Prussia, negotiated by Mr. Adams himself, in 1799, how can the Secretary of State say now that "if British vessels enjoyed in the ports of Louisiana *any gratuitous favor*, undoubtedly French vessels would, by the terms of the treaty, be entitled to the same?"

France, I repeat it, has a right to enjoy, in the ports of Louisiana, the treatment of *the most favored nation*, whether this nation be favored *gratuitously* or *conditionally;* she has a right to enjoy it, inasmuch as the 8th article stipulates expressly that "*in future and forever French ships shall be treated upon the footing of the most favored nation in the ports of the territory ceded by France.*" To pretend that she is to obtain this treatment in case only that it shall be conceded *gratuitously* to another nation, is subjecting the 8th article to an arbitrary interpretation; it is going in the face of a doctrine generally received; it is interpreting what requires no interpretation; it amounts, in fine, to the creation of a new conventional law of nations peculiar to the ports of Louisiana.

I now pass, sir, to the entirely new interpretation which you give in your letter of the 15th of this month to this same article. You make it express that, after the expiration of this special privilege, that, if the seventh article thus limited to the ports of the ceded territory, French vessels should be forever, *in the ports of the ceded territory*, on the footing of the most favored nation in the same ports.

If the question were only to new-mould the article, nothing could be more easy, as I have already made it appear, than to give it the sense which is now attempted to be ascribed to it; but we must adhere to its letter if we mean ever to come to an understanding.

It is certain that French vessels are to be treated upon the footing of the most favored nation; but where are they to be so treated? I answer, in the ports of the territory ceded by France; and this *ipso facto*, *gratis*, whatever be the title under which *the most favored nations* may enjoy the same treatment, has it been meant by the article to say, *the nation most favored in the said ports, exclusively in the said ports?* Finally, are we to read, as you now for the first time propose, *the most favored nation in the ports of the ceded territory?* Doubtless, no; the last member of the period has no reference to *the most favored nation;* it can have no relation except to *the treatment of French vessels:* "*In future and forever French vessels shall be treated upon the footing of the most favored nation.*" Here the sense is complete, with regard to the words *most favored nation*. All instruments found in public law clearly show what is meant by *the most favored nation*. There can, therefore, be no misconception in this respect. But this is not the case with the other member of the sentence. It is not sufficient to stipulate that French vessels shall, *in future and forever, be treated upon the footing of the most favored nation;* it is necessary, moreover, to specify *where* they shall be so treated; for, otherwise, the sense would be incomplete, and the article would have no meaning at all.

I shall avoid all grammatical discussion; but, if the sense of the article did not evidently bear me out, and if I were under the necessity of showing, by its construction, that it cannot have the meaning which you attribute to it, I could cite in favor of my assertion several phrases of your last note, and would prove, by their correctness, that the 8th article, such as it has been drawn and worded in the treaty, cannot admit the argument made by you in the concluding words of the sentence.

It concerns not France to examine if any nation enjoys, in the ports of the territory ceded by her, any right or privilege *as a special favor exclusively in those ports;* she has only to inquire whether any nation is there treated upon the footing of the most favored nation; or, in other words, if the treatment she receives is more favorable than that of French vessels in the said ports. It is matter of small importance to her to know whether such nation, being the most favored in Louisiana, is at the same time the most favored in Baltimore, New York, or Boston, or to know by what title such favor is granted in the ports of Louisiana. The fact alone, when ascertained, is of itself sufficient ground for claiming, as her due, the fulfilment of the 8th article of the Louisiana treaty, which stipulates *that, in future and forever, after the expiration of the twelve years, French vessels shall be treated upon the footing of the most favored nations in the ports above mentioned.*

Which, without gloss or comment, expressly means "in future and forever, after the expiration of the twelve years aforesaid, French vessels shall be treated, in the ports above mentioned, (that is, in the ports of Louisiana territory ceded by France,) upon the footing of the most favored nations."

It would be needless to add anything to this explanation, since the sense is complete. And it would be vain to seek, even in a forced wording (redaction) of the article, the *special favor exclusively* in those ports. The article neither expresses nor could express any such thing. It does not express it, as has been just proved. It could not express it.

This, sir, you would constantly prove by objecting that, "according to the Constitution, no preference shall be given, by any regulations of commerce or revenue, to the ports of one State over those of another." From this it clearly follows, in your own opinion, that no nation can receive *a special favor in a special port*, and exclusively in that port. What is not allowable at this time could not surely be done in 1803; and how can it be conceived that the only end of the American negotiators was to grant to France nothing but an illusive advantage, a privilege which she could *never be put into possession of* consistently with the Constitution? How could the French negotiators have claimed or accepted such a favor? How is it possible to reconcile the idea of a claim, which would amount to a mere *mockery*, with expressions so solemn as these, *in future and forever?* It cannot, I repeat it, be presumed that discreet and sensible men, making a treaty and a solemn conveyance, have intended to make a mere nullity. Let us examine what is likely to have taken place, what certainly did occur, during the negotiation, and we shall find that it is not at all necessary to torture the expressions of the article, in order to establish its true and positive meaning.

France was about to cede a vast territory in order to render an important service to a friendly nation; that territory was her property; she, therefore, had a right to settle the clauses and conditions of the contract. This was not the case of a favor granted, nor of a commercial regulation to be made by the United States; but, on the contrary, of a favor to be received, of a very important acquisition to be made by them. This bargain could not but be very advantageous in every respect to the United States; France was not to gain as much by it; this she knew, but although she willingly consented to make so great a sacrifice, was she entirely to neglect her own interests? The French Government knew at the same time that difficulties had arisen already between the two countries, and the convention of 1800 testified that the parties had not been able to come to an understanding on the treaties of 1778; the provisional convention of 1800 was to remain in force only five years more; it might possibly be renewed; the parties might come to an understanding on the various points in dispute; but, at the same time, it was also possible that other discussions should produce injurious measures, impolitic steps, and lead to a state of things equally injurious to both nations.

Experience seems to have proved how prudent it was in them to foresee, and how wise to act in prevention. Such being the state of things, how was it proper for France to act? I will answer, just as she did act, and this course was too obvious not to have been pursued. She was about to cede an immense colony, the inhabitants of which spoke the French language, and were likely not to lose French tastes, or to abandon French fashions; it particularly behooved her to secure *forever* such a market for her productions;* Mr. Livingston *told her so;* policy and common sense led her to do so. It was, therefore, that the French Government, while ceding Louisiana, in order to give the United States a remarkable proof of friendship, and to do away every cause of rivalship between the two nations, reserved, in the ports of the territory ceded, a right or privilege, the full and entire enjoyment of which should be independent of all general arrangements of commerce or navigation existing at that time, or which might subsequently be made by the two nations; that the privilege should secure to French merchants the advantage of being *forever* treated in Louisiana upon the footing of the most favored nation, whatever might be the footing upon which they should be received in the other ports of the United States; therefore did France demand that, after the expiration of the twelve years, during which both Spain and herself were to enjoy an equal privilege, she, France, should have *alone*, in future and *forever*, a right to be treated in the ports of Louisiana upon the footing of the most favored nation; not of the nation most favored exclusively in the said ports, (which, most assuredly, the 8th article does not say,) but of the most favored nation by whatever title, which the article may be said to stipulate expressly, since no condition is annexed to the favor. It cannot, at all events, be asserted that this is a forced interpretation, since it agrees so perfectly with the text and letter of the article, which is, moreover, abundantly explained by antecedent facts, by the circumstances of the case, and by subsequent events. It appeared to me, sir, that, in my letter of May 15, I had clearly replaced, upon its proper footing, the question relating to a supposed error in that of June 16, 1818. I thought it was proved that, whether there were or were not such an error in my letter, there would still remain the same force in the argument which, alone, it was material to attack; but since you have thought it proper, sir, again to return to this citation, which, I repeat it, even if erroneous, would not alter my argument in the least, let us again examine, with minute attention, if there really be any mistake on my part.

There are eight treaties, compacts, or conventions between France and the United States; four of these are of such a nature as not to admit the clause in question. The four others, being such as to allow its insertion, are: the treaty of amity and commerce of September, 1778; the consular convention of November 9, 1778; the commercial convention of ——, 1800; and, last, the Louisiana treaty of ——, 1803. In the treaty of 1778, stipulating that both countries shall enjoy, each in the ports of the other, the treatment of the most favored nation, the very same expression which I have used will be found in the second, third, and fourth articles. The convention of 9th of November refers to the second, third, and fourth articles of the said preceding treaty. Two, therefore, out of these four treaties state precisely what I have attributed to them, viz: that each nation shall enjoy, in the ports of the other, the treatment of the most favored nation *freely*, if freely granted, or conditionally, if the concession be *conditional*.

The third treaty (of 1800) stipulates expressly that the two nations shall, reciprocally, enjoy the treatment of the most favored nation, both as regards the rights and privileges of consular agents (article 10), and with respect to all privileges, immunities, liberties, and exemptions in trade, navigation, and commerce, and as to duties or imposts, of what nature soever they may be, or by what name soever called. An attentive examination of these two articles will surely suffice to produce an absolute conviction that, when the condition of reciprocity is thus expressed, nations are reciprocally to enjoy the treatment of the most favored nations, upon the condition generally understood. Thus the convention of 1800 does state, in *equivalent* terms, what is stipulated expressly in the treaties of 1778. I therefore concur in your opinion, sir, on one point. In truth, *who can doubt that this was implied in the article?* but I cannot go on to say, with you, *though not expressed*, since it does not appear to me possible to express anything more clearly in equivalent terms. Last remains the Louisiana treaty, and it is precisely because the treatment of the most favored nation is secured to France, *without reciprocity on her part*, that a discussion has arisen on these points. Where, then, have I committed any error? Perhaps it would have been more rigorously exact to have said the *treaties*, instead of *all the treaties*, since the reference was but to four treaties. But I would ask, sir, if that single word *all* was of such moment as to fix so repeatedly your attention? Sir, I repeat it, all the treaties between France and the United States, (those, it is understood, which could admit of such a clause,) all the treaties between the United States and European nations, wherein the treatment of the most favored nation is mentioned, stipulate that it shall be *reciprocal;* and, on examining the other compacts between nations, I find the same stipulation of reciprocal advantages in every case, except where, as in the Louisiana treaty, there is some charge imposed by one party on the other, or a privilege reserved.

*See the end of Mr. Livingston's memorial.

Whence is it that one treaty, that of 1803, should alone mention, *without reciprocity*, the treatment of the most favored nation? The reason becomes obvious, if we consider that it is the only treaty of the United States, *sui generis*, which does not relate to commercial arrangements. A commercial convention, grounded on expected contingencies, and stipulating mutual services and advantages, which do not require any advances, has no sort of analogy with a *contract of sale*, a *mere bargain*. In this last case the vendor conveys his property to the vendee, who binds himself for the stipulated consideration, consisting in the other clauses, charges, and conditions of the bargain, as well as in the funds to be paid at hand or by instalments. The right of the vendor, *his only right*, as you observed, sir, in 1803, *is to require that the conditions stipulated be punctually and faithfully performed*. This is all France desires. She has enjoyed, or might have enjoyed, during the space of twelve years, the right secured to her by the seventh article, and she now demands the fulfilment of the eighth article; which, as well as the seventh, is "a part of the price of the territory, a mere condition of the purchase." In your letter of the 15th you say: "Of the numerous extracts which you have taken the trouble of introducing in your letter of the 15th ultimo from the speeches of individual members of Congress, reported in the *National Intelligencer* as having been delivered at the debates on the passage of the laws for carrying the Louisiana treaties into execution, I regret not to have been able to discover *one* which has any bearing whatever upon the question between us, which is of the true import of the eighth article of the treaty; they all have reference to the seventh."

Suffer me, sir, to observe that, in thus taking the trouble to cite these very respectable opinions, my principal object was to answer the following passage of your letter of the 15th of March: "From the obvious purport of the seventh and eighth articles, it is apparent that *neither* of them was considered in any respect as forming a part of the equivalent for the cession of Louisiana." I was, therefore, right in not separating them when my object was to prove that neither of them was considered in any respect as forming a part of the equivalents for the cession of Louisiana; and although the question of constitutionality cannot, in any case, concern France, it was proper that I should establish its having been completely settled in 1803; and that I was not alone of opinion that Louisiana was property ceded *"with particular reservation, with a condition which the party ceding had a right to require, and to which the United States had a right to assent."* It makes but little difference what particular article of the treaty gave rise to the speeches cited, if they had a full bearing on the whole convention, and if every argument adduced on the seventh article is, *a fortiori*, applicable to the eighth. The seventh and eighth articles are both *a part of the equivalents for the cession*, or, rather, they are reservations of rights of property. France owed no reciprocity, and therefore it is that no reciprocity was stipulated on her part; it was no error or omission of the negotiators.

I read, sir, in your letter of the 15th, "in the latter part of your letter of the 30th of March, without abandoning this demand of *exclusive* favor, you *seem to admit* that the diminution of duties, conceded to the vessels of several nations" in the ports of this Union, is not a favor, but a bargain. Now, sir, I admit nothing of the kind in my letter of the 30th; far from *seeming to admit*, my expressions in the very phrase cited by you, sir, are *Je ne saurais admettre*, I cannot admit.

As to the question treated of in that letter, I shall confine myself to expressing again my surprise that France should be denied, in the ports of the territory ceded by her, even those advantages which are granted to nations having no treaty or convention with the United States. *Those nations you say, sir, have passed no laws excluding the vessels of the United States from carrying to their ports the productions of their own soil, by the excessive aggravation of surcharges.* To this I shall answer, that France has done no such thing; and that her discriminating duties are far from having *operated like magic in favor of the ship owners* of France, and have not even secured to her navigation a due share in the carrying trade. And after all, where is it stipulated that France shall be treated in Louisiana upon the footing of the most favored nation, (as by the 8th article,) only in case she shall make no regulations on navigation, injurious to the interest of the United States, or which might be supposed contrary thereto? Is not every nation free to regulate her own commerce and navigation as she sees fit? If her laws amount to prohibitions, if they appear unjust, if they are deemed injurious, it is, no doubt, allowable to adopt similar countervailing measures; but such measures, on her part, cannot make it justifiable to lose sight of the respect due to a sacred right of property, which is absolute in its nature, and is independent of all regulations of commerce and navigation. Observe, moreover, sir, that French vessels are not treated in the ports of Louisiana either *upon the footing of the most favored nations, nor upon that of nations having no treaty or convention with the United States,*† nor even *upon the footing of those in whose ports the vessels of the United States are not ordinarily permitted to go and trade.* This requires no comment. You have stated, sir, that all the speeches cited by me tend to prove that there was no inconsistency between the Federal Constitution and certain conditions of the treaty of cession, "because Louisiana was acquired, not as a State, but as a Territory; so that while she continued in the territorial or colonial condition regulations of commerce, different from those prescribed for the States of the Union, might be established in their ports without contravening the Constitution." I have already answered this argument by stating the fact that the 7th article, which, in your opinion, was judged to be compatible with the Constitution so long only as Louisiana should continue to be a colony, received its full execution *during three years after Louisiana had become a State.*

To this you reply, that in this there was, in truth, a violation of the Constitution, "from which France has received no wrong, and of which she can have no motive to complain." But if we have adopted in Europe, as a monarchical principle, that *the King can do no wrong*, we also expressly ^{a}dm^{l}t, with Mr. Griswold, that the legislature *cannot violate the Constitution even for a day*. I look upon it as certain and indubitable, that Congress had not the desire, as it had not the power, to violate, *intentionally*, the Constitution for a *day*, *nor even for an hour*. Besides, how can it be considered as a *transient*, *inadvertent departure* from the Constitution, that the unconstitutional execution of the 7th article should have place, not for a day, but for three years, while all the discussion which the speeches referred to had tended only to establish that in such case there would, in fact, be a violation of the Constitution? You add, sir, "there was not, in any one of those speeches, the intimation of a doubt but that, when Louisiana should be admitted as a *State* into the Union, the regulations in her ports must be the same as in the ports of all her sister States;" and in another part of your letter you again repeat, "that by the admission of

_____

*These extra charges were sufficient to drive from our ports the greatest proportion of the foreign tonnage. All foreign nations were affected by the system we had adopted. It seemed to operate like magic in favor of the ship owners of the United States.—(Dr. Seybert on the American discriminating duties.)

†American tonnage law, article 1.

Louisiana into the Union, her ports became subject to that provision of the Constitution which interdicts all preference to the ports of one State over those of another."

I think I have shown that this article of the Constitution is not, in any case, applicable to the express stipulations of a sale and conveyance of property, and that it did not belong to France to examine that question. I could, perhaps, prove also that the last two assertions are not, in every point, rigorously correct. You will find, sir, that in those very speeches it has been questioned whether *all* the ports of the United States were at that time subject to the same commercial regulations. "By turning to our statute books, says Mr. Randolph, it will be perceived that at present there are some port**s** entitled to benefits which other ports do not enjoy." He shows in another place, referring to a treaty between the United States and Great Britain, that several ports of the State of New York have a system of custom and duties peculiar to themselves; and "in this he says gentlemen could not avail themselves of the distinction taken between a Territory and State, even if they were so disposed, since the ports in question were *ports of a State*."*

We see, besides, that Mr. Rodney's principal argument is grounded, not on the article of the Constitution mentioned by you, but on that which gives to Congress the power to *provide for the general welfare*.

Let us conclude from these various instances that the question of constitutionality is foreign to that which we now discuss; that it is of little moment to know whether a State may or may not modify its administration of customs and duties; that even this point was discussed in 1803; that, whether questioned or not, the right of France remains still the same, because it is a right of property, *not a favor, but a bargain;* and finally, that the least doubtful point in all human transactions is the necessity of fulfilling, *punctually* and *faithfully*, all their conditions and stipulations.

As to the memoir of Mr. Livingston, its object, in your opinion, sir, was to convince the French Government that it was its interest, instead of taking possession of Louisiana, to put New Orleans into the hands of the United States. In the first place, I shall ask, what would then have become of the territory, and whether in such case Mr. Livingston's object, which was to prevent every collision, to remove every motive of rivalship between the two nations, would have been fully accomplished? but every discussion on that subject would, I think, be quite useless, the perusal of the memoir being sufficient alone to remove every doubt. Its very basis is this question: "Is it the interest of France to take possession of Louisiana?"

It runs from beginning to end on that subject and no other. If in one paragraph it proposes to put the United States in possession of New Orleans, it is palpable from that very paragraph, and from the following, that the memoir refers not to New Orleans alone, but to the whole of Louisiana. Let us cite some passages. "Who, then, will be willing to cultivate *Louisiana* with slaves?" "*Louisiana* is surrounded by an immense wilderness." "What advantage can France derive from settling *that colony?*" "The productions of *Louisiana* being the same with those of the Antilles, &c., &c., it grows to evidence that, with respect to commerce, the settling (colonization) of Louisiana would be prejudicial to France, since it would deprive her other colonies of capitals which might be more usefully employed there."

"The possession of *Louisiana* is, however, very important to France, if she applies it to the only use which sound policy would seem to approve. I speak of *Louisiana* only, and in this I do not mean to comprehend the Floridas, because I think they are no part of the cession, as she can acquire by this cession the right to carry on the Mississippi a free trade," &c., &c.

Further, after having taken pains to explain all the advantages which France is to derive from the cession of *Louisiana* to the United States, Mr. Livingston adds: "All this can take place only by the cession of New Orleans to the United States, with the reserve of the right of entry at all times, free from all other duties than those paid by American vessels, together with the right of navigation on the Mississippi."

It becomes evident that he means the cession of the whole of Louisiana, since he advises France to secure to herself the navigation on the Mississippi; for how could this stipulation have been necessary if she were to have retained possession of the western shore? In which cases does Mr. Livingston mention New Orleans only? It is when he speaks of a free port, and of securing a free access to French vessels and merchandise. And in these particulars it is plain that he could not express himself otherwise, New Orleans being at that time the only port in Louisiana.

But what is the object of all the arguments of the minister of the United States? To dissuade France from taking possession of *Louisiana;* to prove that under her Government *Louisiana* never would nor ever could flourish; that not only in relation to commerce, but also with respect to policy, the settling of Louisiana could not be profitable to her; that she would find greater advantages in securing to herself the solid friendship of the United States than in the acquisition of a territory which would become a source of *rivalship;* that she ought not to change a natural ally from a warm friend into a suspicious and jealous neighbor, &c., &c. What is Mr. Livingston's conclusion? That, by adopting his opinion, France would easily be able to introduce into the western country the products of her manufactures, which the United States would have no interest to prevent, every cause of *rivalship* between the two nations being thus removed.

What more, I ask, can be wanting to prove that the memoir relates, not to the cession of New Orleans alone, but to that of the whole territory of Louisiana?

You observe that Mr. Livingston proposes to France to cede New Orleans to the United States, to be taken possession of by them, not as an independent and sovereign State, but *merely* on the same colonial condition it was held in by Spain, and as it would have been held by France had she taken and retained possession of the province.

To this I can make no other answer than that I have not been able, even on the closest examination, to discover any such thing expressed in the memoir. The word *merely* is not to be seen there any more than the word *exclusively* in the eighth article of the treaty. There is nothing in the memorial that could suggest the idea of Louisiana continuing under the colonial condition when belonging to the United States.

You do me honor to state, sir, that Mr. Livingston's memoir was presented to the French Government in August, 1802, and yet I read in another part of your letter that it was written at a time when even the treaty ceding Louisiana to France was not concluded. In this there is error of date, since the treaty of St. Ildephonso, by which Spain ceded the colony or province of Louisiana to France, was

---

*Mr. Randolph said that he did not mean to affirm that this exemption made by the treaty of London was constitutional; to solve that question was not his object; he would, however, observe that France had a view in signing the treaty to ascertain whether all its articles were constitutional or not; since here, as well as elsewhere, the most enlightened men frequently disagree on certain points of legislation.

signed on the 1st of October, 1800, as is stated in the convention of 1803, and in all the other documents of that period, which give it a date more than twenty months anterior to Mr. Livingston's memoir.

The error which you think you have found in the citation of page 32 of my letter of the 15th of May does not exist. I have now the honor to send you a copy of the original memoir, addressed in Mr. Livingston's own handwriting to the French Government; you will there find the word *possession*, and not *cession*, of Louisiana, in the paragraph alluded to.

In my letter of the 15th of May I called to mind what, even at the time of the cession, was the acknowledged value of the territory ceded by France, and cited not only the opinions of various writers, but also those of several distinguished members of Congress. To this you reply that "all those estimates were formed under impressions that the extent of the Louisiana cession was vastly more comprehensive than the subsequent declarations and efforts of the French Government would have made it."

I do not know to what subsequent declaration you allude.

In the first article of the treaty it is expressly stated that the French Government cedes Louisiana "*in order to give the United States a remarkable proof of friendship.*" In all these subsequent declarations I find expressions of the same good will and friendly dispositions, combined with a sense of justice, from which even friendship should never depart. As to the *efforts of the French Government*, as you do not specify them, nor indicate of what description they were, I wish to persuade myself, sir, that you thereby allude to those efforts which, on more than one important occasion within the last forty-three years, France has taken a pleasure in making to promote the prosperity of the United States.

What were the real motives which induced the French Government not to retain Louisiana? I see no other, nor can discover any but those expressed in the treaty, and, therefore, I shall not discuss this point. I can, however, safely assert that France has at all times proved that she could do much for her friends, and had little fear of her enemies. For this reason, "the opinion *so forcibly urged*" in the memoir of Mr. Livingston has made but little impression on my mind, and, if such a question were not irrelevant to the present subject of discussion, I believe that I could easily show that France could have retained her territory of Louisiana as well in war as in peace.

I cannot conclude better than by citing, in support of my cause, the words of a celebrated statesman, whose opinions I have already had occasion to quote, and must be received as authority everywhere, and on every occasion.

Opinion of Mr. Madison in 1794.

"The fifteenth article, Mr. Chairman, has another extraordinary feature which I should imagine must strike every observer. In the treaties which profess to put us on the footing of the most favored nation, it is stipulated that, where new favors are granted to a particular nation in return for favors received, the party claiming the new favors shall pay the price of it. This is just and proper where the footing of the most favored nation is established at all. But this article gives to Great Britain the full benefit of all privileges that may be granted to any other nation, without requiring from her the same equivalent privileges with those granted by such nation. Hence, it would happen that if Spain, Portugal, or France should open their colonial ports to the United States, in consideration of certain privileges in our trade, the same privileges would result *gratis* and *ipso facto* to Great Britain."*

The present claim of France is the same, or rather it is better, since it grows not out of a commercial convention, but out of a contract of sale, and since France has, in fact, already paid for her privilege, while England, in the instance cited, would have given no consideration; still, however, Mr. Madison says that England must, by the terms of the article, obtain *gratis* and *ipso facto* every right or privilege granted to any other nation, whether *gratuitously* or for an *equivalent*. From all which, I conclude, sir, that France has a right to enjoy *gratis* and *ipso facto* the privilege reserved to her by the 8th article of the Louisiana treaty.

When so able an advocate as Mr. Madison has taken up my defence I need say no more.

I have the honor to be, &c., &c.

G. HYDE DE NEUVILLE.

No. 20.

Baron de Neuville to the Secretary of State.

[Translation.]

WASHINGTON, *October* 15, 1821.

SIR: I have received fresh instructions from my Government requiring me to insist upon the execution of the 8th article of the Louisiana treaty, or to demand, at least, that in the meantime our shipping be made to enjoy, in the ports of the territory ceded by France, all the privileges and advantages which are granted in the same ports to such nations as have no treaty or convention with the United States.

On this subject I must again refer to my letter of the 30th of March last. Considering, however, that, at the date of these instructions, my Government was not informed of the present state of the negotiation, and being solicitous to make all possible exertion for the removal of every difficulty to the negotiation, I have the honor again to propose (in case you should persist in your opinion on the Louisiana question, as I adhere to mine) that we enter into the agreement suggested in my letter of June 30 and of August 3.

Accept, &c., &c., &c.

G. HYDE DE NEUVILLE.

o Mr. Madison's speech, British treaty, April 15, 1792.

No. 21.

Extract of a letter (No. 233) from Mr. Gallatin to Mr. Adams, dated September 24, 1822.

"I had yesterday a conference with Mr. de Villèle on the subject of our claims. He expressed his wish that a general arrangement might take place, embracing all the subjects of discussion between the two countries; stated those to be the reclamations of the United States for spoliations on their trade; those of France on account of Beaumarchais' claim, and of the vessels captured on the coast of Africa, and the question arising under the Louisiana treaty; and asked whether I was prepared to negotiate upon all these points. I answered that I was ready to discuss them all, but that I must object to uniting the Louisiana question to that of claims for indemnity, as they were essentially distinct, and as I thought that, after all that had passed, we had a right to expect that no further obstacle should be thrown in the discussion of our claims by connecting it with subjects foreign to them. Mr. de Villèle appeared to acquiesce in that observation."

No. 22.

Extract of a letter (No. 236) from Mr. Gallatin to Mr. Adams, dated November 13, 1822.

"I received, on the 8th instant, a letter of Mr. de Villèle of the 6th, a copy of which is inclosed, together with that of my answer of the 12th.

"There is no doubt that the attempt to blend the discussion respecting the claims with that concerning the construction of the eighth article of the Louisiana treaty, is intended to postpone if not to defeat the first object. It must have been presumed that I could not have powers on the Louisiana question; and that, in case I had, they could not be such as to authorize me to acquiesce in the construction contended for by France. From the tenor of the letter, as well as from other circumstances, I am inclined to think that Government will persevere in insisting that the two subjects should be united in the same negotiation. I had received a suggestion to that effect from a respectable quarter, and I beg leave, also, to refer to the semi-official article in the Journal des Débats, of the 8th instant, observing that that paper is considered as the organ of Mr. de Villèle's sentiments.

"It will now remain for the President to decide whether it is proper to send me powers on the subject of the Louisiana treaty; and, in that case, whether it is for the interest of the United States to purchase the annulation of the eighth article. That this Government means to make their claim under it an offset against the just demands of our citizens, is obvious to me. Yet, as I may be mistaken, and as a change of ministry or some unforeseen circumstances may, unexpectedly, give an opportunity of making an arrangement, I beg leave again to refer to the several letters in which I have applied for instructions on that subject."

No. 22, (a.)

Mr. Villèle to Mr. Gallatin.

[Translation.]

PARIS, *November 6, 1822.*

SIR: The convention concluded at Washington on the 24th of June last has removed the obstacles which momentarily fettered the relations of commerce between France and the United States. Although this convention is only temporary, it produces the expectation of a treaty more extensive and more durable. It is intended to leave proper time for discussing and establishing this treaty upon bases the most conformable to the interests of the two States. The communications are already opened on both sides upon the most amicable footing. His Majesty has seen, with satisfaction, this happy effect of the arrangement concluded in his name, and in the name of the United States.

If any partial difficulties still remain to be cleared, they will be easily settled between two powers that are sincerely desirous of establishing their relations on the most perfect equity.

It is in this spirit of reciprocal justice I have received the claims which you have done me the honor to transmit to me, and that, without prejudging anything in their regard, I ought, above all, sir, to remark to you that France has also claims pending, or to produce, against the Government of the United States. It would appear agreeable to the interests of the two parties, and to the reciprocity of justice and of protection to which the subjects of the two States have equally a right, that these affairs should be examined and arranged in concert by way of negotiation.

The intention of his Majesty would be, that these claims and the other points in question, on which the convention of the 24th of June has not pronounced, might be the object of that negotiation, in order to terminate, simultaneously and in a definitive manner, every dispute between the two States, especially that which concerns the duties received in Louisiana upon the French commerce, contrary to the tenor of the eighth article of the treaty of cession.

You will see, sir, in this intention of his Majesty only the most steadfast desire of leaving, in future, no cause or pretext of misunderstanding or of complaints between the two States, and on the part of their respective subjects.

If you are authorized, sir, to pursue this march, I pray you to let me know it, and I will hasten to demand of the King the powers necessary for a negotiator charged to treat of it with you.

If you are also authorized to sign a consular convention, the same plenipotentiary would receive the powers, *ad hoc*, for pursuing also the negotiation.

Accept, sir, the assurances of the high consideration, &c.

JH. DE VILLELE,
The Minister of Finance, charged ad interim with the Portfolio of Foreign Affairs.

No. 22, (b.)

Mr. Gallatin to Mr. de Villèle.

PARIS, *November* 12, 1822.

SIR: I had the honor to receive your excellency's letter of the 6th instant.

I have special powers to negotiate a convention providing for the just claims of citizens of the United States against France, as also for the like claims of French subjects against the United States, with such person or persons as may have a like authority from his most Christian Majesty.

As minister of the United States, I am authorized to discuss the question respecting the construction of the 8th article of the Louisiana treaty, and to give and receive explanations on that subject. But the negotiation on that point having been transferred to Washington, no special powers in that respect have been transmitted to me. I had understood, in the course of the conference I had the honor to have with your excellency on the 23d of September, and had accordingly written to my Government, that it was not intended to insist that that subject should be blended with that of private claims. It is, indeed, obvious that it would be utterly unjust to make the admission of these to depend on the result of a negotiation on a subject with which they have no connexion whatever, and the difficulties respecting which are of a date posterior to that of the claims.

All the representations which his Majesty's Government has made to that of the United States, whether on private or on public subjects, have uniformly been taken into consideration, and received that attention to which they were so justly entitled. In no instance has the Government of the United States declined to open a discussion on any subject thus offered to their consideration by France, or made it a preliminary condition that the discussion should also embrace some other subject in which they might happen to take a greater interest. The question respecting the 8th article of the Louisiana treaty has, in particular, been the subject of a voluminous correspondence, in the course of which, the arguments in support of the construction insisted on by each party, respectively, were made known to the other. I have, in the meanwhile, for six years, made unceasing application to his Majesty's Government for the settlement of claims to a vast amount, affecting the interest of numerous individuals, and arising from flagrant violations of the law of nations and of the rights of the United States, without having ever been able to obtain, to this day, satisfaction in a single instance, or even that the subject should be taken into consideration and discussed. After so many vexatious delays, for which different causes have, at different times been assigned, it cannot now be intended again to postpone the investigation of that subject, by insisting that it should be treated in connexion with one foreign to it, and which has already been discussed. The United States have, at least, the right to ask that their demands should also be examined and discussed, and I trust that, since I am authorized to treat as well concerning the claims of French subjects against the United States, as respecting those of American citizens against France, a distinct negotiation to that effect will be opened without any further delay.

Permit me, at the same time, to renew to your excellency the assurances that the United States have the most earnest desire that every subject of difference between the two countries should be amicably arranged, and their commercial and political relations placed on the most friendly and solid footing. They will be ready to open again negotiations on the subject of the 8th article of the Louisiana treaty, and on every other which remains to be adjusted, and will have no objection that the seat of those negotiations should be transferred from Washington to this place.

Although my powers to treat respecting every subject connected with the commerce of the two countries may embrace that of a consular convention, yet, as this had not been contemplated by my Government, I am not, at this time, prepared to conclude an arrangement for that purpose.

I request your excellency to accept the assurance, &c.

ALBERT GALLATIN.

No. 23.

Mr. Gallatin to Mr. Adams, No. 237.

PARIS, *November* 19, 1822.

SIR: I received last night, and have the honor to inclose, a copy of Mr. de Villèle's answer, (dated 15th instant,) to my letter of the 12th. You will perceive that, without taking any notice of the reasons I had urged why a distinct negotiation should be immediately opened on the subject of the claims against both Governments, he insists that this shall be treated in connexion with the question respecting the construction of the 8th article of the Louisiana treaty. The object is too obvious to require any comments on my part, and this final decision leaves me no other course than to refer the whole to my Government.

I have the honor to be, with great respect, sir, your most obedient servant,

ALBERT GALLATIN.

No. 23, (a.)

Mr. de Villèle to Mr. Gallatin.

[Translation.]

PARIS, *November* 15, 1822.

SIR: You have done me the honor to announce to me, on the 12th of this month, that you were authorized to negotiate a convention relative to the claims of American citizens against France, and to those of France against the United States, but that you have received no power to enter upon a negotiation concerning the interpretation of the 8th article of the Louisiana treaty.

The discussions which have ensued upon this last point between your Government and the Minister Plenipotentiary of the King to the United States having come to nothing, and this question remaining thus undecided, it is as proper as it is just to renew the examination of it; it touches upon too great interests not to be treated with renewed attention and to be abandoned.

If a new arrangement takes place for the claims which are still in question, it ought to embrace them all, and the desire of the King's Government is to permit no difficulty to remain, and to leave nothing undecided in the relations of the two countries.

With this very motive, sir, I have demanded in the letter which I had the honor of addressing to you on the 6th of this month, that the negotiation to be opened upon the respective claims should likewise include a consular convention. If your powers for discussing these different points should not appear to you sufficiently extended for making them the object of a negotiation, I think, sir, that you will judge it proper to demand of your Government supplementary authority for coming to an arrangement which can only have the utility proposed by the two Governments, by its embracing all the questions and claims which are still in dispute.

I can only refer, sir, upon this subject, to the communications which I have had the honor of making to you on the 6th of this month, and with which you have doubtless made your Government acquainted.

Accept, sir, the assurance of my high consideration.

JH. DE VILLELE,
The Minister of Finance, charged ad interim with the Portfolio of Foreign Affairs.

No. 24.

Mr. Gallatin to Mr. Adams, No. 241.

PARIS, *January* 5, 1823.

SIR: I had, after his return from Verona, a conversation with the Duke of Montmorency on our claims; I complained in strong terms of the decision taken by Mr. de Villèle, and said, that his insisting to connect that subject with the discussion respecting the construction of the 8th article of the Louisiana treaty would be considered in the United States as an attempt to avoid altogether the payment of the indemnities due to our citizens. I then stated that the reluctance evinced by the Government of France to make a general arrangement on that subject had induced the President to authorize me to make a separate application for the Antwerp claims; that what had now taken place afforded an additional proof of the difficulties which stood in the way of a general transaction; and that, whilst this seemed indefinitely postponed, I hoped that the special application would at least be attended to, and receive a favorable decision.

The Duke, after some general observations on the earnest desire of France that all the subjects of difference between the two countries should be definitively arranged, and declaring that this was the only motive for insisting on a negotiation embracing all those points, said that to take up at this time any special claim appeared to him inconsistent with the official communication made to me by Mr. de Villèle, and that we must wait at least till I had received an answer from my Government, to whom I must of course have transmitted the correspondence. He promised, however, to lay my request before the King's council, but without giving me any expectation that it would be favorably received.

It is probable that even this has been prevented by the Duke's resignation, which took place a few days after our conversation; and I think it quite useless to renew, at this time, the application to his successor Mr. de Chateaubriand. I will therefore wait till I receive your instructions in answer to my several despatches on this subject.

I have the honor to be, with great respect, sir, your most obedient servant,

ALBERT GALLATIN.

No. 25.

Mr. Gallatin to Mr. Adams, No. 250.

PARIS, *February* 27, 1823.

SIR: I had designedly abstained from answering Mr. de Villèle's last letter, of the 15th of November in order to be able to avail myself of any change in the ministry, or of any other favorable circumstance which might arise. The more I have reflected on the ground assumed by this Government on the subject of our claims, and on the attempt to connect their discussion with the question arising under the eighth article of the Louisiana treaty, the more I have felt satisfied that it was impossible that the United States should depart from the true construction of that article, and acquiesce in that contended for by France, and that a renewed discussion on that subject would be unprofitable, and lead to no result whatever. As a last but, I believe, unavailing effort, I have concluded to express that conviction to the French Government, and have, accordingly, addressed this day to Mr. de Chateaubriand the letter of which I have the honor to inclose a copy.

I have no doubt that there is not at this time any disposition to do us justice, and that if we were even to make some concessions, with respect to the article above mentioned, we could not succeed in making an arrangement on the subject of the claims satisfactory to the parties, or such as the Government of the United States would feel justified to accept. With that view of the subject, it appears to me evident that it is less disadvantageous to let the question rest for the present as it is than to entangle ourselves by consenting to blend it with the discussion of the Louisiana treaty; whilst, on the other hand, the communication of this determination, coming from me before any specific instructions can have been received from you, is less peremptory than if founded on these instructions, does not commit Government, and leaves the United States at liberty to resume, at a more favorable time, the negotiation on the ground which may then appear most eligible.

Independent of unforeseen circumstances which may alter the dispositions of this Government, I can perceive but one mode calculated to produce some effect. It is that the parties interested should petition Congress, and that there should be some marked expression of the sentiments of that body in their favor. The apathy of the great mass of the claimants, and the silence preserved in that respect during so many years in all our public discussions have, undoubtedly, produced here the impression that very little interest was felt on that subject, and, in some degree, contributed in rendering our efforts to obtain justice unavailing.

I have the honor to be, with great respect, sir, your most obedient servant,

ALBERT GALLATIN.

No. 25, (a.)

Mr. Gallatin to Viscount de Chateaubriand.

PARIS, *February* 27, 1823.

SIR: I had the honor to receive his excellency Count de Villèle's letter of the 15th of November last, by which, notwithstanding the remonstrances contained in mine of the 12th, his excellency being at that time charged with the Department of Foreign Affairs, still insisted that the discussion of the claims of individuals of both nations upon the two Governments, respectively, should not take place unless it was connected with a renewed negotiation on the 8th article of the Louisiana treaty.

A conversation I had the honor to have with his excellency the Duke de Montmorency, after his return from Verona, induced me to hope, although he did not encourage any expectation of a different result, that he would, however, again lay the subject before his Majesty's council of ministers. This circumstance, the subsequent change in the Department of Foreign Affairs, and the objects of primary importance which have heretofore necessarily engrossed your excellency's attention, have prevented an earlier official answer to his excellency Count de Villèle's letter.

It has, together with the others on the same subject, as he had naturally anticipated, been of course transmitted to my Government. But, on a review of the correspondence of Mr. Adams with Mr. Hyde de Neuville and with myself, I must express my perfect conviction that the subject having been maturely examined and thoroughly discussed, there cannot be the least expectation that the United States will alter their view of it, or acquiesce in the construction put by his Majesty's minister on the 8th article of the Louisiana treaty.

It is not my intention at this moment to renew a discussion which seems to have been already exhausted, but I will beg leave simply to state the question to your excellency:

It was agreed by the article above mentioned that the ships of France should forever be treated upon the footing of the most favored nation in the ports of Louisiana.

Vessels of certain foreign nations being now treated in the ports of the United States (including those of Louisiana) on the same footing with American vessels, in consideration of the American vessels being treated in the ports of those nations on the same footing with their own vessels, France has required that French vessels should, by virtue of the said article, be treated in the ports of Louisiana on the same footing with the vessels of those nations, without allowing on her part the consideration or reciprocal condition by virtue of which those vessels are thus treated.

The United States contend that the right to be treated upon the footing of the most favored nation, when not otherwise defined, and when expressed only in those words, is that, and can only be that, of being entitled to that treatment gratuitously, if such nation enjoys it gratuitously, and on paying the same equivalent, if it has been granted in consideration of an equivalent. Setting aside every collateral matter and subsidiary argument, they say that the article in question, expressed as it is, can have no other meaning, is susceptible of no other construction, for this plain and incontrovertible reason: that, if the French vessels were allowed to receive gratuitously the same treatment which those of certain other nations receive only in consideration of an equivalent, they would not be treated as the most favored nation, but more favorably than any other nation. And since the article must necessarily have the meaning contended for by the United States, and no other, the omission or insertion of words to define it is wholly immaterial, a definition being necessary only when the expressions used are of doubtful import, and the insertion of words to that effect in some other treaties, belonging to that class of explanatory but superfluous phrases of which instances are to be found in so many treaties.

It might, indeed, have been sufficient to say that, in point of fact, there was no most favored nation in the United States; the right enjoyed by the vessels of certain foreign nations to be treated in the ports of the United States as American vessels, in consideration of American vessels receiving a similar treatment in the ports of those nations, not being a favor but a mere act of reciprocity.

Let me also observe that the pretension of France would, if admitted, leave no alternative to the

United States than either to suffer the whole commerce between France and Louisiana to be carried exclusively in French vessels, or to renounce the right of making arrangements with other nations deemed essential to our prosperity, and having for object not to lay restrictions on commerce but to remove them. If the meaning of the eighth article of the Louisiana treaty was such indeed as has been contended for on the part of France, the United States, bound to fulfil their engagements, must submit to the consequences, whatever these might be. But this having been proven not to be the case, the observation is made only to show that the United States never can, either for the sake of obtaining indemnities for their citizens or from their anxious desire to settle, by conciliatory arrangements, all their differences with France, be brought to acquiesce in the erroneous construction put upon the article in question.

The proposal made by his excellency Mr. de Villèle in his letter of the 15th, can, therefore, have no other effect than to produce unnecessary delays, and would, if persisted in, be tantamount to an indefinite postponement of the examination and settlement of the claims of the citizens of the United States. It will remain for his Majesty's Government to decide whether this determination be consistent with justice; whether the reclamations of private individuals should be thus adjourned because the two Governments happen to differ in opinion on a subject altogether foreign to those claims. Having nothing to add to my reiterated and unavailing applications on that subject, my only object at this moment has been to show that I cannot expect any instructions from my Government that will alter the state of the question.

I request your excellency to accept the assurance, &c.

ALBERT GALLATIN.

No. 26.

Mr. Brown to Mr. Adams, No. 17.

PARIS, *November* 29, 1824.

SIR: Not having received any answer to the letter which, on the 22d ultimo, I addressed to the Minister of Foreign Affairs, I sent him a note, requesting that he would favor me with a conference at as early a day as his convenience would permit, and received his answer, appointing the 25th instant for that purpose.

I waited upon him at the appointed hour, and after an interchange of the customary salutations, I reminded him that I had signified to him my wish to converse freely with him on the subject of the claims of American citizens on the Government of France, and that the state of my health alone had prevented me from asking a conference on that topic prior to the transmission of my letter of the 22d ultimo. I then, in a concise manner, called his attention to the state of the negotiation, and expressed my hope that the French Government would no longer arrest the progress of the discussion by insisting on connecting it with the question arising out of the eighth article of the Louisiana treaty. The two subjects, I contended, were entirely dissimilar in their nature, and therefore could not, with any degree of propriety, be embraced in the same discussion. In the one case, American citizens ask indemnity for their property, which has been taken from them under the authority of the French Government and in opposition to the plainest principles of law and justice; in the other, the Governments of the United States and France disagree in their construction of an article in a treaty which has no relation to the question of claims. The justice of the claims of American citizens has never been denied by France, while the United States have not hitherto seen any reason to admit the validity of their just claim under the eighth article of the Louisiana treaty. I asked him whether it was either just or reasonable that these claims should remain unsatisfied until the two Governments could agree in their interpretation of the treaty? Although the United States have been always ready to continue to discuss with France the question on the treaty, yet they cannot consent to connect it with claims for indemnity. I reminded him that in every instance in which France had presented a claim, either on behalf of the Government or her citizens, founded on any supposed injury done by the United States, the claim had been carefully considered, without entangling it with any other question, and, when well founded, had been admitted and settled; that the United States had a right to expect a corresponding course of fair conduct on the part of France, and, therefore, had seen with deep regret the ground assumed in the present instance and the delay consequent upon it. I concluded by expressing a hope that the negotiation for our claims, so long suspended, would be resumed, and repeated the offer already made, to embrace in the same negotiation any claims on the part of French subjects against the Government of the United States.

The Baron de Damas replied, that the time which had elapsed since he had been placed at the head of the Department of Foreign Affairs had been so short, and his immediate and indispensable duties so numerous, that he had not been able to make himself acquainted with the subject; that the correspondence was voluminous; and that, with the most earnest desire to answer my letter, he had not hitherto had the necessary time allowed him to give it even a cursory perusal; that, being unacquainted with the subject, he could not discuss it with me on equal ground, but that he hoped very shortly to give it a careful examination and to send me a definitive answer. I asked him if I could hope for it in time to send by the next vessel. He said that he could not promise to send me an answer the next week, nor could he precisely say at what time I might expect it, but that I should have it as soon as he could find time to prepare it. I assigned as a reason for wishing to be furnished with an early answer, the call made on the President by the House of Representatives at the last session. He said he was already informed of the proceedings of that branch of our legislature, and felt every disposition to bring the questions of difference between the two countries to a close as speedily as possible. The conference here terminated without the attainment of the object which induced me to ask it. I do not know at what precise time I may expect an answer to my letter, nor can I anticipate, from anything which passed at the interview, what will be the nature of the answer which I may receive.

I have the honor to be, with great respect, sir, your most obedient and very humble servant,

JAMES BROWN.

CAPTURE AND DETENTION BY BRITISH ARMED VESSELS OF AMERICAN FISHERMEN.

COMMUNICATED TO THE HOUSE OF REPRESENTATIVES FEBRUARY 18, 1825.

To the Speaker of the House of Representatives:

I transmit to the House of Representatives a report from the Secretary of State, containing the information called for by their resolution of the first of this month, touching the capture and detention of American fishermen during the last season.

JAMES MONROE.

WASHINGTON, *February* 16, 1825.

DEPARTMENT OF STATE, *Washington, February* 16, 1825.

The Secretary of State, to whom has been referred a resolution of the House of Representatives of the 1st instant, requesting the President of the United States to cause to be laid before it such information as might be in his possession, and which, in his opinion, it would be proper to communicate, touching the capture and detention of American fishermen the last season in the Bay of Fundy, and what progress has been made in obtaining redress, has the honor respectfully to submit to the President copies of the letters and documents in this office which contain the information called for by the resolution referred to.

JOHN QUINCY ADAMS.

List of papers.

Mr. Brent to Mr. Addington, September 8, 1824.
Memorial of Aaron Hayden and others, July 27, 1824, (inclosure.)
Affidavit of Robert Small, July 27, 1824, (inclosure.)
Affidavit of Elias Ficket, July 27, 1824, (inclosure.)
Memorial of Hayden, Kilby, and others, August 16, 1824, (inclosure.)
Memorial of J. G. Faxon, August 16, 1824, (inclosure.)
Protest of Harding, Clark, and others, July 22, 1824, (inclosure.)
Affidavit of Charles Tabbuts, July 23, 1824, (inclosure.)
Protest of Hubbard, Hantz, and others, July 24, 1824, (inclosure.)
Protest of James Woodward, sen., and others, August 7, 1824, (inclosure.)
Mr. Brent to Mr. Addington, September 21, 1824.
Messrs. Wass and Nash to Mr. Adams, September 6, 1824, (inclosure.)
S. Emery, for Wilmot Wass, to Mr. Adams, September 6, 1824, (inclosure.)
Protest of Charles Talbut and others, September 23, 1824, (inclosure.)
Mr. Brent to Mr. Shepley, October 8, 1824.
Mr. Addington to Mr. Adams, October 5, 1824.
R. A. Lake to Mr. Addington, September 9, 1824, (inclosure.)
Captain Hoare to R. A. Lake, August 26, 1824, (inclosure.)
Captain Hoare to R. A. Lake, September 2, 1824, (inclosure.)
Captain Hoare to R. A. Lake, September 2, 1824, (inclosure.)
Mr. Shepley to Mr. Adams, November 6, 1824.
Affidavit of Robert Small, November 5, 1824, (inclosure.)
Affidavit of Paul Johnson, November 5, 1824, (inclosure.)
Affidavit of Hebbert, Hunt, and others, November 5 and 6, 1824, (inclosure.)
Affidavit of Jones Wass and John Wright, November 1, 1824, (inclosure.)
Affidavit of Charles Tabbut and Josiah W. Perry, November 2, 1824, (inclosure.)
Affidavit of Christopher Wass and Jones Wass, November 1, 1824, (inclosure.)
Affidavit of Joel McKinsey, November 3, 1824, (inclosure.)
Affidavit of Otis Bryant and Moses Smith, November 3, 1824, (inclosure.)
Affidavit of Jacob Winslow, November 5, 1824, (inclosure.)
Affidavit of William Howard, Benjamin Newman, and Thomas Brown, November 6, 1824, (inclosure.)
Affidavit of Elisha Small and Benjamin Small, November 6, 1824, (inclosure.)
Affidavit of B. W. Coggins and Henry Coggins, November 5, 1824, (inclosure.)
Affidavit of Harding Clark, November 7, 1824, (inclosure.)
Affidavit of William Rumery and Robert Rumney, November 6, 1824, (inclosure.)
Mr. Emery to the Secretary of State, September 27, 1824, (copy.)
Protest, Jones Wass and John Wright, in case of schooner "Rebecca," (copy.)

Mr. Brent to Mr. Addington, dated September 8, 1824.

SIR: I have the honor to transmit to you three memorials from sundry citizens of the United States, belonging to the State of Maine, accompanied by seven protests and affidavits, which exhibit the nature and extent of the facts referred to by the memorialists, complaining of the interruption which they have experienced during the present season in their accustomed and lawful employment of taking and curing fish in the Bay of Fundy and upon the Grand Banks, by the British armed brig Dotterel, commanded by Captain Hoar, and another vessel, a provincial cutter of New Brunswick, acting under the orders of that officer; and earnestly soliciting the interposition of this Government to procure for them suitable redress.

With this view I was charged by the Secretary, before his late departure from this city, to communicate to you the above papers, and to request your good offices towards obtaining for the sufferers the indemnity. to which they appear to be so well entitled, not only from the peculiar nature and extent of the injuries and losses of which they complain, proved and illustrated as they are by the series of protests and depositions accompanying their memorials, but from the serious violation of the rights and liberties of the citizens of the United States which they involve, in the use of the same fisheries; and I have the honor, accordingly, to request that you will have the goodness to make such representations to the commanding officer of the naval forces of your Government on that station, or to the colonial Government of New Brunswick, as may be available, not only for the relief of the memorialists, but for the prevention of similar interruptions in future.

I have the honor to be, with distinguished consideration, sir, your obedient and very humble servant,

DANIEL BRENT.

Inclosures.

Memorial of Aaron Hayden, Kilby, and others, July 27, 1824.
Memorial of J. G. Faxon.
Memorial of Aaron Hayden, John Burgin, and others.

To the Hon. JOHN QUINCY ADAMS, *Secretary of State for the United States:*

The memorial of the undersigned, merchants and ship owners, residing at Eastport, in the county of Washington and State of Maine, respectfully represents:

That your memorialists during the present year have invested a larger amount of property in vessels than they have heretofore done, for the purpose of carrying on the business of fishing; that the industry and enterprise of our seamen have been unusually directed to the employment of taking and curing fish, under the encouraging and beneficial laws of their country; and that, without interruption from a foreign power, their labors would have been crowned with success, and they would have enjoyed the fruits of their toil.

But your memorialists have to regret the necessity which compels them to state to the honorable Secretary their grievances, and requires of them to seek redress, through him, for the many acts of violence and injustice which have been committed by his Britannic Majesty's brig Dotterel, commanded by Captain Hoar, in total disregard and in violation of the subsisting treaty between the two Governments. Your memorialists, premising that the American fishermen in the Bay of Fundy, for these two or three years last past, have been interrupted and taken by British armed vessels, while fishing agreeably to the provisions of the treaty, beg leave respectfully to state that, during the present year, the British armed brig Dotterel has captured nine sail of fishing vessels and sent some of them into the province of New Brunswick for adjudication, while others have been converted into tenders, without trial, for the purpose of better molesting our fishermen. They have insulted and abused the crews, turned them on shore in a foreign country, entirely destitute and without the means of returning to their homes, and have said, repeatedly, that they would take American fishermen wherever they were to be found, and without regard to the treaty.

That the brig's barge has come into the wharf at Eastport, and taken and carried away two boats laden with flour.

That the American fishermen have been so molested on the fishing ground in the Bay of Fundy, common to both countries, that they dare not again attempt to avail themselves of the rights and privileges secured to them by treaty, and which are well defined and well understood by every fisherman; and inasmuch as they are debarred the privilege of making a harbor, for the purposes of shelter, and to purchase wood and procure water, it operates as a deprivation of a great and important benefit, which they feel that they have a right to enjoy without interruption.

That, unless something be done for the protection of our fishermen, your memorialists believe that many vessels of this and the neighboring States will be captured or thrown out of employ, with great injury to private interest, and not without an infringement of public rights.

Referring the honorable Secretary, therefore, to the annexed affidavits of the masters of three of the captured vessels, and holding ourselves responsible for the truth of the above allegations, your memorialists respectfully request that some prompt and efficient measures may be adopted by our Government to protect us in our rights and pursuits, and that our fishermen may not be molested, nor our shores invaded with impunity by the subjects of any foreign power.

Aaron Hayden,	John Davis,
John Burgin,	Bucknam & Gunnison,
Samuel Wheeler,	Daniel Kilty,
George Hobbs,	Samuel Sturns,
Elijah D. Green,	O. S. Livermore,
Joseph C. Noyes,	Edward Baker,
N. F. Deering,	G. Lamprey,
H. T. Emery,	Benjamin B. Leavitt,
Lorenzo Sabing,	James M. Lincoln,
Jonathan Buck,	John T. Jones,
Ezekiel Prince,	Nathan Bucknam,
Isaac Hobbs,	Thomas Green,
John Webster,	Benjamin Bucknam,
Edward Ilsley,	John Shaw,
John Norton,	Caleb Chace,
Charles Brooks,	W. Eustis,
Jerry Bunain,	William M. Brooks.
Abel Stephens,	
JULY 27, 1824.	

EASTPORT, *July* 27, 1824.

I, Robert Small, master of the schooner Reindeer, of Lubec, do testify, declare, and say: That I sailed from Lubec, in the State of Maine, in the above schooner, on July 22, 1824, on a fishing voyage in the Bay of Fundy. On Sunday, July 25, finding our water very bad, went into a harbor in an uninhabited place called "Two Islands," near Grand Menan, for the purpose of procuring a fresh supply of wood and water. That we picked up about one cord of drift wood from off the beach of said island and filled two barrels of water from a spring or brook on said island. And on Monday morning following, about four o'clock, got under way and towed out of the harbor, it being calm; and when from one to two miles from the shore we were boarded by a barge from the British man-of-war brig Dotterel, containing nine men with arms, &c., commanded by an officer from said brig of the name of Jones, who took possession of my vessel and papers, and brought her to anchor, menacing myself and crew with violence, threatening our lives, &c. They then took out all our crew with the exception of myself, put them on board the schooner Friend, Coggins, of Lubec, which vessel they also captured and made a cartel of, as they termed it, manned my vessel and ordered her for St. Andrew's, New Brunswick.

While on our voyage we had caught no fish within from six to eighteen miles from shore. We had no goods or merchandise on board, nor did we go into a harbor for any other purpose than to procure wood and water.

ROBERT SMALL.

STATE OF MAINE, *Washington*, ss.

Then personally appeared the said Robert Small, and made solemn oath that the foregoing statement by him subscribed was true. Before me,

FREDERICK HOBBS, *Justice of the Peace.*

EASTPORT, *July* 27, 1824.

I, Elisha Small, of Lubec, Maine, on oath declare and say: That on the 7th of July instant I left Lubec as master of the schooner Ruby, on a fishing voyage in the Bay of Fundy; and on the 25th of July, being nearly destitute of wood and water, we made for the outer islands lying near Grand Menan, and, finding the sea so heavy that we could not land, we went into the harbor of the "Two Islands," so called, to get a supply. We got in there between three and four o'clock p. m., when I sent my boat and seven hands to fill water and get wood. We got one boat load of drift wood and filled four barrels of water, when daylight shut in and we had not time to get more. The wind died away calm, and we could not get out of the harbor again that night. The next morning we got under way with a very light wind, and got out of the harbor, and it died away calm again. We were then boarded by a barge belonging to the British armed brig Dotterel, commanded by an officer of said brig by the name of Jones, and having on board nine men armed with guns, cutlasses, dirks, and pistols. Jones demanded my papers, which I delivered up, and ordered my crew forward; told his men to go down and search the vessel; they found nothing but fish, and salt, and fishing gear. He then told my crew to take their dunnage, ordered them on board the fishing schooner Diligent, which had previously been taken, and sent Captain Ficket of the Diligent to Lubec with the men. We had no merchandise on board the said schooner Ruby; had not caught a fish or attempted to catch one within five miles from the shore, nor had we been into any harbor until the one above named.

ELISHA SMALL.

STATE OF MAINE, *Washington*, ss.

Then personally appeared the said Elisha Small, and made oath that the foregoing statement by him subscribed was true. Before me,

FREDERICK HOBBS, *Justice of the Peace.*

EASTPORT, *July* 27, 1824.

I, Elias Ficket, master of the schooner Diligent, of Harrington, Maine, do testify, declare, and say: That on the sixteenth of July, eighteen hundred and twenty-four, I left Eastport, Maine, in the above schooner, for a fishing voyage in the Bay of Fundy; that on Sunday, the twenty-fifth of July, being nearly destitute of water, we repaired to a place called "Two Islands," lying to the southward of Grand Menan about three-fourths of a mile; and on which there are no inhabitants, and procured two barrels of water from a spring or brook on said island. On Monday morning, got under way, and, the wind being light, towed out of the harbor, and when about one and a half mile from the shore, while attempting to get on the fishing ground (which is six to nine miles from any shore) we were boarded by a barge from the British man-of-war brig Dotterel, commanded by a sailing master whose name was Jones, and having on board nine men, taken possession of, and ordered to receive on board the crew of the schooner Ruby, of Lubec, which vessel they had previously captured, and to sail immediately to Lubec, as a cartel; thereby interrupting us in our lawful employment and destroying our fishery. I further declare that we had no goods or merchandise on board our schooner; that we did not go into a harbor for any other purpose than to obtain a supply of water.

We were not fishing where we were captured, nor had we attempted to catch fish within more than six miles from the shore while on our voyage. I further declare that we were badly used by the barge's officers, threatening to shoot us, &c., &c. And they said their orders were to capture all Americans they met with, right or wrong; that there was no treaty, and that Americans should not fish in British waters.

ELIAS FICKET.

STATE OF MAINE, *Washington*, ss.

Then personally appeared the said Elias Ficket, and made solemn oath that the foregoing statement by him subscribed was true. Before me,

FREDERICK HOBBS, *Justice of the Peace.*

To the Hon. JOHN Q. ADAMS, *Secretary of State:*

The undersigned, inhabitants of the county of Washington, in the State of Maine, interested in the fisheries in the Bay of Fundy, beg leave to represent:

That although till the present year the privileges reserved and confirmed to American fishermen by the convention of 1818 have been enjoyed with but few interruptions, they are now, in a great measure, cut off and prostrated by the piratical conduct of the commander of his Britannic Majesty's brig Dotterel and the officers under his command, aided by the provincial cutter attached to the port of St. Andrew's.

That the officer having the charge of the armed boats ordered to cruise round Grand Menan and Campo Bello has written instructions, which have been exhibited to our citizens, from the commander of the Dotterel, to seize and send into St. Andrews's all American fishermen found within three marine miles of said islands. That under these orders that officer, without any pretence other than such instructions, has seized the following vessels:

Schooner Pilgrim, of Lubec, Woodward master; schooner Hero, of Denneyville, Clark master; schooner Rebecca, of Addison, Wass master; schooner Galeon, of Lubec, Hunt master; schooner William, of Addison, Tabbut master; schooner Ruby, of Lubec, E. Small master; schooner Reindeer, of Lubec, R. Small master.

The Pilgrim and the Hero were captured while under sail, standing for Lubec in distress, and more than three miles from said Grand Menan. And, although this capture took place on the sixteenth day of June last, said schooner Hero has not been sent in for trial, but has been armed, and is still used as a tender to said brig Dotterel, the more easily to decoy other fishing vessels. The Rebecca went into Grand Menan in distress for wood and water, and, having obtained a supply, was preparing to return to the fishing ground, when she was taken. The Galeon, with seventy quintals of fish on board, went in for the same purpose, and, within a few minutes after she had accomplished her object, it being quite late in the evening, and the fog extremely dense, she was taken and sent to St. Andrew's. The William, with one hundred and twenty quintals of fish on board, left the fishing ground in distress for want of water, and had come to anchor near the shore of Grand Menan, her sails were not handed, nor was her boat launched from the deck to go on shore, when she was seized and taken to St. Andrew's. The Ruby and Reindeer went into Two Island harbor for wood and water, near Grand Menan, and were immediately seized.

We beg leave here to observe that American fishermen have no occasion nor inducement to violate the provisions of the aforesaid convention, nor have they, as we firmly believe, in any instance, given just cause for complaint.

The protest of the master and crew of the Galeon has already been forwarded you. Those of the Hero and Pilgrim will accompany this memorial, and will, we trust, establish the facts relative to the wanton detention of those vessels, as well as show the indignities cast upon the American flag and the insults offered the citizens of the United States by the British officers of the Dotterel and provincial cutter.

To claim these vessels in the Vice Admiralty courts in New Brunswick would be worse than a total loss; for, besides the fact that the claimant must give bonds to the amount of £60, currency of New Brunswick, to pay costs of libel, whether condemnation takes place or not, his vessel, should he prevail in a claim, (proverbially hopeless,) will come to his hands in a dismantled, and ruinous state. No care is taken of American vessels seized for a pretended violation of British revenue laws; for, as they can never sail under British papers, but must be broken up or taken from the country, the seizing officer has no inducement to keep them in good repair, with the expectation of being remunerated for particular attention by a more advantageous sale. Certificate of reasonable cause of seizure, to prevent a suit for damages, is never refused by the Vice Admiralty judge of New Brunswick to a British naval officer, when the proper application is made. To appeal, therefore, to the provincial courts for redress would be worse than unavailing. It would only aggravate the damages already sustained.

To the successful advocate of the rights of American fishermen, it need not be urged that this state of things is peculiarly vexatious and ruinous. To the owners and crews of the vessels detained, and to their families, it is in many instances oppressive and distressing, and they are left without redress unless their own Government interpose. To that Government they appeal, and they do it with full confidence that their complaints will be heard and their wrongs redressed.

AUGUST 16, 1824.

Sol. Thayer,	Darius Pearn,
Hayden & Killey,	Buck & Tinkham,
John Norton & Co.,	Benj. B. Leawell,
John A. Baskum,	James M. Lincoln,
Benj. Bucknam,	Bucknan & Gunnison,
Ethel Olmstead,	John G. Faxon,
John Webster,	Joseph Sumner,
A. Barnard,	Davenport Tucker,
Oliver & James Glover,	Jeremiah Fowler,
Daniel Young,	Moses Fuller,
Daniel Pease,	F. A. & O. Burrall,
William H. Tyler,	Calvin Gibbs,
Joseph Whitney,	Darms & Noyes,
A. P. Mills,	William M. Brooks,
Joshua Gibbs,	Samuel B. Wadsworth,
Samuel Myers,	T. Pilsbury,
J. Boynton,	John Faxon,
George & Isaac Hobbs,	William Wass,
Samuel Wheeler,	William Nash,
Green & Shaw,	Jery Bevan,
W. Eustis,	Lewis Putnam.

To the Hon. John Q. Adams, *Secretary of State of the United States:*

The memorial of John Gardiner Faxon, merchant, of Lubec, in the State of Maine, humbly showeth:

That the said John G. Faxon is sole owner of the schooner called the Galeon, of said Lubec. The said scho·ner, being on a fishing voyage in the Bay of Fundy, was seized and detained by part of the officers and crew of the British armed brig Dotterel, and is still detained in the British port of St. Andrew's, by the authority of the commander of said brig, under the circumstances set forth in the protest annexed, which seizure and detention is to the great damage of the said John G. Faxon; wherefore your memorialist humbly prays that the honorable Secretary will cause such proceedings relative to the said premises as he may think proper to relieve the said owner and crew of the said schooner Galeon. And your memo. rialist will ever.pray, &c.

And your memorialist further states that the just value of the schooner Galeon, with her cargo and equipments, at the time of her capture and detention as aforesaid, was fifteen hundred dollars.

JOHN G. FAXON.

United States of America, *State of Maine, Washington, ss.*

Be it known to all to whom these presents may come: That on this 22d day of July, in the year of our Lord one thousand eight hundred and twenty-four, before me, Solomon Thayer, notary public, by legal authority duly commissioned and sworn, and dwelling at Lubec, county and State aforesaid, personally appeared Harding Clark, master of the pink-sterned schooner Hero, of Dennysville, Ephraim Clark, and William H. N. Brown, fishermen on board said schooner, who, being severally sworn, do depose, declare, and say: That on the 11th day of June, now last past, they sailed from Dennysville in said schooner Hero, fitted for a fishing cruise of six weeks, and arrived on Monday morning, being the 14th of said June, on the fishing ground called the Grand Menan Banks, from nine to twelve marine miles from land, and commenced fishing; that they continued to fish till Wednesday, the 16th day of said month, when the schooner struck adrift. It was then about 9 o'clock a. m. Got under way immediately and attempted to regain the fishing ground, but could not effect it by reason of a strong tide. Kept beating to windward towards the fishing ground, and, the tide slacking, got within about half a mile of it, and from six to nine miles from any land, when an armed boat, said to belong to the British armed brig Dotterel, fired two muskets, loaded with balls, across said schooner Hero. She was rounded to, and an officer came on board and took forcible possession of the vessel and her papers.

The declarants further depose and say, that they were kept sometimes on board said schooner, sometimes on board the Dotterel or some of her boats, from that time till the twenty-ninth day of said June, and were allowed for a part of this time only one meal per day. That they were every night in harbor and near home; but though they earnestly solicited to be set on shore, it was not granted them, but were forced, by threats and menaces that they would be cut in pieces in case of refusal, to do the same duty as the common British sailors. They were at last landed at St. John, a distance of eighty miles from Dennysville, and even subjected to great expense and distress in getting home.

The declarants further say, that said schooner Hero has been manned and armed, and is still made use of as a tender for said brig Dotterel, and has never been libelled or sent in for trial. And the said Harding Clark for himself saith, that when he was set on shore at St. John his pocket book and private papers were taken from him and detained.

Wherefore they do protest, and I, the said notary, in their behalf, do solemnly protest, against the winds, seas, tides, armed boats, pirates, the wanton and flagrant abuse of power, and whatsoever else that caused the seizure and detention of said schooner Hero, and for all damages, costs, and expenses sustained, and to be sustained, by reason of such illegal and wanton detention of said schooner as aforesaid; and I, the said notary, do aver that the same was caused, not by a breach of the revenue laws of Great Britain and the United States respecting the fisheries, done, made, or committed by said schooner Hero, but was wholly without any fault on the part of said schooner, or any person thereof, but an act of piracy committed on the high seas without a pretence of authority.

In faith whereof, I, the said notary, have hereunto set my hand and affixed my seal of office the day and year first above written.

SOLOMON THAYER, *Notary Public.*
HARDING CLARK.
WILLIAM H. N. BROWN.
EPHRAIM CLARK.

United States of America, *State of Maine, Washington, ss.*

To all whom it may or doth concern: Know ye that on the twenty-third day of July, in the year of our Lord eighteen hundred and twenty-four, before me, Solomon Thayer, notary public, by legal authority duly appointed, commissioned, and sworn, and dwelling in Lubec, State and county aforesaid, personally appeared Charles Tabbut, master of the fishing schooner William, of Addison, and noted his protest; and now, on the twenty-third day of August, anno Domini eighteen hundred and twenty-four, he again appears to extend the same, and with him also appear Thomas Wright, Benjamin Reynolds, and Josiah W. Perry, fishermen belonging to said schooner William, who, being severally sworn, do declare and say: That, on the first day of July, now last past, they sailed in said schooner William on a fishing cruise in the Bay of Fundy, and anchored between what is called Mur-ground and the Grand Menan Banks, a distance from nine to fifteen miles from land; that they continued there at anchor and fishing till the fourteenth day of said July, when, having only fifteen gallons of water on board, and that unfit for use, it was thought prudent and necessary to run into Gull Cove, Grand Menan, and obtain a supply. Arrived at Gull Cove on the fifteenth of said July, at 2 p. m., and came to anchor, the fog being extremely dense. The sails of the William were not handed, as it was intended to obtain water with all possible despatch and return to the fishing ground. They had gone below, and were taking dinner, and not more than ten minutes from the time of anchoring, the boat not having been launched from the deck to go on shore, when they were boarded by an armed launch, commanded by one Jones, an officer of the English gun brig Dotterel, who demanded their business, their papers, and took forcible possession of the vessel. Jones sent his men below to examine the water casks and ascertain what quantity of water there was on board the William. They reported there were three half casks of water below, one empty barrel, and one with the hoops off. Mr. Jones was then told by these declarants that the report of his men was incorrect, that one barrel only had any water in it, and that but fifteen gallons, completely unfit for use; that besides this there was a half barrel of molasses and a barrel with five or six gallons of beer. Mr. Jones ordered the William under way, took her in nearer the shore, moored her in a dangerous place and stripped her, and took the William's boat, carried it on shore, and gave out word that if any of the William's crew attempted to go on shore, or if any boat was called alongside, or if he heard any noise on board, he would shoot them. They were thus left till near sunset without a drop of water fit to drink; though they frequently hailed Mr. Jones as he passed and repassed, and stated to him their distress and begged for water, their prayer was wholly disregarded. About sunsetting a vessel from Campo Bello anchored alongside, and by permission of the captain thereof they obtained from the shore a two-gallon keg filled with water.

These declarants further say, that when Mr. Jones became satisfied there was no water fit for use on board the William, in a violent rage, he said "the American fishermen had been damned saucy to the inhabitants on Grand Menan." The master of the William, one of these declarants, replied that such an allegation did not apply to his vessel; that he had always used the inhabitants as he wished to be treated himself. Jones then said "it was damned well for him he had done so, for otherwise he should have confined him to the deck and cut him into ounce pieces." To this the master of the William replied he should not give himself any uneasiness on that account. Jones, with an oath, replied to this, "damn you, I will confine you to the deck and lash a pump brake across your mouth."

The declarants further say that, on the next day, the William was got under way, and taken to St. Andrew's and stripped; that she had over one hundred and twenty quintals of fish on board when she was captured. Wherefore, they do protest, and I, the said notary, in their behalf, do solemnly protest, against said Jones and the armed men under his command, against pirates and piratical seizures, and detentions of American fishermen, and whatsoever else caused the forcible detention of said schooner William, and for all expenses, costs, charges, and damages paid or sustained, or to be paid, or sustained, by reason of said detention. And I, the said notary, do solemnly aver and declare that said detention was not by reason of any breach of the revenue laws of Great Britain, or of the province of New Brunswick, done or committed by said schooner William, or any one on board thereof, but an unauthorized, a wanton, a piratical act of the said Jones and his abettors.

CHARLES TABBUT.
BENJAMIN REYNOLDS.
JOSIAH W. PERRY.
THOMAS WRIGHT.

In faith whereof, I have hereunto affixed my seal of office, this twenty-third day of August, anno Domini eighteen hundred and twenty-four.

UNITED STATES OF AMERICA, *State of Maine, Washington,* ss.

Be it known to all to whom these presents may come: That on this twenty-fourth day of July, in the year of our Lord one thousand eight hundred and twenty-four, before me, Solomon Thayer, notary public, by legal authority duly commissioned and sworn, and residing at Lubec, State and county aforesaid, personally appeared Hubbard Hunt, junior, mate of the schooner Galeon, of Lubec, Nehemiah Small, Daniel Jay, junior, John Hunt, and Edwin Hunt, sharesmen, belonging to said schooner, who, being severally sworn, do depose and say: That on the first day of July, now current, they sailed in the said schooner from Lubec on a fishing cruise to the Grand Menan Banks. On their way thither, and while doubling round the southerly end of Grand Menan, distant about six miles, with their colors at masthead, they were fired into by the St. Andrew's cutter, McMaster commander, and ordered to come under said cutter's lee. Mr. Baxter, an officer of said cutter, came on board and demanded her papers, sent his men into the hold to search her, and went himself for the same purpose into the cabin. After detaining the Galeon about half an hour, she was permitted to proceed. Arrived on the Banks the same day and commenced fishing; on the fifteenth day of said month, having only five gallons of water on board and no wood, run in for Grand Menan to get a supply. Arrived at Beal's Passage about half-past 7 p. m.; fog quite thick; went on shore and got two barrels of water and a boat load of wood by permission of Charles Blumorten, the owner; it was then about 9 o'clock of the same evening. Having got supper, and intending to get under way as soon as the landmarks could be discerned to return to the Banks, they were boarded by an armed boat belonging to the English brig Dotterell, and their papers demanded and taken. The vessel was immediately got under way by order of Mr. Jones, the commander of the armed boat, and run into Gull Cove. The next day the Galeon was taken to St. Andrew's, stripped, and made fast in the King's dock.

The declarants further depose and say, that from the time they left Lubec, on the first day of said July, until they run in in distress for want of wood and water, on the evening of the fifteenth of said month, they had never been within three marine miles of Grand Menan, nor caught, or attempted to catch, any fish within from ten to twenty miles thereof. That after they were taken, the officer, Mr. Jones, positively promised them that he would release the Galeon as soon as she arrived at St. Andrew's; and it was their reliance on his promise, and the belief he could not be so wanton as to add insult to injury, but that he would redeem his word, that they have not protested before. She is still retained. Wherefore they now protest, and I, the said notary, in their behalf, do solemnly protest, against the flagrant abuse of law (and the right granted to American fishermen by treaty) by armed boats under the British flag, without a pretence of authority; against pirates, the winds, seas, and whatsoever else may have been the cause of the capture and detention of the Galeon; and I do aver that the capture and detention was not by reason of a violation of any revenue law of Great Britain, or an infraction of any privileges granted by the convention, done or committed by said Galeon or any of her crew, but was done without a pretence of right, and substantially an act of piracy.

HUBBARD HUNT, Jr.
NEHEMIAH SMALL.
DANIEL TAYLOR, Jr.
JOHN HUNT.
EDWIN HUNT.

In faith whereof, I, the said notary, have hereunto set my hand and seal of office, the day and year first above written.

SOLOMON THAYER, *Notary Public.*

UNITED STATES OF AMERICA, *State of Maine, Washington, ss.*

To all to whom this public instrument of protest may come: Be it known, that on the 22d day of June, now last past, before me, Solomon Thayer, notary public, by legal authority duly commissioned and sworn, and dwelling at Lubec, county and State aforesaid, personally appeared James Woodward, master of the fishing schooner Pilgrim, of Lubec, and noted his protest; and now, on this 7th day of August, in the year of our Lord one thousand eight hundred and twenty-four, he again appears, and with him also appear Jacob Winslow and James Woodward, jr., fishermen, who, being severally sworn, do depose, declare, and say: That on the 8th day of June aforesaid they sailed from Lubec on a fishing voyage to the Grand Menan Bank, so called, but, owing to thick weather and head winds, did not get on the fishing ground till Monday, the 14th day of said June. They then came to anchor (the wind blowing quite fresh and a high sea) twelve miles from any land. At 4 p. m. of the same day they found the vessel drifting; hauled in the cable, and found the anchor broke close to the stock. Made sail and got on to another part of the fishing ground, nine miles from land, and then continued to fish till Wednesday, the 16th day of said June; but finding their only remaining anchor too light to hold the vessel in so strong a current, weighed it and stood for Lubec to obtain a new one. The same day, at about 3 p. m., were fired upon and brought to by an armed boat belonging to the English armed brig Dotterel, who took their papers, and ordered Jacob Winslow and Benjamin Scott, fishermen, on board the tender, putting one seaman and one marine on board the Pilgrim. This was done while the Pilgrim was under way, and from four to six miles from land. The seamen in the Pilgrim were ordered to follow the tender, which then steered east and still further from land, and took forcible possession of the American schooner Hero, Harding Clark master, also under sail and standing for Lubec. Both vessels were then taken into Flagg's Cove, Grand Menan, and anchored. On Thursday, the 17th of said June, asked permission to be set on shore, but were denied. On the 18th got under way and stood for the Wolf islands; at 6 p. m. both vessels were ordered to heave to, and the Pilgrim's boat to be sent on board the tender. The officer then compelled one of these declarants, James Woodward, jr., only seventeen years of age, to row the boat alone, cross-handed, a distance of not less than four miles, to board vessels lying at the easterly part of the Wolf islands, and then to row back again to the tender. On the officer's return to the tender he ordered the Pilgrim to stand in for the eastern Wolf island; and these declarants were compelled to row her (it being then a dead calm) for four miles to gain said place, where she was anchored for the night. On the 19th, at 8 a. m., got under way and stood to Beaver harbor, and came to anchor; were then forced to unbend the sails of the Pilgrim and stow them below. On the 20th, at 8 a. m., were ordered to bend the sails and get under way, which was done; and, after beating with the wind S.SE. and a flood tide for three hours, were ordered back to Beaver harbor. On the 21st, at 6 a. m., were ordered to get under way; beat all day against a strong head wind, and at night anchored in Mason's Bay.

At 1 o'clock the next morning, these declarants, knowing that the Pilgrim had violated no law, nor any treaty or convention between the United States and Great Britain, and that they were detained without the pretence of authority on the part of the officer of the armed boat, got said Pilgrim under way without orders, and stood for Lubec, where they arrived on the said 22d day of June, with the loss of boat, papers, a fowling-piece, a pistol, and a great quantity of powder and shot, which were plundered from them by said armed boat.

Wherefore they do protest, and I, the said notary, in their behalf, do solemnly protest against said armed boat and the officer and men on board thereof; against pirates and unlawful captures on the high seas; against winds, tides, and whatsoever else caused the detention of said schooner Pilgrim and the loss of her papers, boat, &c.; and I, the said notary, do aver that it was not by reason of a violation of any revenue law of Great Britain, committed by said schooner Pilgrim, or any of her crew, but a wanton insult upon the American flag, on the high seas, without a shadow of excuse, by an officer of the British Navy.

JAMES WOODWARD, Sr.
JACOB WINSLOW.
JAMES WOODWARD, Jr.

In faith whereof, I have hereunto set my hand and affixed my seal of office, this seventh day of August, [L. s.] in the year of our Lord one thousand eight hundred and twenty-four.

SOLOMON THAYER, *Notary Public.*

Mr. Brent to Mr. Addington, dated September 21, 1824.

SIR: I have the honor to transmit to you copies of some additional papers which have been received at this office, upon the subject of the interruption, likewise given by the same armed British brig Dotterel, to vessels of the United States, employed in the prosecution of the fishery in the bay of Passamaquoddy, and elsewhere in the same neighborhood, as particularly exemplified in the cases of the two schooners, William and Rebecca, which are fully stated in the inclosures, and to pray the interposition of your good offices in behalf also of the owners of these vessels towards obtaining for them the indemnity to which they may be justly entitled.

I have the honor to be, with high consideration, sir, your obedient and humble servant,

DANIEL BRENT.

STATE OF MAINE, *County of Washington.*

COLUMBIA, *September 6, 1824.*

SIR: Inclosed is a protest on account of the capture of the fishing schooner William, of Addison, in the county aforesaid, belonging to and owned by the subscribers, citizens of the United States. These papers are inclosed for the purpose of procuring redress for the injury and loss sustained. The said schooner William was forty-one tons burden and but four years old, with a new suit of sails and rigging, cables, anchors, &c., valued at $1,000 00
120 quintals fish on board, at $3 per quintal... 360 00
Bounty for said schooner... 162 62
Damages in consequence of said capture.. 500 00

                                                                            2,022 62

All requisite evidence, should further be needed, will be furnished; and the subscribers pray that such measures may be adopted as shall lead to a redress for the loss and damage by them sustained.

WILLIAM WASS.
WILLIAM NASH.

Hon. JOHN Q. ADAMS, *Secretary of the Department of State.*

STATE OF MAINE, *County of Washington.*

COLUMBIA, *September 6, 1824.*

SIR: The unjustifiable seizure and confiscation of certain fishing vessels in the waters of Passamaquoddy bay, it is hoped, will deserve and receive the attention of Government. Inclosed is a protest against the capture of the schooner Rebecca, of Addison, in the county aforesaid, the property of Wilmot Wass, of the said Addison, a citizen of the United States.
The schooner Rebecca, valued at.. $600 00
25 quintals fish, at $3.. 75 00
Bounty 94 50
Damage in consequence of capture.. 300 00

                                                                            1,069 50

In behalf of said Wass, I have to request that such measures may be adopted as will lead to redress of the loss and injury sustained by him.

STEPHEN EMERY, for
WILMOT WASS.

Hon. JOHN Q. ADAMS, *Secretary of the Department of State.*

Charles Tabbuts, master of the schooner William, of Addison, on oath, deposeth and saith: That he sailed on board said schooner, on a fishing cruise, on the 1st day of July, 1824; anchored between what is called the Grand Menan Banks and the Mur-ground; continued at anchor and fishing till the 14th of July, when, having on board only fifteen gallons of water, and that unfit for use, it was determined best to run into Gull Cove and obtain a barrel of water; arrived there on the 15th, about 2 p. m., and came to anchor; the fog very thick; did not hand the sails, as we intended to get the water on board and go back. While below and taking dinner, and not more than ten minutes from the time of anchoring, our boat still on deck, we were boarded by a Mr. Jones, an officer of the Dotterel, our papers demanded and taken into his possession. He demanded our reasons for being there, and was told them. He sent his men below to see how much water we had; they reported that there were three and a half barrels of water below, one empty barrel, and one with the hoops off. Mr. Jones was then told by me that there was no cask but one that had any water in it, and that had only fifteen gallons, and so bad it could not be used; that there was one half barrel of molasses, and a barrel with five or six gallons of beer. Mr. Jones ordered the William under way, took her in towards the shore, moored her in a dangerous place, and stripped her; took the boat and carried her on shore, and gave orders that if any of the William's crew went on shore, or any boat was called alongside, or if he heard any noise on board, he would shoot us. We were thus left without a drop of water fit to drink till sunset; though we frequently hailed Mr. Jones, and stated our distress, as he passed us, we were wholly disregarded. About sunset a vessel from Campo Bello anchored alongside, and, by permission of the master, the deponent went on shore and got a two-gallon keg of   e . On the 16th instant the William was got under way by Mr. Jones and taken to St. Andrew's at r

The deponent further saith, that when Mr. Jones found there was no water on board fit for use, in a violent rage he told this deponent that the American fishermen had been damned saucy to the inhabitants. The deponent replied that he had not been saucy to the inhabitants, but had always used them as he wished to be used himself. Jones replied that it was damned well for me that I had been so, or he would otherwise confine me to the deck and cut me into ounce pieces. I told him that I should not give myself any uneasiness on that account. Then, with an oath, he said, damn you, I will confine you to the deck and lash a pump-brake across your mouth.

CHARLES TABBUTS.

STATE OF MAINE, *Washington, ss.*

On this 23d day of July, 1824, personally appeared before me Charles Tabbuts, and made solemn oath to the truth of the foregoing statement by him subscribed.

' SOLOMON THAYER,
Justice of the Peace and Notary Public.

Mr. Brent to Mr. Shepley, Attorney of United States for the District of Maine.

DEPARTMENT OF STATE, *Washington, October 8, 1824.*

SIR: In the absence of the Secretary, I have the honor to transmit to you the inclosed copy of a letter from Mr. Addington, the British chargé d'affaires at this place, in answer to remonstrances from this Department, upon the complaints which were lately exhibited to it by sundry citizens of the United States, residing in the State of Maine, and engaged in the fisheries, against the commander of the British armed brig Dotterel, for interruptions and other injuries which they state to have experienced at the instance and under the orders of that officer, in the prosecution of their accustomed employment during the present season, and requesting his good offices towards obtaining for them the redress to which they may be entitled; and I beg leave, at the same time, to trouble you with copies of the letters and documents referred to, and inclosed in Mr. Addington's letter, which exhibit serious complaints on the part of the British authorities against all or very many of the same individuals, in reference to the subject-matter of their own complaints. I do this with the request that, as soon as convenient, you would have the goodness to institute an inquiry into the circumstances particularly complained of by the British chargé d'affaires, and communicate the result to this Department, that the Secretary may be enabled, with the advantage of the counter statement to be thus expected, as I doubt not he will, to give Mr. Addington satisfactory explanations in relation to the transactions complained of by him; or otherwise to direct such proceedings to be had as the circumstances of the whole case shall render advisable and proper.

I am, with great respect, sir, your obedient and humble servant,

DANIEL BRENT.

Mr. Addington to Mr. Adams.

WASHINGTON, *October 5, 1824.*

SIR: I have the honor to acknowledge the receipt of two letters, one dated the 8th and the other the 21st ultimo, which Mr. Brent addressed to me, in pursuance of instructions from you, relative to certain American fishing vessels averred to have been detained, in violation of the terms of the convention of 1818, by his Majesty's sloop Dotterel, in the Bay of Fundy, in the months of June and July last.

I shall not fail to communicate, without loss of time, the whole of the papers relative to this matter to the Admiral commanding his Majesty's naval forces at Halifax; and in so doing shall strongly recommend that a full and impartial investigation be made into the merits of the various cases therein reported, the result of which shall be forthwith imparted to you whenever it comes to my knowledge.

Meantime, sir, I must inform you that a report of those very occurrences, of a nature very different from that made by the individuals to you, has reached me from Rear-Admiral Lake, of whose letter, together with its inclosures, I have the honor to transmit to you copies herewith.

It is therein made to appear that the fishing vessels above mentioned were detained by the Dotterel solely on account of their having been detected in the commission of a direct infraction of the treaties existing between the two nations, having, in fact, been found pursuing their occupation without the view of the boundaries assigned to them by the terms of the convention of 1818.

On this point, however, the parties are at issue, each stating his case according to his own view of it. Thus far, therefore, there is ground for a candid and impartial investigation on both sides. Such I have recommended to Admiral Lake, and such, I trust, you will also cause to be instituted here.

But there is another point, sir, on which I lament that there should be no ground for doubt or hesitation as to the course which I have to pursue.

By a perusal of the inclosed documents you will perceive that, after the detention of the Reindeer and Ruby by the master of the Dotterel, and while on their way to St. Andrew's, "an attack was made on those vessels by two schooners and an open boat, *under American colors, full of armed men, with muskets and fixed bayonets,* amounting to about one hundred, headed by a Mr. Howard, of Eastport, who is said to be a captain in the United States militia, in consequence of which the master thought it most prudent to surrender to such superior force."

This, sir, is an outrage of such a nature as to leave me no other alternative than to make a formal demand from the American Government for the infliction of punishment on the offenders.

Whether the vessels were legally detained or not, such an act of violence will bear no justification. If individuals are permitted to expound the stipulations of treaties for themselves, with arms in their hands, the preservation of harmony and good understanding between nations can no longer be hoped for.

I am disposed (no person can be more so) to act fairly and openly by the citizens of this Republic, wherever they have just ground of complaint against British authorities, and shall accordingly take every measure for ascertaining whether the detention of the vessels in question was legal or not.

If it was not legal, you have abundant proof, sir, in your own hands of the disposition of his Majesty's Government to afford the most prompt and equitable redress to the parties aggrieved. I allude to the case of the American schooner Charles, detained and employed as a tender last year by his Majesty's sloop Argus. That act, you will recollect, was condemned as illegal by his Majesty's ministers, and restitution ordered to be made to the parties who suffered through the exercise of it, although otherwise liable, by the illegality of their conduct, to the entire loss of their property.

But in the meantime, sir, it becomes my duty to demand reparation, by the punishment of the transgressors, for the act of violence perpetrated on persons bearing his Majesty's commission, while engaged in the discharge of their public duties.

I feel confident, sir, that you will view this outrage in the same light as myself, and consider such conduct equally dangerous to the peace and well being of the two countries; and I have no doubt that you will see the expediency of causing immediate proceedings to be instituted against the principal actors in this disgraceful scene.

I beg, sir, that you will accept the renewed assurances of my distinguished consideration,

H. U. ADDINGTON.

Rear-Admiral Lake to Mr. Addington.

HALIFAX, *September* 9, 1824.

SIR: I have the honor to transmit to you a copy of a letter, dated 26th ultimo, from Captain Hoare, of his Majesty's sloop Dotterel, with its inclosure from Mr. John Jones, master of that sloop; also copies of two letters from Captain Hoare, dated the 2d instant, one of them containing a copy of the affidavit therein mentioned.

By the first of these communications you will perceive that two American vessels, called the Reindeer and Ruby, were seized by the master of the Dotterel in Two Island harbor, Grand Menan, on the 26th of July, for a breach of the treaty between Great Britain and the United States; and that on the evening of the same day, when abreast of Harbor de Lute, proceeding to St. Andrew's, an attack was made on the vessels in question by two schooners and an open boat, under American colors, full of armed men, with muskets and fixed bayonets, amounting to about one hundred, having the appearance of militia men, and headed by a Mr. Howard, of Eastport, who is said to be a captain in the United States militia; in consequence of which, the master thought it most prudent to surrender to such superior force.

Captain Hoare's next letter mentions his having, on the 29th ultimo, on his passage to Halifax, fallen in with the American schooner Madison, (by her papers, Ansel Coggins master,) which he was informed was one of the vessels to which the men belonged who rescued the before mentioned vessels from his master; and that, finding on board this vessel a man, named Daniel Rumney, whom one of the marines of the Dotterel identified as one of the persons concerned in the rescue, Captain Hoare thought proper to detain the vessel, and take Rumney on board the Dotterel as a prisoner.

Captain Hoare's other letter refers to the Pilgrim, an American fishing vessel, seized by him at Grand Menan, in June last, for a breach of the treaty; which vessel was afterwards rescued by some of her crew, in conjunction with one of the men whom Captain Hoare had put in charge of her; and the said vessel having been fallen in with on the 29th ultimo, and a man named Winslow, who, Captain Hoare was informed, was one of those actively engaged in the forcible rescue of the said vessel, she was taken possession of, and the man (Winslow) put on board the Dotterel as a prisoner.

As in these transactions his Majesty's officers have been assaulted in the execution of their duty by armed subjects of the United States, and the property of which they had, in his Majesty's name, taken lawful possession, rescued from them, in violation of the treaty subsisting between Great Britain and the United States, I consider it necessary that the subject should be brought officially before the American Government, in order that steps may be taken to prevent the continuance of such proceedings, and therefore request you will be pleased to adopt such measures on the occasion as shall appear to you to be necessary.

I have the honor to be, &c.,

W. T. LAKE, *Rear-Admiral and Commander-in-chief.*

Captain Hoare to Rear-Admiral Lake.

HIS MAJESTY'S SLOOP DOTTEREL, *August* 26, 1824.

SIR: I have the honor to inclose the copy of a letter from the master of his Majesty's sloop under my command, detailing the circumstances of his having been attacked off Campo Bello by two armed schooners under American colors, and that two American fishing vessels he had detained were taken from him and carried into Eastport.

I have the honor, &c.,

RICHARD HOARE, *Commander.*

John Jones, master, to Captain Hoare, of His Majesty's Sloop Dotterel.

HIS MAJESTY'S SLOOP DOTTEREL'S BOAT, *St. Andrew's, N. B., July* 27, 1824.

SIR: I beg leave to represent that on the 25th instant, when cruising in the yawl, in pursuance of your orders, off the Grand Menan for the protection of our fisheries, I received information of several American fishing vessels being at anchor at Two Island harbor, and that two of them, namely, Reindeer and Ruby, of Lubec, were at White Island harbor on the 24th, where they got their wood and water, and that, on their anchoring, they fired their muskets, and told the inhabitants they were armed, and would not allow any man-of-war's boat to board them; and after they had their supplies they shifted to Two Island harbor, Grand Menan.

I made sail from Gull Cove, and at daylight, the 26th, observed four schooners at anchor at Two Island harbor, which vessels got under way on our appearing; when I got close to three of them they lashed alongside each other, and all hands, about thirty in number, went on board the middle one with their fire-arms and fish spears. I desired them to separate, which they refused to do until I threatened to fire on them. On boarding, they proved to be the Reindeer, master's name Small, and Ruby, master's name Small, (brothers,) of Lubec, two fishing vessels, and Friend's shallop, of the same place.

It being fine weather, and they not being in want of wood or water, I detained the Reindeer and Ruby, and put their crew, with the exception of their masters, on board the two Americans chooners, with provisions, for a passage to Lubec, and made sail in the Reindeer and Ruby for St. Andrew's, through East Quoddy. About 6 p. m., when abreast of Harbor de Lute, I observed two schooners and an open boat, full of armed men, muskets and fixed bayonets, hoisting American colors; one of them went alongside. Mr. Towneau, in the Ruby, boarded and took the arms from him and his three men; the one abreast of me was kept off for about a quarter of an hour, when they commenced firing into us. Though with great reluctance, I thought it most prudent to surrender to such superior force, having but four men, one musket, and three cutlasses. On delivering them up, I found there were in the two schooners about a hundred armed men, including the crews of the schooners, about thirty in number, the rest having the appearance of l   men, and headed by a Mr. Howard, of Eastport, said to be a captain in the United States mililiaitia

I have the honor to be, &c., .

JOHN JONES, *Master*.

Captain Hoare to Rear-Admiral Lake.

His Majesty's Sloop Dotterel, *Halifax Harbor, September 2,* 1824.

Sir: I have the honor to inform you that, while running past the Outer Bank of the Grand Menan, on the 29th ultimo, on my passage to this place, I fell in with the Madison, American fishing schooner, (by her papers, Ansel Coggins master,) and as I was informed by Winslow, one of the crew of the Pilgrim, American fishing vessel, and who was then on board the Dotterel, that she was one of the schooners that attacked the master off Harbor de Lute on the 26th of July, and the master having affirmed that the name of the vessel that attacked him was the Madison, though he cannot swear to the vessel, as all that description of vessels are so much alike, but he believes her to be the same; and, on the crew coming on board the Dotterel, one of them, Daniel Rumney, was immediately recognized by William Vickery, one of the marines in the boat with the master, as being one of those who were in and took an active part in the vessel that attacked them, and on boarding the said Madison it was discovered the master had left her, and, as she had her boat out, I have no doubt he had gone on board one of the other fishing vessels to escape detection, as he would have been immediately recognized by the master; and as some dates on the back of the papers relative to her arrival and leaving Lubec at different periods prove her to have been at Lubec about the time of the master's having been attacked; these circumstances, together, left no doubt in my mind of her being the Madison, that, with another schooner, named the Diligence, attacked the master off Harbor de Lute on the 26th of July, and I therefore took possession of her, and ordered her to this port; as it appears to me, sir, that the circumstance of two armed schooners attacking and taking from a British officer and boat's crew two vessels he had legally detained is an act of piracy, and all those concerned therein ought to be punished.

I have, for the present, detained Daniel Rumney on board, and I have to request you will be pleased to solicit the advice of the Attorney General on this important subject, that I may be guided thereby in my proceedings relative to the said Daniel Rumney.

I have the honor to be, &c.,

RICHARD HOARE, *Commander.*

Captain Hoare to Admiral Lake.

His Majesty's Sloop Dotterel, *Halifax, September 2,* 1824.

Sir: I have the honor to inform you that, while running past the Outer Bank of the Grand Menan, on the 29th ultimo, on my way to this port, I fell in with the Pilgrim, American fishing schooner, and as this vessel had been taken by one of my boats on the 16th of June, at Grand Menan, for infringing the treaty, but was retaken by the crew, aided by James Martin, one of the two men put in charge of her, I have taken possession of, and ordered her to this port.

Inclosed, sir, is the copy of an affidavit, made by William Paine (marine) and the other man in charge of the Pilgrim, on their arrival at Lubec, by which affidavit you will see, sir, that a man by the name of Winslow, one of the crew of the Pilgrim, was the most active person in retaking her, and that he forced the cutlass from William Paine and obliged him to go below. Under these circumstances, I felt I should be justified in considering him a prisoner, and, as such, he now remains on board the Dotterel. That he ought to be punished in some way that may deter others of his nation from committing the same offence under similar circumstances, I am sure, sir, you will think necessary.

I have, therefore, to request you will be pleased to solicit the advice of the Attorney General on this important point, that I may be governed thereby in my proceedings.

I have the honor to be, &c., &c.,

RICHARD HOARE, *Commander.*

Admiral Lake.

Copy of the inclosure in the foregoing letter.

William Paine, one of the marines belonging to his Britannic Majesty's brig the Dotterel, maketh oath and saith: That, on Wednesday last, the American fishing boat Pilgrim was seized for a violation of the treaty between the United States and Great Britain, and the deponent, with James Martin, seaman, put on board to take charge of her; that on the night of the 21st instant, between the hours of 11 and 12, it being Martin's watch, he, this deponent, was awoke from sleep by the roll of the vessel; that he attempted to go on deck, but found the companion doors shut; this deponent then broke open the companion doors, armed himself, and went on deck, and ordered Captain Woodward, the master of the boat, then at the helm, to put the boat about; he refused; Martin was rowing; this deponent went forward and ordered him to drop the oar; but he would not, till this deponent threatened to cut his head off if he did not; while this deponent was thus endeavoring to get the vessel about, Winslow and Martin suddenly sprung upon him, and obliged him to go below. This deponent was then brought to this place in the said boat Pilgrim against his will, and against all the exertions in his power to make.

his

WILLIAM ⋈ PAINE.

mark.

Benjamin Scott, one of the hands on board the Pilgrim, on oath, saith: That the foregoing statement of Mr. William Paine is, according to his best knowledge and belief, substantially true; that he was below when Mr. Paine armed himself and went on deck, and soon after he returned, and said he had been overpowered and his arms taken from him; that the Pilgrim was taken by Woodward and Winslow, aided by Martin, to Lubec. This deponent further saith that Woodward and Winslow both acknowledge that Mr. Paine discharged his duty to the utmost of his power; that superior force alone caused him to surrender his arms.

BENJAMIN SCOTT.

STATE OF MAINE, *Washington, ss.*

To all to whom these presents may come: Know ye, that on this twenty-second day of June, anno Domini 1824, before me, Solomon Thayer, notary public, by legal authority duly commissioned and sworn, and residing at Lubec, personally appeared the aforenamed William Paine and Benjamin Scott, and made solemn oath that the declarations by them personally made and signed were just and true.

In testimonium veritatis,

SOLOMON THAYER, *Notary Public.*

NEW BRUNSWICK, *Charlotte County, ss.*

HALIFAX, *September* 2, 1824.

I, the undersigned, one of his Majesty's justices of the peace in and for the said county, residing in Campo Bello, do hereby certify that on the twenty-third day of June, 1824, William Paine, the person in the annexed instrument mentioned, appeared before me, and declared the facts therein contained, which appear to me to be correct. That Solomon Thayer is a notary public for the county of Washington, in the Province of Maine, United States, duly appointed, and that full faith and credit may be given to his attestation.

D. OWEN, *J. P.*

RICHARD HOARE, *Commander of his Majesty's sloop Dotterel.*

Mr. Shepley to Mr. Adams.

SACO, *November* 16, 1824.

SIR: Having been requested by letter from Mr. Brent, under date of the seventh of October last, to institute an inquiry into the circumstances particularly complained of by the British chargé d'affaires, and to communicate the result to the Department, I have now the honor to inform you that I repaired to and near to the places of residence of the parties to those transactions, called upon them and took their statements under oath, which are herewith inclosed, and by which you will be enabled to understand fully and correctly the whole history, not only of the circumstances complained of, but of all the proceedings of the captain of the British armed brig Dotterel in relation to our fishermen, and their proceedings to protect themselves, as they supposed, from the losses occasioned by the conduct of the captain of the Dotterel.

It may, I think, sir, with safety be affirmed that the inclosed documents (being the affidavits of twenty-seven individuals, and relating to thirteen schooners and boats and one small boat,) present a fair and faithful history of all the proceedings this season between our fishermen and the officers of that vessel.

I have been particularly cautious, in taking the testimony, to give it without coloring it by the feelings of excitement manifested by our citizens.

Inclosed, also, is a bill of services and expenses for attending to the business.

With the highest respect, I am, sir, your most obedient servant,

ETHER SHEPLEY, *District Attorney.*

I, Robert Small, master of the schooner Reindeer, of Lubec, on oath, testify and say: That it is my practice, in fitting out for the fisheries, to fill the barrels which I use for oil barrels with water, and, as I use the water and empty the barrels, to fill them with oil. I purchased the barrels while fitting out this cruise, and did not see them till after filled; there were eight filled with water. We left the harbor the twenty-sixth day of July, and proceeded on the fishing ground near Grand Menan Bank; continued to fish two or three days, and then discovered that the water in six of my barrels was salt, so that I could not use it, the barrels having been used for salting beef and pork. Finding my water all bad and expended, ran in to Two Island harbor for water, and went on shore and obtained my water; laid there till the next morning, becalmed; then made sail for the Banks; got out about a mile and a half or two miles, and the wind died away and left me becalmed again; soon discovered the barge of the British armed brig Dotterel, the Ruby, the Friend, and boat Diligence, lying in the same harbor, and near me; the barge came up and fired; ordered the anchor to be dropped, which was done; the master of the barge then ordered us to part— the Ruby and Reindeer being connected by a small line—which was obeyed; the vessels parted; he then ordered the Ruby to drop her anchor, which was done; he then came on board our vessel, the Reindeer, in a great rage; he demanded the papers, which were given him; they then threatened to carve us up like a turkey or a piece of beef, brandishing their cutlasses about our heads; took the crew all out and put them on board the schooner Friend; then took out the crew of the Ruby and put them on board of the schooner Diligence, and ordered the Friend and Diligence off; told them to go off and about their business; then got the Reindeer under way, bound for St. Andrew's, and ordered the Ruby to follow; passing up a little past Harbor de Lute, two other vessels hove down upon us; one, the schooner Madison, came down upon the Reindeer, there being about twenty men on her deck with muskets, but no bayonets upon them; Jones, the master of the barge, being on board of the Reindeer, ordered all hands and directed them to fire into the Madison; I then said to him, if you fire into that vessel, every man of you will be shot; he said, I believe it; he then said, what do they want, and who are they? I said to him, they are my neighbors; they want this vessel, and they will have her; he then laid down his sword and said, I surrender; unlocked his trunk, took out the papers of my vessel and the Ruby and gave them to me; Skipper Coggins then invited him on board the Madison; and upon my assuring him that he might go with perfect safety, he went on board, drank with us, shook hands, and parted with us; went on board his barge, and went off; the Reindeer and Ruby then went home; the vessel has been laid up since, as I did not dare to let her go out; and the crew has been upon charges also; the injury to the owner and crew has been fifteen hundred dollars. I was in no other British harbor, except at Buck's Rock, in Grand Menan, where I went in the night in a heavy blow, and went out again before morning. I saw no person; was not on shore; never fired any musket on the island, nor did I ever state that I was armed or intended to resist; had only one old musket on board; fishermen always carry one or two; the crews of the vessels Reindeer, Ruby, and Diligence, were not on board the middle one or any one of the vessels, nor was there any show of fire-arms or fish spears on board of either of the vessels; they were not lashed together for resistance. This is not only a common practice, but is necessary in this bay, where the tide is very strong and runs in different directions. There was not a gun fired into the Reindeer or at her while in Jones' possession, nor was there a gun fired at all till after Mr. Jones had gone on board the Madison, and then only as an expression of joy; nor was there any gun fired at the Ruby; nor did the Diligence or any person on board of her demand or take any arms from those on board the Ruby when she was retaken; they did ask for one of their own muskets which the barge had taken from them, and it was brought to them; this was after the Ruby had been surrendered. I have not fished any within five to six miles of the land this year. There is no fishing ground nearer the shore, nor any object in going near shore, except for wood and water.

                                                                ROBERT SMALL.
      Sworn to before—   ETHER SHEPLEY.
      NOVEMBER 5, 1824.

Paul Johnson, jr., master of the schooner Sally, of Eastport, on oath, declares: That he sailed the 13th day of May last, fitted out for the fishery on the Labrador coast, and proceeded on the voyage; on the 4th of June, the wind being east and weather coming on thick, thought it prudent to make a harbor, and ran into Shelburne, on the south side of Nova Scotia, and anchored, and was boarded by a boat from the British armed brig Dotterel; was asked what business I had there? I told him I was bound to Labrador, and thought I had a right to make a harbor. The Sally was then ordered under way and carried alongside the brig, and an officer came on board and searched us; was told I had broken the treaty, and should be detained. The next morning my whole crew were taken out and put on board the Dotterel, and my vessel was manned from the Dotterel and sent on a cruise to Cape Negro harbor, about nine miles; there several small vessels were boarded from us; continued there two days, then got under way and proceeded back to Shelburne, and anchored alongside the Dotterel. The captain then sent for me to come on board the brig; went on board; was asked if I was master of the Sally; answered that I was. He said he did not know but my vessel would be condemned if he carried her in, but he should let me go; was told I must pay for my men's rations while they were on board the Dotterel, and I sent on board the Dotterel fifteen pounds of pork and eighteen pounds of bread, and then took my men on board again and proceeded on my voyage.

                                                                PAUL JOHNSON, JR.
      Sworn to before—   ETHER SHEPLEY.
      NOVEMBER 5, 1824.

I, Hebberd Hunt, skipper of the schooner Galeon, of Lubec, Daniel Joy, jr., Nehemiah Small, and John Hunt, hands on board, on oath, testify and say: That we sailed in said schooner from Lubec on the 1st day of July last, fitted out for the fisheries, and proceeded for the fishing ground near Grand Menan Bank; being on the passage, and six miles distant from the southwest head of the island of Great Menan, the provincial revenue cutter, Mr. McMasters master, came down upon us and fired upon us; ordered us under his lee. We hove to under his lee; he sent his boat aboard; demanded the papers, which were delivered; searched the vessel, and then dismissed us, saying we might proceed on to the Banks. We then proceeded to the Bank, and continued to fish fifteen days on and near the Bank, from fifteen to eighteen miles distant from the land; then, being in want of water, having lost part of our water by injury accidentally happening to one of the casks, and being also in want of wood, found it necessary to make a port to obtain wood and water; ran for the island of Grand Menan, and made it a little to the north of Woodward's Cove; obtained our water, and then proceeded to the mouth of Beale's Passage, to obtain wood, being unable to obtain it where we did our water, and there obtained a boat load of drift wood; towards night, being below, eating our only meal for the day, having neither wood nor water to cook before, were boarded from the barge of the British armed brig Dotterel; was asked where the vessel belonged; our papers were demanded and delivered, and the vessel was immediately ordered under way. The skipper stated to the master of the barge that he came only for wood and water; that he had not fished any near the land, and thought he had done nothing which he was not authorized to do by the treaty. The master of the barge said, what is the use of talking about the treaty—damn the treaty; I did not come here to learn my lesson—I learned it before I came. One of the hands, named Joy, was threatened to have his mouth gagged with the pump bolt for conversing with some of the crew of the barge, and was sent on shore on White Head island; the vessel and remainder of the crew were carried to St. Andrew's; the vessel was afterwards sold at St. Andrew's; the crew were turned out of the vessel and everything detained but our wearing apparel. The loss to the owners and crew has been as much as one thousand dollars. We have been on board of the schooner during all the time she was employed this season until taken, and do positively aver that we have not fished at any time within more than six miles of the land, and have not, at any other time, been within any British harbor.

We also testify that, about the middle of June last, being on the gravelly ground about nine miles southeast of the island of Grand Menan, Jacob Winslow came on board of us from the schooner Pilgrim to borrow an anchor, stating that they had lost their anchor; having broken one anchor, could not lend him one. The next day the Pilgrim, being at anchor about half a mile outside of us, and more than nine miles from the land, soon got under way to go home and obtain an anchor; and, having passed us nearly a mile toward the land, a tender to the Dotterel came down upon her, and fired upon her, and took possession of her, she then being eight miles to the southeast of Grand Menan. The same day, about an hour after, the tender took possession of the schooner Hero, of Dennisville, Clark master, she being at the time about a mile outside of us, and ten miles southeast of the island of Grand Menan.

HEBBERD HUNT.
NEHEMIAH SMALL.
DANIEL JOY, Jr.
JOHN HUNT.

Sworn to before—   ETHER SHEPLEY.
November 5, 1824.

John G, Faxon, of Lubec, on oath, declares: That he was the owner of the Galeon when she was captured by a barge of the brig Dotterel. On or about the seventeenth day of July last, the Galeon having been captured and lying in Snug Cove, in Campo Bello, I went on board of her to learn the reasons of her capture. The master, Jones, informed me that he had no other reason for the capture than finding her in a British harbor in Grand Menan. I then asked him if he was not aware that we had a right to go in for wood and water; he said he knew we had that right, but his orders were such that he was obliged to take all, whether in for that purpose or not. I asked if he had known or suspected my vessel had fished near the land. He said he never had. I then asked him if he had no reason to believe they were in want of wood and water when they went in. He said he had, for the wood and water was on deck, not stowed away, when he took them. I then asked him how long he supposed they had been lying at anchor. He said the men told him three-quarters of an hour, and he had no reason to believe otherwise. I then said, by your own statement you ought not to have taken her. He said he should not have taken the Galeon if he had not before taken the William, and should have let her go if he could have done it without excusing the William. He then said, as I have them thus far I must carry them to St. Andrew's, but I give you my word your vessel will not be detained two hours. I then rehearsed that part of the treaty to him authorizing our vessels to go in for wood and water. He said they were authorized to take all vessels within three miles of the land. I afterwards obtained the orders given by the captain to Jones read; they directed him very nearly, and I believe exactly, as follows: "You will consider your cruising ground to be the Menan islands, Campo Bello, and the island of Lubec. You will take all American fishermen found within three miles of the land, except in extreme cases of distress, and carry them to St. Andrew's, there take an inventory of the articles on board and deliver the same to the custom-house."

JOHN G. FAXON.

Sworn to before—   ETHER SHEPLEY.
November 6, 1824.

I further state that I sent an attorney to St. Andrew's to ascertain the expediency of defending the vessel; that I learned through him that I must first give a bond of seventy pounds to pay costs. That the costs must be paid by me whether the defence was successful or not, and that there was little prospect of obtaining a decree of restoration without having an appeal entered; and that the expense attending the trial would probably exceed the value of the property, and therefore declined making any defence.

JOHN G. FAXON.

Sworn to before me,   ETHER SHEPLEY.
November 6, 1824.

I, Jones Wass, of Addison, in the State of Maine, testify and say: That I was master of the schooner Rebecca, of Addison, of the burden of about twenty-seven tons; that I sailed from Addison on the first day of July, 1824, in the said schooner, fitted out for the fisheries; that I proceeded in said schooner and made the "Mur-ground," about fifteen miles southeast of the island of Grand Menan, the same day, and anchored the next morning; caught a few quintals of fish; it came on to blow fresh, and I went in and anchored about half a mile from land, under the island of Grand Menan; went on shore in a boat with a barrel and obtained a barrel of water, for which I went to the island; and having put the water on board, got under way, and, standing off. to the fishing ground, perceived the barge of the British gun brig Dotterel giving chase, and continued to proceed on the same course, the barge still pursuing till evening, it being about 3 o'clock p. m. when we left the island, the barge firing a number of times; at dark we lost sight of the barge, being then near the Nova Scotia shore; then returned partly back to the fishing ground and hove to under the foresail, and the next morning came in and anchored at Gull Cove, in the island of Grand Menan, where were six other American vessels; got under way again an hour after sunrise and stood out to sea; the wind blew so fresh that we could not anchor on the fishing ground that day, and we returned and anchored again at Gull Cove. The next morning, being the fourth of July, got under way and proceeded to the fishing ground first mentioned, and on Monday, the fifth, continued on the Mur-ground, fishing; on Tuesday, the sixth of. July, in the morning, the wind blowing fresh, we hove up and laid to under her foresail,.and about 8 o'clock a. m., weather being thick, and nearly out of wood, went into or near Gull Cove. About 10 o'clock the barge came alongside, all hands being employed in dressing fish, and ordered us under way, and said he was going to carry us into St. John's; demanded my papers, which were given up. I declined navigating my vessel by order from the barge, and the master of the barge directed his own crew to get her under way, which was done. We were carried to St. John's in the Rebecca, and put ashore, and we made the best of our way home, leaving the vessel. She now lies at the wharf in St. John's. No libel or proceedings have ever been instituted against the Rebecca that I can learn; and have learned from the Collector of the port of St..Andrew's that a few days since she had not been libelled. The Rebecca was owned wholly in Addison by Wilmot Wass, Lemuel Wass, and myself. The place in Grand Menan called Gull Cove had been formerly pointed out by the British authorities, on the island as well as on the water, as the place where we should be permitted to anchor and throw the "gurry" overboard. The loss to the owners must be at least seven hundred dollars.

·   ·   : ·· JONES WASS. .

Sworn to before me,   ETHER SHEPLEY.
November 1, 1824. .

I, John Wright, on oath, declare: That I was mate on board of the Rebecca, and that all the facts above stated in the affidavit of Jones Wass, which has been read to me, are true.

JOHN WRIGHT.

Sworn to before me,   ETHER SHEPLEY.
November 1, 1824.

I, Charles Tabbut, on òàth, declare: That I was master of. the schooner William, of Addison; that I sailed on or about the 27th day of June, 1824, fitted out for the fisheries, and proceeded to the fishing ground, on and near Grand Menan Bank, and continued to fish, from fifteen to eighteen miles distant from Grand Menan, until the thirteenth day of July, and on the fourteenth, having lost some of our water, found ourselves in want of water, having only half a barrel on board, and that too bad for use; then ran into Grand Menan for water, that being the only place, as the weather then was, where we could obtain it, and on the fifteenth anchored at Gull Cove, in Grand Menan; had been at anchor about ten minutes; when we were boarded from the barge of the British armed brig Dotterel; the papers were demanded and delivered, and the men from the barge were ordered below to search for arms, (found two muskets;) took the arms and knives. I asked the master of the barge what he was going to do with us? He answered that we had been damned saucy to the inhabitants. To which I replied that I had never been ill used by the inhabitants, nor ill used them; I had never before been in to the land, and could not have used them ill. The master of the barge then threatened to cut me into ounce pieces, to lash me to the deck, and to gag me with the pump bolt or pump brake. The vessel was then got under way, carried near the shore and moored and stripped, the boat taken away, and we were left on board the vessel thus stripped, and deprived of the boat, and without water, and lying in a dangerous place. The master of the barge said if we called a boat, or landed, or made any noise, he would shoot us. He passed us several times, and I called to him and asked for water; he answered that he would come to our assistance, but did not. Despairing of obtaining any from the barge, I called to the master of an English vessel, who aided me with a boat to go on shore and obtain a little water; I went, and obtained a few gallons. The next morning the master of the barge came on board again, and carried the vessel to St. Andrew's, and reported to the Collector there that we were found in Grand Menan, in want of neither wood nor water. After endeavoring to obtain a release of the vessel, without success, was ordered to leave the vessel, and did leave her. I asked the master of the barge how he could detain my vessel contrary to the treaty? He damned the treaty, and them that made it. The vessel was owned by William Wass and William Nash. She was libelled, deemed forfeit, and sold, no person appearing to claim her; and the reason that no person claimed her was, that the costs and expenses attending it would be as much as the vessel was worth. The loss to the owners and crew must be near two thousand dollars.

CHARLES TABBUT.

Sworn to before—   ETHER SHEPLEY.
November 2, 1824.

I, Josiah W. Perry, on oath, declare: That I was a hand on board the schooner William; that the facts as stated by Charles Tabbut are wholly true, the same having been read to me.

JOSIAH W. PERRY.

Sworn to before—   ETHER SHEPLEY.
November 2, 1824.

I, Christopher Wass, on oath, declare: That I was managing master of the schooner Sea Flower, of Addison, my son being master, and sick on shore, and the vessel having, during the previous part of the season, been employed in the fisheries, and sailed on the twentieth of September, on the Grand Menan Bank, and continued there fishing on Tuesday and Wednesday; and about 8 o'clock p. m., Wednesday, blowing fresh from the west, hove up the anchor and laid to under the foresail. The wind during the night drew into the northwest and blew very heavy and split her foresail; reefed the sail above the rent and set it again, and laid till daylight; then stood to the northward and eastward, and made the southwest head of Grand Menan, bearing north by east; made the Mur Rocks and obliged to go between them, and fetched in to Kent's island, near Grand Menan, being Thursday morning. Friday and Saturday, blowing fresh and storming, could not mend our sail. Sunday, continuing to blow fresh, laid still. Monday went out on to the outer part of the rips, five or six miles from the land; caught a few fish, and, continuing to blow so that we could not anchor, came in and anchored again at Kent's island. Tuesday went out to the rips again, still blowing fresh and raining, and heavy sea from the eastward; could not anchor; caught only a few fish, and in running in carried away our fore-shrouds; hauled down the foresail and ran into the same harbor again. Wednesday morning was boarded from a tender to the British armed brig Dotterel; papers were demanded and delivered; asked what business we had there, and was answered that we were riding out the gale with both anchors ahead. The master of the tender, after much entreaty, consented to give up to us most of the fish and salt, and next morning set all hands on shore at Kent's island, and carried the vessel to St. Andrew's, where she now lies. No proceedings have been instituted against her that I can learn. She was owned wholly by me, and my loss will be as much as seven hundred dollars. I have never heard of any complaints against the vessel, other than that she was found in the harbor, and was accused of going in too frequently during the last few days.

                                                           CHRISTOPHER WASS.
Sworn to before—   ETHER SHEPLEY.
November 1, 1824.

I, Jones Wass, mate of the Sea Flower at the time above mentioned, and have heard the affidavit signed by Christopher Wass read, and, on oath, declare the facts therein stated are wholly true.

                                                           JONES WASS.
Sworn to before—   ETHER SHEPLEY.
November 1, 1824.

I, Joel McKinsey, on oath, declare: That I was a hand on board the boat Rover, of Addison, fitted out for the fisheries; that we sailed the first part of the month of October, 1824, and proceeded as far as Little river, where we lay about nine days wind bound, and caught some herring; went out on Friday morning for the Seal islands, but, finding the wind unfavorable, concluded to proceed to the southwest head of Grand Menan, and laid to six or seven miles from the island, to the westward, fishing; while lying in this situation a tender to the British armed brig Dotterel passed between us and Grand Menan, eastward, and went round the point of the island out of sight; we continued fishing, and drifted nearer to the island, and the tender, about the middle of the day, returned and fired a gun towards us, we being then to the westward of the island, and distant from it four or five miles; the tender came up and spoke to the skipper of the boat, and asked him what business he had there; he answered that he had a right to fish there, for he was in our own waters; our papers were taken, and we were ordered to follow the tender, and followed her into Seal Cove, in the western end of Grand Menan, where we were sent on shore, and the boat started for St. Andrew's. The boat was owned by William Nash. The loss to the owner will be about two hundred and fifty dollars.

                                                           JOEL McKINSEY.
Sworn to before—   ETHER SHEPLEY.
November 3, 1824.

I, Otis Bryant, of Jonesborough, on oath, declare: That I was skipper of the boat Escape, of Jonesborough, belonging to Jeremiah Smith, and sailed the forepart of October, fitted for the fisheries; proceeded to Little river, and, wind being ahead and blowing heavy, could not proceed on to the fishing grounds, and remained in Little river eight days, and then proceeded toward the island of Grand Menan; being from three to four miles distant from the southwest point of the island, the tender of the British armed brig Dotterel came down upon us and fired at us, and put a man on board and directed us to follow; took the papers and carried us into Seal Cove, in Grand Menan. The next morning we were directed to leave the boat and go ashore, and did so; the boat started for St. Andrew's. The loss to the owner and crew must be two hundred and fifty dollars.

                                                           OTIS BRYANT.
Sworn to before—   ETHER SHEPLEY.
November 2, 1824.

Moses Smith, on oath, declares: That he has attended to and heard read the statement signed by Otis Bryant, and, being a hand on board the boat, knows the facts therein stated are true.

                                                           MOSES SMITH.
Sworn to before—   ETHER SHEPLEY
November 3, 1824.

I, Jacob Winslow, of Dennysville, being a hand on board of the schooner Pilgrim, of Dennysville, James Woodward master, sailed from Lubec about the 11th day of June last, and proceeded on to the outer grounds of the island of Grand Menan, and began to fish the 14th, being then from 10 to 12 miles distant from the island, wind blowing fresh and tide strong; broke an anchor and struck adrift; got under way and dressed our fish. The next day went on board of the Galeon, Hunt, to borrow an anchor, and could not obtain one; next morning anchored on the ground called the Gravelly Bottom, near the schooners Galeon and Hero, and distant from 8 to 10 miles from the island; caught from 10 to 12 quintals of fish, and then struck adrift; then finding ourselves unable to work to advantage with one anchor, and that a light one, concluded to go home to get one; about half an hour after a vessel from the southeast came down upon us, and fired several times; came on board, and proved to be a tender to the British armed brig Dotterel; demanded and took our papers, and took out two of the hands, myself and Benjamin Scott, and put us on board the tender; asked us what we were doing there, and answered that we had been fishing; master of the tender said we had no business to fish there in British waters, and would make us smart for it this year; he asked me what land it was in sight? said he had never seen it before; was told it was the island of Grand Menan; asked if there was any harbor into which I could pilot him, and being informed there was, asked me to pilot him in, which I did; before he was carried in, the master of the tender asked what vessel was ahead of us: told him I did not know; he said he would know, and bore down upon her, directing the Pilgrim to follow; he ordered a marine to fire upon the vessel, and he fired several times; soon came up with her, and she proved to be the schooner Hero, and boarded her; inquired why they did not heave to at the first fire; master of the Hero answered him that no colors were shown, and he did not know that anything was wanted of him; the papers of the Hero were then demanded and delivered, and one man taken from her and put on board the tender, and two of the tender's men put on board the schooner; the tender was then piloted into a harbor by me, taking with her the Pilgrim and Hero; the master of the tender inquired if there was any custom-house officer of his Majesty on the island; being informed there was not, then asked if there was any other King's officer, and was told there was not except the pilot; then went ashore and examined till about 11 o'clock at night, when with difficulty he came on board again, and was very violent; laid there three days; then got under way and went up to the Wolves islands, and went ashore; tarried there a short time, then asked me to pilot him into Beaver harbor; there ordered all sails of his own and the two other vessels unbent and carried on shore; then asked him to permit me to go home, as I had done before, but he refused; told him I would give him a bill of sale of the boat if he would let me go, she being mine, but he declined; I complained of hard treatment, and he threatened to shoot me and to tie me; next morning directed sails brought on board and bent; got under way and beat out of the harbor, bound, as he said, to St. John's; saw a vessel, and inquired if I had seen an armed brig; being answered that I had seen her at St. John's, we returned to Beaver harbor and tarried that night, then started again for St. John's; beat up about halfway to St. John's, and anchored in a place called Mason's Bay in the evening; about 10 o'clock the coxswain came on board the Pilgrim, I having been previously sent on board of her to sleep, and brought a pint of rum, and ordered the men to keep a strict watch, and left us; as soon as the lights were out on board the tender, one of the men on board of us from the tender being below asleep, the other one proposed going away with the Pilgrim to the United States. We soon got the Pilgrim under way and started for Lubec. The man who was below asleep then came on deck and asked where we were going. I told him to Lubec. He told me as there was but little wind he thought we should be caught, and had better go back. I said we would keep out of their reach. He said, if taken, they would shoot him; and then went below, and soon came up with two cutlasses, and said he would split any man's brains out, in the King's name, that offered to resist him. This it was advised that he should do to clear him from harm in case we should be taken, he having agreed before we started to the adventure; and he ordered the man to desist who was rowing, then knocked off Captain Woodward's hat. I then went and took one of the swords from him, and the other he laid down and went below. We came on home to Lubec with the vessel, obtained an anchor, and in four or five days after sailed again on to the Bank of Grand Menan, fifteen miles or more distant from the island, and continued there fishing four or five days, one of the men who came from the Dotterel still continuing with us by his own desire. Was informed that the schooner Hero, an American vessel which had been captured, was fitting out and armed by the British to take me; saw the Hero soon after boarding several vessels, and got under way and went up to Mount Desert, and fished there four or five weeks, and then returned to Dennysville and washed out our fish, and eight days after sailed again, and went on to Marblehead Bank, so called, and began to fish, the island of Grand Menan bearing north northeast, eighteen leagues distant, and continued to fish there six or eight days; then stood into Grand Menan Bank, being five or six leagues distant from the island, and anchored, and laid to, being Sunday, and all turned in. Soon the Brig Dotterel came upon us, and sent a boat with five men on board, with cutlasses drawn; inquired for Martin, the man who had come away with us, and continued to fish with us. I told him I did not know; believed he had gone to Boston; asked me if I was skipper of the vessel, and answered I was in place of one; asked for the papers, and I declined delivering them; told him they had one set of her papers; was told to get into the boat and go on board the brig, and did so. They then got the Pilgrim under way; the captain of the Dotterel asked my name; was told it; said he had got a pretty good history of my character; told him I had not robbed anybody, or killed any one, or stole anything; he asked for Martin; was told I did not know; believed he had gone to Boston; then said to him, if you are going to keep the vessel, if you will put me on board one of these fishermen, that I may go home, I shall be much obliged to you. Home! said he; yes, if you want to go home, I will carry you home to Halifax, where I will have you tried and hung. I asked him to let me go on board the Pilgrim and get my clothes. He said no, damn you, you shan't have any clothes; asked again for my clothes, and was permitted to go and get them; asked him if he was to give me anything to eat; he said no; asked him if I should fetch some provisions from my own vessel, and how much; he said fetch a week's provision; went aboard the Pilgrim, and was putting up some provision, when Jones, who was on board, and had command of the Pilgrim, called me up; told him the captain told me to get some provision, but he would not permit me to have more than twelve or fourteen biscuit, and four or five pounds of pork; was ordered to get into the boat and go on board the brig. By this time they had searched in the hold of the vessel, and found Martin hid there, and put him in the boat. When we went on board the brig, found five or six marines, with muskets and fixed bayonets. They took Martin and carried him below. I was sent aft, and kept there, guarded by marines, till 8 or 9 o'clock in the evening. Soon after, was sent down the after hatchway, and shackles put upon my ankles, and a large bar of iron put through them and fastened to the deck, and an old sail, with the ropes in it, given me to lie on; and thus I was kept four days, then took out and carried me, under guard, upon the quarter deck, where I found the officers paraded. Captain charged me with threatening their men's lives, and threatening to throw them overboard; I told him I had done no such thing; he said Paine (who was the man on board the Pilgrim that came up with the swords) had told him so, and that I would have done so, unless I had been prevented by Scott, one of my own men. I told him I could not have used a brother better than I did Paine. Captain then said if I would tell him where the Ruby and Reindeer were he would let me go with my vessel. Told him I did not know, and if I did, would not tell him. We had now arrived at Halifax; asked the captain what he should do with me; he said I should be carried to St. John's and hanged. Asked him for something to eat, telling him my own provisions were all gone; he said I ought not to have anything to eat. The next day I asked him again for something to eat, having had nothing; said he had not yet seen the Admiral, and I could have nothing till he had seen him. I then told him I had robbed no one, was no pirate, but thought he was; for if I was to be put to death he should do it like a man, and not starve me to death; told him I wished to go ashore and be put in prison. On the fourth day after I made application for food, and had none for all this time; was taken on deck, and told I was to go to St. John's to be hung, and two-thirds of a sailor's allowance given me, and continued this way sixteen days, and then came out and came on to the Banks of Grand Menan, and the next morning made a harbor in New Brunswick; then went to St. John's, and captain went on shore and came back, and sent the pilot down to me, who told me to go to the captain and tell him that you will give him a bond for sixty dollars to bring the vessel to St. John's, and he will give you an order for her, and you take good care not to fetch her here. I went up, and captain said, I suppose you want to go home, don't you? I answered yes. I suppose if you went home you would give me a pretty name, would you? Told him I would give him no worse name than he deserved. Then asked if ever I was in jail there. Told him no. He said I should be before night. Told him I should prefer that to being on board. He then told me if I had any friends in St. John's that would give him a bond for forty dollars, I might go to Halifax and get my vessel, and bring her to St. John's. I went ashore in his boat, procured a bond, and brought it to him; he then told me I must not give him a bad name, but be thankful that he had let me go and given me my vessel; he took the bond for forty dollars to deliver the vessel there in thirty days, and gave me an order for my vessel; said, you will take care, I suppose, not to come with her. Told him thought I should. I then quit his vessel, and came directly home. The vessel is still at Halifax, I suppose; I have not been after her. The above is a true history of the whole proceedings of the Pilgrim this season. I have been in her all the time. She has never been in any British harbor except where mentioned, nor fished in any other place than is above stated. The loss of property is one thousand dollars.

                                                                   JACOB WINSLOW.
Sworn to before—   ETHER SHEPLEY.
November 5, 1824.

William Howard, aged fourteen, on oath, declares: That he, with two other boys, aged seventeen and thirteen, last August took a small boat belonging to Mr. Thomas Brown, the boat having about fifteen feet keel, and went down the bay a fishing, and passed by the little island called the Thumb-Cap, about half a mile, and fished there about an hour, and a half; then went towards Casco Bay island, and fished perhaps three-quarters of an hour, then started to come home; got up to Friar's Bay, in Campo Bello, and the Dotterel hailed us; we went up and on board the Dotterel, and they took our boat and moored her alongside, kept us until next morning, and then set us on shore on Campo Bello; they have detained the boat and used her, and still do, as a boat for the Dotterel. Have often seen the boat passing in the waters with the Dotterel's men. We went out for pleasure fishing, and to get a fresh fish for our own use. William Howard is an apprentice to a blacksmith.

                                                       WILLIAM HOWARD.
Sworn to before—   ETHER SHEPLEY.
November 6, 1824.

Benjamin Newman, on oath, declares: That he has heard the statement signed by William Howard read to him, and that the facts therein stated, except so far as they relate to the use of the boat by the Dotterel, are wholly true.

                                                       BENJAMIN NEWMAN.
Sworn to before—   ETHER SHEPLEY.
November 6, 1824.

———

Thomas Brown, on oath, declares: That he was the owner of a small boat which William Howard and two other boys took and went out to fish in. They came back without the boat, and said she was taken from them by the Dotterel. I went to St. Andrew's to find her, and asked one of the officers of the Dotterel to let me have the boat, but was told I could not have her. I then applied to Mr. Dunn, the Comptroller of the Customs at St. Andrew's, to get him to intercede with the captain of the Dotterel for the boat. He answered me that he could not; that no report of such a seizure had been made to him; that the captain was a bad fellow, and had the day before insulted the custom-house. I returned without the boat; have since observed her to be used by the Dotterel's men, and believe she is still in use as a boat to the Dotterel. She cost me about twenty-two or three dollars, with the apparatus.

                                                       THOMAS BROWN.
Sworn to before—   ETHER SHEPLEY.
November 6, 1824.

I, Elisha Small, master of the schooner Ruby, of Lubec, on oath, testify and declare: That I sailed the eighth day of July, fitted out for the fisheries, and went on and near to the Grand Menan Bank, and continued there to fish sixteen or seventeen days; then ascertained that our wood and water were expended: the wind blew heavy from the north, and after attempting, without success; to gain the American shore, put in to Grand Menan, in Two Island harbor, to procure wood and water; this was the twenty-fifth day of July, in the afternoon, and laid there till the next morning, having obtained my wood and water; and by 5 o'clock next morning got under way to go out of the harbor; soon saw the barge of the Dotterel lying under the Green islands, and said to the others we should be taken; the wind died away; we were becalmed, and the barge came down upon us and took us. The Reindeer, the Friend, and the Diligence being near, small lines were passed from my vessel to the Reindeer and the Diligence, I being between them. When the barge came within, say one hundred rods, she fired over our heads, and then a second time near us, without speaking us; then came near and ordered the Reindeer to let go her anchor, and all to cast apart; the anchor was let go; then he went and boarded the Friend, which lay thirty or forty rods distant; then came again with their arms for action, and ordered us to cast apart, which was done; the reason we did not cast apart at first was, that we did not fully understand the order; then took possession of the Reindeer. I then went on board the Reindeer; he then came and took possession of the Ruby. I asked why he took me, and asked him if I was not allowed to go in for wood and water; he said I was, but it was time I was out; told him I had departed before I had obtained as much as I wanted. I mentioned to him that the treaty allowed us to go in for wood and water; he said he did not care a damn for the treaty; every vessel he caught within three miles of the land he would make a prize of; he took out the crews and put my crew on board the Diligence, and the Reindeer's crew on board the Friend, and told the Friend and Diligence they might go; put a midshipman and three men on board the Ruby, and directed them to follow him to St. Andrew's, he being on board the Reindeer. We beat up round East Quoddy, and got up opposite Indian island, when the Diligence and Madison came upon us. The Diligence came upon the Ruby, having her own crew and five of my crew and two men from Eastport, twelve in all, on board, armed with muskets, and hailed us and told us to give up the vessel. I told the midshipman I would go below; he asked me not to go; said he would give up the vessel; he gave up the vessel. The Diligence took possession of her, and the midshipman and his men went on board the barge. The Ruby was brought in. The crews of the three vessels, which were connected in Two Island harbor, were never collected on board of my vessel, she being the middle one, with muskets and fish spears; nor was there any such show of resistance made, or any such collection of men on board of either vessel. When the vessels were retaken, there was not a gun fired till after they were both retaken, and then only by way of rejoicing. They gave out that they would have the Reindeer and Ruby if they had to burn Moose island. I did not, therefore, think it prudent to trust her at sea again. The loss to the owner and crew will be five hundred dollars.

ELISHA SMALL.

Sworn to before—   ETHER SHEPLEY
NOVEMBER 6, 1824.

I, Benjamin Small, on oath, declare: That I was a hand on board the schooner Ruby when she was taken by the Dotterel; that the statement of facts signed by Elisha Small has been read to me, and I know all the facts to be true which are related to have taken place before I came away in the Diligence. We came in the Diligence direct to Eastport. I went to Elisha D. Green, of Eastport, and told him I wanted ten muskets—it having been agreed between the Ruby's crew and the Diligence crew that we would retake the Ruby; he and another gentleman obtained for us seven muskets, and the two clerks in Green's store, one named Howard and the other Fields, said they would go with us. They went on board with me; there being then twelve in all on board, having seven muskets and two pistols, and two bayonets only, and went down behind Indian island, waiting for them; laid there about half an hour, and saw the Madison coming down; she spoke us, and Fields and Howard went on board the Madison and then returned, having agreed that the Madison should attack the Reindeer, and the Diligence the Ruby. Then all went below but three men; ran down and passed the Reindeer, and the Madison approached the Reindeer, and we the Ruby; I hailed the Ruby and told her to heave to, being only three of us on deck; I hailed again, and they did not obey; then the crew came up; then the men on board the Ruby let go the jib sheets and fetched her up into the wind; then our crew, and the two clerks, and James Leighton, skipper of the Diligence, went on board the Ruby and took possession of her; the men belonging to the barge left her and went on board the barge; we then hoisted American colors, discharged our muskets, and ran into Eastport. No muskets were fired till after the vessels were retaken and the men belonging to the barge had left them.

BENJAMIM SMALL.

Sworn to before—   ETHER SHEPLEY.
NOVEMBER 6, 1824.

Benjamin W. Coggins, of Lubec, master of the schooner Friend, of Lubec, on oath, declares: That he sailed from Lubec the 20th of July last, and went on to the fishing ground, four or five leagues from Grand Menan. On the 25th, seeing Small, of the Reindeer, going in, and wind blowing fresh, and water short, followed him into Two Island harbor, and anchored there about 4 o'clock p. m.; went ashore and obtained what water I could, and got it on board about 9 same evening; wind had then died away; I could not get out. At 5 next morning a light breeze from northwest; got under way, and went out in company with the Reindeer, Ruby, and Diligence; wind died away, and vessel floated with the current. Barge of the Dotterel soon came upon us; the other three lay together, and barge fired over them; directed one to let go her anchor, and then came to me; asked me what business I had there. I told him I was becalmed, and could not get out. He said that is a damned pretty answer to give me, when the wind was blowing here a gale all day yesterday. I said yesterday I went to Two Island harbor to obtain water. He then directed my sails to be hauled down and my anchor to be let go, which was done. He then left me, and directed the other vessels to cast apart; they did so, and came to anchor; he boarded the Reindeer and took possession of her, and sent her crew on board of me, and they asked him, what if I would not take them? He told them to take my vessel then, and go to Lubec; and I then took my boat and went to see Jones, and asked him if he was going to send me to Lubec with the men? · He said he was, and told me he would give me orders when I should get under way. In about half or three-quarters of an hour he gave me a signal to get under way. I did so, and, after getting out of sight, told the Reindeer's crew that if I could get up to Lubec before they got up, would get some assistance there, and go with the Friend and retake the Reindeer. Came up as fast as I could, and my vessel grounded before I got in; then hove out the boat, and Reindeer's crew got into the boat with me and one of my crew, and the Diligence towed us up to Lubec. Then went to the revenue cutter, Smith; told him the story, and asked him if he could not go and retake them as they came in by East Quoddy? He said he could not, but gave me a line to the Collector; the Collector refused to let the cutter go. Then went to the wharf and hailed my brother, who was master of the Madison, and asked him if he would let the Madison go and retake the Reindeer, if I could obtain a crew; he said he would. I called round to get men to go on board; got four, and two rifles, and two muskets, and two pistols, and powder and ball; took the men on board the Madison, and went to Eastport, then having seven men and four muskets, my brother having the command. When at Eastport, hailed the men on the wharves, and asked them to send us two more muskets; they did send us two, and a man came with them; then ran down and spoke the Diligence. Mr. Howard and Mr. Fields came on board, and it was agreed that they should board the Ruby, and me the Reindeer. We then ran down for the Reindeer, and they for the Ruby. We boarded the Reindeer first, my brother having charge, and being on deck with one man and one boy, the rest below. Brother hailed him, and told him to heave to. Mr. Jones called his men to quarters; brother told him he would give him five minutes to consider whether to give the vessel up before he compelled him to do so, and run his vessel so near that we could step from one vessel to the other. · Jones said, the first man that steps his foot on this vessel shall be a dead man. Brother then called all hands from below, and we went up with our muskets, seven of us, there being only ten men on board, besides two or three boys. Jones then laid his sword down and said, the vessel is yours. We put four men on board, and told skipper Small to make his way to Eastport. Jones then went on board his barge with his men. Then brother hailed him; asked him to come on board the Madison and take something to drink, and he did. He then said we were good fellows for having retaken them; he took them according to his orders, but without any provocation, and was glad we had got them; he then went his way, and we ours. There was no gun fired till after the vessels were recaptured. Mr. Howard is a lad, 17 or 18 years old; has never been a captain of any company of militia. I have heard that he was captain of a company of boys, in Eastport, who trained with wooden guns and swords.

On the 29th of August last, being on Grand Menan Bank, saw the Dotterel take possession of the Pilgrim, she being then about nine leagues distant from the Grand Menan. The Madison was also captured at the same time and place.

The injury to me, by breaking up my fishing cruise, has been five hundred dollars.

B. W. COGGINS.

Sworn to before—
NOVEMBER 6, 1824.

ETHER SHEPLEY.

Henry Coggins, on oath, says: He has heard the statement signed by B. W. Coggins read; is acquainted with the whole transactions on board the Friend, and knows them to be truly stated. Saw the Pilgrim and Madison taken, the 29th of August, on the Bank, nine leagues distant from the island.

HENRY COGGINS.

Sworn to before—
NOVEMBER 6, 1824.

ETHER SHEPLEY.

NOVEMBER 7, 1824.

I, Harding Clark, of Dennysville, master of the schooner Hero, of Dennysville, on oath, do testify and say: That I sailed on the thirteenth day of June last, fitted out for the fishery, and proceeded on to Grand Menan Bank, and continued to fish until the sixteenth; then struck adrift in the forepart of the day; made an attempt to regain our ground, but not succeeding, the barge of the brig Dotterel came upon us, fired and boarded us; demanded our papers, which were given up, and took possession of the vessel, she being then from six to nine miles distant from the land. Two of my men were taken out and two of his put on board my vessel, and I was directed to follow him. I did follow and wait his movements for fourteen days, during which time he was employed in boarding vessels. Was during the time in Beaver and other harbors. Often asked him to let me and my crew go home, there being opportunities, but was denied. One of the men being sick, was detained on board the barge, and did duty there as did the other. At the expiration of the fourteen days arrived at St John's; were all there put on board the Dotterel; were detained there two days with only one meal of victuals, and then put on shore and dismissed. Captain told me he had given the vessel up to the custom-house; went to the custom-house; was there told he had not. Asked if I could see the captain again, and he was sent for, and he came; asked him to give up the vessel, telling him I did not consider her liable to seizure; he said he would think of it; said he wanted her for about a fortnight's cruise, and did not know but he should give her up to me then. I returned home, and went there in a fortnight, as he desired me. The Hero came in from a cruise three days after I arrived there, having been out cruising thirteen days. She then took in supplies for another fortnight's cruise, and sailed again the same day, under the command of the pilot of the brig. Saw the Captain, and asked him if he would let me have the vessel, as he had agreed to; he said he had made a new arrangement, and should not let me have the vessel. I came home again and left her. When last at St. John's, I applied to Messrs. Crookshanks and Johnson, merchants of St. John's, to ascertain when she was libelled or proceeded against; and about three weeks ago received a letter from them stating that the Hero had not been libelled, but had been employed as a tender to the Dotterel. The vessel was owned by Manning Clark and myself. The loss is not less than nine hundred dollars. I have not been out before this season; this being the first and only cruise this season.

HARDING CLARK.

Sworn to before—   ETHER SHEPLEY.

I, William Rumery, of Lubec, testify and say: That I was a hand on board the schooner Madison, of Lubec, fitted out for the fisheries; that we sailed about the 25th of August last, and went on to Grand Menan Bank, about twenty-one miles or more from land, and fished till the 29th of the same month; saw a brig bearing down upon us; soon hailed us; asked the name of the vessel; skipper not being then on board, I answered, the Madison; sent a boat aboard and ordered all the crew aboard the boat, and carried us on board the brig Dotterel; ordered the Madison under way for Halifax; ordered us under the fore-castle deck, among the goats and fowls, where we remained four days; gave bread and water to us once a day; arrived fourth day at Halifax, and set us all ashore but Robert Rumery; told us we must get a passage home as we could; we got a passage and came home, leaving the Madison at Halifax, where I suppose she is now. The fish and salt they sold out of her, in harbors on the way, before they arrived in Halifax. The injury and loss is about nine hundred dollars. I saw Winslow in irons at Halifax.

WILLIAM RUMERY.

Sworn to before—   ETHER SHEPLEY.
NOVEMBER 6, 1824.

I, Robert Rumery, on oath, declare: That I have heard the statement signed by William Rumery read, and know that it is wholly true. I further state, that after the remainder of the Madison's crew left us, I continued on board the Dotterel sixteen days; my brother William left me a little provision; after that was gone, I had nothing for two days; then had two-thirds of a seaman's ration, except grog; then got under way and came to L'Etau harbor, Deer island; asked lieutenant what he was going to do with me; said I should be carried to St. John's and put in prison until my trial, and, no doubt, I should be hung; then got under way and went to St. John's; laid there four days, then was told I might go on shore; went ashore and thence home.

I was a hand on board the Madison when she was going out and met the Diligence and Friend bringing in the crews of the Reindeer and Ruby that had been captured. After learning the facts, we put about and ran into Lubec and anchored. Benjamin Small wanted us to go with them and help take the Reindeer and Ruby, as the Friend had got aground, and Captain Ansel Coggins, of the Madison, agreed to go, and all the crew but one, and took on board seven or eight others; there were not more than twelve or, at most, fifteen on board; had a number of muskets, but no bayonets; then went down upon the Reindeer; our skipper hailed them, and told them to heave to; Jones told his men to prepare for action; we hailed a second time, and Jones ordered the fore sheet cast off, and told Robert Small that he might take charge of his vessel and carry her to Eastport. Jones and his men went aboard the barge, having first come on board of us and drank some grog by invitation, and we went to Eastport. No guns were fired till after the Reindeer was retaken and Jones had left us and gone on board of his barge, and then only by way of rejoicing.

ROBERT RUMERY.

Sworn to before—   ETHER SHEPLEY.
NOVEMBER 6, 1824.

DR.   *The United States to Ether Shepley.*

November 16, 1824.—To services making inquiry relating to the difficulties between our fishermen and the officers of the British armed brig Dotterel; travelled 540 miles; took twenty-seven depositions; absent nineteen days, and expenses, $250.

Received payment,

ETHER SHEPLEY.

COLUMBIA, *September* 27, 1824.

SIR: Inclosed is a regular protest in relation to the capture of the schooner Rebecca, which case, with others, it is hoped, will receive the attention of Government.

Respectfully your obedient servant,

STEPHEN EMERY.

Hon. JOHN QUINCY ADAMS, *Secretary of State.*

UNITED STATES OF AMERICA, *State of Maine, Washington, ss.*

Be it known, that on the twelfth day of July, in the year of our Lord one thousand eight hundred and twenty-four, personally appeared before me, Solomon Thayer, notary public, by legal authority duly admitted and sworn, and dwelling at Lubec, State and county aforesaid, Jones Wass, master of the schooner Rebecca, of Addison, and, noted his protest. And now, on this ninth day of September, anno Domini 1824, he again appears to extend the same; and with him also appears John Wright, fisherman, belonging to the said schooner, who, being severally sworn, do depose and say: That on the twenty-ninth day of June, now last past, they sailed in said schooner Rebecca from Addison on a fishing cruise on the Grand Menan Banks, and arrived there on Thursday, the first day of July, and commenced fishing at a distance of fifteen miles from land; continued to fish during that day. On the next night, the wind springing up quite fresh, were obliged to run into Grand Menan for a harbor. Arrived at Duck island, so called, and anchored at 2 o'clock Friday morning; went on shore and obtained a barrel of water, having a half barrel only on board. In about an hour from the time of anchoring saw an armed boat making towards us; up anchor and stood to sea. The armed boat gave chase, and continued it all the next day, frequently firing muskets at the schooner Rebecca. As soon as it came on dark she lost sight of us; we were then near the Nova Scotia shore. We then put back to Grand Menan, and arrived there the next morning. Immediately made for the fishing banks and continued to fish there that day. At night, the wind blowing quite fresh, run in for a harbor. The next day, being the fourth of July, and Sunday, went on to the Banks and anchored; the next morning commenced fishing, and caught twenty quintals. The following night, wind fresh, hove up and laid to under our foresail until morning; then run into Bucks Rock, so called, near Grand Menan, to procure wood and to dress our fish. In about half an hour after we arrived the same boat that had chased us on Friday came upon us, and took forcible possession of the Rebecca and her papers, ordered her underway, and took her to the city of St. John's and stripped her.

The declarants further say, that during said cruise they did not fish within from twelve to fifteen miles of Grand Menan, nor run in near the land, unless to get water, purchase wood, and from stress of weather.

The said Jones Wass, for himself, saith: That on the seventh day of September, now current, he left the city of St. John's, where he had been to solicit the liberation of the said schooner Rebecca, but that said schooner had not then been libelled for trial, and that he was told by Charles J. Peters, the judge of the Vice Admiralty courts for the province of New Brunswick, it was uncertain when she would be.

Wherefore, they do protest, and I, the said notary, in their behalf, do solemnly protest against said armed boat; against pirates, and the wanton abuse of power, by armed boats on the high seas under pretence of authority; against being deprived of rights confirmed to American fishermen by the convention with Great Britain of 1818; and against winds, seas, and tides, and whatsoever else may have caused the capture and wanton detention of the said schooner Rebecca, of Addison.

JONES WASS.
JOHN WRIGHT.

In faith whereof, I have hereunto affixed my seal and subscribed my name, the ninth day of September, anno Domini eighteen hundred and twenty-four.
[SEAL.]

SOLOMON THAYER, *Notary Public.*

GENERAL CONVENTION OF PEACE, AMITY, NAVIGATION AND COMMERCE WITH THE REPUBLIC OF COLOMBIA, OF OCTOBER 3, 1824, WITH THE DOCUMENTS APPERTAINING TO THE NEGOTIATION OF THE SAME.

COMMUNICATED TO THE SENATE, IN EXECUTIVE SESSION, FEBRUARY 22, 1825, AND THE INJUNCTION OF SECRECY SINCE REMOVED.

To the President of the Senate, pro tempore:

I transmit to the Senate a convention of general peace, amity, navigation and commerce, signed by the plenipotentiaries of the United States and of the Republic of Colombia, at Bogota, on the 3d of October, 1824, together with the documents appertaining to the negotiation of the same, for the constitutional consideration of the Senate, with regard to its ratification.

JAMES MONROE.

WASHINGTON, *February 21, 1825.*

General convention of peace, amity, navigation and commerce between the United States of America and the Republic of Colombia.	Convencion jeneral de paz, amistad, navegacion y commercio entre la República de Colombia y los Estados Unidos de America, Año de 1824.
IN THE NAME OF GOD, AUTHOR AND LEGISLATOR OF THE UNIVERSE.	EN EL NOMBRE DE DIOS, AUTOR Y LEJISLADOR DEL UNIVERSO.
The United States of America and the Republic of Colombia, desiring to make lasting and firm the friendship and good understanding which happily prevails between both nations, have resolved to fix, in a manner clear, distinct, and positive, the rules	La Republica de Colombia y los Estados-Unidos de America, deseando hacer duradera y firme la amistad y buena intelligencia, que felizmente existe entre ambas potencias, han resuelto fijar de una manera clara, distinta y positiva las reglas que deben

which shall in future be religiously observed between the one and the other, by means of a treaty or general convention of peace, friendship, commerce, and navigation.

For this most desirable object, the President of the United States of America has conferred full powers on RICHARD CLOUGH ANDERSON, junior, a citizen of the said States, and their Minister Plenipotentiary to the said Republic; and the Vice President of the Republic of Colombia, charged with the Executive power, on PEDRO GAUL, Secretary of State and of Foreign Relations; who, after having exchanged their said full powers in due and proper form, have agreed to the following articles:

ARTICLE 1. There shall be a perfect, firm, and inviolable peace and sincere friendship between the United States of America and the Republic of Colombia, in all the extent of their possessions and territories, and between their people and citizens, respectively, without distinction of persons or places.

ARTICLE 2. The United States of America and the Republic of Colombia, desiring to live in peace and harmony with all the other nations of the earth, by means of a policy frank and equally friendly with all, engage mutually not to grant any particular favor to other nations, in respect of commerce and navigation, which shall not immediately become common to the other party, who shall enjoy the same freely, if the concession was freely made, or on allowing the same compensation, if the concession was conditional.

ARTICLE 3. The citizens of the United States may frequent all the coasts and countries of the Republic of Colombia, and reside and trade there in all sorts of produce, manufactures, and merchandise, and shall pay no other or greater duties, charges, or fees whatsoever, than the most favored nation is or shall be obliged to pay; and they shall enjoy all the rights, privileges, and exemptions, in navigation and commerce which the most favored nation does or shall enjoy, submitting themselves, nevertheless, to the laws, decrees, and usages there established, and to which are submitted the subjects and citizens of the most favored nations.

In like manner the citizens of the Republic of Colombia may frequent all the coasts and countries of the United States, and reside and trade there in all sorts of produce, manufactures, and merchandise, and shall pay no other or greater duties, charges, or fees whatsoever, than the most favored nation is or shall be obliged to pay; and they shall enjoy all the rights, privileges, and exemptions in navigation and commerce which the most favored nation does or shall enjoy, submitting themselves, nevertheless, to the laws, decrees, and usages there established, and to which are submitted the subjects and citizens of the most favored nations.

ARTICLE 4. It is likewise agreed that it shall be wholly free for all merchants, commanders of ships, and other citizens of both countries, to manage themselves their own business in all the ports and places subject to the jurisdiction of each other, as well with respect to the consignment and sale of their goods and merchandise by wholesale or retail, as with respect to the loading, unloading, and sending off their ships; they being in all these cases to be treated as citizens of the country in which they reside, or at least to be placed on a footing with the subjects or citizens of the most favored nation.

ARTICLE 5. The citizens of neither of the contracting parties shall be liable to any embargo, nor be detained with their vessels, cargoes, merchandises, or effects, for any military expedition, nor for any public or private purpose whatever, without allowing to those interested a sufficient indemnification.

ARTICLE 6. Whenever the citizens of either of the contracting parties shall be forced to seek refuge or

observar religiosamente en lo venidero, por medio de un tratado o convencion general de paz, amistad, comercio y navegacion.

Con este muy, deseable objeto, el Vice Presidente de la Republica de Colombia encargado del podèr Ejecutivo, ha conferido plenos poderes á PEDRO GAUL, Secretario de Estado y del Despacho de Relaciones Esteriores de la misma, y el Presidente de los Estados Unidos de America, á RICARDO CLOUGH ANDERSON, el menor, cuidadano de dichos Estados, y su Ministro Plenipotenciario cerca de la dicha Republica; quienes despues de haber canjeado sus espresados plenos poderes en debida y buena forma, han convenido en los articulos siguientes.

ARTICULO 1. Habra una paz, perfecta, firme, é inviolable y amistad sincera entre la Republica de Colombia y los Estados Unidos de America, en toda la estencion de sus possessiones y territorios, y entre sus pueblos y ciudadanos respectivamente sin distincion de personas, ni lugares.

ARTICULO 2. La Republica de Colombia y los Estados Unidos de America, deseando vivir en paz y harmonia con las demas naciones de la tierra por medio de una politica franca, é igualmente amistosa con todas, se obligan mutuamente á no conceder favores particulares, á otras naciones, con respecto á comercio y navigacion, que no se hagan inmediatamente comun á una ú otra, quien gozara de los mismos libremente, si la concesion fuese hecha libremente ó prestando la misma compensacion, si la concesion fuere condicional.

ARTICULO 3. Los ciudadanos de la Republica de Colombia podràn frecuentar todas las costas y paises de los Estados Unidos de America, y residir, y traficar en ellos con toda suerte de producciones, manufacturas, y mercaderias, y no pagaràn otros, ó mayores derechos, impuestos, ó emolumentos cualesquiera que los ques las naciones mas favorecidas están ó estuvieren obligadas á pagar; y gozaràn todos los derechos, previlejios y esenciones, que gozan ó gozaren los de la nacion mas favorecida, sometiendose, no obstante, á las leyes, decretos, y usos establecidos, á las cuales estan sujetos los subditos ó ciudadanos de las naciones mas favorecidas. Del mismo modo los ciudadanos de los Estados Unidos de America podràn frecuentar todas las costas y paises de la Republica de Colombia, y residir y traficar en ellos con toda suerte de producciones, manufacturas, y mercaderias, y no pagaràn otros ó mayores derechos, impuestos, ó emolumentos cualesquiera, que los que las naciones mas favorecidas, estàn ó estuvieren obligadas á pagàr y gozaràn de todos los derechos privilejios y esenciones, que gozan ó gozaren los de la nacion mas favorecida con respecto á navegacion y comercio, sometiendose, no obstante á las leyes, decretos y usos establecidos á los cuales estan sujetos los subditos ó ciudadanos de las naciones mas favorecidas.

ARTICULO 4. Se conviene ademas, que serà enteramente libre y permitido, á los comerciantes, comandantes de buques, y otros ciudadanos de ambos paises el manejar sus negocios, por si mismos, en todos los puertos y lugares sujetos á la jurisdiccion de uno ù otro, asi respecto á las consignaciones y ventas por mayor y menor de sus efectos y mercaderias, como de la carga, descarga y despacho de sus buques, debiendo en todos estos casos, ser tratados como ciudadanos del pais en que residan, ó al menos puestos sobre un pie igual con los subditos ó ciudadanos de las naciones mas favorecidas.

ARTICULO 5. Los ciudadanos de una ù otra parte, no podràn ser embargados ni detenidos con sus embarcaciones, tripulaciones, mercaderias, y efectos comerciales de su pertenencia, para alguna espedicion militar, usos publicos, ó particulares cualesquiera que sean, sin conceder à los interesados una suficiente indemnizacion.

ARTICULO 6. Siempre que los ciudadanos de alguna de las partes contratantes se vieren precisados à

asylum in the rivers, bays, ports, or dominions of the other, with their vessels, whether merchants or of war, public or private, through stress of weather, pursuit of pirates or enemies, they shall be received and treated with humanity, giving to them all favor and protection for repairing their ships, procuring provisions, and placing themselves in a situation to continue their voyage without obstacle or hindrance of any kind.

Article 7. All the ships, merchandise, and effects belonging to the citizens of one of the contracting parties, which may be captured by pirates, whether within the limits of its jurisdiction or on the high seas, and may be carried or found in the rivers, roads, bays, ports, or dominions of the other, shall be delivered up to the owners, they proving, in due and proper form, their rights before the competent tribunals; it being well understood that the claim should be made within the term of one year by the parties themselves, their attorneys, or agents of the respective Governments.

Article 8. When any vessel belonging to the citizens of either of the contracting parties shall be wrecked, foundered, or shall suffer any damage on the coasts, or within the dominions of the other, there shall be given to them all assistance and protection, in the same manner which is usual and customary with the vessels of the nation where the damage happens, permitting them to unload the said vessel, if necessary, of its merchandise and effects, without exacting for it any duty, impost, or contribution whatever, until they may be exported.

Article 9. The citizens of each of the contracting parties shall have power to dispose of their personal goods within the jurisdiction of the other, by sale, donation, testament, or otherwise; and their representatives, being citizens of the other party, shall succeed to their said personal goods, whether by testament or *ab intestato*, and they may take possession thereof, either by themselves or others acting for them, and dispose of the same at their will, paying such dues only as the inhabitants of the country wherein said goods are shall be subject to pay in like cases; and if, in the case of real estate, the said heirs would be prevented from entering into the possession of the inheritance on account of their character of aliens, there shall be granted to them the term of three years to dispose of the same as they may think proper, and to withdraw the proceeds without molestation, and exempt from all rights of detraction on the part of the Government of the respective States.

Article 10. Both the contracting parties promise and engage formally to give their special protection to the persons and property of the citizens of each other, of all occupations, who may be in the territories subject to the jurisdiction of the one or the other, transient or dwelling therein, leaving open and free to them the tribunals of justice for their judicial recourse, on the same terms which are usual and customary with the natives or citizens of the country in which they may be; for which they may employ, in defence of their rights, such advocates, solicitors, notaries, agents and factors, as they may judge proper in all their trials at law; and such citizens or agents shall have free opportunity to be present at the decisions and sentences of the tribunals in all cases which may concern them, and likewise at the taking of all examinations and evidence which may be exhibited in the said trials.

Article 11. It is likewise agreed that the most perfect and entire security of conscience shall be enjoyed by the citizens of both the contracting parties in the countries subject to the jurisdiction of the one and the other, without their being liable to be disturbed or molested on account of their religious belief, so long as they respect the laws and established usages of the country. Moreover, the bodies of the citizens of one of the contracting parties who may die in the territories of the other shall

buscàr refujio, ó asilo en los rios, bahias, puertos, ó dominios de la otra, con sus buques, ya sean mercantes, ó de guerra, publicos ó particulares, por mal tiempo, persecucion de piratas ó enemigos, seràn recibidos y tratados con humanidad, dandoles todo favor y proteccion, para reparar sus buques, procuràr viveres, y ponerse en situacion de continuar su viaje, sin obstaculo ó estorbo de ningun genero.

Articulo 7. Todos los buques, mercaderias y efectos pertenecientes a los ciudadanos de una de las partes contratantes, que sean apresados por piratas, bien sea dentro de los limites de su jurisdiccion, ó en alta mar, y fueren llevados, ó hallados en los rios, radas, bahias, puertos, ó dominios de la otra, seràn entregados à sus dueños, probando estos en la forma propia y debida sus derechos ante los tribunales competentes; bien entendido que el reclama ha de hacerse dentro del termino de un año, por las mismas partes, sus apoderados ó agentes de los respectivos Gobiernos.

Articulo 8. Cuando algun buque perteneciente à los ciudadanos de alguna de las partes contratantes, naufrague, encalle, ó sufra alguna averia, en las costas, ó dentro de los dominios de la otra, se les darà toda ayuda y proteccion, del mismo modo que es uso y costumbre, con los buques de la nacion en donde suceda la averia; permitiendoles descargàr el dicho buque (si fuere necesario) de sus mercaderias y efectos, sin cobrar por esto hasta que sean esportados, ningun derecho, impuesto ó contribucion.

Articulo 9. Los ciudadanos de cada una de las partes contratantes, tendrán pleno podér para disponér de sus bienes personales dentro de la jurisdiccion de la otra, por venta, donacion testamento, ó de otro modo; y sus representantes, siendo ciudadanos de la otra parte, succederán á sus dichos bienes personales, ya sea por testamento ó *ab intestato*, y podran tomar posecion de ellos, ya sea por si mismos ó por otros, que obren por ellos, y disponér de los mismos, segun su voluntad, pagando aquellas cargas, solamente, que los habitantes del pais en donde estan los referidos bienes, estuvieren sujetos á pagar en iguales casos; y si en el caso de bienes raices, los dichos herederos fuesen impedidos de entrár en la posecion de la herencia por razon de su caracter de estrangeros, se les darà el termino de tres años, para disponér de ella como juzguen conveniente, y para estraér el producto sin molestia, y esentos de todo derecho de deduccion, por parte del Gobierno de los respectivos Estados.

Articulo 10. Ambas partes contratantes se comprometen y obligan formalmente á dar su proteccion especial á las personas y propiedades de los ciudadanos de cada una reciprocamente transeuntes ó habitantes de todas ocupaciones, en los territorios sujetos á la jurisdiccion de una y otra, dejandoles abiertos y libres los tribunales de justicia, para sus recursos judiciales, en los mismos terminos que son de uso y costumbre para los naturales ó ciudadanos del pais en que residan; para lo cual, podrán emplear en defensa de sus derechos aquellos abogados, procuradores, escribanos, agentes, ó factores que juzguen conveniente, en todos sus asuntos y litigios; y dichos ciudadanos ó agentes tendrán la libre facultad de estar presentes en las decisiones y sentencias de los tribunales, en todos los casos que les conciernan, como igualmente al tomar todos los examenes y declaraciones que se ofrezcan en los dichos litigios.

Articulo 11. Se conviene igualmente en que los ciudadanos de ambas partes contratantes gozen la mas perfecta y entera seguridad de consciencia en los paises sujetos á la jurisdiccion da una ù otra, sin quedar por ello espuestos á ser inquietados ó molestados en razon de su creencia religiosa, mientras que respeten las leyes y usos establecidos. Ademas de esto, podrán sepultarse los cadaveres de los ciudadanos de una de las partes contratantes, que fallecieren en los territorios de la otra, en los cementerios

be buried in the usual burying grounds, or in other decent and suitable places, and shall be protected from violation or disturbance.

Article 12. It shall be lawful for the citizens of the United States of America and of the Republic of Colombia to sail with their ships with all manner of liberty and security, no distinction being made who are the proprietors of the merchandises laden thereon, from any port to the places of those who are now, or hereafter shall be, at enmity with either of the contracting parties. It shall likewise be lawful for the citizens aforesaid to sail with the ships and merchandises before mentioned, and to trade with the same liberty and security from the places, ports, and havens of those who are enemies of both or either party, without any opposition or disturbance whatsoever, not only directly from the places of the enemy before mentioned to neutral places, but also from one place belonging to an enemy to another place belonging to an enemy, whether they be under the jurisdiction of one power or under several. And it is hereby stipulated that free ships shall also give freedom to goods, and that everything shall be deemed to be free and exempt which shall be found on board the ships belonging to the citizens of either of the contracting parties, although the whole lading, or any part thereof, should appertain to the enemies of either, contraband goods being always excepted. It is also agreed in like manner that the same liberty be extended to persons who are on board a free ship, with this effect, that, although they be enemies to both or either party, they are not to be taken out of that free ship unless they are officers and soldiers, and in the actual service of the enemies: *Provided, however, and it is hereby agreed,* That the stipulations in this article contained, declaring that the flag shall cover the property, shall be understood as applying to those powers only who recognize this principle; but if either of the two contracting parties shall be at war with a third, and the other neutral, the flag of the neutral shall cover the property of enemies whose Governments acknowledge this principle, and not of others.

Article 13. It is likewise agreed, that, in the case where the neutral flag of one of the contracting parties shall protect the property of the enemies of the other by virtue of the above stipulation, it shall always be understood that the neutral property found on board such enemy's vessels shall be held and considered as enemy's property, and as such shall be liable to detention and confiscation, except such property as was put on board such vessel before the declaration of war, or even afterwards, if it were done without the knowledge of it; but the contracting parties agree that two months having elapsed after the declaration, their citizens shall not plead ignorance thereof. On the contrary, if the flag of the neutral does not protect the enemy's property, in that case the goods and merchandises of the neutral embarked in such enemy's ships shall be free.

Article 14. This liberty of navigation and commerce shall extend to all kinds of merchandises, excepting those only which are distinguished by the name of contraband, and under this name of contraband or prohibited goods shall be comprehended—

1st. Cannons, mortars, howitzers, swivels, blunderbusses, muskets, fuzees, rifles, carbines, pistols, pikes, swords, sabres, lances, spears, halberds, and granades, bombs, powder, matches, balls, and all other things belonging to the use of these arms.

2d. Bucklers, helmets, breast plates, coats of mail, infantry belts, and clothes made up in the form and for a military use.

3d. Cavalry belts and horses with their furniture.

4th. And generally all kinds of arms and instruments of iron, steel, brass, and copper, or of any

acostumbrados, ó en otros lugares decentes, y adecuados, los cuales, serán protejidos contra toda violacion ó trastorno.

Artículo 12. Será lícito a los ciudadanos de la Republica de Colombia, y de los Estados Unidos de America, navegár con sus buques, con toda seguridad y libertad, de cualquiera puerto á las plazas ó lugares de los que son ó fueren en adelante enemigos de cualquiera de las dos partes contratantes, sin hacerse distincion de quienes son los dueños de las mercaderias cargadas en ellos. Será igualmente lícito á los referidos ciudadanos navegár con sus buques y mercaderias mencionadas y traficár con la misma libertad y seguridad, de los lugares, puertos y enseñadas de los enemigos de ambas partes, ó de alguna de ellas, sin ninguna oposicion, ó disturbio cualquiera, no solo directamente de los lugares de enemigo arriba mencionados á lugares neutros, sino tambien de un lugar perteneciente á un enemigo, á otro enemigo, ya sea que esten bajo la jurisdiccion de una potencia, ó bajo la de diversas. Y queda aqui estipulado, que los buques libres, dan tambien libertad á las mercaderias, y que se ha de considerar libre y esento todo lo que se hallare á bordo de los buques pertenecientes á los ciudadanos de cualquiera de las partes contratantes, aunque toda la carga ó parte de ella pertenezca á enemigos de una ú otra, eceptuando siempre los articulos de contrabando de guerra. Se conviene tambien del mismo modo, en que la misma libertad se estienda á las personas que se encuentren á bordo de buques libres, con el fin de que aunque dichas personas sean enemigos de ambas partes ó de alguna de ellas, no deban ser estraidos de los buques libres, á menos que sean oficiales ó soldados en actual servicio de los enemigos: á condicion no obstante, y se conviene aqui en esto, que las estipulaciones contenidas en el presente articulo, declarando que el pabellon cubre la propiedad, se entenderàn aplicables solamente á aquellas potencias que reconocen este principio; pero si alguna de las dos partes contratantes, estuviere en guerra con una tercera, y la otra permaneciese neutral, la bandera de la permaneciente neutral, cubrirá la propiedad de los enemigos, cuyos Gobiernos reconozcan este principio y no de otros.

Artículo 13. Se conviene igualmente que en el caso de que la bandera neutrál de una de las partes contratantes protega las propiedades de los enemigos de la otra en virtud de lo estipulado arriba, deberá siempre entenderse, que las propiedades neutrales encontradas á bordo de tales buques enemigos, han de tenerse y considerarse como propiedades enemigas, y como tales, estaràn sujetas á detencion, y confiscacion; eseptuando solamente aquellas propiedades que hubiesen sido puestas á bordo de tales buques antes de la declaracion de la guerra, y aun despues, si hubiesen sido embarcadas en dichos buques, sin tenèr noticia de la guerra; y se conviene, que pasados dos meses despues de la declaracion, los ciudadanos de una y otra parte no podrán elegàr que la ignoraban. Por el contrario, si la bandera neutral, no protegiese las propiedades enemigos, entonces seràn libres los efectos y mercaderias de la parte neutràl embarcadas en buques enemigos.

Artículo 14. Esta libertad de navegacion y comercio se estenderá a todo genero de mercaderias, eceptuando aquellas solamente, que se distinguen con el nombre de contrabando, y bajo este nombre de *contrabando* ó efectos prohibidos se comprenderán:

1°. Cañones, morteros, obuces, pedreros, trabucos, mosquetes, fusiles, rifles, carabinas, pistolas, picas, espadas, sables, lanzas, chuzos, alabardas, y granadas, bombas, polvora, mechas, balas, con las demas cosas correspondientes al uso de estas armas.

2°. Escudos, casquetes, corazas, cotas de malla, fornituras, y vestidos hechos en forma, y á usanza militar.

3°. Bandoleras, y caballos junto con sus armas y arneses.

4°. Y generalmente toda especie de armas, é instrumentos de hierro, acero, bronce, cobre, y otras

other materials manufactured, prepared, and formed expressly to make war by sea or land.

ARTICLE 15. All other merchandises and things not comprehended in the articles of contraband explicitly enumerated and classified as above shall be held and considered as free, and subjects of free and lawful commerce, so that they may be carried and transported in the freest manner by both the contracting parties, even to places belonging to an enemy, excepting only those places which are at that time besieged or blockaded up; and to avoid all doubt in this particular, it is declared that those places only are besieged or blockaded which are actually attacked by a belligerent force capable of preventing the entry of the neutral.

ARTICLE 16. The articles of contraband before enumerated and classified, which may be found in a vessel bound for an enemy's port, shall be subject to detention and confiscation, leaving free the rest of the cargo and the ship, that the owners may dispose of them as they see proper. No vessel of either of the two nations shall be detained on the high seas on account of having on board articles of contraband, whenever the master, captain, or supercargo of said vessel will deliver up the articles of contraband to the captor, unless the quantity of such articles be so great and of so large a bulk that they cannot be received on board the capturing ship without great inconvenience; but, in this and in all other cases of just detention, the vessel detained shall be sent to the nearest convenient and safe port, for trial and judgment, according to law.

ARTICLE 17. And whereas it frequently happens that vessels sail for a port or place belonging to an enemy without knowing that the same is besieged, blockaded, or invested, it is agreed that every vessel so circumstanced may be turned away from such port or place, but shall not be detained, nor shall any part of her cargo, if not contraband, be confiscated, unless, after warning of such blockade or investment from the commanding officer of the blockading forces, she shall again attempt to enter; but she shall be permitted to go to any other port or place she may think proper. Nor shall any vessel of either, that may have entered into such port before the same was actually besieged, blockaded, or invested by the other, be restrained from quitting such place with her cargo, nor, if found therein after the reduction and surrender, shall such vessel or her cargo be liable to confiscation, but they shall be restored to the owners thereof.

ARTICLE 18 In order to prevent all kind of disorder in the visiting and examination of the ships and cargoes of both the contracting parties on the high seas, they have agreed mutually, that whenever a vessel-of-war, public or private, shall meet with a neutral of the other contracting party, the first shall remain out of cannon shot, and may send its boat, with two or three men only, in order to execute the said examination of the papers concerning the ownership and cargo of the vessel, without causing the least extortion, violence, or ill treatment, for which the commanders of the said armed ships shall be responsible with their persons and property; for which purpose, the commanders of said private armed vessels shall, before receiving their commissions, give sufficient security to answer for all the damages they may commit. And it is expressly agreed that the neutral party shall in no case be required to go on board the examining vessel for the purpose of exhibiting her papers, or for any other purpose whatever.

ARTICLE 19 To avoid all kind of vexation and abuse in the examination of the papers relating to the ownership of the vessels belonging to the citizens of the two contracting parties, they have agreed, and

materias cualesquiera, manufacturadas, preparadas, y formadas espresamente para hacer la guerra por mar, ó tierra.

ARTICULO 15. Todas las demas mercaderias, y efectos no comprendidos en los artículos de contrabando esplícitamente enumerados, y clasificados en el artículo anterior, serán tenidos y reputados por libres, y de lícito y libre comercio, de modo, que ellos puedan sér transportados, y llevados, de la manera mas libre, por los ciudadanos de ambas partes contratantes, aun á los lugares pertenecientes á un enemigo de una ù otra, eceptuando solamente aquellos lugares ó plazas, que están al mismo tiempo sitiadas ó bloqueadas; y para evitar toda duda en el particular, se declaran sitiadas ó bloqueadas aquellas plazas, que en la actualidad estuviesen átacadas por una fuerza de un beligerante capaz de impedir la entrada del neutral.

ARTICULO 16. Los artículos de contrabando antes enumerados y clasificados, que se hallen en un buque destinado à detencion y confiscacion; dejando libre el resto del cargamento y el buque, para que los dueños puedan disponer de ellos como lo crean conveniente. Ningun buque de cualquiera de las dos naciones, será detenido, por tener á bordo artículos de contrabando, siempre que el maestre, capitan, ó sobrecargo de dicho buque quiera entregar los artículos de contrabando al apresador, à menos que la cantidad de estos artículos sea tan grande y de tanto volumen, que no puedan sér recibidos à bordo del buque apresador, sin grandes inconvenientes; pero en este, como en todos los otros casos de justa detencion, el buque detenido será enviado al puerto mas inmediato, comodo, y seguro, para ser juzgado y sentenciado conforme à las leyes.

ARTICULO 17. Y por cuanto frecuentemente sucede que los buques navegan para un puerto ó lugar perteneciente à un enemigo, sin saber que aquel esté sitiado, bloqueado ó envestido, se conviene en que todo buque en estas circunstancias se pueda hacer volver de dicho puerto, ó lugar; pero no será detenido, ni confiscada parte alguna de su cargamento, no siendo contrabando; à menos que despues de la intimacion de semejante bloqueo ó ataque, por el comandante de las fuerzas bloqueadoras, intentase otra vez entrar; pero le será permitido ir à qualquiera otro puerto ó lugar que juzgue conveniente. Ni ningun buque de una de las partes, que haya entrado en semejante puerto, ó lugar, antes que estuviese sitiado, bloqueado, ó envestido por la otra, sera impedido de dejar el tal lugar con su cargamento, ni si fuere hallado alli despues de la rendicion y entrega de semejante lugar, estará el tal buque ó su cargamento sujeto à confiscacion, sino que serán restituidos à sus dueños.

ARTICULO 18. Para evitar toda clase de desorden en la visita, y examen de los buques y cargamentos de ambas partes contratantes en alta mar, han convenido mutuamente, que siempre que un buque de guerra, publico ó particular se emontrase con un neutral de la otra parte contrante, el primero permanecerà fuera de tiro de cañon, y podrá mandàr su bote, condos ó tres hombres solamente, para ejecutár el dicho examen de los papeles concernientes à la propiedad y carga del buque, sin ocasionàr la menor estorcion violencia ó mal tratamiento, por lo que los comandantes del dicho buque armado serán responsables, con sus personas y bienes; à cuyo efecto los comandantes de buques armados, por cuenta de particulares, estarán obligados antes de entregarseles sus comisiones ó patentes, à dar fianza suficiente para responder de los perjuicios que causen. Y se ha convenido espresamente, que en ningun caso se exigira à la parte neutrál, que vaya à bórdo del buque examinadór con el fin de exibir sus papeles, ó para cualquiera otro objeto sea el que fuere.

ARTICULO 19. Para evitar toda clase de vejamen y abuso en el examen de los papeles relativos à la propiedad de los buques pertenecientes à los ciudanos de las dos partes contratantes, han convenido

do agree, that in case one of them should be engaged in war, the ships and vessels belonging to the citizens of the other must be furnished with sea letters, or passports, expressing the name, property, and bulk of the ship, as also the name and place of habitation of the master or commander of said vessel, in order that it may thereby appear that the ship really and truly belongs to the citizens of one of the parties; they have likewise agreed that, such ships being laden, besides the said sea letters or passports, shall also be provided with certificates, containing the several particulars of the cargo, and the place whence the ship sailed, so that it may be known whether any forbidden or contraband goods be on board the same; which certificates shall be made out by the officers of the place whence the ship sailed, in the accustomed form; without which requisites, said vessel may be detained, to be adjudged by the competent tribunal, and may be declared legal prize, unless the said defects shall be satisfied or supplied by testimony entirely equivalent.

ARTICLE 20. It is further agreed, that the stipulations above expressed, relative to the visiting and examination of vessels, shall apply only to those which sail without convoy; and when said vessels shall be under convoy, the verbal declaration of the commander of the convoy, on his word of honor, that the vessels under his protection belong to the nation whose flag he carries, and, when they are bound to an enemy's port, that they have no contraband goods on board, shall be sufficient.

ARTICLE 21. It is further agreed, that in all cases the established courts for the prize causes, in the country to which the prizes may be conducted, shall alone take cognizance of them. And whenever such tribunal of either party shall pronounce judgment against any vessel or goods or property claimed by the citizens of the other party, the sentence or decree shall mention the reasons or motives on which the same shall have been founded, and an authenticated copy of the sentence or decree, and of all the proceedings in the case, shall, if demanded, be delivered to the commander or agent of said vessel without any delay, he paying the legal fees for the same.

ARTICLE 22. Whenever one of the contracting parties shall be engaged in war with another State, no citizen of the other contracting party shall accept a commission, or letter of marque, for the purpose of assisting or co-operating hostilely with the said enemy against the said party so at war, under the pain of being treated as a pirate.

ARTICLE 23. If, by any fatality, which cannot be expected, and which God forbid, the two contracting parties should be engaged in war with each other, they have agreed, and do agree, now for then, that there shall be allowed the term of six months to the merchants residing on the coasts and in the ports of each other, and the term of one year to those who dwell in the interior, to arrange their business and transport their effects wherever they please, giving to them the safe conduct necessary for it, which may serve as a sufficient protection until they arrive at the designated port. The citizens of all other occupations, who may be established in the territories or dominions of the United States and of the Republic of Colombia, shall be respected and maintained in the full enjoyment of their personal liberty and property, unless their particular conduct shall cause them to forfeit this protection, which, in consideration of humanity, the contracting parties engage to give them.

ARTICLE 24. Neither the debts due from individuals of the one nation to the individuals of the other, nor shares or moneys which they may have in public funds, nor in public or private banks, shall ever, in any event of war or of national difference, be sequestered or confiscated.

y convenien, que en caso de que una de ellas estuviere en guerra, los buques, y bajeles pertenecientes á los ciudadanos de la otra, serán provistos con letras de màr, ó pasaportes, espresando el nombre, propiedad y tamaño del buque, como tambien el nombre y lugar de la residencia del maestre, ó comandante, á fin de que se vea que el buque, real y verdaderamente, pertenece á los ciudadanos de una de las partes; y han convenido igualmente, que estando cargados los espresados buques, ademas de las letras de mar, ó pasaportes, estarán tambien provistos de certificatos, que contengan los por menores del cargamento, y el lugar de donde salió el buque, para que asi pueda saberse, si hay á su bordo algunos efectos prohibidos ó de contrabando, cuyos certificatos serán hechos por los oficiales del lugár de la procedencia del buque, en la forma acostumbrada, sin cuyos requisitos el dicho buque puede ser detenido, para ser juzgado por el Tribunal competente, y puede ser declarado buena presa, à menos que satisfagan, ó suplan el defecto con testimonios enteramente equivalentes.

ARTICULO 20. Se ha convenido ademas, que las estipulaciones anteriores, relativas al examen y visita de buques, se aplicarán solamente á los que navegan sin conboy y que cuando los dichos buques estuvieren bajo de conboy, será bastante la declaracion verbal del comandante del conboy, bajo su palabra de honór, de que los buques que están bajo su proteccion pertenecen a la nacion, cuya bandera llevan, y cuando se dirijen á un puerto enemigo, que los dichos buques no tienen á su bordo articulos de contrabando de guerra.

ARTICULO 21. Se ha convenido ademas, que en todos los casos que ocurran, solo los Tribunales establecidos para causas de presas, en el pais á que las presas sean conducidas, tomarán conocimiento de ellas. Y siempre que semejante tribunal de cualquiera de las partes, pronunciase sentencia contra algun buque ó efectos, ó propiedad reclamada por los ciudadanos de la otra parte, la sentencia ó decreto harà mencion de las razones ó motivos en que aquella se haya fundado, y se entregará sin demora alguna al comandante ó agente de dicho buque, si lo solicitase, un testimonio autentico de la sentencia, ó decreto, ó de todo el proceso, pagando por él los derechos legales.

ARTICULO 22. Siempre que una de las partes contratantes estuviere empeñada en guerra, con otro Estado, ningun ciudadano de la otra parte contratante aceptara una comision ó letra de marca para el objeto de ayudár ó co-operar hostilmente con el dicho enemigo, contra la dicha parte que esté asi en guerra, bajo la pena de ser tratado como pirata.

ARTICULO 23. Si por alguna fatalidad, que no puede esperarse, y que Dios no permita, las dos partes contratantes se viesen empeñadas en guerra una con otra, han convenido y convienen de ahora para entonces, que se concederá el termino de seis meses á los comerciantes residentes en las costas y en los puertos de entrambas, y el termino de un año á los que habitan en el interior, para arreglár sus negocios, y transportár sus efectos á donde quieran, dandoles el salvo conducto necesario para ello, que les sirva de suficiente proteccion hasta que lleguen al puerto que designen. Los ciudadanos de otras ocupaciones, que se hallen establecidos en los territorios ó dominios de la Republica de Colombia, ó los Estados Unidos de America, serán respetados, y mantenidos en el pleno goze de su libertad personal y propiedad, á menos que su conducta particular les haga perdér esta proteccion, que en consideracion á la humanidad, las partes contratantes se comprometen á prestarles.

ARTICULO 24. Ni las deudas contraidas por los individuos de una nacion, con los individuos de la otra, ni las acciones ó dineros, que puedan tenér en los fondos publicos, ó en los bancos publicos, ó privados, serán jamas secuestrados ó confiscados en ningun caso de guerra, ó diferencia nacional.

ARTICLE 25. Both the contracting parties, being desirous of avoiding all inequality in relation to their public communications and official intercourse, have agreed, and do agree, to grant to the envoys, ministers, and other public agents, the same favors, immunities, and exemptions which those of the most favored nation do or shall enjoy; it being understood that whatever favors, immunities, or privileges the United States of America or the Republic of Colombia may find it proper to give to the ministers and public agents of any other power, shall by the same act be extended to those of each of the contracting parties.

ARTICLE 26. To make more effectual the protection which the United States and the Republic of Colombia shall afford in future to the navigation and commerce of the citizens of each other, they agree to receive and admit consuls and vice consuls in all the ports open to foreign commerce, who shall enjoy in them all the rights, prerogatives, and immunities of the consuls and vice consuls of the most favored nation, each contracting party, however, remaining at liberty to except those ports and places in which the admission and residence of such consuls may not seem convenient.

ARTICLE 27. In order that the consuls and vice consuls of the two contracting parties may enjoy the rights, prerogatives, and immunities which belong to them by their public character, they shall, before entering on the exercise of their functions, exhibit their commission or patent in due form to the Government to which they are accredited, and having obtained their *exequatur*, they shall be held and considered as such by all the authorities, magistrates, and inhabitants in the consular district in which they reside.

ARTICLE 28. It is likewise agreed that the consuls, their secretaries, officers, and persons attached to the service of consuls, they not being citizens of the country in which the consul resides, shall be exempt from all public service, and also from all kind of taxes, imposts, and contributions, except those which they shall be obliged to pay on account of commerce or their property, to which the citizens and inhabitants, native and foreign, of the country in which they reside are subject, being in everything besides subject to the laws of the respective States. The archives and papers of the consulate shall be respected inviolably, and under no pretext whatever shall any magistrate seize or in any way interfere with them.

ARTICLE 29. The said consuls shall have power to require the assistance of the authorities of the country for the arrest, detention, and custody of deserters from the public and private vessels of their country; and for that purpose they shall address themselves to the courts, judges, and officers competent, and shall demand the said deserters in writing, proving, by an exhibition of the registers of the vessel's or ship's roll, or other public documents, that those men were part of the said crews; and on this demand, so proved, (saving, however, where the contrary is proved,) the delivery shall not be refused. Such deserters, when arrested, shall be put at the disposal of the said consuls, and may be put in the public prisons at the request and expense of those who reclaim them, to be sent to the ships to which they belonged, or to others of the same nation. But if they be not sent back within two months, to be counted from the day of their arrest, they shall be set at liberty, and shall be no more arrested for the same cause.

ARTICLE 30. For the purpose of more effectually protecting their commerce and navigation, the two contracting parties do hereby agree, as soon hereafter as circumstances will permit them, to form a consular convention, which shall declare specially

ARTICULO 25. Deseando ambas partes contratantes, evitár toda diferencia, relativa á etiqueta en sus comunicaciones, y correspondencias diplomaticas han convenido así mismo, y convienen en conceder á sus enviados, ministros, y otros agentes diplomaticos, los mismos favores, inmunidades, y esenciones de que gozan, ó gozaren en lo venidero los de las naciones mas favorecidas, bien entendido que cualquier favór, inmunidad ó privilegio, que la Republica de Colombia ó los Estados Unidos de America, tengan por conveniente dispensár á los enviados, ministros, y agentes diplomaticos de otras potencias, se haga por el mismo hecho estensivo á los de una y otra de las partes contratantes.

ARTICULO 26. Para hacér mas efectiva la proteccion, que la Republica de Colombia, y los Estados Unidos de America, darán en adelante á la navegacion y comercio de los ciudadanos de una y otra, se convienen en recibir y admitir consules, y vice consules en todos los puertos abiertos al comercio estrangero, quienes gozarán en ellos todos los derechos, prerrogativas é inmunidades de los consules, y vice consules de la nacion mas favorecida, quedando no obstante en libertad cada parte contratante, para eceptuar aquellos puertos y lugares en que la admision y residencia de semejantes consules, y vice consules no parezca conveniente.

ARTICULO 27. Para que los consules y vice consules de las dos parte contratantes, puedan gozar los derechos, prerrogativas, é inmunidades, que les corresponden por su caracter publico, ántes de entrár en el ejercicio de sus funciones, presentarán su comision ó patente en la forma debida, al Gobierno con quien esten acreditados, y habiendo obtenido el *exequatur*, serán tenidos, y considerados como tales, por todas las autoridades, majistrados y habitantes del distrito consular en que residan.

ARTICULO 28. Se ha convenido igualmente, que los consules, sus secretarios, oficiales y personas agregadas al servicio de los consulados (no siendo estas personas ciudadanos del pais en que el consul reside) estarán esentos de todo servicio publico, y tambien de toda especie de pechos, impuestos, y contribuciones, eceptuando aquellas que esten obligados á pagar por razon de comercio, o propiedad y á las cuales estan sujetos los ciudadanos, y habitantes naturales, y estrangeros del pais en que residen, quedando en todo lo demas, sujetos a las leyes de los respectivos Estados. Los archivos y papeles de los consulados serán respetados inviolablemente, y bajo ningun pretesto los occupara majistrado alguno, ni tendrá en ellos ninguna intervencion.

ARTICULO 29. Los dichos consules tendrán podér de requerir el auxilio de las autoridades locales, para la prision, detencion y custodia de los desertores de buques publicos y particulares de su pais, y para este objeto se dirigirán á los tribunales, jueces, y oficiales competentes, y pedirán los dichos desertores por escrito, probando por una presentacion de los registres de los buques, rol del equipage, ù otros documentos publicos, que aquellos, hombres eran parte de las dichas tripulaciones, y á esta demanda asi probada (menos no obstante cuando seprobare lo contrario) no se reusará la entrega. Semijantes desertores, luego que sean arrestados, se pondrán á disposicion de los dichos consules, y pueden ser depositados en las prisiones publicas, a solicitud y espensas de los que los reclamen, para ser enviados á los buques á que corresponden, ó á otros de la misma nacion. Pero si nó fueren mandados dentro de dos meses contados des de el dia de su arresto, serán puestos en libertad, y no volverán a ser presos por la misma causa.

ARTICULO 30. Para protegér mas efectivamente su comercio y navigacion, las dos partes contratantes se convienen en formar luego que las circunstancias lo permitan, una convencion consular, que declare mas especialmente los poderes é inmunidades de los

the powers and immunities of the consuls and vice consuls of the respective parties.

ARTICLE 31. The United States of America and the Republic of Colombia, desiring to make as durable as circumstances will permit the relations which are to be established between the two parties by virtue of this treaty or general convention of peace, amity, commerce, and navigation, have declared solemnly and do agree to the following points:

1st. The present treaty shall remain in full force and virtue for the term of twelve years, to be counted from the day of the exchange of the ratifications, in all the parts relating to commerce and navigation; and in all those parts which relate to peace and friendship, it shall be permanently and perpetually binding on both powers.

2d. If any one or more of the citizens of either party shall infringe any of the articles of this treaty, such citizen shall be held personally responsible for the same, and the harmony and good correspondence between the two nations shall not be interrupted thereby; each party engaging in no way to protect the offender or sanction such violation.

3d. If, (what, indeed, cannot be expected,) unfortunately, any of the articles contained in the present treaty shall be violated or infringed in any other way whatever, it is expressly stipulated that neither of the contracting parties will order or authorize any acts of reprisal, nor declare war against the other, on complaints of injuries or damages, until the said party considering itself offended shall first have presented to the other a statement of such injuries or damages, verified by competent proof, and demanded justice and satisfaction, and the same shall have been either refused or unreasonably delayed.

4th. Nothing in this treaty contained shall, however, be construed or operate contrary to former and existing public treaties with other sovereigns or States.

The present treaty of peace, amity, commerce, and navigation, shall be approved and ratified by the President of the United States of America, by and with the advice and consent of the Senate thereof, and by the President of the Republic of Colombia, with the consent and approbation of the Congress of the same, and the ratifications shall be exchanged in the city of Washington, within eight months, to be counted from the date of the signature hereof, or sooner if possible.

In faith whereof, we, the plenipotentiaries of the United States of America and of the Republic of Colombia, have signed and sealed these presents.

Done in the city of Bogota, on the third day of October, in the year of our Lord one thousand eight hundred and twenty-four, in the forty-ninth year of the Independence of the United States of America and the fourteenth of that of the Republic of Colombia.

[L. S.]   RICHARD C. ANDERSON, JR.
[L. S.]   PEDRO GUAL.

consules y vice consules de las partes respectivas.

ARTICULO 31. La Republica de Colombia y los Estados Unidos de America, deseando hacer tan duraderas y firmes, como las circunstancias lo permitan las relaciones que han de establecerse entre las dos potencias, en virtud del presente tratado ó convencion general de paz, amistad, navegacion, y comercio, han declarado solennemente y convienen en los puntos siguientes:

1°. El presente tratado permanencerá en su fuerza y vigor por el termino de doce años contados desde el dia del cange de las ratificaciones, en todos los puntos concernientes á comercio y navegacion, y en todos los demas puntos que se refieren á paz y amistad, será permanente, y perpetuamente obligatorio para ambas potencias.

2°. Si alguno, ó algunos de los ciudadanos de una ú otra parte infringiesen alguno de los articulos contenidos en el presente tratado, dichos ciudadanos serán personalmente responsables, sin que por esto se interrumpa la harmonia y buena correspondencia entre las dos naciones, comprometiendose cada una á no protegér de modo alguno al ofensor, ó sancionár semejante violacion.

3°. Si (lo que á la verdad no puede esperarse) desgraciadamente, alguno de los articulos contenidos en el presente tratado, fuesen en alguna otra manera violados, ó infringidos, se estipula espresamente que ninguna de las dos partes contratantes, ordenará, ó autorizará ningunos actos de represalia, ni declarará la guerra contra la otra por quejas de injurias, ó daños, hasta que la parte que se crea ofendida, haya antes presentado á la otra una esposicion de aquellas injurias, ó daños, verificada con pruebas y testimonios competentes, exigiendo justicia y satisfaccion, y esto haya sido negado, ó diferido sin razon.

4°. Nada de cuanto se contiene en el presente tratado, se construirá sin embargo, en contra de otros tratados publicos anteriores, y existentes con otros soberanos ó Estados.

El presente tratado de paz, amistad, navegacion, y comercio, será ratificado por el Presidente ó Vice Presidente de la Republica de Colombia, encargado del poder Ejecutivo, con consentimiento y aprobacion del Congreso de la misma, y por el Presidente de los Estados Unidos de America, con consejo, y consentimiento del Senado de los mismos; y las ratificaciones serán cangeadas en la ciudad de Washington dentro de ocho meses contados desde este dia, ó antes si fuese posible.

En fe de lo cual nosotros los plenipotenciarios de la Republica de Colombia, y de los Estados Unidos de America hemos firmado y sellado las presentes.

Dadas en la ciudad de Bogota el dia tres de Octubre del año del Señor mil ocho cientos veintecuatro, decimo cuarto de la Independencia de la Republica de Colombia y cuadragesimo nono de la de los Estados Unidos de America.

PEDRO GUAL.
RICHARD C. ANDERSON, JR.

No. 14.

BOGOTA, *August* 20, 1824.

SIR: I now inclose to you copies of the several letters of the Secretary of Foreign Relations to me, on the subject of the negotiation pending between us, together with copies of my answers. In a separate letter of this date, No. 15, I will inclose to you copies of two other letters addressed by me to him, and the answers to them, on the subjects referred to in my letter of the 18th instant.*

His two notes of the 20th and 26th of May, you will see, were either merely introductory to the negotiation, or served only to accompany his projet, presented with the last.

*These letters and the above mentioned despatch, No. 15, related to other subjects than those included in the negotiations for the treaty.

The letter of the 1st of July presents his reasons for wishing to avoid in the convention the declaration of the principle that free ships should give freedom to goods, and, indeed, for wishing to insert, in form, the contrary declaration. My answer of the 7th of July urges and insists on the propriety and necessity of adopting the principle proposed by me. To this answer, which was transmitted immediately after its date, no official response has yet been made; but I understand, from a private conversation with the Secretary, that in a few days I shall either receive a communication or be invited to a conference on that and the subjects of the negotiation generally. He also said that the delay had been produced by having ascertained that it was impracticable to complete the negotiation during the late session of Congress, and that after the adjournment the necessity for any extraordinary despatch had ceased.

I am confirmed in the belief that this Government will not insist on the ground *first assumed* in relation to the saving character of a neutral ship; but in the conversation to which I have just alluded, the Secretary said that his Government had a difficulty of this kind to encounter; that it apprehended that Spain would not admit that any foreign flag could protect the goods of a citizen of this country against her rights; that, notwithstanding the language of the treaty between the United States and Spain, by which it was declared that "the flag should cover the property, with respect to those powers who recognize the principle," it was apprehended that the Spanish Government would not admit that Colombia was 'a power," in the sense of the treaty, but was still her colony. He then said that, in such a case, the article which I proposed would be wholly inoperative, or operate against Colombia. During the conversation he expressed a wish that, in the event a treaty should be concluded on the principle urged by me, the United States should ascertain from Spain, at a very early day, in what way she regarded her own stipulation; and he asked what course the United States would adopt, if, after the conclusion of a treaty, a Spanish cruiser should capture Colombian property in one of her vessels? With all the reluctance which I must ever feel to answer, even informally, any question involving difficulty or importance, without proper consideration and authority, still, on this occasion, I did not hesitate to answer promptly, that the United States would resist such capture in the same way in which she would resist any other infraction of a treaty; that having recognized Colombia as a sovereign State, she would not admit that the property of Colombian citizens was not as effectually protected by her flag, even against Spanish capture, as the property of the subject of any other Government which had acceded to the principle. I infer from the manner and the language of the conversation that when the subject is again renewed some proposition for explanation or further assurance will be made.

You will observe in the letter of the Secretary of the 1st of July, reference is made to the provisional ordinance of this country, in which the principle that "free ships shall not make free goods" is declared, and that in my answer I notice it only in the following language: "You will see that I have restricted my observations to an examination of the expediency of adopting one of two proposed rules, without referring to the provisional ordinance of this country, to which you allude as being in force. I have abstained from any investigation of the legality of that ordinance, from a belief that the present discussion did not require it, and from an ardent hope that no future occurrence may take place which shall render such an examination necessary."

No occasion has yet occurred which produced the necessity of raising the question how far this Government was already bound by the stipulations of our treaty with Spain, made while Colombia was a component part of the monarchy. When I left the United States, it was supposed that the case had then occurred by the capture of the cargo of the Caravan, which required an immediate demand for the restitution of Spanish property taken on board an American vessel, and a portion of my instructions was devoted to an examination of the subject. The property had, by the court of admiralty, been declared "Spanish," and it was believed that the Caravan was a vessel of the United States; but before my arrival at Laguayra the definitive sentence of the court had condemned both vessel and cargo as Spanish property. From this sentence there has been no appeal; the citizens of the United States at Caraccas differed in their representations of the case. Some thought that it was an unjust condemnation, while others had no doubt that the vessel and cargo were really the property of the subjects of Spain. While the decision of the court was unreversed, and I had no authority to allege anything against it, I considered the original ground of demand for restitution, which existed in the event that the vessel was the property of citizens of the United States, as taken from me.

I have recently seen in the gazettes of the United States accounts of several captures of vessels having Spanish property on board, but I have as yet received no representation on which I could act, nor, indeed, have I any information of the fact except what the newspapers give.

I have not, of course, these certain means of knowing what will be the course of this Government on a demand for the restoration of property captured under such circumstances, which an official note would give; but from the reference in the late letter to me to the ordinance now said to be in force, and from observations made on different occasions since my residence in this country, I am satisfied that the restitution will be refused, or at least resisted with great pertinacity; and that the ground will be assumed that on the declaration of independence, or of the promulgation of their ordinance, (for I have heard both dates alluded to,) this country was absolved from all the engagements of the treaty between Spain and the United States. I have not failed, upon all such occasions, to intimate as strongly as the course of conversation with propriety admitted, and with a distinctness which could not be misunderstood, that the propriety of such conclusions was not admitted by the United States. I know very well the peril of speculating on the future course of a Government, but in this case the indications have been so strong that I have considered it proper to apprise you, by anticipation, of what I expect.

The *projet* and *contre projet* are not inclosed, on account of their bulk, and because it is believed that they were not necessary to the understanding of anything in this despatch. They will be sent by the next conveyance.

I have the honor to be, with great respect, your obedient servant,

R. C. ANDERSON, Jr.

Hon. John Quincy Adams, *Secretary of State.*

P. S. The copies are not distributed between the packages in the manner intended, but all of them are in the one or the other.

BOGOTA, *May* 24, 1824.

SIR: Your note of the 20th instant has been received, informing me that the Executive had conferred on you full powers for negotiating and concluding a treaty of amity, commerce, and navigation with the United States, and requesting to know at what time and place it would be agreeable to me to enter on the subject.

I cannot deny to myself the satisfaction of expressing the personal pleasure with which I received the information that the negotiation of a treaty on the part of this Republic had been confided to you, and in answer to your request, I beg leave to say that I shall be happy to commence our conferences on the subject to-morrow at 11 o'clock, at my office.

I have the honor to be, with great respect, your obedient servant,

R. C. ANDERSON, JR.

Hon. PEDRO GUAL, *Secretary of Foreign Relations.*

BOGOTA, *June* 2, 1824.

SIR: I have had the honor of receiving from you a project of a treaty of amity, commerce, and navigation between the United States of America and the Republic of Colombia, and having attentively and respectfully considered the same, have now the honor to submit to you a counter project, and to state to you that it will be very agreeable to me to enter on a discussion of the points involved in the project and counter project at any time it may suit your convenience.

I have the honor to be, with great respect and esteem, your obedient servant,

R. C. ANDERSON, JR.

Hon. PEDRO GUAL, *Secretary of State and Foreign Relations.*

BOGOTA, *July* 7, 1824.

SIR: I have had the honor of receiving your letter of the 1st instant, and have given to the reasons therein urged, in vindication of the fourteenth article of the project of a treaty, submitted by you, the most attentive consideration.

That article contains a principle so important in its effects, and so repugnant to the rule which I wish to establish in the proposed convention, that I must be indulged in making some observations in support of the article by which it is desired to supersede it. It will not be my purpose at this time, nor indeed does the occasion in any way demand it, to enter into an examination of the question "Whether a neutral bottom does of right, where no compact exists, protect the goods of a belligerent power." If this examination were necessary, I should in my own feelings find abundant incentive to support the affirmative of the proposition, and to maintain that the rule, which humanity, peace, and the policy of commercial nations all prescribe as the true rule, was really and already a part of the public law. But the nature of the present negotiation does not impose that duty on me. We have now only to declare what *shall be* the rule for ourselves, without inquiring what *has been* the rule for others. It is, however, my purpose to show that our highest obligations to the pacific and commercial habits of our citizens, to the spirit of our political institutions, and to the physical situation of our country, do demand of us to declare in language unambiguous, and as energetic as our command of language will permit us, "that free ships shall make free goods."

Whatever may be the present usage of some of the maritime nations of the world, or however far belligerent usurpation may have suppressed neutral right, we should be inexcusable in voluntarily permitting the sanction of two independent nations to foster a usurpation, the origin of which was superior force, and the continuance of which depends only on the continuance of that force. To withdraw from neutral rights that moral aid which the force of our example in making this declaration would give, would render us accessary to future mischiefs and vexations, which, though enormous, can only be equal to those which neutral and commercial nations have already suffered from the effects of the opposite doctrine; it would be equivalent to the high offence of refusing to an honest party the benefit of our testimony in a just cause. Such a course would, in that great contest which has been waging for a series of years for the purpose of ascertaining with precision the true boundaries of belligerent and neutral rights, be placing our Governments on that side which their interests and the spirit of commerce alike reject; for in that contest the interests of all those whose policy is peace, and whose prosperity rests on the culture of the soil or the commerce of the ocean, must impel them to take that side which gives the most enlarged enjoyment to the rights of neutral navigation. Any course which would, however remotely or indirectly, give countenance to the existence of a principle so palpably hostile to neutral commerce, should be carefully avoided by those whose interests are inseparably connected with it; but the express and public declaration (as is now proposed) on the face of a treaty, that the vessels of a friend shall not protect the goods with which they are laden, would not only be, it is respectfully submitted, a flagrant surrender of the just immunities of neutrals, but would suppose a total blindness to all the lights of modern improvement.

It is impossible to see what motive can operate on us to become the voluntary auxiliaries of those who maintain this claim, and to lend, gratuitously, the weight of the American example to those whose interest it may be to enlarge the circle of belligerent pretensions, and, of course, to narrow the just rights of those whose practice as well as profession is peace. I do not propose to propagate this, the favorite doctrine of my country, by the sword, but I urge the propriety of propagating it by all those moral means which, upon enlightened and Christian nations, have an effect so much stronger than the sword; of giving our disinterested testimony in its behalf; of inviting all others to adopt and pursue it by the forcible argument of pursuing it ourselves.

The history of the last century declares to us that there is nothing within the range of international transactions more certainly calculated to create dissentions between nations otherwise friendly, than the exercise of the right of search for the various purposes and in the various ways in which it has been claimed; and it declares to us, too, that neutral and pacific nations have ever been the unoffending victims of that vexatious branch of it involved in the present discussion, and which would be legitimated by the article you propose. It has generally been maintained by those who had arms and, of course, the requisite ability in their hands to enforce it beyond right, and to that single cause must be ascribed the fact that the usage has become general enough to assume the name of law. It is not enough to say that it is a matter of strict right to annoy an enemy in every practicable way, to do everything which may impair his strength or reduce him to peace. It is not sufficient to say so, because it is not true. Although nothing may be lawful which does not conduce to end the war, still it is not true that everything is allowed which tends to that end. The same reasoning would justify you in poisoning an adversary or refusing quarter to a prisoner. These rights, if ever they existed, have long since been abandoned with other barbarisms of those ages which gave them birth, and it is no more than just now to abandon others which, if not of equal, are of kindred barbarity. And if this claim which has no foundation in reason, which is supported only by arms, and can be exercised only by invading the jurisdiction of a friend, is yet allowed by the public law among the family of nations, it is time that every civilized member of that family should simultaneously concur in erasing the page which sanctions it.

There is no maxim of the public law more firmly established, none to which the sense of mankind has more universally compelled all nations to submit, than that a belligerent cannot pursue or capture his enemy or seize his property in the jurisdiction of a neutral. That rule, if unqualified, would close the question without the necessity of a special compact, as the right in contest is always exercised by a trespass on that jurisdiction; and it is believed that a practice violatory of this general rule would never have been instituted or continued long enough to assume the name or semblance of a law if, as has been suggested, the belligerent had not always in his hands the means of enforcing his pretensions, while the neutral, defenceless and incapable of resistance, is obliged, for peace or temporary preservation, to submit to the usurpation and to yield, not from a sense of justice, but from a sense of imbecility. It is believed that an examination of the subject will lead to the conviction that this was the original and sole foundation, and that it is, (with the exception of Colombia,) continued and supported now by those only who, feeling power and forgetting right, think proper to enforce what others cannot resist. Upon no other ground can we account for this anomalous practice, wholly violating the general spirit of the law of nations, which in almost every other case so carefully guards the jurisdiction of a neutral; while by this usage a party at war assumes the power of stopping, searching, and unlading the vessel of a friend.

There are other considerations connected with this subject, all tending to show that magnanimous nations should willingly make the concession, if that can be denominated concession which is in truth but an assent to a plain principle of natural justice. The character of the property on which the right is exercised would seem, with all those who regard reason in the acquisition of gain, to forbid any extraordinary eagerness in seizing it; it is generally the property of private and unoffending individuals— of persons who have, probably, not at all participated in the original wrong which gave rise to the war. Such is the spirit of this age, that many philanthropic statesmen, and the chiefs of some nations also, among whom I take high satisfaction in naming the President of the United States, have urged the propriety of expunging from the catalogue of belligerent rights that of capturing private property, and of giving to such property on the ocean the same exemption which it has for ages enjoyed on the land. The nature of this discussion does not require of me to go so far, but it may be fairly inferred that the relinquishment of this branch of the pretension will be no longer resisted when it is remembered that the property which is the object of it belongs to individuals and not to the hostile Government; that it is in a course of lawful commerce, and that the vessels which bear it, and must be assailed in order to enforce the claim, belong to neutrals and friends. This consideration gives to the question various aspects, and under each aspect it does seem to me that its morality, as well as policy, is wholly incapable of vindication.

The interests of those who are engaged in the peaceful pursuits of civil life form the predominating interest which should control the councils of every well regulated Government. A regard for that interest forbids us from adding to the ordinary and unavoidable calamities of war any unnecessary aggravation, and requires of us so to regulate its rules as in every practicable way to diminish the number of individuals operated on by it, and who may thereby be permitted to pursue their ordinary and useful occupations. But the right now claimed is precisely of that character, the execution of which is certainly, perhaps, unavoidably attended by the greatest degree of harshness; the bare detention of a vessel on the high seas, pursuing its lawful commerce and protected by the flag of peace, in itself involves harshness; but when it is remembered that the detention is always under the menace of a superior and warlike force, and that the consequent seizure and search are too often executed in the vexatious spirit which that superiority of force inspires, the appeal to our feelings for the entire abrogation of the practice is too strong to be resisted. One most powerful objection to its continuance is, that it can be exercised only at a distance from all supervising authority, when it may well be believed, as all experience too fully justifies, that the licentious and violent manner of its execution will be but too certainly proportioned to the distance from the sovereign eye, and to the difficulty and uncertainty of redress on the part of the neutral. It is always executed on a theatre to which the vigilance of the high authorities of the country cannot reach, and frequently, from the nature of things, by those who have not that responsibility from character or station which is sufficient to restrain them from unnecessary violence and actual oppression. If this high power of stopping and searching a neutral vessel, and taking therefrom goods which the avidity of an interested party may lead him to think belongs to an enemy, was confined, in practice, to officers commanding the public ships of their Government, it would be less intolerable; but when it is confided to any one who can procure the commission of a privateer, it becomes a system of insufferable vexation and mischief; and it is no sufficient answer to declare that some of these mischiefs do also result from the undoubted right of searching a neutral vessel for contraband goods; such a reply bringing to my recollection that I could not exterminate all, would only animate me more strongly to urge the suppression of this most fruitful source of irritation and national animosity. A reference to one evil, however incurable, can never furnish an argument for tolerating another.

Under this view, it does seem to me that every nation which, in estimating the value of an abstract right, has any regard to the means by which it is to be enforced, is urged irresistibly to abandon on the altar of peace a claim which is doubtful in its existence and odious in its exercise, always executed in violence and sometimes in bloodshed, one which is of all others most highly calculated to disturb the harmony of nations, and to make foes of those whom an identity of feelings, interests, and political institutions invite to be friends.

But, apart from the general reasons which should invite all nations to accede to the benign rule which I propose, is there not, in the peculiar situation of our respective countries, something which should impel us joyfully to embrace it, and to seize this occasion of giving our aid to the creation of a system of international law, which, omitting all those barbarous features that the cupidity or violence of other nations may have retained, shall admit those only which the true interests of our fellow-man and the best feelings of his nature can sanction? This is the first occasion on which a negotiation has ever been opened between the United States and any of her sister Republics; it is probably the first time at which this subject has been canvassed between American parties, and probably, too, it is the very first time at which it has ever been mentioned by the representatives of two nations whose Governments were republican and free. Does not this consideration warn us to be particularly ·cautious in giving counte-nance to any doctrine so hostile to the general spirit of our republican institutions? While in the internal organization of our Governments the greatest care has been displayed to protect all the arts of peace, and to foster all the occupations to which war and its usages are so inimical, shall we, in our exterior arrangements, voluntarily engraft a principle so hostile to the spirit and the practice of peace. If the monarchies of the Old World shall pertinaciously adhere to a pretension founded on and sustained alone by superior power, let the Republics of America recognize only those rights which are founded on reason and humanity, and are consonant to the genius of their constitutions and the habits of their people. In all negotiations with European powers that system of policy must, I admit, be pursued on this as on all other subjects which each independent nation shall think will best promote its interests, or which the pressure of temporary and calamitous circumstances may impose on it; but when two Republics on this continent are, for the first time, creating the rules which shall govern the intercourse of their citizens, why should they, unshackled by the policy and unawed by the power of others, prescribe any rules but those which good sense and humanity dictate? And I consider the introduction of the principle for which I contend as eminently important, when it is remembered (and it may be done without incurring the imputation of much national vanity) that the stipulation now to be made between us will probably furnish a formula for all the free Governments of America in their negotiations on this subject. It may readily be believed that the rule now formed will be regarded in a manner which will almost certainly insure its adoption by them. Nothing, surely, could be more mortifying than the future reflection that, under the influence of our pernicious example, they had pursued an unwise policy, and had surrendered one of the favorite immunities of neutrality.

The usages of modern warfare, with few exceptions, tend to restrict the limits of its operation and to liberate from its calamities the non-combatant and neutral. If at this period of increasing liberality we reject a principle which it is believed almost every nation of Europe has at some one time admitted, we should be rejecting the light from our eyes; we should be throwing back our nations on the darkness of those ages when I might admit that this principle was unknown; but when you will remember that the principles that gave birth to our Governments were alike unknown, or if known, not admitted. And even if I were now contending that the position that "free ships made free goods" was a part of the admitted law of nations, it would not be regarded by me as a fair argument in opposition, to be told that many of the powerful Governments of the world deny this principle, when it is known that some of them deny the plainest principles of human rights; that they deny the principles upon which your Government and mine are founded, and without the establishment of which, under the auspices of Almighty God, neither you nor I would have the power of negotiating this day.

But it may be stated that all the maritime powers of Europe have, at some time, admitted the enormity of the adverse principle by making conventional stipulations against it. Even Great Britain has recognized, at long intervals of time, in her treaties with France, and also with Spain, and with the United Provinces, the doctrine that neutral ships shall cover the goods. And you well recollect that the excitement produced by the enormities committed in enforcing the contrary principle was a prominent reason for forming that celebrated association denominated the Armed Neutrality. Whether or not this confederacy of neutrals, by the resistance which they displayed to maritime usurpation, and by promulgating the rules by which alone they would abide, succeeded in creating or changing the law they surely succeeded in giving to the world the highest evidence that it should be changed. I take great pleasure in citing the course of the United States on this subject. Her policy has been unchanged. It has been invariably that of liberating free trade from all unnecessary shackles. She has eagerly sought every occasion which her negotiations with the maritime powers of the world would afford to give her testimony in behalf of the superior policy and benignity of the rule which imparts to the goods the saving character of the ship. At a very early period of her history she succeeded in establishing it in her treaties with France, the Netherlands, Sweden, and Prussia, and at a later period with Spain. If my country could, for a moment, have forgotten the claims of humanity and fair commerce, and have attended only to her interests in a state of war, recollecting the enterprise and gallantry of her officers and seamen, she might well have supposed that no nation could have inflicted greater or more essential injury on an enemy under the authority of the opposite doctrine; but she has never permitted herself to estimate an action by the amount of injury it would inflict on an enemy, when that injury must fall in a less degree but in a manner equally certain on a friend. While her course on this question is not cited by me to furnish a controlling example for the government of others, I refer to it to show that, after an experience of nearly half a century, she still bears evidence to the superior reasonableness and justice of the rule she has adopted.

The stipulation now proposed is perfectly equal and fair. If one nation surrenders the right of taking her enemy's goods from the ships of another, she gets the equivalent in the corresponding concession from that other. She procures an immunity for her own property at the slight expense of agreeing not to seize another's. Under this view, I cannot feel the weight of the consideration suggested by you, that this Republic, being at war with Spain, has an interest different from that she would have in peace, when it is remembered that the same compact which will save Spanish property from Colombian cruisers will protect the property of your citizens, similarly situated, against capture from your enemy. And surely the exemption of the property of your citizens, and the increased commerce of the Republic, together with the impulse thereby given to agriculture and all other kinds of industry, form most ample equivalents for the miserable pittance of Spanish property which your privateers might catch upon the ocean. So that, even in a state of war, there is no loss in the course proposed; even in pecuniary interest the balance is at least equal; but when the calls of humanity, peace, and the harmony of nations are heard, considerations which with you will ever have the greatest weight, there cannot be any longer ground for hesitation. .

The accidental circumstance of being engaged in war cannot alter the justice of the principle, nor in any way affect its permanent policy. It is one which should be embraced by every nation whose permanent policy is peace, who does not fashion her internal institutions nor exterior arrangements for a system of continued and aggressive warfare. The contrary course should not be adopted even in the case that one of the contracting parties should, at the moment of negotiation, be engaged in war, as that situation must, of course, be temporary; and no wise or pacific nation would regulate her policy by the belief that war, instead of commerce, would be the trade of her citizens. Although the situation of the United States, to which you have been pleased to refer, is, at this time, most happily, one of universal peace, still her views of this subject have never varied; indeed, the policy of a nation on this subject must be permanent; it cannot be varied, from time to time, to suit all the changes which her political attitude with foreign nations may assume. If, in a state of war, she refuses to enter into wholesome regulations, evidently beneficial to her citizens in time of peace, the same course of reasoning would prevent her from adopting them on the return of peace, inasmuch as war might and probably would again come. The result would be, that, between the existence of an actual and the fear of a coming war, the stipulation now proposed might never be adopted.

While it would not become me to enter into an examination of the course which the peculiar interests of Colombia should direct her to pursue in relation to her commercial economy, still, under the suggestions of your letter, referring to the existing war in which she is engaged, I may be permitted to observe that surely the physical situation of no country more certainly directs the views of its Government and citizens to agriculture and commerce than that of Colombia; the variety of its climates, the fertility of its ample territory, but, above all, the great extent of its seacoast, lying on two oceans, having the remaining parts of this and two other entire continents at accessible and convenient distances, all declare that the lasting prosperity of its citizens must rest on the arts of peace, and that the permanent policy of its Government should be such as to foster and sustain those arts, regarding the occasional occurrences of war as events in no way to affect the general system.

Under the qualifications which I propose to annex to the stipulation, it does seem to me that it will be one of unmixed good—one wholly unexceptionable. I propose that it shall be declared that a ship of one of the contracting parties, being neutral, shall protect the goods with which it is laden against the vessels of the other party, being belligerent, *whenever such goods belong to a nation recognizing this principle.* This is, in truth, the whole extent to which any nation can go without manifest injury to itself. Without such a modification, a belligerent nation, holding aloof from the recognition of the principle, would enjoy all its benefits without the corresponding concessions. The truth of this position and the propriety of the modification are easily illustrated by the present relative situation of Colombia and her enemy. If the treaty between Spain and the United States declared simply " that free ships should make free goods," omitting the proposed qualification, the result would have been that all goods belonging to citizens of this Republic found on board vessels of the United States would have been protected against Spanish cruisers, while the goods of Spanish subjects, in like situation, would be liable to capture by Colombian ships, supposing (for illustration) that the Government did not recognize the principle. But, under the language of the treaty, as recently modified, this consequence does not follow, as it is there declared that " if either of the two contracting parties shall be at war with a third party, and the other neutral, the flag of the neutral shall cover the property of enemies whose Government acknowledge this principle, and not of others." It is to this extent that I invite you most earnestly to go ; to declare in the proposed convention that the vessels of our countries, respectively, shall convey, free from molestation, the goods of all nations who will assent to this salutary rule.

You will see that I have restricted my observations to an examination of the expediency of adopting one of two proposed rules, without referring to the provisional ordinance of this country, to which you allude as being now in force. I have abstained from any investigation of the legality of that ordinance, from a belief that the present discussion did not require it, and from an ardent hope that no future occurrence may take place which shall render such an examination necessary.

While I declare with unaffected sincerity my anxious wishes that you may concur with me in the views herein expressed, and that no occurrence may intervene to check the progress and happy completion of the negotiation between us, I will add that it would be a source of extreme and particular regret that the negotiation should be arrested by anything connected with the subject now involved in discussion, inasmuch as I should consider that any radical difference of opinion between two Republics of America on any important point of commercial or general policy would have at this time an unfavorable effect on the reputation and progress of all free Governments.

These considerations are submitted with the most profound respect for all those who entertain a different opinion, but with all the zeal which a most thorough conviction of their truth can inspire.

I have the honor to renew to you the assurances of my profound consideration and respect.

R. C. ANDERSON, Jr.

Hon. PEDRO GUAL, *Secretary of State and of Foreign Relations.*

No. 16.

BOGOTA, *September* 17, 1824.

SIR: Copies of the projet and of the contre projet of a treaty of navigation and commerce, as interchanged between the plenipotentiary of Colombia and myself, referred to in my letter No. 14 of the 20th of August, are herewith inclosed.

Soon after the date of my last letter I was invited to a renewal of the negotiation by verbal conference; these conferences have been frequent, and I am happy to inform you that we have agreed on all the articles to form a treaty. These articles have not, however, been reduced to their destined order, and it is possible that some verbal alterations may yet take place. I know of nothing which will probably prevent its conclusion in a few days. At this time I can inform you that the first three articles of my contre projet, by which the situation of the most favored nation is assured to each party, are adopted without alteration; and that the tenth article, establishing the principle that the flag shall cover the property, under the qualification recommended in my instructions, has been agreed to, also without alteration. In other respects the form of the contre projet is a good deal altered, though in substance it s retained. In most of the changes I think there has been an improvement, and indeed several of them

were made on my own suggestion. If the treaty should be agreed to and signed, I will immediately transmit to you a copy, together with the protocols of our conferences and such explanations as will put you in full possession of everything attending the negotiation. The treaty itself would be reserved for some safer conveyance than the casualties of the ordinary conveyances here afford. My letter numbered 8 gave you information that soon after my arrival in this capital I complied with your instructions by communicating to the Government of Colombia copies of the several acts of the Congress of the United States on the subject of the African slave trade. Although no indisposition has been manifested by this Government to adopt the most effectual measures for the suppression of that trade, and indeed every indication has been given in conversation of a perfect readiness to adopt, in co-operation with the United States, the most energetic measures for its extinction, still I have not yet made any specific proposition on the subject. With every anxiety to carry into effect what is understood to be the wishes of the President and the House of Representatives, and indeed to gratify my own and the feelings of my country, I have hitherto been prevented, solely by the difficulties I encountered, in framing articles for such a convention satisfactory to myself. Very recently I have seen the convention signed in London, and the proceedings of the Senate on it; and I intend, at an early day, to avail myself of the lights which these proceedings furnish to introduce the subject here. As the articles embracing the proper stipulations and restrictions will be more numerous than I had at first supposed necessary, I infer that the authority given in your instructions will be as properly executed by embodying those articles in a separate instrument, as by connecting them with a treaty of commerce.

I have the honor to be, with great respect, your obedient servant,

R. C. ANDERSON, JR.

Hon. JOHN QUINCY ADAMS, *Secretary of State.*

Projet of a Treaty of Friendship, Commerce, and Navigation, between the Republic of Colombia and the United States of America.

[Translation.]

BOGOTA, *May* 18, 1824.

In the name of God, the Author and Lawgiver of the Universe: The Republic of Colombia and the United States of America, desirous of confirming and perpetuating the friendship and good understanding that happily subsist between the two powers, have determined to establish, in a clear, distinct, and positive manner, the regulations to be in future sacredly observed by both, by means of a treaty or convention of peace, friendship, commerce, and navigation.

For this desirable object, the Vice President of the Republic, charged with the executive power, by virtue of an article of the constitution of said Republic, has conferred on the honorable Pedro Gual, Secretary of State and of Foreign Relations, full powers; and the President of the United States of America has conferred them on the honorable Richard C. Anderson, Minister Plenipotentiary near the said Republic; who, having exchanged the said powers in good and proper form, have agreed upon the following articles:

ARTICLE 1. There shall be a perfect, lasting, and inviolable peace and true friendship between the Republic of Colombia and the United States of America, throughout the whole extent of their possessions and territories, and between their people, citizens and subjects, without distinction of persons or places.

ARTICLE 2. The Republic of Colombia and the United States, desirous of remaining in peace and friendship with all other civilized nations of the earth, by means of an open policy, equally friendly to all, bind themselves hereafter not to grant any special favor or particular and exclusive privileges to any nation of which each of the contracting parties shall not immediately participate.

ARTICLE 3. The citizens and subjects of the United States shall have liberty to frequent at pleasure, with their own vessels, the coasts and ports of the Republic of Colombia, and to trade therein with all manner of productions, goods, and merchandise whose importation and exportation shall not be absolutely prohibited, and of whom greater imposts, contributions, and duties shall not be exacted than those usually paid by the most favored nations. The citizens and subjects of the Republic of Colombia shall also enjoy the same liberty on the coasts and in the ports of the United States, without any distinction; it being understood that to enjoy this liberty of commerce, trade, and navigation, the citizens and subjects of both parties shall observe the laws and regulations to which the subjects and citizens of the most favored nations are subject.

ARTICLE 4. The citizens and subjects of both contracting parties, in the territories subject to their jurisdiction, shall have the free power to dispose of their personal, landed, movable, or moving property, by rents, donations, testaments, or in any other way. The property of the citizens and subjects of both parties, who shall die *ab intestato* in any of the countries subject to their respective jurisdictions, shall pass to their legitimate heirs, in conformity with the laws of the country in which they shall have died. And if said heirs shall be disqualified from entering upon the possession of their inheritance on account of their being foreigners, the term of three years shall be allowed for any arrangement that may best suit them.

ARTICLE 5. The Republic of Colombia and the United States promise and oblige themselves formally to afford their special protection to the persons and property of citizens and subjects, traders or professors of any liberal or mechanical art, whether residents or visitors, who may be found in their respective territories, opening and offering the courts of justice for their legal resort upon the same terms as to the native or naturalized citizens of the country in which they may be.

ARTICLE 6. The citizens and subjects of neither party shall be obstructed or detained with their vessels, crews, goods, and merchandise, belonging to them, under pretext of military expeditions, public or private uses of whatever kind, without granting to those interested a sufficient indemnification; but the citizens and subjects of other liberal or mechanical professions of the Republic of Colombia and the United States of America, who shall reside in the countries subject to the jurisdiction of one or the other State, shall remain subject to the same laws, charges, imposts, and contributions, to which the native and naturalized citizens are, of the country in which they reside.

ARTICLE 7. Whenever the citizens and subjects of either party are obliged to seek refuge and safety in its rivers, bays, roads, ports, and jurisdiction, with their vessels, whether merchantmen or ships-of-war, public or private, on account of the weather, or the pursuit of pirates or enemies, they shall be admitted and treated with humanity, affording them every favor and protection in repairing and refitting them, procuring provisions, and placing them in a condition to continue their voyage without any obstruction or hindrance.

ARTICLE 8. All the vessels, goods, and effects of the citizens and subjects of one of the contracting parties that shall be captured by pirates, whether within the limits of its jurisdiction or on the high sea, and shall be conducted to, or found in, the rivers, bays, roads, ports, and jurisdiction of the other, shall be returned to their owners, their claims being proved in due form before the proper tribunals; provided the claim be made within the precise term of one year by the owners themselves, their attorneys or agents of their respective nations.

ARTICLE 9. In case a vessel belonging to the citizens and subjects of one of the contracting parties be wrecked, stranded, or injured in any way, on the coasts and within the jurisdiction of the other, every assistance and protection shall be afforded her, as is usual towards vessels of the nation where the accident may have happened, permitting her to unload her goods and effects without exacting therefor any duty, impost, or contribution, until they be reshipped.

ARTICLE 10. The citizens and subjects of both contracting parties shall have perfect and absolute liberty of sailing, directly, with their vessels, goods, and merchandise, from one neutral port to another, and from a neutral port to an enemy's, although it may belong to one or many chiefs or States at war with either of the two nations, excepting, in these last two cases, the articles of contraband declared to be such in the following enumeration, viz: cannons, mortars, howitzers, swivels, blunderbusses, muskets, fusils, rifles, pistols, pikes, swords, sabres, lances, halberts, grenades, bombs, fusees, balls, and other articles belonging to the use of these or any other description of arms; powder, saltpetre, matches, lead in bars, shields, helmets, cuirasses, and other suitable armor for the equipment of soldiers; colors, horses and their trappings; and, in general, every kind of ready-made clothing, the equipments and appointments of troops, or apparatus for prosecuting war by land or sea.

ARTICLE 11. In all other goods and merchandise, articles of commerce whose importation and exportation shall not have been generally prohibited, the citizens and subjects of both parties shall enjoy the perfect liberty of trading, comprehending every description of provisions and articles of the first necessity for life, excepting only to those ports besieged and blockaded. And, to avoid all doubt, it is expressly declared that those ports alone are besieged or blockaded which are attacked by the forces of one or more belligerents capable of preventing the entrance and departure of neutrals.

ARTICLE 12. And forasmuch as it frequently happens that neutral vessels sail from their respective ports bound for an enemy's port, not knowing that said port has been declared to be in a state of blockade, and is actually besieged or blockaded, the contracting parties have agreed that if these neutral vessels, before their attempt to enter, be informed of the port being blockaded, and, after having received this intimation, should disregard it, or attempt to enter, these vessels and their cargoes, although not consisting of articles of contraband, shall be detained, sequestered; and confiscated. After the blockade shall be raised, the place surrendering to the blockading forces, all the neutral vessels and their cargoes found in the port captured shall also be detained, sequestered, and confiscated, if they shall have entered therein after the blockade had been declared and executed; but the neutrals that shall have entered the said port before the blockade, being ignorant of it, shall be respected.

ARTICLE 13. The articles of contraband above specified that shall be found on the high sea, or within the limits of the jurisdiction of one of the two nations, on board one of their vessels, bound for a country the enemy of one of them, shall be detained, sequestered, and confiscated, leaving the rest of the cargo and the vessel free for whatever disposition may suit the owners. No vessel of the two nations shall be detained on the high sea on account of contrabands, if the master, captain, or supercargo of said vessel shall place the articles of contraband at the disposition of the captain, unless such articles be so numerous and of such quantity as to render it impossible to transport them on board of the capturing vessel without serious inconveniences; but in this case, as well as in those of just detention, the vessels detained shall be sent to the nearest, safest, and most convenient port, for trial and corresponding adjudication, according to law.

ARTICLE 14. In like manner the goods and merchandise belonging to enemies of one of the contracting parties, and found on board of neutral vessels of the other, shall be detained, sequestered, and declared to be good prize, whatever may be their destination; and the goods and merchandise of the neutral party, found on board of enemies' vessels captured, shall be also free.

ARTICLE 15. To prevent all disorder in visiting and examining the vessels and cargoes of both contracting parties on the high sea, they have mutually agreed that whenever a public or private armed vessel shall fall in with a neutral, the first shall remain beyond cannon shot from the second, and order its boat, with two or three men, to make the visit and examination of the papers concerning the property and cargo of the vessel, without causing the least extortion, violence, or ill treatment, for which the commanders and officers of the said armed vessel shall be responsible.

ARTICLE 16. To avoid all grievance and abuse in the examination of the papers concerning the property of the vessels of the citizens and subjects of both powers, they have agreed that, one of them being at war with the vessels belonging to the citizens and subjects of the other shall be obliged to carry with them sea patents or passports, expressing the name, property, and burden of the vessel, as well as the name and residence of the owner and commandant of said vessel, so that it may in this manner appear whether she really and actually belongs to citizens or subjects of the other. They have agreed in like manner that the vessels above mentioned, in addition to their being provided with the sea patents or passports, shall also carry certificates containing the invoice of the cargo, the place whence the vessel has sailed, and a declaration of the goods on board the vessel, whether contraband or not, with a specification of the owner to whom they belong, without which requisite the said vessels shall be detained, to be tried by the competent tribunal, and declared good prize, unless they shall satisfy or repair the deficiency by testimony equivalent in every respect.

ARTICLE 17. Whenever either of the contracting parties shall be engaged in war with another State, no citizen or subject of Colombia, or of the United States, shall accept a commission, or privateering commission, to aid or co-operate with the enemies of one or the other contracting party in a hostile manner, under the penalty of being treated as a pirate.

ARTICLE 18. If, by accident, it should happen that both contracting parties should be engaged in war at the same time with a common enemy, the following regulations shall be mutually observed:

1. The vessels and cargoes of each, that may be captured by the private armed vessels-of-war of

the other, shall be returned to their owners whenever they shall not have remained in the power of the enemy more than four and twenty hours, giving to the captors the third of their value. But if the four and twenty hours shall have been passed over, the vessel and her cargo shall belong entirely to the captor.

2. The vessels and cargoes recaptured by the vessels-of-war of both powers shall be restored to their owners, allowing to the captors the thirtieth part of their whole value, if the vessels captured have not remained in the power of the enemy more than four and twenty hours, and the tenth part if that time have passed by.

3. In these cases the restitution shall be made after the property has been properly proved, previously allowing to the captors the part belonging to them.

4. The public and private armed vessels of both nations shall be admitted, with their prizes, into the ports of the other; but these prizes shall not be unloaded or sold until the proper tribunal of the captor shall have decided upon their legality.

ARTICLE 19. If, by a fatality which cannot be expected, the two high contracting parties shall make war on each other, they have agreed, and do agree, now for then, that there shall be granted the term of six months to the merchants residing on the coasts and at the ports of each, and one year to those living in the interior, to settle their business and transport their merchandise where they may please, granting them for this purpose the necessary safe conduct until they reach the port they have designated.

The citizens and subjects of other professions that may be established in the territories and dominions of the Republic of Colombia and the United States shall be respected and secured in the full enjoyment of their personal liberty and of their property, unless their private conduct render them unworthy this protection, which, in regard for humanity, the two contracting parties oblige themselves to afford them.

ARTICLE 20. To make more effective the protection which the Republic of Colombia or the United States are to furnish in future to the navigation and commerce of their respective citizens and subjects, they agree to receive and admit consuls and vice consuls in the ports fitted for foreign commerce, of both contracting parties, who shall enjoy therein all the privileges, prerogatives, and immunities of the consuls and vice consuls of the most favored nations; each remaining at liberty to except those ports, stations, and places where the admission and residence of the said consuls and vice consuls may not be deemed convenient.

ARTICLE 21. That the consuls and vice consuls of both parties may enjoy the privileges, prerogatives, and immunities belonging to them from their public character, they shall receive, before entering upon their functions, their authority or diploma in due form from the Government, so that, being accredited, and the *exequatur* obtained, they may be esteemed and considered as such consuls by all the authorities, magistrates, and inhabitants of the consular district in which they reside, as soon as they affix the arms of their nation upon the door of the house in which their office may be kept.

ARTICLE 22. It has also been agreed that the consuls, their secretaries, officers, and persons attached to the service of the consulates, shall be exempted from all public service and from every description of taxes, imposts, and contributions, excepting what should be paid on account of commerce, lucrative profession, and landed property, and to which the inhabitants and natives or naturalized citizens of the country where they reside are subject; in every other respect they shall remain subject to the laws in force of the respective State. The archives and papers of the consulates shall be preserved inviolate, and under no pretext shall any magistrate enter to inspect them, by way of domiciliary visits, or on any other ground.

ARTICLE 23. The contracting parties have also agreed, for the better understanding of the 21st article, that the United States shall admit consuls or vice consuls of Colombia in those ports of their territories and dominions in which, until now, the consuls of the most favored nations have been admitted and received; and the Republic of Colombia will admit and receive consuls of the United States in the city of Santo Torras de Angostura, whose consular district shall extend to the ports fitted, or which shall be fitted, for foreign commerce on the river Orinoco; in the city of Cumana, whose consular district shall embrace the ports that are adapted, or which shall be, in the provinces of Cumana, Barcelona, and the island of Margarita; in Laguayra or Puerto Cabello, whose consular district shall embrace the ports fitted, or which shall be fitted, for foreign commerce in the province of Caraccas; in the town of Maracaibo, whose consular district shall extend to the ports that are fitted, or which shall be, in the provinces of Coro and Maracaibo; in the town of Cartagena, whose consular district shall extend to the ports that are, or shall be fitted, in the provinces of Rio Hacha, Santa Marta, and Cartagena; in the town of Panama, whose consular district shall extend to the ports that are, or which shall be fitted, in the provinces of Porto Bello, Veraguas, Panama; in the town of Guayaquil, whose consular district shall embrace the ports that are, or which shall be fitted, on the coasts of the department of the same name, to the confines of Colombia and Peru. The Government of Colombia also agrees that the consuls of the United States may change their residence from the ports above mentioned to other proper ports of their consular district which they may think to be better adapted to the discharge of their offices, on account of their health, location, and mercantile relations, provided they shall previously obtain the consent and approbation of the said Government of Colombia.

ARTICLE 24. The consuls of both parties shall have power to appoint vice consuls or consular agents among the citizens, subjects or foreigners, resident in the other fit ports of their consular districts; but they shall not commence the exercise of their functions until the approbation of the Government of the Republic of Colombia and of the United States be obtained. The functions of said vice consuls or consular agents shall be limited to giving protection and aid to merchants, vessels, public and private property of both nations, with the obligation of giving account to the consuls of whom they shall have obtained their appointments of whatever may have required their intervention; and they shall remain beyond this, subject to the laws, charges, imposts and contributions, as the native and naturalized citizens or foreigners of the country where they may have settled.

ARTICLE 25. The citizens and subjects of both contracting parties shall have the power to make their testaments, codicils, contracts, obligations, protests, and other acts for death, or among the living, mutually obligatory upon themselves, before the consuls of the respective nations; and the testimonies of said acts *inter vivos*, or as last wills, being signed by the said consuls and authorized with their proper seals, shall have full faith and credit before the courts of the United States and those of the Republic of Colombia.

ARTICLE 26. It has also been agreed that the interposition of consuls in the successions and inheritances of the citizens and subjects of the one party who may have died *intestate* in the territory of the other, or the executors or legitimate heirs according to the *testament*, being found absent, shall be confined solely to appearing for the heirs, citizens, or subjects of their respective nation, before the courts of the country in everything proper for the security and preservation of the goods and property, movable and landed, which the deceased may have left; to the settlement of accounts, the payment of debts, and the collection of dues, until the succession or inheritance pass to the legitimate heirs, according to the laws.

ARTICLE 27. They moreover agree that the consuls of both parties may exercise sufficient power and jurisdiction on board of the merchant vessels of their respective nations to decide, in a summary manner, every dispute or altercation that may, in any way, destroy good order between the captains, masters, supercargoes, and crews; which acts the consul shall exercise on board the said vessels, without its being understood from this that the municipal regulations and ordinances of the respective ports are to cease to be observed, but which shall be observed and executed with all their force and effect.

ARTICLE 28. Beyond the vessels themselves, the power and jurisdiction of the consuls, in controverted matters, shall only reach to the cognizance and determination of the differences and disputes that may arise between the citizens and subjects of both contracting parties in relation to the pay of sailors and other persons belonging to the crews and complements, and as to the conditions of the contracts in their engagements, the settlement of pay and passages; the trial and decision of which, the consuls shall make without any expense to the parties, in case they do not wish to determine the matter by arbitration, which mode should be preferred to all others.

ARTICLE 29. The consuls shall moreover have power to demand the aid of the territorial authorities for the detention, custody, and arrest of the deserters of the public and private vessels of both nations; for which purpose they shall present to the said authorities the roll of equipage of the vessels to which they may belong, by which roll it may appear that the deserter or deserters whom they claim compose a part of their crews. As soon as these deserters shall have been taken, they shall be placed at the disposition of the respective consuls to be restored to the vessels to which they previously belonged, or to others of their nation; but the detention or arrest shall not continue for more than two months, after which they shall be set at liberty, and the claim shall not be renewed.

ARTICLE 30. The Republic of Colombia and the United States, desirous of making as durable as circumstances may permit the relations happily to be established between both powers by virtue of the present definitive treaty of friendship, commerce, and navigation, have solemnly proposed and agreed to the following points:

1. The present treaty between the Republic of Colombia and the United States shall continue for the term of ———— years, in everything that concerns commerce and navigation, it being understood to be perpetually and lastingly obligatory as to what it contains in relation to the peace and friendship between the two nations.

2. If any citizen or citizens and subjects of either party shall infringe any of the articles of the present treaty, said citizens and subjects shall be personally responsible, and punished to the satisfaction of the party offended; but this shall not interrupt the good feeling and intercourse between the contracting parties.

3. If, which cannot be expected, any article or articles contained in the present treaty shall be infringed by either of the contracting parties, the rest shall remain in their full force and effect, and shall be observed religiously and inviolably, as if such infraction had not been committed; which shall be submitted to an amicable discussion by both parties; and if no decision can be had, it shall then be referred to a sovereign or Government friendly to the Republic of Colombia and the United States.

The present treaty of friendship, commerce, and navigation, shall be approved and ratified by the Republic of Colombia, with the advice and consent of the Congress of the said Republic, within the term of ————, and by the United States within ————.

In faith of which, we, the plenipotentiaries of the Republic of Colombia and the United States of America, have signed and sealed the present.

Given, &c.

Contre Projet.

In the name of God, Author and Legislator of the Universe: The United States of America and the Republic of Colombia, desirous to make lasting and firm the friendship and good understanding which happily prevails between both nations, have resolved to fix in a manner clear, distinct, and positive, the rules which shall, in future, be religiously observed between the one and the other, by means of a treaty or general convention of peace, friendship, commerce, and navigation.

For this most desirable object, the President of the United States of America has conferred full powers on Richard Clough Anderson, junior, a citizen of the said States, and their Minister Plenipotentiary to the said Republic; and the Vice President of the Republic of Colombia, charged with the executive power, by virtue of the ——— article of the constitution, on the honorable Pedro Gual, Secretary of State and of Foreign Relations; who, having exchanged their said full powers in due and proper form, have agreed to the following articles:

ARTICLE 1. There shall be a perfect, firm, and inviolable peace and sincere friendship between the United States of America and the Republic of Colombia, in all the extent of their possessions and territories, and between their people and citizens, respectively, without distinction of persons or places.

ARTICLE 2. The United States of America and the Republic of Colombia, desiring to live in peace with all the other nations of the earth, by means of a policy frank and equally friendly with all, engage mutually not to grant any particular favor to other nations, in respect of commerce and navigation, which shall not immediately become common to the other party, who shall enjoy the same freely, if the concession was freely made, or on allowing the same compensation, if the concession was conditional.

ARTICLE 3. The citizens of the United States may frequent all the coasts and countries of the Republic of Colombia, and reside and trade therein in all sorts of produce, manufactures, and merchandise, and shall pay no other or greater duties, charges, or fees whatsoever than the most favored nation is or shall be obliged to pay, and they shall enjoy all the rights, privileges, and exemptions in navigation and

commerce which the most favored nation does or shall enjoy, submitting themselves, nevertheless, to the laws and usages there established, and to which are subjected the subjects or citizens of the most favored nations. In like manner the citizens of the Republic of Colombia may frequent all the coasts and countries of the United States, and reside and trade there in all sorts of produce, manufactures, and merchandise, and shall pay no other or greater duties, charges, or fees than the most favored nation is or shall be obliged to pay; and they shall enjoy all the rights, privileges, and exemptions in navigation and commerce which the most favored nation does or shall enjoy, submitting themselves, nevertheless, to the laws and usages there established, and to which are submitted the subjects and citizens of the most favored nations.

ARTICLE 4. The citizens of each of the contracting parties shall have full power to dispose of their personal goods within the jurisdiction of the other by sale, donation, testament, or otherwise, and their representatives, being citizens of the other party, shall succeed to their said personal goods, whether by testament or *ab intestato*, and they may take possession thereof, either by themselves or others acting for them, and dispose of the same at their will, paying such dues only as the inhabitants of the country, wherein the said goods are, shall be subject to pay in like cases. And if, in the case of real estate, the said heirs would be prevented from entering into the possession of the inheritance on account of their character of aliens, there shall be granted to them the term of three years to dispose of the same as they may think proper, and to withdraw the proceeds without molestation and exempt from all rights of detraction on the part of the Government of the respective States.

ARTICLE 5. The United States of America and the Republic of Colombia promise and engage, formally, to give their special protection to the persons and property of the citizens of each other, traders or professors of any liberal or mechanical art, who may be in their respective territories, commorant or transient, leaving open and free to them the tribunals of justice for their judicial recourse, on the same terms which are usual and customary with the natives or naturalized citizens of the country in which they may be. The most perfect freedom of conscience and of worship is granted to the citizens of either party within the jurisdiction of the other, without being liable to molestation in that respect for any cause other than an insult on the religion of others. Moreover, when the citizens of one party shall die within the jurisdiction of the other, their bodies shall be buried in the usual burying grounds or other decent and suitable place, and shall be protected from violation or disturbance.

ARTICLE 6. The citizens of neither of the contracting parties shall be liable to any embargo, nor be detained with their vessels, cargoes, merchandise, or effects, under pretext of any military expedition, nor for any public or private purpose whatever, without allowing to those interested a sufficient indemnification. But the citizens of all professions, liberal or mechanical, of one of the said contracting parties, who may be dwelling in the countries subject to the jurisdiction of the other, shall remain subject to the same laws, charges, contributions, and taxes, to which are subject the citizens, native and naturalized, of the country in which they reside.

ARTICLE 7. Whenever the citizens of either of the contracting parties shall be forced to seek refuge or asylum in the rivers, bays, roads, ports, or dominions of the other with their vessels, whether merchant or of war, public or private, through stress of weather, pursuit of pirates or enemies, they shall be received and treated with humanity, giving to them all favor and protection for repairing their vessels, procuring provisions, and placing themselves in a situation to continue their voyage, without obstacle or hindrance of any kind.

ARTICLE 8. All the ships, merchandise, and effects, belonging to the citizens of one of the contracting parties, which may be captured by pirates, whether within the limits of its jurisdiction or on the high seas, and may be carried or found in the rivers, roads, bays, ports, or dominions of the other, shall be delivered up to the owners, they proving, in due and proper form, their rights before the competent tribunals; it being well understood that the claim should be made within the term of one year, by the parties themselves, their attorneys or agents, of the respective Governments.

ARTICLE 9. When any vessel belonging to the citizens of either of the contracting parties shall be wrecked, foundered, or shall suffer damage, on the coasts or within the dominions of the other, there shall be given to them all assistance and protection, in the same manner which is usual and customary with the vessels of the nation where the damage happens, permitting them to unload the said vessel (if necessary) of its merchandise and effects without exacting for it any duty, impost, or contribution, until they may be exported.

ARTICLE 10. It shall be lawful for all and singular the citizens of the United States of America and of the Republic of Colombia to sail with their ships with all manner of liberty and security, no distinction being made, who are the proprietors of the merchandise laden thereon, from any port to the places of those who now or hereafter may be at enmity with the said United States or the said Republic of Colombia. It shall likewise be lawful for the citizens aforesaid to sail with the ships and merchandise aforementioned, and to trade with the same liberty and security, from the places, ports, and havens of those who are enemies of both or either party, without any opposition or disturbance whatsoever; not only directly from the places of the enemy aforementioned to neutral places, but also from one place belonging to an enemy to another place belonging to an enemy, whether they be under the jurisdiction of one State or under several. And it is hereby stipulated that free ships shall also give a freedom to goods, and that everything shall be deemed to be free and exempt which shall be found on board the ships belonging to the citizens of either of the contracting parties, although the whole or any part thereof should appertain to the enemies of either, contraband goods being always excepted. It is also agreed, in like manner, that the same liberty be extended to persons who are on board a free ship, with this effect, that although they be enemies of either party, they are not to be taken out of that free ship, unless they are soldiers, and in actual service of the enemies: *Provided, however*, and it is hereby agreed, That the stipulations herein contained, declaring that the flag shall cover the property, shall be understood as applying to those powers only who recognize this principle; but if either of the two contracting parties shall be at war with a third party, and the other neutral, the flag of the neutral shall cover the property of enemies whose Governments acknowledge this principle, and not of others.

ARTICLE 11. This liberty of navigation and commerce shall extend to all kinds of merchandise, excepting those only which are distinguished by the name of contraband; and under this name of contraband or prohibited goods shall be comprehended arms, great guns, bombs, with the fusees and other things belonging to them, cannon ball, gunpowder, match pikes, swords, lances, spears, halberds, mortars, petards, grenades, muskets, musket ball, bucklers, helmets, breast plates, coats of mail, and the like kinds of arms proper for arming soldiers, musket vests, belts, and all other warlike instruments whatever. These merchandises which follow shall not be reckoned among contraband or prohibited goods: that is to say, all sorts of cloths, and all other manufactures woven of any wool, flax, silk, cotton, or any other materials whatever; all kinds of wearing apparel, together with the species whereof they are used to be made, gold and silver, as well coined as uncoined, tin, iron, latten, copper, brass, coals, as also wheat and barley, and any other kind of corn and pulse; tobacco, and likewise all manner of spices; salted and smoked flesh, salted fish, cheese and butter, beer, oils, wines, sugars, and all sorts of salts, and, in general, all provisions which serve for the nourishment of mankind and the sustenance of life; furthermore, all kinds of cotton, hemp, flax, tar, pitch, repes, cables, sails, sail cloths, anchors, also ship masts, planks, boards and beams of what trees soever, and all other things proper either for building or repairing ships, and all other goods whatever which have not been worked into the form of any instrument or thing prepared for war, by land or by sea, shall not be reputed contraband, much less such as have been already wrought and made up for any other use; all which shall be wholly reckoned among free goods, as likewise all other merchandise and things which are not comprehended and particularly mentioned in the foregoing enumeration of contraband goods, so that they may be transported and carried in the freest manner by the citizens of both the contracting parties, even to places belonging to an enemy, such towns or places being only excepted as are at that time besieged, blocked up, or invested. And to avoid all doubt in this particular, it is declared that those places only shall be considered as besieged or blocked up which shall be attacked by a force of the belligerent capable of preventing the entry of the neutral.

ARTICLE 12. And whereas it frequently happens that vessels sail for a port or place belonging to an enemy without knowing that the same is either besieged, blockaded, or invested, it is agreed that every vessel so circumstanced may be turned away from such port or place, but she shall not be detained nor any part of her cargo, if not contraband, be confiscated, unless after notice of such blockade or investment she shall again attempt to enter; but she shall be permitted to go to any other port or place she shall think proper. Nor shall any vessel of either, that may have entered into such port or place before the same was actually besieged, blockaded or invested by the other, be restrained from quitting such place with her cargo, nor if found therein after the reduction and surrender of such place, shall such vessel or cargo be liable to confiscation, but they shall be restored to the owners thereof.

ARTICLE 13. The articles of contraband before enumerated, which may be found on the high seas in a vessel bound for an enemy's port, shall be subject to detention and confiscation, leaving free the rest of the cargo and the ship, that the owners may dispose of them as they see proper. No vessel of either of the two nations shall be detained on the high seas on account of having on board articles of contraband, whenever the master, commander, or supercargo of said vessel will deliver up the articles of contraband to the captor, unless the quantity of such articles be so great and of so large a bulk that they cannot be received on board of the capturing ship without great inconvenience; but in this and in all other cases of just detention, the vessels detained shall be sent to the nearest convenient and safe port, for trial and judgment according to law.

ARTICLE 14. In order to prevent all kind of disorder in the visiting and examination of the ships and cargoes of both the contracting parties on the high seas, they have agreed, mutually, that whenever a vessel-of-war, public or private, shall meet with a neutral of the other contracting party, the first shall remain out of cannon shot, and may send its boat with two or three men only, in order to execute the said examination of the papers concerning the ownership and cargo of the vessel, without causing the least extortion, violence or ill treatment, for which the commanders and officers of the said armed ship shall be responsible with their persons and property. And it is expressly agreed that the neutral party shall in no case be required to go on board the examining vessel for the purpose of exhibiting his papers, or for any other examination whatever.

ARTICLE 15. To avoid all kind of vexation and abuse in the examination of the papers relating to the ownership of the vessels belonging to the citizens of the two contracting parties, they have agreed, and do agree, that in case one of them should be engaged in war, the ships and vessels belonging to the citizens of the other must be furnished with sea letters or passports, expressing the name, property, and bulk of the ship, as also the name and place of habitation of the master or commander of said vessel, in order that it may thereby appear that the ship really and truly belongs to citizens of one of the parties; they have likewise agreed that such ships being laden, shall, besides the said sea letters or passports, also be provided with certificates containing the several particulars of the cargo, the place whence the ship sailed, so that it may be known whether any forbidden or contraband goods be on board the same, which certificate shall be made out by the officers of the place whence the ship sailed, in the accustomed form; and if any one shall think it fit or advisable to express in the said certificates the person to whom the goods on board belong, he may freely do so; without which requisites said vessels may be detained to be adjudged by the competent tribunal, and may be declared legal prize, unless they shall satisfy or supply the defect by testimony entirely equivalent.

ARTICLE 16. And it is further agreed, that in all cases the established courts for prize causes, in the country to which the prize may be conducted, shall alone take cognizance. And whenever such tribunal of either of the parties shall pronounce judgment against any vessel, or goods, or property claimed by the citizens of the other party, the sentence or decree shall mention the reasons or motives on which the same shall have been founded, and an authenticated copy of the sentence or decree, and of all the proceedings in the case, shall, if demanded, be delivered to the commander or agent of the said vessel without delay, he paying the legal fees for the same. The citizens of both parties shall be allowed to employ such advocates, solicitors, notaries, agents, and factors, as they may judge proper in all their affairs, and in all their trials at law, in which they may be concerned before the tribunals of the other party; and such agents shall have free access to be present at the proceedings in such cases, and at the taking of all examinations and evidences which may be exhibited in the said trials.

ARTICLE 17. Whenever one of the contracting parties shall be engaged in war with another State, no citizen of the other contracting party shall accept a commission or letter of marque for the purpose of assisting or co-operating hostilely with said enemy against the said party so at war, under the pain of being treated as a pirate.

ARTICLE 18. If, by any fatality which cannot be expected, and which God forbid, the two contracting parties should be engaged in war with each other, they have agreed, and do agree, now for then, that there shall be allowed the term of six months to the merchants resident on the coasts and in the ports of each other, and the term of one year to those who dwell in the interior, to arrange and transport their effects wherever they please, giving to them the safe conduct necessary for it, which may serve as a sufficient protection until they arrive at the designated port. The citizens of other professions, who may be established in the territories or dominions of the United States and of the Republic of Colombia, shall be respected and maintained in the full enjoyment of their personal liberty and property, unless their particular conduct shall cause them to forfeit this protection, which, in consideration of humanity, the contracting parties engage to give them.

ARTICLE 19. Neither the debts due from individuals of the one nation to individuals of the other nor shares nor moneys which they may have in public funds, or in the public or private banks, shall ever, in any event of war or of national difference, be sequestered or confiscated.

ARTICLE 20. To make more effectual the protection which the United States and the Republic of Colombia shall afford in future to the navigation and commerce of the citizens of each other, they agree to receive and admit consuls and vice consuls in all the ports open to foreign commerce, who shall enjoy in them all the rights, prerogatives, and immunities of the consuls and vice consuls of the most favored nation: each contracting party, however, remaining at liberty to except those ports and places in which the admission and residence of such consuls may not seem convenient.

ARTICLE 21. In order that the consuls and vice consuls of the two contracting parties may enjoy the rights, prerogatives, and immunities which belong to them by their public characters, they shall, before entering on the exercise of their functions, exhibit their commissions or patent in due form to the Government to which they are accredited, and, having obtained their exequatur, they shall be held and considered as such by all the authorities, magistrates, and inhabitants in the consular district in which they reside.

ARTICLE 22. It is likewise agreed that the consuls, their secretaries, officers, and persons attached to the service of consuls, such persons not being citizens of the country in which the consul resides, shall be exempt from all public service, and also from all kind of taxes, imposts, and contributions, except those which they shall be obliged to pay on account of commerce, some lucrative profession, or their property, to which the citizens and inhabitants, native and foreign, of the country in which they reside, are subject; being in everything besides subject to the laws of the respective States. The archives and papers of the consulates shall be respected inviolably, and under no pretext whatever shall any magistrate seize or in any way interfere with them.

ARTICLE 23. The said consuls shall have power to require the assistance of the territorial authorities for the arrest, detention, and custody of deserters from the public and private vessels of their country; and for that purpose they shall address themselves to the courts, judges, and officers competent, and shall demand the said deserters in writing, proving, by an exhibition of the registers of the vessels or ship's roll, that those men were part of the said crew; and on this demand, so proved, (saving, however, where the contrary is proved,) the delivery shall not be refused. Such deserters, as soon as they shall be arrested, shall be put at the disposition of the said consuls, to be sent to the ships to which they belonged, or to others of the same nation. But if they be not sent back within two months from the day of their arrest, they shall be set at liberty, and shall be no more arrested for the same cause.

ARTICLE 24. For the purpose of more effectually protecting their commerce and navigation, the two contracting parties do hereby agree, as soon hereafter as circumstances will permit them, to form a consular convention, which shall declare specially the powers and immunities of the consuls and vice consuls of the respective parties.

ARTICLE 25. The United States of America and the Republic of Colombia, desiring to make as durable as circumstances will permit the relations which are to be established between the two parties by virtue of this treaty of amity, commerce, and navigation, have declared solemnly and do agree to the following points:

1. The present treaty between the said parties shall continue for the term of twelve years in all the parts relating to commerce and navigation, and in all those parts which relate to peace and friendship it shall be permanently and perpetually binding on the parties. It being, however, understood that nothing herein contained shall in any way violate or impugn the fifteenth article of a treaty between the United States and Spain, signed on the twenty-second day of February, one thousand eight hundred and nineteen.

2. If any one of the citizens of either of the contracting parties shall infringe or violate any of the articles of this treaty, such citizen shall be held personally responsible for the same, and the harmony and good correspondence between the contracting parties shall not be interrupted thereby, each party engaging in no way to protect the offender or sanction such violation.

3. If, (what, indeed, cannot be expected,) unfortunately, any of the articles contained in the present treaty should be in any way violated by either of the contracting parties, it is expressly stipulated that neither of the said contracting parties will order or authorize any acts of reprisal against the other, on complaint of injuries or damages, until the said party shall first have presented to the other a statement thereof, verified by competent proof and evidence, and demanded justice and satisfaction, and the same shall either have been refused or unreasonably delayed.

The present treaty of amity, commerce, and navigation shall be approved and ratified by the President of the United States, by and with the advice and consent of the Senate thereof, and by ————, of the Republic of Colombia; and the said ratifications shall be exchanged, in the city of Washington, within ———— months from the date hereof, or sooner, if possible.

In faith whereof, we, the plenipotentiaries of the United States of America and of the Republic of Colombia, have signed and sealed these presents.

Done at Bogota, this ———— day of ————, in the year of our Lord one thousand eight hundred and twenty-four.

No. 17.

BOGOTA, *October* 3, 1824.

SIR: Having on this day signed a treaty of amity, commerce, and navigation with the plenipotentiary of Colombia, a copy is herewith transmitted to you. I also transmit copies of his note of the 24th of August, inviting a continuance of the negotiation by verbal conference, and of the protocols of those conferences. I propose, in this letter, to make such observations on the progress of the negotiation as will, with the aid of the accompanying copies and those heretofore sent, present to you a correct and somewhat minute history of the several mutations which the propositions originally made have undergone during the discussion, and of the manner in which we arrived at the conclusion. In a separate letter, under the date of to-morrow, I will, by special reference to each article, give an explanation of them as they stand adopted, without any allusion to the previous discussion or mode by which we arrived at that adoption.

Immediately after the exchange of our respective full powers it was agreed that the Colombian Commissioner should present to me a *projet* embracing such articles and subjects as he wished might form the basis of a convention between the two countries, and that I should respond to his proposition, either by observations addressed to each article separately, with such additions as might be deemed proper, or should present a contre projet. The latter mode was adopted by me, and the one was presented, of which a copy was inclosed in my letter of the 17th September, and which you will be so good as to advert to, in connexion with this letter, for the correct understanding of it.

Although there were many points of difference on minor subjects between the two propositions respectively offered for consideration, the only one which seemed to excite much attention was that in relation to the protection which a neutral flag should give to the property it covered. To this subject the letter of the first of July, and my answer of the seventh, were directed. Several informal conversations were in the meantime held; but no official communication again took place until the conference of the 27th of August, held by virtue of the preceding invitation. The protocol of that conference will show to you that it was agreed to take up the contre projet, as presented by me, and to make it the text for our consideration and remarks, and that the preamble and first four articles were agreed to without alteration. In noticing the differences between articles on corresponding subjects in the two propositions, and between them and the convention as ultimately adopted, I will omit those merely verbal and those which were made solely with a view to attain greater distinctness of expression, and advert only to those which involve something of principle. The only difference worthy of particular remark here consists in the introduction by me of the words "commerce and navigation" in the second article, whereby the reciprocity of favors referred to was restricted to those subjects, according to the manner of all our former treaties; and also in the omission of the word "generally," in the third article, the insertion of which, it seemed to me, would have produced a principle essentially different from the one desired, inasmuch as, under such a stipulation, neither of the contracting parties would have been elevated entirely to the grade of the most favored nation; at least, the introduction of the word was objectionable, as it deprived the sentence of that precision which it was desirable that one of the most important articles of the treaty should have. The substance of the article was not otherwise changed by me, although, in form, it is altered and probably improved. You will readily know whence I borrowed the clause.

In the fourth article (always bearing in mind that the numbers, unless otherwise expressed, refer to the contre projet) no changes have occurred which it is thought require any explanation.

In the first member of the fifth article you will see that an immaterial alteration was made. In the second member of the article, in relation to the freedom of conscience and worship, an alteration was made, and one to which I did not assent without some regret. I had proposed the eleventh article of the treaty with Prussia, as containing everything which I thought desirable on the subject. The protocol of the second conference will show to you the objections made by the Colombian plenipotentiary. When I felt assured of the sincerity of his observations, and of the liberal sentiments of all the chief officers of the Executive Government on this subject, I could not resist the belief that an unaffected apprehension was entertained that the insertion of the article, in the proposed shape, might create unpleasant difficulties in the Congress. The only difference consists in the omission of all express reference to "worship," and it is believed that the article now concedes as much as any Catholic country has hitherto assented to in a public treaty. In the projet the subject was not introduced at all.

The first sentence of the sixth article, in relation to an embargo on vessels and persons, has undergone no alteration whatever in any stage of the negotiation. I refer you to my letter, No. 18, for an explanation of my views on this subject. The second clause was struck out at my own suggestion, everything that was valuable in it being contained in other parts of the convention, and in one respect it seemed a deviation from the general tenor of the treaty. While the other stipulations had a reference to the principle of the most favored nation, this adopted the rule of placing the parties, as to this single purpose, on the footing of the native citizen.

In the seventh, eighth, and ninth articles, all designed to secure the ordinary rights of humanity to unfortunate mariners and merchants of either party, no essential changes have been made from the form in which they were first proposed.

My observations on many of the subsequent articles cannot be addressed to them in strict numerical order, as the corresponding numbers do not always present corresponding subjects; but it is believed that all confusion will be avoided by grouping them in the manner here adopted.

Articles numbered 10, 11, 12, 13, and 14 of the projet embraced the following analogous subjects: an enumeration of the articles of contraband; a definition of blockade; a declaration of the necessity of warning a vessel of the existence of a blockade before she was rendered liable to capture; the liability of contraband articles to capture, saving the ship and the rest of the cargo the right to pursue the voyage on the surrender of the prohibited goods; a declaration of the principle that enemy's goods on board a neutral ship were liable to capture, and that neutral property in an enemy's ship was free. There were some other provisions, which, for the present purpose, need not be mentioned; they may form the subject of some future remarks. The numbers 10, 11, 12, 13 of the contre projet contained all which I thought necessary to introduce on these subjects, not in the order in which they have been mentioned, but in the order which it was supposed their proper connexion rendered most judicious for the true understanding of them. The tenth article contained a declaration of the principle that "free ships should give freedom to goods," expressed in the most approved language which a careful examination of all the treaties heretofore formed by the United States on the subject could furnish to me, but qualified, after the manner of the late treaty with Spain, by restricting the benefits of the rule to those who will submit to its privations. The correspondence heretofore transmitted, and the memoranda of the second and third conferences, will put you in full possession of everything which has taken place on this question. You will see that a readiness was expressed to abandon the first rule as proposed, and to adopt mine, if some explanation could pass in relation to the effect of the rule in the event that Spain should refuse to recognize in this Republic such a Government as would fill the idea of "a power" as expressed in the 12th article of her last treaty with the United States. In answer to the observations made, I stated that, in the event that Spain, disregarding the obligations of her treaty with the United States, or denying that Colombia was a power in the contemplation of that treaty, should attempt to take Colombian property from vessels of the

United States, it was my clear understanding of the proposed convention that the United States would resist such attempts, and would be liable to the same responsibilities in relation to the property, whatever they might be, to which she would be liable if it were the property of the subjects of any other sovereign power who had acknowledged the principle, or, in other words, to the same responsibility to which Colombia would be subject if she, as a neutral, was carrying the property of the citizens of the United States when at war, and such property was taken from her vessels under like circumstances. In giving this opinion I did not design, as I declared, in any way to enlarge the operation of the article, but to express what was considered by me its true and only meaning. I carefully forbore, as was fully explained, to mention 'the nature or character of the responsibility which each nation incurred by entering into the stipulation, in the event that a third party, regardless of its treaties, should seize the property of the one in the vessels of the other. This point was not necessary for us to settle. If the case occurred, the nature of the liability would be adjusted by the proper principles. I only thought proper to say that Colombia would have the same advantage by assenting to the rule which any other nation would have, or which my country would have with her in like cases. The case appeared to me to be too plain to require any explanation, but, as a strong apprehension seemed to be entertained, and I believe is now, that Spain would not, in practice, admit that Colombia was a power in the contemplation of her treaty, I had no hesitation in expressing my understanding of the operation of the clause. The apprehension entertained is bottomed on the idea that Spain will still contend that the countries forming the Republic of Colombia are her colonies; or, varying the ground a little, she will contend that Colombia was not such a power as was contemplated, she not having been recognized by the United States at the date of the treaty. It is not proper for me to indulge in any conjecture as to the course Spain may pursue, but, after having invited Colombia to assent to the salutary and pacific rule contained in this article, it is impossible that the United States can regard her in any light different from that in which she would regard any other power which had assented to it.

The practical operation of the rule will, I hope, be very advantageous to the shipping interest of the ' United States, as the preparations which this Government is now making, under her recently acquired credit in the money market, towards the building and purchasing of ships to operate as cruisers, will soon produce the effect of giving to our vessels the transportation of all Spanish property. · Indeed, under the ordinance of this country declaring that enemies' property is subject to capture in a neutral bottom, no foreign vessels, except those of the United States, will save property from her capture.

The form of the 11th article, embracing an enumeration of contraband goods, and now forming the 14th of the treaty, has been entirely changed, without, however, much altering the enumeration. I was anxious to exclude "lead, saltpetre, and horses, with their furniture," all which it had, as you will see, been proposed to comprehend. The article, as finally agreed to, excludes the two former and retains the last. The whole negotiation was conducted on both sides with a distinct understanding, as is fully expressed in the memorandum of the second and fourth conferences, that neither party had the remotest wish to embrace in the prohibited list articles of first necessity for the sustenance of life, materials for ship-building, gold, silver, or any of those articles which have so frequently formed the topics of irritated discussions. The only anxiety was to give such precision to the language in which the enumeration was expressed as to draw around it a boundary too distinct to be mistaken. "Horses, with their furniture," is the only thing embraced of which the exclusion could with any propriety be urged; and when I ascertained that they were comprehended in every treaty hitherto formed by the United States, and particularly in her treaty with Spain, it was not thought judicious to insist on the omission. According to the form of many treaties, a long list of articles which should not be deemed contraband was at first inserted by me, but, on reflection, the idea of omitting it was readily approved and adopted. I considered that a partial enumeration of free articles, instead of giving any additional strength, might really impair the energy of the strong words of negation which were employed to exclude everything "not explicitly enumerated and classified." And, if anything extrinsic were necessary to explain or fortify the exclusion, which, however, it is believed is not the case, it will be found in the strong language used at the second conference, designed to disclaim all intention of embracing any article of a controverted character.

The definition of blockade has not been materially changed from the language in which it was first proposed. It will be the subject of some observations in my next letter.

The article declaring that a vessel shall not be liable to capture unless she shall again attempt to enter a blockaded port, after notice of the blockade, received several alterations in the course of the negotiation, and at each successive one, I think, received improvement. But a short time before the signature of the treaty, the word "warning" and the corresponding Castilian word "intimacion" were substituted for "notice" and "notitia," at my instance, and words were also introduced requiring that the warning should come from the commanding officer of the blockading forces.

Those provisions in the preceding articles which declare the vessel and the rest of the cargo, in cases where a portion of it was contraband, free, and those which prescribe rules for the government of officers examining vessels at sea, have undergone no material alteration.

· ·· The only difference of importance between the 15th article of the *contre* and the corresponding 16th of the original *projet*, which prescribe the papers a neutral vessel shall bear, to show her character and give evidence of her ownership, is in this: that, in the latter, the clause was framed to form a constituent part of a treaty subjecting enemy's goods to capture in a neutral vessel, while the former was, according to my stipulation, framed to suit itself to the adverse principle, and, of course, that part requiring the exhibition of a certificate, showing to whom the property composing the cargo belonged, was omitted by me. This change has been adopted in consequence of the change in the principal article.

The 16th article contains a provision which was entirely omitted in the proposition of the Commissioner of this Government. The third conference will show that the first part of it, requiring that the established courts only should take cognizance of all cases of capture, and that, in cases of decisions adverse to the prizes, the reasons of the judgments should be expressed, and, moreover, requiring that an authenticated copy of the decree should be furnished on demand, was adopted without objection; it will also show that to the latter part of the article an objection was made which, at first, produced in me unaffected surprise, and would probably in any one who was familiar only with judicial forms as exhibited in courts of common law. The Commissioner of Colombia declared that the effect would be, to give to the citizens of the United States a privilege which a citizen of Colombia did not enjoy; that the forensic forms of this country did not give a litigant "free access to the proceedings" in the manner in which he apprehended that I understood the phrase. Finally, an alteration has been made by which the words "sentences and decisions" are substituted for "proceedings;" and the clause having been incorporated with another, which secures to the citizens of each, in the tribunals of justice, the same rights which the native citizen has, it is thought that everything desirable has been attained. The subject forms the 10th article of the treaty.

The 17th article, prohibiting the citizens of each of the contracting parties from accepting commissions or letters of marque from the enemies of the other, has been subjected to no change whatever.

The same observation is true with regard to the 18th, with an immaterial qualification.

The 19th, in relation to the security of debts due from the individuals of the one nation, or the nation to the individuals of the other, was a new one proposed by me, and agreed to without objection or observation.

The 20th article, providing for the mutual reception of consuls, merits no particular remark, as no alteration has been imposed on it; the same is nearly true with respect to the 21st, containing provisions on the same subject. The 22d, in relation to the clerks and others attached to the offices of consuls, is the same with the one first proposed, except in an alteration, proposed by me and since adopted, by which the exemptions therein given are denied to persons who are citizens of the country in which the consul resides; it not being thought proper to permit a citizen of the United States to release himself from militia and other personal duties by becoming the clerk of a consul.

The 23d article provides for the restoration of deserting seamen. The only material alteration made to this article was, in requiring the deserters to be secured in the prisons of the country until an opportunity occurs (not, however, beyond two months) of sending them off. This addition was made on my suggestion, and, indeed, the necessity for it arose from an inadvertent omission in my original draft.

The 24th article was proposed by me in substitution of the 23d, 24th, 25th, 26th, 27th and 28th of the projet of the Colombian plenipotentiary. The articles, collectively, formed a consular convention. Many of the provisions you will probably deem judicious, others would have required correction. However, I felt myself relieved from the necessity of examining them with much attention, by the language of your instructions to me, which, if not mandatory, very distinctly advised a postponement of the subject in the manner adopted. Indeed, there are such intrinsic difficulties in the way of forming a convention, prescribing the powers and immunities of consuls, which, while it shall secure to them any valuable privilege, shall not conflict with the municipal authorities of the country, that I willingly waived the subject. It is, however, one on which some solicitude is felt here, and the articles offered for my acceptance, and rejected, will serve to give you the view of the matter entertained by this Government, and what is considered by it as desirable on the subject.

The 25th article corresponds with the 30th as originally proposed, and with the last article of the treaty as adopted, and consists of three distinct clauses, in relation to the duration of the treaty and the modes which should be adopted to postpone or avert hostilities in case of violation. The blank in the projet for the duration of the commercial part of the convention indicated a disposition that the treaty should be temporary; this disposition was in entire accordance with my own views of the subject, which led me to think that the commercial and political situation of this country was too new for us to desire the creation of permanent stipulations at this time. Under this opinion I filled the blank with "twelve years," a term which I considered sufficiently long to insure all the advantages which a treaty can insure, and a term long enough to disclose to each party not only the alterations which they might beneficially make in these stipulations, but also to disclose to them new subjects for advantageous negotiation, developed by the new attitudes which this country might assume. It occurred to me that within the period of that time, under the progress which things have recently made, commerce might take channels so essentially different from those which now exist or can be foreseen, that stipulations might then be judicious which would now be thought wholly improper or not thought of at all.

A proviso was offered by me to this article, declaring that nothing in the treaty should be construed in any way to affect the 15th article of our late treaty with Spain, designing in this way to preserve inviolate the exclusive privileges given to that power in the ports of St. Augustine and Pensacola. You will see that at the second conference a wish was expressed to omit the proviso, under the suggestion that, as the provisions of the previous treaty were known to the parties, such an insertion was not necessary. I believe the controlling reason was an indisposition to refer in the body of the treaty, by name, to any foreign nation, but particularly to Spain. I immediately assented to the omission, and have since presented, in an official note, a copy of that article of the treaty. And still thinking it best to show to Spain, on the face of the treaty, that her rights were not forgotten, I have had inserted the clause which stands as the fourth paragraph in the last article of the treaty. This clause is nearly in the language of the one used by Messrs. Monroe and Pinckney,* in the treaty with England in 1806, on an occasion exactly similar, where it was to be provided that nothing therein should affect the exclusive rights of France in the ports of Louisiana.

The third paragraph of this article, as presented by me, omitted a principle contained in the projet, for retaining which a good deal of solicitude had been indicated. It had provided that all cases of differences, or alleged infractions of the instrument, should be submitted to the decision of a friendly power. I had some repugnance, certainly, to oppose anything which even seemed calculated to avert or postpone an angry or capricious resort to arms; still I thought it most prudent to propose, in lieu of it, a declaration that neither party should order or authorize acts of reprisal against the other, unless a statement of the alleged injuries had been previously presented, and justice had been denied or unreasonably delayed. This was a course sanctioned by precedent, and seemed in every way a safe and honorable one. During the conversation which arose on the subject, I stated that there was probably no nation with which such a stipulation was less necessary than with the United States; that her whole history had declared that there was no nation more slow to provoke hostility, none more patient in seeking redress by negotiation, nor more willing, when any difference actually occurred, to refer it to friendly decision; but that I did not deem it proper to bind our Governments, in anticipation, to submit to the sense of others unknown questions which might affect their honor or sovereignty. The clause, as proposed by me, was adopted on adding the words which forbid a declaration of war until satisfaction shall have been demanded and refused. To this addition, it was thought by me that there could be no objection, not only as the contrary course would probably never be pursued by the United States, but as the article had already interdicted reprisals until the pacific step referred to had been taken; that in itself seemed to exclude the idea of declaring war, the last and highest act of hostile intention, until the same effort towards the preservation of peace had been made. The preceding part of this letter has given to you a review of the negotiation connected with all the subjects presented in the counter project. Several articles have since

* See Vol. 6 State Papers, page 347.

been offered and adopted, which have their appropriate places in the treaty. Most of them were introduced by the plenipotentiary of Colombia, and they form the Nos. 4, 13, and 25, one only forming the 20th, and some corrections rendered necessary by previous alterations, were suggested by myself. To these articles some observations will be particularly directed in my letter of to-morrow; the design being now to state to you the time and circumstances under which they were introduced.

After we had arrived at a perfect agreement on the articles which should form the convention, many of them were transposed from their original situation, with the design of giving to them that order which a proper connexion of the several subjects indicated; so that there is now but little coincidence between the numbers of the articles in the treaty, and the numbers representing the same subjects in either of the original propositions.

On examining the projet of the Commissioner of this Government, you will observe that the 18th article proposed the adoption of rules in relation to captures at sea, made in the course of a war in which the two contracting parties might be engaged against a common enemy. This subject was entirely omitted by me, and nothing has been since said on it. Such a provision was considered by me as wholly unnecessary, because it supposed a case which I hoped would not soon occur, and if it did occur, the necessary regulations could be very promptly adopted. Moreover, I thought it might at this time have a menacing aspect, which, whatever may be our courage or determination, it is never judicious to assume.

You will also observe in the concluding part of the letter of Mr. Gual, of the first of July, that an allusion is made to the treaties heretofore concluded by this Government with the new State on the American continent, and to his intention of proposing some article on the subject. In mine, of the 7th of July, which was an answer to his letter of the 1st, I omitted all notice of this allusion; the subject was mentioned so indistinctly that I did not comprehend the effect which it was designed that the intimated addition should have, and I wished to ascertain with exactness the object in view before my official answer was given. With this intention, on a fit occasion which soon presented itself, I mentioned the subject, and stated that I did not entirely understand the effect intended, but that if the proposition was in any way to impair the effect of those clauses of the treaty which would place the United States on the footing of the most favored nation, the proposition would be wholly inadmissible. I understood him as saying that no such effect was intended, and the subject is now altogether unimportant, inasmuch as the alteration or addition suggested has never been proposed or mentioned again; and it is now referred to only from a wish that there may be nothing seen in the correspondence, however immaterial, that is not fully explained.

The memorial of the second conference will show you that a copy of the decree of this Government was furnished to me, prohibiting the introduction of the produce or manufactures of Spain into the ports of this country. This decree was issued in January, 1823, and is well known to all who have commercial connexion with the country. However, the communication of the decree was taken in good part by me, the prohibition contained in it being one which every nation has a right to enforce without giving cause of complaint to any one. You cannot have failed to observe that throughout the whole negotiation, as presented by the correspondence, all the propositions and suggestions of amendment made by me were marked by an inclination to give to neutral commerce its most enlarged enjoyment, and of course to restrict in all dubious cases the boundaries of belligerent claims. To this course I was impelled, not more by my own feelings than by the conviction that the rights of peace were those on which the interests of our country essentially depended, and that a nation at war has but rarely an occasion to invoke the aid of treaty stipulations to enforce its claims against one at peace, having always in its hands, from other sources, an ability fully equal to the extent of its rights. It would be unjust to intimate that any improper tardiness was displayed by this Government in acceding to this system. The original proposition of its representative will show that some of the articles most liberal and most beneficial to neutral commerce are to be found in it. It was probably not to be expected that a party at war, and with no immediate prospect of peace, would be as eager in seeking or as prompt in proposing stipulations solely designed for the protection of neutral rights as the party who had long enjoyed the prosperity of peace, and whose policy gave as strong a security for its continuance as human wisdom can give. It is hoped that the convention, taken in all its parts, will give evidence that both parties were animated by a sincere desire to foster those arts to which good men are devoted, in preference to those which are so hostile to peace and its employments.

I have the honor to be, with great respect and esteem, your obedient servant,

R. C. ANDERSON, JR.

Hon. JOHN QUINCY ADAMS, *Secretary of State.*

P. S. The copy of the treaty inclosed, although not so fair as I could have wished it, is perfectly correct, except that in the original the numbers of the articles are written at length, while in the copy they are designated by figures.

REPUBLIC OF COLOMBIA.

OFFICE OF STATE OF FOREIGN RELATIONS,
Government Palace in the capital of Bogota, May 20, 1824.

SIR: I have the honor to inform you that, having submitted to the Executive your note of the 17th instant, in reply to mine of the 14th, he has been pleased to confer on me full power and authority to negotiate, arrange, conclude and confirm with you a treaty of friendship, navigation, and commerce.

For this object I hope you will have the goodness to make known to me the day, place, and hour, at which you may judge other preliminaries to these conferences convenient. With regard to myself, I have the pleasure to assure you that I highly esteem the honor the Executive has done me, and which offers me the occasion of confirming the sentiments of the perfect esteem and regard with which I am your very obedient servant,

P. GUAL.

Hon. RICHARD C. ANDERSON, *Minister Plenipotentiary from the United States of America.*

Bogota, *May* 26, 1824.

Sir: Having had, yesterday, the pleasure to make (verificar) with you the exchange of our respective full powers by means of compared copies of both, it now remains for us to fix upon the mode by which the negotiation may most readily arrive at a happy and speedy termination.

The project of a treaty of friendship, navigation and commerce, which I have the honor herewith to send you, discloses the principles which, if they be adopted, will, in the opinion of my Government, place the relations of Colombia and the United States upon a footing of reciprocal utility and advantage.

Have the goodness, sir, to examine it and give me your opinions, that we may enter upon the discussion of the different points therein contained, whether by means of conferences, communications, verbal or written, as may best meet your convenience.

I remain, in the meantime, with the greatest consideration and regard, your very obedient and humble servant,

P. GUAL.

Hon. RICHARD C. ANDERSON, *Minister Plenipotentiary of the United States, &c.*

Bogota, *July* 1, 1824.

Sir: The press of business which has lately occurred in the Department of State, under my charge, together with an affection of the eyes that has troubled me considerably, have prevented me from having the honor to reply to your note of the 2d of June, which was accompanied by a counter project of a treaty of friendship, commerce and navigation, between the Republic of Colombia and the United States of America. As my project and yours differ essentially in a point of great importance, namely, whether free vessels make the goods free or not, I proceed to lay down the reasons which have induced me to adopt the second opinion, which I believe to be more conformable to the established principles of the law of nations, and to the state of war in which this country is still unfortunately found.

When the Government of Colombia, in the 14th article of the provisional ordinance relative to privateers, which is at present in full force and operation, laid down the principle that free vessels do not make their goods free, this subject was examined with great deliberation. In the practice of all civilized nations, as well as among writers of the highest authority, this doctrine was found established in a manner clear and distinct. Neutrals have undoubtedly the right of carrying on their usual commerce with the enemy, and also to convey the property of an enemy without exposing their vessels or the neutral goods that may be found on board to confiscation. So, also, neutral goods remain free that are found on board a captured vessel of the enemy, notwithstanding the venerable Grotius has affirmed that whatever may be found on board an enemy's vessel should be considered as belonging to an enemy.

Vattel, whose opinions are respectable, asserts, Lib. III. sec. 15, that the property of an enemy found on board of a neutral is subject to confiscation by the law (derecho) of war. Burlamaqui, maintaining the opinion of Grotius, further asserts, sec. 4, chap. 7, 823, that friends' vessels are not good prize, even if they have enemy's goods on board, unless the said goods have been received by consent of the captain or master, in which case, he appears to have violated neutrality, and given just reasons to be treated as an enemy. And although Martens, in his Compendium of the Law of Nations, inclines to the contrary doctrine, he confounds the right of a neutral to his property existing in the territory under the jurisdiction of an enemy, with that which is now under consideration, and which, consequently, being on the high sea, cannot be considered under any sort of jurisdiction. Messrs. Pinckney, Marshall and Gerry so triumphantly demonstrated this truth to the French ministry in 1798, at the direction of the Government of the United States, that, trespassing no longer upon your attention with respect to the right, I will only refer to that important correspondence.

With regard to advantage, that is to say, to what interests Colombia in her present state of war, I hope you will agree with me in the necessity of our pursuing and annihilating Spanish commerce by all legal means within our power. It is commerce, certainly, that has enabled the Catholic King to wage against us a war so ruinous and protracted. It is commerce, exclusively, that supplied the means for the expedition of General Morillo and of whatever prior or subsequent expeditions sailed from Cadiz against America. It is, in fact, Spanish commerce, which, not having lost hope of recovering its former monopoly over these countries, is still, at this moment, disposed to continue its sacrifices to involve us in fresh calamities.

If, then, this be so, as I can assure you, it follows that the United States being in perfect peace with the whole world, and Colombia in war for her independence, the policy and the inclinations of the two countries cannot fail on this subject to be essentially different. The United States have an immense interest in freeing their extensive commerce from whatever obstructions may be conceived of; Colombia, in lessening the means of her obstinate enemy to make war upon her, and reducing him to a condition for soliciting peace. You will at once perceive, by this difference of situations, how dangerous it would be for us to open, at this time, our channels to the manufactures and productions of Spain. Left, as we are, to our own resources, our duty, on the contrary, is to close them as far as we may be able, until the power of the States, formerly her colonies, is caused to be felt.

Agreeing, however, in the humanity (humanidad) of the principle that free ships make the goods free, I could desire, if it be possible, that you would be pleased to determine to conclude the treaty according to what I proposed in article 14. As soon as Spain shall recognize the Republic of Colombia, the negotiation may be renewed, and the contrary principle acknowledged in the treaty which may be then made. The interests of both countries may thus be perfectly secured, without remaining longer exposed to the inconveniences and errors arising from indefinite and unsettled relations.

At the conclusion of this note, I believe I owe it to candor and sincerity to propose an important (substancial) addition to the 25th article of the counter project, namely, "that the present treaty shall not infringe or violate in any manner the treaties which the Republic of Colombia has concluded with the Republics of Peru and Chile, made at Lima on July 6, 1822, and at Santiago de Chile, on the 21st of October of the same year; nor those which it may make and conclude upon the same principles with the other States of formerly Spanish America."

The situation of all the States of America, formerly Spanish, has been so peculiar in past years, that it has been necessary to contract alliances, and to secure permanently the advantages of those mercantile relations to which they were accustomed, when all conjointly were equally subject to the same laws.

In relation to the points contained in the counter project, some slight alterations, I believe, are only required, upon which, I flatter myself, you and I will agree without great difficulty.

With sentiments of perfect esteem and respect, I have the honor to be your very respectful and obedient servant,

P. GUAL.

Hon. RICHARD C. ANDERSON, *Minister Plenipotentiary from the United States.*

REPUBLIC OF COLOMBIA.

OFFICE OF STATE FOR FOREIGN RELATIONS,
Government Palace in the capital of Bogota, July 23, 1824—14.

SIR: I had the honor to receive and submit to the Executive your communication of the 21st instant, relating to the deduction which had not been made by the custom-house at Santa Marta of the five per cent. of duties for the importation of the cargo of the American schooner Hibernia, according to the law of June 23, 1823; attentive to which, the said vessel was freighted at Baltimore for St. Domingo, but did not nevertheless touch her port,* and continued her voyage directly from Baltimore to Santa Marta with her complete original cargo.

I am pleased, sir, to inform you, in reply, that the case having been examined by the Executive from the documents that you had the goodness to submit, it has been determined that the cargo of the Hibernia should be embraced in the benefit of the law of the 23d of June, 1823. With this view, as well as on account of the cases of similar nature which may hereafter occur, orders have been directed to be circulated by the Treasury Department that every importation from the United States and Europe made in vessels which, although they may have been fitted out for some other port, shall arrive directly at the ports of Colombia with their complete original cargoes, shall be considered as direct. To-day this order will be issued to the Intendant of Magdalena, and particularly to the Governor of Santa Marta, that he may cause the extra duties exacted by that custom-house upon the cargo of the American schooner Hibernia to be returned.

I remain, in the meanwhile, with the utmost consideration and respect, your very obedient servant,

P. GUAL.

Hon. RICHARD C. ANDERSON, *Minister Plenipotentiary from the United States of America.*

REPUBLIC OF COLOMBIA.

OFFICE OF STATE FOR FOREIGN AFFAIRS,
Government Palace in the capital of Bogota, August 3, 1824.

In reply to your note of the 20th of July last, in which you have the goodness to make known to me that the consuls of the United States at Laguayra and Santa Marta were not permitted to receive and keep registers of the American vessels arriving at those ports; and secondly, you advert to the consignments of foreign vessels which have heretofore been usually made to citizens of this country, claiming in both cases a reciprocity in favor of said consuls according to the practice of the United States, I have the pleasure herewith to send you the decrees of the 28th and 30th of the last month, which satisfy the desires and remarks you make in the above note to which I have the honor to reply. In the last document you will find that not only the consuls, but any other citizen of the United States established among us, may transact and conclude his mercantile business as the citizens of this country.

Permit me also to avail myself of this opportunity to send you the Colombian Gazettes, Nos. 93, 94, 14, 143, in which are published the treaties concluded between the Republic of Colombia and those of Peru, Chile, Buenos Ayres, and Mexico, of which I had the honor, heretofore, to speak to you.

I remain, with every consideration, your very obedient and humble servant,

P. GUAL.

Hon. RICHARD C. ANDERSON, *Minister Plenipotentiary of the United States.*

No. 18.

BOGOTA, *October 4, 1824.*

SIR: Having in my letter of yesterday given to you a history of the recent negotiation and of the several changes to which the various propositions were subjected before their final adoption, this letter will be devoted to the articles of the treaty as they are now adopted, on each of which I beg leave to make such observations as they seem to require, and such as it is hoped will be satisfactory to the President, omitting, however, those articles where the design and the language are so palpable as to require no explanation.

Preamble—Article 1. It is thought that the preamble and the first article require no particular observation.

Article 2. With the exception of the prefatory words, this article has been copied entirely from the

o Literally: But did not touch *in said sail.*

second article of our treaty with France in 1778. The same language has been used in most of our subsequent treaties on this subject.

Article 3. This article is copied from the treaty with Prussia. It is believed that the language is as little susceptible of mistake or misinterpretation as any which could have been employed, and on this subject I was unwilling to venture so far as to use any language, however unexceptionable it might seem to be, which had not been submitted to previous trial and approbation.

Article 4. This article is very much like the 9th of our treaty with the Netherlands. It was not one which I thought of any importance, as everything valuable in it was expressed or implied in other provisions. But its insertion was requested in obedience to a late law of this Government, which, placing all citizens of friendly powers on the footing of natives with regard to the receiving of consignments and the transaction of internal commerce, directed the Executive by negotiation to seek reciprocal stipulations with foreign powers.

Article 5. On the subject of this article there has been shown such a contrariety of purpose by the United States at different times that I have felt some difficulty in ascertaining her present policy from her former negotiations. While she has, by legislative authority, more than once imposed an embargo* on foreign vessels within her ports, she has interdicted to herself this right in her first treaty with Prussia, and in her treaties with the Netherlands, Sweden, and Spain; the last two of which are now in force. With England and France all stipulation on the subject is omitted, and with them, and with all nations with whom there is no treaty, the right is retained. In the 16th article of the last treaty with Prussia the right is expressly reserved, in opposition to the provision of the first. The article now presented reserves the right, under the same qualification, of giving an indemnity to the parties interested. It was not thought judicious by me, without instruction, to interdict entirely to my Government this high act of sovereign power, nor did I wish, by omitting the article altogether, to leave its arbitrary exercise to another. The course adopted, while it restrains us from using without giving indemnity—a right which probably we shall not wish to exercise soon, secures our citizens from its capricious exercise by another, who, being at war, is much more likely to resort to it. A further difficulty in omitting it arose from the fact that, having by treaty agreed not to impose an embargo on Spanish vessels in our ports, Colombia could reasonably demand of us to make the same stipulation with her, or at least to qualify the right reserved in the manner adopted.

Article 6. It is thought that no explanation of the principle or of the language of this article is necessary.

Article 7. Nor of this, except that I have inserted one year, the time within which the demand for the restoration of the captured property shall be made, instead of "a reasonable time," usually inserted in such cases. It is believed, in every case of the kind, if a period sufficiently long for the desired purpose is secured, that it is better to limit that period with precision than to leave it to the vagueness of that common expression.

Article 8. The design of this, like the two preceding articles, being altogether obvious and humane, it is submitted without remark.

Article 9. The principle of this article is found in almost every treaty negotiated by the United States. In language it corresponds, so far as it goes, with the eleventh article of our treaty of 1795 with Spain, except in the concluding sentence. In that treaty, "a reasonable time" is allowed for aliens, in the event that the municipal laws of the country do not permit them to hold real estate, to sell it, and to withdraw the proceeds; in the present treaty that time is limited to three years. This period was considered sufficiently long for the object, and upon this and all analogous subjects it was thought better to fix the time definitely than to leave it to the discretion of the parties. The laws of Colombia do not at present prevent an alien from holding lands; indeed, the existing policy of the Government seems to be to invite the purchase of land by foreigners, and neither naturalization nor removal to the country is made a condition of transmitting it by inheritance.

Article 10. As the citizens of all other countries are sure to enjoy the benefits of this article in the United States without any treaty, I thought that it could not be amiss to secure to our citizens in this way the enjoyment of like benefits.

Article 11. This article is not so ample in its concessions, nor indeed so good, as the corresponding article in our treaty with Prussia, which I wished to have inserted, but it is believed that it contains all that the Colombian Government can safely grant at this time.

Article 12. This article, with the exception of the necessary alterations in the style of the contracting parties, and of the introduction of the word "officers" in the sentence preceding the proviso, presents an exact copy of the twenty-third article of our first treaty with France, and of the fifteenth of our existing treaty with Spain, so far as those articles go. The qualification at the end of the article, to the extent of the principle declared in it, "that free ships should make free goods," was subjoined by me conformably to your instructions.

Article 13. The principle contained in this article, that neutral goods shall be subject to capture in an enemy's vessel, seems in all our treaties (with the exception of the one with Spain) to be considered as the necessary consequence of the principle established in the preceding article, that neutral vessels shall save the goods of an enemy. The latter part of the article is designed to express what is considered to be the law of nations with regard to those who refuse to assent to that principle. No precedent of an article combining the alternatives is probably to be found, because the qualification inserted in our late treaty with Spain, and in the one now offered, declaring that the principle that "the flag shall cover the goods" shall be applicable to those powers only who assent to the principle; being only of recent introduction, the case has, of course, but recently arisen, in which it was necessary for a negotiating party to declare one state of the law with one nation, while a different one was declared with another. Possibly in this case there was no absolute necessity for this article, but it is believed that the first part only declares what is generally stipulated in like cases; and that the second member only expresses what is generally understood to be the law in the case therein embraced where there is no stipulation.

Article 14. It is believed that the enumeration of contraband goods here contained is as favorable, always considering the shortest list as the most favorable, as any which can be found in any treaty whatever. In language it does not exactly correspond with any which has been heretofore negotiated by the United States, but it is hoped that in accuracy of description it will be found without objection. "Saltpetre and sulphur" are both here omitted; the first of which is found even in our most favorable treaty, and the last in most of them. Indeed, I think there is no article embraced which is not one designed

<hr>

* See 2d vol. Laws United States, pp. 413, 448.

exclusively for war, unless it be "horses with their furniture;" and you will agree with me that I had but little ground to stand on in urging the exclusion of them, when not a single treaty could be found in which they were omitted.

The last paragraph was inserted in preference to the phrase, "and all other warlike instruments whatever," which is found in most of our treaties. Although there is certainly no material difference, whatever does exist is thought to be in favor of the one used.

Article 15. The first part of this is to be considered in connexion with the last article, as its only object is by strong words to negative the idea that anything not "explicitly enumerated and classified" therein can be considered as prohibited.

The latter part defines a blockaded port. I have ventured to adopt a definition which I have not seen in any treaty, but the policy of the United States on this subject has been so steady and well declared that I thought I could not err in limiting the idea of a blockaded place to one which was "actually attacked by a belligerent force capable of preventing the entry of the neutral." My object was in strict accordance with the uniform policy of pacific nations, to restrict as far as possible the number of cases in which a neutral vessel could subject itself to capture for violating a blockade, by giving to that blockade the most limited boundaries. Although it is probably impossible to guard in any case against determined prevarication, it is hoped that the language here used, fortified as it is by the seventeenth article, will be considered as very little liable to misinterpretation from a candid mind.

Article 16. This article contains several usual but valuable provisions, all calculated to liberate neutral commerce from unnecessary and vexatious restraints.

Article 17. This article was at first copied by me from the last clause of the twelfth article of our treaty with France, in the year 1800, but it has since received amendments which greatly improve it. It is now required that the "warning" should be given by the commanding officer of the blockading forces to the neutral vessel. This was thought important by me, not so much because any particular importance was attached to the individual from whom the "warning" should come, but because it supposes the actual existence and presence of a blockading force.

It is hoped that this article, taken in connexion with the former one, will place the subject nearly on as good a footing as it could be placed, and probably on a better one than any of our former negotiations have placed it.

Article 18. The rules prescribed in this article for the government of examining officers at sea are not unusual, and all of them, it is thought, will tend to save neutral vessels from vexation and insult.

Article 19. This is nearly, in language and substance, a copy of the seventeenth article of our treaty with Spain; the following case, however, presents an exception: In that treaty it was required that the passport or sea letter, which the neutral vessel should bear to declare her character, should be made out according to an annexed form. Here that requisition is omitted, in order that the papers might not be unnecessarily multiplied, and that those now in ordinary use might comply with the stipulation. Similar provisions are to be found in many of our treaties.

Article 20. This was another article designed by me solely to diminish the opportunities for vexatious examinations at sea, and to save the feelings of our naval officers from the mortification of being obliged to witness the detention and examination of vessels under their protection by those who would disregard their declaration, on honor, that the vessels belonged to the nation whose flag they bore. The principle, you know, is not a new one, even in our own treaties.

Article 21. This was thought by me to contain a valuable provision. It grants nothing which our laws and usages do not already assure to all foreigners, and seemed to me to be an important stipulation with all new countries which have but recently passed through the process of a revolution, and where it might be apprehended the prevailing notions on the subject of judicial proceedings had not become so correct and stable as time will render them.

Article 22. This article is the same, substantially, as the fourteenth of the first treaty with Spain, and being there and in force, the insertion of the same could not have been reasonably refused here, even if it had not been in our treaties with several other powers.

Article 23. This is only the usual expression of humanity in like cases.

Article 24. It is not believed that this article requires any explanation or vindication.

Article 25. This article was not considered at all necessary by me; but it is one of those so perfectly inoffensive, that if the insertion of them is urged with much earnestness, it would indicate some degree of incivility, and might create a suspicion that some secret objection existed which was not expressed to insist on their rejection. In this way the article was inserted. Its introduction in the treaty seemed to be desired, from an apprehension that some of the Governments of Europe might, in the establishment of their relations with this country, set up pretensions on this subject inconsistent with perfect equality, and this Republic wished, by the previous insertion of this article, to destroy all such expectations.

Article 26. This article contains an agreement for the mutual reception of consuls very much in the usual way.

Article 27. This requires no explanation.

Article 28. Under the qualifications which are imposed on this article, it gives very few exemptions to those attached to the offices of consuls. An exemption from militia duty and a capitation tax are probably all that the qualifications leave; and when those persons are citizens of the country in which the consul resides, even these are denied to them. The last clause, in relation to the security of the archives against all seizure or municipal interference, merited insertion, I thought, under the same suggestions which you will see applied in this letter to the 21st article.

Article 29. This article is not an exact copy of the one on the same subject in the late convention with France, which I should have preferred, but it is nearly so. There is no difference worthy of notice, except in the time during which a deserter may be detained in prison before he is sent out of the country; in that treaty the time is three and in this two months.

Article 30. This article, as was mentioned in my letter of yesterday, was inserted by me in substitution of several articles proposed by the Commissioner of Colombia, which declared with much explicitness and a good deal of detail the rights and duties of the consuls.

Article 31. Respecting this article I have nothing to add to what was contained in my letter No. 17, in which you will find whatever was thought necessary to explain its several parts.

Having addressed to each article distinctly the observations which it was thought they merited, I will confine myself to a single remark, which may be applicable to many of them. It may have occurred to you, as indeed it has to me, that several of them might have been omitted without much disadvantage to either of the contracting parties; that, as some of them merely stipulate for the exercise of common humanity, their enforcement might .have been left to the spirit of the age in which we live; that others, which are exclusively declaratory of what is known to be the law among civilized nations, might safely have been left for their execution to those correct feelings which so generally prevail among enlightened societies. To this I will only reply, that all articles of this kind are so perfectly harmless in their nature, all contain truths so palpable, that when they are offered and urged by a friendly power it is difficult to find reasons to insist on their rejection. And it may be observed, too, that precise stipulations, however obvious may be the rule which they declare, can scarcely ever fail to be of service on some occasions.

With an anxious wish that the President may find in the result of my exertions something to promote and nothing to impair the interests of our country, I have the honor to be, with very great respect, your obedient servant,

R. C. ANDERSON, Jr.

Hon. John Quincy Adams, *Secretary of State, Washington.*

No. 19.

Bogota, *October* 8, 1824.

Sir: Copies of the following papers are herein inclosed, viz:

Of the full powers under which the plenipotentiary of this Republic acted in the late negotiation; of his note of the 24th August last, omitted in my inclosure of the 3d instant; of my note of the 26th September, containing a copy of the 15th article of our last treaty with Spain in relation to the reserved privileges in the ports of St. Augustine and Pensacola; and of the note of the 1st October acknowledging the receipt of it..

These last are transmitted under the idea that possibly it may be deemed proper, in the event of the ratification of the treaty, to subjoin them to it in the publication, as explanatory of its meaning.

I also transmit to you copies of the treaties heretofore concluded by this Republic and the States of Chile, Peru, Buenos Ayres, and Mexico. They are newspaper copies, and such as were furnished to me by the Department of Foreign Relations. They are necessary to enable you to determine the extent and operation of the treaty just concluded in those articles, which place each contracting party on the footing of the most favored nations, and to ascertain whether any legislative or other measures be necessarily consequent on the ratification of it.

I have the honor to be, with great respect, your obedient servant,

R. C. ANDERSON, Jr.

Hon. John Quincy Adams, *Secretary of State, Washington.*

Bogota, *September* 26, 1824.

The undersigned, minister plenipotentiary of the United States of America, has the honor of communicating to the plenipotentiary of Colombia a copy of the fifteenth article of a treaty concluded at Washington between the United States and Spain on the twenty-second day of February, in the year one thousand eight hundred and nineteen, which article is in the following words, to wit: "Article XV. The United States, to give his Catholic Majesty a proof of their desire to cement the relations of amity subsisting between the two nations, and to favor the commerce of the subjects of his Catholic Majesty, agree that Spanish vessels coming laden only with productions of Spanish growth or manufactures, directly from the ports of Spain or of her colonies, shall be admitted for the term of twelve years to the ports of Pensacola and St. Augustine, in the Floridas, without paying other or higher duties on their cargoes or of tonnage than will be paid by the vessels of the United States. During the said term no other nation shall enjoy the same privilege within the ceded territories. The twelve years shall commence three months after the exchange of the ratifications of this treaty," and to inform him that the said ratifications were exchanged on the twenty-second day of February, one thousand eight hundred and twenty-one.

The undersigned avails himself of this occasion of renewing to the plenipotentiary of Colombia the assurance of his high consideration.

R. C. ANDERSON, Jr.

Bogota, *Agosto* 24, 1824.

Mi Estimado Señor: Despues de haber meditado deteniday respetosamente sobre las ultimas observaciones de Vs. relativas á la convencion de que estamos encargados por nuestros respectivos gobiernos, me parece que nuestras opiniones podrán al fin convenirse con algunas lijeras alteraciones. Creo por tanto, que ya podimos continuar la negociacion pendiente en conferencias verbales, segun los deseos que Vs. tuvo la bondad de manifestarme al principio. Si V. piensa todavia de la misma manera, yo agradeceria infinitamente de que V. se sirviese ase gurarme dia, hora, y lugar en que discutir amistosamte algunos puntos de la referida convencion segun el proyecto y contra-proyecto propuesto.

Entretanto ruego a V. acepte las seguridades de perfecta estimacion y respeto con que quedo de V. muy obedte. y humilde servr.

P. GUAL.

Bogotá, *Octobre* 1, de 1824
El infrascrito tiene la honra de acusar el recibo de la nota, que el ministro plenipotenciario de los Estados Unidos, se sirvió dirigirle con fecha de 26 Setiembre ultimo, transcribiendole literalmente el articulo XV del tratado celebrado entre los estados Unidos y España el dia 22 de Febrero, de 1819, y cuyas ratificaciones fueron cangeadas el dia 22 de Febrero, de 1821.

Con este motivo el infrascrito tiene el honor de renovar al plenipotenciario de los Estados Unidos sus seguridades de distinguida consideracion.

P. GUAL.

Republica de Colombia: Francisco de Paula Santander, general de division de los ejercitos de Colombia, de los libertadores de Venezuela y Cundinamarca, condecorado de la Cruz de Boyaca, Vice Presidente de la Republica encargado del poder ejecutivo, &c., &c.

A todos los que la presente vieren, salud:

Por cuanto el Gobierno de los Estados Unidos de America ha nombrado y constituido al honorable Ricardo C. Anderson su ministro plenipotenciario cerca del de la Republica de Colombia, dandole pleno poder y autoridad para negociar, ajustar, concluir, y firmar, en esta capital, un tratado ó tratados de amistad, comercio, y navegacion, que ponga en claro y afiance de una manera permanente y positiva las relaciones de perfecta corespondencia y buena harmonia que felizmente existen entre ambas potencias. Por tanto, teniendo entera confianza en la capacidad, zelo, y probidad del honorable Pedro Gual, Secretario de Estado y del despacho de relaciones esteriores, he venido en conferirle, como por las presentes le confiero pleno poder y autoridad para que negocie, ajuste, concluya, y firme, con el referido ministro plenipotenciario de los Estados Unidos de America, el espresado tratado ó tratados de amistad, comercio, y navegacion, obligandome á darle ó darles su ratificacion, final con previo consentimiento y aprobacion del congresso de la dicha Republica de Colombia.

En fé de lo cual, doy y firmo de mi mano la presente, sellada con el sello de la Republica de Colombia, y refrendada por el secretario de estado y del despacho del interior, en esta Ciudad de Bogota, á diesiocho de Mayo, del año del Señor mil ochocientos veintecuatro, decimocuatro de la independencia.
[Hay un sello.]   FRANCISCO DE PAULA SANTANDER.

Por su Ex'a el Vice Presidente de la Republica encargado del poder ejecutivo, el Secretario de Estado del Despacho del Interior.

JOSÉ MANUEL RESTREPO.

[Translation.]

Republic of Colombia: Francisco de Paula Santander, general of division of the armies of Colombia, of the liberators of Venezuela and Cundinamarca, decorated with the Cross of Boyaca, Vice President of the Republic, charged with the executive power, &c., &c.

To all those to whom these presents shall come, greeting:

Whereas the Government of the United States of America has constituted and appointed the honorable Richard C. Anderson its minister plenipotentiary near that of the Republic of Colombia, giving him full power and authority to negotiate, arrange, conclude and sign, in this capital, a treaty or treaties of friendship, commerce, and navigation, that may clearly establish and permanently secure the relations of perfect friendship and intercourse which happily exist between both powers: Therefore, having entire confidence in the ability, zeal, and integrity of the honorable Pedro Gual, Secretary of State and of the Despatch of Foreign Affairs, I have conferred upon him, as by these presents I do confer on him, full power and authority to negotiate, arrange, conclude, and sign, with the aforesaid minister plenipotentiary of the United States of America, the above treaty or treaties of friendship, commerce, and navigation, obliging myself to its or their ratification, with the previous consent and approbation of the Congress of the said Republic of Colombia.

In faith of which, I give and sign the present with my hand, sealed with the seal of the Republic of Colombia, and countersigned by the Secretary of State and of the Despatch of the Interior, in this city of Bogota, the 18th of May, of the year of our Lord one thousand eight hundred and twenty-four, fourteenth of independence.
[Locus Sigilli.]   FRANCISCO DE PAULA SANTANDER.

By his excellency the Vice President of the Republic charged with the executive power, the Secretary of State of the Despatch of the Interior.

JOSÉ MANUEL RESTREPO.

Protocol of the first conference of the plenipotentiaries of the United States and of Colombia, held by verbal agreement at the office of Mr. Anderson, August 27, 1824.

Present: the plenipotentiaries.
It was agreed to take up and read, for discussion, by articles, the contre projet proposed by the plenipotentiary of the United States.

The preamble and first four articles were then read and agreed to, without alteration.

In the fifth article, it was agreed that the first member should be so altered as to embrace persons of "all occupations." In the second member of the article, the plenipotentiary of Colombia proposed an alteration relating to "the freedom of worship," and it was agreed that he should present an amendment for consideration.

In the sixth article, it was agreed that the last clause be stricken out.

The seventh, eighth, and ninth articles were read and agreed to, without alteration.

The principle of the tenth article was agreed to, but it was desired by the plenipotentiaries of Colombia that an addition or alteration be made, declaring more explicitly that the provisions of this article should not save the goods of any power which did not respect the goods of the United States and Colombia, respectively, in the vessels of the other, and particularly the merchandise of Spain, who, not having as yet acknowledged the Republic of Colombia, might not, perhaps, acknowledge the principle that "free ships make free goods," with respect to her; and it was agreed to postpone a proposition to that effect for consideration.

It was agreed to postpone the further consideration of the subject, and to meet again on the 28th instant, at the same place.

R. C. ANDERSON, Jr.
P. GUAL.

Protocol of the second conference of the plenipotentiaries of the United States and of Colombia, held on August 31, 1824, at the same place.

Present: the plenipotentiaries.

On the 28th, the conference was postponed until the 31st, on account of the indisposition of the plenipotentiary of Colombia.

On the 31st, the plenipotentiaries met, and the conference was renewed on the points which had remained pending at the former one. The plenipotentiary of Colombia said, in his opinion, the fifth article should be divided so as to form two, in order that the alteration of which he had spoken should appear more clearly, and he presented the following project of an article:

Separate article.—"There is granted to the citizens of Colombia and of the United States of America the most perfect and entire security of conscience in the countries subject to the jurisdiction of both powers, without being thereby subject to be disturbed or molested on account of their religious belief, so long as they shall respect the laws and established usages and customs. Likewise, the bodies of the citizens of one of the contracting parties, who may die in the territories of the other, shall be buried in public, decent, and adequate burying grounds, and their bodies shall be protected from all violation and disturbance."

He further said that this article was conformable to the laws of the Republic; that he felt, in truth, it was not so liberal as the clause proposed to him; he desired the alteration, as well from respect to the present laws, as because the present administration did not consider it judicious to take a premature step on a subject so delicate, which, far from being useful, might find some difficulties in its execution. The plenipotentiary of the United States agreed to take the article into consideration.

With regard to the tenth article, the plenipotentiary of Colombia said that he had the pleasure of repeating, as he had said before, that he no longer considered it improper to assent to the principle that "a neutral flag should protect the property," after having deliberated and respectfully considered the observations and explanations made by the plenipotentiary of the United States in his letter of July 7; but that it ought to be understood that this principle should not be obligatory on the Republic of Colombia after the conclusion and ratification of the treaty, until Spain had declared formally to the United States that she acknowledged this principle with regard to this Republic, or that the United States would declare that they were resolved to protect Colombian property on board her ships, and to answer for it against the depredations of Spain, in case of her refusing the declaration. He further observed that it was necessary to remember that, by a decree of this Government of January 20, 1823, it is not permitted to introduce into its ports, during the war, the manufactures and native productions of Spain and its colonies, and that, consequently, the citizens of the United States will not be authorized to introduce into this country said manufactures or productions on account of Spanish subjects, or even if they may have become by legal means the property of neutrals. After various observations, the plenipotentiary of the United States agreed to take into consideration the manner and terms in which he would make a declaration of the obligations which the parties were about to assume, saying that he did not deem it necessary to insert anything further in the treaty; that it would be equivalent to express, by a formal declaration, the obligations which the United States and Colombia were respectively about to contract. With regard to the decree of January, 1823, he did not consider it necessary to make any observation, as it was certainly a measure which every country had a right to adopt against its enemy.

The discussion being continued, the plenipotentiary of Colombia proposed that, in his opinion, the eleventh article should be divided, having in the first an enumeration, as minute as possible, of the articles called contraband of war, and in the second declaring, with respect to other goods not embraced in that enumeration, an absolute liberty of commerce and navigation, in the same terms in which it is expressed in the final clause of the counter projet, from the words "so that" to the end. He said this alteration appeared proper to him, because it would be very difficult to enumerate all the articles of commerce which were of an innocent nature, and because, if there could be any dispute on the subject, it would be with regard to gold, silver, articles of first necessity for the sustenance of life, and things proper for ship building, which, although some writers consider as contraband, he was disposed to exclude. The plenipotentiary of the United States offered to present a new article, it appearing to him that there were no objections to the suggestions. The plenipotentiary of Colombia also expressed a wish that "military clothing, made up," should be embraced in the articles of contraband, which had been omitted in the *counter projet.*

The articles numbers twelve, thirteen, fourteen, fifteen, and sixteen, were then successively read and agreed to, without alteration, except the last clause of the last member of the sixteenth article, which commences with the words, "The citizens of both parties," &c. "Would to God," said the plenipotentiary of

Colombia, " that the legislation of this country was as perfect as that of the United States, in order to accede without hesitation to this article. But that advocates, proctors, agents, and factors should be present at all the proceedings of the tribunal in such cases, and at the taking of all the examinations and declarations in the suits, would not fail to offer some difficulties in the forensic practices of this country." He promised, however, to examine the subject anew, and to resume it at the next conference.

The seventeenth and eighteenth articles were then read, and it was agreed to suppress the words " other professions," and substitute " other occupations," in the last article.

The nineteenth, twentieth, twenty-first, and twenty-second articles were then read and agreed to, with the exception of the words " some lucrative profession," in the last, they being considered somewhat vague and susceptible of unpleasant interpretations; and, consequently, this part of the article was made to read: " Excepting those which they may be obliged to pay on account of commerce or their property."

The twenty-third article being read, it was agreed, for greater certainty, to insert, after the word " arrested," in the last clause, the words " in the public prisons, at the request and at the expense of those who reclaim them."

The twenty-fourth and twenty-fifth articles were then read, and the plenipotentiary of Colombia observed that, as to the first declaration of the last article, it seemed to him best to omit the second part of it, commencing with the words " It being understood," &c., to the end, because, in his opinion, (as he had heard the plenipotentiary of the United States also say,) the treaty they were then negotiating could not in any way affect any treaties previously concluded with other powers by the United States or Colombia, provided they were previously known to the parties.

The conference was then suspended, and it was agreed that the plenipotentiary of the United States should assign a day for the next, whenever he should think proper.

R. C. ANDERSON, Jr.
P. GUAL.

Protocol of the third conference, held by agreement at the same place, on September 3, by the plenipotentiaries of the United States and Colombia.

Present: the plenipotentiaries.

The proposition to divide the fifth article into two was agreed to; and the modification, as to the right of worship, was also agreed to, as proposed in the second conference. With regard to the article No. 10, and to the observations made by the plenipotentiary of Colombia at the last conference on the principle of said article, and on the necessity of a clear understanding of its effects, the plenipotentiary of the United States said that he was ready to declare, and now declares, that in the event that Spain, disregarding the obligations of her treaty with the United States, or denying that Colombia was such a "power" as was contemplated by the twelfth article of that treaty, should attempt to take Colombian property from vessels of the United States, it was his clear understanding of the proposed convention that the United States would resist such attempts, and would be subject to the same responsibilities to Colombia in relation to the property, whatever they might be, to which she would be liable if it were the property of the subjects of any other sovereign power who had acknowledged that principle; or, in other words, to the same responsibility to which Colombia would be subject if she, as a neutral, was carrying the property of citizens of the United States, when at war, and such property were taken from her vessels under similar circumstances.

The plenipotentiary of Colombia said, that all his Government desired was, that the obligations she was contracting and the rights she was acquiring should be clearly expressed, and said that the declaration he had just heard satisfied that desire.

The article in relation to contraband was then considered, and, after various observations, it was agreed to postpone its further consideration until the next meeting.

It was then agreed to modify the sixteenth article by omitting the words " the proceedings," and inserting " decisions and sentences."

In the twenty-fifth article it was agreed to strike out the words in the first declaration of this article, beginning with " It being understood," &c., to the end, as was proposed in the last conference.

The plenipotentiaries then read and agreed to the second declaration of that article; and the third declaration being read, the plenipotentiary of Colombia proposed that the third declaration of the thirtieth article of his original projet should be here inserted, which submitted to the arbitration of friendly powers the decision of any difference which might arise to produce hostilities between the parties. "The history of Europe," said he, "leaves on this subject lessons as terrible as they may be advantageous to America. Frequently simple caprice has caused those nations to prefer the calamities of war to the blessings of peace." America should always live in peace, and it appeared to him proper to apply henceforth suitable preventives against war, and none seemed to him so adequate as the proposed arbitration. The plenipotentiary of the United States observed, that it was a very delicate subject to submit the sovereign rights of a nation to the arbitration of others; that the past history of his country declared that there was no nation which, after she had received an injury, would show more forbearance in enforcing her rights, nor none which was more ready to submit differences to friendly decision; but he did not deem it judicious, in anticipation, to bind his Government to arbitrate questions which might involve her character and sovereignty; and further said, that the decision of the friendly power would either be obligatory or not; that in the first case the United States and Colombia would, by this act, have deprived themselves of exercising their judgments, (even in similar cases,) which it was to be supposed would always be guided by justice; that, if not binding, the reference would be useless. The plenipotentiary of Colombia answered, that, even if the decision of the friendly power was not obligatory, the proposed declaration would produce a very salutary moral effect on the peace of both nations; since, it being once decided that justice was on the one or the other side, it would require a great effort to make and justify a declaration of war against that decision. After various observations, it was determined not to insert the third declaration of the original projet; and the plenipotentiary of Colombia then proposed that, in case of adopting the declaration of the *counter projet*, the words " not declare war" should be inserted before the words "nor order reprisals." This addition was, in his opinion, of some importance towards the preservation of peace, because it would at least produce the necessity of a previous explanation upon the causes of the complaints or injuries existing, during which it was most probable that everything would be amicably adjusted.

No objection being seen to the proposed addition, it was inserted.

The conference was adjourned, and it was agreed to meet again on the 10th instant, at the same place.

R. C. ANDERSON, Ja.
P. GUAL.

Protocol of the fourth conference, held by agreement at the same place, September 10, 1824.

Present: the plenipotentiaries.

The plenipotentiary of the United States opened the conference by saying that it appeared to him proper to add a fourth declaration to the 25th article of the contre projet, the better to explain the observation made at the close of the second conference, which might be expressed in these words: "Nothing in this treaty contained shall, however, be construed or operate contrary to former and existing public treaties with other sovereigns or States." The plenipotentiary of Colombia assented to the adoption of it. With regard to the 11th article, which remained undetermined at the second and third conferences, the plenipotentiary of the United States observed that he would assent to the enumeration of articles of contraband contained in the tenth of the original project if general expressions were avoided which would give rise to vague interpretations, and if the words "saltpetre, lead, and horses, with their furniture," were omitted, including, however, "military clothing," as was proposed. The plenipotentiary of Colombia replied, that at present he had not much difficulty in omitting "saltpetre" and "lead," but that certainly "horses embarked with their military harness" was an article properly and exclusively for war; because, when horses are embarked as an object of innocent speculation, they do not go accompanied by their appropriate military furniture. Finally, he agreed to the impropriety of using vague and undefined expressions, in the enumeration of which they were treating, and added that it appeared to him, in the impossibility of detailing particularly all instruments destructive of mankind, in the invention of which men were unfortunately too ingenious, and in the determination in which both parties were to indulge in no unnecessary or confused latitude in making an enumeration of contraband articles, that the following clause might be adopted at the close of the article: "And generally all kinds of arms and instruments of iron, steel, brass, and copper, or any other materials manufactured, prepared, and formed expressly to make war by sea or land." After various observations on the subject, the two articles were reduced to the following form:

ARTICLE 11. This liberty of navigation and commerce shall extend to all kinds of merchandise, excepting those only which are distinguished by the name of contraband; and under this name, or of prohibited goods, shall be comprehended—

1st. Cannons, mortars, howitzers, swivels, blunderbusses, muskets, fusees, rifles, carbines, pistols, pikes, swords, sabres, lances, spears, halberds, and grenades, bombs, powder, matches, balls, with other things belonging to the use of those arms.

2d. Bucklers, helmets, breastplates, coats of mail, infantry belts, and clothes made up in the form and for a military use.

3d. Cavalry belts and horses with their furniture.

4th. And generally all kinds of arms and instruments of war, steel, brass, and copper, or any other materials manufactured, prepared, and formed expressly to make war by sea or land.

ARTICLE 12. All other merchandises and things not comprehended in the articles of contraband explicitly enumerated and classified as above, shall be held and considered as free and as subjects of free and lawful commerce, so that they may be transported and carried in the freest manner by the citizens of both the contracting parties, even to places belonging to an enemy, excepting only such towns or places as may be actually besieged or blockaded; and to avoid all doubt in this particular, it is declared that those places only are besieged or blockaded which are actually attacked by a force of the belligerent capable of preventing the entry of the neutral.

The conference was then suspended, the plenipotentiary of Colombia agreeing to introduce at the next, which should be held on the 13th instant, some additional articles. The plenipotentiary of the United States also declared his intention of proposing some others.

R. C. ANDERSON, Jr.
P. GUAL.

Protocol of the fifth conference of the plenipotentiaries of the United States and of Colombia, held by verbal agreement at the same place, September 13, 1824.

Present: the plenipotentiaries.

In conformity with what the plenipotentiary of Colombia had offered at the last conference, he presented three additional articles to be inserted in their appropriate places in the treaty: The first had for its object to declare two principles, which were consequent on the one which they had adopted, declaring "that the flag should protect the property;" the second related to a reciprocity with regard to consignments of goods and merchandises between the citizens of the two countries, according to the recommendation of the Congress of Colombia to the Executive, by the 2d article of the law of the 28th of July last; and the third was upon the privileges of the envoys, ministers, and other diplomatic agents of both powers.

The plenipotentiary of the United States proposed that two additions be made to the treaty: the first obliging the commanders of private armed vessels to give sufficient security to answer for any damages which they might commit; secondly, that vessels sailing under convoy might be exempt from all visits and examination of their papers; that full faith be given to the verbal declaration of the commanders of the convoy, under their word of honor, in such cases.

The plenipotentiaries made no objection to the insertion of these articles and additions respectively proposed.

The conference was suspended, the plenipotentiaries agreeing to make a transposition and correction of the articles agreeably to what had been determined.

R. C. ANDERSON, Jr.
P. GUAL.

Protocol of the sixth conference of the plenipotentiaries of the United States and Colombia, held by verbal agreement at the same place, on the 2d of October, 1824.

Present: The plenipotentiaries.

In compliance with what had been said at the close of the fifth conference, the two plenipotentiaries presented in English and Castilian, as previously agreed and corrected, the treaty or general convention of peace, amity, navigation, and commerce, in the terms in which it had been arranged, and having examined it carefully and compared the English with the Castilian copy, they found them correct and conformable to the alterations and additions which had been respectively proposed in the course of the negotiation, and thereupon they resolved to place their signatures and affix their seals the next day, that is to say, to two distinct originals, the one in the English, the other in the Castilian language, of which copies shall be interchanged mutually, certified and compared with the originals.

R. C. ANDERSON, Jr.
P. GUAL.

CONVENTION NEGOTIATED WITH THE REPUBLIC OF COLOMBIA FOR THE SUPPRESSION OF THE AFRICAN SLAVE TRADE, DECEMBER 10, 1824, BUT NOT RATIFIED.

COMMUNICATED TO THE SENATE, IN EXECUTIVE SESSION, FEBRUARY 22, 1825, AND THE INJUNCTION OF SECRECY SINCE REMOVED.

To the President of the Senate pro tempore:

I transmit to the Senate a convention signed by the plenipotentiaries of the United States and of the Republic of Colombia, at Bogota, on the 10th of December, 1824, together with the documents appertaining to the negotiation of the same, for the constitutional consideration of the Senate, with regard to its ratification.

JAMES MONROE.

WASHINGTON, *February* 21, 1825.

Mr. Anderson to Don Pedro Gual.

BOGOTA, *January* 10, 1824.

SIR: I have the honor of communicating to you herewith a resolution of the House of Representatives of the United States, requesting the President to open such negotiations with the maritime powers of Europe and America as he may deem expedient for the effectual abolition of the African slave trade, and its ultimate denunciation as piracy, under the laws of nations, by the civilized world. I also transmit to you copies of the several acts of Congress on that subject, requesting your particular attention to the 4th and 5th sections of the act of May 15, 1820, by the provisions of which you will see that, so far as legislative enactments can go, the United States have done everything in their power for the suppression of that trade, by subjecting to the penalties of piracy every citizen of the United States who shall be guilty of active participation in it.

These documents are communicated in the certain belief that the Republic of Colombia will not permit herself to be behind any Government in the civilized world in the adoption of energetic measures for the suppression of this disgraceful traffic.

I have the honor to be your obedient servant,

RICHARD C. ANDERSON.

Hon. PEDRO GUAL, *Secretary of State and Foreign Relations.*

Don Pedro Gual to Mr. Anderson.

[Translation.]

REPUBLIC OF COLOMBIA.

OFFICE OF STATE AND OF FOREIGN RELATIONS,
Palace of the Government in the capital of Bogota, January 22, 1824—14.

SIR: I have had the honor of receiving and laying before the Executive your communication of the tenth instant, with a copy of the resolution of the House of Representatives of the United States, requesting the President to enter upon negotiations with the maritime powers of Europe and America relative to the abolition of the slave trade, by denouncing it ultimately as piracy, under the law of civilized nations; and of the acts of the 3d of March, 1813, and of the 15th of May, 1820, particularly calling the attention of this Government to the 4th and 5th articles of this last act.

Nothing is so much for the interest of this country as the entire extirpation of the abominable traffic in Africans, by which Europe has caused incalculable evil to this continent. Influenced by these sentiments, the Congress of Colombia passed the law of the 19th of July, 1821, prohibiting, by article 7th, the introduction of slaves in any manner whatsoever. It should be highly gratifying to the friends of humanity to know that a measure like this has not met with the least opposition among the citizens of this country. But, very much to the contrary, all, without any distinction, have aided to execute it religiously, without there having occurred, to this moment, in the tribunals of justice, one single case of infraction.

Nevertheless, the Executive, desirous, on his part, of contributing to the promotion of the views and laudable policy of the United States on this subject, will with pleasure propose to the next Legislature additional measures analogous to those which have been adopted by your Government. Moreover, he is willing to open any negotiation whatsoever relative to the extermination of this traffic of human flesh. You may be assured that the Republic of Colombia will not be less zealous and active to accomplish it than any other power whatsoever, of Europe or America. . . . . . .

Be pleased, sir, to communicate this to the Government of the United States, and to accept, in the meantime, the assurances of perfect esteem and respect with which I have the honor to remain your very obedient servant,

PEDRO GUAL.

Hon. RICHARD C. ANDERSON, *Minister Plenipotentiary of the United States of America.*

No. 20.

BOGOTA, *November 9, 1824.*

SIR: In my letter of the 8th of October I informed you of my intention of calling the notice of this Government to the subject of the African slave trade at some early day, and in conformity with that intention a note was prepared by me. However, before the design was executed, the Secretary of Foreign Relations gave me to understand, in the course of a conversation recently held with him, that he intended to address to me a letter on the subject, suggesting that it would be agreeable to this Government to receive from me a projet containing the principles on which the Government of the United States would be willing to conclude a convention. Accordingly, I have received from him a letter, in which he states that the Executive had recommended to the last Congress the passage of a law declaring the trade piratical, and that the pressure of urgent business only prevented the Congress from executing the recommendation; that the Government, under the presumption that such a law would pass at the next session, wished that a particular convention should, in the meanwhile, be concluded, determining the manner in which the two Governments should henceforward concur in their efforts to abolish that traffic. The letter, moreover, selected me to make known the principles on which such a convention would be acceptable to the Government of the United States.

In compliance with this request, I have offered to him, as a proposition containing provisions which would be desirable, a set of articles similar to those signed in London, in March last, modified according to the alterations proposed in the Senate. I thought I could not err in offering articles which had passed the various tests to which these had been subjected. On this subject, involving some considerations of delicacy and difficulty in which the guards and restrictions should be expressed in language well considered and accurately defined, I would not venture to make any alteration in the substance or language. As I shall feel but little disposition to assent to any change, unless it be one manifestly unimportant, it is probable that in a few days I shall be able to inform you definitively of the result. If there seems to be a probability of a convention being signed during this month, the messenger, to whom it is intended to entrust the conveyance of the treaty of commerce, will be detained by me until the end of it.

A copy of Doctor Gual's letter to me is herewith inclosed, with a translation, and also a copy of mine in answer thereto, accompanying the projet. You will see from my letter the intimation is distinctly made to him that the negotiation is conducted entirely on the idea that the laws of the United States declaring the slave trade piratical are to be met by corresponding enactments on the part of this country, and that the proposition presented by me is made on the faith of that understanding.

I have the honor to be, with great respect, your obedient servant,

R. C. ANDERSON, JR.

Hon. JOHN QUINCY ADAMS, *Secretary of State, Washington.*

REPUBLIC OF COLOMBIA.

OFFICE OF THE SECRETARY OF STATE OF FOREIGN RELATIONS,
Palace of the Government in the capital of Bogota, October 30, 1824—of independence 14.

SIR: On the 4th day of May last the Executive recommended to Congress again to take into consideration the law which prohibits the trade in African slaves, for the purpose of declaring the perpetrators therein guilty of the crime of piracy, in conformity with the documents which you had the goodness to transmit to me on the tenth of the preceding January, by order of your Government. The multiplicity of business which occupied the attention of Congress during its last sittings did not permit it to adopt measures equivalent to those which the United States have so laudably sanctioned in favor of humanity

As it is to be presumed that this will be done in the course of the next session, my Government thinks that in the meantime it would be convenient to fix, by means of a particular treaty, the manner and terms on which both powers shall concur, in future, in making more effectual the abolition of the said traffic. If, then, you have instructions on the subject, I would infinitely thank you to be so good as to inform me if you are disposed to enter into the negotiation, and under what principles it could be concluded.

I remain, with the greatest respect and consideration, your very obedient and very humble servant,

P. GUAL.

Hon. RICHARD C. ANDERSON, Jr., *Minister Plenipotentiary of the United States, &c.*

BOGOTA, *November* 4, 1824.

The undersigned, Minister Plenipotentiary of the United States of America, has had the honor of receiving the letter of the Secretary of State and of Foreign Relations, of the 30th of October, referring to the communication of the undersigned of the 10th of January last, on the subject of the African slave trade, and giving to him the information that the Government of this Republic is desirous, by a particular convention, to declare the manner and terms by which the two Governments are disposed in future to concur in their efforts to abolish that disreputable and inhuman traffic. It is seen with very great pleasure that this Government has received the communication heretofore made, by order of the President of the United States, in the spirit in which it was designed, and one which gives the amplest assurances of a harmonious concurrence in the measures to be adopted. It is a subject on which the Government of the United States feels much solicitude, and to which its anxieties and exertions are directed in a manner that it is hoped will ultimately produce complete success by a universal acquiescence in the wisdom and humanity of its course. While all those directing its administration must ever have the enjoyment of the feelings which a recollection of these exertions will inspire, the undersigned cannot refuse to himself the satisfaction of expressing the pleasure with which he learns that the Executive of Colombia has united its efforts in the same humane cause, by recommending to the proper authorities the passage of a law affixing to this odious crime the name and the penalties of piracy.

In compliance with the request expressed in the note of the 30th ultimo, desiring that the principles on which a negotiation on this subject might be concluded should be presented, the undersigned has now the honor of transmitting a proposition at length containing those principles; this mode of acceding to the request is adopted under the belief that it is at once the most frank and the most despatchful. It is thought that the articles now offered contain provisions which will be eminently successful in attaining the desired end, while they do not impose any duty or privation on either party which it will not most willingly incur in a cause sanctioned and cheered by the approbation of all Christian men.

It will be immediately perceived that the negotiation is conducted on the predication that the trade to be affected by it is to be declared by the legislative enactments of both the contracting parties piratical, and subject to the ordinary penalties of that high offence; the articles now presented are expressed in language suited only to that state of the law, and would indeed have an application in no other case.

The undersigned will not close this communication without expressing his hope that the Government of Colombia will see in the convention now proposed those principles only which are strictly consistent with its honor, and such as may be considered well calculated to attain the great object in view.

The undersigned avails himself of this occasion to offer the assurances of his consideration and respect.

R. C. ANDERSON, JR.

Hon. PEDRO GUAL, *Secretary of State and of Foreign Relations.*

No. 21.

Mr. Anderson to Mr. Adams.

BOGOTA, *December* 14, 1824.

SIR: On the 10th day of this month I concluded and signed, with the plenipotentiary of this Republic, a convention on the subject of the African slave trade.

Both parties being animated by a common and sincere desire to bring the negotiation to a prompt and happy conclusion, those wishes have been accomplished in a way which I hope may be satisfactory to the President of the United States.

In my letter (No. 20) you were informed that, under the invitation of the Secretary of Foreign Relations, I had presented, as a projet containing principles which would be acceptable to the Government of the United States, a transcript of the articles signed at London in March last, modified according to the manner in which they had received the approbation of the Senate. In a few days afterwards I received a note informing me that the leading principles of the system were considered as unexceptionable, and desiring a conference for the further consideration of the subject. This conference was held, and at it a few alterations were proposed, discussed, and adjusted.

The convention, as signed, presents no difference between the proposition first offered by me and it, except in the following points, which, although they are not considered as material, are mentioned merely as they do constitute a difference. The first consists in a slight alteration of the language of the preamble, which, being obviously unimportant, requires no comment. The second point of difference is presented in the first article, and is one which, in language, though probably not at all in substance, goes to enlarge the operation of the convention. The original proposition, in designating the officers to whom the power of executing the provisions of the convention should be confided, gave that authority "to the commanders and commissioned officers of each of the two high contracting parties, duly authorized under the regulations and instructions of their Governments, to cruise on the *coasts of Africa and the West Indies* for the suppression of the slave trade." This language has been changed, you will observe, so as to extend the authority to those who are authorized " to cruise on the *seas and coasts of Africa and of the West India islands.*" This was an alteration suggested by the Commissioner of Colombia, who urged the opinion that the word " coast," if used alone, might be considered as conveying a sense so narrow as to defeat, in a great degree, the object of the parties; and that, indeed, it might even be considered as embracing only so much of the ocean as was included within the jurisdiction of the power holding the adjacent lands; but that, in either case, the addition proposed would, when qualified by the words showing what seas were in contemplation, not enlarge the theatre of action beyond that which was in the intention of the parties.

Upon a careful consideration of the subject, and of the different articles of the convention, I could not think that there was any objection to the introduction of the proposed word. Although I might not assent to the opinion that the "coasts" embraced only that portion of the seas which was included within the jurisdiction of the contiguous territorial power, still, as it was considered by me not to be within the particular intention of the parties to exclude the seas of Africa and the West Indies, I did not think it objectionable to vary the language in any way which would still maintain the beneficent design of the parties. Indeed, it is seen that the design of the first part of this article is principally to designate the officers to whom the powers of executing the provisions of the convention shall be intrusted; but it is manifest, from the first member of the second article, that the theatre on which these powers are to be executed is not restricted to the " coasts" of Africa and the West Indies, nor to any *coast* in its narrow sense, as the case is there provided for in which " an officer of either of the two contracting parties shall, *on the high seas, or anywhere not within the exclusive jurisdiction of either party,*" board, or cause to be boarded, any merchant vessel," &c. From this, I think, it will obviously appear that the consistency of the different parts of the instrument has not been at all disturbed by the alteration allowed.

In the same sentence the expression " West India islands" has been used in substitution of "West Indies," under the statement of the plenipotentiary of this Government, that, in the works of Spanish historians, and, indeed, throughout the Castilian language, the phrase "West Indies" is used in reference to the whole continent of America, and not to the islands exclusively. As it was desirable to employ no phrase which was in any way indefinite or ambiguous in either language, the change was readily adopted.

The only other alteration from the projet as first presented by me occurs in the eighth article. It is there provided that " copies of the laws of both countries which *are or may be in force* for the suppression of the slave trade shall be furnished to the commanders," &c. This mode of expression was substituted for that first proposed, by which it was declared that copies of the laws " *actually in force*" should be furnished, from an idea that the latter expression might possibly be considered as having reference to the time of signing the convention, in exclusion of all other periods of time; and as there was no law of this Government now in force on the subject, the expression might involve some inaccuracy of fact.

This explanation of the alterations which have been indulged in has been made, not from a belief that they do in any manner affect the sense of the treaty either by enlarging or restricting its operation, or that they are in any way essential, but from an inclination to present with the greatest precision the course and the result of the negotiation.

It is intended on the part of this Government to give the final ratification to the convention, (which, under the constitution of Colombia, is an act of the Congress,) and to pass the laws necessary to fulfil it simultaneously. A copy of those laws will accompany the instrument of ratification to the United States, to be ready for delivery, duly authenticated, on the exchange of the ratifications.

A copy of the convention is herewith inclosed, together with a copy of the letter of the Secretary of Foreign Relations to me, of December 3. The convention itself will be sent by the same messenger to whom will be intrusted the treaty of commerce and navigation, who will leave Bogota during the next week, and will, I hope, arrive in Washington nearly as soon as this despatch.

I have the honor to be, with very great respect, your obedient servant,

R. C. ANDERSON, Jr.

Hon. John Q. Adams, *Secretary of State.*

Don Pedro Gual to Mr. Anderson.

[Translation.]

Bogota, *December 3, 1824.*

The undersigned, Secretary of State and Foreign Relations, has the honor to inform the honorable Minister Plenipotentiary of the United States that the Vice President of the Republic of Colombia having very seriously considered the projet of a convention which was subjoined to your valuable note of 4th November last, upon the illicit trade of slaves of Africa, his Excellency has thought proper to confer upon the undersigned a full power (copy of which is herewith sent) to conclude and sign said convention in the name of this country.

The undersigned has the very great satisfaction of assuring the honorable Minister Plenipotentiary of the United States that the instructions which he has received with that power differ almost in nothing from the cardinal principles of the projet; he will, therefore, have much pleasure in agreeing to a conference with the honorable Minister Plenipotentiary the day and hour which he will have the goodness to appoint, fully expecting that then this important negotiation will be terminated to the satisfaction of both parties.

The undersigned renews to the honorable Minister Plenipotentiary of the United States the assurances of his most distinguished consideration.

P. GUAL.

Extract from a letter (No. 23) from R. C. Anderson, Jr., Esq., to the Secretary of State, dated

BOGOTA, *December* 27, 1824.

"Mr. L. Anderson, who will deliver this letter to you, is the bearer employed by·me to convey to the United States the treaty of navigation and commerce signed in·October last, and also the convention on the African slave trade, more recently concluded and signed with the plenipotentiary of this Government."

"The treaty signed in October would have been transmitted at an earlier day, but no suitable messen‐ger.could be found here, and the state of the mails, either by Caraccas or down the Magdelena, is such as to render the transmission of such documents by them entirely ineligible and unsafe."

"I have directed Mr. Anderson to proceed, without delay, to the coast, and thence to the United States by the earliest conveyance."

In the name of God, Author and Legislator of the Universe: The United States of America and the Republic of Colombia being desirous to co-operate for the complete suppression of the African slave trade, by making the law of piracy, as applied to that traffic under the statutes of their respective Legislatures, immediately and reciprocally operative on the vessels and citizens of each other, have, respectively, furnished to their plenipotentiaries the necessary and full powers to conclude a convention for that purpose: that is to say, the United States of America, to Richard Clough Anderson, Jr., a citizen of said States, and their Minister Plenipotentiary to the said Republic; and the Republic of Colombia, to Pedro Gual, Secretary of State and of Foreign Relations; who, after a reciprocal communication of their respective full powers, have agreed upon. and concluded the following articles:

ARTICLE 1. The commanders and commissioned officers of each of the two high·contracting parties, duly authorized under the regulations and instructions of their respective Governments to cruise on the seas and coasts of Africa,· and of the West India islands, for the suppression of the slave trade, shall be empowered under the conditions, limitations and restrictions hereinafter specified, to detain, examine, capture and deliver over for trial and adjudication, by some competent tribunal of whichever of the two countries it shall be found on examination to belong to, any ship or vessel concerned in the illicit traffic of slaves, and carrying the flag of the other, or owned by any citizens of either of the two contracting parties, except when in the presence of a ship-of-war of its own nation; and it is further agreed that any ship or vessel so captured shall either be carried or sent by the capturing officer to some port of the country to which it belongs, and there given up to the competent authorities, or be delivered for the same purpose to any duly commissioned officer of the other party, it being the intention of the high contracting powers that any ship or vessel within the purview of this convention, and seized on that account, shall be tried and adjudged by the tribunals of the captured party, and not by the captor.

ARTICLE II. Whenever any naval commander or commissioned officer of either of the two contracting parties shall, on the high seas, or anywhere not within the exclusive jurisdiction of either party, board, or cause to be boarded, any merchant vessel bearing the flag of the other power, and visit the same as a slave trader, or on suspicion of her being concerned in the slave trade—in every such case, whether the vessel so visited shall or shall not be captured and delivered over, or sent into the ports of her own country for trial and adjudication, the boarding officer shall deliver to the master or commander of the visited vessel a certificate in writing, signed by the said boarding officer, and specifying his rank in the Navy of his country, together with the names of the commander by whose orders he is acting and of the national vessel commanded by him; and the said certificate shall further contain a declaration purporting that the only object of the visit is to ascertain whether the merchant vessel in question is engaged in the slave trade or not; and, if found to be so engaged, to take and deliver her to the officers and tribunals of her own country, being that of one of the two contracting parties, for trial and adjudication.

In all such cases the commander of the national vessel, whether belonging to the United States or to the Republic of Colombia, shall, when he makes delivery of his capture, either to the officers or to the tribunals of the other power, deliver.all the papers found on board the captured vessel indicating her national character and the objects of her voyage, and, together with them, a certificate, as above, of the visit, signed with his name and specifying his rank in the Navy of his country, as well as the name of the vessel commanded by him,.together with the name and professional rank of the boarding officer by whom the said visit has been made. .

This certificate shall also contain a list of all the papers received from the master of the vessel detained or visited, as well as those found. on board .the said vessel; it shall also contain an exact. description of the state in which the vessel was found when detained, and a statement of the changes, if any,.which have taken place in it,.and of the number of slaves, if any, found on board at the moment of the detention.

ARTICLE III. Whenever any merchant vessel of either nation shall. be visited, under this convention, on suspicion of such vessel being engaged in the slave trade, no search shall, in any such case, be made on board the said vessel, except what is necessary for ascertaining, by due and sufficient proofs, whether she is or is not engaged in that illicit traffic. No person shall be taken out of the vessel so visited, though such reasonable restraints as may be indispensable for the detention and safe delivery of the vessel may be used against the crew by the commanding officer of the visiting vessel, or under his orders; nor shall any part of the cargo of the visited vessel be taken out of her till after her delivery to the officers or tribunals of her own nation, excepting only when a removal of all or a part of the slaves, if any, found on board the visited vessel shall be indispensable, either for the preservation of their lives or from any other urgent consideration of humanity, or for the safety of the person charged with the navigation of the said vessel after her capture. And any of the slaves so removed shall be duly accounted for to the Government of that country to which the visited vessel belongs, and shall be disposed of according to the laws of the country into which they are carried; the regular bounty or head-money allowed by law being in each instance secured to the captors, for their use and benefit, by the receiving Government. .

ARTICLE IV. Whenever any merchant vessel of either nation shall be captured under this convention. it shall be the duty of the commander of any ship belonging to the public service of the other;.charged with the instructions of his Government for·carrying into execution the provisions of this convention, at the requisition of the commander of the capturing vessel, to receive into his custody the vessel so captured, and to carry or send the same for trial and adjudication into some port of his country or its dependencies. In every such case, at the time of the delivery of the vessel, an authentic declaration shall be drawn up, in triplicate, and signed by the commanders, both of the delivering and receiving vessels; one copy, signed by both, to be kept by each of them, stating the circumstances of the delivery, the condition of the captured vessel at the time of delivery, including the name of her master or commander, and of every other person not a slave on board at that time, and exhibiting the number of the slaves, if any, then on board her, and a list of all the papers received or found on board at the time of capture and delivered over with her. The third copy of the said declaration shall be left in the captured vessel, with the papers found on board, to be produced before the tribunal charged with the adjudication of the capture. And the commander of the capturing vessel shall be authorized to send any one of the officers under his command, and one or two of his crew, with the captured vessel, to appear before the competent tribunal as witnesses of the facts regarding her detention and capture; the reasonable expenses of such witnesses in proceeding to the place of trial, during their detention there, and for their return to their own country, or to their station in its service, shall be allowed by the court of adjudication and defrayed, in the event of the vessel being condemned, out of the proceeds of its sale. In case of the acquittal of the vessel, the expenses, as above specified, of these witnesses shall be defrayed by the Government of the capturing officer.

ARTICLE V. Whenever any capture shall be made under this convention by the officers of either of the contracting parties, and no national vessel of that country to which the captured vessel belongs is cruising on the same station where the capture takes place, the commander of the capturing vessel shall, in such case, either carry or send his prize to some convenient port of its own country, or of any of its dependencies, where a court of Vice Admiralty has jurisdiction, and there give it up to competent authorities for trial and adjudication. The captured vessel shall then be libelled according to the practice of the court taking cognizance of the case; and, if condemned, the proceeds of the sale thereof, and its cargo, if also condemned, shall be paid to the commander of the capturing vessel for the benefit of the captors, to be distributed among them according to the rules of their service respecting prize money.

ARTICLE VI. The commander and crew of any vessel captured under this convention, and sent in for trial, shall be proceeded against, conformably to the laws of the country whereinto they shall be brought, as pirates engaged in the African slave trade; but every witness belonging to the capturing vessel shall, upon the criminal trial for piracy, be liable to be challenged by the accused person, and set aside as incompetent, unless he shall release his claim to any part of the prize money, upon the condemnation of the vessel and cargo.

ARTICLE VII. The right reciprocally conceded by the two contracting parties of visiting, capturing, and delivering over for trial, the merchant vessels of the other, engaged in the traffic of slaves, shall be exercised only by such commissioned officers of their respective navies as shall be furnished with instructions for executing the laws of their respective countries against the slave trade.

For every vexatious and abusive exercise of this right the boarding officer and the commander of the capturing or searching vessel shall, in each case, be personally liable, in costs and damages, to the master and owners of any merchant vessel delivered over, detained or visited by them, under the provisions of this convention.

Whatever court of admiralty shall have cognizance of the cause, as regards the captured vessel, in each case the same court shall be competent to hear the complaint of the master or owners, or of any person or persons on board the said vessel, or interested in the property of her cargo at the time of her detention; and on due and sufficient proof being given to the court of any vexation and abuse having been practiced during the search or detention of the said vessel, contrary to the provisions and meaning of this convention, to award reasonable costs and damages to the sufferers, to be paid by the commanding or boarding officer convicted of such misconduct.

The Government of the party thus cast in damages and costs shall cause the amount of the same to be paid, in each instance, agreeably to the judgment of the court, within twelve months from the date thereof.

In case of any such vexation and abuse occurring in the detention or search of a vessel detained under this convention, and not afterwards delivered over for trial, the persons aggrieved, being such as are specified above, or any of them, shall be heard by any court of admiralty of the country of the captors before which they make complaint thereof; and the commander and boarding officer of the detaining vessel shall, in such instance, be liable, as above, in costs and damages to the complainants, according to the judgment of the court; and their Government shall equally cause payment of the same to be made within twelve months from the time when such judgment shall have been pronounced.

ARTICLE VIII. Copies of this convention and of the laws of both countries which are or may be in force for the prohibition and suppression of the African slave trade shall be furnished to every commander of the national vessels of either party charged with the execution of those laws; and in case any such commanding officer shall be accused by either of the two Governments of having deviated, in any respect, from the provisions of this convention and the instructions of his own Government in conformity thereto, the Government to which such complaint shall be addressed agrees hereby to make inquiry into the circumstances of the case, and to inflict on the officer complained of, in the event of his appearing to deserve it, a punishment adequate to his transgression.

ARTICLE IX. The high contracting parties declare that the right which, in the foregoing articles, they have each reciprocally conceded, of detaining, visiting, capturing and delivering over for trial, the merchant vessels of the other engaged in the African slave trade, is wholly and exclusively grounded on the consideration of their having made that traffic piracy by their respective laws; and further, that the reciprocal concession of the said right, as guarded, limited and regulated by this convention, shall not be construed so as to authorize the detention or search of the merchant vessels of either nation by the officers of the Navy of the other, except vessels engaged, or suspected to be engaged, in the African slave trade; or for any other purpose whatever than that of seizing and delivering up the persons and vessels concerned in that traffic for trial and adjudication by the tribunals and laws of their own country, nor to be taken to affect in any other way the existing rights of either of the high contracting parties. And they do also hereby agree and engage to use their influence, respectively, with other maritime and civilized powers, to the end that the African slave trade may be declared to be piracy under the law of nations.

ARTICLE X. It is further agreed by the contracting parties that it shall be allowed and free to either of them to renounce this convention, and all the rights and liabilities created by it, at any time, on giving six months' notice thereof to the other contracting party.

ARTICLE XI. The present convention, consisting of eleven articles, shall be ratified, and the ratifications exchanged in the city of Washington within the term of six months from the signature hereof, or sooner, if possible.

In witness whereof, the respective plenipotentiaries have signed the same, and affixed thereunto their seals.

Done at the city of Bogota, this tenth day of December, in the year of our Lord one thousand eight hundred and twenty-four, of the Independence of the United States of America the forty-ninth, and of the Independence of the Republic of Colombia the fourteenth.

RICHARD CLOUGH ANDERSON, JR.
PEDRO GUAL.

IN THE SENATE OF THE UNITED STATES, *Wednesday, March* 9, 1825.

[The preceding convention was rejected and the injunction of secrecy removed by the Senate this day.]

18TH CONGRESS.]   **No. 408.**   [2D SESSION.

CAPTURE AND DETENTION OF AMERICAN FISHERMEN BY THE BRITISH AUTHORITIES IN THE BAY OF FUNDY.

COMMUNICATED TO THE HOUSE OF REPRESENTATIVES FEBRUARY 26, 1825.

To the Speaker of the House of Representatives:

I transmit to the House of Representatives a further report from the Secretary of State, in pursuance of their resolution of the 1st instant, with the papers to which it refers, upon the subject of the capture and detention of American fishermen, the last season, in the Bay of Fundy.

JAMES MONROE.

WASHINGTON, *February* 23, 1825.

DEPARTMENT OF STATE, *Washington, February* 23, 1825.

The Secretary of State has the honor to lay before the President of the United States the copy of a letter dated the 19th instant, received from Mr. Addington, chargé d'affaires from Great Britain, together with copies of the papers by which it was accompanied, as offering additional information upon the subject of the capture and detention of American fishermen, the last season, in the Bay of Fundy; all respectfully submitted to the President, as a supplement to his report of the 16th, pursuant to a resolution of the House of Representatives of the 1st instant.

JOHN QUINCY ADAMS.

Inclosures.

Mr. Addington to Mr. Adams, February 19, 1825. Copy.
Evidence of Mr. Touzeau, midshipman, and others, relative to the detention of the Rebecca.
Same, relative to the detention of the schooners William, Galeon, Hero, and Pilgrim.
Same, relative to the detention of the schooners Reindeer and Ruby.
Mr. Jones to Captain Hoare, of the Dotterel, November 8, 1824. Copy.
Mr. Protheroe to the same, November 9, 1824. Copy.
Captain Hoare to Rear Admiral Lake, November 25, 1824. Copy.

Mr. Addington to Mr. Adams.

WASHINGTON, *February* 19, 1825.

SIR: On the 8th and 21st of September last I had the honor of receiving, from the Department of State, two letters, in which my good offices were requested in behalf of certain individuals, of the State of Maine, engaged in the fishing trade, who desired redress and reparation for injury done them by the seizure of their vessels, by his Majesty's sloop Dotterel, while employed in cruising on the coasts of his Majesty's North American possessions.

I informed you, sir, in reply to these communications, that I should forthwith address an application to the British naval commander-in-chief on the North American station, recommending.that a full and impartial investigation should be instituted into the various cases which formed the grounds of complaint on the part of the American Government.

I have the honor to transmit to you, herewith, copies of a correspondence which took place, in consequence of my application, between Captain Hoare, commanding his Majesty's sloop Dotterel, and Rear Admiral Lake, in reference to the cases set forth in your letters above mentioned. The depositions of the officers and men concerned in the capture of the Rebecca, Ruby, Reindeer, William, Galeon, Pilgrim, and Hero—vessels therein enumerated—are also annexed.

By a perusal of these documents it will, I trust, sir, most conclusively appear to you that the complainants have no just ground of accusation against the officers of the Dotterel; nor are entitled to reparation for the loss they have sustained; that, on the contrary, they rendered themselves, by the wilful irregularity of their own conduct, justly obnoxious to the severity exercised against them, having been taken, some *flagrante delicto*, and others in such a position, and under such circumstances, as rendered it absolutely impossible that they could have had any other intention than that of pursuing their avocations as fishermen within the lines laid down by treaty as forming the boundaries within which such pursuit was interdicted to them.

With regard to the charge preferred against Captain Hoare, of his having converted detained American vessels, prior to their adjudication in the courts, into tenders for assisting him in his operations against the vessels of the same country, I have only to observe, that that officer broadly, and in the most explicit terms, denies ever having committed or authorized one such act; and in respect to the other accusation, adduced by the complainants, of·maltreatment by the British officers of those persons whose vessels had been detained, I trust that a perusal of the inclosed papers will make it equally clear to you that that charge is entirely unfounded.

I cannot but apprehend, sir, that the acrimony with which the proceedings of Captain Hoare have been viewed by the citizens of the State of Maine, employed in the fishing trade on the British North American coasts, may be justly ascribed to the· circumstance of the recent substitution of vigilance, on the part of British cruisers, for the laxity which appears to have prevailed heretofore, in guarding those coasts from the intrusions of foreign fishermen and smugglers; and I doubt not that, if those persons could be prevailed upon to confine themselves within the limits prescribed to them by treaty, no cause of dissension or complaint would ever arise between the individuals or vessels of the two nations.

It remains for me to observe, that, in one case, in which, by the ignorance of the midshipman employed in the service, the territory of the United States had been violated, by the pursuit and seizure of an American vessel within the American boundaries, Captain Hoare made all the reparation in his power for his officer's misconduct, by delivering up to the Americans the boat which had been detained and paying all the expenses incident to her detention.

I have the honor to be, with distinguished consideration, sir, your most obedient humble servant,

· H. U. ADDINGTON.

Evidence of Mr. Touzeau, midshipman, and the crew of the yawl boat belonging to his Majesty's sloop Dotterel, relative to the detention of the American schooner Rebecca.

Mr. Touzeau, midshipman, examined relative to the detention of the American schooner Rebecca.

Question. Were you in the yawl when Mr. Jones detained the American schooner Rebecca?
Answer. Yes.
Question. Do you know Mr. Jones' reason for detaining her?
Answer. Mr. Jones went down to search an English schooner, and one of the men who was on board, by the name of Wright, as pilot, belonging to an American schooner, told Mr. Jones that his vessel came in for wood and water, at which Mr. Jones appeared to be satisfied; and, on leaving the schooner, saw the American schooner getting under way; ran down and fired several shot across her bows to bring her to; she not heaving to, chased her across the Bay of Fundy. About 8 p. m. of the same day lost sight of her. Some days after, observed the same schooner at anchor near Gull Cove, cleaning fish and heaving the gurry overboard. Mr. Jones detained her, and she was subsequently taken to St. John's.
Question. How was the weather?
Answer. Perfectly clear and fine weather, with a moderate breeze.
Question. Was it fair wind to the fishing ground?
Answer. Yes; we sailed in that direction.

Thomas Richardson examined,

Question. Do you remember the circumstances relative to the detention of the American schooner Rebecca?
Answer. Yes.
Question. Relate all you know about her.
Answer. When we first intended to board her she made sail from us; we then chased her over to the Nova Scotia shore, where we lost sight of her about 11 p. m. About three or four days after, we again saw her at the Grand Menan, lying about a mile from the shore, cleaning fish, throwing the gurry everboard. Mr. Jones then detained her, and carried her to St. John's.
Question. Where was she lying?
Answer. In some harbor at the Menan; but cannot recollect the name.
Question. What quantity of wood and water do you think she had on board?
Answer. About three or four forty-gallon casks, and about two cords of wood.
Question. How was the weather when you boarded her?
Answer. Fine weather and clear, with a moderate breeze.
Question. Do you know whether the wind was fair for the fishing ground?
Answer. Yes; the wind was fair.

Felix Shaw, private marine, examined.

Question. Were you in the yawl with Mr. Jones when he detained the American schooner Rebecca?
Answer. Yes.
Question. Relate what you know about her.
Answer. She came to anchor with another schooner in a small harbor in the Grand Menan. While we were lying there, the foretopsail schooner got under way, and we boarded her. While on board of her. the other weighed and made sail. We then made sail after her, and chased her across the Bay of Fundy over to the Nova Scotia shore, where we lost her after dark. Some days after, we saw her again, at anchor within a mile of the shore, near Gull Cove, throwing the gurry overboard. Mr. Jones seized her and took her to St. John's.
Question. What quantity of wood and water had she on board?
Answer. I do not recollect.
Question. How was the weather when you detained her?
Answer. The weather was fine and clear, with a light breeze.
Question. Was the wind fair for the fishing ground?
Answer. I do not know the position of the fishing ground.

James Lloyd, private marine, examined.

Question. Were you in the yawl with Mr. Jones when he seized the American schooner Rebecca?
Answer. Yes, I was.
Question. Relate what you know about the detention of her.
Answer. While lying at anchor in the harbor—I believe the Grand Menan—I saw the schooner come in and anchor. While Mr. Jones was boarding another vessel under English colors, observed the master and two men go off to the schooner, and immediately got under way. When they got round the point of land, lost sight of her.
Question. Where were you when you lost sight of her?
Answer. On shore, cooking the boat's crew's provisions.
Question. How do you know it was the master who went on board the vessel?
Answer. The people at the store told me so, and said he had been there frequently, and had asked them for water, which they had refused him. His reply was, if he could not have it by fair play, he would be damned if he would not have it by foul.
Question. When did you again see the schooner?
Answer. I never saw her again.
Question. When did you rejoin the yawl?
Answer. Next morning.
Question. Do you remember the schooner Rebecca being detained?
Answer. I was put on board a vessel, and, with the rest of the crew, carried her to St. John's. I believe her name was Rebecca, but am not certain.
Question. Do you remember when this vessel was detained?
Answer. I do not exactly recollect, but believe it to be a week or more after rejoining the yawl.
Question. What quantity of wood and water had she on board?
Answer. I believe there was then a half hogshead three parts full, and a considerable quantity of wood.
Question. How was the weather?
Answer. Quite fine and clear, with moderate breezes.
Question. Do you know the position of the fishing ground?
Answer. I do not.

John Cammish, (S.,) examined.

Question. Were you in the yawl when Mr. Jones detained the American schooner Rebecca?
Answer. Yes.
Question. Relate all you know about her.
Answer. The first time I saw her she was at anchor in a small harbor in the Grand Menan; and when we made after her, she got under way, and we chased her, keeping her in sight, till about 11 p. m., when we lost sight of her on the Nova Scotia shore.
Question. Did you see her again afterwards?
Answer. Yes, about three days afterwards.
Question. Relate where she was then, and what she was doing.
Answer. She was lying in a small harbor, about four or five miles from Gull Cove, cleaning her fish.
Question. What quantity of wood and water had she on board?
Answer. She had plenty of both when we detained her.
Question. Do you know the quantity in casks?
Answer. Two and a half hogsheads.
Question. How was the weather when you boarded her?
Answer. Fine weather, with a little breeze.
Question. Do you know how the wind was?
Answer. I am not positive, but believe it was from the northwest.

Richard Newland, (S.,) examined.

Question. Were you in the yawl when Mr. Jones seized the American schooner Rebecca?
Answer. Yes, I was.
Question. Relate the circumstances.
Answer. She came in and anchored while we were lying in the Grand Menan, when, going to board her, she got under way and made sail; we chased her across the Bay of Fundy, over to the Nova Scotia shore, where we lost sight of her about 11 p. m. Three days afterwards we again saw her at anchor near Beal's Passage, cleaning her fish and heaving the gurry overboard. We boarded her and took her to Gull Cove.

Question. What distance was she from the land when she was taken possession of?
Answer. About a quarter of a mile.
Question. Did you hear Mr. Jones ask what they were doing there?
Answer. Yes, and said they came in for water.
Question. What quantity of wood and water had they on board?
Answer. About two barrels and a half of water, and about a cord or a cord and a half of wood.
Question. How was the weather when you boarded her?
Answer. Fine, clear weather, with little breezes.
Question. Do you remember if it was a fair wind for the fishing ground?
Answer. Yes, it was.

William Vickery, marine, examined.

Question. Were you in the yawl when Mr. Jones seized the American schooner Rebecca?
Answer. Yes, I was.
Question. Relate what you remember respecting her.
Answer. On boarding an English schooner, at or near Gull Cove, we saw another laying there; while going on board observed another getting under way, and made sail; we chased her across the Bay of Fundy, and lost sight of her between 9 and 10 o'clock p. m.
Question. When did you again see the schooner?
Answer. About three or four days afterwards, at anchor within Gull Cove, within half a mile of land, cleaning fish; Mr. Jones boarded her and took possession of her.
Question. Did Mr. Jones ask what they were doing there?
Answer. Yes, he did, and they said they came for wood and water.
Question. What quantity of wood and water had they on board?
Answer. I believe, about a barrel and a half of water, and about a cord and a half of wood.
Question. How did you know it was the Rebecca?
Answer. I was informed by one of the crew that it was the same vessel we chased across the bay, and that they would have hove to, but did not know we were in chase of them; and that the captain said had he not returned, but made the best of his way home, he should not have been taken.
Question. Did you fire at her to bring her to?
Answer. Yes; I was ordered by Mr. Jones to fire across her bows, and I fired several times.
Question. How was the weather when you detained her?
Answer. Fine weather, with a nice breeze.
Question. Do you know if it was a fair wind to the fishing ground?
Answer. No, I do not.

John Lloyd, (S.,) examined ·

Question. Were you in the yawl with Mr. Jones when he seized the American schooner Rebecca?
Answer. Yes, I was.
Question. Relate what you know of the circumstances.
Answer. When lying in Gull Cove, I heard two or three men, who I believe were fishermen belonging to the island of Grand Menan, say that the schooner we had chased across the Bay of Fundy, two or three days before, was then at anchor between two islands, about a mile and a half around the point. We boarded her and detained her. She was then cleaning fish.
Question. Did you hear Mr. Jones ask what they were doing there?
Answer. Yes, they said they came in for wood, water, and to land their gurry.
Question. What quantity of wood and water had they on board?
Answer. They had as much wood as would last them for a fortnight, and a full cask of water on deck, and some below, but cannot say how much, besides beer.
Question. How was the weather when you detained her?
Answer. It was fine weather, with a moderate breeze.

John Cheese, (S.,) examined.

Question. Were you in the yawl when Mr. Jones detained the American schooner Rebecca?
Answer. Yes, I was.
Question. Relate what you recollect relative to the detention of her.
Answer. We were lying alongside a wharf in a harbour in the Menan, and observed two schooners at anchor under the land. We went out and boarded an English schooner, on board 'of which was a man belonging to the Rebecca, acting as pilot; while on board the schooner got under way and ran across the Bay of Fundy. We gave chase to her, and fired several shots across her bows to bring her to; at about half past 10 o'clock p. m. lost sight of her; on the fourth day afterwards we again fell in with her at anchor in a narrow passage in the Menan, boarded her and found them cleaning their fish, and throwing the gurry overboard. Mr. Jones asked what they were doing there; they said they had come in for wood and water.
Question. What quantity of wood and water had they on board?
Answer. Two quarter casks full on deck and some in the hold, but do not know the quantity, and had about a cord and a half of wood.
Question. How was the weather when you detained her?
Answer. Fine weather and a light breeze.
Question. Do you know if the wind was fair for going to the fishing ground?
Answer. Yes, it was.

We, the undersigned, have examined the aforesaid persons, belonging to his Majesty's sloop Dotterel, taking the minutes of their depositions respecting the detention of the American fishing schooner Rebecca; and we do declare that their evidence has been taken in a very impartial manner, and the persons aforesaid have not been biased in any way whatever.

JOHN COOKE,
Senior Lieutenant of his Majesty sloop Dotterel.
JAMES AZZARD,
Purser of his Majesty's sloop Dotterel.
RICHARD HOARE. *Commander.*

Evidence of Mr. Touzeau, midshipman, and the crew of the yawl boat belonging to his Majesty's sloop Dotterel, relative to the detention of the American fishing schooner " William."

Mr. Touzeau, midshipman, examined relative to the detention of the American schooner "William;"
Question. Were you in the yawl when Mr. Jones detained the American schooner " William?"
Answer. Yes.
Question. State the particulars.
Answer. Mr. Jones sent me with James Lloyd, marine, on a point of land to look out; we saw two or three vessels working up; observed one of them anchor in the Gull Cove. Mr. Jones went out in the small boat to board her; he hailed us to come alongside in the yawl, which we did, and found Mr. Jones had detained her. We then took their fish knives from them, having heard by some people, both on shore and on board some English vessels, that they would oppose us in boarding. We unbent her sails and took them with us in the yawl; also her boat.
Question. Do you know Mr. Jones' reason for taking her boat?
Answer. Yes; to prevent her crew going on shore to exchange fish for rum, knowing that another American fishing vessel had done the like with Mr. Fowler, at Gull Cove, the same day; also, to prevent their getting water, as the American fishermen generally make that a pretext for coming in.
Question. What quantity of wood and water had she on board?
Answer. I cannot say the exact quantity, but there was sufficient for her crew and ours to carry her to St. Andrew's, at which place we did not arrive till several days after her detention.
Question. How was the weather?
Answer. Very fine, with a moderate breeze; but after she anchored it came on foggy.

Thomas Richardson examined.

Question. Were you in the yawl with Mr. Jones when he detained the American schooner "William?"
Answer. Yes.
Question. Relate all you know respecting her.
Answer. I went with Mr. Jones in the small boat to board her; went below and overhauled what quantity of wood and water she had on board.
Question. What quantity of wood and water had she?
Answer. About sixty gallons of water below and thirty on deck, and about a cord and a half of wood.
Question. How was the weather?
Answer. The weather was moderate and hazy, but after she anchored it came on foggy.

James Lloyd, marine, examined.

Question. Were you in the yawl when Mr. Jones detained the American schooner "William?"
Answer. I cannot recollect the vessel's name, having detained several.

Felix Shaw, marine, examined.

Question. Were you in the yawl when Mr. Jones detained the American schooner "William?"
Answer. Yes.
Question. Relate the circumstances you know about her.
Answer. I cannot recollect any of the particulars, as we detained several.

John Cammish, seaman, examined.

Question. Were you in the yawl when Mr. Jones detained the American schooner " William?"
Answer. Yes.
Question. Relate what you know of the circumstances.
Answer. It is so long since I cannot recollect the particulars.

Richard Newland, seaman, examined.

Question. Were you in the yawl with Mr. Jones when he detained the American schooner "William?"
Answer. Yes.
Question. Relate what you know respecting her detention.
Answer. When we fell in with the "William" she was lying in Gull Cove. Mr. Jones asked what they were doing there. They said they came in for wood and water. Mr. Jones detained her, unbent her sails, and took them with us on shore in the yawl, and likewise took their small boat with us.
Question. Do you know the reason why Mr. Jones unbent her sails?
Answer. To prevent her, I believe, from going to sea during the night.
Question. What quantity of wood and water had she on board?
Answer. About three barrels of water and a cord of wood.
Question. How was the weather?
Answer. Fine weather, with a light breeze.
Question. Do you know the position of the fishing ground?
Answer. I do not know the bearing of it by compass, but I could see the vessels at anchor on the fishing ground.
Question. Was the wind fair for going on it?
Answer. Yes, it was.
Question. Were you in the small boat when Mr. Jones boarded her?
Answer. Yes, I was.
Question. Did you hear the master of the vessel assign any reason for coming in there?
Answer. He said they came in for wood and water.

William Vickery, marine, examined.

Question. Were you in the yawl when Mr. Jones detained the American schooner William?
Answer. Yes, I was.
Question. Relate what you know respecting her detention.
Answer. I observed a schooner come in and anchor within a mile of the shore. Mr. Jones went out to board her, and brought her in the cove and anchored.
Question. Were you on board the schooner?
Answer. Yes.
Question. What quantity of wood and water had she on board?
Answer. I know there was two barrels, but cannot say whether there was any more; was not down in the hold, and cannot say what wood there was.
Question. How do you know it was the William?
Answer. I saw the "William, of Addison," on her stern.

John Lloyd, seaman, examined.

Question. Were you in the yawl when Mr. Jones detained the American schooner William?
Answer. Yes, I was.
Question. Relate the particulars.
Answer. I was, with the greater part of the crew, encamped on a point of land; observed a schooner come in and anchor. She was boarded, but cannot recollect whether it was by Mr. Jones or Mr. Touzeau.
Question. Were you on board the schooner?
Answer. Yes, I was. I went off and assisted in unbending her sails.
Question. Do you remember what quantity of wood and water she had on board?
Answer. I do not perfectly recollect the quantity, but there was one cask handed up half full, which they said they were going to get filled on shore, but were prevented by Mr. Jones.
Question. Did you hear any of the crew say their reason for coming in?
Answer. Yes, for wood and water.
Question. How was the weather?
Answer. Fine weather and a fresh breeze.

John Cheese, seaman, examined.

Question. Were you in the yawl with Mr. Jones when he detained the American schooner William?
Answer. Yes, I was.
Question. Relate all you know about her.
Answer. I was sick in a tent on shore, and do not know any of the particulars.

William Payne, marine, examined.

Question. Were you in the yawl with Mr. Jones when he detained the American schooner William?
Answer. Yes.
Question. Relate all you know of the particulars.
Answer. I went on board with Mr. Jones, in the small boat, to examine her. Mr. Jones detained her, unbent her sails and took them on shore.
Question. Do you know what wood and water she had on board?
Answer. I cannot say.
Question. Did you drink any of the water on board of her?
Answer. Yes, I did.
Question. How was the weather?
Answer. Fine, with a strong breeze.

We, the undersigned, have examined the aforesaid persons, belonging to his Majesty's sloop Dotterel, taken the minutes of their depositions respecting the detention of the American fishing schooner William; and we do declare that their evidence has been taken in a very impartial manner, and that the persons aforesaid have not been biased in any way whatsoever.

JOHN COOKE,
Senior Lieutenant of his Majesty's sloop Dotterel.
JAS. AZZARD,
Purser of his Majesty's sloop Dotterel.

Evidence of Mr. Touzeau, midshipman, and the crew of the yawl boat belonging to his Majesty's sloop Dotterel, relative to the detention of the American fishing schooner Galeon.

Mr. Touzeau examined.

Question. Were you in the yawl when Mr. Jones detained the American schooner Galeon?
Answer. Yes, I was.
Question. Relate the particulars respecting her detention?
Answer. While at Gull Cove, Mr. Jones went out one evening in a small boat to cruise. About 11 p. m. Mr. Jones returned with an American schooner which he had detained. Next morning, about 8 o'clock, Mr. Jones sent me on board the Galeon to take charge of her; about 9 o'clock we got under way, and made sail for St. Andrew's.

Question. Do you know Mr. Jones' reason for detaining her?

Answer. I believe for their having broken the treaty; but do not know the particulars, as I was left on shore in charge of the yawl.

Question. How was the weather?

Answer. I believe it was a fine clear night.

Question What quantity of wood and water had she on board?

Answer. I cannot state the quantity; but we used from it for some days' after her detention.

Question. How was the wind?

Answer. From the northward, and I think north by west.

Thomas Richardson examined.

Question. Were you in the yawl with Mr. Jones when he detained the American schooner Galeon?

Answer. Yes.

Question. Relate what you know respecting her detention.

Answer. I went in a small boat with Mr. Jones, and pulled out of Gull Cove; boarded two English schooners, who informed us that an American schooner was lying under the land, which vessel we boarded, and found the crew below asleep. Mr. Jones asked them what they came in for; their reply was, for wood and water, and that they had got it that afternoon. Mr. Jones then asked them their reason for not going away; they said they were waiting for wind and tide. We then got her under way, and ran her to Gull Cove, which place lay between us and the fishing ground.

Question. Do you know the position of the fishing ground?

Answer. Yes; I could see it from Gull Cove.

Question. Was the wind fair for the Galeon to proceed to the banks?

Answer. Yes, it was.

Question. Do you know the passage from Gull Cove to the fishing banks?

Answer. Yes; a clear passage outside the Black Kedge towards the banks.

Question. What kind of weather was it?

Answer. Very fine and clear, with moderate breezes.

Question. What quantity of wood and water had the Galeon on board?

Answer. I do not know the quantity; but observed three or four casks, and a quantity of wood.

William Payne, marine, examined.

Question. Were you in the yawl with Mr. Jones when he detained the American schooner Galeon?

Answer. Yes.

Question. Relate the particulars respecting her detention.

Answer. I went with Mr. Jones in a small boat in the afternoon, (the day of the month I do not remember) and boarded an English schooner, where we were informed an American fishing schooner was lying under the land. We boarded her, and found the crew all below; Mr. Jones asked them their reason for being there; they replied, they came in for wood and water. He then asked them why they did not go away when they had got it. They said they were going at daylight. We detained the schooner, and took her to Gull Cove, and on the following morning got under way for St. Andrew's.

Question. Do you know the position of the fishing banks?

Answer. Yes; I could see the vessel on the banks.

Question. Was the wind fair for the Galeon to proceed to the banks?

Answer. Yes; for the banks lie nearly in a line with Gull Cove, from where we detained the Galeon.

Question. On what quarter was the wind when you ran towards Gull Cove?

Answer. Very near before the wind; we came close to the Cove, and then we hauled up into the Cove.

Question. How was the weather?

Answer. Fine, clear weather, and fresh breezes.

Question. What quantity of wood and water had the Galeon on board when detained?

Answer. She had two casks of water on deck, and a great quantity of wood.

Felix Shaw, marine, examined.

Question. Were you in the yawl with Mr. Jones when he detained the American schooner Galeon?

Answer. Yes.

Question. Relate the particulars.

Answer. I was one of the crew of the small boat that went out with Mr. Jones in the afternoon, (the day of the month I do not recollect;) boarded an English schooner near Gull Cove, who said that we had better keep a good lookout, or we should get a good handspiking from the American schooner then lying in shore. We shortly after boarded the American schooner Galeon. Mr. Jones asked them what they were doing there. They said they came in for wood and water, and had got it that afternoon. Mr. Jones asked them if they had their wood and water, why they had not gone to sea. Their reply was, they did not think it worth while to go to sea that night, and the master requested Mr. Jones to let him go that time, and he would not come in again. We then got under way, and took her to Gull Cove for that night. One of the crew was very abusive. We afterwards carried her to St. Andrew's.

Question. Do you know the position of the fishing grounds?

Answer. No, I do not.

Question. How was the wind when you ran for Gull Cove?

Answer. A fair wind, and fine, clear weather.

John Lloyd, seaman, examined.

Question. Were you in the yawl with Mr. Jones when he detained the American schooner Galeon?

Answer. Yes.

Question. Relate the particulars respecting her detention.

Answer. When at Gull Cove we observed a schooner run in and anchor. We boarded her in the small boat, which proved to be English. They told us that the Galeon, American fishing schooner, was lying at an anchorage then about three or four miles off. We then left the English schooner and boarded the Galeon. I was left as boat keeper, and cannot state what passed on board. Shortly after she was got under way and ran to Gull Cove. One of the crew of the Galeon was very abusive to us. She was afterwards taken to St. Andrew's by Mr. Jones.

Question. Do you know the position of the fishing ground?

Answer. No, I do not.

Question. How was the wind for Gull Cove?

Answer. A fair wind.

Question. How was the weather?

Answer. Fine, clear weather.

Question. What quantity of wood and water had the Galeon on board?

Answer. I do not know.

James Lloyd, marine, examined.

Question. Were you in the yawl with Mr. Jones when he detained the American schooner Galeon?

Answer. I was in the yawl when he detained some American fishing schooners, but cannot recollect their names.

John Cammish, seaman, examined.

Question. Were you in the yawl with Mr. Jones when he detained the American schooner Galeon?

Answer. Yes.

Question. Relate what you know respecting her.

Answer. It is so long since that I cannot recollect any particulars.

Richard Newland, seaman, examined.

Question. Were you in the yawl with Mr. Jones when he detained the American schooner Galeon?

Answer. Yes.

Question. Relate what you know respecting her detention.

Answer. I was left in a tent on shore at Gull Cove, and recollect Mr. Jones going out in a small boat and bringing the Galeon into Gull Cove.

Question. How was the weather?

Answer. Fine weather, with a light breeze.

Question. Did you go in the Galeon to St. Andrew's?

Answer. Yes.

Question. Do you know what quantity of wood and water she had on board?

Answer. She had four casks of water, and about two cords of wood.

John Cheese, seaman, examined.

Question. Were you in the yawl with Mr. Jones when he detained the American schooner Galeon?

Answer. Yes.

Question. Relate all you know respecting her detention.

Answer. I cannot state the particulars, as I was in a tent sick on shore.

William Vickery, marine, examined.

Question. Were you in the yawl with Mr. Jones when he detained the American schooner Galeon?

Answer. Yes.

Question. Relate what you know respecting her detention.

Answer. I was left on shore in the tent; Mr. Jones went out in the small boat, and brought in the Galeon in the evening.

Question. How was the weather?

Answer. Fine weather.

Question. Were you one of the crew that took the Galeon to St. Andrew's?

Answer. Yes.

Question. What quantity of wood and water had she on board?

Answer. Two casks of water on deck and one in the hold, and plenty of wood.

We, the undersigned, have examined the aforesaid persons, belonging to his Majesty's sloop Dotterel, taking the minutes of their depositions respecting the detention of the American fishing schooner Galeon; and we do declare that their evidence has been taken in a very impartial manner, and that they have not been biased in any way whatever.

> JOHN COOKE,
> *Senior Lieut. of his Majesty's sloop Dotterel.*
> JAS. AZZARD,
> *Purser of his Majesty's sloop Dotterel.*
> RICHARD HOARE, *Commander.*

Evidence of the crew of the Dotterel's tender, relative to the detention of the American fishing schooners Hero and Pilgrim.

William Payne, marine, examined.

Question. Were you in the Dotterel's tender with Mr. S. R. Protheroe when he detained the American fishing schooners Hero and Pilgrim?

Answer. Yes.

Question. Relate the particulars respecting their detention.

Answer. I first saw the Pilgrim about two miles from the land, fishing; made the best of our way to close her, and boarded her, having live fish on her deck. Mr. Protheroe asked them what business they had to fish in our waters. They replied they thought it was not in our waters. Mr. Protheroe then said, "I shall detain you and take you to St. John's." I was directed by Mr. Protheroe to take charge of the Pilgrim, with another seaman, and to follow him; I afterwards observed the tender board another schooner, which proved to be the Hero.

Question. What distance was the Hero from the land when Mr. Protheroe boarded her?

Answer. About two miles.

Question. State what followed after leaving the Menan.

Answer. We anchored in Beaver harbor with the Hero and tender, and afterwards proceeded the same day and anchored in Mason's Bay. Late one evening Mr. Protheroe sent us our evening's grog, and my having the middle watch I went below and laid down on the lockers to sleep. In the middle of the night I was awoke by the motion of the vessel and endeavored to get on deck, but could not, as the companion hatch was secured down against me. I then forced it open and went on deck, and found the vessel under way in the possession of the Americans. The seaman with me refusing his assistance, I was obliged to submit, and forcibly carried to Lubec, where they allowed me to go on shore. From thence I made the best of my way to St. John's and rejoined the Dotterel.

Question. Did you at any time hear Mr. Protheroe make use of any abusive language to the Americans?

Answer. No.

Question. Did you hear or know that Mr. Protheroe at any time compelled the Americans to assist in working the vessel?

Answer. No; but they did assist of their own free will.

John Donovan, seaman, examined.

Question. Were you in the Dotterel's tender with Mr. Protheroe when he detained the American schooners Hero and Pilgrim?

Answer. Yes.

Question. Relate all the particulars you know relative to their detention?

Answer. We fell in with the Pilgrim while running into the Menans. I think she was about a mile and a half from the land; saw them hauling up fish, and, on boarding her, found live fish on her deck. Mr. Protheroe said he should detain her for fishing in our waters. We sent two men on board her to take charge. We then made sail for another schooner, which proved to be the Hero. When we boarded her she was about a mile and a half from the land, with lines overboard, fishing, and had live fish in the hold. Mr. Protheroe asked them what they had been doing close in shore with their sails down. A man named Wilson said they had been cleaning fish on shore. I was sent on board the Hero, with another man, to take charge, and to follow the tender and Pilgrim, which we did, anchoring each night till our arrival in Mason's Bay, at which place the Pilgrim made her escape in the night. We afterwards proceeded, anchoring each night, till we arrived at St. John's.

Question. What quantity of wood and water had the Hero on board?

Answer. Two casks of water and some wood; the quantity I cannot say.

Question. Did you at any time hear Mr. Protheroe make use of any abusive language towards the Americans?

Answer. No, I did not.

Question. Did Mr. Protheroe compel any Americans to work?

Answer. No, not to my knowledge; but they continued assisting the working of the vessel with their own free will.

Thomas Cassady, seaman, examined.

Question. Were you in the Dotterel's tender with Mr. Protheroe when he detained the American schooners Hero and Pilgrim?

Answer. Yes.

Question. Relate all the particulars?

Answer. We were running in for the Menan and boarded the Pilgrim, American schooner, about a mile or a mile and a quarter from the land, fishing. Mr. Protheroe asked what business they had fishing there, as they were within three miles of the land. The answer was, they did not know they were within the limits. Mr. Protheroe detained her, and put two men on board to take charge, and we proceeded to board another schooner, which proved to be the Hero, about two miles from the land.

Question. Did you hear Mr. Protheroe ask the master of the Hero if he could assign any reason for being so near the land with her sails down?

Answer. Yes, but did not hear the reply.

Question. What became of the Hero?

Answer. Mr. Protheroe sent two men on board her to take charge, and we proceeded to Mason's Bay, anchoring each night in the tender, with the Hero and Pilgrim in company, at which place the Pilgrim made her escape in the night. Afterwards we proceeded to St. John's in the tender, with the Hero, where she was delivered over to the customs.

Question. Did you at any time hear Mr. Protheroe use any abusive language to the Americans?

Answer. No. I did not.

Question. Did Mr. Protheroe compel the Americans in the tender to work?

Answer. No, he did not, but they sometimes voluntarily assisted in working the tender.

Question. Did you, at any time, know Mr. Protheroe to put the Americans on one meal a day, or know them to fare worse than the tender's crew?

Answer. No, we all messed alike, having the allowance of the British Navy, excepting spirits, for part of the time, which was all used, and I know Mr. Protheroe to have frequently given them rum from his own private stock.

Thomas Russel, seaman, examined.

Question. Were you in the Dotterel's tender with Mr. Protheroe when he detained the American schooners Hero and Pilgrim?

Answer. Yes.

Question. Relate the particulars.

Answer. In running from Grand Passage to Grand Menan, observed two schooners lying at anchor, one of which got under way and stood in shore. We made the best of our way to close her. I observed her with lines overboard, fishing. We then boarded her, which proved to be the Pilgrim, American fishing schooner. She had at the time live fish on her deck. Mr. Protheroe detained her, and put two hands on board to take charge, she then being within a mile of the shore. Observed another schooner make sail from in shore, from the northward; stood for her, fired, brought to, and boarded the American fishing schooner Hero. Mr. Protheroe then asked the master what they had been doing in shore; a man named Wilson said, we have been on shore cleaning fish. Mr. Protheroe detained her. On our way to St. John's anchored under the Eastern Wolves; as we were going in, observed two schooners about a mile off us. Mr. Protheroe hailed the Pilgrim for her boat, which was brought to us in the tender by a boy, who requested Mr. Protheroe to be allowed to pull him on board the aforesaid schooners. Mr. Protheroe, with a man and the boy, proceeded to board these vessels. We then, with the Hero and Pilgrim in company, proceeded for St. John's, anchoring each night till we arrived in Mason's Bay, where the Pilgrim effected her escape during the night. Afterwards we proceeded in the tender, Hero in company, to St. John's, where the Hero was delivered up to the custom-house.

Question. Did you, at any time, hear Mr. Protheroe make use of abusive language to the Americans?

Answer. No.

Question. Did you, at any time, hear Mr. Protheroe threaten to ill-use or maltreat the Americans on board the tender?

Answer. No, I did not.

Question. Did Mr. Protheroe compel the Americans to work in the tender?

Answer. No, but they did sometimes assist voluntarily.

Question. Did you, at any time, know Mr. Protheroe to put the Americans on one meal a day, or know them to fare worse than the tender's crew?

Answer. No. Mr. Protheroe never interfered about the prisoners, and we all messed alike, having the established allowance of the British Navy, excepting spirits for part of the time, which had been all used; and I know Mr. Protheroe to have frequently given them rum from his own private stock.

Samuel Goodanew, marine, examined.

Question. Were you in the Dotterel's tender with Mr. Protheroe when he detained the American schooners Hero and Pilgrim?

Answer. Yes.

Question. Relate all the particulars respecting their detention.

Answer. In standing over from Grand Passage to Grand Menan, observed two schooners at anchor, one of which got under way and stood in shore; made the best of our way and boarded the Pilgrim about two miles from the land, to the best of my judgment. I did not go on board of her, but she was detained by Mr. Protheroe, and two hands put on board to take charge. We then made sail and boarded the Hero, then about a mile and a half from the shore. Mr. Protheroe inquired what they had been doing in shore with their sails down. A man by the name of Wilson said, they had been on shore cleaning their fish. Mr. Protheroe detained her, and put two hands on board to take charge. Proceeded, anchoring each night, to the Eastern Wolves. In going in, observed two schooners about two miles from us; took the Pilgrim's small boat and boarded them. Mr. Protheroe, myself, and the American boy, who [we] brought on board the boat, who was allowed to go by his own request. We then proceeded to Mason's Bay, anchoring each night, with the Hero and Pilgrim in company, at which place the Pilgrim got away during the night. We afterwards proceeded to St. John's, with the Hero in company, which vessel was delivered to the custom-house at that place.

Question. Did you, at any time, hear Mr. Protheroe make use of any abusive language to the Americans?

Answer. No, I did not. I must have heard it had it taken place, as I never left the tender.

Question. Did Mr. Protheroe compel the Americans in the tender to work?

Answer. No, they sometimes assisted with their own consent.

Question. Did you, at any time, hear Mr. Protheroe threaten to ill-use or maltreat the Americans on board the tender?

Answer. No, I did not, but must have heard it had it happened.

Question. Did you, at any time, know Mr. Protheroe to put the Americans on one meal a day, or to fare worse than the tender's crew?

Answer. No. We messed all alike, having the established allowance of the British Navy, excepting spirits, which we drank during the bad weather. I know Mr. Protheroe to have given them spirits from his own stock. I was the person who attended Mr. Protheroe, and gave the spirits to them myself, by his direction.

John Wake, mariner, examined.

Question. Were you in the Dotterel's tender when Mr. Protheroe detained the American schooners Hero and Pilgrim?

Answer. Yes, I was.

Question. Relate all the particulars respecting their detention.

Answer. In running from Grand Passage to the Grand Menan, observed two schooners lying at anchor; one of which got under way and stood in shore, which vessel was chased; observed her fishing and hauling live fish in; boarded her, which proved to be the American schooner Pilgrim. She had, at the time, live fish on her deck. Mr. Protheroe detained her, and put on board two hands to take charge of her, she then being about two miles from the shore, to the best of my judgment. We then chased another schooner which had made sail in from shore; boarded her, then about a mile and a half from the land; proved to be the Hero, American fishing schooner. Mr. Protheroe asked them what they were doing in shore; a man by the name of Wilson said they had been on shore cleaning their fish. Mr. Protheroe detained her, and put two hands on board in charge of her. We then proceeded with the schooner to Mason's Bay, anchoring each night, when the Pilgrim made her escape in the night. We then proceeded to St. John's in the tender, with the Hero in company, at which place she was delivered over to the custom house.

Question. Did you, at any time, hear Mr. Protheroe make use of any abusive language to the Americans on board the tender?

Answer. No, I did not.

Question. Did Mr. Protheroe compel the Americans in the tender to work?

Answer. No, he did not; they helped to work the tender by their own accord.

Question. Did you know Mr. Protheroe ill-use or maltreat the Americans on board the tender?

Answer. No.

Question. Did you know him put the Americans on one meal a day, or fare worse than the tender's crew?

Answer. No, they ate and drank with us. We had the established allowance of the British Navy, except spirits, part of the time, which had been used during the bad weather. I recollect, once, Mr. Protheroe giving them a part from his own private stock.

John Cole, seaman, examined.

Question. Were you in the Dotterel's tender with Mr. Protheroe when he detained the American schooners Hero and Pilgrim?

Answer. Yes.

Question. Relate all the particulars you know respecting their detention?

Answer. When running from Grand Passage to the Grand Menan, observed a schooner about two miles from the land, fishing. We boarded her, which proved to be the Pilgrim, American fishing schooner. I saw live fish on her deck. Mr. Protheroe detained her, and put two hands on board to take charge of her. We then made sail and boarded another schooner, the Hero. Mr. Protheroe detained her also.

Question. Do you know what Mr. Protheroe detained her for?

Answer. No, I do not. I did not hear any questions put, as I was getting my clothes to go on board the Hero. We then made sail, in company with the tender and Pilgrim, and proceeded to Mason's Bay, at which place the Pilgrim effected her escape during the night. We afterwards went to St. John's, with the tender and Hero in company, at which place the Hero was delivered over to the custom house.

We, the undersigned, have examined the aforesaid persons, belonging to his Majesty's sloop Dotterel, taking the minutes of their depositions respecting the detention of the American fishing schooners "Hero" and "Pilgrim;" and we declare that their evidence has been taken in a very impartial manner, and the persons aforesaid have not been biased in any way whatever.

JOHN COOKE, *Senior Lieutenant, his Majesty's sloop Dotterel.*
JAMES AZZARD, *Purser.*
RICHARD HOARE, *Commander.*

Evidence of Mr. Touzeau, midshipman, and the crew of the yawl boat belonging to his Majesty's sloop Dotterel, relative to the detention of the American fishing schooners " Reindeer" and " Ruby."

Mr. Touzeau examined.

Question. Were you in the yawl with Mr. Jones when he detained the American schooners Reindeer and Ruby?

Answer. Yes.

Question. Relate all the particulars relative to their detention?

Answer. I recollect, while in Gull Cove, of having received information, on a Sunday, from some men and a Mr. Franklin that several American fishing vessels were at anchor in Whitehead harbor, and that they anchored there the evening before; that, on their anchoring, one of them fired three muskets, and said they were armed and manned, and would oppose our boarding them. I acquainted Mr. Jones of the information I had received, who went immediately in the small boat to cruise, and returned in the evening. He told me that he had boarded an English fishing schooner (Industry) near Whitehead, who gave him information that several American schooners were at anchor at Two Island harbor, and that they got their wood and water at Whitehead; they fired several muskets on their anchoring, and told the crew of the Industry they would not allow a man-of-war's boat to board them; and, after they completed their wood and water, they shifted to Two Island harbor. We got under way the yawl about 9 o'clock in the evening, and went towards Two Island harbor, and anchored about 2 o'clock in the morning. At daylight we observed several vessels at anchor at Two Island harbor, and shortly after got under way, when we chased them; observed three of them lashed together, and all the crews collected on board the middle one. We ordered them to separate, which at first they refused to do, until Mr. Jones threatened to fire on them. They dropped clear of each other; we boarded them, and detained the American schooners Reindeer and Ruby. Mr. Jones asked the masters of the other two American shallops if they were willing to take the crews of the Reindeer and Ruby on board for a passage home. They answered they were willing to do so. Mr. Jones gave them as much provisions as they chose to take, and put them on board, with the exception of the masters. About 8 o'clock we made sail, Mr. Jones in the Reindeer and myself in the Ruby, for St. Andrew's. While beating up through East Quoddy, about 6 p. m., when abreast the harbor Delute, observed two schooners coming down towards us, full of armed men and wearing American colors, one of them making towards me, and the other to Mr. Jones. The one abreast of me ran alongside and boarded, with about forty-five men with pistols, swords, and muskets, and fixed bayonets. When they got on board they took possession of the Ruby, and took the arms from my crew. One of the men, with his musket and fixed bayonet, made a thrust at one of my men, named James Lloyd, (marine,) but Mr. Howard, leader of their party, parried the thrust off. The man again attempted to knock the marine down with the butt end of his musket, which Mr. Howard again parried off, and ordered him not to use violence against any of my men, as he had got possession of the vessel, and which was all they wanted. They then fired off all their muskets and pistols, which were loaded. I observed the other schooner fire off muskets likewise; then I asked for the arms of my crew, which they gave me. We then shoved off, and left them. After we had left, and rejoined the yawl, they fired several volleys of musketry on board both schooners all the way to Eastport.

Question. What quantity of wood and water had the Ruby on board?

Answer. There were two casks with water on deck; but cannot say whether there was any below, nor can I say what quantity of wood there was on board.

Question. How was the wind?

Answer. A moderate breeze from northwest.

Question. How was the weather?

Answer. Fine, clear weather till we had possession of the schooners, and then it came on foggy, and cleared off again in the afternoon.

Thomas Richardson, seaman, examined.

Question. Were you in the yawl with Mr. Jones when he detained the American schooners Reindeer and Ruby?

Answer. Yes.

Question. Relate what you know respecting their detention.

Answer. I remember going in the small boat with Mr. Jones. After pulling some time we launched the boat over a bar, about half a mile broad, between two islands, and afterwards we boarded an English fishing schooner. The crew informed us that the schooners at anchor off Two Island harbor were American fishing vessels, and had, the night before, fired two guns and defied any man-of-war's boat boarding them, and advised us not to attempt to board them in the small boat we were then in. We then returned to Gull Cove, and that night, with the whole of the crew in the yawl, pulled during the whole of that night, and at daylight we were within three miles from four schooners, at anchor, a little more than a mile from shore. We observed them get under way, and three of them lashed alongside each other. Mr. Jones then desired them to separate, which they did not do for some time, when Mr. Jones threatened to fire on them. They then separated, and dropped astern of each other and anchored. We then boarded them, and took possession of the Reindeer and Ruby, and the crews, as I understood, with their own consent, went on board of two other vessels. We then got the Reindeer and Ruby under way, and made sail for St. Andrew's. When in East Quoddy, two schooners came towards us, fired a gun, and hoisted American colors; observed one of the schooners take possession of the Ruby, and the other came close to us and desired us to heave to. I was at the helm when they fired at us, and the shot came close to me and Mr. Jones. There was but one musket on board us, which Payne (a marine) wanted to fire, but Mr. Jones desired him not. I observed the American schooner's deck full of armed men, with muskets, pistols, and carbines. After they fired at us, Mr. Jones gave up the papers to the master of the Reindeer, who held them up in his hand not to fire, as he had possession of the vessel. We then went in the yawl for St. Andrew's. Some of the Americans would insist on taking the yawl with us. I observed them fire volleys of muskets till after they had anchored the Reindeer and Ruby in Eastport.

Question. How was the weather when Mr. Jones detained the Reindeer and Ruby?

Answer. It was clear weather till after they were detained, when it became foggy.

Question. Do you know what quantity of wood and water the Reindeer had on board?

Answer. The quantity I cannot recollect, but we used from both.

James Lloyd, marine, examined.

Question. Were you in the yawl with Mr. Jones when he detained the American schooners Reindeer and Ruby?

Answer. Yes.

Question. Relate the particulars respecting their detention.

Answer. I remember a man, at Gull Cove, giving information of some schooners, (American;) the particulars I do not know. We got under way that evening in the yawl, and pulled all night; after daylight we got close to four schooners, and observed three of them lashed alongside of each other, and the crews of these vessels on board the large one in the centre. Mr. Jones ordered them to separate several times, and at length he said he would fire into them; they were very abusive to us; after a considerable time they separated and we boarded them. Mr. Jones then sent me below to see if there were any fire-arms on board the Reindeer; I found a musket, with a double charge and primed, and two powder horns full of powder, and about twelve or fourteen pistol balls. Mr. Jones detained two of them, with the consent of the masters of the other two vessels and the crew of the two detained; they were allowed to go on board and take what provisions they pleased; the masters of the vessels came on board and took green fish, pork, tea, and butter, molasses, flour, and bread. I was sent, with Mr. Touzeau, on board one of them, and got under way in company with the one Mr. Jones was on board of; and, in the afternoon of the same day, while beating up to St. Andrew's, abreast of Campo Bello, I observed three schooners and two boats; one of the schooners went towards Mr. Jones and fired several muskets; went below to get my dinner, when Mr. Touzeau called us up to our arms, and asked me if my musket was loaded; I told him it was and primed; he told me he thought they were American armed vessels coming to take us. I then asked Mr. Touzeau if I should fire; he said not till he gave me the orders. They came nearly alongside of us, and ordered us to heave to; they presented their muskets, with fixed bayonets, at us, and said, damn your eyes, if you don't heave to we will fire into you. They sung out to the man at the helm if he did not put the helm down and lower the peak they would shoot him dead on the spot. They then came alongside and boarded us, I think about forty men in number; all with muskets and fixed bayonets except one, for our deck was full of armed men. They told me to deliver up my arms or they would run me through; damn your eyes said one; and another said I will blow your brains out. I replied, I am a King's man, and will not deliver up my arms; their leader drew his sword and had a brace of pistols; desired the Americans not to hurt any of us; at that time a man made a thrust at me with fixed bayonet, which their leader parried off; the same man again made a blow at me with the butt end of his musket, which their leader again parried off; then their leader tol'l me that I had better give up my arms, and he would be answerable for them, which I did; about this time they fired volleys of musketry. We then went on board of our boat and observed them continue to fire as they were returning to Eastport.

Question. What kind of weather was it when Mr. Jones detained the Reindeer and Ruby?
Answer. Fine weather, with a light breeze, but came foggy after.
Question. Do you know what quantity of wood and water was in the schooner you were on board of?
Answer. Two casks and a half of water and about a cord of wood.

John Cammish, seaman, examined.

Question. Were you in the yawl with Mr. Jones when he detained the American schooners Reindeer and Ruby?
Answer. I was.
Question. Relate the particulars.
Answer. I recollect Mr. Jones going out from Gull Cove in the small boat and returned in the evening. I heard him say that he had information of some American schooners. We were ordered to get our things in the yawl from the tent, and went out that evening. We pulled the greater part of the night, and anchored for about an hour and a half. At daylight observed five vessels lying at anchor. When they saw us they got under way. When we came near them one of the vessels dropped her anchor, and two others lashed alongside her; and the crews of these vessels went on board the centre one with their fish spears. Mr. Jones desired them to separate, which they did not do for a considerable time, until Mr. Jones threatened several times to fire into them; they separated, and we boarded the Reindeer, where I remained. Mr. Jones detained her and another vessel. By the wish of the crews of these vessels, and by the consent of the masters of the other two vessels not detained, they were sent on board, with as much provisions as they wished. The masters of the two vessels not detained came on board us in their own boats, and took the crews, with as much provision as they chose, on board. We then got under way; the Reindeer for St. Andrew's, the Ruby in company. In the afternoon of the same day observed two armed vessels. One of them came towards us and gave three cheers and hoisted American colors; they called to us to heave to, and threatened to fire into us. Her decks were full of armed men, with muskets and fixed bayonets; there was also in company a large armed boat. The schooner fired two musket balls across our deck, and then Mr. Jones gave up the papers to the master of the Reindeer, who held them up in his hand-and called to the Americans not to fire, as he had possession of the vessel. The American schooner was then about half pistol shot from us. We were then ordered into the yawl by Mr. Jones, and observed them, in going to Eastport, fire volleys of musketry.
Question. What quantity of wood and water had the Reindeer?
Answer. Three barrels of water and a great deal of wood.
Question. What weather was it when the two vessels were detained?
Answer. Fine weather and light winds from northward and westward.

Richard Newland, seaman, examined.

Question. Were you in the yawl with Mr. Jones when he detained the American schooners Reindeer and Ruby?
Answer. Yes, I was.
Question. Relate the particulars.
Answer. I recollect a man coming to Mr. Jones, at the tent at Gull Cove, and informing him that some American fishing schooners had come into an anchorage not far from us, and fired their muskets, and said they would not allow any man-of-war's boat to board them. They got their wood and water there, and got under way and ran to Two Island harbor; laid there one day and a night. I was left on shore in the tent, and remember Mr. Jones going out in a small boat with four hands, and returned the same afternoon. We got under way that evening in the yawl, and stood for Two Island harbor. The next morning we fell in with four American schooners and one English. When I first saw them they were at anchor, about half a mile from the land, in Two Island harbor. After they saw us they got under way. On our chasing them, we fired to bring them to; but instead of complying, three of them ran alongside each other and lashed together. When we came close to them, Mr. Jones desired them to separate and bring up. They refused to do so, and would not allow us to board, until Mr. Jones repeatedly threatened to fire into them; they dropped clear of each other; we then boarded the Reindeer, and Mr. Jones asked what they were doing there? They said they came in to land their gurry and offal of the fish, and get wood and water. Mr. Jones told them they had time enough to get their wood and water at White island. Mr. Jones detained the Reindeer, and then boarded the Ruby, which vessel he detained also; and I was sent below in the Ruby to search for arms; found none; but found a frying-pan full of hot lead and a spoon in it, and some musket balls quite warm. I asked the master of the Ruby where his arms were? He said he had none, except one fowling-piece I then asked him where it was. His reply was, he could not say, unless his boy had lost it or stowed it away in the salt room. When I asked their reason for lashing together and running the musket balls, they said they intended to keep us off; with their five-and-thirty men and eight muskets they would easily have done so. I then asked them where their eight muskets were? They answered, they had eight muskets. The masters of the two schooners which were not detained came on board the Ruby and took their crew, with their clothes, and as much provisions as they wished for a passage to their home, by their own wish, and sanction of Mr. Jones. Afterwards we got under way in the Reindeer and Ruby for St. Andrew's; and the same afternoon, between Indian island and Campo Bello, two schooners came towards us full of armed men. The one abreast of the Ruby gave three cheers and hoisted American colors, bore down and ordered us to heave to, which we refused doing until they threatened to fire into us. They came alongside, and boarded with muskets and fixed bayonets, cutlasses and pistols. I do not know the number of men, but our decks were full. They took our arms from us and discharged their own. We then were ordered into our boat, and I observed them firing volleys of musketry going in, and after they had anchored at Eastport.
Question. Did you search the salt room of the Ruby for arms?
Answer. No; I had not time.

Question. Hów was the weather when the Reindeer and Ruby were detained?
Answer. Fine, clear weather, with a little breeze, but came on foggy afterwards for two hours.
Question. How was the wind?
Answer. I cannot recollect.

William Vickery, marine, examined.

Question. Were ýou in the yawl with Mr. Jones when he detained the American schooners Reindeer and Ruby?
Answer. Yes.
Question. Relate all the particulars you know respecting their detention?
Answer. I recollect going out in the small boat from Gull Cove with Mr. Jones, and, after pulling for a short time, we launched the boat over a bar between two islands, and boarded an English fishing schooner. The crew informed us that two American schooners had anchored the night before, not far from where we laid, and that they fired their muskets and defied any man-of-war's boat to board them. The crew of the English schooner told us that we had better be well armed, as the Americans were prepared for us. We returned to Gull Cove, and in the evening went out with all the crew in the yawl; we pulled till about 4 o'clock in the morning. At daylight observed some schooners at anchor, which vessels, shortly afterwards, got under way; and as we went down towards them, I fired, by the direction of Mr. Jones, to bring them to. As we closed the vessels, three of them lashed alongside each other, and put their crews on board the middle one. Mr. Jones desired them to cast off from each other, which they refused to do for some time, until he threatened to fire into them, when they separated, and we boarded the Reindeer; and Lloyd, a marine, was sent down to search for arms; he found one musket, loaded. Mr. Jones asked the master where the arms were that he saw. He said he had none. Mr. Jones then detained the Reindeer and Ruby; and by the wish of the crews of the vessels, with the exception of the masters, they were put on board the other two Americans not detained, with the consent of the masters, taking with them as much provisions as they chose. We then got under way in the Reindeer, with the Ruby in company. In the afternoon of the same day, when abreast of Campo Bello, I saw two schooners, one of which came towards us, fired a gun, and hoisted American colors, and ordered us to heave to, which we refused to do; and after we tacked they fired across our deck. After this, Mr. Jones delivered up the papers to the master of the Reindeer, who held them up to the Americans, and desired them not to fire. We were then ordered by Mr. Jones into the yawl, and I observed them fire several muskets at a time, and the balls falling into the water, as they were going into Eastport.
Question. What arms had the Americans?
Answer. I observed some men with cross-belts, bright muskets, and fixed bayonets; others with muskets, swords, and pistols.
Question. What quantity of wood and water had the Reindeer on board?
Answer. A cask full below, some on deck, and plenty of wood.
Question. How was the weather when the Reindeer and Ruby were detained?
Answer. Fine weather, with fine breezes.
Question. How was the wind?
Answer. I do not recollect.
Question. Did you search the salt room on board the Reindeer for arms?
Answer. No, I did not.

John Lloyd, seaman, examined.

Question. Were you in the yawl with Mr. Jones when he detained the American schooners Reindeer and Ruby?
Answer. Yes.
Question. Relate the particulars.
Answer. I went out with Mr. Jones from Gull Cove in a small boat, and, after pulling for some time, we launched the boat over a bar about a quarter of a mile broad, between Two islands, and boarded an English schooner (Industry) of Grand Menan, and I heard the master inform Mr. Jones that some American fishing schooners had been in there on the last Saturday, and discharged three guns, and that several were now lying in a bay further on, when Mr. Jones proposed to go after them in the small boat. The master of the Industry advised not to do so, as they were well manned. We returned to Gull Cove the same day, and in the evening went out with all the arms in the yawl, and at daylight next morning observed five schooners getting under way; we ran down to them and fired; observed three of them made fast to each other, the largest of them in the middle, with the crews collected on board of her. Mr. Jones ordered them to separate, which they hesitated to do for some time, and they appeared to be consulting together. After Mr. Jones threatened to fire into them they separated. We boarded two of them, the Reindeer and Ruby, and the crews of these vessels, with the exception of the masters, went on board the two schooners not detained, with as much provisions as they pleased; after this we got under way in the Ruby, and Reindeer in company, for St. Andrew's. On the afternoon of the same day, when abreast of harbor Delute, observed two schooners coming down from Eastport, full of men; óne of them came towards us, and all hands hailing us to heave to, or they would fire into us; they ran alongside and boarded us with about 30 or 40 men, with muskets and bayonets; as they were shearing up alongside, some of them sung out to fire at the officers, and fire at the man at the helm; they had their muskets levelled at us, when their leader, a young man, came among them and said, don't fire at all, and parried their muskets off. They took our arms from us and drove us forward. I saw a scuffle between James Lloyd, a marine, and one of the Americans who wanted to take his arms from him. Mr. Touzeau told us to get into our boat, and I observed them firing volleys of musketry and cheering on their way to Eastport; also observed firing on shore at Eastport.
Question. What quantity of wood and water had the Ruby on board when detained?
Answer. Two or three casks, with plenty of wood.
Question. How was the weather?
Answer. Very fine, with light breezes.

William Payne, marine, examined.

Question. Were you in the yawl with Mr. Jones when he detained the American schooners Reindeer and Ruby?

Answer. Yes, I was.

Question. Relate the particulars respecting her detention.

Answer. I recollect on Sunday going out from Gull Cove, with Mr. Jones, in a small boat, and, after pulling for some time, hauled the boat over a bar; shortly after boarded an English fishing schooner belonging to Grand Menan; the crew gave us information that some American schooners anchored there on Saturday night, fired their guns, and said that they did not care for any man-of-war's boat whatever, as they were as well armed as the men-of-war's boats. I saw the schooners at Two Island harbor, at anchor, when on board the Industry; and her crew said we had better not go to them in the small boat; that it was their determination to kill us. We then returned to Gull Cove, and in the evening of the same day got under way in the yawl, with all the crew, and proceeded to Two Island harbor. About daylight next morning observed them get under way; we closed them, and fired to bring them to. I then saw them closing together, and three of them lashed alongside each other; we ordered them to separate, which they seemed not willing to do. Mr. Jones threatened to fire into them; we had our muskets, two in number, pointed to the vessel; after being threatened several times, two of them, the Reindeer and Ruby, Mr. Jones asked them what brought them there; their answer was, they came for wood and water; Mr. Jones then said, when you had got it, what was their reason for not going away; their reply was, the breeze was so light they could not get out; the crews of their vessels, with the exception of the masters, by their own request, went on board the two other schooners not detained, and were allowed to take what quantity of provisions they thought proper. I then went below, with Thomas Richardson, to search for arms, by the direction of Mr. Jones; found a musket, loaded, in the cabin. Mr. Jones asked the master what became of their arms; he said they were below; we then went again below for the same purpose. Mr. Jones again asked the master of the Reindeer what became of the arms; his answer was, that they must have been hove overboard; he said we had got them yesterday killing ducks. Shortly after we got the Reindeer and Ruby under way, and proceeded for St. Andrew's; in the afternoon of the same day, when abreast of Campo Bello, saw a schooner coming down and ran close alongside the Ruby, hoisted American colors; observed another standing towards us in the Reindeer; they gave three cheers, hoisted American colors, and hailed us to drop the peak of the mainsail; the master of the Reindeer said to us, you had better not fire on them, as they will kill every man of you, and he ran below; they came near us, and Mr. Jones said, come alongside of us, which they were willing to do. I had my musket ready to fire, and asked Mr. Jones if I should do so, to which he objected, and said, let them come alongside first; they then fired, and a ball passed close to us. Mr. Jones gave the papers up to the master of the Reindeer, who held them up to those on board the American schooner, desired them not to fire, and said that we would quit the vessel as soon as possible. We then got into the yawl, and observed them firing different times going into Eastport.

Question. When the schooner with American colors flying came close, did you observe they were armed?

Answer. Yes, they were, and the deck full of men, armed with muskets and fixed bayonets, carbines, blunderbusses, pistols, and swords.

Question. How was the weather when the Reindeer and Ruby were detained?

Answer. Fine weather and a fine breeze.

Question. What quantity of wood and water had the Reindeer on board?

Answer. Two casks of water on deck and plenty of wood.

Question. Did you search the salt room and the hold for arms?

Answer. No; I did not search the salt room aft, but did forward.

John Cheese, seaman, examined.

Question. Were you with Mr. Jones, in the yawl, when he detained the American schooners Reindeer and Ruby?

Answer. No, I was not; I was one of his boat's crew, but was left behind at St. Andrew's.

We, the undersigned, have examined the aforesaid persons, belonging to his Majesty's sloop Dotterel, taking the minutes of their depositions respecting the detention of the American fishing schooners Reindeer and Ruby; and we do declare that their evidence has been taken in a very impartial manner, and that the persons aforesaid have not been biased in any way whatever.

          JOHN COOKE, *Senior Lieutenant, &c.,*
          JAMES AZZARD, *Purser,*
          RICHARD HOARE, *Commander,*
               His Majesty's sloop Dotterel.

His MAJESTY'S SLOOP DOTTEREL, *Halifax, November 8, 1824.*

SIR: I beg leave to represent, in obedience to your orders of this day's date, directing me to give a statement of the facts, and under what circumstances I detained the American fishing schooners at different anchorages at the Grand Menan, while cruising in the yawl, in pursuance of your orders, for the protection of our fisheries, that on the 2d day of July last, on boarding an English vessel, I found a man named Wright officiating as pilot, to carry her to Grand Harbor, who told me that he belonged to the American fishing schooner Rebecca, then at anchor at Woodward's Cove, and that they came there for water. Satisfied with his assertion, I continued cruising, and, shortly after, I observed the American vessel getting under way, leaving the said man (Wright) behind. I ran down towards her; they not heaving to after we fired several shots across their bow, I chased her over to the Nova Scotia shore, where I lost sight of her. On the 6th following, I found the said American schooner Rebecca at anchor, cleaning fish, and throwing the offals overboard, and the aforesaid man (Wright) on board. It being fine weather, and they having three barrels of water on board, with a sufficient quantity of wood, I detained her and took her to St. John's.

On the 15th of the same month I found the American fishing schooner William anchoring in Gull Cove; the weather was fine until after she got in, when it came on foggy with light breezes; and. they having two barrels of water on board, which myself, Mr. Touzeau, and the boat's crew, subsequently used from, and plenty of wood, I detained her. Having found the American schooner Rover, of Addison, Crowley master, landing a great part of her cargo of green fish to a Mr. Fowler's, at Gull Cove, I made the William's boat fast to the yawl for the night, to prevent their crew from doing the same. As for their getting water about sunset, and a vessel to anchor alongside of them, Mr. Touzeau and I know it to be impossible, as I had a sentry planted on shore about two cables' length from them; and if they received any water after dark, it was done as a pretext, for the boat's crew were witnesses to the water I found on board when I first boarded her; and that I threatened to confine the master to the deck and lash a pump brake across his mouth, as stated in their protest, is false. On my first boarding her, with only three men in our small boat, they were very abusive to us, and one of them said, if they were all of his mind, they would heave that fellow overboard, pointing to me. I told him if he did not keep quiet I would lash him to the deck. At 3 p. m., same day, 15th, I received information from the fishermen at Gull Cove, as well as from the master and crew of the fishing schooner Minerva, of Grand Menan, that an American schooner was at anchor at Beal's Passage. I went out from Gull Cove and saw her there; at 9 o'clock .in the evening I boarded her, which proved to be the American fishing schooner Galeon, and found all the crew asleep. On questioning the master the reason of his being there, he told me that he came to throw the gurry, offal of the fish, overboard. They not being in want of wood or water, and a fine fair wind for them, I detained her, got her under way and ran for Gull Cove, a direct course for their fishing ground. What the crew of the last mentioned vessel asserted in their protest is not true; I never said that I would release their vessel, but told them it was not in my power to do it, as they had decidedly violated the treaty of convention between England and the United States; but as they pleaded poverty, saying their vessel was their sole support, I told them I would recommend their case to Captain Hoare, of the Dotterel, my commanding officer. Both schooners, William and Galeon, I took to St. Andrew's the next day. On the 25th of the same month I received information from the master and crew of the fishing schooner Industry, of Grand Menan, that several American fishing schooners were at anchor at Two Island harbor, and that two of them, namely, Reindeer and Ruby, of Lubec, were at White Island harbor on the 24th, where they got their wood and water, and that, on their anchoring there, they told them and the inhabitants they were armed, and would not allow any man-of-war's boat to board them; and, after they had their supplies, they shifted to Two Island harbor. At daylight, the 26th, observed four schooners at anchor at Two Island harbor, which got under way on our appearance. When I got close, three of them they lashed alongside each other, and all hands, about thirty in number, went on board the middle one with fire-arms and fish spears. I desired them to separate, which they refused to do until I threatened to fire on them. On boarding them, they proved to be the Reindeer, Ruby, Friends, and Diligent, American fishing schooners. It being fine weather, and they not in want of wood or water, I detained the Reindeer and Ruby, and, by the sanction of the masters of the Diligent and Friends, I put the crews of the Reindeer and Ruby on board of them, with as much provisions as they wished to take, and on our passage to St. Andrew's the said schooners Reindeer and Ruby were forcibly taken from me by armed vessels, under American colors, as stated in my letter of the 27th of July last.

I have the honor to be, &c., &c.,

JOHN JONES,
Master of his Majesty's sloop Dotterel.

Richard Hoare, *Commander.*

His Majesty's Sloop Dotterel, *November 9, 1824.*

Sir: In obedience to your orders, I herewith add a statement of the Pilgrim and Hero, American fishing schooners.

On the 16th of June last I observed these schooners lying off the Grand Menan, and upon approaching them, one of the schooners got under way and stood in for the shore; 3.30 p. m. observed the schooner under way heave her lines overboard and haul in fish, the schooner then within one and a half mile of the island; 3.40, fired and brought to the schooner; 3.45, boarded the Pilgrim, then about one mile or one mile and a quarter from the shore. She had on board fish, alive; took possession of her for a breach of the treaty. I then stood to the N. ¼ E. and boarded the Hero, who had made sail from in shore. Whilst I was on board the Pilgrim, and finding she was in want of nothing, I inquired what she had been doing so near the shore with her sails down, to which I was informed by one of the crew they had been cleaning their fish on shore; in consequence of which, and having seen her within one mile of the land, I took possession of her also; stood in, and anchored in Long Island harbor. Thursday, the 17th, being for the most part of the day calm, I remained at anchor. Friday, the 18th, at 7 a. m., weighed and stood for Beaver harbor; from 9 to 12, calm; 3 p. m. observed two schooners under the Eastern Wolf, then about one mile distant. It being calm at the time, I ordered the master of the Pilgrim to send me her small boat, not having one myself; upon receiving which, I ordered one of my seamen and one marine, armed, into her. The boy who brought the boat I told to remain on board until I returned; but on his expressing a wish to go, and knowing he was more acquainted with her than any of my men could be, I agreed that he should pull, and ordered my seaman on board; part of the way I pulled, and part of the way the marine pulled with the boy. When I returned, there being no appearance of wind, I ordered the schooners Pilgrim and Hero to follow me and anchor under the Eastern Wolf for the night. Saturday, the 19th, it being calm, did not weigh until 11 a. m., then a light breeze; stood for Beaver harbor, where I anchored at 3 p. m. with an intention of waiting for the Dotterel's arrival; therefore, unbent sails and caused the Pilgrim and Hero to do the same. Sunday, the 20th, 11 a. m., observed the Dotterel pass in the offing to the eastward; bent sails and desired the Pilgrim and Hero to do the same. 12.20 p. m. weighed, schooners in. company, beat out of the harbor; but finding the Pilgrim and Hero could not, I bore up, stood in, and anchored, schooners in company. Monday, the 21st, at 7 a. m., weighed, with light airs, schooners in company; beat up and anchored in Mason's Bay at 8.30 p. m. Tuesday, the 22d, at 2.30 a. m., the sentry reported one of the schooners was gone. Wednesday, the 23d, fresh gales until 10 a. m., then light airs with heavy rain; still at anchor. Thursday, the 24th, at 9 a. m. weighed, with light airs, and stood for Point La Pro, Hero in company, but, falling calm, were obliged to put into Dipper harbor. Friday, the 25th, heavy rains, with strong breezes from the eastward; remained at anchor. Saturday, the 26th, weighed, but were obliged to put back again. Sunday, the 27th, weighed and ran up to St. John's.

I further beg leave to state that I did detain on board the crews of the Pilgrim and Hero, having no authority for acting otherwise; that Winslow, in Beaver harbor, said he was aware of having fished within the limits, and if I would allow him and crew to go home he would give up his schooner and never again ask for her. Part of the men were at times on board my boat and living the same as my boat's crew, who had the allowance of the British Navy, excepting spirits, which had been all used; to make up for which, I gave from my private stock to those of the schooners who were on board my boat. I never asked them to do any duty on board my boat; nor did I, at any time, make use of harsh or menacing language. The duty done by the persons taken out of one or either of the said schooners was a perfect voluntary act of their own. The arms spoken of were taken from the Pilgrim, through expressions made use of by Winslow, for safety. Powder, a quarter of a pound; shot, about one pound. The arms were delivered to the gunner. The papers of each schooner were delivered to the custom-house at St. John's.

I have the honor to be, &c.,

S. R. PROTHEROE, *Mate.*

R. HOARE, *Commander.*

His MAJESTY'S SLOOP DOTTEREL, *Halifax, November* 25, 1824.

SIR: According to your direction, I have made the strictest investigation, and inclose the reports of Mr. Jones, master, and Mr. Protheroe, mate; also, the testimony of the several men belonging to their boats, relative to the several American fishing vessels they had seized, which I trust will be sufficient proof of the propriety of detaining those vessels; and, as the American fishermen do not keep any journal or log, there cannot be possibly any proof but the crews of the boats detaining them and the Americans; it is not to be supposed that the latter will acknowledge to have violated the treaty existing between the two Governments relative to the fisheries. I think you will perceive a consistency throughout the several reports of Messrs. Jones and Protheroe that will bear the stamp of truth. Why should they detain these vessels if they had not violated the laws? It could not be for their value, they had little or nothing in, and they knew if they were condemned and sold they would sell for a mere trifle, the best of them not more than forty dollars; there were many other American fishing vessels of much more value, which they might have seized, if it was merely to annoy them, or for the sake of what they might sell for; but it is known everywhere in the Bay of Fundy that the American fishermen have invariably made use of the several harbors in the Menan as if those islands formed a part of the United States; they come in and haul their nets, and there are many instances of their having cut away the nets of the islanders; and I was informed by the fishermen at the Menan, previous to leaving the Bay of Fundy, that they had taken treble the quantity of fish this year to that of any preceding year since the war, and they ascribed it entirely to the American fishermen having been kept without the distance prescribed by treaty (three marine miles) from the shore. The former cruisers in the Bay of Fundy (*vide* Captain Arabin's letter, dated his Majesty's sloop Argus, off Bermuda, December 17, 1822,) have not paid much attention to the fisheries off Menan, and consequently the American fishermen have gone into the harbors whenever they pleased, and being more numerous than the inhabitants have overawed them; but I have been informed by some of the fishermen resident there that more than once they have had it in contemplation to represent the conduct of, and the injury they have sustained from, the American fishermen, but their living remote from each other, and no educated persons among them, they have been at a loss how to draw up a petition, or who to apply to for redress.

As all the vessels alluded to in the papers sent by Mr. Addington were taken by the boats, I cannot, myself, make any observations on their capture, but shall confine myself to a few remarks on the protests of the American fishermen, and to answer the complaint you have called my particular attention to.

Why do not the crews or owners of the American fishing vessels, detained for violating the treaty, come forward when these vessels are adjudged in the Vice Admiralty court, and produce such evidence as would clear them? they say, to claim their vessels in the Vice Admiralty court of New Brunswick would be a total loss; the fact is, it would not answer their purpose so well; they are well aware that witnesses could be produced that would falsify their testimony; the fishermen at the Menan would immediately come forward to witness the facts of their being in their harbors, and drawing their nets, when not in want of an article of provisions or fuel; but the Americans are aware that when their protest comes before the commander-in-chief of this station, the vessel-of-war will have left the Bay of Fundy, and that there will remain but the testimony of the officer and boat's crew that detained them, which they will take care to outnumber. If the Vice Admiralty courts of New Brunswick are conducted illegally and wrong, should they not make a representation to the British Government, that they may be better conducted? How is the captain of a man-of-war, stationed in the Bay of Fundy, to act, if the proceedings in the Vice Admiralty court are to be considered illegal and void, merely from the protest of some American fishermen?

What are the Vice Admiralty courts instituted for, but to try causes, and decide whether the capture is just; and I should conceive that where they have passed judgment, the captain of the seizing vessel is released from further responsibility; sufficient time is allowed all parties to procure and produce evidence, and if they do not come forward, is it not a tacit acknowledgment of the badness of their cause—and such is the case with these American fishing vessels; they have asserted many things that are wholly false. It is said in the memorial A, "that nine sail of American fishermen had been captured and sent into the province of New Brunswick, while others had been converted into tenders, without trial, for the purpose of molesting our fishermen; they have insulted and abused the crews, turned them on shore in a foreign country, entirely destitute, and without the means of returning to their homes."

That any American fishing vessel detained by the Dotterel, or her boats, has been converted into a tender for the better molesting their fishermen, is wholly false; that the crews have, to my knowledge, been insulted and abused, must be a gross and wilful perjury; it had always been the custom, I understood, to allow the crews of the vessels detained to take their clothes and such provisions as they pleased, and find their way to the States. I have sometimes offered to carry them back, when I returned to Passamaquoddy; they have invariably been allowed to take away everything they could claim as their private property, and the whole of their provisions on board their vessel, with which they paid their passage back to their country.

And in the memorial C it is said "that the American fishermen have no occasion nor inducement to violate the provisions of the aforesaid convention, nor have they, as we firmly believe, given in any instance just cause of complaint."

It is a well known fact that the American fishermen leave their fishing ground every Saturday, (when there is not a man-of-war or her boats in the neighborhood,) and anchor in some of the harbors of the Menan until the Monday, bringing in the fish offal with them, and throwing it overboard on the inner banks, by which they drive the fish off those banks, and they haul their nets during the Sunday, and catch sufficient bait for the ensuing week. This they suppose is not known; for they are not ignorant that this is a violation of the provisions of the convention; the fact is, they want, by causing much trouble, to deter the man-of-war stationed in the Bay of Fundy from interfering with them at all.

That the brig's barge has come into the wharf at Eastport and taken and carried away two boats laden with flour, Lieutenant Driffield's letter on that subject will, I think, completely invalidate that charge.

That the Hero, American fishing vessel, captured on the 16th of June, has not been sent in for trial, but is armed, and is still used as a tender to the Dotterel, is entirely false. She was not used by me to annoy a single American vessel; and on her arrival at St. John's was delivered over to the Collector of the Customs, and ought long ere this to have been adjudged in the Vice Admiralty court. "That the officers having charge of the armed boats of the Dotterel, ordered to cruise round Grand Menan and Campo Bello, have written instructions, which have been exhibited, to seize and send into St. Andrew's all American fishing vessels found within three marine miles of the said island." My order to the officers of the boats has been, that any American vessels they may find within three marine miles of the shore, except in evident cases of distress or in want of wood or water, they are to detain and send or carry them to St. Andrew's.

I have the honor to be, &c., &c.,

RICHARD HOARE, *Commander.*

Rear Admiral LAKE, &c., &c.

CLAIM OF RICHARD W. MEADE ON THE SPANISH GOVERNMENT.

COMMUNICATED TO THE SENATE FEBRUARY 28, 1825.

DEPARTMENT OF STATE, *Washington, February* 28, 1825.

The Secretary of State, to whom, by a resolution of the Senate of the 15th instant, the memorial of Richard W. Meade, with the accompanying documents, was referred to consider and report thereon, has the honor of reporting that the views taken by him of Mr. Meade's claims upon the Spanish Government, and the extent in which they were considered by him as embraced by the treaty of February 22, 1819, have been set forth in various papers heretofore submitted to the Senate, and particularly in the general instructions to the minister of the United States now residing in Spain, dated April 28, 1823, and in a letter of the succeeding day to the chargé d'affaires of Spain, Mr. Salmon; both which were communicated to the Senate among the documents referred to in the message of the President of the United States to both Houses of Congress at the opening of the present session.

To these papers he asks leave to refer, and prays that they may be taken as a part of this report. Since that time, however, the Commission instituted under the stipulations of the above mentioned treaty have closed their sessions, the claims of Mr. Meade having been excluded altogether from a participation of the indemnities awarded by the Commission conformably to the stipulations of the treaty. How far this exclusion was attributable to a definitive opinion of the Commissioners that the claims of Mr. Meade were not included in the provisions of the treaty at all, and how far to the inability of Mr. Meade to adduce the evidence essential to the establishment of his claims, the Secretary of State is not informed. If it rested altogether upon the deficiency of evidence, it is believed the facts are correctly stated in Mr. Meade's memorial, which deprived him of the means of obtaining from the Spanish Government the documents which they were bound to furnish in season to lay before the Commissioners previous to the closing of their sessions. If, as appears to be alleged by the memorialist, the Commissioners, upon the evidence produced by him, admitted the *validity* of his claim as embraced by the treaty, and rejected the whole only upon the deficiency of proof sufficiently specific and particular of the items and of the amount, it remains for Congress to determine how far this can constitute a claim for which the United States are under any obligation to provide an indemnity. As an appeal to the generosity of the nation, it must stand upon this ground alone, and will be, doubtless, decided upon principles equally applicable to all other claimants alike situated.

All which is respectfully submitted.

JOHN QUINCY ADAMS.

The PRESIDENT OF THE SENATE, *pro tempore.*

INAUGURAL ADDRESS OF JOHN QUINCY ADAMS, PRESIDENT OF THE UNITED STATES.

MADE ON THE 4TH OF MARCH, 1825.

The President of the United States, being attended by the ex-President of the United States, the Vice President, the Judges of the Supreme Court, the Senators, and the marshals of the day, then proceeded from the Senate Chamber to the Hall of the House of Representatives, where he addressed the audience as follows:

In compliance with a usage coeval with the existence of our Federal Constitution, and sanctioned by the example of my predecessors in the career upon which I am about to enter, I appear, my fellow-citizens, in your presence, and in that of Heaven, to bind myself by the solemnities of religious obligation to the faithful performance of the duties allotted to me in the station to which I have been called.

In unfolding to my countrymen the principles by which I shall be governed in the fulfilment of those duties, my first resort will be to that Constitution which I shall swear, to the best of my ability, to preserve, protect, and defend. That revered instrument enumerates the powers and prescribes the duties of the Executive Magistrate; and, in its first words, declares the purposes to which these and the whole action of the Government instituted by it should be invariably and sacredly devoted—to form a more perfect union, establish justice, insure domestic tranquillity, provide for the common defence, promote the general welfare, and secure the blessings of liberty to the people of this Union in their successive generations. Since the adoption of this social compact one of these generations has passed away. It is the work of our forefathers. Administered by some of the most eminent men who contributed to its formation, through a most eventful period in the annals of the world, and through all the vicissitudes of peace and war, incidental to the condition of associated man, it has not disappointed the hopes and aspirations of those illustrious benefactors of their age and nation. It has promoted the lasting welfare of that country so dear to us all; it has, to an extent far beyond the ordinary lot of humanity, secured the freedom and happiness of this people. We now receive it as a precious inheritance from those to whom we are indebted for its establishment; doubly bound by the examples which they have left us, and by the blessings which we have enjoyed as the fruits of their labors, to transmit the same, unimpaired, to the succeeding generation.

In the compass of thirty-six years since this great national covenant was instituted, a body of laws, enacted under its authority, and in conformity with its provisions, has unfolded its powers and carried into practical operation its effective energies. Subordinate departments have distributed the executive functions in their various relations to foreign affairs, to the revenue and expenditures, and to the military force of the Union by land and sea. A co-ordinate department of the Judiciary has expounded the Constitution and the laws; settling, in harmonious coincidence with the legislative will, numerous weighty questions of construction, which the imperfection of human language had rendered unavoidable. The year of jubilee since the first formation of our Union has just elapsed: that of the Declaration of our Independence is at hand. The consummation of both was effected by this Constitution.

Since that period, a population of four millions has multiplied to twelve; a territory bounded by the Mississippi has been extended from sea to sea; new States have been admitted to the Union, in numbers nearly equal to those of the first confederation; treaties of peace, amity, and commerce, have been concluded with the principal dominions of the earth; the people of other nations, inhabitants of regions acquired, not by conquest, but by compact, have been united with us in the participation of our rights and duties, of our burdens and blessings; the forest has fallen by the axe of our woodsmen; the soil has been made to teem by the tillage of our farmers; our commerce has whitened every ocean; the dominion of man over physical nature has been extended by the invention of our artists; liberty and law have marched hand in hand; all the purposes of human association have been accomplished as effectively as under any other Government on the globe, and at a cost little exceeding, in a whole generation, the expenditure of other nations in a single year.

Such is the unexaggerated picture of our condition, under a Constitution founded upon the republican principle of equal rights. To admit that this picture has its shades, is but to say it is still the condition of men upon earth. From evil, physical, moral, and political, it is not our claim to be exempt. We have suffered, sometimes by the visitation of Heaven, through disease; often by the wrongs and injustice of other nations, even to the extremities of war; and lastly, by dissensions among ourselves—dissensions, perhaps, inseparable from the enjoyment of freedom, but which have, more than once, appeared to threaten the dissolution of the Union, and with it, the overthrow of all the enjoyments of our present lot, and all our earthly hopes of the future. The causes of these dissensions have been various, founded upon differences of speculation in the theory of republican Government; upon conflicting views of policy in our relations with foreign nations; upon jealousies of partial and sectional interests, aggravated by prejudices and prepossessions which strangers to each other are ever apt to entertain.

It is a source of gratification and of encouragement to me to observe that the great result of this experiment upon the theory of human rights has, at the close of that generation by which it was formed, been crowned with success, equal to the most sanguine expectations of its founder. Union, justice, tranquillity, the common defence, the general welfare, and the blessings of liberty, all have been promoted by the Government under which we have lived. Standing at this point of time, looking back to that generation which has gone by, and forward to that which is advancing, we may at once indulge in grateful exultation and in cheering hope. From the experience of the past we derive instructive lessons for the future. Of the two great political parties which have divided the opinions and feelings of our country, the candid and the just will now admit that both have contributed splendid talents, spotless integrity, ardent patriotism, and disinterested sacrifices, to the formation and administration of this Government, and that both have required a liberal indulgence for a portion of human infirmity and error. The revolutionary wars of Europe, commencing precisely at the moment when the Government of the United States first went into operation under this Constitution, excited a collision of sentiments and of sympathies, which kindled all the passions, and embittered the conflict of parties, till the nation was involved in war, and the Union was shaken to its centre.

This time of trial embraced a period of five and twenty years, during which the policy of the Union in its relations with Europe constituted the principal basis of our political divisions, and the most arduous part of the action of our Federal Government. With the catastrophe in which the wars of the French revolution terminated, and our own subsequent peace with Great Britain, this baneful weed of party strife was uprooted. From that time no difference of principle connected either with the theory of Government or with our intercourse with foreign nations has existed, or been called forth, in force sufficient to sustain a continued combination of parties, or to give more than wholesome animation to public sentiment or legislative debate. Our political creed is without a dissenting voice that can be heard; that the will of the people is the source, and the happiness of the people the end, of all legitimate Government upon earth; that the best security for the beneficence, and the best guaranty against the abuse of power, consists in the freedom, the purity, and the frequency of popular elections; that the General Government of the Union and the separate Governments of the States are all sovereignties of limited powers— fellow servants of the same masters—uncontrolled within their respective spheres—uncontrollable by encroachments upon each other; that the firmest security of peace is the preparation, during peace, of the defences of war; that a rigorous economy and accountability of public expenditures should guard against the aggravation, and alleviate, when possible, the burden of taxation; that the military should be kept in strict subordination to the civil power; that the freedom of the press and of religious opinion should be inviolate; that the policy of our country is peace, and the ark of our salvation union, are articles of faith upon which we are all now agreed. If there have been those who doubted whether a confederated representative democracy were a Government competent to the wise and orderly management of the common concerns of a mighty nation, those doubts have been dispelled. If there have been projects of partial confederacies to be erected upon the ruins of the Union, they have been scattered to the winds. If there have been dangerous attachments to one foreign nation, and antipathies against another, they have been extinguished. Ten years of peace, at home and abroad, have assuaged the animosities of political contention, and blended into harmony the most discordant elements of public opinion. There still remains one effort of magnanimity, one sacrifice of prejudice and passion to be made by the individuals throughout the nation who have heretofore followed the standards of political party: it is that of discarding every remnant of rancor against each other; of embracing as countrymen and friends, and of yielding to talents and virtue alone that confidence which in times of contention for principle was bestowed only upon those who bore the badge of party communion.

The collisions of party spirit which originate in speculative opinions or in different views of administrative policy are, in their nature, transitory. Those which are founded on geographical divisions, adverse interests of soil, climate, and modes of domestic life, are more permanent, and therefore perhaps more dangerous. It is this which gives inestimable value to the character of our Government at once federal and national. It holds out to us a perpetual admonition to preserve alike, and with equal anxiety, the rights of each individual State in its own Government, and the rights of the whole nation in that of the Union. Whatsoever is of domestic concernment, unconnected with the other members of the Union, or with foreign lands, belongs exclusively to the administration of the State Governments. Whatsoever directly involves the rights and interests of the federative fraternity, or of foreign powers, is of the resort of this General Government. The duties of both are obvious in the general principle, though sometimes perplexed with difficulties in the detail. To respect the rights of the State Governments is the inviolable duty of that of the Union; the Government of every State will feel its own obligation to respect and preserve the rights of the whole. The prejudices, everywhere too commonly entertained against distant strangers, are worn away, and the jealousies of jarring interests are allayed by the composition and functions of the great national councils annually assembled from all quarters of the Union at this place. Here the distinguished men from every section of our country, while meeting to deliberate upon the great interests of those by whom they are deputed, learn to estimate the talents and do justice to the virtues of each other. The harmony of the nation is promoted, and the whole Union is knit together by the sentiments of mutual respect, the habits of social intercourse and the ties of personal friendship, formed between the representatives of its several parts, in the performance of their service at this metropolis.

Passing from this general review of the purposes and injunctions of the Federal Constitution, and their results as indicating the first traces of the path of duty in the discharge of my public trust, I turn to the administration of my immediate predecessor as the second. It has passed away in a period of profound peace; how much to the satisfaction of our country, and to the honor of our country's name, is known to you all. The great features of its policy in general concurrence with the will of the Legislature have been, to cherish peace while preparing for defensive war; to yield exact justice to other nations, and maintain the rights of our own; to cherish the principles of freedom and of equal rights wherever they were proclaimed; to discharge, with all possible promptitude, the national debt; to reduce, within the narrowest limits of efficiency, the military force; to improve the organization and discipline of the Army; to provide and sustain a school of military science; to extend equal protection to all the great interests of the nation; to promote the civilization of the Indian tribes, and to proceed in the great system of internal improvements within the limits of the constitutional power of the Union. Under the pledge of these promises, made by that eminent citizen at the time of his first induction to this office, in his career of eight years, the internal taxes have been repealed; sixty millions of the public debt have been discharged; provision has been made for the comfort and relief of the aged and indigent among the surviving warriors of the Revolution; the regular armed force has been reduced, and its constitution revised and perfected; the accountability for the expenditures of public moneys has been made more effective; the Floridas have been peaceably acquired; and our boundary has been extended to the Pacific Ocean; the independence of the southern nations of this hemisphere has been recognized and recommended by example and by counsel to the potentates of Europe; progress has been made in the defence of the country, by fortifications, and the increase of the Navy; towards the effectual suppression of the African traffic in slaves; in alluring the aboriginal hunters of our land to the cultivation of the soil and of the mind; in exploring the interior regions of the Union; and in preparing, by scientific researches and surveys, for the further application of our national resorces to the internal improvement of our country.

In this brief outline of the promise and performance of my immediate predecessor the line of duty for his successor is clearly delineated. To pursue, to their consummation, those purposes of improvement in our common condition, instituted or recommended by him, will embrace the whole sphere of my obligations. To the topic of internal improvement, emphatically urged by him at his inauguration, I recur with peculiar satisfaction. It is that from which I am convinced that the unborn millions of our posterity who are, in future ages, to people this continent, will derive their most fervent gratitude to the founders of the Union; that, in which the beneficent action of its Government will be most deeply felt and acknowledged. The magnificence and splendor of their public works are among the imperishable glories of the ancient Republics. The roads and aqueducts of Rome have been the admiration of all after ages, and have survived thousands of years after all her conquests have been swallowed up in despotism or become the spoil of barbarians. Some diversity of opinion has prevailed with regard to the powers of Congress for legislation upon objects of this nature. The most respectful deference is due to doubts originating in pure patriotism and sustained by venerated authority. But nearly twenty years have passed since the construction of the first national road was commenced. The authority for its construction was then questioned. To how many thousands of our countrymen has it proved a benefit? To what single individual has it ever proved an injury? Repeated, liberal, and candid discussions in the Legislature have conciliated the sentiments and approximated the opinions of enlightened minds upon the question of constitutional power. I cannot but hope that, by the same process of friendly, patient, and persevering deliberation, all constitutional objections will ultimately be removed. The extent and limitation of the powers of the General Government, in relation to this transcendently important interest, will be settled and acknowledged to the common satisfaction of all, and every speculative scruple will be solved by a practical public blessing.

Fellow-citizens, you are acquainted with the peculiar circumstances of the recent election which have resulted in affording me the opportunity of addressing you at this time. You have heard the exposition of the principles which will direct me in the fulfilment of the high and solemn trust imposed upon me in this station. Less possessed of your confidence, in advance, than any of my predecessors, I am deeply conscious of the prospect that I shall stand more and oftener in need of your indulgence. Intentions upright and pure, a heart devoted to the welfare of our country, and the unceasing application of all the faculties allotted to me to her service, are all the pledges that I can give for the faithful performance of the arduous duties I am to undertake. To the guidance of the legislative councils; to the assistance of the Executive and subordinate Departments; to the friendly co-operation of the respective State Govern. ments; to the candid and liberal support of the people, so far as it may be deserved by honest industry and zeal, I shall look for whatever success may attend my public service; and knowing that, except the Lord keep the city, the watchman waketh but in vain, with fervent supplications for His favor, to His overruling providence I commit, with humble but fearless confidence, my own fate, and the future destinies of my country.

After which the oath of office was administered to the President of the United States by the Chief Justice.

SPECIAL SESSION.]   **No. 411.**   [SENATE.

OPINION OF THE ATTORNEY GENERAL (W. WIRT) ON ALLOWANCES OF SALARIES AND OUTFITS TO PUBLIC MINISTERS OF THE UNITED STATES TO FOREIGN COUNTRIES.

THE INJUNCTION OF SECRECY REMOVED BY THE SENATE FROM ITS PROCEEDINGS ON THE NOMINATION OF HENRY CLAY AS SECRETARY OF STATE, MARCH 8, 1825.

OFFICE OF THE ATTORNEY GENERAL OF THE UNITED STATES, *October* 1, 1821.

SIR: I have, according to your request, reconsidered the opinion expressed by me in March last, on the claim of Mr. Clay, and have the honor now to submit to you the result of this new and more deliberate examination of the subject.

Mr. Clay left the United States, in 1814, on two special missions: first, to treat of peace with Great Britain, and secondly, in the event of peace, to treat of commerce with the same nation. In execution of the first commission, he proceeded to Gottenburg, where it was supposed the negotiation would take place, and made arrangements there which he was soon compelled to relinquish on the transfer of the negotiations to Ghent. At this latter place the treaty of peace was formed, and Mr. Clay proceeded on his second commission to London, where he also assisted in forming the commercial convention.

On his return to this country his account was settled as it was presented by himself. He was allowed a full outfit of nine thousand dollars, his full salary at the rate of nine thousand dollars *per annum*, and one quarter's salary, as usual, to cover the expense of his return. He was also allowed the expense and losses sustained by him on changing the seat of negotiation from Gottenburg to Ghent, and his expenses from Ghent to London, his salary running on all the while, to the moment of his departure from the latter place, at the rate of nine thousand dollars *per annum*.

His account, as presented by himself, contains no charge of half outfit under his second commission— that to treat of commerce at London—but believing himself entitled to make this charge, it is now presented; and it is this claim which you require me to examine.

The case presents a preliminary question: is he stopped from making the claim at this time by the account settled at the Treasury on his own statement? I do not think that a bare omission to present the claim constitutes a bar to it. Settlements are not conclusive, when it can be shown that a just charge has been erroneously omitted. A party may, for a valuable consideration, relinquish a just claim, but the fact of relinquishment must be proved; a mere omission to make the charge will not, *per se*, warrant the inference of relinquishment for valuable consideration; and the mere absence of the charge being all that is shown to me, I am of the opinion that if the claim was just at the time of the settlement, it is just still. Its justice, therefore, is fairly presented for your consideration.

If there be a real foundation for this claim, we must find it either in our laws or the usage under them; let us examine the claim under both these heads.

1. The first act of Congress on this subject is that of July 1, 1790, providing the means of intercourse between the United States and foreign nations; and by this act the provision was, "that exclusive of an outfit, which shall in no case exceed the amount of one full year's salary to the minister plenipotentiary or chargé d'affaires to whom the same may be allowed, the President shall not allow to any minister plenipotentiary a greater sum than at the rate of nine thousand dollars per annum as a compensation for all his personal services and other expenses, nor a greater sum for the same than four thousand five hundred dollars to a chargé d'affaires," &c. It will be observed that this act prescribes merely the *maximum* of the allowance under each head, leaving it to the absolute discretion of the President to disallow, either wholly, or to reduce the amount of either or both according to the particular circumstances of each case—a discretion which, it will be presently seen, the President has always exercised freely, without feeling himself absolutely concluded by past precedents, or requiring the authority of a precedent in a new case, which, from the strength of its circumstances, was itself entitled to become a precedent. That the latitude of discretion thus given to the President was advisedly and deliberately conferred, and for the express purpose of enabling him to accommodate both the outfit and salary to the just demands of each case, will be manifest by referring to the second debates on the bill before it became a law, and which will be found in the third volume of Lloyd's Debates, pp. 113, 172, 181. This act continued in force for twenty years, and among other usages under it several cases had occurred in which ministers who had received an outfit on their first appointment were transferred from one court of Europe to another, receiving on such transfer either a whole outfit, or, as was more common, half an outfit; and it is not improbable that it was with reference to this practice, and with a view of putting an end to it, that the act of May 1 1810, "fixing the compensation of public ministers," &c., after declaring in the express terms of the original act "that the President of the United States shall not allow to any minister plenipotentiary *a greater sum* than at the rate of nine thousand dollars per annum as a compensation for all his personal services and expenses," has the following proviso on the subject of outfit: "*Provided*, That it shall be lawful for the President to allow to a minister plenipotentiary, *on going from the United States to any foreign country*, an outfit which shall in no case exceed one year's full salary of such minister," &c. If, however, it was the intention of this act to put an end to the practice of allowing outfit to a minister who should, while abroad, be transferred from one court to another, that intention has not been answered with sufficient distinctness to produce the effect, for the act, as it stands, is susceptible of the construction of looking to and providing, by its express terms, for the case only of a minister proceeding from the *United States on a single mission to some one foreign court.* But, since it cannot be considered as having been intended by Congress to constrain the President to adopt the more expensive course of sending a minister from the United States whenever diplomatic services might be required at a foreign court, while the cheaper expedient of making use of a minister at some neighboring court so readily presented itself, nor to restrict his choice to citizens in the United States while a preferable one might at the time be travelling abroad; nor, in the latter case at least, to require the citizen to accept the appointment without the usual emoluments; and since there are no prohibitory terms in the act to preclude the resort to either of these latter causes, the act may be fairly interpreted, and has been interpreted, as leaving them open to the adoption of the President, and as drawing with them, by an equitable construction, the provisions of the act as to outfit and salary. This construction was given to the act by the administration under which it passed. The question arose in 1815, in the case of Mr. J. Q. Adams, whom the Government was desirous of transferring from the court of St. Petersburg to that of London. It was doubted whether, under those restrictive terms of the act, as to outfit, "*on going from the United States,*" outfit could be allowed on such a transfer. It was the subject of most deliberate consideration, as you will be reminded by the accompanying extract from the letter of the Secretary of State to that gentleman, dated November 19, 1815, (No. 1,) and it was finally decided that outfit might be allowed, and it was allowed. This construction, too, received the subsequent sanction of Congress in the case, who ratified the allowance of outfit by their appropriation, although they differed with the President as to the amount.

I. Under this construction, the act of Congress of 1810 leaves the whole subject of salary and outfit where it found it under the act of 1790; that is to say, completely in the power of the President, without any other restriction than the *maximum* prescribed by the act. And, as the act authorizes salary and outfit in the case of a single mission, so where there are several successive missions thrown upon the same individual, the President is left at liberty, *by the law,* to consider each mission as a separate one, and to allow for each as if it stood alone. I say he is at *liberty,* by the law, to do this, and there may be cases in which it would be proper to do it: as where a minister resident abroad is transferred, at considerable intervals of time, to several courts in succession. The whole outfit may be as necessary and proper in the last case as the first, and in the intermediate cases as in either of the former. The subject, therefore, is by the law properly referred to the discretion of the President, in the confidence that he will adapt the allowance to the particular case. There is nothing, therefore, I think, *in the law* to forbid this allowance to Mr. Clay, if the President shall think it reasonable on the circumstances of the case.

II. With regard to the usage, the President has at all times exercised very freely the discretion given to him by the law, both as to the salary and outfit.

1. As to salary. The bill, which finally became the act of 1790, as reported to the House, (Lloyd's Debates, *qua supra*,) contemplated three grades of diplomatic agents: the minister plenipotentiary, at a *maximum* of salary and outfit of $9,000; the *minister resident,* at a *maximum* of $5,000; and chargé d'affaires, at $3,000. The law, as passed, dropped the *minister resident,* and retained the other two, advancing the chargé d'affaires to a *maximum* of $4,500; yet the President, in the exercise of his discretion, virtually restored the *minister resident* to the law, and the greater part of the ministers employed under the first two Presidents were *ministers resident,* at the salary and outfit of chargé d'affaires, $4,500.

Another instance of the exercise of this discretion as to salary occurred in the case of Mr. Jay, Envoy Extraordinary and Minister Plenipotentiary to London, 1794, who received nothing in the name of salary. His expenses were allowed, and they amounted to $12,000, (see his account in the Book A;) another in the case of G. W. Erving, appointed special minister to Sweden, in 1811, at a salary of $6,000.

2. As to outfit. We shall, perhaps, find a key to the practice under this head, by considering the reason of the allowance. It means *preparatory equipment,* and seems to have been intended to cover the *extra expense* which every one must necessarily encounter who goes as a minister to a foreign court. But the *quantum* of this expense would be very different in missions of different characters. A minister who goes to *reside permanently* near a foreign court must have a domestic establishment, and that whether he have a family or not, as we may see by the example of the ministers among us from the primary courts of Europe. A

minister, on the contrary, who goes *on a special and short-lived mission* has no occasion for any such establishment; without degrading either himself or his country, he lives in a hotel, as Mr. Jay did in London, in 1794. Now, as outfit is pointed to this very expense, it is manifest that the allowance of equal outfit to ministers so differently circumstanced would be unnecessary, unequal, and consequently unjust; and the usage, so far as I can trace it, has conformed to this obvious and simple distinction.

I have examined critically all the accounts of our ministers since the period of the adoption of our Constitution, together with the printed State papers, and the correspondence in the Department of State and of the Treasury, so far as they could throw light on the practice, and the following appear to me to to be the *general rules* which have been followed in the allowance of outfit.

I. All ministers who *go to reside* at a foreign court are, in the first instance, allowed the amount of a full year's salary as outfit. At whatever sum the President fixes the salary, the same sum is allowed as outfit.

Examples.

London, Thomas Pinkney, 1792—1796, salary and outfit, each $9,000.
London, Rufus King, 1796—1803, same allowance.
London, James Monroe, 1803—1807, same allowance.
Paris, Gouverneur Morris, 1792—1794, same allowance.
Paris, James Monroe, 1794—1796, same allowance.
Paris, C. C. Pinkney, 1796—1798, same allowance.
Paris, R. R. Livingston, 1801—1804, same allowance.
Paris, J. Armstrong, 1804—1810, same allowance.
Madrid, William Short, 1794—1796, minister resident, salary and outfit, each $4,500.
Madrid, C. Pinkney, 1801—1805, minister resident, salary and outfit, each $9,000.
Madrid, J. Bowdoin, 1805—1807, same allowance.
Lisbon, D. Humphreys, 1791—1797, minister resident, salary and outfit, each $4,500.
Lisbon, William Smith, 1797—1801, minister plenipotentiary, salary and outfit, each $9,000.
Hague, J. Q. Adams, 1794—1797, minister resident, salary and outfit, each $4,500.
Hague, William Vans Murray, 1797—1801, minister resident, same allowance.
St. Petersburg, J. Q. Adams, 1813—1815, minister plenipotentiary, salary and outfit, each $9,000.
St. Petersburg, William Pinkney, 1816, same allowance.

II. Ministers *residing at one court*, and *transferred to reside at another*, receive half an outfit; and if transferred to reside in a new and higher grade of character, they receive half the year's salary of the new and higher grade. The rule probably arose from the increased expense which would unavoidably attend the making a new establishment at the new court. The only written notice of this rule which I can find in the Department of State is in a letter from the Secretary of State to Mr. J. Q. Adams, on his transfer from his residence at the Hague to be minister plenipotentiary at Lisbon and Berlin. The letter is dated February 17, 1797, and the following is the extract: "In estimating *the sum necessary* for maintaining the intercourse of the United States with foreign nations, it was considered that your appointment and that of Colonel Humphreys to the office of minister plenipotentiary *not being original*, and an *outfit of* $4,500 *to each as minister resident having been already allowed, the principle on which the outfit is provided* authorized the Executive to make to each of you the further allowance of $4,500 *only to complete the outfit of the advanced grade;* and the estimate and appropriation conformed to this idea." The only *principle* which I can understand as being here alluded to is, that the outfit shall equal the year's salary of the grade to which the minister is advanced; but that, in order to make up such outfit, the outfit which he had received in his former grade shall be taken into the account. But, according to this rule, it would seem to follow that if the minister is transferred in the same character which he had previously held, and on his former appointment had received his full outfit, he would not be entitled to outfit at all *on his transfer.* The rule, however, is that which I have stated.

Examples.

1797.—David Humphreys, minister resident at Lisbon, transferred as minister plenipotentiary to Madrid, half outfit, $4,500.
1797.—J. Q. Adams, minister resident at the Hague, transferred to Lisbon and Berlin as minister plenipotentiary, same allowance.
1815.—J. Q. Adams, minister plenipotentiary at St. Petersburg, transferred to London; Congress allowed half outfit, $4,500.—(See his account herewith.)
So much for resident and stationary appointments.

III. A *special mission* is not entitled to outfit at all, whether it stands alone as a single original mission from the United States to a foreign court, or whether it be connected with another and a permanent mission; the rule is as to *special missions* being, to allow only the *actual expenses* attending them.

Examples of single and original special missions.

1.—1793. Mr. Jay to London; no outfit allowed nor salary; his expenses were borne, *(see ante.)* This was probably the effect of arrangement before he went out; but so far as outfit is concerned, it conforms with the rule as distinctly announced in other cases.
2.—1808. Mr. Short to Prussia; no outfit allowed. Here we are not left to infer the rule from the mere fact of disallowance, because the correspondence shows that it was founded avowedly on *the special character* of the mission.—(See Mr. Short's letter to President Jefferson, No. 2.)
3.—1811. Mr. George W. Erving to Denmark; no outfit. The Secretary of State says to him, in his letter of January 3, 1811, (No. 3:) "*In conformity to the rule which has hitherto prevailed in cases of special missions, you will not have an outfit.*" Here we have *the rule* explicitly announced; but there are several exceptions to it.

Exceptions.

1708.—Messrs. Marshal, Gerry, and Pinkney to France; outfit allowed.
1800.—Messrs. Ellsworth and Davie to the same court; same allowance.

If these cases are *exceptions*, a reason may be found for them in the superior splendor and expensiveness of the court to which these gentlemen were sent. If they are not to be regarded as exceptions to a rule, but as announcing in themselves a substantive rule, they only prove that the rule during the second Presidency was different from that which we have seen unequivocally announced during the third and fourth Presidencies.

According to this *rule*, the allowance which had been already made of an outfit to Mr. Clay and his associates, on their mission to Ghent, was improper, and can be justified only *as an exception* on the particular circumstances of the case.

Examples of the disallowance of outfit to a special mission, where it has been connected with a permanent one.

1. Where the minister has gone out from the United States with two missions in view, the one *special*, the other *permanent.*

1803.—Mr. Monroe, special envoy to Paris, with a permanent commission to London. I refer to this case for the purpose of showing that the rule in such a case was to allow only the *actual expenses* on the *special* mission. This rule is understood as having been announced to him before he left the country, and as having been opposed to his claim of outfit on this mission after his return; and it is understood as having been waived *as to him*, at last, only on the ground that *the actual expenses of the special mission* would have equalled, if not surpassed, the amount of outfit.

The substantial ground of the allowance, therefore, was the *actual expenses*. The case at once affords proof of the rule, and operates as an exception to it. 1814.—Mr. Russell was united with Mr. Clay and others to treat of peace at Ghent; and with this commission he had another as *stationary minister* to Sweden. In announcing these appointments to him, the Secretary of State, in his letter of the 7th of February, 1814, (No. 6,) says: "In blending the appointment of minister extraordinary to treat with Great Britain with that of minister plenipotentiary to the court of Sweden, no *expense to the public, beyond the ordinary allowance of a minister plenipotentiary, was contemplated, and hence one outfit to cover the expense of both.*"

It is true Mr. Russell did not accept; but this does not invalidate the proof of the practice which this letter affords. The letter announces a principle which, if applied to the case of Mr. Clay, is certainly unfavorable, at least to any further demand of outfit. It will be observed that the letter attaches the outfit to the permanent mission to Sweden, that of *minister plenipotentiary to the court of Sweden*, to which the commission to treat of peace is merely an incidental annexation.

1816.—Mr. William Pinkney, appointed stationary minister to Russia, with an incidental and special mission at the same time to Naples, received only one outfit, which was attached to his stationary appointment; on the special mission to Naples he received his *actual expenses* to the amount of another outfit; not, however, in the name of *outfit*, which was positively refused, but as *actual expenses; the measure of* an outfit is assumed as a limit to the expenses of the special mission.

If the out-of-doors history of this mission be correct, (which you must, of course, know if it be so,) the case affords strong proof of the rule that *outfit* does not properly attach to a special mission, but that the appropriate compensation on such a mission, beyond the salary, is *the actual expenses*; for it is said that Mr. Pinkney made the allowance of *outfit* to Naples the *sine quâ non* of his acceptance of the double mission; which was refused by the Government; but he was assured at the same time that the *actual expenses* of the special mission would be paid, provided they did not exceed the *amount of an outfit.*

Now, as there was no difference in the two propositions, except in name, (as the result showed,) it is not discerned why this difference *in form* was insisted on, unless upon the ground that the rule (as announced so distinctly to Mr. Erving) stood in the way of the allowance of *outfit* on a *special mission*, while at the same time it admitted of the allowance of *actual expenses* without limit. Examples of this disallowance of *outfit* on a special mission, under another form of connexion with a permanent mission, to wit: where a minister stationed at one court is sent on a *special mission* to another.

1792.—Mr. William Short, stationed as a chargé d'affaires at Paris, was sent on a *special mission*, as "commissioner plenipotentiary," to Madrid, to treat of the navigation of the Mississippi. The selection of a person already abroad was made to avoid the expense of an original mission from the United States, as I learn from the report made by Mr. Jefferson, then Secretary of State, to the President, on the 11th of January, 1792.—(Vol. 10, State Papers, p. 102.) Mr. Jefferson, in announcing to him this new appointment in his letter of the 23d of the same month, (No. 4,) tells him: "The salary of your new grade being the same as of your former one," [*i. e.*, as the President chose to make it so,] "and *your services continued, though the scene of them is changed*, there will be no intermission of salary." "*For the same reason there can be but one allowance of outfit*," &c. For what reason? Because his salary continued the same under both appointments, and because his services were continued, though the scene of them was changed. It is not necessary for me to apply this reasoning to the case of Mr. Clay; the exactness of the application is obvious.

Mr. Short was entitled to an outfit as chargé d'affaires at Paris, in the settlement of his accounts he received only this one outfit and his *actual expenses* on the special mission to Madrid.

Besides this special mission to Madrid, Mr. Short went on several others to Holland, as appears by the settlement of his accounts, never receiving any outfit but his *expenses merely*.—(See document No. 5)

1794-'5.—Mr. J. Q. Adams, being minister resident at the Hague, proceeded on a special mission [to London, and was allowed no outfit but his actual expenses, amounting to $3,449 45.

1795-'6.—Mr. Thomas Pinkney, minister plenipotentiary at London, proceeded on a special mission to Madrid, where he made a treaty. He received no outfit, but was allowed his actual expenses, amounting to $7,737 49.

1803-'4.—Mr. James Monroe, minister at London, proceeded on a *special mission* to Spain, the circumstances attending which are detailed at large in the Book of Ministers' Accounts, marked "B, July 30, 1813, France." For this mission he received no outfit but his actual expenses, $10,598 28.

Exceptions.

1800.—Mr. William Vans Murray, minister resident at the Hague, at a salary and outfit of $4,500 each, was associated, as minister plenipotentiary, with Messrs. Ellsworth and Davie, in a special mission to Paris. The two latter gentlemen proceeded from the United States at a salary and outfit of $9,000 each. It was thought proper that Mr. Murray, going to meet these gentlemen, and appear with them in the same character, at the same court, (which is said to be one of uncommon splendor at that period,) should be put on a footing with them in point of emolument; and on this ground expressly (that is, to *place him on a footing with his associates*) the Auditor is directed, by a note from the Secretary of State, to allow him *the full outfit* which they had received, which was done accordingly.—(See the Secretary's note at the end of Mr. Murray's Account Book C.)

1812–'13.—Mr. Adams, minister plenipotentiary, and stationed at St. Petersburg, was united with Mr. Clay and others to treat of peace with Great Britain, under the mediation of the Emperor of Russia. It was expected that the negotiation would be held at St. Petersburg, and that, in consequence of it, the stationary minister would be put to considerable increase of expense; *for this reason* the President allowed him the *entire outfit* which his associates had received. The negotiation was not held at Ghent, but this does not change the ground on which the allowance was made by the Executive. One-half of the outfit thus allowed has been appropriated by Congress.

I take the reason for this allowance, by the President, to Mr. Adams, from your recollection, sir. In turning to the letter addressed by the Secretary of State to Mr. Adams on the 26th of April, 1813, making the allowance, I find the reason no further developed than by the following sentence: "In the joint commissions, the character of envoy extraordinary has been adopted; *and, as you will all be exposed to considerable expense, an outfit has been allowed to each.*"—(Document No. 1.) This letter presents to us two inferences: that the allowance was not a thing of course, but rather a departure from the common cause, or otherwise no reason would have been assigned for it, and that *one outfit alone* was then contemplated for both negotiators—that is, the treaty of peace at Ghent, and of commerce at London. The letter is such a one as would have been expected, where outfit was allowed in violation of a general rule, the case being supposed to form an exception to the rule, but is entirely unadapted to an allowance which was a thing of course.

There remains only one other case to be noticed, which is of a character so anomalous that I have not been able to class it under either of the preceding heads.

While Mr. Monroe was minister plenipotentiary and stationed at London, on May 12, 1806, a joint commission issued to himself and Mr. Wm. Pinkney constituting them Commissioners Plenipotentiary and Extraordinary for the purpose of settling all matters of differences between the United States and Great Britain, relative to wrongs committed by the parties on the high seas and other waters, and for establishing the principles of navigation and commerce between them. By a separate commission of the same date Mr. Pinkney was appointed minister plenipotentiary to the court of London in the usual form. He received a full outfit on the first commission; and when, by Mr. Monroe's return, he was left to act alone on his separate commission, he received a half outfit. From the phraseology of the first commission (see the document No. 6) it is not very easy to distinguish whether it is to be considered as a general or special commission. If, as I suppose it must be considered, it was a *special commission*, the allowance of full outfit falls within the principle of the exception in Mr. Murray's case, for Mr. Pinkney, too, was going to join another minister who had received a full outfit, and to appear with him in the same character, at the same court, which is understood as being one of the most expensive in Europe.

Having received this outfit when Mr. Monroe's return left him to act alone, which it did in one year afterwards, and when he entered on the execution of his second and *permanent* commission, he conceived himself entitled to *a full outfit* on the ground that one outfit to the full amount of a year's salary has *never* been withheld from *a permanent* appointment; he still considers himself entitled to it, and the *general rule* is certainly in his favor, for this is the only *permanent* and *stationary appointment* which has been made since the adoption of our Constitution from which such an outfit has been separated. But as an exception had been recently made in his favor in attaching a full outfit to his special commission *to the same court*, I *presume* that the President considered himself justified in making an exception also against him, in regard to his permanent commission; still, however, so far respecting the general rule as to allow half an outfit in the latter instance. I cannot discover on what other ground at all consistent with the scheme of practice presented by the documents before me the last allowance could have been made. If it was made on the ground of the inadequacy of the compensation allowed by the law, and the desire of the President to compensate that inadequacy by the allowance of outfit whenever separate and successive commissions will permit it, the reason applies to Mr. Clay's case, in common with all others like it which may come before the President; and in every case of the kind he may, if he think fit, allow the full outfit, or any part of it.

Having had no experience myself in diplomatic life, and having never been in a situation to observe the practice as it relates to others, nor in one which required me to know it, the duty of exploring and endeavoring to learn the practice, as it is to be extracted from the mass of accounts and documents in the Department of State and of the Treasury, has, to me, been equally new and laborious. I have spared no labor in the analysis, yet it is very possible that I have mistaken some of the cases, and built up an uneven theory of rules on them. At first and for a long time these cases appeared to me to present a hopeless chaos, utterly unsusceptible of being reduced to order, and it is not improbable that my desire to disengage them from this confusion and discover something like plan or system in the practice may have betrayed me into the belief of a theory which has no foundation in fact.

But, if I am not mistaken, the tendency of the practice has always been to withhold outfit in the case of special missions, and to allow the expenses whether the special mission has stood alone or been connected with a permanent one.

It appears, also, where outfit has been allowed in special missions, it has been by way of exception to the general rule, and upon reasons which do not operate in the case of Mr. Clay, on the mission from Ghent to London.

That there has been no instance of double outfit in *two special missions*, on both of which the citizen leaves the United States at the same time; and that no rule, or exception to a rule, according to the practice which has heretofore obtained countenances such an allowance.

That it certainly was not contemplated in the particular case, as is already manifested by the letter to Messrs. Adams and Russell.

That it has not been received or asked by any of Mr. Clay's associates, so far as I am informed.

Yet, although such has been the general usage and such the facts of this particular case, if, by reason of the general inadequacy of the compensation, or for any reasons existing in the particular case, and satisfactory to your own mind, the allowance ought to be made, I have no doubt that it is within your legal discretion to make it, and that the law makes you the only and final judge on the subject.

I have the honor to remain, sir, very respectfully your obedient servant,

WM. WIRT.

The PRESIDENT *of the United States.*

MESSAGE OF THE PRESIDENT AT THE COMMENCEMENT OF THE SESSION—PROCLAMATION
OF TREATY WITH THE REPUBLIC OF COLOMBIA OF OCTOBER 3, 1824.

COMMUNICATED TO CONGRESS DECEMBER 6, 1825.

Fellow-citizens of the Senate and of the House of Representatives:

In taking a general survey of the concerns of our beloved country, with reference to subjects interesting to the common welfare, the first sentiment which impresses itself upon the mind is of gratitude to the Omnipotent Disposer of all Good for the continuance of the signal blessings of his Providence, and especially for that health which, to an unusual extent, has prevailed within our borders, and for that abundance which, in the vicissitudes of the seasons, has been scattered with profusion over our land. Nor ought we less to ascribe to Him the glory that we are permitted to enjoy the bounties of His hand in peace and tranquillity—in peace with all the other nations of the earth, in tranquillity among ourselves. There has, indeed, rarely been a period in the history of civilized man in which the general condition of the Christian nations has been marked so extensively by peace and prosperity.

Europe, with a few partial and unhappy exceptions, has enjoyed ten years of peace, during which all her Governments, whatever the theory of their constitutions may have been, are successively taught to feel that the end of their institution is the happiness of their people, and that the exercise of power among men can be justified only by the blessings it confers upon those over whom it is extended.

During the same period our intercourse with all those nations has been pacific and friendly; it so continues. Since the close of your last session no material variation has occurred in our relations with any one of them. In the commercial and navigation system of Great Britain important changes of municipal regulation have recently been sanctioned by acts of Parliament, the effect of which upon the interests of other nations, and particularly upon ours, has not yet been fully developed. In the recent renewal of the diplomatic missions, on both sides, between the two Governments, assurances have been given and received of the continuance and increase of the mutual confidence and cordiality by which the adjustment of many points of difference had already been effected, and which affords the surest pledge for the ultimate satisfactory adjustment of those which still remain open, or may hereafter arise.

The policy of the United States in their commercial intercourse with other nations has always been of the most liberal character. In the mutual exchange of their respective productions they have abstained altogether from prohibitions; they have interdicted themselves the power of laying taxes upon exports, and whenever they have favored their own shipping, by special preferences, or exclusive privileges in their own ports, it has been only with a view to countervail similar favors and exclusions granted by the nations with whom we have been engaged in traffic to their own people or shipping, and to the disadvantage of ours. Immediately after the close of the last war a proposal was fairly made by the act of Congress of the 3d of March, 1815, to all the maritime nations to lay aside the system of retaliating restrictions and exclusions, and to place the shipping of both parties to the common trade on a footing of equality in respect to the duties of tonnage and impost. This offer was partially and successively accepted by Great Britain, Sweden, the Netherlands, the Hanseatic cities, Prussia, Sardinia, the Duke of Oldenburg, and Russia. It was also adopted, under certain modifications, in our late commercial convention with France. And by the act of Congress of the 8th of January, 1824, it has received a new confirmation with all the nations who had acceded to it, and has been offered again to all those who are, or who may hereafter be willing to abide in reciprocity by it. But all these regulations, whether established by treaty or by municipal enactments, are still subject to one important restriction.

The removal of discriminating duties of tonnage and of impost is limited to articles of the growth, produce, or manufacture of the country to which the vessel belongs, or to such articles as are most usually first shipped from her ports. It will deserve the serious consideration of Congress whether even this remnant of restriction may not be safely abandoned, and whether the general tender of equal competition made in the act of January, 1824, may not be extended to include all articles of merchandise not prohibited, of what country soever they may be the produce or manufacture. Propositions to this effect have already been made to us by more than one European Government, and it is probable that, if once established by legislation or compact with any distinguished maritime State, it would recommend itself, by the experience of its advantages, to the general accession of all.

The convention of commerce and navigation between the United States and France, concluded on the 24th of June, 1822, was, in the understanding and intent of both parties, as appears upon its face, only a temporary arrangement of the points of difference between them of the most immediate and pressing urgency. It was limited, in the first instance, to two years from the 1st of October, 1822, but with a proviso that it should further continue in force till the conclusion of a general and definitive treaty of commerce, unless terminated by a notice six months in advance of either of the parties to the other. Its operation, so far as it extended, has been mutually advantageous, and it still continues in force by common consent; but it left unadjusted several objects of great interest to the citizens and subjects of both countries, and particularly a mass of claims, to considerable amount, of citizens of the United States upon the Government of France, of indemnity for property taken or destroyed under circumstances of the most aggravated and outrageous character. In the long period during which continual and earnest appeals have been made to the equity and magnanimity of France, in behalf of these claims, their justice has not been, as it could not be, denied. It was hoped that the accession of a new sovereign to the throne would have afforded a favorable opportunity for presenting them to the consideration of his Government. They have been presented and urged hitherto without effect. The repeated and earnest representations of our minister at the court of France remain, as yet, even without an answer. Were the demands of nations upon the justice of each other susceptible of adjudication by the sentence of an impartial tribunal, those to which I now refer would long since have been settled, and adequate indemnity would have been obtained. There are large amounts of similar claims upon the Netherlands, Naples, and Denmark. For those upon Spain prior to one thousand eight hundred and nineteen, indemnity was, after many years of patient forbearance, obtained, and those upon Sweden have been lately compromised by a private settlement, in which the claimants themselves have acquiesced. The Governments of Denmark and of Naples have been recently reminded of those yet existing against them; nor will any of them be forgotten while a hope may be indulged of obtaining justice by the means within the constitutional power of the Executive, and without resorting to those measures of self-redress which, as well as the time, circumstances, and occasion which may require them, are within the exclusive competency of the Legislature.

It is with great satisfaction that I am enabled to bear witness to the liberal spirit with which the Republic of Colombia has made satisfaction for well established claims of a similar character. And among the documents now communicated to Congress will be distinguished a treaty of commerce and navigation with that Republic, the ratifications of which have been exchanged since the last recess of the Legislature. The negotiation of similar treaties with all the independent South American States has been contemplated, and may yet be accomplished. The basis of them all, as proposed by the United States, has been laid in two principles: the one, of entire and unqualified reciprocity; the other, the mutual obligation of the parties to place each other permanently upon the footing of the most favored nation. These principles are, indeed, indispensable to the effectual emancipation of the American hemisphere from the thraldom of colonizing monopolies and exclusions—an event rapidly realizing in the progress of human affairs, and which the resistance still opposed in certain parts of Europe to the acknowledgment of the Southern American Republics as independent States, will, it is believed, contribute more effectually to accomplish. The time has been, and that not remote, when some of those States might, in their anxious desire to obtain a nominal recognition, have accepted of a nominal independence, clogged with burdensome conditions, and exclusive commercial privileges granted to the nation from which they had separated, to the disadvantage of all others. They are now all aware that such concessions to any European nation would be incompatible with that independence which they have declared and maintained.

Among the measures which have been suggested to them by the new relations with one another, resulting from the recent changes in their condition, is that of assembling, at the Isthmus of Panama, a Congress, at which each of them should be represented, to deliberate upon objects important to the welfare of all. The Republics of Colombia, of Mexico, and of Central America, have already deputed plenipotentiaries to such a meeting, and they have invited the United States to be also represented there by their ministers. The invitation has been accepted, and ministers on the part of the United States will be commissioned to attend at those deliberations, and to take part in them, so far as may be compatible with that neutrality from which it is neither our intention nor the desire of the other American States that we should depart.

The Commissioners under the seventh article of the treaty of Ghent have so nearly completed their arduous labors, that, by the report recently received from the agent on the part of the United States, there is reason to expect that the Commission will be closed at their next session, appointed for the 22d of May of the ensuing year.

The other Commission, appointed to ascertain the indemnities due for slaves carried away from the United States after the close of the late war, have met with some difficulty, which has delayed their progress in the inquiry. A reference has been made to the British Government on the subject, which, it may be hoped, will tend to hasten the decision of the Commissioners, or serve as a substitute for it.

Among the powers specifically granted to Congress by the Constitution are those of establishing uniform laws on the subject of bankruptcies throughout the United States, and of providing for organizing, arming, and disciplining the militia, and for governing such part of them as may be employed in the service of the United States. The magnitude and complexity of the interests affected by legislation upon these subjects may account for the fact that, long and often as both of them have occupied the attention and animated the debates of Congress, no systems have yet been devised for fulfilling, to the satisfaction of the community, the duties prescribed by these grants of power. To conciliate the claim of the individual citizen to the enjoyment of personal liberty, with the effective obligation of private contracts, is the difficult problem to be solved by a law of bankruptcy. These are objects of the deepest interest to society: affecting all that is precious in the existence of multitudes of persons, many of them in the classes essentially dependent and helpless; of the age requiring nurture, and of the sex entitled to protection, from the free agency of the parent and the husband. The organization of the militia is yet more indispensable to the liberties of the country. It is only by an effective militia that we can at once enjoy the repose of peace, and bid defiance to foreign aggression; it is by the militia that we are constituted an armed nation, standing in perpetual panoply of defence in the presence of all the other nations of the earth. To this end it would be necessary, if possible, so to shape its organization as to give it a more united and active energy. There are laws for establishing a uniform militia throughout the United States, and for arming and equipping its whole body. But it is a body of dislocated members, without the vigor of unity, and having little of uniformity but the name. To infuse into this most important institution the power of which it is susceptible, and to make it available for the defence of the Union at the shortest notice and at the smallest expense possible of time, of life, and of treasure, are among the benefits to be expected from the persevering deliberations of Congress.

Among the unequivocal indications of our national prosperity is the flourishing state of our finances. The revenues of the present year, from all their principal sources, will exceed the anticipations of the last. The balance in the Treasury on the 1st of January last was a little short of two million of dollars, exclusive of two million and a half, being the moiety of the loan of five million, authorized by the act of May 26, 1824. The receipts into the Treasury, from the 1st of January to the 30th of September, exclusive of the other moiety of the same loan, are estimated at sixteen million five hundred thousand dollars, and it is expected that those of the current quarter will exceed five million of dollars: forming an aggregate of receipts of nearly twenty-two million, independent of the loan. The expenditures of the year will not exceed that sum more than two million. By those expenditures nearly eight million of the principal of the public debt have been discharged. More than a million and a half has been devoted to the debt of gratitude to the warriors of the Revolution; a nearly equal sum to the construction of fortifications and the acquisition of ordnance, and other permanent preparations of national defence; half a million to the gradual increase of the Navy; an equal sum for purchases of territory from the Indians, and payment of annuities to them; and upwards of a million for objects of internal improvement, authorized by special acts of the last Congress. If we add to these four million of dollars for payment of interest upon the public debt, there remains a sum of about seven million, which have defrayed the whole expense of the administration of Government, in its Legislative, Executive, and Judiciary Departments, including the support of the Military and Naval Establishments, and all the occasional contingencies of a Government co-extensive with the Union.

The amount of duties secured on merchandise imported since the commencement of the year is about twenty-five million and a half, and that which will accrue during the current quarter is estimated at five million and a half; from these thirty-one million, deducting the drawbacks, estimated at less than seven million, a sum exceeding twenty-four million will constitute the revenue of the year, and will exceed the whole expenditures of the year. The entire amount of public debt remaining due on the 1st of January next will be short of eighty-one million of dollars.

By an act of Congress of the 3d of March last a loan of twelve million of dollars was authorized, at four and a half per cent., or an exchange of stock to that amount of four and a half per cent. for a stock of six per cent., to create a fund for extinguishing an equal amount of the public debt, bearing an interest of six per cent., redeemable in the year 1826. An account of the measures taken to give effect to this act will be laid before you by the Secretary of the Treasury. As the object which it had in view has been but partially accomplished, it will be for the consideration of Congress whether the power with which it clothed the Executive should not be renewed at an early day of the present session, and under what modifications.

The act of Congress of the 3d of March last, directing the Secretary of the Treasury to subscribe, in the name and for the use of the United States, for one thousand five hundred shares of the capital stock of the Chesapeake and Delaware Canal Company, has been executed by the actual subscription for the amount specified; and such other measures have been adopted by that officer, under the act, as the fulfilment of its intentions requires. The latest accounts received of this important undertaking authorize the belief that it is in successful progress.

The payments into the Treasury from proceeds of the sales of the public lands during the present year were estimated at one million of dollars. The actual receipts of the first two quarters have fallen very little short of that sum. It is not expected that the second half of the year will be equally productive; but the income of the year, from that source, may now be safely estimated at a million and a half. The act of Congress of May 18, 1824, to provide for the extinguishment of the debt due to the United States by the purchasers of public lands, was limited, in its operation of relief to the purchaser, to the 10th of April last. Its effect at the end of the quarter, during which it expired, was to reduce that debt from ten to seven million. By the operation of similar prior laws of relief, from and since that of March 2, 1821, the debt had been reduced from upwards of twenty-two million to ten. It is exceedingly desirable that it should be extinguished altogether; and, to facilitate that consummation, I recommend to Congress the revival, for one year more, of the act of May 18, 1824, with such provisional modification as may be necessary to guard the public interests against fraudulent practices in the resale of the relinquished land. The purchasers of public lands are among the most useful of our fellow-citizens; and, since the system of sales for cash alone has been introduced, great indulgence has been justly extended to those who had previously purchased upon credit. The debt which had been contracted under the credit sales had become unwieldy, and its extinction was alike advantageous to the purchaser and the public. Under the system of sales, matured, as it has been, by experience, and adapted to the exigencies of the times, the lands will continue, as they have become, an abundant source of revenue; and when the pledge of them to the public creditor shall have been redeemed, by the entire discharge of the national debt, the swelling tide of wealth, with which they replenish the common treasury, may be made to reflow in unfailing streams of improvement, from the Atlantic to the Pacific Ocean.

The condition of the various branches of the public service resorting from the Department of War, and their administration during the current year, will be exhibited in the report of the Secretary of War, and the accompanying documents, herewith communicated. The organization and discipline of the Army are effective and satisfactory. To counteract the prevalence of desertion among the troops, it has been suggested to withhold from the men a small portion of their monthly pay until the period of their discharge; and some expedient appears to be necessary to preserve and maintain among the officers so much of the art of horsemanship as could scarcely fail to be found wanting on the possible sudden eruption of a war, which should overtake us unprovided with a single corps of cavalry. The Military Academy at West Point, under the restrictions of a severe but paternal superintendence, recommends itself more and more to the patronage of the nation; and the number of meritorious officers which it forms and introduces to the public service furnishes the means of multiplying the undertakings of public improvements, to which their acquirements at that institution are peculiarly adapted. The school of artillery practice established at Fortress Monroe is well suited to the same purpose, and may need the aid of further legislative provision to the same end. The reports of the various officers at the head of the administrative branches of the military service, connected with the quartering, clothing, subsistence, health, and pay of the Army, exhibit the assiduous vigilance of those officers in the performance of their respective duties, and the faithful accountability which has pervaded every part of the system.

Our relations with the numerous tribes of aboriginal natives of this country, scattered over its extensive surface, and so dependent, even for their existence, upon our power, have been, during the present year, highly interesting. An act of Congress of May 25, 1824, made an appropriation to defray the expenses of making treaties of trade and friendship with the Indian tribes beyond the Mississippi. An act of March 3, 1825, authorized treaties to be made with the Indians for their consent to the making of a road from the frontier of Missouri to that of New Mexico; and another act, of the same date, provided for defraying the expenses of holding treaties with the Sioux, Chippewas, Menomonees, Sauks, Foxes, &c., for the purpose of establishing boundaries and promoting peace between said tribes. The first and the last objects of these acts have been accomplished, and the second is yet in a process of execution. The treaties which, since the last session of Congress, have been concluded with the several tribes will be laid before the Senate, for their consideration, conformably to the Constitution. They comprise large and valuable acquisitions of territory, and they secure an adjustment of boundaries and give pledges of permanent peace between several tribes which had been long waging bloody wars against each other.

On the 12th of February last a treaty was signed, at the Indian Springs, between Commissioners appointed on the part of the United States and certain chiefs and individuals of the Creek Nation of Indians, which was received at the seat of Government only a very few days before the close of the last session of Congress and of the late administration. The advice and consent of the Senate were given to it on the 3d of March, too late for it to receive the ratification of the then President of the United States. It was ratified on the 7th of March, under the unsuspecting impression that it had been negotiated in good faith, and in the confidence inspired by the recommendation of the Senate. The subsequent transactions in relation to this treaty will form the subject of a separate message.

The appropriations made by Congress for public works, as well as in the construction of fortifications as for purposes of internal improvement, so far as they have been expended, have been faithfully applied.

Their progress has been delayed by the want of suitable officers for superintending them. An increase of both the Corps of Engineers, military and topographical, was recommended by my predecessor at the last session of Congress. The reasons upon which that recommendation was founded subsist in all their force, and have acquired additional urgency since that time. It may also be expedient to organize the Topographical Engineers into a corps similar to the present establishment of the Corps of Engineers. The Military Academy at West Point will furnish, from the cadets annually graduated there, officers well qualified for carrying this measure into effect.

The Board of Engineers for Internal Improvement, appointed for carrying into execution the act of Congress of April 30, 1824, "to procure the necessary surveys, plans and estimates on the subject of roads and canals," have been actively engaged in that service from the close of the last session of Congress. They have completed the surveys necessary for ascertaining the practicability of a canal from the Chesapeake bay to the Ohio river, and are preparing a full report on that subject, which, when completed, will be laid before you. The same observation is to be made with regard to the two other objects of national importance upon which the Board have been occupied, namely: the accomplishment of a national road from this city to New Orleans, and the practicability of uniting the waters of Lake Memphramagog with Connecticut river, and the improvement of the navigation of that river. The surveys have been made and are nearly completed. The report may be expected at an early period during the present session of Congress.

The acts of Congress of the last session relative to the surveying, marking, or laying out roads in the Territory of Florida, Arkansas, and Michigan, from Missouri to Mexico, and for the continuation of the Cumberland road, are, some of them, fully executed, and others in the process of execution. Those for completing or commencing fortifications have been delayed only so far as the Corps of Engineers has been inadequate to furnish officers for the necessary superintendence of the works. Under the act confirming the statutes of Virginia and Maryland, incorporating the Chesapeake and Ohio Canal Company, three Commissioners, on the part of the United States, have been appointed for opening books and receiving subscriptions, in concert with a like number of Commissioners appointed on the part of each of those States. A meeting of the Commissioners has been postponed, to await the definitive report of the Board of Engineers. The light-houses and monuments for the safety of our commerce and mariners; the works for the security of Plymouth Beach, and for the preservation of the islands in Boston harbor, have received the attention required by the laws relating to those objects, respectively. The continuation of the Cumberland road, the most important of them all, after surmounting no inconsiderable difficulty in fixing upon the direction of the road, has commenced, under the most promising auspices, with the improvements of recent invention in the mode of construction, and with the advantage of a great reduction in the comparative cost of the work.

The operation of the laws relating to the revolutionary pensioners may deserve the renewed consideration of Congress. The act of the eighteenth of March, eighteen hundred and eighteen, while it made provision for many meritorious and indigent citizens who had served in the war of independence, opened a door to numerous abuses and impositions. To remedy this, the act of the first of May, eighteen hundred and twenty, exacted proofs of absolute indigence, which many really in want were unable, and all, susceptible of that delicacy which is allied to many virtues, must be deeply reluctant to give. The result has been, that some among the least deserving have been retained, and some in whom the requisites both of worth and want were combined have been stricken from the list. As the numbers of these venerable relics of an age gone by diminish; as the decays of body, mind, and estate, of those who survive, must, in the common course of nature, increase, should not a more liberal portion of indulgence be dealt out to them? May not the want, in most instances, be inferred from the demand, when the service can be duly proved; and may not the last days of human infirmity be spared the mortification of purchasing a pittance of relief only by the exposure of its own necessities? I submit to Congress the expediency of providing for individual cases of this description by special enactment, or of revising the act of the first of May, eighteen hundred and twenty, with a view to mitigate the rigor of its exclusions, in favor of persons to whom charity, now bestowed, can scarcely discharge the debt of justice.

The portion of the naval force of the Union in actual service has been chiefly employed on three stations: The Mediterranean, the coasts of South America bordering on the Pacific Ocean, and the West Indies. An occasional cruiser has been sent to range along the African shores most polluted by the traffic of slaves; one armed vessel has been stationed on the coast of our eastern boundary, to cruise along the fishing grounds in Hudson's Bay and on the coast of Labrador; and the first service of a new frigate has been performed in restoring to his native soil and domestic enjoyments the veteran hero whose youthful blood and treasure had freely flowed in the cause of our country's independence, and whose whole life had been a series of services and sacrifices to the improvement of his fellow-men. The visit of General Lafayette, alike honorable to himself and to our country, closed, as it had commenced, with the most affecting testimonials of devoted attachment on his part, and of unbounded gratitude of this people to him in return. It will form, hereafter, a pleasing incident in the annals of our Union, giving to real history the intense interest of romance, and signally marking the unpurchaseable tribute of a great nation's social affections to the disinterested champion of the liberties of human kind.

The constant maintenance of a small squadron in the Mediterranean is a necessary substitute for the humiliating alternative of paying tribute for the security of our commerce in that sea, and for a precarious peace, at the mercy of every caprice of four Barbary States, by whom it was liable to be violated. An additional motive for keeping a respectable force stationed there at this time is found in the maritime war raging between the Greeks and the Turks, and in which the neutral navigation of this Union is always in danger of outrage and depredation. A few instances have occurred of such depredations upon our merchant vessels by privateers or pirates wearing the Grecian flag, but without real authority from the Greek or any other Government. The heroic struggles of the Greeks themselves, in which our warmest sympathies as freemen and Christians have been engaged, have continued to be maintained with vicissitudes of success adverse and favorable.

Similar motives have rendered expedient the keeping of a like force on the coasts of Peru and Chile, on the Pacific. The irregular and convulsive character of the war upon the shores has been extended to the conflicts upon the ocean. An active warfare has been kept up for years, with alternate success, though generally to the advantage of the American Patriots. But their naval forces have not always been under the control of their own Governments. Blockades, unjustifiable upon any acknowledged principles of international law, have been proclaimed by officers in command; and though disavowed by the supreme authorities, the protection of our own commerce against them has been made cause of complaint and of erroneous imputations against some of the most gallant officers of our Navy. Complaints equally groundless have been made by the commanders of the Spanish royal forces in those seas; but the most effective protection to our commerce has been the flag, and the firmness of our own commanding officers. The cessation of the war, by the complete triumph of the Patriot cause, has removed, it is hoped, all cause of dissension with one party, and all vestige of force of the other. But an unsettled coast of many degrees of latitude, forming a part of our own territory, and a flourishing commerce and fishery, extending to the islands of the Pacific and to China, still require that the protecting power of the Union should be displayed under its flag, as well upon the ocean as upon the land.

The objects of the West India squadron have been to carry into execution the laws for the suppression of the African slave trade; for the protection of our commerce against vessels of piratical character, though bearing commissions from either of the belligerent parties; for its protection against open and unequivocal pirates. These objects, during the present year, have been accomplished more effectually than at any former period. The African slave trade has long been excluded from the use of our flag; and if some few citizens of our country have continued to set the laws of the Union, as well as those of nature and humanity, at defiance, by persevering in that abominable traffic, it has been only by sheltering themselves under the banners of other nations less earnest for the total extinction of the trade than ours. The irregular privateers have, within the last year, been, in a great measure, banished from those seas; and the pirates, for months past, appear to have been almost entirely swept away from the borders and the shores of the two Spanish islands in those regions. The active, persevering, and unremitted energy of Captain Warrington, and of the officers and men under his command, on that trying and perilous service, have been crowned with signal success, and are entitled to the approbation of their country. But experience has shown that not even a temporary suspension or relaxation from assiduity can be indulged on that station without reproducing piracy and murder in all their horrors; nor is it probable that for years to come our immensely valuable commerce in those seas can navigate in security without the steady continuance of an armed force devoted to its protection.

It were, indeed, a vain and dangerous illusion to believe that, in the present or probable condition of human society, a commerce so extensive and so rich as ours could exist and be pursued in safety without the continual support of a military marine, the only arm by which the power of this Confederacy can be estimated or felt by foreign nations, and the only standing military force which can never be dangerous to our own liberties at home. A permanent naval peace establishment, therefore, adapted to our present condition, and adaptable to that gigantic growth with which the nation is advancing in its career, is among the subjects which have already occupied the foresight of the last Congress, and which will deserve your serious deliberations. Our Navy, commenced at an early period of our present political organization upon a scale commensurate with the incipient energies, the scanty resources, and the comparative indigence of our infancy, was even then found adequate to cope with all the powers of Barbary, save the first, and with one of the principal maritime powers of Europe. At a period of further advancement, but with little accession of strength, it not only sustained with honor the most unequal of conflicts, but covered itself and our country with unfading glory. But it is only since the close of the late war that, by the number and force of the ships of which it was composed, it could deserve the name of a Navy. Yet it retains nearly the same organization as when it consisted of only five frigates. The rules and regulations by which it is governed earnestly call for revision; and the want of a naval school of instruction, corresponding with the Military Academy at West Point, for the formation of scientific and accomplished officers, is felt with daily increasing aggravation.

The act of Congress of 26th May, 1824, authorizing an examination and survey of the harbor of Charleston, in South Carolina, of St. Mary's, in Georgia, and of the coast of Florida, and for other purposes, has been executed, so far as the appropriation would admit. Those of the 3d of March last, authorizing the establishment of a navy yard and depot on the coast of Florida, in the Gulf of Mexico, and authorizing the building of ten sloops-of-war, and for other purposes, are in the course of execution; for the particulars of which, and other objects connected with this Department, I refer to the report of the Secretary of the Navy, herewith communicated.

A report from the Postmaster General is also submitted, exhibiting the present flourishing condition of that Department. For the first time for many years the receipts for the year ending on the first of July last exceeded the expenditures during the same period to the amount of more than forty-five thousand dollars. Other facts, equally creditable to the administration of this Department, are, that in two years from the first of July, 1823, an improvement of more than one hundred and eighty-five thousand dollars in its pecuniary affairs has been realized; that, in the same interval, the increase of the transportation of the mail has exceeded one million five hundred thousand miles, annually; and that one thousand and forty new post offices have been established. It hence appears that under judicious management the income from this establishment may be relied on as fully adequate to defray its expenses; and that by the discontinuance of post roads altogether unproductive, others of more useful character may be opened, till the circulation of the mail shall keep pace with the spread of our population, and the comforts of friendly correspondence, the exchanges of internal traffic, and the lights of the periodical press, shall be distributed to the remotest corners of the Union, at a charge scarcely perceptible to any individual, and without the cost of a dollar to the public treasury.

Upon this first occasion of addressing the Legislature of the Union, with which I have been honored, in presenting to their view the execution, so far as it has been effected, of the measures sanctioned by them for promoting the internal improvement of our country, I cannot close the communication without recommending to their calm and persevering consideration the general principle in a more enlarged extent. The great object of the institution of civil government is the improvement of the condition of those who are parties to the social compact. And no Government, in whatever form constituted, can accomplish the lawful ends of its institution but in proportion as it improves the condition of those over whom it is established. Roads and canals, by multiplying and facilitating the communications and intercourse between distant regions and multitudes of men, are among the most important means of improvement. But moral, political, intellectual improvement, are duties assigned by the Author of our existence to social, no less than to individual man. For the fulfilment of those duties Governments are invested with power; and to the attainment of the end, the progressive improvement of the condition of the governed, the exercise of delegated power is a duty as sacred and indispensable as the usurpation of power not granted is criminal and odious. Among the first, perhaps the very first instrument for the improvement of the condition of men, is knowledge; and to the acquisition of much of the knowledge adapted to the wants, the comforts, and enjoyments of human life, public institutions and seminaries of learning are essential. So convinced of this was the first of my predecessors in this office, now first in the memory, as, living, he was first in the hearts of our country, that once and again, in his addresses to the Congresses with whom he co-operated in the public service, he earnestly recommended the establishment of seminaries of learning, to prepare for all the emergencies of peace and war—a National University and a Military Academy. With respect to the latter, had he lived to the present day, in turning his eyes to the institution at West Point he would have enjoyed the gratification of his most earnest wishes. But in surveying the city which has been honored with his name, he would have seen the spot of earth which he had destined and bequeathed to the use and benefit of his country as the site for an university still bare and barren.

In assuming her station among the civilized nations of the ear th, it would seem that our country had contracted the engagement to contribute her share of mind, of labor, and of expense, to the improvement of those parts of knowledge which lie beyond the reach of individual acquisition, and particularly to geographical and astronomical science. Looking back to the history only of the half century since the declaration of our independence, and observing the generous emulation with which the Governments of France, Great Britain, and Russia, have devoted the genius, the intelligence, the treasures of their respective nations to the common improvement of the species in these branches of science, is it not incumbent upon us to inquire whether we are not bound by obligations of a high and honorable character to contribute our portion of energy and exertion to the common stock? The voyages of discovery prosecuted in the course of that time at the expense of those nations have not only redounded to their glory, but to the improvement of human knowledge. We have been partakers of that improvement, and owe for it a sacred debt, not only of gratitude, but of equal or proportional exertion in the same common cause. Of the cost of these undertakings, if the mere expenditures of outfit, equipment, and completion of the expeditions were to be considered the only charges, it would be unworthy of a great and generous nation to take a second thought. One hundred expeditions of circumnavigation, like those of Cook and La Perouse, would not burden the exchequer of the nation fitting them out so much as the ways and means of defraying a single campaign in war. But if we take into the account the lives of those benefactors of mankind, of which their services in the cause of their species were the purchase, how shall the cost of those heroic enterprises be estimated? And what compensation can be made to them, or to their countries for them? Is it not by bearing them in affectionate remembrance? Is it not still more by imitating their example? by enabling countrymen of our own to pursue the same career, and to hazard their lives in the same cause?

In inviting the attention of Congress to the subject of internal improvements upon a view thus enlarged, it is not my design to recommend the equipment of an expedition for circumnavigating the globe for purposes of scientific research and inquiry. We have objects of useful investigation nearer home, and to which our cares may be more beneficially applied. The interior of our own territories has yet been very imperfectly explored. Our coasts, along many degrees of latitude upon the shores of the Pacific Ocean, though much frequented by our spirited commercial navigators, have been barely visited by our public ships. The river of the west, first fully discovered and navigated by a countryman of our own, still bears the name of the ship in which he ascended its waters, and claims the protection of our armed national flag at its mouth. With the establishment of a military post there, or at some other point of that coast, recommended by my predecessor, and already matured, in the deliberations of the last Congress, I would suggest the expediency of connecting the equipment of a public ship for the exploration of the whole northwest coast of this continent.

The establishment of an uniform standard of weights and measures was one of the specific objects contemplated in the formation of our Constitution, and to fix that standard was one of the powers delegated by express terms in that instrument to Congress. The Governments of Great Britain and France have scarcely ceased to be occupied with inquiries and speculations on the same subject since the existence of our Constitution; and with them it has expanded into profound, laborious, and expensive researches into the figure of the earth, and the comparative length of the pendulum vibrating seconds in various latitudes, from the equator to the pole. These researches have resulted in the composition and publication of several works highly interesting to the cause of science. The experiments are yet in the process of performance. Some of them have recently been made on our own shores, within the walls of one of our own colleges, and partly by one of our own fellow-citizens. It would be honorable to our country if the sequel of the same experiments should be countenanced by the patronage of our Government, as they have hitherto been by those of France and Britain.

Connected with the establishment of an university, or separate from it, might be undertaken the erection of an astronomical observatory, with provision for the support of an astronomer to be in constant attendance, of observations upon the phenomena of the heavens, and for the periodical publication of his observations. It is with no feeling of pride, as an American, that the remark may be made that on the comparatively small territorial surface of Europe there are existing upwards of one hundred and thirty of these light-houses of the skies, while throughout the whole American hemisphere there is not one. If we reflect a moment upon the discoveries which, in the last four centuries, have been made in the physical constitution of the universe by the means of these buildings, and of observers stationed in them, shall we doubt of their usefulness to every nation? And while scarcely a year passes over our head without bringing some new astronomical discovery to light, which we must fain receive at second hand from Europe, are we not cutting ourselves off from the means of returning light for light, while we have neither observatory nor observer upon our half of the globe, and the earth revolves in perpetual darkness to our unsearching eyes?

When, on October 25, 1791, the first President of the United States announced to Congress the result of the first enumeration of the inhabitants of this Union, he informed them that the returns gave the pleasing assurance that the population of the United States bordered on four millions of persons. At the distance of thirty years from that time, the last enumeration, five years since completed, presented a population bordering upon ten millions. Perhaps, of all the evidences of a prosperous and happy condition of human society, the rapidity of the increase of population is the most unequivocal. But the demonstration of our prosperity rests not alone upon this indication. Our commerce, our wealth, and the extent of our territories, have increased in corresponding proportions; and the number of independent communities associated in our Federal Union has since that time nearly doubled. The legislative representation of the States and people in the two Houses of Congress has grown with the growth of their constituent bodies. The House, which then consisted of sixty-five members, now numbers upwards of two hundred. The Senate, which consisted of twenty-six members, has now forty-eight. But the Executive, and still more the Judiciary Departments, are yet in a great measure confined to their primitive organization, and are now not adequate to the urgent wants of a still growing community.

The naval armaments, which at an early period forced themselves upon the necessities of the Union, soon led to the establishment of a Department of the Navy. But the Departments of Foreign Affairs and of the Interior, which early after the formation of the Government had been united in one, continue so united at this time, to the unquestionable detriment of the public service. The multiplication of our relations with the nations and Governments of the Old World has kept pace with that of our population and commerce, while, within the last ten years, a new family of nations in our own hemisphere has arisen among the inhabitants of the earth, with whom our intercourse, commercial and political, would of itself furnish occupation to an active and industrious Department. The constitution of the Judiciary, experimental and imperfect as it was even in the infancy of our existing Government, is yet more inadequate to the administration of national justice at our present maturity. Nine years have elapsed since a predecessor in this office, now not the last, the citizen who, perhaps, of all others throughout the Union, contributed most to the formation and establishment of our Constitution, in his valedictory address to Congress, immediately preceding his retirement from public life, urgently recommended the revision of the Judiciary and the establishment of an additional Executive Department. The exigencies of the public service, and its unavoidable deficiencies, as now in exercise, have added yearly cumulative weight to the considerations presented by him as persuasive to the measure; and in recommending it to your deliberations, I am happy to have the influence of his high authority in aid of the undoubting convictions of my own experience.

The laws relating to the administration of the Patent Office are deserving of much consideration, and, perhaps, susceptible of some improvement. The grant of power to regulate the action of Congress on this subject has specified both the end to be obtained and the means by which it is to be effected—" to promote the progress of science and useful arts by securing for limited times to authors and inventors the exclusive right to their respective writings and discoveries." If an honest pride might be indulged in the reflection that on the records of that office are already found inventions the usefulness of which has scarcely been transcended in the annals of human ingenuity, would not its exultation be allayed by the inquiry, whether the laws have effectually insured to the inventors the reward destined to them by the Constitution—even a limited term of exclusive right to their discoveries?

On December 24, 1799, it was resolved by Congress that a marble monument should be erected by the United States in the Capitol, at the city of Washington; that the family of General Washington should be requested to permit his body to be deposited under it; and that the monument be so designed as to commemorate the great events of his military and political life. In reminding Congress of this resolution, and that the monument contemplated by it remains yet without execution, I shall indulge only the remarks that the works at the Capitol are approaching to completion; that the consent of the family desired by the resolution was requested and obtained; that a monument has been recently erected in this city over the remains of another distinguished patriot of the Revolution; and that a spot has been reserved within the walls where you are deliberating for the benefit of this and future ages, in which the mortal remains may be deposited of him whose spirit hovers over you, and listens with delight to every act of the representatives of his nation which can tend to exalt and adorn his and their country.

The Constitution under which you are assembled is a charter of limited powers. After full and solemn deliberation upon all or any of the objects which, urged by an irresistible sense of my own duty, I have recommended to your attention, should you come to the conclusion that, however desirable in themselves, the enactment of laws for effecting them would transcend the powers committed to you by that venerable instrument which we are all bound to support, let no consideration induce you to assume the exercise of powers not granted to you by the people. But, if the power to exercise exclusive legislation in all cases whatsoever over the District of Columbia; if the power to lay and collect taxes, duties, imposts, and excises, to pay the debts and provide for the common defence and general welfare of the United States; if the power to regulate commerce with foreign nations and among the several States, and with the Indian tribes; to fix the standard of weights and measures; to establish post offices and post roads; to declare war; to raise and support armies; to provide and maintain a Navy; to dispose of and make all needful rules and regulations respecting the territory or other property belonging to the United States; and to make all laws which shall be necessary and proper for carrying these powers into execution: If these powers and others enumerated in the Constitution be effectually brought into action by laws promoting the improvement of agriculture, commerce, and manufactures, the cultivation and encouragement of the mechanic and of the elegant arts, the advancement of literature, and the progress of the sciences, ornamental and profound,—to refrain from exercising them for the benefit of the people themselves, would be to hide in the earth the talent committed to our charge—would be treachery to the most sacred of trusts.

The spirit of improvement is abroad upon the earth. It stimulates the heart and sharpens the faculties, not of our fellow-citizens alone, but of the nations of Europe and of their rulers. While dwelling with pleasing satisfaction upon the superior excellence of our political institutions, let us not be unmindful that liberty is power; that the nation blessed with the largest portion of liberty must, in proportion to its numbers, be the most powerful nation upon earth; and that the tenure of power by man is, in the moral purposes of his Creator, upon condition that it shall be exercised to ends of beneficence, to improve the condition of himself and his fellow-men. While foreign nations, less blessed with that freedom which is power than ourselves, are advancing with gigantic strides in the career of public improvement, were we to slumber in indolence, or fold up our arms and proclaim to the world that we are palsied by the will of our constituents, would it not be to cast away the bounties of Providence, and doom ourselves to perpetual inferiority? In the course of the year now drawing to its close we have beheld, under the auspices and at the expense of one State of this Union, a new university unfolding its portals to the sons of science, and holding up the torch of human improvement to eyes that seek the light. We have seen, under the persevering and enlightened enterprise of another State, the waters of our western lakes mingled with those of the ocean. If undertakings like these have been accomplished in the compass of a few years, by the authority of single members of our Confederation, can we, the representative authorities of the whole Union, fall behind our fellow-servants in the exercise of the trust committed to us for the benefit of our common sovereign, by the accomplishment of works important to the whole, and to which neither the authority nor the resources of any one State can be adequate?

Finally, fellow-citizens, I shall await with cheering hope and faithful co-operation the result of your deliberations; assured that, without encroaching upon the powers reserved to the authorities of the respective States or to the people, you will, with a due sense of your obligations to your country, and of the high responsibilities weighing upon yourselves, give efficacy to the means committed to you for the common good. And may He who searches the hearts of the children of men prosper your exertions to secure the blessings of peace and promote the highest welfare of our country.

WASHINGTON, *December* 6, 1825.

JOHN QUINCY ADAMS.

COMMUNICATED TO CONGRESS WITH THE MESSAGE OF THE PRESIDENT, AT THE COMMENCEMENT OF THE 1ST SESSION, 19TH CONGRESS, FROM THE STATE DEPARTMENT.

BY THE PRESIDENT OF THE UNITED STATES OF AMERICA.

A PROCLAMATION.

Whereas a general convention of peace, amity, navigation, and commerce, between the United States of America and the Republic of Colombia, was concluded and signed at Bogota, on the third day of October, in the year of our Lord one thousand eight hundred and twenty-four; which convention, being in the English and Spanish languages, is word for word, as follows:

General convention of peace, amity, navigation, and commerce, between the United States of America and the Republic of Colombia.	*Convencion jeneral de paz, amistad, navegacion, y comercio, entre la Republica de Colombia y los Estados Unidos de America, Año de 1824.*
IN THE NAME OF GOD, AUTHOR AND LEGISLATOR OF THE UNIVERSE.	EN EL NOMBRE DE DIOS, AUTOR Y LEJISLADOR DEL UNIVERSO.

The United States of America and the Republic of Colombia, desiring to make lasting and firm the friendship and good understanding which happily prevail between both nations, have resolved to fix, in a manner clear, distinct, and positive, the rules which shall in future be religiously observed between the one and the other, by means of a treaty or general convention of peace, friendship, commerce, and navigation.

For this most desirable object, the President of the United States of America has conferred full powers on RICHARD CLOUGH ANDERSON, junior, a citizen of the said States, and their Minister Plenipotentiary to the said republic; and the Vice President of the Republic of Colombia, charged with the Executive power, on PEDRO GUAL, Secretary of State and of Foreign Relations; who, after having exchanged their said full powers in due and proper form, have agreed to the following articles:

ARTICLE 1. There shall be a perfect, firm, and inviolable peace and sincere friendship between the United States of America and the Republic of Colombia, in all the extent of their possessions and territories, and between their people and citizens, respectively, without distinction of persons or places.

ARTICLE 2. The United States of America and the Republic of Colombia, desiring to live in peace and harmony with all the other nations of the earth, by means of a policy frank and equally friendly with all, engage mutually not to grant any particular favor to other nations, in respect of commerce and navigation, which shall not immediately become common to the other party, who shall enjoy the same freely, if the concession was freely made, or on allowing the same compensation, if the concession was conditional.

ARTICLE 3. The citizens of the United States may frequent all the coasts and countries of the Republic of Colombia, and reside and trade there in all sorts of produce, manufactures, and merchandise, and shall pay no other or greater duties, charges, or fees whatsoever, than the most favored nation is or shall be obliged to pay; and they shall enjoy all the rights, privileges, and exemptions, in navigation and commerce which the most favored nation does or shall enjoy, submitting themselves, nevertheless, to the laws, decrees, and usages there established, and to which are submitted the subjects and citizens of the most favored nations.

In like manner the citizens of the Republic of

La Republica de Colombia, y los Estados Unidos de America, deseando hacer duradera y firme la amistad y buena inteligencia que felizmente existe entre ambas Potencias, han resuelto fijar de una manera clara, distinta y positiva las reglas que deben observar religiosamente en lo venidero, por medio de un tradado o convencion jeneral de paz, amistad, comercio, y navegacion.

Con este muy deseable objeto, el Vice-Presidente de la Republica de Colombia encargado del podér Ejecutivo, ha conferido plenos poderes á PEDRO GUAL, Secretario de Estado y del Despacho de Relaciones Esteriores de la misma, y el Presidente de los Estados Unidos de America, á RICARDO CLOUGH ANDERSON, el menor, ciudadano de dichos Estados, y su Ministro Plenipotenciario cerca de la dicha Republica; quienes despues de haber canjeado sus espresados plenos poderes en debida y buena forma, han convenido en los articulos siguientes:

ARTICULO 1. Habra una paz, perfecta, firme, é inviolable y amistad sincera entre la Republica de Colombia y los Estados Unidos de America, en toda la estencion de sus possessiones y territorios, y entre sus pueblos y ciudadanos respectivamente sin distincion de personas, ni lugares.

ARTICULO 2. La Republica de Colombia y los Estados Unidos de America, deseando vivir en paz y harmonia con las demas naciones de la tierra por medio de una politica franca, é igualmente amistosa con todas, se obligan mutuamente à no conceder favores particulares, à otras naciones, con respecto à comercio y navegacion, que no se hagan inmediatamente comun á una ú otra, quien gozara de los mismos libremente, si la concesion fuese hecha libremente ó prestando la misma compensacion, si la concesion fuere condicional.

ARTICULO 3. Los ciudadanos de la Republica de Colombia podràn frecuentar todas las costas y paises de los Estados Unidos de America, y residir, y traficar en ellos con toda suerte de producciones, manufacturas, y mercaderias, y no pagaràn otros, ó mayores derechos, impuestos, ó emolumentos cualesquiera que los ques las naciones mas favorecidas están ó estuvieren obligadas à pagar; y gozaràn todos los derechos, previlejios y esenciones, que gozan ó gozaren los de la nacion mas favorecida, con respecto à navegacion y comercio, sometiendose, no obstante, à las leyes, decretos, y usos establecidos, à los cuales estan sujetos los subditos ó ciudadanos de las naciones mas favorecidas. Del mis-

Colombia may frequent all the coasts and countries of the United States, and reside and trade there in all sorts of produce, manufactures, and merchandise, and shall pay no other or greater duties, charges, or fees whatsoever, than the most favored nation is or shall be obliged to pay; and they shall enjoy all the rights, privileges, and exemptions in navigation and commerce which the most favored nation does or shall enjoy, submitting themselves, nevertheless, to the laws, decrees, and usages there established, and to which are submitted the subjects and citizens of the most favored nations.

ARTICLE 4. It is likewise agreed that it shall be wholly free for all merchants, commanders of ships, and other citizens of both countries, to manage themselves their own business in all the ports and places subject to the jurisdiction of each other, as well with respect to the consignment and sale of their goods and merchandise by wholesale or retail, as with respect to the loading, unloading, and sending off their ships; they being in all these cases to be treated as citizens of the country in which they reside, or at least to be placed on a footing with the subjects or citizens of the most favored nation.

ARTICLE 5. The citizens of neither of the contracting parties shall be liable to any embargo, nor be detained with their vessels, cargoes, merchandises, or effects, for any military expedition, nor for any public or private purpose whatever, without allowing to those interested a sufficient indemnification.

ARTICLE 6. Whenever the citizens of either of the contracting parties shall be forced to seek refuge or asylum in the rivers, bays, ports, or dominions of the other, with their vessels, whether merchants or of war, public or private, through stress of weather, pursuit of pirates or enemies, they shall be received and treated with humanity, giving to them all favor and protection for repairing their ships, procuring provisions, and placing themselves in a situation to continue their voyage without obstacle or hindrance of any kind.

ARTICLE 7. All the ships, merchandise, and effects belonging to the citizens of one of the contracting parties, which may be captured by pirates, whether within the limits of its jurisdiction or on the high seas, and may be carried or found in the rivers, roads, bays, ports, or dominions of the other, shall be delivered up to the owners, they proving, in due and proper form, their rights before the competent tribunals; it being well understood that the claim should be made within the term of one year by the parties themselves, their attorneys, or agents of the respective Governments.

ARTICLE 8. When any vessel belonging to the citizens of either of the contracting parties shall be wrecked, foundered, or shall suffer any damage on the coasts, or within the dominions of the other, there shall be given to them all assistance and protection, in the same manner which is usual and customary with the vessels of the nation where the damage happens, permitting them to unload the said vessel, if necessary, of its merchandise and effects, without exacting for it any duty, impost, or contribution whatever, until they may be exported.

ARTICLE 9. The citizens of each of the contracting parties shall have power to dispose of their personal goods within the jurisdiction of the other, by sale, donation, testament, or otherwise; and their representatives, being citizens of the other party, shall succeed to their said personal goods, whether by testament or *ab intestato*, and they may take possession thereof, either by themselves or others acting for them, and dispose of the same at their will, paying such dues only as the inhabitants of the country wherein said goods are shall be subject to pay in like cases; and if, in the case of real estate, the said heirs would be prevented from entering into the

mo modo los ciudadanos de los Estados Unidos de America podràn frecuentar todas las costas y paises de la Republica de Colombia, y residir y traficàr en ellos con toda suerte de producciones, manufacturas, y mercaderias, y no pagaràn otros ó mayores derechos, impuestos, ó emolumentos cualesquiera, que los que las naciones mas favorecidas, estàn ó estuvieren obligadas à pagàr y gozaràn de todos los derechos privilejios y esenciones, que gozan ó gozaren los de la nacion mas favorecida con respecto à navegacion y comercio, sometiendose, no obstante à las leyes, decretos y usos establecidos à los cuales estan sujetos los subditos ó ciudadanos de las naciones mas favorecidas.

ARTICULO 4. Se conviene ademas, que serà enteramente libre y permitido, a los comerciantes, comandantes de buques, y otros ciudadanos de ambos paises el manejar sus negocios, por si mismos, en todos los puertos y lugares sujetos à la jurisdiccion de uno ù otro, asi respecto à las consignaciones y ventas por mayor y menor de sus efectos y mercaderias, como de la carga, descarga y despacho de sus buques, debiendo en todos estos casos, ser tratados como ciudadanos del pais en que residan, ó al menos puestos sobre un pie igual con los subditos ó ciudadanos de las naciones mas favorecidas.

ARTICULO 5. Los ciudadanos de una ù otra parte, no podràn ser embargados ni detenidos con sus embarcaciones, tripulaciones, mercaderias, y efectos comerciales de su pertenencia, para alguna espedicion militàr, usos publicos, ó particulares cualesquiera que sean, sin conceder à los interesados una suficiente indemnizacion.

ARTICULO 6. Siempre que los ciudadanos de alguna de las partes contratantes se vieren precisados à buscàr refujio, ó asilo en los rios, bahias, puertos, ó dominios de la otra, con sus buques, ya sean mercantes, ó de guerra, publicos ó particulares, por mal tiempo, persecucion de piratas ó enemigos, seràn recibidos y tratados con humanidad, dandoles todo favor y proteccion, para reparar sus buques, procuràr viveres, y ponerse en situacion de continuar su viaje, sin obstaculo ó estorbo de ningun genero.

ARTICULO 7. Todos los buques, mercaderias y efectos pertenecientes a los ciudadanos de una de las partes contratantes, que sean apresados por piratas, bien sea dentro de los limites de su jurisdiccion, ó en alta mar, y fueren llevados, ó hallados en los rios, radas, bahias, puertos, ó dominios de la otra, seràn entregados à sus dueños, probando estos en la forma propia y debida sus derechos ante los tribunales competentes; bien entendido que el reclama ha de hacerse dentro del termino de un año, por las mismas partes, sus apoderados ó agentes de los respectivos Gobiernos.

ARTICULO 8. Cuando algun buque perteneciente à los ciudadanos de alguna de las partes contratantes, naufrague, encalle, ó sufra alguna averia, en las costas, ó dentro de los dominios de la otra, se les darà toda ayuda y proteccion, del mismo modo que es uso y costumbre, con los buques de la nacion en donde suceda la averia; permitiendoles descargàr el dicho buque (si fuere necesario) de sus mercaderias y efectos, sin cobrar por esto hasta que sean esportados, ningun derecho, impuesto ó contribucion.

ARTICULO 9. Los ciudadanos de cada una de las partes contratantes, tendràn pleno podér para disponér de sus bienes personales dentro de la jurisdiccion de la otra, por venta, donacion testamento, ó de otro modo; y sus representantes, siendo ciudadanos de la otra parte, succederán à sus dichos bienes personales, ya sea por testamento ó *ab intestato*, y podran tomar posecion de ellos, ya sea por si mismos ó por otros, que obren por ellos, y disponér de los mismos, segun su voluntad, pagando aquellas cargas, solamente, que los habitantes del pais en donde estan los referidos bienes, estuvieren sujetos à pagar en iguales casos; y si en el caso de bienes

possession of the inheritance on account of their character of aliens, there shall be granted to them the term of three years to dispose of the same as they may think proper, and to withdraw the proceeds without molestation, and exempt from all rights of detraction on the part of the Government of the respective States.

ARTICLE 10. Both the contracting parties promise and engage formally to give their special protection to the persons and property of the citizens of each other, of all occupations, who may be in the territories subject to the jurisdiction of the one or the other, transient or dwelling therein, leaving open and free to them the tribunals of justice for their judicial recourse, on the same terms which are usual and customary with the natives or citizens of the country in which they may be; for which they may employ, in defence of their rights, such advocates, solicitors, notaries, agents and factors, as they may judge proper in all their trials at law; and such citizens or agents shall have free opportunity to be present at the decisions and sentences of the tribunals in all cases which may concern them, and likewise at the taking of all examinations and evidence which may be exhibited in the said trials.

ARTICLE 11. It is likewise agreed that the most perfect and entire security of conscience shall be enjoyed by the citizens of both the contracting parties in the countries subject to the jurisdiction of the one and the other, without their being liable to be disturbed or molested on account of their religious belief, so long as they respect the laws and established usages of the country. Moreover, the bodies of the citizens of one of the contracting parties who may die in the territories of the other shall be buried in the usual burying grounds, or in other decent and suitable places, and shall be protected from violation or disturbance.

ARTICLE 12. It shall be lawful for the citizens of the United States of America and of the Republic of Colombia to sail with their ships with all manner of liberty and security, no distinction being made who are the proprietors of the merchandises laden thereon, from any port to the places of those who are now, or hereafter shall be, at enmity with either of the contracting parties. It shall likewise be lawful for the citizens aforesaid to sail with the ships and merchandises before mentioned, and to trade with the same liberty and security from the places, ports, and havens of those who are enemies of both or either party, without any opposition or disturbance whatsoever, not only directly from the places of the enemy before mentioned to neutral places, but also from one place belonging to an enemy to another place belonging to an enemy, whether they be under the jurisdiction of one power or under several. And it is hereby stipulated that free ships shall also give freedom to goods, and that everything shall be deemed to be free and exempt which shall be found on board the ships belonging to the citizens of either of the contracting parties, although the whole lading, or any part thereof, should appertain to the enemies of either, contraband goods being always excepted. It is also agreed in like manner that the same liberty be extended to persons who are on board a free ship, with this effect, that, although they be enemies to both or either party, they are not to be taken out of that free ship unless they are officers and soldiers, and in the actual service of the enemies: *Provided, however, and it is hereby agreed,* That the stipulations in this article contained, declaring that the flag shall cover the property, shall be understood as applying to those powers only who recognize this principle; but if either of the two contracting parties shall be at war with a third, and the other neutral, the flag of the neutral shall cover the property of enemies whose Governments acknowledge this principle, and not of others.

raices, los dichos herederos fuesen impedidos de entrár en la posecion de la herencia por razon de su caracter de estrangeros, se les dará el termino de tres años, para dispónér de ella como juzguen conveniente, y para estraér el producto sin molestia, y esentos de todo derecho de deduccion, por parte del Gobierno de los respectivos Estados.

ARTICULO 10. Ambas partes contratantes se comprometen y obligan formalmente á dar su proteccion especial á las personas y propiedades de los ciudadanos de cada una reciprocamente transeuntes ó habitantes de todas ocupaciones, en los territorios sujetos á la jurisdiccion de una y otra, dejandoles abiertos y libres los tribunales de justicia, para sus recursos judiciales, en los mismos terminos que son de uso y costumbre para los naturales ó ciudadanos del pais en que residan; para lo cual, podrán emplear en defensa de sus derechos aquellos abogados, procuradores, escribanos, agentes, ó factores que juzguen conveniente, en todos sus asuntos y litigios; y dichos ciudadanos ó agentes tendrán la libre facultad de estar presentes en las decisiones y sentencias de los tribunales, en todos los casos que les conciernan, como igualmente al tomar todos los examenes y declaraciones que se ofrezcan en los dichos litigios.

ARTICULO 11. Se conviene igualmente en que los ciudadanos de ambas partes contratantes gozen la mas perfecta y entera seguridad de consciencia en los paises sujetos á la jurisdiccion da una ù otra, sin quedar por ello espuestos á ser inquietados ó molestados en razon de su creencia religiosa, mientras que respeten las leyes y usos establecidos. Ademas de esto, podrán sepultarse los cadaveres de los ciudadanos de una de las partes contratantes, que fallecieren en los territorios de la otra, en los cementerios acostumbrados, ó en otros lugares decentes, y adecuados, los cuales, serán protejidos contra toda violacion ó trastorno.

ARTICULO 12. Será licito a los ciudadanos de la Republica de Colombia, y de los Estados Unidos de America, navegár con sus buques, con toda seguridad y libertad, de cualquiera puerto á las plazas ó lugares de los que son ó fueren en adelante enemigos de cualquiera de las dos partes contratantes, sin hacerse distinçion de quienes son los dueños de las mercaderias cargadas en ellos. Será igualmente licito á los referidos ciudadanos navegár con sus buques y mercaderias mencionadas y traficár con la misma libertad y seguridad, de los lugares, puertos y ense ñadas de los enemigos de ambas partes, ó de alguna de ellas, sin ninguna oposicion, ó disturbio cualquiera, no solo directamente de los lugares de enemigo arriba mencionados á lugares neutros, sino tambien de un lugar perteneciente á un enemigo, á otro enemigo, ya sea que esten bajo la jurisdiccion de una potencia, ó bajo la de diversas. Y queda aqui estipulado, que los buques libres, dan tambien libertad á las mercaderias, y que se ha de considerar libre y esento todo lo que se hallare á bordo de los buques pertenecientes á los ciudadanos de cualquiera de las partes contratantes, aunque toda la carga ó parte de ella pertenezca á enemigos de una ù otra, eceptuando siempre los articulos de contrabando de guerra. Se conviene tambien del mismo modo, en que la misma libertad se estienda á las personas que se encuentren á bordo de buques libres, con el fin de que aunque dichas personas sean enemigos de ambas partes ó de alguna de ellas, no deban ser estraidos de los buques libres, à menos que sean oficiales ó soldados en actual servicio de los enemigos: á condicion no obstante, y se conviene aqui en esto, que las estipulaciones contenidas en el presente articulo, declarando que el pabellon cubre la propiedad, se entenderán aplicables solamente á aquellas potencias que reconocen este principio; pero si alguna de las dos partes contratantes, estuviere en guerra con una tercera, y la otra permaneciese neutral, la bandera de la neutral cubrirá la propiedad de los enemigos, cuyos Gobiernos reconozcan este principio y no de otros.

ARTICLE 13. It is likewise agreed, that, in the case where the neutral flag of one of the contracting parties shall protect the property of the enemies of the other by virtue of the above stipulation, it shall always be understood that the neutral property found on board such enemy's vessels shall be held and considered as enemy's property, and as such shall be liable to detention and confiscation, except such property as was put on board such vessel before the declaration of war, or even afterwards, if it were done without the knowledge of it; but the contracting parties agree that two months having elapsed after the declaration, their citizens shall not plead ignorance thereof. On the contrary, if the flag of the neutral does not protect the enemy's property, in that case the goods and merchandises of the neutral embarked in such enemy's ships shall be free.

ARTICLE 14. This liberty of navigation and commerce shall extend to all kinds of merchandises, excepting those only which are distinguished by the name of contraband, and under this name of contraband or prohibited goods shall be comprehended—

1st. Cannons, mortars, howitzers, swivels, blunderbusses, muskets, fuzees, rifles, carbines, pistols, pikes, swords, sabres, lances, spears, halberds, and granades, bombs, powder, matches, balls, and all other things belonging to the use of these arms.

2d. Bucklers, helmets, breast plates, coats of mail, infantry belts, and clothes made up in the form and for a military use.

3d. Cavalry belts and horses with their furniture.

4th. And generally all kinds of arms and instruments of iron, steel, brass, and copper, or of any other materials manufactured, prepared, and formed expressly to make war by sea or land.

ARTICLE 15. All other merchandises and things not comprehended in the articles of contraband explicitly enumerated and classified as above shall be held and considered as free, and subjects of free and lawful commerce, so that they may be carried and transported in the freest manner by both the contracting parties, even to places belonging to an enemy, excepting only those places which are at that time besieged or blockaded up; and to avoid all doubt in this particular, it is declared that those places only are besieged or blockaded which are actually attacked by a belligerent force capable of preventing the entry of the neutral.

ARTICLE 16. The articles of contraband before enumerated and classified, which may be found in a vessel bound for an enemy's port, shall be subject to detention and confiscation, leaving free the rest of the cargo and the ship, that the owners may dispose of them as they see proper. No vessel of either of the two nations shall be detained on the high seas on account of having on board articles of contraband, whenever the master, captain, or supercargo of said vessel will deliver up the articles of contraband to the captor, unless the quantity of such articles be so great and of so large a bulk that they cannot be received on board the capturing ship without great inconvenience; but, in this and in all other cases of just detention, the vessel detained shall be sent to the nearest convenient and safe port, for trial and judgment, according to law.

ARTICLE 17. And whereas it frequently happens that vessels sail for a port or place belonging to an enemy without knowing that the same is besieged, blockaded, or invested, it is agreed that every vessel so circumstanced may be turned away from such port or place, but shall not be detained, nor shall any part of her cargo, if not contraband, be confiscated, unless, after warning of such blockade or investment from the commanding officer of the blockading forces, she

ARTÍCULO 13. So conviene igualmente que en el caso de que la bandera neutrál de una de las partes contratantes protega las propiedades de los enemigos de la otra en virtud de lo estipulado arriba, deberá siempre entenderse, que las propiedades neutrales encontradas á bordo de tales buques enemigos, han de tenerse y considerarse como propiedades enemigos, y como tales, estarán sujetas á detencion, y confiscacion; eseptuando solamente aquellas propiedades que hubiesen sido puestas à bordo de tales buques antes de la declaracion de la guerra, y aun despues, si hubiesen sido embarcadas en dichos buques, sin tenèr noticia de la guerra; y se conviene, que pasados dos meses despues de la declaracion, los ciudadanos de una y otra parte no podrán elegàr que la ignoraban. Por el contrario, si la bandera neutral, no protegiese las propiedades enemigos, entonces seràn libres los efectos y mercaderias de la parte neutrál embarcadas en buques enemigos.

ARTÍCULO 14. Esta libertad de navegacion y comercio se estenderá a todo genero de mercaderias, eceptuando aquellas solamente, que se distinguen con el nombre de contrabando, y bajo este nombre de contrabando ó efectos prohibidos se comprenderán:

1°. Cañones, morteros, obuces, pedreros, trabucos, mosquetes, fusiles, rifles, carabinas, pistolas, picas, espadas, sables, lanzas, chuzos, alabardas, y granadas, bombas, polvóra, mechas, balas, con las demas cosas correspondientes al uso de estas armas.

2°. Escudos, casquetes, corazas, cotas de malla, fornituras, y vestidos hechos en forma, y á usanza militar.

3°. Bandoleras, y caballos junto con sus armas y arneses.

4°. Y generalmente toda especie de armas, é instrumentos de hierro, acero, bronce, cobre, y otras materias cualesquiera, manufacturadas, preparadas, y formadas espresamente para hacér la guerra por mar, ó tierra.

ARTÍCULO 15. Todas las demas mercaderias, y efectos no comprendidos en los articulos de contrabando esplicitamente enumerados, y clasificados en el articulo anterior, serán tenidos y reputados por libres, y de licito y libre comercio, de modo, que ellos puedan sér transportados, y llevados, de la manera mas libre, por los ciudadanos de ambas partes contratantes, aun á los lugares pertenecientes á un enemigo de una ù otra, eceptuando solamente aquellos lugares ó plazas, que estàn al mismo tiempo sitiadas ó bloqueadas; y para evitar toda duda en el particulàr, se declaran sitiadas ó bloqueadas àquellas plazas, que en la actualidad estuviesen átacadas por una fuerza de un beligerante capaz de impedir la entrada del neutral.

ARTÍCULO 16. Los articulos de contrabando antes enumerados y clasificados, que se hallen en un buque destinado à detencion y confiscacion; dejando libre el resto del cargamento y el buque, para que los dueños puedan disponer de ellos como lo crean conveniente. Ningun buque de cualquiera de las dos naciones, será detenido, por tener à bordo articulos de contrabando, siempre que el maestre, capitan, ó sobrecargo de dicho buque quiera entregar los articulos de contrabando al apresador, à menos que la cantidad de estos articulos sea tan grande y de tanto volumen, que no puedan sér recibidos à bordo del buque apresadòr, sin grandes inconvenientes; pero en este, como en todos los otros casos de justa detencion, el buque detenido serà enviado al puerto mas inmediato, comodo, y seguro, para sér juzgado y sentenciado conforme à las leyes.

ARTÍCULO 17. Y por cuanto frecuentemente sucede que los buques navegan para un puerto ó lugàr perteneciente à un enemigo, sin saber que aquel esté sitiado, bloqueado ó envestido, se conviene en que todo buque en estas circunstancias se pueda hacer volver de dicho puerto, ó lugar; pero no serà detenido, ni confiscada parte alguna de su cargamento, no siendo contrabando; à menos que despues de la intimacion de semejante bloqueo ó ataque, por el coman-

shall again attempt to enter; but she shall be permitted to go to any other port or place she shall think proper. Nor shall any vessel of either, that may have entered into such port before the same was actually besieged, blockaded, or invested by the other, be restrained from quitting such place with her cargo, nor, if found therein after the reduction and surrender, shall such vessel or her cargo be liable to confiscation, but they shall be restored to the owners thereof.

ARTICLE 18. In order to prevent all kind of disorder in the visiting and examination of the ships and cargoes of both the contracting parties on the high seas, they have agreed mutually, that whenever a vessel-of-war, public or private, shall meet with a neutral of the other contracting party, the first shall remain out of cannon shot, and may send its boat, with two or three men only, in order to execute the said examination of the papers concerning the ownership and cargo of the vessel, without causing the least extortion, violence, or ill treatment, for which the commanders of the said armed ships shall be responsible with their persons and property; for which purpose, the commanders of said private armed vessels shall, before receiving their commissions, give sufficient security to answer for all the damages they may commit. And it is expressly agreed that the neutral party shall in no case be required to go on board the examining vessel for the purpose of exhibiting her papers, or for any other purpose whatever.

ARTICLE 19. To avoid all kind of vexation and abuse in the examination of the papers relating to the ownership of the vessels belonging to the citizens of the two contracting parties, they have agreed, and do agree, that in case one of them should be engaged in war, the ships and vessels belonging to the citizens of the other must be furnished with sea letters, or passports, expressing the name, property, and bulk of the ship, as also the name and place of habitation of the master or commander of said vessel, in order that it may thereby appear that the ship really and truly belongs to the citizens of one of the parties; they have likewise agreed that, such ships being laden, besides the said sea letters or passports, shall also be provided with certificates, containing the several particulars of the cargo, and the place whence the ship sailed, so that it may be known whether any forbidden or contraband goods be on board the same; which certificates shall be made out by the officers of the place whence the ship sailed, in the accustomed form; without which requisites, said vessel may be detained, to be adjudged by the competent tribunal, and may be declared legal prize, unless the said defects shall be satisfied or supplied by testimony entirely equivalent.

ARTICLE 20. It is further agreed, that the stipulations above expressed, relative to the visiting and examination of vessels, shall apply only to those which sail without convoy; and when said vessels shall be under convoy, the verbal declaration of the commander of the convoy, on his word of honor, that the vessels under his protection belong to the nation whose flag he carries, and, when they are bound to an enemy's port, that they have no contraband goods on board, shall be sufficient.

ARTICLE 21. It is further agreed, that in all cases the established courts for the prize causes, in the country to which the prizes may be conducted, shall alone take cognizance of them. And whenever such tribunal of either party shall pronounce judgment against any vessel or goods or property claimed by the citizens of the other party, the sentence or decree shall mention the reasons or motives on which the same shall have been founded, and an authenticated copy of the sentence or decree, and of all the proceedings in the case, shall, if demanded,

dante de las fuerzas bloqueadoras, intentase otra vez entrar; pero le será permitido ir à qualquiera otro puerto ó lugar que juzque conveniente. Ni ningun buque de una de las partes, que haya entrado en semejante puerto, ó lugar, antes que estuviese sitiado, bloqueado, ó envestido por la otra, sera impedido de dejar el tal lugar con su cargamento, ni si fuere hallado alli despues de la rendicion y entrega de semejante lugàr, estará el tal buque ó su cargamento sujeto à confiscacion, sino que seràn restituidos à sus dueños.

ARTICULO 18. Para evitar todo genero de desorden en la visita, y examen de los buques y cargamentos de ambas partes contratantes en alta mar, han convenido mutuamente, que siempre que un buque de guerra, publico ó particular se emontrase con un neutral de la otra parte contrante, el primero permanecerà fuera de tiro de cañon, y podrà mandàr su bote, condos ó tres hombres solamente, para ejecutár el dicho examen de los papeles concernientes à la propiedad y carga del buque, sin ocasionàr la menor estorcion violencia·ó mal tratamiento, por lo que los comandantes del dicho buque armado serán responsables, con sus personas y bienes; à cuyo efecto los comandantes de buques armados, por cuenta de particulares, estaràn obligados antes de entregarseles sus comisiones ó patentes, à dar fianza suficiente para responder de los perjuicios que causen. Y se ha convenido espresamente, que en ningun caso se exigira à la parte neutrál, que vaya à bordo del buque examinadór con el fin de exibir sus papeles, ó para cualquiera otro objeto sea el que fuere.

ARTICULO 19. Para evitar toda clase de vejamen y abuso en el examen de los papeles relativos à la propiedad de los buques pertenecientes à los ciudadanos de las dos partes contratantes, han convenido y convenien, que en caso de que una de ellas estuviere en guerra, los buques, y bajeles pertenecientes à los ciudadanos de la otra, seràn provistos con letras de màr, ó pasaportes, espresando el nombre, propiedad y tamaño del buque, como tambien el nombre y lugar de la residencia del maestre, ó comandante, à fin de que se vea que el buque, real y verdaderamente, pertenece à los ciudadanos de una de las partes; y han convenido igualmente, que estando cargados los espresados buques, ademas de las letras de mar, ó pasaportes, estaràn tambien provistos de certificatos, que contengan los por menores del cargamento, y el lugar de donde salió el buque, para que asi pueda saberse, si hay à su bordo algunos efectos prohibidos ó de contrabando, cuyos certificatos seràn hechos per los oficiales del lugár de la procedencia del buque, en la forma acostumbrada, sin cuyos requisitos el dicho buque puede ser detenido, para ser juzgado por el Tribunal competente, y puede ser declarado buena presa, à menos que satisfagan, ó suplan el defecto con testimonios enteramente equivalentes.

ARTICULO 20. Se ha convenido ademas, que las estipulaciones anteriores, relativas al examen y visita de buques, se aplicarán solamente á los que navegan sin conboy y que cuando los dichos buques estuvieren bajo de conboy, será bastante la declaracion verbal del comandanté del conboy, bajo su palabra de honór, de que los buques que están bajo su proteccion pertenecen a la nacion, cuya bandera llevan, y cuando se dirijen á un puerto enemigo, que los dichos buques no tienen á su bordo articulos de contrabando de guerra.

ARTICULO 21. Se ha convenido ademas, que en todos los casos que ocurran, solo los Tribunales establecidos para causas de presas, en el pais á que las presas sean conducidas, tomarán conocimiento de ellas. Y siempre que semejante tribunal de cualquiera de las partes, pronunciase sentencia contra algun buque ó efectos, ó propiedad reclamada por los ciudadanos de la otra parte, la sentencia ó decreto harà mencion de las razones ó motivos en que aquella se haya fundado, y se entregará sin demora alguna al comandante ó agente de dicho

be delivered to the commander or agent. of said vessel without any delay, he paying the legal fees for the same.

ARTICLE 22. Whenever. one of the contracting parties shall be engaged in war with another State, no citizen of the other contracting party shall accept a commission, or letter of marque, for the purpose of assisting or co-operating hostilely with the said enemy against the said party so at war, under the pain of being treated as a pirate.

ARTICLE 23. If, by any fatality, which cannot be expected, and which God forbid, the two contracting parties should be engaged in war with each other, they have agreed, and do agree, now for· then, that there shall be allowed the term of six months to the merchants residing on the coasts and in the· ports of each other, and the term of one year to those· who dwell in the interior, to arrange their business and transport their effects wherever they please, giving to them the safe conduct necessary for it, which may serve as a sufficient protection until they arrive at the designated port. The citizens of all other occupations, who may be established in the territories or dominions of the United States and of the Republic of Colombia, shall ·be respected and maintained in the full enjoyment of their personal liberty and property, unless their particular conduct shall cause them to forfeit this protection, which, in consideration of humanity, the· contracting parties' engage to give them.

ARTICLE 24. Neither the debts due from individuals of the one nation to the individuals of the other, nor shares nor moneys which they may have in public funds, nor in public or private banks, shall ever, in any event of war· or of national difference, be sequestered or confiscated.

ARTICLE 25. Both the contracting parties, being desirous of avoiding all inequality in relation· to their public communications and official intercourse, have agreed, and do agree, to grant to the envoys,' ministers, and other public agents, the same favors,' immunities, and exemptions which those of the most favored nation do or shall enjoy; it being understood that whatever favors, immunities, or privileges the United States of America or the Republic of Colombia may find it proper to give to the ministers and public agents of any other power, shall by the same act be extended to. those of each of the contracting· parties. .

ARTICLE 26. To make more effectual the protection which the United States and the Republic·of Colombia shall afford in future to the navigation and commerce·of the citizens of each other, they agree to receive and admit consuls and vice consuls in all the ports open to foreign·commerce, who shall enjoy in them all the rights, prerogatives, and immunities of the consuls and vice consuls of the most favored nation, each contracting party, however, remaining at liberty to except those ports and places in which the admission and residence of such consuls may not seem convenient. ·

ARTICLE 27. In order that the consuls· and vice consuls of the two contracting parties may enjoy the rights, prerogatives, and immunities· which belong to them by their public character, they shall, before entering on the exercise of their functions, exhibit their commission or patent in due form to the Government to which they are accredited, and having obtained ·their exequatur, they shall be held and considered as such by all the authorities, magistrates, and inhabitants in the consular district in which they reside.

ARTICLE 28. It is likewise agreed that the consuls, their secretaries, officers, and persons attached to the service of consuls, they not being citizens of the country in which the consul resides, shall be exempt from all, public service, and also from all kind of taxes, imposts, and contributions, except those which

buque, si lo solicitase, un testimonio autentico de la·. sentencia, ó decreto, ó de todo el proceso, pagando por él los derechos legales.

ARTICULO 22. Siempre que una de las partes contratantes estuviere empeñada en' guerra, con otro Estado, ningun ciudadano de la otra parte contratante· aceptara una comisión ó letra de marca para el objeto de ayudar ó co-operar hostilmente con el dicho enemigo, contra la dicha parte que esté asi en guerra, bajo la pena de ser tratado como pirata.

ARTICULO 23. Si por alguna fatalidad, que no puede esperarse, y que Dios no permita, las dos partes contratantes se viesen· empeñadas en guerra una con otra, han convenido y convienen de ahora para entonces, que se concederá el termino de seis meses á los comerciantes residentes en las costas y en los puertos de entrambas, y el· termino de un año á los que habitan en el interior, para arreglár sus negocios, y transportár· sus efectos á donde quieran, dandoles el salvo conducto necesario para ello, que les sirva de suficiente proteccion hasta que lleguen al puerto que designen. Los ciudadanos de otras ocupaciones, que se hallen establecidos en los territorios ó·dominios de·la Republica de Colombia, ó los Estados Unidos· de America, serán respetados, y mantenidos en el pleno goze de su libertad personal y propiedad, á menos que su conducta particular les haga perdér esta proteccion, que en consideracion á la humanidad, las partes contratantes se comprometen á prestarles.

ARTICULO 24. Ni las deudas contraidas por· los individuos de una nacion, .con los individuos de la otra, ni las acciones ó dineros, que puedan tenér en los fondos publicos, ó en los bancos. publicos, ó privados, serán jamas secuestrados ó confiscados en ningun caso de guerra, ó diferencia nacional. ·

ARTICULO 25. Deseando ambas partes contratantes, evitár toda diferencia, relativa á etiqueta en sus comunicaciones, y correspondencias diplomaticas han convenido asi mismo, y convienen en conceder á sus enviados, ministros, y otros 'agentes diplomaticos, los mismos favores, inmunidades, y esenciones de que gozan, ó gozaren en lo venidero de las naciones mas favorecidas, bien entendido que cualquier favór, inmunidad ó privilegio, que la Republica de Colombia· ó los Estados Unidos de America, tengan por conveniente dispensár á los enviados, ministros, y agentes diplomaticos de otras potencias, se haga por el mismo hecho estensivo á los de una y otra de las partes contratantes.

ARTICULO 26· Para hacér mas efectiva la proteccion, que la Republica de Colombia, y los Estados Unidos de America, darán en adelante á la navegacion y comercio de los ciudadanos de una y otra, se convienen en recibir y admitir consules, y vice consules· en todos los puertos abiertos al comercio estrangero; quienes gozarán en ellos todos los derechos, prerrogativas é inmunidades de los consules, y vice consules de la nacion mas favorecida, quedando no obstante en libertad 'cada parte contra., tante, para eceptuar aquellos· puertos y lugares en que la admision y residencia de semejantes consules, y vice consules no parezca· conveniente.

ARTICULO 27. Para que· los consules ·y· vice consules· de las dos partes contratantes, puedan gozar los·derechos, prerrogativas, é inmunidades, que les corresponden por su caracter. publico, antes de entrár en el ejercicio de sus funciones, presentarán su comision ó patente en la forma debida, al Gobierno con quien esten acreditados, y habiendó obtenidó el exequatur, serán tenidos, y considerados como tales, por todas· las autoridades, majistrados y habitantes del distrito consular en que residan.

. ARTICULO 28. ·Se ha convenido igualmente, que los consules, sus secretarios, oficiales y personas agre_gadas al servicio de los consulados (no siendo estas personas ciudadanos del pais en que el consul reside) estarán esentos de todo servicio' publico, y tambien de toda especie de pechos, impuestos, y contribu-

they shall be obliged to pay on account of commerce or their property, to which the citizens and inhabitants, native and foreign, of the country in which they reside are subject, being in everything besides subject to the laws of the respective States. The archives and papers of the consulate shall be respected inviolably, and under no pretext whatever shall any magistrate seize or in any way interfere with them.

Article 29. The said consuls shall have power to require the assistance of the authorities of the country for the arrest, detention, and custody of deserters from the public and private vessels of their country; and for that purpose they shall address themselves to the courts, judges, and officers competent, and shall demand the said deserters in writing, proving, by an exhibition of the registers of the vessel's or ship's roll, or other public documents, that those men were part of the said crews; and on this demand, so proved, (saving, however, where the contrary is proved,) the delivery shall not be refused. Such deserters, when arrested, shall be put at the disposal of the said consuls, and may be put in the public prisons at the request and expense of those who reclaim them, to be sent to the ships to which they belonged, or to others of the same nation. But if they be not sent back within two months, to be counted from the day of their arrest, they shall be set at liberty, and shall be no more arrested for the same cause.

Article 30. For the purpose of more effectually protecting their commerce and navigation, the two contracting parties do hereby agree, as soon hereafter as circumstances will permit them, to form a consular convention, which shall declare specially the powers and immunities of the consuls and vice consuls of the respective parties.

Article 31. The United States of America and the Republic of Colombia, desiring to make as durable as circumstances will permit the relations which are to be established between the two parties by virtue of this treaty or general convention of peace, amity, commerce, and navigation, have declared solemnly and do agree to the following points:

1st. The present treaty shall remain in full force and virtue for the term of twelve years, to be counted from the day of the exchange of the ratifications, in all he parts relating to commerce and navigation; and in all those parts which relate to peace and friendship, it shall be permanently and perpetually binding on both powers.

2d. If any one or more of the citizens of either party shall infringe any of the articles of this treaty, such citizen shall be held personally responsible for the same, and the harmony and good correspondence between the two nations shall not be interrupted thereby; each party engaging in no way to protect the offender or sanction such violation.

3d. If, (what, indeed, cannot be expected,) unfortunately, any of the articles contained in the present treaty shall be violated or infringed in any other way whatever, it is expressly stipulated that neither of the contracting parties will order or authorize any acts of reprisal, nor declare war against the other, on complaints of injuries or damages, until the said party considering itself offended shall first have presented to the other a statement of such injuries or damages, verified by competent proof, and demanded justice and satisfaction, and the same shall have been either refused or unreasonably delayed.

4th. Nothing in this treaty contained shall, however, be construed or operate contrary to former and existing public treaties with other sovereigns or States.

The present treaty, of peace, amity, commerce, and navigation, shall be approved and ratified by the President of the United States of America, by

ciones, eceptuando aquellas que esten obligadas á pagar por razon de comercio, o propiedad y á las cuales estan sujetos los ciudadanos, y habitantes naturales, y estrangeros del pais en que residen, quedando en todo lo demas, sujetos a las leyes de los respectivos Estados. Los archivos y papeles de los consulados serán respetados inviolablemente, y bajo ningun pretesto los occupara magistrado alguno, ni tendrá en ellos ninguna intervencion.

Articulo 29. Los dichos consules tendrán podér de requerir el auxilio de las autoridades locales, para la prision, detencion y custodia de los desertores de buques publicos y particulares de su pais, y para este objeto so dirigirán á los tribunales, jueces, y oficiales competentes, y pedirán los dichos desertores por escrito, probando por una presentacion de los registros de los buques, rol del equipage, ù otros documentos publicos, que aquellos, hombres eran parte de las dichas tripulaciones, y á esta demanda asi probada (menos no obstante cuando seprobare lo contrario) no se reusará la entrega. Semijantes desertores, luego que sean arrestados, se pondrán á disposicion de los dichos consules, y pueden ser depositados en las prisiones publicas, a solicitud y espensas de los que los reclaman, para ser enviados á los buques á que corresponden, ó á otros de la misma nacion. Pero si no fueren mandados dentro de dos meses contados des de el dia de su arresto, serán puestos en libertad, y no volverán a ser presos por la misma causa.

Articulo 30. Para protegér mas efectivamente su comercio y navigacion, las dos partes contratantes se convienen en formar luego que las circunstancias lo permitan, una convencion consular, que declare mas especialmente los poderes é inmunidades de los consules y vice consules de las partes respectivas.

Articulo 31. La Republica de Colombia y los Estados Unidos de America, deseando hacer tan duraderas y firmes, como las circunstancias lo permitan las relaciones que han de establecerse entre las dos potencias, en virtud del presente tratado ó convencion general de paz, amistad, navegacion, y comercio, han declarado solennemente y convienen en los puntos siguientes:

1°. El presente tratado permanencerá en su fuerza y vigor por el termino de doce años contados desde el dia del cange de las ratificaciones, en todos los puntos concernientes à comercio y navegacion, y en todos los demas puntos que se refieren á paz y amistad, será permanente, y perpetuamente obligatorio para ambas potencias.

2°. Si alguno, ó algunos de los ciudadanos de una ù otra parte infringiesen alguno de los articulos contenidos en el presente tratado, dichos ciudadanos serán personalmente responsables, sin que por esto se interrumpa la harmonia y buena correspondencia entre las dos naciones, comprometiendose cada una à no protegér de modo alguno al ofensor, ó sancionár semejante violacion.

3°. Si (lo que á la verdad no puede esperarse) desgraciadamente, alguno de los articulos contenidos en el presente tratado, fuesen en alguna otra manera violados, ó infringidos, se estipula espresamente que ninguna de las dos partes contratantes, ordenará, ó autorizará ningunos actos de represalia, ni declarará la guerra contra la otra por quejas de injurias, ó daños, hasta que la parte que se crea ofendida, haya antes presentado á la otra una esposicion de aquellas injurias, ó daños, verificada con pruebas y testimonios competentes, exigiendo justicia y satisfaccion, y esto haya sido negado, ó diferido sin razon.

4°. Nada de cuanto se contiene en el presente tratado, se construirá sin embargo, ni obrará, en contra de otros tratados publicos anteriores, y existentes con otros soberanos ó Estados.

El presente tratado de paz, amistad, navegacion, y comercio, será ratificado por el Presidente ó Vice Presidente de la Republica de Colombia, encar-

and with the advice and consent of the Senate thereof, and by the President of the Republic of Colombia, with the consent and approbation of the Congress of the same, and the ratifications shall be exchanged in the city of Washington, within eight months, to be counted from the date of the signature hereof, or sooner if possible.

In faith whereof, we, the plenipotentiaries of the United States of America and of the Republic of Colombia, have signed and sealed these presents.

Done in the city of Bogota, on the third day of October, in the year of our Lord one thousand eight hundred and twenty-four, in the forty-ninth year of the Independence of the United States of America and the fourteenth of that of the Republic of Colombia.

[L. S.]　　RICHARD C. ANDERSON, JR.
[L. S.]　　·PEDRO GUAL. .

gado del poder Ejecutivo, con consentimiento y aprobacion del Congreso de la misma, y por el Presidente .de los Estados Unidos de America, con consejo, y consentimiento del Senado de los mismos; y las ratificaciones serán cangeadas en la ciudad de Washington dentro de ocho meses contados desde este dia, ó antes si fuese posible.

En fe de lo cual. nosotros los plenipotenciarios de la Republica de Colombia, y de los Estados Unidos de America hemos firmado y sellado las presentes.

Dadas en la. ciudad de Bogota el dia tres de Octubre del año del Señor mil ocho cientos veinte-cuatro, decimo cuarto de la Independencia de la Republica de Colombia y cuadragesimo nono de la de los Estados Unidos de America.

PEDRO GUAL. ·
RICHARD C. ANDERSON, JR.

And whereas the said convention has been duly ratified on both parts, and the respective ratifications of the same were exchanged at Washington, on the twenty-seventh day of the present month, by Daniel Brent, Chief Clerk of the Department of State, and José Maria Salazar, LL. D., Fiscal of the High Court of Justice of the Republic of Colombia, and Envoy Extraordinary and Minister Plenipotentiary thereof, near the Government of the United States of America, on the part of their respective Governments:

Now, therefore, be it known that I, John Quincy Adams, President of the United States, have caused the said convention to be made public, to the end that the same, and every clause and article thereof, may be observed and fulfilled with good faith by the United States and the citizens thereof.

In witness whereof, I have hereunto set my hand, and caused the seal of the United States to be affixed. Done at the city of Washington, this thirty-first day of May, in the year of our Lord one [L. S.] thousand eight hundred and twenty-five, and of the Independence of the United States the forty-ninth.

　　　　　　　　　　　　　　　　　　　　JOHN QUINCY ADAMS.

By the President:
　H. CLAY, Secretary of State.

19TH CONGRESS.]　　　　　　　　No. 413.　　　　　　　[1ST SESSION.

GENERAL ·CONVENTION OF PEACE, AMITY, COMMERCE, AND NAVIGATION, WITH THE FEDERATION OF THE CENTRE OF AMERICA.

COMMUNICATED TO THE SENATE, IN EXECUTIVE SESSION, DECEMBER 15, 1825, AND THE INJUNCTION OF SECRECY SINCE REMOVED.

To the Senate of the United States:

I transmit herewith to the Senate, for its consideration, in reference to its ratification, a general: convention of peace, amity,.commerce, and navigation, between the United States of America and the Federation of the Centre of America, signed at this place, on the fifth instant, by the Secretary of State and the Minister Plenipotentiary from the Republic of Central America to the United States.

　　　　　　　　　　　　　　　　　　　　JOHN QUINCY ADAMS.

WASHINGTON, *December* 15, 1825.

General convention of peace, amity, commerce, and navigation, between the United States of America and the Federation of the Centre of America.

. The United States of America and the Federation of the Centre of America, desiring to make firm and permanent the peace and friendship which happily prevails between both nations, have resolved to fix, in. a manner clear, distinct, and positive, the rules which shall in future be religiously observed between the one and the other, by means of a treaty or general convention of peace, friendship, commerce, and navigation.

For this most desirable object, the President of the United States of America has conferred full powers on HENRY CLAY, their Secretary of State; and the Executive Power of the Federation of the Centre of America, on ANTONIO JOSÉ CANAS, a Deputy of the Constituent National Assembly for the Province of San Salvador, and Envoy Extraordinary and Minister Plenipotentiary of that Republic near the United

Convencion general de paz, amistad, commercio, y navegacion, entre la Confederacion de Centro-America i los Estados Unidos de America.

. La Federacion de Centro-America i los Estados-Unidos de America, deseando hacer firme i permanente la paz i amistad que felizmente existe entre · ambas potencias, han resuelto fijar, de una manera clara, distinta, y positiva, las reglas que deben observar religiosamente en lo venidero, per medio du un tratado ó convencion general de paz, amistad, comercio, y navegacion.

Con este muy deseable objeto, el Poder Ejecutivo de la Federacion de Centro-America ha conferidos plenos poderes à ANTONIO JOSÉ CANAS, Diputado de la Assemblea Nacional Constituyente por la Provincia de San Salvador, i Enviado Extraordinario i Ministro Plenipotenciario de la aquella Republica cerca de los Estados Unidos; y el Presidente de los Estados Unidos de America á HENRICO CLAY, su Secretario

States; who, after having exchanged their said full powers in due and proper form, have agreed to the following articles:

ARTICLE 1. There shall be a perfect, firm, and inviolable peace and sincere friendship between the United States of America and the Federation of the Centre of America, in all the extent of their possessions and territories, and between their people and citizens, respectively, without distinction of persons or places.

ARTICLE 2. The United States of America and the Federation of the Centre of America, desiring to live in peace and harmony with all the other nations of the earth, by means of a policy frank and equally friendly with all, engage mutually not to grant any particular favor to other nations, in respect of commerce and navigation, which shall not immediately become common to the other party, who shall enjoy the same freely, if the concession was freely made, or on allowing the same compensation, if the concession was conditional.

ARTICLE 3. The two high contracting parties, being likewise desirous of placing the commerce and navigation of their respective countries on the liberal basis of perfect equality and reciprocity, mutually agree that the citizens of each may frequent all the coasts and countries of the other, and reside and trade there, in all kind of produce, manufactures, and merchandise, and they shall enjoy all the rights, privileges, and exemptions, in navigation and commerce, which native citizens do or shall enjoy, submitting themselves to the laws, decrees, and usages there established, to which native citizens are subjected. But it is understood that this article does not include the coasting trade of either country, the regulation of which is reserved by the parties, respectively, according to their own separate laws.

ARTICLE 4. They likewise agree that whatever kind of produce, manufacture, or merchandise, of any foreign country, can be, from time to time, lawfully imported into the United States, in their own vessels, may be also imported in vessels of the Federation of the Centre of America; and that no higher or other duties, upon the tonnage of the vessel, or her cargo, shall be levied and collected, whether the importation be made in vessels of the one country or of the other; and, in like manner, that whatever kind of produce, manufactures, or merchandise, of any foreign country, can be, from time to time, lawfully imported into the Central Republic, in its own vessels, may be also imported in vessels of the United States, and that no higher or other duties, upon the tonnage of the vessel, or her cargo, shall be levied and collected, whether the importation be made in vessels of the one country or of the other. And they further agree, that whatever may be lawfully exported or re-exported, from the one country, in its own vessels, to any foreign country, may, in like manner, be exported or re-exported in the vessels of the other country. And the same bounties, duties, and drawbacks shall be allowed and collected, whether such exportation or re-exportation be made in vessels of the United States or of the Central Republic.

ARTICLE 5. No higher or other duties shall be imposed on the importation into the United States of any articles the produce or manufactures of the Federation of the Centre of America, and no higher or other duties shall be imposed on the importation into the Federation of the Centre of America of any articles the produce or manufactures of the United States than are, or shall be, payable on the like articles, being the produce or manufactures of any other foreign country; nor shall any higher or other duties or charges be imposed, in either of the two countries, on the exportation of any articles to the United States or to the Federation of the Centre of America, respectively, than such as are payable on the exportation of the like articles to any other foreign

de Estado, quienes, despues de haber canjeado sus espresados plenos poderes en debida¶i buena forma, han convenido en los articulos siguientes:

ARTICULO 1. Habra una paz, perfecta, firme, é inviolable, y amistad sincera entre la Federacion de Centro-America y los Estados Unidos de America, en todo la estencion de sus posesiones y territorios, y entre sus pueblos y ciudadanos, respectivamente, sin distincion de personas ni lugares.

ARTICULO 2. La Federacion de Centro-America y los Estados Unidos de America, deseando vivir en paz y harmonia con las demas naciones de la tierra, por medio de una politica franca é igualmente amistosa con todas, se obligan mutuamente à no conceder favores particulares à otras naciones, con respecto à comercio y navegacion, que no se hagan inmediatamente comun á una ù otra, quien gozará de los mismos libremente si la concesion fuese hecha libremente, ó prestando la misma compensacion si la concesion fuere condicional.

ARTICULO 3. Las dos altas partes contratantes, deseando tambien establecer el comercio y navegacion de sus respectivos paises sobre las liberales bases de perfecta igualdad y reciprocidad, convienen mutuamente que los ciudadanos de cada una podran frecuentar todas las costas y paises de la otra, y residir i traficar en ellos con toda clase de producciones, manufacturas, i mercaderias; i gozaran de todos los derechos, privilegios, y esempciones, con respecto à navegacion i commercio, que gozan ó gozaren los ciudadanos nativos, sometiendose á las leyes, decretos, é usos establecidos, á que estan sujetos dichos ciudadanos nativos. Pero debe entenderse que este articulo no comprende el comercio de costa de cada uno de los dos paises, cuya regulacion es reservada á las partes, respectivamente, segun sus propias i peculiares leyes.

ARTICULO 4. Igualmente convienen, que cualquiera clase de producciones, manufacturas ó mercaderias estrangeras que puedan ser, en cualquier tiempo, legalmente introducidas en la Republica Central en sus propios buques, puedan tambien ser introducidas en los buques de los Estados Unidos; i que no se impondran ó cobraran otras ó mayores derechos de tonelada ó por el cargamento, ya sea que la importacion se haga en buques de la una ó de la otra. De la misma manera que cualesquiera clase de producciones, manufacturas ó mercaderias estrangeras que pueden ser en cualquier tiempo legalmente introducidas en los Estados Unidos en sus propios buques, puedan tambien ser introducidas en los buques de la Federacion de Centro-America; i que no se impondran ó cobraran otros ó mayores derechos de tonelada ó por el cargamento ya sea que la importacion se haga en buques de la una ó de la otra. Convienen ademas, que todo lo que pueda ser legalmente esportado ó re-esportado de uno de los dos paises, en sus buques propios para un pais estrangero pueda de la misma manera ser esportado ó re-esportado en los buques de el otro. Y los mismos derechos, premios ó descuentos se concederan i cobraran ya sea que tal exportacion, ó re-exportacion se haga en los buques de la Republica Central ó de los Estados Unidos.

ARTICULO 5. No se impondran otros ó mayores derechos sobre la importacion de cualquier articulo, produccion ó manufactura de los Estados Unidos en la Federacion de Centro-America, i no se impondran otros ó mayores derechos sobre la importacion de cualquier articulo, produccion ó manufactura de la Federacion de Centro-America en los Estados Unidos, que los que se pagan ó pagaren en adelante por iguales articulos, produccion ó manufactura de cualquiera pais estrangero; ni se impondran otros ó mayores derechos ó cargas en cualquiera de los dos paises sobre la esportacion de cualesquiera articulos para la Federacion de Centro-America ó para los Estados Unidos respectivamente, que los que se pagan ó pagaren en adelante por la esportacion de

country; nor shall any prohibition be imposed on the exportation or importation of any articles the produce or manufactures of the United States, or of the Federation of the Centre of America, to or from the territories of the United States, or to or from the territories of the Federation of the Centre of America, which shall not equally extend to all other nations.

ARTICLE 6. It is likewise agreed that it shall be wholly free for all merchants, commanders of ships, and other citizens of both countries, to manage themselves, their own business in all the ports and places subject to the jurisdiction of each other, as well with respect to the consignment and sale of their goods and merchandise by wholesale or retail, as with respect to the loading, unloading, and sending off their ships; they being, in all these cases, to be treated as citizens of the country in which they reside, or at least to be placed on a footing with the subjects or citizens of the most favored nation.

ARTICLE 7. The citizens of neither of the contracting parties shall be liable to any embargo, nor be detained with their vessels, cargoes, merchandise, or effects, for any military expedition, nor for any public or private purpose whatever, without allowing to those interested a sufficient indemnification.

ARTICLE 8. Whenever the citizens of either of the contracting parties shall be forced to seek refuge or asylum in the rivers, bays, ports, or dominions, of the other, with their vessels, whether merchant or of war, public or private, through stress of weather, pursuit of pirates or enemies, they shall be received and treated with humanity, giving to them all favor and protection for repairing their ships, procuring provisions, and placing themselves in a situation to continue their voyage without obstacle or hindrance of any kind.

ARTICLE 9. All the ships, merchandise, and effects belonging to the citizens of one of the contracting parties, which may be captured by pirates, whether within the limits of its jurisdiction or on the high seas, and may be carried or found in the rivers, roads, bays, ports, or dominions, of the other, shall be delivered up to the owners, they proving, in due and proper form, their rights before the competent tribunals; it being well understood that the claim should be made within the term of one year by the parties themselves, their attorneys, or agents of the respective Governments.

ARTICLE 10. When any vessel belonging to the citizens of either of the contracting parties shall be wrecked, foundered, or shall suffer any damage on the coasts, or within the dominions of the other, there shall be given to them all assistance and protection, in the same manner which is usual and customary with the vessels of the nation where the damage happens, permitting them to unload the said vessel, if necessary, of its merchandise and effects, without exacting for it any duty, impost, or contribution whatever, until they may be exported.

ARTICLE 11. The citizens of each of the contracting parties shall have power to dispose of their personal goods within the jurisdiction of the other, by sale, donation, testament, or otherwise; and their representatives, being citizens of the other party, shall succeed to their said personal goods, whether by testament or ab intestato, and they may take possession thereof, either by themselves or others acting for them, and dispose of the same at their will, paying such dues only as the inhabitants of the country wherein said goods are shall be subject to pay in like cases. And if, in the case of real estate, the said heirs would be prevented from entering into the possession of the inheritance on account of their character of aliens, there shall be granted to them the term of three years to dispose of the same, as they may think proper, and to withdraw the proceeds without molestation, and

iguales articulos para cualquiera otro pais estrangero; ni se establecera prohivicion sobre la importacion ó esportacion de cualesquiera articulos, produccion ó manufactura de los territorios de la Federacion de Centro-America para los de los Estados Unidos, ó de los territorios de los Estados Unidos para los de la Federacion de Centro-America, que no sea igualmente estensiva á las otras naciones.

ARTICULO 6. Se conviene ademas, que será enteramente libre y permitido, a los comerciantes, comandahtes de buques, y otros ciudadanos de ambos paises. el manejar sus negocios, por si mismos, en todos los puertos y lugares sujetos à la jurisdiccion de uno ù otro, asi respecto à las consignaciones y ventas por mayor y menor de sus efectos y mercaderias, como de la carga, descarga y despacho de sus buques, debiendo en todos estos casos, ser tratados como ciudadanos del pais en que residan, ó al menos puestos sobre un pie igual con los subditos ó ciudadanos de las naciones mas favorecidas.

ARTICULO 7. Los ciudadanos de una ù otra parte, no podràn ser embargados ni detenidos con sus embarcaciones, tripulaciones, mercaderias, y efectos comerciales de su pertenencia, para alguna espedicion militàr, usos publicos, ó particulares cualesquiera que sean, sin conceder à los interesados una suficiente indemnizacion.

ARTICULO 8. Siempre que los ciudadanos de alguna de las partes contratantes se vieren precisados à buscar refujio, ó asilo en los rios, bahias, puertos, ó dominios de la otra, consus buques, ya sean mercantes, ó de guerra, publicos ó particulares, por mal tiempo, persecucion de piratas ó enemigos, seràn recibidos y tratados con humanidad, dandoles todo favor y proteccion, para reparar sus buques, procurar viveres, y ponerse en situacion de continuar su viaje, sin obstaculo ó estorbo de ningun genero.

ARTICULO 9. Todos los buques, mercaderias y efectos pertenecientes a los ciudadanos de una de las partes contratantes, que sean apresados por piratas, bien sea dentro de los limites de su jurisdiccion, ó en alta mar, y fueren llevados, ó hallados en los rios, radas, bahias, puertos, ó dominios de la otra, seràn entregados à sus dueños, probando estos en la forma propia y debida sus derechos ante los tribunales competentes; bien entendido que el reclamo ha de hacerse dentro del termino de un año por las mismas partes, sus apoderados ó agentes de los respectivos Gobiernos.

ARTICULO 10. Cuando algun buque perteneciente à los ciudadanos de alguna de las partes contratantes, naufrague, encalle, ó sufra alguna averia, en las costas, ó dentro de los dominios de la otra, se les dará toda ayuda y proteccion, del mismo modo que es uso y costumbre, con los buques de la nacion en donde suceda la averia, permitiendoles descargar el dicho buque (si fuere necesario) de sus mercaderias y efectos, sin cobrar por esto hasta que sean esportados, ningun derecho, impuesto ó contribucion.

ARTICULO 11. Los ciudadanos de cada una de las partes contratantes, tendran pleno poder para disponer de sus bienes personales dentro de la jurisdiction de la otra, por venta, donacion, testamento, ó de otro modo; y sus representantes, siendo ciudadanos de la otra parte, succederán à sus dichos bienes personales, ya sea por testamento ó ab intestato, y podran tomar posecion de ellos, ya sea por si mismos ó por otros, que obren por ellos, y disponer de los mismos, segun su voluntad, pagando aquellas cargas, solamente, que los habitantes del pais en donde estan los referidos bienes, estuvieren sujetos á pagar en iguales casos. Y si en el caso de bienes raices, los dichos herederos fuesen impedidos de entrà en la posecion de la herencia por razon de su caracter de estrangeros, se les dará el termino de tres años para disponer de ella como juzguen convenientе, y para estraér el producto sin

exempt from all duties of detraction, on the part of the Government of the respective States.

ARTICLE 12. Both the contracting parties promise and engage formally to give their special protection to the persons and property of the citizens of each other, of all occupations, who may be in the territories subject to the jurisdiction of the one or the other, transient or dwelling therein, leaving open and free to them the- tribunals of justice for their judicial recourse, on the same terms which are usual and customary with the natives or citizens of the country in which they may be; for which they may employ, in defence of their rights, such advocates, solicitors, notaries, agents, and factors, as they may judge proper in all their trials at law; and such citizens or agents shall have free opportunity to be present at the decisions and sentences of the tribunals in all cases which may concern them, and likewise at the taking of all examinations and evidence which may be exhibited in the said trials.

ARTICLE 13. It is likewise agreed that the most perfect and entire security of conscience shall be enjoyed by the citizens of both the contracting parties in the countries subject to the jurisdiction of the one and the other, without their being liable to be disturbed or molested on account of their religious belief, so long as they respect the laws and established usages of the country. Moreover, the bodies of the citizens of one of the contracting parties who may die in the territories of the other shall be buried in the usual burying grounds, or in other decent and suitable places, and shall be protected from violation or disturbance.

ARTICLE 14. It shall be lawful for the citizens of the United States of America and of the Federation of the Centre of America to sail with their ships with all manner of liberty and security, no distinction being made who are the proprietors of the merchandise laden thereon, from any port to the places of those who are now, or hereafter shall be, at enmity with either of the contracting parties. It shall likewise be lawful for the citizens aforesaid to sail with the ships and merchandise before mentioned, and to trade with the same liberty and security from the places, ports, and havens of those who are enemies of both or either party, without any opposition or disturbance whatsoever, not only directly from the places of the enemy before mentioned to neutral places, but also from one place belonging to an enemy to another place belonging to an enemy, whether they be under the jurisdiction of one power or under several. And it is hereby stipulated that free ships shall also give freedom to goods, and that everything shall be deemed to be free and exempt which shall be found on board the ships belonging to the citizens of either of the contracting parties, although the whole lading, or any part thereof, should appertain to the enemies of either, contraband goods being always excepted. It is also agreed in like manner that the same liberty be extended to persons who are on a free ship, with this effect, that, although they be enemies to both or either party, they are not to be taken out of that free ship, unless they are officers or soldiers, and in the actual service of the enemies: Provided, however, and it is hereby agreed, that the stipulations in this article contained, declaring that the flag shall cover the property, shall be understood as applying to those powers only who recognize this principle; but if either of the two contracting parties shall be at war with a third, and the other neutral, the flag of the neutral shall cover the property of enemies whose Governments acknowledge this principle, and not of others.

ARTICLE 15. It is likewise agreed, that, in the case where the neutral flag of one of the contracting parties shall protect the property of the enemies of the other by virtue of the above stipulation, it shall

molestia, y escutos de todo derecho de deduccion, por parte del Gobierno de los respectivos Estados.

ARTICULO 12. Ambas partes contratantes se comprometen y obligan formalmente á dar su proteccion especial á las personas y propiedades de los ciudadanos de cada una reciprocamente transeuntes ó habitantes detodas occupaciones, en los territorios sujetos á la jurisdiccion de una y otra, dejandoles abiertos y libres los tribunales de justicia, para sus recursos judiciales, en los mismos terminos que son de uso y costumbre para los naturales ó ciudadanos del pais en que residan; para lo cual, podrán emplear en defensa de sus derechos aquellos abogados, procuradores, escribanos, agentes, ó factores que juzguen conveniente, en todos sus asuntos y litigios; y dichos ciudadanos ó agentes tendrán la libre facultad de estar presentes en las decisiones y sentencias de los tribunales, en todos los casos que les conciernan, como igualmente al tomar todos los examenes y declaraciones que se ofrezcan en- los dichos litigios.

ARTICULO 13. Se conviene igualmente en que los ciudadanos de ambas partes contratantes gozen la mas perfecta y entera seguridad de conciencia en los paises sugetos á la jurisdiccion da una ù otra, sin quedar por ello espuestos á ser inquietados ó molestados en razon de su creencia religiosa, mientras que respeten las leyes y usos establecidos. Ademas de esto, podrán sepultarse los cadaveres de los ciudadanos de una de las partes contratantes, que fallecieren en los territorios de la otra, en los cementerios acostumbrados, ó en otros lugares decentes, y adecuados, los cuales, serán protejidos contra toda violacion ó trastorno.

ARTICULO 14. Será licito á los ciudadanos de la Federacion de Centro-America, y de los Estados Unidos de America, navegár con sus buques, con toda seguridad y libertad, de cualquiera puerto á las plazas ó lugares de los que son ó fueren en adelante enemigos de cualquiera de las dos partes contratantes, sin hacerse distincion de quienes son los dueños de las mercaderias cargadas en ellos. Será igualmente licito á los referidos ciudadanos navegár con sus buques y mercaderias mencionadas y traficár con la misma libertad y seguridad, de los lugares, puertos y enseñadas de los enemigos de ambas partes, ó de alguna de ellas, sin ninguna oposicion, ó disturbio cualquiera, no solo directamente de los lugares de enemigo arriba mencionados á lugares neutros, sino tambien de un lugar perteneciente á unáenemigo, á otro enemigo, ya sea que esten bajo la jurisdiccion de una potencia, ó bajo la de diversas. Y queda aqui estipulado, que los buques libres, dan tambien libertad á las mercaderias, y que se ha de considerar libre y esento todo lo que se hallare á bordo de los buques pertenecientes á los ciudadanos de cualquiera de las partes contratantes, aunque toda la carga ó parte de ella pertenezca á enemigos de una ù otra, eceptuando siempre los articulos de contrabando de guerra. Se conviene tambien del mismo modo, en que la misma libertadáse estienda á las personas que se encuentren á bordo de buques libres, con el fin de que aunque dichas personas sean enemigos de ambas partes ó de alguna de ellas, no deban ser estraidos de los buques libres, ó menos que sean oficiales ó soldados en actual servicio de los enemigos: á condicion no obstante, y se conviene aqui en esto, que las estipulaciones contenidas en el presente articulo, declarando que el pabellon cubre la propiedad, se entenderán aplicables solamente á aquellas potencias que reconocen este principio; pero si alguna de los dos partes contratantes, estuviere en guerra con una tercera, y la otra permaneciese neutrál, la bandera de la neutrál cubrira la propiedad de los enemigos, cuyos Gobiernos reconozcan este principio y no de otros.

ARTICULO 15. Se conviene igualmente que en el caso de que la bandera neutrál de una de las partes contratantes protega las propiedades de los enemigos de la otra en virtud de lo estipulado arriba,

always be understood that the neutral property found on board such enemy's vessels shall be held and considered as enemy's property, and as such shall be liable to detention and confiscation, except such property as was put on board such vessel before the declaration of war, or even afterwards, if it were done without the knowledge of it; but the contracting parties agree that, two months having elapsed after the declaration, their citizens shall not plead ignorance thereof. On the contrary, if the flag of the neutral does not protect the enemy's property, in that case the goods and merchandise of the neutral embarked in such enemy's ships shall be free.

ARTICLE 16. This liberty of navigation and commerce shall extend to all kinds of merchandise, excepting those only which are distinguished by the name of contraband, and under this name of contraband or prohibited goods shall be comprehended—

1st. Cannons, mortars, howitzers, swivels, blunderbusses, muskets, fuzees, rifles, carbines, pistols, pikes, swords, sabres, lances, spears, halberds, and granades, bombs, powder, matches, balls, and all other things belonging to the use of these arms.

2dly. Bucklers, helmets, breast plates, coats of mail, infantry belts, and clothes made up in the form and for military use.

3dly. Cavalry belts and horses, with their furniture.

4thly. And generally all kinds of arms and instruments of iron, steel, brass, and copper, or of any other materials manufactured, prepared, and formed expressly to make war by sea or land.

ARTICLE 17. All other merchandise and things not comprehended in the articles of contraband explicitly enumerated and classified as above shall be held and considered as free, and subjects of free and lawful commerce, so that they may be carried and transported in the freest manner by both the contracting parties, even to places belonging to an enemy, excepting only those which are at that time besieged or blockaded; and to avoid all doubt in this particular, it is declared that those only are besieged or blockaded which are actually attacked by a belligerent force capable of preventing the entry of the neutral.

ARTICLE 18. The articles of contraband before enumerated and classified, which may be found in a vessel bound for an enemy's port, shall be subject to detention and confiscation, leaving free the rest of the cargo and the ship, that the owners may dispose of them as they see proper. No vessel of either of the two nations shall be detained on the high seas on account of having on board articles of contraband, whenever the master, captain, or supercargo of said vessel will deliver up the articles of contraband to the captor, unless the quantity of such articles be so great and of so large a bulk that they cannot be received on board the capturing ship without great inconvenience; but, in this and in all other cases of just detention, the vessel detained shall be sent to the nearest convenient and safe port, for trial and judgment according to law.

ARTICLE 19. And whereas it frequently happens that vessels sail for a port or place belonging to an enemy without knowing that the same is besieged, blockaded, or invested, it is agreed that every vessel so circumstanced may be turned away from such port or place, but shall not be detained, nor shall any part of her cargo, if not contraband, be confiscated, unless, after warning of such blockade or investment from the commanding officer of the blockading forces, she shall again attempt to enter; but she shall be permitted to go to any other port or place she shall think proper. Nor shall any vessel of either, that may

deberá siempre entenderse, que las propiedades neutrales encontradas á bordo de tales buques enemigos, han de tenerse y considerarse como propiedades · enemigas, y como tales, estarán sujetas á detencion, y confiscacion; eseptuando solomente aquellas propiedades que hubiesen sido puestas à bordo de tales buques antes de la declaracion de la guerra, y aun despues, si hubiesen sido embarcadas en dichos buques, sin tenèr noticia de la guerra; y se conviene, que pasados dos meses despues de la declaracion, los ciudadanos de una y otra parte no podrán alegà que la ignoraban. Por el contrario, si la bandera neutral, no protegiese las propiedades enemigas, entonces serán libres los efectos y mercaderias de la parte neutrál, embarcadas en buques enemigos.   ;

ARTICULO 16. Esta libertad de navigacion y comercio se estenderà á todo genero de mercaderias, eceptuando aquellas solamente, que ´se distinguen con el nombre de contrabando, y bajo este nombre de contrabando ó efectos prohibidos se comprenderán:

1°. Cañones, morteros, obuces, pedreros, trabucos, mosquetes, fusiles, rifles, carabinas, pistolas, picas, espados, sables, lanzas, chuzos, alabardas, y granadas, bombas, polvoro, mechas, balas, con las demas cosas correspondientes al uso de estas armas.

2°. Escudos, casquetes, corazas,· cotas de malla, fornituras, y vestidos hechos en forma, y á usanza militar.

3°. Bandoleras, y caballos junto con sus armas y arneses.

4°. Y generalmente toda especie de armas é instrumentos de hierro, acero, bronce, cobre, y otras materias cualesquiera, manufacturadas, preparadas´, y formadas espresamente para hacér la guerra por mar ó tierra.

ARTICULO 17. Todas las demas mercaderias, y efectos no comprendidos en los articulos de contrabando esplicitamente enumerados, y classificados en el articulo anterior, serán tenidos, y reputados por libres, y de licito y libre comercio de modo, que ellos puedan sér transportados, y´llevados de la manera mas libre, por los ciudadanos de ambas partes contratantes, aun á los lugares pertenecientes á un enemigo de una ù otra, eceptuando solamente aquellos lugares ó plazas, que estàn al mismo tiempo sitiadas ó bloqueados; y para evitar toda duda en el particulàr, se declaran sitiadas ó bloqueadas àquellas plazas, que en la actualidad estuviesen átacadas por una fuerza de un beligerante capaz de impedir la entrada del neutral.

ARTICULO 18. Los articùlos de contrabando antes enumerados y classificados, que se hallen en un buque destinado à puerto enemigo estarán sujetos à detencion y confiscacion; dejando libre el resto del cargamento y ell buque, para que los dueños puedan disponer de ellos como lo crean conveniente. Ningun buque de cualquiera de las dos naciones, serà detenido, por tener à bordo articulos de contrabando, siempre que el maestre, capitan, ó sobrecargo de dicho buque quiera entregar los articulos de contrabando al apresador, à ménos que la cantidad de estos articulos sea tan grande y de tanto volumen, que no puedan sér recibidos à bordo del buque apresadór, sin grandes inconvenientes; pero en este, como en todos los otros casos de justa detencion, el buque detenido serà enviado al puerto mas inmediato, comodo, y seguro, para ser juzgado y sentenciado conforme à las leyes.

ARTICULO 19. Y por cuanto frecuentemente sucede que los buques navegan para un puerto ó lugàr perteneciente à un enemigo, sin saber que aquel esté sitiado, bloqueado ó envestido, se conviene en que todo buque en estas circumstancias se pueda hacer volver de dicho puerto, ó lugar; pero no serà detenido, ni confiscada parte alguna de su cargamento, no siendo contrabando; à ménos que despues de la intimacion de semejante bloqueo ó ataque, por el comandante de las fuerzas bloqueadoras, intentase otra vez entrar; pero le serà permitido ir à qualquiera otro puerto ó lugar que juzque conveniente. Ni

have entered into such port before the same was actually besieged, blockaded, or invested by the other, be restrained from quitting such place with her cargo, nor, if found therein after the reduction and surrender, shall such vessel or her cargo be liable to confiscation, but they shall be restored to the owners thereof.

Article 20. In order to prevent all kind of disorder in the visiting and examination of the ships and cargoes of both the contracting parties on the high seas, they have agreed mutually, that whenever a vessel of war, public or private, shall meet with a neutral of the other contracting party, the first shall remain out of cannon shot, and may send its boat, with two or three men only, in order to execute the said examination of the papers concerning the ownership and cargo of the vessel, without causing the least extortion, violence, or ill treatment, for which the commanders of the said armed ships shall be responsible with their persons and property; for which purpose, the commanders of said private armed vessels shall, before receiving their commissions, give sufficient security to answer for all the damages they may commit. And it is expressly agreed that the neutral party shall in no case be required to go on board the examining vessel for the purpose of exhibiting her papers, or for any other purpose whatever.

Article 21. To avoid all kinds of vexation and abuse in the examination of the papers relating to the ownership of the vessels belonging to the citizens of the two contracting parties, they have agreed, and do agree, that in case one of them should be engaged in war, the ships and vessels belonging to the citizens of the other must be furnished with sea letters or passports, expressing the name, property, and bulk of the ship, as also the name and place of habitation of the master or commander of said vessel, in order that it may thereby appear that the ship really and truly belongs to the citizens of one of the parties; they have likewise agreed that, such ships being laden, besides the said sea letters or passports, shall also be provided with certificates, containing the several particulars of the cargo, and the place whence the ships sailed, so that it may be known whether any forbidden or contraband goods be on board the same; which certificates shall be made out by the officers of the place whence the ship sailed, in the accustomed form; without which requisites, said vessel may be detained, to be adjudged by the competent tribunal, and may be declared legal prize unless the said defects shall be satisfied, or supplied by testimony entirely equivalent.

Article 22. It is further agreed, that the stipulations above expressed, relative to the visiting and examination of vessels, shall apply only to those which sail without convoy; and when said vessels shall be under convoy, the verbal declaration of the commander of the convoy, on his word of honor, that the vessels under his protection belong to the nation whose flag he carries, and, when they are bound to an enemy's port, that they have no contraband goods on board, shall be sufficient.

Article 23. It is further agreed, that in all cases the established courts for prize causes, in the country to which the prizes may be conducted, shall alone take cognizance of them. And whenever such tribunal of either party shall pronounce judgment against any vessel or goods or property claimed by the citizens of the other party, the sentence or decree shall mention the reasons or motives on which the same shall have been founded, and an authenticated copy of the sentence or decree, and of all the proceedings in the case, shall, if demanded, be delivered to the commander or agent of said vessel without any delay, he paying the legal fees for the same.

ningun buque de una de las partes, que haya entrado en semejante puerto, ó lugar, antes que estuviese sitiado, bloqueado, ó envestido por la otra, sera impedido de dejar el tal lugar con su cargamento, ni si fuere hallado alli despues de la rendicion y entrega de semejante lugàr, estarà el tal buque ó su cargamento sujeto à confiscacion, sino que serán restituidos á sus dueños.

Articulo 20. Para evitar todo genero de desorden en la visita, y examen de los buques y cargamentos de ambas partes contratantes en alta mar, han convenido mutuamente, que siempre que un buque de guerra, publico ó particular se emontrase con un neutral de la otra parte contrante, el primero permanecerà fuera de tiro de cañon, y podrà mandàr su bote, con dos ó tres hombres solamente, para ejecutár el dicho examen de los papeles concernientes à la propiedad y carga del buque, sin ocasionàr la menor estorcion violencia á mal tratamiento, por lo que los comandantes del dicho buque armado seràn responsables, con sus personas y bienes; à cuyo efecto los comandantes de buques armados, por cuenta de particulares, estaràn obligados antes de entregarseles sus comisiones ó patentes, à dar fianza suficiente para respondér de los perjuicios que causen. Y se ha convenido espresamente, que en ningun caso se exigira à la parte neutrál, que vaya à bordo del buque examinadór con el fin dé exibir sus papeles, ó para cualquiera otro objeto sea el que fuere.

Articulo 21. Para evitar toda clase de vejamen y abuso en el examen de los papeles relativos à la propiedad de los buques pertenecientes à los ciudadanos de las dos partes contratantes, han convenido y convienen, que en caso de que una de ellas estuviere en guerra, los buques, y bajeles pertenecientes à los ciudadanos de la otra, seràn provistos con letras de màr, ó pasaportes, espresando el nombre, propiedad y tamaño del buque, como tambien el nombre y lugar de la residencia del maestre ó comandante, à fin de que se vea que el buque, real y verdaderamente pertenece à los ciudadanos de una de las partes; y han convenido igualmente, que estando cargados los espresados buques, ademas de las letras de mar, ó pasaportes, estaràn tambien provistos de certificatos, que contengan los por menores del cargamento, y el lugar de donde salió el buque, parà que asi pueda saberse, si hay à su bordo algunos efectos prohibidos ó de contrabando, cuyos certificatos seràn hechos per los oficiales del lugár de la procedencia del buque, en la forma acostombrada, sin cuyos requisitos el dicho buque puede ser detenido, para ser juzgado por el tri bunal competente, y puede ser declarado buena presa, à menos que satisfagan, ó suplan el defecto con testimonios enteramente equivalentes.

Articulo 22. Se ha convenido ademas, que las estipulaciones anteriores, relativas al examen y visita de buques, se aplicarán solamente á los que navegan sin conboy y que cuando los dichos buques estuvieren bajo de conboy, será bastante la declaracion verbal del comandante del conboy, bajo su palabra de honór, de que los buques que están bajo su proteccion pertenecen a la nacion, cuya bandera llevan, y cuando se dirijen á un puerto enemigo, que los dichos buques no tienen à su bordo articulos de contrabando de guerra.

Articulo 23. Se ha convenido ademas que en todos los casos que ocurran, solo los tribunales establecidos para causas de presas, en el pais á que las presas sean conducidas, tomarán conocimiento de ellas. Y siempre que semejante tribunal de cualquiera de las partes, pronunciase sentencia contra algun buque, ó efectos, ó propiedad reclamada por los ciudadanos de la otra parte, la sentencia ó decreto harà mencion de las razones ó motivos en que aquella se haya fundado, y se entregarà sin demora alguna al comandante ó agente de dicho buque, si lo solicitase, un testimonio autentico de la sentencia, ó decreto, ó de todo el proceso, pagando por él los derechos legales.

ARTICLE 24. Whenever one of the contracting parties shall be engaged in war with another State, no citizen of the other contracting party shall accept a commission, or letter of marque, for the purpose of assisting or co-operating hostilely with the said party so at war, under the pain of being treated as a pirate.

ARTICLE 25. If, by any fatality which cannot be expected, and which God forbid, the two contracting parties should be engaged in a war with each other, they have agreed, and do agree, now for then, that there shall be allowed the term of six months to the merchants residing on the coasts and in the ports of each other, and the term of one year to those who dwell in the interior, to arrange their business, and transport their effects wherever they please, giving to them the safe conduct necessary for it, which may serve as a sufficient protection until they arrive at the designated port. The citizens of all other occupations, who may be established in the territories or dominions of the United States and of the Federation of the Centre of America, shall be respected and maintained in the full enjoyment of their personal liberty and property, unless their particular conduct shall cause them to forfeit this protection, which, in consideration of humanity, the contracting parties engage to give them.

ARTICLE 26. Neither the debts due from individuals of the one nation to the individuals of the other, nor shares, nor moneys which they may have in public funds, nor in public or private banks, shall ever, in any event of war or of national difference, be sequestered or confiscated.

ARTICLE 27. Both the contracting parties, being desirous of avoiding all inequality in relation to their public communications and official intercourse, have agreed, and do agree, to grant to the envoys, ministers, and other public agents, the same favors, immunities, and exemptions, which those of the most favored nation do or shall enjoy; it being understood that whatever favors, immunities, or privileges the United States of America or the Federation of the Centre of America may find it proper to give to the ministers and public agents of any other power, shall by the same act be extended to those of each of the contracting parties.

ARTICLE 28. To make more effectual the protection which the United States and the Federation of the Centre of America shall afford in future to the navigation and commerce of the citizens of each other, they agree to receive and admit consuls and vice consuls in all the ports open to foreign commerce, who shall enjoy in them all the rights, prerogatives, and immunities of the consuls and vice consuls of the most favored nation; each contracting party, however, remaining at liberty to except those ports and places in which the admission and residence of such consuls may not seem convenient.

ARTICLE 29. In order that the consuls and vice consuls of the two contracting parties may enjoy the rights, prerogatives, and immunities which belong to them by their public character, they shall, before entering on the exercise of their functions, exhibit their commission or patent in due form to the Government to which they are accredited; and having obtained their *exequatur*, they shall be held and considered as such by all the authorities, magistrates, and inhabitants in the consular district in which they reside.

ARTICLE 30. It is likewise agreed that the consuls, their secretaries, officers, and persons attached to the service of consuls, they not being citizens of the country in which the consul resides, shall be exempt from all public service, and also from all kind of taxes, imposts, and contributions, except those which they shall be obliged to pay on account of commerce or their property, to which the citizens and inhabitants, native and foreign, of the country in which

ARTICULO 24. Siempre que una de las partes contratantes estuviere empeñada en guerra, con otro Estado, ningun ciudadano de la otra parte contratante aceptara una comision ó letra de marca para el objeto de ayudár ó co-operar hostilmente con el dicho enemigo, contra la dicha parte que esté así en guerra, bajo la pena de ser tratado como pirata.

ARTICULO 25. Si por alguna fatalidad, que no puede esperarse, y que Dios no permita, las dos partes contratantes se viesen empeñadas en guerra una con otra, han convenido y convienen de ahora para entonces, que se concederá el termino de seis meses á los comerciantes residentes en las costas y en los puertos de entrambas, y el termino de un año á los que habitan en el interior, para arreglár sus negocios, y transportár sus efectos á donde quieran, dandoles el salvo conducto necesario para ello, que les sirva de suficiente proteccion hasta que lleguen al puerto que designen. Los ciudadanos de otras ocupaciones, que se hallen establecidos en los territorios ó dominios de la Federacion de Centro-America, ó los Estados Unidos de America, serán respetados, y mantenidos en el pleno goze de su libertad personal y propiedad, á menos que su conducta particular les haga perdér esta proteccion, que en consideracion á la humanidad, las partes contratantes se comprometen á prestarles.

ARTICULO 26. Ni las deudas contraidas por los individuous de una Nacion, con los individuous de la otra, ni las acciones ó dineros, que puedan tenér en los fondos publicos, ó en los bancos publicos, ó privados, serán jamas secuestrados ó confiscados en ningun caso de guerra, ó diferencia nacional.

ARTICULO 27. Deseando ambas partes contratántes, evitár, toda diferencia, relativa á etiqueta en sus comunicaciones, y correspondencias diplomaticas han convenido asi mismo, y convienen en conceder á sus enviados, ministros, y otros agentos diplomaticos, los mismos favores, inmunidades, y esenciones de que gozan, ó gozarén en lo venidero los de las naciones mas favorecidas, bien entendido que cualquier favór, inmunidad ó privilegio, que la Federacion de Centro-America, ó los Estados Unidos de America, tengan por conveniente dispensár á los enviados, ministros, y agentos diplomaticos de otras potencias, se haga por el mismo hecho estensivo á los de una y otra de las partes contratantes.

ARTICULO 28. Para hacér mas efectiva la proteccion, que la Federacion de Centro-America, y los Etados Unidos de America, darán en adelante á la navegacion y comercio de los ciudadanos de una y otra, se convienen en recibir y admitir consules y vice consules en todos los puertos abiertos al comercio estrangero, quienes gozarán en ellos todos los derechos, prerrogativas é inmunidades de los consules y vice consules de la nacion mas favorecida quedando no obstante en libertad cada parte contratante, para eceptuar aquellos puertos y lugares en que la admision y residencia de semejantes consules y vice-consules no parezca conveniente.

ARTICULO 29. Para que los consules y vice consules de las dos partes contratantes puedan gozar los derechos, prerrogativas, é inmunidades que les correspoden por su caracter publico, antes de entrár en el ejercicio de sus funciones, presentarán su comision ó patente en la forma debida, al Gobierno con quien esten acreditados; y habiendo obtenido el *exequatur*, serán tenidos y considerados como tales por todas las autoridades, majistrados, y habitantes del distrito consular en que residan.

ARTICULO 30. Se ha convenido igualmente, que los consules, sus secretarios, oficiales y personas agregadas al servicio de los consulados (no siendo estas personas ciudadanos del pais en que el consul reside) estarán esentos de todo servicio publico, y tambien de toda especie de pechos, impuestos, y contribuciones, eceptuando aquellas que esten obligados á pagar por razon de comercia, ó propiedad, y á las cuales estan sujetos los ciudadanos, y habi-

they reside are subject, being in everything besides subject to the laws of the respective States. The archives and papers of the consulate shall be respected inviolably, and under no pretext whatever shall any magistrate seize or in any way interfere with them.

ARTICLE 31. The said consuls shall have power to require the assistance of the authorities of the country for the arrest, detention, and custody of deserters from the public and private vessels of their country; and for that purpose they shall address themselves to the courts, judges, and officers competent, and shall demand the said deserters in writing, proving, by an exhibition of the registers of the vessel's or ship's roll, or other public documents, that those men were part of the said crews; and on this demand, so proved, (saving, however, where the contrary is proved,) the delivery shall not be refused. Such deserters, when arrested, shall be put at the disposal of the said consuls, and may be put in the public prisons at the request and expense of those who reclaim them, to be sent to the ships to which they belonged, or to others of the same nation. But if they be not sent back within two months, to be counted from the day of their arrest, they shall be set at liberty, and shall be no more arrested for the same cause.

ARTICLE 32. For the purpose of more effectually protecting their commerce and navigation, the two contracting parties do hereby agree, as soon hereafter as circumstances will permit them, to form a consular convention, which shall declare specially the powers and immunities of the consuls and vice consuls of the respective parties.

ARTICLE 33. The United States of America and the Federation of the Centre of America, desiring to make as durable as circumstances will permit the relations which are to be established between the two parties by virtue of this treaty or general convention of peace, amity, commerce, and navigation, have declared solemnly and do agree to the following points:

1. The present treaty shall remain in full force and virtue for the term of twelve years, to be counted from the day of the exchange of the ratifications, in all the parts relating to commerce and navigation; and in all those parts which relate to peace and friendship, it shall be permanently and perpetually binding on both powers.

2. If any one or more of the citizens of either party shall infringe any of the articles of this treaty, such citizen shall be held personally responsible for the same, and the harmony and good correspondence between the two nations shall not be interrupted thereby, each party engaging in no way to protect the offender or sanction such violation.

3. If, (which, indeed, cannot be expected,) unfortunately, any of the articles contained in the present treaty shall be violated or infringed in any other way whatever, it is expressly stipulated that neither of the contracting parties will order or authorize any acts of reprisal, nor declare war against the other, on complaints of injuries or damages, until the said party considering itself offended shall first have presented to the other a statement of such injuries or damages, verified by competent proof, and demanded justice and satisfaction, and the same shall have been either refused or unreasonably delayed.

4. Nothing in this treaty contained shall, however, be construed or operate contrary to former and existing public treaties with other sovereigns or States.

The present treaty of peace, amity, commerce, and navigation, shall be approved and ratified by the President of the United States of America, by and with the advice and consent of the Senate thereof, and by the Government of the Federation of the Centre of America, and the ratifications shall

tantes naturales, y estrangeros del pais en que residen, quedando en todo lo demas, sujetos a las leyes de los respectivos Estados. Los archivos y papeles de los consulados serán respetados inviolablemente, y bajo ningun pretesto los occupará magistrado alguno, ni tendrá en ellos ninguna intervencion.

ARTICULO 31. Los dichos consules tendrán podér de requerir el auxilio de las autoridades locales, para la prision, detencion y custodia de los desertores de buques publicos y particulares de su pais, y para este objeto se dirigirán á los tribúnales, jueces, y oficiales competentes, y pedirán los dichos desertores por escrito, probando por una presentacion de los registros de los buques, rol del equipage, ù otros documentos publicos, que aquellos hombres eran parte de las dichas tripulaciones, y á esta demanda asi probada (menos no obstante cuando se probare lo contrario) no se reusará la entrega. Semijantes desertores, luego que sean arrestados, se pondrán á disposicion de los dichos consules, y pueden ser depositados en las prisiones publicas, à solicitud y espensas de los que los reclamen, para ser enviados á los buques á que corresponden, ó á otros de la misma nacion. Pero si no fueren mandados dentro de dos meses contados des de el dia de su arresto, serán puestos en libertad, y no volverán a ser presos por la misma causa.

ARTICULO 32. Para protegér mas efectivamente su comercio y navegacion, las dos partes contratantes se convienen en formar luego que las circunstancias lo permitan, una convencion consulár, que declare mas especialmente los poderes é inmunidades de los consules y vice consules de las partes respectivas.

ARTICULO 33. La Federacion de Centro-America, y los Estados Unidos de America, deseando hacer tan duraderas y firmes, como las circunstancias lo permitan las relaciones que han de establecerse entre entre las dos potencias, en virtud del presente tratado ó convencion general de paz, amistad, navegacion, y comercio, han declarado solennemente y convienen en los puntos siguientes:

1. El presente tratado permanecerá en su fuerza y vigor por el termino de doce años contados desde el dia del cange de las ratificaciones, en todos los puntos concernientes à comercio y navegacion, y en todos los demas puntos que se refieren á paz y amistad, será permanente, y perpetuamente obligatorio para ambas potencias.

2. Si alguno, ó algunos de los ciudadanos de una ù otra parte infringiesen algun de los articulos contenidos en el presente tratado, dichos ciudadanos serán personalmente responsables, sin que por esto se interrumpa la harmonia y buena correspondencia entre las dos naciones, comprometiendose cada una à no protegér de modo alguno al ofenser ó sancionár semejante violacion.

3. Si (lo que á la verdad no puede esperarse) desgraciadamente, alguno de los articulos contenidos en el presente tratado, fuesen én alguna otra manera violados, ó infringidos, se estipula espresamente que ninguna de las dos partes contratantes, ordenará, ó autorizará ningunos actos de represalia, ni declarará la guerra contra la otra por quejas de injurias, ó daños, hasta que la parte que se crea ofendida, haya antes presentado á la otra una esposicion de aquellas injurias, ó daños, verificada con pruebas y testimonios competentes, exigiendo justicia y satisfaccion, y esto haya sido negado, ó diferido sin razon.

4. Nada de cuanto se contiene en el presente tratado, se construirá sin embargo, ni obrará, en contra de otros tratados publicos anteriores, y existentes con otros soberanos ó Estados.

El presente tratado de paz, amistad, comercio, y navegacion, será ratificado por el Gobierno de la Federacion de Centro America y por el Presidente de los Estados Unidos de America, con consejo, y consentimiento del Senado de los mismos; y las ratificaciones serán cangeadas en la ciudad de Guate-

be exchanged in the city of Guatemala, within eight months from the date of the signature hereof, or sooner, if possible.

In faith whereof, we, the plenipotentiaries of the United States of America and of the Federation of the Centre of America have signed and sealed these presents.

Done in the city of Washington, on the fifth day of December, in the year of our Lord one thousand eight hundred and twenty-five, in the fiftieth year of the independence of the United States of America, and the fifth of that of the Federation of the Centre of America, in duplicate.

H. CLAY.   [L. S.]
ANTONIO JOSÉ CANAS. [L. S.]

mala dentro de ocho meses contados desde este dia, ó antes si fuese posible.

En fe de lo cual nosotros los plenipotentiarios de la Federacion de Centro-America, y de los Estados Unidos de America hemos firmado y sellado las presentes.

Dadas en la ciudad de Washington, el dia cinco de Deciembre del año del Señor mil ocho cientos veinti cinco quinto de la independencia de la Federacion de Centro-America y quinquagesimo de la de los Estados Unidos de America, por duplicado.

ANTONIO JOSÉ CANAS. [L. S.]
H. CLAY.   [L. S.]

CORRESPONDENCE WITH GREAT BRITAIN RELATIVE TO THE SUPPRESSION OF THE SLAVE TRADE.

COMMUNICATED TO THE HOUSE OF REPRESENTATIVES DECEMBER 27, 1825.

To the House of Representatives of the United States:

In compliance with a resolution of the House of Representatives of the 20th instant, I transmit, herewith, a report from the Secretary of State, with copies of such portions of the correspondence between the United States and Great Britain, on the subject of the convention for suppressing the slave trade, as have not heretofore been and which can be communicated without detriment to the public interest.

JOHN QUINCY ADAMS.

WASHINGTON, *December 27, 1825.*

DEPARTMENT OF STATE, *Washington, December 22, 1825.*

The Secretary of State, in compliance with a resolution of the House of Representatives of the 20th instant, which has been referred to him, requesting the President of the United States to communicate to that House copies of such portions of the correspondence between the United States and Great Britain, on the subject of the convention for suppressing the slave trade, as have not heretofore been and which can be communicated without detriment to the public interest, has the honor to submit, herewith, to the President, copies of all the correspondence upon that subject which is embraced by the call of the House.

Respectfully submitted.

H. CLAY.

Papers sent.

Mr. Addington to Mr. Adams, March 2, 1825. (Copy.)
Mr. Clay to Mr. Addington, April 6, 1825. (Copy.)
Mr. Addington to Mr. Clay, April 9, 1825. (Copy.)

Mr. Addington to Mr. Adams.

WASHINGTON, *March 2, 1825.*

SIR: On the 6th of November last I had the honor to inform you that I had received full powers from his Majesty to conclude and sign, with this Government, a convention, *verbatim* the same as that entered into on the 13th March, last year, between Great Britain and the United States, with all the amendments subsequently effected in it by the Senate, the erasure of the words "and America," in the first article, excepted.

In reply to that communication, you did me the honor to acquaint me that the President had decided upon referring the whole subject to Congress, whereby it became necessary for you to postpone giving a definitive answer to my proposal.

This resolution of the President was, at the commencement of the session, carried into effect; and I understand that the subject has been under the consideration of Congress. You will, therefore, I trust, sir, allow me now to request to be made acquainted with the definitive intention of the President with respect to the proposition submitted by me on behalf of his Majesty's Government.

I have the honor to be, with distinguished consideration, sir, your most obedient humble servant,

H. U. ADDINGTON.

Hon. JOHN QUINCY ADAMS.

Mr. Clay to Mr. Addington.

DEPARTMENT OF STATE, *Washington, April* 6, 1825.

SIR: I have the honor to inform you that the delay in the transmission of a definitive answer to your note of the 6th of November last has proceeded from an anxious desire on the part of the late President of the United States to ascertain the practicability of reconciling, if possible, the views of the Government of the United States with those which are entertained by that of his Britannic Majesty in respect to the convention for more effectually suppressing the slave trade. With that object, the correspondence with your Government, and the convention in which it terminated, together with what has since passed between the two Governments, both here and at London, were submitted to Congress during its late session. Of that reference you were apprised by the note of my predecessor of the 4th December last. It has so happened that neither the Senate nor the House of Representatives has expressed, directly, any opinion on the subject. But, on another convention, having the same object, concluded with the Republic of Colombia on the 10th day of December, 1824, which was formed after the model of that which is pending between the Governments of the United States and Great Bitrain, the Senate has expressed a very decided opinion. In the Colombian convention, the coasts of America were excepted from its operation, and yet, notwithstanding this conciliating feature, the Senate, after full deliberation, in the exercise of its proper constitutional powers, has, by a large majority, deemed it inexpedient to consent to and advise the ratification of this convention.

The Government of his Britannic Majesty is well acquainted with the provision of the Constitution of the United States, by which the Senate is a component part of the treaty-making power; and that the consent and advice of that branch of Congress are indispensable in the formation of all treaties. According to the practice of this Government, the Senate is not ordinarily consulted in the initiatory state of a negotiation, but its consent and advice are only invoked, after a treaty is concluded, under the direction of the President, and submitted to its consideration. Each of the two branches of the treaty-making authority is independent of the other, whilst both are responsible to the States and to the people, the common sources of their respective powers. It results, from this organization, that, in the progress of the Government, instances may sometimes occur of a difference of opinion between the Senate and the Executive as to the expediency of a projected treaty, of which the rejection of the Colombian convention affords an example. The people of the United States have justly considered that, if there be any inconveniences in this arrangement of their executive powers, those inconveniences are more than counterbalanced, by the greater security of their interests, which is effected by the mutual checks which are thus interposed. But it is not believed that there are any inconveniences to foreign powers of which they can with propriety complain. To give validity to any treaty, the consent of the contracting parties is necessary. As to the mode by which that consent shall be expressed, it must necessarily depend with each upon its own peculiar constitutional arrangement. All that can rightly be demanded in treating is to know the contingencies on the happening of which that consent is to be regarded as sufficiently testified. This information the Government of the United States has always communicated to the foreign powers with which it treats, and to none more fully than to the United Kingdom of Great Britain and Ireland. Nor can it be admitted that any just cause of complaint can arise out of the rejection by one party of a treaty which the other has previously ratified. When such a case occurs, it only proves that the consent of both, according to the constitutional precautions which have been provided for manifesting that consent, is wanting to make the treaty valid. One must necessarily precede the other in the act of ratification; and if, after a treaty be ratified by one party, a ratification of it be withheld by the other, it merely shows that one is, and the other is not, willing to come under the obligations of the proposed treaty.

I am instructed by the President to accompany these frank and friendly explanations by the expression of his sincere regret that, from the views which are entertained by the Senate of the United States, it would seem to be unnecessary and inexpedient any longer to continue the negotiation respecting the slave convention, with any hope that it can be made to assume a form satisfactory to both parties. The Government of his Britannic Majesty insists, as an indispensable condition, that the regulated right of search, proposed in the convention, should be extended to the American coasts as well as to those of Africa and the West Indies. The Senate, even with the omission of America, thinks it unadvisable to ratify the Colombian convention. And it is, therefore, clearly to be inferred that a convention with his Britannic Majesty, with a similar omission, would not receive the approbation of the Senate. The decision of the Senate shows that it has made up its deliberate judgment, without any regard to the relative state of the military or commercial marine, for all the considerations belonging to a view of that subject would have urged the Senate to an acceptance of the Colombian convention. It is hoped, therefore, that his Britannic Majesty cannot fail to perceive that the Senate has been guided by no unfriendly feeling towards Great Britain.

Before closing this note, I must express my regret that I am unable to concur with you in the view which you have been pleased to present of the act of the British Parliament, by which it has denounced as piratical the slave trade, when exercised by British subjects. It is acknowledged that the Government of the United States considered such a denunciation as expedient, preliminary to the conclusion of the projected convention. But the British Parliament, doubtless upon its own sense of the enormity of the offence, deemed it proper to affix to it the character and penalties of piracy. However much it may be supposed to have been actuated by an accommodating spirit towards the United States, it can hardly be imagined that it would have given that denomination to the fact of trading in slaves from motives of concession merely, contrary to its own estimate of the moral character of that act. The Executive of the United States believed that it might conduce to the success of the negotiation, if the British Parliament would previously declare, as the United States had done, the slave trade to be piratical. But it did not follow, from the passage of that act, that any treaty, in which the negotiation might terminate, was to be taken out of the ordinary rule by which all treaties are finally submitted to the scrutiny and sanction of the respective Governments. No peculiar advantage has accrued to the United States from the enactment of that British law. Its continued existence, moreover, now depends upon the pleasure of the British Parliament.

But there is no disposition to dwell longer on this subject. The true character of the whole negotiation cannot be misconceived. Great Britain and the United States have had in view a common end of great humanity, entitled to their highest and best exertions. With respect to the desire of attaining that end, there is no difference of opinion between the Government of his Britannic Majesty and that of the United States in any of its branches. But the Senate has thought that the proposed convention was an instrument not adapted to the accomplishment of that end, or that it was otherwise objectionable. And, without the concurrence of the Senate, the convention cannot receive the constitutional sanctions of the United States. Without indulging, therefore, unavailing regrets, it is the anxious hope of the President that the Government of his Britannic Majesty should see, in all that has occurred, nothing towards it unfriendly on the part of the United States, and nothing that ought to slacken their separate or united exertions in the employment of all other practical modes to effectuate the great object, so dear to both, of an entire extirpation of a traffic which is condemned by reason, religion, and humanity.

I pray you, sir, to accept the assurance of my distinguished consideration.

H. CLAY.

HENRY U. ADDINGTON, Esq., *Chargé d'Affaires from Great Britain.*

Mr. Addington to Mr. Clay.

WASHINGTON, *April* 9, 1825.

SIR: I have the honor to acknowledge the receipt of your letter of the 6th instant, in which you announce to me the definitive decision of the President with regard to the convention for the more effectual suppression of the slave trade, which I had the honor to submit for the acceptance of this Government on the 6th of November last.

In expressing my regret at the failure of the benevolent efforts which have been employed in a cause so dear to humanity, I may venture to assure you that, however deeply his Majesty's Government may deplore the present disappointment of their hopes, they will consider the unfortunate issue of this business as in nowise affecting the friendly feelings which exist between the two Governments, and will accept, with pleasure, the expression of the President's desire that every exertion should still be used for effecting the entire extirpation of that odious traffic which the convention was designed to suppress.

I cannot dismiss this subject without a brief observation on that part of your letter in which you animadvert upon the argument employed in mine of the 6th of November last, relative to the act passed by the British Parliament for denouncing the slave trade as piracy. The expressions used by you would lead to the belief that I had represented the passage of that act, on the part of Great Britain, as rendering it *imperative* on the American Government to accede to the convention, even at the expense of a sacrifice of their constitutional prerogatives.

A reference to the expressions of my letter will, I apprehend, at once demonstrate the erroneousness of this impression, by showing that I put the case as a point of conscience, not one of right, and that I urged the argument above alluded to in the form of an appeal, not of a demand.

The denunciation of the slave trade as piracy by the British statute was made by this Government a *sine qua non* to the signature of the convention. As far as Great Britain was concerned, that proceeding, although perfectly conformable to the views of Parliament, *quo ad morality*, was one of pure supererogation, and conferred no power towards the suppression of the slave trade not possessed before. Had the Government of the United States not expressly desired the enactment of that statute it would never have been passed; but, being passed, its revocation, although certainly within the competence of Parliament, is now, by the interposition of subsequent events, rendered tantamount to morally impracticable.

These circumstances will, I apprehend, amply justify both the form of the argument which I built upon then, and the warmth with which I urged it.

I offer the preceding remarks, not by any means with a view to invite to further discussion, but simply in order to obviate all misconstruction of the meaning of words already employed by me.

I have the honor, sir, to renew to you the assurance of my distinguished consideration.

H. U. ADDINGTON.

Hon. HENRY CLAY, *Secretary of State.*

19TH CONGRESS.]   No. 415.   [1ST SESSION.

CLAIMS OF ELIPHALET LOUD, SAMUEL BAILEY, AND ISRAEL THORNDIKE, ON THE RUSSIAN GOVERNMENT.

COMMUNICATED TO THE HOUSE OF REPRESENTATIVES JANUARY 6, 1826.

Mr. FORSYTH, from the Committee on Foreign Affairs, to whom, by a resolution of the House of the 9th of December last, was referred the petition of Eliphalet Loud and Samuel Bailey; and, by a resolution of the House of the 3d of January instant, the claim of Israel Thorndike on the Russian Government, have had the said petition and claim under consideration, and report:

That Eliphalet Loud and Samuel Bailey, inhabitants of the town of Weymouth, Massachusetts, represent themselves as the principal owners of the ship Commerce; that, in the year 1807, the said ship sailed from Boston to Leghorn, where she discharged her cargo; that she proceeded thence to Manfredonia, in the Gulf of Venice, and loaded with a cargo of wheat for Lisbon, under a contract with a merchant of Leghorn; that on her passage from Manfredonia to Lisbon the vessel was in distress by reason of the choking of the pumps, and consequently attempted to put into the island of Corfu; that in so doing she was captured by a Russian gun-boat, and condemned by a prize court sitting in Corfu, to which court neither the captain of the Commerce, nor any of the ship's company, nor counsel on their behalf, was admitted; that the ship's crew was left wholly destitute of money or means of return to America; that appeal was made from the decision of the prize court to the court of St. Petersburg, through Leavit Harris, esq., the American consul in that city; and that the successive ministers of the United States to the court of St. Petersburg have been charged by the American Government to present this case to the consideration of his Imperial Majesty the Emperor of all the Russias for indemnity.

The committee further report, that the claim of Israel Thorndike, of Boston, is for indemnity for the loss of the brigantine Hector and her cargo, the property of the said Thorndike; that this vessel, while pursuing, as the claimant is fully persuaded, a lawful commerce, was captured by his Imperial Majesty's frigate Venus, and carried into the island of Tenedos; that she was, with her cargo, condemned by the officers of the Russian fleet, in the cabin of the Admiral's ship, assuming the functions of a prize court, to which irregular court the captain of the Hector was not admitted; that due appeal was made to the court at St. Petersburg, through the American consul, Leavit Harris, esq., and that application has been made, in behalf of the claimants, by the successive ministers of the United States at St. Petersburg, to the Russian Government, up to the year 1819.

By a report of John Quincy Adams, esq., then Secretary of State, bearing date April 17, 1820,* it appears that the foregoing representations of the claimants are believed to be true; and from the same report it appears that, including the appeal made to the Russian Government by Mr. Harris, the American consul at St. Petersburg, at least three distinct representations of these cases had been made by the ministers of the United States of America to the Government of his Imperial Majesty the Emperor of all the Russias. The last of these being a memorial addressed by Mr. G. W. Campbell to Count Nesselrode, the Russian Minister of Foreign Affairs, under date of June 6, 1819, was communicated to the Senate of the United States with the report of the Secretary of State just mentioned. From this report, and from a communication made by the present Secretary of State to the Committee of Foreign Affairs, on the 27th of December last, the committee learn that no answer has ever been returned by the Russian Government to these representations, made to that Government by our ministers under the special instructions of the President of the United States.

More than six years having elapsed since the last of these representations was made, no answer to it from the Russian Government can now be expected; and the committee infer, from the note of the Secretary of State last alluded to, that the Executive has desisted from the repetition of appeals to the justice of his Imperial Majesty, which have so long remained not only unsuccessful but unnoticed. Whether a happier effect might be produced by a representation directly made by the Executive of the United States to the Russian minister in this country, it is not the province of the Committee of Foreign Affairs to decide. Under this view of the subject, not deeming it advisable to recommend any legislative measure to the House, the Committee of Foreign Affairs submit the following resolution:

Resolved, That Eliphalet Loud and Samuel Bailey have leave to withdraw their petition, and that the Committee of Foreign Affairs be discharged from the further consideration of the claim of Israel Thorndike.

COMMITTEE OF FOREIGN RELATIONS, HOUSE OF REPRESENTATIVES, *December* 23, 1825.

SIR: By order of the Committee of Foreign Relations, of the House of Representatives, I have to request a copy, from the Department of State, of the statement presented in October, 1809, to the Government of Russia, by Leavit Harris, Consul General of the United States, of the claims of the owners of the ship Commerce, Captain Tirrell, captured by an Imperial privateer, carried into, and condemned in, Corfu, in 1807, by the committee of prizes of that island; also, the answer of the Russian Government to the reclamation of our minister in favor of the owners of said vessel.

I am, sir, respectfully, your most obedient,

JOHN FORSYTH, C. C. F. R., H. of R.

Hon. H. CLAY, *Secretary of State.*

DEPARTMENT OF STATE, *Washington, December* 27, 1825.

SIR: I have the honor to state, for the information of the committee, and in reference to the request in your letter of the 23d instant, that a search has been made through the letters from Mr. Leavit Harris, formerly Consul General of the United States at St. Petersburg, to this Department, and that the statement to which you refer is not to be found here. It would seem probable, indeed, that a transcript of it was communicated directly by Mr. Harris to the legation of the United States at St. Petersburg, and that it was never sent to this office. On the 6th of June, 1819, Mr. Campbell presented a note to the Russian Government, in relation to the claim to which the statement refers—the claim of the Weymouth Importing Company—as Mr. Adams, his predecessor, had done before; to which note no answer has since been received from that Government, nor was any ever given to the note of Mr. Adams.

I am, with great respect, sir, your obedient and very humble servant,

H. CLAY.

Hon. JOHN FORSYTH, *Chairman of Committee of Foreign Relations of the House of Representatives of the United States.*

* This report and the memorial of G. W. Campbell will be found in volume 4 Foreign Relations, page 635.

No. 416.

CORRESPONDENCE WITH FRANCE RELATIVE TO DESERTIONS FROM FRENCH SHIPS IN THE UNITED STATES.

COMMUNICATED TO THE HOUSE OF REPRESENTATIVES JANUARY 23, 1826.

DEPARTMENT OF STATE, *January 5, 1826.*

SIR: In reply to your letter of the 3d instant, transmitting a copy of a resolution of the House of Representatives, instructing the Committee of Foreign Relations to inquire into the expediency of making provision, by law, for the more complete execution of the 6th article of the convention with France, of June 24, 1822, touching the delivery of deserters, and requesting any information in the Department of State on the subject of that resolution, I have the honor now to communicate—

1st. Copy of a correspondence which has taken place with the French minister, in regard to the interpretation and execution of the 6th article of the convention;

2d. Copy of a letter from the Department of State, addressed to the mayor of Norfolk; and

3d. Copy of a letter, under date of 29th December, 1825, from the mayor of Norfolk to Mr. Hersant, vice consul of France at Norfolk.

The above correspondence shows that, from the opinion in which both the Executive of the United States and the representative of France concur, as to the meaning of the 6th article of the convention, the mayor of Norfolk dissents; and, according to his letter to Mr. Hersant, that the attorney general of Virginia, to whom he had appealed for advice, has confirmed the correctness of his declaration, that he did not possess the authority to lend his official assistance in the recovery of French sailors who had deserted from the public ships of France. Not having seen the opinion of that law officer of Virginia, the ground upon which it is placed, or the extent of its scope, cannot be now stated. Whatever they may be, it is presumed that the magistracy of that State will act in conformity to his opinion, and will decline, in the cases in which he thinks they ought to withhold, their co-operation in the recovery of French deserters.

I have the honor to be, with great respect, your obedient servant,

H. CLAY.

Hon. JOHN FORSYTH, *Chairman of the Committee of Foreign Relations,*
House of Representatives, United States.

Inclosures.

No. 1. Baron de Mareuil to Mr. Adams, October 3, 1824, (translation.)
No. 2. Same to Mr. Clay, October 4, 1825, (translation.)
No. 3. Mr. Holt to Mr. Hersant, September 29, 1825, (copy.)
No. 4. Mr. Wright to same, September 29, 1825, (copy.)
No. 5. Mr. Clay to Mr. Holt and Mr. Wright, November 7, 1825, (copy.)
No. 6. Same to Baron de Mareuil, November 7, 1825, (copy.)
No. 7. Baron de Mareuil to Mr. Clay, November 16, 1825, (translation.)
No. 8. Mr. Clay to Baron de Mareuil, December 19, 1825, (copy.)
No. 9. Baron de Mareuil to Mr. Clay, December 24, 1825, (translation.)
No. 10. Mr. Holt to Mr. Hersant, December 16, 1825, (copy.)
No. 11. Same to same, December 29, 1825, (copy.)

The Baron de Mareuil to Mr. Adams.

[Translation.]

WASHINGTON, *October 3, 1824.*

SIR: The French squadron which is in Hampton Roads has experienced some desertion in their crews. The vice consul of France residing at Norfolk took the necessary steps to obtain the arrest of these deserters, agreeably to the 6th article of the maritime and commercial convention of the 24th of June, 1822; and having only, on this subject, to acknowledge the readiness of the magistrates to whom he applied, he attributes his want of success hitherto to a circumstance of form, with which I have the honor to make you acquainted.

The convention stipulates that, to obtain the delivery of deserters, the respective consuls must address themselves to the *courts, judges, and officers competent:* consequently, the consul must address himself to the magistrate of the county in which the vessel is stationed from which the desertion took place; but it happens, from the very division of the territory of each State, that the particular competence of each magistrate being restricted, the deserters may easily, in the space of a day, shift from the counties several times, and the mandate obtained in the one being of no force in the other, it is very easy for them to escape the researches directed against them.

The same inconvenience does not exist in France, where the tribunals are permanent, where their competence is less limited, and where, moreover, their mandates, by means of a simple formality, have force through the whole Kingdom.

It is therefore true, that the intention of the 6th article of the convention to give, in a just and complete reciprocity, to the commerce of the two countries a sufficient protection, is partly eluded, to the detriment of France, and it becomes indispensable that the Federal Government be pleased to find means for re-establishing, in this regard, the perfect equality which the spirit of the treaty demands.

With this view I have thought it my duty to address you, sir, and to request you to call all the attention, which the President cannot fail to give it, to a point which so nearly touches the commercial interests of the two countries.

Accept, sir, the assurances of my very high consideration.

BARON DE MAREUIL.

The Baron de Mareuil to Mr. Clay.

[Translation.]

WASHINGTON, *October* 4, 1825.

SIR: On the 3d of October, last year, I had the honor to address the Department of State, to call its attention to certain difficulties relative to the execution of the 6th article of the convention of 1822, and to measures to be taken in the States of the Union, for securing the surrender of marine deserters. My letter still remaining without answer, I proposed to revert to this matter, when a fact still more grave should put me to the necessity of demanding of you an immediate explanation.

During the stay of the French brig, the Endymion, at Norfolk, one of her sailors having disappeared from on board, the vice consul of France immediately applied to the mayor of the city and to the judge of the county, from the one the assistance, and from the other the warrant necessary for the seizure of the deserter and sending him on board. Both formally refused it, and under the pretext, equally new and unexpected, that the 6th article of the convention was only applicable to the sailors of merchant vessels, and not to those of ships-of-war.

As this is the first time in three years that a distinction so strange has been advanced, and as I cannot believe that it had the approbation of the Government, I shall abstain from discussing it; but I pray you, sir, to be pleased to put me right in this regard, and to cause the necessary orders to be given, that a similar refusal on the part of the local authorities may no more fetter the execution of stipulation, so formal and so important to the maritime interests of the two States.

I send herewith a copy of the two answers made to Mr. Hersant.

Accept, sir, the assurances of my very high consideration.

BARON DE MAREUIL.

VICE CONSULATE OF FRANCE AT NORFOLK.

Copy of a letter addressed to the Vice Consul of France, at Norfolk, by Mr. Holt, Mayor of said city.

NORFOLK, *September* 29, 1825.

SIR: I have to acknowledge the receipt of your letter of the 28th instant, informing me of the desertion of a sailor from his most Catholic Majesty's brig Endymion, and requesting me to issue an order for his arrest and delivery to that vessel, in conformity to the convention between France and the United States, signed on the 22d of June, 1822.

There exists no law of our General and State Government that authorizes a magistrate of this Commonwealth to cause a deserter from a foreign national or private vessel-of-war to be apprehended and restored to such vessel; nor is it presumed that the convention to which you refer confers the power, but is solely applicable to cases of desertion from those employed between the two countries for the purposes of commerce. The sixth article provides that "the contracting parties, wishing to favor their mutual commerce, by affording in their ports every necessary assistance to their respective vessels, have agreed that the consuls and vice consuls may cause to be arrested the sailors, being part of the crews of the vessels of their respective nations, who shall have deserted from the said vessels, in order," &c.

I have the honor to be, sir, with great respect, your very obedient servant,

JOHN E. HOLT.

A true copy.   HERSANT.

VICE CONSULATE OF FRANCE AT NORFOLK.

Copy of a letter addressed by Mr. Stephen Wright, Judge of the county of Norfolk, to the Vice Consul of France, in said city.

NORFOLK COUNTY, *September* 29, 1825.

SIR: I have the honor, in reply to your note of yesterday requesting a warrant to apprehend a deserter from the Endymion, a French vessel-of-war, to state that the construction given to the sixth article of the convention by the Commonwealth's attorney does not relate to deserters from vessels-of-war. This opinion I feel myself bound to respect. Your application to the higher authorities may produce a more liberal construction.

Accept, sir, an assurance of my high respect and consideration. Respectfully, your obedient servant,

STEPHEN WRIGHT.

A true copy.   HERSANT.

Mr. Clay to Mr. Holt and Mr. Wright

DEPARTMENT OF STATE, *November* 7, 1825.

SIR: The Baron de Mareuil, the minister of France, has presented a complaint to the Government, founded upon your refusal, on the 29th of September last, to afford your official co-operation for the recovery of a sailor who had deserted from the Endymion. It has been laid before the President, who conceives that the sixth article of the convention with France of the 24th day of June, 1822, comprehends as well deserters from public ships as from merchant vessels. The inducement which operated with the parties to agree to the sixth article was that of favoring their mutual commerce; that the stipulation itself makes no exception of public vessels; on the contrary, it applies to all vessels of the respective parties, and to all deserting sailors, being part of the crews of those vessels. Besides, it cannot be said that the surrender of the deserter from the public vessel has no tendency to favor commerce. This is believed to be the true construction of the treaty; and if we have to extend the benefit of it to French vessels, public as well as private, in our ports, it should not be forgotten that we derive a corresponding benefit in the ports of France. Assuming this to be the meaning of the treaty, all observation is presumed to be unnecessary to show that it is the law of the land.

I have the honor to be, with great respect, your obedient servant.

Mr. Clay to the Baron de Mareuil.

DEPARTMENT OF STATE, *November* 7, 1825.

SIR: I have the honor to acknowledge the receipt of your note of the 4th ultimo, which has been submitted to the President. In respect to that of the third of same month of the previous year, I understand, in this Department, that an answer was not sent to it, in consequence of some conversation which passed between my predecessor and you, which appeared to render one unnecessary. If any misconception prevailed in that particular, and you should desire a written reply, it will afford me pleasure to furnish one.

In regard to the refusal of the mayor of Norfolk, and the justice of the peace of Norfolk county, to afford the requisite aid to the recovery of the sailor who deserted from the Endymion, that refusal, so far as it was founded upon the interpretation which those officers gave to the sixth article of the convention of 1822, ought not to have occurred. The President believes that, according to the true construction of that article, sailors deserting from public ships are comprehended as well as those from vessels in the merchant service. The error of those officers might have been corrected by resort to the tribunals of the United States, which will ever be ready to afford their co-operation, when questions are regularly brought before them, in carrying into effect the engagements of the United States with foreign nations, with all the precision and good faith which the President desires should characterize their execution. I have, in the meantime, communicated to the mayor of Norfolk, and to the justice of the peace of Norfolk county, the opinion of the President as to the erroneous construction of the convention which they have adopted, and doubt not that if their authority should again be invoked it will not be withheld upon the ground heretofore assumed by them.

I avail myself of the occasion to repeat to you assurances of the distinguished consideration of your obedient servant.

The Baron de Mareuil to Mr. Clay.

[Translation.]

WASHINGTON, *November* 16, 1825.

SIR: The letter under date of the 7th of this month, which you did me the honor to write me in answer to mine of October 3, 1824, and of October 4, of the present year, places me under the necessity of making you acquainted with, and of recommending also to your benevolent attention, two important observations.

The first is relative to that conversation, of which you remind me, that took place last year between your predecessor and me, and in which I do not remember that there was any other question than the difficulties arising from the division of territories, and that of jurisdiction for the very execution of the 6th article of our convention; so that it appeared to have been intended that the Attorney General of the United States should be consulted upon the means of procuring a more easy execution of the stipulation relative to deserters in the ports and countries of the American Confederacy.

This is the result of that consultation which I solicited, and which I still solicit, for the purpose of establishing upon this subject a complete reciprocity between the two countries.

My second observation will bear upon that part of your letter where, after having acknowledged that the interpretation given by the mayor of Norfolk and the magistrate of the county to the same article of the convention is erroneous, and that this article applies to deserters from ships-of-war, as well as to those from merchant vessels; announcing to me, moreover, that, according to the orders of the President, you have transmitted to Norfolk the necessary information, that a difficulty of the same nature may not again take place. You, in the meantime, add, that there would be an appeal in the matter from this first decision to the tribunals of the United States. On this subject, sir, it is impossible for me not to remark that, from Government to Government, in all that concerns the general interests of the respective States, the execution of treaties can never afford matter for juridical actions; that it belongs to each Government to procure, in its territory, the full and entire execution of stipulations which bind it towards foreign Governments; and that, in the case in question, for example, if the consuls of France shall be always bound to pursue before the courts the arrest and return of deserters, there will result a loss of time and expense which would render illusory the stipulation made for the mutual interest of the navigation and commerce of the two States.

Be pleased to receive these two observations as emanating from the very duties of my station, and the sincere desire which I shall always have to contribute all in my power to the maintenance of a perfect understanding; which no one appreciates more than I do.

Accept, sir, the assurances of my very high consideration.

BARON DE MAREUIL.

Mr. Clay to the Baron de Mareuil.

DEPARTMENT OF STATE, *Washington, December* 19, 1825.

SIR: In answer to the note which you did me the honor to address to me on the 16th ultimo, it is quite unnecessary to repeat the assurance already given of an anxious disposition on the part of the Government of the United States to fulfil its engagements with France, in their true spirit, and to their utmost extent. With respect to the desertion of sailors from the vessels of one of the two countries in the ports of the other, the instances cannot be so numerous as to require the establishment of any new tribunals or the creation of any new officers to enforce the provisions of the 6th article of the convention. The facilities for apprehending deserters necessarily depend, in some degree, upon the density of population and other circumstances at the place where a desertion happens; and they are greater at some ports than at others. This observation is applicable to both countries. It is believed that the suggestion is not well founded, that any difficulty in arresting and securing such deserters is to be attributed to the form of our Confederacy. "The courts, judges, and officers competent," referred to in the above article, comprehend those of the several States, as well as of the General Government; and one or other of the two descriptions of officers are to be found in sufficient number at all places. Besides, both nations contemplated, at the time of contracting, the actual forms of their respective Governments.

In regard to the second observation which you have done me the honor to make in your note, I have to remark, that, whatever may be the case with treaties generally between State and State, the above article of the convention, so far from being withdrawn from judicial action, expressly refers itself to judicial means for its execution; and from the very nature of the facts to be examined, the intervention of judicial functionaries was indispensable.

I pray you, sir, to accept renewed assurances of my high consideration.

H. CLAY.

The Baron DE MAREUIL, *Envoy Extraordinary and*
                         Minister Plenipotentiary from France.

The Baron de Mareuil to Mr. Clay.

[Translation.]

WASHINGTON, *December* 24, 1825.

SIR: When, on the 3d October, 1824, I submitted to your honorable predecessor some difficulties which obstructed the execution of the 6th article of the convention of 1822, relative to the mutual surrender of deserters, I did not require that there should be, on that account, new courts of justice established or new functionaries created for the execution of said article; but I only showed the desire that means might be found of rendering effective, from one county to another of the same State, the warrant obtained from the magistrate residing in the port where the desertion took place, in order to obtain the reciprocity of what is practiced in France on the same occasion.

I regret, without doubt, to learn that the Federal Government has not discovered any means of procuring this perfect equality in the execution of a stipulation so interesting to the navigation of the two countries.

But an object more important has engaged me since then, and to which I find myself obliged to recur, as, on the one hand, we are not entirely agreed on the sense itself of the convention, and on the other, the assurances given in your letter of the 7th of November last are not sufficient to prevent a new refusal of the mayor of Norfolk, which you will see expressed, sir, in the letter of which a copy is sent.

It is, besides, evident to me that the 6th article of the convention in enumerating the *tribunals, judges, and officers competent,* has principally had in view to specify, according to the organization of each country, the different authorities to which the consuls and vice consuls ought to address themselves for the arrest and surrender of deserters; but that it has not supposed that there ever was, in this circumstance, a ground of procedure to appeal from one jurisdiction to another, unless in the case where one party appeared, denying the very fact of the desertion. The question from the beginning, therefore, has been, to know what was, in the ports of the United States, the competent authority to which the French consuls ought to address themselves. Now it had appeared, until now, that the magistrate or justice of the peace granted the *warrant,* and that the mayor attended to the execution of it. Several examples have already presented themselves, where those of Norfolk had attended to the requisitions of the consul. Still it is not their competence that they refuse to acknowledge; it is not the justice of the requisition that they discuss; it is the very application of the treaty; it is its interpretation that they contest; and in this case, as in those of which I spoke in my letter of the 17th of November, it is impossible for me to admit that the consul ought to address himself to the court of the United States. It appeared to me, on the contrary, that his representation could only come to the minister of his Government, and that it was my part to make it the object of a direct representation to the Federal Government; for if, definitively, (and the new letter of the mayor of Norfork afforded the idea,) the directions of the cabinet were not sufficient to regulate the conduct of this magistrate, there was a necessity, in the system of the country, to cause judgment to be given by the court of the United States, it would be for the Federal Government to cause it.

I can only, therefore, through your means, sir, refer myself to the justice of the President, and to the express intention which I, without doubt, acknowledge that he has to contribute all in his power to the full and entire execution of the engagements which subsist between France and the United States.

Accept, sir, the assurances of the high consideration with which I have the honor to be your most humble and obedient servant,

BARON DE MAREUIL.

Copy of a letter addressed by Mr. Holt, Mayor of Norfolk, to Mr. Hersant, eleve Vice Consul, officiating as Vice Consul of France in the said city.

NORFOLK, December, 16, 1825.

SIR: I have to acknowledge the receipt of your letters of the 8th instant and of this date, in which you desire me to cause two deserters from his most Catholic Majesty's brig Endymion to be apprehended and confined, subject to your order. I had the honor to communicate to you, in answer to your former note on this subject, my impression that the 6th article of the convention of navigation and commerce between the United States and France provided for cases of desertion from vessels engaged in their mutual commerce, and not from their ships-of-war. This construction still appears to me to be correct, and I must therefore decline for the present complying with your request. I have, however, applied to the attorney general of the State for his interpretation of the article above alluded to, which, when received, shall be communicated to you, and your demand complied with, if sustained by his opinion.

I am, sir, with the greatest respect, your most obedient servant,

JOHN E. HOLT.

A true copy.

HERSANT,
The eleve Vice Consul, officiating as Vice Consul of France at Norfolk.

VICE CONSULATE OF FRANCE AT NORFOLK.

Copy of a letter addressed to Mr. Hersant, eleve Vice Consul, officiating as Vice Consul of France at Norfolk, by Mr. John Holt, Mayor of that city.

NORFOLK, December 29, 1825.

SIR: In the note I had the honor to address you on the 16th instant, you were apprised I had submitted to the consideration of the attorney general of the State your application to me to cause two deserters from his most Catholic Majesty's brig Endymion to be arrested and confined, subject to your order, and that I had desired his opinion as to the propriety of my affording my official co-operation for their recovery. His answer to my letter has confirmed me in the correctness of the declaration contained in the note above alluded to, that I did not possess the authority to comply with your request.

I am, sir, &c.,

JOHN E. HOLT.

A true copy.

HERSANT.

19TH CONGRESS.]   **No. 417.**   [1ST SESSION.

CORRESPONDENCE WITH THE BRITISH GOVERNMENT RELATIVE TO THE BOUNDARY OF THE UNITED STATES ON THE PACIFIC COAST.

COMMUNICATED TO THE HOUSE OF REPRESENTATIVES JANUARY 31, 1826.

To the House of Representatives of the United States:

In compliance with a resolution of the House of Representatives of the 18th instant, I transmit a report from the Secretary of State, with the correspondence with the British Government, relating to the boundary of the United States on the Pacific Ocean, desired by the resolution.

JOHN QUINCY ADAMS.

WASHINGTON, *January* 31, 1826.

DEPARTMENT OF STATE, Washington, January 30, 1826.

The Secretary of State, to whom was referred the resolution of the House of Representatives of January 18, 1826, requesting the President to communicate to that House all the correspondence between the Government of the United States and the Government of Great Britain, respecting the boundary of that part of the territory of the United States which is situated upon the Pacific Ocean, and which has not already been communicated, or so much thereof as may be compatible with the public interest to disclose, has the honor to report to the President, as coming within the purview of the resolution, copies of—

1. A letter from Mr. Adams, late Secretary of State, to Mr. Rush, under date July 22, 1823.
2. An extract from a despatch of Mr. Rush to the Secretary of State, under date August 12, 1823.
3. Copy of the protocol of the 11th conference of the American and British Plenipotentiaries, held at the Board of Trade, (in London,) on April 1, 1824.
4. Copy of the protocol of the 12th conference.
5. Copy of the protocol of the 20th conference.
6. Extract from the protocol of the 23d conference.
7. Copy of paper marked F, American paper, on the Northwest Coast of America.
8. Copy of paper marked P, British paper, on the Northwest Coast of America.
Respectfully submitted.

H. CLAY.

Mr. Adams to Mr. Rush.

DEPARTMENT OF STATE, *Washington, July 22*, 1823.
SIR: Among the subjects of negotiation with Great Britain which are pressing upon the attention of this Government is the present condition of the Northwest Coast of this continent. This interest is connected in a manner becoming from day to day more important with our territorial rights; with the whole system of our intercourse with the Indian tribes; with the boundary relations between us and the British North American dominions; with the fur trade; the fisheries in the Pacific Ocean; the commerce with the Sandwich Islands and China; with our boundary upon Mexico; and lastly, with our political standing and intercourse with the Russian Empire.

By the third article of the convention between the United States and Great Britain of October 20, 1818, it is agreed that "any country that may be claimed by either party on the Northwest Coast of America, westward of the Stony mountains, shall, together with its harbors, bays, and creeks, and the navigation of all rivers of the same, be free and open, for the term of ten years from the date of the signature of the convention, to the vessels, citizens, and subjects of the two powers. It being well understood that this agreement is not to be construed to the prejudice of any claim which either of the two high contracting parties may have to any part of the said country, nor shall it be taken to affect the claims of any other power or State to any part of the said country, the only object of the high contracting parties in that respect being to prevent disputes and differences among themselves."

On the 6th of October, 1818, fourteen days before the signature of this convention, the settlement at the mouth of Columbia river had been formally restored to the United States by order of the British Government.—(Message of the President of the United States to the House of Representatives, April 15, 1822, page 13. Letter of Mr. Prevost to the Secretary of State of November 11, 1818.)

By the treaty of amity, settlement, and limits, between the United States and Spain, of February 22, 1819, the boundary line between them was fixed at the 42° of latitude from the source of the Arkansas river to the South Sea. By which treaty the United States acquired all the right of Spain north of that parallel.

The right of the United States to the Columbia river, and to the interior territory washed by its waters, rests upon its discovery from the sea and nomination by a citizen of the United States; upon its exploration to the sea by Captains Lewis and Clarke; upon the settlement of Astoria, made under the protection of the United States, and thus restored to them in 1818; and upon the subsequent acquisition of all the rights of Spain, the only European power who, prior to the discovery of the river, had *any* pretensions to territorial rights on the Northwest Coast of America.

The waters of the Columbia river extend by the Multnomah to the 42° of latitude, where its source approaches within a few miles of those of Platte and Arkansas, and by Clarke's river to the 50th or 51st degree of latitude; thence descending southward till its sources almost intersect those of the Missouri.

To the territory thus watered and immediately contiguous to the original possessions of the United States, as first bounded by the Mississippi, they consider their right to be now established by all the principles which have ever been applied to European settlements upon the American hemisphere.

By the ukase of the Emperor Alexander of September 4, (16,) 1821, an exclusive territorial right, on the Northwest Coast of America, is asserted as belonging to Russia, and as extending from the northern extremity of the continent to latitude 51°, and the navigation and fishery of all other nations are interdicted by the same ukase to the extent of 100 Italian miles from the coast.

When Mr. Poletica, the late Russian minister here, was called upon to set forth the grounds of right, conformable to the laws of nations which authorized the issuing of this decree, he answered in his letters of February 28 and April 2, 1822, by alleging, first, discovery, occupancy, and uninterrupted *possession*.

It appears upon examination that these claims have no foundation in fact. The right of *discovery* on this continent, claimed by Russia, is reduced to the probability that in 1741 Captain Tchirikoff saw from the sea the mountain called St. Elias, in about the 59th degree of north latitude. The Spanish navigators, as early as 1582, had discovered as far north as 57° 30′.

As to occupancy, Captain Cook, in 1779, had the express declaration of Mr. Ismaloff, the chief of the Russian settlement at Oonalaska, that they *knew nothing* of the continent in America; and in the Nootka Sound controversy, between Spain and Great Britain, it is explicitly stated in the Spanish documents that Russia had disclaimed all pretension to interfere with the Spanish exclusive rights *to beyond* Prince William's Sound, latitude 61°. No evidence has been exhibited of any Russian settlement on this continent, south and east of Prince William's Sound, to this day, with the exception of that in California, made in 1816.

It never has been admitted by the various European nations which have formed settlements in this hemisphere that the occupation of an *island* gave any claim whatever to territorial possessions on the continent to which it was adjoining. The recognized principle has rather been the reverse, as, by the law of nature, islands must be rather considered as appendages to continents than continents to islands.

The only color of claim alleged by Mr. Poletica, which has an appearance of plausibility, is that which he asserts as an authentic fact, "that in 1789 the Spanish packet St. Charles, commanded by Captain Haro, found, in latitude 48° and 49°, Russian settlements to the number of eight, consisting, in the whole, of twenty families, and 462 individuals." But more than twenty years since Fleurieu had shown, in his introduction to the voyage of Marchand, that in this statement there was a mistake of at least ten degrees of latitude, and that instead of 48° and 49°, it should read 58° and 59°. This is, probably, not the only mistake in the account. It rests altogether upon the credit of two private letters—one written from St. Blas, and the other from the city of Mexico, to Spain, there communicated to a French consul in one of the Spanish ports, and by him to the French Minister of Marine. They were written in October, 1788, and August, 1789. We have seen that in 1790 Russia explicitly disclaimed interfering with the exclusive rights of Spain to *beyond* Prince William's Sound, in latitude 61°; and Vancouver, in 1794, was informed by the Russians on the spot that their most *eastern* settlement there was on Hinchinbrook island, at Port Etches, which *had been established in the course of the preceding summer*, and that the adjacent continent was a *sterile and uninhabited country*. Until the Nootka Sound contest, Great Britain had never advanced any claim to territory upon the Northwest Coast of America by right of occupation. Under the treaties of 1763 her territorial rights were bounded by the Mississippi.

On the 22d July, 1793, Mackenzie reached the shores of the Pacific, by land, from Canada, in latitude 52° 21′ north, longitude 128° 2′ west of Greenwich.

It is stated in the 52d number of the Quarterly Review, in the article upon Kotzebue's voyage, "that the whole country, from latitude 56° 30′ to the United States, in latitude 38°, or thereabouts, is now, and has long been, in the actual possession of the British Northwest Company;" that this company have a post on the borders of a river in latitude 54° 30′ north, longitude 125° west, and that in latitude 55° 15′ north, longitude 129° 44′ west, "by this time (March, 1822) the United Company of the Northwest and Hudson's Bay have, in all probability, formed an establishment."

It is not imaginable that, in the present condition of the world, *any* European nation should entertain the project of settling a *colony* on the Northwest Coast of America; that the United States should form establishments there, with views of absolute territorial right and inland communication, is not only to be expected, but is pointed out by the finger of nature, and has been for years a subject of serious deliberation in Congress. A plan has, for several sessions, been before them for establishing a territorial government on the borders of Columbia river. It will, undoubtedly, be resumed at their next session, and even if then again postponed, there cannot be a doubt that, in the course of a very few years, it must be carried into effect. As yet, however, the only useful purposes to which the Northwest Coast of America has been or can be made subservient to the settlements of civilized men are the fisheries on its adjoining seas, and trade with the aboriginal inhabitants of the country. These have hitherto been enjoyed in common by the people of the United States and by the British and Russian nations. The Spanish, Portuguese, and French nations have also participated in them hitherto, without other annoyance than that which resulted from the exclusive territorial claims of Spain, so long as they were insisted on by her.

The United States and Great Britain have both protested against the Russian Imperial ukase of September 4, (16,) 1821. At the proposal of the Russian Government, a full power and instructions are now transmitted to Mr. Middleton for the adjustment, by amicable negotiation, of the conflicting claims of the parties on this subject.

We have been informed by the Baron de Tuyll that a similar authority has been given on the part of the British Government to Sir Charles Bagot.

Previous to the restoration of the settlement at the mouth of Columbia river in 1818, and again upon the first introduction in Congress of the plan for constituting a territorial government there, some disposition was manifested by Sir Charles Bagot and Mr. Canning to dispute the *right* of the United States to that establishment; and some vague intimation was given of British claims on the Northwest Coast. The restoration of the place, and the convention of 1818, were considered as a final disposal of Mr. Bagot's objections, and Mr. Canning declined committing to paper those which he had intimated in conversation.

The discussion of the Russian pretensions in the negotiation now proposed necessarily involves the interests of the three powers, and renders it manifestly proper that the United States and Great Britain should come to a mutual understanding with respect to *their* respective pretensions as well as upon their joint views with reference to those of Russia. Copies of the instructions to Mr. Middleton are, therefore, herewith transmitted to you; and the President wishes you to confer freely with the British Government on the subject.

The principles settled by the Nootka Sound convention of October 28, 1790, were—

1st. That the right of fishing in the South Seas; of trading with the natives of the Northwest Coast of America; and of making settlements on the coast itself, for the purposes of that trade, north of the *actual* settlements of Spain, were common to all the European nations, and, of course, to the United States.

2d. That, so far as the *actual* settlements of Spain had extended, she possessed the exclusive rights, territorial, and of navigation and fishery, extending to the distance of ten miles from the coasts so *actually occupied*.

3d. That, on the coasts of *South America* and the adjacent islands *south* of the parts already occupied by Spain, no settlement should thereafter be made either by British or Spanish subjects; but, on both sides, should be retained the liberty of landing and of erecting temporary buildings for the purposes of the fishery. These rights were also, of course, enjoyed by the people of the United States.

The exclusive rights of Spain to any part of the American continents have ceased. That portion of the convention, therefore, which recognizes the exclusive colonial rights of Spain on these continents, though confirmed, as between Great Britain and Spain, by the first additional article to the treaty of the 5th of July, 1814, has been extinguished by the fact of the independence of the South American nations and of Mexico. The independent nations will possess the rights incident to that condition, and their territories will, of course, be subject to no *exclusive* right of navigation in their vicinity, or of access to them, by any foreign nation.

A necessary consequence of this state of things will be, that the American continents, henceforth, will no longer be subject to *colonization*. Occupied by civilized, independent nations, they will be accessible to Europeans, and to each other, on that footing alone; and the Pacific Ocean, in every part of it, will remain open to the navigation of all nations, in like manner with the Atlantic.

Incidental to the condition of national independence and sovereignty, the rights of interior navigation of their rivers will belong to each of the American nations within its own territories.

The application of colonial principles of exclusion, therefore, cannot be admitted by the United States as lawful, upon any part of the Northwest Coast of America, or as belonging to any European nation. Their own settlements there, when organized as territorial Governments, will be adapted to the freedom of their own institutions, and, as constituent parts of the Union, be subject to the principles and provisions of their Constitution.

The right of carrying on trade with the natives throughout the Northwest Coast they cannot renounce. With the Russian settlements at Kodiack, or at New Archangel, they may fairly claim the advantage of a fur trade, having so long enjoyed it unmolested, and because it has been, and would continue to be, as advantageous, at least, to those settlements as to them. But they will not contest the right of Russia to prohibit the traffic, as strictly confined to the Russian settlement itself, and not extending to the original natives of the coast.

If the British Northwest and the Hudson's Bay Companies have any posts on the coast, as suggested in the article of the Quarterly Review, above cited, the 3d article of the convention of the 20th October, 1818, is applicable to them. Mr. Middleton is authorized by his instructions to propose an article of similar import, to be inserted in a joint convention between the United States, Great Britain, and Russia, for a term of ten years from its signature. You are authorized to make the same proposal to the British Government, and, with a view to draw a definite line of demarkation for the future, to stipulate that no settlement shall hereafter be made on the Northwest Coast, or on any of the islands thereto adjoining, by Russian subjects, south of latitude 55°; by citizens of the United States, north of latitude 51°; or by British subjects, either south of 51° or north of 55°. I mention the latitude of 51° as the bound within which we are willing to limit the future settlement of the United States, because it is not to be doubted that the Columbia river branches as far north as 51°, although it is most probably not the Tacoutche Tesse of Mackenzie. As, however, the line already runs in latitude 49° to the Stony mountains, should it be earnestly insisted upon by Great Britain, we will consent to carry it in continuance on the same parallel to the sea. Copies of this instruction will likewise be forwarded to Mr. Middleton, with whom you will freely, but cautiously, correspond on this subject, as well as in relation to your negotiation respecting the suppression of the slave trade.

I have the honor to be, with great respect, sir, your very humble and obedient servant,

JOHN QUINCY ADAMS.

Hon. RICHARD RUSH, *Envoy Extraordinary and*
Minister Plenipotentiary of the United States, London.

Extract of a letter from Mr. Rush to Mr. Adams, dated August 12, 1824.

No. 10.

VI. Northwest Coast of America.

(For this extract see No. 396 of this volume, being the 6th article of the letter from Mr. Rush of 12th August, 1824.)

Protocol of the Eleventh Conference of the American and British Plenipotentiaries, held at the Board of Trade, on the 1st of April, 1824.

(For this Protocol see No. 396 of this volume.)

Protocol of the Twelfth Conference of the American and British Plenipotentiaries, held at the Board of Trade, on the 2d of April, 1824.

(For this Protocol see No. 396 of this volume.)

Protocol of the Twentieth Conference of the American and British Plenipotentiaries, held at the Board of Trade, on the 29th of June, 1824.

(For this Protocol see No. 396 of this volume.)

Extract from Protocol of the Twenty-third Conference of the American and British Plenipotentiaries, held at the Board of Trade, on the 13th of July, 1824.

(For this Protocol see No. 396 of this volume.)

F.

American papers on the Northwest Coast of America, (twelfth Protocol.)

(For this paper see No. 396 of this volume.)

P.

British paper on the Northwest Coast of America, (twenty-third Protocol.)

(For this paper see No. 396 of this volume.)

No. 418.

RELATIVE TO THE INTERVENTION OF FOREIGN GOVERNMENTS TO INDUCE SPAIN TO ACKNOWLEDGE THE INDEPENDENCE OF THE SOUTH AMERICAN GOVERNMENTS.

COMMUNICATED TO THE SENATE, IN EXECUTIVE SESSION, FEBRUARY 2, 1826, AND THE INJUNCTION OF SECRECY SINCE REMOVED.

To the Senate of the United States:

In compliance with a resolution of the Senate of the 30th ultimo, I communicate herewith, in confidence, a report from the Secretary of State, with the documents containing the information desired by the resolution.

JOHN QUINCY ADAMS.

WASHINGTON, *February* 1, 1826..

The Secretary of State, to whom the President has referred the resolution of the Senate of January 30, 1826, requesting him to inform the Senate whether the Government of Spain has been informed of the application made by our Government for the intervention of the Emperor of Russia to induce Spain to recognize the independence of the South American States, and to lay before the Senate the correspondence, if any has taken place, between our minister at Madrid and the Spanish Government, and also between such minister and our Government on the subject of such intervention and recognition, has the honor to report—

An extract of a letter from this Department to Mr. Everett, dated Department of State, April 27, 1825.

An extract from the notes of a conversation between Mr. Everett and Mr. Zea, communicated with a despatch from Mr. Everett to this Department, dated September 25, 1825.

An extract of a despatch from Mr. Everett to this Department, of October 20, 1825.

All which is respectfully submitted.

H. CLAY.

Extract of a letter from Mr. Clay to Mr. Everett, dated

DEPARTMENT OF STATE, *April* 27, 1825.

"Besides the preceding objects, to which your attention will be directed, others of great interest will also claim it. Of these, that of the highest importance is the present war between Spain and her former colonies on this continent. The President wishes you to bring this subject in the most conciliating manner possible before the Spanish Government. It would be as unnecessary as unprofitable to look to the past, except for the purpose of guiding future conduct. True wisdom dictates that Spain, without indulging in unavailing regrets on account of what she has irretrievably lost, should employ the means of retaining what she may yet preserve from the wreck of her former possessions. The war upon the continent is, in fact, at an end. Not a solitary foot of land from the western limit of the United States to Cape Horn owns her sway; not a bayonet in all that vast extent remains to sustain her cause. And the Peninsula is utterly incompetent to replace those armies which have been vanquished and annihilated by the victorious forces of the new Republics. What possible object, then, can remain to Spain to protract a war which she can no longer maintain, and to the conclusion of which, in form, there is only wanting the recognition of the new Governments by treaties of peace? If there were left the most distant prospect of her reconquering her continental provinces, which have achieved their independence, there might be a motive for her perseverance. But every expectation of such reconquest, it is manifest, must be perfectly chimerical. If she can entertain no rational hope to recover what has been forced from her grasp, is there not great danger of her losing what she yet but feebly holds? It should be borne in mind that the armies of the new States, flushed with victory, have no longer employment on the continent, and yet, whilst the war continues, if it be only in name, they cannot be disbanded without a disregard of all the maxims of just precaution. To what object, then, will the new Republics direct their powerful and victorious armies? They have a common interest and a common enemy, and let it be supposed that that enemy, weak and exhausted as he is, refuses to make peace, will they not strike wherever they can reach? and from the proximity and great value of Cuba and Porto Rico, is it not to be anticipated that they will aim, and aim a successful blow too, at those Spanish islands? Whilst they would operate from without, means would doubtless be, at the same time, employed to stimulate the population within to a revolt. And that the disposition exists among the inhabitants, to a considerable extent, to throw off the Spanish authority, is well known. It is due to the United States to declare that they have constantly declined to give any countenance to that disposition.

It is not, then, for the new Republics that the President wishes you to urge upon Spain the expediency of concluding the war. Their interest is probably on the side of its continuance, if any nation can ever have an interest in a state of war. But, it is for Spain herself, for the cause of humanity, for the general repose of the world, that you are required, with all the delicacy which belongs to the subject, to use every topic of persuasion to impress upon the councils of Spain the propriety, by a formal pacification, of terminating the war. And as the views and policy of the United States in regard to those islands may possibly have some influence, you are authorized, frankly and fully, to disclose them. The United States are satisfied with the present condition of those islands in the hands of Spain, and with their ports open to our commerce, as they are now open. This Government desires no political change of that condition. The population itself of the islands is incompetent at present, from its composition and its amount, to maintain self-government. The maritime force of the neighboring Republics of Mexico and Colombia is not now, nor is it likely shortly to be, adequate to the protection of those islands, if the conquest of them were effected. The United States would entertain constant apprehension of their passing from their possession to that of some less friendly sovereignty; and of all the European powers, this country prefers that Cuba and Porto Rico should remain dependent on Spain. If the war should continue between Spain and the new Republics, and those islands should become the object and the theatre of it, their fortunes have such a connexion with the prosperity of the United States that they could not be indifferent spectators; and the possible contingencies of such a protracted war might bring upon the Government of the United States duties and obligations, the performance of which, however painful it should be, they might not be at liberty to decline. A subsidiary consideration in favor of peace, deserving some weight, is, that as the war has been the parent cause of the shocking piracies in the West Indies, its termination would be, probably, followed by their cessation; and thus the Government of Spain, by one act, would fulfil the double obligation under which it lies to foreign Governments, of repressing enormities, the perpetrators of which find refuge, if not succor, in Spanish territory; and that to the Spanish nation itself, of promoting its real interests.

Extract from the notes of a conversation between Mr. Everett and Mr. Zea, communicated with a despatch (No. 7) from Mr. Everett to Mr. Clay, dated

MADRID, *September* 25, 1825.

"In the course of this conversation upon matters touching so nearly the independence of the colonies, there were, of course, frequent opportunities of alluding to that question, and the minister seemed to feel no delicacy or reserve in expressing his sentiments upon it. He remarked, repeatedly, that the King would never abandon his claim to these his ancient and rightful possessions; that the cause was a good one; and that, however unfavorable their prospect might appear at present, they had a right to suppose that they should, in the end, succeed; that we had seen, of late, revolutions in political affairs at least as violent as this would be—for example, the overthrow of Bonaparte and the restoration of Louis XVIII to the throne of his ancestors; that the party in the colonies in favor of independence, though dominant and apparently unresisted, was not, in reality, so strong as was generally supposed; that it consisted of a busy and active, but in reality feeble minority; that the mass of the good citizens, constituting a great majority of the population, were in favor of the King, and were only waiting for some suitable occasion to come out in their strength and to put down the insurgents, and, finally, that the cause being a just one, they had a right to suppose that they should be assisted, sooner or later, by an interference of Providence.

"I did not think it necessary to enter very fully into the argument with Mr. Zea.

"I said to him, however, that I regretted to hear from him so decisive a declaration of the King's resolution not to acknowledge the new States; that my Government had hoped that the battle of Ayacucho, and the recognition of England, would have been considered by his Majesty as settling the question, and that he would have been induced to put an end to the violent state of things now existing, which was more or less injurious to all Christian nations; that enlightened men of all classes, parties, and opinions in most of the civilized countries of Europe, and in the United States, were now satisfied that Spain could never recover her authority over the colonies. As a single instance, I mentioned to him the opinion of the Bishop of Hermopolis, minister of church affairs in France, and well known throughout Europe as one of the ablest and most decided adherents of the anti-liberal sect, whom I had seen at Paris on my way, and who had told me expressly that he regarded the affair of South America as settled.

"To this he made answer that the Bishop had also, in the time of Bonaparte, despaired of the possibility of the King's restoraton, and that he might be as much in the wrong now as he was then. I remarked that there were evident symptoms in the proceedings of the French Government of an intention to recognize the new States at no very distant period. He said that France had hitherto stood by them faithfully in all their troubles; that he could not say how long she would be true to them, but should she even desert them, the King would still adhere firmly to his principles; that the standing and invariable rule of conduct observed by his Majesty upon all occasions was that of strict justice; that he made no concessions to expediency, acknowledged no distinction between politics and morals, and was prepared to sacrifice everything rather than surrender what he knew to be his right. He then recurred to his favorite example of Louis XVIII; said that they were by no means reduced to so low a point as he had been; that he, too, often had been solicited to abandon his claims to the French throne; but that, by firmly rejecting all such propositions, and tenaciously adhering to his purpose, he had finally succeeded in recovering everything.

"It struck me that the example of Bonaparte, who had lost all by obstinately refusing to make a timely surrender of a part, would have been rather more to the point, but I did not think it worth while to press this subject at present. I told him that I was not called upon to advise his Majesty's ministers upon this or any other question, and that what I had said had been thrown out incidentally in reply to his remarks."

No. 10.

Extract of a letter from Mr. Everett to the Secretary of State, dated

MADRID, *October* 20, 1825.

"It was reported here very confidentially, a few days ago, that the new Consulative Junta, or Council of Government, was occupied in preparing the way for an arrangement with the South American States. Upon tracing this rumor to its origin, I found that it arose from the fact that the council had deputed some of its members to confer with two Spanish officers who lately arrived from South America by way of the Havana and New York, and are the same that were sent out by the constitutional Government to Buenos Ayres as Commissioners. They landed at Bordeaux from New York, and came on immediately to this place; remained here about three weeks, during which time they had occasional conferences with members of the council, and afterwards proceeded to Cadiz. These facts being known, and it being also understood that the council had been requested by the minister to give their opinion upon the measures proper to be taken in regard to the colonies, it was natural enough to draw the conclusion that the conferences in question had some connexion with this subject, and that the persons with whom they were held might, perhaps, have gone to Cadiz, on their way to America, as private agents of the Government. Another, and a more probable construction of the fact, would be, that the council had no other object in conferring with these gentlemen than to obtain information respecting the state of the colonies.

"About the time when this report was in circulation I went to the Escurial, in order to be present at the celebration of the King's birthday, and when there had, of course, frequent opportunities of seeing the minister. In one of the conversations which I had with him I inquired of him what foundation there was for this rumor, and whether there was any change of policy contemplated in regard to the American States. To this question he replied most decidedly in the negative, and entered anew, and very readily, at great length, into an exposition of the intentions of the Government, repeating, in substance, the same remarks which he had made to me at San Ildefonso. He declared that the King would never abandon his rights; that it was a matter of conscience with him to transmit his hereditary possessions to his successors; that the Royalist cause was not so desperate as we supposed; that there were even now symptoms of a return of these provinces to their ancient loyalty; and that such an event would not be at all strange, considering what violent and sudden revolutions have been constantly occurring during the last thirty years. From all that he said upon the subject I was quite satisfied that the reports of an intended arrangement were entirely groundless, and that the detention and examination of the above mentioned officers were merely for the purpose of obtaining information as to facts.

"The tone and manner of the minister during this conversation were such as to induce me to doubt the correctness of the opinion which I had entertained and expressed to you as to his private sentiments upon this subject. He spoke with so much decision and apparent openness of the probability of reconquering the colonies that I found myself bound to give him credit for his sincerity, at the expense of his sagacity and good sense. He inquired of me at this time whether I had any knowledge of the communications that had lately been made by my Government upon that subject to the Emperor of Russia. I replied in the affirmative, and he then said that he had received the day before, for the first time, upon his return to the Escurial from Madrid, an intimation (probably from one of the ministers abroad) that some overtures had been made in that quarter, and requested me to give him such information respecting them as I might think it proper to communicate. I was not quite so fully prepared upon this subject myself as I could have wished, not having obtained any answer from Mr. King to the request which I made him for a copy of the instructions to Mr. Middleton, probably because he has had no good private occasion to send it. I, however, told him that my Government made no secret of their policy in regard to this business, and that I had no objection to inform him that our minister at St. Petersburg had been directed to express to the Emperor their full conviction that the contest between Spain and the colonies must be considered as finally settled in favor of the latter party; their persuasion that the interest of Spain and the general good of the civilized world would be promoted by the early acquiescence of his Catholic Majesty in this result, and their wish that the Emperor, should he also entertain these opinions, would unite with them in advising and requesting the Spanish Government to put an end to the war by an acknowledgment of the independence of the colonies. I took this opportunity of informing the minister, more precisely than I had done before, that what I had already suggested to him in favor of this measure must be considered as expressing the wishes and policy of my Government, and not my own individual sentiments, which I should not, of course, think of intruding upon his Majesty's cabinet. I told him that I was formally instructed to avail myself of any suitable occasion to suggest to him, with the delicacy required by the nature of the subject, the earnest desire of the Government of the United States to see this long struggle brought to an amicable conclusion, and their complete conviction that all further effort on the part of Spain to recover the colonies must be wholly fruitless, and more injurious to herself than to them.

"Mr. Zea seemed to be a good deal struck with these remarks, and I was inclined to suppose, from his manner, that he had considered what I had said to him before upon the subject as a merely personal communication. He replied, that these proceedings of the Government of the United States placed him under the necessity of declaring, in the most positive manner, the King's unalterable resolution never to abandon his rights, and to reject all offers of mediation, or of amicable intervention, which should contemplate an acknowledgment of the independence of the new States. He said that they were, and always had been, ready and willing to accept any proposal for mediation, or to treat directly with the colonies, upon the basis of their previous submission to the King's sovereign power; but that they would never consent to negotiate in any way upon any other terms; that the King, being once satisfied on this head, would doubtless be disposed to grant his subjects in America every favor and indulgence which they could possibly wish, but that they must begin by proving their loyalty and their confidence in his Majesty's justice and good intentions. He wondered that, among the offers of mediation that had been made from time to time, especially by England, none had ever been proposed upon this basis. I told him that the reason probably was, that the British Government, as well as that of the United States, considered the independence of the new States as now firmly established, and were well aware that they would never treat upon any other terms than an acknowledgment of it by Spain. I added, however, that I should be well pleased to know, if he were disposed to inform me, what concessions the King would be willing to grant to the Americans, in the event of their return to their allegiance; as, for example, whether he would allow them to make their own laws, in legislative assemblies of their own choice? My object in asking this question was, of course, merely to obtain a more complete view of the intentions and dispositions of the Government upon the whole subject. He replied, that, as to legislative assemblies, he was far from being satisfied that they would suit the condition of the colonies, and that, in general, he thought the only safe course for the Americans would be to trust entirely and implicitly to the King's known good character. I should have thought, from this answer, that my question did not make a very favorable impression upon him. At the close, however, of the conversation he recurred to it in such a way as induced me to think that he would have been glad to consider it as an indirect overture from some of the colonies. He said, after I arose to go, that the conversation had turned upon a number of delicate and interesting topics; that on such occasions it was not always possible to distinguish between remarks that were merely of a private and personal description and such as were official, and that, in order to avoid mistakes upon that point, he should be glad if I would state, in writing, what my instructions required me to communicate to him as the opinions and intentions of the Government, and especially any propositions that I might be authorized to make, in the nature of an overture from the colonies, founded on the basis of submission. I told him that I had no authority, from any quarter, to make propositions of that description; but that I would, with pleasure, if he wished it, give him an official statement of what I had said to him, by order of my Government, in favor of the acknowledgment of the independence of the new States. He replied that he was ready to receive any note that I might send him; but that on that head the King's mind was completely made up beyond the possibility of change. Notwithstanding this, I have thoughts of preparing and transmitting to the minister a pretty detailed communication upon this subject. Such a paper, if it does not produce much immediate effect upon the Spanish cabinet, may, perhaps, in one way or another, have a favorable bearing on the general question.

"Previously to this interview with Mr. Zea I had availed myself of such occasions as offered to converse upon the same subject with the British and Russian ministers. The former is Mr. Frederick Lamb, brother of Lord Melbourne, a gentleman of about forty-five years of age, regularly trained to the diplomatic line, and apparently well fitted for it by his talents and information. The latter is Mr. D'Oubril, who has also passed his life in the employment of a foreign minister, and has now reached the age of about sixty. He seems to enjoy the confidence of his Government, and last year took the place of Count Nesselrode, as Minister of Foreign Affairs, during an absence of the latter from St. Petersburg, which lasted several months. Both these gentlemen have shown, since my arrival here, every disposition to be on friendly terms with me, and have plainly manifested, by their attentions, the high esteem in which they hold the American nation and character. Mr. D'Oubril, in particular, has been more civil than any other of the diplomatic body with whom I was not previously acquainted.

"Mr. Lamb's sentiments in regard to the South American question are, of course, precisely the same with ours. I was desirous to ascertain whether the British Government had lately made any attempts to urge Spain to a recognition of the new States, and questioned Mr. Lamb upon this point. He said he had had one or two conversations with Mr. Zea soon after his arrival, (he has been here about five months,) and stated the substance of what had passed between them. The minister, it seems, gave to him the same answer which he has since given to me, and cited, to illustrate his argument, the same examples of Louis XVIII and Bonaparte. No offer of formal mediation has been made by England since her recognition. Indeed her interest as a commercial and manufacturing country is now on the other side. The longer the war continues, the longer she enjoys a monopoly of the Spanish American market for her fabrics, and the more difficult will Spain find it to recover her natural advantages upon the return of peace. England will therefore, probably, be very easy in regard to this matter, and will leave Spain to pursue, unmolested, the course she may think expedient. I suggested this point both to Mr. Zea and to the Russian minister, and was inclined to think, from what they said of it, that it had more weight with them than any other consideration in favor of recognition. They both admitted the justice of my remarks and the great inconvenience that resulted in this way from the present state of things, and could only avoid the proper conclusion by reverting to their common places of the probability of a return of the colonies to their allegiance, which they really seem to imagine will come about sooner or later, without any effort on the part of either Spain or her allies, and by the aid of some unlooked for intervention of Divine Providence. I learned nothing material from Mr. L., excepting the fact that the British Government is now quiet in regard to this matter, and makes no attempts to influence the decision of Spain. He professed to have but little information as to the state of the Spanish settlements in America; and, having passed the greater part of his life, including the last eight or ten years, on the continent, has been, in fact, rather out of the way of obtaining it.

"Mr. D'Oubril was somewhat guarded in his language, and did not seem quite willing to admit that it was the decided intention of the Emperor to encourage Spain in her present system. He said that, individually, he did not by any means take the same view of the subject which the Spanish Government did, and yet that he was not completely satisfied that an immediate recognition was the true policy. He cited, in his turn, the old instance of Louis XVIII and Bonaparte, and was far from being sure that the internal divisions which did or would distract the colonies might not bring them again under the Spanish Government. He was aware, nevertheless, that Spain was daily and yearly suffering great injury from the effects of the present system, and that, by continuing it, she would probably lose her remaining possessions in America and her chance of ever obtaining a due share in the trade with that continent, besides endangering her national existence at home. This was making out a pretty strong case in favor of recognition, but he still returned to his former text, that he considered the question as extremely doubtful. In all that he said upon it he professed to declare merely his own personal opinions and feelings, and, if I recollect right, did not say directly what language he was ordered to hold in his communications with this Government. It is understood, however, that the influence of the Emperor has been employed in support of the present system, and the general impression which I received from his remarks coincided with this opinion. Mr. D'Oubril's private sentiments may possibly be different. Both he and Mr. L. inquired of me respecting the late overtures made by the President's order at St. Petersburg, and appeared to have some though not a very minute acquaintance with the language of your instructions to Mr. Middleton. The representatives of France, Holland, Sweden, Saxony, and Prussia, whom I have had more or less conversation on this subject, have all expressed themselves strongly in opposition to the policy of Spain. Even the Pope's Nuncio and the ambassador from Naples seem to be of the American party. The French, I suspect, are making pretty strong efforts in favor of the new States, but on this point I have, at present, no very precise information."

No. 419.

CLAIMS ON ACCOUNT OF SPANISH SPOLIATIONS UNDER TREATY WITH SPAIN FOR
THE CESSION OF FLORIDA.

COMMUNICATED TO THE HOUSE OF REPRESENTATIVES FEBRUARY 7, 1826.

To the Senate and House of Representatives of the United States of America:

The memorial of the subscribers most respectfully represents:

That the property of the citizens of the United States, while peaceably and honestly engaged in their lawful commerce and business, was, to a very great amount, at various times and under various pretences, forcibly taken from them by means and under circumstances which rendered the Government of Spain responsible for the losses thus sustained; and, of consequence, gave to the sufferers an undoubted right to the direct and efficient aid of their own Government to obtain a just indemnity from Spain. The Government of the United States never denied or shrunk from this great duty of protection which was due to her citizens, but in every form of complaint or remonstrance continued, without ceasing, to urge the Government of Spain to make reparation for the wrongs committed under her authority.

After many years of tedious negotiations and ruinous delay, a provision was made for the satisfaction of those claims in the treaty concluded between the United States and Spain for the purchase and cession of Florida, and a Board of Commissioners was constituted to examine and judicially decide upon the validity of the claims which should be preferred to them.

In this manner the United States received from Spain what was admitted to be an equivalent for the claims of our citizens upon Spain, and by assuming these claims our Government became discharged from their obligation to enforce the payment of them by Spain. This arrangement was a just one only on the supposition that it was the intention of our Government to take upon itself to pay all that Spain was bound to pay; for it could justly cancel the claims of our citizens upon Spain on no other terms; and such would be the justice of the case, even if no consideration had been received from Spain; but it is made much stronger from the circumstance that the United States have actually received from Spain the cession of a country of immense value and extent, for which no consideration has been given to Spain but the assumption of these claims by the United States, and the discharge of Spain from all future responsibility in relation to them. Your memorialists, therefore, take for granted that it was *bona fide* the intention of their Government to place itself precisely, as to these claims, in the situation of the debtor, thus discharged by its interference, to pay whatever that debtor was bound to pay, and to make the same satisfaction to the injured citizens of the United States which Spain was bound to make. Your memorialists do not conceive that the limitation of a certain sum in the treaty should be intended to impeach or evade a principle of justice so unquestionable as that above referred to; that is, that he who steps between me and my debtor takes upon himself the whole responsibility of the debtor, most especially when he receives from the debtor a full consideration for doing so.

The limitation of the sum, your memorialists respectfully suggest, was introduced as a measure of precaution, to prevent that carelessness in the admission of claims which might prevail, if the whole Treasury of the United States was thrown open to them, and to raise an interest amongst just and honest claimants to lend their assistance to detect and exclude every attempt at imposition. This was a fair and perhaps a necessary policy; and as an extension of the sum allowed would always be in the power of the Government, it held the means in its own hands of preventing any injustice being done by this limitation. Your memorialists confidently take this position, that when the sum of five millions of dollars was assumed by the treaty as the limit of the responsibility of the United States, it was honestly and truly believed that this sum would be sufficient to pay and satisfy all the claims which could be substantiated under the treaty; and calculations, intended to be just and liberal, were made from the materials in the possession of the Government which justified this limitation. But it never was the intention of the Government—it is inconsistent with its honor and justice to imagine it—to save itself an inconsiderable sum of money by deducting eight or ten per cent., or any other amount, from the honest claims of its citizens.

After a patient and severe scrutiny by a tribunal selected and constituted by the Government itself, in whose investigations the utmost circumspection and rigor, as well as learning and ability, are manifest, it turns out that the estimate of the claims made by the Government was too low, the amount established by said tribunal as positively due requiring a deduction of one-twelfth part, or eight and one-third per cent., in order to bring it within the sum stipulated in the treaty. It is, indeed, surprising that it was so near the truth. Your memorialists, therefore, respectfully request that this mistake may be corrected; that the original intention of Government in assuming these claims may be carried into effect; and that provision may be made to make good the unexpected deficiency in the fund appropriated to the payment of these debts.

Your memorialists beg leave respectfully to call your attention to another subject connected with these claims. The Commissioners, after much argument and deliberation, decided that the principal only of the claims admitted should be paid, and rejected every application for interest. The interest for delay of payment has become so inseparably connected with the debt, both in our judicial proceedings and the common understanding, that a difference between them is scarcely recognized; to establish the debt is to establish a right to interest from the period when the debt ought to have been paid. Thus only can equal justice be administered, and the creditor of twenty years' standing be placed on as favorable a footing as one of yesterday. It is understood that the Commissioners departed from this obvious rule of equality principally, if not altogether, on the ground that they had but a limited fund to distribute; that it should first be applied to the debts or claims admitted; and that, by allowing interest, they would take the principal of one claimant to pay the interest of another. Without discussing the soundness of this reasoning, which does not consider the interest as a part of the debt, your memorialists are content to remark, that it can have no force or application to the case as presented to Congress, who are not fettered in the administration of justice by the narrowness of their means, but have ample room and power to give to the claimants all they shall believe they are justly entitled to. Whether the payment of interest should be at once and absolutely assumed by our Government, or be made contingent upon the sales of the lands in Florida, your memorialists submit to your wisdom and justice, being assured that, if the property received by the United States in commutation for the claims held by our citizens against Spain shall yield to our Treasury an amount sufficient to pay the interest as well as the principal of the claims, both will be paid with the same exactitude which the law would enforce between individual creditors and debtors.

Your memorialists are not unmindful of, or unthankful for, what has been already done for them in this behalf; nor do they mean to make it a ground for any unreasonable importunity for more. They truly intend to limit their demands to that mere indemnity which was always their right, and which their country has so long and urgently labored to obtain for them; and they confidently believe the measure of that indemnity will be the same, whether it is to be made by Spain or the United States.

Resting on the hope that their request will be viewed by your honorable bodies as just and proper, your memorialists will, as in duty bound, ever pray.

JOHN INSKEEP,
President, for the Insurance Company of North America.
JOHN ASHLEY,
President, for the Insurance Company of Philadelphia.
CHAND. PRICE,
President, for the Insurance Company of the United States.
JOHN LEAMY,
President, for the Marine Insurance Company.
SAMUEL MIFFLIN,
Agent and Attorney for the Private Underwriters of Philadelphia.
CLEMENT C. BIDDLE.
F. DUSAR.
R. S. McALESTER,
President, for the Insurance Company of Pennsylvania.
DAVID LEWIS,
President of the Phœnix Insurance Company of ·Philadelphia.
HUGH COLHOUN,
President, for the Union Insurance Company of Philadelphia.
JAMES YARD.
JOS. DONATH.
ROBERT RALSTON.
SAMUEL R. FISHER.
DAVID H. CONYNGHAM.
JACOB RIDGWAY,
For himself and Smith & Ridgway.
SAMUEL R. FISHER,
Attorney for Wm. Rotch, jr. and Dan'l Wing, executors of Paul E. Cush, of Westport, Mass.; and att'y of Othniel Trip, adm'r of Lem'l Milk, of same place.
JOHN JAMES.
PAUL BECK, JR.
F. DUSAR,
As executor to the late L. D. Carpentier, esq.
SAM. KEITH.
W. JONES.
GEO. DAVIDSON.
JOHN GREINER. ·
JAMES M. BROOM,
Executor of J. Broom, deceased.
RICHARD WILLING,
Executor of T. M. Willing, who was the surviving partner of Willing & Francis, and Willings & Francis.
F. BREUIL.

PHILADELPHIA, *January 16, 1826.*

(For report on this memorial see No. 433.)

RELATIVE TO DESERTIONS FROM SHIPS OF THE NETHERLANDS IN THE UNITED STATES.

COMMUNICATED TO THE HOUSE OF REPRESENTATIVES FEBRUARY 13, 1826.

The Chevalier Huygens to the Secretary of State.

[Translation.]

WASHINGTON, *December 27, 1825.*

The Dutch ship Anna Elizabeth, commanded by Captain Brunow, arrived lately at New York from Curaçoa, has experienced in that port inconveniences from a legislation entirely singular, at least unusual among the commercial nations of Europe, but which appears in force in that State.

The ship has been detained there by a mandate of arrest, issuing from the marine court sitting in that city, against the master, who, being cited before that court to bear and defend himself against the complaints of one of his crew, on account of his having corrected him on board, and on the high sea, had to pass through the forms, and await the issue of a process, the termination of which, fortunately, turned out favorable to him; but after having obtained the judgment, he has incurred the charge of a second mandate of arrest upon the complaints of another sailor of his crew. This last, however, being unable to support the charge, has fled from his duty, and, in fine, the two men have broken their obligations contracted in the role, and have deserted.

The master immediately making application to the court of police to obtain their arrest, has been refused; after this he applied to the mayor with the same success; then going to Judge Thompson, of the Supreme Court of 'the United States, he was told by him that he knew of no treaties or arrangements between the United States and the Netherlands to sanction this requisition, nor any law to authorize it.

The consequence of all this was, that the ship was retarded in her voyage; that the master and his crew were engaged four days in appearing before the court, thereby losing their time; that the first was attended with great expense, and that if he had not found sufficient security he would have certainly been sent to prison; and, finally, that he was obliged to depart with his crew weakened by the loss of two men.

The simple exposition of the facts, more fully detailed in the subjoined report of the master's lawyer, will doubtless suffice to show how contrary this state of things is to the liberty of navigation, which may be stopped and troubled by the complaint of a single man of the crew, contrary to the liberty of nations, which gives the right of being judged by their own tribunals; in fine, contrary to the interest of commerce, which risks all if a captain loses authority over his crew, and has no support to maintain the integrity of his role.

To watch for this maintenance, and to judge the differences between captains and their crews, is one of the attributes which the laws of the Kingdom assign to the consuls, and which their admission in the ports of the United States should secure to them. Yet Mr. Zimmerman, the consul of the Netherlands at New York, was deprived of his attributes by the competence which the marine court exercises in the causes of the crews of his nation, to which circumstance is added the facility of desertion, and the refusal of the authorities to act against deserters, as has happened in the present case.

When, during this summer, two ships of the royal marine touched and sojourned in American ports, and when the commanders as well as the consuls called for the interposition of the authorities against deserters, the refusal was not pronounced, but what was equivalent took place, inasmuch as of a great number of men, the greater part of whom, were, moreover, accused of thefts, not one was arrested, or justice rendered to these commanders. Their reports upon this subject, having already fixed the attention of the Government of the Netherlands, that upon the affair of the crew of the ship Ann Elizabeth will doubtless cause a painful impression, as it will compel the belief that the system of the marine court of New York is that of the United States.

The undersigned, Envoy Extraordinary and Minister Plenipotentiary of his Majesty the King of the Netherlands, being authorized to inform the Government of the United States of the great inconveniences which result from this facility, and a sort of protection granted to desertion, and to agree upon the means of remedying it, seizes this moment to submit to it his representations, and to demand of it the adoption of a system analogous to that which is followed in the Netherlands.

Coincident with this demand, the undersigned is authorized, at the same time, to assure that his Government makes no difficulty in satisfying the claims of American consuls in regard to their marine deserters, which he has just proved by the restoration of four men engaged on board a ship-of-war.

As it is a matter of public notoriety that the American consuls in the ports of the Netherlands enjoy the right of determining the differences between the crews of their nation, the undersigned flatters himself that the President, by the admission of consuls of the Netherlands in the ports of the United States, will see fit to recognize in their attributes the same authority.

The undersigned, on this occasion, prays Mr. Clay to accept the assurance of his high consideration.

C. D. E. I. BANGEMAN HUYGENS.

INDEMNITIES DUE UNDER THE AWARD OF THE EMPEROR OF RUSSIA, FOR SLAVES AND OTHER PRIVATE PROPERTY CARRIED AWAY BY THE BRITISH FORCES IN VIOLATION OF THE TREATY OF GHENT.

COMMUNICATED TO THE HOUSE OF REPRESENTATIVES MARCH 8, 1826.

To the House of Representatives of the United States:

In compliance with the resolution of the House of Representatives of the 10th ultimo, requesting information relating to the proceedings of the joint commission of indemnities, due under the award of the Emperor of Russia, for slaves and other private property carried away by the British forces in violation of the treaty of Ghent, I transmit herewith a report from the Secretary of State, and documents containing the information desired by the resolution.

JOHN QUINCY ADAMS.

WASHINGTON, *March* 8, 1826.

DEPARTMENT OF STATE, *Washington, March* 7, 1826.

The Secretary of State, to whom has been referred by the President the resolution of the House of Representatives of the 10th of February, 1826, requesting certain information therein described in relation to the mixed American and British commission, respecting the indemnity due under the award of the Emperor of Russia, for slaves and other private property, transported by the British forces, in violation of the treaty of Ghent, has the honor to submit the following report:

1. A copy of the list of slaves and other private property carried away, which has been submitted to the Commissioners, together with a statement of the amount of the several claims, as far as it is practicable to prepare such a statement.

2. That no claim has been finally acted upon and allowed by the Commissioners.

3. That none has been finally rejected, and all yet remain to be determined.

4. That "the causes which have delayed the complete adjustment of those claims" are, first, the time which was consumed in procuring the necessary testimony to establish their amount and validity; and, secondly, disagreement in opinion between the American and British Commissioners in the execution of the commission. One of the questions on which they disagree (that of interest) applies to every claim for indemnity which is presented to the Board. Another extends to all, or nearly all, of the slaves belonging to citizens of Louisiana, for the loss of which they claim to be indemnified. These disagreements occurred in the course of the last spring. By the first article of the convention, concluded and signed at St. Petersburg in June, 1822, under the mediation of the late Emperor of Russia, provision is made for the appointment of two arbitrators, as well as of two Commissioners, for the purpose of ascertaining and determining the amount of indemnification which may be due to citizens of the United States, under the decision of his Imperial Majesty. And, by the fifth article of the same convention, it is stipulated that "in the event of the two Commissioners not agreeing in any particular case under examination, or of their disagreement upon any question which may result from the stipulations of this convention, then, and in that case, they shall draw, by lot, the name of one of the two arbitrators, who, after having given due consideration to the matter contested, shall consult with the Commissioners, and a final decision shall be given conformably to the opinion of the majority of the two Commissioners and of the arbitrator so drawn by lot. The American Commissioner has offered, on his part, to give effect to that article, in the several cases in which the two Commissioners have disagreed, by proceeding to designate one of the arbitrators in the mode prescribed; but the British Commissioner has declined to concur in the selection of an arbitrator, upon the ground taken by him that the cases on which the Commissioners differ in their judgment are not comprehended in the decision of the Emperor of Russia and the terms of the convention. This ground being deemed wholly inadmissible, instructions adapted to the circumstances of the commission were given during the last spring to the minister of the United States at the court of London to bring the subject before the British Government. A negotiation was accordingly opened as soon as it was practicable; but, at the date of the last despatches from Mr. King, (the 25th day of December, 1825,) it was not brought to a close; and it is now submitted to the President whether the progress which had been then made in it be such as to admit of any other notice of the negotiation than that which is now respectfully presented.

With respect to the inquiry, ' at what period said commission will probably terminate," no satisfactory answer can be given. The commission does not depend upon the sole will of one party, but upon that of two. Its progress is now obstructed by the non-concurrence of the two Commissioners. That obstacle to the execution of the business, and the consequent termination of the commission, can only be removed by a change of opinion of one of the Commissioners, or by the American or British Government operating upon its Commissioner. One of the objects of the negotiation at London is to remove that obstacle; and when that negotiation, the precise duration of which cannot be anticipated, is brought to a conclusion, some probable estimate may be made of the subsequent continuation of the commission. The hope is indulged that the issue of that negotiation may be known here before the adjournment of Congress.

All which is respectfully submitted.

H. CLAY.

Number of the slaves, and amount, conformably to the average value agreed upon and fixed by the Commission.

States, &c.	Slaves.	Average value.	Amount.	Total value.
Maryland	714	$280	$199,920 00	
Virginia	1,721	280	481,880 00	
South Carolina	10	390	3,900 00	
Georgia	833	390	324,870 00	
Louisiana	259	580	150,220 00	
Mississippi	22	280	6,160 00	
Delaware	2	280	560 00	
Alabama	18	390	7,020 00	
Alexandria, District of Columbia	3	280	840 00	
				$1,175,370 00
Amount of property other than slaves, with the estimated value, viz :				
Maryland			83,256 22	
Virginia			47,553 97½	
Georgia			158,946 68½	
Delaware			250 00	
Maine			16,934 00	
Alexandria, District of Columbia			113,108 77	
				420,049 65
Total of average and estimated value				1,595,419 65

List of slaves stated to have been carried off by the British forces from the State of Maryland; with an alphabetical list of the claimants, and the average value of the said slaves.

Claimants.	Names of slaves.	Proof.
A.		
Abell, Francis	Theophilus	Oath of owner.
Alloway, Mary	Priscilla	Oath of owner and deposition of James Benton.
Avis, David	Phillis; Tom	Oath of owner.
Allen, Benjamin W	Dennis; Sam; Tom; David	Oath of owner and one deposition.
Addison, Anthony	Jim	
B.		
Ballard, Leven W	Charles	Oath of the owner and deposition of J. W. Reynolds.
Ballard, Elizabeth	Adam; Mary; Sarah; Rebecca; Betta; Suck; Phillis; Fanna; Eve; Sophia; Elizabeth; Juliet; Jane.	Deposition of S. W. Ballard and J. W. Reynolds.
Barnes, Thomas W	James	Deposition of the owner and of John Goodhand.
Beall, Aquila	Tom	Deposition of the owner.
Board, Rebecca	George	Deposition of the owner and of John Elliott.
Benton, James	Perry; Emory	Deposition of the owner.
Beauchamp, Isaac	Mentor; Jack	Oath of the owner and two depositions.
Beauchamp, Samuel, for estate of T. Beauchamp, deceased.	Elijah; Stephen	Oath of the claimant and two depositions.
Berry, Zachariah, sen	Richard; Harkless; Mikell	Oath of the owner and three depositions.
Billingsby, Thomas	Joseph	Oath of the owner and one deposition.
Blake, Mary, administratrix of Thos. Blake, deceased.	Ned Green; Jerry	Oath of the claimant and one deposition.
Biscoe, G. W., for G. Biscoe, dec'd	Robert	Do. do.
Biscoe, Josiah	Harry; Tom	Oath of owner and two depositions as to value.
Biscoe, Margaret, widow of Thomas Biscoe, deceased.	Betty; Clem; Charles; Margaret; Mary	Oath of the claimant and deposition of James Jarbes.
Bond, John T	Bob; Moses	Five depositions.
Bourne, James E	Bill; David; Dorcas; Charlotte; Clarissa	Oath of the owner and one deposition.
Bourner, James I	Jim	Oath of the owner and four depositions.
Bowie, C., adm'x of J. Bowie, dec'd	Phil	Four depositions.
Bowen, Isaac	Ben; Easton; Hillely	Oath of the owner and two depositions.
Bowen, Peregrine	Polly Cross; Mahaly; Clarissa	Do. do.
Bowie, Thomas	Jerry; William	Oath of owner and four depositions.
Bowler, H. S	Judson	Oath of owner and three depositions.
Broome, James M., for self and John Mackall.	Jelly; Harry Hammett; Jeffery; Jim; Little Harry; Stephen; Daniel; Nan; Rachel; Ginn; Lucy; Betty; Emmory; Toby; Leonard; Ephraim; Emanuel; Violet; Hannah.	Oath of claimant and four depositions.
Broome, John	Isenath; Joseph	One deposition.
Broome, Alexander	Clarissa; Sarah	Two depositions.
Bspok, John J	James; Matthew; Benjamin	Four depositions.
Bullet, Henry	Phill	Oath of the owner.
Bowie, Charles, and Bowie, Ursula	Osborn; Toby; Sam	Oath of owners and one deposition, and letter from Toby.
Barrow, Charles D., by Mulray, H. M., and J. Glenn, attorneys.	Line and child	Oath of the owner and three depositions.
Barnhouse, Eliza	Joe Sprigg	Three depositions; two depositions as to value.
Blook, Harriet	Ben	Deposition of Mrs. Kelly.
Brown, J. H	Jenny	Do. do.
Barns, John, ex'r, and Bond, Samuel.	Amos; James; Nathan	Two depositions.
Briam, Richard	Philomon; Sewall	See B. L. Lear's list.
C.		
Calvert, Edward H	Tom; Charles; John; William	Oath of owner and one deposition.
Carroll, Juliana	Daniel	Oath of the owner.
Carroll, Henry John, for Carroll, Charles John.	Adam; Phillip; Sandy; Lewis; Beck	Oath of the claimant and two depositions.
Carroll, Thomas K	Dollar; Keah	Oath of the owner and two depositions. (Vide W. Sudler's deposition in Beauchamp's claim.)
Carroll, Margaret A. A	Betty; Henry; Calista	Oath of the owner.
Causin, Nicholas	Andrew	Two depositions.
Cheseldine, K., for Cheseldine, Seneca, deceased.	Dick	Oath of the claimant and deposition as to value.
Chew, Ann, executrix of P. L. Chew, deceased.	James	Oath of claimant and one deposition.
Chew, John H	Harry; David London	Oath of owner and deposition as to value. See, also, his letter of November 25, 1822, to Colonel Ashton: received October 20, 1823.
Clagett, Charles	Romulus; Heneges	Oath of the owner and two depositions.
Clarke, Mathias	Nathaniel	Four depositions and oath of the owner.
Clockel, Benjamin	Henry	Three depositions.
Coberth, Hezekiah	Hoppal; David; Jane; Rosetty; Betty	Oath of owner and one deposition.
Cook, Thomas, executor of Helen Water, deceased.	Benjamin; Cecilia	One deposition.
Colhoun, Edward	Bob	Two depositions.
Cox, Sarah	Alexander	Oath of owner and deposition as to value.

MARYLAND—Continued.

Claimants.	Names of slaves.	Proof.
Cooms, Mary M....................	Sampson; Letty; Letty, (daughter;) Nancy; Dick; Priss; Bill; Priscilla; Maria; Milley; Welley; Thomas; Adeline; James; Betty; Laura.	Oath of owner and two depositions.
Callis, H. A........................	Three slaves..	See Thomas Johnson's letter.
Canby, J. S........................	Six slaves..	
Coad, John, by T. Johnson, agent for the representatives.	Isaac.	Thomas Johnson's letter and list of articles, oath of claimant and three depositions.
Calvel, Edward, heirs of.............	Jacob..	See B. L. Lear's list.
D.		
Dyson, Sarah......................	Reuben..	Oath of owner and two depositions.
Dare, Ann.........................	Dick; Will...	Two depositions.
Dawkins, William C................	Hannah; Beck; Sal; Clem; Mila; John; Sam; George; Peg; Augustus; Chancey; Maria; Hannah.	Oath of owner and three depositions.
Dawson, James.....................	Frisby..	Oath of owner and one deposition.
Deer, Dr. John.....................	William..	Two depositions.
Denton, James D...................	Racel..	One deposition.
Dixon, William.....................	Bob; Hally; Mary....................................	Oath of owner and three depositions.
Duke, James, sr....................	James; Thomas; Jenny; Priscilla; James, (vide claim;) Salth; Minty; John; Maly.	Four depositions.
Dunkinson, Robert.................	Abram; Jacob..	Oath of owner and deposition as to value; five depositions.
Duval, Howard	Moses...	Oath of owner and two depositions.
Dangerfield, Henry P..............	Ned Carey; Stephen..................................	Oath of claimant and deposition of J. Allison and J. Lindsay.
E.		
Earecson, William.................	Tom...	Oath of owner and one deposition.
Edwards, Jesse	Phil...	Oath of owner.
Edelon, Water Estate, by Jenkins, R. S., executor.	Aaron...	Three depositions.
Edelon, Jeremiah	Dony	Oath of claimant and one deposition.
F.		
Ford, Josias B.....................	Peter; Fidelio.......................................	Oath of owner and two depositions.
Fenwick, Athanasius		
Fontaine, Henry....................	Corbin..	Oath of owner and two depositions. (Vide W. Sudler's deposition in Beauchamp's claim.)
Frisby, Richard....................	William; Ephraim; Solomon; Peregrine................	Oath of owner, two depositions as to value, and order of Adl. C. filed among the records of Congress.
Freeland, Jacob....................	Monday	Oath of claimant and three depositions.
Fitzhugh, John	John..	Oath of claimant and one deposition.
Fendall, Benjamin T...............	James; Summerville; Brooks; Lloyd; Townshend; Carter.	Oath of owner and two depositions.
G.		
Gale, John P., for his mother	Daniel; Nathan......................................	Oath of claimant and two depositions.
Gant, Thomas C...................	Richard Gant; Robert................................	Oath of owner and depositions.
Gant, Thos. C., trustee for Edward Gant, deceased.	Basil; Harry...	Four depositions.
Gant, Elizabeth....................	Bett; Sarah	Three depositions.
Gist, Mary........................	Mary; Matilda.......................................	Oath of the owner.
Goodhand, John....................	Pere; Emory	Do.
Gray, John M......................	Doll Handy; Sophy...................................	Oath of the owner and one deposition.
Green, Josiah......................	Sam...	Do.　　do.
Gardner, Robert....................	Milcah; Charlotte....................................	Oath of claimant and of James Benton.
Greer, Alexander...................	Joshua; York; Moses	Oath of owner and two depositions.
H.		
Hammett, Robert	George	Oath of owner and three depositions.
Hammett, Richard	Jane..	Do.　　do.
Hance, Benjamin	William; Mary	Oath of owner and one deposition as to value.
Handy, Joseph.....................	Levin..	Oath of owner and one deposition. (Vide Sudler's deposition in Beauchamp's claim.)
Hambleton, Harriet................	George..	Vide B. L. Lear's list.
Harris, Wm., deceased..............	Frisby	Two depositions.
Heard, Edmond....................	Tone..	Oaths of owner and deposition as to value.
Heard, Winifred	Joe..	Do.　　do.
Harwood, Thomas	Harry; Toby	Oath of owner and three depositions.
Hellen, Rebecca....................	Bob...	One deposition.
Hungerford, Eliza J	Daniel...	Oath of owner and two depositions.
Hungerford, Mary..................	Rachel and two children..............................	One deposition.
Hungerford, Thos. B................	Tom..	Do.
Hungerford, Violetta, deceased, by Juliet Hungerford, John W. Hungerford, and Thos. Tubman, her heirs.	Hendly and wife.....................................	Two depositions.
Hopewell, Angelica, executrix of Jas. Hopewell, deceased.	Wm. Handy..	Mr. Plater's letter and two depositions.
Harrison, Jona., by H. M. Murray and J. Glenn, attorneys.	Thomas; Peter; Bill; Anne; Poll and child............	Oath of claimant and three depositions.

MARYLAND—Continued.

Claimants.	Names of slaves.	Proof.
Hatton, Nathaniel......................	Charles..	Oath of owner and four depositions.
Same, as executor of Martha Hutton.	Baptist..	Oath of claimant and four depositions.
Hatton, Basil	James...	Deposition of Francis Dyer.
Hall, Richard T......................	Ben...	One deposition.
Hedges, John.........................	Washington..	Oath of claimant and one deposition.
Hillery, Tilghman.....................	Peter Redout; Andrew Redout.........................	
Hatton, Henry D......................	Henry; Nance..	Two depositions.
J.		
Jackson, John K......................	Joseph...	Two depositions.
Johnson, Ann E.......................	Charles; Bill; Barnett.................................	
Jones, Arthur T......................	Jacob; George; Abraham; Elijah; John; Delila; Polly; Hannah.	Three depositions; three depositions received October 24, 1823.
Jones, Mordecai	Isaac..	Three depositions and oath of claimant.
Jones, Caleb..........................	Job; Peter; Luce; Buck; James; Abraham; Jack; Jenny	
Ireland, John C.......................	Tom...	Two depositions.
Johns, Aquilla........................	About twenty slaves....................................	See Thos. Johnson's letter, filed with H. A. Charles' claim.
Jenkins, John M., by John G. Brooke, attorney.	Bob; Harry...	One deposition and exhibition as to deposition, filed with the claim.
Johnson, Ann E.......................	Charles; Bill; Barnett.................................	Three depositions.
Johnson, Renalde, estate of, by Jos. Kent, administrator.	Three slaves..	Joseph Kent's statement.
K.		
Kilgour, William......................	Dick; Jacob; John; Richard...........................	Oath of owner and two depositions.
King, Joshua..........................	Anthony; Lucy; Mary; Joseph.........................	Three depositions.
King, Thomas E	Sam..	Oath of owner and one deposition.
L.		
Legg, Harris..........................	Jacob...	Oath of claimant and one deposition.
Locker, George........................	Leah; Margaret; Lucy; Jelly; Litty; Elizabeth; Letty; Juliana.	Various depositions and documents.
Lowry, Margaret......................	Peter...	Oath of the owner.
Lynch, Thomas, jr....................	Guy; Jacob..	Oath of owner and two depositions.
M.		
M'Kay, Eliza K.......................	Matilda; Levi; Henney; Mary; Jenney.................	Oath of claimant and deposition of Leven W. Ballard.
Mackall, John G	Michael...	Oath of owner and two depositions.
Mackall, Ann..........................	Mary..	One deposition.
Mackall, Benj. H......................	Harry; Sall; Tamar; Ben; Dick; Charles; Fanny; Bennet; Benson; Annanias; Ishael; Nazareth; Rachael; Eleanor; Milley; Alley; Esau; Ann; Rocney; Sarah.	Oath of owner and one deposition.
Maddun, Prisey	Joe...	Do. do.
M'Krowin, Daniel.....................	John Dublin...	Oath of owner.
Miles, John...........................	David...	Oath of owner and one deposition.
Morgan, Jonathan, deceased	Chany; Cate...	Two depositions.
Mason, Richard B.....................	Abram Green; Lydia Green; Harry Green...............	Letter of Com. Barry to Colonel Fenwick.
Magruder, J. Read	Clem; Polly and child; Phillis..........................	
Marshal, Sarah	Dick..	One deposition.
Moreland, Mary, executrix of T. B. Moreland.	Peter Johnson...	Oath of claimant and one deposition.
Maccubbin, Thomas L...............	Isaac	Do. do.
N.		
Neth, Lewis...........................	Wm. Ross, alias Rolla	Do. do.
Nelson, Aquilla.......................	Peter; George; March; Primus	Oath of owner and four depositions.
Norris, Daniel........................	Gerard	Oath of claimant.
O.		
Ogle, Benjamin, for H. M. Ogle, deceased, and F. Closs.	Bob; Ben; Jacob; John; Bill; Flora; Sarah; Clara; Deborah; Sam; Tom; eight children.	Two depositions and letter of Captain Dix.
Osburn, Keziah........................	Minta; Fill; Sewell....................................	Oath of owner and one deposition.
P.		
Parrann, Jane	Davy; Jim; Damon; Amey; Pegg; Sophy	Deposition, and Captain Nourse's certificate and note.
Plater, John R	Stephen Courcey; Abram Wood; Crowley Young; John Young; Daniel Young; Henry Young; James Thomas; John Seale; John Seale, jr.; Wm. Hammer; Isaac Hammer; Mathew Courcey; James; Benjamin Seale; Francis Hammer; Prince Young; Peter Campbell; Lewis Monroe; Gerald Monroe; Richard Monroe; Lewis Monroe; Susanah Courcey; Maria Seale; Carey Hammer; Sophia Seale; Maria Seale; Frankey Seale; Maria Wood; Jesse Wood; Henney Williams; Mary Young; Catharine Young; Elizabeth Hammer; Teney Merritt; Louisa Thomas; Mary Hammer; Patty Seale; Peggy Seale; Eder Seale; Peggy Courcey; Mary Ann Young; Grace Monroe; Ester Monroe; Kitty Monroe; Perregrine Young; Ignatius Seale; James Bowie; Joseph Wood; Cornelius.	

MARYLAND—Continued.

Claimants.	Names of slaves.	Proof.
Parker, George......................	Washington..	Two depositions.
Pumphrey, James....................	Archibald...	Memorial and letter.
Phillips, Benjamin	Jerry; Martha; Joseph; Mary; Jerry....................	Oath of claimant and five depositions.
Parker, Elisha	Bob	Deposition of Collins.
R.		
Rawlings, Juliet	Mary; Harriet; Sidney...........................	Oath of the owner and one deposition.
Rawlings, Susanna..................	Minty; Sawney; Peter	Do. do.
Rawlings, Sarah, now Sarah Sedwick	Monday, with wife and children.....................	Oath of the owner and one deposition.
Rawlings, Isaac, for Isaac Rawlings, jr.	Charles...	Two depositions.
Reynolds, Thomas	Gen. Saunders	Oath of owner and one deposition as to value.
Ringgold, Edward...................	Jesse; Deborah..	Oath of owner and one deposition.
Ringgold, Samuel W., administrator of Jacob Ringgold, deceased.	Jesse	Oath of owner and one deposition as to value.
Ross, Richard	Thomas Perks	Do. do.
Reeder, William	Richard...	Oath of owner and deposition of two persons.
S.		
Sampson, Elizabeth W., executrix of Josiah W. Heath, deceased.	Monday; Violet..	Oath of the claimant and two depositions.
Sasscer, Thomas, executor of Wm. Sasscer, deceased.	Andrew...	Oath of claimant and three depositions as to value.
Shaw, Neal H	John	Oath of owner and one deposition.
Shaw, Richard, husband of Mary Shaw, widow and administratrix of Bernard Todd, deceased.	Able; Sam	Oath of claimant and two depositions.
Scott, Edward, executor of Thomas Lewis, deceased.	Kitty	Do. do.
Schoolfield, Wm. A.................	Bob	Oath of owner and one deposition.
Scrivener, John.....................	Jacob Carter; Brista Murdock..........................	Oath of owner and two depositions.
Skinner, Artemisa	Moses...	Oath of owner and one deposition.
Skinner, Andrew	Thomas Johnson..	One deposition.
Skinner, Alexander, executor of Leven Skinner, deceased.	Jacob	
Studert, John T.....................	Priamus; Hally..	Do.
Sewell, Robert, deceased...........	Tobias; Polly; Charles; Nancy; Sophy; Magdaline; Tobias; Fanny; Hally; James; Sooky; Sally; Mary; Jenny; Harriet; Rachel; Abraham.	Two depositions and a letter to R. S.
Smith, William......................	Nace..	Six depositions.
Sollers, James M....................	Monday..	Oath of owner and three depositions.
Sollers, Ann........................	David Armstrong; Jacob Goler; Hammond Goler; Rosetta Goler.	Oath of owner and two depositions.
Somerville, W. C., for self and H. V. Somerville, dec'd. W. C. S.	Ben; Jim; Ellick; Rawleigh or Rolla; Jenney; Henney; Robbin.	Oath of owner.
Somerville, W. C., for self and father, W. Somerville, dec'd. H. V. S.	Basil; Folman; Jack; Peter; Hezekiah; Charles; Nat; Frisby; Bill; Peg; Bet; Rachael; Sook; Anna; Minto; Clarissa; Fanny.	Oath of claimant and four depositions.
Sprigg, Ann, deceased, by Ishael T. Canby, executor.	Charles; Tom; Maria, and her daughter; Kitty, and her son.	Oath of owner and three depositions.
Sudler, William.....................	Arnold; Severn...	Oath of owner and one deposition.
Sewall, Mary, widow of Nicholas, deceased.	Jim; Beck; John; George; Louisa; Ghee; Isaac; Caroline; Peg; Jim; Charles; John; Moses; Enoch; a child of Jack; Grace; Bridget; a child of Ghee; Peg; Milley; Jack; Toby; George.	Oath of claimant and two depositions.
Simons, Thomas T..................	Isaac	Oath of claimant and one deposition.
Smith, Thomas......................	Dick..	Do. do.
T.		
Taney, Michael, sen., deceased......	Joe; Jesse; Charles; Ben; Tom; Joseph; Cloe; Priss; Ann; Letty; Hannah; Sall; Jenny; Veney; and ten or twelve children.	Oath of owner and three depositions.
Tanner, Keziah, widow of Philemon Tanner, deceased.	Ghee; Deborah; Charles; Daniel; Alla..............	Oath of owner and one deposition.
Taylor, James M.....................	Ned...	Oath of owner and two depositions.
Thompson, Peter W., husband of Larine Thompson, lately Larine Deni, widow of Dr. Hezekiah Dent, deceased.	Jim; Job; Davy; Bill; Henry...........................	Four depositions.
Tucker, John........................	Gideon; Pet; Mary Ann...................................	Oath of owner and two depositions.
Tucker, John........................	Jim	One deposition.
Turner, Samuel	Ben; Stephen...	Oath of owner and two depositions.
Tyler, Trueman......................	George; Chatham...	Oath of owner and one deposition.
Tolson's, Jacob, heirs...............	Priss..	See B. L. Lear's list.
W.		
Washington, Nathaniel	Bill...	Oath of owner and one deposition.
Wells, Walter.......................	Aaron; Gabriel; Jane......................................	Oath of owner and two depositions.
Weems, Gustavus....................	Harry	Oath of owner and one deposition.

MARYLAND—Continued.

Claimants.	Names of slaves.	Proof.
Whittington, William	Nace Leach; Wm. Hockton; George Leach; Samuel Leach.	Oath of owner and one deposition.
Wilkinson, George...:..............	Ned; Daniel; Jacob; Maly; Pegg; Plus	Oath of owner and three depositions.
Williams, Thomas	Tom....................:.....................	Oath of owner and one deposition.
Williams, Wm...:.................	Milly	Do. do.
Williams, Benjamin................	Prince; Betty; Mial; Rac,ae,; John; Nan; Letty; Kitty; Holdsworth; Sophia; Jacob; Cong; Rosetty; David; Tracy; Crecy; Perry; Gideon; Dalinda; Annach.	Oath of owner and three depositions.
Whittington, Thomas	Jane; Levice; Willoughby; Levincey; John; Eliza; Louisa; Ezekiel; Isaiah.	Do. do.
Wilson; Martha....................	Sam; Colonel; Deb; Jenny; Abby; Sillah; Vienna; Flunk; Holsey; Cato; Sab; Sidney; Milley; Margaret.	Oath of claimant.
		Oath of owner and five depositions.
Wise, Miel.....................	Shadrick; Winney; Charlotte; Louisa................	Oath of owner and one deposition as to value.
Wood, John...................	Daniel; Bet; Sampson; London; Gabe	Oath of owner and two depositions.
White, Walter K., husband of Mrs. White, representative of Malmaduke Goodhand, deceased.	Sam; Thomas; Minta; Nestor......................	Oath of claimant and one deposition.
Wrightson, Francis	Daniel...................................	Oath of owner and one deposition.
Ward, William	Alexander Cook.............................	Four depositions.
Y.		
Young, Robt. L. Ward, of Henry S. Hawkins.	Philip.....................................	Three depositions.
Do.......................	Robert; Malla; Stephen; Thomas....................	Two depositions, received October 20, 1823.

RECAPITULATION.

714 slaves; which, at the average value agreed upon and fixed by the Commissioners, viz., $280, amount to the sum of $199,920.

Inventory of property, other than that of slaves, stated to have been carried off by the British forces from the State of Maryland; with an alphabetical list of the claimants, and the estimated value of the said property.

Claimants.	Property.	Estimated value.	Proof.
A.			
Armstrong, George..............	80 hhds. of tobacco................	$8,566 74	Various documents inclosed in George Armstrong's memorial, proving the loss and ascertaining the value of the tobacco.
Alloway, Mary.................	Sheep and other property...........	157 00	Vide her claim for slaves, in which the various articles are enumerated and the proof exhibited.
B.			
Beckham, John..................	Furniture.........................	261 67	Oath of claimant.
Biscoe, George W	17 hhds. tobacco..................	649 13	Oath of claimant and two depositions.
Biscoe, George W., and Wm. L. Schmitt.	Schooner Speedwell...............	2,000 00	Oath of claimant, two depositions, and bill of sale.
Beall, Rebecca..................	Sheep and other property.........	50 00	See her claim for slaves, &c.
Benton, James..................	Sheep and other property.........	168 20	See his claim for slaves, &c.
Bryan, Ann....................	Horse, &c...:...................	137 00	Oath of claimant.
Butler, Henry..................	Cattle, &c.....................	502 00	Oath of claimant.
Baden, John....................	3 hhds. tobacco	331 00	Deposition of James Baden.
Baden, James..................	1 hhd. tobacco................	107 00	One deposition.
C.			
Carter, Richard..................	Sheep, &c.....................	85 00	Oath of claimant.
Coad, John, by T. Johnson, agent for the representatives.	Cattle and other articles enumerated in the schedule furnished herewith.	620 00	Th. Johnson's letter and list of articles, oath of claimant, and three depositions.
Crackland, John	1 horse	80 00	Oath of claimant and one deposition.
D.			
Donn, John....................	Coach and other articles............	1,021 22	Oath of claimant and four depositions.
Diggs, Mary...................	Mule, horse, &c................	200 00	Deposition of Daniel C. Sim.
E.			
Elliott, John...................	Cattle, &c.....................	159 50	Oath of claimant.
Earickson, William...:.........	7 cattle......................	84 00	See his claim for slaves.
Edelen, John	2 hhds. tobacco	214 00	See Vincent & Ferguson's list.
Evans, Jesse..................	1 horse	100 00	Deposition of D. C. Sim.
Edwards, Jesse.................	2 oxen	50 00	Oath of claimant; vide his claim for slave Phil.
Estep, Rezin..................	44 hhds. tobacco................	4,508 00	See his documents.
F.			
Fendall, Benj. T.................	1 schooner....................	1,200 00	See his list of property.

MARYLAND—Continued.

Claimants.	Property.	Estimated value.	Proof.
G.			
Gant, Edward, deceased, by Th. C. Gant, his ex'r.	14 hhds. tobacco	$1,120 00	Deposition and other papers.
Gist, Mary	11 cattle	188 00	See her claim for slaves, &c.
Goodhand, John	Horses, &c.	373 00	See his claim for slaves, &c.
Green, Josias	2 horses	150 00	See his claim for slaves, &c.
Griffin, Edward	Schooner Happy Return	1,000 00	Oath of claimant, two depositions, and bill of sale.
Gardner, Joseph	7 hhds. tobacco	560 00	
H.			
Hampton, John	Cattle, &c.	359 50	Oath of claimant,
Harwood, Thomas	Mule, &c.	469 00	See his claim for slaves, &c.
Hodges & Lansdale	335 hhds. tobacco	23,450 00	Their letter and memorial.
Hodgkins, W. C.	Horse, furniture, &c.	349 53	His letter.
Hoxter, James	Cattle, &c.	91 00	Oath of claimant.
J.			
Joiner, William	Cattle, &c.	138 25	Oath of claimant
Johnson, Ann E., estate of	54 hhds. tobacco	3,780 00	Deposition of T. R. Johnson (and tobacco notes inclosed.)
Johnson, Rinaldo, estate of, by Jos. Kent, adm'r.	80 hhds. tobacco	8,000 00	See Jos. Kent's memorial relative to three slaves belonging to R. Johnson's estate.
	Plate	500 00	
K.			
Knotts, Mark	Cattle, &c.	452 50	Oath of claimant
L.			
Legg, John C.	Cattle, &c.	489 50	Oath of claimant.
Legg, Harris	Horse, &c.	176 00	See his claim for slaves, &c.
M.			
McKrowin, Daniel	1 carriage	400 00	Oath of claimant.
McFaden & Harris, insurance agents.	Sloop Chance	690 00	Declaration of McFaden, policy of insurance.
Mackall, Benjamin H	Bacon, &c.	167 00	Oath of claimant.
O.			
Osburn, Kesia	Cattle, &c.	330 00	See his claim for slaves, &c.
P.			
Plater, James R., guardian of Plater, Ann E.	15 hhds. tobacco	1,050 00	Oath of claimant and one deposition.
R.			
Richardson, James	Cattle, &c.	636 75	Oath of claimant.
Ringgold, Edward	Sheep, &c.	201 00	See his claim for slaves, &c.
Ringgold, Samuel W., adm'r of Jacob Ringgold, dec'd.	Horse, &c.	262 50	See his claim for slaves, &c.
Rodness, John	Cattle, &c.	156 63	Oath of claimant.
S.			
Sudler, Mary Ann	Cattle, &c.	390 00	One deposition.
Stanley, Charles	Oxen, &c.	305 75	Oath of claimant.
Scrivener, John	Tobacco		
Sim, Daniel C.	Horse, &c.	165 00	Deposition of Mary Diggs.
T.			
Taney, Michael	Cattle, &c.	200 00	See his claim for slaves, &c.
Tanner, Keziah, widow of Philemon Tanner, deceased.	Sheep, &c.	82 00	See her claim for slaves, &c.
Tolson, Benjamin	Cattle, &c.	103 50	Oath of claimant
Tiernan, Michael, by Edward Fitzgerald, agent and former owner.	Schooner Caroline, int.	3,217 37	Documents inclosed in Mr. Fitzgerald's letter.
W.			
Walker, John	Cattle, &c.	230 00	Oath of claimant.
Weedon, Henry	Horse and saddle.	198 00	Oath of claimant.
Wilson, Wm., & Sons, for selves and Hodges & Lansdale.	116 hhds. tobacco	7,061 51	Their letter and memorial.
Winchester, Isaac	Cattle, &c.	41 50	Certificate of Lieutenant Pearce.
Woolahand, Margaret	Cattle, &c.	453 00	Oath of claimant.
Woolahand, Thomas	Household goods	33 25	Oath of claimant.
Wright, John	Corn, fodder, &c.	268 00	Oath of claimant.
V.			
Vincent & Ferguson, by John Ferguson, surviving partner.	56 hhds. tobacco	3,416 00	See John Ferguson's letter.
Vicker's Joel	Goods lost by capture of the sloop Chance.	449 12	Deposition of claimant, protest of Captain Mitchell, &c.

RECAPITULATION.

Amount of property per estimated value.... .... $83,256 22

List of slaves stated to have been carried off by the British forces from the State of Virginia, with an alphabetical list of the claimants, and the average value of the said slaves.

Claimants.	Names of slaves.	Proof.
A.		
Alderman, William	Adam	Oath of claimant and depositions of John D. White and S. Baker.
Alexander, Benjamin, deceased	Tom	Three depositions. (Paper No. 6.)
Allen, Thomas	Dan	Three depositions. (Paper No. 4.)
Anderson, Seney or Sena	John; Dick	Depositions of Philip Sale, Robert Hagens, and Matthew Anderson. (Paper No. 14.)
Armistead, Ralph	Lewis; Toby; Cain	Two depositions.
Armistead, Anthony	Nat; Essex; Peter; Pender	One deposition.
Armistead, Robert	Billy	One deposition. (See paper No. 2.)
Ashton, George	Nancy; Hampstead; Betsey	Deposition of Abraham B. Hooe.
Ashton, George D	Harry	Depositions of William Settle, Daniel Carmichael, and J. W. Hungerford.
Ashton, Mary	Sucky; Clary; Thornton	Deposition of George Rogers.
Austin, Chapman	Guy	Deposition of G. Davis.
Atwell, Eliz., representative of Richard Atwell	William	Deposition of Elliot Minor.
B.		
Baker, Elijah	Daniel; William; Dilly; Peggy; Esther; Joe	Five depositions.
Baker, Thomas B	Wilson	One deposition. (See paper No. 1.)
Badger, Thomas	Robin	Do. do.
Bailey, Robert	Isaac; Toney; Moore; Brister; Affey; Margaret; Nancy; Lucy; Milley; Letty; Sam; Julia; Maria; Cæsar; Humphrey.	Depositions of A. Rozin and J. B. Stevens.
Ball, James	John, alias John Hall*; Daniel, alias D. Jessup; Lee, alias Lee Williams.	Two depositions.
Ball, Joseph, jr.	Isaac	Depositions of James Hurst and Josias Ingram.
Ball, Thomas, deceased	Joe; Beswick	Depositions of Jas. Hurst, Thos. E. Nutt, Wm. Harding, Jno. D. Ficklin, and J. C. Edwards. (Paper No. 25.)
Ball, Mottrom	Betty; Barbara; Flora†; Tim; Barbara and children	Deposition of William Ball.
Ball, William	Robin	Deposition of Thomas H. Jett.
Ball, David	Rhodam; James; Robin; Isaac; Humphra	Deposition of Josias Ingram.
Baines, Stephen	Pleasant; Philes; Fanny; Filler; Jack; Matilda; Judith; Lucind; Clariss.; Leah; William.	Depositions of Vincent and Alfred Kirkham.
Barber or Baber, Thos. B. B.	Wilson	Deposition of A. B. Hooe.
Barnett, George	Edward Barnet	Mr. Bailey's list.
Barron, James	Joe	Depositions of Wm. Cooper and Ann Cooper. (Paper No. 2.)
Barrot, George	Ned	Deposition of George Haydon.
Baynham, Richard, deceased	Emanuel	Deposition of Thomas Hudgins. (Paper No. 20.)
Beacham, Thomas	Silvia; Betty; Eliza; Adam; Silvia; Sam; Will; Daniel; Harry; Will; James.	Deposition of John King.
Beacham, Daniel W	Abraham; Jenny; George	Deposition of Thomas Beacham.
Beacham, Bushrod M'F.	Isaac; Job Townsend	Deposition of Elijah Williams; M. Bailey's list.
Beacham, Polly F.	Dick	Deposition of Thomas Brann.
Beale, Alice O.	Anthony; Isaac	Depositions of Thaddeus Forrester and B. H. Leland.
Beard, Matthew, deceased	Harry	Depositions of George Schirer, Thomas H. Kellam, and John C. Kellam.
Belfield, Sydner	Lucy; Sally	Deposition of George Saunders.
Bell, Charles	Mary	Depositions of Thomas M. Cox and John Hardwick.
Berryman, Alexander	Phil or Philip Lee	Deposition of William Berryman.
Bell, Thomas	George	Deposition in case of Benj. Turner. See paper in case of Langley, (paper No. 24.)
Berry, Ann W	Samuel Shadock; Nancy Lewis and four children; Jeremiah Wilcox; James Sprigg; George Hains; Judy Hudgins.	Depositions of Philip Sale and Henry Griffin. (See papers in case of John Sutton; see paper No. 9.)
Berryman, Willoughby N	Rachel; Winney; Vincent	Depositions of John Winstead and Thomas Kirkham.
Berryman, Francis	George; Isaac; Ned	Depositions of John H. Washington, T. T. Fitzhugh, and Benjamin Grymes.
Belote, Leven	Nat	Deposition of Elias Dunton. (See paper No. 1.)
Biggs, Thomas, deceased	Jacob; Sam	Depositions of Walker Suker and Leven Scott. (See paper No. 1.)
Blackwell, George	Milley	Deposition of William Prosser.
Billups, Sally	Bill	Deposition of William L. Smith.
Blake, James	Frank	Deposition of Thomas R. Yeatman. (Paper No. 21.)
Bohannon, William, deceased	Jack	Depositions of Philip Sale, Robt. Hugins, and J. Patterson.
Booker, George	Not mentioned	Deposition of Paul D. Luke. (Paper No. 27.)
Booth, John	Elijah	Deposition of William Way.
Bradford, John B.	Ansley; Margaret	Depositions of Thomas Walker and John B. Bradford.
Bray, Winter	James	Deposition of William Davis.
Bray, Polly	Sam	Do. do.
Brickhouse, George	Sam; Sarah; Grace	Deposition of Johannis Johnson and of William Dixon. (See paper No. 1.)
Briscoe, Ann	Able	Deposition of Christopher Hartley.

* Returned home from Jamaica.   † Flora is said to have belonged to J. Turberville, sen., and is enumerated among his slaves.

VIRGINIA—Continued.

Claimants.	Names of slaves.	Proof.
Brokenborough, A	Solomon; Stephen..	Deposition of Benjamin Blake.
Bucker, Elizabeth, reversionary interest in Thomas Miller.	Jude; Charlotte; Delia; Lavinia; Tom; Billar; Hannah*; Ben*; Tom*; Lucy; Hannah; Anthony; Mary; Phelicia; Easther; Winney; Phelicia; James; Charles; Mingo; Harry; James; Ned; Simon.	Deposition of Jas. R. Miller; deposition of A. B. Hoos.†
Bull, or Ball, Joseph, deceased........	Fielding; Harry..	Deposition of John Cattrell.
Barwell, James, deceased	James..	Deposition of Thomas Fowles.
Braxton, Carter, deceased...............	Solomon; Scipio..	Deposition of John Harmon.
Bunting, Jonathan	Jacob..	Deposition of M. S. Pitts. (See paper No. 1.)
Brown, Richard T........................	Henry..	Deposition of J. Hazard and R. Pierce. (See papers in case of R. H. Lee and E. A. Lee.)
Boush, William........................	Berry; Friday; Mingo; Jack; Anthony; Ned; Cato; John; Tom; Sarah; Eddy; Fanny; Nice; Comfort; Mary; Alice; Joshua.	John Cowper's list.
Boraure, Mary	George; Harry..	John Cowper's list; deposition of J. M. Bude.
Boraure, John........................	Dick; Isaac..	Do.　　　do.
Bernard, William........................	Charles..	Deposition of Robert Scott.
Brooks, John	Humphrey..	J. Cowper's list; deposition of Thomas R. Yeatman.
Bailey, Susannah	Michael; Reuben; Milley..	Deposition of Allen S. Dozier.

C.

Claimants.	Names of slaves.	Proof.
Cabell, Joseph C., subject to Mrs. Tucker's dower.	Dick; Sukey; Morocco; George; James; Solomon; Tom Saunders; Hannah Marks; Delila; Joe; Joseph; Edenborough; Hollace; Fanny; Dinah; Nancy; Charles; Alfred; Lucinda; Ezekiel; Nelly; China; Betty Bush; Spencer; Betty Stevins; Willoughby; Rodner; Nancy; Peter; George; Amy; Young; James; George and an infant; Jim Bull; Billy Saunders; Sarah; Sucky; Cordelia; Joe; Cannada.	Depositions of John Richardson, James J. White, and Charles Carter.
Carter, Charles	Henry Saunders; Henry Lee; Charles James; Dean Bunday; Henry Lee; Talbot Cox; Tom Browne; Joe Browne; Robert Lee; Gabriel Lowry; Peyton Cox; Aggy Brown; Frankey Cox; Suckey Brown; Unity Lee; Suckey Brown; Sarah Ann Moore; Merinda Saunders; Charity Brown; Chris. Lee; Dinah Dennis; Nelly Cox; Nelly Lee; Emily Lee; Nancy Lowry; Fanny Saunders; James Cox.	Depositions of George Robertson, James J. White, and John Richardson.
Campbell, John......................	Henry; Caty; Cornelia; Finness......................	Depositions of Nathaniel Lafevre and James Montgomery.
Catmichael, Daniel......................	Alech; Palker..	Depositions of J. Paine and William Berryman.
Carpenter, John, deceased...............	Ned..	Depositions of John Kimm, Richard Hutchins, and John Rogers.
Carpenter, John......................	Jim; Ladus..	Depositions of John Scott, Robert James, and William B. Clarke. (Paper No. 3.)
Carpenter, William......................	Pyrrmus; Inse; Manuel......................	Depositions of Eppy Norris and C. Tapscott. (Paper No. 11.)
Carter, Joseph, jr......................	Isaac..	Deposition of George Hathaway.
Carter, Landon, deceased...............	Sally; Mendith..	A. Neale's list; deposition of John D. Ficklin; Mr. Bailey's list.
Carter, Nancy......................	John Gibson	Mr. Bailey's list.
Carter, James, jr., deceased...........	Wat; Sam..	Depositions of Griffin Edwards and George L. Corbin.
Carter, Charles B., deceased...........	Attwell; John; Bob; Charles	Depositions of W. Settle and William Stanley.
Cary, Miles..........	Nat; Abraham; Davy; Harry; Cæsar; Rose; Lucy, and four children.	Depositions of Charles Jennings, William Ham, James Burke, Thomas Lattimer, and Paul D. Luke. (Paper No. 27.)
Cottrell, or Cockrell, Peter..........	Amy; William; James; Eliza; Roxy......................	Deposition of James Harcum.
Cottrell, or Cockrell, John	Levi; Ezekiel; Joe; Isaac; Jacob; Timity; Bill; Jesse; George; Andrew; Abraham; Judith, and two children; William.	Depositions of Joseph Conway, Walker Anderson, Samuel Blunder, and Matthew Hudson.
Cox, Peter P......................	Sam; Manuel; House Joe; Little Joe; Mima; Daniel; Anna; Fanny; John; Criss; Patty; Molly; Sukey; Hannah; James; Bill; Jess; Winney; Davy; Tom; Suckey; Nancy; Rose; Frankey; Charles; Bill; Mary.	Depositions of Daniel Nealy and Benedict Lampkin.
Cox, Polly......................	Nelly..	Deposition of Daniel Nealy.
Cox, Downing	Spencer..	Depositions of Daniel Nealy and William Middleton.
Cox, Elizabeth, guardian of Carlos Cox.	Richard; Phillis; Solomon; Metham; Catsby; Betty; Martin; Julius.	Deposition of Samuel Barnes, jr.
Cox, Ann......................	Charles..	Deposition of Thomas Brown.
Cox, Peter, deceased......................	Meshick; Bill; James......................	Deposition of Samuel Burnes.
Cox, Thomas M......................	Thornton; Andrew; John; Sinah; Job; Stephen.......	Depositions of John Hardwick, Peter Morgan, John King, and Jeremiah Middleton; also oath of claimant. (Paper No. 11.)
Cox, Sally J......................	Andrew; Robert; Silvia; Rawleigh; Minco; Nelson; Betsey, Winney.	Deposition of P. Claughton.
Costin, William, sen........	Joe; Harry; Rhoda; Lucy; Sarah; Ned; and Silvia....	Deposition of Arthur Simpkin. (See paper No. 1.)
Castin, Abraham......................	Daniel	Deposition of S. Spady. (See paper No. 1.)

＊ See A. B. Hooe's deposition.　　　　　　　　　　　　† For this latter deposition see papers of Thomas Miller.

VIRGINIA—Continued.

Claimants.	Names of slaves.	Proof.
Chandler, Thomas	Fortunatus; Troy; Stephen; Pertilly; William; Jane; Lucy; Kitty; and Fill.	Deposition of William Chandler.
Chandler, John.	Lavinia; Suckey; Frankey...........................	Depositions of Wm. C. Chandler and Nath'l V. Clópton.
Chandler, William C................	George; .George; Nancy, and child; Eliza; Henry; James.	Depositions of Wm. Pillion, A. Parker, and John C. Chandler.
Chilton, Cyrus......................	Adam..	Depositions of Eppa Norris, L. R. Dobyns, and oath of claimant. (Paper No. 11.)
Chowning, Wm. C., jr................	Billy...	Deposition of Thomas Stowens. (Paper No. 29.)
Chowning, James................,......	Bartlett..	Deposition of S. Candiff, (filed in the case of J. Satton.)
Christopher, John, deceased........	Robin; Adam; Joe; Royston..........................	Deposition of Washington Haynie.
Clarke, Samuel	Charlotte; Alfred; Harriet; Polly; Louisa.............	Deposition of Richard Walker.
Claughton, Pemberton, jr., deceased..	Rodham; Lucinda; Hannah; Mahala..................	Depositions of Thomas Beacham and Thomas Bell.
Claughton, Pemberton	Sam; Jerry; Hannalon; Phillis; Jenny; Laticia; Epamanondas; Thomas; Leluius; Rachel; Britannia; Abraham; Into; John.	Depositions of Kenner W. Kralle and Richard Knott.
Claughton, Betty and Kitty..........	Solomon; Spencer; George; Jacob; Sam.............	Depositions of P. C. Rice and Thomas Beacham.
Clements, Lucy......................	Janot..	Deposition of Henry Young.
Cochrane, Samuel	William Gilmor...	M. Bailey's list.
Cockerill, Joshua, deceased	Bill...	Deposition of Joseph Doulin.
Coleman, Ann......................	Harry; Jim; Robin....................................	Depositions of Dolly Elliot and Thomas Pitcher.
Coles, Richard, deceased............	Bill; Samuel; Daniel; Peter.........................	Deposition of Christopher Heartley.
Coles, Joseph	Eppa; Solomon..................	Deposition of Matthew Hudson.
Coles, Rodham......................	James..	Depositions of W. Anderson and Richard Nelmes.
Coles, Ann	Abel	Do. do. do.
Coles, Elizabeth	Bill; Sam; Dan; Peter.................................	Do. do. do.
Coles, Edward, deceased............	James..	Deposition of Christopher Heartley.
Collard, Samuel	Sophia...	Oath of claimant, and depositions of W. L. Barrell and B. Rogers.
Conway, Thomas....................	Peter or P. Crancy...............	Depositions of Jos. Doulin and John Hayes; M. Baily's list.
Conway, Joseph, deceased..........	Ned; Peter; Patty; Judy; Nisey; Charles; Siller; Nancy; Solomon; Dick.	Deposition of John Cottrell.
Conway, Eliza......................	Gabriel..	Deposition of Thomas Conway.
Cooper, John, deceased	Bray; Jack; Milley; Hannah, and child; Austin; Pompey; Betty; Isaac; Malvina; Bill; Nancy; Milley; Orenau.	Deposition of Charles M. Cullier and two depositions of William Cooper. (Papers No. 2 and 15.)
Corbin, Gowin......................	Davy; Henry..	Deposition of George L. Corbin.
Cooper, James N....................	Scipio; Jim; Sail; Lavinia; Lydia....................	Depositions of William Cooper and Ann Cooper. (See papers of T. and R. Wornum; paper No. 2.)
Cornlek, Thomas....................	Sarah Riggs and her two children.:...................	Depositions of John T. Keeling and John Cornick, filed in papers of the case of L. Shepherd. (Papers No. 16.)
Cornick, Thomas, jr................	Will; Lewis; Daniel........................	Depositions of John Cornick and Samuel Cornick.
Cornick, Adam, deceased..........	Davey...	Depositions of John T. Keeling and John Cornick. (See Speed's case; paper No. 16.)
Cornick, Lemuel....................	Tom; Roger; Peter Riggs; Peter, jr..................	Depositions of John T. Keeling and John Cornick.
Cornick, John	Isaac..	Depositions of John T. Keeling and Samuel Cornick.
Cornick, James....................	Owen..	Depositions of John T. Keeling and John Cornick.
Cornick, James....................	William Moore..	J. Cooper's list.
Cornick, Elizabeth	Nanny	Depositions of William D. Woodhouse.
Cornick, Margaret	Moody...	Depositions of Adam Keeling and Wm. D. Woodhouse.
Cornick, William B., deceased		Depositions of John Kellum and Wm. D. Woodhouse.
Cralle, John, jr....................	Tom; Armstead; Matilda..............................	Deposition of Kenner W. Cralle.
Cralle, Keuner W..................	Jerry; Sam; Job; Harry; John; Milley; Letty; Molly; Sally. Brown; Pharnie; Letia; Winney; Hannah; James; Charlotte; Paul; Frederick; Vilet; Rachel; Peggy; Stephen.	Deposition of John Winstead.
Crawford, Carter....................	Peter..	Depositions of Charles Jones, John Jones, and William Jones, filed with the case of Burnett Wood. (Paper No. 4.)
Cricher's, John, estate..............	Hannah..	Deposition of Thomas Stowens. (Paper No. 29.)
Crandle, John......................	Billy..	Deposition of John Young, H. R. Dunn, and Richard Young, filed with William Digg's papers. (No 23.)
Crow, Fielding	Charles..	Five depositions filed with Wm. Taylor's papers. (Paper No. 6.)
Chrisman, Martha..................	Hannah; Charles ...:..................................	Depositions of Wm. Cowper and Ann Cowper. (See T. & R. Wornum's paper; see paper No. 2.)
Crowder, Nancy	Hapy..	Deposition of Josias Ingram.
Cundiff, Nelly......................	Ephraim...	Depositions of John Davenport, Steptoe Taylor, and Thomas Hughlett.
Curtes, Henry, deceased............	Billy.....	Deposition of George Stubblefield, (paper No. 10,) filed with the papers of B. Stubblefield.
Custis, Thomas, deceased..........	Isaac..	Deposition of Edmund R. Curtis and Ethel Lyon.
Custis, John......................	Charles..	Oath of claimant and depositions of Stephen Hopkins and Spencer Lewis.
Custis, Wm. P......................	Joshua; Nathaniel......................................	Letter of claimant.
Crump, John C	Moses; Anthony; Abourdeen; Roger; Jacob.............	Deposition of Arthur Smith and oath of claimant.
Chichester, Daniel M'C......,.......	Martin; Daniel ......;..................................	See letter of Thomas Johnson.

VIRGINIA—Continued.

Claimants.	Names of slaves.	Proofs.
Cary, Thomas	Hercules; Flora; Buckey	Memorandum of Thomas Cary, and depositions of Wm. T. Tilledge, Wm. Moor, Thomas C. Tillege, and John Hobday.
D.		
Dade, Francis T	Dick	Depositions of Charles Massey, Jr.
Dade, Langhorne	Charles; Billy	Deposition of Wm. H. Hooe.
Dade, Townshend S.	Phill	Deposition of Charles Massey, Jr.
Dawson, Thomas	Charles	J. Cowper's list; deposition of J. Patterson.
Dangerfield, John	Billy	Deposition of Overton Meader.
Darley, John and Eliza C	Charles; Edmond; Jesse	Deposition of Horace Welford, John R. T. Corbin, and George Davis.
Davenport, D. F	Jerry; Charles	Deposition of William Paine.
Davenport, Lindsay O	James	Deposition of Willis W. Hudnall.
Davis, John, deceased	Lazarus	Deposition of Thomas Bills.
Davis, Edward	Abraham	Deposition of Thos. Davis and John Watkins.
Dean, Josiah L., deceased	Tom; Sam; Adam	Deposition of Thomas Hagins and Thomas Davis. (See papers No. 14 and No. 20.)
Demerit, Molly	Thaddeus	A. Neale's list.
Diggs, John T	Spencer; Sukey; Anne	Deposition of John Ingram.
Diggs, William, deceased	Tom	Deposition of John Young, H. R. Dunn, and Richard Young. (No. 23.)
Dixon, Wm., jr	James; Kit	Deposition of J. S. Pitts and Thomas Jacobs. (See paper No. 1.)
Dixon, Wm., sr	Rose; Sarah; Sabra; Isaac	Depositions of John T. Elliott and John W. Dixon. (See papers No. 1 and 3.)
Doggett, Clem	Bill	Deposition of William Elkridge and Winder Ellison.
Dobyns, Thomas	Bradley; Solomon; Nassau; Simon; William	Depositions of Vincent Garland and Daniel Garland.
Dobyns, Le Roy	Carter; Absolem; Jerry; Newman; Bill; Sam; George; Solomon; James; Joe; Ned; Milley; Shadrack; Amelia; Sylvia; Betty; Thresby; Lydia; Bob; Betty; Lewis; Jemima; Nelly; Emily; Charlotte; Pat; Ariana; Polly; Rachel; Jenny; Isaac.	Depositions of Henry Meskell, Christopher L. Dobyns, and William Dobyns.
Dolemon, John H	Charles	Deposition of James Scate.
Downman, H. J	Bond	Deposition of B. M. Leland.
Downman, J. W. P	Genny	Do. do.
Downman, H. J., A. O. Beale, and O. Downman.	Manuel; Robin; Dick; Tabb; Randall	Deposition of Priscilla Brown and Eppa Norris.
Downman, R. R	Daniel; Robin; Abel; Joe; Charles; Nassau;* Andrew; Ben; Nell; Alice; Cyrus.	Depositions of Joseph B. Downman, L. Stamper, and James and Fanny Ball; correspondence between Lt. Col. Chowing and Capt. Barrie.
Downman, Fanny	Jesse	A. Neale's list.
Downing, Samuel	Solomon; Jerry	Depositions of Elias Hudnall and D. Hayner.
Doulin, Joseph	George; Joe; Emanuel	Depositions of Thomas Conway and John Hays.
Downing, Edward	James	Depositions of William Ball and Samuel Blackwell.
Downing, Winnifred	Roger	Deposition of John Hughtell.
Downing, Thos. D	Rawleigh; James	Depositions of Joseph Rogers and F. Bates.
Doxier, Allen J	Jenny; Abraham	Deposition of William C. Chandler.
Dudley, John	David; Amen; George; Harry; Billy; Thrisby; Winney; Billy; Mary; Robin; Milley; Bob; Joe.	Depositions of Martin Session and George Davis.
Dungan, Nancy B	Rachel; Silva; Sillar; Lavinia; George	Deposition of Pemberton Claughton.
Dunton, John	Dinah; Rose	Deposition of Kendal Groton. (Paper No. 1.)
Dunton, William	Peter	Deposition of John D. Turpin. (Paper No. 3.)
Dunn, Robert	Watt; Maria	See list furnished by S. Whitehead.
Davis, Arthur L	Beckey; Mary; Mordecai; Lucy; William; an infant; Phillis; Warner; Henry; Louisa.	Oath of claimant.
Day, Davis		Deposition of A. Smith and J. C. Crump.
E.		
Edwards, Thomas	Peter	J. Cowper's list.
Elliott, John R	George	Oaths of Philip Sale, Robert Hudgens, and J. Patterson.
Elliot, John	Daniel	Deposition of Thomas G. Scott. (Paper No. 1.)
Elleston, Frances	Michael	Deposition of William Eakridge and Clement Doggett.
Eakridge, William	Jack; Samuel; Betty; Anne; Richard; Fanny	Deposition of Clement Doggett and Winder Elliston.
Eustice, William, deceased	Daniel	Deposition of James Brent and Thomas James.
Evans, Kemp	Simon; Isaac	Two depositions of George Saunders.
Edwall, James	David; Josiah	Depositions of Richard H. Gaskins and Thos. Gaskins.
Eyre, William, deceased	Daniel; Lewis; Jenny and child; Luke; Abraham	Deposition of Curtis Willis. (See paper No. 1.)
Eyre, John	Billy; Jonathan; Jim; John; Mingo; Nim Carter; Bill; Esau.	Two depositions of Curtis Willis. (See paper No. 1.)
F.		
Fairfax, Henry	Tom	Oath of claimant and depositions of Thomas Turner and Jesse Bobs.
Fitchett, Salathiel	Amos	Depositions of Thos. Fitchett & Thos. R. Yeatman, and Thomas Fitchett. (Papers Nos. 14 and 20.)
Fitchett, James N	Isaac	Deposition of John B. Thomas. (Paper No. 1.)
Fitchett, Joshua	Joe; Parker; Jack; Matthew	Deposition of Arthur Simpkins. (See paper No. 1.)
Fitchett, Joshua, (of Matthews county)	Hannah; Davy; William; Courtney	J. Cowper's list.
Fitchett, Richard	John	Deposition of Thomas R. Yeatman. (Paper No. 20.)

* Returned, having escaped from Bermuda.

VIRGINIA—Continued.

Claimants.	Names of slaves.	Proof.
Flannery, Rebecca........................	Bob...	
Fletcher, Thomas, deceased.............	Isaac; James; Isaac, jr.; Frederick; Benjamin; Bandy; Hannah and child; Etsay; Ann; Rachel.	Deposition of Henry Fletcher, administrator.
Forrester, William H..................	Rachel...	Deposition of Richard Knott.
Fox, Joseph............................	Joshua; Henry...	Deposition of Richard Monroe and William Berryman.
Farrow, Benjamin......................	Jesse...	Letter of Joseph S. Barbour.
Floyd, John K.........................	Jack; Pat; Jacob; Sam; Tinney; Chocolate; Elisha; Maria; Betty; Southey; Lucy; John Morris; Matthew.	
G.		
Garland, Griffin, deceased............	Billy; Joe..	Depositions of John Garland and Nimrod Rochester.
Garner, William.......................	Jenny; Hannah; Alice; Kate; George; Jacob; James; Dilly; an infant.	Deposition of Thomas Stowers and Willis Garner.
Garner, William S.....................	Will; Henry; Roger; Jerd; Darley; Anthony; William, jr.; George; Silar; Sinah; Ruth; Betty; Hannah; Jane; Winney; Moriah; Lavinia; Ann; Malinday Grace; Pollard; Budd; John; Anthony, jr.; James.	Deposition of Thomas Kirkham, John Winstead, and Thomas Beacham.
Gaskins, Henry L.....................	Betty; Nanny; Nelly; Maria; Tabley; Alice; Rose	Deposition of Thomas Taylor.
Gaskins, Richard H..................	Harry..	Deposition of James Ewell and Thomas Gaskins.
Gayle, Joseph........................	Jim..	J. Cowper's list.
Gibbons, Elizabeth...................	Prince...	Two depositions of Thos. Archer, of Thos. Griffin, and of Samuel Griffin. (Filed with papers of Griffin.)
Gibson, William.....................	Ned, or Nace, or Nathan	Depositions of John Hunt and James Bunt.
Gibson, John, deceased..............	Jesse..	Do. do.
Glascock, Richard M................	Dennis...	Depositions of Charles Palmer and Joseph Dale.
Goffigan, John......................	Sam; Mack..	Depositions of Peter Wilkins and S. E. Nottingham. (Paper No. 3.)
Goffigan, James.....................	Daniel...	Deposition of L. Nottingham.
Goffigan, Francis...................	James..	Deposition of Thomas G. Scott. (See paper No. 1.)
Griffin, Thomas.....................	Lewis; James; Bob; Billy; Jack	Deposition of Thos. Archer and two of Sam'l S. Griffin.
Griffin, Lampkin....................	Nelson Lampkin...	Mr. Bailey's list.
Grimstead, John.....................	Joseph...	Deposition of P. C. Rice.
Grymes, Benjamin...................	Carry..	Depositions of D. Lewis, R. Lyle, and B. Stewart.
Groton, Kindall.....................	Daniel...	Oath of L. Bilote. (See paper No. 1.)
H.		
Haile, Benjamin R., deceased........	Lucy; Betty...	Deposition of Richard Knott.
Hallett, William....................	Gundy...	Deposition of Arthur Simpkins. (Paper No. 1.)
Hansborough, John, deceased.........	James; Ephraim...	Depositions of James Bent, John Murphy, Wm. Clarke; and Theophilus Bowie.
Harcum, William, deceased...........	Gabriel..	Deposition of William Hudnall.
Hannanson, John H..................	Adah and her 2 children....................................	Deposition of John W. Dixon.
Harvey, Thomas, deceased...........	Bill; Michael; Rawleigh; Jim; Burgess; Polly; Darkey	Depositions of William B. Kent and Sephorus Harvey.
Harvey, James, deceased............	Daniel...	Depositions of Richard Monroe and William Berryman.
Hathaway, Thomas...................	Emanuel; Jesse; Phil.......................................	Deposition of George Myers.
Hayes, John.........................	Rose; Martin; Spencer; Winder; Effy	Depositions of Joseph Doulin and Samuel Webb.
Hayden, George.....................	Mark...	Deposition of George Barrot.
Haynes, James......................	America Sparrow; Anthony Johnson; George White-house; Bash.	Letter of Mr. Cowper. (Paper No. 5.)
Haynie, Bridgar.....................	Jesse..	Deposition of Mary Nightingale.
Haynie, William D..................	Deane...	Depositions of George Davis and Joseph Decamps; (Paper No. 11.)
Hazard, William....................	Charles; Edmund..	Two depositions of William Stowers. (Paper No. 29.)
Headly, James, sen.................	Job; Isaac; Mima; Moriah; Jera........................	Deposition of G. Headly.
Henderson, William.................	Abel...	Depositions of S. W. East and T. Henderson.
Henderson, John....................	William Moore...	Mr. Bailey's list.
Holland, Thomas....................	Gilbert..	S. Whitehead's list.
Hooe, Abraham B....................	Mary; Bartlett; Peter; Prince; Aaron; Gust; Frank; Betsey; Jack; John; Paul.	Depositions of Benjamin Grimes and Geo. M. Grimes.
Howard, Henry......................	Melchisedeck..	Two depositions of R. Shield. (Paper No. 17.)
Howard, Calthorpe..................	Ned..	Do. do.
Hudgins, Robert....................	Sam...	Depositions of Philip Sale and Robert Hudgins.
Hudgins, Houlder...................	Philis Johnson; John Hutchings; Tom Johnson; Mary Wright; Nancy Lewis. George.. Phil; Jane; Sam. John..	Mr. Bailey's list. (Paper No. 6.) Deposition of H. Griffin.
Hudgins, John L....................	Carrill; Davy...	Depositions of J. Patterson and H. Griffin. (Paper No. 8.) J. Cowper's list.
Hudgins, John......................	William Hudgins..	Mr. Bailey's list.
Hudnall, Richard...................	Sarah; Winney; Armstead; Sam; Lavinia...............	Deposition of Thomas Hudnall.
Hudnall, Thomas....................	Spencer; Jack..	Deposition of Richard Hudnall.
Hudnall, Polly.....................	Betty; Thomas; Solomon*; Cooper*	Depositions of Thomas Fowler, J. Rogers, and Thomas H. Gett. (Papers No. 7 and 21.)
Hudnall, William...................	James..	Depositions of Henry L. Gookins and Geo. Blackwell.
Hudnall, Warner....................	Tom..	Deposition of Joseph Rogers.
Hughlett, Esther...................	Mark; Daniel; Armstead..................................	Depositions of John Hughlell, Ann F. Rust, and Wm. Haynie.

* A. Neale's list.

VIRGINIA—Continued.

Claimants.	Names of slaves.	Proof.
Hughlett, Thomas W.	Joe; Bill.	Deposition of John Ingraham.
	Daniel Taylor.	Mr. Bailey's list.
Hughlett, John	Jacob; Daniel; James; Lucy	Deposition of William Haynie and Ann T. Rust.
Hull, J., deceased	Isaiah	Mr. Bailey's list.
	Aaron; Joe; Weaver	Deposition of John Catrell.
Holt, George	Beck, and her child Elenor; Joshua	Depositions of Wm. Kelium, J. W. Dixon, and T. Groton. (Paper No. 3.)
Hunt, Obadiah	Ezekiel.	Deposition of L. Nottingham.
Hunter, James	John or Jack.	Depositions of James M. Garnett, Edward Rowze, W. M. Garnett, John R. Matthews, and Thos. Matthews.
Hunter, Nancy	Travis.	Depositions of Nathaniel P. Clopton and John Hunter.
Hurst, Isaac	Suckey.	Depositions of James Hurst and Joseph Ball.
Hull, Maria.	Peter; Hannah; Aggy; John; Sally; Betsey; Patty; Peter; Robin; Elliott.	Depositions of R. B. Hutt, William Y. Sterman, and Thomas W. Hutt. (Paper No. 22.)
Hipkins, William A., deceased.	Cyrus	Deposition of James Miller.
Haynes, John, deceased	Argyle; George; Betty; Peggy	Depositions of Eliz. Lee, J. Drayton, H. Haines, and John Mills.
Hall, Pitt.	David.	
Hunt, John.	Ezekiel	S. Whitehead's list.
I & J.		
Jacob, Thomas.	Levi; Nanny.	Deposition of M. S. Pitts. (See paper No. 1.)
Ingram, Sally.	Robin.	Deposition of J. Hurst. (Paper No. 26.)
Ingram, Josias.	Phill; Nero.	Depositions of Jos. Ball, jr. and James Hurst.
Ingram, John	Lewis; Matilda.	Depositions of James Hurst and Josias Ingraham.
Johnson, Thomas.	Bill.	Depositions of James and William Johnson.
Johnson, James.	Jim.	Deposition of S. Killum.
Johnson, John.	Jim and Tom.	S. Whitehead's list.
Jones, Armistead, deceased.	Jacob; Jerry, or Jerry Page.	Depositions of Thomas James and William Games.
Jones, John.	Peter; Zachariah Rundall.	Deposition of H. Brown. Mr. Bailey's list.
Jones, Thomas.	Jack.	Depositions of H. Browne and William Games.
Jones, Walter.	Solomon; Daniel; Manuel; Stephen; Ben; John; Rachael; Lucy; Tom; Joseph; Job; Presley.*	Deposition of J. Hudson. *Deposition of Robt. Murphey.
Jones, John, deceased.	Zachary	Deposition of Judy Baxendine.
Joynes, William	Mark.	Deposition of S. Hopkins.
Iveson, George D.	Ben.	Depositions of H. Diggs, sen., and Thomas Hodgins. (Papers Nos. 14 and 20.)
Jervis, Francis	Will.	J. Cowper's list. Deposition of T. R. Yeatman.
K.		
Keeling, John T	Argyle; Will; Isaac; Adam; Mary; Levy; James.	Depositions of John Cormick and Samuel Cormick.
Keg, William	Daniel.	Deposition of William Kirk.
Kellum, Walter.	Isaac; Joshua.	Depositions of J. D. Turpin and H. Simpkins. (Papers Nos. 1 and 3.)
King, Philip	Ben.	Depositions of Thomas Stowers and S. Potter.
Knott, Richard.	Bob; Rachael; Ryal; Bill; Minor.	Deposition of Richard Knott.
Keeling, Adam, deceased.	Charles; Tully; Europe; Minor.	S. Whitehead's list.
L.		
Lackey, Mary	Steward; Rachel.	Deposition of Thomas Conway.
Lampkin, Rebecca.	Nelson.	Depositions of Richard Roult and James Neale.
Lampkin, Griffin.	Nelson Lambkin.	Mr. Bailey's list.
Land, Hillary, deceased.	Cudjo.	Depositions of William Whitehurst and P. Land, jr.
Lane, William, sen.	Esau; Tom, child of Ada; Isaac; Nathaniel; Adah and two children; Barney.	Depositions of Thomas R. Yeatman, Philip Sale, Robt. Hudgins, and H. Griffin. (Papers Nos. 8 and 20.) J. Cowper's list, and deposition of William H. Ransome.
Langley, William G.	Job.	Deposition of B. Turner. (Paper No. 24.)
Langley, Philip	Miram	Do. do. do.
Landsell, Benjamin, deceased.	Bob; Daniel	Deposition of H. Haynie.
Landell, John, sen.	Peter.	Deposition of Thomas Berry.
Lee, Richard.		Depositions of W. Harding, J. C. Edwards, and John D. Fitchliu. (Paper No. 25.)
Lee, Richard.	Lewis; Jesse.	Depositions of P. Spiller, James Hurst, and Jonas Ingram.
Lee, Richard, and Eleanor Ann Lee, deceased.	Bob; Newyear; Charles; Jacob; Stephen; Reuben; Gray; Thornton; Henry; Pompey; George; William; Jordon; James; Perry; Matilda; Peggy; Minorca; Caty; Jemima; Joan; Lucy; Judy; Esther; Mimy; Milley; Rose; Betty; Joyce; Polly; Siley; Lotty; Harriet; Arienor; Henry; Moriah; Lucy; Molena; Mary; Celina.	Depositions of Josias Hazard and R. Pierce.
Leland, B. M.	George.	Deposition of Cyrus Coppedge. (Paper No. 7.)
Leland, Charles, deceased.	Perimus.	Deposition of Thomas Fowler.
Lewis, Samuel.	Charles; Reuben; Bob; Frank; Emanuel; Ampry; William; Randall; Milley; Polly; Henry; Ellen; Abram; James; Sally; Nancy; Barbara; Hannah; George; Betsey; James; Matty; Lucy; Matilda; Lucy; Molly.	Depositions of Thos. Howard, Josiah Hazzard, J. Turberville, James H. Bailey, Jno. Redman, and A. B. Hooe. (For the deposition of A. B. Hooe see papers of T. Stowers.)

VIRGINIA—Continued.

Claimants.	Names of slaves.	Proof.
Letterell, Thomas........................	Sam..	Deposition of Richard Roult.
Lowry, Catharine W................	Ben; Landall; Jerry; Nancy; Bob; and two men and one woman; names not remembered.	Deposition of P. D. Luke and letter of J. Cowper. (Paper No. 27.)
Lyle, John...........................	James Essicks; Reuben Walker......................	Depositions of William Morgan, S. Redmond, and S. H. Baley.
Lyon, Ethel........................	Peter...	Oath of claimant and depositions of S. Waple and Tully R. Wise.
Lovet, John J., sr., deceased........	Charles; Hector; Owen..............................	S. Whitehead's list.
Lovett, John J., jr.................	Harry, alias Harry Oakes; Nat, called Nat Stewart; Nancy Stone.	Do.
Lewis, John........................	Billy Buck; Billy Cooke; Peter Jackson; Ben; Rose, or Rosetta Sparta and child; Daphlin; Nancy.	Oath of claimant and deposition of Thomas Haskins.
Lewis, Lawrence....................	Michael..	Four depositions.
Levy, Ezekiel, deceased.............	Billy; Sam; Sally; Miney; Bob; Jack...............	Do.
Lewis, Richard.....................	Phillis; Judah; Ned...............................	Oath of claimant and depositions of William Alderson and Samuel Baker.
Lampkin, Samuel...................	Nance..	Deposition of William Lampkin.
M.		
McAlpin, James....................	Penima Fuller.....................................	S. Whitehead's list.
McClanahan, J. M..................	Jesse..	Deposition of John Ingraham and John T. Diggs.
McClanahan, James.................	Sam...	Deposition of S. Barnes.
McClanahan, Eliz..................	Billy; Dinah; Lucy; Adam; Alice; Daniel; Sam.......	Deposition of Thomas Beacham.
McCarthy, Ann R. and Elizabeth.....	Tom; Judy; Milley; Hanney; Old Sall; Spencer; Peggy; Joan; Old Milley; Daniel; Louis; Frank; Joan; Bet; Elizabeth; Kitty; William; Old Prince; Anthony; Charles; John.	Deposition of Samuel Lyell.
McCarthy, Ann R. and Elizabeth	Harry; George; Lue; Phil; John; Adam; Joshua; Anthony; Cate; Bener; Mary; Joe..................	Deposition of D. Lyell.
McCarty, Tarpley..................	Godfrey; Nassau; Joe...............................	Deposition of B. McCarty. (Paper No. 11.)
McCarty, Bartholomew..............	Dick; Sam...	Deposition of G. Summers. (Paper No. 11.)
McCarty, Elizabeth	Vincent; Sally.....................................	Depositions of M. G. Yearly and B. McCarty. (Papers Nos. 11 and 13.)
McIntosh, Thomas..................	Will; Bill, or Billy Lee............................	Depositions of William Mitchell, C. L. Sears, and Cornelius Wells.
McCarty, Sydnor, deceased.........	Billy..	Depositions of William D. McCarty and B. McCarty. (Paper No. 11.)
McKenny, Jesse	Samuel..	Deposition of J. Fox.
McNemara, Timothy................	Adam..	Depositions of H. C. Lawful and R. Carrol.
Major, William	Abel...	Oath of claimant and deposition of Thomas Walter.
Malicote, Thomas..................	Sam...	Deposition of John Young.
Malicote, George, deceased.........	Anthony; Ben; Stepney.............................	Depositions of Dixon Brown, John Young, H. R. Duhn, and John Hughes.
Manson, John, deceased............	Ben...	Depositions of Charles Jones, J. Jones, and W. Jones. (Paper No. 4.)
Marchant, Ambrose................	Dick...	Depositions of H. Griffin and J. Patterson. (Paper No. 8.)
Marmaduke, Joseph................	Daniel; Lavinia and child; Dick....................	Deposition of Thomas W. Clark.
Massey, Lee, deceased.............	Tom; Will; Harry..................................	Depositions of Nancy Massey and George Mason.
Mason, N. H.......................	Moses Edwards; Minerva Edwards..................	Mr. Bailey's list.
Mason, Thompson..................	Bet...	Oath of claimant and depositions of Richard C. Mason and B. Rogers.
Mason, John B., deceased	Dana; Lucy; Minerva; Moses......................	Deposition of A. B. Hooe.
Matthews, William	Willis...	Depositions of C. Matthews and William Kirby.
Mayo, Susanna	Harry..	J. Cowper's list.
Meredith, Catharine...............	George; Solomon	Mr. Neale's list.
Middleton, John	James..	Deposition of William Roult.
Miller, Thomas	Diana Ray; James Ray; Sam.......................	Deposition of A. B. Hooe. (Diana Ray and James Ray are said to have been the property of Lucy R. Miller, and are enumerated among her slaves.) (See papers in case of Thomas Stowers.)
Miller, Lucy R.....................	Dinah; Ciss; James................................	Deposition of J. R. Miller.
Miller, James......................	John...	Depositions of H. Hudgins, Francis Jarvis, and H. Griffin. (Paper No. 14.)
Miskell, Newman..................	Jerry; Stewart.....................................	Depositions of M. Saunders and R. Street.
Mitchell, William, deceased........	James; Bond	Oath of James Neale.
Montgomery, Andrew..............	Harry..	Depositions of R. Pierce and James Montgomery.
Morris, John.......................	Bill; Harry; Nelson................................	Deposition of T. Johnson.
Moseley, or Moxley, Nancy.........	Bill...	Deposition of E. Spence.
Mountfuth, Francis................	Ned...	Depositions of C. Jones, W. Jones, and J. Jones. (Paper No. 4.)
Muse, Lawrence....................	Sandy; Bill; Howard; Richard; Lucy; Sally.........	Deposition of John Harman.
Muse, James, jr...................	Edmund...	Dolly Elliott's deposition.
Muse, Charles	Henry..	Deposition of John W. Hungerford.
Myers, Thomas....................	Patrick; Jesse; Pyramus; Aaron....................	Deposition of Charles Rogers.
N.		
Neale, Parsly	Mima and child; Winney..........................	Deposition of Charles Rogers and George F. Myers.
Neuson, Epp. L....................	Gratie; Paramus...................................	Deposition of Cyrus Chilton. (Paper No. 18.)
Nelms, Edwin, deceased	Cooper; George; Simon; Solomon; Hiram...........	Deposition of S. Blackwell.

VIRGINIA—Continued.

Claimants.	Names of slaves.	Proof.
Nelms, Peter..........................	Lucy..	Depositions of John Conway and J. Walker.
Nelson, Thomas	York..	Depositions of Charles Jones, John Jones, and William Jones. (Paper No. 4.)
Nelson, John	Guy..	Deposition of A. Simpkins. (See papers in case of B. Wood; see paper No. 1.)
Norris, William	John..	Deposition of G. Westead.
Northem, George	Abram; Joe	Deposition of A. G. Saunders.
Northum, Edward M	Sam..	List of A. Neale; depositions of W. Dobyns and H. Miskell.
Nottingham, Jacob, deceased........	Isaac; George	Deposition of John Widgron. (See paper No. 1.)
Nottingham, William.................	Solomon; Lyddy; Luke; Eke; Peter; Jacob; Rhoda; Mary.	Deposition of N. Widgron.
Nottingham, William, sen...........	Sam..	Deposition of William Savage.
Nottingham, Leven	Nat...	Deposition of Jacob Nottingham.
Nottingham, John....................	James	Do. do.
Nutt, Walter.........................	Hiram; Esther; Shadrack	Depositions of George Simpson and Thomas Lunsford.
Nutt, Sarah	John; Josiah	Depositions of Thomas E. Nutt and Thomas Beacham.
Narcum, ——.	One negro man	Deposition of J. Smith. (See case of James Smith.)¶
Nimmo, Elizabeth J	Jim, alias Jim Bousber; Jim Nimmo	
Nicholson, G. D., estate of, by Healy, Robert, administrator.	Tom..	Two depositions.
Nottingham, William, jr.............	James; Jacob	J. Cowper's list.
O.		
Opie, Hiram L.......................	Daniel..	Deposition of P. Claughton.
P.		
Paine, John	Charles; Will.....................................	Deposition of G. Robinson.
Palmer, Charles......................	Joe...	Depositions of A. Chilton and E. Norris. (Paper No. 18.)
Palmer, Elizabeth, now Dobyns	James	Depositions of C. Palmer, C. Chilton, and E. Norris.
Palmer, Elizabeth, deceased	No name or value.................................	A. Neale's list.
Palmer, William.....................	Winney; Sukey; Sally; Fanny; John; Charles; Amey; Eliza; Jefferson; Winney; Rose; Patty; Fanny; Polly; Moses.	Depositions of Cyrus Chilton and Charles Palmer.
Palmer, Rawleigh	Moses..	Depositions of A. J. Palmer and O. Dunaway.
Panish, Nathaniel....................	Davy...	Deposition of N. Collin. (Paper No. 27.)
Parker, Alexander	Phill; Stafford; Winslow	Deposition of E. S. Miner.
Parker, George......................	Tom; Nanny; Eliza; James; Morris	Deposition of John Evans and oath of claimant.
Parramore, Thomas, jr	Abraham	Depositions of M. S. Pitts and Th. Jacobs. (Paper No. 1.)
Parramore, John, jr	Edmund	Do do. do.
Parramore, John, sen................	Abel..	Deposition of Thomas Parramore. (Paper No. 1.)
Parsons, William	Letty...	Deposition of Sally Reed.
Patterson, John	Ned; Hull; Sci; Sam; Nancy.....................	Letter of claimant and depositions of Thomas R. Yeatman, Thomas Hudgins, and of J. McBride. (Paper No. 20.)
Parsons, Margaret...................	Ben..	Deposition of William White, jr. (Paper No. 1.)
Parsons, Elizabeth	George..	Deposition of William W. Wilson. (Paper No. 1.)
Parsons, William	Eits; Lety	Depositions of A. Simpkins and Sally Reed. (Paper No. 1; see paper No. 3.)
Peck, Emanuel	Solomon..	Deposition of V. T. Branson.
Peck, Harriet	Rose; Matilda	Depositions of William L. Lee and John C. Peck.
Peck, John C	Sam; Tom; Judy; Louisa.........................	Oath of claimant and depositions of J. Graham and Vincent T. Branson.
Pearce or Penn, Ransdell............	William Lawson...................................	Depositions of Andrew and James Montgomery.
Pinchard, Cyrus.....................	Harry; Sam	Deposition of James Hurst.
Plummer, John	Billy..	Yide A. Neale's list; depositions of H. Meskell and W. Dobyns.
Pope, Thaddeus......................	Mary...	Deposition of William Palmer.
Powell, Mary........................	Sam..	Deposition of A. Simpkins. (Paper No. 1.)
Powell, John........................	Jim...	Depositions of H. Griffin and Thomas R. Yeatman. (Papers Nos. 8 and 20.)
Powell, James	Babel; Lige; Jane; Teap; Charlotte; Silly..........	Deposition of Charles M. Collin. (Paper No. 27.)
Pursell, Sarah.......................	George..	Deposition of Thomas Stowers.
Pointer, Michael.....................		
Parker, Jacob G.....................	Peter; Jacob	J. Cooper's list.
Powell, George......................	Sam..	S. Whitehead's list.
R.		
Ransome, William H	Jack..	Depositions of Wm. H. Wistr and Th. Hudgins. (Papers Nos. 14 and 20.)
Redman, John, deceased	Manuel; Jemy; Little Manuel......................	A. Neale's list.
Ruri, Sarah B........................	Levi..	Deposition of Z. Paul.
Rice, Peter C........................	Sampson; Isaac; Rodham	Depositions of Richard Roult.
Richards, Ann, deceased	James	Deposition of H. Young.
Rogers, George......................	Willoughby	Deposition of G. D. Ashton.
Robins, John........................	Adah and child; Henrietta; Daniel; Harry..........	Deposition of L. Kendall, jr. (Paper No. 1.)
Robins, Temple......................	Jacob...	Do. do. do.
Roberts, Zerobabel..................	Luke..	Deposition of S. Bunting. (Paper No. 2)
Robb, Robert G	Lewis...	Deposition of William Williams and John Payne.

VIRGINIA—Continued.

Claimants.	Names of slaves.	Proof.
Roult, William	Stephen	Deposition of John Middleton.
Roy, James H	William; Gabriel; Davy	Depositions of Thomas Hudgins and Lewis B. Wiatt, and certificate of Capt. Barrie. (Papers Nos. 14 and 20.) Also deposition of H. Griffin.
Royster, Thomas	Emanuel	Deposition of James H. Roy. (Paper No. 19.)
Rose, Margaret	Frederick; George; Pristly; James; Alexander; Jack; Ripley, sen.; Sally; Jenny; Ripley, jr.; Frank; Charity; Matilda; Nancy.	Depositions of Andrew Stephenson, John Payne, and John Ashton.
Robertson, William	Letty	Deposition of Robert Bailey.
S.		
Sadwick, Benjamin	Len	Deposition of L. Dade.
Sanford, Charles	Lewis; Judith	Depositions of V. Marmaduke and Thomas Clarke.
Sandy, Nancy	Caty; John	Deposition of Sampson Potter.
Saunders, Edward	Winney; Polly; Hannah; Peg; Nancy; Violet; Patty; Horace; Manuel; Dorinda; Sukey; Joe; Crisa; Amey; Minerva; Willoughby; Daniel; Billy; Judy; George; John; Nell; Sam; Simon; Letty; Jerry; Bob, alias Robin; Rawleigh.	Depositions of George Saunders and Eppa Norris.
Savage, Mary Ann	Jacob; Lucinda; Ellen	Depositions of G. Parker, J. Evans, and Thomas Groton. (Paper No. 3.)
Savage, William	Elijah; George	Deposition of Nathaniel Widgeon. (Paper No. 1.)
Savage, Severn	Letty	Deposition of D. Topping. (Paper No. 1)
Self, Job	Ben	Depositions of Richard Straughan and Richard Knott.
Shackleford, R. L	Ned	Deposition of William Stanley.
Silverthorn, John	George; Joshua	Depositions of William Linton and J. Sterling.
Shield, Robert	Tom; Jacob; Charles	Depositions of R. Shield and H. Howard. (Paper No. 17.)
Shield, Samuel, deceased	Sam	Do. do. do. do.
Sheppard, Smith	Argyle; Frank	Depositions of T. Keeling and John Cornick. (Paper No. 16.)
Scott, George	George	Deposition of William Savage, jr. (Paper No. 1.)
Sherman, Joseph	Bob; Billy; Perimus	Deposition of E. G. Sherman.
Smith, John M	Molly; Eddy; Leonora; Matilda; Gabriel	Depositions of J. K. Ball and R. Downman.
Smith, Catharine	Solomon	Depositions of R. W. McCarty and B. McCarty. (Paper No. 11.)
Smith, W. B	Jacob; Bill	Depositions of James Smith and T. Barber.
Smith, James	Peter; Jack; Jesse; Mary	Oath of claimant; and depositions of W. L. Smith, C. Moore, W. Morrison, S. Blackwell, and others, filed by A. Neile.
Smith, Joseph	George Doolan, alias Smith; Joe Smith; Manuel Smith	Mr. Bailey's list.
Smith, James	Jacob	J. Cowper's list.
Smith, George	Sam	Deposition of A. Simpkins. (Paper No. 1.)
Spady, Thomas	Judy	Deposition of W. Castin, sen. (Paper No. 1.)
Spence, Edward	Winney	Depositions of J. Jett and Owen Brinnon.
Stratton, John, deceased	Joe	Deposition of L. Nottingham. (Paper No. 3.)
Stratton, Benjamin	Mathew; Southey	Depositions of W. Thomas and G. Scott. (Paper No.1.)
Steele, John B	Sam	Depositions of John Winstead and Thomas Kirkham.
Stowers, Thomas	Eley Butler;* Hannah Butler;* George Neal;* Jenny Butler;* Nelly Weaver;* Charity and child; Daniel; Core; Solomon Redmond.	Depositions of William Garner, V. T. Branson, and A. B. Hooe.
Stuart, John G	Mingo; Ampy; Davy	Depositions of Benjamin Grimes and Robert Lyle.
Stuart, David	Robin; Lewis	Depositions of B. Grimes, R. Lyle, and J. Crismond.
Stuart, John	Kinna	Depositions of A. B. Hooe and James Cox.
Stubblefield, Simon	Reuben	Depositions of G. Stubblefield and John Jones. (Paper No. 10.)
Stubblefield, Beverly	Charles	Do. do. do. do.
Sutton, John	Cephus	Depositions of G. Cindiff and H. Grippin. (Paper No. 9.)
Sutton, Judith	Cyner	Deposition of C. Sutton.
Sydnor, Duanna	(No name)	Deposition of A. Neale. (See papers of G. Yearly; paper No. 13.)
Skinner, John	Bill; Anthony; Nann; Rachel, and Bridget	Deposition of C. M. Collier. (Paper No. 27. See papers in case of Shield. S. Whitehead's list.)
Sydnor, John	(No name)	A. Neale's list.
Stubblefield, John, deceased	Noah; Patty; Eliza; Jefferson; Betsy	Oath of Mary Pointer; depositions of B. F. and F. M. Stubblefield.
Smith, John B	David, or David Boush; Tully, or Tully Boush	
Seymour, Edward	Jim, or Jim Keeling	
Savage, Littleton	Paul; Tony; Sam; Shadrick	J. Cowper's list.
Seldon, Elizabeth, administratrix of Richard Seldon.	Peter	See Eliz. Selden's letter.
T.		
Tabb, Thomas	Jack; William; Isaac; Bob; Harry; Ned	Deposition of H. Griffin. (Paper No. 8.)
Tabb, Philip	Charles	Letter of J. Cowper and deposition of S. R. Yeatman. (Paper No. 5.)
Taylor, Edmund	Jim	Seven depositions. (Paper No. 6.)
Tiffey, Pope, deceased	Jesse	Deposition of J. H. Doleman.
Tignor, Philip, deceased	George	Deposition of S. Blundon.

*Mr. Bailey's list.

VIRGINIA—Continued.

Claimants.	Names of slaves.	Proof.
Thomas, Benjamin	James; Emanuel	Depositions of William Berryman and John Redman.
Thomas, John B	Milley; Edmund; Mary	Deposition of J. N. Fitchett. (Paper No. 1.)
Thomas, William	Ned; Daniel	Deposition of L. Kendall. (Paper No. 1.)
Thompson, Frances	Grace	Depositions of Thomas H. Jett, Ellis Hudnall, and T. Fowles. (Paper No. 7.)
Thompson, Ann	Sail	Deposition of E. Brown.
Thurnton, George F	Will; Jack	Deposition of Thomas Martin.
Tomlin, Moore F	Cyrus; Lucy; Sarah; Mary; Lucy; Charity; Sam	Depositions of B. McCarty and Jeremiah Garland. (Paper No. 11.)
Towles, Thomas, deceased	Jack; Charles	Depositions of J. Rogers and Thomas H. Jett, and oath of claimant. (Papers Nos. 7 and 21.)
Travers, Henry	Eve	Deposition of Thomas Bell.
Turberville, John, sen	Flora; Charles; Keziah; Lilly; Edmond; Nancy; Lucy; Jenny; Lotty; Phœbe; Judy; Lilly; Suckey, (60 years old;) Reuben; Elcy; Andrew; Caty; Anna; Vincent; Mary; Cressey; Alloway; Nancy; Caty, (70 years old;) Frankey; Alice; Harriet; Molly; Felicia; Peggy; Patty; Barbara; Martha; Peggy, (75 years old.)	Deposition of Trussal B. Hall.
Turner, Benjamin	Betty; Caroline	Deposition of T. Bell.
Turpin, John D	Rachel	Deposition of O. White. (Papers Nos. 1 and 3.)
Turpin, John	Jacob	Deposition of S. M. Pitts. (Papers Nos. 1 and 3.)
Tyson, John	Nebo; Jacob; Jack	Deposition of Nathaniel Wigeon. (Paper No. 1.)
Todd, Mallory	Bob, perhaps Bob Goodson	S. Whitehead's list.
Truss, William	Dick	Do.
Tomlin, Williamson B	Sypbax	
Taliffers, William	Ralph; Sally, or Sall; Cornelius; Henderson and an infant; Anthony; Patty.	Deposition of Thomas Yeatman and oath of claimant.
Thompson, George, deceased	Edward	Deposition of George Douglas.
Thompson, Eliza, deceased	Edward	B. L. Lear's list. (See account for property.)

U.

Underhill, Nancy	Gabe and Caleb	Deposition of A. Underhill. (Paper No. 1.)

Y.

Yeatman, John, sen., deceased	Will; Jane; Funny	Deposition of William Morgan and Thomas Barber.
Yerly, Thomas, jr., deceased	Lishey; Sam	Deposition of R. Dudnall.
Yerly, William G	Johnson	Samuel Bailey's deposition.
Yerbey, George, deceased	No name, one boy	Deposition of A. Neall. (Paper No. 13.)
Yearby, Nancy, deceased	Emanual; Lee	Deposition of W. G. Yerly and William D. McCarty. (Papers Nos. 11 and 12.)
Young, Henry	Bob	Deposition of William Young.
Young, Williamson	Beverly	Deposition of H. Young.

W.

Waddy, George F	Lucy	A. Neale's list.
Waddy, Shapleigh N	Peter; Charlotte; Ezekiel	Deposition of Clem Dogget and William Ellison.
Waddy, Elizabeth	No name	Depositions of Ingram and John T. Diggs.
Waddy, C. N	Peter Cullers	M. Bailey's list.
Waples, Samuel	Arthur	Oath of claimant and depositions of S. Hopkins, E. Lyon, and T. R. Wise.
Waring, Wm., jr., deceased	Isaac; Scipio; Jerry; Randall; Bill Perry; Billy; Sam; Lewis; Anthony; Benjamin; Harry; Mary; Lucy; Rachel; Aney; Burrell.	Depositions of James Morris, Lewis and C. Edmondson.
Waring, William	Jesse; Jim; Love or Lewis	Do. do. do.
Warner, William	Lewis Jackson	Mr. Bailey's list.
Washington, Sarah	Gus	Deposition of Charles Muse.
Washington, John Hooe	Phil; John; Frank, wife of John	Depositions of H. F. Washington, William H. Hooe, and John Massey.
Watts, Thomas, deceased	Will; Jack; Jupiter; Peter; Lydia; Bob; Cesar; Joe; Adam; Mary; Frank.	Depositions of James Altmand and R. Lively.
Watson, Edmund	George	Deposition of J. N. Fitchell. (Paper No. 1.)
Weathers, John	Prince	Deposition of D. Garland.
West, Hezekiah	Mack	Deposition of J. N. Fitchill. (Paper No. 1.)
Wheeler, Thomas	Sam	Deposition of H. L. Gaskins.
White, Obedience	Dinah; Peggy	Deposition of D. Turpin and M. S. Pitts. (Papers Nos. 1 and 3.)
White, Mary, deceased	Simon; Rachel; Sylvia; Priscilla; Lavinia; George	Deposition of J. G. White. (Paper No. 11.)
Whittington, Thomas	George; Jane; Leviticus; Willoughby; Leviney; John; Eliza; Louisia; Isaac; Ezekiel.	Deposition of J. Grinsted and J. Dashields.
Winder, John	George; Leven; Spence; Joe; Hannibal; Ben; Violet; Eliza and 2 children; Caleb; Will; Arnold; Bob; Nelson.	Deposition of William G. Winder.
Winder, John H	Ben	Do. do.
Widgeon, Nathaniel	Sam; Jacob; Joe	Depositions of W. Savage and J. Tyson, sr. (Paper No. 1.)
Wishart, Sidney	Frank	Oath of claimant.
Widgeon, Westerhouse	Jacob	Deposition of J. Widgeon. (Paper No. 1.)
Wilkins, Peter	Bill; Jane	Deposition of Thomas G. Scott. (Paper No. 1.)
Wilkins, Robert	Ben; Luke; Isaac	Deposition of W. Savage. (Paper No. 1.)

VIRGINIA—Continued.

Claimants.	Names of slaves.	Proof.
Wilkins, John....................	Bill..	Deposition of A. Simkins. (Paper No. 1.)
Williams, Peggy	Peter; Ben....................................	Do. do.
Williams, John, sen.............	Ben; Edmund................................	Do. do.
Williams, Samuel S..............	Joshua; Rachel and two children	Deposition of John Rayfield. (Paper No. 1.)
Williams, W. S...................	Luke; James..................................	Deposition of Walter Luker and L. Scott. (Paper No. 1.)
Wilson, James R.................	Harry..	S. Whitehead's list.
Wise, Tully, deceased...........	Jacob, sen.; Jacob, jun.; David; Leven; Phillis; Hannah; Esther; Peggy; Nancy; Polly; Rose; Grace; Letty; Jenny; Cyrus; Lucy; Edy; Rachel; Tom; Susy; George.	Depositions of T. L. Wise, John Finney, John Nelson, and E. Lyon.
Wise, J. J........................	Southey; Charles.............................	Oath of claimant and depositions of S. Hopkins and James F. Mister.
Wise, Tully R....................	Isaac..	Deposition of William White, jr. (Paper No. 1.)
Willis, Mary.....................	Hannah...	Deposition of William and Ann Cooper. (Paper No. 2.)
Wood, Bennett...................	Sam..	Deposition of Charles Jones. (Paper No. 4.)
Woodhouse, Wm. D..............	Adam; Harry; John; James; Charles; James Keeling; Grace.	Deposition of H. Keeling, jr., and Samuel Cornick.
Wornun, Samuel, deceased......	Ned..	Deposition of William and Ann Cooper. (Paper No. 2.)
Wroe, William	James; Cloe; Lilly............................	Deposition of John King.
Williams, Thomas...............	Quack...	J. Cowper's list.
Whiting, Henry, deceased.......	Dunman; Eliza................................	Oath of A. L. Davis.
Waddy, Chapman................	Charlotte; Chance............................	M. Bailey's list.
Williams, John	William...	

RECAPITULATION.

1,721 slaves, which, at the average value agreed upon and fixed by the commission, viz., $280, amount to the sum of.......... $481,880.

Inventory of property, other than slaves, stated to have been carried off by the British forces from the State of Virginia; with an alphabetical list of the claimants, and the estimated value of the said property.

Claimants.	Property.	Estimated value.	Proof.
B.			
Barrick, Robert	Schooner Independence..................	$4,000 00	Deposition of H. Griffin. (See paper No. 8.)
Beachman, Thomas..................	Barn, &c., burnt..........................	568 00	Deposition of C. Claughton and Wm. Damnon.
Buckner, E., Mrs...................	Horse, not valued; horse, sheep, hogs, &c., household furniture, plate, &c.	1,800 00	Mr. Bailey's list and A. B. Hooe's deposition. (See Mrs. Buckner for slaves; Tho. Miller's deposition.)
C.			
Chilton, Blackwell..................	Sloop Harriet	600 00	Deposition of Spencer Mallins.
	10 cords tan bark, per cord.............	11 12½	Do. do.
Cary, Miles.........................	65 sheep...................................	250 00	Deposition of Fault D. Luke. (See papers for slaves.)
Chandler, Thomas	4 hhds. tobacco, net weight 4,767 lbs., at $7 per cwt.	297 93	Wm. C. Chandler. (Refer to slave papers.)
D.			
Dameron, William..................	Dwelling-house	800 00	
	Corn-house	20 00	
	......do....................................	15 00	
	Desk	7 00	
	Walnut table	2 50	
	3 chests	3 00	
	2 bedsteads and cords	2 00	
	Looking-glass.............................	2 00	
	3 pictures	6 00	
	10 pounds wool	5 00	
	Pair of boots.............................	7 00	
	Spinning wheel	2 50	
	2 jugs	1 75	
	3 tight barrels...........................	3 00	
	Saddle	8 00	
		884 75	Deposition of Th. Beacham & Pemberton Claughton.
Dameron. Luke, sen.	Dwelling-house	500 00	
	Cow-house	15 00	
	5 barrels of corn	15 00	
	3 beds	60 00	
	30 yards cloth in the loom	15 00	
	Chest, with clothing......................	20 00	
	Looking-glass.............................	3 00	
	Cash in the chest	2 50	

VIRGINIA—Continued.

Claimants.	Property.	Estimated value.	Proof.
Dameron, Luke, sen.—Continued....	Parcel of iron.............................	$4 25	
	Parcel of pewter.........................	2 00	
	Parcel of earthen ware..................	2 50	
		639 25	
Dozier, Allen S.....................	1 Beeve..................................	30 00	Deposition of Wm. C. Claughton. (See slave papers.)
Dobyns, H. M.......................	3,002 pounds of tobacco	300 00	A. Neale's list.
Dudley, John, deceased	Boat, anchor, and cable	300 00	Deposition of G. Davis and Mr. Session. (See slave papers.)
E.			
Eskridge, William	Battenu	30 00	Depositions of C. Doggett and W. Elliston. (See slave papers.)
F.			
Ficklin, J. D......................	2 hhds. tobacco, of 2,034 pounds.........	137 10	
G.			
Gaskins, R. H......................	Furniture...............................	200 00	J. Edwell and Thos. Gaskins. (See slave papers.)
Gordon, William....................	33,567 pounds tobacco....................	2,098 00	
Gilman, Ephraim	Merchandise, &c.........................	3,135 29	
H.			
Hall, Nancy	Chest	2 00	
	4 habits	12 00	
	2 petticoats	3 00	
	Bonnet...................................	2 00	
	2 yards I. cotton	1 00	
	Pair of stockings........................	1 00	
	Counterpane, 2 sheets....................	9 00	
	Lot of earthen ware.....................	1 25	
	Counterpane.............................	2 00	
	Hair comb	50	
	Sugar box and sugar.....................	50	
	5 pounds bacon, &c	1 50	
		35 75	Deposition of Mary Williams
Hathaway, Mary....................	Trunk and clothes........................	100 00	Oath of claimant.
	A quantity of china ware.................	40 00	Do.
	Several articles of furniture	150 00	Do.
Hamborough, John..................	Small boat and a vessel	2,000 00	Theophilus Bowie, James Want, John Murphey, and William Clarke, deponents.
Hazzard, Josiah	Furniture, &c............................	617 01	D. Lyle and Thomas Muse, deponents.
Hughlett, John.....................	8 beds, at $30...........................	240 00	Ann T. Rust and N. Haynes, deponents.
	16 counterpanes, at $7 50	120 00	Do.　　do.　　do.
	16 blankets, at $8 per pair	64 00	Do.　　do.　　do.
	Sheets, table-cloths, &c.	100 00	Do.　　do.　　do.
L.			
Liland, Charles	Gun, silver cup, and ladle	50 00	A. Neale's list.
	3,000 pounds bacon, and other articles....	450 00	Do.
Lewis, Samuel	Furniture, &c. (See list)	300 00	Lucy R. Miller's deposition.
	Dwelling-house	1,000 00	Five depositions. (See slave papers.)
M.			
Middleton, John	Horse, saddle and bridle.................	200 00	Deposition of William Roult.
McCarty, Daniel	1 horse and 3 mules	275 00	Deposition of Samuel Lyell.
Moore, Elijah......................	Carpenters' tools........................	100 00	Deposition of R. R. Kirk.
McCarty, B........................	Gig.....................................	100 00	Oath of claimant; paper No. 11.
P.			
Parker, Col.	Horse	80 00	Mr. Bailey's list.
Parish, Nathaniel	The boat Brothers.......................	500 00	George Hoy's deposition.
R.			
Redman, Caleb	Schooner Harriet	700 00	S. Bunting's deposition.
Roberts, Z........................	24 sheep, corn, clothing, beds, &c........	1,119 00	Do.　　do.
	8 head of cattle	160 00	Do.　　do.
S.			
Stewart, Mrs......................	2 hhds. tobacco	140 00	
Smith, James......................	House and furniture......................	6,500 00	
	Overseer's house, barn, &c..............	3,333 33	
	Flooring plank	930 00	
	Crop, &c	300 00	
		11,063 33	Deposit'n of E. Moore & Morrison. (See slave papers.)
Sanford, Robert....................	House, barn, &c	3,090 00	Samuel Lewis, J. Hazard, Thomas Skinner, and George Glascock's depositions.
Shield, John.......................	Gun, canoe, furniture, &c	120 00	S. Bunting's deposition. (See slave papers No. 27.)
	Also 1 pilot boat	800 00	Deposition of U. Dobyns.

VIRGINIA—Continued.

Claimants.	Property.	Estimated value.	Proof.
T.			
Thomas, Joel........................	Schooner U. States	$1,500 00	J. Cowper's list; deposition of H. Griffin.
Teacle, Savage & Co...............	Pilot boat Comet.........	1,000 00	Deposition of T. Parker, Wm. Jennings, and Thomas Hope.
Thomas, Joel........................	Vessel, from 20 to 30 tons.................	400 00	John Patterson's list.
Tune, Lewis	2 hhds. tobacco	140 00	A. Neale's list.
Thompson, Elizabeth G.	Furniture, &c....;.........................	2,449 50	Deposition of James Douglas.
Thompson, Elizabeth	......do...................................	3,239 50	
W.			
William, Elijah.., ...	Cash and sundry articles	58 00	Nancy Purcell's deposition.

RECAPITULATION.

Amount of property, per estimated value...$47,553 97¾.

List of slaves stated to have been carried off by the British forces from the State of South Carolina, with an alphabetical list of the claimants, and the estimated value of the said slaves.

Claimants.	Names of slaves.	Proof.
B.		
Bingley, Captain N..................	Not mentioned, being part of the crew of the Abby Ann, of Charleston, South Carolina.	A deposition.
C.		
Cochran, Charles B.................	Renot Cochran, Cymon Cochran, and Saby Cochran, captured in the schooner Sally Jefferson.	No statement but his own.
H.		
Hatch, Mary, and Hatch, James R...	Robert...	Deposition of owner and one other.
M.		
McNeill, Daniel......................	Jack Watkins; Harvey; Jim; captured in a sloop commanded by Captain Bingley, within the waters of the United States.	Do. do.
P.		
Parker, Samuel......................	Not stated...	One certificate.
W.		
Waring, Morton A..................	Bristol	Oath of claimant and two depositions.

RECAPITULATION.

10 slaves, which, at the average value agreed upon and fixed by the commission, viz., $390, amount to the sum of...........$3,900.

A list of slaves stated to have been carried off by the British forces from the State of Georgia, with an alphabetical list of the claimants, and the estimated value of the said slaves.

Claimants.	Names of slaves.	Proof.
A.		
Armstrong, Thomas, estate of........	James Hyatt....;...	S. Armstrong's statement and one deposition.
Andrews, Thomas	Jim; Harry; Titus; Hannah; Susan; Adam............	Oath and two depositions.
Atwater, Elisha.....................	Sabro...	Claimant's oath and five depositions.
Atkinson, George....................	Trumpeter...	Claimant's oath and two depositions.
Atkinson, Andrew	Andrew..	Two depositions.
Abrahams, Isaac.....................	Joe..	Claimant's statement on oath.
B.		
Bailey, George	Isaac; Kent; Frederick; Hector; Daniel; Aaron; Patrick; January.	Claimant's statement on oath, two depositions, and letter from Mr. Spalding.
Brailsford, M.......................	Harry; Isaac	One deposition.
Babcock, Clarissa Ann..............	Cuffy...	Claimant's statement on oath and one deposition.

GEORGIA—Continued.

Claimants.	Names of slaves.	Proof.
Butler, Pierce......................	Gabriel; Isaac; Isaac, jr.; Renter; Harry; George; John; Jeffery; Gabriel; Billy; Frank; William; Sampson; Sam; Abraham; George; March; Cesar; Cuffy; Joe; Charles; Daniel; Moses; Richard; Bram; Hector; June; Justice; Job; Briamus; Hardy; Cato; Joe; Joe, jr.; Hope; Pompey; Abraham; Sawney; George; John; Sambo; Cato; Joe; John; Billy; Stepney; Charles; Negar; Edmund; Tabby; Peter; Keen; Bram; Philip; Hardy; William; Elisha; Lewey; John; Squire; Andrew; Sam, old; Billy, old; Esther; Daphne; Diana; Bina; Tabby; Die; Cetira; Sue; Peggy; Lucy; Evander; Molly; Winney; Anne; Winney; Judy; Clara; Nelly; Juba; Doll; Celia; Bina; Patty; Tina; Diana; Bess; Peggy; Suckey; Rose; Nelly; Tabby; Aggy; Hagar; Linda; Celia; Dids; Selina; Linda; Sidney; Luna; Jean; Elsey; Tesse; Jean; Delia; Cate; Cresse; Abigail; Charlotte; Casey; Sally; Panby; Molly; Hagar; Peggy; Lucy; Violet; Daphne; Matilda; Jane; Insey; Jemima; Hester; Bess; Bina; Venus; Fanny; Cate; Selina, old; Lucy, old; Cressy, old; Daphne; Lucy; Peggy; Cate.	Letter to Secretary Adams. Two statements by the claimant.
Bullock, J. S.......................	Charles Bullock; Lucy Bullock; John Bullock..........	Thomas Johnson's letter.
Burnet, Reml...	One slave, and other property......................	The papers in this case were received at the Department of State May 31, 1821, but cannot now be found.
Bachlots, John, sr., for the estate of Francis Leroy.	Philip; Hannah; Lewis; Dick; William; Mingo.......	Oath of claimant and two depositions.
C.		
Clarke, John.......................	Fuller..	Claimant's oath and one deposition.
Clark, Archibald...................	Jack; Andrew; Stepney.............................	Claimant's oath and three depositions.
Copp, Daniel......................	Nelson; Collin; Cary; Ned	Letter to the Secretary, three statements and three depositions.
Creighton, John....................	Dick; Jim; Joe; Tony; Bob; Nanny; George; Jacob; Sandy; Clarissa; Mary; Will.	Claimant's statement on oath and five depositions.
Campbell, John....................	Cato..	Claimant's statement on oath and one deposition.
Cowper, John......................	Roger; George; Charles; Hannibal; Scipio; Bob; Smart; Timothy; John; Quash, jr.; Cuffey; March; Leicester; Cesar; London; Ben; Plenty; Horace; Hopkins; Fortune; Sunbury; Alick; Sandy; Darion; Titus; Jack, Gen.; Quash, sr.; Cudjoe; Jack Galla; Peter; Bonny Tom; Frank; Gabriel; Hard Times; Hannah; Charlotte; Nelly; Pennanis; Grœe Johnst; Nanny; Clarissa; Eliza; Flora; Minty; Nanny Quash; Susey; Sarah; Lamie; Polly; Lucy; Abraham; Phœbe; Luke; Judy; Eve.	Claimant's statement on oath, letter to Secretary Adams, and four depositions.
Cohen, Mordecai, assignee of Chas. B. Cochran.	Pierrot Cochrane; Simon Cochran; Saby Cochran.......	J. B. Cochrane's memorial, and deposition inclosed in it.
D.		
Destar, Benjamin W....	Will..	Claimant's oath and one deposition.
Delany, Daniel S...................	Cesar	Claimant's statement.
Delany, Robert S....................	Grandison	Claimant's oath and one deposition.
Duvall, Suzette	Ned	Claimant's statement and two depositions.
Dubignon, Poulain	Big Peter; Little Peter; Adam; Alexis; Jack; S. Esperance; Martinique; Charles; Pierre Paul; Noel; Tom; Hillary; Ben; Little John; Alexander; Sam; Paul; Frederick; Louis; Cato; Rosetta; Nanny; Mary; Lucy; Vilette; Rose; Tanis; Suzette.	Claimant's statement and two depositions.
E.		
Ellis, Thomas	Ben...	Claimant's oath and two depositions. For further proof see John Campbell's document.
F.		
Floyd, Charles and John............	William; Cesar; Charlotte; Priscilla; Polydore; Tarquin.	Claimant's statement and four depositions.
Frazer, John......................	Cesar; Dundee; Jekyl; Moses; Sawney; Smart; Will; Charlotte; Diana; Daphne; Fatima; Jebbo; Sarah; Sylvia.	See John Cooper's document; his statement on oath.
Fayley, Joshua.....................	Prince	Claimant's statement on oath and two depositions.
G.		
Grant's, Daniel, estate..............	Isaac, sr.; Isaac, jr.; Nelly; Jenny; Philip; Peggy; Arch; Dinah; Betsey; William; Frank.	Claimant's statement and four depositions. Certificates of magistrates.
Gibson, William	Nero; Cuffy.......................................	Claimant's statement on oath and one deposition.
Goodbread, Thomas	Hannah	Claimant's oath and two depositions.
Goodbread, Philip..................	Bob; Bristol; Will	Claimant's oath and one deposition.
Gickie, James H....................	Will; Nicholas; Charles; Bob; Edmund; Chloe; Betty; Juno; Phillis; Child, 7; Child, 5.	Claimant's statement and oath; letter to Secretary Adams; two depositions; certificates of magistrates and clerks.
Grant, Robert......................	Negro woman and two children......................	R. Grant's memoranda.

GEORGIA—Continued.

Claimants.	Names of slaves.	Proof.
H.		
Harris', William, estate, by J. Harris, agent.	Hunter	Claimant's statement and four depositions.
Hubnal, Ezekiel	Cook	Claimant's statement and two depositions.
Horry, Mrs.....	Three slaves...................................	No names, oath, or deposition.
Howell, Catharine	Jack Watkins...........................	See John Ross' letter to Thomas Spalding; Admiral Cockburn's passport.
*Hamilton, James...................	Bob; Leannie; Jacob; Sambo; Tenah; Quamina; Scipio; Betty; Polly; Brass; Harriet; Jesse; Brutus; Brass, (boy;) Toney; Sarah; Sampson; Dick; Patty; Katey; Lawrence and Ned, (boys;) Ben; Reyna; Dick; John; Edward; Sally; Tim; Sam; Reuben; Amey; Frederick; Minerva; Sarah; Reuben, Jr.; Gabriel; Jule; Peggy; Nancy; Rose; Fatima; Medina; Willie; Diana; Philliday; Henrick; Grace; Israel; Polly; Jack; Fanny; Thomas; Violet; Jeannie; Judy; Abraham; Robin; Harry; Betty; Joe; Kate; Alli; Allinate; Mali; Mary; Jonny; Hannah; Peter; Elizabeth; James; Delia; Bell; Sylvester; Philip; Ebo; Margaret; Alice; Tim; Joe; Ditty; Ester; Joe; Susan; Hector; Sophy; Jack; Sophy; Maman; Schadi; Lucy; Toney; Sam; Fatima; Jeffery; William; Lawrence; Tim; Judy; Adam; Syke; Maria; Gumba; Jack; Daniel; Linda; Quash; Sarah; Nat; Sue; Molly; Sam; Harry; Tom; James; Mary; Peggy; Dick; Judy; Phillis; Lydia; Jeannie; Bob; Nanny; Hendrick; Molly; Will; Nanny; Robin; Betsey; Will; Jerico; Solomon; Aaron; Patty; Maria; Caithness; Jeannie; Cathness, jr.; Sam; James; Chloe; Pompey; Tenah; Auran; Phillis; Paddy; Moses; Polydore; Mary; Manuel; Alice; Yarico; Statira; Elsey; John; Elsey; Rachel; Louisa; John; Joseph; Calamus; Charity; Prince; Toby; Bill; Mary; Sandy; William; Johnny; Bella; Toper; Phillis; Amoretta; Memba; Nanny; Hannah; Jupiter; Tenah; Sally; Mariana; Peter; Benny; Ado.	Claimant's statement and four depositions. (See documents Nos. 1, 2, 3.)
J.		
Johnston, William, estate of........	George; Hagar; London; Hester.....................	Claimant's oath and one deposition.
Johnston, Charles...................	Frank; April..	Claimant's statement and one deposition.
Jenkins, Royal.....................	Harry...	Oath of claimant.
K.		
King, Thomas, estate of.............	Sam; John; Lewis; Johnson; Bob; Jim; Corporal; Will; Jonah; Peggy; Sarah; Maria; Eliza; Patience; Millery; Sarah; Fanny.	Statement of Kelly, W. F., executor, two depositions, &c.
King, Boswell, sen..................	Harry.	One deposition.
L.		
Lehoy, Francis, estate of............	Mingo; Hannah; Lewis; Dick; William; Philip	Two depositions and notarial certificate.
M.		
McNish, William...................	Polydore; Nancy; Betsey; Eve; Alich; Diana; Will; Pegg; Helen; Sukey; Brutus; Ruobie; Jane; July; Sally; Jerry; Juno.	Claimant's statement on oath and four depositions.
McGillis, Randolph.................	Emanuel; Sukey	Claimant's statement and one deposition.
McFarlane, Sarah...................	Notwick	Do. do.
Moody, Solomon....................	Isaac	Do. do.
Mickler, Peter......................		No list, oath, or valuation.
Matthews, Edmund.................	Bob; Cudjoe; Prince; William; Jack; Isaac; Lindy; Lucy; Juba; Chloe; L. Mary; B. Mary; Selina; Cinda; Nancy; Molly; Maria; L. Maria; Rhina; Doll; Jenny; Sarah; Prissey; Smart; Phœbe; Sampson.	Statement and two depositions.
McIntosh, John H..................	Leah; Eve; Juno; Sally; boy, 5.......................	Claimant's statement and one deposition.
Massie, Peter......................	Tom; Sam; Mose; Duncan; George; Nanny; Hetty; Simon; Mary; Violet; Peggy; Jenny; Nanny.	Do. do.
McClure, Cochrane and William.....	April; July; Cooke; Cæsar; Edward; Dick; Sampson; March; Mary; Dinah; Rose; two children, (April's;) one child, (Dinah's;) two children, (Jaly's;) one child, Cæsar.	See Cowper's, John, statement.
Maxwell, Joseph....................	Sam; Toby; Sally; Harriet; Nancy......	Claimant's statement and one deposition.
Mather, William H..................	Fuller	Letter of W. H. M. and one deposition.
O.		
Ogilby, William, and wife...........	Brandy; Henry; Rachel; Benjamin; Sarah; Pierre; Mingo; Ben.	Claimant's statement on oath; two depositions; three certificates.
	Cuffy...	One deposition.

* Mr. Frost, agent of Mr. Hamilton, states that the name of one of the slaves claimed by his principal is omitted upon this list, and that it can be supplied by a reference to a document now in possession of the commission under the St. Petersburg convention, March 25, 1824.

GEORGIA—Continued.

Claimants.	Names of slaves.	Proof.
P.		
Parker, John*	Jack; Betty; Nanny; Sandy; Juba; Ned; Minda; Harry.	Claimant's statement on oath and four depositions.
Page, William	Louis; Tom; Sarah; Mary; child	Claimant's statement on oath and two depositions.
Pratt, Abraham	Rose; Nan; Malo, child	Claimant's statement on oath and one deposition.
Parland, John	Will; Mary; January	Do. do.
Parmer, William		One certificate.
Parker, Samuel	Big Frank; Little Frank; Anthony; L. Anthony; Sunday; Adam; Dowey; Baggy; Sambo; Aquilla; Boston; John; Careless; Jenny; Eliza; Cumbo; Jenny; Nancy; Margana; Clarinda; Delia; Phœbe; Charlotte; Clarissa; Delia; Dinah; Mary; Binah; Elsey; Silvia.	Claimant's statement and four depositions.
Pelot, James	Caroline; Dick; Allen; Edward; Serjoe; Glarissa; Billy; Nanny; Chloe; Infant; Cora; Jack; Abraham; Ned.	Claimant's statement on oath; two depositions; one certificate.
Piles, John, estate of	Harry; Lucy; Harriet; Venus; Kate; Princess	Statement and five depositions.
Piles, William	Harry; Lucy; Princess; Harriet; Venus; Kate†	Claimant's statement on oath; one deposition; certificate of nine persons.
Piles, James	Jim; Molly; Tom	
R.		
Ross, John, estate of, Betton A. Copp, administrator.	Sam	Statement, three depositions, and certificate.
Russell, John, estate of, Robt. Leach, executor.	Bob	Statement of executor, and two certificates.
Ross, Hugh	Jim; Dick; Frank; Lymns; Cork; Comfort; Ryna; Patience; Davy; Sarah; Harriet; Jack.	No valuation or deposition; letter to Messrs. Newell and Spalding.
S.		
Smith, Jas., and Mary, his widow	Derry; Harris; Tony	Two statements on oath and one deposition.
Stewart, Sarah	Joe	Claimant's statement and one deposition.
Stewart, Danl., G. Kerr, administrator	Grandison	One deposition.
Shaw, Louisa C.	Sancho	See her statement and oath in the supplement.
Scott, William, estate of, Elisha Atwater, administrator.	Jerry; Ben	Four depositions and claimant's statement.
Sadler, Henry	Patsey; Betsey; Letty; Mary; Geoffry; George	Claimant's statement on oath and six depositions.
Seals, Margaret, now Bailey, M	Ellis; Sylvia	Statement on oath and two depositions.
Shearman, Edward	Jenny; Cuffy; Tom; Belfast	Deposition of Whipple Oldrich.
T.		
Timmons, Mary	Tom	Claimant's oath and two depositions.
Tisdale, John	Jack	Deposition of D. Thompson. (See also further proof of the loss of this slave in J. F.'s claim for property.)
V.		
Victory, Thomas	Willis	Claimant's statement and oath letters to the Secretaries, and five depositions.
W.		
Wright, Rebecca	Male slave	No valuation.
‡Williamson, James, estate of Edward Shearman, trustee.	Jenny; Cuffey; Belfast; Tom	Claimant's statement on oath and three depositions.
Williamson, Elizabeth	Aaron; Tom Moor; Jack Tatnal; Dilsey; Kate	Statement and one deposition.
Wood, John	Fly; Hagar; Dick; Bengey; Lewis; Prince	
Wardrobe, H. L.	Hector; Patrick; Donald; Aaron; January	Oath of claimant.
Wiley, Alexander C	Charles; Wallie; Alney; Daphne; Aggy; Franky; Lubin; Phœbe; Kitty; Monday; January; Deal; Jenny; Sam; Priscilla; Guinea Joe; Betty; Big Joe; Peggy; Joe, child; Hannah, child; Nero; John; Sam; Judy; Moses; Cyrus; Sally; Nanny; Jenny; Lucius; Sue; Duncan; Boatswain; Betty; Sophy; Suckey; Jack; Prince; Dick; Charles; Sue.	Claimant's statement, and valuation by four persons; two letters to Secretary.
Y.		
Yonge, Henry	Bob; Rolla; Alfred	Claimant's statement on oath and three depositions.

RECAPITULATION.

833 slaves, which, at the average value agreed upon and fixed by the commission, viz., $390, amount to the sum of.............. $394,870.

* Since this claim has been transmitted, with other papers, to Mr. J. Baker, secretary, &c., a letter from Mr. Parker to Mr. Seldon (on file in this office) states the loss of two other slaves, viz: Joe and Molly. No proof accompanied the letter, which is exhibited with the claims recently received from Georgia.
† These slaves are claimed above with a different valuation. (See John Piles.)
‡ See E. Shearman.

Inventory of property, other than that of slaves, stated to have been carried off by the British forces from the State of Georgia, with an alphabetical list of the claimants, and the estimated value of the said property.

Claimants.	Property.	Estimated value.	Proof.
A.			
Aldricks, Whipple..................	20,000 lbs. sole leather.....................	$500 00	Statement and eight depositions.
B.			
Buller, Pierce......................	Cotton and merchandise....................	2,500 00	One deposition.
	Provisions, &c.........	500 00	
Brunelte, Remi......................	Merchandise.......................	2,327 75	
Backlott, John, sr.	Sugar and other articles	2,410 50	Oath of claimant and four depositions.
Backlott, John, jr., surviving partner of J. & J. Backlott.	Sugar, &c................................	1,763 00	Oath of claimant and two depositions.
Boog, John	Wine and other articles	1,337 50	Three depositions.
Beyer, G. F....................... ..	Gin and other articles....................	3,336 00	Oath of claimant and one deposition.
C.			
Couper, John	Eight bales of cotton	1,900 00	Claimant's statement on oath.
	Loss of crop and labor....................	3,000 00	William Hunter's letter to John Bailey.
Oster, Benjamin F..................	Six bags of cotton...........	1,066 50	Claimant's statement and two depositions.
D.			
Dubignon, Poulain	Cotton, plate, crops, cattle and provisions...	10,000 00	Three statements included in the claimant's list of slaves lost.
Dufour, Louis......................	Merchandise......................	3,474 00	Claimant's statement and two affidavits.
Demere, Raymond	Cotton, &c.	....	See his letter to J. Cowper.
G.			
Gibson, William....................	Merchandise......................	346 00	See his statement on oath.
Glekie, James H..............	Loss of crop and labor...........	730 91	See his statement in slave list.
Grant, Robert......................	Four bales of Sea Island cotton	660 00	See R. Grant's memorial for the loss of negro woman and two children.
H.			
Hipkins, Susan...........	Furniture.......................	720 00	Statement on oath and one deposition.
Hopkins, Timothy....................	Nineteen sweeps....................	28 50	See William Gibson's statement.
Havens & Bilbo....................	Quantity of steel....................	689 08	Do. do.
Harding, Robert....................	Barque Maria Theresa...............	3,000 00	Claimant's statement.
Hamilton, James....................	Cotton, provision, and furniture, &c........	7,392 98	Statement by J. M. Davis, and two depositions; also, document No. 3, in his list of slaves lost.
K.			
Keane, Alexander....................	Merchandise....................	1,613 43	Certificate of J. Campbell.
L.			
Lewis, Levi	Flour and furniture....................	1,000 00	Claimant's statement and oath.
Lassee, Lewis......................	Goods, &c......................	1,200 12½	Two affidavits.
M.			
Maxwell, Joseph....................	Loss of crop and labor....................	1,000 00	See his statement with slaves, two letters to Secretary Adams, and claimants statement on oath.
Matthews, Edmund..................	Six bales of cotton	1,110 00	
	A cotton gin	140 00	
	Two saddles and bridles....................	30 00	
		1,280 00	
O.			
O'Neal, James T....................	Loss of crop and labor..........	1,500 00	Claimant's statement and one deposition.
Ogilby, William....................	A boat........................	180 00	See his list of slaves lost; see also John Cowper's documents.
P.			
Page, William	Seven bags of cotton	1,347 50	Claimant's statement on oath.
Potter, John	Furniture and house injured	250 00	Three depositions.
Pelot, James......................	Loss of crop and labor	1,500 00	Claimant's statement; one deposition : letter to Secretary Adams.
R.			
Ross, John........................	Merchandise......................	963 50	Claimant's statement.
Ripley, Robert......................	Sugar, &c.........	1,439 05	Oath of claimant and one deposition.
S.			
Sands, Ray.....	Cotton and horses........	7,230 00	Statement on oath and one deposition.
Shaw, Louisa C..................	Cotton, buildings, and provisions..........	19,348 00	Statement on oath and two depositions.
Bonsedale, John....................	Provisions and furniture	500 00	
Sheafe, Daniel R..................	Captured ship Calliope	}	
Sheafe, Jacob......................	........do........................	2,000 00	Statement by claimants; letter to Secretary Adams.
Sheafe, Jacob, jr......................	........do........................	}	
Shearman, Edward, for Edw'd Shearman, jr., and Uzial Shearman.	Cotton and merchandise....................	1,601 00	Claimant's statement and four depositions.
Sinclair, William..................	Cotton........................	36,363 60	Claim filed by Selden and Frost.
	Tobacco........................	23,940 00	
		60,303 60	

GEORGIA—Continued.

Claimants.	Property.	Estimated value.	Proof.
T.			
Talbot....................................	Cordage....................................	$20 00	See William Gibson's statement.
Tisdale, John..........................	Cotton, &c.................................	3,849 00	Depositions, &c.
V.			
Vocelle, Jacque.......................	Merchandise...............................	960 68	Claimant's statement and one affidavit.
Vincent, James, for Smith & Vincent.	Leather, &c..............................	4,680 00	Three depositions.
W.			
Wood, Jacob.............................	2,168 lbs. cotton...........................	975 60	Letter to Secretary Adams, claimant's statement, and five depositions.
Wylly, Alexander C...................	Loss of crop and labor....................	1,500 00	See his statement, and three depositions in his list of slaves lost.

RECAPITULATION.

Amount of property, per estimated value.. $158,946 68¼.

A list of slaves stated to have been carried off by the British forces from the State of Louisiana; with an alphabetical list of the claimants, and the estimated value of the said slaves.

Claimants.	Names of slaves.	Proof.
B.		
Barjac, Mrs. P.......................	Edward....................................	Oath of claimant and two depositions.
Beauregard, Lewis F.................	Billy; Henry..............................	Oath of claimant and three depositions.
Berquier, Francisco & Baptiste......	Pierre; Marteguille; Georges; Victor....................	Do. do.
Bienvena, Antoine, sr................	Laurent; Baptiste; Jim; Thomas; Antoine; Mariga; Mongo; Pierre; Lewis; Jacques; Cesar; Allen; Robert.	Do. do.
Bienvena, Mrs. H., heirs of..........	Lewis.....................................	Four depositions.
C.		
Chancerel, Marie.....................	Louis.....................................	Oath of claimant and three depositions.
Canon, Jean...........................	Jean Baptiste.............................	Oath of claimant and two depositions.
Chiapella, Celestin..................	Bill; Christopher; Ado; Charity; Samby; Peter; Michael; Isaac; Hector; Prince; Harris; Honore; Soulas; Coisey; Friday; Coffy; James; Zephyr; Rabasse; Gallo; Jean Baptiste; Joe; Lapaix; James Corego; William; Henry; Fine; Sophie; Denise; Rosalie; Azimia; Françoise; Felicite; Rosette; Bahet; Josephine; Suzane; Jean; Vincent; Rougean; Louis; Petit Charles; Charles Soussier.	Four depositions.
Coison, John Joseph..................	Yoys; John................................	Oath of claimant and three depositions.
D.		
Ducres, Rodolphe J...................	Sande; Lindor; Pierre; Jioglis; Billy; Linder; Marianne.	Oath of claimant and two depositions.
Dufossat, Jean Baptiste..............	Thomas....................................	Do. do.
Delaroude, Pierre Donis..............	Petit Pierre; Joseph; Jean; Antoine; Colos; Telemaque; Jean Baptiste; Alexis; Apollon; Minan; Nicholas; Chuma; Babet; Rosalie; Catiche; Hersonne.	Do. do.
Delasseize, Valery J.................	Baptiste Coulomb; Bambara; Honore; Lindor; Edward; Alexandre.	Oath of claimant and three depositions.
G.		
Gosselin, Basile.....................	Benjamin..................................	Do. do.
H.		
Howard, ————.......................	Jim; Ned; Sampson; Will; Bob; Cesar; Eilick; Charlotte; Esther; Jude; Susan; Lucy; Bet; Reuben; Mary.	Oath of claimant and two depositions.
Hedge, Lewis.........................	George; Sall; Bob; Jinny; Dick; Mary; Chloe; Matilda; Parlor; Peter; Charles; Ben; Leah; Bet; Jim; Richard; Hiram; Schern; Stephen; Reuben; Bill; John; Hanna; Rose; Sukey; Julia; Anna; Tom.	Oath of claimant and one deposition.
J.		
Jourdan Brothers.....................	Jean; Narcissus..........................	Three depositions.
K.		
Kernion, Ch. Lab.....................	Jean Baptiste.............................	Oath of claimant and two depositions.

LOUISIANA—Continued.

Claimants.	Names of slaves.	Proof.
L.		
Lacoste, Pierre	Jacques; Valentin; Jasmin; Manuel; Valere; François Congo; Louis Bambara; Antoine; Françoise; Rose; Marietta; Angelique; Rosalie.	Oath of claimant and one deposition.
Lacoste, Leandre....................	Carter; Pierre; Ana.....................................	Oath of claimant and three depositions.
M.		
Macarty, Louis B....................	Redmond.....................................	Do. do.
Mendez, Antonio....................	Baptiste; Philippe; Pielîe; Hanna.....................	Do. do.
Morgan, Benjamin ··················	Moses.....................................	Four depositions.
O.		
Overton, John.....................	Jeff; Primus; Ike; Ned; Rose; Lucy; Nell............	Do.
P.		
Philippon, Antoine..................	Jean Baptiste; Alexander; Marie; Caroline............	Oath of claimant and one deposition.
R.		
Reggio, Louis.....................	John; Tom; Joe.....................................	Oath of claimant and three depositions.
V.		
Villers, Jumonville de.............	Narcisse; Jean; Figarro; Bazille; Thomas; Narcisse; Isidore; Valentin; Mars; Alexis; Sampson; Amadis; Pierre; Quinton; Saturnin; Cesar; Jacques; Bambard; Pompee; Manon.	Oath of claimant and six depositions.
Villere, James	Lindor; Allain; Milion; Thiary; Isedore; La Fortune; Michael; Appollon; Antoine; Joe; Scapin; Castor; Charlite; Paul; Petion; Porus; Momus; Dick; Azael; Moses; Blase; Auguste; Isaac; Lubin; Alexis; Azor; Mars; Lamour; Vendredi; Polidor; Larame; Phill; Apollon Minan; Mercure; Vulcaine; Bon Homme; Françoise; Joseph; Gregoire; Annette; Louisa; Julie; Denise; Agathe; Hanna; Manette; Betsi; Sophie; Rosine; Esther; Clarisse; Laurette; Celesta.	Oath of claimant and six depositions.
Veillon, Pierre....................		
Villon, Silvain....................		
Solis, Manuel....................		
Cure, Martin	Pompee; Jacques; Francisque; Jean Baptiste; George..	Two depositions.
Versailles, François..............		
By Pierre Lacoste, their attorney in fact.		

RECAPITULATION.

259 slaves, which, at the average value agreed upon and fixed by the commission, viz., $580, amount to the sum of.............. $150,220.

List of slaves stated to have been carried off by the British forces from the State of Mississippi; with an alphabetical list of the claimants, and the estimated value of the said slaves.

Claimants.	Names of slaves.	Proof.
Ellis, Mary B.................	Jerry; Ben; John; Will; Sam; Big Dick; Little Dick; Tom; Abram; King; Sally.	Oath of owner and two depositions.
Gaines, Ann, administratrix of Ambrose Gaines, deceased, by E. W. Ripley, attorney.	Four slaves...............................	See General Ripley's letters.
Jourdan, John Joseph, by John Conrad, his attorney.	Cæsar Castillon; Cæsar Panton; Daniel; Raphael; Polly; Raphael, son; Marie.	Oath of claimant and two depositions.

RECAPITULATION.

22 slaves, at the average value agreed upon and fixed by the commission, viz., $280, amount to the sum of $6,160.

List of slaves stated to have been carried off by the British forces from the State of Delaware.

Claimants.	Names of slaves.	Proof.
Primrose, Thomas..................	Jerry.....................................	Depositions of Edmund Bailey, Thomas Peterkin, and Elias Primrose.
Wood, John.......................	Peter.....................................	Do. do. do.

RECAPITULATION.

2 slaves, which, at the average Value agreed upon and fixed by the commission, viz., $280, amount to the sum of $560.

Inventory of property, other than that of slaves, stated to have been carried off by the British forces from the State of Delaware; with the names of the claimants, and estimated value of the property.

Claimants.	Property.	Estimated value.	Proof.
Holleges, Thomas......................	4 oxen, at $25............................	$100 00	Six depositions.
Williams, Aaron.......................	10 cattle, at $15........................	150 00	Do.

RECAPITULATION.

Amount of property, per estimated value, $250.

List of slaves stated to have been carried off by the British forces from the State of Alabama; with an alphabetical list of the claimants, and the estimated value of the said slaves.

Claimants.	Names of slaves.	Proof.
B.		
Bazarge, John B........	Tom..	Deposition of owner and three others
C.		
Cook, Nicholas.....................	William..................................	Deposition of owner and five others.
Colin, Honore........................	Tom	Deposition of owner and two others.
D.		
Dolives, Louis......................	Hector; Michael; Isidore	Deposition of owner and four others.
Dubroca, Hague.....................	Dominique; Sally; Carmelite, (F;) Charles; Infant.....	Deposition of owner and six others.
E.		
Eslava, Miguel......................	Challes; Isabella........................	Deposition of owner and four others.
F.		
Fee, Samuel........................	Not stated...................................	No statement but his own.
H.		
Hardridge, James....................	Affee; Kitta............................	Two depositions and Mr. Crowell's letter.
Hall, Charles.......................	John......................................	Claim put in by Mr. G. S. Bulfinch, July 15, but no papers or proof filed.
L.		
Lacoste, Augustine...................	Ransom of 14 slaves...............	Two depositions.
M.		
McDonald, Archibald................	Dick..................	Deposition of James Gould.

RECAPITULATION.

18 slaves, which, at the average value agreed upon and fixed by the commission, viz., $390, amount to the sum of $7,020.

Inventory of property stated to have been carried off by the British forces from the State of Maine; with an alphabetical list of the claimants, and the estimated value of the said property.

Claimants.	Property.	Estimated value.	Proof.
Cave & Richaud	Ship Victory........................	$6,000 00	See W. M. Worthington's letter, his memorial, and Mr. Whitman's letter.
Chadburn, James................	50 half barrels of beef...............	400 00	
Chadburn, James, for himself, and, as attorney, for William Francis.	1,600 barrels of flour...............	7,034 00	Do. do. do.
O'Brien, Jeremiah, and O'Brien, Gideon, for themselves, and as attorneys for Wm. O'Brien, deceased, and John Holway.	Schooner Washington..............	1,500 00	Four depositions and copy of enrolment, and James Penniman, jr.'s, deposition, received October 18, 1823.

RECAPITULATION.

Amount of property, per estimated value, $16,934.

A list of slaves stated to have been carried off by the British forces from the town of Alexandria, District of Columbia.

Claimants.	Names of slaves.	Proof.
Carson, Nehemiah.................	One slave	See documents.
Halton, Basil.........................	One slave	Do.
Perry, Henrietta.....................	Samuel...	Deposition of Thomas Travers.

RECAPITULATION.

Three slaves, at the average value agreed upon and fixed by the commission, viz., $280, amounts to the sum of..................... $840.

List of property, other than that of slaves, stated to have been carried off by the British forces from the town of Alexandria and the District of Columbia ; with an alphabetical list of the claimants, and the estimated value of the said property.

Claimants.	Property.	Estimated value.	Proof.
B.			
Bennett, Charles.................	86 hhds. tobacco	$4,400 00	Claimant refers to J. Muncaster's affidavit.
Butler, Silas, & Co.......	100 bbls. flour.....................	400 00	See Newton Keene's deposition.
Barnes, John.....................	43 hhds. tobacco	2,200 00	Memorial.
C.			
Callett, Charles I.....	101 hhds. tobacco	1,515 00	Oath of claimant and deposition of J. Muncaster and R. Coe.
	1,656 bbls. flour.....................	6,694 00	
Carson, Nehemiah..............	1 hhd. tobacco.....................	51 00	Included in his claim for the loss of a slave.
Coleman, George,..............	Various articles,....................	1,261 09	See his account.
D.			
Dean, Joseph	1,500 bbls. flour...........:	6,000 00	Oath of claimant.
	11 bbls. Orleans sugar	330 00	
	13 bbls. pickled shad..................	65 00	
	3 hhds. pickled fish..................	30 00	
	1 pipe Lisbon wine..................	150 00	
	And other articles not ascertained correctly.	100 00	
Deneale, James C...............	Flour.............................	14,496 00	Oath of claimant.
F.			
Fendall, Benjamin T...........	Schooner Little Eliza	2,000 00	Letter of Thomas Johnson, agent.
Forrest, Joseph	Schooner Citizen....................	4,000 00	Do. do.
Fowle, William, surviving partner of Lawrason & Fowle.	3 brigs	7,500 00	See William Fowler's letter.
	1 schooner..........................	1,500 00	
	2,500 bbls. flour	10,000 00	
	50 hhds. tobacco	2,600 00	
G.			
Greer, Alexander.................	36 hhds. tobacco	1,872 00	See his schedule and manifests of inspectors.
H.			
Hunter, John....................	Suit of sails for a brig	830 50	Letter of Thomas Johnson, agent.
J.			
Janney, John, for self and James Keith.	745 bbls. flour.....................	2,980 00	Affirmation of claimant.
	2 hhds. tobacco....................	104 00	
Janney, Joseph	80 hhds. tobacco......:........	4,160 00	See his schedule.
Janney, Thomas, & Co.........	32 hhds. tobacco....................	1,664 00	Depositions of R. Coe and J. Muncaster.
Janney, Thomas, & Co..........	44 hhds. tobacco....................	2,288 00	See their schedule.
Jameson, Robert, executor of Andrew Jameson, deceased.	113 kegs of crackers..............	363 59	Oath of claimant.
K.			
Keene, Newton..................	163 bbls. flour.....................	652 00	Oath of claimant.
L.			
Lloyd, John.....................	352 bbls. flour	1,408 00	Oath of claimant.
M.			
Mark, Samuel, & Co...........	79 hhds. tobacco.....................	4,108 00	Depositions of J. Muncaster and R. Coe.
	79 hhds. tobacco	4,108 00	
Mason, Thompson.....	90½ bbls. flour..........·..........	112 75	See his deposition filed with his claim for slaves lost from Virginia.
M'Pherson, Daniel..............	Brig Hunter.......................	2,000 00	Letter of Thomas Johnson, agent.
	And 1,300 bbls. flour................	5,200 00	
N.			
Neale, ·C., trustee of J. & G. Plummer.	156 hhds. tobacco	· 8,112 00	Affirmation of G. Plumer.
Newton, Augustine, administrator of Wm. Newton, deceased.	Flour, wine, &c..................	500 00	

ALEXANDRIA AND THE DISTRICT OF COLUMBIA—Continued.

Claimants.	Property.	Estimated value.	Proof.
P.			
Page, C., Cashier of the Bank of Potomac.	Ship William and John............	815,000 00	C. Page's letter.
R.			
Reed, S. & D.,..................	12 hhds. tobacco	624 00	Their letter to Mr. Berryman.
V.			
Veitch, Richard, surviving partner of R. Veitch & Co.	Sails, rigging, &c., of the brig Columbia.	2,000 00	R. Veitch's memorandum.

RECAPITULATION.

Amount of property, per estimated value... · 8113,106 77.

CLAIMS OF THE INHABITANTS OF EAST FLORIDA FOR PROPERTY LOST AND DESTROYED
BY TROOPS OF THE UNITED STATES IN 1812.

COMMUNICATED TO THE HOUSE OF REPRESENTATIVES MARCH 10, 1826.

Mr. FORSYTH, from the Committee of Foreign Relations, on the memorial of sundry persons, inhabitants of
East Florida previous to the cession of it to the United States, reported:

That the petitioners state that they suffered greatly by the invasion and occupation of a part of the
province of East Florida, in 1812, by troops under the command of General Matthews, a Commissioner of
the United States, and they pray Congress to adopt the proper means to ascertain the amount of their
respective losses, and provide for. the speedy payment of them when ascertained.   No evidence accompanies the memorial; but the committee have not thought it necessary to call for evidence, as their
judgment is unfavorable to the claimants, on the admission of the truth of the principal facts stated by
them.   The attempted revolution in East Florida, in 1812, is well remembered; the part said to have
been taken in it by General Matthews, the disavowal of his conduct, and the revocation of his authority
by the President, are equally well known.   The transactions of that day formed a part of complicated
negotiations with Spain, which were terminated by the treaty of cession of February 22, 1819.   As
individuals, the Spanish inhabitants of East Florida had no claim upon the United States.   The question
of indemnity, arising out of the events of,1812, was purely international, urged by Spain, doubtless, for
the benefit of the sufferers.   What were the obligations of the United States to Spain for the transaction
of 1812 the committee do not think it necessary to inquire; an agreement, mutually satisfactory to the
parties, was made, and to that agreement a resort must be had to ascertain the foundation of the claims
of the petitioners upon the United States.   Such part of the 9th article of the treaty of the 22d of February,
1819, which relates to the various transactions in Florida, is as follows:
"And the high contracting parties, respectively, renounce all claim to indemnities for any of the
recent events or transactions of their respective commanders and officers in the Floridas.
"The United States will cause satisfaction to be made for the injuries, if any, which, by process of
law, shall be established to have been suffered by the Spanish officers and individual Spanish inhabitants
by the late operations of the American army in Florida.
Soon after the Floridas were delivered to the United States, to fulfil the obligations under this article
of the treaty of cession, an act was passed, on the 3d day of March, 1823, authorizing the judges of the
Territory to receive evidence of the several claims under it; to report them to the Secretary of the
Treasury, who was directed to re-examine them, and to pay those which were approved out of any moneys
in the Treasury not specially appropriated to some other object.   Various claims were presented,
established by authentic evidence, and transmitted to the Treasury Department.   Upon all those presented
before March last the late Secretary of the Treasury decided.   Three classes of cases have been presented,
arising in 1812, 1814, and 1818.   It appears, by the records of the Treasury Department, that all those
of 1812 and 1814 were rejected as not embraced by the treaty.   It is understood by the committee that,
before a final decision upon them, the late Secretary of the Treasury applied to the Chief Magistrate,
under whose instructions the treaty was framed, and was confirmed in the opinion previously entertained
by him, that no cases were within the scope of the 9th article which occurred prior to 1818.
An application has been lately made on behalf of claimants for losses sustained in 1812 and 1814,
and the opinion of the present coincides with that of the preceding administration.   The only question
for the committee to consider is, whether that decision is justified by the 9th article of the treaty, the
words of which have been already quoted.   In the judgment of the committee, the word *late* operations
refers only to the last operations of the American army.   Prior to 1812 no operations are known to have
occurred; to include 1812, 1814, and 1818, three distinct periods, under the term *late*, would be using a
latitude of construction not warranted by the letter or spirit of the article.   If "late operations" do not

exclude any "operations," why was the term used? It is alleged, however, in the very ingenious and elaborate argument of the delegate of Florida, which accompanies this report, that the 9th article in the English differs from the Spanish, no qualifying word equivalent to "late" being used in the Spanish. The English and Spanish are equally originals, and it cannot be important to ascertain which is the translation of the other. On a careful comparison of the English and Spanish, the committee are of opinion, however, that the same idea is conveyed in both languages, and that the same construction may be put on the Spanish as upon the English. The Spanish is as follows:

"Las altas partes contratantes renuncian reciprocamente todos sus derechos á indemnizaciones por qualquiera de los ultimos a contecimientos y transacciones de sus respectivos comandantes y oficiales en las Floridas."

"Y los Estados Unidos satisfarán los perjuicios, si los hubiese habido, que los habitantes y oficiales Españoles justifiquen legalmente haber sufrido por las operaciones del Exercito Americano en ellas."

The words "por las operaciones del Exercito Americano en ellas" refer to the "ultimos a contecimientos y transacciones." The whole should form but one sentence; there is evidently a mistake in the punctuation. The copulative conjunction y (and) unites the two parts of the sentence together. "Las Floridas" should be followed by a semicolon, otherwise the relative pronoun "ellas," which concludes the whole, would be without an antecedent.

The committee recommend, therefore, to the House, not to disturb the decision made under the treaty and the law to carry it into effect, and offer the following resolution:

Resolved, That the inhabitants of East Florida, who pray indemnity for injuries sustained in 1812, in the then province, have leave to withdraw their memorial and the accompanying documents.

To the honorable the Senate and House of Representatives of the United States in Congress assembled:

The memorial of the subscribers, Spanish subjects, resident in East Florida previous to the cession of that province to the United States, respectfully showeth:

That on the 17th of March, 1812, an invasion of the said province, and the capture of the town of Fernandina, within its limits, took place, by a naval force of the United States, consisting of several gun-boats, under the command of Commodore Campbell, and a body of men from Georgia, among whom were the Savannah Guards and Blues, under the direction of General George Matthews, Commissioner on the part of the United States; that said body of men were joined by regular troops of the United States, under the command of Colonel Thomas Smith, and proceeded through the province to the city of St. Augustine, which they invested, and continued before, from the 25th of March to the middle of September, during which time the American flag was constantly flying; that they were obliged to retreat from thence to St. John's river, where they remained until the United States troops were finally withdrawn, in consequence of the convention between Governor Kindelan and General Thomas Pinckney, in the May following.

Your memorialists beg leave further to represent: That at the time of the aforesaid invasion they were subjects of the Crown of Spain, a power then at peace with the United States, and in the enjoyment of prosperity and domestic comfort; that the officers and troops of the United States, with those associated with them, did, under the sanction of the American flag, burn the houses of your memorialists; destroy their cattle and other property; and that the Indians, let loose upon the country in consequence of the invasion, did complete the ruin of your memorialists, by carrying off their negroes and destroying all that remained of their property; that, in consequence of these unprovoked hostilities and atrocities, they are involved in distress and poverty; their debts have accumulated; their creditors are coming down upon them; they are deprived of the means of paying them; and the remnant of their property is seized and sacrificed to satisfy their demands; in one word, they have nothing before them but distress and ruin. That your memorialists did look forward with confidence to remuneration for the pecuniary losses they have sustained by the aforesaid invasion; those of their domestic comforts, and the prospects of their families, can never be repaired; hitherto their expectations have been disappointed; they therefore pray your honorable body will take such measures as to your wisdom may seem fit, in order that the amount of said losses may be ascertained, and means taken for their speedy liquidation; and your memorialists will ever pray, &c.

F. J. Fatio,	Pablo Sabate,
F. M. Arredondo, senior,	B. de Castro y Ferrer,
F. M. Arredondo, junior,	Per John A. Cavedo,
F. J. Fatio, for the heirs of Jos. M. Arredondo,	Juan Gianoply,
Geo. F. Clarke,	Antonio Andreu,
John Geiofer,	Prudence Plummer,
F. P. Fatio,	James Hall,
L. Fleming,	Sarah Faulk,
Geo. Fleming,	Wm. Bardin,
Mateo Solano,	Henry Hartley,
William Harvy,	Moses Bowden,
Wm. Hollingsworth,	Farq. Bethune.
Edward Wanton,	

St. Augustine, *January* 14, 1826.

Letter from Joseph M. White to Mr. Rush.

Washington, *November* 28, 1825.

Sir: By an act of Congress approved March 3, 1823, the claims of Spanish officers and individual Spanish inhabitants, under the 9th article of the treaty between Spain and the United States, concluded at Washington on the 22d of February, 1819, were referred to the judges of the superior courts of East and

West Florida, for examination and adjustment, and a provision made for their payment, upon the approval of the Secretary of the Treasury of the United States. These claims were submitted and judicially investigated by the judges, in obedience to the requisitions of the act, and reported during the last winter, at a time when it is believed the health of your predecessor was such as to prevent his giving that attention to the subject which its magnitude and importance required. A list has been furnished by one of the clerks of your Department, purporting to be an account of the number admitted and those rejected, without giving the reason of the decision against the latter, with which some of my constituents, particularly in East Florida, are greatly and (in my humble opinion, although it is uttered with deference and respect,) justly dissatisfied.

It therefore becomes my duty, as the representative of that Territory, to invite your attention to the subject, under a firm conviction that upon an examination of the facts and the treaty itself you cannot fail, by the application of those principles of rational construction with which you are so familiar, to give such an interpretation as will do ample justice to the claimants and preserve the honor and faith of the nation, without subjecting them to the necessity of appealing to Congress to institute an inquiry whether any further provision is necessary to carry into effect that article of the treaty. The amount of the claims dwindle into comparative insignificance when the great principles involved in their determination are considered by a Government that possesses the proud pre-eminence of a national character, unsullied by injustice or punic faith, and when it is recollected that these claimants are not foreign subjects, having a Government to interpose its negotiations in their behalf; by the treaty they have been made citizens of the United States, and are now relying on the magnanimity of their own adopted rulers, and, appealing only to the standard of reason and national law, expect by that to be judged. It is said, in a letter written to East Florida, that the claims in that section of the Territory were rejected because they were not embraced by the provisions of the treaty. The claims for losses in West Florida occasioned by the invasion of 1814 were no doubt doomed to the same fate and for the same reason. By this construction the operation of the treaty is only confined to the losses occasioned by the operations of the army in 1818, when it is known that in that year there were few losses, in consequence of the strict discipline and uncommon prudence of the commanding general and his officers, and when the quartermaster had not only stores, but money, adequate to the demands of the army, with the exception, perhaps, of a few instances, which resulted more from the consequences of the consternation occasioned by an invasion than the immediate destruction of the soldiery.

I shall endeavor, however, to inquire, in the first place, what were the obligations incurred by the United States in consequence of the invasion of Florida, independently of any treaty on the subject; and in the second, to prove that those losses, such as might be established by the decision of the judges, were embraced by it, and so intended by the contracting parties. It will be recollected by you, sir, that, for many years previously to the occupation of the province of East Florida by the American troops, there had been various questions of controversy between the Spanish monarchy and the Government of the United States in relation to limits, the right of deposit at New Orleans, the navigation of the Mississippi, and particularly the Spanish spoliations on our commerce and the condemnation of prizes captured by French privateers in the ports of Spain, for the latter of which our Government claimed an indemnity, which was provided for in the convention of 1802. My object in referring to these facts, so prominent in the diplomatic history of our country and so perfectly familiar to you, is to present a view of the relations of the two Governments previous to the passage of the secret act of Congress of 1811. I do not pretend that the Spanish Government had not violated the laws of nations and the convention they had solemnly entered into. These are questions that it would be useless to discuss. Whatever may have been the undoubted rights, equitable claims, and just complaints of the United States on the one hand, and the fraud, injustice, and perfidy of the Spanish Government on the other, it will be obvious that the inhabitants of East Florida could not incur no responsibility, and that their private fortunes could not be appropriated to the satisfaction of these spoliations or the support of an American army in pursuit of redress within the acknowledged limits of the Spanish territory, without previous declaration of war by the constitutional authorities. Even in case there had been an open war existing at the time of the invasion between the two Governments, according to the well settled principles of all civilized nations, the private property of the inhabitants of the belligerent parties would be free from molestation or injury. This question is of too recent occurrence in our own Government to admit of controversy; in the late war with England the United States asserted successfully her claims for the deportation of slaves, taken from individuals by the enemy in time of open and declared war. There was, however, no war between Spain and the United States when despatches were issued in 1811 to General Matthews, directing him to "repair with all possible expedition, concealing from general observation the trust committed," and directing him, if the local authorities were willing to surrender the country, to take possession, and in case a foreign power should be suspected of a design to take it, "to preoccupy by force the territory," and if a "military force" should be required, they are placed under his command. Under these instructions General Matthews entered the country with an army, took possession of Amelia island, contrary to the declared will and in defiance of the Spanish authority, and against their loudest protestations. Many of the inhabitants of that country, seeing an American general, bearing the commission of the President of the United States, and upon his "assurances" that the United States intended to hold possession, joined his standard, or declared the province independent of the Spanish monarchy, and made a formal delivery of it to the United States, and placed themselves under its protection. All the confusion and consequent loss of property, of both the inhabitants and what has been denominated the Patriots, was to be attributed directly to the invasion of General Matthews.

The Patriots, seeing from his instructions that he was authorized to receive it from the local authorities, proclaimed a revolution, that they, the dominant party in the country, might surrender the province. The proceedings of General Matthews were, however, disavowed, his powers revoked, and finally conferred on General Mitchell, of Georgia; and in the official communication to this gentleman, the Government seem to be sensible that the inhabitants who had declared the province independent "placed reliance on the countenance and support of the Government of the United States. In subsequent instructions from the Department of State, bearing date May 27, 1812, the following language is employed: "It is not expected, if you find it proper to withdraw the troops, that you will interfere to compel the Patriots to surrender the country, or any part of it, to the Spanish authorities; the United States are responsible for their own acts only." Here is an explicit declaration that, although the Government admits that the Patriots were encouraged by the countenance and support of its officers, yet they will only be responsible for their own acts. It is submitted for your consideration, sir, whether this position is defensible, and whether it was not abandoned in the formation of the treaty? I humbly conceive that they were, in *foro conscientiæ*, liable for all the injuries to the property of both the Spanish subjects and Patriots, resulting from the alternate conflicts of both parties. The United States, although they disavow the acts of General Matthews and dismiss him from service, still maintain his position in the interior of a country with which we are at peace, and say, "we are responsible for our own acts," by which it is evidently meant they intend "to hold the ground occupied," and settle with the King of Spain for the hostile entry, and the inhabitants for any injury to their personal property.

All these proceedings took place prior to the declaration of war against England, and when there was no apprehension of Indian hostility in that quarter to justify such precautionary measures. At the succeeding session of Congress a bill was introduced to authorize the forcible possession of the Floridas, which was rejected in the Senate, and, notwithstanding, the position was still maintained. The Governor of Georgia seemed to have understood the diplomatic instructions he had received, and in his letter of the 17th July, 1812, he says: "I have carefully avoided making any proposition for withdrawing the troops, under the fullest conviction that such a step was not intended." Here, although General Matthews was dismissed for transcending orders, as it was alleged, his position is maintained by a subsequent commander, under the fullest conviction that it was not the intention that he should recede from it. That possession of the country was forcibly held, against the wishes and entreaties of the Spanish officers and inhabitants, will be seen by a letter from Governor Kindelan to Governor Mitchell, forwarded to the Department of State, in which the former protests against a longer continuance of the troops in the Spanish dominions, and against the destruction of the property of the inhabitants. As an evidence of the great destruction of property "in consequence of the operations of the Army," reference is requested to the letter of Colonel Smith, the commander of the United States troops, dated "Camp, twenty miles north of St. Augustine, September 22, 1812;" he says: "the inhabitants have all abandoned their houses, with as much of their movables as they could carry with them;" and again, "the province will soon become a desert." This letter was written to General Mitchell and sent to the Government. Here is the most unequivocal proof of the American commander that, on account of the operations of the Army, and the consequences resulting from it, the whole country was abandoned and exhibited a spectacle of desolation. I know it has been alleged that the occupation was persisted in, in consequence of an attack which resulted in the death of one man, made upon a scouting party, doubtless in defence of the lives or property of the inhabitants.

In all the negotiations of the two Governments up to the conclusion of the treaty, it will be seen that the Spanish minister insists for reparation for what he calls the war in East Florida upon a neighboring and friendly power; and again, "I protest against the occupation of Amelia island by the naval and military forces of this Republic," &c. It is apparent, sir, from the foregoing, that there have been "losses" occasioned by the operations of the American Army in the provinces of a country with which we were at peace, at a time when we cannot impute the sin of encouraging or abetting the enemy, against the known will and in defiance of the repeated protestations of the authorities and the peaceful and unoffending inhabitants. For these losses the Spanish minister insisted upon reparation up to the time of concluding the treaty. I humbly conceive that without any stipulation on the subject, but upon the immutable principles of justice and good faith, and the precedents established by the practice of our own Government, the United States are bound to pay for these "losses."

It has been said that interest and ambition are the pole star and magnet of nations, but the United States has heretofore, and we hope will hereafter be considered the great exemplar of liberal principles and liberal establishments, and that the escutcheon of its fame will never be tarnished with injustice, with or without the obligations of treaty stipulations.

If it has been assumed as a position by your predecessor, deemed supported by the phraseology of the treaty, that under its provisions the United States were only bound to pay for the losses occasioned by the entry of the Army in pursuit of the enemy in 1818, the question naturally presents itself, why were the others not provided for? The considerations that impelled the invasion in either of the other instances were not more pressing or powerful than the one in 1818. In the one made in 1814, it was by the same Army, for the same purpose; if Spain had a right to demand indemnity and satisfaction for the injuries of her subjects, and the United States acquiesced in the justice and legality of her demand in the one case, with what color of propriety could they claim an exemption from it in the other? The same rights existed on the part of Spain, and the same moral and political obligations were imposed on the United States; whilst in East Florida the obligation was increased fourfold, from the fact that at the time of the hostile entry into that province there was no war, no enemy fostered and encouraged by the local authorities, no Indians furnished with ammunition and weapons to be used against us; none of these extenuating circumstances existed; the movement was a political one altogether, and the object to seize the province as an indemnity for spoliations, with which these inhabitants had nothing to do; and to that, as the immediate and not remote cause, may be attributed all the consequences of the revolution, and proceedings of the Patriots, the sortie of Sir Gregor McGregor, and the excursions of the visionary Aury, in addition to the devastations of our own Army. A proposition of this kind, successfully advanced, would result in the establishment of a principle of this kind, that the United States have a right to invade the provinces of a friendly or neutral power, destroy the property of the inhabitants without making any compensation, without its being forced upon them by the stipulations of a treaty. Such an argument would not only be indefensible, but incompatible with the honor and magnanimity of the nation. No one, it is presumed, will contend that, according to the usages and laws of war, the private property of an enemy could be appropriated or destroyed by an invader without incurring a just liability to make compensation, and if it is not made by the aggressor the Government ought to remunerate her own citizens or subjects, and continue the war until the object is accomplished; a contrary doctrine would subvert established principles, and make a new chapter in the code of nations that few civilized communities would deem it politic to adopt.

If, then, the private property of an enemy is sacred in time of war, the argument applies much more forcibly in favor of a friendly or neutral power. The British seem to have been so sensible of the application of this principle, that after the arrival of their troops in the West Indies they despatched an officer to pay for all losses occasioned by their troops during the temporary occupation of Pensacola; in addition to this, the British Government, upon the representations of the Spanish ministers, have constituted a commission in England to receive and adjust all claims of Spanish subjects against that Government for property, and particularly negroes, carried off in British vessels. Instances of a similar character are not wanting in our own Government; when the Northwestern Army invaded Canada, and were reduced to considerable extremities, to carry on the war more vigorously, destroyed the individual property of the enemy, an American agent was despatched to Frenchtown to adjust all claims and pay for the losses occasioned by the operations of the Army.. So far as the decision of the Emperor of all the Russias may be quoted as an exposition of national law, it was made in our favor in the controversy with England in regard to the deportation of slaves. Governments should not be unmindful of the benign maxim, "to do unto others as they would have others do unto them."

I have endeavored to prove that the United States were bound to pay for these losses, without the injunctions of a treaty. I beg leave now to refer to that instrument itself, as constituting a positive covenant that has not been discharged; the words in the English copy are as follows: "The United States will cause satisfaction to be made for injuries, if any, which by process of law shall be established to have been suffered by the Spanish officers and individual Spanish inhabitants by the late operations of the American Army in Florida." To establish these claims, an act of Congress was passed, referring them to the judges of East and West Florida, who have performed that service, and have reported them to the Secretary of the Treasury, who is authorized to exercise appellate jurisdiction over the decisions of the judges in pronouncing upon the interpretation of the treaty. It appears, however, that the Secretary, if he examined the claims at all, has overruled and reversed their opinions, and confined the treaty to 1818. If it had ever occurred to Congress that such an interpretation could fairly be given to that article, they would have only invested the judge of West Florida with authority, inasmuch as the "operation" of that year was in that province only; and had the contracting parties intended it to be confined to that year, they would have said the "late operations in West Florida," and not "in Florida," which comprehends both provinces; besides, sir, the word "late," in the English copy, does not, by any principle of construction, apply to one invasion; it may refer to one, or to a half a dozen operations with equal propriety. In the correspondence between the plenipotentiaries of the two Governments, they speak of the "late events," and late "operations," referring to a variety, and comprehending all the transactions connected with the invasion of Florida, East and West. Taken in connexion with this part of the subject, the correspondence of the Chevalier de Onis, pending the negotiations which resulted in the conclusion of a treaty, in which he uniformly claimed reparation for the injuries sustained in East Florida, it is satisfactorily demonstrated that the "late operations," comprising a period of six years, in which these expeditions were projected and carried on, were intended by the contracting parties, and the United States are bound to pay for all that may be established.

If, however, I should be mistaken in supposing that the word "late" could not be made legitimately to apply to any proceedings prior to the campaign of 1818, there is another ground deemed incontrovertible. In the Spanish copy of the treaty, to be found in the 6th volume of the Laws of the United States, there is no word employed to signify "late." The phraseology is, "por las operaciones," "by the operations" of the Army in Florida, applying to East as well as to West; and as this is one of the few covenants in favor of Spain, it must be taken most strongly against the grantor. How this difference between the two copies occurred I am at a loss to conjecture, unless it be a mistake of the translator, in turning that article into English, as it is probable it was proposed in the Spanish language.

However that may be, the Spanish negotiator believed at the time that the rights of these claimants were provided for; and as I have endeavored to show that the United States were bound, by the unchanging and unchangeable obligations of justice, to pay for them, and when there are such strong arguments in favor of that construction, I think they cannot hesitate to do so.

I do not know the nature or amount of the claims in East Florida; it is the principle alone for which I contend, leaving it to the judges, who are fully competent to the duties assigned them, and who have, no doubt, examined them with the strictest scrutiny, and to you, sir, in whose judgment I have the most implicit confidence, to say whether they were embraced by the treaty.

That illegitimate claims should be presented under this law excites no surprise, and is of frequent occurrence, as is shown by the frequent rejections at your own Department; that these claims have been thoroughly examined, and the good separated from the fraudulent, we may have every confidence, from the high character of the tribunals to whom they were referred, and they having received their examination in pursuance of law, ought not now to be questioned by the United States.

In West Florida, having been engaged as counsel for some of the claimants, I had occasion to attend the examination of the judge, and in that district the claims were submitted to the ordeal of the strictest investigation; it was proved by all the witnesses examined that every effort was made by the commanding general and his officers to preserve the property of the inhabitants inviõlate, and you will observe, by an inspection of these claims, that they resulted more from the consternation and flight of the inhabitants than the excesses of the militia, and that there was no such desolation as followed the invasion of East Florida. I trust that every suspicious claim will be promptly rejected; that the honest sufferer alone shall be provided for, and the fraudulent claimant repulsed.

The negotiations in regard to the treaty terminated so soon after the campaign of 1818, the losses were comparatively so insignificant, and the paucity of complaints on the subject, that the conclusion is inevitable that the treaty was intended to embrace those of 1812 and 1814.

I have thus endeavored to call your attention to a subject in which my constituents are deeply interested with the zeal due to their interests, and with a freedom that confidence in the justice of their claims inspires; if I have mistaken any of the facts or principles of legal construction arising from them, you will please to ascribe it to error of judgment and a sincere desire to do justice to those I have the honor to represent. My views have been expressed with frankness and, at the same time, with all possible respect and unlimited confidence in the constituted authorities, and from a belief that your predecessor could never have examined them.

I have the honor to be, with high considerations of respect, your obedient servant,

JOS. M. WHITE.

Hon. RICHARD RUSH, *Secretary of the Treasury.*

TREASURY DEPARTMENT, *December* 16, 1825.

SIR: I received, and have not failed to lay before the President, your communication of the 28th of last month, relative to the construction of the ninth article of the treaty between the United States and Spain, of the 22d of February, 1819.

I am directed to state to you, in reply, that the President's opinion is, that the article in question does not embrace claims for injuries suffered prior to the campaign of 1818; and that this was also the opinion entertained by the Government during the late administration, at which time the question was fully considered.

I have the honor to remain, with great respect, your obedient servant,

RICHARD RUSH.

Hon. JOSEPH M. WHITE, *Delegate from Florida.*

19TH CONGRESS.]   No. 423.   [1ST SESSION.

MESSAGES AND DOCUMENTS COMMUNICATED TO THE SENATE AND HOUSE OF REPRE-
SENTATIVES, AND THE EXECUTIVE PROCEEDINGS OF THE SENATE, FROM WHICH THE
INJUNCTION OF SECRECY HAS BEEN REMOVED, ON THE SUBJECT OF THE MISSION
TO THE CONGRESS AT PANAMA.

IN EXECUTIVE SESSION, SENATE UNITED STATES, TUESDAY, MARCH 21, 1826.

Resolved, That the injunction of secrecy be removed from the President's message of December 26, 1825, relative to the proposed Assembly of American Nations at Panama, and from all Executive communications made and documents sent to the Senate in relation thereto, and from all proceedings in the Senate upon that subject, from which the injunction of secrecy has not yet been removed, and that six thousand copies of the whole be printed. Also, that the injunction of secrecy be removed from all communications relative thereto received from the Executive since the Senate's decision upon the mission, and that an equal number thereof be printed as an appendix to the proceedings had and documents first sent. Also, that all papers and documents sent and communications made by the Executive to the House of Representatives, shall not sent or made to the Senate, be printed in a second appendix, distinguishing the papers and passages sent to the House and not to the Senate, and those sent to the Senate and not to the House. Also, that the resolution of December 28 shall be transferred to the Legislative Journal of the Senate.

The following message was received from the President of the United States, by Mr. John Adams, jr.:

To the Senate of the United States:

In the message to both Houses of Congress at the commencement of the session it was mentioned that the Governments of the Republics of Colombia, of Mexico, and of Central America, had severally invited the Government of the United States to be represented at the Congress of American Nations, to be assembled at Panama, to deliberate upon objects of peculiar concernment to this hemisphere, and that this invitation had been accepted.

Although this measure was deemed to be within the constitutional competency of the Executive, I have not thought proper to take any step in it before ascertaining that my opinion of its expediency will concur with that of both branches of the Legislature: first, by the decision of the Senate upon the nominations to be laid before them; and, secondly, by the sanction of both Houses to the appropriations, without which it cannot be carried into effect.

A report from the Secretary of State, and copies of the correspondence with the South American Governments on this subject, since the invitation given by them, are herewith transmitted to the Senate. They will disclose the objects of importance which are expected to form a subject of discussion at this meeting, in which interests of high importance to this Union are involved. It will be seen that the United States neither intend nor are expected to take part in any deliberations of a belligerent character; that the motive of their attendance is neither to contract alliances, nor to engage in any undertaking or project importing hostility to any other nation.

But the Southern American nations, in the infancy of their independence, often find themselves in positions, with reference to other countries, with the principles applicable to which, derivable from the state of independence itself, they have not been familiarized by experience. The result of this has been, that, sometimes in their intercourse with the United States, they have manifested dispositions to reserve a right of granting special favors and privileges to the Spanish nation as the price of their recognition; at others they have actually established duties and impositions, operating unfavorably to the United States, to the advantage of other European powers; and sometimes they have appeared to consider that they might interchange, among themselves, mutual concessions of exclusive favor, to which neither European powers nor the United States should be admitted. In most of these cases, their regulations unfavorable to us have yielded to friendly expostulation and remonstrance; but it is believed to be of infinite moment that the principles of a liberal commercial intercourse should be exhibited to them, and urged, with disinterested and friendly persuasion, upon them, when all assembled for the avowed purpose of consulting together upon the establishment of such principles as may have an important bearing upon their future welfare.

The consentaneous adoption of principles of maritime neutrality, and favorable to the navigation of peace and commerce, in time of war, will also form a subject of consideration to this Congress. The doctrine that free ships make free goods, and the restrictions of reason upon the extent of blockades, may be established, by general agreement, with far more ease, and perhaps with less danger, by the general engagement to adhere to them, concerted at such a meeting, than by partial treaties or conventions with each of the nations separately. An agreement between all the parties represented at the meeting, that each will guard, by its own means, against the establishment of any future European colony within its borders, may be found advisable. This was, more than two years since, announced by my predecessor to the world as a principle resulting from the emancipation of both the American continents. It may be so developed to the new Southern nations that they will all feel it as an essential appendage to their independence.

There is yet another subject upon which, without entering into any treaty, the moral influence of the United States may, perhaps, be exerted with beneficial consequences at such a meeting—the advancement of religious liberty. Some of the Southern nations are, even yet, so far under the dominion of prejudice that they have incorporated with their political constitutions an exclusive church, without toleration of any other than the dominant sect. The abandonment of this last badge of religious bigotry and oppression may be pressed more effectually by the united exertions of those who concur in the principles of freedom of conscience upon those who are yet to be convinced of their justice and wisdom, than by the solitary efforts of a minister to any one of the separate Governments.

The indirect influence which the United States may exercise upon any projects or purposes originating in the war in which the Southern Republics are still engaged, which might seriously affect the interests of this Union, and the good offices by which the United States may ultimately contribute to bring that war to a speedier termination, though among the motives which have convinced me of the propriety of complying with this invitation, are so far contingent and eventual that it would be improper to dwell upon them more at large.

In fine, a decisive inducement with me for acceding to the measure is to show, by this token of respect to the Southern Republics, the interest that we take in their welfare, and our disposition to comply with their wishes. Having been the first to recognize their independence, and sympathized with them, so far as was compatible with our neutral duties, in all their struggles and sufferings to acquire it, we have laid the foundation of our future intercourse with them in the broadest principles of reciprocity and the most cordial feelings of fraternal friendship. To extend those principles to all our commercial relations with them, and to hand down that friendship to future ages, is congenial to the highest policy of the Union, as it will be to that of all those nations and their posterity. In the confidence that these sentiments will meet the approbation of the Senate, I nominate RICHARD C. ANDERSON, of Kentucky, and JOHN SERGEANT, of Pennsylvania, to be Envoys Extraordinary and Ministers Plenipotentiary to the Assembly of American Nations at Panama; and WILLIAM B. ROCHESTER, of New York, to be secretary to the mission.

JOHN QUINCY ADAMS.

WASHINGTON, *December* 26, 1825.

DEPARTMENT OF STATE, Washington, December 20, 1825.

SIR: Agreeably to your direction, that a statement should be presented to you of what passed in the Department of State, with the ministers of the Republics of Colombia, Mexico, and Central America, in respect to the invitation to the United States to be represented in the Congress at Panama, I have the honor now to report:

That during the last spring I held separate conferences on the same day with the respective ministers of Mexico and Colombia, at their request, in the course of which each of them verbally stated that his Government was desirous that the United States should be represented at the proposed Congress, and that he was instructed to communicate an invitation to their Government to send representatives to it. But that as his Government did not know whether it would or would not be agreeable to the United States to receive such an invitation, and as he did not wish to occasion any embarrassment, he was charged informally to inquire, previous to the delivery of the invitation, whether it would be accepted if given by both of the Republics of Mexico and Colombia. It was also stated, by each of those ministers, that his Government did not expect that the United States would change their present neutral policy, nor was it desired that they should take part in such of the deliberations of the proposed Congress as might relate to the prosecution of the present war.

Having laid before you what transpired at these conferences, I received, about a week after they had been held, your direction to inform the ministers of Mexico and Colombia, and I accordingly did inform them, that their communication was received with due sensibility to the friendly consideration of the United States by which it had been dictated; that, of course, they could not make themselves a party to the existing war with Spain, nor to councils for deliberating on the means of its further prosecution; that the President believed such a Congress as was proposed might be highly useful in settling several important disputed questions of public law, and in arranging other matters of deep interest to the American continent, and strengthening the friendship and amicable intercourse between the American powers; that, before such a Congress, however, assembled, it appeared to him to be expedient to adjust, between the different powers to be represented, several preliminary points, such as the subjects to which the attention of the Congress was to be directed, the nature and the form of the powers to be given to the diplomatic agents who were to compose it, and the mode of its organization and action. If these preliminary points could be arranged in a manner satisfactory to the United States, the ministers from Colombia and Mexico were informed that the President thought the United States ought to be represented at Panama. Each of those ministers undertook to transmit to his Government the answer which was thus given.

In this posture the affair remained until the letters were received which accompany this report, from the ministers of the Republics of Mexico and Colombia, under date of the 3d and 2d of November last. To both of those letters the same answer was returned, in official notes, a copy of one of which is with this report.

The first and only communication from the minister of the Republic of Central America to this

Department, in regard to the Congress at Panama, is contained in his official note, a copy of which, together with a copy of the answer which was returned by your directions, will be found along with this report.

I have the honor to be, with great respect, your obedient servant,

H. CLAY.

The PRESIDENT *of the United States.*

Mr. Obregon to Mr. Clay.

[Translation.]

LEGATION OF THE UNITED STATES OF MEXICO, *Washington, November 3, 1825.*

The underwritten minister plenipotentiary has the honor of informing the honorable Secretary of State that he has communicated to his Government the conversations which occurred between them on his making known to him the determination of the Governments of Colombia and Mexico to form a Congress of representatives from the new States of the continent, who, to that end, had been invited; in which were to be discussed subjects of general interest to all the American powers, as well as those which might be particularly suggested by the existence and actual position of the new powers; and in the meeting of which it was thought proper, by the Government of the subscriber, that the United States of America, by means of their Commissioners, should constitute and take part, as being much interested in the first and principal subject upon which the Congress would be engaged.

In consequence of which, being informed of the concurrence of this Government in the idea of discussing the first point in a Congress, as was desired; and that it would send representatives to it, under condition that the neutrality in which it stood towards Spain should not be violated, and that it should be invited thereto by the Republics of Mexico and Colombia, who should, moreover, signify the affairs with which it was to be occupied to promote its object, and the necessary uniformity of credentials, or authorization of the respective representatives, the President of the United States of Mexico has charged and commissioned anew the underwritten to make the invitation, and to point out the affairs as stated.

The Government of the subscriber never supposed nor desired that the United States of America would take part in the Congress about to be held, in other matters than those which, from their nature and importance, the late administration pointed out and characterized as being of general interest to the continent; for which reason, one of the subjects which will occupy the attention of the Congress will be the resistance or opposition to the interference of any neutral nation in the question and war of independence between the new powers of the continent and Spain.

The Government of the undersigned apprehends that, as the powers of America are of accord as to resistance, it behooves them to discuss the means of giving to that resistance all possible force, that the evil may be met, if it cannot be avoided; and the only means of accomplishing this object is by a previous concert as to the mode in which each of them shall lend its co-operation; for otherwise, resistance would operate but partially, and in a manner much less certain and effective.

The opposition to colonization in America by the European powers will be another of the questions which may be discussed, and which is in like predicament with the foregoing.

After these two principal subjects, the representatives of the United States of America may be occupied upon others to which the existence of the new States may give rise, and which it is not easy to point out or enumerate; for which the Government of the United States of Mexico will give instructions and ample powers to its Commissioners, and it trusts that those from the other powers may bear the same.

The Congress is to be assembled in Panama, at which city the representatives from Colombia, Peru, Guatemala, and Mexico, will have already arrived at the date of this; they will be engaged upon the preliminary rules of the Assembly, and likewise upon questions which belong exclusively to the belligerents.

The United States of America may send their representatives to that city to take part in those questions which, long since, they were the first in declaring to the world they regarded as of transcendent importance to the interests of all America; and in others, to which the formation of the new States will give rise, the concurrence in which will, moreover, accomplish the object so much desired by their respective Governments, of manifesting, by deeds, the disposition and facility which the powers of this continent possess to act in concert in the common cause. To which end, and in compliance with the tenor of the conversations held with the honorable Secretary of State, the underwritten minister plenipotentiary invites this Government to send representatives to the Congress of Panama, with authorities as aforesaid, and with express instructions in their credentials upon the two principal questions; in which step, he is likewise joined by the minister of Colombia, and with which, he trusts, he has fulfilled all that was stipulated to this end.

The subscriber has the honor, on this occasion, to present to the honorable Secretary of State his respects and highest consideration.

PABLO OBREGON.

Hon. HENRY CLAY, *Secretary of State.*

Mr. Salazar to the Secretary of State.

[Translation.]

LEGATION OF COLOMBIA, NEAR THE UNITED STATES OF NORTH AMERICA,
Washington, November 2, 1825.

The undersigned has the honor to communicate to the Hon. Henry Clay, for the information of his Government and the attainment of the objects proposed, that the assembly of American plenipotentiaries, in relation to which the minister from Mexico and the undersigned have held some verbal conferences with the Secretary of State, at their previous request, will shortly be organized; as the plenipotentiaries from Peru are already at the Isthmus of .Panama, the place appointed for the Congress, and those from Colombia and other American Republics are on their way to this Assembly, which they have provided for by public treaties.

The honorable Secretary having intimated, in the name of his Government, that the United States, if formally invited by Mexico and Colombia, and apprised of the subjects to be discussed, would, on their part, appoint a person to represent them, if these subjects should be approved by the United States, the undersigned is accordingly authorized by his Government to address this invitation which he now makes by this note in all due form. He is also assured that the minister from Mexico will present the same invitation on the part of his Government, and the minister from Guatemala has just received similar instructions from his Government.

Of the points which will be under discussion by the Assembly of Panama the undersigned is unable to give a minute enumeration, as they will evidently arise out of the deliberations of the Congress. He is, however, authorized by his Government to assure the United States that these points have no tendency to violate their professed principles of neutrality. The undersigned has also been instructed to suggest some subjects that will form useful matter of discussion in the Congress.

These subjects constitute two classes:

1st. Matters peculiarly and exclusively concerning the belligerents;

2d. Matters between the belligerents and neutrals.

As the United States will not take part in the discussion of subjects of the first description, we will confine ourselves to the latter.

At Panama, the best and most opportune occasion is offered to the United States to fix some principles of international law, the unsettled state of which has caused much evil to humanity. It is to be presumed, that this Government possesses more light upon the subject than the other States of our hemisphere, both from its experience during the wars that succeeded the French revolution, and from its negotiations now on foot with Great Britain and other nations relative to these principles. It belongs to each of the concurring parties to propose their views, but the voice of the United States will be heard with the respect and deference which its early labors in a work of such importance will merit.

The manner in which all colonization of European powers on the American continent shall be resisted, and their interference in the present contest between Spain and her former colonies prevented, are other points of great interest. Were it proper, an eventual alliance, in case these events should occur, which is within the range of possibilities, and the treaty, of which no use should be made until the *casus fœderis* should happen to remain secret; or, if this should seem premature, a convention so anticipated would be different means to secure the same end of preventing foreign influence. This is a matter of immediate utility to the American States that are at war with Spain, and is in accordance with the repeated declarations and protests of the cabinet at Washington. The conferences held on this subject being confidential, would increase mutual friendship and promote the respective interests of the parties.

The consideration of the means to be adopted for the entire abolition of the African slave trade is a subject sacred to humanity and interesting to the policy of the American States. To effect it, their energetic, general, and uniform co-operation is desirable. At the proposition of the United States, Colombia made a convention with them on this subject, which has not been ratified by the Government of the United States. Would that America, which does not think politic what is unjust, would contribute in union, and with common consent, to the good of Africa!

The descendants of this portion of the globe have succeeded in founding an independent Republic, whose Government is now recognized by its ancient metropolis. On what basis the relations of Hayti, and of other parts of our hemisphere that shall hereafter be in like circumstances, are to be placed, is a question simple at first view, but attended with serious difficulties when closely examined. These arise from the different manner of regarding Africans, and from their different rights in Hayti, the United States, and in other American States. This question will be determined at the Isthmus, and, if possible, a uniform rule of conduct adopted in regard to it, or those modifications that may be demanded by circumstances.

The undersigned merely makes these suggestions by way of example; it is left to the wisdom of the Governments and the judgments of their representatives to propose whatever may be esteemed of common good to the new hemisphere. Inviting the United States, in the name of Colombia, to a Congress, the mere assembling of which will increase the political importance of America, and show the facility with which she can combine her resources in defence of common rights when necessary, the undersigned hopes that the United States will make an early appointment of a person or persons to represent them in this Assembly, as the conditions that were required have been fulfilled.

The undersigned has the honor to offer to the Hon. Henry Clay his most distinguished consideration.

JOSÉ MARIA SALAZAR.

Mr. Clay to Mr. Obregon.

DEPARTMENT OF STATE, *Washington,. November* 30, 1825.

SIR: I have the honor to acknowledge the receipt of your official note of the 3d instant, communicating a formal invitation from the Government of the United States of Mexico to that of the United States to send deputies to the contemplated Congress of Panama, and particularizing several subjects which your Government conceives may be proper for the consideration of that Congress; and I have laid your note before the President of the United States.

When, at your instance, during the last spring, I had the honor of receiving you at the Department of State, and conferring with you, verbally, in regard to the proposed Congress, and to the friendly wish entertained by your Government that ours should be represented at it, I stated to you, by direction of the President, that it appeared to him to be necessary, before the assembling of such a Congress, to settle between the different powers to be represented several preliminary points, such as the subjects to which the attention of the Congress should be directed; the substance and the form of the powers to be given to the respective representatives, and the mode of organizing the Congress; and that if these points should be satisfactorily arranged, the President would be disposed to accept, in behalf of the United States, the invitation with which you were provisionally charged.

In your note there is not recognized so exact a compliance with the conditions on which the President expressed his willingness that the United States should be represented at Panama as could have been desired. It would have been, perhaps, better if there had been a full understanding between all the American powers who may assemble, by their representatives, of the precise questions on which they are to deliberate; and that some other matters, respecting the powers of the deputies and the organization of the Congress, should have been distinctly arranged prior to the opening of its deliberations. But as the want of the adjustment of these preliminaries, if it should occasion any inconvenience, could be only productive of some delay, the President has determined at once to manifest the sensibility of the United States to whatever concerns the prosperity of the American hemisphere, and to the friendly motives which have actuated your Government in transmitting the invitation which you have communicated. He has therefore resolved, should the Senate of the United States, now expected to assemble in a few days, give their advice and consent, to send Commissioners to the Congress at Panama. While they will not be authorized to enter upon any deliberations, or to concur in any acts inconsistent with the present neutral position of the United States and its obligations, they will be fully empowered and instructed upon all questions likely to arise in the Congress on subjects in which the nations of America have a common interest. All unnecessary delay will be avoided in the departure of these Commissioners from the United States for the point of their destination.

I avail myself of the occasion to offer you assurances of my distinguished consideration.

H. CLAY.

Don PABLO OBREGON,
Envoy Extraordinary and Minister Plenipotentiary from Mexico.

Mr. Clay to Mr. Salazar.

DEPARTMENT OF STATE, *Washington, November 30, 1825.*

SIR: I have the honor to acknowledge the receipt of your official note of the third instant, communicating a formal invitation from the Government of Colombia to that of the United States to send deputies to the contemplated Congress at Panama, and particularizing several subjects which your Government conceives may be proper for the consideration of that Congress; and I have laid your note before the President of the United States.

When, at your instance, during the last spring, I had the honor of receiving you at the Department of State, and conferring with you, verbally, in regard to the proposed Congress, and to the friendly wish entertained by your Government that ours should be represented at it, I stated to you, by the direction of the President, that it appeared to him to be necessary, before the assembling of such a Congress, to settle between the different powers to be represented several preliminary points, such as the subjects to which the attention of the Congress should be directed; the substance and the form of the powers to be given to the respective representatives, and the mode of organizing the Congress; and that if these points should be satisfactorily arranged, the President would be disposed to accept, in behalf of the United States, the invitation with which you were provisionally charged.

In your note there is not recognized so exact a compliance with the conditions on which the President expressed his willingness that the United States should be represented at Panama as could have been desired. It would have been, perhaps, better if there had been a full understanding between all the American powers who may assemble, by their representatives, of the precise questions on which they are to deliberate; and that some other matters, respecting the powers of the deputies and the organization of the Congress, should have been distinctly arranged prior to the opening of its deliberations. But as the want of the adjustment of these preliminaries, if it should occasion any inconvenience, could be only productive of some delay, the President has determined at once to manifest the sensibility of the United States to whatever concerns the prosperity of the American hemisphere, and to the friendly motives which have actuated your Government in transmitting the invitation which you have communicated. He has therefore resolved, should the Senate of the United States, now expected to assemble in a few days, give their advice and consent, to send Commissioners to the Congress at Panama. While they will not be authorized to enter upon any deliberations, or to concur in any acts inconsistent with the present neutral position of the United States and its obligations, they will be fully empowered and instructed upon all questions likely to arise in the Congress on subjects in which the nations of America have a common interest. All unnecessary delay will be avoided in the departure of these Commissioners from the United States for the point of their destination.

I avail myself of the occasion to offer you assurances of my distinguished consideration.

H. CLAY.

Don JOSÉ MARIA SALAZAR,
Envoy Extraordinary and Minister Plenipotentiary from Colombia.

Mr. Canaz to the Secretary of State.

[Translation.]

WASHINGTON, *November 14, 1825.*

The Government of Central America, which I have the honor to represent, as early as the year 1821 was sensible of the importance to the independent nations of this continent of a general Congress of their representatives, at some central point, which might consider upon and adopt the best plan for defending the States of the New World from foreign aggression, and, by treaties of alliance, commerce, and friendship, raise them to that elevation of wealth and power which, from their resources, they may attain. It also acknowledged that, as Europe had formed a *continental system*, and held a Congress whenever questions affecting its interests were to be discussed, America should form a system for itself, and assemble, by its representatives, in Cortes, whenever circumstances of necessity and great importance should demand it.

Entertaining these views, the Government of Central America voluntarily expressed its willingness to appoint its deputies for such an object. Sensible of its importance, which has also been felt by the Governments of South America, it has resolved to send plenipotentiaries to a general Congress, to be formed for the purposes of preserving the territorial integrity, and firmly establishing the absolute independence of each of the American Republics. On the 19th of March last the Government of Central America formed a convention with that of Colombia providing for this object; and I, as its representative, have been instructed to express to the Government of the United States the desire entertained by my Government that it should send a representative to the general Congress.

To fulfil the wishes of my Government, and convinced, at the same time, of the importance and respectability which would attach to the general Congress of the American Republics, from the presence of envoys from the United States of America, I now address this high Government upon this subject, in the name of Central America. I am anxious, therefore, to know if this Republic, which has ever shown itself the generous friend of the new American States, is disposed to send its envoys to the general Congress, the object of which is to preserve and confirm the absolute independence of these Republics, and to promote the general good, and *which will not require that the representatives of the United States should, in the least, compromit their present neutrality, harmony, and good intelligence with other nations*. This my Government has deemed it necessary to state distinctly in making the present invitation.

Be pleased, sir, to accept expressions of the high consideration with which I am, respectfully, your obedient servant,

ANTONIO JOSÉ CANAZ.

The Hon. SECRETARY OF STATE.

Mr. Clay to Mr. Canaz.

DEPARTMENT OF STATE, *Washington, November* 30, 1825.

SIR: I have the honor to acknowledge the receipt of your official note of the 14th instant, communicating an invitation from the Government of the Federation of the Centre of America to that of the United States to the contemplated Congress at Panama. Having laid it before the President, I am instructed by him to say that the United States, always feeling the deepest interest in whatever concerns the prosperity of the American hemisphere, and receiving with great sensibility this new proof of the friendly esteem of the Government of the Central Republic, will be represented at that Congress, if the Senate of the United States should so advise and consent. That body will assemble in the course of a few days, and, if it concur with the President, Commissioners from the United States will be deputed to Panama without any unnecessary delay. These Commissioners will be empowered and instructed upon all questions which may appear to this Government to be likely to arise in the Congress on subjects in which the nations of America may be supposed to have a common interest.

I avail myself of the occasion to offer you, sir, assurances of my distinguished consideration.

H. CLAY.

Don ANTONIO JOSÉ CANAZ,
   Envoy Extraordinary and Minister Plenipotentiary from Central America.

The message and the accompanying documents were read.
Ordered, That they be printed, in confidence, for the use of the Senate.

WEDNESDAY, DECEMBER 28, 1826.

On motion,
Ordered, That the message of the President of the United States, of the 26th instant, nominating Richard C. Anderson and John Sergeant to be Envoys Extraordinary and Ministers Plenipotentiary to the Assembly of American Nations at Panama, be referred to the Committee on Foreign Relations to consider and report thereon.

Mr. Branch submitted the following motion for consideration; which was read and ordered to be printed, in confidence, for the use of the Senate:

Whereas the President of the United States, in his opening message to Congress, asserts that "invitations had been accepted, and that ministers on the part of the United States would be commissioned to attend the deliberations at Panama," without submitting said nominations to the Senate; and whereas, in an Executive communication of the 26th day of December, 1825, although he submits the nominations, yet maintains the right, previously announced in his opening message, that he possesses an authority to make such appointments, and to commission them without the advice and consent of the Senate; and whereas a silent acquiescence on the part of this body may, at some future time, be drawn into dangerous precedent: Therefore,

Resolved, That the President of the United States does not constitutionally possess either the right or the power to appoint ambassadors or other public ministers but with the advice and consent of the Senate, except when vacancies may happen in the recess.

TUESDAY, JANUARY 3, 1826.

. The Senate proceeded to the consideration of the motion, submitted on the 28th of December, relative to the extent of the Executive power; and
Ordered, That it lie on the table.

WEDNESDAY, JANUARY 4, 1826.

On motion of Mr. Macon,
Resolved, That the President of the United States be requested to communicate to the Senate, confidentially, any conventions in possession of the Executive between any of the new States of America relative to the proposed Congress of Panama; and also any other information upon that subject not heretofore communicated tending to show the propriety of the United States sending ministers to said Congress.

TUESDAY, JANUARY 10, 1826.

The following message was received from the President of the United States, by Mr. John Adams, jr.:

To the Senate of the United States:

In compliance with a resolution of the Senate of the 3d instant, I communicate herewith, in confidence, a report from the Secretary of State, with translations of the conventions and documents containing information of the nature referred to in the said resolution.

JOHN QUINCY ADAMS.

WASHINGTON, *January 9,* 1826.

DEPARTMENT OF STATE, *Washington, January* 9, 1826.

The Secretary of State, to whom the President has referred the resolution of the Senate of the 3d of January, 1826, requesting him to communicate to the Senate, confidentially, any conventions in possession of the Executive between any of the new States of America relative to the proposed Congress of Panama; and also any other information upon that subject not before communicated tending to show the propriety of the United States sending ministers to said Congress, has the honor to report:

That, in compliance with the first part of the resolution, conventions are herewith presented between—
The Republic of Colombia and that of Chile;
The Republic of Colombia and Peru;
The Republic of Colombia and the Federation of the Centre of America; and
The Republic of Colombia and the United Mexican States.

That the latter part of the resolution of the Senate opens a wide field, and might be made to embrace all the foreign relations, American and European, of the United States; but it is presumed that it was not intended to have this extended scope. Under this impression, certain parts of the correspondence between the Executive Government of the United States and the Governments of Russia, France, Colombia, and Mexico, of which a descriptive list accompanies this report, and which are supposed to have such a connexion with the resolution of the Senate as to render their communication acceptable, are now respectfully laid before the President. The negotiations to which a portion of this correspondence relates being yet in progress, the propriety of the confidential restriction which the Senate itself has suggested must be quite evident.

All which is respectfully submitted.

H. CLAY.

Inclosures.

The four treaties referred to, (translations.)
Mr. Clay to Mr. Middleton, May 10, 1825, (copy.)
Mr. Middleton to Mr. Clay, July 15, (27,) 1825, (copy.)
Mr. Middleton to Mr. Clay, August 27, (September 8,) 1825, (copy.)
Count Nesselrode to Mr. Middleton, August 20, 1825, (translation.)
Mr. Clay to Mr. Middleton, December 26, 1825, (copy.)
Mr. Clay to Mr. Salazar, December 20, 1825, (copy.)
Mr. Poinsett to Mr. Clay, September 30, 1825, (extract.)
Mr. Poinsett to Mr. Clay, September 28, 1825, (extract.)
Mr. Clay to Mr. Poinsett, November 9, 1825, (copy.)
Mr. Clay to Mr. Brown, October 25, 1825, (copy.)
Mr. Clay to Mr. Obregon,* December 20, 1825, (copy.)
Mr. Salazar to Mr. Clay, December 30, 1825, (translation.)
Mr. Obregon to Mr. Clay, January 4, 1826, (translation.)

° Copy of the note to Mr. Obregon not sent, being in substance the same as that to Mr. Salazar, of the same date.

COLOMBIA AND CHILE.

[Translation.]

Francisco de Paula Santander, of the Liberators of Venezuela and Cundinamarca, decorated with the cross of Boyacá, General of Division of the Armies of Colombia, Vice President of the Republic, charged with the Executive power, &c., &c., &c.

To all who shall see these presents, greeting:

Whereas there has been concluded and signed, in the city of Santiago de Chile, on the twenty-first day of October, in the year of Grace one thousand eight hundred and twenty-two, between the Republic of Colombia and the State of Chile, by means of plenipotentiaries sufficiently authorized by both parties, a treaty of perpetual union, league, and confederation, the tenor whereof is, word for word, as follows:

In the name of God, the Author and Legislator of the Universe: The Government of the Republic of Colombia on the one part, and on the other that of the State of Chile, animated with the most sincere desire of putting a speedy termination to the calamities of the present war, to which they have been incited by the Government of his Catholic Majesty the King of Spain, by effectually co-operating for so important an object, with all their influence, resources, and forces, by sea and land, to secure forever to their respective people, subjects, and citizens, the precious enjoyments of their internal tranquillity, of their liberty and national independence: and his excellency the Liberator, President of Colombia, having for that purpose conferred full powers upon the honorable Joaquin Mosquera and Arbolida, member of the Senate of the Republic of the same name; and his excellency the Supreme Director of the State of Chile, upon his Minister of State in the Departments of Government and Foreign Relations, D. Joaquin de Echeverria, and in those of Finance and War, D. José Antonio Rodriguez; they, after having exchanged, in good and due form, the said powers, have agreed on the following articles:

ARTICLE 1. The Republic of Colombia and the State of Chile are united, bound, and confederated, in peace and war, to maintain with their influences and forces, by sea and land, as far as circumstances permit, their independence of the Spanish nation, and of any other foreign domination whatsoever, and to secure, after that is recognized, their mutual prosperity, the greatest harmony and good understanding, as well between their people, subjects, and citizens, as with other powers with which they may enter into relations.

ARTICLE 2. The Republic of Colombia and the State of Chile, therefore, voluntarily promise and contract a league of close alliance and firm and constant friendship for the common defence, for the security of their independence and liberty, for their reciprocal and general good, and for their internal tranquillity, obliging themselves to succor each other, and to repel, in common, every attack or invasion which may in any manner threaten their political existence.

ARTICLE 3. In order to contribute to the objects pointed out in the foregoing articles, the Republic of Colombia binds itself to assist with the disposable sea and land forces, of which the number or its equivalent shall be fixed at a meeting of plenipotentiaries.

ARTICLE 4. The State of Chile shall also contribute with the disposable sea and land forces, of which the number or its equivalent shall be likewise fixed at the said meeting.

ARTICLE 5. In cases of sudden invasion, both parties shall be empowered to act in a hostile manner in the territories of the dependence of either, whenever circumstances of moment prevent their acting in concert with the Government to which the sovereignty of the invaded territory belongs. But the party so acting shall fulfil, and caused to be fulfilled, the statutes, ordinances, and laws of the respective States, so far as circumstances permit, and cause its Government to be respected and obeyed. The expenses which shall be incurred in these operations, and others which may be incurred in consequence of the third and fourth articles, shall be liquidated by separate conventions, and shall be made good one year after the conclusion of the present war.

ARTICLE 6. To secure and perpetuate in the best mode possible the good friendship and correspondence between both States, their subjects and citizens, they shall have free entrance and departure in their ports and territories, and shall enjoy there all the civil rights and privileges of trade and commerce, being subjected only to the duties, imposts, and restrictions to which the subjects and citizens of each of the contracting parties shall be subject.

ARTICLE 7. In virtue hereof, the vessels and territorial productions of each of the contracting parties shall pay no higher duties of importation, exportation, anchorage, and tonnage than those established, or to be established, for those of the nation in the ports of each State, according to the existing laws; that is to say, that the vessels and productions of Colombia shall pay the duties of entering and departure in the ports of the State of Chile as Chileans, and those of the State of Chile as Colombians in those of Colombia.

ARTICLE 8. Both contracting parties oblige themselves to furnish what assistance may be in their power to the ships-of-war and merchant vessels that may come to the ports belonging to them on account of damage or for any other cause, and as such they shall be empowered to careen, repair, provision, arm, augment their armament and their crews, so as to enable them to continue their voyages or cruises at the expense of the State or individuals to whom they belong.

ARTICLE 9. In order to avoid the scandalous abuses which may be caused by privateers, armed on account of individuals, to the injury of the national commerce and neutrals, both parties agree in extending the jurisdiction of their maritime courts to the privateers which sail under the flag of either, and their prizes indiscriminately, whenever they are unable to sail easily to the ports of their destination, or when there are appearances of their having committed excesses against the commerce of neutral nations with whom both States are desirous of cultivating the greatest harmony and good understanding.

ARTICLE 10. If by misfortune the internal tranquillity be disturbed in any part of the States mentioned by men turbulent, seditious, and enemies of the Governments lawfully constituted by the voice of the people, freely, quietly, and peaceably expressed in virtue of their laws, both parties solemnly and formally bind themselves to make common cause against them, assisting each other with whatever means are in their power till they obtain the re-establishment of order and the empire of their laws.

ARTICLE 11. If any person guilty or accused of treason, sedition, or other grievous crime, flee from justice and be found in the territory of any of the States mentioned, he shall be delivered up and sent back at the disposal of the Government which has cognizance of the crime, and in whose jurisdiction he ought to be tried, as soon as the offended party has made his claim in form. Deserters from the national armies and marine of either party are also comprehended in this article.

ARTICLE 12. To draw more closely the bonds which ought in future to unite both States, and to remove any difficulty which may present itself, or interrupt in any manner their good correspondence and harmony, an assembly shall be formed, composed of two plenipotentiaries for each party, in the same terms and with the same formalities which, in conformity to established usages, ought to be observed for the appointment of the ministers of equal class near the Governments of foreign nations.

ARTICLE 13. Both parties oblige themselves to interpose their good offices with the Governments of the other States of America, formerly Spanish, to enter into this compact of union, league, and confederation.

ARTICLE 14. As soon as this great and important object has been attained, a general assembly of the American States shall be convened, composed of their plenipotentiaries, with the charge of cementing, in the most solid and stable manner, the intimate relations which ought to exist between all and every one of them, and who may serve as a council in the great conflicts, as a rallying point in the common dangers, as a faithful interpreter of their public treaties when difficulties occur, and as an umpire and conciliator in their disputes and differences.

ARTICLE 15. The Republic of Colombia and the State of Chile bind themselves cheerfully to afford to the plenipotentiaries who may compose the assembly of the American States all the aids which hospitality among brotherly people and the sacred and inviolable character of their persons demand, whenever the plenipotentiaries shall choose their place of meeting in any part of the territory of Colombia or that of Chile.

ARTICLE 16. This compact of union, league, and confederation shall in nowise interrupt the exercise of the national sovereignty of each of the contracting parties, as well as to what regards their laws and the establishment and form of their respective Governments, as to what regards their relations with other foreign nations. But they expressly and irrevocably bind themselves not to yield to the demands of indemnifications, tributes, or exactions which the Spanish Government may bring for the loss of her ancient supremacy over these countries, or any other nation whatever, in her name and stead, nor enter into any treaty with Spain, or any other nation, to the prejudice and diminution of this independence, maintaining on all occasions, and in all places, their reciprocal interests with the dignity and energy of nations free, independent, friendly, brotherly, and confederated.

ARTICLE 17. This treaty, or convention, of amity, league, and confederation shall be ratified within the third day by the Government of the State of Chile, with the advice of the honorable National Convention, in conformity to article 4, chapter 3, title 3, of the Provisional Constitution, and by that of the Republic of Colombia as soon as it can obtain the approbation of the Senate, in virtue of the resolution by the law of Congress of October 13, 1821; and in case, by any accident, it cannot assemble, it shall be ratified in the next Congress, agreeably to the provision of the Constitution of the Republic, in article 55, section 18. The ratifications shall be exchanged without delay, and in the period which the distance that separates both Governments permits.

In faith whereof, the respective plenipotentiaries have signed these presents, and sealed them with the seals of the States which they represent.

Done in the city of Santiago de Chile, on the twenty-first day of the month of October, in the year of Grace one thousand eight hundred and twenty-two, twelfth of the independence of Colombia, thirteenth of the liberty of Chile, and fifth of its independence.

JOAQUIN MOSQUERA. [L. S.]
JOAQUIN DE ECHEVERRIA.
JOSÉ ANTONIO RODRIGUEZ. [L. S.]

ADDITIONAL ARTICLE. The honorable National Convention of Chile having terminated its sessions on the twenty-third day of October last, and not having, on that account, had time sufficient for the discussions by which the present treaty ought to be ratified in the time which was agreed upon by the 17th article, and the honorable Minister Plenipotentiary of Colombia having proposed to their excellencies the Ministers Plenipotentiary of Chile that a new period for the ratifications should be appointed, they consulted the most excellent Supreme Court of Representatives, with whose consent they have agreed with the honorable Minister Plenipotentiary of Colombia on the following article:

The present treaty, concluded in Santiago de Chile on the 21st of October, 1822, shall be ratified in the space of four months, which shall be counted from this day, or sooner if possible, and the ratifications shall be exchanged without delay in the time which the distance that separates both Governments permits.

In faith whereof, the respective plenipotentiaries sign this, and seal it with the seals of the Governments which they represent.

Done at Santiago de Chile, the twentieth of November, of the year of Grace one thousand eight hundred and twenty-two, twelfth of the independence of Colombia, and fifth of that of Chile.

JOAQUIN MOSQUERA. [L. S.]
JOAQUIN DE ECHEVERRIA.
JOSÉ ANTONIO RODRIGUEZ. [L. S.]

Therefore, having seen and examined the said treaty of union, league, and confederation, the consent and approbation of the Congress of the Republic being first had, agreeably to article 55, section 18, of the Constitution, I make use of the power conferred upon me by the 120th article of the same Constitution in ratifying it, and by these presents I ratify it and hold it as valid, grateful, and firm, in all its articles and clauses, with the exception of the words: and *for their internal tranquillity*, of article 2d; all those which the 10th article expresses, and those which follow of the 11th article, to wit: *If any person guilty, or accused of treason, sedition, or other grievous crime, flee from justice and be found in the territory of any of the States mentioned, he shall be delivered up and sent back to the disposal of the Government which has cognizance of the crime, and in whose jurisdiction he ought to be tried, as soon as the offended party has made his claim in form.* And for its fulfilment and exact observance on our part, I solemnly engage and comprimit the national honor. In faith whereof, I have caused issue these presents, signed with my hand, sealed with the great seal of the Republic, and countersigned by the Secretary of State and of the Despatch of Foreign Relations, in the capital of Bogota, the twelfth of July, of the year of Grace one thousand eight hundred and twenty-three, thirteenth of our independence.

FRANCISCO DE P. SANTANDER.

By his excellency the Vice President of the Republic, charged with the Executive power.

PEDRO GUAL,
The Secretary of State for Foreign Relations.

COLOMBIA AND PERU.

[Translation.]

Francisco de Paula Santander, of the Liberators of Venezuela and Cundinamarca, decorated with the cross of Boyacá, General of Division of the Armies of Colombia, Vice President of the Republic, charged with the Executive power, &c., &c., &c.

To all who shall see these presents, greeting:

Whereas there has been concluded and signed, between the Republic of Colombia and the State of Peru, a treaty additional to that of perpetual union, league, and confederation, on the 6th day of July, of the year of Grace one thousand eight hundred and twenty-two, by means of plenipotentiaries sufficiently authorized by both parties, the tenor whereof, word for word, is as follows:

In the name of God, the Sovereign Ruler of the Universe: The Government of the Republic of Colombia on the one part, and on the other that of the State of Peru, animated with the most sincere desires of terminating the calamities of the present war, to which they have been provoked by the Government of his Catholic Majesty the King of Spain, determined with all their resources and forces by sea and land to maintain effectually their liberty and independence, and desirous that this league be general between all the States of the America, formerly Spanish, that united, strong, and powerful, they may maintain in common the cause of their independence, which is the primary object of the present contest, have appointed plenipotentiaries to discuss, arrange, and conclude a treaty of union, league, and confederation, to wit:

His excellency the Liberator, President of Colombia, the honorable Joaquin Mosquera, member of the Senate of the Republic of the same name; and his excellency the Supreme Delegate of the State of Peru, the most illustrious and honorable Colonel Dn. Bernardo Monteagudo, Counsellor and Minister of State and Foreign Relations, founder and member of the great Council of the order of the Sun, and Secretary thereof, decorated with the medal of the Liberator Army, Superintendent of the finances of the General Post Office, and President of the Patriotic Society; who, after having exchanged their full powers, found in good and due form, have agreed on the following articles:

1. To draw more closely the bonds which ought in future to unite both States, and to remove any difficulty which may present itself, and interrupt in any manner their good correspondence and harmony, an assembly shall be formed, composed of two plenipotentiaries for each party, in the terms and with the same formalities which, in conformity to established usages, ought to be observed for the appointment of the ministers of equal class near the Governments of foreign nations.

2. Both parties oblige themselves to interpose their good offices with the Governments of the other States of America, formerly Spanish, to enter into this compact of perpetual union, league, and confederation.

3. As soon as this great and important object has been attained, a general assemby of the American States shall be convened, composed of their plenipotentiaries, with the charge of cementing, in a manner the most solid, and of establishing the intimate relations which ought to exist between all and every one of them, and who may serve as a council in the great conflicts, as a rallying point in the common dangers, as a faithful interpreter of their public treaties when difficulties occur, and as an umpire and conciliator in their disputes and differences.

4. The Isthmus of Panama being an integral part of Colombia, and the most adequate for that august assembly, this Republic cheerfully obliges itself to afford to the plenipotentiaries who may compose the assembly of the American States all the aids which hospitality among brotherly people and the sacred and inviolable character of their persons demand.

5. The State of Peru, from this time, contracts the same obligation, whenever, by the casualties of the war or by the consent of the majority of the American States, the said assembly may meet in the territory of its dependence, in the same terms as the Republic of Colombia has obliged itself in the former article, as well with respect to the Isthmus of Panama as any other point of its jurisdiction, which may be believed for the purpose to this most interesting end by its central position between the States of the north and of the south of this America, formerly Spanish.

6. This compact of perpetual union, league, and confederation, shall in nowise interrupt the exercise of the national sovereignty of each of the contracting parties, as well as to what regards their laws and the establishment and form of their respective Governments, as with respect to their relations with other foreign nations. But they expressly and irrevocably bind themselves not to accede to the demands of tributes or exactions which the Spanish Government may bring for the loss of her ancient supremacy over these countries, or any other nation whatever, in her name and stead, nor enter into any treaty with Spain, or any other nation, to the prejudice and diminution of this independence, maintaining on all occasions, and in all places, their reciprocal interests, with the dignity and energy of nations, free, independent, friendly, brotherly, and confederated.

7. The Republic of Colombia specially obliges itself to raise and maintain on foot a force of four thousand men, armed and equipped, in order to concur in the objects pointed out in the preceding articles. Her national marine, whatever it may be, shall be also directed to the fulfilment of those stipulations.

8. The State of Peru shall contribute on its part with its maritime forces, whatever they may be, and with an equal number of troops as the Republic of Colombia.

9. This treaty shall be ratified by the Government of the State of Peru in the space of ten days, and approved by the next constituent Congress, if in the time of their session they should think good to publish it; and by that of the Republic of Colombia as soon as the approbation of the Senate can be obtained, according to the provision of the law of Congress of October 13, 1821; and if, by some occurrence, it be not extraordinarily assembled, it shall be ratified in the next Congress, agreeably to the resolution of the Constitution of the Republic in article 55, section 18. The ratification shall be exchanged without delay, in the space which the distance separating both Governments permits.

In faith whereof, the respective plenipotentiaries have signed this, and sealed it with the seals of the States which they represent.

Done in the city of the Free of Lima, the sixth of July, of the year of Grace one thousand eight hundred and twenty-two, twelfth of the independence of Colombia, and third of that of Peru.

[L. s.]   BERNARDO MONTEAGUDO.
[L. s.]   JOAQUIN MOSQUERA.

Therefore, having seen and examined the said additional treaty of perpetual union, league, and confederation, the consent and approbation of the Congress of the Republic being previously had, agreeably to section 18 of the 55th article of the Constitution, I make use of the power which the 120th article of the same Constitution grants me in ratifying it, as by these presents I ratify it, and hold it as valid, grateful and firm, and for its fulfilment and exact observance I solemnly engage and compromit the honor of the Republic. In faith whereof, I have caused issue these presents, signed with my hand, sealed with the great seal of the Republic, and countersigned by the Secretary of State and the Despatch of Foreign Relations, in the city of Bogota, the twelfth of July, in the year of Grace one thousand eight hundred and twenty-three, thirteenth of independence.

[L. s.]   FRANCISCO DE P. SANTANDER.

By his excellency the Vice President of the Republic, charged with the Executive power.

PEDRO GUAL.

COLOMBIA AND GUATEMALA.

Treaty of perpetual union, league, and confederation, between the Republic of Colombia and the United Provinces of Central America.

[Translation.]

The Republic of Colombia and the United Provinces of Central America, desirous of putting a speedy termination to the calamitous war in which they are engaged with the King of Spain, and both contracting powers being disposed to unite all their resources with their naval and land forces, and to identify their principles and interests in peace and war, have resolved to form a treaty of perpetual union, league, and confederation, which shall forever secure to them the advantages of liberty and independence.

For this desirable object, Pedro Gual, Minister of Foreign Relations of the Republic of Colombia, and Pedro Molina, Plenipotentiary of the United Provinces of Central America, being respectively furnished with full powers, and in due form, have agreed to the following articles:

1. The Republic of Colombia and the United Provinces of Central America bind themselves to a perpetual union, league, and confederation, in peace and war, to defend their independence of the Spanish nation, and every other, by naval and land forces, and thus to secure their mutual prosperity, to promote harmony and good intelligence with each other, and with other nations.

2. The Republic of Colombia and the Provinces of Central America, therefore, promise and freely contract a firm and constant friendship and a permanent alliance, which shall be intimate and binding for their common defence, the security of their independence and liberty, and for their reciprocal and general good. They oblige themselves mutually to aid in repelling every attack or invasion from the enemies of either that may in anywise affect their political existence.

3. That the objects contemplated by the preceding articles may be carried into effect, the Republic of Colombia engages to aid the United Provinces of Central America with that amount of its disposable naval and land forces which shall be determined by the Congress of Plenipotentiaries to be mentioned hereafter.

4. The United Provinces of Central America shall, in like manner, aid the Republic of Colombia with their disposable naval and land forces, or its equivalent, which shall be fixed by the aforesaid Congress.

5. The contracting parties guaranty, mutually, the integrity of their respective territories as they existed prior to the present war of independence, against the designs and invasions of the subjects of the King of Spain and his adherents.

6. In case, therefore, of sudden invasion, each party shall be at liberty to act against the enemy, within the territory of the other, whenever circumstances will not allow of a communication with the Government to which the sovereignty of the country invaded belongs. But the party so acting shall observe, and cause to be observed, the statutes, ordinances, and laws of the State, as far as circumstances may permit, and cause its Government to be respected and obeyed. The expenses of these operations, and whatever may be incurred in consequence of articles third and fourth, shall be settled by separate conventions, and paid one year after the conclusion of the present war.

7. The Republic of Colombia and the United Provinces of Central America promise and oblige themselves, formally, to respect the limits of each other as they now exist; and agree, as soon as circumstances will permit, to settle, in a friendly manner, by a special convention, the line of demarkation between the two States, or whenever one of the parties shall be disposed to enter on this negotiation.

8. To facilitate the progress and happy termination of the negotiation about limits; as in the preceding article, both parties shall be at liberty to appoint Commissioners, who shall survey the whole frontier for the purpose of fixing the boundary line. The local authorities shall not offer them the least obstruction, but shall, on the contrary, furnish every protection and aid for the proper execution of their object, provided they exhibit the passport of their Governments authorizing their operations.

9. The contracting parties, desirous, in the meantime, of providing against the evils that might arise to both, from unauthorized colonies of adventurers on that part of the Mosquito shore between Cape Gracias a Dios and the river Chagres, promise and oblige themselves to employ their naval and land forces against any individual or individuals who shall attempt to form establishments on the above coast without having previously obtained permission from the Government to which it may belong.

10. To make the union and alliance contracted by the present convention more intimate and close, it is moreover stipulated and agreed that the citizens and inhabitants of each State shall have free entrance to, and departure from, the ports and territories of the other, and shall enjoy therein all the civil rights and privileges of traffic and commerce; but they shall be subject to the same duties, imposts, and restrictions, as the citizens and inhabitants of the State themselves.

11. In consequence of this, their vessels and cargoes, composed of productions or merchandise, domestic or foreign, and registered at the custom-houses of either of the contracting parties, shall not pay in the ports of the other greater duties of importation, exportation, anchorage, or tonnage, than those already established, or which may be established for its own vessels and cargoes; that is to say, vessels and cargoes from Colombia shall pay the same duties of importation, exportation, anchorage, and tonnage in the ports of the United Provinces of Central America as if they belonged to these United Provinces; and those from the United Provinces of Central America shall pay in the ports of Colombia the same duty as Colombians.

12. The contracting parties oblige themselves to afford every aid in their power to the merchant and national vessels of each other that may go into port to repair any damage they may have received. They shall there be at liberty to refit, increase their armaments and crews, so as to be able to continue their voyage or cruise. The expense of these repairs shall be sustained by the State or individuals to whom they may belong.

13. To suppress the shameful abuses that may be committed on the high seas by armed privateers upon neutrals and the national commerce, the contracting parties agree to extend the jurisdiction of their maritime courts to the privateers and their prizes, of each other indiscriminately, whenever they shall not be able to reach the port of their departure, or suspicions may be excited of their having committed abuses against the commerce of neutral nations with whom both States desire to cultivate lasting harmony and good intelligence.

14. To prevent all disorder in the Army and Navy of each other, the contracting parties moreover agree that, if any soldiers or sailors shall desert from the service of one to the territory of the other, even

if the latter belong to merchant vessels, they shall be immediately restored by the tribunal or authority within whose jurisdiction they may be found; provided, the reclamation of the commander, or of the captain of the vessel, as the case may be, shall previously be made, giving a description of the individual or individuals, with their names, and that of the corps or vessel from which they may have deserted. Until the demand be made in form, they shall be confined in the public prisons.

15. To cement the bonds of future union between the two States, and remove every difficulty that may occur to interrupt their good correspondence and harmony, there shall be formed a Congress, composed of two plenipotentiaries from each contracting party, who shall be appointed with the same formalities as are required by established usages in the commission of ministers of equal character among other nations.

16. The contracting parties oblige themselves to interpose their good offices with the other ci-devant Spanish States of America to induce them to unite in this compact of perpetual union, league, and confederation.

17. As soon as this great and important object shall be accomplished, a general Congress shall be assembled, composed of plenipotentiaries from the American States, for the purpose of establishing, on a more solid basis, the intimate relations which should exist between them all, individually and collectively, and that it may serve as a council in great events, as a point of union and common danger, as a faithful interpreter of public treaties when difficulties may arise, and as an arbitrator and conciliator in their disputes and differences.

18. This compact of union, league, and confederation shall not affect in any manner the exercise of the national sovereignty of the contracting parties in regard to their laws and the establishment and form of their respective Governments, nor in regard to their relations with other nations; but they bind themselves, irrevocably, not to accede to any demands of indemnity or tribute from the Spanish Government, or any other in its name, for the loss of its supremacy over these countries. They also bind themselves not to enter into any treaty with Spain, or any other nation, that shall in the least prejudice their independence, but to maintain their mutual interests on all occasions with the dignity and energy of free, independent, friendly, and confederate nations.

19. As the Isthmus of Panama is an integral part of Colombia, and the point best suited for this august assembly, this Republic freely engages to afford to the plenipotentiaries of the American States composing it all the attentions which are required by hospitality among sister States, and by the sacred and inviolable character of their persons.

20. The United Provinces of Central America oblige themselves, in like manner, whenever the events of war, or by the voice of a majority of the American States, the Congress shall assemble within their territory, at the Isthmus of Panama, or any point of their territory which, from its central position between the States of North and South America, may be fixed on as best suited for this most interesting object.

21. The Republic of Colombia and the United Provinces of Central America, desirous of avoiding all interpretation contrary to their intentions, declare that any advantages which either power may gain from the preceding stipulations are, and shall be, considered as compensation for the obligations they contract in the present compact of perpetual union, league, and confederation.

22. The present perpetual treaty of union, league, and confederation shall be ratified by the President or Vice President of the Republic of Colombia, charged with the executive power, with the consent and approbation of the Congress, within thirty days; and by the Government of the United Provinces of Central America as early as possible, regarding the distance; and the ratifications shall be exchanged in the city of Guatemala within six months from the date hereof, or sooner, if possible.

In faith of which, we, the plenipotentiaries from the Republic of Colombia and of the United Provinces of Central America, have signed and sealed the present, in the city of Bogota, on this fifteenth day of March, in the year of our Lord 1825, fifteenth of Colombian independence, and fifth of that of the United Provinces of Central America.

[L. S.]   PEDRO GUAL.
[L. S.]   PEDRO MOLINA.

Ratified by the Vice President of Colombia, Francisco de P. Santander, on the twelfth day of April, 1825, and fifteenth of independence, with the previous consent and approbation of the Congress.

COLOMBIA AND MEXICO.

Treaty of perpetual union, league, and confederation, between Colombia and Mexico, published at the city of Mexico on the 20th of September, 1825.

The Government of the Republic of Colombia on the one part, and that of Mexico on the other, sincerely desirous of terminating the evils of the present war, into which they have been forced by the King of Spain, and having determined to employ their whole naval and land forces in defence of their liberty; and anxious, also, that this league should be general among all the States of Spanish America, that they may contribute their united strength and resources to maintain the common cause of their independence, have appointed plenipotentiaries, who have concluded the following treaty of union, league, and confederation:

ARTICLE 1. The Republics of Colombia and Mexico unite, league, and confederate forever, in peace and war, to maintain, with their naval and land forces, as far as circumstances may permit, their independence of Spain and all other foreign dominion, and, after the recognition of their independence, to assure their mutual prosperity, harmony, and good intelligence, both among their people and citizens and the States with which they may institute relations.

ARTICLE 2. The Republics of Colombia and Mexico, therefore, enter into and mutually form a perpetual compact of alliance and firm and constant friendship for their common defence, obliging themselves to aid each other, and mutually repel any attack or invasion that may in any manner menace the security of their independence and liberty, affect their interests, or disturb their peace: Provided that, in the last case, requisition be made by one or other of two Governments legally established.

Article 3. To effect the objects of the preceding article, the contracting parties promise to aid each other with the amount of land forces that may be fixed upon by special conventions, as the circumstances may demand, and during the continuance of the occasion.

Article 4. The military Navy of both contracting parties shall also be in fulfilment of the preceding convention.

Article 5. In cases where aid is suddenly required, each party shall operate against the enemy with all the disposable forces within the territories of the other, if time be not allowed for concert between both Governments. But the party thus operating shall observe the laws and ordinances of the State, as far as circumstances may permit, and shall respect and obey its Government. The expenses thus incurred shall be fixed by separate conventions, and be paid one year after the conclusion of the present war.

Article 6. The contracting parties oblige themselves to furnish whatever assistance they may be able to the military and mercantile vessels arriving at the ports of each other from distress or other cause; and they shall have power to repair, refit, provision, arm, and increase their armament and crews, so as to be able to continue their voyages or cruises, at the expense of the State or individuals to whom they may belong.

Article 7. To avoid abuses by armed privateers of the commerce of the State and that of neutrals, the contracting parties agree to extend the jurisdiction of the maritime $co^n{}_{rts}$ of each other to their privateers and prizes indifferently, when they cannot readily ascertain their port of departure, and abuses shall be suspected of the commerce of neutral nations.

Article 8. The contracting parties mutually guaranty to each other the integrity of their respective territories as they existed before the present war, recognizing also, as part of this territory, what was not included in the Viceroyalties of Mexico and New Granada, but is now a component part of it.

Article 9. The component parts of the territory of both parties shall be defined and recognized.

Article 10. If internal quiet should unfortunately be disturbed in the territory of either party by disorderly men and enemies of legal government, the contracting parties engage to make common cause against them until order and the empire of law be re-established. Their forces shall be furnished as provided by articles 2 and 3.

Article 11. All persons taking arms against either Government, legally established, and fleeing from justice, if found within the territory of either contracting party, shall be delivered up to be tried by the Government against which the offence has been committed. Deserters from the Army and Navy are included in this article.

Article 12. To strengthen the bonds of future union between the two States, and to prevent every interruption of their friendship and good intelligence, a Congress shall be formed, to which each party shall send two plenipotentiaries, commissioned in the same form and manner as are observed towards ministers of equal grade to foreign nations.

Article 13. Both parties oblige themselves to solicit the other ci-devant Spanish States of America to enter into this compact of perpetual union, league, and confederation.

Article 14. As soon as this important purpose shall have been attained, a general Congress of the American States shall assemble, composed of their plenipotentiaries. Its object will be to confirm and establish intimate relations between the whole and each one of the States. It will serve as a council on great occasions, a point of union in common danger, a faithful interpreter of public treaties in cases of misunderstanding, and as an arbitrator and conciliator of disputes and differences.

Article 15. The Isthmus of Panama being an integral part of Colombia, and the most suitable point for the meeting of the Congress, this Republic promises to furnish to plenipotentiaries of the Congress all the facilities demanded by hospitality among a kindred people, and by the sacred character of ambassadors.

Article 16. Mexico agrees to the same obligation, if ever, by the accidents of war or the consent of a majority of the States, the Congress should meet within her jurisdiction.

Article 17. This compact of perpetual union, league, and confederation shall not in any wise affect the exercise of the national sovereignty of either contracting party in regard to its laws and form of government, or its foreign relations. But the parties bind themselves positively not to accede to any demand of indemnity, tribute, or impost from Spain for the loss of her former supremacy over these countries, or from any other nation in her name. They also agree not to enter into any treaty with Spain, or any other nation, to the prejudice of their independence; but to maintain at all times their mutual interests, with the dignity and energy proper to free, independent, friendly, and confederate States.

Article 18 provides for the time of ratification of this treaty.

The foregoing treaty has been duly ratified.

GAUDALUPE VICTORIA.

By the President:
Lucas Alaman.

Note.—The foregoing is the copy of the only translation, as far as it goes, in possession of the Department of State, of the treaty between Colombia and Mexico.

Mr. Clay to Mr. Middleton.

Department of State, *May* 10, 1825.

Sir: I am directed by the President to instruct you to endeavor to engage the Russian Government to contribute its best exertions towards terminating the existing contest between Spain and her colonies.

Among the interests which, at this period, should most command the serious attention of the nations of the Old and New World, no one is believed to have a claim so paramount as that of the present war. It has existed, in greater or less extent, seventeen years. Its earlier stages were marked by the most shocking excesses, and, throughout, it has been attended by an almost incalculable waste of blood and treasure. During its continuance whole generations have passed away without living to see its close, while others have succeeded them, growing up from infancy to majority without ever tasting the blessings of peace. The conclusion of that war, whatever and whenever it may be, must have a great effect upon Europe and America. Russia is so situated, as that, while she will be less directly affected than other parts of Christendom, her weight and her councils must have a controlling influence on its useless protraction or its happy termination. If this peculiar attitude secures her impartiality, it draws to it great responsibility in the decision which she may feel it proper to make. The predominance of the power of the Emperor is everywhere felt. Europe, America, and Asia, all own it. It is with a perfect knowledge of its vast extent, and the profoundest respect for the wisdom and the justice of the august personage who wields it, that his enlightened and humane councils are now invoked.

In considering that war, as in considering all others, we should look back upon the past, deliberately survey its present condition, and endeavor, if possible, to catch a view of what is to come. With respect to the first branch of the subject, it is, perhaps, of the least practical importance. No statesman can have contemplated the colonial relations of Europe and continental America without foreseeing that the time must come when they would cease. That time might have been retarded or accelerated, but come it must, in the great march of human events. An attempt of the British Parliament to tax, without their consent, the former British colonies, now these United States, produced the war of our Revolution, and led to the establishment of that independence and freedom which we now so justly prize. Moderation and forbearance on the part of Great Britain might have postponed, but could not have prevented our ultimate separation. The attempt of Bonaparte to subvert the ancient dynasty of Spain, and to place on its throne a member of his own family, no doubt, hastened the independence of the Spanish colonies. If he had not been urged, by his ambition, to the conquest of the Peninsula, those colonies, for a long time to come, might have continued quietly to submit to the parental sway. But they must have inevitably thrown it off, sooner or later. We may imagine that a vast continent, uninhabited, or thinly peopled by a savage and untutored race, may be governed by a remote country, blessed with the lights and possessed of the power of civilization; but it is absurd to suppose that this same continent, in extent twenty times greater than that of the parent country, and doubling it in a population equally civilized, should not be able, when it chooses to make the effort, to cast off the distant authority. When the epoch of separation between a parent State and its colony, from whatever cause, arrives, the struggle for self-government on the one hand, and for the preservation of power on the other, produces mutual exasperation, and leads to a most embittered and ferocious war. It is then that it becomes the duty of third powers to interpose their humane offices, and calm the passions and enlighten the councils of the parties. And the necessity of their efforts is greatest with the parent country, whose pride, and whose wealth and power, swelled by the colonial contributions, create the most repugnance to an acquiescence in a severance which has been ordained by Providence.

In the war which has been so long raging between Spain and her colonies the United States have taken no part, either to produce or to sustain it. They have been inactive and neutral spectators of the passing scenes. Their frankness forbids, however, that they should say that they have beheld those scenes with feelings of indifference. They have, on the contrary, anxiously desired that other parts of this continent should acquire and enjoy that independence with which, by the valor and the patriotism of the founders of their liberty, they have been, under the smiles of Heaven, so greatly blessed.

But, in the indulgence of this sympathetic feeling, they have not for one moment been unmindful of the duties of that neutrality which they had deliberately announced. And the best proof of the fidelity with which they have strictly fulfilled its obligations is furnished in the fact that, during the progress of the war, they have been unjustly accused, by both parties, of violating their declared neutrality. But it is now of little consequence to retrace the causes, remote or proximate, of the revolt of the Spanish colonies. The great and much more important consideration which will, no doubt, attract the attention of his Imperial Majesty is the present state of the contest. The principles which produced the war, and those which may be incorporated in the institutions of the new States, may divide the opinions of men. Principles, unhappily, are too often the subject of controversy; but notorious facts are incontestible. They speak a language which silences all speculation, and should determine the judgment and the conduct of States, whatever may be the school in which their rulers are brought up or practiced, and whatever the social forms which they would desire to see established. And it is to the voice of such facts that Europe and America are now called upon patiently to listen.

And in contemplating the present state of the war, what are the circumstances which must forcibly strike every reflecting observer? Throughout both continents, from the western limits of the United States to Cape Horn, the Spanish power is subdued. The recent decisive victory of Ayachuco has annihilated the last remains of the Spanish force. Not a foot of territory in all that vast extent owns the dominion, not a bayonet sustains the cause of Spain. The war, in truth, has ended. It has been a war between a contracted corner of Europe and an entire continent; between ten millions of people, amidst their own extraordinary convulsions, fighting, at a distance across an ocean of three thousand miles in extent, against twenty millions contending at home for their lives, their liberty, and their property. Henceforward it will present only the image of a war between an exhausted dwarf struggling for power and empire, against a refreshed giant combating for freedom and existence. Too much confidence is reposed in the enlightened judgment of his Imperial Majesty to allow of the belief that he will permit any abatement of his desire to see such a war formally terminated, and the blessings of peace restored, from sympathies which he may feel, however strong, for the unhappy condition of Spain. These very sympathies will naturally lead his Imperial Majesty to give her the best and most friendly advice in her actual posture. And in what does that consist? His Imperial Majesty must be the exclusive, as he is the most competent judge. But it will not be deemed inconsistent with respect to inquire if it be possible to believe that Spain can bring the new States again under her dominion: Where does the remotest prospect of her success break out? In Colombia, Mexico, or Peru? The reconquest of the United States by Great Britain would not be a more mad and hopeless enterprise than that of the restoration of the Spanish power on these continents. Some of the most considerable of the new States have established Governments, which are in full and successful operation, regularly collecting large revenues, levying and maintaining numerous and well appointed armies, and already laying the foundations of respectable marines. Whilst they are consolidating their institutions at home, they are strengthening themselves abroad by treaties of alliance among themselves, and of amity and commerce with foreign States. Is the vain hope indulged that intestine divisions within the new States will arise, which may lead to the recall of the Spanish power, as the Stuarts were recalled in England, and the Bourbons in France, at the close of their respective revolutions?

We should not deceive ourselves. Amidst all the political changes of which the new States are destined to be the theatre, whatever party or power may be uppermost, one spirit will animate them all, and that is, an invincible aversion from all political connexion with Spain, and an unconquerable desire of independence. It could not be otherwise. They have already tasted the fruits of independence. And the contrast between what their condition now is in the possession of free commerce, liberal institutions, and all the faculties of their country, and its population allowed full physical and moral development, and what it was under Spain, cramped, debased, and degraded, must be fatal to the chimerical hope of that monarchy, if it be cherished, by any means whatever to re-establish her power. The cord which binds a colony to its parent country being broken is never repaired. A recollection of what was inflicted and what was borne during the existence of that relation, the pride of the former governing power, and the sacrifices of the interests of the colony to those of the parent, widen and render the breach between them, whenever it occurs, perpetual. And if, as we may justly suppose, the embittered feelings excited by an experience of that unequal connexion are in proportion to the severity of the parental rule, they must operate with irresistible force on the rupture which has taken place between Spain and her colonies, since in no other instance has it been exerted with such unmitigated rigor.

Viewing the war as practically terminated, so far at least as relates to Spanish exertion on the continent, in considering the third branch of the inquiry which I proposed, let us endeavor to anticipate what may be expected to happen if Spain obstinately perseveres in the refusal to conclude a peace. If the war has only a nominal continuance, the new Republics cannot disband their victorious armies without culpable neglect of all the maxims of prudence and precaution. And the first observation that occurs is, that this protracted war must totally change its character and its objects. Instead of being a war of offensive operations, in which Spain has been carrying on hostilities in the bosom of the new States, it will become one to her of a defensive nature, in which all her future exertions must be directed to the protection and defence of her remaining insular possessions. And thus the Peninsula, instead of deriving the revenue and the aid so necessary to the revival of its prosperity from Cuba and Porto Rico, must be further drained to succor those islands. For it cannot be doubted that the new States will direct their combined and unemployed forces to the reduction of those valuable islands. They will naturally strike their enemy wherever they can reach him. And they will be stimulated to the attack by the double motive arising from the richness of the prize, and from the fact that those islands constitute the rendez-vous of Spain, where are concentrated and from which issue all the means of annoying them which remain to her. The success of the enterprise is by no means improbable. Their proximity to the islands, and their armies being perfectly acclimated, will give to the united efforts of the Republics great advantages. And if with these be taken into the estimate the important and well known fact that a large portion of the inhabitants of the islands is predisposed to a separation from Spain, and would therefore form a powerful auxiliary to the republican arms, their success becomes almost certain. But even if they should prove incompetent to the reduction of the islands, there can be but little doubt that the shattered remains of Spanish commerce would be swept from the ocean. The advantages of the positions of Colombia and Mexico for annoying that commerce in the Gulf of Mexico and the Caribbean sea must be evident from the slightest observation. · In fact, Cuba is in the mouth of a sack, which is held by Colombia and the United Mexican States. And if, unhappily for the repose of the world, the war should be continued, the coasts of the Peninsula itself may be expected soon to swarm with the privateers of the Republics. If, on the contrary, Spain should consent to put an end to the war, she might yet preserve what remains of her former American possessions. And surely the retention of such islands as Cuba and Porto Rico is eminently worthy of serious consideration, and should satisfy a reasonable ambition. The possessions of Spain in the West Indies would be still more valuable than those of any other power. The war ended, her commerce would revive, and there is every reason to anticipate, from the habits, prejudices, and tastes of the new Republics, that she would find, in the consumption of their population, a constantly augmenting demand for the produce of her industry, now excluded from its best markets. And her experience, like that of Great Britain with the United States, would demonstrate that the value of the commercial intercourse would more than indemnify the loss, while it is unburdened with the expense incident to political connexion.

A subordinate consideration, which should not be overlooked, is, that large estates are owned by Spanish subjects, resident in Spain, which may possibly be confiscated if the war be wantonly continued. If that measure of rigor shall not be adopted, their incomes must be greatly diminished during a state of war. These incomes, upon the restoration of peace, or the proceeds of the sales of the estates themselves, might be drawn to Spain, and would greatly contribute towards raising her from her present condition of embarrassment and languishment. If peace should be longer deferred, and the war should take the probable direction which has been supposed, during its further progress other powers not now parties may be collaterally drawn into it. From much less considerable causes the peace of the world has been often disturbed. From the vicinity of Cuba to the United States, its valuable commerce and the nature of its population, their Government cannot be indifferent to any political change to which that island may be destined. Great Britain and France also have deep interests in its fortunes, which must keep them wide awake to all those changes. In short, what European State has not much at stake, direct or indirect, in the destiny, be it what it may, of that most valuable of all the West India islands? The reflections and the experience of the Emperor on the vicissitudes of war must have impressed him with the solemn duty of all Governments to guard against even the distant approach of that most terrible of all scourges by every precaution with which human prudence and foresight can surround the repose and safety of States.

Such is the view of the war between Spain and the new Republics which the President desires you most earnestly, but respectfully, to present to his Imperial Majesty. From this view it is evident that it is not so much for the new States themselves as for Spain that peace has become absolutely necessary. Their independence of her, whatever intestine divisions may, if intestine divisions shall, yet unhappily await them, is fixed and irrevocable. She may, indeed, by a blind and fatal protraction of the war, yet lose more: gain, for her, is impossible. In becoming the advocate for peace, one is the true advocate of Spain. If the Emperor shall, by his wisdom, enlighten the councils of Spain, and bring home to them a conviction of her real interests, there can be no fears of the success of his powerful interposition. You are authorized, in that spirit of the most perfect frankness and friendship which have ever characterized all the relations between Russia and the United States, to disclose, without reserve, the feelings and the wishes of the United States in respect to Cuba and Porto Rico. They are satisfied with the present condition of those islands, now open to the commerce and enterprise of their citizens. They desire for themselves no political change in them. If Cuba were to declare itself independent, the amount and the character of its population render it improbable that it could maintain its independence.

Such a premature declaration might bring about a renewal of those shocking scenes of which a neighboring island was the afflicting theatre. There could be no effectual preventive of those scenes, but in the guaranty, and in a large resident force of foreign powers. The terms of such a guaranty, and the quotas which each should contribute of such a force, would create perplexing questions of very difficult adjustment, to say nothing of the continual jealousies which would be in operation. In the state of possession which Spain has, there would be a ready acquiescence of those very foreign powers, all of whom would be put into angry activity upon the smallest prospect of a transfer of those islands. The United States could not, with indifference, see such a transfer to any European power. And if the new Republics, or either of them, were to conquer them, their maritime force as it now is, or for a long time to come is likely to be, would keep up constant apprehensions of their safety. Nor is it believed that the new States desire, or will attempt, the acquisition, unless they shall be compelled, in their own defence, to make it, by the unnecessary prolongation of the war. Acting on the policy which is here unfolded, the Government of the United States, although they would have been justified to have seized Cuba and Porto Rico, in the just protection of the lives and the commerce of their citizens, which have been a prey to infamous pirates finding succor and refuge in Spanish territory, have signally displayed their patience and moderation by a scrupulous respect of the sovereignty of Spain, who was herself bound, but has utterly failed, to repress those enormities.

Finally, the President cherishes the hope that the Emperor's devotion to peace, no less than his friendship for Spain, will induce him to lend the high authority of his name to the conclusion of a war the further prosecution of which must have the certain effect of an useless waste of human life. No power has displayed more solicitude for the repose of the world than Russia, who has recently given the strongest evidence of her unwillingness to disturb it, in the East, by unexampled moderation and forbearance. By extending to America the blessings of that peace which, under the auspices of his Imperial Majesty, Europe now enjoys, all parts of this continent will have grateful occasion for regarding him, as the United States ever have done, as their most potent and faithful friend.

This despatch is confided to your discretion, to be communicated in extenso, or its contents disclosed in such other manner to the Government of Russia as shall appear to you most likely to accomplish its object.

I have the honor to be, sir, with great respect, you obedient and very humble servant.

No. 48.

Mr. Middleton to Mr. Clay.

St. Petersburg, *July* 15, (27,) 1825.

Sir: I had the honor of receiving your despatch No. 1 on the 28th June, (O. S.) The Emperor was, at that period, absent from this residence, but expected about the 5th of the present month. Count Nesselrode had preceded him by a few days, and had announced, by a circular letter, dated June 24, that he had resumed the direction of the Imperial Ministry of Foreign Affairs.

I conceive it would be best to lose no time in opening the matter committed to my care by your instructions in the despatch above mentioned. After having carefully weighed what would be the best mode of proceeding, I mentioned to the count the purport of the instructions. He gave me, at first, no great encouragement, adverting to the essential difference in our way of thinking on the question between Spain and her colonies. I begged leave, however, to furnish him with a copy of the despatch, (as you had permitted,) in order that he might lay it before the Emperor. Accordingly, on the second of July, a copy of your instructions, together with a short introductory note, was sent in. (See the accompanying paper.)

I conclude, from my knowledge of the modes of proceeding in all matters of general concern, that the proposition is in consideration between *the allies*, it being a fundamental maxim with them not to take any determination in matters affecting the general policy without the mutual consent of the parties to this alliance.

I trust that I need not add that every endeavor shall be made, on my part, to give effect to your proposition.

I have the honor to be, sir, very faithfully, your obedient servant,

HENRY MIDDLETON.

No. 49.

Mr. Middleton to Mr. Clay.

St. Petersburg, *August* 27, (*September* 8,) 1825.

Sir: I have the honor to forward herewith a copy of the answer of the Russian Secretary of State to my note of 2d July last, by which I had communicated to this Government, *in extenso*, the instructions I had received by your despatch No. 1.

I think I am warranted in considering this answer to be, *in substance*, (when divested of diplomatic garb,) in every respect as favorable to the views developed in your despatch as could possibly be expected to be given by this Government, standing in the predicament it now does. We are left to infer from it that the proposal that the Emperor shall lend his aid towards the conclusion of the war between Spain and her colonies, by interposing his good offices in the form of pacific counsel to the mother country, has been communicated to the allied cabinets, and I am fully of opinion that the majority, if not the whole of them, will agree to it. If such should be the event, the diplomatic committee sitting at Paris will be instructed accordingly. The chief difficulty to be overcome will be in the cabinet of the King of Spain, where it is understood that *all parties* are opposed to the independence of the colonies. The necessity of the case, however, begins to be so crying that a hope may be entertained that even there the counsels of wisdom may ere long be listened to. For obvious reasons we must not expect to learn, *officially*, that such advice as that alluded to above has been given, unless it should be attended to.

I have the honor to be, sir, very faithfully, your very obedient servant,

HENRY MIDDLETON.

The SECRETARY OF STATE, &c., &c., &c.

Count Nesselrode to Mr. Middleton.

[Translation of a paper with Mr. Middleton's No. 49.]

ST. PETERSBURG, *August* 20, 1825.

The undersigned, Secretary of State, directing the Imperial Administration of Foreign Affairs, hastened to submit to the Emperor the note with which Mr. Middleton, Envoy Extraordinary and Minister Plenipotentiary of the United States of America, did the honor to address him on the 2d of July last, accompanying a copy of the despatch from Mr. Clay, in which that minister, in the name of the cabinet at Washington, urges the necessity of confirming the general peace by terminating the contest of the Spanish colonies against the Government of his Catholic Majesty, of securing to Spain the peaceful possession of the islands of Cuba and Porto Rico, and of effecting these objects by the impartial intervention of Russia.

The principles of the Emperor were sufficiently known to the Government of the United States to justify the perfect confidence that, in expressing a wish for the continuance and confirmation of the peace enjoyed by the world, it did but represent the most sincere desire of his Imperial Majesty; that, in professing a generous solicitude for the rights of Spain over her islands in the West Indies, it avowed principles that had long since been adopted by Russia as the bases of her political system; and that, in anticipating perfect impartiality and true disinterestedness from her intervention, it was not deceived as to the sentiments of the Emperor in relation to all arrangements in which foreign powers might be pleased to claim or admit his good offices.

His Imperial Majesty felicitates himself with having inspired this confidence in the United States of America, and the undersigned is charged to invite Mr. Middleton to convey to his Government the assurance of the high value at which the Emperor estimates those sentiments, of which new evidence is furnished by its present propositions.

The opinions of his Imperial Majesty as to the question discussed by Mr. Clay in his despatch cannot be concealed from the cabinet of Washington. His Imperial Majesty has ever thought that justice, the law of nations, and the general interest in having the indisputable titles of sovereignty respected, could not allow the determinations of the mother country in this important case to be prejudged or anticipated. On the other side, whenever Spain has wished to discuss the future condition of South America, she has addressed overtures to all the allied powers of Europe. It will not be possible, therefore, for his Imperial Majesty to change principles in this negotiation, nor to institute it separately (isolement); and until positive information has been received of the ulterior views of Spain in regard to her American possessions, of her decision upon the proposition of the United States, and of the opinions of her allies in relation to the same subject, Russia cannot give a definitive answer.

She is, however, in the meanwhile, pleased to hope that the United States, becoming every day more convinced of the evils and dangers that would result to Cuba and Porto Rico from a change of Government, being satisfied, as Mr. Clay has said in his despatch, with the present commercial legislation of these two islands, and deriving an additional motive of security from the honorable resolution of Spain not to grant to them any longer letters of marque, will use their influence in defeating, as far as may be in their power, every enterprise against these islands; in securing to the rights of his Catholic Majesty constant and proper respect; in maintaining the only state of things that can preserve a just balance of power in the sea of the Antilles, prevent shocking examples, and, as the cabinet of Washington has remarked, secure to the general peace salutary guarantees.

The undersigned seizes, with pleasure, this occasion to repeat to Mr. Middleton the assurances of his very distinguished consideration.

NESSELRODE.

No. 2.

Mr. Clay to Mr. Middleton.

DEPARTMENT OF STATE, *Washington, December* 26, 1825.

SIR: Your despatches (Nos. 48 and 49) have been duly received and submitted to the President. He sees with much satisfaction that the appeal which has been made through you to the Emperor of Russia, to employ his friendly offices in the endeavor to bring about a peace between Spain and the new American Republics, has not been without favorable effect. Considering the intimate and friendly relations which exist between the Emperor and his allies, it was perhaps not to be expected that, previous to a consultation with them, language more explicit should be held than that which is contained in Count Nesselrode's note. Although very guarded, it authorizes the belief that the preponderating influence of Russia has been thrown into the scale of peace. Notwithstanding the predictions of a contrary result, confidently made by Mr. Secretary Canning, this decision of the Emperor corresponds with the anticipations which have been constantly entertained here ever since the President resolved to invoke his intervention. It affords strong evidence both of his humanity and his enlightened judgment. All events out of Spain seem now to unite in their tendency towards peace; and the fall of the Castle of St. Juan d'Ulloa, which capitulated on the eighteenth day of last month, cannot fail to have a powerful effect within that Kingdom. We are informed that when information of it reached the Havana it produced great and general sensation; and that the local Government immediately despatched a fast sailing vessel to Cadiz to communicate the event, and, in its name, to implore the King immediately to terminate the war and acknowledge the new Republics, as the only means left of preserving Cuba to the Monarchy.

In considering what further measures could be adopted by this Government to second the pacific exertions which, it is not doubted, the Emperor is now employing, it has appeared to the President that a suspension of any military expedition which both or either of the Republics of Colombia and Mexico may be preparing against Cuba and Porto Rico might have a good auxiliary influence. Such a suspension, indeed, seemed to be due to the friendly purposes of the Emperor. I have accordingly addressed official notes to the ministers of those Republics accredited here, recommending it to their Governments, an extract from one of which (the other being substantially the same) is herewith transmitted. You will observe it intimated in those notes that other Governments may feel themselves urged, by a sense of their interests and duties, to interpose in the event of an invasion of the islands, or of contingencies which may accompany or follow it. On this subject it is proper that we should be perfectly understood by Russia. For ourselves, we desire no change in the possession of Cuba, as has been heretofore stated. We cannot allow a transfer of the island to any European Power. But if Spain should refuse to conclude a peace, and obstinately resolve on continuing the war, although we do not desire that either Colombia or Mexico should acquire the island of Cuba, the President cannot see any justifiable ground on which we can forcibly interfere. Upon the hypothesis of an unnecessary protraction of the war, imputable to Spain, it is evident that Cuba will be her only *point d'appui* in this hemisphere. How can we interpose, on that supposition, against the party clearly having right on his side, in order to restrain or defeat a lawful operation of war? If the war against the islands should be conducted by those Republics in a desolating manner; if, contrary to all expectation, they should put arms into the hands of one race of the inhabitants to destroy the lives of another; if, in short, they should countenance and encourage excesses and examples, the contagion of which, from our neighborhood, would be dangerous to our quiet and safety, the Government of the United States might feel itself called upon to interpose its power. But it is not apprehended that any of those contingencies will arise, and, consequently, it is most probable that the United States, should the war continue, will remain hereafter, as they have been heretofore, neutral observers of the progress of its events.

You will be pleased to communicate the contents of this despatch to the Russian Government. And as, from the very nature of the object which has induced the President to recommend to the Governments of Colombia and Mexico a suspension of their expeditions against the Spanish islands, no definite time could be suggested for the duration of that suspension, if it should be acceded to, it must be allowed, on all hands, that it ought not to be unnecessarily protracted. Therefore, you will represent to the Government of Russia the expediency of obtaining a decision from Spain as early as possible in respect to its disposition to conclude a peace.

I am your obedient servant,

H. CLAY.

HENRY MIDDLETON, *Envoy Extraordinary and*
Minister Plenipotentiary United States, St. Petersburg.

Mr. Clay to Mr. Salazar.

DEPARTMENT OF STATE, *Washington, December 20, 1825.*

SIR: During the last spring I had the honor to state to you that the Government of the United States had addressed that of Russia with the view of engaging the employment of its friendly offices to bring about a peace, if possible, between Spain and the new American Republics, founded upon the basis of their independence; and the despatch from this Department to the American minister at St. Petersburg, having that object, was read to you. I have now the satisfaction to state that it appears, by late advices just received from St. Petersburg, that this appeal to the Emperor of Russia has not been without good effect, and that there is reason to believe that he is now exerting his friendly endeavors to put an end to the war. The first would be naturally directed to his allies, between whom and his Imperial Majesty it was desirable that there should be, on that interesting subject, concurrence of opinion and concert in action. Our information from Europe authorizes the belief that all the great powers are now favorably inclined towards peace, and that, separately or conjointly, they will give pacific counsels to Spain. When all the difficulties exterior to Spain in the way of peace are overcome, the hope is confidently indulged that those within the Peninsula cannot long withstand the general wish. But some time is necessary for the operation of these exertions to terminate the war, and to ascertain their effect upon the Spanish Government.

Under these circumstances, the President believes that a suspension, for a limited time, of the sailing of the expedition against Cuba or Porto Rico, which is understood to be fitting out at Carthagena, or of any other expedition which may be contemplated against either of those islands by Colombia or Mexico, would have a salutary influence on the great work of peace. Such a suspension would afford time to ascertain if Spain, resisting the powerful motives which unite themselves on the side of peace, obstinately resolves upon a protraction of the war. The suspension is due to the enlightened intentions of the Emperor of Russia, upon whom it could not fail to have the happiest effect. It would also postpone, if not forever render unnecessary, all consideration which other powers may, by an irresistible sense of their essential interests, be called upon to entertain of their duties in the event of the contemplated invasion of those islands, and of other contingencies which may accompany or follow it. I am directed, therefore, by the President, to request that you will forthwith communicate the views here disclosed to the Government of the Republic of Colombia, which, he hopes, will see the expediency, in the actual posture of affairs, of forbearing to attack those islands until a sufficient time has elapsed to ascertain the result of the pacific efforts which the great powers are believed to be now making on Spain.

I seize, with pleasure, the occasion to renew to you assurances of my distinguished consideration.

H. CLAY.

Don JOSÉ MARIE SALAZAR, *Envoy Extraordinary and Minister Plenipotentiary from Colombia.*

No. 18.

Extract of a letter from Mr. Joel R. Poinsett to Mr. Clay, dated

MEXICO, *September* 13, 1825.

"I had this morning a second conference with the plenipotentiaries of this Government, and, as some difficulties have been presented that may retard the progress of the negotiation, I am anxious that you should be made acquainted with them as early as possible, and lose no time, therefore, in laying them before you.

"The project of the treaty was drawn up by me, and of course contains the principle of perfect reciprocity in the commerce and navigation of the two countries, according to the spirit of the act of January 7, 1824. This was objected to, as might have been expected, and an effort made to introduce the fourth article of their treaty with Great Britain, which contains an exeption, in my opinion, highly objectionable. It is at the close of that article, in these words: 'Excepting only the American nations which were formerly Spanish possessions, to which, on account of the fraternal relations that unite them to the United Mexican States, the latter may grant special privileges which shall not be extended to the dominions and subjects of his Britannic Majesty.' It was agreed to reserve the point of perfect reciprocity in the commercial relations between the two countries, but I most strenuously opposed the exception above cited, and, as at present advised, will never sign a treaty on such terms.

"The mail leaves the city in a few hours, so that I have not time to give you the arguments which were urged for and against it. My principal objections are the impolicy of admitting any distinctions in the interests of the American States which would tend to unite these more closely and place us, in some contingencies, without the pale. Treaties, in all probability, by this time, have been concluded between the United States and Buenos Ayres and Chile, on such terms as would render a provision of this nature nugatory in time of peace; but in the event of a war between the United States and either of those powers, an event which, however remote, ought to be provided against, such an exception would enable this country to assist very materially our enemies without violating the treaty. With these impressions, and with this view of the subject, I will not agree to this provision; and as I know the plenipotentiaries and the President of the Mexican States to be obstinately bent on carrying this point, I earnestly solicit that you will instruct me if you think I ought to yield it."

Extract of a letter (No. 22) from Mr. Poinsett to Mr. Clay, dated

MEXICO, *September* 28, 1825.

"Anxious to conclude the pending negotiations in time for the President to communicate the result in his message to the next Congress, I urged the. President of these States either to permit Alaman to continue them, or to appoint another plenipotentiary. He preferred the latter alternative, and has given powers to Don José Gomez Pedraza, the Secretary of War, who now holds the portfolio of the Minister of Foreign Relations *ad interim*. The Secretary of the Treasury, being about to leave town for the coast, on business connected with the capture of the castle of Ulloa, a desire was expressed to complete the negotiations before his departure. In consequence we have had two conferences, yesterday and to-day, but the exception contained in the fourth article of the treaty between Great Britain and Mexico, to which I alluded in my communication No. 18, and to which the Mexican plenipotentiaries pertinaciously adhere, has prevented our coming to any conclusion.

"They continue to urge the fraternal ties by which they are bound to the American nations which formerly were Spanish possessions, and the treaties of alliance, offensive and defensive, which have been made between them. But what really prevents them from yielding the point is their having succeeded in persuading the British negotiators to consent to insert this exception in their treaty. I will, however, give you a succinct account of what passed at our several conferences on this subject.

"I first objected to the exception in favor of the American nations formerly Spanish possessions, on the ground that no distinctions ought to be made between any of the members of the great American family; that Great Britain, having consented to such a provision, ought not to influence the United States, because the Republics of America were united by one and the same interest, and that it was the interest of the European powers to cause such distinctions to be made as would divide it into small confederacies, and if possible to prevent us from so uniting as to present one front against the attempts of Europe upon our republican institutions. That it might, therefore, have been considered by the British plenipotentiaries important to lay the foundation of distinctions which must disunite us; but that it was much more mani-. festly our interest that all the States of America should be united as intimately as possible, an union which could only exist on the basis of the most perfect equality and reciprocity.

"The plenipotentiaries of Mexico observed, in reply, that Mexico was united by fraternal ties and strong sympathies to the nations which had, like themselves, shaken off the yoke of Spain; and that they had concluded with them an offensive and defensive alliance which united them more intimately, and placed them on a different footing from that on which they stood towards the United States. To which I rejoined, that the policy we had observed towards these countries gave us a right to expect that no such distinctions as those sought to be introduced into the treaty should be made in our case, and entitled us to be considered on at least an equal footing with any of the American Republics. And further, that this exception could now avail them nothing, as our treaty with Colombia, and those probably, by this time, concluded with Buenos Ayres and Chile, contained no such provision. The plenipotentiaries of Mexico hastily remarked that a war might dissolve any one of those treaties, and in such an event they thought Mexico ought to possess the power to evince her sympathies in favor of either of the American nations which had been formerly Spanish possessions without violating her neutrality. To this observation I replied that I considered this argument conclusive why the United States should not accede to the insertion of such a provision in the treaty; that I regarded a war between the United States and any of the other Republics of America as a very remote and improbable event; but that I never would consent, by treaty, to place the former in a less favorable situation than their enemies, if, unfortunately, those Republics should ever become so. This was the substance of our discussion at the first conference on this subject. It has been alluded to since, in conversation, in a manner that induced me to believe they were bent on carrying their point, and they must have perceived that I was equally decided not to yield it.

"Yesterday, after adjusting all other disputed points, inserting an article similar to the 15th article of our treaty with Spain, signed at San Lorenzo el Real in 1795, and one on the arrest, detention, and delivery of fugitive slaves, this subject was again renewed. The President, they said, was so decided on the subject that they feared there could be no treaty without it. I replied that I was perfectly aware what would be the view my Government would take of this subject, and I could not agree to a provision which would cause the treaty to be rejected at Washington; that such distinctions were entirely contrary to the course of policy we were desirous America should pursue, and that, by persisting in them, Mexico placed herself in opposition to the interests of all the other American Republics, and that uselessly, because, whatever advantage she had promised herself from such an exception in favor of the former Spanish colonies, it was now manifest that she could derive none, as the other American States had made their treaties on a different basis. I remarked, too, that it appeared to me very singular that they should persist in their desire to insert a provision in this treaty which had already occasioned the non-ratification of the first Mexico had entered into; certainly exposed the second to be rejected by England, for the plenipotentiaries of that power had consented to it only because the treaty with Colombia had been made and ratified here, and which would insure the rejection of this treaty at Washington if I were to consent to it.

"The plenipotentiaries replied that all the Spanish American Republics had not made their treaties, and instanced Peru and Guatemala. They readily admitted that Peru would, in all probability, follow the example of Colombia; and I then observed that, after what had so lately passed between Mexico and Guatemala, by which it was evident that the latter had more to fear than to hope from the former, she would scarcely adopt a line of policy which would place her in closer union with Mexico, and separate her from the other States of America. As it was late before this subject was touched upon, little more passed yesterday.

"This morning, early, I received a visit from Don Ramos Arispe, a priest and an intimate of mine, who brought me a proposal from the plenipotentiaries to annex a condition that the exception should extend only to those Spanish American nations who would treat with Mexico on the same terms. I told him that I must persist in my objection, and would not admit the principle at all; that I believed the exception Mexico insisted upon making would avail her nothing, for no other American nation would agree to it; but that any distinctions at all among the nations of America were, in my opinion, destructive of the best interests of this hemisphere. As I knew that he is appointed one of the plenipotentiaries of this Government to the Congress at Panama, I hinted to him that the course of policy Mexico appeared determined to pursue would leave her at that Congress entirely alone; for it was to be expected that those American-Republics who stood towards each other on the same footing, and whose interests were identical, would be united more closely among themselves than with a third, which had thought proper to pursue a separate line of policy, and to unite herself more closely with a European power than with them, notwithstanding they had, obviously, all the same interests. After some further discussion, in which I went over the whole course of policy pursued by the United States towards these countries, and recapitulated the reasons which induced me to believe that the great interests of America required us all to be intimately united, he either was or pretended to be convinced, and promised to use his influence to induce the President and the plenipotentiaries to yield to this point.

"We met at noon, and the plenipotentiaries of this Government commenced the conference by saying that, as I had had the day before expressed an opinion that their they had now one to submit to me, which they presumed I could not refuse, as I had the day before expressed an opinion that their treaty with Great Britain would be rejected, in London, on the ground of this exception. They then proposed to insert the following words: 'with respect to the exception contained in the —— article, which speaks of the Republics which formerly were Spanish possessions, it shall be understood in the same terms which finally shall be agreed upon, in relation to this subject, between Mexico and England.'

"To this proposal I instantly replied that I would prefer agreeing to the article as it stood rather than consent to be governed by the decision of Great Britain; that our interests were separate and distinct; that nation formed one of the European powers, and the United States were the head of the American powers; and that, in treaties which were intended to strengthen the interests of the latter, no allusion ought to be made to those made with the former. Great Britain had concluded a treaty with these States in order to secure a profitable commerce with the Americans, but her interests were European, whereas ours were strictly American. With respect to the opinion I had advanced, that their treaty with England would not be ratified in London, I had been induced to suppose so from the fact that one of the plenipotentiaries of that Government had assured me the exception in question never would have been agreed to by them if they had not been shown the treaty with Colombia, which contained this principle of exclusive alliance among the Spanish American States. It had been ratified here, and they supposed it would be ratified in Colombia, and therefore consented to what they considered irremediable, satisfied that we were excluded as well as themselves. If, therefore, this state of things constituted their only motive for agreeing to it, and they had so declared to their Government, I had a right to suppose, as the principle was not sanctioned by Colombia, that the treaty with that condition would not be ratified in London; and I knew that the chargé d'affaires of her Britannic Majesty had sent in a note to explain the only reasons why the British plenipotentiaries had agreed to that provision in the treaty, and to declare that, as the treaty between Mexico and Colombia had not been ratified by the latter, those reasons no longer existed, and the exception ought to be expunged. If the cabinet of London took the same view of it, the alteration would be insisted upon; but, on the contrary, if it should appear to them more important in a political than in a commercial view, they might not object, as an European power, to the establishment of such distinctions as those proposed, because these must necessarily separate the interests of the American Republics, and that nothing but the policy Great Britain might be disposed to adopt towards America, as one of the European powers, could induce them to make so unnecessary a sacrifice of their commercial interests.

"The plenipotentiaries of this Government then asked what would be their situation if their treaty with Great Britain should arrive ratified, after they had signed one with us without inserting this exception. Aware that this was the real difficulty as well as the source of this obstinacy on their part, I replied that, in my opinion, as the plenipotentiaries of Great Britain had been induced to consent to this exception from the mistaken belief that the treaty with Colombia, in which the principle was established, would be ratified by both parties, and that, therefore, they must admit it, however objectionable, or make no treaty at all with Mexico, and as these motives had fallen to the ground with the rejection of the treaty by Colombia, it would be not only decorous but honorable in the Mexican Government to agree, at once, to expunge that exceptionable provision of their treaty with Great Britain. One of the plenipotentiaries who had assisted at the conferences with those of Great Britain protested that the motive alleged by the British plenipotentiaries had not been the only one. I could only repeat that one of the British plenipotentiaries has assured me it was entered on the protocol of the conferences that the previous treaty of Mexico with Colombia was the only motive which induced them to accede to this exception in favor of the Spanish American States.

"They continued to insist that they were bound by fraternal ties to the Spanish American States, and that it was natural they should unite themselves more intimately with States in their infancy, whose interests were identified with theirs from the peculiar circumstances in which they mutually stood towards Spain, than with a nation already in adolescence, and which had to pursue a different policy towards Spain on account of the relations they had with the other powers of Europe. To these observations I replied, that against the power of Spain they had given sufficient proof that they required no assistance, and the United States had pledged themselves not to permit any other power to interfere either with their independence or form of government; and that, as, in the event of such an attempt being made by the powers of Europe, we would be compelled to take the most active and efficient part and to bear the brunt of the contest, it was not just that we should be placed on a less favorable footing than the other Republics of America, whose existence we were ready to support at such hazards. They interrupted me by stating that we had no right to insist upon being placed on the same footing with the Spanish American States, unless we were willing to take part with them in their contest with Spain. I told them that such an act would be in the highest degree impolitic towards all parties; it was true that the power of the United States was sufficient not only at once to put an end to this contest, but, if the nations of Europe did not interfere, to crush and annihilate that of Spain. This measure, however, which they now proposed, would infallibly produce what it was so much our interest to avoid, the alliance of the great powers of Europe against the liberties of America. I then recapitulated the course of policy pursued towards the Spanish colonies by our Government, which had so largely contributed to secure their independence and to enable them to take their station among the nations of the earth, and declared what further we were ready to do in order to defend their rights and liberties, but that this could only be expected from us, and could only be accomplished, by a strict union of all the American Republics on terms of perfect equality and reciprocity; and repeated that it was the obvious policy of Europe to divide us into small confederacies, with separate and distinct interests, and as manifestly ours to form a single great confederacy, which might oppose one united front to the attacks of our enemies.

" As this conference had already lasted some hours, for Spanish eloquence is diffuse, and as I understood their motives for insisting on this provision in the treaty, I broke it up, with a positive declaration that, putting out of view my duty as representative of the United States, I regarded the proposed exception in favor of the nations which were formerly Spanish possessions so contrary to the best interests of the Americas that I never would agree to its insertion in a treaty between the United States and any of the American Republics."

Mr. Clay to Mr. Poinsett.

DEPARTMENT OF STATE, *Washington, November 9, 1825.*

SIR: Since the date of my letter of the 26th of September last, your despatches to No. 21 have been received. That of the 13th of September, 1825, was received yesterday. They have all been laid before the President, and I shall now make the remarks which appear to be called for by the last, being the only one which seems to require particular notice. In that you state that, in the course of your conferences with the plenipotentiaries of the United Mexican States, on the subject of the proposed commercial convention, a point of difficulty has arisen which has been agreed to be reserved. The point is an exception in favor of the American nations which were formerly Spanish possessions, to which, on account of the fraternal relations that unite them to the United Mexican States, the latter may grant special privileges which shall not be extended to the dominions and citizens of the United States. The President approves of your refusal to accede to that exception.

The United States have neither desired nor sought to obtain for themselves, in their commercial relations with the new States, any privileges which were not common to other nations. They have proposed and only wished to establish, as the basis of all their commercial treaties, those of equality and reciprocity. They can consent to no other. Ready, themselves, to extend to the United Mexican States any favors which they have granted to other nations, the United States feel themselves authorized to demand, in this respect, a perfect reciprocity. They could not agree to treat on the principle of a concession to any European power of commercial privileges which has been denied to them. They would feel even more repugnance to the adoption of such a principle in respect to any American nations, because, by placing the United States, in some degree, out of the pale of that American system of which they form no unessential part, it would naturally wound the sensibility of the people of the United States. As you had not time, at the date of your despatch, to communicate the reasons which were urged in support of this extraordinary exception, they can only be collected from the tenor of the clause inserted in the British treaty, which you have cited. That clause asserts as the motives for the exception: first, that the new States, in whose favor it is to be applied, were formerly Spanish possessions; and second, that certain fraternal relations unite them to the Mexican States. The validity of neither of these reasons can be perceived. What is there in the nature of the fact that those nations were once bound by a common allegiance to Spain to justify the exception? Can any rule be fairly deduced from a colonial condition which should govern independent nations no longer bound by any common tie? Is there not something derogatory from the character of free States and free men in seeking to find a rule for their commercial intercourse in their emancipated condition from a retrospect of their colonial state, which was one of dependence and vassalage? What is to be the limit of this principle? If the accident of a colonial connexion under a common sovereign is to justify a peculiar rule for the emancipated colonies, may not that common sovereign also insist, on the ground of ancient relations, upon special privileges? And then it would. be incumbent upon the United States to consider if they had not been premature in their recognition of the independence of the United Mexican States. But if the fact of the Spanish dominion having once stretched over the new States is to create an exception of commercial privileges in their behalf, the United States, upon a similar ground, have a right to demand the benefit of it. For the same Spanish dominion once, and at no very distant day, extended over the larger part of their territories, and all that part which is conterminous with those of the United Mexican States.

With respect to the second reason, deducible from the clause in the British treaty, there is no statement of the nature of those fraternal relations which are supposed to warrant the exception. Certainly, as between the United Mexican States and the other new nations carved out of the former Spanish colonies, none are known to the world which can sanction the exception. The United Mexican States have, it is true, been waging war with Spain contemporaneously with the other States, but hitherto there has been no co-operation of arms between them. The United Mexican States have alone sustained their contest. If the idea of those fraternal relations is to be sought for in the sympathy between the American belligerents, this sympathy has been equally felt and constantly expressed throughout the whole struggle by the United States. They have not, indeed, taken up arms in support of the independence of the new States, but the neutrality which they have maintained has enabled them, more efficaciously, to serve the cause of independence than they could have done by taking part in the war. Had they become a belligerent, they would, probably, have drawn into the war, on the other side, parties whose force would have neutralized if it had not overbalanced their exertions. By maintaining neutral ground, they have entitled themselves to speak out with effect, and they have constantly so spoken to the powers of Europe. They disconcerted the designs of the European alliance upon the new States by the uncalculating declarations which they made in the face of the world. They were the first to hasten to acknowledge the independence of the United Mexican States, and by their example drew after them Great Britain.

It has, no doubt, not escaped your observation that, in the case of the treaty which has been concluded between the United States and the Republic of Colombia, (and of which a printed authentic copy, as it has been ratified by the two Governments, is herewith transmitted) no such exception was set up by that Republic. On the contrary, it is expressly stipulated in the second article that the parties "engage, mutually, not to grant any particular favor to other nations, in respect of commerce and navigation, which shall not immediately become common to the other party, who shall enjoy the same freely, if the concession was freely made, or on allowing the same compensation, if the concession was conditional."

There is a striking inconsistency in the line of policy which the United Mexican States would seem disposed to pursue towards the United States. They would regard these States as an American nation or not, accordingly as it shall suit their own purposes. In respect to commerce, they would look upon us as an European nation, to be excluded from the enjoyment of privileges conceded to other American nations. But when an attack is imagined to be menaced by Europe upon the independence of the United Mexican States, then an appeal is made to those fraternal sympathies which are justly supposed to belong to our condition as a member of the American family. No longer than about three months ago, when an invasion by France of the island of Cuba was believed at Mexico, the United Mexican Government promptly called upon the Government of the United States, through you, to fulfil the memorable pledge of the President of the United States in his message to Congress of December, 1823. What they would have done had the contingency happened may be inferred from a despatch to the American minister at Paris, a copy of which is herewith sent, which you are authorized to read to the plenipotentiaries of the United Mexican States. Again, the United Mexican Government has invited that of the United States to be represented at the Congress of Panama, and the President has determined to accept the invitation. Such an invitation has been given to no European power, and it ought not to have been given to this if it is not to be considered as one of the American nations.

The President indulges the confident expectation that, upon reconsideration, the Mexican Government will withdraw the exception. But, if it should continue to insist upon it, you will, upon that ground, abstain from concluding any treaty, and put an end to the negotiation. It is deemed better to have no treaty and abide by the respective commercial laws of the two countries, than to subscribe to a principle wholly inadmissible, and which, being assented to in the case of Mexico, might form a precedent to be extended to others of the new States.

I am your obedient servant,

H. CLAY.

JOEL·R. POINSETT, *Envoy Extraordinary and Minister Plenipotentiary United States, Mexico.*

Mr. Clay to Mr. Brown.

DEPARTMENT OF STATE, *Washington, October* 25, 1825.

SIR: During the last summer a large French fleet visited the American seas and the coast of the United States. Its object naturally gave rise to much speculation. Neither here nor through you at Paris was the Government of the United States made acquainted with the views of that of France in sending out so considerable an armament. The President conceives it due to the friendly relations which happily subsist between the two nations, and to the frankness by which he wishes all their intercourse to be characterized, that the purpose of any similar movement hereafter, made in a season of peace, should be communicated to this Government. You will therefore inform the French Government of his expectation that such a communication will, in future, be accordingly made. The reasonableness of it, in a time of peace, of which France shall enjoy the blessings, must be quite apparent. The United States having, at the present period, constantly to maintain, in the Gulf of Mexico and on the coasts of Cuba and Porto Rico, a naval force on a service beneficial to all commercial nations, it would appear to be quite reasonable that, if the commanders of any American squadron, charged with the duty of suppressing piracy, should meet with those of a French squadron, the respective objects of both should be known to each. Another consideration to which you will advert, in a friendly manner, is the present condition of the islands of Cuba and Porto Rico. The views of the Executive of the United States in regard to them have been already disclosed to France by you on the occasion of inviting its co-operation to bring about peace between Spain and her former colonies in a spirit of great frankness. It was stated to the French Government that the United States could not see, with indifference, those islands passing from Spain to any other European power; and that, for ourselves, no change was desired in their present political and commercial condition, nor in the possession which Spain has of them. In the same spirit, and with the hope of guarding beforehand against any possible difficulties on that subject that may arise, you will now add that we could not consent to the occupation of those islands by any other European power than Spain under any contingency whatever. Cherishing no designs on them ourselves, we have a fair claim to an unreserved knowledge of the views of other great maritime powers in respect to them. If any sensibility should be manifested to what the French minister may choose to regard as suspicions entertained here of a disposition on the part of France to indulge a passion of aggrandisement, you may disavow any such suspicions, and say that the President cannot suppose a state of things in which either of the great maritime powers of Europe, with or without the consent of Spain, would feel itself justified to occupy or attempt the occupation of Cuba or Porto Rico without the concurrence or, at least, the knowledge of the United States. You may add, if the tenor of your communications with the French minister should seem to make it necessary, that, in the course of the past summer, rumors reached this country, not merely of its being the design of the French fleet to take possession of the island of Cuba, but that it had, in fact, taken possession of that island. If the confidence in the Government of France, entertained by that of the United States, could not allow it to credit these rumors, it must be admitted that they derived some countenance from the weakness of Spain, the intimate connexion between that monarchy and France, and the general ignorance that prevailed as to the ultimate destination and object of a fleet greatly disproportionate, in the extent of its armament, to any of the ordinary purposes of a peaceful commerce.

You are at liberty to communicate the subject of this note to the French Government, in conference or in writing, as you may think most proper; but in either case it is the President's wish that it should be done in the most conciliatory and friendly manner.

I am, with great respect, sir, your obedient servant,

H. CLAY.

JAMES BROWN, *Envoy Extraordinary and*
Minister Plenipotentiary of the United States to France.

Don José Maria Salazar to the Secretary of State.

[Translation.]

LEGATION OF COLOMBIA, *New York, December 30, 1825.*

I have the honor to inform you that I received the note of the 20th current, in which you are pleased to communicate to me the hopes of a favorable result to the good offices of his Majesty the Emperor of Russia with the great powers of Europe and with Spain to put an end to the war of America. The Government of Colombia, being informed by me of the instructions given to the American minister at St. Petersburg, which you had the goodness to read to me last spring, has seen, with the greatest satisfaction, this measure of real friendship and love of humanity of the Government of the United States, and charged me to declare its gratitude, as well as its anxiety for the continuance of those good offices with the other powers of the continent of Europe.

As to the views of the President of the United States for suspending the invasion of the islands of Cuba and Porto Rico until the result is obtained of the mediation of the great powers with Spain, I shall have the honor of transmitting them to my Government by the first opportunity, being able, in the meantime, to assure you that neither by official communications nor by my private letters from Colombia have I any knowledge relative to the expedition which is preparing at Carthagena. I am consequently inclined to believe that what is said upon that matter is founded on vague conjecture or, perhaps, on the convenience and opportunity of invasion. I ought likewise to add, in confirmation of my private opinion, that, as I have been informed, there are at Carthagena only the troops necessary to garrison the place, such as is requisite in these times, when new expeditions have sailed from the ports of the Peninsula, and are announced against America, and when the Spanish army in the islands of Cuba and Porto Rico has been augmented. When the great facility is considered of acting against the territory of Colombia or Mexico by the advantageous situation of said islands, their great resources, and, what is more important, the superiority of the marine which has assembled there, it will not be denied that Colombia has sufficient causes of alarm. It is true, in support of said conjectures on the approaching invasion of Cuba and Porto Rico, the necessity presents itself, under which the Government of Colombia is, of withdrawing the auxiliary forces from Peru by the way of Panama and Carthagena, which is the most convenient, ready, and economical way to place them on the Atlantic in an attitude of giving immediate succor to any point of our territory, or of that of our allies, which may be invaded; but it is clear that this military operation is rather the necessary effect of the geographical situation of Colombia and Peru than a meditated plan of an expedition without the continent.

To these reasons, which, in my private opinion, and for want of official communications from my Government upon the subject, sufficiently explain the movements of troops which are going on in Colombia, permit me to repeat to you what I said upon another occasion, that this military attitude, extremely grievous to our people, is a necessary consequence of the obstinacy of the Spanish Government in prolonging a useless war, and in declining every idea of treating with independent America, no less than the lamentably equivocal policy of the great continental powers which, notwithstanding they see our independence irrevocably established by force of arms, and upon the solid basis of general opinion and of just and moderate Governments, refuse the formal recognition of the new Republics, pretending to misunderstand what their own interest, justice, reason, and humanity demand. In this situation of justly inspired doubt and inquietude, when the obstinacy of Spain and the indifference of the rest of Europe have convinced us even that we are engaged in a question of fact, when the nations of America have displayed all the vigor of youth, and know the value of their forces and combined resources, and when our armies have gloriously terminated the campaign which has forever secured the liberty of the South, it will not appear to many reasonable to renounce all these favorable circumstances, to terminate at once the evils of war, and dictate conditions of peace, with the manifest advantage of the American system, in the absolute expulsion of one European nation from the important islands of Cuba and Porto Rico, which, in the precarious and miserable situation of Spain, are not without the possibility of falling into the power of some of the great powers of Europe.

·It will appear even less reasonable that Colombia and her allies should have to continue in a state of inaction, enduring the heavy expenses and grievous inconveniences which accompany the maintenance of the army and the marine upon a war footing, not being able to rely upon a guarantee of suspension from armaments and attacks·on the part of Spain, which, in spite of its nullity, does not cease in its efforts to augment the army of America so far as to induce us to suspect that a foreign hand affords these aids, which are by no means in harmony with the scantiness of the resources of the Peninsula.

I can likewise assure you that my Government has always regarded, with all due circumspection, the consequences which might result from an ill directed expedition against Cuba and Porto Rico; and, notwithstanding the urgent necessity which it has had to attack the headquarters (if I may so speak) of our enemies, and the opportunity which oftener than once has presented itself for that purpose, it has preferred to suffer repeated invasions from those islands, waiting for the favorable moment to attack them with a certainty of success by the greater forces which the alliance of all the sections of the south and Mexico will procure to us, and by the state, every day advancing, of the opinion for independence in the inhabitants of said islands, who have repeatedly implored our aid. By this prudent slowness it has wished to give time to the Spanish Government to reflect upon its own interest, and, consequently, to take the just resolution of recognizing the independence of the States of the continent to save the rest of her colonies; but the time has passed in vain, and Spain, in spite of the repeated reverses which she has suffered in the course of this year, shows herself as proud and indignant at every idea of accommodation as at the commencement of the contest. Already a plan of conciliation has been seen inadmissible by the independent States, presented by the Minister Zea, in. which were proposed some slight modifications of the ancient colonial regimen, and which, however, were rejected by King Ferdinand as too liberal.

In fine, by the same risks and lamentable consequences which would happen from the invasion of Cuba and Porto Rico if the result is not secured by the combination of superior forces, at least of the nations most interested, Colombia and Mexico, and the plan of operations for this campaign be regulated by common consent, I think that the fortune of said islands must be decided in the Congress of the Isthmus of Panama, which gives time sufficient to receive positive accounts of the final result of the good offices of his Majesty the Emperor of Russia; and I doubt not that, in attention to the friendship which his Imperial Majesty professes to the United States, which have requested his high mediation, and the glory of attributing to the great work of peace, a boon so important will be obtained, or the recognition of our political existence by Russia and the other powers, which is the object of the most ardent desires of the new Governments of America.

I have the honor to offer you the sentiments of the most distinguished consideration, with which I am your very obedient servant,

JOSÉ MARIA SALAZAR.

Hon. HENRY CLAY, *Secretary of State.*

Don Pablo Obregon to the Secretary of State.

[Translation.]

LEGATION OF THE ·UNITED STATES OF MEXICO, *Washington, January 4, 1826.*

SIR: I have the honor of answering your note of the 20th ultimo, in which you communicate to me the favorable hope of a happy issue in the negotiation undertaken by this Government with the Russian Cabinet, through its minister at St. Petersburg, to solicit of his Imperial Majesty his interposition in promoting peace between Spain and the powers of the American continent formerly a part of that monarchy, and in using his influence with his allies towards a general recognition, all of which you communicated to me in the month of May last, by reading to me the instructions which had been given to that effect to the American minister near his Imperial Majesty. I imparted to my Government a step so friendly and agreeable to the philanthropy and position of these States, and, although I have as yet received no answer thereto, I repeat to you what I had the honor to mention verbally, that Mexico was only desirous of peace, and that I·acknowledged to this Government its interest and mode of acting in the cause of the continent and of liberty. .

I shall make known to my Government the wishes of the President that any other expedition be suspended which may be projected, as well as that which is said to be fitting out at Carthagena, to assist the independence of one or both the islands of Cuba and Porto Rico, as the means best adapted to obtain the.negotiation mentioned.

I avail myself of this occasion to present to you my respects and most distinguished consideration, repeating myself to be your obedient servant,

PABLO OBREGON.

The message and the report and documents therein referred to were read.

Ordered, That they be referred to the Committee on Foreign Relations to consider and report thereon.

MONDAY, JANUARY 16, 1826.

Mr. MACON, from the Committee on Foreign Relations, to whom was referred on the 28th of December the message of the President of the United States, nominating Richard C. Anderson and John Sergeant to be Envoys Extraordinary and Ministers Plenipotentiary to the Assembly of the American Nations at Panama; and on the 10th instant, the message communicating certain documents relating thereto, submitted the following report:

That they have examined the subject to them referred with the most profound attention, and have bestowed upon it all the consideration demanded by its novelty, delicacy, and high importance to the character and future destinies of the United States. In making this examination the committee found themselves not a little embarrassed at first by the circumstance announced by the President in his message to both Houses of Congress, at the commencement of the present session, that he had *already accepted* the invitation given to the United States by some of the American Republics to be represented at the contemplated Congress of American nations about to be assembled at Panama. But seeing in the several communications made by the Secretary of State to the different ministers of these Republics that an express reference was made to the concurrence of the Senate as the indispensable preliminary to the acceptance of this invitation, and finding in the present message of the President the explicit assurance that he had not thought proper to take any step in carrying this measure into effect until he could ascertain that his opinion of its expediency would concur with that of both branches of the Legislature, the committee believed it became a part of the duty they owed to the Senate, and would be evidence of the proper respect due to the President, that they should fully and freely examine into the propriety of the proposed measure, the expediency of adopting which was the subject that the Senate was thus invited to deliberate upon, and to make known their opinion.

Considerations of much higher importance than even these induced the committee to adopt this course. In the ordinary progress of their proceedings the Senate can rarely, if ever, find it either necessary or proper to inquire as to the objects expected to be attained by appointments to which their advice and consent is asked. As to all offices created by statute in which these objects are defined, and their attainment positively required, the single question arising before the Senate must ever refer merely to the fitness of the persons nominated by the President to fulfill such duties. The same will generally be found the sole inquiry necessary to be made in filling up vacancies happening in pre-existing foreign missions, designed to maintain the customary relations and intercourse of friendship and commerce between the United States and other nations. Very different, however, is the case when it is proposed to create new offices by nomination, or to despatch ministers to foreign States, for the first time, or to accomplish by such missions objects not specially disclosed, or under circumstances new, peculiar, and highly important. In all these cases, instead of confining their inquiries to the mere fitness of the persons nominated to fill such offices, it is not only the right, but the duty of the Senate to determine previously as to the necessity and propriety of creating the offices themselves; and in deciding these questions not only the objects for the accomplishment by which it is proposed to create them, but every other circumstance connected with such a measure must necessarily and unavoidably become a subject of their serious examination.

This right conferred by the Constitution upon the Senate is the only *direct* check upon the power possessed by the President in this respect which, relieved from this restraint, would authorize him to create and consummate all the political relations of the United States at his mere will. And as in the theory of their Government the high destinies of the people of the United States are never to be confided to the unrestrained discretion of any single man, even the wisest and best of their fellow-citizens, it becomes a solemn duty which the Senate owe to the sovereign States here represented most seriously to investigate all the circumstances connected with the novel measure now proposed by the President, as to the expediency of adopting which they have been invited to aid him with their counsel and advice.

Entertaining these opinions in the performance of the duty which they believe has been required by the Senate, and anxious to manifest to the President their high respect by complying fully with the wish which he has expressed upon this subject, the committee will proceed to investigate the circumstances connected with the measure proposed and disclosed by the documents to them referred, most deeply impressed with the importance of the consequences that may very probably result from it.

The first question which suggested itself to the committee, at the very threshold of their investigation, was, what cogent reasons now existed for adopting this new and untried measure, so much in conflict with the whole course of policy uniformly and happily pursued by the United States from almost the very creation of this Government to the present hour? By the principles of this policy, inculcated by our wisest statesmen in former days, and approved by the experience of all subsequent time, the true interest of the United States was supposed to be promoted by avoiding all entangling connexions with any other nation whatsoever. Steadily pursuing this course, while they have been desirous to manifest the most cordial good will to all nations, and to maintain with each relations of perfect amity, and of commerce, regulated and adjusted by rules of the most fair, equal, and just reciprocity, the United States have hitherto sedulously abstained from associating themselves in any other way, even with those nations for whose welfare the most lively sensibility has been at all times felt and otherwise manifested.

During the conflict for freedom and independence, in which these new States of America were so long engaged with their former sovereign, although every heart in the United States beat high in sympathy with them, and fervent aspirations were hourly put up for their success, and although the relations then existing with Spain were well calculated to excite strong irritation and resentment on our part, yet the Government of the United States, convinced of the propriety of a strict adherence to the principles it had ever proclaimed as the rule of its conduct in relation to other nations, forebore to take any part in this struggle, and maintained the most exact neutrality between these belligerents. Nor would it ever recognize the independence of these new Republics until they had become independent in fact, and the situation of their ancient sovereign in relation to them was such as to manifest that he ought no longer to be held responsible for their acts. So soon as this occurred the United States most gladly embraced the opportunity, and in being the first to proclaim the sovereignty and independence of these States gave to them the strongest pledge of respect and cordial friendship and sincere anxiety for their prosperity.

Since that event ministers have been despatched to each of these new Republics, instructed to declare the sentiments sincerely and warmly felt for them by the United States, and empowered to conclude treaties with them, the objects of which should be to establish, upon principles of the most perfect justice and equity, all the ordinary relations that exist between nations. Thus much was due not less to them than to ourselves; and in going so far we did all that our feelings dictated and the interests of either seemed then to require. What necessity has since arisen to do more? What cause exists now to prompt the United States to establish new and stronger relations with them, and so to abandon that rule of conduct which has hitherto been here so steadily and happily pursued?

These inquiries necessarily called the attention of the committee to a minute examination of all the documents to them referred, in order that they might therein discover the reasons assigned by the new States of America for desiring the United States to be represented at the Congress about to be assembled at Panama, and the motives of the President for intimating his willingness to accept this invitation. And in making such an examination many reflections presented themselves as connected with the proposed measure, all of which the committee will now state to the Senate.

In a Government constituted as is that of the United States, in which the sentiment so natural to freemen prompts them to scrutinize most exactly the extent of all the powers they grant, and to limit this extent by the objects desired to be accomplished by their exercise, the strongest anxiety is (and it is to be hoped always will be) felt to learn distinctly what is the precise object desired to be attained, and what are the precise means proposed for its attainment. Even the confidence reposed in the long-tried patriotism and well-proved wisdom of our own best citizens does not and ought not to suffice to quiet this anxiety, or to remove this jealousy inspired by an ardent attachment to our rights and privileges. It was therefore much to be desired, and certainly to have been expected, that before the destinies of the United States should be committed to the deliberation and decision of a Congress composed not of our own citizens but of the representatives of many different nations, that the objects of such deliberations should be most accurately stated and defined, and the manner of their accomplishment clearly and distinctly marked out.

In this opinion the President himself seems to have concurred at the commencement of this negotiation, for in the report made to him on the 20th of December last by the Secretary of State this officer states that, agreeably to his directions, he had informed the ministers by whom the invitation to the proposed Congress at Panama was given; that "before such a Congress assembled it appeared to the President to be expedient to adjust, between the different powers to be represented, several preliminary points, such as the subjects to which the attention of the Congress was to be directed, the nature and the form of the powers to be given to the diplomatic agents who were to compose it, and the mode of its organization and action." And it was made an express and previous condition to the acceptance of the invitation proposed to be given that "these preliminary points should be arranged in a manner satisfactory to the United States."

It was, therefore, not without much surprise and great regret that the committee discovered that although in none of the communications subsequently made to this Government by either of the ministers of the several States by whom this invitation was given are these preliminary points even stated, and although the want of "a compliance with these conditions" is expressly noticed in the reply made to them by the Secretary of State, yet they were therein told that the President had determined "at once" to send Commissioners to this Congress at Panama, provided the Senate would advise and consent to such a measure.

If, then, the Senate should now demand of this committee to inform them what are the objects to be accomplished at this Congress, and what are the means by which their accomplishment is to be effected—although as to objects the documents referred to them will enable the committee to name a few—yet as to all others they must answer, in the language of the communication made by the Mexican minister, that they are those "to which the existence of the new States may give rise, and which it is not easy to point out or enumerate." As to the means, however, the committee can only reply that, while it seems to be expected that the United States are to clothe their representatives with "ample powers" to accomplish all the enumerated, and these other undefined objects also, yet the mode in which these powers, if granted, are to be used and exercised, is nowhere even hinted at.

One great question, therefore, upon which the decision of the Senate is called for, will be whether, in the existing state of things, it is wise or expedient that the United States should be represented at a Congress of American nations by agents endowed with undefined powers to accomplish undefined objects? And this committee feel no hesitation in stating, as their opinion, that, if ever it may be proper to adopt such a measure, there is nothing known to them that requires or justifies it at this time.

It is true the power confided to the Senate to ratify or reject any agreement that may be entered into by such agents would constitute some safeguard to the important interests of the United States. But long experience must have informed the Senate that it is generally exceedingly difficult, and sometimes even impossible, to escape from the embarrassments produced by the mere act of entering into a negotiation, and that it is much better to abstain from doing so until its objects are distinctly known and approved than to confide in the power of the Senate, in the last resort, to refuse their assent to the ratification of an agreement after it is adjusted by means of such negotiation.

In the present case, if the measures to be accomplished by the proposed Congress, whatever may be their object or character, should not meet the concurring opinion of all the parties there to be represented, we need not the lights of history to inform us that many consequences, mischievous in themselves, and greatly to be deplored, not only may, but most probably will, result. And that a difference of opinion will exist in regard to measures so important in themselves, and so various and diversified in their effects upon nations differing from each other in almost every particular, is much to be apprehended. The power possessed by the Senate of withholding its assent ought not, therefore, to be regarded as furnishing sufficient assurance against the possible and probable effects of the proposed measure.

Turning from the undefined objects of this Congress, so imperfectly disclosed in the vague description given of them, that, if seen at all, they are presented most indistinctly to their view, and regarding those which are particularly mentioned and described with more precision, this committee have not been able to discover in any one of these last a single subject concerning which the United States ought to enter into any negotiation with the States of America to be assembled at the contemplated Congress at Panama.

Before proceeding to the enumeration of these objects the committee cannot refrain from calling the attention of the Senate to a singular circumstance, disclosed by the documents to them referred, although an enumeration of the subjects to which the attention of the proposed Congress was to be directed was explicitly stated as a condition preliminary to the acceptance by the United States of the invitation given to them to be there represented; although each of the ministers giving this invitation had communicated this to his Government, and received its instructions relative thereto; yet great diversities will be found in the enumeration of these subjects, made by each of these ministers in pursuance of such instructions. And, what is still more remarkable, while many of the subjects of intended discussion, so enumerated by each of these ministers, are not referred to in the message of the President to the Senate, others are therein stated, as matters for the deliberation of the proposed Congress, to which not the slightest allusion seems ever to have been made by any one of the American ministers in any of their communications to this Government; nay, one of the subjects (the most important, probably, of any which the United States are desirous to discuss at this Congress) is neither noticed in the communications made to this Government by any of the American States nor in the message of the President to the Senate, and is to be only inferred from the documents last referred to this committee, received under the call made by the Senate for further information; all which will be very clearly shown by the details which the committee will now lay before the Senate.

The first subject stated by the Mexican minister as one which would occupy the attention of the contemplated Congress, and in the deliberations concerning which the United States are expected to take a part, is "The resistance or opposition to be made to the interference of any neutral. nation in the question and war of independence between the new powers of this. continent and Spain." And in the deliberations upon this subject it seems to be proposed " to discuss the means of giving to that resistance all possible force," and so to adjust, by previous concert, the mode in which each of the States represented at the Congress " shall lend its co-operation."

The same subject is also stated by the minister of Colombia, and in terms still more explicit. He suggests as a matter of useful discussion in the Congress· the formation of " an·eventual alliance" of the States there to be represented, for the purpose of preventing any European power from interfering in the present contest between Spain and her former colonies, and that the treaty for this purpose should " remain secret until the *casus fœderis* should happen."

Notwithstanding this is so stated by both of these ministers, as the first- and great object of the proposed Congress, yet the President, in his message, assures the Senate ."that the motive of the attendance of the United States is neither to contract·alliances nor to engage in any undertaking or project importing hostility to any other nation." It thus appears that in relation to this first and most important point, which seems to have given birth to the scheme of this Congress, the views and. motives of the United States differ essentially from those of the other parties. And this difference of opinion occurring as to the very first proposition, which is said to be " a matter of immediate utility to the American States that are at war with Spain," and is believed by them to be in accordance with the repeated declarations and protests of the Cabinet at Washington," must unavoidably excite doubts as to " the interest we take in their welfare and our disposition to comply with their wishes," and would so contribute not a.little to defeat other objects.

The next subject stated by the Mexican minister, as presenting ."another of the questions which may be discussed," and which he considers as being "in like predicament with the foregoing," is, "the opposition to colonization in America by the European powers."

The minister of Colombia concurs in this enumeration. He places "the manner in which all colonization of European powers on the American continent shall be resisted " at the very head of all the subjects of proposed discussion; and couples this with the former, as an object to be effected by the joint and united efforts of all the States to be represented at the Congress, who should be bound by a solemn convention to secure this end.

The President concurs in part in the opinion as to the propriety of attaining this end, but differs radically as to the mode of accomplishing it. "An agreement between all the parties represented at the meeting, that each will guard, by its own means, against the establishment of any future European colony within its borders," he thinks, "may be found advisable." Now, if this be meant, that each nation shall, by its own means, protect its own territories against all encroachments upon them attempted by any European or other foreign State whatsoever, the committee cannot discern either the necessity or expediency of entering into any formal agreement with other States to that effect, more than exists for reducing to treaty stipulations any other of the high, just, and universally admitted rights of all nations. Such an idea, however, is obviously not that suggested by the ministers of Mexico and Colombia; and if more is meant to be comprehended in the agreement, which the President thinks may be found advisable, every other article it would contain must, in the opinion of this committee, violate all the well-settled principles of the policy of the United States, and put at hazard their best interests, without any adequate motive for so novel an experiment. In the one case the views and motives of the President differ again essentially from those of the other parties to be represented at this Congress; and from the disclosure of these repeated differences of opinion no good can possibly result. And in the other, should the views of the President concur with those of the other American States, (which the committee do not believe,) the mutual stipulations growing out of such an agreement would, in the opinion of this committee, prove fatal to the best interests of the United States should the *casus fœderis* ever happen.

To adjust the means of most effectual resistance to the interference of neutral nations in the war of independence between the new powers of this continent and Spain, and of opposition to colonization in America by the European powers, are said by the Mexican minister to be " the two principal subjects" of intended discussion at the contemplated Congress; and, indeed, are all the subjects of discussion which he particularly states. The minister of Colombia, however, extends his enumeration of the subjects of intended discussion somewhat further; and after mentioning those before stated adds, as another, ."the consideration of the means to be adopted for the entire abolition of the African slave trade."

To this subject the President makes no allusion in his message; and, after the examination which it has received in the Senate during two successive years, this committee deem it quite unnecessary to say much in relation to it at this time. Some of the sovereign States here represented were the first in the world to proclaim their abhorrence of this traffic. Since the formation of this Government the United States have exerted (and, as this committee believe, have exerted effectually) all the means in their power to arrest its progress, so far as their own citizens were concerned; and, if all other nations, and especially those nations holding possessions in America, would follow their example, the African slave trade would no longer exist. The United States, however, have not certainly the right, and ought never to feel the inclination to dictate to others who may differ with them upon this subject, nor do the committee see the expediency of insulting other States, with whom we are maintaining relations of perfect amity, by ascending the moral chair, and proclaiming from thence mere abstract principles, of the rectitude of which each nation enjoys the perfect right of deciding for itself.

The minister of Colombia states, as another subject of discussion at the contemplated Congress, "on what basis the relations of Hayti, and of other parts of our hemisphere that shall hereafter be in like circumstances, are to be placed." To this matter, also, the President makes no allusion in his message. And, surely, if there is any subject within the whole circle of political relations, as to which it is the interest and the duty of all States to keep themselves perfectly free and unshackled by any previous stipulation, it is that which regards their future connexions with any other people not parties to such an agreement. Of the propriety or impropriety of such connexions each must ever be permitted to judge freely for itself, because the benefit or disadvantage to result from them must be peculiar, and very different to each; and that relation which is highly desirable at one time may become hurtful at another. In the opinion of this committee, therefore, the United States should never permit themselves to enter into discussion with any foreign State whatever as to the relations they should be obliged to establish with any other people not parties to such discussions. And the objections to such a course become infinitely stronger when the discussions are intended to refer not only to those who then exist, but also to others who may hereafter be considered as placed "in like circumstances."

These are all the points particularly suggested by the minister of Colombia as subjects of discussion at the contemplated Congress. The minister of Guatemala (who also unites in the invitation given to the United States) has stated no particular subject as matter of discussion at this Congress. He intimates, however, "that as Europe had formed a *Continental System*, and held a Congress whenever questions affecting its interests were to be discussed, America should also form a system for itself."

How far this general suggestion meets the views of the President the committee are not enabled, by any document to them referred, to decide; but they will present to the Senate their own ideas in relation to it, the rather because it seems now to be the prominent object of the proposed Congress, the magnitude and variety of details belonging to which defied present enumeration and particular specification.

Without adverting to the great and obvious diversities existing between the States of this continent and those of Europe, by which the system here alluded-to has been established, diversities growing out of the situation of their people, the nature of their governments, and the positions they occupy, not only in relation to each other but to the rest of the civilized world, this committee will state, as their opinion, that no effect yet produced by the continental system of Europe is of a character to invite the States of this continent to take that system as a model or example fit for their imitation. The great object of the continental system of Europe is to preserve ancient institutions, and relations long known and well understood, in the position which they now occupy and for many centuries have done.

The operation of this system is, by the combination of powers and the application of mere force, to arrest the progress of improvement in the science of government and in the condition of society. Ends which all free States must reprobate as much as they do the means employed for their accomplishment. If this were not so, however, a system formed for this continent for the same, or even different objects, would most probably produce the worst effects. The short political existence of all the States on this continent, even of the United States themselves, the most ancient of any, hath enabled them to profit so little as yet by experience that it would seem rash to proclaim their perfection at this time or to pledge any of them to perpetuate either their present institutions or existing political relations. Our own excellent Constitution is based upon the supposition of its own probable imperfections, and most wisely provides for its amendment whenever such defects shall be discovered to exist. We cannot, therefore, stipulate to preserve it as it is; and no compact with other States can be necessary to bestow upon each the power it now possesses to effect any change which experience may hereafter show to be beneficial to itself; and a stipulation to make such changes as the good of any others may hereafter require, would either be futile in itself or must inevitably lead to discord and to wars.

This committee doubt, moreover, the authority of the Government of the United States to enter into any negotiation with foreign nations for the purpose of settling and promulgating either principles of internal polity or mere abstract propositions as parts of the public law. And if the proposed Congress is viewed but as a convenient mode of conducting a summary negotiation relative to existing interests important to this continent alone, it not only may, but most probably will, be considered by all other civilized nations as a confederacy of the States therein represented for purposes as prejudicial to the interests of the Old as they are supposed to be beneficial to those of the New World. Many of the provisions in the different conventions already concluded between some of the new States relative to this very Congress, and which are now public, are well calculated to create such a suspicion, even if they do not justify a belief in its truth. And whensoever this suspicion shall be entertained by the nations of the Old World, and especially by those who still hold possessions on this continent, it must be obvious to all that consequences much to be deplored will unavoidably result.

Nothing that can be done thereafter by any department of this Government in refusing to sanction the stipulations concluded at a Congress regarded in this light will suffice to avert the calamity. And the United States, who have grown up in happiness to their present prosperity by a strict observance of their old well known course of policy, and by manifesting entire good will and most profound respect for all other nations, must prepare to embark their future destinies upon an unknown and turbulent ocean, directed by little experience, and destined for no certain haven. In such a voyage, the dissimilitude existing between themselves and their associates in interest, character, language, religion, manners, customs, habits, laws, and almost every other particular, and the rivalship these discrepancies must surely produce among them, would generate discords which, if they did not destroy all hope of its successful termination, would make even success itself the ultimate cause of new and direful conflicts between themselves. Such has been the issue of all such enterprises in past time, and we have therefore strong reasons to expect in the future similar results from similar causes.

The committee, having thus examined the several subjects of proposed discussions stated or alluded to by each of the ministers of the new States of America as subjects of deliberation at the contemplated Congress, will now proceed to the investigation of others not mentioned or referred to by any of them, but exhibited in the message of the President.

The committee see nothing in the documents to them referred to prove that the States who originated the project of this Congress, and settled the subjects proper for its deliberation, and who most probably have already adjusted "the preliminary rules of that assembly," will admit as fit matters of discussion any other than those which they themselves have so previously announced. Should this be the case, the degraded position which the United States must then occupy at the Congress must be apparent to all. Without adverting further, however, at this time to this consideration, the committee will enter into the examination of the several topics suggested by the President, as though the discussion of them was a matter settled and already agreed.

The first of these subjects stated by the President is, "the establishment of principles of a liberal commercial intercourse." The motives for desiring this are stated to be, that "the Southern American nations in their intercourse with the United States have sometimes manifested dispositions to reserve a right of granting special favors and privileges to the Spanish nation as the price of their recognition; at others, they have actually established duties and impositions, operating unfavorably to the United States, to the advantage of other European powers; and sometimes they have appeared to consider that they might interchange among themselves mutual concessions of exclusive favor, to which neither European powers nor the United States should be admitted."

In considering these reasons it cannot escape the observation of any that, in manifesting dispositions to establish such commercial relations, the Southern American nations must have been actuated by the only motive that ever operates either upon nations or individuals, in regard to their mere commercial intercourse, a desire fairly to advance their own interests, and a belief that they could, by such means, properly accomplish this end. If, in this belief, these nations are right, then the United States can scarcely be viewed as acting towards them in that spirit of generous kindness and fraternal friendship they have professed, when they should strive to induce them to establish as liberal principles such as would be injurious to the interests of these southern nations themselves. And if they are wrong, it seems to this committee that the task of exhibiting their errors may be much better performed, as hitherto it hath been, by particular discussions with each separately than by general demonstrations made to all, assembled as a Congress.

The interests of commerce are necessarily peculiar; they grow out of numerous circumstances, produced by locality, climate, population, manners, customs, and other causes, no one of which exists alike in any two nations on the globe. Few general principles, therefore, can ever apply, with equal truth, to so many peculiarities; and such as do so apply need not the sanction of solemn compact to give them effect. They may be very safely confided to the natural disposition of man promptly to discover and eagerly to advance his own best interests.

Whatever dispositions, then, may have been manifested by the southern nations of America, this committee think that their effects, both upon themselves and the United States, will constitute subjects much more fit for separate discussions with each than of general investigation before all. And the committee are the more confirmed in this opinion by the assurance given by the President in this message, that "in most of these cases their regulations unfavorable to us have already yielded to friendly expostulation and remonstrance;" and by the fact that the treaties recently concluded between these States contain express stipulations that in no event will they agree or enter into any treaty with Spain, or any other nation, to the prejudice of their independence, but to maintain, at all times, their mutual interests with the dignity and energy proper to free independent States.

It is true a difference of opinion appears to exist at present between the United States and one of the new Republics of America in relation to a single principle of their commercial intercourse. When the Senate recollect, however, that treaties have been already concluded between the United States and three others of these Republics, in each of which treaties this point has been settled, as the United States themselves think, right, the committee believe that the Senate will concur with them in the opinion that it is much better to continue the discussion of this subject with the dissenting State singly, urging upon her the example of her sister States, than to put in hazard the stipulations already secured by voluntarily entering into an examination of their expediency before the contemplated Congress.

"The consentaneous adoption of principles of maritime neutrality, favorable to the navigation of peace and commerce in time of war," is the next object which, in the opinion of the President, should "also form a subject of consideration to this Congress." In relation to this, so far as it regards the commerce of peace, the committee have already expressed their opinion; and, so far as it is intended to settle the rules of war, as applicable to navigation, the committee will only remark that there exists so much risk of compromising and destroying the relations of neutrality, which the United States are now maintaining, should they involve themselves, by any compact, relative to belligerent rights, entered into with only one of the parties to the present war, during its continuance, that, in their opinion, it would be highly inexpedient to make such an experiment at this time. Any principle relating to the rights of war, which one of the parties in the existing contest might be willing to adopt, as promoting its interests, could scarcely be regarded with indifference by the other. And the great maritime States of Europe would most probably consider that the United States had seized the occasion of this war to enter into a confederacy with the other States of this continent now actually engaged in it for the purpose of settling principles intended to affect materially their future interests.

It is well known to the Senate, moreover, that treaties already exist between the United States and several of the new States of this continent, in which all the subjects alluded to by the President, in this part of his message are already settled; and no reason is known to this committee to excite the slightest doubt that the others of these States, with whom treaties are not yet concluded, will feel any disinclination to enter into similar stipulations for themselves.

"There is yet another subject, (says the President,) upon which, without entering into any treaty, the moral influence of the United States may, perhaps, be exerted with beneficial consequences at such a meeting—the advancement of religious liberty." And, as a motive for making an effort to accomplish this object, he states that "an exclusive church has been incorporated with the political constitutions of some of the southern nations, without toleration of any other than the dominant sect."

In the opinion of this committee there is no proposition concerning which the people of the United States are now and ever have been more unanimous than that which denies not merely the expediency but the right of intermeddling with the internal affairs of other States; and especially of seeking to alter any provision they may have thought proper to adopt as a fundamental law or may have incorporated with their political constitutions. And if there be any such subject more sacred and delicate than another, as to which the United States ought never to intermeddle even by obtrusive advice, it is that which concerns religious liberty. The most cruel and devastating wars have been produced by such interferences, the blood of man has been poured out in torrents, and, from the days of the crusades to the present hour, no benefit has resulted to the human family from discussions carried on by nations upon such subjects. Among the variety even of Christian nations which now inhabit the earth, rare, indeed, are the examples to be found of States who have not established an exclusive church, and to far the greater number of these toleration is yet unknown. In none of the communications which have taken place is the most distant allusion made to this delicate subject by any of the ministers who have given this invitation; and the committee feel very confident in the opinion that if ever an intimation shall be made to the sovereignties they represent that it was the purpose of the United States to discuss at the proposed Congress their plans of internal civil polity, or anything touching the supposed interests of their religious establishments, the invitation given would soon be withdrawn.

The committee have thus exhibited to the Senate in detail all the subjects which they have been enabled to find particularly stated either by the President in his first message or by any of the ministers of the new States of America as matters intended to be discussed at the contemplated Congress. In reviewing these they will repeat, that a concurrence of opinion does not seem to exist between the different parties as to the subjects of deliberation; nor has the mode of discussion or decision been in any way settled between them. In relation to some of the subjects alluded to as fit matters for consideration, differences of opinion, radical and irreconcileable, seem already to exist, which discussion may aggravate but cannot assuage. As to others, their very agitation, in this mode, threatens seriously the compromitment of the neutral relations which the United States are now maintaining and have so carefully observed throughout this whole contest. Others, again, are unfit subjects for deliberation in this mode at all times, and any agreement resulting from their discussion must impair that freedom of action which it is so necessary for the United States to preserve as to these; and as to the residue, they are either not of sufficient importance to require the adoption of this new and untried experiment of a Congress of nations, or may be much better adjusted and settled in separate negotiations with each than in a general conference with all. For these reasons, if there were none other, this committee should regard the adoption of the measure proposed by the President as highly inexpedient at this time.

Although in the message of the President of the 9th instant no new subject of deliberation at the contemplated Congress is specially stated, yet, from the documents accompanying that message and therein referred to as containing information tending to show the expediency of adopting the proposed measure, it appears to this committee that the present and future condition of the remaining Spanish possessions in America are considered as proper matters to be there agitated and settled. Such being the inference of the committee they will proceed to lay before the Senate their opinion upon this subject also.

The committee are well aware that the United States can never regard with indifference the situation and probable destiny of the neighboring Spanish islands of Cuba and Puerto Rico; but so far from believing it expedient to discuss these subjects at a Congress of all the American States, and especially at this time, the committee consider the great probability that such a discussion might be *forced* upon the United States, if they are there represented, as a circumstance furnishing in itself the strongest objections to the adoption of the measure proposed.

If the existing war between Spain and the new States of America continues, the United States could scarcely endeavor to arrest the progress of that war, in the only direction it can hereafter take, or prevail upon one of the belligerents not to strike their enemy, where alone he is now assailable and most vulnerable by them, without announcing a determination to take part in the contest; and if peace shall happily be restored all apprehension of the effects of such a blow must cease of course. Why, then, discuss the merits of such a question, which it seems probable may never arise ? Or why place the United States in a situation where, if the question does arise and they must speak, the language which they utter must be regarded as equally unfriendly to all the new States, and where, if the United States keep silence, this very silence will be misinterpreted ?

Should the situation or policy of the United States induce them to look with indifference upon the new direction that the existing war may take and to abstain from all interference in it, even though the neighboring islands of Cuba and Puerto Rico may be threatened or assailed, then the very annunciation of such a purpose must contribute much to accelerate an event that cannot be desired by us. In whatever light, therefore, this subject is viewed, it does not seem to be one which the United States should discuss with the other American States assembled as a Congress. The inexpediency of pursuing such a course appeared more obvious to this committee when they considered that many of the nations of Europe must also feel that their interests were materially involved in its decision, and that they would not abstain from making some movement in relation to it which must greatly embarrass any course that the United States may wish hereafter to pursue.

While the United States retain the position which they have hitherto occupied, and manifest a constant determination not to mingle their interests with those of the other States of America, they may continue to employ the influence they possess and have already happily exerted with the nations of Europe in favor of these new Republics ; but if ever the United States permit themselves to be associated with these nations in any general Congress assembled for the discussion of common plans in any way affecting European interests, they will, by such an act, not only deprive themselves of the ability they now possess of rendering useful assistance to the other American States, but also produce other effects prejudicial to their own interests. Then the powers of Europe, who have hitherto confided in the sagacity, vigilance, and impartiality of the United States to watch, detect, announce, and restrain any disposition that the heat of the existing contest might excite in the new States of America to extend their empires beyond their own limits, and who have, therefore, considered their possessions and commerce in America safe, while so guarded, would no longer feel this confidence. Each would, therefore, endeavor to secure its own interests by its own means ; and the power of Spain not being considered by any as equal to the protection of her remaining American possessions, a struggle would probably commence who should first obtain the islands of Cuba and Puerto Rico, the possession of which must ever be of the last importance to the commerce of this hemisphere. Or, if such should not be the case, the interest of many European nations might seem to require that they should make common cause with Spain for the purpose of preventing these islands from falling into other hands. To the United States it would be of little moment which of these events should occur ; for it cannot be expected that any such contest could be carried on so near them without the most imminent danger to their neutrality.

The very situation of Cuba and Puerto Rico, therefore, furnishes the strongest inducement to the United States not to take a place at the contemplated Congress, since, by so doing, they must be considered as changing the attitude in which they hitherto have stood as impartial spectators of the passing scenes, and identifying themselves with the new Republics.

These reasons, strong as they have appeared to this committee, are not the only objections to the proposed measure disclosed by the documents to them referred. The manner in which this invitation has been given of itself furnishes many forcible obstacles to its acceptance ; and, in the opinion of this committee, the United States will neither consult their own dignity nor what is due to the proper respect they have a right to claim from all nations, and especially from the new States of America, if they now agree to co-operate in carrying this proposed measure into effect.

The history of the transaction, so far as it is disclosed to this committee, seems to be this: So early as the year 1821 the project of assembling a General Congress of their representatives to consider and adopt the best plan for defending the States of the New World from foreign aggression, and to conclude treaties of alliance, commerce, and friendship for the promotion of their happiness and prosperity, appears to have been conceived by one at least of the new States of America. This scheme of forming a continental system for America, to resemble that already formed in Europe, was communicated to the others of these States, who, concurring in the project, negotiations were instituted between them for the purpose of concluding conventions to provide for this object.

The plan being so far matured the United States were for the first time informally applied to, during the last spring, by the ministers of two of the new States, separately, to learn whether an invitation to be represented at this Congress, if given by both these Republics, would be accepted. To this communication, informally made, the President as informally replied, that he believed such a Congress as was proposed might be highly useful for several purposes, but that, before it assembled, it appeared to him expedient to adjust, between the powers to be represented, several preliminary points, such as the subjects to be discussed, the nature of the powers to be given to the agents who were to compose it, and the mode of its organization and action. And if these preliminary points could be arranged in a manner satisfactory to the United States the ministers to whom this communication was made were informed that the President thought the United States ought to be represented at the contemplated Congress. Each minister undertook to transmit to his Government this answer thus given.

The affair remaining in this posture as to the United States, the negotiations previously entered into between the new States were brought to a close, and conventions providing for the objects of the proposed Congress were actually concluded, some of them so far back as the 6th day of July, 1822.

After the conclusion of all these conventions, and only a few weeks since, during the month of November last, separate formal communications were made to the United States by the ministers of Mexico, Colombia, and Guatemala, respectively, disclosing some of the objects intended to be discussed at the proposed Congress in the manner already stated by the committee, and giving the invitation to the United States to be there represented. In some of these communications the United States were informed that instructions and ample powers for the attainment of the proposed objects would be given by at least one of the new Republics, and a wish was expressed that the agents of all the others might bear the same. In none, however, is any mention made either of the mode of organization or action of the Congress, nor is it anywhere stated who would be the parties, or what representatives were either invited, expected, or would be received. But, in the very communication which conveys the information already stated, the United States are told that at the date of that communication (November 3) the representatives from Colombia, Peru, Guatemala, and Mexico would have arrived at Panama, the agreed place of assembling, and would be engaged in settling the preliminary rules of the assembly, and in discussing the questions which should be supposed by them to belong exclusively to the belligerents.

It thus appears that after everything relative to the meeting of the proposed Congress had been settled by formal negotiations and treaties between themselves, the United States have been thus loosely invited by the other American States, as if in mere courtesy, to attend its deliberations. Should the United States accept such an invitation the deputies whom they may send to Panama will there be associated with they know not whom, or for what purposes, or in what mode. When these deputies shall inquire of the Congress as to any of these important particulars they will receive the information they ask in resolutions and compacts adjusted and concluded before their arrival. And if, waiving all these things, which none ought to consider as mere ceremonials, the agents of the United States shall take the places previously assigned them, and propose to take a part in the discussions, they will find all the leading principal topics for deliberation already passed upon and concluded.

The committee are well aware that the interest and character of free States should never be permitted to rest upon matters of mere fastidious etiquette and ceremonious observance; but even in the intercourse between individuals, and much more in that between sovereignties, there is a point at which form becomes substance, and when scrupulous attention to the most minute ceremonials that comity and respect exact is due to the sacred character and dignity of the Republic. At that point the committee believe the United States should ever make a stand, and resting there, should always exact, even from the most ancient and puissant sovereign of the earth, everything required by their own self respect. Nor should anything be then waived even to manifest their sensibility to whatever concerns the prosperity of the American hemisphere or the sincere friendship which they feel for these new Republics.

As the most ancient State in the New World; the first acknowledged, sincere friend of those more recently existing; as a State from whose greater experience more light is said to be expected to be shed upon the subjects to be discussed and the principles to be established at the contemplated Congress than from the other States, the United States had a right to expect that when this project of a Congress of American nations was conceived, it should have been communicated to them as early as to any others whose presence, by their representatives, was deemed desirable. That they too should have been asked whether such a measure would be acceptable. That they too should have been consulted as to the time the place, and the manner of assembling such a Congress. That they too should have been permitted to assist in the enumeration of the subjects to which its attention might properly be directed; in the adjustment of the nature and form of the powers to be given to the diplomatic agents who were to compose it; in the mode of its organization and action; and, above all others, in the settlement of the great question, who should be invited to take a part in its deliberations. The United States had also a right to expect that the result of all such consultations should be fixed and secured by solemn pacts and conventions, in which they too should be parties.

Such, the committee believe, ought to have been, and would have been the course pursued by the United States, if the project of convening a Congress of American nations had occurred to us as a measure useful and beneficial to the American continent; and being never disposed to exact from others more respect than in like circumstances they are willing themselves to pay, the United States, in the opinion of this committee, owe it to themselves, even if an opinion should be entertained that anything exists requiring the adoption of such a measure at this time, courteously to decline the invitation given under the circumstances stated, and to institute the proper proceedings necessary to its consummation, in the mode which friendship, comity, and deference to others require. Such a movement belongs to the high character which the United States enjoy in the estimation of all the world, the merit of which is accorded to them by none more willingly than by the new born States of this continent; and, if it be not now made, the time will go by when the position may ever hereafter be properly assumed.

The committee would not be understood as suggesting the expediency of any such measure at this time. In their opinion there exists no adequate motive to induce its adoption. Every spot known or habitable in America is already appropriated by different nations, whose rights of territory all recognize; and if trifling differences may exist between any upon the subject of mere common boundary these differences constitute fit matter of friendly discussion between them alone. The idea of colonization in America, therefore, no longer exists; and in the present posture of nations there is little reason to apprehend the willful encroachment of any upon the American possessions of another. Each passing hour strengthens the just claims which the new States of America have preferred to be recognized as sovereign and independent by all other nations; and the quiet efflux of time, if it has not already done so, must very soon place their sovereignty upon the same basis on which rests that of the most ancient nations of the earth. Spain possesses not the ability to give any of them cause of serious concern; and enjoying the friendship and proclaimed recognition of Great Britain and of the United States, there is no sufficient reason to apprehend the interference of any European nation in the question and war of their independence. Compacts have been already concluded, or are now negotiating, between each of the States of this continent, wherein their mutual interests, both general and particular, will be firmly fixed, upon principles of the most perfect justice and liberal equity. And no common subject now remains of sufficient magnitude to require a movement so new and important as the assembling of a Congress of all the American nations, which cannot but excite suspicion and jealousy in the other hemisphere, and might so affect injuriously the interests of the new States themselves.

Should this happy state of things ever change, the lively interest which the United States have ever taken in the welfare of these their sister sovereignties ought to be regarded by them as the surest pledge that we cannot be indifferent to anything that concerns them. An eye the most vigilant we shall ever direct to their prosperity; the appearance of the first cloud, rising to obscure its light, will be announced to them; and the United States will then manifest the deep interest which they feel in the elevation and happiness of all the nations of the New World.

When such an event shall occur the United States will probably be the first to solicit the assembling a Congress of American States, and the invitations which they shall then give to others to be there represented will be such as their friendship and respect shall dictate, and upon terms which the most fair and liberal principles of policy require. The same, this committee have no doubt, would have been the character of the invitation given to the United States upon this occasion, if the new States of America, when they conceived or matured the scheme for assembling the Congress at Panama, had entertained the most remote idea that the United States either would or ought to be there represented. All the conventions concluded between these States, however, prove, beyond doubt, that even at the date of the most recent of all their compacts, none others were expected or desired to be represented at this Congress but the States of America who had formerly been colonies of Spain, and who were then engaged in war with that power; that the great object of this Congress was, to adjust between themselves the most effectual means of conducting this war to the most speedy and happy conclusion; and that the presence of no neutral State could, therefore, be anticipated.

Before they conclude their report, the committee beg leave to remark that the intimation given by the President, in his first message to the Senate, that this measure, in which he had thought proper to take no step before ascertaining that his opinion of its expediency would concur with that of both branches of the Legislature, was, nevertheless, "deemed by him to be within the constitutional competency of the Executive," did not escape their observation. But, as the correctness of this opinion, entertained and expressed by the President, will constitute proper matter for the deliberation and decision of the Senate, when they shall enter upon the consideration of a resolution now lying on their table, and not referred to this committee, they did not believe that they were authorized by the Senate to consider this subject. The committee, therefore, forbear from saying anything in relation thereto.

The committee feel most sensibly the embarrassing situation in which they are placed. On the one hand, the duty which they owe to themselves, and to the Senate, and to the President, required that they should examine fully and freely the measure proposed, and should state the reasons that lead to the conclusion which they felt themselves bound to adopt; on the other, they were well aware that the adoption of this conclusion, and the assignment of the reasons which produced it, might contribute not a little to embarrass the President, whose acceptance of the invitation given was already announced. Placed in this delicate situation, after bestowing upon the subject the most mature consideration—believing it to be a sacred duty, which the Senate owed to the sovereign States that they here represent, to exercise the constitutional power conferred upon them, by examining, at this time, every feature of this new project, and deciding upon its expediency or inexpediency as to them might seem right—the committee could not hesitate to disclose all their views in relation to this important matter, in order that these, being fully exhibited to the Senate, might be by them either adopted or corrected. The committee were induced to adopt this course with less reluctance by the assurance given by the President that, until he could be aided by the advice and consent of the Senate, he would take no step to carry the measure which he had proposed into effect. Most willingly would the committee recommend to the Senate to abstain from pronouncing any opinion upon this now delicate subject, if they could permit themselves to propose to this body a dereliction of its bounden duty, or the adoption of any course that might lead it to shrink from its high responsibility. But, convinced that the Senate had the right, and were bound to decide *directly* upon the expediency of this new scheme, without limiting their decision to the mere nominations incidentally connected with it, and convinced that the project itself, viewed in any light, was highly inexpedient at this time, the committee thought it better to exhibit these their views, and to advise the expression of the opinion of the Senate, in relation thereto, in the first instance. Abstaining, therefore, from any remark at present as to the nominations to them referred, the committee recommend to the Senate the adoption of the following resolution:

Resolved, That it is not expedient, at this time, for the United States to send any ministers to the Congress of American nations, assembled at Panama.

The report and resolution were read.

On motion by Mr. Macon,

Ordered, That the report, with the documents accompanying the message of the 10th instant, be printed, in confidence, for the use of the members.

TUESDAY, JANUARY 24, 1826.

The Senate proceeded to consider the resolution, reported by the Committee on Foreign Relations, in relation to the expediency of sending ministers to the Congress at Panama; and

Ordered, That the further consideration thereof be postponed to, and made the order of the day for, Wednesday, the 1st of February.

MONDAY, JANUARY 30, 1826.

On motion by Mr. Van Buren,

Resolved, That the President of the United States be requested to inform the Senate whether the Government of Spain has been informed of the application made by our Government for the intervention of the Emperor of Russia to induce Spain to recognize the independence of the South American States, and to lay before the Senate the correspondence, if any has taken place, between our minister at Madrid and the Spanish Government, and also between such ministers and our own Government on the subject of such intervention and recognition.

MONDAY, FEBRUARY 2, 1826.

The following message was received from the President of the United States, by Mr. John Adams, jr.:

To the Senate of the United States:
In compliance with a resolution of the Senate of the 30th ultimo, I communicate herewith, in confidence, a report from the Secretary of State, with the documents containing the information desired by the resolution.

JOHN QUINCY ADAMS.

WASHINGTON, *February* 1, 1826.

The Secretary of State, to whom the President has referred the resolution of the Senate of the 30th January, 1826, requesting him to inform the Senate whether the Government of Spain has been informed of the application made by our Government for the intervention of the Emperor of Russia to induce Spain to recognize the independence of the South American States, and to lay before the Senate the correspondence, if any has taken place, between our minister at Madrid and the Spanish Government, and also between such minister and our Government, on the subject of such intervention and recognition, has the honor to report—

An extract of a letter from this Department to Mr. Everett, dated Department of State, April 27, 1825.

An extract from the notes of a conversation between Mr. Everett and Mr. Zea, communicated with a despatch from Mr. Everett to this Department, dated September 25, 1825.

An extract of a despatch from Mr. Everett to this Department of the 20th October, 1825.

All which is respectfully submitted.

H. CLAY.

Extract of a letter from Mr. Clay to Mr. Everett, dated

"DEPARTMENT OF STATE, *April* 27, 1825.

"Besides the preceding objects to which your attention will be directed, others of great interest will also claim it. Of these, that of the highest importance is the present war between Spain and her former colonies on this continent. The President wishes you to bring this subject, in the most conciliating manner possible, before the Spanish Government. It would be as unnecessary as unprofitable to look to the past, except for the purpose of guiding future conduct. True wisdom dictates that Spain, without indulging in unavailing regrets on account of what she has irretrievably lost, should employ the means of retaining what she may yet preserve from the wreck of her former possessions. The war upon the continent is, in fact, at an end. Not a solitary foot of land from the western limit of the United States to Cape Horn owns her sway; not a bayonet in all that vast extent remains to sustain her cause; and the Peninsula is utterly incompetent to replace those armies which have been vanquished and annihilated by the victorious forces of the new Republics. What possible object, then, can remain to Spain to protract a war which she can no longer maintain, and to the conclusion of which, in form, there is only wanting the recognition of the new Governments by treaties of peace? If there were left the most distant prospect of her reconquering her continental provinces, which have achieved their independence, there might be a motive for her perseverance. But every expectation of such reconquest, it is manifest, must be perfectly chimerical. If she can entertain no rational hope to recover what has been forced from her grasp, is there not great danger of her losing what she yet but feebly holds? It should be borne in mind that the armies of the new States, flushed with victory, have no longer employment on the continent; and yet, whilst the war continues, if it be only in name, they cannot be disbanded, without a disregard of all the maxims of just precaution. To what object, then, will the new Republics direct their powerful and victorious armies? They have a common interest and a common enemy; and let it be supposed that that enemy, weak and exhausted as he is, refuses to make peace, will they not strike wherever they can reach? and, from the proximity and great value of Cuba and Porto Rico, is it not to be anticipated that they will aim, and aim a successful blow too, at those Spanish islands? Whilst they would operate from without, means would doubtless be, at the same time, employed to stimulate the population within to a revolt; and that the disposition exists among the inhabitants, to a considerable extent, to throw off the Spanish authority is well known. It is due to the United States to declare that they have constantly declined to give any countenance to that disposition.

"It is not, then, for the new Republics that the President wishes you to urge upon Spain the expediency of concluding the war. Their interest is, probably, on the side of its continuance, if any nation can ever have an interest in a state of war. But it is for Spain herself, for the cause of humanity, for the general repose of the world, that you are required, with all the delicacy which belongs to the subject, to use every topic of persuasion to impress upon the councils of Spain the propriety, by a formal pacification, of terminating the war. And as the views and policy of the United States in regard to those islands may possibly have some influence, you are authorized frankly and fully to disclose them. The United States are satisfied with the present condition of those islands, in the hands of Spain, and with their ports open to our commerce, as they are now open. This Government desires no political change of that condition. The population itself of the islands is incompetent at present, from its composition and its amount, to maintain self-government. The maritime force of the neighboring Republics of Mexico and Colombia is not now, nor is it likely shortly to be, adequate to the protection of those islands, if the conquest of them were effected. The United States would entertain constant apprehension of their passing from their possession to that of some less friendly sovereignty; and of all the European powers, this country prefers that Cuba and Porto Rico should remain dependent on Spain. If the war should continue between Spain and the new Republics, and those islands should become the object and the theatre of it, their fortunes have such a connexion with the prosperity of the United States that they could not be indifferent spectators ; and the possible contingencies of such a protracted war might bring upon the Government of the United States duties and obligations, the performance of which, however painful it should be, they might not be at liberty to decline. A subsidiary consideration in favor of peace, deserving some weight, is, that as the war has been the parent cause of the shocking piracies in the West Indies, its termination would be, probably, followed by their cessation : and thus the Government of Spain, by one act, would fulfil the double obligation under which it lies to foreign Governments, of repressing enormities, the perpetrators of which find refuge, if not succor, in Spanish territory ; and that to the Spanish nation itself of promoting its real interests."

Extract from the notes of a conversation between Mr. Everett and Mr. Zea, communicated with a despatch (No. 7.) from Mr. Everett to Mr. Clay, dated

"MADRID, *September* 25, 1825.

"In the course of this conversation upon matters touching so nearly the independence of the colonies, there were, of course, frequent opportunities of alluding to that question, and the minister seemed to feel no delicacy or reserve in expressing his sentiments upon it. He remarked, repeatedly, that the King would never abandon his claim to these his ancient and rightful possessions ; that the cause was a good one ; and that however unfavorable their prospect might appear at present, they had a right to suppose that they should, in the end, succeed; that we had seen of late revolutions in political affairs at least as violent as this would be—for example, the overthrow of Bonaparte and the restoration of Louis the XVIII to the throne of his ancestors ; that the party in the colonies in favor of independence, though dominant, and apparently unresisted, was not in reality so strong as was generally supposed; that it consisted of a busy and active, but in reality feeble minority; that the mass of the good citizens, constituting a great majority of the population, were in favor of the King, and were only waiting for some suitable occasion to come out in their strength and to put down the insurgents; and, finally, that the cause being a just one, they had a right to suppose that they should be assisted, sooner or later, by an interference of Providence.

"I did not think it necessary to enter very fully into the argument with Mr. Zea. I said to him, however, that I regretted to hear from him so decisive a declaration of the King's resolution not to acknowledge the new States; that my Government had hoped that the battle of Ayacucho, and the recognition of England, would have been considered by his Majesty as settling the question, and that he would have been induced to put an end to the violent state of things now existing, which was more or less injurious to all Christian nations; that enlightened men of all classes, parties, and opinions, in most of the civilized countries of Europe, and in the United States, were now satisfied that Spain could never recover her authority over the colonies. As a single instance, I mentioned to him the opinion of the Bishop of Hermopolis, minister of church affairs in France, and well known throughout Europe as one of the ablest and most decided adherents of the anti-liberal sect, whom I had seen at Paris on my way, and who had told me expressly that they regarded the affair of South America as settled.

"To this he made answer that the Bishop had also, in the time of Bonaparte, despaired of the possibility of the King's restoration, and that he might be as much in the wrong now as he was then. I remarked that there were evident symptoms in the proceedings of the French Government of an intention to recognize the new States at no very distant period. He said that France had hitherto stood by them faithfully in all their troubles; that he could not say how long she would be true to them, but should she even desert them, the King would still adhere firmly to his principles; that the standing and invariable rule of conduct observed by his Majesty upon all occasions was that of strict justice ; that he made no concessions to expediency, acknowledged no distinction between politics and morals, and was prepared to sacrifice everything rather than surrender what he knew to be his right. He then recurred to his favorite example of Louis the XVIII; said that they were by no means reduced to so low a point as he had been; that he, too, often had been solicited to abandon his claims to the French throne; but that, by firmly rejecting all such propositions, and tenaciously adhering to his purpose, he had finally succeeded in recovering everything.

"It struck me that the example of Bonaparte, who had lost all by obstinately refusing to make a timely surrender of a part, would have been rather more to the point; but I did not think it worth while to press this subject at present. I told him that I was not called upon to advise his Majesty's ministers upon this or any other question, and that what I had said had been thrown out incidentally in reply to his remarks."

No. 10.

Extract of a letter from Mr. Everett to the Secretary of State, dated

* MADRID, *October* 20, 1825.

"It was reported here very confidently, a few days ago, that the new Consulative Junta or Council of Government was occupied in preparing the way for an arrangement with the South American States. Upon tracing this rumor to its origin, I found that it arose from the fact that the council had deputed some of its members to confer with two Spanish officers who lately arrived from South America, by way of the Havana and New York, and are the same that were sent out by the Constitutional Government to Buenos Ayres as Commissioners. They landed at Bordeaux from New York, and came on immediately to this place; remained here about three weeks, during which time they had occasional conferences with members of the council, and afterwards proceeded to Cadiz. These facts being known, and it being also understood that the council had been requested by the minister to give their opinion upon the measures proper to be taken in regard to the colonies, it was natural enough to draw the conclusion that the conferences in question had some connexion with this subject, and that the persons with whom they were held might perhaps have gone to Cadiz, on their way to America, as private agents of the Government. Another and a more probable construction of the fact would be, that the council had no other object in conferring with these gentlemen than to obtain information respecting the state of the colonies.

"About the time when this report was in circulation I went to the Escurial, in order to be present at the celebration of the King's birth-day, and when there had, of course, frequent opportunities of seeing the minister. In one of the conversations which I had with him I inquired of him what foundation there was for this rumor, and whether there was any change of policy contemplated in regard to the American States? To this question he replied most decidedly in the negative, and entered anew and very readily, at great length, into an exposition of the intentions of the Government, repeating in substance the same remarks which he had made to me at San Ildefonso. He declared that the King would never abandon his rights; that it was a matter of conscience with him to transmit his hereditary possessions to his successors; that the Royalist cause was not so desperate as we supposed; that there were even now symptoms of a return of these provinces to their ancient loyalty; and that such an event would not be at all strange, considering what violent and sudden revolutions have been constantly occurring during the last thirty years. From all that he said upon the subject I was quite satisfied that the reports of an intended arrangement were entirely groundless, and that the detention and examination of the above mentioned officers were merely for the purpose of obtaining information as to facts.

"The tone and manner of the minister during this conversation were such as to induce me to doubt the correctness of the opinion which I had entertained and expressed to you as to his private sentiments upon this subject. He spoke with so much decision and apparent openness of the probability of reconquering the colonies that I found myself bound to give him credit for his sincerity at the expense of his sagacity and good sense. He inquired of me at this time whether I had any knowledge of the communications that had lately been made by my Government upon that subject to the Emperor of Russia. I replied in the affirmative; and he then said that he had received the day before, for the first time, upon his return to the Escurial from Madrid, an intimation (probably from one of the ministers abroad) that some overtures had been made in that quarter, and requested me to give him such information respecting them as I might think it proper to communicate. I was not quite so fully prepared upon this subject myself as I could have wished, not having obtained any answer from Mr. King to the request which I made him for a copy of the instructions to Mr. Middleton, probably because he has had no good private occasion to send it. I, however, told him that my Government made no secret of their policy in regard to this business, and that I had no objection to inform him that our minister at St. Petersburg had been directed to express to the Emperor their full conviction that the contest between Spain and the colonies must be considered as finally settled in favor of the latter party; their persuasion that the interest of Spain and the general good of the civilized world would be promoted by the early acquiescence of his Catholic Majesty in this result, and their wish that the Emperor, should he also entertain these opinions, would unite with them in advising and requesting the Spanish Government to put an end to the war by an acknowledgment of the independence of the colonies. I took this opportunity of informing the minister, more precisely than I had done before, that what I had already suggested to him in favor of this measure must be considered as expressing the wishes and policy of my Government, and not my own individual sentiments, which I should not, of course, think of intruding upon his Majesty's cabinet. I told him that I was formally instructed to avail myself of any suitable occasion to suggest to him, with the delicacy required by the nature of the subject, the earnest desire of the Government of the United States to see this long struggle brought to an amicable conclusion, and their complete conviction that all further efforts on the part of Spain to recover the colonies must be wholly fruitless, and more injurious to herself than to them.

"Mr. Zea seemed to be a good deal struck with these remarks, and I was inclined to suppose, from his manner, that he had considered what I had said to him before upon the subject as a merely personal communication. He replied, that these proceedings of the Government of the United States placed him under the necessity of declaring, in the most positive manner, the King's unalterable resolution never to abandon his rights, and to reject all offers of mediation, or of amicable intervention, which should contemplate an acknowledgment of the independence of the new States. He said that they were, and always had been, ready and willing to accept any proposal for mediation, or to treat directly with the colonies, upon the basis of their previous submission to the King's sovereign power, but that they would never consent to negotiate in any way upon any other terms; that the King, being once satisfied on this head, would doubtless be disposed to grant his subjects in America every favor and indulgence which they could possibly wish, but that they must begin by proving their loyalty, and their confidence in his Majesty's justice and good intentions. He wondered that, among the offers of mediation that had been made from time to time, especially by England, none had ever been proposed upon this basis. I told him that the reason probably was, that the British Government, as well as that of the United States, considered the independence of the new States as now firmly established, and were well aware that they would never treat upon any other terms than an acknowledgment of it by Spain. I added, however, that I should be well pleased to know, if he were disposed to inform me, what concessions the King would be willing to grant to the Americans in the event of their return to their allegiance: as, for example, whether he would allow them to make their own laws in legislative assemblies of their own choice? My object in asking this question was, of course, merely to obtain a more complete view of the intentions and dispositions of the Government upon the whole subject. He replied that, as to legislative assemblies, he was far from being satisfied that they would suit the condition of the colonies, and that, in general, he thought the only safe course for the Americans would be to trust entirely and implicitly to the King's known good character. I should have thought from this answer that my question did not make a very favorable impression upon him. At the close, however, of the conversation, he recurred to it in such a way as induced me to think that he would have been glad to consider it as an indirect overture from some of the colonies. He said, after I arose to go, that the conversation had turned upon a number of delicate and interesting topics; that on such occasions it was not always possible to distinguish between remarks that were merely of a private and personal description and such as were official; and that in order to avoid mistakes upon that point, he should be glad if I would state, in writing, what my instructions required me to communicate to him as the opinions and intentions of the Government, and especially any propositions that I might be authorized to make, in the nature of an overture from the colonies, founded on the basis of submission. I told him that I had no authority from any quarter to make propositions of that description, but that I would, with pleasure, if he wished it, give him an official statement of what I had said to him, by order of my Government, in favor of the acknowledgment of the independence of the new States. He replied that he was ready to receive any note that I might send him, but that on that head the King's mind was completely made up beyond the possibility of change. Notwithstanding this, I have thoughts of preparing and transmitting to the minister a pretty detailed communication upon this subject. Such a paper, if it does not produce much immediate effect upon the Spanish cabinet, may, perhaps, in one way or another, have a favorable bearing on the general question.

"Previously to this interview with Mr. Zea I had availed myself of such occasions as offered to converse upon the same subject with the British and Russian ministers. The former is Mr. Frederick Lamb, brother of Lord Melbourne, a gentleman of about forty-five years of age, regularly trained to the diplomatic line, and apparently well fitted for it by his talents and information. The latter is Mr. D'Oubril, who has also passed his life in the employment of a foreign minister, and has now reached the age of about sixty. He seems to enjoy the confidence of his Government, and last year took the place of Count Nesselrode, as Minister of Foreign Affairs, during an absence of the latter from St. Petersburg, which lasted several months. Both these gentlemen have shown, since my arrival here, every disposition to be on friendly terms with me, and have plainly manifested, by their attentions, the high esteem in which they hold the American nation and character. Mr. D'Oubril, in particular, has been more civil than any other of the diplomatic body with whom I was not previously acquainted.

"Mr. Lamb's sentiments in regard to the South American question are, of course, precisely the same with ours. I was desirous to ascertain whether the British Government had lately made any attempts to urge Spain to a recognition of the new States, and questioned Mr. Lamb upon this point. He said he had had one or two conversations with Mr. Zea soon after his arrival, (he has been here about five months,) and stated the substance of what had passed between them. The minister, it seems, gave to him the same answer which he has since given to me, and cited, to illustrate his argument, the same examples of Louis XVIII and Bonaparte. No offer of formal mediation has been made by England since her recognition. Indeed, her interest as a commercial and manufacturing country is now on the other side. The longer the war continues, the longer she enjoys a monopoly of the Spanish American market for her fabrics, and the more difficult will Spain find it to recover her natural advantages upon the return of peace. England will, therefore, probably be very easy in regard to this matter, and will leave Spain to pursue, unmolested, the course she may think expedient. I suggested this point both to Mr. Zea and to the Russian minister, and was inclined to think, from what they said of it, that it had more weight with them than any other consideration in favor of recognition. They both admitted the justice of my remarks, and the great inconvenience that resulted in this way from the present state of things, and could only avoid the proper conclusion, by reverting to their common places, of the probability of a return of the colonies to their allegiance, which they really seem to imagine will come about sooner or later, without any effort on the part of either Spain or her allies, and by the aid of some unlooked-for intervention of Divine Providence. I learned nothing material from Mr. L., excepting the fact that the British Government is now quiet in regard to this matter, and makes no attempts to influence the decision of Spain. He professed to have but little information as to the state of the Spanish settlements in America, and having passed the greater part of his life, including the last eight or ten years, on the continent, has been, in fact, rather out of the way of obtaining it.

"Mr. D'Oubril was somewhat guarded in his language, and did not seem quite willing to admit that it was the decided intention of the Emperor to encourage Spain in her present system. He said that, individually, he did not by any means take the same view of the subject which the Spanish Government did, and yet that he was not completely satisfied that an immediate recognition was the true policy. He cited, in his turn, the old instance of Louis XVIII and Bonaparte, and was far from being sure that the internal divisions which did or would distract the colonies might not bring them again under the Spanish Government. He was aware, nevertheless, that Spain was daily and yearly suffering great injury from the effects of the present system, and that, by continuing it, she would probably lose her remaining possessions in America, and her chance of ever obtaining a due share in the trade with that continent, besides endangering her national existence at home. This was making out a pretty strong case in favor of recognition, but he still returned to his former text, that he considered the question as extremely doubtful. In all that he said upon it he professed to declare merely his own personal opinions and feelings, and, if I recollect right, did not say directly what language he was ordered to hold in his communications with this Government. It is understood, however, that the influence of the Emperor has been employed in support of the present system; and the general impression which I received from his remarks coincided with this opinion. Mr. D'Oubril's private sentiments may possibly be different. Both he and Mr. L. inquired of me respecting the late overtures made by the President's order at St. Petersburg, and appeared to have some, though not a very minute acquaintance with the language of your instructions to Mr. Middleton. The representatives of France, Holland, Sweden, Saxony, and Prussia, with whom I have had more or less conversation upon this subject, have all expressed themselves strongly in opposition to the policy of Spain. Even the Pope's Nuncio and the ambassador from Naples seem to be of the American party. The French, I suspect, are making pretty strong efforts in favor of the new States, but on this point I have, at present, no very precise information."

The message and accompanying documents were read.
Ordered, That they be printed, in confidence, for the use of the members.

MONDAY, February 6, 1826.

Agreeably to the order of the day, the Senate resumed the consideration of the resolution reported by the Committee on Foreign Relations, relative to the expediency of sending ministers to the Congress at Panama.
On motion by Mr. White,
That the resolution lie on the table,

It was determined in the affirmative—yeas 23, nays 22.

On motion by Mr. Harrison,

The yeas and nays being desired by one-fifth of the Senators present,

Those who voted in the affirmative are—

Messrs. Benton, Berrien, Branch, Chandler, Cobb, Dickerson, Eaton, Ellis, Findlay, Hayne, Holmes, Johnson, of Kentucky, Kane, King, Macon, Randolph, Rowan, Smith, Tazewell, Van Buren, White, Williams, Woodbury—23.

Those who voted in the negative are—

Messrs. Barton, Bell, Bouligny, Chase, Clayton, Edwards, Harrison, Hendricks, Johnston, Louis, Knight, Lloyd, McIlvaine, Marks, Mills, Noble, Robbins, Ruggles, Sanford, Seymour, Thomas, Van Dyke, Willey—22.

THURSDAY, February 9, 1826.

On motion by Mr. Mills,

That the Senate resume the consideration of the resolution, reported by the Committee on Foreign Relations, relative to the expediency of sending ministers to the Congress at Panama.

A debate ensued; and

On motion by Mr. Lloyd,

The Senate adjourned.

WEDNESDAY, February 15, 1826.

Mr. Mills had leave to withdraw the motion submitted on the 9th instant, that the Senate resume the consideration of the resolution relative to the expediency of sending ministers to the Congress at Panama.

Mr. Van Buren submitted the following resolutions :

Resolved, That, upon the question whether the United States shall be represented in the Congress of Panama, the Senate ought to act with open doors, unless it shall appear that the publication of documents necessary to be referred to in debate will be prejudicial to existing negotiations.

Resolved, That the President be respectfully requested to inform the Senate whether such objection exists to the publication of the documents communicated by the Executive, or any portion of them; and, if so, to specify the parts the publication of which would, for that reason, be objectionable.

On the question to agree thereto.

It was determined in the affirmative—yeas 23, nays 20.

The yeas and nays being desired by one-fifth of the senators present,

Those who voted in the affirmative are—

Messrs. Benton, Berrien, Branch, Chandler, Cobb, Dickerson, Eaton, Ellis, Harrison, Hayne, Hendricks, Holmes, Johnson, of Kentucky, Kane, King, Macon, Randolph, Rowan, Ruggles, Van Buren, White, Williams, Woodbury.

Those who voted in the negative are—

Messrs. Barton, Bell, Bouligny, Chase, Clayton, Edwards, Findlay, Johnston, of Louisiana, Knight, Lloyd, McIlvaine, Marks, Mills, Noble, Robbins, Sanford, Seymour, Thomas, Van Dyke, Willey.

Ordered, That the Secretary lay the said resolutions before the President of the United States.

FRIDAY, February 17, 1826.

The following message was received from the President of the United States, by Mr. John Adams, jr.:

To the Senate of the United States:

In answer to the two resolutions of the Senate of the 15th instant, marked Executive, and which I have received, I state, respectfully, that all the communications from me to the Senate relating to the Congress at Panama have been made, like all other communications upon Executive business, in *confidence*, and most of them in compliance with a resolution of the Senate requesting them confidentially. Believing that the established usage of free confidential communications between the Executive and the Senate ought, for the public interest, to be preserved unimpaired, I deem it my indispensable duty to leave to the Senate itself the decision of a question involving a departure hitherto, so far as I am informed, without example, from that usage, and upon the motives for which, not being informed of them, I do not feel myself competent to decide.

JOHN QUINCY ADAMS.

Washington, *February* 16, 1826.

The message was read.

On motion, by Mr. Van Buren,

Ordered, That the said message, with the resolutions therein referred to, be printed, in confidence, for the use of the Senate.

Mr. Berrien submitted the following motion:

Resolved, That the communication of the President of the United States, in answer to the resolutions of the Senate of the 15th instant, and the said resolutions, be referred to a select committee, with instructions to report what is the usage of the Senate in relation to the publication of Executive communications, and the documents accompanying such communications. And that they be further instructed to report whether the publication of the documents necessary to be referred to in debate on the report of the Committee on Foreign Relations on the message of the President of the United States nominating ministers to the Congress at Panama will be prejudicial to existing negotiations, and to specify the parts, if any, the publication of which will be so prejudicial.

The Senate proceeded to consider the motion.

On motion, by Mr. Noble,

It was agreed that when the question be taken, it be by yeas and nays.

On motion by Mr. Sanford,

The Senate adjourned.

MONDAY, February 20, 1826.

The Senate resumed the consideration of the motion submitted on the 17th instant by Mr. Berrien, and
On his motion,
Ordered, That it lie on the table.

Mr. Rowan submitted the following motion :

Resolved, That it is the unquestionable right of the Senate to call, in respectful terms, upon the
President of the United States for such information as may be in his possession, and which the Senate
deem necessary to the faithful discharge of the duties imposed upon it by the Constitution; and, more
especially, the duties resulting from matters which the Constitution makes it the duty of the President
to submit to the Senate for their advice and consent.

Resolved, That the two following resolutions of the 15th instant, viz: "Resolved, That, upon the
question whether the United States shall be represented in the Congress at Panama, the Senate ought to
act with open doors, unless it shall appear that the publication of documents necessary to be referred to
in debate will be prejudicial to existing negotiations;" "Resolved, That the President be respectfully
requested to inform the Senate whether such objection exists to the publication of the documents communicated by the Executive, or any portion of them; and, if so, to specify the parts the publication of
which would, for that reason, be objectionable"—requested information in the possession of the Executive, and in his possession only, which the Senate deemed important to guide its decision on a subject
within the scope of its advising powers, and deeply interesting to the States and to the people of this
Union.

Resolved, That the Senate regret that they do not perceive in the President's message of the seventeenth
either a compliance with the call made by its resolutions of the fifteenth instant or the assignment of any
reason for withholding the same: Therefore,

Resolved, That the Senate cannot, consistently with a proper regard for its constitutional rights, nor
without a manifest dereliction of the duties which it owes to the States and the people of the United
States, proceed further to consider the subject, in any aspect of it, to which the call upon the President
for information relates, until he shall have afforded the information, or assigned some satisfactory reason
for withholding it.

The Senate proceeded to consider the motion.

Mr. Holmes proposed the following amendment:

Strike out the two last resolutions, and insert the following:

Resolved, That, as the Senate have not been able to learn from the President whether the publication
of the documents in relation to the proposed mission to the Congress at Panama would affect any pending
negotiations, it is expedient to proceed to the discussion of the subject of that mission with closed doors.

On motion by Mr. Smith,
The Senate adjourned.

TUESDAY, February 21, 1826.

The Senate resumed the consideration of the motion submitted yesterday by Mr. Rowan, together
with the amendment proposed by Mr. Holmes.

Mr. Holmes had leave to withdraw his amendment.

On motion by Mr. Hayne,
The Senate adjourned.

WEDNESDAY, February 22, 1826.

The Senate resumed the consideration of the motion submitted by Mr. Rowan on the 20th instant;
and the same having been modified, at the instance of Mr. Woodbury, as follows:

Resolved, That it is the unquestionable right of the Senate to call, in respectful terms, upon the
President of the United States for such information as may be in his possession, and which the Senate
deem necessary to the faithful discharge of the duties imposed upon it by the Constitution, and, more
especially, the duties resulting from matters which the Constitution makes it the duty of the President to
submit to the Senate for its advice and consent.

Resolved, That the two following resolutions, of the 15th instant, viz: "Resolved, That, upon the question whether the United States shall be represented in the Congress of Panama, the Senate ought to act
with open doors, unless it shall appear that the publication of documents necessary to be referred to in
debate will be prejudicial to existing negotiations;" "Resolved, That the President be respectfully requested
to inform the Senate whether such objection exists to the publication of the documents communicated by
the Executive, or any portion of them; and, if so, to specify the parts the publication of which would, for
that reason, be objectionable"—requested information in the possession of the Executive, and in his
possession only, which the Senate deemed important to guide its decision on a subject within the scope of
its advising powers, and deeply interesting to the States and to the people of this Union.

Resolved, That the message of the President, in the following words, viz: "In answer to the two
resolutions of the Senate of the 15th instant, marked (Executive,) and which I have received, I state,
respectfully, that all the communications from me to the Senate relating to the Congress at Panama have
been made, like all other communications upon Executive business, in confidence, and most of them in
compliance with a resolution of the Senate requesting them confidentially. Believing that the established
usage of free confidential communications between the Executive and the Senate ought, for the public
interest, to be preserved unimpaired, I deem it my indispensable duty to leave to the Senate itself the
decision of a question involving a departure hitherto, so far as I am informed, without example, from that
usage, and upon the motives for which, not being informed of them, I do not feel myself competent to
decide," does not give to the Senate the information requested, "whether the publication of the documents," or "any portion of them," communicated by the Executive, as to the mission to Panama, "would
be prejudicial to existing negotiations."

Resolved, That the Senate has the sole right, in all cases, to determine what shall be the "rules of its
proceedings;" and that the President cannot interfere with the same without violating the constitutional
privileges of the Senate.

Resolved, That the Senate has the sole right to determine what are its existing "rules of proceedings," whether founded on "usage" or positive written regulations; and that the President cannot officially decide what those rules are, or whether any proposed mode of acting is a "departure" from them "without example," or whether it is essential to the "public interest" that some supposed "usage" of the Senate should be "preserved unimpaired."

Resolved, That it is not competent for the President, on a call from the Senate, to decline giving information whether "the publication of documents necessary to be referred to in debate will be prejudicial to existing negotiations," on the ground that he disapproves of the mode of proceeding which the Senate proposes to follow on the subject to which those documents relate.

On motion by Mr. Barton, to postpone the same indefinitely, a division of the question was called for.

On the question to postpone indefinitely the *first* resolution,

It was decided in the affirmative—yeas 24, nays 20.

On motion by Mr. Cobb,

The yeas and nays being desired by one-fifth of the Senators present,

Those who voted in the affirmative are—.

Messrs. Barton, Bell, Bouligny, Chambers, Chase, Clayton, Edwards, Harrison, Hendricks, Holmes, Johnston, of Louisiana, Knight, Lloyd, Marks, Mills, Noble, Robbins, Ruggles, Sanford, Seymour, Smith, Thomas, Van Dyke, Willey—24.

Those who voted in the negative are—

Messrs. Benton, Berrien, Branch, Chandler, Cobb, Dickerson, Eaton, Ellis, Findlay, Hayne, Johnson, of Kentucky, Kane, King, Macon, Randolph, Rowan, Van Buren, White, Williams, Woodbury—20.

On the question to postpone indefinitely the second resolution,

It was determined in the affirmative—yeas 24, nays 20.

The yeas and nays being desired by one-fifth of the Senators present,

Those who voted in the affirmative are—

Messrs. Barton, Bell, Bouligny, Chambers, Chase, Clayton, Edwards, Harrison, Hendricks, Holmes, Johnston, of Louisiana, Knight, Lloyd, Marks, Mills, Noble, Robbins, Ruggles, Sanford, Seymour, Smith, Thomas, Van Dyke, Willey—24.

Those who voted in the negative are—

Messrs. Benton, Berrien, Branch, Chandler, Cobb, Dickerson, Eaton, Ellis, Findlay, Hayne, Johnson, of Kentucky, Kane, King, Macon, Randolph, Rowan, Van Buren, White, Williams, Woodbury—20.

On the question to postpone indefinitely the *third* resolution,

It was determined in the affirmative—yeas 24, nays 20.

The yeas and nays being desired by one-fifth of the Senators present,

Those who voted in the affirmative are—.

Messrs. Barton, Bell, Bouligny, Chambers, Chase, Clayton, Edwards, Harrison, Hendricks, Holmes, Johnston, of Louisiana, Knight, Lloyd, Marks, Mills, Noble, Robbins, Ruggles, Sanford, Seymour, Smith, Thomas, Van Dyke, Willey—24.

Those who voted in the negative are—

Messrs. Benton, Berrien, Branch, Chandler, Cobb, Dickerson, Eaton, Ellis, Findlay, Hayne, Johnson, of Kentucky, Kane, King, Macon, Randolph, Rowan, Van Buren, White, Williams, Woodbury—20.

On the question to postpone indefinitely the *fourth* resolution,

It was determined in the affirmative—yeas 24, nays 20.

The yeas and nays being desired by one-fifth of the Senators present,

Those who voted in the affirmative are—

Messrs. Barton, Bell, Bouligny, Chambers, Chase, Clayton, Edwards, Harrison, Hendricks, Holmes, Johnston, of Louisiana, Knight, Lloyd, Marks, Mills, Noble, Robbins, Ruggles, Sanford, Seymour, Smith, Thomas, Van Dyke, Willey—24.

Those who voted in the negative are—

Messrs. Benton, Berrien, Branch, Chandler, Cobb, Dickerson, Eaton, Ellis, Findlay, Hayne, Johnson, of Kentucky, Kane, King, Macon, Randolph, Rowan, Van Buren, White, Williams, Woodbury—20.

On the question to postpone indefinitely the *fifth* resolution,

It was determined in the affirmative—yeas 24, nays 20.

The yeas and nays being desired by one-fifth of the Senators present,

Those who voted in the affirmative are—

Messrs. Barton, Bell, Bouligny, Chambers, Chase, Clayton, Edwards, Harrison, Hendricks, Holmes, Johnston, of Louisiana, Knight, Lloyd, Marks, Mills, Noble, Robbins, Ruggles, Sanford, Seymour, Smith, Thomas, Van Dyke, Willey—24.

Those who voted in the negative are—

Messrs. Benton, Berrien, Branch, Chandler, Cobb, Dickerson, Eaton, Ellis, Findlay, Hayne, Johnson, of Kentucky, Kane, King, Macon, Randolph, Rowan, Van Buren, White, Williams, Woodbury—20.

On the question to postpone indefinitely the *sixth* resolution,

It was determined in the affirmative—yeas 24, nays 20.

The yeas and nays being desired by one-fifth of the Senators present, .

Those who voted in the affirmative are—

Messrs. Barton, Bell, Bouligny, Chambers, Chase, Clayton, Edwards, Harrison, Hendricks, Holmes, Johnston, of Louisiana, Knight, Lloyd, Marks, Mills, Noble, Robbins, Ruggles, Sanford, Seymour, Smith, Thomas, Van Dyke, Willey—24.

Those who voted in the negative are—

Messrs. Benton, Berrien, Branch, Chandler, Cobb, Dickerson, Eaton, Ellis, Findlay, Hayne, Johnson, of Kentucky, Kane, King, Macon, Randolph, Rowan, Van Buren, White, Williams, Woodbury—20.

Mr. Holmes submitted the following motion:

Resolved, That the Senate having, on the 15th day of February, passed the following resolutions:

"*Resolved*, That, upon the question whether the United States shall be represented in the Congress of Panama, the Senate ought to act with open doors, unless it shall appear that the publication of documents necessary to be referred to in debate will be prejudicial to existing negotiations.

"*Resolved*, That the President be respectfully requested to inform the Senate whether such objection exists to the publication of the documents communicated by the Executive, or any portion of them; and, if so, to specify the parts the publication of which would, for that reason, be objectionable."

To which the President returned the following message in answer, viz:

" *To the Senate of the United States:*

" " In answer to the two resolutions of the Senate of the 15th instant, marked 'Executive,' and which I have received, I state respectfully that all communications from me to the Senate relating to the Congress at Panama have been made, like all other communications upon Executive business, in *confidence*, and most of them in compliance with a resolution of the Senate requesting them confidentially. Believing that the established usage of free confidential communications between the Executive and the Senate ought, for the public interest, to be preserved unimpaired, I deem it my indispensable duty to leave to the Senate itself the decision' of a question involving a departure hitherto, so far as I am informed, without example, from that usage, and upon the motives for which, not being informed of them, I do not feel myself competent to decide.

                                        "JOHN QUINCY ADAMS.

" Washington, *February* 15, 1826."

Resolved, That as the Senate have not been informed by the President whether the publication of the documents in relation to the proposed mission to the Congress at Panama would affect any pending negotiations, it is expedient to proceed to the discussion of the subject of that mission with closed doors.
      On motion by Mr. King,
   The Senate adjourned.

THURSDAY, February 23, 1826.

    The Senate resumed the consideration of the motion submitted yesterday by Mr. Holmes, in relation to the proposed mission to the Congress at Panama.
    On motion by Mr. Dickerson, to amend the same by striking out all after the word "*Resolved,*" where it first occurs, and inserting in lieu thereof the following:
    Resolved, That although the Senate cannot find in the answer of the President of the United States to their resolutions of the 15th instant, relative to the proposed mission to Panama, any distinct information that the publication of the communications alluded to in said resolutions would or would not be prejudicial to existing negotiations, they find a strong objection on the part of the President to the publication of those communications, inasmuch as they were made "in confidence, and most of them in compliance with a resolution of the Senate requesting them confidentially." And although the Senate have the right to publish communications so made, and to discuss the same with open doors, without the assent of the President, when in their opinion the public interest may require such publication and such discussion, they do not think that present circumstances require the exercise of this right, so far as respects a discussion of those confidential communications with open doors. Therefore,
    Resolved, That the discussion upon the proposed mission to Panama and the confidential communications upon the same be held with closed doors.
    A motion was made by Mr. Lloyd to postpone indefinitely the original motion; and
    It was determined in the negative—yeas 15, nays 29.
    The yeas and nays being desired by one-fifth of the Senators present,
    Those who voted in the affirmative are—
    Messrs. Bouligny, Branch, Chambers, Chase, Edwards, Johnston, of Louisiana, King, Knight, Lloyd, Mills, Sanford, Smith, Van Dyke, White, Willey—15.
    Those who voted in the negative are—
    Messrs. Barton, Bell, Benton, Berrien, Chandler, Clayton, Cobb, Dickerson, Eaton, Ellis, Findlay, Harrison, Hayne, Hendricks, Holmes, Johnson, of Kentucky, Kane, Macon, Marks, Noble, Randolph, Robbins, Rowan, Ruggles, Seymour, Thomas, Van Buren, Williams, Woodbury—29.
    On motion by Mr. White, to amend the proposed amendment by striking out the following words:
    "*Resolved,* That the discussion upon the proposed mission to Panama and the confidential communications upon the same be held with closed doors," and inserting, "*Resolved,* That the Senate cannot, consistently with the duty which it owes to the United States and to itself, proceed to consider the expediency of appointing ministers to attend the Congress at Panama until it can receive the information necessary to enable it to determine whether the consideration of that question ought to be with open or with closed doors."
    On the question, "Will the Senate agree to this amendment to the proposed amendment," a division of the question was called for; and it was taken on *striking out*, and determined in the affirmative—yeas 27, nays 17.
    On motion by Mr. Cobb, the yeas and nays being desired by one-fifth of the Senators present,
    Those who voted in the affirmative are—
    Messrs. Bell, Benton, Berrien, Branch, Chase, Cobb, Eaton, Edwards, Ellis, Findlay, Harrison, Hayne, Holmes, Johnson, of Kentucky, King, Macon, Mills, Randolph, Rowan, Ruggles, Sanford, Seymour, Thomas, Van Buren, White, Williams, Woodbury—27.
    Those who voted in the negative are—
    Messrs. Barton, Bouligny, Chambers, Chandler, Clayton, Dickerson, Hendricks, Johnston, of Louisiana, Kane, Knight, Lloyd, Marks, Noble, Robbins, Smith, Van Dyke, Willey—17.
    On the question to insert the amendment last proposed, it was determined in the negative—yeas 13, nays 31.
    The yeas and nays being desired by one-fifth of the Senators present,
    Those who voted in the affirmative are—
    Messrs. Berrien, Cobb, Eaton, Ellis, Hayne, King, Macon, Randolph, Rowan, Van Buren, White, Williams, Woodbury—13.
    Those who voted in the negative are—
    Messrs. Barton, Bell, Benton, Bouligny, Branch, Chambers, Chandler, Chase, Clayton, Dickerson, Edwards, Findlay, Harrison, Hendricks, Holmes, Johnson, of Kentucky, Johnston, of Louisiana, Kane, Knight, Lloyd, Marks, Mills, Noble, Robbins, Ruggles, Sanford, Seymour, Smith, Thomas, Van Dyke, Willey—31.
    The question recurring on the adoption of the amendment first proposed to the original motion, amended by striking out the last clause:

On the question, "Will the Senate agree to this amendment?" a division of the question was called for; and,

On the question to *strike out* all the original motion after the word "*Resolved,*" where it first occurs, it was determined in the affirmative—yeas 31, nays 13.

The yeas and nays being desired by one-fifth of the Senators present,

Those who voted in the affirmative are—

· Messrs. Barton, Benton, Berrien, Branch, Chambers, Chandler, Cobb, Dickerson, Eaton, Edwards, Ellis, Findlay, Hayne, Hendricks, Johnson, of Kentucky, Kane, King, Macon, Marks, Mills, Randolph, Robbins, Rowan, Ruggles, Sanford, Van Buren, Van Dyke, White, Willey, Williams, Woodbury—31.

Those who voted in the negative are—

Messrs. Bell, Bouligny, Chase, Clayton, Harrison, Holmes, Johnson, of Louisiana, Knight, Lloyd, Noble, Seymour, Smith, Thomas—13.

On the question to insert the proposed amendment, it was determined in the affirmative—yeas 27, nays 16.

The yeas and nays being desired by one-fifth of the Senators present,

Those who voted in the affirmative are—

Messrs. Barton, Benton, Berrien, Bouligny, Chandler, Clayton, Cobb, Dickerson, Findlay, Harrison, Hayne, Hendricks, Holmes, Johnson, of Kentucky, Kane, King, Marks, Randolph, Robbins, Rowan, Ruggles, Seymour, Smith, Van Buren, Willey, Williams, Woodbury—27.

Those who voted in the negative are—

Messrs. Branch, Chambers, Chase, Eaton, Edwards, Ellis, Johnston, of Louisiana, Knight, Lloyd, Macon, Mills, Noble, Sanford, Thomas, Van Dyke, White—16.

So it was

Resolved, That although the Senate cannot find in the answer of the President of the United States to their resolutions of the 15th instant, relative to the proposed mission to Panama, any distinct information that the publication of the communications alluded to in said resolutions would not be prejudicial to existing negotiations, they find a strong objection on the part of the President to the publication of those communications, inasmuch as they were made "in confidence, and most of them in compliance with a resolution of the Senate requesting them confidentially." And although the Senate have the right to publish communications so made, and to discuss the same with open doors, without the assent of the President, when, in their opinion, the public interest may require such publication and such discussion, they do not think that present circumstances require the exercise of this right so far as respects a discussion of those confidential communications with open doors.

On motion by Mr. Randolph,

Ordered, That the motion submitted by Mr. Rowan, as modified on the 21st instant, relating to the mission at Panama, and the resolution of this day, be printed, in confidence, for the use of the members.

FRIDAY, FEBRUARY 24, 1826.

On motion by Mr. Lloyd, that the Senate proceed to consider the resolution reported by the Committee on Foreign Relations, in relation to the expediency of sending ministers to the Congress of Panama, it was determined in the affirmative—yeas 32, nays 12.

The yeas and nays being desired by one-fifth of the Senators present,

Those who voted in the affirmative are—

Messrs. Barton, Bell, Benton, Bouligny, Branch, Chambers, Chandler, Chase, Clayton, Dickerson, Edwards, Findlay, Harrison, Hendricks, Holmes, Johnson, of Louisiana, Johnston, of Louisiana, Kane, Knight, Lloyd, Marks, Mills, Noble, Robbins, Ruggles, Sanford, Seymour, Smith, Thomas, Van Dyke, Willey—32.

Those who voted in the negative are—

Messrs. Berrien, Cobb, Eaton, Ellis, Hayne, Macon, Randolph, Rowan, Van Buren, White, Williams, Woodbury—12.

On motion by Mr. Hayne,

Ordered, That the further consideration of the resolution be postponed to, and made the order of the day for, Monday next.

WEDNESDAY, MARCH 1, 1826.

Agreeably to the order of the day, the Senate resumed the consideration of the resolution reported by the Committee on Foreign Relations, in relation to the expediency of sending ministers to the Congress at Panama; and, after debate,

On motion by Mr. Randolph,

The Senate adjourned.

THURSDAY, MARCH 2, 1826.

The Senate resumed the consideration of the resolution reported by the Committee on Foreign Relations, in relation to the expediency of sending ministers to the Congress at Panama.

On motion by Mr. Holmes,

It was agreed that when the question be taken, it be by yeas and nays.

On motion by Mr. Chandler,

The Senate adjourned.

FRIDAY, MARCH 3, 1826.

The Senate resumed the consideration of the resolution reported by the Committee on Foreign Relations, in relation to the expediency of sending ministers to the Congress at Panama; and, after debate,

On motion by Mr. King,

The Senate adjourned.

MONDAY, March 6, 1826.

The Senate resumed the consideration of the resolution reported by the Committee on Foreign Relations, in relation to the expediency of sending ministers to the Congress at Panama; and, after debate,
On motion by Mr. Dickerson,
The Senate adjourned.

TUESDAY, March 7, 1826.

The Senate resumed the consideration of the resolution reported by the Committee on Foreign Relations, in relation to the expediency of sending ministers to the Congress at Panama; and, after debate,
On motion by Mr. Van Buren,
The Senate adjourned.

THURSDAY, March 9, 1826.

The Senate resumed the consideration of the resolution reported by the Committee on Foreign Relations, relative to the expediency of sending ministers to the Congress at Panama; and, after debate,
Ordered, That it lie on the table.

FRIDAY, March 10, 1826.

The Senate resumed the consideration of the resolution reported by the Committee on Foreign Relations, relative to the expediency of sending ministers to the Congress at Panama; and, after debate,
On motion by Mr. Chandler, that the Senate adjourn,
It was determined in the negative—yeas 21, nays 23.
On motion by Mr. Noble,
The yeas and nays being desired by one-fifth of the Senators present,
Those who voted in the affirmative are—
Messrs. Benton, Berrien, Branch, Chandler, Cobb, Dickerson, Eaton, Ellis, Findlay, Hayne, Holmes, Johnson, of Kentucky, Kane, King, Macon, Randolph, Rowan, Van Buren, White, Williams, Woodbury—21.
Those who voted in the negative are—
Messrs. Barton, Bell, Bouligny, Chambers, Chase, Clayton, Edwards, Harrison, Hendricks, Johnston, of Louisiana, Knight, Lloyd, Mark, Mills, Noble, Robbins, Ruggles, Sanford, Seymour, Smith, Thomas, Van Dyke, Willey—23.
On motion by Mr. Dickerson,
The Senate adjourned.

SATURDAY, March 11, 1826.

The Senate resumed the consideration of the resolution reported by the Committee on Foreign Relations, relative to the expediency of sending ministers to the Congress at Panama; and, after debate,
On motion by Mr. Dickerson, that the Senate adjourn,
It was determined in the affirmative—yeas 23, nays 21.
On motion by Mr. Bell,
The yeas and nays being desired by one-fifth of the Senators present,
Those who voted in the affirmative are—
Messrs. Benton, Berrien, Branch, Chandler, Cobb, Dickerson, Eaton, Findlay, Hayne, Holmes, Johnson, of Kentucky, Johnston, of Louisiana, Kane, King, Macon, Randolph, Reed, Rowan, Van Buren, White, Williams, Woodbury—23.
Those who voted in the negative are—
Messrs. Barton, Bell, Chambers, Chase, Clayton, Edwards, Harrison, Hendricks, Knight, Lloyd, Marks, Mills, Noble, Robbins, Ruggles, Sanford, Seymour, Smith, Thomas, Van Dyke, Willey—21.

MONDAY, March 13, 1826.

The Senate resumed the consideration of the resolution reported by the Committee on Foreign Relations, relative to the expediency of sending ministers to the Congress of Panama.
A motion was made by Mr. Benton to amend the said resolution, by striking out all after "*Resolved*," and inserting, "That the Senate cannot advise that it is expedient for the Government of the United States to send ministers to the Congress of American nations at Panama before it shall have received satisfactory information upon the following points: First. The subjects to which the attention of that Congress will be directed. Second. The substance and form of the powers to be given to the respective representatives. Third. The mode of organizing the Congress. Fourth. The mode of action in deciding the questions which may be submitted to it."
On motion by Mr. Hayne,
The Senate adjourned.

TUESDAY, March 14, 1826.

The Senate resumed the consideration of the resolution reported by the Committee on Foreign Relations, relative to the expediency of sending ministers to the Congress of Panama; together with the amendment proposed thereto by Mr. Benton.
On motion by Mr. Benton, the said amendment was modified as follows: Strike out all after "*Resolved*," and insert, "That it is not expedient for the United States to send any ministers to the Congress of American nations assembled at Panama before it shall have received satisfactory information

upon the following points: First. The subjects to which the attention of the Congress will be directed. Second. The substance and form of the powers to be given to the respective representatives. Third. The mode of organizing the Congress. Fourth. The mode of action in deciding the questions which may be submitted to it."

On motion by Mr. Hayne, that the further consideration of the resolution with the proposed amendment be postponed to Friday next, it was determined in the negative—yeas 20, nays 25.

The yeas and nays being desired by one-fifth of the Senators present,

Those who voted in the affirmative are—

Messrs. Benton, Berrien, Branch, Chandler, Cobb, Dickerson, Eaton, Findlay, Hayne, Johnson, of Kentucky, Kane, King, Macon, Randolph, Reed, Rowan, Van Buren, White, Williams, Woodbury—20.

Those who voted in the negative are—

Messrs. Barton, Bell, Bouligny, Chambers, Chase, Clayton, Edwards, Harrison, Hendricks, Holmes, Johnston, of Louisiana, Knight, Lloyd, McIlvaine, Marks, Mills, Noble, Robbins, Ruggles, Sanford, Seymour, Smith, Thomas, Van Dyke, Willey—25.

On motion by Mr. Reed, that he be excused from voting on the proposed amendment, it was determined in the affirmative—yeas 32, nays 12.

The yeas and nays being desired by one-fifth of the Senators present,

Those who voted in the affirmative are—

Messrs. Barton, Bell, Benton, Berrien, Bouligny, Branch, Chambers, Chase, Clayton, Dickerson, Edwards, Findlay, Harrison, Hendricks, Holmes, Johnston, of Louisiana, Knight, Lloyd, McIlvaine, Macon, Marks, Mills, Noble, Robbins, Ruggles, Sanford, Seymour, Smith, Thomas, Van Dyke, Willey, Williams—32.

Those who voted in the negative are—

Messrs. Chandler, Cobb, Eaton, Hayne, Johnson, of Kentucky, Kane, King, Randolph, Rowan, Van Buren, White, Woodbury—12.

On the question to agree to the proposed amendment to the resolution, it was determined in the negative—yeas 19, nays 24.

The yeas and nays being desired by one-fifth of the Senators present,

Those who voted in the affirmative are—

Messrs. Benton, Berrien, Branch, Chandler, Cobb, Dickerson, Eaton, Findlay, Hayne, Holmes, Kane, King, Macon, Randolph, Rowan, Van Buren, White, Williams, Woodbury—19.

Those who voted in the negative are—

Messrs. Barton, Bell, Bouligny, Chambers, Chase, Clayton, Edwards, Harrison, Hendricks, Johnson, of Kentucky, Johnston, of Louisiana, Knight, Lloyd, Marks, Mills, Noble, Robbins, Ruggles, Sanford, Seymour, Smith, Thomas, Van Dyke, Willey—24.

A motion was made by Mr. Van Buren to amend the resolution, by adding thereto the following:

Resolved, That the Constitution of the United States, in authorizing the President of the United States to nominate and, by and with the advice and consent of the Senate, to appoint "ambassadors and other public ministers," authorizes the nomination and appointment to offices of a diplomatic character only, existing by virtue of international laws, and does not authorize the nomination and appointment (under the name of ministers) of representatives to an Assembly of Nations like the proposed Congress of Panama, who, from the nature of their appointment, must be mere deputies, unknown to the law of nations and without diplomatic character or privilege.

Resolved, That the power of forming or entering (in any manner whatever) into new political associations or confederacies belongs to the people of the United States in their sovereign character, being one of the powers which, not having been delegated to the Government, is reserved to the States or people; and that it is not within the constitutional power of the Federal Government to appoint deputies or representatives of any description to represent the United States in the Congress of Panama, or to participate in the deliberation, or discussion, or recommendation of acts of that Congress.

Resolved, As the opinion of the Senate, that (waiving the question of constitutional power) the appointment of deputies to the Congress of Panama by the United States, according to the invitation given and its conditional acceptance, would be a departure from that wise and settled policy by which the intercourse of the United States with foreign nations has hitherto been regulated, and may endanger the friendly relations which now happily exist between us and the Spanish American States, by creating expectations that engagements will be entered into by us at that Congress which the Senate could not ratify, and of which the people of the United States would not approve.

Resolved, That the advantages of the proposed mission to the Congress of Panama (if attainable) would, in the opinion of the Senate, be better obtained without such hazard, by the attendance of one of our present ministers near either of the Spanish Governments, authorized to express the deep interest we feel in their prosperity, and instructed fully to explain (when requested) the great principles of our policy, but without being a member of that Congress, and without power to commit the United States to any stipulated mode of enforcing those principles in any supposed or possible state of the world.

And, on the question to agree thereto, it was determined in the negative—yeas 19, nays 24.

The yeas and nays being desired by one-fifth of the Senators present,

Those who voted in the affirmative are—

Messrs. Benton, Berrien, Branch, Chandler, Cobb, Dickerson, Eaton, Findlay, Hayne, Holmes, Kane, King, Macon, Randolph, Rowan, Van Buren, White, Williams, Woodbury—19.

Those who voted in the negative are—

Messrs. Barton, Bell, Bouligny, Chambers, Chase, Clayton, Edwards, Harrison, Hendricks, Johnson, of Kentucky, Johnston, of Louisiana, Knight, Lloyd, Marks, Mills, Noble, Robbins, Ruggles, Sanford, Seymour, Smith, Thomas, Van Dyke, Willey—24.

On the question to agree to the resolution reported by the committee, in the following words:

Resolved, That it is not expedient at this time for the United States to send any ministers to the Congress of American Nations assembled at Panama,

It was determined in the negative—yeas 19, nays 24.

The yeas and nays being desired by one-fifth of the Senators present,

Those who voted in the affirmative are—

Messrs. Benton, Berrien, Branch, Chandler, Cobb, Dickerson, Eaton, Findlay, Hayne, Holmes, Kane, King, Macon, Randolph, Rowan, Van Buren, White, Williams, Woodbury—19.

Those who voted in the negative are—

Messrs. Barton, Bell, Bouligny, Chambers, Chase, Clayton, Edwards, Harrison, Hendricks, Johnson, of Kentucky, Johnston, of Louisiana, Knight, Lloyd, Marks, Mills, Noble, Robbins, Ruggles, Sanford, Seymour, Smith, Thomas, Van Dyke, Willey—24.

On motion by Mr. Chase, that the Committee on Foreign Relations be discharged from the further consideration of the message of the President of the United States of the 26th December, nominating Richard C. Anderson, John Sergeant, and William B. Rochester to the appointments therein mentioned, it was determined in the affirmative—yeas 38, nays 6.

The yeas and nays being desired by one-fifth of the Senators present,

Those who voted in the affirmative are—

Messrs. Barton, Bell, Benton, Berrien, Bouligny, Branch, Chambers, Chandler, Chase, Clayton, Cobb, Dickerson, Edwards, Findlay, Harrison, Hendricks, Holmes, Johnson, of Kentucky, Johnston, of Louisiana, Kane, King, Knight, Lloyd, Macon, Marks, Mills, Noble, Reed, Robbins, Ruggles, Sanford, Seymour, Smith, Thomas, Van Buren, Van Dyke, White, Willey—38.

Those who voted in the negative are—

Messrs. Eaton, Hayne, Randolph, Rowan, Williams, and Woodbury—6.

On motion by Mr. Chandler, that, it being ten minutes past 12 o'clock, the Senate do adjourn, it was determined in the negative—yeas 15, nays 29.

The yeas and nays being desired by one-fifth of the Senators present,

Those who voted in the affirmative are—

Messrs. Benton, Branch, Chandler, Cobb, Dickerson, Findlay, Hayne, Holmes, Johnson, of Kentucky, King, Macon, Reed, Rowan, Williams, and Woodbury—15.

Those who voted in the negative are—

Messrs. Barton, Bell, Berrien, Bouligny, Chambers, Chase, Clayton, Eaton, Edwards, Harrison, Hendricks, Johnston, of Louisiana, Kane, Knight, Lloyd, Marks, Mills, Noble, Randolph, Robbins, Ruggles, Sanford, Seymour, Smith, Thomas, Van Buren, Van Dyke, White, Willey—29.

On motion by Mr. Mills, that the Senate proceed to consider the nominations of Richard C. Anderson, John Sergeant, and William B. Rochester, contained in the message of the 26th December, it was determined in the affirmative—yeas 25, nays 19.

The yeas and nays being desired by one-fifth of the Senators present,

Those who voted in the affirmative are—

Messrs. Barton, Bell, Bouligny, Chambers, Chase, Clayton, Edwards, Harrison, Hendricks, Johnson, of Kentucky, Johnston, of Louisiana, Knight, Lloyd, Marks, Mills, Noble, Reed, Robbins, Ruggles, Sanford, Seymour, Smith, Thomas, Van Dyke, Willey—25.

Those who voted in the negative are—

Messrs. Benton, Berrien, Branch, Chandler, Cobb, Dickerson, Eaton, Findlay, Hayne, Holmes, Kane, King, Macon, Randolph, Rowan, Van Buren, White, Williams, Woodbury—19.

On the question, "Will the Senate advise and consent to the appointment of Richard C. Anderson?" it was determined in the affirmative—yeas 27, nays 17.

The yeas and nays being desired by one-fifth of the Senators present,

Those who voted in the affirmative are—

Messrs. Barton, Bell, Benton, Bouligny, Chambers, Chase, Clayton, Edwards, Harrison, Hendricks, Johnson, of Kentucky, Johnston, of Louisiana, Kane, Knight, Lloyd, of Massachusetts, Marks, Mills, Noble, Reed, Robbins, Ruggles, Sanford, Seymour, Smith, Thomas, Van Dyke, Willey—27.

Those who voted in the negative are—

Messrs. Berrien, Branch, Chandler, Cobb, Dickerson, Eaton, Findlay, Hayne, Holmes, King, Macon, Randolph, Rowan, Van Buren, White, Williams, Woodbury—17.

On the question, "Will the Senate advise and consent to the appointment of John Sergeant?" it was determined in the affirmative—yeas 26, nays 18.

The yeas and nays being desired by one-fifth of the Senators present,

Those who voted in the affirmative are—

Messrs. Barton, Bell, Bouligny, Chambers, Chase, Clayton, Edwards, Findlay, Harrison, Hendricks, Johnson, of Kentucky, Johnston, of Louisiana, Kane, Knight, Lloyd, Marks, Mills, Noble, Robbins, Ruggles, Sanford, Seymour, Smith, Thomas, Van Dyke, Willey—26.

Those who voted in the negative are—

Messrs. Benton, Berrien, Branch, Chandler, Cobb, Dickerson, Eaton, Hayne, Holmes, King, Macon, Randolph, Reed, Rowan, Van Buren, White, Williams, Woodbury—18.

On the question, "Will the Senate advise and consent to the appointment of Wm. B. Rochester?" it was determined in the affirmative—yeas 28, nays 16.

The yeas and nays being desired by one-fifth of the Senators present,

Those who voted in the affirmative are—

Messrs. Barton, Bell, Benton, Bouligny, Chambers, Chase, Clayton, Edwards, Findlay, Harrison, Hendricks, Johnson, of Kentucky, Johnston, of Louisiana, Kane, Knight, Lloyd, Marks, Mills, Noble, Reed, Robbins, Ruggles, Sanford, Seymour, Smith, Thomas, Van Dyke, Willey—28.

Those who voted in the negative are—

Messrs. Berrien, Branch, Chandler, Cobb, Dickerson, Eaton, Hayne, Holmes, King, Macon, Randolph, Rowan, Van Buren, White, Williams, Woodbury—16.

So it was

Resolved, That the Senate advise and consent to the appointments of Richard C. Anderson, John Sergeant, and William B. Rochester, agreeably to their nominations respectively.

Mr. Berrien submitted the following resolution:

Resolved, That the injunction of secrecy be removed from the journal of the Senate on the subject of sending ministers to the Assembly of American Nations at Panama, and that the Secretary of the Senate cause the same to be published, viz:

Resolutions of the Senate of the 15th of February, and proceedings thereon. Proceedings of the Senate of the 22d, 23d, and 24th February, and of the 13th and 14th of March.

The Senate proceeded to consider the resolution.

On motion by Mr. Bell that the Senate adjourn, it was determined in the negative—yeas 13, nays 29.

On motion by Mr. Van Buren, the yeas and nays being desired by one-fifth of the Senators present,

Those who voted in the affirmative are—
Messrs. Barton, Bell, Chase, Clayton, Edwards, Knight, Macon, Marks, Noble, Reed, Robbins, Sanford, Seymour—13.
Those who voted in the negative are—
Messrs. Benton, Berrien, Bouligny, Branch, Chambers, Chandler, Cobb, Dickerson, Eaton, Findlay, Harrison, Hayne, Hendricks, Holmes, Johnson, of Kentucky, Johnston, of Louisiana, Kane, King, Lloyd, Mills, Rowan, Ruggles, Smith, Thomas, Van Buren, White, Willey, Williams, Woodbury—29.
On the question "Will the Senate agree to the resolution?" it was determined in the affirmative—yeas 37.
The yeas and nays being desired by one-fifth of the Senators present,
Those who voted in the affirmative are—
Messrs. Barton, Benton, Berrien, Bouligny, Branch, Chambers, Chandler, Chase, Cobb, Dickerson, Eaton, Edwards, Findlay, Harrison, Hayne, Hendricks, Holmes, Johnson, of Kentucky, Johnston, of Louisiana, Kane, King, Lloyd, Macon, Marks, Mills, Noble, Reed, Rowan, Ruggles, Sanford, Seymour, Smith, Van Buren, White, Willey, Williams, Woodbury—37.
So it was
Resolved, That the injunction of secrecy be removed from the journal of the Senate on the subject of sending ministers to the Assembly of American Nations at Panama, and that the Secretary of the Senate cause the same to be published, viz:
Resolutions of the Senate of the 15th of February, and proceedings thereon. Proceedings of the Senate of the 22d, 23d, and 24th February, and of the 13th and 14th of March.

FRIDAY, MARCH 17.

On motion by Mr. Randolph, and by unanimous consent,
Ordered, That the following motion, submitted by Mr. Randolph on the 21st of February, and withdrawn on the 22d of February, be inserted on the journal.
Resolved, That the Senate having, on the 15th day of February, passed the following resolutions:
"*Resolved*, That upon the question whether the United States shall be represented in the Congress of Panama the Senate ought to act with open doors, unless it shall appear that the publication of documents necessary to be referred to in debate will be prejudicial to existing negotiations.
"*Resolved*, That the President be respectfully requested to inform the Senate whether such objection exists to the publication of the documents communicated by the Executive, or any portion of them; and if so, to specify the parts the publication of which would, for that reason, be objectionable."
To which the President returned the following message in answer, viz:

"*To the Senate of the United States:*
"In answer to the two resolutions of the Senate of the 15th instant, marked 'Executive,' and which I have received, I state respectfully that all the communications from me to the Senate relating to the Congress at Panama have been made, like all other communications on Executive business, in *confidence*, and most of them in compliance with a resolution of the Senate requesting them confidentially. Believing that the established usage of free confidential communications between the Executive and the Senate ought, for the public interest, to be preserved unimpaired, I deem it to be my indispensable duty to leave to the Senate itself the decision of a question involving a departure, hitherto, so far as I am informed, without example, from that usage, and upon the motives for which, not being informed of them, I do not feel myself competent to decide.
"JOHN QUINCY ADAMS.
"WASHINGTON, *February* 16, 1826."

Resolved, That the Senate cannot, consistently with a due sense of its constitutional rights and duties, proceed, under the circumstances of the case, to a further consideration of the question whether or not it be expedient for the United States to send a mission to the Congress at Panama.
On motion by Mr. Randolph, and by unanimous consent,
Ordered, That the following motion, made by Mr Randolph on the 14th of March, and afterwards withdrawn, be entered on the journal.
Resolved, That the States of South Carolina and Alabama, being unrepresented in consequence of the death of John Gaillard and of Henry Chambers; and the State of Virginia being also unrepresented by the unavoidable absence of Littleton Waller Tazewell; and the State of Mississippi, by the vote that Thomas B. Reed, one of the Senators, be excused from voting, he not having had time to make up his opinion so as to be prepared to vote understandingly on the question, the Senate cannot, on a question involving the dignity and neutrality of the United States, and the fundamental principles of their union, and the peace and security of a great subdivision of the Confederacy, proceed to consider the nominations until the States shall be more fully represented.
On motion by Mr. Hayne,
Ordered, That the injunction of secrecy be removed from the foregoing proceedings, and that the Secretary cause the same to be published.

TUESDAY, MARCH 21' 1826.

Mr. Benton submitted the following resolution for consideration:
Resolved, That the injunction of secrecy be removed from the President's message of December 26, 1825, relative to the proposed Assembly of American Nations at Panama, and from all Executive communications made and documents sent to the Senate in relation thereto, and from all proceedings in the Senate upon that subject from which the injunction of secrecy has not yet been removed, and that six thousand copies of the whole be printed. Also, that the injunction of secrecy be removed from all communications relative thereto received from the Executive since the Senate's decision upon the mission, and that an equal number thereof be printed as an appendix to the proceedings had and documents first sent. Also, that all papers and documents sent and communications made by the Executive to the House of Representatives, and not sent or made to the Senate, shall, in like manner, be printed in a second appendix, distinguishing the papers and passages sent to the House and not to the Senate, and those sent to the

Senate and not to the House. Also, that the resolution of December 28 shall be transferred to the legislative journal of the Senate.

The Senate proceeded to the consideration thereof.

On motion by Mr. Mills, that the further consideration thereof be postponed until to-morrow, it was determined in the negative—yeas 6, nays 30.

The yeas and nays being desired by one-fifth of the Senators present,

Those who voted in the affirmative are—

Messrs. Barton, Chase, Edwards, Mills, Sanford, Seymour—6.

Those who voted in the negative are—

Messrs. Benton, Berrien, Bouligny, Chandler, Clayton, Cobb, Dickerson, Eaton, Findlay, Harrison, Hayne, Hendricks, Holmes, Johnson, of Kentucky, Johnston, of Louisiana, Kane, King, Knight, Macon, Marks, Noble, Reed, Robbins, Rowan, Ruggles, Smith, Van Buren, White, Willey, Woodbury—30.

On the question to agree to the resolution, it was determined in the affirmative—yeas 33, nays 3.

The yeas and nays being desired by one-fifth of the Senators present,

Those voted in the affirmative are—

Messrs. Barton, Benton, Berrien, Bouligny, Chandler, Chase, Clayton, Cobb, Dickerson, Eaton, Findlay, Harrison, Hayne, Hendricks, Holmes, Johnson, of Kentucky, Johnston, of Louisiana, Kane, King, Knight, Macon, Marks, Noble, Reed, Robbins, Rowan, Ruggles, Sanford, Smith, Van Buren, White, Willey, Woodbury—33.

Those who voted in the negative are—

Messrs. Edwards, Mills, Seymour—3.

Attest: WALTER LOWRIE, *Secretary.*

APPENDIX No. 1.

The following message and documents were communicated to the Senate on Friday the 17th March, 1826, after their final decision on the mission to Panama, which decision took place on the 14th March.

To the Senate of the United States:

Some additional documents, having relation to the objects of the mission to the Congress at Panama, and received since the communication of those heretofore sent, are now transmitted to the Senate.

JOHN QUINCY ADAMS.

WASHINGTON, *March* 16, 1826.

Papers sent.

No. 1. Mr. Everett to Mr. Clay, (No. 15,) November 21, 1825.   (Extract.)
No. 2. Same to same, (No. 17,) December 12, 1825.   (Extract.)
No. 3. Same to same, (No. 18,) January 1, 1826.   (Copy.)
No. 4. Mr. Brown to same, (No. 42,) January 10, 1826.   (Copy.)
   (a.) Same to Baron de Damas, (No. 42,) January 2, 1826.   (Copy.)

No. 1.

Extract of a letter (No. 15) *from Mr. Everett, minister to Spain, to the Secretary of State, dated*

MADRID, *November* 21, 1825.

"After conversing with the Duke (del Infantado) as much as was necessary upon the direct relations between the two countries, the opportunity being favorable for a longer interview, I availed myself of it to introduce the subject of the colonies, upon which I had not before said anything to him. I told him that it was a part of my instructions to intimate to his Majesty's Government, in the most delicate manner possible, the full conviction of that of the United States that the question of the independence of the colonies was, in point of fact, settled; and their strong desire that the war might, as soon as possible, be brought to a close. I inquired of him whether there was at present any disposition in his Majesty's cabinet towards a change of policy upon this subject. He replied in the negative, but did not express himself to this effect with the same fullness and decision that I had observed in Mr. Zea's communications. I presume, however, that this difference, which was certainly very perceptible and obvious, is rather owing to the difference in the characters of the men and their habit of expressing themselves than to any actual intention in the cabinet to yield; at least I do not learn from any other quarter that such an intention is supposed to exist. The Duke said that the matter was a delicate one; that he could easily imagine how inconvenient and injurious it must be to the United States to have this struggle constantly going on at their doors; that he was not surprised or dissatisfied that they should exert their influence in endeavoring to procure the termination of it in the way which they thought just; but that the King could not yet resolve to abandon his rights, or give up the hope that these countries would in one way or another be ultimately brought back to their allegiance. I then suggested to him particularly the opinion entertained by the Government of the United States that the loss of the islands of Cuba and Porto Rico would be the inevitable effect of the continuance of the struggle for two or three years longer; but that Spain, by making peace at once, might very probably retain them. When I made this remark to Mr. Zea, he answered that the King did not consider these islands as in danger in any event, and that his Majesty confidently trusted that he should not only retain them, but reconquer very shortly all the other American provinces. The Duke's answer was quite different. He inquired of me, in reply, upon what evidence the American Government founded the opinion that Spain would be able to retain these islands in case of her recognizing the independence of the other colonies. This question seemed to suppose the persuasion that the islands must at all events be lost unless the King should recover the whole of his American possessions. I replied that the principal circumstance in favor of this opinion was the fact that no symptoms of a disposition to separate from the mother country had yet appeared in the islands, and that as their situation, in consequence of the opening of the ports, was extremely flourishing, there was room to suppose that they were contented with it. He acquiesced in this remark, and expressed his deep regret that a similar system of allowing a full freedom of trade had not been adopted in season in regard to the other colonies. This was the substance of our conversation. The general impression I received from it was, that there is at present no direct intention in the cabinet to change their policy; but that there is at least as much probability of a recognition now as before the late ministerial revolution. I mentioned to the Duke that Mr. Zea had expressed a wish that I would give him in writing what I had to say by order of my Government upon this subject, and inquired of him whether this would also be agreeable to him. He said that he had no objection whatever to receive such a communication, and I shall accordingly at my leisure prepare and transmit one."

No. 2.

Extract of a letter (No. 17) from Mr. Everett to the Secretary of State, dated at

MADRID, *December* 12, 1825.

"I received two or three days ago from Mr. King a copy of the instructions to Mr. Middleton on the affairs of Spanish America. It came very opportunely, while I was engaged in preparing the note which I intend to address to this Government upon the same subject. This communication, as it requires to be drawn up with care and caution, does not admit of being hastened, and will not probably be ready before the first of January. I learn with much pleasure, through the medium of Mr. Brown, that the overture made by Mr. Middleton at St. Petersburg has been well received and is likely to produce a favorable effect. I shall take an early opportunity of conversing anew with Mr. D'Oubril upon the subject and of ascertaining what are his present instructions."

No. 3.

Mr. Everett to the Secretary of State, No. 18.

MADRID, *January* 1, 1826.

SIR: I have the honor to transmit herewith a translation of a decree which has just been published for establishing a Council of State. A council has already existed, I believe, ever since the King's return, bearing the same name, composed of nearly the same persons, and charged with substantially the same duties as this, but the King has not been in the habit of calling them together. The only thing, therefore, really new in the decree is the part which declares that the council shall meet every day and remain in session three hours. How far this regulation is likely to be observed is, of course, a matter of mere conjecture. It is rather singular that no allusion is made to an existing council, and that the decree purports to be for the establishment of an entirely new one. The measure is considered here as pretty important, but I do not see that it is likely to introduce any very great changes either in the principles or proceedings of the Government. The latent object of the institution is, probably, to get rid of the Ministerial Council established by Mr. Zea; no allusion is, however, made to the latter in the decree which thus supercedes two of these high state corporations, without naming either. Some of the most considerable members of Mr. Zea's council are transferred to the new one, including the President, General Castanos, a person much respected by all parties, and of known liberal sentiments. He told me yesterday that this was the fifth council to which he had been called, as they were successively instituted. He does not appear to anticipate any very important consequences from the innovation.

There are some things, however, in the decree, and in the composition of the council, which may be construed into indications that the measure has been taken with a view to a more careful consideration of the great question of America. Among the members named who, exclusively of the ministers, only amount to fourteen or fifteen, are the Archbishop of Mexico, the Viceroys of Mexico, Venegas, and Apodaca, under new names, the Duke de San Carlos, an American, and Father Cyril, who has been in America. The last is considered the ablest man in the council. It is worthy of remark, that none of these, except San Carlos, were of the old Council of State. General Castanos is friendly to the recognition of the independence of America. Provision seems to have been made in this way for bringing into the meeting a great deal of positive information upon American affairs. The decree also mentions that this question is one to which the attention of the council is to be particularly called; and speaks of it in terms which will bear a favorable interpretation, although they do not necessarily require it. Among other things deserving consideration are enumerated "the weighty affairs of the colonies in America, which are endeavoring to separate from the mother country, by a necessary effect of the dangers to which the Crown has been exposed." To acknowledge the necessity of the separation on any account seems to be a large step towards the acknowledgment of the new States, and to call the effort to separate a necessary effect of the late political crisis is, perhaps, to give the best possible justification of it. The passage may, however, be interpreted in a different sense; and there is, at present, no other evidence of any recent change on this subject, in the disposition of this Government The French newspapers abound, as usual, with accounts, apparently authentic, of constant efforts made here by the foreign powers, especially the British minister, in favor of the colonies, but these accounts are also, as usual, without the slightest foundation. Mr. Lamb and myself converse, habitually, on this subject, with perfect freedom, and I am certain that he has said and done almost nothing for the Americans since I have been here; the others never interfere with the subject, excepting, perhaps, the French ambassador, who has recently arrived, and with whose proceedings I am not so well acquainted.

I lately read to the Duke del Infantado a part of a letter I had received from New York, which spoke with great confidence of the probability of an early and successful attack upon the Island of Cuba by the Mexicans and Colombians. The intelligence evidently made an impression upon him. He asked me, among other things, as he has done before, what security there would be for the possession of Cuba in the event of recognising the colonies. I replied by stating the general reasons why they should not wish to separate. It has since occurred to me that the Duke, by his repeated questions to this effect, intended to intimate a desire that a guaranty for the fidelity of Cuba should be offered by the United States, or by the Spanish American powers. This was proposed directly by Mr. Zea to Mr. Nelson and to me as a consideration for admitting our consul at the Havana.

Since I wrote to you last I have been principally engaged in preparing my note upon the affairs of the colonies. It is now nearly ready, and I shall probably send you a copy of it with my next despatches. The other affairs remain in the same state. The intelligence of the death of the Emperor of Russia arrived here about ten days ago, and was soon followed by that of the quiet succession of his brother Constantine. It does not appear that the change will produce any immediate effect upon the state of political affairs. The money market is exceedingly depressed in France and England, and the distress among the merchants is greater than was almost ever known before; but the crisis appears to have arisen, in part, from pure panic and will, in all probability, pass off very soon, leaving the value of public stocks somewhat lower, perhaps, than it stood before. The French Parliament is summoned for the 31st of this month.

I have the honor to transmit herewith copies of the notes which I have addressed to the minister since my last despatches, and of some official articles of general interest, and remain, with high respect, sir, your most obedient humble servant,

A. H. EVERETT.

P. S.—Upon looking again at the decree upon the Council of State, which was out of my hands when I was writing the above, I find that the council is not described as a new institution in such distinct terms as I had supposed and stated. The impression I had upon the subject was partly derived from conversation. The existence of the council had been pretty generally forgotten, and this revival of it has been commonly mentioned as the establishment of an entirely new one; in effect it is, as the King never called the members together under the former system.

Hon. HENRY CLAY, *Secretary of State.*

No. 4.

No. 42.—*Mr. Brown to Mr. Clay.*

PARIS, *January* 10, 1826.

SIR: In order to comply with the instructions contained in your despatch No. 3, I obtained an interview with his excellency the Baron de Damas, on the 2d instant. I reminded him that, in the month of July last, I had, in a spirit of frankness, disclosed to him the views of the President of the United States in relation to the islands of Cuba and Porto Rico, and that I had then stated to him that the United States could not see with indifference those islands passing from Spain to any other European Government; and that, for the United States, no change was desired in their political or commercial condition, nor in the possession which Spain had of them. I informed him that I was now instructed to add, in the same frank and friendly spirit, and in order to guard against all possible difficulties that might arise on that subject, that we could not consent to the occupation of those islands by any other European power than Spain under any contingency whatever. Disclaiming, as we now did, all designs on them ourselves, we believed we might justly claim an unreserved communication of the views of other great maritime States in relation to them. I observed that the President could not suppose a state of things in which it would be right or proper that possessions so important should be occupied by either England or France without the concurrence, or, at least, the knowledge, of the United States.

The Baron de Damas appeared to concur entirely in the view which I took of the subject, and inquired whether it had been mentioned to the British Government. I told him that a similar communication had been made to Mr. Canning, and I had sufficient reason to think that the British Government concurred with the President in the policy of not disturbing the possession of those islands in favor of either of the great maritime nations.

I then, in the most delicate and friendly manner, alluded to the French squadron which had appeared in the West Indies and on the American coast last summer, and stated that my Government would expect that, in case France should again send out a naval force disproportionate in the extent of its armament to the ordinary purpose of a peace establishment, its design and object should be communicated to the Government of the United States. The Baron de Damas answered that the vessels composing that squadron had been stationed at different places, where the number on each station was not more than sufficient for the service of protecting French commerce and their West India islands; that it had become necessary definitively to settle the relations between France and St. Domingo; that this squadron was hastily collected for that object, and that the nature of the service required secrecy. He said that it was not only right in itself, but had been customary with the French Government to communicate to friendly Governments, in time of peace, the objects of considerable fleets sent on distant service; that the peculiar circumstances in the instance I alluded to had occasioned a departure from the rule, but that, in future, the United States should be duly apprised of the objects of every such squadron sent into their vicinity. The Baron de Damas closed the conference by saying that he would communicate what had passed to the King, to whom, he was sure, it would give great satisfaction.

On the same day I addressed a short note to the Baron de Damas, of which I inclose a copy; and meeting him in the evening I told him, in an informal manner, that I had written it with the design of avoiding any mistake in my communication to the President of what had passed at the conference. He said he was well satisfied that no mistake existed on either side, and that he had communicated our conversation to the King.

I have the honor to be, with great respect, sir, your most obedient and humble servant,

JAMES BROWN.

A.

Mr. Brown to the Baron de Damas.

PARIS, *January 2,* 1826.

SIR: In the month of July last I had the honor to state to your excellency, with the utmost frankness, the views of the President of the United States in relation to the Spanish islands of Cuba and Porto Rico. I informed you that the United States could not see with indifference those islands passing from Spain to any other European power, and that the United States desired no change in their political or commercial condition, nor in the possession which Spain had of them. In the conference with which your excellency honored me on this day I repeated the same assurances, and added, in a spirit of friendship, and with a view of guarding beforehand against any possible difficulties on the subject which might arise, that my Government could not consent to the occupation of those islands by any other European power than Spain under any contingency whatever.

Having understood your excellency to say that the policy and views of the United States, as disclosed by me, corresponded with those of his Majesty's Government, I shall not fail to communicate the information to the President, who will feel happy in finding the two nations agreeing on a point of so much importance to the tranquillity of that portion of the globe.

I request your excellency to accept, &c.

JAMES BROWN.

His Excellency BARON DE DAMAS, *Minister of Foreign Affairs, &c., &c.*

APPENDIX—No. 2.

COMMUNICATED TO THE HOUSE OF REPRESENTATIVES MARCH 17, 1826.

To the House of Representatives of the United States:

In compliance with the resolution of the House of the 5th ultimo, requesting me to cause to be laid before the House so much of the correspondence between the Government of the United States and the new States of America, or their ministers, respecting the proposed Congress or meeting of diplomatic agents at Panama, and such information respecting the general character of that expected Congress, as may be in my possession, and as may, in my opinion, be communicated without prejudice to the public interest, and also to inform the House, so far as in my opinion the public interest may allow, in regard to what objects the agents of the United States are expected to take part in the deliberations of that Congress, I now transmit to the House a report from the Secretary of State, with the correspondence and information requested by the resolution.

With regard to the objects in which the agents of the United States are expected to take part in the deliberations of that Congress, I deem it proper to premise that these objects did not form the only nor even the principal motive for my acceptance of the invitation. My first and greatest inducement was to meet in the spirit of kindness and friendship an overture made in that spirit by three sister Republics of this hemisphere.

The great revolution in human affairs which has brought into existence, nearly at the same time, eight sovereign and independent nations in our own quarter of the globe, has placed the United States in a situation not less novel, and scarcely less interesting, than that in which they had found themselves by their own transition from a cluster of colonies to a nation of sovereign States. The deliverance of the Southern American Republics from the oppression under which they had been so long afflicted was hailed, with great unanimity, by the people of this Union, as among the most auspicious events of the age. On the 4th of May, 1822, an act of Congress made an appropriation of one hundred thousand dollars "for such missions to the independent nations on the American continent as the President of the United States might deem proper."

In exercising the authority recognized by this act, my predecessor, by and with the advice and consent of the Senate, appointed, successively, ministers plenipotentiary to the Republics of Colombia, Buenos Ayres, Chile, and Mexico. Unwilling to raise among the fraternity of freedom questions of precedency and etiquette, which even the European monarchs had of late found it necessary in a great measure to discard, he despatched these ministers to Colombia, Buenos Ayres, and Chile, without exacting from those Republics, as by the ancient principals of political primogeniture he might have done, that the compliment of a plenipotentiary mission should have been paid *first* by them to the United States. The instructions, prepared under his direction, to Mr. Anderson, the first of our ministers to the southern continent, contain, at much length, the general principles upon which he thought it desirable that our relations, political and commercial, with these our new neighbors, should be established for their benefit and ours, and that of the future ages of our posterity.   A copy of so much of these instructions as relates to these general subjects is among the papers now transmitted to the House.   Similar instructions were furnished to the ministers appointed to Buenos Ayres, Chile, and Mexico, and the system of social intercourse which it was the purpose of those missions to establish, from the first opening of our diplomatic relations with those rising nations, is the most effective exposition of the principles upon which the invitation to the Congress at Panama has been accepted by me, as well as of the objects of negotiation at that meeting, in which it was expected that our plenipotentiaries should take part.

The House will perceive that, even at the date of these instructions, the first treaties between some of the southern Republics had been concluded, by which they had stipulated among themselves this diplomatic assembly at Panama.   And it will be seen with what caution, so far as it might concern the policy of the United States, and at the same time with what frankness and good will towards those nations, he gave countenance to their design of inviting the United States to this high assembly for consultation upon *American interests*.   It was not considered a conclusive reason for declining this invitation that the proposal for assembling such a Congress had not first been made by ourselves.   It had sprung from the urgent, immediate, and momentous common interests of the great communities struggling for independence, and, as it were, quickening into life.   From them the proposition to us appeared respectful and friendly ; from us to them it could scarcely have been made without exposing ourselves to suspicions of purposes of ambition, if not of domination, more suited to rouse resistance and excite distrust than to conciliate favor and friendship.   The first and paramount principle upon which it was deemed wise and just to lay the corner-stone of all our future relations with them was *disinterestedness;* the next was cordial good will to them; the third was a claim of fair and equal reciprocity.   Under these impressions, when the invitation was formally and earnestly given, had it even been doubtful whether *any* of the objects proposed for consideration and discussion at the Congress were such as that immediate and important interests of the United States would be affected by the issue, I should, nevertheless, have determined, so far as it depended upon me, to have accepted the invitation, and to have appointed ministers to attend the meeting.   The proposal itself implied that the Republics by whom it was made *believed* that important interests of ours or of theirs rendered our attendance there desirable.   They had given us notice that, in the novelty of their situation, and in the spirit of deference to our experience, they would be pleased to have the benefit of our friendly counsel.   To meet the temper with which this proposal was made with a cold repulse was not thought congenial to that warm interest in their welfare with which the people and Government of the Union had hitherto gone hand in hand through the whole progress of their revolution.   To insult them by a refusal of their overture, and then invite them to a similar assembly, to be called by ourselves, was an expedient which never presented itself to the mind.   I would have sent ministers to the meeting had it been merely to give them such advice as they might have desired, even with reference to *their own* interests, not involving ours.   I would have sent them had it been merely to explain and set forth to them our reasons for *declining* any proposal of specific measures to which they might desire our concurrence, but which we might deem incompatible with our interests or our duties.   In the intercourse between nations temper is a missionary perhaps more powerful than talent.   Nothing was ever lost by kind treatment.   Nothing can be gained by sullen repulses and aspiring pretensions.

But objects of the highest importance, not only to the future welfare of the whole human race, but bearing directly upon the special interests of this Union, *will* engage the deliberations of the Congress of Panama whether we are represented there or not.   Others, if we are represented, may be offered by our plenipotentiaries for consideration, having in view both these great results—our own interests and the improvement of the condition of man upon earth.   It may be that, in the lapse of many centuries, no other opportunity so favorable will be presented to the Government of the United States to subserve the benevolent purposes of Divine Providence, to dispense the promised blessings of the Redeemer of mankind, to promote the prevalence in future ages of peace on earth and good will to man, as will now be placed in their power by participating in the deliberations of this Congress.

Among the topics enumerated in official papers published by the Republic of Colombia, and adverted to in the correspondence now communicated to the House, as intended to be presented for discussion at Panama, there is scarcely one in which the *result* of the meeting will not deeply affect the interests of the United States.   Even those in which the belligerent States alone will take an active part will have a powerful effect upon the state of our relations with the American, and probably with the principal European States.   Were it merely that we might be correctly and speedily informed of the proceedings of the Congress, and of the progress and issue of their negotiations, I should hold it advisable that we should have an accredited agency with them, placed in such confidential relations with the other members as would insure the authenticity and the safe and early transmission of its reports.   Of the same enumerated topics are the preparation of a manifesto setting forth to the world the justice of their cause and the relations they desire to hold with other Christian powers, and to form a convention of navigation and commerce applicable both to the confederated States and to their allies.

It will be within the recollection of the House that, immediately after the close of the war of our independence, a measure closely analogous to this Congress of Panama was adopted by the Congress of our confederation, and for purposes of precisely the same character.   Three commissioners, with plenipotentiary powers, were appointed to negotiate treaties of amity, navigation, and commerce with the principal powers of Europe.   They met and resided for that purpose about one year at Paris, and the only result of their negotiations at that time was the first treaty between the United States and Prussia—memorable in the diplomatic annals of the world, and precious as a monument of the principles, in relation to commerce and maritime warfare, with which our country entered upon her career as a member of the great family of independent nations.   This treaty, prepared in conformity with the instructions of the American plenipotentiaries, consecrated three fundamental principles of the foreign intercourse which the Congress of that period were desirous of establishing.   First, equal reciprocity and the mutual stipulation of the privileges of the most favored nation in the commercial exchanges of peace; secondly, the abolition of private war upon the ocean; and thirdly, restrictions favorable to neutral commerce upon belligerent practices with regard to contraband of war and blockades.   A painful, it may be said a calamitous, experience of more than forty years has demonstrated the deep importance of these same principles to the peace and prosperity of this nation, and to the welfare of all maritime States, and has illustrated the profound wisdom with which they were assumed as cardinal points of the policy of the Union.

At that time, in the infancy of their political existence, under the influence of those principles of liberty and of right so congenial to the cause in which they had just fought and triumphed, they were able but to obtain the sanction of one great and philosophical, though absolute sovereign, in Europe to their liberal and enlightened principles. They could obtain no more. Since then a political hurricane has gone over three-fourths of the civilized portions of the earth; the desolation of which, it may with confidence be expected, is passing away, leaving at least the American atmosphere purified and refreshed. And now, at this propitious moment, the new-born nations of this hemisphere, assembling by their representatives at the isthmus between its two continents, to settle the principles of their future international intercourse with other nations and with us, ask, in this great exigency, for our advice upon those very fundamental maxims which we from our cradle at first proclaimed, and partially succeeded to introduce into the code of national law.

Without recurring to that total prostration of all neutral and commercial rights which marked the progress of the late European wars, and which finally involved the United States in them, and adverting only to our political relations with these American nations, it is observable that while, in all other respects, those relations have been uniformly, and without exception, of the most friendly and mutually satisfactory character, the only causes of difference and dissension between us and them which have ever arisen originated in those never-failing fountains of discord and irritation, discriminations of commercial favor to other nations, licentious privateers, and paper blockades. I cannot, without doing injustice to the Republics of Buenos Ayres and Colombia, forbear to acknowledge the candid and conciliatory spirit with which they have repeatedly yielded to our friendly representations and remonstrances on those subjects, in repealing discriminative laws which operated to our disadvantage, and in revoking the commissions of their privateers; to which Colombia has added the magnanimity of making reparation for unlawful captures by some of her cruisers, and of assenting, in the midst of war, to treaty stipulations favorable to neutral navigation. But the recurrence of these occasions of complaint has rendered the renewal of the discussions which result in the removal of them necessary, while in the mean time injuries are sustained by merchants and other individuals of the United States which cannot be repaired, and the remedy lingers in overtaking the pernicious operation of the mischief. The settlement of general principles, pervading with equal efficacy all the American States, can alone put an end to these evils, and can alone be accomplished at the proposed assembly.

If it be true that the noblest treaty of peace ever mentioned in history is that by which the Carthaginians were bound to abolish the practice of sacrificing their own children, *because it was stipulated in favor of human nature*, I cannot exaggerate to myself the unfading glory with which these United States will go forth in the memory of future ages if, by their friendly counsel, by their moral influence, by the power of argument and persuasion alone, they can prevail upon the American nations at Panama to stipulate, by general agreement among themselves, and so far as any of them may be concerned, the perpetual abolition of private war upon the ocean. And if we cannot yet flatter ourselves that this may be accomplished as advances towards it, the establishment of the principle that the friendly flag shall cover the cargo, the curtailment of contraband of war, and the proscription of fictitious paper blockades—engagements which we may reasonably hope will not prove impracticable—will, if successfully inculcated, redound proportionally to our honor, and drain the fountain of many a future sanguinary war.

The late President of the United States, in his message to Congress of December 2, 1823, while announcing the negotiation then pending with Russia, relating to the Northwest Coast of this Continent, observed that the occasion of the discussions to which that incident had given rise had been taken for asserting, as a principle, in which the rights and interests of the United States were involved, that the American continents, by the free and independent condition which they had assumed and maintained, were thenceforward not to be considered as subjects for future colonization by any European power. The principle had first been assumed in that negotiation with Russia. It rested upon a course of reasoning equally simple and conclusive. With the exception of the existing European colonies, which it was in nowise intended to disturb, the two continents consisted of several sovereign and independent nations, whose territories covered their whole surface. By this their independent condition the United States enjoyed the right of commercial intercourse with every part of their possessions. To attempt the establishment of a colony in those possessions would be to usurp, to the exclusion of others, a commercial intercourse, which was the common possession of all. It could not be done without encroaching upon existing rights of the United States. The Government of Russia has never disputed these positions, nor manifested the slightest dissatisfaction at their having been taken. Most of the new American Republics have declared their entire assent to them; and they now propose, among the subjects of consultation at Panama, to take into consideration the means of making effectual the assertion of that principle, as well as the means of resisting interference from abroad with the domestic concerns of the American Governments.

In alluding to these means it would obviously be premature at this time to anticipate that which is offered merely as matter for consultation, or to pronounce upon those measures which have been or may be suggested. The purpose of this Government is to concur in none which would import hostility to Europe, or justly excite resentment in any of her States. Should it be deemed advisable to contract any conventional engagement on this topic, our views would extend no further than to a mutual pledge of the parties to the compact to maintain the principle in application to its own territory, and to permit no colonial lodgments or establishments of European jurisdiction upon its own soil; and, with respect to the obtrusive interference from abroad, if its future character may be inferred from that which has been and perhaps still is exercised in more than one of the new States, a joint declaration of its character, and exposure of it to the world, may be probably all that the occasion would require. Whether the United States should or should not be parties to such a declaration may justly form a part of the deliberation. That there is an evil to be remedied needs little insight into the secret history of late years to know, and that this remedy may best be concerted at the Panama meeting deserves at least the experiment of consideration. A concert of measures, having reference to the more effectual abolition of the African slave trade, and the consideration of the light in which the political condition of the Island of Hayti is to be regarded, are also among the subjects mentioned by the minister from the Republic of Colombia, as believed to be suitable for deliberation at the Congress. The failure of the negotiations with that Republic, undertaken during the late administration, for the suppression of that trade, in compliance with a resolution of the House of Representatives, indicates the expediency of listening, with respectful attention, to propositions which may contribute to the accomplishment of the great end which was the purpose of that resolution, while the result of those negotiations will serve as admonition to abstain from pledging this Government to any arrangement which might be expected to fail of obtaining the advice and consent of the Senate by a constitutional majority to its ratification:

Whether the political condition of the island of Hayti shall be brought at all into discussion at the meeting may be a question for preliminary advisement. There are in the political constitution of Govern. ment of that people circumstances which have hitherto forbidden the acknowledgment of them by the Government of the United States as sovereign and independent. Additional reasons for withholding that acknowledgment have recently been seen in their acceptance of a nominal sovereign by the *grant* of a foreign prince, under conditions equivalent to the concession by them of exclusive commercial advantages to one nation, adapted altogether to the state of colonial vassalage, and retaining little of independence but the name. Our plenipotentiaries will be instructed to present these views to the assembly at Panama, and, should they not be concurred in, to decline acceding to any arrangement which may be proposed upon different principles.

The condition of the islands of Cuba and Porto Rico is of deeper import and more immediate bearing upon the present interests and future prospects of our Union. The correspondence herewith transmitted will show how earnestly it has engaged the attention of this Government. The invasion of both those islands by the united forces of Mexico and Colombia is avowedly among the objects to be matured by the belligerent States at Panama. The convulsions to which, from the peculiar composition of their population, they would be liable in the event of such an invasion, and the danger therefrom resulting of their falling ultimately into the hands of some European power other than Spain, will not admit of our looking at the consequences to which the Congress at Panama may lead with indifference. It is unnecessary to enlarge upon this topic, or to say more than that all our efforts in reference to this interest will be to preserve the existing state of things, the tranquillity of the islands, and the peace and security of their inhabitants.

And lastly, the Congress of Panama is believed to present a fair occasion for urging upon all the new nations of the South the just and liberal principles of religious liberty. Not by any interference whatever in their internal concerns, but by claiming for our citizens, whose occupations or interests may call them to occasional residence in their territories, the inestimable privilege of worshipping their Creator according to the dictates of their own consciences. This privilege, sanctioned by the customary law of nations, and secured by treaty stipulations in numerous national compacts—secured even to our own citizens in the treaties with Colombia and with the Federation of Central America—is yet to be obtained in the other South American States and Mexico. Existing prejudices are still struggling against it, which may, perhaps, be more successfully combatted at this general meeting than at the separate seats of Government of each Republic.

I can scarcely deem it otherwise than superfluous to observe that the assembly will be in its nature diplomatic and not legislative. That nothing can be transacted there obligatory upon any one of the States to be represented at the meeting, unless with the express concurrence of its own representatives; nor even then, but subject to the ratification of its constitutional authority at home. The faith of the United States to foreign powers cannot otherwise be pledged. I shall, indeed, in the first instance, consider the assembly as merely *consultative;* and although the plenipotentiaries of the United States will be empowered to receive and refer to the consideration of their Government any proposition from the other parties to the meeting, they will be authorized to conclude nothing unless subject to the definitive sanction of this Government in all its constitutional forms. It has, therefore, seemed to me unnecessary to insist that every object to be discussed at the meeting should be specified with the precision of a judicial sentence, or enumerated with the exactness of a mathematical demonstration. The purpose of the meeting itself is to deliberate upon the great and common *interests* of several new and neighboring nations. If the measure is new and without precedent, so is the situation of the parties to it. That the purposes of the meeting are somewhat indefinite, far from being an objection to it, is among the cogent reasons for its adoption. It is not the establishment of principles of intercourse with one, but with seven or eight nations at once. That, before they have had the means of exchanging ideas and communicating with one another in common upon these topics, they should have definitively settled and arranged them in concert is to require that the effect should precede the cause. It is to exact, as a preliminary to the meeting, that for the accomplishment of which the meeting itself is designed.

Among the inquiries which were thought entitled to consideration before the determination was taken to accept the invitation was that, whether the measure might not have a tendency to change the policy, hitherto invariably pursued by the United States, of avoiding all entangling alliances and all unnecessary foreign connexions.

Mindful of the advice given by the Father of our Country in his farewell address that the great rule of conduct for us in regard to foreign nations is, in extending our foreign relations, to have with them as little political connexion as possible, and faithfully adhering to the spirit of that admonition, I cannot overlook the reflection that the counsel of Washington, in that instance, like all the counsels of wisdom, was founded upon the circumstances in which our country and the world around us were situated at the time when it was given. That the reasons assigned by him for his advice were, that Europe had a set of primary interests which to us had none, or a very remote relation. That hence she must be engaged in frequent controversies, the cause of which were essentially foreign to our concerns. That our *detached* and *distant* situation invited and enabled us to pursue a different course. That by our union and rapid growth, with an efficient Government, the period was not far distant when we might defy material injury from external annoyance—when we might take such an attitude as would cause our neutrality to be respected, and, with reference to belligerent nations, might choose peace or war, as our interests, guided by justice, should counsel.

Compare our situation and the circumstances of that time with those of the present day, and what, from the very words of Washington then, would be his counsels to his countrymen now? Europe has still her set of primary interests with which we have little or a remote relation. Our distant and detached situation with reference to Europe remains the same. But we were then the only independent nation of this hemisphere; and we were surrounded by European colonies, with the greater part of which we had no more intercourse than with the inhabitants of another planet. Those colonies have now been transformed into eight independent nations, extending to our very borders. Seven of them Republics like ourselves; with whom we have an immensely growing commercial, and *must* have, and have, already important political connexions; with reference to whom our situation is neither distant nor detached; whose political principles and systems of Government, congenial with our own, must and will have an action and counteraction upon us and ours to which we cannot be indifferent if we would.

The rapidity of our growth 'and the consequent increase of our strength has more than realized the anticipations of this admirable political legacy. Thirty years have nearly elapsed since it was written, and in the interval our population, our wealth, our territorial extension, our power, physical and moral, have nearly trebled. Reasoning upon this state of things from the sound and judicious principles of Washington, and must we not say that the period which he predicted as then not far off has arrived? That *America* has a set of primary interests which have none or a remote relation to Europe. That the interference of Europe, therefore, in those concerns, should be spontaneously withheld by her upon the same principles that we have never interfered with hers; and that if she should interfere, as she may by measures which may have a great and dangerous recoil upon ourselves, we might be called, in defence of our own altars and firesides, to take an attitude which would cause our neutrality to be respected, and choose peace or war, as our interest, guided by justice, should counsel.

The acceptance of this invitation, therefore, far from conflicting with the counsel or the policy of Washington, is directly deducible from and comformable to it. Nor is it less conformable to the views of my immediate predecessor, as declared in his annual message to Congress of December 2, 1823, to which I have already adverted, and to an important passage of which I invite the attention of the House. "The citizens of the United States," said he, "cherish sentiments the most friendly in favor of the liberty and happiness of their fellow men on that (the European) side of the Atlantic. In the wars of the European Powers, in matters relating to themselves, we have never taken any part, nor does it comport with our policy so to do. It is only when our rights are invaded or seriously menaced that we resent injuries or make preparation for our defence. With the movements in this hemisphere we are of necessity more immediately connected, and by causes which must be obvious to all enlightened and impartial observers. The political system of the allied powers is essentially different in this respect from that of America. This difference proceeds from that which exists in their respective Governments. And to the defence of our own, which has been achieved by the loss of so much blood and treasure, and matured by the wisdom of their most enlightened citizens, and under which we have enjoyed unexampled felicity, this whole nation is devoted. We owe it, therefore, to candor and to the amicable relations subsisting between the United States and those powers, to declare that we should consider any attempt on their part to extend their system to any portion of this hemisphere as dangerous to our peace and safety. With the existing colonies or dependencies of any European power we have not interfered, and shall not interfere. But with the Governments who have declared their independence and maintained it, and whose independence we have, on great consideration and on just principles, acknowledged, we could not view any interposition, for the purposes of oppressing them or controlling in any other manner their destiny by any European power, in any other light than as the manifestation of an unfriendly disposition towards the United States. In the war between those new Governments and Spain we declared our neutrality at the time of their recognition, and to this we have adhered and shall continue to adhere, provided no change shall occur which, in the judgment of the competent authorities of this Government, shall make a corresponding change on the part of the United States indispensable to their security."

To the question which may be asked, whether this meeting and the principles which may be adjusted and settled by it as rules of intercourse between the American nations may not give umbrage to the Holy League of European powers or offence to Spain, it is deemed a sufficient answer that our attendance at Panama can give no *just cause* of umbrage or offence to either; and that the United States will stipulate nothing there which can give such cause. Here the right of inquiry into our purposes and measures must stop. The Holy League of Europe itself was formed without inquiring of the United States whether it would or would not give umbrage to them. The fear of giving umbrage to the Holy League of Europe was urged as a motive for denying to the American nations the acknowledgment of their independence. That it would be viewed by Spain as hostility to her was not only urged but directly declared by herself. The Congress and administration of that day consulted their rights and duties, and not their fears. Fully determined to give no needless displeasure to any foreign power, the United States can estimate the probability of their giving it only by the right which any foreign State could have to take it from their measures. Neither the representation of the United States at Panama, nor any measure to which their assent may be yielded there, will give to the Holy League, or any of its members, nor to Spain, the right to take offence. For the rest the United States must still, as heretofore, take counsel from their duties rather than their fears.

Such are the objects in which it is expected that the plenipotentiaries of the United States, when commissioned to attend the meeting at the Isthmus, will take part; and such are the motives and purposes with which the invitation of the three Republics was accepted. It was, however, as the House will perceive from the correspondence, accepted only upon condition that the nomination of Commissioners for the mission should receive the advice and consent of the Senate.

The concurrence of the House to the measure, by the appropriations necessary for carrying it into effect, is alike subject to its free determination and indispensable to the fulfilment of the intention.

That the Congress at Panama will accomplish all or even any of the transcendent benefits to the human race which warmed the conceptions of its first proposer, it were, perhaps, indulging too sanguine a forecast of events to promise. It is, in its nature, a measure speculative and experimental. The blessing of Heaven may turn it to the account of human improvement. Accidents unforseen and mischances not to be anticipated may baffle all its high purposes and disappoint its fairest expectations. But the design is great, is benevolent, is humane.

It looks to the melioration of the condition of man. It is congenial with that spirit which prompted the Declaration of our Independence; which inspired the preamble of our first treaty with France; which dictated our first treaty with Prussia, and the instructions under which it was negotiated; which filled the hearts and fired the souls of the immortal founders of our Revolution.

With this unrestricted exposition of the motives by which I have been governed in this transaction as well as of the objects to be discussed and of the ends, if possible, to be attained by our representation at the proposed Congress, I submit the propriety of an appropriation to the candid consideration and enlightened patriotism of the Legislature.

JOHN QUINCY ADAMS.

WASHINGTON, *March* 15, 1826.

DEPARTMENT OF STATE, *March* 14, 1826.

The Secretary of State, to whom the President has referred that part of the resolution of the House of Representatives of the 3d instant which requests that he would cause to be laid before that House "so much of the correspondence between the Government of the United States and the new States of America, or their ministers, respecting the proposed Congress or meeting of diplomatic agents at Panama, and of such information respecting the general character of that expected Congress as may be in his possession," has the honor now to report:

That during the last spring he held, at the Department of State, separate conferences, on the same day, with the respective ministers of Colombia and Mexico, in the course of which each of them verbally stated that his Government was desirous that the United States should be represented at the proposed Congress, and that he was instructed to communicate an invitation to their Government to send representatives to it; but that, as his Government did not know whether it would be agreeable or not to the United States to receive such an invitation, and as it was not wished to occasion any embarrassment to them, he was charged informally to inquire, previous to the delivery of the invitation, whether it would be accepted, if given, by both of the Republics of Mexico and Colombia. It was also stated by each of those ministers that his Government did not expect that the United States would change their present neutral policy, nor was it desired that they should take part in such of the deliberations of the proposed Congress as might relate to the prosecution of the existing war with Spain.

Having laid before the President what transpired at these conferences, his direction was received, about a week after they had been held, to inform the ministers of Mexico and Colombia, and they were accordingly informed, that their communication was received with due sensibility to the friendly consideration of the United States by which it had been dictated; that of course they could not make themselves a party to the war between the new States and Spain, nor to councils for deliberating on the means of its further prosecution; that the President believed that such a Congress as was contemplated might be highly useful in settling several important disputed questions of public law, in arranging other matters of deep interest to the American continent, and in strengthening the friendship and amicable intercourse between the American powers; that before such a Congress, however, assembled, it appeared to the President to be expedient to adjust, between the different powers to be represented, several preliminary points, such as the subjects to which the attention of the Congress was to be directed, the nature and the form of the powers to be given to the diplomatic agents who were to compose it, and the mode of its organization and its action. If these preliminary points could be arranged in a manner satisfactory to the United States, the ministers from Colombia and Mexico were informed that the President thought that the United States ought to be represented at Panama. Each of those ministers undertook to transmit to his Government the answer which was thus given to both.

In this posture the overture remained until the letters were received, which accompany this report, from the ministers of the Republics of Mexico and Colombia, under date of the 2d and 3d of November, 1825. A similar answer was returned to each of those letters in official notes, a copy of one of which is with this report.

The first and only communication from the minister of the Republic of Central America to this Department in regard to the Congress at Panama is contained in his official note, a copy of which, together with a copy of the answer which was returned, will be found along with this report.

Copies of conventions, containing stipulations respecting the intended Congress, are herewith reported between—

The Republic of Colombia and that of Chile;
The Republic of Colombia and Peru;
The Republic of Colombia and the Federation of the Centre of America; and
The Republic of Colombia and the United Mexican States.*

The Secretary of State has also the honor to report to the President extracts from the instructions which were given by the Department of State to Mr. Anderson on the 27th day of May, 1823; and copies of certain parts of the correspondence which, since the last session of Congress, has taken place between the Executive of the United States and the Governments of Russia, France, Spain, and Mexico, of which a descriptive list accompanies this report. In respect to the negotiation which Mr. Middleton was authorized, by the despatch of the 10th of May last,† (one of the papers now reported,) to institute at St. Petersburg, considering the lapse of time and the great and lamented event which has lately occurred in Europe, perhaps there is no adequate reason for refraining from a communication of it to the House, which is recommended by its intimate connexion with the interests of the new Republics. About the same period with the date of that despatch instructions were given to Mr. Everett to inculcate on Spain the necessity of peace, and to our ministers in France and England to invite the Cabinets of Paris and London to co-operate in the same work. The hope, not yet abandoned, was indulged that, by a united exertion of all the great powers, and especially of Russia, Spain might be brought to see her true interests in terminating the existing war. Other negotiations, growing out of and subordinate to that which was authorized in the before-mentioned despatch of the 10th of May to Mr. Middleton, have been more recently commenced. They have for their object the prevention of disorder in the Spanish islands of Cuba and Porto Rico, and also to guard the United States against the danger of bad examples and excesses, of which, in the course of events, those islands might become the theatre, as well as the conservation of our commercial and navigating interests.

All of which is respectfully submitted.

H. CLAY.

---

* These conventions were communicated to the Senate in a report of the Secretary of State accompanying the President's message to the Senate of the 10th of January, 1826, in answer to a resolution of the Senate of the 3d of January, 1826.

† This letter to Mr. Middleton, of the 10th of May, 1825, was communicated, *with others*, (see following list,) to the Senate, at the same time with the conventions above mentioned.

N. B. All the documents mentioned in the above list were communicated to the Senate and will be found in the preceding pages of this number, with the exception of the first on the above list, which is here inserted, as follows:

The following document was not communicated to the Senate:

Extracts of a letter from Mr. Adams, Secretary of State, to Mr. Anderson, Minister Plenipotentiary to Colombia, dated May 27, 1823.

' The revolution which has severed the colonies of Spanish America from European thraldom, and left them to form self-dependent Governments as members of the society of civilized nations, is among the most important events in modern history. As a general movement in human affairs it is perhaps no more than a development of principles first brought into action by the separation of these States from Great Britain, and by the practical illustration, given in the formation and establishment of our Union, to the doctrine that voluntary agreement is the only legitimate source of authority among men, and that all just Government is a compact. It was impossible that such a system as Spain had established over her colonies should stand before the progressive improvement of the understanding in this age, or that the light shed upon the whole earth by the results of our Revolution should leave in utter darkness the regions immediately adjoining upon ourselves. The independence of the Spanish colonies, however, has proceeded from other causes, and has been achieved upon principles in many respects different from ours. In our Revolution the principle of the social compact was, from the beginning, in immediate issue. It originated in a question of *right* between the Government in Europe and the subject in America. Our *independence* was declared in defence of our *liberties*, and the attempt to make the yoke a yoke of oppression was the cause and the justification for casting it off.

"The revolution of the Spanish colonies was not caused by the oppression under which they had been held, however great it had been. Their independence was first forced upon them by the temporary subjugation of Spain herself to a foreign power. They were, by that event, cast upon themselves, and compelled to establish Governments of their own. Spain, through all the vicissitudes of her own revolutions, has clung to the desperate hope of retaining or reclaiming them to her own control, and has waged, to the extent of her power, a disastrous war to that intent. In the mind of every rational man it has been for years apparent that Spain can never succeed to recover her dominion where it has been abjured, nor is it probable that she can long retain the small remnant of her authority yet acknowledged in some spots of the South American continent.

"The political course of the United States, from the first dawning of South American independence, has been such as was prescribed by their relative duties to all the parties. Being on terms of peace and amity with Spain through all the changes of her own Government, they have considered the struggles of the colonies for independence as a case of civil war, to which their national obligations prescribed to them to remain neutral. Their policy, their interest, and their feelings, all concurred to favor the cause of the colonies; and the principles upon which the right of independence has been maintained by the South American patriots have been approved, not only as identical with those upon which our own independence was asserted and achieved, but as involving the whole theory of Government on the emphatically American foundation of the sovereignty of the people and the unalienable rights of man. To a cause reposing upon this basis the people of this country never could be indifferent, and their sympathies have accordingly been, with great unanimity and constancy, enlisted in its favor. The sentiments of the Government of the United States have been in perfect harmony with those of their people, and while forbearing, as their duties of neutrality prescribed, from every measure which could justly be construed as hostile to Spain, they have exercised all the moral influence which they possessed to countenance and promote the cause of independence. So long as a contest of arms, with a rational or even remote prospect of eventual success, was maintained by Spain, the United States could not recognise the independence of the colonies as existing *de facto* without trespassing on their duties to Spain by assuming as decided that which was precisely the question of the war. In the history of South American independence there are

.two periods, clearly distinguishable from each other: the first, that of its origin, when it was rather a war of independence against France than against Spain; and the second, from the restoration of Ferdinand VII, in 1814. Since that period the territories now constituting the Republic of Colombia have been the only theatre upon which Spain has been able to maintain the conflict offensively, with even a probable color of ultimate success. But when, in 1815, she made her greatest effort, in the expedition from Cadiz, commanded by Morillo, Mexico, Peru, and Chile were yet under her authority; and had she succeeded in reducing the coast of Terra Firma and New Granada, the provinces of La Plata, divided among themselves, and weakened by the Portuguese occupation of Montevideo, would probably not have held out against her long. This, at least, was the calculation of her policy; and from the geographical position of those countries, which may be termed the heart of South America, the conclusion might well be drawn that if the power of Spain could not be firmly reseated there, it must be, on her part, a fruitless struggle to maintain her supremacy in any part of the American continent. The expedition of Morillo, on its first arrival, was attended with signal success. Carthagena was taken, the whole coast of Terra Firma was occupied, and New Granada was entirely subdued. A remnant of Patriots in Venezuela, with their leader, Bolivar, returning from expulsion, revived the cause of independence; and after the campaign of 1819, in which they reconquered the whole of New Granada, the demonstration became complete, that every effort of Spain to recover the South American continent must thenceforward be a desperate waste of her own resources, and that the truest friendship of other nations to her would consist in making her sensible that her own interest would be best consulted by the acknowledgment of that independence which she could no longer effectually dispute.

To this conclusion the Government of the United States had at an earlier period arrived. But from that emergency, the President has considered the question of recognition, both in a moral and political view, as merely a question of the proper *time*. While Spain could entertain a reasonable hope of maintaining the war and of recovering her authority, the acknowledgment of the colonies as independent States would have been a wrong to her; but she had no right, upon the strength of this principle, to maintain the pretension after she was manifestly disabled from maintaining the contest, and, by unreasonably withholding her acknowledgment, to deprive the Independents of their right to demand the acknowledgment of others. To fix upon the precise *time* when the duty to respect the prior sovereign right of Spain should cease, and that of yielding to the claim of acknowledgment would commence, was a subject of great delicacy, and, to the President, of constant and anxious solicitude. It naturally became, in the first instance, a proper subject of consultation with other powers having relations of interest to themselves with the newly opened countries as well as influence in the general affairs of Europe. In August, 1818, a formal proposal was made to the British Government for a concerted and cotemporary recognition of the independence of Buenos Ayres, then the only one of the South American States which, having declared independence, had no *Spanish* force contending against it within its borders; and where it therefore most unequivocally existed *in fact*. The British Government declined accepting the proposal themselves, without, however, expressing any disapprobation of it; without discussing it as a question of principle, and without assigning any reason for the refusal, other than that it did not then suit with their policy. It became a subject of consideration at the deliberations of the Congress of Aix-la-Chapelle, in October, 1818. There is reason to believe that it disconcerted projects which were there entertained of engaging the European Alliance in actual operations against the South Americans, as it is well known that a plan for their joint mediation between Spain and her colonies, for restoring them to her authority, was actually matured and finally failed at that place, only by the refusal of Great Britain to accede to the condition of employing *force* eventually against the South Americans for its accomplishment. Some dissatisfaction was manifested by several members of the Congress at Aix-la-Chapelle at this avowal on the part of the United States of their readiness to recognize the independence of Buenos Ayres.

The reconquest, in the campaign of 1819, of New Granada to the Patriot cause was immediately followed by the formation of the Republic of Colombia, consisting of three great divisions of the preceding Spanish Government: Venezuela, Cundinamarca, and Quito. It was soon succeeded by the dissolution of the Spanish authority in Mexico; by the revolution in Spain itself; and by the military operations which resulted in the declaration of independence in Peru. In November, 1820, was concluded the armistice between the Generals Morillo and Bolivar, together with a subsequent treaty, stipulating that, in case of the renewal of the war, the parties would abstain from all hostilities and practices not consistent with the modern law of nations and the humane maxims of civilization. In February, 1821, the partial independence of Mexico was proclaimed at Yguala; and in August of the same year was recognized by the Spanish Viceroy and Captain General O'Donoju, at Cordova.

The formation of the Republic of Colombia, by the fundamental law of the 17th of December, 1819, was notified to this Government by its agent, the late Don Manuel Torres, on the 20th of February, 1821, with a request that it might be recognized by the Government of the United States, and a proposal for the negotiation of treaties of commerce and navigation, *founded upon the bases of reciprocal utility and perfect equality*, as the most efficacious means of strengthening and increasing the relations of amity between the two Republics.

The request and proposal were renewed in a letter from Mr. Torres, of the 30th of November, 1821, and again repeated on the 2d of January, 1822. In the interval since the first demand, the General Congress of the new Republic had assembled, and formed a constitution, founded upon the principles of popular representation, and divided into legislative, executive, and judicial authorities. The Government under this constitution had been organized and was in full operation; while, during the same period, the principal remnant of the Spanish force had been destroyed by the battle of Carabobo, and its last fragments were confined to the two places of Porto Cabello and Panama.

Under these circumstances, a resolution of the House of Representatives of the United States, on the 30th of January, 1822, requested of the President to lay before the House the communications from the agents of the United States with the Governments south of the United States which had declared their independence, and those from the agents of such Governments here with the Secretary of State, tending to show the political condition of their Governments and the state of the war between them and Spain. In transmitting to the House the papers called for by this resolution, the President, by his message of the 8th of March, 1822, declared his own persuasion that the time had arrived when, in strict conformity to the law of nations and in the fulfilment of the duties of equal and impartial justice to all parties, the acknowledgment of the independence declared by the Spanish American colonies could no longer be withheld. Both Houses of Congress having almost unanimously concurred with these views of the President, an appropriation was made by law (4th of May, 1822,) for such missions to the independent nations on the American continent as the President should deem proper.

On the day after the President's message of the 8th of March, the Spanish minister, Anduaga, addressed to this Department a remonstrance against the measure which it recommended, and a solemn protest against the recognition of the Governments mentioned of the insurgent Spanish provinces of America. He was answered on the 6th of April, by a letter recapitulating the circumstances under which the Government of the United States had "yielded to an obligation of duty of the highest order, by recognizing as independent States nations which, after deliberately asserting their right to that character, had maintained and established it against all the resistance which had been or could be brought to oppose it." On the 24th of April he gave information that the Spanish Government had disavowed the treaty of the 24th of August, 1821, between the Captain General O'Donoju and Colonel Iturbide, and had denied the authority of the former to conclude it.

On the 12th of February, 1822, the Spanish Extraordinary Cortes adopted the report of a committee proposing the appointment of Commissioners to proceed to South America to negotiate with the revolutionary Patriots concerning the relations to be established thereafter in regard to their connexion with Spain. They declared, at the same time, all treaties made with them before that time by Spanish commanders, implying any acknowledgment of their independence, null and void, as not having been authorized by the Cortes; and on the next day they passed three resolutions, the first annulling expressly the treaty between O'Donoju and Iturbide.

The second, "That the Spanish Government, by a declaration to all others with which it has friendly relations, make known to them that the Spanish nation will regard, *at any epoch*, as a violation of the treaties, the recognition, either partial or absolute, of the independence of the Spanish provinces of Ultramer, so long as the dissensions which exist between some of them and the Metropolis *are not terminated*, with whatever else may serve to convince foreign Governments that Spain has not yet renounced any of the rights belonging to it in those countries."

The third resolution recommended to the Government to take all necessary measures, and to apply to the Cortes for the needed resources to preserve and recover the authority of Spain in the ultramarine provinces.

These measures of the Cortes were not known to the President of the United States when he sent to Congress his message of the 8th of March; but information of them was received while the bill making an appropriation for the missions was before Congress, and on the 25th of April a resolution of the Senate requested of the President any information he might have, proper to be disclosed, from our minister at Madrid, or from the Spanish minister resident in this country, concerning the views of Spain relative to the recognition of the independence of the South American colonies and of the dictamen of the Spanish Cortes. In answer to this resolution, the letter from Mr. Anduaga, protesting against the recognition, and one from Mr. Forsyth, inclosing a translation of the dictamen, were transmitted to the Senate, which, with all these documents before them, gave their concurrent sanction, with that of the House of Representatives, to the passage of the bill of appropriation.

This review of the proceedings of the Government of the United States in relation to the independence of Spanish America has been taken to show the consistency of the principles by which they were uniformly dictated, and that they have been always eminently friendly to the new Republics, and disinterested. While Spain maintained a doubtful contest with arms to recover her dominion it was regarded as a civil war. When that contest became so manifestly desperate that Spanish Viceroys, Governors, and Captain Generals themselves, concluded treaties with the insurgents, virtually acknowledging their independence, the United States frankly and unreservedly recognized the fact, without making their acknowledgment the price of any favor to themselves, and although at the hazard of incurring the displeasure of Spain. In this measure they have taken the lead of the whole civilized world; for, although the Portuguese Brazilian Government had, a few months before, recognized the revolutionary Government of Buenos Ayres, it was at a moment when a projected declaration of their own independence made the question substantially their own cause, and it was presented as an equivalent for a reciprocal recognition of their own much more questionable right to the eastern shore of La Plata.

On the 17th day of June, 1822, Mr. Manuel Torres was received by the President of the United States as the chargé d'affaires from the Republic of Colombia, and the immediate consequence of our recognition was the admission of the vessels of the South American nations, under their own colors, into the ports of the principal maritime nations of Europe.

The European alliance of Emperors and Kings have assumed, as the foundation of human society, the doctrine of unalienable *allegiance.* Our doctrine is founded upon the principle of unalienable *right.* The European allies, therefore, have viewed the *cause* of the South Americans as rebellion against their lawful sovereign. We have considered it as the assertion of natural right. They have invariably shown their disapprobation of the revolution, and their wishes for the restoration of the Spanish power. We have as constantly favored the standard of independence and of America. In contrasting the principles and the motives of the European powers, as manifested in their policy towards South America, with those of the United States, it has not been my intention to boast of our superior purity, or to lay a claim of merit to any extraordinary favor from South America in return. Disinterestedness must be its own reward; but in the establishment of our future political and commercial intercourse with the new Republics it will be necessary to recur often to the principles in which it originated; they will serve to mark the boundaries of the rights which we may justly claim in our future relations with them, and to counteract the efforts which it cannot be doubted European negotiators will continue to make in the furtherance of their monarchical and monopolizing contemplations.

Upon a territory by one-half more extensive than the whole inhabited part of the United States, with a population of less than four millions of souls, the Republic of Colombia has undertaken to establish a single, and not a confederated Government.

Whether this attempt will be found practicable in execution may be susceptible of doubt; but in the new organization of society upon this hemisphere, even unsuccessful experiments lead to results by which the science of Government is advanced and the happiness of man is promoted. The Republic of Colombia has a constitution deliberately formed and adopted upon principles entirely republican, with an elective Legislature in two branches, a distribution of the powers of Government, with the exception of the federative character, almost identical with our own, and articles declaratory of the natural rights of the citizen to personal security, property, and reputation, and of the inviolable liberty of the press. With such a constitution, in such a country, the modifications which experience may prove to be necessary for rendering the political institutions most effectually competent to the ends of civil Government, will make their own way by peaceable and gradual conquests of public opinion. If a single Government should be found inadequate to secure and protect the rights of the people living under it, a federation of Republics may, without difficulty, be substituted in its place. Practical effect having once been given to the principle that lawful government is a compact and not a grant, the pretences for resorting to force for effecting political revolutions disappear. The subordination of the military to the civil power is the only principle yet remaining to be established in Colombia to insure the liberties of the future genera-. tions as well as those of the present age; and that subordination, although not directly guarantied by their present constitution, is altogether conformable to its spirit.

In the letter of February 20, 1821, from the late Mr. Torres, demanding the recognition of the Republic of Colombia, it has been observed that the additional proposal was made of negotiating "*treaties of navigation and commerce*, founded upon the bases of reciprocal utility and perfect equality, as the most efficacious means of strengthening and increasing the relations of amity between the two Republics."

In compliance with this proposal, among the documents furnished you, for proceeding upon the mission to which you have been appointed, of minister plenipotentiary to the Republic of Colombia, is a full power which will authorize you to negotiate with any plenipotentiary or plenipotentiaries of that Government, duly provided with like powers, such a treaty. The President wishes, however, that every step in such negotiation should be taken with full deliberation. The treaty, if concluded, must, as you are aware, be reserved subject to ratification here, with the advice and consent of the Senate, by the constitutional majority of two-thirds, as by the constitution of Colombia (article 120) their treaties, to be valid, must receive the consent and approbation of their Congress.

Our commercial relations with the Colombian territory are of so recent origin, and have depended so much upon the revolutionary condition of that country, under which they have arisen, that our know-ledge of their state and character is very imperfect, although we are certain that they are altogether different from those which may be expected to arise from permanent interests, when the independence of the Republic shall be universally recognized, and a free trade shall be opened to its inhabitants with all parts of the world. The only important point now to be settled, as the radical principle of all our future commercial intercourse, is the basis proposed by Mr. Torres, of *reciprocal utility and perfect equality*. As the necessary consequence of which, you will claim that, without waiting for the conclusion of a treaty, the commerce and navigation of the United States, in the ports of the Colombian Republic, should be received on the footing of equality with the most favored nation. It is hoped, indeed, that on your arrival at the place of your destination you will find the principle already settled, assurances to that effect having been given by the Minister of Foreign Relations to Mr. Todd.

By an act of the Congress of Colombia of the 25th of September, 1821, an impost duty of $7\frac{1}{2}$ per cent. was laid upon all articles imported from any part of America, *additional* to the duty upon the like articles imported from Europe. This discrimination was mentioned to Mr. Torres at the time of his reception. He thought it had arisen only from an inadvertency, and promised to write concerning it to his Government. Mr. Todd was instructed to remonstrate against it, which he accordingly did. From his correspondence and conferences relating to it with the Colombian Minister of Foreign Relations, Dr. Gual, it appears that the object of the law was to burden with heavier duties the indirect trade from Great Britain and France, carried on through the medium of the West India islands, and thereby to present to those powers an inducement to acknowledge the independence of the Republic. However just or reasonable this expedient might be with reference to the relations between the Colombian people and European nations, it was manifestly injurious to the United States; nor was its injustice in any manner compensated by the provisions of another law of the Congress of September 27, 1821, allowing a draw-back of duties upon re-exportations *in their own vessels* of provisions imported from the United States. It is alleged by Dr. Gual that the object of this latter law was to favor the United States by facilitating the indirect trade between them and the British colonies in the West Indies, the direct trade being then interdicted by the laws of the United States and of Great Britain. But this trade was carried on more advantageously to the United States by the way of the Swedish, Danish, and Dutch islands, than it could be by that of the Colombian ports, and the object of favoring their own shipping appears more obviously as the motive of the law, than that of favoring the commerce of the United States. The opening of the direct trade between the United States and the British islands has, at all events, rendered all the provisions of the Colombian law of September 27, 1821, inoperative; and assurances have been given by Dr. Gual that, at the meeting of the Congress which was to take place in March last, measures would be taken for procuring the immediate repeal of the discrimination, to the disadvantage of the United States, prescribed by the law of the 25th of September.

The spirit of the Colombian constitution is explicitly that of entire and unqualified independence, and the sentiments expressed by Dr. Gual to Mr. Todd have been altogether conformable to it. He has declared that the intention of the Government is to treat all *foreign* nations upon the footing of equal favor and of perfect reciprocity. This is all that the United States will require, and this, so far as their interests are concerned, they have a right to exact.

It had been, in the first instance, proposed by Mr. Torres that the treaty of commerce and navigation should be negotiated *here*, and he informed me that a minister would be appointed with powers and instructions sufficient for concluding it at this place. Dr. Gual has informed Mr. Todd that the views of the Colombian Government have since undergone a change; and although they have appointed Mr. Salazar as Envoy Extraordinary and Minister Plenipotentiary to the United States, and in March last he was under instructions to proceed forthwith upon his mission to this country, they were, nevertheless, exceed· ingly desirous that the *treaty* should be negotiated there.

The President deems it of no material importance to the United States whether the treaty shall be negotiated at Washington or at Bogota; but the proposal having first been made for concluding it here, it was natural to inquire what it was that produced the change in the wishes of the Colombian Government with regard to the seat of the negotiation. Dr. Gual intimated confidentially to Mr. Todd that it had proceeded from two causes: one, the desire to establish a *precedent* which might prevail upon the great *European* Governments to negotiate likewise with the Republic at its own capital, and thereby hasten them to the recognition of Colombian independence; and the other, a jealousy of their own negotiators in Europe, who were apt to become themselves entangled with European intrigues, and to involve the Republic in unsuitable and perplexing engagements. With regard to the second of these causes, what-ever occasion may have been given to the distrust of their own agents which it avows, it could have no application to their transactions with the United States. By assuming the principles of independence, equality, and reciprocity as the foundations of all our negotiations, we discard all the incentives and all the opportunities for double dealing, overreaching, and corrupt caballing. We shall ask nothing which the Colombian Republic can have any interest to deny. We shall offer nothing for which she may be unwilling to yield the fair equivalent. To the other reason, however, the President the more readily accedes, because, perceiving its full force, it gives him an opportunity of manifesting in action the friendly disposition of the United States towards the Republic, and their readiness to promote by all proper means the recognition of its independence by the great European powers.

In the negotiation of all commercial treaties there is undoubtedly an advantage, at least of convenience, enjoyed by the party which treats *at home;* and this advantage acquires greater importance when, as is now the case with both parties, the treaty, to become valid, must obtain the assent of legislative assemblies. This advantage, in the ordinary course of things, accrues to the party to whom the proposal of negotiation is first made. Independent, then, of all questions of precedence, and without resorting to the example of the first treaties negotiated by the United States, both of which considerations have been mentioned by Mr. Todd to Dr. Gual, the United States might insist upon having the negotiation concluded *here,* not only as the first proposal of it was made to them, but because the proposal itself was that it should be concluded here. The President, however, is well aware of the stimulus which a treaty negotiated, and even a negotiation known to be in progress at Bogota, will apply to the attention of European interests, and has no doubt that it will press them to the recognition more powerfully than they have been urged by the example, or are likely to be by the exhortations of the North American Government. You are accordingly furnished, by his direction, with the full power necessary for the conclusion of the treaty.

Dr. Gual informed Mr. Todd that the project of the treaty was already prepared, and that a copy of it would be committed to Mr. Salazar, with powers and instructions authorizing him to conclude the negotiation, if this Government should insist upon its being completed here. The arrival of Mr. Salazar may be expected from day to day. In the meantime, we are yet unacquainted with the particular objects of commercial intercourse which the Colombian Government wishes to regulate with us by treaty. The only object which we shall have much at heart in the negotiation will be the sanction by solemn compact of the broad and liberal principles of *independence, equal favors,* and *reciprocity.* With this view I recommend to your particular attention the preamble and first four articles of the first treaty of amity and commerce between the United States and France, concluded on the 6th of February, 1778. The preamble is believed to be the first instance on the diplomatic record of nations upon which the true principles of all fair commercial negotiation between independent States were laid down and proclaimed to the world. That preamble was to the foundation of our commercial intercourse with the rest of mankind what the Declaration of Independence was to that of our internal Government. The two instruments were parts of one and the same system, matured by long and anxious deliberation of the founders of this Union in the ever memorable Congress of 1776; and as the Declaration of Independence was the fountain of all our municipal institutions, the preamble to the treaty with France laid the corner stone for all our subsequent transactions of intercourse with foreign nations. Its principles should be therefore deeply impressed upon the mind of every statesman and negotiator of this Union, and the first four articles of the treaty with France contain the practical exposition of those principles which may serve as models for insertion in the projected treaty, or in any other that we may hereafter negotiate with any of the rising Republics of the south.

There is indeed a principle of still more expansive liberality, which may be assumed as the basis of commercial intercourse between nation and nation. It is that of placing the *foreigner,* in regard to all objects of navigation and commerce, upon a footing of equal favor with the *native* citizen, and, to that end, of abolishing all discriminating duties and charges whatsoever. This principle is altogether congenial to the spirit of our institutions, and the main obstacle to its adoption consists in this: that the fairness of its operation depends upon its being admitted *universally.* For while two maritime and commercial nations should bind themselves to it as a compact operative only between *them,* a third power might avail itself of its own restrictive and discriminating regulations to secure advantages to its own people, at the expense of both the parties to the treaty. The United States have, nevertheless, made considerable advances in their proposals to other nations towards the general establishment of this most liberal of all principles of commercial intercourse.

On the 3d of March, 1815, immediately after the conclusion of our late war with Great Britain, an act of Congress (United States Laws, vol. 4, p. 824) repealed *so much* of the discriminating duties of tonnage and impost as were imposed on foreign vessels and merchandise beyond the duties imposed on the same in our own vessels; *so far* as they respected the *produce or manufacture of the nation to which the foreign vessel might belong.* The repeal to take effect in favor of *any* foreign nation whenever the President of the United States should be satisfied that the discriminating or countervailing duties of such foreign nation, so far as they operated to the disadvantage of the United States, had been abolished.

On the 3d of July, 1815, (United States Laws, vol. 6, p. 603,) a convention was concluded with Great Britain, by the second article of which this principle was adopted for the commercial intercourse between the United States and the British territories *in Europe,* so far as related to duties and charges of tonnage, impost, export, and bounties upon articles of the produce or manufacture of the two countries, respectively. It was partially admitted for *drawbacks.* But the intercourse between the United States and the British possessions in India was differently regulated by another article of the same convention, and that between the United States and the British colonies in America was expressly excepted from the convention, leaving each party to the exercise, in this respect, of its own rights. This convention, originally limited to four years, was afterwards, by the convention of October 20, 1818, (United States Laws, vol. 6, p. 607,) extended for the term of ten years from that time.

On the 4th of September, 1816, (United States Laws, vol. 6, p. 642,) a treaty with Sweden and Norway was concluded and extended to the Swedish island of St. Bartholomew, in the West Indies; by the second article of which the same principle is established of equal duties and charges, of tonnage, impost, export, and prohibition, upon vessels and their cargoes, being of the produce or manufacture of the respective countries, whether in vessels of the foreigner or the native. The duration of this treaty is limited to the 25th of September, 1826.

On the 20th of April, 1818, (United States Laws, vol. 6, p. 344,) an act of Congress repealed all discriminating duties of tonnage and impost in favor of the vessels of the *Netherlands* and their cargoes, being of the produce or manufacture of the Territories *in Europe,* of the King of the Netherlands, or "*such produce and manufactures as can only be or most usually are first shipped from a port or place in the Kingdom aforesaid.*" Such repeal to take effect from the time the Government of the Netherlands had abolished its discriminating duties upon the vessels of the United States, and on merchandise imported in them, being of the produce or manufacture of the United States.

By an act of March 3, 1819, in addition to the above, (United States Laws, vol. 6, p. 411,) it was extended in all its provisions and limitations to the vessels of *Prussia*, of the city of *Hamburg*, and of the city of *Bremen*.

This same act of March 3, 1819, limited its own duration and that of the act to which it was in addition, and the act of March 3, 1815, itself, to the first of January, 1824.

The provisions of the 3d March, 1815, have been extended by proclamations of the President of the United States, as follows:

1818, July 24, to the Free and Hanseatic city of Bremen.—(United States Laws, vol. 6, p. 599.)
August 1, to the Free and Hanseatic city of Hamburg.—p. 600.
1820, May 4, the Free and Hanseatic city of Hamburg.—p. 601.
1821, August 20, to the Kingdom of Norway.—p. 602.
November 22, to the Dukedom of Oldenburg.—p. 774.

You will observe that the act of March 3, 1819, admitted the vessels of *Hamburg* and *Bremen* to advantages more extensive than those offered by the act of March, 3 1815, and which had already been secured to them by the proclamations of July 24, and August 1, 1818. The same enlargement of the favors offered by the act of March 3, 1815, is extended to the vessels of the Netherlands and of Prussia; while Norway has the double security, of the principle offered in the act of March 3, 1815, by the stipulation in the treaty with Sweden, and by the President's proclamation under the act.

The proclamation with regard to Norway was founded on an act of the Government of that Kingdom, not extending, however, to Sweden, abolishing all discriminating duties whatsoever in the Norwegian ports between their own vessels and vessels of the United States, and upon their cargoes of whatsoever origin, and whencesoever coming. This is the consummation of the principle of treating the foreigner, in respect to navigation and foreign commerce, upon a footing of equal favor with the native. The Government of Norway, in adopting this regulation, required that it should be reciprocally granted to Norwegian vessels and their cargoes in the ports of the United States. This, however, could be granted only by an act of Congress; and the proclamation could only extend to them under the *law* that to which they were already entitled by the *treaty*.

The subject was submitted to Congress by a message from the President towards the close of the first session of the 17th Congress, (May 1, 1822,) and the general policy of our commercial system, with particular reference to the act of March 3, 1815, and the subsequent measures resulting from it, had been reviewed in the message of December 5, 1821, at the commencement of the same session. The principle offered by the Norwegian Government could not, however, then have been accepted without great disadvantage to the United States. Our direct trade with the British colonies in America was interdicted by our own and British laws. That with France was under countervailing regulations of both parties, equivalent to interdiction. To have granted then to Norwegian vessels unrestricted admission into our ports upon the same terms with our own would, in fact, have granted them privileges which our own did not and could not enjoy; our own being under the operation of restrictions and prohibitions, ordained by Britain and France, from which the Norwegian vessels would have been exempt.

Our direct trade with the British American colonies has since been opened, and that with France has been restored; both, however, shackled with countervailing restrictions and regulations, burdensome to those by whom it may be carried on. As the act of Congress of March 3, 1815, and all the regulations founded upon it, will expire on the first of January next, the whole subject will again be before that body at their next session for revisal. In this state of things, it may be perhaps most prudent, in the commercial negotiations with the Republic of Colombia, to adhere to the principle of *equal favor to the most friendly nation*, leaving that of *equal favor with the native* for future consideration and concert between the parties.

To the same extent, however, as we are already bound by treaty with Great Britain until October, 1828, and with Sweden until September, 1826, you may safely proceed; taking the second article of each of those compacts for a model, and forming an article embracing the stipulations of both. Thus far we may safely go with any one or more foreign nations, without endangering, by the liberality of our engagements with them, the interests of our own country, to be affected by the restrictive ordinances of others. An exception must be made with regard to the ports of St. Augustine and Pensacola, where, by the 15th article of the late treaty with Spain, special privileges are secured to Spanish vessels until the 22d of May, 1833.

Among the usual objects of negotiation in treaties of commerce and navigation are the liberty of conscience and of religious worship. Articles to this effect have been seldom admitted in Roman Catholic countries, and are even interdicted by the present constitution of Spain. The South American Republics have been too much under the influence of the same intolerant spirit; but the Colombian constitution is honorably distinguished by exemption from it. The 10th and 11th articles of our treaty with Prussia, or articles to the like effect, may be proposed for insertion in the projected treaty; and after setting the first example in South America of a constitution unsullied by prohibitions of religious liberty, Colombia will deserve new honors in the veneration of present and future ages by giving her *positive* sanction to the freedom of conscience, and by stipulating it in her first treaty with these United States. It is, in truth, an essential part of the system of American independence. Civil, political, commercial, and religious liberty, are but various modifications of one great principle, founded in the unalienable rights of human nature, and before the universal application of which the colonial domination of Europe over the American hemisphere has fallen, and is crumbling into dust. *Civil* liberty *can* be established on no foundation of human reason which will not at the same time demonstrate the *right* to religious freedom. The tendency of the spirit of the age is so strong towards religious liberty that we cannot doubt it will soon banish from the constitutions of the southern Republics of this hemisphere all those intolerant religious establishments with which they have hitherto been trammelled. Religious and military coercion will be alike discarded from all the institutions framed for the protection of human rights in civil society of independent nations, and the freedom of opinion and of faith will be guarantied by the same sanction as the rights to personal liberty and security. To promote this event by all the moral influence which we can exercise, whether of example, of friendly counsel, or of persuasion, is among the duties which devolve upon us in the formation of our future relations with our southern neighbors; and in the intercourse which is hereafter to subsist between us, as their citizens who may visit or transiently reside with us will enjoy the benefit of religious freedom in its utmost latitude, we are bound to claim for our countrymen who may occasionally dwell for a time with them the reciprocal exercise of the same natural rights.

In the present imperfect state of our information with regard to the existing commerce between the two countries, and the uncertainty as to what its future and permanent relations may be, it would be useless to enter into any further detail of articles which it may be proper to propose for the intended treaty of commerce. The Republic of Colombia, if permanently organized to embrace the whole territory which it now claims, and blessed with a Government effectually protective of the rights of its people, is undoubtedly destined to become hereafter one of the mightiest nations of the earth. Its central position upon the surface of the globe, directly communicating at once with the Pacific and Atlantic Oceans, north and south, with the Caribbean Sea and the Gulf of Mexico, brings it into relations of proximity with every other part of the world; while the number and variety of its ports on every sea by which it is surrounded, the magnitude and extent of its navigable rivers, three of which, the Amazon, the Orinoco, and the Magdalena, are among the largest in the world, intersecting with numberless tributary streams, and in every direction the continent of South America, and furnishing the means of water communication from every point of its circumference to every spot upon its surface; the fertility of its soil; the general healthiness and beauty of its climate; the profusion with which it breeds and bears the precious and the useful metals, present a combination of elements unparalleled in the location of the human race, and relieve, at least from all charge of enthusiasm, the sentiment expressed by the late Mr. Torres, that this republic appeared to have been destined by the Author of Nature "as the centre and the *empire* of the human family."

But it is to *man*, placed in a Paradise like this, that Nature, with her loudest, voice exclaims: "God to *thee* has done his part—do thine;" and the part of man, so gifted and so endowed, is to enjoy and to communicate the bounties of Providence so largely lavished upon him, and not to fancy himself destined to the *empire* of the human family. If the natural advantages bestowed upon the Colombian territory were to be improved by its inhabitants only for purposes of empire, that which nature has bestowed as a blessing upon them would, in its consequences prove a curse inflicted upon the rest of mankind. The territory of Colombia contains, at this moment, little more than three million and a half of souls. Were it only as populous as its late parent country, Spain, it would bear one hundred millions; and if as populous as France, nearly three times that number. At the most rapid rate of increase which human population has ever attained, even a doubling every quarter of a century, the Republic of Colombia, for two hundred years to come, may devote all her exertions to the improvement of her internal means of subsistence for the multiplying myriads of her people, without seeking support from the extension of her empire beyond her own borders. Let her look to *commerce* and *navigation*, and not to empire, as her means of communication with the rest of the human family. These are the principles upon which *our* confederated Republic is founded, and they are those upon which we hope our sisters of the southern continent will ultimately perceive it to be for their own welfare, no less than for that of the world, that they should found themselves.

The *materials* of commercial intercourse between the United States and the Colombian Republic are at present not many. Our exports to it hitherto have been confined to flour, rice, salted provisions, lumber, a few manufactured articles, warlike stores, and arms, and some East India productions, for which we have received cocoa, coffee, indigo, hides, copper, and specie. Much of this trade has originated and has continued only by the war in which that country has been engaged, and will cease with it. As producing and navigating nations, the United States and Colombia will be rather competitors and rivals than customers to each other. But as navigators and manufacturers, *we* are already so far advanced in a career upon which *they* are yet to enter, that we may, for many years after the conclusion of the war, maintain with them a commercial intercourse, highly beneficial to both parties, as *carriers* to and for them of numerous articles of manufacture and of foreign produce. It is the nature of commerce, when unobstructed by interference of authority, to find its own channels and to make its own way. Let us only not undertake to regulate that which will best regulate itself.

In the conferences between Dr. Gual and Mr. Todd, the Colombian Minister of Foreign Affairs has spoken of treaties, *almost* treaties of alliance, concluded by the Colombian plenipotentiary, Mosquera, with the Governments of Peru and Chile, and which he expected would also be shortly concluded with Buenos Ayres. The purport of these treaties was mentioned by Dr. Gual only in general terms, but he said that Mr. Salazar would be authorized to communicate copies of them to this Government, and eventually to propose that the United States should accede to them, or take a part in the system which it was their purpose to originate. In January last, about the same time when Dr. Gual was making this confidential communication to Mr. Todd, we learn, by despatches from Mr. Forbes, that Mr. Mosquera was at Buenos Ayres, and had made his proposals of negotiation to the Government there. Mr. Forbes speaks doubtfully of his prospects of success. The general intention, but not the specific purport of the treaties had also been communicated by Mr. Mosquera to Mr. Forbes. But the Colombian minister had been more confidential with Mr. Prevost, who, in a despatch dated the 14th of December last, states that he had obtained a sight of the original treaty. He describes it in a preceding letter as a treaty of alliance, offensive and defensive, containing "a pledge from each of the contracting parties to send deputies to the Isthmus, within a limited time, for the double purpose of effecting an union in support of a representative system throughout, and of preventing partial associations with any one of the powers of Europe. An agent (he adds) has gone to Mexico with the same object; and it is in contemplation, as soon as the several treaties shall be ratified by Colombia, to invite a representation from the United States to preside at a meeting intended to assimilate the politics of the south with those of the north;" and in a letter of 14th December, after having seen the treaty, he says: "It embraces in the most express terms the several objects to which I alluded, together with a stipulation not to enter into partial arrangements with Spain, and not to listen to overtures on her part unaccompanied with an acknowledgment of the independence of all."

Mr. Prevost, as well as Dr. Gual, entertains higher expectations of the success of this negotiation at Buenos Ayres than Mr. Forbes. Mr. Prevost thinks that it must succeed, although the Government of Buenos Ayres is secretly averse to it, and implicated in secret intrigues with the Portuguese Government and General Le Cor for a confederacy of a different character. Dr. Gual told Mr. Todd that proposals had been made by the Portuguese Government at Lisbon, to Colombia, for a general confederacy of all America, North and South, together with the Constitutional Governments of *Portugal* and Spain, as a counterpoise to the European *Holy Alliance;* but he said they had been rejected on account of their *European aspect.* Loose and indefinite projects of the same kind have been presented by the present

Portuguese Government to us, but they have never been considered even as objects of deliberation. Brazil has declared its own independence of Portugal, and constituted itself into an Empire, with an Emperor at its head. General Le Cor has lost the real command of his own army, and has been, or cannot fail shortly to be, compelled to embark, with all his European Portuguese troops, for Lisbon. Then will come the question between Buenos Ayres and Brazil, for Montevideo and the Oriental Band of La Plata.

Of this mighty movement in human affairs, mightier far than that of the downfall of the Roman Empire, the United States may continue to be, as they have been hitherto, the tranquil but deeply attentive spectators. They *may*, also, in the various vicissitudes by which it must be followed, be called to assume a more active and leading part in its progress. Floating, undigested purposes of this great American confederation have been for some time fermenting in the imaginations of many speculative statesmen; nor is the idea to be disdainfully rejected because its magnitude may appal the understanding of politicians accustomed to the more minute but more complicated machinery of a contracted political standard.

So far as the proposed Colombian confederacy has for its object a combined system of total and unqualified *independence* of Europe, to the exclusion of all partial compositions of any one of the emancipated colonies with Spain, it will have the entire approbation and good wishes of the United States, but will require no special agency of theirs to carry it into effect.

So far as its purposes may be to concert a general system of popular representation for the government of the several independent States which are floating from the wreck of the Spanish power in America, the United States will still cheer it with their approbation, and speed with their good wishes its success.

And so far as its objects may be to accomplish a meeting, at which the United States should preside, to assimilate the politics of the south with those of the north, a more particular and definite view of the end proposed by this design, and of the means by which it is to be effected, will be necessary to enable us to determine upon our concurrence with it. An agent from France, named Molien, and Mr. Lorich, the Consul General of Sweden in the United States, arrived at Bogota in January last. Dr. Gual told Mr. Todd that Molien had no letters or avowed powers, though he had intimated he was there by authority; that he was considered as a spy on behalf of a faction in France. "He had insinuated that the United States were *influenced by interested motives* in recognizing the new Governments in South America; *that our influence in Europe had been impaired* by a measure which *was considered premature;* and that he supposed we were now endeavoring to procure exclusive advantages for having been the first to recognize." And Dr. Gual added, that Mr. Molien undertook "to give him some advice as to our views"—Mr. Lorich came with authority.

The political systems of Europe are all founded upon partial rights and *exclusive* privileges. The colonial system had no other basis; and having no generous or liberal views of their own, it is not surprising that they should entertain and disseminate suspicions of the disinterestedness of others. The French Government sends an agent to Bogota, without daring to trust him with a credential or an avowed power; and he executes his commission by misrepresenting our motives, upon *suspicions* which those to whom he makes the misrepresentation know to be unfounded, and by testifying to those who were benefitted by our recognition that we had made it by the sacrifice of some part of our influence in Europe. It must be admitted that the address of the agent in the performance of his trust was upon a level with the candor and frankness in which it originated.

We are well aware that our recognition of South American independence was not palatable to the taste of any of the European Governments. But we felt that it was a subject upon which it became us to take the lead, and as we knew that the European Governments, sooner or later, must and would, whether with good or with bad grace, follow our example, we determined that both Europe and America should have the benefit of it. We hope, also, and this is the only return which we ask, and have a right to ask, from the South Americans for our forwardness in their favor, that Europe will be compelled to follow the whole of our example—that is, to recognize without condition and without equivalent. We claim no exclusive privilege for ourselves. We trust to the sense of justice, as well as to the interest of the South Americans, the denial of all exclusive privileges to others. The Colombian Government, at various times, have manifested a desire that the United States should take some further and active part in obtaining the recognition of their independence by the European Governments, and particularly by Great Britain. This has been done even before it was solicited. All the ministers of the United States in Europe have, for many years, been instructed to promote the cause, by any means consistent with propriety and adapted to their end, at the respective places of their residence. The formal proposal of a concerted recognition was made to Great Britain before the Congress of Aix-la-Chapelle. At the request of Mr. Torres, on his dying bed, and signified to us after his decease, Mr. Rush was instructed to give every aid in his power, without offence to the British Government, to obtain the admission of Mr. Ravenga; of which instruction we have recent assurances from Mr. Rush that he is constantly mindful. Our own recognition undoubtedly opened all the ports of Europe to the Colombian flag, and your mission to Colombia, as well as those to Buenos Ayres and Chile, cannot fail to stimulate the cabinets of maritime Europe, if not by the liberal motives which influenced us, at least by selfish impulses, to a direct, simple, and unconditional recognition. We shall pursue this policy steadily through all the changes to be foreseen of European affairs. There is every reason to believe that the preponderating tendency of the war in Spain will be to promote the universal recognition of all the South American Governments; and, at all events, our course will be to promote it by whatever influence we may possess."

"One of the complaints of Mr. Lowry was relative to the case of the ship Caravan, from Providence, captured by a Colombian cruiser and carried into Laguayra, where the vessel had been cleared as neutral, and the cargo condemned as enemy's property. Mr. Lowry had invoked the stipulations of various treaties, establishing and recognizing the principle that free ships make free goods, the application of which is denied by Dr. Gual, who appealed to the instructions from Mr. Pickering, in 1797, to Messrs. Marshall, Pinckney, and Gerry, our envoys to France.

By the general *usage* of nations, independent of treaty stipulations, the property of an enemy is liable to capture in the vessel of a friend. It is not possible to justify this rule upon any sound principle of the law of nature; for by that law the belligerent party has no right to pursue or attack his enemy without the jurisdiction of either of them. The high seas are a general jurisdiction common to all, qualified by a special jurisdiction of each nation over its own vessels. As the theatre of general and common jurisdiction, the vessels of one nation and their commanders have no right to exercise over those of another any act of authority whatsoever. This is universally admitted in time of peace. War gives the belligerent a right to pursue his enemy within the jurisdiction common to both, but not into the special jurisdiction of the neutral party. If the belligerent has a right to take the property of his enemy on the seas, the neutral has a right to carry *and protect* the property of his friend on the same element. War gives the belligerent no natural right to take the property of his enemy from the vessel of his friend. But as the belligerent is armed, and the neutral, as such, is defenceless, it has grown into *usage* that the belligerent should take the property of his enemy; paying the neutral his freight and submitting the question of facts to the tribunals of the belligerent party. It is evident, however, that this *usage* has no foundation in natural right, but has arisen merely from *force* used by the belligerent, and which the neutral in the origin did not resist because he had not the power. But it is a usage harsh and cruel in its operation and unjust in its nature; and it never fails in time of maritime war to produce irritation and animosity between the belligerent and the neutral. So universally has this been found to be its consequence, that *all* the maritime nations of modern Europe have shown their sense of it by stipulating in treaties the contrary principle, namely, that the property of an enemy shall be *protected* in the vessel of a friend. Great Britain, herself the most unwilling to admit this principle, because the most enabled to use the *force* upon which the usage is founded, has recognized the superior justice and expediency of the other principle, by stipulating it at distant intervals of time in two treaties with France: the treaty of Utrecht and the treaty of commerce of 1786. In the seven years' war, the King of Prussia resisted the capture by British vessels of the property of their enemies in the vessels of his subjects, then neutrals, and made reprisals upon British property for such captures. The question was then ultimately settled by a compromise, under which the British Government paid a large sum of money for indemnity to the Prussian subjects who had suffered by those captures. The armed neutrality of the American war is a memorable example of the testimony by all the civilized nations of the world to the principle, that the protection of all property, excepting contraband of war, on board of neutral vessels, by neutral force, is of *natural* right; and of this principle there can be no question. If, however, a belligerent power, founded upon the *usage* which has superseded the natural right, practices the seizure and condemnation of enemy's property found in the vessel of a friend, it remains for the neutral to decide whether he will acquiesce in the usage, or whether he will maintain his natural right by force. No neutral nation is bound to submit to the usage; for it has none of the properties which can give to any usage the sanction of obligatory law. It is not reasonable. It is not conformable to the law of nature. It is not *uninterrupted.* But reduced to the option of maintaining its right by force, or of acquiescing in the disturbance of it, which has been usual, the neutral nation may yield at one time to the usage, without sacrificing her right to vindicate by force the security of her flag at another. And the belligerent nation, although disposed to admit the right of neutrals to protect the property of her enemy upon the seas, may yet justly refuse the benefit of this principle, unless admitted also by the enemy for the protection of her property by the same neutral flag. Thus stands the state of this question upon the foundation of *natural, voluntary,* and *customary* law. How stands it between us and the Republic of Colombia on the ground of *conventional* law? By a treaty between the United States and Spain, concluded at a time when Colombia was a part of the Spanish dominions, and, so far as the *Spanish* laws would admit, enjoyed the benefit of its stipulations, the principle that free ships make free goods was expressly recognized and established. Is it asserted that, by her declaration of independence, Colombia has been entirely released from all the obligations by which, as a part of the Spanish nation, she was bound to other nations? This principle is not tenable. To all the engagements of Spain with other nations, affecting their rights and interests, Colombia, so far as she was affected by them, remains bound in honor and in justice. The stipulation now referred to is of that character, and the United States, besides the natural right of protecting by force, in their vessels on the seas, the property of their friends, though enemies of the Republic of Colombia, have the additional claim to the benefit of the principle by an express compact with Spain, made when Colombia was a Spanish country. Again, by the late treaty of February 22, 1819, between the United States and Spain, it is agreed that the 15th article of the treaty of 1795, in which it is stipulated that the flag shall cover the property, shall be so understood with respect to those powers who recognize the principle; but if either of the two contracting parties shall be at war with a third party, and the other neutral, the flag of the neutral shall cover the property of enemies whose Governments acknowledge the principle, and not of others.

This treaty having been concluded after the territories now composing the Republic of Colombia had ceased to acknowledge the authority of Spain, they are not parties to it, but their rights and duties in relation to the subject-matter remain as they had existed before it was made. Nor will she be affected by it at all, if she continues to acknowledge in her new national character, and with reference to the United States, the principle that free ships make free goods, which was the conventional law between them while Colombia was a part of Spain.

You will urge all these considerations upon the Colombian Minister of Foreign Affairs, to obtain restitution of the cargo of the Caravan, or indemnity for it. The claim rests upon foundations so solid that it is earnestly hoped your representations in its favor will be successful; and in the negotiation of the treaty you will press in like manner for the insertion of an article of the same purport as that of our last treaty with Spain above recited. This principle can with safety be recognized only to that extent; and to that extent the United States would willingly assent to it with every other nation. It is a principle favorable to the rights of peace, and of pacific spirit and tendency. It is recommended by every humane and liberal consideration as a rule of universal application. But the nation which would enjoy the benefit of it as a neutral, or as a passive belligerent resorting to the neutral flag, must also recognize it as an active belligerent, and suffer the property of her enemy to be conveyed safely by the same flag which safely conveys hers; otherwise the liberal principle of itself is turned to the advantage of the belligerent which rejects it, and the mild spirit of peace is made subservient to the unfeeling rapacity of war.

A resolution of the House of Representatives, of the late session of Congress, requests the President of the United States to enter upon and to prosecute from time to time such negotiations with the several maritime powers of Europe and America as he may deem expedient, for the effectual abolition of the African slave trade, and its ultimate denunciation as *piracy,* under the law of nations, by the consent of the civilized world.

In pursuance of this object, you will communicate to the Colombian Government copies of the several acts of our Congress, for the suppression of the slave trade, of the 20th of April, 1818, (United States Laws, vol. vi, p. 325,) of March 3, 1819, (p. 435,) and of May 15, 1820, (p. 529,) pointing their attention particularly to the fourth and fifth sections of the last, which subject to the penalties of piracy every citizen of the United States guilty of active participation in the African slave trade. The adoption of this principle in the legislative code of all the maritime nations would, of itself, probably suffice for the suppression of the trade. But as it would yet not authorize the armed vessel of any one nation to capture those of another engaged in the trade, a stipulation to that effect may be agreed to by the treaty, conditioned that the captor shall deliver over the captured party to the tribunals of his own country for trial, to which should be added some guard of responsibility upon the capturing officer to prevent the abusive exercise of his power.

There are several cases of claims by the citizens of the United States upon the Colombian Government, which were given in charge to Mr. Todd, and concerning which he has been often promised by Dr. Gual that satisfactory proceedings would be had. Some of them are already of several years' standing, and indemnity was acknowledged to be due upon them so long since as when the late Commodore Perry was at Angostura. Mr. Todd will put you in possession of the papers relating to them, and you will follow up the demand of indemnities with all the earnestness and perseverance which their justice and the delays already interposed may require.

Most of them are complaints which have arisen from maritime captures. Before the establishment of the Republic of Colombia, the Venezuelan revolutionary authorities for some time countenanced an irregular system of maritime warfare, which soon degenerated into absolute piracy. It became a subject of very earnest remonstrance by the Government of the United States, whose citizens suffered severely under its depredations, whose laws were continually outraged by its operative agents, and whose good faith and justice towards other nations it tended very seriously to implicate. Since the organization of the new Republic there has been less reason for complaints, but satisfaction has not yet been made for those which had arisen before. A list of the cases committed to Mr. Todd, and copies of papers recently received at this Department from the Delaware Insurance Company at Philadelphia, relating to the schooner Minerva, are now furnished you.

In this case of the Minerva, the sentence is given by an *assessor*, acting as a Court of Admiralty, and confirmed by the Commandant General of Marine at Santa Martha. It refers to the 19th article of an ordinance of March 4, 1817, which is no doubt a law relating to prizes. You are requested to procure and transmit to this Department a copy of that ordinance, and also exact information of the organization of the Admiralty Courts, and any laws relating to prize or privateering which may be in force, whether Spanish law continued or new law promulgated since the revolution.

Our intercourse with the Republic of Colombia, and with the territories of which it is composed, is of recent origin, formed while their own condition was altogether revolutionary and continually changing its aspect. Our information concerning them is imperfect, and among the most important objects of your mission will be that of adding to its stores; of exploring the untrodden ground, and of collecting and transmitting to us the knowledge by which the friendly relations between the two countries may be extended and harmonized to promote the welfare of both, with due regard to the peace and good will of the whole family of civilized man. It is highly important that the first foundations of the permanent future intercourse between the two countries should be laid in principles benevolent and liberal in themselves, congenial to the spirit of our institutions, and consistent with the duties of universal philanthropy.

In all your consultations with the Government to which you will be accredited, bearing upon its political relations with this Union, your unvarying standard will be the spirit of independence and of freedom, as *equality* of rights and favors will be that of its commercial relations. The emancipation of the South American continent opens to the whole race of man prospects of futurity, in which this Union will be called, in the discharge of its duties to itself and to unnumbered ages of posterity, to take a conspicuous and leading part. It involves all that is precious in hope, and all that is desirable in existence, to the countless millions of our fellow creatures which, in the progressive revolution of time, this hemisphere is destined to rear and to maintain.

That the fabric of our social connexions with our southern neighbors may rise, in the lapse of years, with a grandeur and harmony of proportion corresponding with the magnificence of the means placed by Providence in our power, and in that of our descendants, its foundations must be laid in principles of politics and of morals new and distasteful to the thrones and dominations of the elder world, but co-extensive with the surface of the globe, and lasting as the changes of time.

APPROPRIATION TO CARRY INTO EFFECT A MISSION TO PANAMA.

COMMUNICATED TO CONGRESS MARCH 17, 1826.

To the Senate and House of Representatives of the United States:

I now submit to the consideration of Congress the propriety of making the appropriation necessary for carrying into effect the appointment of a mission to the Congress at Panama.

JOHN QUINCY ADAMS.

WASHINGTON, *March* 15, 1826.

No. 424.   [1ST SESSION.

CLAIM OF RICHARD W. MEADE ON THE SPANISH GOVERNMENT.

COMMUNICATED TO THE SENATE MARCH 21, 1826.

Mr. CLAYTON, from the Select Committee, to whom was referred the memorial of Richard W. Meade, reported:

That, by the fifth clause of the ninth article of the treaty between the United States and Spain, by which Florida was ceded to the United States, the Government of the United States renounced to Spain "all claims of citizens of the United States upon the Spanish Government, statements of which, soliciting the interposition of the Government of the United States, have been presented to the Department of State, or to the minister of the United States in Spain, since the date of the convention of 1802, and until the signature of the treaty."

By the eleventh article of that treaty the United States undertook to make satisfaction for these claims to an amount not exceeding five millions of dollars. To ascertain the full amount and validity of these claims, it was stipulated that a commission, to consist of three Commissioners, should be appointed by the President, by and with the advice and consent of the Senate, which commission should meet at the City of Washington, and, within the space of three years from the time of their first meeting, should receive, examine, and decide upon the amount and validity of all claims included within the renunciations of the treaty.

The Commissioners were accordingly appointed, and they commenced their sessions in June, 1821, and closed them in June, 1824. Mr. Meade, among others, presented his claims on the Spanish Government to the Commissioners for ascertainment and decision. The sum claimed at that time was $491,153 62; and it was conceded that Mr. Meade had presented a statement of his claims on the Spanish Government to the Department of State, and to the minister of the United States in Spain, soliciting the interposition of the Government of the United States, since the date of the convention of 1802, and before the signature of the treaty of 1819; and that, therefore, if he could establish the amount and validity of his claims by "suitable authentic testimony," he came within the fifth clause of the ninth article, above recited. Mr. Meade failed, in the opinion of the Commissioners, to prove, by sufficient evidence, the amount and validity of his claims, and they were, therefore, on the 7th of June, 1824, finally rejected.

Under these circumstances, it is not deemed necessary that the committee should go into an investigation of the claims of Mr. Meade, nor to inquire whether the evidence adduced to the Commissioners was sufficient to establish the validity of his claims, because the Commissioners, in the opinion of the committee, were constituted the sole and exclusive judges of that question.

It will be proper to inquire what were the obligations imposed by the treaty on the Government of the United States. It assumed the payment of the claims of its citizens to an amount not exceeding five millions of dollars. To distribute this sum among its citizens, proportionate to their respective claims, it undertook to establish a commission, to be composed of three of its citizens, to ascertain, by "suitable authentic testimony," the full amount and validity of these claims; and it may be conceded that a further obligation was imposed on the Government, not, indeed, in terms, but impliedly, to be careful in appointing persons to form the commission, to select men of known intelligence, integrity, and learning; and when the claims presented to the Commissioners for decision had been adjusted and admitted, to pay them, provided they did not exceed five millions of dollars; and if they did exceed that sum, to pay them pro rata. All these obligations the government has performed with the utmost sincerity and good faith.

It will not be pretended that the Government stipulated that the decisions of the Commissioners should be infallible; it is enough that the commission was composed of learned and discreet men, whose decisions would be respected in all parts of the world. But it is by no means intended to insinuate that the correctness of the final rejection of Mr. Meade's memorial is questioned, because the committee have not permitted themselves to go into a consideration of that matter. By undertaking to review the proceedings of the Commissioners a wide door would be opened to a flood of claims to an amount which it was not in the contemplation of the Government to pay when it entered into the stipulations of the treaty. A fund of five millions of dollars was provided, to be distributed, by the adjudication of the Commissioners, among citizens having valid claims on the Spanish Government. This distribution has been made, and the whole fund is exhausted. The amount of claims exhibited to the Commissioners, the committee are informed, exceeded forty millions of dollars; so that, if the proceedings of the Board are to be reviewed and investigated anew, as but about five and a half millions of dollars were allowed, claims to the amount of thirty-five millions more are yet to be investigated and provided for. In such a course of proceeding there is no mutuality of advantage between the Government and the claimants; for if an erroneous decision shall have been made against the Government, there is no possible means by which the injury can be redressed.

It is insisted that the United States, having renounced these claims to the Spanish Government, are under a moral obligation to discharge them all, without regard to the limited sum specified in the treaty. But without the aid of the Government these claims on the Spanish nation never could have been enforced. Its aid was invoked; it was extended to them; and the most beneficial terms of compromise were made which could be obtained without the sacrifice of a much larger sum than prudence would authorize to be given for the ceded territory. Nor should it be forgotten that the sum of five millions was not the only consideration given for the cession of Florida. We, at the same time, surrendered a large and valuable territory lying beyond our present southern limits; and without this treaty all the claims would have remained unpaid to a much more distant day than the present; and if we looked to the exhausted state of the Spanish treasury and its impoverished resources, perhaps that period never would have arrived. Statements of these claims were presented to the Government, soliciting its interposition in their favor, and the consequence was the treaty of 1819, by which the Government assumed the payment of these claims to an amount not exceeding five millions of dollars. Had the aid of the Government not been asked, the fate of the claimants must have rested altogether upon the honor and justice of the Spanish nation; but the interposition of the Government being required, the claimants were bound to submit either to the fate of war or to such amicable compromise as could be made in their behalf. And it may be truly said that, in estimating the value of these claims, their nominal amount is not to be looked to only; but the *spes recuperandi* is the standard by which their just value is to be estimated. The *certainty* of having a smaller sum paid by this Government would, by a prudent man, be valued higher than the *contingent* prospect of obtaining a larger sum from Spain.

But a further view of this case, from the facts presented, is required. Mr. Meade's claim was disallowed by the Commissioners because the evidence which he adduced to them was not sufficient to prove the amount or validity of his claim; and it is believed they went so far as to say that it was incompetent evidence, and wholly inadmissible to prove anything before them. This was a matter of which they, by the treaty, were made the exclusive judges. This opinion was rendered on the 16th of April, 1823; and on the next day Mr. Meade filed a specification of the documents which he requested the Commissioners to demand of the Spanish Government, under the following clause of the 11th article of the treaty, viz: "And the Spanish Government shall furnish all such documents and elucidations as may be in their possession for the adjustment of the said claims according to the principles of justice, the laws of nations, and the stipulations of the treaty between the two parties, of October 27, 1795; the said documents to be specified when demanded at the instance of the said Commissioners;" and on the following day the Commissioners requested the Secretary of State to adopt such means as he should think proper to require of the Spanish authorities the documents so specified. On the 13th of May the Secretary of State instructed Mr. Nelson, who was then about to depart this country as minister to Spain, to demand the specified documents from the Spanish Government. These documents were accordingly demanded; but owing to the distracted situation of the country, being then recently overrun by French troops, the documents were not obtained so as to enable Mr. Meade to lay further proof before the Board before the termination of the commission; nor has the demand of our Government for these proofs yet been complied with. The consequence has been, that the Commissioners, adhering to their decision of the 16th of April, 1823, and no further proof being presented to them, on the 7th of June, the day previous to the close of their sessions, finally rejected the claim. This statement is made to show that no negligence is imputable to the Government of the United States, in performing its duty under the treaty, to demand the desired documents; for the earliest opportunity was taken by the Secretary of State to instruct our minister to make the demand; and if there has been a failure of duty anywhere, it is attributable to Spain. That Government engaged to furnish the documents when demanded, *and it has not furnished them.* If, therefore, a fair claim (about which the committee express no opinion) has been lost through the fault of the Spanish authorities, who ought to make good that loss? Spain, or the United States, to whom no blame or negligence can be imputed?

Every suitor prepares his cause for the hearing. He comes to it, if unprepared, at *his* peril. It is not the duty of the tribunal which is to decide his cause to instruct him beforehand as to the nature of the evidence which it will require to sustain his case. That is the duty of others; and if he is erroneously advised, it is his misfortune. The documents, which it is alleged are to be found in the Spanish archives, and which, it is contended, would sustain Mr. Meade's claim, were not specified to the Commissioners until the 17th of April, 1823, when nearly two-thirds of the time limited for the duration of the Board had expired. Had the specification of the documents been made at the commencement of the sessions, as Spain was at that time, and for a long time after, free from invasion, the probability is, that all the documents relating to the claim might have been procured in season to have enabled the Commissioners to judge whether they would sustain the claim, or any part of it. That these documents were not earlier demanded was not the fault of any agent of the Government. The Commissioners, after having decided the cause against Mr. Meade, upon the evidence on which he relied, indulged him to the last moment to enable him to produce further proof; and upon his failing to do so, they finally dismissed his memorial. The committee, therefore, submit the following resolution:

Resolved, That the prayer of the memorialist ought not to be granted.

EXPENSE OF THE MISSION TO PANAMA.

COMMUNICATED TO THE HOUSE OF REPRESENTATIVES MARCH 23, 1826.

DEPARTMENT OF STATE, *Washington, March 23, 1826.*

SIR: In compliance with the request which you made yesterday, at the instance of the Committee of Ways and Means of the House of Representatives, I have the honor to transmit the following estimate of the sum which it may be proper to appropriate for the proposed mission to Panama, agreeably to the recommendation of the President, viz:

For the outfits of two Envoys Extraordinary and Ministers Plenipotentiary	$18,000
Salaries for the same, at $9,000 a year, for one year	18,000
Secretary of the mission, at $2,000 a year, for one year	2,000
Contingent expenses of the mission	2,000
	40,000

I am, sir, respectfully, your obedient servant,

H. CLAY.

Hon. LOUIS MCLANE,
　　Chairman of the Committee of Ways and Means of the House of Representatives.

DEPARTMENT OF STATE, *Washington, March* 24, 1826.

SIR: In reply to the note which you did me the honor to address to me this morning, by direction of the Committee of Ways and Means, I have to state that it is not contemplated by the President to allow Mr. Anderson more than *one* salary during his service in the proposed mission to Panama. The affairs of the legation at Bogota will be placed in charge of some other person during Mr. Anderson's absence, and he will not then receive his salary as minister to Colombia.

In respect to the other inquiry contained in your note, as to the "usual allowance for outfit made to a minister abroad, when transferred temporarily to another Court, or on a new mission," I have the honor to state that the practice has always been to allow a full outfit where the transfer has been temporary, but the amount of the allowance has varied according to circumstances. The general rule has been, to allow a full outfit when the transfer from one mission to another has been permanent. If the requisite authority be conferred, the President is disposed, considering the importance and the peculiarity of the mission to Panama, to allow to Mr. Anderson a full outfit.

I have the honor to be your obedient servant,

H. CLAY.

Hon. LOUIS McLANE,
Chairman of the Committee of Ways and Means of the House of Representatives.

DEPARTMENT OF STATE, *Washington, April* 19, 1826.

SIR: In answer to the letter which you addressed to me this day, I have the honor to state that no information is possessed in this Department which enables me to determine the probable duration of the Congress at Panama, and the continuance of ministers who may be sent there from the United States. Upon the supposition that the instructions with which the ministers from the several powers may be charged embrace all the matters to be treated of in their negotiations, I should imagine that a period of six months after they have entered on their conferences might be sufficient to bring them to a close. But the arrival of some of them at Panama may be delayed; they may have occasion to send home for fresh instructions; and these or other causes may prolong the Congress beyond that period. In asking an appropriation for the term of one year, the hope was indulged that in the course of that time the negotiations might be completed, including the time of the ministers going and returning. As their salaries are annual, if the mission should terminate in less than a year, less than a year's salary would be paid. If it requires a longer time, the House of Representatives would, of course, have to pass upon any additional appropriation that might be required.

With respect to the outfit to Mr. Anderson, in proposing it the Department has been guided by what has been most usual in the case of the transfer of a minister from one Government to another, and by considerations connected with the importance of the mission, the place where the Congress is to be held, and unavoidable expenses which may be incurred in the interchanges of civility and hospitality, which may be more frequent among the ministers who attend the Congress, in consequence of the place not being the seat of any Government. Circumstances may also occur to require, for the preservation of their health, the removal of the Congress to some place in that respect more eligible.

I am, with great respect, your obedient servant,   H. CLAY.

Hon. LOUIS McLANE,
Chairman of the Committee of Ways and Means of the House of Representatives.

19TH CONGRESS.]   No. 426.   [1ST SESSION.

ON THE MISSION TO PANAMA.

COMMUNICATED TO THE HOUSE OF REPRESENTATIVES MARCH 25, 1826.

Mr. CROWNINSHIELD, from the Committee on Foreign Affairs, to whom was referred the message of the President of the United States to the House of Representatives, of the 15th instant, with the documents accompanying it, having had the same under consideration, reported:

That it appears from the above named message and papers that an invitation has been received by the United States from the Republics of Colombia, Central America, and Mexico, to attend the Congress about to be held at Panama. It appears that this invitation was accepted by the President, on the condition that the nomination of Commissioners for the mission should receive the advice and consent of the Senate. This advice and consent having been constitutionally expressed, in the confirmation of the ministers nominated by the President, the Concurrence of the House of Representatives is requested, as necessary to carry the mission into effect, by an appropriation to defray the expense of it. This concurrence being "subject to the free determination" of the House, the committee have regarded it as their duty to the House to inquire into the expediency of accepting this invitation. The ordinary courtesy of nations in friendship with each other, and the peculiar interest which, for the strongest reasons, the people of the United States have ever felt, and must ever feel, in the new American Republics, would seem to dictate the propriety of accepting this invitation, unless there were sufficient reasons for declining it. No such reasons are believed by the Committee on Foreign Affairs to exist.

In order to present the subject in its true light to the House, the committee would first make a remark on the general nature of the assembly designated by the name of the Congress of Panama. The term Congress, it need scarcely be observed, is by no means to be here understood in the sense in which it is applied to some other political assemblies. The Congress of Panama is not a representative delegation, forming a branch of a Government, like the present Congress of the United States. It is not a body in which the government of several confederated sovereign States is deposited, like the old American Congress. Neither is it a personal meeting of Sovereigns, like the recent Congresses of Europe. It is an assembly of diplomatic agents, clothed with no powers except to discuss and to negotiate, deputed by Governments whose constitutions require that all engagements with foreign powers shall be subject to the ratification of some organic body at home; and the more effectually to guard against mistake, even of *the design* in which this Congress has been proposed, it is stipulated, in the several treaties formed by Colombia with the other new Republics, that this meeting at Panama "shall not affect in any manner the exercise of the national sovereignty of the contracting parties in regard to their laws and the establishment and form of their respective Governments."

Such is the general *nature* of the proposed Congress, as appears from the papers referred to this committee. Of its *objects* the committee will, in the course of this report, more particularly speak. They are, in general, all subjects interesting to the powers represented at the Congress, and susceptible of discussion at such a meeting. The minister of the Colombian Republic, with the liberal design, as it would appear, of excluding the supposition that his own Government, or those which joined it, in inviting us to the Congress, had any wish to exercise a dictation as to what subjects should exclusively be discussed, has observed, in his letter to the Secretary of State of November 2, 1825, that the topics of discussion therein enumerated are designed merely " as suggestions by way of example," while " it is left to the wisdom of the Governments and the judgment of their representatives to propose whatever may be esteemed of common good to the new hemisphere." In the same letter of the Colombian minister to the Secretary of State the following remarks also occur : " At Panama the best and most opportune occasion is offered to the United States to fix some principles of international law, the unsettled state of which has caused much evil to humanity. It is to be presumed that this Government (the United States of America) possesses more light upon the subject than the other States of our hemisphere, both from its experience during the wars that succeeded the French revolution, and from its negotiations now on foot with Great Britain and other nations relative to these principles. It belongs to each of the concurring parties to propose their views ; but the voice of the United States will be heard with the respect and deference which its early labors in a work of such importance will merit." The sentiments here expressed by the minister of Colombia are in accordance with those of the ministers of Mexico and of Central America, as contained in their respective letters to the Secretary of State, on the subject of the invitation to attend the Congress.

The objects of this body, therefore, as far as the United States are concerned, are all subjects which the United States may deem it for their interest to propose for discussion. They embrace, consequently, in general terms, our political and commercial relations with the new American Republics.

The Committee on Foreign Affairs has, accordingly, been led to inquire what *the principle* of our diplomatic intercourse with other Governments has been? The answer to this inquiry is, that it has ever been the policy of the United States to maintain diplomatic relations with those powers, and those only, with which we have important political and commercial relations. We have not formed diplomatic connexions with very powerful States, such as Austria and the Porte, where no great political, no extensive commercial relations required such connexions; while, with powers not of the first class, such as Holland and Spain, important political and commercial relations have led the United States to the establishment of permanent missions.

This being the principle of our diplomatic intercourse, the committee conceive it to apply with great force in the present instance, and to require the attendance of our agents at the Congress of Panama. In that body questions directly involving our most important political and commercial interests are to be discussed. Though the new Republics there represented are so many separate Governments, our relations with them are not merely those which we hold toward each, individually; they form one whole family in language, religion, law, historical fortunes, and present political alliance. From this family, as far as the enumerated circumstances go, we are necessarily excluded; out of this exclusion springs an entire class of political and commercial relations between us, on the one side, and a large family of new Republics on the other. This family of Republics has thought it expedient to convene an assembly of plenipotentiaries at Panama. As an important part of their public relations are those in which they stand to us, they have invited us to send our ministers to this assembly. The law of nations warrants them in thus designating the place and mode of treating with friendly powers, and, if we refuse to accept the invitation, takes from us the right of complaining of any result, however inconsistent with our interests.

Under the circumstances in which this subject is before the House, the committee deem it their duty to consider some of the objections which may be urged against the acceptance by the United States of this invitation. These may be, among others: that such acceptance is unconstitutional; that all the objects of the Congress, as far as we are concerned, may be attained by negotiations with the separate States; that the subjects of discussion, the powers of the ministers, the mode of organizing the Congress, and the mode of deciding questions, are not sufficiently settled to authorize our accepting the invitation; that our attendance would endanger our neutrality toward Spain; that it might involve us in an entangling alliance with the new States; that our attendance would be a novel and unprecedented measure; that there is, in a Congress of States, something essentially pernicious, as proved by the example of Europe in its recent history.

The first objection may be, that the attendance of the United States at the Congress of Panama would be unconstitutional. To this objection the committee would reply, that they are not acquainted with any restriction in the Constitution on the appointment of foreign ministers by the proper authority. It may not, however, be superfluous to add, that this objection proceeds on the assumption that the Congress at Panama is either a Government, a branch of a Government, or a confederacy of Governments, and that the United States, by attending this assembly, unite themselves to the said Government or Confederacy. Neither part of this assumption is true. The Congress is a meeting of diplomatic agents from independent Governments; and, granting for a moment that the Congress at Panama were a Government or a Confederacy, our attendance at it by diplomatic ministers would be no entrance into such Confederacy—no union with such Government. It need scarcely be urged that the United States do not enter into confederacy, do not form a union with a foreign power, or any number of powers, by sending a minister to treat with such power or powers.

It may, in the next place, be objected to our attendance at this meeting, that all its objects may be attained by separate negotiations with the several States. It may admit a doubt whether this could, by possibility, be the case. It is questionable whether separate and disconnected negotiations between States geographically so remote, and in various respects politically so different from each other, could be brought to the same harmonious and systematic result as a discussion in an assembly of diplomatic agents, promptly communicating with each other information, counsel, and argument. At all events, it may safely be affirmed that the same result may be far more expeditiously and conveniently attained by a conference with the assembled ministers of States so remote from each other that an interchange of intelligence with their respective capitals could not take place more than twice in a twelvemonth. This objection, going only to the convenience of the measure, need not be more particularly weighed.

The third objection may be, that the subjects of discussion, the powers of the ministers, the mode of organizing the Congress, and mode of deciding questions, are not yet sufficiently settled to justify our attendance. From the papers submitted to the committee it appears that this consideration engaged the attention of the Executive when the invitation was made to this Government, last spring, by the ministers of Mexico and Colombia. It was then required by the President that previous satisfaction should be given on these points. The replies of those ministers, after having consulted their Governments, do not enter into minute detail on all these points, yet the committee are of opinion that they are satisfactory. As to the subjects in general to be discussed, there is no limitation to the disadvantage of any Government represented; and the meeting being one of diplomatic agents, and it being stipulated in the Colombian treaties that the ministers to the Congress are to go with the usual diplomatic powers and instructions, it follows that their mode of proceeding must be that of diplomatic discussion and conference, and their mode of deciding that which can alone exist between diplomatic agents—the mutual reference of whatever convention or pact may be negotiated to the constitutional authorities at home. That such is to be the case with respect to our ministers is particularly stated in the message of the President, as also that they are to be bound by no decision of the Congress without their own consent. While the committee are of opinion that these details are of no great importance, they apprehend that, as far as they are of importance, the omission to fix them, or to propose them for acceptance to the United States, is rather favorable than disadvantageous to us. The committee are persuaded that, on these details, as well as in the leading business of the Congress, the new States are desirous to have the advantage of our experience. This sentiment is repeatedly expressed in the letters of the ministers of the new States communicating the invitation.

The next objection may be, that our attendance at this Congress may put to hazard our neutrality. To this it may be answered that, having already acknowledged the independence of the new States, we have established the right of treating them as free and independent States, as well toward Spain as all the rest of the world. These States are nominally at war with Spain, and Spain alone. Her allies have taken no part in this war. The most powerful of those allies, Great Britain, has formally acknowledged the independence of several of these States, and has established diplomatic relations with them. To these acts on our part and that of Great Britain Spain submits, although they not only essentially weaken her as a belligerent, but directly violate her colonial laws. But if our recognition of each of the States represented at the Congress, and our trading with them in direct contravention of the colonial laws of Spain be no breach, as it is none, of our neutrality, so neither is our attendance at a diplomatic council of all those States united a breach of neutrality. This is particularly true when it is added that the United States, instead of going to the Congress to animate the war against Spain, will go as mediators and peacemakers, to promote by every means a termination of the contest on terms honorable to the new States and advantageous to Spain. This power has already received the strongest pledges that such is the policy of the United States. The committee are clearly of opinion that, if our attendance at this Congress be desirable on the part of the new States, it is not less so on the part of Spain.

The next objection that may be urged against our attendance at the Congress of Panama is, that it may involve us in an entangling alliance with the new States. To this it may be answered that the project of such an alliance is expressly disclaimed by the President in the message referred to the committee. In the next place, the Congress is neither a Government nor a confederacy of Governments with which we could, by possibility, in the first instance, enter into an alliance, entangling or not; and lastly, even if a negotiation for such an alliance were entered into by our ministers, contrary to the principles on which it appears from the message of the President that the invitation was accepted, it would still remain for the treaty of alliance to be submitted to the constitutional ratifying powers in this country. Whether, under these circumstances, our acceptance of the invitation can be considered even as an approach to an alliance, the committee need not say.

If it be still objected that, from the nature of this assembly, there is danger that we, by our attendance, may be drawn into an alliance, it may be replied that there is no other danger of the formation of an entangling alliance, in consequence of this mission, than that which is incident to any mission to any power. We have ministers to France, to Russia, to England. We have had ministers to European countries at periods when very strong temptations of momentary interest existed for forming alliances with foreign powers. The committee are not aware that it ever was suggested that the least danger existed of the formation of such an alliance in consequence of such missions. Our minister to France followed the march of the French Emperor to the confines of Russia, but no one surmised that we projected an alliance with him, although we were at the time engaged in a war with his other chief enemy, Great Britain. Yet it is plain that the way to an alliance is much more direct in an ordinary mission than in that proposed. When our minister is accredited to a foreign Sovereign, particularly an absolute one, he is accredited to a party competent to form an alliance without further delay or ulterior responsibility. While, on the other hand, our ministers to Panama will be accredited to other ministers no more competent than our own to pledge their Governments.

Further, it is particularly to be observed that an alliance with any one of the new Republics would be fully as entangling as an alliance with them all. They are all at war, and with the same enemy. They stand in an alliance, offensive and defensive, with each other. Precisely the same consequences, therefore, would result from the formation of an alliance with either of them (Colombia, for instance) as with all of them. If, then, the danger of being drawn into an alliance requires us to abstain from attending the Congress at Panama, the same danger, with equal force, requires us to withdraw all diplomatic connexion with these new States.

But, in truth, this suggestion of the danger of an alliance, incident to a diplomatic mission, carries with it so direct a reflection on the wisdom and fidelity of the treaty-making power, as lodged in the hands of the President and Senate, that the committee, out of proper respect to the co-ordinate branches of the Government, will not longer consider it.

Another objection to the proposed mission may be, that the Congress is an unprecedented measure, and that our attendance at it would, on our part, be a novel and unprecedented step. A little reflection will show that this assumption, as far as it forms an objection to our attendance at the Congress, involves a confusion of ideas. The establishment of several new Republics at once may be called an unprecedented event, and, as a historical occurrence, without a parallel in the history of the world. But the committee cannot admit that every subsequent political act of these new States, or of other States in reference to them, is therefore to be called novel and unprecedented, and that in an injurious sense of the words. On the contrary, it appears to the committee exceedingly natural that these States should hold diplomatic conferences with each other and neighboring nations who have important relations with them. Nothing, perhaps, is more frequent in political history than similar meetings among friendly States.

Nor, when the subject is correctly viewed, is there anything *in principle* novel or unprecedented in our attendance at the proposed Congress. As a merely historical event, indeed, it may be considered as without an exact precedent, although the negotiations between the United States, France, and Great Britain, in 1782, which resulted in the treaties of peace between the several countries, were of the nature of the conferences of a meeting of diplomatic agents. It will also not escape the reflection of the House that, had this Government ever acted on the principle that exact precedent was necessary to authorize its measures, no one of the most important measures of the Government since the date of the Constitution could have been adopted. Whatever weight there is in the mere argument of want of exact precedents, applied, in full force, to the adoption of the Federal Constitution itself. The whole history of the world contained no precedent of such a Government.

But, in point of principle, there is no novelty in our attendance at the proposed Congress at Panama. Our ministers will carry with them the same powers, no larger, no more discretionary, than have ever been vested in the foreign ministers of the United States. It has been the characteristic policy of the United States to ask no questions about the quality or constitution of the power to which our ministers were sent. We have rested for our security, not on a timid calculation of the powers of the Government or of the body with which our ministers were to treat, but on constitutional safeguards at home. It has been indifferent to us whether Europe were at peace or at war, or by what titles her Sovereigns filled their thrones. To instance in a single case: we have sent missions to France, alike under the ancient absolute monarchy, limited monarchy, and revolutionary anarchy; to the Convention and to the Directory, to the Consular and the Imperial despotisms, and to the present Constitutional Government. The posture of affairs which our ministers found in that country has often been novel; their personal position unprecedented; the scenes they witnessed strange and unexampled. But of none of our successive missions could it have been said, in any important sense, that the mission itself was novel; that is, that it opened a door to any relaxation of the constitutional checks in the administration of any foreign affairs of the Government at home. In like manner the mission to Panama is in the strictest conformity with our whole international policy, which is to be represented wherever we have important political and commercial connexions. Our Commissioners will go there to do the business of the country. Their appearance at that meeting cannot surely have the effect of breaking down the Senate and House of Representatives, and, by a kind of dictatorial power unknown to the Constitution, of binding the country in a foreign alliance.

Lastly, it may be objected that, in a Congress of assembled powers, there is something essentially pernicious, which this country, instead of approaching, ought to shun; and the existing organization in Continental Europe may be quoted as the illustration. The committee deem it hardly necessary to remark, that the pernicious character of the late European Congresses, or of any European Congresses, does not consist in the act of assembling and treating together, but in the character of the Governments assembled, and in the objects effected or aimed at. A Congress of despotic powers, wielding the force of large standing armies, and meeting to concert measures for violent interference in the internal affairs of other States, is certainly a pernicious assembly. In other words, despotic Governments, standing armies, and unprovoked invasion, are pernicious in a single State, and proportionably more so when several despotic Governments league their forces to prevent the establishment of liberal institutions in any country not beyond their reach. But if the States of Europe were free Republics, blessed with popular Governments, written laws, elective magistrates, and senatorial bodies beyond the reach of corruption, the committee do not perceive that a meeting of the diplomatic agents of such Governments, to form treaties and conventions on their mutual interests and concerns, that are to be sent home to their constitutional ratifying functionaries, would be in any degree alarming. Moreover, it is an obvious reflection that this argument against the mission to Panama, if it prove anything, proves too much. If the pernicious character of the power to which the mission is to be sent form a reason for not sending it, it would be impossible for the United States to maintain a single mission in Europe. Our ministers there are, in every case, accredited to Governments constructed, as we think, on principles which could not be introduced here without immediate national ruin. If it be safe for us to hold diplomatic intercourse with the unlimited monarchy of Russia, it cannot be dangerous to hold the same kind of intercourse with an assembly of the agents of our neighboring Republics.

Having thus considered the objections which may exist to this measure, and endeavored to show that it is strictly within the line of the international policy of the United States, the committee regard it as their duty to the House, on the present occasion, to dwell for a moment on the subjects of discussion at the Congress of Panama.

By the terms of the invitation, as well as the nature of the case, the discussions at Panama are to extend to all subjects of importance—

To the new States, as among each other;

Or, as between them and Spain;

Or of importance directly to us, in our connexion with them.

Each power is at liberty to propose what subject for discussion or negotiation it may please, the only limitation being that which the United States impose upon themselves, with the understanding of the other powers, that we are to engage in no discussions inconsistent with an entire neutrality.

Although, in different degrees, the three classes of subjects above enumerated are interesting to the people of the United States, the relations of the new States to each other are very important to us.

They are our near neighbors.   One of them has an immense landed frontier on our territory, and, together with the two next in geographical succession, lies on the waters into which the great internal communications of the United States are discharged.   With the others we have no direct geographical, but we have highly important commercial, connexions.   At present there are eight or nine independent States formed out of the late Spanish and Portuguese colonies; seven of these, viz: Mexico, Guatemala, Colombia, the Provinces of La Plata, Chile, Peru, and Upper Peru, have adopted republican Governments.   Now, it is to us a matter of very great interest how these States shall stand towards each other.   Should they fall into dissensions and wars, those great advantages which we have reasonably promised ourselves from their growth and prosperity could not be realized.   The great drawbacks on the progress of these States and on the extension of advantageous commercial relations with them, arising from the war with Spain, would be perpetuated by the growth of feuds and conflicts with each other.   It would have been as well for us and for themselves that the mother country had continued to rule them, as that their energies should be wasted in civil wars.   The committee do not intend to augur unfavorably for the peace and harmony of these States; but it is obvious that the simultaneous rise of so many neighboring independent Republics must be attended with its hazards.   Rival claims to portions of territory may form a subject of contention among the new States, as they did in our own Confederacy after the war of the Revolution.   A controversy of this kind has actually arisen between Mexico and Guatemala, which the committee trust will be settled by friendly compromise, for few events could be more deprecated by us than a war between two States lying on and near the Gulf of Mexico.   Unfortunately, a controversy of the same kind has broken out into a war between Brazil and the United Provinces of La Plata, for the disputed possession of the Banda Oriental.   The effect of this war on us has been instantaneous.   It has already become necessary to ask for an additional appropriation for the naval service of the year of near one hundred thousand dollars, to protect the property and lives of our citizens from the dangers to which, in the progress of this war, they will be exposed.   Now, it has been expressly provided in the treaties which led to the formation of the Congress of Panama that the ministers there assembled should exercise the office of mediators when such differences shall arise.   Brazil and La Plata have both been invited to the Congress; and had it been in active operation, it certainly is within the reach of political probability that this unfortunate controversy might, by friendly mediation, have been prevented from ripening into the fatal issue of war.   To the work of mediation, in all such cases, the United States would come as the most disinterested party; and, as we ourselves have experienced the benefits of the mediation of a foreign friendly power, it may happen that we may render the like good office to our sister States.   Could we but in a single instance avert or terminate a war, it would itself form a sufficient motive for accepting the invitation.   We claim no right of interference; we do not obtrude ourselves as umpires.   We are invited to a Congress where we are told these national differences, if any arise, will be discussed; we are told that our presence, counsel, and experience are desired.   No maxim of the most cautious political prudence bids us stand aloof.   Next to peace on our own part, their peace and prosperity are our leading interest; and the policy of maintaining peace through the instrumentality of friendly mediation is entirely congenial with the principles and feelings of the people of the United States of America, and sanctioned by their practice.

   The next general class of subjects to be discussed at the Congress of Panama are the relations of the new States with Spain.   This subject, it is expressly stipulated, is only to be approached by our ministers under the reservation of strict neutrality.   More than this, our great efforts will be directed to pacification.   The policy of the United States, in this respect, is sufficiently unfolded in the letter of the Secretary of State to Mr. Middleton, dated May 10, 1825, and the letter of the Secretary of State to Mr. Salazar, dated December 20, 1825.   Pacification between the belligerents is an object which it is our most decided interest to pursue.   No single political event, perhaps, could be named more desirable to the United States, in reference to their industrious interests, than the termination of the present contest.   We suffer every way by its continuance; our commerce with Spain languishes, and it is impossible that it should assume a profitable expansion with the new States.

   Connected with the belligerent relations between Spain and the new States is the fate of the Spanish islands, particularly Cuba.   If the war continues, the invasion of that island will be attempted; it is an avowed subject of discussion at the Congress.   This is a subject of the greatest moment to the United States in every respect.   We have an intercourse with that island, which acts upon our industry in all its branches.   The Moro may be regarded as a fortress at the mouth of the Mississippi; and what is infinitely more important, unless Cuba should be invaded by an overwhelming force, (such a force as the new States will hardly be able to organize,) that invaluable island may renew, almost within sight of our shores, the terrific example of San Domingo.   Any effort on the part of the United States to avert such a catastrophe would be cheaply made; none could justifiably be omitted.   Had the Government of the United States, after being invited to attend a conference of the ministers of the powers by whom that invasion is projected, declined to be present, they would have been heavily responsible to the people for whatever disastrous effects our friendly interference might have averted or delayed.

   The last general class of subjects to be discussed and treated at Panama are the direct interests between the United States and the new Republics; unquestionably, as far as we are concerned, the most important branch of the negotiations.   With several of these powers we have no treaty whatever.   With Mexico, as appears from the correspondence between the Secretary of State and Mr. Poinsett, we have been unable, as yet, to form a treaty on satisfactory conditions; and the obstacles which have hitherto prevented this from being done are precisely such as are most likely to be removed at a conference of ministers of all the new States.   At such a conference we shall of course possess the best opportunity of establishing uniform and liberal relations with all.   The arrangements to be made with them comprehend the great principles of belligerent, neutral, and commercial law, as set forth in the general instructions to Mr. Anderson by the then Secretary of State.   The United States have long been laboring to introduce into every branch of public law principles of liberality, equality, and humanity, hitherto unknown in its codes.   The various respects in which our policy, in many leading points of the laws of war and trade, differs from that of Europe, are well known to the House, and need not here be stated.   The Republic of Colombia, in inviting our attendance at the Congress, has asked for herself and her sister Republics the benefits of our experience in the great school of international politics.   To refuse our attendance at the Congress, when urged on this ground, would be to neglect to seize, perhaps, the fairest opportunity which the history of the world ever afforded of giving a wide and prompt diffusion to liberal doctrines of public law.   It would certainly put it out of our power to complain of any policy these States might adopt, however unfriendly toward our interests, and however vicious in principle,

Such are the views of the committee with respect to the several classes of subjects which will be discussed at this Congress. It is a very obvious reflection that our attendance may have a powerful effect in giving a character to the assembly itself. Our presence is particularly requested by one of the new States, who have joined in the invitation, on the ground of the "importance and respectability" which would thence attach to the Congress. The committee do not foresee the possibility that, under any circumstances, the Congress could become an inconvenient or dangerous assembly. But, if it be thought by any one that evil consequences are likely to flow from it, the prospect of such consequences would furnish new reasons why we should be represented at it. Whatever opinions may be held of the expediency of such a meeting, in itself, it would seem that there could be but one opinion as to the duty of our attendance at the Congress, to correct the pernicious tendency which it may be feared to have. To neglect to attend the Congress because it was a combination of unfriendly aspect, would be to neglect the ordinary preparations of defence, precisely because there was danger of war. Viewing the Congress at Panama in this unfavorable light, (for which, however, the committee apprehend there is no reason,) no administration of the Executive Government would stand justified to the country, without taking measures most promptly to be informed of its proceedings. If not invited to send authorized and accredited ministers, it would have been their duty to send private political agents.

The committee have felt it their duty to consider this question chiefly on strict grounds of political expediency, and in reference to the principle of our diplomatic intercourse. They, however, accord in sentiment with the President, that a sufficient inducement to accept the invitation would have been "to meet in the spirit of kindness and friendship an overture made in that spirit by three sister Republics of this hemisphere." It will not escape the consideration of the House that the conduct of the United States toward the new Republics has ever been regulated by the maxims of a frank and liberal policy. Had we acted toward them even as we have felt it our duty to act toward Europe, our course would have been essentially different. Had our feelings toward them been the same as those which our political fathers have inculcated toward Europe, we should certainly have regarded it rather as an evil than a benefit, that so many new Republics, of which the greater part must be powerful States, are rising into existence on the same side of the water as ourselves. We are henceforward to be without that which has formerly been regarded as the great bulwark of our national security, our geographical distance from every other powerful State. But we have not hesitated to break down this bulwark. We have gone to meet and welcome the new Republics. We have ourselves assisted to exchange weak colonial for powerful sovereign neighbors. As far as it depended on us, we have chosen to place the regions on our immense southwestern frontier beneath the government of vigorous republican institutions, instead of having them under the safe and enervating despotism of Spain. In the judgment of the committee, this has been a sound, a great, an auspicious policy. It was not rashly adopted; it was long deliberated, well weighed, and at length received its sanction in the unanimous voice of this House and the acclamations of the people. From this policy it is now too late to recede. We cannot now do much to obstruct the growth of the new States; we can do everything to conciliate and attach them, or to estrange and disgust them. The first course will promote the general cause of liberty, will perpetuate friendly relations between the two great portions of this continent, to the mutual advantage of both, and will render us more and more independent of Europe. The latter course will tend to revive in the New World the false and pernicious maxims of the Old; to teach neighboring Republics to fix on each other the fatal name of natural enemies; to create piratical and border wars; to generate systems of exclusion; and, finally, to establish in this hemisphere those political principles and habits which have caused the downfall of so many foreign States, and made so many others stationary and languishing, and checked the growth of all. We are now to consider whether we will take the first step in an unfriendly and repulsive policy, by refusing to accept the courteous invitation of three most respectable neighboring Governments, tendered in a manner equally creditable to their delicacy and flattering to the United States. Nothing but a certainty of pernicious consequences to result from our attendance at the Congress would, in the opinion of the committee, be sufficient to justify our refusal to accept such an invitation. As our attendance at the Congress, instead of being prejudicial to the public interests, is, in the judgment of the committee, a measure of the most obvious political expedience; as it is stipulated to bring into no hazard the neutrality of the United States, as all fears of an entangling alliance have been shown to be unfounded; in a word, as the Congress will be regarded by the Executive of the United States as purely a consultative meeting, and as the objects of consultation are of primary importance to the country, the Committee on Foreign Affairs are of opinion that the mission to Panama ought to receive the sanction of the House of Representatives, and they accordingly recommend the adoption of the following resolution:

Resolved, That, in the opinion of the House, it is expedient to appropriate the funds necessary to enable the President of the United States to send ministers to the Congress of Panama.

19TH CONGRESS.]   No. 427.   [1ST SESSION.

GENERAL CONVENTION OF FRIENDSHIP, COMMERCE, AND NAVIGATION, WITH DENMARK.

COMMUNICATED TO THE SENATE, IN EXECUTIVE SESSION, APRIL 28, 1826, AND THE INJUNCTION OF SECRECY SINCE REMOVED.

To the Senate of the United States:

I transmit herewith to the Senate, for their advice concerning its ratification, a general convention of friendship, commerce, and navigation, between the United States and his Majesty the King of Denmark, signed by the Secretary of State and the Danish minister on the 26th instant; a copy of the convention and a note from the Secretary of State, together with Mr. Pedersen's answer, respecting the claims of the citizens of the United States upon the Danish Government, are likewise communicated.

JOHN QUINCY ADAMS.

WASHINGTON, *April* 28, 1826.

The following convention was read twice by unanimous consent, referred to the Committee on Foreign Relations, and, together with the accompanying documents, ordered to be printed in confidence for the use of the Senate.

General Convention of Friendship, Commerce, and Navigation, between the United States of America and His Majesty the King of Denmark.

The United States of America and his Majesty the King of Denmark being desirous to make firm and permanent the peace and friendship which happily prevail between the two nations, and to extend the commercial relations which subsist between their respective territories and people, have agreed to fix, in a manner clear and positive, the rules which shall in future be observed between the one and the other party, by means of a general convention of friendship, commerce, and navigation. With that object, the President of the United States of America has conferred full powers on HENRY CLAY, their Secretary of State, and his Majesty the King of Denmark has conferred like powers on PETER PEDERSEN, his Privy Counsellor of Legation and Minister Resident near the said States, Knight of the Danneborg; who, after having exchanged their said full powers, found to be in due and proper form, have agreed to the following articles:

ARTICLE 1. The contracting parties, desiring to live in peace and harmony with all the other nations of the earth, by means of a policy frank and equally friendly with all, engage, mutually, not to grant any particular favor to other nations, in respect of commerce and navigation, which shall not immediately become common to the other party, who shall enjoy the same freely, if the concession were freely made, or on allowing the same compensation, if the concession were conditional.

ARTICLE 2. The contracting parties being likewise desirous of placing the commerce and navigation of their respective countries on the liberal basis of perfect equality and reciprocity, mutually agree that the citizens and subjects of each may frequent all the coasts and countries of the other, (with the exception hereafter provided for in the sixth article,) and reside and trade there in all kinds of produce, manufactures, and merchandise; and they shall enjoy all the rights, privileges, and exemptions, in navigation and commerce, which native citizens or subjects do or shall enjoy, submitting themselves to the laws, decrees, and usages there established to which native citizens or subjects are subjected. But it is understood that this article does not include the coasting trade of either country, the regulation of which is reserved by the parties, respectively, according to their own separate laws.

ARTICLE 3. They likewise agree that whatever kind of produce, manufacture, or merchandise, of any foreign country, can be, from time to time, lawfully imported into the United States in vessels belonging wholly to the citizens thereof, may be also imported in vessels wholly belonging to the subjects of Denmark; and that no higher or other duties upon the tonnage of the vessel or her cargo shall be levied and collected, whether the importation be made in vessels of the one country or of the other. And, in like manner, that whatever kind of produce, manufacture, or merchandise, of any foreign country, can be, from time to time, lawfully imported into the dominions of the King of Denmark in the vessels thereof, (with the exception hereafter mentioned in the sixth article,) may be also imported in vessels of the United States; and that no higher or other duties upon the tonnage of the vessel or her cargo shall be levied and collected, whether the importation be made in vessels of the one country or of the other. And they further agree that whatever may be lawfully exported or re-exported from the one country in its own vessels to any foreign country may, in like manner, be exported or re-exported in the vessels of the other country. And the same bounties, duties, and drawbacks shall be allowed and collected, whether such exportation or re-exportation be made in vessels of the United States or of Denmark. Nor shall higher or other charges of any kind be imposed in the ports of one party on vessels of the other, than are or shall be payable in the same ports by native vessels.

ARTICLE 4. No higher or other duties shall be imposed on the importation into the United States of any article the produce or manufacture of the dominions of his Majesty the King of Denmark; and no higher or other duties shall be imposed on the importation into the said dominions of any article the produce or manufacture of the United States than are or shall be payable on the like articles being the produce or manufacture of any other foreign country. Nor shall any higher or other duties or charges be imposed in either of the two countries on the exportation of any articles to the United States, or to the dominions of his Majesty the King of Denmark, respectively, than such as are or may be payable on the exportation of the like articles to any other foreign country. Nor shall any prohibition be imposed on the exportation or importation of any articles the produce or manufacture of the United States, or of the dominions of his Majesty the King of Denmark, to or from the territories of the United States, or to or from the said dominions, which shall not equally extend to all other nations.

ARTICLE 5. Neither the vessels of the United States nor their cargoes shall, when they pass the Sound or the Belts, pay higher or other duties than those which are or may be paid by the most favored nation.

ARTICLE 6. The present convention shall not apply to the northern possessions of his Majesty the King of Denmark—that is to say, Iceland, the Feroe Islands, and Greenland—nor to places situated beyond the Cape of Good Hope, the right to regulate the direct intercourse with which possessions and places is reserved by the parties respectively. And it is further agreed that this convention is not to extend to the direct trade between Denmark and the West India colonies of his Danish Majesty; but in the intercourse with those colonies it is agreed that whatever can be lawfully imported into or exported from the said colonies in vessels of one party from or to the ports of the United States, or from or to the ports of any other foreign country, may, in like manner, and with the same duties and charges, applicable to vessel and cargo, be imported into or exported from the said colonies in vessels of the other party.

ARTICLE 7. The United States and his Danish Majesty mutually agree that no higher or other duties, charges, or taxes of any kind, shall be levied in the territories or dominions of either party upon any personal property, money, or effects of their respective citizens or subjects on the removal of the same from their territories or dominions reciprocally, either upon the inheritance of such property, money, or effects, or otherwise, than are or shall be payable in each State upon the same when removed by a citizen or subject of such State, respectively.

ARTICLE 8. To make more effectual the protection which the United States and his Danish Majesty shall afford in future to the navigation and commerce of their respective citizens and subjects, they agree mutually to receive and admit consuls and vice consuls in all the ports open to foreign commerce, who shall enjoy in them all the rights, privileges, and immunities of the consuls and vice consuls of the most favored nation; each contracting party, however, remaining at liberty to except those ports and places in which the admission and residence of such consuls may not seem convenient.

ARTICLE 9. In order that the consuls and vice consuls of the contracting parties may enjoy the rights, privileges, and immunities which belong to them by their public character, they shall, before entering on the exercise of their functions, exhibit their commission or patent in due form to the Government to which they are accredited; and having obtained their exequatur, which shall be granted gratis, they shall be held and considered as such by all the authorities, magistrates, and inhabitants in the consular district in which they reside.

ARTICLE 10. It is likewise agreed that the consuls and persons attached to their necessary service, they not being natives of the country in which the consul resides, shall be exempt from all public service, and also from all kind of taxes, imposts, and contributions, except those which they shall be obliged to pay on account of commerce or their property, to which inhabitants, native and foreign, of the country in which such consuls reside are subject; being in everything besides subject to the laws of the respective States. The archives and papers of the consulate shall be respected inviolably, and, under no pretext whatever, shall any magistrate seize or in any way interfere with them.

ARTICLE 11. The present convention shall be in force for ten years from the date hereof, and further until the end of one year after either of the contracting parties shall have given notice to the other of its intention to terminate the same; each of the contracting parties reserving to itself the right of giving such notice to the other at the end of the said term of ten years; and it is hereby agreed between them that, on the expiration of one year after such notice shall have been received by either from the other party, this convention, and all the provisions thereof, shall altogether cease and determine.

ARTICLE 12. This convention shall be approved and ratified by the President of the United States, by and with the advice and consent of the Senate thereof, and by his Majesty the King of Denmark, and the ratifications shall be exchanged in the city of Copenhagen within eight months from the date of the signature hereof, or sooner, if possible.

In faith whereof, we, the plenipotentiaries of the United States of America and of his Danish Majesty, have signed and sealed these presents.

Done in triplicate, at the city of Washington, on the twenty-sixth day of April, in the year of our Lord one thousand eight hundred and twenty-six, in the fiftieth year of the Independence of the United States of America.

H. CLAY.
PR. PEDERSEN.

Mr. Clay to Mr. Pedersen.

DEPARTMENT OF STATE, *Washington, April 25,* 1826.

The undersigned, Secretary of State of the United States, by direction of the President thereof, has the honor to state to Mr. Pedersen, minister resident of his Majesty the King of Denmark, that it would have been satisfactory to the Government of the United States if Mr. Pedersen had been charged with instructions in the negotiation which has just terminated to treat of the indemnities due to citizens of the United States, in consequence of the seizure, detention, and condemnation of their property in the ports of his Danish Majesty. But as he has no instructions to that effect, the undersigned is directed, at and before proceeding to the signature of the treaty of friendship, commerce, and navigation, on which they have agreed, explicitly to declare that the omission to provide for those indemnities is not hereafter to be interpreted as a waiver or abandonment of them by the Government of the United States, which, on the contrary, is firmly resolved to persevere in the pursuit of them until they shall be finally arranged upon principles of equity and justice. And, to guard against any misconception of the fact of the silence of the treaty in the above particular, or of the views of the American Government, the undersigned requests that Mr. Pedersen will transmit this official declaration to the Government of Denmark. And he avails himself of this occasion to tender to Mr. Pedersen assurances of his distinguished consideration.

H. CLAY.

Chevalier PEDERSEN, *Minister Resident from Denmark.*

The Chevalier Peter Pedersen to Mr. Clay.

WASHINGTON, *April* 26, 1826.

The undersigned, minister resident of his Majesty the King of Denmark, has the honor herewith to acknowledge having received Mr. Clay's official note of this day, declaratory of the advanced claims against Denmark not being waived on the part of the United States by the convention agreed upon and about to be signed, which note he, as requested, will transmit to his Government. And he avails himself of this occasion to renew to Mr. Clay assurances of his distinguished consideration.

P. PEDERSEN.

Hon. HENRY CLAY, *Secretary of State of the United States.*

19TH CONGRESS.]   **No. 428.**   [1ST SESSION.

RELATIVE TO INSTRUCTIONS TO MINISTERS OF THE UNITED STATES, AND CONCERNING ANY PLEDGE GIVEN ON THE PART OF THE GOVERNMENT TO MEXICO AND SOUTH AMERICA.

COMMUNICATED TO THE HOUSE OF REPRESENTATIVES MARCH 30, 1826.

To the House of Representatives of the United States:

In compliance with a resolution of the House of Representatives of the 27th instant, requesting a copy of such parts of the answer of the Secretary of State to Mr. Poinsett's letter to Mr. Clay, dated

Mexico, September 28, 1825, No. 22, as relates to the pledge of the United States therein mentioned; and also requesting me to inform the House whether the United States have, in any manner, made any pledge to the Governments of Mexico and South America; that the United States would not permit the interference of any foreign power with the independence or form of government of those nations; and, if so, when, in what manner, and to what effect; and also to communicate to the House a copy of the communication from our minister at Mexico, in which he informed the Government of the United States that the Mexican Government called upon this Government to fulfil the memorable pledge of the President of the United States, in his message to Congress of December, 1823, I transmit to the House a report from the Secretary of State, with documents containing the information desired by the resolution.

JOHN QUINCY ADAMS.

WASHINGTON, *March* 30, 1826.

DEPARTMENT OF STATE, *Washington, March* 29, 1826.

The Secretary of State, to whom has been referred, by the President, the resolution of the House of Representatives of the 27th March, 1826, requesting him to transmit to that House certain parts of the correspondence between the Department of State and the minister of the United States at Mexico, and to communicate certain information therein mentioned, has the honor to report:

That no answer was transmitted from this Department to the letter of Mr. Poinsett, No. 22, under date at Mexico, of the 28th September, 1825; that No. 18, from Mr. Poinsett, under date of the 13th of the same month, and No. 22, relate to the same subject; the first stating the obstacle which had occurred to the conclusion of the commercial treaty in the pretension brought forward by Mexico to grant to the American nations of Spanish origin special privileges which were not to be enjoyed by other nations; and the second narrating the arguments which were urged for and against it in the conferences between Mr. Poinsett and the Mexican ministers; that No. 22 was received on the 9th of December last, and the answer, of the 9th of November, 1825, from this Department to No. 18, having been prepared and transmitted, superseded the necessity, as was believed, of any more particular reply to No. 22.

That extracts from the general instructions to Mr. Poinsett, under date the 25th March, 1825, are herewith reported, marked A; that the United States have contracted no engagement, nor made any pledge to the Governments of Mexico and South America, or to either of them, that the United States would not permit the interference of any foreign power with the independence or form of government of those nations, nor have any instructions been issued authorizing any such engagement or pledge. It will be seen that the message of the late President of the United States of the 2d of December, 1823, is adverted to in the extracts now furnished from the instructions to Mr. Poinsett, and that he is directed to impress its principles upon the Government of the United Mexican States. All apprehensions of the danger to which Mr. Monroe alludes, of an interference by the allied powers of Europe to introduce their political systems into this hemisphere, have ceased. If, indeed, an attempt by force had been made by allied Europe to subvert the liberties of the southern nations on this continent, and to erect upon the ruins of their free institutions monarchical systems, the people of the United States would have stood pledged, in the opinion of their Executive, not to any foreign State, but to themselves and to their posterity, by their dearest interests and highest duties, to resist to the utmost such attempt; and it is to a pledge of that character that Mr. Poinsett alone refers.

That extracts from a despatch of Mr. Poinsett, under date the 21st August, 1825, marked B, are also herewith reported, relating to the movements of the French fleet in the West India seas during the last summer; that his previous letter, to which he refers, on the same subject, with the accompanying papers, is accidentally mislaid, and cannot, therefore, now be communicated, which is less regretted because the information contained in that now reported, it is presumed, will be entirely satisfactory.

All which is respectfully submitted.

H. CLAY.

A.

Extracts from the general instructions of Mr. Clay, Secretary of State, to Mr. Poinsett, appointed Envoy Extraordinary and Minister Plenipotentiary of the United States to Mexico, dated

DEPARTMENT OF STATE, *Washington, March* 25, 1825.

"The mission on which the President wishes you, with all practicable despatch, to depart, would at any time be highly important, but possesses at this moment a peculiar interest. Everywhere on this continent, but on the side of the United Mexican States, the United States are touched by the colonial territories of some Sovereign authority fixed in Europe. You are the first minister actually leaving the United States to reside near a Sovereign power established and exerted on this continent whose territories are conterminous with our own. You will probably be the first minister received by that power from any foreign State, except from those which have recently sprung out of Spanish America. The United Mexican States, whether we regard their present fortune, or recall to our recollection their ancient history and fortunes, are entitled to high consideration. In point of population, position, and resources, they must be allowed to rank among the first powers of America. In contemplating the progress in them towards civilization which the aborigines had made at the epoch of the Spanish invasion, and the incidents connected with the Spanish conquest which ensued, an irresistible interest is excited which is not surpassed, if it be equalled, by that which is awakened in perusing the early history of any other part of America. But what gives, with the President, to your mission peculiar importance at this time is, that it has for its principal object to lay for the first time the foundations of an intercourse of amity, commerce, navigation, and neighborhood, which may exert a powerful influence for a long period upon the prosperity of both States.

"In more particularly inviting your attention to the objects which should engage it on your mission, I will, in the first place, refer you to the general instructions which were given by my predecessor on the 27th May, 1823, to Mr. Anderson, the minister of the United States at Colombia, of which a copy is annexed, and which are to be considered as incorporated in these. So far as they are applicable alike to the condition of Colombia and of Mexico, and shall not be varied in this or subsequent letters, you will view them as forming a guide for your conduct. In that letter of the 27th of May the principles which have regulated the course of this Government in respect to the contest between Spanish America and Spain, from its origin, are clearly stated, explained, and indicated, and the bases of those upon which it is desirable to place the future intercourse between the United States and the several Governments which have been established in Spanish America are laid down. So that, although that letter was intended to furnish instructions for the American minister deputed to one of those Governments only, it should be contemplated as unfolding a system of relations which it is expedient to establish with all of them.

"From that letter, as well as from notorious public facts, it clearly appears that the people and the Government of the United States have alike, throughout all the stages of the struggle between Spain and the former colonies, cherished the warmest feelings and the strongest sympathies towards the latter; that the establishment of their independence and freedom has been anxiously desired; that the recognition of that independence was made as early as it was possible, consistently with those just considerations of policy and duty which this Government felt itself bound to entertain towards both parties; and that, in point of fact, with the exception of the act of the Portuguese Brazilian Government, to which it was prompted by self-interest, and which preceded that of the United States only a few months, this Government has been the first to assume the responsibility and encounter the hazard of recognizing the Governments which have been formed out of Spanish America. If there ever were any ground for imputing tardiness to the United States in making that recognition, as it respects other parts of what was formerly Spanish America, there is not the slightest pretext for such a suggestion in relation to Mexico. For, within a little more than a year after its independence was proclaimed, the United States hastened to acknowledge it. They have never claimed, and do not now claim, any peculiar favor or concession to their commerce or navigation, as the consideration of the liberal policy which they have observed towards those Governments. But the President does confidently expect that the priority of movement, on our part, which has disconcerted plans which the European allies were contemplating against the independent Governments, and which has no doubt tended to accelerate similar acts of recognition by the European powers, and especially that of Great Britain, will form a powerful motive with our southern neighbors, and particularly with Mexico, for denying to the commerce and navigation of those European States any favors or privileges which shall not be equally extended to us."

"You will bring to the notice of the Mexican Government the message of the late President of the United States to their Congress, on the 2d December, 1823, asserting certain important principles of intercontinental law, in the relations of Europe and America. The first principle asserted in that message is, that the American continents are not henceforth to be considered as subjects for future colonization by any European powers. In the maintenance of that principle all the independent Governments of America have an interest; but that of the United States has probably the least. Whatever foundation may have existed three centuries ago, or even at a later period, when all this continent was under European subjection, for the establishment of a rule, founded on priority of discovery and occupation, for apportioning among the powers of Europe parts of this continent, none can be now admitted as applicable to its present condition. There is no disposition to disturb the colonial possessions, as they may now exist, of any of the European powers; but it is against the establishment of new European colonies, upon this continent that the principle is directed. The countries in which any such new establishments might be attempted are now open to the enterprise and commerce of all Americans. And the justice or propriety cannot be recognized, of arbitrarily limiting and circumscribing that enterprise and commerce, by the act of voluntarily planting a new colony, without the consent of America, under the auspices of foreign powers, belonging to another and a distant continent. Europe would be indignant at any American attempt to plant a colony on any part of her shores, and her justice must perceive, in the rule contended for, only perfect reciprocity.

"The other principle asserted in the message is, that whilst we do not desire to interfere in Europe with the political system of the allied powers, we should regard as dangerous to our peace and safety any attempt, on their part, to extend their system to any portion of this hemisphere. The political systems of the two continents are essentially different. Each has an exclusive right to judge for itself what is best suited to its own condition and most likely to promote its happiness; but neither has a right to enforce upon the other the establishment of its peculiar system. This principle was declared in the face of the world, at a moment when there was reason to apprehend that the allied powers were entertaining designs inimical to the freedom if not the independence of the new Governments. There is ground for believing that the declaration of it had considerable effect in preventing the maturity, if not in producing the abandonment, of all such designs. Both principles were laid down, after much and anxious deliberation, on the part of the late administration. The President, who then formed a part of it, continues entirely to coincide in both. And you will urge upon the Government of Mexico the utility and expediency of asserting the same principles on all proper occasions."

B.

Extracts of a letter from Mr. Poinsett, Envoy Extraordinary and Minister Plenipotentiary of the United States to Mexico, to Mr. Clay, Secretary of State, dated

"MEXICO, August 21, 1825.

"The correspondence respecting the reported movements of the French fleet on the West India seas, which accompanied my last letter, was attended with circumstances which I had not then time to communicate.

"The intelligence was received on the 15th instant by the Secretary of State. On the morning of the 16th he called upon the chargé d'affaires of his Britannic Majesty and showed him the letters from the agent of this Government at Jamaica. Mr. Ward came immediately to me to consult what was to be done, and expressed a wish that we should act in concert. As I had not seen the Secretary nor the letters to which he alluded, I could only reply that I was perfectly willing to do so, provided this Government, in their communications with us, placed both our Governments on precisely the same footing. He immediately went to the palace and saw the Secretary of State, to whom he explained his desire that the notes to be addressed to us should be *verbatim et literatim* the same. Late in the afternoon the Secretary called on me and exhibited the letters he had received from Jamaica, and which induced him to believe that France entertained hostile intentions against this country. In this conversation I assured him of the friendly disposition of the United States, and that they would not view with indifference the occupation of the island of Cuba by France, especially if it was the result of any hostile views towards Mexico; but, at the same time, hinted that the imprudent conduct of some of their commanders might have induced Spain to cede that island to the French, rather than have it wrested from her in the manner proposed by Santa Anna, of which they were fully aware."

"When Mr. Ward was informed that the Secretary had said nothing to me of his interview with him, nor of his intention to make the notes to be addressed to us on this subject similar, he waited on the President and reiterated his request. The President, after assuring him that this should be done, declared that he himself was ignorant of the arrival of this important intelligence until he saw it published in the Sol."

"On the ensuing day, notes, couched in exactly the same words, were received by both Mr. Ward and myself. I objected to the language, and waited upon Mr. Alaman to state my objections. The original note—after stating that we had declared, in the most solemn manner, that we would never consent that any third power should interpose in the question between Spain and her former colonies, and that the conduct of France, on this occasion, is certainly an interposition, which, however cloaked, is not the less inexcusable—goes on to say: 'The President, therefore, instructs me to inform your excellency of these important occurrences, so that, by bringing them to the notice of your Government, it may demand of his Most Catholic Majesty such explanations as the case requires.'

"I told the Secretary that the declaration of the President and the known friendly disposition of the Government and of the people of the United States towards these countries did not confer upon this Government the privilege of demanding our interference as a right. He expressed his readiness to alter the phraseology of the note, and it was done." "The note to his Britannic Majesty's chargé d'affaires was afterwards altered in the same terms, and the substance of our answers corresponded."

19TH CONGRESS.]   **No. 429.**   [1ST SESSION.

COMMERCIAL RELATIONS WITH COLOMBIA.

COMMUNICATED TO THE HOUSE OF REPRESENTATIVES MARCH 31, 1826.

To the Senate and House of Representatives of the United States:

By the second article of the general convention of peace, amity, navigation, and commerce, between the United States and the Republic of Colombia, concluded at Bogota on the 3d of October, 1824, it was stipulated that the parties engaged, mutually, not to grant any particular favor to other nations, in respect of commerce and navigation, which should not immediately become common to the other party, who should enjoy the same freely, if the concession was freely made, or on allowing the same compensation, if the concession was conditional.

And, in the third article of the same convention, it was agreed that the citizens of the United States might frequent all the coasts and countries of the Republic of Colombia, and reside and trade there in all sorts of produce, manufactures, and merchandise, and should pay no other or greater duties, charges, or fees whatsoever than the most favored nation should be obliged to pay; and should enjoy all the rights, privileges, and exemptions, in navigation and commerce, which the most favored nation should enjoy, submitting themselves, nevertheless, to the laws, decrees, and usages there established, and to which were submitted the subjects and citizens of the most favored nations, with a reciprocal stipulation in favor of the citizens of the Republic of Colombia in the United States.

Subsequently to the conclusion of this convention, a treaty was negotiated between the Republic of Colombia and Great Britain, by which it was stipulated that no other or higher duties, on account of tonnage, light or harbor dues, should be imposed in the ports of Colombia on British vessels than those payable in the same ports by Colombian vessels; and that the same duties should be paid on the importation into the territory of Colombia of any article the growth, produce, or manufacture of his Britannic Majesty's dominions, whether such importation should be in Colombian or in British vessels, and that the same duties should be paid, and the same discount (drawbacks) and bounties allowed on the exportation of any articles the growth, produce, or manufacture of Colombia, to his Britannic Majesty's dominions, whether such exportation were in Colombian or British vessels.

The minister of the United States to the Republic of Colombia having claimed, by virtue of the second and third articles of the convention between the two Republics, that the benefit of these subsequent stipulations should be alike extended to the citizens of the United States, upon the condition of reciprocity provided for by the convention, the application of those engagements was readily acceded to by the Colombian Government, and a decree was issued by the Executive authority of that Republic, on the 30th of January last, a copy and translation of which are herewith communicated, securing to the citizens of the United States in the Republic of Colombia the same advantages, in regard to commerce and navigation, which had been conceded to British subjects in the Colombian treaty with Great Britain.

It remains for the Government of the United States to secure to the citizens of the Republic of Colombia the reciprocal advantages to which they are entitled by the terms of the convention, to commence from the 30th of January last; for the accomplishment of which, I invite the favorable consideration of the Legislature.

JOHN QUINCY ADAMS.

Washington, *March* 30, 1826.

List of papers sent.

No. 1. Mr. Clay to Mr. Anderson, September 16, 1825. (Extract.)
No. 2. Mr. Watts to Mr. Clay, January 17, 1826. (Extract.)
   (*a*.) Same to Mr. Revenga, January 15, 1826. (Copy.)
No. 3. Mr. Anderson to Mr. Clay, February 1, 1826. (Copy.)
   (*a*.) Same to Mr. Revenga, January, 1826. (Copy.)
   (*b*.) Mr. Revenga to Mr. Anderson, January 31, 1826. (Translation.)
   (*c*.) Decree of the Republic of Colombia, January 31, 1826. (Translation.)

No. 1.

Extracts of a letter from Mr. Clay to Mr. Anderson, dated

Department of State, *Washington, September* 16, 1825.

"By the treaty recently concluded between Great Britain and Colombia, it is understood that the vessels of the two countries, and their cargoes, are admitted into their respective ports upon the payment, without discrimination, of the same duties of impost and tonnage, whenever the cargo consists of the produce of the country to which the vessel belongs. Colombia having adopted the system of protecting her own tonnage by subjecting native vessels, and their cargoes, to a less rate of duty than that which is demanded on foreign vessels and their cargoes, these discriminating duties are paid by all foreign nations with which she has not agreed to equalize them. But the treaty between the United States and Colombia has not stipulated for the equalization of those duties, and, consequently, the vessel and its cargo, of each country, now remain subject, in the ports of the other, to alien duties. The United States would have had just cause to complain of the advantage conceded to Great Britain, if, by the second article of our treaty with Colombia, we had not a right to demand the same concession; and, if Mr. Gual had not, in a friendly spirit, in the course of the month of June last, informed Mr. Watts 'that the United States, whenever its Government desired, would be invested with all the privileges and powers which had been surrendered to England.' The President wishes, and you are authorized to propose, a mutual abolition of those discriminating duties. No difficulty, on the part of the Government of Colombia, in acceding to this proposal is anticipated; and it is only necessary to inquire into the best way of accomplishing the object. This may be done in either of the two following modes: 1st. By the fourth section of the act of Congress of January 7, 1824, it is enacted 'That, upon satisfactory evidence being given to the President of the United States by the Government of any foreign nation that no discriminating duties of tonnage or impost are imposed or levied within the ports of the said nation upon vessels wholly belonging to citizens of the United States, or upon merchandise, the produce or manufacture thereof, imported in the same, the President is hereby authorized to issue his proclamation, declaring that the foreign discriminating duties of tonnage and impost within the United States are and shall be suspended and discontinued, so far as respects the vessels of the said nation, and, consequently, the vessel and its cargo, *of its produce or manufacture*, imported into the United States in the same; the said suspension to take effect from the time of such notification being given to the President of the United States, and to continue so long as the reciprocal exemption of vessels belonging to citizens of the United States, and merchandise, as aforesaid, thereon laden, shall be continued and no longer.'

"This act, conceived in a genuine spirit of liberality, makes a general proposition to all nations. The same offer had been made by a previous act of Congress, and it has been embraced by the King of the Netherlands, Prussia, the Imperial Hanseatic cities of Hamburg, Lubec, and Bremen, the Dukedom of Oldenburg, Norway, Sardinia, and Russia. A convention between the United States and Great Britain and a treaty with Sweden adopt the same principle; and Mr. Poinsett has been instructed to propose it to Mexico. The President is desirous that all nations would see and appreciate the fairness of the principle of reciprocity and competition upon which the act of Congress is based. To enable the President to give effect, as it respects any particular foreign nation, to the act, by issuing the proclamation for which it provides, all that is requisite is, that *satisfactory evidence* should be given to him ' that no discriminating duties of tonnage or impost are imposed or levied within the ports of the said nation upon vessels wholly belonging to citizens of the United States, or upon merchandise, the produce or manufacture thereof, imported in the same.' In regard to Colombia, an act of its Congress abolishing all such discriminating duties, or a diplomatic note from its Minister of Foreign Affairs, declaring that no such discriminating duties exist against the United States, would be deemed by the President evidence sufficiently satisfactory to authorize the issuing of his proclamation; and it would, accordingly, upon the production of such evidence, be by him issued.

"Secondly. A convention might be concluded between the two powers effecting the proposed mutual abolition of alien duties; and, in that case, the second article of that which, on July 3, 1815, was formed between the United States and Great Britain, (6th vol. of the Laws of the United States, page 603,) will supply a model that may be safely followed. It is not very important which of these two modes be adopted; but the President rather prefers the latter, because the proposed equalization of duties would not, when depending upon compact, be so liable to a sudden termination as if it rested on separate acts of the two parties, revocable at the pleasure of either. But if a strong inclination to the other mode should be manifested by the Government of Colombia, you are authorized to accède to it. A commission empowering you to conclude and sign a convention, if that should be the form selected, accompanies these instructions."

No. 2.

Extract of a letter from Mr. Watts to Mr. Clay, Secretary of State, dated

"Bogotá, *January* 17, 1826.

"I have the honor to inclose you a copy of my note addressed to the Secretary of Foreign Affairs, growing out of the treaty recently ratified between this Republic and his Majesty the King of Great Britain.

"This morning I had a short interview with M. Revenga, when he apologized for not answering my note of the 15th, but gave me assurances that vessels of the United States, trading to the territories of Colombia, would be treated by the authorities of his Government as in possession of all the privileges granted to the Colombian and English vessels, upon a reciprocal equality, and that orders would immediately issue to the officers of the customs directing them to observe the same."

(a.)

Mr. Watts to Mr. Revenga.

Bogotá, *January* 15, 1826.

Sir: Since your excellency has been pleased to communicate to me the ratification of the treaty entered into between the Republic of Colombia and his Majesty the King of Great Britain, it becomes my duty to call your attention to the second and third articles of the treaty made and ratified between this Republic and the United States, wherein it is declared that the contracting parties engage, mutually, not to grant any particular favor to other nations which shall not immediately become common to the other party. In the treaty between Colombia and his Britannic Majesty, it is stipulated that no other or higher duties or imposts shall be levied on account of tonnage, light-house dues, port fees, &c., in the territories of Colombia, on British vessels, than the payments made for the same by Colombian vessels, and the same discount and bounties granted, whether in British or Colombian vessels.

May I therefore, sir, remind you of the promise made by your predecessor, Dr. Gual, and subsequently renewed by yourself, that, whenever it should be officially communicated to your Government that the treaty with Colombia and Great Britain had been ratified, that, simultaneously thereafter, orders would be issued placing the United States in all the privileges of the most favored nations.

I have the honor to repeat to your excellency the assurances of my high regard.
BEAUFORT T. WATTS.

His Excellency Joseph R. Revenga, *Secretary of Foreign Relations.*

No. 3.

Mr. Anderson to Mr. Clay.

Bogotá, *February* 1, 1826.

Sir: Agreeably to the expectation intimated in my letter No. 32' no difficulty has occurred in procuring from this Government its assent to a mutual and immediate renunciation of the countervailing duties to which the commerce and navigation of the two countries have been heretofore subjected in the ports of each other, and a few days only were occupied in concerting the means of accomplishing that end. Not having ascertained, with distinctness, in the conversation which I had with the Secretary of Foreign Relations on this subject, the views of his Government in relation to the mode of effecting the desired object, I determined to submit, at once, in a formal manner, the alternative suggested in your instructions, of effecting the abolition either by a convention, or by an order to that end, to be issued by Colombia, in anticipation of a corresponding order from the Government of the United States.

To this mode I was led from a wish to exclude, without delay, a subject which, in truth, admitted no delay without great injury to our commerce, and, also, because, although an inclination had been indicated to adopt the course of mutual Executive orders, no such distinct preference had been announced as to justify me in forbearing to make the proposition to effect the object by treaty. This Government has, however, elected to abolish the duties under consideration, by a decree of the Executive, a copy of which, together with the official note accompanying it, is herewith transmitted to you. The thing is, I believe, satisfactory and complete. The decree, in recapitulating the different motives and obligations which moved the Executive to issue it, has gone into a recital much more minute than was necessary for our purpose, but probably not more so than was necessary to show, on its face, the authority of the Vice President for acting in the case.

The late convention between Colombia and Great Britain, which has been assumed, in this case, as the standard for affixing the regulations to be established with us, embraces the following principles ;
1st. It equalizes the tonnage and other port duties on the vessels of the two countries.
2d. It equalizes the duties on the importation of goods, whether it be in the vessels of the one or the other country, provided those goods are of the produce or manufacture of the country from which the importation is made.
3d. The duty ; and
4th. The bounty on exportation are made equal, whether the exportation be made in Colombian or British vessels.
It is on this footing that the recent order has placed our navigation, and it is to this extent, no doubt, that Colombia expects an entire reciprocity from the United States. But you will observe that, in this respect, the inclosed decree is broader than the act of Congress to which you refer me, as giving the President authority to reciprocate the abolition. The fourth section of the act of the 7th of January, 1824, authorizes the President, in certain events, to declare discontinued and suspended the duties of tonnage and *impost*. I am aware that no difficulty can, at any time, occur with regard to a duty on exportation, as none by our laws, has been or can be imposed; but, inasmuch as it is within the competency of Congress to legislate at any time on the subject of a *bounty* on exports, I considered it proper to call your attention to the extent of the arrangement on the part of Colombia, in order that the reciprocity which I believe will exist under our laws as they now are may not be violated by future legislation.
In that part of the decree which refers to my letter of the 28th of January to the Secretary of Foreign Relations, as giving an assurance that there will be a mutual abrogation of the corresponding duties in the United States, it is stated that this abolition will take place from the day on which the suspension occurs in Colombia. You will see that this is not the language of my note. My expressions conform more nearly to the language of the law, which says: "The suspension shall take effect from the time of the notification being given to the President of the United States." But well knowing the liberal spirit which governs our conduct on analogous occasions, I did not doubt that, if a Colombian vessel should arrive in our ports under the faith of that construction, the excess between the alien and domestic duties would be refunded. I have therefore permitted the subject to pass without notice, under the certain belief that no difficulty can arise out of it.
I have the honor to be, with great respect, your obedient servant,

R. C. ANDERSON, Jr.

Hon. HENRY CLAY, *Secretary of State, Washington.*

P. S. A copy of my letter to the Secretary of Foreign Relations is herein also inclosed.

(*a.*)

Mr. Anderson to Mr. Revenga.

BOGOTA, *January,* 1826.

SIR: The propriety of abolishing the discriminating duties of imposts and tonnage, hitherto imposed by the laws of our respective countries on the vessels and merchandise of the one in the ports of the other, has been a subject of correspondence between yourself and Mr. Watts, chargé d'affaires of the United States near this Republic. It is with great pleasure I learn from that correspondence that the Government of Colombia is not indisposed to make a mutual abolition of those duties; and it is with still further satisfaction I learned from you, in conversation on Thursday last, that this Government was now ready, in confirmation of its previous declaration, to make an immediate arrangement which would place the commerce and navigation of the two States on so eligible a foundation. In that conversation I had the honor of stating to you that two modes occurred to me, by either of which the same beneficial result would probably be produced, but that there were considerations connected with one of them which seemed to give claims to its adoption beyond the other.
The one mode of accomplishing the object is that referred to in your letter to Mr. Watts, of the 20th of the present month, in which you declare the readiness of Colombia to extend, by a decree of the Government, to the vessels and merchandise of the United States, the same rights and exemptions which have been recently granted to Great Britain. This course will be in fulfilment of those clauses of the treaty between the United States and Colombia, signed on the 3d of October, 1824, by which each has assured to the commerce and navigation of the other the footing of the most favored nation. This principle, then, taken in connexion with the provisions of the late convention between this Government and the Government of Great Britain, under which the vessels of those countries and their cargoes pay only, in the ports of each other, the duties demanded in like cases from native vessels and their cargoes.
If this shall be the mode preferred to be made to the United States, I am authorized to say, and I desire that this may be deemed the necessary declaration, that, immediately on receiving the information that the duties in question have been abolished here, the President of the United States will issue his proclamation declaring a mutual and immediate abolition of the corresponding duties with regard to Colombia in the ports of the United States.
Another mode suggesting itself for effecting the desired object is, a convention between the two powers declaring a mutual abolition of alien duties. This mode is recommended by its superior simplicity. A single instrument would then show the whole rule governing the commerce of the two countries. A convention would declare on its face, without reference for explanation to any other treaty or public document, the duties demandable in the ports of the one from the citizens of the other nation.
The relations produced in this way would be more permanent, inasmuch as they would not rest for their existence or continuance on any arrangement made with a third power, which would necessarily be the case if the first course referred to be adopted.
Under this view, it is respectfully submitted whether it is not more desirable to effect an object directly, and by express stipulation, than to reach it by a circuity, and then to permit it to depend for its

·duration on the continuance of an arrangement to which one of our Governments is no party. It does not occur to me that any objection can exist on the part of Colombia to make the same stipulations with the United States, and in the same form, too, in which they have been recently made between this Government and that of his Britannic Majesty; and especially, as whatever objection to the principle or precedent of such a compact may once have existed is now destroyed by the adoption and ratification of that convention.

In the event that the manner here last suggested should be preferred by this Government, it will give me great pleasure, under the full powers with which I have been furnished for the purpose, to enter on the negotiation at as early a day as it may be convenient.

I have the honor to assure you of my high consideration and respect.

R. C. ANDERSON, Jr.

· Hon. Joseph R. Revenga, *Secretary of Foreign Affairs.*

(b.)

Don Joseph R. Revenga to Mr. Anderson.

[Translation.]

REPUBLIC OF COLOMBIA.

Department of State and Foreign Relations,
Bogota, January 31, 1826.

Sir: I have had the honor to receive and to lay before the Vice President your communication of the 28th ultimo, in which, after referring to that addressed by this Department to Mr. Watts, chargé d'affaires of the United States, on the 20th, you are pleased to propose a treaty in addition to that which was concluded between Colombia and the United States on the 3d October, 1824, as the most simple means of extending to their vessels, productions, and manufactures, the privileges which, by the treaty concluded here in April last, were granted to the vessels, productions, and manufactures of the dominions of his Britannic Majesty.

The Vice President agrees in opinion with you, that a treaty which should abolish all the duties to which foreign vessels are subject in the mutual commerce of our respective countries would facilitate the comprehension of the rules to be observed in our mutual mercantile relations; but he judges, at the same time, that this object is no less attainable by a simple declaration, and that this being in the power of the Executive of both countries, in virtue of the said treaty of October, the adoption of what you propose would only have the effect of deferring it.

The copy with which you were pleased to accompany your above-mentioned communication has inspired the Vice President with the agreeable persuasion that, for this purpose, a decree, such as that which I have the honor to inclose, would be entirely satisfactory to the Government of the United States. And the apprehension that the duration of these new privileges would be thus more ephemeral has appeared to his excellency to be removed, as he flatters himself that those States endeavor, no less than Colombia, to strengthen and cultivate, mutually, the most frank, friendly, and benevolent relations. These sentiments have induced the Vice President to order me to communicate that decree to the proper persons, that it may be observed as a law of the Republic; and I am gratified in adding that I this day fulfil that order.

I pray you, sir, to accept my assurances of perfect respect, and the sentiments of high esteem with which I have the honor to be your obedient humble servant.

JOSEPH R. REVENGA.

(c.)

Translation of the decree.

Francisco de Paula Santander, Vice President, charged with the Executive authority of the Republic of Colombia.

The ratifications of the treaty of friendship, commerce, and navigation, concluded in this city on the eighteenth of April, one thousand eight hundred and twenty-five, between Colombia and his Majesty the King of the United Kingdom of Great Britain and Ireland, having been exchanged, as is duly known; in which treaty it is declared, in the fifth article, "that no other or higher duties on account of tonnage, ·light or harbor dues, shall be imposed in the ports of Colombia on British vessels than those payable in the same ports by Colombian vessels;" and, also, in the sixth article, "that the same duties shall be paid on the importation into the territories of Colombia of any article the growth, produce, or manufacture of his Britannic Majesty's dominions, whether such importation shall be in Colombian or British vessels; and the same duties shall be paid, and the same discount (drawback) and bounties allowed on the exportation of any articles the growth, produce, or manufacture of Colombia, to his Britannic Majesty's dominions, whether such exportation be in Colombian or British vessels."

And it being stipulated in the third article of the general convention of peace, amity, navigation, and commerce, concluded in this city on the third day of October, in the year one thousand eight hundred and twenty-four, between Colombia and the United States of America, the ratifications of which were exchanged on the twenty-seventh of May, one thousand eight hundred and twenty-five, "that the citizens of the United States of America shall pay no other or greater duties, charges, or fees, whatsoever, than the most favored nation is or shall be obliged to pay; and they shall enjoy all the rights, privileges, and exemptions, in navigation and commerce, which the most favored nation does or shall enjoy."

And the honorable Richard C. Anderson, Envoy Extraordinary and Minister Plenipotentiary of the United States near the Government of Colombia, having made known, in a communication dated on the twenty-eighth day of the present month of January, that the President of the said United States is ready to concede, or cause to be conceded, to the vessels, productions, and manufactures of Colombia, the same exemptions which, by the before-mentioned treaty, are granted to the vessels, productions, and manufac. tures of the dominions of his Britannic Majesty, which may be introduced into the ports and territories of Colombia; and that those exemptions will be granted from the day in which, in Colombia, there shall be extended to the commerce of the citizens of the United States the privileges which are granted to British commerce.

And it being obligatory on Colombia, by the second and third articles of the before-mentioned general convention, "not to grant any particular favor to other nations, in respect to commerce and navigation, which shall not become common to the United States:"

Wherefore, and the condition of which the said second article speaks being considered as complied with, and in the execution of the laws of the Republic, I declare:

Article 1. That there shall be paid the same duties on the importation into the territories of Colombia of any article whatever of the growth, produce, or manufacture of the United States of America and of the territories subject to the Government of the United States; and that there shall be paid the same duties, and there shall be granted the same discounts and bounties on the exportation of any article the growth, produce, or manufacture of Colombia to the United States, or to the territories of the same, whether the said importation or exportation be made in Colombian vessels or in vessels of the said United States.

Article 2. The vessels of the United States which may enter into the ports of the Republic of Colombia shall not pay other or higher duties or charges, on account of tonnage, light, or harbor dues, or other local charges, than shall be payable in the same ports by Colombian vessels.

Article 3. The Secretary of State in the despatch of foreign affairs is charged with communicating this declaration.

Done in the city of Bogota, this thirtieth day of January, one thousand eight hundred and twenty-six, in the sixteenth of independence.

FRANCISCO DE PAULA SANTANDER.

By the Vice President, charged with the Executive power :

JOSEPH R. REVENGA,
Secretary of State in the despatch of Foreign Relations.

FRANCISCO DE PAULA SANTANDER, *Vice Presidente, encargado del poder Ejecutivo de la Republica de Colombia:*

Canjeadas como se sabe que han sido las ratificaciones del tratado de amistad, comercio y navegacion concludio en esta ciudad en diez y ocho de Abril de mil ochocientos veinte y cinco, entre Colombia y S. M. el Rey del Reyno-Unido de la Gran Bretaña é Irlanda, en cuyo tratada se dispone al Articulo V. "Que no se impondrán otros ó mas altos derechos por razon de tonelada, fanal ó emolumentos de puerto, en. los puertos de Colombia á los buques Británicos que los pagaderos en los mismos puertos por buques Colombianos;" y al articulo VI., "Que se pagaran los mismos derechos á la importacion en los territorios de Colombia de cualquier articulo del producto natural, producciones ó manufacturas de los dominios de S. M. B. ya sea que esta importacion se haga en buques Colombianos ó en Británicos: y que se pagaran los mismos derechos, y se concederan los mismos descuentos y gratificaciones á la exportacion de cualesquiera articulos del producto natural, producciones ó manufacturas de Colombia para los dominios de S. M. B. ya sea que esta exportacion se haga en buques Británicos ó en Colombianos."

Y habiendose estipulado en el articulo III de la convencion jeneral de paz, amistad, navegacion y comercio, concluida en esta ciudad á tres de Octubre del año de mil ochocientos veinte y cuatro, entre Colombia y los Estados-Unidos de America cuyas ratificaciones fueron canjeadas en veinte y siete de Mayo de mil ochocientos veinte y cinco: "Que los ciudadanos de los Estados-Unidos de America no pagarán otros ó mayores derechos, impuestos ó emolumentos cualesquiera que los que las naciones mas favorecidas estan ó estuvieren obligadas á pagar, y gozarán de todos los derechos, privilejios y exenciones que gozan ó gozaren los de la nacion mas favorecida con respeto á navegacion y comercio."

Y habiendo manifestado el Honorable Sr. R. C. Anderson, enviado extraordinario y ministro plenipotenciario de los Estados Unidos cerca del Gobierno de Colombia en comunicacion fecha á veinte y ocho del corriente mes de Enero que el Presidente de dichos Estados-Unidos está pronto á conceder ó á hacer que se conceda en ellos, á los buques, producciones y manufacturas Colombianas los mismos goces que por el sobre-dicho tratado se conceden á los buques, producciones, y manufacturas de los dominios de S. M. B. que se introduzcan en los puertos y territorios Colombianos; y que los concedera ó hará que se concedan desde el dia en que en Colombia se estiendan al comercio de los cuidadanos de los Estados-Unidos los goces concedidos al comercio Británico.

Y siendo obligatorio á Colombia por los articulos II y III de la sobre-dicha convencion general "el no conceder favores particulares á otras nacions con respecto á comercio y navegacion que no se hagan comunes" á los Estados-Unidos:

Por tanto; y cumplida ya como se concidera la condicion de que habla el citado articulo II, en ejecucion de las leyes de la Republica, declaro:

Articulo 1º. Se pagaran los mismos derechos á la importacion en los territorios de Colombia de cualquier articulo del producto natural, producciones ó manufacturas de los Estados-Unidos de America y de los territorios sujetos al Gobierno de los Estados-Unidos; y se pagaran los mismos derechos, y se concederan los mismos descuentos y gratificaciones á la exportacion de cualesquiera articulos del producto natural, producciones ó manufacturas de Colombia, para los Estados-Unidos ó para los territorios de los, Estados-Unidos; ya sea que la importacion se haga en buques Colombianos ó en buques de dichos Estados-Unidos.

Articulo 2º. No pagaran los buques de los Estados-Unidos que entren en puertos de la República de´

Colombia otros ó mas altos derechos ó impuestos por razon de tonelada, fanal ó emolumentos de puerto, ú otros gastos locales, que los pagaderos en los mismos puertos por buques Colombianos.

Articulo 3°. El Secretario de Estado en el despacho de relaciones exteriores queda encargado de comunicar esta declaracion.

Dado en la ciudad de Bogotá, á treinta de Enero, de mil ochocientos veinte y seis—decimo sexto de la independencia.

(Firmado)   FRANCISCO DE PAULA SANTANDER.

Por el Vice Presidente, encargado del poder Ejecutivo de la Republica,
                                                 JOSEPH R. RAVENGA,
                      El Secretario de Estado en el despacho de Relaciones Exteriores.

CORRESPONDENCE RELATIVE TO THE CONGRESS AT PANAMA.

COMMUNICATED TO THE HOUSE OF REPRESENTATIVES APRIL 5, 1826.

To the House of Representatives of the United States:

In compliance with a resolution of the House of the 30th ultimo, I transmit to the House a report from the Secretary of State, with the documents desired by the resolution, and also a copy of the letter from the Secretary of State to Mr. Poinsett, acknowledging the receipt of his despatch No. 22, accidentally overlooked in the answer to the resolution of the House of the 27th ultimo.

                                                 JOHN QUINCY ADAMS.

WASHINGTON, *April* 5, 1826.

DEPARTMENT OF STATE, *Washington, April* 3, 1826.

The Secretary of State, to whom has been referred by the President the resolution of the House of Representatives of the 30th ultimo, requesting him to transmit to the House "a copy of Mr. Middleton's letter of the 2d of July to Count Nesselrode, communicated with the despatch of the Secretary of State of the 10th of May, 1825, and so much of the instructions from the Department of State to the ministers of the United States to Buenos Ayres, Chile, and Mexico, as relates to a proposed or contemplated Congress of the Spanish American States," has the honor to report:

1. A copy of the letter of Mr. Middleton, requested, with a copy of a translation of it into English.

2. An extract from a despatch from the late Secretary of State to Mr. Rodney, under date of 17th day of May, 1823, containing the only instructions given to any minister of the United States at Buenos Ayres respecting the contemplated Congress; and

3. An extract from a despatch from the Department of State, under date of the 24th of September, 1825, embracing the only instructions given to the minister of the United States at Mexico in relation to the Congress.

That no instructions have been given to the minister of the United States at Chile in relation to the proposed Congress.

The Secretary of State asks permission to take this occasion to state that, when his report of the 29th ultimo was made, in obedience to the resolution of the House of Representatives of the 27th ultimo, it was overlooked in the office; that in a despatch to Mr. Poinsett of the 9th of December last, communicating the conclusion of a treaty with the Central Republic, the receipt was acknowledged of Mr. Poinsett's despatch, No. 22. Although, in fact, nothing is contained in that despatch of the 9th of December falling within the scope of the resolution of the House, a copy of it is, nevertheless, now laid before the President, that he may decide on the propriety of its being communicated to the House. The Secretary also begs leave to add that Mr. Poinsett has been requested to furnish to this Department a duplicate of the despatch referred to by him in his letter of the 21st of August, 1825, which was accidentally mislaid, as stated in the above report of the 29th ultimo.

All which is respectfully submitted.

                                                 H. CLAY.

Mr. Middleton to Count Nesselrode.

À ST. PETERSBOURG, *ce* 2 (14) *Juillet*, 1825.

Le soussigné, Envoyé Extraordinaire et Ministre Plénipotentiaire des Etats-Unis d'Amérique à l'honneur de prévenir son Excellence Monsieur le Comte de Nesselrode, qu' à fin de remplir les intentions de son Gouvernement, il croit ne pouvoir mieux faire que de lui envoyer ci-près copie d'une dépêche en forme d'instruction qu'il vient de recevoir, et de la prier de vouloir bien la mettre sous les yeux de sa Majesté l'Empereur, dont intervention amicale, invoquée avec succès dans plus d'une occasion, peut encore en ce moment servir à la fois les intérêts de l'Europe et de l'Amérique.

Le soussigné est d'autant plus porté à faire cette démarche, qu'il est dans la persuasion que sa Majesté Impériale trouvera consignées, dans la dépêche sus-mentionnée, de nouvelles preuves ajoutées à tant d'autres, des sentimens de haute estime et de confiance qu'elle inspire au Gouvernement des Etats-Unis, et par conséquent, qu'elle daignera accueillir avec bienveillance les vœux qu'il à émis.

Dans la guerre actuelle entre l'Espagne et ses ci-devant possessions d'outremer, les Etats-Unis n'ont jamais pris de part, ni pour l'exciter ni pour l'alimenter; ils ont toujours observé la neutralité la plus stricte. On ne peut pas dire, à la verité, qu'ils aient été des spectateurs indifferents aux événements qui se passaient sous leur yeux. Dans des vues raisonnées de commerce, ils ont toujours désiré que ces nations placées sur la même continent qu'ils habitent pussent établir une indépendence politique dont ils avoient eux même ressenti l'heureuse influence; mais ce sentiment n'a jamais faussé la neutralité qu'ils avaient déclarée. La preuve de la fidélité avec laquelle ils en ont rempli les obligations est, que dans le cours de la guerre actuelle, les deux parties belligérantes se sont également et faussement plaintes de la violation de cette neutralité.

Mais si les Etats-Unis ont vû avec satisfaction les efforts des nations du Continent Américain pour se soustraire au joug de la domination Espagnole, il n'en est pas de même pour ci qui regarde les isles de Cuba et de Porto Rico. Le caractère de la population de ces isles rend extrêmement problématique leur capacité de maintenir l'independence. Une déclaration prématurée n'aurait probablement pour résultat, que la répétition affligéante des scénes désastreuses de St. Domingue.

Contre un telle catastrophe il ne puit y avoir d'autre garantie que celle de la présence d'une force armée fournie par quelque puissance protectrice. Si les noveaux Etats, ou quelques uns d'entre eux, faisaient la conquête de ces îles, leurs moyens militaires et maritimes ne sauraient rassurer contre l'occurrence de scénes sanglantes et déplorables.

Ayant égard donc aux circonstances, et sous le point de vue commercial, des Etats-Unis sont parfaitement satisfaits de le condition politique de ces iles sous la domination de leur metropole; mais ils ne pourraient envisager comme indifférent à leurs intérêts l'intervention armée d'aucune autre nation.

Toutes les puissances qui ont des possessions dans l'archipel Américain ont un intérêt pressant d'empecher le bouleversement de l'ordre existant dans ces iles. Quoique la Russie ne se trouve pas dans cette catégorie, le caractère bienveillant de sa Majesté Impériale et son penchant décidé pour le maintien de toutes les legitimités, font espérer qu'elle ne refusera pas de préter son puissant appui au *seul moyen* qui parait s'offrir pour éviter un surcroit de malheurs pour l'Espagne et le monde civilisé.

Ce moyen se trouve indiqué dans l'écrit dont copie ci-prés.

Le Gouvernement des Etats Unis plus à portée par sa position géographique et par les informations qu'il a prises sur la condition actuelle des nouveaux états de juger des chances probables de cette guerre, que ne le sont des Gouvernements moins rapprochés, peut sans témérité se croire autorisé à mettre son opinion sur la meilleure maniére de tarir une source deja abondante de maux pour l'humanité et qui menace incessamment de redoubler d'activité.

Dans toute cette question il ne s'agit pas de considérer qu'ils peuvent être le vrais principes du droit. En cela il peut y avoir, pas, ou n'y avoir dissentiment d'opinion. Il s'agit ici de constater les faits. Où les faits ont prononce, le droit se trouve anéanti. Il n'est question donc que de faire le bien qui soit encore possible, lorsqu'on ne peut pas accomplir tout le bien qu'on aurait désiré. Mais si l'on ne sa hâte en ce moment de sauver pour l'Espagne les derniéres colonies qui lui restent, l'occasion en sera peut-être à jamais perdue.

En appelant une attention sériéuse sur l'urgence du cas qui se presente, il ne reste au soussigné qu'à priér son Excellence M. le Comté dè Nesselrode de vouloir bien agreér l'assurance renouvellée de sa haute considération.

H. MIDDLETON.

Mr. Middleton to Count Nesselrode.

[Translation.]

Sт. Petersburg, *July* 2, (14,) 1825.

The undersigned, Envoy Extraordinary and Minister Plenipotentiary of the United States of America, has the honor to inform his excellency the Count de Nesselrode that, in order to fulfil the intentions of his Government, he thinks he cannot do better than send him a copy of a despatch, in the form of an instruction, which he has just received, and pray him to be pleased to lay it before his Majesty the Emperor, whose friendly interposition, invoked with success on more than one occasion, may still at this moment subserve at once the interests of Europe and of America.

The undersigned is, moreover, the more inclined to do this, as he is persuaded that his Imperial Majesty will find recorded, in the above-mentioned despatch, new proofs, in addition to so many others, of the sentiments of high esteem and confidence with which he inspires the Government of the United States, and consequently that he will deign to receive with kindness the wishes therein expressed.

In the present war between Spain and her late ultramar possessions the United States have never taken a part, either to excite or foster it; they have always observed the strictest neutrality. It cannot, in truth, be said that they have been indifferent spectators of the events passing under their view. In the reasonable views of commerce they have always desired that the nations placed upon the same continent with them might establish a political independence, the happy influence of which they themselves had felt, but this sentiment has never infringed the neutrality which they had declared. It is a proof of the fidelity with which they have fulfilled its obligations, that, in the course of the existing war, the two belligerent parties have equally and erroneously complained of the violation of that neutrality.

But if the United States have seen with satisfaction the efforts of the nations of the American continent to withdraw themselves from the yoke of Spanish domination, it is not so with regard to the islands of Cuba and Porto Rico. The character of the population of these islands renders extremely problematical their capacity to maintain independence. A premature declaration would probably result only in the afflicting repetition of the disastrous scenes of St. Domingo.

Against such a catastrophe there can be no other security than that of the presence of an armed force furnished by some protecting power. If the new States, or any of them, were to make conquest of these islands, their military and naval means could be no security against the occurrence of bloody and deplorable scenes. Having regard, therefore, to the circumstances, and in a commercial point of view, the United States are perfectly satisfied with the political condition of these islands under the dominion of their mother country; but they could not see, as indifferent to their interests, the armed intervention of any other nation.

All the powers that have possessions in the American archipelago have an urgent interest in preventing the overthrow of the existing order in these islands. Although Russia is not in that predicament, the benevolent character of his Imperial Majesty and his decided inclination for the maintenance of all legitimacies create a hope that he will not refuse to lend his powerful aid to the *only means* which appear to offer for averting an increase of misfortunes from Spain and the civilized world.

These means are pointed out in the writing of which a copy is inclosed.

The Government of the United States, better able, by their geographical position, and by the information which they receive of the actual condition of the new States, to judge of the probable chances of this war than those Governments at a greater distance, may, without temerity, think themselves authorized to give their opinion upon the best manner of drying up a source, already overflowing, of evils to mankind, and which incessantly threatens to be redoubled in activity.

In all this question there enters no consideration of what may be the true principles of right. In that there may or may not be a difference of opinion. Here there is only a verification of facts. When facts have decided, the question of right has vanished. It remains, therefore, only to do the good which is still possible, when all the good which may be desired cannot be accomplished. But if haste be not made at present to save to Spain the last colonies which remain to her, the opportunity of doing so will be perhaps forever lost.

In calling a serious attention to the urgency of the case which is presented, it only remains for the undersigned to pray his excellency Count Nesselrode to be pleased to accept the renewed assurances of his high consideration.

HENRY MIDDLETON.

Extract of a letter from Mr. Adams, Secretary of State, to Mr. Cæsar A. Rodney, Minister Plenipotentiary of the United States at Buenos Ayres, dated .

MAY 17, 1823.

"In the meantime a more extensive confederation has been projected under the auspices of the new Government of the Republic of Colombia. In the last despatch received from Mr. Forbes, dated the 27th of January last, he mentions the arrival and reception, at Buenos Ayres, of Mr. Joaquin Mosquera y Arbolada, senator of the Republic of Colombia, and their Minister Plenipotentiary and Extraordinary, upon a mission, the general object of which, he informed Mr. Forbes, was to engage the other independent Governments of *Spanish* America to unite with Colombia in a Congress, to be held at such point as might be agreed on, to settle a general system of *American policy* in relation to Europe, leaving to each section of the country the perfect liberty of independent self-government. For this purpose he had already signed a treaty with Peru, of which he promised Mr. Forbes the perusal; but there were some doubts with regard to the character of his associations and the personal influence to which he was accessible at Buenos Ayres, and Mr. Forbes had not much expectation of his success in prevailing on that Government to enter into his project of extensive federation.

"By letters of a previous date, November, 1822, received from Mr. Prevost, it appears that the project is yet more extensive than Mr. Mosquera had made known to Mr. Forbes. It embraces North as well as South America, and a formal proposal to join and take the lead in it is to be made known to the Government of the United States.

"Intimations of the same design have been given to Mr. Todd at Bogota. It will be time for this Government to deliberate concerning it when it shall be presented in a more definite and specific form. At present it indicates more distinctly a purpose on the part of the Colombian Republic to assume a leading character in this hemisphere than any practicable objects of utility which can be discovered by us. With relation to *Europe*, there is perceived to be only one object in which the interests and wishes of the United States can be the same as those of the Southern American nations, and that is, that they should all be governed by republican institutions, politically and commercially independent of Europe. To any confederation of Spanish American provinces for that end the United States would yield their approbation and cordial good wishes. If more should be asked of them, the proposition will be received and considered in a friendly spirit, and with a due sense of its importance."

Extract of a letter from Mr. Clay, Secretary of State, to Mr. Poinsett, Minister of the United States to Mexico, dated

DEPARTMENT OF STATE, *September* 24, 1825.

"During the last spring the ministers of Mexico and Colombia near this Government made separate, but nearly simultaneous, communications to this Department in relation to the contemplated Congress at Panama. Each of them stated that he was instructed by his Government to say that it would be very agreeable to it that the United States should be represented at that Congress; that it was not expected they would take any part in its deliberations, or measures of concert, in respect to the existing war against Spain, but that other great interests, affecting the continent of America and the friendly intercourse between the independent nations established on it, might be considered and regulated at the Congress; and that, not knowing what might be the views of the United States, a previous inquiry was directed to be made whether they would, if invited by Mexico or Colombia, be represented at Panama, and, if an affirmative answer were given, each of those ministers stated that the United States would be accordingly invited to be represented there. The President directed me to say, and I accordingly replied, that the communication was received with great sensibility to the friendly consideration of the United States by which it had been dictated; that of course they could not make themselves any party to the existing war with Spain, or to councils for deliberating on the means of its further prosecution; that he believed such a Congress as was proposed might be highly useful in settling several important controverted questions of public law, and in arranging other matters of deep interest to the American continent, and to the friendly intercourse between the American powers; that before such a Congress assembled, however, it appeared to him to be necessary to arrange between the different powers to be represented several preliminary points, such as the subjects to which the attention of the Congress should be directed, the nature and the form of the powers to be given to the ministers, and the mode of organizing the Congress. If these preliminary points could be adjusted in a manner satisfactory to the United States, the ministers from Mexico and Colombia were informed that the United States would be represented at the Congress. Upon inquiry if these preliminary points had yet engaged the attention of either the Government of Mexico or Colombia, they were unable to inform me that they had, whilst both appeared to admit the expediency of their being settled. Each of them undertook to communicate to his Government the answer which I delivered to their invitations, and nothing further has since transpired. It is deemed proper that you should be made acquainted with what has occurred here on this matter, in order that, if it should be touched upon by the Mexican Government, you may, if necessary, be able to communicate what passed. We shall make no further movement in it until we hear from the Governments of Mexico or Colombia."

Mr. Clay to Mr. Poinsett, No. 8.

DEPARTMENT OF STATE, *December* 9, 1825.

SIR: Your despatch No. 22, under date of September 28, 1825, is this day received. By mine of the 9th ultimo you will have learned that the President approves of your rejection of the exception in the proposed commercial treaty, which the Mexican Government insists upon making, of favors in behalf of the new Governments established within what was formerly Spanish territory, and that you are instructed to break off the negotiation rather than accede to that exception. It is therefore seen with regret that the Mexican Government perseveres in an exception which is so inadmissible. On the 5th instant a treaty of peace, amity, commerce, and navigation was concluded and signed here with the Central Republic, which will be submitted to the Senate for its advice and consent in a day or two. This treaty embraces the same articles as that which we have made with Colombia, and three others, (one a modification of a similar article in that treaty, and two new ones,) of which copies are herewith sent. It contains no exception of favors to any of the American Republics carved out of former Spanish territory. On the contrary, no such pretension was ever advanced in the progress of the negotiation. It has been brought forward by no American power but Mexico. The treaty with the Republic of the Centre is characterized by the greatest liberality and by a true American spirit; and it expressly provides that whatever favors shall be granted to any foreign power (of course American as well as European) by either of the high contracting parties shall extend to and be enjoyed by the other.

Our information here in regard to the treaty negotiated by Great Britain with Mexico is, that the objection taken to it in England was that it embraced the principle that free ships should make free goods, to which Great Britain is not prepared to subscribe.

I am your obedient servant,

H. CLAY.

JOEL R. POINSETT, *Envoy Extraordinary and Minister Plenipotentiary
of the United States to Mexico.*

19TH CONGRESS.]　　　　　No. 431.　　　　　[1ST SESSION.

RELATIVE TO WHAT GOVERNMENTS ARE EXPECTED TO BE REPRESENTED AT THE CONGRESS OF PANAMA.

COMMUNICATED TO THE HOUSE OF REPRESENTATIVES APRIL 15, 1826.

To the House of Representatives of the United States:

In compliance with a resolution of the House of the 11th instant, I transmit herewith a report from the Secretary of State and documents containing the information desired by the resolution.

JOHN QUINCY ADAMS.

WASHINGTON, *April* 15, 1826.

The Secretary of State, to whom has been referred by the President the resolution of the House of Representatives of the 11th instant, requesting him to inform that House ("if within his power") whether any Government, except the Government of the United States, has been invited to send ministers to the Congress at Panama, and, also, whether he has any reason to expect that any other Government or Governments, in addition to the independent Governments of Spanish America and the Government of the United States of North America, (and, if any, what other Government or Governments,) will be represented in or at the Congress at Panama," has the honor to report:

1. A copy of a note from Mr. Salazar, addressed to the Secretary of State from New York, under date of March 10, 1826, with a copy of the note to which it refers, from the Chevalier de Gamiero to Mr. Hurtado, under date at Park Crescent, in London, October 30, 1825.

2. An extract from a despatch from Mr. Raguet, chargé d'affaires of the United States to Brazil, under date of February 14, 1826; and

3. An extract from a letter of Mr. Poinsett, under date at Mexico, January 18, 1826.

The Secretary has also the honor to state that other information, though not in an official form, has reached this Department of the intention of Great Britain to have an agent present at the Congress at Panama; and the Department has also been informed that France (whether with or without invitation is not known here) will likewise have an agent there. But it is not believed that these agents of Great Britain and France are expected to take any part in the conferences or negotiations of the Congress. No information is possessed in the Department of the intention of any other Government to be represented in or at the Congress of Panama, except the independent Governments of Spanish America, the United States Great Britain, France, and the Emperor of Brazil.

All which is respectfully submitted.

H. CLAY.

Don José Maria Salazar to the Secretary of State.

[Translation.]

LEGATION OF COLOMBIA NEAR THE UNITED STATES OF NORTH AMERICA,
New York, March 10, 1826.

SIR: I have just received the orders of my Government to communicate to that of the United States that his Majesty the Emperor of Brazil has accepted a formal invitation, given by the Government of Colombia, to come to the Congress of Panama, and it has been resolved to send plenipotentiaries to take part in the deliberations of general interest, and which may be compatible with the neutrality which Brazil has observed in the war of America with Spain.

The plenipotentiary of his Majesty the Emperor of Brazil near his Britannic Majesty has made this declaration to the Hon. Manuel José Hurtado, minister of Colombia at the said court, by a note, dated the 30th of October last, a copy of which I have the honor to inclose.

The Government of Colombia has seen with the greatest pleasure this disposition of his Majesty the Emperor of Brazil to enter into relations of friendship with the new Republics, and to labor in concert for the general prosperity of America, at the same time that he puts an end to the sinister interpretations which have been given in Europe to the objects of the Congress of Panama.

I avail myself of this occasion to renew to you, sir, the assurances of my distinguished consideration.
JOSÉ MÁRIA SALAZAR.

The Chevalier de Gamiero to Mr. Hurtado.

[Translation.]

PARK CRESCENT, *October* 30, 1825.

SIR: I fulfil to-day a very agreeable duty in announcing to you that the Emperor, my master, to whom I made known the note which you addressed to me on the 7th of June last, has been pleased to accept the formal invitation, which the Government of Colombia gave to him, that Brazil should join the other States of America, about to assemble at Panama, to arrange in common their mutual relations, and fix their respective political and commercial system.

The policy of the Emperor is so generous and benevolent that he will always be ready to contribute to the repose, the happiness, and the glory of America. And as soon as the negotiation relative to the recognition of the empire shall be honorably terminated at Rio de Janeiro he will send a plenipotentiary to the Congress to take part in the deliberations of general interest, which shall be compatible with the strict neutrality which he observes *between the belligerent States of America and Spain.*

Such, sir, is the answer which I am charged to make you, adding that the Emperor appreciates the friendship of the Colombian Government, and it will give him pleasure to cultivate it.

Happy to be the organ of the sentiments of my august master, I pray you to accept the renewed assurances of the high consideration with which I have the honor to be your most humble and most obedient servant,
CHEVALIER DE GAMIERO.

His Excellency Mr. HURTADO, *Minister Plenipotentiary of the Republic of Colombia, London.*

A true copy: J. M. GOMEZ, *Secretary of Legation.*

Extract of a letter to Mr. Clay, Secretary of State, from Mr. Condy Raguet, Chargé d'Affaires of the United States, Brazil, dated

"RIO DE JANEIRO, *February* 14, 1826.

"By decree of January 25 Theodoro Jose Brancardi, chief clerk of the Home Department, was appointed plenipotentiary of this Government to the Congress at Panama, in which his Majesty was invited by the Government of Colombia, through the Brazilian minister at London, to take a part."

Extract of a letter from Mr. Poinsett to Mr. Clay, Secretary of State, dated

"MEXICO, *January* 18, 1826.

"The chargé d'affaires of the United Mexican States at Bogota has very lately sent an official communication to this Government, from that of Colombia, setting forth that the Emperor of Brazil had been invited to send plenipotentiaries to the Congress of Panama, and his Majesty the King of Great Britain to send an agent there. Nothing is said as to the precise character of the latter."

INDEX TO FOREIGN RELATIONS

VOLUME V.

G.

Lightning Source UK Ltd.
Milton Keynes UK
UKHW050235200219
337528UK00025B/537/P